KU-533-099

The Works of Jonathan Edwards

Jonathan Edwards

The Works of Jonathan Edwards

with a memoir by
SERENO E. DWIGHT

revised and corrected by
EDWARD HICKMAN

VOLUME ONE

The Banner of Truth Trust

THE BANNER OF TRUTH TRUST
3 *Murrayfield Road, Edinburgh* EH12 6EL
PO Box 621, *Carlisle, Pennsylvania* 17013, USA

*

First published 1834
This edition published 1974
Reprinted 1976
Reprinted 1979

ISBN 0 85157 216 X

*

Printed in Great Britain by offset lithography by
Billing & Sons Limited, Guildford, London and Worcester

ADVERTISEMENT

The present Edition of the Works of Jonathan Edwards will be found more complete than any other previously submitted to the Public.

1. It contains all the matter included in the first collected American edition—that which was published at Worcester, and is regarded in the United States as the only one entitled to confidence.

2. The various original extracts from the diary and papers of Edwards, first published in America, by his descendant Sereno E. Dwight, in the year 1830, are here incorporated.

3. Several smaller pieces, printed originally in a separate form, and not hitherto included in any collection of the Works, are here introduced.

4. The valuable notes of Dr. Williams have been added.

5. The whole has been carefully revised by collation of all the previous editions.

Bungay, January, 1834.

CONTENTS

III. APPENDIX TO MEMOIRS.

IV. A CAREFUL AND STRICT INQUIRY INTO THE PREVAILING NOTIONS OF THE FREEDOM OF WILL.

CONTENTS.

MEMOIRS

OF

JONATHAN EDWARDS, A.M.

CHAPTER I.

BIRTH—PARENTAGE—EARLY RELIGIOUS ADVANTAGES—SERIOUS IMPRESSIONS AND ACCOUNT OF HIS EXPERIENCE.

FEW individuals ever appeared in the church of God who have merited, and actually received, higher tributes of respect than Jonathan Edwards. His intellectual powers were of no common order, and his industry in the cultivation of those powers is strongly marked in that wide extent of most important knowledge which he possessed. If we consider him as ranking with Hartley, Locke, and Bacon, in the scale of intellect, we shall have little apprehension of his title to such distinction being disputed. His mighty mind grasped with ease those subjects at which others faltered. He saw truth almost intuitively, and was equally keen in the detection of error in all its varied shades.—This distinguished man claims admiration, not merely on the ground of uncommon strength of intellectual powers, and intense application of mind, rewarded by proportionate acquirements, but also as a most humble and devoted servant of Christ; bringing all he had received into his service, and living only to him. His soul was indeed a temple of the Holy Spirit, and his life uniformly manifested all the simplicity, purity, disinterestedness, and elevated character of the gospel of Christ. The glory of God was his supreme object, whether engaged in his devotional exercises, his studies, his social intercourse, the discharge of his public ministry, or in the publication of his writings. All inferior motives seem to have been without any discernible influence upon him. He entered fully into the expressive language of Paul—"The love of Christ constraineth me." "For me to live is Christ." His personal example will long instruct, excite, and encourage, and his writings will necessarily be most highly esteemed so long as the love of truth prevails.

It has been justly observed, "The number of those men, who have produced great and permanent changes in the character and condition of mankind, and stamped their own image on the minds of succeeding generations, is comparatively small; and, even of this small number, the great body have been indebted for their superior efficiency, at least in part, to extraneous circumstances, while very few can ascribe it to the simple strength of their own intellect. Yet here and there an individual can be found, who, by his mere mental energy, has changed the course of human thought and feeling, and led mankind onward in that new and better path which he had opened to their view. Such an individual was *Jonathan Edwards*. Born in an obscure colony, in the midst of a wilderness, and educated at a seminary just commencing its existence; passing the better part of his life as the pastor of a frontier village, and the residue as an Indian missionary in a still humbler hamlet; he discovered, and unfolded, a system of the divine moral government, so new, so clear, so full, that while at its first disclosure it needed no aid from its friends, and feared no opposition from its enemies, it has at length constrained a reluctant world to bow in homage to its truth."*

Jonathan Edwards was born on the 5th of October, 1703, at Windsor, on the banks of the Connecticut. His father, the Rev. Timothy Edwards, was minister of that place about 60 years.† He died in January, 1758, in the 89th year of his age, not two months before this his only son. He was a man of great piety and usefulness. On November 6th, 1694, he married Esther Stoddard, daughter of the reverend and celebrated Solomon Stoddard, of Northampton, in the 23rd year of her age. They lived together in the married state above sixty-three years. Mrs. Edwards, our author's mother, was born June 2nd, 1672, and lived to about ninety years of age, (some years after her son,) a remarkable instance of the small decay of mental powers at so advanced an age. This venerable couple had eleven children; one son, the subject of these memoirs, and ten daughters, four of whom were older, and six younger, than himself.

From the highly spiritual character and intellectual attainments of his parents, it might naturally be expected that his early education would be attended with no common

* Life prefixed to the American edition of the Works of Jonathan Edwards, 1830.

† Appendix, No. I.

advantages; this was the fact. Many were the prayers presented by parental affection that this only and beloved son might be filled with the Holy Spirit; from a child know the Holy Scriptures; and be great in the sight of the Lord. They who thus fervently and constantly commended him to God, manifested equal diligence in training him up for God. Prayer excited to exertion, and exertion again was encouraged by prayer. The domestic circle was a scene of supplication, and it was a scene of instruction. In the abode of such exemplary servants of God, instruction abounded; that which the eye saw, as well as that which the ear heard, formed a lesson. There was nothing in the example of those who taught to diminish the force of instruction; there was nothing in social habits which counteracted the lessons of wisdom, and infused those principles which in after-years produced the fruit of folly and sin. On the contrary, there was every thing to enlarge, to purify, and to elevate the heart, and at the same time to train the mind, to those exercises of thought from which alone eminent attainments can be expected.

The faithful religious instructions of his parents "rendered him when a child familiarly conversant with God and Christ, with his own character and duty, with the way of salvation, and with the nature of that eternal life which, begun on earth, is perfected in heaven." Their prayers were not forgotten, and their efforts did not remain without effect. In the progress of childhood he was in several instances the subject of strong religious impressions. "This was particularly true some years before he went to college, during a powerful revival of religion in his father's congregation. He, and two other lads of his own age, who had the same feelings with himself, erected a booth in a very retired spot in a swamp, for an oratory, and resorted to it regularly for social prayer. This continued for a long period; but the impressions ultimately disappeared, and in his own view, were followed by no permanent effects of a salutary nature." The precise period when he regarded himself as entering on a religious life he no where mentions, nor has any record been found of the time when he made a publick profession of religion. Even the church with which he became connected would not certainly be known, were it not that on one occasion he alludes to himself as a member of the church in East Windsor. From various circumstances, it seems that the time of his uniting himself to it was not far from the time of his leaving college. Of the views and feelings of his mind, on this most important subject, both before and after this event, there is a most satisfactory and instructive account, which was found among his papers in his own hand-writing, and which was written near twenty years afterwards for his own private benefit. It is as follows:

"I had a variety of concerns and exercises about my soul from my childhood; but I had two more remarkable seasons of awakening, before I met with that change by which I was brought to those new dispositions, and that new sense of things, that I have since had. The first time was when I was a boy, some years before I went to college,* at a time of remarkable awakening in my father's congregation. I was then very much affected for many months, and concerned about the things of religion, and my soul's salvation; and was abundant in religious duties. I used to pray five times a day in secret, and to spend much time in religious conversation with other boys; and used to meet with them to pray together. I experienced I know not what kind of delight in religion. My mind was much engaged in it, and had much self-righteous pleasure, and it was my delight to abound in religious duties. I, with some of my school-mates, joined together and built a booth in a swamp, in a very retired spot, for a place of prayer.† And besides, I had particular secret places of my own in the woods, where I used to retire by myself; and was from time to time much affected. My affections seemed to be lively and easily moved, and I seemed to be in my element when I engaged in religious duties. And I am ready to think, many are deceived with such affections, and such a kind of delight as I then had in religion, and mistake it for grace.

"But, in progress of time, my convictions and affections wore off, and I entirely lost all those affections and delights, and left off secret prayer, at least as to any constant preference of it; and returned like a dog to his vomit, and went on in the ways of sin. Indeed, I was at times very uneasy, especially towards the latter part of my time at college, when it pleased God to seize me with a pleurisy; in which he brought me nigh to the grave, and shook me over the pit of hell. And yet it was not long after my recovery, before I fell again into my old ways of sin. But God would not suffer me to go on with any quietness; I had great and violent inward struggles, till after many conflicts with wicked inclinations, repeated resolutions, and bonds that I laid myself under by a kind of vows to God, I was brought wholly to break off all former wicked ways, and all ways of known outward sin; and to apply myself to seek salvation, and practise many religious duties, but without that kind of affection and delight which I had formerly experienced. My concern now wrought more by inward struggles and conflicts, and self-reflection. I made seeking my salvation the main business of my life. But yet, it seems to me, I sought it after a miserable manner, which has made me sometimes since to question, whether ever it issued in that which was saving; being ready to doubt whether such miserable seeking ever succeeded. I was indeed brought to seek salvation, in a manner that I never was before; I felt a spirit to part with all things in the world, for an interest in Christ. My concern continued, and prevailed, with many exercising thoughts and inward struggles; but yet it never seemed to be proper, to express that concern by the name of terror.

"From my childhood up, my mind had been full of objections against the doctrine of God's sovereignty, in choosing whom he would to eternal life; and rejecting whom he pleased; leaving them eternally to perish, and be everlastingly tormented in hell. It used to appear like a horrible doctrine to me. But I remember the time very well when I seemed to be convinced, and fully satisfied, as to this sovereignty of God, and his justice in thus eternally disposing of men, according to his sovereign pleasure. But never could give an account how, or by what means, I was thus convinced, not in the least imagining at the time, nor a long time after, that there was any extraordinary influence of God's Spirit in it; but only that now I saw further, and my reason apprehended the justice and reasonableness of it. However, my mind rested in it; and it put an end to all those cavils and objections. And there has been a wonderful alteration in my mind, with respect to the doctrine of God's sovereignty, from that day to this; so that

* As he entered college at twelve years of age, this was probably when he was seven or eight.

† The place where the booth was built is known at East Windsor.

I scarce ever have found so much as the rising of an objection against it, in the most absolute sense, in God showing mercy to whom he will show mercy, and hardening whom he will. God's absolute sovereignty and justice, with respect to salvation and damnation, is what my mind seems to rest assured of, as much as of any thing that I see with my eyes; at least it is so at times. But I have often, since that first conviction, had quite another kind of sense of God's sovereignty than I had then. I have often since had not only a conviction, but a *delightful* conviction. The doctrine has very often appeared exceedingly pleasant, bright, and sweet. Absolute sovereignty is what I love to ascribe to God. But my first conviction was not so.

" The first instance, that I remember, of that sort of inward, sweet delight in God and divine things, that I have lived much in since, was on reading those words, 1 Tim. i. 17. *Now unto the King eternal, immortal, invisible, the only wise God, be honour and glory for ever and ever. Amen.* As I read the words, there came into my soul, and was as it were diffused through it, a sense of the glory of the Divine Being; a new sense, quite different from any thing I ever experienced before. Never any words of Scripture seemed to me as these words did. I thought with myself, how excellent a Being that was, and how happy I should be, if I might enjoy that God, and be rapt up to him in heaven; and be as it were swallowed up in him for ever! I kept saying, and as it were singing, over these words of Scripture to myself; and went to pray to God that I might enjoy him; and prayed in a manner quite different from what I used to do, with a new sort of affection. But it never came into my thought, that there was any thing spiritual, or of a saving nature, in this.

" From about that time I began to have a new kind of apprehensions and ideas of Christ, and the work of redemption, and the glorious way of salvation by him. An inward, sweet sense of these things, at times, came into my heart; and my soul was led away in pleasant views and contemplations of them. And my mind was greatly engaged to spend my time in reading and meditating on Christ, on the beauty and excellency of his person, and the lovely way of salvation by free grace in him. I found no books so delightful to me, as those that treated of these subjects. Those words Cant. ii. 1. used to be abundantly with me, *I am the rose of Sharon, and the lily of the valleys.* The words seemed to me sweetly to represent the loveliness and beauty of Jesus Christ. The whole book of Canticles used to be pleasant to me, and I used to be much in reading it, about that time; and found from time to time an inward sweetness, that would carry me away in my contemplations. This I know not how to express otherwise, than by a calm, sweet abstraction of soul from all the concerns of this world; and sometimes a kind of vision, or fixed ideas and imaginations, of being alone in the mountains, or some solitary wilderness, far from all mankind, sweetly conversing with Christ, and wrapt and swallowed up in God. The sense I had of divine things, would often of a sudden kindle up, as it were, a sweet burning in my heart, an ardour of soul, that I know not how to express.

" Not long after I first began to experience these things, I gave an account to my father of some things that had passed in my mind. I was pretty much affected by the discourse we had together; and when the discourse was ended, I walked abroad alone, in a solitary place in my father's pasture, for contemplation. And as I was walking there, and looking upon the sky and clouds, there came into my mind so sweet a sense of the glorious *majesty* and *grace* of God, as I know not how to express.—I seemed to see them both in a sweet conjunction; majesty and meekness joined together: it was a sweet, and gentle, and holy majesty; and also a majestic meekness; an awful sweetness; a high, and great, and holy gentleness.

" After this my sense of divine things gradually increased, and became more and more lively, and had more of that inward sweetness. The appearance of every thing was altered; there seemed to be, as it were, a calm, sweet cast or appearance of divine glory, in almost every thing. God's excellency, his wisdom, his purity, and love, seemed to appear in every thing; in the sun, moon, and stars; in the clouds and blue sky; in the grass, flowers, trees; in the water and all nature; which used greatly to fix my mind. I often used to sit and view the moon for a long time; and in the day, spent much time in viewing the clouds and sky, to behold the sweet glory of God in these things: in the mean time singing forth, with a low voice, my contemplations of the Creator and Redeemer. And scarce any thing, among all the works of nature, was so sweet to me as thunder and lightning: formerly nothing had been so terrible to me. Before, I used to be uncommonly terrified with thunder, and to be struck with terror when I saw a thunder-storm rising; but now, on the contrary, it rejoiced me. I felt God, if I may so speak, at the first appearance of a thunder-storm; and used to take the opportunity, at such times, to fix myself in order to view the clouds, and see the lightnings play, and hear the majestic and awful voice of God's thunders, which oftentimes was exceedingly entertaining, leading me to sweet contemplations of my great and glorious God. While thus engaged, it always seemed natural for me to sing or chant forth my meditations; or, to speak my thoughts in soliloquies with a singing voice.

" I felt then great satisfaction as to my good estate; but that did not content me. I had vehement longings of soul after God and Christ, and after more holiness, wherewith my heart seemed to be full, and ready to break; which often brought to my mind the words of the psalmist, Ps. cxix. 28. *My soul breaketh for the longing it hath.* I often felt a mourning and lamenting in my heart, that I had not turned to God sooner, that I might have had more time to grow in grace. My mind was greatly fixed on divine things; almost perpetually in the contemplation of them. I spent most of my time in thinking of divine things, year after year; often walking alone in the woods, and solitary places, for meditation, soliloquy, and prayer, and converse with God; and it was always my manner, at such times, to sing forth my contemplations. I was almost constantly in ejaculatory prayer, wherever I was. Prayer seemed to be natural to me, as the breath by which the inward burnings of my heart had vent. The delights which I now felt in the things of religion, were of an exceedingly different kind from those before mentioned, that I had when a boy; and what then I had no more notion of, than one born blind has of pleasant and beautiful colours. They were of a more inward, pure, soul-animating, and refreshing nature. Those former delights never reached the heart; and did not arise from any sight of the divine excellency of the things of God; or any taste of the soul-satisfying and life-giving good there is in them.

" My sense of divine things seemed gradually to increase, till I went to preach at New York; which was about a year and a half after they began: and while I was there I felt them very sensibly, in a much higher degree than I had done before. My longings after God and holiness were much increased. Pure and humble, holy and heavenly, Christianity appeared exceedingly amiable to me. I felt a burning desire to be, in every thing, a complete Christian; and conformed to the blessed image of Christ; and that I might live, in all things, according to the pure, sweet, and blessed rules of the gospel. I had an eager thirsting after progress in these things; which put me upon pursuing and pressing after them. It was my continual strife, day and night, and constant inquiry, how I should *be* more holy, and *live* more holily, and more becoming a child of God, and a disciple of Christ. I now sought an increase of grace and holiness, and a holy life, with much more earnestness than ever I sought grace before I had it. I used to be continually examining myself, and studying and contriving for likely ways and means how I should live holily, with far greater diligence and earnestness than ever I pursued any thing in my life; but yet with too great a dependence on my own strength; which afterwards proved a great damage to me. My experience had not then taught me, as it has done since, my extreme feebleness and impotence, every manner of way; and the bottomless depths of secret corruption and deceit there was in my heart. However, I went on with my eager pursuit after more holiness and conformity to Christ.

" The heaven I desired was a heaven of holiness; to be with God, and to spend my eternity in divine love, and holy communion with Christ. My mind was very much taken up with contemplations on heaven, and the enjoyments there; and living there in perfect holiness, humility, and love; and it used at that time to appear a great part of the happiness of heaven, that there the saints could express their love to Christ. It appeared to me a great clog and burden, that what I felt within I could not express as I desired. The inward ardour of my soul seemed to be hindered and pent up, and could not freely flame out as it would. I used often to think, how in heaven this principle should freely and fully vent and express itself. Heaven appeared exceedingly delightful, as a world of love; and that all happiness consisted in living in pure, humble, heavenly, divine love.

" I remember the thoughts I used then to have of holiness; and said sometimes to myself, 'I do certainly know that I love holiness, such as the gospel prescribes.' It appeared to me, that there was nothing in it but what was ravishingly lovely; the highest beauty and amiableness—a *divine* beauty; far purer than any thing here upon earth; and that every thing else was like mire and defilement in comparison of it.

" Holiness, as I then wrote down some of my contemplations on it, appeared to me to be of a sweet, pleasant, charming, serene, calm nature; which brought an inexpressible purity, brightness, peacefulness, and ravishment to the soul. In other words, that it made the soul like a field or garden of God, with all manner of pleasant flowers; enjoying a sweet calm, and the gently vivifying beams of the sun. The soul of a true Christian, as I then wrote my meditations, appeared like such a little white flower as we see in the spring of the year; low and humble on the ground, opening its bosom to receive the pleasant beams of the sun's glory; rejoicing, as it were, in a calm rapture; diffusing around a sweet fragrancy; standing peacefully and lovingly, in the midst of other flowers round about; all in like manner opening their bosoms to drink in the light of the sun. There was no part of creature-holiness that I had so great a sense of its loveliness, as humility, brokenness of heart, and poverty of spirit; and there was nothing that I so earnestly longed for. My heart panted after this—to lie low before God, as in the dust; that I might be nothing, and that God might be *all*, that I might become as a little child.

" While at New York, I sometimes was much affected with reflections on my past life, considering how late it was before I began to be truly religious; and how wickedly I had lived till then: and once so as to weep abundantly, and for a considerable time together.

" On January 12, 1723, I made a solemn dedication of myself to God, and wrote it down; giving up myself, and all that I had, to God; to be for the future in no respect my own; to act as one that had no right to himself, in any respect. And solemnly vowed to take God for my whole portion and felicity, looking on nothing else as any part of my happiness, nor acting as it were; and his law for the constant rule of my obedience; engaging to fight with all my might against the world, the flesh, and the devil, to the end of my life. But I have reason to be infinitely humbled, when I consider how much I have failed of answering my obligation.

" I had, then, abundance of sweet religious conversation, in the family where I lived, with Mr. John Smith, and his pious mother. My heart was knit in affection to those in whom were appearances of true piety; and I could bear the thoughts of no other companions, but such as were holy, and the disciples of the blessed Jesus. I had great longings for the advancement of Christ's kingdom in the world; and my secret prayers used to be, in great part, taken up in praying for it. If I heard the least hint of any thing that happened in any part of the world, that appeared, in some respect or other, to have a favourable aspect on the interests of Christ's kingdom, my soul eagerly catched at it, and it would much animate and refresh me. I used to be eager to read public news-letters, mainly for that end; to see if I could not find some news favourable to the interest of religion in the world.

" I very frequently used to retire into a solitary place, on the banks of Hudson's river, at some distance from the city, for contemplation on divine things and secret converse with God; and had many sweet hours there. Sometimes Mr. Smith and I walked there together, to converse on the things of God; and our conversation used to turn much on the advancement of Christ's kingdom in the world, and the glorious things that God would accomplish for his church in the latter days. I had then, and at other times, the greatest delight in the Holy Scriptures of any book whatsoever. Oftentimes in reading it every word seemed to touch my heart. I felt a harmony between something in my heart, and those sweet and powerful words. I seemed often to see so much light exhibited by every sentence, and such a refreshing food communicated, that I could not get along in reading; often dwelling long on one sentence, to see the wonders contained in it; and yet almost every sentence seemed to be full of wonders.

" I came away from New York in the month of *April*, 1723, and had a most bitter parting with Madam Smith and her son. My heart seemed to sink within me, at leaving the family and city, where I had enjoyed so many sweet and pleasant days. I went from New York to Wethersfield by water; and as I sailed away, I kept sight of the city as long as I could. However, that night, after this sorrowful parting, I was greatly comforted in God at West Chester, where we went ashore to lodge: and had a pleasant time of it all the voyage to Saybrook. It was sweet to me to think of meeting dear Christians in heaven, where we should never part more. At Saybrook we went ashore to lodge on Saturday, and there kept the sabbath; where I had a sweet and refreshing season walking alone in the fields.

"After I came home to Windsor, I remained much in a like frame of mind as when at New York; only sometimes I felt my heart ready to sink with the thoughts of my friends at New York. My support was in contemplations on the heavenly state; as I find in my diary of May 1, 1723. It was a comfort to think of that state, where there is fulness of joy; where reigns heavenly, calm and delightful love, without alloy; where there are continually the dearest expressions of this love; where is the enjoyment of the persons loved, without ever parting; where those persons who appear so lovely in this world, will really be inexpressibly more lovely, and full of love to us. And how secretly will the mutual lovers join together, to sing the praises of God and the Lamb! How will it fill us with joy to think, that this enjoyment, these sweet exercises, will never cease, but will last to all eternity!"

Thus deep, decided, and powerful were the operations of divine grace upon the mind of this eminent servant of Christ. That his understanding was much enlightened in the things of God, and his heart deeply affected by them, are circumstances which will immediately strike the attention of every serious observer. There was in him a holy anxiety to obtain the most satisfactory testimony to a change of heart: for this purpose he closely and diligently examined himself; he had no inclination to shun this self-inquiry. Personal examination seems to have been considered by him as a pleasing as well as a momentous exercise. Many professors revolt at the thought of such inward survey; they content themselves with looking (and that hastily) at external matters, but they will not look *within*, though this neglect be at the peril of eternal good. The feelings with which men regard the duty of personal examination, may justly be viewed as an accurate criterion of their spiritual state, for in proportion to their concern for eternity, will be their disposition to try themselves; or in other words, in the same measure in which grace exists, will there be a desire of fully ascertaining its existence and progress. Upon a review of the statement given by Mr. Edwards as to his early religious experience, it is evident, that he was not one who could satisfy himself upon any insufficient grounds: not a symptom of carelessness or of presumption can be discerned; he looked upon himself with a holy jealousy; he thought, he read, he conversed, and above all he prayed, that he might be enabled more accurately to search his own heart, and thus escape the danger of self-deception, and be convinced by proofs which would stand the test of the judgment of God, that he was a child of light, a subject of holiness, and an heir of glory. And thus studying himself under the penetrating light of the word, and the gracious influences of the Spirit of God, he acquired that exact knowledge of the various inward exercises and outward displays of the christian character, which enabled him in after-years, with such skill, to separate delusive appearances from those which are solid, and to mark the strong difference between the mere professor of the name of Christ, and the actual partaker of the power of the gospel. It was in these early years of his life that those correct views were formed which afterwards expanded in his admirable treatise on Religious Affections.

CHAPTER II.

INTELLECTUAL PROGRESS—EARLIEST PRODUCTIONS—ENTRANCE AT COLLEGE—MENTAL HABITS.

A STATEMENT has been given principally from the pen of Mr. Edwards himself of his religious views in youth, and it will be proper before that subject be resumed, to advert to his intellectual progress at the same period. It is delightful to contemplate the simultaneous advancement of knowledge in the mind and of piety in the heart. None can reasonably imagine that there is an opposition between these things; and all whose minds are open to conviction will be persuaded, that the growth of piety is most conducive to the increase of the best treasures of earthly wisdom. Religion strengthens the powers of man; it never enfeebles them. It at once cuts off those guilty pleasures, and those unworthy pursuits, which not merely impede the progress of the understanding, but in many cases are absolutely fatal to its energies; and it forms those mental habits, as well as produces that outward propriety of conduct, which are most favourable to the cultivation of man's noblest faculties. It would be easy to record a lengthened list of names enrolled with never-fading honour, both in the schools of science, and in the church of God. The gospel of Christ has uniformly been the friend of solid learning, nor are those persons the judicious friends of the gospel, who are disposed to disparage the exertions and acquirements of intellect. The christian church dreads the veil of darkness, but it rejoices in the light.

The same parental kindness and wisdom, which, under God, guided the mind of Jonathan Edwards to the knowledge and love of things eternal, were also much discovered in the direction of his powers to useful objects of earthly science. When only six years of age, the study of the Latin language engaged his attention under the care of his father, and occasionally that of his elder sisters. No account is preserved of his progress in his studies at that early period, but his high standing as a scholar on his admission to college, as well as afterwards, and his thorough knowledge of the Latin, Greek, and Hebrew, prove at once his own diligence as a student at this time, and the accuracy and fidelity of his father's instructions.

"From his remaining manuscripts, it is evident that his father's family were fond of the use of the pen, and that he and his sisters were early encouraged by their parents to make attempts, not only in letter writing, but in other species of composition. This course, though rarely pursued with children, is eminently advantageous; and in the case before us, was obviously followed by the best results. While it increased the mutual affection of the brother and the sisters, it also served to strengthen their minds, and to impart exactness both of thought and expression. The earliest effort of his pen appears to have been written on the following occasion. Some one in the vicinity, probably an older boy than himself, had advanced the opinion, *that the soul was material, and remained with the body till the resurrection;* and had endeavoured to convince him of its correctness. Struck with the absurdity of the notion, he sat down and wrote the following reply; which, as a specimen both of wit and reasoning in a child of about ten years of age, may fairly claim to be preserved. It is without date, and without pointing, or any division into sentences; and has every appearance of having been written by a boy just after he had learned to write.

"I am informed that you have advanced a notion, that the soul is material, and attends the body till the resurrection; as I am a professed lover of novelty, you must imagine I am very much entertained by this discovery; (which, however old in some parts of the world, is new to us;) but suffer my curiosity a little further. I would know the manner of the kingdom before I swear allegiance: 1st, I would know whether this material soul keeps with (the body) in the coffin, and *if* so, whether it might not be convenient to build a repository for it; in order to which I would know what shape it is of, whether round, triangular, or four-square; or whether it is a number of long fine strings reaching from the head to the foot; and whether it does not live a very discontented life. I am afraid when the coffin gives way, the earth will fall in and crush it; but if it should choose to live above-ground, and hover about the grave, how big is it?—whether it covers all the body; what it does when another body is laid upon it: whether the first gives way; and if so where is the place of retreat. But suppose that souls are not so big but that ten or a dozen of them may be about one body; whether they will not quarrel for the highest place; and, as I insist much upon my honour and property, I would know whether I must quit my dear head, if a superior soul comes in the way: but above all, I am concerned to know what they do, where a burying-place has been filled twenty, thirty, or an hundred times. If they are a-top of one another, the uppermost will be so far off, that it can take no care of the body. I strongly suspect they must march off every time there comes a new set. I hope there is some other place provided for them but dust. The undergoing so much hardship, and being deprived of the body at last, will make them ill-tempered. I leave it with your physical genius to determine, whether some medicinal applications might not be proper in such cases, and subscribe your proselyte, when I can have solution of these matters."

The following letter to one of his sisters, written at twelve years of age, is the earliest *dated* effort of his pen which has been discovered.

"To Miss Mary Edwards, at Hadley.

"*Windsor, May* 10, 1716.

"Dear Sister,

"Through the wonderful goodness and mercy of God, there has been in this place a very remarkable outpouring of the Spirit of God. It still continues, but I think I have reason to think is in some measure diminished, yet I hope not much. Three have joined the church since you last heard; five now stand propounded for admission; and I think above thirty persons come commonly on Mondays to converse with father about the condition of their souls. It is a time of general health here. Abigail, Hannah, and Lucy have had the chicken pox and are recovered. Jerusha is almost well. Except her, the whole family is well.

"Sister, I am glad to hear of your welfare so often as I do, I should be glad to hear from you by letter, and therein how it is with you as to your crookedness.

"Your loving brother,

"JONATHAN E."

He was educated, until he entered college, at home, and under his father's personal instruction; while his older sisters were daily pursuing their respective branches of study in his immediate presence. Their father having been distinguished as a scholar, was able to give them, and actually gave them, a superior education. In all their various pursuits, the mind of their brother, as it opened, would of course be more and more interested; and thus at length he would easily and insensibly acquire a mass of information far beyond his years. The course of his education may in this way have been less systematic, indeed, and less conformed to rule, than that ordinarily given in the school. At the same time it was more safe; forming him to softer manners, gentler feelings, and purer affections. In his circumstances, also, it was obviously more comprehensive and universal; and while it brought him acquainted with many things which are not usually communicated until a later period, it also served to unfold the original traits of his mind, and to give it that expansion, which is the result of information alone. One characteristic, of which he has not generally been suspected, but which he possessed in an unusual degree, was a fondness minutely and critically to investigate the works of nature. This propensity was not only discovered in youth and manhood, but was fully developed in childhood, and at that early period was encouraged and cherished by the fostering hand of parental care.

He entered Yale college in New-Haven, in September, 1716, before he was thirteen years of age. The college was then in its infancy, and various untoward circumstances had greatly impeded its growth. It was first planted at Saybrook, and then partially removed to Kenilworth, to the house of its first rector, until his death in 1707. From that time the Rev. Mr. Andrews, of Milford, one of the trustees, was rector *pro tempore*, upwards of twelve years; and the location of the college was a constant theme of contention between the towns of New-Haven, Saybrook, Wethersfield, and Hartford, until 1716; when the vote of the trustees, the donation of Mr. Yale, and the vote of the legislature of the colony, fixed it permanently at New-Haven. In the collegiate year 1716-1717, thirteen of the students resided at New-Haven, fourteen at Wethersfield, and four at Saybrook. The temporary presidency of Mr. Andrews continued until 1719; and as he was the acting minister of Milford, his oversight of the college, and his influence over the students, must of course have been exceedingly imperfect. The government of the institution, virtually and necessarily, was chiefly in the hands of the tutors: who, as young men without experience and a knowledge of mankind, could not usually be found qualified for so difficult a trust. Some time in the year 1717, the extreme unpopularity of one of the tutors occasioned a general insurrection of the students, who were at New-Haven, against the government of the college; and in one body they withdrew from New-Haven, and joined their companions at Wethersfield. At the commencement in that year, eight of the senior class returned to New-Haven, to receive their degrees of the regular college government; while five received theirs irregularly at Wethersfield. There is no evidence that Jonathan Edwards took part in these disturbances. He went however with his companions to Wethersfield, and continued there until 1719. While there, he gained a high character and standing in his class. His father, writing to one of his daughters, under date of Jan. 27, 1718, says, "I have not heard but that your brother Jonathan is also well. He has a very good name at Wethersfield, both as to his carriage and his learning." While at Wethersfield, he wrote to one of his sisters the following letter; which, as it is a document relating to an interesting event in the history of the college, may not improperly be preserved.

"To Miss Mary Edwards at Northampton.

"*Wethersfield, March* 26, 1719.

"Dear Sister,

"Of all the many sisters I have, I think I never had one so long out of my hearing as yourself; inasmuch as I cannot remember, that I ever heard one tittle from you, from the time you last went up the country, until the last week, by Mr. B. who then came from Northampton. When he came in, I truly rejoiced to see him, because I fully expected to receive a letter from you by him. But being disappointed, and that not a little, I was willing to make that, which I hoped would be an opportunity of receiving, the same of sending. For I thought it was a pity, that there should not be the least correspondence between us, or communication from one to another, when at no farther distance. I hope also that this may be a means of exciting the same in yourself; and so, having more charity for you than to believe that I am quite out of your mind, or that you are not at all concerned for me, I think it fit that I should give you some account of my condition, relative to the school. I suppose you are fully acquainted with our coming away from New-Haven, and the circumstances of it. Since then we have been in a more prosperous condition, as I think, than ever. But the council and trustees, having lately had a meeting at New-Haven concerning it, have removed that which was the cause of our coming away, *viz.* Mr. Johnson, from the place of a tutor, and have put in Mr. Cutler, pastor of Canterbury, president; who, as we hear, intends very speedily to be resident at Yale college, so that all the scholars belonging to our school expect to return there, as soon as our vacancy after the election is over.

"I am your loving brother in good health,

"JONATHAN EDWARDS."

While a member of college, he was distinguished for the uniform sobriety and correctness of his behaviour, for diligent application to his studies, and for rapid and thorough attainments in learning. In the second year of his collegiate course, while at Wethersfield, he read Locke on the Human Understanding, with peculiar pleasure. The uncommon strength and penetration of his mind, which admirably qualified him for profound thought and metaphysical investigation, began to be discovered and exerted even at this early age. From his own account of the subject, he was inexpressibly entertained and delighted with that profound work, when he read it at the age of fourteen, enjoying a far higher pleasure in the perusal of its pages, "than the most greedy miser finds, when gathering up handfuls of silver and gold, from some newly discovered treasure." To studies of this class he from that time devoted himself, as to those in which he felt the most intense interest. Still, however, he applied himself, with so much diligence and success, to the performance of his assigned duties, as to sustain the first standing in his class, and to secure the highest approbation of his instructors.

Mr. Cutler went to New-Haven early in June 1719, at the opening of the summer term, to enter on the duties of his office as rector; and the students, among whom was Jonathan Edwards, returned to the college. The following letter from the rector to his father, will show the character which he had acquired while at Wethersfield, and the trying circumstances of the college.

"*New-Haven, June* 30, 1719.

"Rev. Sir,

"Your letter came to my hands by your son. I congratulate you upon his promising abilities and advances in learning. He is now under my care, and probably may continue so, and doubtless will so do if he should remain here, and I be settled in the business I am now in. I can assure you, Rev. Sir, that your good affection to me in this affair, and that of the ministers around you, is no small inducement to me; and if I am prevailed on thereby, it shall be a strong motive to me to improve my poor abilities, in the service of such hopeful youths as are with us. They may suffer much from my weakness, but they shall not from my neglect. I am no party man, but shall carry it, with an equal hand and affection, to the whole college; and I doubt not, but the difficulty and importance of the business will secure me your prayers, and those of all good men, which I do much value and desire.

"I remain, under the earnest hope and expectation of your prayers,

"Your humble servant,

"T. CUTLER."

The following characteristical letter, written to his father in his third collegiate year, will not be uninteresting to the reader.

"To the Rev. Timothy Edwards, Pastor of the Church at East Windsor.

"*New-Haven, July* 21, 1719.

"Ever honoured Sir,

"I received, with two books, a letter from yourself, bearing the date of July 7th; and therein I received, with the greatest gratitude, your wholesome advice and counsel; and I hope I shall, God helping of me, use my utmost endeavours to put the same in practice. I am sensible of the preciousness of my time, and am resolved it shall not be through any neglect of mine, if it slips without the greatest advantage. I take very great content under my present tuition, as all the rest of the scholars seem to do under theirs. Mr. Cutler is extraordinarily courteous to us, has a very good spirit of government, keeps the school in excellent order, seems to increase in learning, is loved and respected by all who are under him; and when he is spoken of in the school or town, he generally has the title of President. The scholars all live in very good peace with the people of the town, and there is not a word said about our former carryings on, except now and then by aunt Mather. I have diligently searched into the circumstances of Stiles's examination, which was very short, and as far as I can understand, was to no other disadvantage than that he was examined in Tully's Orations; in which, though he had never construed before he came to New-Haven, yet he committed no error in that or any other book, whether Latin, Greek, or Hebrew, except in Virgil, wherein he could not tell the preteritum of requiesco. He is very well treated among the scholars, and accepted in the college as a member of it by every body, and also as a freshman; neither, as I think, is he inferior, as to learning, to any of his classmates. I have inquired of Mr. Cutler what books we shall have need of the next year. He answered, he would have me to get against that time, Alstead's Geometry and Gassendus's Astronomy; with which I would entreat you to get a pair of dividers, or mathematician's compasses, and a scale, which are absolutely necessary in order to learning mathematics; and also the Art of Thinking, which, I am persuaded, would be no less profitable, than the other necessary, to me who am

"Your most dutiful son,

"JONATHAN EDWARDS."

"P. S. What we give a week for our board is £0 5*s*. 0*d*."

"The habits of study, which Edwards formed in very early youth, were not only strict and severe, and this in every branch of literature, but in one respect peculiar. Even while a boy, he began to study *with his pen in his hand*; not for the purpose of copying off the thoughts of others, but for the purpose of writing down, and preserving, the thought suggested to his own mind, from the course of study which he was pursuing. This most useful practice he commenced in several branches of study very early; and he steadily pursued it in all his studies through life. His pen appears to have been in a sense always in his hand. From this practice steadily persevered in, he derived the very great advantages of thinking continually during each period of study; of thinking accurately; of thinking connectedly; of thinking habitually at all times; of banishing from his mind every subject, which was not worthy of continued and systematic thought; of pursuing each given subject of thought as far as he was able, at the happy moment when it opened spontaneously on his mind; of pursuing every such subject afterwards, in regular sequence, starting anew from the point where he had previously left off, when again it opened upon him in some new and interesting light; of preserving his best thoughts, associations, and images, and then arranging them under their proper heads, ready for subsequent use; of regularly strengthening the faculty of thinking and reasoning, by constant and powerful exercise; and above all, of gradually moulding himself into a thinking being—a being, who instead of regarding thinking and reasoning as labour, could find no high enjoyment but in intense, systematic, and certain thought. In this view of the subject, when we remember how few students comparatively, from want of this mental discipline, think at all; how few of those who think at all, think habitually; how few of those who think habitually, think to purpose; and how few of those who think to purpose, attain to the fulness of the measure of the stature, to which, as thinking beings, they might have attained; it will not I think be doubted, that the practice in question was the principal means of the ultimate development of his mental superiority."*

CHAPTER III.

EARLY RELIGIOUS PRODUCTIONS—"MISCELLANIES"—NOTES ON THE SCRIPTURES—COMMENCEMENT OF HIS PREACHING—RESOLUTIONS.

A CONSCIENTIOUS regard to duty appeared greatly in the early as well as in the latter days of Jonathan Edwards. As a child, the spirit of love and obedience uniformly guided him; and as a pupil, he discovered every disposition honourable to himself, encouraging to those who anxiously watched over his progress, and which was justly considered as the earnest of uncommon attainments. The child, the youth, the man, all presented to view the same superior mind, in different degrees of advancement, but still alike indicative of the same general excellencies.

While at college, he paid a most assiduous and successful attention to his assigned duties, and particularly to the study of mental and physical philosophy; yet he still found time for pursuits of a more elevated and spiritual character. His whole education from early infancy, and the counsels of his parents, as well as his own feelings, prompted him to these pursuits. "To read the Bible daily, and to read it in connexion with other religious books, diligently and attentively, on the sabbath, was made, in the earlier days of New England, the habitual duty of every child; and his father's family, though not inattentive to the due cultivation of mind and manners, had lost none of the strictness, or conscientiousness, which characterized the pilgrims. The books which he found in his father's house, the conversation of ministers often resorting to the house, the custom of the times, as well as the more immediate influence of parental instruction and example, naturally prompted a mind like his to the early contemplation and investigation of many of the truths and principles of theology. He had also witnessed in his father's congregation, before his admission to college, several extensive revivals of religion; and in two of them the impressions made on his own mind had been unusually deep and solemn. The name familiarly given by the plain people of New England to these events—"A religious *attention*," and "A *general attention* to religion"—indicates their nature; and those personally acquainted with them need not be informed, that during their progress, the

* For a specimen of the early papers of Jonathan Edwards, see Appendix, No. IV.

great truths of religion, as taught in the Scriptures, and as explained in the writings of theologians, become the objects of general and intense interest, and of close practical study; or that the knowledge, acquired by a whole people at such a time, in a comparatively little period, often exceeds the acquisitions of many previous years. With all these things in view, it is not surprising, that, to these two kinds of reading, he devoted himself early, with great diligence and with great success."

Two of his early "Resolutions" relate to this subject, in which he proposes "to study the Scriptures so steadily, constantly, and frequently, as that I may find and plainly perceive myself to grow in the knowledge of the same." He never lost sight of this resolution. On the 8th of June, 1723, he also proposes, whenever he finds himself in a dull, listless frame, to read over his own "Remarks and Reflections of a Religious Nature," in order to quicken him in his duty. These "Remarks and Reflections" were very numerous. The first manuscript of his "Miscellanies" is in folio, and consists of forty-four sheets of foolscap, written separately, and stitched together. When he began the work, he had obviously no suspicion of the size to which it was to grow, nor had he formed his ultimate plan of arrangement. He headed his first article, "Of holiness;" and having finished it, and drawn a line of separation across the page, he commenced the second, "Of Christ's mediation and satisfaction." The same is done with the third and fourth. The fifth he writes, without a line of separation, in larger letters, "*Spiritual Happiness.*" After that the subject of each new article is printed, or written, in larger letters. His first article was written on the second page of a loose sheet of paper; and having written over the second, third, and fourth pages, he went back to the first. He began to number his articles by the letters of the alphabet, a, b, c, and having gone through, he commenced with a double alphabet, a a, b b, c c; when this was finished, finding his work enlarge, he took the regular numbers, 1, 2, 3, &c. and this plan, both as to subjects and numbers, is afterwards continued.

The beginning of the work is written in a remarkably small round hand, nearly the same with that in which his earliest productions are written. This extends through about the first 150 articles, and is soon after perceptibly changed, into a hand somewhat more formed and flowing. These appear obviously to have been written during the last years of his college life, and the two years of his residence at college as Bachelor of Arts. Large extracts from this work will be found in the present edition of his Works, and a number of them from the earlier articles. Such are the Miscellaneous Observations, and the Miscellaneous Remarks, vol. ii. page 459. and the Miscellanies, page 525. In these will be found many of his most original and most profound thoughts and discussions on theological subjects.

"His regular and diligent study of the sacred Scriptures, led him early to discover, that they opened before him an almost boundless field of investigation and inquiry. Some passages he found to be incorrectly rendered; many were very obscure, and difficult in explanation; in many there were apparent inconsistencies and contradictions; many had been long employed, as proofs of doctrines and principles, to which they had no possible reference; the words and phrases, as well as the sentiments and narratives, of one part, he saw illustrated, and interpreted those of another. The Old Testament, in its language, history, doctrines, and worship, in its allusions to manners and customs, in its prophecies, types, and images, he perceived to be introductory and explanatory of the New; while the New, by presenting the full completion of the whole plan and design of their common Author, unfolded the real drift and bearing of every part of the Old. Regarding the sacred volume with the highest veneration, he appears to have resolved, while a member of college, that he would, as far as possible, possess himself, in every part of it which he read, of the true meaning of its Author. With this view he commenced his "*Notes on the Scriptures;*" obviously making it his standing rule, to study every passage which he read, which presented the least difficulty to his own mind, or which he had known to be regarded as difficult by others, until such difficulty was satisfactorily removed. The result of his investigations he regularly, and at the time, committed to writing; at first in separate half-sheets, folded in 4to; but having found the inconvenience of this in his other juvenile writings, he soon formed small pamphlets of sheets, which were ultimately made into volumes. A few of the articles, to the number of about fifty, appear to have been written while he was in college; the rest, while preparing for the ministry, and during his subsequent life. That he had no suspicion when he began of the size to which the work would grow, is plain, and whether he afterwards formed the design of publishing it, as an illustration of the more difficult and obscure passages of the Bible, perhaps cannot be determined with certainty. A few of the articles of an historical or mythological nature, are marked as quotations from the writings of others, and are omitted in the present edition of his Works. The reader, after perusing the work, will be satisfied that they are the fruit of his own investigations; and that his mode of removing difficulties was,—not as it too often is, by disguising or misstating them, but by giving them their full force, and meeting them with fair argument. Perhaps no collection of notes on the Scriptures so entirely original can be found. From the number prefixed to each article, it will be found easy to select those which were the result of his early labours. Such a plan of investigating and explaining the difficulties of the sacred volume, at so early a period of life, was probably never formed in any other instance, and evinces a maturity of intellectual and moral attainments, not often paralleled. Among the most interesting and able of these investigations, will be found the discussion on the *sacrifice of the daughter of Jephtha*, Judg. xi. 29—40.; and that on the principle advanced by Paul, in Romans viii. 28. *That all things work together for good to them that love God;* which as being contained in his letter to Mr. Gillespie, of Sept. 4, 1747, is omitted in the notes on the Scriptures."

The class of which Edwards was a member, finished their regular collegiate course, in Sept. 1720, before he was seventeen years of age. At that period, and for a long time afterwards, the only exercise, except the Latin Theses, given at the public commencement, to the class of Bachelors, was the Salutatory, which was also a Valedictory, Oration in Latin. This exercise was awarded to Edwards, as sustaining the highest rank as a scholar among the members of the class.

He resided at college nearly two years after he took his first degree, preparing himself for the work of the ministry; after which, having passed the customary trials, he received a licence to preach: this was in the nineteenth year of his age. In consequence of an application from a number of ministers in New England, who were intrusted to act in behalf of the presbyterians in New York, he went to that city in the beginning of August, 1722, and preached there with great acceptance, about eight months. While there he found a most happy residence in the house of a Mrs. Smith; whom, as well as her son Mr. John Smith, he regarded as persons of uncommon piety and purity of life, and with whom he formed an intimate christian friendship. There also he found a considerable number of persons, among the members of that church, exhibiting the same character; with whom he enjoyed, in a high degree, all the pleasures and advantages of christian intercourse. His personal attachment to them became strong; and their interest in him as a man and a preacher was such, that they warmly solicited him to remain with them for life. To decline their candid invitation was most distressing to his feelings; but on account of the smallness of that congregation, and some peculiar difficulties which attended it, he did not think there was a rational prospect of usefulness and comfort. After a most painful parting with the kind friends, under whose hospitable roof he had so long and happily resided, he left the city on Friday, the 26th of April, by water, and reached his father's house on Wednesday, the 1st of May. Here he spent the summer in close study, during which he was again earnestly requested, by the congregation in New York, to return to that city, and settle among them; but his former views were not altered; and therefore, though strongly inclined from his own feelings to gratify them, he could not comply with their wishes. Probably in no part of his life had he higher advantage for spiritual contemplation and enjoyment, than in the period first mentioned. He went to New York in a delightful frame of mind. He found there a little flock of Christ, constrained from a sense of their own weakness to "dwell together in unity," and to feel a practical sense of their dependence on God. He was in the midst of a family, whose daily influence served only to refresh and to sanctify. He had also much leisure for religious reading, meditation, and prayer. In these circumstances the presence of the Comforter appears to have been a daily reality; the evidence of which he found in that purity of heart which enables its possessor to see God, in the peace which passeth all understanding, and the joy with which a stranger intermeddleth not.

During his preparation for the ministry, his residence in New York, and his subsequent residence in his father's house, he formed a series of *resolutions,* to the number of seventy, intended obviously for himself alone, to regulate his own heart and life, but fitted also, from their christian simplicity and spiritual-mindedness, to be eminently useful to others. Of these the first thirty-four* were written before Dec. 18, 1722, the time in which his Diary, as it now exists, commences. The particular time and occasion of making many of the rest, will be found in that most interesting narrative, in which also are many other rules and resolutions, intended for the regulation of his own affections, of perhaps equal excellence. It should be remembered they were all written before he was twenty years of age. As he was wholly averse to all profession and ostentation; and as these resolutions themselves were plainly intended for no other eye than his own, except the eye that is omniscient; they may be justly considered as the basis of his conduct and character, the plan by which he governed the secret as well as the publick actions of his life. As such they will deeply interest the reader, not only as they unfold the inmost mind of their author, but as they also show, in a manner most striking and convincing to the conscience, what is the true foundation of great and distinguished excellence.

He was too well acquainted with human weakness and frailty, even where the intentions are most sincere, to enter on any resolutions rashly, or from a reliance on his own strength. He therefore in the outset looked to God for aid, who alone can afford success in the use of the best means, and in the intended accomplishment of the best purposes. This he places at the head of all his other important rules, that his whole dependence was on the grace of God, while he still proposes to recur to a frequent and serious perusal of them, in order that they might become the habitual directory of his life.

RESOLUTIONS.

"Being sensible that I am unable to do any thing without God's help, I do humbly entreat him, by his grace, to enable me to keep these Resolutions, so far as they are agreeable to his will, for Christ's sake.

Remember to read over these Resolutions once a week.

1. *Resolved,* That *I will do whatsoever* I think to be most to the glory of God, and my own good, profit, and pleasure, in the whole of my duration; without any consideration of the time, whether now, or never so many myriads of ages hence. *Resolved,* to do whatever I think to be my *duty,* and most for the good and advantage of mankind in general. *Resolved,* so to do, whatever *difficulties* I meet with, how many soever, and how great soever.

2. *Resolved,* To be continually endeavouring to find out some *new contrivance* and invention to promote the forementioned things.

3. *Resolved,* If ever I shall fall and grow dull, so as to neglect to keep any part of these Resolutions, to repent of all I can remember, when I come to myself again.

4. *Resolved,* Never *to do* any manner of thing, whether in soul or body, less or more, but what tends to the glory of God, nor *be,* nor *suffer* it, if I can possibly avoid it.

5. *Resolved,* Never to lose one moment of time, but to improve it in the most profitable way I possibly can.

6. *Resolved,* To live with all my might, while I do live.

7. *Resolved,* Never to do any thing, which I should be afraid to do if it were the last hour of my life.

8. *Resolved,* To act, in all respects, both speaking and doing, as if nobody had been so vile as I, and as if I had committed the same sins, or had the same infirmities or failings, as others; and that I will let the knowledge of their failings promote nothing but shame in myself, and prove only an occasion of my confessing my own sins and misery to God. *Vid.* July 30.

9. *Resolved,* To think much, on all occasions, of my dying, and of the common circumstances which attend death.

10. *Resolved,* When I feel pain, to think of the pains of martyrdom, and of hell.

11. *Resolved,* When I think of any theorem in divinity to be solved, immediately to do what I can towards solving it, if circumstances do not hinder.

* The first twenty-one were written at once, with the same pen; as were the next ten, at a subsequent sitting. The rest were written occasionally. They are all on two detached pieces of paper.

12. *Resolved,* If I take delight in it as a gratification of pride, or vanity, or on any such account, immediately to throw it by.

13. *Resolved,* To be endeavouring to find out fit objects of liberality and charity.

14. *Resolved,* Never to do any thing out of revenge.

15. *Resolved,* Never to suffer the least motions of anger towards irrational beings.

16. *Resolved,* Never to speak evil of any one, so that it shall tend to his dishonour, more or less, upon no account except for some real good.

17. *Resolved,* That I will live so, as I shall wish I had done when I come to die.

18. *Resolved,* To live so, at all times, as I think is best in my most devout frames, and when I have the clearest notions of the things of the gospel, and another world.

19. *Resolved,* Never to do any thing, which I should be afraid to do, if I expected it would not be above an hour before I should hear the last trump.

20. *Resolved,* To maintain the strictest temperance in eating and drinking.

21. *Resolved,* Never to do any thing, which if I should see in another, I should count a just occasion to despise him for, or to think any way the more meanly of him.

22. *Resolved,* To endeavour to obtain for myself as much happiness in the other world as I possibly can, with all the power, might, vigour, and vehemence, yea violence, I am capable of, or can bring myself to exert, in any way that can be thought of.

23. *Resolved,* Frequently to take some deliberate action, which seems most unlikely to be done, for the glory of God, and trace it back to the original intention, designs, and ends of it; and if I find it not to be for God's glory, to repute it as a breach of the fourth Resolution.

24. *Resolved,* Whenever I do any conspicuously evil action, to trace it back, till I come to the original cause; and then, both carefully endeavour to do so no more, and to fight and pray with all my might against the original of it.

25. *Resolved,* To examine carefully and constantly, what that one thing in me is, which causes me in the least to doubt of the love of God; and so direct all my forces against it.

26. *Resolved,* To cast away such things as I find do abate my assurance.

27. *Resolved,* Never wilfully to omit any thing, except the omission be for the glory of God; and frequently to examine my omissions.

28. *Resolved,* To study the Scriptures so steadily, constantly, and frequently, as that I may find, and plainly perceive, myself to grow in the knowledge of the same.

29. *Resolved,* Never to count that a prayer, nor to let that pass as a prayer, nor that as a petition of a prayer, which is so made, that I cannot hope that God will answer it; nor that as a confession which I cannot hope God will accept.

30. *Resolved,* To strive every week to be brought higher in religion, and to a higher exercise of grace, than I was the week before.

31. *Resolved,* Never to say any thing at all against any body, but when it is perfectly agreeable to the highest degree of christian honour, and of love to mankind, agreeable to the lowest humility, and sense of my own faults and failings, and agreeable to the golden rule; often, when I have said any thing against any one, to bring it to, and try it strictly by, the test of this Resolution.

32. *Resolved,* To be strictly and firmly faithful to my trust, that that, in Prov. xx. 6. 'A faithful man, who can find?' may not be partly fulfilled in me.

33. *Resolved,* To do always what I can towards making, maintaining, and preserving peace, when it can be done without an overbalancing detriment in other respects. Dec. 26, 1722.

34. *Resolved,* In narrations, never to speak any thing but the pure and simple verity.

35. *Resolved,* Whenever I so much question whether I have done my duty, as that my quiet and calm is thereby disturbed, to set it down, and also how the question was resolved. Dec. 18, 1722.

36. *Resolved,* Never to speak evil of any, except I have some particular good call to it. Dec. 19, 1722.

37. *Resolved,* To inquire every night, as I am going to bed, wherein I have been negligent,—what sin I have committed,—and wherein I have denied myself;—also, at the end of every week, month, and year. Dec. 22 and 26, 1722.

38. *Resolved,* Never to utter any thing that is sportive, or matter of laughter, on a Lord's day. Sabbath evening, Dec. 23, 1722.

39. *Resolved,* Never to do any thing, of which I so much question the lawfulness, as that I intend, at the same time, to consider and examine afterwards, whether it be lawful or not; unless I as much question the lawfulness of the omission.

40. *Resolved,* To inquire every night before I go to bed, whether I have acted in the best way I possibly could, with respect to eating and drinking. Jan. 7, 1723.

41. *Resolved,* To ask myself, at the end of every day, week, month, and year, wherein I could possibly, in any respect, have done better. Jan. 11, 1723.

42. *Resolved,* Frequently to renew the dedication of myself to God, which was made at my baptism, which I solemnly renewed when I was received into the communion of the church, and which I have solemnly re-made this 12th day of January, 1723.

43. *Resolved,* Never, henceforward, till I die, to act as if I were any way my own, but entirely and altogether God's; agreeably to what is to be found in Saturday, Jan. 12th. *Jan.* 12, 1723.

44. *Resolved,* That no other end but religion shall have any influence at all on any of my actions; and that no action shall be, in the least circumstance, any otherwise than the religious end will carry it. Jan. 12, 1723.

45. *Resolved,* Never to allow any pleasure or grief, joy or sorrow, nor any affection at all, nor any degree of affection, nor any circumstance relating to it, but what helps religion. Jan. 12 and 13, 1723.

46. *Resolved,* Never to allow the least measure of any fretting or uneasiness at my father or mother. *Resolved,* to suffer no effects of it, so much as in the least alteration of speech, or motion of my eye; and to be especially careful of it with respect to any of our family.

47. *Resolved,* To endeavour, to my utmost, to deny whatever is not most agreeable to a good and universally sweet and benevolent, quiet, peaceable, contented and easy, compassionate and generous, humble and meek, submissive and obliging, diligent and industrious, charitable and even, patient, moderate, forgiving, and sincere, temper; and to do, at all times, what such a temper would

lead me to; and to examine strictly, at the end of every week, whether I have so done. Sabbath morning, May 5, 1723.

48. *Resolved,* Constantly, with the utmost niceness and diligence, and the strictest scrutiny, to be looking into the state of my soul, that I may know whether I have truly an interest in Christ or not; that when I come to die, I may not have any negligence respecting this to repent of. May 26, 1723.

49. *Resolved,* That this never shall be, if I can help it.

50. *Resolved,* That I will act so, as I think I shall judge would have been best, and most prudent, when I come into the future world. July 5, 1723.

51. *Resolved,* That I will act so, in every respect, as I think I shall wish I had done, if I should at last be damned. July 8, 1723.

52. I frequently hear persons in old age say how they would live, if they were to live their lives over again: *Resolved,* That I will live just so as I can think I shall wish I had done, supposing I live to old age. July 8, 1723.

53. *Resolved,* To improve every opportunity, when I am in the best and happiest frame of mind, to cast and venture my soul on the Lord Jesus Christ, to trust and confide in him, and consecrate myself wholly to him; that from this I may have assurance of my safety, knowing that I confide in my Redeemer. July 8, 1723.

54. *Resolved,* Whenever I hear anything spoken in commendation of any person, if I think it would be praiseworthy in me, that I will endeavour to imitate it. July 8, 1723.

55. *Resolved,* To endeavour, to my utmost, so to act, as I can think I should do, if I had already seen the happiness of heaven and hell torments. July 8, 1723.

56. *Resolved,* Never to give over, nor in the least to slacken, my fight with my corruptions, however unsuccessful I may be.

57. *Resolved,* When I fear misfortunes and adversity, to examine whether I have done my duty, and resolve to do it, and let the event be just as Providence orders it. I will, as far as I can, be concerned about nothing but my duty and my sin. June 9, and July 13, 1723.

58. *Resolved,* Not only to refrain from an air of dislike, fretfulness, and anger in conversation, but to exhibit an air of love, cheerfulness, and benignity. May 27, and July 13, 1723.

59. *Resolved,* When I am most conscious of provocations to ill nature and anger, that I will strive most to feel and act good-naturedly; yea, at such times, to manifest good nature, though I think that in other respects it would be disadvantageous, and so as would be imprudent at other times. May 12, July 11, and July 13.

60. *Resolved,* Whenever my feelings begin to appear in the least out of order, when I am conscious of the least uneasiness within, or the least irregularity without, I will then subject myself to the strictest examination. July 4 and 13, 1723.

61. *Resolved,* That I will not give way to that listlessness which I find unbends and relaxes my mind from being fully and fixedly set on religion, whatever excuse I may have for it—that what my listlessness inclines me to do, is best to be done, &c. May 21, and July 13, 1723.

62. *Resolved,* Never to do any thing but my duty, and then, according to Eph. vi. 6—8. to do it willingly and cheerfully, as unto the Lord, and not to man: knowing that whatever good thing any man doth, the same shall he receive of the Lord. June 25, and July 13, 1723.

63. On the supposition, that there never was to be but one individual in the world, at any one time, who was properly a complete Christian, in all respects of a right stamp, having Christianity always shining in its true lustre, and appearing excellent and lovely, from whatever part and under whatever character viewed: *Resolved,* To act just as I would do, if I strove with all my might to be that one, who should live in my time. Jan. 14, and July 13, 1723.

64. *Resolved,* When I find those "*groanings which cannot be uttered,*" of which the apostle speaks, and those "*breathings of soul* for the longing it hath," of which the psalmist speaks, Psalm cxix. 20. that I will promote them to the utmost of my power; and that I will not be weary of earnestly endeavouring to vent my desires, nor of the repetitions of such earnestness. July 23, and Aug. 10, 1723.

65. *Resolved,* Very much to exercise myself in this, all my life long, *viz.* with the greatest openness of which I am capable, to declare my ways to God, and lay open my soul to him, all my sins, temptations, difficulties, sorrows, fears, hopes, desires, and every thing, and every circumstance, according to Dr. Manton's Sermon on the 119th Psalm. July 26, and Aug. 10, 1723.

66. *Resolved,* That I will endeavour always to keep a benign aspect, and air of acting and speaking, in all places, and in all companies, except it should so happen that duty requires otherwise.

67. *Resolved,* After afflictions, to inquire, what I am the better for them; what good I have got by them; and, what I might have got by them.

68. *Resolved,* To confess frankly to myself, all that which I find in myself, either infirmity or sin; and, if it be what concerns religion, also to confess the whole case to God, and implore needed help. July 23, and August 10, 1723.

69. *Resolved,* Always to do that, which I shall wish I had done when I see others do it. Aug. 11, 1723.

70. Let there be something of benevolence in all that I speak. Aug. 17, 1723."

Such were the excellent Resolutions formed by Jonathan Edwards at an early period of life, and which in succeeding years were regarded by him, not as unimportant records, but as containing the great principles of the spiritual life, A deep and extensive knowledge of the heart is manifest in these Resolutions, a conviction of its defects, a lively apprehension of its dangers, and an intense concern that all its tendencies should be towards God, and towards every thing required by his holy will. There is a remarkable tenderness of conscience discovered in every particular which has been stated. The man who could thus write, was not one who could easily trifle with sin, or who could enter any of its paths without the immediate reproofs of an offended conscience. This holy man trembled even at the distant view of sin; he could not willingly come near and survey its enticements. Accustomed to breathe in a holy atmosphere, the least taint of corruption immediately affected his spiritual frame. He knew no happiness except that connected with a conscience void of offence. All these rules were the suggestions of a conscience of a highly enlightened character.——They also indicate a constant sense of the presence and exact observations of the Searcher of all hearts. The writer lived as seeing him who is invisible; he set the Lord always before him; encouraging upon all occasions an earnest concern for the glory of God, the grand object for which he desired to live both upon earth and in heaven, an object compared with which all other things seemed in his view but trifles. If this were attained, all his desires were satisfied; but if this were lost or imperfectly gained, his soul was filled with anguish. These Resolutions afford ample testimony how much the author had entered into the spirit of 1 Cor. x. 31. *Whether therefore ye eat, or drink, or whatsoever ye do, do all to the glory of God.* They also illustrate his views of the importance of consistency of character. He was not content with accurate views of truth, or any kind of outward profession, apart from holy consistency of character. He studied, he admired, and he exhibited the influence of the gospel; a walk "worthy of the vocation wherewith he was called" was the elevated object at which he ardently aimed. He well knew that the followers of Christ are required "to hold forth the word of life," to shine as lights in the world, to instruct by their examples as well as by their words; and he desired to honour God by presenting to the view of the members of the spiritual kingdom, and also of the world, an example which might declare the reality and the beauty of religion. It is further manifest from these Resolutions, that his mind was most anxious for daily advancement in every branch of holiness. An active spiritual principle existed in him, which caused him to press forward, whatever might be the obstacles in his way. He could not be contented while one sin remained in him, while one grace was defective, or a single duty engaged in but imperfectly. He longed for the holy perfection of the heavenly world, and anticipated with joy that day when he should awake with the Divine likeness. It cannot be a matter of surprise, that with these sentiments and feelings he attained an exaltation of character seldom equalled and perhaps never surpassed.

The Resolutions which have given rise to these reflections are probably, "to persons of every age, but especially to the young, the best uninspired summary of christian duty, the best directory to high attainment in evangelical virtue, which the mind of man has hitherto been able to form." They disclose the writer's own character, and they are admirably calculated to improve the character of every reader who fears to sin, and rejoices in the purity of the Divine will.

CHAPTER IV.

HIS DIARY.

THE views and practices of men of equal excellence have differed considerably in regard to the keeping of a diary. Many have never attempted it; some who at one period of life commenced it have afterwards from various causes declined it; and others have steadily adhered to a custom which certainly has the sanction of some of the most eminent names in the church of God. It is at once admitted that many diaries have been kept in the most injudicious manner, and it is still more an object of deep regret that these records have in some instances been published, not merely to the grief of serious and intelligent minds, but to the injury of religion itself, and the exciting a prejudice against all similar records. There are, however, some published journals of excellent men, which evince so much solid judgment as well as fervent piety, and have been the sources of so much usefulness, that a more than equal balance is presented against works in part of an opposite description. No one is disposed to lament the publication of parts of the Diaries of Philip and Matthew Henry, Brainerd, Doddridge, or Joseph Williams and some others; writings which illustrate the inward and outward power of godliness, reflect honour upon the individuals themselves, and yield a powerful and holy stimulus to the minds of other Christians. The Diary of Jonathan Edwards corresponds in its excellencies with those to which reference is thus made, and will be perused with the same feelings, and lead it is hoped to the like beneficial effects.—This Diary begins Dec. 18, 1722, when he was nineteen years of age. As far as to Jan. 15th, at night, it is written on two detached slips of paper; and the remainder in a book.* As it commences abruptly, and as near as possible to the top of that paper, the beginning of it is undoubtedly lost; and it is not improbable, that, as he originally wrote it, it may have reached back, at least to the period of his preparation for the ministry. It was intended, as will at once be perceived, for his own private use exclusively; and had it been with him at the close of life, it is not unlikely it might have been destroyed. "Still, whatever is calculated to do good, and is perfectly consistent with an author's real reputation, may be published with honour, whatever his design might be while writing. The best of men, indeed, have thoughts, and opinions, and feelings, which are perfectly proper and right in themselves, which yet it would be wholly improper for them to disclose to others. But a man of sound discretion will take care that nothing of this nature is placed within the reach of accident. What Mr. Edwards wished to have concealed from every eye but his own, he wrote in *short hand;* and on one occasion, after having written to a considerable extent in that character, he adds this remark in his customary hand, 'Remember to act according to Prov. xii. 23. A prudent man concealeth knowledge.'"

† "The reader, while perusing the Diary in its various parts, will be struck with it as possessing the following characteristics. It consists of facts; and of solid thought, dictated by deep religious feeling; and not of the mere expressions of feeling, or of common-place moral reflections or exhortations. It was intended for his own eyes exclusively; and not chiefly for those of his friends and of the public. It is an exhibition of the simple thinking,

* He mentions, Jan. 14, his making the book, and annexing the loose papers to it.

† Dwight.

feeling, and acting of a man, who is unconscious how he appears, except to himself and to God; and not the remarks of one, who is desirous of being thought humble, respecting his own humility. If we suppose a man of christian simplicity and godly sincerity to bring all the secret movements of his own soul under the clear, strong light of heaven, and there to survey them with a piercing and an honest eye, and a contrite heart, in order to humble himself, and make himself better; it is just the account which such a man would write."

DIARY.—*December*, 1722.

" *Dec.* 18. This day made the 35th Resolution. The reason why I in the least question my interest in God's love and favour, is,—1. Because I cannot speak so fully to my experience of that preparatory work, of which divines speak:—2. I do not remember that I experienced regeneration, exactly in those steps, in which divines say it is generally wrought:—3. I do not feel the christian graces sensibly enough, particularly faith. I fear they are only such hypocritical outside affections, which wicked men may feel as well as others. They do not seem to be sufficiently inward, full, sincere, entire, and hearty. They do not seem so substantial, and so wrought into my very nature, as I could wish.—4. Because I am sometimes guilty of sins of omission and commission. Lately I have doubted, whether I do not transgress in evil speaking. This day, resolved, No.

Dec. 19. This day made the 36th Resolution. Lately I have been very much perplexed, by seeing the doctrine of different degrees in glory questioned; but now have almost got over the difficulty.

Dec. 20. This day somewhat questioned, whether ₋ had not been guilty of negligence yesterday, and this morning; but resolved, No.

Dec. 21, *Friday.* This day and yesterday, I was exceedingly dull, dry, and dead.

Dec. 22, *Saturday.* This day, revived by God's Holy Spirit; affected with the sense of the excellency of holiness; felt more exercise of love to Christ, than usual. Have, also, felt sensible repentance for sin, because it was committed against so merciful and good a God. This night made the 37th Resolution.

Sabbath night, *Dec.* 23. Made the 38th Resolution.

Monday, *Dec.* 24. Higher thoughts than usual of the excellency of Christ and his kingdom.—Concluded to observe, at the end of every month, the number of breaches of resolutions, to see whether they increase or diminish, to begin from this day, and to compute from that the weekly account my monthly increase, and out of the whole, my yearly increase, beginning from new-year days.

Wednesday, *Dec.* 26. Early in the morning yesterday, was hindered by the head-ache all day; though I hope I did not lose much. Made an addition to the 37th Resolution, concerning weeks, months, and years.—*At night.* Made the 33d Resolution.

Saturday, *Dec.* 29. About sunset this day, dull and lifeless.

1722-23, *Tuesday*, *Jan.* 1. Have been dull for several days. Examined whether I have not been guilty of negligence to-day; and resolved, No.

Wednesday, *Jan.* 2. Dull. I find, by experience, that, let me make resolutions, and do what I will, with never so many inventions, it is all nothing, and to no purpose at all, without the motions of the Spirit of God; for if the Spirit of God should be as much withdrawn from me always, as for the week past, notwithstanding all I do, I should not grow, but should languish, and miserably fade away. I perceive, if God should withdraw his Spirit a little more, I should not hesitate to break my resolutions, and should soon arrive at my old state. There is no dependence on myself. Our resolutions may be at the highest one day, and yet, the next day, we may be in a miserable dead condition, not at all like the same person who resolved. So that it is to no purpose to resolve, except we depend on the grace of God. For, if it were not for his mere grace, one might be a very good man one day, and a very wicked one the next. I find also by experience, that there is no guessing out the ends of Providence, in particular dispensations towards me—any otherwise than as afflictions come as corrections for sin, and God intends when we meet with them, to desire us to look back on our ways, and see wherein we have done amiss, and lament that particular sin, and all our sins, before him:—knowing this, also, that all things shall work together for our good; not knowing in what way, indeed, but trusting in God.

Saturday evening, *Jan.* 5. A little redeemed from a long dreadful dulness, about reading the Scriptures. This week, have been unhappily low in the weekly account:—and what are the reasons of it?—abundance of listlessness and sloth; and, if this should continue much longer, I perceive that other sins will begin to discover themselves. It used to appear to me, that I had not much sin remaining; but now, I perceive that there are great remainders of sin. Where may it not bring me to, if God should leave me? Sin is not enough mortified. Without the influences of the Spirit of God, the old serpent would begin to rouse up himself from his frozen state, and would come to life again. *Resolved,* that I have been negligent in two things:—in not striving enough in duty; and in not forcing myself upon religious thoughts.

Sabbath, *Jan.* 6. *At night.* Much concerned about the improvement of precious time. Intend to live in continual mortification, without ceasing, and even to weary myself thereby, as long as I am in this world, and never to expect or desire any worldly ease or pleasure.

Monday, *Jan.* 7. At night, made the 40th Resolution.

Tuesday, *Jan.* 8. In the morning, had higher thoughts than usual of the excellency of Christ, and felt an unusual repentance of sin therefrom.

Wednesday, *Jan.* 9. *At night.* Decayed. I am sometimes apt to think, that I have a great deal more of holiness than I really have. I find now and then that abominable corruption, which is directly contrary to what I read of eminent Christians. I do not seem to be half so careful to improve time, to do every thing quick, and in as short a time as I possibly can, nor to be perpetually engaged to think about religion, as I was yesterday and the day before, nor indeed as I have been at certain times, perhaps a twelvemonth ago. If my resolutions of that nature, from that time, had always been kept alive and awake, how much better might I have been than I now am! How deceitful is my heart! I take up a strong resolution, but how soon doth it weaken!

Thursday. Jan. 10, *About noon.* Recovering. It is a great dishonour to Christ, in whom I hope I have an interest, to be uneasy at my worldly state and condition; or when I see the prosperity of others, and that all things go easy with them, the world is smooth to them, and they are very happy in many respects, and very prosperous, or are advanced to much honour; to grudge them their prosperity, or envy them on account of it, or to be in the least uneasy at it, to wish and long for the same prosperity, and to desire that it should ever be so with me. Wherefore, concluded always to rejoice in every one's prosperity, and not to pretend to expect or desire it for myself; and to expect no happiness of that nature, as long as I live; but to depend on afflictions, and to betake myself entirely to another happiness.—I think I find myself much more sprightly and healthy, both in body and mind, for my self-denial in eating, drinking, and sleeping. I think it would be advantageous, every morning to consider my business and temptations, and the sins to which I shall be exposed on that day, and to make a resolution how to improve the day, and avoid those sins; and so at the beginning of every week, month, and year. I never knew before what was meant, by not setting our hearts on those things. It is, not to care about them, nor to depend upon them, nor to afflict ourselves with the fear of losing them, nor to please ourselves with the expectation of obtaining them, or with the hopes of their continuance.—*At night*. Made the 41st Resolution.

Saturday, Jan. 12. *In the morning*. I have, this day, solemnly renewed my baptismal covenant and self-dedication, which I renewed when I was taken into the communion of the church. I have been before God, and have given myself, all that I am and have, to God; so that I am not, in any respect, my own. I can challenge no right in this understanding, this will, these affections, which are in me. Neither have I any right to this body, or any of its members—no right to this tongue, these hands, these feet; no right to these senses, these eyes, these ears, this smell, or this taste. I have given myself clear away, and have not retained any thing as my own. I gave myself to God in my baptism, and I have been this morning to him, and told him, that I gave myself *wholly* to him. I have given every power to him; so that, for the future, I'll challenge no right in myself, in no respect whatever. I have expressly promised him, and I do now promise Almighty God, that by his grace I will not. I have this morning told him that I did take him for my whole portion and felicity, looking on nothing else as any part of my happiness, nor acting as if it were; and his law, for the constant rule of my obedience; and would fight with all my might against the world, the flesh, and the devil, to the end of my life; and that I did believe in Jesus Christ, and did receive him as a Prince and Saviour; and that I would adhere to the faith and obedience of the gospel, however hazardous and difficult the confession and practice of it may be; and that I did receive the blessed Spirit as my Teacher, Sanctifier, and only Comforter, and cherish all his motions to enlighten, purify, confirm, comfort, and assist me. This, I have done; and I pray God, for the sake of Christ, to look upon it as a self-dedication, and to receive me now as entirely his own, and to deal with me, in all respects, as such, whether he afflicts me or prospers me, or whatever he pleases to do with me, who am his. Now, henceforth, I am not to act, in any respect, as my own.—I shall act as my own, if I ever make use of any of my powers to any thing that is not to the glory of God, and do not make the glorifying of him my whole and entire business:—if I murmur in the least at affliction; if I grieve at the prosperity of others; if I am in any way uncharitable; if I am angry because of injuries; if I revenge them; if I do any thing purely to please myself, or if I avoid any thing for the sake of my own ease; if I omit any thing because it is great self-denial; if I trust to myself; if I take any of the praise of the good that I do, or that God doth by me; or if I am in any way proud. This day, made the 42nd and 43rd Resolutions.—Whether or no, any other end ought to have any influence at all on any of my actions; or whether any action ought to be any otherwise, in any respect, than it would be, if nothing else but religion had the least influence on my mind. Wherefore I make the 44th Resolution.

Query: Whether any delight or satisfaction ought to be allowed, because any other end is obtained beside a religious one.—*In the afternoon*. I answer, Yes, because, if we should never suffer ourselves to rejoice, but because we have obtained a religious end, we should never rejoice at the sight of friends, we should not allow ourselves any pleasure in our food, whereby the animal spirits would be withdrawn, and good digestion hindered. But the query is to be answered thus:—We never ought to allow any joy or sorrow, but what helps religion. Wherefore, I make the 45th Resolution.

The reason why I so soon grow lifeless, and unfit for the business I am about, I have found out, is only because I have been used to suffer myself to leave off, for the sake of ease, and so I have acquired a habit of expecting ease; and therefore, when I think I have exercised myself a great while, I cannot keep myself to it any longer, because I expect to be released, as my due and right. And then I am deceived, as if I were really tired and weary, whereas, if I did not expect ease, and was resolved to occupy myself by business as much as I could, I should continue with the same vigour at my business, without vacation time to rest. Thus I have found it in reading the Scriptures; and thus I have found it in prayer; and thus I believe it to be in getting sermons by heart, and in other things.

At night. This week, the weekly account rose higher than ordinary. It is suggested to me, that too constant a mortification, and too vigorous application to religion, may be prejudicial to health; but nevertheless, I will plainly feel it and experience it, before I cease on this account. It is no matter how much tired and weary I am, if my health is not impaired.

Sabbath day, Jan. 13. I plainly feel, that if I should continue to go on, as from the beginning of the last week hitherto, I should continually grow and increase in grace. After the afternoon meeting, made an addition to the 45th Resolution.—*At noon*. I remember I thought that I loved to be a member of Christ, and not any thing distinct, but only a part, so as to have no separate interest or pleasure of my own.—*At night*. Resolved to endeavour fully to understand 1 Cor. vii. 29—32. and to act according to it.

Monday, Jan. 14. About 10 o'clock in the morning made this book, and put these papers in it.* The dedication, which I made of myself to God on Saturday last, has been exceedingly useful to me. I thought I had a more spiritual insight into the Scriptures, when reading the 8th of Romans, than ever before.—*At night*. Great instances of mortification are deep wounds given to the body of sin; hard blows, which make him stagger and reel. We thereby get strong ground and footing against him, he is the weaker ever after, and we have easier work

* He refers to slips of paper on which the first part of the Diary is written; as far as Jan. 15, *at night*.

with him the next time. He grows cowardly; and we can easily cause him to give way, until at length we find it easy work with him, and can kill him at pleasure. While we live without great instances of mortification and self-denial, the old man keeps about where he was; for he is sturdy and obstinate, and will not stir for small blows. This, without doubt, is one great reason why many Christians do not sensibly increase in grace. After the greatest mortifications, I always find the greatest comfort. Wrote the 63rd Resolution. Such little things as Christians commonly do, will not evince much increase of grace. We must do great things for God.—It will be best, when I find that I have lost any former ancient good motions or actions, to take notice of it, if I can remember them.

Tuesday, Jan. 15. *About two or three o'clock.* I have been all this time decaying. It seemed yesterday, the day before, and Saturday, that I should always retain the same resolutions to the same height. But alas! how soon do I decay! O how weak, how infirm, how unable to do any thing of myself! What a poor inconsistent being! What a miserable wretch, without the assistance of the Spirit of God! While I stand, I am ready to think that I stand by my own strength, and upon my own legs; and I am ready to triumph over my spiritual enemies, as if it were I myself that caused them to flee:—when alas! I am but a poor infant, upheld by Jesus Christ; who holds me up, and gives me liberty to smile to see my enemies flee, when he drives them before me. And so I laugh, as though I myself did it, when it is only Jesus Christ leads me along, and fights himself against my enemies. And now the Lord has a little left me, how weak do I find myself! O let it teach me to depend less on myself, to be more humble, and to give more of the praise of my ability to Jesus Christ! The heart of man is deceitful above all things, and desperately wicked; who can know it?—The occasion of my decaying, is a little melancholy. My spirits are depressed, because I fear that I lost some friendship the last night; and, my spirits being depressed, my resolutions have lost their strength. I differ to-day from yesterday in these things: I do not resolve anything to-day half so strongly. I am not so perpetually thinking of renewing my resolutions as I was then. I am not half so vigorous as I was then; nor am I half so careful to do every thing with vigour. Then, I kept continually acting; but now, I do things slowly, and satisfy myself by thinking of religion in the mean time. I am not so careful to go from one business to another.—I felt humiliation about sun-set. What shall I do, in order that I may, with a good grace, fall into christian discourse and conversation?—*At night.* The next time I am in such a lifeless frame, I will force myself to go rapidly from one thing to another, and to do those things with vigour, in which vigour would ever be useful. The things which take off my mind, when bent on religion, are commonly some remarkable change or alteration—journeys, change of place, change of business, change of studies, and change of other circumstances; or something that makes me melancholy; or some sin.

Thursday, Jan. 17. About three o'clock, overwhelmed with melancholy.

Friday, Jan. 18. *At night.* Beginning to endeavour to recover out of the death I have been in for these several days.

Sabbath day, Jan. 20. *At night.* The last week I was sunk so low, that I fear it will be a long time before I am recovered. I fell exceedingly low in the weekly account. I find my heart so deceitful, that I am almost discouraged from making any more resolutions.—Wherein have I been negligent in the week past; and how could I have done better, to help the dreadful low estate in which I am sunk?

Monday Jan. 21. Before sunrise, answered the preceding questions thus: I ought to have spent my time in bewailing my sins, and in singing psalms—especially psalms or hymns of penitence; these duties being most suited to the frame I was in. I do not spend time enough in endeavouring to affect myself with the glories of Christianity.—Fell short in the monthly account. It seems to me, that I am fallen from my former sense of the pleasantness of religion.

Tuesday, Feb. 5. *At night.* I have thought that this being so exceedingly careful, and so particularly anxious, to force myself to think of religion at all times, has exceedingly distracted my mind, and made me altogether unfit for that and every thing else. I have thought that this caused the dreadful low condition I was in on the 15th of January. I think that I stretched myself further than I could bear, and so broke.—But now it seems to me, though I know not why, that I do not do enough to prepare for another world. I do not seem to press forward, to fight and wrestle, as the apostles used to speak. I do not seem so greatly and constantly to mortify and deny myself, as the mortification of which they speak represents. Therefore, wherein ought I to do more in this way?—I answer: I am again grown too careless about eating, drinking, and sleeping—not careful enough about evil-speaking.

Saturday, Feb. 16. I do certainly know that I love holiness, such as the gospel prescribes.—*At night.* For the time past of my life, I have been negligent, in that I have not sufficiently kept up that part of divine worship, singing the praise of God in secret and with company.—I have been negligent this month past, in these three things: I have not been watchful enough over my appetites, in eating and drinking; in rising too late in the morning; and in not applying myself with sufficient application to the duty of secret prayer.

Sabbath day, Feb. 17. *Near sunset.* Renewedly promised, that I will accept of God for my whole portion, and that I will be contented, whatever else I am denied. I will not murmur, nor be grieved, whatever prosperity upon any account I see others enjoy and I am denied. To this I have lately acted contrary.

Thursday, Feb. 21. I perceive that I never yet have adequately known what was meant by being weaned from the world, by not laying up treasure on earth, but in heaven, by not having our portion in this life, by making the concerns of another life our whole business, by taking God for our whole portion. I find my heart in great part yet adheres to the earth. O that it might be quite separated from thence. I find when I have power and reputation as others, I am uneasy, and it does not satisfy me to tell me, that I have chosen God for my whole portion, and that I have promised to rest entirely contented with him.

Saturday, Feb. 23. I find myself miserably negligent, and that I might do twice the business that I do, if I were set upon it. See how soon my thoughts of this matter will be differing from what they are now. I have been indulging a horrid laziness a good while, and did not know it. I can do seven times as much in the same time now, as I can at other times, not because my faculties are in better tune; but because of the fire of diligence that I feel burning within me. If I could but always continue so, I should not meet with one quarter of the trouble. I should run the christian race much better, and should go out of the world a much better man.

Saturday, March 2. O how much more base and vile am I, when I feel pride working in me, than when I am in a more humble disposition of mind! How much, how exceedingly much, more lovely is an humble than a proud disposition! I now plainly perceive it, and am really sensible of it. How immensely more pleasant is an humble delight, than a high thought of myself! How much better do I feel, when I am truly humbling myself, than when I am pleasing myself with my own perfections! O how much pleasanter is humility than pride! O that God would fill me with exceeding great humility, and that he would evermore keep me from all pride! The pleasures of humility are really the most refined, inward, and exquisite delights in the world. How hateful is a proud man! How hateful is a worm, that lifts up itself with pride! What a foolish, silly, miserable, blind, deceived poor worm am I, when pride works!—*At night*. I have lately been negligent as to reading the Scriptures. Notwithstanding my resolutions on Saturday was se'night, I have not been sedulous and diligent enough.

Wednesday, March 6. *Near sunset*. Regarded the doctrines of election, free grace, our inability to do any thing without the grace of God, and that holiness is entirely, throughout, the work of the Spirit of God, with greater pleasure than ever before.

Thursday, March 7. I think I now suffer from not forcing myself enough on religious thoughts.

Saturday night, March 24. I intend, if I am ever settled, to concert measures, and study methods, of doing good in the world, and to draw up rules of acting in this matter, in writing, of all the methods I can possibly devise, by which I can in any respect do good.

Saturday night, March 31. This week I have been too careless about eating.

Monday morning, April 2. I think it best not to allow myself to laugh at the faults, follies, and infirmities of others.

Saturday night, April 7. This week I found myself so far gone, that it seemed to me I should never recover more. Let God of his mercy return unto me, and no more leave me thus to sink and decay! I know, O Lord, that without thy help I shall fall, innumerable times, notwithstanding all my resolutions, how often soever repeated.

Saturday night, April 14. I could pray more heartily this night for the forgiveness of my enemies, than ever before.—I am somewhat apt, after having asked one petition over many times, to be weary of it; but I am now resolved not to give way to such a disposition.

Wednesday forenoon, May 1. Last night I came home, after my melancholy parting from New York.

I have always in every different state of life I have hitherto been in, thought that the troubles and difficulties of that state were greater than those of any other state that I proposed to be in; and when I have altered, with assurance of mending myself, I have still thought the same, yea that the difficulties of that state are greater than those of that I left last. Lord, grant that from hence I may learn to withdraw thoughts, affections, desires, and expectations entirely from the world, and may fix them upon the heavenly state, where there is fulness of joy; where reigns heavenly, sweet, calm, and delightful love without alloy; where there are continually the dearest expressions of this love; where there is the enjoyment of this love without ever parting; and where those persons, who appear so lovely in this world, will be inexpressibly more lovely, and full of love to us. How sweetly will those, who thus mutually love, join together in singing the praises of God and the Lamb. How full will it fill us with joy, to think that this enjoyment, these sweet exercises, will never cease or come to an end, but will last to all eternity. Remember after journeys, removals, overturnings, and alterations in the state of my life, to reflect and consider, whether therein I have managed the best way possible respecting my soul; and before such alterations, if foreseen, to resolve how to act.

Thursday, May 2. *Afternoon*. I observe this, that when I was at New York, when I meditated on things of a religious nature, I used to conceive of myself as walking in the fields at home; but now I am at home, I conceive of myself as walking in the fields which I used to frequent at New York. I think it a very good way, to examine dreams every morning when I awake; what are the nature, circumstance, principles, and ends of my imaginary actions and passions in them; in order to discern what are my prevailing inclinations, &c.

Saturday night, May 4. Although I have, in some measure, subdued a disposition to chide and fret, yet I find a certain inclination, which is not agreeable to christian sweetness of temper and conversation: either too much dogmaticalness or too much egotism; a disposition to manifest my own dislike and scorn, and my own freedom from those which are innocent, sinless, yea common infirmities of men, and many other such like things. O that God would help me to discover all the flaws and defects of my temper and conversation, and help me in the difficult work of amending them; and that he would grant me so full a measure of vital Christianity, that the foundation of all those disagreeable irregularities may be destroyed, and the contrary sweetnesses and beauties may of themselves naturally follow.

Sabbath morning, May 5. Made the 47th Resolution.

Monday morning, May 6. I think it best commonly to come before God three times in a day, except I find a great inaptitude to that duty.

Saturday night, May 11. I have been to blame, the month past, in not laying violence enough to my inclination, to force myself to a better improvement of time. Have been tardy with respect to the 47th Resolution. Have also been negligent about keeping my thoughts, when joining with others in prayer.

Sabbath-day morning, May 12. I have lost that relish of the Scriptures, and other good books, which I had five or six months ago. *Resolved*, When I find in myself the least disposition to exercise good nature, that I will then strive most to feel good-naturedly.—*At noon*. Observe to remember the meditations which I had at West Chester, as I was coming from New York; and those which I had in the orchard; and those under the oak-tree. This day, and the last night, I read over and reviewed those reflections and remarks, which I find to be a very beneficial thing to me.—*After the afternoon meeting*. I think I find in my heart to be glad from the hopes I have, that my eternity is to be spent in spiritual and holy joys, arising from the manifestation of God's love, and the exercise of holiness, and burning love to him.

Saturday night, May 18. This week past, spent in journeying to Norwich, and the towns thereabouts. This day returned, and received a letter from my dear friend, Mr. John Smith.—The last Wednesday, took up a resolution to refrain from all manner of evil speaking, for one week to try it, and see the effect of it: hoping, if that evil speaking, which I used to allow myself in, and to account lawful, agreeably to the resolutions I have formed concerning it, were not lawful, or best, I should hereby discover it, and get the advantage of temptations to it, and so deceive myself into a strict adherence to my duty, respecting that matter;—that that corruption, which I cannot conquer by main strength, I may get the victory of by stratagem. I find the effect of it already to be, to make me apt to take it for granted, that what I have resolved on this week, is a duty to be observed for ever.

I now plainly perceive, what great obligations I am under to love and honour my parents. I have great reason to believe, that their counsel and education have been my making; though, in the time of it, it seemed to do me so little good. I have good reason to hope, that their prayers for me have been, in many things, very powerful and prevalent, that God has, in many things, taken me under his care and guidance, provision and direction, in answer to their prayers for me. I was never made so sensible of it as now.

I think it the best way, in general, not to seek for honour, in any other way, than by seeking to be good and to do good. I may pursue knowledge, religion, the glory of God, and the good of mankind with the utmost vigour; but am to leave the honour of it entirely at God's disposal, as a thing with which I have no immediate concern; no, not although, by possessing that honour, I have the greater opportunity to do good.

Mem. To be particularly careful, lest I should be tardy in any point wherein I have been negligent, or have erred, in days, weeks, months, or years past.

Sabbath-day morning, May 19. With respect to my journey last week, I was not careful enough to watch opportunities of solemnly approaching to God three times a day. The last week, when I was about to take up the Wednesday Resolution, it was proposed to me, in my thought, to omit it till I got home again, because there would be a more convenient opportunity. Thus am I ready to look at any thing as an excuse, to grow slack in my christian course.—*At night.* Concluded to add to my inquiries, as to the spending of time.—At the beginning of the day, or the period, What can I do for the good of men?—and at the end, What have I done for their good?

Tuesday morning, May 21. My conscience is, undoubtedly, more calm, since my last Wednesday Resolution, than it was before.

Wednesday morning, May 22. *Memorandum.* To take special care of the following things: evil speaking, fretting, eating, drinking, and sleeping, speaking simple verity, joining in prayer, slightiness in secret prayer, listlessness and negligence, and thoughts that cherish sin.

Saturday morning, May 25. As I was this morning reading the 17th Resolution, it was suggested to me, that if I were now to die, I should wish that I had prayed more that God would make me know my state, whether it be good or bad, and that I had taken more pains and care, to see and narrowly search into that matter. Wherefore, *Mem*, for the future, most nicely and diligently to look into the opinions of our old divines, concerning conversion. This morning made the 48th Resolution.

Monday afternoon, May 27. *Memorandum.* Not only to keep from an air of dislike, anger, and fretfulness, in discourse or conversation; but, let me also have as much of an appearance of love, cheerfulness, and benignity, as may be, with a good grace. These following things especially to beware of, in order to the better observation of the 47th Resolution: distrust, discontent, uneasiness and a complaining temper, self-opinion, self-confidence, melancholy, moroseness, slight antipathy, privacy, indolence, and want of resolution—to beware of any thing in discourse or conversation that savours of these.

Saturday night, June 8. *At Boston.* When I find myself listless and dull, and not easily affected by reading religious books, then to read my resolutions, remarks, reflections, &c.—One thing that would be of great advantage to me, in reading to my profit, would be, the endeavouring, with all my might, *to keep the image and picture of the thing in my mind*, and be careful that I do not lose it in the chain of the discourse.

Sabbath day, June 9, *after the afternoon meeting. Mem.* When I fear misfortune, to examine whether I have done my duty; and at the same time, to resolve to do it, and let it go, and be concerned about nothing, but my duty and my sin.

Saturday morning, June 15. *At Windsor.* Have been to blame, this journey, with respect to strict temperance, in eating, drinking, and sleeping, and in suffering too small matters to give interruption to my wonted chain of religious exercises.—Concluded to protract the Wednesday Resolution to the end of my life.

Tuesday morning, June 18. *Mem.* To do that part, which I conveniently can, of my stated exercise, while about other business, such as self-examination, resolutions, &c. that I may do the remainder in less time.

Friday afternoon, June 21. I have abundant cause, O my merciful Father, to love thee ardently, and greatly, to bless and praise thee, that thou hast heard me, in my earnest request, and so hast answered my prayer, for mercy, to keep me from decay and sinking. O, graciously of thy mere goodness, still continue to pity my misery, by reason of my sinfulness. O, my dear Redeemer, I commit myself, together with my prayer and thanksgiving, into thine hand.

Saturday morning, June 22. Altered the 36th Resolution, to make it the same with the Wednesday Resolution. If I should take special care, every day, to rise above, or not to fall below, or to fall as little as I possibly could below, what I was the day before, it would be of great advantage to me.—I take notice that most of these determinations, when I first resolve them, seem as if they would be much more beneficial than I find them.

Tuesday morning, June 25. Last sabbath, at Boston, reading the 6th, 7th, and 8th verses of the 6th to the Ephesians, concluded that it would be much to my advantage, to take the greatest care, never to do any thing but my duty, and then to do it willingly, cheerfully, and gladly, whatever danger or unpleasant circumstances it may be attended with; with good-will doing it, as to the Lord, not as pleasing man, or myself; knowing that whatsoever good thing any man doth, the same shall he receive of the Lord.

Saturday morning, June 29. It is best to be careful in prayer, not to put up those petitions, of which I do not feel a sincere desire: thereby my prayer is rendered less sincere, less acceptable to God, and less useful to myself.

Monday noon, July 1. I find I am not careful enough, to keep out all thoughts but religious ones on the sabbath. When I find the least uneasiness in doing my duty, to fly to the 43rd Resolution.

Wednesday night, July 3. I am too negligent, with respect to improving petty opportunities of doing good; thinking, that the good will be very small and unextended, and not worth the pains. *Resolved*, to regulate this, as that which is wrong, and what ought not to be.—Again confirmed by experience, of the happy effects of a strict temperance, with respect both to body and mind.

Thursday morning, July 4. The last night, in bed, when thinking of death, I thought if I was then to die, that which would make me die in the least degree fearfully, would be the want of a trusting and relying on Jesus Christ, so distinctly and plainly, as has been described by divines; my not having experienced so particular a venturing, and entirely trusting my soul on Christ, after the fears of hell, and terrors of the Lord, encouraged by the mercy, faithfulness, and promises of God, and the gracious invitations of Christ. Then I thought I could go out of the world, as much assured of my salvation, as I was of Christ's faithfulness, knowing that if Christ did not fail me, he would save me who had trusted in him on his word.—*At night*. Whenever things begin to seem to be in the least out of order, when things begin to feel uneasy within, or irregular without, then to examine myself by the strictest examination.—*Resolved*, for the future to observe rather more of meekness, moderation, and temper in disputes.

Friday morning, July 5. Last night, when thinking what I should wish I had done, that I had not done, if I was then to die; I thought I should wish, that I had been more importunate with God to fit me for death, and lead me into all truth, and that I might not be deceived about the state of my soul.—In the forenoon made the 50th Resolution.

Thursday night, July 11. This day, too impatient at the church meeting. Snares and briers have been in my way this afternoon. It is good at such times for one to manifest good nature, even to one's disadvantage, and so as would be imprudent at other times.

Saturday morning, July 13. Transferred the conclusion of June 9, to the Resolution, No. 57; and the conclusion of May 27, to No. 58; and May 12, and July 11, to No. 59; and of July 4, *at night*, to No. 60; and of May 24, to No. 61; and of June 25, to No. 62; and about noon, the Resolution of January 14, to No. 63.—In times past, I have been too free in judging of the hearts of men from their actions.

Thursday, July 18. *Near sunset*. Resolved, to make sure of that sign, which the apostle James gives of a perfect man: James iii. 2. "If any man offend not in word, the same is a perfect man, and able, also, to bridle the whole body."

Friday afternoon, July 19. 1 Peter ii. 18. "Servants, be subject to your masters, with all fear; not only to the good and gentle, but also to the froward:" how then ought children to honour their parents!—This verse, together with the two following, *viz.* "For this is thankworthy, if a man for conscience toward God endure grief, suffering wrongfully. For what glory is it, if, when ye be buffeted for your faults, ye shall take it patiently? but if, when ye do well, and suffer for it, ye take it patiently, this is acceptable with God."

Saturday noon, July 20. Dr. Manton's Sermon, on the 119th Psalm, pp. 140, 141. Of Evil-speaking, Use 2d. To them that either devise or receive reproaches. Both are very sinful. Hypocrites, and men that put themselves into a garb of religion, are all for censuring, take a mighty freedom that way: these men betray the rottenness of their hearts.—Alas, in our own sight, we should be the worst of men. The children of God do ever thus speak of themselves, as the least of saints, the greatest of sinners—"more brutish than any man"—"of sinners, whereof I am the chief." You rob them of the most precious treasure. He that robs thee of thy name, is the worst kind of thief. Prov. xxii. 1. "A good name is rather to be chosen than great riches."—Object. But must we, in no case, speak evil of another; or may we not speak of another's sin in any case?—Solution 1. It is a very hard matter to speak evil of another without sin.—In one way or another, we shall dash upon the command: better let it alone.—If you speak of the failings of another, it should be with tenderness and grief; as, when they are incorrigible, and likely to infect others; or when it is for the manifest glory of God.—To them that receive the slander, he is a slanderer, who wrongs his neighbour's credit, by upholding an ill report against him.

Monday afternoon, July 22. I find it would be desirable, on many accounts, always to endeavour to wear a benign aspect and air of acting and speaking, in all companies, except it should so happen, that duty requires it otherwise.—I am afraid I am now defective, in not doing whatever my hand finds to do, with my might, with respect to my particular affairs. Remember to watch, see, and know how it is. *Vid.* Aug. 31.—I see there is danger, of my being drawn into transgression, by the power of such temptations, as the fear of seeming uncivil, and of offending friends. Watch against it.—I might still help myself, and yet not hurt myself, by going with greater expedition from one thing to another, without being quite so nice.

Tuesday afternoon, July 23. When I find those *groanings which cannot be uttered*, of which the apostle speaks, and those soul-breakings for the longing it hath, of which the psalmist speaks, (Ps. cxix. 20.) *resolved*, to favour and promote them, to the utmost of my power, and not to be weary of earnestly endeavouring to vent my desires, and not to be weary of the repetitions of such earnestness.

To count it all joy, when I have occasions of great self-denial; because, then, I have a glorious opportunity of giving deadly wounds to the body of sin, and of greatly confirming and establishing the new creature. I seek to mortify sin, and increase in holiness. These are the best opportunities, according to Jan. 14.

To improve afflictions, of all kinds, as blessed opportunities of forcibly bearing on, in my christian course, notwithstanding that which is so very apt to discourage me, and to damp the vigour of my mind, and to make me lifeless; also, as opportunities of trusting and confiding in God, and getting a habit of so doing, according to the 57th Resolution; and as an opportunity of rending my heart off from the world, and setting it on heaven alone, according to Jan. 10. and the 43d and 45th Resolutions; and according to Jan. 12. Feb. 17 and 21. and May 1.—To improve them, also, as opportunities to repent of and bewail my sin, and abhor myself; and as a blessed opportunity to exercise patience, to trust in God, and divest my mind from the affliction, by fixing myself in religious exercises. Also, let me comfort myself, that it is the very nature of afflictions, to make the heart better; and, if I am made better by them, what need I be concerned, however grievous they seem for the present.

Wednesday night, July 24. I begin to find the success of my striving, in joining with others, in the worship of God; insomuch that there is a prospect of making it easy and delightful, and very profitable, in time. Wherefore, *Resolved* not to cease striving, but to continue it, and redouble it.

Thursday morning, July 25. Altered, and anew established, the 8th Resolution; also established my determination of April 1.—*Memorandum.* At a convenient time, to make an alphabet of these Resolutions and Remarks, that I may be able to educe them on proper occasions, suitable to the condition I am in, and the duty I am engaged in.

Friday afternoon, July 26. To be particularly careful, to keep up, inviolably, a trust and reliance, ease and entire rest in God, in all conditions, according to the 57th Resolution; for this I have found to be wonderfully advantageous to me.—*At night. Resolved*, very much to exercise myself in this, all my life long: *viz.* with the greatest openness, of which I am capable, to declare my ways to God, and lay open my soul to him:—all my sins, temptations, difficulties, sorrows, fears, hopes, desires, and every thing and every circumstance, according to Dr. Manton's 27th Sermon, on the 119th Psalm.

Saturday forenoon, July 27. When I am violently beset with temptation, or cannot rid myself of evil thoughts, to do something in arithmetic, or geometry, or some other study, which necessarily engages all my thoughts, and unavoidably keeps them from wandering.

Monday afternoon, July 29. When I am concerned how I shall prepare any thing to public acceptance, to be very careful that I have it very clear to me, to do what is duty and prudence in the matter.—I sometimes find myself able to trust God, and to be pretty easy when the event is uncertain, but I find it difficult when I am convinced beforehand, that the event will be adverse. I find that this arises, 1. From my want of faith, to believe that that particular advantage will be more to my advantage than disadvantage: 2. From the want of a due sense of the real preferableness of that good, which will be obtained, to that which is lost: 3. From the want of a spirit of adoption.

Tuesday night, July 30. Have concluded to endeavour to work myself into duties by searching and tracing back all the real reasons why I do them not, and narrowly searching out all the subtle subterfuges of my thoughts, and answering them to the utmost of my power, that I may know what are the very first originals of my defect, as with respect to want of repentance, love to God, loathing of myself,—to do this sometimes in sermons.—*Vid.* Resolution 8. Especially, to take occasion therefrom, to bewail those sins of which I have been guilty, that are akin to them; as for instance, from pride in others, to take occasion to bewail my pride; from their malice, to take occasion to bewail my evil speaking: and so of other sins. *Mem.* To receive slanders and reproaches, as glorious opportunities of doing this.

Wednesday afternoon, July 31. After afflictions, to inquire what I am the better for them; what good I have got by them; and what I might have got by them.—Never in the least to seek to hear sarcastical relations of others' faults. Never to give credit to any thing said against others, except there is very plain reason for it; nor to behave in any respect otherwise for it.

Sabbath morning, Aug. 4. Concluded at last, at those times when I am in the best frames, to set down the aspirations of my heart, as soon as I can get time.

Tuesday afternoon, Aug. 6. Very much convinced of the extraordinary deceitfulness of the heart, and how exceedingly affection or appetite blinds the mind, and brings it into entire subjection. There are many things which I should really think to be my duty, if I had the same affections, as when I first came from New York; which now I think not to be so. How doth appetite stretch the reason, to bring both ends together.

Wednesday forenoon, Aug. 7. To esteem it as some advantage, that the duties of religion are difficult, and that many difficulties are sometimes to be gone through, in the way of duty. Religion is the sweeter, and what is gained by labour is abundantly more precious, as a woman loves her child the more for having brought it forth with travail; and even to Christ Jesus himself his mediatorial glory, his victory and triumph, the kingdom which he hath obtained, how much more glorious is it, how much more excellent and precious, for his having wrought it out with such agonies.

Friday afternoon, Aug. 9. With respect to the important business which I have now in hand,* *Resolved*, To do whatever I think to be duty, prudence, and diligence in the matter, and to avoid ostentation; and if I succeed not, and how many disappointments soever I meet with, to be entirely easy; only to take occasion to acknowledge my unworthiness; and if it should actually not succeed, and should not find acceptance, as I expected, yet not to afflict myself about it, according to the 57th Resolution.—*At night.* One thing that may be a good help towards thinking profitably in times of vacation, is, when I find a profitable thought that I can fix my mind on, to follow it as far as I possibly can to advantage.—I missed it when a graduate at college, both in point of duty and prudence, in going against a universal benevolence and good nature.

Saturday morning, Aug. 10. Transferred my determination of July 23, to the 64th Resolution, and that of July 26, to the 65th.—*About sunset.* As a help against that inward shameful hypocrisy, to confess frankly to myself all that which I find in myself, either infirmity or sin; also to confess to God, and open the whole case to him, when it is what concerns religion, and humbly and earnestly implore of him the help that is needed; not in the least to endeavour to smother what is in my heart, but to bring it all out to God and my conscience. By this means, I may arrive at a greater knowledge of my own heart.—When I find difficulty in finding a subject of religious meditation, in vacancies, to pitch at random on what alights to my thoughts, and to go from that to other things which that shall bring into my mind, and follow this progression as a clue, till I come to what I can meditate on with profit and attention, and then to follow that, according to last Thursday's determination.

Sabbath afternoon, Aug. 11. Resolved always to do that, which I shall wish I had done when I see others do it; as for instance, sometimes I argue with myself, that such an act of good nature, kindness, forbearance, or forgiveness, &c. is not my duty, because it will have such and such consequences: yet when I see others do it, then

* Perhaps the preparation of a public exercise for the college commencement, when he received his Master's degree.

it appears amiable to me, and I wish I had done it, and see that none of these feared inconveniences follow.

Monday morning, Aug. 12. The chief thing, that now makes me in any measure to question my good estate, is my not having experienced conversion in those particular steps, wherein the people of New England, and anciently the dissenters of Old England, used to experience it. Wherefore, now resolved, never to leave searching, till I have satisfyingly found out the very bottom and foundation, the real reason, why they used to be converted in those steps.

Tuesday morning, Aug. 13. Have sinned, in not being careful enough to please my parents.—*Afternoon.* I find it would be very much to my advantage, to be thoroughly acquainted with the Scriptures. When I am reading doctrinal books, or books of controversy, I can proceed with abundantly more confidence; can see on what footing and foundation I stand.

Saturday noon, Aug. 17. Let there, in the general, be something of benevolence in all that I speak.

Tuesday night, Aug. 20. Not careful enough in watching opportunities of bringing in christian discourse with a good grace. Do not exercise myself half enough in this holy art; neither have I courage enough to carry it on with a good grace. *Vide* Sept. 2.

Saturday morning, Aug. 24. Have not practised quite right about revenge; though I have not done any thing directly out of revenge, yet I have perhaps omitted some things that I should otherwise have done; or have altered the circumstances and manner of my actions, hoping for a secret sort of revenge thereby. I have felt a little sort of satisfaction, when I thought that such an evil would happen to them by my actions, as would make them repent what they have done. To be satisfied for their repenting, when they repent from a sense of their error, is right. But a satisfaction in their repentance, because of the evil that is brought upon them, is revenge. This is in some measure a taking the matter out of God's hands when he was about to manage it, who is better able to plead it for me. Well, therefore, may he leave me to boggle at it.—*Near sunset.* I yet find a want of dependence on God, to look unto him for success, and to have my eyes unto him for his gracious disposal of the matter; for want of a sense of God's particular influence, in ordering and directing all affairs and businesses, of whatever nature, however naturally, or fortuitously, they may seem to succeed; and for want of a sense of those great advantages, that would follow therefrom: not considering that God will grant success, or make the contrary more to my advantage; or will make the advantage accruing from the unsuccessfulness more sensible and apparent; or will make it of less present and outward disadvantage; or will some way so order the circumstances, as to make the unsuccessfulness more easy to bear: or several, or all of these. This want of dependence, is likewise for want of the things mentioned, July 29.—Remember to examine all narrations I can call to mind; whether they are exactly according to verity.

Wednesday night, Aug. 28. When I want books to read; yea, when I have not very good books, not to spend time in reading them, but in reading the Scriptures, in perusing Resolutions, Reflections, &c. in writing on types of the Scripture, and other things, in studying the languages, and in spending more time in private duties. To do this, when there is a prospect of wanting time for the purpose. Remember, as soon as I can to get a piece of *slate*, or something, whereon I can make short memorandums while travelling.

Thursday, Aug. 29. Two great quærenda with me now are: How shall I make advantage of all the time I spend in journeys? and how shall I make a glorious improvement of afflictions?

Saturday night, Aug. 31. The objection which my corruptions make against doing whatever my hands find to do with my might, is, that it is a constant mortification. Let this objection by no means ever prevail.

Sabbath morning, Sept. 1. When I am violently beset with worldly thoughts, for a relief, to think of death, and the doleful circumstances of it.

Monday afternoon, Sept. 2. To help me to enter with a good grace into religious conversation; when I am conversing on morality, to turn it over by application, exemplification, or otherwise, to Christianity. *Vid.* Aug. 28, and Jan. 15.—*At night.* There is much folly, when I am quite sure I am in the right, and others are positive in contradicting me, in entering into a vehement or long debate upon it.

Saturday, Sept. 7. Concluded no more to suffer myself to be interrupted, or diverted from important business, by those things from which I expect, though some, yet but little, profit.

Sabbath morning, Sept. 8. I have been much to blame, for expressing so much impatience for delays in journeys, and the like.

Sabbath evening, Sept. 22. To praise God by singing psalms in prose, and by singing forth the meditations of my heart in prose.

Monday, Sept. 23. I observe that old men seldom have any advantage of new discoveries, because they are beside the way of thinking to which they have been so long used. *Resolved*, if ever I live to years, that I will be impartial to hear the reasons of all pretended discoveries, and receive them if rational, how long soever I have been used to another way of thinking. My time is so short, that I have not time to perfect myself in all studies; wherefore resolved, to omit and put off all but the most important and needful studies."

Keep thy heart with all diligence, for out of it are the issues of life,—was the maxim of the wisest of men, and it was founded upon the most solid reason. This maxim has ever been considered as most important by all the possessors of true wisdom and piety who have strenuously aimed at daily spiritual advancement. It has never been regarded without the greatest advantages, nor neglected without the most extensive injury. The views which were entertained of this lesson of spiritual wisdom by Jonathan Edwards are sufficiently apparent in all the extracts now presented from his Diary, and the advantages which he derived from its practice are equally manifest. He lived in the sight of God; he lived in the constant and faithful survey of his own heart and conduct, and he arose to the highest class of the followers of Christ, whose religion is eminently that of the heart. Let others pursue the same steps, and they will surely find the same precious results.

CHAPTER V

HIS TUTORSHIP—SICKNESS—INVITATION TO NORTHAMPTON—PERSONAL NARRATIVE CONTINUED—DIARY CONCLUDED.

In Sept. 1723, Mr. Edwards went to New-Haven, and received his degree of Master of Arts, when he was elected a tutor in the college. About this time, several congregations invited him to become their minister; but being fond of study, and conscious how much it would promote his usefulness, he declined their proposals. As there was no immediate vacancy in the office of tutor, he passed the ensuing winter and spring at New-Haven, in study, and in the occasional discharge of the active duties of his profession, and in the beginning of June, 1724, entered on the instruction of a class in the college.

The period of his tutorship was a period of great difficulty. For a long time before the election of Mr. Cutler to the office of rector, the college had been in a state of open revolt against the legal government, and had withdrawn from New-Haven. Two years after his election, in Jan. 1721, there was an universal insurrection of the students, which though, after considerable effort, apparently quieted, resulted in a state of extreme disorder and insubordination, beyond any thing that had been known before. In 1722, Mr. Cutler, one of the tutors, and two of the neighbouring ministers, renounced their connexion with the presbyterian church, and publicly declared themselves episcopalians. The shock, occasioned by this event, was very great in the college, in the town, and throughout the colony; and a series of controversies grew out of it, which lasted for many years. In consequence of this, the offices of these gentlemen were vacated, and the college was left for four years without a head; the trustees residing by turns at the college, and each in rotation acting as vice-rector for a month. Fortunately however for the institution, during this bereavement, it had three gentlemen in the office of tutor, of distinguished talents and scholarship, and of great resolution and firmness of character:—Mr. William Smith, of the class of 1719, and chosen tutor in 1722; Mr. Edwards; and Mr. Daniel Edwards, his uncle, class-mate and room-mate, who was chosen in Sept. 1724. On these three gentlemen, all of whom were young men, devolved almost exclusively the government and instruction of the college; yet, by their union, energy, and faithfulness, they introduced among the students, in the room of their former negligence and misrule, habits of close study and exact subordination; and in no great length of time, rendered the institution flourishing and prosperous beyond what it had long been. The late President Stiles, who, though a member of college a considerable time after this period, was personally acquainted with the three gentlemen, and knew well the history of their administration, has left an eulogy on the three united, of the highest character. "The Honourable William Smith, the Honourable Daniel Edwards, and the Rev. President Edwards, were the pillar tutors, and the glory of the college, at the critical period between Rector Cutler and Rector Williams. Their tutorial renown was great and excellent. They filled and sustained their offices with great ability, dignity, and honour. For the honour of literature these things ought not to be forgotten."

In Sept. 1725, immediately after the commencement, as he was preparing to set out for his father's house, he was taken suddenly ill, at New-Haven; but hoping that the illness was not severe, and anxious to be at home if he was to be sick, he set out for Windsor. The fatigue of travelling only increased his illness, and he was compelled to stop at North-Haven, at the house of the Rev. Mr. Stiles, where he was confined, by severe sickness, about three months: during the greater part of this time, his mother was constantly with him. Her husband, writing to her on the 20th of October, begs her to spare herself. "I am afraid you are taking too great a burden on yourself, in tending your son both day and night. I beg of you, therefore, not only to take care of him, but of yourself also. Accept, rather, of the kindness of the neighbours, in watching over again, than outbid your own strength, which is but small, by overdoing." She could not leave him till about the middle of November; and it was some time in the winter before he could go to his father's house. In this sickness, he speaks of himself as having enjoyed new, and most refreshing, manifestations of the presence and grace of God.

After he had held the office of tutor upwards of two years, with the highest reputation, he received proposals from the people of Northampton to become their minister. Many circumstances conspired to prompt his acceptance. He was familiarly acquainted with the place and people. The Rev. Mr. Stoddard, his grandfather, a man of great dignity, and of singular weight and influence in the churches, in consequence of his advanced age, stood in need of his assistance, and wished him to be his colleague. His parents and his other friends all desired it. The situation was in itself respectable, and the town unusually pleasant. He therefore resigned his tutorship, in Sept. 1726, and accepted of the invitation.

"Those who are conversant with the instruction and government of a college, will readily be aware that the period, of which we have now been speaking, was a very busy portion of Mr. Edwards's life; and if they call to mind the circumstances of the institution, and the habits of the students, when he entered on his office, they will not need to be informed, that the discharge of his official duties must have been accompanied with painful anxiety. It is a rare event in Providence, that so heavy a responsibility is thrown on three individuals so young, so destitute of experience, and of the knowledge of mankind; and the business of instruction and government must have occupied their whole time, and exhausted their whole strength."

"In such a state of things, it was not possible that he should find the same leisure for spiritual exercises as he had found at New York. There his business was chiefly to enjoy; here it was to act. There the persons with whom he continually associated were possessed of uncommon excellence; here their characters were very different. There his attention was drawn, by the objects around him, to heavenly things; here it was necessarily confined almost all the time to this world. There, when retiring for prayer and heavenly contemplation, his mind sought communion with God in all its energy and freshness; here, when it was worn out by toil and exhausted by perplexities. The change in the current of thought and feeling must, therefore, have been great; and (so much is the mind prone to measure its religious state by the amount of daily enjoyment, and so little by the readiness to encounter trials, and to perform laborious and self-denying duties) it is not surprising, that he should have regarded this change, as evidence of perceptible and lamentable declension in religion. Such he in fact regarded it; as we shall find, both from his Narrative and Diary; yet it is by no means certain, that his views of the subject were altogether correct."

"The young Christian has usually a season of leisure, given him in the providence of God, in which to become acquainted with the members of that family into which he has lately been introduced, and with those objects with which as a spiritual being he is in future to be conversant. His time and his strength are given chiefly to the Scriptures, to prayer, to meditation, and to religious conversation; and he is delightfully conscious that his communion is with the Father, and the Son Jesus Christ, through the fellowship of the Holy Spirit, as well as with 'the whole family both on earth and in heaven.' The design of this is to open to him his new state of existence, to enable him to understand its relations and duties, and to give him an earnest of better things in reversion. It is a most refreshing and happy period of his life, and, were he designed for contemplation merely, might well be protracted to its close. But, as we are taught most explicitly, in the word and Providence of God, his great worth lies in action--in imitating him whose rule it was—'I must *do the work* of him that sent me while it is day;' and whose practice it was, that 'he went about *doing* good.' The Scriptures are given by the inspiration of God, and are profitable for doctrine, for reproof, for correction, and for instruction in righteousness.—Wherefore? that the man of God may be perfected, being thoroughly furnished unto every good *work*. Probably no year in the life of Mr. Edwards was spent more usefully, than that in which he was occupied, with his associates, in laying the foundation of sober habits and sound morals, in the seminary now intrusted to their care. Probably in no equal period did he more effectually serve God and his generation. And if, in its progress, he found less of that enjoyment which grows out of spiritual contemplation; he must have had the more delightful consciousness, that in the midst of great difficulties and crosses, he had honestly endeavoured to serve God, and to perform his duty."

There may therefore be reason for doubt, whether the change in his feelings, of which he speaks in the succeeding parts of his Narrative and Diary, was not a declension in this particular species of religious enjoyment, necessarily growing out of the circumstances in which he was placed, rather than a declension in the life and power of religion.

"I continued," he observes, "much in the same frame, in the general, as when at New York, till I went to New-Haven as tutor of the college; particularly once at Bolton, on a journey from Boston, while walking out alone in the fields. After I went to New-Haven, I sunk in religion, my mind being diverted from my eager pursuits after holiness, by some affairs that greatly perplexed and distracted my thoughts.

"In September, 1725, I was taken ill at New-Haven, and while endeavouring to go home to Windsor, was so ill at the North Village, that I could go no further; where I lay sick, for about a quarter of a year. In this sickness, God was pleased to visit me again with the sweet influences of his Spirit. My mind was greatly engaged there, on divine and pleasant contemplations, and longings of soul. I observed, that those who watched with me, would often be looking out wishfully for the morning; which brought to my mind those words of the psalmist, and which my soul with delight made its own language; 'My soul waiteth for the Lord, more than they that watch for the morning; I say, more than they that watch for the morning;' and when the light of day came in at the window, it refreshed my soul, from one morning to another. It seemed to be some image of the light of God's glory."

"I remember, about that time, I used greatly to long for the conversion of some that I was concerned with; I could gladly honour them, and with delight be a servant to them, and lie at their feet, if they were but truly holy. But some time after this, I was again greatly diverted with some temporal concerns, that exceedingly took up my thoughts, greatly to the wounding of my soul; and went on, through various exercises, that it would be tedious to relate, which gave me much more experience of my own heart than I ever had before."

That the mind of Mr. Edwards was not injured as to its spirituality, by his official engagements and trials, is sufficiently evident from these extracts. He was still a holy man of God, whose heart was in heaven, and with whom converse with God was the highest delight.——The remainder of his Diary is chiefly confined to the period of his life which has now been reviewed, and is therefore inserted here. It is only to be regretted, that through the multiplicity of his affairs, he should have found it necessary to discontinue it.

REMAINDER OF DIARY.

"*Thursday forenoon, Oct.* 4, 1723. Have this day fixed and established it, that Christ Jesus has promised me faithfully, that, if I will do what is my duty, and according to the best of my prudence in the matter, that my condition in this world shall be better for me than any other condition whatever, and more to my welfare to all eternity. And, therefore, whatever my condition shall be, I will esteem it to be such: and if I find need of faith in the matter, that I will confess it as impiety before God. *Vid.* Resolution 57, and June 9.

Sabbath night, Oct. 7. Have lately erred, in not allowing time enough for conversation.

Friday night, Oct. 12. I see there are some things quite contrary to the soundness and perfection of Christianity, in which almost all good men do allow themselves, and where innate corruption has an unrestrained secret vent, which they never take notice of, or think to be no hurt, or cloak under the name of virtue; which things exceedingly darken the brightness, and hide the loveliness, of Christianity. Who can understand his errors? O that I might be kept from secret faults!

Sabbath morning, Oct. 14. Narrowly to observe after what manner I act when I am in a hurry, and to act as much so at other times as I can without prejudice to the business.

Monday morning, Oct. 15. I seem to be afraid, after errors and decays, to give myself the full exercise of spiritual meditation:—Not to give way to such fears.

Thursday, Oct. 18. To follow the example of Mr. B. who though he meets with great difficulties, yet undertakes them with a smiling countenance, as though he thought them but little; and speaks of them as if they were very small.

Friday night, Nov. 1. When I am unfit for other business to perfect myself in writing *characters.**

Friday afternoon, Nov. 22. For the time to come, when I am in a lifeless frame in secret prayer, to force myself to expatiate, as if I were praying before others, more than I used to do.

Tuesday forenoon, Nov. 26. It is a most evil and pernicious practice, in meditations on afflictions, to sit ruminating on the aggravations of the affliction, and reckoning up the evil, dark circumstances thereof, and dwelling long on the dark side: it doubles and trebles the affliction. And so when speaking of them to others, to make them as bad as we can, and use our eloquence to set forth our own troubles, is to be all the while making new trouble, and feeding and pampering the old; whereas the contrary practice would starve our affliction. If we dwelt on the bright side of things in our thoughts, and extenuated them all that we possibly could, when speaking of them, we should think little of them ourselves, and the affliction would really, in a great measure, vanish away.

Friday night, Nov. 29. As a help to attention in social prayer, to take special care to make a particular remark at the beginning of every petition, confession, &c.

Monday morning, Dec. 9. To observe, whether I express any kind of fretting emotion, for the next three weeks.

Thursday night, Dec. 12. If, at any time, I am forced to tell others wherein I think they are somewhat to blame; in order to avoid the important evil that would otherwise ensue, not to tell it to them so, that there shall be a probability of their taking it as the effect of little, fretting, angry emotions of mind.—*Vid.* Aug. 28. When I do want, or am likely to want, good books, to spend time in studying mathematics, and in reviewing other kinds of old learning; to spend more time in visiting friends, in the more private duties of a pastor, in taking care of worldly business, in going abroad, and other things that I may contrive.

Friday morning, Dec. 27. At the end of every month, to examine my behaviour strictly by some chapter in the New Testament, more especially made up of rules of life.—At the end of the year, to examine my behaviour by the rules of the New Testament in general, reading many chapters. It would also be convenient some time at the end of the year, to read for this purpose in the book of Proverbs.

Tuesday night, Dec. 31. Concluded never to suffer nor express any angry emotions of mind, more or less, except the honour of God calls for it in zeal for him, or to preserve myself from being trampled on.

1724. *Wednesday, Jan.* 1. Not to spend too much time in thinking, even of important and necessary worldly business, and to allow every thing its proportion of thought, according to its urgency and importance.

Thursday night, Jan. 2. These things established,—That time gained in things of lesser importance, is as much gained in things of greater; that a minute gained in times of confusion, conversation, or in a journey, is as good as a minute gained in my study, at my most retired times; and so, in general, that a minute gained at one time is as good as at another.

Friday night, Jan. 3. The time and pains laid out in seeking the world, is to be proportioned to the necessity, usefulness, and importance of it, with respect to another world, together with the uncertainty of living, and of retaining; provided, that nothing that our duty enjoins, or that is amiable, be omitted, and nothing sinful or unbecoming be done for the sake of it.

Friday, Jan. 10. (After having written to a considerable extent in short hand, which he used, when he wished what he wrote to be effectually concealed from every one but himself, he adds the following.) Remember to act according to Prov. xii. 23. *A prudent man concealeth knowledge.*

Monday, Jan. 20. I have been very much to blame, in that I have not been as full, and plain, and downright, in my standing up for virtue and religion, when I have had fair occasion, before those who seemed to take no delight in such things. If such conversation would not be agreeable to them, I have in some degree minced the matter, that I might not displease, and might not speak against the grain, more than I should have loved to have done with others, to whom it would be agreeable to speak for religion. I ought to be exceedingly bold with such persons, not talking in a melancholy strain, but in one confident and fearless, assured of the truth and excellence of the cause.

Monday, Feb. 3. Let every thing have the value now which it will have upon a sick bed: and frequently, in my pursuits of whatever kind, let this question come into my mind. 'How much shall I value this upon my death-bed?'

Wednesday, Feb. 5. I have not in times past, in my prayers, enough insisted on the glorifying of God in the world, on the advancement of the kingdom of Christ, the prosperity of the church, and the good of man. Determined that this objection is without weight, *viz.* that it is not likely that God will make great alterations in the whole world, and overturnings in kingdoms and nations, only for the prayers of one obscure person, seeing such things used to be done in answer to the united prayers of the whole church; and that if my prayers should have some influence, it would be but imperceptible and small.

Thursday, Feb. 6. More convinced than ever, of the usefulness of free religious conversation. I find by conversing on natural philosophy, that I gain knowledge abundantly faster, and see the reasons of things much more clearly, than in private study: wherefore, earnestly to seek at all times for religious conversation; for those with whom I can at all times, with profit and delight, and with freedom, so converse.

Friday, Feb. 7. *Resolved,* If God will assist me to it, that I will not care about things, when, upon any account, I have prospect of ill success or adversity; and that I will not think about it, any further than just to do what prudence directs to for prevention, according to Phil. iv. 6. Be careful for nothing; to 1 Pet. v. 7. Cast all your care upon God, for he careth for you; and again, Take no thought for the morrow; and again, Take no thought, saying, What shall I eat, and what shall I drink, and wherewithal shall I be clothed: seek ye first the kingdom of God, and all these things shall be added unto you.

Saturday night, Feb. 15. I find that when eating, I cannot be convinced in the time of it, that if I should eat more, I should exceed the bounds of strict temperance,

* He probably refers to short-hand characters.

though I have had the experience of two years of the like; and yet as soon as I have done, in three minutes I am convinced of it. But yet when I eat again, and remember it, still while eating I am fully convinced that I have not eaten what is but for nature, nor can I be convinced, that my appetite and feeling is as it was before. It seems to me that I shall be somewhat faint if I leave off then; but when I have finished, I am convinced again, and so it is from time to time.—I have observed that more really seems to be truth, when it makes for my interest, or is in other respects according to my inclination, than it seems if it be otherwise; and it seems to me, that the words in which I express it are more than the thing will properly bear. But if the thing be against my interest, the words of different import seem as much as the thing will properly bear.—Though there is some little seeming indecorum, as if it looked like affectation, in religious conversation as there is also in acts of kindness, yet this is to be broke through.

Tuesday, Feb. 18. *Resolved,* to act with sweetness and benevolence, and according to the 47th Resolution, in all bodily dispositions,—sick or well, at ease or in pain, sleepy or watchful; and not to suffer discomposure of body to discompose my mind.

Saturday, Feb. 22. I observe that there are some evil habits, which do increase and grow stronger, even in some good people, as they grow older; habits that much obscure the beauty of Christianity: some things which are according to their natural tempers, which in some measure prevail when they are young in Christ, and the evil disposition having an unobserved control, the habit at last grows very strong, and commonly regulates the practice until death. By this means, old Christians are very commonly, in some respects, more unreasonable than those who are young. I am afraid of contracting such habits, particularly of grudging to give, and to do, and of procrastinating.

Sabbath, Feb. 23. I must be contented, where I have any thing strange or remarkable to tell, not to make it appear so remarkable as it is indeed; lest through fear of this, and the desire of making a thing appear very remarkable, I should exceed the bounds of simple verity. When I am at a feast, or a meal, that very well pleases my appetite, I must not merely take care to leave off with as much of an appetite as at ordinary meals; for when there is a great variety of dishes, I may do that, after I have eaten twice as much as at other meals is sufficient. If I act according to my resolution, I shall desire riches no otherwise, than as they are helpful to religion. But this I determine, as what is really evident from many parts of Scripture, that to fallen man, they have a greater tendency to hurt religion.

Monday, March 16. To practise this sort of self-denial, when, as sometimes on fair days, I find myself more particularly disposed to regard the glories of the world, than to betake myself to the study of serious religion.

Saturday, May 23. How it comes about I know not, but I have remarked it hitherto, that at those times when I have read the Scriptures most, I have evermore been most lively and in the best frame.

AT YALE COLLEGE.

Saturday night, June 6. This week has been a very remarkable week with me, with respect to despondencies, fears, perplexities, multitudes of cares, and distraction of mind: it being the week I came hither to New-Haven, in order to entrance upon the office of tutor of the college. I have now abundant reason to be convinced of the troublesomeness and vexation of the world, and that it will never be another kind of world.

Tuesday, July 7. When I am giving the relation of a thing, remember to abstain from altering either in the matter or manner of speaking, so much, as that if every one, afterwards, should alter as much, it would at last come to be properly false.

Tuesday, Sept. 2. By a sparingness in diet, and eating as much as may be what is light and easy of digestion, I shall doubtless be able to think more clearly, and shall gain time; 1. By lengthening out my life; 2. Shall need less time for digestion, after meals; 3. Shall be able to study more closely, without injury to my health; 4. Shall need less time for sleep; 5. Shall more seldom be troubled with the head-ache.

Saturday night, Sept. 12. Crosses of the nature of that which I met with this week, thrust me quite below all comforts in religion. They appear no more than vanity and stubble, especially when I meet with them so unprepared for them. I shall not be fit to encounter them, except I have a far stronger and more permanent faith, hope, and love.

Wednesday, Sept. 30. It has been a prevailing thought with me, to which I have given place in practice, that it is best sometimes to eat or drink, when it will do me no good, because the hurt that it will do me, will not be equal to the trouble of denying myself. But I have determined to suffer that thought to prevail no longer. The hurries of commencement and diversion of the vacancy, has been the occasion of my sinking so exceedingly, as in the last three weeks.

Monday, Oct. 5. I believe it is a good way, when prone to unprofitable thoughts, to deny myself and break off my thoughts by keeping diligently to my study, that they may not have time to operate to work me to such a listless frame. I am apt to think it a good way when I am indisposed to reading and study, to read of my own remarks, the fruit of my study in divinity, &c. to set me a going again.

Friday, Nov. 6. Felt sensibly somewhat of that trust and affiance in Christ, and with delight committing of my soul to him, of which our divines used to speak, and about which I have been somewhat in doubt.

Tuesday, Nov. 10. To mark all that I say in conversation merely to beget in others a good opinion of myself, and examine it.

Sabbath, Nov. 15. Determined, when I am indisposed to prayer, always to premeditate what to pray for; and that it is better, that the prayer should be of almost any shortness, than that my mind should be almost continually off from what I say.

Sabbath, Nov. 22. Considering that by-standers always copy some faults, which we do not see ourselves, or of which at least we are not so fully sensible; and that there are many secret workings of corruption, which escape our sight, and of which others only are sensible: *Resolved,* therefore, that I will if I can by any convenient means, learn what faults others find in me, or what things they see in me, that appear any way blameworthy, unlovely, or unbecoming.

Friday, Feb. 12, 1725. The very thing I now want, to give me a clearer and more immediate view of the perfections and glory of God, is as clear a knowledge of the manner of God's exerting himself, with respect to spirits and mind, as I have of his operations concerning matter and bodies.

Tuesday, Feb. 16. A virtue which I need in a higher degree, to give a beauty and lustre to my behaviour, is gentleness. If I had more of an air of gentleness, I should be much mended.

Friday, May 21. If ever I am inclined to turn to the opinion of any other sect: *Resolved,* beside the most deliberate consideration, earnest prayer, &c. privately to desire all the help that can possibly be afforded me, from some of the most judicious men in the country, together with the prayers of wise and holy men, however strongly persuaded I may seem to be that I am in the right.

Saturday, May 22. When I reprove for faults, whereby I am in any way injured, to defer till the thing is quite over and done with; for that is the way, both to reprove aright, and without the least mixture of spirit, or passion, and to have reproofs effectual, and not suspected.

Friday, May 28. It seems to me, that whether I am now converted or not, I am so settled in the state I am in, that I shall go on in it all my life. But, however settled I may be, yet I will continue to pray to God, not to suffer me to be deceived about it, nor to sleep in an unsafe condition; and ever and anon, will call all into question and try myself, using for helps some of our old divines, that God may have opportunities to answer my prayers, and the Spirit of God to show me my error, if I am in one.

Saturday night, June 6. I am sometimes in a frame so listless, that there is no other way of profitably improving time, but conversation, visiting, or recreation, or some bodily exercise. However, it may be best in the first place, before resorting to either of these, to try the whole circle of my mental employments.

Nov. 16. When confined at Mr. Stiles's. I think it would be of special advantage to me, with respect to my truer interest, as near as I can in my studies, to observe this rule: To let half a day's, or at most a day's, study in other things, be succeeded by half a day's or a day's study in divinity.

One thing wherein I have erred, as I would be complete in all social duties, is, in neglecting to write letters to friends. And I would be forewarned of the danger of neglecting to visit my friends and relations when we are parted.

When one suppresses thoughts that tend to divert the run of the mind's operations from religion, whether they are melancholy, or anxious, or passionate, or any others; there is this good effect of it, that it keeps the mind in its freedom. Those thoughts are stopped in the beginning, that would have set the mind a going in that stream.

There are a great many exercises, that for the present seem not to help, but rather impede, religious meditation and affections, the fruit of which is reaped afterwards, and is of far greater worth than what is lost; for thereby the mind is only for the present diverted; but what is attained is, upon occasion, of use for the whole life-time.

Sept. 26, 1726. Tis just about three years, that I have been for the most part in a low sunk estate and condition, miserably senseless, to what I used to be, about spiritual things. 'Twas three years ago, the week before commencement; just about the same time this year, I began to be somewhat as I used to be.

Jan. 1728. I think Christ has recommended rising early in the morning, by his rising from the grave very early.

Jan. 22, 1734. I judge that it is best, when I am in a good frame for divine contemplation, or engaged in reading the Scriptures, or any study of divine subjects, that, ordinarily, I will not be interrupted by going to dinner, but will forego my dinner, rather than be broke off.

April 4, 1735. When at any time I have a sense of any divine thing, then to turn it in my thoughts to a practical improvement. As for instance, when I am in my mind, on some argument for the truth of religion, the reality of a future state, and the like, then to think with myself, how safely I may venture to sell all, for a future good. So when at any time I have a more than ordinary sense of the glory of the saints in another world, to think how well it is worth my while to deny myself, and to sell all that I have, for this glory, &c.

May 18. My mind at present is, never to suffer my thoughts and meditations at all to ruminate.

June 11. To set apart days of meditation on particular subjects; as, sometimes to set apart a day for the consideration of the greatness of my sins; at another, to consider the dreadfulness and certainty of the future misery of ungodly men; at another, the truth and certainty of religion; and so, of the great future things promised and threatened in the Scriptures."

CHAPTER VI.

SETTLEMENT IN THE MINISTRY AT NORTHAMPTON—SITUATION OF THINGS AT THE TIME OF HIS SETTLEMENT—ATTENTION TO RELIGION IN THE PARISH—COURSE OF STUDY—HABITS OF LIFE—MARRIAGE—DEATH AND CHARACTER OF MR. STODDARD—SICKNESS OF MR. EDWARDS—DEATH AND CHARACTER OF HIS SISTER JERUSHA—HIS FIRST PUBLICATION.

On the 15th of February, 1727, Mr. Edwards was ordained as a minister of the gospel, and placed over the church and congregation at Northampton, as the colleague of his grandfather, the Rev. Mr. Stoddard. He was now entering on the business of life, in a profession attended with many difficulties, and presenting a field sufficiently ample for the employment of the highest faculties ever conferred on man. It may not be improper, therefore, to stop a moment, and review the circumstances in which he was placed.

He was twenty-three years of age. His constitution was naturally so tender and feeble, as to be preserved, even in tolerable health, only with unceasing care. He had passed through the successive periods of childhood, youth, and early manhood, not only without reproach, but in such a manner, as to secure the high esteem and approbation of all who knew him. His filial piety, and fraternal affection, had been most exemplary, and had rendered him a centre of strong attraction to the united family. Originally of a grave and sober character, he had been the subject of early, frequent, and strong religious impressions; which, if they did not result in saving conversion in his childhood, yet rendered him conscientious, and solemnly and habitually mindful of eternal things. For a considerable period, he had not only felt the life and power of religion, but had appeared imbued with an unusually large measure of the grace of God. Few persons, of the same age, discover a piety so pure, so practical, or so pervading.

He had been devoted to books from his infancy, and appears of his own accord, from an early period, to have formed habits of severe and successful application. His mind, originally possessed of uncommon powers, and fraught with an intense desire of knowledge, was qualified for eminence, as we have already seen, not in a single pursuit merely, but in every walk of literature and science. Though probably the youngest member of his class, he had been acknowledged as its first scholar, in the distribution of its honours. He had not been distinguished for his attainments in Latin, Greek, or Hebrew literature only, but still more in those studies which require the application of stronger powers—in mathematics and logic, in natural and mental philosophy, and the higher principles of theology. In these, he had not simply proved himself capable of comprehending the discoveries of others, but had ventured out, where there was no path nor guide, into new and unexplored regions of the spiritual * world, with a success, which might well have prompted him to bold and fearless enterprise. As officers of the college, the peculiar difficulties in which they were placed, had given him, and his associates, an opportunity to acquire uncommon reputation, not only as instructors and governors of youths, but as men of unshaken firmness, and unwavering integrity. His mind was now rich in its attainments; its views were already, for the period in which he lived, singularly expanded and comprehensive; and its powers were under thorough discipline, and yielded an exact and persevering obedience. His habits of study were completely formed, and were of the most severe and unbending character.

Theology had been, for years, his favourite study. For it he had deliberately relinquished, not only the varied pursuits of natural science, but in a measure, also, those investigations into the nature and operations of mind, by which, at an earlier period, his whole attention had been engrossed. He had already discovered, that much of what he found in systems and commentaries, was a mere mass of rubbish; and that many of the great principles, which constitute the foundation of the science, were yet to be established. He had studied theology, not chiefly in systems or commentaries, but in the Bible, and in the character and mutual relations of God and his creatures, from which all its principles are derived; and had already entered on a series of investigations, which, if ultimately found correct, would effectuate most important changes in the opinions of the christian world.

The ministry had long been the profession of his choice, and was doubtless the only profession which he had ever thought of pursuing. Few persons, probably, enter the sacred office with more just views of its elevation and importance. His work he appears to have regarded simply as the work of salvation;—the same work, on which HE, whose commission he bore, came down to this lower world;—and to the accomplishment of it, the surrendry of himself appears to have been deliberate and entire. His reception as a preacher had certainly been flattering. Repeated and urgent proposals had been made to him for settlement; and, as far as he was known, he was obviously regarded as a young man of uncommon promise.

Northampton, the place of his settlement, is in its natural situation uncommonly pleasant, was then the shire town of a county, embracing nearly one half of the area of the colony, and embodied within its limits, more than the ordinary share of refinement and polish. The church was large, and, with the congregation, was united. Both were united in him, and earnestly desirous that he should become their minister. From his childhood he had familiarly known both the place and the people. His parents were the familiar friends of many of the inhabitants; and they, with his connexions in the place, regarded his settlement there as a most pleasing event.

He was also the individual, whom probably, of all others, his grandfather desired, for his colleague and successor. That venerable man, then in his 84th year, had been the minister of Northampton 55 years; and by his piety, his great energy of character, and his knowledge of mankind, had early acquired, and maintained through a long life, a singular degree of weight among the ministers and churches of New England. Though a close student, and an able and faithful preacher, he was in character a man of business, and of action; and, in all the important ecclesiastical bodies of Massachusetts, he had for many years an influence, which usually was not contested, and almost always was paramount. In Northampton he had been a faithful and successful minister. Under his preaching, the place had repeatedly witnessed revivals of religion; particularly in 1679, 1683, 1690, 1712, and 1718. Those in 1683, 1690, and 1712, were distinguished for their extent, and for the accessions made to the number of communicants. While the existing members of the church, with scarcely an exception, regarded him as their spiritual father, all the acting inhabitants of the town had grown up under his ministry, and had been accustomed, from infancy, to pay a respect to his person and character, and a deference to his opinions, such as children pay to those of a loved and venerated parent.

One circumstance, relating to the actual condition of the church at Northampton, deserves to be mentioned here, as it had an ultimate bearing on some of the most important events recorded in these pages. That church, like the other early churches of New England, according to its original platform, admitted none to the sacrament of the Lord's supper, except those who, after due examination, were regarded in the judgment of christian charity as regenerate persons. Such was the uniform practice of the church, from the time of its formation, during the life of Mr. Mather, and for upwards of thirty years after the settlement of Mr. Stoddard. How early Mr. Stoddard changed his own views on this subject, cannot probably be ascertained; but he attempted, in 1704, and, though not without opposition, yet with ultimate success, to introduce a

* I use *spiritual* here in its original and most appropriate sense, as opposed to *material.*

corresponding change in the practice of the church. Though no vote was then taken to alter the rules of admission, yet the point of practice was yielded. The sacrament, from that time, was viewed as a converting ordinance, and those who were not regarded, either by themselves or others, as possessed of piety, were encouraged to unite themselves to the church.

The attention to religion in 1718, was neither extensive, nor of long continuance, and appears not to have terminated happily. During the nine years which intervened between that event and the settlement of Mr. Edwards, Mr. Stoddard witnessed "a far more degenerate time among his people, particularly among the young, than ever before," in which the means of salvation were attended with little or no visible efficacy. The young became addicted to habits of dissipation and licentiousness; family government too generally failed; the sabbath was extensively profaned; and the decorum of the sanctuary was not unfrequently disturbed. There had also long prevailed in the town a spirit of contention between two parties, into which they had for many years been divided, which kept alive a mutual jealousy, and prepared them to oppose one another in all public affairs.

Such were the circumstances in which Mr. Edwards entered on his ministry at Northampton.

At this time, Mr. Stoddard, though so much advanced in years, had a good degree of strength, both of body and mind; and, for a considerable period after the settlement of his grandson, he was able to officiate in the desk the half of every sabbath. Almost immediately after that event, he was permitted to witness a work of divine grace among some of his people; in the course of which about twenty were believed to be savingly converted. This was to him a most pleasing circumstance, as well as most useful to his colleague; who observes, "I have reason to bless God for the great advantage I had by it." No doubt it was intended to prepare him for more important and interesting scenes. The attention to religion, though at no time very extensive, continued for about two years, and was followed by several years of general inattention and indifference.

Immediately after his settlement, Mr. Edwards commenced the practice of preparing two discourses weekly; one of which was preached as a lecture, on an evening in the week. This he continued for several years. Though he regarded preaching the gospel as the great duty of a minister, and would on no account offer to God, or deliver to his people, that which was not the fruit of toil and labour; yet he resolved, from the commencement of his ministry, not to devote the time of each week exclusively to the preparation of his sermons, but to spend a large portion of it in the study of the Bible, and in the investigation of the more difficult and important subjects of theology. His mode of study with the pen has been described, and was now vigorously pursued, in the continuation of his "Miscellanies," and his "Notes on the Scriptures," as well as of a work, entitled, "The Types of the Messiah in the Old Testament," which he appears to have commenced while a candidate for the ministry. With an infirm constitution, and health ordinarily feeble, it was obviously impossible, however, to carry this resolution into practice, without the most strict attention to diet, exercise, and method; but in all these points, his habits had long been formed, and persevered in, with a direct reference to the best improvement of time, and the greatest efficiency of his intellectual powers. In eating and drinking, he was unusually abstemious, and constantly watchful. He carefully observed the effects of the different sorts of food, and selected those which best suited his constitution, and rendered him most fit for mental labour. Having also ascertained the quantity of food, which, while it sustained his bodily strength, left his mind most sprightly and active, he most scrupulously and exactly confined himself to the prescribed limits; regarding it as a shame and a sin, to waste his time, and his mental strength, by animal indulgence. In this respect, he lived *by rule*, and constantly practised great self-denial; as he did, also, with regard to the time passed in sleep. He accustomed himself to rise at four, or between four and five, in the morning, and, in winter, spent several of those hours in study which are commonly wasted in slumber. In the evening, he usually allowed himself a season of relaxation, in the midst of his family.

His most usual diversion in summer, was riding on horseback, and walking; and in his solitary rides and walks, he appears to have decided, before leaving home, on what subjects to meditate. He would commonly, unless diverted by company, ride two or three miles after dinner, to some lonely grove, where he would dismount and walk awhile. At such times, he generally carried his pen and ink with him, to note any thought that might be suggested, and which promised some light on any important subject. In winter, he was accustomed, almost daily, to take his axe, and cut wood moderately, for the space of half an hour or more. In solitary rides of considerable length, he adopted a kind of artificial memory. Having pursued a given subject of thought to its proper results, he would pin a small piece of paper on a given spot in his coat, and charge his mind to associate the subject and the piece of paper. He would then repeat the same process with a second subject of thought, fastening the token in a different place, and then a third, and a fourth, as the time might permit. From a ride of several days, he would usually bring home a considerable number of these remembrancers; and, on going to his study, would take them off, one by one, in regular order, and write down the train of thought of which each was intended to remind him.

"He did not," observes Dr. Hopkins, "make it his custom to visit his people in their own houses, unless he was sent for by the sick, or he heard that they were under some special affliction. Instead of visiting from house to house, he used to preach frequently at private meetings, in particular neighbourhoods; and often call the young people and children to his own house, when he used to pray with them, and treat with them in a manner suited to their years and circumstances; and he catechized the children in public, every sabbath in the forenoon. And he used, sometimes, to propose questions to particular young persons, in writing, for them to answer, after a proper time given to them to prepare. In putting out these questions, he endeavoured to suit them to the age, genius, and ability of those, to whom they were given. His questions were generally such, as required but a short answer; and yet, could not be answered without a particular knowledge of some historical part of the Scriptures; and therefore led, and even obliged, persons to study the Bible.

"He did not neglect visiting his people from house to house, because he did not look upon it, in ordinary cases, to be one important part of the work of a gospel minister; but, because he supposed that ministers should, with respect to this, consult their own talents and circumstances, and visit more or less, according to the degree in which they could hope thereby to promote the great ends of the ministry. He observed, that some had a talent for entertaining and profiting by occasional visits among their people. They have words at command, and a facility at introducing profitable religious discourse, in a manner free, natural, and familiar, and apparently without design or contrivance. He supposed, that such had a call to spend a great deal of their time in visiting their people; but he looked on his own talents to be quite otherwise. He was not able to enter into a free conversation with every person he met, and, in an easy manner, turn it to whatever topic he pleased, without the help of others, and it may be, against their inclinations. He therefore found, that his visits of this kind must be, in a great degree, unprofitable. And as he was settled in a large parish, it would have taken up a great part of his time to visit from house to house, which he thought he could spend, in his study, to much more valuable purposes, and so better promote the great ends of his ministry. For it appeared to him, that he could do the greatest good to the souls of men, and most promote the cause of Christ, by preaching and writing, and conversing with persons under religious impressions, in his study; whither he encouraged all such to repair; where they might be sure, in ordinary cases, to find him, and to be allowed easy access to him; and where they were treated with all desirable tenderness, kindness, and familiarity."

Owing to his constant watchfulness and self-denial in food and sleep, and his regular attention to bodily exercise, notwithstanding the feebleness of his constitution, few students are capable of more close or more long-continued application than he was. He commonly spent thirteen hours every day in his study; and these hours were passed, not in perusing or treasuring up the thoughts of others, but in employments far more exhausting—in the investigation of difficult subjects, in the origination and arrangement of thoughts, in the invention of arguments, and in the discovery of truths and principles. Nor was his exact method, in the distribution of his time, of less essential service. In consequence of his uniform regularity and self-denial, and the force of habit, the powers of his mind were always at his command, and would do their prescribed task in the time appointed. This enabled him to assign the preparation of his sermons, each week, to given days, and specific subjects of investigation to other given days; and except in cases of sickness, or journeying, or some other extraordinary interruption, it was rare, indeed, that he failed of accomplishing every part of his weekly task, or that he was pressed for time in the accomplishment. So exact was the distribution of his time, and so perfect the command of his mental powers, that in addition to his preparation of two discourses in each week, his stated and occasional lectures, and his customary pastoral duties, he continued regularly his "Notes on the Scriptures," his "Miscellanies," his "Types of the Messiah," and a work which he soon commenced, entitled, "Prophecies of the Messiah in the Old Testament, and their Fulfilment."

On the 28th of July, 1727, Mr. Edwards was married, at New-Haven, to Miss Sarah Pierrepont. Her paternal grandfather, John Pierrepont, Esq. who came from England and resided in Roxbury, Massachusetts, was a younger branch of a most distinguished family in his own country. Her father, the Rev. James Pierrepont, was "an eminent, pious, and useful minister, at New-Haven." He married Mary, the daughter of the Rev. Samuel Hooker, of Farmington, who was the son of the Rev. Thomas Hooker, of Hartford, familiarly denominated "the father of the Connecticut churches," and "well known, in the churches of England, for his distinguished talents and most ardent piety." Mr. Pierrepont was one of the principal founders, and one of the trustees, of Yale college; and, to help forward the seminary, read lectures to the students, for some considerable time, as professor of Moral Philosophy. The Platform of the Connecticut Churches, established at Saybrook, in 1708, is ascribed to his pen. Miss Pierrepont was born on the 9th of January, 1710, and at the time of her marriage was in the 18th year of her age. She was a young lady of uncommon beauty. Not only is this the language of tradition; but Dr. Hopkins, who first saw her when the mother of seven children, says she was more than ordinarily beautiful; and her portrait, taken by a respectable English painter,* while it presents a form and features not often rivalled, exhibits also that peculiar loveliness of expression, which is the combined result of intelligence, cheerfulness, and benevolence. The native powers of her mind were of a superior order; and her parents being in easy circumstances, and of liberal views, provided for their children all the advantages of an enlightened and polished education. In her manners she was gentle and courteous, amiable in her behaviour, and the law of kindness appeared to govern all her conversation and conduct. She was also a rare example of early piety; having exhibited the life and power of religion, and that in a remarkable manner, when only five years of age;† and having also confirmed the hopes which her friends then cherished, by the uniform and increasing excellence of her character, in childhood and youth. So warm and animated were her religious feelings, in every period of life, that they might perhaps have been regarded as enthusiastic, had they not been under the control of true delicacy and sound discretion. Mr. Edwards had known her several years before their marriage, and from the following passage, written on a blank leaf, in 1723, it is obvious, that even then her uncommon piety, at least, had arrested his attention. "They say there is a young lady in [New-Haven] who is loved of that Great Being, who made and rules the world, and that there are certain seasons in which this Great Being, in some way or other invisible, comes to her and fills her mind with exceeding sweet delight; and that she hardly cares for any thing, except to meditate on him—that she expects after a while to be received up where he is, to be raised up out of the world and caught up into heaven; being assured that he loves her too well to let her remain at a distance from him always. There she is to dwell with him, and to be ravished with his love and delight for ever. Therefore, if you present all the world before her, with the richest of its treasures, she disregards it and cares not for it, and is unmindful of any pain or affliction. She has a strange sweetness in her mind, and singular purity in her

* The Rev. Dr. Erskine, the warm friend and the correspondent of Mr. Edwards, being desirous of procuring a correct portrait, both of him and his wife, and hearing that a respectable English painter was in Boston, forwarded to his agent in that town, the sum requisite, not only for the portraits, but for the expenses of the journey. They were taken in 1740; and after the death of Dr. Erskine, were very kindly transmitted by his executor to Dr. Edwards.

† Hopkins's Life of Edwards. Dr. H. resided in the family a considerable time.

affections; is most just and conscientious in all her conduct; and you could not persuade her to do any thing wrong or sinful, if you would give her all the world, lest she should offend this Great Being. She is of a wonderful sweetness, calmness, and universal benevolence of mind; especially after this Great God has manifested himself to her mind. She will sometimes go about from place to place, singing sweetly; and seems to be always full of joy and pleasure; and no one knows for what. She loves to be alone, walking in the fields and groves, and seems to have some one invisible always conversing with her." After due allowance is made for animation of feeling, the reader will be convinced, that such a testimony, concerning a young lady of thirteen, could not have been given, by so competent a judge, had there not been something unusual in the purity and elevation of her mind, and the excellence of her life. Few persons, we are convinced, no older than she was at the time of her marriage, have made equal progress in holiness; and rare, very rare, is the instance, in which such a connexion results in a purer or more uninterrupted happiness. It was a union founded on high personal esteem, and on a mutual affection, which continually grew, and ripened, and mellowed for the time of harvest. The station, which she was called to fill at this early age, is one of great delicacy, as well as responsibility, and is attended with many difficulties. She entered on the performance of the various duties to her family and the people, to which it summoned her, with a firm reliance on the guidance and support of God; and perhaps no stronger evidence can be given of her substantial worth, than that from the first she discharged them in such a manner, as to secure the high and increasing approbation of all who knew her.

The attention to religion, which has been mentioned as commencing about the period of Mr. Edwards's ordination, though at no time extensive, continued about two years, and was followed by several years of inattention and indifference. His public labours were continued with faithfulness, but with no peculiar success; and he had reason to lament the too perceptible declension of his people, both in religion and morals.

On the 11th of February, 1729, his venerable colleague was removed from the scene of his earthly labours. This event was sincerely and tenderly lamented by the people of Northampton, as well as extensively throughout the province. His funeral sermon was preached by his son-in-law, the Rev. William Williams, of Hatfield; and numerous ministers, in their own pulpits, paid a similar tribute of respect to his memory.

In the spring of the same year, the health of Mr. Edwards, in consequence of too close application, so far failed him, that he was obliged to be absent from his people several months. Early in May he was at New-Haven, in company with Mrs. Edwards and their infant child, a daughter born Aug. 25th, 1728. In September, his father, in a letter to one of his daughters, expresses the hope that the health of his son is so far restored, as to enable him to resume his labours, and to preach twice on the sabbath. The summer was probably passed, partly at Northampton, and partly in travelling.

His visit to Windsor, in September, gave him his last opportunity of seeing his sister Jerusha, whom he tenderly loved; and who a little while before had passed a considerable time with her friends in Northampton. She was attacked with a malignant fever in December, and on the 22d of that month died at her father's house. The uncommon strength and excellence of her character, rendered her peculiarly dear to all her relatives and friends; and from the testimonials of her father, of four of her sisters, and of a friend of the family at a distance, written soon after her death,* I have ascertained the following particulars. She was born in June, 1710, and, on the testimony of that friend, was a young lady of great sweetness of temper, of a fine understanding, and of a beautiful countenance. She was devoted to reading from childhood, and though fond of books of taste and amusement, she customarily preferred those which require close thought, and are fitted to strengthen and inform the mind. Like her sisters, she had received a thorough education, both English and classical, and by her proficiency, had justified the views of her father, and sustained the honour and claims of her sex. In conversation, she was solid and instructive beyond her years, yet, at the same time, was sprightly and active, and had an uncommon share of native wit and humour. Her wit was always delicate and kind, and used merely for recreation. According to the rule she prescribed to another, it constituted "the sauce, and not the food, in the entertainment." Being fond of retirement and meditation from early life, she passed much of her leisure time in solitary walks in the groves behind her father's house; and the richness of her mind, in moral reflection and philosophical remark, proved that these hours were not wasted in reverie, but occupied by solid thought and profitable contemplation. Habitually serene and cheerful, she was contented and happy; not envious of others, not desirous of admiration, not ambitious nor aspiring: and while she valued highly the esteem of her friends and of the wise and good, she was firmly convinced that her happiness depended, chiefly and ultimately, on the state of her own mind. She appeared to have gained the entire government of her temper and her passions, discovered uncommon equanimity and firmness under trials, and while, in difficult cases, she sought the best advice, yet ultimately acted for herself. Her religious life began in childhood; and from that time, meditation, prayer, and reading the sacred Scriptures, were not a prescribed task, but a coveted enjoyment. Her sisters, who knew how much of her time she daily passed alone, had the best reason to believe that no place was so pleasant to her as her own retirement, and no society so delightful as solitude with God. She read theology, as a science, with the deepest interest, and pursued the systematic study of the Scriptures, by the help of the best commentaries. Her observance of the sabbath was exemplary, in solemnly preparing for it, in allotting to it the prescribed hours, and in devoting it only to sacred employments; and in the solemn and entire devotion of her mind to the duties of the sanctuary, she appeared, habitually, to feel with David, "Holiness becometh thine house for ever." Few persons attend more closely to preaching, or judge more correctly concerning it, or have higher pleasure in that which is solid, pungent, and practical. She saw and conversed with God, in his works of creation and providence. Her religious joy was, at times, intense and elevated. After telling one of her sisters, on a particular occasion, that she could not describe it, she observed to her, that it seemed like a streak of light shining in a dark place; and reminded her of a line in Watts's Lyrics,

"And sudden, from the cleaving skies, a gleam of glory broke."

* This last was published.

Her conscience was truly enlightened, and her conduct appeared to be governed by principle. She approved of the best things; discovered great reverence for religion, and strong attachment to the truly pious and conscientious; was severe in her estimate of herself, and charitable in judging of others; was not easily provoked, and usually tried to excuse the provocation; was unapt to cherish prejudices, and lamented, and strove to conceal, the faults of Christians.

On the testimony of those who knew her best, "She was a remarkably loving, dutiful, obedient daughter, and a very kind and loving sister," "very helpful and serviceable in the family, and willingly labouring with her own hands," very "kind and friendly to her neighbours," attentive to the sick, charitable to the poor, prone to sympathize with the afflicted, and merciful to the brutes; and at the same time, respectful to superiors, obliging to equals, condescending and affable to inferiors, and manifesting sincere good will to all mankind. Courteous and easy in her manners, she was also modest, unostentatious, and retiring; and, while she uniformly respected herself, she commanded the respect of all who saw her. She was fond of all that was comely in dress, but averse to every thing gay and gaudy. She loved peace, and strove to reconcile those who were at variance; was delicately attentive to those of her sex, who were slighted by others; received reproofs with meekness, and told others of their faults with so much sweetness and faithfulness, as to increase their esteem and affection for herself. She detested all guile, and management, and deception, all flattery and falsehood, and wholly refused to associate with those who exhibited this character. She was most careful and select in her friendships, and most true and faithful to her friends—highly valuing their affection, and discovering the deepest interest in their welfare. Her conversation and conduct indicated uncommon innocence and purity of mind; and she avoided many things, which are thought correct by multitudes who are strictly virtuous. During her sickness she was not forsaken. A day or two before its termination, she manifested a remarkable admiration of the grace and mercy of God, through Jesus Christ, to sinners, and particularly to herself: saying, "It is wonderful, it surprises me." A part of the time she was in some degree delirious; but, when her mind wandered, it seemed to wander heavenward. Just before her death, she attempted to sing a hymn, entitled, "The Absence of Christ," and died, in the full possession of her rational powers, expressing her hope of eternal salvation through his blood. This first example of the ravages of death, in this numerous family, was a most trying event to all its members; and the tenderness with which they cherished the memory of her who was gone, probably terminated only with life.

The second daughter of Mr. and Mrs. Edwards, was born on the 16th of the following April, and named Jerusha, after their deceased sister.

In July, 1731, Mr. Edwards being in Boston, delivered a sermon at the public lecture, entitled, "God glorified in Man's Dependence," from 1 Cor. i. 29, 30. "That no flesh should glory in his presence. But of him are ye in Christ Jesus, who of God is made unto us wisdom, and righteousness, and sanctification, and redemption. That according as it is written, He that glorieth, let him glory in the Lord." It was published, at the request of several ministers, and others who heard it, and preceded by a preface by the Rev. Messrs. Prince and Cooper, of Boston. This was his first publication, and is scarcely known to the American reader of his works. The subject was at that time novel, as exhibited by the preacher, and made a deep impression on the audience, and on the reverend gentlemen who were particularly active in procuring its publication. "It was with no small difficulty," say they, "that the author's youth and modesty were prevailed on, to let him appear a preacher in our public lecture, and afterwards to give us a copy of his discourse, at the desire of divers ministers, and others who heard it. But, as we quickly found him to be a workman that need not be ashamed before his brethren, our satisfaction was the greater, to see him pitching upon so noble a subject, and treating it with so much strength and clearness, as the judicious will perceive in the following composure: a subject, which secures to God his great design, in the work of fallen man's redemption by the Lord Jesus Christ, which is evidently so laid out, as that the glory of the whole should return to him the blessed ordainer, purchaser, and applier; a subject, which enters deep into practical religion; without the belief of which, that must soon die in the hearts and lives of men."

The following is the testimony, borne by these excellent men, to the talents and piety of the author:

"We cannot, therefore, but express our joy and thankfulness, that the great Head of the church is pleased still to raise up, from among the children of his people, for the supply of his churches, those who assert and maintain these evangelical principles; and that our churches, notwithstanding all their degeneracies, have still a high value for just principles, and for those who publicly own and teach them. And, as we cannot but wish and pray, that the college in the neighbouring colony, as well as our own, may be a fruitful mother of many such sons as the author; so we heartily rejoice, in the special favour of Providence, in bestowing such a rich gift on the happy church of Northampton, which has, for so many lustres of years, flourished under the influence of such pious doctrines, taught them in the excellent ministry of their late venerable pastor, whose gift and spirit we hope will long live and shine in his grandson, to the end that they may abound in all the lovely fruits of evangelical humility and thankfulness, to the glory of God."

The discourse itself deserves this high commendation. It was the commencement of a series of efforts, on the part of the author, to illustrate the glory of God, as appearing in the greatest of all his works, the work of man's redemption. Rare indeed is the instance, in which a first publication is equally rich in condensed thought, or in new and elevated conceptions.

The third child of Mr. and Mrs. Edwards, also a daughter, was born February 13th, 1732, and received the name of Esther, after his mother and Mrs. Stoddard.

CHAPTER VII.

REMARKABLE REVIVAL OF RELIGION, IN 1734, AND 1735—ITS EXTENT AND POWER—MANNER OF TREATING AWAKENED SINNERS—CAUSES OF ITS DECLINE—RELIGIOUS CONTROVERSY IN HAMPSHIRE—DEATH OF HIS SISTER LUCY—CHARACTERISTICS OF MRS. EDWARDS—REMAINDER OF PERSONAL NARRATIVE.

Early in 1732, the state of religion in Northampton, which had been for several years on the decline, began gradually, and perceptibly, to grow better; and an obvious check was given to the open prevalence of disorder and licentiousness. Immoral practices, which had long been customary, were regarded as disgraceful, and extensively renounced. The young, who had been the chief abettors of these disorders, and on whom the means of grace had exerted no salutary influence, discovered more of a disposition to hearken to the counsels of their parents, and the admonitions of the gospel, relinquished by degrees their more gross and public sins, and attended on the worship of the sabbath more generally, and with greater decorum and seriousness of mind; and, among the people as a body, there was a larger number than before, who manifested a personal interest in their own salvation. This desirable change in the congregation became more and more perceptible, throughout that and the following year. At the latter end of 1733, there appeared a very unusual flexibleness, and a disposition to yield to advice, in the young of both sexes; on an occasion, too, and under circumstances, where it was wholly unexpected. It had long, and perhaps always, been the custom in Northampton, to devote the sabbath evening, and the evening after the stated public lecture, to visiting and diversion. On a sabbath preceding one of the public lectures, Mr. Edwards preached a sermon on the subject, explaining the mischievous consequences of this unhappy practice, exhorting the young to a reformation; and calling on parents and masters, universally, to come to an explicit agreement with one another, to govern their families in this respect, and on these evenings to keep their children and servants at home. The following evening, it so happened that, among a considerable number visiting at his house, there were individuals from every part of the town; and he took that occasion, to propose to those who were present, that they should, in his name, request the heads of families in their respective neighbourhoods, to assemble the next day, and converse upon the subject, and agree, every one, to restrain his own family. They did so. Such a meeting was accordingly held in each neighbourhood, and the proposal was universally complied with. But, when they made known this agreement to their families, they found little or no restraint necessary; for the young people, almost without exception, declared that they were convinced, by what they had heard from the pulpit, of the impropriety of the practice, and were ready cheerfully to relinquish it. From that time forward, it was given up, and there was an immediate and thorough reformation of those disorders and immoralities, which it had occasioned. This unexpected occurrence tenderly affected the minds of the people, and happily prepared them for events of still deeper interest.

Just after this, there began to be an unusual concern on the subject of religion, at a little hamlet called Pascommuck, consisting of a few farm houses, about three miles from the principal settlement; and a number of persons, at that place, appeared to be savingly converted. In the ensuing spring, the sudden and awful death of a young man, who became immediately delirious, and continued so until he died; followed by that of a young married woman, who, after great mental suffering, appeared to find peace with God, and died full of comfort, in a most earnest and affecting manner warning and counselling others; contributed extensively, and powerfully, to impress the minds of the young, and to excite a deeper interest on the subject of religion, throughout the congregation.

The fourth child and daughter of Mr. and Mrs. Edwards was born April 7th, 1734, and baptized by the name of Mary.

In the autumn, Mr. Edwards recommended to the young people, on the day of each stated public lecture, to assemble in various parts of the town, and spend the evening in prayer, and the other duties of social religion. This they readily did, and their example was followed by those who were older.

The solemnity of mind, which now began to pervade the church and congregation, and which was constantly increasing, had a visible re-action on all the labours of Mr. Edwards, public as well as private; and it will not be easy to find discourses in any language, more solemn, spiritual, or powerful, than many of those which he now delivered. One of these, from Matt. xvi. 17. entitled, "A Divine and Supernatural Light immediately imparted to the Soul by the Spirit of God, shown to be both a Scriptural and Rational Doctrine," excited uncommon interest in the hearers, and, at their request, was now published. As an exhibition of religion, as existing within the soul, in one of its peculiar forms or aspects, it will be found, in the perusal, remarkably adapted to enlighten, to refresh, and to sanctify; while the evidence of the reality of such a light, as derived both from the Scriptures and from reason, will convince every unprejudiced mind.

At this time, a violent controversy, respecting Arminianism, prevailed extensively over that part of New England, and the friends of vital piety in Northampton regarded it as likely to have a most unhappy bearing on the interests of religion in that place; but, contrary to their fears, it was powerfully overruled for its promotion. Mr. Edwards, well knowing that the points at issue had an immediate bearing on the great subject of salvation, and that mankind never can be so powerfully affected by any subject, as when their attention to it has been strongly excited; determined, in opposition to the fears and the counsels of many of his friends, to explain his own views to his people, from the pulpit. Accordingly, he preached a series of sermons, on the various points relating to the controversy, and among others, his well-known Discourses on the great doctrine of Justification by Faith alone. For this he was sincerely censured by numbers on the spot, as well as ridiculed by many elsewhere.* The event, however, proved that he had judged wisely. In his discourses, he explained the scriptural conditions of salvation, and exposed the errors then prevalent with regard to them, with so much force of argument, and in a manner so solemn and practical, that it was attended with a signal blessing from heaven, on the people of his charge. Many, who had cherished these errors, were convinced that they could be justified only by the righteousness of Christ; while others, who had not, were brought to feel that they must be renewed by the Holy Spirit; and the minds of both were led the more earnestly to seek that they might be accepted of God. In the latter part of December, five or six individuals appeared to be very suddenly and savingly converted, one after another; and some of them in a manner so remarkable, as to awaken very great numbers, of all ages and conditions.

The year 1735 opened on Northampton in a most auspicious manner. A deep and solemn interest in the great truths of religion, had become universal in all parts of the town, and among all classes of people. This was the only subject of conversation in every company; and almost the only business of the people appeared to be, to secure their salvation. So extensive was the influence of the Spirit of God, that there was scarcely an individual in the town, either old or young, who was left unconcerned about the great things of the eternal world. This was true of the gayest, of the most licentious, and of the most hostile to religion. And in the midst of this universal attention, the work of conversion was carried on in the most astonishing manner. Every day witnessed its triumphs; and so great was the alteration in the appearance of the town, that in the spring and summer following, it appeared to be full of the presence of God. There was scarcely a house which did not furnish the tokens of his presence, and scarcely a family which did not present the trophies of his grace. "The town," says Mr. Edwards, "was never so full of love, nor so full of joy, nor yet so full of distress, as it was then." Whenever he met the people in the sanctuary, he not only saw the house crowded, but every hearer earnest to receive the truth of God, and often the whole assembly dissolved in tears: some weeping for sorrow, others for joy, and others from compassion. In the months of March and April, when the work of God was carried on with the greatest power, he supposes the number, apparently of genuine conversions, to have been at least four a day, or nearly thirty a week, take one week with another, for five or six weeks together.

During the winter and spring, many persons from the neighbouring towns came to Northampton, to attend the stated lectures of Mr. Edwards; many others, on business, or on visits; and many others, from a distance, having heard contradictory reports of the state of things, came to see and examine for themselves. Of these, great numbers had their consciences awakened, were savingly wrought upon, and went home rejoicing in the forgiving love of God. This appeared to be the means of spreading the same influence in the adjacent towns, and in places more remote, so that no less than ten towns in the same county, and seventeen in the adjoining colony of Connecticut, within a short time, were favoured with revivals of religion.

This was undoubtedly one of the most remarkable events of the kind, that has occurred since the canon of the New Testament was finished. It was so on account of its universality: no class, nor age, nor description, was exempt. Upwards of fifty persons above forty years of age, and ten above ninety, near thirty between ten and fourteen, and one of four,† became, in the view of Mr. Edwards, the subjects of the renewing grace of God. It was so on account of the unusual numbers, who appeared to become Christians; amounting to more than three hundred persons, in half a year, and about as many of them males as females. Previous to one sacrament, about one hundred were received to the communion, and near sixty previous to another; and the whole number of communicants, at one time, was about six hundred and twenty, including almost all the adult population of the town. It was so in its rapid progress, in its amazing power, in the depth of the convictions felt, and in the degree of light, of love, and of joy communicated; as well as in its great extent, and in its swift propagation from place to place.

Early in the progress of this work of grace, Mr. Edwards seems to have decided for himself, the manner in which he was bound to treat awakened sinners:—to urge repentance on every such sinner, as his immediate duty; to insist that God is under no manner of obligation to any unrenewed man; and that a man can challenge nothing, either in absolute justice, or by free promise, on account of any thing he does before he repents and believes. He was fully convinced that if he had taught those, who came to consult him in their spiritual troubles, any other doctrines, he should have taken the most direct course to have utterly undone them. The discourses, which, beyond measure more than any others which he preached, "had an immediate saving effect," were several from Rom. iii. 19. "That every mouth may be stopped,"—in which he endeavoured to show that it would be just with God, for ever to reject, and cast off, mere natural men.

Though it had not been the custom, as we have already seen, for a long period at Northampton, to require of candidates for admission to the church, a credible relation of the evidences of their own conversion, because, if unconverted, they were supposed to have a right to the sacrament of the Lord's supper, as a converting ordinance; yet Mr. Edwards supposed he had very "sufficient evidence" of the conversion of those who were now admitted. There can be but little doubt, however, that, if the rules of the church had required, in every case, a thorough examination of the candidate's piety, the period of probation would have been longer, the danger of a false profession more solemnly realized, and the examination of each individual, by the pastor of the church, as well as by himself, far more strict; or that many, at first, regarded, both by themselves and others, as unquestionably Christians, would not, at that time, have made a profession of re-

* Among those who opposed Mr. Edwards on this occasion, were several members of a family, in a neighbouring town, nearly connected with his own, and possessing, from its numbers, wealth, and respectability, a considerable share of influence. Their religious sentiments differed widely from his, and their opposition to him, in the course which he now pursued, became direct and violent. As his defence of his own opinions was regarded as triumphant, they appear to have felt, in some degree, the shame and mortification of a defeat; and their opposition to Mr. Edwards, though he resorted to every honourable method of conciliation, became, on their part, a settled personal hostility. It is probable, that their advice to Mr. Edwards, to refrain from the controversy, and particularly, not to publish his sentiments with regard to it, was given somewhat categorically, and with a full expectation that he, young as he was, would comply with it. His refusal so to do, was an offence not to be forgiven. We shall have occasion to recur to this subject again.

† Of the conversion of this child, whose name was Phebe Bartlett, a most minute and interesting account is given in the "Narrative of Surprising Conversions." Dr. Edwards, under date of March 30, 1789, in a letter to Dr. Ryland, says, "In answer to your inquiry, in a former letter, concerning Phebe Bartlett, I have to inform you, that she is yet living, and has uniformly maintained the character of a true convert."

ligion. But unfortunately he had never fully examined the scriptural ground for admission to the Lord's supper, and, like many others, had taken it for granted, that Mr. Stoddard's views of the subject were just. Had he investigated it as thoroughly, at that important crisis, as he did afterwards, there can be but little doubt that, in the high state of religious feeling then prevalent, the church would readily have changed its practice, or that all the candidates for admission would have consented to a thorough examination. Had such indeed been the issue, Mr. Edwards himself would have been saved from many trials, and the church and people of Northampton from great and incalculable evils: still it may well be doubted, whether the actual result has not occasioned a far greater amount of good to the church at large.

In the latter part of May, 1735, this great work of the Spirit of God began obviously to decline, and the instances of conversion to be less numerous, both at Northampton and in the neighbouring villages. One principal cause of this declension, is undoubtedly to be found in the fact, that in all these places, both among ministers and private christians, the *physical excitement* had been greater than the human constitution can, for a long period, endure. Nothing, it should be remembered, exhausts the strength and the animal spirits, like *feeling*. One hour of intense joy, or of intense sorrow, will more entirely prostrate the frame, than weeks of close study. In revivals of religion, as they have hitherto appeared, the nerves of the whole man—of body, mind, and heart,—are kept continually on the stretch, from month to month; until at length they are relaxed, and become non-elastic; and then all feeling and energy, of every kind, is gone. Another reason is undoubtedly to be found in the fact, that those, who had so long witnessed this remarkable work of God, without renouncing their sins, had at length become hardened and hopeless in their impenitence. Mr. Edwards also attributes it, in part, to two striking events of Providence, at Northampton, and to two remarkable instances of enthusiastic delusion, in two of the neighbouring villages.

He mentions also a third cause, and one far more powerful, and more extensive in its influence, than either of the two last. This was an ecclesiastical controversy, growing out of the settlement of a minister at Springfield, in which he himself was ultimately compelled, though with great reluctance, to take a part; which agitated, not only the county of Hampshire, but the more remote churches of the province. Of this, a bare mention would alone be necessary, did we not find his connexion with it referred to, at a subsequent and most interesting period of his life.

In 1735, the first church in Springfield, having elected a pastor, invited the churches in the southern part of Hampshire, by their pastors and delegates in council, to proceed to his ordination. The council, when convened, after examining the qualifications of the candidate, refused to ordain him, and assigned two reasons for this refusal—youthful immorality, and anti-scriptural tenets. Mr. Edwards, though invited to this council, for some reason or other, was not present. The church, in August, called a second council, consisting chiefly of ministers and delegates from the churches in Boston, which, without delay, proceeded to the ordination. The first council, finding their own measures thus openly impeached, published a pamphlet entitled, "A Narrative and Defence of the Proceedings of the Ministers of Hampshire," &c. justifying their own conduct, and censuring that of their brethren. The second council defended themselves in a pamphlet entitled, "An Answer to the Hampshire Narrative." Mr. Edwards, at the request of the first council, and particularly of his uncle, the Rev. Mr. Williams, of Hatfield, who was its moderator, wrote a reply to this, entitled, "A Letter to the Author of the Pamphlet called, An Answer to the Hampshire Narrative."—This reply, viewed either as an argument upon the law and the facts, or as an answer to his opponents, is an exhibition of logic, not often met with in similar discussions, and appears to have concluded the controversy. This series of events occurred during the revival of religion in the churches of that county, and was thought, by too powerfully engrossing the attention, both of ministers and people, in various places, to have hastened its conclusion. And there can be no doubt that this opinion was correct. A revival of religion is nothing but the *immediate result* of an uncommon *attention*, on the part of a church and congregation, to the truth of God;—particularly to the great truths, which disclose the worth of the soul, and the only way in which it can be saved. Whenever, and wherever, the members of a church pay the due attention to these truths, by giving them their proper influence on their hearts, religion revives immediately in their affections and their conduct; and when the impenitent pay such attention, the kingdom of heaven immediately "suffereth violence, and the violent take it by force." The only effectual way to put a stop to such a work of grace, is, therefore, *to divert the attention* of Christians and sinners from those truths which bear immediately on the work of salvation.

In the latter part of the summer, Mr. and Mrs. Edwards were called to mourn the death of another of his sisters, named Lucy, the youngest but one of his father's children; who was born in 1715, and died August 21, 1736,* at the age of 21. After her they named their fifth child, who was born August 31, of the same year.

It was a peculiarly favourable dispensation of Providence, that, amid the multiplied cares and labours of this period, the health of Mr. Edwards was graciously preserved. A revival of religion to a minister, like the period of harvest to the husbandman, is the most busy and the most exhausting of all seasons; and during the progress of that, which he had just witnessed, not only was the whole time of Mr. Edwards fully occupied, but all the powers of his mind were laboriously employed, and all the feelings of his heart kept, from month to month, in high and powerful excitement. In addition to his ordinary duties as a teacher and pastor, his public lectures were now multiplied, private lectures were weekly appointed in different parts of the town, and his study was almost daily thronged by multitudes, looking to him as their spiritual guide. From the adjacent villages, also, great numbers resorted to him, for the same purpose, having the highest confidence in his wisdom and experience; and numerous ministers from various parts of the country, came to his house, to witness the triumphs of divine grace, and to gain, from his counsels and his measures, more just conceptions of the best manner of discharging the highest and most sacred duties of their office.

In the midst of these complicated labours, as well as at all times, he found at home one, who was in every sense a *help meet* for him; one who made their common dwelling the abode of order and neatness, of peace and comfort,

* I have discovered no papers or letters of the family, of a date near this, and no mention of this young lady, except on her tombstone.

of harmony and love, to all its inmates, and of kindness and hospitality to the friend, the visitant, and the stranger. "While she uniformly paid a becoming deference to her husband, and treated him with entire respect, she spared no pains in conforming to his inclinations, and rendering every thing in the family agreeable and pleasant: accounting it her greatest glory, and that wherein she could best serve God and her generation, to be the means, in this way, of promoting his usefulness and happiness. As he was of a weakly, infirm constitution, and was necessarily peculiarly exact in his diet, she was a tender nurse to him, cheerfully attending upon him at all times, and in all things ministering to his comfort. And no person of discernment could be conversant in the family, without observing, and admiring, the perfect harmony, and mutual love and esteem, that subsisted between them. At the same time, when she herself laboured under bodily disorders and pains, which was not unfrequently the case, instead of troubling those around her with her complaints, and wearing a sour or dejected countenance, as if out of humour with every body, and every thing around her, because she was disregarded and neglected; she was accustomed to bear up under them, not only with patience, but with cheerfulness and good humour."

Devoted as Mr. Edwards was to study, and to the duties of his profession, it was necessary for him at all times, but especially in a season like this, of multiplied toils and anxieties, to be relieved from attention to all secular concerns; and it was a most happy circumstance, that he could trust every thing of this nature to the care of Mrs. Edwards, with entire safety, and with undoubting confidence. "She was a most judicious and faithful mistress of a family, habitually industrious, a sound economist, managing her household affairs with diligence and discretion. She was conscientiously careful that nothing should be wasted and lost; and often when she herself took care to save any thing *of trifling value*, or directed her children or others to do so, or when she saw them *waste* any thing, she would repeat the words of our Saviour—'THAT NOTHING BE LOST;' which words she said she often thought of, as containing a maxim worth remembering, especially when considered as the reason alleged by Christ, why his disciples should gather up the fragments of that bread which he had just before *created with a word*. She took almost the whole direction of the temporal affairs of the family without doors and within, managing them with great wisdom and prudence as well as cheerfulness; and in this was particularly suited to the disposition as well as the habits and necessities of her husband, who chose to have no care, if possible, of any worldly business."

But there are other duties, of a still more tender and difficult nature, which none but a parent can adequately perform; and it was an unspeakable privilege to Mr. Edwards, now surrounded by a young and growing family, that when his duties to his people, especially in seasons like this, necessarily occupied his whole attention, he could safely commit his children to the wisdom and piety, the love and faithfulness, of their mother. Her views of the responsibility of parents were large and comprehensive. "She thought that, as a parent, she had great and important duties to do towards her children, before they were capable of government and instruction. For them, she constantly and earnestly prayed, and bore them on her heart before God, in all her secret and most solemn addresses to him; and that, even before they were born. The prospect of her becoming the mother of a rational immortal creature, which came into existence in an undone and infinitely dreadful state, was sufficient to lead her to bow before God daily, for his blessing on it—even redemption and eternal life by Jesus Christ. So that, through all the pain, labour, and sorrow, which attended her being the mother of children, she was in travail for them, that they might be born of God."

She regularly prayed with her children, from a very early period, and, as there is the best reason to believe, with great earnestness and importunity. Being thoroughly sensible that, in many respects, the chief care of forming children by government and instruction naturally lies on mothers, as they are most with their children at an age when they commonly receive impressions that are permanent, and have great influence in forming the character for life, she was very careful to do her part in this important business. When she foresaw or met with any special difficulty in this matter, she was wont to apply to her husband for advice and assistance; and on such occasions, they would both attend to it as a matter of the utmost importance. She had an excellent way of governing her children: she knew how to make them regard and obey her cheerfully, without loud angry words, much less, heavy blows. She seldom punished them; and in speaking to them used gentle and pleasant words. If any correction was necessary, she did not administer it in a passion; and when she had occasion to reprove and rebuke, she would do it in few words, without warmth and noise, and with all calmness and gentleness of mind. In her directions and reproofs in matters of importance, she would address herself to the reason of her children, that they might not only know her inclination and will, but at the same time be convinced of the reasonableness of it. She had need to speak but once; she was cheerfully obeyed; murmuring and answering again were not known among them. In their manners, they were uncommonly respectful to their parents. When their parents came into the room, they all rose instinctively from their seats, and never resumed them until their parents were seated; and when either parent was speaking, no matter with whom they had been conversing, they were all immediately silent and attentive. The kind and gentle treatment they received from their mother, while she strictly and punctiliously maintained her parental authority, seemed naturally to beget and promote a filial respect and affection, and to lead them to a mild, tender treatment of each other. Quarrelling and contention, which too frequently take place among children, were in her family wholly unknown. She carefully observed the first appearance of resentment and ill will in her young children, towards any person whatever, and did not connive at it, as many who have the care of children do, but was careful to show her displeasure, and suppress it to the utmost; yet not by angry, wrathful words, which often provoke children to wrath, and stir up their irascible passions, rather than abate them. Her system of discipline was begun at a very early age, and it was her rule to resist the first, as well as every subsequent, exhibition of temper or disobedience in the child, however young, until its will was brought into submission to the will of its parents; wisely reflecting, that until a child will obey his parents, he can never be brought to obey God.

Fond as Mr. Edwards was of welcoming the friend and

the stranger, and much as his house was a favourite place of resort, to ministers and others; it was absolutely necessary at all times, and peculiarly so in seasons of religious attention like this, that some one, well knowing how to perform the rites of hospitality, and to pay all the civilities and charities of life, should relieve him from these attentions, during those hours which were consecrated to his professional duties; and here, also, he could most advantageously avail himself of the assistance of Mrs. Edwards. Educated in the midst of polished life, familiar from childhood with the rules of decorum and good breeding, affable and easy in her manners, and governed by the feelings of liberality and benevolence, she was remarkable for her kindness to her friends, and to the visitants who resorted to Mr. Edwards; sparing no pains to make them welcome, and to provide for their convenience and comfort. She was also peculiarly kind to strangers who came to her house. By her sweet and winning manners and ready conversation, she soon became acquainted with them, and brought them to feel acquainted with herself; and showed such concern for their comfort, and so kindly offered what she thought they needed, that while her friendly attentions discovered at once that she knew the feelings of a stranger, they also made their way directly to his heart, and gaining his confidence, led him immediately to feel as if he were at home, in the midst of near and affectionate friends.

"She made it her rule to speak well of all, so far as she could with truth and justice to herself and others. She was not wont to dwell with delight on the imperfections and failings of any; and when she heard persons speaking ill of others, she would say what she thought she could with truth and justice in their excuse, or divert the obloquy, by mentioning those things that were commendable in them. Thus she was tender of every one's character, even of those who injured and spoke evil of her; and carefully guarded against the too common vice of evil speaking and backbiting. She could bear injuries and reproach with great calmness, without any disposition to render evil for evil; but, on the contrary, was ready to pity and forgive those who appeared to be her enemies." This course of conduct, steadily pursued, secured, in an unusual degree, the affection and confidence of those who knew her.

She proved, also, an invaluable auxiliary to Mr. Edwards, in the duties of his profession, not only by her excellent example, but by her active efforts in doing good. "She was," says Dr. Hopkins, "eminent for her piety, and for experimental religion. Religious conversation was her delight; and, as far as propriety permitted, she promoted it in all companies. Her religious conversation showed at once her clear comprehension of spiritual and divine things, and the deep impression which they had made upon her mind." It was not merely conversation *about* religion—about its truths, or duties, or its actual state—its doctrines or triumphs—or the character and conduct of its friends and ministers: it was religion itself;—that supreme love to God, to his kingdom and his glory, which, abounding in the heart, flows forth spontaneously, in the daily conversation and the daily life.

The friends of vital Christianity, those who delighted in its great and essential truths, who showed its practical influence on their lives, and who were most engaged in promoting its prosperity, were her chosen friends and intimates. With such persons, she would converse freely and confidentially, telling them of the exercises of her own heart, and the happiness she had experienced in a life of religion, for their encouragement in the christian course. Her mind appeared to attend to spiritual and divine things constantly, on all occasions, and in every condition and business of life. Secret prayer was her uniform practice, and appeared to be the source of daily enjoyment. She was a constant attendant on public worship, and always exhibited the deepest solemnity and reverence in the house of God. She always prized highly the privilege of social worship, not only in the family, but in the private meetings of christians. Such meetings, on the part of females *only*, for prayer and religious conversation, have at times been objected to, as, both in their nature and results, inconsistent with the true delicacy of the sex. Her own judgment, formed deliberately, and in coincidence with that of her husband, was in favour of these meetings; and accordingly, she regularly encouraged and promoted them, during the revival of religion of which we have been speaking, as well as at other times; attending on them herself, and not declining to take her proper share in the performance of their various duties. In this way, she exerted an important influence among her own sex, and over the young; an influence always salutary in promoting union, ardour, and spiritual-mindedness, but especially powerful in seasons of uncommon attention to religion.

One circumstance, which served essentially to extend and increase this influence, was the fact, that her religion had nothing gloomy or forbidding in its character. Unusual as it was in degree, it was eminently the religion of joy. On the testimony of Mr. Edwards, it possessed this character, even when she was a little child of about five or six years of age, as well as customarily in after-life. At the commencement of this remarkable work of grace, she appears to have dedicated herself anew to God, with more entire devotion of heart to his service and glory, than she had ever been conscious of before; and during its progress, as well as afterwards, she experienced a degree of religious enjoyment, not previously known to herself, and not often vouchsafed to others. But on this subject, we may have occasion to speak more fully hereafter.

What, during this interesting work of grace, was the state of Mr. Edwards's own feelings on the subject of religion, must be gathered chiefly from his sermons written at the time, from the "Narrative of Surprising Conversions," and from that high character for moral excellence, which he enjoyed not only among his own people, but among the ministers. Yet the remainder of his Personal Narrative, extending from his settlement, until a date somewhat later than this, and of course including this period, presents a general view of the subject, in a high degree interesting, and most proper to be inserted here.

REMAINDER OF PERSONAL NARRATIVE.

"Since I came to Northampton, I have often had sweet complacency in God, in views of his glorious perfections, and of the excellency of Jesus Christ. God has appeared to me a glorious and lovely Being, chiefly on account of his holiness. The holiness of God has always appeared to me the most lovely of all his attributes. The doctrines of God's absolute sovereignty, and free grace, in showing mercy to whom he would show mercy; and man's absolute dependence on the operations of God's Holy Spirit, have very often appeared to me as sweet and glorious doctrines These doctrines have been much my delight. God's sovereignty has ever appeared to me a great part of his glory. It has often been my delight to approach God, and adore him as a sovereign God, and ask sovereign mercy of him.

"I have loved the doctrines of the gospel; they have been to my soul like green pastures. The gospel has seemed to me the richest treasure; the treasure that I have most desired, and longed that it might dwell richly in me. The way of salvation by Christ has appeared, in a general way, glorious and excellent, most pleasant and most beautiful. It has often seemed to me, that it would, in a great measure, spoil heaven, to receive it in any other way. That text has often been affecting and delightful to me, Isa. xxxii. 2. 'A man shall be an hiding place from the wind, and a covert from the tempest,' &c.

"It has often appeared to me delightful, to be united to Christ; to have him for my Head, and to be a member of his body; also to have Christ for my Teacher and Prophet. I very often think with sweetness, and longings, and pantings of soul, of being a little child, taking hold of Christ, to be led by him through the wilderness of this world. That text, Matt. xviii. 3. has often been sweet to me, 'Except ye be converted, and become as little children,' &c. I love to think of coming to Christ, to receive salvation of him, poor in spirit, and quite empty of self, humbly exalting him alone; cut off entirely from my own root, in order to grow into and out of Christ: to have God in Christ to be all in all; and to live, by faith on the Son of God, a life of humble, unfeigned confidence in him. That scripture has often been sweet to me, Ps. cxv. 1. 'Not unto us, O Lord, not unto us, but unto thy name give glory, for thy mercy, and for thy truth's sake.' And those words of Christ, Luke x. 21. 'In that hour Jesus rejoiced in spirit, and said, I thank thee, O Father, Lord of heaven and earth, that thou hast hid these things from the wise and prudent, and hast revealed them unto babes: even so, Father, for so it seemed good in thy sight.' That sovereignty of God, which Christ rejoiced in, seemed to me worthy of such joy; and that rejoicing seemed to show the excellency of Christ, and of what spirit he was.

"Sometimes, only mentioning a single word caused my heart to burn within me; or only seeing the name of Christ, or the name of some attribute of God. And God has appeared glorious to me, on account of the Trinity. It has made me have exalting thoughts of God, that he subsists in three persons; Father, Son, and Holy Ghost. The sweetest joys and delights I have experienced, have not been those that have arisen from a hope of my own good estate; but in a direct view of the glorious things of the gospel. When I enjoy this sweetness, it seems to carry me above the thoughts of my own estate; it seems, at such times, a loss that I cannot bear, to take off my eye from the glorious, pleasant object I behold without me, to turn my eye in upon myself, and my own good estate.

"My heart has been much on the advancement of Christ's kingdom in the world. The histories of the past advancement of Christ's kingdom have been sweet to me. When I have read histories of past ages, the pleasantest thing, in all my reading, has been, to read of the kingdom of Christ being promoted. And when I have expected, in my reading, to come to any such thing, I have rejoiced in the prospect, all the way as I read. And my mind has been much entertained and delighted with the scripture promises and prophecies, which relate to the future glorious advancement of Christ's kingdom upon earth.

"I have sometimes had a sense of the excellent fulness of Christ, and his meetness and suitableness as a Saviour; whereby he has appeared to me, far above all, the chief of ten thousands. His blood and atonement have appeared sweet, and his righteousness sweet; which was always accompanied with ardency of spirit; and inward strugglings and breathings, and groanings that cannot be uttered, to be emptied of myself, and swallowed up in Christ.

"Once, as I rode out into the woods for my health, in 1737, having alighted from my horse in a retired place, as my manner commonly has been, to walk for divine contemplation and prayer, I had a view, that for me was extraordinary, of the glory of the Son of God, as Mediator between God and man, and his wonderful, great, full, pure and sweet grace and love, and meek and gentle condescension. This grace that appeared so calm and sweet, appeared also great above the heavens. The person of Christ appeared ineffably excellent, with an excellency great enough to swallow up all thought and conception—which continued, as near as I can judge, about an hour; which kept me the greater part of the time in a flood of tears, and weeping aloud. I felt an ardency of soul to be, what I know not otherwise how to express, emptied and annihilated; to lie in the dust, and to be full of Christ alone; to love him with a holy and pure love; to trust in him; to live upon him; to serve and follow him; and to be perfectly sanctified and made pure, with a divine and heavenly purity. I have several other times had views very much of the same nature, and which have had the same effects.

"I have, many times, had a sense of the glory of the Third Person in the Trinity, and his office as Sanctifier; in his holy operations, communicating divine light and life to the soul. God in the communications of his Holy Spirit, has appeared as an infinite fountain of divine glory and sweetness; being full, and sufficient to fill and satisfy the soul; pouring forth itself in sweet communications; like the sun in its glory, sweetly and pleasantly diffusing light and life. And I have sometimes an affecting sense of the excellency of the word of God as a word of life; as the light of life; a sweet, excellent, life-giving word; accompanied with a thirsting after that word, that it might dwell richly in my heart.

"Often, since I lived in this town, I have had very affecting views of my own sinfulness and vileness; very frequently to such a degree, as to hold me in a kind of loud weeping, sometimes for a considerable time together; so that I have often been forced to shut myself up. I have had a vastly greater sense of my own wickedness, and the badness of my heart, than ever I had before my conversion.* It has often appeared to me, that if God should mark iniquity against me, I should appear the very worst of all mankind; of all that have been since the beginning of the world to this time: and that I should have by far the lowest place in hell. When others, that have come to talk with me about their soul-concerns, have expressed

* Our author does not say, that he *had* more wickedness, and badness of heart, since his conversion, than he had before; but that he had a greater *sense* thereof. Thus a blind man may *have* his garden *full* of noxious weeds, and yet not *see* or be *sensible* of them. But should the garden be in great part cleared of these, and furnished with many beautiful and salutary plants; and supposing the owner now to have the power of discriminating objects of sight; in this case, he would *have* less, but would *see* and have a *sense* of more. And thus it was that St. Paul, though greatly freed from sin, yet *saw* and *felt* himself as "the chief of sinners." To which may be added, that the better the organ, and clearer the light may be, the stronger will be the *sense* excited by sin or holiness.

the sense they have had of their own wickedness, by saying, that it seemed to them, that they were as bad as the devil himself; I thought their expressions seemed exceeding faint and feeble, to represent my wickedness.

"My wickedness, as I am in myself, has long appeared to me perfectly ineffable, and swallowing up all thought and imagination; like an infinite deluge, or mountains over my head. I know not how to express better what my sins appear to me to be, than by heaping infinite upon infinite, and multiplying infinite by infinite. Very often, for these many years, these expressions are in my mind, and in my mouth, 'Infinite upon infinite—Infinite upon infinite!' When I look into my heart, and take a view of my wickedness, it looks like an abyss, infinitely deeper than hell. And it appears to me, that were it not for free grace, exalted and raised up to the infinite height of all the fulness and glory of the great Jehovah, and the arm of his power and grace stretched forth in all the majesty of his power, and in all the glory of his sovereignty, I should appear sunk down in my sins below hell itself; far beyond the sight of every thing, but the eye of sovereign grace, that can pierce even down to such a depth. And yet, it seems to me that my conviction of sin is exceedingly small and faint; it is enough to amaze me, that I have no more sense of my sin. I know certainly, that I have very little sense of my sinfulness. When I have had turns of weeping and crying for my sins, I thought I knew at the time, that my repentance was nothing to my sin.

"I have greatly longed of late for a broken heart, and to lie low before God; and, when I ask for humility, I cannot bear the thoughts of being no more humble than other Christians. It seems to me, that though their degrees of humility may be suitable for them, yet it would be a vile self-exaltation in me, not to be the lowest in humility of all mankind. Others speak of their longing to be 'humbled to the dust;' that may be a proper expression for them, but I always think of myself, that I ought, and it is an expression that has long been natural for me to use in prayer, 'to lie infinitely low before God.' And it is affecting to think, how ignorant I was, when a young Christian, of the bottomless, infinite depths of wickedness, pride, hypocrisy, and deceit, left in my heart.

"I have a much greater sense of my universal, exceeding dependence on God's grace and strength, and mere good pleasure, of late, than I used formerly to have; and have experienced more of an abhorrence of my own righteousness. The very thought of any joy arising in me, on any consideration of my own amiableness, performances, or experiences, or any goodness of heart or life, is nauseous and detestable to me. And yet, I am greatly afflicted with a proud and self-righteous spirit, much more sensibly than I used to be formerly. I see that serpent rising and putting forth its head continually, every where, all around me.

"Though it seems to me, that in some respects I was a far better Christian, for two or three years after my first conversion, than I am now; and lived in a more constant delight and pleasure; yet of late years, I have had a more full and constant sense of the absolute sovereignty of God, and a delight in that sovereignty; and have had more of a sense of the glory of Christ, as a Mediator revealed in the gospel. On one Saturday night, in particular, I had such a discovery of the excellency of the gospel above all other doctrines, that I could not but say to myself, 'This is my chosen light, my chosen doctrine;' and of Christ, 'This is my chosen Prophet.' It appeared sweet, beyond all expression, to follow Christ, and to be taught, and enlightened, and instructed by him; to learn of him, and live to him. Another Saturday night, (*Jan.* 1739,) I had such a sense, how sweet and blessed a thing it was to walk in the way of duty; to do that which was right and meet to be done, and agreeable to the holy mind of God; that it caused me to break forth into a kind of loud weeping, which held me some time, so that I was forced to shut myself up, and fasten the doors. I could not but, as it were, cry out, 'How happy are they, who do that which is right in the sight of God! They are blessed indeed, *they* are the happy ones!' I had, at the same time, a very affecting sense, how meet and suitable it was that God should govern the world, and order all things according to his own pleasure; and I rejoiced in it, that God reigned, and that his will was done."

CHAPTER VIII.

"NARRATIVE OF SURPRISING CONVERSIONS"—HIS VIEWS OF REVIVALS OF RELIGION—REMARKABLE PROVIDENCE AT NORTHAMPTON—"FIVE DISCOURSES"—MR BELLAMY A RESIDENT OF HIS FAMILY—HISTORY OF REDEMPTION—EXTRA-PAROCHIAL LABOURS OF MR. EDWARDS—SERMON AT ENFIELD—FUNERAL SERMON ON THE REV. W WILLIAMS.

On the 30th of May, 1735, Mr. Edwards, in answer to a letter from the Rev. Dr. Colman, of Boston, wrote a succinct account of the work of Divine grace at Northampton; which, being published by him, and forwarded to the Rev. Dr. Watts and the Rev. Dr. Guyse, in London, those gentlemen discovered so much interest in the facts recited, detailing them on several occasions before large assemblies, that the author, at the request of his correspondent, was induced to prepare a much fuller statement, in a letter to the same gentleman, bearing date, Nov. 6, 1736. This was published in London, under the title of "Narrative of Surprising Conversions," with an Introduction by Dr. Watts and Dr. Guyse; and was read very extensively, and with very lively emotions, by Christians in England. There, this mark of Divine grace was regarded, not only with very deep interest, but with surprise and wonder: nothing like it, for its extent and power, having been witnessed in that country, for many previous years. Those excellent men observe, "We are abundantly satisfied of the truth of this narrative, not only from the character of the writer, but from the concurrent testimony of many other persons in New England; *for this thing was not done in a corner*. There is a spot of ground, as we are here informed, wherein there are twelve or fourteen towns and villages, chiefly situate in the county of Hampshire, near the banks of the river Connecticut, within the compass of thirty miles, wherein it pleased God, two years ago, to display his sovereign mercy, in the conversion of a great multitude of souls, in a short space of time; turning them from a formal, cold, and careless profession of Christianity, to the lively exercise of every christian grace, and the powerful practice of our holy religion. The great God has seemed to act over again the miracle of Gideon's fleece, which was plentifully watered with the dew of heaven, while the rest of the earth round about it was dry, and had no such remarkable blessing.

"There has been a great and just complaint, for many years, among the ministers and churches of Old England, and in New, (except about the time of the late earthquake there,) that the work of conversion goes on very slowly, that the Spirit of God, in his saving influences, is much withdrawn from the ministrations of his word; and there are few that receive the ministrations of the gospel, with any eminent success upon their hearts. But as the gospel is the same divine instrument of grace still, as ever it was in the days of the apostles, so our ascended Saviour, now and then, takes a special occasion to manifest the divinity of this gospel, by a plentiful effusion of his Spirit where it is preached: then sinners are turned into saints in numbers, and there is a new face of things spread over a town or country. The wilderness and the solitary places are glad, the desert rejoices and blossoms as the rose; and surely, concerning this instance, we may add, that they have seen the glory of the Lord there, and the excellency of our God; they have seen the outgoings of God our King in his sanctuary."

This work was the first of a series of publications from Mr. Edwards, intended to explain the nature and effects of saving conversion, and the nature of a genuine work of the Holy Spirit in a community. As a religious narrative, it is one of the most interesting I have hitherto met with; having all that exactness of description and vividness of colouring, which attend the account of an eye-witness, when drawn up, not from recollection, but in the very passing of the scenes which he describes. It proved a most useful and seasonable publication. For a long period, revivals of religion had been chiefly unknown, both in Great Britain and on the continent of Europe. The church at large had generally ceased to expect events of this nature, regarding them as confined to apostolic times, and to the ultimate triumphs of Christianity; and appear to have entertained very imperfect views of their causes, their nature, and the manner in which they ought to be regarded. In no previous publication had these important subjects been adequately explained. The particular event, which Mr. Edwards had the privilege of recording, viewed as a remarkable work of Divine grace, has, to this day, scarcely a parallel in the modern annals of the church. His own views of these subjects were alike removed from the apathy of unbelief, and the wildness of enthusiasm; they were derived, not merely from his familiarity with the facts, but from just conceptions of the intellectual and moral faculties of man, and from a thorough knowledge of the word of God. And while the "Narrative of Surprising Conversions" served to inspire the church at large with a new and higher kind of faith, and hope, and zeal, it also proved a safe directory of their views and their conduct. In a short time it was extensively circulated, both in England and Scotland; and in the latter country, as we shall soon have occasion to remark, its diffusion was speedily followed by salutary and important consequences.

It may not be improper to insert in this place the following letter of Mr. Edwards, giving an account of a surprising and alarming providence, which attended the people of Northampton, in the early part of 1737.

"*Northampton, March* 19, 1737.

"We in this town were, the last Lord's day, (March 13th,) the spectators, and many of us the subjects, of one of the most amazing instances of Divine preservation, that perhaps was ever known in the world. Our meeting-house is old and decayed, so that we have been for some time building a new one, which is yet unfinished. It has been observed of late, that the house we have hitherto met in, has gradually spread at the bottom; the sills and walls giving way, especially in the foreside, by reason of the weight of timber at top pressing on the braces, that are inserted into the posts and beams of the house. It has done so more than ordinarily this spring: which seems to have been occasioned by the heaving of the ground, through the extreme frosts of the winter past, and its now settling again on that side which is next the sun, by the spring thaws. By this means, the underpinning has been considerably disordered, which people were not sensible of, till the ends of the joists, which bore up the front gallery, were drawn off from the girts on which they rested, by the walls giving way. So that in the midst of the public exercise in the forenoon, soon after the beginning of the sermon, the whole gallery—full of people, with all the seats and timbers, suddenly, and without any warning—sunk, and fell down, with the most amazing noise, upon the heads of those that sat under, to the astonishment of the congregation. The house was filled with dolorous shrieking and crying; and nothing else was expected than to find many people dead, or dashed to pieces.

"The gallery, in falling, seemed to break and sink first in the middle; so that those who were upon it were thrown together in heaps before the front door. But the whole was so sudden, that many of those who fell, knew nothing what it was, at the time, that had befallen them. Others in the congregation thought it had been an amazing clap of thunder. The falling gallery seemed to be broken all to pieces before it got down; so that some who fell with it, as well as those who were under, were buried in the ruins; and were found pressed under heavy loads of timber, and could do nothing to help themselves.

"But so mysteriously and wonderfully did it come to pass, that every life was preserved; and though many were greatly bruised, and their flesh torn, yet there is not, as I can understand, one bone broken, or so much as put out of joint, among them all. Some, who were thought to be almost dead at first, are greatly recovered; and but one young woman seems yet to remain in dangerous circumstances, by an inward hurt in her breast; but of late there appears more hope of her recovery.

"None can give an account, or conceive, by what means people's lives and limbs should be thus preserved, when so great a multitude were thus imminently exposed. It looked as though it was impossible, but that great numbers must instantly be crushed to death, or dashed in pieces. It seems unreasonable to ascribe it to any thing else but the care of Providence, in disposing the motions of every piece of timber, and the precise place of safety where every one should sit and fall, when none were in any capacity to care for their own preservation. The preservation seems to be most wonderful, with respect to the women and children in the middle alley, under the gallery, where it came down first, and with greatest force, and where there was nothing to break the force of the falling weight.

"Such an event may be a sufficient argument of a Divine providence over the lives of men. We thought ourselves called on to set apart a day to be spent in the solemn worship of God, to humble ourselves under such a rebuke of God upon us, in time of public service in his house, by so dangerous and surprising an accident; and to praise his name for so wonderful, and as it were miraculous, a preservation. The last Wednesday was kept by us to that end; and a mercy, in which the hand of God is so remarkably evident, may be well worthy to affect the hearts of all who hear it."

In 1738, the "Narrative of Surprising Conversions" was republished in Boston, with a preface by four of the senior ministers of that town.

To it were prefixed five discourses, on the following subjects:

I. Justification by Faith alone. Rom. iv. 5.

II. Pressing into the Kingdom of God. Luke xvi. 16.

III. Ruth's Resolution. Ruth i. 16.

IV. The Justice of God in the Damnation of Sinners. Rom. iii. 19.

V. The Excellency of Jesus Christ. Rev. v. 5, 6.

The first four of these discourses were delivered during the revival of religion, and were published at the earnest desire of those to whom they were preached. In fixing on the particular discourses, necessary to make up the volume, he was guided by the choice of the people. "What has determined them in this choice," he observes, "is the experience of special benefit to their souls from *these discourses*. Their desire to have them in their hands, from the press, has been long manifested, and often expressed to me; their earnestness in it is evident from this, that though it be a year to them of the greatest charge that ever has been, by reason of the expense of building a new meeting-house, yet they chose rather to be at this additional expense now, though it be very considerable, than to have it delayed another year." In publishing the discourse on "Justification," he was also influenced by the urgent request of several ministers, who were present when a part of it was delivered, and whose opinion and advice he thought deserving of great respect. This discourse, though when first written of a much less size than as it is printed, was preached at two successive public lectures, in the latter part of 1734. It was at a time, when the minds of the people, in all that section of country, were very much agitated by a controversy on that very subject; when some were brought to doubt of that way of acceptance with God, which they had been taught from their infancy was the only way; and when many were engaged in looking more thoroughly into the grounds of those doctrines in which they had been educated; that this discourse seemed to be remarkably blessed, not only in establishing the judgments of men in this truth, but in engaging their hearts in a more earnest pursuit of justification, by faith in the righteousness of Christ. "*At that time*," says the author, "while I was greatly reproached for defending this doctrine in the pulpit, and just upon my suffering a very open abuse for it, God's work wonderfully broke forth among us, and souls began to flock to Christ, as the Saviour in whose righteousness alone they hoped to be justified. So that this was the doctrine, on which this work, in its beginning, was founded, as it evidently was in the whole progress of it." He regarded these facts as a remarkable testimony of God's approbation of the doctrine of justification by faith alone.

This discourse, which is really a treatise of more than one hundred closely printed pages, exhibited the subject in a light so new, clear, and convincing, and so effectually removed the difficulties with which, till then, it was supposed to be attended, that on its first publication it met a very welcome reception, and from that time to the present has been regarded as the common text-book of students in theology. It would not be easy to find another treatise on the same subject, equally able and conclusive.

There are individuals, who, having received their theological views from the straitest sect of a given class of theologians, regard the sermon on "Pressing into the kingdom of God," as inconsistent with those principles of moral agency, which are established in the treatise on the "Freedom of the Will;" and charitably impute the error to the imperfect views of the author at this period. While a member of college, however, Mr. Edwards, in investigating the subject of *Power*, as he was reading the Essay of Locke, came to the settled conclusion, that men have, *in the physical sense*, the power of repenting and turning to God. A further examination might perhaps evince, that the points in question are less consistent with some peculiar views of theology, of a more modern date, than with any, logically deducible from the treatise on the "Will." The sermon itself, like the rest, has uncommon ardour, unction, and solemnity, and was one of the most useful which he delivered.

The sermon on the "Justice of God in the Damnation of Sinners," in the language of the text, literally *stops the mouth* of every reader, and compels him, as he stands before his Judge, to admit, if he does not feel, the justice of his sentence. I know not where to find, in any language, a discourse so well adapted to strip the impenitent sinner of every excuse, to convince him of his guilt, and to bring him low before the justice and holiness of God. According to the estimate of Mr. Edwards, it was far the most powerful and effectual of his discourses; and we scarcely know of any other sermon which has been favoured with equal success.

The sermon on the "Excellency of Christ," was selected by Mr. Edwards himself, partly because he had been importuned to publish it by individuals in another town, in whose hearing it was occasionally preached; and partly because he thought that a discourse on such an evangelical subject, would properly follow others that were chiefly awakening; and that something of the excellency of the *Saviour* was proper to succeed those things, that were to show the necessity of *salvation*. No one who reads it will hesitate to believe, that it was most happily selected. I have met with no sermon hitherto, so admirably adapted to the circumstances of a sinner, when, on the commencement of his repentance, he renounces every other object of trust, but the righteousness of Christ. Taking the whole volume, as thus printed, the Narrative and the Five Discourses, we suppose it to have been one of the most effectual, in promoting the work of salvation, which has hitherto issued from the press.

The sixth child, and eldest son, of Mr. and Mrs. Edwards was born July 25, 1738, and after *his* father was baptized by the name of Timothy.

About this period, Mr. Joseph Bellamy, afterwards the Rev. Dr. Bellamy of Bethlem, Connecticut, went to Northampton to pursue his theological studies under Mr. Edwards, and resided for a considerable period in his family. The very high respect which he cherished for the eminent talents and piety of Mr. Edwards, and which drew him to Northampton, was reciprocated by the latter; and a friendship commenced between them, which terminated only with life.*

In the beginning of March, 1739, Mr. Edwards commenced a series of sermons from Isaiah li. 8. "For the moth shall eat them up like a garment, and the worm shall eat them like wool; but my righteousness shall be for ever, and my salvation from generation to generation." The eight first were delivered during that month, the eight next in the two following months, and the whole series, thirty in all, was completed before the close of August. After explaining the text, he derives from it the following doctrine: "The work of redemption is a work, which carries on from the fall of man to the end of the world." The subject was one in which Mr. Edwards felt the deepest interest; but he appears never to have repeated the series of discourses to his people. What his ultimate intentions were, we may learn, however, from the following extract of a letter, written by him many years afterwards: "I have had on my mind and heart (which I long ago began, not with any view to publication) a great work, which I call, *a History of the Work of Redemption*, a body of divinity in an entire new method, being thrown into the form of a history, considering the affair of christian theology, as the whole of it, in each part, stands in reference to the great work of redemption by Jesus Christ, which I suppose is to be the grand design of all God's designs, and the *summum* and *ultimum* of all God's operations and decrees, particularly considering all parts of the grand scheme in their historical order;—The order of their existence, or their being brought forth to view, in the course of divine dispensations, or the wonderful series of successive acts and events; beginning from eternity and descending from thence to the great work and successive dispensations of the infinitely wise God in time, considering the chief events coming to pass in the church of God, and revolutions in the world of mankind, affecting the state of the church and the affair of redemption, which we have an account of in history or prophecy, till at last we come to the general resurrection, last judgment, and consummation of all things, when it shall be said, *It is done*, I am Alpha and Omega, the Beginning and *the End;* concluding my work, with the consideration of that perfect state of things, which shall be finally settled to last for eternity.—This history will be carried on with regard to all three worlds,—heaven, earth, and hell; considering the connected successive events and alterations in each, so far as the Scriptures give any light; introducing all parts of divinity in that order which is most scriptural and most natural; which is a method which appears to me the most beautiful and entertaining, wherein every doctrine will appear to the greatest advantage, in the brightest light, in the most striking manner, showing the admirable contexture and harmony of the whole."

From this it is obvious, that he long cherished the intention of re-writing and enlarging the work, and of turning it into a regular treatise; but this design he never accomplished. We shall have occasion to allude to this work hereafter.

The sixth daughter of Mr. and Mrs. Edwards was born June 24, 1740, and named Susannah.

The circumstances which caused the remarkable attention to religion, which began in 1734, to decline, were chiefly local in their nature, and limited in their influence, either to Northampton, or to the county of Hampshire. The consequence was, that it continued to exist, in various sections of the country, to the east, the south, and the west, during the five following years. By the astonishing work of grace at Northampton, an impulse had been given to the churches of this whole western world, which could not soon be lost. The history of that event, having been extensively circulated, had produced a general conviction in the minds of Christians, that the preaching of the gospel might be attended by effects, not less surprising, than those which followed it in apostolic times. This conviction produced an important change in the views, and conduct, both of ministers and churches. The style of preaching was altered: it became, extensively, more direct and pungent, and more adapted to awaken the feelings and convince the conscience. The prayers of good men, both in public and private, indicated more intense desires for the prevalence of religion, and a stronger expectation that the word of God would be attended with an immediate blessing. As the natural result of such a change, revivals of religion were witnessed in numerous villages in New Jersey, Connecticut, and the eastern parts of New England; and even where this was not the case, religion was so extensively and unusually the object of attention, during the period specified, that the church at large seemed preparing for events of a more interesting nature, than any that had yet been witnessed.

In consequence of the high reputation, which Mr. Edwards had acquired as a powerful and successful preacher, and as a safe and wise counsellor to the anxious and inquiring, he received frequent invitations from churches, near and more remote, to come and labour among them for a little period; and with the consent of his people, (his own pulpit always being supplied,) he often went forth on these missionary tours, and found an ample reward in the abundant success which crowned his labours. In this, his example was soon followed by several distinguished ministers in Connecticut and New Jersey. In one of these excursions, he spent some little time at Enfield in Connecticut, where he preached, on the 8th of July, 1741, the well-known sermon, entitled, "*Sinners in the hands of an angry God*," from Deut. xxxii. 35.; which was the cause of an immediate and general revival of religion throughout the place. It was soon afterwards published.

On the 2d of September following, he preached the sermon, entitled, "The Sorrows of the Bereaved spread before Jesus," at the funeral of his uncle, the Rev. William Williams of Hatfield, a gentleman highly respected for his sound understanding, piety, and faithfulness as a minister. This sermon was immediately afterwards published.

* Mr. Bellamy was settled at Bethlem in the spring of 1740, in the midst of a general attention to religion, on the part of the people of that place.

CHAPTER IX.

COMMENCEMENT OF A SECOND GREAT REVIVAL OF RELIGION, IN THE SPRING AND SUMMER OF 1740—VISIT OF MR. WHITEFIELD AT NORTHAMPTON—IMPULSES—JUDGING OF THE RELIGIOUS CHARACTER OF OTHERS—LETTER TO MR. WHEELOCK—GREAT EFFECTS OF A PRIVATE LECTURE OF MR. E.—LETTER TO HIS DAUGHTER—LETTER TO A YOUNG LADY IN CONNECTICUT—LAY PREACHING—LETTER OF REV. G. TENNENT—SERMON AT NEW-HAVEN—"DISTINGUISHING MARKS OF A WORK OF THE SPIRIT OF GOD"—PREFACES BY MR. COOPER AND MR. WILLISON—MR. SAMUEL HOPKINS.

While Mr. Edwards was thus occasionally serving his Divine Master abroad, he found, also, that his labours at home began to be attended with similar success. A great reformation in morals, as well as religion, had been the consequence of the preceding revival of religion. Associations for prayer and social religion had been regularly kept up, and a few instances of awakening and conversion had all along been known, even at the season of the greatest stupidity. In the spring of 1740, there was a perceptible alteration for the better; and the influence of the Spirit of God was most obvious on the minds of the people, particularly on those of the young, in causing greater seriousness and solemnity, and in prompting them to make religion far more generally the subject of conversation. Improprieties of conduct, too often allowed, were more generally avoided; greater numbers resorted to Mr. Edwards to converse with him respecting their salvation; and, in particular individuals, there appeared satisfactory evidence of an entire change of character. This state of things continued through the summer and autumn.

On the evening of Thursday, the 16th of October, 1740, Mr. Whitefield came to Northampton to see Mr. Edwards, and to converse with him respecting the work of God in 1735, and remained there until the morning of the 20th. In this interval he preached five sermons, adapted to the circumstances of the town, reproving the backslidings of some, the obstinate impenitence of others, and summoning all, by the mercies with which the town had been distinguished, to return to God. His visit was followed by an awakening among professors of religion, and soon afterwards by a deep concern among the young, and there were some instances of hopeful conversion. This increased during the winter; and in the spring of 1741 religion became the object of general attention.

On Monday, Mr. Edwards, with the Rev. Mr. Hopkins of West Springfield, his brother-in-law, and several other gentlemen, accompanied Mr. Whitefield on the east side of the river as far as East Windsor, to the house of his father, the Rev. Timothy Edwards. While they were thus together, he took an opportunity to converse with Mr. Whitefield alone, at some length, on the subject of *impulses*, and assigned the reasons which he had to think, that he gave too much heed to such things. Mr. Whitefield received it kindly, but did not seem inclined to have much conversation on the subject, and in the time of it, did not appear convinced by any thing which he heard. He also took occasion in the presence of others, to converse with Mr. Whitefield at some length, about his too customary practice of *judging other persons to be unconverted;* examined the scriptural warrant for such judgments, and expressed his own decided disapprobation of the practice. Mr. Whitefield, at the same time, mentioned to Mr. Edwards his design of bringing over a number of young men from England, into New Jersey and Pennsylvania, to be ordained by the two Mr. Tennents. Their whole interview was an exceedingly kind and affectionate one; yet Mr. Edwards supposed that Mr. Whitefield regarded him somewhat less as an intimate and confidential friend, than he would have done, had he not opposed him in two favourite points of his own practice, for which no one can be at a loss to perceive that he could find no scriptural justification. Each however regarded the other with great affection and esteem, as a highly favoured servant of God; and Mr. Edwards, as we shall soon see, speaks of Mr. Whitefield's visit to Northampton in terms of the warmest approbation.

In the month of May, a private lecture of Mr. Edwards's was attended with very powerful effects on the audience, and ultimately upon the young of both sexes, and on children throughout the town; and during the summer, and the early part of the autumn, there was a glorious progress in the work of God on the hearts of sinners in conviction and conversion, and great numbers appeared to become the real disciples of Christ.

Among the ministers, who at this period occasionally left their own congregations, and went forth as labourers into the common field to gather in the harvest, one of those who were most distinguished for their activity and success, was the Rev. Mr. Wheelock, of Lebanon, afterwards the president of Dartmouth college. In the following letter from Mr. Edwards to this gentleman, he urges him to visit Scantic, a feeble settlement in the northern part of his father's parish: the inhabitants of which were too remote to attend public worship regularly at East Windsor, and yet too few and feeble to maintain it themselves.

"*Northampton, June* 9, 1741.

"Rev. and Dear Sir,

"The special occasion of my now writing to you, is a desire I have of two things; one is, that you and your brother Pomeroy would go to Scantic, in my father's parish, and preach there as often as the people will be willing to hear you, and continue so doing as long as the concerns of your own parishes will allow of your being absent. You know the wretched circumstances of that society; and if ever they are healed, I believe it must be by a reviving and prevailing of true religion among them. By all that I can understand, they are wholly dead, in this extraordinary day of God's gracious visitation. You have lately been so remarkably blessed elsewhere, that I cannot but hope you would have success there also. I have written to my father, to inform him that I have desired this of you.

"Another thing that I desire of you is, that you would come up hither and help us, both you and Mr. Pomeroy. There has been a reviving of religion among us of late; but your labours have been much more remarkably blessed than mine. Other ministers, I have heard, have shut up their pulpits against you; but here I engage you shall find one open. May God send you hither, with the like blessing as he has sent you to some other places; and may your coming be a means to humble me, for my barrenness and unprofitableness, and a means of my instruction and enlivening. I want an opportunity to concert measures with you, for the advancement of the kingdom and glory of our Redeemer. Please to communicate what I write to Mr. Pomeroy, and give my service to him. I desire the prayers of you both, that God will give me more of that holy spirit, and happy success, with which you are replenished.

I am, Dear Sir, your unworthy brother
and fellow-labourer,
JONATHAN EDWARDS."

As very few of Mr. Edwards's letters to his own family are preserved, it is proper to give those few to the reader, even when they are not otherwise interesting, in order to exhibit his true character, as an affectionate and faithful christian father. The following was addressed to his eldest daughter, in her thirteenth year, while residing with her aunt, Mrs. Huntington, at Lebanon.

"To Miss Sarah Edwards, Lebanon.

Northampton, June 25th, 1741.

My dear Child,

Your mother has received two letters from you, since you went away. We rejoice to hear of your welfare, and of the flourishing state of religion in Lebanon. I hope you will well improve the great advantage God is thereby putting into your hands, for the good of your own soul. You have very weak and infirm health, and I am afraid are always like to have; and it may be, are not to be long-lived; and while you do live, are not like to enjoy so much of the comforts of this life as others do, by reason of your want of health; and therefore, if you have no better portion, will be miserable indeed. But, if your soul prospers, you will be a happy, blessed person, whatever becomes of your body. I wish you much of the presence of Christ, and of communion with him, and that you might live so as to give him honour, in the place where you are, by an amiable behaviour towards all.

Your mother would have you go on with your work, if you can, and she would be glad if your aunt would set you to work something of hers, though you do but little in a day. She would have you send word by Mr. Wheelock, who I suppose will come up the next week, or the week after, whether you are well enough to make lace: if you are, she will send you a lace and bobbins.

The flourishing of religion in this town, and in these parts of the country, has rather increased since you went away. Your mother joins with me in giving her love to you, and to your uncle and aunt. Your sisters give their love to you, and their duty to them. The whole family is glad, when we hear from you. Recommending you to the continual care and mercy of heaven, I remain your loving father,

JONATHAN EDWARDS."

Some time in the course of the year, a young lady, residing at S——, in Connecticut, who had lately made a public profession of religion, requested Mr. Edwards to give her some advice, as to the best manner of maintaining a religious life. In reply, he addressed to her the following letter; which will be found eminently useful to all persons just entering on the christian course.

Letter addressed to a Young Lady at S——, Conn. in the year 1741.

"My dear young Friend,

As you desired me to send you, in writing, some directions how to conduct yourself in your christian course, I would now answer your request. The sweet remembrance of the great things I have lately seen at S——, inclines me to do any thing in my power, to contribute to the spiritual joy and prosperity of God's people there.

1. I would advise you to keep up as great a strife and earnestness in religion, as if you knew yourself to be in a state of nature, and were seeking conversion. We advise persons under conviction, to be earnest and violent for the kingdom of heaven; but when they have attained to conversion, they ought not to be the less watchful, laborious, and earnest, in the whole work of religion, but the more so; for they are under infinitely greater obligations. For want of this, many persons, in a few months after their conversion, have begun to lose their sweet and lively sense of spiritual things, and to grow cold and dark, and have 'pierced themselves through with many sorrows;' whereas, if they had done as the apostle did, (Phil. iii. 12—14.) their path would have been 'as the shining light, that shines more and more unto the perfect day.'

2. Do not leave off seeking, striving, and praying for the very same things that we exhort unconverted persons to strive for, and a degree of which you have had already in conversion. Pray that your eyes may be opened, that you may receive sight, that you may know yourself, and be brought to God's footstool; and that you may see the glory of God and Christ, and may be raised from the dead, and have the love of Christ shed abroad in your heart. Those who have most of these things, have need still to pray for them; for there is so much blindness and hardness, pride and death remaining, that they still need to have that work of God wrought upon them, further to enlighten and enliven them, that shall be bringing them out of darkness into God's marvellous light, and be a kind of new conversion and resurrection from the dead. There are very few requests that are proper for an impenitent man, that are not also, in some sense, proper for the godly.

3. When you hear a sermon, hear for yourself. Though what is spoken may be more especially directed to the unconverted, or to those that, in other respects, are in different circumstances from yourself; yet, let the chief intent of your mind be to consider, 'In what respect is this applicable to me? and what improvement ought I to make of this, for my own soul's good?'

4. Though God has forgiven and forgotten your past sins, yet do not forget them yourself: often remember, what a wretched bond-slave you were in the land of Egypt. Often bring to mind your particular acts of sin before conversion; as the blessed apostle Paul is often mentioning his old blaspheming, persecuting spirit, and his injuriousness to the renewed; humbling his heart, and acknowledging that he was 'the least of the apostles,' and not worthy 'to be called an apostle,' and the 'least of all saints,' and the 'chief of sinners;' and be often confessing your old sins to God, and let that text be often in your mind, (Ezek. xvi. 63.) 'that thou mayest remember and be confounded, and never open thy mouth any more, be-

cause of thy shame, when I am pacified toward thee for all that thou hast done, saith the Lord God.'

5. Remember, that you have more cause, on some accounts, a thousand times, to lament and humble yourself for sins that have been committed since conversion, than before, because of the infinitely greater obligations that are upon you to live to God, and to look upon the faithfulness of Christ, in unchangeably continuing his loving-kindness, notwithstanding all your great unworthiness since your conversion.

6. Be always greatly abased for your remaining sin, and never think that you lie low enough for it; but yet be not discouraged or disheartened by it; for, though we are exceeding sinful, yet we have an Advocate with the Father, Jesus Christ the righteous; the preciousness of whose blood, the merit of whose righteousness, and the greatness of whose love and faithfulness, infinitely overtop the highest mountains of our sins.

7. When you engage in the duty of prayer, or come to the Lord's supper, or attend any other duty of divine worship, come to Christ as Mary Magdalen* did; (Luke vii. 37, 38.) come, and cast yourself at his feet, and kiss them, and pour forth upon him the sweet perfumed ointment of divine love, out of a pure and broken heart, as she poured the precious ointment out of her pure broken alabaster box.

8. Remember, that pride is the worst viper that is in the heart, the greatest disturber of the soul's peace, and of sweet communion with Christ: it was the first sin committed, and lies lowest in the foundation of Satan's whole building, and is with the greatest difficulty rooted out, and is the most hidden, secret, and deceitful of all lusts, and often creeps insensibly into the midst of religion, even, sometimes, under the disguise of humility itself.

9. That you may pass a correct judgment concerning yourself, always look upon those as the best discoveries, and the best comforts, that have most of these two effects: those that make you least and lowest, and most like a child; and those that most engage and fix your heart, in a full and firm disposition to deny yourself for God, and to spend and be spent for him.

10. If at any time you fall into doubts about the state of your soul, in dark and dull frames of mind, it is proper to review your past experience; but do not consume too much time and strength in this way: rather apply yourself, with all your might, to an earnest pursuit after renewed experience, new light, and new lively acts of faith and love. One new discovery of the glory of Christ's face, will do more toward scattering clouds of darkness in one minute, than examining old experience, by the best marks that can be given, through a whole year.

11. When the exercise of grace is low, and corruption prevails, and by that means fear prevails; do not desire to have fear cast out any other way, than by the reviving and prevailing of love in the heart: by this, fear will be effectually expelled, as darkness in a room vanishes away, when the pleasant beams of the sun are let into it.

12. When you counsel and warn others, do it earnestly, and affectionately, and thoroughly; and when you are speaking to your equals, let your warnings be intermixed with expressions of your sense of your own unworthiness, and of the sovereign grace that makes you differ.

* This is a very common mistake. The woman here mentioned was not Mary Magdalen.

13. If you would set up religious meetings of young women by yourselves, to be attended once in a while, besides the other meetings that you attend, I should think it would be very proper and profitable.

14. Under special difficulties, or when in great need of, or great longings after, any particular mercy, for yourself or others, set apart a day for secret prayer and fasting by yourself alone; and let the day be spent, not only in petitions for the mercies you desire, but in searching your heart, and in looking over your past life, and confessing your sins before God, not as is wont to be done in public prayer, but by a very particular rehearsal before God of the sins of your past life, from your childhood hitherto, before and after conversion, with the circumstances and aggravations attending them, and spreading all the abominations of your heart very particularly, and fully as possible, before him.

15. Do not let the adversaries of the cross have occasion to reproach religion on your account. How holily should the children of God, the redeemed and the beloved of the Son of God, behave themselves. Therefore, 'walk as children of the light, and of the day,' and 'adorn the doctrine of God your Saviour;' and especially, abound in what are called the christian virtues, and make you like the Lamb of God: be meek and lowly of heart, and full of pure, heavenly, and humble love to all; abound in deeds of love to others, and self-denial for others; and let there be in you a disposition to account others better than yourself.

16. In all your course, walk with God, and follow Christ, as a little, poor, helpless child, taking hold of Christ's hand, keeping your eye on the marks of the wounds in his hands and side, whence came the blood that cleanses you from sin, and hiding your nakedness under the skirt of the white shining robes of his righteousness.

17. Pray much for the ministers and the church of God; especially, that he would carry on his glorious work which he has now begun, till the world shall be full of his glory."

About this period, a considerable number of lay members of the church began, in various parts of New England, to hold religious meetings, and to preach and exhort in the manner of ministers. They were usually men of worth, and desirous of doing good; but having much zeal, and little knowledge, and often but little discretion, the church, at that period, had certainly very little reason to rejoice in their labours. The following letter of the Rev. Gilbert Tennent, written probably in the autumn of 1741, explains his own views on this subject.†

"Rev. and dear Sir,

I rejoice to hear that my poor labours have been of any service to any in New England. All glory be to the great and glorious God, when out of the mouths of babes and sucklings, he is pleased sometimes to ordain praise. I rejoice to hear the progress of God's work among you, this last summer, and that there are any appearances of its continuance: Blessed be God, dear brother! As to the subject you mention, of *laymen being sent out to exhort and to teach*, supposing them to be real converts, I cannot but think, if it be encouraged and continued, it will be of dreadful consequence to the church's peace and soundness in the faith. I will not gainsay but that private persons may be

† The superscription and date are gone from the MS. but having Mr. Edwards's hand-writing on the back, I suppose the letter to have been written to him.

of service to the church of God by private, humble, fraternal reproof, and exhortations; and no doubt it is their duty to be faithful in these things. But in the mean time if christian prudence and humility do not attend their essays, they are like to be prejudicial to the church's real well-being. But for ignorant young converts to take upon them authoritatively to instruct and exhort publicly, tends to introduce the greatest errors and the grossest anarchy and confusion. The ministers of Christ should be apt to teach and able to convince gainsayers, and it is dangerous to the pure church of God, when those are novices, whose lips should preserve knowledge. It is base presumption, whatever zeal be pretended to, notwithstanding, for any persons to take this honour to themselves, unless they be called of God, as Aaron. I know most young zealots are apt, through ignorance, inconsideration, and pride of heart, to undertake what they have no proper qualifications for: and, through their imprudences and enthusiasm, the church of God suffers. I think all that fear God, should rise up and crush the enthusiastic creature in the egg. Dear brother, the times we live in are dangerous. The churches in America and elsewhere are in great hazard of enthusiasm: we have need to think of the maxim, *principiis obsta*. May Zion's King protect his church! I add no more, but love, and beg a remembrance in your prayers.

GILBERT TENNENT."

In the September following, Mr. Edwards attended the public commencement at New-Haven, and on the 10th of that month preached his celebrated sermon entitled, "Distinguishing Marks of a Work of the Spirit of God," which, in consequence of a general request from the clergy, and other gentlemen attending the commencement, was published soon after at Boston, accompanied with a Preface from the Rev. Mr. Cooper; and in Scotland the ensuing year, with a preface from the Rev. Mr. Willison. This sermon, by exhibiting the distinguishing marks between an imaginary and a real work of the Spirit of God, and by applying those marks to the work of grace then begun, and rapidly spreading throughout the northern and middle colonies, became an unanswerable defence, not only of that, but of all genuine revivals of religion. It was indeed the object of immediate and reiterated attacks from the press; but being built on the foundation of the apostles and the prophets, it stands sure, while those attacks and their authors are forgotten. It exhibits the scriptural evidences of a genuine revival of religion, in much the same manner, as his subsequent treatise on "Religious Affections," does those of a genuine conversion. Mr. Cooper thus introduces it to the Christians of New England:

"If any are disposed to receive conviction, have a mind open to light, and are really willing to know of the present work, whether it be of God; it is with great satisfaction and pleasure I can recommend to them the following sheets, in which they will find the "distinguishing marks" of such a work, as they are to be found in the Holy Scriptures, applied to the uncommon operation that has been on the minds of many in this land. Here the matter is tried by the infallible touchstone of the Holy Scriptures, and is weighed in the balance of the sanctuary with great judgment and impartiality.

"A performance of this kind is seasonable and necessary; and I desire heartily to bless God, who inclined this, his servant, to undertake it, and has greatly assisted him in it. The reverend author is known to be 'a scribe instructed unto the kingdom of heaven;' the place where he has been called to exercise his ministry has been famous for experimental religion; and he has had opportunities to observe this work in many places where it has powerfully appeared, and to converse with numbers that have been the subjects of it. These things qualify him for this undertaking, above most. His arguments in favour of the work, are strongly drawn from Scripture, reason, and experience: and I shall believe every candid, judicious reader will say, he writes very free from an enthusiastic or a party spirit. The use of human learning is asserted; a methodical way of preaching, the fruit of study as well as prayer, is recommended; and the exercise of charity, in judging others, pressed and urged: and those things, which are esteemed the blemishes, and are like to be the hinderances, of the work, are with great faithfulness cautioned and warned against.—Many, I believe, will be thankful for this publication. Those who have already entertained favourable thoughts of this work, will be confirmed by it; and the doubting may be convinced and satisfied. But if there be any, after all, who cannot see the signatures of a Divine hand on the work, it is to be hoped they will be prevailed on to spare their censures, and stop their oppositions, lest 'haply they should be found to fight against God.'—I will only add my prayer, That the worthy author of this discourse may long be continued a burning and a shining light, in the golden candlestick where Christ has placed him, and from thence diffuse his light throughout these provinces! That the Divine Spirit, whose cause is here espoused, would accompany this, and the other valuable publications of his servant, with his powerful influences; that they may promote the Redeemer's interests, serve the ends of vital religion, and so add to the author's present joy and future crown!"

The following is the testimony of the Rev. Mr. Willison, to the churches of Scotland. "The ensuing treatise, by the Rev. Mr. Edwards, of Northampton, in New England, concerning the work and operation of the Holy Spirit on men's consciences, is, in my humble opinion, a most excellent, solid, judicious, and scriptural performance; which I hope, through the Divine blessing, will prove most useful to the church, for discerning a true and real work of the Spirit of God, and for guarding against delusions and mistakes. It is certainly a great mercy to the church, that this subject hath been undertaken and handled by such an experienced, well furnished scribe, that hath been long acquainted with the Spirit of God's dealings with the souls of men, in his own congregation, and the country where he lives. And seeing the extraordinary work there at present, though several thousand miles distant from Scotland, is of the same kind with that at Cambuslang and other places about, and meets with the same opposition; the author doth, with great judgment, answer the common objections which are made against the work, both here and there, so that scarce any thing further needs be added. He warns people very warmly against opposing or reproaching the work of the Holy Spirit. He being the Third Person of the glorious Trinity, and God equal with the Father and the Son, and the great applier of the redemption purchased for us; it becomes all men highly to honour him and his work, and to look upon it as highly dangerous to speak a word against him, according to Matt. xii. 32.—I shall add no more, but my fervent prayers to

God, to bless both the author and his discourse, and that he would pour out his Spirit yet more abundantly, both on America and all the British dominions; and that he would hasten the glory of the latter days, when the Jews shall be brought in with the fulness of the Gentiles, and that all the kingdoms of the world may become the kingdoms of the Lord and of his Christ, that he may reign for ever and ever! Amen and Amen."

It was during this visit to New-Haven, that Mr. Hopkins,* then about to receive the degree of A. B. at Yale college, first saw Mr. Edwards. He soon after became his pupil, and continued his intimate friend through life, and was ultimately his biographer. The impression made on his mind, may be gathered from the following account of the subject, in the Memoirs of his own life. "When I heard Mr. Tennent," [the Rev. Gilbert Tennent, who had preached often at New-Haven in the preceding March.] "I thought he was the greatest and best man, and the best preacher, that I had ever seen or heard. His words were to me 'like apples of gold in pictures of silver.' And I thought that, when I should leave the college, as I was then in my last year, I would go and live with him, wherever I should find him. But just before the commencement in September, when I was to take my degree, on the seventeenth day of which month I was twenty years old, Mr. Edwards, of Northampton, came to New-Haven, and preached. He then preached the sermon on *The Trial of the Spirits*, which was afterwards printed. I had before read his sermons on Justification, &c., and his Narrative of Remarkable Conversions at Northampton, which took place about seven years before this. Though I then did not obtain any personal acquaintance with him, any further than by hearing him preach; yet I conceived such an esteem of him, and was so pleased with his preaching, that I altered my former determination with respect to Mr. Tennent, and concluded to go and live with Mr. Edwards, as soon as I should have opportunity, though he lived about eighty miles from my father's house."

CHAPTER X.

TEMPORARY ABATEMENT OF RELIGIOUS ATTENTION—LETTER TO MR. BELLAMY—MISSIONARY TOUR—SUCCESS AT LEICESTER—MR. HOPKINS BECOMES A MEMBER OF HIS FAMILY—MR. BUELL'S SUCCESSFUL LABOURS AT NORTHAMPTON—MR. EDWARDS'S NARRATIVE OF THE REVIVAL AT NORTHAMPTON, IN 1740-1742—COVENANT ENTERED INTO BY THE CHURCH.

For about three months, or from November to January, there was an obvious abatement in the attention to religion at Northampton; and although there were instances of conversion from time to time through the winter, yet they were less frequent than before. Mr. Edwards alludes to this fact, in the following letter to Mr. Bellamy, of Bethlem.

"*Northampton, Jan.* 21, 1742.

Rev. and dear Sir,

I received yours of Jan. 11, for which I thank you. Religion, in this and the neighbouring towns, has now of late been on the decaying hand. I desire your prayers, that God would quicken and revive us again; and particularly, that he would greatly humble, and pardon, and quicken me, and fill me with his own fulness; and, if it may consist with his will, improve me as an instrument to revive his work. There has been, the year past, the most wonderful work among children here, by far, that ever was. God has seemed almost wholly to take a new generation, that are come on since the late great work, seven years ago.—Neither earth nor hell can hinder his work, that is going on in the country. Christ gloriously triumphs at this day. You have probably before now heard of the great and wonderful things that have lately been wrought at Portsmouth, the chief town in New Hampshire. There are also appearing great things at Ipswich and Newbury, the two largest towns in this province except Boston, and several other towns beyond Boston, and some towns nearer. By what I can understand, the work of God is greater at this day in the land, than it has been at any time. O what cause have we, with exulting hearts, to agree to give glory to him, who thus rides forth in the chariot of his salvation, conquering and to conquer; and earnestly to pray, that now the Sun of righteousness would come forth like a bridegroom, rejoicing as a giant, to run his race from one end of the heavens to the other, that nothing may be hid from the light and heat thereof.

It is not probable that I shall be able to attend your meeting at Guilford. I have lately been so much gone from my people, and don't know but I must be obliged to leave 'em again next week about a fortnight, being called to Leicester, a town about half way to Boston, where a great work of grace has lately commenced; and probably soon after that to another place; and having at this time some extraordinary affairs to attend to at home. I pray that Christ, our good Shepherd, will be with you, and direct you, and greatly strengthen and bless you.

Dear Sir, I have none of those books you speak of, to sell. I have only a few, that I intend to send to some of my friends. I have already sent you one of my New-Haven sermons, by Mr. ——. Nevertheless, I have herewith sent another, which I desire you to give to Mr. Mills, if he has none; but if he has, dispose of it where you think it will do most good. I have also sent one of those sermons I preached at Enfield; as to the other, I have but one of them in the world.

I am, dear Sir, your affectionate and unworthy brother, and fellow-labourer,

JONATHAN EDWARDS."

The absence from his people, alluded to in the preceding letter, occurred in consequence of a missionary tour of some length, in the two preceding months; during which

* Afterwards the Rev. Samuel Hopkins, D. D. of Newport, author of the System of Divinity.

he visited various places, to which he had been invited, in consequence of an unusual attention to religion there, among the people. His own congregation, readily admitting that, at such a time, there was a louder call for his services in those places, than in Northampton, consented, in the true spirit of christian benevolence, that he should listen to these calls of Providence, and go forth into other fields of labour. In so doing, they soon found a fulfilment of the promise, that *he who watereth shall be watered himself*. On Monday the 25th of January, Mr. Edwards set out for Leicester, and remained there several weeks, preaching with remarkable success. The revival of religion almost immediately pervaded the whole congregation, and great numbers were believed to be the subjects of hopeful conversion. On Wednesday, January 27th, Mr. Buell, a class-mate of Mr. Hopkins, who, though he left college in the September preceding, had already been preaching some time, and had gained the reputation of an uncommonly engaged and animated preacher, came to Northampton, to preach during the absence of Mr. Edwards. Immediately the work of grace, which had for a season declined, was again carried on with even greater power than before. A high degree of religious feeling was excited in the church; a solemn, anxious attention to the salvation of the soul, was witnessed extensively among the congregation; and, soon after the return of Mr. Edwards, the work of conviction and conversion again went forward with renewed success.

Mr. Hopkins alludes to these events, in his own narrative. "In the month of December," he observes, "being furnished with a horse, I set out for Northampton, with a view to live with Mr. Edwards, where I was an utter stranger. When I arrived there, Mr. Edwards was not at home; but I was received with great kindness by Mrs. Edwards and the family, and had encouragement that I might live there during the winter. Mr. Edwards was absent on a preaching tour, as people in general were greatly attentive to religion and preaching, which was attended with remarkable effects, in the conviction and supposed conversion of multitudes. I was very gloomy, and was most of the time retired in my chamber. After some days, Mrs. Edwards came into my chamber, and said, "As I was now become a member of the family for a season, she felt herself interested in my welfare; and, as she observed that I appeared gloomy and dejected, she hoped I would not think she intruded, by her desiring to know, and asking me what was the occasion of it, or to that purpose. I told her the freedom she used was agreeable to me; that the occasion of the appearance which she mentioned, was the state in which I considered myself. I was in a Christless, graceless state, and had been under a degree of conviction and concern for myself, for a number of months; had got no relief, and my case, instead of growing better, appeared to grow worse. Upon which we entered into a free conversation; and on the whole she told me, that she had peculiar exercises in prayer respecting me, since I had been in the family; that she trusted I should receive light and comfort, and doubted not that God intended yet to do great things by me.

"Religion was now at a lower ebb at Northampton than it had been of late, and than it appeared to be in the neighbouring towns, and in New England in general. In the month of January, Mr. Buell, my class-mate, came to Northampton, having commenced a zealous preacher of the gospel; and was the means of greatly reviving the people to zeal in religion. He preached every day, and sometimes twice a day, publicly, Mr. Edwards being out of town, preaching in distant towns. Professing Christians appeared greatly revived and comforted; and a number were under conviction; and I think there were some hopeful new converts. After Mr. Buell had been in Northampton a week or two, he set out on a tour towards Boston."*

Having thus alluded to the religious state of Northampton at this period, so far as was necessary to exhibit the order and connexion of events; we now proceed to give Mr. Edwards's own account of the revival of religion in that town, in 1740—1742, as communicated in a letter to a minister of Boston.

"*Northampton, Dec.* 12, 1743.

Rev. and dear Sir,

Ever since the great work of God, that was wrought here about nine years ago, there has been a great and abiding alteration in this town, in many respects. There has been vastly more religion kept up in the town, among all sorts of persons, in religious exercises, and in common conversation; there has been a great alteration among the youth of the town, with respect to revelry, frolicking, profane and licentious conversation, and lewd songs; and there has also been a great alteration, amongst both old and young, with regard to tavern-haunting. I suppose the town has been in no measure so free of vice in these respects, for any long time together, for sixty years, as it has been these nine years past. There has also been an evident alteration, with respect to a charitable spirit to the poor; though I think with regard to this, we in this town, as well as the land in general, come far short of gospel rules. And though after that great work nine years ago, there has been a very lamentable decay of religious affections, and the engagedness of people's spirit in religion; yet many societies for prayer and social worship were all along kept up, and there were some few instances of awakening, and deep concern about the things of another world, even in the most dead time.

In the year 1740, in the spring before Mr. Whitefield came to this town, there was a visible alteration: there was more seriousness and religious conversation, especially among young people; those things that were of ill tendency among them, were forborne; and it was a very frequent thing for persons to consult their minister upon the salvation of their souls; and in some particular persons there appeared a great attention, about that time. And thus it continued, until Mr. Whitefield came to town, which was about the middle of October following: he preached here four sermons in the meeting-house, (besides a private lecture at my house,) one on Friday, another on Saturday, and two upon the sabbath. The congregation was extraordinarily melted by every sermon; almost the whole assembly being in tears for a great part of sermon time. Mr. Whitefield's sermons were suitable to the circumstances of the town; containing a just reproof of our backslidings, and in a most moving and affecting manner, making use of our great professions, and great mercies, as arguments with us to return to God, from whom we had departed. Immediately after this, the minds

* Mr. Hopkins continued to pursue his studies with Mr. Edwards, until the next autumn, and again for a short period in the spring, after which he was settled at *Housatonnuck*, then a part of Stockbridge, now called Great Barrington.

of the people in general appeared more engaged in religion, showing a greater forwardness to make religion the subject of their conversation, and to meet frequently for religious purposes, and to embrace all opportunities to hear the word preached. The revival at first appeared chiefly among professors, and those that had entertained hope that they were in a state of salvation, to whom Mr. Whitefield chiefly addressed himself; but in a very short time, there appeared an awakening and deep concern among some young persons, that looked upon themselves in a Christless state; and there were some hopeful appearances of conversion, and some professors were greatly revived. In about a month or six weeks, there was a great attention in the town, both as to the revival of professors and the awakening of others. By the middle of December, a considerable work of God appeared among those that were very young; and the revival of religion continued to increase, so that in the spring an engagedness of spirit, about the things of religion, was become very general amongst young people and children, and religious subjects almost wholly took up their conversation when they were together.

In the month of May, 1741, a sermon was preached to a company, at a private house. Near the conclusion of the discourse, one or two persons, that were professors, were so greatly affected with a sense of the greatness and glory of divine things, and the infinite importance of the things of eternity, that they were not able to conceal it—the affection of their minds overcoming their strength, and having a very visible effect upon their bodies. When the exercises were over, the young people that were present removed into the other room for religious conference; and particularly that they might have opportunity to inquire of those, that were thus affected, what apprehensions they had, and what things they were that thus deeply impressed their minds; and there soon appeared a very great effect of their conversation; the affection was quickly propagated throughout the room; many of the young people and children, that were professors, appeared to be overcome with a sense of the greatness and glory of divine things, and with admiration, love, joy, and praise, and compassion to others, that looked upon themselves as in a state of nature; and many others at the same time were overcome with distress, about their sinful and miserable estate and condition; so that the whole room was full of nothing but outcries, faintings, and the like. Others soon heard of it in several parts of the town, and came to them; and what they saw and heard there, was greatly affecting to them, so that many of them were overpowered in like manner, and it continued thus for some hours; the time being spent in prayer, singing, counselling, and conferring. There seemed to be a consequent happy effect of that meeting, to several particular persons, and on the state of religion in the town in general. After this, were meetings from time to time, attended with like appearances. But a little after it, at the conclusion of the public exercises on the sabbath, I appointed the children that were under seventeen years of age, to go from the meeting-house to a neighbouring house, that I might there further enforce what they had heard in public, and might give in some counsels proper for their age. The children were there very generally and greatly affected with the warnings and counsels that were given them, and many exceedingly overcome; and the room was filled with cries; and when they were dismissed, they almost all of them went home crying aloud through the streets, to all parts of the town. The like appearances attended several such meetings of children, that were appointed. But their affections appeared by what followed, to be of a very different nature: in many, they appeared indeed but childish affections, and in a day or two would leave them as they were before; others were deeply impressed; their convictions took fast hold of them, and abode by them: and there were some that, from one meeting to another, seemed extraordinarily affected for some time, to but little purpose, their affections presently vanishing from time to time; but yet afterwards, were seized with abiding convictions, and their affections became durable.

About the middle of the summer, I called together the young people that were communicants, from sixteen to twenty-six years of age, to my house; which proved to be a most happy meeting: many seemed to be very greatly and most agreeably affected with those views, which excited humility, self-condemnation, self-abhorrence, love, and joy: many fainted under these affections. We had several meetings that summer, of young people, attended with like appearances. It was about that time, that there first began to be cryings out in the meeting-house; which several times occasioned many of the congregation to stay in the house after the public exercises were over, to confer with those who seemed to be overcome with religious convictions and affections, which was found to tend much to the propagation of their impressions, with lasting effect upon many; conference being, at these times, commonly joined with prayer and singing. In the summer and autumn, the children in various parts of the town had religious meetings by themselves, for prayer, sometimes joined with fasting; wherein many of them seemed to be greatly and properly affected, and I hope some of them savingly wrought upon.

The months of August and September were the most remarkable of any this year, for appearances of the conviction and conversion of sinners, and great revivings, quickenings, and comforts of professors, and for extraordinary external effects of these things. It was a very frequent thing, to see a house full of outcries, faintings, convulsions, and such like, both with distress, and also with admiration and joy. It was not the manner here, to hold meetings all night, as in some places, nor was it common to continue them till very late in the night; but it was pretty often so, that there were some that were so affected, and their bodies so overcome, that they could not go home, but were obliged to stay all night where they were. There was no difference, that I know of here, with regard to these extraordinary effects, in meetings in the night and in the day time: the meetings in which these effects appeared in the evening, being commonly begun, and their extraordinary effects, in the day, and continued in the evening; and some meetings have been very remarkable for such extraordinary effects, that were both begun and finished in the day time. There was an appearance of a glorious progress of the work of God upon the hearts of sinners, in conviction and conversion, this summer and autumn, and great numbers, I think we have reason to hope, were brought savingly home to Christ. But this was remarkable: the work of God in his influences of this nature, seemed to be almost wholly upon a new generation—those that were not come to years of discretion in that wonderful season, nine years ago; children, or those that were then children: others, who had enjoyed that former glorious opportunity, without any appearance of saving benefit, seemed now to be almost wholly passed over and let alone. But now we had the most wonderful work among children, that ever was in Northampton. The former outpouring of the Spirit was remarkable for influences upon the minds of children, beyond all that had ever been before; but this far exceeded that. Indeed, as to influences on the minds of professors, this work was by no means confined to a new generation. Many, of all ages, partook of it; but yet, in this respect, it was more general on those that were of the young sort. Many, who had been formerly wrought upon, and in the time of our declension had fallen into decays, and had in a great measure left God, and gone after the world, now passed under a very remarkable new work of the Spirit of God, as if they had been the subjects of a second conversion. They were first led into the wilderness, and had a work of conviction; having much deeper convictions of the sins of both nature and practice, than ever before; though with some new circumstances, and something new in the kind of conviction in some, with great distress, beyond what they had felt before their first conversion. Under these convictions, they were excited to strive for salvation, and the kingdom of heaven suffered violence from some of them, in a far more remarkable manner than before; and after great convictions and humblings, and agonizing with God, they had Christ discovered to them anew, as an all-sufficient Saviour, and in the glories of his grace, and in a far more clear manner than before; and with greater humility, self-emptiness, and brokenness of heart, and a purer, a higher joy, and greater desires after holiness of life; but with greater self-diffidence and distrust of their treacherous hearts. One circumstance, wherein this work differed from that, which had been in the towns five or six years before, was, that conversions were frequently wrought more sensibly and visibly; the impressions stronger, and more manifest by their external effects; the progress of the Spirit of God in conviction, from step to step, more apparent; and the transition from one state to another, more sensible and plain; so that it might, in many instances, be as it were seen by bystanders. The preceding season had been very remarkable on this account, beyond what had been before; but this more remarkable than that. And in this season, these apparent or visible conversions, (if I may so call them,) were more frequently in the presence of others, at religious meetings, where the appearances of what was wrought on the heart fell under public observation.

After September, 1741, there seemed to be some abatement of these extraordinary appearances, yet they did not wholly cease, but there was something of them, from time to time, all winter. About the beginning of February, 1742, Mr. Buell came to this town. I was then absent from home, and continued so till about a fortnight after. Mr. Buell preached from day to day, almost every day, in the meeting-house.—I had left to him the free use of my pulpit, having heard of his designed visit, before I went from home. He spent almost the whole time in religious exercises with the people, either in public or private, the people continually thronging him. When he first came, there came with him a number of the zealous people from Suffield, who continued here for some time. There were very extraordinary effects of Mr. Buell's labours; the people were exceedingly moved, crying out in great numbers in the meeting-house, and a great part of the congregation commonly staying in the house of God, for hours after the public service. Many also were exceedingly moved in private meetings, where Mr. Buell was: almost the whole town seemed to be in a great and continual commotion, day and night, and there was indeed a very great revival of religion. But it was principally among professors; the appearances of a work of conversion were in no measure as great, as they had been the summer before. When I came home, I found the town in very extraordinary circumstances, such as, in some respects, I never saw it in before. Mr. Buell continued here a fortnight or three weeks after I returned: there being still great appearances attending his labours; many in their religious affections being raised far beyond what they had ever been before: and there were some instances of persons lying in a sort of trance, remaining perhaps for a whole twenty-four hours motionless, and with their senses locked up; but in the mean time under strong imaginations, as though they went to heaven, and had there a vision of glorious and delightful objects. But when the people were raised to this height, Satan took the advantage, and his interposition, in many instances, soon became very apparent: and a great deal of caution and pains were found necessary, to keep the people, many of them, from running wild.

In the month of March, I led the people into a solemn public renewal of their covenant with God. To that end, having made a draft of a covenant, I first proposed it to some of the principal men in the church; then to the people, in their several religious associations in various parts of the town; then to the whole congregation in public; and then I deposited a copy of it in the hands of each of the four deacons, that all who desired it might resort to them, and have opportunity to view and consider it. Then the people in general, that were above fourteen years of age, first subscribed the covenant with their hands; and then, on a day of fasting and prayer, all together presented themselves before the Lord in his house, and stood up, and solemnly manifested their consent to it, as their vow to God. The covenant was as follows:

COPY OF A COVENANT,

Entered into and subscribed, by the people of God at Northampton, and owned before God in his house as their vow to the Lord, and made a solemn act of public worship, by the congregation in general that were above fourteen years of age, on a day of fasting and prayer for the continuance and increase of the gracious presence of God in that place.

March 16th, 1742. Acknowledging God's great goodness to us, a sinful, unworthy people, in the blessed manifestations and fruits of his gracious presence in this town, both formerly and lately, and particularly in the very late spiritual revival; and adoring the glorious majesty, power, and grace of God, manifested in the present wonderful outpouring of his Spirit, in many parts of this land, in this place; and lamenting our past backslidings and ungrateful departings from God, and humbly begging of God that he would not mark our iniquities, but, for Christ's sake, come over the mountains of our sins, and visit us with his salvation, and continue the tokens of his presence with us, and yet more gloriously pour out his blessed Spirit upon us, and make us all partakers of the divine blessings he is, at this day, bestowing here, and in many parts of this land; we do this day present ourselves before the Lord, to renounce our evil ways, we put away our abominations from before God's eyes, and with one accord, to renew our engagements to seek and serve God: and particularly do now solemnly promise and vow to the Lord as follows:—

In all our conversation, concerns, and dealings with our neighbour, we will have a strict regard to rules of honesty, justice, and uprightness, that we don't overreach or defraud our neighbour in any matter, and either wilfully, or through want of care, injure him in any of his honest possessions or rights; and in all our communication will have a tender respect, not only to our own interest, but also to the interest of our neighbour; and will carefully endeavour, in every thing, to do to others as we should expect, or think reasonable, that they should do to us, if we were in their case, and they in ours.

And particularly we will endeavour to render every one his due, and will take heed to ourselves, that we don't injure our neighbour, and give him just cause of offence, by wilfully or negligently forbearing to pay our honest debts.

And wherein any of us, upon strict examination of our past behaviour, may be conscious to ourselves, that we have by any means wronged any of our neighbours in their outward estate, we will not rest, till we have made that restitution, or given that satisfaction, which the rules of moral equity require; or if we are, on a strict and impartial search, conscious to ourselves, that we have in any other respect considerably injured our neighbour, we will truly endeavour to do that, which we in our consciences suppose christian rules require, in order to a reparation of the injury, and removing the offence given thereby.

And furthermore we promise, that we will not allow ourselves in backbiting; and that we will take great heed to ourselves to avoid all violations of those christian rules, Tit. iii. 2. 'Speak evil of no man;' Jam. iv. 11. 'Speak not evil one of another, brethren;' and 2 Cor. xii. 20. 'Let there be no strifes, backbitings, whisperings;' and that we will not only not slander our neighbour, but also will not feed a spirit of bitterness, ill will, or secret grudge against our neighbour, insist on his real faults needlessly, and when not called to it, or from such a spirit, speak of his failings and blemishes with ridicule, or an air of contempt.

And we promise, that we will be very careful to avoid doing any thing to our neighbour from a spirit of revenge. And that we will take great care that we do not, for private interest or our own honour, or to maintain ourselves against those of a contrary party, or to get our wills, or to promote any design in opposition to others, do those things which we, on the most impartial consideration are capable of, can think in our consciences will tend to wound religion, and the interests of Christ's kingdom.

And particularly, that so far as any of us, by Divine Providence, have any special influence upon others, to lead them in the management of public affairs, we will not make our own worldly gain, or honour, or interest in the affections of others, or getting the better of any of a contrary party, that are in any respect our competitors, or the bringing or keeping them down, our governing aim, to the prejudice of the interest of religion, and the honour of Christ.

And in the management of any public affair, wherever there is a difference of opinions, concerning any outward possessions, privileges, rights, or properties, we will not willingly violate justice for private interest: and with the greatest strictness and watchfulness, will avoid all unchristian bitterness, vehemence, and heat of spirit; yea, though we should think ourselves injured by a contrary party; and in the time of the management of such affairs, will especially watch over ourselves, our spirits, and our tongues, to avoid all unchristian inveighings, reproachings, bitter reflectings, judging and ridiculing others, either in public meetings or in private conversation, either to men's faces, or behind their backs; but will greatly endeavour, so far as we are concerned, that all should be managed with christian humility, gentleness, quietness, and love.

And furthermore we promise, that we will not tolerate the exercise of enmity and ill will, or revenge in our hearts, against any of our neighbours; and we will often be strictly searching and examining our own hearts with respect to that matter.

And if any of us find that we have an old secret grudge against any of our neighbours, we will not gratify it, but cross it, and endeavour to our utmost to root it out, crying to God for his help; and that we will make it our true and faithful endeavour, in our places, that a party spirit may not be kept up amongst us, but that it may utterly cease; that for the future, we may all be one, united in undisturbed peace and unfeigned love.

And those of us that are in youth, do promise, never to allow ourselves in any diversions or pastimes, in meetings, or companies of young people, that we, in our consciences, upon sober consideration, judge not well to consist with, or would sinfully tend to hinder, the devoutest and most engaged spirit in religion, or indispose the mind for that devout and profitable attendance on the duties of the closet, which is most agreeable to God's will, or that we, in our most impartial judgment, can think tends to rob God of that honour which he expects, by our orderly serious attendance on family worship.

And furthermore we promise, that we will strictly avoid all freedoms and familiarities in company, so tending either to stir up or gratify a lust of lasciviousness, that we cannot in our consciences think will be approved by the infinitely pure and holy eye of God, or that we can think, on serious and impartial consideration, we should be afraid to practise, if we expected in a few hours to appear before that holy God, to give an account of ourselves to him, as fearing they would be condemned by him as unlawful and impure.

We also promise, with great watchfulness, to perform relative duties, required by christian rules, in the families we belong to, as we stand related respectively, towards parents and children, husbands and wives, brothers and sisters, masters or mistresses, and servants.

And we now appear before God, depending on Divine grace and assistance, solemnly to devote our whole lives, to be laboriously spent in the business of religion; ever making it our greatest business, without backsliding from such a way of living, not hearkening to the solicitations of our sloth, and other corrupt inclinations, or the temptations of the world, that tend to draw us off from it; and particularly, that we will not abuse a hope or opinion that any of us may have, of our being interested in Christ, to indulge ourselves in sloth, or the more easily to yield to the solicitations of any sinful inclinations; but will run with perseverance the race that is set before us, and work out our own salvation with fear and trembling.

And because we are sensible that the keeping these

solemn vows may hereafter, in many cases, be very contrary to our corrupt inclinations and carnal interests, we do now therefore appear before God to make a surrender of all to him, and to make a sacrifice of every carnal inclination and interest, to the great business of religion and the interest of our souls.

And being sensible of our weakness, and the deceitfulness of our own hearts, and our proneness to forget our most solemn vows, and lose our resolutions, we promise to be often strictly examining ourselves by these promises, especially before the sacrament of the Lord's supper; and beg of God that he would, for Christ's sake, keep us from wickedly dissembling in these our solemn vows; and that he who searches our hearts, and ponders the path of our feet, would, from time to time, help us in trying ourselves by this covenant, and help us to keep covenant with him, and not leave us to our own foolish, wicked, and treacherous hearts.

In the beginning of the summer of 1742, there seemed to be an abatement of the liveliness of people's affections in religion; but yet many were often in a great height of them. And in the fall and winter following, there were at times extraordinary appearances. But in the general, people's engagedness in religion, and the liveliness of their affections, have been on the decline; and some of the young people especially, have shamefully lost their liveliness and vigour in religion, and much of the seriousness and solemnity of their spirits. But there are many that walk as becometh saints; and to this day there are a considerable number in town that seem to be near to God, and maintain much of the life of religion, and enjoy many of the sensible tokens and fruits of his gracious presence.

With respect to the late season of revival of religion amongst us for three or four years past, it has been observable, that in the former part of it, in the years 1740 and 1741, the work seemed to be much more pure, having less of a corrupt mixture than in the former great outpouring of the Spirit, in 1735 and 1736. Persons seemed to be sensible of their former errors, and had learned more of their own hearts, and experience had taught them more of the tendency and consequences of things. They were now better guarded, and their affections were not only stronger, but attended with greater solemnity, and greater humility and self-distrust, and greater engagedness after holy living and perseverance: and there were fewer errors in conduct. But in the latter part of it, in the year 1742, it was otherwise: the work continued more pure till we were infected from abroad: our people hearing of, and some of them seeing, the work in other places, where there was a greater visible commotion than here, and the outward appearances were more extraordinary, were ready to think that the work in those places far excelled what was amongst us, and their eyes were dazzled with the high profession and great show that some made, who came hither from other places.

That those people went so far beyond them in raptures and violent emotions of the affections, and a vehement zeal, and what they call *boldness for Christ*, our people were ready to think was owing to far greater attainments in grace, and intimacy with heaven: they looked little in their own eyes in comparison with them, and were ready to submit themselves to them, and yield themselves up to their conduct, taking it for granted, that every thing was right that they said and did. These things had a strange influence on the people, and gave many of them a deep and unhappy tincture, from which it was a hard and long labour to deliver them, and from which some of them are not fully delivered to this day.

The *effects* and *consequences* of things among us plainly show the following things, *viz.* That the degree of *grace* is by no means to be judged of by the degree of *joy*, or the degree of *zeal;* and that indeed we cannot at all determine by these things, who are gracious and who are not; and that it is not the *degree* of religious affections, but the *nature* of them, that is chiefly to be looked at. *Some* that have had very great raptures of joy, and have been extraordinarily *filled*, (as the vulgar phrase is,) and have had their bodies overcome, and that very often, have manifested far less of the temper of Christians in their conduct since, than some others that have been still, and have made no great outward show. But then again, there are *many others*, that have had extraordinary joys and emotions of mind, with frequent great effects upon their bodies, that behave themselves stedfastly, as humble, amiable, eminent Christians.

'Tis evident that there may be great religious affections in individuals, which may in show and appearance resemble gracious affections, and have the same effects upon their bodies, but are far from having the same effect on the temper of their minds and the course of their lives. And likewise there is nothing more manifest, by what appears amongst us, than that the good estate of individuals is not chiefly to be judged of by any exactness of steps, and method of experiences, in what is supposed to be the first conversion; but that we must judge by the spirit that breathes, the effect wrought upon the temper of the soul in the time of the work and remaining afterwards. Though there have been very few instances among professors, amongst us, of what is ordinarily called scandalous sins, known to me; yet the temper that some of them show, and the behaviour they have been of, together with some things in the nature and circumstances of their experiences, make me much afraid lest there be a considerable number that have woefully deceived themselves. Though, on the other hand, there is a great number whose temper and conversation is such, as justly confirms the charity of others towards them; and not a few, in whose disposition and walk there are amiable appearances of eminent grace. And notwithstanding all the corrupt mixtures that have been in the late work here, there are not only many blessed fruits of it, in particular persons that yet remain, but some good effects of it upon the town in general. A spirit of party has more extensively subsided. I suppose there has been less appearance these three or four years past, of that division of the town into two parties, which has long been our bane, than has been at any time during the preceding thirty years; and the people have apparently had much more caution, and a greater guard on their spirit and their tongues, to avoid contention and unchristian heats, in town-meetings, and on other occasions. And 'tis a thing greatly to be rejoiced in, that the people very lately came to an agreement and final issue, with respect to their grand controversy relating to their common lands; which has been, above any other particular thing, a source of mutual prejudices, jealousies, and debates, for fifteen or sixteen years past. The people also seem to be much more sensible of the danger of resting in old experiences, or what they were subjects of at their supposed first conversion; and to be more fully convinced of the necessity of forgetting the things that are behind, and pressing forward and maintaining earnest labour, watchfulness, and prayerfulness, as long as they live.

I am, Rev. Sir,

Your friend and brother,

JONATHAN EDWARDS"

CHAPTER XI.

MRS. EDWARDS—HER SOLEMN SELF-DEDICATIONS—HER UNCOMMON DISCOVERIES OF THE DIVINE PERFECTIONS AND GLORY; AND OF THE EXCELLENCY OF CHRIST—REMARKS CONCERNING THEM.

In speaking of Mrs. Edwards, we have already had occasion to remark, that her piety appears to have been in no ordinary degree pure, intense, and elevated, and that her views of spiritual and heavenly things were uncommonly clear and joyful. Near the close of the year 1738, according to the testimony of Mr. Edwards, she was led, under an uncommon discovery of God's excellency, and in an high exercise of love to God, and of rest and joy in him, to make a new and most solemn dedication of herself to his service and glory, an entire renunciation of the world, and a resignation of all to God. After this, she had often such views of the glory of the divine perfections, and of Christ's excellencies, and at times, for hours together, without any interruption, that she was overwhelmed, and as it were swallowed up, in the light and joy of the love of God. In the summer of 1740, after a new and more perfect resignation of herself to God, with yet greater fervency, her views of the glory of God, and of the excellency of Christ, became still more clear and transporting; and in the following winter, after a similar but more perfect resignation of herself, and acceptance of God as the only portion and happiness of her soul, God appeared to vouchsafe to her, for a long period, a degree of spiritual light and enjoyment, which seemed to be, in reality, an anticipation of the joys of the heavenly world. There was so much that was unusual and striking in this state of mind, that her husband requested her to draw up an exact statement of it; which, having been preserved, is now presented to the reader.

"On Tuesday night, Jan. 19, 1742," observes Mrs. Edwards, "I felt very uneasy and unhappy, at my being so low in grace. I thought I very much needed help from God, and found a spirit of earnestness to seek help of him, that I might have more holiness. When I had for a time been earnestly wrestling with God for it, I felt within myself great quietness of spirit, unusual submission to God, and willingness to wait upon him, with respect to the time and manner in which he should help me, and wished that he should take his own time, and his own way, to do it.

"The next morning I found a degree of uneasiness in my mind, at Mr. Edwards's suggesting, that he thought I had failed in some measure in point of prudence, in some conversation I had with Mr. Williams, of Hadley, the day before. I found, that it seemed to bereave me of the quietness and calm of my mind, in any respect not to have the good opinion of my husband. This, I much disliked in myself, as arguing a want of a sufficient rest in God, and felt a disposition to fight against it, and look to God for his help, that I might have a more full and entire rest in him, independent of all other things. I continued in this frame, from early in the morning until about 10 o'clock, at which time the Rev. Mr. Reynolds went to prayer in the family.

"I had, before this, so entirely given myself up to God, and resigned up every thing into his hands, that I had, for a long time, felt myself quite alone in the world; so that the peace and calm of my mind, and my rest in God, as my only and all-sufficient happiness, seemed sensibly above the reach of disturbance from any thing but these two: 1st. My own good name and fair reputation among men, and especially the esteem and just treatment of the people of this town; 2dly. And more especially, the esteem, and love, and kind treatment of my husband. At times, indeed, I had seemed to be considerably elevated above the influence of even these things; yet I had not found my calm, and peace, and rest in God so sensibly, fully, and constantly, above the reach of disturbance from them, until now.

"While Mr. Reynolds was at prayer in the family this morning, I felt an earnest desire that, in calling on God, he should say, *Father*, or that he should address the Almighty under that appellation: on which the thought turned in my mind—Why can I say, *Father?*—Can I now at this time, with the confidence of a child, and without the least misgiving of heart, call God my Father?—This brought to my mind two lines of Mr. Erskine's sonnet:

'I see him lay his vengeance by,
'And smile in Jesus' face.'

"I was thus deeply sensible, that my sins did loudly call for vengeance; but I then by faith saw God 'lay his vengeance by, and smile in Jesus' face.' It appeared to be real and certain that he did so. I had not the least doubt, that he then sweetly smiled upon me, with the look of forgiveness and love, having laid aside all his displeasure towards me, for Jesus' sake; which made me feel very weak, and somewhat faint.

"In consequence of this, I felt a strong desire to be alone with God, to go to him, without having any one to interrupt the silent and soft communion, which I earnestly desired between God and my own soul; and accordingly withdrew to my chamber. It should have been mentioned that, before I retired, while Mr. Reynolds was praying, these words, in Rom. viii. 34. came into my mind, 'Who is he that condemneth; it is Christ that died, yea rather that is risen again, who is even at the right hand of God, who also maketh intercession for us;' as well as the following words, 'Who shall separate us from the love of Christ,' &c.; which occasioned great sweetness and delight in my soul. But when I was alone, the words came to my mind with far greater power and sweetness; upon which I took the Bible, and read the words to the end of the chapter, when they were impressed on my heart with vastly greater power and sweetness still. They appeared to me with undoubted certainty as the words of God, and as words which God did pronounce concerning me. I had no more doubt of it, than I had of my being. I seemed as it were to hear the great God proclaiming thus to the world concerning me; 'Who shall lay any thing to thy charge,' &c.; and had it strongly impressed on me, how impossible it was for any thing in heaven or earth, in this world or the future, ever to separate me from the love of God which was in Christ Jesus. I cannot find language to express, how *certain* this appeared—the everlasting mountains and hills were but shadows to it. My safety, and happiness, and eternal enjoyment of God's immutable love, seemed as durable and unchangeable as God himself. Melted and overcome by the sweetness of this assurance, I fell into a great flow of tears, and could not forbear weeping aloud. It appeared certain to me that God was my Father, and Christ my Lord and Saviour, that he was mine and I his. Under a delightful sense of the immediate presence and love of God, these words seemed to come over and over in my mind, 'My God, my all; my God, my all.' The presence of God was so near, and so real, that I seemed scarcely conscious of any thing else. God the Father, and the Lord Jesus Christ, seemed as distinct persons, both manifesting their inconceivable loveliness, and mildness, and gentleness, and their great and immutable love to me. I seemed to be taken under the care and charge of my God and Saviour, in an inexpressibly endearing manner; and Christ appeared to me as a mighty Saviour, under the character of the Lion of the tribe of Judah, taking my heart, with all its corruptions, under his care, and putting it at his feet. In all things, which concerned me, I felt myself safe under the protection of the Father and the Saviour; who appeared with supreme kindness to keep a record of every thing that I did, and of every thing that was done to me, purely for my good.

"The peace and happiness, which I hereupon felt, was altogether inexpressible. It seemed to be that which came from heaven; to be eternal and unchangeable. I seemed to be lifted above earth and hell, out of the reach of every thing here below, so that I could look on all the rage and enmity of men or devils, with a kind of holy indifference, and an undisturbed tranquillity. At the same time, I felt compassion and love for all mankind, and a deep abasement of soul, under a sense of my own unworthiness. I thought of the ministers who were in the house, and felt willing to undergo any labour and self-denial, if they would but come to the help of the Lord. I also felt myself more perfectly weaned from all things here below, than ever before. The whole world, with all its enjoyments, and all its troubles, seemed to be nothing:—My God was my all, my only portion. No possible suffering appeared to be worth regarding: all persecutions and torments were a mere nothing. I seemed to dwell on high, and the place of defence to be the munition of rocks.

"After some time, the two evils mentioned above, as those which I should have been least able to bear, came to my mind—the ill treatment of the town, and the ill will of my husband; but now I was carried exceedingly above even such things as these, and I could feel that, if I were exposed to them both, they would seem comparatively nothing. There was then a deep snow on the ground, and I could think of being driven from my home into the cold and snow, of being chased from the town with the utmost contempt and malice, and of being left to perish with the cold, as cast out by all the world, with perfect calmness and serenity. It appeared to me, that it would not move me, or in the least disturb the inexpressible happiness and peace of my soul. My mind seemed as much above all such things, as the sun is above the earth.

"I continued in a very sweet and lively sense of divine things, day and night, sleeping and waking, until Saturday, Jan. 23. On Saturday morning, I had a most solemn and deep impression on my mind of the eye of God as fixed upon me, to observe what improvement I made of those spiritual communications I had received from him; as well as of the respect shown Mr. Edwards, who had then been sent for to preach at Leicester. I was sensible that I was sinful enough to bestow it on my pride, or on my sloth, which seemed exceedingly dreadful to me. At night, my soul seemed to be filled with an inexpressibly sweet and pure love to God, and to the children of God; with a refreshing consolation and solace of soul, which made me willing to lie on the earth, at the feet of the servants of God, to declare his gracious dealings with me, and breathe forth before them my love, and gratitude, and praise.

"The next day, which was the sabbath, I enjoyed a sweet, and lively, and assured sense of God's infinite grace, and favour, and love to me, in taking me out of the depths of hell, and exalting me to the heavenly glory, and the dignity of a royal priesthood.

"On Monday night, Mr. Edwards, being gone that day to Leicester, I heard that Mr. Buell was coming to this town, and from what I had heard of him, and of his success, I had strong hopes that there would be great effects from his labours here. At the same time, I had a deep and affecting impression, that the eye of God was ever upon my heart, and that it greatly concerned me to watch my heart, and see to it that I was perfectly resigned to God, with respect to the instruments he should make use of to revive religion in this town, and be entirely willing, if it was God's pleasure, that he should make use of Mr. Buell; and also that other Christians should appear to excel me in christian experience, and in the benefit they should derive from ministers. I was conscious, that it would be exceedingly provoking to God if I should not be thus resigned, and earnestly endeavoured to watch my heart, that no feelings of a contrary nature might arise; and was enabled, as I thought, to exercise full resignation, and acquiescence in God's pleasure, as to these things. I was sensible what great cause I had to bless God, for the use he had made of Mr. Edwards hitherto; but thought, if he never blessed his labours any more, and should greatly bless the labours of other ministers, I could entirely acquiesce in his will. It appeared to me meet and proper, that God should employ babes and sucklings to advance his kingdom. When I thought of these things, it was my instinctive feeling to say, 'Amen, Lord Jesus! Amen, Lord Jesus!' This seemed to be the sweet and instinctive language of my soul.

"On Tuesday, I remained in a sweet and lively exercise of this resignation, and love to and rest in God, seeming to be in my heart from day to day, far above the reach of every thing here below. On Tuesday night, especially the latter part of it, I felt a great earnestness of soul and engagedness in seeking God for the town, that religion might now revive, and that God would bless Mr. Buell to that end. God seemed to be very near to me while I was thus striving with him for these things, and I had a strong hope that what I sought of him would be granted. There seemed naturally and unavoidably to arise in my mind an assurance that now God would do great things for Northampton.

"On Wednesday morning, I heard that Mr. Buell arrived the night before at Mr. Phelps's, and that there seemed to be great tokens and effects of the presence of God there, which greatly encouraged and rejoiced me. About an hour and a half after, Mr. Buell came to our house; I sat still in entire resignedness to God, and willingness that God should bless his labours here as much as he pleased; though it were to the enlivening of every saint, and to the conversion of every sinner, in the town. These feelings continued afterwards, when I saw his great success; as I never felt the least rising of heart to the contrary, but my submission was even and uniform, without interruption or disturbance. I rejoiced when I saw the honour which God put upon him, and the respect paid him by the people, and the greater success attending his preaching, than had followed the preaching of Mr. Edwards immediately before he went to Leicester. I found rest and rejoicing in it, and the sweet language of my soul continually was, 'Amen, Lord Jesus! Amen, Lord Jesus!'

"At 3 o'clock in the afternoon, a lecture was preached by Mr. Buell. In the latter part of the sermon, one or two appeared much moved, and after the blessing, when the people were going out, several others. To my mind there was the clearest evidence, that God was present in the congregation, on the work of redeeming love; and in the clear view of this, I was all at once filled with such intense admiration of the wonderful condescension and grace of God, in returning again to Northampton, as overwhelmed my soul, and immediately took away my bodily strength. This was accompanied with an earnest longing, that those of us, who were the children of God, might now arise and strive. It appeared to me, that the angels in heaven sung praises, for such wonderful, free, and sovereign grace, and my heart was lifted up in adoration and praise. I continued to have clear views of the future world, of eternal happiness and misery, and my heart full of love to the souls of men. On seeing some, that I found were in a natural condition, I felt a most tender compassion for them; but especially was I, while I remained in the meeting-house, from time to time overcome, and my strength taken away, by the sight of one and another, whom I regarded as the children of God, and who, I had heard, were lively and animated in religion. We remained in the meeting-house about three hours, after the public exercises were over. During most of the time, my bodily strength was overcome; and the joy and thankfulness, which were excited in my mind, as I contemplated the great goodness of God, led me to converse with those who were near me, in a very earnest manner.

"When I came home, I found Mr. Buell, Mr. Christophers, Mr. Hopkins, Mrs. Eleanor Dwight, the wife of Mr. Joseph Allen, and Mr. Job Strong, at the house. Seeing and conversing with them on the Divine goodness, renewed my former feelings, and filled me with an intense desire that we might all arise, and with an active, flowing, and fervent heart give glory to God. The intenseness of my feelings again took away my bodily strength. The words of one of Dr. Watts's Hosannas powerfully affected me; and in the course of the conversation, I uttered them as the real language of my heart, with great earnestness and emotion.

> 'Hosanna to King David's Son,
> Who reigns on a superior throne,' &c.

And while I was uttering the words, my mind was so deeply impressed with the love of Christ, and a sense of his immediate presence, that I could with difficulty refrain from rising from my seat, and leaping for joy. I continued to enjoy this intense, and lively, and refreshing sense of divine things, accompanied with strong emotions, for nearly an hour; after which, I experienced a delightful calm, and peace and rest in God, until I retired for the night; and during the night, both waking and sleeping, I had joyful views of divine things, and a complacential rest of soul in God. I awoke in the morning of Thursday, Jan. 28th, in the same happy frame of mind, and engaged in the duties of my family with a sweet consciousness, that God was present with me, and with earnest longings of soul for the continuance and increase of the blessed fruits of the Holy Spirit in the town. About nine o'clock, these desires became so exceedingly intense, when I saw numbers of the people coming into the house, with an appearance of deep interest in religion, that my bodily strength was much weakened, and it was with difficulty that I could pursue my ordinary avocations. About 11 o'clock, as I accidentally went into the room where Mr. Buell was conversing with some of the people, I heard him say, 'O that we, who are the children of God, should be cold and lifeless in religion!' and I felt such a sense of the deep ingratitude manifested by the children of God, in such coldness and deadness, that my strength was immediately taken away, and I sunk down on the spot. Those who were near raised me, and placed me in a chair; and from the fulness of my heart, I expressed to them, in a very earnest manner, the deep sense I had of the wonderful grace of Christ towards me, of the assurance I had of his having saved me from hell, of my happiness running parallel with eternity, of the duty of giving up all to God, and of the peace and joy inspired by an entire dependence on his mercy and grace. Mr. Buell then read a melting hymn of Dr. Watts's,* concerning the loveliness of Christ, the enjoyments and employments of heaven, and the Christian's earnest desire of heavenly things; and the truth and reality of the things mentioned in the hymn, made so strong an impression on my mind, and my soul was drawn so powerfully towards Christ and heaven, that I leaped unconsciously from my chair. I seemed to be drawn upwards, soul and body, from the earth towards heaven; and it appeared to me that I must naturally and necessarily ascend thither. These feelings continued while the hymn was reading, and during the prayer of Mr. Christophers, which followed. After the prayer, Mr. Buell read two other hymns, on the glories of heaven, which moved me so exceedingly, and drew me so strongly heavenward, that it seemed as it were to draw my body upwards, and I felt as if I must necessarily ascend thither. At length my strength failed me, and I sunk down; when they took me up and laid me on the bed, where I lay for a considerable time, faint with joy, while contemplating the glories of the heavenly world. After I had lain a while, I felt more perfectly subdued and weaned from the world, and more fully resigned to God, than I had ever been con-

* Probably the 91st Hymn of the 2d Book, beginning with
"O the delights, the heavenly joys,
The glories of the place."

scious of before. I felt an entire indifference to the opinions, and representations, and conduct of mankind respecting me; and a perfect willingness, that God should employ some other instrument than Mr. Edwards, in advancing the work of grace in Northampton. I was entirely swallowed up in God, as my only portion, and his honour and glory was the object of my supreme desire and delight. At the same time, I felt a far greater love to the children of God, than ever before. I seemed to love them as my own soul; and when I saw them, my heart went out towards them, with an inexpressible endearedness and sweetness. I beheld them by faith in their risen and glorified state, with spiritual bodies re-fashioned after the image of Christ's glorious body, and arrayed in the beauty of heaven. The time when they would be so appeared very near, by faith it seemed as if it were present. This was accompanied with a ravishing sense of the unspeakable joys of the upper world. They appeared to my mind in all their reality and certainty, and as it were in actual and distinct vision; so plain and evident were they to the eye of my faith, I seemed to regard them as begun. These anticipations were renewed over and over, while I lay on the bed, from twelve o'clock till four, being too much exhausted by emotions of joy, to rise and sit up; and during most of the time, my feelings prompted me to converse very earnestly with one and another of the pious women, who were present, on those spiritual and heavenly objects, of which I had so deep an impression. A little while before I arose, Mr. Buell and the people went to meeting.

"I continued in a sweet and lively sense of divine things, until I retired to rest. That night, which was Thursday night, Jan. 28, was the sweetest night I ever had in my life. I never before, for so long a time together, enjoyed so much of the light, and rest, and sweetness of heaven in my soul, but without the least agitation of body during the whole time. The great part of the night I lay awake, sometimes asleep, and sometimes between sleeping and waking. But all night I continued in a constant, clear, and lively sense of the heavenly sweetness of Christ's excellent and transcendent love, of his nearness to me, and of my dearness to him; with an inexpressibly sweet calmness of soul in an entire rest in him. I seemed to myself to perceive a glow of divine love come down from the heart of Christ in heaven, into my heart, in a constant stream, like a stream or pencil of sweet light. At the same time, my heart and soul all flowed out in love to Christ; so that there seemed to be a constant flowing and reflowing of heavenly and divine love, from Christ's heart to mine; and I appeared to myself to float or swim, in these bright, sweet beams of the love of Christ, like the motes swimming in the beams of the sun, or the streams of his light which come in at the window. My soul remained in a kind of heavenly elysium. So far as I am capable of making a comparison, I think that what I felt each minute, during the continuance of the whole time, was worth more than all the outward comfort and pleasure, which I had enjoyed in my whole life put together. It was a pure delight, which fed and satisfied the soul. It was pleasure, without the least sting, or any interruption. It was a sweetness, which my soul was lost in. It seemed to be all that my feeble frame could sustain, of that fulness of joy, which is felt by those, who behold the face of Christ, and share his love in the heavenly world. There was but little difference, whether I was asleep or awake, so deep was the impression made on my soul; but if there was any difference, the sweetness was greatest and most uninterrupted while I was asleep.

"As I awoke early the next morning, which was Friday, I was led to think of Mr. Williams of Hadley preaching that day in the town, as had been appointed; and to examine my heart, whether I was willing that he, who was a neighbouring minister, should be extraordinarily blessed, and made a greater instrument of good in the town, than Mr. Edwards; and was enabled to say, with respect to that matter, 'Amen, Lord Jesus!' and to be entirely willing, if God pleased, that he should be the instrument of converting every soul in the town. My soul acquiesced fully in the will of God, as to the instrument, if his work of renewing grace did but go on.

"This lively sense of the beauty and excellency of divine things continued during the morning, accompanied with peculiar sweetness and delight. To my own imagination, my soul seemed to be gone out of me to God and Christ in heaven, and to have very little relation to my body. God and Christ were so present to me, and so near me, that I seemed removed from myself. The spiritual beauty of the Father and the Saviour, seemed to engross my whole mind; and it was the instinctive feeling of my heart, 'Thou art; and there is none beside thee.' I never felt such an entire emptiness of self-love, or any regard to any private, selfish interest of my own. It seemed to me, that I had entirely done with myself. I felt that the opinions of the world concerning me were nothing, and that I had no more to do with any outward interest of my own, than with that of a person whom I never saw. The glory of God seemed to be all, and in all, and to swallow up every wish and desire of my heart.

"Mr. Sheldon came into the house about 10 o'clock, and said to me as he came in, 'The Sun of righteousness arose on my soul this morning, before day;' upon which I said to him in reply, 'That Sun has not set upon my soul all this night; I have dwelt on high in the heavenly mansions; the light of divine love has surrounded me; my soul has been lost in God, and has almost left the body.' This conversation only served to give me a still livelier sense of the reality and excellence of divine things, and that to such a degree, as again to take away my strength, and occasion great agitation of body. So strong were my feelings, I could not refrain from conversing with those around me, in a very earnest manner, for about a quarter of an hour, on the infinite riches of divine love in the work of salvation; when, my strength entirely failing, my flesh grew very cold, and they carried me and set me by the fire. As I sat there, I had a most affecting sense of the mighty power of Christ, which had been exerted in what he had done for my soul, and in sustaining and keeping down the native corruptions of my heart, and of the glorious and wonderful grace of God in causing the ark to return to Northampton. So intense were my feelings, when speaking of these things, that I could not forbear rising up and leaping with joy and exultation. I felt at the same time an exceedingly strong and tender affection for the children of God, and realized, in a manner exceedingly sweet and ravishing, the meaning of Christ's prayer, in John xvii. 21. 'That they all may be one, as thou Father art in me, and I in thee, that they also may be one in us.' This union appeared to me an inconceivable, excellent, and sweet oneness; and at the same time I felt that oneness in my soul, with the children of God who were present. Mr. Christophers then read the hymn out of the Penitential Cries, beginning with

'My soul doth magnify the Lord,
My spirit doth rejoice;'

The whole hymn was deeply affecting to my feelings: but when these words were read,

'My sighs at length are turn'd to songs,
The Comforter is come:'—

so conscious was I of the joyful presence of the Holy Spirit, I could scarcely refrain from leaping with transports of joy. This happy frame of mind continued until two o'clock, when Mr. Williams came in, and we soon went to meeting. He preached on the subject of the assurance of faith. The whole sermon was affecting to me, but especially when he came to show the way in which assurance was obtained, and to point out its happy fruits. When I heard him say, that *those who have assurance, have a foretaste of heavenly glory*, I knew the truth of it from what I then felt: I knew that I then tasted the clusters of the heavenly Canaan: my soul was filled and overwhelmed with light, and love, and joy in the Holy Ghost, and seemed just ready to go away from the body. I could scarcely refrain from expressing my joy aloud, in the midst of the service. I had, in the mean time, an overwhelming sense of the glory of God, as the Great Eternal All, and of the happiness of having my own will entirely subdued to his will. I knew that the foretaste of glory, which I then had in my soul, came from him, that I certainly should go to him, and should, as it were, drop into the Divine Being, and be swallowed up in God.

"After meeting was done, the congregation waited while Mr. Buell went home, to prepare to give them a lecture. It was almost dark before he came, and, in the mean time, I conversed in a very earnest and joyful manner, with those who were with me in the pew. My mind dwelt on the thought, that the Lord God Omnipotent reigneth, and it appeared to me that he was going to set up a reign of love on the earth, and that heaven and earth were, as it were, coming together; which so exceedingly moved me that I could not forbear expressing aloud, to those near me, my exultation of soul. This subsided into a heavenly calm, and a rest of soul in God, which was even sweeter than what preceded it. Afterwards, Mr. Buell came and preached; and the same happy frame of mind continued during the evening, and night, and the next day. In the forenoon, I was thinking of the manner in which the children of God had been treated in the world—particularly of their being shut up in prison—and the folly of such attempts to make them miserable, seemed to surprise me. It appeared astonishing, that men should think, by this means, to injure those who had such a kingdom within them. Towards night being informed that Mrs. P—— had expressed her fears lest I should die before Mr. Edwards's return, and he should think the people had killed his wife; I told those who were present, that I chose to die in the way that was most agreeable to God's will, and that I should be willing to die in darkness and horror, if it was most for the glory of God.

"In the evening, I read those chapters in John, which contain Christ's dying discourse with his disciples, and his prayer with them. After I had done reading, and was in my retirement, a little before bed-time, thinking on what I had read, my soul was so filled with love to Christ, and love to his people, that I fainted under the intenseness of the feeling. I felt, while reading, a delightful acquiescence in the petition to the Father—'I pray not that thou shouldst take them out of the world, but that thou shouldst keep them from the evil.' Though it seemed to me infinitely better to die to go to Christ, yet I felt an entire willingness to continue in this world so long as God pleased, to do and suffer what he would have me.

"After retiring to rest and sleeping a little while, I awoke and had a very lively consciousness of God's being near me. I had an idea of a shining way, or path of light, between heaven and my soul, somewhat as on Thursday night, except that God seemed nearer to me, and as it were close by, and the way seemed more open, and the communication more immediate and more free. I lay awake most of the night, with a constant delightful sense of God's great love and infinite condescension, and with a continual view of God as *near*, and as *my God*. My soul remained, as on Thursday night, in a kind of heavenly elysium. Whether waking or sleeping, there was no interruption, throughout the night, to the views of my soul, to its heavenly light, and divine, inexpressible sweetness. It was without any agitation or motion of the body. I was led to reflect on God's mercy to me, in giving me, for many years, a willingness to die; and after that, for more than two years past, in making me willing to live, that I might do and suffer whatever he called me to here; whereas, before that, I often used to feel impatient at the thought of living. This then appeared to me, as it had often done before, what gave me much the greatest sense of thankfulness to God. I also thought how God had graciously given me, for a great while, an entire resignation to his will, with respect to the kind and manner of death that I should die; having been made willing to die on the rack, or at the stake, or any other tormenting death, and, if it were God's will, to die in darkness: and how I had that day been made very sensible and fully willing, if it was God's pleasure and for his glory, to die in horror. But now it occurred to me, that when I had thus been made willing to live, and to be kept on this dark abode, I used to think of living no longer than to the ordinary age of man. Upon this I was led to ask myself, Whether I was not willing to be kept out of heaven even longer; and my whole heart seemed immediately to reply, 'Yes, a thousand years, if it be God's will, and for his honour and glory:' and then my heart, in the language of resignation, went further, and with great alacrity and sweetness, to answer as it were over and over again, 'Yes, and live a thousand years in horror, if it be most for the glory of God: yea, I am willing to live a thousand years a hell upon earth, if it be most for the honour of God.' But then I considered with myself, What this would be, to live a hell upon earth, for so long a time; and I thought of the torment of my body being so great, awful, and overwhelming, that none could bear to live in the country where the spectacle was seen, and of the torment and horror of my mind being vastly greater than the torment of my body; and it seemed to me that I found a perfect willingness, and sweet quietness and alacrity of soul, in consenting that it should be so, if it were most for the glory of God; so that there was no hesitation, doubt, or darkness in my mind, attending the thoughts of it, but my resignation seemed to be clear, like a light that shone through my soul. I continued saying, 'Amen, Lord Jesus! Amen, Lord Jesus! glorify thyself in me, in my body and my soul,'—with a calm and sweetness of soul, which banished all reluctance. The glory of God seemed to overcome me and swallow me up, and every conceivable suffering, and every thing that was terrible to my nature, seemed to shrink to nothing before it. This resignation continued in its clearness and brightness the rest of the night, and all the next day, and the night following, and on Monday in the forenoon, without interruption or abatement. All this while, whenever I thought of it, the language of my soul was, with the greatest fulness and alacrity, 'Amen, Lord Jesus! Amen, Lord Jesus!' In the afternoon of Monday, it was not quite so perceptible and lively, but my mind remained so much in a similar frame, for more than a week, that I could never think of it without an inexpressible sweetness in my soul.

"After I had felt this resignation on Saturday night, for some time as I lay in bed, I felt such a disposition to rejoice in God, that I wished to have the world join me in praising him; and was ready to wonder how the world of mankind could lie and sleep, when there was such a God to praise, and rejoice in, and could scarcely forbear calling out to those who were asleep in the house, to arise, and rejoice, and praise God. When I arose on the morning of the sabbath, I felt a love to all mankind, wholly peculiar in its strength and sweetness, far beyond all that I had ever felt before. The power of that love seemed to be inexpressible. I thought, if I were surrounded by enemies, who were venting their malice and cruelty upon me, in tormenting me, it would still be impossible that I should cherish any feelings towards them but those of love, and pity, and ardent desires for their happiness. At the same time I thought, if I were cast off by my nearest and dearest friends, and if the feelings and conduct of my husband were to be changed from tenderness and affection, to extreme hatred and cruelty, and that every day, I could so rest in God, that it would not touch my heart, or diminish my happiness. I could still go on with alacrity in the performance of every act of duty, and my happiness remain undiminished and entire.

"I never before felt so far from a disposition to judge and censure others, with respect to the state of their hearts, their sincerity, or their attainments in holiness, as I did that morning. To do this, seemed abhorrent to every feeling of my heart. I realized also, in an unusual and very lively manner, how great a part of Christianity lies in the performance of our social and relative duties to one another. The same lively and joyful sense of spiritual and divine things continued throughout the day—a sweet love to God and all mankind, and such an entire rest of soul in God, that it seemed as if nothing that could be said of me, or done to me, could touch my heart, or disturb my enjoyment. The road between heaven and my soul seemed open and wide, all the day long; and the consciousness I had of the reality and excellence of heavenly things was so clear, and the affections they excited so intense, that it overcame my strength, and kept my body weak and faint, the great part of the day, so that I could not stand or go without help. The night also was comforting and refreshing.

"This delightful frame of mind was continued on Monday. About noon, one of the neighbours who was conversing with me, expressed himself thus, 'One smile from Christ is worth a thousand million pounds,' and the words affected me exceedingly, and in a manner which I cannot express. I had a strong sense of the infinite worth of Christ's approbation and love, and at the same time of the grossness of the comparison; and it only astonished me, that any one could compare a smile of Christ to any earthly treasure.—Towards night, I had a deep sense of the awful greatness of God, and felt with what humility and reverence we ought to behave ourselves before him. Just then Mr. W—— came in, and spoke with a somewhat light, smiling air, of the flourishing state of religion in the town; which I could scarcely bear to see. It seemed to me, that we ought greatly to revere the presence of God, and to behave ourselves with the utmost solemnity and humility, when so great and holy a God was so remarkably present, and to rejoice before him with trembling.—In the evening, these words, in the Penitential Cries,—'THE COMFORTER IS COME!'—were accompanied to my soul with such conscious certainty, and such intense joy, that immediately it took away my strength, and I was falling to the floor; when some of those who were near me caught me and held me up. And when I repeated the words to the by-standers, the strength of my feelings was increased. The name—'THE COMFORTER'—seemed to denote that the Holy Spirit was the only and infinite Fountain of comfort and joy, and this seemed real and certain to my mind. These words—'THE COMFORTER'—seemed as it were immensely great, enough to fill heaven and earth.

"On Tuesday after dinner, Mr. Buell, as he sat at table, began to discourse about the glories of the upper world; which greatly affected me, so as to take away my strength. The views and feelings of the preceding evening, respecting the Great Comforter, were renewed in the most lively and joyful manner; so that my limbs grew cold, and I continued to a considerable degree overcome for about an hour, earnestly expressing to those around me, my deep and joyful sense of the presence and divine excellence of the Comforter, and of the glories of heaven.

"It was either on Tuesday or Wednesday, that Mr. W—— came to the house, and informed what account Mr. Lyman, who was just then come from Leicester, on his way from Boston, gave of Mr. Edwards's success, in making peace and promoting religion at Leicester. The intelligence inspired me with such an admiring sense of the great goodness of God, in using Mr. Edwards as the instrument of doing good, and promoting the work of salvation, that it immediately overcame me, and took away my strength, so that I could no longer stand on my feet. On Wednesday night, Mr. Clark, coming in with Mr. Buell and some of the people, asked me how I felt. I told him that I did not feel at all times alike, but this I thought I could say, that I had given up all to God; and there is nothing like it, nothing like giving up all to him, esteeming all to be his, and resigning all at his call. I told him that, many a time within a twelvemonth, I had asked myself when I lay down, How I should feel, if our house and all our property in it should be burnt up, and we should that night be turned out naked; whether I could cheerfully resign all to God; and whether I so saw that all was his, that I could fully consent to his will, in being deprived of it? and that I found, so far as I could judge, an entire resignation to his will, and felt that, if he should thus strip me of every thing, I had nothing to say, but should, I thought, have an entire calm and rest in God, for it was his own, and not mine. After this, Mr. Phelps gave us an account of his own feelings, during a journey from which he had just returned; and then Mr. Pomeroy broke forth in the language of joy, and thankfulness, and praise, and continued speaking to us nearly an hour, leading us all the time to rejoice in the visible presence of God, and to adore his infinite goodness and condescension. He concluded by saying, 'I would say more if I could; but words were not made to express these things.' This reminded me of the words of Mrs. Rowe:

> 'More I would speak, but all my words are faint:
> Celestial Love, what eloquence can paint?
> No more, by mortal words, can be expressed;
> But vast Eternity shall tell the rest:'

and my former impressions of heavenly and divine things were renewed with so much power, and life, and joy, that my strength all failed me, and I remained for some time faint and exhausted. After the people had retired, I had a still more lively and joyful sense of the goodness and all-sufficiency of God, of the pleasure of loving him, and of being alive and active in his service, so that I could not sit still, but walked the room for some time, in a kind of transport. The contemplation was so refreshing and delightful, so much like a heavenly feast within the soul, that I felt an absolute indifference as to any external circumstances; and, according to my best remembrance, this enlivening of my spirit continued so, that I slept but little that night.

"The next day, being Thursday, between ten and eleven o'clock, and a room full of people being collected, I heard two persons give a minute account of the enlivening and joyful influences of the Holy Spirit on their own hearts. It was sweet to me to see others before me in their divine attainments, and to follow after them to heaven. I thought I should rejoice to follow the negro servants in the town to heaven. While I was thus listening, the consideration of the blessed appearances there were of God's being there with us, affected me so powerfully, that the joy and transport of the preceding night were again renewed. After this they sang a hymn, which greatly moved me, especially the latter part of it, which speaks of the ungratefulness of not having the praises of Christ always on our tongues. Those last words of the hymn seemed to fasten on my mind, and as I repeated them over, I felt such intense love to Christ, and so much delight in praising him, that I could hardly forbear leaping from my chair and singing aloud for joy and exultation. I continued thus extraordinarily moved until about one o'clock, when the people went away."

I am well aware, that very different views will be formed of the preceding narrative, by different individuals. Those who have no conception of what is meant by the religion of the heart, will doubtless pronounce it the offspring of a diseased body, or a distempered brain. Others, who profess the religion of Christ, but whose minds usually come in contact with nothing which is not merely *palpable*—with nothing but what they can either see, or hear, or feel, or taste—will probably regard it as the effect of mere enthusiasm. While others, who are both more intellectual and more spiritual in their objects of contemplation, will at once perceive that the state of mind therein described, is one to which they themselves are chiefly or wholly strangers; and will therefore very naturally and rationally wish to learn somewhat more minutely the circumstances of the individual, who was the subject of these spiritual discoveries, as well as their actual effect upon her character. On these points, the testimony of Mr. Edwards is full and explicit; and from his authority we state the following facts.

At this time, Mrs. Edwards had been long, in an uncommon manner, growing in grace, and rising by very sensible degrees to higher love to God, weanedness from the world, and mastery over sin and temptation, through great trials and conflicts, and long-continued struggling and fighting with sin, and earnest and constant prayer and labour in religion, and engagedness of mind in the use of all means, attended with a great exactness of life; and this growth had been attended not only with a great increase of religious affections, but with a most visible alteration of outward behaviour; particularly in living above the world, and in a greater degree of stedfastness and strength in the way of duty and self-denial: maintaining the christian conflict against temptations, and conquering from time to time under great trials; persisting in an unmoved, untouched calm and rest, under the changes and accidents of time, such as seasons of extreme pain and apparent hazard of immediate death. These transports did not arise from bodily weakness, but were greatest in the best state of health. They were accompanied with a lively sense of the greatness of God, and her own littleness and vileness; and had abiding effects in the increase of the sweetness, rest, and humility, which they left upon the soul, and in a new engagedness of heart to live to the honour of God, and to watch and fight against sin. They were attended with no enthusiastical disposition to follow impulses or supposed revelations, nor with any appearance of spiritual pride; but on the contrary with a very great increase of meekness and humility, and a disposition in honour to prefer others, as well as with a great aversion to judging others, and a strong sense of the importance of moral, social duties. They were accompanied with an extraordinary sense of the awful majesty of God, so as frequently to take away the bodily strength; with a sense of the holiness of God, as of a flame infinitely pure and bright, so as oftentimes to overwhelm soul and body, with an extraordinary view of the infinite terribleness of his wrath, of the exceeding sinfulness of her own heart, and of a desert of that wrath for ever; with an intense sorrow for sin, so as entirely to prostrate the strength of the body; with a clear certainty of the truth of the great things revealed in the gospel; with an overwhelming sense of the glory of the work of redemption, and the way of salvation by Jesus Christ, of the glorious harmony of the divine attributes appearing therein, as that wherein mercy and truth are met together, and righteousness and peace have kissed each other; with a sight of the glorious sufficiency of Christ, a constant immovable trust in God, an overwhelming sense of his glorious unsearchable wisdom, a sweet rejoicing at his being infinitely and unchangeably happy, independent, and all-sufficient, at his reigning over all, and doing his own will with uncontrollable power and sovereignty; with a delightful sense of the glory of the Holy Spirit as the great Comforter; with intense desires for the honour and glory of God's name, a clear and constant preference of it, not only to her own temporal interests, but to her spiritual comfort; with a willingness to live and die in spiritual darkness, if the honour of God required it, a great lamenting of ingratitude, intense longings and faintings after higher love to Christ, and greater conformity to him—particularly to be more perfect in humility and adoration; with great delight in singing praises to God and Jesus Christ, a desire that this present life might be one continued song of praise, and an overcoming pleasure at the thought of spending eternity in that exercise; with a living by faith in a very unusual manner; with a uniform distrust of her own strength, and a great dependence on God for help; with intense longings that all Christians might be fervent in love, and active in the service of God; with taking pleasure in watchfulness and toil, self-denial and bearing the cross; with a melting compassion for those who were in a state of nature, and for Christians under darkness, a universal benevolence to all mankind, a willingness to endure any suffering for the conversion of the impenitent—her compassion for them being often to that degree, that she could find no support nor rest, but in going to God and pouring out her soul in prayer for them; with earnest desires that the then existing work of Divine grace might be carried on with greater purity, and freedom from all bitter zeal, censoriousness, spiritual pride, and angry controversy, and that the kingdom of Christ might be established through the earth, as a kingdom of holiness, peace, and joy; with unspeakable delight in the thoughts of heaven, as a world of love, where love shall be the saints' eternal food, where they shall dwell in the light of love, and where the very air and breath will be nothing but love; with intense love to the people of God, as to those who will soon wear his perfect image; with earnest desires that others might love God better than herself, and attain to higher degrees of holiness; with a delight in conversing on the most spiritual and heavenly things in religion, often engaging in such conversation, with a degree of feeling too intense to be long endured; and with a lively sense of the importance of charity to the poor, as well as of the need which ministers have of the influences of the Holy Spirit, and earnest longings and wrestlings with God for them in prayer. She had also, according to Mr. Edwards, the greatest, fullest, longest continued, and most constant assurance of the favour of God, and of a title to future glory, that he ever saw any appearance of, in any person;—enjoying, especially near the time in which he made this statement, to use her own expression, THE RICHES OF FULL ASSURANCE; as well as an uninterrupted, entire resignation to God, with respect to health or sickness, ease or pain, life or death, and an entire resignation of the lives of her nearest earthly friends. These things were attended with a constant, sweet peace and serenity of soul, without a cloud to interrupt it, a continual rejoicing in all the works of nature and providence, a wonderful access to God by prayer, sensibly conversing with him, as much as if Christ were here on earth; frequent, plain, sensible, and immediate answers of prayer, all tears wiped away, all former troubles and sorrows of life forgotten, excepting sorrow for sin, doing every thing for God and his glory, doing it as the service of love, with a continual uninterrupted cheerfulness, peace, and joy. "O how good," she once observed, "is it to work for God in the day time, and at night to lie down under his smiles." Instead of slighting the means of grace in consequence of these discoveries, she was never more sensible of her need of instruction; instead of regarding herself as free from sin, she was led by her clearer sight of the Divine holiness, to perceive more fully the sinfulness of her own heart; instead of neglecting the business of life, she performed it with greater alacrity, as a part of the service of God—declaring that, when thus done, it was as delightful as prayer itself. At the same time, she discovered an extreme anxiety to avoid every sin, and to discharge every moral obligation, was most exemplary in the performance of every social and relative duty, exhibited great inoffensiveness of life and conversation, great meekness, gentleness, and benevolence of spirit, and avoided, with remarkable conscientiousness, all those things which she regarded as failings in her own character.

To those who, after reading this statement of facts, still regard the preceding narrative as the offspring of enthusiasm, we shall draw our reply from Mr. Edwards himself: "Now if such things are enthusiasm, and the offspring of a distempered brain; let my brain be possessed evermore of that happy distemper! If this be distraction; I pray God that the world of mankind may all be seized with this benign, meek, beneficent, beatific, glorious distraction! What notion have they of true religion, who reject what has here been described? What shall we find to correspond with these expressions of Scripture, *The peace of God, that passeth all understanding: Rejoicing with joy unspeakable, and full of glory: God's shining into our hearts, to give the light of the knowledge of the glory of God, in the face of Jesus Christ: With open face, beholding as in a glass the glory of God, and being changed into the same image, from glory to glory, even as by the Spirit of the Lord: Being called out of darkness into marvellous light: and having the day-star arise in our hearts?* What, let me ask, if these things that have been mentioned do not correspond with these expressions; what else can we find that does correspond with them?"

Mr. Edwards adds, that he had witnessed many instances, in Northampton and elsewhere, of other persons, which were in general of the same kind with these, though not so high in degree, in any instance; and, in many of them, not so pure and unmixed, or so well regulated. In some individuals, who discovered very intense religious affections, there was obviously a great mixture of nature with grace, and in some a sad degenerating of religious affections; yet, in most instances, they were uniform in their character, and obviously the result of fervent piety.

That such full and clear discoveries of the Divine excellency and glory, as those recited in the preceding narrative, are uncommon, is unhappily too true: still they are far from being singular; for accounts of a similar nature may be found in the private diaries of men of distinguished piety, in almost every age of the church.* They are not however probably more uncommon, than are great attainments in piety; and, when enjoyed by those who have made such attainments, ought, in no respect, to be regarded as surprising. There is certainly in God a goodness and a glory, infinitely surpassing the comprehension of the highest created beings. This goodness and glory, which constitutes the Divine beauty and loveliness, God is able to reveal to the mind of every intelligent creature, as far as his faculties extend. If the mind, to which this revelation is made, has a supreme relish for holiness; the discovery of this spiritual beauty of the Divine mind will communicate to it an enjoyment, which is pure and heavenly in its nature; and the degree of this enjoyment, in every case, will be proportioned to the measure of the faculties, and to the fulness of the discovery. This is obviously true in the heavenly world. God there reveals his glory—not in all its infinite brightness: this, he cannot do to a created intelligence: he reveals it—in as strong

* As examples of this nature, the reader is referred to the writings of Flavel, L. Baxter, and Brainerd, and of Mr. Edwards himself.

an effulgence as the minds of saints and angels can endure. Were a revelation, equally clear and full, to be made to one of us here on earth, it would obviously overwhelm and destroy the life of the body; for John, even when he beheld the glorified body of Christ, fell at his feet as dead. In proportion as an individual is possessed of holiness, so much more near does he come to God, and so much more clear and distinct is his perception of his true character. "If a man love me," says Christ, "he will keep my words; and my Father will love him, and we will come unto him, and make our abode with him." Such discoveries of the Divine beauty and glory are therefore the *promised reward*, as well as the natural consequence, of distinguished holiness; and a well authenticated narrative, of the manner in which they were made, in a given instance, even if they were unusual in degree, instead of exciting our distrust or surprise, should lead us, with a noble emulation, to "press forward towards the mark, for the prize of the high calling of God in Christ Jesus."

CHAPTER XII.

EXTENT OF THE REVIVAL OF 1740-1742—AUSPICIOUS OPENING—OPPOSED BY ITS ENEMIES: AND INJURED BY ITS FRIENDS—"THOUGHTS ON THE REVIVAL IN NEW ENGLAND"—ATTESTATIONS OF NUMEROUS MINISTERS—CAUSES OF ITS DECLINE—INFLUENCE OF MR. WHITEFIELD, MR. TENNENT, AND OTHERS—INFLUENCE OF MR. EDWARDS'S PUBLICATIONS IN SCOTLAND—GREAT REVIVAL OF RELIGION THERE—HIS CORRESPONDENTS IN THAT COUNTRY—LETTER TO MR. M'CULLOCH—ANSWER TO DO.—LETTER FROM MR. ROBE.

THE reader can scarcely need to be informed, that the revival of religion, of which we have been speaking, was not confined to Northampton. It began there, and at Boston, and many other places, in 1740, and in that, and the three following years, prevailed, to a greater or less degree, in more than one hundred and fifty congregations in New England, New York, New Jersey, and Pennsylvania; as well as in a considerable number more, in Maryland and Virginia, in 1744. At its commencement, it appears to have been, to an unusual degree, a silent, powerful, and glorious work of the Spirit of God—the simple effect of truth applied to the conscience, and accompanied by his converting grace. So auspicious indeed was the opening of this memorable work of God, and so rapid its progress, that the promised reign of Christ on the earth was believed, by many, to be actually begun. Had it continued of this unmixed character, so extensive was its prevalence, and so powerful its operation, it would seem that in no great length of time, it would have pervaded the western world. As is usual in such cases, it was opposed by the enemies of vital religion, and with a violence proportioned to its prevalence and power. But its worst enemies were found among its most zealous friends: and Mr. Edwards appear to have been early aware, that the measures too generally resorted to, by many of them, to extend its influence over the whole country, as well as throughout every town and village where it was actually begun, were only adapted to introduce confusion and disorder, as far as they prevailed. To check these commencing evils, if possible, and to bear his own testimony to the work as a genuine work of the Holy Spirit, he prepared and published his "Thoughts on the Revival of Religion in New England, in 1740." In this treatise, after presenting evidence most clear and convincing that the attention to religion, of which he speaks, was a glorious work of God, and showing the obligations which all were under, to acknowledge and promote it, as well as the danger of the contrary conduct; he points out various particulars in which its friends had been injuriously blamed, then exhibits the errors and mistakes into which they had actually fallen, and concludes by showing positively, what ought to be done to promote it. This work, which was published in 1742, excited a very deep interest in the American churches, and was immediately republished in Scotland. The author, from his uncommon acquaintance with the Scriptures, the soundness of his theological views, his intuitive discernment of the operations of the mind, his knowledge of the human heart both before and after its renovation by the Spirit of God, his familiarity with revivals of religion, his freedom from enthusiasm, and his utter aversion to extravagance and disorder, was admirably qualified to execute it in the happiest manner: and, from the time of its first publication, it has been, to a very wide extent, the common text-book of evangelical divines, on the subject of which it treats. If the reader will examine the various accounts of revivals of religion, he will find that no one of them, anterior to this, furnishes an explanation of the subject, in accordance with the acknowledged principles of mental philosophy.

In 1743, about one hundred and sixty ministers published their attestations to this work, as in their own view a genuine work of the Spirit of God, and as having been extraordinary and remarkable; on account of the numbers who discovered a deep anxiety for their salvation; on account of its rapid progress from place to place; and on account of the power with which it was carried on. Yet, while they bear witness to the great numbers who appeared to have become real Christians, to the extensive reformation of morals which it occasioned, and to a greater prevalence of religion than they had before witnessed; many of them also regret the extravagances and irregularities, which in some places had been permitted to accompany it. Among these, they particularly point out—a disposition to make secret impulses on the mind a rule of duty—laymen invading the ministerial office, and under a pretence of exhorting, setting up preaching—ministers invading each other's provinces—indiscreet young men rushing into particular places, and preaching on all occasions—unscriptural separations of churches, and of ministers from their churches—a rash judging of the religious state of others—and a controversial, uncharitable, and censorious spirit.

There can be no doubt, that both parts of this statement

are true. Although this most extensive work of grace opened on New England, in 1740 and 1741, in a manner eminently auspicious; yet in the two following years, it assumed, in various places, a somewhat different aspect, and was unhappily marked with irregularity and disorder. This was doubtless owing, in some degree, to the fact, that many ministers of wisdom and sound discretion, not adverting sufficiently to the extent and importance of the apostolic exhortation, "Let all things be done decently and in order," either encouraged, or did not effectually suppress, outcries, falling down and swooning, in the time of public and social worship, the speaking and praying of women in the church and in mixed assemblies, the meeting of children by themselves for religious worship, and singing and praying aloud in the streets; but far more to the unrestrained zeal of a considerable number of misguided men—some of them preachers of the gospel, and others lay exhorters—who, intending to take Mr. Whitefield as their model, travelled from place to place, preaching and exhorting wherever they could collect an audience; pronounced definitively and unhesitatingly with respect to the piety of individuals, both ministers and private Christians; and whenever they judged a minister, or a majority of his church, destitute of piety—which they usually did, not on account of their false principles or their irreligious life, but for their want of an ardour and zeal equal to their own—advised, in the one case, the whole church to withdraw from the minister; and in the other, a minority to separate themselves from the majority, and to form a distinct church and congregation. This indiscreet advice had, at times, too much influence, and occasioned in some places the sundering of churches and congregations, in others the removal of ministers, and in others the separation of individuals from the communion of their brethren. It thus introduced contentions and quarrels into churches and families, alienated ministers from each other, and from their people, and produced, in the places where these consequences were most discernible, a wide-spread and rivetted prejudice against revivals of religion. It is deserving perhaps of inquiry, Whether the subsequent slumber of the American church, for nearly seventy years, may not be ascribed, in an important degree, to the fatal re-action of these unhappy measures.

There can be no doubt that on Mr. Whitefield (although by his multiplied and successful labours he was the means of incalculable good to the churches of America, as well as to those of England and Scotland) these evils are, to a considerable degree, to be charged, as having first led the way in this career of irregularity and disorder. He did not go as far as some of his followers; but he opened a wide door, and went great lengths, in these forbidden paths; and his imitators, having less discretion and experience, ventured, under the cover of his example, even beyond the limits which he himself was afraid to pass. His published journals show, that he was accustomed to decide too authoritatively, whether others, particularly ministers, were converted; as well as to insist that churches ought to remove those, whom they regarded as unconverted ministers; and that individual Christians or minorities of churches, where a majority refused to do this, were bound to separate themselves. Mr. Edwards, wholly disapproving of this conduct, conversed with Mr. Whitefield freely, in the presence of others, about his practice of pronouncing ministers, and other members of the christian church, unconverted; and declares that he supposed him to be of the opinion, that unconverted ministers ought not to be continued in the ministry; and that he supposed that he endeavoured to propagate this opinion, and a practice agreeable thereto. The same may be said, in substance, of Mr. G. Tennent, Mr. Finley, and Mr. Davenport, all of whom became early convinced of their error, and with christian sincerity openly acknowledged it. At the same time, while these things were to be regretted in themselves, and still more so in their unhappy consequences, the evidence is clear that, in far the greater number of places, these irregularities and disorders, if in any degree prevalent, were never predominant; and that the attention to religion in these places, while it continued, was most obviously a great and powerful work of the Spirit of God. The testimony of the ministers of those places, on these points, is explicit. It is given with great caution, and with the utmost candour; it acknowledges frankly the evils then experienced; and it details the actual moral change wrought in individuals and in society at large, in such a manner, that no one, who believes in regeneration as the work of the Holy Spirit, can doubt that this change was effected by the finger of God.

Though the attention to religion, at this period, was more powerful and more universal at Northampton, than in almost any other congregation, there was yet scarcely one in which so few of these evils were experienced. The reason was, that their spiritual guide had already formed, in his own mind, settled principles respecting a genuine revival of religion—as to its cause, its nature, and in the most important points, as to the manner in which it was to be treated. He regarded it as caused—not by appeals to the feelings or the passions, but—by the truth of God brought home to the mind, in a subordinate sense by the preaching of the gospel, but in a far higher sense by the immediate agency of the Holy Spirit. He considered such an event, so far as man is concerned, as the simple effect of a practical attention to truth, on the conscience and the heart. He felt it to be his great, and in a sense his only, duty, therefore, to urge divine truth on the feelings and consciences of his hearers, with all possible solemnity and power. How he in fact urged it, his published sermons will show.

Yet even in Northampton many things occurred, which not only were deviations from decorum and good sense, but were directly calculated, as far as they prevailed, to change that which, in its commencement, was, to an uncommon degree, a silent and powerful work of Divine grace, into a scene of confusion and disorder. This was owing chiefly to contagion from without. "The former part of the revival of religion, in 1740 and 1741, seemed to be much more pure, having less of a corrupt mixture than in that of 1735 and 1736.—But in 1742, it was otherwise: the work continued more pure till we were infected from abroad. Our people hearing of, and some of them seeing, the work in other places, where there was a greater visible commotion than here, and the outward appearances were more extraordinary, their eyes were dazzled with the high professions and great show that some made, who came in hither from other places. That these people went so far before them in raptures and violent emotions of the affections, and a vehement zeal, and what they called *boldness for Christ*, our people were ready to think was owing to far greater attainments in grace and intimacy with heaven. These things had a strange influence on the people, and gave many of them a deep and unhappy tincture, from which it was a hard and long labour to deliver them, and from which some of them are not fully delivered to this day."

In many parishes, where the attention to religion commenced in 1742, it was extensively, if not chiefly, of this unhappy character. This was particularly true in the eastern part of Connecticut, and in the eastern and south-eastern part, and some of the more central parishes, of Massachusetts. Churches and congregations were torn asunder, many ministers were dismissed, churches of a separatical character were formed, the peace of society was permanently broken up, and a revival of religion became extensively, in the view of the community, another name for the prevalence of fanaticism, disorder, and misrule. This unhappy and surprising change should prove an everlasting beacon to the church of God.

I have already had occasion to remark, that the "Narrative of Surprising Conversions" was repeatedly published, and extensively circulated, throughout England and Scotland. The same was true of Mr. Edwards's Five Sermons preached during the revival of religion in 1734-5, and of his discourse on "the Distinguishing Marks of a Work of the Spirit of God." The effect of these publications, particularly of the first, was in the latter country great and salutary. The eyes both of ministers and Christians were extensively opened to the fact, that an effusion of the Spirit, resembling in some good degree those recorded in the Acts of the Apostles, might take place, and might rationally be expected to take place, in modern times, in consequence of the direct and powerful application of similar means. Scotland was at that time favoured with the labours of many clergymen, greatly respected for their piety and talents; among whom were the Rev. William M'Culloch of Cambuslang, the Rev. John Robe of Kilsyth, the Rev. John M'Laurin of Glasgow, the Rev. Thomas Gillespie of Carnoch, the Rev. John Willison of Dundee, and the Rev. John Erskine of Kirkintilloch, afterwards Dr. Erskine of Edinburgh. These gentlemen, and many of their associates in the ministry, appear, at the time of which we are speaking, to have preached, not only with great plainness and fervency, but with the strongest confidence of immediate and great success; and, as a natural consequence, the church of Scotland soon witnessed a state of things, to which she had long been a stranger.

In February, 1742, a revival of religion began at Cambuslang, the parish of Mr. M'Culloch, four miles from Glasgow, resembling in its power and rapidity, and the number of conversions, that in Northampton, in 1734-5; and in the course of that year, scenes of a similar nature were witnessed in Kilsyth, Glasgow, Dundee, Carnock, Kirkintilloch, Edinburgh, Aberdeen, and upwards of thirty towns and villages, in various parts of that kingdom. Thus the darkness which covers the earth was dispersed, for a season, from over these two countries, and the clear light of heaven shone down upon them, with no intervening cloud. In such circumstances, it might naturally be expected, that the prominent clergymen in both, feeling a common interest, and being engaged in similar labours, would soon open a mutual correspondence.

The first of Mr. Edwards's correspondents in Scotland, was the Rev. Mr. M'Laurin of Glasgow; but, unfortunately, I have been able to procure none of the letters which passed between them. That gentleman, in the early part of 1743, having informed Mr. Edwards that his friend, Mr. M'Culloch of Cambuslang, had intended to write to him with a view of offering a correspondence, but had failed of the expected opportunity; Mr. Edwards addressed to the latter the following letter.

"To the Rev. William M'Culloch, Cambuslang.

Northampton, May 12, 1743.

Rev. and dear Sir,

Mr. M'Laurin of Glasgow, in a letter he has lately sent me, informs me of your proposing to write a letter to me, and of your being prevented by the failing of the expected opportunity. I thank you, Rev. Sir, that you had such a thing in your heart. We were informed last year, by the printed and well attested narrative, of the glorious work of God in your parish; which we have since understood has spread into many other towns and parishes in that part of Scotland; especially are we informed of this by Mr. Robe's Narrative, and I perceive by some papers of the Weekly History, sent me by Mr. M'Laurin of Glasgow, that the work has continued to make glorious progress at Cambuslang, even till it has prevailed to a wonderful degree indeed. God has highly favoured and honoured you, dear Sir, which may justly render your name precious to all that love our Lord Jesus Christ. We live in a day wherein God is doing marvellous things: in that respect, we are distinguished from former generations. God has wrought great things in New England, which, though exceedingly glorious, have all along been attended with some threatening clouds; which, from the beginning, caused me to apprehend some great stop or check to be put to the work, before it should be begun and carried on in its genuine purity and beauty, to subdue all before it, and to prevail with an irresistible and continual progress and triumph; and it is come to pass according to my apprehensions. But yet I cannot think otherwise, than that what has now been doing, is the forerunner of something vastly greater, more pure, and more extensive. I can't think that God has come down from heaven, and done such great things before our eyes, and gone so much beside and beyond his usual way of working, and wrought so wonderfully, and that he has gone away with a design to leave things thus. Who hath heard such a thing? Who hath seen such things? And will God, when he has wrought so wonderfully, and made the earth to bring forth in one day, bring to the birth and not cause to bring forth? And shall he cause to bring forth, and shut the womb? Isaiah lxvi. 8, 9. I live upon the brink of the grave, in great infirmity of body, and nothing is more uncertain, than whether I shall live to see it: but, I believe God will revive his work again before long, and that it will not wholly cease till it has subdued the whole earth. But God is now going and returning to his place, till we acknowledge our offence, and, I hope, to humble his church in New England, and purify it, and so fit it for yet greater comfort, that he designs in due time to bestow upon it. God may deal with his church, as he deals with a particular saint; commonly, after his first comfort, the clouds return, and there is a season of remarkable darkness, and hiding of God's face, and buffetings of Satan; but all to fit for greater mercy; and as it was with Christ himself, who, presently after the heavens were opened above his head, and the Spirit was poured out upon him, and God wonderfully testified his love to him, was driven into the wilderness to be tempted of the devil forty days. I hope God will show us our errors, and teach us wisdom by his present withdrawings. Now in the day of adversity, we have time and cause to consider, and begin now to have opportunity to see, the consequences of our conduct. I wish that God's ministers and people, every where, would take warning by our errors, and the calamities that are the issue of them. I have mentioned several things, in my letters to Mr. M'Laurin and Mr. Robe; another I might have mentioned, that most evidently proves of ill consequence, that is, we have run from one extreme to another, with respect to talking of experiences; that whereas formerly there was too great a reservedness in this matter, of late many have gone to an unbounded openness, frequency, and constancy, in talking of their experiences, declaring almost every thing that passes between God and their own souls, every where and before every body. Among other ill consequences of such a practice, this is one, that religion runs all into that channel; and religion is placed very much in it, so that the strength of it seems to be spent in it; that other duties, that are of vastly greater importance, have been looked upon as light in comparison of this, so that other parts of religion have been really much injured thereby: as when we see a tree excessively full of leaves, we find so much less fruit; and when a cloud arises with an excessive degree of wind, we have the less rain. How much, dear Sir, does God's church at such a day need the constant gracious care and guidance of our good Shepherd; and especially, we that are ministers.

I should be glad, dear Sir, of a remembrance in your prayers, and also of your help, by informations and instructions, by what you find in your experience in Scotland. I believe it to be the duty of one part of the church of God thus to help another.

I am, dear Sir, your affectionate
Brother and servant in Jesus Christ,
JONATHAN EDWARDS."

The following is the answer of Mr. M'Culloch to the preceding letter.

"*Cambuslang, Aug.* 13, 1743.

REV. AND DEAR SIR,

The happy period in which we live, and the times of refreshing from the presence of the Lord, wherewith you first were visited, in Northampton, in the year 1734; and then, more generally, in New England, in 1740, and 1741; and then we, in several places in Scotland, in 1742, and 1743; and the strong opposition made to this work, with you and with us, checked by an infinitely superior power; often brings to my mind that prophecy, Isa. lix. 19. "So shall they fear the name of the Lord from the west, and his glory from the rising of the sun. When the enemy shall come in as a flood, the Spirit of the Lord shall lift up a standard against him." I cannot help thinking that this prophecy eminently points at our times; and begins to be fulfilled in the multitudes of souls that are bringing in to fear the Lord, to worship God in Christ, in whom his name is, and to see his glory in his sanctuary. And it is, to me, pretty remarkable, that the prophet here foretells they should do so, in the period he points at, not from east to west, but from west to east; mentioning the west before the east, contrary to the usual way of speaking in other prophecies, as where Malachi foretells, that the name of the Lord should be great among the Gentiles, from the rising of the sun to the west, (Mal. i. 11.) and our Lord Jesus, that many should come from the east and west, &c. (Matt. viii. 11.) And in this order it was, that the light of the gospel came to dawn on the several nations, in the propagation of it through the world. But the prophet here, under the conduct of the Holy Spirit, who chooses all his words in infinite wisdom, puts the west before the east; intending, as I conceive, thereby to signify, that the glorious revival of religion, and the wide and diffusive spread of vital Christianity, in the latter times of the gospel, should begin in the more *westerly* parts, and proceed to these more *easterly*. And while it should be doing so, or shortly after, great opposition should arise, *the enemy should come in as a flood:* Satan should, with great violence, assault particular believing souls; and stir up men to malign and reproach the work of God; and, it's likely also, raise a terrible persecution against the church. But while the enemy might seem, for a time, to be thus carrying all before him, *the Spirit of the Lord should lift up a standard against him;* give a banner to them that fear him, and animate them to display it for the truth, and make his word mightily to prevail, and bear down all opposing power. For on what side soever the Almighty and Eternal Spirit of Jehovah lifts up a standard, there the victory is certain; and we may be sure he will lift it up in defence of his own work. The Chaldee paraphrase makes the words in the latter part of this verse, to allude to the river Euphrates, when it breaks over all its banks, and overflows the adjacent plains: thus when persecutors shall come in, as the inundation of the river Euphrates, they shall be broke in pieces by the word of the Lord.

The whole of this verse seems to me to have an aspect to the present and past times, for some years. The Sun of righteousness has been making his course from west to east, and shedding his benign and quickening influences, on poor forlorn and benighted souls, in places vastly distant from one another. But clouds have arisen and intercepted his reviving beams. The enemy of salvation has broke in as an overflowing flood, almost overwhelmed poor souls, newly come into the spiritual world, after they had got some glimpse of the glory of Christ, with a deluge of temptations; floods of ungodly men, stirred up by Satan, and their natural enmity at religion, have affrighted them; mistaken and prejudiced friends have disowned them. Many such things have already befallen the subjects of this glorious work of God of late years. But I apprehend more general and formidable trials are yet to come: and that the enemy's coming in as a flood, may relate to a flood of errors or persecutions of fierce enemies, rushing in upon the church and threatening to swallow her up. But our comfort is, that the Spirit of the Lord of hosts will lift up a standard, against all the combined powers of earth and hell, and put them to flight; and Christ having begun to conquer, so remarkably, will go on from conquering to conquer, till the whole earth be filled with his glory. Rev. xii. 15. Isa. xvii. 12, 13.

I mention these things, dear Sir, not for your information, for I know that I can add nothing to you; but to show my agreement with you, in what you express as your sentiments, that what has now been a doing is the forerunner of something vastly greater, more pure, and more extensive, and that God will revive his work again, ere long, and that it will not wholly cease, till it has subdued the whole earth: and, without pretending to prophecy, to hint a little at the ground of my expectations. Only I'm afraid (which is a thing you do not hint at) that before these glorious times, some dreadful stroke or trial may yet be abiding us. May the Lord prepare us for it. But as to this, I cannot and dare not peremptorily determine. All things I give up to farther light, without pretending to fix the times and seasons for God's great and wonderful works, which he has reserved in his own power, and the certain knowledge of which he has locked up in his own breast."

The same conveyance brought Mr. Edwards the following letter, from the Rev. Mr. Robe, of Kilsyth.

"*Kilsyth, Aug.* 16, 1743.

Rev. Sir, and very dear Brother,

We acknowledge, with praise and thanks, the Lord's keeping his work hitherto, *with us*, free from those errors and disorders, which, through the subtilty of the serpent, and corruptions even of good men, were mixed with it in New England. As this was no more just ground of objection against what was among you, being a real work of the Holy Spirit, than the same things were against the work of God in Corinth, and other places, at the first conversion of the pagans, and afterwards at the reformation from popery; so the many adversaries to this blessed work here, have as fully made use of all those errors, disorders, and blemishes, against it *there*, as objections, as if they had really been *here*. The most unseasonable accounts from America, the most scurrilous and bitter pamphlets, and representations from mistaking brethren, were much and zealously propagated. Only it was overruled by Providence, that those letters and papers dropped what was a real testimony to the goodness of the work they designed to defame and render odious. Many thinking persons concluded, from the gross calumnies forged and spread against the Lord's work here, within a few miles of them, that such stories from America could not be much depended upon.

What you write about the trial of extraordinary joys and raptures, by their concomitants and effects, is most solid; and our practice, by all I know, hath been conformable to it. It hath been in the strongest manner declared, that no degree of such rapturous joys evidenced them to be from God, unless they led to God, and carried with them those things which accompany salvation. Such conditional applications of the promises of grace and glory as you justly recommend, hath been all along our manner. A holy fear of caution and watchfulness, hath been much pressed upon the subjects of this work, who appeared to believe through grace. And what is greatly comfortable, and reason of great praise to our God, is, that there is, as is yet known to any one in these bounds, no certain instance of what can be called apostacy; and not above four instances of any who have fallen into any gross sin.

As to the state and progress of this blessed work here, and in other places, it is as followeth. Since the account given in the several prints of my Narrative, which I understand is or will be at Boston; the awakening of secure sinners hath and doth continue in this congregation; but not in such multitudes as last year, neither can it be reasonably expected. What is ground of joy and praise is, that there scarce hath been two or three weeks, but wherein I have some instance of persons newly awakened, besides several come to my knowledge who have been awakened, and appear in a most hopeful state, before they were known to me. Of which I had an instance yesterday, of a girl awakened, as she saith, in October last. I have, at writing this, an instance of a woman who appears to have obtained a good issue of her awakening last year; though I supposed it had come to nothing, through her intermitting to come to me of a long time. There is this difference in this parish betwixt the awakening last year and now; that some of their bodies have been affected by their fears, in a convulsive or hysteric way; and yet the inward distress of some of them hath been very sharp. I have seen two or three, who have fainted under apprehension of the hiding of God's face, or of their having received the Lord's supper unworthily. In some of the neighbouring congregations, where this blessed work was last year, there are instances of discernible awakenings this summer. In the large parish of St. Ninians, to the north of this, I was witness to the awakening of some, and conversed with others awakened, the middle of July last. In the parish of Sintrie to the west of St. Ninians there were several newly awakened at the giving the Lord's supper, about the end of July. In Gargunnock, Kippen, Killern, farther north and west, the Lord's work is yet discernible. At Muthel, which is about twenty miles north from this, the minister wrote me about the middle of July, that this blessed work, which hath appeared there since last summer as at Cambuslang, yet continued; and hath spread into other parishes, and reacheth even to the Highlands bordering upon that parish.

I am not without hopes of having good accounts of the outpouring of the Holy Spirit in the shires of Rosse and Nairn among the northernmost parts of Scotland. There was more than ordinary seriousness, in some parishes, in hearing the word, and in a concern about their souls, in the spring, when I saw some godly ministers from those bounds. This more than ordinary seriousness in hearing, and about communion times, is observable in several parts in Scotland, this summer. Societies for prayer setting up where there were none, and in other places increasing. A concern among the young are in some of the least hopeful places in Scotland, particularly in the Meuse near the English borders. There is a great likelihood of the Lord's doing good by the gospel, in this discernible way, in those bounds. Mr. M'Laurin, my dear brother, gives you an account of the progress of this work to the west of Glasgow, and other places. There have been very extraordinary manifestations of the love of God, in Christ Jesus, unto his people, in the use of the holy supper, and in the dispensation of the word about that time, this summer; which hath made the Lord's people desire it a second time in these congregations during the summer season. It was given here upon the first sabbath of July, and is to be given here next Lord's day, a second time, upon such a desire.

Your affectionate brother and servant

In our dearest Lord,

JAMES ROBE."

CHAPTER XIII.

FIRST INTERVIEW WITH DAVID BRAINERD—SEPARATIONS FROM CHURCHES—LETTER TO REV. MR. WHITMAN—CORRESPONDENCE WITH MR. CLAP—CHARACTER OF THAT GENTLEMAN—SERMON AT THE ORDINATION OF MR. ABERCROMBIE—LETTER TO MR. M'CULLOCH—VIEWS OF THE PROPHECIES RELATIVE TO THE CHURCH—SERMON AT THE ORDINATION OF MR. BUELL.

In September, 1743, Mr. Edwards, while attending the public commencement at New-Haven, first became acquainted with David Brainerd, then a missionary at Kaunaumeek. Brainerd, when a sophomore in college, in consequence of some indiscreet remarks, uttered in the ardour of his religious zeal, respecting the opposition of two of the faculty to the preaching of Mr. Whitefield, but which a generous mind would have wholly disregarded, had been expelled from the college. As this was the commencement, at which his class were to receive the degree of A. B., he came to New-Haven to attempt a reconciliation with the faculty, and made to them a truly humble and christian acknowledgment of his fault. "I was witness," says Mr. Edwards, "to the very christian spirit which Brainerd showed at that time; being then at New-Haven, and one whom he thought fit to consult on that occasion. There truly appeared in him a great degree of calmness and humility; without the least appearance of rising of spirit for any ill-treatment which he supposed he had suffered, or the least backwardness to abase himself before those, who, as he thought, had wronged him. What he did was without any objection or appearance of reluctance, even in private to his friends, to whom he freely opened himself. Earnest application was made on his behalf, that he might have his degree then given him; and particularly by the Rev. Mr. Burr of Newark, one of the correspondents of the Honourable Society in Scotland; he being sent from New Jersey to New-Haven, by the rest of the commissioners, for that end; and many arguments were used, but without success. He desired his degree, as he thought it would tend to his being more extensively useful; but still, when he was denied it, he manifested no disappointment nor resentment."

I have already alluded to the numerous separations of individual members, from the churches to which they belonged, which occurred about this period, and usually for the alleged want of piety, either of the minister or of the church. As these commonly took place without a regular dismission, it became a practical question of some interest, how the withdrawing members should be treated. Mr. Edwards, having been consulted on this subject, with reference to some of the members of the second church in Hartford, who had thus withdrawn, addressed the following letter to the minister of that church.

"To the Rev. Elnathan Whitman, of Hartford, Connecticut.

Northampton, Feb. 9, 1744.

Rev. and dear Sir,

Mr. P—— was here this week, and requested my opinion, with respect to the proper treatment of a number of persons, who have absented themselves from your meeting, and have since attended public worship in W——. I declined giving any opinion, except a very general one, to him; but, on reflection, have concluded to express my thoughts to you, as a friend, leaving you to attach to them such weight as you may see cause.

"As to differences, among professing Christians, of opinion and practice, about things that appertain to religion, and the worship of God, I am ready to think that you and I are agreed, as to the general principles of liberty of conscience; and that men's using methods with their neighbours, to oblige them to a conformity to their sentiments or way, is in nothing so unreasonable, as in the worship of God; because that is a business, in which each person acts for himself, with his Creator and Supreme Judge, as one concerned for his own acceptance with him; and on which depends his own, and not his neighbour's, eternal happiness, and salvation from everlasting ruin. And it is an affair, wherein every man is infinitely more concerned with his Creator than he is with his neighbour. And so I suppose that it will be allowed, that every man ought to be left to his own conscience, in what he judges will be most acceptable to God, or what he supposes is the will of God, as to the kind, or manner, or means of worship, or the society of worshippers he should join with in worship. Not but that a great abuse may be made of this doctrine of liberty of conscience in the worship of God. I know that many are ready to justify every thing in their own conduct, from this doctrine, and I do not suppose that men's pretence of conscience is always to be regarded, when made use of to justify their charging the society of worshippers they unite with, or the means of their worship, or indeed the kind or manner of their worship. Men may make this pretence at times under such circumstances, that they may, obviously, be worthy of no credit in what they pretend. It may be manifest from the nature and circumstances of the case, and their own manner of behaviour, that it is not conscience, but petulancy, and malice, and wilfulness, and obstinacy, that influence them. And, therefore, it seems to me evident, that, when such pleas are made, those that are especially concerned with them as persons that are peculiarly obliged to take care of their souls, have no other way to do, but to consider the nature and circumstances of the case, and from thence to judge whether the case be such as will admit of such a plea, or whether the nature of things will admit of such a supposition, that the men act conscientiously in what they do, considering all things that appertain to the case. And in this, I conceive, many things are to be considered and laid together, as—the nature of that thing that is the subject of controversy, or wherein they differ from others, or have changed their own practice—the degree in which it is disputable, or how it may be supposed liable to diversity of opinion, one way or the other, as to its agreeableness to the word of God, and as to the importance of it, with regard to men's salvation or the good of their souls—the degree of knowledge or ignorance of the persons, the advantages they had for information, or the disadvantages they have been under, and what has been in their circumstances that might mislead the judgment—the principles that have been instilled into them—the instructions they have received from those, of whose piety and wisdom they have had a high opinion, which might misguide the judgment of persons of real honesty, and sincerity, and tender conscience—the example of others—the diversity of opinion among ministers—the general state of things in the land—the character of the persons themselves—and the manner of their behaviour in the particular affair in debate.

Now, Sir, with regard to those persons that have gone from you, to W——, however you may look upon their behaviour herein as very disorderly, yet, if you suppose (the case being considered with all its circumstances) that there was any room for charity, that it might be through infirmity, ignorance, and error of judgment, so that they might be truly conscientious in it; that is, might really believe it to be their duty, and what God required of them, to do as they have done; you would, I imagine, by no means think, that they ought to be proceeded with, in the use of such means as are proper to be used with contumacious offenders, or those that are stubborn and obstinate in scandalous vice and wilful wickedness; or that you would think it proper to proceed with persons, towards whom there is this room left for charity, that possibly they may be honest and truly conscientious, acting as persons afraid to offend God, so as to cut them off from the communion of the Lord, and cast them forth into the visible kingdom of Satan, to be as harlots and publicans.

Now, it may be well to examine, whether it can positively be determined, when all things are taken into consideration with respect to these persons, who have absented themselves from your assembly, that it is not possible in their case, that this might really be their honest judgment, that it was their duty to do so, and that God required it of them, and that they should greatly expose the welfare of their own souls, in attending no other public worship but that in your congregation. I suppose these persons are not much versed in casuistical divinity. They are of the common people, whose judgments, in all nations and ages, are exceedingly led and swayed. They are not very capable of viewing things in the extent of their consequences, and of estimating things in their true weight and importance. And you know, dear Sir, the state that things have been in, in the country. You know what opinions have lately prevailed, and have been maintained and propagated, by those that have been lifted up to heaven, in their reputation for piety and great knowledge in spiritual things, with a great part of the people of New England. I do not pretend to know what has influenced these people, in particular; but I think, under these circumstances, it would be no strange thing, if great numbers of the common people in the country, who are really conscientious, and concerned to be accepted with God, and to take the best course for the good of their souls, should really think in their hearts that God requires them to attend the ministry of those that are called *New Light Ministers,* and that it would be dangerous to their souls, and what God approved not of, ordinarily to attend the ministry of others; yea, I should think it strange if it were otherwise. It ought to be considered, how public controversy, and a great and general cry in matters of religion, strongly influences the conduct of multitudes of the common people, how it blinds their minds, and wonderfully misleads their judgments. And the rules of the gospel, and the example of the apostles, most certainly require that great allowances be made in such cases. And particularly the example of the apostle Paul, with regard to great numbers of professing Christians, in the church of Corinth; who, in a time of great and general confusion in that church, through the evil instructions of teachers whom they admired, who misled and blinded their judgments, ran into many and great disorders in their worship, and woeful schisms and divisions among themselves—particularly with regard to ministers, and even with regard to the apostle Paul himself, whom many of them seem for a time to have forsaken, to follow others who set up themselves in opposition to him; though, as he says, he had been their father who begat them through the gospel. Yet with how much gentleness does the apostle treat them, still acknowledging them as brethren; and though he required church censures to be used with regard to the incestuous person, yet there is no intimation of the apostle taking any such course, with those that had been misled by these false teachers, or with any that had been guilty of these disorders, except with the false teachers themselves. But as soon as they are brought off from following these false apostles any longer, he embraces them without further ado, with all the love and tenderness of a father; burying all their censoriousness, and schisms, and disorders, at the Lord's supper, as well as their ill treatment of him, the extraordinary messenger of Christ to them. And, indeed, the apostle never so much as gave any direction for the suspension of any one member from the Lord's supper, on account of these disorders, or from any other part of the public worship of God; but instead of this, gives them directions how they shall go on to attend the Lord's supper, and other parts of worship, in a better manner. And he himself, without suspension or interruption, goes on to call and treat them as beloved brethren, Christians, sanctified in Christ Jesus, called to be saints; and praises God in their behalf, for the grace that is given to them by Christ Jesus; and often and abundantly exhibits his charity towards them, in innumerable expressions which I might mention. And nothing is more apparent than that he does not treat them as persons, with respect to whom there lies a bar in the way of others treating them with the charity that belongs to saints, and good and honest members of the christian church, until the bar be removed by a church process. And, indeed, the insisting on a church process with every member that has behaved disorderly, in such a state of general confusion, is not a way to build up the church of God, (which is the end of church discipline,) but to pull it down. It will not be the way to cure a diseased member, but to bring a disease on the whole body.

I am not alone in these sentiments; but I have reason to think that Col. Stoddard, from the conversation I have had with him, is in the like way of thinking. There came hither, the last fall, two young men belonging to the church at New-Haven, who had been members of Mr. Noyes's church, but had left it and joined the separate church, and entered into covenant with it, when that church was embodied. This was looked upon as a crime, that ought not to be passed over, by Mr. Noyes and the rector. They declared themselves willing to return to Mr. Noyes's meeting; but a particular confession was required of them in the meeting-house. Accordingly, each of them had offered a confession, but it was not thought sufficient; but it was required that they should add some things, of which they thought hard; and they consulting me about it, I acquainted Col. Stoddard with the affair, and desired his thoughts. He said he looked upon it unreasonable to require any confession at all; and that, considering the general state of confusion that had existed, and the instructions and examples these young men had had, it might well be looked upon enough, that they were now willing to change their practice, and return again to Mr. Noyes's meeting. Not that you, Rev. Sir, are obliged to think as Col. Stoddard does; yet I think, considering his character and relation, his judgment may well be of so much weight, as to engage you the more to attend to and weigh the reasons he gives.

The objections, that these persons may have had against ordinarily attending your meeting, may be very trivial; but yet I suppose that, through infirmity, the case may be so with truly honest Christians, that trivial things may have great weight in their consciences, so as to have fast hold of them, until they are better enlightened: as in the former times of the country, it was with respect to the controversy between presbyterians and congregationalists. It was, as I have heard, in those days real matter of question with some, whether a presbyterian, living and dying such, could be saved. Some presbyterians, that have lived with us, have desired baptism for their children, who yet lived in neglect of the ordinances of the Lord Jesus Christ, because of a difference in some trivial circumstances of the administration, from the method of the church of Scotland. This matter being discoursed of, it was thought by Col. Stoddard in particular, that their neglect ought to be borne with, and they ought to be looked upon as Christians, and their children received to baptism; because, however trivial the foundation of their scruples were, yet through ignorance they might be honest and conscientious in them.

As to the church covenant, that these persons have entered into, wherein they have obliged themselves ordinarily to join in the worship of that church; I suppose none interpret the promises of a church covenant in such a sense, as to exclude all reserves of liberty, in case of an alteration of the judgment, in the affairs of conscience and religion, in one respect or another. As if a person, after incorporating with a congregational church, should become a conscientious episcopalian, or anabaptist, or should, by any change of judgment, come to think the means or manner of worship unlawful; and so in other respects that might be mentioned.

And if it be so that these persons, in some of their conversation and behaviour, have manifested a contentious, froward spirit, at the time of their withdrawing from your church; I confess this gives greater ground of suspicion of the sincerity of their plea of conscience; yet, as to this, I humbly conceive allowances must be made. It must be considered, that it is possible that persons, in an affair of this nature, may, in the thing itself, be conscientious, and yet, in the course of the management of it, may be guilty of very corrupt mixtures of passion and every evil disposition; as indeed is commonly the case with men, in long controversies of whatever nature, and even with conscientious men. And therefore it appears to me, that if persons in such a case are not obstinate, in what is amiss in them in this respect, and don't attempt to justify their frowardness and unchristian speeches, they notwithstanding may deserve credit, when they profess themselves conscientious in the affair in general.

Thus, dear Sir, I have freely communicated to you some of my thoughts, with regard to some of the concerns of this difficult day, which prove a trouble to you; not however with any aim at directing your conduct, but merely to comply with the request to which I have alluded. I am fully sensible, that I am not the pastor of the second church of Hartford; and I only desire you would impartially consider the reasons I have offered. Begging of Christ, our common Lord, that he would direct you in your theory and practice, to that which will be acceptable in his sight,

I remain, Rev. Sir,
Your friend and brother,
JONATHAN EDWARDS."

In May, 1743, Mr. Edwards went, as he often did, to Boston, to attend the convention of the clergy, which is held the day after the General Election. He was on horseback, and had his eldest daughter on a pillion behind him. At Brookfield, they fell in company with the Rev. Mr. Clap, rector of Yale College, his wife and son-in-law, also on horseback, with several others, all travelling in the same direction; and Mr. Edwards, joining the company, rode side by side with Mr. Clap, during a considerable part of the journey. At the commencement of Harvard college in the following year, 1744, Mr. Clap stated, before a large number of gentlemen, both at Boston and Cambridge, that, while riding through Leicester, in May of the year preceding, he was informed by Mr. Edwards, that Mr. Whitefield *told him*, "that he had the design of turning out of their places the greater part of the ministers of New England, and of supplying their pulpits with ministers from England, Scotland, and Ireland." This statement surprised those who heard it; yet, coming from such a source, it was believed, and extensively circulated. Mr. Edwards heard of it with astonishment, and without hesitation denied that he had said so. Mr. Clap, hearing of this denial, addressed a letter to Mr. Edwards, dated Oct. 12, 1744, in which he stated anew the alleged conversation, in the same terms; but before the latter received it, he had forwarded a letter to Mr. Clap, dated Oct. 18, 1744, showing him his mistake, and calling on him to correct it. On Oct. 29th, he wrote a reply to Mr. Clap's letter of the 12th; and receiving another, dated Oct. 28th, before he sent it, he replied to that also in the postscript, under date of Nov. 3d. Mr. Clap, finding that Mr. Edwards's contradiction of his statement was believed; and having heard, though incorrectly, that Mr. Edwards was about to publish such a contradiction; incautiously published a letter to his friend in Boston, in which he not only re-asserted his former statement, but declared that Mr. Edwards, in his private correspondence with him on the subject, had made a declaration, *equally full and strong*, to the same point. Mr. Edwards published a reply, in a letter to his friend in Boston, dated Feb. 4, 1745; in which he gave his two letters of Oct. 18, and Oct. 29, with the postscript of Nov. 3; from which it appears that, instead of admitting the truth of Mr. Clap's statement, he had most explicitly and solemnly denied it; and, in order to show how Mr. Clap might have been led into the mistake, acknowledged that he himself *supposed* that Mr. Whitefield was formerly of the opinion, that unconverted ministers ought not to be continued in the ministry; and that he himself *supposed* that Mr. Whitefield endeavoured to propagate this opinion, and a practice agreeable to it; and that all he had ever stated to any one was, his *own opinion* merely, and not any *declared design* of Mr. Whitefield. He also admitted, that Mr. Whitefield told him he intended to bring over a number of young men, to be ordained by the Messrs. Tennents, in New Jersey. He then asks, whether this is the same thing as Mr. Clap asserted, and suggests a variety of arguments, which seem absolutely conclusive, that he could never have made such a statement.

Mr. Clap, in reply to this, in a letter to Mr. Edwards, dated April 1, 1745, enters seriously upon the task of showing that Mr. Edwards's assertion—"that Mr. Whitefield *told* him, that he intended to bring over a number of young men, to be ordained by the Messrs. Tennents, in New Jersey"—connected with the assertion—that Mr. Edwards himself *supposed*, that Mr. Whitefield was formerly of the opinion, that unconverted ministers ought not to be continued in the ministry, and that Mr. Edwards himself *supposed* that Mr. Whitefield endeavoured to propagate this opinion, and a practice agreeable to it—was equivalent to Mr. Edwards's saying, that Mr. Whitefield *told him*, "that he had the design of turning out of their places the greater part of the ministers of New England, and of supplying their places with ministers from England, Scotland, and Ireland."

Mr. Edwards, in a letter to Mr. Clap, of May 20, 1745, after exposing in a few words the desperate absurdity of this attempt, enters on the discussion of the question—Whether he ever made such a statement to Mr. Clap?—with as much calmness as he afterwards exhibited in examining the question of a self-determining power; and with such logical precision of argument, that probably no one of his readers ever had a doubt left upon his mind, with regard to it;—no, not even his antagonist himself; for he never thought proper to attempt a reply; and in the public protest of the faculty of Yale college, against Mr. Whitefield, he and his associates in office say, in alluding to this very conversation, "You told the Rev. Mr. Edwards of Northampton, that you intended to bring over a number of young men from England, to be ordained by the Tennents." Those who have an opportunity of reading these communications, will find, in those of Mr. Edwards, an example of a personal controversy, conducted throughout, and to a very uncommon degree, in the spirit of the gentleman and the Christian.

This occurred at a period of great excitement, when many ministers had been removed, and many churches rent asunder; and when the minds of men were of course prepared beforehand to believe every thing that favoured their own side of the question. Mr. Clap was in this case obviously mistaken; still he was truly a man of respectability and worth. He had a powerful mind, rich in invention, and stored with knowledge, was profoundly versed in mathematics, physics, and astronomy, as well as the principles of law, and proved an able instructor and governor of the institution over which he presided. He was elected by a board of trustees, exclusively Arminian in sentiment, and all his associates in office held the same tenets. At the same time, though he entered warmly into the controversy relative to Mr. Whitefield, from a full conviction that it was his design to occasion the separation of churches, and to procure as far as possible the ejectment of all whom he regarded as unconverted ministers; and was doubtless happy in supposing himself able to prove that such was his avowed design, on the testimony of one of his warmest friends; yet he was far from taking the low ground of orthodoxy assumed by many on the same side, but always adhered to the doctrines of grace, and ultimately became their champion. Some time after this, he showed his magnanimity, by introducing the Essay on the Freedom of the Will, as a classic in the college.

In August, 1744, Mr. Edwards preached the sermon entitled, "The True Excellency of a Gospel Minister," at the ordination of Mr. Robert Abercrombie, to the ministry of the gospel, at Pelham. This gentleman was from Scotland, having been made known to Mr. Edwards by his correspondents in that country; and through his kind offices was introduced to the people at Pelham. The sermon was immediately published.

The reader will probably recollect, that Mr. M'Culloch, in his letter of August 13, 1743, had expressed the opinion, that the church of God, previous to her ultimate extension and triumph, was destined to meet with "more extensive and formidable trials," than she had ever before experienced. Mr. Edwards, from a minute investigation of the scriptural prophecies, having been convinced that this, which was at that time the commonly received opinion of the church, was erroneous; expresses his dissent from it in the following answer.

"To the Rev. Mr. M'Culloch.

Northampton, March 5, 1744.

Rev. and dear Sir,

I return you thanks for your most obliging, entertaining, and instructive letter, dated Aug. 13, 1743, which I received about the latter end of October: my answering which has been unhappily delayed, by reason of my distance from Boston, and not being able to find any opportunity to send thither, till the ship was gone that brought your letter; which I much regretted. My delaying to answer has been far from arising from any indifference with respect to this correspondence, by which I am sensible I am highly honoured and privileged.

'Tis probable that you have been informed, by other correspondents, before now, what the present state of things in New England is: it is, indeed, on many accounts very melancholy; there is a vast alteration within these two years; for about so long I think it is, since the Spirit of God began to withdraw, and this great work has been on the decline. Great numbers in the land, about two years ago, were raised to an exceedingly great height in joy and elevation of mind; and through want of watchfulness, and sensibleness of the danger and temptation that there is in such circumstances, many were greatly exposed, and the devil taking the advantage, multitudes were soon, and to themselves insensibly, led far away from God and their duty; God was provoked that he was not sanctified in this height of advancement, as he ought to have been; he saw our spiritual pride and self-confidence, and the polluted flames that arose of intemperate, unhallowed zeal; and he soon, in a great measure, withdrew from us; and the consequence has been, that the enemy has come in like a flood, in various respects, until the deluge has overwhelmed the whole land. There had from the beginning been a great mixture, especially in some places, of false experiences, and false religion with true; but from about this time, the mixture became much greater, many were led away with sad delusions; and this opened the door for the enemy to come in like a flood in another respect, it gave great advantages to these enemies and opposers of this work, furnished them with weapons and gave them new courage, and has laid the friends of the work under such disadvantage, that nothing that they could do would avail any thing to withstand their violence. And now it is come to that, that the work is put to a stop every where, and it is a day of the enemy's triumph; but I believe also a day of God's people's humiliation, which will be better to them in the end than their elevations and raptures. The time has been amongst us when the sower went forth to sow, and we have seen the spring wherein the seed sprang up in different sorts of ground, appearing then fair and flourishing; but this spring is past, and we now see the summer, wherein the sun is up with a burning heat, that tries the sorts of ground; and now appears the difference, the seed in stony ground, where there was only a thin layer of earth on a rock, withers away, the moisture being dried out; and the hidden seeds and roots of thorns, in unsubdued ground, now spring up and choke the seed of the word. Many high professors are fallen, some into gross immoralities, some into a rooted spiritual pride, enthusiasm, and an incorrigible wildness of behaviour, some into a cold frame of mind, showing a great indifference to the things of religion. But there are many, and I hope those the greater part of those that were professed converts, who appear hitherto like the good ground, and notwithstanding the thick and dark clouds, that so soon follow that blessed sunshine that we have had; yet I cannot but stedfastly maintain a hope and persuasion that God will revive his work, and that what has been so great and very extraordinary, is a forerunner of a yet more glorious and extensive work.—It has been slanderously reported and printed concerning me, that I have often said, that the Millennium was already begun, and that it began at Northampton. A doctor of divinity in New England has ventured to publish this report to the world, from a single person, who is concealed and kept behind the curtain: but the report is very diverse from what I have ever said. Indeed I have often said, as I say now, that I looked upon the late wonderful revivals of religion as forerunners of those glorious times so often prophesied of in the Scripture, and that this was the first dawning of that light, and beginning of that work, which, in the progress and issue of it, would at last bring on the church's latter-day glory; but there are many that know that I have from time to time added, that there would probably be many sore conflicts and terrible convulsions, and many changes, revivings, and intermissions, and returns of dark clouds, and threatening appearances, before this work shall have subdued the world, and Christ's kingdom shall be every where established and settled in peace, which will be the lengthening of the Millennium or day of the church's peace, rejoicing, and triumph on earth, so often spoken of. I was much entertained and delighted, dear Sir, with your thoughts on that text in Isa. lix. 19. which you signify in your letter, and so have many others been to whom I have communicated them; and as to what you say of some dreadful stroke or trial yet abiding, before the happy days of the promised peace and prosperity of the church, I so far agree with you, that I believe that, before the church of God shall have obtained the conquest, and the visible kingdom of Satan on earth shall receive its overthrow, and Christ's kingdom of grace be every where established on its ruins, there shall be a great and mighty struggle between the kingdom of Christ and the kingdom of Satan, attended with the greatest and most extensive convulsions and commotion, that ever were upon the face of the earth, wherein doubtless many particular Christians will suffer, and perhaps some parts of the church.

" But that the enemies of the church of God should ever gain such advantages against her any more, as they have done in times past, that the victory should ever any more be on their side, or that it shall ever be given to the beast again to make war with the saints, and to prevail against them, and overcome them, (as in Rev. xiii. 7. and xi. 7. and Dan. vii. 21.) to such a degree as has been heretofore, is otherwise than I hope. Though in this I would be far from setting up my own judgment, in opposition to others, who are more skilled in the prophecies of Scripture than I am. I think that what has mainly induced many divines to be of that opinion, is what is said in Revelation chap. xi. concerning the slaying of the witnesses, ver. 7, 8. 'And when they shall have finished their testimony, the beast, that ascendeth out of the bottomless pit, shall make war against them, and shall overcome them, and kill them. And their dead bodies shall lie in the street of the great city,' &c.

The event here spoken of, seems evidently to be that wherein the enemies of the church gain the greatest advantage against her that ever they have, and have the greatest conquest of her that ever they obtained, and bring the church nearest to a total extinction. For a long time the church is very small, represented by two witnesses, and they had been long in a very low state, prophesying in sackcloth; but now they are dead and their enemies triumph over them, as having gotten a complete victory, and look upon it that they are now past all possibility of recovery, there being less prospect of the church's restoration than ever there was before. But are we to expect this, dear Sir, that Satan will ever find means to bring things to pass, that after all the increase of light that has been in the world, since the Reformation, there shall be a return of a more dark time than in the depth of the darkness of popery, before the Reformation, when the church of God shall be nearer to a total extinction, and have less of visibility, all true religion and light be more blotted out of the memories of mankind, Satan's kingdom of darkness be more firmly established, all monuments of true religion be more abolished, and that the state of the world should be such, that it should appear further from any hope of a revival of true religion than it ever has done; is this conceivable or possible, as the state of things now is all over the world, even among papists themselves, without a miracle, a greater than any power short of divine can effect, without a long tract of time, gradually to bring it to pass, to introduce the grossest ignorance and extinguish all memory and monuments of truth; which was the case in that great extinction of true religion that was before the Reformation. And besides, if we suppose this war of the beast that ascends out of the bottomless pit with the witnesses, wherein he overcomes them and kills them, to be that last war which the church shall have with the beast, that great and mighty conflict that shall be just before the final overthrow of antichrist, that we read of in the 16th chap. the 13th and following verses, and in the 19th chapter; how shall we make them consist together? In the 11th chapter the church conflicts in sorrow, clothed in sackcloth, and in blood; in the 19th chap. the saints are not represented as fighting in sorrow and blood, though the battle be exceedingly great, but in strength, glory, and triumph. Their Captain goes forth to this battle, in great pomp and magnificence, on a white horse, and on his head many crowns, and on his vesture and on his thigh a name written, KING OF KINGS AND LORD OF LORDS; and the saints follow him, not in sackcloth, but coming forth on white horses, clothed in pure linen, clean and white, the raiment of triumph, the same raiment that the saints appear in, Rev. vii. 14. when they appear with palms in their hands, after they had washed their robes, that had been stained with their own blood, and made themselves white in the blood of the Lamb. In the conflict spoken of in chap. xi. the beast makes war with the witnesses, and overcomes them, and kills them: the same is foretold, Dan. vii. 21. and Rev. xiii. 7. But in that last great battle, just before the fall of antichrist, we find the reverse of this; the church shall obtain a glorious victory over the beast, and the beast is taken and cast into the lake of fire. Rev. xvii. 14. 'These shall make war with the Lamb; and the Lamb shall overcome them; for he is Lord of Lords and King of Kings; and they that are with him are called, and chosen, and faithful;' compared with chap. xix. 16, to the end, and chap. xvi. 16, 17. In that conflict, chap. xi. the beast has war with the witnesses, and kills them, and their dead bodies lie unburied, as if it were to be meat for the beasts of the earth and fowls of heaven; but in that last conflict, Christ and his church shall slay their enemies, and give their dead bodies to be meat for the beasts of the earth and fowls of heaven, chap. xix. 17, &c. There is no manner of appearance in the descriptions that are given of that great battle, of any great advantages gained in it against the church, before the enemy is overcome, but all appearance of the contrary. The descriptions in the 16th and 19th chapters of Rev. will by no means allow of such an advantage, as that of the overcoming and slaying of the church, or people of God, and their lying for some time unburied, that their dead bodies may be for their enemies to abuse and trample on, and make sport with. In the 16th chap. we have an account of their being gathered together into the place called Armageddon; and then the first thing we hear of after that, is the pouring out of the seventh vial of God's wrath, and a voice saying, It is done; and so in chap. xix. we read of the beast, and the kings of the earth and their armies being gathered together, to make war against him that sat on the horse, and against his army; and then the next thing we hear of is the beast's being taken, &c. The event of the conflict of the beast with the church, chap. xi. is the triumph of the church's enemies, when they of the people, and kindred, and tongues, and nations, and they that dwell on the earth, shall see the dead bodies of the saints lying in the streets, and shall rejoice over them, and make merry, and send gifts one to another. But the event of that great and last battle, before the fall of antichrist, is quite the reverse of this, even the church's triumphing over their enemies, as being utterly destroyed. Those events, that are consequent on the issue of the war with the witnesses, chap. xi. do in no wise answer to those, that are represented as consequent on that last conflict of antichrist with the church. 'Tis said that when the witnesses ascended into heaven, the same hour there was an earthquake, and the tenth part of the city fell; and in the earthquake were slain of men seven thousand! but this don't seem at all to answer what is described, chap. xvi. and xix. The great city was divided into three parts, and the cities of the nations fell; and great Babylon came in remembrance before God, to give her the cup of the wine of the fierceness of his wrath; and every island fled away, and the mountains were not found. And it had been said before, that there was a great earthquake, such as was not since men were upon the earth, so mighty an earthquake, and so great. And in chap. xix. instead of slaying seven thousand men, it seems as if there was a general slaughter of all the enemies of the church, through the world. And besides, if we read this 11th chapter through, we shall see that the falling of the tenth part of the city and the rising of the witnesses, and their standing on their feet and ascending into heaven, are represented there as entirely distinct from the accomplishment of the church's glory, after the fall of antichrist, and God's judging and destroying the enemies of the church. The judgment here spoken of, as executed on God's enemies, are under another *woe*, and the benefits bestowed on the church, are under another *trumpet:* for immediately after the account of the rising and ascending of the witnesses, and its consequences, follow these words, ver. 14, 15. 'The second woe is past, and behold the third woe cometh quickly. And the seventh angel sounded, and there were great voices in heaven, saying, The kingdoms of this world are become the kingdoms of our Lord and of his Christ, and he shall reign for ever and ever.' And in the following verses, we have an account of the praises sung to God on the occasion; and in the last verse we have a brief hint of that same great earthquake, and the great hail, and those thunders, and lightnings, and voices, that we have an account of in the latter part of chap. xvi. so that the earthquake mentioned in the last verse of chap. xi. seems to be the great earthquake, that attends the last great conflict of the church and her enemies, rather than that mentioned ver. 13.

The grand objection against all this is, that it is said, that the witnesses should prophesy one thousand two hundred and sixty days, clothed in sackcloth; and when they have finished their testimony, the beast should make war against them, and kill them, &c. and that it seems manifest that after this they are no longer in sackcloth; for henceforward they are in an exalted state in heaven: and that therefore, seeing the time of their wearing sackcloth is one thousand two hundred and sixty days, *i. e.* during the time of the continuance of antichrist; hence their being slain, and their rising again, must be at the conclusion of this period, at the end of antichrist's reign.

In answer to which I would say, with submission to better judgments, that I humbly conceive that we can justly infer no more from this prophecy than this, *viz.* that the one thousand two hundred and sixty days is the proper time (as it were) of the church's trouble and bondage, or being clothed in sackcloth, because it is the appointed time of the reign of antichrist; but this don't hinder but that God, out of great compassion to his church, should, in some respect, shorten the days, and grant that his church should in some measure anticipate the appointed great deliverance that should be at an end of these days, as he has in fact done in the Reformation; whereby his church has had a great degree of restoration granted her, from the darkness, power, and dominion of antichrist, before their proper time of restoration, which is at the end of the one thousand two hundred and sixty days; and so the church, through the compassion of her Father and Redeemer, anticipates her deliverance from her sorrows; and has, in some respects, an end put to her testifying in sackcloth, as many parts of the church are henceforward brought out from under the dominion of the antichristian powers, into a state of liberty; though in other respects, the church may be said still to continue in her sackcloth, and in the wilderness, (as chap. xii. 14.) till the end of the days. And as to the witnesses standing on their feet, and ascending into heaven; I would propose that it may be considered, Whether any more can be understood by it, than the protestant church's being now (at least as to many parts of it) able to stand on her own legs, and in her own defence, and being raised to such a state, that she henceforward is out of the reach of the Romish powers; that, let them do what they will, they shall never any more be able to get the church under their power, as they had before; as oftentimes in the Scriptures God's people dwelling in safety, out of the reach of their enemies, is represented by their dwelling on high, or being set on high; Ps. lix. 1. Isa. xxxiii. 16. Ps. lxix. 29. and xci. 14. and cvii. 41. Prov. xxix. 25.; and the children of Israel, when brought out of Egypt, were said to be carried on eagle's wings, that is lofty in its flight, flies away towards heaven where none of her enemies can reach her.

I might here observe, that we have other instances of God's shortening the days of his church's captivity and bondage, either at the beginning or latter end, in some measure parallel with this. Thus the proper time of the bondage of the posterity of Abraham, in a strange land, was four hundred years, Gen. xv. 13.; but yet God in mercy delayed their bondage, whereby the time was much shortened at the beginning. So the time wherein it was foretold, that the whole land of Israel should be a desolation and an astonishment, and the land should not enjoy her sabbaths, was seventy years, Jer. xxv. 11, 12.; and these seventy years are dated in 2 Chron. xxxvi. 20, 21. from Zedekiah's captivity; and yet from that captivity to Cyrus's decree was about fifty-two years, though it was indeed about seventy years before the temple was finished. So the proper time of the oppression of Antiochus Epiphanes, wherein both the sanctuary and the host should be trodden under-foot by him, was two thousand and three hundred days, Dan. vii. 13, 14. and yet God gave Israel a degree of deliverance by the Maccabees, and they were holpen with a little help, and the host ceased to be trodden under-foot before that time was expired. Dan. xi. 32, 34.

But in these things, dear Sir, I am by no means dogmatical; I do but humbly offer my thoughts on what you suggested in your letter, submitting them to your censure. 'Tis pity that we should expect such a terrible devastation of the church, before her last and most glorious deliverance, if there be no such thing to be expected. It may be a temptation to some of the people of God, the less earnestly to wish and pray for the near approach of the church's glorious day, and the less to rejoice in the signs of its approach.

But, let us go on what scheme we will, it is most apparent from the Scriptures, that there are mighty strugglings to be expected, between the church of God and her enemies, before her great victory; and there may be many lesser strugglings before that last, and greatest, and universal conflict. Experience seems to show that the church of God, according to God's method of dealing with her, needs a great deal gradually to prepare her for that prosperity and glory that he has promised her on earth; as the growth of the earth, after winter, needs gradually to be prepared for the summer heat: I have known instances, wherein by the heat's coming on suddenly in the spring, without intermissions of cold to check the growth, the branches, many of them, by a too hasty growth, have afterwards died. And perhaps God may bring on a spiritual spring as he does the natural, with now and then a pleasant sunshiny season, and then an interruption by clouds and stormy winds, till at length, by the sun more and more approaching, and the light increasing, the strength of the winter is broken. We are extremely apt to get out of the right way. A very great increase of comfort that is sudden, without time and experience, in many instances, has appeared to wound the soul, in some respects, though it seems to profit it in others. Sometimes, at the same time that the soul seems wonderfully delivered from those lusts, that are more carnal and earthly, there is an insensible increase of those that are more spiritual; as God told the children of Israel, that he would put out the former inhabitants of the land of Canaan, by little and little, and would not consume them at once, lest the beasts of the field should increase upon them.—We need much experience, to teach us the innumerable ways that we are liable to err, and to show us the evil and pernicious consequences of those errors. If it should please God, before many years, to grant another great revival of religion in New England, we should perhaps be much upon our guard against such errors as we have run into, and which have undone us this time, but yet might run insensibly into other errors that now we think not of.

You inquire of me, Rev. Sir, whether I reject all those for counterfeits that speak of visions and trances. I am far from doing of it: I am and always have been, in that matter, of the same opinion that Mr. Robe expresses, in some of those pamphlets Mr. M'Laurin sent me, that persons are neither to be rejected nor approved on such a foundation. I have expressed the same thing in my discourse on 'the Marks of a Work of the True Spirit,' and have not changed my mind.

I am afraid, dear Sir, that I have been too bold with you, in being so lengthy and tedious, and have been too impertinent and forward to express my opinion upon this and that; but I consider myself as writing to a candid, christian friend and brother, with whom I may be free and bold, and from whom I may promise myself excuse and forgiveness. Dear brother, asking your earnest prayers for me and for New England, I am your affectionate brother, and engaged friend and servant,

JONATHAN EDWARDS."

The opinion here expressed by Mr. Edwards, was not the result of a slight and cursory examination of the subject in discussion. He had a considerable time before examined, at great length, the prophecies of Daniel and John, with regard to this very point; and, as we shall soon have occasion to remark, had been convinced that the opinion, then commonly received, *that the severest trials of the church were yet future, was erroneous.*

The Rev. Samuel Buell, whom I have already mentioned, as having preached at Northampton during the absence of Mr. Edwards, in January, 1742, with uncommon fervour and success, continued his labours, as an evangelist among the churches, upwards of four years; and at length accepted of an invitation from the people of East Hampton, a village in the S. E. corner of Long Island, to become their minister. At his request, Mr. Edwards went to East Hampton, and there preached his installation sermon, on the 19th of September, 1746, from Isaiah lxii. 4, 5.

CHAPTER XIV.

MISTAKES EXTENSIVELY PREVALENT AT THIS TIME, AS TO THE NATURE AND EVIDENCES OF TRUE GODLINESS—"TREATISE ON RELIGIOUS AFFECTIONS"—DESIGN AND CHARACTER OF THE WORK—REPUBLISHED ABROAD—LETTER FROM MR. GILLESPIE CONCERNING IT—LETTER FROM MR. EDWARDS TO MR. M'CULLOCH—REPLY TO MR. GILLESPIE—PROPOSAL MADE IN SCOTLAND, FOR UNITED EXTRAORDINARY PRAYER—EFFORTS OF MR. EDWARDS TO PROMOTE IT—LETTER TO MR. M'CULLOCH—"HUMBLE ATTEMPT TO PROMOTE EXTRAORDINARY PRAYER."

From the facts already recited, it will be obvious to the reader, that few ministers, even in the course of a long ministry, have as full an opportunity of learning, from their own observation, the true nature of a revival of religion, and the differences between imaginary and saving conversion, as Mr. Edwards had now enjoyed. He had early discovered, that there was a radical difficulty attending not only every revival of religion, but, in a greater or less degree, also, every instance of supposed conversion:—a difficulty arising from erroneous conceptions, so generally entertained, respecting the question, *What is the nature of true religion?* or, *What are the distinguishing marks of that holiness, which is acceptable in the sight of God?*—Perceiving, at an early period of his christian life, that no other subject was equally important to man, that no other was more frequently or variously illustrated by the scriptural writers, and yet, that on no other had professing Christians been less agreed; his attention, as he himself informs us, had been particularly directed to it, from his first commencement of the study of theology; and he was led to examine it with all the diligence, and care, and exactness of search and inquiry, of which his mind was capable. In addition to this, he had not only witnessed, in two successive instances, a solemn and universal attention to religion, among the young as well as among grown persons in his own congregation, and in both, almost all of the latter, as well as very many of the former, gathered into the church; but he had been the spiritual counsellor and guide of multitudes in other congregations, where he had occasionally laboured, as well as of great numbers who visited him for this purpose at Northampton. These advantages of observation, it may easily be believed, were not lost on a mind like his.

This subject, at the time of which we are speaking, had become, also, a subject of warm and extended controversy. The advocates of revivals of religion, had too generally been accustomed to attach to the mere circumstances of conversion—to the time, place, manner, and means, in and by which it was supposed to be effected—an importance, no where given them in the Scriptures; as well as to conclude, that all affections which were high in degree, and accompanied with great apparent zeal and ardour, were of course gracious in their nature; while their opposers insisted, that true religion did not consist at all in the affections, but wholly in the external conduct. The latter class attributed the uncommon attention to religion, which they could not deny had existed for four years in New England, to artificial excitement merely; while the former saw nothing in it, or in the measures taken to promote it, to condemn, but every thing to approve. Mr. Edwards, in his views of the subject, differed materially from both classes. As he knew from his own experience, that sin and the saving grace of God might dwell in the same heart; so he had learned, both from observation and testimony, that much false religion might prevail during a powerful revival of true religion, and that at such a time, multitudes of hypocrites might spring up among real Christians. Thus it was in the revival of religion in the time of Josiah, in that which attended the preaching of John the Baptist, in those which occurred under the preaching of Christ, in the remarkable outpouring of the Spirit in the days of the apostles, and in that which existed in the time of the Reformation. He clearly saw, that it was this mixture of counterfeit religion with true, which in all ages had given the devil his chief advantage against the kingdom of Christ. "By this," observes Mr. Edwards, "he hurt the cause of Christianity, in and after the apostolic age, much more, than by all the persecutions of both Jews and heathens. By this he prevailed against the Reformation, to put a stop to its progress, more than by all the bloody persecutions of the church of Rome. By this he prevailed against the revivals of religion, that have occurred since the Reformation. By this he prevailed against New England, to quench the love of her espousals, about a hundred years ago. And I think I have had opportunity enough to see plainly, that by this the devil has prevailed against the late great revival of religion in New England, so happy and promising in its beginning. I have seen the devil prevail in this way, against two great revivings of religion in this country. By perverting us from the simplicity that is in Christ, he hath suddenly prevailed to deprive us of that fair prospect we had a little while ago, of a kind of paradisaic state of the church of God in New England."

These evils, it was obvious, must exist in the church, until their cause was removed, and men had learned to distinguish accurately between true and false religion. To contribute his own best endeavours for the accomplishment of this end, Mr. Edwards prepared and published his "Treatise on Religious Affections." The great design of this treatise is, to show, in what true religion consists, and what are its distinguishing marks and evidences; and thus to enable every man, who will be honest and faithful with himself, to decide whether he is, or is not, a real Christian. Similar attempts had been made, by many earlier writers; but it may, I believe, safely be asserted, that no one of their efforts, taken as a whole, and viewed as an investigation of the entire subject would now be regarded as in any high degree important or valuable. The subject itself is one of the most difficult which theology presents; and demands for its full investigation, not only ardent piety, and a most intimate acquaintance with the Scriptures, but an exact and metaphysical inspection of the faculties and operations of the human mind; which unfortunately few, very few, writers on experimental religion have hitherto discovered. The work of Mr. Edwards is at once a scriptural and a philosophical view of the subject;—as truly scientific in its arrangement, and logical in its deductions, as any work on the exact sciences. That it is also a thorough and complete view of it, we have this decisive evidence —that no work of the kind, of any value, has appeared since, for which the author has not been indebted, *substantially*, to the "Treatise on the Affections;" or which has not been that very treatise, in part, or in whole, *diluted* to the capacity of weaker understandings. The trial, to which the mind of the honest, attentive, and prayerful reader of its pages is subjected, is the very trial of the final day. He who can endure the trial of the "Treatise on the Affections," will stand unhurt amidst a dissolving universe; and he who cannot will assuredly perish in its ruins. It ought to be the *vade mecum*, not only of every minister, and every Christian, but of every man, who has sobriety of thought enough to realize, that he has any interest in a coming eternity. Every minister should take effectual care that it is well dispersed among the people of his own charge, and that none of them is admitted to a profession of religion, until, after a thorough study of this treatise, he can satisfy both himself and his spiritual guide, not only that he does not rely upon the mere *negative signs* of holiness, but that he finds within himself those distinguishing marks and evidences of its *positive* existence, which the Divine Author of holiness has pronounced sure and unerring. It is indeed said, that anxious inquirers will often be discouraged by this course—particularly by a perusal of the Second Part of the treatise—from making a profession of religion, and led to renounce the hope of their own conversion; and the answer is, that he, who, on finding himself discouraged from a profession of religion by the Second Part, is not encouraged to make it by a perusal of the Third Part, should of course, unless his views are perverted by disease or melancholy, consider the call *to repent and believe the gospel*, as still addressed immediately to himself; and that he, who on the perusal of this Treatise, is led to renounce the hope which he had cherished of his own piety, while he has the best reason to regard it as a false hope, will find almost of course that that hope is soon succeeded by one which will endure the strictest scrutiny. It is also said that many persons cannot understand this treatise; and the answer is, that he who is too young to understand it in its *substance*, is too young to make a profession of religion; and that he whose mind is too feeble to receive it substantially, when communicated by a kind and faithful pastor, cannot understandingly make such a profession. Pre-eminently is this treatise necessary to every congregation during a revival of religion. It was especially designed by its author to be used on every such occasion; and the minister who then uses it as he ought, will find it like a fan in his hand, winnowing the chaff from the wheat. And until ministers, laying aside the miserable vanity which leads them, in the mere number of those whom they denominate their 'spiritual children,' to find an occasion of boasting, and of course to swell that number as much as they can, shall be willing thus faithfully and honestly to make a separation among their inquirers; every revival of religion will open a great and effectual door, through which the enemies as well as the friends of religion, will gain an admission into the house of God. And when they are thus admitted, and the ardour of animal feeling has once subsided, the minister will generally find not only that he has wounded Christ in the house of his friends, but that he has destroyed his own peace, and that of his church, and prepared the way for his own speedy separation from his people.

To prevent this miserable system of deception on the part of ministers and churches, as well as of candidates for a profession of religion, Mr. Edwards wrote the treatise in question. As at first prepared, it was a series of sermons, which he preached from his own pulpit, from the text still prefixed to it, 1 Peter i. 8. "Whom having not seen, ye love: in whom, though now ye see him not, yet believing, ye rejoice with joy unspeakable and full of glory." It was thus written and preached, probably in the years 1742 and 1743. Being afterwards thrown into the form of a treatise by the author, it was published early in 1746. In its style it is the least correct of any of the works of Mr. Edwards, published in his life-time; but, as a work exhibiting genuine Christianity in distinction from all its counterfeits, it possesses such singular excellence, that were the books on earth destined to a destruction so nearly universal, that only one beside the Bible could be saved; the church of Christ, if aiming to preserve the volume of the greatest value to man, that which would best unfold to a bereaved posterity the real nature of true religion, would unquestionably select for preservation, the "Treatise on the Affections."

This treatise was immediately republished in England and Scotland, and was cordially welcomed by all the friends of evangelical religion in those countries, as well as in America. Its appearance in Scotland gave rise to an interesting correspondence, between Mr. Edwards and the Rev. Thomas Gillespie, of Carnock, near Edinburgh; which was commenced by the latter gentleman with the following letter.

Letter from Mr. Gillespie.

"*Carnock, Nov.* 24, 1746.

Very dear Sir,

I have ever honoured you for your work's sake, and what the great Shepherd made you the instrument of, from the time you published the then very extraordinary account of the revival of religion at Northampton, I think in the year 1735. The two performances you published on the subject of the late glorious work in New England, well adapted to that in Scotland, gave me great satisfaction, especially the last of them, for peculiar reasons. This much I think myself bound to say. I have many a time, for some years, designed to claim humbly the privilege of correspondence with you. What has made me defer doing it so long, when some of my brethren and good acquaintances have been favoured with it for a considerable time, it is needless now to mention. I shall only say, I have blamed myself for neglect in that matter. I do now earnestly desire a room in your prayers and friendship, and a letter from you sometimes, when you have occasion to write to Scotland; and I shall wish to be as regular as I can in making a return. With your permission, I propose to trouble you now and then with the proposal of doubts and difficulties that I meet with, and am exercised by; as for other reasons, so because some solutions in the two mentioned performances were peculiarly agreeable to me, and I find from these discourses, that wherein I have differed in some things from many others, my sentiments have harmonized with Mr. Edwards. This especially was the case in some things contained in your '*Thoughts concerning the Revival of Religion in New England.*' All the apology I make for using such freedom, though altogether unacquainted, is that you will find from my short attestation in Mr. Robe's Narrative, I am no enemy to you or to the work you have been engaged in, and which you have defended in a way I could not but much approve of. Also my friend and countryman, the Rev. Mr. Robert Abercrombie, will inform you about me, if you have occasion to see him or hear from him.

I longed to see somewhat about impressions respecting facts and future events, &c. whether by scripture texts or otherwise, made on the minds of good people, and supposed to be from the Lord; for I have had too good occasion to know the hurtful, yea, pernicious tendency of this principle, as commonly managed, upon many persons in manifold instances and various respects. It has indeed surprised me much, that wise, holy, and learned divines, as well as others, have supposed this a spiritual experience, an answer of prayers, an evidence of being highly favoured by the Lord, &c. and I was exceeding glad, that the Lord had directed you to give so seasonable a caveat against what I am assured you had the best reason to term, 'A handle in the hand of the devil,' &c. I was only sorry your then design had not permitted you to say more on that point. It merits a volume; and the proper full discussion of it would be one of the most seasonable and effectual services done the church of Christ, and interest of vital religion through the world, that I know of. I rejoice to find there is a good deal more on that subject interspersed in your '*Treatise of Religious Affections,*' which I have got, but could not as yet regularly peruse. I humbly think the Lord calls you, dear Sir, to consider every part of that point in the most critical manner, and to represent fully the consequences resulting from the several principles in that matter, which good people, as well as others, have been so fond of. And as (if I do not mistake) Providence has already put that in your hand as a part of your generation-work, so it will give me, as well as others, vast satisfaction to find more said on the subject by you, if you do not find what is in the mentioned treatises sufficient, as to which I can form no judgment, because, for myself, I have not as yet considered it. If any other author has treated that subject, I do not remember to have met with it, and I believe hell has been no less delighted than surprised, that a regular attack has not been made on them on that side before now. I doubt not they dread the consequences of such assault with exquisite horror. The neglect or oversight, if not the mistakes, of so many learned authors, who have insisted on doctrines that bear similitude or relation to this matter, while it was passed over, I humbly think should teach us humility, and some other useful lessons I need not name to Mr. Edwards.

I hope, dear Sir, it will not offend you, that I humbly offer some remarks, with all due deference, upon what I have observed in looking into your '*Treatise on Religious Affections*:' and, upon further perusal, shall frankly represent what I may find difficulty about, if any such passage should cast up; expecting you will be so good as to set me right, if I shall mistake or not perceive your meaning.

Pages 78, 79,* there are several passages I do not well understand. Page 78, line 6, *ad finem*, you say, 'That they should confidently believe and trust, while they yet remain without spiritual light or sight, is an antiscriptural and absurd doctrine you are refuting.' But this doctrine, as it is understood by many, is, that Christians ought firmly to believe and trust in Christ without light or sight, and though they are in a dark, dead frame, and for the present having no spiritual experiences and discoveries. Had you said they could not or would not believe or trust without spiritual light or sight, this is what could not be doubted: but I humbly apprehend, the position will not hold as you have laid it, whether it is applied to a sinner or a saint, as I suppose you understand it; for though the sinner never will believe on the Lord Jesus, till he has received a saving manifestation of his glory by the work of the Spirit, yet every sinner, we know, is indispensably bound, at all seasons, by the divine authority, to believe instantly on the Lord Jesus. The command of the Lord, 1 John iii. 23. that we should believe on the name of his Son Jesus Christ, no less binds the sinner to immediate performance, than the command not to kill, to keep the sabbath day, or any other duty, as to the present performance of which, in way of duty, all agree, the sinner is bound. I suppose none of us think we are authorized, or will adventure to preach, that the sinner should delay to attempt to believe in the Saviour, till he finds light from heaven shining into his mind, or has got a saving sight or discovery of the Lord Jesus, though it is certain he cannot believe, nor will do it eventually, till favoured with such light or sight; because we should, in that event, put in a qualification where the apostle Paul and Silas did put none; such is their exhortation to the jailor, Acts xvi. 31. Also, as it may be the last call the sinner is to receive, in the dispensation of the word, we are bound to require him *instantly* to believe, whatever he does or does not feel in himself. If you did intend not the sinner, but the saint, in the before-mentioned positions, as I am apt to think your scope plainly intimates, still I apprehend these your assertions are not tenable; for I humbly suppose the Christian is bound to trust the divine faithfulness plighted in the promise for needful blessings, be his case with respect to light or darkness, sight, &c. what it will; and that no situation the saint can be in, looses him from obligation to glorify the Lord on all occasions, by trusting in him and expecting the fulfilment of his word suiting his case. Also I would imagine, in Isa. l. 10. the saint is required to believe, in the precise circumstances mentioned in your assertion above mentioned. Pardon my freedom. You do indeed say, 'It is truly the duty of those who are thus in darkness to come out of darkness into light and believe,' page 78, line 5; but how to reconcile that with the mentioned assertion that immediately follows, or with Isa. l. 10. or other scriptures, or said assertions, and the other, of which before, I am indeed at a loss. Sometimes I think it is not believing the promise, or trusting the Lord, and trusting in him, you mean in the positions I have cited; but the belief of the goodness of one's state that he is a saint. If that was what you intended, I heartily wish you had said so much in the book; but as this is not ordinarily what is

* See vol. i. pp. 258, 259.

meant by believing in Scripture, I must suppose it was not the idea affixed to your words; and an expression of yours seems to make it evident. Had you plainly stated the distinction, betwixt the impossibility of one's actually believing, and its yet being his duty to believe, in the circumstances you mentioned, danger of mistake and a handle for cavil had been cut off.

Page 78, line 20, &c., you say, 'To press and urge them to believe, without any spiritual light or sight, tends greatly to help forward the delusions of the prince of darkness.' Had you said, to press them to believe that the Lord was their God, when going on in a course of sin, or when sinning presumptuously, was of such tendency, which probably was in part what you designed, it would, in my humble apprehension, have been much more safe, for the reasons given. Also, as it is ordinarily and justly observed, that they who are most humbled think they are least so, when under a saving work of the Spirit, perhaps in like manner, spiritual light and sight may, in some instances, be mistaken or not duly apprehended; in which case, the person, upon admitting and proceeding upon your suppositions, may perhaps be apt to give way to unbelief, and to say, If I am not to be urged by the Lord's servants to believe in my present circumstances, it would surely be presumptuous in me to entertain thoughts of attempting it. Or, it may be, he shall think he has not that degree of spiritual light or sight, that is absolutely necessary in order to his believing; and thus the evil heart of unbelief shall make him depart from the living God, and neglect to set to his seal that he is true, perhaps from the apprehension that it is his duty to remain as he is, or at least in the persuasion it would be in vain to essay to believe, till matters be otherwise with him. If I have deduced consequences from your words and manner of reasoning, which you think they do not justly bear, I will be glad to be rectified by you, dear Sir, and would be satisfied to know from you, how the practice you remark upon in the fore-mentioned passage tends to help forward the delusions of Satan. I am apt to believe the grounds upon which you proceed, in the whole paragraph I have mentioned, is, that you have with you real Antinomians, who teach things about faith and believing, subversive of new obedience and gospel holiness, and inconsistent with the scripture doctrines concerning them. But as we have few, if any such at all, (I believe I might say more,) in this country, and at the same time have numbers who would have the most accurate and judicious evangelical preachers to insist a great deal more upon *doing*, and less upon *believing*, Mark x. 17—23. for what reasons you will perceive, I am afraid your words will be misrepresented by them, and a sense put upon your expressions, which you were far from intending. I expect a mighty clamour by the Seceders, if the book shall fall into their hands. All I shall say about what is expressed by you, page 78, line 32, &c. is, that I have frequently heard it taught by those accounted the most orthodox, that the believer was bound to trust in the Lord, in the very worst frame he could be in, and that the exercise of faith was the way to be delivered from darkness, deadness, backsliding, &c. It is impossible one should err, who follows the course prescribed by the Lord in his word. I suppose no person is bound or allowed to defer believing one single moment, because he finds himself in a bad situation, because the Spirit breathes not on him, or he finds not actual influence from heaven communicated to him at that season, rendering him capable or meet for it; for this reason, that not our ability or fitness, but the Lord's command, is the rule of duty, &c. It merits consideration, whether the believer should ever doubt of his state, on any account whatever; because doubting, as opposed to believing, is absolutely sinful. I know the opposite has been prescribed, when the saint is plunged in prevailing iniquity; but does not doubting strengthen corruption? is not unbelief the leading sin, as faith is the leading grace?

Page 258, (Note,) you cite as an authority Mr. Stoddard, affirming, 'One way of sin is exception enough against men's salvation, though their temptations be great.' I well remember the singularly judicious Dr. Owen somewhere says to this effect, 'Prevalence of a particular sin over a person for a considerable time, shows him to be no saint, except when under the power of a strong temptation.' I would suppose such texts as Isaiah lxiv. 6. page 65, 3, &c. warranted the Doctor to assert as he did. It is, I own, no small difficulty to steer the middle course, betwixt affording hypocrites ground unwarrantably to presume on the one hand, and wounding the Lord's dear children on the other; and all the little knowledge of the Scriptures I would hope the Lord has given me, makes me think Mr. Shepherd, good and great man as he was, verged not a little to the last extreme, with whom, if I mistake not, Mr. Stoddard symbolizes in the above assertion; for such as I have mentioned, I apprehend is the drift and tendency of Mr. Shepherd's principles. In some instances, daily experience and observation confirm me still more, that we should be very cautious and modest when asserting on that head, and should take care to go no further in the matter, than we have plain Scripture to bear us out. The consideration, that indwelling sin sometimes certainly gets such ascendant, that the new creature is, for the time the Lord seems meet, as fire buried under ashes, undiscerned and inactive, lays foundation, in my humble apprehension, for saying somewhat stronger on that point, than I would choose to utter in public teaching; and how long a saint may have been in the case now hinted, I suppose it belongs not to us precisely to determine.

Page 259, you say, 'Nor can a true saint ever fall away, so that it shall come to this, that ordinarily there shall be no remarkable difference in his walk and behaviour since his conversion, from what was before.' I do not remember that the Scripture any where mentions, that David or Solomon were sanctified from the womb. I think the contrary may be presumed; and it is evident for a considerable time, with the first ordinarily, and for a long time, in the case of the latter ordinarily, there was a remarkable difference for the worse, in the walk and behaviour of both of them, when we are sure they were saints, from what it appears it had been in their younger years. Besides, let us suppose a person of a good natural disposition, bred up in aversion to all vicious practices, by a religious education and example, and virtuous inclination thus cultivated in him, 2 Peter ii. 20. and he is converted when come to maturity, and afterwards corruption in him meets with peculiar temptations; I doubt much if there would be a remarkable difference betwixt his then conversation and walk, and that in unregeneracy. The contrary I think is found in experience, and the principles laid down leave room to suppose it.

I own in what I have above said I have perhaps gone further than becomes a man of my standing in writing to one of Mr. Edwards's experience, and am heartily sorry my first letter to you is in such a strain, and on such a subject. But love to you, dear Sir, and concern lest you should be thought to patronize what I am sure you do not, and to oppose what are your real sentiments, made me write with such freedom, and break over restraints, which modesty, decency, &c. should otherwise have laid me under, that you might have an opportunity to know in what light these things I mention to you appear to some who are your real friends in this country. A valuable minister, in looking into what is noticed in pages 78 and 79, said to me, it would be right some should write you about it; and I take this first opportunity, that you may have access to judge of the matter, and what it may be proper for you to do or not to do in it.

I will expect an answer with your convenience. I hope you will deal freely with me; for I can say, I would sit down and learn at your feet, dear Sir, accounting myself as a child in knowledge of the Scriptures, when compared with others I will not name, and the longer I live I see the greater advantage in improvements of that kind. Conceal nothing that you think will tend to put me right if you find my views are not just. I proposed in the beginning of this letter to trouble you with some questions or doubts, and shall mention one or two at present. What should one do who is incessantly harassed by Satan; can by no means keep him out of his mind; has used all means prescribed in Scripture and suggested by divines for resistance known to him, in vain; it may be for a long time has cried to Christ, but he hears not, seems not to regard him; all his efforts are swallowed up in the deluge of the foe; do what he will, seems to gain no ground against the powers of darkness; is apt to dread he shall sink under the load, and never shall be delivered in this world? What would you advise such a person to do? What construction, think you, should be put on the sovereign conduct and dispensation of Heaven toward him? I have occasion to be conversant about this case practically demonstrated, of many years continuance, without interruption; and will therefore be glad to have your mind about it in a particular manner, and as much at large as you conveniently can. It is said, all things work for good, &c. As degrees of glory will be in proportion to those of grace, how can it be made appear it is for one's good what sometimes happens to saints, their being permitted to fall under backslidings and spiritual decays, and to die in that state, perhaps after continuing in it a considerable while, and when their situation has been attended with the melancholy circumstances and consequences that sometimes have place in that state of matters? The solution of this I would gladly receive from you.

Are the works of the great Mr. Boston known in your country, *viz.* the Fourfold State of Man, View of the Covenant of Grace, and a Discourse on Afflictions, and Church Communion, &c. If not, inform me by your letter. I have now need to own my fault in troubling you with so long a letter, and so I shall end," &c.

Letter from Mr. Edwards to Mr. M'Culloch, of Cambuslang.

"To the Rev. Mr. M'Culloch.

Northampton, Jan. 21, 1747.

Rev. and dear Brother,

The time seems long to me since I have received a letter from you; I have had two letters from each of my other correspondents in Scotland since I have had any from you. Our correspondence has been to me very pleasant, and I am very loth it should fail.

Great changes have been, dear Sir, since I have had a letter from you, and God has done great things, both in Scotland and America; though not of the same nature, with those that were wrought some years ago, by the outpourings of his Spirit, yet those wherein his providence is on many accounts exceedingly remarkable: in Scotland, in the suppression of the late rebellion; and in America, in our preservation from the great French armada, from Brest, and their utter disappointment and confusion, by the immediate and wonderful hand of Heaven against them, without any interposition of any arm of flesh. The nearest akin to God's wonderful works of old, in the defence of his people in Moses's, Joshua's, and Hezekiah's time, perhaps of any that have been in these latter ages of the world. I have been writing some account of it to Mr. M'Laurin; but since then I have seen a thanksgiving sermon of Mr. Prince's, preached on that occasion; in which is a much more distinct, particular, and (I suppose) exact account of the matter (which sermon you will doubtless see). Though there is something that I observed in my letter to Mr. M'Laurin, of the coming of that fleet, its being overruled for our preservation, in this part of the land where I dwell, when eminently exposed, and when we have all reason to think our enemies in Canada had formed designs against us, that Mr. Prince does not mention.

In my last letter to you, I wrote you some thoughts and notions I had entertained, concerning the pouring out of the sixth vial on the river Euphrates, and the approach of the happy day of the church's prosperity and glory, and the utter destruction of antichrist, and other enemies of the church, so often spoken of in the Holy Scriptures: I signified it as what appeared to me probable, that one main thing intended by the drying up the river Euphrates, was the drying up the temporal supplies and income of the antichristian church and kingdom; and suggested it to consideration whether God, appearing so wonderfully for the taking Cape Breton, and the American fishery, thereon depending, out of the hands of the French, and thereby drying up so great a fountain of the wealth of the kingdom of France, might not be looked upon as one effect of the sixth vial. I would now also propose it to be considered, whether God's so extraordinarily appearing to baffle the great attempt of the French nation, to repossess themselves of this place, be not some confirmation of it; and whether or no the almost ruining the French East India trade, by the dreadful hand of Heaven, in burying their stores at Port L'Orient, and the taking so many of their ships by Commodore Barnet, and also the taking so many of their South Sea ships, vastly rich, and several other things of like nature, that might be mentioned, may not probably be further effects of this vial. But whatever be thought of these particular events, and the application of the prophecies to them; yet it appears to me, that God's late dealings, both with Great Britain and the American plantations, if they be duly considered, as they are in themselves and circumstances, afford just reason to hope that a day is approaching for the peculiar triumphs of divine mercy and sovereign grace, over all the unworthiness, and most aggravated provocations of men. If it be considered what God's past dealings have been with England and Scotland for two centuries past, what obligations he has laid those nations under, and particularly the mercies bestowed more lately; and we then well consider the kind, manner, and degree, of the provocations and wickedness of those nations, and yet that God so spares them, and has of late so remarkably delivered them, when so exposed to deserved destruction: and if it be also considered what God's dealings have been with this land, on its first settlement, and from its beginning hitherto, and how long we have been revolting and growing worse, and what great mercy he has lately granted us, on the late remarkable striving of his Spirit with us, and how his Spirit has been treated, his mercy and grace despised, and bitterly opposed, how greatly we have backslidden, what a degree of stupidity we are sunk into, and how full the land has been of such kinds of wickedness, as have approached so near to the unpardonable sin against the Holy Ghost, and how obstinate we are still in our wickedness, without the least appearances of repentance or reformation; and it be then considered how God has of late made his arm bare, in almost miraculous dispensations of his providence, in our behalf, to succeed us against our enemies, and defend us from them:—I say, if these things be considered, it appears evident to me, not only that God's mercies are infinitely above the mercies of men; but also that he has, in these things, gone quite out of the usual course of his providence and manner of dealings with his professing people, and I confess, it gives me great hope that God's appointed time is approaching, for the triumphs and displays of his infinite, sovereign grace, beyond all that ever has been before, from the beginning of the world; at least I think there is much in these things, considered together with other remarkable things God has lately done, to encourage and animate God's people unitedly to cry to God, that he would appear for the bringing on those glorious effects of his mercy, so often foretold to be in the latter days; and particularly to continue that concert for prayer, set on foot in Scotland, and which it is now proposed to continue seven years longer. My wife and children join with me in respectful, cordial salutations to you and yours.

That we may be remembered in your prayers, is the request, dear Sir, of your affectionate brother,

JONATHAN EDWARDS."

To the letter from Mr. Gillespie, Mr. Edwards returned the following answer.

"*Northampton, Sept.* 4, 1747.

Rev. and dear Sir,

I received your letter of Nov. 24, 1746, though very long after it was written. I thank you for it, and for your proposing a correspondence. Such an offer I shall gladly embrace, and esteem it a great privilege, more especially from the character I have received of you from Mr. Abercrombie, who I perceive was intimately acquainted with you.

As to the objections you make against some things contained in my work *on Religious Affections*, I am sorry you did not read the book through before you made them; if you had, perhaps the difficulties would not have appeared quite so great. As to what is contained in the 78th and 79th pages, I suppose there is not the least difference of opinion between you and me, unless it be concerning the signification and propriety of expressions. I am fully of your mind, and always was without the least doubt of it; 'That every one, both saint and sinner, is indispensably bound, at all seasons, by the Divine authority, to believe instantly on the Lord Jesus; and that the command of the Lord, 1 John iii. 23. that we should believe on the name of his Son Jesus Christ, as it is a prescription of the moral law, no less binds the sinner to immediate performance, than the commandment not to kill, to keep the sabbath day, or any other duty, as to the *present* performance of which, in way of duty, all agree the sinner is bound; and that men are bound to trust the divine faithfulness, be their case with respect to light and darkness, sight, &c. what it will; and that no situation they can be in, looses them from obligation to glorify the Lord at all seasons, and to expect the fulfilment of his words; and that the sinner who is without spiritual light or sight is bound to believe, and that it is a duty *at that very time* incumbent on him to believe.' But I conceive that there is a great deal of difference between these two things, *viz.* its being the duty of a man, who is without spiritual light or sight, to believe, and its being his duty to believe without spiritual light or sight, or to believe while he yet remains without spiritual light or sight. Just the same difference, which there is between these two things, *viz.* its being *his* duty who has no faith to believe, and its being his duty to believe without faith, or to believe without believing. I trust none will assert the latter, because of the contradiction which it implies. As it is not proper to say, it is a man's duty to believe without faith, because it implies a contradiction; so I think it equally improper to say, it is a man's duty to believe without those things which are essentially implied in faith, because that also implies a contradiction. But a spiritual sight of Christ, or knowledge of Christ, is essentially implied in the very nature and notion of faith; and therefore it is absurd to talk of believing on Christ, without spiritual light or sight. It is the duty of a man, who is without those things which essentially belong to faith, to believe; and it is the duty of a man, who is without those things which essentially belong to love, to love God; because it is an indispensable obligation that lies on all men at all times, and in all circumstances, to love God: but yet it is not a duty to love God without loving him, or continuing without those things which essentially belong to his love. It is the duty of those who have no sense of the loveliness of God and have no esteem of him, to love him, and they are not in the least excused, by the want of this sense and esteem in not loving him one moment; but yet it would be properly nonsense to say it is their duty to love him, without any sense of his loveliness, or esteem of him. It is indeed their duty this moment to come out of their disesteem, and stupid wicked insensibility of his loveliness, and to love him. I made the distinction (I thought) very plainly, in the midst of those sentences you quote as exceptionable. I say expressly, p. 74, 'It is truly the *duty* of those who are in darkness, to *come out* of darkness into light and *believe;* but, that they should confidently believe and trust, while they yet remain *without* spiritual light or sight, is an anti-scriptural and absurd doctrine.' The misunderstanding between us, dear Sir, I suppose to be in the different application of the particle *without*, in my use of it, and your understanding of it, or what we understand as spoken of and supposed in the expression, *without spiritual light or sight*. As I use it, I apply it to the *act* of believing, and I suppose it to be very absurd to talk of an act of faith *without* spiritual light or sight, wherein I suppose you will allow me to be in the right.

As you understand it, it is applied to *duty* or *obligation*, and you suppose it to be not at all absurd, to talk of an obligation to believe without spiritual light or sight, but that the obligation remains full, where there is no spiritual light or sight, wherein I allow you are in the right. I think, Sir, if you read what I have said in my book on this head again, it will be exceedingly apparent to you, that it is thus that I apply the preposition *without*, and not as you before understood it. I thought I had very plainly manifested, that what I meant by *being in darkness* was *being in spiritual blindness*, and so in a dead, stupid, and unchristian frame, and not what is commonly called being without the light of God's countenance, under the hidings of his face. Great numbers in this country proceed on the supposition, in their opinions and practice, that there really is such a manner of believing, such a kind of faith as this, *viz.* a confident believing and firm trusting in God in the dark, in the sense just mentioned, which is the subject matter of Divine prescription, and which many actually have. Indeed there are innumerable instances of such as are apparently in a most negligent, apostate, and every way unchristian and wicked frame; who yet, encouraged by this principle, retain a strong confidence of their piety, and imagine that herein they do their duty and glorify God, under the notion of trusting God in the dark, and hoping against hope, and not relying on their own righteousness; and they suppose it would show a legal spirit to do otherwise. I thought it would be manifest to every reader that I was arguing against such persons as these.

You say, 'It merits consideration, whether the believer should ever doubt of his state, on any account whatever, because doubting, as opposed to believing, is absolutely sinful.' Here, Sir, you seem to suppose that a person's *doubting of his own good estate*, is the proper opposite of *faith;* and these and some other expressions in your letter seem to suppose that *doubting of one's good estate*, and *unbelief*, are the same thing; and so, that *confidence in one's good estate*, and *faith*, are the same thing. This, I acknowledge, I do not understand; I do not suppose *faith*, and *a person's believing that he has faith*, to be the same thing. Nor do I take *unbelief*, or being without faith, and *doubting whether he has it*, to be the same thing, but entirely different. I should have been glad either that you had taken a little more notice of what I say on this head, p. 79, 80, or that you had said something to convince me that I am wrong in this point. *The exercise of faith is doubtless the way to be delivered from darkness, deadness, backsliding, &c.* or rather is the deliverance; as forsaking sin is the way to deliverance from sin, and is the deliverance itself. The exercise of grace is doubtless the way to deliverance from a graceless frame, which consists in the want of the exercise of grace. But as to what you say, or seem to intimate, that a person's being confident of his own good estate, is the way to be delivered from darkness, deadness, backsliding, and prevailing iniquity; I think, whoever supposes this to be God's method of delivering his saints, when sunk into an evil, careless, carnal, and unchristian frame, first to assure them of their good estate and his favour, while they yet remain in such a frame, and to make *that* the means of their deliverance, does surely mistake God's method of dealing with such persons. Among all the multitudes I have had opportunity to observe, I never knew one dealt with after this manner. I have known many brought back from great declension, who appeared to me to be real saints; but it was in a way very different from this. *In the first place*, conscience has been awakened, and they have been brought into distressing fears of the wrath of God. Thus they have become the subjects of a new work of humiliation, and have been led deeply to feel that they deserve his wrath, even while they have feared it, before God has delivered them from their apprehensions, and comforted them with a renewed sense of his favour.

As to what I say of the necessity of *universal obedience*, or of *one way of known sin, (i. e.* so as properly to be said to be the way and manner of the man,) being exception enough against a man's salvation; I should have known better what to have said further about it, if you had briefly shown how the passages of Scripture which I mention, and the arguments which I deduce from them, are insufficient for the proof of this point. I confess they appear to me to approve it as fully, as any thing concerning the necessary qualifications of a Christian can be proved from Scripture.

You object against my saying, p. 259, 'Nor can a true saint ever fall away to such a degree, that ordinarily there shall be no remarkable difference between his behaviour, after his conversion, and before." This, I think, implies no more than that his behaviour, in similar circumstances, and under similar trials, will have a remarkable difference. As to the instances of David and Solomon, I am not aware that the Scriptures give us any where so full a history of their behaviour before their conversion, as to enable us to compare it with their subsequent life. These examples are uncertain. But I think those doctrines of the Scriptures are not uncertain, which I mention in the passage you cite, to prove that converts are new men, new creatures, that they are renewed not only within but without, that old things are passed away and all things become new, that they walk in newness of life, that the members of their bodies are new, that whereas they before were the servants of sin, and yielded their members servants of iniquity, now they yield them servants of righteousness unto holiness.

As to the doubts and cases of difficulty you mention, I think it needless for a divine of your character, to apply for the solution of them to one, who ought rather to take the attitude of a learner. However, since you are pleased to insist on my giving my mind upon them, I would observe, with regard to the first case you mention, that of a person incessantly harassed by Satan, &c. you do not point out the nature of the temptations with which he is harassed; and without this, I think it impossible to give proper advice and directions concerning it. Satan is to be resisted in a very different manner, in different kinds of onsets. When persons are harassed with those strange, horrid impressions, to which persons afflicted with hypochondria are often subject, he is to be resisted in a very different manner, from what is proper in cases of violent temptation to gratify some worldly lust. In the former case, I should by no means advise men to resist the devil by entering the lists with him, and engaging in a violent struggle with the grand adversary; but rather by diverting the mind from his frightful suggestions, by going on stedfastly and diligently in the ordinary course of duty, without allowing themselves time and leisure to attend to his sophistry, and by committing themselves to God in prayer. That is the best way of resisting the devil, which crosses his design most; and he more effectually disappoints him in such cases, who treats him with neglect, than he who engages in a direct conflict, and tries his strength and skill with him, in a violent dispute or combat. The latter course rather gives him an advantage; and if he can get persons thus engaged in a violent struggle, he gains a great point. He knows that hypochondriacal persons are not qualified to maintain it. By this he diverts him from the ordinary course of duty; and having gained his attention to what he says, he has opportunity to use all his craft and subtilty. By such a struggle he raises a deeper melancholy, weakens the mind still more, gets the unhappy man faster and faster in his snares, and increases his anxiety of mind; which is the very thing by which he mainly accomplishes all his purposes with such persons.

As to the difficulty of verifying Rom. viii. 28. 'All things shall work together for good to them that love God,' in the case of a Christian who falls under backsliding and spiritual decays; it is not perfectly obvious how this is to be interpreted, and how far it may hence be inferred, that the temptations of Christians from Satan and an evil world, and their declensions and sins, shall surely work for their good. However, since you desire my thoughts, I will endeavour to express them.

Two things may be laid down, as certain and indubitable, concerning this doctrine of the apostle.

First. The meaning cannot be that God's actual dispensations towards each Christian are the best for him *of all that are possible;* or that all things which are ordered for him, or done with respect to him, are in all respects better for him than any thing which God could have ordered or done, issuing in the highest good and happiness to which he can possibly be brought; for that implies that God will confer on every one of his elect as much happiness as he can confer, in the utmost exercise of his omnipotence; and this sets aside all those different degrees of grace and holiness here, and glory hereafter, which he bestows according to his sovereign pleasure.

All things work together for good to the saints; all may have a concurring tendency to their happiness, and may finally issue in it, and yet not tend to, or issue in, the highest possible degree of happiness. There is a certain measure of holiness and happiness, to which each one of the elect is eternally appointed, and all things that relate to him work together to bring to pass *this appointed measure of good.* The text and context speak of God's *eternal purpose* of good to the elect, predestinating them to a conformity to his Son in holiness and happiness; and the implicit reasoning of the apostle leads us to suppose that all things will purely concur to bring to effect God's eternal purpose. Hence from his reasoning it may be inferred, that all things will tend to, and work together to accomplish, that degree of good which God has purposed to bestow upon them, and not any more. Indeed it would be in itself unreasonable to suppose any thing else; for as God is the supreme orderer of all things, doubtless all things shall be so ordered, that with one consent they shall help to bring to pass his ends and purposes; but surely not to bring to pass what de does not aim at, and never intended. God, in his government of the world, is carrying on his own designs in every thing; but he is not carrying on that which is not his design, and therefore there is no need of supposing, that all the circumstances, means, and advantages of every saint, are the best in every respect that God could have ordered for him, or that there could have been no circumstances or means of which he could have been the subject, which would with God's usual blessing have issued in his greater good. Every Christian is a living stone, that, in this present state of preparation, is fitting for the place appointed for him in the heavenly temple. In this sense all things undoubtedly work together for good to every one who is called according to God's promise. He is, all the while he lives in this world, by all the dispensations of Providence towards him, fitting for the particular mansion in glory which is appointed and prepared for him.

Secondly. When it is said, that 'all things work together for good to them that love God,' it cannot be intended that all things, *both positive and negative, are best for them;* in other words, that not only every positive thing, of which Christians are the subjects, or in which they are concerned, will work for their good, but also, that when any thing is absent or withheld from them by God in his providence, that absence or withholding is also for their good, in such a sense, as to be better for them than the presence or bestowment would have been; for this would have the same absurd consequence which was mentioned before, *viz.* That God makes every Christian as happy as he possibly can make him. And if so, it would follow that God's withholding from his people greater degrees of the sanctifying influences of his Spirit, is for their good, and that it is best for them to live and die with so small a measure of piety as they actually possess, which is the same as to say, that it is for their good to have no more good, or that it is for their happiness to have no more happiness here and hereafter. If we carefully examine the apostle's discourse in Rom. viii. it will be apparent that his words imply no such thing. All God's creatures, and all that he does in disposing of them, is for the good of the Christian; but it will not thence follow, that all God's forbearing to do is also for his good, or that it is best for him that God does no more for him.

Hence, with regard to the position, that the sins and temptations of Christians are for their good; I suppose the following things to be true:

1. That all things, whatsoever, are for their good, things negative as well as positive, in this sense, that *God intends that some benefit to them shall arise from every thing,* so that somewhat of the grace and love of God will hereafter be seen to have been exercised towards them in every thing. At the same time, the sovereignty of God will also be seen, with regard to the measure of the good or benefit aimed at, in that some other things, if God had seen cause to order them, would have produced a higher benefit. And with regard to negative disposals—consisting, not in God's doing, but forbearing to do, not in giving, but withholding—some benefit, in some respect or other, will ever accrue to them, even from these; though sometimes the benefit will not be equal to the benefit withheld, if it had been bestowed. As for instance, when a Christian lives and dies comparatively low in grace; some good improvement shall be made even of this, in his eternal state, whereby he shall receive a real benefit, though the benefit shall not be equal to the benefit of a higher degree of holiness, if God had bestowed it.

2. God carries on a design of love to his people, and to each individual Christian, not only in all things of which they are the subjects while they live, but also in all his works and dispensations, and in all his acts from eternity to eternity.

3. That the sin, in general, of Christians, is for their good, in this respect, *viz.* that through the sovereign grace and infinite wisdom of God, the fact that they have been sinful fallen creatures, and not from the beginning perfectly innocent and holy as the elect angels, will issue in a high advancement of their eternal happiness; and that they shall obtain some additional good, on occasion of all the sin of which they have been the subjects, or have committed, beyond what they would have had if they never had been fallen creatures.

4. The sin of Christians cannot in this sense be for their good, that it should finally be best for them, that while they lived in this world, their restoration and recovery from the corruption to which they became subject by the fall, was no greater, that the mortification of sin, and spiritual vivification of the soul, was carried on to no higher degree, that they were so deficient in love to God, love to men, humility, and heavenly-mindedness, that they did so few good works, and consequently, that in general, they had so much sin, and so little holiness; for in proportion as one of these is more, the other will be less, as infallibly, as darkness is more or less, in proportion to the diminution or increase of light. It cannot finally be better for Christians, that in general, while they live, they had so much sin of heart and life, rather than more holiness of heart and life; because the reward of all at last will be *according to their works.* He that sowed sparingly shall reap sparingly, and he that sowed bountifully shall reap also bountifully; and he that builds wood, hay, and stubble, shall finally suffer loss, and have a less reward, than if he had built gold, silver, and precious stones, though he himself shall be saved. But notwithstanding this,

5. The sins and falls of Christians may be for their good, and for the better, in this respect, that the issue may be better than if the temptation had not *happened,* and so the occasion not given, either for the sin of yielding to the temptation, or the virtue of overcoming it: and yet not in this respect, (with regard to their sins or falls in general,) that it should be better for them in the issue, that they have *yielded* to the temptation offered, than if they had *overcome.* For the fewer victories they obtain over temptation, the fewer are their good works, and particularly of that kind of good works to which a distinguished reward is promised in Rev. ii. and iii. and in many other parts of Scripture. The word of God represents the work of a Christian in this world as a warfare, and it is evident in the Scriptures, that he who acquits himself as the best soldier, shall win the greatest prize. Therefore, when Christians are brought into backslidings and decays, by being overcome by temptations, the issue of their backslidings may be some good to them, beyond what they would have received if the temptations had never existed; and yet their backslidings in general may be a great loss to them in this respect, that they shall have much less reward, than if the temptations had been *overcome,* and they had persevered in spiritual vigour and diligence. But yet this don't hinder, but that,

6. It may be so ordered by a sovereign and all-wise God, that the falls and backslidings of Christians, through their being overcome by temptations in some particular instances, may prove best for them, not only because the issue may be greater good to them, than they would have received if the temptation had not *happened,* but even greater in that instance, than if the temptation had been *overcome.* It may be so ordered, that their being overcome by that temptation, shall be the occasion of their having greater strength, and on the whole, obtaining more and greater victories, than if they had not fallen in that instance. But this is no where promised, nor can it be so, that, in the general, it should prove better for them that they were foiled so much, and did overcome so little, in the course of their lives, and that finally their decay is so great, or their progress so small. From these things it appears,

7. That the saying of the apostle, *all things work together for good to them that love God,* though it be fulfilled in some respects to all Christians, at all times and in all circumstances, yet it is fulfilled more especially and eminently to Christians *continuing in the exercise of love to God,* not falling from the exercises, or failing in the fruits of divine love in times of trial. Then it is, that temptations, enemies, and suffering, will be best for them, working that which is most for their good every way; and they shall be more than conquerors over tribulation, distress, persecution, famine, nakedness, peril, and sword, Rom. viii. 35—37.

8. As God is carrying on a design of love to each individual Christian, in all his works and dispensations whatsoever, so the particular design of love to them which he is carrying on, is to fit them for and bring them to their appointed place in the heavenly temple, or to that identical degree of happiness and glory in heaven, which his eternal love designed for them, and no other. For God's design of love or of happiness to them, is only just what it is, and is not different from itself; and to fulfil this particular design of love, every thing which God does, or in any respect disposes, whether it be positive, privative, or negative, contributes; because, doubtless, every thing which God does, or in any respect offers, tends to fulfil his aims and designs. Therefore, undoubtedly,

9. All the while the Christian lives in the world, he is preparing for his appointed mansion in glory, and fitting for his place in the heavenly building. All his temptations, though they may occasion, for the present, great spiritual injuries, yet at last shall be an occasion of his being more fitted for his place in glory. Hence we may determine, that however the Christian may die in some respects under the decay of spiritual comfort, and of some religious affections, yet every Christian dies at that time when his habitual fitness for his place in the heavenly temple is most complete, because otherwise, all things which happen to him while he lives, would not work together to fit him for that place.

10. God brings his people, at the end of their lives, to this greatest fitness for their place in heaven, not by diminishing holiness in their hearts, but by increasing it, and carrying on the work of grace in their souls. If it be not so, that cannot be true, that where God *has begun a good work he will perform it, or carry it on to the day of Christ;* for if they die with a less degree of holiness than they had before, then it ceases to be carried on before the day of Christ comes. If holiness finally decreases, then Satan so far finally obtains the victory. He finally prevails to diminish the fire in the smoking flax; and then how is that promise verified, that God *will not quench the smoking flax, till he bring forth judgment unto victory?* So that it must needs be, that although Christians may die under decay, *in some respects,* yet they never die under a real habitual decay of the work of grace *in general.* If

they fall, they shall rise again before they die, and rise higher than before, if not in joy, and some other affections, yet in greater degrees of spiritual knowledge, self-abasement, trust in God, and solidity and ripeness of grace.

If these things which have been observed are true, then we may infer from them these corollaries.

1. That notwithstanding the truth of the apostle's declaration in Rom. viii. 28. Christians have cause to lament their leanness and unfruitfulness, and the fact that they are guilty of so much sin, not only as it is to the dishonour of God, but also as it is likely to redound to their own eternal loss and damage.

2. That nothing can be inferred from this promise, which is calculated to set aside or make void the influence of motives to earnest endeavours to avoid all sin, to increase in holiness, and abound in good works, from an aim at a high and eminent degree of glory and happiness in a future world.

3. That though it is to the eternal damage of Christians, ordinarily, when they yield to and are overcome by temptations; yet Satan and the other enemies of Christians, from whom these temptations come, are always wholly disappointed in the temptation, and baffled in their design to hurt them, inasmuch as the temptation and the sin which it occasions, are for the saints' good, and they receive a greater benefit in the issue, than if the temptation had not been, and yet less than if the temptation had been overcome.

As to Mr. Boston's *View of the Covenant of Grace*, I have had some opportunity to examine it, and I confess I do not understand the scheme of thought presented in that book. I have read his *Fourfold State of Man*, and liked it exceedingly well. I think, in that, he shows himself to be a truly great divine.

Hoping that you will accept my letter with candour, and remember me in your prayers, I subscribe myself

Your affectionate and obliged
brother and servant,
JONATHAN EDWARDS."

In October, 1744, a number of ministers in Scotland, among whom, I believe, were all the correspondents of Mr. Edwards in that country, thinking that the state of the church and the world called loudly for united extraordinary prayer to God, that he would deliver the nations from their miseries, and fill the earth with his glory; proposed that Christians universally should, for the two years then next ensuing, set apart a portion of time, on Saturday evening and sabbath morning, every week, to be spent in prayer for this purpose; and that they should still more solemnly devote the first Tuesday in the last month of each quarter of the year, to be spent either in private, social, or public prayer to God, for the bestowment of those blessings on the world. Mr. Edwards not only welcomed the proposal as soon as he received it, but did all in his power to promote its general acceptance by the American churches; and the following letter, alluding to a more particular account of the subject in one to Mr. M'Laurin, which I have not been able to procure, will in some measure apprize the reader of the efforts which he made for this purpose.

"To the Rev. William M'Culloch.

Northampton, Sept. 23, 1747.

Rev. and dear Sir,

I thank you for your letter of March 12, 1747, which I suppose lay a long while at Mr. Prince's in Boston, before I received it, through Mr. Prince's forgetfulness. It seems he had forgotten that he had any such letter; and when I sent a messenger to his house, on purpose to inquire whether I had any letter lodged there for me from Scotland, he told him no; when I suppose this letter had been long in his house: and I should probably never have had it at last, had not one of my daughters had occasion to go to Boston, who made a visit at the house, and made a more full inquiry.

I am sorry to hear of your affliction, through your indisposition that you speak of, and desire to be thankful to the God of all mercy for his goodness, in restoring you again to health.

I have, in my letter to Mr. M'Laurin, given a particular account of what I know, concerning the propagation of the Concert for United Prayer, in America; which you will doubtless have opportunity to see. The propagation of it is but slow; but yet so many do fall in with it, and there is that prospect of its being further spread, that it is a great encouragement to me. I earnestly hope, that they, that have begun extraordinary prayer for the outpouring of the Spirit of God, and the coming of Christ's kingdom, will not fail, or grow dull and lifeless, in such an affair, but rather that they will increase more and more in their fervency. I have taken a great deal of pains to promote this concert here in America, and shall not cease to do so, if God spares my life, as I have opportunity, in all ways that I can devise. I have written largely on the subject, insisting on persuasions, and answering objections; and what I have written is gone to the press. The undertaker for the publication encourages me that it shall speedily be printed. I have sent to Mr. M'Laurin a particular account of it.

You desire to hear how it was with the people of New England, when we were threatened with an invasion by the French fleet, the last summer. As to the particular circumstances of that wonderful deliverance, the fullest and best account I have ever seen of it, is in Mr. Prince's Thanksgiving Sermon on that occasion; which, in all probability, you have seen long before this time. Nor need you be informed by me, of the repeated mercy of God to us, in confounding our enemies in their renewed attempt this year, by delivering up their fleet, in its way hither, into the hands of the English. In all probability, that fleet was intended for the execution of a very extensive design, against the English colonies, in conjunction with the French forces in Canada. For there was an army lay waiting at Nova Scotia, which, on the news of the sailing of their fleet, immediately left the country, and returned to Canada, over the lake Champlain, towards New England and New York; and they, or a part of them, attacked Fort Saratoga, in New York government, and killed or took about fifty men that were drawn out of the fort; but desisted from any further attempts, about the time we may suppose they received the news of the defeat of their fleet. And very soon after they received this news in Canada, the French there released most of our captives, and sent one ship loaded with them, to the number of about one hundred and seventy, to Boston, and another ship with about sixty, if I remember right, to Louisburg. The reasons that induced them so to do, are not known, and can only be guessed at by us; but, by their doing it very soon after they received the news of the loss of their fleet, it looks as though that had great influence in the affair. New England has had many other surprising deliverances from the French and Indians; some of which I have given a particular account of, in my letter to Mr. M'Laurin; which it would be needless for me to repeat, seeing you have such frequent opportunities with him. These deliverances are very wonderful and affecting; our enemies own that the heavens are on our side, and fight for us; but there are no such effects of these mercies upon us that are the subjects of them, as God requires, and most justly expects. The mercies are acknowledged in words, but we are not led to repentance by them; there appears no such thing as any reformation or revival of religion in the land. God's so wonderfully protecting and delivering a people, whose provocations have been so great, and who do so continue in apostasy and provocation, is very marvellous; and I can think of no account that can be given of it, so probable as this, that God has a design of mercy to the rising generation, and that there are a great number of the elect among our children, born and unborn, and that for these elect's sake, God will not suffer us to be destroyed, having a design to bring forth a seed of the posterity of this people, to inherit and dwell in this land, that shall be a holy seed, and a generation of his servants. And so that those words are applicable to us, Isa. lxv. 8, 9. 'Thus saith the Lord, As the new wine is found in the cluster, and one saith, Destroy it not, for a blessing is in it; so will I do for my servants' sakes, that I may not destroy them all. And I will bring forth a seed out of Jacob, and out of Judah an inheritor of my mountains; and mine elect shall inherit it, and my servants shall dwell there.' I am full of apprehensions, that God has no design of mercy to those that were left unconverted, of the generation that were on the stage, in the time of the late extraordinary religious commotion, and striving of God's Spirit; unless it be perhaps a small gleaning from among them. But it may be, when their little ones, the generation that was then in their childhood, are brought fully on the stage of action, God will abundantly pour out his Spirit, and revive and carry on his work, here and elsewhere in the christian world.*

I thank you for taking the pains of writing to me your thoughts of the forty-two months of the treading down of the holy city, which are new and entertaining. The chief objection against what you propose, that I can think of, is, that the forty-two months of the treading down the holy city, seems to be the same period with the one thousand two hundred and sixty days of the witnesses prophesying in sackcloth, mentioned in the very next verse, in immediate connexion with this; and *that* the same with the one thousand two hundred and sixty days of the woman's being in the wilderness, chap. xii. 6.; and *that* the same with the time, times, and an half of the woman's being in the wilderness, v. 14.; and that the same with the time, times, and an half of the reign of the little horn, Dan. vii. 25.; and with the forty-two months of the reign of the beast, Rev. xiii. 5.; and that this evidently signifies the duration of the reign of antichrist; which is a thing entirely diverse from the sum of the times of the city of Jerusalem's being under the dominion of pagans, Saracens, Persians, and Turks, as you represent. However, it is possible that what you mention may be one way wherein that prophecy, Rev. xi. 2. may be fulfilled. For God's word is oftentimes fulfilled in various ways: as one way, wherein the prophetical representation of the beast with the seven heads is fulfilled, is in the seven successive forms of government that idolatrous Rome is under; and another way that it was fulfilled, was by Rome's being built on seven hills. One way that the seventy years captivity of the Jews was fulfilled, was in its being seventy years from Jehoiachim's captivity to Cyrus's decree; and another way that it was fulfilled, was in its being seventy years from Zedekiah's captivity to Darius's decree, Ezra 6.; and another way that it was fulfilled, was in its being seventy years from the last carrying away of all, Jer. lii. 30. to the finishing and dedication of the temple. But I expect no certainty as to these things, or any of the various conjectures concerning the time of the calling of the Jews, and the fall of the kingdom of the beast, till time and fulfilment shall decide the matter. However, I cannot think otherwise, than that we have a great deal of reason to suppose, that the beginning of that glorious work of God's Spirit, which, before it is finished, shall accomplish these things, is not very far off; and there is very much in the word of God, and in the present aspects of Divine Providence, to encourage us greatly in our begun concert for extraordinary united prayer for the coming of Christ's kingdom. Let us therefore go on with what we have begun in that respect, and continue instant in prayer, with all perseverance, and increase more and more in faith and fervency; and not keep silence, nor give God any rest, till he establish, and make Jerusalem a praise in the earth.

And remember in your prayers, dear Sir,

Yours, in great esteem and affection,

JONATHAN EDWARDS."

The continuation of this concert for united and extraordinary prayer was proposed in a Memorial from Scotland, dated August 26, 1746, signed by twelve clergymen of that country, and circulated soon after in all the American colonies. To secure the general adoption of the proposed measure, Mr. Edwards first preached to his people a series of sermons in its favour, and then published them in the form of a treatise, with the title, "An Humble Attempt to promote Explicit Agreement and Visible Union among God's People, in Extraordinary Prayer for the Revival of Religion, and the Advancement of Christ's Kingdom on Earth, pursuant to Scripture Promises, and Prophecies concerning the Last Time." This work was immediately republished in England and Scotland, and extensively circulated in both countries, as well as in America, and had great influence in securing the general adoption of the measures proposed—a measure which was pursued for more than half a century by many of the American churches, and only discontinued on the adoption of a more frequent concert—the monthly concert—for united and extraordinary prayer, for the same great object, proposed at an association of the ministers of the Baptist churches, in the counties of Northampton, Leicester, &c. held at Nottingham in 1784, and observed the first Monday evening of each month; and now extensively adopted throughout the christian world.

In the course of this treatise, Mr. Edwards was led, in

* It was postponed to the time of the children of the generation here referred to.

answering objections, to examine an interpretation of prophecy, until then most generally if not universally received: *viz. That the kingdom of Christ could not come, until there had previously been a time of most extreme calamity to the church of God, and prevalence of her antichristian enemies against her, as represented in* Rev. xi. *by the slaying of the witnesses.* Some years before this, Mr. Edwards had examined the Apocalypse with great care, in connexion with the prophecy of Daniel; in order to satisfy himself whether the *slaying of the witnesses* was to be regarded as past or future. This he did with his pen in his hand; and a brief abstract of his views on this point, is found in the answers to the 4th and 5th objections in the Humble Attempt. The views of prophecy, here presented by Mr. Edwards, were, I believe, at the time wholly new to the christian world, and were at first regarded by many as doubtful if not erroneous; but have since produced the general conviction that the downfall of popery and the ultimate extension of the kingdom of Christ, are far less distant than has been supposed—a conviction remarkably supported by the whole series of providential dispensations. And there can be no doubt that this conviction has been a prime cause of the present concentrated movement of the whole church of God, to hasten forward the reign of the Messiah. As long as it was the commonly received opinion of Christians that the church was yet destined to experience far more severe and overwhelming calamities, than any she had hitherto known—calamities amounting to an almost total extinction—before the time of her final prosperity; the efforts and the prayers of Christians for the arrival of that period of prosperity were chiefly prevented: inasmuch as it was, in effect, to labour and pray for the almost total extinction of the church of Christ, during a period of indefinite extent, as well as to labour and pray, if speedy success should crown their efforts, for the destruction, if not of their own lives, yet of those of their children and immediate descendants. In the sections referred to, he endeavours to show, and by arguments which are yet unanswered, that the severest trials announced in prophecy against the church of God were already past, that her warfare was even then almost accomplished, and that the day of her redemption was drawing nigh. By establishing this point; and by presenting the arguments in a manner so clear and convincing, as wholly to supersede the necessity of any subsequent treatise on the subject; the work in question, through the Divine blessing, has exerted an influence, singularly powerful, in rousing the church o. Christ to that series of efforts which is to result in her final victory.

CHAPTER XV.

ARRIVAL OF DAVID BRAINERD AT NORTHAMPTON—HIS SICKNESS AND DEATH AT THE HOUSE OF MR. EDWARDS—HIS PAPERS—DEATH OF JERUSHA, THE SECOND DAUGHTER OF MR. E.—HER CHARACTER—CORRESPONDENCE OF MR. E. WITH REV. JOHN ERSKINE—ABSTRACT OF MR. E.'S FIRST LETTER TO MR. ERSKINE—PLAN CONCEIVED OF THE FREEDOM OF THE WILL—DEATH OF COL. STODDARD—KINDNESS OF MR. ERSKINE—LETTER OF MR. E. TO HIM—SECOND LETTER FROM MR. GILLESPIE—LETTER TO MR. M'CULLOCH—LETTER TO MR. ERSKINE—LETTER FROM MR. WILLISON—LIFE AND DIARY OF BRAINERD—LETTERS TO MESSRS. ERSKINE, M'CULLOCH, AND ROBE—ORDINATION OF REV. JOB STRONG—ANECDOTE OF REV. MR. MOODY—LETTER OF MR. E. TO HIS DAUGHTER MARY—SECOND LETTER TO MR. GILLESPIE.

THE reader will recollect, that while Mr. Edwards was at New-Haven, in September, 1743, he formed an acquaintance with DAVID BRAINERD, then a missionary to the Indians at *Kaunaumeek*,* and became his counsellor at a most interesting period of his life. In March 1747, Brainerd, in consequence of extreme ill health, took leave of his Indians in New Jersey, and in April came into New England; when he was invited by Mr. Edwards to take up his abode in his own house. He came there on the 28th of May, apparently very much improved in health, cheerful in his spirits, and free from melancholy, yet at that time probably in a confirmed consumption. Mr. Edwards had now an opportunity of becoming most intimately acquainted with him, and regarded his residence under his roof as a peculiar blessing to himself and his family. "We enjoyed," he observes, "not only the benefit of his conversation, but had the comfort and advantage of having him pray in the family from time to time." He was at this time very feeble in health; but in consequence of the advice of his physician, he left Northampton for Boston, on the 9th of June, in company with the second daughter of Mr. Edwards. They arrived on the evening of the 12th, among the family relatives of Mr. Edwards in Boston, and for a few days the health of Brainerd appeared much amended; but a relapse on the 18th convinced his friends that his recovery was hopeless. Contrary to their expectations, however, he so far revived, that on the 20th of July they were able to leave Boston, in company with his brother, Mr. Israel Brainerd, and on the 25th they reached Northampton. Here his health continued gradually to decline, until early in October it was obvious that he would not long survive. "On the morning of Lord's day, Oct.

* *Kaunaumeek* was an Indian settlement, about five miles N. W. from New Lebanon, on the main road from that village to Albany. The place is now called *Brainerd's Bridge*, and is a village of a few houses, on the *Kayaderosseras creek*, where that road crosses it. It was thus named, not after the missionary, but after a relative of his of the name of Brainerd, who some years since planted himself in this spot, and built the bridge across the creek, now a toll bridge. The mountain, about a mile N. W. of the bridge, still bears the name of Kaunaumeek. The creek winds beautifully in the valley beneath, and forms a delightful meadow. In 1823, I found an aged negro on the spot, about one hundred years of age, who had passed his life in the vicinity. He was about twenty-one years old when Brainerd resided at Kaunaumeek, but never saw him. He told me that the house which Brainerd built here stood on the first little knowl, or hillock on the left of the road, and on the W. or N. W. side of the creek immediately after passing the bridge; and that the Indian settlement was down in the meadow, at some distance below the bridge. On following the stream, I discovered an old Indian orchard, the trees of an Indian burying ground, and the ruins of several buildings of long standing. He also informed me, that the Indians had often told him, that Mr. Brainerd was "a very holy man," and that he resided at Kaunaumeek but a short time.

4," says Mr. Edwards, "as my daughter Jerusha, who chiefly attended him, came into the room, he looked on her very pleasantly, and said, 'Dear Jerusha, are you willing to part with me?—I am quite willing to part with you: I am willing to part with all my friends: though if I thought I should not see you and be happy with you in another world, I could not bear to part with you. But we shall spend a happy eternity together." He died on Friday, Oct. 9, 1747, and on the Monday following, Mr. Edwards preached the sermon at his funeral, from 2 Cor. v. 8. entitled, "True Saints when absent from the Body are present with the Lord;" which was published in the December following.

Brainerd, after destroying the early part of his Diary, left the residue in the hands of Mr. Edwards, to dispose of as he thought best. Mr. Edwards concluded to publish it, in connexion with a brief Memoir of his life.

In the ensuing February, Jerusha, the second daughter of Mr. and Mrs. Edwards, was removed by death. Her father, in a note to the Memoirs of Brainerd, thus alludes to this distressing event. "Since this, it has pleased a holy and sovereign God, to take away this my dear child by death, on the 14th of February, next following, after a short illness of five days, in the 18th year of her age. She was a person of much the same spirit with Brainerd. She had constantly taken care of and attended him in his sickness, for nineteen weeks before his death; devoting herself to it with great delight, because she looked on him as an eminent servant of Jesus Christ. In this time, he had much conversation with her on the things of religion; and, in his dying state, often expressed to us, her parents, his great satisfaction concerning her true piety, and his confidence that he should meet her in heaven, and his high opinion of her not only as a real Christian, but as a very eminent saint: one whose soul was uncommonly fed and entertained with things which pertain to the most spiritual, experimental, and distinguishing parts of religion: and one, who, by the temper of her mind, was fitted to deny herself for God, and to do good, beyond any young woman whatsoever whom he knew. She had manifested a heart uncommonly devoted to God in the course of her life, many years before her death; and said on her death-bed, that *she had not seen one minute, for several years, wherein she desired to live one minute longer, for the sake of any other good in life, but doing good, living to God, and doing what might be for his glory*."

In the course of the year 1747, an epistolary correspondence was commenced between Mr. Edwards and the Rev. John Erskine of Kirkintilloch, afterwards the Rev. Dr. Erskine of Edinburgh, which was continued to the close of Mr. Edwards's life. This gentleman, possessing superior talents, and having every advantage of birth, fortune, and education, made choice of the clerical profession, in opposition to the prevailing wishes of his family; and in May, 1744, took charge of the parish of Kirkintilloch near Glasgow. In 1753, he was translated to a parish in the borough of Culross, and, in the autumn of 1758, to one of the parishes in Edinburgh. Distinguished alike for his learning and piety, for his honourable and munificent spirit, and for his firm attachment to evangelical religion, he adorned every station which he filled by a faithful and conscientious discharge of its various duties—private, social, and public;—enjoyed the high respect of the wise and good, not only in Great Britain, but extensively in both continents; and died in 1803, in his 82d year, having been the correspondent, successively, of President Edwards, of his son Dr. Edwards, president of Union College, and of his grandson President Dwight, for the period of fifty-six years.

Mr. Erskine began the correspondence with Mr. Edwards early in 1747, through the intervention of Mr. M'Laurin of Glasgow, by sending him the "Remains of Mr. Hall"—a memoir, written by himself, of a most respectable and beloved fellow-student in theology, a young gentleman of uncommon promise. I have none of the letters of Mr. Erskine to Mr. Edwards, and not having been able to procure the first letter of Mr. Edwards to Mr. Erskine, written in the summer of 1747, must be indebted for the following account of it to the "Life of Dr. Erskine," by the Hon. and Rev. Sir H. M. Wellwood.—"On this occasion Mr. Edwards expressed, with great tenderness and delicacy, his sympathy with one, who had lost his most intimate and estimable friend in the prime of life, the companion of his youth, and, for a considerable time before his death, the delightful and affectionate associate of his studies and of his piety.

"In a postscript to this letter, he mentioned his book on Religious Affections, then just published, and at the same time sent his correspondent a copy of it in a book of which it is not too much to say, that it is not only worthy of the talents and sincerity of its author, but that while it shows that he was neither forward nor rash in estimating striking or sudden impressions of religion, it contains more sound instruction on its particular subject, and lays down more intelligible and definite rules to distinguish true from false religion, and to ascertain by distinct characters the genuine spirit of vital piety, separated from all fanatical delusions, than any other book which has yet been given to the world.

"In the same postscript to Mr. Edwards's first letter to Dr. Erskine, he gave him a general sketch of a plan which he had then formed, and which he afterwards executed with so much ability in his book on the Freedom of the Will;—a book which, whether his opinions be questioned or adopted, has certainly given him an eminent station both among philosophers and divines. 'I have thought,' he says, 'of writing something particularly and largely on the Arminian controversy in distinct discourses on the various points in dispute, to be published successively, beginning first with a discourse concerning the Freedom of the Will, and Moral Agency; endeavouring fully and thoroughly to state and discuss those points of liberty and necessity, moral and physical inability, efficacious grace, and the ground of virtue and vice, reward and punishment, blame and praise, with regard to the dispositions and actions of reasonable creatures.'

"Such was the first idea of a work from which Mr. Edwards afterwards derived his chief celebrity as an author; but a considerable time intervened before he found it possible to make any progress in his design."

The death of Col. Stoddard, which occurred at Boston, on the 19th of June this year, was a loss severely felt, not only by Mr. Edwards and the people of Northampton, but by the county and the province at large. He was eminently distinguished for his strength of understanding and energy of character, and had for a long period unrivalled influence in the council of the province. He was also a man of decided piety, and a uniform friend and supporter of sound morals and evangelical religion. Mr.

Edwards preached a sermon on his death from Ezek. xix. 12. which was immediately published.

Early in the next year Mr. Edwards received from Mr. Erskine a number of books which he valued very highly, as containing the ablest exhibition and defence of the system of doctrines usually styled *Arminianism*, which had at that time appeared before the public. In the following letter he acknowledges the kindness of his correspondent, and at the same time alludes to the decease of his daughter.

"To the Rev. John Erskine

Northampton, Aug. 31, 1748.

Rev. and dear Sir,

I this summer received your kind letter of Feb. 9, 1748, with your most acceptable present of *Taylor on Original Sin*, and his *Key to the Apostolic Writings*, with his *Paraphrase on the Epistle to the Romans;* together with your Sermons and Answer to Doct. Campbell. I had your Sermons before, sent either by you or Mr. M'Laurin. I am exceedingly glad of those two books of Taylor's. I had before borrowed and read Taylor on Original Sin; but am very glad to have one of my own; if you had not sent it, I intended to have sought opportunity to buy it. The other book, his Paraphrase, &c. I had not heard of; if I had I should not have been easy till I had seen it, and been possessed of it. These books, if I should live, may probably be of great use to me. Such kindness from you was unexpected. I hoped to receive a letter from you, which alone I should have received as a special favour.

I have for the present been diverted from the design I hinted to you, *of publishing something against some of the Arminian tenets*, by something else that Divine Providence unexpectedly laid in my way, and seemed to render unavoidable, *viz.* publishing Mr. Brainerd's Life, of which the enclosed paper of proposals give some account.

It might be of particular advantage to me, here in this remote part of the world, to better informed what books there are that are published on the other side of the Atlantic; and especially if there be any thing that comes out that is very remarkable. I have seen many notable things that have been written in this country against the truth, but nothing very notable on our side of the controversies of the present day, at least of the Arminian controversy. You would much oblige me, if you would inform me what are the best books that have lately been written in defence of Calvinism.

I have herewith sent the two books of Mr. Stoddard's you desired. The lesser of the two was my own; and though I have no other, yet you have laid me under such obligations that I am glad I have it to send to you. The other I procured of one of my neighbours.

I have lately heard some things that have excited hope in me, that God was about to cause there to be a turn in England, with regard to the state of religion there for the better; particularly what we have heard, that one Mr. West, a clerk of the privy council, has written in defence of Christianity, though once a notorious deist; and also what Mr. Littleton, a member of the house of commons, has written. I should be glad if you would inform me more particularly in your next concerning this affair, and what the present state of infidelity in Great Britain is.

It has pleased God, since I wrote my last to you, sorely to afflict this family, by taking away by death, the last February, my second daughter, in the eighteenth year of her age; a very pleasant and useful member of this family, and one that was esteemed the flower of the family. Herein we have a great loss; but the remembrance of the remarkable appearances of piety in her, from her childhood, in life, and also at her death, are very comfortable to us, and give us great reason to mingle thanksgiving with our mourning. I desire your prayers, dear Sir, that God would make up our great loss to us in himself.

Please to accept of one of my sermons on Mr. Brainerd's death, and also one of my sermons on Mr. Buell's instalment. I desire that for the future your letters to me may be directed to be left with Mr. Edward Bromfield, merchant in Boston. My wife joins with me in respectful and affectionate salutations to you and Mrs. Erskine. Desiring that we may meet often at the throne of grace in supplications for each other,

I am, dear brother, your obliged friend,

Fellow labourer, and humble servant,

JONATHAN EDWARDS."

"P. S. I desired Mr. Prince to send to you one of my books on the subject of the concert for prayer for a general revival of religion the last year; and he engaged to do it; but I perceive he forgot it, and it was long neglected. But I have since taken some further care to have the book conveyed; so that I hope that ere this time you have received it.

In the conclusion of your letter of Feb. 9, you mention a design of writing to me again by a ship that was to sail the next month for Boston. That letter I have not received."

Mr. Gillespie, imagining that the difficulties which he had stated in his former letter, were not satisfactorily cleared up in the answer of Mr. Edwards, addressed to him the following reply.

Letter from Mr. Gillespie.

"*Sept.* 19, 1748.

Rev. and very dear Sir,

I had the favour of yours in spring last, for which I heartily thank you. I did not want inclination to make you a return long ago, as I prize your correspondence, but some things concurred that effectually prevented me, which has given me concern.

It was my desire to be informed, and my inclination to make you understand, how some passages in your book on Religious Affections did appear to me and some others, your real friends and well-wishers in this country, that determined me to presume to offer you some few remarks on the passages mentioned in my former letter; and desire of further information engages me now, with all respect, to make some observations upon some things in your letter. I hope you will pardon my freedom, and bear with me in it, and set me right wherein you may find me to misapprehend your meaning, or to mistake in any other respect.

You say, 'You conceive that there is a great difference between these two things, *viz.* its being a man's duty, who is without spiritual light or sight, to believe; and its being his duty to believe without spiritual light or sight, or to believe while he yet remains without spiritual light or sight: it is not proper to say, it is a man's duty to believe *without* faith,' &c. Now, dear Sir, the difference here, I am not able to conceive; for all are bound to believe the divine testimony and to trust in Christ, which you acknowledge; and the want of spiritual light or sight does not loose from the obligation one is laid under by the divine command to believe instantly on Christ, and at all seasons, as his circumstances shall require, nor does it excuse him in any degree for not believing. I own that a person who has no spiritual light or sight cannot eventually believe, if by light or sight is meant the influence or grace of the Spirit, by which one's mind is irradiated to take up the object and grounds of faith, so as to be made to have a spiritual sight of Christ, and to act that grace; yet still, even when one wants this, it is his duty, and he is bound to believe, for we know it is a maxim, '*ability is not the rule of duty*.' I also acknowledge, that no person who is, and always has been, without spiritual light or sight, is bound, nor is it his duty, to believe that he has actually believed, or to conclude he is really a partaker of the faith of God's elect. I have some apprehension this is all you meant by the expressions I have noticed, and the reasoning in consequence of them; or else certainly different ideas are affixed to words with you and among us. There is indeed a great deal of difference betwixt its being one's duty to believe, or to act faith, and its being his duty to believe he has believed, or has acted divine faith; *i. e.* you say *you* apply the particle *without*, respecting spiritual light or sight, to the act of believing, by which I suppose you intend, 'all *should* believe, though none *do* really believe, *without* spiritual light or sight;' in which I entirely agree with you. The word *duty* indeed, which you use when treating that matter, is ordinarily supposed to signify the obligation the person is under by the divine authority to believe, as applied to the *matter* of faith, and not to the *act* of faith put forth in consequence of such obligation. Had I not supposed you plainly meant by the expressions I quoted from the book, the *duty* or *obligation* to believe, and not an act of faith exerted, I should have made no remarks on them. It is indeed as absurd for one to conclude he has really believed without spiritual light or sight, as to say one should believe he had believed, without those things that are essentially implied in faith. But I must differ from you in thinking it is not very proper to say, it is a man's duty to believe *without* faith, *i. e.* while he yet remains without spiritual light or sight, or to put forth an act of faith on the Saviour, however void of spiritual light or sight; for if this was not the truth, the finally impenitent sinner could not be condemned for unbelief, as the Holy Ghost declares he will be, John iii. 19, 20, 24. and that notwithstanding the power of the Spirit of faith must make him believe. I should be glad to know the precise idea you affix to the words *faith* and *believing*. I do not remember a person's reflecting on his act of faith, any where in Scripture termed believing. You remark, 'That I seem to suppose that a person's doubting of his good estate is the proper opposite of faith;' and I own, as it is a believer's duty to expect salvation through Christ, which, in other words, is to believe his good estate, Acts xv. 11. Gal. ii. 20. Eph. ii. 4. Job xix. 25. doubting of it must be his sin, an effect of unbelief, a part of it, and thus the proper opposite of faith, considered in its full compass and latitude. Thus once doubting of his good estate by a true believer, and unbelief in one branch of it, or one part and manner of its acting, are the same thing. Faith and unbelief are opposed in Scripture, and what is the opposite of one ingredient in unbelief must be faith in one part of it,—one thing that belongs to its exercise. A person's believing that the Lord will never leave nor forsake him, who is in a gracious state, Heb. xiii. 5. is owned to be his indispensable duty, and this comprehends or supposes his being confident of his good estate, and is properly divine faith, because it has the divine testimony now cited, on which it bottoms, Jer. iii. 19. The Lord says, 'Thou shalt call me, My father, and shalt not turn away from me;' which is evidently faith, and no less manifestly belief of one's good estate, or being confident of it, because the expression must denote the continued exercise of faith, in not turning away from the Lord. Crying *Abba Father*, Rom. viii. 15. is faith in the Lord as one's father, which must have a being confident of one's good estate inseparable from it, or rather enwrapped in it. I suppose what I have mentioned is very consistent with what you say, 'That faith, and persons believing that they have faith, are not the same;' for one's believing that he has faith, simply and by itself, has for its object the man's inward frame, or the actings and exercises of his spirit, and not a divine testimony. This is not divine faith; but, as I have laid the matter, a being confident of one's good estate has for its foundation the word of God, Heb. xiii. 5, &c. ultimately, —at least; to be sure this is *one* way in which faith is acted, or one thing in its exercise. I am far from thinking unbelief, or being without faith, and doubting whether they have faith, to be the same thing in an unconverted sinner, whom your words, '*being without faith*,' must mean, and therein we entirely agree. But I must think, as to the believer, his doubting whether or not he has faith, is sinful, because it is belying the Holy Ghost, denying his work in him, so there is no sin to which that doubting can so properly be reduced as unbelief. You know, dear Sir, doubting and believing are opposed in Scripture, Matt. xiv. 31. xxi. 21. Mark xi. 23. and I cannot exclude from the idea of doubting, a questioning the truth and reality of a work of grace on one's soul; for the Holy Ghost requires us to believe the reality of his work in us, in all its parts, just as it is, and never would allow us, much less call us to sin, or to believe a falsehood, that one is void of grace, when he has it, that good might come of it, *i. e.* that the person might be awakened from security, &c. 1 John iii. 3. 'Every man that hath this hope in him purifieth himself, as he is pure;' I think intimates, that in proportion to the degree of one's hope, that the Lord is his Father, will be his aim after sanctification, and his attainment of it; if so, to renounce this hope, to throw it up at any season, on any account, must be unlawful; whence I infer, for the believer to doubt of his gracious state, to call it in question for any reason whatever, so as to raze it, it is simply sinful, 1 John ii. 12, 15. 'I write unto you, little children, because your sins are forgiven you, *viz.* Love not the world.' Here forgiveness of sin is used as a motive or incitement not to love the world; and this reasoning of the apostle would lose all its force, were it incumbent on a believer, at some seasons, to think he was not within the bond of the new covenant,—he is bound ever to hold that conclusion fixed. The exhortation, not to cast away one's confidence, certainly comprehends a call to persevere in believing in our interest in the Lord, and to practise it at all seasons, Heb. x. 35. Job's friends endeavoured to make him question, whether the root of the matter was in him, and to conclude that he was a hypocrite. He resolved, though the Lord should slay him, he would trust in him, chap. xiii. 15. being confident of his own good estate, chap. xxvii. 3, 5. 'All the while my breath is in me;' and ver. 5. 'Till I die, I will not remove my integrity from me;' and we see, from the whole tenor of his book, what there he resolved, he actually did practise; he never entertained the thought of supposing the Lord was not his God, notwithstanding the grievous eruptions of iniquity in him, in quarrelling with the sovereignty of God, &c. And in the end, the Lord condemned his friends for speaking of him 'the things that were not right,' and pronounced that Job, his servant, had said of him the thing 'that is right,' Job iv. 1.; from which, it is to be presumed, he was approved in guarding against razing his state.* Also, 2 Cor. i. 12. what the apostle terms there, 'his rejoicing,' was what supposed his being confident of his good estate, that he was participant of a principle of grace, which made him capable of acting, as he did, with godly sincerity. All which, with other considerations, do satisfy me, that a believer never should raze his state on any account whatever; and that, as has been mentioned, doubting of his gracious state is sinful, one way of unbelief, its acting in him, though not the direct and immediate opposite of that acting of faith by which a person renounces his own righteousness and closes with Christ, yet the opposite of the posterior exercise of faith *in* him, and *upon* the promise, in certain respects. Your book is now lent, and therefore I cannot take notice, as you wish and I incline, of what you say on this head, p. 80, 81. more particularly than I have done. However, I have, I think, touched the precise point in difference between us.

You observe, I seem to intimate, 'A person's being confident of his own good estate is the way to be delivered from darkness, deadness, backsliding, and prevailing iniquity.' And you add, that 'you think whoever supposes this to be God's method of delivering his saints, when sunk into an evil, careless, carnal, and unchristian frame, first to assure them of their good estate and his favour, while they yet remain in such a frame, and so to make *that* the means of their deliverance, does surely mistake God's method of dealing with such persons.' Here I think you represent the case too strong; for the words in my letter to which you refer, were, 'I have heard it taught that the believer was bound to trust in the Lord in the very worst frame he could be in, and that the exercise of faith was the way to be delivered from darkness, deadness, backsliding,' &c. And afterwards, I said, when questioning whether the believer should ever doubt of his estate on any account whatever, 'I know the opposite has been prescribed; when the saint is plunged in the mire of prevailing iniquity.' Now, as a believer may be thus plunged, and yet sin at that instant be his grief and burden, Rom. vii. 24. and he may have the hope and expectation of being relieved from it even then, Psalm lxv. 3. I do not think my words convey the idea you affix to them. Also you will observe, I do not say, 'that a person's being confident of his own good estate is the way to be delivered from,' &c. but 'that the believer was bound to trust the Lord in the worst frame,' &c. This I mention, precisely to state my words, and they are, I think, very defensible; for the believer is called 'to trust in the Lord for ever,' Isa. xxvi. 4. If so, when in the situation mentioned; for this is a trusting in the Lord as one's God. The woman with the issue of blood, her touching Christ, and the success, is, I suppose, a call and encouragement to touch him by faith, for having the worst soul-maladies healed, Mark v. 25. Trusting in the Lord for needful blessings, in the situation mentioned, gives him the glory of his faithfulness, and engages him to act in the believer's behalf; thus to do, it is both duty and interest. Jonah, when in a course of grievous rebellion, and under awful chastisement for it, when perhaps he had actually disclaimed interest in the Lord, or was in danger of it, said, 'he would look again toward the Lord's holy temple,' chap. ii. 4. evidently in exercise of faith in the Lord as his God, the Lord assuring him of his good estate and his favour, by the operation of the Spirit causing him so to act, and to be conscious of it; and, verse 7. 'when my soul fainted within me, I remembered the Lord, and my prayer came in unto thee, into thine holy temple.' Here is my assertion exemplified in practice, by a believer, I may venture to say, in an evil frame, when the Spirit breathed upon him. Though a prophet, he deliberately disobeyed the express instructions of his Lord, chap. i. 2, 3. and in a careless frame, for he slept securely in the sides of the ship, during a tempest raised for his sake, and when the heathen mariners every one called upon his god, chap. i. 5, 6. So far was he from dreading, as he had reason to do, that the Lord would plead a controversy with him for the part he acted, that dismal security, awful carelessness, and a carnal frame had seized him; for he declared to the Lord, that he said to him in his country, he would repent of the evil he had said he would do to the Ninevites, if they turned from their evil way, and assigned that for the reason why he fled to Tarshish, chap. iv. 2.; and thus would rather that the Lord should want the honour, that would redound to his name by the repentance, though only outward, of the Ninevites, than that the whole city should be destroyed, one of the largest the sun shone upon, and the most populous, and that himself should lose the honour and comfort of being the instrument of its preservation, than that *he* should fall under the imputation of being a false prophet, for which there would yet have been no foundation. Horrid carnality this! for as it was dreadful selfishness, it may, in that view, be termed carnality,—astonishing pride! this 'filthiness of the spirit' is worse than that of the flesh; and, all circumstances of his conduct considered, he was not only in an ungodly frame, but in an inhumane one, and he sinned presumptuously in one of the highest degrees, we may suppose, in which it is possible for a believer so to act; notwithstanding it appears the happy turn was begun in him, under the influence of the Spirit, by renewing his faith in the Lord as his God, and being confident of his good estate; upon which he prayed, as already mentioned, and was heard by his God, see verses 7, 8. was delivered out of his then dismal and dangerous circumstances, chap. ii. 12.—Thus I have done more than I was bound to do, and have proved the point, not only in the manner in which I expressed it, but in the strong light your words, a comment on mine, had set it; for one plain scripture instance, such certainly as that I have given, is sufficient, as agreed, to prove any thing. It is so far from being a mistaking of God's method of dealing with such persons, as you suggest, (pardon me, dear Sir,) to say, that it is 'the Lord's method of delivering his saints when in a backsliding condition, first to assure them of their good estate and his favour, and so to make that the means of their deliverance;' that I give you the words of the Holy Ghost for it is as express and full as any thing possibly can be, Jer. iii. 12, 13, 14.; verse 14. 'Turn, O backsliding children, saith the Lord, for I *am married unto you*.' This was, to be sure, the Lord's intimating the new covenant relation in

* This, and several other Scotticisms, I do not feel at liberty to alter.

which he stood to the spiritual Israel among them; and, verse 22 of that chapter, the Lord says, 'Return, ye backsliding *children*, and I will heal your backslidings;' and in the close of the verse, we have the Lord's thus assuring them of their good estate and his favour, shown to be the effectual mean of the backsliding being healed: 'Behold, we come unto thee; for thou art *the Lord our God*.' Hos. xiv. 4. 'O Israel, return unto *the Lord thy God;* for thou hast fallen by thine iniquity.' Here the first words of the Lord's message to his *spiritual* Israel, are, that '*the Lord was their God*,' and the expression, 'fallen by iniquity,' conveys a very strong idea, when applied to a believer, perhaps as strong, as is comprehended in your words, '*evil, &c. frame;*' and I must think this verse is so expressed to work on holy ingenuousness in them, for its revival when under the ashes of corruption. It would perhaps be no difficult matter to multiply scripture testimonies of such kind; but these adduced are, I think, full proof of the point, for confirmation of which they are brought. The love of Christ constrains the believer to return from folly, as well as to other things in other respects, 2 Cor. v. 14. I might argue here from the efficacy of the love of God apprehended, the genius of the new creature, and nature in believers, and a variety of other topics, but choose, without expatiating, to confine myself to precise scripture testimonies. As to what you say, that 'among all the multitudes you have had opportunity to observe, you never knew one dealt with in this manner, but have known many brought back from great declensions, that appeared to be true saints, but it was in a very diverse way from this: first conscience awakened; they brought into great fear of the wrath of God; his favour hid; the subjects of a kind of new work of humiliation; brought to great sense of deserving God's wrath, while they yet feared it, before God had delivered them from apprehension of it, and comforted with a renewed sense of his favour.' All I observe upon this is, that the way I have laid down, is obviously that which the Lord declares in his word, he takes, for bringing back his people from declensions, and thus that in it mercy is to be expected, whatever the Lord may be pleased to do in sovereignty, and he will not be limited; also, persons do not perceive every thing that passes within them, far less are they capable to give a full distinct account of every thing of each kind. Experiences of Christians are to be brought to the touch-stone of the infallible bar, and to stand or fall by it; the Bible is not to be brought to their test, and judged of by them. I own we may mistake the sense of Scripture, but it is so obvious in the passages I have quoted, that I cannot see how it can be misapprehended.

I cannot say any thing now, about the other remarks I made on your book, touched on in your letter, because I have not now the book to look into. I understand the passages about prevalence of sin, so as to denominate a person not in a gracious state, better, by what you have wrote; and, if any difficulty shall remain after comparing your book and letter, I may come to propose it to you afterwards.

What you wrote about the case of temptation was very agreeable, and I thank you for it. I shall now state the case more plainly, because I want much your further thoughts upon it. It is precisely this. A person finds himself beset by evil angels, what if I remember right *Voetius* terms *obsessio*, and one in that situation *obsessus;* they incessantly break into his body and mind, sometimes by vain, at other seasons by vile thoughts, now by the thoughts of a business neglected, which was a seasonable thing to be done, then by a scripture text, or an engaging thought of some spiritual truth, when entrance is not to be had another way, and by a variety of other methods. They do all they can, perpetually to teaze, defile, and discourage; he is conscious of the whole transaction, and finds his spirit broken by it, and goes not about to reason with Satan, knows the expediency of this course, is aware Satan wants no better, than that he pray much and long against his temptations, and so wont pray himself out of breath, by his instigation; is convinced the remedy is to get them kept out of body and mind; trusts, in dependence on the Lord, to the use of medical, moral, and religious means for that end, because experience shows all of them are expedient and advantageous in their place; but all is in vain, no relief for him, relish of divine things wore off the mind, no comfort, is rendered callous by cruel constant buffetings, he cries, but the Lord hears not. By what I understand, this is a just representation of the case, and will lead you to the knowledge of other circumstances in it. What would you advise such a person to do? How shall he recover savour of spiritual truths and objects?

I wondered you said nothing in your letter, about what I mentioned in mine, respecting *supposed immediate revelations of facts and future events*, as special favours conferred on some special favourites of heaven. I give in to your sentiments on that point, expressed in the three treatises you have published, and greatly like what Mr. Brainerd said on the subject, as mentioned, I think, by you, in the funeral sermon on him, which I perused with a great deal of pleasure; and shall now mention some things, said in favour of that principle, of which people are very tenacious, that I may have your answers to them, which will be a singular favour done me, for certain reasons: for example, John xvi. 13. is affirmed to be an express promise of such a thing;—it is urged, the thing is not contrary to Scripture, and therefore, *may be;*—it is urged, John xiii. 24—27. is an example of it, an intimation what the Lord will do in such kind when it pleaseth him, till the end of time. It is pretended, and indeed this is the strength of the cause, that the thing is a matter of fact, has nothing to do with the Bible, therefore nothing about it is to be expected in Scripture, and simply to deny it in all cases, is daringly to limit the power of God. The Lord has not said he will *not* grant it, and how dare any say it cannot be? It is reasoned, there are numbers of well attested instances of the thing in different ages and places, facts are stubborn things, and to deny them all is shocking, an overturning of all moral evidence. It is insisted on, that the thing *has been* formerly; it is confessed, and why may it not be now? We are told, a considerable time before a thing happened, that it has been impressed on the mind in all its circumstances, which exactly happened in every point; if when asked, what one can say to this, he says, perhaps it was from Satan, to this it is answered, does *he* know future contingent events? The reply is at hand, it is not above him to figure a thing on the fancy long before, which he is resolved by some means to bring about; but to all this it is answered by advocates for immediate revelations, such reasoning tends to sap one of the main pillars of evidence of the divinity of the scripture prophecies.

I have, by what I remember, given you the force of the argument, to establish what has had, I too well know, very bad effects, as commonly managed, in Britain, as well as in New England; a history of instances of them would not be without its use, and materials for it are not wanting. I will long much to see what you say in way of reply to all this. I am sure you cannot employ time better than in framing it. I should have mentioned that the authority of eminent divines is brought to bear upon them, whose stomachs stand at swallowing things, like additions to the Bible,—Mr. Fleming, in *the Fulfilling of the Scriptures*, Dr. Goodwin, &c. But on this, it has been pleasantly observed, that the authority of the worthies in the eleventh of the Hebrews, would have done a good deal better. I have some apprehension this is a point of truth, which the Lord is to clear up in this age.

I have read your *Humble Attempt*, and with much satisfaction; was charmed with the scriptures of the latter day of glory set in one point of light. I do think humbly your observations on *Lowman* have great strength of reason. The killing of the witnesses, as yet to come, has been to me a grievous temptation; for which reason, I peruse with peculiar pleasure what you say on this subject; but if you answer the objection, 'It would appear that the seventh trumpet is to sound soon after the resurrection of the witnesses, and the kingdoms of the world, &c. but that has not happened, therefore the witnesses are not killed;' I say, if this you answer, I have forgot.

I should have also mentioned, that it seems evident, the doctrine of immediate revelations must be simply denied as unscriptural, and thus well-founded in *no* case; or it must be allowed in its full compass and latitude, let the consequences of it be what they will, for if the thing is allowed *possible*, reasonings about its effects will not conclude nor avail; I can see no middle way between the two things. That principle taken for granted by almost all, in all times past, is, as I mentioned in my last letter, to me a surprising thing.

Mr. Whitefield arrived at Edinburgh Wednesday last, and was to preach on Thursday evening; but as I am fifteen miles from that city, of which two miles by sea, I have not yet heard of the effects of his preaching, or the number of the audiences; I wish they may be as frequent as when he was last here. May Divine power specially attend his ministrations! We need it much, as we are generally fallen under great deadness. I believe he will find use for all his prudence and patience in dealing with us, for different reasons. With great pleasure, friends to vital religion, and to him, are informed he is to make no collections at this time! I was glad to hear you write, that he laboured with success in New England, in rectifying mistakes he had favoured, about intimations made by the Lord to his people, &c. and heartily wish he may be directed to apply an antidote here, where it is also needed.

I have tired you with a long epistle, and shall therefore now break off. What you was pleased to favour me with, upon the difficulty started from Rom. viii. 28. was very acceptable, and I thank you much for it. I will expect a letter from you the first opportunity after this comes to hand; and in it all the news of New England, particularly some account of the state of religion with you. It gives me pleasure to think, I may write you my sentiments upon every thing without reserve. Please make my affectionate compliments to my friend Mr. Abercrombie, when you see him, or write to him, and tell him, I remember I am in his debt for a letter. I hope the ship I am informed of, for carrying this, is not sailed, and therefore it will not be so long in coming to your hand, after being writ, as my last.

I am, &c."

Letter to Mr. M'Culloch.

"To the Rev. Mr. M'Culloch.

Northampton, Oct. 7, 1748.

Rev. and dear Sir,

I thank you for your letter of Feb. 19, 1748, which I received the week before last. I had also, long before that, received the letter you speak of, which you wrote the spring before, dated March 12, 1747, which I wrote an answer to, and sent it to Mr. Prince of Boston, and committed it to his care; and am very sorry that you never received it. I am far from being weary of our correspondence. I ever looked on myself as greatly honoured and obliged by you, in your beginning this correspondence; and have found it pleasant and profitable; and particularly your last letter, that I have but now received, has been very agreeable and entertaining; especially on account of the good news it contains. I cannot but think many things mentioned in your letter, and the letters of my other correspondents in Scotland, which came with yours, are great things, worthy to be greatly taken notice of, and to be an occasion of much rejoicing and praise to all that love Zion: *viz.* The remarkable change in one of the clerks of the privy council; God's stirring up him and Mr. Littleton to write in defence of Christianity; the good effect of this among men of figure and character; the good disposition of the king, and the Prince and Princess of Wales; the late awakening of two of the princesses, Amelia and Caroline, and the hopeful conversion of one or both of them; the hopeful, real piety of the Archbishop of Canterbury, and his good disposition towards experimental religion and the dissenters; several of the clergy of the church of England lately appearing to preach the doctrines of grace; several of the magistrates, in various towns in England, exerting themselves with uncommon zeal to put the laws in execution against vice; and the eminent piety of the Prince of Orange, now the stadtholder of the Seven United Provinces. These things (at least some of them) are great in themselves, and are of that nature that they have a most promising aspect on the interests of Zion, and appear to be happy presages and forerunners of yet better and greater things that are coming. They look as if the tide was turning, and glorious things approaching, by the revolution of the wheel of God's providence. I think we, and all others, who have lately united by explicit agreement in extraordinary prayer for a general revival of religion and the coming of Christ's kingdom, may, without presumption, be greatly encouraged and animated in the duty we have engaged in, by the appearance of such a dawning of light from such great darkness; and should be ungrateful if we did not acknowledge God's great goodness in these things, and faithfulness in fulfilling the promises of his word; such as these in particular, 'If any two of you shall agree on earth as touching any thing you shall ask, it shall be done of my Father which is in heaven;' and, 'Before they call, I will answer; and while they are yet speaking, I will hear.' I have already communicated these things to some belonging to this town, and other places; some have appeared much affected with them; and one that belongs to another town, has taken extracts of these passages. I design, God willing, to communicate these things to my congregation, before the next quarterly day for prayer, and also to the neighbouring ministers, who, according to our stated agreement, will be met together on that day, to spend the former part of the day in prayer among ourselves, and the latter part in public services in one of our congregations; and shall also probably communicate these things to some of my correspondents in New Jersey and elsewhere, and I cannot but think they will tend to do a great deal of good, in various respects; and particularly will tend to promote the Concert for Prayer, in these parts of the world. I desired Mr. Prince of Boston to send you one of my books on the Concert, soon after it was published; who engaged to do it; but long forgot it, as I perceived afterwards to my surprise; but since that more thorough care has been taken about that matter; and I hope you, and each of my other correspondents in Scotland, have before now received one of those books.

I thank you, dear Sir, for sending me your thoughts on some things in the prophecies of the Revelation of St. John, and for being at so much trouble as to send it twice (supposing the first letter had miscarried.) This I take as a particular mark of respect, for which I am obliged to you. I received, as I said before, your former letter, (which contained the same observations,) and sent an answer to it, wherein I gave you my thoughts, such as they were, on those subjects. But if you have received my book on United Prayer, &c. therein you have seen more fully my thoughts on some things in the Revelation, that have a near relation to the same matter that you write about; the substance of which I before had written to you in a large letter, desiring your opinion of what I wrote.

The letter I think you received, by some intimations contained in yours of March 12, 1747. But you was not pleased to favour me with any thing at all of your thoughts of what I had so largely communicated to you, to that end, that I might have your opinion. But I am not the less willing again to communicate my thoughts on your remarks.

As to what you observe concerning the number *six hundred and sixty-six*, and that number being found in the name of the present king of France; it is indeed something remarkable, that that number should be found both in his Latin and French names, as you observe; and I do not know but that the omniscient Spirit of God (who doubtless in his predictions has sometimes his eye on several things in which he knows they will be fulfilled) might have some respect to his name in the prophecy; but I can hardly think that this individual king of France, or any other particular prince in Europe, is what is chiefly intended by the beast, so largely described in the 13th chapter of Revelation, whose number is said to be six hundred and sixty-six. Of all the conjectures concerning the number of the beast, that I have lit on in my small reading, that of Mr. Potter's seems to me the most *ingenious*, who supposes the true meaning is to be found by extracting the root of the number. But after all, I have ever suspected that the thing chiefly aimed at by the Holy Spirit, was never yet found out, and that the discovery is reserved for later times. Yet one reason why Mr. Potter's conjecture does not fully satisfy me, is, the difficulty about adjusting the fractions in the root, when extracted. With respect to your very ingenious conjectures, concerning the period of *forty-two months*, or *one thousand two hundred and sixty days*, of the outer court and holy city's being trodden under-foot of the Gentiles; you know, Sir, that that forty-two months, or one thousand two hundred and sixty days, spoken of Rev. xi. 2. has been universally understood, as being the very same period with the 1260 days of the witnesses prophesying in sackcloth, spoken of in the next verse; and the one thousand two hundred and sixty days of the woman's being led in the wilderness, chap. xiii. 6. and the time, times, and half a time, of her being nourished in the wilderness from the face of the serpent, ver. 14. and the forty-two months of the continuance of the beast, chap. xiii. 5. But it does not appear to me probable that these forty-two months of the continuance of the beast, means the sum of the diverse periods in which the *plat of ground*, whereon the ancient literal Jerusalem stood, was under the dominion of the Romans, Saracens, Persians, and Turks; but the space of time during which the reign of antichrist or the popish hierarchy continues; and as to the particular time of the downfall of antichrist, you see my reasons in the forementioned pamphlet, why I think it certain that it will not be known till it be accomplished: I cannot but think that the Scripture is plain in that matter, and that it does, in effect, require us to rest satisfied in ignorance till *the time of the end* comes.

However, I should be very foolish, if I were dogmatical in my thoughts concerning the interpretation of the prophecies: especially in opposition to those who have had so much more opportunity to be well acquainted with things of this nature. But since you have insisted on my thoughts, I conclude you will not be displeased that I have mentioned them, though not altogether agreeable to yours. I am nevertheless greatly obliged to you for your condescension in communicating your thoughts to me. If we do not exactly agree in our thoughts about these things, yet in our prayers for the accomplishment of these glorious events in God's time, and for God's gracious presence with us, and his assistance in endeavours to promote his kingdom and interests, in the mean time, we may be entirely agreed and united. That we may be so, is the earnest desire of, dear Sir,

Your affectionate brother and servant,
in our common Lord,
JONATHAN EDWARDS."

In perusing the following letter, while the reader will deeply regret the loss of that from Mr. Erskine to which it is an answer, he will feel a lively interest in the mass of religious intelligence which it contains, as well as in the interesting development which it gives of the character of Governor Belcher.

"To the Rev. Mr. Erskine.

Northampton, Oct. 14, 1748.

Rev. and dear Sir,

A little while ago I wrote a letter to you, wherein I acknowledged the receipt of your letter, and the books that came with it, *viz. Taylor on Original Sin*; and *on the Romans*: with your sermons, and *Answer to Mr. Campbell*; for which most acceptable presents I would most heartily and renewedly thank you.

I sent my letter to Boston, together with one of Mr. Stoddard's *Benefit of the Gospel to the Wounded in Spirit*, and his *Nature of Saving Conversion*, with a sermon on Mr. Brainerd's death, and some account of a history of his life now in the press, to be sent to Scotland by the first opportunity; whether there has been any opportunity or no, I cannot tell. I have very lately received another letter from you, dated April 4, 1748, which was indeed exceedingly acceptable, by reason of the remarkable and joyful accounts it contains of things, that have a blessed aspect on the interests of Christ's kingdom in the world: such as the good effects of the writings of Mr. West and Mr. Littleton on some at court, and the religious concern in Mr. Randy's and Mr. Gray's parishes, the hopeful true piety of the Archbishop of Canterbury; this and the king's disposition, not only to tolerate but comprehend the dissenters; and their indifference with respect to the liturgy, ceremonies, and espiscopal ordination; the piety of the prince who is now advanced to the stadtholdership, and has it established in his family for ever; the awakening of the Princess Caroline; and the good disposition of the Princess of Wales. I think it very fit that those, who have lately entered into an union of extraordinary prayer for the coming of Christ's kingdom and the prosperity of Zion, should inform one another of things which they know of, that pertain to the prosperity of Zion, and whereby their prayers are in some degree answered; that they may be united in joy and thanksgiving, as well as in supplication; and that they may be encouraged and animated in their prayers for the future, and engaged to continue instant therein with all perseverance. I think these things forementioned, which you have sent me an account of, are worthy greatly to be observed, by those that are united in the Concert for Prayer, for their comfort, praise, and encouragement. I intend to communicate these things to my own people, before the next quarterly season for prayer, and to the neighbouring ministers, who are united in this affair; and also to my correspondents in this province, and other provinces of America. I doubt not but they will have a happy tendency and influence in many respects. I hope, dear Sir, you will continue still to give me particular information of things that appear, relative to the state of Zion and the interests of religion, in Great Britain or other parts of Europe. In so doing, you will not only inform me, but I shall industriously communicate any important informations of that kind, and spread them amongst God's people in this part of the world; and shall endeavour to my utmost to make such a use of them, as shall tend most to promote the interest of religion. And among other things I should be glad to be informed of any books that come out, remarkably tending either to the illustration or defence of that truth, or the promoting the power of godliness, or in any respect peculiarly tending to advance true religion.

I have given an account of some things, which have a favourable aspect on the interests of religion, in these American parts of the world, in my letters to Mr. Robe, and Mr. M'Laurin, sent with this; which you will have opportunity to see.

In your last letter you desired to be particularly informed of the present state of New Jersey college, and of things remarkable of a religious nature respecting the Indians. As to the former, *viz.* the state of New Jersey college: by the last accounts I had, it was in somewhat of an unsettled state. Governor Belcher had a mind to give them a new charter, that he thought would be more for the benefit of the society. Accordingly a draft of a new charter was drawn; wherein it was proposed to make considerable alteration in the corporation of trustees; to leave out some of the former trustees; and that the governor, for the time being, should be a trustee, and three or four of the council of that province. Those two things made considerable uneasiness, *viz.* leaving out some of the former trustees, and making it a part of the constitution that the governor and so many of the council should be members of the corporation. Some feared that this would not be for the health of the society; because the men in chief authority in that province have, for the most part, been men of no religion, and many of them open and professed contemners of it. How this matter has been settled, or whether these difficulties are got over, I have not been informed. As to Governor Belcher himself, he appears thoroughly engaged to promote virtue and vital religion in those parts, which already has had some good effects; vice and open profaneness, by the means, is become less fashionable among the great men, and virtue and religion more creditable. The disposition of Governor Belcher may in some measure be seen, by the following extract of a letter from him, in answer to one I wrote to him on a special occasion.

'*Burlington, New Jersey, Feb.* 5, 1748.

You will, Sir, be sure of me as a friend and father to the missionaries this way, and of all my might and encouragement for spreading the everlasting gospel of God our Saviour, in all parts and places where God shall honour me with any power or influence.

As to myself, Sir, it is impossible to express the warm sentiments of my heart, for the mercies without number with which I have been loaded, by the God who has fed me all my life long to this day; and my reflection upon his goodness covers me with shame and blushing, for I know my utter unworthiness, and that I am less than the least of all his mercies. I would therefore abhor myself, and repent in dust and ashes. You are sensible, my good friend, that governors stand in a glaring light, and their conduct is narrowly watched by friends and enemies: the one often unreasonably applaud them, while the other perhaps too justly censure them. Yet in this I am not anxious; but to approve myself to the Searcher of hearts, from whose mouth I must hear pronounced, at the great and general audit, those joyful words, Enter thou, &c.—or that terrible sentence, Depart from me, &c. Join with me then in thankfulness to God, for all the blessings and talents he has intrusted me with, and in prayer that I may employ them to his honour and glory, to the good of the people over whom he hath placed me, and so to the comfort of my own soul: that I may always remember that he that ruleth over men, must be just, ruling in the fear of God.'

In another letter which I have received, dated Burlington, N. J. May 31, 1748, he says as follows.

'I will prostrate myself before my God and Saviour, and on the bended knees of my soul, (abhorring myself in every view,) I will beg for a measure of divine grace and wisdom; that so I may be honoured, in being an instrument of advancing the kingdom of the blessed Jesus in this world, and in that way be bringing forth fruit in old age * I bless God, my heavenly Father, that I am not ashamed of the cross of Christ; and I humbly ask the assistance of sovereign grace, that, in times of tempta-

* He was 66 years old, the 8th day of January last.

tion, I may never be a shame to it, I mean that my conversation may always be such as becometh the gospel of Christ. And I tell you again, that all such as minister at the altar, and in the course of their ministry approve themselves faithful to the great Head of the church, will not only find my countenance and protection, but my love and esteem.

'As to our embryo college, it is a noble design; and if God pleases, may prove an extensive blessing. I have adopted it for a daughter, and hope it may in time become an Alma Mater, to this and the neighbouring provinces. I am getting the best advice and assistance I can in the draught of a charter, which I intend to give to our infant college, and I thank you, Sir, for all the kind hints you have given me, for the service of this excellent undertaking: and as St. Luke says of Mary, *She kept all these things, and pondered them in her heart;* so you may depend, what you have said about the college will not be lost with me; but, as far as God shall enable me, I shall exert and lay out myself in every way to bring it to maturity, and then to advance its future welfare and prosperity; for this I believe will be acceptable in the sight of God our Saviour; a relish for true religion and piety, being great strangers to this part of America. The accounts I receive from time to time, give me too much reason to fear that Arminianism, Arianism, and even Socinianism, in destruction to the doctrines of free grace, are daily propagated in the New England colleges. How horribly and how wickedly, are these poisonous notions rooting out those noble pious principles, on which our excellent ancestors founded those seminaries! and how base a return is it of the present generation, to that God, who is constantly surrounding them with goodness and mercy! and how offensive is it in the eyes of that God, who is jealous of his glory, and will take vengeance on his adversaries, and reserveth wrath for his enemies! And from these things I am led to thank you for your book, wrote in consequence of the Memorial from Scotland, for promoting a Concert in Prayer. I am much pleased with this proposal and imitation to all good Christians, and with your arguments to encourage and corroborate the design. The two missionaries you mention, Messrs. Spencer and Strong, I am told are at present at Boston. I have once and again desired Mr. Brainerd to assure them of my kindness and respect. But their affairs have not yet led them this way. I rejoice in their being appointed to carry the gospel, in its purity, to the Six Nations; and when Mr. Brainerd and they proceed to Susquehannah, they shall have all my assistance and encouragement; by letters to the king's governors where they may pass, and my letters to the sachem or chief of those Indians.'

With regard to the missionaries, Governor Belcher mentions: 'The commissioners in Boston, of the corporation in London, for the propagation of the gospel among the Indians in New England and parts adjacent, a little before Mr. David Brainerd went to Boston, the summer before his death, had received a sum of money from the estate left by the famous Dr. Williams, for the maintenance of two missionaries among the Six Nations: and having entertained a very great esteem of Mr. Brainerd, from the opportunity they had of acquaintance with him while in Boston, the committee intrusted to him the affair of finding and recommending the persons proper to be employed in this business.' Accordingly he, after much deliberation, recommended one Mr. Spencer, belonging to Haddam, his native town; and Mr. Strong, belonging to this town, Northampton; who are undoubtedly well qualified persons, of good abilities and learning, and of pious dispositions. The commissioners, on his recommendation, accepted these persons; and after Mr. Brainerd's death, sent to them; and they went down to Boston, and accepted the mission. But the commissioners did not think proper immediately to send them forth among the Six Nations; but ordered them to go and live, during the winter, in New Jersey with Mr. John Brainerd, among the christian Indians, there to follow their studies, and get acquaintance with the manners and customs of Indians; and in the spring to go with Mr. Brainerd to Susquehannah, to instruct the Indians on that river, before they went to the Six Nations. Accordingly they went and lived in New Jersey; but were discouraged as to their intended journey to Susquehannah; for they understood that the Susquehannah Indians greatly objected against entertaining missionaries, without the consent of the Six Nations, (to whom they are subject, and of whom they stand it seems in great fear,) and insisted that the missionaries should go to the Six Nations first. Therefore, in the spring, Messrs. Spencer and Strong returned to Boston, for new orders from the commissioners; who saw cause to order them to come and live at my house, till the time of an appointed interview of the governors of Boston and New York with the chiefs of the Six Nations, at Albany, in the latter part of the summer; when it was proposed that some, that should go to Albany with Gov. Shirley, should, on the behalf of the commissioners, treat with the Six Nations concerning their receiving missionaries. Messrs. Spencer and Strong did accordingly; they lived with me in the summer, and went to Albany at the time of the treaty; and the nation of the Oneidas, in particular, were dealt with concerning receiving these missionaries; who appeared free and forward in the matter. Messrs. Spencer and Strong, at that time, got some acquaintance with the chiefs of the tribe; who appeared fond of them, and very desirous of their going with them. But the grand difficulty then in the way, was the want of an interpreter; which occasioned their not going with the Indians at that time, but returning again to New England. Mr. Strong, also, was taken much out of health, which discouraged him from entertaining any thoughts of throwing himself into the fatigues and hardships of their undertaking, till the next spring. But the difficulty of the want of an interpreter is now got over; a very good one has been found; and Mr. Spencer was ordained on the 14th of the last month, and is gone with the interpreter, to go to the country of the Oneidas, about 170 miles beyond Albany, and about 130 miles distant from all settlements of the white people.

It is a thing, that has a favourable aspect on the design of propagating the gospel among the Indians, that many of late have been remarkably spirited to promote it, and liberally to open their hands in order to it. Mr. Brainerd's going to Boston before his death, and people there having some acquaintance with him, and with his labours and success among the Indians, gave occasion to a considerable number in Boston, men of good substance and of the best character, and some of them principal men in the town, to form themselves into a charitable society, that by their joint endeavours and contributions, they might promote the instruction and spiritual good of the Indians;

who have done some very liberal things for the Indians in New Jersey, and also for the Six Nations. The people of Northampton have also had their hearts remarkably opened, to contribute to the maintenance of Mr. Spencer's interpreter; and one individual at Springfield, has been moved to devote a considerable part of his estate, to promote the propagation of the gospel among the Six Nations.

As to my writing against Arminianism; I have hitherto been remarkably hindered; so that probably it will be a considerable time before I shall have any thing ready for the press; but do intend, God allowing and assisting, to prosecute that design: and I desire your prayers for the Divine assistance in it. The books you sent me, will be a great help to me; I would on no account have been without them.

I condole with you and Mrs. Erskine, on the loss of your noble and excellent father; which is doubtless a great loss to the church of God. But the glorious King of Zion, who was dead, is alive, and lives for evermore, and can raise up others in exalted stations to favour Zion; and seems to be so doing at this day, by things you give an account of in your letter. I have been the subject of an afflictive dispensation of late, tending to teach me how to sympathize with the afflicted; which I think I mentioned in my last letter to you, *viz.* the death of my second daughter, the last February.

Please to present my most affectionate and respectful salutations to your dear consort. That I and mine may be remembered in your and her prayers, is the request of

Your affectionate and obliged
Friend and brother,
JONATHAN EDWARDS."

Letter from Mr. Willison to Mr. Edwards.

" To the Rev. Mr. Edwards.

Dundee, March 17, 1749.

Rev. and dear Brother,

I thank you for yours of October last, with your two sermons, which Mr. M'Laurin sent me; which two sermons give me cause to sing of mercy as well as of judgment, that as one shining and successful youth is laid aside from labouring in the gospel, another is sent forth to it. Indeed, worthy Mr. Brainerd was one among a thousand, for carrying the gospel among the heathen, as appears by the account you give of him in your sermon, and by his Journals which have been published here, and prefaced by Dr. Doddridge, and dedicated by him to the Society at Edinburgh. We must be silent; seeing He who hath removed him is holy, just, and wise. We must also lay our hands on our mouths, with respect to the loss of our great and eminent men, such as Dr. Watts, Dr. Colman, Mr. Cowper, and others. But O, it is no loss to be absent from the body, to them who are present with the Lord. Great need have we to cry to the Lord of the vineyard, to send forth others in their room: it is easy for him to do it, from places we little expect. These are hopeful and promising accounts, which you have from your correspondents in Scotland, mentioned in your letter. May they all hold true, and be the forerunners of greater things, and the dawnings of the glory of the latter days. I may add to them, the rising of a burning and shining light of a church of England minister, in Dr. Doddridge's neighbourhood, *viz.* Mr. Hervey; for he dates his writings from Weston Favel, near Northampton. He has lately published two volumes of Meditations on all kinds of subjects, in a most orthodox, Calvinistic, and evangelical strain, in which he takes all kinds of occasions of exalting and commending his glorious Master, Christ, in a most rhetorical way, and in a style I think inimitable, and in the most moving expressions, so that it is not easy to read him without tears. He freely taxes his brethren of that church, for departing from the doctrines of grace, and of justification by imputed righteousness, &c. which were taught by the Reformers, and their own articles and homilies. And notwithstanding this uncommon freedom, which he uses with his brethren, great men, &c. never had any books such a run in England, as his; for in a year and a half's time, or thereabouts, there are five editions of them published at London, and still they are greedily bought and read, especially by persons of distinction; the style being a little too high and poetical for the vulgar. His name is James Hervey, A. B. Some say he is of noble descent, from the Earl of Bristol; but I am not sure of this. It is thought he is the man that Dr. Doddridge points at, in the life of Col. Gardiner, pages 37, 38. It looks well, that so many in England should become fond of sound evangelical writings. No doubt the books may have reached Boston by this time. Let us therefore still wait and pray in hope. I should be glad to do any thing in my power, for promoting the Concert for United Prayer, and oh that it were spread both far and near; it would be a token of a general revival of religion to be fast approaching. I know nothing that hath a greater tendency to promote the aforesaid happy Concert, than the book you lately published about it (a copy whereof you sent me, for which I humbly thank you). I wish it were universally spread, for I both love and admire the performance upon subjects so uncommon. I approve your remarks on Mr. Lowman. His reason for beginning antichrist's reign so late as the year 756, is weak, *viz.* because then King Pepin invested the pope in his temporal dominion over that province in Italy, called St. Peter's Patrimony—when it is evident that the pope had usurped his tyrannical dominion over Christ's church long before, which is the main ground of his being called antichrist; yea, the pope's usurped power was greater before King Pepin's time, than it is at this day—as for instance, in Pope Symmachus' time, anno 501; in Pope Hormisdas' time, anno 516; in Pope Boniface 3d's time, anno 606; in Pope Constantine's time, anno 713. Yea, Mr. Lowman himself gives a dreadful instance of the pope's tyranny and usurpation, both over the church and the emperor, in page 97 of his book, which happened anno 726, thirty years before he begins antichrist's reign; when Pope Gregory 2d excommunicated the Emperor Leo, for ordering images to be removed out of the churches, and forbad obedience or paying of taxes to him. Was not antichrist's reign far advanced by that time? And we have several instances of the pope's tyranny, similar to this, recorded by historians, before that which Mr. Lowman mentions; which more directly denominate him antichrist, than his temporal doings in Italy. We see how easy it is for the best of writers to slip into mistakes and wrong schemes. I agree with you, that antichrist's fall will be gradual, in the way you explain it.

I am sorry to hear of Arminianism growing in New England. But I rejoice to hear of Gov. Belcher's zeal for religion in New Jersey; may the Lord spare him and bless him. As also I am glad to hear of the hopeful prospect of the gospel's growing among the Six Nations of

Indians; and of such a youth as Mr. Spencer being sent among them: may the Lord prosper him as he did Mr. Brainerd. I sympathize with you under that affliction of your daughter's death; but it is comfortable she was helped so to live and die, as to afford such grounds of hope concerning her. And though she was the flower of your family, yet the remembering of the gracious hand, that *painted the flower*, will engage your worthy spouse and you to a becoming silence, like Aaron. As he will do what he will, let us join and say always, *Let his will be done.* I would fain be at this in my own case: may the Lord help me to more of christian submission and resignation. I am now entered into the 69th year of my age, and fallen under several distresses, whereby I have been shaken over the grave these many months past, and am laid aside from preaching. May the Lord assist me in my preparation for the dissolution of this tabernacle. I find it no easy matter to die, and to die in faith, and to die like Simeon with Jesus in his arms. I very much need your prayers for me. I am glad to hear, dear brother, that your parents are both alive, and that they hold the abilities of both body and mind so remarkably at so great an age; and particularly that your father, at seventy-nine years of age, and now near eighty, performs the whole of his ministerial work so constantly, without feeling it burdensome, and was able to travel forty miles to see you: he is indeed a wonder of his age, and would be reckoned so in this country, where few ministers come near to that age and vigour. May the Lord still spare him, with your mother, and make them still flourishing in old age; may they be blessed with much of God's gracious presence, and with the consolations and fruits of the Spirit, in their aged and declining days. I still kindly remember your worthy spouse and children remaining, and pray they may long be continued for comforts to you, and you continued for a blessing to them, to your flock, and to many others, as you already have been.

I remain, Rev. and dear brother,

Your most affectionate brother, and serv't

In our Lord,

J. WILLISON."

"P. S. The Rev. Mr. Whitefield came to Scotland in September last, and preached about two months in and about Edinburgh and Glasgow. But some brethren who employed him, being challenged for it in synods and presbyteries, and debates arising thereupon, Mr. Whitefield returned to London. To give a view of the substance of these debates, and what passed thereupon in the synod of Glasgow, I have sent you herewith a printed pamphlet containing the same, with two other books, as a small acknowledgment of your favours."

The three following letters went in the same packet to Scotland. The religious intelligence, which they communicated, will be found highly interesting at the present day. In the first of the three, is the earliest allusion, on the part of Mr. Edwards, which I have met with, to a most painful subject; the mention of which I have purposely forborne, that all which relates to it may be presented together.

Letter to Mr. Erskine.

"*Northampton, May* 20, 1749.

Rev. and dear Sir,

The day before yesterday, I received your letter of February 14th, with a pacquet, containing the pamphlets you mention in your letter; for which I am greatly obliged to you. I have not yet had opportunity to read these books, but promise myself much entertainment by them, from the occasions on which they were written, and the subject they are upon. The last letter I received from you before this, was dated April 6, 1748, so that I suppose the two letters you say you wrote to me, since those which I acknowledge the receipt of, have miscarried, which I much regret, as I much value what comes from your hand.

In one of your last letters which came to hand, you desire to be particularly informed concerning the state of religion, in these parts of the world, and particularly concerning the mission to the Indians, and the infant college in New Jersey. As to the affair of preaching the gospel to the Indians, Mr. Spencer went, the last fall, far into the western wilderness; to the Oneidas, one of the tribes of Indians called the Six Nations, living on Susquehannah river, towards the head of the river; to a place called by the Indians *Onohohquauga*, about 180 miles south-west from Albany on Hudson's river, where he continued through the winter; and went through many difficulties and hardships, with little or no success, through the failing of his interpreter; who was a woman that had formerly been a captive among the Caghnawauga Indians in Canady, who speak the same language with those Oneidas, excepting some small variation of dialect. She went with her husband, an Englishman, and is one of the people we here call *Separatists;* who showed the spirit he was of there in that wilderness, beyond what was known before. He differed with and opposed Mr. Spencer in his measures, and had an ill influence on his wife; who I fear was very unfaithful, refusing to interpret for Mr. Spencer more than one discourse in a week, a sermon upon the sabbath; and utterly declined assisting him in discoursing and conversing with the Indians in the week time. And her interpretations on the sabbath were performed very unfaithfully, as at last appeared. So that Mr. Spencer came away in discouragement in the spring, and returned to Boston, and gave the corporation there, who employed him, an account of his unexpected difficulties and disappointments; and became obliged to them to wait three months, to see if they could procure a fellow missionary, and another interpreter, to go with him to the Indians; which I believe is not much expected. If these are not obtained within the limited time, Mr. Spencer is free from any further engagements to them. Mr. Spencer is now preaching at Elizabeth-town in New Jersey, in the pulpit of the late Mr. Dickinson; and I believe is likely to settle there. He is a person of very promising qualifications: and will hopefully in some measure make up the great loss that people have sustained by the death of their former pastor.

As to the mission in New Jersey, we have from time to time had comfortable accounts of it; and Mr. John Brainerd, who has the care of the congregation of christian Indians there, was about three weeks ago at my house; and informed me of the increase of his congregation, and of their being added to from time to time, by the coming of Indians from distant places, and settling in the Indian town at *Cranberry*, for the sake of hearing the gospel; and of something of a work of awakening being all along carried on among the Indians to this day; and of some of the new comers being awakened; and of there being instances, from time to time, of hopeful conversion among them; and of a general good and pious behaviour of the professing Indians. But he gave an account also of some trouble the Indians meet with, from some of the white people; and particularly from Mr. Maurice, the chief justice of the province, a professed deist; who is sueing them for their lands under pretext of a will, made by their former king; which was undoubtedly forged. However, he is a man of such craft and influence, that it is not known how the matter will issue.

I have heard nothing new that is very remarkable concerning the college in New Jersey. It is in its infancy; there has been considerable difficulty about settling their charter. Gov. Belcher, who gave the charter, is willing to encourage and promote the college to his utmost; but differs in his opinion concerning the constitution, which will tend most to its prosperity, from some of the principal ministers that have been concerned in founding the society. He insists upon it that the governor, for the time being, and four of His Majesty's council for the province, should always be of the corporation of trustees; and that the governor should always be the president of the corporation. The ministers are all very willing that the present governor, who is a religious man, should be in this standing; but their difficulty is with respect to future governors, who they suppose are as likely to be men of no religion, and deists, as otherwise. However, so the matter is settled, to the great uneasiness of Mr. Gilbert Tennent in particular, who it is feared will have no further concern with the college on this account. Mr. Burr, the president of the college, is a man of religion and singular learning, and I hope the college will flourish under his care.

I have taken a great deal of pains in communicating to others, in various parts, the pleasing accounts you and my other correspondents in Scotland gave me last year of things of promising aspect on the interest of religion, on your side of the ocean: which have been very affecting to pious ministers and people in New England, and also in the provinces of New York and New Jersey; and hope some considerable good has been done by such tidings; particularly in animating many in the duty of extraordinary united prayer for a general revival of religion, and promoting the Concert for Prayer proposed from Scotland; which prevails more and more in these parts of the world; which, together with some other things in some places, are cause of thankfulness, and bode well to the interests of Zion, (of which I have given a more particular account in my letters to Mr. M'Laurin, Mr. Robe, and Mr. M'Culloch, sent with this,) though it be in general a very dead time as to religion, and a time of the prevailing of all manner of iniquity.

I shall send orders to Boston, that one of my books on Mr. Brainerd's life may be sent to you with this letter; if any of them are ready, as I hope they are, or will be very speedily.

I have nothing very comfortable to inform you of concerning the present state of religion in this place. A very great difficulty has arisen between my people, relating to qualifications for communion at the Lord's table. My honoured grandfather Stoddard, my predecessor in the ministry over this church, strenuously maintained the Lord's supper to be *a converting ordinance;* and urged all to come, who were not of scandalous life, though they knew themselves to be unconverted. I formerly conformed to his practice; but I have had difficulties with respect to it, which have been long increasing; till I dared no longer to proceed in the former way; which has occasioned great uneasiness among my people, and has filled all the country with noise, which has obliged me to write something on the subject, which is now in the press. I know not but this affair will issue in a separation between me and my people. I desire your prayers, that God would guide me in every step of this affair. My wife joins with me in respectful salutations to you and your consort.

I am, dear Sir, your obliged and affectionate

Brother and servant,

JONATHAN EDWARDS."

Letter to Mr. M'Culloch.

" *Northampton, May* 23, 1749.

REV. AND DEAR BROTHER,

The last letter I received from you was dated Feb. 10, 1748, to which I wrote an answer the latter end of last summer; which I suppose you received, because I perceive by letters sent me this spring, by some others of my correspondents, your neighbours, they had received letters I sent to them at the same time, and in the same packet. Your letters to me have been very acceptable; I should be glad to receive them oftener.

The letter I last received from you, and others that came with it, were peculiarly agreeable, on account of the good news they contained concerning Messrs. West and Littleton, the Archbishop of Canterbury, some in the royal family, the stadtholder, &c. These things I have taken a great deal of pains to communicate to others; and they have been very entertaining, and I hope profitable to many. I was at the pains to extract from all the letters I received at that time, those things which appeared with a favourable aspect on the interest of religion in the world, and to draw various copies to send to different parts, to such as I supposed would be most likely to be entertained and improved by them, and to do good with them; and I believe they have been of great benefit, particularly to excite and encourage God's people, in the great duty of praying for the coming of Christ's kingdom, and to promote extraordinary united prayer, in the method proposed in the Memorial from Scotland. I read these articles of good news to my own congregation, and also to the association of ministers to which I belong, when met on one of the quarterly seasons for prayer; and read them occasionally to many others; and sent a copy of one of the forementioned abstracts to Connecticut, which was carried into various parts of that government, and shown to several ministers there. I sent one to Mr. Hall of Sutton, a pious minister about the middle of this province; who, according to my desire, communicated it to other ministers, and I suppose to his people. I sent a copy to Mr. Rogers of Kittery, I suppose about seventy miles to the eastward of Boston; who in reply wrote to me, and in his letter says as follows: 'Yours of the 22d Dec. came not to my hand till the 19th of this; with which I was well pleased, and had some sweet sense of the sovereign free grace of God in the instances you mentioned, with some going forth of heart after further displays of it, in the mighty and noble of our nation, and the great ones of our own country; and indeed, that the kingdom of our exalted Redeemer might prevail in all the world. And, dear Sir, I am full in the belief, that so many of the Lord's people agreeing upon a time to unite in prayer for the pouring out of the Holy Spirit, and the coming of the Redeemer's kingdom, is from the Lord; and cannot but hope the day draws near, when he will pour out water upon the thirsty, and floods upon the dry ground; as also, that all his ministers and people, who are engaged in so delightful a work, for so noble an end, will give him no rest, till he shall make his Jerusalem a quiet habitation, a name and a praise in the earth.'

I sent another copy into New Jersey to Mr. John Brainerd, missionary to the Indians there, with a desire that he would communicate it to others as he thought would be most serviceable.

He writes in answer, March 4, 1748, as follows: 'I received yours of Jan. 12, on sabbath morning Feb. 5, and desire to acknowledge your kindness with much thankfulness and gratitude. It was a great resuscitant, as well as encouragement, to me; and I trust, has been so to many others, in these parts, who are concerned for the prosperity of Zion. The next Tuesday after, (as perhaps, Sir, you may remember,) was the quarterly day appointed for extraordinary prayer; upon which I called my people together, and gave them information of the most notable things contained in your letter. And since I have endeavoured to communicate the same to several of my neighbouring ministers, and sundry private Christians, as I had opportunity. I have also thought it my duty to send an extract, or rather a copy of it, to Gov. Belcher. I have likewise (for want of time to transcribe) sent the original to Philadelphia by a careful hand, that the Rev. Mr. Gilbert Tennent might have the perusal of it; where a copy was taken, and the original safely returned to me again. I cannot but hope that this letter, as it contains many things wherein the power and goodness of God do appear in a most conspicuous manner, will be greatly serviceable in stirring up the people of God in these parts, and encouraging their hearts to seek his face and favour, and to cry mightily to him, for the further outpouring of a gracious Spirit upon his church in the world. For my part, I think the remarkable things which your letter contains, might be sufficient to put new life into any one who is not past feeling; and as a means to excite a spirit of prayer and praise, in all those who are not buried in ignorance, or under the power of a lethargic stupor. And it is looked upon, by those whom I have had opportunity to converse with, whether ministers or private Christians, that what God has done is matter of great thankfulness and praise, and might well encourage his people to lift up the hand of prayer, and be instant therein.'

Mr. Davenport, minister of a church in Elizabeth-town in New Jersey, writes thus upon it, in a letter dated April 1, 1749: 'I thank you for sending your letter to our Brainerd open, that I might see it, which I took a copy of; and have found it again and again refreshing and animating. I read it to the ministers who met at my house for prayer, on the first Tuesday of February, and sent it afterwards to Long Island: Mr. Rivel took a copy of it, and read it in his congregation on the Island.'

I hope, dear Sir, these things will encourage you to continue your correspondence, and to go on to give me information of whatever appears in your parts of the world favourable to the interests of the kingdom of Christ. It will not only be entertaining to me; but I shall endeavour, whenever I receive such tidings, to communicate it for the entertainment and profit of God's people, as I have opportunity. I must refer you, dear Sir, to my letters to other correspondents in your neighbourhood, for other particulars relating to the state of religion in these parts of the world. And hope, when you are before the throne of grace, you will not forget

Your very affectionate friend,
And brother and servant,
JONATHAN EDWARDS."

Letter to Mr. Robe.

"*Northampton, May* 23, 1749.

REV. AND DEAR SIR,

Mr. M'Laurin, in a letter I received from him the last week, dated March 10th, 1749, informs me of a letter you had written to me, sent to him; which he had taken care of. This letter, by some means or other, has failed, and has never reached me. I intend to make inquiry after it, to see if it has not been left at Boston, and forgotten to be sent. I have reason to hope (though I have not received your letter) that you and your family are well, because Mr. M'Laurin and Mr. Erskine (the only correspondents from whom I have received letters this time) inform me of nothing to the contrary.

As to the present state of religion in these parts of the world, it is in the general very dark and melancholy. But yet there are some things which appear comfortable and hopeful; particularly, the Concert for extraordinary Prayer for the coming of Christ's kingdom, is spreading and prevailing—and we hear of awakenings and revivals of religion in some places. We have had accounts, from time to time, of religion's being in a flourishing state, in the Indian congregation in New Jersey, under the care of Mr. John Brainerd; of the congregation's increasing, by the access of Indians from distant parts; of a work of awakening carried on among the unconverted, and additions made to the number of the hopefully converted, and the christian behaviour of professors there. Mr. Brainerd was at my house a little while ago, and represented this to be the present state of things in that congregation. I had a letter from Mr. Davenport, (who is settled now as a minister over a congregation belonging to Elizabeth-town, in New Jersey,) dated April 1, 1749, wherein he says as follows: 'Mr. Lewis told me, that there has been a remarkable work of conviction prevailing in his place, ever since last December. I think he spoke of about forty under soul concern, a considerable number of them under strong convictions, and some hopefully converted. I heard lately a credible account of a remarkable work of conviction and conversion, among whites and negroes, at Hanover in Virginia, under the ministry of Mr. Davies, who is lately settled there, and has the character of a very ingenious and pious young man; whose support, in his preparation for service, Mr. Robinson* contributed much, if not mostly to; and on his death-bed gave him his books, &c.

* This Mr. Robinson was a young minister of eminent gifts and graces; I think, belonging to Pennsylvania, but had some time preached, with great success, in Virginia, in various parts; but died a few years ago in his youth

Mr. Buell, of East Hampton, on Long Island, was here last week, and gave me an account of a very considerable work of awakening at this time in his congregation, especially among the young people; and also of a yet greater work at Bridgehampton, under the ministry of one Mr. Brown, a very pious and prudent young man, lately settled there. These congregations are both pretty large. He also gave an account of religion's continuing in a very prosperous state at a part of Huntington, another town on Long Island, where was a great and general awakening, last year.

An association of ministers, between this and Boston, seem of late to have applied themselves somewhat earnestly, to invent means for promoting religion. The following is a copy of something they have agreed upon for this end, as it was sent to me, by a minister that lives that way.

"The sum and substance of the answers, given by the association, to this question, What things shall be done by us, for preventing the awful threatening degeneracy and backsliding in religion, in the present day?

These, we apprehend, may be reduced to the following heads, *viz.* Those that respect ourselves personally; those which concern the association, as such; and those which relate to our people, in our respective churches and congregations.

I. As to what respects ourselves personally.

1. We ought surely to get a deep and affecting sense of this: Whether there is not in ourselves defection, and great danger of further degeneracy; for otherwise, we shall with little heartiness undertake, or earnestness endeavour after, reformation.

2. We are not to think it amiss, that we ourselves be excited to look, with a proper attention and concern, into our own estate, into our own experiences in the divine life, and into what little proficiency we make, or declension we fall into, ourselves.

3. We must by all means see to it, that we be sound and clear in the great doctrines of the gospel, which are the life of our holy religion; (we here intend, those doctrines which are exhibited in our excellent Westminster Catechism and Confession of Faith;) and that we all boldly and impartially appear in the defence thereof: at the same time we must take heed and beware of the dangerous errors which many have run into; particularly the Arminian and Neonomian on the one hand, and the Antinomian and Enthusiastical on the other.

4. We must be very faithful in every part of our ministerial works, and make conscience to magnify our office. In a particular manner, we must take good heed to our preaching; that it be not only sound, but instructive, savoury, spiritual, very awakening and searching, well adapted to the times and seasons which pass over us; labouring earnestly herein. We must therefore dwell much upon the doctrines of repentance and conversion, the nature, necessity, and evidence thereof; and much urge the duty of self-examination, and open the deceits of the heart; bringing the unconverted under the work of the law, that they may be prepared to embrace the offer of the gospel. Moral duties must be treated of in an evangelical strain; and we must give unto every one his portion, and not shrink from it, under the notion of prudence; particularly, in the important duty of reproving sinners of all sorts, be they who they will. Again, we must not be slighty in our private conference with souls, and examining candidates for the communion, or other special privileges; and we must carefully and wisely suit our endeavours to the several ages and conditions of persons, the elder and younger; and in a very particular manner, we must set ourselves to promote religion among our young people. And, in a word, we must see whether we are animated to all these things by the grace of God in us.

5. We are impartially to see what evils are to be found among ourselves, and remove them. Let us be seriously thoughtful, whether (among our defects) we have not been, in some respect or other, the blamable means of discouragement to those who have been under religious concern; or whether we have not given strength and boldness to the ungodly, when we have been testifying against the extravagances and disorders of the late times.

6. We must be conscientiously exemplary in our whole behaviour and conversation. It is necessary that we be serious and grave, as what highly becomes gospel bishops. And especially, we must be very watchful over our frame and conduct on the Lord's day. We must therefore look well to our sabbatizing, both at home and abroad, both before our own and other people. Our example is of vast consequence, in magnifying our office before recommended.

7. We ought to stir up the gifts which are in us, and to grow more and more, according to the sacred injunction, 2 Tim. i. 6.

8. We should follow all our endeavours with fervent prayer to God; especially our labours in preaching and teaching: the seed of the word is to be steeped in tears.

II. As to what concerns the association as such.

1. We must lay aside disgusts one with another, and study brotherly love, that it may revive and continue; we must endeavour to be as near as we can of one mind, and go on harmoniously; and then we shall be the more strongly united in all, but especially in our present proceedings. There must be respectful treatment one of another, of the persons and character of one another; and we must be careful of ministerial character; which is of greater consequence than at first sight may appear. And when we have occasion to dispute, let it be under a very strict guard, avoiding all censuring reflections.

2. That we manifest our approbation of the Westminster Assembly's Catechism, as containing an excellent system of divinity; and we purpose to preach agreeably to the doctrines of the Bible exhibited therein.

3. As we must be very careful of our conversation in general as above said; so especially must we be respecting our conduct while together in association.

4. It is proposed that a course of our association be turned into fasts, upon this great account.

5. We agree to be more especially fervent, in continual prayer for the advancement of the kingdom of Christ.

6. Some special, new, and prudent care must be taken to guard our pulpits.

7. It is proposed, that we agree to endeavour to introduce the public reading of the Holy Scriptures. The manner and time to be left to discretion.

III. With regard to what may be done among the people we stand related to.

1. We conceive that whatever public exercises are to be agreed on, or whatever concerns the public, the people are to be informed and acquainted with our design.

2. That it be earnestly recommended to the people, to consider the worth of their privileges, and the danger of being deprived of them; which there is, partly by the spreading of evil doctrines among them, and partly by the conduct of too many people towards their ministers.

3. Let pragmatical, factious spirits, fomenting division, be duly frowned upon.

4. We must guard them against the temptations of their several employments, and the special seasons wherein they are most exposed.

5. We must consider what evils there are to be found among them, which do especially need reforming; as the profanation of the Lord's day, which is enough to destroy all religion; tavern-haunting, company-keeping, chambering, uncleanness, profaneness, &c.; and we ought loudly to testify against them. And that what we do may be effectual, let us endeavour to convince their consciences of the evil of sin, and of these sins.—We are not to fail to warn people solemnly against the dreadful guilt of unthankfulness under God's signal mercies, and of incorrigibleness under heavy and sore judgments. Could we in wisdom do it, we should also warn them against their oppressing the Lord's ministers in their maintenance.

6. Let us endeavour to revive good customs and practices among them; particularly, the ancient good practice of catechising, family order, worship, and government, religious societies under good regulation, godly conference and conversation among Christians; and in brief, whatever is laudable and of good tendency.

7. Church discipline should be revived; brotherly watchfulness, and admonition; nor are we to forget to take special care of the children and youths of the flock.

8. We may do well to engage, as far as we are able, all persons of distinction and influence to unite with us in this work of reformation; *e. g.* justices, school-masters, candidates for the ministry; and especially to assist us by their example.

9. Solemn renewal of covenant hath been advised to, as very useful upon this occasion; (vid. Synod, 1679, for Reformation;) but we leave this to each one's discretion.

Finally, in these things we should think ourselves bound to exert ourselves, and use uncommon fervency, to preserve what remains of religion, and prevent further decay.

October, 1748.

Thus far this association.

The members of this association, as their names were sent to me, are as follows:

The Rev. Messrs. Loring, of Sudbury; Cushing, of Shrewsbury; Parkman, of Westborough; Gardiner, of Stow; Martyn, of Westborough; Stone, of Southborough; Seecomb, of Harvard; Morse, of Shrewsbury; Smith, of Marlborough; Goss, of Boston; Buckminster, of Rutland; Davis, of Holden.

I must refer you, dear Sir, for other particulars relating to the state of religion, in these parts of the world, to my letters to my other correspondents in your neighbourhood.

My wife and family join with me in very affectionate and respectful salutations to you and yours. Desiring an interest in your prayers for us all, and for this part of the Zion of God,

I remain, dear Sir,

Your affectionate brother,

And obliged friend and servant,

JONATHAN EDWARDS."

In the Memoirs of Brainerd, under the date of Sept. 13, 1747, the reader will find mention of a Mr. Job Strong, a candidate for the ministry, whom Brainerd, immediately before his death, recommended to the commissioners in Boston, as a missionary to the Indians; and in the 4th Reflection on those Memoirs, an interesting letter of his, giving an account of the Indian mission at Bethel, in New Jersey, in Jan. 1748. This young gentleman, having ultimately declined that appointment, accepted proposals of settlement in the ministry, the following year, from a church in Portsmouth, New Hampshire, and invited Mr. Edwards to preach the sermon at his ordination, which was appointed for the 28th of June. Mary, the fourth daughter of Mr. Edwards, then a young lady of fifteen, went before her father to Portsmouth, to visit some of the friends of the family in that place. From her I learned the following anecdote.—The Rev. Mr. Moody, of York, a gentleman of unquestioned talents and piety, but perfectly unique in his manners, had agreed, in case of Mr. Edwards's failure, to be his substitute in preaching the sermon. On the morning of the appointed day, Mr. Edwards not having arrived, the council delayed the ordination as long as they well could, and then proceeded to the church; where Mr. Moody had been regularly appointed to make the introductory prayer, which is the prayer immediately before the sermon. That gentleman, knowing that a numerous and highly respectable audience had been drawn together by a strong desire to hear Mr. Edwards, rose up to pray under the not very pleasant impression, that he must stand in his place; and offered a prayer, which was wholly characteristic of himself, and in some degree also of the times in which he lived. In that part of it, in which it was proper for him to allude to the exercises of the day, he besought the Lord, that they might be suitably humbled under the frown of his providence, in not being permitted to hear on that occasion, a discourse, as they had all fondly expected, from "that eminent servant of God, the Rev. Mr. Edwards, of Northampton;" and proceeded to thank God, for having raised him up, to be such a burning and shining light, for his uncommon piety, for his great excellence as a preacher, for the remarkable success which had attended his ministry, in other congregations as well as his own, for the superior talents and wisdom with which he was endowed as a writer, and for the great amount of good which his works had already done, and still promised to do, to the church and to the world. He then prayed that God would spare his life, and endow him with still higher gifts and graces, and render him still more eminent and useful than he had been; and concluded this part of his prayer, by supplicating the divine blessing on the daughter of Mr. Edwards, (then in the house,) who, though a very worthy and amiable young lady, was still, as they had reason to believe, without the grace of God, and in an unconverted state; that God would bring her to repentance, and forgive her sins, and not suffer the peculiar privileges which she enjoyed to be the means of a more aggravated condemnation. Mr. Edwards, who travelled on horseback, and had been unexpectedly detained on the road, arrived at the church a short time after the commencement of the exercises, and entered the door just after Mr. Moody began his prayer. Being remarkably still in all his movements, and particularly in the house of God, he ascended the stairs, and entered the pulpit so silently, that Mr. Moody did not hear him; and of course was necessitated, before a very numerous audience, to listen to the very high character given of himself by Mr. Moody. As soon as the prayer was closed, Mr. Moody turned round, and saw Mr. Edwards behind him; and, without leaving his place, gave him his right hand, and addressed him as follows: " Brother Edwards, we are all of us much rejoiced to see you here to-day, and nobody, probably, as much so as myself; but I wish that you might have got in a little sooner, or a little later, or else that I might have heard you when you came in, and known that you were here. I didn't intend to flatter you to your face; but there's one thing I'll tell you: They say that your wife is a going to heaven by a shorter road than yourself." Mr. Edwards bowed, and after reading the Psalm, went on with the sermon. His text was John xiii. 15, 16. and his subject, " Christ the Example of Ministers." It was soon after published.

To his daughter, who prolonged her visit some time after the return of her father, he addressed, during her visit at Portsmouth, the following letter.

" To Miss Mary Edwards,* at Portsmouth.

Northampton, July 26, 1749.

My dear Child,

You may well think it is natural for a parent to be concerned for a child at so great a distance, so far out of view, and so far out of the reach of communication; where, if you should be taken with any dangerous sickness, that should issue in death, you might probably be in your grave before we could hear of your danger. But yet, my greatest concern is not for your health, or temporal welfare, but for the good of your soul. Though you are at so great a distance from us, yet God is every where. You are much out of the reach of our care, but you are every moment in His hands. We have not the comfort of seeing you, but He sees you. His eye is always upon you. And if you may but live sensibly near to God, and have his gracious presence, it is no matter if you are far distant from us. I had rather you should remain hundreds of miles distant from us, and have God near to you by his Spirit, than to have you always with us, and live at a distance from God. And if the next news we should hear of you, should be of your death, though that would be very melancholy; yet, if at the same time we should receive such intelligence concerning you, as should give us the best grounds to hope, that you had died in the Lord, how much more comfortable would this be, though we should have no opportunity to see you, or to take our leave of you in your sickness, than if we should be with you during all its progress, and have much opportunity to attend upon you, and converse and pray with you, and take an affectionate leave of you, and after all have reason to apprehend, that you died without the grace and favour of God! It is comfortable to have the presence of earthly friends, especially in sickness, and on a death-bed; but the great thing is to have God our friend, and to be united to Christ, who can never die any more, and from whom our own death cannot separate us.

My desire and daily prayer is, that you may, if it may consist with the holy will of God, meet with God where you are, and have much of his divine influences on your heart, wherever you may be; and that, in God's due time, you may be returned to us again, in all respects under the smiles of Heaven, and especially, in prosperous circumstances in your soul, and that you may find us all alive and well. But that is uncertain; for you know what a dying time it has been with us in this town, about this season of the year, in years past. There is not much sickness prevailing among us as yet, but we fear whether mortal sickness is not now commencing. Yesterday, the only remaining son of Mr. C—— died of a fever, and is to be buried to-day. May God fit us all for his will!

I hope that you will maintain a strict and constant watch over yourself, against all temptations, that you do not forsake and forget God, and particularly, that you do not grow slack in secret religion. Retire often from this vain world, from all its bubbles and empty shadows, and vain amusements, and converse with God alone; and seek effectually for that divine grace and comfort, the least drop of which is worth more than all the riches, gaiety, pleasures, and entertainments of the whole world.

If Mrs. S——, of Boston, or any of that family, should send to you, to invite you to come and remain there, on your return from Portsmouth, until there is opportunity for you to come home, I would have you accept the invitation. I think it probable they will invite you. But if otherwise, I would have you go to Mr. Bromfield's. He and Mrs. B. both told me you should be welcome. After you are come to Boston, I would have you send us word of it by the first opportunity, that we may send for you without delay.

We are all, through the Divine goodness, in a tolerable state of health. The ferment in the town runs very high, concerning my opinion about the sacrament; but I am no more able to foretell the issue, than when I last saw you. But the whole family has indeed much to put us in mind, and make us sensible, of our dependence on the care and kindness of God, and of the vanity of all human dependences; and we are very loudly called upon to seek his face, to trust in him, and walk closely with him. Commending you to the care and special favour of our heavenly Father, I am

Your very affectionate father,

JONATHAN EDWARDS.

Your mother and all the family give their love to you."

The following letter of Mr. Edwards to Mr. Gillespie, is in reply to the second letter of that gentleman, written in the autumn of 1748.†

" *Northampton, April* 2, 1750.

Rev. and dear Sir,

I received your favour of September 19, 1748, the last summer, and would now heartily thank you for it. I suppose it may have come in the same ship with letters I had from my other correspondents in Scotland, which I answered the last summer; but it did not come to hand till a long time after most of the others, and after I had finished and sent away my answers to them, and that opportunity for answering was past. I have had no leisure or opportunity to write any letters to Scotland, from that time till now, by reason of my peculiar and very extraordinary circumstances, on account of the controversy which has arisen between me and my people, concerning the profession which ought to be made by persons who come to christian sacraments; which is likely speedily to issue in a separation between me and my congregation. This controversy, in the progress of it, has proved not only a

* Afterwards Mrs. Dwight, of Northampton.

† See page cxxxvii.

controversy between me and my people, but between me and a great part of New England; there being many far and near who are warmly engaged in it. This affair has unavoidably engaged my mind, and filled up my time, and taken me off from other things. I need the prayers of my friends, that God would be with me, and direct and assist me in such a time of trial, and mercifully order the issue.

As to the epistolary controversy, dear Sir, between you and me, about FAITH and DOUBTING, I am sorry it should *seem* to be greater than it is, through misunderstanding of one another's meaning, and that the *real* difference between us is so great as it is, in some part of the controversy.

As to the dispute *about believing without spiritual light or sight*, I thought I expressed my meaning in my last letter very plainly; but I kept no copy, and it might perhaps be owing to my dulness that I thought so. However, I perceive I was not understood. I cannot find out by any thing you say to me on this head, that we really differ in sentiments, but only in words. I acknowledge with you that 'all are bound to believe the divine testimony, and trust in Christ; and that want of spiritual light or sight does not loose from the obligation one is laid under by the divine command, to believe instantly on Christ, and at all seasons, nor excuse him, in any degree, for not believing. Even when one wants the influence and grace of the Spirit, still he is bound to believe.' I think the obligation to believe, lies on a person *who is remaining without spiritual light or sight*, or even in darkness. No darkness, no blindness, no carnality or stupidity, excuses him a moment for not having as strong and lively a faith and love, as ever was exercised by the apostle Paul, or rather renders it not sinful in him, that he is at that same moment without such a faith and love;—and yet I believe it is absurd, and of a very hurtful consequence, to urge persons *to believe in the dark*, in the manner, and in the sense, in which many hundreds have done in *America*, who plainly intend, a believing with such a sort of strong faith or confidence, as is consistent with continuing still, even in the time of these strong acts of faith, without spiritual light, carnal, stupid, careless, and senseless. Their doctrine evidently comes to this, both in sense and effect, that it is a man's duty strongly to believe with a lightless and sightless faith; or to have a confident, although a blind, dark, and stupid faith. Such a faith has indeed been promoted exceedingly by their doctrine, and has prevailed with its dreadful effects, answerable to the nature of the cause. We have had, and have to this day, multitudes of such firm believers, whose bold, presumptuous confidence, attended with a very wicked behaviour, has given the greatest wound to the cause of truth and vital religion, which it has ever suffered in America.

As to what follows in your letter, that *a person's believing himself to be in a good estate is properly of the nature of faith;* in this there seems to be some real difference between us. But perhaps there would be none, if distinctness were well observed in the use of words. If by *a man's believing that he is in a good estate,* be meant no more than *his believing that he does believe in Christ, does love God, &c.* I think there is nothing of the nature of faith in it; because knowing it or believing it, depends on our own immediate sensation or consciousness, and not on divine testimony. True believers, in the hope they entertain of salvation, make use of the following syllogism: *Whosoever believes shall be saved: I believe: Therefore, I shall be saved.* Assenting to the major proposition,—*Whosoever believes shall be saved,*—is properly of the nature of faith; because the ground of my assent to that, is divine testimony; but my assent to the minor proposition,—*I believe,*—is, as I humbly conceive, not of the nature of faith, because that is not grounded on the divine testimony, but on my own consciousness. The testimony, which is the proper ground of faith, is in the word of God, Romans x. 17. 'Faith cometh by hearing, and hearing by the word of God.' There is a testimony given us in the word of God, that '*he that believeth shall be saved.*' But there is no testimony in the word of God, that a *given individual, in such a town in Scotland, or New England, believes.* There is such a proposition in the Scriptures, as that *Christ loves those that love him;* and this, therefore, every one is bound to believe and affirm: and believing this, on the divine testimony, is properly of the nature of faith, while for any one to doubt it, is properly the heinous sin of unbelief. But there is no such proposition in the Scriptures, nor is it any part of the gospel of Christ, that *such an individual person in Northampton loves Christ.* If I know that I have complacency in Christ, I know it the same way that I know I have complacency in my wife and children, *viz.* by the testimony of my own heart, or my inward consciousness. *Evangelical faith* has the gospel of Christ for its foundation; but the proposition, *that I love Christ,* is a proposition not contained in the gospel of Christ.

Hence, that we may not dispute in the dark, it is necessary, that we should explain what we mean by *a person's believing that he is in a good estate.* If thereby we mean only believing the minor of the foregoing syllogism, or similar syllogisms,—*I believe;* or, *I love God;*—it is not of the nature of faith. But if by a man's believing himself to be in a good estate, be understood his believing not only the minor but the consequence, *therefore I shall be saved,* or, *therefore God will never leave me nor forsake me;* then a man's believing his good estate, partakes of the nature of faith; for these consequences depend on divine testimony in the word of God and the gospel of Jesus Christ. Yea, I would observe further, that a man's judging of the faith or love which he actually finds in himself, whether it is that sort of faith or love which he finds to be saving, may depend on his reliance on scripture rules and marks, which are divine testimonies, on which he may be tempted not to rely, from the consideration of his great unworthiness. But his judging that he *has* those individual inward acts of understanding, and exercises of heart, depends on inward sensations, and not on any testimony of the word of God. The knowing of his present acts depends on immediate consciousness, and the knowing of his past acts depends on memory. Hence the fulness of my satisfaction, that I now have such an inward act or exercise of mind, depends on the strength of the sensation; and my satisfaction, that I have had them heretofore, depends on the clearness of my memory, and not on the strength of my reliance on any divine testimony. So likewise, my doubting whether I have, or have had, such individual inward acts, is not of itself of the nature of unbelief, though it may arise from unbelief *indirectly;* because, if I had had more faith, the actings of it would have been more sensible, and the memory of them more lear, and so I should have been better satisfied that I had them.

God appears to have given Abraham's servant a revelaion, that the damsel in whom he found certain marks,—

her coming to draw water with a pitcher to that well, and her readiness to give him and his camels drink,—should be Isaac's wife; and therefore his assenting to *this*, was of the nature of faith, having divine testimony for its foundation. But his believing that Rebekah was the damsel who had these individual marks, his knowing that she came to draw water, and that she let down her pitcher, was not of the nature of faith. His knowing *this* was not from divine testimony, but from the testimony of his own senses. (Vide Gen. xxiv.)

You speak of 'a saint's doubting of his good estate, as a part of unbelief, and the opposite of faith, considered in its full compass and latitude, as one branch of unbelief, one ingredient in unbelief; and of assurance of a man's good estate, as one thing that belongs to the exercise of faith.' I do not know whether I take your meaning in these expressions. If you mean, that a person's believing himself to be in a good estate, is one thing which appertains to the essence of saving faith, or that saving faith, in all that belongs to its essence, yea its perfection, cannot be without implying it, I must humbly ask leave to differ from you. That my believing that I am in a good estate, is no part or ingredient in the essence of saving faith, is evident from this, that the essence of saving faith must be complete in me, *before it can be true* that I am in a good estate. If I have not as yet acted faith, yea if there be any thing wanting in me to make up the essence of saving faith, then I am not as yet in a state of salvation, and therefore can have no ground to believe that I am so. Any thing that belongs to the essence of saving faith is prior, in the order of nature, to a man's being in a state of salvation, because it is saving faith which brings him into such a state. And therefore believing that he is in such a state, cannot be one thing which is essential or necessary, in order to his being in such a state; for that would imply a contradiction. It would be to suppose a man's believing that he is in a good estate, to be *prior*, in the order of nature, to his being in a good estate. But a thing cannot be both prior and posterior, antecedent and consequent, with respect to the very same thing. The real truth of a proposition is in the order of nature first, before its being believed to be true. But, till a man has already all that belongs to the essence of saving faith, that proposition, *that he is in a good estate*, is not as yet true. All the propositions contained in the gospel, all divine testimonies that we have in God's word, are true already, are already laid for a foundation for faith, and were laid long ago. But that proposition, *I am in a good estate*, not being one of them, is not true till I have first believed; and therefore this proposition, as it *is* not true, cannot be *believed* to be true, till saving faith be first complete. Therefore the completeness of the act of saving faith will not make it take in a belief of this proposition, nor will the strength or perfection of the act cause it to imply this. If a man, in his first act of faith, has ever so full a conviction of God's sufficiency and faithfulness, and ever so strong and perfect a reliance on the divine testimony; all will have no tendency to make him believe that this proposition, *I am in a good estate*, is true, until it is true; which is not the fact, till the first act of faith is complete, and has made it true. A belief of divine testimony, in the first act of faith, may be to an assignable degree of strength and perfection, without believing the proposition, for there is no such divine testimony then extant, nor is there any such truth extant, but in consequence of the first act of faith. Therefore, (as I said,) saving faith may exist, with all that belongs to its essence, and that in the highest perfection, without implying a belief of my own good estate. I do not say that it can exist without having this immediate *effect*. But it is rather the *effect* of faith, than a *part*, *branch*, or *ingredient* of faith. So I do not dispute whether a man's doubting of his good estate, may be a consequence of unbelief, and I doubt not but it is in those who are in a good estate; because, if men had the exercise of faith in such a degree as they ought to have, it could not but be very sensible and plain that they had it. But yet I think this doubting of one's good estate, is entirely a different thing from the sin of unbelief itself, and has nothing of the nature of unbelief in it, *i. e.* if we take doubting one's good estate in the sense in which I have before explained it, *viz. doubting whether I have such individual principles and acts in my soul.* Take it in a complex sense, and it may have the sin of unbelief in it; *e. g.* If, although I doubt not that I have such and such qualifications, I yet doubt of those *consequences*, for which I have divine testimony or promise; as when a person doubts not that he loves Christ, yet doubts whether *he shall receive a crown of life.* The doubting of this consequence is properly the sin of unbelief.

You say, dear Sir, 'the Holy Ghost requires us to believe the reality of its works in us in all its parts just as it is;' and a little before, 'the believer's doubting whether or not he has faith, is sinful; because it is belying the Holy Ghost, denying his work in him, so there is no sin to which that doubting can so properly be reduced as unbelief.'

Here I would ask leave thus to express my thoughts, in a diversity from yours. I think, if it be allowed to be sinful for a believer to doubt whether he has faith, that this doubting is not the sin of unbelief on any such account as you mention, *viz.* as belying or denying any testimony of the Holy Ghost. There is a difference between doubting of the being of some *work* of the Holy Ghost, and denying the *testimony* of the Holy Ghost; as there is a difference between doubting concerning some other works of God, and denying the testimony of God. It is the work of God to give a man great natural abilities; and if we suppose that God requires a man thus endowed *to believe the reality of his work in all its parts just as it is*, and therefore, that it is sinful for him at all to doubt of his natural abilities being just as good as they are; yet this is no belying any testimony of God, though it be doubting of a work of God, and so is diverse from the sin of unbelief. So, if we suppose that a very eminent Christian is to blame, in doubting whether he has so much holiness as he really has; he indeed *does not believe the reality of God's work in him, in all its parts just as it is*, yet he is not therein guilty of the sin of unbelief, against any testimony of God, any more than the other.

I acknowledge, that for a true saint, in a carnal and careless frame, to doubt of his good state, is sinful, *more indirectly*, as the cause of it is sinful, *viz.* the lowness and insensibility of the actings of grace in him, and the prevalence of carnality and stupidity. 'Tis sinful to be without assurance, or, (as we say,) *it is his own fault;* he sinfully deprives himself of it, or foregoes it; as a servant's being without his tools is his sin, when he has carelessly lost them, or as it is his sin to be without strength of body, or without the sight of his eyes, when he has deprived himself of these by intemperance. Not that weakness or blindness of body, in their own nature, are sin, for they are qualities of the body, and not of mind, the subject in which sin is inherent. It is indirectly the duty of a true saint *always* to rejoice in the light of God's countenance, because sin is the cause of his being without this joy at any time; and therefore it was *indirectly* David's sin that he was not rejoicing in the light of God's countenance, at that very time when he was committing the great iniquities of adultery and murder. But yet it is not directly a believer's duty to rejoice in the light of God's countenance, when God hides his face. But it rather then becomes him to be troubled and to mourn. So there are, perhaps, many other privileges of saints that are their duty indirectly, and the want of them is sinful, not simply, but complexly considered. Of this kind I take the want of assurance of my good estate to be.

I think no words of mine, either in my book or letter, implied that a person's deliverance from a bad frame, does not begin with renewed acts of faith or trusting in God. If they did, they implied what I never intended. Doubtless if a saint comes out of an ill frame, wherein grace is asleep and inactive, it must be by renewed actings of grace. It is very plainly impossible, that grace should begin to cease to be inactive, in any other way than by its beginning to be active. It must begin with the renewed actings of some grace or other; and I know nothing that I have said to the contrary, but that the grace which shall first begin sensibly to revive shall be faith, and that this shall lead the way to the renewed acting of all other graces, and to the further acting of faith itself. But a person's coming out of a carnal, careless, dead frame, by, or in the reviving of, grace in his soul, is quite another thing from a saint's having a strong exercise of faith, or strong hope, or strong exercise of any grace, while yet remaining in a carnal, careless, dead frame; or, in other words, in a frame wherein grace is so far from being in strong exercise, that it is asleep, and in a great measure without exercise.

There is a *holy hope*, a truly *christian hope*, of which the Scriptures speak, that is reckoned among the graces of the Spirit. And I think I should never desire or seek any other hope but such an one; for I believe no other hope has any holy or good tendency. Therefore *this* hope, *this* grace of hope alone, can properly be called a duty. But it is just as absurd to talk of the exercises of this holy hope, the strong exercise of this grace of the Spirit, in a carnal, stupid, careless frame, *such a frame yet remaining*, as it would be to talk of the strong exercises of love to God, or heavenly-mindedness, or any other grace, while remaining in such a frame. It is doubtless proper, earnestly to exhort those who are in such a frame to come out of it, in and by the strong exercise of every grace; but I should not think it proper to press a man earnestly to maintain strong hope, *notwithstanding* the prevailing and continuance of great carnality and stupidity, which is plainly the case of the people I opposed. For this is plainly to press people to an unholy hope, to a strong hope which is no christian grace, but strong and wicked presumption; and the promoting of this has most evidently been the effect of such a method of dealing with souls in innumerable multitudes of awful instances.

You seem, Sir, to suppose, that God's manner of dealing with his people, *while in a secure and careless frame*, is *first* to give assurance of their good state *while they remain in such a frame*, and to make use of that assurance as a mean to bring them out of such a frame. Here, again, I must beg leave to differ from you, and to think, that none of the instances or texts you adduce from Scripture, do at all prove the point. I think it is his manner, first to awaken their consciences, to bring them to reflect upon themselves, to feel their own calamity which they have brought upon themselves by so departing from God, by which an end is put to their carelessness and security, and again earnestly and carefully to seek God's face before they find him, and before God restores the comfortable and joyful sense of his favour; and I think this is abundantly evident both from Scripture and experience. You much insist on the case of *Jonah* as a clear instance of the thing you lay down. You observe that he says, chap. ii. 'I said I am cast out of thy sight, yet I will look again towards thy holy temple.' Ver. 5, 7. 'When my soul fainted within me, I remembered the Lord, and my prayer came in unto thee, even into thine holy temple.' You speak of these words as expressing an assurance of his good state and of God's favour; (I will not now dispute whether they do or not;) and you speak of this exercise of assurance, as *his practice in an evil frame and in a careless frame; for he slept securely in the sides of the ship*, manifesting *dismal security, awful carelessness in a carnal frame.* That Jonah was in a careless secure frame when he was asleep in the sides of the ship, I do not deny. But, my dear Sir, does that prove that he remained still in a careless secure frame, when in his heart he said these things in the belly of the fish; does it prove that he remained careless after he was awakened, and saw the furious storm, and owned it was the fruit of God's anger towards him for his sins; and does it prove, that he still remained careless after the whale had swallowed him, when he seemed to himself to be *in the belly of hell*, when *the water compassed him about, even to the soul*, and, as he says, *all God's waters and billows passed over him, and he was ready to despair when he went down to the bottoms of the mountains*, was ready to think God had cast him out of his sight, and confined him in a prison, that he could never escape, *when the earth with her bars was about him for ever, and his soul fainted within him?* He was brought into *this* condition *after* his sleeping securely in the sides of the ship, *before* he said, 'I will look again towards thine holy temple,' &c. He was evidently first awakened out of carelessness and security, and brought into distress, before he was comforted.

The other place you also must insist on, concerning the people of Israel, is very similar. Before God comforted them with the testimonies of his favour after their backslidings, he first, by severe chastisements, together with the awakening influences of his Spirit, brought them out of their *carelessness* and carnal *security.* It appears by many passages of Scripture, that this was God's way of dealing with that people. In Hos. chap. ii. we are told that God first 'hedged up her ways with thorns, and made a wall that she could not find her paths. And took away her corn and wine, and wool and flax, destroyed her vines and fig-trees, and caused her mirth to cease.' By this means, he roused her from her security, carelessness, and deep sleep, and brought her to herself, very much as the prodigal son was brought to himself: thus God 'brought her first into the wilderness, before he spake comfortably to her, and opened to her a door of hope.' By her distress he first led her to say, 'I wil go and return to my first husband;' and then when God spake comfortably to her, she called him '*Ishi*, my husband;' and God did as it were renewedly betroth her unto him. This passage is parallel with Jer. iii. They serve well to illustrate and explain each other, and show that it was God's way of dealing with his people Israel, after their apostacy, *first* to awaken them, and under a sense of their sense and misery, to bring them solicitously to seek his face, before he gave them sensible evidence of his favour; and not first to manifest his favour to them, in order to awaken them out of their security.*

In Jer. iii. the prophecy is not concerning the recovery of backsliding *saints*, or the mystical church, which, though she had corrupted herself, still continued to be figuratively God's wife. It is concerning apostate Israel, who had forsaken and renounced her husband, and gone after other lovers, and whom God had renounced, put away, and given her a bill of divorce; (verse 8.) so that her recovery could not be, by giving her assurance of her good estate as still remaining his wife, and that God was already married unto her, for that was not true, and is not consistent with the context. And whereas it is said, verse 14. 'Return, O backsliding children, saith the Lord; for I am married unto you, and I will take you one of a city;' *I am married*, in the Hebrew, is in the *preter-perfect* tense; but you know, Sir, that in the language of prophecy, the *preter tense* is very commonly put for the *future*. And whereas it is said, verse 19. 'How shall I put thee among the children? And I said, Thou shalt call me My father;' I acknowledge this expression here, *My Father*, and in Rom. viii. 15. is the language of faith. It is so two ways: 1st. It is such language of the soul, as is the immediate effect of a lively faith. I acknowledge, that the lively exercises of faith do naturally produce satisfaction of a good state, *as their immediate effect*. 2d. It is a language which, in another sense, does properly and naturally express the very act of faith itself, yea, the first act of faith in a sinner, before which he never was in a good state. As thus, supposing a man in distress, pursued by his enemies that sought his life, should have the gates of several fortresses set open before him, and should be called to from each of them to fly thither for refuge; and viewing them all, and one appearing strong and safe, but the rest insufficient, he should accept the invitation to that one, and fly thither with this language, 'This is my fortress; this is my refuge. In vain is salvation looked for from others. Behold I come to thee; this is my sure defence.' Not that he means that he is already within the fortress, and so in a good estate. But, this is my chosen fortress, in the strength of which I trust, and to which I betake myself for safety. So if a woman were solicited by many lovers, to give herself to them in marriage, and beholding the superiority of one to all the rest, should betake herself to him, with this language, 'This is my husband, behold I come unto thee, thou art my spouse;' not that she means that she is already married to him, but that he is her chosen husband, &c. Thus God offers himself to sinners as their Saviour, their God and Father; and the language of the heart of him who accepts the offer by faith, is, 'Thou art my Saviour; in vain is salvation hoped for from others: thou art my God and Father.' Not that he is already his child, but he chooses him, and comes to him, that he may be one of his children; as in Jer. iii. 19. Israel calls God his Father, as the way to be *put among the children*, and to be one of them, and not as being one already; and in verses 21, 22, 23. she is not brought out of a careless and secure state, by knowing that the Lord is her God, but she is first brought to consideration and sense of her sin and misery, weeping and supplications for mercy, and conviction of the vanity of other saviours and refuges, not only before she has assurance of her good estate, but before she is brought to fly to God for refuge, that she may be in a good estate.

As to the instance of Job, I would only observe, that while in his state of sore affliction, though he had some painful exercises of infirmity and impatience under his extreme trials, yet he was very far from being in such a frame as I intended, when I spoke of a *secure, careless, carnal* frame. I doubt not, nor did I ever question it, that the saints' hope and knowledge of their good estate, is in many cases of great use to help them against temptation, and the exercises of corruption.

With regard to the case of extraordinary temptations and buffetings of Satan, which you mention, I do not very well know what to say further. I have often found my own insufficiency as a counsellor in cases where melancholy and bodily distemper have so much influence, and give Satan so great advantage, as appears to me in the case you mention. If the Lord do not help, whence should we help? If some christian friends of such afflicted and (as it were) possessed persons, would, from time to time, pray and fast for them, it might be a proper exercise of christian charity, and the likeliest way I know for relief. I kept no copy of my former letter to you, and so do not remember fully what I have already said concerning this case. But this I have often found with such melancholy people, that the greatest difficulty does not lie in giving them good advice, but in persuading them to take it. One thing I think of great importance, which is, that such persons should go on in a steady course of performance of all duties, both of their general and particular calling, without suffering themselves to be diverted from it by any violence of Satan, or specious pretence of his whatsoever, properly ordering, proportioning, and timing, all sorts of duties, duties to God, public, private, and secret, and duties to man, relative duties of business and conversation, family duties, duties of friendship and good neighbourhood, duly proportioning labour and rest, intentness and relaxation, without suffering one duty to crowd out or intrench upon another. If such persons could be persuaded to this, I think in this way they would be best guarded against the devil, and he would soonest be discouraged, and a good state of body would be most likely to be gained, and persons would act most as if they trusted and rested in God, and would be most in the way of his help and blessing.

With regard to what you write concerning immediate revelations, I have thought of it, and I find I cannot say any thing to purpose, without drawing out this letter to a very extraordinary length, and I am already got to such length, that I had need to ask your excuse. I have written enough to tire your patience.

It has indeed been with great difficulty that I have found time to write much. If you knew my extraordinary circumstances, I doubt not you would excuse my not writing any more. I acknowledge the subject you mention is very important. Probably if God spares my life, and gives me opportunity, I may write largely upon it. I know not how Providence will dispose of me; I am going to be cast on the wide world, with my large family of ten

* This is evident by many passages of Scripture; as, Lev. xxvi. 40—42. Deut. xxxii. 36—39. 1 Kings viii. 21, 22. chap. i. 4—8. Ezek. xx. 35, 36, 37. Hos. v. 15. with chap. vi. 1—3. chap. xiii 9, 10. chap. xiv. throughout.

children.—I humbly request your prayers for me under my difficulties and trials.

As to the state of religion in this place and this land, it is at present very sorrowful and dark. But I must, for a more particular account of things, refer you to my letter to Mr. M'Laurin of Glasgow, and Mr. Robe. So, asking a remembrance in your prayers, I must conclude by subscribing myself, with much esteem and respect,

Your obliged brother and servant,

JONATHAN EDWARDS."*

CHAPTER XVI.

COMMENCEMENT OF DIFFICULTIES AT NORTHAMPTON.

THAT this world is not a place of rest even to the most excellent of men, is a fact proved by the history of all past ages. How few who have been in prominent situations of usefulness but have experienced a variety of bitter disappointments; which though mysterious in themselves, disgraceful to those who have been the occasions of them, and most distressing to those who have felt their weight, yet have presented to the reflecting mind no unimportant lessons, and have tended to results little anticipated by any party connected with them. Nor should it seem strange to us that neither the world, nor the church of God itself, in its present imperfect state, can be considered as affording a resting-place. All the instruments employed by God in the promotion of his work, have been greatly tried; their labours have been mingled with their tears; and they have not only suffered from their own personal share of human imperfection, but have found in the ignorance, the perverse dispositions, and the unholy practices of others, their sharpest sorrows. They have been grieved by foes, but more injured and vexed by pretended friends. Divine grace has however enabled them honourably to stand amidst these perilous conflicts, and though the storm has fiercely raged around them, they have at length found a calm which can never be endangered; and they place before those who succeed them this grand lesson, that the faithful pursuit of the path of duty, whatever may be its difficulties and trials, will end well; and that this is the only course which can be reviewed with any satisfaction amidst the solemnities of a dying scene.

If any individual might have expected freedom from painful opposition, Mr. Edwards was that person; if unblemished holinesss of character, if fervent desires of usefulness in all its varied and delightful forms, and if constant devotedness to every object connected with man's present and eternal good, could have insured uninterrupted satisfaction here, how large was the measure of enjoyment which would have fallen to the lot of this excellent man! All that he was, and all he had, he was disposed to sacrifice upon the altar of God, and to dedicate to the service of his fellow-creatures. No disposition to spare himself, to exalt himself, or place burdens upon others which he was unwilling to share, could be discovered in him; yet afflictions of no common extent attended him; but still he could say, "*None of these things move me, neither count I my life dear unto myself, so that I might finish my course with joy, and the ministry which I have received of the Lord Jesus, to testify the gospel of the grace of God.*"

Mr. Edwards was for many years unusually happy in the esteem and love of his people; and there was during that period the greatest prospect of his living and dying in the same state of harmony. So admirably was he qualified for the discharge of his official duties, and so faithful in the actual discharge of them, that he was probably the last minister in New England, who would have been thought likely to be opposed and rejected by the people of his charge. His uniform kindness, and that of Mrs. Edwards, had won their affection, and the exemplary piety of both, had secured their confidence; his very able and original exhibitions of truth on the sabbath, had enlightened their understandings and their consciences; his published works had gained him a reputation for powerful talents, both in Europe and America, which left him without a competitor, either in the colonies or the mother country; his labours had been remarkably blessed, he had been the means of gathering one of the largest churches on earth; and of such of the members as had any real evidence of their own piety, the great body ascribed their conversion to his instrumentality. But the event teaches us the instability of all earthly things, and proves how incompetent we are to calculate those consequences, which depend on a cause so uncertain and changeable as the will of man.

In the year 1744, about six years before the final separation, Mr. Edwards was informed, that some young persons in the town, who were members of the church, had licentious books in their possession which they employed to promote obscene conversation among the young people at home. Upon further inquiry, a number of persons testified that they had heard one and another of them, from time to time, talk obscenely; as what they were led to, by reading books of this gross character which they had in circulation among them. On the evidence thus presented to him, Mr. Edwards thought, that the brethren of the church ought to look into the matter; and in order to introduce it to their attention, he preached a sermon from Heb. xii. 15, 16. "Looking diligently, lest any man fail of the grace of God, lest any root of bitterness springing up trouble you, and thereby many be defiled: lest there be any fornicator, or profane person, as Esau, who for one morsel of meat sold his birthright." After sermon, he desired the brethren of the church to stop, told them what information he had received, and put the question to them in form, whether the church, on the evidence before them, thought proper to take any measures to examine into the matter? The members of the church, with one consent and with much zeal, manifested it to be their opinion that

* The postscript of this letter, under date of July 6, 1750, is reserved for a subsequent page.

it ought to be inquired into; and proceeded to choose a number of individuals as a committee of inquiry, to assist their pastor in examining into the affair. After this Mr. Edwards appointed the time for the committee of the church to meet at his house; and then read to the church a catalogue of the names of the young persons, whom he desired to come to his house at the same time. Some of those whose names were thus read, were the persons accused, and some were witnesses; but through mere forgetfulness or inadvertence on his part, he did not state to the church, in which of these two classes any particular individual was included; or in what character he was requested to meet the committee, whether as one of the accused, or a witness.

When the names were thus published, it appeared that there were but few of the considerable families in the town, to which some of the persons named, either did not belong, or were not nearly related. Many of the church, however, having heard the names read, condemned what they had done, before they got home to their own houses; and whether this disclosure of the names, accompanied with the apprehension, that some of their own connexions were included in the list of offenders, was the occasion of the alteration or not, it is certain that, before the day appointed for the meeting of the committee arrived, a great number of heads of families altered their minds, and declared they did not think proper to proceed as they had begun, and that their children should not be called to an account in such a way for such conduct; and the town was suddenly all in a blaze. This strengthened the hands of the accused: some refused to appear; others who did appear, behaved with a great degree of insolence, and contempt of the authority of the church; and little or nothing could be done further in the affair.

This was the occasion of weakening Mr. Edwards's hands in the work of the ministry, especially among the young people, with whom, by this means, he greatly lost his influence. It seemed in a great measure to put an end to his usefulness at Northampton, and doubtless laid a foundation for his removal, and will help to account for the surprising events which we are about to relate. He certainly had no great visible success after this; the influences of the Holy Spirit were chiefly withheld, and stupidity and worldly-mindedness were greatly increased among them. That great and singular degree of good order, sound morals, and visible religion, which had for years prevailed at Northampton, soon began gradually to decay, and the young people obviously became from that time more dissolute.*

There was another difficulty of a far more serious nature. The church of Northampton, like the other early churches of New England, was formed on the plan of *strict communion:* in other words, none were admitted to the Lord's supper, but those who, after due examination, were regarded as regenerate persons. Such was the uniform practice of the church from its formation during the ministry of Mr. Mather, and for a considerable period after the settlement of Mr. Stoddard, the predecessor of Mr. Edwards. Mr. Stoddard publicly avowed a change in his opinions in 1704, when he had been in the ministry at Northampton *thirty-two years,* and endeavoured at that time to introduce a corresponding change in the practice of the church. He then declared himself, in the language of Dr. Hopkins, to be "of the opinion, that unconverted persons, considered as such, had a right in the sight of God, or by his appointment, to the sacrament of the Lord's supper; that thereby it was their *duty* to come to that ordinance, though they knew they had no true goodness or evangelical holiness. He maintained that visible Christianity does not consist in a profession, or appearance of that wherein true holiness, or real Christianity, consists; that therefore the profession, which persons make, in order to be received as visible members of Christ's church, ought not to be such as to express or imply a real compliance with, or consent to, the terms of this covenant of grace, or a hearty embracing of the gospel: so that they who really reject Jesus Christ, and dislike the gospel way of salvation in their hearts, and know that this is true of themselves, may make the profession without lying and hypocrisy," [on the principle that they regard the sacrament as a converting ordinance, and partake of it with the hope of obtaining conversion.] "He formed a short profession for persons to make, in order to be admitted into the church, and to the sacrament, on these terms. Mr. Stoddard's principle at first made a great noise in the country; and he was opposed, as introducing something contrary to the principles and the practice of almost all the churches in New England, and the matter was publicly controverted between him and Dr. Increase Mather of Northampton. However, through Mr. Stoddard's great influence over the people of Northampton, it was introduced there, though not without opposition: by degrees it spread very much among ministers and people in that county, and in other parts of New England."

At the settlement of Mr. Edwards, in 1727, this alteration in the qualifications required for admission into the church had been in operation about twenty-two or three years; a period during which the great body of the members of any church will be changed. This lax plan of admission has no where been adopted by a church, for any considerable length of time, without introducing a large proportion of members who are destitute of piety; and although Mr. Stoddard was in other respects so faithful a minister, and so truly desirous of the conversion and salvation of his people, there can be no doubt that such must have been the result during so long a period in the church at Northampton.

"Mr. Edwards," observes Dr. Hopkins, "had some hesitation about this matter when he first settled at Northampton, but did not receive such a degree of conviction, as to prevent his adopting it with a good conscience, for some years. But at length his doubts increased; which put him upon examining it thoroughly, by searching the Scriptures, and reading such books as were written on the subject. The result was, a full conviction that it was wrong, and that he could not retain the practice with a good conscience. He was fully convinced that to be a *visible* Christian, was to put on the visibility or appearance of a *real* Christian; that a profession of Christianity was a profession of that wherein real Christianity consists; and therefore that no person, who rejected Christ in his heart, could make such a profession consistently with truth. And as the ordinance of the Lord's supper was instituted for none but *visible* professing Christians, that none but those who are *real* Christians have a right, in the sight of God, to come to that ordinance: and, conse-

* What an awful warning to all professors, and especially to young people! Behold, how great a matter a little fire kindleth! Little do the giddy and the gay think how their levities operate, and what seeds of distress and sorrow they are sowing for themselves and others. Woe unto you that *thus* laugh now, for ye shall mourn and weep! How desirable it should be *penitentially* here, and not *despairingly* hereafter.—DR. WILLIAMS.

quently, that none ought to be admitted thereto, who do not make a profession of real Christianity, and so can be received, in a judgment of charity, as true friends to Jesus Christ.

"When Mr. Edwards's sentiments were generally known in the spring of the year 1749, it gave great offence, and the town was put into a great ferment; and before he was heard in his own defence, or it was known by many what his principles were, the general cry was to have him dismissed, as what would alone satisfy them. This was evident from the whole tenor of their conduct, as they neglected and opposed the most proper means of calmly considering, and so of thoroughly understanding, the matter in dispute, and persisted in a refusal to attend to what Mr. Edwards had to say, in defence of his principles. From the beginning to the end, they opposed the measures, which had the best tendency to compromise and heal the difficulty; and with much zeal pursued those, which were calculated to make a separation certain and speedy. He thought of preaching on the subject, that they might know what were his sentiments and the grounds of them, (of both which he was sensible that most of them were quite ignorant,) before they took any steps for a separation. But that he might do nothing to increase the tumult, he first proposed the thing to the standing committee of the church; supposing, that if he entered on the subject publicly with their consent, it would prevent the ill consequences, which otherwise he feared would follow. But the most of them strenuously opposed it. Upon which he gave it over for the present, as what, in such circumstances, would rather blow up the fire to a greater height, than answer the good ends proposed."

Mr. Edwards was sensible that his principles were not understood, but misrepresented through the country; and finding that his people were too warm, calmly to attend to the matter in controversy, he proposed to print what he had to say on the point, as this seemed the only way left him to have a fair hearing. Accordingly his people consented to put off calling a council, till what he should write was published. With this view he began immediately to prepare a statement and defence of his own sentiments, and in the latter part of April, about two months from the time of its commencement, sent it to the press—an instance of rapidity of composition almost unexampled in an individual, who was at once occupied by the duties of an extensive parish, and involved in the embarrassments of a most perplexing controversy. Notwithstanding the efforts of Mr. Edwards, the printing of the work was not completed until August. It was entitled, "An Humble Inquiry into the Rules of the Word of God, concerning the Qualifications requisite to a Complete Standing and Full Communion in the Visible Christian Church;" and contains a discussion of the question agitated between himself and his people, "Whether any persons ought to be admitted to full communion in the christian church, but such as, in the eye of a reasonable judgment, are truly Christians?"—a discussion so thorough and conclusive, that it has been the standard work with evangelical divines from that time to the present.

It was a very painful consideration to Mr. Edwards, that, while the circumstances in which he was placed, constrained him to declare his sentiments from the press, the "*Appeal to the Learned*," the production of a man so much loved and venerated at Northampton, and so much respected throughout New England, his own colleague too, and his own grandfather, was the work, and the only work of any respectability, on the opposite side of the question, which he should be obliged publicly to examine and refute. But his feelings on this subject he has himself explained. "It is far from a pleasing circumstance of this publication, that it is against what my honoured grandfather strenuously maintained, both from the pulpit and the press. I can truly say, on account of this and some other considerations, it is what I engage in with the greatest reluctance that ever I undertook any public service in my life. But the state of things with me is so ordered by the sovereign disposal of the great Governor of the world, that my doing this appears to me very necessary, and altogether unavoidable. I am conscious that not only is the interest of religion concerned in this affair, but my own reputation, future usefulness, and my very subsistence, all seem to depend on my freely opening and defending myself as to my principles, and agreeable conduct in my pastoral charge, and on my doing it from the press: in which way alone am I able to state, and justify my opinion to any purpose, before the country, (which is full of noise, misrepresentations, and many censures concerning this affair,) or even before my own people, as all would be fully sensible, if they knew the exact state of the case.—I have been brought to this necessity in Divine Providence, by such a situation of affairs, and coincidence of circumstances and events, as I choose at present to be silent about; and which it is not needful, nor perhaps expedient, for me to publish to the world."

The people of Northampton manifested great uneasiness in waiting for this publication, before it came out of the press; and when it was published, some of the leading men, afraid of its ultimate effect on the minds of the people, did their utmost to prevent its extensive perusal, and it was read by comparatively a small number. Some of those who read it, of a more cool and dispassionate temper, were led to doubt whether they had not been mistaken.

Mr. Edwards, as Dr. Hopkins observes, being sensible that his treatise had been read but by very few of the people, renewed his proposal to preach upon the subject, and at a meeting of the brethren of the church asked their consent in the following terms: "I desire that the brethren would manifest their consent, that I should declare the reasons of my opinion, relating to full communion in the church, in lectures appointed for that end: not as an act of authority, or as putting the power of declaring the whole counsel of God out of my hands; but for peace sake and to prevent occasion for strife." This was answered in the negative.—He then proposed that it should be left to a few of the neighbouring ministers, whether it was not, all things considered, reasonable, that he should be heard in this matter from the pulpit, before the affair should be brought to an issue. But this also passed in the negative.

However, having had the advice of the ministers and messengers of the neighbouring churches who met at Northampton, to advise them under their difficulties, he proceeded to appoint a lecture, in order to preach on the subject, proposing to do so weekly till he had finished what he had to say. On Monday there was a society meeting, in which a vote was passed to choose a committee to go to Mr. Edwards, and desire him not to preach lectures on the subject in controversy, according to his declaration and appointment; in consequence of which a committee of three men, chosen for that purpose, waited upon him. However, Mr. Edwards thought proper to proceed according to his proposal, and accordingly preached a number of sermons, till he had finished what he had to say on the subject. These lectures were very thinly attended by his own people; but great numbers of strangers from the neighbouring towns attended them, so many as to make above half the congregation. This was in February and March, 1750.

The calling of a decisive council, to determine the matter of difference, was now more particularly attended to on both sides. Mr. Edwards had before this insisted, from time to time, that they were by no means ripe for such a procedure; as they had not yet given him a fair hearing, whereby perhaps the need of such a council would be superseded. He observed, "That it was exceedingly unbecoming to manage religious affairs of the greatest importance in a ferment and tumult, which ought to be managed with great solemnity, deep humiliation, submission to the awful frowns of Heaven, humble dependence on God, with fervent prayer and supplication to him: that therefore for them to go about such an affair as they did, would be greatly to the dishonour of God and religion; a way in which a people cannot expect a blessing." Thus having used all means to bring them to a calm and charitable temper without effect, he consented that a decisive council should be called without any further delay.

But a difficulty attended the choice of a council, which was for some time insuperable. It was agreed, that the council should be mutually chosen, one half by the pastor, and the other half by the church, but the people insisted upon it, that he should be confined to the county for his choice. Mr. Edwards thought this an unreasonable restraint upon him, as it was known that the ministers and churches in that county were almost universally against him in the controversy. He indeed did not suppose that the business of the proposed council would be to determine whether his opinion was right or not; but whether any possible way could be devised for an accommodation between pastor and people, and to use their wisdom and endeavour in order to effect it. And if they found this impracticable, they must determine, whether what ought in justice to be done had already actually been attempted, so that there was nothing further to be demanded by either of the parties concerned, before a separation should take place. And if he was dismissed by them, it would be their business to set forth to the world in what manner, and for what cause, he was dismissed: all which were matters of great importance to him, and required upright and impartial judges. Now considering the great influence a difference in religious opinions has to prejudice men one against another, and the close connexion of the point, in which most of the ministers and churches in the county differed from him, with the matter to be judged of, he did not think they could be reasonably looked upon so impartial judges, as that the matter ought to be left wholly to them. Besides, he thought that the case, being so new and extraordinary, required the ablest judges in the land. For these, and some other reasons which he offered, he insisted upon liberty to go out of the county, for those members of the proposed council in which he was to have a choice. In this the people strenuously and obstinately opposed him. At length they agreed to leave the matter to a council consisting of the *ministers* and *messengers* of the five neighbouring churches; who after they had met twice upon it, and had the case largely debated before them, were *equally divided*, and therefore left the matter undetermined.

However, they were all agreed, that Mr. Edwards ought to have liberty to go out of the county for *some* of the council. And at the next church meeting, which was on the 26th of March, Mr. Edwards offered to join with them in calling a council, if they would consent that he should choose *two* of the churches out of the county, in case the council consisted of but *ten* churches. The church however refused to comply with this, at one meeting after another repeatedly; and proceeded to warn a church meeting and choose a moderator, in order to act without their pastor. But to pass by many particulars, at length, at a meeting of the church, warned by their pastor, May 3rd, they voted their consent to his proposal of going out of the county for two of the churches that should be applied to. And they then proceeded to make choice of the ten ministers and churches of which the council should consist.

CHAPTER XVII.

ACCOUNT OF DIFFICULTIES AT NORTHAMPTON CONTINUED.

On Friday afternoon, June 22nd, 1750, the result of the council, and the protest of the minority, were publicly read to the people assembled in the church. On the next sabbath but one, July 1st Mr. Edwards delivered to them his *Farewell Sermon*, which was soon afterwards published, at the request of some of the hearers. This sermon has been extensively and deservedly styled, "the best farewell sermon that was ever written;" and has been the source from which subsequent discourses, on occasions and in circumstances generally similar, have, to a great extent, been substantially derived. Had it been written in the case of an indifferent person, instead of his own, it could not have discovered less of passion or of irritation, or have breathed a more calm and excellent spirit. Instead of indicating anger under a sense of multiplied injuries, it appears in every sentence to have been dictated by meekness and forgiveness. At the same time, it presents an exhibition of the scenes of the last judgment, singularly solemn and awful. Few, indeed, are the compositions which furnish so many or so unequivocal marks of uncommon excellence in their author; and very few are so well adapted to be practically useful to churches and congregations.

The following postscript to the letter to Mr. Gillespie,*

* For the letter itself see page cli.

of April 2, 1750, and the letters to Mr. Erskine and Mr. M'Culloch, all written immediately after the separation of Mr. Edwards from his people, exhibit also, in a very striking manner, the calm and tranquil state of his mind at the time when they were written.

"P. S. July 3, 1750. Having had no leisure to finish the preparation of my letters to Scotland, before this time, by reason of the extraordinary troubles, hurries, and confusions of my unusual circumstances, I can now inform you, that the controversy between me and my people, which I mentioned in the beginning of my letter, has issued in a separation. An ecclesiastical council was called on the affair, who sat here the week before last, and by a majority of one voice determined an immediate separation to be necessary; and accordingly my pastoral relation to my people was dissolved, on June 22nd. If I can procure the printed accounts from Boston of the proceedings of the council, I will give orders to my friend there, to enclose them with this letter, and direct them to you.—I desire your prayers, that I may take a suitable notice of the frowns of Heaven on me and this people, between whom there once existed so great a union, in bringing to pass such a separation between us; that these troubles may be sanctified to me; that God would overrule the event for his own glory (in which doubtless many adversaries will rejoice and triumph); that he would open a door for my future usefulness, provide for me and my numerous family, and take a fatherly care of us in our present unsettled, uncertain circumstances, being cast on the wide world.

J. E."

"To the Rev. Mr. Erskine.

Northampton, July 5, 1750.

Rev. and dear Brother,

I now acknowledge the receipt of three letters from you since I last wrote to you; one of Sept. 12, another of Sept. 20, another of Dec. 22; all of the year 1749. The two first I received in the winter, with Mr. Glass's Notes on Scripture Texts, Ridgeley on Original Sin, Wheatley's Schools of the Prophets, Davidson's Sermon occasioned by the death of Mr. Harrison, and Mr. M'Raile's Sermon. Your letter written in December, I received a little while ago. I have greatly regretted the want of opportunity to answer you till now; but such have been my extraordinary circumstances, the multitude of distracting troubles and hurries that I have been involved in, (which I cannot easily represent to you,) that I have had no leisure. I have been very uneasy in neglecting to write to my correspondents in Scotland; and about two months ago I set myself to the business, but was soon broken off; and have not been able to return to it again till now. And now, my dear Sir, I thank you for your letters and presents. The books you sent me were entertaining to me, and some of them will be of advantage to me, if God should give me opportunity to prosecute the studies I had begun on the Arminian controversy. There were various things pleasing to me in Glass's Notes, tending to give some new light into the sense of Scripture. He seems to be a man of ability; though I cannot fall in with all his singularities.

The account you say Mr. Davidson gave of the absurdities of the Moravians, are not very surprising to me. I have seen here in America so much of the tendency and issue of such kind of notions, and such sort of religion, as are in vogue among them, and among others in many respects like them, that I expect no other than that sin, folly, absurdity, and things to the last degree reproachful to Christianity, will for ever be the consequence of such things. It seems to me, that enough and enough of this kind has lately appeared, greatly to awaken the attention of christian divines, and make them suspect that the devil's devices in the various counterfeits of vital, experimental religion, have not been sufficiently attended to, and the exact distinctions between the saving operations of the Spirit of God and its false appearances not sufficiently observed. There is something now in the press at Boston, largely handling the subject. I have had opportunity to read the manuscript, and, in my humble opinion, it has a tendency to give as much light in this matter, as any thing that ever I saw. It was written by Mr. Bellamy, minister of Bethlehem, in Connecticut; the minister whom Mr. Brainerd sometimes speaks of as his peculiarly dear and intimate friend (as possibly you may have observed in reading his life). He was of about Mr. Brainerd's age, and it might have been well, if he had had more years over his head. But as he is one of the most intimate friends that I have in the world, and one that I have much acquaintance with, I can say this of him, that he is one of very great experience in religion, as to what has passed between God and his own soul; one of very good natural abilities, of closeness of thought, of extraordinary diligence in his studies, and earnest care exactly to know the truth in these matters. He has long applied his mind to the subject he has wrote upon, and used all possible helps of conversation and reading. And though his style is not such as is like to please the polite world, yet if his youth, and the obscurity of his original, and the place that he lives in, &c. do not prevent his being much taken notice of, I am persuaded his book might serve to give the church of God considerable light as to the nature of true religion, and many important doctrines of Christianity. From the knowledge I have of him, I am fully satisfied that his aim in this publication is not his own fame and reputation in the world; but the glory of God, and the advancement of the kingdom of his Redeemer.

I suspect the follies of some of the Seceders, which you mention in both your letters of Sept. 20, and Dec. 22, arise, in considerable measure, from the same cause with the follies of the Moravians, and the followers of the Wesleys, and many extravagant people in America, *viz.* false religion, counterfeit conversions, and the want of a genuine renovation of the spirit of their minds. I say, as to many of them, not to condemn all in the gross. The spirit seems to be exactly the same with what appears in many, who apparently, by their own account, have had a false conversion. I am a great enemy to censoriousness, and have opposed it very much in my preaching and writings. But yet I think we should avoid that bastard, mischievous charity, by which Satan keeps men asleep, and hides their eyes from those snares and crafty works of his, which it is of the utmost consequence to the church of God to discern and be aware of; and by which, for want of their being discovered, the devil has often had his greatest advantages against the interest of religion.

The Scriptures often lead us to judge of true religion, and the gracious sincerity of professors, by the genius, the temper, and spirit of their religion: Jam. iii. 17. Eph. v. 9. Gal. v. 19. 25. 1 Cor. xiii. 4, &c. Rom. viii. 9.

1 John iv. 16. John xiii. 35. 1 John ii. 10. 1 John iii. 14, and 18, 19, and 23, 24. chap. iv. 7. v. 12, 13. and very many other places. I have been greatly grieved at a spirit of censoriousness; but yet I heartily wish that some sorts of charity were utterly abolished.

The accounts you give of Archbishop Herring, of the moderate, generous, truly catholic and christian principles appearing in him, and some other of the dignified clergy, and other persons of distinction in the church of England, are very agreeable. It is to be hoped that these things are forerunners of something good and great to be brought to pass for the church of God.

I have seen some accounts in our public prints, published here in America, of those conversions and baptisms in the Russian empire, which you mention in your last letter; and should be glad of further information about that matter. We have had published here, an extract of a letter, written by Dr. Doddridge to Mr. Pearsall of Taunton, in Somersetshire, and transmitted by him to Boston, in a letter to Mr. Prince; giving a surprising account of a very wonderful person, a German by nation, a preacher of the gospel to the Jews, lately in London; whom he (Dr. Doddridge) saw and conversed with, and heard preach (or rather repeat) a sermon there; who had had great success in preaching to those miserable people in Germany, Poland, Holland, Lithuania, Hungary, and other parts; God having so blessed his labours that, in the various parts through which he had travelled, he had been the instrument of the conversion of about six hundred Jews; many of whom are expressing their great concern to bring others of their brethren to the knowledge of the great and blessed Redeemer, and beseeching him to instruct their children, that they may preach Christ also. I should be glad if you hear any thing further of the affair, to be informed of it by you. I think such things may well be improved to animate and encourage those who have engaged in the Concert for Prayer for the reviving of Religion. I rejoice to hear what you write of some appearances of awakening in Mr. Gillies's church in Glasgow, and if it continues should be glad to be informed.

I am very glad to hear of what Mr. M'Laurin informs me of the encouragements likely to be given from Scotland to New Jersey college; a very hopeful society; and I believe what is done for that seminary is doing good in an eminent manner. Mr. M'Laurin tells me of some prospect of your being removed to a congregation in Edinburgh, which I am pleased with, because I hope there you will act in a larger sphere, and will have more opportunity to exert the disposition that appears in you, to promote good public designs for Zion's prosperity.

I thank you for the concern you manifest for me under my difficulties and troubles, by reason of the controversy between me and my people, about the terms of christian communion.

This controversy has now had that issue which I expected; it has ended in a separation between me and my people. Many things have appeared, that have been exceedingly unhappy and uncomfortable in the course of this controversy. The great power of prejudices from education, established custom, and the traditions of ancestors and certain admired teachers, and the exceeding unhappy influence of bigotry, has remarkably appeared in the management of this affair. The spirit, that has actuated and engaged my people in this affair, is evidently the same that has appeared in your own people in their opposition to winter communions, but only risen to a much higher degree; and some of the arguments, that have been greatly insisted on here, have been very much of the same sort with some of those urged by your people in your affair. There have been many things said and done, during our controversy, that I shall not now declare. But would only say in the general, that there has been that prejudice, and spirit of jealousy, and increasing engagedness of spirit and fixedness of resolution, to gain the point in view, *viz.* my dismission from my pastoral office over them, upheld and cherished by a persuasion that herein they only stood for the truth, and did their duty, that it has been an exceedingly difficult thing for me to say or do any thing at all in order to their being enlightened, or brought to a more calm and sedate consideration of things, without its being misinterpreted, and turned to an occasion of increasing jealousy and prejudice; even those things wherein I have yielded most, and done most to gratify the people, and assuage their spirits and win their charity. I have often declared to the people, and gave it to them under my hand, that if, after all proper means used, and regular steps taken, they continued averse to remaining under my ministry, I had no inclination to do any thing, as attempting to oblige them to it. But I looked on myself bound in conscience, before I left them, (as I was afraid they were in the way to ruin,) to do my endeavour, that proper means should be used to bring them to a suitable temper, and so to a capacity of proceeding considerately, and with their eyes open; properly, and calmly, and prayerfully examining the point in controversy, and also weighing the consequences of things. To this end I have insisted much on an impartial council, in which should be some of the elderly ministers of the land, to look fully into our state, and to view it with all its circumstances, with full liberty to give both me and them such advice as they should think requisite and proper. And therefore I insisted, that the council should not wholly consist of ministers and churches that were professedly *against me* in the point in controversy; and that it should not consist wholly of ministers and churches of this neighbourhood, who were almost altogether in opposition to me; but that some should be brought from abroad. This I also insisted on, as I thought it most likely an impartial council would do me justice, in the public representation they would make of our affairs, in their result. The people insisted that the council should be wholly of the neighbourhood; undoubtedly because they supposed themselves most sure, that their judgment and advice would be favourable and agreeable to them. I stood the more against it, because in this country we have no such thing as appeals from one council to another, from a lesser to a larger; and also, because the neighbouring ministers were all youngerly men. These things were long the subject matter of uncomfortable troubles and contests. Many were the proposals I made. At last they complied with this proposal, (after great and long-continued opposition to it,) *viz.* That I should nominate two churches to be of the council, who were not within the bounds of this county. And so it was agreed that a council of ten churches should be called, mutually chosen; and that two of my half should be called from abroad. I might have observed before, that there was a great and long dispute about the business of the council, or what should be left to them; and particularly, whether it should be left to them, or they should have liberty, to give us what advice they pleased for a remedy from our calamities. This I insisted on, not that I desired that we should bind ourselves beforehand to stand to their advice, let it be what it would; but I thought it absurd to tie up and limit the council, that they should not exercise their own judgment, and give us their advice, according to their own mind. The people were willing the council should make proposals for an accommodation; but that, if they did not like them, the council should be obliged immediately to separate us, and would not have them have any liberty to advise to wait longer, or use any further means for light, or to take any further or other course for a remedy from our calamities. At last a vote was passed in these words,—'That a council should be called to give us their last advice, for a remedy from the calamities arising from the present unsettled, broken state of the church, by reason of the controversy here subsisting, concerning the qualifications for full communion in the church: and if upon the whole of what they see and find in our circumstances, they judge it best that pastor and people be immediately separated, that they proceed to dissolve the relation between them.' Accordingly a council was agreed upon, to meet here on this business, on June 19th. I nominated two out of this county; of which Mr. Foxcroft's church in Boston was one. But others were nominated provisionally, in case these should fail. Those that came, were Mr. Hall's church of Sutton, and Mr. Hobby's church in Reading. One of the churches that I nominated within the county, refused to send a delegate, *viz.* Mr. Billing's church of Cold Spring. However, Mr. Billing himself (though with some difficulty) was admitted into the council. The people, in managing this affair on their side, have made chief use of a young gentleman of liberal education and notable abilities, and a fluent speaker, of about seven or eight and twenty years of age, my grandfather Stoddard's grandson, being my mother's sister's son; a man of lax principles in religion, falling in, in some essential things, with Arminians, and is very open and bold in it. He was improved as one of the agents for the church, and was their chief spokesman before the council. He very strenuously urged before the council the necessity of an immediate separation; and I knowing the church, the most of them, to be inflexibly bent on this event, informed the council that I should not enter into the dispute, but should refer the matter wholly to the council's judgment; I signified, that I had no desire to leave my people, on any other consideration, any other than their aversion to my being their minister any longer; but, they continuing so averse, had no inclination or desire that they should be compelled, but yet should refer myself to their advice. When the church was convened, in order to the council's knowing their minds with respect to my continuance, about twenty-three appeared for it, others staid away, choosing not to act either way; but the generality of the church, which consists of about 230 male members, voted for my dismission. My dismission was carried in the council by a majority of one voice. The ministers were equally divided, but of the delegates one more was for it than against it, and it so happened that all those of the council, who came from the churches of the people's choosing, voted for my dismission; but all those who came from the churches that I chose, were against it, and there happening to be one fewer of these than of the other, by the church of Cold Spring not sending a delegate, (which was through that people's prejudice against my opinion,) the vote was carried that way by the voice of one delegate. However, on the 22d of the last month, the relation between me and this people was dissolved. I suppose that the Result of the Council, and the Protestation of some of the members, are printed in Boston by this time. I shall endeavour to procure one of the printed accounts, to be sent with this letter to you, together with one of my books on the point that has been in controversy between me and my people. Two of the members of the council, who dissented from the Result, yet did not sign the Protestation, *viz.* Mr. Reynolds and his delegate, which I suppose was owing to Mr. Reynolds's extraordinarily cautious and timorous temper. The last sabbath I preached my farewell sermon. Many in the congregation seemed to be much affected, and some are exceedingly grieved. Some few, I believe, have some relentings of heart, that voted me away. But there is no great probability that the leading part of the church will ever change. Beside their own fixedness of resolution, there are many in the neighbouring towns to support their resolution, both in the ministry and civil magistracy; without whose influence I believe the people never would have been so violent as they have been.

I desire that such a time of awful changes, dark clouds, and great frowns of Heaven on me and my people, may be a time of serious consideration, thorough self-reflection and examination, and deep humiliation with me. I desire your fervent prayers for me, and for those who have heretofore been my people. I know not what will become of them. There seems to be the utmost danger, that the younger generation will be carried away with Arminianism as with a flood. The young gentleman I spoke of, is high in their esteem, and is become the most leading man in the town; and is very bold in declaiming and disputing for his opinions; and we have none able to confront and withstand him in dispute; and some of the young people already show a disposition to fall in with his notions. And it is not likely that the people will obtain any young gentleman of Calvinistic sentiments, to settle with them in the ministry, who will have courage and ability to make head against him. And as to the older people, there never appeared so great an indifference among them, about things of this nature. They will at present be much more likely to be thorough in their care to settle a minister of principles contrary to mine, as to terms of communion, than to settle one that is sound in the doctrines of grace. The great concern of the leading part of the town, at present, will probably be, to come off with flying colours, in the issue of the controversy they have had with me, and of what they have done in it; for which they know many condemn them.

An end is put for the present, by these troubles, to the studies I was before engaged in, and my design of writing against Arminianism. I had made considerable preparation, and was deeply engaged in the prosecution of this design, before I was rent off from it by these difficulties, and if ever God should give me opportunity, I would again resume that affair. But I am now, as it were, thrown upon the wide ocean of the world, and know not what will become of me, and my numerous and chargeable family. Nor have I any particular door in view that I depend upon to be opened for my future serviceableness. Most places in New England that want a minister, would not be forward to invite one with so chargeable a family, nor one so far advanced in years—being 46 the 5th day of last October. I am fitted for no other business but study. I should make a poor hand at getting a living by any secular employment. We are in the hands of God, and I bless him, I am not anxious concerning his disposal of us. I hope I shall not distrust him, nor be unwilling to submit to his will. And I have cause of thankfulness, that there seems also to be such a disposition in my family. You are pleased, dear Sir, very kindly to ask me, whether I could sign the Westminster Confession of Faith, and submit to the presbyterian form of church government; and to offer to use your influence to procure a call for me, to some congregation in Scotland. I should be very ungrateful, if I were not thankful for such kindness and friendship. As to my subscribing to the substance of the Westminster Confession, there would be no difficulty; and as to the presbyterian government, I have long been perfectly out of conceit of our unsettled, independent, confused way of church government in this land; and the presbyterian way has ever appeared to me most agreeable to the word of God, and the reason and nature of things; though I cannot say that I think, that the presbyterian government of the church of Scotland is so perfect, that it cannot, in some respects, be mended. But as to my removing, with my numerous family, over the Atlantic, it is, I acknowledge, attended with many difficulties that I shrink at. Among other things, this is very considerable, that it would be on uncertainties, whether my gifts and administrations would suit my congregation, that should send for me without trial; and so great a thing as such a removal, had need to be on some certainty as to that matter. If the expectations of a congregation were so great, and they were so confident of my qualifications, as to call me at a venture, having never seen nor heard me; their disappointment might possibly be so much the greater, and they the more uneasy after acquaintance and trial. My own country is not so dear to me, but that, if there were an evident prospect of being more serviceable to Zion's interests elsewhere, I could forsake it. And I think my wife is fully of this disposition.

I forgot to mention, that, in this evil time in Northampton, there are some of the young people under awakenings; and I hope two or three have lately been converted: two very lately, besides two or three hopefully brought home the last year.

My wife and family join with me in most respectful and cordial salutations to you, and your consort; and we desire the prayers of you both for us, under our present circumstances. My youngest child but one has long been in a very infirm, afflicted, and decaying state with the rickets, and some other disorders. I desire your prayers for it.

I am, dear Sir,
Your most affectionate and obliged
Friend and brother,
JONATHAN EDWARDS."

"P. S. For accounts of the state of religion in America, and some reasons of my conduct in this controversy with my people, I must refer you to my letters to Mr. Robe and Mr. M'Laurin."

CHAPTER XVIII.

LETTER TO MR. M'CULLOCH—TO MR. ERSKINE—AN ACCOUNT OF THE TROUBLES AT NORTHAMPTON CONCLUDED.

THE correspondence of Mr. Edwards with some eminent ministers in Scotland, already introduced, has probably been found among the most interesting parts of this Memoir; equally creditable to Mr. Edwards, and to the excellent men, whose enlightened minds at once discerned his uncommon worth. The admirers of Mr. Edwards are under the deepest obligations to Mr. (afterwards Dr.) Erskine, whose name so frequently has occurred, as the individual through whose exertions the various works which principally form these volumes were first introduced in this kingdom.—The letters which are found in this chapter will not diminish the interest already felt by the pious and intelligent reader.

"To the Rev. Mr. M'Culloch.

Northampton, July 6, 1750.

REV. AND DEAR SIR,

It is now long since I have received a letter from you: the last was dated March 10, 1749. However, you having heretofore manifested that our correspondence was not unacceptable to you, I would not omit to do my part towards the continuance of it. Perhaps one reason of your neglecting to write, may be the failing of such agreeable matter for correspondence, as we had some years ago, when religion was flourishing in Scotland and America, and we had joyful information to give each other, of things pertaining to the city of our God. It is indeed now a sorrowful time on this side of the ocean. Iniquity abounds, and the love of many waxes cold. Multitudes of fair and high professors, in one place and another, have sadly backslidden; sinners are desperately hardened; experimental religion is more than ever out of credit, with the far greater part, and the doctrines of grace, and those principles in religion that do chiefly concern the power of godliness, are far more than ever discarded. Arminianism and Pelagianism have made a strange progress within a few years. The church of England, in New England, is I suppose treble of what it was seven years ago. Many professors are gone off to great lengths in the enthusiasms and extravagance, in their notions and practices. Great contentions, separations, and confusions, in our religious state, prevail in many parts of the land. Some of our main pillars are broken; one of which was Mr. Webb of Boston, who died in the latter part of last April. Much of the glory of the town of Boston is gone with him; and if the bereavements of that town should be added to, by the death of two or three more of their remaining elder ministers, that place would be in a very sorrowful state indeed, like a city whose walls are broken down, and like a large flock without a shepherd, encompassed with wolves, and many in the midst of it.

These are the dark things that appear. But on the other hand, there are some things that have a different aspect. There have in some places appeared revivals of religion. Some little revivings have been in some places towards Boston. There has been some reformation, not long since, in one of our colleges; and by what I hear there has been much more of this nature in some other parts of the province of New York, near Bedford river; something in several parts of New Jersey, particularly through the labours of Mr. Greenman, a young gentleman educated by the charitable expenses of the pious and eminent Mr. David Brainerd, mentioned in his Life, which I think I sent to you the last summer. And since I last wrote to Scotland, I have had accounts of the prevailing of a religious concern in some parts of Virginia.

And I must not forget to inform you, that, although I think it has of late been the darkest time in Northampton, that ever was since the town stood, yet there have been some overturnings on the minds of some of the young people here, and two or three instances of hopeful conversion the last summer, and as many very lately.

When I speak of its being a dark time here, I have a special reference to the great controversy that has subsisted here, for about a year and a half, between me and my people, about the forms of communion in the visible church; which has even at length issued in a separation between me and my people; for a more particular account of which, I must refer you to my letters to Mr. Robe and Mr. Erskine.—Besides, I shall endeavour to procure the printed copies of the Result of the Council, that sat here the week before last, with the Protestation of some of the members, that these may be sent to you with this letter, together with one of my books, published on the point in debate between me and my people; of which I crave your acceptance.

I am now separated from the people between whom and me there was once the greatest union. Remarkable is the providence of God in this matter. In this event we have a striking instance of the instability and uncertainty of all things here below. The dispensation is indeed awful in many respects, calling for serious reflection and deep humiliation in me and my people. The enemy, far and near, will now triumph; but God can overrule all for his own glory. I have now nothing visible to depend upon for my future usefulness, or the subsistence of my numerous family. But I hope we have an all-sufficient, faithful, covenant God, to depend upon. I desire that I may ever submit to him, walk humbly before him, and put my trust wholly in him. I desire, dear Sir, your prayers for us, under our present circumstances.

I am, Sir, your respectful
and affectionate friend and brother,

JONATHAN EDWARDS."

"P. S. My wife and family join with me in cordial salutations to you and yours."

After Mr. Edwards was dismissed from his people, several months elapsed before he received any proposals of settlement. During this interval, the committee of the church found it very difficult to procure a regular supply of the pulpit. When no other preacher could be procured, Mr. Edwards was for a time applied to by the committee, to preach for them; but always with apparent reluctance, and only for the given sabbath. He alludes to these circumstances in the following letter; in which the reader will find, that he was a decided advocate for the celebration of the Lord's supper every Lord's day.

Letter to Mr. Erskine.

"*Northampton, Nov.* 15, 1750.

Rev. and dear Sir,

Some time in July last I wrote to you, and ordered one of my books on the Qualifications for Communion in the Church, to be sent to you from Boston, with the letter. In my letter I informed you of what had come to pass, in the issue of the late controversy between me and my people, in the dissolution of my pastoral relation to them; and ordered the printed Result of the Ecclesiastical Council, that sat upon our affairs, and the Protest against the said Result, to be put up with the letter; and also, at the same time, sent letters to my other correspondents in Scotland, with the books, &c. I have as yet had no call to any stated business elsewhere in the ministry; there has been some prospect of my having invitations to one or two places. The people of Northampton are hitherto destitute of a minister. They have exerted themselves very much, to obtain some candidate to come and preach to them on probation, and have sent to many different places; but have hitherto been disappointed, and seem to be very much nonplussed. But the major part of them seem to continue without any relenting or misgiving of heart, concerning what has been done; at least the major part of the leading men in the congregation. But there is a number whose hearts are broken at what has come to pass; and I believe are more deeply affected than ever they were at any temporal bereavement. It is thus with one of the principal men in the parish, *viz.* Col. Dwight; and another of our principal men, *viz.* Dr. Mather, adheres very much to me; and there are more women of this sort, than men; and I doubt not but there is a number, who in their hearts are with me, who durst not appear, by reason of the great resolution, and high hand, with which things are carried in the opposition, by the prevailing part. Such is the state of things among us, that a person cannot appear on my side, without greatly exposing himself to the resentments of his friends and neighbours, and being the object of much odium. The committee, that have the care of supplying the pulpit, have asked me to preach, the greater part of the time since my dismission, when I have been at home; but it has seemed to be with much reluctance that they have come to me, and only because they could not get the pulpit supplied otherwise; and they have asked me only from sabbath to sabbath. In the mean time, they have taken much pains to get somebody else to preach to them.

Since I wrote to you in July last, I received your letter, dated the 30th of April last, with your generous and acceptable presents of Fraser's Treatise of Justifying Faith, Mr. Crawford's Manual against Infidelity, Mr. Randal's Letters on Frequent Communicating, Mr. Blair's Sermon before the Society for propagating Christian Knowledge, with an account of the Society, and the Bishop of London's Letters to the Cities of London and Westminster. The view the last mentioned gives of the wickedness of those cities, is very affecting; and the patience of God towards such cities, so full of wickedness, so heinous and horrid in its kinds, and attended with such aggravations, is very astonishing. That those cities and the nation, and indeed Christendom in general, are come to such a pass as they are, seems to me to argue that some very remarkable dispensation of Divine Providence is nigh, either of mercy or of judgment, or perhaps both; of mercy to an elect number, and great wrath and vengeance towards others; and that those very things you take notice of in Isa. lix. are approaching, appears to me very probable. However, I cannot but think, that, at such a day, all such as truly love Zion, and lament the wickedness that prevails in the earth, are very loudly called upon to united and earnest prayer to God, to arise and plead his own cause, that he would make bare his arm, that *that* may bring salvation; that now when the enemy comes in as a flood, the Spirit of the Lord may lift up a standard against him. When the church of Christ is like the ship, wherein Christ and his disciples were, when it was tossed with a dreadful tempest, and even covered with waves, and Christ was asleep; certainly it becomes Christians (though not with doubting and unbelief) to call on their Redeemer, that he would awake out of sleep, and rebuke the winds and waves. There are some things that afford a degree of comfort and hope, in this dark day, respecting the state of Zion. I cannot but rejoice at some things which I have seen, that have been lately published in England, and the reception they have met with in so corrupt a time and nation. Some things of Dr. Doddridge's, (who seems to have his heart truly engaged for the interests of religion,) particularly his Rise and Progress, and Col. Gardiner's Life, and also Mr. Hervey's Meditations. And I confess it is a thing that gives me much hope, that there are so many on this side the ocean united in the Concert for Prayer, proposed from Scotland; of which I may give a more particular account in a letter to Mr. M'Laurin, which I intend shall be sent with this. I had lately a letter from Governor Belcher, and in the postscript he sent me the following extract of a letter he had lately received from Dr. Doddridge. 'Nor did I ever know a finer class of young preachers, for its number, than that which God has given me this year, to send out into the churches. Yet are not all the supplies, here as elsewhere, adequate to their necessities; but I hope God will prosper the schemes we are forming for their assistance. I bless God, that in these middle parts of our island, peace and truth prevail in sweet harmony; and I think God is reviving our cause, or rather his own, sensibly, though in a gentle and almost unobserved manner.'

This which the Doctor speaks of, I hope is a revival of religion; though many things, in many places, have been boasted of as glorious revivals, which have been but counterparts of religion; so it has been with many things that were intermingled with and followed our late happy revival. There have been in New England, within these eight years past, many hundreds, if not thousands, of instances very much like that of the boy at Tiptry Heath, mentioned by Mr. Davidson, as you give account in your letter. We ought not only to praise God for every thing that appears favourable to the interests of religion, and to pray earnestly for a general revival, but also to use means that are proper in order to it; and one proper means must be allowed to be, a due administration of Christ's ordinances: one instance of which is that, which you and Mr. Randal have been striving for; *viz.* a restoring the primitive practice of frequent communicating. I should much wonder (had it not been for what I have myself lately seen of the force of bigotry and prejudice, arising from education and custom) how such arguments and persuasions, as Mr. Randal uses, could be withstood; but however they may be resisted for the present, yet I hope those who have begun will continue to plead the cause of Christ's institutions; and whatever opposition is made, I should think it would be best for them to plead nothing at all short of Christ's institutions, *viz.* the administration of the Lord's supper every Lord's day:—it must come to that at last; and why should Christ's ministers and people, by resting in a partial reformation, lay a foundation for a new struggle, an uncomfortable labour and conflict, in some future generation, in order to a full restoration of the primitive practice.

I should be greatly gratified, dear Sir, by the continuance of your correspondence, and by being informed by you of the state of things, relating to the interests of religion in Europe, and especially in Great Britain; and particularly whether the affair of a comprehension is like to go on, or whether the test act is like to be taken off, or if there be any thing else done, or published, in England or Scotland, that remarkably affects the interests of religion.

I have, with this letter, sent Mr. Bellamy's *True Religion Delineated,* with a Sermon of mine at Mr. Strong's ordination; of which I ask your acceptance, as a small testimony of gratitude for your numerous favours to me. I ask a constant remembrance in your prayers, that I may have the presence of God under my unusual trials, and that I may make a good improvement of all God's dealings with me. My wife joins with me in most cordial salutations to you and Mrs. Erskine.

I am, dear Sir,

your affectionate and obliged

friend and brother,

"Mr. Erskine." JONATHAN EDWARDS."

"At length," observes Dr. Hopkins, "a great uneasiness was manifested, by many of the people of Northampton, that Mr. Edwards should preach there at all. Upon which the committee for supplying the pulpit called the town together, to know their minds with respect to that matter, when they voted, *That it was not agreeable to their minds that he should preach among them.* Accordingly, while Mr. Edwards was in the town, and they had no other minister to preach to them, they carried on public worship among themselves, and without any preaching, rather than invite him.*

"Every one must be sensible," remarks Dr. Hopkins, who was himself an occasional eye-witness of these scenes, "that this was a great trial to Mr. Edwards. He had been nearly twenty-four years among that people; and his labours had been, to all appearance, from time to time greatly blessed among them: and a great number looked on him as their spiritual father, who had been the happy instrument of turning them from darkness to light, and plucking them as brands out of the burning. And they had from time to time professed that they looked upon it as one of their greatest privileges to have such a minister, and manifested their great love and esteem of him, to such

* This vote appears to have been passed in the latter part of November, a few weeks only before Mr. Edwards received proposals of settlement, which he ultimately accepted.

a degree, that, (as St. Paul says of the Galatians,) "if it had been possible, they would have plucked out their own eyes, and given them to him." And they had a great interest in *his* affection: he had borne them on his heart, and carried them in his bosom for many years; exercising a tender concern and love for them: for their good he was always writing, contriving, labouring; for them he had poured out ten thousand fervent prayers; in their good he had rejoiced as one that findeth great spoil; and they were dear to him above any other people under heaven.—Now to have *this people* turn against him, and thrust him out from among them, stopping their ears, and running upon him with furious zeal, not allowing him to defend himself by giving him a fair hearing; and even refusing so much as to hear him preach; many of them surmising and publicly speaking many ill things as to his ends and designs! surely this must come very near to him, and try his spirit. The words of the psalmist seem applicable to this case: "It was not an enemy that reproached me, that did magnify himself against me, then I would have hid myself from him. But it was *thou*—my guide and mine acquaintance. We took sweet counsel together, and walked unto the house of God in company."

"Let us therefore now *behold the man!*—The calm sedateness of his mind; his meekness and humility in great and violent opposition, and injurious treatment; his resolution and steady conduct through all this dark and terrible storm; were truly wonderful, and cannot be set in so beautiful and affecting a light by any description, as they appeared in to his friends, who were eye-witnesses.

"Mr. Edwards had a numerous and chargeable family, and little or no income, exclusive of his salary; and considering how far he was advanced in years; the general disposition of people, who want a minister, to prefer a young man, who has never been settled, to one who has been dismissed from his people; and what misrepresentations were made of his principles through the country; it looked to him not at all probable, that he should ever have opportunity to be settled again in the work of the ministry, if he was dismissed from Northampton: and he was not inclined, or able, to take any other course, or go into any other business to get a living: so that beggary as well as disgrace stared him full in the face, if he persisted in his principles. When he was fixed in his principles, and before they were publicly known, he told some of his friends, that if he discovered and persisted in them, it would most likely issue in his dismission and disgrace; and the ruin of himself and family, as to their *temporal* interests. He therefore first sat down and counted the cost, and deliberately took up the cross, when it was set before him in its full weight and magnitude; and in direct opposition to all *worldly* views and motives. And therefore his conduct, in these circumstances, was a remarkable exercise and discovery of his conscientiousness; and of his readiness to deny himself, and to forsake all that he had, to follow Christ.—A man must have a considerable degree of the spirit of a martyr, to go on with the stedfastness and resolution with which he did. He ventured wherever truth and duty appeared to lead him, unmoved at the threatening dangers on every side.

"However, God did not forsake him. As he gave him those inward supports, by which he was able in patience to possess his soul, and courageously row on in the storm, in the face of boisterous winds beating hard upon him, and in the midst of gaping waves threatening to swallow him up; so he soon appeared for him in his providence, even beyond all his expectations. His correspondents, and other friends in Scotland, hearing of his dismission, and fearing it might be the means of bringing him into worldly straits, generously contributed a considerable sum, and sent it over to him.

"And God did not leave him without tender and valuable friends at Northampton. For a small number of his people, who opposed his dismission from the beginning, and some, who acted on neither side, but after his dismission adhered to him, under the influence of their great esteem and love of Mr. Edwards, were willing, and thought themselves able, to maintain him: and insisted upon it, that it was his duty to stay among them, as a distinct and separate congregation from the body of the town who had rejected him.

"Mr. Edwards could not see it to be his duty to remain among them, as this would probably be a means of perpetuating an unhappy division in the town; and there was to him no prospect of doing the good there, which would counterbalance the evil. However, that he might do all he could to satisfy his tender and afflicted friends, he consented to ask the advice of an ecclesiastical council. Accordingly a council was called, and met at Northampton on the 15th of May, 1751.—The town on this occasion was put into a great tumult. They, who were active in the dismission of Mr. Edwards, supposed, though without any good ground, that he was contriving with his friends again to introduce himself at Northampton." A meeting of the church was summoned, and a committee of the church appointed; who, in the name of the church, drew up a remonstrance against the proceedings of the council, and laid it before that body. The character of this instrument may be learned, from the subsequent confession of one of the committee of the church that signed it, who was principally concerned in drawing it up, and very active in bringing the church to accept of it, and to vote that it should be presented to the council. To use his own language, it was "every where interlarded with unchristian bitterness, and sarcastical and unmannerly insinuations. It contained divers direct, grievous, and criminal charges and allegations against Mr. Edwards, which, I have since good reason to suppose, were all founded on jealous and uncharitable mistakes, and so were really gross slanders; also many heavy and reproachful charges upon divers of Mr. Edwards's adherents, and some severe censures of them all indiscriminately; all of which, if not wholly false and groundless, yet were altogether unnecessary, and therefore highly criminal. Indeed I am fully convinced that the whole of that composure, excepting the small part of it relating to the expediency of Mr. Edwards's resettlement at Northampton, was totally unchristian,—a scandalous, abusive, injurious libel against Mr. Edwards and his particular friends, especially the former, and highly provoking and detestable in the sight of God; for which I am heartily sorry and ashamed; and pray I may remember it, with deep abasement and penitence, all my days."

After this remonstrance of the church had been read before the council, they immediately invited *the committee*, by whom it was signed, to come forward, and prove the numerous allegations and insinuations which it contained; but they refused to appear and support any of their charges, or so much as to give the gentlemen of the council any opportunity to confer with them, about the affair depending, though it was diligently sought; and though, by presenting the remonstrance, they had virtually given the council jurisdiction, as to the charges it contained, yet they utterly refused to acknowledge them to be an ecclesiastical council. The council then invited *the church*, as a body, to a friendly conference, to see if some measures could not be devised for the removal of the difficulties, in which the ecclesiastical affairs of the town were involved; but although this was earnestly and repeatedly moved for, on the part of the council, it was repeatedly and finally denied on the part of the church.

The council having heard what Mr. Edwards, and those who adhered to him, had to say, advised, agreeably to the judgment of Mr. Edwards, that he should leave Northampton, and accept of the invitations which he had received, to take charge of the Indian mission, as well as of the church and congregation, at Stockbridge; of which a more particular account will be given.

As a proper close to this melancholy story, and to confirm and illustrate what has been related, the following *letter* from Joseph Hawley, Esq. to the Rev. Mr. Hall, of Sutton, published in a weekly newspaper in Boston, May 9, 1760, is here inserted. This gentleman was a near kinsman of Mr. Edwards,* though his active opponent; he was a lawyer of distinguished talents and eloquence.

"To the Rev. Mr. Hall, of Sutton.

Northampton, May 9, 1760.

Rev. Sir,

I have often wished that every member of the two ecclesiastical councils, that formerly sat in Northampton, upon the unhappy differences, between our former most worthy and reverend pastor, Mr. Jonathan Edwards, and the church here, whereof you were a member; I say, Sir, I have often wished every one of them truly knew my real sense of my own conduct in the affair, that the one and the other of the said councils are privy to. As I have long apprehended it to be my duty, not only to humble myself before God, for what was unchristian and sinful in my conduct before the said councils, but also to confess my faults to *them*, and take shame to myself before them; so I have often studied with myself, in what manner it was practicable for me to do it. When I understood that you, Sir, and Mr. Eaton, were to be at Cold-Spring at the time of the late council, I resolved to improve the opportunity, fully to open my mind there to you and him thereon; and thought that probably some method might be then thought of, in which my reflections on myself, touching the matters above hinted at, might be communicated to most, if not all, the gentlemen aforesaid, who did not reside in this county. But you know, Sir, how difficult it was for us to converse together by ourselves, when at Cold-Spring, without giving umbrage to that people; I therefore proposed writing to you upon the matters, which I had then opportunity only most summarily to suggest; which you, Sir, signified would be agreeable to you. I therefore now undertake what I then proposed, in which I humbly ask the divine aid; and that I may be made most freely willing, fully to confess my sin and guilt to you and the world, in those instances, which I have reason to suppose fell under your notice, as they were public and notorious transactions, and on account whereof, therefore, you, Sir, and all others who had knowledge thereof, had just cause to be offended at me.

And in the first place, Sir, I apprehend that, with the church and people of Northampton, I sinned and erred exceedingly, in consenting and labouring, that there should be so early a dismission of Mr. Edwards from his pastoral relation to us, even upon the supposition that he was really in a mistake in the disputed point; not only because the dispute was upon matters so very disputable in themselves, and at the greatest remove from fundamental, but because Mr. Edwards so long had approved himself a most faithful and painful pastor to the said church. He also changed his sentiments, in that point, wholly from a tender regard to what appeared to him to be truth; and had made known his sentiments with great moderation, and upon great deliberation, against all worldly motives, from mere fidelity to his great Master, and a tender regard to the souls of his flock, as we had the highest reason to judge. These considerations now seem to me sufficient; and would (if we had been of a right spirit) have greatly endeared him to his people, and made us to the last degree reluctant to part with him, and disposed us to the exercise of the greatest candour, gentleness, and moderation. How much of the reverse whereof appeared in us I need not tell you, Sir, who were an eye-witness of our temper and conduct.

And, although it does not become me to pronounce decisively, on a point so disputable, as was then in dispute; yet I beg leave to say, that I really apprehend, that it is of the highest moment to the body of this church, and to me in particular, most solicitously to inquire, whether, like the Pharisees and lawyers in John Baptist's time, we did not reject the counsel of God against ourselves, in rejecting Mr. Edwards and his doctrine, which was the ground of his dismission. And I humbly conceive, that it highly imports us all of this church, most seriously and impartially to examine what that most worthy and able divine published, about that time, in support of the same, whereby he being dead yet speaketh. But there were three things, Sir, especially, in my own particular conduct before the first council, which have been justly matter of great grief and much trouble to me, almost ever since; *viz.*

In the first place, I confess, Sir, that I acted very immodestly and abusively to you, as well as injuriously to the church and myself, when with much zeal and unbecoming assurance, I moved the council that they would interpose to silence and stop you, in an address you were making one morning to the people, wherein you were, if I do not forget, briefly exhorting them to a tender remembrance of the former affection and harmony, that had long subsisted between them and their reverend pastor, and the great comfort and profit which they apprehended that they had received from his ministry; for which, Sir, I heartily ask your forgiveness; and I think, that we ought, instead of opposing an exhortation of that nature, to have received it with all thankfulness.

Another particular of my conduct before that council, which I now apprehend was criminal, and was owing to the want of that tender affection, and reverend respect and esteem for Mr. Edwards, which he had highly merited of me, was my strenuously opposing the adjournment of the matters submitted to that council for about two months; for which I declare myself unfeignedly sorry; and I with shame remember, that I did it in a peremptory, decisive, vehement, and very immodest manner.

But, Sir, the most criminal part of my conduct at that

* The father of Mr. Hawley married Rebekah, the fifth daughter of the Rev. Mr. Stoddard, the sister of Mr. Edwards's mother.

time, that I am conscious of, was my exhibiting to that council a set of arguments in writing, the drift whereof was to prove the reasonableness and necessity of Mr. Edwards's dismission, in case no accommodation was then effected with mutual consent; which writing, by clear implication, contained some severe, uncharitable, and, if I remember right, groundless and slanderous imputations on Mr. Edwards, expressed in bitter language. And although the original draft thereof was not done by me, yet I foolishly and sinfully consented to copy it; and, as agent for the church, to read it, and deliver it to the council; which I could never have done, if I had not had a wicked relish for perverse things: which conduct of mine I confess was very sinful, and highly provoking to God; for which I am ashamed, confounded, and have nothing to answer.

As to the church's remonstrance, as it was called, which their committee preferred to the last of the said councils; (to all which I was consenting, and in the composing whereof I was very active, as also in bringing the church to their vote upon it;) I would, in the first place, only observe, that I do not remember any thing, in that small part of it, which was plainly discursive of the expediency of Mr. Edwards's re-settlement here, as pastor to a part of the church, which was very exceptionable. But as to all the residue, which was much the greatest part thereof, (and I am not certain that any part was wholly free,) it was every where interlarded with unchristian bitterness, sarcastical and unmannerly insinuations. It contained divers direct, grievous, and criminal charges and allegations against Mr. Edwards, which, I have since good reason to suppose, were all founded on jealous and uncharitable mistakes, and so were really gross slanders; also many heavy and reproachful charges upon divers of Mr. Edwards's adherents, and some severe censures of them all indiscriminately; all of which, if not wholly false and groundless, were altogether unnecessary, and therefore highly criminal. Indeed, I am fully convinced, that the whole of that composure, excepting the small part thereof above mentioned, was totally unchristian—a scandalous, abusive, injurious libel, against Mr. Edwards and his particular friends, especially the former, and highly provoking and detestable in the sight of God; for which I am heartily sorry and ashamed; and pray that I may remember it with deep abasement and penitence all my days. Nor do I now think, that the church's conduct in refusing to appear, and attend before that council, to support the charges and allegations in the said remonstrance against Mr. Edwards and the said brethren, which they demanded, was ever vindicated, by all the subtle answers that were given to the said demand; nor do I think that our conduct in that instance was capable of a defence. For it appears to me, that, by making such charges against them before the said council, we necessarily so far gave that council jurisdiction; and I own with sorrow and regret, that I zealously endeavoured, that the church should perseveringly refuse to appear before the said council, for the purpose aforesaid; which I humbly pray God to forgive.

Another part of my conduct, Sir, of which I have long repented, and for which I hereby declare my hearty sorrow, was my obstinate opposition to the last council's having any conference with the church; which the said council earnestly and repeatedly moved for, and which the church, as you know, finally denied. I think it discovered a great deal of pride and vain sufficiency in the church, and showed them to be very opinionative, especially the chief sticklers, one of whom I was; and think it was running a most presumptuous risk, and acting the part of proud scorners, for us to refuse hearing, and candidly and seriously considering, what that council could say or oppose to us; among whom, there were divers justly in great reputation for grace and wisdom.

In these instances, Sir, of my conduct, and in others, (to which you were not privy,) in the course of that most melancholy contention with Mr. Edwards, I now see that I was very much influenced by vast pride, self-sufficiency, ambition, and vanity. I appear to myself vile, and doubtless much more so to others, who are more impartial; and do, in the review thereof, abhor myself, and repent sorely: and if my own heart condemns me, it behoves me solemnly to remember, that God is greater and knoweth all things. I hereby own, Sir, that such treatment of Mr. Edwards, wherein I was so deeply concerned and active, was particularly and very aggravatedly sinful and ungrateful in me, because I was not only under the common obligations of each individual of the society to him, as a most able, diligent, and faithful pastor; but I had also received many instances of his tenderness, goodness, and generosity to me as a young kinsman, whom he was disposed to treat in a most friendly manner.

Indeed, Sir, I must own, that, by my conduct in consulting and acting against Mr. Edwards, within the time of our most unhappy disputes with him, and especially in and about that abominable 'remonstrance,' I have so far symbolized with Balaam, Ahitophel, and Judas, that I am confounded and filled with terror, oftentimes, when I attend to the most painful similitude. And I freely confess, that, on account of my conduct above mentioned, I have the greatest reason to tremble at those most solemn and awful words of our Saviour, Matt. xviii. 6. 'Whoso shall offend one of these little ones, which believe in me, it were better for him that a mill-stone were hanged about his neck, and that he were drowned in the depth of the sea;' and those in Luke x. 16. 'He that despiseth you, despiseth me; and he that despiseth me, despiseth him that sent me;' and I am most sorely sensible that nothing but that infinite grace and mercy, which saved some of the betrayers and murderers of our blessed Lord, and the persecutors of his martyrs, can pardon me; in which alone I hope for pardon, for the sake of Christ, whose blood, blessed be God, cleanseth from all sin. On the whole, Sir, I am convinced, that I have the greatest reason to say as David, 'Have mercy upon me, O God, according to thy loving-kindness, according to the multitude of thy tender mercies, blot out my transgressions; wash me thoroughly from mine iniquity, and cleanse me from my sin: for I acknowledge my transgressions, and my sin is ever before me. Hide thy face from my sins, and blot out all mine iniquities; create in me a clean heart, O God, and renew a right spirit within me; cast me not away from thy presence, and take not thy Holy Spirit from me; restore unto me the joy of thy salvation, and uphold me with thy free Spirit.' (Ps. li. 1—3, 9—12.)

And I humbly apprehend, that it greatly concerns the church of Northampton most seriously to examine, whether the many hard speeches, spoken by many particular members against their former pastor, some of which the church really countenanced, (and especially those spoken by the church as a body, in that most vile 'remonstrance,') are not so odious and ungodly, as to be utterly incapable of defence; whether the said church were not guilty of a great sin, in being so willing and disposed, for so slight a cause, to part with so faithful and godly a minister as Mr. Edwards was; and whether ever God will hold us guiltless, till we cry to him for Christ's sake to pardon and save us from that judgment, which such ungodly deeds deserve. And I most heartily wish and pray, that the town and church of Northampton would seriously and carefully examine, Whether they have not abundant cause to judge, that they are now lying under great guilt in the sight of God; and whether those of us, who were concerned in that most awful contention with Mr. Edwards, can ever more reasonably expect God's favour and blessing, till our eyes are opened, and we become thoroughly convinced that we have greatly provoked the Most High, and have been injurious to one of the best of men; and until we shall be thoroughly convinced, that we have dreadfully persecuted Christ, by persecuting and vexing that just man, and servant of Christ; until we shall be humble as in the dust on account of it, and till we openly, in full terms, and without baulking the matter, confess the same before the world, and most humbly and earnestly seek forgiveness of God, and do what we can to honour the memory of Mr. Edwards, and clear it of all the aspersions which we unjustly cast upon him; since God has been pleased to put it beyond our power to ask his forgiveness. Such terms, I am persuaded, the great and righteous God will hold us to, and that it will be vain for us to hope to escape with impunity in any other way. This I am convinced of with regard to myself, and this way I most solemnly propose to take myself (if God in his mercy shall give me opportunity); that so, by making free confession to God and man of my sin and guilt, and publicly taking shame to myself, I may give glory to the God of Israel, and do what in me lies to clear the memory of that venerable man from the wrongs and injuries I was so active in bringing on his reputation and character; and I thank God, that he has been pleased to spare my life to this time, and am sorry that I have delayed the affair so long.

Although I made the substance of almost all the foregoing reflections in writing, but not exactly in the same manner, to Mr. Edwards and the brethren who adhered to him, in Mr. Edwards's life, and before he removed from Stockbridge, and I have reason to believe that he, from his great candour and charity, heartily forgave me and prayed for me; yet, because that was not generally known, I look on myself obliged to take further steps; for *while I kept silence my bones waxed old, &c.* For all these my great sins, therefore, in the first place, I humbly and most earnestly ask forgiveness of God; in the next place, of the relatives and near friends of Mr. Edwards. I also ask the forgiveness of all those, who were called Mr. Edwards's adherents; and of all the members of the ecclesiastical councils above mentioned; and lastly, of all christian people, who have had any knowledge of these matters.

I have no desire, Sir, that you should make any secret of this letter; but that you would communicate the same to whom you shall judge proper: and I purpose, if God shall give me opportunity, to procure it to be published in some one of the public newspapers; for I cannot devise any other way of making known my sentiments of the foregoing matters to all who ought to be acquainted therewith, and therefore I think I ought to do it, whatever remarks I may foresee will be made thereon. Probably, when it comes out, some of my acquaintance will pronounce me quite overrun with vapours; others will be furnished with matter for mirth and pleasantry; others will cursorily pass it over, as relating to matters quite stale; but some, I am persuaded, will rejoice to see me brought to a sense of my sin and duty; and I myself shall be conscious, that I have done something of what the nature of the case admits, towards undoing what is, and long has been, to my greatest remorse and trouble, that it was ever done.

Sir, I desire that none would entertain a thought, from my having spoken respectfully of Mr. Edwards, that I am disaffected to our present pastor; for the very reverse is true; and I have a reverend esteem, real value, and hearty affection for him; and bless God, that he has, notwithstanding all our former unworthiness, given us one to succeed Mr. Edwards, who, as I have reason to hope, is truly faithful.

I conclude this long letter, by heartily desiring your prayers, that my repentance of my sins above mentioned may be unfeigned and genuine, and such as God in infinite mercy, for Christ's sake, will accept; and I beg leave to subscribe myself,

Sir, your real, though very unworthy friend,
and obedient servant,
JOSEPH HAWLEY."

On the whole it is evident, that while the dismission of Mr. Edwards was, *in itself considered*, an event greatly to be regretted, it was at the same time, in every part of it, most honourable to himself, and proved in its ultimate consequences an essential blessing to the church of God. Probably no one event, of apparently malignant aspect, ever did so much towards reforming the churches of New England. Many difficult subjects of theology, also, needed at that time to be thoroughly examined and illustrated; and to this end, some individual of expanded views and profound penetration, as well as of correct faith and elevated piety, was to be found, who could give the strength of his talents and his time to these investigations. The providence of God had selected Mr. Edwards for this important office; but so numerous and engrossing were the duties of the ministry at Northampton, that, had he remained there, he could not have fulfilled it but in part. To give him abundant opportunity and advantage for the work assigned him, he was taken from that busy field at the best time of life, when his powers had gained their greatest energy, when the field of thought and inquiry had been already extensively surveyed, and when the labours of the pulpit were fully provided for and anticipated; and was transferred to the retirement and leisure of a remote frontier village. There he prepared, within a little period, four of the ablest and most valuable works which the church of Christ has in its possession.

CHAPTER XIX.

PROPOSALS FROM STOCKBRIDGE, AND FROM THE COMMISSIONERS—VISIT TO STOCKBRIDGE—INDIAN MISSION—HOUSATONNUCKS—MOHAWKS—DISSENSIONS OF ENGLISH INHABITANTS—MR. HOLLIS'S MUNIFICENCE.

Early in December, 1750, Mr. Edwards received proposals from the church and congregation at Stockbridge, to become their minister; and about the same time, similar proposals from the commissioners, at Boston, of the "Society in London, for Propagating the Gospel in New England, and the Parts adjacent," to become the missionary of the *Housatonnucks*, or River Indians, a tribe at that time located in Stockbridge and its immediate vicinity. Before deciding on these proposals, he went to Stockbridge, in the beginning of January, 1751, and continued there during the remainder of the winter, and the early part of the spring, preaching both to the English inhabitants, and, by the aid of an interpreter, to the Indians. Soon after his return, he accepted of the invitation both of the commissioners and of the people of Stockbridge.

The Indian mission at Stockbridge commenced in 1735; when the Rev. John Sergeant was ordained their missionary. He continued to reside there until his death, July 27th, 1749. His Indian congregation, originally about fifty in number, gradually increased, by accessions from the neighbouring settlements on the Housatonnuck river, to the number of two hundred and fifty—the actual number in 1751. Mr. Sergeant devoted much of his time to the study of their language; (the Moheekanneew;*) yet, at the close of his life, he had not made such progress, that he could preach in it, or even pray in it, except by a form. He ultimately regretted the time and labour thus lost, and expressed the conviction, that it would be far better for his successor not to learn the language, but to preach by an interpreter, and to teach the children of the Indians the English language, by the aid of schoolmasters. Very little success appears to have attended his labours, either among the Indians or the English congregation.

A school was established, for the instruction of the Indian children, at the commencement of the mission, and placed under the care of Timothy Woodbridge, Esq. one of the original settlers of Stockbridge, and characterized by Mr. Edwards, as "a man of very good abilities, of a manly, honest, and generous disposition, and as having, by his upright conduct and agreeable manners, secured the affections and confidence of the Indians." He was supported by the government of the province, and devoted himself faithfully to the business of instructing the Indian children; yet for a long period, like Mr. Sergeant, he had to lament that so little success attended his labours. This was owing to various causes. The Indians lived in a village by themselves, at a small distance from the English settlement. Their children lived at home with their parents, and not in a boarding-school, and of course made little or no progress in the English language; and they had no books in their own. The English traders sold large quantities of ardent spirits to the Indians, and in this way constantly counteracted the efforts made to do them good. There were also unfortunate dissensions among the people of Stockbridge. The settlement of the town was begun, with a direct reference to the intellectual and moral improvement of the Indians, in the immediate vicinity. The lands of the Indians, comprising a very extensive tract, were secured to them; and important privileges were granted to the families of the original settlers, by the provincial legislature, with reference to this very object. Unfortunately, one of the most wealthy of those settlers appears to have removed to Stockbridge, with the design of amassing a still larger fortune by his intercourse with the Indian settlement. With this view, he formed a large trading establishment in the neighbourhood. From his wealth and his locality, affairs of some moment, relating to the Indians at Stockbridge, were on various occasions intrusted to his management; in one of which Mr. Woodbridge regarded him as doing so great and palpable an injury, both to the Indians and the province, that, taking it in connexion with the general tenor of his conduct, he felt himself bound to prevent, as far as lay in his power, all intercourse between him and the Indian settlement, as well as all influence which he might attempt to exert over the affairs of the Indians. In return, he endeavoured, in the first instance, to prevent the Indians from sending their children to the school, and to render those parents who actually sent them dissatisfied with Mr. Woodbridge; and at length to procure the dismission of that gentleman from his appointment. This controversy was of long continuance, and affected the whole settlement. The result was, that although he amassed considerable wealth, he entirely lost the confidence of the Indians; and so completely alienated the minds of the English inhabitants, that every family in the place, his own excepted, sided with his antagonist. This controversy, for a long time, had a most inauspicious effect on the school of Mr. Woodbridge and on the mission of Mr. Sergeant.

In 1739, Mr. Sergeant, despairing of any considerable success under the existing plan of instruction, attempted the establishment of an Indian boarding-school, to be kept at the expense of the English. He proposed, that the children should live in the family of their instructor, and learn the English language; and that their time should be divided between work and study, under different masters. For some time, he made but little progress in raising funds for this purpose, but at length was aided in his design, by the benevolence of the Rev. Isaac Hollis, a clergyman near London, who most generously offered to defray the expense of the board, clothing, and instruction of twelve Indian children. At this time no boarding-house was built; and for a long period, Mr. Serjeant found it impossible to procure a person duly qualified to take charge of the school. To begin the work, however, Mr. Serjeant hired as a temporary teacher, until a competent one could be procured, a Capt. Martin Kellogg, an illiterate man, originally a farmer, and subsequently a soldier, about sixty years of age, very lame, and wholly unaccustomed to the business of instruction. His sister,

* The common language of all the Indians in New England, New York, New Jersey, Pennsylvania, and Delaware, except the Iroquois.

Mrs. Ashley, the wife of a Capt. Ashley, of Suffield, who had been taken prisoner, when a child, by the Iroquois, and perfectly understood their language, was the interpreter of the English at Stockbridge; and her brother having come to reside there, in consequence of having no regular business, was employed temporarily by Mr. Sergeant, for the want of a better instructor, because he was on the spot. A school had just been commenced under his auspices, (not however as a boarding-school, as no house could be procured for the purpose,) when the French war of 1744 broke it up; and Capt. Kellogg, that he might continue to receive the money of Mr. Hollis, carried several of the Indian boys to Newington, in Connecticut, where he had previously resided.

After the close of the war, in 1748, Mr. Sergeant began the erection of a house for a boarding-school. He also wrote a letter to the nation of the Mohawks, then residing on the Mohawk river, about forty miles west of Albany, inviting them to bring their children to Stockbridge for instruction. But he did not live to see either of these designs accomplished. At his death, in 1749, several Indian boys were left in the hands of Capt. Kellogg, who in the autumn of 1750, not having heard from Mr. Hollis for a considerable period, and supposing him to be dead, dismissed them for a time, and gave up his attempt to form a school.

In consequence of the letter of Mr. Sergeant to the Mohawk tribe, which had been accompanied by a very kind invitation from the Housatonnuck Indians, offering them a portion of their lands for a place of settlement, if they would come and reside in Stockbridge, about twenty of them, old and young, came to that place in 1750, a short time before the removal of Mr. Edwards and his family. The provincial legislature, learning this fact, made provision for the support and maintenance of the children, and Capt. Kellogg, unfortunately, was employed as the instructor. He never established a regular school, however, but taught the boys occasionally, and incidentally, and employed them chiefly in cultivating his own lands. He was then 65 years of age.

Near the close of Mr. Serjeant's life, the school for the Housatonnuck children, under Mr. Woodbridge, became much more flourishing. His salary was increased, the number of his pupils augmented, and himself left to act with less restraint. The Indians also became less inclined to intemperance. The influence of the —— family was likewise extinct; the English inhabitants having to a man taken the opposite side in the controversy; and the Indians regarding Mr. Woodbridge as their best friend, and his opponent as their worst enemy. Mr. Woodbridge was also, at this period, able to avail himself of the assistance of a young Housatonnuck, educated by himself, of the name of John Wonwanonpequunnonnt, a man of uncommon talents and attainments, as well as of sincere piety; who appears to have been raised up by Providence, that he might become the interpreter of Mr. Edwards, in preaching to his countrymen.

Mr. Hollis, having heard of the arrival of the Mohawks at Stockbridge, and supposing that a regular boarding-school was established under the care of Capt. Kellogg, wrote to him to increase the number of the children to twenty-four, who were to be maintained and instructed at his expense. During the winter of 1750-51, the number of Mohawks, who came to reside at Stockbridge, was increased to about ninety; among whom were Hendrick, and Nicholas, and several others of their chiefs.

Such was the state of things at Stockbridge, and such the state of the Indian mission, and of the Indian schools, when Mr. Edwards was invited to remove to that place. The —— family at first exerted their whole influence, to prevent his receiving an invitation from the people at Stockbridge; but, finding that the church and parish (themselves excepted) were unanimous in giving the invitation, and very anxious that he should accept it, that there was no chance of producing a change in the minds of the commissioners in Boston, and that continued opposition must terminate in their own utter discomfiture, they changed their course, and professed to be highly gratified that he was coming among them.

After his return to Northampton, in the spring of 1751, Mr. Edwards, before coming to a final decision, paid a visit to his Excellency Sir William Pepperell, at Kittery, to learn the actual views of the government, with regard to the Indian establishment at Stockbridge; and having received satisfactory assurances on this subject, he soon after announced to the people of Stockbridge, and to the commissioners in Boston, his acceptance of their respective invitations. In the third week of June, he went again to Stockbridge, and remained there during the greater part of the ensuing month.

While at Stockbridge, he addressed the following letter to the Rev. Mr. Erskine.

"*Stockbridge, June* 28, 1751.

Rev. and dear Brother,

I have lately received the 'Treatise on the Restoration of the Jews,' and a pamphlet entitled, 'A Serious Address to the Church of Scotland,' and a 'Sermon on the Qualifications of the Teachers of Christianity,' preached by you before the Synod, with Glass's Notes on Scripture Texts, No. 5. These pamphlets were enclosed in a wrapper, superscribed by your hand. There was also in the packet, a brief advertisement concerning one of the pamphlets, written in your hand, though without any date or name, or any letter in the packet. But yet, I conclude these pamphlets were sent by you, and accordingly I now thank you for them. Your discourse on the Qualifications of Teachers of Christianity, is a very acceptable present. Glass's Notes on Scripture Texts contain some things that are very curious, and discover close study, and a critical genius. The Treatise on the Restoration of the Jews, if written by a christian divine, is a strange and unaccountable thing; by reason of there being nothing at all said, or hinted, about the Jews' conversion to the christian faith, or so much as one mention of Jesus Christ; and his supporting that the prophecies of Ezekiel are to be literally fulfilled, in the building of such a temple and city as is there described, and the springing of such a river from the threshold of the temple, and its running into the east sea, and the Jews offering sacrifices, and observing other rites spoken of in Ezekiel; and that the Messiah is yet to come, and to reign in Jerusalem as a temporal prince, &c. And I am wholly at a loss, as to the author's real design, whether it was, to promote Judaism, or deism, or only to amuse his readers.

Since I received these pamphlets, I have received letters from all my other correspondents in Scotland; but none from you. Mr. M'Laurin speaks of your writing, or designing to write; but suggests that possibly your letter would not arrive so soon as the rest; so that I hope I shall yet, ere long, receive a letter from you. The letters I have received from my other correspondents, make mention of a great revival of religion in Guelderland, and Mr. M'Laurin has sent me printed accounts of it, published, as I understand, by Mr. Gillies, his son-in-law, being extracts of letters from Holland. I had some notice of it before, in a letter from Mr. Davenport, who, for the most part, resides in New Jersey. The account he wrote, was brought over from Holland by a young Dutch minister, whose name is John Frielinghausen, born in New Jersey, second son to an eminent Dutch minister there. His elder brother is settled at Albany, and by all accounts, is an able and faithful minister. This second son has been in Holland two years, I suppose to perfect his education in one of their universities, where his brother at Albany had his education. He came over into America the last summer, having just been married and ordained in Holland, in order to take the pastoral charge of some of the places that had been under his father's care.

The accounts Mr. Davenport gives from him, are not so particular, as those that are published by Mr. Gillies. But there is one material and important circumstance, which he mentions, not taken notice of in the accounts from Scotland, *viz.* that the STADTHOLDER was much pleased with the work.

At the same time, that we rejoice in that glorious work, and praise God for it, it concerns us carefully to pray, that God's ministers and people there may be directed in such a state of things, wherein wisdom and great discretion are so exceedingly needed, and great care and skill, to distinguish between true and false religion; between those inward experiences, which are from the saving influence of the Spirit of God, and those that are from Satan, transforming himself into an angel of light. Without this, it may be expected, that the great deceiver will gradually insinuate himself; acting under disguise, he will pretend to be a zealous assistant in building the temple, yea, the chief architect, when his real design will be, to bring all to the ground, and to build Babel, instead of the temple of God, finally to the great reproach and grief of all true friends of religion, and the haughty triumph of its adversaries. If I may be allowed my conjecture in this affair, *there* lies the greatest danger of the people in Guelderland, who are concerned in this work. I wish they had all the benefit of the late experience of this part of the church of God, here in America. Mr. M'Laurin informs me, dear Sir, that you have a correspondence in the Netherlands; and, as you know something of the calamities we have suffered from this quarter, I wish you would give them some kind admonitions. They will need all the warnings that can be given them. For the temptation to religious people, in such a state of things, to countenance the glaring, shining counterparts of religion, without distinguishing them from the reality, what is true and genuine, is so strong, that they are very hardly indeed restrained from it. They will at last find the consequences not to be good, of an abundant declaring and proclaiming their experience, on all occasions, and before all companies, if they get into that way, as they will be very likely to do, without special caution in their guides. I am not so much concerned about any danger, the interest of the revival of religion in Guelderland may be in, from violent open opposition, as from the secret, subtle, undiscerned guile of the old serpent. I perceive, pious ministers in the Netherlands are concerned to obtain attestations to the good abiding effect of the awakenings in Scotland and America. I think it is fit they should know the very truth of the case, and that things should be represented neither better nor worse than they are. If they should be represented worse, that would give encouragement to unreasonable opposers; if better, that might prevent a most necessary caution, of the true friends of the awakening. There are, undoubtedly, very many instances in New England, in the whole, of the perseverance of such, as were thought to have received the saving benefits of the late revival of religion; and of their continuing to walk in newness of life, and as becomes saints; instances, which are incontestable, and which men must be most obstinately blind not to see; but I believe the proportion here is not so great as in Scotland. I cannot say, that the greater part of supposed converts give reason, by their conversation, to suppose that they are true converts. The proportion may, perhaps, be more truly represented, by the proportion of the blossoms on a tree which abide and come to mature fruit, to the whole number of blossoms in the spring.

In the forementioned letter, which I lately received from Mr. Davenport, he mentions some degrees of awakening in some places of New Jersey. The following are extracts from his letter. 'I returned last month from Cape May, where I had been labouring some time, with little or no success, as to the unregenerate; except somewhat encouraging, the last day of my preaching among them. Yet, blessed be God, I hear of the success of several ministers in the Jerseys, and the revival of religion in some places; though it is very dull times in most. Mr. Reed, of Boundbrook, has, I hear, some encouragement, by reason of a few in that place being under conviction. Mr. Kennedy, who is likely to settle at Baskingridge, I hear, has still more encouragement; and Mr. John Frielinghausen more yet, among the Dutch. He is the second son of the Mr. Frielinghausen, mentioned in your narrative, who died a few years ago. This second son came over from Holland, where he had been two years, and was ordained a little before he came over, the last summer. Pious ministers among the Dutch, this way, I think increase faster of late, than among other people. I was at the house of such an one, Mr. Varbryk, as I came along in this journey; who was ordained last fall, about five miles beyond Dobbs's Ferry, in New York government. Mr. William Tennent told me, that Mr. John Light, a pious young Dutch minister in New Jersey, was translating the accounts from Holland into English. Mr. Brainerd has had some special success lately, through mercy; so that nine or ten Indians appear to be under conviction, as he tells me; and about twelve of the white people near them, that used to be stupid like the very heathen; and many others more thoughtful and serious. Mr. Sacket has lately been favoured with peculiar success, in reducing a number drawn away and infected by the separatists; and some endeavours I have used since that, and with him, have, I trust, not been altogether in vain. The good Lord grant, that false religion may cease, and true religion prevail through the earth!' This letter of Mr. Davenport was dated April 26, 1751.

The Dutch people in the provinces of New York and New Jersey, have been famed for being generally exceedingly ignorant, stupid, and profane, little better than the savages of our American deserts. But it is remarkable, that things should now begin to appear more hopeful among them, about the same time that religion is reviving among the Dutch in their mother country; and certainly the revivals of religion which have very lately appeared, especially among the Dutch in Europe, do verify God's holy word, which not only gives such great encouragement to those who have engaged in the Concert for United Prayer, begun in Scotland, to go forward, but binds it strongly upon them so to do; and shows that it will be an aggravated fault, if, after God does such glorious things so soon after we have begun in an extraordinary manner to ask them, we should grow cold and slack, and begin to faint. And I think what God has now done, may well cause those, who seemed at first, with some zeal, to engage in the affair, but have grown careless about it, and have left off, to reflect on themselves with blushing and confusion. What if you, dear Sir, and other ministers in Scotland, who have been engaged in this affair, should now take occasion to inform ministers in the Netherlands of it, and move them to come into it, and join with us, in our united and extraordinary prayers, for an universal revival of religion?

As to my present circumstances, I came the last week to this place, having undertaken the business of a missionary to the Indians here; having been chosen the pastor of this church, and chosen missionary by the commissioners for Indian affairs in Boston. My instalment is appointed to be on the second Thursday in the next month.* I don't expect to get ready to remove my family till winter. But I must refer you, dear Sir, to my letters to Mr. M'Laurin and Mr. Robe, for a more full account of my circumstances, and of the things which have passed relating to them. I have, with this, sent you the Gazette, containing the Result of the late Council at Northampton, and intend to order one of my Farewell Sermons to be put up for you. My family were in their usual state of health when I left them, excepting my youngest child, who had something like an intermitting fever.

Please to present my cordial respects, and christian love, to your dear consort, and remember me in your prayers, with regard to the trials and changes I am called to pass through, and the new important business I have undertaken.

I am, dear Sir, your most
united and obliged friend and brother,
JONATHAN EDWARDS."

From Mr. Gillespie he received, about this period, a letter most grateful to his own feelings, expressing a lively and affectionate sympathy in his afflictions, as well as surprise and astonishment at the conduct of the people of Northampton. Mr. Edwards, in his reply, communicates a series of facts respecting them, which not only were adapted at the time to remove these impressions of his friend; but will be found, also, to contain a most important and salutary lesson of instruction, to every minister and every church. The solemn caution of the apostle, in 1 Cor. iii. 10—15. to every minister, to take care how he builds up the temple of God, of which Jesus Christ is the foundation—a caution, which refers not only to the nature of the *doctrines* which he teaches, but also, and even more especially, (as will be obvious from verses 16 and 17.) to the character of the *members* whom he adds to the church of Christ, which is the temple of God;—is here enforced most solemnly, by arguments derived from experience.

* This part of the letter must have been written in July, as the installation took place in August.

"To the Rev. Thomas Gillespie, Carnock.

Stockbridge, July 1, 1751.

Rev. and very dear Sir,

I am very greatly obliged to you for your most kind, affectionate, comfortable, and profitable letter of Feb. 2, 1751. I thank you, dear Sir, for your sympathy with me, under my troubles, so amply testified, and the many suitable and proper considerations you suggest me, for my comfort and improvement. May God enable me to make a right improvement of them.

It is not to be wondered at, dear Sir, that you are shocked and surprised at what has happened between me and the people of Northampton. It is surprising to all impartial and considerate persons that live near, and have the greatest advantage to know the circumstances of the affair, and the things that preceded the event, and made way for it. But no wonder if it be much more so to strangers at a distance. I doubt not, but that God intends his own glory, and the safety and prosperity of Zion, and the advancement of the interests of religion, in the issue of this event.

But it is best, that the true state of the case should be known, and that it should be viewed as it is, in order to receiving that instruction which Divine Providence holds forth in it, and in order to proper reflections and right improvement.

As there is a difference among particular persons, as to their natural temper, so there is some difference of this kind to be observed in different countries, and also in different cities and towns. The people of Northampton have, ever since I can remember, been famed for a high-spirited people, and of a difficult and turbulent temper. However, though in some respects they have been a stiff-necked people, yet God has been pleased, in times past, to bestow many distinguishing favours upon them. The town has stood now near one hundred years. Their first minister, Mr. Eleazar Mather, brother to Dr. Increase Mather of Boston, and Mr. Samuel Mather of Dublin, Ireland; was a very eminent man of God. After him came Mr. Stoddard, my grandfather, a very great man, of strong powers of mind, of great grace and great authority, of a masterly countenance, speech, and behaviour. He had much success in his ministry; there being many seasons in his day, of general awakening among his people. He continued in the ministry, at Northampton, about sixty years. But God was pleased, in some respects, especially, to manifest his power in the weakness of his successor; there having been a more remarkable awakening, since his death, than ever had been till then, in that town: although since that, also, a greater declension, and more awful departures from God, in some respects, than ever before; and so the last minister has had more to humble him, than either of his predecessors. May the effect be answerable to God's just expectations.

The people have, from the beginning, been well instructed; having had a name, for a long time, for a very knowing people; and many have appeared among them, persons of good abilities; and many, born in the town, have been promoted to places of public trust: they have been a people distinguished on this account. These things have been manifestly abused to nourish the pride of their natural temper, which had made them more difficult and unmanageable. There were some mighty contests and controversies among them, in Mr. Stoddard's day; which were managed with great heat and violence: some great quarrels in the church, wherein Mr. Stoddard, great as his authority was, knew not what to do with them. In one ecclesiastical controversy in Mr. Stoddard's day, wherein the church was divided into two parties, the heat of spirit was raised to such a degree, that it came to hard blows. A member of one party met the head of the opposite party, and assaulted him, and beat him unmercifully. In latter times, the people have had more to feed their pride. They have grown a much greater and more wealthy people than formerly, and are become more extensively famous in the world, as a people that have excelled in gifts and grace, and had God extraordinarily among them; which has insensibly engendered and nourished spiritual pride, that grand inlet of the devil in the hearts of men, and avenue of all manner of mischief among a professing people. Spiritual pride is a most monstrous thing. If it be not discerned, and vigorously opposed, in the beginning, it very often soon raises persons above their teachers, and supposed spiritual fathers, and sets them out of the reach of all rule and instruction, as I have seen in innumerable instances. And there is this inconvenience, attending the publishing of narratives of a work of God among a people, (such is the corruption that is in the hearts of men, and even of good men,) that there is great danger of their making it an occasion of spiritual pride. There is great reason to think that the Northampton people have provoked God greatly against them, by trusting in their privileges and attainments. And the consequences may well be a warning to all God's people, far and near, that hear of them.

Another thing, which probably has contributed in some measure to the unhappiness of the people's manners, was, that Mr. Stoddard, though an eminently holy man, was naturally of a dogmatical temper; and the people being brought up under him, and with a high veneration for him, were naturally led to imitate him. Especially their officers and leading men, seemed to think it an excellency, to be like him in this respect.

It has been a very great wound to the church of Northampton, that there has been for forty or fifty years, a sort of settled division of the people into two parties, somewhat like the *Court* and *Country party*, in England (if I may compare small things with great). There have been some of the chief men in the town, of chief authority and wealth, that have been great proprietors of their lands, who have had one party with them. And the other party, which has commonly been the greatest, have been of those, who have been jealous of them, apt to envy them, and afraid of their having too much power and influence in town and church. This has been a foundation of innumerable contentions among the people, from time to time, which have been exceedingly grievous to me, and by which doubtless God has been dreadfully provoked, and his Spirit grieved and quenched, and much confusion and many evil works have been introduced.

Another thing, that evidently has contributed to our calamities, is, that the people had got so established in certain wrong notions and ways in religion, which I found them in, and could never beat them out of. Particularly; it was too much their method to lay almost all the stress of their hopes in religion, on the particular shape and method of their first work; *i. e.* the first work of the Spirit of God on their hearts, in their conviction and conversion; and to look but little at the abiding sense and temper of their hearts, and the course of their exercises, and trials of grace, for evidences of their good estate. Nor had they learned, and many of them never could be made to learn, to distinguish between impressions on the imagination, and lively spiritual experience; and when I came among them, I found it to be too much a custom among them without discretion, or distinction of occasions, places, or companies, to declare and publish their own experiences; and oftentimes to do it in a light manner, without any air of solemnity. This custom has not a little contributed to spiritual pride and many other evils. When I first settled among the people, being young and of little experience, I was not thoroughly aware of the ill consequences of such a custom, and so allowed or at least did not testify against it, as I ought to have done.

And here I desire it may be observed, that I would be far from so laying all the blame of the sorrowful things, that have come to pass, to the people, as to suppose that I have no cause of self-reflection and humiliation before God, on this occasion. I am sensible that it becomes me to look on what has lately happened, as an awful frown of heaven on me, as well as on the people. God knows the sinfulness of my heart, and the great and sinful deficiencies and offences, which I have been guilty of, in the course of my ministry at Northampton. I desire that God would discover them to me more and more, and that now he would effectually humble me, and mortify my pride and self-confidence, and empty me entirely of myself, and make me to know how that I deserve to be cast away, as an abominable branch, and as a vessel wherein is no pleasure; and, if it may consist with his holy will, that he would sanctify me, and make me a vessel more meet for my Master's use; and yet improve me as an instrument of his glory, and the good of the souls of mankind.

One thing, that has contributed to bring things to such a pass at Northampton, was my youth, and want of more judgment and experience, in the time of that extraordinary awakening, about sixteen years ago.* Instead of a youth, there was want of a giant, in judgment and discretion, among a people in such an extraordinary state of things. In some respects, doubtless, my confidence in myself was a great injury to me; but in other respects my diffidence of myself injured me. It was such, that I durst not act my own judgment, and had no strength to oppose received notions, and established customs, and to testify boldly against some glaring false appearances, and counterfeits of religion, till it was too late. And by this means, as well as others, many things got footing, which have proved a dreadful source of spiritual pride, and other things that are exceedingly contrary to true Christianity. If I had had more experience, and ripeness of judgment and courage, I should have guided my people in a better manner, and should have guarded them better from Satan's devices, and prevented the spiritual calamity of many souls, and perhaps the eternal ruin of some of them; and have done what would have tended to lengthen out the tranquillity of the town.

However, doubtless at that time, there was a very glorious work of God wrought in Northampton, and there

* In 1734-35.

were numerous instances of saving conversion; though undoubtedly many were deceived, and deceived others; and the number of true converts was not so great as was then imagined. Many may be ready, from things that are lately come to pass, to determine, that all Northampton religion is come to nothing; and that all the famed awakenings, and revivals of religion in that place, prove to be nothing but strange tides of a melancholy and whimsical humour. But they would draw no such conclusion, if they exactly knew the true state of the case, and would judge of it with full calmness and impartiality of mind.

There are many things to be considered in the case of Northampton:

1. That many of those, who have been most violently engaged, and have chiefly led and excited others in it, though they have been leading men in the town, and have been esteemed considerable for their knowledge, estate, and age, and have been professors of religion, yet have not been the most famed for piety.

2. The leading men, who have been the most engaged in this matter, who have taken vast pains to stir up others that are inferior, have had this great advantage in their hands, that the controversy was a religious controversy; that that, which I opposed, was what they always had supposed to be a part of divine truth, a precious and important doctrine of the word of God; and, that the cause of my opposers was the cause of God. This has led the more ignorant and less considerate people to look on their zeal against me as virtue, and to christen even their passions and bitterness in such a cause with sanctified names, and to let them loose, and prosecute the views of their bitterness and violence without a check of conscience.

3. They have also had the great advantage of the vast veneration the people had for Mr. Stoddard's memory; which was such, that many looked on him almost as a sort of deity. They were all, (*i. e.* except the young people,) born and brought up under his ministry, and had been used from their infancy to esteem his sayings all as oracles. And he, they knew, maintained that doctrine which I oppose, with great positiveness and zeal, and opposed the contrary, which I maintain, as an exceedingly pernicious doctrine. Under these circumstances, I naturally appear as a dangerous opposer of the cause of God, and my teaching and insisting on the doctrine, which Mr. Stoddard opposed, appears to them a sort of horrid profaneness.

4. Crafty designing men have abundantly filled the ears of the more ignorant with suggestions, that my opinion tends to overthrow all religion, and to ruin the present and future generations, and to make all heathens, shutting them out of the church of Christ.

5. Not only many of the leading men of Northampton have used their utmost endeavours, to engage the minds of the common people in this controversy, but they have also been put forward, by the neighbouring ministers all round. My opposers have also been assisted and edged on by some at a great distance, persons of note; and some great men in civil authority have had a great hand in it.

6. It is to be considered, that the contrary opinion to mine, had not only long been established in Northampton without so much as one opposer to it; but it had also been fully and quietly established, for a long time, in all the neighbouring churches and congregations, and in all the country round, even to a great distance; so that my opinion when first broached, appeared to the people exceedingly singular. Their views being very narrow, it appeared to them, that all the world, almost, was against me. And my most crafty opposers improved this advantage, and abundantly represented me as all alone in my opinion.

7. Many of the people, who at length came to have their spirits much raised, and were brought to join in violent measures, yet came slowly into it, after being long practised with, and indefatigable endeavours used, to engage and influence them.

8. There are about twenty heads of families, besides others, women and young people, who ever appeared openly against the proceedings of the town, and many others have appeared friendly to me. And there is not a little reason to think, that there are many more, especially women and youths, that would appear so, if they dare. For a person, by appearing my friend at Northampton, even so much so as openly to discountenance my being turned out of the pulpit, exposes himself to the immediate persecution of his neighbours, and perhaps of his nearest friends. I mean, he falls under their great resentment, loses all their friendship, and is every where the object of reproach.

9. It is to be considered, that these things have happened when God is greatly withdrawn, and religion was very low, not only at Northampton, but all over New England.

10. I believe the devil is greatly alarmed, by the opposition made to the lax doctrine of admission to the christian church, and to the corresponding practice, which had been so long established at Northampton, and so extensively in the country; in which he found his account, and hoped for more important consequences, and more agreeable to him. And God, for wise ends, has suffered him to exert himself, in an extraordinary manner, in opposition; as God ordinarily does, when truth is in the birth.

But I am drawn out to an unexpected length in my observations on these things, and have not left myself room, nor time, for some other things, that I would willingly write, and must therefore refer you to my letters to my other correspondents in Scotland; particularly, Mr. M'Laurin, Mr. Robe, Mr. M'Culloch, and Mr. Erskine. To some of them, I have sent a particular account of my present circumstances, and of things which have lately passed, relating to them. I would only say in general, that I have had a call to settle in Stockbridge, a place in the western borders of New England, next to the province of New York, about thirty-six miles from Albany, and about forty miles from Northampton, the place where Mr. Sergeant was minister and missionary to the Indians. I am both called by the church here, constituted partly of Indians and partly of English, and am appointed missionary to the Indians, by the commissioners of Indian affairs, in Boston; agreeably to what you suggest in your letter, as though you had been able to foresee future events, when you say,—" Perhaps you are to be employed where the gospel has been little understood or attended to." I suppose this place will, for the future, be the place of my ordinary abode, though it will be some months before I can remove my family. I have no leisure, at present, to write on the subject you speak of, *viz. impressions, and supposed immediate revelations*, though I own the vast importance of the subject. I had begun to write something against the Arminians, before the late controversy; and now lately, Mr. Williams has written a book, in answer to mine on that subject; which I think myself obliged to answer, if God give me opportunity.

I have much to teach me to behave like a pilgrim and stranger in the earth. But in the midst of troubles and difficulties, I receive many mercies. Particularly, I have great reason, with abundant thankfulness, to take notice of the great kindness of my friends in Scotland. Blessed be God, who never forsakes those that trust in him; and never wants instruments, for the conveyance of his goodness and liberality to those who suffer in his cause!

I shall take care, that there be conveyed, with this letter, to you, one of my Farewell Sermons, and the Result of the Council that sat at Northampton the last May. Remember me, dear Sir, at the throne of grace, with regard to all my trials; and with regard to my new circumstances, and the important service I have undertaken in this place;—and please, in your next, to inform me, what family you have, and of their state.

I am, dear Sir, your most
affectionate friend and brother,
JONATHAN EDWARDS."

The following letter of Mr. Edwards to the Rev. Isaac Hollis, the patron of one of the Indian schools at Stockbridge, will explain some of the difficulties to which they were subjected.

"To Mr. Hollis.

Stockbridge, July 2, 1751.

Rev. and honoured Sir,

Having seen your late letter to Mr. Prince of Boston, and another to Capt. Kellogg, received this summer, and having lately been appointed missionary to the Indians in this place, I thought myself obliged to take the first opportunity to write to you, who have exerted yourself, in so extraordinary a manner, to promote our interests here, to serve which I am now devoted; partly to offer you my thanks for what you have done, and have lately offered to do, with so fervent and enlarged a heart, and bountiful a hand, for the advancement and enlargement of Christ's kingdom of grace among this poor people, and the eternal welfare of their souls; which may well excite the joy and admiration of all good Christians, the thanks of all who make the interests of Zion their own, and especially of him who has the souls of the Indians committed to his own more immediate care.

I write, also, partly to inform you of what I have had opportunity to observe, of the state of things here, relating to the affair of the instruction of the Indians, which you have a right to know; it being an affair in which you have been pleased so greatly to interest yourself, and which depends so much on the effects of your most generous christian beneficence. I have had considerable opportunity to observe the state of things; for though it is but about a month since I came here, after I had undertaken the work of the ministry here, as the stated missionary, yet I had been here before, two months in the winter, and then spent much time with the Indians, particularly with the Mohawks under the care of Capt. Kellogg.

There are here two schools for the instruction of Indian children: one under the care of Mr. Timothy Woodbridge, which began soon after Mr. Sergeant began to preach to these Indians,—this school consists wholly of the proper *Housatonnuck* Indians; the other, under the care of Capt. Kellogg, which he began with the *Housatonnucks*, on the plan which Mr. Sergeant projected; but, in the changeable unsettled state, in which things have been since Mr. Sergeant's death, it has been altered from that form, and the *Housatonnuck* boys have left it, and it now consists wholly of *Mohawk* children, which have been brought down hither by their parents, from their own proper country, about eighty miles, to this end, that they might be taught to read, and write, and be instructed in the christian religion.

There are some things, which give a hopeful prospect with regard to these Mohawk Indians; particularly the forward inclination of the children and their aptness to learn. But that, which has evidently been the greatest defect from the beginning in the method of instruction here, is, that no more proper and effectual measures have been taken, to bring the children that are here to the knowledge of the English tongue. For want of this, all the labour and cost, which have been expended in schools here, for about fourteen years, have been consequently to but little effect or benefit. When the children are taught to read, many of them, for want of the English language, know nothing of what they read; their books being all in English. They merely learn to make such and such sounds, on the sight of such and such marks, but know not *the meaning* of the words, and so have neither profit nor pleasure in reading, and will therefore be apt soon to lose even what they have learned, having no benefit or entertainment in the use of it.

It is on many other accounts of great importance, that they should be brought to know the English language. This would greatly tend to forward their instruction; their own barbarous languages being exceedingly barren, and very unfit to express moral and divine things. It would likewise open their minds, and, by means of their acquaintance and conversation with the English, would tend to advance them in knowledge and civilization. Some pains has been taken to teach the children the English tongue, but nothing very considerable has been accomplished. And I can think of but two ways in which it can be effected:—either by introducing a number of English children into the schools, to learn with them, and be their mates; or by distributing the Indian children into English families, to live there a year or two, where they must be allowed to speak the English and nothing else, and then return into the Indian schools, to perfect them in reading and writing, and the knowledge of the principles of religion, and all other useful knowledge. The latter, if their parents can be persuaded to consent to it, as probably they may, will be much the most effectual.

I would therefore, Sir, humbly propose, that some such method should be taken with regard to the children, who have the benefit of your liberality; and that part of your benefaction should be expended in this way, under the care of prudent and faithful trustees; for, in order to the business being managed thoroughly in future, a great deal of care and activity will be necessary, vastly more than the schoolmaster can have leisure for. There are many things pertaining to the regulation of the affairs of the instruction of the Indian children, which seem greatly to require the care of a number of persons, who shall be intrusted to dispose things according to the best of their discretion; sending from time to time a particular and exact account of the manner in which they have laid out your money.

I thought myself obliged to give you these intimations; you being at a great distance, and not capable of knowing the exact state of things, any otherwise, than by the information of those who are on the spot; and it being fit that you should know those circumstances, which are of so much importance to the affair, that, without a proper regard to them, the great expense which you incur, is liable to be in a great measure in vain.

I humbly request your prayers to the Fountain of all light and grace, for his guidance and assistance in this important service, which I have lately undertaken in this place.

I am, Honoured Sir,
Your most humble servant,
And affectionate brother in the gospel ministry,
JONATHAN EDWARDS."

A conference was appointed to be held at Albany, the last week in June, 1751, between the commissioners of the governments of Massachusetts, Connecticut, and New York, and the chiefs of the Iroquois, or Six Nations, for the purpose of making a treaty. The commissioners of Massachusetts were directed to pass through Stockbridge, on their way to Albany, for the purpose of conferring with the Mohawks already there, about their settlement in New England. On their arrival they found that Hendrick, and almost all the heads of families, on account of their disgust at the neglect of their children, on the part of Capt. Kellogg, had returned to their own country. In consequence of this, they requested Mr. Edwards to go to Albany, and be present at the conference; whither he accordingly went the first week in July. In an interview with Hendrick and Nicholas, he endeavoured to persuade them to influence as many of the Mohawk chiefs, as possible, to go to Stockbridge, and there treat of their removal to New England. This being urged upon them afterwards, by the commissioners of Massachusetts, was agreed to by them and the other chiefs; and a conference appointed to be held at Stockbridge in August. Mr. Edwards then returned to Stockbridge, and in the latter part of July, to his family in Northampton.

The first week in August, he removed his family and effects from Northampton to Stockbridge; and on Thursday, Aug. 8th, was regularly installed as the minister of the congregation in that place, and inducted into the office of missionary to the Indians residing in its vicinity. His salary was derived from three sources: from the parish of Stockbridge; from the Society in London, for Propagating the Gospel in New England, and the Parts adjacent, whose missionary he was, through their commissioners at Boston; and from the legislature of the colony, as a part of the annual fund devoted to the civilization of the Indians. This latter sum was paid, of course, to the individual, who held the office of minister and missionary at Stockbridge, although the government had no voice in his appointment.

On Tuesday, Aug. 13th, the chiefs of the Mohawks came from their two principal settlements to Stockbridge, and met the commissioners of the province. The chiefs expressed a very strong desire that their children might be instructed; but objected to the removal to Stockbridge, on the ground that the affairs of the Mohawks there were left in the utmost confusion, that no regular school was established, and no thorough means taken for the education of their children. After reminding the commissioners how often the English had failed to fulfil their promises, and disappointed the hopes which they had encouraged them to entertain, they requested them *to promise nothing, but what the government would certainly perform.* The commissioners agreed among themselves, that in consequence of the utter incompetency of Capt. Kellogg, another instructor, a man of learning and skill, must be procured for the Mohawk school; and promised the chiefs that a regular school should be established for their children, and a competent instructor speedily procured. After this, the chiefs declared their acceptance of the proposals made to them, of sending their children to Stockbridge for instruction, and of coming, a number of them, to reside there; and tendered a belt of wampum to the commissioners, in confirmation of the agreement, which was accepted. On Thursday, Aug. 22, the council was dissolved, and the chiefs went home.

The *Mohawks* at this time discovered a very strong desire to promote the education of their children, and an unusual willingness to receive religious instruction; as did also a part of the tribe of the *Oneiyutas*, or *Oneidas*, residing at *Onohohquauga*, or *Onohquauga*, a settlement on the Susquehannah. The French having been apprized of the efforts making by the English, in behalf of the Mohawks, were busily occupied in seducing them, and the other tribes of the Iroquois, to emigrate into Canada; and were actually erecting a chain of forts extending from Canada through New York, Pennsylvania, and the wilderness beyond to the Mississippi. Mr. Edwards, believing that if the utmost good faith was not kept with the Mohawks the whole plan of instructing them would be defeated, and regarding the period as a most critical one for the welfare of the British colonies, addressed a letter on the subject of the Indians, to the Hon. Thomas Hubbard, Speaker of the House of Assembly. In this letter he gave an account of the council held with the chiefs of the Mohawks, at Stockbridge, and their agreement to encourage the education of their children at that place; mentioned the interest felt in the subject by the Mohawks and the Oneiyutas, and by some of the Tuscaroras; stated the vast importance of the existing crisis, for securing the friendship of the Six Nations; recited the machinations of the French, to seduce them from the English interest, and their hostile movements in the west; pointed out the religious and literary instruction of the Indians as the only means of securing their attachment to the British cause; and detailed the measures necessary to be pursued at Stockbridge, to promote these great objects.*

When Mr. Edwards had removed his family to Stockbridge, he found himself exceedingly embarrassed, from the difficulty of procuring the land necessary for his own immediate accommodation. When the town was first settled, it was granted to the Housatonnucks, except *six portions*, to the late missionary, the school-master, and four other settlers. These portions were now distributed among *fourteen* proprietors, and could be purchased only at a very high price. He therefore presented a petition to the General Court, at their session in October, 1751, asking leave to purchase the necessary lands, for his own accommodation—a homestead in the centre of the town,

* I regret that the length of this interesting letter renders its insertion impracticable.

and a piece of wood-land in the outskirts. The legislature granted him leave to purchase the homesteads, and recommended to the English inhabitants, to provide the necessary wood-land for their minister.

On the tract of land, which he purchased, near the centre of the town, Mr. Edwards, soon after, erected a commodious dwelling, which is still standing.

CHAPTER XX.

LETTER TO SIR W. PEPPERELL—LETTER TO LADY PEPPERELL—LETTER TO HIS FATHER—ARRIVAL OF MR. HAWLEY—INCREASING IMPORTANCE OF INDIAN ESTABLISHMENT—SCHEMES OF ITS ENEMIES—FIRM STAND TAKEN BY MR. EDWARDS—LETTER TO MR. OLIVER—LETTER TO COMMISSIONERS—DIFFICULTIES TO THE MISSION—ANSWER TO MR. WILLIAMS—LETTER TO THE PEOPLE OF NORTHAMPTON—MARRIAGE OF MR. AND MRS. BURR—LETTER TO MR. ERSKINE—LETTER TO MR. HOLLIS—LETTER TO MR. HUBBARD.

The Indian establishment at Stockbridge, being gradually more and more known, excited more and more the attention, and interest, of the benevolent of England. Among these, Joshua Paine, Esq. of London, addressed a letter to Sir William Pepperell, the governor of the province; requesting the information, as to the proper plan of a school for Indian girls at that place. An extract from that letter was forwarded to Mr. Edwards from Sir William, through the secretary of the commissioners, with a request that he would write to Sir William on the subject. He accordingly addressed to him the following letter.

" *Stockbridge, Nov.* 28, 1751.

Honoured Sir,

When I had the opportunity the last spring of waiting on your Excellency at your seat at Kittery, and was there gratified and honoured by the kind and hospitable entertainment of your house, I was favoured with some conversation with you, concerning the affairs of the Indians at Stockbridge, and the business of the mission here, to which I had then been invited. And you were then pleased generously to assure me of your good offices, in affording me any assistance in this employment, which you could render me, through your acquaintance and correspondence in London.

I have lately been favoured with a letter from the Hon. Andrew Oliver, of Boston, wherein he was pleased to send me an extract of a letter to you from Joshua Paine, Esq. of London, concerning a proper plan of a school for Indian girls in this place, and to propose to me to write to you on the subject of the said extract. This encourages me to hope that a letter from me, on this subject, to your Excellency will be kindly received.

With this hope, I would take leave to say, that I think that, as the boarding-schools here are now in their commencement, and are yet to receive their form and character, and that among a people hitherto unaccustomed to any method of instruction whatever, it is a great pity but that the method actually adopted should be free from the gross defects of the ordinary method of teaching among the English.

One of these grand defects, as I humbly conceive, is this, that children are habituated to learning without understanding. In the common method of teaching, so far as my observation extends, children, when they are taught to read, are so much accustomed to reading, without any kind of knowledge of the meaning of what they read, that they continue reading without understanding, even a long time after they are capable of understanding, were it not for a habit of making such and such sounds, on the sight of such and such letters, with a perfect inattentiveness to any meaning. In like manner they are taught their catechism, saying over the words by rote, which they began to say, before they were capable of easily and readily comprehending them. Being long habituated to make sounds without connecting any ideas with them, they so continue, until they come to be capable of well understanding the words, and would perhaps have the ideas, properly signified by the words, naturally excited in their minds on hearing the words, were it not for an habitual hearing and speaking them without any ideas; so that, if the question were put in phraseology somewhat new, to which they have not been accustomed, they would not know what to answer. Thus it happens to children, even with regard to the plainest printed catechisms, even those which have been contrived with great care and art, so that they might be adapted to the lowest capacities.

I should therefore think that, in these boarding-schools, the children should never read a lesson, without the master or mistress taking care, that the child be made to attend to, and understand, the meaning of the words and sentences which it reads; at least after the child begins to read without spelling, and perhaps in some degree before. And the child should be taught to understand *things*, as well as *words*. After it begins to read in a Psalter, Testament, or Bible, not only the words and phrases should be explained, but the things which the lesson treats of should be, in a familiar manner, opened to the child's understanding; and the master or mistress should enter into conversation with the child about them. Familiar questions should be put to the child about the subjects of the lesson; and the child should be encouraged, and drawn on, to speak freely, and in his turn also to ask questions, for the resolution of his own doubts.

Many advantages would arise from this method. By this means, the child's learning will be rendered pleasant, entertaining, and profitable, as his mind will gradually open and expand with knowledge, and his capacity for reasoning be improved. His lesson will cease to be a dull, wearisome task, without any suitable pleasure or benefit. This will be a rational way of teaching. Assisting the child's reason enables him to see the use, and end, and benefit of reading, at the same time that he takes pains from day to day to read. It is the way also to accustom the child from its infancy to think and reflect, and to beget in it an early taste for knowledge, and a regularly increasing appetite for it.

So also, with regard to the method of catechizing children; beside obliging them to give the answers in the printed catechism, or in any stated form of words, questions should be asked them from time to time, in the same familiar manner, as they are asked questions commonly about their ordinary affairs, with familiar instructions, explanations, and rehearsals of things, intermixed; and if it be possible, the child should be led, by wise and skilful management, into the habit of conversation on divine things, and should gradually be divested of that shyness and backwardness, usually discovered in children, to converse on such topics with their superiors. And when the printed catechisms are used, as I am far from thinking they ought to be entirely neglected, care should be taken, that the child should attend to the meaning of the words, and be able to understand them; to this end, not only explaining the words and sentences, but also from time to time varying the phraseology, putting the question in different words of the same sense, and also intermixing with the questions and answers, whether printed or not, some improvement or application, in counsels and warnings given to them, founded on the answers that have been given.

Beside the things already mentioned, there are other things, which, as it appears to me, ought to be done, with regard to the education of children in general, wherein the common methods of instruction in New England are grossly defective. The teacher, in familiar discourses, might, in a little time, give the children a short general scheme of the scriptural history, beginning with the creation of the world, and descending through the various periods of that history, informing them of the larger divisions, and more important events of the story, and giving them some idea of their connexion one with another;—first, of the history of the Old Testament, and then of the New. And when the children had in their heads this general scheme, then the teacher might, at certain times, entertain them, in like familiar discourse, with the particular stories of the Scriptures, sometimes with one story, and then with another, before they can obtain the knowledge of them themselves, by reading; for example, at one time the story of the creation, at another time the story of the flood, then the dispersion of the nations, the calling of Abraham, the story of Joseph, the bringing of the children of Israel out of Egypt: and in the New Testament, the birth of Christ, some of the chief acts of his life, his death, his resurrection, his ascension, the effusion of the Holy Spirit at the day of Pentecost, and some of the chief of the acts of the apostles; withal, pointing out to them the place which each event has in the general scheme, and the connexion it has with other main parts of it. The teacher, in a familiar manner, should apply the events of the story discoursed upon, with the design of informing the child's understanding, influencing his heart, and directing his practice. A child, who is able to read his Bible, might be set to read a particular scriptural history, sometimes one, and sometimes another, diligently observing it, and examining for himself all that is said concerning it. And when he has done, he might be called to the master or mistress, and inquired of, concerning the particulars of the history, to see that he has paid attention, and is able to give a good account of it.

And I can see no good reason, why children in general, beside the scriptural history, should not, in a like familiar manner of conversation, be taught something of the great successive changes and events, in the Jewish nation, and the world at large, which connect the history of the Old and New Testaments. Thus, they might be informed, in short, of the manner in which the four great monarchies succeeded each other, the persecutions which the Jews suffered from Antiochus Epiphanes, and the principal changes which happened to their church and state, before the coming of Christ. And they might be shown, how such and such events were a fulfilment of such and such prophecies. And when they learn the history of the New Testament, they might, with much profit and entertainment, have pointed out to them many plain prophecies of the Old Testament, which have their fulfilment in him. And I can see no good reason, why children cannot, or may not, be taught something in general of ecclesiastical history, and be informed how things, with regard to the state of religion and the church of God, have gone on, as to some of the main events, from the time when the scriptural history ended, to the present time; and how given prophecies of the Scriptures have been fulfilled in some of these events; or why they may not be told, what may yet be expected to come to pass according to the scriptural prophecies, from this time, to the end of the world.

It appears to me obvious, also, that, in connexion with all this, they should be taught somewhat relating to the chronology of events, which would make the story so much the more distinct and entertaining. Thus, they may be taught how long it was from the creation of the world to the coming of Christ; how long from the creation to the flood; how long from the flood to the calling of Abraham, &c.; how long David lived before Christ; how long before the captivity in Babylon; how long the captivity, before Christ, &c.; how long since the birth of Christ; how old he was when he began to preach, and when he was crucified; how long after his resurrection, before he ascended; how long, also, after the destruction of Jerusalem by Nebuchadnezzar, until Babylon was destroyed by Cyrus; how long after the Persian empire, before that empire was overthrown by Alexander; when was the great oppression of the Jews by Antiochus Epiphanes; when Judea was conquered by the Romans; how long after Christ's resurrection before the destruction of Jerusalem; and how long before the empire became christian; how long after Christ before the popes claimed such and such powers; when the worship of images was introduced; how long before the Reformation, &c. &c. All children are capable of being informed, and having an idea of these things, and can much more easily learn them, if endeavours were used to that end, than many things which they do learn.

And with like ease, and with equal benefit, they might be taught some of the main things in geography: which way the land of Canaan lies from this; how far it is; which way Egypt lay from Canaan; which way Babylon lay from Jerusalem, and how far; which way Padan-Aram was from Canaan; where Rome lay from Jerusalem; where Antioch, &c. &c.

And I cannot but think it might be a pretty easy thing, if proper means were taken, to teach children to spell well, and *girls* as well as *boys*. I should think it may be worth the while, on various accounts, to teach them to write, and also to teach them a little of arithmetic, some of the first and plainest rules. Or, if it be judged, that it is needless to teach all the children all these things, some difference might be made in children of different genius, and children of the best genius might be taught more things than others. And all would serve, the more speedily and effectually, to change the taste of Indians, and to bring them off from their barbarism and brutality, to a relish for those things which belong to civilization and refinement.

Another thing, which properly belongs to a christian education, and which would be unusually popular with them, and which would in several respects have a powerful influence, in promoting the great end in view, of leading them to renounce the coarseness, and filth, and degradation, of savage life, for cleanliness, refinement, and good morals, is teaching them to sing. Music, especially sacred music, has a powerful efficacy to soften the heart into tenderness, to harmonize the affections, and to give the mind a relish for objects of a superior character.

In order to promote the salvation of the children, which is the main design of the whole Indian establishment at this place, I think that, beside their attending public worship on the sabbath, and the daily worship of the family, and catechizing in the school, and frequent counsels and warnings given them, when all together, by their teachers; each child should, from time to time, be dealt with singly, particularly, and closely, about the state and concerns of his soul; and particular care should be taken to teach and direct each child, concerning the duty of *secret prayer*, and the duty pressed and enforced on every one; and care should be taken, that all may have proper opportunity and convenience for it.

I need say nothing concerning buildings, lodgings, household stuff, cattle, servants, husbandry instruments, and utensils for the children's work; as it is agreed on all hands, that these are necessary; and the providing of them will doubtless be left to the care and discretion of the trustees that shall be appointed.

But I would beg leave to say further, with regard to methods to forward the proficiency of the children in their learning, that I cannot but think measures might be devised, greatly to encourage and animate them in it, and excite a laudable ambition to excel. One thing I have thought of, which, as appears to me, might have a happy tendency this way, in each of the boarding-schools: at certain periods, there should be a sort of public examination in the school, on a day appointed for the purpose, which shall be attended by all the trustees, and all in the town who are in any respect connected with Indian affairs, and some of the neighbouring ministers, and gentlemen and ladies; and also that the chiefs of the Indians be invited to attend; at which there shall be a public trial of the proficiency which each one has made, in the various branches which have been taught, as in reading, writing, spelling, arithmetic, knowledge in the principles of religion, knowledge of church history, &c.; and that a premium shall be given to such as are found to excel, which may be done in something that will very much please Indian children, with but little expense. And likewise, that the works of the children be then produced, to be judged of, that it may be determined who has made the greatest proficiency in learning to sew, to spin, to knit, &c.; and that a reward be given to such as have excelled. And perhaps, also, that a reward be then given to such, as, by the testimony of their teachers and governors, have excelled in virtue or diligence, in care to speak the truth, in strictly observing the sabbath, in good manners, in respect to their superiors, &c. And that, in the day of public trial, there be somewhat of an entertainment made for the members of the school, and those who are invited to attend. This not only might tend greatly to stimulate the children in their learning, but would be very pleasing and animating to the tribes of Indians, and would have great influence in rendering them very favourably disposed to the affairs of the schools.

But your Excellency will easily see that, in order to the practicableness of these things, in any tolerable degree and manner, it is necessary that the children should be taught the English tongue; and indeed this is of the most absolute necessity, on almost every account. The Indian languages are extremely barbarous and barren, and very ill fitted for communicating things moral and divine, or even things speculative and abstract. In short, they are wholly unfit for a people possessed of civilization, knowledge, and refinement.

Besides, without their learning English, their learning to read will be in vain; for the Indians have not the Bible, nor any other book, in their own language. Without this, their teachers cannot converse with them, and so can have no advantage to instruct them. Hence, all possible means must be used, in the first place, to introduce the English tongue among the children. To this end, much pains should be taken to teach them the English name for every thing, and English words that signify such and such actions; and an interpreter might be used for a while, to interpret their lessons to them, and to teach them to construe them, or turn them into Indian. And a number of English children might be put into the school with the Indian children. But the most effectual method of all would be, to put out some of the Indian children, first, into some good English families, one at a place, to live there a year or two, before they are brought into the school; which would not only be above all others the most successful method, but would be absolutely necessary, at least at first; but truly a great deal of care must be taken to find good places for them, and to look well to them, and to see that they are well taken care of, in the families to which they are sent. It is probable, that the parents of the children might, with proper endeavours, be persuaded to such a measure.

But it will doubtless be very easily and quickly determined, by your Excellency, that, if such methods as those which have been mentioned, or any like them, or indeed any other effectual measures, are taken, it will be absolutely necessary that the school should be under the constant care and inspection of trustees, who live upon the spot, or very near at hand. It will be in vain for any to expect that any woman can look after such a school, and provide for and govern so large a family, and take care continually to order and regulate so many and great affairs pertaining to it, within doors and without, without much assistance of some always at hand, who are able and faithful, and are interested and duly empowered. If she has under her a second, or a kind of usher, and has servants of both sexes, yet still she will be under the necessity of having some superior assistance. And as to the precise method of teaching, and regulating the discipline of the school and family, it must be left very much to their discretion; for experience alone can certainly determine the fittest methods of ordering such an establishment, so new and untried, though very probable conjectures may be made. And experience will doubtless direct to some new measures, which cannot now be thought of. Hoping that your Excellency will excuse the particularity and minuteness into which I have unintentionally been led on a subject about which I cannot but feel the deepest interest,

I remain,
With very high respect,
Your most humble servant,
JONATHAN EDWARDS."

In the package to Sir William, Mr. Edwards, in consequence of her own request, forwarded to Lady Pepperell, who was then in very deep affliction, the following letter; which will probably be regarded as one of the happiest specimens of christian sympathy and condolence, to be found in epistolary writing.

" To Lady Pepperell.

Stockbridge, Nov. 28, 1751.

MADAM,

When I was at your house in Kittery, the last spring, among other instances of your kind and condescending treatment to me, was this, that, when I had some conversation with Sir William, concerning Stockbridge and the affairs of the Indians, and he generously offered me any assistance, in the business of my mission here, which his acquaintance and correspondence in London enabled him to afford me, and proposed my writing to him on our affairs; you were also pleased to invite me to write to you at the same time. If I should neglect to do as you then proposed, I should fail not only of discharging my duty, but of doing myself a great honour. But as I am well assured, even from the small acquaintance I had with you, that a letter of mere compliments would not be agreeable to a lady of your disposition and feelings, especially under your present melancholy circumstances; so the writing of such a letter is very far from my intention or inclination.

When I saw the evidences of your deep sorrow, under the awful frown of Heaven in the death of your only son, it made an impression on my mind not easily forgotten; and when you spoke of my writing to you, I soon determined what should be the subject of my letter. It was that which appeared to me to be the most proper subject of contemplation for one in your circumstances; that, which I thought, above all others, would furnish you a proper and sufficient source of consolation, under your heavy affliction; and this was the Lord Jesus Christ:—particularly the amiableness of his character, which renders him worthy that we should love him, and take him for our only portion, our rest, hope, and joy; and his great and unparalleled love towards us.—And I have been of the same mind ever since; being determined, if God favoured me with an opportunity to write to your Ladyship, that those things should be the subject of my letter. For what other subject is so well calculated to prove a balm to the wounded spirit.

Let us then, dear Madam, contemplate the loveliness of our blessed Redeemer, which entitles him to our highest love; and, when clearly seen, leads us to find a sweet complacency and satisfaction of soul in him, of whatever else we are deprived. The Scriptures assure us that He, who came into the world in our nature, and freely laid down his life for us, was truly possessed of all the fulness of the Godhead, of his infinite greatness, majesty, and glory, his infinite wisdom, purity, and holiness, his infinite righteousness and goodness. He is called 'the brightness of God's glory, and the express image of his person.' He is the Image, the Expression, of infinite beauty; in the contemplation of which, God the Father had all his unspeakable happiness from eternity. That eternal and unspeakable happiness of the Deity is represented as a kind of social happiness, in the society of the persons of the Trinity; Prov. viii. 30. 'Then I was by him, as one brought up with him; I was daily his delight, rejoicing always before him.' This glorious Person came down from heaven to be 'the Light of the world,' that by him the beauty of the Deity might shine forth, in the brightest and fullest manner, to the children of men.

Infinite Wisdom also has contrived that we should behold the glory of the Deity, in the face of Jesus Christ, to the greatest advantage, in such a manner as should be best adapted to the capacity of poor feeble man; in such a manner, too, as is best fitted to engage our attention, and allure our hearts, as well as to inspire us with the most perfect complacency and delight. For Christ having, by his incarnation, come down from his infinite exaltation above us, has become one of our kinsmen and brothers. And his glory shining upon us through his human nature, the manifestation is wonderfully adapted to the strength of the human vision; so that, though it appears in all its effulgence, it is yet attempered to our sight. He is indeed possessed of infinite majesty, to inspire us with reverence and adoration; yet that majesty need not terrify us, for we behold it blended with humility, meekness, and sweet condescension. We may feel the most profound reverence and self-abasement, and yet our hearts be drawn forth sweetly and powerfully into an intimacy the most free, confidential, and delightful. The dread, so naturally inspired by his greatness, is dispelled by the contemplation of his gentleness and humility; while the familiarity, which might otherwise arise from the view of the loveliness of his character merely, is ever prevented by the consciousness of his infinite majesty and glory; and the sight of all his perfections united fills us with sweet surprise and humble confidence, with reverential love and delightful adoration.

This glory of Christ is properly, and in the highest sense, divine. He shines in all the brightness of glory that is inherent in the Deity. Such is the exceeding brightness of this Sun of righteousness, that, in comparison of it, the light of the natural sun is as darkness; and hence, when he shall appear in his glory, the brightness of the sun shall disappear, as the brightness of the little stars do when the sun rises. So says the prophet Isaiah, 'Then the moon shall be confounded, and the sun shall be ashamed, when the Lord of hosts shall reign in Mount Zion, and before his ancients gloriously,' Isa. xxiv. 23. But, although his light is thus bright, and his beams go forth with infinite strength; yet, as they proceed from the Lamb of God, and shine through his meek and lowly human nature, they are supremely soft and mild, and, instead of dazzling and overpowering our feeble sight, like a smooth ointment or a gentle eye-salve, are vivifying and healing. Thus on them, who fear God's name, 'the Sun of righteousness arises, with healing in his beams,' Mal. iv. 2. It is like the light of the morning, a morning without clouds, as the dew on the grass, under whose influence the souls of his people are as the tender grass springing out of the earth, by clear shining after rain. Thus are the beams of his beauty and brightness fitted for the support and reviving of the afflicted. He heals the broken in spirit, and bindeth up their wounds. When the spirits of his people are cut down by the scythe, he comes down upon them, in a sweet and heavenly influence, like rain on the mown grass, and like showers that water the earth. (Psal. lxxii. 6.)

But especially are the beams of Christ's glory infinitely softened and sweetened by his love to men, the love that passeth knowledge. The glory of his person consists, pre-eminently, in that infinite goodness and grace, of which he made so wonderful a manifestation, in his love to us. The apostle John tells us, that God is light; (1 John i. 5.) and again, that God is love; (1 John iv. 8.) and the light of his glory is an infinitely sweet light, because it is the light of love. But especially does it appear so, in the person of our Redeemer, who was infinitely the most wonderful example of love that was ever witnessed. All the perfections of the Deity have their highest manifestation in the work of redemption, vastly more than in the work of creation. In other works, we see him indirectly; but here, we see the immediate glory of his face. (2 Cor. iii. 18.) In his other works, we behold him at a distance; but in this, we come near, and behold the infinite treasures of his heart. (Eph. iii. 8, 9, 10.) It is a work of love *to us*, and a work of which *Christ* is the author. His loveliness, and his love, have both their greatest and most affecting manifestation in those sufferings, which he endured *for us* at his death. Therein, above all, appeared his holiness, his love to God, and his hatred of sin, in that, when he desired to save sinners, rather than that a sensible testimony should not be seen against sin, and the justice of God be vindicated, he chose to become obedient unto death, even the death of the cross. Thus, in the same act, he manifests, in the highest conceivable degree, his infinite hatred of sin, and his infinite love to sinners. His holiness appeared like a fire, burning with infinite vehemence against sin; at the same time, that his love to sinners appeared like a sweet flame, burning with an infinite fervency of benevolence. It is the glory and beauty of his love to us, polluted sinners, that it is an infinitely pure love; and it is the peculiar sweetness and endearment of his holiness, that it has its most glorious manifestation in such an act of love to us. All the excellencies of Christ, both divine and human, have their highest manifestation in this wonderful act of his love to men—his offering up himself a sacrifice for us, under these extreme sufferings. Herein have abounded toward us the riches of his grace, in all wisdom and prudence. (Eph. i. 8.) Herein appears his perfect justice. Herein, too, was the great display of his humility, in being willing to descend so low for us. In his last sufferings, appeared his obedience to God, his submission to his disposing will, his patience, and his meekness, when he went as a lamb to the slaughter, and opened not his mouth, but in a prayer that God would forgive his crucifiers. And how affecting this manifestation of his excellency and amiableness to our minds, when it chiefly shines forth in such an act of love to us.

The love of Christ to men, in another way, sweetens and endears all his excellencies and virtues; as it has brought him into so near a relation to us, as our Friend, our elder Brother, and our Redeemer; and has brought us into so strict an union with him, that we are his friends, yea, members of his body, of his flesh, and of his bones. (Eph. v. 30.)

We see then, dear Madam, how rich and how adequate is the provision, which God has made for our consolation, in all our afflictions, in giving us a Redeemer of such glory, and such love; especially, when it is considered, what were the ends of this great manifestation of beauty and love in his death. He suffered, that we might be delivered. His soul was exceeding sorrowful, even unto death, to take away the sting of sorrow, and to impart everlasting consolation. He was oppressed and afflicted, that we might be supported. He was overwhelmed in the darkness of death, that we might have the light of life. He was cast into the furnace of God's wrath, that we might drink of the rivers of his pleasures. His soul was overwhelmed with a flood of sorrow, that our hearts might be overwhelmed with a flood of eternal joy.

We may also well remember, in what circumstances our Redeemer now is. He was dead; but he is alive, and he lives for evermore. Death may deprive us of our friends here, but it cannot deprive us of this our best Friend. We have this best of friends, this mighty Redeemer, to go to, in all our afflictions; and he is not one who cannot be touched with the feeling of our infirmities. He has suffered far greater sorrows than we have ever suffered; and if we are actually united to him, the union can never be broken, but will continue when we die, and when heaven and earth are dissolved. Therefore, in this we may be confident, though the earth be removed, in him we shall triumph with everlasting joy. Now, when storms and tempests arise, we may resort to him, who is a hiding-place from the storm, and a covert from the tempest. When we thirst, we may come to him, who is as rivers of water in a dry place. When we are weary, we may go to him, who is as the shadow of a great rock in a weary land. Having found him, who is as the apple-tree among the trees of the wood, we may sit under his shadow with great delight, and his fruit will be sweet to our taste. Christ said to his disciples, 'In the world ye shall have tribulation; but in me ye shall have peace.' If we are united to him, we shall be like a tree planted by the waters, and that spreadeth out its roots by the river, that shall not see when heat cometh, but its leaf shall ever be green, and it shall not be careful in the year of drought, neither shall it cease from yielding fruit. He will now be our light in darkness; our morning-star, shining as the sure harbinger of approaching day. In a little time, he will arise on our souls, as the sun in his glory; and our sun shall no more go down, and there shall be no interposing cloud—no veil on his face, or on our hearts; but the Lord shall be our everlasting light, and our Redeemer our glory.

That this glorious Redeemer would manifest his glory and love to your mind, and apply what little I have said on this subject to your consolation, in all your afflictions, and abundantly reward your kindness and generosity to me while I was at Kittery, is the fervent prayer, Madam, of

Your Ladyship's most obliged
and affectionate friend,
and most humble servant,
JONATHAN EDWARDS."

The repeated afflictions of a widowed sister, in the beginning of the next year, occasioned the following letter to his father, containing some allusions to the state and circumstances of his own family.

"To the Reverend Timothy Edwards, East Windsor.

Stockbridge, Jan. 27, 1752.

Honoured Sir,

We have lately heard the sorrowful tidings of the death of two of sister Backus's* children, as we are informed, both at your house; which is the occasion of cousin Eunice returning from Stockbridge at this time; she having a desire to see her mother and surviving sisters at Windsor, on this melancholy occasion. We are much affected with sister's great and heavy afflictions, and lament the death of two such likely, promising children, in their early youth. It is my earnest desire, that it may be sanctified to us of this family. I desire your prayers, that it may be so; particularly to those that are young in the family; that they may be awakened by it to diligent preparation for death; and that we all may take notice of our distinguished mercies, with a becoming thankfulness to God. I look upon it as a great favour of Heaven, that you, my parents, are still preserved in the land of the living, to so great an age. I hope, by the leave of Divine Providence, to make you and sister Backus a visit in the spring. We are, through mercy, in our ordinary state of health, except that little Betty don't seem of late to be so well as she was in the summer. If she lives till spring, I believe we must be obliged to come again to the use of the cold bath with her. My wife and children are well pleased with our present situation. They like the place far better than they expected. Here, at present, we live in peace; which has of long time been an unusual thing with us. The Indians seem much pleased with my family, especially my wife. They are generally more sober and serious than they used to be. Beside the Stockbridge Indians, here are above sixty of the Six Nations, who live here for the sake of instruction. Twenty are lately come to dwell here, who came from about two hundred miles beyond Albany. We expect our son and daughter Parsons will remove hither in a short time. Many of their goods are already brought up.

[After alluding to the indigent circumstances of his sister Mrs. Backus and her family, and mentioning that himself and Mrs. Edwards had done every thing for his niece which was in their power, he proceeds.]

I hope some of her friends will be kind to her in this respect. There are perhaps none of her uncles but are much better able to help her than I am at this time; who, by reason of lately marrying two children, and the charge of buying, building, and removing, am, I suppose, about £2000 in debt, in this province money.† I should be glad if sister Mary would suggest it to brother Ellsworth to do something for her. If she don't care to do it in her own name, let her do it in mine, as doing the errand from me. Please to give my duty to my mother, and my love to sister Mary. My wife is at this moment from home. My children give their duty to their grandparents, and aunts, and love and affectionate condolence to their mournful surviving cousins.

I am, honoured Sir,
Your dutiful son,
JONATHAN EDWARDS."

The allusion to his pecuniary circumstances, made by Mr. Edwards in the preceding letter, requires explanation. What was the actual amount of his salary at Northampton, I have not been able to ascertain; but he speaks of it, in one of his letters, as "the largest salary of any country minister in New England." Soon after his settlement there, he purchased a valuable homestead, with the requisite lands for pasturage and fuel, and erected a commodious dwelling-house. These, by the strictest economy, had all been paid for before his dismission. It was several years, however, after his removal to Stockbridge, before he could sell his property at Northampton. In the mean time, he was under the necessity of purchasing another homestead, and of erecting another dwelling-house at Stockbridge. The debt thus incurred, added to the expense of removing his family, subjected them for a time to very serious pecuniary embarrassments; and his daughters, who had received not only an enlightened, but a polished, education, readily lent their aid, to relieve the family from the existing pressure. For this purpose, they occupied their leisure in making lace and embroidering, in tambouring and other ornamental work, and in making and painting fans; all of which, in the existing state of the country, found a ready market at Boston.‡ At length, the sale of his property in Northampton relieved him from debt, and placed his family in more pleasant circumstances.

On the 5th of February, O. S. Mr. Gideon Hawley, a young gentleman of a liberal education, and of great prudence, firmness, and integrity, arrived at Stockbridge. He had been appointed, by the commissioners, the schoolmaster of the Mohawk and other Iroquois children, and entered immediately on the duties of his office. He was ordained as a minister and missionary, July 31, 1754, N. S. Mr. Edwards found him a most faithful and useful coadjutor. He also occasionally preached to the Iroquois, as did Mr. Edwards once every sabbath.

Soon after the removal of Mr. Edwards to Stockbridge, in consequence of the misunderstandings and jealousies, subsisting between some of the principal English inhabitants of the town, and the confusion in which he saw the Indian affairs involved, he was led, in a letter to the Hon. Mr. Hubbard, of Aug. 31, 1751, to recommend the appointment of two or more trustees, "men perfectly impartial, no way interested in, related to, or engaged with, the contending parties." The absolute necessity of this step to the welfare of the mission, and of the Indian schools, soon became apparent.§ In consequence of the increasing importance of the Indian establishment at Stockbridge, and the increasing attention of the public to the mission and the schools; the benefactions of the legislature and of indivi-

* Mrs. Backus, the fifth sister of Mr. Edwards, was now a widow. Her husband, the Rev. Simon Backus of Newington, (Wethersfield,) was designated by the Connecticut legislature, as chaplain to the troops sent to Louisburgh in 1746, to prevent its recapture by the French. He died there soon after his arrival. The vessel, containing his effects, and a considerable sum contributed by the gentlemen of the army for his family, was cast away on its return; and the family were left in very indigent circumstances.

† I suppose that this means £2000 *old tenor*, as it was then called; the value of which continually varied, but has been commonly estimated at 6*s.* 8*d.* sterling to the pound.

‡ So severe was this pressure, for a considerable time, that Mr. Edwards found himself necessitated to practise the most rigid economy, in every thing—even in the article of *paper*. Much of what he now wrote, for his own use, was written on the margins of useless pamphlets, the covers of letters, and the remnants of the silk paper used in making fans.

§ A representation having been made to the legislature, in pursuance of this recommendation, three trustees or commissioners were appointed in behalf of the province.

duals, were increasing, and still likely to increase. By the augmented numbers of the *Housatonnucks*, and the accession of a *Mohawk* colony, it had become the principal mission of the Society for Propagating the Gospel in New England, and appeared destined to receive the chief amount of its revenue; Mr. Hollis had increased his annual stipend to £160, stg.; Mr. Paine was proposing to support a female boarding-school; the legislature of the province had just voted £500, provincial currency, for the school-house, and would probably aid in the support of the mistress; an adequate support was now given to the instructor of the Housatonnuck school; an annual stipend was given to the *Housatonnucks*, to be expended at Stockbridge for their benefit; a similar stipend was to be paid for the *Mohawks*, if they removed in considerable numbers to Stockbridge; a school, to be supported by the colony, for the education of their children, was not only pledged, but actually begun; and hopes were indulged that the yearly stipend of £500, stg. granted by the king, to the Mohawks, might be expended under the direction of an agent, residing at Stockbridge, and not as before at Albany. It needed no great discernment to discover, that the amount of these numerous items must be great; and the bare possibility of engrossing the agency, through which this large aggregate must pass, and of turning it into a source of great private emolument, might easily excite the strong cupidity of individuals, and lead them to resort to every measure in their power, to secure that emolument to themselves. The opponent of Mr. Woodbridge, (whose influence in the town, and with the Indians, had been long chiefly extinct,) in consequence of the strong recommendation, given of him, by his nephew, while in London, to the directors of the Society for Propagating the Gospel in New England, had been appointed one of the board of commissioners of that society; as had the nephew himself, another of the same board; one of his family, through the same recommendation, had been *conditionally* nominated as the teacher of the female school;* one of the trustees of the Indian establishment was about to connect himself with the family; and, if the nomination should be confirmed, it was his intention to remove to Stockbridge, in order to take a superintendence of Indian affairs, which, in the absence of his colleagues, would be sole and exclusive. So fair was the prospect at this time, in the view of these individuals, of engrossing the profit and the direction of the whole establishment in their own hands, that they threw off their wonted caution, and made known their purpose of removing every obstacle in the way of their designs.

Mr. Edwards well knew, that the influence of these individuals was most formidable: two of them being now members of the board of commissioners, on which, as Indian missionary, he was dependent; one of them being one of the trustees for the Indians at Stockbridge; one of them being personally acquainted with the directors in London; and two of them having considerable influence with the principal men in the provincial government. Yet he saw, just as clearly, that, if their plans succeeded, the funds appropriated to the literary and moral improvement of the Indians, would be perverted to the purpose of individual aggrandizement. In such a state of things, he was not at a loss as to his own duty. The question, whether the individual nominated by the board of directors in London, as the teacher of the female school, should be appointed, having been thus submitted, for final decision, to the board of commissioners in Boston; their secretary wrote to Mr. Edwards, for an explicit statement of the facts relating to the subject. Thus called upon, he did not hesitate to present the whole case, in a reply to the secretary, bearing date Feb. 18, 1752.

In this letter, after stating it to be absolutely necessary, that his correspondent should be let into some of the secrets of the affairs of Stockbridge, and after alluding to his having, on account of the controversy there subsisting, recommended, formerly, the appointment of "two or more impartial trustees, no way interested in, or related to, the contending parties," to inspect those affairs; he states, among other things, the following particulars:—When he recommended the appointment of these trustees, he little suspected, that one of them would prove the farthest of any person whatever, from possessing the indispensable qualification of *impartiality*, in consequence of his being about to become the son-in-law of one of the contending parties.—The preceding year, a very formal pacification took place, between Mr. Woodbridge and his opponent, with solemn promises made by the latter, that he would thenceforward live peacefully with Mr. W., and no more speak ill of him, nor in any wise molest him. But the proposed alliance, the nomination of one of his family as teacher of the female school, and the appointment of himself and his nephew to the board of commissioners, had so elated him, that those promises appeared to be wholly forgotten. A sudden and strange alteration had also appeared, in the temper and conduct of his intended son-in-law, who, in the absence of his colleagues, claimed the sole management of all Indian affairs, so that nothing was done but he was the doer of it.—The Indians had a most unfavourable opinion of the opponent of Mr. Woodbridge, and the deepest prejudice against him, in consequence of his having often molested them, with respect to their lands, and other affairs, and, as they thought, having done very unjustly by them. This prejudice was extended to the family; and that to such a degree, that, after offering to feed and clothe such of their children, as should be sent to the school, attempted to be established, only *four* could be procured, three Housatonnucks and one Mohawk; and the parents of these four complained loudly of the treatment of their children. Whether this prejudice was well or ill founded, it was too deep to be eradicated.—Very improper use had been made of the money given by Mr. Hollis. He had made large remittances, and to no good purpose; and was kept in entire ignorance, as to the actual state of things at Stockbridge. The individual who received his money, and boarded, and professed to instruct, the children, had never established a regular school, and had never kept any regular accounts of his expenditures. No government was maintained, little attention paid to the manners of the children, and all was suffered to go on in wildness, filth, and confusion, to the great offence of such as visited the place. The generous design of Mr. Hollis had been totally defeated, and the large sums of money he had given, had been wholly lost, and worse than lost. The same boys, without this additional expense, would have been far better instructed and governed at the school of Mr. Woodbridge. There, they would have been taught reading, cleanliness, good manners, and good morals; all of which had been wholly neglected, on the part of their professed instructor, who had himself been absent from

* That is, provided the commissioners, in Boston, approved of the appointment.

Stockbridge for a long period.—This irregularity, and disorderly management, led the Mohawks to take all their children away from him, after the arrival of Mr. Hawley, and to place them under the care of the latter. Yet the former, wishing some pretext for drawing the money of Mr. Hollis, and not being able to procure any of the Indian boys to form a school, went regularly into the school kept by Mr. Hawley, and proceeded to treat the boys as if they were under his own care; alleging, that he was the superintendent of the male school.—No one had been more open and abundant, in speaking of his uselessness, his exceeding unfitness for the business of an instructor, and the disorder and filthiness in which things were kept under his care, or in declaring, that it was high time that he was dismissed from the employment, than the resident trustee; but, in consequence of his new connexion, he had suddenly changed his mind, and now declared, that he must be retained.—A similar change had taken place in his treatment of Mr. Edwards. For many years he had constantly professed the highest respect for him, far beyond what the latter could, with any modesty, expect. He had often expressed a higher esteem of him than of any minister in New England, as well as a very strong desire of living under his ministry. Yet, although Mr. Edwards had never had a word of difference with him, or his new connexions, his whole conduct was suddenly and entirely changed, and he had sided with them, in all their measures of opposition and violence.

Very singular management had been used, with respect to Mr. Hawley. Before his arrival, dark representations were carried to him,—misrepresentations of the actual state of things at Stockbridge,—to discourage him from accepting his appointment. Soon after his arrival, it was openly given out, that he would soon be removed. Had it not been for his firmness, prudence, and steadiness of temper, he would have been laid under great and permanent disadvantages. The resident trustee had warned him not to depend on Mr. Edwards, and challenged to himself the whole authority of directing the school, and the affairs of the Indians.—When the society in London recommended the proposed teacher of the female school, they could not have been aware, that her nearest kinsmen were to be the committee to examine her accounts. But the actual state of things was soon to be still more preposterous. She being the mistress, her nearest relatives were to be her council, and her husband the sole committee to examine her accounts, and make report to the legislature.

Mr. Edwards then adds, "I write these things, honoured Sir, because I am satisfied you have not heretofore been enlightened, in the true state of things, as you ought to have been. It was my knowledge of some of these matters, though but little in comparison, which occasioned me, when last in Boston, so earnestly to press the commissioners frequently to visit this place. I have been slow to speak. My disposition has been entirely to suppress what I knew, that would be to the disadvantage of any of the people here. But I dare not hold my peace any longer. You doubtless will own, Sir, that it is but doing you justice, for somebody or other to let you know the true state of things, in a matter of such vast importance, which is under your care, and which you being at so great a distance never can know, but by the information of some that live here; and I know of no one from whom you can more reasonably expect it, than from the missionary you have sent here, to have the special care of the interests of religion among the Indians. I did not intend to interfere with the affair of the teacher of the female school, or to say any thing that should tend to hinder it; and therefore avoided every thing of that nature, in my letter to Sir William Pepperell. But being now questioned again by the honourable commissioners, and the tendency of the measure more and more appearing, I thought that this was the time when God called on me to speak, and that if I should hold my peace now, I should perhaps lay a foundation for great uneasiness to my conscience all my life after; when I might deeply lament the continued consequences of my silence, and when it would be too late to speak."

The next day Mr. Edwards addressed a letter to the commissioners in Boston, in which, after announcing the arrival of Mr. Hawley, and the high gratification of the Mohawks at the establishment of a regular school for their boys, he states the number of his scholars to be at that time thirty-six, mentions his happy qualifications as an instructor, and in compliance with their request gives, very summarily, his own views respecting a proper teacher for the female boarding-school.

During the spring of 1752, the state of affairs in Stockbridge, instead of improving, only grew worse. The interference of the former school-master with the school of Mr. Hawley, produced so much confusion, that, in the latter part of April, one half of the Mohawks left Stockbridge in utter disgust with him and his friends, and fully resolved never to return. A few days after their departure an intimate friend of the former school-master and his associates, visiting the male Mohawk school, under the care of Mr. Hawley, struck a child of the chief sachem of the Onohquaugas on the head with his cane, without any manner of provocation. The mother of this child was a woman of remarkable piety. This unhappy occurrence excited the universal indignation of the remaining Iroquois; and they appeared resolved, all of them, to pack up their effects immediately, and be gone. Mr. Hawley and the interpreter, finding it impossible to calm them, came to Mr. Edwards for advice; but he, having been often blamed for interfering with the affairs of the Iroquois, and told that, in doing so, he meddled with that which was none of his business, referred them to the resident trustee; advising them to represent the whole affair to him, that he might use proper means to prevent the fatal consequences which were feared. Their doing so was, however, regarded as the result of a disposition to find fault with him and his friends. The chiefs of the Onohquaugas, finding no redress, went to Mr. Edwards to make their complaint for this violent assault. There they found the aggressor; who, in order to pacify them, was persuaded to pay them a sum of money. The resident trustee, angry at what had occurred, went to the boarding-school, and proceeded to abuse Mr. Hawley in the presence of the whole school, in a very fervid manner; telling him that he was a man of no judgment, and of no prudence, and that he was unfit for the business he was in; and continued this abuse for three hours together. As his conversation was very loud, the Iroquois heard it, and came to the spot, expressing their fears for the personal safety of Mr. Hawley, to whom they had become much attached. Apprehending that, in consequence of this violence, he might be induced to leave Stockbridge, they declared, in a body, that, if he went away, they would go also. By these occurrences, the Indians were as effectually alienated from the resident trustee, as they had previously been from his new friends.

In consequence of these unhappy measures, and of a settled determination, on *his* part, to take, in the absence of his colleagues, the whole management of Indian affairs on himself; *they* also were disgusted. One of them relinquished all connexion with the business, and ceased to visit Stockbridge altogether. The other openly announced his entire discouragement, and declared that he would do his utmost to induce the government to withdraw their support from the establishment of the Iroquois. This led to an attempt to procure the dismission of the latter, and the appointment of a connexion of the resident trustee; which however proved unsuccessful. At the same time, it was publicly and repeatedly announced, that Mr. Edwards himself would be removed from his mission; and, as soon after appeared, a vigorous attempt was actually made to accomplish this object.*

Having stated these facts in a letter to the secretary of the commissioners, of May, 1752, Mr. Edwards proceeds, —"But still I think there is no necessity of the Iroquois establishment being broken up, unless its enemies are resolved to have it so. The dependence of the establishment, as to continuance and prosperity, is chiefly on the Onohquaugas, who are much the best disposed of any of the Iroquois, and most likely to come in considerable numbers. They have not been here so long as the others, to see so much to discourage them, and they alone are willing to settle at the Hop-lands. The affair is not at all desperate as to them, nor as to some of the Mohawks, if there be a speedy alteration. But if the two individuals, who challenge to themselves the whole direction of the affairs of the Iroquois, continue here, there is no hope of the continuance of Mr. Hawley, or of Mr. Ashley and his wife. They will not continue under one whom they regard as so despotic an inspector. And there will be no way to retain any of the Indians, unless it be some who are entirely mercenary, who may be persuaded to stay for the sake of the presents that are made them, and to be maintained and live here in mere idleness. This, it is now very apparent, is all that moves many of the Conneenchees, in being and continuing here."

"The resident trustee† has plainly discovered many designs, tending to bring money into his own pocket: *viz.* a design of taking care of Mr. Hollis's boys himself; a design of being steward of both boarding-schools, by which he will have the opportunity of supplying the Indians out of his own shop, and of getting his pay from the British funds; a design of introducing his son, as the master of the boarding-school, under the idea of a present supply, another proper person not appearing; and an expectation of diverting the king's bounty, of £500 sterling, to the Six Nations, from New York. The former school-master has given hints of an agreement, between himself and him, to resign the care of Mr. Hollis's scholars to him, when things are ripe for it; he providing for their maintenance, and taking care of their instruction by his son. Beside these things, his wife is to be mistress of the female school; and two of their sons to be maintained and educated at the public expense; and two of their girls, in like manner, to be maintained in the female school; and one of his family to be his wife's usher; and his servants to be paid for, under the character of servants employed in the affairs of the female school; and the house for the boarding-school set on his wife's land; and then the farm to be bought by the country for the school, with the advantage of selling it at a high rate; and yet the family in a great measure to be maintained on the produce of it; beside the advantage of carrying on a trade, both with the Stockbridge Indians and the Mohawks. A man had need to have a great stock of assuredness, to urge a public affair, under so manifold temptations of private interest."

The time of Mr. Edwards had been so much occupied by his removal from Northampton, the comfortable establishment of his family at Stockbridge, the ordinary duties of his parish and his mission, the claims of the Mohawks, the concerns of the various Indian schools, and the unhappy contentions of the whites; that he had, at first, no leisure to attend to the Reply of Mr. Williams. In the latter part of the spring, however, he began an answer to that gentleman, which he sent to the press the beginning of July,‡ with the following title: "Misrepresentations Corrected, and Truth Vindicated, in a Reply to the Rev. Mr. Solomon Williams's Book, entitled, *The True State of the Question, concerning the Qualifications necessary to Lawful Communion in the Christian Sacraments.*" It was read with deep interest by both parties, was admitted by both to be a triumphant answer to the "True State of the Question," and, taken in connexion with the "Humble Attempt," was regarded by the friends of strict communion, at that time, as it has ever since been, as an unanswerable defence of their system. If the opposers of that system have not so regarded it, they have not publicly avowed the opposite opinion; as no attempt to answer it has hitherto appeared. Mr. Williams is said to have asked the advice of some of his friends, among the clergy, whether he had better commence a reply; but, finding that no one would encourage him to an attempt, which must end in reiterated defeat, he is reported to have sat down in mortified silence.

Appended to this publication was a letter from Mr. Edwards to his late flock at Northampton. They had published Mr. Williams's pamphlet at their own expense, and distributed it to every family in the town. That pamphlet, though so unsuccessful an attempt to answer Mr. Edwards, was yet filled with many lax and sceptical notions, derived from the writings of Dr. Taylor of Norwich, and apparently adopted by Mr. Williams, in the existing emergency, though in direct opposition, not only to Mr. Stoddard, whom he professed at once to venerate and defend, but to his own former publications. Though Mr. Edwards knew that the work of Mr. W. must soon go to its proper place, yet he also knew the state of fervid excitement in which his former congregation had long been; that they had printed and dispersed the pamphlet of Mr. W., (even without knowing its contents,) as an answer to his own treatise, and thus, in a sense, had *adopted* it before the world as their own work. These circumstances led him to fear, that the fatal errors abounding in the work of Mr. Williams might, at a period when the prin-

* With reluctance I have yielded to the necessity of this minuteness of detail; but the fact, that Mr. Edwards had no very marked success in his Stockbridge mission, cannot otherwise be adequately explained; and the failure of the Iroquois establishment at Stockbridge cannot otherwise be accounted for. Unhappily the Indians at that place, like all other Indians in the vicinity of the whites, were exposed to the impositions, the seductions, and the oppressions, of their civilized neighbours. In these counteracting causes, both the friends and the enemies of Indian missions may learn, why it is so difficult to reform and christianize savages.

† I have regarded the use of the *antonomasia* as correct in this and some other quotations.

‡ It was not published until November.

ciples of Dr. Taylor of Norwich were gaining many converts in the colonies, mislead many, especially of the young, among his former people. To save them from this danger, he addressed to them an affectionate and truly pastoral letter, which will be found at the close of the Answer to Mr. Williams.*

On the 29th of June, 1752, Mr. Edwards married his third daughter, Esther, to the Rev. Aaron Burr, of Newark, president of the college of New Jersey, then established in that town, and a few years afterwards removed to Princeton.

In the following letter to Mr. Erskine, which is rich in intelligence, as well as thought, the reader will find one fact not generally known,—that Mr. Edwards, in the latter part of the summer of 1751, was applied to, with much earnestness, by some parish in Virginia, to go and settle with them in the ministry. They offered him a handsome support, and sent a messenger with the offer, but his instalment at Stockbridge had taken place before his arrival.

"To the Rev. John Erskine.

Stockbridge, July 7, 1752.

Rev. and dear Brother,

The last spring I received a letter from you, dated, at the beginning, July 17, and at the end, Sept. 5, 1751; and the week before last I received another letter, dated Feb. 11, 1752, with a packet, containing Arnauld de la fréquente Communion; Goodwin's Sermon at the Ordination of Mr. Pickering; Mr. Jarvis's Sermon on Methods for reviving Religion; Reasons of Dissent from the Sentence of the General Assembly; Edwards on Christ, God-man; Mr. Hartley's Sermon; Parish on the Assembly's Catechism; and Dr. Gill's Sermon on Isaiah xi. 12. I heartily thank you for these letters and pamphlets. Arnauld on frequent Communion will not be very profitable to me, by reason of my not understanding the French. But several of the rest have been very agreeable to me. That letter which you mention in your last, dated Feb. 11, as sent about a twelve-month before, containing some Remarks on the Decay of the Power of the Papal Clergy, and an Abstract of Venema's Reasonings to prove that Judas was not present at the Lord's Supper, I never received, and regret it much that I missed it, and request that you would still send me those Remarks on the Decay of the Papal Clergy.

I am obliged to you for the particular information you have given me, concerning Mr. Adam of Falkirk's affair. Though it is a pity so deserving a person should suffer at all from his brethren, only for not acting contrary to his conscience; yet it is matter of thankfulness, that the Assembly of the year 51 showed so much better temper than that of the preceding year. I shall be glad to hear concerning the temper and conduct of the Assembly of this present year, 1752.

I am sorry to learn, that there is so much reason to fear, that the revival of religion in the Netherlands will be hindered, and brought under a cloud, through the prevailing of imprudences. It is what I was afraid I should hear. I should be glad to see the Pastoral Letter you mention against Fanaticism, though written by one disaffected to the revival. I wish I could see a *History of Enthusiasm* through all ages, written by some good hand, a hearty friend of vital religion, a person of accurate judgment, and large acquaintance with ecclesiastical history. Such a history, well written, might doubtless be exceedingly useful and instructive, and of great benefit to the church of God; especially, if there were united with it a proper account and history of true religion. I should therefore choose, that the work should be a history of true, vital, and experimental religion, and enthusiasm: bringing down the history from age to age, judiciously and clearly making the distinction between one and the other; observing the difference of source, progress, and issue; properly pointing out the limits, and doing justice to each, in every age, and at each remarkable period. I don't know that there is any such thing extant, or any thing that would, in any good measure, answer the same purpose. If there be, I should be glad to hear of it.

I thank you for the account you give me of Mr. Taylor's writings, and of the things which he is doing to propagate his opinions. It now appears to be a remarkable time in the christian world; perhaps such an one, as never has been before: things are going down-hill so fast, and truth and religion, both of heart and practice, are departing by such swift steps, that I think it must needs be, that a crisis is not very far off; and what will then appear, I will not pretend to determine.

The last week I sent away my answer to Mr. Williams. If I live till it is published, I will endeavour to send one to you, and some other friends in Scotland. I hope now, in a short time, to be at leisure to resume my design, of writing something on the Arminian controversy. I have no thought of going through with all parts of the controversy at once; but the subject which I intended, God willing, first to write something upon, was *Free-will and Moral Agency;* endeavouring, with as much exactness as I am able, to consider the nature of that freedom of moral agents, which makes them the proper subjects of moral government, moral precepts, councils, calls, motives, persuasions, promises and threatenings, praise and blame, rewards and punishments: strictly examining the modern notions of these things, endeavouring to demonstrate their most palpable inconsistency and absurdity; endeavouring also to bring the late great objections and outcries against Calvinistic divinity, from these topics, to the test of the strictest reasoning; and particularly that great objection, in which the modern writers have so much gloried, so long triumphed, with so great a degree of insult towards the most excellent divines, and in effect against the gospel of Jesus Christ:—*viz.* That the Calvinistic notions of God's moral government are contrary to the common sense of mankind. In this Essay, I propose to take particular notice of the writings of Dr. Whitby, and Mr. Chubb, and the writings of some others, who, though not properly Pelagians, nor Arminians, yet in their notions of the freedom of the will, have, in the main, gone into the same scheme. But, if I live to prosecute my design, I shall send you a more particular account of my plan after it is perfected.

I suppose there has been a trial before now, whether a national collection can be obtained in Scotland, for New Jersey college: unless it has been thought prudent, by such as are friends of the affair, to put it off a year longer; as some things I have seen seem to argue. There was a design of Mr. Pemberton's going to England and Scotland. He was desired by the trustees, and it was his

* This excellent letter, omitted here for want of room, will be found in vol. i. pp. 529—531, and should be read in this place.

settled purpose, to have gone the last year; but his people, and his colleague, Mr. Cummings, hindered it. His intention of going occasioned great uneasiness among his people, and created some dissatisfaction towards him, in the minds of some of them. Since that President Burr has been desired to go, by the unanimous voice of the trustees. Nevertheless, I believe there is little probability of his consenting to it; partly, on the account of his having lately entered into a married state. On the 29th of last month, he was married to my third daughter.

What you write of the appointment of a gentleman, to the office of lieut. governour, of Virginia, who is a friend of religion, is an event that the friends of religion in America have great reason to rejoice in; by reason of the late revival of religion in that province, and the opposition that has been made against it, and the great endeavours to crush it, by many of the chief men of the province. Mr. Davies, in a letter I lately received from him, dated March 2, 1752, mentions the same thing. His words are, 'we have a new governor; who is a candid, condescending gentleman. And, as he has been educated in the church of Scotland, he has a respect for the presbyterians; which I hope is a happy omen.' I was in the latter part of the last summer applied to, with much earnestness and importunity, by some of the people of Virginia, to come and settle among them, in the work of the ministry; who subscribed handsomely for my encouragement and support, and sent a messenger to me with their request and subscriptions; but I was installed at Stockbridge before the messenger came. I have written some account of the state of things at Stockbridge to Mr. M'Laurin; which you doubtless will have opportunity to see.

July 24. The people of Northampton are still destitute of a minister, and in broken, sorrowful circumstances. They had the last winter Mr. Farrand, a young gentleman from New Jersey college; but contended much about him, so that he has left them. They are now in a state of contention; my warmest opposers are quarrelling among themselves. I hear they have lately sent for a young preacher, a Mr. Green of Barnstable, who is soon expected; but I know nothing of his character.

Another minister has lately been dismissed from his people, on the same account that I was dismissed from Northampton: *viz.* Mr. Billings of Cold Spring. Many of the Cold Spring people were originally of Northampton, were educated in the principles, and have followed the example, of the people there.

I heartily thank you for the accounts you have from time to time sent me of new books, that are published in Great Britain. I desire you would continue such a favour. I am fond of knowing how things are going on in the literary world.

Mr. John Wright, a member of New Jersey college; who is to take the degree of Bachelor of Arts, the next September; is now at my house. He was born in Scotland; has lived in Virginia; is a friend and acquaintance of Mr. Davies; has a great interest in the esteem of the religious people of Virginia, and is peculiarly esteemed by President Burr; has been admitted to special intimacy with him; and is a person of very good character for his understanding, prudence, and piety. He has a desire to have a correspondence with some divine of his native country, and has chosen you for his correspondent, if he may be admitted to such a favour. He intends to send you a letter with this, of which I would ask a favourable reception, as he has laid me under some special obligations.

My wife joins with me in affectionate salutations to you, and Mrs. Erskine. Hoping that we shall continue to remember each other at the throne of grace, I am,

Dear Sir,
Your affectionate and obliged
Brother and servant,
JONATHAN EDWARDS."

Soon after he had entered on the mission at Stockbridge, Mr. Edwards addressed the Rev. Mr. Hollis, by letter, concerning the Indian schools, and the state of the mission at large. The observations of a year had now brought him far more intimately acquainted with the actual state of things, and particularly, with the manner in which the annual benefactions of that gentleman had been expended; and he felt himself bound, at whatever hazard, to make the facts known. In doing this, he presented him, in a letter bearing date July 17, 1752, with a succinct and well drawn history of the mission, and stated, in general terms, the unhappy disagreement subsisting among the English inhabitants of Stockbridge, as well as various other circumstances of malignant aspect, which threatened ruin to the mission, and to the Indian schools. Want of room forbids its insertion. With this letter, he forwarded to Mr. Hollis a certificate, from a large number of the most respectable people of the town, stating the actual conduct of his agent, or instructor, the condition of the Indian boys, and the manner in which his benefactions had been perverted.

The firm and undeviating course of conduct pursued by Mr. Edwards, with regard to the Indian schools, and the general concerns of the mission, at length convinced the resident trustee, and his new friends, that they had nothing to hope from any compliances on his part. They resolved, therefore, if possible, to effect his removal from Stockbridge. With this view, that gentleman repaired to Boston, and endeavoured, in conversation, not only with the commissioners, but with some of the principal men in the government, (and among others, with the secretary of the province,) to produce in their minds very unfavourable impressions concerning him: particularly, that he was a man of an unyielding character, and unwilling to be reconciled to those from whom he had differed; and that, by this course, he was likely to ruin the Indian mission. The friends of Mr. Edwards, in Boston, giving him timely notice of this attempt; he addressed a letter to the Hon. Mr. Willard, in his own defence, bearing date July 17, 1752; in which he so effectually refuted these representations, that the influence of that gentleman was permanently secured, in favour of the mission, and its real friends.

CHAPTER XXI.

VOTE OF THANKS OF COMMISSIONERS—SERMON AT NEWARK—MEASURES OF THE ENEMIES OF THE MISSION DEFEATED—LETTER TO MR. OLIVER—FREEDOM OF THE WILL—LETTER TO MR. ERSKINE—DEPOSITION OF MR. GILLESPIE—LETTER TO DO.—LETTER TO MR. M'CULLOCH—REPORT OF INDIAN AGENT—REPLY OF MR. EDWARDS—FURTHER DEFEAT OF THE ENEMIES OF THE MISSION.

On the 29th of June, the secretary of the commissioners in Boston forwarded, by their direction, to Mr. Edwards and Mr. Hawley, an official expression of the approbation, entertained by that board, of the firmness and integrity manifested by them, in their conduct relative to the Stockbridge mission.* The commissioners knew of the attempt made, to shake their own confidence, and that of the public, in their agents in that mission; and doubtless intended, by this prompt and unequivocal act of justice, at once to sustain the hearts of these gentlemen, under their severe trials, and to make it manifest to all men, that, notwithstanding that attempt, they continued to repose in them an undiminished confidence. In his reply, bearing date Aug. 27, 1752, Mr. Edwards, after returning his thanks to those gentlemen, for this very decisive expression of their favourable opinion, made to their secretary his regular report of the state of the mission.

After observing, that the people of the town, both English and Indians, notwithstanding repeated and vigorous efforts to break up their union, and, particularly, to excite a disaffection in them towards their ministers, were all happily united in opinion and affection, except one individual and his family; he mentions the alliance of the resident trustee with his family, which took place soon after the arrival at Stockbridge of his nephew from Connecticut. The latter gentleman soon called on Mr. Edwards, and, after alluding to the fact, that he was opposed to the appointment of his cousin, as superintendent of the female boarding-school, insisted, as a member of the society in London, and of the board of commissioners, on knowing his reasons; and, at the same time, offered to be the instrument of settling the differences subsisting at Stockbridge. Mr. Edwards, preferring to answer this demand by letter, declined to make a representation of the case before him, but offered to join with him, in an earnest representation to the board of commissioners, that they would appoint a committee, to come on the spot, to inquire into the existing difficulties; on the ground, that it was more proper to have such a committee, as judges or mediators, than an individual, who was very nearly related to the family chiefly interested in these contentions; and proposed, that the commissioners, by their committee, should be desired to look into the management of the affairs at Stockbridge, from the beginning, by all the living inhabitants and residents of the town, who had had any hand in them, in any respect; declaring himself ready to open himself with freedom before such a committee.—His correspondent, in reply, declined this proposal, reasserted his right to know the objections to the proposed teacher of the boarding-school, and intimated the regret which he should feel, if obliged to inform the society in London of the existing state of things at Stockbridge.—Mr. Edwards, in his answer, insisted anew on his former proposal, of referring the case to the commissioners, declared himself not satisfied, that his correspondent, acting *singly*, had authority to demand the reasons of his judgment, as to the teacher of the female school, whatever the society in London, or their commissioners in Boston, acting as *a body*, might have; and concluded, by referring himself again to the commissioners, who were his constituents, and who had, a little before, informed him, that they looked upon their agents as accountable *to them only*.

The arrival of this gentleman, and the assurances he gave them of his influence with the society in London, revived for a time the drooping courage of his friends, particularly of the resident trustee, and of the agent of Mr. Hollis, who had, just before that event, resolved on removing from Stockbridge.—Having thus alluded to the mischievous consequences growing out of this unhappy state of things, Mr. Edwards proceeds,—"Thus things go on, in a state of confusion, of which those at a distance can scarcely have any idea. In the mean time, the affair of the Six Nations is languishing to death. The affair of the *Mohawks* is, I fear, past recovery, and in a manner dead. They seem to be discouraged, are most of them gone, and I do not expect will come up again; unless it be to get presents, and satisfy their hunger, in the present time of great scarcity in their own country. They have apparently very much given up the idea of coming hither for instruction. The *Onohquaugas* have not been here so long, to be discouraged by our management. But if things go on in this manner, it may be expected that they will be discouraged also. The management of things has a great while been in wrong hands. They ought to be conducted exclusively by the commissioners, who have had the care of Stockbridge affairs; but here are others, who seem to aim to engross all to themselves, to be indefatigably active in prosecuting their particular designs, and impatient of every thing that stands in their way.

"Very much depends on the appointment of a teacher of the female school. If that affair is settled to their minds, their influence here is well established. They are sensible that affairs depend very much on this simple point, and therefore this is the point they drive at with all their might. The wisdom of the commissioners will easily discover, that this is the juncture, in which the foundation is to be laid of the future state of things in Stockbridge; of their prosperity or adversity; and perhaps with no opportunity of future redress. I look upon myself as called upon to speak somewhat freely at such a juncture; and therefore I hope my so doing will be candidly interpreted by the commissioners. I do not think that our affairs will ever prosper, if they must be under the hands of the resident trustee and his friends."

In the month of September, Mr. Edwards went into New Jersey, and, on the 28th of that month, preached a

* The copy designed for Mr. Hawley was enclosed in the letter to Mr. Edwards. Probably a similar vote was forwarded *directly* to Mr. Woodbridge, as that gentleman always enjoyed their fullest confidence.

sermon from James ii. 19. before the synod at Newark, entitled, "True Grace distinguished from the Experience of Devils," which was published at their request. It is a clear, condensed, and powerful exhibition of the differences between real religion and its counterfeits, and will be found eminently useful, as a criterion of christian character.

In the unhappy controversy, between Mr. Woodbridge and his opponent, perhaps no one circumstance had been more mortifying to the latter, or had had a more direct tendency to defeat all his measures, than the fact, that the white inhabitants of the town, (his own immediate family connexions excepted,) as well as the Indians of both nations, were, to a man, opposed to himself, and friendly to his antagonist. This rendered his daily life uncomfortable; it discouraged every attempt to forward his plans at the public meetings of the town; and when any point in controversy was to be decided, or any measure attempted, at Boston, he found that Mr. Woodbridge had a host of substantial witnesses on the spot, who gave in their testimony without fear. In this way, hitherto, every important design had been frustrated.

The winter, that was approaching, was regarded by both parties as a most important and interesting period; during which, in all probability, the affairs of the mission, and of the town, would be brought to a crisis. Those opposed to Mr. Woodbridge, were not ignorant, that, if Mr. Edwards were continued as the missionary at Stockbridge, such was his influence at Boston, and his general weight of character, there was too much probability, that Mr. Woodbridge would be continued the school-master of the Housatonnucks, and Mr. Hawley of the Iroquois. In that case, there was but little chance of the female school being placed in the desired hands; if that failed, the stewardship of all the schools would fail; and then the whole system of measures, apparently so happily conceived, would be defeated. But if Mr. Edwards could be removed from Stockbridge, the removal of Mr. Woodbridge would be attended with less difficulty; that of Mr. Hawley, a young man, would follow of course, which would make way for the son of the resident trustee: these changes would almost necessarily insure the female school, as well as the stewardship and agency, in the family; and then the other objects in view could scarcely fail to be accomplished. As so much depended on the fact, whether Mr. Edwards was continued at Stockbridge, or not; there seemed to be held out, to minds capable of being influenced by them, very strong inducements to make one vigorous effort to effect his removal. This was accordingly resolved on, and, by some of the persons concerned, incautiously proclaimed.

One of the steps taken to accomplish this so desired object, is mentioned in the following letter. Whether it was one of the measures *concerted*, or was the *self-suggested* plan of the individual, who attempted to execute it, does not certainly appear. Could he have succeeded, could the English inhabitants of the town have been changed, and a new set of inhabitants have been introduced, all of them his adherents; no event probably would have so much furthered the objects in view. The almost utter impossibility of its success, connected with its total and immediate discomfiture, rendered the attempt supremely ridiculous, and covered the individual making it, and his party, with confusion.

"To Andrew Oliver, Esquire.

Stockbridge, Oct. 1752.

Sir,

Since my letter of Aug. 27, various things have occurred among us, of which it may not be improper to inform you. It seems as though there was a resolution, in the people on the hill, to carry their schemes into effect, though the earth should be removed for it. The opponent of Mr. Woodbridge has lately made a vigorous and vehement attempt, suddenly to change the English inhabitants of the town, by *buying out*, at once, the old inhabitants in general. To this end, he arose very early in the morning, and went out before day, and called some of them out of their beds, offering *to buy their farms.* In this manner, he went from one to another, until he had been to almost all the inhabitants in that forenoon; offering *very high prices,* and *cash in hand;* vehemently pressing that the bargain should be immediately closed, and the writings drawn, and the affair completed, without delay; urging it most pressingly on each one. One of the inhabitants completed and finished the affair with him. Some others came to a verbal agreement, on conditions. But, notwithstanding the great and extraordinary vigour, with which this matter was carried on, yet the design was discovered, before it could be completed, and so disappointed; and then his friends, and he himself too, were glad to lay this conduct to *distraction.*

A scheme is plainly laid, entirely to thrust Mr. Hawley out of the schools; let his friends and constituents do what they will to prevent it. The resident trustee has told Mr. Hawley, that it is the design of Mr. Hollis's former school-master, to set up a distinct independent school, under another teacher, whom he shall provide to keep the school on Mr. Hollis's behalf, and that he intends to take up all boys who come, to board them and clothe them well, better than heretofore. Probably he presumes, that the clothing and presents that will be offered, will tempt them all to subject themselves to himself, rather than to Mr. Hawley.

I have lately been a journey to Newark, in New Jersey, where I saw Mr. Hazzard, a merchant in New York, who told me that he, the last June, received and answered two bills from him, drawn on Mr. Hollis, of £80 sterling apiece. By this, it appears, that he has drawn full pay from Mr. Hollis, for the two years past, as much as he had in the preceding years, without clothing the boys in the least; imposing on Mr. Hollis, in an almost unprecedented manner, considering the greatness of the injury, the plainness of the case, and the obstinacy with which he has proceeded to such a step, after this part of the country had been, so long a time, so full of objections to his being here at Mr. Hollis's expense, without being engaged in the business to which Mr. Hollis appointed him, and for which he agreed to send him his money. In the beginning of the year before last, he professedly threw up Mr. Hollis's school, and dismissed all his boys, supposing that Mr. Hollis was dead; it having been long since he heard any thing from him. In what he did afterwards, in teaching the Mohawks, he did not pretend to proceed on Mr. Hollis's plan, or with any expectation of any pay from him. And he never pretended to take up any boys on Mr. Hollis's account, till about a year afterwards, *viz.* the last autumn, after he had received a letter from Mr. Hollis; and it is but little he has done since. The charge he has been at, in clothing the boys, is but a trifle. He has never really kept any school at all, though sometimes he has pretended to teach some children to read, in a most confused manner. But, through a great part of the last year, he has not done even that. He has been absent, at least one third of the year; and the greater part of the time that he has been here, he has not had so much as the shadow of a school, nor been in any business whatsoever.

I some time ago wrote a letter to Mr. Hollis, giving him some account of the state of his affairs here, accompanied with letters from some of the inhabitants of Stockbridge. I desired Mr. Prince to show those letters to some of the commissioners.

One of the trustees has lately been here, but staid only two or three days. While he was here, there was little else but altercation, and warm contest, between his colleague and him, concerning the mode of managing affairs, and concerning the female school. And he is gone away entirely discouraged, with a resolution to have no more to do with the affairs of Stockbridge, which, he says, are blown up already. If it be not altogether so, yet I think it is high time the hon. commissioners had full information of the state of things among us. We have long waited for an opportunity to send, but none has presented. Mr. Hawley meets with many things to discourage him; his circumstances here are very difficult and precarious; he greatly needs the advice of the commissioners; he has a strong inclination to see the commissioners himself, and to confer with them, freely and fully, about the affairs in which he is concerned; and it appears to me necessary that he should do this, both for the public interest, and on his own account. He is kept out of business, and probably very good business, in which he might settle elsewhere, and I do not wonder that he is uneasy, and thinks it necessary to talk with the commissioners. We have had thoughts of his staying, until Mr. Woodbridge went to the general court, the necessity of whose going appears more and more apparent; but the court being prorogued, and we not knowing for how long a time; and the important matters of intelligence to the commissioners, and to Mr. Hollis, having been so long delayed for want of opportunity, which so much require their speedy notice; our calamities also continuing, and growing worse and worse; and it being now a time, wherein most of the Mohawks are gone, and so a time in which Mr. Hawley can be absent, with far less inconvenience than some time hence, when many of the Mohawks are expected down, in consequence of the want of provisions in their own country; and considering that probably the commissioners might have a more free opportunity to hear and consider Mr. Hawley's representations now, than in the time of the sitting of the court; and likewise, that it might be some convenience to the commissioners, to have notice of the state of our affairs, so as to ripen their thoughts with regard to them, before the sitting of the court;—I say, considering these things, it was thought advisable for Mr. Hawley not to delay his journey. That the Most High would give wisdom, and counsel, and success to the commissioners, in their consultations on our affairs, and direct and aid those who are here employed, in so important a service, is the humble and earnest prayer of

Their most obedient servant,

JONATHAN EDWARDS."

From these scenes of unsuccessful intrigue, and disappointed avarice, all notice of which, could the life of Mr. Edwards, as a missionary at Stockbridge, have been fairly exhibited without thus detailing them, would have been most gladly dispensed with; the reader will turn with pleasure, even for a short interval, to communications prompted by friendship, and relating to the more general interests of the church.

Some years before this, through the kindness of Mr. Erskine, he had received the writings of some of the more considerable Arminian writers, particularly of Dr. Taylor of Norwich, and Dr. Turnbull; which, with those of Dr. Whitby and those of Chubb and Tindal, already in his possession, furnished him with the means of examining their whole system. This examination he commenced, in form, a considerable time before he left Northampton; and in the summer of 1747, as we have already seen, he announced, in his first letter to Mr. Erskine, the general plan of a Discourse on the Freedom of the Will, and Moral Agency. This subject drew his attention, even while he was a member of college; and, from an investigation of the nature of *Power*, to which he was led by reading the article, in the Essay on the Human Understanding, relating to that subject, he derived the all-important principle, THAT MEN, IN A PROPER SENSE, MAY BE SAID TO HAVE POWER TO ABSTAIN FROM SIN, AND TO REPENT, TO DO GOOD WORKS, AND TO LIVE HOLILY; BECAUSE IT DEPENDS ON THEIR WILL.—After Mr. Edwards had thus announced his plan, his attention was necessarily diverted from its execution, during his residence in Northampton, by the controversy respecting the Qualifications for Communion, his Treatise on that subject, and the many perplexities and embarrassments, which terminated in his dismission. His removal from Northampton, the establishment of his family at Stockbridge, the Answer to Mr. Williams, and his ordinary duties as minister and missionary, and the unhappy controversy subsisting respecting the mission, engrossed his whole time, until July, 1752. In August following, he entered upon the work, and pursued it a short time; but the violence of that controversy, and the attempts of the party hostile to Mr. Woodbridge, to force him from Stockbridge, compelled him to intermit his labours. Some of these circumstances are alluded to, in the following letter to Mr. Erskine, in which the reader will also find some interesting details, relative to the Dutch church, and to the state of religion in New Jersey.

" *Stockbridge, November* 23, *N. S.* 1752.

REV. AND DEAR BROTHER,

In August last I wrote to you, and sent away the letter, (with letters to some of my other correspondents,) to Boston, to be conveyed to Scotland. Therein I acknowledged the receipt of two letters from you, one of July 17, 1751; another of Feb. 11, 1752; with the pamphlets, put with the last letter; and now acknowledge the receipt of another letter from you of May 14, 1752; and the pamphlets you sent with the last. The letter I received the latter end of September: the pamphlets I did not receive till very lately: they were forgotten by Mr. Prince. The Treatise against Fanaticism I shall have no benefit from, because I am not acquainted with the French language. What the Jewish convert has published of his conversion, &c. is very agreeable. And I now heartily thank you for this letter and packet. I am very glad to see what you write concerning the state of religion in the Netherlands. But I believe there is more of a mixture of what is bad with the good, that appears in that land, than

Mr. Kennedy, and many other ministers there, are aware of; and that they will find, that the consequences of their not carefully and critically distinguishing between the good and bad, and guarding with the utmost caution and diligence against the latter, will prove worse than they now conceive of. By your account, it is now exactly with Mr. Kennedy, as it was with many pious ministers in America, in the time of the great religious moving here. They looked upon critical inquiries, into the difference between true grace and its counterfeits, or at least a being very busy in such inquiries, and spending time in them, to be impertinent and unseasonable; tending rather to damp the work of the Spirit of God, than promote it; diverting their own minds, and the minds of others, as they supposed, from that to which God, at such an extraordinary time, did loudly call them more especially to attend. The cry was, O, *there is no danger, if we are but lively in religion, and full of God's Spirit, and live by faith, of being misled! If we do but follow God, there is no danger of being led wrong! 'Tis the cold, carnal, and lifeless, that are most likely to be blind, and walk in darkness. Let us press forward, and not stay and hinder the good work, by standing and spending time in these criticisms and carnal reasoning! &c. &c.* This was the language of many, till they ran on deep into the wilderness, and were taught by the briers and thorns of the wilderness. However, 'tis no wonder that divines in Europe will not lay very much weight on the admonitions they receive from so obscure a part of the world. Other parts of the church of God must be taught as we have been; and when they see and feel, then they will believe. Not that I apprehend there is in any measure so much enthusiasm and disorder, mixed with the work in Holland, as was in many parts of America, in the time of the last revival of religion here. But yet I believe the work must be more pure, and the people more thoroughly guarded from his wiles, who beguiled Eve through his subtilty, and who corrupts the minds of zealous people from the simplicity that is in Christ, before the work goes on to a general conquest, and is maintained in its power and glory for a great length of time. But God will have his own way:—'Who, being his counsellor, hath taught Him?' We must expect confusion and uproar, before we have that abundance of peace and truth, which the Scriptures speak of: many must run to and fro, and knowledge will be increased.

The Dutch ministers in America, whom you mention, whom I have acquaintance with, are some of the younger ministers, and such as were born in America, though several of them have had part of their education in Holland. I have not acquaintance enough with them, to know their sentiments, particularly, about those corrupt mixtures above mentioned, and the care which is to be used in guarding against them. However, 'tis not very likely, if some of them should write to their brethren in Holland, that their letters would have more influence upon them than letters from you, and some others of the ministers of Scotland. Nevertheless, there is a prospect, that there will in time be very happy effects of the growing acquaintance and union, there is between a very considerable number of very hopeful and pious Dutch ministers, in the province of New York and New Jersey, and many English and Scotch ministers in America. The number of well disposed Dutch ministers in these provinces, has of late remarkably increased; so that I think when they meet together in their Cœtus, they make the major part. Some of the elder ministers seem to be of quite contrary sentiment and disposition, not appearing friendly, as the others, to what they esteem the power of religion, nor approving of awakening, searching, strict, and experimental preaching; which has occasioned various contests among them. However, the stricter sort being the prevailing part, are like to carry the day.

The Dutch churches in these provinces have hitherto been so dependent on the Classis in Holland, that, whenever any among them have been educated for the ministry, and any churches have been desirous of their administrations, they could not receive their orders on this side of the water, but have been obliged to go to Holland for ordination: which has been a great encumbrance, that has attended the settlement of ministers among them, and has undoubtedly been one occasion of such multitudes of the Dutch being wholly without ministers. Application was made not long since, through the influence of the forementioned serious young ministers, (as I take it,) by the Cœtus here, to the Classis in Holland, for their consent, that they might unite themselves to the presbyterian synod of New York, which now consists of English and Scotch. But the success of their application was prevented, by a letter written by one of the elder ministers, remonstrating against it, very falsely representing the New York synod, as no proper presbyterian synod, but rather a company of independents. On which, the Classis of Holland advised them, by no means, to unite themselves with that synod.

The last September I went a journey into New Jersey, and had opportunity, in my journey, of seeing some of these young ministers, and conversing with them on the subject. They seem resolved, by some means or other, to disengage themselves and their churches from the forementioned great encumbrance, of being obliged to cross the ocean for the ordination of every minister. I was much gratified, during the little opportunity I had, to observe the agreeable disposition of these ministers.

There were, also, many other things I had opportunity to observe in those parts, which were very agreeable. I was there, at the time of the public commencement in the college, and the time of the meeting of the trustees of the college, the time of the meeting of the correspondents of the society for propagating christian knowledge, and the time of the meeting of the New York synod; so that I had opportunity to converse with ministers from Long-Island, New York, New Jersey, Pennsylvania, and Virginia. The college is in flourishing circumstances; increases apace; and is happily regulated. The trustees seem engaged to their utmost to promote learning, virtue, and true religion, in it; and none more so than Governor Belcher; who is the president of the trustees, and was at the commencement, and at the trustees' meeting. But they very much want further supplies, for the convenient support of the college. I had considerable opportunity to converse with Governor Belcher; and was several times at his house at Elizabeth-town. He labours under many of the infirmities of age, but savours much of a spirit of religion, and seems very desirous of doing all the good he can, while he lives. The New York synod is in flourishing circumstances: much more so than the Philadelphia synod. They have the greatest body of ministers now, and increase much faster than the other. They are in higher credit with the people in almost all parts, and are chiefly sought to for supplies by distant congregations.

With respect to the proceedings of the correspondents, they have dismissed Mr. Horton from his mission on Long-Island, and he is about to settle in a congregation in New Jersey. He was dismissed by reason of his very much failing of employment: many of the clans of Indians, he used to preach to, having dwindled away, by death or dispersion, and there being but little prospect of success among others that remain, and some being so situated, that they may conveniently be taken care of by other ministers. The correspondents have it in their view to employ the money, by which he used to be supported, to support a mission among the Six Nations; after they have found a suitable person to undertake the business of such a mission, and he is fitted for it by learning the language. They used endeavours to obtain a suitable person for the business, in New Jersey; but, meeting with no success, they voted to empower Mr. Bellamy, Mr. Hopkins of Sheffield, and myself, to procure a suitable person, if we can find such an one, in New England, for the present, to come and live at Stockbridge, to be here learning the Mohawk language with Mr. Hawley, our school-master for the Mohawks, to fit him for the mission. Persons proper to be employed, and such as may be obtained, are very scarce; and 'tis doubtful whether we shall be able to obtain one.

There is a very dark cloud, that at present attends the affair, relating to the Indians at Stockbridge, occasioned very much by one of the agents of the province, (who lives at Stockbridge,) pursuing measures very contrary to the measures of the commissioners of the society in London. The opposition is maintained, not with a small degree of stiffness and resolution; and the contest is become so great that it has brought things into very great confusion. This gentleman is a man of some note; and his wife's relations earnestly engage with him, and many of them are persons of considerable figure in the country. The commissioners all very much dislike his conduct. This contest occasions no misunderstandings among the people in Stockbridge, in general: all, excepting those nearly related to the family, both English and Indians, are happily united to me and my family. It would be very tedious for me to write, and for you to read, all the particulars of this uncomfortable affair. The commissioners are exerting themselves to relieve us of this calamity; and it is probable they will be successful.

I thank you for the account you give of some valuable books published: I desire you would continue to favour me in this manner. I began the last August to write a little on the Arminian controversy, but was soon broke off: and such have been my extraordinary avocations and hinderances, that I have not had time to set pen to paper about this matter since. But I hope that God, in his providence, will favour me with opportunity to prosecute the design. And I desire your prayers, that God would assist me in it, and in all the work I am called to, and enable me to conduct my life to his glory and acceptance, under all difficulties and trials.

My wife joins with me in most hearty and affectionate salutation to you, and Mrs. Erskine.

I am, dear Sir,

Your affectionate and obliged

Brother and servant,

JONATHAN EDWARDS."

"P. S. I propose with this, to send you Mr. Hobart's second address to the members of the episcopal church in New England, and my answer to Mr. Williams, which I would desire you to give your neighbours, my correspondents, opportunity to read, if they desire it."

The correspondence of Mr. Edwards and the Rev. Thomas Gillespie of Carnock, in Scotland, has already interested the attention of the reader. This gentleman was born in 1708, pursued his theological studies under Dr. Doddridge, and was ordained and settled in the parish of Carnock, in 1741. He was a faithful and indefatigable minister.—"I never (says Dr. Erskine, who was several months his stated hearer at Carnock, and often heard his occasional efforts in other places) sat under a minister better calculated to awaken the thoughtless and secure, to caution convinced sinners against what would stifle their convictions and prevent their issuing in conversion, and to point out the differences between vital Christianity and specious, counterfeit appearances of it."—His popularity and usefulness were very great, not only in his own parish, but in Edinburgh and the west of Scotland. In 1752 an event occurred, which forms an era in the ecclesiastical history of that country. The Rev. Andrew Richardson of Broughton was presented to the charge of the town of Inverkeithing, by the lay patron of the parish—*the individual who had that living in his gift.*—The inhabitants refused to receive him as their minister. The case was appealed from court to court, until the General Assembly, in May, 1752, directed the presbytery of Dunfermline to admit Mr. R. to the charge of Inverkeithing, and appointed Mr. Gillespie to preside on the occasion. Mr. Gillespie, and several others in the presbytery, had conscientious scruples on the subject of lay patronage, and fully believed that no one, on the principles of the gospel, could have any right to place a clergyman over a parish but the people themselves.* He therefore, and those who thought with him, declined obedience to the mandate: and while *they* were subjected to various ecclesiastical censures, *he* was deposed from the ministry, and removed from the parish of Carnock. When called to the bar to receive his sentence, he replied, "Moderator, I receive this sentence of the General Assembly with reverence and awe. But I rejoice that it is given to me, on the behalf of Christ, not only to believe on his name, but to suffer for his sake."

For about a year he preached to his people out of doors, hoping that the sentence would be reversed; at the close of which, a church having been purchased for him in Dunfermline, a short distance from Carnock, he preached there, as an independent, about six years, unconnected with any associate in the ministry. In 1758 he united with the Rev. Thomas Boston, Jr., and formed a new establishment, called, *The Presbytery of Relief;* to which some dissenting ministers of England soon acceded. The congregations at present connected with them, and known, as an ecclesiastical body, by the name of THE RELIEF, are 65 in number, are found in all the principal towns, and many of the country parishes, of Scotland, and are computed to consist of towards 60,000 individuals.† They provide ministers for the inhabitants of those parishes, which do not submit to ministers introduced by *lay patronage;* and readily admit to ministerial and church

* Lay patronage was wholly rejected by the Scotch reformers, and was not introduced by law until 1711. For a long period, the law was regarded as a public grievance, but is now submitted to.

† "Mr. Gillespie died, Jan. 19th, 1774, in serenity of mind, and good hope through grace."

communion, evangelical ministers of the church of Scotland, and of the church of England.

The correspondents of Mr. Edwards had forwarded to him various publications relative to the deposition of Mr. Gillespie; and the views which he formed with regard to it, as expressed in the following letter, while they must, at the time, have been consoling and supporting to the excellent man to whom they were sent, will also probably harmonize with those of every reader of these pages.

"To the Rev. Thomas Gillespie, Carnock.

Stockbridge, Nov. 24, 1752.

Rev. and dear Brother,

In letters and pamphlets lately forwarded to me, by some of my correspondents in Scotland, I have received the affecting and surprising account of your deposition, for not assisting in the settlement of Mr. Richardson, at Inverkeithing. The circumstances of which affair seem to be such, as abundantly manifest your cause to be good; at the same time that they plainly show the persecuting spirit with which you have been proceeded against. It is strange, that a protestant church should condemn and depose one of her ministers, for conscientiously declining to act in a forced settlement of a minister, over a congregation that have not chosen him as their pastor, but are utterly averse to his administrations, at least as to a stated attendance upon them. It is to be wondered at, that such a church, at this time of day, after the cause of liberty in matters of conscience has been so abundantly defended, should arrogate to herself such a kind of authority over the consciences of both ministers and people, and use it in such a manner, by such severity, to establish that, which is not only contrary to the liberty of Christians, wherewith Christ has made them free; but so directly contrary to her own professed principles, acts, and resolutions, entered on public record. The several steps of this proceeding, and some singular measures taken, and the hastiness and vehemence of the proceeding, are such, as savour very strongly of the very spirit of persecution, and must be greatly to the dishonour of the church of Scotland; and are such, as will naturally engage the friends of God's people, abroad in the world, in your favour, as suffering very injuriously. It is wonderful, that a church, which has itself suffered so much by persecution, should be guilty of so much persecution. This proceeding gives reason to suspect, that the church of Scotland, which was once so famous, is not what it once was. It appears probable to me, at this distance, that there is something else at the bottom, besides a zeal to uphold the authority of the church. Perhaps many of the clergy of the church of Scotland have their minds secretly infected with those lax principles of the new divinity, and have imbibed the *liberal* doctrines, as they are accounted, which are so much in vogue at the present day, and so contrary to the strict, mysterious, spiritual, soul-humbling principles of our forefathers. I have observed, that these modern fashionable opinions, however called noble and liberal, are commonly attended, not only with a haughty contempt, but an inward malignant bitterness of heart, towards all the zealous professors and defenders of the contrary spiritual principles, that do so nearly concern the vitals of religion, and the power of experimental godliness. This, be sure, has been the case in this land. I have known many gentlemen, (especially in the ministry,) tainted with these liberal principles; who, though none seem to be such warm advocates as they, for liberty and freedom of thought, or condemn a narrow and persecuting spirit so much as they; yet, in the course of things, have made it manifest, that they themselves had no small share of a persecuting spirit. They were, indeed, against any body's restraining *their* liberties, and pretending to control *them* in their thinking and professing as they please; and that is what they mean, truly, when they plead for liberty. But they have that inward enmity of spirit towards those others mentioned, that, if they see an opportunity to persecute them under some good cloak, and with some false pretext, they will eagerly embrace it, and proceed with great severity and vehemence. Thus far, perhaps, if the truth were known, it would appear, that some of your most strenuous persecutors hate you much more for something else, than they do for your not obeying the orders of the general assembly. I do not pretend to know how the case is. I only speak from what I have seen and found, here in America, in cases somewhat similar. However, it is beyond doubt, that this proceeding will stand on the records of future time, for the lasting reproach of your persecutors; and your conduct, for which you have suffered, will be to your lasting honour in the church of God. And what is much more, that, which has been condemned in you by man, and for which you have suffered from him, is doubtless approved by God, and I trust you will have a glorious reward from him. For the cause you suffer in, is the cause of God; and if God be for us, who can be against us? If he justifies, what need we care who condemns? Not only is the mercy of God, dear brother, manifested, in its being granted you to suffer for his sake, but his mercy is to be taken notice of, in many of the circumstances of this suffering. Particularly, that he has excited so many to appear for you: that you had the major part of the presbytery, which you belong to, with you in the affair, though God has honoured you above all the rest, in calling you to suffer for his name: that the major part of the commission of the General Assembly did in effect approve of the conduct of the presbytery, judging it no censurable fault: that no greater part of the Assembly had a hand in your deposition: that so many of God's people have, on this occasion, very boldly appeared to befriend you, as suffering in a righteous cause, openly condemning the conduct of your most bitter prosecutors, and testifying an abhorrence of their conduct: and that many have appeared, liberally to contribute to your outward support; so that, by what I understand, you are likely to be no loser in that respect; by which, your enemies will, perhaps, be entirely disappointed. And, above all, that you have been enabled, through the whole of this affair, to conduct yourself with so much christian meekness, decency, humility, proper deference to authority, and composure and fortitude of mind; which is an evident token that God will appear for you, and also, that he will appear against your enemies. When I received your kind letter, soon after my dismission from Northampton, so full of expressions of sympathy towards me under what I suffered, I little thought of your being brought so soon under sufferings so similar. But, seeing God has so ordered it in his providence, my prayer and hope is, that he would abundantly reward your sympathy in my case. '*Blessed are the merciful, for they shall obtain mercy.*'

As to myself, I still meet with difficulties in my new station, which arise partly from private views (as it is to be feared) of some particular persons of some note and distinction, who are concerned with the affair of the Mohawks here, and partly from the same spirit and the same persons, and others nearly related to them, who fomented the contention with me at Northampton. However, all the people, both Indians and English, except the very few of the above-mentioned connexion, are firmly united to me: and the commissioners in Boston, who are my constituents, and from whom I have my support, are altogether on my side; and are endeavouring to the utmost to remove the difficulties that attend our affairs; by which the cause of religion here, especially among the Mohawks, suffers much more than I do, or am like to do, in my personal and temporal interests. These difficulties which have arisen, have, indeed, almost brought the Mohawk affair to ruin, which the last year was attended with so glorious a prospect. It would be very tedious to relate the particulars of this unhappy affair. I think that God, by these sufferings, calls me to expect no other than to meet with difficulties and trials while in this world. And what am I better than my fathers, that I should expect to fare better in the world, than the generality of Christ's followers in all past generations. May all our trials be for our justification, and our being more and more meet for our Master's use, and prepared to enter into the joy of our Lord, in a world where all tears shall be wiped from the eyes of God's people. Let us, dear Sir, earnestly pray one for another, that it may be thus with us; and that, however we may be called to labour and to suffer, we may see peace on God's Israel, and hereafter eternally glory and triumph with his inheritance. God has of late mercifully preserved my wife and youngest daughter, in time of very sore and dangerous sickness, and restored them again. My eldest daughter has also been sick, and is restored in a considerable degree.

The Northampton people remain in sorrowful circumstances, destitute of a settled minister, and without any prospect of a settlement; having met with many disappointments. But all don't as yet seem to be effectual, to bring them to a suitable temper of mind. I much desire to hear from you, and to be informed of your present circumstances.

I am, dear Sir,
Your affectionate brother
in the gospel,
JONATHAN EDWARDS."

With the preceding letter was sent the following to Mr. M'Culloch.

" *Stockbridge, Nov.* 24, 1752.

Rev. and dear Sir,

I thank you for your letter of March 3, 1752, which I received this fall. I thank you for your friendly and instructive observations, on God's dealings with me and my family. Though God's dispensations towards me, have been attended with some distinguishing trials, yet the end of the Lord has been very gracious. He has ever manifested himself very pitiful and of tender mercy, in the midst of difficulties we have met with, in merciful circumstances with which they have been attended, and also in the event of them. Our circumstances, here at Stockbridge, are in many respects comfortable. We here live in peace and friendship, with the generality of the people. But we are not without our difficulties and troubles here. The Indian affair, which the last year was attended with so pleasing and glorious a prospect, has since been unspeakably embarrassed, through the particular schemes of certain individuals, who are opposed, in their counsels and measures, to the commissioners of the Society in London, and are, to their utmost, striving to accomplish their designs in opposition to them; and in this great contest I am looked on as a person not a little obnoxious. They belong to a family of some note, who vigorously abetted and set forward my opposers at Northampton, and were a chief occasion of my removal from that town; to whom my settlement at Stockbridge was very grievous; who now take occasion to exert themselves to the utmost to weaken my interest and influence; and I have all reason to think, would, if it were possible, undermine me, and procure my removal far hence. Many endeavours have been used to disaffect my people towards me, but all in vain. They are all firmly united to me, excepting the forementioned family. Endeavours have been used, also, to disaffect some of the commissioners; but wholly in vain. They seem to have their eyes very wide open, as to their particular designs and schemes, and the true spring of their opposition. We hope for an end of this lamentable contest before long. But its effects hitherto have been very sorrowful, especially with regard to the Mohawks. Some other things have happened, which have much prejudiced the cause of religion among the Indians; and among other things, the discovery of the famous Tartarian root, described in Chambers's dictionary, called *Ginseng*, which was found in our woods the last summer, and is since found in the woods in many of these western parts of New England, and in the country of the Six Nations. The traders in Albany have been eager to purchase all that they could, of this root, to send to England; where they make great profit by it. This has occasioned our Indians of all sorts, young and old, to spend abundance of time in wandering about the woods, and sometimes to a great distance, in the neglect of public worship, and of their husbandry; and also in going much to Albany, to sell their roots, (which proves worse to them than their going into the woods,) where they are always much in the way of temptation and drunkenness; especially when they have money in their pockets. The consequence has been that many of them have laid out their money, which they have got for their roots of Ginseng, for rum; wherewith they have intoxicated themselves.

God has been very gracious to my family of late, when some of them have been visited with sore sickness. My wife has lately been very dangerously sick, so as to be brought to the very brink of the grave. She had very little expectation of life, but seemed to be assisted to an unweaned resignation to the Divine will, and an unshaken peace and joy in God, in the expectation of a speedy departure. But God was pleased to preserve her, and mercifully to restore her to a pretty good state of health. My youngest daughter also, who has been a very infirm child, was brought nigh unto death by a sore fit of sickness, and is now also restored to her former state. My daughter Parsons, my eldest daughter, who with her husband has removed from Northampton, and dwells in Stockbridge, has also very lately been very sick, but is in a considerable measure restored. My daughter Esther's marriage with President Burr, of Newark, seems to be very much to the satisfaction of ministers and people in those parts, and also of our friends in Boston, and other parts of New England.

As to the state of religion in America, I have but little to write that is comfortable; but there seems to be better appearances in some other colonies than in New England. When I was lately in New Jersey, in the time of the synod there, I was informed of some small movings and revivals in some places on Long-Island and New Jersey. I there had the comfort of a short interview with Mr. Davies of Virginia, and was much pleased with him and his conversation. He appears to be a man of very solid understanding, discreet in his behaviour, and polished and gentlemanly in his manners, as well as fervent and zealous in religion. He gave an account of the probability of the settlement of a Mr. Todd, a young man of good learning and of a pious disposition, in a part of Virginia near to him. Mr. Davies represented before the synod, the great necessities of the people in the back parts of Virginia, where multitudes were remarkably awakened and reformed several years ago, and ever since have been thirsting after the ordinances of God. The people are chiefly from Ireland, of Scotch extraction. The synod appointed two men to go down and preach among these people; *viz.* Mr. Henry, a Scotchman, who has lately taken a degree at New Jersey college, and Mr. Greenman, the young man who was educated at the charge of Mr. David Brainerd.

The people of Northampton are in sorrowful circumstances, are still destitute of a minister, and have met with a long series of disappointments in their attempts for a resettlement of the ministry among them. My opposers have had warm contentions among themselves. Of late, they have been wholly destitute of anybody to preach steadily among them. They sometimes meet to read and pray among themselves, and at other times set travellers or transient persons to preach, that are hardly fit to be employed.

My wife joins with me in most respectful salutations to you and yours. Desiring your prayers, that God would be with us in all our wanderings through the wilderness of this world,

I am, dear Sir,
Your most affectionate brother,
In the labours of the gospel,
JONATHAN EDWARDS."

The chagrin and mortification, and entire loss of influence and respect, consequent upon the indiscreet attempt to force Mr. Edwards from Stockbridge, by buying out all the English inhabitants, and upon its utter discomfiture, had, in its connexion with the infirmities of age, such an effect upon the individual who made it, that he was soon after induced to part with his property in that town, and remove to a distance. His children, though somewhat disheartened by so untoward an event, and now assured that if help came to them, it could not come from Stockbridge, appear however to have resolved, that they would not lose all their labour, and all their hopes, without a struggle. The commissioners in Boston, of the Society in London, were now to a man firmly opposed to them, and resolved to resist them to the utmost. But their kinsman who was a member of the Society in London, was well acquainted with its board of directors, and had written to them in behalf of his cousin. He had also applied to Mr. Hollis, to secure to her husband the management of his benefactions. The latter gentleman also, and the brother of the former, had considerable influence at Boston, and this influence had now been exerted for a considerable period, to procure the removal of Mr. Edwards. At the opening of the general court, in the autumn, all the influence and all the efforts of the family, and its friends, were brought to bear on this one point; and representations most unfavourable to the character and qualifications of Mr. E. were made to many of the principal men of the province. The Annual Report of the resident trustee was drawn up with a direct and immediate reference to this subject, and was read to the legislature, when Mr. Edwards knew nothing of its contents, and when, being at the distance of one hundred and fifty miles, he of course could not at once answer it. Mr. Woodbridge, however, was on the spot, as were the honourable commissioners of the Society in London, and they made such counteracting statements, as the circumstances rendered proper. Of this Report we shall take notice further on.

While Mr. Woodbridge was at Boston, he was informed, and that too most incautiously, by the son of his opponent, who went thither in company with his brother-in-law, the author of the Report, that the latter had solicited his Excellency, Sir William Pepperell, governor of the province, to write to England, and to use his influence, with the corporation in London, that Mr. Edwards might be removed from the office of missionary; and that Sir William had engaged to do it. On this information, coming so directly, Mr. Edwards felt himself bound, from a regard to his own reputation, and to the welfare of his family, to address Sir William on the subject; which he did in a letter, bearing date January 30, 1753.* In this letter, after reciting the preceding facts, as his apology for writing it, and mentioning the great disadvantage under which he lay, in attempting to defend himself, at such a distance, when he did not know what had been said to his prejudice, he states, among other things, the following: That, since the revival of religion in 1734, the family, with which the writer of the Report was now connected, had discovered an unceasing hostility towards himself, and his own family, notwithstanding the best endeavours he could use to remove it; that they deeply engaged themselves in the controversy at Northampton, on the side of his opposers, upholding, directing, and animating them, in all their measures; that two of them, especially, had been the confidential advisers of the opposition, in procuring his dismission; that when his removal to Stockbridge was proposed, the whole family, there and elsewhere, opposed it, with great vehemence, though, when they saw an entire union and universal engagedness in all the rest of the inhabitants, both English and Indians, for his settlement there, and that there was no hope of preventing it, they appeared as though their minds were changed;—that the author of the Report, during the whole controversy at Northampton, in direct opposition to the family, with which he was now connected, had remained his zealous friend and advocate; that he warmly advocated his removal to Stockbridge, and expressed a strong desire of living under his ministry; (for the evidence of which facts, he refers Sir William to two of the most respectable gentlemen in the province;) that this confidential friendship lasted until his connexion with that family, and then was suddenly changed, first into secret, and afterwards into open opposition; that he had personally blamed him

* This letter is too long for insertion.

for preaching to the Mohawks, as *intermeddling with what was none of his business*, although Mr. E. produced the note of the commissioners, *expressly desiring him to preach to the Mohawks, until a distinct missionary was appointed over them;* that the reason, openly assigned for the very great resentment of the author of the Report, and that of his friends, against Mr. Edwards, was, his having opposed the appointment of the wife of that gentleman, as teacher of the female school, although he neither said nor did any thing respecting it, until his opinion was expressly desired in writing by the commissioners, and then, that he opposed it on the ground, that it was impossible for an individual, who had the care of two numerous families of children, to instruct and govern the children of an Indian school;—and that, as to his qualifications for the business of a missionary, his *communicative faculty*, &c. which were now denied, he could only appeal to those, who had the best opportunity of judging, from their own experience,—particularly, to every man, woman, and child, in Stockbridge, that had any understanding, both English and Indians, except the families of the opponent of Mr. Woodbridge, and of the author of the Report. Mr. Edwards then adds, " Now, Sir, I humbly request, that, if you had resolved on endeavouring to have me removed from my present employment here, you would once more take the matter into your impartial consideration. And I would pray you to consider, Sir, what disadvantages I am under; not knowing what has been said of me in conversation; not knowing, therefore, the accusation, or what to answer to. The ruin of my usefulness, and the ruin of my family, which has greatly suffered in years past, for righteousness' sake, are not indeed things of equal consideration with the public good. Yet, certainly, I should first have an equal, impartial, and candid hearing, before I am executed for the public good. I must leave the matter, dear Sir, to your justice and christian prudence; committing the affair to Him, who knows all the injuries I have suffered, and how wrongfully I now suffer, and who is the Great Protector of the innocent and oppressed; beseeching him to guide you in your determination, and mercifully to order the end."

In the month of February, 1753, the building erected for the instruction of the Mohawk boys, usually denominated the *boarding-school*, took fire in a way unknown, and, with considerable furniture in it, was reduced to ashes. Mr. Hawley had furnished a chamber in the building, and resided in it. By this calamity, he lost his clothing, books, and furniture. It was supposed, with some grounds, to have been set on fire by design; and its destruction was, for the time, a very serious interruption to the labours of Mr. Hawley.

The Report of the Indian agent was read early in the session. It contained various insinuations and charges, of a general nature, against Mr. Edwards. Other charges were busily circulated among the members, with the hope of procuring his removal. But it was well understood, that Mr. Edwards was at a great distance, and had had no notice of these charges. He had likewise a character for integrity, too well established, to be shaken by general insinuations, or covert attacks. Mr. Woodbridge, and the commissioners, were also on the spot, and took care that the real state of things should be made known, and the conduct of Mr. Edwards adequately defended. So effectually and satisfactorily was this done, that, when Mr. Edwards received a copy of the Report by Mr. Woodbridge, he appears also to have been apprized, by his friends in Boston, that the design of his enemies, in this attack, had been completely frustrated. What these insinuations and charges were, we learn from his letter to the Speaker of the House of Representatives, written for the purpose of being communicated, if he thought necessary, to the legislature. It deserves here to be mentioned, as a singular and very kind dispensation of Providence, that the author of the Report had, some time before, addressed a letter to Mr. Edwards, while he was his friend, and when he hoped for his co-operation; particularly, in the appointment of his son as school-master to the Mohawks; in which he had either furnished the means of contradicting the statements made in the Report, or had expressly requested Mr. Edwards to do the very things, which he now complained of, and made the ground of complaint. Of this letter Mr. Edwards enclosed a copy; offering to forward the original, if desired, and, at the same time, to substantiate every part of his own statement, by numerous witnesses, of the most unexceptionable character.

From his letter to the Speaker, it appears, that the writer of the Report charged him—with introducing Mr. Hawley into the school;—with introducing a master, in his absence, and when there was reason to expect his return;—with doing this, when he had been at the expense of a journey of his son of 260 miles, to procure Mr. Hawley as master of the boys;—with introducing Mr. Ashley, the interpreter, as assistant instructor;—and with opposing the appointment of his wife, as teacher of the female school;—and that he also alleged, that the school was in very desirable circumstances, until Mr. Hawley took it, and that it then declined;—that the Mohawks had been discouraged, through the conduct of the agents of the mission;—and that Mr. Edwards was not qualified for his office, because, on account of his age, he could not learn the language of the Indians.

To these charges Mr. Edwards replied,—that he introduced Mr. Hawley, because he was directed so to do, by the letter of the commissioners, of Dec. 31, 1751;—that he introduced a master, in the absence of the author of the Report, for two reasons, 1. Because he knew not when he was to return; and, 2. Because the author of the Report, himself, in a letter sent him by his son, requested him, *at that very time*, to introduce a master into the school; of which letter he enclosed a copy, with the offer of forwarding the original, if desired;—that, when the author of the Report sent his son on the specified journey, *it was not* to procure *Mr. Hawley* to be a master for the boys, but *it was*, that *the son himself* might be the master; for evidence of which, appeal is also made to the copy of the same letter;—that, as to the appointment of teacher of the female school, he said nothing about it, until expressly requested to give his opinion by the commissioners;—that so far was the school from being in desirable circumstances, before the introduction of Mr. Hawley, that the author of the Report had, himself, represented it as having been, until that time, in most lamentable circumstances, in the very letter of which he enclosed a copy, in which he requested Mr. Edwards to introduce his son into the school, in the room of the former master;—that the school continued to flourish under Mr. Hawley, until his opposers used their utmost endeavours to destroy it; for evidence of which, he offers the testimony of the substantial inhabitants of the town;—that Hendrick, and the other chiefs, and the Mohawks generally, had expressly assigned their dissatisfaction with the conduct of these individuals, as the reason of their leaving Stockbridge; for evidence of which, he offers the same testimony;—and, as to his learning the Housatonnuck language, that the author of the Report knew how the case would be, before he recommended him to the office of missionary; and that Mr. Sergeant, after fourteen years study, had never been able to preach in it, nor even to pray in it except by a form, and had often expressed the opinion, previous to his death, that his successor ought not to trouble himself in learning the language. He then requests, that the Speaker would communicate his letter to the Assembly, and prays that honourable body, if they proposed to take any order on the case, first to give him opportunity to meet his accuser face to face.

I have no means of ascertaining whether the preceding letter was, or was not, read to the legislature. If not, it was because the honourable Speaker, who was a personal friend of Mr. Edwards, found it to be wholly unnecessary. And it can scarcely be necessary to inform the reader, that the attack, made thus directly upon Mr. Edwards, and indirectly upon all his associates in the mission, not only failed altogether of its intended effect; but, by leading to a development of the mercenary scheme, devised to divert, to the purposes of private emolument, the consecrated charities of the province and of individuals, recoiled with increased violence upon its authors.

Thus far the individuals, opposed to the Stockbridge missionaries, had met with little success to encourage their efforts. They had looked for help to various sources; to the Indians and to the people of Stockbridge, to the commissioners and to the provincial legislature, to Mr. Hollis and to the Society in London; and in every instance, so far as the result was known, they had looked in vain. The Housatonnucks had refused all intercourse with them. From disgust at their management, a part of the Mohawks had actually retired, and the rest were threatening to retire, to their own country. The people of Stockbridge had, to a man, united against them. The commissioners were equally unanimous, in sustaining the individuals whose overthrow they had attempted. And now, before the provincial legislature, they had made their great and united effort, and had failed. In the mean time, Mr. Edwards was even more firmly established as the Indian missionary, and Mr. Woodbridge as the schoolmaster of the Housatonnucks; Mr. Hawley had not been compelled to resign his place to the son of the resident trustee; the female school had not as yet been secured to his wife, and obviously could not now be, unless secured to her in London; and the stewardship of the three schools was not likely to be conferred on himself. Such was the state of things in the spring of 1753. It looked as though the great struggle was over; and that the party, which had hitherto acted on the offensive, would thenceforward be quiet, from a conviction, that every hostile movement must issue in defeat. The result justified this conclusion.

To Mr. Edwards, and his associates in the mission, as well as to their friends, this result must have been in a high degree satisfactory. On his arrival in Stockbridge, he found this controversy waging, and soon discovered that it was a controversy between the friends and enemies of the mission; between those who aimed at the real welfare of the Indians, and those who endeavoured to use them as instruments of their own private emolument; that one party relied on wealth, and office, and influence, to carry its measures; and the other, on personal integrity, a conscientious discharge of duty, and the protection of God. For a time he avoided taking any part in it; and his own temporal comfort, and the welfare of his family, seemed to require, that he should persevere in the same course. But his conscience forbade it. He must either sit quietly by, and see the charities of the province, of the Society in London, and of Mr. Hollis, diverted from their appointed course, to fill the coffers of private avarice; or he must unite with those who were exerting their whole influence to prevent it. In such a state of things, he could not deliberate; and, through the divine blessing, he and his associates were now permitted to see, that they had not toiled and suffered in vain.

CHAPTER XXII.

LETTER TO HIS ELDEST SON—RETURN OF GREATER PART OF THE MOHAWKS—LETTER TO COMMISSIONERS—MISSION OF MR. HAWLEY TO ONOHQUAUGA—REMAINDER OF MOHAWKS DIRECTED TO RETURN—"FREEDOM OF THE WILL"—LETTER TO MR. ERSKINE—PROPOSAL OF SOCIETY IN LONDON—LETTER TO MR. GILLESPIE—DESIGN AND CHARACTER OF THE "FREEDOM OF THE WILL"—LETTERS FROM MR. HOLLIS—SURRENDER OF MOHAWK SCHOOL TO MR. EDWARDS—ENTIRE DEFEAT OF ENEMIES OF MISSION—RETURN OF REMAINING MOHAWKS.

Early in the ensuing spring, the eldest son of Mr. Edwards, then a lad of fourteen, went to New York, and thence to New Jersey; and on his way was much exposed to the small-pox. On his return to New York, he was seized with a violent fever. His father hearing this, and not knowing whether it was an ordinary fever, or the small-pox, addressed to him the following letter; which, like all his letters to his children, indicates that his chief anxiety was for their salvation.

"To Master Timothy Edwards, at New York.

Stockbridge, April, 1753.

My dear Child,

Before you will receive this letter, the matter will doubtless be determined, as to your having the small-pox. You will either be sick with that distemper, or will be past danger of having it, from any infection taken in your voyage. But whether you are sick or well, like to die or like to live, I hope you are earnestly seeking your salvation. I am sure there is a great deal of reason it should be so, considering the warnings you have had in word and in providence. That which you met with, in your passage from New York to Newark, which was the occasion of your fever, was indeed a remarkable warning, a dispensation full of instruction, and a very loud call of God to you, to make haste, and not to delay in the great business of religion. If you now have that distemper, which you have been threatened with, you are separated from your earthly friends, as none of them can come to see you; and if you should die of it, you have already taken a final and everlasting leave of them while you are yet alive, so as not to have the comfort of their presence and immediate care, and never to see them again in the land of the living. And if you have escaped that distemper, it is by a remarkable providence that you are preserved. And your having been so exposed to it, must certainly be a loud call of God, not to trust in earthly friends or any thing here below. Young persons are very apt to trust in parents and friends when they think of being on a death-bed. But this providence remarkably teaches you the need of a better Friend, and a better Parent, than earthly parents are; one who is every where present, and all-sufficient, that cannot be kept off by infectious distempers, who is able to save from death, or to make happy in death, to save from eternal misery, and to bestow eternal life. It is indeed comfortable, when one is in great pain, and languishing under sore sickness, to have the presence, and kind care, of near and dear earthly friends; but this is a very small thing, in comparison of what it is, to have the presence of a heavenly Father, and a compassionate and almighty Redeemer. In God's favour is life, and his loving-kindness is better than life. Whether you are in sickness or health, you infinitely need this. But you must know, however great need you stand in of it, you do not deserve it: neither is God the more obliged to bestow it upon you, for your standing in need of it, your earnest desiring of it, your crying to him constantly for it from fear of misery, and taking much pains. Till you have savingly believed in Christ, all your desires, and pains, and prayers lay God under no obligation; and, if they were ten thousand times as great as they are, you must still know, that you would be in the hands of a sovereign God, who hath mercy on whom he will have mercy. Indeed, God often hears the poor miserable cries of sinful vile creatures, who have no manner of true regard to Him in their hearts; for he is a God of infinite mercy, and he delights to show mercy for his Son's sake, who is worthy, though you are unworthy, who came to save the sinful and the miserable, yea, some of the chief of sinners. Therefore, there is your only hope; and in him must be your refuge, who invites you to come to him, and says, 'Him that cometh to me, I will in no wise cast out.' Whatever your circumstances are, it is your duty not to despair, but to hope in infinite mercy, through a Redeemer. For God makes it your duty to pray to him for mercy; which would not be your duty, if it was allowable for you to despair. We are expressly commanded to call upon God in the day of trouble, and when we are afflicted, then to pray. But, if I hear that you have escaped,—either that you have not been sick, or are restored,—though I shall rejoice, and have great cause of thankfulness, yet I shall be concerned for you. If your escape should be followed with carelessness and security, and forgetting the remarkable warning you have had, and God's great mercy in your deliverance, it would in some respects be more awful than sore sickness. It would be very provoking to God, and would probably issue in an increasing hardness of heart; and, it may be, divine vengeance may soon overtake you. I have known various instances of persons being remarkably warned, in providence, by being brought into very dangerous circumstances, and escaping, and afterwards death has soon followed in another way. I earnestly desire, that God would make you wise to salvation, and that he would be merciful and gracious to you in every respect, according as he knows your circumstances require. And this is the daily prayer of

Your affectionate and tender father,

JONATHAN EDWARDS."

"P. S. Your mother and all the family send their love to you, as being tenderly concerned for you."

At length the event, so long predicted by Mr. Edwards, actually took place. The Mohawks, who had manifested exemplary patience under the vexations and embarrassments to which they had been subjected by the whites, were at last wearied out; and, in the month of April, the greater part of them relinquished their lands and settlements at Stockbridge, and returned finally to their own country. After a brief allusion to this fact, in a letter to the commissioners, Mr. Edwards communicated to them a variety of interesting intelligence relative to the Iroquois, and to the mission proposed to be established among them.

"To the Commissioners in Boston.

Stockbridge, April 12, 1753.

Gentlemen,

The last Tuesday, about two-thirds of the Mohawks, young and old, went away from Stockbridge, and are never likely to return again. They have long manifested a great uneasiness at the management of affairs here, and at the conduct of those persons on whom their affairs have almost wholly fallen; and have shown themselves very much grieved, that others, who used to be concerned, have been excluded. They have, once and again, represented the grounds of their uneasiness to the provincial agent, but without redress. They have been dissatisfied with his answers, and there has appeared in them a growing dislike of the family, who have lately left their own house, and taken up their constant abode among them, in the female boarding-school.

The correspondents, in New York and New Jersey, of the Society in Scotland for propagating Christian Knowledge, have determined, if Providence favours, to settle a mission among the Six Nations. To that end, they have chosen Mr. Gordon, a pious young gentleman, who has lately been a tutor at New Jersey college, to come to Stockbridge, and remain here with Mr. Hawley, to learn the Mohawk language with him, in order to his being fitted for the business. Mr. Gordon is expected here to prosecute this design in the beginning of May.

In addition to this, Mr. Brainerd, the pastor of the Indian congregation at Bethel in New Jersey, who is supported by the correspondents, having met with much trouble from the enemies of religion in those parts; and his Indians being greatly disturbed, with regard to the possession and improvement of their lands; the correspondents have of late had a disposition, that he, with his school-master and whole congregation, should remove, if a door might be opened, and take up a new settlement, somewhere in the country of the Six Nations. Mr. Hawley has seen Mr. Brainerd, and conversed with him on the subject, this spring. He manifests an inclination to such a removal, and says his Indians will be ready for it. If such a thing as this could be brought to pass, it would probably tend greatly to the introduction of the gospel, and the promotion of the interests of religion, among the Six Nations; as his congregation are, I suppose, the most virtuous and religious collection of Indians in America, and some of them have now been long established in religion and virtue.

According to the best information I can get, of the country of the Six Nations, the most convenient place, to be chosen as the chief seat of missionary operations, is the country about *Onohquauga*, near the head of the Susquehannah river.

I apprehend, from some things of which Mr. Woodbridge informed me, that the commissioners have had very wrong information concerning the Onohquauga Indians, as though they were a very despicable company, a kind of renegadoes, scarcely to be reckoned as of the Six Nations, living out of the country of those nations. There are, indeed, some here, who have sometimes spoken very contemptuously of them; which seems to have been, not from any manner of ground in fact, or so much as any colour of reason; but merely because these Indians appeared peculiarly attached to Mr. Ashley and his wife, and under their influence. But there are other persons in Stockbridge, who have had as much opportunity to know what is the true state of these people, as they. The *Onohquauga* Indians, who have been here, are properly, not only of the Six Nations, but of the Five Nations, who are the original united tribes of the Iroquois. All, but one or two of them, are of the nation of the *Oneiutas;* and they appear not to be looked upon as contemptible, by the rest of the Five Nations, from what was once openly said of them, at a public council, by the sachems of the *Conneenchees*, or proper *Mohawks*, who advised us to treat the Onohquaugas with peculiar care and kindness, as excelling their own tribe in religion and virtue; giving at the same time many instances of their virtue. We have found the testimony which they gave of them to be true. They appear to be far the best disposed Indians with which we have had any connexion. They would be inclined to the utmost, to assist, encourage, and strengthen, the hands of missionaries and instructors, should any be sent among them, and to do all they could to forward their success, among themselves, and the other Indians round about.

There seems to be no room for a missionary, in the country of the Conneenchees. The Society for Propagating the Gospel in Foreign Parts, have long since taken them under their care, and pretended to support a mission among them. A mission from the commissioners in Boston would not be borne by them, nor by the Dutch, who are always among them. And as to the country of the *Quinquas*,* and the original seat of the *Oneiutas*, they seem not to be convenient places for settling a mission, on two accounts. They are in the road to Oswego, where the Dutch are incessantly passing and repassing with their rum; with which they are continually making them drunk, and would be, in many other respects, a continual hinderance and affliction to a missionary; for they are exceedingly opposed to the New England people having any thing to do with the Iroquois. The nation of the *Quinquas*, also, are mostly in the French interest, as well as many of the *Oneiutas;* so that a missionary would there be afflicted, and perhaps in danger, by the French. And it is very evident, that the country of the *Onoontaugas*, is no country for our missionaries to attempt to establish a mission in. It would be like establishing a mission in Canada; for that nation have entirely gone over to the French interest. They are in the road of the French, as they go up a trading to Mississippi, and their distant settlements, and the nations on the great lakes; and the French have of late built a fort in their country, and have in effect annexed it to Canada. And the country of the *Senecas* will not be much more convenient for the purpose, both by reason of its very good distance, and also because most of the nation are firmly united to the French, who constantly maintain their missionaries among them.

Onohquauga is within the territory of the Five Nations, and not so far from the other settlements, but that it may be convenient for making excursions to the several tribes; as convenient perhaps as any place that can be found. It is, I suppose, as near to the heart of the country as any place, unless *Oneiuta* and *Quinquah*. They are also much out of the way of the French, and considerably out of the way of the Dutch, are in a pleasant fruitful country, surrounded by many settlements of Indians on every side, and where the way is open by an easy passage down the river, which runs through one of the most pleasant and fruitful parts of America, for four or five hundred miles, exceedingly well peopled on both sides, and on its several branches, by Indians. Onohquauga is the road, by which several of the nations pass, as they go to war with the southern nations. And there will be this advantage, which missionaries will have, that the Onohquauga Indians are fast friends to the English; and though some of the Dutch have tried much to disaffect them to the English, their attempts have been in vain. They are very desirous of instruction, and to have the gospel established in their country.

There are several towns of the Onohquaugas; and several missionaries might probably find sufficient employment in those parts. If Mr. Brainerd should settle somewhere in that country, with his christian Indians, and one or two more missionaries, not at a great distance, they might be under advantage to assist one another; as they will greatly need one another's company and assistance, in so difficult a work, in such a strange distant land. They might be under advantage to consult one another, and to act in concert, and to help one another, in any case of peculiar difficulty. Many English people would be found to go from New England, and settle there; and the greatest difficulty would be, that there would be danger of too many English settlers, and of such as are not fit for the place.

But, in order to accomplish this; especially in order to such a body of new Indians coming from the Jerseys, and settling in the country of the Six Nations; the consent of those nations, or at least of several of them, must be obtained. The method which Mr. Woodbridge, Mr. Hawley, and I, have thought of, which we submit to the

* Now called the *Cayugas*.

wisdom of the commissioners, is this,—that Mr. Woodbridge, and Mr. Ashley and his wife, should go, as speedily as possible, into the country of the Conneenchees;—they being the first tribe in honour, though not in numbers;—and there spend some weeks, perhaps a month, among them, to get acquainted with them, and endeavour to gain their approbation of a mission, for settling the gospel in the country of the Six Nations.—Mr. Hawley, in the mean time, to keep Mr. Woodbridge's school. Then, that Mr. Hawley and Mr. Gordon should join them there, and go with them from thence to Onohquauga; and when they have acquainted themselves well with the people, and the state of the country, and find things agreeable, and see a hopeful prospect, then for Mr. Woodbridge to return, and leave Mr. Hawley and Mr. Gordon there, and forthwith send word to Mr. Brainerd, and propose to him to come up, with some of his chief Indians, to see the country. And if, on the observations they make, and the acquaintance they get with the people and country, they think there is an encouraging prospect, then to endeavour to gain a conference with some of the chiefs of the Five Nations, at an appointed time, to know whether they will consent to their coming to settle in their territories. All this will occupy some considerable time; so that, if they can obtain their consent, Mr. Brainerd must return home; and he and his chief Indians must come again to the treaty, at the time and place appointed.

You will easily perceive, Gentlemen, that these things will require time, and that, in order to carry these various measures into effect this year, there will be need of expedition, which may show the reason why we think it necessary, that Mr. Hawley should come to Boston; for, if these things are to be done this year, we had need speedily to know the minds of the commissioners, and therefore that the case would not allow of waiting for, and depending on, uncertain accidental opportunities, of sending to them, and hearing from them. It is also proper, that the commissioners should have opportunity to agree with Mr. Hawley, concerning the reward of his services.

Mr. Brainerd told Mr. Hawley, that, if he removed with his Indians, he should choose to do it speedily; and that, the longer it was delayed, the more difficult it would be, by reason of his building, and the Indians increasing their buildings and improvements at Bethel. Probably, if the removal cannot be brought about the next year, it never will be. And if his Indians remove the next year, it will be necessary that they remove as early as the spring, in order to plant there that year. And if so much needs to be done this summer, it is as much as it will be possible to find time for.

Though we project the measures mentioned above, we are sensible they will be attended with much uncertainty. *Man's heart deviseth his way, but the Lord directeth his steps. Many are the desires of men's hearts, but the counsel of the Lord, that shall stand.* Unthought of difficulties may arise, to confound all our projects; as unforeseen difficulties have dashed all the pleasing hopes we entertained, and the fair prospects we had, concerning the affairs of the Mohawks at Stockbridge, the year before last. And I would humbly propose it for consideration, whether it will not be necessary, to leave these affairs, in some measure at discretion, to be determined as the complicated, uncertain, changing state of things shall require; to save the trouble and expense of frequently going or sending to Boston, for new instructions; and to prevent the disadvantages, under which our affairs may be laid, through the lengthy, uncertain way of sending for and receiving new orders, by occasional opportunities.

There will be a necessity of Mrs. Ashley's going as an interpreter, and of her husband going with her. He will be qualified to instruct the Indians in their husbandry; having been well instructed in it himself. I believe he will not be very difficult as to his wages, though probably he expects to know what they will be.

I have the honour to be,

Gentlemen,

Your obliged and obedient servant,

JONATHAN EDWARDS."

During the month of April, Mr. Hawley received a letter from the commissioners, directing him to go to Onohquauga, for the purpose of commencing a new mission at that place. He left Stockbridge May 22d, in company with Mr. Woodbridge, and Mr. and Mrs. Ashley, travelling through the wilderness, and on the 4th of June arrived at the place of their destination. The Indians received the intelligence of their proposed mission with strong expressions of satisfaction. Mr. Woodbridge returned soon after to Stockbridge. Mr. Hawley appears to have remained, with his interpreter; and his labours, as a missionary, were attended with considerable success.

In the course of the summer, not long after the return of the larger part of the Mohawks, from Stockbridge to their own country, a general council of the nation was held, at their principal settlement on the Mohawk; in which, after due examination of the facts, it was decided, That the rest of the Mohawks, at Stockbridge, should return early in the spring, as soon as the hunting season was over. Instructions, to this effect, were immediately transmitted, from the chief sachem of the tribe, to the residue of the little colony, and made known to the people of Stockbridge.

About this time, the agent of Mr. Hollis, discouraged, doubtless, by the state of things, as far as it was known, and probably auguring no very favourable result to himself, or his friends, from the application to Mr. Hollis, quitted Stockbridge, and went back to Newington; leaving the few boys, whom, by offering to board and clothe them gratuitously, he had persuaded to live with him, in the hands of the resident trustee.

This unhappy controversy, now drawing to its close, which, during its continuance, had threatened to subvert the whole Indian mission, and to destroy the prosperity of the village, and the temporal welfare of Mr. Edwards and his family, must have occupied so much of his attention, that when our readers remember, that he preached two discourses a week to the whites, as well as one, by an interpreter, to the *Housatonnucks*, and one to the *Mohawks;* and also catechised the children of the whites, the *Housatonnucks*, and the *Mohawks;* they will be ready to believe, that he found no time for any additional labours. And when they also recollect, that, on the 23d of November, 1752, he says, in his letter to Mr. Erskine,—"I began, the last August, to write a little on the Arminian controversy, but was soon broken off: and such have been my extraordinary avocations and hinderances, that I have not had time to set pen to paper, about this matter, since. But I hope God, in his providence, will favour me with opportunity to prosecute the design, and I desire your prayers, that God would assist me in it;"—and that this proposed work, on the Arminian controversy, was none other, than the TREATISE ON THE FREEDOM OF THE WILL; they will conclude, of course, that the execution of it must have been deferred to some happier period, when, amid the leisure and tranquillity of retirement, he could give his uninterrupted attention, and his individual strength, to its accomplishment. What then will be their surprise, when they find him opening his next letter to Mr. Erskine, under the date of April 14th, 1753, with the following annunciation.—"After many hinderances, delays, and interruptions, Divine Providence has so far favoured me, and smiled on my design of writing on the Arminian controversy, that I have almost finished the first draught of what I first intended; and am now sending the proposals for subscription, to Boston, to be printed." Let it be remembered, that the Essay on the Freedom of the Will, which, in the opinion of Dugald Stewart, raises its author to the same rank as a metaphysician with Locke and Leibnitz, was written within the space of four months and a half; and those, not months of leisure, but demanding the additional duties of a parish, and of two distinct Indian missions; and presenting, also, all the cares, perplexities, and embarrassments of a furious controversy, the design of which was to deprive the author, and his family, of their daily bread. So far as I am aware, no similar example, of power and rapidity united, is to be found on the annals of mental effort.*

"*Stockbridge, April* 14, 1753.

REV. AND DEAR SIR,

After many hinderances, delays, and interruptions, Divine Providence has so far favoured me, and smiled on my design of writing on the Arminian controversy, that I have almost finished the first draught of what I first intended; and am now sending the proposals for subscription to Boston to be printed; with a letter of Mr. Foxcroft, to send thirty of those proposals to Mr. M'Laurin, with a letter to him; in which I have desired him to deliver half of them to you, as you have manifested yourself ready to use endeavours to get subscriptions in Scotland. The printing will be delayed to wait for subscriptions from thence. I therefore request that you endeavour to promote and expedite the affair.

Stockbridge affairs, relating to the Indians, are, in many respects, under a very dark cloud. The affair of the Iroquois, or Six Nations, here is almost at an end, as I have given a more particular account to Mr. M'Laurin. The commissioners in Boston, I believe, are discouraged about it, and have thoughts of sending and settling a missionary in their own country. The correspondents of the Society in Scotland, have also determined to send a missionary there, and have chosen Mr. Gordon a tutor of the college at Newark, for that end. Mr. Gordon is expected here at the beginning of May, to live at my house with Mr. Hawley, in order to learn the Iroquois language with him. It is probable that he and Mr. Hawley will go up, and spend the summer, in the Iroquois country.

The correspondents have also a disposition, that Mr. Brainerd should remove, with the whole congregation of Indians, to settle somewhere in the country of the Six Nations; and he himself and his Indians, are ready for it. 'Tis probable that something will be done to prepare the way for it; and at least to see, whether the way can be prepared, or any door opened for it, this summer. Some of these Indians have a great desire, that the gospel should be introduced and settled in their country.

Some of the Stockbridge Indians have of late been under considerable awakenings,—two or three elderly men, that used to be vicious persons. My family is now in usual health. My daughter Burr, in New Jersey, has been very ill all the winter past. We last heard from her about five weeks ago; when it was hoped there was some amendment.

My wife joins with me, in respectful and affectionate salutations to you and Mrs. Erskine. Desiring a remembrance in your prayers,

I am, dear Sir,

Your affectionate brother,

and obliged friend and servant,

JONATHAN EDWARDS."

The representations of the nephew of the opponent of Mr. Woodbridge, and those of the commissioners of Boston, to the Society in London, the former hostile, and the latter friendly, to Mr. Edwards and his associates, were sent forward, and arrived at their place of destination, in due season. That gentleman had entertained an overweening estimate of his own influence with the board of directors of the Society in London. They gave full credit to the statements of their own commissioners, and sustained them in upholding their missionaries and instructers. Perceiving, however, that an unhappy controversy subsisted at Stockbridge, relative to the mission, and knowing that their commissioners at Boston were 150 miles distant; they endeavoured to devise a plan, by which the existing evils might be remedied. Mr. Edwards, in his letter to Mr. Mauduit, one of their number, had observed, "What renders it the more necessary, that things here should be under the immediate care of trustees on the spot, is, the misunderstanding and jealousy here subsisting, between some of the chief of the present English inhabitants of the town, which is one of our greatest calamities. Things, on this account, do much need careful inspection; and therefore, the gentlemen intrusted ought to be such, as are perfectly impartial, and no way interested in, or related to, these contending parties." The plan suggested by the directors was this, That eleven persons,—two in New York, two in Albany, one in Wethersfield, two in Hartford, one in Windsor, one in Suffield, one in Hadley, and one in Stockbridge,—should be a board of consultation, to advise their agents at Stockbridge, and to act, by correspondence, with the commissioners; and they counted upon the preceding extract, as what had confirmed them in the measure.† At the request of the Hon. Mr. Brom-

* Sir Henry Moncrieff Wellwood, who had the MS. Letters of Mr. Edwards to Dr. Erskine in his possession, while writing his Life of the latter, observes, "It was not, however, till the month of July, 1752, that he [Mr. Edwards] appears to have resumed his studies, on the subject of Free-will; for, on the 7th of that month, he writes Dr. Erskine, that *he hoped soon to be at leisure, to resume his design.*" He then adds, "Whatever opinion may be held, with regard to Mr. Edwards's argument, it must appear astonishing to those, who are capable of appreciating the difficulty of his subject, that, in *nine* months from the date of this letter, (on the 14th of April, 1753,) he could write Dr. Erskine, *that he had almost finished the first draught of what he originally intended.*" The passage, in Mr. Edwards's letter of Nov. 23, 1752, announcing, that he began to write in August, but was soon broke off; and had not, from that time, been able to put pen to paper, about the matter; and that he hoped, that God, in his providence, would favour him with an opportunity to prosecute the design; obviously escaped Sir Henry's notice. If he regarded it as astonishing, that Mr. Edwards should have been able to write the work in *nine* months; what would have been his views of the subject, if, after first reading the details of the Stockbridge controversy, he had then discovered, that it was written, not in *nine* months, but in *four and a half.*

† The directors, knowing the characters of the respective individuals residing in these places, whom they designated; and perceiving, from an inspection of the map, that Stockbridge was nearly central to most of the places mentioned; appear to have supposed, that they might all meet there, without inconvenience.

field, one of the commissioners, Mr. Edwards, in a letter, dated Oct. 19, 1753, expressed his own views of the plan, and pointed out its inconvenience, if not utter impracticability. The commissioners having expressed similar views to the directors; the plan was relinquished. This was the result of the application to the Society in London.*

The General Assembly of the church of Scotland, for the year 1753, having refused, by a very small majority, to restore Mr. Gillespie to the ministry in the kirk, and to his parish of Carnock;—an act of plain justice, which he would not ask them to render him;—Mr. Edwards addressed to him the following letter; a part of which must have been sweet and consoling to the feelings of suffering piety.

"*Stockbridge, October* 18, 1753.

Rev. and dear Sir,

The last November I wrote you a letter, and desired Mr. Foxcroft to put up with it, for you, one of my Answers to Mr. Williams. After that, in the latter part of the winter, I received a letter from you, dated June 15th, 1752, with Milton on Hirelings; and duplicates of a Letter from a Gentleman in Town, &c.; and Answers to the Reasons of Dissent, &c. I now return you my hearty thanks for these things. Since that, I have received letters from Mr. M'Laurin and Mr. Erskine, with various pamphlets and prints relative to your extraordinary affair. I think, dear Sir, although your sufferings are like to continue, the General Assembly having refused to restore you to your former station and employments in the church of Scotland; yet they are attended with many manifestations of the goodness, and fatherly kindness, and favour of the great Governor of the world, in the many alleviations and supporting circumstances of your persecutions; in that so many of God's ministers and people have appeared to be so much concerned for you; and have so zealously, and yet so properly, exerted themselves in your behalf; and have so many ways given their testimony to the goodness of the cause in which you suffer, and the unrighteousness of the hardships which you have been subjected to; and that even so great a part of the General Assembly, themselves, have, in effect, given this testimony for you, there being but a very small majority, but what openly appeared for the taking off of the censure of the former Assembly, without any recantation on your part, or so much as an application from you, desiring them so to do. You have some peculiar reasons to rejoice in your sufferings, and to glorify God on account of them. They having been so greatly taken notice of by so many of the people of God, and there being so much written concerning them, tends to render them, with their circumstances, and particularly the patience and meekness with which you have suffered, so much the more extensively and durably to the glory of the name of your blessed Lord, for whom you suffer. God is rewarding you for laying a foundation, in what has been said and done and written concerning your sufferings, for glory to his own name, and honour to you, in his church, in future generations. Your name will doubtless be mentioned hereafter with peculiar respect, on the account of these sufferings, in ecclesiastical history; as they are now the occasion of a peculiar notice, which saints and angels in heaven take of you, and of their praises to God on your account; and will be the occasion of a peculiar reward, which God will bestow upon you, when you shall be united to their assembly.

As to my own circumstances, I still meet with trouble, and expect no other, as long as I live in this world. Some men of influence have much opposed my continuing a missionary at Stockbridge, and have taken occasion abundantly to reproach me, and endeavour my removal. But I desire to bless God, he seems in some respects to set me out of their reach. He raises me up friends, who are exerting themselves to counteract the designs of my opposers; particularly the commissioners for Indian affairs in Boston; with whom innumerable artifices have been used, to disaffect them towards me; but altogether in vain. Governor Belcher, also, has seen cause much to exert himself, in my behalf, on occasion of the opposition made to me. My people, both English and Indians, stedfastly adhere to me; excepting the family with whom the opposition began, and those related to them; which family greatly opposed me while at Northampton. Most numerous, continued, and indefatigable endeavours have been used, to undermine me, by attempting to alienate my people from me; innumerable mean artifices have been used with one another, with young and old, men and women, Indians and English: but hitherto they have been greatly disappointed. But yet they are not weary.

As we, dear Sir, have great reason to sympathize, one with another, with peculiar tenderness; our circumstances being in many respects similar; so I hope I shall partake of the benefit of your fervent prayers for me. Let us then endeavour to help one another, though at a great distance, in travelling through this wide wilderness; that we may have the more joyful meeting in the land of rest, when we have finished our weary pilgrimage.

I am, dear Sir,
Your most affectionate brother,
and fellow-servant,
JONATHAN EDWARDS."

"P. S. My wife joins in most affectionate regards to you and yours."

The proposals for publishing the Essay on the Freedom of the Will, were issued in Massachusetts, in 1753; but in consequence of the kind offer of Mr. Erskine and Mr. M'Laurin, to circulate the papers, and procure subscribers for it in Scotland, the printing was postponed until the success of their efforts was known. What that success was, probably cannot now be ascertained. The work was published early in the year 1754, under the title of "A careful and strict Inquiry into the modern prevailing Notions of that Freedom of the Will, which is supposed to be essential to Moral Agency, Virtue and Vice, Reward and Punishment, Praise and Blame." This work is justly considered as the most laboured and important of the metaphysical investigations undertaken by the author. The subject, as will be obvious from the preceding title, lies at the very foundation of all religion and of all morality. That it was also a subject of no ordinary difficulty, appears generally to have been felt, and in effect acknowledged; for until the time of Mr. Edwards, it had never been thoroughly investigated either by philosophers or theologians, though it was constantly recurring in their reasonings on the great principles connected with the

* On this account only, is the plan worthy of being mentioned here.

moral government of God, and the character of man. Calvin, in his chapter on the Slavery of the Will, may be taken as an example of the most that had been done to settle the opinions of the orthodox, and refute their opposers on this subject before this period. His defect, and that of his followers, until the time of Mr. Edwards, is seen in this one thing; that they insisted on the great fact, merely that the will of man was not in a state of indifference, but so strongly fixed in its choice as to require supernatural grace for conversion; overlooking in a great measure the nature of moral agency, and what is essential to its nature. Their opposers, on the contrary, were constantly affirming, that freedom of will was necessary to moral agency, and carried their views to the extent that the will *determined itself*, and could not be enslaved. In this state of ethical and theological science, Mr. Edwards set himself to the task of examining the great subject of moral agency, as connected with the human will; and by the precision of his definitions and statements, the cogency of his reasonings, the fulness of his illustrations, the thorough handling of all objections, and the application of his views to many scriptural truths, he placed the grand points of his subject in a light so overwhelmingly convincing, as to leave little room for any doubt or dispute afterwards.

In this treatise it is contended, that *the power of choosing*, or *willing*, does itself constitute freedom of agency; and that particular acts of will are determined, *i. e.* are rendered certain, or become such as they are, rather than otherwise, by some sufficient cause or reason, in perfect consistency with their being acts of will, or in perfect consistency with that power of willing which constitutes freedom of agency. On the ground that the power of willing pertains to man, the author asserts a *natural ability*, which is the just occasion of precept, invitation, &c. or of the will of God being addressed to him; and on the ground that his acts of will are rendered certain, by a sufficient cause, the author asserts a *moral inability*. The principal point contended for, and which is most essential to the defence of the Calvinistic scheme of faith, in distinction from the Arminian, is the latter one, *that the acts of the will are rendered certain by some other cause than the mere power of willing*. What the particular cause or causes may be, is not particularly considered; but this question is dismissed with a few brief remarks. The fact, that there is and must be, some such cause, is the great subject argued, and most powerfully demonstrated. This cause he asserts is the foundation of *necessity*, in the sense merely of *certainty* of action, and does not therefore destroy natural ability or the power of choice, nor imply that man acts otherwise than electively, or by choice; so that it is a necessity consistent with accountability, demerit, or the contrary and so with rewards and punishments. He asserts that all such terms as *must*, *cannot*, *impossible*, *unable*, *irresistible*, *unavoidable*, *invincible*, *&c.* when applied here, are not applied in their proper signification, and are either used nonsensically, and with perfect insignificance, or in a sense quite diverse from their proper and original meaning, and their use in common speech; and that such a necessity as attends the acts of men's wills, is more properly called *certainty* than *necessity*.

Rightly to understand this controversy, it must be observed, that he and his opponents, alike, considered sin to consist in acts of will. Had this not been the case, it would have been idle for Mr. Edwards to have confined himself, in his whole treatise, to acts of choice, and the manner in which they are determined, *i. e.* rendered certain. He must, in that case, have agitated the previous question, respecting acts of choice themselves; and have asserted and maintained, that something else of specifically a different nature, enters into moral character, and forms the ground of praise and blame, or retribution. But the question which he considered to be at issue, is this: *Does the mind will, in any given manner, without a motive, cause or ground, which renders the given choice, rather than a different choice, certain.* Whitby, the writer whom he especially has in view, in his remarks on the freedom of man, asserts, that man, by his own activity alone, decides the choice. Mr. Edwards acknowledges that man chooses; but asserts, in opposition to the opinion of Whitby, and those who side with him, that there must be some other ground or cause, beside the mere activity of man, or his power of choosing, which occasions his choosing in one manner, rather than another. He asserts, that "doubtless common sense requires men's being the authors of their own acts of will, in order to their being esteemed worthy of praise or dispraise, on account of them." The very act of volition itself, is, doubtless, a determination; *i. e.* it is the mind's drawing up a conclusion, or coming to a choice, between two things or more, proposed to it. But determining among external objects of choice, is not the same as determining the act of choice itself, among various possible acts of choice. The question is, What influences, directs, or determines, the mind or will, to such a conclusion or choice as it does form? Or what is the cause, ground, or reason, why it concludes thus, and not otherwise? This is the question, on his own statement.

In the latter part of February, 1754, a letter was received from Mr. Hollis, by Mr. Edwards, containing his explicit directions as to the school, for which he had expended so much money, to so little purpose. By this letter, Mr. Hollis withdrew the care of the school, and the expenditure of his benefactions, from the hands of those who had had the charge of them, and placed them in the hands of Mr. Edwards.* On the 25th, Mr. Edwards enclosed a copy of this letter, in a note to the provincial agent, requesting, from him, an account of the existing state of the school, and of the furniture and books belonging to it. On the 27th, he went to the school, to examine into its actual condition, and found in it *six* Indian boys. The following day, he mentioned this fact, in a second note to the agent, and informed him, that, as the Mohawks had long had the resolution to leave Stockbridge, early in the spring, he had appointed a conference with them, on the 1st of March, to learn whether they still persisted in that resolution; to the end, that, if they did so, he might suspend any further expense upon them, on Mr. Hollis's account. At this conference, which was held with all the Mohawks, men, women, and children, in the presence of many of the people of the town, they informed him, that they had all agreed in the autumn, that they would return, in the spring, to their own country; and that this agreement was owing to the determination of the council of their nation, the sachems of the *Connenchees*, and could not be altered, unless by a new determination of their sa-

* Many benevolent men, on being apprized of such a wanton and shameful perversion of the funds, appropriated by themselves to a given charity, would, at once, have wholly discontinued their benefactions; but the benevolence of Mr. Hollis, like a living and copious fountain, could neither be dried up, nor obstructed.

chems. Of this he gave the agent due notice the day following, as well as of his purpose to expend none of Mr. Hollis's money upon them, so long as they persisted in that resolution.

As the general court had interested themselves in the affairs of Mr. Hollis, and had waited to know his mind concerning them, that they might order their own measures accordingly; Mr. Edwards, in a letter to the secretary of the province, dated March 8th, enclosed an extract from the letter of Mr. Hollis, and informed him of the actual state of the school, of the determination of the council of the Mohawks, and the consequent resolution of the little colony to return to their own country, and of the notice he had given the agent, that he should withhold any subsequent expense of Mr. Hollis's money upon them. He likewise informed him, that some of the Mohawks had, since the conference, brought their children to him, and earnestly requested that they might be instructed; offering to take the charge of their maintenance themselves; and that he had consented to receive them.* He also asks the advice of the secretary, whether he might still occupy the school-house, which had been built on the lands of the Indians, at the expense of the province, for the benefit of Mr. Hollis's school.

The individuals opposed to Mr. Edwards and Mr. Woodbridge, thus found every plan, which they had formed of connecting themselves with the Stockbridge mission, defeated, and their last hope extinguished. In 1750, the prospects of the mission, in consequence of the arrival of the two detachments of the Mohawks and Onohquaugas, which seemed to be mere harbingers of still larger colonies of their countrymen, were uncommonly bright and promising. And could the benevolent intentions of Mr. Hollis, of the Society in London, and of the provincial legislature, in behalf of the Iroquois, have been carried forward to their full completion, with no obstructions thrown in their way, by greedy avarice or unhallowed ambition; it is difficult to conceive of the amount of good which might have been accomplished. A large and flourishing colony of the Iroquois would soon have been established at Stockbridge, drawn thither for the education of their children, and brought directly within the reach of the means of salvation. What would have been the ultimate effect of such a colony on their countrymen at home, and on the more remote Indian tribes, can only be conjectured. By the stedfast resolution of those persons to oppose these plans of benevolence, unless the management of the funds by which they were to be accomplished could be placed in their own hands, this whole system of beneficence towards the Iroquois, which would only have enlarged with the opportunity of exerting it, was frustrated finally and for ever. We will not cherish the belief, that the disappointed individuals found any thing in this melancholy result, to console them under the shame and mortification of their own defeat; although they thus effectually prevented the benevolent efforts of their opponents, by driving the intended objects of them beyond their reach. A short time after the letter of Mr. Hollis was received, the individual, in whose hands the Mohawk school had been left by the former teacher, removed with his family to his former place of residence; leaving behind him only one of his associates at Stockbridge.

CHAPTER XXIII.

SICKNESS OF MR. EDWARDS—"GOD'S LAST END IN CREATION"—"NATURE OF VIRTUE"—MR. EDWARDS'S SECOND SON RESIDES AT ONOHQUAUGA—DANGERS OF THE WAR—LETTER TO MR. ERSKINE—LETTER TO COL. WILLIAMS—LORD KAIMES—LETTER TO MR. ERSKINE—LETTER TO MR. M'CULLOCH—LETTER OF DR. BELLAMY—"TREATISE ON ORIGINAL SIN"—LETTER TO HIS FATHER—LETTER TO MR. ERSKINE.

In July, 1754, Mr. Edwards had a most severe attack of the ague and fever, which lasted until January. It wholly disqualified him from writing even to his correspondents, and greatly enfeebled his constitution. In the course of the spring following, he began the preparation of two other treatises, which were entitled, "A Dissertation concerning the End for which God created the World;" and "A Dissertation concerning the Nature of True Virtue." These two subjects are fundamental in a system of theology. On the first, many writers had hazarded occasional remarks; yet it has rarely occupied the space even of a chapter or a section in theological systems; and I know not whether any writer before Mr. Edwards had made it the subject of a formal and separate treatise. From the purest principles of reason, as well as from the fountain of revealed truth, he demonstrates that the *chief* and *ultimate* end of the Supreme Being, in the works of creation and providence, was the manifestation of his own glory, in the highest happiness of his creatures. The treatise was left by the author, as at first written, without being prepared for the press; yet it exhibits the subject in a manner so clear and convincing, that it has been the manual of theologians from the time of its publication to the present.

The nature of virtue has been a frequent subject of discussion among ethical writers of almost every class,—heathen, infidel, and christian. Aristotle, and other ancient moralists, supposed virtue to consist in avoiding *extremes*, and in following *the mean* in every thing. Others of the ancients defined virtue to be *living according to nature*. Balguy and Doddridge represent it as consisting in *acting agreeably to the moral fitness of things*. Wollaston places it in *regard to truth*. Hutcheson defines it to be "*a quality apprehended in some actions which produces approbation and love towards the actor, from those who receive no benefit from the action.*" Many writers,

* These children of the Mohawks, and the children of the Onohquaugas, constituted, from this time, the male Iroquois boarding-school at Stockbridge. How long it was continued I have not been able to ascertain; but suppose it was removed to Onohquauga, soon after the establishment of the mission of Mr. Hawley at that place.

ancient and modern, have placed virtue in *imitation of God;* and many others in *obedience to the will of God.* Waterland, Rutherforth, and (John) Brown, have placed it in *a wise regard to our own interest.* Bishop Butler says, that "a due concern about our own interest or happiness, and a reasonable endeavour to promote it, is virtue;" and that "benevolence, singly considered, is in no sort the whole of virtue." Hume, who appears to have read several of the works of Edwards, and to have made use of them in accommodation to his own views, includes in his description of virtue, *whatever is agreeable and useful to ourselves and others.* Adam Smith refers it to *the principle of sympathy.* Paley, who read Edwards with care, defines virtue to be "*The doing good to mankind in obedience to the will of God, and for the sake of everlasting happiness.*" Cumberland, in his *Laws of Nature,* justly regards it as consisting in *the love of God, and of our fellow-creatures;* and explains himself thus; "The foundation of all natural law is *the greatest benevolence of every rational agent towards all.*

Mr. Edwards represents virtue as founded in HAPPINESS; and as being *love to the greatest happiness,* or *love to the happiness of universal being.* He describes it, as leading its possessor to desire, and to promote, as far as in him lies, the happiness of all beings, and a greater degree of happiness in preference to a less. His account of the subject is in exact accordance with the decision of reason. Happiness is the *end,* for which intelligent beings were made, the perfection of their existence; and therefore virtue, or moral excellence, must be love to that happiness. It is also in exact accordance with the Scriptures. The sum of our duty is unquestionably virtue. But Moses sums up our duty in two commands, "*Thou shalt love the Lord thy God with all thy heart,*" and "*Thou shalt love thy neighbour as thyself:*" in other words, *Thou shalt love the happiness of universal being.*

When the Scriptures had so plainly pointed out the nature of virtue, as consisting in love; and its foundation, as being happiness; it is not a little remarkable, that so many acute writers, with the Scriptures in their hands, should have formed views either so obscure, or so erroneous, of these subjects; and, perhaps not less remarkable, that Mr. Edwards should have been able to discover its true nature, and its real foundation, at a very early age, as clearly as he did in after-life. That this was the case, no one will want evidence, who reads the various articles under the head of Excellency, particularly the last, in the Notes on the Mind.*

These two treatises were first published together in a pamphlet, in Boston, in 1788, without alteration from the rough draught of the author. He designed them both for publication, but never prepared either of them for the press. Though conceived and expressed with great perspicuity, they treat of subjects, which demand close thought in the reader, as well as the writer; and, on this account, have often been imperfectly comprehended, even by divines. But wherever they have been read and understood, they have to such a degree formed and regulated the views of theologians, with regard to the subjects of which they treat, that other treatises are consulted, rather as objects of curiosity, or history, than as guides of opinions and principles.†

In February, or early in March, this year, Mr. Edwards sent his second son, Jonathan,‡ then a lad of nine years of age, to Onohquauga, to reside with Mr. Hawley, that he might learn more perfectly the language of the Iroquois. He continued there about a twelvemonth; when, in consequence of the war with France, the danger of attack from the Indians became so imminent, that Mr. Hawley returned with him to his father's house.

The war of 1754 was most disastrous to the colonies; and the frontier settlements of New England, of which Stockbridge was one, were exposed to unceasing anxiety and alarm, from their constant liability to attack from the French savages. In the autumn, several of the inhabitants of Stockbridge were killed by these marauders; in consequence of which it became a garrisoned town; and every family had quartered upon it its own quota of the soldiers, necessary for the defence of the place. The state of things, in this respect, may be learned from the following letter of Mr. Edwards, to the officer who had the command of the troops in that part of the county.

"*Stockbridge, Feb.* 26, 1755.

SIR,

We have not lodgings and provisions, so as to board and lodge more than four soldiers; and being in a low state as to my health, and not able to go much abroad, and upon that and other accounts, under much greater disadvantages than others to get provisions, it is for this reason, and not because I have a disposition to make difficulty, that I told the soldiers of this province, who had hitherto been provided for here, that we could not board them any longer. I have often been told that you had intimated, that you have other business for them in a short time. Capt. Hosmer has sent three of his men to lodge at my house, whom I am willing to entertain, as I choose to board such as are likely to be continued for our defence in times of danger. Stebbins has manifested to us a desire to continue here. Him, therefore, I am willing to entertain, with your consent. Requesting your candid construction of that, which is not intended in any inconsistence with my having all proper honour and respect, I am

Your humble servant,

JONATHAN EDWARDS."

The subsequent letter to Mr. Erskine will show, still more fully, the state of alarm and terror then existing at Stockbridge.

"*Stockbridge, April* 15, 1755.

REV. AND DEAR SIR,

The last year, in the spring, I received, without a letter, a packet containing the following books: Casaubon on Enthusiasm; Warburton's Principles of Natural and Revealed Religion; Merrick on Christ the True Vine; Campbell's Apostles no Enthusiasts; Discourse on the Prevailing Evils of the Present Time; Remarks on Apostles no Enthusiasts; Moncrieff's Review and Examination of some Principles in Campbell's Apostles no

* See Appendix IV. In several of the articles under the head of Excellency, the reader will find, if I mistake not, as striking specimens of powerful metaphysical reasoning, as any to be found in the Essay on the Freedom of the Will.

† Bishop Butler has left a "Dissertation on the Nature of Virtue," which the curious reader will do well to examine in connexion with Mr. Edwards's "Dissertation on the Nature of True Virtue;" if he wishes to compare the powers of these two distinguished men, when endeavouring to grasp the same subject.

‡ Afterwards the Rev. Jonathan Edwards, D. D. President of Union College, Schenectady. He was familiarly acquainted with the Housatonnuck and the Iroquois; in early life, more so than with the English

Enthusiasts; Gilbert on the Guilt and Pardon of Sin; Hervey on the Cross of Christ; An Account of the Orphan School, &c. at Edinburgh; Memorial Concerning the Surgeon's Hospital; Gairdner's Account of the Old People's Hospital; State of the Society in Scotland for Propagating Christian Knowledge; Abridgment of the Rules of said Society; Regulations of the Town's Hospital at Glasgow; and Annals of the Persecution of the Protestants in France.

In the beginning of last December, I received another packet without a letter; the wrapper superscribed with your hand. In this were the following pamphlets: A Sermon by a Lay Elder, before the Commission; A Letter to a Gentleman at Edinburgh; Resolutions of the General Assembly, of May 22d, 1736; Rutherford's Power of Faith and Prayer; Inquiry into the Method of Settling Parishes; The Nature of the Covenant and Constitution of the Church of Scotland; Essay on Gospel and Legal Preaching; Necessity of Zeal for the Truth; A Vindication of the Protestant Doctrine of Justification, against the Charge of Antinomianism. The last week I received a letter from you, dated 11th July, 1754; which was found at Mr. Prince's by one that went to Boston from hence, and had lain there Mr. Prince could not tell how long. In this letter you make mention of these last-mentioned pamphlets, received last December. I now return you my hearty thanks for this letter, and these generous presents. I should have written to you long ago, had I not been prevented by the longest and most tedious sickness that ever I had in my life: It being followed with fits of ague which came upon me about the middle of last July, and were for a long time very severe, and exceedingly wasted my flesh and strength, so that I became like a skeleton. I had several intermissions of the fits by the use of the Peruvian bark; but they never wholly left me till the middle of last January. In the mean time, I several times attempted to write letters to some of my friends about affairs of importance, but found that I could bear but little of such writing. Once, in attempting to write a letter to Mr. Burr, a fit of the ague came upon me while I was writing, so that I was obliged to lay by my pen. When my fits left me they left me in a poor weak state, so that I feared whether I was not going into a dropsy. Nevertheless, I have of late gradually gained strength.

I lately received a letter from Mr. M'Laurin, dated Aug. 13, 1754; which Mr. Prince sent me, with a letter from himself, wherein he informed me that a captain of a ship from Glasgow, then lately arrived, brought an account of Mr. M'Laurin's death; that he died very suddenly, with an apoplexy, a little before he left Glasgow. Since I received that letter, I sent to Mr. Prince, desiring to know more of the certainty of the account. This is an affecting piece of news. It is an instance of death which I have much cause to lament. He has long shown himself to be a very worthy, kind, and obliging friend and correspondent of mine. And doubtless, the church of Scotland has much cause to lament his death. There is reason to think that he was one of them that stood in the gap to make up the hedge in these evil times. He was a wise, steady, and most faithful friend of gospel truth and vital piety, in these days of great corruption. I wish that I may take warning by it, as well as by my own late sickness, to prepare for my own departure hence.

I have nothing very comfortable to write respecting my own success in this place. The business of the Indian mission, since I have been here, has been attended with strange embarrassments, such as I never could have expected, or so much as once dreamed of; of such a nature, and coming from such a quarter, that I take no delight in being very particular and explicit upon it. But, beside what I especially refer to, some things have lately happened that have occasioned great disturbance among the Indians, and have tended to alienate them from the English. As particularly, the killing of one of them in the woods, by a couple of travellers, white men, who met him, and contended with him. And though the men were apprehended and imprisoned; yet on their trial they escaped the sentence of death: one of them only receiving a lighter punishment, as guilty of manslaughter: by which these Indians, and also the Indians of some other tribes, were greatly displeased, and disaffected towards the English. Since the last fall, some Indians from Canada, doubtless instigated by the French, broke in upon us, on the sabbath, between meetings, and fell upon an English family, and killed three of them; and about an hour after killed another man, coming into the town from some distant houses; which occasioned a great alarm in the town, and in the country. Multitudes came from various parts, for our defence, that night, and the next day; and many of these conducted very foolishly towards our Indians on this occasion, suspecting them to be guilty of doing the mischief, charging them with it, and threatening to kill them, and the like. After this, a reward being offered by some private gentlemen, to some that came this way as soldiers, if they would bring them the scalp of a Canada Indian; two men were so extremely foolish and wicked, that they, in the night, dug up one of our Indians, that had then lately died, out of his grave, to take off his scalp; that, by pretending that to be a scalp of a Canada Indian, whom they had met and killed in the woods, they might get the promised reward. When this was discovered, the men were punished. But this did not hinder, but that such an act greatly increased the jealousy and disaffection of the Indians, towards the English. Added to these things, we have many white people, that will, at all times, without any restraint, give them ardent spirits, which is a constant temptation to their most predominant lust.

Though I have but little success, and many discouragements, here at Stockbridge, yet Mr. Hawley, now a missionary among the Six Nations, who went from New-England to Onohquauga, a place more than 200 miles distant from hence, has, of late, had much encouragement. Religion seems to be a growing, spreading thing, among the savages in that part of America, by his means. And there is a hopeful prospect, of way being made for another missionary in those parts, which may have happy consequences, unless the Six Nations should go over to the French; which there is the greatest reason to expect, unless the English should exert themselves, vigorously and successfully, against the French, in America, this year. They seem to be waiting to see whether this will be so or no, in order to determine, whether they will entirely desert the English, and cleave to the French. And if the Six Nations should forsake the English, it may be expected, that the Stockbridge Indians, and almost all the nations of Indians in North America, will follow them. It seems to be the most critical season, with the British dominions in America, that ever was seen, since the first settlement of these colonies; and all, probably, will depend on the warlike transactions of the present year. What will be done I cannot tell. We are all in commotion, from one end of British America to the other; and various expeditions are projected, and preparing for; one to Ohio, another to the French Forts in Nova Scotia, another to Crown Point. But these affairs are not free from embarrassments: great difficulties arise, in our present most important affairs, through the dispirited state of the several governments. It is hard for them to agree upon means and measures. And we have no reason to think that the French are behind us in their activity and preparations. A dark cloud seems to hang over us: we need the prayers of all our friends, and all friends to the protestant interest. Stockbridge is a place much exposed; and what will become of us, in the struggles that are coming on, God only knows. I have heard that Messrs. Tennent and Davies are arrived in America, having had good success in the errand they went upon. Mr. Bellamy is not likely to go to New York, principally by reason of the opposition of some of the congregation, and also of some of the neighbouring ministers. I have heard, they have lately unanimously agreed to apply themselves to Mr. M'Gregor, of New Londonderry, alias Nutfield, in New England, to be their minister; who is a gentleman that, I think, if they can obtain him, will be likely to suit them, and competent to fill the place. And I have heard, that there has been some difference in his own congregation, that has lately made his situation there uneasy. If so, he will be more likely to consent to the motion from New York.

My wife joins with me in respectful and affectionate salutations to you and Mrs. Erskine.

I am, dear Sir, your affectionate and obliged brother,

JONATHAN EDWARDS."

"P. S. In a journey I went to Northampton, the last April, I carried the foregoing letter, with others for Scotland, so far, seeking an opportunity to send them from thence to Boston; and there I met another letter from Mr. Prince, with a joyful contradiction of his former account of Mr. M'Laurin's death; which occasioned my bringing my packet home again. Nevertheless, after I had broken open and perused this letter, I thought best to send it along, enclosed in a wrapper to Mr. M'Laurin; who, I hope, is yet living, and will convey it to you.

J. E.

Stockbridge, June 2, 1755."

In the beginning of September, the danger became so imminent, that Mr. Edwards, at the request of the people of the town, addressed the following urgent letter to the colonel of the county.

"To Col. Israel Williams.

Stockbridge, Sept. 5, 1755.

Sir,

Yesterday the English inhabitants of the town sent away a letter, directed to you, to be conveyed to Hatfield, respecting the state of the town, stating that it was left very greatly exposed, by the drawing off of all the Connecticut soldiers; that Governor Shirley, by his urgency, had persuaded away almost all the Indian inhabitants fit for war, who objected much against going, on that account, that the departure of so many would leave the town, and their wives and children too, defenceless; that the governor removed their objection, by promising that a sufficient number of English soldiers should be maintained here, during their absence, for the defence of the town; and also, that we had just now information sent in writing, from Mr. Vanschaak, that two large parties of Indians are lately gone out of Crown Point, against our frontiers; and so entreating that soldiers may be speedily sent. But being informed to-day, that you are gone from Hatfield, and not knowing whether you will seasonably receive the aforementioned letter, I now, at the desire of the people, give you this brief information of what was therein written; earnestly desiring, that we may not be left so easy and open a prey to our enemies, who, we have reason to think, have the means of learning our situation, and are certainly preparing to attack some of the most defenceless of the frontier villages. We hope that the troops may be forwarded immediately; for, having no adequate means of repelling an attack, we have no security for a single day.

I am respectfully,

Your obedient servant,

JONATHAN EDWARDS."

In 1751, an anonymous work was published in Edinburgh, entitled "Essays on the Principles of Morality and Natural Religion,"* of which Henry Home,† Esq. soon avowed himself the author. These essays, though written by a member of the church of Scotland, were regarded as decidedly sceptical in their tendency, and brought the author into some difficulties with the particular church with which he was connected. This led to a public discussion of the character of the work at large—particularly of the Essay on Liberty and Necessity. When this discussion was commencing, the Essay on the Freedom of the Will arrived in Scotland. It was extensively read by men of speculative minds; and, though presenting a view of the subject wholly new, gave great satisfaction to men of all classes. Lord Kaimes and his friends, having read the work of Mr. Edwards, endeavoured to show that the view of liberty and necessity, in the Freedom of the Will, was substantially the same with that given by his lordship. Mr. Erskine apprized Mr. Edwards of this fact. In the following letter, the latter barely alludes to the work of Lord Kaimes, as a work of corrupt tendency. In a subsequent letter to his friends, written in the summer of the following year, and now appended to the Treatise on the Freedom of the Will,‡ he examines the views of liberty and necessity by his lordship, shows their entire discordance with his own views, as exhibited in the Freedom of the Will, and exposes their inconsistency, not only with reason but with each other. This letter, from a sense of justice to its author, was immediately published, in the form of a pamphlet, by Mr. Erskine, and produced a universal conviction, that Lord Kaimes had wholly misunderstood the view taken of liberty and necessity by Mr. Edwards; and that his own views of it were at war, alike with reason and revela-

* The subjects treated of in this volume were, Attachment to objects of Distress. Law of Nature. Law of Necessity. Belief. Personal Identity. Authority of our Senses. Idea of Power. Knowledge of Future Events. Dread of Supernatural Powers in the Dark. Our Knowledge of the Deity.

† Soon after created a lord of session, with the title of Lord Kaimes.

‡ See vol. i. pp. 89—93. Lord Kaimes had a much higher reputation, as a writer, fifty years ago than at present. The perusal of his Essay on Liberty and Necessity, and of the remarks upon it, in the letter of Mr. Edwards, here referred to, will inevitably lead to the conviction, that, as a metaphysician, he was neither accurate nor profound.

tion. Indeed, his lordship himself appears to have been of the same opinion; for, in a subsequent edition, the Essay on Liberty and Necessity is said to have been much changed, as to present essentially different views of those important subjects.

"To the Rev. John Erskine, Minister of the Gospel, at Culross, Scotland.

Stockbridge, Dec. 11, 1755.

REV. AND DEAR SIR,

I last wrote to you July 24th, 1755. Since that I received a letter from you, dated June 23, 1755, together with the *Essays on the Principles of Morality and Natural Religion*,* from Mr. Hogg, and the Analysis of the Moral and Religious Sentiments of Sopho, from yourself. I thank you for your letter and present, and shall write a letter of thanks to Mr. Hogg, for his present by your hand, added to former instances of his generosity. I had before read that book of Essays, having borrowed Mr. Bellamy's, and also that book of Mr. David Hume's, which you speak of. I am glad of an opportunity to read such corrupt books, especially when written by men of considerable genius; that I may have an idea of the notions that prevail in our nation. You say that some people say, that Lord Kaimes's being made a Lord of Session would have been prevented, if Chancellor Hardwick and Archbishop Herring had seasonably seen his book. I should be glad to know who this Chancellor Hardwick is, and what is his character. By your mentioning him in such a manner, I am ready to suppose he may be, in some respects, of good character; and it is a matter of thankfulness, if a man of good character, and a friend to religion, be Lord Chancellor.

As to our warlike concerns, I have not heretofore been very particular in writing about them, in my letters to Scotland, supposing it highly probable that you would have earlier accounts from Boston, New York, and Philadelphia, than any I can send you, living at so great a distance from any of the sea-ports. Nevertheless, seeing you propose my sending you some account of the present posture of affairs, I would say, that it appears to me that notwithstanding some remarkable favours of Heaven, of which we are very unworthy, it has in the general been a year of great frowns of Providence on British America. Notwithstanding our success at Nova Scotia, and in having the better in the battle near Lake George, and taking the French general prisoner; yet, considering the advantages the enemy hath obtained against us, by General Braddock's defeat, especially in gaining over and confirming the Indians on their side, and disheartening and weakening our friends, and what we have suffered from our enemies, and how greatly we are weakened and almost sunk with our vast expenses, especially in New England, and the blood as well as money we have expended; I say, considering these things, and how little we have gained by our loss and trouble, our case is no better, but far worse than it was in the beginning of the year. At least, I think it certain, that we have attained no advantage, in any wise, to balance our trouble and expense of blood and treasure. The expedition to the eastward has been remarkably successful; but the other three expeditions, that against the French forts on the Ohio, that against Niagara, and that against Crown Point, have all been unsuccessful, as to their main designs. And though the army under General Johnson had a kind of victory over the French, and took the Baron Dieskau, their general, prisoner; yet we suffered very greatly in the battle, and the taking of the French general probably was the saving of his army. For, by telling a lie to our army, *viz.* that the French were in constant expectation of being greatly enforced by a large body, that marched another way, and had appointed to meet them near that place, our army was prevented from pursuing the enemy, after they had repelled them; which, if they had done, the French might have been under great advantages to have cut them off, and prevented the return of almost all of them to Crown Point, which could be no otherwise than through the water in their batteaux. Our army never proceeded any farther than the place of their engagement; but, having built a fort there, near Lake George, *alias* Lake St. Sacrament, after they had built another near Hudson's river, about fourteen miles on this side, and left garrisons, has lately returned. As also has the army under General Shirley, (who went with designs against Niagara,) after having built some vessels of force in the lake Ontario, and strengthened the fortifications at Oswego, and sent for the remains of General Braddock's army to Albany, there to go into winter quarters. The governors of the several provinces, in the latter part of the last month, had a meeting to confer together, concerning our warlike affairs, and to agree on a plan of operations to be recommended to the government at home for the next year. But I have heard nothing of their determinations. The Indians have not done much mischief on the frontiers of New England, since our army have been about us; but have been dreadful in their ravages, on the back settlements of Virginia and Pennsylvania.

It is apparent that the ministry at home miss it very much, in sending over British forces to fight with Indians in America, and in sending over British officers, to have the command of our American forces. Let them send us arms, ammunition, money, and shipping; and let New England men manage the business in their own way, who alone understand it. To appoint British officers over them, is nothing but a hinderance and discouragement to them. Let them be well supplied, and supported, and defended by sea, and then let them go forth under their own officers and manage in their own way, as they did in the expedition against Cape Breton. All the provinces in America seem to be fully sensible, that New England men are the only men to be employed against Canada; as I had opportunity abundantly to observe, in my late journey to New York, New Jersey, and Philadelphia. However, we ought to remember that neither New England men, nor any other, are any thing unless God be with us; and when we have done all, at finding fault with men and instruments employed, we cannot expect prosperity, unless the accursed thing be removed from our camp.

God has lately frowned on my family, in taking away a faithful servant, who was a great help to us; and one of my children has been under threatening infirmities, but is somewhat better. I desire your prayers for us all.

My wife joins with me in affectionate and respectful salutations to you and Mrs. Erskine.

I am, Rev. and dear Sir,
Your obliged brother,
and affectionate friend,
JONATHAN EDWARDS."

* By Lord Kaime

The effect of the war on the Indian mission will be seen from the following letter to Mr. M'Culloch.

"*Stockbridge, April* 10, 1756.

Rev. and dear Sir,

I thank you for your favour of August, 1755, with Mr. Imries's letter, which came to hand in the latter part of the last month. It recommends a man, especially a minister of the gospel, to me, to see in him evidences of a disposition to be searching into the prophecies of Scripture, relating to the future advancement of Christ's kingdom on earth. It looks as though he was a man, who felt concern for Christ's kingdom and interests in the world; as though he were one of those, who took pleasure in the stones, and favoured the dust of Zion. But it has proved by events, that many divines, who have been of this character, have been over-forward to fix the times and the seasons, which the Father hath put in his own power. However, I will not positively charge Mr. Imries with this, before I see what he has to offer, in proof of those things which he has advanced. I think that neither I nor any other person, that knows no more than what is contained in his letter, of the reasons that he builds his opinions upon, have any opportunity to judge of those opinions. And therefore I should think it a pity that his private letter to Mr. Hogg was published to the world, before his reasons were prepared for the press. This letter has been reprinted in Boston; but coming abroad, with so little mention of the grounds of his opinion, it gives occasion to the profane to reproach and ridicule it, and its author.

With respect to Mr. Hawley, and Mr. Brainerd, and their Indians, concerning which you desire to be informed; the correspondents have altered their determination, from time to time, with respect to Mr. Brainerd and his Indians. They seemed inclined at first to their removal to *Wawwoming*, alias *Wyoming*, and then to Onohquauga, and then to Wyoming again; and finally, about a twelvemonth ago, they wholly dismissed him from employ as a missionary to the Indians, and pastor to the Indian church at Bethel. I cannot say I am fully satisfied with their conduct in doing this so hastily; nor do I pretend to know so much, concerning the reasons of their conduct, as to have sufficient grounds positively to condemn their proceedings. However, the congregation is not wholly left as sheep without a shepherd, and are in part committed to the care of Mr. William Tennent, who lives not far off, and is a faithful, zealous minister, who visits them, and preaches to them, once a week; but I think not often upon the sabbath. The last fall, I was in New Jersey and Philadelphia, and was present at a meeting of the correspondents; when Mr. Tennent gave an agreeable account of the then present state of these Indians, with respect to religion, and also of their being in better circumstances, as to their lands, than they had been. Mr. Brainerd was then at Newark with his family, where he had been preaching, as a probationer for settlement, ever since Mr. Burr's dismission from that place, on account of his business as president of the college. But whether Mr. Brainerd is settled, or like to settle there, I have not heard. At the forementioned meeting of the correspondents, I used some arguments, to induce them to re-establish Mr. Brainerd, in his former employ with his Indians, and to send them to Onohquauga. But I soon found it would be fruitless to urge the matter. What was chiefly insisted on, as an insuperable obstacle to Mr. Brainerd's going, with his family, so far into the wilderness, was Mrs. Brainerd's very infirm state. Whether there was indeed any sufficient objection to such a removal, at that time, or no; Divine Providence has, since that, so ordered the state and consequences of the war, subsisting here in America, that insuperable obstacles are laid in the way of their removal, either to Onohquauga, Wawwoming, or any other parts of America, that way. The French, by their indefatigable endeavours with the nation of the *Delawares*, so called, from their ancient seat about Delaware river, though now chiefly residing on the Susquehannah and its branches, have stirred them up to make war on the English; and dreadful have been the ravages and desolations, which they have made of late, on the back parts of Pennsylvania and New Jersey. They are the principal nation inhabiting the parts about Susquehannah river, on which both Wyoming and Onohquauga stand. The latter indeed is above the bounds of their country, but yet not very far from them; and the Delaware Indians are frequently there, as they go to and fro; on which account there is great danger, that Mr. Hawley's mission and ministry there will be entirely broken up. Mr. Hawley came from there about two months ago, with one of my sons, about ten years old; who had been there with him near a twelvemonth, to learn the Mohawk language. He has since been to Boston, to consult the commissioners for Indian affairs, that have employed him, and returned: and yesterday went from my house, to meet some of his Indians, at an appointed time and place in the Mohawk country; to determine with them, whether it will be safe for him to return to abide with them. If not, yet will he be under the pay of the commissioners till next fall, and the issue be seen of the two expeditions now in prosecution, one against Crown Point, the other against the French forts at Frontenac and Niagara, near Lake Ontario; which may possibly make a great alteration, as to the state of the war with the Indians. If Mr. Hawley determines not to return to Onohquauga this spring, he will probably go as chaplain to the Indians, in General Shirley's army, in the expedition to Lake Ontario.

You speak of the vast superiority of the numbers of the English, in America, to those of the French; and that some therefore think, the settlements of the former are in no great danger from the latter. Though it be true, that the French are twenty times less than we are in number, yet it may be a question, whether other things, in which they exceed us, when all jointly considered, will not more than counterbalance all our excess of numbers. They vastly exceed us in subtilty and intrigue, in vigilance and activity, in speed and secrecy; in acquaintance with the continent of North America, in all parts west of the British settlements, for many hundred leagues, the rivers, lakes, and mountains, the avenues and passes; and also in the influence they have among the various tribes and nations of Indians, and in their constant skill and indefatigable diligence in managing them, to alienate them from the English, attach them firmly to themselves, and employ them as their tools. Beside the vast advantage they have, in time of war, in having all united under the absolute command of one man, the governor of Canada; while we are divided into a great many distinct governments, independent one of another, and, in some respects, of clashing interests: interests, which unspeakably clog and embarrass our affairs, and make us, though a great, yet an unwieldy, unmanageable body, and an easy prey to our vigilant, secret, subtle, swift and active, though comparatively small, enemy.

As to a description of the situation of those parts you mention, I can give you no better than you have, in many that abound in Great Britain. With respect to the situation of Stockbridge, it is not in the province of New York, as you have been informed, but in the utmost border of the province of Massachusetts, on the west, next to the province of New York; about 40 miles west of Connecticut river, about 25 miles east of Hudson's river, and about 35 miles south east from Albany: a place exposed in this time of war. Four persons were killed here, in the beginning of September, 1754, by Canada Indians; which occasioned a great alarm to us, and to a great part of New England. Since then we have had many alarms; but God has preserved us.

I desire your prayers that we may still be preserved, and that God would be with me and my family, and people, and bless us in all respects. My wife and family join with me, in their respects to you and yours.

I am, dear Sir,

Your affectionate brother and servant,

JONATHAN EDWARDS."

In consequence of the ill success attending the British arms, during the campaign of 1756, the danger of the frontiers became extreme, and the friends of Mr. Edwards were, for a time, exceedingly anxious for his personal safety. Mr. Bellamy, at this period, sent him the following kind invitation, to look to Bethlem, as the place of retreat, for himself and his family.

"*Bethlem, May* 31, 1756.

DEAR SIR,

I am in pain, fearing our army against Crown Point will be defeated. God only knows how it will be. Your own discretion will make you sufficiently speedy, to secure yourself and family. We stand as ready to receive you, and any of your family, to all the comforts our house affords, as if you were our children. I am greatly interested in your safety.—I am concerned for Mr. Hawley. I fear he will be too venturesome, and fling away his life for nothing.—I wish, if you know how to get one along, you would send him a letter.—Our youngest child still remains somewhat unwell. The Indian boys grow more and more easy and content, but they love play too well—are very ignorant—and very stupid, as to the things of religion—and in arithmetic, when I would teach them any thing that is a little difficult, they are soon discouraged, and don't love to try. So I take them off, and put them to writing again—designing, by little and little, to get them along. They will not endure hardship, and bend their minds to business, like English boys. It seems they were never taught their catechism. Shall I teach it? I have got three Bibles; but have not yet given them to the boys, they are so ignorant. I expect you will give me any instructions you think proper; and remain, Rev. Sir,

Your unworthy friend and servant,

J. BELLAMY."

It is probable that Mr. Edwards began his Treatise on Original Sin about this period, and that he devoted the leisure hours of the summer, autumn, and winter, to the preparation of that work. The date of the author's preface, May 26, 1757, shows the time when it was finished for the press.

The views of Mr. Edwards, in this treatise, are these: that there is a tendency in human nature, prevailing and effectual, to that sin, which implies the utter ruin of all; that this tendency originates in the sin of Adam, of which the whole race are imputed the partakers; and that this tendency consists, in their being left of God, at their original, in the possession of merely human appetites and passions, in themselves "innocent," and without the influx of those superior principles, which come from divine influences. The only guilt, attributed by him to mankind, before they come to the exercise of moral agency themselves, is that of participating in the apostasy of Adam, in consequence of the original constitution of God, which made him and his race "*one*."

He supposes this tendency to sin, pertaining to men, at their original, to constitute the subject of it a sinner, only, because he regards him as a participator in that sin, by which Adam apostatized, with his whole race. This tendency he calls "sinful," "corrupt," "odious," &c., because it is a tendency "to that *moral evil*, by which the subject of it becomes odious in the sight of God." (Part I. Chap. II. Sect. III.) He supposes that infants, who have this tendency in their nature, are, as yet, "sinners, only by the one act or offence of Adam;" and, that "they have not renewed the act of sin themselves." (Part I. Chap. IV.) He utterly denies any positive agency of God, in producing sin; and resolves the tendency to sin, into the "innocent principles" of human nature; (which God might create, without sin;) and the withholding of that positive influence, from which spring superior and divine principles:—which act of withholding, is not infusing, or positively creating, any thing. These "innocent principles"—such as hunger and thirst, love and hatred, desire and fear, joy and sorrow, and self-love, as distinguished from *selfishness*,—which are necessary to the nature of man, and belong to him, whether holy or sinful, are not, in his view, *sin*. They barely constitute the *ground of certainty*, that the being, who has them, will sin, as soon as he is capable of sinning, if that positive influence, from which spring superior and divine principles, is withheld; and, in this relation, they are spoken of, under the general designation, "a tendency," "a propensity," &c. to sin.

The views of Imputation, contained in this work, are such, as had been long and extensively entertained; yet some of them, certainly, are not generally received, at present. With this exception, the Treatise on Original Sin is regarded as the standard work, on the subject of which it treats; and is doubtless the ablest defence of the doctrine of human depravity, and of the doctrine that that depravity is the consequence of the sin of Adam, which has hitherto appeared.

The father of Mr. Edwards, as the reader may remember, on account of the increasing infirmities of age, had requested his people to settle a colleague in the ministry in 1752, but continued to preach to them regularly until the summer of 1755, when he was in his eighty-seventh year. The following letter, probably the last ever written to him by his son, shows the gradual decline of his health and strength, during the two following years.

"To the Rev. Timothy Edwards, East Windsor.

Stockbridge, March 24, 1757.

Honoured Sir,

I take this opportunity just to inform you, that, through the goodness of God, we are all in a comfortable state of health, and that we have heard, not long since, of the welfare of our children in New Jersey and Northampton. I intend, God willing, to be at Windsor some time near the beginning of June; proposing then to go a journey to Boston. I intended to have gone sooner; but I foresee such hinderances, as will probably prevent my going till that time. We rejoice much to hear, by Mr. Andrewson, of your being so well as to be able to baptize a child at your own house the sabbath before last. We all unite in duty to you and my honoured mother, and in respectful and affectionate salutations to sisters and cousins; and in a request of a constant remembrance in your prayers.

I am, honoured Sir,
Your dutiful son,
JONATHAN EDWARDS."

Not long after Mr. Edwards had forwarded to Mr. Erskine his vindication of himself,* against the charge of having advanced, in the Freedom of the Will, the same views of liberty and necessity, with those exhibited by Lord Kaimes; he received from his friend a pamphlet, entitled "Objections to the Essays on the Principles of Morality and Natural Religion examined;" in which the opinion was directly advanced, that, if it were really true, (as Mr. Edwards had insisted and demonstrated in the Freedom of the Will,) that there is no *liberty of contingence*, nor *self-determining power in the will*, as opposed to *moral necessity*, or the *certain connexion between motives and volitions;* yet it was best for mankind, that the truth, in this respect, should not be known, because, in that case, they would not regard either themselves, or others, as deserving of praise or blame for their conduct. In the following letter, Mr. Edwards exposes the folly and absurdity of this opinion; and explains, in a remarkably clear and convincing manner, *the practical bearing* of the great principles advanced in the Freedom of the Will, on the subject of salvation. This letter might well have been published at the time, and circulated through the church at large. And we recommend it to the frequent and prayerful perusal both of those ministers, who cannot clearly comprehend the distinction between *physical* and *moral* inability, and of those who do not perceive the importance of explaining and enforcing this distinction from the pulpit; as exhibiting the consequences of representing impenitent sinners, to be possessed of any other inability to repent and believe, than mere *unwillingness*, in a manner too awful to be resisted, by a conscientious mind.

"To Mr. Erskine.

Stockbridge, August 3, 1757.

Rev. and dear Sir,

In June last, I received a letter from you, dated January 22, 1757, with 'Mr. Anderson's Complaint verified,' and 'Objections to the Essays† examined.' For these things, I now return you my hearty thanks.

The conduct of the vindicator of the 'Essays,' from objections made against them, seems to be very odd. Many things are produced from Calvin, and several Calvinistic writers, to defend what is not objected against. His book is almost wholly taken up about that which is nothing to the purpose; perhaps only to amuse and blind the common people. According to your proposal, I have drawn up something, stating the difference between my hypothesis, and that of the Essays; which I have sent to you, to be printed in Scotland, if it be thought best; or to be disposed of as you think proper.‡ I have written it in a letter to you; and if it be published, it may be as 'A letter from me to a minister in Scotland.' Lord Kaimes's notion of God's deceiving mankind, by a kind of invincible or natural instinct or feeling, leading them to suppose, that they have a liberty of *contingence* and *self-determination of will*, in order to make them believe themselves and others worthy to be blamed or praised for what they do, is a strange notion indeed; and it is hard for me to conjecture, what his views could be, in publishing such things to the world.

However, by what I have heard, some others seem to be so far of the same mind, that they think, that if it be really true, that there is no self-determining power in the will, as opposed to any such moral necessity, as I speak of, consisting in a certain connexion between motives and volitions, it is of a mischievous tendency to say any thing of it; and that it is best that the truth in this matter should not be known by any means. I cannot but be of an extremely different mind. On the contrary, I think that the notion of liberty, consisting in a *contingent self-determination of the will*, as necessary to the morality of men's dispositions and actions, is almost inconceivably pernicious; and that the contrary truth is one of the most important truths of moral philosophy, that ever was discussed, and most necessary to be known; and that for want of it, those schemes of morality and religion, which are a kind of infidel schemes, entirely diverse from the virtue and religion of the Bible, and wholly inconsistent with, and subversive of, the main things belonging to the gospel scheme, have so vastly and so long prevailed, and have stood in such strength. And I think, whoever imagines that he, or any body else, shall ever see the doctrines of grace effectually maintained against these adversaries, till the truth in this matter be settled, imagines a vain thing. For, allow these adversaries what they maintain in this point, and I think they have strict demonstration against us. And not only have these errors a most pernicious influence, in the public religious controversies that are maintained in the world; but such sort of notions have a more fatal influence many ways, on the minds of all ranks, in all transactions between God and their souls. The longer I live, and the more I have to do with the souls of men, in the work of the ministry, the more I see of this. Notions of this sort are one of the main hinderances of the success of the preaching of the word, and other means of grace, in the conversion of sinners. This especially appears, when the minds of sinners are affected with some concern for their souls, and they are stirred up to seek their salvation. Nothing is more necessary for men, in such circumstances, than thorough conviction and humiliation; than that their consciences should be properly convinced of their real guilt and sinfulness in the sight of God, and

* See Vol. I. pp. 89—93.

† Essays on the principles of Morality and Natural Religion, by Lord Kaimes.

‡ See the letter in Vol. I. pp. 8.

their deserving of his wrath. But who is there, that has had experience of the work of a minister, in dealing with souls in such circumstances, that does not find that the thing, that mainly prevents this, is men's excusing themselves with their own inability, and the moral necessity of those things, wherein their exceeding guilt and sinfulness in the sight of God most fundamentally and mainly consist: such as, living from day to day without one spark of true love to the God of infinite glory, and the fountain of all good; their having greater complacency in the little vile things of this world, than in him; their living in a rejection of Christ, with all his glorious benefits and dying love; and after all the exhibition of his glory and grace, having their hearts still as cold as a stone towards him; and their living in such ingratitude, for that infinite mercy of his laying down his life for sinners. They, it may be, think of some instances of lewd behaviour, lying, dishonesty, intemperance, profaneness, &c. But the grand principles of iniquity, constantly abiding and reigning, from whence all proceeds, are all overlooked. Conscience does not condemn them for those things, because *they cannot love God of themselves, they cannot believe of themselves*, and the like. They rather lay the blame of these things, and their other reigning wicked dispositions of heart, to God, and secretly charge him with all the blame. These things are very much for want of being thoroughly instructed in that great and important truth, *that a bad will, or an evil disposition of heart, itself, is wickedness.* It is wickedness, in its very being, nature, and essence, and not merely the occasion of it, or the determining influence, that it was at first owing to. Some, it may be, will say, 'they own it is their fault that they have so bad a heart, that they have no love to God, no true faith in Christ, no gratitude to him, because they have been careless and slothful in times past, and have not used means to obtain a better heart, as they should have done.' And it may be, they are taught, 'that they are to blame for their wickedness of heart, because they, as it were, brought it on themselves, in Adam, by the sin which he voluntarily committed, which sin is justly charged to their account;' which perhaps they do not deny. But how far are these things from being a proper conviction of their wickedness, in their enmity to God and Christ. To be convinced of the sin of something that, long ago, was the occasion of their enmity to God; and to be convinced of the wickedness of the enmity itself; are quite two things. And if sinners, under some awakening, find the exercise of corruption of heart, as it appears in a great many ways; in their meditations, prayers, and other religious duties, and on occasion of their fears of hell, &c. &c.; still, this notion of their inability to help it, excusing them, will keep them from proper conviction of sin herein. Fears of hell tend to convince men of the hardness of their hearts. But then, when they find how hard their hearts are, and how far from a proper sensibility and affection in things of religion; they are kept from properly condemning themselves for it, from the *moral necessity*, or *inability*, which attends it. For the very notion of hardness of heart implies moral inability. The harder the heart is, the more dead is it in sin, and the more unable to exert good affections and acts. Thus the strength of sin is made the excuse for sin. And thus I have known many under fears of hell, justifying, or excusing, themselves, at least implicitly, in horrid workings of enmity against God, in blasphemous thoughts, &c.

It is of great importance, that they that are seeking their salvation, should be brought off from all dependence on their own righteousness; but these notions above all things prevent it. They justify themselves in the sincerity of their endeavours. They say to themselves, that they do what they can; they take great pains; and though there be great imperfection in what they do, and many evil workings of heart arise, yet these they cannot help: here moral necessity, or inability, comes in as an excuse. Things of this kind have visibly been the main hinderance of the true humiliation and conversion of sinners, in the times of awakening that have been in this land, every where, in all parts, as I have had opportunity to observe, in very many places. When the gospel is preached, and its offers and invitations and motives most powerfully urged, and some hearts stand out, here is their strong hold, their sheet-anchor. Were it not for this, they would either comply, or their hearts would condemn them for their horrid guilt in not complying. And if the law of God be preached in its strictness and spirituality, yet conscience is not properly convinced by it. They justify themselves with their *inability;* and the design and end of the law, as a school-master to fit them for Christ, is defeated. Thus both the law and the gospel are prevented from having their proper effect.

The doctrine of a self-determining will, as the ground of all moral good and evil, tends to prevent any proper exercises of faith in God and Christ, in the affair of our salvation, as it tends to prevent all dependence upon them. For, instead of this, it teaches a kind of absolute independence on all those things, that are of chief importance in this affair; our righteousness depending originally on our own acts, as self-determined. Thus our own holiness is from ourselves, as its determining cause, and its original and highest source. And as for imputed righteousness, that should have any merit at all in it, to be sure there can be no such thing. For self-determination is necessary to praise and merit. But what is imputed from another is not from our self-determination or action. And truly, in this scheme, man is not dependent on God; but God is rather dependent on man in this affair: for he only operates consequentially in acts, in which he depends on what he sees we determine and do first.

The nature of true faith implies a disposition to give all the glory of our salvation to God and Christ. But this notion is inconsistent with it, for it in effect gives the glory wholly to man. For that is the very doctrine that is taught, that the merit and praise is his, whose is the original and effectual determination of the praiseworthy deed. So that, on the whole, I think it must be a miracle, if ever men are converted that have imbibed such notions as these, and are under their influence in their religious concerns.

Yea, these notions tend effectually to prevent men's ever seeking after conversion, with any earnestness. It is manifest that men never will be in earnest in this matter, till their consciences are awakened, and they are made sensible of God's anger, and their danger of suffering the terrible effects of it. But that stupidity, which is opposed to this awakening, is upheld chiefly by these two things: their insensibility of their guilt, in what is past and present; and their flattering themselves, as to what is future. These notions of liberty of indifference, contingence, and self-determination, as essential to guilt or merit, tend to preclude all sense of any great guilt for past or present wickedness. As has been observed already, all wickedness of heart is excused, as what, in itself considered, brings no guilt. And all that the conscience has to recur to, to find any guilt, is the first wrong determination of the will, in some bad conduct, before that wickedness of heart existed, that was the occasion of introducing or confirming it. Which determination arose contingently from a state of indifference. And how small a matter does this at once bring men's guilt to, when all the main things, wherein their wickedness consists, are passed over. And indeed the more these principles are pursued, the more and more must guilt vanish, till at last it comes to nothing, as may easily be shown.

And with respect to self-flattery and presumption, as to what is future, nothing can possibly be conceived more directly tending to it, than a notion of liberty, at all times possessed, consisting in a power to determine one's own will to good or evil; which implies a power men have, at all times, to determine them to repent and turn to God. And what can more effectually encourage the sinner, in present delays and neglects, and imbolden him to go on in sin, in a presumption of having his own salvation at all times at his command? And this notion of self-determination and self-dependence, tends to prevent, or enervate, all prayer to God for converting grace; for why should men earnestly cry to God for his grace, to determine their hearts to that which they must be determined to of themselves. And indeed it destroys the very notion of conversion itself. There can properly be no such thing, or any thing akin to what the Scripture speaks of conversion, renovation of the heart, regeneration, &c. if growing good, by a number of self-determined acts, are all that is required, or to be expected.

Excuse me, Sir, for troubling you with so much on this head. I speak from the fulness of my heart. What I have long seen of the dreadful consequences of these prevalent notions every where, and what I am convinced will still be their consequences so long as they continue to prevail, fills me with concern. I therefore wish that the affair were more thoroughly looked into, and searched to the very bottom.

I have reserved a copy of this letter, and also of my other to you, dated July 25, intending to send them to Mr. Burr, to be by him conveyed, by the way of New York or Philadelphia. Looking on these letters as of special importance, I send duplicates, lest one copy should fail. The packet, in which I enclose this, I cover to Mr. Gillies, and send to Boston, to the care of Mr. Hyslop, to be conveyed to Mr. Gillies. But yet have desired him, if he has a more direct opportunity, to convey the packet to Edinburgh, by the way of London, then to put a wrapper over the whole, inscribed to you; and to write to you, desiring you to break open the packet, and take out the letters which belong to you.

You will see, Sir, something of our sorrowful state, on this side of the water, by my letter to Mr. M'Culloch. O, Sir, pray for us; and pray in particular, for

Your affectionate and obliged

Friend and brother,

JONATHAN EDWARDS."

CHAPTER XXIV.

DEATH OF PRESIDENT BURR—HIS CHARACTER—MR. EDWARDS CHOSEN HIS SUCCESSOR—LETTERS OF MRS. BURR—TO A GENTLEMAN IN SCOTLAND—TO A GENTLEMAN IN BOSTON—TO HER MOTHER—LETTER OF MR. EDWARDS, TO THE TRUSTEES OF THE COLLEGE—LETTER OF MRS. BURR, TO HER FATHER—LETTER TO DR. BELLAMY—COUNCIL DISMISS MR. EDWARDS—INAUGURATION AS PRESIDENT—FIRST SERMON AT PRINCETON—SICKNESS—DEATH—LETTER OF DR. SHIPPEN—LETTERS OF MRS. EDWARDS, AND OF HER DAUGHTER, TO MRS. BURR—DEATH OF MRS. BURR—DEATH OF MRS. EDWARDS.

The Rev. Aaron Burr, president of the college at Princeton, and the son-in-law of Mr. Edwards, died, on the 24th of September, 1757, two days before the public commencement. He was a native of Fairfield, Connecticut, was born in 1716, and was graduated at Yale college in 1735. In 1738, he was ordained, as pastor of the presbyterian church at Newark. In 1748, he was unanimously elected president of the college, as successor to Mr. Dickinson. Though possessed of a slender and delicate constitution, he joined, to uncommon talents for the despatch of business, a constancy of mind, that commonly secured to him success. The flourishing state of the college, at the time of his death, was chiefly owing to his great and assiduous exertions. Until the autumn of 1755, he discharged the duties, both of president and pastor of the church.* Mr. Burr was greatly respected, in every station and relation of life. He was a man of acknowledged talents, of sound, practical good sense, of unimpeachable integrity, and of ardent piety. Polished in his manners, he had uncommon powers in conversation, and possessed the happy art of inspiring all around him with cheerfulness. As a reasoner, he was clear and solid; and as a preacher, animated, judicious, fervent, and successful. He had warm affections, was greatly endeared to his family and friends, and was open, fair, and honourable in all his intercourse with mankind. During the period of his presidency, he secured the high esteem and confidence of all who were interested in the college.—In the latter part of July, or the beginning of August, being in a low state of health, he made a rapid and exhausting visit to Stockbridge, in a very hot, sultry season. He soon returned to Princeton, and went immediately to Elizabethtown; where, on the 19th of August, he made an attempt, before the legislature, to procure the legal exemption of the students from military duty. On the 21st, at Newark, being much indisposed, he preached an extemporaneous funeral sermon, in consequence of a death in the family of his successor. He then returned to Princeton, and, in a

* In the autumn of 1756, or early in 1757, the college was removed to Princeton.

few days, went to Philadelphia, on the business of the college. On the way, his disorder took the form of an intermittent fever. On his return, he learned that his friend, Governor Belcher, died at Elizabeth-town, on the 31st of August, and that he had been designated to preach the funeral sermon. His wife, perceiving his increasing illness, besought him to spare himself, and decline the undertaking; but he felt himself bound, if possible, to perform it. Having devoted the afternoon of Sept. 2d, to the task of preparing the sermon, in the midst of a high fever, which was succeeded by delirium in the night, he rode the next day to Elizabeth-town, about forty miles, and, on the 4th, in a state of extreme languor and exhaustion, when it was obvious to every one, that he ought to have been confined to a sick bed, he with great difficulty preached the sermon. He returned to Princeton the following day; and his disorder immediately assumed the character of a fixed and violent fever, seated on the nerves. At the approach of death, that gospel, which he had preached to others, gave him unfailing support. He was patient and resigned, and cheered with the liveliest hope of a happy immortality.

The corporation of the college met, two days after his death, and on the same day made choice of Mr. Edwards as his successor.

Some of the circumstances, connected with the sickness and death of her husband, are alluded to in the following letter from Mrs. Burr, to a gentleman in Scotland, written soon after Mr. Burr's decease.

" Honoured Sir,

I flatter myself I shall not be thought intrusive, if I acknowledge, in a few lines, the receipt of your letter, dated in August, to my late dear husband, which reached me after he was beyond the reach of all mortal things. The affectionate regard that you express for one, who was dearer to me than my own life, was extremely affecting to me; nor can I forgive myself, if I neglect to acknowledge it, in terms of lively gratitude. You, Sir, had a large share, with me, in that dear good man's heart, which he often expressed, with the warmest affection. I thought it might not be improper, to lay your letter before the trustees, as they were then convened, and it chiefly concerned the college; and then I sent it to my honoured father, the Rev. Mr. Edwards, who is chosen to succeed my dear husband; which, I hope, will be grateful to the friends of the college, in Scotland. I here enclose you, Sir, the last attempt my dear husband made to serve God in public, and to do good to his fellow-creatures—a Sermon, that he preached at the funeral of our late excellent governor. You will not think it strange, if it has imperfections; when I tell you, that all he wrote on the subject, was done in a part of one afternoon and evening, when he had a violent fever on him, and the whole night after, he was irrational.

Give me leave to beg an interest in your prayers, at the throne of grace, for a poor, disconsolate widow, and two fatherless orphans. Please to present, with great respect, my kindest regard to your lady and daughters.

I am, honoured Sir,

Your most obliged and humble servant,

ESTHER BURR."

The two following extracts from letters, written soon after the death of Mr. Burr, will show the strength of her own feelings, as well as her religious sentiments, and the exercises of her heart. The first is from a letter to a near friend of the family, in Boston.

" Your most kind letter of condolence gave me inexpressible delight, and at the same time set open afresh all the avenues of grief, and again probed the deep wound death has given me. My loss—Shall I attempt to say how great my loss is—God only can know—And to him alone would I carry my complaint.—Indeed, Sir, I have lost all that was or could be desirable in a creature.—I have lost all that ever I set my heart on in this world.—I need not enlarge on the innumerable amiable qualities of my late dear husband, to one that was so well acquainted with him, as you were; however pleasing it is to me to dwell on them.—Had not God supported me by these two considerations; first, by showing the right he has to his own creatures, to dispose of them when and in what manner he pleases; and secondly, by enabling me to follow him beyond the grave, into the eternal world, and there to view him in unspeakable glory and happiness, freed from all sin and sorrow; I should, long before this, have been sunk among the dead, and been covered with the clods of the valley.—God has wise ends in all that he doth. This thing did not come upon me by chance; and I rejoice that I am in the hands of such a God."

The other is from a letter to her mother, dated at Princeton, Oct. 7, 1757. After giving some account of Mr. Burr's death, and representing the sense she had of the greatness of the loss, which she and her children had sustained; she writes in the following words:

" No doubt, dear Madam, it will be some comfort to you to hear, that God has not utterly forsaken, although he has cast down. I would speak it to the glory of God's name, that I think he has, in an uncommon degree, discovered himself to be an all-sufficient God, a full fountain of all good. Although all streams were cut off, yet the fountain is left full.—I think I have been enabled to cast my care upon him, and have found great peace and calmness in my mind, such as this world cannot give nor take.—I have had uncommon freedom and nearness to the throne of grace. God has seemed sensibly near in such a supporting and comfortable manner, that I think I have never experienced the like. God has helped me to review my past and present mercies, with some heart-affecting degree of thankfulness.

I think God has given me such a sense of the vanity of the world, and uncertainty of all sublunary enjoyments, as I never had before. The world vanishes out of my sight! Heavenly and eternal things appear much more real and important than ever before. I feel myself to be under much greater obligations to be the Lord's, than before this sore affliction.—The way of salvation by faith in Jesus Christ, has appeared more clear and excellent; and I have been constrained to venture my all upon him; and have found great peace of soul in what I hope have been the actings of faith. Some parts of the Psalms have been very comforting and refreshing to my soul.—I hope God has helped me to eye his hand, in this awful dispensation; and to see the infinite right he has to his own, and to dispose of them as he pleases.

Thus, dear Madam, I have given you some broken hints of the exercises and supports of my mind, since the death of him, whose memory and example will ever be precious to me as my own life. O, dear Madam! I doubt not but I have your and my honoured father's prayers daily for me; but give me leave to entreat you both, to request earnestly of the Lord, that I may never despise his chastenings, nor faint under this his severe stroke; of which I am sensible there is great danger, if God should only deny me the supports that he has hitherto graciously granted.

O, I am afraid I shall conduct myself so, as to bring dishonour on my God, and the religion which I profess! No, rather let me die this moment, than be left to bring dishonour on God's holy name.—I am overcome—I must conclude, with once more begging, that, as my dear parents remember themselves, they would not forget their greatly afflicted daughter, (now a lonely widow,) nor her fatherless children.—My duty to my ever dear and honoured parents, and love to my brothers and sisters.

From, dear madam,

Your dutiful and affectionate daughter,

ESTHER BURR."

"The news of his appointment to the presidency," says Dr. Hopkins, "was quite unexpected, and not a little surprising, to Mr. Edwards. He looked on himself in many respects, so unqualified for that business, that he wondered that gentlemen of so good judgment, and so well acquainted with him, as he knew some of the trustees were, should think of *him* for that place. He had many objections in his own mind, against undertaking the business, both from his unfitness and his particular circumstances; yet could not certainly determine that it was not his duty to accept it. The following extract of a letter which he wrote to the trustees, will give the reader a view of his sentiments and exercises on this occasion, as well as of the great designs he was deeply engaged in and zealously prosecuting."

"*Stockbridge, Oct.* 19, 1757.

Rev. and hon. Gentlemen,

I was not a little surprised on receiving the unexpected notice of your having made choice of me to succeed the late President Burr, as the Head of Nassau Hall.—I am much in doubt, whether I am called to undertake the business which you have done me the unmerited honour to choose me for.—If some regard may be had to my outward comfort, I might mention the many inconveniences and great detriment, which may be sustained by my removing with my numerous family, so far from all the estate I have in the world, (without any prospect of disposing of it, under present circumstances, but with great loss,) now when we have scarcely got over the trouble and damage sustained by our removal from Northampton, and have but just begun to have our affairs in a comfortable situation, for a subsistence in this place; and the expense I must immediately be at to put myself into circumstances tolerably comporting with the needful support of the honours of the office I am invited to; which will not well consist with my ability.

But this is not my main objection. The chief difficulties in my mind, in the way of accepting this important and arduous office, are these two: First, my own defects unfitting me for such an undertaking, many of which are generally known; beside others of which my own heart is conscious.—I have a constitution, in many respects, peculiarly unhappy, attended with flaccid solids, vapid, sizy, and scarce fluids, and a low tide of spirits; often occasioning a kind of childish weakness and contemptibleness of speech, presence, and demeanour, with a disagreeable dulness and stiffness, much unfitting me for conversation, but more especially for the government of a college.—This makes me shrink at the thoughts of taking upon me, in the decline of life, such a new and great business, attended with such a multiplicity of cares, and requiring such a degree of activity, alertness, and spirit of government; especially as succeeding one so remarkably well qualified in these respects, giving occasion to every one to remark the wide difference. I am also deficient in some parts of learning, particularly in algebra, and the higher parts of mathematics, and the Greek classics; my Greek learning having been chiefly in the New Testament.—The other thing is this; that my engaging in this business will not well consist with those views, and that course of employ in my study, which have long engaged and swallowed up my mind, and been the chief entertainment and delight of my life.

And here, honoured Sirs, (imboldened by the testimony I have now received of your unmerited esteem, to rely on your candour,) I will with freedom open myself to you.

My method of study, from my first beginning the work of the ministry, has been very much by writing; applying myself, in this way, to improve every important hint; pursuing the clue to my utmost, when any thing in reading, meditation, or conversation, has been suggested to my mind, that seemed to promise light in any weighty point; thus penning what appeared to me my best thoughts, on innumerable subjects, for my own benefit.—The longer I prosecuted my studies in this method, the more habitual it became, and the more pleasant and profitable I found it.—The farther I travelled in this way, the more and wider the field opened, which has occasioned my laying out many things in my mind, to do this in manner, if God should spare my life, which my heart hath been much upon; particularly many things against most of the prevailing errors of the present day, which I cannot with any patience see maintained, (to the utter subverting of the gospel of Christ,) with so high a hand, and so long continued a triumph, with so little control, when it appears so evident to me, that there is truly no foundation for any of this glorying and insult. I have already published something on one of the main points in dispute between the Arminians and Calvinists; and have it in view, God willing, (as I have already signified to the public,) in like manner to consider all the other controverted points, and have done much towards a preparation for it.—But beside these, I have had on my mind and heart (which I long ago began, not with any view to publication) a great work, which I call a *History of the Work of Redemption*, a body of divinity in an entire new method, being thrown into the form of a history; considering the affair of christian theology, as the whole of it, in each part, stands in reference to the great work of redemption by Jesus Christ; which I suppose to be, of all others, the grand design of God, and the *summum* and *ultimum* of all the divine operations and decrees; particularly considering all parts of the grand scheme, in their historical order.—The order of their existence, or their being brought forth to view, in the course of divine dispensations, or the wonderful series of successive acts and events; beginning from eternity, and descending from thence to the great work and successive dispensations of the infinitely wise God, in time; considering the chief events coming to pass in the church of God, and revolutions in the world of mankind, affecting the state of the church and the affair of redemption, which we have an account of in history or prophecy; till, at last, we come to the general resurrection, last judgment, and consummation of all things; when it shall be said, *It is done. I am Alpha and Omega, the beginning and the end.*—Concluding my work, with the consideration of that perfect state of things, which shall be finally settled, to last for eternity.—This history will be carried on with regard to all three worlds, heaven, earth, and hell; considering the connected, successive events and alterations in each, so far as the Scriptures give any light; introducing all parts of divinity in that order which is most scriptural and most natural; a method which appears to me the most beautiful and entertaining, wherein every divine doctrine will appear to the greatest advantage, in the brightest light, in the most striking manner, showing the admirable contexture and harmony of the whole.

I have also, for my own profit and entertainment, done much towards another great work, which I call the *Harmony of the Old and New Testament*, in three parts. The first, considering the prophecies of the Messiah, his redemption and kingdom; the evidences of their references to the Messiah, &c. comparing them all one with another, demonstrating their agreement, true scope, and sense; also considering all the various particulars wherein those prophecies have their exact fulfilment; showing the universal, precise, and admirable correspondence between predictions and events. The second part, considering the types of the Old Testament, showing the evidence of their being intended as representations of the great things of the gospel of Christ; and the agreement of the type with the antitype. The third and great part, considering the harmony of the Old and New Testament, as to doctrine and precept. In the course of this work, I find there will be occasion for an explanation of a very great part of the Holy Scriptures; which may, in such a view, be explained in a method, which to me seems the most entertaining and profitable, best tending to lead the mind to a view of the true spirit, design, life, and soul of the Scriptures, as well as their proper use and improvement.—I have also many other things in hand, in some of which I have made great progress, which I will not trouble you with an account of. Some of these things, if Divine Providence favour, I should be willing to attempt a publication of. So far as I myself am able to judge of what talents I have, for benefiting my fellow-creatures by word, I think I can write better than I can speak.

My heart is so much in these studies, that I cannot find it in my heart to be willing to put myself into an incapacity to pursue them any more in the future part of my life, to such a degree as I must, if I undertake to go through the same course of employ, in the office of president, that Mr. Burr did, instructing in all the languages, and taking the whole care of the instruction of one of the classes, in all parts of learning, besides his other labours. If I should see light to determine me to accept the place offered me, I should be willing to take upon me the work of a president, so far as it consists in the general inspection of the whole society; and to be subservient to the school, as to their order and methods of study and instruction, assisting, myself, in the immediate instruction in the arts and sciences, (as discretion should direct, and occasion serve, and the state of things require,) especially of the senior class; and added to all, should be willing to do the whole work of a professor of divinity, in public and private lectures, proposing questions to be answered, and some to be discussed in writing and free conversation, in meetings of graduates, and others, appointed in proper seasons, for these ends. It would be now out of my way, to spend time in a constant teaching of the languages; unless it be the Hebrew tongue; which I should be willing to improve myself in, by instructing others.

On the whole, I am much at a loss, with respect to the way of duty, in this important affair: I am in doubt, whether, if I should engage in it, I should not do what both you and I would be sorry for afterwards. Nevertheless, I think the greatness of the affair, and the regard due to so worthy and venerable a body, as that of the trustees of Nassau Hall, requires my taking the matter into serious consideration, And unless you should appear to be discouraged, by the things which I have now represented, as to any further expectation from me, I shall proceed to ask advice, of such as I esteem most wise, friendly, and faithful; if, after the mind of the commissioners in Boston is known, it appears that they consent to leave me at liberty, with respect to the business they have employed me in here."

Soon after the death of President Burr, Mr. Edwards addressed a letter to his greatly afflicted daughter, fraught with all the affectionate instruction and consolation which such a father could impart.* To this she returned the following answer:

"To the Rev. Jonathan Edwards, Stockbridge.

Princeton, Nov. 2, 1757.

To my ever honoured father.

Honoured Sir,

Your most affectionate, comforting letter, by my brother Parsons, was exceeding refreshing to me; although I was somewhat damped by hearing, that I should not see you until spring.† But it is my comfort in this disappointment, as well us under all my affliction, that God knows what is best for me, and for his own glory. Perhaps I counted too much on the company, and conversation, of such a near and dear affectionate father and guide. I cannot doubt but all is for the best; and I am satisfied that God should order the affair of your removal, as shall be for his glory, whatever becomes of me.

Since I wrote my mother a letter, God has carried me through new trials, and given me new supports. My little son has been sick with a slow fever, ever since my brother left us, and has been brought to the brink of the grave; but, I hope in mercy, God is bringing him back again. I was enabled after a severe struggle with nature, to resign the child with the greatest freedom. God showed me that the children were not my own, but his, and that he had a right to recall what he had lent, whenever he thought fit; and that I had no reason to complain, or say that God was hard with me. This silenced me. But O how good is God. He not only kept me from complaining, but comforted me, by enabling me to offer up my child by

* Unfortunately this letter is lost.

† When Mr. Edwards wrote the letter to which she refers, he did not think of going to Princeton till spring; but he afterwards determined otherwise.

faith, if ever I acted faith. I saw the fulness there was in Christ for little infants, and his willingness to accept of such as were offered to him. 'Suffer little children to come unto me, and forbid them not,' were comforting words. God also showed me, in such a lively manner, the fulness there was in himself of all spiritual blessings, tnat I said, 'Although all streams were cut off, yet so long as my God lives, I have enough.' He enabled me to say, 'Although thou slay me, yet will I trust in thee.' In this time of trial, I was led to enter into a renewed and explicit covenant with God, in a more solemn manner than ever before; and with the greatest freedom and delight, after much self-examination and prayer, I did give myself and my children to God, with my whole heart. Never, until then, had I an adequate sense of the privilege we are allowed in covenanting with God. This act of soul left my mind in a great calm, and steady trust in God. A few days after this, one evening, in talking of the glorious state my dear departed husband must be in, my soul was carried out in such large desires after that glorious state, that I was forced to retire from the family to conceal my joy. When alone I was so transported, and my soul carried out in such eager desires after perfection and the full enjoyment of God, and to serve him uninterruptedly, that I think my nature would not have borne much more. I think, dear Sir, I had that night a foretaste of heaven. This frame continued, in some good degree, the whole night. I slept but little, and when I did, my dreams were all of heavenly and divine things. Frequently since, I have felt the same in kind, though not in degree. This was about the time that God called me to give up my child. Thus a kind and gracious God has been with me, in six troubles and in seven.

But O, Sir, what cause of deep humiliation and abasement of soul have I, on account of remaining corruption, which I see working continually in me, especially pride. O, how many shapes does pride cloak itself in. Satan is also busy, shooting his darts. But blessed be God, those temptations of his, that used to overthrow me, as yet have not touched me. I will just hint at one or two, if I am not tedious as to length.—When I was about to renew my covenant with God, the suggestion seemed to arise in my mind, 'It is better you should not renew it, than break it when you have: what a dreadful thing it will be, if you do not keep it!' My reply was, 'I did not do it in my own strength.' Then the suggestion would return, 'How do you know that God will help you to keep it.' But it did not shake me in the least.—Oh, to be delivered from the power of Satan, as well as sin! I cannot help hoping the time is near. God is certainly fitting me for himself; and when I think that it will be soon that I shall be called hence, the thought is transporting.

I am afraid I have tired out your patience, and will beg leave only to add my need of the earnest prayers of my dear and honoured parents, and all good people, that I may not at last be a cast-away; but that God would constantly grant me new supplies of divine grace. I am tenderly concerned for my dear brother Timothy, but I hope his sickness will not be unto death, but for the glory of God.—Please to give my duty to my honoured mother, and my love to all my brothers and sisters.

I am, honoured and dear Sir,
With the greatest respect,
Your affectionate and dutiful daughter,
ESTHER BURR."

While Mr. Edwards was in the state of suspense alluded to in his letter to the trustees of the college, he determined to ask the advice of a number of gentlemen in the ministry, on whose judgment and friendship he could rely, and to act accordingly. One of those invited, on this occasion, was his old and faithful friend, and former pupil, Mr. Bellamy, of Bethlem; to whom, having received from him, on the last day of November, two letters, dated on the 12th and 17th of that month, he returned, on the next day, the following answer; which, while it refers to the subject of the council, shows also, in a very striking manner, with what ease and readiness he could throw a clear and certain light on any dark and difficult passage of the word of God.

"*Stockbridge, Dec.* 1, 1757.

REV. AND DEAR SIR,

Yesterday I received your two letters, of the 12th and 17th of Nov.; but I saw and heard nothing of Mr. Hill. I thank you for your concern, that I may be useful in the world.—I lately wrote you a letter, informing you of our choice of a council, to sit here on the 21st of this month; and enclosed in it a letter missive to Mr. Brinsmade, who is one of the council. I hope, before this time, you have received it. Don't fail of letting me see you here; for I never wanted to see you more.

As to the question you ask, about Christ's argument, in John x. 34—36. I observe,

First, That it is not *all princes* of the earth, who are called *gods*, in the Old Testament; but only the *princes of Israel*, who ruled over God's people. The princes, who are called gods, in Psalm lxxxii. here referred to, are, in the same sentence, distinguished from the *princes of the nations of the world*.—'I have said, Ye are *gods*; but ye shall die like men, and fall like one of the *princes*.'

Secondly, That the reason why these princes of Israel were called *gods*, was, that they, as the rulers and judges of God's Israel, were types and figures of Him, who is the true King of the Jews, and the Prince of God's people, who is to rule over the house of Jacob for ever, the Prince and Saviour of God's church, or spiritual Israel, gathered from all nations of the earth; who is God indeed. The throne of Israel, or of God's people, properly belonged to Christ. He only was the proper Heir to that throne; and therefore, the princes of Israel are said to sit upon *the throne of the Lord*, 1 Chron. xxix. 23.; and the kingdom of Israel, under the kings of the house of David, is called *the kingdom of the Lord*, 2 Chron. xiii. 8. And because Christ took the throne, as the *Antitype* of those kings, therefore he is said, Luke i. 32. to sit upon *their throne*.—Thus, the princes of Israel, in the 82nd Psalm, are called *gods*, and *sons of God*, or 'all of them *children of the Most High*;' being appointed *types* and remarkable representations of the true Son of God, and in him of the true God. They were called *gods*, and *sons of God*, in the same manner as the Levitical sacrifices were called an *atonement* for sin, and in the same manner as the manna was called the *bread of heaven*, and *angels' food*. These things represented, and, by special divine designation, were *figures* of, the true Atonement, and of Him who was the true Bread of heaven, and the true angels' food; in the same sense as Saul, the person especially pointed out in the 82nd Psalm, is called '*the Lord's anointed*,' or (as it is in the original) *Messiah*, or *Christ*, which are the same. And it is to be observed, that these typical gods, and judges of Israel, are particularly distinguished from the true God, and true Judge, in the next sentence, Psal. lxxxii. 8. 'Arise, O GOD, thou JUDGE of the earth; for thou shalt inherit all nations.'—This is a wish for the coming of that King, that should reign in righteousness, and judge righteously; who was to inherit the Gentiles, as well as the Jews; and the words, as they stand in connexion with the two preceding verses, import thus much—'As to you, the temporal princes and judges of Israel, you are called gods, and sons of God, being exalted to the place of kings, judges, and saviours of God's people, the kingdom and heritage of Christ; but you shall die like men, and fall like other princes; whereby it appears that you are truly no gods, nor any one of you the true Son of God, which your injustice and oppression also shows. But oh, that He who is truly God, the Judge of the earth, the true and just Judge and Saviour, who is to be King over Gentiles as well as Jews, would come and reign!'—It is to be observed, that when it is said in this verse—'Arise, O *God*' —the word rendered *God*, is *Elohim*—the same used in verse 6. 'I have said, Ye are *gods*,'—I have said, Ye are *elohim*.

Thirdly, As to the words of Christ, in John x. 35. 'If he called them gods, unto whom the word of God came,' I suppose that, by the *word of God coming* to these princes of Israel, is meant, their being set forth by special and express divine designation, to be types or figurative significations of God's mind. Those things which God had appointed to be types, to signify the mind of God, were a *visible word*. Types are called *the word of the Lord*—as in Zech. xi. 10, 11. and in Zech. iv. 4—6.—The word of God came to the princes of Israel, both as they, by God's ordering, became subjects of a typical representation of a divine thing, which was a visible word of God; and also, as this was done by express divine designation, as they were marked out to this end, by an express, audible, and legible word, as in Exod. xxii. 28. and Psal. lxxxii. 1.; and besides, the thing, of which they were appointed types, was Christ, who is called '*the word of God*.'—Thus, the word of God came to Jacob, as a type of Christ, 1 Kings xviii. 31. 'And Elijah took twelve stones, according to the number of the tribes of Jacob, UNTO WHOM THE WORD OF THE LORD CAME, saying, *Israel* shall be thy name.'—The word Israel is PRINCE OF GOD: —Jacob being, by that express divine designation, appointed as a type of Christ, the true Prince of God, (who is called, in Isa. xlix. 3. by the name of *Israel*,) in his prevailing in his wrestling with God, to save himself and his family from destruction by Esau, who was then coming against him, and obtaining the blessing for himself and his seed.—Now,

Fourthly, Christ's argument lies in these words, *The Scripture cannot be broken*. That word of God, by which they are called gods, as *types* of Him who is truly God, must be verified, which they cannot be, unless the *Antitype* be truly God.—They are so called, as types of the Messiah, or of the *Anointed One*, (which is the same,) or the *Sanctified* or *Holy One*, or Him that was to be *sent*; which were all known names among the Jews for the Messiah. (See Dan. ix. 24, 25. Psal. lxxxix. 19, 20. Psal. xvi. 10. John ix. 7.) But it was on this account, that those types or images of the Messiah were called gods, because He, whom they represented, was God indeed. If he were not God, the word by which they were called gods could not be verified, and must be broken. As the word, by which the legal sacrifices were called an atonement, and are said to atone for sin, was true in no other sense, than as they had relation to the sacrifice of Christ the true atonement. If Christ's sacrifice had not truly atoned for sin; the word, which called the types or representations of it an atonement, could not be verified. So, if Jesus Christ had not been the true Bread from heaven, and angels' food indeed; the scripture which called the type of him, the bread from heaven, and angels' food, would not have been verified, but would have been broken.

These, Sir, are my thoughts on John x. 34, &c.

I am yours, most affectionately,

J. EDWARDS."

"*P. S. Dec.* 5.—The opportunity for the conveyance of my letters to the ministers chosen to be of the council, your way, not being very good, I here send other letters, desiring you to take the charge of conveying them with all possible care and speed."

The gentlemen invited to the council, at his desire, and that of his people, met at Stockbridge, January 4, 1758;* and, having heard the application of the agents of the college, and their reasons in support of it;† Mr. Edwards's own representation of the matter; and what his people had to say, by way of objection, against his removal; determined that it was his duty to accept of the invitation to the presidency of the college. When they published their judgment and advice to Mr. Edwards and his people, he appeared uncommonly moved and affected with it, and fell into tears on the occasion, which was very unusual for him, in the presence of others; and soon after, he said to the gentlemen who had given their advice, that it was matter of wonder to him, that they could so easily, as they appeared to do, get over the objections he had made against his removal.‡ But, as he thought it his duty to be directed by their advice, he should now endeavour cheerfully to undertake it, believing he was in the way of his duty.

"Accordingly, having had, by the application of the trustees of the college, the consent of the commissioners of the 'Society in London, for Propagating the Gospel, in New England and the Parts adjacent,' to resign their mission; he girded up his loins, and set off from Stockbridge for Princeton, in January. He left his family at Stockbridge, not to be removed till the spring. He had two daughters at Princeton; Mrs. Burr, and Lucy, his eldest daughter that was unmarried. His arrival at Princeton was to the great satisfaction and joy of the college. And indeed all the greatest friends of the college, and to the interests of religion, were highly satisfied and pleased with the appointment."

It was a singular fact, that, soon after his arrival at

* I have ascertained the names of only three of the members of the council—Mr. Bellamy, Mr. Brinsmade, and Mr. Hopkins. This date is right, though it differs from that mentioned in the letter to Mr. Bellamy.

† The agents of the college were Rev. Messrs. Caleb Smith and John Brainerd.

‡ The council, at the request both of the English and Indian congregations at Stockbridge, addressed a letter to the commissioners in Boston, requesting that the Rev. John Brainerd might be appointed Mr. Edwards's successor;—the Housatonnucks offering land for a settlement to the Indian congregation at Cranberry, New Jersey, if they would remove to Stockbridge;—and another letter to the trustees of the college, requesting that they would use their collective and individual influence, to procure the appointment of Mr. Brainerd, and his removal to Stockbridge.

Princeton, he heard the melancholy tidings of the death of his father. It occurred on the 27th of January, 1758, in the 89th year of his age.

"The corporation met as soon as could be with convenience, after his arrival at the college, when he was by them fixed in the president's chair. While at Princeton, before his sickness, he preached in the college-hall, sabbath after sabbath, to the great acceptance of the hearers;* but did nothing as president, unless it was to give out some questions in divinity to the senior class, to be answered before him; each one having opportunity to study and write what he thought proper upon them. When they came together to answer them, they found so much entertainment and profit by it, especially by the light and instruction Mr. Edwards communicated, in what he said upon the questions, when they had delivered what they had to say, that they spoke of it with the greatest satisfaction and wonder.

"During this time, Mr. Edwards seemed to enjoy an uncommon degree of the presence of God. He told his daughters he once had great exercise, concern, and fear, relative to his engaging in that business; but since it now appeared, so far as he could see, that he was called of God to that place and work, he did cheerfully devote himself to it, leaving himself and the event with God to order what seemed to him good.

"The small-pox had now become very common in the country, and was then at Princeton, and likely to spread. And as Mr. Edwards had never had it, and inoculation was then practised with great success in those parts, he proposed to be inoculated, if the physician should advise to it, and the corporation would give their consent. Accordingly, by the advice of the physician, and the consent of the corporation, he was inoculated February 13th. He had it favourably, and it was thought all danger was over; but a secondary fever set in, and, by reason of a number of pustules in his throat, the obstruction was such, that the medicines necessary to check the fever could not be administered. It therefore raged till it put an end to his life, on the 22d of March, 1758, in the 55th year of his age.

"After he was sensible that he could not survive that sickness, a little before his death, he called his daughter to him, who attended him in his sickness, and addressed her in a few words, which were immediately taken down in writing, as near as could be recollected, and are as follows:—'Dear Lucy, It seems to me to be the will of God, that I must shortly leave you; therefore give my kindest love to my dear wife, and tell her, that the uncommon union, which has so long subsisted between us, has been of such a nature, as I trust is spiritual, and therefore will continue for ever: and I hope she will be supported under so great a trial, and submit cheerfully to the will of God. And as to my children, you are now like to be left fatherless; which I hope will be an inducement to you all, to seek a Father who will never fail you. And as to my funeral, I would have it to be like Mr. Burr's; and any additional sum of money, that might be expected to be laid out that way, I would have it disposed of to charitable uses.'†

"He said but very little in his sickness; but was an admirable instance of patience and resignation, to the last. Just at the close of his life, as some persons, who stood by, expecting he would breathe his last in a few minutes, were lamenting his death, not only as a great frown on the college, but as having a dark aspect on the interest of religion in general; to their surprise, not imagining that he heard, or ever would speak another word, he said, 'Trust in God, and ye need not fear.' These were his last words. What could have been more suitable to the occasion? And what need of more? In these there is as much matter of instruction and support, as if he had written a volume. This was the only consolation to his bereaved friends, deeply sensible as they were of the loss which they and the church of Christ had sustained in his death: GOD IS ALL-SUFFICIENT, AND STILL HAS THE CARE OF HIS CHURCH.‡

"He appeared to have the uninterrupted use of his reason to the last, and died with as much calmness and composure, to all appearance, as that with which one goes to sleep."

The physician, who inoculated and constantly attended him, in his sickness, addressed the following letter to Mrs. Edwards, on this occasion:

"To Mrs. Sarah Edwards, Stockbridge.

Princeton, March 22, 1758.

MOST DEAR AND VERY WORTHY MADAM,

I am heartily sorry for the occasion of writing to you, by this express, but I know you have been informed, by a line from your excellent, lovely, and pious husband, that I was brought here to inoculate him, and your dear daughter Esther, and her children, for the small-pox, which was then spreading fast in Princeton; and that, after the most deliberate and serious consultation, with his nearest and most religious friends, he was accordingly inoculated with them, the 23d of last month; and although he had the small-pox favourably, yet, having a number of them in the roof of his mouth and throat, he could not possibly swallow a sufficient quantity of drink, to keep off a secondary fever, which has proved too strong for his feeble frame; and this afternoon, between two and three o'clock, it pleased God to let him sleep in that dear Lord Jesus, whose kingdom and interest he has been faithfully and painfully serving all his life. And never did any mortal man more fully and clearly evidence the sincerity of all his professions, by one continued, universal, calm, cheerful resignation, and patient submission to the Divine will, through every stage of his disease, than he; not so much as one discontented expression, nor the least appearance of murmuring, through the whole. And never did any person expire with more perfect freedom from pain;—not so much as one distorted hair—but in the most proper sense of the words, he fell asleep. Death had certainly lost its sting, as to him.

Your daughter, Mrs. Burr, and her children, through

* The first sermon, which he preached at Princeton, was on the Unchangeableness of Christ, in Vol. II. p. 949. It was upwards of two hours in the delivery; but is said to have been listened to with such profound attention, and deep interest, by the audience, that they were unconscious of the lapse of time, and surprised that it closed so soon.

† President Burr ordered, on his death-bed, that his funeral should not be attended with pomp and cost; that nothing should be expended but what was agreeable to the dictates of christian decency; and that the sum which must be expended at a fashionable funeral, above the necessary cost of a decent one, should be given to the poor, out of his estate.

‡ The reader may wish to see the notice taken of the death of Mr. Edwards, at the time when it occurred. The following is the account of it, in the Boston Gazette, of April 10, 1750.—"On Wednesday, the 22d of last month, died, by inoculation, at Nassau Hall, an eminent servant of God, the Rev. pious, Mr. Jonathan Edwards, president of the college of New Jersey; a gentleman of distinguished abilities, and a heavenly temper of mind: a most rational, generous, catholic, and exemplary Christian, admired by all who knew him, for his uncommon candour and disinterested benevolence; a pattern of temperance, meekness, patience, and charity; always steady, calm, and serene; a very judicious and instructive preacher, and a most excellent divine. And, as he lived, cheerfully resigned to the will of Heaven, so he died, or rather, as the Scriptures emphatically express it, with respect to good men, *he fell asleep in Jesus*, without the least appearance of pain."

the mercy of God, are safely over the disease, and she desires me to send her duty to you, the best of mothers. She has had the small-pox the heaviest of all whom I have inoculated, and little Sally far the lightest; she has but three in her face. I am sure it will prove serviceable to her future health.

I conclude, with my hearty prayer, dear Madam, that you may be enabled to look to that God, whose love and goodness you have experienced a thousand times, for direction and help, under this most afflictive dispensation of his providence, and under every other difficulty, you may meet with here, in order to your being more perfectly fitted for the joys of heaven hereafter.

I am, dear Madam,
Your most sympathizing
And affectionate friend,
And very humble servant,
WILLIAM SHIPPEN."

This letter reached Mrs. Edwards while in a feeble state of health, when she was preparing to pay a visit, first to her sister, Mrs. Hopkins, at West Springfield, and then to her mother, Mrs. Edwards, of Windsor, in consequence of the death of Mr. Edwards's father. What her feelings were, and those of her family, under this unexpected and overwhelming dispensation, can be more easily conceived than described.

" She had long told her intimate friends, that she had, after long struggles and exercises, obtained, by God's grace, an habitual willingness to die herself, or part with any of her most near relatives. That she was willing to bring forth children for death; and to resign up him, whom she esteemed so great a blessing to her and her family, her nearest partner, to the stroke of death, whenever God should see fit to take him. And when she had the greatest trial, in the death of Mr. Edwards, she found the help and comfort of such a disposition. Her conduct on this occasion was such as to excite the admiration of her friends; it discovered that she was sensible of the great loss, which she and her children had sustained in his death; and, at the same time, showed that she was quiet and resigned, and had those invisible supports, which enabled her to trust in God with quietness, hope, and humble joy."

A few days afterwards, she addressed the following letter to Mrs. Burr.

" *Stockbridge, April* 3, 1758.

My very dear Child,

What shall I say? A holy and good God has covered us with a dark cloud. O that we may kiss the rod, and lay our hands on our mouths! The Lord has done it. He has made me adore his goodness, that we had him so long. But my God lives; and he has my heart. O what a legacy my husband, and your father, has left us! We are all given to God; and there I am, and love to be.

Your ever affectionate mother,
SARAH EDWARDS."

On the same sheet was the following letter from one of her daughters.

" My dear Sister,

My mother wrote this with a great deal of pain in her neck, which disabled her from writing any more. She thought you would be glad of these few lines from her own hand.

O, sister, how many calls have we, one upon the back of another. O, I beg your prayers, that we, who are young in this family, may be awakened and excited to call more earnestly on God, that he would be our Father and Friend for ever.

My father took leave of all his people and family as affectionately as if he knew he should not come again. On the sabbath afternoon he preached from these words,—*We have no continuing city, therefore let us seek one to come.* The chapter that he read was Acts the 20th. O, how proper; what could he have done more? When he had got out of doors he turned about,—'I commit you to God,'—said he.—I doubt not but God will take a fatherly care of us, if we do not forget him.

I am your affectionate sister,
SUSANNAH EDWARDS.

Stockbridge, April 3, 1758."

" Mrs. Burr and her children were inoculated at the same time that her father was, and had recovered when he died. But after she was perfectly recovered, to all appearance, she was suddenly seized with a violent disorder, which carried her off in a few days; and which, the physician said, he could call by no name, but that of *a messenger, sent suddenly, to call her out of the world.* She died April 7, 1758, sixteen days after her father, in the 27th year of her age. She was married to Mr. Burr June 29, 1752. They had two children, a son and a daughter.

" Mrs. Burr exceeded most of her sex in the beauty of her person, as well as in her behaviour and conversation. She discovered an unaffected, natural freedom, towards persons of all ranks, with whom she conversed. Her genius was much more than common. She had a lively, sprightly imagination, a quick and penetrating discernment, and a good judgment. She possessed an uncommon degree of wit and vivacity; which yet was consistent with pleasantness and good nature; and she knew how to be facetious and sportive, without trespassing on the bounds of decorum, or of strict and serious religion. In short, she seemed formed to please, and especially to please one of Mr. Burr's taste and character, in whom he was exceedingly happy. But what crowned all her excellencies, and was her chief glory, was religion. She appeared to be the subject of divine impressions, when seven or eight years old; and she made a public profession of religion, when about fifteen. Her conversation, until her death, was exemplary, as becometh godliness."—She was, in every respect, an ornament to her sex, being equally distinguished for the suavity of her manners, her literary accomplishments, and her unfeigned regard to religion. Her religion did not cast a gloom over her mind, but made her cheerful and happy, and rendered the thought of death transporting. She left a number of manuscripts, on interesting subjects, and it was hoped they would have been made public; but they are now lost.

Mrs. Edwards did not long survive her husband. In September she set out, in good health, on a journey to Philadelphia, to take care of her two orphan grand-children, which were now in that city; and had been, since the death of Mrs. Burr. As they had no relations in those parts, Mrs. Edwards proposed to take them into her own family. She arrived there, by the way of Princeton, Sept. 21, in good health, having had a comfortable journey.

But, in a few days, she was seized with a violent dysentery, which, on the fifth day, put an end to her life, October 2d, 1758, in the 49th year of her age. She said not much in her sickness; being exercised, most of the time, with violent pain. On the morning of the day she died, she apprehended her death was near, when she expressed her entire resignation to God, and her desire that he might be glorified in all things; and that she might be enabled to glorify him to the last: and continued in such a temper, calm and resigned, till she died.

Her remains were carried to Princeton, and deposited with those of Mr. Edwards. Thus they who were in their lives remarkably lovely and pleasant, in their death were not much divided. Here, the father and mother, the son and daughter, were laid together in the grave, within the space of a little more than a year; though a few months before their dwelling was more than 150 miles apart:—two presidents of the same college, and their consorts, than whom it will doubtless be hard to find four persons more valuable and useful!

By these repeated strokes, following in quick succession, the American church, within a few months, sustained a loss, which probably, in so short a space of time, will never be equalled.

Mr. and Mrs. Edwards lived together, in the married state, above thirty years; in which time they had eleven children, three sons and eight daughters. The second daughter died Feb. 14, 1748. The third daughter was Mrs. Burr. The youngest daughter, Elizabeth, died soon after her parents.*

The trustees of the college erected a marble monument over the grave of Mr. Edwards, which has the following inscription:

M. S.
Reverendi admodum Viri,
JONATHAN EDWARDS, A. M.
Collegii Novæ Cæsariæ Præsidis.
Natus apud Windsor Connecticutensium V. Octobris.
A. D. MDCCIII, S. V.
Patre Reverendo Timotheo Edwards oriundus,
Collegio Yalensi educatus;
Apud Northampton Sacris initiatus, XV Februarii,
MDCCXXVI-VII.
Illinc dimissus XXII Junii, MDCCL.
Et Munus Barbaros instituendi accepit.
Præses Aulæ Nassovicæ creatus XVI Februarii.
MDCCLVIII.
Defunctus in hoc Vico XXII Martii sequentis, S. N.
Ætatis LV, heu nimis brevis!
Hic jacet mortalis pars.
Qualis Persona quæris, Viator?
Vir Corpore procero, sed gracili,
Studiis intensissimis, Abstinentia, et Sedulitate,
Attenuato.
Ingenii acumine, Judicio acri, et Prudentiâ,
Secundus Nemini Mortalium.
Artium liberalium et Scientiarum peritia insignis,
Criticorum sacrorum optimus, Theologus eximius,
Ut vix alter æqualis; Disputator candidus;
Fidei Christianæ Propugnator validus et invictus;
Conciniator gravis, serius, discriminans;
Et, Deo ferente, Successu
Felicissimus.
Pietate præclarus, Moribus suis severus,
Ast aliis æquus et benignus.
Vixit dilectus, veneratus—
Sed, ah! lugendus
Moriebatur.
Quantos Gemitus discedens ciebat!
Heu Sapientia tanta! heu Doctrina et Religio!
Amissum plorat Collegium, plorat et Ecclesia:
At, eo recepto, gaudet
Cœlum.
Abi, Viator, et pia sequere Vestigia.

* See Appendix, No. 5.

CHAPTER XXV.

CONCLUDING REMARKS.

The writer of the preceding pages regrets, at least as sincerely as any of his readers, that the collection of facts, which they contain, is not more full and complete; yet, in consequence of the long interval which has elapsed since the death of President Edwards, they are all, which after much time, and labour, and travel, he has been able to discover. Such as they are, they constitute, with his writings, the body of materials from which we are to form our estimate of his character, as an intelligent and moral being.

In reviewing them, it is delightful to remember, in the outset, that so far as the human eye could judge, the individuals of both the families from which he derived his descent, were, as far back as we can trace them, distinguished for their piety. Each married pair, in both lines, with that care and conscientiousness which so generally marked the pilgrims of New England, and their puritan ancestors, trained up their children in the fear of God, and continued through life to supplicate daily the divine favour on them and their descendants, in all succeeding generations. Their prayers, ascending separately and successively indeed, were yet embodied in their influence, and from Him, who "showeth mercy to thousands of generations of them that love him, and keep his commandments," called down concentrated blessings on their common offspring. So full, so rich, were these blessings, as bestowed on the subject of this Memoir, that, perhaps, no one example on record furnishes a stronger encouragement to parents, to wrestle with God for the holiness and the salvation of their posterity.

It was owing to the moral influence thus exerted, and to the divine favour thus secured, that when we review the childhood and youth of Mr. Edwards, we find them not only passing without a stain upon his memory, but marked by a purity and excellence rarely witnessed at so early a period of life. The religious impressions made upon his mind in childhood, were certainly frequent, deep, and of long continuance, and had a powerful effect upon his ultimate character; yet the estimate formed of their real nature by different persons will probably be different. His own estimate of them was, unquestionably, that they were not the result of real religion.

The circumstances which led him to this conclusion, were these two:—First, That, after he had cherished the hope of his own conversion, for a considerable period, and had experienced a high degree of joy, in what he regarded as communion with God, he lost imperceptibly this spirituality of mind, relinquished for a season the "constant performance" of the practice of secret prayer, and cherished many affections of a worldly and sinful character:—Secondly, That when he recovered from this state of declension, his views of divine truth, particularly those connected with the sovereignty of God, were in many respects new, and far more clear and delightful than any which he had previously formed.

Without calling in question the fact, that a given individual has, on some accounts, decidedly superior advantages for judging of his own christian character, than others enjoy; and without presuming to decide on the correctness of the estimate, thus formed by Mr. Edwards; it may not be improper to state various circumstances, which lead me to suspect, that it may perhaps have been erroneous. 1. The declension, of which he complains, appears to have been chiefly, or wholly, a declension in the state of the affections. 2. Those impressions began when he was seven or eight years of age, and were so powerful and lasting, as to render religion the great object of attention, for a number of years. As made on the mind of such a child, they were very remarkable, even if we suppose them to have resulted in piety. 3. The season of his declension commenced soon after his admission to college, when he was twelve years of age. That a truly pious child, in consequence of leaving his early religious connexions and associations, and especially the altar and the incense of the parental sanctuary; of removing to a new place of residence, of entering on a new course of life, of forming new acquaintances and attachments, of feeling the strong attractions of study, and the powerful incentives of ambition, and of being exposed to the new and untried temptations of a public seminary; should, for a season, so far decline from his previous spirituality, as to lose all hope of his own conversion, is so far from being a surprising event, that, in ordinary cases, it is perhaps to be expected. Piety, at its commencement in the mind, is usually feeble; and especially is it so, in the mind of a child. How often are similar declensions witnessed, even at a later age. Yet the subject of such backsliding, though, during its continuance, he may well renounce the hope of his conversion, does not usually regard the period of his recovery as the commencement of his christian life.—4. He had not, at this period, made a public profession of religion; and, of course, was not restrained from such declension by his own covenant, by communion with Christians, or by the consciousness, that, as a visible Christian, his faults were subjected to the inspection and the censure of the surrounding world. 5. Though charitable in judging others, he was at least equally severe in judging himself. 6. He appears, at a very early period, to have formed views of the purity of the christian character—of the degree of freedom from sin, and of the degree of actual holiness, requisite to justify the hope of conversion—altogether more elevated in their nature, than the truth will warrant. 7. That his views of divine truth—particularly of the sovereignty of God—should have opened, after the age of twelve, with so much greater clearness and beauty, as to appear wholly new, was to have been expected from the nature of the case. 8. At a subsequent period, when his mind was incessantly occupied by the unusual perplexities of his tutorship, he complained of a similar declension. 9. The purity, strength, and comprehensiveness of his piety, as exhibited *immediately after* his public profession of Christianity, was so much superior to what is frequently witnessed, in Christians of an advanced standing, as almost to force upon us the conviction that it commenced—not a few months before, at the time of his supposed conversion, but—at a much earlier period of life. Rare indeed is the fact, that holiness is not, at its commencement in the soul, "as a grain of mustard-seed, which is the least of all seeds;" and though in the rapidity of its growth, it differs widely in different soils, yet *time* is indispensably necessary, before its fruits can cover the full-grown plant, like the clusters on the vine.—These considerations, and particularly the last, have led me to believe, that the early religious impressions of Mr. Edwards are to be regarded, as having been the result of a gracious operation of the Spirit of God upon his heart.

Under this happy influence, exerted in childhood, his character was formed. It prompted him then to study the Scriptures, to love prayer, to sanctify the sabbath, and to pay an unusual attention to the duties of religion. It inspired him with reverence towards God, and made him afraid to sin. It rendered him conscientious in the performance of every relative duty, in manifesting love and gratitude, honour and obedience, towards his parents, kindness and courteousness towards his sisters, and the other companions of his childhood, respect and deference to his superiors, and good will to all around him. It led him also, at a very early period, to overcome that aversion to mental labour, which is so natural to man, and to devote himself with exemplary assiduity to the great duty, daily assigned him, of storing his mind with useful knowledge. Some of our readers, we are aware, may perhaps regard the recollections of his earlier years, as of little importance; but those, who cherish common sympathies, with the whole body of evangelical Christians, in the deep interest which they feel in his character and efforts, and who reflect, that the foundation of that character and of those efforts was then laid, will require of us no apology for thus exhibiting the comparative innocence and purity, the docility and amiableness, the tenderness of conscience, the exemplary industry, and the ardent thirst for knowledge, which characterized this vernal season of his life.

The development of mental superiority, in the childhood and youth of Mr. Edwards, was certainly uncommon, if not singular. Boys of the age of eleven and twelve, even when receiving every aid from their parents and instructors, and when feeling the influence of all the motives, which *they* can present, are usually unwilling, in any branch of natural science, to examine, so as thoroughly to comprehend, the discoveries and investigations of others.

Still more unwilling are they to make this examination, when no such aid is furnished, and no such inducements are presented. But rare indeed is the instance, in which the attention of such a boy has been so far arrested, by any of the interesting phenomena, in either of the kingdoms of nature, that he has been led, without prompting, and without aid, to pursue a series of exact observations and discoveries, as to the facts themselves; to search out their causes; and, as the result of the whole, to draw up and present a lucid, systematic, and well digested report of his investigations.

After the lapse of a little more than a year, just as he attained the age of fourteen, we find him entering on pursuits of a still higher character. Few boys of that age have sufficient strength of intellect to comprehend the Essay on the Human Understanding. Of those who have, but a small proportion can be persuaded to read it; and a much smaller, still, are found to read it voluntarily, and of choice. We find Edwards, however, at this period of life, not only entering on this work of his own accord, and with deep interest, but at once relinquishing every other pursuit, that he may devote himself wholly to the philosophy of the mind; and, to use his own language, " enjoying a far higher pleasure in the perusal of its pages, than the most greedy miser finds, when gathering up handfuls of silver and gold, from some newly discovered treasure." Nor is this all. While reading the work of Locke, he presents himself before us, not as a pupil, nor simply as a critic; but in the higher character of an investigator, exploring for himself the universe of minds, and making new and interesting discoveries. Fortunately his investigations are preserved, and may be compared with the efforts of other distinguished men, at the same period of life, in other countries and in other ages. And if any one of all those efforts discovers greater perspicacity and mental energy, than the " Notes on the Mind;" particularly, the articles entitled, *Being*, *Space*, *Motion*, *Genus*, *the Will*, *and Excellency;* we are yet to learn where it is to be found, and who was its author. The discussion of the very important and difficult question, in the last of these articles, What is the foundation of excellency,—of excellency in its most enlarged acceptation, in things material and spiritual, in things intellectual, imaginative, and moral,—is not only original, as to its youthful author, and profound, but is even now, we believe, in various respects, new to the investigations of philosophy.* The Notes on Natural Science, furnish similar proofs of high mental superiority; and, by their variety of topics, their general accuracy, and their originality, evince a power and comprehension, discovered by only here and there an individual, when possessed of the full maturity of his faculties. His habits of thinking and reasoning, at this time of life, appear to have been as severe, as exact, and as successful, as those of the most accomplished scholars usually are, in the vigour of manhood. The plan of study, itself, which he then formed,—of studying with his pen; and of immediately, and of course, employing the principles of the science he was examining, which had been already detailed and demonstrated by others, in the discovery of new principles,—is at least equal evidence of the same superiority. So vigorous was the mental soil, that the seeds of thought could not be implanted therein, without being quickened at once, and made to grow into a rich and abundant harvest. Looking at these two series of Notes, in connexion with the plan of study under which they grew, and then comparing them, by the aid of recollection, witn the efforts of other children and youths of uncommon promise; we instinctively ask, When, and where, has the individual lived, who has left behind him substantial proofs, that he has possessed, at the same age, a mind more powerful, comprehensive, or creative?

These conclusions are only confirmed by the survey of his succeeding years. Though drawn away from the entire devotion of his mind to his collegiate studies, by (what were to him) the alluring blandishments of mental philosophy, he yet sustained in his class the first standing as a scholar; and, though leaving college when sixteen, he was not too young to receive its highest honours. Having entered the pulpit at eighteen, he was, after a few trials, designated by a number of gentlemen of a superior character, for a very important and difficult station; to which, as well as to various other interesting fields of labour, he received most pressing invitations.

The extraordinary difficulties and perplexities of the college, while he was one of its officers, sufficient as they were to have overwhelmed a common mind, only served to furnish him and his colleagues a fairer opportunity, to show forth the superiority of their own character. By their wisdom and fidelity, the college was preserved and enlarged, when in imminent danger of ruin; and the period of their administration will ever be regarded as one of the most important eras in its history.

While the review of the childhood and youth of Mr. Edwards thus forces upon us the conviction, that, in the early development of extraordinary mental powers, he has had few equals; and enables us to reflect, with pleasure, that these powers were never prostituted to folly, or to vice, but from the beginning were faithfully devoted to the great end for which they were given; it also leads us to remark, that his character, as a moral being, was thoroughly formed and established, at a very early period of life. Like a dutiful child, he listened, indeed, to the counsels of his parents, as to the principles by which his conduct should be regulated; but he also examined for himself the foundations of those principles, and, having discovered that they were firm and immovable, formed out of them a series of rules, for the systematic regulation of his own conduct. These rules, particularly as exemplified in the journal of his daily life, evince not only a pure and transparent sincerity, and the greatest openness of soul towards God; as well as an inspection, metaphysically accurate, of his own mind, and a thorough acquaintance with his own heart; but a knowledge of his duty,—to God, his fellow-men, and himself,—and a conscientiousness in performing it, which are usually the result of great wisdom and piety, combined with long experience. They grew, obviously, out of a disposition to turn every occurrence of life to a religious use, and thus to grow wiser and better, continually, under the course of discipline to which the providence of God subjected him. They appear to have been made under the immediate inspection of the Omniscient eye, with a solemn conviction that he was an immortal being, formed to act on the same theatre with God, and angels, and the just made perfect, in carrying forward the kingdom of holiness and joy, in its ever enlarging progress. Viewing himself as just entering on this career of glory, he adopted, for the permanent direction of his course, the best and noblest resolution, that an

* The last article under this head, is obviously the foundation of the author's subsequent Treatise on the Nature of True Virtue.

intelligent being can form :—" Resolved, That I will do *whatsoever* I think to be most to the glory of God, and my own good, profit, and pleasure, in the whole of my duration; without any consideration of *the time*, whether now, or never so many myriads of ages hence: resolved, to do whatsoever I think to be my *duty*, and most for the good and advantage of mankind in general: resolved, so to do, whatever *difficulties* I meet with, how many soever, and how great soever." In the spirit of this resolution, we find him, with all the earnestness of which he was capable, giving up himself to God,—all that he was, and all that he possessed,—so as habitually to feel that he was in no respect his own, and could challenge no right to the faculties of his body, to the powers of his mind, or the affections of his heart; receiving Christ as a Prince and a Saviour, under a solemn covenant to adhere to the faith and obedience of the gospel, however hazardous and difficult the profession and practice of it might be; and taking the Holy Spirit as his Teacher, Sanctifier, and only Comforter. And, in accordance with both, we find him, at this time, regularly making the glory of God the great end for which he lived; habitually trusting in God, to such a degree, as to feel no uneasiness about his worldly condition; maintaining the most open and confidential intercourse with his Maker; cherishing exalted thoughts of Christ and his salvation; feeling himself to be a part of Christ, and to have no separate interest from his; exercising a filial and delightful sense of dependence on the Holy Spirit, for the daily communication of his grace; regarding communion with God as the very life and sustenance of the soul; delighting in praising God, and in singing his praises, and as much when alone, as in the company of others; often observing days of secret fasting, that he might discover, and repent of, and renounce every sin; maintaining a constant warfare against sin and temptation; frequently renewing his dedication of himself to God; conversing daily and familiarly with his own death and his own final trial; rejoicing habitually in the divine perfections and the divine government; reverentially acknowledging the divine hand in all the works of nature, and in all the events of providence; exhibiting a calm and sweet submission to the divine will under all the afflictions of life, so that he could regard afflictions as real and great blessings; and enabled so to live with God, from day to day, and from hour to hour, as to be delightfully conscious of his presence, to refer his inmost mind to the inspection of his eye, to value his approbation above all things else, to cherish a joyful sense of union to him, to converse with him, as a father, concerning his wants, infirmities, and sins, his dangers, duties, and trials, his joys and sorrows, his fears and desires, his hopes and prospects, and to commune with him in all his works and dispensations, in his perfections and his glory. And, as the result of this, we find the Spirit of God unfolding to him the wonders of divine truth; vouchsafing to him joyful and glorious discoveries of the perfections of God, as the Father, the Son, and the Holy Spirit; enabling him to live, as in the immediate presence and vision of the things that are unseen and eternal; and communicating to him a joyful assurance of the favour of God, and of a title to future glory.

This state of his heart towards God, prepared him for a just estimate of his own character, for the formation of the best habits, and for a conscientious and faithful government over himself. The daily and careful survey of his sins, by the light of the divine holiness, enabled him to discover the deceitfulness of his own heart, and led him habitually to abhor himself, to form none but humbling and abasing views of his own attainments in piety, and to esteem others better than himself. There was something extremely delicate in his constitution; which always obliged him to the exactest rules of temperance, and every method of cautious and prudent living. His temperance was the result of principle. It was not the mere ordinary care and watchfulness of temperate people, but such a degree of self-denial, both as to the quantity and quality of his food, as left his mind, in every part of the day, alike unclouded in its views, and unembarrassed in its movements. We have seen, from his diary, that he rose at a very early hour, throughout the year; that, in the morning, he considered well the business and studies of the day, resolved to pursue that which was the most important; that his habits of punctuality were exact and thorough; that he husbanded his time, as the miser guards his choicest treasures; not losing it even in his walks, his rides, or his journeys; and not allowing himself to leave his study for the table, if his mind would thereby lose its brighter moments, and its happier sequences of thought and discovery; and that, in consequence of this regularity of life, and an exact and punctilious regard to bodily exercise, he was enabled to spend an unusual portion of every day, in severe and laborious mental application.* Let it also be remembered, by every minister, that notwithstanding the exact discipline to which his mind had been subjected, by the course of his education, and by his long devotion to metaphysical pursuits, he continued his attention to *mathematical* studies, as a source, alike, of recreation and improvement, throughout the whole of his ministerial life.

The habits of his religious life, which he formed in his youth, were not less thorough and exact. His observation of the sabbath was such as to make it, throughout, a day of real religion; so that not only were his conversation and reading conformed to the great design of the day, but he allowed himself in no thoughts or meditations, which were not decidedly of a religious character. It was his rule, not only to search the Scriptures daily, but to study them so steadily, constantly, and frequently, as that he might perceive a regular and obvious growth in his knowledge of them. By prayer and self-application, he took constant care to render them the means of progressive sanctification. He made a secret of his private devotions, observes Dr. Hopkins, and therefore they cannot be particularly known; though there is much evidence that he was punctual, constant, and frequent in secret prayer, and often kept days of fasting and prayer in secret, and set apart time for serious, devout meditations on spiritual and eternal things, as part of his religious exercises in secret. It appears from his diary, that his *stated* seasons of secret prayer were, from his youth, three times a day,—in his journeys, as well as at home. He was, so far as can be known, much on his knees in secret, and in devout reading of God's word, and meditation upon it. And his constant, solemn converse with God, in these exercises of secret religion, made his face, as it were, to shine before others. His appearance, his countenance, his words, and whole demeanour, were attended with a seriousness,

* On a preceding page it is stated, on the authority of Dr. Hopkins, that he regularly spent *thirteen hours*, every day, in close study. After receiving the invitation to Princeton, he told his eldest son, that he had for many years spent *fourteen hours* a day in study; and mentioned the necessity of giving up a part of this time to other pursuits, as one of his chief objections against accepting the office of president.

gravity and solemnity, which was the natural, genuine indication and expression, of a deep abiding sense of divine things on his mind, and of his living constantly in the fear of God. His watchfulness over himself—over his external conduct and over his secret thoughts and purposes—was most thorough and exemplary. The fear of God, and a consciousness of his own weakness, made him habitually apprehensive of sin, and led him most carefully to avoid every temptation. His self-examination was regular, universal, and in a sense constant. Every morning he endeavoured to foresee, and to guard against, the dangers of the day. Every night he carefully reviewed the conduct of his mind, during its progress, and inquired, wherein he had been negligent; what sin he had committed; wherein he had denied himself; and regularly kept an account of every thing which he found to be wrong. This record he reviewed at the close of the week, of the month, and of the year, and on the occurrence of every important change in life; that he might know his own condition, and that he might carry his sins in humble confession before God. Whenever he so much questioned whether he had done his duty, as that the quiet of his mind was thereby disturbed, he regularly set it down, that he might examine its real nature; and, if found in any respect to be wrong, might put it away. Every course of conduct, which led him in the least to doubt of the love of God; every action of his mind, the review of which would give him uneasiness in the hour of death, and on his final trial; he endeavoured, with all his strength, to avoid. Every obvious sin he traced back to its original, that he might afterward know where his danger lay. Every desire, which might prove the occasion of sin,—the desire of wealth, of ease, of pleasure, of influence, of fame, of popularity,—as well as every bodily appetite, he strove not only to watch against, but habitually and unceasingly to mortify; regarding occasions of great self-denial as glorious opportunities of destroying sin, and of confirming himself in holiness; and uniformly finding that his greatest mortifications were succeeded by the greatest comforts. On the approach of affliction, he searched out the sin, which he ought especially to regard, as calling for such a testimony of the divine displeasure, that he might receive the chastisement with entire submission, and be concerned about nothing but his duty and his sin. The virtues and sins of others led him to examine himself, whether he possessed the former, and whether he did not practise the latter. Thus his whole life was a continued course of self-examination; and in the duty of secret fasting, and humiliation, which he very frequently observed,—a duty enjoined by Christ, on his followers, as explicitly, and in the same terms, as the duty of secret prayer; enjoined too, for the very purpose of discovery, confession, and purification,—he was accustomed, with the greatest unreservedness of which he was capable, to declare his ways to God, and to lay open his soul before him, all his sins, temptations, difficulties, sorrows, and fears, as well as his desires and hopes; that the light of God's countenance might shine upon him without obstruction.

The fear of God had a controlling influence, also, in regulating his intercourse with mankind. The basis of that intercourse, in all the relations of life, and indeed of his whole character, was *evangelical integrity*,—a settled unbending resolution to do what he thought right, whatever self-denial or sacrifices it might cost him. This trait of character he early discovered, in the unfavourable estimate, which he formed, of his youthful attainments in religion; and in the severe judgment, which he passed upon the period of his official connexion with college, as a period of marked declension in his christian life. He discovered it, during that connexion, in his most conscientious and honourable efforts to promote the welfare of that institution, under uncommon difficulties and trials. He discovered it during his ministry at Northampton, in the very laborious performance of every ministerial duty, and in his firm and fearless defence of the truth, in opposition to numbers, power, and influence. He discovered it eminently in the affair of his dismission. His conscience at first hesitated, as to the lawfulness of the prevailing mode of admission to the church. Still, he regarded the question as altogether doubtful. It had been once publicly discussed; his own colleague and grandfather, who had introduced it at Northampton, being one of the combatants; and the victory had been supposed to be on *his* side, and in favour of the existing mode. The churches of the county had adopted it; and the whole current of public opinion,—the united voice of wealth, fashion, numbers, learning, and influence,—was in its favour. If he decided against continuing the practice, all these would certainly be combined against him; his people would demand his dismission, before a tribunal which had prejudged the case; his only means of supporting a young and numerous family would be taken away, at a time of life, when an adequate provision for their wants would probably involve him in extreme embarrassment. Yet none of these things moved him; and his only anxiety was, to ascertain and to perform his duty. He discovered it, in the same manner, in the controversy at Stockbridge. There, the same influence, which, in the former case, had effected his dismission, he knew would be combined against him, with increased hostility, and in all probability would deprive his family a second time of their support; unless he sat quietly, and saw the charities of christian philanthropy perverted to sources of private emolument. But in such a crisis he could not deliberate for a moment.

" He had a strict and inviolable regard to justice, in all his dealings with his neighbours, and was very careful to provide things honest in the sight of all men; so that scarcely a man had any dealings with him, who was not conscious of his uprightness.

" His great benevolence to mankind discovered itself, among other ways, by the uncommon regard he showed to liberality, and charity to the poor and distressed. He was much in recommending this, both in his public discourses, and in private conversation. He often declared it to be his opinion, that professed Christians were greatly deficient in this duty, and much more so than in most other parts of external Christianity. He often observed how much this is spoken of, recommended, and encouraged, in the Holy Scriptures, especially in the New Testament. And it was his opinion, that every particular church ought, by frequent and liberal contributions, to maintain a public stock, that might be ready for the poor and necessitous members of that church; and that the principal business of deacons is, to take care of the poor, in the faithful and judicious improvement and distribution of the church's contributions, lodged in their hands. And he did not content himself with merely recommending charity to others, but practised it much himself: though, according to his Master's advice, he took great care to conceal his acts of charity; by which means, doubtless, most of his alms-deeds will be unknown till the resurrection, but which, if known, would prove him to have been as honourable an example of charity, as almost any that can be produced. This is not mere conjecture, but is evident many ways. He was forward to give, on all public occasions of charity; though, when it could properly be done, he always concealed the sum given. And some instances of his giving more privately have accidentally come to the knowledge of others, in which his liberality appeared in a very extraordinary degree. One of the instances was this: upon his hearing that a poor obscure man, whom he never saw, or any of his kindred, was, by an extraordinary bodily disorder, brought to great straits; he, unasked, gave a considerable sum to a friend, to be delivered to the distressed person; having first required a promise of him, that he would let neither the person, who was the object of his charity, nor any one else, know by whom it was given. This may serve both as an instance of his extraordinary charity, and of his great care to conceal it."*

Not less exemplary was his practice of the kindred virtue of hospitality, so much enjoined on all Christians, in the sacred Scriptures. As his acquaintance was very extensive, his house was the frequent resort of gentlemen from all parts of the colonies; and the friend, and the stranger of worth, ever found a kind and cordial welcome at his table, and in the midst of his family.

"He was thought by some to be *distant* and *unsociable* in his manners; but this was owing to the want of a better acquaintance. He was not, indeed, a man of many words, and was somewhat reserved in the company of strangers, and of those, on whose candour and friendship he did not know that he could rely. And this was probably owing to two causes. First, the strict guard he set over his tongue, from his youth. From experience and observation he early discovered, that the sins of the tongue make up a very formidable proportion of all the sins committed by men, and lead to a very large proportion of their remaining sins. He therefore resolved to take the utmost care, *never to sin with his tongue;* to avoid not only uttering reproaches himself, but receiving them, and listening to them from others; to say nothing for the sake of giving pain, or wounding the feelings or reputation of others; to say nothing evil concerning them, except when an obvious duty required him to do it, and then to speak, as if nobody had been as vile as himself, and as if he had committed the same sins, or had the same infirmities or failings, as others; never to employ himself in idle, trivial, and impertinent talk, which generally makes up a great part of the conversation of those, who are full of words, in all companies; and to make sure of that mark of a perfect man, given by James, 'If any man offend not *in word*, the same is a perfect man, and able, also, to bridle the whole body.' He was sensible, that 'in the multitude of words there wanteth not sin;' and therefore refrained his lips, and habituated himself to *think* before he *spoke*, and to propose some good end in all his words; which led him, conformably to an apostolic precept, to be, above many others, *slow to speak*.—Secondly, this was in part the effect of his bodily constitution. He possessed but a comparatively small stock of animal life: his spirits were low, and he had neither the vivacity nor strength of lungs to spare, that would have been requisite in order to render him what might be called an affable, sprightly companion, in all circles. They who have a great flow of animal spirits, and so can speak with more ease, and less expense and exhaustion, than others, may doubtless lawfully engage in free conversation, in all companies, for a lower end than that which he proposed: *e. g.* to please, or to render themselves agreeable to others. But not so he who has not such an abundant supply: it becomes him to reserve what he has for higher and more important service. Besides, the want of animal spirit lays a man under a *natural* inability of exercising that freedom of conversation, at all times, and in whatever company he is, which those possessed of more vivacity naturally and easily glide into; and the greatest degree of humility and benevolence, of good sense and social feeling, will not remove this obstacle.

"He was not forward to enter into any dispute before strangers, and in companies where there might be persons of different sentiments; being sensible that such disputes are generally unprofitable, and often sinful, and of bad consequence. He thought he could dispute to the best advantage with his pen; yet he was always free to give his sentiments, on any subject proposed to him, and to remove any difficulties or objections offered by way of inquiry, as lying in the way of what he looked upon to be the truth. But how groundless, with regard to him, the imputation of being *distant* and *unsociable* was, his known and tried friends best knew. They always found him easy of access, kind and condescending; and though not talkative, yet affable and free. Among those, whose candour and friendship he had experienced, he threw off all that, which to others had the appearance of reserve, and was most open and communicative; and was always patient of contradiction, while the utmost opposition was made to his sentiments, that could be made by any arguments or objections, whether plausible or solid. And indeed he was, on all occasions, quite sociable and free with all who had any special business with him.

"His conversation with his friends was always savoury and profitable: in this he was remarkable, and almost singular. He was not accustomed to spend his time with them in evil speaking, or foolish jesting, idle chit-chat, and telling stories; but his mouth was that of the just, which bringeth forth wisdom, and whose lips dispense knowledge. His tongue was as the pen of a ready writer, while he conversed about important heavenly and divine things, of which his heart was so full, in a manner so new and original, so natural and familiar, as to be most entertaining and instructive; so that none of his friends could enjoy his company without instruction and profit, unless it was by their own fault.

"He was cautious in choosing his *intimate friends*, and therefore had not many that might properly be called such; but to them he showed himself friendly in a peculiar manner. He was, indeed, a faithful friend, and able above most others to keep a secret. To them he discovered himself, more than to others, and led them into his views and ends in his conduct in particular instances: by which they had abundant evidence that he well understood human nature, and that his general reservedness, and many particular instances of his conduct, which a stranger might

* "As both the giver, and the object of his charity, are dead, and all the ends of the proposed secrecy are answered; it is thought not inconsistent with the above-mentioned promise, to make known the fact, as it is here related."

impute to ignorance of men, were really owing to his uncommon knowledge of mankind.

"In his family, he practised that conscientious exactness, which was conspicuous in all his ways. He maintained a great esteem and regard for his amiable and excellent consort. Much of the tender and affectionate was expressed in his conversation with her, and in all his conduct towards her. He was often visited by her in his study, and conversed freely with her on matters of religion; and he used commonly to pray with her in his study, at least once a day, unless something extraordinary prevented. The season for this, commonly, was in the evening, after prayers in the family, just before going to bed. As he rose very early himself, he was wont to have his family up betimes in the morning; after which, before they entered on the business of the day, he attended on family prayers; when a chapter in the Bible was read, commonly by candle-light in the winter; upon which he asked his children questions, according to their age and capacity; and took occasion to explain some passages in it, or enforce any duty recommended, as he thought most proper.

He was careful and thorough in the government of his children; and, as a consequence of this, they reverenced, esteemed, and loved him. He took the utmost care to begin his government of them, when they were very young. When they first discovered any degree of self-will and stubbornness, he would attend to them, until he had thoroughly subdued them, and brought them to submit. Such prudent discipline, exercised with the greatest calmness, being repeated once or twice, was generally sufficient for that child; and effectually established his parental authority, and produced a cheerful obedience ever after.

"He kept a watchful eye over his children, that he might admonish them of the first wrong step, and direct them in the right way. He took opportunities to converse with them singly and closely, about the concerns of their souls, and to give them warnings, exhortations, and directions, as he saw them severally need." The salvation of his children was his chief and constant desire, and aim, and effort concerning them. In the evening, after tea, he customarily sat in the parlour, with his family, for an hour, unbending from the severity of study, entering freely into the feelings and concerns of his children, and relaxing into cheerful and animated conversation, accompanied frequently with sprightly remarks, and sallies of wit and humour. But, before retiring to his study, he usually gave the conversation, by degrees, a more serious turn, addressing his children, with great tenderness and earnestness, on the subject of their salvation; when the thought that they were still strangers to religion would often affect him so powerfully, as to oblige him to withdraw, in order to conceal his emotions.—"He took much pains to instruct his children in the principles and duties of religion, in which he made use of the Assembly's Shorter Catechism: not merely by taking care that they learned it by heart, but by leading them into an understanding of the doctrines therein taught, by asking them questions on each answer, and explaining it to them. His usual time to attend to this was on the evening before the sabbath. And, as he believed that the sabbath, or holy time, began at sunset, on the evening preceding the first day of the week, he ordered his family to finish all their secular business by that time, or before; when all were called together, a psalm was sung, and prayer offered, as an introduction to the sanctification of the sabbath. This care and exactness effectually prevented that intruding on holy time, by attending to secular business, which is too common even in families where the evening before the sabbath is professedly observed.

"He was utterly opposed to every thing like unseasonable hours, on the part of young people, in their visiting and amusements; which he regarded as a dangerous step towards corrupting them, and bringing them to ruin. And he thought the excuse offered by many parents, for tolerating this practice in their children,—*that it is the custom, and that the children of other people are allowed thus to practise, and therefore it is difficult, and even impossible, to restrain theirs,*—was insufficient and frivolous, and manifested a great degree of stupidity, on the supposition that the practice was hurtful and pernicious to their souls. And when his children grew up, he found no difficulty in restraining them from this improper and mischievous practice; but they cheerfully complied with the will of their parents. He allowed none of his children to be absent from home after nine o'clock at night, when they went abroad to see their friends and companions; neither were they allowed to sit up much after that time, in his own house, when any of their friends came to visit them. If any gentleman desired to address either of his daughters, after the requisite introduction and preliminaries, he was allowed all proper opportunities of becoming thoroughly acquainted with the manners and disposition of the young lady, but must not intrude on the customary hours of rest and sleep, nor on the religion and order of the family."

Perhaps there never was a man more constantly retired from the world, giving himself to reading and contemplation; and it was a wonder that his feeble frame could subsist under such fatigues, daily repeated, and so long continued. Yet, upon this being alluded to by one of his friends, only a few months before his death, he said to him, "I do not find but that I now am as well able to bear the closest study, as I was thirty years ago; and can go through the exercises of the pulpit with as little uneasiness or difficulty."—In his youth he appeared healthy, and with a good degree of vivacity, but was never robust. In middle life he appeared very much emaciated, by severe study, and intense mental application. In his person he was tall of stature, and of a slender form.* He had a high, broad, bold forehead, and an eye unusually piercing and luminous; and on his whole countenance the features of his mind—perspicacity, sincerity, and benevolence—were so strongly impressed, that no one could behold it without at once discovering the clearest indications of great intellectual and moral elevation. His manners were those of the christian gentleman, easy, tranquil, modest, and dignified; yet they were the manners of the student, grave, sedate, and contemplative; and evinced an exact sense of propriety, and an undeviating attention to the rules of decorum. "He had," observes one of his contemporaries, "a natural steadiness of temper, and fortitude of mind; which, being sanctified by the Spirit of God, was ever of vast advantage to him, to carry him through difficult services, and to support him under trying afflictions in the course of his life.—Personal injuries he bore with a becoming meekness and patience, and a disposition to forgiveness." According to Dr. Hopkins, him-

* His height was about six feet one inch.

self an eye-witness, these traits of character were eminently discovered, throughout the whole of his long-continued trials at Northampton. His own narrative of that transaction, his remarks before the council, his letters relating to it, and his farewell sermon, all written in the midst of the passing occurrences, bespeak as calm, and meek, and unperturbed a state of mind, as they would have done, had they been written by a third person, long after the events took place.—"The humility, modesty, and serenity of his behaviour, much endeared him to his acquaintance, and made him appear amiable in the eyes of such as had the privilege of conversing with them.—The several relations sustained by him, he adorned with exemplary fidelity; and was solicitous to fill every station with its proper duty.—In his private walk as a Christian, he appeared an example of truly rational, consistent, uniform religion and virtue; a shining instance of the power and efficacy of that holy faith, to which he was so firmly attached, and of which he was so zealous a defender. He exhibited much of spirituality, and a heavenly bent of soul. In him one saw the loveliest appearance—a rare assemblage of christian graces, united with the richest gifts, and mutually subserving and recommending one another."

"He had an uncommon thirst for knowledge, in the pursuit of which he spared no cost nor pains. He read all the books, especially books treating of theology, that he could procure, from which he could hope to derive any assistance in the discovery of truth. And in this, he did not confine himself to authors of any particular sect or denomination; but even took much pains to procure the works of the most distinguished writers, who advanced views of religion or morals most contrary to his own principles; particularly the ablest Arminian, Socinian, and infidel writers. But he studied the Bible more than all other books, and more than most other divines do." He studied the Bible, to receive implicitly what it teaches; but he read other books to examine their soundness, and to employ them as helps in the investigation of principles, and the discovery of truth. His uncommon acquaintance with the Bible, appears in his sermons, in his treatises,—particularly in the treatises on the Affections, on the History of Redemption, on United and Extraordinary Prayer, on the Types of the Messiah, on the Qualifications for Communion, and on God's Last End in the Creation,—in his Notes on the Scriptures, and in his Miscellaneous Observations and Remarks. Any person who will read his works with close attention, and then will compare them with those of other theological writers, since the days of the apostles, will easily be satisfied that no other divine has as yet appeared, who has studied the Scriptures more thoroughly, or who has been more successful in discovering the mind of the Holy Spirit. He took his religious principles from the Bible, and not from treatises, or systems of theology, or any work of man. On the maturest examination of the different schemes of faith, prevailing in the world, and on comparing them with the sacred Scriptures, he adhered to the main articles of the reformed religion, with an unshaken firmness and with a fervent zeal, yet tempered with charity and candour, and governed by discretion. Few men are less under the bias of education, or the influence of bigotry: few receive the articles of their creed so little upon trust, or discover so much liberality or thoroughness in examining their foundation. His principles have been extensively styled *Calvinistic*, yet they differ widely from what has usually been denominated *Calvinism*, in various important points; particularly, in all immediately connected with moral agency; and he followed implicitly, if any man ever followed, the apostolic injunction, to *call no man, Father*, by receiving nothing on human authority, and examining scrupulously every principle which he adopted. He thought, and investigated, and judged for himself; and from the strength of his reasoning powers, as well as from his very plan of study, he became truly an *original* writer. As we have already sufficiently seen, *reading* was not the only, nor the chief, method which he took of improving his mind; but he devoted the strength of his time and of his faculties to *writing*, without which no student, and, be it remembered, no minister, can make improvements to the best advantage. He preached extensively on subjects, continued through a series of discourses;—many of his treatises having been a course of sermons actually delivered from the desk. In this practice, every minister who has a mind fitted for investigation, would do well to follow him. "Agreeably to the 11th Resolution, he applied himself, with all his might, to find out truth: he searched for it as for silver, and digged for it as for hidden treasures. Every thought, on any subject, which appeared to him worth pursuing and preserving, he pursued as far as he then could, with a pen in his hand. Thus he was, all his days, like the industrious bee, collecting honey from every opening flower, and storing up a stock of knowledge, which was indeed sweet to him, as honey and the honey-comb."

"As a scholar, his intellectual furniture exceeded what was common, under the disadvantages experienced at that time, in these remote colonies. He had an extensive acquaintance with the arts and sciences—with classical and Hebrew literature, with physics, mathematics, history, chronology, ethics, and mental philosophy. By the blessing of God on his indefatigable labours, to the last, he was constantly treasuring up useful knowledge, both human and divine.

"Thus he appears to have been uncommonly accomplished for the arduous and momentous province to which he was finally called. And had his precious life been spared, there is every reason to believe, that he would have graced the station on which he had but entered, and proved a signal blessing to the college of New Jersey, and therein extensively served his generation according to the will of God."

His inattention to his style is certainly to be regretted. In earlier life, he appears to have thought neatness and correctness in writing of little consequence,* and to have sent his works to the press very much in the state in which they were first written. Let it here be remembered, that the cultivation of style was not then attended to in the colonies; that the people at large were accustomed to discourses written in the plainest manner; and that it is extremely doubtful, whether, in the then existing state of the country, it would have been possible for him to have devoted much attention to the style of his sermons, without greatly diminishing their amount of impression. About the time of his leaving Northampton, he received one of the works of Richardson,† which he read with deep interest, and regarded as wholly favourable to good morals and purity of character. The perusal of it led him to at-

* See Preface to Five Sermons, vol. i. p. 621.

† Sir Charles Grandison. I had this anecdote through his eldest son.

tempt the formation of a more correct style, his previous inattention to which he then deeply regretted; and in this attempt he had much success. The style of the Freedom of the Will, though obviously that of a student, and not of a man of the world, is otherwise as correct as that of most of the metaphysical treatises to be found in the language. The same is true, generally, of the Treatise on Original Sin; although it was in the press when he died, and never received his last corrections.* In the two highest excellences of style, perspicuity and precision, he was probably never excelled.

Of the powers of his mind, enough, perhaps, has been said already. They were certainly very varied, and fitted him for high distinction in any of the pursuits of learning or science.—His memory was strong, exact, uniform, and comprehensive.—His imagination was rich and powerful. I know that the contrary opinion has extensively prevailed, and that for three reasons. First, he paid little or no attention to his style of writing. Secondly, he never cultivated his imagination, and never indulged it but sparingly, and probably in no instance, for mere ornament. Thirdly, his great works are treatises on *metaphysical* subjects. A writer without imagination, always thinks and writes in a *dry* manner; and, if his powers are great, like those of Aristotle, he writes like a pure intelligence. Those who are conversant with the writings of Edwards, need not be informed that all his works, even the most metaphysical, are rich in illustration, or that his sermons abound with imagery of every kind, adapted to make a powerful and lasting impression. In his earlier writings, this faculty of his mind was suffered to act with less restraint. The first production of his pen, on the materiality of the soul, is a constant play of imagination and wit. The boy who could speak of the spiders of the forest, as "those wondrous animals, from whose glistening web so much of the wisdom of the Creator shines;"—who, in describing their operations, could say, "I have seen a vast multitude of little shining webs, and glistening strings, brightly reflecting the sun-beams, and some of them of great length, and of such a height, that one would think they were tacked to the vault of the heavens, and would be burnt like tow in the sun;"—and who, in exposing the absurdity of the supposition, that there can be absolutely nothing, observes, "When we go to form an idea of perfect nothing, we must not suffer our thoughts to take sanctuary in a mathematical point, but we must think of the same, that *the sleeping rocks do dream of;*"—possessed an imagination at once rich, brilliant, and creative.—His taste, if we do not refer to style of writing, but merely to the judgment of the mind, concerning all the varieties of sublimity and beauty, was at once delicate and correct.—Few of mankind, hitherto, have possessed either invention, ratiocination, or judgment in so high a degree; and it is difficult to say for which of these he is most distinguished. In comparing him with the metaphysicians of the old world, we must not forget his and their respective advantages for the culture of the mind. He was born in an obscure village, in which the ancient reign of barbarism was only beginning to yield to the inroads of culture and civilization; in a colony comprising but here and there a settlement; and in a country literally in its infancy, constituting with the exception of now and then a white plantation, one vast continuous forest, and distant three thousand miles from Europe, the seat of arts, refinement, and knowledge. He was educated at a seminary but three years older than himself; which had as yet no domicil, and which furnished advantages totally inferior to those now enjoyed at the respectable academies of New England. The rest of his life was passed amid the cares of a most laborious profession, and on the very frontiers (and the latter part of it in the very midst) of savage life; with no libraries to explore, and with no men of eminence with whose minds his could come into daily contact. His greatest work was written *in four months and a half*, while each sabbath he delivered two sermons to his English flock, and two others by interpreters, to two distinct auditories of Indians, and catechised the children of both tribes, and carried on all the correspondence of the mission, and was forced to guard against the measures of a powerful combination, busily occupied in endeavouring to drive him from his office, and thus to deprive his family of their daily bread.—With these things in view, instead of drawing any such comparison myself, I will refer my readers to the opinion of a writer of no light authority on such a subject,—I mean Dugald Stewart;—who, after having detailed the systems of Locke, and Leibnitz, and Berkeley, and Condillac, speaks thus of the subject of this Memoir:—"There is, however, *one* metaphysician, of whom America has to boast, who, in logical acuteness and subtilty, does not yield to any disputant bred in the universities of Europe. I need not say that I allude to Jonathan Edwards."

Mr. Edwards acquired a very high character, as a divine and as a preacher, during his life. "Among the luminaries of the church, in these American regions," says one of his contemporaries,† "he was justly reputed a star of the first magnitude; thoroughly versed in all the branches of theology, didactic, polemic, casuistic, experimental, and practical. In point of divine knowledge and skill, he had few equals, and perhaps no superior; at least in those foreign parts."—"Mr. Edwards," says Dr. Hopkins, "had the most universal character of a *good preacher*, of almost any minister in America. There were but few that heard him, who did not call him a good preacher, however they might dislike his religious principles, and be much offended at the same truths when delivered by others; and most people admired him above all the preachers that ever they heard." His character as a laborious and faithful minister, and especially as a powerful and successful preacher, if we may judge from the history of his life, and of the time in which he lived, was such for many years before his death, as to leave him here without a competitor.‡ This was owing chiefly to his preaching and pastoral labours; for most of his laboured productions were published either a little before, or after, his death; yet, long ere this, his fame as a preacher and minister of Christ, had pervaded the colo-

* The treatises on the Affections, and on United Extraordinary Prayer, are the most incorrect of all his works, published by himself. In his sermons, published in his life-time, somewhat of the *limæ labor* is discernible. The works, published by his son, Dr. Edwards, in this country, are but little altered from the rough draught; but those first published in Edinburgh, are, generally, more so. The History of Redemption was considerably corrected by my father, and afterwards thrown into the form of a treatise by Dr. Erskine. The sermons published by Dr. Hopkins, are the least correct of all his works.

† I suppose the writer referred to here, and in various other places, to have been Dr. Finley

‡ For many of the remarks on the character of Mr. Edwards, as a preacher and writer, I am indebted to a well written review of the Worcester edition of his Works, in the Christian Spectator; but they are usually so blended with my own, that it is impossible to designate the passages.

nies, and was extensively known in Great Britain. Until within these few years, there were many living witnesses, who had heard him in their youth, and who distinctly remembered the powerful impressions left on their minds by his preaching, and particularly described his appearance in the pulpit, the still, unmoved solemnity of his manner, the weight of his sentiments first fixing the attention, and then overwhelming the feelings, of his audience. One of his youthful auditors, afterwards a gentleman of great respectability, informed my father that he was present, when he delivered the sermon in the History of Redemption, in which he describes the day of judgment; and that so vivid and solemn was the impression made on his own mind, that he fully supposed, that as soon as Mr. Edwards should close his discourse, the Judge would descend, and the final separation take place. The late Dr. West, of Stockbridge, who heard him in his childhood, in that village, gave me an account generally similar of the effects of his preaching. On one occasion, when the sermon exceeded two hours in its length, he told me that from the time that Mr. Edwards had fairly unfolded his subject, the attention of the audience was fixed and motionless, until its close; when they seemed disappointed that it should terminate so soon. There was such a bearing down of truth upon the mind, he observed, that there was no resisting it.—In his own congregation, the visible effects of his preaching were such as were never paralleled in New England. Often, also, he was invited to great distances to preach; and these occasional sermons sometimes produced a wonderful effect. One of these instances, which occurred at Enfield, at a time of great religious indifference there, is thus mentioned by the Rev. Dr. Trumbull. "When they went into the meeting-house, the appearance of the assembly was thoughtless and vain. The people hardly conducted themselves with common decency. The Rev. Mr. Edwards, of Northampton, preached; and before the sermon was ended, the assembly appeared deeply impressed, and bowed down with an awful conviction of their sin and danger. There was such a breathing of distress and weeping, that the preacher was obliged to speak to the people and desire silence, that he might be heard." This was the commencement of a general and powerful revival of religion.

To what, it may not improperly be asked, are this reputation and this success to be ascribed? It was not to his style of writing: that had no claims to elegance, or even to neatness.—It was not to his voice: that, far from being strong and full, was, in consequence of his feeble health, a little languid, and too low for a large assembly; though relieved and aided by a proper emphasis, just cadence, well placed pauses, and great clearness, distinctness, and precision of enunciation.—It was not owing to attitude or gesture, to his appearance in the pulpit, or to any of the customary arts of eloquence. His appearance in the pulpit was with a good grace, and his delivery easy, perfectly natural, and very solemn. He *wrote* his sermons; and in so fine and so illegible a hand, that they could be read only by being brought near to the eye. "He carried his notes with him into the pulpit, and read most that he wrote: still, he was not confined to them; and if some thoughts were suggested to him while he was preaching, which did not occur to him when writing, and appeared pertinent, he would deliver them with as great propriety and fluency, and often with greater pathos, and attended with a more sensibly good effect on his hearers, than what he had written."* While preaching, he customarily stood, holding his small manuscript volume in his left hand, the elbow resting on the cushion or the Bible, his right hand rarely raised but to turn the leaves, and his person almost motionless.—It was not owing to the pictures of fancy, or to any ostentation of learning, or of talents. In his preaching, usually all was plain, familiar, sententious, and practical.

One of the positive causes of his high character, and great success, as a preacher, was the deep and pervading solemnity of his mind. He had, at all times, a solemn consciousness of the presence of God. This was visible in his looks and general demeanour. It obviously had a controlling influence over all his preparations for the pulpit; and was most manifest in all his public services. Its effect on an audience is immediate, and not to be resisted. "He appeared," says Dr. Hopkins, "with such gravity and solemnity, and his words were so full of ideas, that few speakers have been able to command the attention of an audience as he did."—His knowledge of the Bible, evinced in his sermons—in the number of relevant passages which he brings to enforce every position, in his exact discernment of the true scope of each, in his familiar acquaintance with the drift of the whole Scriptures on the subject, and in the logical precision with which he derives his principles from them—is probably unrivalled.—His knowledge of the human heart, and its operations, has scarcely been equalled by that of any uninspired preacher. He derived this knowledge from his familiarity with the testimony of God concerning it in the Bible; from his thorough acquaintance with his own heart; and from his profound knowledge of mental philosophy. The effect of it was, to enable him to speak to the *consciousness* of every one who heard him; so that each one was compelled to reflect, in language like that of the woman of Sychar, "Here is a man, who is revealing to me the secrets of my own heart and life: is not this man from God?"—His knowledge of theology was so exact and universal, and the extensiveness of his views and of his information was so great, that while he could shed unusual variety and richness of thought over every discourse, he could also bring the most striking and impressive truths, facts, and circumstances, to bear upon the point, which he was endeavouring to illustrate or enforce.—His aim, in preparing and delivering his sermons, was *single*. This is so obvious, that no man probably ever suspected him of writing or delivering a sermon, for the sake of display, or reputation. From the first step to the last, he aimed at nothing but the salvation of his hearers, and at the glory of God as revealed in it. This enabled him to bring all his powers of mind and heart to bear on this one object.—His feelings on this subject were most intense. The love

* "Though, as has been observed," says Dr. Hopkins, "he was wont to read so considerable a part of what he delivered, yet he was far from thinking this the best way of preaching in general; and looked upon using his notes, so much as he did, a deficiency and infirmity, and in the latter part of his life, he was inclined to think it had been better, if he had never been accustomed to use his notes at all. It appeared to him, that preaching wholly without notes, agreeably to the custom in most protestant countries, and in what seems evidently to have been the manner of the apostles and primitive ministers of the gospel, was by far the most natural way, and had the greatest tendency, on the whole, to answer the end of preaching; and supposed that no one, who had talents, equal to the work of the ministry, was incapable of speaking *memoriter*, if he took suitable pains for this attainment from his youth. He would have the young preacher write all his sermons, or at least most of them, out, at large; and, instead of reading them to his hearers, take pains to commit them to memory: which, though it would require a great deal of labour at first, yet would soon become easier by use, and help him to speak more correctly and freely, and be of great service to him all his days."

of Christ constrained him; and the strong desire of his soul was, that they for whom Christ died might live for Him who died for them. "His words," says Dr. Hopkins, "often discovered a great degree of inward fervour, without much noise or external emotion, and fell with great weight on the minds of his hearers; and he spake so as to reveal the strong emotions of his own heart, which tended, in the most natural and effectual manner, to move and affect others."—The plan of his sermons is most excellent. In his introduction, which is always an *explanation of the passage*, he exhibits uncommon skill, and the sagacity with which he discovers, and the power with which he seizes at once, the whole drift and meaning of the passage in all its bearings, has rarely if ever been equalled. In the body of the discourse, he never attempts an elaborate proof of his doctrine, from revelation and reason; but rather gives an explanation of the doctrine, or places the truth on which he is discoursing directly before the mind, as a *fact*, and paints it to the imagination of his hearers. In the application, where he usually lays out his strength, he addresses himself with peculiar plainness to the consciences of his hearers, takes up and applies to them minutely all the important ideas contained in the body of the discourse, and appropriates them to persons of different characters and situations in life, by a particular explanation of their duties and their dangers; and lastly, by a solemn, earnest, and impressive appeal to every feeling and active principle of our nature. He counsels, exhorts, warns, expostulates, as if he were determined not to suffer his hearers to depart, until they were convinced of their duty, and persuaded to choose and to perform it.—His *graphic* manner of exhibiting truth, is, perhaps, his peculiar excellence. The doctrines of the gospel, in his hands, are not mere abstract propositions, but living realities, distinctly seen by the author's faith, and painted with so much truth, and life, and warmth of colouring, as cannot fail to give his hearers the same strong impression of them, which already exists in his own mind.—With all this, he preached the real truth of God, in its simplicity and purity, keeping nothing back, with so much weight of thought and argument, so much strength of feeling, and such sincerity of purpose, as must enlighten every understanding, convince every conscience, and almost convert every heart.—I inquired of Dr. West, Whether Mr. Edwards was an *eloquent* preacher. He replied, "If you mean, by eloquence, what is usually intended by it in our cities; he had no pretensions to it. He had no studied varieties of the voice, and no strong emphasis. He scarcely gestured, or even moved; and he made no attempt, by the elegance of his style, or the beauty of his pictures, to gratify the taste, and fascinate the imagination. But, if you mean by eloquence, the power of presenting an important truth before an audience, with overwhelming weight of argument, and with such intenseness of feeling, that the whole soul of the speaker is thrown into every part of the conception and delivery; so that the solemn attention of the whole audience is rivetted, from the beginning to the close, and impressions are left that cannot be effaced; Mr. Edwards was the most eloquent man I ever heard speak."—As the result of the whole, we are led to regard him as, beyond most others, an instructive preacher, a solemn and faithful preacher, an animated and earnest preacher, a most powerful and impressive preacher, in the sense explained, and the only true sense, a singularly eloquent preacher, and, through the blessing of God, one of the most successful preachers since the days of the apostles. It ought here to be added, that the sermons of Mr. Edwards have been, to his immediate pupils, and to his followers, the models of a style of preaching, which has been most signally blessed by God to the conversion of sinners, and which should be looked to as a standard, by those who wish, like him, to turn many to righteousness, that with him they may shine, as the stars, for ever and ever.

"His prayers," says Dr. Hopkins, "were indeed *extempore*. He was the farthest from any appearance of a form, as to his words and manner of expression, of almost any man. He was quite singular and inimitable in this, by any, who have not a spirit of real and undissembled devotion; yet he always expressed himself with decency and propriety. He appeared to have much of the grace and spirit of prayer; to pray with the spirit and with the understanding; and he performed this part of duty much to the acceptance and edification of those who joined with him. He was not wont, in ordinary cases, to be *long* in his prayers: an error which, he observed, was often hurtful to public and social prayer, as it tends rather to damp, than to promote, true devotion."

His practice, not to visit his people in their own houses, except in cases of sickness or affliction, is an example, not of course to be imitated by all. That, on this subject, ministers ought to consult their own talents and circumstances, and visit more or less, according to the degree in which they can thereby promote the great ends of their ministry, cannot be doubted. That *his* time was too precious to the church at large, to have been devoted, in any considerable degree, to visiting, all will admit. Yet it is highly probable, that, if he had been somewhat less in his study, and seen his people occasionally in the midst of their families, and known more of their circumstances and wants, and entered more into their feelings, his hold on their affections would have been stronger, and more permanent. Certainly this will be true with ministers at large.—In other pastoral duties, in preaching public and private lectures, in extraordinary labours during seasons of attention to religion, and in conversing with the anxious and inquiring, he was an uncommon example of faithfulness and success. "At such seasons, his study was thronged with persons, who came to lay open their spiritual concerns to him, and seek his advice and direction. He was a peculiarly skilful guide to those who were under spiritual difficulties; and was therefore sought unto, not only by his own people, but by many at a great distance." For this duty he was eminently fitted, from his own deep personal experience of religion, from his unwearied study of the word of God, from his having had so much intercourse with those who were in spiritual troubles, from his uncommon acquaintance with the human heart, with the nature of conversion, and with revivals of religion, and from his skill in detecting and exposing every thing like enthusiasm and counterfeit religion. How great a blessing was it to a church, to a people, and to every anxious inquirer, to enjoy the counsels and the prayers of such a minister!

But it is the theological treatises of Mr. Edwards, especially, by which he is most extensively known, to which he owes his commanding influence, and on which his highest reputation will ultimately depend. It is proper, therefore, before we conclude, to sketch his character as a theologian and controversialist, and to state the actual effects of his writings.

As a theologian, he is distinguished for his *scriptural*

views of divine truth. Even the casual reader of his works can scarcely fail to perceive that, with great labour, patience, and skill, he derived his principles from an extensive and most accurate observation of the word of God. The number of passages which he adduces from the Scriptures, on every important doctrine, the critical attention he has evidently given them, the labour in arranging them, and the skill and integrity with which he derives his general conclusions from them, is truly astonishing. We see no intermixture of his own hypotheses; no confidence in his own reason, except as applied to the interpretation of the oracles of God; nor even that disposition to make extended and momentous inferences, which characterizes some of his successors and admirers.

Another characteristic of his theology, is the *extensiveness* of his views. In his theology, as in his mind, there was nothing narrow; no partial, contracted views of a subject: all was simple, great, and sublime. His mind was too expanded to regard the distinctions of sects and churches. He belonged, in his feelings, to no church but the church of Christ; he contended for nothing but the truth; he aimed at nothing but to promote holiness and salvation. The effect of his labours so exactly coincides with the effects of the gospel, that no denomination can ever appropriate his name to itself, or claim him as its own.

Viewing Mr. Edwards as a controversialist, the most excellent, if not the most striking, trait in his character, is his *integrity*. Those who have been most opposed to his conclusions, and have most powerfully felt the force of his arguments, have acknowledged that he is a perfectly *fair* disputant. He saw so certainly the truth of his positions, and had such confidence in his ability to defend them by fair means, that the thought of employing *sophistry* in their defence never occurred to him. But, if he had felt the want of sound arguments, he would not have employed it. His conscience was too enlightened, and his mind too sincere. His aim, in all his investigations, was the discovery and the defence of truth. He valued his positions, only because they were true; and he gave them up at once, when he found that they were not supported by argument and evidence.

Another trait in his character, as a reasoner, is *originality*, or *invention*. Before his time, the theological writers of each given class or party, had, with scarcely an exception, followed on, one after another, in the same beaten path; and, whenever any one had deviated from it, he had soon lost himself in the mazes of error. Mr. Edwards had a mind too creative to be thus dependent on others. If the reader will examine carefully his controversial and other theological works, and compare them with those of his predecessors on the same subjects; he will find that his positions are new, that his definitions are new, that his plans are new, that his arguments are new, that his conclusions are new, that his mode of reasoning and his methods of discovering truth are perfectly his own; and that he has done more to render theology a new science, than, with perhaps one or two exceptions, all the writers who have lived since the days of the Fathers.

Another characteristic of his controversial writings, is the *excellent spirit* which every where pervades them. So strikingly is this true, that we cannot but urge every one, who peruses them, to examine for himself, whether he can discover, in them all, a solitary deviation from christian kindness and sincerity. By such an examination he will discover in them, if I mistake not, a fairness in proposing the real point in dispute, a candour in examining the arguments of his opponents, in stating their objections, and in suggesting others which had escaped them, and a care in avoiding every thing like personality, and the imputation of unworthy motives, rarely paralleled in the annals of controversy. It should here be remembered, that he wrote his treatise on the Affections, and his several works on revivals of religion, in the very heat of a violent contest, which divided and agitated this whole country; that in his treatises on the Freedom of the Will, on Original Sin, and on Justification, he handles subjects, which unavoidably awaken the most bitter opposition in the human heart, and opposes those, who had boasted of their victories over what he believed to be the cause of truth, "with no little glorying and insult;" that his treatise on the Qualifications for Communion, was written amid all the violence, and abuse, and injury of a furious parochial controversy; and that, in the Answer to Williams, he was called to reply to the most gross personalities, and to the most palpable misrepresentations of his arguments, his principles, and his motives.

He has, I know, been charged sometimes with handling his antagonists with needless severity. But let it be remembered, that his severity is never directed against their personal character, but merely against their principles and arguments; that his wit is only an irresistible exposition of the *absurdity* which he is opposing;* that he stood forth as the champion of truth, and the opponent of error; and that, in this character, it was his duty not merely to prostrate error, but to give it a death-blow, that it might never rise again.

But the characteristic of his controversial, and indeed of all his theological, writings, which gives them their chief value and effect, is the *unanswerableness of his arguments.* He not only drives his enemy from the field, but he erects a rampart, so strong and impregnable, that no one afterwards has any courage to assail it; and his companions in arms find the great work of defending the positions, which he has occupied, already done to their hands.

* Few men have possessed a greater fund of genuine wit, than Mr. Edwards. In early life, he found it difficult to restrain it. The clear *reductio ad absurdum*, to which he subjects every scheme and argument of his antagonists, in the Freedom of the Will, is usually a brilliant example of true logical wit. The Answer to Williams abounds with it. I doubt whether the annals of metaphysics can show a finer specimen of it, than the following; which is the conclusion of his exposure of the metaphysical notion of an *action* or *act*, as defined by Chubb, and his associates:

"So that, according to their notion of an act, considered with regard to its consequences, these following things are all essential to it; *viz.* That it should *be* necessary, and yet *not* necessary; that it should be *from* a cause, and yet from *no* cause; that it should *be* the fruit of choice and design, and yet *not* the fruit of choice and design; that it should be *the beginning* of motion or exertion, and yet *consequent on previous* exertion; that it should *be before* it *is;* that it should spring immediately out of *indifference* and *equilibrium*, and yet be the effect of *preponderation;* that it should be *self*-originated, and also have its original from *something else;* that it is what the mind causes *itself* of its own will, and *can* produce or prevent according to its choice or pleasure, and yet what the mind *has no power* to prevent, precluding all previous choice in the affair.

"So that an act, according to their metaphysical notion of it, is something of which there is no idea; it is nothing but a confusion of the mind, excited by words without any distinct meaning, and is an absolute non entity; and that in two respects: 1. There is *nothing* in the world that ever was, is, or can be, to answer the *things* which must belong to its description, according to what they suppose to be essential to it. And, 2. There neither is, nor ever was, nor can be, any *notion* or *idea* to answer the *word*, as they use and explain it. For if we should suppose any such notion, it would many ways destroy itself. But it is impossible that any idea or notion should subsist in the mind, whose very nature and essence, which constitutes it, destroys it.—If some learned philosopher, who has been abroad, in giving an account of the curious observations he had made in his travels, should say, 'He had been in *Terra del Fuego*, and there had seen an animal, which he calls by a certain name, that begat and brought forth himself, and yet had a sire and dam distinct from himself; that he had an appetite, and was hungry, before he had a being; that his master, who led him, and governed him at his pleasure, was always governed by him, and driven by him where he pleased; that when he moved, he always took a step before the first step; that he went with his head first, and yet always went tail foremost, and this, though he had neither head nor tail:' it would be no impudence at all to tell such a traveller, though a man of profound learning, that he himself had no idea of such an animal as he gave an account of, and never had, nor ever would have."

This impossibility of answering his arguments, arises, in the first place, from the *strength* and *conclusiveness* of his reasoning. By first fixing in his own mind, and then exactly defining, the meaning of his terms, by stating his propositions with logical precision, and by clearly discerning and stating the connexion between his premises and conclusions, he has given to *metaphysical* reasoning very much of the exactness and certainty of mathematical demonstration.

Another cause of the unanswerable character of his reasonings, is, that he usually follows several distinct trains of argument, which all terminate in the same conclusion. Each of them is satisfactory; but the union of all, commencing at different points, and arriving at the same identical result, cannot fail to convince the mind, that that result is not to be shaken.

A third cause of this is, that he himself anticipates, and effectually answers, not only all the objections that have been made, but all that apparently can be made, to the points for which he contends. These he places in the strongest light, and examines under every shape which they can assume in the hands of an evasive antagonist, and shows that, in every possible form, they are wholly inconclusive.

A fourth cause is his method of treating the opinions of his opponents. It is *the identical method of Euclid.* Assuming them as premises, he with great ingenuity shows, that they lead to palpable absurdity. He demonstrates that his opponents are inconsistent with themselves, as well as with truth and common sense;—and rarely stops, until he has exposed their error to contempt and ridicule.

This unanswerableness of Mr. Edwards's reasonings, in his controversial works, has been most publicly confessed. The Essay on the Will treats of subjects the most contested within the limits of theology; and, unless it can be answered, prostrates in the dust the scheme of doctrines, for which his antagonists so earnestly contend. Yet, hitherto, it stands unmoved and unassailed; and the waves of controversy break harmless at its base.* The treatise on Original Sin, though written chiefly to overthrow the hypothesis of an individual, is perhaps not less conclusive in its reasonings. That he succeeded in that design, as well as in establishing the great principles for which he contends, will not be doubted by any one who examines the controversy; and is said to have been virtually confessed, in a melancholy manner, by Taylor himself. He had indiscreetly boasted, in his larger work, that it never would be answered. The answer was so complete, that it admitted of no reply. His consequent mortification is said to have shortened his days. Whether it was true, or not, that the grasp of his antagonist was literally death, it was at least death to the controversy. The treatise on the Qualifications for Communion, attacked the most favourite scheme of all the lax religionists of this country, the only plausible scheme, ever yet devised, of establishing a communion between light and darkness, between Christ and Belial. They regarded this attack with indignation, from one end of the country to the other. One solitary combatant appeared in the field; and, being left in a state of irrecoverable prostration, he has hitherto found no one adventurous enough to come to his aid. The Treatise, and Reply, of Mr. Edwards, by the conclusiveness of their reasonings, have so changed the opinion and practice of the ministers, and the churches, of New England, that a mode of admission, once almost universal, now scarcely finds a solitary advocate.

But it may not unnaturally be asked, What are the changes in theology, which have been affected by the writings of President Edwards. It gives me peculiar pleasure that I can answer this question, in the words of his son, the late Dr. Edwards, President of Union College, Schenectady.

"CLEARER STATEMENTS

OF THEOLOGICAL TRUTH,

MADE BY PRESIDENT EDWARDS, AND THOSE WHO HAVE FOLLOWED HIS COURSE OF THOUGHT.

"1. The important question, concerning the *ultimate end of the creation*, is a question, upon which Mr. Edwards has shed much light. For ages it had been disputed, whether the end of creation was *the happiness of creatures* themselves, or *the declarative glory of the Creator*. Nor did it appear that the dispute was likely to be brought to an issue. On the one hand, it was urged, that reason declared in favour of the former hypothesis. It was said that, as God is a benevolent being, he doubtless acted under the influence of his own infinite benevolence in the creation; and that he could not but form creatures for the purpose of making them happy. Many passages of Scripture also were quoted in support of this opinion. On the other hand, numerous and very explicit declarations of Scripture were produced to prove that God made all things for his own glory. Mr. Edwards was the first, who clearly showed, that both these were the ultimate end of the creation, that they are only one end, and that they are really one and the same thing. According to him, the declarative glory of God *is* the creation, taken, not distributively, but collectively, as a system raised to a high degree of happiness. The creation, thus raised and preserved, is the *declarative* glory of God. In other words, it is the exhibition of his *essential* glory.

"2. On the great subject of *Liberty and Necessity*, Mr. Edwards made very important improvements. Before him, the *Calvinists* were nearly driven out of the field, by the *Arminians, Pelagians, and Socinians*. The Calvinists, it is true, appealed to Scripture, the best of all authority, in support of their peculiar tenets. But how was the Scripture to be understood? They were pressed and embarrassed by the objection,—*That the sense, in which they interpreted the sacred writings, was inconsistent with human liberty, moral agency, accountableness, praise and blame.* It was consequently inconsistent with all command and exhortation, with all reward and punishment. Their interpretation must of course be erroneous, and an entire perversion of Scripture. How absurd, it was urged, that a man totally dead, should be called upon to arise and perform the duties of the living and sound—that we should need a divine influence to give us a new heart, and yet be commanded to make us a new heart, and a right spirit—that a man has no power to come to Christ, and yet be commanded to come to him on pain of damnation! The Calvinists themselves began to be ashamed of their own cause and to give it up, so far at least as relates to liberty and necessity. This was true especially of Dr. Watts and Doddridge, who, in their day, were accounted leaders

* Dugald Stewart, alluding to it in conversation, is said, on good authority, to have spoken of it thus:—"Edwards on the Will, a work which never was answered, and which never will be answered."

of the Calvinists. They must needs bow in the house of Rimmon, and admit the *self-determining power;* which, once admitted and pursued to its ultimate results, entirely overthrows the doctrines of regeneration, of our dependence for renewing and sanctifying grace, of absolute decrees, of the saints' perseverance, and the whole system of doctrines, usually denominated the *doctrines of grace.*—But Mr. Edwards put an end to this seeming triumph of those, who were thus hostile to that system of doctrines. This he accomplished, by pointing out the difference between *natural* and *moral,* necessity and inability, by showing the absurdity, the manifold contradictions, the inconceivableness, and the impossibility, of a *self-determining power,* and by proving that *the essence* of the virtue and vice, existing in the disposition of the heart and the acts of the will, lies not in their *cause,* but in their *nature.* Therefore, though we are *not* the efficient causes of our own acts of will, yet they may be either virtuous or vicious; and also that *liberty of contingence,* as it is an exemption from all previous certainty, implies that free actions have no cause, and come into existence by mere chance. But if we admit that any event may come into existence by chance, and without a cause, the existence of the world may be accounted for in this same way; and atheism is established.—Mr. Edwards and his followers have further illustrated this subject by showing, that *free action* consists in *volition* itself, and that *liberty* consists in *spontaneity.* Wherever, therefore, there is volition, there is free action; wherever there is spontaneity there is liberty; however and by whomsoever that liberty and spontaneity are caused. *Beasts,* therefore, according to their measure of intelligence, are as free as *men. Intelligence,* therefore, and not *liberty,* is the only thing wanting, to constitute them moral agents.—The power of self-determination, alone, cannot answer the purpose of them who undertake its defence; for self-determination must be free from all control and previous certainty, as to its operations, otherwise it must be subject to what its advocates denominate a fatal necessity, and therefore must act by contingence and mere chance. But even the defenders of self-determination themselves, are not willing to allow the principle, that our actions, in order to be free, must happen *by chance.*—Thus Mr. Edwards and his followers understand, that the whole controversy concerning liberty and necessity, depends on the explanation of the word *liberty,* or the sense in which that word is used. They find that all the senses in which the word has been used, with respect to the mind and its acts, may be reduced to these two: 1. Either *an entire exemption from previous certainty,* or the certain futurity of the acts which it will perform: or, 2. *Spontaneity.*—Those, who use it in the former sense, cannot avoid the consequence, that, in order to act freely, we must act by chance, which is absurd, and what no man will dare to avow. If then liberty means an exemption from an influence, to which the will is or can be opposed, every *volition* is free, whatever may be the manner of its coming into existence. If, furthermore, God, by his grace, create in man a clean heart and holy volitions, such volitions being, by the very signification of the term itself, *voluntary,* and in no sense opposed to the divine influence which causes them, they are evidently as free as they could have been, if they had come into existence by mere chance and without cause. We have, of course, no need of being the efficient causes of those acts, which our wills perform, to render them either virtuous or vicious. As to the liberty, then, of self-determination or contingence, it implies, as already observed, that actions, in order to be free, must have no cause; but are brought into existence by chance. Thus have they illustrated the real and wide difference between *natural* and *moral* necessity. They have proved that this difference consists, not *in the degree of previous certainty* that an action will be performed—but in the fact, that *natural necessity* admits an entire *opposition* of the will, while *moral necessity* implies, and, in all cases, secures, the *consent* of the will. It follows that all necessity of the will, and of its acts, is of the *moral* kind; and that *natural* necessity cannot possibly affect the will or any of its exercises. It likewise follows, that if liberty, as applied to a moral agent, mean an exemption from all *previous certainty* that an action will be performed, then no action of man or any other creature can be free; for on this supposition, every action must come to pass without divine prescience, by mere chance, and consequently without a cause.—Now, therefore, the Calvinists find themselves placed upon firm and high ground. They fear not the attacks of their opponents. They face them on the ground of reason, as well as of Scripture. They act not merely on the defensive. Rather they have carried the war into Italy, and to the very gates of Rome.—But all this is peculiar to America; except that a few European writers have adopted, from American authors, the sentiments here stated. Even the famous Assembly of Divines had very imperfect views of this subject. This they prove, when they say, "Our first parents, *being left to the freedom of their own will,* fell from the state wherein they were created;"—and "God foreordained whatsoever comes to pass, so as *the contingency* of second causes is not taken away, but rather established."—These divines unquestionably meant, that our first parents, in the instance, at least, of their fall, acted from self-determination, and by mere contingence or chance. But there is no more reason to believe or even suppose this, than there is to suppose it true of every sinner, in every sin which he commits.

"3. Mr. Edwards very happily illustrated and explained *The nature of True Virtue, or Holiness.*—What is the nature of true virtue, or holiness?—In what does it consist?—and, Whence arises our obligation to be truly virtuous or holy?—are questions which moral writers have agitated in all past ages. Some have placed virtue in *self-love;*—some in *acting agreeable to the fitness of things;*—some in *following conscience,* or *moral sense;*—some in *following truth;*—and some in *acting agreeably to the will of God.* Those who place or found virtue in *fitness,* and those who found it in *truth,* do but use one synonymous word for another. For they doubtless mean *moral* fitness, and *moral* truth; these are no other than *virtuous* fitness, and *virtuous* truth. No one would pretend that it is a virtuous action to give a man poison, because it is a *fit* or direct mode of destroying his life. No person will pretend that the crucifying of Christ was virtuous, because it was *true,* compared with the ancient prophecies.—To found virtue *in acting agreeably to conscience,* or *moral sense,* justifies the persecutions of Christians by Saul of Tarsus, as well as a great proportion of heathenish idolatry.—If we found virtue in *the will of God,* the question arises, Whether the will of God be our rule, because it is in fact what it is, *wise, good, and benevolent;* or whether it be our rule, merely *because it is his will,* without any consideration of its nature and tendency;

and whether it would be a rule equally binding, as to observance, if it were foolish and malicious?—Mr. Edwards teaches, that virtue consists in *benevolence*. He proves that every *voluntary action*, which, in its general tendency and ultimate consequences, leads *to happiness*, is virtuous; and that every such action, which has not this tendency, and does not lead to this consequence, is vicious. By happiness, in this case, he does not mean the happiness of *the agent* only, or principally, but happiness *in general*, happiness *on the large scale*. Virtuous or holy benevolence embraces both the agent himself and others—all intelligences, wherever found, who are capable of a rational and moral blessedness. All actions, proceeding from such a principle, he holds to be *fit*, or *agreeable to the fitness of things*—agreeable equally to *reason*, and, *to a well-informed conscience*, or *moral sense*, and to *moral truth*;—and agreeable especially to *the will of God*, who "is love," or benevolence.—In this scheme of virtue or holiness, Mr. Edwards appears to have been original. Much indeed has been said, by most moral writers, in favour of benevolence. Many things they had published, which imply, in their consequences, Mr. Edwards's scheme of virtue. But no one before him had traced these consequences to their proper issue. No one had formed a system of virtue, and of morals, built on that foundation.

"4. Mr. Edwards has thrown much light on the inquiry concerning *The Origin of Moral Evil*. This question, comprehending the influence which the Deity had in the event of moral evil, has always been esteemed most difficult and intricate. That God is *the author of sin*, has been constantly objected to the Calvinists, as the consequence of their principles, by their opponents. To avoid this objection, some have holden that God is the author of the sinful *act*, which the sinner commits, but that the sinner himself is the author of its *sinfulness*. But how we shall abstract the sinfulness of a malicious act from the malicious act itself; and how God can be the author of a malicious *act*, and not be the author of the *malice*, which is the sinfulness of that act; is hard to be conceived. Mr. Edwards rejects, with abhorrence, the idea that God either is, or can be, the agent, or actor, of sin. He illustrates and explains this difficult subject, by showing that God may dispose things in such a manner, that sin will certainly take place in consequence of such a disposal. In maintaining this, he only adheres to his own important doctrine of *moral necessity*. The divine disposal, by which sin certainly comes into existence, is only establishing a certainty of its future existence. If that *certainty*, which is no other than moral necessity, be not inconsistent with human liberty; then surely the *cause* of that certainty, which is no other than *the divine disposal*, cannot be inconsistent with such liberty.

"5. The followers of Mr. Edwards have thrown new and important light upon *The Doctrine of Atonement*. It has been commonly represented, that the atonement which Christ made was *the payment of a debt*, due from his people. By this payment, they were purchased from slavery and condemnation. Hence arose this question,—If the sinner's *debt* be paid, how does it appear that there is any *pardon* or *grace* in his deliverance?—The followers of Mr. Edwards have proved, that the atonement does not consist in the payment of a debt, properly so called. It consists rather in doing that, which, for the purpose of establishing the authority of the divine law, and of supporting in due tone the divine government, is equivalent to the punishment of the sinner according to the letter of the law. Now, therefore, God, without the prostration of his authority and government, can pardon and save those who believe. As what was done to support the divine government, was not done *by the sinner*, so it does not at all diminish the free grace of his pardon and salvation.*

"6. With respect to *The Imputation of Adam's Sin*, and *The Imputation of Christ's Righteousness*, their statements also have been more accurate. The common doctrine had been, that *Adam's* sin is so *transferred* to his posterity, that it properly becomes *their* sin. The righteousness *of Christ*, likewise, is so *transferred* or *made over* to the believer, that it properly becomes *his* righteousness. To the believer it is reckoned in the divine account.—On this the question arises, How can the righteousness or good conduct of one person be the righteousness or good conduct of another? If, in truth, it cannot be the conduct of that other; how can God, who is omniscient, and cannot mistake, reckon, judge, or think it to be the conduct of that other?—The followers of Mr. Edwards find relief from this difficulty, by proving that *to impute righteousness*, is, in the language of Scripture, *to justify*; and that, *to impute the righteousness of Christ*, is to justify *on account of* Christ's righteousness. The *imputation* of righteousness can, therefore, be no *transfer* of righteousness. They are *the beneficial consequences* of righteousness, which are transferred. Not therefore *the righteousness* of Christ *itself*, but its beneficial consequences and advantages, are transferred to the believer.—In the same manner they reason with respect to the imputation of *Adam's sin*. The baneful consequences of Adam's sin, which came upon *himself*, came also upon *his posterity*. These consequences were, that, after his first transgression, God left him *to an habitual disposition to sin*, to *a series of actual transgressions*, and to *a liableness to the curse of the law, denounced against such transgression*.—The same consequences took place with regard to Adam's *posterity*. By divine constitution, they, as descending from Adam, become, like himself, the subjects of an habitual disposition to sin. This disposition is commonly called *original depravity*. Under its influence they sin, as soon as, in a moral point of view, they act at all. This depravity, this disposition to sin, leads them naturally to a series of actual transgressions, and exposes them to the whole curse of the law.—On this subject two questions have been much agitated in the christian world:—1. Do the posterity of Adam, unless saved by Christ, suffer final damnation on account of Adam's sin?—and, if this be asserted, how can it be reconciled with justice?—2. How shall we reconcile it with justice, that Adam's posterity should be doomed, in consequence of his sin, to come into the world, with an habitual disposition themselves to sin?—On the former of these questions, the common doctrine has been, that Adam's posterity, unless saved by Christ, are damned on account of Adam's sin, and that this is just, because his sin is imputed or transferred to them. By imputation, *his* sin becomes *their* sin. When the justice of such a transfer is demanded, it is said that the constitution, which God has established, makes the transfer just.—To this it may be replied, that in the same way it may be proved to be just, to damn a man without any sin at all, either personal

* It is proper to remark, that the above statement is not altogether correct. The same views of the atonement appear in Bates on the Harmony of the Divine Attributes in Redemption; in the writings of Howe, Baxter, and some other eminent divines of the seventeenth century.

or imputed. We need only resolve it into a sovereign constitution of God. From this difficulty the followers of Mr. Edwards relieve themselves, by holding that, though Adam was so constituted the federal head of his posterity, that in consequence of his sin they all sin or become sinners, yet they are damned on account of *their own personal sin merely*, and not on account of *Adam's sin*, as though they were individually guilty of his identical transgression. This leads us to the second question stated above:—viz. How shall we reconcile it with perfect justice, that Adam's posterity should, by a divine constitution, be depraved and sinful, or become sinners, in consequence of Adam's apostacy?—But this question involves no difficulty, beside that, which attends the doctrine of divine decrees. And this is satisfactory; because for God to decree that an event shall take place, is, in other words, the same thing as if he make a constitution, under the operation of which that event shall take place. If God has decreed whatever comes to pass, he decreed the fall of Adam. It is obvious that, in equal consistency with justice, he may decree any other sin. Consequently he may decree that every man shall sin; and this too, as soon as he shall become capable of moral action. Now if God could, consistently with justice, establish, decree, or make a constitution, according to which this depravity, this sinfulness of disposition, should exist, *without* any respect to Adam's sin, he might evidently, with the same justice, decree that it should take place *in consequence* of Adam's sin. If God might consistently with justice decree, that the Jews should crucify Christ, without the treachery of Judas preceding, he might with the same justice decree, that they should do the same evil deed, in consequence of that treachery.—Thus the whole difficulty, attending the connexion between Adam and his posterity, is resolved into the doctrine of the divine decrees; and the followers of Mr. Edwards feel themselves placed upon strong ground—ground upon which they are willing, at any time, to meet their opponents.—They conceive, furthermore, that, by resolving several complicated difficulties into one simple vindicable principle, a very considerable improvement is made in the representations of theological truth. Since the discovery and elucidation of the distinction, between natural and moral necessity, and inability; and since the effectual confutation of that doctrine, which founds moral liberty on self-determination; they do not feel themselves pressed with the objections, which are made to divine and absolute decrees.

"7. With respect to *The State of the Unregenerate*, *The Use of Means*, and *The Exhortations, which ought to be addressed to the Impenitent*, the disciples of Mr. Edwards, founding themselves on the great principles of moral agency, established in the Freedom of the Will, have since his day made considerable improvement upon former views.—This improvement was chiefly occasioned by the writings of Robert Sandeman, a Scotchman, which were published after the death of Mr. Edwards. Sandeman, in the most striking colours, pointed out the inconsistency of the *popular preachers*, as he called them; by whom he meant Calvinistic divines in general. He proved them inconsistent, in teaching that the unregenerate are, by total depravity, 'dead in trespasses and sins,'—and yet supposing that such sinners do often attain those sincere desires, make those sincere resolutions, and offer those sincere prayers, which are well pleasing in the sight of God, and which are the sure presages of renewing grace and salvation. He argued, that, if the unregenerate be dead in sin, then all that they do must be sin; and that sin can never be pleasing and acceptable to God. Hence he taught, not only that all the exercises and strivings of the unregenerate are abominable in the Divine view, but that there is no more likelihood, in consequence of their strictest attendance on the means of grace, that they will become partakers of salvation, than there would be in the total neglect of those means. These sentiments were entirely new. As soon as they were published, they gave a prodigious shock to all serious men, both ministers and others. The addresses to the unregenerate, which had hitherto consisted chiefly in exhortations to attend on the outward means of grace, and to form such resolutions, and put forth such desires, as all supposed consistent with unregeneracy, were examined. It appearing that such exhortations were addresses to no real spiritual good; many ministers refrained from all exhortations to the unregenerate. The perplexing inquiry with such sinners consequently was—'*What then have we to do? All we do is sin. To sin is certainly wrong. We ought therefore to remain still, doing nothing, until God bestow upon us renewing grace.*' In this state of things, Dr. Hopkins took up the subject. He inquired particularly into the exhortations delivered by the inspired writers. He published several pieces on *The character of the Unregenerate*; on *Using the Means of Grace*; and on *The Exhortations, which ought to be addressed to the Unregenerate*. He clearly showed that, although they are dead in depravity and sin, yet, as this lays them under a mere *moral inability* to the exercise and practice of true holiness,—and as such exercise and practice are their unquestionable duty,—to *this* duty they are to be exhorted. To this duty only, and to those things which imply it, the inspired writers constantly exhort the unregenerate. Every thing short of this duty is sin. Nevertheless, 'as faith cometh by hearing,' those who 'hear,' and attend on the means of grace, even in their unregeneracy, and from natural principles, are more likely than others to become the subjects of divine grace. The Scriptures sufficiently prove, that this is the constitution which Christ has established. It likewise accords perfectly with experience and observation, both in apostolic and subsequent ages.

"8. Mr. Edwards greatly illustrated *The Nature of Experimental Religion*. He pointed out, more clearly than had been done before, the distinguishing marks of genuine christian experience, and those religious affections and exercises, which are peculiar to the true Christian. The accounts of christian affection and experience, which had before been given, both by American and European writers, were general, indiscriminate, and confused They seldom, if ever, distinguished the exercises of *self-love, natural conscience, and other natural principles of the human mind under conviction of divine truth*, from *those of the new nature, given in regeneration*. In other words, they seldom distinguished the exercises of the sinner under the law work, and the joys afterwards often derived from a groundless persuasion of his forgiveness, from those sincere and evangelical affections, which are peculiar to the real convert. They did not show *how far* the unregenerate sinner can proceed in religious exercises, and yet fall short of saving grace. But this whole subject, and the necessary distinctions with respect to it, are set in a striking light by Mr. Edwards, in his treatise concerning Religious Affections.

"9. Mr. Edwards has thrown much light upon the subject of affection as disinterested. The word *disinterested*, is, indeed, capable of such a sense, as affords a ground of argument against disinterested affections; and scarcely perhaps is an instance of its use to be found, in which it does not admit of an equivocation. It seems to be a mere equivocation to say, that disinterested affection is an impossibility; and that, if we are not interested in favour of religion, we are indifferent with respect to it, and do not love it at all. But who ever thought that, when a person professes a disinterested regard for another, he has no regard for him at all.* The plain meaning is, that his regard for him is *direct* and benevolent, *not selfish*, nor arising from selfish motives. In this sense, Mr. Edwards maintained that our religious affections, if genuine, are disinterested; that our love to God arises chiefly—not from the motive that God has bestowed, or is about to bestow, on us favours, whether temporal or eternal, but—from his own infinite excellence and glory. The same explanation applies to the love which every truly pious person feels for the Lord Jesus Christ, for every truth of divine revelation, and for the whole scheme of the gospel. Very different from this is the representation given by most theological writers before Mr. Edwards. The motives presented by them, to persuade men to love and serve God, to come unto Christ, to repent of their sins, and to embrace and practise religion, are chiefly of the selfish kind. There is, in their works, no careful and exact discrimination upon this subject.

"10. He has thrown great light on the important doctrine of *Regeneration*. Most writers before him treat this subject very loosely. They do indeed describe a variety of awakenings and convictions, fears and distresses, comforts and joys, as implied in it; and they call the whole, *regeneration*. They represent the man before regeneration as dead, and no more capable of spiritual action, than a man naturally dead is capable of performing those deeds, which require natural life and strength. From their description, a person is led to conceive, that the former is as excusable, in his omission of those holy exercises, which constitute the christian character and life, as the latter is, in the neglect of those labours, which cannot be performed without natural life. From their account, no one can determine *in what* the change, effected by regeneration, consists. They do not show the inquirer, whether every awakened and convinced sinner, who afterwards has lively gratitude and joy, is regenerated; or whether a gracious change of heart implies joys of a peculiar kind: neither, if the renewed have joys peculiar to themselves, do the teachers, now referred to, describe that peculiarity; nor do they tell from what motives the joys, that are evidence of regeneration, arise. They represent the whole man, his understanding, and his sensitive faculties, as renewed, no less than his heart and affections. According to them generally, this change is effected by *light*. As to this indeed they are not perfectly agreed. Some of them hold, that the change is produced by the bare light and motives exhibited in the gospel. Others pretend, that a man is persuaded to become a Christian, as he is persuaded to become a friend to republican government. Yet others there are, who hold that regeneration is caused by a supernatural and divine light immediately communicated. Their representation of this seems to imply, and their readers understand it as implying, an immediate and new revelation. But according to Mr. Edwards, and those who adopt his views of the subject, regeneration consists in *the communication of a new spiritual sense or taste*. In other words, a new heart is given. This communication is made, this work is accomplished, by the Spirit of God. It is their opinion, that *the intellect*, and *the sensitive faculties*, are not the *immediate* subject of any change in regeneration. They believe, however, that, in consequence of the change which the renewed heart experiences, and of its reconciliation to God, light breaks in upon the understanding. The subject of regeneration sees, therefore, the glory of God's character, and the glory of all divine truth. This may be an illustration. A man becomes cordially reconciled to his neighbour, against whom he had previously felt a strong enmity. He now sees the real excellencies of his neighbour's character, to which he was blinded before by enmity and prejudice. These new views of his neighbour, and these different feelings towards him, are the *consequence* of the change: its *evidence*, but not *the change itself*.—At the same time, Mr. Edwards and others believe, that in saving experience, the sensitive faculties are brought under the due regulation by the new heart or holy temper. None of the *awakenings*, *fears*, and *convictions*, which precede the new heart, are, according to this scheme, any part of regeneration; though they are, in some sense, a preparation for it, as all doctrinal knowledge is. The sinner, before regeneration, is allowed to be totally dead to the exercises and duties of the spiritual life. He is nevertheless accounted a moral agent. He is therefore entirely blamable in his impenitence, his unbelief, and his alienation from God. He is therefore, with perfect propriety, exhorted to repent, to become reconciled to God in Christ, and to arise from his spiritual death, that "Christ may give him light."—According to this system, regeneration is produced, neither by moral suasion, *i. e.* by the arguments and motives of the gospel, nor by any supernatural, spiritual light; but by the immediate agency of the Holy Spirit. Yet the light and knowledge of the gospel are, by divine constitution, usually necessary to regeneration, as the blowing of the rams' horns was necessary to the falling of the walls of Jericho; and the moving of the stone from the mouth of the sepulchre, was necessary to the raising of Lazarus."

THUS it appears, that Mr. Edwards taught us in his writings, in a manner so clear, that mankind have hitherto been satisfied with the instruction, Why God created this material and spiritual universe;—What is the nature of that government which he exercises over minds, and how it is consistent with their perfect freedom;—What is the nature of that virtue, which they must possess, if they are to secure his approbation;—What is the nature, the source, the extent, and the evidences of that depravity, which characterizes man, as a fallen being;—What is the series of events by which his redemption is accomplished;—What are the qualifications for that church, to which the redeemed belong;—What are the grounds on which they are justified;—What are the nature and evidences of that religion, which is imparted to them by the Spirit of grace;—What are the nature and effects of that revival of religion which accompanies an effusion of his

* The whole difficulty is removed by reflecting that *disinterested* is the converse of *selfish*; and *uninterested*, the converse of *interested*.

divine influences on a people;—And what are the inducements to united and extraordinary prayer, that such effusions may be abundantly enjoyed by the church of God.*—By what is thus said, we do not intend, that all his reasonings are solid, or all his opinions sound and scriptural; but we know of no writer, since the days of the apostles, who has better comprehended the word of God; who has more fully unfolded the nature and design of the revelation of his mind, which it contains; who has more ably explained and defended the great doctrines which it teaches; who has more clearly illustrated the religion which it requires; who has done more for the purification and enlargement of that church which it establishes; or who, in consequence of his unfoldings of divine truth, will find, when the work of every man is weighed in the balances of eternity, a larger number to be "his hope, and joy, and crown of rejoicing in that day."—And when we remember, in addition to all this, that we can probably select no individual, of all who have lived in that long period, who has manifested a more ardent or elevated piety towards God, a warmer or more expanded benevolence towards man, or greater purity, or disinterestedness, or integrity of character—one, who gave the concentrated strength of all his powers, more absolutely, to the one end of glorifying God in the salvation of man;—and then reflect, that at the age of *fifty-four*, in the highest vigour of all his faculties, in the fulness of his usefulness, when he was just entering on the most important station of his life, he yielded to the stroke of death; we look towards his grave, in mute astonishment, unable to penetrate those clouds and darkness, which hover around it. One of his weeping friends † thus explained this most surprising dispensation:—" He was pouring in a flood of light upon mankind, which their eyes, as yet, were too feeble to bear."—If this was not the reason; we can only say—" Even so, Father! for so it seemed good in thy sight."

* For a Catalogue of the works of Mr. Edwards, published previous to this edition, see Appendix, No. VI.

† Dr. Finley

A FAREWELL SERMON,

PREACHED AT THE

FIRST PRECINCT AT NORTHAMPTON,

AFTER THE PEOPLE'S PUBLIC REJECTION OF THEIR MINISTER, AND RENOUNCING THEIR RELATION TO HIM AS PASTOR OF THE CHURCH THERE,

ON JUNE 22, 1750;

OCCASIONED BY DIFFERENCE OF SENTIMENTS, CONCERNING THE REQUISITE QUALIFICATIONS OF MEMBERS OF THE CHURCH IN COMPLETE STANDING.

Acts xx. 18. Ye know, from the first day that I came into Asia, after what manner I have been with you at all seasons.
Ver. 20. And how I kept back nothing that was profitable unto you, but have showed you, and have taught you publicly, and from house to house.
Ver. 26, 27. Wherefore I take you to record this day, that I am pure from the blood of all men. For I have not shunned to declare unto you all the counsel of God.
Gal. iv. 15, 16. Where is then the blessedness ye spake of? For I bear you record, that if it had been possible, ye would have plucked out your own eyes, and have given them to me. Am I therefore become your enemy, because I tell you the truth?

PREFACE.

It is not unlikely, that some of the readers of the following Sermon may be inquisitive concerning the circumstances of the difference between me and the people of Northampton, that issued in that separation between me and them, which occasioned the preaching of this Farewell Sermon.—There is, by no means, room here for a full account of that matter: but yet it seems to be proper, and even necessary, here to correct some gross misrepresentations, which have been abundantly, and (it is to be feared) by some affectedly and industriously made, of that difference. Such as, that I insisted on persons being assured of their being in a state of salvation, in order to my admitting them into the church; that I required a particular relation of the method and order of a person's inward experience, and of the time and manner of his conversion, as the test of his fitness for christian communion; yea, that I have undertaken to set up a pure church, and to make an exact and certain distinction between saints and hypocrites, by a pretended infallible discerning the state of men's souls; that in these things I had fallen in with those wild people, who have lately appeared in New England, called Separatists; and that I myself was become a grand separatist; that I arrogated all the power of judging of the qualifications of candidates for communion wholly to myself, and insisted on acting by my sole authority, in the admission of members into the church, &c.

In opposition to these slanderous representations, I shall at present only give my reader an account of some things which I laid before the council that separated between me and my people, in order to their having a just and full account of my principles, relating to the affair in controversy.—Long before the sitting of the council, my people had sent to the Reverend Mr. Clark of Salem village, desiring him to write in opposition to my principles. Which gave me occasion to write to Mr. Clark, that he might have true information what my principles were. And in the time of the sitting of the council, I did, for their information, make a public declaration of my principles before them and the church, in the meeting-house, of the same import with that in my letter to Mr. Clark, and very much in the same words. And then, afterwards, sent in to the council in writing, an extract of that letter, containing the information I had given Mr. Clark, in the very words of my letter to him, that the council might read and consider it at their leisure, and have a more certain and satisfactory knowledge what my principles were. The extract which I sent in to them was in the following words:

"I am often, and I do not know but pretty generally in the country, represented as of a new and odd opinion with respect to the terms of christian communion, and as being for introducing a peculiar way of my own.—Whereas, I do not perceive that I differ at all from the scheme of Dr. Watts, in his book entitled, *The rational Foundation of a Christian Church, and the Terms of Christian Communion;* which, he says, is the common sentiment and practice of all reformed churches. I had not seen this book of Dr. Watts's when I published what I have written on the subject. But yet, I think, my sentiments, as I have expressed them, are as exactly agreeable to what he lays down, as if I had been his pupil. Nor do I at all go beyond what Dr. Doddridge plainly shows to be his sentiments, in his *Rise and Progress of Religion*, and his *Sermons on Regeneration*, and his Paraphrase and Notes on the New Testament. Nor indeed, Sir, when I consider the sentiments you have expressed in your letters to Major Pomroy and Mr. Billing, can I perceive but that they come exactly to the same thing that I maintain. You suppose, the sacraments are not converting ordinances: but that, *as seals of the covenant, they presuppose conversion, especially in the adult; and that it is visible saintship, or, in other words, a credible profession of faith and repentance, a solemn consent to the gospel-covenant, joined with a good conversation, and competent measure of christian knowledge, is what gives a gospel-right to all sacred ordinances: but that it is necessary to those that come to these ordinances, and in those that profess a consent to the gospel covenant, that they be sincere in their profession*, or at least should think themselves so.——The great thing which I have scrupled in the established method of this church's proceeding, and which I dare no longer go on in, is their publicly assenting to the form of words rehearsed on occasion of their admission to the communion, without pretending thereby to mean any such thing as a hearty consent to the terms of the gospel-covenant, or to mean any such faith or repentance as belong to the covenant of grace, and are the grand conditions of that covenant. It being, at the same time that the words are used, their known and established principle, which they openly profess and proceed upon, that men may and ought to use these words, and mean no such thing, but something else of a nature far inferior; which I think they have no distinct determinate notion of; but something consistent with their knowing that they do not choose God as their chief good, but love the world more than him, and that they do not give themselves up entirely to God. but make reserves; and in short, knowing that they do not heartily consent to the gospel-covenant, but live still under the reigning power of the love of the world, and enmity to God and Christ. So that the words of their public profession, according to their openly established use, cease to be of the nature of any profession of gospel faith and repentance, or any proper compliance with the covenant. For it is their profession, that the words, as used, mean no such thing. The words used under these circumstances, do at least fail of being a credible profession of these things.—I can conceive of no such virtue in a certain set of words, that it is proper, merely on the making these sounds, to admit persons to christian sacraments, without any regard to any pretended meaning of these sounds. Nor can I think, that any institution of Christ has established any such terms of admission into the christian church.—It does not belong to the controversy between me and my people, how particular or large the profession should be, that is required. I should not choose to be confined to exact limits as to that matter: but rather than contend, I should content myself with a few words, briefly expressing the cardinal virtues or acts implied in a hearty compliance with the covenant, made (as should appear by inquiry into the person's doctrinal knowledge) understandingly; if there were an external conversation agreeable thereto. Yea, I should think, that such a person, solemnly making such a profession, had a right to be received as the object of a public charity, however he himself might scruple his own conversion, on account of his not remembering the time, not knowing the method, of his conversion, or finding so much remaining sin, &c. And (if his own scruples did not hinder his coming to the Lord's table) I should think the minister or church had no right to debar such a professor, though he should say he did not think himself converted. For I call that a profession of godliness, which is a profession of the great things wherein godliness consists, and not a profession of his own opinion of his good estate.

"*Northampton, May* 7, 1750."

The council having heard that I had made certain draughts of the covenant, or forms of a public profession of religion which I stood ready to accept of from the candidates for church communion, they, for their further information, sent for them. Accordingly I sent them four distinct draughts or forms, which I had drawn up about a twelvemonth before, as what I stood ready to accept of (any one of them) rather than contend, and break with my people.—The two shortest of these forms are here inserted for the satisfaction of the reader.—They are as follows:

"I hope I do truly find a heart to give up myself wholly to God, according to the tenor of that covenant of grace which was sealed in my baptism; and to walk in a way of that obedience to all the commandments of God, which the covenant of grace requires, as long as I live."

Another,

"I hope I truly find in my heart a willingness to comply with all the commandments of God, which require me to give up myself wholly to him, and to serve him with my body and my spirit. And do accordingly now promise to walk in a way of obedience to all the commandments of God, as long as I live."

Such kind of professions as these I stood ready to accept, rather than contend and break with my people. Not but that I think it much more convenient, that ordinarily the public profession of religion that is made by Christians, should be much fuller and more particular. And that (as I hinted in my letter to Mr. Clark) I should not choose to be tied up to any certain form of words, but to have liberty to vary the expressions of a public profession, the more exactly to suit the sentiments and experience of the professor, that it might be a more just and free expression of what each one finds in his heart.—Moreover, it must be noted, that I ever insisted on it, that it belonged to me as a pastor, before a profession was accepted, to have full liberty to instruct the candidate in the meaning of the terms of it, and in the nature of the things proposed to be professed; and to inquire into his doctrinal understanding of these things, according to my best discretion; and to caution the person, as I should think needful, against rashness in making such a profession, or doing it mainly for the credit of himself or his family, or from any secular views whatsoever, and to put him on serious self-examination, and searching his own heart, and prayer to God to search and enlighten him, that he may not be hypocritical and deceived in the profession he makes; withal pointing forth to him the many ways in which professors are liable to be deceived.

Nor do I think it improper for a minister in such a case, to inquire and know of the candidate what can be remembered of the circumstances of his christian experience; as this may tend much to illustrate his profession, and give a minister great advantage for proper instructions: though a particular knowledge and remembrance of the time and method of the first conversion to God, is not to be made the test of a person's sincerity, nor insisted on as necessary in order to his being received into full charity. Not that I think it at all improper or unprofitable, that in some special cases, a declaration of the particular circumstances of a person's first awakening, and the manner of his convictions, illuminations, and comforts, should be publicly exhibited before the whole congregation, on occasion of his admission into the church; though this be not demanded as necessary to admission. I ever declared against insisting on a relation of experiences, in this sense, (*viz.* a relation of the particular time and steps of the operation of the Spirit, in first conversion,) as the term of communion: yet, if by a relation of experiences, be meant a declaration of experience of the great things wrought, wherein true grace and the essential acts and habits of holiness consist; in this sense, I think an account of a person's experiences necessary in order to his admission into full communion in the church. But that in whatever inquiries are made, and whatever account is given, neither minister nor church are to set up themselves as searchers of hearts, but are to accept the serious solemn profession of the well-instructed professor, of a good life, as best able to determine what he finds in his own heart. These things may serve in some measure to set right those of my readers who have been misled in their apprehensions of the state of the controversy between me and my people, by the forementioned misrepresentations.

A
FAREWELL SERMON.

2 Corinthians i. 14.

As also you have acknowledged us in part, that we are your rejoicing, even as ye also are ours in the day of the Lord Jesus.

The apostle, in the preceding part of the chapter, declares what great troubles he met with in the course of his ministry. In the text, and two foregoing verses, he declares what were his comforts and supports under the troubles he met with. There are four things in particular.

1. That he had approved himself to his own conscience, verse 12. "For our rejoicing is this, the testimony of our conscience, that in simplicity and godly sincerity, not with fleshly wisdom, but by the grace of God, we have had our conversation in the world, and more abundantly to you-wards."

2. Another thing he speaks of as matter of comfort, is, that as he had approved himself to his own conscience, so he had also to the consciences of his hearers, the Corinthians, to whom he now wrote, and that they should approve of him at the day of judgment.

3. The hope he had of seeing the blessed fruit of his labours and sufferings in the ministry, in their happiness and glory, in that great day of accounts.

4. That in his ministry among the Corinthians, he had approved himself to his Judge, who would approve and reward his faithfulness in that day.

These three last particulars are signified in my text, and the preceding verse; and indeed all the four are implied in the text. It is implied, that the Corinthians had acknowledged him as their spiritual father, and as one that had been faithful among them, and as the means of their future joy and glory at the day of judgment. It is implied, that the apostle expected at that time to have a joyful meeting with them before the Judge, and with joy to behold their glory, as the fruit of his labours; and so they would be his rejoicing. It is implied also, that he then expected to be approved of the great Judge, when he and they should meet together before him; and that he would then acknowledge his fidelity, and that this had been the means of their glory; and that thus he would, as it were, give them to him as his crown of rejoicing. But this the apostle could not hope for, unless he had the testimony of his own conscience in his favour. And therefore the words do imply, in the strongest manner, that he had approved himself to his own conscience.

There is one thing implied in each of these particulars, and in every part of the text, which I shall make the subject of my present discourse, *viz.*

Doctrine. Ministers, and the people that have been under their care, must meet one another before Christ's tribunal at the day of judgment.

Ministers, and the people that have been under their care, must be parted in this world, how well soever they have been united. If they are not separated before, they must be parted by death; and they may be separated while life is continued. We live in a world of change, where nothing is certain or stable; and where a little time, a few revolutions of the sun, brings to pass strange things, surprising alterations, in particular persons, in families, in towns and churches, in countries and nations. It often happens, that those who seem most united, in a little time are most disunited, and at the greatest distance. Thus ministers and people, between whom there has been the greatest mutual regard and strictest union, may not only differ in their judgments, and be alienated in affection, but one may rend from the other, and all relation between them be dissolved; the minister may be removed to a distant place, and they may never have any more to do one with another in this world. But if it be so, there is one meeting more that they must have, and that is in the last great day of accounts. Here I would show,

I. In what *manner* ministers, and the people which have been under their care, shall meet one another at the day of judgment.

II. For what *purposes*.

III. For what *reasons* God has so ordered it, that ministers and their people shall then meet together in such a manner, and for such purposes.

I. I would show, in some particulars, in what manner ministers and the people which have been under their care, shall meet one another at the day of judgment.

1. They shall not meet at that day merely as all the world must then meet together. I would observe a difference in two things.

(1.) As to a clear actual view, and distinct knowledge and notice, of each other.

Although the whole world will be then present, all mankind of all generations gathered in one vast assembly, with all of the angelic nature, both elect and fallen angels; yet we need not suppose that every one will have a distinct and particular knowledge of each individual of the whole assembled multitude, which will undoubtedly consist of many millions of millions. Though it is probable that men's capacities will be much greater than in their present state, yet they will not be infinite. Though their understanding and comprehension will be vastly extended, yet men will not be deified. There will probably be a very enlarged view that particular persons will have of the various parts and members of that vast assembly, and so of the proceedings of that great day; but yet it must needs be, that according to the nature of finite minds, some persons and some things, at that day, shall fall more under the notice of particular persons than others; and this (as we may well suppose) according as they shall have a nearer concern with some than others in the transactions of the day. There will be special reason why those who have had special concerns together in this world, in their state of probation, and whose mutual affairs will be then to be tried and judged, should especially be set in one another's view. Thus we may suppose, that rulers and subjects, earthly judges and those whom they have judged, neighbours who have had mutual converse, dealings, and contests, heads of families and their children and servants, shall then meet, and in a peculiar distinction be set together. And especially will it be thus with ministers and their people. It is evident by the text, that these shall be in each other's view, shall distinctly know each other, and shall have particular notice one of another at that time.

(2.) They shall meet together, as having special concern one with another in the great transactions of that day.

Although they shall meet the whole world at that time, yet they will not have any immediate and particular concern with all. Yea, the far greater part of those who shall then be gathered together, will be such as they have had no intercourse with in their state of probation, and so will have no mutual concerns to be judged of. But as to ministers and the people that have been under their care, they will be such as have had much immediate concern one with another, in matters of the greatest moment. Therefore they especially must meet, and be brought together before the Judge, as having special concern one with another in the design and business of that great day of accounts.—Thus their meeting, as to the manner of it, will be diverse from the meeting of mankind in general.

2. Their meeting at the day of judgment will be very diverse from their meetings one with another in this world.

Ministers and their people, while their relation continues, often meet together in this world. They are wont to meet from sabbath to sabbath, and at other times, for the public worship of God, and administration of ordinances, and the solemn services of God's house. And besides these meetings, they have also occasions to meet for the determining and managing their ecclesiastical affairs, for the exercise of church discipline, and the settling and adjusting those things which concern the purity and good order of public administrations. But their meeting at the day of judgment will be exceeding diverse, in its manner and circumstances, from any meetings and interviews they have one with another in the present state. I would observe how, in a few particulars.

(1.) Now they meet together in a preparatory mutable state, but then in an unchangeable state.

Now *sinners* in the congregation meet their minister in a state wherein they are capable of a saving change, capable of being turned, through God's blessing on the ministrations and labours of their pastor, from the power of Satan unto God; and being brought out of a state of guilt, condemnation, and wrath, to a state of peace and favour with God, to the enjoyment of the privileges of his children, and a title to their eternal inheritance. And *saints* now meet their minister with great remains of corruption, and sometimes under great spiritual difficulties and affliction: and therefore are yet the proper subjects of means for a happy alteration of their state, which they have reason to hope for in the attendance on ordinances, and of which God is pleased commonly to make his ministers the instruments. Ministers and their people now meet in order to the bringing to pass such happy changes: they are the great benefits sought in their solemn meetings.

But when they shall meet together at the day of judgment, it will be far otherwise. They will all meet in an unchangeable state. *Sinners* will be in an unchangeable state. They who then shall be under the guilt and power of sin, and have the wrath of God abiding on them, shall be beyond all remedy or possibility of change, and shall meet their ministers without any hopes of relief or remedy, or getting any good by their means. And as for the *saints*, they will be already perfectly delivered from all their corruption, temptation, and calamities of every kind, and set for ever out of their reach; and no deliverance, no happy alteration, will remain to be accomplished in the use of means of grace, under the administrations of ministers. It will then be pronounced, "He that is unjust, let him be unjust still; and he that is filthy, let him be filthy still; and he that is righteous, let him be righteous still; and he that is holy, let him be holy still."

(2.) Then they shall meet together in a state of clear, certain, and infallible light.

Ministers are set as guides and teachers, and are represented in Scripture as lights set up in the churches; and in the present state meet their people, from time to time, in order to instruct and enlighten them, to correct their mistakes, and to be a voice behind them, when they turn aside to the right hand or the left, saying, "This is the way, walk ye in it;" to evince and confirm the truth by exhibiting the proper evidences of it, and to refute errors and corrupt opinions, to convince the erroneous, and establish the doubting. But when Christ shall come to judgment, every error and false opinion shall be detected; all deceit and delusion shall vanish away before the light of that day, as the darkness of the night vanishes at the appearance of the rising sun; and every doctrine of the word of God shall then appear in full evidence, and none shall remain unconvinced. All shall know the truth with the greatest certainty, and there shall be no mistakes to rectify.

Now ministers and their people may disagree in their judgments concerning some matters of religion, and may sometimes meet to confer together concerning those things wherein they differ, and to hear the reasons that may be offered on one side and the other; and all may be ineffectual as to any conviction of the truth. They may meet and part again, no more agreed than before; and that side which was in the wrong, may remain so still. Sometimes the meetings of ministers with their people, in such a case of disagreeing sentiments, are attended with unhappy debate and controversy, managed with much prejudice and want of candour; not tending to light and conviction, but rather to confirm and increase darkness, and establish opposition to the truth, and alienation of affection one from another. But when they shall meet together at the day of judgment, before the tribunal of the great Judge, the mind and will of Christ will be made known; and there shall no longer be any debate or difference of opinions. The evidence of the truth shall appear beyond all dispute, and all controversies shall be finally and for ever decided.

Now ministers meet their people in order to enlighten and awaken the consciences of sinners; setting before them the great evil and danger of sin, the strictness of God's law, their own wickedness of heart and practice, the great guilt they are under, the wrath that abides upon them, and their impotence, blindness, poverty, and helpless and undone condition. But all is often in vain; they remain still, notwithstanding all their ministers can say, stupid and unawakened, and their consciences unconvinced. But it will not be so at their last meeting at the day of judgment; sinners, when they shall meet their minister before their great Judge, will not meet him with a stupid conscience. They will then be fully convinced of the truth of those things which they formerly heard from him, concerning the greatness and terrible majesty of God, his holiness, and hatred of sin, and his awful justice in punishing it; the strictness of his law, and the dreadfulness and truth of his threatenings, and their own unspeakable guilt and misery. And they shall never more be insensible of these things. The eyes of conscience will now be fully enlightened, and never shall be blinded again. The mouth of conscience shall now be opened, and never shall be shut any more.

Now ministers meet with their people, in public and private, in order to enlighten them concerning the state of their souls; to open and apply the rules of God's word to them, in order to their searching their own hearts, and discerning their state. But now ministers have no infallible discernment of the state of their people; and the most skilful of them are liable to mistakes, and often are mistaken in things of this nature. Nor are the people able certainly to know the state of their minister, or one another's state: very often those pass among them for saints, and it may be eminent saints, that are grand hypocrites; and on the other hand, those are sometimes censured, or hardly received into their charity, that are indeed some of God's jewels. And nothing is more common than for men to be mistaken concerning their *own* state. Many that are abominable to God, and the children of his wrath, think highly of themselves, as his precious saints and dear children. Yea, there is reason to think, that often some that are most bold in their confidence of their safe and happy state, and think themselves not only true saints, but the most eminent saints in the congregation, are in a peculiar manner a smoke in God's nostrils. And thus it undoubtedly often is in those congregations where the word of God is most faithfully dispensed, notwithstanding all that ministers can say in their clearest explications, and most searching applications of the doctrines and rules of God's word to the souls of their hearers. But in the day of judgment they shall have another sort of meeting; then the secrets of every heart shall be made manifest, and every man's state shall be perfectly known. 1 Cor. iv. 5. "Therefore judge nothing before the time, until the Lord come, who both will bring to light the hidden things of darkness, and will make manifest the counsels of the hearts: and then shall every man have praise of God."

Then none shall be deceived concerning his own state, nor shall be any more in doubt about it. There shall be an eternal end to all the self-conceit and vain hopes of deluded hypocrites, and all the doubts and fears of sincere Christians. And then shall all know the state of one another's souls. The people shall know whether their minister has been sincere and faithful, and the minister shall know the state of every one of their people, and to whom the word and ordinances of God have been a savour of life unto life, and to whom a savour of death unto death.

Now in this present state it often happens, that when ministers and people meet together to debate and manage their ecclesiastical affairs, especially in a state of controversy, they are ready to judge and censure with regard to each other's views and designs, and the principles and ends by which each is influenced; and are greatly mistaken in their judgment, and wrong one another in their censures. But at that future meeting, things will be set in a true and perfect light, and the principles and aims that every one has acted from, shall be certainly known: and there will be an end to all errors of this kind, and all unrighteous censures.

(3.) In this world, ministers and their people often meet together to hear of and wait upon an unseen Lord; but at the judgment, they shall meet in his most immediate and visible presence.

Ministers, who now often meet their people to preach to them the King eternal, immortal, and invisible, to convince them that there is a God, and declare to them what manner of being he is, and to convince them that he governs, and will judge the world, and that there is a future state of rewards and punishments—and to preach to them a Christ in heaven, at the right hand of God, in an unseen world—shall then meet their people in the most immediate sensible presence of this great God, Saviour, and Judge, appearing in the most plain, visible, and open manner, with great glory, with all his holy angels, before them and the whole world. They shall not meet them to hear about an absent Christ, an unseen Lord, and future Judge; but to appear before that Judge—being set together in the presence of that supreme Lord—in his immense glory and awful majesty, of whom they have heard so often in their meetings together on earth.

(4.) The meeting at the last day, of ministers and the people that have been under their care, will not be attended by any one with a careless, heedless heart.

With such a heart are their meetings often attended in this world by many persons, having little regard to him whom they pretend unitedly to adore in the solemn duties of his public worship, taking little heed to their own thoughts or frame of their minds, not attending to the business they are engaged in, or considering the end for which they are come together. But at that great day there will not be one careless heart, no sleeping, no wandering of mind from the great concern of the meeting, no inattentiveness to the business of the day, no regardlessness of the presence they are in, or of those great things which they shall hear from Christ, or that they formerly heard from him, and of him, by their ministers, in their state of trial, or which they shall now hear their ministers declaring concerning them before their Judge.

Having observed these things, concerning the manner and circumstances of this future meeting, before the tribunal of Christ at the day of judgment, I now proceed,

II. To observe to what *purposes* they shall then meet.

1. To give an account, before the great Judge, of their behaviour one to another, in the relation they bore to each other in this world.

Ministers are sent forth by Christ to their people on his business. They are his servants and messengers; and, when they have finished their service, they must return to their master to give him an account of what they have done, and of the entertainment they have had in performing their ministry. Thus we find, in Luke xiv. 16—21. that when the servant who was sent forth to call the guests to the great supper, had finished his appointed service, he returned to his master, and gave him an account of what he had done, and of the entertainment he had received. And when the master, being angry, sent his servant to others, he returns again, and gives his master an account of his conduct and success. So we read, in Heb. xiii. 17. of ministers or rulers in the house of God, that "they watch for souls, as those that must give account." And we see by the fore-mentioned Luke xiv. that ministers must give an account to their master, not only of their own behaviour in the discharge of their office, but also of their people's reception of them, and of the treatment they have met with among them.

Faithful ministers will then give an account with joy, concerning those who have received them well, and made a good improvement of their ministry; and these will be given them, at that day, as their crown of rejoicing. And, at the same time, they will give an account of the ill treatment of such as have not well received them and their messages from Christ: they will meet these, not as they used to do in this world, to counsel and warn them, but to bear witness against them; as their judges, and assessors with Christ, to condemn them. And, on the other hand, the people will at that day rise up in judgment against wicked and unfaithful ministers, who have sought their own temporal interest more than the good of the souls of their flock.

2. At that time ministers, and the people who have been under their care, shall meet together before Christ, that he may judge between them, as to any controversies which have subsisted between them in this world.

It often comes to pass in this evil world, that great differences and controversies arise between ministers and the people under their pastoral care. Though they are under the greatest obligations to live in peace, above persons in almost any relation whatever; and although contests and dissensions between persons so related are the most unhappy and terrible in their consequences, on many accounts, of any sort of contentions; yet how frequent have such contentions been! Sometimes a people contest with their ministers about their doctrine, sometimes about their administrations and conduct, and sometimes about their maintenance. Sometimes such contests continue a long time; and sometimes they are decided in this world, according to the prevailing interest of one party or the other, rather than by the word of God, and the reason of things; and sometimes such controversies never have any proper determination in this world.

But at the day of judgment there will be a full, perfect, and everlasting decision of them. The infallible Judge, the infinite fountain of light, truth, and justice, will judge between the contending parties, and will declare what is the truth, who is in the right, and what is agreeable to his mind and will. And in order hereto, the parties must stand together before him at the last day; which will be the great day of finishing and determining all controversies, rectifying all mistakes, and abolishing all unrighteous judgments, errors, and confusions, which have before subsisted in the world of mankind.

3. Ministers, and the people that have been under their care, must meet together at that time to receive an eternal sentence and retribution from the Judge, in the presence of each other, according to their behaviour in the relation they stood in one to another in the present state.

The Judge will not only declare justice, but he will do justice between ministers and their people. He will declare what is right between them, approving him that has been just and faithful, and condemning the unjust; and perfect truth and equity shall take place in the sentence which he passes, in the rewards he bestows, and the punishments which he inflicts. There shall be a glorious reward to faithful ministers; to those who have been successful. Dan. xii. 3. "And they that be wise shall shine as the brightness of the firmament, and they that turn many to righteousness, as the stars for ever and ever:" and also to those who have been faithful, and yet not successful; Isa. xlix. 4. "Then I said, I have laboured in vain, I have spent my strength for nought; yet surely my judgment is with the Lord, and my reward with my God." And those who have well received and entertained them shall be gloriously rewarded; Matt. x. 40, 41. "He that receiveth you, receiveth me; and he that receiveth me, receiveth him that sent me. He that receiveth a prophet in the name of a prophet, shall receive a prophet's reward; and he that receiveth a righteous man, in the name of a righteous man, shall receive a righteous man's reward." Such people, and their faithful ministers, shall be each other's crown of rejoicing. 1 Thess. ii. 19, 20. "For what is our hope, or joy, or crown of rejoicing? Are not even ye in the presence of our Lord Jesus Christ at his coming? For ye are our glory and joy." And in the text, "We are your rejoicing, as ye also are ours, in the day of the Lord Jesus." But they that evil entreat Christ's faithful ministers, especially in that wherein they are faithful, shall be severely punished; Matt. x. 14, 15. "And whosoever shall not receive you, nor hear your words, when ye depart out of that house or city, shake off the dust of your feet. Verily I say unto you, it shall be more tolerable for the sinners of Sodom and Gomorrah, in the day of judgment, than for that city." Deut. xxxiii. 8—11. "And of Levi he said, Let thy Thummim and thy Urim be with thy holy one. They shall teach Jacob thy judgments, and Israel thy law. Bless, Lord, his substance, and accept the work of his hands; smite through the loins of them that rise against him, and of them that hate him, that they rise not again." On the other hand, those ministers who are found to have been unfaithful, shall have a most terrible punishment. See Ezek. xxxiii. 6. Matt. xxiii. 1—33.

Thus justice shall be administered at the great day to ministers and their people: and to that end they shall meet together, that they may not only receive justice to themselves, but see justice done to the other party. For this is the end of that great day, to reveal or declare the righteous judgment of God; Rom. ii. 5. Ministers shall have justice done them, and they shall see justice done to their people. And the people shall receive justice themselves from their Judge, and shall see justice done to their minister. And so all things will be adjusted and settled for ever between them; every one being sentenced and recompensed according to his works, either in receiving and wearing a crown of eternal joy and glory, or in suffering everlasting shame and pain.—I come now to the next thing proposed, *viz.*

III. To give some *reasons* why we may suppose God has so ordered it, that ministers, and the people that have been under their care, shall meet together at the day of judgment, in such a manner and for such purposes.

There are two things which I would now observe.

1. The mutual concerns of ministers and their people are of the greatest importance.

The Scripture declares, that God will bring every work into judgment, with every secret thing, whether it be good, or whether it be evil. It is fit that all the concerns and all the behaviour of mankind, both public and private, should be brought at last before God's tribunal, and finally determined by an infallible Judge. But it is especially requisite that it should be thus, as to affairs of very great importance.

Now the mutual concerns of a christian minister and his church and congregation, are of the highest importance; in many respects, of much greater moment than the temporal concerns of the greatest earthly monarchs, and their kingdoms or empires. It is of vast consequence, how ministers discharge their office, and conduct themselves towards their people in the work of the ministry, and in affairs appertaining to it. It is also a matter of vast importance, how a people receive and entertain a faithful minister of Christ, and what improvement they make of his ministry. These things have a more immediate and direct respect to the great and last end for which man was made, and the eternal welfare of mankind, than any of the temporal concerns of men, whether private or public. And therefore it is especially fit that these affairs should be brought into judgment, and openly determined and settled in truth and righteousness; and that to this end, ministers and their people should meet together before the omniscient and infallible Judge.

2. The mutual concerns of ministers and their people have a special relation to the main things appertaining to the day of judgment.

They have a special relation to that great and divine person who will then appear as Judge. Ministers are his messengers, sent forth by him; and, in their office and administrations among their people, represent his person, stand in his stead, as those that are sent to declare his mind, to do his work, and to speak and act in his name. And therefore it is especially fit, that they should return to him to give an account of their work and success. The king is judge of all his subjects, they are all accountable to him. But it is more especially requisite that the king's ministers, who are especially intrusted with the administrations of his kingdom, and who are sent forth on some special negociation, should return to him, to give an account of themselves, and their discharge of their trust, and the reception they have met with.

Ministers are not only messengers of the person who at the last day will appear as Judge, but the errand they are sent upon, and the affairs they have committed to them as his ministers, most immediately concern his honour, and the interest of his kingdom. The work they are sent upon is to promote the designs of his administration and government; and therefore their business with their people has a near relation to the day of judgment; for the great end of that day is completely to settle and establish the affairs of his kingdom, to adjust all things that pertain to it, that every thing which is opposite to the interests of his kingdom may be removed, and that every thing which contributes to the completeness and glory of it may be perfected and confirmed, that this great king may receive his due honour and glory.

Again, the mutual concerns of ministers and their people have a direct relation to the concerns of the day of judgment, as the business of ministers with their people is to promote the eternal salvation of the souls of men, and their escape from eternal damnation; and the day of judgment is appointed for that end, openly to decide and settle men's eternal state, to fix some in a state of eternal salvation, and to bring their salvation to its utmost consummation, and to fix others in a state of everlasting damnation and most perfect misery. The mutual concerns of ministers and people have a most direct relation to the day of judgment, as the very design of the work of the ministry is the people's preparation for that day: ministers are sent to warn them of the approach of that day, to forewarn them of the dreadful sentence then to be pronounced on the wicked, and declare to them the blessed sentence then to be pronounced on the righteous, and to use means with them that they may escape the wrath which is then to come on the ungodly, and obtain the reward then to be bestowed on the saints.

And as the mutual concerns of ministers and their people have so near and direct a relation to that day, it is especially fit that those concerns should be there settled and issued; and that, in order to this, ministers and their people should meet and appear together before the great Judge at that day.

APPLICATION.

The improvement I would make of the subject, is to lead the people here present, who have been under my pastoral care, to some reflections, and give them some advice suitable to our present circumstances; relating to what has been lately done in order to our being separated, but expecting to meet each other before the great tribunal at the day of judgment.

The deep and serious consideration of our future solemn meeting, is certainly most suitable at such a time as this; there having so lately been that done, which, in all probability, will (as to the relation we have heretofore stood in) be followed with an everlasting separation.

How often have we met together in the house of God in this relation! how often have I spoke to you, instructed, counselled, warned, directed, and fed you, and administered ordinances among you, as the people which were committed to my care, and of whose precious souls I had the charge! But in all probability, this never will be again.

The prophet Jeremiah, (chap. xxv. 3.) puts the people in mind how long he had laboured among them in the work of the ministry: "From the thirteenth year of Josiah, the son of Amon, king of Judah, even unto this day, (that is, the three and twentieth year,) the word of the Lord came unto me, and I have spoken unto you, rising early and speaking." I am not about to compare myself with the prophet Jeremiah; but in this respect I can say as he did, that "I have spoken the word of God to you, unto the three and twentieth year, rising early and speaking." It was three and twenty years, the 15th day of last February, since I have laboured in the work of the ministry, in the relation of a pastor to this church and congregation. And though my strength has been weakness, having always laboured under great infirmity of body, besides my insufficiency for so great a charge in other respects, yet I have not spared my feeble strength, but have exerted it for the good of your souls. I can appeal to you, as the apostle does to his hearers, Gal. iv. 13. "Ye know how through infirmity of the flesh, I preached the gospel unto you." I have spent the prime of my life and strength in labours for your eternal welfare. You are my witnesses, that what strength I have had, I have not neglected in idleness, nor laid out in prosecuting worldly schemes, and managing temporal affairs, for the advancement of my outward estate, and aggrandizing myself and family; but have given myself to the work of the ministry, labouring in it night and day, rising early, and applying myself to this great business to which Christ has appointed me. I have found the work of the ministry among you to be a great work indeed, a work of exceeding care, labour, and difficulty. Many have been the heavy burdens that I have borne in it, to which my strength has been very unequal. God called me to bear these burdens; and I bless his name, that he has so supported me as to keep me from sinking under them, and that his power herein has been manifested in my weakness; so that although I have often been troubled on every side, yet I have not been distressed; perplexed, but not in despair; cast down, but not destroyed.—But now I have reason to think my work is finished which I had to do as your minister: you have publicly rejected me, and my opportunities cease.

How highly therefore does it now become us, to consider of that time when we must meet one another before the chief Shepherd! When I must give an account of my stewardship, of the service I have done, and the reception and treatment I have had among the people to whom he sent me. And you must give an account of your own conduct towards me, and the improvement you have made of these three and twenty years of my ministry. For then both you and I must appear together, and we both must give an account, in order to an infallible righteous and eternal sentence to be passed upon us, by him who will judge us with respect to all that we have said or done in our meetings here, all our conduct one towards another, in the house of God and elsewhere; who will try our hearts, and manifest our thoughts, and the principles and frames of our minds. He will judge us with respect to all the controversies which have subsisted between us, with the strictest impartiality, and will examine our treatment of each other in those controversies. There is nothing covered, that shall not be revealed, nor hid, which shall not be known; all will be examined in the searching penetrating light of God's omniscience and glory, and by him whose eyes are as a flame of fire; and truth and right shall be made plainly to appear, being stript of every veil. All error, falsehood, unrighteousness, and injury shall be laid open, stripped of every disguise; every specious pretence, every cavil, and all false reasoning, shall vanish in a moment, as not being able to bear the light of that day. And then our hearts will be turned inside out, and the secrets of them will be made more plainly to appear than our outward actions do now. Then it shall appear what the ends are which we have aimed at, what have been the governing principles which we have acted from, and what have been the dispositions we have exercised in our ecclesiastical disputes and contests. Then it will appear, whether I acted uprightly, and from a truly conscientious careful regard to my duty to my great Lord and master, in some former ecclesiastical controversies, which have been attended with exceeding unhappy circumstances and consequences. It will then appear whether there was any just cause for the resentment which was manifested on those occasions. And then our late grand controversy, concerning the qualifications necessary for admission to the privileges of members in complete standing, in the visible church of Christ, will be examined and judged in all its parts and circumstances, and the whole set forth in a clear, certain, and perfect light. Then it will appear whether the doctrine which I have preached and published concerning this matter be Christ's own doctrine, whether he will not own it as one of the precious truths which have proceeded from his own mouth, and vindicate and honour as such before the whole universe. Then it will appear what is meant by "the man that comes without the wedding-garment;" for that is the day spoken of, Matt. xxii. 13. wherein such an one shall be "bound hand and foot, and cast into outer darkness, where shall be weeping and gnashing of teeth." And then it will appear whether, in declaring this doctrine, and acting agreeably to it, and in my general conduct in the affair, I have been influenced from any regard to my own temporal interest, or honour, or desire to appear wiser than others; or have acted from any sinister secular views whatsoever; and whether what I have done has not been from a careful, strict, and tender regard to the will of my Lord and Master, and because I dare not offend him, being satisfied what his will was, after a long, diligent, impartial, and prayerful inquiry. Then it will be seen, whether I had this constantly in view and prospect, to engage me to great solicitude not rashly to determine the question, that such a determination would not be for my temporal interest, but every way against it, bringing a long series of extreme difficulties, and plunging me into an abyss of trouble and sorrow. And then it will appear whether my people have done their duty to their pastor with respect to this matter; whether they have shown a right temper and spirit on this occasion; whether they have done me justice in hearing, attending to, and considering what I had to say in evidence of what I believed and taught as part of the counsel of God; whether I have been treated with that impartiality, candour, and regard which the just Judge esteemed due; and whether, in the many steps which have been taken, and the many things that have been said and done in the course of this controversy, righteousness, and charity, and christian decorum have been maintained; or if otherwise, to how great a degree these things have been violated. Then every step of the conduct of each of us in this affair, from first to last, and the spirit we have exercised in all, shall be examined and manifested, and our own consciences will speak plain and loud, and each of us shall be convinced, and the world shall know; and never shall there be any more mistake, misrepresentation, or misapprehension of the affair to eternity.

This controversy is now probably brought to an issue between you and me as to this world; it has issued in the event of the week before last: but it must have another decision at that great day, which certainly will come, when you and I shall meet together before the great judgment seat: and therefore I leave it to that time, and shall say no more about it at present.—But I would now proceed to address myself particularly to several sorts of persons.

I. To those who are *professors* of godliness amongst us.

I would now call you to a serious consideration of that great day wherein you must meet him who has heretofore been your pastor, before the Judge whose eyes are as a flame of fire.—I have endeavoured, according to my best ability, to search the word of God, with regard to the distinguishing notes of true piety, those by which persons might best discover their state, and most surely and clearly judge of themselves. And these rules and marks I have from time to time applied to you, in the preaching of the word, to the utmost of my skill, and in the most plain and searching manner that I have been able, in order to the detecting of the deceived hypocrite, and establishing the hopes and comforts of the sincere. And yet it is to be feared, that after all that I have done, I now leave some of you in a deceived, deluded state; for it is not to be supposed that among several hundred professors, none are deceived.

Henceforward I am like to have no more opportunity to take the care and charge of your souls, to examine and search them. But still I entreat you to remember and consider the rules which I have often laid down to you during my ministry, with a solemn regard to the future day when you and I must meet together before our Judge; when the uses of examination you have heard from me must be rehearsed again before you, and those rules of trial must be tried, and it will appear whether they have been good or not. It will also appear whether you have impartially heard them, and tried yourselves by them; and the Judge himself, who is infallible, will try both you and me. After this none will be deceived concerning the state of their souls.

I have often put you in mind, that whatever your pretences to experiences, discoveries, comforts, and joys have been, at that day every one will be judged according to his works; and then you will find it so. May you have a minister of greater knowledge of the word of God, and better acquaintance with soul cases, and of greater skill in applying himself to souls, whose discourses may be more searching and convincing; that such of you as have held fast deceit under my preaching, may have your eyes opened by his; that you may be undeceived before that great day.

What means and helps for instruction and self-examination you may hereafter have is uncertain; but one thing is certain, that the time is short, your opportunity for rectifying mistakes in so important a concern will soon come to an end. We live in a world of great changes. There is now a great change come to pass; you have withdrawn yourselves from my ministry, under which you have continued for so many years. But the time is coming, and will soon come, when you will pass out of time into eternity; and so will pass from under all means of grace whatsoever.

The greater part of you who are professors of godliness have (to use the phrase of the apostle) "acknowledged me in part." You have heretofore acknowledged me to be your spiritual father, the instrument of the greatest good to you that can be obtained by any of the children of men. Consider of that day when you and I shall meet before our Judge, when it shall be examined whether you have had from me the treatment which is due to spiritual children, and whether you have treated me as you ought to have treated a spiritual father.—As the relation of a natural parent brings great obligations on children in the sight of God; so much more, in many respects, does the relation of a spiritual father bring great obligations on such of whose conversion and eternal salvation they suppose God has made them the instruments: 1 Cor. iv. 15. "For though you have ten thousand instructors in Christ, yet have ye not many fathers: for in Christ Jesus, I have begotten you through the gospel."

II. Now I am taking my leave of this people, I would apply myself to such among them as I leave in a *Christless*, graceless condition; and would call on such seriously to consider of that solemn day when they and I must meet before the Judge of the world.

My parting with you is in some respects, in a peculiar manner, a melancholy parting; inasmuch as I leave you in most melancholy circumstances; because I leave you in the gall of bitterness and bond of iniquity, having the wrath of God abiding on you, and remaining under condemnation to everlasting misery and destruction. Seeing I must leave you, it would have been a comfortable and happy circumstance of our parting, if I had left you in Christ, safe and blessed in that sure refuge and glorious rest of the saints. But it is otherwise, I leave you far off, aliens and strangers, wretched subjects and captives of sin and Satan, and prisoners of vindictive justice; without Christ, and without God in the world.

Your consciences bear me witness, that while I had opportunity, I have not ceased to warn you, and set before you your danger. I have studied to represent the misery of your circumstances in the clearest manner possible. I have tried all ways that I could think of tending to awaken your consciences, and make you sensible of the necessity of improving your time, and being speedy in fleeing from the wrath to come, and thorough in the use of means for your escape and safety. I have diligently endeavoured to find out and use the most powerful motives to persuade you to take care for your own welfare and salvation. I have not only endeavoured to awaken you, that you might be moved with fear, but I have used my utmost endeavours to win you. I have sought out acceptable words, that if possible I might prevail upon you to forsake sin, and turn to God, and accept of Christ as your Saviour and Lord. I have spent my strength very much in these things. But yet, with regard to you whom I am now addressing, I have not been successful: but have this day reason to complain in those words, Jer. vi. 29. "The bellows are burnt, the lead is consumed of the fire, the founder melteth in vain, for the wicked are not plucked away." It is to be feared that all my labours, as to many of you, have served to no other purpose but to harden you; and that the word which I have preached, instead of being a savour of life unto life, has been a savour of death unto death. Though I shall not have any account to give for the future of such as have openly and resolutely renounced my ministry, as of a trust committed to me; yet remember you must give account for yourselves, of your care of your own souls, and your improvement of all means past and future, through your whole lives. God only knows what will become of your poor perishing souls, what means you may hereafter enjoy, or what disadvantages and temptations you may be under. May God in mercy grant, that however all past means have been unsuccessful, you may have future means which may have a new effect; and that the word of God as it shall be hereafter dispensed to you, may prove as the fire and the hammer that breaketh the rock in pieces. However, let me now at parting exhort and beseech you not wholly to forget the warnings you have had while under my ministry. When you and I shall meet at the day of judgment, then you will remember them. The sight of me your former minister, on that occasion, will soon revive them in your memory; and that in a very affecting manner. O do not let that be the first time that they are so revived.

You and I are now parting one from another as to this world; let us labour that we may not be parted after our meeting at the last day. If I have been your faithful pastor, (which will that day appear whether I have or no,) then I shall be acquitted, and shall ascend with Christ. O do your part, that in such a case, you may not be forced eternally to part from me, and all that have been faithful in Christ Jesus. *This* is a sorrowful parting, but *that* would be more sorrowful.—This you may perhaps bear without being much affected with it, if you are not glad of it; but such a parting in that day will most deeply, sensibly, and dreadfully affect you.

III. I would address myself to those who are under some *awakenings*.

Blessed be God that there are some such, and that (although I have reason to fear I leave multitudes in this large congregation in a Christless state) I do not leave them all in total stupidity and carelessness about their souls. Some of you, that I have reason to hope are under some awakenings, have acquainted me with your circumstances; which has a tendency to cause me, now I am leaving, to take my leave with peculiar concern for you. What will be the issue of your present exercise of mind I know not; but it will be known at that day, when you and I shall meet before the judgment-seat of Christ. Therefore now be much in consideration of that day.

Now I am parting with this flock, I would once more press upon you the counsels I have heretofore given, to take heed of slighting so great a concern, to be thorough and in good earnest in the affair, to beware of backsliding, and to hold on and hold out to the end. And cry mightily to God, that these great changes which pass over this church and congregation do not prove your overthrow. There is great temptation in them; and the devil will undoubtedly seek to make his advantage of them, if possible, to cause your present convictions and endeavours to be abortive. You had need to double your diligence, and watch and pray, lest you be overcome by temptations.

Whoever may hereafter stand related to you as your spiritual guide, my desire and prayer is, that the great Shepherd of the sheep would have a special respect to you, and be your guide, (for there is none teacheth like him,) and that he who is the infinite fountain of light, would "open your eyes, and turn you from darkness unto light, and from the power of Satan unto God; that you may receive forgiveness of sins, and inheritance among them that are sanctified, through faith that is in Christ:" that so, in that great day, when I shall meet you again before your Judge and mine, we may meet in joyful and glorious circumstances, never to be separated any more.

IV. I would apply myself to the *young* people of the congregation.

Since I have been settled in the work of the ministry in this place, I have ever had a peculiar concern for the souls of the young people, and a desire that religion might flourish among them; and have especially exerted myself in order to it; because I knew the special opportunity they had beyond others, and that ordinarily those for whom God intended mercy, were brought to fear and love him in their youth. And it has ever appeared to me a peculiarly amiable thing, to see young people walking in the ways of virtue and Christian piety, having their hearts purified and sweetened with a principle of divine love. How exceeding beautiful, and how conducive to the adorning and happiness of the town, if the young people could be persuaded, when they meet together, to converse as Christians, and as the children of God; avoiding impurity, levity, and extravagance; keeping strictly to rules of virtue, and conversing together of the things of God, and Christ, and heaven! This is what I have longed for: and it has been exceedingly grievous to me when I have heard of vice, vanity, and disorder among our youth. And so far as I know my heart, it was from hence that I formerly led this church to some measures, for the suppressing vice among our young people, which gave so great offence, and by which I became so obnoxious. I have sought the good and not the hurt of our young people. I have desired their truest honour and happiness, and not their reproach; knowing that true virtue and religion tended not only to the glory and felicity of young people in another world, but their greatest peace and prosperity, and highest dignity and honour, in this world; and above all things to sweeten, and render pleasant and delightful, even the days of youth.

But whether I have loved you, and sought your good more or less, now committing your souls to him who once committed the pastoral care of them to me—nothing remains, but only (as I am now taking my leave of you) earnestly to beseech you, from love to yourselves, if you have none to me, not to despise and forget the warnings and counsels I have so often given you; remembering the day when you and I must meet again before the great Judge of quick and dead; when it will appear whether the things I have taught you were true, whether the counsels I have given you were good, and whether I truly sought your welfare, and whether you have well improved my endeavours.

I have, from time to time, earnestly warned you against *frolicking*, (as it is called,) and some other liberties commonly taken by young people in the land. And whatever some may say in justification of such liberties and customs, and may laugh at warnings against them, I now leave you my parting testimony against such things; not doubting but God will approve and confirm it in that day when we shall meet before him.

V. I would apply myself to the *children* of the congregation, the lambs of this flock, who have been so long under my care.

I have just now said that I have had a peculiar concern for the young people; and in so saying, I did not intend to exclude you. You are in youth, and in the most early youth; and therefore I have been sensible, that if those that were young had a precious opportunity for their souls' good, you who are very young had, in many respects, a peculiarly precious opportunity. And accordingly I have not neglected you: I have endeavoured to do the part of a faithful shepherd, in feeding the lambs as well as the sheep. Christ did once commit the care of your souls to me as your minister; and you know, dear children, how I have instructed you, and warned you from time to time. You know how I have often called you together for that end; and some of you, sometimes, have seemed to be affected with what I have said to you. But I am afraid it has had no saving effect as to many of you; but that you remain still in an unconverted condition, without any real saving work wrought in your souls, convincing you thoroughly of your sin and misery, causing you to see the great evil of sin, and to mourn for it, and hate it above all things; and giving you a sense of the excellency of the Lord Jesus Christ, bringing you with all your hearts to cleave to him as your Saviour, weaning your hearts from the world, and causing you to love God above all, and to delight in holiness more than in all the pleasant things of this earth. And I must now leave you in a miserable condition, having no interest in Christ, and so under the awful displeasure and anger of God, and in danger of going down to the pit of eternal misery.—Now I must bid you farewell: I must leave you in the hands of God. I can do no more than pray for you. Only I desire you not to forget, but often think of the counsels and warnings I have given you, and the endeavours I have used, that your souls might be saved from everlasting destruction.

Dear children, I leave you in an evil world, that is full of snares and temptations. God only knows what will become of you. This the Scripture has told us, that there are but few saved; and we have abundant confirmation of it from what we see. This we see, that children die as well as others. Multitudes die before they grow up; and of those that grow up, comparatively few ever give good evidence of saving conversion to God. I pray God to pity you, and take care of you, and provide for you the best means for the good of your souls; and that God himself would undertake for you, to be your heavenly Father, and the mighty Redeemer of your immortal souls. Do not neglect to pray for yourselves. Take heed you be not of the number of those who cast off fear, and restrain prayer before God. Constantly pray to God in secret; and often remember that great day when you must appear before the judgment-seat of Christ, and meet your minister there, who has so often counselled and warned you.

I conclude with a few words of advice to all in general, in some particulars, which are of great importance in order to the future welfare and prosperity of this church and congregation.

1. One thing that greatly concerns you, as you would be a happy people, is the maintaining of *family order*.

We have had great disputes how the church ought to be regulated; and indeed the subject of these disputes was of great importance: but the due regulation of your families is of no less, and, in some respects, of much greater importance. Every christian family ought to be as it were a little church, consecrated to Christ, and wholly influenced and governed by his rules. And family education and order are some of the chief of the means of grace. If these fail, all other means are likely to prove ineffectual. If these are duly maintained, all the means of grace will be likely to prosper and be successful.

Let me now therefore, once more, before I finally cease to speak to this congregation, repeat, and earnestly press the counsel which I have often urged on heads of families, while I was their pastor, to great painfulness in teaching, warning, and directing their children; bringing them up in the nurture and admonition of the Lord; beginning early, where there is yet opportunity, and maintaining a constant diligence in labours of this kind. Remember that, as you would not have all your instructions and counsels ineffectual, there must be government as well as instructions, which must be maintained with an even hand, and steady resolution, as a guard to the religion and morals of the family, and the support of its good order. Take heed that it be not with any of you as it was with Eli of old, who reproved his children, but restrained them not; and that, by this means, you do not bring the like curse on your families as he did on his.

And let children obey their parents, and yield to their instructions, and submit to their orders, as they would inherit a blessing and not a curse. For we have reason to think, from many things in the word of God, that nothing has a greater tendency to bring a curse on persons in this world, and on all their temporal concerns, than an undutiful, unsubmissive, disorderly behaviour in children towards their parents.

2. As you would seek the future prosperity of this society, it is of vast importance that you should avoid contention.

A contentious people will be a miserable people. The contentions which have been among you, since I first became your pastor, have been one of the greatest burdens I have laboured under in the course of my ministry—not only the contentions you have had with me, but those which you have had one with another, about your lands, and other concerns—because I knew that contention, heat of spirit, evil speaking, and things of the like nature, were directly contrary to the spirit of Christianity, and did, in a peculiar manner, tend to drive away God's Spirit from a people, and to render all means of grace ineffectual, as well as to destroy a people's outward comfort and welfare.

Let me therefore earnestly exhort you, as you would seek your own future good, hereafter to watch against a contentious spirit. "If you would see good days, seek peace, and ensue it." 1 Pet. iii. 10, 11. Let the late contention about the terms of christian communion, as it has been the greatest, be the last. I would, now I am preaching my farewell sermon, say to you, as the apostle to the Corinthians, 2 Cor. xiii. 11. "Finally, brethren, farewell. Be perfect, be of one mind, live in peace; and the God of love and peace shall be with you."

And here I would particularly advise those that have adhered to me in the late controversy, to watch over their spirits, and avoid all bitterness towards others. Your temptations are, in some respects, the greatest; because what has been lately done is grievous to you. But however wrong you may think others have done, maintain, with great diligence and watchfulness, a christian meekness and sedateness of spirit; and labour, in this respect, to excel others who are of the contrary part. And this will be the best victory: for "he that rules his spirit, is better than he that takes a city." Therefore let nothing be done through strife or vain-glory. Indulge no revengeful spirit in any wise; but watch and pray against it: and, by all means in your power, seek the prosperity of this town. And never think you behave yourselves as becomes Christians, but when you sincerely, sensibly, and fervently love all men, of whatever party or opinion, and whether friendly or unkind, just or injurious, to you or your friends, or to the cause and kingdom of Christ.

3. Another thing that vastly concerns the future prosperity of the town, is, that you should watch against the encroachments of error; and particularly Arminianism, and doctrines of like tendency.

You were, many of you, as I well remember, much alarmed with the apprehension of the danger of the prevailing of these corrupt principles, near sixteen years ago. But the danger then was small in comparison of what appears now. These doctrines at this day are much more prevalent than they were then. The progress they have made in the land, within this seven years, seems to have been vastly greater than at any time in the like space before. And they are still prevailing and creeping into almost all parts of the land, threatening the utter ruin of the credit of those doctrines which are the peculiar glory of the gospel, and the interests of vital piety. And I have of late perceived some things among yourselves, that show that you are far from being out of danger, but on the contrary remarkably exposed. The elder people may perhaps think themselves sufficiently fortified against infection. But it is fit that all should beware of self-confidence and carnal security, and should remember those needful warnings of sacred writ, "Be not high minded, but fear; and let him that stands, take heed lest he fall." But let the case of the elder people be as it will, the rising generation are doubtless greatly exposed. These principles are exceeding taking with corrupt nature, and what young people, at least such as have not their hearts established with grace, are easily led away with.

And if these principles should greatly prevail in this town, as they very lately have done in another large town I could name, formerly greatly noted for religion, for a long time, it will threaten the spiritual and eternal ruin of this people, in the present and future generations. Therefore you have need of the greatest and most diligent care and watchfulness with respect to this matter.

4. Another thing which I would advise to, that you may hereafter be a prosperous people, is, that you would give yourselves much to prayer.

God is the fountain of all blessing and prosperity, and he will be sought to for his blessing. I would therefore advise you not only to be constant in secret and family prayer, and in the public worship of God in his house, but also often to assemble yourselves in private praying societies. I would advise all such as are grieved for the afflictions of Joseph, and sensibly affected with the calamities of this town, of whatever opinion they be with relation to the subject of our late controversy, often to meet together for prayer, and cry to God for his mercy to themselves, and mercy to this town, and mercy to Zion and the people of God in general through the world.

5. The last article of advice I would give (which doubtless does greatly concern your prosperity) is, that you would take great care with regard to the settlement of a minister; and particularly in these two respects.

(1.) That he be a man of thoroughly sound principles, in the scheme of doctrine which he maintains.

Of this you will stand in the greatest need, especially at such a day of corruption as this is. And in order to obtain such a one, you had need to exercise extraordinary care and prudence.—I know the danger.—I know the manner of many young gentlemen of corrupt principles, their ways of concealing themselves, the fair specious disguises they are wont to put on, by which they deceive others, to maintain their own credit, and get themselves into others' confidence, and establish their own interest, until they see a convenient opportunity to begin more openly to broach and propagate their corrupt tenets.

(2.) Labour to obtain a man who has an established character, as a person of serious religion and fervent piety.

It is of vast importance that those who are settled in this work should be men of true piety, at all times, and in all places; but more especially at some times, and in some towns and churches. And this present time, wherein religion is in danger, by so many corruptions in doctrine and practice, is in a peculiar manner a day wherein such ministers are necessary. Nothing else but sincere piety of heart is at all to be depended on, as a security to a young man, just coming into the world, from the prevailing infection, or thoroughly to engage him in proper and successful endeavours to withstand and oppose the torrent of error and prejudice, against the high mysterious evangelical doctrines of the religion of Jesus Christ, and their genuine effects in true experimental religion. And this is a place that does peculiarly need such a minister, for reasons obvious to all.

If you should happen to settle a minister who knows nothing truly of Christ, and the way of salvation by him, nothing experimentally of the nature of vital religion; alas, how will you be exposed as sheep without a shepherd! Here is need of one who shall be eminently fit to stand in the gap, and make up the hedge, and who shall be as the chariots of Israel, and the horsemen thereof. You need one that shall stand as a champion in the cause of truth and the power of godliness.

Having briefly mentioned these important articles of advice, nothing remains, but that I now take my leave of you, and bid you all, *farewell;* wishing and praying for your best prosperity. I would now commend your immortal souls to him, who formerly committed them to me, expecting the day when I must meet you again before him, who is the Judge of quick and dead. I desire that I may never forget this people, who have been so long my special charge, and that I may never cease fervently to pray for your prosperity. May God bless you with a faithful pastor, one that is well acquainted with his mind and will, thoroughly warning sinners, wisely and skilfully searching professors, and conducting you in the way to eternal blessedness. May you have truly a burning and shining light set up in this candlestick; and may you, not only for a season, but during his whole life, that a long life, be willing to rejoice in his light.

And let me be remembered in the prayers of all God's people that are of a calm spirit, and are peaceable and faithful in Israel, of whatever opinion they may be with respect to terms of church communion. And let us all remember, and never forget our future solemn meeting on that great day of the Lord; the day of infallible decision, and of the everlasting and unalterable sentence. Amen.

APPENDIX, No. I.

The following interesting particulars of the ancestors of Jonathan Edwards will be acceptable to the reader. They are introduced in this separate form, that the thread of the narration may not be interrupted; and this plan will be adopted for a similar reason in other instances.

The family of Edwards is of Welch origin. The Rev. Richard Edwards, the great-great-grandfather, and earliest known ancestor of President Edwards, was a clergyman in London, in the time of Queen Elizabeth. He came, according to the family tradition, from Wales to the metropolis, but in what county his family lived, or of what church in London he was minister, is not known. His wife, Mrs. Ann Edwards, after the death of her husband, married Mr. James Coles; who with her son, William Edwards, then young and unmarried, accompanied her to Hartford in Connecticut about the year 1640, where they both died.

William Edwards, Esquire, the *great-grandfather*, resided in Hartford, and is supposed to have been by profession a merchant. His wife, whose christian name was Agnes, and who came when a young lady with her parents to America, had two brothers in England—one the mayor of Exeter, the other the mayor of Barnstable. Their marriage occurred probably about the year 1645. It is not known whether they had more than one child.

Richard Edwards, Esquire, the *grandfather*, and, so far as can now be ascertained, the only child of William and Agnes Edwards, was born at Hartford in May, 1647, and resided in that town during his life.* He also was a merchant, and a man of wealth and respectability. At an early age he became a communicant in the presbyterian church in Hartford, and adorned his profession by a long life of conscientious integrity, and unusual devotedness to the prosperity of religion. He married Elizabeth Tuthill, the daughter of William and Elizabeth Tuthill, who came from Northamptonshire in England. Mr. Tuthill was a merchant of New-Haven, and one of the proprietors of the colony attempted on Delaware Bay. By this connexion Mr. Edwards had seven children, the eldest of whom was the Rev. Timothy Edwards. After her decease, he married a Miss Talcot, of Hartford, sister of the Hon. John Talcot, by whom he had six children. He died April 20, 1718, in the 71st year of his age; exhibiting, during his last sickness, a bright example of christian resignation and triumphant faith.

The family of Stoddard is of English descent. Anthony Stoddard, Esquire, the *maternal great-grandfather* of President Edwards, and the first of the family in America, emigrated from the west of England to Boston. He had five wives; the first of whom, Mary Downing, the sister of Sir George Downing, was the mother of the Rev. Solomon Stoddard of Northampton. His other children were Anthony, Simeon, Samson, and Israel.

The Rev. Solomon Stoddard, his eldest child, and the *maternal grandfather* of President Edwards, was born in 1643, and received the degree of A. B. at Harvard college in 1662. Soon after his licensure, the first minister of Northampton, the Rev. Eleazar Mather, then a young man, died,† and the parish applied to one of the ministers of Boston to designate a successor. He advised them at all hazards to secure Mr. Stoddard. When the parish committee applied to him, he had already taken his passage for London, and put his effects on board the ship with the expectation of sailing the next day; but through the earnest solicitation of the gentlemen who had recommended him, he was induced to relinquish the voyage and go to Northampton. He began to preach there in 1669, soon after the death of Mr. Mather, and on the 4th of March, 1670, received a unanimous call from the church and people of that village to become their minister; but was not ordained until September 11, 1672. On the 8th of March, 1670, he married Mrs. Esther Mather, originally Miss Warham, the youngest child of Rev. John Warham, of Windsor in Connecticut,‡ and widow of his predecessor, who had left three children. Mr. and Mrs. Stoddard had twelve children; six sons and six daughters. He was a man celebrated throughout the colonies for his capacity, his knowledge of men, his influence in the churches, and his zeal for vital religion; and will long be remembered for his valuable writings, which have often been published on both sides of the Atlantic.§ He was the minister of Northampton from 1672 until his death in 1729, and left impressions of a character strongly marked for originality, for talents, for energy, and for piety, on the minds of its inhabitants, which the lapse of a century has scarcely begun to diminish.

The Rev. Timothy Edwards, the *father* of President Edwards, was born at Hartford, May 14, 1669, and pursued his studies preparatory to his admission to college, under the Rev. Mr. Glover of Springfield, a gentleman distinguished for his classical attainments. In 1687, he entered Harvard college, at that time the only seminary in the colonies; and received the two degrees of Bachelor and Master of Arts on the same day, July 4, 1691, one in the morning, and the other in the afternoon, "an uncommon mark of respect paid to his extraordinary proficiency in learning," such is the statement in the records of East Windsor. After the usual course of theological study, at that time longer and more thorough than it was during the latter half of the following century, he was ordained to the ministry of the gospel in the east parish of Windsor in Connecticut, in May, 1694.

* See Appendix, No. II.

† Mr. Mather was ordained June 18, 1661, and died July 24, 1669.

‡ The Rev. John Warham was originally one of the ministers of Exeter, "He was distinguished for piety and the strictest morals; yet at times was subject to great religious melancholy. Such were his doubts and fears, at some times, that when he administered the Lord's supper to his brethren, he did not participate with them, fearing that the seals of the covenant did not belong to him. It is said he was the first minister in New England who used *notes* in preaching; yet he was applauded by his hearers, as one of the most animated and energetic preachers of the day. He was considered as one of the principal fathers and pillars of the churches of Connecticut." Trumbull's Hist. of Connecticut, I. 467.

§ The following is a list of the publications of the Rev. Mr. Stoddard.

1. The Trial of Assurance . . . 1696.
2. The Doctrine of Instituted Churches . . . 1700.
3. The Necessity of acknowledging Offences . . . 1701.
4. The Danger of Degeneracy . . . 1702.
5. Election Sermon . . . 1703.
6. A Sermon on the Lord's Supper, Ex. xii. 47, 48. . . . 1707.
7. A Sermon at the Ordination of the Rev. Joseph Willard of Swampfield . . . 1708.
8. The Inexcusableness of Neglecting the Worship of God . . . 1708.
9. The Falseness of the Hopes of many Professors . . . 1708.
10. An Appeal to the Learned on the Lord's Supper . . . 1709.
11. A plea for Tythes: Divine Teachings render Persons blessed 1712.
12. A Guide to Christ . . . 1714.
13. Three Sermons: The Virtue of Christ's Blood; Natural Men under the Government of Self-love; The Gospel the Means of Conversion; and a fourth to stir up young men and maidens 1717.
14. Sermon at the Ordination of Mr. Thomas Cheney . . . 1718.
15. Treatise concerning Conversion . . . 1719.
16. Answer to Cases of Conscience . . . 1722.
17. Inquiry whether God is not angry with the Country? . . . 1723.
18. Safety of appearing in the Righteousness of Christ . . . ——

Windsor was the earliest settlement in that colony, the first house having been erected there in Oct. 1633. The original inhabitants came from Devonshire, Dorsetshire, and Somersetshire in England. They arrived at Boston in the beginning of the year 1630 ; and planting themselves at Dorchester in Massachusetts, were there formed into a congregational church on the 20th of March ; when the Rev. John Warham, previously a distinguished clergyman in Exeter, but ejected as a nonconformist, was installed their pastor. Finding themselves straitened for room at that place, in consequence of the great number of emigrants from England, the church with their minister left Dorchester, and planted themselves in Windsor, in the summer of 1635. This town, lying immediately north of Hartford, and delightfully situated in the valley of Connecticut, originally comprehended a very large tract of land on both sides of the river, and is distinguished for the fertility of its soil, and the beauty of its scenery. The inhabitants constituted one parish until the year 1694; when those residing on the eastern side of the Connecticut, finding it inconvenient to cross the river, and being grown sufficiently numerous to support public worship among themselves, proceeded to build a church, which stood near to the present burying ground, and invited Mr. Timothy Edwards, son of Richard Edwards, Esquire, of Hartford, to be their minister.

Mr. Edwards was married, on the 6th day of November, 1694, to Esther Stoddard, the second child of the Rev. Solomon Stoddard, who was born in 1672. His father, immediately after his settlement, purchased for him a farm of moderate extent, and built him a house, which was regarded, at the time of its erection, as a handsome residence. It was still standing in 1803 ; it was a solid, substantial house of moderate dimensions, had one chimney in the middle, and was entered, like all other houses at that period, by stepping over the sill. In this house his children were born, and he and Mrs. Edwards resided during their lives. They had one son and ten daughters, whose names follow in the order of their births :—Esther, Elizabeth, Anne, Mary, Jonathan, Eunice, Abigail, Jerusha, Hannah, Lucy, and Martha.*

In the spring of 1711, Mr. Edwards and the Rev. Mr. Buckingham of Milford, were appointed by the legislature of the colony, the chaplains of the Connecticut troops in a military expedition, designed for Canada. He left Windsor for New-Haven in July. A fleet, consisting of twenty men of war and eighty transports, sailed from Canada on the 30th of that month. Three companies under the command of Lieut. Col. Livingston, marched from New-Haven for Albany on the 9th of August, with whom went Mr. Edwards and Mr. Buckingham. The country through which their march lay, was at that time chiefly uncleared ; and the troops were obliged to lie out two nights in the forest. They reached Albany on the 15th, and found there, including their own regiment, about 1100 whites, and 120 Indians. The following letter, addressed to Mr. Edwards from Albany, not only details the state of the expedition, but unfolds the character of the writer, and the circumstances of his family.

"To Mrs. Esther Edwards, on the east side of Connecticut river, in Windsor.

Albany, August 17, 1711.

My dear and loving Wife,

The last Wednesday we came to this place. That we might not travel too hard for the footmen of our troops, (which consisted but of half the regiment, the rest not marching out of New-Haven when we did,) we spent seven days in the journey, which Col. Livingston judges to be about 160 miles, and I am apt to think it may not be much short of it. I lay with our troops two nights in the woods. I took cold in my journey, and have something of a cough, and am otherwise not much amiss. Notwithstanding this I am able to travel, and hope I shall be so through the whole journey. Col. Livingston has been very careful of me, so that through the whole march, both as to diet and lodging, I fared as well in the main as himself. The rest of the officers and the troops carry themselves as well to me as I can expect or desire.

Here are about 1100 white men, (or will be, at least, when the rest of the regiment come up, whom we expect to-night,) and 120 Indians, beside what are expected of the Five Nations, which many here think will be 1600 or 1800 men, but Col. Schuyler told me that he did not expect more than 1000. About 200 or 250 more whites are expected ; so that the whole army that goes to Canada is like to be about 2500 men ; to carry whom over the lake, there are provided, as I am told here, 350 batteaux and 40 or 50 bark canoes. The Governor of New York and the General are here. The General is in great haste to have the forces on their march ; so that Col. Schuyler's regiment was, as I understand, ordered to march out of town yesterday ; but as I slept last night, and still am, on the east side of the river, I am uncertain whether they are yet gone. The General told Col. Livingston and me also afterwards, that we must march for Wood Creek to-morrow, but I am apt to think we shall hardly march till Monday.

Whether I shall have any time to write to you after this I know not ; but however that may be, I would not have you discouraged or over anxious concerning me, for I am not so about myself. I have still strong hopes of seeing thee and our dear children once again. I cannot but hope that I have had the gracious presence of God with me since I left home, encouraging and strengthening my soul, as well as preserving my life. I have been much cheered and refreshed respecting this great undertaking, in which I verily expect to proceed, and that I shall, before many weeks are at an end, see Canada ; but I trust in the Lord that he will have mercy on me, and thee, my dear, and all our dear children, and that God has more work for me to do in the place where I have dwelt for many years, and that you and I shall yet live together on earth, as well as dwell together for ever in heaven with the Lord Jesus Christ, and all his saints, with whom to be is best of all.

Remember my love to each of the children, to Esther, Elizabeth, Anne, Mary, Jonathan, Eunice, and Abigail. The Lord have mercy on and eternally save them all, with our dear little Jerusha ! The Lord bind up their souls with thine and mine in the bundle of life. Tell the children, that I would have them, if they desire to see their father again, to pray daily for me in secret ; and above all things to seek the favour of God in Christ Jesus, and that while they are young.

I would have you very careful of my books and account of rates. I sent you from New-Haven a 40*s*. bill in a letter by Lieut. Willis, and since that ordered the treasurer to deliver to my father six pounds more for you. You may call for it, or send for it by some sure hand.

Though for a while we must be absent from each other, yet I desire that we may often meet at the throne of grace in our earnest prayers one for another, and have great hopes that God will hear and answer our prayers. The God of grace be with you.

I am, thy loving husband,

TIMOTHY EDWARDS."

On Monday, August 20th, they marched for Wood Creek. At Saratoga, in consequence of the fatigues and exposure of the march, Mr. Edwards was taken severely ill. On the 4th of September, being unable to proceed with the army, he was conveyed in a boat to Stillwater. Thence he was carried back through the woods to Albany, where he arrived in three days in a state of extreme danger. On the 10th he wrote to Mrs. Edwards as follows :

"To Mrs. Esther Edwards in Windsor, New England.

Albany, Sept. 10, 1711.

My dear,

I came last Tuesday from Saratoga towards Albany, very ill, in order to return home ; having been ill more than a month, and growing at last so weak that I could

* See Appendix, No. III.

go no further than that place, which is near fifty miles above Albany. I came to Albany in a waggon, lying along in a bed, prepared for me, last Thursday night. Since then I have been at the house of Madam Vandyke, a Dutch gentlewoman, where I have been so kindly taken care of, that I am much better, and daily gain strength, and my lost appetite is somewhat recovered. I hope to be able to ride homeward next week.

Last Friday I sent Mr. Hezekiah Mason to New England, to acquaint my father and my friends at Windsor how it is with me, and to desire three or four of them to come hither and to bring an easy horse with them for me to ride upon, and to come provided to carry home my effects, and to bring a blanket or two with them in case we should be forced to sleep in the woods. I should have written by him, but was too ill to do it. This is the first day I have been able to sit up. If the neighbours have not started when you receive this, speak to Mr. Drake that they set out as soon as possible.

I rejoice to learn, by a letter from my father, that you were all well on the 2d, and hope in the mercy of God to see you all ere long.

Lieut. Silvy, sent over by the queen to serve in this expedition, a stout, active young man, who came sick with me in another waggon from the camp to Albany, died this evening just by my lodgings. We came together from the camp sick, we lay together in one room by the way sick, we lodged just by one another several days in this town sick—but he is dead, and I am alive and recovering. Blessed be God for his distinguishing and undeserved grace to me! Remember my love to all the children. Give my respects to Mr. Colton, who I understand stays with you. I wish you to provide something for my cough, which is the worst I ever had in my life. Remember my love to sister Staughton, and my duty to my father and mother, if you have opportunity.

I am your very affectionately loving husband,

TIMOTHY EDWARDS."

Owing to the lateness of the season and to numerous disappointments, the expedition was soon after relinquished; and in the course of the month Mr. Edwards returned home.

Mr. and Mrs. Edwards lived together in the married state upwards of sixty-three years. Mr. Edwards was about five feet ten inches in height, of a fair complexion; of a strong robust frame, full, but not corpulent. He was a man of polished manners, and particularly attentive to his external appearance.—The management not only of his domestic concerns, but of his property generally, was intrusted to the care of Mrs. Edwards, who discharged the duties of a wife and a mother with singular fidelity and success. In strength of character she resembled her father, and like him she left behind her, in the place where she resided for seventy-six years, that "good name which is better than precious ointment."

"On a visit to East Windsor, in the summer of 1823," remarks Mr. Dwight, "I found a considerable number of persons advanced in years, who had been well acquainted with Mrs. Edwards, and two upwards of ninety, who had been pupils of her husband. From them I learned that she received a superior education in Boston, was tall, dignified, and commanding in her appearance, affable and gentle in her manners, and was regarded as surpassing her husband in native vigour of understanding. They all united in speaking of her as possessed of remarkable judgment and prudence, of an exact sense of propriety, of extensive information, of a thorough knowledge of the Scriptures and theology, and of singular conscientiousness, piety, and excellence of character. By her careful attention to all his domestic concerns, her husband was left at full liberty to devote himself to the proper duties of his profession. Like many of the ministers of the gospel of that early period in New England, he was well acquainted with Hebrew literature, and was regarded as a man of more than usual learning; but was particularly distinguished for his accurate knowledge of the Greek and Roman classics. In addition to his other duties, he annually prepared a number of pupils for college, there being at that time no public schools endowed for this purpose. One of my aged informants, who pursued his preparatory studies under him, told me, that on his admission to college, when the officers had learned with whom he had studied, they remarked to him, that there was no need of examining Mr. Edwards's scholars."

He was for that period unusually liberal and enlightened, with regard to the education of his children; preparing not only his son but each of his daughters also for college. In a letter, bearing date Aug. 3, 1711, while absent on the expedition to Canada, he wishes that Jonathan and the girls may continue to prosecute the study of Latin; and in another of Aug. 7, that he may continue to recite his Latin to his elder sisters. When his daughters were of the proper age, he sent them to Boston, to finish their education. Both he and Mrs. Edwards were exemplary in their care of their religious instruction; and, as the reward of their parental fidelity, were permitted to see the fruits of piety in them all during their youth.

He always preached extemporaneously, and, until he was upwards of seventy, without noting down the heads of his discourse. After that time, he commonly wrote the divisions on small slips of paper, which, as they occasionally appeared beyond the leaves of the Bible that he held in his hand, his parishioners called, "Mr. Edwards's thumb papers." Apologizing for this one day to one of his pupils, he remarked to him, that he found his memory beginning to fail, but that he thought his judgment as sound as ever; and this was likewise the opinion of his people, till near the close of his life. He is not known to have written out but a single sermon, which was preached at the general election, in 1732, and was published. It is a solemn and faithful application of the doctrine of a general judgment to his hearers, particularly as legislators and magistrates. As he lived till within a few months of his son's decease, the latter often visited his father, and preached in his desk. It was the customary remark of the people, that "although Mr. *Edwards* was perhaps the more learned man, and more animated in his manner, yet Mr. *Jonathan* was the deeper preacher."

His influence over his congregation was commanding, and was steadily exerted on the side of truth and righteousness. When he knew of any division among them, he went immediately to see that the parties were reconciled; and when he heard of any improper conduct on the part of any individuals, it was his uniform custom to go and reprove them. Under his preaching, the gospel was attended with a regular, uniform efficacy, and in frequent instances, with revivals of religion, yet no record is preserved of the actual admissions to the church. From some of the family letters, evidence appears of a revival of religion existing in 1715 and 1716; during which Mrs. Edwards, and two of her daughters, made a profession of their christian faith; and several others of the family are spoken of, as "travelling towards Zion, with their faces thitherward." His son observes, in 1737, that he had known of no parish in the west of New England, except Northampton, which had as often been favoured with revivals of religion, as that of his father.

During the whole of his ministry, he was regarded by his people with great respect and affection; no symptoms of dissatisfaction having been manifested by them for sixty-three years. In the summer of 1752, on account of his increasing infirmities, he proposed to them the settlement of a colleague; and they actually settled one, the Rev. Joseph Perry, June 11, 1755; but continued his salary until his death, which took place Jan. 27, 1758, when he was eighty-nine years of age.

Mrs. Edwards survived him twelve years; her fourth daughter, Mary, residing with her and watching over the infirmities of age. "From a lady in East Windsor, far advanced in life, I learned," says Mr. Dwight, "the following facts.—'Mrs. Edwards was always fond of books, and discovered a very extensive acquaintance with them in her conversation; particularly with the best theological writers. After the death of her husband, her family being small, a large portion of her time was devoted to reading. A table always stood in the middle of her parlour, on which lay a large quarto Bible, and treatises on doctrinal and experimental religion. In the afternoon, at a stated hour, such of the ladies of the neighbourhood as found it convenient, went customarily to her house, accompanied not unfrequently by their children. Her daughter regularly read a chapter of the Bible, and then a passage of some religious author; but was often stopped by the comments of her mother, who always closed the interview with prayer. On these occasions it was a favourite point with the neighbouring females, even with those who were young, to be present; all of them regularly attending when they were able, and many of them, among whom was my informant, dating their first permanent attention to religion from the impressions there made. In this way she was regarded with a respect bordering on veneration, and was often spoken of by Mr. Perry, as one of his most efficient auxiliaries. She died Jan. 19, 1770, in the 99th year of her age, retaining her mental faculties until the close of her life. Her daughter Mary spent many years of her early life at Northampton with Mr. and Mrs. Stoddard; and returning thence to her father's house, she was the nurse and attendant, and I may almost say, support of her aged parents. She was a woman of most amiable disposition, fine understanding, and uncommon attainments, had read much, and appeared to have made the best improvement of the knowledge that she obtained.* She survived her mother six years."

APPENDIX, No. II.

PARTICULARS AS TO THE LIFE AND DEATH OF MR. RICHARD EDWARDS, THE GRANDFATHER OF JONATHAN EDWARDS.

A CLOSELY written manuscript of ninety-six pages, foolscap 8vo, by the Rev. Timothy Edwards, of East Windsor, and eldest son of Richard Edwards, Esquire, is still preserved, headed, "Some things written for my own use and comfort, concerning the life and death of my very dear and honoured father, Mr. Richard Edwards, late of Hartford, who died April 20, 1718, on the sabbath, in the forenoon, being the ninth day of his sickness, and the 71st year of his age, he being then very near seventy-one years old, having been born in May, 1647."

The following brief abstract of this account will not be uninteresting to those who respect the memory of departed piety and worth; especially as it is an accurate moral picture of the man who moulded the character of the father and instructor of President Edwards. As far as is consistent with brevity, the language of the original is exactly preserved.

"He was naturally of a strong healthy constitution, well formed and comely, and of uncommon vigour, activity, and nimbleness of body—characteristics, for which he was distinguished until the close of life. He had a clear voice and ready utterance, and expressed himself not only with ease and propriety, but with uncommon energy and effect. He was naturally cheerful, sprightly, and sweet tempered, of a ready wit, had a mind well stored with knowledge, particularly the knowledge of history and theology, and in conversation was uncommonly pleasant and entertaining. He was sober and considerate, a man of great courage, resolution, and perseverance; had a clear and strong understanding, a sound judgment, and a quick, sharp insight into men and things, and was capable of almost any kind of business. He was in the full sense of the phrase *a man of business*, distinguished for his wisdom and forecast; had uncommon prudence and discretion in the management of his own affairs, and was extensively consulted in matters of weight and difficulty by others.

Though natively quick and warm when provoked or affronted, he had acquired the self-government, which became him as a man and a Christian; though firm and inflexible in the discharge of his duty, he was yet easy to be entreated. He was candid and charitable in his estimate of the conduct of others, kind and affectionate in his feelings, liberal and generous in the use of his property, obliging in his disposition, willing to devote his time and services to the good of his fellow-men, readily forgiving injuries on the slightest acknowledgment, but yielding nothing to pride and haughtiness of spirit. He was uniformly courteous, affable, and easy of access; free and familiar with his children and servants, and with the poorest and humblest of his neighbours; and at the same time tender-hearted and compassionate, easily melting into tears, while witnessing either examples of kindness and generosity, or scenes of affliction and sorrow, and doing what lay in his power to relieve the wants and distresses of others. He had a manly, ingenuous spirit, was accustomed to deal very faithfully and thoroughly with his fellow-men about their faults and miscarriages, and did not fear, on any proper occasion, to tell any man plainly what he saw amiss in his conduct.

He was a sincere and faithful friend, never disappointing those who trusted in him; and it was no difficult thing for any honest man, however humble his circumstances, in a just cause, especially if he was oppressed and unable to defend himself, to secure his friendship. Such confidence, says the writer, have I in my father's faithfulness, that, under God, I could venture my estate, my good name, and even my life, in the hands of such a friend. In all his dealings with his fellow-men he was eminently just and upright. Though his business was very extensive, and continued through a long life, and though I had the best opportunity of knowing his concerns, I never knew him attempt to wrong any individual, or to do any thing which discovered the least shadow of deceit or dishonesty. On the contrary, he abhorred all base underhand management, scorned all that was little, unfair, and unworthy, and in freedom from dissimulation, hypocrisy, and any design to do wrong, was among those who excel.

"In all the relations of life his character was truly estimable. He was hospitable and courteous to strangers, and charitable to the poor, and was ever ready to sympathize with the afflicted, to plead the cause of the widow and the fatherless, and to help those who wanted both friends and money to help themselves. He was an affectionate, tender, careful husband, one of the best of fathers to his children, a just and kind master, esteemed and beloved by his neighbours, a good and punctual paymaster, and of a credit always unimpeached. He was not only faithful in managing the concerns of others; but equitable, in his demands for services rendered, often indeed rendering them for nothing; just and moderate in his profits, gentle and accommodating towards his debtors, often bearing with them, year after year, if they were poor and honest. He was also merciful to his beast.

He had an excellent spirit of government—having wisdom to govern not only himself, but others—so that he was both feared and loved, by his children, and servants, and all who were under his control. I cannot say that he discovered no infirmities, but they were much outweighed by his virtues.

In the existence and constant presence of God, he appeared not only to believe, but to delight. The fear of God seemed habitually before his eyes, so that probably nothing would have tempted him to do that, which he really thought would offend him. Twice every day he worshipped God in his house, by reading the Scriptures and prayer. Other religious books were read in their season

* From the letter of an excellent lady in Middletown, in whose family she resided several years.

in the family, and that to an extent rarely surpassed. His conversation with, and his letters to, his children, were full of religious instruction. He laid great stress on the promises of God to the righteous, and his threatenings to the wicked; fully expecting and looking for the accomplishment of both. He habitually and attentively observed the dispensations of Providence; ever acknowledging with thankfulness his goodness to him and his; and regarding every affliction as an immediate chastisement from God, so that he heard the voice of the rod, and him that appointed it. Rarely does any Christian express so solemn and heart-affecting a sense of the great and awful dispensations of Providence, towards individuals, or towards the world at large.

He hated vice and wickedness, wherever he saw it, and abhorred to justify or make light of sin, whether committed by strangers, or by his own near relatives: always discovering in this respect a just, conscientious, impartial spirit, and appearing to frown upon it even more in his children than in others.

In prayer he seemed to draw very near to God with peculiar solemnity and reverence, with exalted views of his greatness and goodness, and with a supreme regard to his glory. He appeared to cherish an admiring sense of the wisdom, the power, and the goodness of God, in contemplating the works of creation and providence, and the riches of his grace as unfolded in the work of redemption. The truth of God he studied and understood, as well as loved and obeyed.

Few men administered christian admonition and reproof with so much faithfulness, discretion, and solemnity, or with so much success; and few received it with more humility, meekness, and self-application. His feelings on religious subjects were at once strong and tender; often discovering themselves at public worship, in family prayer, and in religious reading and conversation.

He took peculiar care, that his family sanctified the sabbath, and appeared himself conscientiously to keep it holy. On the morning of every sacramental sabbath, he regularly spent a long time alone, in religious retirement. He was abundant in his religious instructions and admonitions to his family, on every proper occasion, and regularly on every sabbath afternoon in enforcing the sermons of the day, and the instructions of the book which was then read. From my own observation of other religious families, with which I have been familiarly acquainted, I have reason to believe that few children, even of christian parents, have been as much counselled and instructed. He loved and honoured the faithful ministers of Christ, for their work's sake; and was a sincere and hearty friend to his own minister; actively and zealously exciting others to help and befriend him, and resolutely and successfully opposing and bearing down those who arrayed themselves against him.

In his religion he was far from being ostentatious, and the applause of men he regarded as nothing, in comparison with that testimony of a good conscience, which would enable him to appeal to the heart-searching God, for the sincerity and uprightness of his conduct. He appeared to love the real disciples of Christ, for their piety; disregarding the distinctions of sect and party, and receiving all his brethren who were received by Christ.

Though possessed of property, he realized, in an unusual degree, the vanity of worldly good, and placed but a slight dependence upon riches, honours, or pleasures as the means of permanent happiness. Surely, says his son, this world was not my father's god; his chief good was something better and nobler, than this present world can afford. He appeared habitually sensible of the frailty of his nature, and of the nearness of his own death, often conversing on death and the judgment, in a truly devout and edifying manner, and frequently observing, near the close of life, 'I carry my life in my hand every day; I am daily looking and waiting until my change come.' Few Christians, indeed, seem more conversant with their own death, more careful to prepare for it, or more ready to meet it.

In the government of God he seemed habitually to rejoice. His sense of the evil of sin was peculiarly deep; he was patient and submissive under sufferings, was willing to suffer for Christ's sake, and was free from the fear of death. He appeared to be truly humbled under a sense of his own sins, to mourn over sin, and to wage a constant warfare against it, to love the way of salvation revealed in the gospel, to cherish a sacred regard to the glory of God and the interests of religion, and to entertain exalted views of the character and glory of Christ. Though he never, says his son, gave me an account of his conversion at large; yet on various occasions, in conversation, he has alluded to the great change then wrought in his views and affections, with regard to temporal and spiritual objects, particularly to worldly good, the warfare with sin, the hope of reconciliation to God, and a title to eternal life. He appeared eminently to trust in God, to cherish a deep sense of his dependence, and to lead a life of faith. Though I have now been in the ministry, he adds, nearly four and twenty years, and, during that period, have often had much private conversation with many of the truly pious, I do not remember that I have met with any, who seemed more truly to lead such a life, than my dear father; and to such a life he habitually advised and directed his children, both in his conversation and in his letters. Writing to me on an important subject, he says—'I leave you in this, and all your affairs, to the direction and guidance of the Fountain of wisdom and goodness, who, I doubt not, will guide you into the best and safest course, if you trust in him, and by faith commit your ways to him. Make the glory of God your main end, and depend on him by a lively faith in his promise; for He is faithful who hath promised, that they who wait on him shall not want any good thing—that is, any that is really good for them.'—In a letter addressed to me when I was with the army at Albany,* then on an expedition to Canada, he thus writes —'I have nothing new to write to you, but merely to revive what I have said formerly, that, since God, in his all-wise providence, has called you to this present service, you put your whole trust in *him*, to carry you through it, who never fails any who put their trust in him. You may expect to meet with difficulties, but still God is all-sufficient —the same God in all places, and in all conditions,—therefore commit yourself wholly to his merciful providence, who is a faithful God to all his people, in all their ways. So I leave you to the blessing, guidance, and keeping of a gracious and faithful God and Father.'—I have cause to say, 'Blessed be God, that once I had a father, thus disposed to counsel his children!'

In all affairs of weight and difficulty, he appeared, in an unusual degree, to commit himself to God, to wait on him for direction and for help, to leave the event in his hands, and then to be at peace. He has sometimes told me, says his son, that when his mind has been much agitated in consequence of some great trouble and perplexity, in which he could see no means of help or relief, so that he could get no rest for a great part of a night, it has been his customary course, to cast it entirely on God, and leave it in his hands; and then, said he, I can at once go to sleep.

God was his great refuge in times of trouble, and I have good reason to believe that the declaration in Deut. xxxiii. 27. The eternal God is thy refuge, and underneath thee are the everlasting arms—might be applied to him with truth. In the time of health he trusted in God, and strongly relied on his providential care and goodness, to provide for himself and his family. This was peculiarly observable in seasons of affliction and distress. In sickness he stayed himself on God, and looked to the Lord Jesus Christ, to carry him safely through, however it might issue. In the very dreadful mortality in 1711, when great numbers of the inhabitants died, he was dangerously sick of the distemper; and when the crisis was passed, he gave us the following account of his reflections, during the first night of his sickness: 'When I was first taken ill, I concluded that I had the prevailing fever; and was strongly impressed with the belief that I should die of it. During the former part of the night, I felt considerable anxiety respecting it, but in the latter part of it, the

* In August, 1711.

disquiet of my mind passed away, and I was willing to leave myself with God. I found myself not so much concerned about the issue of my sickness; but thought I was satisfied that it should be as he pleased.'—This, during his whole sickness, gave him inward peace and rest in God, and comfortably freed him from the terrors of death.

The language of his last will, written near the close of life, strongly exhibits the good man, who trusteth in the Lord, and whose hope the Lord is:—'I, Richard Edwards of Hartford, being weak in body, yet, through God's goodness, my understanding and memory remaining good, being sensible of my own mortality, and not knowing how suddenly the Lord may put a period to this short life, do therefore make this my last will and testament. And first, I commit my soul into the bosom of my most merciful God and Father, and ever blessed Redeemer, Jesus Christ, hoping for eternal life and salvation through the merits, mediation, and intercession of my Lord and Saviour Jesus Christ; and my body to the earth, to be buried, nothing doubting but that it shall be raised again, and re-united to my soul, by the mighty power of God, at the last day, and so rest in hopes of a glorious resurrection, through Jesus Christ our Lord.'

The piety and evangelical excellence, which had characterized his life, were even more conspicuous in his last sickness, and at his death.—Towards one whom he regarded as having greatly injured him, he expressed feelings of kindness and good will; and while he declared, that in the review of his conduct towards him, he had peace of conscience, that he could safely die upon what he had done in it, and that under the approach of death, he felt no trouble lying upon his mind, with reference to it, yet he declared he could truly say, he heartily wished him the best good. He took great care that no wrong should be done through mistake, with respect to what had been due, or was still due, to him from others. To one of his neighbours who came and, whispering in his ear, asked his forgiveness, he readily and promptly replied, 'I forgive you, I forgive you;' and this so kindly and heartily, that the man was melted into tears. He repeatedly charged his children, on no consideration to take advantage of the law against any, who had mortgaged their lands or estates to him, and whose mortgages were out and their debts unpaid.

When his children came around his bed, weeping at the apprehension of his approaching death, and their incalculable loss, he said to them, 'This time I have long expected, this scene I have looked for, and now it is come.' As some of us who lived at a distance came into his sick chamber for the first time, he said, 'I can but look upon you, my children, I can't speak to you; I have a great deal to say, but I can't say it; God now denies me that liberty.' When I first saw him, (April 16th,) he expressed a hope, that he should meet me with joy, at the right hand of Christ in the great day. Something being said to him, with reference to death, he replied, 'Death, indeed, is terrible to nature, but I hope God will strengthen me, and carry me through it, and help me to submit to his will; I lie at the feet of God.'—While he was praying to God by himself, he was overheard to say, 'Lord, I come to thee with my naked soul; I desire to bow under thy chastizing hand, and hope it is a good chastisement.' As we sat weeping by his bed-side, April 16th, he said to us,—'Come, children, moderate your grief, for such things must be, and the will of God is best. I freely submit myself to the will of God, whether in life or death, to do with me as he pleases.' He said to me on the 17th,—'Though I seem to be better to-day, yet I am of the opinion that this sickness will be my last; and I am very willing that the will of God should be done, I am not at all anxious about it: I rely on the Lord Jesus Christ; I have chosen him for my Saviour and mighty Redeemer.' On my observing, 'This must be a great support, Sir, to your mind;'—he replied, 'It is so.' As I was sitting by him on the 17th, I heard him say,—'O my poor, frail, mortal body, methinks, sometimes I should be glad to slip away from thee!' In the midst of most severe pain, he expressed himself very desirous, that God would enable him to bear his afflicting hand, and quietly submit to his will, even to the end; and that he might not at any time, by impatience, be left to sin against him, and for this he desired our prayers, that God would, in this respect, strengthen him more and more; and in a very humble manner, when he had scarce strength to speak, he thus, in a short ejaculation, prayed to God, 'O Lord, increase thy grace, and strengthen thy servant's faith!' During his whole sickness, he appeared to be almost always praying to God; far more than is commonly witnessed on the death-bed of the Christian.

He solemnly exhorted and charged his son John, to carry on the worship of God in his family, after his death. To one of his daughters, he said, as she stood weeping over him, 'I must say to you, as Mr. Whiting said to his daughter Sybil, Through wet and dry, through thick and thin, keep steady for that port.' On the 18th, as his good friend Mr. Austin, and myself, sat by him, and we observed him troubled with hiccoughs, one of us remarked that the hiccoughs were very distressing, and he replied, 'God must take his own way, and use his own means, and I desire to submit to his holy will, and hope I can do it freely.' He expressed to me his conviction, that it was better for him to depart and be with Christ, than to continue with his family. On my reminding him, that he had many friends, he replied,—'I know that I have many friends, but there is one Friend that is better than all;' and when one of us spoke of making his bed easy; he replied,—'The favour of Jesus Christ will make my bed easy; the bosom of Jesus Christ is the best resting-place, for a man in my condition.'—To one of my sisters he said, 'Weep for yourself, my child, as I have wept for myself, I have laid hold of the rock of ages, I hope my anchor is within the veil;'—and to another, as she observed him in very great pain—'The passage may prove rough, but the shore is safe, and the bottom will bear me.' In reply to a remark of mine, he said,—'I trust in the Lord Jesus Christ, and have ventured my soul upon him for eternity, and I desire to do so more and more.' On the night of the 18th, when his distemper was most violent, he expressed his full conviction, that he had chosen God for his portion, and that he would grant him a favourable issue.

He expressed high and honourable thoughts of God, in the midst of his greatest distress. On Wednesday, observing his uncommon patience and resignation under extreme suffering, I was led to remark, that to submit quietly and patiently to the will of God, when sorely afflicted by him, was one of the hardest lessons a Christian had to learn. His reply was striking and affecting:—'Alas! there is no room nor cause to complain of God, for he is infinitely good, yea goodness itself, and the fountain of it; I should be very ungrateful indeed, if I should complain of him who has been so good to me all my days.'

On Saturday, the 19th of April, and the last day but one of his life, when he lay rattling in his throat, much oppressed for want of breath, and in great pain, so that he seemed to me to be in the very pangs of death, he expressed some fear that he might lie long in that condition, and so endure great pain and misery before he died, and therefore seemed to desire that God would mercifully shorten the time of his sufferings, by taking him quickly out of the world. Mrs. Talcot said to him, 'But you are willing to wait God's time:'—to which he replied,—'O yes, O yes.' At a time when he appeared to be fast sinking, Major Talcot informed him, that he was ready to think death was upon him, he was so very low; and I added,—'I hope that God will never leave you nor forsake you:'—with great readiness, and with an air of much inward satisfaction, he replied,—'I don't fear it, I don't fear it!'—When he was hardly able to speak, he told me, in answer to a question, that—his hope of eternal life, through the infinite mercy of God in Jesus Christ, was still firm; that he trusted all would be well with him in a short time, and that then he should think of his present afflictions and sufferings with pleasure!—In the former part of the night, he told us that he was comforted with the hope of going to heaven. On my asking him if he did not wish to recover, he replied:—'To recover! No; I am better as I am, I have no desire to go back, I have left myself with God!'—In the latter part of the night, having lain down for a little sleep, I was called up, as he appeared to be dying. I asked him if his hope of salvation continued. He said—'Yes.'—I asked him whether he still had good thoughts of God, and he replied—'Yes, Yes!'—In the morning of the sabbath, a few hours before his death, I went to him, and told him, I would make one more prayer with him, if he thought he could attend; he was only able to say—'Yes'—and at the same time nodded his head; and, when it was concluded, gave me the same sign, that he had been able to understand and unite with me. In the prayer, I spoke of him as dying; and expressing my hope to him afterwards, that he was going to keep sabbath with saints and angels in heaven, and inquiring whether he had that hope to sustain him, he gave me the customary sign that such was the fact.

In this manner he lived and died, glorifying God both in his life and in his death, and leaving behind him that good name, which is better than precious ointment."

APPENDIX, No. III.

ACCOUNT OF THE CHILDREN OF TIMOTHY AND ESTHER EDWARDS.

The following particular statement of the children of Timothy and Esther Edwards, will probably interest some readers.

1. *Esther*, born in 1695; married Rev. Samuel Hopkins of West Springfield. They had several children: Hannah, married in 1740, to Hon. John Worthington, L. L. D. of Springfield. They had two sons, who died in infancy; and four daughters: *Mary*, who married Hon. Jonathan Bliss, chief justice of the province of New Brunswick; *Hannah*, who married Hon. Thomas Dwight of Springfield; *Frances*, who married Hon. Fisher Ames, L. L. D.; and *Sophia*, who married John Williams, Esq. of Weathersfield.

2. *Elizabeth*, born 1697; married Col. Jabez Huntington of Windham. They had four daughters: 1. *Jerusha*, married Dr. Clark of Lebanon. 2. *Sarah*, married Hezekiah Wetmore of Middletown, and had two children; and after his death married Samuel Beers of Stratford, and had three children: Lucy, married to George Smith of Smith-town, L. Island; Sarah Anne, married David Burr, Esq. of Fairfield; and William Pitt Beers, Esq. of Albany, who married Anne, daughter of Hon. Jonathan Sturges of Fairfield. 3. *Elizabeth*, married Rev. Abraham Davenport of Stamford, and had two children; Hon. Jon. Davenport, M. C. and Hon. James Davenport, a judge of the supreme court of Connecticut.

3. *Anne*, born in 1699, married John Ellworth, Esq. of East Windsor, and died in 1798, aged 99. They had four children: 1. John, born Aug. 24, 1735, and had five children; 2. Solomon, born April 3, 1737, and had twelve children; 3. Frederick; 4. Anne, who married Mr. John Stoughton of East Windsor, and had six children.

4. *Mary*, born in 1701, and died single, Sept. 17, 1776, in the 76th year of her age.

5. *Jonathan*, the subject of the present Memoir. *For his children, see Appendix, No. VI.*

6. *Eunice*, born in 1706, married, in Oct. 1729, Rev. Simon Backus of Newington, who went as chaplain of the Connecticut troops to Louisburg, in 1745, and died there in 1746. They had seven children: 1. Unknown. 2. Eunice, born in 1732, died unmarried, aged 75. 3. Elizabeth, born in 1734, married David Bissell of East Windsor. They had two children. 4. Esther, married Benjamin Ely of West Springfield, and had fourteen children. 5. Rev. Simon Backus, A. B. of Yale, in 1759, married Rachel Moseley of East Haddam, and had nine children. 6. Jerusha, married Mr. Smith Bailey, and had four children. 7. Mary, died unmarried.

7. *Abigail*, born in 1708; married William Metcalf, Esq. of Lebanon, and A. B. of Harvard college. She died in 1754. They had five children: 1. Abigail, married Moses Bliss, Esq. of Springfield, and had eight children, Hon. George Bliss, Moses, William Metcalf, Lucy, married Dr. Hezekiah Clark of Lebanon, Abigail, married Hon. William Ely of Springfield, Frances, married Rev. William Rowland of Windsor, Emily, and Harriet. 2. William, and 3. Eliphalet, who died young. 4. Lucy, who married Mr. John Huntington of East Haddam, and had seven children. 5. Eliphalet, born Dec. 6, 1748, married Mary West of Lebanon.

8. *Jerusha*, born in 1710 and died Dec. 22, 1729, aged about 19 years.

9. *Hannah*, born in 1712, and married Seth Wetmore, Esq. of Middletown, Conn.

10. *Lucy*, born in 1715, and died unmarried in East Windsor, Aug. 21, 1736, aged 21.

11. *Martha*, born in 1716, married Rev. Moses Tuthill of Granville, Mass. and died Feb. 1794, aged 77.

APPENDIX, No. IV.

REMARKS IN MENTAL PHILOSOPHY—THE MIND.

There are four distinct series of these manuscript Notes or Remarks, which from the handwriting, as well as from other evidence, were obviously commenced by him during his collegiate life, and as nearly as can be judged in the following order. The first, entitled "*The Mind*," is a brief collection of discussions and remarks in mental philosophy. The second is without a title, and consists of "*Notes on Natural Science.*" The third is entitled "*Notes on the Scriptures.*" The fourth is entitled, "*Miscellanies*," and consists chiefly of observations on the doctrines of the Scriptures. The two last he continued through life.

The following series of remarks, entitled "The Mind," appears to have been composed either during, or soon after, his perusal of Locke's Essay on the Human Understanding.

"THE MIND."

TITLE. The Natural History of the Mental World, or of the Internal World: being a Particular Inquiry into the Nature of the Human Mind, with respect to both its Faculties—the Understanding and the Will—and its various Instincts, and Active and Passive Powers.

INTRODUCTION. Concerning the two worlds—the External and the Internal: the External, the subject of Natural Philosophy; the Internal, our own Minds. How the

Knowledge of the latter is, in many respects, the most important. Of what great use the true knowledge of this is; and of what dangerous consequence errors, here, are more than in the other.

Subjects to be handled in the Treatise on the Mind.

1. Concerning the difference between Pleasure and Pain, and Ideas, or the vast difference between the Understanding and the Will.

2. Concerning Prejudices; the influence of Prejudice to cloud the mind. The various sorts of prejudices in particular, and how they come to cloud the mind; particularly Prejudices of Interest—the true reason why they cloud the judgment.—Prejudices of Education and Custom. Their universal influence on wise, and learned, and rational, as well as other men; demonstrated from fact and experience—of their insensible influence, how it is insensible on great men.—How difficultly a people are got out of their old customs. In husbandry, how difficult to persuade that a new way is better.—Another prejudice is the general cry, and fashion, and vogue, of an age. Its exceeding strong influence, like a strong stream, that carries all that way. This influence on great men. Prejudices of People, in favour of individual great men, to the contempt of others.—Again, the voice of men in power, riches, or honourable place.—How some Churches would laugh at their ceremonies, if they were without them.—How a man's being rich, or in high place, gives great weight to his word.—How much more weighty a man's sayings are, after he becomes a Bishop, than before—another prejudice is from ridicule, or an high, strong, overbearing, contemptuous style.

3. Either after or before this, to have a dissertation concerning the exceeding vanity, blindness, and weakness of the mind of man.—What poor fallible creatures men are. How every man is insensible of his own; thinks himself best.—Concerning the Pride of men; how ready to think they shall be great men, and to promise themselves great things.

4. How some men have Strong Reason, but not Good Judgment.

5. Concerning Certainty and Assurance. How many things that are demonstrations in themselves, are not demonstrations to men, and yet are strong arguments; no more demonstrations than a boy may have, that a cube of two inches may be cut into eight cubes of one inch, for want of proper clearness, and full comprehension of the ideas. How assurance is capable of infinite degrees.—How none have such a degree, but that it might be heightened—even of that, that two and two make four. It may be increased by a stronger sight, or a greater clearness of ideas. Minds of clearer and stronger sight may be more assured of it, than those of more obscure vision. There may be beings of a thousand times stronger sight than we are. How God's sight only is infinitely clear and strong. That which is demonstration at one time, may be only probable reasoning at another, by reason of different degrees of clearness and comprehension. It is almost impossible, that a long demonstration should beget so great assurance as a short one; because many ideas cannot be so clearly comprehended at one time, as a few. A very long demonstration may beget assurance, by a particular examination of each link of the chain, and so by recollection, that we were very careful and assured in the time of it; but this is less immediate, and less clear.

6. Why it is proper for Orators and Preachers to move the Passions—needful to show earnestness, &c. how this tends to convince the judgment, and many other ways is good and absolutely necessary.

7. Of the nature of the Affections or Passions—how only strong and lively exercises of the Will, together with the effect on the Animal nature.

8. In treating of Human Nature, treat first of Being in general, and show what in Human Nature, necessarily existing from the nature of Entity. And then, concerning Perceiving or Intelligent Beings, in particular, and show what arises from the nature of such. And then Animal Nature, and what from that.

9. Concerning Enthusiasm, Inspiration, Grace, &c.

10. Concerning a two-fold ground of Assurance of the Judgment—a reducing things to an Identity or Contradiction, as in Mathematical demonstrations,—and by a natural, invincible inclination to a connexion, as when we see any Effect to conclude a Cause—an opposition to believe a thing can begin without a Cause. This is not the same with the other, and cannot be reduced to a contradiction.

11. Difference between Natural Appetites and Rational Desires.

12. Whether any difference between the Will and Inclination. Imperate acts of the Will, nothing but the prevailing Inclination, concerning what should be done that moment. So hath God ordained that the motions of the Body should follow that.

13. Concerning the Influence which Nearness, or Remoteness, of Time has in Determining the Will, and the Reason of it.

14. Concerning Speculative Understanding, and Sense of Heart. Whether any difference between the Sense of the Heart, and the Will or Inclination. How the Scriptures are ignorant of the Philosophic distinction of the Understanding, and the Will; and how the Sense of the Heart is there called *Knowledge*, or *Understanding*.

15. Of what nature are Ideas of what is Internal or Spiritual. How they are the same thing over again.

16. Concerning Liberty, wherein it consists.

17. Concerning the prime and proper foundation of Blame.

18. How far men may be to blame for their Judgments; or for Believing, or Not Believing, this or that.

19. Concerning great Prejudices from the ambiguous and equivocal use of Words—such as Liberty, Force, Power, &c. How from this many things seem to be, and are called, Natural Notions, that are not so.

20. Concerning Beauty and Deformity, Love and Hatred, the nature of Excellency or Virtue, &c.

21. Whether or no Self-Love be the ground of all Love.

22. Concerning the Corruption of Man's Nature. How it comes to be corrupt. What is the positive cause of corruption.

23. How greatly things lose their influence on the mind, through persons being used to them; as Miracles, and the Evidence of the Being of God, which we daily behold. The greatest Demonstrations—most plain and direct Proofs. Use makes things fail of their influence on the Understanding, so on the Will and Affections—things most satisfying and convincing—things otherwise most moving.

24. Consider of what nature is that inward sensation, that a man has when he Almost thinks of a thing—a name or the like—when we say it is *at our tongue's end*.

25. Concerning Moral Sense: what Moral Sense is Natural.

26. How Natural men have a Taste of, and Delight in, that External Beauty, that is a resemblance to Love.

27. Sensitive Appetites: How far they consist in some Present Pain, attended with the idea of Ease, habitually connected, or associated, with the idea of such an object—Whether the sight of Food excites the appetite of one who is hungry, any other way.

By what means persons come to long after a particular thing; either from an idea of Pleasure, or the Removal of Pain, associated.

Not immediately after the Thing itself, but only the pleasure, or the removal of pain.

28. Judgment. Wherein an Act of the judgment consists, or an Assent to a thing as true, or a Dissent from it as false. Show it to be different from mere Perception, such as is in the mere presence of an idea in the mind: and so not the Perception of the Agreement and Disagreement of Ideas.

29. Sensation. How far all acts of the mind are from Sensation. All ideas begin from thence; and there never can be any idea, thought, or act of the mind, unless the mind first received some ideas from Sensation, or some other way equivalent, wherein the mind is wholly passive in receiving them.

30. Separate State. How far the Soul, in a Separate

State, must depend on Sensation, or some way of passively receiving ideas equivalent to Sensation, in order to conversing with other minds, to the knowing of any occurrence, to beholding any of the works of God, and to its further improvement in knowledge.

31. Sensation. Whether all ideas, wherein the mind is merely passive, and which are received immediately without any dependence on Reflexion, are not ideas of Sensation, or External ideas? Whether there be any difference between these? Whether it be possible for the Soul of man, in this manner, to be originally, and without dependence on Reflexion, capable of receiving any other ideas than those of sensation, or something equivalent, and so some external idea? And whether the first ideas of the ANGELS, must not be of some such kind?

32. Angels. Separate Spirits. How far the Angels and Separate Spirits, being in some respects *in place*, in the Third Heaven, where the body of Christ is; their removing from place to place; their coming down from Heaven, then ascending to Heaven; their being with Christ at the Day of Judgment; their seeing bodies; their beholding the Creation of the Material Universe; their having, in their ministry, to do with the bodies of men, with the body of Christ, and other material things; and their seeing God's works of Providence, relating to the Material Universe;—how far these things necessarily imply, that they have some kind of Sensations like ours; and, Whether these things do not show that, by some laws or other, they are united to some kind of Matter?

33. Concerning the great Weakness and Fallibility of the Human Mind, in its present state.

34. Concerning Beauty.

35. How the Affections will suggest words, and expressions, and thoughts, and make eloquent.

36. The manifest analogy between the Nature of the Human Soul and the Nature of other things. How Laws of nature take place alike. How it is Laws, that constitute all permanent being, in created things, both corporeal and spiritual.

37. Wherein there is an agreement between Men and Beasts. How many things, in Men, are like instincts in Brutes.

38. Whether the mind perceives more than One object at a time.

39. How far the mind may perceive, without adverting to what it perceived; as in the winking of the eyelids, and many other like things.

40. How far there may be Acts of the Will, without our adverting to it; as in walking, the act of the will for each individual step, and the like.

41. The agreement between Objects of Sight, and Objects of Feeling; or Visible Magnitude and Figure, and Tangible Magnitude and Figure, as to Number and Proportion.

42. How far Imagination is unavoidable, in all Thinking; and Why?

43. Connexion of Ideas. Concerning the Laws by which Ideas follow each other, or call up one another, in which one thing comes into the mind after another, in the course of our thinking. How far this is owing to the Association of ideas; and how far, to any Relation of Cause and Effect, or any other Relation. And whether the whole may not be reduced to these following: *Association of Ideas; Resemblance of some kind;* and that *Natural Disposition* in us, when we see any thing begin to be, to suppose it owing to a Cause.—Observe how these laws, by which one idea suggests and brings in another, are a kind of mutual attraction of ideas.—Concerning the importance, and necessity, of this mutual attraction and adhesion of ideas—how rarely our minds would serve us, if it were not for this. How the mind would be without ideas, except as suggested by the Senses. How far Reasoning, Contemplation, &c. depend on this.

44. How far the Love of Happiness is the same with the Faculty of the Will? It is not distinct from the mere Capacity of enjoying and suffering, and the Faculty of the Will is no other.

45. Whether it be possible for a man to love any thing better than himself; and in what sense it is so.

46. Example To inquire, What are the true reasons of so strong an inclination, in mankind, to follow Example. How great its influence over men, in their opinions, their judgment, their taste, and the whole man. How by this means, at certain times, a particular thing will come to be in great vogue, and men's passions will all, as it were, be moved at once, as the trees in the wood, by the same wind, or as things floating with the tide, the same way. Men follow one another like a flock of sheep. How sometimes the vogue lasts an age; at other times, but a short time; and the reason of this difference.

47. In what respects men may be, and often are, ignorant of their own hearts; and how this comes to pass.

48. Concerning the Soul's Union with the Body, its Laws, and Consequences.

49. One section, particularly to show wherein Men differ from Beasts.

50. In how many respects the very Being of Created things depends on Laws, or stated methods, fixed by God, of events following one another.

51. Whether all the Immediate Objects of the mind are properly called Ideas; and what inconvenience and confusion arises from giving every Subjective Thought that name. What prejudices and mistakes it leads to.

52. In what respects Ideas, or thoughts, and judgments, may be said to be *Innate*, and in what respects not.

53. Whether there could have ever been any such thing as Thought, without External Ideas, immediately impressed by God, either according to some law, or otherwise. Whether any Spirit, or Angel, could have any Thought, if it had not been for this. Here particularly explain what I mean by *External Ideas.*

54. How words came to have such a mighty influence on thought and judgment, by virtue of the Association of Ideas, or from Ideas being habitually tied to words.

55. How far, through Habit, men move their bodies without thought or consciousness.

56. Whether Beauty, (Natural and Moral,) and the pleasure that arises from it, in ourselves or others, be not the only object of the Will; or whether Truth be not also the object of the Will.*

THE MIND.

[12.] BEING. It seems strange sometimes to me, that there should be Being from all Eternity; and I am ready to say, What need was there that any thing should be? I should then ask myself, Whether it seems strange that there should be either Something, or Nothing? If so, it is not strange that there should BE; for that necessity of there being Something, or Nothing, implies it.

[26.] CAUSE is that, after or upon the existence of which, or the existence of it after such a manner, the existence of another thing follows.

[27.] EXISTENCE. If we had only the sense of Seeing, we should not be as ready to conclude the visible world to have been an existence independent of perception, as we do; because the ideas we have by the sense of Feeling, are as much mere ideas, as those we have by the sense of Seeing. But we know, that the things that are objects of this sense, all that the mind views by Seeing, are merely mental Existences; because all these things, with all their modes, do exist in a looking-glass, where all will acknowledge, they exist only mentally.

IT is now agreed upon by every knowing philosopher, that Colours are not really in the things, no more than pain is in a needle; but strictly no where else but in the mind. But yet I think that Colour may have an existence out of the mind, with equal reason as any thing in Body has any existence out of the mind, beside the very substance of the body itself, which is nothing but the Divine

* The preceding articles were set down from time to time at the close of the work, in two series; the first, ending with No. 26.

power, or rather the Constant Exertion of it. For what idea is that, which we call by the name of Body? I find Colour has the chief share in it. 'Tis nothing but Colour, and Figure, which is the termination of this Colour, together with some powers, such as the power of resisting, and motion, &c. that wholly makes up what we call Body. And if that, which we principally mean by the thing itself, cannot be said to be in the thing itself, I think nothing can be. If Colour exists not out of the mind, then nothing belonging to Body exists out of the mind but Resistance, which is Solidity, and the termination of this Resistance, with its relations, which is Figure, and the communication of this Resistance, from space to space, which is Motion; though the latter are nothing but modes of the former. Therefore, there is nothing out of the mind but Resistance. And not that neither, when nothing is actually resisted. Then, there is nothing but the Power of Resistance. And as Resistance is nothing else but the actual exertion of God's power, so the Power can be nothing else, but the constant Law or Method of that actual exertion. And how is there any Resistance, except it be in some mind, in idea? What is it that is resisted? It is not Colour. And what else is it? It is ridiculous to say, that Resistance is resisted. That does not tell us at all what is to be resisted. There must be something resisted before there can be Resistance; but to say Resistance is resisted, is ridiculously to suppose Resistance, before there is any thing to be resisted. Let us suppose two globes only existing, and no mind. There is nothing there, *ex confesso*, but Resistance. That is, there is such a Law, that the space within the limits of a globular figure shall resist. Therefore, there is nothing there but a power, or an establishment. And if there be any Resistance really out of the mind, one power and establishment must resist another establishment and law of Resistance, which is exceedingly ridiculous. But yet it cannot be otherwise, if any way out of the mind. But now it is easy to conceive of Resistance, as a mode of an idea. It is easy to conceive of such a power, or constant manner of stopping or resisting a colour. The idea may be resisted, it may move, and stop, and rebound; but how a mere power, which is nothing real, can move and stop, is inconceivable, and it is impossible to say a word about it without contradiction. The world is therefore an ideal one; and the Law of creating, and the succession, of these ideas is constant and regular.

[28.] *Coroll.* 1. How impossible is it, that the world should exist from Eternity, without a Mind.

[30.] *Coroll.* 2. Since it is so, and that absolute Nothing is such a dreadful contradiction; hence we learn the necessity of the Eternal Existence of an All-comprehending Mind; and that it is the complication of all contradictions to deny such a mind.

[34.] WHEN we say that the World, *i. e.* the material Universe, exists no where but in the mind, we have got to such a degree of strictness and abstraction, that we must be exceedingly careful, that we do not confound and lose ourselves by misapprehension. That is impossible, that it should be meant, that all the world is contained in the narrow compass of a few inches of space, in little ideas in the place of the brain; for that would be a contradiction; for we are to remember that the human body, and the brain itself, exist only mentally, in the same sense that other things do; and so that, which we call *place*, is an idea too. Therefore things are truly in those places; for what we mean, when we say so, is only, that this mode of our idea of place appertains to such an idea. We would not therefore be understood to deny, that things are where they seem to be. For the principles we lay down, if they are narrowly looked into, do not infer that. Nor will it be found, that they at all make void Natural Philosophy, or the science of the Causes or Reasons of corporeal changes; for to find out the reasons of things, in Natural Philosophy, is only to find out the proportion of God's acting. And the case is the same, as to such proportions, whether we suppose the World only mental, in our sense, or no.

THOUGH we suppose, that the existence of the whole material Universe is absolutely dependent on Idea, yet we may speak in the old way, and as properly and truly as ever. God, in the beginning, created such a certain number of Atoms, of such a determinate bulk and figure, which they yet maintain and always will, and gave them such a motion, of such a direction, and of such a degree of velocity; from whence arise all the Natural changes in the Universe, for ever, in a continued series. Yet, perhaps all this does not exist any where perfectly, but in the Divine Mind. But then, if it be inquired, What exists in the Divine Mind; and how these things exist there? I answer, There is his determination, his care, and his design, that Ideas shall be united for ever, just so, and in such a manner, as is agreeable to such a series. For instance, all the ideas that ever were, or ever shall be to all eternity, in any created mind, are answerable to the existence of such a peculiar Atom in the beginning of the Creation, of such a determinate figure and size, and have such a motion given it: That is, they are all such, as Infinite Wisdom sees would follow, according to the series of nature, from such an Atom, so moved. That is, all ideal changes of creatures are just so, as if just such a particular Atom had actually all along existed even in some finite mind, and never had been out of that mind, and had, in that mind, caused these effects, which are exactly according to nature, that is, according to the nature of other matter, that is actually perceived by the mind. God supposes its existence; that is, he causes all changes to arise, as if all these things had actually existed in such a series, in some created mind, and as if created minds had comprehended all things perfectly. And, although created minds do not; yet, the Divine Mind doth; and he orders all things according to his mind, and his ideas. And these hidden things do not only exist in the Divine idea, but in a sense in created idea; for that exists in created idea, which necessarily supposes it. If a ball of lead were supposed to be let fall from the clouds, and no eye saw it, till it got within ten rods of the ground, and then its motion and celerity was perfectly discerned in its exact proportion; if it were not for the imperfection and slowness of our minds, the perfect idea of the rest of the motion would immediately, and of itself, arise in the mind, as well as that which is there. So, were our thoughts comprehensive and perfect enough, our view of the present state of the world would excite in us a perfect idea of all past changes.

And we need not perplex our minds with a thousand questions and doubts that will seem to arise: as, To what purpose is this way of exciting ideas? and, What advantage is there in observing such a series? I answer, It is just all one, as to any benefit or advantage, any end that we can suppose was proposed by the Creator, as if the Material Universe were existent in the same manner as is vulgarly thought. For the corporeal world is to no advantage but to the spiritual; and it is exactly the same advantage this way as the other, for it is all one, as to any thing excited in the mind.

[51.] IT is hardly proper to say, that the dependence of ideas of sensation upon the organs of the body, is only the dependence of some of our ideas upon others. For the organs of our bodies are not our ideas, in a proper sense, though their existence be only mental. Yet there is no necessity of their existing actually in our minds, but they exist mentally, in the same manner as has been explained. *See above, No.* 34. The dependence of our ideas upon the organs, is the dependence of our ideas on our bodies, after the manner there explained, mentally existing. And if it be inquired, To what purpose is this way of exciting ideas? I answer, To exactly the same purpose as can be supposed, if our organs are actually existing, in the manner vulgarly conceived, as to any manner of benefit, or end, that can be mentioned.

IT is not proper at all, nor doth it express the thing we would, to say *that bodies do not exist without the mind*. For the scheme will not allow the mind to be supposed determined to any place, in such a manner as to make that proper; for *Place itself* is mental, and *Within* and *Without* are mere mental conceptions. Therefore, that way of expressing, will lead us into a thousand difficulties and perplexities. But when I say, the Material Universe exists only in the mind, I mean, that it is absolutely dependent on the conception of the mind for its existence, and does not exist as Spirits do, whose existence does not consist in, nor in dependence on, the conception of other minds. We must be exceedingly careful, lest we confound ourselves in these by mere imagination. It is from hence I expect the greatest opposition. It will appear a ridiculous thing, I suppose, that the material world exists no where, but in the soul of man, confined within his skull; but we must again remember what sort of existence the head and brain have.—The soul, in a sense, has its seat in the brain; and so, in a sense, the visible world is existent out of the mind, for it certainly, in the most proper sense, exists out of the brain.

[36.] Things, as to God, exist from all Eternity, alike; that is, the idea is always the same, and after the same mode. The existence of things, therefore, that are not actually in created minds, consists only in Power, or in the Determination of God, that such and such ideas shall be raised in created minds, upon such conditions.

[40.] Since all material existence is only idea, this question may be asked, In what sense may those things be said to exist, which are supposed, and yet are in no actual idea of any Created minds? I answer, they existed only in Uncreated idea. But how do they exist, otherwise than they did from all Eternity, for they always were in Uncreated idea and Divine appointment? I answer, They did exist from all Eternity in Uncreated idea, as did every thing else, and as they do at present, but not in Created idea. But it may be asked, How do those things exist, which have an actual existence, but of which no created mind is conscious?—For instance, the Furniture of this room, when we are absent, and the room is shut up, and no created mind perceives it; How do these things exist?—I answer, There has been in times past such a course and succession of existences, that these things must be supposed to make the series complete, according to Divine appointment, of the order of things. And there will be innumerable things consequential, which will be out of joint, out of their constituted series, without the supposition of these. For, upon the supposition of these things, are infinite numbers of things otherwise than they would be, if these were not by God thus supposed. Yea, the whole Universe would be otherwise; such an influence have these things, by their attraction and otherwise. Yea, there must be a universal attraction, in the whole system of things, from the beginning of the world to the end; and, to speak more strictly and metaphysically, we must say, in the whole system and series of ideas in all Created minds; so that these things must necessarily be put in, to make complete the system of the ideal world. That is, they must be supposed, if the train of ideas be, in the order and course, settled by the Supreme mind. So that we may answer in short, That the existence of these things is in God's supposing of them, in order to the rendering complete the series of things, (to speak more strictly, *the series of ideas*,) according to his own settled order, and that harmony of things, which he has appointed.—The supposition of God, which we speak of, is nothing else but God's acting, in the course and series of his exciting ideas, as if they (the things supposed) were in actual idea.

But you may object, But there are many things so infinitely small, that their influence is altogether insensible; so that, whether they are supposed or not, there will no alteration be made in the series of Ideas. Answer, But though the influence is so small, that *we* do not perceive, yet, who knows how penetrating other spirits may be, to perceive the minutest alterations. And whether the alterations be sensible, or not, at present, yet the effect of the least influence will be sensible, in time. For instance, Let there be supposed to be a Leaden Globe, of a mile in diameter, to be moving in a right line, with the swiftness of a cannon ball, in the Infinite Void, and let it pass by a very small Atom, supposed to be at rest. This Atom will somewhat retard this Leaden Globe in its motion, though at first, and perhaps for many ages, the difference is altogether insensible. But let it be never so little, in time it will become very sensible. For if the motion is made so much slower, that in a million of years it shall have moved one inch less than it would have done otherwise, in a million million it will have moved a million inches less. So now the least Atom, by its existence or motion, causes an alteration, more or less, in every other Atom in the Universe; so the alteration in time will become very sensible; so the whole Universe, in time, will become all over different from what it would otherwise have been. For if every other Atom is supposed to be either retarded, or accelerated, or diverted; every Atom, however small for the present, will cause great alterations, as we have shown already, of Retardation. The case is the same as to Acceleration; and so as to Diversion, or varying the direction of the motion. For let the course of the body be never so little changed, this course, in time, may carry it to a place immensely distant from what the other would have carried it to, as is evident enough. And the case is the same still, if the motion that before was never so slow is wholly stopped; the difference in time will be immense; for this slow motion would have carried it to an immense distance, if it were continued.

But the Objector will say, I acknowledge it would be thus, if the bodies, in which these insensible alterations are made, were free, and alone, in an Infinite Void; but I do not know but the case may be far otherwise, when an insensible alteration is made in a body, that is among innumerable others, and subject to infinite jumbles among them.—*Answer.* The case is the same, whether the bodies be alone in a Void, or in a System of other bodies; for the influence of this insensible alteration continues as steadily for ever, through all its various interchanges and collisions with other bodies, as it would if it were alone in an Infinite Void: so that in time, a particle of matter, that shall be on this side of the Universe, might have been on the other. The existence and motion of every Atom, has influence, more or less, on the motion of all other bodies in the Universe, great or small, as is most demonstrable from the Laws of Gravity and Motion. An alteration, more or less, as to motion, is made on every Fixed Star, and on all its Planets, Primary and Secondary. Let the alteration made in the Fixed Stars be never so small, yet in time it will make an infinite alteration, from what otherwise would have been. Let the Fixed Stars be supposed, for instance, before to have been in perfect rest; let them now be all set in motion, and this motion be never so small, yet, continued for ever, where will it carry those immense bodies, with their Systems. Let a little alteration be made in the motion of the Planets, either Retardation or Acceleration; this, in time, will make a difference of many millions of Revolutions: and how great a difference will that make in the floating bodies of the Universe.

Coroll. By this we may answer a more difficult question, *viz.* If material existence be only mental, then our bodies and organs are ideas only; and then in what sense is it true, that the Mind receives Ideas by the Organs of Sense; seeing that the Organs of Sense, themselves, exist no where but in the Mind?—*Answer.* Seeing our Organs, themselves, are ideas; the connexion, that our ideas have with such and such a mode of our Organs, is no other than God's constitution, that some of our ideas shall be connected with others, according to such a settled Law and Order, so that some ideas shall follow from others as their cause.—But how can this be, seeing that ideas most commonly arise from Organs, when we have no idea of the mode of Organs, or the manner of external objects being applied to them? I answer, Our Organs, and the motions in them and to them, exist in the manner explained above.

" Plato, in his ' Subterranean Cave,' so famously known, and so elegantly described by him, supposes men tied with their backs towards the Light, placed at a great distance from them, so that they could not turn about their heads to it neither, and therefore could see nothing but the shadows of certain substances behind them, projected from it; which shadows they concluded to be the only substance and realities. And when they heard the sounds made by those bodies, that were betwixt the Light and them, or their reverberated echoes, they imputed them to those shadows which they saw. All this is a description of the state of those men, who take Body to be the only Real and Substantial Thing in the world, and to do all that is done in it; and therefore often impute Sense, Reason, and Understanding, to nothing but Blood and Brains in us."

Cudworth's Intellectual System.

[9.] SPACE. Space, as has been already observed, is a necessary being, if it may be called a being; and yet we have also shown, that all existence is mental, that the existence of all exterior things is ideal. Therefore it is a necessary being, only as it is a necessary idea, so far as it is simple idea, that is necessarily connected with other simple exterior ideas, and is, as it were, their common substance or subject. It is in the same manner a necessary being, as any thing external is a being.

Coroll. It is hence easy to see in what sense that is true, that has been held by some, That, when there is nothing between any two bodies, they unavoidably must touch.

[13.] THE real and necessary existence of Space, and its Infinity, even beyond the Universe, depend upon a like reasoning as the Extension of Spirits, and to the supposition of the reality of the existence of a Successive Duration, before the Universe: even the impossibility of removing the idea out of the mind. If it be asked, If there be Limits of the Creation, whether or no it be not possible that an Intelligent being shall be removed beyond the limits; and then whether or no there would not be distance between that Intelligent being and the limits of the Universe, in the same manner, and as properly, as there is between Intelligent beings and the parts of the Universe, within its limits; I answer, I cannot tell what the Law of Nature, or the Constitution of God, would be in this case.

Coroll. There is, therefore, no difficulty in answering such questions as these, What cause was there why the Universe was placed in such a part of Space? and, Why was the Universe created at such a Time? for, if there be be no Space beyond the Universe, it was impossible that it should be created in another place; and if there was no Time before, it was impossible it should be created at another time.

THE idea we have of Space, and what we call by that name, is only *Coloured Space*, and is entirely taken out of the mind, if Colour be taken away. And so all that we call Extension, Motion, and Figure, is gone, if Colour is gone. As to any idea of Space, Extension, Distance, or Motion, that a man born blind might form, it would be nothing like what we call by those names. All that he could have would be only certain sensations or feelings, that in themselves would be no more like what we intend by Space, Motion, &c. than the pain we have by the scratch of a pin, or than the ideas of taste and smell. And as to the idea of Motion, that such a one could have, it could be only a diversification of those successions in a certain way, by succession as to time. And then there would be an agreement of these successions of sensations, with some ideas we have by sight, as to number and proportions; but yet the ideas, after all, nothing akin to that idea we now give this name to.—And, as it is very plain, Colour is only in the mind, and nothing like it can be out of all mind. Hence it is manifest, there can be nothing like those things we call by the name of Bodies, out of the mind, unless it be in some other mind or minds.

And, indeed, the secret lies here: That, which truly is the Substance of all Bodies, is *the infinitely exact, and precise, and perfectly stable Idea, in God's mind, together with his stable Will, that the same shall gradually be communicated to us, and to other minds, according to certain fixed and exact established Methods and Laws*: or in somewhat different language, *the infinitely exact and precise Divine Idea, together with an answerable, perfectly exact, precise, and stable Will, with respect to correspondent communications to Created Minds, and effects on their minds.*

[61.] SUBSTANCE.* It is intuitively certain, that, if Solidity be removed from Body, nothing is left but empty space. Now, in all things whatsoever, that which cannot be removed without removing the whole thing, that thing which is removed is the thing itself, except it be mere circumstance and manner of existence, such as Time and Place; which are in the general necessary, because it implies a contradiction to existence itself, to suppose that it exists at no time and in no place, and therefore in order to remove time and place in the general, we must remove the thing itself: So if we remove Figure and Bulk and Texture, in the general; which may be reduced to that necessary circumstance of Place.

If, therefore, it implies a contradiction to suppose that body, or any thing appertaining to Body, beside Space, exists, when Solidity is removed; it must be, either because Body is nothing but Solidity and Space, or else, that Solidity is such a mere circumstance and relation of existence, which the thing cannot be without, because whatever exists must exist in some circumstances or other, as at some time or some place. But we know, and every one perceives, it to be a contradiction to suppose, that Body or Matter exists without Solidity, for all the notion we have of Empty Space, is Space without Solidity, and all the notion we have of Full Space, is Space Resisting.

The reason is plain; for if it implies a contradiction to suppose Solidity absent, and the thing existing, it must be because Solidity is that thing, and so it is a contradiction to say the thing is absent from itself; or because it is such a mode, or circumstances, or relation, of the existence, as it is a contradiction to suppose existence at all without it, such as Time and Place, to which both Figure and Texture are reduced. For nothing can be conceived of so necessarily in an existence, that it is a contradiction to suppose it without it, but the Existence itself, and those general Circumstances or Relations of existence, which the very supposition of existence itself implies.

Again, Solidity or Impenetrability is as much Action, or the immediate result of Action, as Gravity. Gravity by all will be confessed to be immediately from some active influence. Being a continual tendency in bodies to move, and being that, which will set them in motion though before at perfect rest, it must be the effect of something acting on that body. And it is as clear and evident, that action is as requisite to stop a body, that is already in motion, as in order to set bodies a moving, that are at perfect rest. Now we see continually, that there is a stopping of all motion, at the limits of such and such parts of Space, only this stoppage is modified and diversified according to certain Laws; for we get the idea and apprehension of Solidity, only and entirely, from the observation we make of that ceasing of motion, at the limits of some parts of Space, that already is, and that beginning of motion, that till now was not, according to a certain constant manner.

And why is it not every whit as reasonable, that we should attribute this action, or effect, to the influence of some Agent, as that other action or effect which we call Gravity; which is likewise derived from our observation of the beginning and ceasing of motion, according to a certain method? In either case, there is nothing observed, but the beginning, increasing, directing, diminishing, and ceasing of motion. And why is it not as reasonable to seek a reason, beside that general one, that it is something; which is no reason at all? I say, Why is it not as reasonable to seek a reason or cause of these actions, as well in one as in the other case? We do not think it sufficient to say, It is the nature of the unknown substance, in the one case; and why should we think it a sufficient explication of the same actions or effects, in the other. By Substance, I suppose it is confessed, we mean only Something; because of Abstract Substance we have no idea, that is more particular than only existence in general. Now why is it not as reasonable, when we see something suspended in the air, set to move with violence towards the Earth, to rest in attributing of it to the nature of the something that is there; as when we see that motion, when it comes to such limits, all on a sudden cease, for

* This article, and the numbers following, *viz.* 62, 63, &c. are inserted in the manuscript distinctly from the rest, and were written probably at a somewhat later period of life.

this is all that we observe in falling bodies. Their falling is the action we call Gravity: their stopping upon the surface of the Earth, the action whence we gain the idea of Solidity. It was before agreed on all hands, that there is something there, that supports that resistance. It must be granted now, that that Something is a Being, that acts there, as much as that Being, that causes bodies to descend towards the centre. Here is something in these parts of space, that of itself produces effects, without previously being acted upon; for that Being that lays an arrest on bodies in motion, and immediately stops them when they come to such limits and bounds, certainly does as much, as that Being that sets a body in motion, that before was at rest. Now this Being, acting altogether of itself, producing new effects, that are perfectly arbitrary, and that are no way necessary of themselves; must be Intelligent and Voluntary. There is no reason, in the nature of the thing itself, why a body, when set in motion, should stop at such limits, more than at any other. It must therefore be some arbitrary, active, and voluntary Being, that determines it. If there were but one body in the Universe, that always in time past had been at rest, and should now, without any alteration, be set in motion; we might certainly conclude, that some voluntary Being set it in motion, because it can certainly be demonstrated, that it can be for no other reason. So with just the same reason, in the same manner, we may conclude, if the body had hitherto been in motion, and is at a certain point of space now stopped. And would it not be every whit as reasonable to conclude, it must be from such an Agent, as if, in certain portions of space, we observed bodies to be attracted a certain way, and so at once to be set into motion, or accelerated in motion. And it is not at all the less remarkable, because we receive the ideas of light and colours from those spaces; for we know that light and colours are not there, and are made entirely by such a resistance, together with attraction, that is antecedent to these qualities, and would be a necessary effect of a mere resistance of space without other substance.

The whole of what we any way observe, whereby we get the idea of Solidity, or Solid Body, are certain parts of Space, from whence we receive the ideas of light and colours; and certain sensations by the sense of feeling; and we observe that the places, whence we receive these sensations, are not constantly the same, but are successively different, and this light and colours are communicated from one part of space to another. And we observe that these parts of Space, from whence we receive these sensations, resist and stop other bodies, which we observe communicated successively through the parts of Space adjacent; and that those that there were before at rest, or existing constantly in one and the same part of Space, after this exist successively in different parts of Space, and these observations are according to certain stated rules. I appeal to any one that takes notice and asks himself, whether this be not all that ever he experienced in the world, whereby he got these ideas; and that this is all that we have or can have any idea of, in relation to bodies. All that we observe of Solidity is, that certain parts of Space, from whence we receive the ideas of light and colours, and a few other sensations, do likewise resist any thing coming within them. It therefore follows, that if we suppose there be any thing else, than what we thus observe, it is but only by way of Inference.

I know that it is nothing but the Imagination will oppose me in this: I will therefore endeavour to help the Imagination thus. Suppose that we received none of the sensible qualities of light, colours, &c. from the resisting parts of Space, (we will suppose it possible for resistance to be without them,) and they were, to appearance, clear and pure; and all that we could possibly observe, was only and merely Resistance; we simply observed that Motion was resisted and stopped, here and there, in particular parts of Infinite Space. Should we not then think it less unreasonable to suppose, that such effects should be produced by some Agent, present in those parts of Space, though Invisible. If we, when walking upon the face of the Earth, were stopped at certain limits, and could not possibly enter into such a part of Space, nor make any body enter into it; and we could observe no other difference, no way, nor at any time, between that and other parts of clear space; should we not be ready to say, What is it stops us? What is it hinders all entrance into that place?

The reason why it is so exceedingly natural to men to suppose that there is some Latent *Substance*, or Something that is altogether hid, that upholds the properties of bodies, is, because all see at first sight, that the properties of bodies are such as need some Cause, that shall every moment have influence to their continuance, as well as a Cause of their first existence. All therefore agree, that there is Something that is there, and upholds these properties. And it is most true, there undoubtedly is; but men are wont to content themselves in saying merely, that it is Something; but that Something is He "by whom all things consist."

[25.] The distribution of the objects of our thoughts, into Substances and Modes, may be proper; if, by Substance, we understand, a complexion of such ideas, which we conceive of as subsisting together, and by themselves; and, by Modes, those simple ideas which cannot be by themselves, or subsist in our mind alone.

[38.] BODY INFINITE? If we dispute, whether Body is capable of being Infinite; let us in the first place put the question, Whether motion can be infinite; that is, Whether there can be a motion infinitely swift. I suppose that every one will see, that, if a body moved with infinite swiftness, it would be in every part of the distance passed through exactly at once, and therefore it could not be said to move from one part of it to another. Infinite motion is therefore a contradiction. Supposing therefore a Body were infinitely great, it could doubtless be moved by Infinite Power, and turned round some point or axis. But if that were possible, it is evident that some part of that Infinite Body would move with Infinite Swiftness; which we have seen is a contradiction. Body therefore cannot be infinite.

[21.] MATTER. THOUGHT. It has been a question with some, Whether or no it was not possible with God, to the other properties or powers of Matter to add that of Thought; whether he could not, if he had pleased, have added Thinking, and the power of Perception, to those other properties of Solidity, Mobility, and Gravitation. The question is not here, Whether the Matter that now is, without the addition of any new primary property, could not be so contrived and modelled, so attenuated, wrought, and moved, as to produce thought; but, whether any Lump of matter, a solid Atom, for instance, is not capable of receiving, by the Almighty Power of God, in addition to the rest of its powers, a new power of thought.

Here, if the question be, Whether or no God cannot cause the faculty of thinking to be so added to any parcel of matter, so as to be in the same place, (if thought can be in place,) and that inseparably, where that matter is, so that by a fixed law, that thought should be where that matter is, and only there, being always bound to solid extension, mobility, and gravity; I do not deny it. But that seems to me quite a different thing from the question, Whether Matter can think; or, Whether God can make Matter think; and is not worth the disputing. For if Thought be in the same place where Matter is, yet, if there be no manner of communication, or dependence, between that and any thing that is material; that is, any of that collection of properties that we call Matter; if none of those properties of Solidity, Extension, &c. wherein Materiality consists;—which are Matter, or at least whereby Matter is Matter;—have any manner of influence towards the exerting of Thought; and if that Thought be no way dependent on Solidity or Mobility, and they no way help the matter, but Thought could be as well without those properties; then Thought is not properly in Matter, though it be in the same place. All the properties, that are properly said to be in Matter, depend on the other properties of Matter, so that they cannot be without them. Thus Figure is in Matter: it depends on Solidity and Extension; and so doth Motion; so doth Gravity; and Extension itself depends on Solidity, in that it is the extension of the Solidity; and Solidity on Extension, for nothing can be solid except it be extended. These ideas have a dependence on one another; but there is no manner of connexion between the ideas of Perception and Solidity, or Motion, or Gravity. They are simple ideas, of which we can have a perfect view; and we know there is no dependence. Nor can there be any dependence, for the ideas in their own nature are independent and aliene one to another. All the others either include the rest, or are included in them; and, except the the property of Thought be included in the properties of Matter, I think it cannot properly be said, that Matter has Thought, or if it can, I see not a possibility of Matter, in any other sense, having Thought.—If Thought's being so fixed to Matter, as to be in the same place where Matter is, be for Thought to be *in Matter;* Thought not only can be in Matter, but actually is, as much as Thought can be, *in place.* It is so connected with the Bodies of men, or, at least, with some parts of their bodies, and will be for ever after the Resurrection.

[65.] MOTION. If Motion be only mental, it seems to follow that there is no difference between Real and Apparent motion, or that Motion is nothing else but the change of position between bodies; and then of two bodies that have their position changed, Motion may with equal reason be ascribed to either of them, and the Sun may as properly be said to move as the Earth. And then returns this difficulty. If it be so, how comes it to pass that the Laws of Centrifugal Force are observed to take place, with respect to the Earth, considered as moving round the Sun, but not with respect to the Sun, considered as moving round the Earth?—I answer, It would be impossible it should be so, and the Laws of gravitation be observed. The Earth cannot be kept at a distance from a body, so strongly attracting it as the Sun, any other way than by such a motion as is supposed. That body therefore must be reputed to move, that can be supposed so to do, according to the Laws of Nature universally observed in other things. It is upon them that God impresses that Centrifugal Force.

N. B. This answers the objection that might be raised from what Newton says of Absolute, and Relative, Motion, and that distinguishing property of absolute Circular Motion, that there was a Centrifugal Force in the body moved; for God causes a Centrifugal Force in that body, that can be supposed to move circularly, consistently with the Laws of Motion, in that and in all other things, on which it has a near, or a remote, dependence, and which must be supposed to move in order to the observance of those Laws in the Universe. For instance, when a bushel, with water in it, is violently whirled round, before the water takes the impression, there is a continual change of position between the water and the parts of the bushel; but yet that must not be supposed to move as fast as that position is altered; because if we follow it, it will not hold out consistent with the Laws of motion in the Universe, for if the Water moves, then the bushel does not move; and if the Bushel does not move, then the Earth moves round the bushel, every time that seems to turn round; but there can be no such alteration in the motion of the Earth created naturally, or in observance of the Laws of Nature.

[2.] PLACE OF MINDS. Our common way of conceiving of what is Spiritual, is very gross, and shadowy, and corporeal, with dimensions and figure, &c. though it be supposed to be very clear, so that we can see through it. If we would get a right notion of what is Spiritual, we must think of Thought, or Inclination, or Delight. How large is that thing in the Mind which they call Thought? Is Love square, or round? Is the surface of Hatred rough, or smooth? Is Joy an inch, or a foot, in diameter? These are Spiritual things; and why should we then form such a ridiculous idea of Spirits, as to think them so long, so thick, or so wide; or to think there is a necessity of their being square, or round, or some other certain figure?

Therefore Spirits cannot be *in place,* in such a sense, that all, within the given limits, shall be where the Spirit is, and all without such a circumscription, where he is not; but in this sense only, that all created Spirits have clearer and more strongly impressed ideas of things, in one place than in another, or can produce effects here, and not there; and as this place alters, so Spirits move. In Spirits united to bodies, the Spirit more strongly perceives things where the body is, and can there immediately produce effects; and in this sense the soul can be said to be *in the same place* where the body is. And this law is, that we call *the Union between soul and body.* So the soul may be said to be *in the brain;* because ideas, that come by the body, immediately ensue, only on alterations that are made there; and the soul most immediately produces effects no where else.

No doubt that all Finite Spirits, united to bodies or not, are thus *in place;* that is, that they perceive, or passively receive, ideas, only of created things, that are in some particular place at a given time. At least a Finite Spirit cannot thus be in all places at a time, equally. And doubtless the change of the place, where they perceive most strongly and produce effects immediately, is regular and successive; which is the motion of Spirits.

[31.] From what is said above, we learn, that the seat of the Soul is not *in the Brain,* any otherwise, than as to its immediate operations, and the immediate operation of things on it. The Soul may also be said to be *in the Heart,* or the Affections, for its immediate operations are there also. Hence we learn the propriety of the Scriptures calling the soul, *the Heart,* when considered with respect to the Will and the Affections.

We seem to think in our heads, because most of the ideas, of which our thoughts are constituted, or about which they are conversant, come by the sensories that are in the head, especially the sight and hearing, or those ideas of Reflection, that arise from hence; and partly because we feel the effects of thought and study in our head.

[35.] Seeing the Brain exists only mentally, I therefore acknowledge, that I speak improperly, when I say, *the Soul is in the Brain, only as to its operations.* For, to speak yet more strictly and abstractly, 'tis nothing but the connexion of the operations of the Soul with these, and those modes of its own ideas, or those mental acts of the Deity; seeing the Brain exists only in idea. But we have got so far beyond those things for which language was chiefly contrived, that, unless we use extreme caution, we cannot speak, except we speak exceeding unintelligibly, without literally contradicting ourselves.—*Coroll.* No wonder, therefore, that the high and abstract mysteries of the Deity, the prime and most abstract of all beings, imply so many seeming contradictions.

[32.] Seeing Human Souls and Finite Spirits are said to be in this place or that, only because they are so as to mutual communications; it follows that the Scripture, when it speaks of God being *in heaven,* of his dwelling *in Israel,* of his dwelling *in the hearts of his people,* does not speak so improperly as has been thought.

[4.] UNION of mind with body. The Mind is so united with the Body, that an alteration is caused in the Body, it is probable, by every action of the Mind. By those acts that are very vigorous, a great alteration is very sensible; at some times, when the vigour of the body is impaired by disease, especially in the head, almost every action causes a sensible alteration of the Body.

[3.] PERCEPTION of separate minds. Our perceptions, or ideas that we passively receive by our bodies, are communicated to us immediately by God, while our minds are united with our bodies; but only we in some measure know *the rule.* We know that, upon such alterations in our minds, there follow such ideas in the mind. It need, therefore, be no difficulty with us, how we shall perceive things when we are Separate. They will be communicated then, also, and according to some rule, no doubt, only we know not what.

[68.] REASON. A person may have a strong Reason and yet not a good Reason. He may have a strength of mind to drive an argument, and yet not have even balances. It is not so much from a defect of the reasoning powers, as from a fault of the disposition. When men of strong Reason do not form an even and just judgment, 'tis for one of these two reasons: either a liableness to Prejudice, through natural temper, or education, or circumstances; or, for want of a great love to Truth, and of fear of Error, that shall cause a watchful circumspection, that nothing, relative to the case in question of any weight, shall escape the observation and just estimation, to distinguish with great exactness between what is real and solid, and what is only colour, and shadow, and words.

Persons of mean capacities may see the Reason of that, which requires a nice and exact attention, and a long discourse, to explain—as the reason why Thunder should be so much feared; and many other things that might be mentioned.

[16.] CONSCIOUSNESS is the mind's perceiving what is in itself,—ideas, actions, passions, and every thing that is there perceptible. It is a sort of feeling within itself. The mind feels when it thinks; so it feels when it discerns, feels when it loves, and feels when it hates.

[69.] MEMORY is the identity, in some degree, of Ideas that we formerly had in our minds, with a consciousness that we formerly had them, and a supposition that their former being in the mind is the cause of their being in us at present. There is not only the presence of the same ideas, that were in our minds formerly, but also, an act of the judgment, that they were there formerly, and that judgment, not properly from proof, but from natural necessity, arising from a Law of nature which God hath fixed.

In Memory, in mental principles, habits, and inclinations, there is something really abiding in the mind, when there are no acts or exercises of them; much in the same manner, as there is a chair in this room, when no mortal perceives it. For when we say, There are chairs in this room, when none perceives it, we mean, that minds would perceive chairs here, according to the Law of Nature in such circumstances. So when we say, A person has these and those things, laid up in his memory, we mean, they would actually be repeated in his mind, upon some certain occasions, according to the Law of Nature; though we cannot describe, particularly, the Law of Nature about these mental acts, so well as we can about other things.

[11.] PERSONAL IDENTITY. Well might Mr. Locke say, that Identity of *person* consisted in identity of consciousness; for he might have said that identity of *spirit*, too, consisted in the same consciousness; for a mind or spirit is nothing else but consciousness, and what is included in it. The same consciousness is, to all intents and purposes, individually, the very same spirit, or substance; as much as the same particle of matter can be the same with itself, at different times.

[72.] IDENTITY of person is what seems never yet to have been explained. It is a mistake, that it consists in sameness, or identity, of consciousness—if, by sameness of consciousness, be meant, having the same ideas hereafter, that I have now, with a notion or apprehension that I had had them before; just in the same manner as I now have the same ideas, that I had in time past, by memory. It is possible, without doubt, in the nature of things, for God to annihilate me, and after my annihilation to create another being that shall have the same ideas in his mind that I have, and with the like apprehension that he had had them before, in like manner as a person has by memory; and yet I be in no way concerned in it, having no reason to fear what that being shall suffer, or to hope for what he shall enjoy.—Can any one deny, that it is possible, after my annihilation, to create two beings in the Universe, both of them having my ideas communicated to them, with such a notion of their having had them before, after the manner of memory, and yet be ignorant one of another; and, in such case, will any one say, that both these are one and the same person, as they must be, if they are both the same person with me. It is possible there may be two such beings, each having all the ideas that are now in my mind, in the same manner that I should have by memory, if my own being were continued; and yet these two beings not only be ignorant one of another, but also be in a very different state, one in a state of enjoyment and pleasure, and the other in a state of great suffering and torment. Yea, there seems to be nothing of impossibility in the Nature of things, but that the Most High could, if he saw fit, cause there to be another being, who should begin to exist in some distant part of the Universe, with the same ideas I now have, after the manner of memory: and should henceforward co-exist with me; we both retaining a consciousness of what was before the moment of his first existence, in like manner; but thenceforward should have a different train of ideas. Will any one say, that he, in such a case, is the same person with me, when I know nothing of his sufferings, and am never the better for his joys.

[29.] POWER. We have explained a Cause to be *that, after, or upon, the Existence of which, or its Existence in such a manner, the existence of another thing follows.* The Connexion between these two existences, or between the Cause and Effect, is what we call Power. Thus the Sun, above the Horizon, enlightens the Atmosphere. So we say the Sun has power to enlighten the Atmosphere. That is, there is such a connexion between the Sun, being above the Horizon, after such a manner, and the Atmosphere being enlightened, that one always follows the other. So the Sun has power to melt wax: That is, the Sun and wax so existing, the melting of the wax follows. There is a connexion between one and the other. So Man has power to do this or that: That is, if he exists after such a manner, there follows the existence of another thing: if he wills this or that, it will be so. God has power to do all things, because there is nothing but what follows upon his willing of it. When Intelligent beings are said to have power to do this or that; by it is meant, the Connexion between this or that, upon this manner of their existing, their willing: in which sense they have power to do many things that they never shall will.

Coroll. Hence it follows, that men, in a very proper sense, may be said to have power to abstain from sin, and to repent, to do good works and to live holily; because it depends on their Will.

[59.] JUDGMENT. The mind passes a judgment, in multitudes of cases, where it has learned to judge by perpetual experience, not only exceedingly quick, as soon as one thought can follow another, but absolutely without any reflection at all, and at the same moment, without any time intervening. Though the thing is not properly self-evident, yet it judges without any ratiocination, merely by force of habit. Thus, when I hear such and such sounds, or see such letters, I judge that such things are signified without reasoning. When I have such ideas coming in by my sense of seeing, appearing after such a manner, I judge without any reasoning, that the things are further off, than others that appear after such a manner. When I see a globe, I judge it to be a globe, though the image impressed on my sensory is only that of a flat circle, appearing variously in various parts. And in ten thousand other cases, the ideas are habitually associated together, and they come into the mind together.—So likewise, in innumerable cases, men act without any proper act of the Will at that time commanding, through habit. As when a man is walking, there is not a new act of the Will every time a man takes up his foot and sets it down.

Coroll. Hence there is no necessity of allowing reason to Beasts, in many of those actions, that many are ready to argue are rational actions. As cattle in a team are wont to act as the driver would have them, upon his making such and such sounds, either to stop or go along, or turn hither or thither, because they have been forced to do it, by the whip, upon the using of such words. It is become habitual, so that they never do it rationally, but either from force or from habit. So of all the actions that beasts are taught to perform, dogs, and horses, and parrots, &c. And those, that they learn of themselves to do, are merely by virtue of appetite and habitual association of ideas. Thus a horse learns to perform such actions for his food, because he has accidentally had the perceptions of such actions, associated with the pleasant perceptions of taste: and so his appetite makes him perform the action, without any reason or judgment.

The main difference between Men and Beasts is, that Men are capable of reflecting upon what passes in their own minds. Beasts have nothing but direct consciousness. Men are capable of viewing what is in themselves, contemplatively. Man was made for spiritual exercises and enjoyments, and therefore is made capable, by reflection, to behold and contemplate spiritual things. Hence it arises that Man is capable of Religion.

A very great difference between Men and Beasts is, that Beasts have no voluntary actions about their own thoughts; for it is in this only, that reasoning differs from mere perception and memory. It is the act of the Will, in bringing its ideas into Contemplation, and ranging and comparing of them in Reflection and Abstraction. The minds of Beasts, if I may call them *minds*, are purely passive with respect to all their ideas. The minds of Men are not only passive, but abundantly active. Herein probably is the most distinguishing difference between Men and Beasts. Herein is the difference between Intellectual, or Rational, Will, and mere Animal Appetite, that the latter is a simple Inclination to, or Aversion from, such and such Sensations, which are the only ideas that they are capable of, that are not active about their ideas: the former is a Will that is active about its own ideas, in disposing of them among themselves, or Appetite towards those ideas that are acquired by such action.

The Association of ideas in Beasts, seems to be much quicker and stronger than in Men: at least in many of them.

It would not suppose any exalted faculty in Beasts, to suppose that like ideas in them, if they have any, excite one another. Nor can I think why it should be so any the less for the weakness and narrowness of their faculties; in such things, where to perceive the argument of ideas, requires neither attention nor comprehension. And experience teaches us, that what we call thought in them, is thus led from one thing to another.

[17.] LOGIC. One reason why, at first, before I knew other Logic, I used to be mightily pleased with the study of the Old Logic, was, because it was very pleasant to see my thoughts, that before lay in my mind jumbled without any distinction, ranged into order and distributed into classes and subdivisions, so that I could tell where they all belonged, and run them up to their general heads. For this Logic consisted much in Distributions and Definitions; and their maxims gave occasion to observe new and strange dependencies of ideas, and a seeming agreement of multitudes of them in the same thing, that I never observed before.

[66.] IDEAS. All sorts of ideas of things are but the repetitions of those very things over again—as well the ideas of colours, figures, solidity, tastes, and smells, as the ideas of thought and mental acts.

[67.] LOVE is not properly said to be an idea, any more than Understanding is said to be an idea. Understanding and Loving are different acts of the mind entirely; and so Pleasure and Pain are not properly ideas.

Though Pleasure and Pain may imply perception in their nature, yet it does not follow, that they are properly ideas. There is an Act of the mind in it. An idea is only a perception, wherein the mind is passive, or rather subjective. The Acts of the mind are not merely ideas. All Acts of the mind, about its ideas, are not themselves mere ideas.

Pleasure and Pain have tneir seat in the Will, and not in the Understanding. The Will, Choice, &c. is nothing else, but the mind's being pleased with an idea, or having a superior pleasedness in something thought of, or a desire of a future thing, or a pleasedness in the thought of our union with the thing, or a pleasedness in such a state of ourselves, and a degree of pain while we are not in that state, or a disagreeable conception of the contrary state at that time when we desire it.

[7.] GENUS. The various distributing and ranking of things, and tying of them together, under one common abstract idea, is, although arbitrary, yet exceedingly useful, and indeed absolutely necessary: for how miserable should we be, if we could think of things only individually, as the beasts do; how slow, narrow, painful, and endless would be the exercise of thought.

What is this putting and tying things together, which is done in abstraction? It is not merely a tying of them under the same name; for I do believe, that deaf and dumb persons abstract and distribute things into kinds. But it is so putting of them together, that the mind resolves hereafter to think of them together, under a common notion, as if they were a collective substance; the mind being as sure, in this proceeding, of reasoning well, as if it were of a particular substance; for it has abstracted that which belongs alike to all, and has a perfect idea, whose relations and properties it can behold, as well as those of the idea of one individual. Although this ranking of things be arbitrary, yet there is much more foundation for some distributions than others. Some are much more useful, and much better serve the purposes of abstraction.

[24.] There is really a difference that the mind makes, in the consideration of an Universal, absolutely considered, and a Species. There is a difference in the two ideas, when we say Man, including simply the abstract idea; and when we say, the Human Sort of Living Creature. There is reference had to an idea more abstract. And there is this act of the mind in distributing an Universal into Species. It ties this abstract idea to two or more less abstract ideas, and supposes it limited by them.

It is not every property that belongs to all the particulars included in, and proper to, a Genus, and that men generally see to be so, that is a part of that complex abstract idea, that represents all the particulars, or that is a part of that nominal essence. But so much is essential, which, if men should see any thing less, they would not call it by the name, by which they call the Genus. This indeed is uncertain, because men never agreed upon fixing exact bounds.

[25.] A PART, is one of those many ideas, which we are wont to think of together. *A whole*, is an idea containing many of these.

[47.] THE FOUNDATION of the most considerable Species or Sorts, in which things are ranked, is the order of the world—the designed distribution of God and nature. When we, in distributing things, differ from that design, we don't know the true essences of things. If the world had been created without any order, or design, or beauty, indeed, all species would be merely arbitrary. There are certain multitudes of things, that God has made to agree, very remarkably in something, either as to their outward appearance, manner of acting, the effects they produce, or that other things produce on them, the manner of their production, or God's disposal concerning them, or some peculiar perpetual circumstances that they are in. Thus diamonds agree in shape; pieces of gold, in that they will be divided in *aqua regia;* loadstones, in innumerable strange effects that they produce; many plants, in the peculiar effects they produce on animal bodies; men, in that they are to remain after this life. That inward conformation, that is the foundation of an agreement in these things, is the real essence of the thing. For instance, that disposition of parts, or whatever it be, in the matter of the loadstone, from whence arises the verticity to the poles, and its influence on other loadstones and iron, is the real essence of the loadstone that is unknown to us.

[41.] As there is great foundation in Nature for those abstract ideas, which we call Universals; so there is great foundation in the common circumstances and necessities of mankind, and the constant method of things proceeding, for such a tying of simple modes together to the constituting such mixed modes. This appears from the agreement of languages; for language is very much made up of the names of Mixed Modes; and we find that almost all those names, in one language, have names that answer to them in other languages. The same Mixed Mode has a name given to it by most nations. Whence it appears that most of the inhabitants of the Earth have agreed upon putting together the same Simple Modes into Mixed ones, and in the same manner. The learned and polished have indeed many more than others: and herein chiefly it is, that languages do not answer one to another.

[42.] THE agreement or similitude of Complex ideas, mostly consists in their precise identity, with respect to some third idea of some of the simples they are compounded of. But if there be any similitude or agreement between simple ideas themselves, it cannot consist in the identity of a third idea that belongs to both; because the ideas are simple; and if you take any thing that belongs to them, you take all. Therefore no agreement between simple ideas can be resolved into Identity, unless it be the identity of Relations. But there seems to be another infallible agreement between simple ideas. Thus some Colours are more like one to another than others, between which there is yet a very manifest difference. So between Sounds, Smells, Tastes, and other Sensations. And what is that common agreement of all these ideas we call colours, whereby we know immediately that that name belongs to them. Certainly all colours have an agreement one to another, that is quite different from any agreement that Sounds can have to them. So is there some common agreement to all Sounds, that Tastes cannot have to any Sound. It cannot be said that the agreement lies only in this, that these simple ideas come all by the ear; so that their agreement consists only in their relation they have to that organ. For if it should have been so that we had lived in the world, and had never found out the way we got these ideas we call Sounds, and never once thought or considered any thing about it, and should hear some new simple sound, I believe nobody would question, but that we should immediately perceive an agreement with other ideas, that used to come by that sense, though we knew not which way one of them came, and should immediately call it a *Sound*, and say we had heard a strange *Noise*. And if we had never had any such sensation as the *Head-ache*, and should have it, I do not think we should call that a new *Sound;* for there would be so manifest a disagreement between those simple ideas, of another kind from what simple ideas have one with another.

I have thought, whether or no the agreement of Colours did not consist, in a Relation they had to the idea of Space; and whether Colour in general might not be defined, *that idea that filled Space*. But I am convinced, that there is another sort of agreement beside that; and the more, because there can no such common relation be thought of, with respect to different Sounds. It is probable that this agreement may be resolved into Identity. If we follow these ideas to their original in their Organs, like sensations may be caused from like motions in the Animal Spirits. Herein the likeness is perceived, after the same manner as the harmony in a simple colour; but if we consider the ideas absolutely, it cannot be.

Coroll. All Universals, therefore, cannot be made up of ideas, abstracted from Particulars; for Colour and Sound are Universals, as much as Man or Horse. But the idea of Colour, or Sound, in general, cannot be made up of ideas, abstracted from particular Colours, or Sounds; for from simple ideas nothing can be abstracted. But these Universals are thus formed. The mind perceives that some of its ideas agree, in a manner very different from all its other ideas. The mind therefore is determined to rank those ideas together in its thoughts; and all new ideas, it receives with the like agreement, it naturally, and habitually, and at once, places to the same rank and order, and calls them by the same name; and by the nature, determination, and habit of the mind, the idea of one excites the idea of others.

[43.] Many of our Universal ideas are not Arbitrary. The tying of ideas together, in Genera and Species, is not merely the calling of them by the same name, but such an union of them, that the consideration of one shall naturally excite the idea of others. But the union of ideas is not always arbitrary, but unavoidably arising from the nature of the Soul; which is such, that the thinking of one thing, of itself, yea, against our wills, excites the thought of other things that are like it. Thus, if a person, a stranger to the Earth, should see and converse with a man, and a long time after should meet with another man, and converse with him; the agreement would immediately excite the idea of that other man, and those two ideas would be together in his mind, for the time to come, yea, in spite of him. So if he should see a third, and afterwards should find multitudes, there would be a Genus, or Universal Idea, formed in his mind, naturally, without his counsel or design. So I cannot doubt but, if a person had been born blind, and should have his eyes opened, and should immediately have *blue* placed before his eyes, and then *red*, then *green*, then *yellow;* I doubt not, they would immediately get into one General Idea—they would be united in his mind without his deliberation.

Coroll. So that God has not only distributed things into species, by evidently manifesting, by his making such an agreement in things, that he designed such and such particulars to be together in the mind; but by making the Soul of such a nature, that those particulars, which he thus made to agree, are unavoidably together in the mind, one naturally exciting and including the others.

[37.] GENUS and Species, indeed, is a mental thing; yet, in a sense, Nature has distributed many things into Species without our minds. That is, God evidently designed such Particulars to be together in the mind, and in other things. But 'tis not so indeed, with respect to all genera. Some therefore may be called *Arbitrary* Genera, others *Natural*. Nature has designedly made a distribution of some things: other distributions are of a mental original.

[56.] NUMBER is a train of differences of ideas, put together in the mind's consideration in orderly succession, and considered with respect to their relations one to another, as in that orderly mental succession. This mental succession is the succession of Time. One may make which they will the first, if it be but the first in consideration. The mind begins where it will, and runs through them successively one after another. It is a collection of differences; for it is its being another, in some respect, that is the very thing that makes it capable of pertaining to multiplicity. They must not merely be put together, in orderly succession; but it's only their being considered with reference to that relation, they have one to another as differences, and in orderly mental succession, that denominates it *Number*.—To be of such a particular number, is for an idea to have such a particular relation, and so considered by the mind, to other differences put together with it, in orderly succession.—So that there is nothing inexplicable in the nature of Number, but what Identity and Diversity is, and what Succession, or Duration, or Priority and Posteriority, is.

[57.] DURATION. *Pastness,* if I may make such a word, is nothing but a Mode of ideas. This Mode, perhaps, is nothing else but a certain *Veterascence*, attending our ideas. When it is, as we say, *Past*, the idea, after a particular manner, fades and grows old. When an idea appears with this mode, we say it is *Past*, and according to the degree of this particular inexpressible mode, so we say the thing is longer or more lately past. As in distance, it is not only by a natural trigonometry of the eyes, or a sort of parallax, that we determine it; because we can judge of distances, as well with one eye, as with two. Nor is it by observing the parallelism or aperture of the rays, for the mind judges by nothing, but the difference it observes in the idea itself, which alone the mind has any notice of. But it judges of distance, by a particular mode of indistinctness, as has been said before. So it is with respect to distance of time, by a certain peculiar inexpressible mode of fading and indistinctness, which I call *Veterascence*.

[65.] I THINK we find by experience, that when we have been in a sound sleep, for many hours together, if we look back to the time when we were last awake, the ideas seem farther off to us, than when we have only ceased thinking a few minutes: which cannot be because we see a longer train of intermediate ideas in one case, than in the other; for I suppose we see none in neither. But there is a sort of Veterascence of ideas, that have been a longer time in the mind. When we look upon them, they do not look just as those that are much nearer. This Veterascence consists, I think, in blotting out the little distinctions, the minute parts, and fine strokes of it. This is one way of judging of the distance of Visible objects. In this respect, a house, a tree, do not look at a little distance, as they do very near. They not only do not appear so big; but a multitude of the little distinctions vanish, that are plain when we are near.

[53.] SENSATION. Our Senses, when sound, and in ordinary circumstances, are not properly fallible in any thing: that is, we mean our Experience by our Senses. If we mean any thing else, neither fallibility nor certainty in any way belongs to the Senses. Nor are our Senses certain in any thing at all, any other way, than by constant experience by our Senses. That is, when our Senses make such or such representations, we constantly experience, that things are in themselves thus or thus. So, when a thing appears after such a manner, I judge it to be at least two rods off, at least two feet broad; but I only know, by constant experience, that a thing, that makes such a representation, is so far off, and so big. And so my senses are as certain in every thing, when I have equal opportunity and occasion to experience. And our senses are said to deceive us in some things, because our situation does not allow us to make trial, or our circumstances do not lead us to it, and so we are apt to judge by our experience, in other and different cases. Thus, our Senses make us think, that the Moon is among the clouds, because we cannot try it so quick, easily, and frequently, as we do the distance of things, that are nearer. But the Senses of an Astronomer, who observes the Parallax of the Moon, do not deceive him, but lead him to the truth. Though the idea of the Moon's distance will never be exercised, so quick and naturally, upon every occasion, because of the tediousness and infrequency of the trial; and there are not so many ways of trial, so many differences in the Moon's appearance, from what a lesser thing amongst the clouds would have, as there are in things nearer. I can remember when I was so young, that seeing two things in the same building, one of which was twice so far off as the other, yet, seeing one over the other, I thought they had been of the same distance, one right over the other. My senses then were deceitful in that thing, though they made the same representations as now, and yet now they are not deceitful. The only difference is in *experience*. Indeed, in some things, our senses make no difference in the representation, where there is a difference in the things. But in those things, our experience by our Senses will lead us not to judge at all, and so they will deceive. We are in danger of being deceived by our Senses, in judging of appearances, by our experience in different things, or by judging where we have had no experience, or the like.

[19.] THINGS, that we know by immediate Sensation, we know intuitively; and they are properly self-evident truths: as, *Grass is green; The Sun shines; Honey is sweet*. When we say that Grass is green, all that we can be supposed to mean by it, is—that, in a constant course, when we see Grass, the idea of green is excited by it; and this we know self-evidently.

[55.] APPETITE of the Mind. As all ideas are wholly in the mind, so is all Appetite. To have Appetite towards a thing is as remote from the nature of Matter, as to have Thought. There are some of the Appetites, that are called Natural Appetites, that are not indeed natural to the Soul; as the Appetite to meat and drink. I believe when the Soul has that sort of pain, which is in hunger and thirst, if the Soul never had experienced that food and drink remove that pain, it would create no Appetite to any thing. A man would be just as incapable of such an Appetite, as he is to food he never smelt nor tasted. So the Appetite of scratching when it itches.

[15.] TRUTH. After all that has been said and done, the only adequate definition of Truth is, The agreement of our ideas with existence. To explain what this existence is, is another thing. In abstract ideas, it is nothing but the ideas themselves; so their truth is their consistency with themselves. In things that are supposed to be without us, it is the determination and fixed mode of God's exciting ideas in us. So that Truth, in these things, is an agreement of our ideas with that series in God. It is existence; and that is all that we can say. It is impossible that we should explain a perfectly abstract and mere idea of existence; only we always find this, by running of it up, that God and Real Existence are the same.

Coroll. Hence we learn how properly it may be said, that God is, and that there is none else; and how proper are these names of the Deity, JEHOVAH, and I AM THAT I AM.

[6.] TRUTH is *The perception of the relations there are between ideas.* Falsehood is *The supposition of relations between ideas that are inconsistent with those ideas themselves;* not *their disagreement with things without.* All truth is in the mind, and only there. It is ideas, or what is in the mind, alone, that can be the object of the mind; and what we call Truth, is a consistent supposition of relations, between what is the object of the mind. Falsehood is an inconsistent supposition of relations. The Truth, that is in a mind, must be in that mind as to its object, and every thing pertaining to it. The only foundation of Error is inadequateness and imperfection of ideas; for, if the idea were perfect, it would be impossible but that all its relations should be perfectly perceived.

[10.] TRUTH, in the general, may be defined, after the most strict and metaphysical manner, *The consistency and agreement of our ideas with the ideas of God.* I confess this, in ordinary conversation, would not half so much tend to enlighten one in the meaning of the word, as to say, *The agreement of our ideas with the things as they are.* But it should be inquired, What is it for our ideas to agree with things as they are? seeing that corporeal things exist no otherwise than mentally; and as for most other things, they are only abstract ideas. Truth, as to external things, is the consistency of our ideas with those ideas, or that train and series of ideas, that are raised in our minds, according to God's stated order and law.

Truth, as to abstract ideas, is the consistency of our ideas with themselves. As when our idea of a circle, or a triangle, or any of their parts, is agreeable to the idea we have stated and agreed to call by the name of a circle, or a triangle. And it may still be said, that Truth is, *the consistency of our ideas with themselves.* Those ideas are false, that are not consistent with the series of ideas, that are raised in our minds, by according to the order of nature.

Coroll. 1. Hence we see, in how strict a sense it may be said, that God is Truth itself.

Coroll. 2. Hence it appears, that Truth consists in having perfect and adequate ideas of things: For instance, if I judge truly how far distant the Moon is from the Earth, we need not say, that this Truth consists, in the perception of the relation, between the two ideas of the Moon and the Earth, but in the adequateness.

Coroll. 3. Hence Certainty is the clear perception of this perfection. Therefore, if we had perfect ideas of all things at once, that is, could have all in one view, we should know all truth at the same moment, and there would be no such thing as Ratiocination, or finding out Truth. And Reasoning is only of use to us, in consequence of the paucity of our ideas, and because we can have but very few in view at once.—Hence it is evident, that all things are *self-evident* to God.

[5.] CERTAINTY. Determined that there are many degrees of certainty, though not indeed of absolute certainty; which is infinitely strong. We are certain of many things upon demonstration, which yet we may be made more certain of by more demonstration; because although, according to the strength of the mind, we see the connexion of the ideas, yet a stronger mind would see the connexion more perfectly and strongly, because it would have the ideas more perfect. We have not such strength of mind, that we can perfectly conceive of but very few things; and some little of the strength of an idea is lost, in a moment of time, as we, in the mind, look successively on the train of ideas in a demonstration.

[8.] RULES OF REASONING. It is no matter how abstracted our notions are—the farther we penetrate and come to the prime reality of the thing, the better; provided we can go to such a degree of abstraction, and carry it out clear. We may go so far in abstraction, that, although we may thereby, in part, see Truth and Reality, and farther than ever was seen before, yet we may not be able more than just to touch it, and to have a few obscure glances. We may not have strength of mind to conceive clearly of the Manner of it. We see farther indeed, but it is very obscurely and indistinctly. We had better stop a degree or two short of this, and abstract no farther than we can conceive of the thing distinctly, and explain it clearly: otherwise we shall be apt to run into error, and confound our minds.

[54.] REASONING. We know our own existence, and the existence of every thing, that we are conscious of in our own minds, intuitively; but all our reasoning, with respect to Real Existence, depends upon that natural, unavoidable, and invariable disposition of the mind, when it sees a thing begin to be, to conclude certainly, that there is a *Cause* of it; or if it sees a thing to be in a very orderly, regular, and exact manner, to conclude that some *Design* regulated and disposed it. That a thing that begins to be should make itself, we know implies a contradiction; for we see intuitively, that the ideas, that such an expression excites, are inconsistent. And that any thing should start up into being, without any cause at all, itself, or any thing else, is what the mind, do what we will, will for ever refuse to receive, but will perpetually reject. When we therefore see any thing begin to be, we intuitively know there is a cause of it, and not by ratiocination, or any kind of argument. This is an innate principle, in that sense, that the soul is born with it—a necessary, fatal propensity, so to conclude, on every occasion.

And this is not only true of every new existence of those we call Substances, but of every alteration that is to be seen: any new existence of any new mode, we necessarily suppose to be from a cause. For instance, if there had been nothing but one globe of solid matter, which in time past had been at perfect rest; if it starts away into motion, we conclude there is some cause of that alteration. Or if that globe, in time past, had been moving in a straight line, and turns short about at right angles with its former direction; or if it had been moving with such a degree of celerity, and all at once moves with but half that swiftness. And it is all one, whether these alterations be in Bodies, or in Spirits, their beginning must have a cause: the first alteration that there is in a Spirit, after it is created, let it be an alteration in what it will; and so the rest. So, if a Spirit always, in times past, had had such an inclination, for instance, always loved and chosen sin, and then has a quite contrary inclination, and loves and chooses holiness; the beginning of this alteration, or the first new existence in that Spirit towards it, whether it were some action, or whatsoever, had some cause.

And, indeed, it is no matter, whether we suppose a being has a beginning or no, if we see it exists in a particular manner, for which way of existing we know that there is no more reason, as to any thing in the thing itself, than any other different manner; the mind necessarily concludes, that there is some cause of its existing, more than any other way. For instance, if there is but one piece of matter existing from all eternity, and that be a square; we unavoidably conclude, there is some cause why it is square, seeing there is nothing in the thing itself that more inclines it to that figure, than to an infinite number of other figures. The same may be said as to rest, or motion, or the manner of motion; and for all other bodies existing, the mind seeks a Cause why.

When the mind sees a being existing very regularly, and in most exact order, especially if the order consists in the exact regulation of a very great multitude of particulars, if it be the best order, as to use and beauty, that the mind can conceive of, that it could have been, the mind unavoidably concludes, that its Cause was a being that had design: for instance, when the mind perceives the beauty and contrivance of the world; for the world might have been one infinite number of confusions, and not have been disposed beautifully and usefully; yea, infinite times an infinite number, and so, if we multiply infinite by infinite, *in infinitum*. So that, if we suppose the world to have existed from all eternity, and to be continually all the while without the guidance of design, passing under different changes; it would have been, according to such a multiplication, infinite to one, whether it would ever have hit upon this form or no. Note—This way of concluding is a sort of ratiocination.

[58.] REASONING does not absolutely differ from Perception, any further than there is the act of the will about it. It appears to be so in demonstrative Reasoning. Because the knowledge of a self-evident truth, it is evident, does not differ from Perception. But all demonstrative knowledge consists in, and may be resolved into, the knowledge of self-evident truths. And it is also evident, that the act of the mind, in other reasoning, is not of a different nature from demonstrative Reasoning.

[71.] KNOWLEDGE is not the perception of the *agreement*, or *disagreement*, of ideas, but rather the perception of the *union*, or *disunion*, of ideas—or the perceiving whether two or more ideas belong to one another.

Coroll. Hence it is not impossible to believe, or know, the Truth of MYSTERIES, or propositions that we cannot comprehend, or see the manner how the several ideas, that belong to the proposition, are united. Perhaps it cannot properly be said, that we see the *agreement* of the ideas, unless we see *how they agree*. But we may perceive that they are *united*, and know that they *belong* one to another; though we do not know the manner *how they are tied together*.

[22.] PREJUDICE. Those ideas, which do not pertain to the prime essence of things,—such as all colours that are every where objected to our eyes; and sounds that are continually in our ears; those that affect the touch, as cold and heats; and all our sensations,—exceedingly clog the mind, in searching into the innermost nature of things, and cast such a mist over things, that there is need of a sharp sight to see clearly through; for these will be continually in the mind, and associated with other ideas, let us be thinking of what we will; and it is a continual care and pains to keep clear of their entanglements, in our scrutinies into things. This is one way, whereby the body and the senses observe the views of the mind. The world seems so differently to our eyes, to our ears, and other senses, from the idea we have of it by reason, that we can hardly realize the latter.

[18.] WORDS. We are used to apply the same words a hundred different ways; and ideas being so much tied and associated with the words, they lead us into a thousand real mistakes; for where we find that the words may be connected, the ideas being by custom tied with them, we think the ideas may be connected likewise, and applied every where, and in every way, as the Words.

[23.] THE reason why the names of Spiritual things are all, or most of them, derived from the names of Sensible or Corporeal ones—as Imagination, Conception, Apprehend, &c.—is, because there was no other way of making others readily understand men's meaning, when they first signified these things by sounds, than by giving of them the names of things sensible, to which they had an analogy.

They could thus point it out with the finger, and so explain themselves as in sensible things.

[48.] DEFINITION. That is not always a true Definition, that tends most to give us to understand the meaning of a word; but that, which would give any one the clearest notion of the meaning of the word, if he had never been in any way acquainted with the thing signified by that word. For instance, if I was to explain the meaning of the word Motion, to one that had seen things move, but was not acquainted with the word; perhaps I should say, Motion is *a thing's going from one place to another.* But, if I was to explain it to one, who had never seen any thing move, (if that could be,) I should say, Motion is *a Body's existing successively in all the immediately contiguous parts of any distance, without continuing any time in any.*

[20.] INSPIRATION. The evidence of immediate Inspiration that the prophets had, when they were immediately inspired by the Spirit of God with any truth, is an absolute sort of certainty; and the knowledge is in a sense intuitive—much in the same manner as Faith, and Spiritual Knowledge of the truth of Religion. Such bright ideas are raised, and such a clear view of a perfect agreement with the excellencies of the Divine Nature, that it is known to be a communication from him. All the Deity appears in the thing, and in every thing pertaining to it. The prophet has so divine a sense, such a divine disposition, such a divine pleasure; and sees so divine an excellency, and so divine a power, in what is revealed, that he sees as immediately that God is there, as we perceive one another's presence, when we are talking together face to face. And our features, our voice, and our shapes, are not so clear manifestations of us, as those spiritual resemblances of God, that are in the Inspiration, are manifestations of him. But yet there are doubtless various degrees in Inspiration.

[21.] THE WILL. It is not that which appears the greatest good, or the greatest apparent good, that determines the Will. It is not the greatest good apprehended, or that which is apprehended to be the greatest good; but the Greatest Apprehension of good. It is not merely by judging that any thing is a great good, that good is apprehended, or appears. There are other ways of apprehending good. The having a clear and sensible idea of any good, is one way of good's appearing, as well as judging that there is good. Therefore, all those things are to be considered—the degree of the judgment, by which a thing is judged to be good, and the contrary evil; the degree of goodness under which it appears, and the evil of the contrary; and the clearness of the idea and strength of the conception of the goodness and of the evil. And that Good, of which there is the greatest apprehension or sense, all those things being taken together, is chosen by the Will And if there be a greater apprehension of good to be obtained, or evil escaped, by doing a thing, than in letting it alone, the Will determines to the doing it. The mind will be for the present most uneasy in neglecting it, and the mind always avoids that, in which it would be for the present most uneasy. The degree of apprehension of good, which I suppose to determine the Will, is composed of the degree of good apprehended, and the degree of apprehension. The degree of apprehension, again, is composed of the strength of the conception, and the judgment.

[60.] WILL, ITS DETERMINATION. The greatest mental existence of Good, the greatest degree of the mind's sense of Good, the greatest degree of apprehension, or perception, or idea of own Good, always determines the Will. Where three things are to be considered, that make up the proportion of mental existence of own good; for it is the proportion compounded of these three proportions that always determines the Will. 1. The degree of good apprehended, or the degree of good represented by idea. This used to be reckoned by many the only thing that determined the Will.—2. The proportion or degree of apprehension or perception—the degree of the view the mind has of it, or the degree of the ideal perceptive presence of the good in the mind. This consists in two things. (1.) In the degree of the judgment. This is different from the first thing we mentioned, which was the judgment of the degree of good; but we speak now of the degree of that judgment, according to the degree of assurance or certainty. (2.) The Deepness of the sense of the goodness; or the clearness, liveliness, and sensibleness of the goodness or sweetness, or the strength of the impression on the mind. As one, that has just tasted honey, has more of an idea of its goodness, than one that never tasted, though he also fully believes that it is very sweet, yea as sweet as it is. And he that has seen a great beauty, has a far more clear and strong idea of it, than he that never saw it. Good, as it is thus most clearly and strongly present to the mind, will proportionally more influence the mind to incline and will.—3. There is to be considered the proportion or degree of the mind's apprehension of the *Propriety* of the good, or of its Own Concernment in it. Thus the soul has a clearer and stronger apprehension of a pleasure, that it may enjoy the next hour, than of the same pleasure that it is sure it may enjoy ten years hence, though the latter doth really as much concern it as the former. There are usually other things concur, to make men choose present, before future, good. They are generally more certain of the good, and have a stronger sense of it. But if they were equally certain, and it were the very same good, and they were sure it would be the same, yet the soul would be most inclined to the nearest, because they have not so lively an apprehension of themselves, and of the good, and of the whole matter. And then there is the pain and uneasiness of enduring such an appetite so long a time, that generally comes in. But yet this matter wants to be made something more clear, why the soul is more strongly inclined to near than distant good.

It is utterly impossible but that it should be so, that the inclination and choice of the mind should always be determined by Good, as mentally or ideally existing. It would be a contradiction to suppose otherwise, for we mean nothing else by Good, but *that which agrees with the inclination and disposition of the mind.* And surely that, which agrees with it, must agree with it. And it also implies a contradiction, to suppose that that good, whose mental or ideal being is greatest, does not always determine the Will; for we mean nothing else, by Greatest Good, but that which agrees most with the inclination and disposition of the soul. It is ridiculous to say, that the soul does not incline to that most, which is most agreeable to the inclination of the soul.—I think I was not mistaken when I said that nothing else is meant by Good, here, but that that agrees with the Inclination and Disposition of the mind. If they do not mean that that strikes the mind, that that is agreeable to it, that that pleases it, and falls in with the disposition of its nature; then I would know, What is meant.

The Will is no otherwise different from the Inclination, than that we commonly call that the Will, that is the Mind's Inclination, with respect to its own Immediate Actions.

[70.] That it is not Uneasiness, in our present circumstances, that always determines the Will, as Mr. Locke supposes, is evident by this, that there may be an Act of the Will, in choosing and determining to forbear to act, or move, when some action is proposed to a man; as well as in choosing to act. Thus, if a man be put upon rising from his seat, and going to a certain place; his voluntary refusal is an act of the Will, which does not arise from any uneasiness in his present circumstances certainly. An act of voluntary refusal is as truly an act of the Will, as an act of choice; and indeed there is an act of choice in an act of refusal. The Will chooses to neglect: it prefers the opposite of that which is refused.

[39.] CONSCIENCE. Beside the two sorts of Assent of the mind, called *Will* and *Judgment*, there is a third, arising from a sense of the General Beauty and Harmony of things, which is *Conscience.* There are some things, which move a kind of horror in the mind, which yet the mind wills and chooses; and some, which are agreeable in this way to its make and constitution, which yet it chooses not. These Assents of Will and Conscience have indeed a common object, which is Excellency. Still they differ. The one is always General Excellency: that is Harmony, taking in its relation to the Whole System of beings. The other, that Excellency which most strongly effects, whether the Excellency be more general or particular. But the degree, wherein we are affected by any Excellency, is in proportion compounded of the Extensiveness, and the Intensiveness, of our view of that Excellency.

[1.] EXCELLENCY. There has nothing been more without a definition, than *Excellency;* although it be what we are more concerned with than any thing else whatsoever: yea, we are concerned with nothing else. But what is this Excellency? Wherein is one thing excellent, and another evil; one beautiful, and another deformed? Some have said that all Excellency is *Harmony, Symmetry,* or *Proportion;* but they have not yet explained it. We would know, Why Proportion is more excellent than Disproportion; that is, why Proportion is pleasant to the mind, and Disproportion unpleasant? Proportion is a thing that may be explained yet further. It is an *Equality,* or *Likeness of ratios;* so that it is the Equality that makes the Proportion. Excellency therefore seems to consist in *Equality.* Thus, if there be two perfect *equal* circles, or globes, together, there is something more of beauty than if they were *unequal,* disproportionate magnitudes. And if two *parallel* lines be drawn, the beauty is greater, than if they were *obliquely* inclined without proportion, because there is equality of distance. And if betwixt two parallel lines, two equal circles be placed, each at the same distance from each parallel line, as in Fig. 1, the beauty is greater, than if they stood at irregular dis-

1 2 3 4

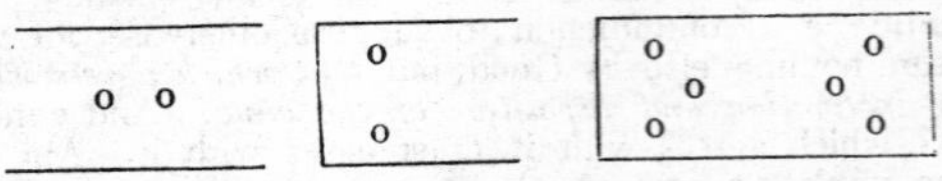

tances from the parallel lines. If they stand, each in a perpendicular line, going from the parallel lines, (Fig. 2,) it is requisite that they should each stand at an equal distance from the perpendicular line next to them; otherwise there is no beauty. If there be three of these circles between two parallel lines, and near to a perpendicular line run between them, (Fig. 3.) the most beautiful form perhaps, that they could be placed in, is in an equilateral triangle with the cross line, because there are most equalities. The distance of the two next to the cross line is equal from that, and also equal from the parallel lines. The distance of the third from each parallel is equal, and its distance from each of the other two circles is equal, and is also equal to their distance from one another, and likewise equal to their distance from each end of the cross line. There are two equilateral triangles: one made by the three circles, and the other made by the cross line and two of the sides of the first protracted till they meet that line. And if there be another like it, on the opposite side, to correspond with it, and it be taken altogether, the beauty is still greater, where the distances from the lines, in the one, are equal to the distances in the other; also the two next to the cross lines are at equal distances from the other two; or, if you go crosswise, from corner to corner. The two cross lines are also parallel, so that all parts are at an equal distance, and innumerable other equalities might be found.

This simple Equality, without Proportion, is the lowest kind of Regularity, and may be called Simple Beauty. All other beauties and excellencies may be resolved into it. Proportion is Complex Beauty. Thus, if we suppose that there are two points, A B, placed at two inches distance, and the next, C, one inch farther; (Fig. 1,)

Fig. 1.

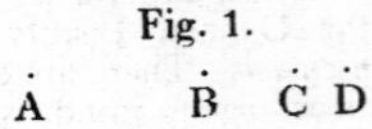

A B C D

Fig. 2.

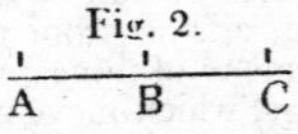

A B C

it is requisite, in order to regularity and beauty, if there be another, D, that it should be at half an inch distance; otherwise there is no regularity, and the last, D, would stand out of its proper place; because now the relation that the space C D bears to B C, is equal to the relation that B C bears to A C; so that B C D is exactly similar to A B C. It is evident, this is a more complicated excellency than that which consisted in Equality, because the terms of the relation are here complex, and before were simple. When there are three points set in a right line, it is requisite, in order to regularity, that they should be set at an equal distance, as A B C, (Fig. 2.) where A B is similar to B C, or the relation of C to B is the same as of B to A. But in the other are three terms necessary in each of the parts, between which is the relation, B C D is as A B C: so that here more simple beauties are omitted, and yet there is a general complex beauty: that is, B C is not as A B, nor is C D as B C, but yet B C D is as A B C. It is requisite that the consent or regularity of C D to B C be omitted, for the sake of the harmony of the whole. For although, if C D was perfectly equal to B C, there would be regularity and beauty with respect to them two; yet, if A B be taken into the idea, there is nothing but confusion. And it might be requisite, if these stood with others, even to omit this proposition, for the sake of one more complex still. Thus, if they stood with other points, where B stood at four inches distance from A, C at two from B, and D at six from C: the place where D must stand in, if A, B, C, D, were alone, *viz.* one inch from C, must be so as to be made proportionate with the other points beneath;

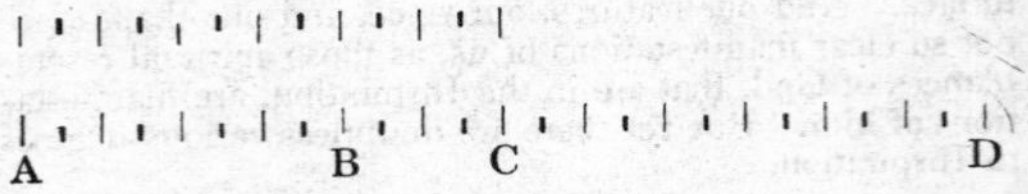

A B C D

A B C D

So that although A, B, C, D, are not proportioned, but are confusion among themselves; yet taken with the whole they are proportioned and beautiful.

All beauty consists in similarness or identity of relation. In identity of relation consists all likeness, and all identity between two consists in identity of relation. Thus, when the distance between two is exactly equal, their distance is their relation one to another, the distance is the same, the bodies are two; wherefore this is their correspondency and beauty. So bodies exactly of the same figure, the bodies are two, the relation between the parts of the extremities is the same, and this is their agreement with them. But if there are two bodies of different shapes, having no similarness of relation between the parts of the extremities; this, considered by itself, is a deformity, because being disagrees with being, which must undoubtedly be disagreeable to perceiving being: because what disagrees with Being, must necessarily be disagreeable to Being in general, to every thing that partakes of Entity, and of course to perceiving being; and what agrees with Being, must be agreeable to Being in general, and therefore to perceiving being. But agreeableness of perceiving being is pleasure, and disagreeableness is pain. Disagreement or contrariety to Being, is evidently an approach to Nothing, or a degree of Nothing; which is nothing else but disagreement or contrariety of Being, and the greatest and only evil: And Entity is the greatest and only good. And by how much more perfect Entity is, that is without mixture of Nothing, by so much the more Excellency. Two beings can agree one with another in nothing else but Relation; because otherwise the notion of their twoness (duality) is destroyed, and they become one.

And so, in every case, what is called Correspondency, Symmetry, Regularity, and the like, may be resolved into Equalities; though the Equalities in a beauty, in any degree complicated, are so numerous, that it would be a most tedious piece of work to enumerate them. There are millions of these Equalities. Of these consist the beautiful shape of flowers, the beauty of the body of man, and of the bodies of other animals. That sort of beauty which is called Natural, as of vines, plants, trees, &c. consists of a very complicated harmony; and all the natural motions, and tendencies, and figures of bodies in the Universe are done according to proportion, and therein is their beauty. Particular disproportions sometimes greatly add to the general beauty, and must necessarily be, in order to a more universal proportion:—So much equality, so much beauty; though it may be noted that the quantity of equality is not to be measured only by the number, but the intenseness, according to the quantity of being. As bodies are shadows of being, so their proportions are shadows of proportion.

The pleasures of the senses, where harmony is not the object of judgment, are the result of equality. Thus in Music, not only in the proportion which the several notes of a tune bear one among another, but in merely two notes there is harmony; whereas it is impossible there should be proportion between only two terms. But the proportion is in the particular vibrations of the air, which strike on the ear. And so, in the pleasantness of light, colours, tastes, smells, and touch, all arise from proportion of motion. The organs are so contrived that, upon the touch of such and such particles, there shall be a regular and harmonious motion of the animal spirits.

Spiritual harmonies are of vastly larger extent: *i. e.* the proportions are vastly oftener redoubled, and respect mere beings, and require a vastly larger view to comprehend them; as some simple notes do more affect one, who has not a comprehensive understanding of Music.

The reason why Equality thus pleases the mind, and Inequality is unpleasing, is because Disproportion, or Inconsistency, is contrary to Being. For Being, if we examine narrowly, is nothing else but Proportion. When one being is inconsistent with another being, then Being is contradicted. But contradiction to Being, is intolerable to perceiving being, and the consent to Being, most pleasing.

Excellency consists in the *Similarness* of one being to another—not merely Equality and Proportion, but any kind of Similarness—thus Similarness of direction. Supposing many globes moving in right lines, it is more beautiful, that they should move all the same way, and according to the same direction, than if they moved disorderly; one, one way, and another, another. This is a universal definition of Excellency:—*The Consent of Being to Being*, or *Being's Consent to Entity*. The more the Consent is, and the more extensive, the greater is the Excellency.

How exceedingly apt are we, when we are sitting still, and accidentally casting our eye upon some marks or spots in the floor or wall, to be ranging of them into regular parcels and figures: and, if we see a mark out of its place, to be placing of it right, by our imagination; and this, even while we are meditating on something else. So we may catch ourselves at observing the rules of harmony and regularity, in the careless motions of our heads or feet, and when playing with our hands, or walking about the room.

Pleasedness, in perceiving Being, always arises, either from a perception of Consent to Being in general, or of Consent to that Being that perceives. As we have shown, that Agreeableness to Entity must be agreeable to perceiving Entity; it is as evident that it is necessary that Agreeableness to that Being must be pleasing to it, if it perceives it. So that Pleasedness does not always arise from a perception of Excellency; [in general;] but the greater a Being is, and the more it has of Entity, the more will Consent to Being in general please it. But God is proper Entity itself, and these two therefore, in Him, become the same; for so far as a thing consents to Being in general, so far it consents to Him; and the more perfect Created Spirits are, the nearer do they come to their Creator, in this regard.

That, which is often called *Self-Love*, is exceedingly improperly called *Love*, for they do not only say that one loves himself, when he sees something amiable in himself, the view of which begets delight. But merely an inclination to pleasure, and averseness to pain, they call Self-Love; so that the devils, and other damned spirits, love themselves, not because they see any thing in themselves which they imagine to be lovely, but merely because they do not incline to pain but to pleasure, or merely because they are capable of pain or pleasure; for pain and pleasure include an inclination to agreeableness, and an aversion to disagreeableness. Now how improper is it to say, that one loves himself, because what is agreeable to him is agreeable to him, and what is disagreeable to him is disagreeable to him: which mere Entity supposes. So that this, that they call Self-Love, is no affection, but only the Entity of the thing, or his being what he is.

One alone, without any reference to any more, cannot be excellent; for in such case, there can be no manner of relation no way, and therefore no such thing as Consent. Indeed what we call *One*, may be excellent because of a consent of parts, or some consent of those in that being, that are distinguished into a plurality some way or other. But in a being that is absolutely without any plurality, there cannot be Excellency, for there can be no such thing as consent or agreement.

One of the highest excellencies is Love. As nothing else has a proper being but Spirits, and as Bodies are but the shadow of being, therefore the consent of bodies one to another, and the harmony that is among them, is but the shadow of Excellency. The highest Excellency therefore must be the consent of Spirits one to another. But the consent of Spirits consists half in their mutual love one to another. And the sweet harmony between the various parts of the Universe, is only an image of mutual love. But yet a lower kind of love may be odious, because it hinders, or is contrary to, a higher and more general. Even a lower proportion is often a deformity, because it is contrary to a more general proportion.

Coroll. 1. If so much of the beauty and excellency of Spirits consists in Love, then the deformity of evil spirits consists as much in hatred and malice.

Coroll. 2. The more any doctrine, or institution, brings to light of the Spiritual World, the more will it urge to Love and Charity.

Happiness strictly consists in the perception of these three things: of the consent of being to its own being; of its own consent to being; and of being's consent to being.

[14.] Excellence, to put it in other words, is that which is beautiful and lovely. That which is beautiful, considered by itself separately, and deformed, considered as a part of something else more extended; or beautiful, only with respect to itself and a few other things, and not as a part of that which contains all things—the Universe;—is false beauty and a confined beauty. That which is beautiful, with respect to the university of things, has a generally extended excellence and a true beauty; and the more extended, or limited, its system is, the more confined or extended is its beauty.

[62.] As bodies, the objects of our external senses are but the shadows of beings; that harmony, wherein consists sensible excellency and beauty, is but the shadow of excellency. That is, it is pleasant to the mind, because it is a shadow of love. When one thing sweetly harmonizes with another, as the Notes in music, the notes are so conformed, and have such proportion one to another, that they seem to have respect one to another, as if they loved one another. So the beauty of figures and motions is, when one part has such consonant proportion with the rest, as represents a general agreeing and consenting together; which is very much the image of Love, in all the parts of a Society, united by a sweet consent and charity of heart. Therein consists the beauty of figures, as of flowers drawn with a pen; and the beauty of the body, and of the features of the face.

There is no other way, that sensible things can consent one to another but by Equality, or by Likeness, or by Proportion. Therefore the lowest or most simple kind of beauty is equality or likeness; because by equality or likeness, one part consents with but one part; but by Proportion one part may sweetly consent to ten thousand different parts; all the parts may consent with all the rest; and not only so, but the parts, taken singly, may consent with the whole taken together. Thus, in the figures or flourishes drawn by an acute penman, every stroke may have such a proportion, both by the place and distance, direction, degree of curvity, &c. that there may be a consent, in the parts of each stroke, one with another, and a harmonious agreement with all the strokes, and with the various parts, composed of many strokes, and an agreeableness to the whole figure taken together.

There is a beauty in Equality, as appears very evident by the very great respect men show to it, in every thing they make or do. How unbeautiful would be the body, if the parts on one side were unequal to those on the other; how unbeautiful would writing be, if the letters were not of an equal height, or the lines of an equal length, or at an equal distance, or if the pages were not of an equal width or height; and how unbeautiful would a building be, if no equality were observed in the correspondent parts.

Existence or Entity is that, into which all Excellency is to be resolved. Being or Existence is what is necessarily agreeable to Being; and when Being perceives it, it will be an agreeable perception; and any contradiction to Being or Existence is what Being, when it perceives, abhors. If Being, in itself considered, were not pleasing, Being's consent to Being would not be pleasing, nor would Being's disagreeing with Being be displeasing. Therefore, not only may *Greatness* be considered as a capacity of Excellency; but a Being, by reason of his greatness considered alone, is the more excellent, because he partakes more of Being. Though if he be great, if he dissents from more general and extensive Being, or from Universal Being; he is the more odious for his greatness, because the dissent or contradiction to Being in general is so much the greater. It is more grating to see much Being dissent from Being than to see little; and his greatness, or the quantity of Being he partakes of, does nothing towards bettering his dissent from Being in general, because there is no proportion between Finite Being, however great, and Universal Being.

Coroll. 1. Hence it is impossible that God should be any otherwise than excellent; for he is the Infinite, Universal, and All-comprehending Existence.

2. Hence God infinitely loves himself, because his Being is Infinite. He is in himself, if I may so say, an Infinite Quantity of Existence.

3. Hence we learn one reason, why persons, who view Death merely as Annihilation, have a great abhorrence of it, though they live a very afflicted life.

[63.] Sensible Things, by virtue of the harmony and proportion that is seen in them, carry the appearance of perceiving and willing being. They evidently show at first blush, the action and governing of understanding and volition. The Notes of a tune or the strokes of an acute penman, for instance, are placed in such exact order, having such mutual respect one to another, that they carry with them, into the mind of him that sees or hears, the conception of an understanding and will exerting itself in these appearances; and were it not that we, by reflection and reasoning, are led to an extrinsic intelligence and will, that was the cause, it would seem to be in the Notes and Strokes themselves. They would appear like a society of so many perceiving beings, sweetly agreeing together. I can conceive of no other reason why *Equality* and *Proportion* should be pleasing to him that perceives, but only that it has an appearance of *Consent*.

[64.] Excellency may be distributed into *Greatness* and *Beauty*. The former is the Degree of Being; the latter is Being's Consent to Being.

[49.] It is reasonable to suppose that the mere perception of Being is agreeable to perceiving Being, as well as Being's consent to Being. If absolute Being were not agreeable to perceiving Being, the contradiction of Being to Being would not be unpleasant. Hence there is in the mind an inclination to perceive the things that are, or the Desire of Truth. The exercise of this disposition of the soul, to a high degree, is the passion of admiration. When the mind beholds a very uncommon object, there is the pleasure of a new perception, with the excitation of the appetite of knowing more of it, as the causes and manner of production and the like, and the uneasiness arising from its being so hidden. These compose that emotion called *Admiration*.

[45.] EXCELLENCE. 1. When we spake of Excellence in Bodies, we were obliged to borrow the word, *Consent*, from Spiritual things; but Excellence in and among Spirits is, in its prime and proper sense, Being's consent to Being. There is no other proper consent but that of *Minds*, even of their Will; which, when it is of Minds towards Minds, it is *Love*, and when of Minds towards other things, it is *Choice*. Wherefore all the Primary and Original beauty or excellence, that is among Minds, is Love; and into this may all be resolved that is found among them.

2. When we spake of External excellency, we said, that *Being's consent to Being* must needs be agreeable to *Perceiving Being*. But now we are speaking of Spiritual things, we may change the phrase, and say, that *Mind's love to Mind* must needs be lovely to *Beholding Mind;* and Being's love to Being, in general, must needs be agreeable to Being that perceives it, because itself is a participation of Being in general.

3. As to the proportion of this Love;—to greater Spirits, more, and to less, less;—it is beautiful, as it is a manifestation of love to Spirit or Being in general. And the want of this proportion is a deformity, because it is a manifestation of a defect of such a love. It shows that it is not Being, in general, but something else, that is loved, when love is not in proportion to the Extensiveness and Excellence of Being.

4. Seeing God has so plainly revealed himself to us; and other minds are made in his image, and are emanations from him; we may judge what is the Excellence of other minds, by what is his, which we have shown is Love. His Infinite Beauty, is His Infinite mutual Love of Himself. Now God is the Prime and Original Being, the First and Last, and the Pattern of all, and has the sum of all perfection. We may therefore, doubtless, conclude, that all that is the perfection of Spirits may be resolved into that which is God's perfection, which is Love.

5. There are several degrees of deformity or disagreeableness of dissent from Being. One is, when there is only merely a dissent from Being. This is disagreeable to Being, (for Perceiving Being only is properly Being). Still more disagreeable is a dissent to very excellent Being, or, as we have explained, to a Being that consents in a high degree to Being, because such a Being by such a consent becomes bigger; and a dissenting from such a Being includes, also, a dissenting from what he consents with, which is other Beings, or Being in general. Another deformity, that is more odious than mere dissent from Being, is, for a Being to dissent from, or not to consent with, a Being who consents with his Being. It is a manifestation of a greater dissent from Being than ordinary; for the Being perceiving, knows that it is natural to Being, to consent with what consents with it, as we have shown It therefore manifests an extraordinary dissent, that consent to itself will not draw its consent. The deformity, for the same reason, is greater still, if there be dissent from consenting Being. There are such contrarieties and jars in Being, as must necessarily produce jarring and horror in perceiving Being.

6. Dissent from such Beings, if that be their fixed nature, is a manifestation of Consent to Being in general; for consent to being is dissent from that which dissents from Being.

7. Wherefore all Virtue, which is the Excellency of minds, is resolved into *Love to Being;* and nothing is virtuous or beautiful in Spirits, any otherwise than as it is an exercise, or fruit, or manifestation, of this love; and nothing is sinful or deformed in Spirits, but as it is the defect of, or contrary to, these.

8. When we speak of Being in general, we may be un-

derstood of the Divine Being, for he is an Infinite Being: therefore all others must necessarily be considered as nothing. As to *Bodies*, we have shown in another place, that they have no proper Being of their own. And as to *Spirits*, they are the communications of the Great Original Spirit; and doubtless, in metaphysical strictness and propriety, He *is*, as there is none else. He is likewise Infinitely Excellent, and all Excellence and Beauty is derived from him, in the same manner as all being. And all other Excellence, is, in strictness only, a shadow of his. We proceed, therefore, to show how all Spiritual Excellence is resolved into Love.

9. As to God's Excellence, it is evident it consists in the *Love of himself*; for he was as excellent before he created the Universe, as he is now. But if the Excellence of Spirits consists in their disposition and action, God could be excellent no other way at that time; for all the exertions of himself were towards himself. But he exerts himself towards himself, no other way, than in infinitely loving and delighting in himself; in the mutual love of the Father and the Son. This makes the Third, the Personal Holy Spirit, or the Holiness of God, which is his infinite Beauty; and this is God's Infinite Consent to Being in general. And his love to the creature is his excellence, or the communication of Himself, his complacency in them, according as they partake of more or less of Excellence and beauty, that is, of holiness (which consists in love); that is, according as he communicates more or less of his Holy Spirit.

10. As to that Excellence, that Created Spirits partake of; that it is all to be resolved into Love, none will doubt, that knows what is the Sum of the Ten Commandments; or believes what the Apostle says, That Love is the fulfilling of the Law; or what Christ says, That on these two, loving God and our neighbour, hang all the Law and the Prophets. This doctrine is often repeated in the New Testament. We are told that the End of the Commandment is Love; that to Love, is to fulfil the Royal Law; and that all the Law is fulfilled in this one word, Love.

11. I know of no difficulties worth insisting on, except pertaining to the spiritual excellence of Justice; but enough has been said already to resolve them. Though Injustice is the greatest of all deformities, yet justice is no otherwise excellent, than as it is the exercise, fruit, and manifestation of the mind's love or consent to Being; nor Injustice deformed any otherwise, than as it is the highest degree of the contrary. Injustice is not to exert ourselves towards any Being as it deserves, or to do it contrary to what it deserves, in doing good or evil, or in acts of Consent or Dissent. There are two ways of deserving our Consent, and the acts of it: (By *deserving* any thing, we are to understand *that the nature of being requires it*:) By extensiveness and excellence; and by consent to that particular being. The reason of the deformity of not proportioning our consent, and the exercise of it, may be seen in paragraphs 3 and 5. As to the beauty of Vindictive Justice, see paragraph 6.

12. 'Tis peculiar to God, that he has beauty *within himself*, consisting in Being's consenting with his own Being, or the love of himself, in his own Holy Spirit. Whereas the excellence of others is in loving others, in loving God, and in the communications of his Spirit.

13. We shall be in danger, when we meditate on this love of God to himself, as being the thing wherein his infinite excellence and loveliness consists, of some alloy to the sweetness of our view, by its appearing with something of the aspect and cast of what we call self-love. But we are to consider that this love includes in it, or rather is the same as, a love to every thing, as they are all communications of himself. So that we are to conceive of Divine Excellence as the Infinite General Love, that which reaches all, proportionally, with perfect purity and sweetness; yea, it includes the true Love of all creatures, for that is his Spirit, or which is the same thing, his Love. And if we take notice, when we are in the best frames meditating on Divine Excellence, our idea of that tranquillity and peace, which seems to be overspread and cast abroad upon the whole Earth, and Universe, naturally dissolves itself into the idea of a General Love and Delight, every where diffused.

14. Conscience is *that Sense the Mind has of this Consent*: Which Sense consists in the Consent of the Perceiving Being, to such a General Consent; (that is, of such perceiving Beings, as are capable of so general a perception, as to have any notion of Being in general;) and the Dissent of his mind to a Dissent from Being in general. We have said already, that it is naturally agreeable to Perceiving Being that Being should consent to Being, and the contrary disagreeable. If by any means, therefore, a particular and restrained love overcomes this General Consent;—the foundation of that Consent yet remaining in the nature, exerts itself again, so that there is the contradiction of one consent to another. And as it is naturally agreeable to every Being, to have being consent to him; the mind, after it has thus exerted an act of dissent to Being in general, has a sense that Being in general dissents from it, which is most disagreeable to it. And as he is conscious of a dissent from Universal Being, and of that Being's dissent from him, wherever he is, he sees what excites horror. And by inclining or doing that, which is against his natural inclination as a Perceiving Being, he must necessarily cause uneasiness, inasmuch as that natural inclination is contradicted. And this is the *Disquiet of Conscience*. And, though the Disposition be changed, the remembrance of his having so done in time past, and the idea being still tied to that of himself, he is uneasy. The notion of such a dissent any where, as we have shown, is odious; but the notion of its being in himself, renders it uneasy and disquieting. But when there is no sense of any such dissent from Being in general, there is no contradiction to the natural inclination of Perceiving Being. And when he reflects, he has a sense that Being in general doth not dissent from him; and then there is *Peace of Conscience*; though he has a remembrance of past dissensions with nature. Yet if by any means it be possible, when he has the idea of it, to conceive of it as not belonging to him, he has the same Peace. And if he has a sense not only of his not dissenting, but of his consenting to Being in general, or Nature, and acting accordingly; he has a sense that Nature, in general, consents to him: he has not only *Peace*, but *Joy, of mind*, wherever he is. These things are obviously invigorated by the knowledge of God and his Constitution about us, and by the light of the Gospel.

[The preceding articles were written as comments on the various subjects treated of, while the author was studying the Essay on the Human Understanding. It is not improbable that some of the later numbers were written while the author was a tutor in College.]

APPENDIX, No. V.

FAMILY AND DESCENDANTS OF PRESIDENT EDWARDS.

First.—FAMILY.

THE following is a copy of the Family Record, in his own hand, in the Family Bible.

"Jonathan Edwards, son of Timothy and Esther Edwards of Windsor in Connecticut.

I was born Oct. 5, 1703.

I was ordained at Northampton, Feb. 15, 1727.

I was married to Miss Sarah Pierrepont, July 28, 1727.

My wife was born Jan. 9, 1710.

My daughter Sarah was born on a sabbath day, between 2 and 3 o'clock in the afternoon, Aug. 25, 1728.

My daughter Jerusha was born on a sabbath day, towards the conclusion of the afternoon exercise, April 26, 1730.

My daughter Esther was born on a sabbath day, between 9 and 10 o'clock in the forenoon, Feb. 13, 1732.

My daughter Mary was born April 7th, 1734, being sabbath day, the sun being about an hour and a half high, in the morning.

My daughter Lucy was born on Tuesday, the last day of Aug. 1736, between 2 and 3 o'clock in the morning.

My son Timothy was born on Tuesday, July 25, 1738, between 6 and 7 o'clock in the morning.

My daughter Susannah was born on Friday, June 20, 1740, at about 3 in the morning.

All the family above named had the measles, at the latter end of the year 1740.

My daughter Eunice was born on Monday morning, May 9, 1743, about half an hour after midnight, and was baptized the sabbath following.

My son Jonathan was born on a sabbath-day night, May 26, 1745, between 9 and 10 o'clock, and was baptized the sabbath following.

My daughter Jerusha died on a sabbath day, Feb. 14, 1747, about 5 o'clock in the morning, aged 17.

My daughter Elizabeth was born on Wednesday, May 6, 1747, between 10 and 11 o'clock at night, and was baptized the sabbath following.

My son Pierrepont was born on a sabbath-day night, April 8, 1750, between 8 and 9 o'clock; and was baptized the sabbath following.

I was dismissed from my pastoral relation to the first church in Northampton, June 22d, 1750.

My daughter Sarah was married to Mr. Elihu Parsons, June 11, 1750.

My daughter Mary was married to Timothy Dwight, Esq. of Northampton, Nov. 8, 1750.

My daughter Esther was married to the Rev. Aaron Burr of Newark, June 29, 1752.

Mr. Burr aforesaid, President of the New Jersey college, died at Princeton, Sept. 24, 1757, of the nervous fever. Mr. Burr was born Jan. 4, 1715.

I was properly initiated President of New Jersey college, by taking the previous oaths, Feb. 16, 1758."

Rev. Jonathan Edwards, President of Nassau Hall, died of the small pox, March 22, 1758, and was buried March 24th.

Esther Burr, wife of Rev. Aaron Burr, died at Princeton, April 7, 1758, of a short illness, aged 26.

Sarah Edwards, wife of Jonathan Edwards, died Oct. 2, 1758, about 12 o'clock, and was buried at Princeton the day following.

Elizabeth Edwards, daughter of Jonathan and Sarah, died at Northampton, Jan. 1, 1762, aged 14.

Lucy Woodbridge died at Stockbridge in Oct. 1786, aged 50.

Rev. Jonathan Edwards, D. D. died at Schenectady, Aug. 1, 1801, aged 56.

Susannah Porter died at Hadley, in the spring of 1802, aged 61.

Sarah Parsons died at Goshen, Mass. May 15, 1805, aged 76.

Mary Dwight died at Northampton, Feb. 1807, aged 72.

Timothy Edwards died at Stockbridge in the autumn of 1813, aged 75.

Eunice Hunt died at Newburn, N. C. in the autumn of 1822, aged 79.

Pierrepont Edwards died at Bridgeport, April 14, 1826, aged 76.

Second.—MORE REMOTE DESCENDANTS.

I. { Elihu Parsons, Esq. / Sarah Edwards, } married June 11, 1750. They lived at Stockbridge, and afterwards at Goshen.

Children.

1. Ebenezer. Died in infancy.
2. Esther, born May 17, 1752, died at Stockbridge, Nov. 17, 1774.
3. Elihu, born Dec. 9, 1753, married Rhoda Hinsdale of Lenox. He died at Goshen in Aug. 1804. They had 6 children.
4. Eliphalet, born Jan. 1756; married Martha Young of Long Island. He died at Chenango, N. Y. in Jan. 1813. They had 5 children.
5. Lydia, born Jan. 15, 1757; married Aaron Ingersoll of Lee. They had 4 children.
6. Lucretia, born Aug. 3, 1759; married Rev. Justin Parsons of Pittsfield, Vt. She died at Goshen in Dec. 1786. They had 1 child.
7. Sarah, born Sept. 8, 1760; married David Ingersoll of Lee, Dec. 13, 1781. They had 13 children.
8. Lucy, born Oct. 14, 1762; married Joshua Ketchum. They had 3 children.
9. Jonathan. Died an infant.
10. Jerusha. Died an infant.
11. Jerusha, born May, 1766; married Ira Seymour of Victor, N. Y. They have had 5 children.

II. Jerusha, died unmarried, at the age of 17.

III. { Rev. Aaron Burr, / Esther Edwards, } married June 29, 1752. They lived at Newark, and Princeton.

Children.

1. Sarah, born May 3, 1754; married Hon. Tapping Reeve of Litchfield, Conn. They had 1 child, Aaron Burr Reeve.
2. Hon. Aaron Burr, Vice President of the United States, born Feb. 6, 1756; married Mrs. Theodosia Prevost. They had one daughter.

IV. { Timothy Dwight, Esq. / Mary Edwards, } married Nov. 8, 1750. They lived at Northampton. He died at Natchez, in 1776; and she, in Feb. 1807, at Northampton.

Children 13.

1. Rev. Timothy Dwight, DD., LL. D., President of Yale college, born May 14, 1752; married Mary, the daughter of Benjamin Woolsey, Esq. of Dorsous, L. I. They had 7 children. He died at New-Haven, Jan. 11, 1817.
2. Sereno Edwards Dwight, M. D., born 1753: married Miss Lyman. They had 2 children. He was lost at sea, on the coast of Nova Scotia, in 1779.
3. Jonathan Dwight, born 1755; married Miss Wright. They had 2 children. He died in 180-.
4. Erastus Dwight, born 1756; died, unmarried, in 1825.

5. Maurice William Dwight, M. D., born in 1758; married Margaret Dewitt. They had 2 children.
6. Sarah, born May 29, 1760; married Seth Storrs of Northampton. She died at Northampton, in 1805.
7. Hon. Theodore Dwight, born in 1762; married Abbey Alsop. They have 3 children.
8. Mary, born in 1764; married Lewis R. Morris. They had 1 child.
9. Delia, born in 1766; married Jonathan Edwards Porter, Esq. They had 3 children.
10. Nathaniel Dwight, M. D., born in 1769; married Miss Robbins. They have 4 children.
11. Elizabeth, born in 1771; married William W. Woolsey, Esq. They had 8 children. She died at New-Haven in the autumn of 1812.
12. Cecil Dwight, born June 10, 1774; married Mary Clap. They have had 11 children.
13. Henry Edwin Dwight, born in 1776; married Electa Keyes. They had 6 children.

V. { Jahleel Woodbridge, Esq. / Lucy Edwards, } married June 1764. They lived at Stockbridge.

Children 7.
1. Jonathan Woodbridge, Esq. born 1766; married Sarah Meach. They had 8 children.
2. Stephen, born 1778, and had several children.
3. Joseph Woodbridge, Esq., born in 1770; married Louisa Hopkins. They had 4 children.
4. Lucy, born in 1772; married Henry Brown. They had 9 or 10 children.
5. John Woodbridge, Esq.
6. Sarah, married a Mr. Leicester of Griswold, Conn. They had 5 children.
7. Rev Timothy Woodbridge, of Green River, N. Y.

VI. { Hon. Timothy Edwards, / Rhoda Ogden, } married Sept. 25, 1760. They lived at Stockbridge.

Children 15. Two died young.
1. Sarah. 2. Edward. 3. Jonathan. 4. Richard. 5. Phebe. 6. William. 7. Robert Ogden. 8. Timothy. 9. Mary Ogden. 10. Rhoda. 11. Mary. 12. Anna. 13. Robert.

VII. { Eleazar Porter, Esq. / Susannah Edwards, } married Sept. 1761. They lived at Hadley.

Children 5.
1. Eleazar. 2. William. 3. Jonathan Edwards. 4. Moses. 5. Pierrepont.

VIII. { Thomas Pollock, Esq. / Eunice Edwards, } married Jan. 1764. They lived at Elizabethtown, N. J.

Children 5.
1. Elizabeth, married ——— Williams, Esq.
2. Hester, died unmarried.
3. Thomas Pollock, Esq.
4. Frances, married John Deveraux, Esq. They have 3 children.
5. George Pollock, Esq.

IX. { Rev. Jonathan Edwards, D. D. / President of Union College, / Sarah Porter, } married in 1770. They lived at New-Haven, and Schenectady.

Children 4. One died young.
1. Mary, married Mr. Hoit, of Schenectady.
2. Jonathan Walter Edwards, Esq. Married Elizabeth Tryon.
3. Jerusha, married Rev. Calvin Chapin, D. D. of Stepney.

X. Elizabeth. Died unmarried, at the age of 14.

XI. { Hon. Pierrepont Edwards, / Frances Ogden, } married May, 1769. They lived at New-Haven.

Children 10. Of whom 4 died in infancy.
1. Susan, married Samuel W. Johnson, Esq. They have had 6 children.
2. Hon. John Starkes Edwards, married Louisa Morris. They had 3 children.
3. Hon. Henry Waggerman Edwards, married Lydia Miller. They have had 8 children.
4. Hon. Ogden Edwards, married Harriet Penfield. They had 10 children.
5. Alfred Edwards, married Deborah Glover.
6. Henrietta Frances, married Eli Whitney, Esq. They had 4 children.

APPENDIX, No. VI.

CATALOGUE OF PRESIDENT EDWARDS'S WORKS, HERETOFORE PUBLISHED.

1731. God glorified in Man's Dependence; A Sermon on 1 Cor. i. 29—31. *Boston.*
1734. A Divine and Supernatural Light imparted to the Soul by the Spirit of God; A Sermon on Matt. xvi. 17. *Boston.*
1735. (Probably.) Curse ye Meroz; A Sermon on Judges v. 33. (This I have not found.)
1736. Narrative of Surprising Conversions. *London.*
1738. Five Discourses prefixed to the first American edition of the preceding. *Boston.*
1741. Sinners in the hands of an angry God; A Sermon on Deut. xxxii. 35. *Boston.*
1741. Sorrows of the Bereaved spread before Jesus; A Sermon at the Funeral of the Rev. William Williams, on Matt. xiv. 12. *Boston.*
1741. Distinguishing Marks of a Work of the True Spirit; A Sermon on 1 John iv. 1. preached at New-Haven, Sept. 10. 1741. *Boston.*
1742. Thoughts on the Revival of Religion in New England in 1740. *Boston.*
1743. The Watchman's Duty and Account; A Sermon on Heb. xiii. 17. at the Ordination of the Rev. Jonathan Judd. *Boston.*
1744. The True Excellency of a Gospel Minister; A Sermon on John v. 35. at the Ordination of the Rev. Robert Abercrombie. *Boston.*
1746. Treatise on Religious Affections. *Boston.*
1747. True Saints, when absent from the Body, present with the Lord; A Sermon on 2 Cor. v. 8. at the Funeral of Rev. David Brainerd. *Boston.*
1748. God's awful Judgments in breaking the Strong Rods of Community; A Sermon on the Death of Col. John Stoddard. *Boston.*
1749. Life and Diary of the Rev. David Brainerd. *Boston.*
1749. Christ the Example of Gospel Ministers; A Sermon on John xiii. 15, 16. at the Ordination of the Rev. Job Strong. *Boston.*
1749. Qualifications for Full Communion in the Visible Church. *Boston.*
1750. Farewell Sermon to the People of Northampton. *Boston.*
1752. True Grace distinguished from the Experience of Devils; A Sermon on James ii. 19. before the Synod of Newark. *New York.*
1754. On the Freedom of the Will. *Boston.*
1758. On Original Sin. *Boston.*
1765. Eighteen Sermons, annexed to the Life by Dr. Hopkins. *Boston.*
1777. The History of Redemption. *Edinburgh.*
1788. Nature of Virtue. *Boston.*
1788. God's Last End in the Creation. *In the same pamphlet as the preceding.*
1788. Practical Sermons. *Edinburgh.*
1789. Twenty Sermons. *Edinburgh.*
1793. Miscellaneous Observations. *Edinburgh.*
1796. Miscellaneous Remarks. *Edinburgh.*

A

CAREFUL AND STRICT INQUIRY

INTO THE

MODERN PREVAILING NOTIONS

OF THAT

FREEDOM OF WILL,

WHICH IS SUPPOSED TO BE ESSENTIAL TO MORAL AGENCY, VIRTUE AND VICE, REWARD AND PUNISHMENT, PRAISE AND BLAME.

Rom. ix. 16. It is not of him that willeth.

PREFACE.

MANY find much fault with calling professing Christians, that differ one from another in some matters of opinion, by distinct *names;* especially calling them by the names of particular men, who have distinguished themselves as maintainers and promoters of those opinions: as calling some professing Christians *Arminians,* from ARMINIUS; others *Arians,* from ARIUS; others *Socinians,* from SOCINUS, and the like. They think it unjust in itself; as it seems to suppose and suggest, that the persons marked out by these names, received those doctrines which they entertain, out of regard *to,* and reliance *on,* those men after whom they are named; as though they made them their rule; in the same manner, as the followers of CHRIST are called *Christians,* after his name, whom they regard and depend upon, as their great Head and Rule. Whereas, this is an unjust and groundless imputation on those that go under the forementioned denominations. Thus, say they, there is not the least ground to suppose, that the chief divines, who embrace the scheme of doctrine which is, by many, called *Arminianism,* believe it the more, because ARMINIUS believed it: and that there is no reason to think any other, than that they sincerely and impartially study the Holy Scriptures, and inquire after the mind of Christ, with as much judgment and sincerity, as any of those that call them by these names; that they seek after truth, and are not careful whether they think exactly as *Arminius* did; yea, that, in some things, they actually differ from him. This practice is also esteemed actually injurious on this account, that it is supposed naturally to lead the multitude to imagine the difference between persons thus named, and others, to be greater than it is; so great, as if they were another species of beings. And they object against it as arising from an uncharitable, narrow, contracted spirit; which, they say, commonly inclines persons to confine all that is good to themselves, and their own party, and to make a wide distinction between themselves and others, and stigmatize those that differ from them with odious names. They say, moreover, that the keeping up such a distinction of names, has a direct tendency to uphold distance and disaffection, and keep alive mutual hatred among Christians, who ought all to be united in friendship and charity, though they cannot, in all things, think alike.

I confess, these things are very plausible; and I will not deny, that there are some unhappy consequences of this distinction of names, and that men's infirmities and evil dispositions often make an ill improvement of it. But yet, I humbly conceive, these objections are carried far beyond reason. The generality of mankind are disposed enough, and a great deal too much, to uncharitableness, and to be censorious and bitter towards those that differ from them in religious opinions: which evil temper of mind will take occasion to exert itself from many things in themselves innocent, useful, and necessary. But yet there is no necessity to suppose, that our thus distinguishing persons of different opinions by different names, arises mainly from an uncharitable spirit. It may arise from the disposition there is in mankind (whom God has distinguished with an ability and inclination for speech) to improve the benefit of language, in the proper use and design of names, given to things of which they have often occasion to speak, which is to enable them to express their ideas with ease and expedition, without being encumbered with an obscure and difficult circumlocution. And our thus distinguishing persons of different opinions in religious matters may not imply any more, than that there is a *difference;* a difference of which we find we have often occasion to take notice: and it is always a defect in language, in such cases, to be obliged to make use of a description, instead of a name. Thus we have often occasion to speak of those who are the descendants of the ancient inhabitants of *France,* in distinction from the descendants of the inhabitants of *Spain;* and find the great convenience of those distinguishing words, *French* and *Spaniards;* by which the signification of our minds is quick and easy, and our speech is delivered from the burden of a continual reiteration of diffuse descriptions, with which it must otherwise be embarrassed.

That there is occasion to speak often concerning the difference of those, who in their general scheme of divinity agree with these two noted men, CALVIN and ARMINIUS, is what the practice of the latter confesses; who are often, in their discourses and writings, taking notice of the supposed absurd and pernicious opinions of the former sort. And therefore the making use of different names in this case cannot reasonably be objected against, as a thing which must come from so bad a cause as they assign. It is easy to be accounted for, without supposing it to arise from any other source, than the exigence of the case, whereby mankind express those things, which they have frequent occasion to mention, by certain distinguishing names. It is an effect, similar to what we see in cases innumerable, where the cause is not at all blameworthy.

Nevertheless, at first, I had thoughts of carefully avoiding the use of the appellation, *Arminian,* in this Treatise. But I soon found I should be put to great difficulty by it; and that my discourse would be too much encumbered with circumlocution, instead of a name, which would better express the thing intended. And therefore I must ask the excuse of such as are apt to be offended with things of this nature, that I have so freely used the term *Arminian* in the following Discourse. I profess it to be without any design to stigmatize persons of any sort with a name of reproach, or at all to make them appear more odious. If, when I had occasion to speak of those divines who are commonly called by this name, I had, instead of styling them *Arminians,* called them "*these men,*" as Dr. WHITBY does *Calvinistic* divines, it probably would not have been taken any better, or thought to show a better temper, or more good manners. I have done as I would be done by, in this matter. However the term *Calvinistic* is, in these days, among most, a term of greater reproach than the term *Arminian;* yet I should not take it at all amiss, to be called a *Calvinist,* for distinction's sake: though I utterly disclaim a dependence on CALVIN, or believing the doctrines which I hold, because he believed and taught them; and cannot justly be charged with believing in every thing just as he taught.

But, lest I should really be an occasion of injury to some persons, I would here give notice, that though I generally speak of that doctrine, concerning free-will and moral agency, which I oppose, as an *Arminian* doctrine; yet I would not be understood as asserting, that every divine or author, whom I have occasion to mention as maintaining that doctrine, was properly an *Arminian*, or one of that sort which is commonly called by that name. Some of them went far beyond the *Arminians*; and I would by no means charge *Arminians* in general with all the corrupt doctrine which these maintained. Thus, for instance, it would be very injurious, if I should rank *Arminian* divines, in general, with such authors as Mr. CHUBB. I doubt not, many of them have some of his doctrines in abhorrence; though he agrees, for the most part, with *Arminians*, in his notion of the Freedom of the Will. And, on the other hand, though I suppose this notion to be a leading article in the *Arminian* scheme, that which, if pursued in its consequences, will truly infer, or naturally lead to all the rest; yet I do not charge all that have held this doctrine, with being *Arminians*. For whatever may be the consequences of the doctrine really, yet some that hold this doctrine, may not own nor see these consequences; and it would be unjust, in many instances, to charge every author with believing and maintaining all the real consequences of his avowed doctrines. And I desire it may be particularly noted, that though I have occasion, in the following Discourse, often to mention the author of the book, entitled *An Essay on the Freedom of the Will, in God and the Creature*,* as holding that notion of Freedom of Will, which I oppose; yet I do not mean to call him an *Arminian*: however, in that doctrine he agrees with *Arminians*, and departs from the current and general opinion of *Calvinists*. If the author of that Essay be the same as it is commonly ascribed to, he doubtless was not one that ought to bear that name. But however good a divine he was in many respects, yet that particular *Arminian* doctrine which he maintained, is never the better for being held by such an one: nor is there less need of opposing it on that account, but rather more; as it will be likely to have the more pernicious influence, for being taught by a divine of his name and character; supposing the doctrine to be wrong, and in itself to be of an ill tendency.

I have nothing further to say by way of preface; but only to bespeak the reader's candour, and calm attention to what I have written. The subject is of such importance, as to *demand* attention, and the most thorough consideration. Of all kinds of knowledge that we can ever obtain, the knowledge of God, and the knowledge of ourselves, are the most important. As religion is the great business for which we are created, and on which our happiness depends; and as religion consists in an intercourse between ourselves and our Maker; and so has its foundation in God's nature and ours, and in the relation that God and we stand in to each other; therefore a true knowledge of both must be needful, in order to true religion. But the knowledge of ourselves consists chiefly in right apprehensions concerning those two chief faculties of our nature, the *understanding* and *will*. Both are very important: yet the science of the latter must be confessed to be of greatest moment; inasmuch as all virtue and religion have their seat more immediately in the will, consisting more especially in right acts and habits of this faculty. And the grand question about the Freedom of the Will, is the main point that belongs to the science of the Will. Therefore, I say, the importance of the subject greatly *demands* the attention of Christians, and especially of divines. But as to my *manner* of handling the subject, I would be far from presuming to say, that it is such as *demands* the attention of the reader to what I have written. I am ready to own, that in this matter I depend on the reader's courtesy. But only thus far I may have some colour for putting in a *claim*; that if the reader be disposed to pass his censure on what I have written, I may be fully and patiently heard, and well attended to, before I am condemned. However, this is what I would humbly *ask* of my readers; together with the prayers of all sincere lovers of truth, that I may have much of that Spirit which Christ promised his disciples, which guides into all truth; and that the blessed and powerful influences of this Spirit would make truth victorious in the world.

A CAREFUL AND STRICT INQUIRY, &c.

PART I.

WHEREIN ARE EXPLAINED AND STATED VARIOUS TERMS AND THINGS BELONGING TO THE SUBJECT OF THE ENSUING DISCOURSE.

SECTION I.

Concerning the Nature of the Will.

It may possibly be thought, that there is no great need of going about to define or describe the *Will*; this word being generally as well understood as any other words we can use to explain it: and so perhaps it would be, had not philosophers, metaphysicians, and polemic divines, brought the matter into obscurity by the things they have said of it. But since it is so, I think it may be of some use, and will tend to greater clearness in the following discourse, to say a few things concerning it.

And therefore I observe, that the *Will* (without any metaphysical refining) is, *That by which the mind chooses any thing*. The faculty of the *Will*, is that power, or principle of mind, by which it is capable of *choosing*: an act of the *Will* is the same as an act of *choosing* or *choice*.

If any think it is a more perfect definition of the Will, to say, that it is that by which the soul either *chooses* or *refuses*; I am content with it: though I think it enough to say, It is that by which the soul chooses: for in every act of Will whatsoever, the mind chooses one thing rather than another; it chooses something rather than the contrary, or rather than the want or non-existence of that thing. So in every act of refusal, the mind chooses the absence of the thing refused; the positive and the negative are set before the mind for its choice, and it chooses the negative; and the mind's making its choice in that case is properly the act of the Will: the Will's determining between the two, is a voluntary determination; but that is the same

* This Essay has been generally ascribed to Dr. Watts, and is included in his works.—W.

thing as making a choice. So that by whatever names we call the act of the Will, choosing, refusing, approving, disapproving, liking, disliking, embracing, rejecting, determining, directing, commanding, forbidding, inclining, or *being* averse, *being* pleased or displeased *with;* all may be reduced to this of *choosing*. For the soul to act *voluntarily*, is evermore to act *electively*.

Mr. Locke* says, "The Will signifies nothing but a power or ability to *prefer* or *choose*." And, in the foregoing page, he says, "The word *preferring* seems best to express the act of volition;" but adds, that "it does it not precisely; for, though a man would *prefer* flying to walking, yet who can say he ever *wills* it?" But the instance he mentions, does not prove that there is any thing else in *willing*, but merely *preferring:* for it should be considered what is the immediate object of the Will, with respect to a man's walking, or any other external action; which is not being removed from one place to another; on the earth, or through the air; these are remoter objects of preference; but such or such an immediate *exertion* of himself. The thing next chosen, or preferred, when a man wills to walk, is not his being removed to such a place where he would be, but such an exertion and motion of his legs and feet, &c. in order to it. And his willing such an alteration in his body in the present moment, is nothing else but his choosing or preferring such an alteration in his body at such a moment, or his liking it better than the forbearance of it. And God has so made and established the human nature, the soul being united to a body in proper state, that the soul preferring or choosing such an immediate exertion or alteration of the body, such an alteration instantaneously follows. There is nothing else in the actions of my mind, that I am conscious of while I walk, but only my preferring or choosing, through successive moments, that there should be such alterations of my external sensations and motions; together with a concurring habitual expectation that it will be so; having ever found by experience, that on such an immediate preference, such sensations and motions do actually, instantaneously, and constantly arise. But it is not so in the case of flying: though a man may be said *remotely* to choose or prefer flying; yet he does not prefer, or desire, under circumstances in view, any *immediate exertion* of the members of his body in order to it; because he has no expectation that he should obtain the desired end by any such exertion; and he does not prefer, or incline to, any bodily exertion, under this apprehended circumstance, of its being wholly in vain. So that if we carefully distinguish the *proper objects* of the several acts of the Will, it will not appear by this, and such like instances, that there is any difference between *volition* and *preference;* or that a man's choosing, liking best, or being best pleased with a thing, are not the same with his *willing* that thing. Thus an act of the Will is commonly expressed by *its pleasing a man* to do thus or thus; and a man doing as he *wills*, and doing as he *pleases*, are in common speech the same thing.

Mr. Locke† says, "The Will is perfectly distinguished from Desire; which in the very same action may have a quite contrary tendency from that which our Wills sets us upon. A man, says he, whom I cannot deny, may oblige me to use persuasions to another, which, at the same time I am speaking, I may wish may not prevail on him. In this case, it is plain the Will and Desire run counter." I do not suppose, that *Will* and *Desire* are words of precisely the same signification: *Will* seems to be a word of a more general signification, extending to things present and absent. *Desire* respects something absent. I may prefer my present situation and posture, suppose sitting still, or having my eyes open, and so may *will* it. But yet I cannot think they are so entirely distinct, that they can ever be properly said to run counter. A man never, in any instance, wills any thing contrary to his desires, or desires any thing contrary to his Will. The forementioned instance, which Mr. Locke produces, is no proof that he ever does. He may, on some consideration or other *will* to utter speeches which have a tendency to persuade another, and still may *desire* that they may not persuade him; but yet his Will and Desire do not run counter at all: the thing which he wills, the very same he desires; and he does not will a thing, and desire the *contrary*, in any particular. In this instance, it is not carefully observed, what is the thing willed, and what is the thing desired: if it were, it would be found, that Will and Desire do not clash in the least. The thing willed on some consideration, is to utter such words; and certainly, the same consideration so influences him, that he does not desire the contrary; all things considered, he chooses to utter such words, and does not desire not to utter them. And so as to the thing which Mr. Locke speaks of as *desired*, viz. That the words, though they tend to persuade, should not be effectual to that end, his Will is not contrary to this; he does not will that they should be effectual, but rather wills that they should not, as he desires. In order to prove that the Will and Desire may run counter, it should be shown that they may be contrary one to the other in the same thing, or with respect to the *very same object* of Will or Desire: but here the objects are two; and in each, taken by themselves, the Will and Desire agree. And it is no wonder that they should not agree in *different* things, though but little distinguished in their nature. The Will may not agree with the Will, nor Desire agree with Desire, in different things. As in this very instance which Mr. Locke mentions, a person may, on *some* consideration, desire to use persuasions, and at the same time may desire they may not prevail; but yet nobody will say, that *Desire* runs counter to *Desire;* or that this proves that *Desire* is perfectly a distinct thing from *Desire*.—The like might be observed of the other instance Mr. Locke produces, of a man's desiring to be eased of pain, &c.

But, not to dwell any longer on this, whether *Desire* and *Will*, and whether *Preference* and *Volition* be precisely the same things, I trust it will be allowed by all, that in every act of *Will* there is an act of *choice;* that in every *volition* there is a *preference*, or a prevailing inclination of the soul, whereby, at that instant, it is out of a state of perfect indifference, with respect to the direct object of the volition. So that in every act, or going forth of the Will, there is some preponderation of the mind, one way rather than another; and the soul had rather *have* or *do* one thing, than another, or than *not* to have or do that thing; and that where there is absolutely no preferring or choosing, but a perfect, continuing equilibrium, there is no volition.

SECT. II.

Concerning the Determination of the Will.

By *determining* the Will, if the phrase be used with any meaning, must be intended, *causing* that the act of the Will or choice should be thus, and not otherwise: and the Will is said to be *determined*, when, in consequence of some action, or influence, its choice is directed to, and fixed upon a particular object. As when we speak of the determination of motion, we mean causing the motion of the body to be in such a direction, rather than another.

The Determination of the Will, supposes an effect, which must have a cause. If the Will be determined, there is a Determiner. This must be supposed to be intended even by them that say, The Will determines itself. If it be so, the Will is both Determiner and determined; it is a cause that acts and produces effects upon itself, and is the object of its own influence and action.

With respect to that grand inquiry, "What determines the Will?" it would be very tedious and unnecessary, at present, to examine all the various opinions, which have been advanced concerning this matter; nor is it needful that I should enter into a particular discussion of all points debated in disputes on that other question, "Whether the Will always follows the last dictate of the understanding?" It is sufficient to my present purpose to say, *It is that motive, which, as it stands in the view of the mind, is the strongest, that determines the Will.* But it may be necessary that I should a little explain my meaning.

* Human Understanding. Edit. 7. vol. i. p. 197.

† Hum. Und. vol. i. p. 203, 204

By *motive*, I mean the whole of that which moves, excites, or invites the mind to volition, whether that be one thing singly, or many things conjunctly. Many particular things may concur, and unite their strength, to induce the mind; and when it is so, all together are as one complex motive. And when I speak of the *strongest* motive, I have respect to the strength of the whole that operates to induce a particular act of volition, whether that be the strength of one thing alone, or of many together.

Whatever is objectively * a motive, in this sense, must be something that is *extant in the view or apprehension of the understanding*, or perceiving faculty. Nothing can induce or invite the mind to will or act any thing, any further than it is perceived, or is some way or other in the mind's view; for what is wholly unperceived and perfectly out of the mind's view, cannot affect the mind at all. It is most evident, that nothing is in the mind, or reaches it, or takes any hold of it, any otherwise than as it is perceived or thought of.

And I think it must also be allowed by all, that every thing that is properly called a motive, excitement, or inducement to a perceiving, willing agent, has some sort and degree of *tendency*, or *advantage* to move or excite the Will, previous to the effect, or to the act of the Will excited. This previous tendency of the motive is what I call the *strength* of the motive. That motive which has a less degree of previous advantage, or tendency to move the Will, or which appears less inviting, as it stands in the view of the mind, is what I call a *weaker* motive. On the contrary, that which appears most inviting, and has, by what appears concerning it to the understanding or apprehension, the greatest degree of previous tendency to excite and induce the choice, is what I call the *strongest* motive. And in this sense, I suppose the Will is always determined by the strongest motive.

Things that exist in the view of the mind have their strength, tendency, or advantage to move, or excite its Will, from many things appertaining to the nature and circumstances of the *thing viewed*, the nature and circumstances of the *mind that views*, and the degree and manner of its *view;* of which it would perhaps be hard to make a perfect enumeration. But so much I think may be determined in general, without room for controversy, that whatever is perceived or apprehended by an intelligent and voluntary agent, which has the nature and influence of a motive to volition or choice, is considered or viewed *as good;* nor has it any tendency to engage the election of the soul in any further degree than it appears such. For to say otherwise, would be to say, that things that appear, have a tendency, by the appearance they make, to engage the mind to elect them, some other way than by their appearing eligible to it; which is absurd. And therefore it must be true, in some sense, that *the Will always is, as the greatest apparent good is.* But only, for the right understanding of this, two things must be well and distinctly observed.

1. It must be observed in what sense I use the term "good;" namely, as of the same import with "agreeable." To appear *good* to the mind, as I use the phrase, is the same as to *appear agreeable*, or *seem pleasing* to the mind. Certainly, nothing appears inviting and eligible to the mind, or tending to engage its inclination and choice, considered as *evil* or *disagreeable;* nor indeed, as *indifferent*, and neither agreeable nor disagreeable. But if it tends to draw the inclination, and move the Will, it must be under the notion of that which *suits* the mind. And therefore that must have the greatest tendency to attract and engage it, which as it stands in the mind's view, suits it best, and pleases it most; and in that sense, is the greatest apparent good: to say otherwise, is little, if any thing, short of a direct and plain contradiction.

The word "good," in this sense, includes in its signification, the removal or avoiding of evil, or of that which is disagreeable and uneasy. It is agreeable and pleasing, to avoid what is disagreeable and displeasing, and to have uneasiness removed. So that here is included what Mr. Locke supposes determines the Will. For when he speaks of "uneasiness," as determining the Will, he must be understood as supposing that the end or aim which governs in the volition or act of preference, is the avoiding or the removal of that uneasiness; and that is the same thing as choosing and seeking what is more easy and agreeable.

2. When I say, that the Will is as the greatest apparent good, or, (as I have explained it,) that volition has always for its object the thing which appears most agreeable; it must be carefully observed, to avoid confusion and needless objection, that I speak of the *direct* and *immediate* object of the act of volition; and not some object to which the act of Will has only an indirect and remote respect. Many acts of volition have some remote relation to an object, that is different from the thing most immediately willed and chosen. Thus, when a drunkard has his liquor before him, and he has to choose whether to drink it, or no; the immediate objects, about which his present volition is conversant, and between which his choice now decides, are his own *acts*, in drinking the liquor, or letting it alone; and this will certainly be done according to what, in the present view of his mind, taken in the whole of it, is most agreeable to him. If he chooses to drink it, and not to let it alone; then this action, as it stands in the view of his mind, with all that belongs to its appearance there, is more agreeable and pleasing than letting it alone.

But the objects to which this act of volition may relate more remotely, and between which his choice may determine more indirectly, are the present pleasure the man expects by drinking, and the future misery which he judges will be the consequence of it: he may judge that this future misery, when it comes, will be more disagreeable and unpleasant, than refraining from drinking now would be. But these two things are not the proper objects that the act of volition spoken of is next conversant about. For the act of Will spoken of, is concerning present drinking, or forbearing to drink. If he wills to drink, then *drinking* is the proper object of the act of his Will; and drinking, on some account or other, now appears most agreeable to him, and suits him best. If he chooses to refrain, then *refraining* is the immediate object of his Will, and is most pleasing to him. If in the choice he makes in the case, he prefers a present pleasure to a future advantage, which he judges will be greater when it comes; then a lesser present pleasure appears more agreeable to him than a greater advantage at a distance. If on the contrary a future advantage is preferred, then that appears most agreeable, and suits him best. And so still, the present volition is, as the greatest apparent good at present is.

I have rather chosen to express myself thus, "that the Will always is as the greatest apparent good," or "as what appears most agreeable," than to say "that the Will *is determined by* the greatest apparent good," or "by what seems most agreeable;" because an appearing most agreeable to the mind, and the mind's preferring, seem scarcely distinct. If strict propriety of speech be insisted on, it may more properly be said, that the *voluntary action*, which is the immediate *consequence* of the mind's choice, is *determined* by that which appears most agreeable, than the choice itself; but that *volition* itself is always determined by that in or about the mind's view of the object, which *causes it to appear* most agreeable. I say, "in or about the mind's view of the object;" because what has influence to render an object in view agreeable, is not only what appears *in* the object viewed, but also *the manner* of the view and *the state and circumstances* of the mind that views. Particularly to enumerate all things pertaining to the mind's view of the objects of volition, which have influence in their appearing agreeable to the mind, would be a matter of no small difficulty, and might require a treatise by itself, and is not necessary to my present purpose. I shall therefore only mention some things in general.

I. One thing that makes an object proposed to choice agreeable, is the *apparent nature* and *circumstances of the*

* This appears to be the author's meaning, in order to preserve a consistency with his professed sentiment of divine influence. He believed that a real Christian's mind is born of the Spirit; and that such a state of mind induces one choice rather than another. But he could not maintain that *divine influence*, which is a *subjective cause* of one volition rather than another, must be "in the view or apprehension of the understanding." For "the wind bloweth where it listeth, and thou hearest the sound thereof, but canst not tell whence it cometh, and whither it goeth: so is every one that is born of the Spirit." Beside, the most proper acceptation of the term "motive" seems to plead in favour of the restriction suggested in the text by the word "objectively;" and the use of this distinction may appear more fully hereafter.—W.

object. And there are various things of this sort, that have influence in rendering the object more or less agreeable; as,

1. That which appears *in* the object, rendering it *beautiful* and pleasant, or *deformed* and irksome to the mind; viewing it as it is *in itself*.

2. The apparent degree of pleasure or trouble *attending* the object, or the *consequence* of it. Such concomitants and consequences being viewed as circumstances of the object, are to be considered as belonging to it; and as it were parts of it, as it stands in the mind's view a proposed object of choice.

3. The *apparent state* of the pleasure or trouble that appears, with respect to *distance of time;* being either nearer or farther off. It is a thing in itself agreeable to the mind, to have pleasure speedily; and disagreeable, to have it delayed: so that if there be two equal degrees of pleasure set in the mind's view, and all other things are equal, but one is beheld as near, and the other afar off; the nearer will appear most agreeable, and so will be chosen. Because, though the agreeableness of the objects be exactly equal, as viewed in themselves, yet not as viewed in their circumstances; one of them having the additional agreeableness of the circumstance of nearness.

II. Another thing that contributes to the agreeableness of an object of choice, as it stands in the mind's view, is the *manner of the view*. If the object be something which appears connected with future pleasure, not only will the degree of apparent pleasure have influence, but also the manner of the view, especially in two respects.

1. With respect to the degree of *assent*, with which the mind judges the pleasure to be future. Because it is more agreeable to have a *certain* happiness, than an *uncertain* one; and a pleasure viewed as more probable, all other things being equal, is more agreeable to the mind, than that which is viewed as less probable.

2. With respect to the degree of the *idea* or apprehension of the future pleasure. With regard to things which are the subject of our thoughts, either past, present, or future, we have much more of an idea or apprehension of some things than others; that is, our idea is much more clear, lively, and strong. Thus the ideas we have of sensible things by immediate sensation, are usually much more lively than those we have by mere imagination, or by contemplation of them when absent. My idea of the sun when I look upon it is more vivid, than when I only think of it. Our idea of the sweet relish of a delicious fruit is usually stronger when we taste it, than when we only imagine it. And sometimes, the idea we have of things by contemplation, are much stronger and clearer, than at other times. Thus, a man at one time has a much stronger idea of the pleasure which is to be enjoyed in eating some sort of food that he loves, than at another. Now the strength of the idea or the sense that men have of future good or evil, is one thing that has great influence on their minds to excite volition. When two kinds of future pleasure are presented for choice, though both are supposed exactly equal by the judgment, and both equally certain, yet of one the mind has a far more lively sense, than of the other; this last has the greatest advantage by far to affect and attract the mind, and move the Will. It is now more agreeable to the mind, to take the pleasure of which it has a strong and lively sense, than that of which it has only a faint idea. The view of the former is attended with the strongest appetite, and the greatest uneasiness attends the want of it; and it is agreeable to the mind to have uneasiness removed, and its appetite gratified. And if several future enjoyments are presented together, as competitors for the choice of the mind, some of them judged to be greater, and others less; the mind also having a more lively idea of the good of some, and of others a less; and some are viewed as of greater certainty or probability than others; and those enjoyments that appear most agreeable in one of these respects, appear least so in others: in this case, all other things being equal, the agreeableness of a proposed object of choice will be in a degree some way compounded of the degree of good supposed by the judgment, the degree of apparent probability or certainty of that good, and the degree of liveliness of the idea the mind has of that good; because all together concur to constitute the degree in which the object appears at present agreeable; and accordingly will volition be determined.

I might further observe, that the *state of the mind* which views a proposed object of choice, is another thing that contributes to the agreeableness or disagreeableness of that object; the particular temper which the mind has by nature, or that has been introduced and established by education, example, custom, or some other means; or the frame or state that the mind is in on a particular occasion. That object which appears agreeable to one, does not so to another. And the same object does not always appear alike agreeable to the same person, at different times. It is most agreeable to some men, to follow their reason; and to others, to follow their appetites: to some men, it is more agreeable to deny a vicious inclination, than to gratify it; others it suits best to gratify the vilest appetites. It is more disagreeable to some men than others, to counteract a former resolution. In these respects, and many others which might be mentioned, different things will be most agreeable to different persons; and not only so, but to the same persons at different times.

But possibly it is needless to mention the "state of the mind," as a ground of the agreeableness of objects distinct from the other two mentioned before; *viz.* The apparent *nature and circumstances* of the objects viewed, and the *manner* of the view. Perhaps, if we strictly consider the matter, the different temper and state of the mind makes no alteration as to the agreeableness of objects, any other way, than as it makes the objects themselves appear differently *beautiful* or *deformed*, having apparent pleasure or pain attending them; and, as it occasions the *manner* of the view to be different, causes the idea of beauty or deformity, pleasure or uneasiness, to be more or less lively.

However, I think so much is certain, that volition, in no one instance that can be mentioned, is otherwise than the greatest apparent good is, in the manner which has been explained. The choice of the mind never departs from that which, at the time, and with respect to the direct and immediate objects of decision, appears most agreeable and pleasing, all things considered. If the immediate objects of the Will are a man's own actions, then those actions which appear most agreeable to him he wills. If it be now most agreeable to him, all things considered, to walk, then he now wills to walk. If it be now, upon the whole of what at present appears to him, most agreeable to speak, then he chooses to speak; if it suits him best to keep silence, then he chooses to keep silence. There is scarcely a plainer and more universal dictate of the sense and experience of mankind, than that, when men act voluntarily, and do what they please, then they do what suits them best, or what is most *agreeable to them*. To say, that they do what *pleases* them, but yet not what is *agreeable* to them, is the same thing as to say, they do what they please, but do not act their pleasure; and that is to say, that they do what they please, and yet do not what they please.

It appears from these things, that in some sense, *the Will always follows the last dictate of the understanding*. But then the *understanding* must be taken in a large sense, as including the whole faculty of perception or apprehension, and not merely what is called *reason* or *judgment*. If by the dictate of the understanding is meant what reason declares to be best, or most for the person's happiness, taking in the whole of its duration, it is not true, that the Will always follows the last dictate of the understanding. Such a dictate of reason is quite a different matter from things appearing now most *agreeable*, all things being put together which pertain to the mind's present perceptions in any respect: although that dictate of reason, when it takes place, has concern in the compound influence which moves the Will; and should be considered in estimating the degree of that appearance of good which the Will always follows; either as having its influence added to other things, or subducted from them. When such dictate of reason concurs with other things, then its weight is added to them, as put into the same scale; but when it is against them, it is as a weight in the opposite scale, resisting the influence of other things: yet its resistance is often overcome by their greater weight, and so the act of the Will is determined in opposition to it.

These things may serve, I hope, in some measure, to illustrate and confirm the position laid down in the beginning of this section, viz. "That the Will is always determined by the strongest motive," or by that view of the mind which has the greatest degree of *previous* tendency to excite volition. But whether I have been so happy as rightly to explain the thing wherein consists the strength of motives, or not, yet my failing in this will not overthrow the position itself; which carries much of its own evidence with it, and is a point of chief importance to the purpose of the ensuing discourse: And the truth of it, I hope, will appear with great clearness, before I have finished what I have to say on the subject of human liberty.

SECT. III.

Concerning the meaning of the terms, Necessity, Impossibility, Inability, &c. and of Contingence.

The words *necessary, impossible, &c.* are abundantly used in controversies about Free-Will and Moral Agency; and therefore the sense in which they are used should be clearly understood.

Here I might say, that a thing is then said to be *necessary*, when it *must* be, and cannot be otherwise. But this would not properly be a definition of Necessity, any more than if I explained the word *must*, by the phrase, there being a Necessity. The words *must, can*, and *cannot*, need explication as much as the words *necessary*, and *impossible*; excepting that the former are words that in earliest life we more commonly use.

The word *necessary*, as used in common speech, is a relative term; and relates to some supposed opposition made to the existence of a thing, which opposition is overcome, or proves insufficient to hinder or alter it. That is necessary, in the original and proper sense of the word, which is, or will be, notwithstanding all supposable opposition. To say, that a thing is necessary, is the same thing as to say, that it is impossible it should not be. But the word *impossible* is manifestly a relative term, and has reference to supposed power exerted to bring a thing to pass, which is insufficient for the effect; as the word *unable* is relative, and has relation to ability, or endeavour, which is insufficient. Also the word *irresistible* is relative, and has always reference to resistance which is made, or may be made, to some force or power tending to an effect, and is insufficient to withstand the power, or hinder the effect. The common notion of Necessity and Impossibility implies something that frustrates endeavour or desire.

Here several things are to be noted.

1. Things are said to be necessary in *general*, which are or will be notwithstanding any supposable opposition from whatever quarter. But things are said to be necessary *to us*, which are or will be notwithstanding all opposition supposable in the case *from us*. The same may be observed of the word *impossible*, and other such like terms.

2. These terms *necessary, impossible, irresistible, &c.* more especially belong to controversies about liberty and moral agency, as used in the latter of the two senses now mentioned, viz. as necessary or impossible *to us*, and with relation to any supposable opposition or endeavour *of ours*.

3. As the word *Necessity*, in its vulgar and common use, is relative, and has always reference to some supposable insufficient opposition; so when we speak of any thing as necessary *to us*, it is with relation to some supposable opposition of *our Wills*, or some voluntary exertion or effort of ours to the contrary. For we do not properly make opposition to an event, any otherwise than as we *voluntarily* oppose it. Things are said to be what must be, or *necessarily* are, *as to us*, when they are, or will be, though we desire or endeavour the contrary, or try to prevent or remove their existence: but such opposition of ours always either consists in, or implies, opposition of our wills.

It is manifest that all such like words and phrases, as vulgarly used, are understood in this manner. A thing is said to be *necessary*, when we cannot help it, let us do what we will. So any thing is said to be *impossible* to us, when we would do it, or would have it brought to pass, and endeavour it; or at least may be supposed to desire and seek it; but all our desires and endeavours are, or would be, vain. And that is said to be *irresistible*, which overcomes all our opposition, resistance, and endeavour to the contrary. And we are said to be *unable* to do a thing, when our supposable desires and endeavours are insufficient.

We are accustomed, in the common use of language, thus to apply and understand these phrases: we grow up with such a habit; which, by the daily use of these terms from our childhood, becomes fixed and settled; so that the idea of a relation to a supposed will, desire, and endeavour of ours, is strongly connected with these terms, whenever we hear the words used. Such ideas, and these words, are so associated, that they unavoidably go together; one suggests the other, and never can be easily separated as long as we live. And though we use the words, as terms of art, in another sense, yet, unless we are exceedingly circumspect, we shall insensibly slide into the vulgar use of them, and so apply the words in a very inconsistent manner, which will deceive and confound us in our reasonings and discourses, even when we pretend to use them as terms of art.

4. It follows from what has been observed, that when these terms *necessary, impossible, irresistible, unable, &c.* are used in cases wherein no insufficient will is supposed, or can be supposed, but the very nature of the supposed case itself excludes any opposition, will, or endeavour, they are then not used in their proper signification. The reason is manifest; in such cases we cannot use the words with reference to a supposable opposition, will, or endeavour. And therefore if any man uses these terms in such cases, he either uses them nonsensically, or in some new sense, diverse from their original and proper meaning. As for instance; if any one should affirm after this manner, That it is *necessary* for a man, or what *must* be, that he should choose virtue rather than vice, during the time that he prefers virtue to vice; and that it is a thing impossible and irresistible, that it should be otherwise than that he should have this choice, so long as this choice continues; such a one would use the terms *must, irresistible, &c.* with either perfect insignificance, or in some new sense, diverse from their common use; which is with reference, as has been observed, to supposable opposition, unwillingness, and resistance; whereas, here, the very supposition excludes and denies any such thing: for the case supposed is that of being willing, and choosing.

5. It appears from what has been said, that these terms *necessary, impossible, &c.* are often used by philosophers and metaphysicians in a sense quite diverse from their common and original signification; for they apply them to many cases in which no opposition is supposable. Thus they use them with respect to God's existence before the creation of the world, when there was no other being; with regard to many of the dispositions and acts of the divine Being, such as his loving himself, his loving righteousness, hating sin, &c. So they apply them to many cases of the inclinations and actions of created intelligent beings wherein all opposition of the Will is excluded in the very supposition of the case.

Metaphysical or *philosophical* Necessity is nothing different from their certainty. I speak not now of the certainty of knowledge, but the certainty that is in things themselves, which is the foundation of the certainty of the knowledge, or that wherein lies the ground of the infallibility of the proposition which affirms them.

What is sometimes given as the definition of philosophical Necessity, namely, "*That by which a thing cannot but be*," or "*whereby it cannot be otherwise*," fails of being a proper explanation of it, on two accounts: *First*, the words *can*, or *cannot*, need explanation as much as the word *Necessity*; and the former may as well be explained by the latter, as the latter by the former. Thus, if any one asked us what we mean, when we say, a thing *cannot but be*, we might explain ourselves by saying, it must necessarily be so; as well as explain Necessity, by saying, it is that by which a thing cannot but be. And *Secondly*, this definition is liable to the fore-mentioned great inconvenience; the words *cannot*, or *unable*, are properly relative, and have relation to power exerted, or that may be exerted, in order to the thing spoken of; to which as I have now observed, the word *Necessity*, as used by philosophers, has no reference.

Philosophical Necessity is really nothing else than the FULL AND FIXED CONNEXION BETWEEN THE THINGS SIGNIFIED BY THE SUBJECT AND PREDICATE OF A PROPOSITION, which affirms something to be true. When there is such a connexion, then the thing affirmed in the proposition is necessary, in a philosophical sense; whether any opposition or contrary effort be supposed, or no. When the subject and predicate of the proposition, which affirms the existence of any thing, either substance, quality, act, or circumstance, have a full and CERTAIN CONNEXION, then the existence or being of that thing is said to be *necessary* in a metaphysical sense. And in this sense I use the word *necessity*, in the following discourse, when I endeavour to prove *that necessity is not inconsistent with liberty*.

The subject and predicate of a proposition, which affirms existence of something, may have a full, fixed, and certain connexion several ways.

(1.) They may have a full and perfect connexion *in and of themselves;* because it may imply a contradiction, or gross absurdity, to suppose them not connected. Thus many things are necessary in their own nature. So the eternal existence of being generally considered, is necessary *in itself:* because it would be in itself the greatest absurdity, to deny the existence of being in general, or to say there was absolute and universal nothing; and is as it were the sum of all contradictions; as might be shown, if this were a proper place for it. So God's infinity and other attributes are necessary. So it is necessary *in its own nature*, that two and two should be four; and it is necessary, that all right lines drawn from the centre of a circle to the circumference should be equal. It is necessary, fit, and suitable, that men should do to others, as they would that they should do to them. So innumerable metaphysical and mathematical truths are necessary *in themselves:* the subject and predicate of the proposition which affirms them, are perfectly connected *of themselves*.

(2.) The connexion of the subject and predicate of a proposition, which affirms the existence of something, may be fixed and made certain, because the existence of that thing is *already* come to pass; and either now is, or has been; and so has, as it were, made sure of existence. And therefore, the proposition which affirms present and past existence of it, may by this means be made certain, and necessarily and unalterably true; the past event has fixed and decided the matter, as to its existence; and has made it impossible but that existence should be truly predicated of it. Thus the existence of whatever is already come to pass, is now become necessary; it is become impossible it should be otherwise than true, that such a thing has been.

(3.) The subject and predicate of a proposition which affirms something to be, may have a real and certain connexion *consequentially;* and so the existence of the thing may be consequentially necessary; as it may be surely and firmly *connected* with something else, that is necessary in one of the former respects. As it is either fully and thoroughly connected with that which is absolutely necessary in its own nature, or with something which has already received and made sure of existence. This Necessity lies *in*, or may be explained *by*, the connexion of two or more propositions one with another.——Things which are *perfectly connected* with other things that are necessary, are necessary themselves, by a Necessity of consequence.

And here it may be observed, that all things which are future, or which will hereafter begin to be, which can be said to be necessary, are necessary only in this last way. Their existence is not necessary *in itself;* for if so, they always would have existed. Nor is their existence become necessary by being *already* come to pass. Therefore, the only way that any thing that is to come to pass hereafter, is or can be necessary, is by a *connexion* with something that is necessary in its own nature, or something that already is, or has been; so that the one being supposed, the other certainly follows.—And this also is the only way that all things past, excepting those which were from eternity, could be necessary *before they come to pass;* and therefore the only way in which any effect or event, or any thing whatsoever that ever has had or will have a beginning, has come into being necessarily, or will hereafter necessarily exist. And therefore *this* is the Necessity which especially belongs to controversies about the acts of the will.

It may be of some use in these controversies, further to observe concerning *metaphysical* Necessity, that (agreeable to the distinction before observed of Necessity, as *vulgarly* understood) things that exist may be said to be necessary, either with a *general* or *particular* Necessity. The existence of a thing may be said to be necessary with a *general* Necessity, when, all things considered, there is a foundation for the certainty of their existence; or when in the most general and universal view of things, the subject and predicate of the proposition, which affirms its existence, would appear with an infallible connexion.

An event, or the existence of a thing, may be said to be necessary with a *particular* Necessity, when nothing that can be taken into consideration, in or about a person, thing, or time, alters the case at all, as to the certainty of an event, or the existence of a thing; or can be of any account at all, in determining the infallibility of the connexion of the subject and predicate in the proposition which affirms the existence of the thing; so that it is all one, as to that person, or thing, at least, at that time, as if the existence were necessary with a Necessity that is most *universal* and *absolute*. Thus there are many things that happen to particular persons, in the existence of which no will of theirs has any concern, at least, at that time; which, whether they are necessary or not, with regard to things in general, yet are necessary to them, and with regard to any volition of theirs at that time; as they prevent all acts of the will about the affair.——I shall have occasion to apply this observation to particular instances in the following discourse.—Whether the same things that are necessary with a *particular* Necessity, be not also necessary with a *general* Necessity, may be a matter of future consideration. Let that be as it will, it alters not the case, as to the use of this distinction of the kinds of Necessity.

These things may be sufficient for the explaining of the terms *necessary* and *Necessity*, as terms of art, and as often used by metaphysicians, and controversial writers in divinity, in a sense diverse from, and more extensive than, their original meaning, in common language, which was before explained.

What has been said to show the meaning of the terms *necessary* and *necessity*, may be sufficient for the explaining of the opposite terms, *impossible* and *impossibility*. For there is no difference, but only the latter are negative, and the former positive. *Impossibility* is the same as *negative Necessity*, or a Necessity that a thing should not be. And it is used as a term of art in a like diversity from the original and vulgar meaning, with Necessity.

The same may be observed concerning the words *unable* and *Inability*. It has been observed, that these terms, in their original and common use, have relation to will and endeavour, as supposable in the case, and as insufficient for the bringing to pass the thing willed and endeavoured. But as these terms are often used by philosophers and divines, especially writers on controversies about Free Will, they are used in a quite different and far more extensive sense, and are applied to many cases wherein no will or endeavour for the bringing of the thing to pass is or can be supposed.

As the words *necessary, impossible, unable, &c.* are used by polemic writers, in a sense diverse from their common signification, the like has happened to the term *contingent*. Any thing is said to be contingent, or to come to pass by chance or accident, in the original meaning of such words, when its connexion with its causes or antecedents, according to the established course of things, is *not discerned;* and so is what we have no means of foreseeing. And especially is any thing said to be contingent, or accidental, with regard to us, when it comes to pass without our foreknowledge, and besides our design and scope.

But the word *contingent* is abundantly used in a very different sense; not for that whose connexion with the series of things we cannot discern, so as to foresee the event, but for something which has absolutely no previous ground or reason, with which its existence has any fixed and certain connexion.

SECT. IV.

Of the distinction of natural and moral Necessity, and Inability.

THAT Necessity which has been explained, consisting in an infallible connexion of the things signified by the subject and predicate of a proposition, as intelligent beings are the subjects of it, is distinguished into *moral* and *natural* Necessity.

I shall not now stand to inquire whether this distinction be a proper and perfect distinction; but shall only explain how these two sorts of Necessity are understood, as the terms are sometimes used, and as they are used in the following discourse.

The phrase, *moral Necessity*, is used variously: sometimes it is used for a Necessity of moral obligation. So we say, a man is under Necessity, when he is under bonds of *duty* and conscience, from which he cannot be discharged. Again, the word *Necessity* is often used for great obligation in point of *interest*. Sometimes by moral Necessity is meant that apparent connexion of things, which is the ground of *moral evidence;* and so is distinguished from *absolute Necessity*, or that sure connexion of things, that is a foundation for *infallible certainty*. In this sense, moral Necessity signifies much the same as that high degree of *probability*, which is ordinarily sufficient to satisfy mankind, in their conduct and behaviour in the world, as they would consult their own safety and interest, and treat others properly as members of society. And sometimes by moral Necessity is meant that Necessity of connexion and *consequence*, which arises from such *moral causes*, as the strength of inclination, or motives, and the connexion which there is in many cases between these and such certain volitions and actions. And it is in *this* sense, that I use the phrase, *moral necessity*, in the following discourse.

By *natural Necessity*, as applied to men, I mean such Necessity as men are under through the force of natural causes; as distinguished from what are called moral causes, such as habits and dispositions of the heart, and moral motives and inducements. Thus men, placed in certain circumstances, are the subjects of particular sensations by Necessity: they feel pain when their bodies are wounded; they see the objects presented before them in a clear light, when their eyes are opened: so they assent to the truth of certain propositions, as soon as the terms are understood; as that two and two make four, that black is not white, that two parallel lines can never cross one another; so by a natural Necessity men's bodies move downwards, when there is nothing to support them.

But here several things may be noted concerning these two kinds of Necessity.

1. Moral Necessity may be as *absolute* as natural Necessity. That is, the effect may be as perfectly connected with its moral cause, as a natural, necessary effect is with its natural cause. Whether the Will in every case is necessarily determined by the strongest motive, or whether the Will ever makes any resistance to such a motive, or can ever oppose the strongest present inclination, or not; if that matter should be controverted, yet I suppose none will deny, but that, in some cases, a previous bias and inclination, or the motive presented, may be so powerful, that the act of the Will may be certainly and indissolubly connected therewith. When motives or previous bias are very strong, all will allow that there is some *difficulty* in going against them. And if they were yet stronger, the difficulty would be still greater. And therefore, if more were still added to their strength, to a certain degree, it would make the difficulty so great, that it would be wholly *impossible* to surmount it; for this plain reason, because whatever power men may be supposed to have to surmount difficulties, yet that power is not infinite; and so goes not beyond certain limits. If a man can surmount ten degrees of difficulty of this kind with twenty degrees of strength, because the degrees of strength are beyond the degrees of difficulty; yet if the difficulty be increased to thirty, or an hundred, or a thousand degrees, and his strength not also increased, his strength will be wholly insufficient to surmount the difficulty. As therefore it must be allowed, that there may be such a thing as a *sure* and *perfect* connexion between moral causes and effects; so this only is what I call by the name of *moral Necessity.*

2. When I use this distinction of *moral* and *natural Necessity,* I would not be understood to suppose, that if any thing come to pass by the former kind of Necessity, the *nature* of things is not concerned in it, as well as in the latter. I do not mean to determine, that when a *moral* habit or motive is so strong, that the act of the Will infallibly follows, this is not owing to the *nature of things.* But *natural* and *moral* are the terms by which these two kinds of Necessity have usually been called; and they must be distinguished by some names, for there is a difference between them, that is very important in its consequences. This difference, however, does not lie so much in the nature of the *connexion,* as in the two terms *connected.* The cause with which the effect is connected, is of a particular kind; *viz.* that which is of a moral nature; either some previous habitual disposition, or some motive exhibited to the understanding. And the effect is also of a particular kind; being likewise of a moral nature; consisting in some inclination or volition of the soul, or voluntary action.

I suppose, that Necessity which is called *natural* in distinction from *moral* Necessity, is so called, because *mere nature,* as the word is vulgarly used, is concerned, without any thing of *choice.* The word *nature* is often used in opposition to *choice;* not because nature has indeed never any hand in our choice; but, probably, because we first get our notion of nature from that obvious course of events, which we observe in many things where our choice has no concern; and especially in the material world; which, in very many parts of it, we easily perceive to be in a settled course; the stated order, and manner of succession, being very apparent. But where we do not readily discern the rule and connexion, (though there be a connexion, according to an established law, truly taking place,) we signify the manner of event by some other name. Even in many things which are seen in the material and inanimate world, which do not obviously come to pass according to any settled course, men do not call the manner of the event by the name of *nature,* but by such names as *accident, chance, contingence, &c.* So men make a distinction between nature and choice; as if they were completely and universally distinct. Whereas, I suppose none will deny but that choice, *in many cases,* arises from nature, as truly as other events. But the connexion between acts of choice, and their causes, according to established laws, is not so obvious. And we observe that choice is, as it were, a new principle of motion and action, different from that established order of things which is most obvious, and seen especially in corporeal things. The choice also often interposes, interrupts, and alters the chain of events in these external objects, and causes them to proceed otherwise than they would do, if let alone. Hence it is spoken of as if it were a principle of motion entirely distinct from nature, and properly set in opposition to it. Names being commonly given to things, according to what is most obvious, and is suggested by what appears to the senses without reflection and research.

3. It must be observed, that in what has been explained, as signified by the name of *moral Necessity,* the word *Necessity* is not used according to the original design and meaning of the word: for, as was observed before, such terms, *necessary, impossible, irresistible, &c.* in common speech, and their most proper sense, are always relative; having reference to some supposable voluntary opposition or endeavour, that is insufficient. But no such opposition, or contrary will and endeavour, is supposable in the case of moral Necessity; which is a certainty of the inclination and will itself; which does not admit of the supposition of a will to oppose and resist it. For it is absurd, to suppose the same individual will to oppose itself, in its present act; or the present choice to be opposite to and resisting present choice: as absurd as it is to talk of two contrary motions, in the same moving body, at the same time.—

And therefore the very case supposed never admits of any trial, whether an opposing or resisting will can overcome this Necessity.

What has been said of natural and moral Necessity, may serve to explain what is intended by natural and moral *Inability.* We are said to be *naturally* unable to do a thing, when we cannot do it if we will, because what is most commonly called *nature* does not allow of it, or because of some impeding defect or obstacle that is extrinsic to the Will; either in the faculty of understanding, constitution of body, or external objects. *Moral* Inability consists not in any of these things; but either in the want of inclination; or the strength of a contrary inclination; or the want of sufficient motives in view, to induce and excite the act of the Will, or the strength of apparent motives to the contrary. Or both these may be resolved into one; and it may be said in one word, that moral Inability consists in the opposition or want of inclination. For when a person is unable to will or choose such a thing, through a defect of motives, or prevalence of contrary motives, it is the same thing as his being unable through the want of an inclination, or the prevalence of a contrary inclination, in such circumstances, and under the influence of such views.

To give some instances of this *moral Inability.*—A woman of great honour and chastity may have a moral Inability to prostitute herself to her slave. A child of great love and duty to his parents, may be thus unable to kill his father. A very lascivious man, in case of certain opportunities and temptations, and in the absence of such and such restraints, may be unable to forbear gratifying his lust. A drunkard, under such and such circumstances, may be unable to forbear taking strong drink. A very malicious man may be unable to exert benevolent acts to an enemy, or to desire his prosperity; yea, some may be so under the power of a vile disposition, that they may be unable to love those who are most worthy of their esteem and affection. A strong habit of virtue, and a great degree of holiness, may cause a moral Inability to love wickedness in general, and may render a man unable to take complacence in wicked persons or things; or to choose a wicked in preference to a virtuous life. And on the other hand, a great degree of habitual wickedness may lay a man under an Inability to love and choose holiness; and render him utterly unable to love an infinitely holy Being, or to choose and cleave to him as his chief good.

Here it may be of use to observe this distinction of moral Inability, viz. of that which is *general and habitual,* and that which is *particular and occasional.* By a *general and habitual* moral Inability, I mean an Inability in the heart to all exercises or acts of will of that kind, through a fixed and habitual inclination, or an habitual and stated defect, or want of a certain kind of inclination. Thus a very ill-natured man may be unable to exert such acts of benevolence, as another, who is full of good nature, commonly exerts; and a man whose heart is habitually void of gratitude, may be unable to exert grateful acts, through that stated defect of a grateful inclination. By *particular and occasional* moral Inability, I mean an Inability of the will or heart to a particular act, through the strength or defect of present motives, or of inducements presented to the view of the understanding, *on this occasion.*—If it be so, that the Will is always determined by the strongest motive, then it must always have an Inability, in this latter sense, to act otherwise than it does; it not being possible, in any case, that the Will should, at present, go against the motive which has now, all things considered, the greatest advantage to induce it.—The former of these kinds of moral Inability is most commonly called by the name of *Inability;* because the word, in its most proper and original signification, has respect to some *stated defect.* And this especially obtains the name of *Inability* also upon another account:—because, as before observed, the word Inability, in its original and most common use, is a relative term; and has respect to will and endeavour, as supposable in the case, and as insufficient to bring to pass the thing desired and endeavoured. Now there may be more of an appearance and shadow of this, with respect to the acts which arise from a fixed and strong habit, than others that arise only from transient occasions and causes. Indeed will and endeavour against, or diverse from *present* acts of the Will are in no case supposable, whether those acts be occasional or habitual; for that would be to suppose the Will, at present, to be otherwise than, at present, it is. But yet there may be will and endeavour against *future* acts of the Will, or volitions that are likely to take place, as viewed at a distance. It is no contradiction, to suppose that the acts of the Will at one time, may be against the acts of the Will at another time; and there may be desires and endeavours to prevent or excite future acts of the Will; but such desires and endeavours are, in many cases, rendered insufficient and vain, through fixedness of habit: when the occasion returns, the strength of habit overcomes and baffles all such opposition. In this respect, a man may be in miserable slavery and bondage to a strong habit. But it may be comparatively easy to make an alteration, with respect to such future acts, as are only occasional and transient; because the occasion or transient cause, if foreseen, may often easily be prevented or avoided. On this account, the moral Inability that attends fixed habits, especially obtains the name of *Inability.* And then, as the Will may remotely and indirectly resist itself, and do it in vain, in the case of strong habits; so reason may resist present acts of the Will, and its resistance be insufficient; and this is more commonly the case also, when the acts arise from strong habit.

But it must be observed concerning moral Inability, in each kind of it, that the word *Inability* is used in a sense very diverse from its original import. The word signifies only a natural Inability, in the proper use of it; and is applied to such cases only wherein a present will or inclination to the thing, with respect to which a person is said to be unable, is supposable. It cannot be truly said, according to the ordinary use of language, that a malicious man, let him be never so malicious, cannot hold his hand from striking, or that he is not able to show his neighbour kindness; or that a drunkard, let his appetite be never so strong, cannot keep the cup from his mouth. In the strictest propriety of speech, a man has a thing in his power, if he has it in his choice, or at his election: and a man cannot be truly said to be unable to do a thing, when he can do it if he will. It is improperly said, that a person cannot perform those external actions, which are dependent on the act of the Will, and which would be easily performed, if the act of the Will were present. And if it be improperly said, that he cannot perform those external voluntary actions, which depend on the Will, it is in some respect more improperly said, that he is unable to exert the acts of the Will themselves; because it is more evidently false, with respect to these, that he cannot if he will: for to say so, is a downright contradiction; it is to say, he *cannot* will, if he *does* will. And in this case, not only is it true, that it is easy for a man to do the thing if he will, but the very willing is the doing; when once he has willed, the thing is performed; and nothing else remains to be done. Therefore, in these things, to ascribe a non-performance to the want of power or ability, is not just; because the thing wanting is not a being *able,* but a being *willing.* There are faculties of mind, and a capacity of nature, and every thing else, sufficient, but a disposition: nothing is wanting but a will.

SECT. V.

Concerning the notion of Liberty, and of moral Agency.

THE plain and obvious meaning of the words *Freedom* and *Liberty,* in common speech, is *The power, opportunity, or advantage, that any one has, to do as he pleases.* Or in other words, his being free from hinderance or impediment in the way of doing, or conducting in any respect, as he wills.*—And the contrary to Liberty, whatever name we call that by, is a person's being hindered or unable to conduct as he will, or being necessitated to do otherwise.

If this which I have mentioned be the meaning of the

* I say not only *doing,* but *conducting;* because a voluntary forbearing to do, sitting still, keeping silence, &c. are instances of persons' *conduct,* about which Liberty is exercised; though they are not so properly called *doing.*

word Liberty, in the ordinary use of language; as I trust that none that has ever learned to talk, and is unprejudiced, will deny; then it will follow, that in propriety of speech, neither Liberty, nor its contrary, can properly be ascribed to any being or thing, but that which has such a faculty, power or property, as is called Will. For that which is possessed of no *will*, cannot have any *power* or *opportunity* of doing *according to its will*, nor be necessitated to act *contrary to its will*, nor be restrained from acting agreeably to it. And therefore to talk of Liberty, or the contrary, as belonging to the *very Will itself*, is not to speak good sense; if we judge of sense, and nonsense, by the original and proper signification of words.—For the *Will itself* is not an Agent that *has a will:* the power of choosing, itself, has not a power of choosing. That which has the power of volition is the man, or the soul, and not the power of volition itself. And he that has the Liberty of doing according to his will, is the Agent who is possessed of the Will; and not the Will which he is possessed of. We say with propriety, that a bird let loose has power and liberty to fly; but not that the bird's power of flying has a power and Liberty of flying. To be free is the property of an Agent, who is possessed of powers and faculties, as much as to be cunning, valiant, bountiful, or zealous. But these qualities are the properties of persons; and not the properties of properties.

There are two things contrary to what is called Liberty in common speech. One is *constraint;* otherwise called *force, compulsion,* and *coaction;* which is a person's being necessitated to do a thing *contrary* to his will. The other is *restraint;* which is, his being hindered, and not having power to do *according* to his will. But that which has no will, cannot be the subject of these things.—I need say the less on this head, Mr. Locke having set the same thing forth, with so great clearness, in his *Essay on the Human Understanding*.

But one thing more I would observe concerning what is vulgarly called *Liberty;* namely, that power and opportunity for one to do and conduct as he will, or according to his choice, is all that is meant by it; without taking into the meaning of the word, any thing of the *cause* of that choice; or at all considering how the person came to have such a volition; whether it was caused by some external motive, or internal habitual bias; whether it was determined by some internal antecedent volition, or whether it happened without a cause; whether it was necessarily connected with something foregoing, or not connected. Let the person come by his choice any how, yet, if he is able, and there is nothing in the way to hinder his pursuing and executing his will, the man is perfectly free, according to the primary and common notion of freedom.

What has been said may be sufficient to show what is meant by *Liberty*, according to the common notions of mankind, and in the usual and primary acceptation of the word: but the word, as used by *Arminians, Pelagians*, and others, who oppose the *Calvinists*, has an entirely different signification.—These several things belong to their notion of Liberty. 1. That it consists in a *self-determining power* in the Will, or a certain sovereignty the Will has over itself, and its own acts, whereby it determines its own volitions; so as not to be dependent, in its determinations, on any cause without itself, nor determined by any thing prior to its own acts. 2. *Indifference* belongs to Liberty in their notion of it, or that the mind, previous to the act of volition, be *in equilibrio*. 3. *Contingence* is another thing that belongs and is essential to it; not in the common acceptation of the word, as that has been already explained, but as opposed to all *necessity*, or any fixed and certain connexion with some previous ground or reason of its existence. They suppose the essence of Liberty so much to consist in these things, that unless the will of man be free in this sense, he has no real freedom, how much soever he may be at Liberty to act according to his will.

A *moral Agent* is a being that is capable of those actions that have a *moral* quality, and which can properly be denominated good or evil in a moral sense, virtuous or vicious, commendable or faulty. To moral Agency belongs a *moral faculty*, or sense of moral good and evil, or of such a thing as desert or worthiness, of praise or blame, reward or punishments; and a capacity which an Agent has of being influenced in his actions by moral inducements or motives, exhibited to the view of understanding and reason, to engage to a conduct agreeable to the moral faculty.

The sun is very excellent and beneficial in its action and influence on the earth, in warming and causing it to bring forth its fruit; but it is not a moral agent: its action, though good, is not virtuous or meritorious. Fire that breaks out in a city, and consumes great part of it, is very mischievous in its operation; but is not a moral Agent: what it does is not faulty or sinful, or deserving of any punishment. The brute creatures are not moral Agents: the actions of some of them are very profitable and pleasant; others are very hurtful: yet seeing they have no moral faculty, or sense of desert, and do not act from choice guided by understanding, or with a capacity of reasoning and reflecting, but only from instinct, and are not capable of being influenced by moral inducements, their actions are not properly sinful or virtuous, nor are they properly the subjects of any such moral treatment for what they do, as moral Agents are for their faults or good deeds.

Here it may be noted, that there is a circumstantial difference between the moral Agency of a *ruler* and a *subject*. I call it *circumstantial*, because it lies only in the difference of moral inducements, by which they are capable of being influenced, arising from the difference of *circumstances*. A *ruler*, acting in that capacity only, is not capable of being influenced by a moral law, and its sanctions of threatenings and promises, rewards and punishments, as the *subject* is; though both may be influenced by a knowledge of moral good and evil. And therefore the moral Agency of the Supreme Being, who acts only in the capacity of a *ruler* towards his creatures, and never as a *subject*, differs in that respect from the moral Agency of created intelligent beings. God's actions, and particularly those which he exerts as a moral governor, have moral qualifications, and are morally good in the highest degree. They are most perfectly holy and righteous; and we must conceive of Him as influenced, in the highest degree, by that which, above all others, is properly a moral inducement; *viz.* the moral good which He sees in such and such things: and therefore He is, in the most proper sense, a moral Agent, the source of all moral ability and Agency, the fountain and rule of all virtue and moral good; though by reason of his being supreme over all, it is not possible He should be under the influence of law or command, promises or threatenings, rewards or punishments, counsels or warnings. The essential qualities of a moral Agent are in God, in the greatest possible perfection; such as understanding to perceive the difference between moral good and evil; a capacity of discerning that moral worthiness and demerit, by which some things are praiseworthy, others deserving of blame and punishment; and also a capacity of choice, and choice guided by understanding, and a power of acting according to his choice or pleasure, and being capable of doing those things which are in the highest sense praiseworthy. And herein does very much consist that image of God wherein he made man, (which we read of, *Gen.* i. 26, 27, and *chap.* ix. 6.) by which God distinguished man from the beasts, *viz.* in those faculties and principles of nature, whereby He is capable of moral Agency. Herein very much consists the *natural* image of God; whereas the *spiritual* and *moral* image, wherein man was made at first, consisted in that moral excellency with which he was endowed.

PART II

WHEREIN IT IS CONSIDERED WHETHER THERE IS OR CAN BE ANY SUCH SORT OF FREEDOM OF WILL, AS THAT WHEREIN ARMINIANS PLACE THE ESSENCE OF THE LIBERTY OF ALL MORAL AGENTS; AND WHETHER ANY SUCH THING EVER WAS OR CAN BE CONCEIVED OF.

SECT. I.

Showing the manifest inconsistence of the Arminian notion of Liberty of Will, consisting in the Will's self-determining Power.

HAVING taken notice of those things which may be necessary to be observed, concerning the meaning of the principal terms and phrases made use of in controversies concerning human liberty, and particularly observed what *Liberty* is according to the common language and general apprehension of mankind, and what it is as understood and maintained by *Arminians;* I proceed to consider the *Arminian* notion of the *Freedom of the Will*, and the supposed necessity of it in order to moral agency, or in order to any one's being capable of virtue or vice, and properly the subject of command or counsel, praise or blame, promises or threatenings, rewards or punishments; or whether that which has been described, as the thing meant by Liberty in common speech, be not sufficient, and the only Liberty, which makes or can make any one a moral agent, and so properly the subject of these things. In *this Part*, I shall consider whether any such thing be possible or conceivable, as that Freedom of Will which *Arminians* insist on; and shall inquire, whether any such sort of Liberty be necessary to moral agency, &c. in the *next* part.

And first of all, I shall consider the notion of *a self-determining Power* in the Will: wherein, according to the *Arminians*, does most essentially consist the Will's freedom; and shall particularly inquire, whether it be not plainly absurd, and a manifest inconsistence, to suppose that *the Will itself determines all the free acts of the Will.*

Here I shall not insist on the great impropriety of such ways of speaking as *the Will determining itself;* because actions are to be ascribed to agents, and not properly to the powers of agents; which improper way of speaking leads to many mistakes, and much confusion, as Mr. Locke observes. But I shall suppose that the *Arminians*, when they speak of the Will's determining itself, do by the *Will* mean the *soul willing*. I shall take it for granted, that when they speak of the Will, as the determiner, they mean *the soul in the exercise of a power of willing*, or acting voluntarily. I shall suppose this to be their meaning, because nothing else can be meant, without the grossest and plainest absurdity. In all cases when we speak of the powers or principles of acting, or doing such things, we mean that the agents which have these Powers of acting, do them, in the exercise of those Powers. So when we say, valour fights courageously, we mean, the man who is under the influence of valour fights courageously. When we say, love seeks the object loved, we mean, the person loving seeks that object. When we say, the understanding discerns, we mean the soul in the exercise of that faculty. So when it is said, the will decides or determines, the meaning must be, that the person, in the exercise of a Power of willing and choosing, or the soul, acting voluntarily, determines.

Therefore, if the Will determines all its own free acts, the *soul* determines them in the exercise of a Power of willing and choosing; or, which is the same thing, it determines them of choice; it *determines* its own acts, by *choosing* its own acts. If the Will determines the Will, then choice orders and determines the choice; and acts of choice are subject to the decision, and follow the conduct of *other* acts of choice. And therefore if the Will determines all its own free acts, then every free act of choice is determined by a preceding act of choice, choosing that act. And if that preceding act of the Will be also a free act, then by these principles, in this act too, the Will is self-determined: that is, this, in like manner, is an act that the soul voluntarily chooses; or, which is the same thing, it is an act determined still by a preceding act of the Will, choosing that. Which brings us directly to a contradiction: for it supposes an act of the Will preceding the first act in the whole train, directing and determining the rest; or a free act of the Will, before the first free act of the Will. Or else we must come at last to an act of the Will, determining the consequent acts, wherein the Will is not self-determined, and so is not a free act, in this notion of freedom: but if the first act in the train, determining and fixing the rest, be not free, none of them all can be free; as is manifest at first view, but shall be demonstrated presently.

If the Will, which we find governs the members of the body, and determines their motions, does also govern itself, and determines its own actions, it doubtless determines them the same way, even by antecedent volitions. The Will determines which way the hands and feet shall move, by an act of choice: and there is no other way of the Will's determining, directing, or commanding any thing at all. Whatsoever the Will commands, it commands by an act of the Will. And if it has itself under its command, and determines itself in its own actions, it doubtless does it the same way that it determines other things which are under its command. So that if the freedom of the Will consists in this, that it has itself and its own actions under its command and direction, and its own volitions are determined by itself, it will follow, that every free volition arises from another antecedent volition, directing and commanding that: and if that *directing* volition be also free, in that also the Will is determined; that is to say, that directing volition is determined by another going before that; and so on, till we come to the first volition in the whole series: and if that first volition be free, and the Will self-determined in it, then that is determined by another volition preceding that. Which is a contradiction; because by the supposition, it can have none before it, to direct or determine it, being the first in the train. But if that first volition is not determined by any preceding act of the Will, then that act is not determined by the Will, and so is not free in the *Arminian* notion of freedom, which consists in the Will's self-determination. And if that first act of the Will which determines and fixes the subsequent acts, be not free, none of the following acts which are determined by it can be free.—If we suppose there are five acts in the train, the fifth and last determined by the fourth, and the fourth by the third, the third by the second, and the second by the first; if the first is not determined by the Will, and so not free, then none of them are truly determined by the Will: that is, that each of them are as they are, and not otherwise, is not first owing to the Will, but to the determination of the first in the series, which is not dependent on the Will, and is that which the Will has no hand in determining. And this being that which decides what the rest shall be, and determines their existence; therefore the first determination of their existence is not from the Will. The case is just the same, if instead of a chain of five acts of the Will, we should suppose a succession of ten, or an hundred, or ten thousand. If the first act be not free, being determined by something out of the Will, and this determines the next to be agreeable to itself, and that the next, and so on; none of them are free, but all originally depend on, and are determined by, some cause out of the Will; and so all freedom in the case is excluded, and no act of the Will can be free, according to this notion of freedom. If we should suppose a long chain of ten thousand links, so connected, that if the first link moves, it will move the next, and that the next; and so the whole chain must be determined to motion, and in the direction of its motion, by the motion of the first link; and that is moved by something else; in this case, though all the links, but one, are moved by other parts of the same chain, yet it appears that the motion of no one, nor the direction of its motion, is from any self-moving or self-determining power in the chain, any more than if every link were immediately moved by something that did not belong to the chain.—If the Will be not free in the first act, which causes the next, then neither is it free in the next, which is caused by that first act; for though indeed the Will caused it, yet it did not cause it freely; because the preceding act, by which it was caused, was not free. And again, if the Will be not free in the second act, so neither can it be in the third, which is caused by that; because in like manner, that third was determined by an act of the Will that was not free. And so we may go on to the next act, and from that to the next; and how long soever the succession of acts is, it is all one: if the first on which the whole chain depends, and which determines all the rest, be not a free act, the Will is not free in causing or determining any one of those acts; because the act by which it determines them all is not a free act; and therefore the Will is no more free in determining them, than if it did not cause them at all.—Thus, this *Arminian* notion of Liberty of the Will, consisting in the Will's *Self-determination*, is repugnant to itself, and shuts itself wholly out of the world.

SECT. II.

Several supposed ways of evading the foregoing reasoning, considered.

If to evade the force of what has been observed, it should be said, that when the *Arminians* speak of the Will determining its own acts, they do not mean that the Will determines them by any preceding act, or that one act of the Will determines another; but only that the faculty or power of Will, or the soul in the use of that power, determines its own volitions; and that it does it without any act going before the act determined; such an evasion would be full of the most gross absurdity.—I confess, it is an evasion of my own inventing; and I do not know but I should wrong the *Arminians*, in supposing that any of them would make use of it. But it being as good a one as I can invent, I would observe upon it a few things.

First, If the power of the will determines an act of volition, or the soul in the *use* or *exercise of that power* determines it, that is the same thing as for the soul to determine volition *by an act of will.* For an *exercise* of the power of will, and an *act* of that power, are the same thing. Therefore to say, that the power of will, or the soul in the *use* or *exercise* of that power, determines volition, without an *act* of will preceding the volition determined, is a contradiction.

Secondly, If a power of will determines the act of the Will, then a power of choosing determines it. For, as was before observed, in every act of will, there is choice, and a power of willing is a power of choosing. But if a power of choosing determines the act of volition, it determines it by choosing it. For it is most absurd to say, that a power of choosing determines one thing rather than another, without choosing any thing. But if a power of choosing determines volition by choosing it, then here is the act of volition determined by an antecedent choice, choosing that volition.

Thirdly, To say, that the faculty, or the soul, determines its own volition, but not by any act, is a contradiction. Because for the soul to *direct, decide*, or *determine* any thing, is to act; and this is supposed: for the soul is here spoken of as being a cause in this affair, doing something; or, which is the same thing, exerting itself in order to an effect, which effect is the determination of volition, or the particular kind and manner of an act of will. But certainly, this action is not the same with the effect, in order to the production of which it is exerted; but must be something prior to it.

The advocates for this notion of the freedom of the Will, speak of a certain *sovereignty* in the Will, whereby it has power to determine its own volitions. And therefore the determination of volition must itself be an act of the Will; for otherwise it can be no exercise of that supposed power and sovereignty. Again, if the Will determines itself, then either the Will is *active* in determining its volitions, or it is not. If active, then the determination is an *act* of the Will; and so there is one act of the Will determining another. But if the Will is not *active* in the determination, then how does it *exercise* any liberty in it? These gentlemen suppose that the thing wherein the Will *exercises* liberty, is in its determining its own acts. But how can this be, if it be not *active* in determining? Certainly the Will, or the soul, cannot *exercise any liberty* in that wherein it doth not *act*, or wherein it doth not *exercise itself*. So that if either part of this dilemma be taken, this scheme of liberty, consisting in self-determining power, is overthrown. If there be an act of the Will in determining all its own free acts, then one free act of the Will is determined by another; and so we have the absurdity of every free act, even the very first, determined by a foregoing free act. But if there be no act or exercise of the Will in determining its own acts, then no liberty is exercised in determining them. From whence it follows, that no liberty consists in the Will's power to determine its own acts: or, which is the same thing, that there is no such thing as liberty consisting in a self-determining power of the Will.

If it should be said, That although it be true, if the soul determines its own volitions, it must be active in so doing, and the determination itself must be an act; yet there is no need of supposing this act to be prior to the volition determined; but the Will or soul determines the act of the Will *in willing;* it determines its own volition, *in* the very act of volition; it directs and limits the act of the Will, causing it to be so and not otherwise, *in* exerting the act, without any preceding act to exert that. If any should say after this manner, they must mean one of these three things: either, (1.) That the determining act, though it be before the act determined in the order of nature, yet is not before it in order of time. Or, (2.) That the determining act is not before the act determined, either in the order of time or nature, nor is truly distinct from it; but that the soul's determining the act of volition is the same thing with its exerting the act of volition: the mind's exerting such a particular act, is its causing and determining the act. Or, (3.) That volition has no cause, and is no effect; but comes into existence, with such a particular determination, without any ground or reason of its existence and determination.—I shall consider these distinctly.

(1.) If all that is meant, be, that the determining act is not before the act determined in order of *time*, it will not help the case at all, though it should be allowed. If it be before the determined act in the order of nature, being the cause or ground of its existence, this as much proves it to be distinct from, and independent on, it, as if it were before in the order of time. As the cause of the particular motion of a natural body in a certain direction, may have no distance as to time, yet cannot be the same with the motion effected by it, but must be as distinct from it, as any other cause, that is before its effect in the order of time: as the architect is distinct from the house which he builds, or the father distinct from the son which he begets. And if the act of the Will determining be distinct from the act determined, and before it in the order of nature, then we can go back from one to another, till we come to the first in the series, which has no act of the Will before it in the order of nature, determining it; and consequently is an act not determined by the Will, and so not a free act, in this notion of freedom. And this being the act which determines all the rest, none of them are free acts. As when there is a chain of many links, the first of which only is taken hold of and drawn by hand; all the rest may follow and be moved at the same instant, without any distance of time; but yet the motion of one link is before that of another in the order of nature; the last is moved by the next, and that by the next, and so till we come to the first; which not being moved by any other, but by something distinct from the whole chain, this as much proves that no part is moved by any self-moving power in the chain, as if the motion of one link followed that of another in the order of time.

(2.) If any should say, that the determining act is not before the determined act, either in the order of time, or of nature, nor is distinct from it; but that the *exertion* of the act is the *determination* of the act; that for the soul to exert a particular volition, is for it to cause and determine that act of volition: I would on this observe, that the thing in question seems to be forgotten, or kept out of sight, in a darkness and unintelligibleness of speech; unless such an objector would mean to contradict himself.—The very act of volition itself is doubtless a determination of mind; i. e. it is the mind's drawing up a conclusion, or coming to a choice between two or more things proposed to it. But determining among external *objects* of choice, is not the same with determining the *act* of choice itself, among various possible acts of choice.—The question is, What influences, directs, or determines the mind or Will to come to such a conclusion or choice as it does? Or what is the cause, ground, or reason, why it concludes thus, and not otherwise? Now it must be answered, according to the *Arminian* notion of freedom, that the Will influences, orders, and determines itself thus to act. And if it does, I say, it must be by some antecedent act. To say, it is caused, influenced, and determined by something, and yet not determined by any thing antecedent, either in order of time or nature, is a contradiction. For that is what is meant by a thing's being prior in the order of nature, that it is someway the cause or reason of the thing, with respect to which it is said to be prior.

If the particular act or exertion of will, which comes into existence, be any thing properly determined at all, then it has some cause of existing, and of existing in such a particular determinate manner, and not another; some cause, whose influence *decides the matter*: which cause is distinct from the effect, and prior to it. But to say, that the Will or mind orders, influences, and determines itself to exert an act by the very exertion itself, is to make the exertion both cause and effect; or the exerting such an act, to be a cause of the exertion of such an act. For the question is, What is the cause and reason of the soul's exerting such an act? To which the answer is, The soul exerts such an act, and that is the cause of it. And so, by this, the exertion must be distinct from, and in the order of nature prior to, itself.

(3.) If the meaning be, that the soul's exertion of such a particular act of will, is a thing that comes to pass *of itself*, without any cause; and that there is absolutely no reason of the soul being determined to exert such a volition, and make such a choice, rather than another; I say, if this be the meaning of *Arminians*, when they contend so earnestly for the Will determining its own acts, and for liberty of Will consisting in self-determining power; they do nothing but confound themselves and others with words without a meaning. In the question, *What determines the Will?* and in their answer, that *the Will determines itself*, and in all the dispute, it seems to be taken for granted, that *something* determines the Will; and the controversy on this head is not, whether its determination has any cause or foundation at all; but where the foundation of it is, whether in the Will itself, or somewhere else. But if the thing intended be what is above mentioned, then nothing at all determines the Will; volition having absolutely no cause or foundation of its existence, either within or without.——There is a great noise made about self-determining power, as the source of all free acts of the Will: but when the matter comes to be explained, the meaning is, that no power at all is the source of these acts, neither self-determining power, nor any other, but they arise from nothing; no cause, no power, no influence, being at all concerned in the matter.

However, this very thing, even that the free acts of the Will are events which come to pass *without* a cause, is certainly implied in the *Arminian* notion of liberty of Will; though it be very inconsistent with many other things in their scheme, and repugnant to some things implied in their notion of liberty. Their opinion implies, that the particular determination of volition is without any cause; because they hold the free acts of the Will to be *contingent* events; and contingence is essential to freedom in their notion of it. But certainly, those things which have a prior ground and reason of their particular existence, a cause which antecedently determines them to be, and determines them to be just as they are, do not happen contingently. If something foregoing, by a casual influence and connexion, determines and fixes precisely their coming to pass, and the manner of it, then it does not remain a contingent thing whether they shall come to pass or no.

And because it is a question in many respects very important in this controversy, *Whether the free acts of the Will are events which come to pass without a cause;* I shall be particular in examining this point in the two following sections.

SECT. III.

Whether any Event whatsoever, and Volition in particular, can come to pass without a Cause of its existence.

BEFORE I enter on any argument on this subject, I would explain how I would be understood, when I use the word *Cause* in this discourse; since, for want of a better word, I shall have occasion to use it in a sense which is more extensive than that in which it is sometimes used. The word is often used in so restrained a sense as to signify only that which has a *positive efficiency* or influence *to produce* a thing, or bring it to pass. But there are many things which have no such positive productive influence; which yet are Causes in this respect, that they have truly the nature of a reason why some things are, rather than others; or why they are thus, rather than otherwise. Thus the absence of the sun in the night, is not the Cause of the fall of dew at that time, in the same manner as its beams are the cause of the ascent of vapours in the day-time; and its withdrawment in the winter, is not in the same manner the Cause of the freezing of the waters, as its approach in the spring is the cause of their thawing. But yet the withdrawment or absence of the sun is an antecedent, with which these effects in the night and winter are connected, and on which they depend; and is one thing that belongs to the ground and reason why they come to pass at that time, rather than at other times; though the absence of the sun is nothing positive, nor has any positive influence.

It may be further observed, that when I speak of *connexion of Causes and effects,* I have respect to *moral* Causes, as well as those that are called *natural* in distinction from them. Moral Causes may be Causes in as proper a sense as any Causes whatsoever; may have as real an influence, and may as truly be the ground and reason of an Event's coming to pass.

Therefore I sometimes use the word *Cause,* in this inquiry, to signify any *antecedent*, either natural or moral, positive or negative, on which an Event, either a thing, or the manner and circumstance of a thing, so depends, that it is the ground and reason, either in whole, or in part, why it is, rather than not; or why it is as it is, rather than otherwise; or, in other words, any antecedent with which a consequent Event is so connected, that it truly belongs to the reason why the proposition which affirms that Event is true; whether it has any positive influence, or not. And agreeably to this, I sometimes use the word effect for the consequence of another thing, which is perhaps rather an occasion than a Cause, most properly speaking.

I am the more careful thus to explain my meaning, that I may cut off occasion, from any that might seek occasion to cavil and object against some things which I may say concerning the dependence of all things which come to pass, on some Cause, and their connexion with their Cause.

Having thus explained what I mean by *Cause,* I assert, that nothing ever comes to pass without a Cause. What is self-existent must be from eternity, and must be unchangeable: but as to all things that *begin to be*, they are not self-existent, and therefore must have some foundation of their existence without themselves.—That whatsoever begins to be, which before was not, must have a Cause why it then begins to exist, seems to be the first dictate of the common and natural sense which God hath implanted in the minds of all mankind, and the main foundation of all our reasonings about the existence of things, past, present, or to come.

And this dictate of common sense equally respects substances and modes, or things and the manner and circumstances of things. Thus, if we see a body which has hitherto been at rest, start out of a state of rest, and begin to move, we do as naturally and necessarily suppose there is some Cause or reason of this new mode of existence, as of the existence of a body itself which had hitherto not existed. And so if a body, which had hitherto moved in a certain direction, should suddenly change the direction of its motion; or if it should put off its old figure, and take a new one; or change its colour: the beginning of these new modes is a new Event, and the human mind necessarily supposes that there is some Cause or reason of them.

If this grand principle of common sense be taken away, all arguing from effects to causes ceaseth, and so all knowledge of any existence, besides what we have by the most direct and immediate intuition, particularly all our proof of the being of God, ceases: we argue His being from our own being, and the being of other things, which we are sensible once were not, but have begun to be; and from the being of the world, with all its constituent parts, and the manner of their existence; all which we see plainly are not necessary in their own nature, and so not self-existent, and therefore must have a Cause. But if things, not in themselves necessary, may begin to be without a Cause, all this arguing is vain.

Indeed, I will not affirm, that there is in the nature of things no foundation for the knowledge of the Being of God, without any evidence of it from his works. I do suppose there is a great absurdity in denying Being in general, and imagining an eternal, absolute, universal nothing: and therefore that there would be, in the nature of things, a foundation of intuitive evidence, that there must be an eternal, infinite, most perfect Being; if we had strength and comprehension of mind sufficient, to have a clear idea of general and universal Being. But then we should not properly come to the knowledge of the Being of God by arguing; our evidence would be intuitive: we should see it, as we see other things that are necessary in themselves, the contraries of which are in their own nature absurd and contradictory; as we see that twice two is four; and as we see that a circle has no angles. If we had as clear an idea of universal, infinite entity, as we have of these other things, I suppose we should most intuitively see the absurdity of supposing such Being not to be; should immediately see there is no room for the question, whether it is possible that Being, in the most general, abstracted notion of it should not be. But we have not that strength and extent of mind, to know this certainly in this intuitive, independent manner: but the way that mankind come to the knowledge of the Being of God, is that which the apostle speaks of, Rom. i. 20. *The invisible things of him, from the creation of the world, are clearly seen; being understood by the things that are made; even his eternal power and Godhead.* We *first ascend*, and prove *a posteriori*, or from effects, that there must be an eternal Cause; and then *secondly*, prove by argumentation, not intuition, that this Being must be necessarily existent; and then *thirdly*, from the proved necessity of his existence, we may *descend*, and prove many of his perfections *a priori*.*

But if once this grand principle of common sense be given up, that *what is not necessary in itself, must have a Cause;* and we begin to maintain, that things which heretofore have not been, may come into existence, and begin to be of themselves, without any cause; all our means of ascending in our arguing from the creature to the Creator, and all our evidence of the Being of God, is cut off at one blow. In this case, we cannot prove that there is a God, either from the Being of the world, and the creatures in it, or from the manner of their Being, their order, beauty, and use. For if things may come into existence without any Cause at all, then they doubtless may without any Cause answerable to the effect. Our minds do alike naturally suppose and determine both these things; namely, that what begins to be has a Cause, and also that it has a Cause proportionable to the effect. The same principle which leads us to determine, that there cannot be any thing coming to pass without a Cause, leads us to determine that there cannot be more in the effect than in the Cause.

Yea, if once it should be allowed, that things may come to pass without a Cause, we should not only have no proof of the Being of God, but we should be without evidence of the existence of any thing whatsoever, but our own immediately present ideas and consciousness. For we have no way to prove any thing else, but by arguing from effects to Causes: from the ideas now immediately in view, we argue other things not immediately in view; from sensations now excited in us, we infer the existence of things without us, as the Causes of these sensations; and from the existence of these things, we argue other things, on which they depend, as effects on Causes. We infer the past existence of ourselves, or any thing else, by memory; only as we argue, that the ideas, which are now in our minds, are the consequences of past ideas and sensations. We immediately perceive nothing else but the ideas which are this moment extant in our minds. We perceive or know other things only *by means* of these, as necessarily connected with others, and dependent on them. But if things may be without Causes, all this necessary connexion and dependence is dissolved, and so all means of our knowledge is gone. If there be no absurdity or difficulty in supposing one thing to start out of non-existence into being, of itself without a Cause; then there is no absurdity or difficulty in supposing the same of millions of millions. For nothing, or no difficulty, multiplied, still is nothing, or no difficulty: nothing multiplied by nothing, does not increase the sum.

And indeed, according to the hypothesis I am opposing, of the acts of the Will coming to pass without a Cause, it is the cause in fact, that millions of millions of Events are continually coming into existence *contingently*, without any Cause or reason why they do so, all over the world, every day and hour, through all ages. So it is in a constant succession, in every moral agent. This contingency, this efficient nothing, this effectual No-Cause, is always ready at hand, to produce this sort of effects, as long as the agent exists, and as often as he has occasion.

If it were so, that things only of one kind, *viz.* acts of the Will, seemed to come to pass of themselves; and it were an Event that was continual, and that happened in a course, wherever were found subjects capable of such Events; this very thing would demonstrate that there was some Cause of them, which made such a difference between this Event and others, and that they did not really happen contingently. For contingence is blind, and does not pick and choose a particular sort of Events. Nothing has no choice. This No-Cause, which causes no existence, cannot cause the existence which comes to pass, to be of one particular sort only, distinguished from all others. Thus, that only one sort of matter drops out of the heavens, even water, and that this comes so often, so constantly and plentifully, all over the world, in all ages, shows that there is some Cause or reason of the falling of water out of the heavens; and that something besides mere contingence has a hand in the matter.

If we should suppose Non-entity to be about to bring forth; and things were coming into existence, without any Cause or antecedent, on which the existence, or kind, or manner of existence depends; or which could at all determine whether the things should be stones, or stars, or beasts, or angels, or human bodies, or souls, or only some new motion or figure in natural bodies, or some new sensations in animals, or new ideas in the human understanding, or new volitions in the Will; or any thing else of all the infinite number of possibles; then certainly it would not be expected, although many millions of millions of things were coming into existence in this manner, all over

* To the inquirer after truth it may here be recommended, as a matter of some consequence, to keep in mind the precise difference between an argument *a priori* and one *a posteriori*, a distinction of considerable use, as well as of long standing, among divines, metaphysicians, and logical writers. An argument from either of these, when *legitimately* applied, may amount to a demonstration, when used, for instance, relatively to the being and perfections of God; but the one should be confined to the *existence* of Deity, while the other is applicable to his *perfections*. By the argument *a posteriori* we rise *from* the effect to the cause, from the stream to the fountain, from what is *posterior* to what is prior; in other words, from what is contingent to what is absolute, from number to unity; that is, from the *manifestation* of God to his *existence*. By the argument *a priori* we descend *from* the cause to the effect, from the fountain to the stream, from what is *prior* to what is posterior; that is, from the necessary existence of God we safely infer certain properties and perfections. To attempt a demonstration of the existence of a first cause, or the Being of God, *a priori*, would be most absurd; for it would be an attempt to prove a *prior* ground or cause of existence of a *first* cause; or, that there is some cause *before* the *very first*. The argument *a priori*, therefore, is not *applicable* to prove the divine *existence*. For *this* end, the argument *a posteriori* alone is legitimate; and its conclusiveness rests on this axiom, that "there can be *no effect without a cause.*"—The absurdity of denying this axiom is abundantly demonstrated by our author.—W.

the face of the earth, that they should all be only of one particular kind, and that it should be thus in all ages, and that this sort of existences should never fail to come to pass where there is room for them, or a subject capable of them, and that constantly, whenever there is occasion.

If any should imagine, there is something in the sort of Event that renders it possible for it to come into existence without a Cause, and should say, that the free acts of the Will are existences of an exceeding *different nature* from other things; by reason of which they may come into existence without any previous ground or reason of it, though other things cannot: if they make this objection in good earnest, it would be an evidence of their strangely forgetting themselves; for they would be giving an account of some ground of the existence of a thing, when at the same time they would maintain there is no ground of its existence. Therefore I would observe, that the particular nature of existence, be it never so diverse from others, can lay no foundation for that thing coming into existence without a Cause; because to suppose this, would be to suppose the *particular nature* of existence to be a thing prior to the existence, and so a thing which makes way for existence, without a cause or reason of existence. But that which in any respect makes way for a thing coming into being, or for any manner or circumstance of its first existence, must be prior to the existence. The distinguished nature of the effect, which is something belonging to the effect, cannot have influence backward, to act before it is. The peculiar nature of that thing called Volition, can do nothing, can have no influence, while it is not. And afterwards it is too late for its influence: for then the thing has made sure of existence already, without its help.

So that it is indeed as repugnant to reason, to suppose that an act of the Will should come into existence without a Cause, as to suppose the human soul, or an angel, or the globe of the earth, or the whole universe, should come into existence without a Cause. And if once we allow, that such a sort of effect as a Volition may come to pass without a Cause, how do we know but that many other sorts of effects may do so too? It is not the particular *kind* of effect that makes the absurdity of supposing it has being without a Cause, but something which is common to all things that ever begin to be, *viz.* That they are not self-existent, or necessary in the nature of things.

SECT. IV.

Whether Volition can arise without a Cause, through the activity of the nature of the soul.

THE author of the *Essay on the Freedom of the Will in God and the Creatures*, in answer to that objection against his doctrine of a self-determining power in the Will, (p. 68—69.) *That nothing is, or comes to pass, without a sufficient reason why it is, and why it is in this manner rather than another*, allows that it is thus in corporeal things, *which are, properly and philosophically speaking, passive being;* but denies it is thus in *spirits, which are beings of an active nature, who have the spring of action within themselves, and can determine themselves.* By which it is plainly supposed, that such an event as an act of the Will, may come to pass in a spirit, without a sufficient reason why it comes to pass, or why it is after this manner, rather than another. But certainly this author, in this matter, must be very unwary and inadvertent. For,

1. The objection or difficulty proposed by him seems to be forgotten in his answer or solution. The very difficulty, as he himself proposes it, is this: How an event can come to pass *without a sufficient reason* why it is, or why it is in this manner rather than another? Instead of solving this difficulty, with regard to Volition, as he proposes, he forgets himself, and answers another question quite diverse, *viz.* What *is a sufficient reason* why it is, and why it is in this manner rather than another? And he assigns the active being's own determination as the Cause, and a Cause sufficient for the effect; and leaves all the difficulty unresolved, even, How the soul's own determination, which he speaks of, came to exist, and to be what it was, *without a Cause?* The *activity* of the soul may enable it to be the *Cause* of effects; but it does not at all enable it to be the subject of effects which have *no Cause;* which is the thing this author supposes concerning acts of the Will. Activity of nature will no more enable a being to produce effects, and determine the manner of their existence, *within* itself, without a Cause, than *out of* itself, in some other being. But if an active being should, through its activity, produce and determine an effect in some external object, how absurd would it be to say, that the effect was produced *without* a Cause!

2. The question is not so much, How a spirit endowed with activity comes to *act*, as why it exerts *such* an act, and not another; or why it acts with such a particular determination? If activity of nature be the Cause why a spirit (the soul of man, for instance) acts, and does not lie still; yet that alone is not the Cause why its action is thus and thus limited, directed, and determined. Active nature is a *general* thing; it is an ability or tendency of nature to action, generally taken; which may be a Cause why the soul acts as occasion or reason is given; but this alone cannot be a sufficient Cause why the soul exerts such a *particular* act, at such a time, rather than others. In order to this there must be something besides a *general* tendency to action; there must also be a *particular* tendency to that individual action.—If it should be asked, why the soul of man uses its activity, in such a manner as it does; and it should be answered, that the soul uses its activity thus, rather than otherwise, because it has activity; would such an answer satisfy a rational man? Would it not rather be looked upon as a very impertinent one?

3. An active being can bring no *effects* to pass by his activity, but what are *consequent* upon his *acting:* he produces nothing by his activity, any other way than by the *exercise* of his activity, and so nothing but the fruits of its exercise: he brings nothing to pass by a dormant activity. But the exercise of his activity is action; and so his action, or exercise of his activity, must be prior to the effects of his activity. If an active being produces an effect in another being, about which his activity is conversant, the effect being the fruit of his activity, his activity must be first exercised or exerted, and the effect of it must follow. So it must be, with equal reason, if the active being is his own object, and his activity is conversant about himself, to produce and determine some effect in himself; still the exercise of his activity must go before the effect, which he brings to pass and determines by it. And therefore his *activity* cannot be the *Cause* of the determination of the first action, or exercise of activity itself, whence the effects of activity arise; for that would imply a contradiction; it would be to say, the first exercise of activity is before the first exercise of activity, and is the Cause of it.

4. That the soul, though an active substance, cannot *diversify* its own acts, but by first acting; or be a determining Cause of *different* acts, or any different effects, sometimes of one kind, and sometimes of another, any other way than in consequence of its own diverse acts, is manifest by this; that if so, then the *same* Cause, the *same* causal influence, *without variation in any respect*, would produce *different* effects at different times. For the same substance of the soul before it acts, and the same active nature of the soul before it is exerted, i. e. before in the order of nature, would be the Cause of different effects, viz. different Volitions at different times. But the substance of the soul before it acts, and its active nature before it is exerted, are the same without variation. For it is some *act* that makes the first variation in the Cause, as to any causal exertion, force, or influence. But if it be so, that the soul has no different causality, or diverse causal influence, in producing these diverse effects; then it is evident, that the soul has no influence in the diversity of the effect; and that the difference of the effect cannot be owing to any thing in the soul; or which is the same thing, the soul does not determine the diversity of the effect; which is contrary to the supposition.—It is true, the substance of the soul before it acts, and before there is any difference in that respect, may be in a different state and circumstances: but those whom I oppose, will not allow the different circumstances of the soul to be the determining Causes of the acts of the Will; as being contrary to their notion of self-determination.

5. Let us suppose, as these divines do, that there are no acts of the soul, strictly speaking, but free Volitions; then it will follow, that the soul is an active being in nothing further than it is a voluntary or elective being; and whenever it produces effects actively, it produces effects voluntarily and electively. But to produce effects thus, is the same thing as to produce effects *in consequence of*, and *according to* its own choice. And if so, then surely the soul does not by its activity produce all its own acts of will or choice themselves; for this, by the supposition, is to produce all its free acts of choice voluntarily and electively, or in consequence of its own free acts of choice, which brings the matter directly to the forementioned contradiction, of a free act of choice *before the first* free act of choice.—According to these gentlemen's own notion of action, if there arises in the mind a Volition without a free act of the Will to produce it, the mind is not the voluntary Cause of that Volition; because it does not arise from, nor is regulated by, choice or design. And therefore it cannot be, that the mind should be the active, voluntary, determining Cause of the first and leading Volition that relates to the affair.—The mind being a *designing* Cause, only enables it to produce effects in consequence of its *design;* it will not enable it to be the designing Cause of all its own designs. The mind being an *elective* Cause, will enable it to produce effects only in consequence of its *elections,* and according to them; but cannot enable it to be the elective Cause of all its own elections; because that supposes an election before the first election. So the mind being an *active* Cause enables it to produce effects in consequence of its own *acts,* but cannot enable it to be the determining Cause of all its own *acts;* for that is, in the same manner, a contradiction; as it supposes a determining act conversant about the first act, and prior to it, having a causal influence on its existence, and manner of existence.

I can conceive of nothing else that can be meant by the soul having power to cause and determine its own Volitions, as a being to whom God has given a power of action, but this; that God has given power to the soul, sometimes at least, to excite Volitions at its pleasure, or according as it chooses. And this certainly supposes, in all such cases, a choice preceding all Volitions which are thus caused, even the first of them. Which runs into the forementioned great absurdity.

Therefore the activity of the nature of the soul affords no relief from the difficulties with which the notion of a self-determining power in the Will is attended, nor will it help, in the least, its absurdities and inconsistences.

SECT. V.

Showing, that if the things asserted in these Evasions should be supposed to be true, they are altogether impertinent, and cannot help the cause of Arminian Liberty; and how, this being the state of the case, Arminian writers are obliged to talk inconsistently.

WHAT was last observed in the preceding section, may show—not only that the active nature of the soul cannot be a reason why an act of the Will is, or why it is in this manner rather than another, but also—that if it could be proved, that volitions are contingent events, their being and manner of being not fixed or determined by any cause, or any thing antecedent; it would not at all serve the purpose of *Arminians,* to establish their notion of freedom, as consisting in the Will's *determination of itself,* which supposes every free act of the Will to be determined by some act of the Will going before; inasmuch as for the *Will* to determine a thing, is the same as for the soul to determine a thing by *willing;* and there is no way that the *Will* can determine an act of the Will, than by willing that act of the Will, or, which is the same thing, *choosing* it. So that here must be two acts of the Will in the case, one going before another, one conversant about the other, and the latter the object of the former, and chosen by the former. If the Will does not cause and determine the act by choice, it does not cause or determine it at all; for that which is not determined by choice, is not determined voluntarily or *willingly:* and to say, that the Will determines something which the soul does not determine willingly, is as much as to say, that something is done by the Will, which the soul doth not with its Will.

So that if *Arminian* liberty of Will, consisting in the Will determining its own acts, be maintained, the old absurdity and contradiction must be maintained, that every free act of Will is caused and determined by a foregoing free act of Will. Which doth not consist with the free acts arising without any cause, and being so contingent, as not to be fixed by any thing foregoing. So that this evasion must be given up, as not at all relieving this sort of liberty, but directly destroying it.

And if it should be supposed, that the soul determines its own acts of Will some other way, than by a foregoing act of Will; still it will help not their cause. If it determines them by an act of the understanding, or some other power, then *the Will* does not determine *itself;* and so the *self-determining* power of the Will is given up. And what liberty is there exercised, according to their own opinion of liberty, by the soul being determined by something besides *its own choice?* The acts of the Will, it is true, may be directed, and effectually determined and fixed; but it is not done by the soul's own Will and pleasure: there is no exercise at all of choice or Will in producing the effect: and if *Will* and choice are not exercised in it, how is the *liberty of the Will* exercised in it?

So that let *Arminians* turn which way they please with their notion of liberty, consisting in the Will determining its own acts, their notion destroys itself. If they hold every free act of Will to be determined by the soul's own free choice, or foregoing free act of Will; *foregoing,* either in the order of time, or nature; it implies that gross contradiction, that the *first* free act belonging to the affair, is determined by a free act which is *before* it. Or if they say, that the free acts of the Will are determined by some *other act* of the soul, and not an act of Will or choice; this also destroys their notion of liberty consisting in the acts of the Will being determined by the *Will itself;* or if they hold that the acts of the Will are determined by *nothing at all* that is prior to them, but that they are contingent in that sense, that they are determined and fixed by no cause at all; this also destroys their notion of liberty, consisting in the Will determining its own acts.

This being the true state of the *Arminian* notion of liberty, the writers who defend it are forced into gross inconsistences, in what they say upon this subject. To instance in Dr. Whitby; he, in his discourse on the freedom of the Will,* opposes the opinion of the *Calvinists,* who place man's liberty *only in a power of doing what he will,* as that wherein they plainly agree with Mr. Hobbes. And yet he himself mentions the very same notion of liberty, as the dictate of *the sense and common reason of mankind, and a rule laid down by the light of nature;* viz. that *liberty is a power of acting from ourselves, or* DOING WHAT WE WILL.† This is indeed, as he says, a thing agreeable to *the sense and common reason of mankind;* and therefore it is not so much to be wondered at, that he unawares acknowledges it against himself: for if liberty does not consist in this, what else can be devised that it should consist in? If it be said, as Dr. Whitby elsewhere insists, that it does not only consist in liberty of *doing what we will,* but also a liberty of willing without necessity; still the question returns, what does that liberty of willing without necessity consist in, but in a power of willing *as we please,* without being impeded by a contrary necessity? or in other words, a liberty for the soul in its willing to act *according to its own choice?* Yea, this very thing the same author seems to allow, and suppose again and again, in the use he makes of sayings of the fathers, whom he quotes as his vouchers. Thus he cites the words of Origen, which he produces as a testimony on his side;‡ "The soul acts by HER OWN CHOICE, and it is free for her to incline to whatever part SHE WILL." And those of Justin Martyr;|| "The doctrine of the Christians is this, that nothing is done or suffered according to fate, but that every man doth good or evil ACCORDING TO HIS OWN FREE CHOICE." And from Eusebius,

* In his Book on the five Points, Second Edit. p. 350, 351, 352.

† Ibid. p. 325, 326. ‡ Ibid. p. 342. || Ibid. p. 360.

these words;* "If fate be established, philosophy and piety are overthrown.—All these things depending upon the necessity introduced *by the stars, and not upon meditation and exercise* PROCEEDING FROM OUR OWN FREE CHOICE." And again, the words of Maccarius;† "God, to preserve the liberty of man's Will, suffered their bodies to die, that it might be IN THEIR CHOICE to turn to good or evil."——"They who are acted by the Holy Spirit, are not held under any necessity, but have liberty to turn themselves, *and* DO WHAT THEY WILL *in this life*."

Thus, the Doctor in effect comes into that very notion of liberty, which the *Calvinists* have; which he at the same time condemns, as agreeing with the opinion of Mr. Hobbes, namely, *The soul acting by its own choice, men doing good or evil according to their own free choice, their being in that exercise which proceeds from their own free choice, having it in their choice to turn to good or evil, and doing what they will.*" So that if men exercise this liberty in the acts of the Will themselves, it must be in exerting acts of Will *according to their own* free *choice*; or, exerting acts of Will *that proceed from their choice*. And if it be so, then let every one judge whether this does not suppose a free choice going before the free act of Will, or whether an act of choice does not go before that act of the Will which *proceeds from it*. And if it be thus with all free acts of the Will, then let every one judge, whether it will not follow that there is a free choice going *before the first* free act of the Will exerted in the case! And finally, let every one judge whether in the scheme of these writers there be any possibility of avoiding these absurdities.

If liberty consists, as Dr. Whitby himself says, in a man's *doing what he will*; and a man exercises this liberty, not only in external actions, but in the *acts* of the Will themselves; then so far as liberty is exercised in the latter, it consists in *willing what he wills*: and if any say so, one of these two things must be meant, either, 1. That a man has power to will, as he does will; because what he wills, he wills; and therefore power to will what he has power to will. If this be their meaning, then all this mighty controversy about freedom of the Will and self-determining power, comes wholly to nothing; all that is contended for being no more than this, that the mind of man does what it does, and is the subject of what it is the subject, or that what is, is; wherein none has any controversy with them. Or, 2. The meaning must be, that a man has power to will as he chooses to will: that is, he has power by one act of choice to choose another; by an antecedent act of Will to choose a consequent act: and therein to execute his own choice. And if this be their meaning, it is nothing but shuffling with those they dispute with, and baffling their own reason. For still the question returns, wherein lies man's liberty in that antecedent act of Will which chose the consequent act. The answer according to the same principles must be, that his liberty in this also lies in his willing as he would, or as he chose, or agreeable to another act of choice preceding that. And so the question returns *in infinitum*, and the like answer must be made *in infinitum*: in order to support their opinion, there must be no beginning, but free acts of Will must have been chosen by foregoing free acts of Will in the soul of every man, without beginning.

SECT. VI.

Concerning the Will determining in things which are perfectly indifferent in the view of the mind.

A GREAT argument for self-determining power, is the supposed experience we universally have of an ability to determine our Wills, in cases wherein no prevailing motive is presented: the Will, as is supposed, has its choice to make between two or more things, that are perfectly equal in the view of the mind; and the Will is apparently altogether indifferent; and yet we find no difficulty in coming to a choice; the Will can instantly determine itself to one, by a sovereign power which it has over itself, without being moved by any preponderating inducement.

Thus the fore-mentioned author of an *Essay on the Freedom of the Will, &c.* (p. 25, 26, 27.) supposes, "That there are many instances, wherein the Will is determined neither by present uneasiness, nor by the greatest apparent good, nor by the last dictate of the understanding, nor by any thing else, but merely by itself, as a sovereign self-determining power of the soul; and that the soul does not will this or that action, in some cases, by any other influence but because it will. Thus, says he, I can turn my face to the south, or the north; I can point with my finger upward, or downward.—And thus, in some cases, the Will determines itself in a very sovereign manner, because it will, without a reason borrowed from the understanding: and hereby it discovers its own perfect power of choice, rising from within itself, and free from all influence or restraint of any kind." And (p. 66, 70, 73, 74.) this author very expressly supposes the Will in many cases to be determined by *no motive at all, and acts altogether without motive, or ground of preference*.—Here I would observe,

1. The very supposition which is here made, directly contradicts and overthrows itself. For the thing supposed, wherein this grand argument consists, is, that among several things the Will actually chooses one before another, at the same time that it is perfectly indifferent; which is the very same thing as to say, the mind has a preference, at the same time that it has no preference. What is meant cannot be, that the mind is indifferent *before* it comes to have a choice, or until it has a preference; for certainly this author did not imagine he had a controversy with any person in supposing this. Besides, it appears in fact, that the thing which he supposes, is—not that the Will chooses one thing before another, concerning which it is indifferent *before it chooses*, but that the Will is indifferent *when* it *chooses*; and that it being otherwise than indifferent is not until afterwards, in consequence of its choice; that the chosen thing appearing preferable, and more agreeable than another, arises from its choice already made. His words are, (p. 30.) "Where the objects which are proposed appear equally fit or good, the Will is left without a guide or director; and therefore must take its own choice, by its own determination; it being properly a self-determining power. And in such cases the Will does as it were make a good to itself by its own choice, i. e. creates its own pleasure or delight in this self-chosen good. Even as a man by seizing upon a spot of unoccupied land, in an uninhabited country, makes it his own possession and property, and as such rejoices in it. Where things were indifferent before, the Will finds nothing to make them more agreeable, considered merely in themselves, but the pleasure it feels *arising from its own choice*, and its perseverance therein. We love many things which we have chosen, *and purely because we chose them*."

This is as much as to say, that we first begin to prefer many things, purely because we have preferred and chosen them before.—These things must needs be spoken inconsiderately by this author. Choice or preference cannot be before itself in the same instance, either in the order of time or nature: It cannot be the foundation of itself, or the consequence of itself. The very act of choosing one thing *rather than another*, is *preferring* that thing, and that is setting a higher value on that thing. But that the mind sets a higher value on one thing than another, is not, in the first place, the *fruit* of its setting a higher value on that thing.

This author says, (p. 36.) "The Will may be perfectly indifferent, and yet the Will may determine itself to choose one or the other." And again, in the same page, "I am entirely indifferent to either; and yet my Will may determine itself to choose." And again, "Which I shall choose must be determined by the mere act of my Will." If the choice is determined by a mere act of Will, then the choice is determined by a mere act of choice. And concerning this matter, *viz.* That the act of the Will itself is determined by act of choice, this writer is express. (p. 72.) Speaking of the case, where there is no superior fitness in objects presented, he has these words: "There it must act by its own CHOICE, and determine itself as it

* In his Book on the five Points, Second Edit. p. 363

† Ibid. p. 369, 370.

pleases." Where it is supposed that the very *determination*, which is the ground and spring of the Will's act, is an act of *choice* and *pleasure*, wherein one act is more agreeable than another; and this *preference* and *superior pleasure* is the ground of all it does in the case. And if so, the mind is not indifferent when it determines itself, but *had rather* determine itself one way than another. And therefore the Will does not act at all in indifference; not so much as in the first step it takes. If it be possible for the *understanding* to act in indifference, yet surely the *Will* never does; because the Will beginning to *act* is the very same thing as it beginning to choose or *prefer*. And if in the very first act of the Will, the mind prefers something, then the idea of that thing preferred, does at that time preponderate, or prevail in the mind: or, which is the same thing, the idea of it has a prevailing influence on the Will. So that this wholly destroys the thing supposed, *viz.* That the mind can by a sovereign power choose one of two or more things, which in the view of the mind are, in every respect, perfectly equal, one of which does not at all preponderate, nor has any prevailing influence on the mind above another.

So that this author, in his grand argument for the ability of the Will to choose one of two or more things, concerning which it is perfectly indifferent, does at the same time, in effect, deny the thing he supposes, even that the Will, in choosing, is subject to no prevailing influence of the view of the thing chosen. And indeed it is impossible to offer this argument without overthrowing it; the thing supposed in it being that which denies itself. To suppose the Will to act at all in a state of perfect indifference, is to assert that the mind chooses without choosing. To say that when it is indifferent, it can do as it pleases, is to say that it can follow its pleasure, when it has no pleasure to follow. And therefore if there be any difficulty in the instances of two cakes, or two eggs, &c. which are exactly alike, one as good as another; concerning which this author supposes the mind in fact has a *choice*, and so in effect supposes that it has a *preference;* it as much concerned himself to solve the difficulty, as it does those whom he opposes. For if these instances prove any thing to his purpose, they prove that a man chooses without choice. And yet this is not to his purpose; because if this is what he asserts, his own words are as much against him, and does as much contradict him, as the words of those he disputes against can do.

2. There is no great difficulty in showing, in such instances as are alleged, not only *that it must needs be so*, that the mind must be influenced in its choice by something that has a preponderating influence upon it, but also *how it is so*. A little attention to our own experience, and a distinct consideration of the acts of our own minds, in such cases, will be sufficient to clear up the matter.

Thus, supposing I have a chess-board before me; and because I am required by a superior, or desired by a friend, or on some other consideration, I am determined to touch some one of the spots or squares on the board with my finger. Not being limited or directed, in the first proposal, to any one in particular; and there being nothing in the squares, in themselves considered, that recommends any one of all the sixty-four, more than another; in this case, my mind determines to give itself up to what is vulgularly called *accident*,* by determining to touch that square which happens to be most in view, which my eye is especially upon at that moment, or which happens to be then most in my mind, or which I shall be directed to by some other such like accident. Here are several *steps* of the mind proceeding (though all may be done, as it were, in a moment). The *first* step is its *general* determination that it will touch one of the squares. The *next* step is another *general* determination to give itself up to accident, in some certain way; as to touch that which shall be most in the eye or mind at that time, or to some other such like accident. The *third* and last step is a *particular* determination to touch a certain individual spot, even that square, which, by that sort of accident the mind has pitched upon, has actually offered itself beyond others. Now it is apparent that in none of these several steps does the mind proceed in absolute indifference, but in each of them is influenced by a preponderating inducement. So it is in the *first* step, the mind's general determination to touch one of the sixty-four spots: the mind is not absolutely indifferent whether it does so or no; it is induced to it, for the sake of making some experiment, or by the desire of a friend, or some other motive that prevails. So it is in the *second* step, the mind determining to give itself up to accident, by touching that which shall be most in the eye, or the idea of which shall be most prevalent in the mind, &c. The mind is not absolutely indifferent whether it proceeds by this rule or no; but chooses it, because it appears at that time a convenient and requisite expedient in order to fulfil the general purpose. And so it is in the *third* and last step, which is determining to touch that individual spot which actually does prevail in the mind's view. The mind is not indifferent concerning this; but is influenced by a prevailing inducement and reason; which is, that this is a prosecution of the preceding determination, which appeared requisite, and was fixed before in the second step.

Accident will ever serve a man, without hindering him a moment, in such a case. Among a number of objects in view, one will prevail in the eye, or in idea, beyond others. When we have our eyes open in the clear sunshine, many objects strike the eye at once, and innumerable images may be at once painted in it by the rays of light; but the attention of the mind is not equal to several of them at once; or if it be, it does not continue so for any time. And so it is with respect to the ideas of the mind in general: several ideas are not in equal strength in the mind's view and notice at once; or at least, does not remain so for any sensible continuance. There is nothing in the world more constantly varying, than the ideas of the mind; they do not remain precisely in the same state for the least perceivable space of time; as is evident by this:—That all time is perceived by the mind, only by the successive changes of its own ideas. Therefore while the perceptions of the mind remain precisely in the same state, there is no perceivable length of time, because no sensible succession at all.

As the acts of the Will, in each step of the forementioned procedure, do not come to pass without a particular cause, but every act is owing to a prevailing inducement; so the accident, as I have called it, or that which happens in the unsearchable course of things, to which the mind yields itself, and by which it is guided, is not any thing that comes to pass without a cause. The mind in determining to be guided by it, is not determined by something that has no cause; any more than if it be determined to be guided by a lot, or the casting of a die. For though the die falling in such a manner be accidental to him that casts it, yet none will suppose that there is no cause why it falls as it does. The involuntary changes in the succession of our ideas, though the cause may not be observed, have as much a cause, as the changeable motions of the motes that float in the air, or the continual, infinitely various, successive changes of the unevennesses on the surface of the water.

There are two things especially, which are probably the occasions of confusion in the minds of them who insist upon it, that the Will acts in a proper indifference, and without being moved by any inducement, in its determinations in such cases as have been mentioned.†

1. They seem to mistake the point in question, or at least not to keep it distinctly in view. The question they dispute about, is, Whether the mind be indifferent about the *objects* presented, one of which is to be taken, touched, pointed to, &c. as two eggs, two cakes, which appear equally good. Whereas the question to be considered, is, Whether the person be indifferent with respect to his own

* I have elsewhere observed, what that is which is vulgarly called *accident;* that it is nothing akin to the *Arminian* metaphysical notion of *contingence*, or something not connected with any thing foregoing; but that it is something that comes to pass in the course of things, unforeseen by men, and not owing to their design.

† The reader is particularly requested to give due attention to these two remarks, especially the former, as being of the utmost importance in the controversy. If he be pleased to examine, with this view, the most popular advocates for the liberty of indifference, he will find them continually confounding the *objects* of choice, and the *acts* of choice. When they have shown, with much plausibility, that there is no perceivable difference, or ground of choice, in the *objects*, they hastily infer the same indifference as applicable to the *acts* of choice.—W.

actions; whether he does not, on some consideration or other, prefer one act with respect to these objects before another. The mind in its determination and choice, in these cases, is not most immediately and directly conversant about the *objects presented;* but *the acts to be done* concerning these objects. The objects may appear equal, and the mind may never properly make any choice between them; but the next act of the Will being about the external actions to be performed, taking, touching, &c. these may not appear equal, and one action may properly be chosen before another. In each step of the mind's progress, the determination is not about the objects, unless indirectly and improperly, but about the actions, which it chooses for other reasons than any preference of the objects, and for reasons not taken at all from the objects.

There is no necessity of supposing, that the mind does ever at all properly choose one of the objects before another; either before it has taken, or afterwards. Indeed the man chooses to *take* or *touch* one rather than another; but not because it chooses the *thing taken*, or *touched*, but from foreign considerations. The case may be so, that of two things offered, a man may, for certain reasons, prefer taking that which he *undervalues*, and choose to neglect that which his mind *prefers*. In such a case, choosing the thing taken, and choosing to take, are diverse: and so they are in a case where the things presented are equal in the mind's esteem, and neither of them preferred. All that fact and experience makes evident, is, that the mind chooses one *action* rather than another. And therefore the arguments which they bring, in order to be to their purpose, should be to prove that the mind chooses the *action* in perfect indifference, with respect to *that action;* and not to prove that the mind chooses the action in perfect indifference with respect to the *object;* which is very possible, and yet the Will not act at all without prevalent inducement, and proper preponderation.

2. Another reason of confusion and difficulty in this matter, seems to be, not distinguishing between a *general* indifference, or an indifference with respect to what is to be done in a more distant and general view of it, and a *particular* indifference, or an indifference with respect to the next immediate act, viewed with its particular and present circumstances. A man may be perfectly indifferent with respect to his own *actions*, in the former respect; and yet not in the latter. Thus in the foregoing instance of touching one of the squares of a chess-board; when it is first proposed that I should touch one of them, I may be perfectly indifferent which I touch; because as yet I view the matter remotely and generally, being but in the first step of the mind's progress in the affair. But yet, when I am actually come to the last step, and the very next thing to be determined is *which* is to be touched, having already determined that I will touch that which happens to be most in my eye or mind, and my mind being now fixed on a particular one, the act of touching that, considered thus immediately, and in these particular present circumstances, is not what my mind is absolutely indifferent about.

SECT. VII.

Concerning the notion of Liberty of Will, consisting in Indifference.

WHAT has been said in the foregoing section, has a tendency in some measure to evince the absurdity of the opinion of such as place Liberty in Indifference, or in that equilibrium whereby the Will is without all antecedent bias; that the determination of the Will to either side may be entirely from itself, and that it may be owing only to its own power, and the sovereignty which it has over itself, that it goes this way rather than that.*

But inasmuch as this has been of such long standing, and has been so generally received, and so much insisted on by *Pelagians, Semi-Pelagians, Jesuits, Socinians, Arminians*, and others, it may deserve a more full consideration. And therefore I shall now proceed to a more particular and thorough inquiry into this notion.

Now lest some should suppose that I do not understand those that place Liberty in Indifference, or should charge me with misrepresenting their opinion, I would signify, that I am sensible, there are some, who, when they talk of Liberty of the Will as consisting in Indifference, express themselves as though they would not be understood to mean the Indifference of the *inclination* or tendency of the Will, but an Indifference of the soul's *power* of willing; or that the Will, with respect to its power or ability to choose, is indifferent, can go either way indifferently, either to the right hand or left, either act or forbear to act, one as well as the other. This indeed seems to be a refining of some particular writers only, and newly invented, which will by no means consist with the manner of expression used by the defenders of Liberty of Indifference in general. I wish such refiners would thoroughly consider, whether they distinctly know their own meaning, when they make a distinction between an Indifference of the soul as to its *power* or *ability* of choosing, and the soul's Indifference as to the preference or choice itself; and whether they do not deceive themselves in imagining that they have any distinct meaning at all. The Indifference of the soul as to its ability or power to will, must be the same thing as the Indifference of the state of the power or faculty of the Will, or the Indifference of the state which the soul itself, which has that power or faculty, hitherto remains in, as to the exercise of that power, in the choice it shall by and by make.

But not to insist any longer on the inexplicable abstruseness of this distinction; let what will be supposed concerning the meaning of them that use it, thus much must at least be intended by *Arminians* when they talk of Indifference as essential to Liberty of Will, if they intend any thing, in any respect to their purpose, *viz.* That it is such an Indifference as leaves the Will not determined already; but free from actual possession, and vacant of predetermination, so far, that there may be room for the exercise of the *self-determining power* of the Will; and that the Will's freedom consists in, or depends upon, this vacancy and opportunity that is left for the Will itself to be the determiner of the act that is to be the free act.

And here I would observe in the *first* place, that to make out this scheme of Liberty, the Indifference must be *perfect* and *absolute;* there must be a perfect freedom from all antecedent preponderation or inclination. Because if the Will be already inclined, before it exerts its own sovereign power on itself, then its inclination is not wholly owing to itself: if when two opposites are proposed to the soul for its choice, the proposal does not find the soul wholly in a state of Indifference, then it is not found in a state of Liberty for mere self-determination.—The least degree of an antecedent bias must be inconsistent with their notion of Liberty. For so long as prior inclination possesses the Will, and is not removed, the former binds the latter, so that it is utterly impossible that the Will should act otherwise than agreeably to it. Surely the Will cannot act or choose contrary to a remaining prevailing inclination of the Will. To suppose otherwise, would be the same thing as to suppose that the Will is *inclined* contrary to its present prevailing *inclination*, or contrary to what it is *inclined* to. That which the Will prefers, to that, all things considered, it preponderates and inclines. It is equally impossible for the Will to choose contrary to its own remaining and present preponderating inclination, as it is to *prefer* contrary to its own present *preference*, or *choose* contrary to its own present *choice*. The Will, therefore, so long as it is under the influence of an old preponderating inclination, is not at Liberty for a new free act; or any, that shall now be an

* Dr. Whitby, and some other *Arminians*, make a distinction of different kinds of freedom; one of God, and perfect spirits above; another of persons in a state of trial. The former Dr. Whitby allows to consist with necessity; the latter he holds to be without necessity: and this latter he supposes to be requisite to our being the subject of praise or dispraise, rewards or punishments, precepts and prohibitions, promises and threats, exhortations and dehortations, and a covenant treaty. And to this freedom he supposes *Indifference* to be requisite. In his Discourse on the five points, (p 299, 300.) he says; "It is a freedom, (speaking of a freedom not only from co-action, but from necessity) requisite, as we conceive, to render us capable of trial or probation, and to render our actions worthy of praise or dispraise, and our persons of rewards or punishments." And in the next page, speaking of the same matter, he says, "Excellent to this purpose, are the words of Mr. Thorndake: *We say not, that Indifference is requisite to all freedom, but to the freedom of man alone in this state of travail and proficience; the ground of which is God's tender of a treaty, and conditions of peace and reconcilement to fallen man, together with those precepts and prohibitions, those promises and threats, those exhortations and dehortations, it is enforced with.*"

act of self-determination. That which is a self-determined free act, must be one which the Will determines in the possession and use of a peculiar sort of Liberty; such as consists in a freedom from *every thing*, which, if it were there, would make it *impossible* that the Will, at that time, should be *otherwise* than that way to which it tends.*

If any one should say, there is no need that the Indifference should be perfect; but although a former inclination still remains, yet, if it be not very strong, possibly the strength of the Will may oppose and overcome it:—This is grossly absurd; for the strength of the Will, let it be never so great, gives it no such sovereignty and command, as to cause itself to prefer and not to prefer at the same time, or to choose contrary to its own present choice.

Therefore, if there be the least degree of antecedent preponderation of the Will, it must be perfectly abolished, before the Will can be at liberty to determine itself the contrary way. And if the Will determines itself the *same* way, it was not a *free determination*, because the Will is not wholly at liberty in so doing; its determination is not altogether *from itself*, but it was partly determined before, in its prior inclination: and all the freedom the Will exercises in the case, is in an increase of inclination, which it gives itself, added to what it had by a foregoing bias; so much is from itself, and so much is from perfect indifference. For though the Will had a previous tendency that way, yet as to that additional degree of inclination, it had no tendency. Therefore the previous tendency is of no consideration, with respect to the act wherein the Will is free. So that it comes to the same thing which was said at first, that as to the act of the Will, wherein the Will is free, there must be *perfect Indifference*, or *equilibrium*.

To illustrate this: suppose a sovereign self-moving power in a natural body; but that the body is in motion already, by an antecedent bias; for instance, gravitation towards the centre of the earth; and has *one degree* of motion by virtue of that previous tendency; but by its self-moving power it *adds one degree more* to its motion, and moves so much more swiftly towards the centre of the earth than it would do by its gravity only: it is evident, all that is owing to a self-moving power in this case, is the *additional* degree of motion; and that the other degree which it had from gravity, is of no consideration in the case; the effect is just the same, as if the body had received from itself *one* degree of motion from a state of perfect rest. So, if we suppose a self-moving power given to the scale of a balance, which has a weight of *one degree* beyond the opposite scale; and if we ascribe to it an ability to add to itself *another degree* of force the same way, by its self-moving power; this is just the same thing as to ascribe to it a power to give itself *one degree* of preponderation from a perfect equilibrium; and so much power as the scale has to give itself an over-balance from a perfect equipoise, so much self-moving self-preponderating power it has, and no more. So that its free power this way is always to be measured from perfect equilibrium.

I need say no more to prove, that if Indifference be essential to Liberty, it must be *perfect* Indifference; and that so far as the Will is destitute of this, so far is it destitute of that freedom by which it is in a capacity of being its own determiner, without being at all passive, or subject to the power and sway of something else, in its motions and determinations.

Having observed these things, let us now try whether this notion of the Liberty of Will consisting in Indifference and equilibrium, and the Will's self-determination in such a state, be not absurd and inconsistent.

And here I would lay down this as an axiom of undoubted truth; *that every free act is done* IN *a state of freedom, and not only* AFTER *such a state*. If an act of the Will be an act wherein the soul is free, it must be exerted in a *state of freedom*, and in the *time of freedom*. It will not suffice, that the act immediately follows a state of Liberty; but Liberty must yet continue, and co-exist with the act; the soul remaining in possession of Liberty. Because that is the notion of a free act of the soul, even an act wherein the soul *uses* or *exercises Liberty*. But if the soul is not, in the very time of the act, in the *possession* of Liberty, it cannot at that time be in the *use* of it.

Now the question is, whether ever the soul of man puts forth an act of Will, while it yet remains in a state of Liberty, *viz.* as implying a state of Indifference; or whether the soul ever exerts an act of preference, while at that very time the Will is in a perfect equilibrium, not inclining one way more than another. The very putting of the question is sufficient to show the absurdity of the affirmative answer: for how ridiculous would it be for any body to insist, that the soul chooses one thing before another, when at the very same instant it is perfectly indifferent with respect to each! This is the same thing as to say, the soul prefers one thing to another, at the very same time that it has no preference.—Choice and preference can no more be in a state of Indifference, than motion can be in a state of rest, or than the preponderation of the scale of a balance can be in a state of equilibrium. Motion may be the next moment after rest; but cannot co-exist with it, in *any*, even the *least*, part of it. So choice may be immediately *after* a state of Indifference, but cannot co-exist with it: even the very beginning of it is not in a state of Indifference. And therefore, if this be Liberty, no act of the Will, in any degree, is ever performed in a state of Liberty, or in the time of Liberty. Volition and Liberty are so far from agreeing together, and being essential one to another, that they are contrary one to another, and one excludes and destroys the other, as much as motion and rest, light and darkness, or life and death. So that the Will acts not at all, does not so much as begin to act, in the time of such Liberty: freedom has ceased to be, at the first moment of action; and therefore Liberty cannot reach the action, to affect, or qualify it, or give it a denomination, any more than if it had ceased to be twenty years before the action began. The moment that Liberty ceases to be, it ceases to be a qualification of any thing. If light and darkness succeed one another instantaneously, light qualifies nothing after it is gone out, to make any thing lightsome or bright, at the first moment of perfect darkness, any more than months or years after. Life denominates nothing *vital*, at the first moment of perfect death. So freedom, if it consists in or implies Indifference, can denominate nothing *free*, at the first moment of preference or preponderation. Therefore it is manifest, that no Liberty which the soul is possessed of, or ever uses, in any of its acts of volition, consists in Indifference; and that the opinion of such as suppose, that Indifference belongs to the very essence of Liberty, is to the highest degree absurd and contradictory.

If any one should imagine, that this manner of arguing is nothing but a trick and delusion; and to evade the reasoning, should say, that the thing wherein the Will exercises its Liberty, is not in the *act* of choice or preponderation itself, but in *determining* itself to a certain choice or preference; that the act of the Will wherein it is free, and uses its own sovereignty, consists in its *causing* or *determining* the *change* or *transition* from a state of indifference to a certain preference or determining to give a certain turn to the balance, which has hitherto been even; and that the Will exerts this act in a state of Liberty, or while the Will yet remains in equilibrium, and perfect master of itself.—I say, if any one chooses to express his notion of Liberty after this, or some such manner, let us see if he can succeed any better than before.

What is asserted is, that the Will, while it yet remains in perfect equilibrium, without preference, *determines* to change itself from that state, and excite in itself a certain choice or preference. Now let us see whether this does not come to the same absurdity we had before. If it be so, that the Will, while it yet remains perfectly indifferent, *determines* to put itself out of that state, and to give itself a certain preponderation; then I would inquire, whether the soul does not determine this of *choice*; or whether the Will coming to a determination to do so, be not the same

* There is a little intricacy in this mode of expression. It may be thus illustrated. Suppose it were asserted, "That it is impossible for the Will to be otherwise at any one given time, than that way to which it tends." Such a proposition one might think, none who understood the terms would controvert; for it would be to controvert this proposition, "The Will is as its tendency." And yet, the advocates for a self-determining power must assert a liberty which denies this plain proposition.—W.

thing as the soul coming to a choice to do so. If the soul does not determine this of choice, or in the exercise of choice, then it does not determine it voluntarily. And if the soul does not determine it voluntarily, or of its own *Will*, then in what sense does its *Will* determine it? And if the Will does not determine it, then how is the *Liberty of the Will* exercised in the determination? What sort of Liberty is exercised by the soul in those determinations, wherein there is no exercise of choice, which are not voluntary, and wherein the Will is not concerned? But if it be allowed, that this determination is an act of choice, and it be insisted on, that the soul, while it yet remains in a state of perfect Indifference, chooses to put itself out of that state, and to turn itself one way; then the soul is already come to a choice; and chooses that way. And so we have the very same absurdity which we had before. Here is the soul in a state of *choice*, and in a state of *equilibrium*, both at the same time: the soul already choosing one way, while it remains in a state of perfect Indifference, and has no choice of one way more than the other.—And indeed this manner of talking, though it may a little hide the absurdity, in the obscurity of expression, increases the inconsistence. To say, the free act of the Will, or the act which the Will exerts in a state of freedom and Indifference, does not imply preference in it, but is what the will does in order to cause or produce a preference, is as much as to say, the soul chooses (for to *will* and to *choose* are the same thing) without choice, and prefers without preference, in order to cause or produce the beginning of a preference, or the first choice. And that is, that the first choice is exerted without choice, in order to produce itself!

If any, to evade these things, should own, that a state of Liberty and a state of Indifference are not the same, and that the former may be without the latter; but should say, that Indifference is still *essential to* freedom, as it is necessary to go immediately *before it;* it being essential to the freedom of an act of Will that it should directly and immediately *arise out* of a state of Indifference; still this will not help the cause of *Arminian* Liberty, or make it consistent with itself. For if the act springs immediately out of a state of Indifference, then it does not arise from *antecedent* choice or preference. But if the act arises directly out of a state of Indifference, without any intervening *choice* to determine it, then the act not being determined by choice, is not determined by the *Will;* the mind exercises no free choice in the affair, and free choice and free Will have no hand in the determination of the act. Which is entirely inconsistent with their notion of the freedom of volition.

If any should suppose, that these absurdities may be avoided, by saying, that the Liberty of the mind consists in a power to *suspend* the act of the Will, and so to keep it in a state of *Indifference*, until there has been opportunity for consideration; and so shall say, that however Indifference is not essential to Liberty in such a manner, that the mind must make its choice in a state of Indifference, which is an inconsistency, or that the act of Will must spring immediately out of Indifference; yet Indifference may be essential to the Liberty of acts of the Will in this respect; *viz.* That Liberty consists in a power of the mind to forbear or suspend the act of volition, and keep the mind in a state of Indifference for the present, until there has been opportunity for proper deliberation: I say, if any one imagines that this helps the matter, it is a great mistake: it reconciles no inconsistency, and relieves no difficulty.—For here the following things must be observed:

1. That this *suspending* of volition, if there be properly any such thing, is itself an act of volition. If the mind determines to suspend its act, it determines it voluntarily; it chooses, on some consideration, to suspend it. And this choice or determination, is an act of the Will: And indeed it is supposed to be so in the very hypothesis; for it is supposed that the Liberty *of the Will* consists in its power to do this, and that its doing it is the very thing wherein *the Will exercises its Liberty*. But how can the Will exercise Liberty in it, if it be not an act of the Will? The Liberty of the Will is not exercised in any thing but what the Will does.

2. This determining to suspend acting is not only an act of the Will, but it is supposed to be the *only* free act of the Will; because it is said, that *this is the thing wherein the Liberty of the Will consists.*—If so, then this is all the act of Will that we have to consider in this controversy. And now, the former question returns upon us; *viz.* Wherein consists the freedom of the will *in those acts* wherein it is free*!* And if this act of determining a suspension be the only act in which the Will is free, then wherein consists the Will's freedom with respect to this act of suspension? And how is Indifference essential to this act? The answer must be, according to what is supposed in the evasion under consideration, that the Liberty of the Will in this act of suspension, consists in a power to suspend even this act, until there has been opportunity for thorough deliberation. But this will be to plunge directly into the grossest nonsense: for it is the act of suspension itself that we are speaking of; and there is no room for a space of deliberation and suspension in order to determine whether we will suspend or no. For that supposes, that even suspension itself may be deferred: which is absurd; for the very deferring the determination of suspension, to consider whether we will suspend or no, will be actually suspending. For during the space of suspension, to consider whether to suspend, the act is, *ipso facto*, suspended. There is no medium between suspending to act, and immediately acting; and therefore no possibility of avoiding either the one or the other one moment.

And besides, this is attended with ridiculous absurdity another way: for now, it seems, Liberty consists wholly in the mind having power to suspend its determination whether to suspend or no; that there may be time for consideration, whether it be best to suspend. And if Liberty consists in this only, then this is the Liberty under consideration. We have to inquire now, how Liberty, with respect to this act of suspending a determination of suspension, consists in Indifference, or how Indifference is essential to it. The answer, according to the hypothesis we are upon, must be, that it consists in a power of suspending even this last-mentioned act, to have time to consider whether to suspend that. And then the same difficulties and inquiries return over again with respect to that; and so on for ever. Which, if it would show any thing, would show only that there is no such thing as a free act. It drives the exercise of freedom back *in infinitum;* and that is to drive it out of the world.

And besides all this, there is a delusion, and a latent gross contradiction in the affair another way; inasmuch as in explaining how, or in what respect, the Will is free, with regard to a particular act of volition, it is said, that its Liberty consists in a power to determine to suspend *that act*, which places Liberty not in *that act* of volition which the inquiry is about, but altogether in another antecedent act. Which contradicts the thing supposed in both the question and answer. The question is, wherein consists the mind's Liberty *in any particular act* of volition? And the answer, in pretending to show wherein lies the mind's Liberty *in that act*, in effect says, it does not lie in that act at all, but in another, *viz.* a volition *to suspend that act.* And therefore the answer is both contradictory, and altogether impertinent and beside the purpose. For it does not show wherein the Liberty of the Will consists in the act in question; instead of that, it supposes it does not consist in that act at all, but in another distinct from it, even a volition to suspend that act, and take time to consider of it. And no account is pretended to be given wherein the mind is free with respect to that act, wherein this answer supposes the Liberty of the mind indeed consists, *viz.* the act of suspension, or of determining the suspension.

On the whole, it is exceeding manifest, that the Liberty of the mind does not consist in Indifference, and that Indifference is not essential or necessary to it, or at all belonging to it, as the *Arminians* suppose; that opinion being full of nothing but self-contradiction.

SECT. VIII.

Concerning the supposed Liberty of the Will, as opposite to all Necessity.

It is chiefly insisted on by *Arminians*, in this controversy, as a thing most important and essential in human

Liberty, that volitions, or the acts of the Will, are *contingent* events; understanding contingence as opposite, not only to constraint, but to all Necessity. Therefore I would particularly consider this matter.

And, *First*, I would inquire, whether there is or can be any such thing, as a volition which is contingent in such a sense, as not only to come to pass without any Necessity of constraint or co-action, but also without a *Necessity of consequence*, or an infallible connexion with any thing foregoing.—*Secondly*, Whether, if it were so, this would at all help the cause of Liberty.

I. I would consider whether volition is a thing that ever does or can come to pass, in this manner, contingently.

And here it must be remembered, that it has been already shown, that nothing can ever come to pass without a cause, or a reason, why it exists in this manner rather than another; and the evidence of this has been particularly applied to the acts of the Will. Now if this be so, it will demonstrably follow, that the acts of the Will are never contingent, or without Necessity, in the sense spoken of; inasmuch as those things which have a cause, or a reason of their existence, must be connected with their cause. This appears by the following considerations.

1. For an event to have a cause and ground of its existence, and yet not to be connected with its cause, is an inconsistence. For if the event be not connected with the cause, it is not dependent on the cause; its existence is as it were loose from its influence, and may attend it, or may not; it being a mere contingence, whether it follows or attends the influence of the cause, or not: And that is the same thing as not to be dependent on it. And to say, the event is not dependent on its cause, is absurd; it is the same thing as to say, it is not its cause, nor the event the effect of it; for dependence on the influence of a cause is the very notion of an effect. If there be no such relation between one thing and another, consisting in the connexion and dependence of one thing on the influence of another, then it is certain there is no such relation between them as is signified by the terms *cause* and *effect*. So far as an event is dependent on a cause, and connected with it, so much causality is there in the case, and no more. The cause does, or brings to pass, no more in any event, than is dependent on it. If we say, the connexion and dependence is not total, but partial, and that the effect, though it has some connexion and dependence, yet is not entirely dependent on it; that is the same thing as to say, that not all that is in the event is an effect of that cause, but that only part of it arises from thence, and part some other way.

2. If there are some events which are not necessarily connected with their causes, then it will follow, that there are some things which come to pass without any cause, contrary to the supposition. For if there be any event which was not necessarily connected with the influence of the cause under such circumstances, then it was contingent whether it would attend or follow the influence of the cause, or no; it might have followed, and it might not, when the cause was the same, its influence the same, and under the same circumstances. And if so, why did it follow, rather than not follow? Of this there is no cause or reason. Therefore here is something without any cause or reason why it is, *viz.* the following of the effect on the influence of the cause, with which it was not necessarily connected. If there be no necessary connexion of the effect on any thing antecedent, then we may suppose that sometimes the event will follow the cause, and sometimes not, when the cause is the same, and in every respect in the same state and circumstances. And what can be the cause and reason of this strange phenomenon, even this diversity, that in one instance, the effect should follow, in another not? It is evident by the supposition, that this is wholly without any cause or ground. Here is something in the present manner of the existence of things, and state of the world, that is absolutely without a cause. Which is contrary to the supposition, and contrary to what has been before demonstrated.

3. To suppose there are some events which have a cause and ground of their existence, that yet are not necessarily connected with their cause, is to suppose that they have a cause which is not their cause. Thus; if the effect be not necessarily connected with the cause, with its influence, and influential circumstances; then, as I observed before, it is a thing possible and supposable, that the cause may sometimes exert the same influence, under the same circumstances, and yet the effect not follow. And if this actually happens in any instance, this instance is a proof, in fact, that the influence of the cause is not sufficient to produce the effect. For if it had been sufficient, it would have done it. And yet, by the supposition, in another instance, the same cause, with perfectly the same influence, and when all circumstances which have any influence are the same, it *was followed* with the effect. By which it is manifest, that the effect in this last instance was not owing to the influence of the cause, but must come to pass some other way. For it was proved before, that the influence of the cause was not sufficient to produce the effect. And if it was not sufficient to produce it, then the production of it could not be owing to that influence, but must be owing to something else, or owing to nothing. And if the effect be not owing to the influence of the cause, then it is not the cause. Which brings us to the contradiction of a cause, and no cause, that which is the ground and reason of the existence of a thing, and at the same time is NOT the ground and reason of its existence.

If the matter be not already so plain as to render any further reasoning upon it impertinent, I would say, that which seems to be the cause in the supposed case, can be no cause; its power and influence having, on a full trial, proved insufficient to produce such an effect: and if it be not sufficient to produce it, then it does not produce it. To say otherwise, is to say, there is power to do that which there is not power to do. If there be in a cause sufficient power exerted, and in circumstances sufficient to produce an effect, and so the effect be actually produced at *one time;* all these things concurring, will produce the effect at *all times*. And so we may turn it the other way; that which proves not sufficient at one time, cannot be sufficient at another, with precisely the same influential circumstances. And therefore if the effect follows, it is not owing to that cause; unless the different time be a circumstance which has influence: but that is contrary to the supposition; for it is supposed that all circumstances that have influence, are the same. And besides, this would be to suppose the time to be the cause; which is contrary to the supposition of the other thing being the cause. But if merely diversity of time has no influence, then it is evident that it is as much of an absurdity to say, the cause was sufficient to produce the effect at one time, and not at another; as to say, that it is sufficient to produce the effect at a certain time, and yet not sufficient to produce the same effect at the same time.

On the whole, it is clearly manifest, that every effect has a necessary connexion with its cause, or with that which is the true ground and reason of its existence. And therefore, if there be no event without a cause, as was proved before, then no event whatsoever is contingent, in the manner that *Arminians* suppose the free acts of the Will to be contingent.

SECT. IX.

Of the Connexion of the Acts of the Will with the Dictates of the Understanding.

IT is manifest, that no Acts of the Will are contingent, in such a sense as to be without all necessity, or so as not to be necessary with a necessity of consequence and Connexion; because every Act of the Will is some way connected with the Understanding, and is as the greatest apparent good is, in the manner which has already been explained; namely, that the soul always wills or chooses that which, in the present view of the mind, considered in the whole of that view, and all that belongs to it, appears most agreeable. Because, as was observed before, nothing is more evident than that, when men act voluntarily, and do what they please, then they do what appears most agreeable to them; and to say otherwise, would be as much as to affirm, that men do not choose what appears to suit them best, or what seems most pleasing to them; or that they do not choose what they prefer. Which brings the matter to a contradiction.

And as it is very evident in itself, that the Acts of the Will have some Connexion with the Dictates or views of the Understanding, so this is allowed by some of the chief of the *Arminian* writers; particularly by Dr. Whitby and Dr. Samuel Clark. Dr. Turnbull, though a great enemy to the doctrine of necessity, allows the same thing. In his *Christian Philosophy*, (p. 196.) he with much approbation cites another philosopher, as of the same mind, in these words: "No man (says an excellent philosopher) sets himself about any thing, but upon some view or other, which serves him for a reason for what he does; and whatsoever faculties he employs, the Understanding, with such light as it has, well or ill formed, constantly leads; and by that light, true or false, all her operative powers are directed. The Will itself, how absolute and incontrollable soever it may be thought, never fails in its obedience to the Dictates of the Understanding. Temples have their sacred images; and we see what influence they have always had over a great part of mankind; but in truth, the ideas and images in men's minds are the invisible powers that constantly govern them; and to these they all pay universally a ready submission." But whether this be in a just consistence with themselves, and their own notions of liberty, I desire may now be impartially considered.

Dr. Whitby plainly supposes, that the Acts and determinations of the Will always follow the Understanding's view of the greatest good to be obtained, or evil to be avoided; or, in other words, that the determinations of the Will constantly and infallibly follow these two things in the Understanding: 1. The *degree of good* to be obtained, and evil to be avoided, proposed to the Understanding, and apprehended, viewed, and taken notice of by it. 2. The *degree of the Understanding's* apprehension of that good or evil; which is increased by attention and consideration. That this is an opinion in which he is exceeding peremptory, (as he is in every opinion which he maintains in his controversy with the *Calvinists,*) with disdain of the contrary opinion, as absurd and self-contradictory, will appear by the following words, in his Discourse on the Five Points.*

"Now, it is certain, that what naturally makes the Understanding to perceive, is evidence proposed, and apprehended, considered or adverted to: for nothing else can be requisite to make us come to the knowledge of the truth. Again, what makes the Will choose, is something approved by the Understanding; and consequently appearing to the soul as good. And whatsoever it refuseth, is something represented by the Understanding, and so appearing to the Will, as evil. Whence all that God requires of us is and can be only this; to refuse the evil, and choose the good. Wherefore, to say that evidence proposed, apprehended, and considered, is not sufficient to make the Understanding approve; or that the greatest good proposed, the greatest evil threatened, when equally believed and reflected on, is not sufficient to engage the Will to choose the good and refuse the evil, is in effect to say, *that which alone doth move the Will to choose or to refuse*, is not sufficient to engage it so to do; which being contradictory to itself, must of necessity be false. Be it then so, that we naturally have an aversion to the truths proposed to us in the gospel; that only can make us indisposed to attend to them, but cannot hinder our conviction, when we do apprehend them, and attend to them.—Be it, that there is in us also a renitency to the good we are to choose; that only can indispose us to believe it is, and to approve it as our chiefest good. Be it, that we are prone to the evil that we should decline; that only can render it the more difficult for us to believe it is the worst of evils. But yet, *what we do really believe to be our chiefest good, will still be chosen; and what we apprehend to be the worst of evils, will, whilst we do continue under that conviction, be refused by us.* It therefore can be only requisite, in order to these ends, that the Good Spirit should so illuminate our Understandings, that we attending to and considering what lies before us, should apprehend and be convinced of our duty; and that the blessings of the gospel should be so propounded to us, as that we may discern them to be our chiefest good; and the miseries it threateneth, so as we may be convinced that they are the worst of evils; that we may choose the one, and refuse the other."

Here let it be observed, how plainly and peremptorily it is asserted, *that the greatest good proposed, and the greatest evil threatened, when equally believed and reflected on, is sufficient to engage the Will to choose the good, and refuse the evil, and is that alone which doth move the Will to choose or to refuse; and that it is contradictory to itself, to suppose otherwise; and therefore must of necessity be false; and then what we do really believe to be our chiefest good will still be chosen, and what we apprehend to be the worst of evils, will, whilst we continue under that conviction, be refused by us.* Nothing could have been said more to the purpose, fully to signify, that the determinations of the Will must evermore follow the illumination, conviction, and notice of the Understanding, with regard to the greatest good and evil proposed, reckoning both the degree of good and evil understood, and the degree of Understanding, notice, and conviction of that proposed good and evil; and that it is thus necessarily, and can be otherwise in no instance: because it is asserted, that it implies a contradiction, to suppose it ever to be otherwise.

I am sensible, the Doctor's aim in these assertions is against the *Calvinists;* to show, in opposition to them, that there is no need of any physical operation of the Spirit of God on the Will, to change and determine that to a good choice, but that God's operation and assistance is only moral, suggesting ideas to the Understanding; which he supposes to be enough, if those ideas are attended to, infallibly to obtain the end. But whatever his design was, nothing can more directly and fully prove, that every determination of the Will, in choosing and refusing, *is necessary;* directly contrary to his own notion of the liberty of the Will. For if the determination of the Will, evermore, in this manner, follows the light, conviction, and view of the Understanding, concerning the greatest good and evil, and this be that alone which moves the Will, and it be a contradiction to suppose otherwise; then it is *necessarily* so, the Will necessarily follows this light or view of the Understanding, not only in some of its acts, but in every act of choosing and refusing. So that the Will does not determine itself in any one of its own acts; but every act of choice and refusal depends on, and is necessarily connected with, some antecedent cause; which cause is not the Will itself, nor any act of its own, nor any thing pertaining to that faculty, but something belonging to another faculty, whose acts go before the Will, in all its acts, and govern and determine them.

Here, if it should be replied, that although it be true, that according to the Doctor, the final determination of the Will always depends upon, and is infallibly connected with, the Understanding's conviction, and notice of the greatest good; yet the Acts of the Will are not necessary; because that conviction of the Understanding is first dependent on a preceding Act of the Will, in determining to take notice of the evidence exhibited; by which means the mind obtains that degree of conviction, which is sufficient and effectual to determine the consequent and ultimate choice of the Will; and that the Will, with regard to that preceding act, whereby it determines whether to attend or no, is not necessary; and that in this, the liberty of the Will consists, that when God holds forth sufficient objective light, the Will is at liberty whether to command the attention of the mind to it or not.

Nothing can be more weak and inconsiderate than such a reply as this. For that preceding Act of the Will, in determining to attend and consider, still is an *Act of the Will;* if the *Liberty of the Will* consists in it, as is supposed, as if it be an Act of the Will, it is an act of *choice* or *refusal*. And therefore, if what the Doctor asserts be true, it is determined by some antecedent light in the Understanding concerning the greatest apparent good or evil. For he asserts, it is that light *which alone doth move the Will to choose or refuse.* And therefore the Will must be moved by that, in choosing to attend to the objective light

* Second Edit. p. 211, 212, 213.

offered, in order to another consequent act of choice: so that this act is no less necessary than the other. And if we suppose another Act of the Will, still preceding both these mentioned, to determine both, still that also must be an Act of the Will, an act of choice; and so must, by the same principles, be infallibly determined by some certain degree of light in the Understanding concerning the greatest good. And let us suppose as many Acts of the Will, one preceding another, as we please, yet are they every one of them necessarily determined by a certain degree of light in the Understanding, concerning the greatest and most eligible good in that case; and so, not one of them free according to Dr. Whitby's notion of freedom. And if it be said, the reason why men do not attend to light held forth, is because of ill habits contracted by evil acts committed before, whereby their minds are indisposed to consider the truth held forth to them, the difficulty is not at all avoided: still the question returns, What determined the Will in those preceding evil acts? It must, by Dr. Whitby's principles, still be the view of the Understanding concerning the greatest good and evil. If this view of the Understanding be *that alone which doth move the Will to choose or refuse*, as the Doctor asserts, then every act of *choice or refusal*, from a man's first existence, is moved and determined by this view; and this view of the Understanding exciting and governing the act, must be before the act. And therefore the Will is necessarily determined, in every one of its acts, from a man's first existence, by a cause beside the Will, and a cause that does not proceed from or depend on any act of the Will at all. Which at once utterly abolishes the Doctor's whole scheme of Liberty of Will; and he, at one stroke, has cut the sinews of all his arguments from the goodness, righteousness, faithfulness, and sincerity of God, in his commands, promises, threatenings, calls, invitations, and expostulations; which he makes use of, under the heads of reprobation, election, universal redemption, sufficient and effectual grace, and the freedom of the Will of man; and has made vain all his exclamations against the doctrine of the *Calvinists*, as charging God with manifest unrighteousness, unfaithfulness, hypocrisy, fallaciousness, and cruelty.

Dr. Samuel Clark, in his Demonstration of the Being and Attributes of God,* to evade the argument to prove the necessity of volition, from its necessary Connexion with the last Dictate of the Understanding, supposes the latter not to be diverse from the Act of the Will itself. But if it be so, it will not alter the case as to the *necessity* of the Act. If the Dictate of the Understanding be the very same with the determination of the Will, as Dr. Clark supposes, then this determination is no *fruit* or *effect of choice;* and if so, no *liberty* of choice has any hand in it: it is *necessary;* that is, choice cannot prevent it. If the last Dictate of the Understanding be the same with the determination of volition itself, then the existence of that determination must be necessary as to volition; in as much as volition can have no opportunity to determine whether it shall exist or no, it having existence already before volition has opportunity to determine any thing. It is itself the very rise and existence of volition. But a thing *after* it exists, has no opportunity to determine as to its own existence; it is too late for that.

If liberty consists in that which *Arminians* suppose, *viz.* in the Will determining its own acts, having free opportunity and being without all necessity; this is the same as to say, that liberty consists in the soul having power and opportunity to have what determinations of the Will it pleases. And if the determinations of the Will, and the last Dictates of the Understanding, be the same thing, then liberty consists in the mind having power and opportunity to choose its own Dictates of Understanding. But this is absurd; for it is to make the determination of choice prior to the Dictate of Understanding, and the ground of it; which cannot consist with the Dictate of the Understanding being the determination of choice itself.

Here is no alternative, but to recur to the old absurdity of one determination before another, and the cause of it; and another before, determining that; and so on *in infinitum.* If the last Dictate of the Understanding be the determination of the Will itself, and the soul be free with regard to that Dictate, in the *Arminian* notion of freedom; then the soul, before that dictate of its Understanding exists, voluntarily and according to its own choice determines, in every case, what that Dictate of the Understanding shall be; otherwise that Dictate, as to the Will, is necessary; and the acts determined by it must also be necessary. So that here is a determination of the mind prior to that Dictate of the Understanding, an act of choice going before it, choosing and determining what that Dictate of the Understanding shall be: and this preceding act of choice, being a free Act of Will, must also be the same with another last Dictate of the Understanding: And if the mind also be free in that Dictate of Understanding, that must be determined still by another; and so on for ever.

Besides, if the Dictate of the Understanding, and determination of the Will be the same, this confounds the Understanding and Will, and makes them the same. Whether they be the same or no, I will not now dispute; but only would observe, that if it be so, and the *Arminian* notion of liberty consists in a self-determining power in the Understanding, free of all necessity; being independent, undetermined by any thing prior to its own acts and determinations; and the more the Understanding is thus independent, and sovereign over its own determinations, the more free: then the freedom of the soul, as a moral agent, must consist in the independence of the Understanding on any *evidence* or appearance of things, or any thing whatsoever that stands forth to the view of the mind, prior to the Understanding's determination. And what a liberty is this! consisting in an ability, freedom, and easiness of judging, either according to evidence, or against it; having a sovereign command over itself at all times, to judge, either agreeably or disagreeably to what is plainly exhibited to its own view. Certainly, it is no liberty that renders persons the proper subjects of persuasive reasoning, arguments, expostulations, and such like moral means and inducements. The use of which with mankind is a main argument of the *Arminians*, to defend their notion of liberty without all necessity. For according to this, the more free men are, the less they are under the government of such means, less subject to the power of evidence and reason, and more independent on their influence, in their determinations.

And whether the Understanding and Will are the same or no, as Dr. Clark seems to suppose, yet in order to maintain the *Arminian* notion of liberty without necessity, the free Will is not determined by the Understanding, nor necessarily connected with the Understanding; and the further from such Connexion, the greater the freedom. And when the liberty is full and complete, the determinations of the Will have no Connexion at all with the Dictates of the Understanding. And if so, in vain are all the applications to the Understanding, in order to induce to any free virtuous act; and so in vain are all instructions, counsels, invitations, expostulations, and all arguments and persuasives whatsoever: for these are but applications to the Understanding, and a clear and lively exhibition of the objects of choice to the mind's view. But if, after all, the Will must be self-determined, and independent on the Understanding, to what purpose are things thus represented to the Understanding, in order to determine the choice?

SECTION X.

Volition necessarily connected with the influence of Motives: with particular observations on the great inconsistence of Mr. Chubb's assertions and reasonings about the Freedom of the Will.

That every act of the Will has some cause, and consequently (by what has been already proved) has a necessary connexion with its cause, and so is necessary by a necessity of connexion and consequence, is evident by this, that every act of the Will whatsoever is excited by some motive: which is manifest, because, if the mind, in willing

* Edit. VI. p. 93.

after the manner it does, is excited by no motive or inducement, then it has no end which it proposes to itself, or pursues in so doing; it aims at nothing, and seeks nothing. And if it seeks nothing, then it does not go after any thing, or exert any inclination or preference towards any thing. Which brings the matter to a contradiction; because for the mind to will something, and for it to go after something by an act of preference and inclination, are the same thing.

But if every act of the Will is excited by a Motive, then that Motive is the cause of the act. If the acts of the Will are excited by Motives, then Motives are the causes of their being excited; or, which is the same thing, the cause of their existence. And if so, the existence of the acts of the Will is properly the effect of their Motives. Motives do nothing, as Motives or inducements, but by their influence; and so much as is done by their influence is the effect of them. For that is the notion of an effect, something that is brought to pass by the influence of something else.

And if volitions are properly the effects of their Motives, then they are necessarily connected with their Motives. Every effect and event being, as was proved before, necessarily connected with that which is the proper ground and reason of its existence. Thus it is manifest, that volition is necessary, and is not from any self-determining power in the Will: the volition, which is caused by previous Motive and inducement, is not caused by the Will exercising a sovereign power over itself, to determine, cause, and excite volitions in itself. This is not consistent with the Will acting in a state of indifference and equilibrium, to determine itself to a preference; for the way in which Motives operate, is by biassing the Will, and giving it a certain inclination or preponderation one way.

Here it may be proper to observe, that Mr. Chubb in his Collection of Tracts on Various Subjects, has advanced a scheme of liberty, which is greatly divided against itself, and thoroughly subversive of itself: and that many ways.

I. He is abundant in asserting, that the Will, in all its acts, is influenced by Motive and excitement; and that this is the *previous ground and reason* of all its acts, and that it is never otherwise in any instance. He says, (p. 262.) "No action can take place without some Motive to excite it." And, (p. 263.) "Volition cannot take place without some PREVIOUS reason or motive to induce it." And, (p. 310.) *Action would not take place without some reason or Motive to induce it; it being absurd to suppose, that the active faculty would be exerted without some* PREVIOUS *reason to dispose the mind to action.*" (So also p. 257.) And he speaks of these things, as what we may be absolutely certain of, and which are the foundation, the only foundation we have of certainty respecting God's moral perfections. (p. 252—255, 261—264.)

And yet, at the same time, by his scheme, the influence of Motives upon us to excite to action, and to be actually a ground of volition, is *consequent* on the volition or choice of the mind. For he very greatly insists upon it, that in all free actions, before the mind is the subject of those volitions, which Motives excite, it chooses to be so. It chooses, whether it will comply with the Motive, which presents itself in view, or not; and when various Motives are presented, it chooses which it will yield to, and which it will reject. (p. 256.) "Every man has power to act, or to refrain from acting, agreeably with, or contrary to, any Motive that presents." (p. 257.) "Every man is at liberty to act, or refrain from acting, agreeably with, or contrary to, what each of these Motives, considered singly, would excite him to.—Man has power, and is as much at liberty, to reject the Motive that does prevail, as he has power, and is at liberty, to reject those Motives that do not." (And so p. 310, 311.) "In order to constitute a moral agent, it is necessary, that he should have power to act, or to refrain from acting, upon such moral Motives, as he pleases." And to the like purpose in many other places. According to these things, the Will acts first, and chooses or refuses to comply with the Motive that is presented, before it falls under its prevailing influence: and it is first determined by the mind's pleasure or choice, what Motives it will be induced by, before it is induced by them.

Now, how can these things hang together? How can the mind first act, and by its act of *volition* and *choice* determine what Motives shall be the ground and reason of its *volition* and *choice?* For this supposes, the choice is already made, before the Motive has its effect; and that the volition is already exerted, before the Motive prevails, so as actually to be the ground of the volition; and make the prevailing of the Motive, the consequence of the volition, of which yet it is the ground. If the mind has *already* chosen to comply with a Motive, and to yield to its excitement, the excitement comes in too late, and is needless afterwards. If the mind has already chosen to yield to a Motive which *invites* to a thing, that implies, and in fact is, a choosing of the thing *invited to;* and the very act of choice is before the influence of the Motive which induces, and is the ground of the choice; the son is before-hand with the father that begets him: the choice is supposed to be the ground of that influence of the Motive, which very influence is supposed to be the ground of the choice. And so *vice versa,* the choice is supposed to be the consequence of the influence of the Motive, which influence of the Motive is the consequence of that very choice.

And besides, if the Will acts first towards the Motive before it falls under its influence, and the prevailing of the Motive upon it to induce it to act and choose, be the fruit and consequence of its act and choice, then how is the Motive "A PREVIOUS ground and reason of the act and choice, so that in the nature of the things, volition cannot take place without some PREVIOUS reason and Motive to induce it;" and that this act is consequent upon, and follows the Motive? Which things Mr. Chubb often asserts, as of certain and undoubted truth. So that the very same Motive is both *previous* and *consequent,* both before and after, both the ground and fruit of the very same thing!

II. Agreeable to the forementioned inconsistent notion of the Will first acting towards the Motive, choosing whether it will comply with it, in order to it becoming a ground of the Will's acting, before any act of volition can take place, Mr. Chubb frequently calls Motives and excitements to the action of the Will, "the passive ground or reason of that action." Which is a remarkable phrase; than which I presume there is none more unintelligible, and void of distinct and consistent meaning, in all the writings of Duns Scotus, or Thomas Aquinas. When he represents the Motive volition as passive, he must mean—passive in that affair, or passive with respect to that action, which he speaks of; otherwise it is nothing to the design of his argument: he must mean, (if that can be called a meaning,) that the Motive to volition is first acted *upon* or *towards* by the volition, choosing to yield to it, making it a ground of action, or determining to fetch its influence from thence; and so to make it a previous ground of its own excitation and existence. Which is the same absurdity, as if one should say, that the soul of man, previous to its existence, chose by what cause it would come into existence, and acted upon its cause, to fetch influence thence, to bring it into being; and so its cause was a passive ground of its existence!

Mr. Chubb very plainly supposes Motive or excitement to be the *ground of the being* of volition. He speaks of it as the ground or reason of the EXERTION of an act of the Will, (p. 391, and 392.) and expressly says, that "volition cannot TAKE PLACE without some *previous* ground or Motive to induce it," (p. 363.) And he speaks of the act as "FROM the Motive, and FROM THE INFLUENCE of the Motive," (p. 352.) "and from the influence that the Motive has on the man, for the PRODUCTION of an action," (p. 317.) Certainly there is no need of multiplying words about this; it is easily judged, whether Motive can be the ground of volition taking place, so that the very production of it is from the influence of the Motive, and yet the Motive, before it becomes the ground of the volition, is passive, or acted upon the volition. But this I will say, that a man, who insists so much on clearness of meaning in others, and is so much in blaming their confusion and inconsistence, ought, if he was able, to have explained his meaning in this phrase of "passive ground of action," so as to show it not to be confused and inconsistent.

If any should suppose, that Mr. Chubb, when he speaks of Motive as a "passive ground of action," does not mean passive with regard to that volition which it is the ground of, but some other antecedent volition, (though his purpose and argument, and whole discourse, will by no means allow of such a supposition,) yet it would not help the matter in the least. For, (1.) If we suppose an act, by which the soul chooses to yield to the invitation of a Motive to another volition; both these supposed volitions are in effect the very same. A volition to yield to the force of a Motive inviting to choose something, comes to just the same thing as choosing the thing which the Motive invites to, as I observed before. So that here can be no room to help the matter, by a distinction of two volitions. (2.) If the Motive be passive, not with respect to the same volition to which the Motive excites, but to one truly distinct and prior; yet, by Mr. Chubb, that prior volition cannot take place without a Motive or excitement, as a *previous ground* of its existence. For he insists, that "it is absurd to suppose any volition should take place without some previous Motive to induce it." So that at last it comes to just the same absurdity: for if *every* volition must have a previous Motive, then the very *first* in the whole series must be excited by a previous Motive; and yet the Motive to that first volition is *passive;* but cannot be passive with regard to another antecedent volition, because, by the supposition, it is the very first: therefore if it be passive with respect to any volition, it must be so with regard to that very volition of which it is the ground, and that is excited by it.

III. Though Mr. Chubb asserts, as above, that every volition has some motive, and that "*in the nature of the thing, no volition can take place without some Motive to induce it;*" yet he asserts, that volition does not always follow the *strongest* Motive; or, in other words, is not governed by any superior strength of the Motive that is followed, beyond Motives to the contrary, previous to the volition itself. His own words (p. 258.) are as follow: "Though with regard to physical causes, that which is strongest always prevails, yet it is otherwise with regard to moral causes. Of these, sometimes the stronger, sometimes the weaker, prevails. And the ground of this difference is evident, namely, that what we call moral causes, strictly speaking, are no causes at all, but barely passive reasons of or excitements to the action, or to the refraining from acting: which excitements we have power, or are at liberty, to comply with or reject, as I have showed above." And so throughout the paragraph, he in a variety of phrases insists, that the Will is not always determined by the strongest Motive, unless by strongest we preposterously mean actually prevailing in the event; which is not in the Motive, but in the Will; but that the Will is not always determined by the Motive which is strongest, by any strength previous to the volition itself. And he elsewhere abundantly asserts, that the Will is determined by no superior strength or advantage, that Motives have, from any constitution or state of things, or any circumstances whatsoever, previous to the actual determination of the Will. And indeed his whole discourse on human liberty implies it, his whole scheme is founded upon it.

But these things cannot stand together. There is a diversity of strength in Motives to choice, previous to the choice itself. Mr. Chubb himself supposes, that they do *previously invite, induce, excite,* and *dispose the mind to action.* This implies, that they have something in themselves that is *inviting,* some tendency to *induce* and *dispose* to volition previous to volition itself. And if they have in themselves this nature and tendency, doubtless they have it in certain limited degrees, which are capable of diversity; and some have it in greater degrees, others in less; and they that have most of this tendency, considered with all their nature and circumstances, previous to volition, are the strongest Motives, and those that have least, are the weakest Motives.

Now if volition sometimes does not follow the Motive which is strongest, or has most previous tendency or advantage, all things considered, to induce or excite it, but follows the weakest, or that which, as it stands previously in the mind's view, has least tendency to induce it; herein the Will apparently acts wholly without Motive, without any previous reason to dispose the mind to it, contrary to what the same author supposes. The act, wherein the Will must proceed without a previous motive to induce it, is the act of preferring the weakest Motive. For how absurd is it to say, the mind sees previous reason in the Motive, to prefer that Motive before the other; and at the same time to suppose, that there is nothing in the Motive, in its nature, state, or any circumstance of it whatsoever, as it stands in the previous view of the mind, that gives it any preference: but on the contrary, the other Motive that stands in competition with it, in all these respects, has most belonging to it that is inviting and moving, and has most of a tendency to choice and preference. This is certainly as much as to say, there is previous ground and reason in the Motive for the act of preference, and yet no previous reason for it. By the supposition, as to all that is in the two rival Motives, which tends to preference, previous to the act of preference, it is not in that which is preferred, but wholly in the other: and yet Mr. Chubb supposes, that the act of preference is from *previous ground and reason* in the Motive which is preferred. But are these things consistent? Can there be previous ground in a thing for an event that takes place, and yet no previous tendency in it to that event? If one thing follows another, without any previous tendency to its following, then I should think it very plain, that it follows it without any manner of previous reason why it should follow.

Yea, in this case, Mr. Chubb supposes, that the event follows an antecedent, as the ground of its existence, which has not only *no tendency* to it, but *a contrary tendency.* The event is the preference, which the mind gives to that Motive, which is weaker, as it stands in the previous view of the mind; the immediate antecedent is the view the mind has of the two rival Motives conjunctly; in which previous view of the mind, all the preferableness, or previous tendency to preference, is supposed to be on the other side, or in the contrary Motive; and all the unworthiness of preference, and so previous tendency to comparative neglect, or undervaluing, is on that side which is preferred: and yet in this view of the mind is supposed to be the *previous ground or reason* of this act of preference, *exciting it, and disposing the mind to it.* Which I leave the reader to judge, whether it be absurd or not. If it be not, then it is not absurd to say, that the previous tendency of an antecedent to a consequent, is the ground and reason why that consequent does not follow; and the want of a previous tendency to an event, yea, a tendency to the contrary, is the true ground and reason why that event does follow.

An act of choice or preference is a comparative act, wherein the mind acts with reference to two or more things that are compared, and stand in competition in the mind's view. If the mind, in this comparative act, prefers that which appears inferior in the comparison, then the mind herein acts absolutely without Motive, or inducement, or any temptation whatsoever. Then, if a hungry man has the offer of two sorts of food, to both which he finds an appetite, but has a stronger appetite to one than the other; and there be no circumstances or excitements whatsoever in the case to induce him to take either the one or the other, but merely his appetite: if in the choice he makes between them, he chooses that which he has least appetite to, and refuses that to which he has the strongest appetite, this is a choice made absolutely without previous Motive, Excitement, Reason, or Temptation, as much as if he were perfectly without all appetite to either; because his volition in this case is a comparative act, following a comparative view of the food, which he chooses, in which view his preference has absolutely no previous ground, yea, is against all previous ground and motive. And if there be any principle in man, from whence an act of choice may arise after this manner, from the same principle volition may arise wholly without Motive on either side. If the mind in its volition can go beyond Motive, then it can go without Motive: for when it is beyond the Motive, it is out of the reach of the Motive, out of the limits of its influence, and so without Motive. If so, this demonstrates the independence of volition on Motive; and no reason can be given for what Mr. Chubb so often asserts, even that "*in the nature of things volition cannot take place without a Motive to induce it.*"

If the Most High should endow a balance with agency or activity of nature, in such a manner, that when unequal weights are put into the scales, its agency could enable it to cause that scale to descend, which has the least weight, and so to raise the greater weight; this would clearly demonstrate, that the motion of the balance does not depend on weights in the scales; at least, as much as if the balance should move itself, when there is no weight in either scale. And the activity of the balance which is sufficient to move itself against the greater weight, must certainly be more than sufficient to move it when there is no weight at all.

Mr. Chubb supposes, that the Will cannot stir at all without some Motive; and also supposes, that if there be a Motive to one thing, and none to the contrary, volition will infallibly follow that Motive. This is virtually to suppose an entire dependence of the Will on Motives; if it were not wholly dependent on them, it could surely help itself a little without them; or help itself a little against a Motive, without help from the strength and weight of a contrary Motive. And yet his supposing that the Will, when it has before it various opposite Motives, can use them as it pleases, and choose its own influence from them, and neglect the strongest, and follow the weakest, supposes it to be wholly independent on Motives.

It further appears, on Mr. Chubb's hypothesis, that volition must be without any previous ground in any Motive, thus: if it be, as he supposes, that the Will is not determined by any previous superior strength of the Motive, but determines and chooses its own Motive, then, when the rival Motives are exactly equal, in all respects, it may follow either; and may, in such a case, sometimes follow one, sometimes the other. And if so, this diversity which appears between the acts of the Will, is plainly without previous ground in either of the Motives; for all that is previously in the Motives, is supposed precisely and perfectly the same, without any diversity whatsoever. Now perfect identity, as to all that is previous in the antecedent, cannot be the ground and reason of diversity in the consequent. Perfect identity in the ground, cannot be a reason why it is not followed with the same consequence. And therefore the source of this diversity of consequence must be sought for elsewhere.

And lastly, it may be observed, that however much Mr. Chubb insists, that no volition can take place without some Motive to induce it, which previously disposes the mind to it; yet, as he also insists that the mind, without reference to any superior strength of Motives, picks and chooses for its Motive to follow; he himself herein plainly supposes, that, with regard to the mind's preference of one Motive before another—it is not the Motive that disposes the Will, but—the Will disposes itself to follow the Motive.

IV. Mr. Chubb supposes necessity to be utterly inconsistent with *agency*; and that to suppose a being to be an agent in that which is necessary, is a plain contradiction, p. 311. and throughout his discourses on the subject of Liberty, he supposes, that necessity cannot consist with agency or freedom; and that to suppose otherwise, is to make Liberty and Necessity, Action and Passion, the same thing. And so he seems to suppose, that there is no action, strictly speaking, but volition; and that as to the effects of volition in body or mind, in themselves considered, being necessary, they are said to be free, only as they are the effects of an act that is not necessary.

And yet, according to him, volition itself is the *effect of volition*; yea, every act of free volition; and therefore every act of free volition must, by what has now been observed from him, be necessary. That every act of free volition is itself the effect of volition, is abundantly supposed by him. In p. 341. he says, " If a man is such a creature as I have proved him to be, that is, if he has in him a power of Liberty of doing either good or evil, and either of these is the subject of his own free choice, so that he might, IF HE HAD PLEASED, have CHOSEN and done the contrary."—Here he supposes all that is good or evil in man is the effect of his choice; and so that his good or evil choice itself is the effect of his pleasure or choice, in these words, "*he might if he had* PLEASED, *have* CHOSEN *the contrary*." So in p 356. " Though it be highly reasonable, that a man should always choose the greater good,—yet he may, if he PLEASE, CHOOSE otherwise." Which is the same thing as if he had said, *he may if he chooses choose otherwise*. And then he goes on,—" that is, he may, *if he pleases, choose* what is good for himself," &c. And again in the same page, " The Will is not confined by the understanding, to any particular sort of good, whether greater or less; but it is at liberty *to choose* what kind of good *it pleases*."—If there be any meaning in the last words, it must be this, that *the Will is at liberty to choose what kind of good it chooses to choose*; supposing the act of choice itself determined by an antecedent choice. The Liberty Mr. Chubb speaks of, is not only a man's power to move his body, agreeable to an antecedent act of choice, but to use or exert the faculties of his soul. Thus, (p. 379.) speaking of the faculties of the mind, he says, " Man has power, and is at liberty to neglect these faculties, to use them aright, or to abuse them, *as he pleases*." And that he supposes an act of choice or exercise of pleasure, properly distinct from, and antecedent to, those acts thus chosen, directing, commanding, and producing the chosen acts, and even the acts of choice themselves, is very plain in p. 283. " He can *command his actions*; and herein consists his Liberty; he can give or deny himself that pleasure, *as he pleases*. And p. 377. If the actions of men—are not the *produce of a free choice*, or election, but spring from a necessity of nature,—he cannot in reason be the object of reward or punishment on their account. Whereas, if action in man, whether good or evil, is *the produce of will or free choice*; so that a man in either case, had it in his power, and was at liberty to have CHOSEN the contrary, he is the proper object of reward or punishment, according as he CHOOSES to behave himself." Here, in these last words, he speaks of *Liberty of* CHOOSING, *according as he* CHOOSES. So that the behaviour which he speaks of as subject to his choice, is his *choosing* itself, as well as his external conduct consequent upon it. And therefore it is evident, he means not only external actions, but the acts of choice themselves, when he speaks of *all free actions, as the* PRODUCE *of free choice*. And this is abundantly evident in what he says elsewhere, (p. 372, 373.)

Now these things imply a twofold great inconsistence.

1. To suppose, as Mr. Chubb plainly does, that every free act of choice is *commanded by*, and is the *produce of, free choice*, is to suppose the first free act of choice belonging to the case, yea, the first free act of choice that ever man exerted, to be *the produce* of an antecedent act of choice. But I hope I need not labour at all to convince my readers, that it is an absurdity to say, the very *first* act is the produce of another act that went *before* it.

2. If it were both possible and real, as Mr. Chubb insists, that every free act of choice were the produce or the effect of a free act of choice; yet even then, according to his principles, no one act of choice would be free, but every one necessary; because, every act of choice being the effect of a foregoing act, every act would be necessarily connected with that foregoing cause. For Mr. Chubb himself says, (p. 389.) " When the self-moving power is exerted, it becomes the necessary cause of its effects."—So that his notion of a free act, that is rewardable or punishable, is a heap of contradictions. It is a free act, and yet, by his own notion of freedom, is necessary; and therefore by him it is a contradiction, to suppose it to be free. According to him, every free act is the produce of a free act; so that there must be an infinite number of free acts in succession, without any beginning, in an agent that has a beginning. And therefore here is an infinite number of free acts, every one of them free; and yet not any one of them free, but every act in the whole infinite chain a necesary effect. All the acts are rewardable or punishable, and yet the agent cannot, in reason, be the object of reward or punishment, on account of any one of these actions. He is active in them all, and passive in none; yet active in none, but passive in all, &c.

V. Mr. Chubb most strenuously denies, that Motives are *causes* of the acts of the Will; or that the moving principle in man is *moved*, or *caused to be exerted* by Motives. His words, (p. 388 and 389.) are, " If the moving principle in man is MOVED, OR CAUSED TO BE EXERTED, by something external to man, *which all Motives are*, then it would not be a self-moving principle, seeing it would be moved by a principle external to itself. And to say, that a self-moving principle is MOVED, or CAUSED TO BE EXERT-

ED, by a cause external to itself, is absurd and a contradiction." &c.—And in the next page, it is particularly and largely insisted, that Motives are causes in no case, that "*they are merely passive in the production of action, and have no causality in the production of it,—no causality, to be the cause of the exertion of the Will.*

Now I desire it may be considered, how this can possibly consist with what he says in other places. Let it be noted here,

1. Mr. Chubb abundantly speaks of Motives as *excitements of the acts of the Will;* and says, that *Motives do excite volition, and induce it,* and that they are necessary to this end; that *in the reason and nature of things, volition cannot take place without Motives to excite it.* But now, if Motives *excite* the Will, they *move* it; and yet he says, it is absurd to say, the Will is moved by Motives. And again, if language is of any significancy at all, if Motives excite volition, then they are the *cause* of its being excited; and to cause volition to be excited, is to cause it to be put forth or *exerted.* Yea, Mr. Chubb says himself, (p. 317.) Motive is necessary to the *exertion* of the active faculty. To excite, is positively to *do* something; and certainly that which does something, is the cause of the thing *done* by it. To create, is to cause to be created; to make, is to cause to be made; to kill, is to cause to be killed; to quicken, is to cause to be quickened; and *to excite,* is *to cause to be excited.* To excite, is to be a cause, in the most proper sense, not merely a negative occasion, but a ground of existence by positive influence. The notion of *exciting,* is exerting influence to cause the effect to arise or come forth into existence.

2. Mr. Chubb himself (p. 317.) speaks of Motives as the ground and reason of action BY INFLUENCE, and BY PREVAILING INFLUENCE. Now, what can be meant by a cause, but something that is the ground and reason of a thing by its influence, an influence that is *prevalent* and effectual?

3. This author not only speaks of Motives as the ground and reason of action, by prevailing influence; but expressly of their *influence as prevailing* FOR THE PRODUCTION of an action, (p. 317.) which makes the inconsistency still more palpable and notorious. The production of an effect is certainly the *causing* of an effect; and *productive influence* is *causal influence,* if any thing is; and that which has this influence prevalently, so as thereby to become the ground of another thing, is a cause of that thing, if there be any such thing as a cause. This influence, Mr. Chubb says, Motives have to produce an action; and yet, he says, it is absurd and a contradiction, to say they are causes.

4. In the same page, he once and again speaks of Motives as *disposing* the Agent to action, *by their influence.* His words are these: "As Motive, which takes place in the understanding, and is the product of intelligence, is NECESSARY to action, that is, to the EXERTION of the active faculty, because that faculty would not be exerted without some PREVIOUS REASON to DISPOSE the mind to action; so from hence it plainly appears, that when a man is said to be *disposed* to one action rather than another, this properly signifies the PREVAILING INFLUENCE that one Motive has upon a man FOR THE PRODUCTION of an action, or for the being at rest, before all other Motives, for the *production* of the contrary. For as motive is the ground and reason of any action, so the Motive that *prevails,* DISPOSES the agent to the performance of that action."

Now, if Motives dispose the mind to action, then they *cause* the mind to be disposed; and to cause the mind to be disposed is to cause it to be willing; and to cause it to be willing is to cause it to will; and that is the same thing as to be the cause of an act of the Will. And yet this same Mr. Chubb holds it to be absurd, to suppose Motive to be a cause of the act of the Will.

And if we compare these things together, we have here again a whole heap of inconsistences. *Motives are the previous ground and reason* of the acts of the Will; yea, the *necessary* ground and reason of *their exertion, without which they will not be exerted, and cannot, in the nature of things, take place;* and they do *excite* these acts of the Will, and do this by *a prevailing influence;* yea, *an influence which prevails for the production of the act* of the Will, and for *the disposing of the mind to it;* and yet it is *absurd,* to suppose *Motive to be a cause* of an act of the Will, or that *a principle of Will is moved or caused to be exerted by it,* or that it has *any causality in the production of it,* or *any causality to be the cause of the exertion of the Will.*

A due consideration of these things which Mr. Chubb has advanced, the strange inconsistences which his notion of Liberty—consisting in the Will's power of self-determination void of all necessity, united with that dictate of common sense, that there can be no volition without a Motive—drove him into, may be sufficient to convince us, that it is utterly impossible ever to make that notion of Liberty consistent with the influence of Motives in volition. And as it is in a manner self-evident, that there can be no act of Will, or preference of the mind, without some Motive or inducement, something in the mind's view which it aims at, and goes after; so it is most manifest, that there is no such Liberty in the universe as *Arminians* insist on; nor any such thing possible, or conceivable.

SECT. XI.

The evidence of God's certain Foreknowledge of the Volitions of moral Agents.

THAT the acts of the Wills of moral Agents are not contingent events, in such a sense, as to be without all necessity, appears by God's certain Foreknowledge of such events.

In handling this argument, I would in the *first* place prove, that God has a certain Foreknowledge of the voluntary acts of moral Agents; and *secondly,* show the consequence, or how it follows from hence, that the Volitions of moral Agents are not contingent, so as to be without necessity of connexion and consequence.

FIRST, I am to prove, that God has an absolute and certain Foreknowledge of the free actions of moral Agents.

One would think it wholly needless to enter on such an argument with any that profess themselves Christians: but so it is; God's certain Foreknowledge of the free acts of moral Agents, is denied by some that pretend to believe the Scriptures to be the Word of God; and especially of late. I therefore shall consider the evidence of such a prescience in the Most High, as fully as the designed limits of this essay will admit; supposing myself herein to have to do with such as own the truth of the Bible.

ARG. I. My *first* argument shall be taken from God's *prediction* of such events. Here I would, in the first place, lay down these two things as axioms.

1. If God does not *foreknow,* He cannot *foretell* such events; that is, He cannot peremptorily and certainly foretell them. If God *has* no more than an uncertain guess concerning events of this kind, then he can *declare* no more than an uncertain guess. Positively to foretell, is to profess to foreknow, or declare positive Foreknowledge.

2. If God does not certainly foreknow the future Volitions of moral Agents, then neither can he certainly foreknow those events which are *dependent* on these Volitions. The existence of the one depending on the existence of the other, the knowledge of the existence of the one depends on the knowledge of the existence of the other; and the one cannot be more certain than the other.

Therefore, how many, how great, and how extensive soever the consequences of the Volitions of moral Agents may be; though they should extend to an alteration of the state of things through the universe, and should be continued in a series of successive events to all eternity, and should in the progress of things branch forth into an infinite number of series, each of them going on in an endless chain of events; God must be as ignorant of all these consequences, as he is of the Volition whence they first take their rise: and the whole state of things depending on them, how important, extensive, and vast soever, must be hid from him.

These positions being such as, I suppose, none will deny, I now proceed to observe the following things.

1. Men's moral conduct and qualities, their virtues and vices, their wickedness and good practice, things rewardable and punishable, have often been foretold by God.—*Pharaoh's* moral conduct, in refusing to obey God's com-

mand, in letting his people go, was foretold. God says to *Moses*, Exod. iii. 19. "I am sure that the king of *Egypt* will not let you go." Here God professes not only to guess at, but to know *Pharaoh's* future disobedience. In chap. vii. 4. God says, "but *Pharaoh* shall not hearken unto you; that I may lay mine hand upon *Egypt*," &c. And chap. ix. 30. *Moses* says to Pharaoh, "as for thee, and thy servants, I KNOW that ye will not fear the Lord." See also chap. xi. 9.—The moral conduct of *Josiah*, by name, in his zealously exerting himself to oppose idolatry, in particular acts, was foretold above three hundred years before he was born, and the prophecy sealed by a miracle, and renewed and confirmed by the words of a second prophet, as what surely would not fail, (1 *Kings* xiii. 1—6, 32.) This prophecy was also in effect a prediction of the moral conduct of the people, in upholding their schismatical and idolatrous worship until that time, and the idolatry of those priests of the high places, which it is foretold *Josiah* should offer upon that altar of *Bethel*. *Micaiah* foretold the foolish and sinful conduct of *Ahab*, in refusing to hearken to the word of the Lord by him, and choosing rather to hearken to the false prophets, in going to *Ramoth-Gilead* to his ruin, (1 *Kings* xxi. 20—22.) The moral conduct of *Hazael* was foretold, in that cruelty he should be guilty of; on which *Hazael* says, "What, is thy servant a dog, that he should do this thing!" The prophet speaks of the event as what he knew, and not what he conjectured, 2 Kings viii. 12. "I know the evil that thou wilt do unto the children of Israel: Thou wilt dash their children, and rip up their women with child." The moral conduct of *Cyrus* is foretold, long before he had a being, in his mercy to God's people, and regard to the true God, in turning the captivity of the *Jews*, and promoting the building of the temple, (Isa. xliv. 28. and lxv. 13. compare 2 *Chron.* xxxvi. 22, 23. and *Ezra* i. 1—4.) How many instances of the moral conduct of the *kings of the North and South*, particular instances of the wicked behaviour of the kings of *Syria* and *Egypt*, are foretold in the 11th chapter of *Daniel!* Their corruption, violence, robbery, treachery, and lies. And particularly, how much is foretold of the horrid wickedness of *Antiochus Epiphanes*, called there "a vile person," instead of *Epiphanes*, or illustrious! In that chapter, and also in chap. viii. ver. 9, 14, 23, to the end, are foretold his flattery, deceit, and lies, his having "his heart set to do mischief," and set "against the holy covenant," his "destroying and treading under foot the holy people," in a marvellous manner, his "having indignation against the holy covenant, setting his heart against it, and conspiring against it," his "polluting the sanctuary of strength, treading it under foot, taking away the daily sacrifice, and placing the abomination that maketh desolate;" his great pride, "magnifying himself against God, and uttering marvellous blasphemies against Him," until God in indignation should destroy him. Withal, the moral conduct of the *Jews*, on occasion of his persecution, is predicted. It is foretold, that "*he should corrupt many by flatteries*," (chap. xi. 32—34.) But that others should behave with a glorious constancy and fortitude, in opposition to him, (ver. 32.) And that some good men should fall and repent, (ver. 35.) Christ foretold *Peter's* sin, in denying his Lord, with its circumstances, in a peremptory manner. And so, that great sin of *Judas*, in betraying his master, and its dreadful and eternal punishment in hell, was foretold in the like positive manner, *Matt.* xxvi. 21—25. and parallel places in the other Evangelists.

2. Many events have been foretold by God, which are dependent on the moral conduct of particular persons, and were accomplished, either by their virtuous or vicious actions. Thus, the children of *Israel's* going down into *Egypt* to dwell there, was foretold to *Abraham*, (Gen. xv.) which was brought about by the wickedness of *Joseph's* brethren in selling him, and the wickedness of *Joseph's* mistress, and his own signal virtue in resisting her temptation. The accomplishment of the thing prefigured in *Joseph's* dream, depended on the same moral conduct. *Jotham's* parable and prophecy, (*Judges* ix. 15—20.) was accomplished by the wicked conduct of *Abimelech*, and the men of *Shechem*. The prophecies against the house of *Eli*, (1 *Sam.* chap. ii. and iii.) were accomplished by the wickedness of *Doeg* the *Edomite*, in accusing the priests; and the great impiety, and extreme cruelty of *Saul* in destroying the priests at *Nob*. (1 *Sam.* xxii.) *Nathan's* prophecy against *David*, (2 *Sam.* xii. 11, 12.) was fulfilled by the horrible wickedness of *Absalom*, in rebelling against his father, seeking his life, and lying with his concubines in the sight of the sun. The prophecy against *Solomon*, (1 *Kings* xi. 11—13.) was fulfilled by *Jeroboam's* rebellion and usurpation, which are spoken of as his wickedness, (2 *Chron.* xiii. 5, 6. compare ver. 18.) The prophecy against *Jeroboam's* family, (1 *Kings* xiv.) was fulfilled by the conspiracy, treason, and cruel murders of *Baasha*, (2 *Kings* xv. 27, &c.) The predictions of the prophet *Jehu* against the house of *Baasha*, (1 *Kings* xvi. at the beginning,) were fulfilled by the treason and parricide of *Zimri*, (1 *Kings* xvi. 9—13, 20.)

3. How often has God foretold the future moral conduct of nations and people, of numbers, bodies, and successions of men; with God's judicial proceedings, and many other events consequent and dependent on their virtues and vices; which could not be foreknown, if the Volitions of men, wherein they acted as *moral Agents*, had not been foreseen! The future cruelty of the *Egyptians* in oppressing *Israel*, and God's judging and punishing them for it, was foretold long before it came to pass, (*Gen.* xv. 13, 14.) The continuance of the iniquity of the *Amorites*, and the increase of it until it *should be full*, and they ripe for destruction, was foretold above four hundred years before, (*Gen.* xv. 16. *Acts* vii. 6, 7.) The prophecies of the destruction of *Jerusalem*, and the land of *Judah*, were absolute; (2 *Kings* xx. 17—19. chap. xxii. 15, to the end.) It was foretold in *Hezekiah's* time, and was abundantly insisted on in the book of the prophet *Isaiah*, who wrote nothing after *Hezekiah's* days. It was foretold in *Josiah's* time, in the beginning of a great reformation, (2 *Kings* xxii.) And it is manifest by innumerable things in the predictions of the prophets, relating to this event, its time, its circumstances, its continuance, and end; the return from the captivity, the restoration of the temple, city, and land, &c. I say, these show plainly, that the prophecies of this great event were *absolute*. And yet this event was connected with, and dependent on, two things in men's moral conduct: first, the injurious rapine and violence of the king of *Babylon* and his people, as the efficient cause; which God often speaks of as what he highly resented, and would severely punish; and secondly, the final obstinacy of the *Jews*. That great event is often spoken of as suspended on this, (*Jer.* iv. 1. and v. 1. vii. 1—7. xi. 1—6. xvii. 24, to the end, xxv. 1—7. xxvi. 1—8, 13. and xxxviii. 17, 18.) Therefore this destruction and captivity could not be foreknown, unless such a moral conduct of the *Chaldeans* and *Jews* had been foreknown. And then it was foretold, that the people *should be finally obstinate*, to the utter desolation of the city and land, (*Isa.* vi. 9—11. *Jer.* i. 18, 19. vii. 27—29. *Ezek.* iii. 7. and xxiv. 13, 14.)

The final obstinacy of those *Jews* who were left in the land of *Israel*, in their idolatry and rejection of the true God, was foretold by him, and the prediction confirmed with an oath, (*Jer.* xliv. 26, 27.) And God tells the people, (*Isa.* xlviii. 3, 4—8.) that he had predicted those things which should be consequent on their treachery and obstinacy, because he knew they would be obstinate; and that he had declared these things beforehand, for their conviction of his being the only true God, &c.

The destruction of *Babylon*, with many of the circumstances of it, was foretold, as the judgment of God for the exceeding pride and haughtiness of the heads of that monarchy, *Nebuchadnezzar* and his successors, and their wickedly destroying other nations, and particularly for their exalting themselves against the true God and his people, before any of these monarchs had a being; (*Isa.* chap. xiii. xiv. xlvii. compare *Habak.* ii. 5, to the end, and *Jer.* chap. l. and li.) That *Babylon's* destruction was to be "a recompence, according to the works of their own hands," appears by *Jer.* xxv. 14.—The immorality of which the people of *Babylon*, and particularly her princes and great men, were guilty, that very night that the city was destroyed, their revelling and drunkenness at *Belshazzar's* idolatrous feast, was foretold, (*Jer.* li. 39, 57.)

The return of the *Jews* from the *Babylonish* captivity is

often very particularly foretold, with many circumstances, and the promises of it are very peremptory: (*Jer.* xxxi. 35—40. and xxxii. 6—15, 41—44. and xxxiii. 24—26.) And the very time of their return was prefixed; (*Jer.* xxv. 11, 12. and xxix. 10, 11. 2 *Chron.* xxxvi. 21. *Ezek.* iv. 6. and *Dan.* ix. 2.) And yet the prophecies represent their return as consequent on their repentance. And their repentance itself is very expressly and particularly foretold, (*Jer.* xxix. 12, 13, 14. xxxi. 8, 9, 18—31. xxxiii. 8. l. 4, 5. *Ezek.* vi. 8, 9, 10. vii. 16. xiv. 22, 23. and xx. 43, 44.)

It was foretold under the Old Testament, that the Messiah should suffer greatly through the malice and cruelty of men; as is largely and fully set forth, *Psal.* xxii. applied to Christ in the New Testament, (*Matt.* xxvii. 35, 43. *Luke* xxiii. 34. *John* xix. 24. *Heb.* ii. 12.) And likewise in *Psal.* lxix. which, it is also evident by the New Testament, is spoken of Christ; (*John* xv. 25. vii. 5, &c. and ii. 17. *Rom.* xv. 3. *Matt.* xxvii. 34, 48. *Mark* xv. 23. *John* xix. 29.) The same thing is also foretold, *Isa.* liii. and l. 6. and *Mic.* v. 1. This cruelty of men was their sin, and what they acted as moral Agents. It was foretold, that there should be an union of heathen and *Jewish* rulers against Christ, (*Psal.* ii. 1, 2. compared with *Acts* iv. 25—28.) It was foretold, that the *Jews* should generally reject and despise the Messiah, (*Isa.* xlix. 5, 6, 7. and liii. 1—3. *Psal.* xxii. 6, 7. and lxix. 4, 8, 19, 20.) And it was foretold, that the body of that nation should be rejected in the Messiah's days, from being God's people, for their obstinacy in sin; (*Isa.* xlix. 4—7. and viii. 14, 15, 16. compared with *Rom.* x. 19. and *Isa.* lxv. at the beginning, compared with *Rom.* x. 20, 21.) It was foretold, that Christ should be rejected by the chief priests and rulers among the *Jews*, (*Psal.* cxviii. 22. compared with *Matt.* xxi. 42. *Acts* iv. 11. 1 *Pet.* ii. 4, 7.)

Christ himself foretold his being delivered into the hands of the elders, chief priests, and scribes, and his being cruelly treated by them, and condemned to death; and that he by them should be *delivered to the Gentiles:* and that he should be *mocked* and *scourged*, and *crucified*, (*Matt.* xvi. 21. and xx. 17—19. *Luke* ix. 22. *John* viii. 28.) and that the people should be concerned in and consenting to his death, (*Luke* xx. 13—18.) especially the inhabitants of *Jerusalem;* (*Luke* xiii. 33—35.) He foretold, that the disciples should all be offended because of him, that night in which he was betrayed, and should forsake him; (*Matt.* xxvi. 31. *John* xvi. 32.) He foretold, that he should be rejected of that generation, even the body of the people, and that they should continue obstinate to their ruin; (*Matt.* xii. 45. xxi. 33—42. and xxii. 1—7. *Luke* xiii. 16, 21, 24. xvii. 25. xix. 14, 27, 41—44. xx. 13—18. and xxiii. 34—39.)

As it was foretold in both the Old Testament and the New that the *Jews* should reject the Messiah, so it was foretold that the *Gentiles* should receive him, and so be admitted to the privileges of God's people; in places too many to be now particularly mentioned. It was foretold in the Old Testament, that the *Jews* should envy the *Gentiles* on this account; (*Deut.* xxxii. 21. compared with *Rom.* x. 19.) Christ himself often foretold, that the *Gentiles* would embrace the true religion, and become his followers and people; (*Matt.* viii. 10, 11, 12. xxi. 41—43. and xxii. 8—10. *Luke* xiii. 28. xiv. 16—24. and xx. 16. *John* x. 16.) He also foretold the *Jews*' envy of the *Gentiles* on this occasion; (*Matt.* xx. 12—16. *Luke* xv. 26, to the end.) He foretold, that they should continue in this opposition and envy, and should manifest it in the cruel persecutions of his followers, to their utter destruction; (*Matt.* xxi. 33—42. xxii. 6. and xxiii. 34—39. *Luke* xi. 49—51.) The obstinacy of the Jews is also foretold, (*Acts* xxii. 18.) Christ often foretold the great persecutions his followers should meet with, both from *Jews* and *Gentiles;* (*Matt.* x. 16—18, 21, 22, 34—36. and xxiv. 9. *Mark* xiii. 9. *Luke* x. 3. xii. 11, 49—53. and xxi. 12, 16, 17. *John* xv. 18—21. and xvi. 1—4, 20—22, 23.) He foretold the martyrdom of particular persons; (*Matt.* xx. 23. *John* xiii. 36. and xxi. 18, 19, 22.) He foretold the great success of the gospel in the city of *Samaria*, as near approaching; which afterwards was fulfilled by the preaching of *Philip*, (*John* iv. 35—38.) He foretold the rising of many deceivers after his departure, (*Matt.* xxiv. 4, 5, 11.) and the apostasy of many of his professed followers; (*Matt.* xxiv. 10, 12.)

The persecutions, which the apostle *Paul* was to meet with in the world, were foretold; (*Acts* ix. 16. xx. 23, and xxi. 11.) The apostle says, to the christian *Ephesians*, Acts xx. 29, 30.) "I know, that after my departure shall grievous wolves enter in among you, not sparing the flock; also of your ownselves shall men arise, speaking perverse things, to draw away disciples after them." The apostle says, *he knew this:* but he did not know it, if God did not know the future actions of moral Agents.

4. Unless God foreknows the future acts of moral Agents, all the prophecies we have in Scripture concerning the great *Antichristian* apostasy; the rise, reign, wicked qualities, and deeds of "the man of sin," and his instruments and adherents; the extent and long continuance of his dominion, his influence on the minds of princes and others, to corrupt them, and draw them away to idolatry, and other foul vices; his great and cruel persecutions; the behaviour of the saints under these great temptations, &c. &c. I say, unless the Volitions of moral Agents are foreseen, all these prophecies are uttered without knowing the things foretold.

The predictions relating to this great apostasy are all of a moral nature, relating to men's virtues and vices, and their exercises, fruits, and consequences, and events depending on them; and are very particular; and most of them often repeated, with many precise characteristics, descriptions, and limitations of qualities, conduct, influence, effects, extent, duration, periods, circumstances, final issue, &c. which it would be tedious to mention particularly. And to suppose, that all these are predicted by God, without any certain knowledge of the future moral behaviour of free Agents, would be to the utmost degree absurd.

5. Unless God foreknows the future acts of men's Wills, and their behaviour as moral Agents, all those great things which are foretold both in the Old Testament and the New, concerning the erection, establishment, and universal extent of the *kingdom* of the *Messiah*, were predicted and promised while God was in ignorance whether any of these things would come to pass or no, and did but guess at them. For that kingdom is not of this world, it does not consist in things external, but is within men, and consists in the dominion of virtue in their hearts, in righteousness, and peace, and joy in the Holy Ghost; and in these things made manifest in practice, to the praise and glory of God. The Messiah came "to save men from their sins, and deliver them from their spiritual enemies; that they might serve him in righteousness and holiness before him: he gave himself for us, that he might redeem us from all iniquity, and purify unto himself a peculiar people, zealous of good works." And therefore his success consists in gaining men's hearts to virtue, in their being made God's willing people in the day of his power. His conquest of his enemies consists in his victory over men's corruptions and vices. And such a victory, and such a dominion is often expressly foretold: that his kingdom shall fill the earth; that all people, nations, and languages should serve and obey him; and so that all nations should go up to the mountain of the house of the Lord, that he might teach them his ways, and that they might walk in his paths; and that all men should be drawn to Christ, and the earth be full of the knowledge of the Lord (true virtue and religion) as the waters cover the seas; that God's laws should be put into men's inward parts, and written in their hearts; and that God's people should be all righteous, &c. &c.

A very great part of the Old-Testament prophecies is taken up in such predictions as these.—And here I would observe, that the prophecies of the universal prevalence of the kingdom of the Messiah, and true religion of Jesus Christ, are delivered in the most peremptory manner, and confirmed by the oath of God, *Isa.* xlv. 22, to the end, "Look unto me, and be ye saved, all the ends of the earth; for I am God, and there is none else. I have SWORN by my Self, the word is gone out of my mouth in righteousness, and shall not return, that unto Me every knee shall bow, and every tongue shall swear. SURELY, shall one say, in the Lord have I righteousness and strength: even to Him shall men come," &c. But, here, this peremptory declaration and great oath of the Most High, are delivered with such mighty solemnity, respecting things which God did not know, if he did not certainly foresee the Volitions of moral Agents.

And all the predictions of Christ and his apostles, to the like purpose, must be without knowledge: as those of our Saviour comparing the kingdom of God to a grain of mustard-seed, growing exceeding great, from a small beginning; and to leaven, hid in three measures of meal, until the whole was leavened, &c.—And the prophecies in the epistles concerning the restoration of the Jewish nation to the true church of God, and bringing in the fulness of the *Gentiles;* and the prophecies in all the *Revelation* concerning the glorious change in the moral state of the world of mankind, attending the destruction of Antichrist, "the kingdoms of the world becoming the kingdoms of our Lord and of his Christ;" and its being granted to the church to be "arrayed in that fine linen, white and clean, which is the righteousness of saints," &c.

Corol. 1. Hence that great promise and oath of God to Abraham, Isaac, and Jacob, so much celebrated in Scripture, both in the Old Testament and the New, namely, "That in their seed all the nations and families of the earth should be blessed," must be made on uncertainties, if God does not certainly foreknow the Volitions of moral Agents. For the fulfilment of this promise consists in that success of Christ in the work of redemption, and that setting up of his spiritual kingdom over the nations of the world, which has been spoken of. Men are "blessed in Christ" no otherwise than as they are brought to acknowledge him, trust in him, love and serve him, as is represented and predicted in *Psal.* lxxii. 11. "All kings shall fall down before him; all nations shall serve him." With ver. 17. "Men shall be blessed in him; all nations shall call him blessed." This oath to Jacob and Abraham is fulfilled in subduing men's iniquities; as is implied in that of the prophet *Micah*, chap. vii. 19, 20.

Corol. 2. Hence also it appears, that the first gospel-promise that ever was made to mankind, that great prediction of the salvation of the Messiah, and his victory over *Satan*, made to our first parents, (*Gen.* iii. 15.) if there be no certain Prescience of the Volitions of moral Agents, must have no better foundation than conjecture. For Christ's victory over *Satan* consists in men's being saved from sin, and in the victory of virtue and holiness over that vice and wickedness which *Satan* by his temptations has introduced, and wherein his kingdom consists.

6. If it be so, that God has not a Prescience of the future actions of moral Agents, it will follow, that the prophecies of Scripture in *general* are without Foreknowledge. For Scripture prophecies, almost all of them, if not universally, are either predictions of the actings and behaviour of moral Agents, or of events depending on them, or some way connected with them; judicial dispensations, judgments on men for their wickedness, or rewards of virtue and righteousness, remarkable manifestations of favour to the righteous, or manifestations of sovereign mercy to sinners, forgiving their iniquities, and magnifying the riches of divine grace; or dispensations of Providence, in some respect or other, relating to the conduct of the subjects of God's moral government, wisely adapted thereto; either providing for what should be in a future state of things, through the Volitions and voluntary actions of moral Agents, or consequent upon them, and regulated and ordered according to them. So that all events that are foretold, are either moral events, or others which are connected with and accommodated to them.

That the predictions of Scripture in general must be without knowledge, if God does not foresee the Volitions of men, will further appear, if it be considered, that almost all events belonging to the future state of the world of mankind, the changes and revolutions which come to pass in empires, kingdoms, and nations, and all societies, depend, in ways innumerable, on the acts of men's Wills; yea, on an innumerable multitude of millions of Volitions. Such is the state and course of things in the world of mankind, that one single event, which appears in itself exceeding inconsiderable, may, in the progress and series of things, occasion a succession of the greatest and most important and extensive events; causing the state of mankind to be vastly different from what it would otherwise have been, for all succeeding generations.

For instance, the coming into existence of those particular men, who have been the great conquerors of the world, which, under God, have had the main hand in all the consequent state of the world, in all after-ages; such as Nebuchadnezzar, Cyrus, Alexander, Pompey, Julius Cæsar, &c. undoubtedly depended on many millions of acts of the Will, in their parents. And perhaps most of these Volitions depended on millions of Volitions in their contemporaries of the same generation; and most of these on millions of millions of Volitions in preceding generations.—As we go back, still the number of Volitions, which were some way the occasion of the event, multiply as the branches of a river, until they come at last, as it were, to an infinite number. This will not seem strange to any one who well considers the matter; if we recollect what philosophers tell us of the innumerable multitudes of those things which are the *principia*, or *stamina vitæ*, concerned in generation; the animalcula in semine masculo, and the ova in the womb of the female; the impregnation or animating of one of these in distinction from all the rest, must depend on things infinitely minute relating to the time and circumstances of the act of the parents, the state of their bodies, &c. which must depend on innumerable foregoing circumstances and occurrences; which must depend, infinite ways, on foregoing acts of their Wills; which are occasioned by innumerable things that happen in the course of their lives, in which their own and their neighbour's behaviour must have a hand, an infinite number of ways. And as the Volitions of others must be so many ways concerned in the conception and birth of such men; so, no less, in their preservation, and circumstances of life, their particular determinations and actions, on which the great revolutions they were the occasions of, depended. As, for instance, when the conspirators in *Persia*, against the *Magi*, were consulting about a succession to the empire, it came into the mind of one of them, to propose, that he whose horse neighed first, when they came together the next morning, should be king. Now, such a thing coming into his mind, might depend on innumerable incidents, wherein the Volitions of mankind had been concerned. But, in consequence of this accident, *Darius*, the son of *Hystaspes*, was king. And if this had not been, probably his successor would not have been the same, and all the circumstances of the *Persian* empire might have been far otherwise: Then perhaps *Alexander* might never have conquered that empire; and then probably the circumstances of the world in all succeeding ages, might have been vastly otherwise. I might further instance in many other occurrences; such as those on which depended *Alexander's* preservation, in the many critical junctures of his life, wherein a small trifle would have turned the scale against him; and the preservation and success of the *Roman* people, in the infancy of their kingdom and commonwealth, and afterwards; upon which all the succeeding changes in their state, and the mighty revolutions that afterwards came to pass in the habitable world, depended. But these hints may be sufficient for every discerning considerate person, to convince him, that the whole state of the world of mankind, in all ages, and the very being of every person who has ever lived in it, in every age, since the times of the ancient prophets, has depended on more Volitions, or acts of the Wills of men, than there are sands on the sea-shore.

And therefore, unless God does most exactly and perfectly foresee the future acts of men's Wills, all the predictions which he ever uttered concerning David, Hezekiah, Josiah, Nebuchadnezzar, Cyrus, Alexander; concerning the four monarchies, and the revolutions in them; and concerning all the wars, commotions, victories, prosperity, and calamities, of any kingdoms, nations, or communities in the world, have all been without knowledge.

So that, according to this notion, God not foreseeing the Volitions and free actions of men, he could foresee nothing appertaining to the state of the world of mankind in future ages; not so much as the being of one person that should live in it; and could foreknow no events, but only such as he would bring to pass himself by the extraordinary interposition of his immediate power; or things which should come to pass in the natural material world, by the laws of motion, and course of nature, wherein that is independent on the actions or works of mankind: that is, as he might, like a very able mathematician and astronomer, with great exactness calculate the revolutions of the heavenly bodies, and the greater wheels of the machine of the external creation.

And if we closely consider the matter, there will appear reason to convince us, that he could not, with any absolute certainty, foresee even these. As to the *first*, namely, things done by the immediate and extraordinary interposition of God's power, these cannot be foreseen, unless it can be foreseen when there shall be occasion for such extraordinary interposition. And that cannot be foreseen, unless the state of the moral world can be foreseen. For whenever God thus interposes, it is with regard to the state of the moral world, requiring such divine interposition. Thus God could not certainly foresee the universal deluge, the calling of Abraham, the destruction of Sodom and Gomorrah, the plagues on Egypt, and Israel's redemption out of it, the expelling of the seven nations of *Canaan*, and the bringing *Israel* into that land; for these all are represented as connected with things belonging to the state of the moral world. Nor can God foreknow the most proper and convenient time of the day of judgment and general conflagration; for that chiefly depends on the course and state of things in the moral world.

Nor, *Secondly*, can we on this supposition reasonably think, that God can certainly foresee what things shall come to pass, in the course of things, in the natural and material world, even those which in an ordinary state of things might be calculated by a good astronomer. For the moral world is the end of the natural world; and the course of things in the former, is undoubtedly subordinate to God's designs with respect to the latter. Therefore he has seen cause, from regard to the state of things in the moral world, extraordinarily to interpose, to interrupt, and lay an arrest on the course of things in the natural world; and unless he can foresee the Volitions of men, and so know something of the future state of the moral world, he cannot know but that he may still have as great occasion to interpose in this manner, as ever he had: nor can he foresee how, or when, he shall have occasion thus to interpose.

Corol. 1. It appears from the things observed, that unless God foresees the Volitions of moral Agents, that cannot be true which is observed by the apostle *James*, (Acts xv. 18.) "Known unto God are all his works from the beginning of the world."

Corol. 2. It appears, that unless God foreknows the Volitions of moral Agents, all the prophecies of Scripture have no better foundation than mere conjecture; and *that*, in most instances, a conjecture which must have the utmost uncertainty; depending on an innumerable multitude of Volitions, which are all, even to God, uncertain events: however, these prophecies are delivered as absolute predictions, and very many of them in the most positive manner, with asseverations; and some of them with the most solemn oaths.

Corol. 3. It also follows, that if this notion of God's ignorance of future Volitions be true, in vain did Christ say, after uttering many great and important predictions, depending on men's moral actions, (*Matt.* xxiv. 35.) "Heaven and earth shall pass away; but my words shall not pass away."

Corol. 4. From the same notion of God's ignorance, it would follow, that in vain has he himself often spoken of the predictions of his word, as evidences of Foreknowledge; of that which is his prerogative as GOD, and his peculiar glory, greatly distinguishing him from all other beings; (as in *Isa.* xli. 22.—26 xliii. 9, 10. xliv. 8. xlv. 21. xlvi. 10. and xlviii. 14.)

Arg. II. If God does not foreknow the Volitions of moral Agents, then he did not foreknow the *fall* of man, nor of angels, and so could not foreknow the great things which are *consequent* on these events; such as his sending his Son into the world to die for sinners, and all things pertaining to the great work of redemption; all the things which were done for four thousand years before Christ came, to prepare the way for it; and the incarnation, life, death, resurrection, and ascension of Christ; setting him at the head of the universe as King of heaven and earth, angels and men; and setting up his church and kingdom in this world, and appointing him the Judge of the world; and all that Satan should do in the world in opposition to the kingdom of Christ: and the great transactions of the day of judgment, &c. And if God was thus ignorant, the following scriptures, and others like them, must be without any meaning, or contrary to truth. (Eph. i. 4.) "According as he hath chosen us in him before the foundation of the world." (1 Pet. i. 20.) "Who verily was foreordained before the foundation of the world." (2 Tim. i. 9.) "Who hath saved us, and called us with an holy calling; not according to our works, but according to his own purpose, and grace, which was given us in Christ Jesus before the world began." So (Eph. iii. 11.) speaking of the wisdom of God in the work of redemption, "according to the eternal purpose which he purposed in Christ Jesus." (Tit. i. 2.) "In hope of eternal life, which God that cannot lie, promised before the world began." (Rom. viii. 29.) "Whom he did foreknow, them he also did predestinate," &c. (1 Pet. i. 2.) "Elect, according to the foreknowledge of God the Father."

If God did not foreknow the fall of man, nor the redemption by Jesus Christ, nor the Volitions of man since the fall; then he did not foreknow the saints in any sense; neither as particular persons, nor as societies or nations; either by election, or by mere foresight of their virtue or good works; or any foresight of any thing about them relating to their salvation; or any benefit they have by Christ, or any manner of concern of theirs with a Redeemer.

Arg. III. On the supposition of God's ignorance of the future Volitions of free Agents, it will follow, that God must in many cases truly *repent* what he has done, so as properly to wish he had done otherwise: by reason that the *event* of things, in those affairs which are most important, viz. the affairs of his moral kingdom, being uncertain and contingent, often happens quite otherwise than he was before aware of. And there would be reason to understand that, in the most literal sense, (*Gen.* vi. 6.) "It repented the Lord, that he had made man on the earth, and it grieved him at his heart," (and 1 *Sam.* xv. 11.) contrary to *Numb.* xxiii. 19. "God is not the son of Man, that he should repent;" and 1 *Sam.* xv. 29. "Also the Strength of Israel will not lie, nor repent; for he is not a man that he should repent." Yea, from this notion it would follow, that God is liable to repent and be grieved at his heart, in a *literal* sense, continually; and is always exposed to an infinite number of real disappointments in governing the world; and to manifold, constant, great perplexity and vexation: but this is not very consistent with his title of "God over all, blessed for evermore;" which represents him as possessed of perfect, constant, and uninterrupted tranquillity and felicity, as God over the universe, and in his management of the affairs of the world, as supreme and universal ruler. (See *Rom.* i. 25. ix. 5. 2 *Cor.* xi. 31. 1 *Tim.* vi. 15.)

Arg. IV. It will also follow from this notion, that as God is liable to be continually repenting of what he has done; so he must be exposed to be constantly *changing* his mind and intentions, as to his future conduct; altering his measures, relinquishing his old designs, and forming new schemes and projects. For his purposes, even as to the main parts of his scheme, such as belong to the state of his moral kingdom, must be always liable to be broken, through want of foresight; and he must be continually putting his system to rights, as it gets out of order, through the contingence of the actions of moral Agents: he must be a Being, who, instead of being absolutely immutable, must necessarily be the subject of infinitely the most numerous acts of repentance, and changes of intention, of any being whatsoever; for this plain reason, that his vastly extensive charge comprehends an infinitely greater number of those things which are to him contingent and uncertain. In such a situation, he must have little else to do, but to mend broken links as well as he can, and be rectifying his disjointed frame and disordered movements, in the best manner the case will allow. The Supreme Lord of all things must needs be under great and miserable disadvantages, in governing the world which he has made, and of which he has the care, through his being utterly unable to find out things of chief importance, which hereafter shall befall his system; for which, if he did but know, he might make seasonable provision. In many cases, there may be very great necessity that he should make provision, in the manner of his ordering and disposing things, for some great events which are to happen, of vast and extensive influence, and endless consequence to the universe; which he may see afterwards, when it is too late, and may wish in vain that he had known before, that he might have ordered his affairs accordingly. And it is in the power of man, on these principles, by his devices, purposes, and actions, thus to disappoint God, break his measures, make him continually change his mind, subject him to vexation, and bring him into confusion.

But how do these things consist with reason, or with the word of God? Which represents, that *all God's works*, all that he has ever to do, the whole scheme and series of his operations, are *from the beginning* perfectly in his view; and declares, that whatever devices and designs are in the hearts of men, "the counsel of the Lord shall stand, and the thoughts of his heart to all generations," (Prov. xix. 21. Psal. xxxiii. 10, 11.) And "that which the Lord of hosts hath purposed, none shall disannul," (Isa. xiv. 27.) And that he cannot be frustrated *in one design or thought*, (Job xlii. 2.) And "that which God doth, it shall be for ever, that nothing can be put to it, or taken from it," (Eccl. iii. 14.) The stability and perpetuity of God's counsels are expressly spoken of as connected with his foreknowledge, (*Isa.* xlvi. 10.) "Declaring the end from the beginning, and from ancient times the things that are not yet done; saying, My counsel shall stand, and I will do my pleasure." —And how are these things consistent with what the Scripture says of God's immutability, which represents him as "without variableness, or shadow of turning;" and speaks of him, most particularly, as unchangeable with regard to his purposes, (*Mal.* iii. 6.) "I am the Lord; I change not; therefore ye sons of Jacob are not consumed." (Exod. iii. 14.) "I AM THAT I AM." (Job xxiii. 13, 14.) "He is in one mind; and who can turn him? And what his soul desireth, even that he doth: for he performeth the thing that is appointed for me."

ARG. V. If this notion of God's ignorance of future Volitions of moral Agents be thoroughly considered in its consequences, it will appear to follow from it, that God, after he had made the world, was liable to be wholly *frustrated of his end* in the creation of it; and so has been, in like manner, liable to be frustrated of his end in all the great works he had wrought. It is manifest, the moral world is the end of the natural: the rest of the creation is but a house which God hath built, with furniture, for moral Agents: and the good or bad state of the moral world depends on the improvement they make of their natural Agency, and so depends on their Volitions. And therefore, if these cannot be foreseen by God, because they are contingent, and subject to no kind of necessity, then the affairs of the moral world are liable to go wrong, to any assignable degree; yea, liable to be utterly ruined. As on this scheme, it may well be supposed to be *literally* said, when mankind, by the abuse of their moral Agency, became very corrupt before the flood, "that the Lord repented that he had made man on the earth, and it grieved him at his heart;" so, when he made the universe, he did not know but that he might be so disappointed in it, that it might grieve him at his heart that he had made it. It actually proved, that all mankind became sinful, and a very great part of the angels apostatized: and how could God know before, that all of them would not? And how could God know but that all mankind, notwithstanding means used to reclaim them, being still left to the freedom of their own Will, would continue in their apostasy, and grow worse and worse, as they of the old world before the flood did?

According to the scheme I am endeavouring to confute, the fall of neither men nor angels could be foreseen, and God must be greatly disappointed in these events; and so the grand contrivance for our redemption, and destroying the works of the devil, by the Messiah, and all the great things God has done in the prosecution of these designs, must be only the fruits of his own disappointment; contrivances to mend, as well as he could, his system, which originally was all very good, and perfectly beautiful; but was broken and confounded by the free Will of angels and men. And still he must be liable to be totally disappointed a second time: he could not know, that he should have his desired success, in the incarnation, life, death, resurrection, and exaltation of his only-begotten Son, and other great works accomplished to restore the state of things: he could not know, after all, whether there would actually be any tolerable measure of restoration; for this depended on the free Will of man. There has been a general great apostasy of almost all the Christian world, to that which was worse than heathenism; which continued for many ages. And how could God, without foreseeing men's Volitions, know whether ever Christendom would return from this apostasy? And which way would he foretell how soon it would begin? The apostle says, it began to work in his time; and how could it be known how far it would proceed in that age? Yea, how could it be known that the gospel which was not effectual for the reformation of the *Jews*, would ever be effectual for the turning of the heathen nations from their heathen apostasy, which they had been confirmed in for so many ages?

It is represented often in Scripture, that God, who made the world for himself, and created it for his pleasure, would infallibly obtain his end in the creation, and in all his works; that as all things are *of* him, so they would all be *to* him; and that in the final issue of things, it would appear that he is "the first, and the last." (Rev. xxi. 6.) "And he said unto me, It is done. I am Alpha and Omega, the beginning and the end, the first and the last." But these things are not consistent with God's liability to be disappointed in all his works, nor indeed with his failing of his end in any thing that he has undertaken.

SECT. XII.

God's certain Foreknowledge of the future volitions of moral agents, inconsistent with such a Contingence of those volitions as is without all Necessity.

HAVING proved, that GOD has a certain and infallible Prescience of the voluntary acts of moral agents, I come now, in the *second* place, to show the consequence; how it follows from hence, that these events are *necessary*, with a Necessity of connexion or consequence.

The chief *Arminian* divines, so far as I have had opportunity to observe, deny this consequence; and affirm, that if such Foreknowledge be allowed, it is no evidence of *any Necessity* of the event foreknown. Now I desire, that this matter may be particularly and thoroughly inquired into. I cannot but think, that on particular and full consideration, it may be perfectly determined, whether it be indeed so or not.

In order to a proper consideration of this matter, I would observe the following things.

I. It is very evident, that, with regard to a thing whose existence is infallibly and indissolubly connected with something which already hath, or has had existence, the existence of that thing is necessary. Here may be noted the following particulars:

1. I observed before, in explaining the nature of Necessity, that in things which are *past*, their past existence is now *necessary*: having already made sure of existence, it is too late for any possibility of alteration in that respect; it is now impossible that it should be otherwise than true, that the thing has existed.

2. If there be any such thing as a divine Foreknowledge of the volitions of free agents, that Foreknowledge, by the supposition, is a thing which already *has*, and long ago *had* existence; and so, now its existence is necessary; it is now utterly impossible to be otherwise, than that this Foreknowledge should be or should have been.

3. It is also very manifest, that those things which are indissolubly connected with other things that are necessary, are themselves necessary. As that proposition whose truth is necessarily connected with another proposition, which is necessarily true, is itself necessarily true. To say otherwise would be a contradiction: it would be in effect to say, that the connexion was indissoluble, and yet was not so, but might be broken. It that, the existence

of which is indissolubly connected with something whose existence is now necessary, is itself not necessary, then it may *possibly not exist*, notwithstanding that indissoluble connexion of its existence.—Whether the absurdity be not glaring, let the reader judge.

4. It is no less evident, that if there be a full, certain, and infallible Foreknowledge of the future existence of the volitions of moral agents, then there is a certain, infallible, and indissoluble connexion between those events and that Foreknowledge; and that therefore, by the preceding observations, those events are necessary events; being infallibly and indissolubly connected with that, whose existence already is, and so is now necessary, and cannot but have been.

To say, the Foreknowledge is certain and infallible, and yet the connexion of the event with that Foreknowledge is dissoluble and fallible, is very absurd. To affirm it, would be the same thing as to affirm, that there is no necessary connexion between a proposition being infallibly known to be true, and its being true indeed. So that it is perfectly demonstrable, that if there be any infallible knowledge of future volitions, the event is *necessary;* or, in other words, that it is *impossible* but the event should come to pass. For if it be not impossible but that it may be otherwise, then it is not impossible but that the proposition which affirms its future coming to pass, may not now be true. There is this absurdity in it, that it is not impossible, but that there now should be no truth in that proposition, which is now infallibly known to be true.

II. That no future event can be certainly foreknown, whose existence is contingent, and without all Necessity, may be proved thus; it is impossible for a thing to be certainly known to any intellect without *evidence*. To suppose otherwise, implies a contradiction: because for a thing to be certainly known to any understanding, is for it to be *evident* to that understanding: and for a thing to be *evident* to any understanding is the same thing, as for that understanding to *see evidence* of it: but no understanding, created or uncreated, can *see evidence* where there is none; for that is the same thing, as to see that to be which is not. And therefore, if there be any truth which is absolutely without evidence, that truth is absolutely unknowable, insomuch that it implies a contradiction to suppose that it is known.

But if there be any future event, whose existence is contingent, without all Necessity, the future existence of the event is absolutely *without evidence*. If there be any evidence of it, it must be one of these two sorts, either *self-evidence* or *proof;* an evident thing must be either evident *in itself*, or evident *in something else*: that is, evident by *connexion* with something else. But a future thing, whose existence is without all Necessity, can have neither of these sorts of evidence. It cannot be *self-evident*: for if it be, it may be now known, by what is now to be seen in the thing itself; its present existence, or the Necessity of its nature: but both these are contrary to the supposition. It is supposed, both that the thing has no present existence to be seen; and also that it is not of such a nature as to be necessarily existent for the future: so that its future existence is not self-evident. And *secondly*, neither is there any *proof*, or evidence *in any thing else*, or evidence of connexion with something else that is evident; for this is also contrary to the supposition. It is supposed that there is now nothing existent, with which the future existence of the *contingent* event is connected. For such a connexion destroys its *contingence*, and supposes Necessity. Thus it is demonstrated, that there is in the nature of things absolutely no evidence at all of the future existence of that event, which is contingent, without all Necessity, (if any such event there be,) neither self-evidence nor proof. And therefore the thing in reality is not evident; and so cannot be seen to be evident, or, which is the same thing, cannot be known.

Let us consider this in an example. Suppose that five thousand seven hundred and sixty years ago, there was no other being but the Divine Being; and then this world, or some particular body or spirit, all at once starts out of nothing into being, and takes on itself a particular nature and form; all in *absolute Contingence*, without any concern of God, or any other cause, in the matter; without any manner of ground or reason of its existence; or any dependence upon, or connexion at all with any thing foregoing: I say, that if this be supposed, there was no evidence of that event beforehand. There was no evidence of it to be seen *in the thing itself;* for the thing itself, as yet, was not. And there was no evidence of it to be seen *in any thing else;* for *evidence in* something else, is *connexion with* something else: but such connexion is contrary to the supposition. There was no evidence before, that this thing *would happen;* for by the supposition, there was no reason why *it should happen*, rather than something else, or rather than nothing. And if so, then all things before were exactly equal, and the same, with respect to that and other possible things; there was no preponderation, no superior weight or value; and therefore, nothing that could be of weight or value to determine any understanding. The thing was absolutely without evidence, and absolutely unknowable. An increase of understanding, or of the capacity of discerning, has no tendency, and makes no advance, towards discerning any signs or evidences of it, let it be increased never so much; yea, if it be increased infinitely. The increase of the strength of sight may have a tendency to enable to discern the evidence which is far off, and very much hid, and deeply involved in clouds and darkness; but it has no tendency to enable to discern evidence where there is none. If the sight be infinitely strong, and the capacity of discerning infinitely great, it will enable to see all that there is, and to see it perfectly, and with ease; yet it has no tendency at all to enable a being to discern that evidence which is not; but on the contrary, it has a tendency to enable to discern with great certainty that there is none.

III. To suppose the future volitions of moral agents not to be necessary events; or, which is the same thing, events which it is not impossible but that they may not come to pass; and yet to suppose that God certainly foreknows them, and knows all things; is to suppose God's knowledge to be inconsistent with itself. For to say, that God certainly, and without all conjecture, knows that a thing will infallibly be, which at the same time he knows to be so *contingent*, that it may possibly not be, is to suppose his knowledge inconsistent with itself; or that one thing he knows, is utterly inconsistent with another thing he knows. It is the same as to say, he now knows a proposition to be of certain infallible truth, which he knows to be of contingent uncertain truth. If a future volition is so without all Necessity, that nothing hinders but it may not be, then the proposition which asserts its future existence, is so uncertain, that nothing hinders, but that the truth of it may entirely fail. And if God knows all things, he knows this proposition to be thus uncertain. And that is inconsistent with his knowing that it is infallibly true; and so inconsistent with his infallibly knowing that it is true. If the thing be indeed contingent, God views it so, and judges it to be contingent, if he views things as they are. If the event be not necessary, then it is possible it may never be: and if it be possible it may never be, God knows it may possibly never be; and that is to know that the proposition, which affirms its existence, may possibly not be true; and that is to know that the truth of it is uncertain; which surely is inconsistent with his knowing it as a certain truth. If volitions are in themselves contingent events, without all Necessity, then it is no argument of perfection of knowledge in any being to determine peremptorily that they will be; but on the contrary, an argument of ignorance and mistake; because it would argue, that he supposes that proposition to be certain, which in its own nature, and all things considered, is uncertain and contingent. To say, in such a case, that God may have ways of knowing contingent events which we cannot conceive of, is ridiculous; as much so, as to say, that God may know contradictions to be true, for ought we know; or that he may know a thing to be certain, and at the same time know it not to be certain, though we cannot conceive how; because he has ways of knowing which we cannot comprehend.

Corol. 1. From what has been observed it is evident, that the absolute *decrees* of God are no more inconsistent with human liberty, on account of any Necessity of the event, which follows from such decrees, than the absolute

Foreknowledge of God. Because the connexion between the event and certain Foreknowledge, is as infallible and indissoluble, as between the event and an absolute decree. That is, it is no more impossible, that the event and decree should not agree together, than that the event and absolute Knowledge should disagree. The connexion between the event and Foreknowledge is absolutely perfect, by the supposition: because it is supposed, that the certainty and infallibility of the Knowledge is absolutely perfect. And it being so, the certainty cannot be increased; and therefore the connexion, between the Knowledge and thing known, cannot be increased; so that if a decree be added to the Foreknowledge, it does not at all increase the connexion, or make it more infallible and indissoluble. If it were not so, the certainty of Knowledge might be increased by the addition of a decree; which is contrary to the supposition, which is, that the Knowledge is absolutely perfect, or perfect to the highest possible degree.

There is as much impossibility but that the things which are infallibly foreknown, should be, or, which is the same thing, as great a Necessity of their future existence, as if the event were already written down, and was known and read by all mankind, through all preceding ages, and there was the most indissoluble and perfect connexion possible between the writing and the thing written. In such a case, it would be as impossible the event should fail of existence, as if it had existed already; and a decree cannot make an event surer or more necessary than this.

And therefore, if there be any such Foreknowledge, as it has been proved there is, then Necessity of connexion and consequence is not at all inconsistent with any liberty which man, or any other creature, enjoys. And from hence it may be inferred, that absolute decrees, which do not at all increase the Necessity, are not inconsistent with the liberty which man enjoys, on any such account, as that they make the event decreed necessary, and render it utterly impossible but that it should come to pass. Therefore, if absolute decrees are inconsistent with man's liberty as a moral agent, or his liberty in a state of probation, or any liberty whatsoever that he enjoys, it is not on account of any *Necessity* which absolute decrees infer.

Dr. Whitby supposes, there is a great difference between God's Foreknowledge, and his decrees, with regard to Necessity of future events. In his Discourse on the five Points, (p. 474, &c.) he says, "God's Prescience has no influence at all on our actions.—Should God, says he, by immediate revelation, give me the knowledge of the event of any man's state or actions, would my knowledge of them have any influence upon his actions? Surely none at all.—Our knowledge doth not affect the things we know, to make them more certain, or more future, than they would be without it. Now, Foreknowledge in God is Knowledge. As therefore Knowledge has no influence on things that are, so neither has Foreknowledge on things that shall be. And consequently, the Foreknowledge of any action that would be otherwise free, cannot alter or diminish that freedom. Whereas God's decree of election is powerful and active, and comprehends the preparation and exhibition of such means, as shall unfrustrably produce the end.—Hence God's Prescience renders no actions necessary." And to this purpose, (p. 473.) he cites Origen, where he says, "*God's Prescience is not the cause of things future, but their being future is the cause of God's Prescience that they will be:*" and Le Blanc, where he says, "*This is the truest resolution of this difficulty, that Prescience is not the cause that things are future; but their being future is the cause they are foreseen.*" In like manner, Dr. Clark, in his Demonstration of the Being and Attributes of God, (p. 95—99.) And the Author of *The Freedom of Will, in God and the Creature,* speaking to the like purpose with Dr. Whitby, represents "*Foreknowledge as having no more influence on things known, to make them necessary, than After-knowledge,*" or to that purpose.

To all which I would say; that what is said about Knowledge, its not having influence on the thing known to make it necessary, is nothing to the purpose, nor does it in the least affect the foregoing reasoning. Whether Prescience be the thing that *makes* the event necessary or no, it alters not the case. Infallible Foreknowledge may *prove* the Necessity of the event foreknown, and yet not be the thing which *causes* the Necessity.* If the Foreknowledge be absolute, this *proves* the event known to be necessary, or proves that it is impossible but that the event should be, by some means or other, either by a decree, or some other way, if there be any other way: because, as was said before, it is absurd to say, that a proposition is known to be certainly and infallibly true, which yet may possibly prove not true.

The whole of the seeming force of this evasion lies in this; that, inasmuch as certain Foreknowledge does not *cause* an event to be necessary, as a decree does; therefore it does not *prove* it to be necessary, as a decree does. But there is no force in this arguing: for it is built wholly on this supposition, that nothing can *prove* or *be an evidence* of a thing being necessary, but that which has *a causal influence to make it so.* But this can never be maintained. If certain Foreknowledge of the future existence of an event be not the thing which first *makes* it impossible that it should fail of existence; yet it may, and certainly does *demonstrate,* that it is impossible it should fail of it, however that impossibility comes. If Foreknowledge be not the cause, but the effect of this impossibility, it may prove that there is such an impossibility, as much as if it were the cause. It is as strong arguing from the effect to the cause, as from the cause to the effect. It is enough, that an existence, which is infallibly foreknown, cannot fail, whether that impossibility arises from the Foreknowledge, or is prior to it. It is as evident as any thing can be, that it is impossible a thing, which is infallibly known to be true, should prove not to be true; therefore there is a *Necessity* that it should be otherwise; whether the Know-

* This distinction is of great importance in the present controversy; and the want of attending to the true ground on which it stands, has been, we presume, the principal cause of Dr. Whitby's objections, and those of most, if not all, other Arminian writers. They seem to consider, in this argument, no other *necessity* but the *decretive*, as maintained by their opponents; and therefore infer, that to allow *any* kind of necessity, is the same as to allow an infallible *decree.* From this view the transition is easy to another conclusion, viz. that if *any thing* is foreknown *because* it is decreed, *every* thing is foreknown on the same ground, or for the same reason.—And then, this proving *too much*—the decretive appointment of all the *evil* in the universe, which they are sure is incompatible with the divine character, and therefore impossible—they reject the whole doctrine of *necessity* as a ground of foreknowledge; and suppose that, though they cannot clearly *disprove* what is advanced against them, they infer that there is somehow a *sophism* in the reasoning of their opponents, or some false principle assumed, were they but happy enough to detect it.

But our author, in this reasoning, does not maintain, that the connexion by which *every* event is evidently certain, and therefore necessary, is so because *decreed.* The truth is, that *some* events are foreknown to be certain *because* foreordained; and *others*, because of the tendency there is in the *nature* of the things themselves.——Should any, in the way of objection, assert, that the nature of things is itself derived from the divine *will*, or decree; we apprehend there is no evidence to support such an assertion. For instance, is it owing to a *decree* that the nature of any created being is *dependent* on the first cause? That a creature, however exalted, is not *infinite?* That any *relation* should subsist between the Creator and a creature? Or that, if equal quantities be taken from equal quantities, the remainders will be equal? Is there any room, in thought, for a supposition of any decree in the case? Nay more, does it appear possible for a decree to have made such things *otherwise?*

Let it be observed, however, that God is the Almighty Sovereign over nature—not indeed so far as to alter the nature of things, which in reality is no object of power, any more than to make spirit to be the *same thing* as matter, and *vice versa*, or the working of contradictions is an object of power, but—by the position of antecedents, and establishing premises. To illustrate this, let it be supposed, IF God create a world, that world *must* depend upon him, as a *necessary* consequence. To deny this, is to deny the nature and identity of things. For what is it to create, but for an independent cause to impart, *ad extra*, a dependent existence? So that to deny dependence, is to deny creation. But though the *consequence* be *necessary*, if the antecedent be established; yet the antecedent itself is not necessary, except from decree; for there is not, *in the nature of things*, any antecedent necessity that a world be created. That is, to suppose its non-existence implies no contradiction, it being evidently the effect of sovereign pleasure. Hence to deny the consequence, on supposition of the antecedent, is to deny the nature of things, and to assert a contradiction, though the antecedent itself be not necessary. And hence also, in the instance now specified among others innumerable, the antecedent is an object of *decree*, but not the consequence. It is as absurd to say, that God *decreed* the dependence of the world upon himself, as it is to say, he decreed that two and two shall be equal to *four*, rather than to *five.*

These remarks, duly considered in their just consequences, will abundantly show, that *some things* are necessary because decreed,—as the creation, the preservation, and the government of the world; the redemption, the purification, and the salvation of the church:—and that other things—as all imperfections, dependence, relations, and especially moral evils—come to be necessary, and so capable of being foreknown, only by connexion, or consequence. That is, if the antecedent, which is under the control of the Almighty Sovereign, be admitted, the consequence follows infallibly *from the nature of things.* But IF *another* antecedent be established, *another consequence* will follow, with equal certainty, also from the nature of things. For instance; IF *holiness* be given and continued to a redeemed creature, as an antecedent; excellence, honour, and happiness are the *necessary* consequences. But IF *sin* operate without control, as the anteceden , dishonour and misery must be the necessary consequence from the same cause.—W.

ledge be the cause of this Necessity, or the Necessity the cause of the Knowledge.

All certain Knowledge, whether it be Foreknowledge or After-knowledge, or concomitant Knowledge, proves the thing known now to be necessary, by some means or other; or proves that it is impossible it should now be otherwise than true.—I freely allow, that Foreknowledge does not prove a thing to be necessary any more than After-knowledge: but then After-knowledge, which is certain and infallible, proves that it is now become impossible but that the proposition known should be true. Certain After-knowledge proves that it is *now*, by some means or other, become impossible but that the proposition, which predicates *past* existence on the event, should be true. And so does certain Foreknowledge prove, that *now*, in the time of the Knowledge, it is, by some means or other, become impossible but that the proposition, which predicates *future* existence on the event, should be true. The necessity of the truth of the propositions, consisting in the present impossibility of the non-existence of the event affirmed, in both cases, is the immediate ground of the certainty of the Knowledge; there can be no certainty of Knowledge without it.

There must be a certainty in things themselves, before they are certainly known, or which is the same thing, known to be certain. For certainty of Knowledge is nothing else but knowing or discerning the certainty there is in the things themselves, which are known. Therefore there must be a certainty in things to be a ground of certainty of Knowledge, and to render things capable of being known to be certain. And there is nothing but the necessity of truth known, or its being impossible but that it should be true; or, in other words, the firm and infallible connexion between the subject and predicate of the proposition that contains that truth. All certainty of Knowledge consists in the view of the firmness of that connexion. So God's certain Foreknowledge of the future existence of any event, is his view of the firm and indissoluble connexion of the subject and predicate of the proposition that affirms its future existence. The subject is that possible event; the predicate is its future existence, but if future existence be firmly and indissolubly connected with that event, then the future existence of that event is necessary. If God certainly knows the future existence of an event which is wholly contingent, and may possibly never be, then, he sees a firm connexion between a subject and predicate that are not firmly connected; which is a contradiction.

I allow what Dr. Whitby says to be true, that *mere Knowledge does not affect the thing known, to make it more certain or more future*. But yet, I say, it *supposes* and *proves* the thing to be *already*, both *future* and *certain;* i. e. necessarily future. Knowledge of *futurity*, supposes *futurity;* and a *certain Knowledge* of futurity, supposes *certain futurity*, antecedent to that certain Knowledge. But there is no other certain futurity of a thing, antecedent to certainty of Knowledge, than a prior impossibility but that the thing should prove true; or, which is the same thing, the *Necessity* of the event.

I would observe one thing further; that if it be as those forementioned writers suppose, that God's Foreknowledge is not the cause, but the effect of the existence of the event foreknown; this is so far from showing that this Foreknowledge doth not infer the Necessity of the existence of that event, that it rather shows the contrary the more plainly. Because it shows the existence of the event to be so settled and firm, that it is as if it had already been; inasmuch as *in effect* it actually exists already; its future existence has already had actual *influence* and *efficiency*, and has *produced an effect*, viz. Prescience: the effect exists already; and as the effect supposes the cause, and depends entirely upon it, therefore it is as if the future event, which is the cause, had existed already. The effect is firm as possible, it having already the possession of existence, and has made sure of it. But the effect cannot be more firm and stable than its cause, ground, and reason. The building cannot be firmer than the foundation.

To illustrate this matter; let us suppose the appearances and images of things in a glass, for instance, a reflecting telescope, to be the real effects of heavenly bodies (at a distance, and out of sight) which they resemble: if it be so, then, as these images in the telescope have had a past actual existence, and it is become utterly impossible now that it should be otherwise than that they have existed; so they being the true effects of the heavenly bodies they resemble, this proves the existence of those heavenly bodies to be as real, infallible, firm, and necessary, as the existence of these effects; the one being connected with, and wholly depending on the other.—Now let us suppose future existences, some way or other, to have influence back, to produce effects beforehand, and cause exact and perfect images of themselves in a glass, a thousand years before they exist, yea, in all preceding ages; but yet that these images are real effects of these future existences, perfectly dependent on, and connected with their cause. These effects and images having already had actual existence, render that matter of their existence perfectly firm and stable, and utterly impossible to be otherwise; and this proves, as in the other instance, that the existence of the things, which are their causes, is also equally sure, firm, and necessary; and that it is alike impossible but that they should be, as if they had been already, as their effects have. And if instead of images in a glass, we suppose the antecedent effects to be perfect ideas of them in the Divine Mind, which have existed there from all eternity, which are as properly effects, as truly and properly connected with their cause, the case is not altered.

Another thing which has been said by some *Arminians*, to take off the force of what is urged from God's Prescience, against the contingence of the volitions of moral agents, is to this purpose; "That when we talk of Foreknowledge in God, there is no strict propriety in our so speaking; and that although it be true, that there is in God the most perfect Knowledge of all events from eternity to eternity, yet there is no such thing as *before* and *after* in God, but he sees all things by one perfect unchangeable view, without any succession."—To this I answer,

1. It has been already shown, that all certain Knowledge proves the Necessity of the truth known; whether it be *before, after*, or *at the same time.*—Though it be true, that there is no succession in God's Knowledge, and the manner of his Knowledge is to us inconceivable, yet thus much we know concerning it, that there is no event, past, present, or to come, that God is ever uncertain of. He never is, never was, and never will be without infallible Knowledge of it; he always sees the existence of it to be certain and infallible. And as he always sees things just as they are in truth; hence there never is in reality any thing contingent in such a sense, as that possibly it may happen never to exist. If, strictly speaking, there is no Foreknowledge in God, it is because those things, which are future to us, are as present to God, as if they already had existence: and that is as much as to say, that future events are always in God's view as evident, clear, sure, and necessary, as if they already were. If there never is a time wherein the existence of the event is not present with God, then there never is a time wherein it is not as much impossible for it to fail of existence, as if its existence were present, and were already come to pass.

God viewing things so perfectly and unchangeably, as that there is no succession in his ideas or judgment, does not hinder but that there is properly *now*, in the mind of God, a certain and perfect Knowledge of the moral actions of men, which to us are an hundred years hence: yea the objection supposes this; and therefore it certainly does not hinder but that, by the foregoing arguments, it is now impossible these moral actions should not come to pass.

We know, that God foreknows the future voluntary actions of men, in such a sense, as that he is able particularly to foretell them, and cause them to be recorded, as he often has done; and therefore that necessary connexion which there is between God's Knowledge and the event known, as much proves the event to be *necessary* beforehand, as if the Divine Knowledge were in the same sense before the event, as the prediction or writing is. If the Knowledge be infallible, then the expression of it in the written prediction is infallible; that is, there is an infallible connexion between that written prediction and the event. And if so, then it is impossible it should ever be otherwise, than that the prediction and the event should agree:

and this is the same thing as to say, it is impossible but that the event should come to pass: and this is the same as to say that its coming to pass is *necessary*.—So that it is manifest, that there being no proper succession in God's mind, makes no alteration as to the Necessity of the existence of the events known. Yea,

2. This is so far from weakening the proof, given of the impossibility of future events known, not coming to pass, as that it establishes the foregoing arguments, and shows the clearness of the evidence. For,

(1.) The very reason, why God's Knowledge is without succession, is, because it is absolutely perfect, to the highest possible degree of clearness and certainty. All things, whether past, present, or to come, being viewed with equal evidence and fulness; future things being seen with as much clearness, as if they were present; the view is always in absolute perfection; and absolute constant perfection admits of no alteration, and so no succession; the actual existence of the thing known, does not at all increase or add to the clearness or certainty of the thing known: God calls the things that are not, as though they were; they are all one to him as if they had already existed. But herein consists the strength of the demonstration before given; that it is as impossible they should fail of existence, as if they existed already. This objection, instead of weakening the argument, sets it in the strongest light; for it supposes it to be so indeed, that the existence of future events is in God's view so much as if it already had been, that when they come actually to exist, it makes not the least alteration or variation in his Knowledge of them.

(2.) The objection is founded on the *immutability* of God's Knowledge: for it is the immutability of Knowledge that makes it to be without succession. But this most directly and plainly demonstrates the thing I insist on, *viz.* that it is utterly impossible the known events should fail of existence. For if that were possible, then a change in God's Knowledge and view of things, were possible. For if the known event should not come into being, as God expected, then he would see it, and so would change his mind, and see his former mistake; and thus there would be change and succession in his Knowledge. But as God is immutable, and it is infinitely impossible that his view should be changed; so it is, for the same reason, just so impossible that the foreknown event should not exist; and that is to be impossible in the highest degree; and therefore the contrary is necessary. Nothing is more impossible than that the immutable God should be changed, by the succession of time; who comprehends all things, from eternity to eternity, in one, most perfect, and unalterable view; so that his whole eternal duration is *vitæ interminabilis, tota, simul et perfecta possessio*.

On the whole, I need not fear to say, that there is no geometrical theorem or proposition whatsoever, more capable of strict demonstration, than that God's certain Prescience of the volitions of moral agents is inconsistent with such a Contingence of these events, as is without all Necessity; and so is inconsistent with the *Arminian* notion of liberty.

Corol. 2. Hence the doctrine of the *Calvinists*, concerning the absolute decrees of God, does not all infer any more *fatality* in things, than will demonstrably follow from the doctrine of the most *Arminian* divines, who acknowledge God's omniscience, and universal Prescience. Therefore all objections they make against the doctrine of the *Calvinists*, as implying Hobbes's doctrine of Necessity, or the *stoical* doctrine of *fate*, lie no more against the doctrine of *Calvinists*, than their own doctrine: and therefore it doth not become those divines, to raise such an outcry against the *Calvinists*, on this account.

Corol. 3. Hence all arguments of *Arminians*, who own God's omniscience, against the doctrine of the inability of unregenerate men to perform the conditions of salvation, and the commands of God requiring spiritual duties, and against the *Calvinistic* doctrine of efficacious grace; on this ground, that those doctrines, though they do not suppose men to be under any constraint or coaction, yet suppose them under *Necessity*, must fall to the ground. And their arguments against the Necessity of men's volitions, taken from the reasonableness of God's commands, promises, and threatenings, and the sincerity of his counsels and invitations; and all objections against any doctrines of the *Calvinists* as being inconsistent with human liberty, because they infer *Necessity;* I say, all these arguments and objections must be justly esteemed vain and frivolous, as coming from them; being levelled against their own doctrine, as well as against that of the *Calvinists*.*

* In these two sections our author has abundantly demonstrated, that foreknowledge *infers* necessity; such a necessity as exists in the connexion of a consequent with its antecedent; and has represented, in various lights, how the most contradictory and absurd conclusions follow from the opposite hypothesis. But as his argument, strictly speaking, did not require a further explanation or distinction of the *principles* on which it rested, which yet are important, it may not be improper in this place briefly to inquire into the *rationale* of those principles; by which his reasoning may appear with additional evidence, and the radical principles themselves confirmed by their connexion with others. As these remarks are presented in the form of a series analytically disposed, we shall prefix to them the corresponding ordinal numbers.

1. *Any* kind of NECESSITY is a sufficient ground of foreknowledge, in the view of omniscience; but as is the *kind* of necessity, or the *nature* of the *connexion* between cause and effect, so is the *nature* of the foreknowledge. But this difference in the nature of the connexion affects—not the *certainty* of the event, but the *mode* of causation; or from what CAUSE the certainty arises.

2. All necessity, or certainty of connexion between antecedent and consequent, must arise from one of these two sources, viz. the NATURE OF THINGS, or, the DECREE OF GOD. Chance is *nothing;* and nothing has no properties, consequently has no causal influence.

3. The necessity which arises from the NATURE OF THINGS, is either *absolute* or *hypothetical.* ABSOLUTE NECESSITY belongs only to the *first* cause, or God. He exists ABSOLUTELY; and to *suppose* him not to exist, or not to have existed, is a contradiction. For the *supposition* itself is made by a confessedly contingent being; but a contingent being necessarily implies an absolute being, with as much certainty as an effect implies a cause; and consequently a *first* cause.

4. The first cause excepted, every other being, or mode of being, or any event whatever, is only of HYPOTHETICAL NECESSITY. Any event is necessary, only on account of its *relation* to the first cause. This relation, or necessary connexion, between an event and the first cause, is either in the way of *contrast*, or in the way of *dependence.*

5. There are two things *necessarily related* to the first cause by way of CONTRAST; *passive power*, which is a *natural* evil—if limited existence, dependence, and insufficiency, *in their necessary tendency*, may be so called—and *sin*, which is a *moral* evil; or something which, in point of *obligation*, *ought not* to be.

6. The other mode of *necessary relation* to the first cause, arising from the nature of things, is that of DEPENDENCE. Every contingent being and event must necessarily depend upon God, as an effect depends upon its cause. Nor is it conceivable without involving the grossest contradiction and absurdity, that any contingent being should *continue* to exist, any more than begin to exist, independent of the first cause. *Sublata causa, tollitur effectus*, is justly entitled to be called an *axiom* in metaphysical science.

7. It was before observed, that all necessity must arise either from the nature of things, or from the decree of God. What arises from the nature of things, as a consequence, has for its *antecedent*, either an *efficient* or a *deficient* cause.

8 A DEFECT, no less than active efficiency, may be an antecedent, as *founded in the nature of things*, from whence a corresponding consequence must follow; but there is no defect in any antecedent but *may* be counteracted by a decree; so far counteracted, as that the defect shall not be an operative cause.

9. The purposes of God are a series of antecedents, from whence follow, by the very *nature of things*, corresponding good consequences, and good only: but the *defect* which is inseparable from created existence, considered in itself, is also a *cause* in the sense of an *antecedent;* otherwise a created existence would be as *indefectible* as the creating or first cause, which involves the most absurd consequences.

10. Defect is either *natural* or *moral;* and each arises from the nature of things, as contradistinguished to decree, but in a different manner. NATURAL DEFECT arises from the nature of things in the way of contrast to God's *natural perfections;* which contrast forms the primary *difference* between creator and creature.

11. This *natural defect* is different from *defectibility;* for defectibility expresses, in strictness, an *effect* not a cause; a *liableness* to defection. But the question returns, WHAT renders a creature *liable* to *defect?* To say, Its *liableness* to defect, or its *defectibility*, assigns no true cause; for the question returns as before, WHAT makes it liable, WHAT makes it defectible?

12. Perhaps there is no term less exceptionable, in order to prevent circumlocution, than PASSIVE POWER, to express that *natural defect*, which exists in a created nature as a *contrast* to the *natural* (not the moral) *perfections* of God.

13. Passive power is as *inapplicable* to God, as it is *applicable* to a creature; for natural perfection is as applicable to him, as natural imperfection is to us.—Therefore to say, that a creature is not the subject of passive power, is the same as to say, that it is perfect and indefectible in its nature as God is; which is the grossest pantheism—the deification of every creature, of every atom that exists.

14. All *antecedents* originate in either *passive power* or the *divine decrees.* From the former proceed, according to the nature of things, all evil consequents; from the latter, all good.

15. MORAL DEFECT, is a contrast to the *moral perfections*, excellence, or holiness of God; and arises, as a *necessary consequence*—not from the divine decree as its antecedent, but—from the *hypothetical nature of things;* that is, passive power, IF not aided by a decretive interposition, and IF also united to liberty of choice in an accountable being.

16. The *removal* of the antecedent is the prerogative of the supreme Lord of nature; but IF the antecedent be not *removed*, that is, altered from what it was as to its *causal influence*, the consequence can no more be prevented, than the nature of things can be changed.

17. That *nature* of things, or that *necessity* of consequence, whereby the effect is *infallibly connected* with its cause, is nothing else but the *essence of* TRUTH, emanating from the first cause, the GOD OF TRUTH, or the TRUE GOD.

18. We now observe, that an event may be necessarily connected with its cause by a divine *decree.* If the divine will contemplate an *end*, and decree accordingly, it necessarily implies that the means, or the *antecedents* to this consequence, are decreed.

SECT. XIII.

Whether we suppose the volitions of moral Agents to be connected with any thing antecedent, or not, yet they must be necessary in such a sense as to overthrow Arminian Liberty.

Every act of the Will has a cause, or it has not. If it has a cause, then, according to what has already been demonstrated, it is not contingent, but necessary; the effect being necessarily dependent and consequent on its cause, let that cause be what it will. If the cause is the Will itself, by antecedent acts choosing and determining; still the *determined caused* act must be a necessary effect. The act, that is the determined effect of the foregoing act which is its cause, cannot prevent the efficiency of its cause; but must be wholly subject to its determination and command, as much as the motions of the hands and feet. The consequent commanded acts of the Will are as passive and as necessary, with respect to the antecedent determining acts, as the parts of the body are to the volitions which determine and command them. And therefore, if all the free acts of the Will are all determined effects determined by the Will itself, that is by antecedent choice, then they are all necessary; they are all subject to, and decisively fixed by, the foregoing act, which is their cause: yea, even the determining act itself; for that must be determined and fixed by another act preceding, if it be a free and voluntary act; and so must be necessary. So that by this, all the free acts of the Will are necessary, and cannot be free unless they are necessary: because they cannot be free, according to the *Arminian* notion of freedom, unless they are determined by the Will; and this is to be determined by antecedent choice, which being their cause, proves them necessary. And yet they say, Necessity is utterly inconsistent with Liberty. So that, by their scheme, the acts of the Will cannot be free unless they are necessary, and yet cannot be free if they be necessary!

But if the other part of the dilemma be taken, that the free acts of the Will have no cause, and are connected with nothing whatsoever that goes before and determines them, in order to maintain their proper and absolute Contingence, and this should be allowed to be possible; still it will not serve their turn. For if the volition come to pass by perfect Contingence, and without any cause at all, then it is certain, no act of the Will, no prior act of the soul, was the cause, no determination or choice of the soul had any hand in it. The Will, or the soul, was indeed the subject of what happened to it accidentally, but was not the cause. The Will is not active in causing or determining, but purely the passive subject; at least, according to their notion of action and passion. In this case, Contingence as much prevents the determination of the Will, as a proper cause; and as to the Will, it was necessary, and could be no otherwise. For to suppose that it could have been otherwise, if the Will or soul had pleased, is to suppose that the act is dependent on some prior act of choice or pleasure, contrary to what is now supposed; it is to suppose that it might have been otherwise, if its cause had ordered it otherwise. But this does not agree to it having no cause or orderer at all. That must be necessary as to the soul, which is dependent on no free act of the soul: but that which is without a cause, is dependent on no free act of the soul; because, by the supposition, it is dependent on nothing, and is connected with nothing. In such a case, the soul is necessarily subjected to what accident brings to pass, from time to time, as much as the earth that is inactive, is necessarily subjected to what falls upon it. But this does not consist with the *Arminian* notion of Liberty, which is the Will's power of determining itself in its own acts, and being wholly active in it, without passiveness, and without being subject to Necessity.—Thus, Contingence belongs to the *Arminian* notion of Liberty, and yet is inconsistent with it.

I would here observe, that the author of the *Essay on the Freedom of Will, in God and the Creature,* (p. 76, 77.) says as follows: "The word *Chance* always means something done without design. Chance and design stand in direct opposition to each other: and Chance can never be properly applied to acts of the Will, which is the spring of all design, and which designs to choose whatsoever it doth choose, whether there be any superior fitness in the thing which it chooses, or no; and it designs to determine itself to one thing, where two things, perfectly equal, are proposed, merely because it will." But herein appears a very great inadvertence. For if *the Will be the spring of all design,* as he says, then certainly it is not always the *effect* of design; and the acts of the Will themselves must sometimes come to pass, when they do not *spring from* design; and consequently come to pass by Chance, according to his own definition of Chance. And if *the Will designs to choose whatsoever it does choose,* and *designs to determine itself,* as he says, then it designs to determine all its designs. Which carries us back from one design to a foregoing design determining that, and to another determining that; and so on *in infinitum.* The very first design must be the effect of foregoing design, or else it must be by Chance, in his notion of it.

Here another alternative may be proposed, relating to the connexion of the acts of the Will with something foregoing that is their cause, not much unlike to the other; which is this: either human liberty may well stand with

19. Hence, an event may be *necessary*, either because virtually *determined* by the divine *will*, IN a series of antecedents; or because the *nature of things* operates without being affected, as to their casual influence, by decretive antecedents.

20. To suppose any sort, or any degree of *defect*, to be *decreed*, is absurd in different ways. It is contrary to an established axiom, that *from good nothing but good can proceed*—and it is absurd to impute that to a divine decree, which antecedently arises from the nature of things.

21. In reality, DIVINE DECREES (as before hinted) are nothing else than a wonderful chain or *series of positions*, which are so many antecedents, *counteracting defects* arising from the hypothetical nature of things. Whence it necessarily follows, that *if there were no* PASSIVE POWER *there could be no* DIVINE DECREES. For if good, and only good, arose from the nature of things; the decree, which has good only for its object, would be superfluous, and therefore unworthy of divine volition.

22. Hence also, whatever event is *in itself good*, is an object of divine decree *in its antecedent;* and the event itself is connected with the decretive position by the very essence of truth. But whatever is *in itself evil* arises from the hypothetical nature of things not counteracted by decretive positions.

23. In God, his absolutely necessary, eternal, infinite, and unchangeable *nature*, is to be regarded as an *antecedent;* from which all possible happiness is the necessary consequence. Such an antecedent is not the result of mere, arbitrary, or decretive *will*, but of *absolute necessity*, but all antecedents in a creature, or every causal influence, of which good, or happiness, whether natural or moral, is the consequence, must be the positions of decretive will, as the only possible mode of securing a good result.

24. As is the antecedent, so is the consequent; for the connexion is formed by eternal truth. If therefore a *good event*—for instance, a virtuous or holy choice—be the consequent, the antecedent is a *decretive position.*

25. In reference to God, the proper and only ground of *infallible certainty* that his choice is *good* and praiseworthy, is the GOODNESS OF HIS NATURE. Were we to admit in thought the possibility of a defectible nature in him, in the same proportion must we admit a possible failure in the goodness of his choice. And in reference to a created being, the proper and only *ground of certainty* that his choice will be good, is the antecedent goodness of his nature or *disposition.* This alone is a sufficient causal influence; but the goodness of a creature's disposition can be secured, as a ground of certainty, only by DECRETIVE INFLUENCE of a nature corresponding with the nature of the effect.

26. From these principles and considerations, which can here be but briefly stated, as necessarily connected with their legitimate consequences, we infer, that God foresees ALL GOOD, in every created being, in every mode, in every event, by the evidence of a DECRETIVE NECESSITY; a necessity resulting from *actual influx*, or perpetual *energy*, in the position of *antecedents*, and the essence of *truth* connecting the causal influence with the effect.

27. From the same principles we learn, that God foresees or foreknows ALL EVIL—however blended with the good, as the different colours in a pencil of light are blended—in every being, and in every event where found, by that necessity which is HYPOTHETICAL only; a necessity resulting from the nature of things left to their own causal influence; which influence, in any given circumstances, will manifest itself either in the way of contrast, of dependence, or both united.

28. Again: *Volitions* are *acts* of the mind, and each voluntary act is compounded of a *natural* and *moral* quality. The NATURAL quality of a voluntary act proceeds from *decretive necessity;* for there is nothing in it but what is good, decreed, and effected by the first cause. The MORAL quality of a voluntary act is either good or evil.

29. A voluntary act *morally* GOOD, is *altogether* of *decretive* necessity, both as to its physical and moral quality; and is therefore foreknown *because* of decretive appointment and energy. But a voluntary act *morally* BAD, is partly of decretive, and partly of hypothetical necessity, or that of consequence.

30. The PHYSICAL QUALITY of a voluntary act *morally bad*, is of decretive necessity, and is foreknown *because* foreappointed; but the MORAL QUALITY of the same act, or its *badness*, is foreknown only by relation, connexion, or consequence. Thus *deformity* is the absence of beauty, and may be known by the standard of beauty from which it deviates. *Weakness* is the absence of strength, and may be known by relation. A *shadow* is known by the interception of rays, and may be known in the same manner. *Darkness* is caused by the absence of light, and may be known by the light excluded.

31. How the BAD *quality* of a moral act may be foreknown by the evidence of relation, will further appear from the consideration of the nature of moral evil itself. For what is moral evil, or sin, but WHAT OUGHT NOT TO BE, in point of *moral obligation?* Now for at all knowing, or foreknowing, what *ought not* to be, which is incapable of being decreed, the proper medium or evidence is the knowledge of what *ought* to be.

32. If therefore *what ought to be*, is known to the omniscient by constituted relations, or voluntary appointment; *what ought not to be* may be known by evident consequences.—W.

volitions being necessarily connected with the views of the understanding, and so is consistent with Necessity; or it is inconsistent with and contrary to such a connexion and Necessity. The former is directly subversive of the *Arminian* notion of Liberty, consisting in freedom from all Necessity. And if the latter be chosen, and it be said, that liberty is inconsistent with any such necessary connexion of volition with foregoing views of the understanding, it consisting in freedom from any such Necessity of the Will as that would imply; then the Liberty of the soul consists, partly at least, in freedom from restraint, limitation, and government, in its actings, by the understanding, and in Liberty and liableness to act contrary to the views and dictates of the understanding: and consequently the more the soul has of this disengagedness in its acting, the more Liberty. Now let it be considered to what this brings the noble principle of human Liberty, particularly when it is possessed and enjoyed in its perfection, *viz.* a full and perfect freedom and liableness to act altogether at random, without the least connexion with, or restraint or government by, any dictate of reason, or any thing whatsoever apprehended, considered, or viewed by the understanding; as being inconsistent with the full and perfect sovereignty of the Will over its own determinations.—The notion mankind have conceived of Liberty, is some dignity or privilege, something worth claiming. But what dignity or privilege is there, in being given up to such a wild Contingence as this, to be perfectly and constantly liable to act unreasonably, and as much without the guidance of understanding, as if we had none, or were as destitute of perception, as the smoke that is driven by the wind!

PART III.

WHEREIN IS INQUIRED, WHETHER ANY SUCH LIBERTY OF WILL AS ARMINIANS HOLD, BE NECESSARY TO MORAL AGENCY, VIRTUE AND VICE, PRAISE AND DISPRAISE, &c.

SECT. I.

God's moral Excellency necessary, yet virtuous and praiseworthy.

Having considered the *first* thing proposed, relating to that freedom of Will which *Arminians* maintain; namely, Whether any such thing does, ever did, or ever can exist, I come now to the *second* thing proposed to be the subject of inquiry, *viz.* Whether any such kind of liberty be requisite to moral agency, virtue and vice, praise and blame, reward and punishment, &c.

I shall begin with some consideration of the virtue and agency of the Supreme moral Agent, and Fountain of all Agency and Virtue.

Dr. Whitby in his Discourse on the five Points, (p. 14.) says, "If all human actions are necessary, virtue and vice must be empty names; we being capable of nothing that is blameworthy, or deserveth praise; for who can blame a person for doing only what he could not help, or judge that he deserveth praise only for what he could not avoid?" To the like purpose he speaks in places innumerable; especially in his Discourse on the *Freedom of the Will;* constantly maintaining, that a *freedom not only from coaction, but necessity,* is absolutely requisite, in order to actions being either worthy of blame, or deserving of praise. And to this agrees, as is well known, the current doctrine of *Arminian* writers, who, in general, hold, that there is no virtue or vice, reward or punishment, nothing to be commended or blamed, without this freedom. And yet Dr. Whitby (p. 300.) allows, that God is without this freedom; and *Arminians,* so far as I have had opportunity to observe, generally acknowledge, that God is necessarily holy, and his will necessarily determined to that which is good.

So that, putting these things together, the infinitely holy God—who always used to be esteemed by God's people not only virtuous, but a Being in whom is all possible virtue, in the most absolute purity and perfection, brightness and amiableness; the most perfect pattern of virtue, and from whom all the virtue of others is but as beams from the sun; and who has been supposed to be, (being thus every where represented in Scripture,) on the account of his virtue and holiness, infinitely more worthy to be esteemed, loved, honoured, admired, commended, extolled, and praised, than any creature—this Being, according to this notion of Dr. Whitby, and other *Arminians,* has no virtue at all; virtue, when ascribed to him, is but *an empty name;* and he is deserving of no commendation or praise; because he is under necessity, he cannot avoid being holy and good as he is; therefore no thanks to him for it. It seems, the holiness, justice, faithfulness, &c. of the Most High, must not be accounted to be of the nature of that which is virtuous and praiseworthy. They will not deny, that these things in God are good; but then we must understand them, that they are no more virtuous, or of the nature of any thing commendable, than the good that is in any other being that is not a moral agent; as the brightness of the sun, and the fertility of the earth, are good, but not virtuous, because these properties are necessary to these bodies, and not the fruit of self-determining power.

There needs no other confutation of this notion, to Christians acquainted with the Bible, but only stating and particularly representing it. To bring texts of Scripture, wherein God is represented, as in every respect, in the highest manner virtuous, and supremely praiseworthy, would be endless, and is altogether needless to such as have been brought up in the light of the gospel.

It were to be wished, that Dr. Whitby and other divines of the same sort, had explained themselves, when they have asserted, that *that* which is necessary, is *not deserving of praise;* at the same time that they have owned God's perfection to be necessary, and so in effect representing God as not deserving praise. Certainly, if their words have any meaning at all, by *praise,* they must mean the exercise or testimony of esteem, respect, or honourable regard. And will they then say, that men are worthy of that esteem, respect, and honour for their virtue, small and imperfect as it is, which yet God is not worthy of, for his infinite righteousness, holiness, and goodness? If so, it must be, because of some sort of peculiar Excellency in the virtuous man, which is his prerogative, wherein he really has the preference; some dignity, that is entirely distinguished from any Excellency or amiableness in God; not in dependence, but in pre-eminence; which therefore he does not receive from God, nor is God the fountain or pattern of it; nor can God, in that respect, stand in competition with him, as the object of honour and regard; but man may claim a peculiar esteem, commendation, and glory, to which God can have no pretension. Yea, God has no right, by virtue of his necessary holiness, to intermeddle with that grateful respect and praise, due to the virtuous man, who chooses virtue, in the exercise of a freedom *ad utrumque;* any more than a precious stone, which cannot avoid being hard and beautiful.

And if it be so, let it be explained what that peculiar respect is, that is due to the virtuous man, which differs in nature and kind, in some way of pre-eminence, from all that is due to God. What is the name or description of that peculiar affection? Is it esteem, love, admiration, honour, praise, or gratitude? The Scripture every where represents God as the highest object of all these: there we read of the soul magnifying the Lord, of "loving him with all the heart, with all the soul, with all the mind, and with all the strength;" *admiring* him, and *his righteous acts,* or greatly regarding them, as *marvellous and wonder-*

ful; honouring, glorifying, exalting, extolling, blessing, thanking, and *praising* him; *giving unto him all the glory* of the good which is done or received, rather than unto men; "that no flesh should glory in his presence;" but that he should be regarded as the Being to whom all glory is due. What then is that respect? What passion, affection, or exercise is it, that *Arminians* call *praise*, diverse from all these things, which men are worthy of for their virtue, and which God is not worthy of, in any degree?

If that necessity which attends God's moral perfections and actions, be as inconsistent with being worthy of praise, as a necessity of co-action; as is plainly implied in, or inferred from, Dr. Whitby's discourse; then why should we thank God for his goodness, any more than if he were forced to be good, or any more than we should thank one of our fellow-creatures who did us good, not freely, and of good will, or from any kindness of heart, but from mere compulsion, or extrinsical necessity? *Arminians* suppose, that God is necessarily a good and gracious Being; for this they make the ground of some of their main arguments against many doctrines maintained by *Calvinists;* they say, these are *certainly* false, and it is *impossible* they should be true, because they are not consistent with the goodness of God. This supposes, that it is *impossible* but that God should be good: for if it be possible that he should be otherwise, then that impossibility of the truth of these doctrines ceases according to their own argument.

That virtue in God is not, in the most proper sense, *rewardable*, is not for want of merit in his moral perfections and actions, sufficient to deserve rewards from his creatures; but because he is infinitely above all capacity of receiving any reward. He is already infinitely and unchangeably happy, and we cannot be profitable unto him. But still he is worthy of our supreme benevolence for his virtue: and would be worthy of our beneficence, which is the fruit and expression of benevolence, if our goodness could extend to him. If God deserves to be thanked and praised for his goodness, he would, for the same reason, deserve that we should also *requite* his kindness, if that were possible. "What shall I render unto the Lord for all his benefits?" is the natural language of thankfulness: and so far as in us lies, it is our duty to *render again according to benefits received.* And that we might have opportunity for so natural an expression of our gratitude to God, as beneficence, notwithstanding his being infinitely above our reach, he has appointed others to be his receivers, and to stand in his stead, as the objects of our beneficence; such are especially our indigent brethren.

SECT. II.

The Acts of the Will of the human soul of Jesus Christ, necessarily holy, yet truly virtuous, praise-worthy, rewardable, &c.

I HAVE already considered how Dr. Whitby insists upon it, that a freedom, not only from coaction, but necessity, is *requisite either to virtue or vice, praise or dispraise, reward or punishment.* He also insists on the same freedom as absolutely requisite to a person being the subject of a *law*, of *precepts*, or *prohibitions;* in the book before mentioned, (p. 301, 314, 328, 339, 340, 341, 342, 347, 361, 373, 410.) And of *promises* and *threatenings*, (p. 298, 301, 305, 311, 339, 340, 363.) And as requisite to *a state of trial*, p. 297, &c.

Now therefore, with an eye to these things, I would inquire into the moral conduct and practices of our Lord Jesus Christ, which he exhibited in his human nature, in his state of humiliation. And *first*, I would show, that his holy behaviour was *necessary;* or that it was *impossible* it should be otherwise, than that he should behave himself holily, and that he should be perfectly holy in each individual act of his life. And *secondly*, that his holy behaviour was properly of the nature of *virtue*, and was *worthy of praise;* and that he was the subject of *law, precept*, or *commands, promises* and *rewards;* and that he was *in a state of trial.*

I. It was *impossible*, that the Acts of the Will of Christ's human soul should, in any instance, degree, or circumstance, be otherwise than holy, and agreeable to God's nature and Will. The following things make this evident.

1. God had promised so effectually to preserve and uphold him by his Spirit, under all his temptations, that he could not fail of the end for which he came into the world; but he would have failed, had he fallen into sin. We have such a promise, (Isa. xliii. 1—4.) "Behold my Servant, whom I uphold; mine Elect, in whom my soul delighteth: I have put my Spirit upon him: he shall bring forth judgment to the Gentiles: he shall not cry, nor lift up, nor cause his voice to be heard in the street.—He shall bring forth judgment unto truth. He shall not fail, nor be discouraged, till he have set judgment in the earth; and the isles shall wait his law." This promise of God's Spirit put upon him, and his not crying and lifting up his voice, &c. relates to the time of Christ's appearance on earth; as is manifest from the nature of the promise, and also the application of it in the New Testament, (Matt. xii. 18.) And the words imply a promise of his being so upheld by God's Spirit, that he should be preserved from sin; particularly from pride and vain-glory; and from being overcome by any temptations he should be under to affect the glory of this world, the pomp of an earthly prince, or the applause and praise of men: and that he should be so upheld, that he should by no means fail of obtaining the end of his coming into the world, of bringing forth judgment unto victory, and establishing his kingdom of grace in the earth. And in the following verses, this promise is confirmed, with the greatest imaginable solemnity. "Thus saith the Lord, he that created the heavens, and stretched them out; he that spread forth the earth, and that which cometh out of it; he that giveth breath unto the people upon it, and spirit to them that walk therein: I the Lord have called thee in righteousness, and will hold thine hand; and will keep thee, and give thee for a Covenant of the people, for a Light of the Gentiles, to open the blind eyes, to bring out the prisoners from the prison, and them that sit in darkness out of the prison-house. I am JEHOVAH, that is my name," &c.

Very parallel with these promises is another, (Isa. xlix. 7, 8, 9.) which also has an apparent respect to the time of Christ's humiliation on earth.—"Thus saith the Lord, the Redeemer of Israel, and his Holy One, to him whom man despiseth, to him whom the nation abhorreth, to a servant of rulers; kings shall see and arise, princes also shall worship; because of the Lord that is faithful, and the Holy One of Israel, and he shall choose thee. Thus saith the Lord, in an acceptable time have I heard thee; in a day of salvation have I helped thee; and I will preserve thee, and give thee for a covenant of the people, to establish the earth," &c.

And in Isa. l. 5, 6. we have the Messiah expressing his assurance, that God would help him, by so opening his ear, or inclining his heart to God's commandments, that he should not be rebellious, but should persevere, and not apostatize, or turn his back: that through God's help, he should be immovable in obedience, under great trials of reproach and suffering; setting his face like a flint: so that he knew he should not be ashamed, or frustrated in his design; and finally should be approved and justified, as having done his work faithfully. "The Lord hath opened mine ear; so that I was not rebellious, neither turned away my back: I gave my back to the smiters, and my cheeks to them that plucked off the hair; I hid not my face from shame and spitting. For the Lord God will help me; therefore shall I not be confounded: therefore have I set my face as a flint, and I know that I shall not be ashamed. He is near that justifieth me: who will contend with me? Let us stand together. Who is mine adversary? Let him come near to me. Behold the Lord God will help me: who is he that shall condemn me? Lo, they shall all wax old as a garment, the moth shall eat them up."

2. The same thing is evident from all the promises which God made to the Messiah, of his future glory, kingdom, and success, in his office and character of a Mediator: which glory could not have been obtained, if his holiness had failed, and he had been guilty of sin. God's absolute promise makes the things promised *necessary*, and their failing to take place absolutely *impossible:* and, in like

manner, it makes those things necessary, on which the thing promised depends, and without which it cannot take effect. Therefore it appears, that it was utterly impossible that Christ's holiness should fail, from such absolute promises as these, (Psal. cx. 4.) " The Lord hath sworn, and will not repent, thou art a priest for ever, after the order of Melchizedec." And from every other promise in that psalm, contained in each verse of it. (And Psal. ii. 6, 7.) " I will declare the decree: The Lord hath said unto me, Thou art my Son, this day have I begotten thee: Ask of me, and I will give thee the heathen for thine inheritance," &c. (Psal. xlv. 3, 4, &c.) " Gird thy sword on thy thigh, O most mighty, with thy glory and thy majesty; and in thy majesty ride prosperously." And so every thing that is said from thence to the end of the psalm. (See Isa. iii. 13—15. and liii. 10—12.) And all those promises which God makes to the Messiah, of success, dominion, and glory in the character of a Redeemer, (Isa. chap. xlix.)

3. It was often promised to the church of God of old, for their comfort, that God would give them a righteous, sinless Saviour. (Jer. xxiii. 5, 6.) " Behold, the days come, saith the Lord, that I will raise up unto David a righteous branch; and a king shall reign and prosper, and shall execute judgment and justice in the earth. In his days shall Judah be saved, and Israel shall dwell safely. And this is the name whereby he shall be called, The Lord our righteousness." (So, Jer. xxxiii. 15.) " I will cause the branch of righteousness to grow up unto David, and he shall execute judgment and righteousness in the land." (Isa. xi. 6, 7.) " For unto us a child is born;—upon the throne of David and of his kingdom, to order it and to establish it with judgment and justice, from henceforth, even for ever: the zeal of the Lord of hosts will do this." (Chap. xi. 1, &c.) " There shall come forth a rod out of the stem of Jesse, and a branch shall grow out of his roots; and the Spirit of the Lord shall rest upon him,—the spirit of knowledge, and the fear of the Lord:—with righteousness shall he judge the poor, and reprove with equity:—Righteousness shall be the girdle of his loins, and faithfulness the girdle of his reins." (Chap. lii. 13.) " My servant shall deal prudently." (Chap. liii. 9.) " Because he had done no violence, neither was guile found in his mouth." If it be impossible, that these promises should fail, and it be easier for heaven and earth to pass away, than for one jot or tittle of them to pass away, then it was impossible that Christ should commit any sin.——Christ himself signified, that it was impossible but that the things which were spoken concerning him, should be fulfilled. (Luke xxiv. 44.) " That all things must be fulfilled, which were written in the law of Moses, and in the prophets, and in the psalms concerning me." (Matt. xxvi. 53, 54.) " But how then shall the scripture be fulfilled, that thus it must be?" (Mark xiv. 49.) " But the scriptures must be fulfilled." And so the apostle, (Acts i. 16, 17.) " This scripture must needs have been fulfilled."

4. All the promises, which were made to the church of old, of the Messiah as a future Saviour, from that made to our first parents in paradise, to that which was delivered by the prophet *Malachi* show it to be impossible that Christ should not have persevered in perfect holiness. The ancient predictions given to God's church, of the Messiah as a Saviour, were of the nature of promises; as is evident by the predictions themselves, and the manner of delivering them. But they are expressly and very often called *promises* in the New Testament; (as in Luke i. 54, 55, 72, 73. Acts xiii. 32, 33. Rom. i. 1—3. and chap. xv. 8. Heb. vi. 13, &c.) These promises were often made with great solemnity, and confirmed with an oath; as, (Gen. xxii. 16, 17.) " By myself have I sworn, saith the Lord, that in blessing I will bless thee, and in multiplying I will multiply thy seed, as the stars of heaven, and as the sand which is upon the sea-shore:——And in thy seed shall all the nations of the earth be blessed." (Compare Luke i. 72, 73. and Gal. iii. 8, 15, 16.) The apostle in Heb. vi. 17, 18. speaking of this promise to *Abraham*, says, " Wherein God willing more abundantly to show to the heirs of promise the immutability of his counsel, confirmed it by an oath; that by two IMMUTABLE things, in which it was IMPOSSIBLE for God to lie, we might have strong consolation." In which words, the *necessity* of the accomplishment, or (which is the same thing) the *impossibility* of the contrary, is fully declared. So God confirmed the promise of the Messiah's great salvation, made to *David*, by an oath; (Psal. lxxxix. 3, 4.) " I have made a covenant with my chosen, I have sworn unto David my servant; thy seed will I establish for ever, and build up thy throne to all generations." There is nothing so abundantly set forth in Scripture, as sure and irrefragable, as this promise and oath to *David*. (See Psal. lxxxix. 34—36. 2 Sam. xxiii. 5. Isa. lv. 4. Acts ii. 29, 30. and xiii. 34.) The Scripture expressly speaks of it as utterly *impossible* that this promise and oath to *David*, concerning the everlasting dominion of the Messiah, should fail. (Jer. xxxiii. 15, &c.) " In those days, and at that time, I will cause the Branch of righteousness to grow up unto David.—For thus saith the Lord, David shall never want a man to sit upon the throne of the house of Israel." (Ver. 20, 21.) " If you can break my covenant of the day, and my covenant of the night, and that there should not be day and night in their season; then may also my covenant be broken with David my servant, that he should not have a son to reign upon his throne." (So in ver. 25, 26.) Thus abundant is the Scripture in representing how *impossible* it was, that the promises made of old concerning the great salvation and kingdom of the Messiah should fail: which implies, that it was impossible that this Messiah, the second *Adam*, the promised seed of *Abraham*, and of *David*, should fall from his integrity, as the first *Adam* did.

5. All the promises that were made to the church of God under the Old Testament, of the great enlargement of the church, and advancement of her glory, in the days of the gospel, after the coming of the Messiah; the increase of her light, liberty, holiness, joy, triumph over her enemies, &c. of which so great a part of the Old Testament consists; which are repeated so often, are so variously exhibited, so frequently introduced with great pomp and solemnity, and are so abundantly sealed with typical and symbolical representations; I say, all these promises imply, that the Messiah should perfect the work of redemption: and this implies, that he should persevere in the work, which the Father had appointed him, being in all things conformed to his Will. These promises were often confirmed by an oath. (See Isa. liv. 9. with the context; chap. lxii. 18.) And it is represented as utterly impossible that these promises should fail. (Isa. xlix. 15. with the context, chap. liv. 10. with the context; chap. li. 4—8. chap. xl. 8. with the context.) And therefore it was *impossible* that the Messiah should fail, or commit sin.

6. It was *impossible* that the Messiah should fail of persevering in integrity and holiness, as the first *Adam* did, because this would have been inconsistent with the promises, which God made to the blessed Virgin, his mother, and to her husband; implying, that he should " save his people from their sins," that God would " give him the throne of his father David," that he should " reign over the house of Jacob for ever;" and that " of his kingdom there shall be no end." These promises were sure, and it was *impossible* they should fail, and therefore the Virgin *Mary*, in trusting fully to them, acted reasonably, having an immovable foundation of her faith; as *Elizabeth* observes, (ver. 45.) " And blessed is she that believeth; for there shall be a performance of those things which were told her from the Lord."

7. That it should have been possible that Christ should sin, and so fail in the work of our redemption, does not consist with the eternal purpose and decree of God, revealed in the Scriptures, that he would provide salvation for fallen man in and by Jesus Christ, and that salvation should be offered to sinners through the preaching of the gospel. Thus much is implied in many scriptures, (as 1 Cor. ii. 7.—Eph. i. 4, 5. and chap. iii. 9—11.—1 Pet. i. 19, 20.) Such an absolute decree as this, *Arminians* allow to be signified in many texts; their election of nations and societies, and general election of the christian church, and conditional election of particular persons, imply this. God could not decree before the foundation of the world, to save all that should believe in and obey Christ, unless he had absolutely decreed, that salvation should be provided,

and effectually wrought out by Christ. And since (as the *Arminians* themselves strenuously maintain) a decree of God infers *necessity;* hence it became *necessary,* that Christ should persevere and actually work out salvation for us, and that he should not fail by the commission of sin.

8. That it should have been possible for Christ's holiness to fail, is not consistent with what God promised to his Son, before all ages. For that salvation should be offered to men, through Christ, and bestowed on all his faithful followers, is at least implied in that certain and infallible promise spoken of by the apostle, (Tit. i. 2.) "In hope of eternal life; which God, that cannot lie, promised before the world began." This does not seem to be controverted by *Arminians.**

9. That it should be possible for Christ to fail of doing his Father's Will, is inconsistent with the promise made to the Father by the Son, the *Logos* that was with the Father from the beginning, before he took the human nature: as may be seen in Ps. xl. 6—8. (compared with the apostle's interpretation, Heb. x. 5—9.) "Sacrifice and offering thou didst not desire: mine ears hast thou opened, (or bored;) burnt-offering and sin-offering thou hast not required. Then said I, Lo, I come; in the volume of the book it is written of me, I delight to do thy Will, O my God, yea, thy law is within my heart." Where is a manifest allusion to the covenant, which the willing servant, who loved his master's service, made with his master, to be his servant for ever, on the day wherein he had his ear bored; which covenant was probably inserted in the public records, called the Volume of the Book, by the judges, who were called to take cognizance of the transaction; (Exod. xxi.) If the *Logos,* who was with the Father before the world, and who made the world, thus engaged in covenant to do the Will of the Father in the human nature, and the promise was as it were recorded, that it might be made sure, doubtless it was *impossible* that it should fail; and so it was *impossible* that Christ should fail of doing the Will of the Father in the human nature.

10. If it was possible for Christ to have failed of doing the Will of his Father, and so to have failed of effectually working out redemption for sinners, then the salvation of all the saints, who were saved from the beginning of the world, to the death of Christ, was not built on a firm foundation. The Messiah, and the redemption which he was to work out by his obedience unto death, was the saving foundation of all that ever were saved. Therefore, if when the Old-Testament saints had the pardon of their sins and the favour of God promised them, and salvation bestowed upon them, still it was possible that the Messiah, when he came, might commit sin, then all this was on a foundation that was not firm and stable, but liable to fail; something which it was possible might never be. God did as it were trust to what his Son had engaged and promised to do in future time, and depended so much upon it, that he proceeded actually to save men on the account of it, though it had been already done. But this trust and dependence of God, on the supposition of Christ's being liable to fail of doing his Will, was leaning on a staff that was weak, and might possibly break. The saints of old trusted on the promises of a future redemption to be wrought out and completed by the Messiah, and built their comfort upon it: *Abraham* saw Christ's day, and rejoiced; and he and the other Patriarchs died in the faith of the promise of it, (Heb. xi. 13.) But on this supposition, their faith, their comfort, and their salvation, was built on a fallible foundation; Christ was not to them "*a tried stone, a sure foundation;*" (Isa. xxviii. 16.) *David* entirely rested on the covenant of God with him, concerning the future glorious dominion and salvation of the Messiah; and said it was all his salvation, and all his desire; and comforts himself that this covenant was an "everlasting covenant, ordered in all things and sure," (2 Sam. xxiii. 5.) But if Christ's virtue might fail, he was mistaken: his great comfort was not built so "sure" as he thought it was, being founded entirely on the determinations of the Free Will of Christ's human soul; which was subject to no necessity, and might be determined either one way or the other. Also the dependence of those, who "*looked for redemption in Jerusalem, and waited for the consolation of Israel,*" (Luke ii. 25, and 38.) and the confidence of the disciples of Jesus, who forsook all and followed him, that they might enjoy the benefits of his future kingdom, were built on a sandy foundation.

11. The man Christ Jesus, before he had finished his course of obedience, and while in the midst of temptations and trials, was abundant in positively predicting his own future glory in his kingdom, and the enlargement of his church, the salvation of the Gentiles through him, &c. and in promises of blessings he would bestow on his true disciples in his future kingdom; on which promises he required the full dependence of his disciples, (John xiv.) But the disciples would have no ground for such dependence, if Christ had been liable to fail in his work: and Christ himself would have been guilty of presumption, in so abounding in peremptory promises of great things, which depended on a mere contingence; viz. the determinations of his Free Will, consisting in a freedom *ad utrumque,* to either sin or holiness, standing in indifference, and incident, in thousands of future instances, to go either one way or the other.

Thus it is evident, that it was *impossible* that the Acts of the Will of the human soul of Christ should be otherwise than holy, and conformed to the Will of the Father; or, in other words, they were necessarily so conformed.

I have been the longer in the proof of this matter, it being a thing denied by some of the greatest *Arminians,* by *Episcopius* in particular; and because I look upon it as a point clearly and absolutely determining the controversy between *Calvinists* and *Arminians,* concerning the necessity of such a freedom of Will as is insisted on by the latter, in order to moral agency, virtue, command or prohibition, promise or threatening, reward or punishment, praise or dispraise, merit or demerit. I now therefore proceed,

II. To consider whether Christ, in his holy behaviour on earth, was not thus a *moral agent,* subject to *commands, promises, &c.*

Dr. Whitby very often speaks of what he calls a freedom ad utrumlibet, without necessity, as requisite to *law and commands:* and speaks of necessity as entirely inconsistent with *injunctions and prohibitions.* But yet we read of Christ being the subject of his Father's commands, (John x. 18. and xv. 10.) And Christ tells us, that every thing that he *said,* or *did,* was in compliance with "commandments he had received of the Father;" (John xii. 49, 50. and xiv. 31.) And we often read of Christ's *obedidience* to his Father's commands, (Rom. v. 19. Phil. ii. 18. Heb. v. 8.)

The forementioned writer represents *promises offered as motives* to persons to do their duty, or *a being moved and induced by promises,* as utterly inconsistent with a state wherein persons have not a liberty *ad utrumlibet,* but are necessarily determined to one. (See particularly, p. 298, and 311.) But the thing which this writer asserts, is demonstrably false, if the christian religion be true. If there be any truth in Christianity or the Holy Scriptures, the man Christ Jesus had his Will infallibly and unalterably determined to good, and that alone; but yet he had promises of glorious rewards made to him, on condition of his persevering in and perfecting the work which God had appointed him; (Isa. liii. 10, 11, 12. Psal. ii. and cx. Isa. xlix. 7, 8, 9.) In Luke xxii. 28, 29. Christ says to his disciples, "Ye are they which have continued with me in my temptations; and I appoint unto you a kingdom, as my Father hath appointed unto me." The word most properly signifies to appoint by covenant, or promise. The plain meaning of Christ's words is this: "As you have partaken of my temptations and trials, and have been stedfast, and have overcome; I promise to make you partakers of my reward, and to give you a kingdom; as the Father has promised me a kingdom for continuing stedfast and overcoming in those trials." And the words are well explained by those in Rev. iii. 21. "To him that overcometh, will I grant to sit with me on my throne; even as I also overcame, and am set down with my Father in his throne." And Christ had not only promises of glorious

* See Dr. Whitby on the five Points, p. 48, 49, 50.

success and rewards made to his obedience and sufferings, but the Scriptures plainly represent him as using these promises for motives and inducements to obey and suffer; and particularly that promise of a kingdom which the Father had appointed him, or sitting with the Father on his throne; (as in Heb. xii. 1, 2.) "Let us lay aside every weight, and the sin which doth easily beset us, and let us run with patience the race that is set before us, looking unto Jesus the author and finisher of our faith; who for the joy that was set before him, endured the cross, despising the shame, and is set down on the right hand of the throne of God."

And how strange would it be to hear any Christian assert, that the holy and excellent temper and behaviour of Jesus Christ, and that obedience which he performed under such great trials, was not *virtuous* or *praiseworthy;* because his Will was not free *ad utrumque,* to either holiness or sin, but was unalterably determined to one; that upon this account, there is no virtue at all in all Christ's humility, meekness, patience, charity, forgiveness of enemies, contempt of the world, heavenly-mindedness, submission to the Will of God, perfect obedience to his commands unto death, even the death of the cross, his great compassion to the afflicted, his unparalleled love to mankind, his faithfulness to God and man, under such great trials; his praying for his enemies, even when nailing him to the cross; that *virtue,* when applied to these things, *is but an empty name;* that there was no merit in any of these things; that is, that Christ was *worthy* of nothing at all on account of them, worthy of no reward, no praise, no honour or respect from God or man; because his Will was not indifferent, and free either to these things, or the contrary; but under such a strong inclination or bias to the things that were excellent, as made it *impossible* that he should choose the contrary; that upon this account, to use Dr. Whitby's language, *it would be sensibly unreasonable* that the human nature should be rewarded for any of these things.

According to this doctrine, that creature who is evidently set forth in Scripture as the *first-born of every creature,* as having *in all things the pre-eminence,* and as the highest of all creatures in virtue, honour, and worthiness of esteem, praise, and glory, on account of his virtue, is less worthy of reward or praise, than the very least of saints; yea, no more worthy than a clock or mere machine, that is purely passive, and moved by natural necessity.

If we judge by scriptural representations of things, we have reason to suppose, that Christ took on him our nature, and dwelt with us in this world, in a suffering state, not only to satisfy for our sins; but that he, being in our nature and circumstances, and under our trials, might be our most fit and proper *example,* leader, and captain, in the exercise of glorious and victorious virtue, and might be a visible instance of the glorious end and reward of it; that we might see in him the beauty, amiableness, and true honour and glory, and exceeding benefit, of that virtue, which it is proper for us human beings to practise; and might thereby learn, and be animated, to seek the like glory and honour, and to obtain the like glorious reward. (See Heb. ii. 9—14. with v. 8, 9. and xii. 1, 2, 3. John xv. 10. Rom. viii. 17. 2 Tim. ii. 11, 12. 1 Pet. ii. 19, 20. and iv. 13.) But if there was nothing of any virtue or merit, or worthiness of any reward, glory, praise, or commendation at all, in all that he did, because it was all necessary, and he could not help it; then how is here any thing so proper to animate and incite us, free creatures, *by patient continuance in well-doing, to seek for honour glory, and virtue?*

God speaks of himself as peculiarly well pleased with the righteousness of this distinguished servant. (Isa. xlii. 21.) "The Lord is well pleased for his righteousness' sake." The sacrifices of old are spoken of as a sweet savour to God, but the obedience of Christ as far more acceptable than they. (Psal. xl. 6, 7.) "Sacrifice and offering thou didst not desire: mine ear hast thou opened [as thy servant performing willing obedience;] burnt-offering and sin-offering hast thou not required. Then said I, Lo, I come, [as a servant that cheerfully answers the calls of his master:] I delight to do thy will, O my God, and thy law is within mine heart." (Matt. xvii. 5.) "This is my beloved Son, in whom I am well-pleased." And Christ tells us expressly, that the Father loves him for that wonderful instance of his obedience, his voluntary yielding himself to death, in compliance with the Father's command, (John x. 17, 18.) "Therefore doth my Father love me, because I lay down my life:—No man taketh it from me; but I lay it down of myself—This commandment received I of my Father."

And if there was no merit in Christ's obedience unto death, if it was not worthy of praise, and of the most glorious rewards, the heavenly hosts were exceedingly mistaken, by the account that is given of them, (Rev. v. 8—12.) "The four beasts, and the four and twenty elders, fell down before the Lamb, having every one of them harps, and golden vials full of odours;—and they sung a new song, saying, Thou art worthy to take the book, and to open the seals thereof; for thou wast slain.—And I beheld, and I heard the voice of many angels round about the throne, and the beasts, and the elders, and the number of them was ten thousand times ten thousand, and thousands of thousands, saying with a loud voice, Worthy is the Lamb that was slain, to receive power, and riches, and wisdom, and strength, and honour, and glory, and blessing."

Christ speaks of the eternal life which he was to receive, as the reward of his obedience to the Father's commandments. (John xii. 49, 50.) "I have not spoken of myself; but the Father which sent me, he gave me a commandment what I should say, and what I should speak: and I know that his commandment is life everlasting: whatsoever I speak therefore, even as the Father said unto me, so I speak."—God promises to divide him a portion with the great, &c. for his being his righteous servant, for his glorious virtue under such great trials and afflictions. (Isa. liii. 11, 12.) "He shall see the travail of his soul and be satisfied: by his knowledge shall my righteous servant justify many; for he shall bear their iniquities. Therefore will I divide him a portion with the great, and he shall divide the spoil with the strong, because he hath poured out his soul unto death." The Scriptures represent God as rewarding him far above all his other servants. (Phil. ii. 7—9.) "He took on him the form of a servant, and was made in the likeness of men: and being found in fashion as a man, he humbled himself, and became obedient unto death, even the death of the cross: wherefore God also hath highly exalted him, and given him a name above every name." (Psal. xlv. 7.) "Thou lovest righteousness, and hatest wickedness; therefore God, thy God, hath anointed thee with the oil of gladness above thy fellows."

There is no room to pretend, that the glorious benefits bestowed in consequence of Christ's obedience, are not properly of the nature of a reward. What is a reward, in the most proper sense, but a benefit bestowed in consequence of something morally excellent in quality or behaviour, in testimony of well-pleasedness in that moral excellency, and of respect and favour on that account? If we consider the nature of a reward most strictly, and make the utmost of it, and add to the things contained in this description proper merit or worthiness, and the bestowment of the benefit in consequence of a promise; still it will be found, there is nothing belonging to it, but what the Scripture most expressly ascribes to the glory bestowed on Christ, after his sufferings; as appears from what has been already observed: there was a glorious benefit bestowed in consequence of something morally excellent, being called *Righteousness* and *Obedience;* there was great favour, love, and well-pleasedness, for this righteousness and obedience, in the bestower; there was proper merit, or worthiness of the benefit, in the obedience; it was bestowed in fulfilment of promises, made to that obedience; and was bestowed *therefore,* or *because* he had performed that obedience.

I may add to all these things, that Jesus Christ, while here in the flesh, was manifestly in a state of trial. The last *Adam,* as Christ is called, (1 Cor. xv. 45. Rom. v. 14.) taking on him the human nature, and so the form of a servant, and being under the law, to stand and act for us, was put into a state of trial, as the first *Adam* was.—Dr. Whitby mentions these three things as evidences of persons being in a state of trial, (on the five Points, p.

298, 299.) namely, their afflictions being spoken of as their trials or temptations, their being the subjects of promises, and their being exposed to Satan's temptations. But Christ was apparently the subject of each of these. Concerning promises made to him, I have spoken already. The difficulties and *afflictions* he met with in the course of his obedience, are called his *temptations* or *trials*, (Luke xxii. 28.) " Ye are they which have continued with me in my temptations *or* trials." (Heb. ii. 18.) " For in that he himself hath suffered, being tempted [or tried,] he is able to succour them that are tempted." And, (chap. iv. 15.) " We have not an high-priest, which cannot be touched with the feeling of our infirmities; but was in all points tempted like as we are, yet without sin." And as to his being tempted by *Satan* it is what none will dispute.

SECT. III.

The case of such as are given up of God to sin, and of fallen man in general, proves moral Necessity and Inability to be consistent with Blameworthiness.

DR. WHITBY asserts freedom, not only from coaction, but Necessity, to be essential to any thing deserving the name of sin, and to an action being *culpable;* in these words, (Discourse on five Points, edit. 3. p. 348.) " If they be thus necessitated, then neither their sins of omission or commission could deserve that name: it being essential to the nature of sin, according to St. Austin's definition, that it be an action *à quo liberum est abstinere.* Three things seem plainly necessary to make an action or omission culpable; 1. That it be in our power to perform or forbear it: for, as Origen, and all the fathers, say, no man is blameworthy for not doing what he could not do." And elsewhere the Doctor insists, that " when any do evil of Necessity, what they do is no vice, that they are guilty of no fault,* are worthy of no blame, dispraise,† or dishonour,‡ but are unblamable."§

If these things are true, in Dr. Whitby's sense of Necessity, they will prove all such to be blameless, who are given up of God to sin, in what they commit after they are thus given up.—That there is such a thing as men being judicially given up to sin, is certain, if the Scripture rightly informs us; such a thing being often there spoken of: as in Psal. lxxxi. 12. " So I gave them up to their own hearts' lust, and they walked in their own counsels." (Acts vii. 42.) " Then God turned, and gave them up to worship the host of heaven." (Rom. i. 24.) " Wherefore, God also gave them up to uncleanness, through the lusts of their own hearts, to dishonour their own bodies between themselves." (Ver. 26.) " For this cause God gave them up to vile affections." (Ver. 28.) " And even as they did not like to retain God in their knowledge, God gave them over to a reprobate mind, to do those things that are not convenient."

It is needless to stand particularly to inquire, what God's "giving men up to their own hearts' lusts" signifies: it is sufficient to observe, that hereby is certainly meant God so ordering or disposing things, in some respect or other, either by doing or forbearing to do, as that the consequence should be men continuing in their sins. So much as men are given up *to*, so much is the consequence of their being given up, whether that be less or more. If God does not order things so, by action or permission, that sin will be the consequence, then the event proves that they are not given up to that consequence. If good be the consequence, instead of evil, then God's mercy is to be acknowledged in that good; which mercy must be contrary to God's judgment in giving up to evil. If the event must prove, that they are given up to evil as the consequence, then the persons, who are the subjects of this judgment, must be the subjects of such an event, and so the event is necessary.

If not only *coaction*, but *all Necessity*, will prove men blameless, then *Judas* was blameless, after Christ had given him over, and had already declared his certain damnation, and that he should *verily* betray him. He was guilty of no sin in betraying his Master, on this supposition; though his so doing is spoken of by Christ as the most aggravated sin, more heinous than the sin of *Pilate* in crucifying him. And the *Jews* in *Egypt*, in *Jeremiah's* time, were guilty of no sin, in their not worshipping the true God, after God had " sworn by his great name, that his name should be no more named in the mouth of any man of Judah, in all the land of Egypt," (Jer. xliv. 26.)

Dr. Whitby (Disc. on five Points, p. 302, 303.) denies, that men, in this world, are ever so given up by God to sin, that their Wills should be necessarily determined to evil; though he owns, that hereby it may become *exceeding difficult* for men to do good, having a strong bent and powerful inclination to what is evil.—But if we should allow the case to be just as he represents, the judgment of giving up to sin will no better agree with his notions of that liberty, which is essential to praise or blame, than if we should suppose it to render the avoiding of sin *impossible.* For if an *impossibility* of avoiding sin wholly excuses a man; then for the same reason, its being difficult to avoid it, excuses him in part; and this just in proportion to the degree of difficulty.—If the influence of *moral* impossibility or inability be the same, to excuse persons in not doing or not avoiding any thing, as that of *natural* inability, (which is supposed,) then undoubtedly, in like manner, *moral difficulty* has the same influence to excuse with *natural difficulty.* But all allow, that natural impossibility wholly excuses, and also that *natural difficulty* excuses in part, and makes the act or omission less blameable in proportion to the difficulty. All *natural difficulty*, according to the plainest dictates of the light of nature, excuses in some degree, so that the neglect is not so blamable, as if there had been no difficulty in the case: and so the greater the difficulty is, still the more excuseable, in proportion to the increase of the difficulty. And as *natural* impossibility wholly excuses, and excludes all blame, so the nearer the difficulty approaches to impossibility, still the nearer a person is to blamelessness in proportion to that approach. And if the case of *moral* impossibility or Necessity, be just the same with *natural* Necessity or coaction, as to its influence to excuse a neglect, then also, for the same reason, the case of natural difficulty does not differ in influence, to excuse a neglect, from moral difficulty, arising from a strong bias or bent to evil, such as Dr. Whitby owns in the case of those that are given up to their own hearts' lusts. So that the fault of such persons must be lessened, in proportion to the difficulty, and approach to impossibility. If ten degrees of moral difficulty make the action quite impossible, and so wholly excuse, then if there be nine degrees of difficulty, the person is in great part excused, and is nine degrees in ten less blameworthy, than if there had been no difficulty at all; and he has but one degree of blameworthiness. The reason is plain, on *Arminian* principles; *viz.* because as difficulty, by antecedent bent and bias on the Will, is increased, liberty of indifference, and self-determination in the Will, is diminished; so much hinderance, impediment is there, in the way of the Will acting freely, by mere self-determination. And if ten degrees of such hinderance take away all such liberty, then nine degrees take away nine parts in ten, and leave but one degree of liberty. And therefore there is but one degree of blameableness, *cæteris paribus*, in the neglect; the man being no further blamable in what he does, or neglects, than he has liberty in that affair: for blame or praise (say they) arises wholly from a good use or abuse of liberty.

From all which it follows, that a strong bent and bias one way, and difficulty of going the contrary, never causes a person to be at all more exposed to sin, or any thing blamable: because, as the difficulty is increased, so much the less is required and expected. Though in one respect, exposedness to sin is increased, *viz.* by an increase of exposedness to the evil action or omission; yet it is diminished in another respect, to balance it; namely, as the sinfulness or blamableness of the action or omission is diminished in the same proportion. So that, on the whole, the affair, as to exposedness to guilt or blame, is left just as it was.

* Discourse on the five Points, p. 347, 360, 361, 377 † 303, 326, 329, and many other places. ‡ 371. § 304, 361.

To illustrate this, let us suppose a scale of a balance to be intelligent, and a free agent, and indued with a self-moving power, by virtue of which it could act and produce effects to a certain degree, *ex. gr.* to move itself up or down with a force equal to a weight of ten pounds; and that it might therefore be required of it, in ordinary circumstances, to move itself down with that force; for which it has power and full liberty, and therefore would be blameworthy if it failed of it. But then let us suppose a weight of ten pounds to be put in the opposite scale, which in force entirely counterbalances its self-moving power, and so renders it impossible for it to move down at all; and therefore wholly excuses it from any such motion. But if we suppose there to be only nine pounds in the opposite scale, this renders its motion not impossible, but yet more difficult; so that it can now only move down with the force of one pound: but however, this is all that is required of it under these circumstances; it is wholly excused from nine parts of its motion: and if the scale, under these circumstances, neglect to move, and remain at rest, all that it will be blamed for, will be its neglect of that one tenth part of its motion; for which it had as much liberty and advantage, as in usual circumstances it has for the greater motion, which in such a case would be required. So that this new difficulty does not at all increase its exposedness to any thing blameworthy.

And thus the very supposition of difficulty in the way of a man's *duty*, or proclivity to sin, through a being given up to hardness of heart, or indeed by any other means whatsoever, is an inconsistence, according to Dr. Whitby's notions of liberty, virtue and vice, blame and praise. The avoiding of sin and blame, and the doing of what is virtuous and praiseworthy, must be always equally easy.

Dr. Whitby's notions of liberty, obligation, virtue, sin, &c. led him into another great inconsistence. He abundantly insists, that necessity is inconsistent with the nature of sin or fault. He says, in the forementioned treatise, (p. 14.) *Who can blame a person for doing what he could not help?* And, (p. 15.) *It being sensibly unjust, to punish any man for doing that which was never in his power to avoid.* And, (p. 341.) to confirm his opinion, he quotes one of the fathers, saying, *Why doth God command, if man hath not free will and power to obey?* And again, in the same and the next page, *Who will not cry out, that it is folly to command him, that hath not liberty to do what is commanded; and that it is unjust to condemn him, that has it not in his power to do what is required?* And, (p. 373.) he cites another saying, *A law is given to him that can turn to both parts;* i. e. *obey or transgress it; but no law can be against him who is bound by nature.*

And yet the same Dr. Whitby asserts, that fallen man is not able to perform perfect obedience. In p. 165, he has these words: "The nature of *Adam* had power to continue innocent, and without sin; whereas, it is certain our nature never had." But if we have not power to continue innocent and without sin, then sin is not inconsistent with Necessity, and we may be sinful in that which we have not power to avoid; and those things cannot be true, which he asserts elsewhere, namely, "That if we be necessitated, neither sins of omission nor commission, would deserve that name," (p. 348.) If we have it not in our power to be innocent, then we have it not in our power to be blameless; and if so, we are under a *Necessity* of being blameworthy. And how does this consist with what he so often asserts, that Necessity is inconsistent with blame or praise? If we have it not in our power to perform perfect obedience to all the commands of God, then we are under a Necessity of breaking some commands, in some degree; having no power to perform so much as is commanded. And if so, why does he cry out of the unreasonableness and folly of commanding beyond what men have power to do?

Arminians in general are very inconsistent with themselves, in what they say of the Inability of fallen man in this respect. They strenuously maintain, that it would be unjust in God, to require any thing of us beyond our present power and ability to perform; and also hold that we are now unable to perform perfect obedience, and that Christ died to satisfy for the *imperfections of our obedience,* and has made way, that our imperfect obedience might be accepted instead of perfect; wherein they seem insensibly to run themselves into the grossest inconsistence. For (as I have observed elsewhere) "they hold that God, in mercy to mankind, has abolished that rigorous constitution or law, that they were under originally, and instead of it, has introduced a more mild constitution, and put us under a new law, which requires no more than imperfect sincere obedience, in compliance with our poor infirm impotent circumstances since the fall."

Now how can these things be made consistent? I would ask, of what law are these imperfections of our obedience a breach? If they are a breach of no law that we were ever under, then they are not sins. And if they be not sins, what need of Christ dying to satisfy for them? But if they are sins, and the breach of some law, what law is it? They cannot be a breach of their new law, for that requires no other than imperfect obedience, or obedience with imperfections: and therefore to have obedience attended with imperfections, is no breach of it; for it is as much as it requires. And they cannot be a breach of their old law: for that, they say, is entirely abolished; and we never were under it.—They say, it would not be just in God to require of us *perfect* obedience, because it would not be just to require more than we can perform, or to punish us for failing of it. And, therefore, by their own scheme, the imperfections of our obedience do not deserve to be punished. What need therefore of Christ dying, to satisfy for them? What need of his *suffering*, to satisfy for that which is no fault, and in its own nature deserves no *suffering?* What need of Christ dying, to purchase, that our *imperfect* obedience should be accepted, when, according to their scheme, it would be unjust in itself, that any other obedience than *imperfect* should be required? What need of Christ dying to make way for God's accepting of such obedience, as it would be unjust in him not to accept? Is there any need of Christ dying to prevail with God not to do unrighteously?—If it be said, that Christ died to satisfy that old law for us, that so we might not be under it, but that there might be room for our being under a more mild law; still I would inquire, what need of Christ dying, that we might not be under a law, which (by their principles) it would be in itself unjust that we should be under, whether Christ had died or no, because, in our present state, we are not able to keep it?

So the *Arminians* are inconsistent with themselves, not only, in what they say of the need of Christ's satisfaction to atone for those imperfections, which we cannot avoid, but also in what they say of the grace of God, granted to enable men to perform the sincere obedience of the new law. "I grant indeed, (says Dr. Stebbing,*) that by original sin, we are utterly disabled for the performance of the condition, without new grace from God. But I say then, that he gives such a grace to all of us, by which the performance of the condition, is truly possible; and upon this ground he may and doth most righteously require it." If Dr. Stebbing intends to speak properly, by *grace* he must mean, that assistance which is of grace, or of free favour and kindness. But yet in the same place he speaks of it as very *unreasonable, unjust,* and *cruel,* for God to require that, as the condition of pardon, that is become impossible by original sin. If it be so, what *grace* is there in giving assistance and ability to perform the condition of pardon? Or why is that called by the name of grace, that is an absolute debt, which God is bound to bestow, and which it would be unjust and cruel in him to withhold, seeing he requires that, *as the condition of pardon,* which he cannot perform without it?

SECT. IV.

Command and Obligation to Obedience, consistent with moral Inability to obey.†

It being so much insisted on by *Arminian* writers, that necessity is inconsistent with law or command, and particularly, that it is absurd to suppose God by his command

* Treatise of the Operations of the Spirit. 2 edit. p. 112, 113.

† The subject of "obligation to obedience," or MORAL OBLIGATION, though

should require that of men which they are unable to do; not allowing in this case for any difference between natural and moral Inability; I would therefore now particularly consider this matter.—And for greater clearness I would distinctly lay down the following things.

I. The Will *itself*, and not only those *actions* which are the effects of the Will, is the proper object of Precept or Command. That is, such a state or acts of men's Wills, are in many cases properly required of them by Commands; and not only those alterations in the state of their bodies or minds that are the consequences of volition. This is most manifest; for it is the soul only that is properly and directly the subject of Precepts or Commands; that only being capable of receiving or perceiving Commands. The motions or state of the body are matter of Command, only as they are subject to the soul, and connected with its acts. But now the soul has no other faculty whereby it can, in the most direct and proper sense, consent, yield to, or comply with any Command, but the faculty of the Will; and it is by this faculty only, that the soul can directly disobey, or refuse compliance: for the very notions of *consenting, yielding, accepting, complying, refusing, rejecting, &c.* are, according to the meaning of the terms, nothing but certain acts of the Will. Obedience, in the primary nature of it, is the submitting and yielding of the Will of one, to the Will of another. Disobedience is the not consenting, not complying of the Will of the commanded, to the manifested Will of the commander. Other acts that are not the acts of the Will, as certain motions of the body and alterations in the soul, are Obedience or Disobedience only indirectly, as they are connected with the state or actions of the Will, according to an established law of nature. So that it is manifest, the Will itself may be required: and the being of a good Will is the most proper, direct, and immediate subject of Command; and if this cannot be prescribed or required by Command or Precept, nothing can; for other things can be required no otherwise than as they depend upon, and are the fruits of a good Will.

Corol. 1. If there be several acts of the Will, or a series of acts, one following another, and one the effect of another, the *first and determining act* is properly the subject of Command, and not only the consequent acts, which are dependent upon it. Yea, this more especially is that to which Command or Precept has a proper respect; because it is this act that determines the whole affair: in this act the Obedience or Disobedience lies, in a peculiar manner; the consequent acts being all governed and determined by

expressed in the title of this section, is not professedly handled by our author, either here or in any other part of the work. His professed object in this place is to prove that obligation to obey commands is not weakened by moral inability. But though this conclusion is established by many considerations, yet the *nature* and *grounds* of obligation are not pointed out, which might afford evidence WHY moral *obligation* is consistent with moral *inability?* The subject is confessedly profound; but, perhaps, the following series of remarks may contribute in some degree to assist our inquiries and to bring them to a satisfactory conclusion.

1. *Obligation*, if we regard the term, is a *binding power*, or an *irresistible force;* but, in reference to morality and voluntary actions, obligation is expressive of a *hypothetical indispensable connexion between an antecedent and a consequent;* or between an end proposed, and the means of obtaining it. Thus, IF a moral agent would attain the *end*, he is *obliged* or bound indispensably, to use the required *means*. And, on the contrary, IF a moral agent adopt a *different* antecedent from what is required, not only he shall not attain to the proposed consequent, but *another* consequent is to follow, indispensably connected with the antecedent actually adopted, by a necessity of consequence. Therefore,

2. The *consequent* or the *end*, which is proposed by the moral Governor, is always a supposed *good;* for it would be unworthy of a governor wise and good to propose any other, especially as the antecedent prescribed and required is indispensably connected with it. But if the connexion be broken by the free agent, by the adoption of an antecedent naturally connected with a different consequent, he then becomes *naturally* obliged, or forced, to sustain a proportionable *evil*.

3. In the system of moral government, it is the prerogative of the supreme Governor to propose the *consequent* of the indispensable connexion; and it is the part of the moral agent, who in the *act of choice* is left *free*, to choose the antecedent, which the governor has objectively furnished, and indispensably required. To this choice he is *morally* or hypothetically bound, yet is *naturally* free; and IF the required choice be made, the *good* follows; but IF NOT, the corresponding evil follows. For instance; if the forgiveness of sin be the consequent proposed, and repentance the antecedent required: the agent is *morally bound* to repent, but *naturally free*. If, however, he break through the moral bond, which is done by abusing his natural freedom, or continuing his wrong choice, forgiveness does not follow, but he stands exposed to the natural and threatened consequence of that wrong choice, or impenitence.

4. Hence it is obvious, that in the system of Providence, and the execution of all decretive designs, it is the prerogative of the Sovereign of the universe to *establish* the chain of all *antecedents*, and the consequents follow from the nature of things: but in the system of moral government, it is equally obvious, the reverse takes place; for here the supreme Governor proposes, and *establishes* objectively, the chain of *consequents*, while the moral agent, or the obligee, establishes *optionally* the antecedents; and as the *actual* choice of an antecedent is, such will be the *actual* consequence. When the moral agent chooses that antecedent which is required, or which is conformable to rectitude, the proposed consequent is obtained by the nature of things; but when that which is not required, or is not conformable to rectitude, is chosen for an antecedent, the evil consequence flows from the same nature of things, that is, from the essence of eternal truth.

5. *Required* antecedents are either *a state of mind*, or *voluntary actions;* according as the particular consequent proposed may be. For example, if *happiness* be the end or consequent proposed, *holiness*, or a *holy state of mind*, is the mean, or antecedent required. If we would *see the Lord*, we must be *holy*, or *pure in heart*, by a new birth unto righteousness. If *justification* be the end proposed, *believing* is a mean required. For to us *righteousness shall be imputed*, IF we *believe*. If a subsequent *favourable treatment* of the obligee be the end proposed; *obedience*, or conformity to rule, is the mean required.

6. When an agent is said to be obliged *in* or *by* any thing or consideration, that thing or consideration *in* or *by* which he is obliged, is to be considered as the *consequent* proposed; and the state or act leading to it is the antecedent required. To be obliged *in conscience, in duty, in law, in honour, &c.* expresses the *end* to be obtained by a certain state or conduct as the mean or antecedent required. Thus, for instance, if *conscience* be *satisfied*, if *duty* be *discharged*, if *law* be *conformed to*, or if *honour* be *secured*, the required antecedent means *must* be adopted, or such acts *must be performed*.

7. If the *required* antecedents be not performed, it is manifest that the free agent has voluntarily established *other* antecedents, and the *injurious consequents* of these last flow (as before observed) from the nature of things; which consequents will be similar or dissimilar to those proposed by the supreme Governor, in proportion as the antecedent established voluntarily by the agent, is similar or dissimilar to what was required. Hence we may see the *true standard* and measure of guilt, and of the different *gradations* of praise or blame.

8. Having considered the NATURE of moral obligation, let us now advert to the SUBJECT of it. This inquiry has more immediately for its object the *qualifications* of the moral agent, or those *considerations* whereby he stands *obliged*, in contradistinction to those beings in the universe that are not moral agents. An attentive and long-continued investigation of the subject has taught us, that they are included in these three particulars: (1.) A natural *capacity* of moral enjoyment. (2.) A sufficiency of suitable *means*. And (3.) A *freedom* from compulsion in the choice of means.—Whatever being is possessed of these qualifications is morally obliged; for he has a *suitable* ability to establish his own antecedents as required, in order that the proposed consequents may follow.

9. The *first* qualification is *a* NATURAL CAPACITY *of moral enjoyments.* This belongs to no being that is not a free agent; but to every being who is so, it inseparably belongs. This, more than any superior degree of reason, (however great, and however forcible the influence from that superiority,) constitutes the chief and *most essential* difference between men and brutes. That such a *capacity* is an indispensably requisite qualification, is clear. For free agency necessarily implies, a consequent moral advantage, or a natural good to be morally enjoyed, either explicitly proposed by the moral Governor, or fairly implied in the system of moral government; but this could not be proposed if there were no capacity of enjoyment as now stated. And this consequent advantage may properly be called the perpetual *enjoyment of God*, the chief good; because the *chief end* of all subordinate enjoyments, as well as of all obedience, and the sum total of all *happiness*, is the conscious enjoyment of *divine favour and excellence.*

10. The *second* qualification is *a sufficiency of suitable* MEANS. This is indispensably requisite; for to require an *end* while the *means* are out of the agent's reach, or *physically out of his power*, and that under the forfeiture of the governor's displeasure, is of the very essence of injustice. But the divine Governor is "a God of truth, and without iniquity; just and right is he." And that these means ought to be *sufficient* and *suitable* in their own nature to attain the end, in other words, that the antecedents required to be adopted by the agent, are *infallibly connected* with the proposed consequent, is equally plain, for the same reason that there should be any means at all. For means *in themselves* insufficient and unsuitable have no true connexion with the end proposed; even as a law *in itself* bad, has morally no obliging power.

11. The *third* qualification is *a* FREEDOM *from constraint and compulsion in the choice of means*, or in the voluntary establishment of antecedents. By "constraint" and "compulsion," we mean a physical interference with the free agent in his *act of choice*, in such a sense, as that the choice would not be *the genuine effect of the motive;* or, that the nature of the fruit should not *correspond* with the nature of the tree; but some extraneous force interposing would make the nature of the volition to be different from the nature of the mind or disposition, which otherwise would be its immediate cause.

12. Divine influence is admitted to be requisite, in order to prepare *the state of the mind* for a right choice, even as a good tree is requisite for good fruit; but this is no interference with *the act of choice* itself, nor has it the least tendency to break the connexion between motive and choice, or between the mind and its volition.—Such *influence*, indeed, forms one glorious link of the decretive chain, which the sovereign Governor has established as so many antecedents; and a *right choice*, in a free agent thus divinely influenced, or formed anew, is the unrestrained and unimpelled *effect* which follows by a *necessity* of consequence. In other words, no bad *choice* can possibly follow, but by a failure in the *cause*, the mind or disposition itself.

13. On this principle it is, that the sovereign Being himself *never errs* in his choice. The *source* from which the act of choice proceeds is perfectly good, (an infinitely holy nature,) and the *connexion* between this cause and the effect, which is a right choice, is infallibly and in the nature of things necessarily secure. Hence it is that we never admit, or suspect, an error in his choice, however great his freedom; and hence we have a firm ground of confidence, that the Judge of the whole earth will do *right*.

14. The three qualifications mentioned belong to man as a *free agent;* but we must not confound this idea with that of *a subject of moral government.* An infant may be the subject of government, both human and divine; but cannot be, properly speaking, a free agent. Hence it follows that the *first* of the qualifications mentioned *alone* is essential to constitute a subject of *moral government*, in the most extensive sense of the term; but in order to constitute that class of subjects who are *also free agents*, the other two are essential.

15. When these *three* qualifications are found in any free agent, *nothing more* is requisite to constitute *moral obligation*. An *end* is proposed—*means* firmly connected with that end are afforded, and required to be used—these means are physically *in the power* of the agent—who is also *free* from all constraint and compulsion in his *act of choice*. If these qualifications are not sufficient *morally to oblige*, we are fully persuaded nothing can be sufficient.—As to the notion, that *moral ability* is necessary to constitute moral obligation, which is maintained alike by many Arminians and most Antinomians, (for extremes will sometimes meet,) our author abundantly demonstrates its futility and absurd contradictions.—W.

it. This governing act must be the proper object of Precept, or none.

Corol. 2. It also follows, from what has been observed, that if there be any act, or exertion of the soul, prior to all free acts of choice in the case, directing and determining what the acts of the Will shall be; that act of the soul cannot properly be subject to any Command or Precept, in any respect whatsoever, either directly or indirectly, immediately or remotely. Such acts cannot be subject to Commands *directly*, because they are no acts of the Will; being by the supposition prior to all acts of the Will, determining and giving rise to all its acts: they not being acts of the Will, there can be in them no consent to or compliance with any Command. Neither can they be subject to Command or Precept *indirectly* or *remotely;* for they are not so much as the *effects* or *consequences* of the Will, being prior to all its acts. So that if there be any Obedience in that original act of the soul, determining all volitions, it is an act of Obedience wherein the Will has no concern at all; it preceding every act of Will. And therefore, if the soul either obeys or disobeys in this act, it is wholly involuntarily; there is no willing Obedience or rebellion, no compliance or opposition of the Will in the affair: and what sort of Obedience or rebellion is this?

And thus the *Arminian* notion of the freedom of the Will consisting in the soul's determining its own acts of Will, instead of being essential to moral agency, and to men being the subjects of moral government, is utterly inconsistent with it. For if the soul determines *all* its acts of Will, it is therein subject to no Command or moral government, as has been now observed; because its original determining act is no act of Will or choice, it being prior, by the supposition, to *every act* of Will. And the soul cannot be the subject of Command in the act of the Will itself, which depends on the foregoing determining act, and is determined by it; inasmuch as this is necessary, being the necessary consequence and effect of that prior determining act, which is not voluntary. Nor can the man be the subject of Command or government in his external actions; because these are all necessary, being the necessary effects of the acts of the Will themselves. So that mankind, according to this scheme, are subjects of Command or moral government in nothing at all; and all their moral agency is entirely excluded, and no room is left for virtue or vice in the world.

So that the *Arminian* scheme, and not that of the *Calvinists*, is utterly inconsistent with moral government, and with all use of laws, precepts, prohibitions, promises, or threatenings. Neither is there any way whatsoever to make their principles consist with these things. For if it be said, that there is no prior determining act of the soul, preceding the acts of the Will, but that volitions are events that come to pass by pure accident, without any determining cause, this is most palpably inconsistent with all use of laws and precepts; for nothing is more plain than that laws can be of no use to direct and regulate perfect accident: which, by the supposition of its being pure accident, is in no case regulated by any thing preceding; but happens, this way or that, perfectly by chance, without any cause or rule. The perfect uselessness of laws and precepts also follows from the *Arminian* notion of indifference, as essential to that liberty, which is requisite to virtue or vice. For the end of laws is to *bind to one side;* and the end of Commands is to turn the Will one way: and therefore they are of no use, unless they turn or bias the Will that way. But if liberty consists in indifference, then their biassing the Will one way only, destroys liberty; as it puts the Will out of equilibrium. So that the will, having a bias, through the influence of binding law, laid upon it, is not wholly left to itself, to determine itself which way it will, without influence from without.

II. Having shown that the Will itself, especially in those acts which are original, leading and determining in any case, is the proper subject of Precept and Command—and not only those alterations in the body, &c. which are the effects of the Will—I now proceed, in the *second* place, to observe, that the very opposition or defect of the Will itself, in its *original and determining act* in the case, to a thing proposed or commanded, or its failing of compliance, implies a moral inability to that thing: or, in other words, whenever a Command requires a certain state or act of the Will, and the person commanded, notwithstanding the Command and the circumstances under which it is exhibited, still finds his Will opposite or wanting, in *that*, belonging to its state or acts, *which is original and determining in the affair*, that man is morally unable to obey that Command.

This is manifest from what was observed in the first part concerning the nature of *moral* Inability, as distinguished from *natural:* where it was observed, that a man may then be said to be morally unable to do a thing, when he is under the influence or prevalence of a contrary inclination, or has a want of inclination, under such circumstances and views. It is also evident, from what has been before proved, that the Will is always, and in every individual act, necessarily determined by the strongest motive;* and so is always unable to go against the motive, which, all things considered, has now the greatest strength and advantage to move the Will.—But not further to insist on these things, the truth of the position now laid down, *viz.* that when the Will is opposite to, or failing of a compliance with, a thing, *in its original determination or act*, it is not able to comply, appears by the consideration of these two things.

1. The Will in the time of that diverse or opposite leading act or inclination, and when actually under its influence, is not able to exert itself to the contrary, to make an alteration, in order to a compliance. The inclination is unable to change itself; and that for this plain reason, that it is unable to incline to change itself. Present choice cannot at present choose to be otherwise: for that would be *at present* to choose something diverse from what is *at present* chosen. If the Will, all things now considered, inclines or chooses to go that way, then it cannot choose, all things now considered, to go the other way, and so cannot choose to be made to go the other way. To suppose that the mind is now sincerely inclined to change itself to a different inclination, is to suppose the mind is now truly inclined otherwise than it is now inclined. The Will may oppose some future remote act that it is exposed to, but not its own present act.

2. As it is impossible that the Will should comply with the thing commanded, with respect to its *leading act*, by any act of its own, in the time of that diverse or opposite *leading and original act*, or after it has actually come under the influence of that *determining choice or inclination;* so it is impossible it should be determined to a compliance by any foregoing act; for, by the very supposition, there is no foregoing act; the opposite or noncomplying act being that act which is *original* and *determining* in the case. Therefore it must be so, that if this *first determining act* be found non-complying, on the proposal of the command, the mind is morally unable to obey. For to suppose it to be able to obey, is to suppose it to be able to determine and cause its *first determining*

* Our author does not mean by "motive," the *object* presented to the mind according to its intrinsic worth; but he takes into the account also the *state* of the mind itself, in reference to that object, according to which will be the *appearance* of it. Therefore, strictly speaking, the *motive*, as he has intimated at the commencement of this work, denotes *the object as it stands in the view of the mind.* If we do not maintain this distinction, the dispute will soon degenerate into a confused logomachy; and we should be forced, in defending this position—that the will is "necessarily determined by the strongest motive"—to adopt this, the most absurd of all conclusions, that the will of every man in the present state always chooses what is really best, or *never errs* in its elections. Whereas the world is full of errors and delusions; things the most excellent in themselves, are commonly rejected, and others the most worthless are preferred. But this could not happen, except on this principle, that the *reality* of worth differs, in those instances, from the *appearance* of it. In such cases, the *difference* is not in the object, but in the mind, when the choice takes place. For instance; suppose the blessed God in his true character as revealed in the Scriptures, the chief and an unchangeable good, be proposed to the contemplation of a wicked man, and his will *rejects* that good. Now, as the mind is incapable of rejecting a good, or of choosing an evil, *as such;* it is plain, that the proper and immediate cause of difference between the reality and the appearance of good, is in the *state* of the mind. Here lies the essence of an erroneous choice,—the will preferring an object which is *apparently* but not *really* preferable. Hence it follows irrefragably, that the *state of the mind* is the true and proper source of a right and wrong choice. This is it that influences the *appearance* of an object, so as to stand in the apprehension and practical judgment of the mind as worse or better than it *really* is. Therefore, the *true state of the mind* and the *real state of the object of choice*, united, are the genuine parents of the *objective appearance* in the mind, morally considered, or according to the qualities of good and evil; and this offspring—OBJECTIVE APPEARANCE—is what our author calls "the strongest motive."—W.

act to be otherwise, and that it has power better to govern and regulate its *first governing and regulating act*, which is absurd; for it is to suppose a prior act of the Will, determining its first determining act; that is, an act prior to the first, and leading and governing the original and governing act of all; which is a contradiction.

Here if it should be said, that although the mind has not any ability to will contrary to what it does will, in the original and leading act of the Will, because there is supposed to be no prior act to determine and order it otherwise, and the Will cannot immediately change itself, because it cannot at present incline to a change; yet the mind has an ability for the present to *forbear* to proceed to action, and taking time for deliberation; which may be an occasion of the change of the inclination.

I answer, (1.) In this objection, that seems to be forgotten which was observed before, *viz.* that the determining to take the matter into consideration, is itself an act of the Will: and if this be all the act wherein the mind exercises ability and freedom, then this, by the supposition, must be all that can be commanded or required by precept. And if this act be the commanding act, then all that has been observed concerning the commanding act of the Will remains true, that the very want of it is a moral Inability to exert it, &c. (2.) We are speaking concerning the first and leading act of the Will about the affair; and if determining to deliberate, or, on the contrary, to proceed immediately without deliberating, be the first and leading act; or whether it be or no, if there be another act before it, which determines that; or whatever be the original and leading act; still the foregoing proof stands good, that the non-compliance of the leading act implies moral Inability to comply.

If it should be objected, that these things make all moral Inability equal, and suppose men morally unable to will otherwise than they actually do will, in all cases, and equally so in every instance.—In answer to this objection, I desire two things may be observed.

First, That if by being *equally* unable, be meant, as *really* unable; then, so far as the Inability is merely moral, it is true; the Will, in every instance, acts by moral necessity, and is morally unable to act otherwise, as truly and properly in one case as another; as, I humbly conceive, has been perfectly and abundantly demonstrated by what has been said in the preceding part of this essay. But yet, in some respect, the Inability may be said to be greater in some instances than others: though the man may be truly unable, (if moral Inability can truly be called Inability,) yet he may be further from being able to do some things than others. As it is in things, which men are naturally unable to do. A person, whose strength is no more than sufficient to lift the weight of one hundred pounds, is as truly and really unable to lift one hundred and one pounds, as ten thousand pounds; but yet he is further from being able to lift the latter weight than the former; and so, according to the common use of speech, has a greater Inability for it. So it is in moral Inability. A man is truly morally unable to choose contrary to a present inclination, which in the least degree prevails; or, contrary to that motive, which, all things considered, has strength and advantage now to move the Will, in the least degree, superior to all other motives in view: but yet he is further from ability to resist a very strong habit, and a violent and deeply rooted inclination, or a motive vastly exceeding all others in strength. And again, the Inability may, in some respects, be called greater in some instances than others, as it may be *more general* and *extensive to all acts of that kind.* So men may be said to be unable in a different sense, and to be further from moral ability, who have that moral Inability which is *general* and *habitual*, than they who have only that Inability which is *occasional* and *particular*.* Thus in cases of natural Inability; he that is born blind may be said to be unable to see, in a different manner, and is, in some respects, further from being able to see, than he whose sight is hindered by a transient cloud or mist.

And besides, that which was observed in the first part of this discourse, concerning the Inability which attends a *strong and settled habit*, should be here remembered; *viz.* that a fixed habit is attended with this peculiar moral Inability, by which it is distinguished from *occasional volition*, namely, that endeavours to avoid future volitions of that kind, which are agreeable to such a habit, much more frequently and commonly prove vain and insufficient. For though it is impossible there should be any sincere endeavours against a present choice, yet there may be against volitions of that kind, when viewed at a distance. A person may desire and use means to prevent future exercises of a certain inclination; and, in order to it, may wish the habit might be removed; but his desires and endeavours may be ineffectual. The man may be said in some sense to be unable; yea, even as the word *unable* is a *relative term*, and has relation to ineffectual endeavours; yet not with regard to present, but remote endeavours.

Secondly, It must be borne in mind, according to what was observed before, that indeed no Inability whatsoever, which is merely moral, is properly called by the name of *Inability;* and that in the strictest propriety of speech, a man may be said to have a thing *in his power*, if he has it at his election, and he cannot be said to be unable to do a thing, when he can, if he now pleases, or whenever he has a proper, direct, and immediate desire for it. As to those desires and endeavours, that may be against the exercises of a strong habit, with regard to which men may be said to be unable to avoid those exercises, they are remote desires and endeavours in two respects. *First*, as to *time;* they are never against present volitions, but only against volitions of such a kind, when viewed at a distance. *Secondly*, as to their *nature;* these opposite desires are not directly and properly against the habit and inclination itself, or the volitions in which it is exercised; for these, in themselves considered, are agreeable: but against something else that attends them, or is their consequence; the opposition of the mind is levelled entirely against this; the volitions themselves are not at all opposed directly, and for their own sake; but only indirectly and remotely, on the account of something foreign.

III. Though the opposition of the Will itself, or the very want of Will to a thing commanded, implies a moral Inability to that thing; yet, if it be, as has been already shown, that the being of a good state or act of Will, is a thing most properly required by Command; then, in some cases, such a state or act of Will may properly be required, which at present is not, and which may also be wanting after it is commanded. And therefore those things may properly be commanded, for which men have a moral Inability.

Such a state or act of the Will, may be required by Command, as does not already exist. For if that volition only may be commanded to be, which already is, there could be no use of precept: Commands in all cases would be perfectly vain and impertinent. And not only may such a Will be required, as is wanting before the Command is given, but also such as may possibly be wanting afterwards; such as the exhibition of the Command may not be effectual to produce or excite. Otherwise, no such thing as disobedience to a proper and rightful Command is possible in any case; and there is no case possible, wherein there can be a faulty disobedience. Which *Arminians* cannot affirm, consistently with their principle: for this makes obedience to just and proper Commands always *necessary*, and disobedience impossible. And so the *Arminian* would overthrow himself, yielding the very point we are upon, which he so strenuously denies, *viz.* that Law and Command are consistent with necessity.

If merely that Inability will excuse disobedience, which is implied in the opposition or defect of inclination, remaining after the Command is exhibited, then wickedness always carries that in it which excuses it. By how much the more wickedness there is in a man's heart, by so much is his inclination to evil the stronger, and by so much the more, therefore, has he of moral Inability to the good required. His moral Inability consisting in the strength of his evil inclination, is the very thing wherein his wickedness consists; and yet, according to *Arminian* principles,

* See this distinction of moral Inability explained in Part I. Sect. IV

it must be a thing inconsistent with wickedness; and by how much the more he has of it, by so much is he the further from wickedness.

Therefore, on the whole, it is manifest, that moral Inability alone (which consists in disinclination) never renders any thing improperly the subject matter of Precept or Command, and never can excuse any person in disobedience, or want of conformity to a command.

Natural Inability, arising from the want of natural capacity, or external hinderance, (which alone is properly called Inability,) without doubt wholly excuses, or makes a thing improperly the matter of Command. If men are excused from doing or acting any good thing, supposed to be commanded, it must be through some defect or obstacle that is not in the Will itself, but either in the capacity of understanding, or body, or outward circumstances.—Here two or three things may be observed,

1. As to spiritual acts, or any good thing in the state or imminent acts of the Will itself, or of the affections, (which are only certain modes of the exercise of the Will,) if persons are justly excused, it must be through want of capacity in the natural faculty of understanding. Thus the same spiritual duties, or holy affections and exercises of heart, cannot be required of men, as may be of angels; the capacity of understanding being so much inferior. So men cannot be required to love those amiable persons, whom they have had no opportunity to see, or hear of, or know in any way agreeable to the natural state and capacity of the human understanding. But the insufficiency of motives will not excuse; unless their being insufficient arises not from the moral state of the Will or inclination itself, but from the state of the natural understanding. The great kindness and generosity of another may be a motive insufficient to excite gratitude in the person that receives the kindness, through his vile and ungrateful temper: in this case, the insufficiency of the motive arises from the state of the Will or inclination of heart, and does not at all excuse. But if this generosity is not sufficient to excite gratitude, being unknown, there being no means of information adequate to the state and measure of the person's faculties, this insufficiency is attended with a natural Inability, which entirely excuses it.

2. As to such motions of body, or exercises and alterations of mind, which do not consist in the imminent acts or state of the Will itself—but are supposed to be required as effects of the Will, in cases wherein there is no want of a capacity of understanding—that Inability, and that only, excuses, which consists in want of connexion between them and the Will. If the Will fully complies, and the proposed effect does not prove, according to the laws of nature, to be connected with his volition, the man is perfectly excused; he has a natural Inability to the thing required. For the Will itself, as has been observed, is all that can be directly and immediately required by Command; and other things only indirectly, as connected with the Will. If therefore, there be a full compliance of Will, the person has done his duty; and if other things do not prove to be connected with his volition, that is not criminally owing to him.

3. Both these kinds of natural Inability, and all Inability that excuses, may be resolved into one thing; namely, want of natural capacity or strength; either capacity of understanding, or external strength. For when there are external defects and obstacles, they would be no obstacles, were it not for the imperfection and limitations of understanding and strength.

Corol. If things for which men have a moral Inability may properly be the matter of Precept or Command, then they may also of invitation and counsel. Commands and invitations come very much to the same thing; the difference is only circumstantial: Commands are as much a manifestation of the Will of him that speaks, as invitations, and as much testimonies of expectation of compliance. The difference between them lies in nothing that touches the affair in hand. The main difference between Command and invitation consists in the enforcement of the Will of him who commands or invites. In the latter it is his *kindness*, the goodness from which his Will arises: in the former it is his *authority*. But whatever be the *ground* of Will in him that speaks, or the *enforcement* of what he says, yet, seeing neither his Will, nor his expectation, is any more testified in the one case than the other; therefore, a person being directed *by invitation*, is no more an evidence of insincerity in him that directs—in manifesting either a Will or expectation which he has not—than a person being known to be morally unable to do what he is directed *by command is* an evidence of insincerity. So that all this grand objection of *Arminians* against the Inability of fallen men to exert faith in Christ, or to perform other spiritual duties, from the sincerity of God's counsels and invitations, must be without force.*

SECT. V.

That Sincerity of Desires and Endeavours, which is supposed to excuse in the non-performance of things in themselves good, particularly considered.

It is much insisted on by many, that some men, though they are not able to perform spiritual duties, such as repentance of sin, love to God, a cordial acceptance of Christ as exhibited and offered in the gospel, &c. yet may sincerely desire and endeavour after these things; and therefore must be excused; it being unreasonable to blame them for the omission of those things, which they sincerely desire and endeavour to do, but cannot. Concerning this matter, the following things may be observed.

1. What is here supposed, is a great mistake, and gross absurdity; even that men may sincerely choose and desire those spiritual duties of love, acceptance, choice, rejection, &c. consisting in the exercise of the Will itself, or in the disposition and inclination of the heart; and yet not able to perform or exert them. This is absurd, because it is absurd to suppose that a man should directly, properly, and sincerely incline to have an inclination, which at the same time is contrary to his inclination: for that is to suppose him not to be inclined to that which he is inclined to. If a man, in the state and acts of his Will and inclination, properly and directly falls in with those duties, he therein performs them: for the duties themselves consist in that very thing; they consist in the state and acts of the Will being so formed and directed. If the soul properly and sincerely falls in with a certain proposed act of Will or choice, the soul therein makes that choice its own. Even as when a moving body falls in with a proposed direction of its motion, that is the same thing as to move in that direction.

* On the subject of Sincerity or Insincerity in prohibitions, commands, counsels, invitations, and the like, in cases where God foreknows that the event will not take place by the compliance of the moral agent addressed, we may remark a few particulars in addition to our author's reasoning:

1. The *sincerity* of prohibitions and commands, counsels and invitations, and the like, is *founded*—not in the *event* of things as good or bad, or the *knowledge* of events, or the *purpose* that secures some, or the *necessity* of consequence from which others flow, nor in the *moral ability* of the agent, but—in the *very nature and tendency* of the things themselves which are prohibited, commanded, or proposed, as *good* or *evil*, either *intrinsically*, if of a moral nature, or else *relatively*, if of positive appointment. Therefore,

2. Whether the *event* be compliance or non-compliance, the command, or invitation, &c. is *perfectly sincere*. For, in truth, these are neither more nor less than *testimonies* respecting the goodness or badness of the things in question, in the sense before mentioned, and the consequent *obligations* of the agent respecting them, under a forfeiture either declared or implied. Consequently,

3. *Insincerity* can attach to a command only on supposition that the goodness or badness of the *event* were the ground of the *signified* will, while at the same time *another event*, diverse from that which actually takes place, was *purposed* by the same will. But,

4. Strictly speaking, *no events*, as such, are the objects of purpose; but rather, the purpose respects the good *antecedents*, whereby good events, following by necessity of consequence, are infallibly secured. Besides,

5. It is highly absurd, as must appear from the nature of law and obligation, to suppose that the sincerity of legislative or inviting will should depend on the *event* of compliance or non-compliance. Surely the *sincerity* of a lawgiver is not affected, whether all obey, or only some, or even none. Legislation is a *testimony* with sanctions, that the thing prohibited is evil, or the thing commanded is good, *to the party*. Hence,

6. The *consequent*, whether good or bad, is *objectively established*, or hypothetically proposed, by the legislator: and the *antecedent* is supposed to be within the reach, or, physically considered, *placed within the power*, of the agent. Therefore,

7. The agent's *abuse* of his physical power, in reference to the antecedent, constitutes the criminality, and the *right use* of it constitutes the virtue, of an action. And then alone is physical power, in fact, *used aright* when it is the instrument of moral rectitude, or a *right state of mind*. Do men gather grapes of thorns, or figs of thistles? Even so, every good tree bringeth forth good fruit; but a corrupt tree bringeth forth evil fruit. A good tree (as such) cannot bring forth evil fruit; neither can a corrupt tree (as such) bring forth good fruit.—W.

2. That which is called a *Desire* and *Willingness* for those inward duties, in such as do not perform them, has respect to these duties only indirectly and remotely, and is improperly so called; not only because (as was observed before) it respects those good volitions only in a distant view, and with respect to future time; but also because evermore, not these things themselves, but something else that is foreign, is the object that terminates these volitions and Desires.

A drunkard, who continues in his drunkenness, being under the power of a violent appetite to strong drink, and without any love to virtue; but being also extremely covetous and close, and very much exercised and grieved at the diminution of his estate, and prospect of poverty, may in a sort *desire* the virtue of temperance; and though his present Will is to gratify his extravagant appetite, yet he may wish he had a heart to forbear future acts of intemperance, and forsake his excesses, through an unwillingness to part with his money: but still he goes on with his drunkenness; his wishes and endeavours are insufficient and ineffectual: such a man has no proper, direct, *sincere Willingness* to forsake this vice, and the vicious deeds which belong to it; for he acts voluntarily in continuing to drink to excess: his Desire is very improperly called a Willingness to be temperate; it is no true Desire of that virtue; for it is not that virtue, that terminates his wishes; nor have they any direct respect at all to it. It is only *the saving of his money*, or the avoiding of poverty, that terminates and exhausts the whole strength of his Desire. The virtue of temperance is regarded only very indirectly and improperly, even as a necessary means of gratifying the vice of covetousness.

So, a man of an exceedingly corrupt and wicked heart, who has no love to God and Jesus Christ, but, on the contrary, being very profanely and carnally inclined, has the greatest distaste of the things of religion, and enmity against them; yet being of a family, that, from one generation to another, have most of them died, in youth, of an hereditary consumption; and so having little hope of living long; and having been instructed in the necessity of a supreme love to Christ, and gratitude for his death and sufferings, in order to his salvation from eternal misery; if under these circumstances he should, through fear of eternal torments, wish he had such a disposition; but his profane and carnal heart remaining, he continues still in his habitual distaste *of*, and enmity *to* God and religion, and wholly without any exercise of that love and gratitude, (as doubtless the very devils themselves, notwithstanding all the devilishness of their temper, would wish for a holy heart, if by that means they could get out of hell:) in this case, there is no sincere Willingness to love Christ and choose him as his chief good: these holy dispositions and exercises are not at all the direct object of the Will: they truly share no part of the inclination or desire of the soul; but all is terminated on deliverance from torment: and these graces and pious volitions, notwithstanding this forced consent, are looked upon as in themselves undesirable; as when a sick man desires a dose he greatly abhors, in order to save his life. From these things it appears,

3. That this indirect Willingness is not that exercise of the Will which the command requires; but is entirely a different one; being a volition of a different nature, and terminated altogether on different objects; wholly falling short of that virtue of Will, to which the command has respect.

4. This other volition, which has only some indirect concern with the duty required, cannot excuse for the want of that good will itself, which is commanded; being not the thing which answers and fulfils the command, and being wholly destitute of the virtue which the command seeks.

Further to illustrate this matter. If a child has a most excellent father that has ever treated him with fatherly kindness and tenderness, and has every way, in the highest degree, merited his love and dutiful regard, and is withal very wealthy; but the son is of so vile a disposition, that he inveterately hates his father; and yet, apprehending that his hatred of him is like to prove his ruin, by bringing him finally to those abject circumstances, which are exceedingly adverse to his avarice and ambition; he, therefore, wishes it were otherwise: but yet remaining under the invincible power of his vile and malignant disposition, he continues still in his settled hatred of his father. Now, if such a son's indirect Willingness to love and honour his father, at all acquits or excuses before God, for his failing of actually exercising these dispositions towards him, which God requires, it must be on one of these accounts. (1.) Either, That it answers and fulfils the command. But this it does not by the supposition; because the thing commanded is love and honour to his worthy parent. If the command be proper and just, as is supposed, then it obliges to the thing commanded; and so nothing else but that can answer the obligation. Or, (2.) It must be at least, because there is that virtue or goodness in his indirect Willingness, that is equivalent to the virtue required; and so balances or countervails it, and makes up for the want of it. But that also is contrary to the supposition. The Willingness the son has merely from a regard to money and honour, has no goodness in it, to countervail the want of the pious filial respect required.

Sincerity and reality, in that indirect Willingness, which has been spoken of, does not make it the better. That which is real and hearty is often called sincere; whether it be in virtue or vice. Some persons are sincerely *bad;* others are sincerely *good;* and others may be sincere and hearty in things, which are in their own nature *indifferent;* as a man may be sincerely desirous of eating when he is hungry. But being sincere, hearty, and in good earnest, is no virtue, unless it be in a thing that is virtuous. A man may be sincere and hearty in joining a crew of pirates, or a gang of robbers. When the devils cried out, and besought Christ not to torment them, it was no mere pretence; they were very hearty in their desires not to be tormented: but this did not make their Will or Desire virtuous. And if men have sincere Desires, which are in their kind and nature no better, it can be no excuse for the want of any required virtue.

And as a man's Sincerity in such an indirect Desire or *willingness* to do his duty, as has been mentioned, cannot excuse for the want of performance; so it is with *Endeavours* arising from such a Willingness. The Endeavours can have no more goodness in them, than the Will of which they are the effect and expression. And, therefore, however sincere and real, and however great a person's Endeavours are; yea, though they should be to the utmost of his ability; unless the Will from which they proceed be truly good and virtuous, they can be of no avail or weight whatsoever in a moral respect. That which is not truly virtuous is, in God's sight, good for nothing: and so can be of no value, or influence, in his account, to make up for any moral defect. For nothing can counterbalance evil, but good. If *evil* be in one scale, and we put a great deal into the other of sincere and earnest Desires, and many and great Endeavours; yet, if there be no real *goodness* in all, there is no weight in it; and so it does nothing towards balancing the real weight, which is in the opposite scale. It is only like substracting a thousand noughts from before a real number, which leaves the sum just as it was.

Indeed such Endeavours may have a *negatively* good influence. Those things, which have no positive virtue, have no positive moral influence; yet they may be an occasion of persons avoiding some positive evils. As if a man were in the water with a neighbour to whom he had ill will, and who could not swim, holding him by his hand; this neighbour was much in debt to him,—the man is tempted to let him sink and drown—but refuses to comply with the temptation; not from love to his neighbour, but from the love of money, and because by his drowning he should lose his debt; that which he does in preserving his neighbour from drowning, is nothing good in the sight of God: yet hereby he avoids the greater guilt that would have been contracted, if he had designedly let his neighbour sink and perish. But when *Arminians*, in their disputes with *Calvinists*, insist so much on sincere Desires and Endeavours, as what must excuse men, must be accepted of God, &c. it is manifest they have respect to some positive moral weight or influence of those Desires and Endeavours. Accepting, justifying, or excusing on the account of sincere Endeavours, (as they are called,) and men doing what they can, &c. has relation to some moral value, something that is accepted as good, and as such, countervailing some defect.

But there is a great and unknown deceit, arising from the ambiguity of the phrase, *sincere Endeavours.* Indeed there is a vast indistinctness and unfixedness in most, or at least very many of the terms used to express things pertaining to moral and spiritual matters. Whence arise innumerable mistakes, strong prejudices, inextricable confusion, and endless controversy.—The word *sincere* is most commonly used to signify something that is good: men are habituated to understand by it the same as *honest* and *upright;* which terms excite an idea of something good in the strictest and highest sense; good in the sight of him, who sees not only the outward appearance, but the heart. And, therefore, men think that if a person be *sincere,* he will certainly be accepted. If it be said that any one is sincere in his Endeavours, this suggests, that his heart is good, that there is no defect of duty, as to virtuous inclination; he *honestly* and *uprightly* desires and endeavours to do as he is required; and this leads them to suppose, that it would be very hard and unreasonable to punish him, only because he is unsuccessful in his Endeavours, the thing endeavoured after being beyond his power.—Whereas it ought to be observed, that the word *sincere* has these different significations.

1. *Sincerity,* as the word is sometimes used, signifies no more than *reality of Will and Endeavour,* with respect to any thing that is professed or pretended; without any consideration of the nature of the principle or aim, whence this real Will and true Endeavour arises. If a man has some *real* Desire either direct or indirect to obtain a thing, or does *really* endeavour after it, he is said *sincerely* to desire or endeavour, without any consideration of the goodness of the principle from which he acts, or any excellency or worthiness of the end for which he acts. Thus a man who is kind to his neighbour's wife, who is sick and languishing, and very helpful in her case, makes a show of desiring and endeavouring her restoration to health and vigour; and not only makes such a show, but there is a reality in his pretence, he does heartily and earnestly desire to have her health restored, and uses his true and utmost Endeavours for it: he is said *sincerely* to desire and endeavour after it, because he does so truly or really; though perhaps the principle he acts from, is no other than a vile and scandalous passion; having lived in adultery with her, he earnestly desires to have her health and vigour restored, that he may return to his criminal pleasures. Or,

2. By *Sincerity* is meant, not merely a *reality* of Will and Endeavour of some sort, and from some consideration or other, but a *virtuous Sincerity.* That is, that in the performance of those particular acts, that are the matter of virtue or duty, there be not only the matter, but the form and essence of virtue, consisting in the aim that governs the act, and the principle exercised in it. There is not only the reality of the act, that is as it were the *body* of the duty; but also the *soul,* which should properly belong to such a body. In this sense, a man is said to be sincere, when he acts with a *pure intention;* not from sinister views: he not only in reality desires and seeks the thing to be done, or qualification to be obtained, for some end or other; but he wills the thing directly and properly, as neither forced nor bribed; the virtue of the thing is properly the object of the Will.

In the former sense, a man is said to be sincere, in opposition to a mere pretence, and *show of the particular thing to be done or exhibited,* without any real Desire or Endeavour at all. In the latter sense, a man is said to be sincere, in opposition to that *show of virtue there is in merely doing the matter of duty,* without the reality of the virtue itself in the soul. A man may be sincere in the former sense, and yet in the latter be in the sight of God, who searches the heart, a vile hypocrite.

In the latter kind of sincerity, only, is there any thing truly valuable or acceptable in the sight of God. And this is what in Scripture is called *Sincerity, uprightness, integrity,* "truth in the inward parts," and "being of a perfect heart." And if there be such a Sincerity, and such a degree of it as there ought to be, and there be any thing further that the man is not able to perform, or which does not prove to be connected with his sincere Desires and Endeavours, the man is wholly excused and acquitted in the sight of God; his Will shall surely be accepted for his deed: and such a sincere Will and Endeavour is all that in strictness is required of him, by any command of God. But as to the other kind of Sincerity of Desires and Endeavours, having no virtue in it, (as was observed before,) it can be of no avail before God, in any case, to recommend, satisfy, or excuse, and has no positive moral weight or influence whatsoever.

Corol. 1. Hence it may be inferred, that nothing in the reason and nature of things appears from the consideration of any moral weight in the former kind of Sincerity, leading us to suppose, that God has made any positive promises of salvation, or grace, or any saving assistance, or any spiritual benefit whatsoever, to any Desires, prayers, Endeavours, striving, or obedience of those, who hitherto have no true virtue or holiness in their hearts; though we should suppose all the Sincerity, and the utmost degree of Endeavour, that is possible to be in a person without holiness.

Some object against God requiring, as the condition of salvation, those holy exercises, which are the result of a supernatural renovation; such as a supreme respect to Christ, love to God, loving holiness for its own sake, &c. that these inward dispositions and exercises are above men's power, as they are by nature; and therefore that we may conclude, that when men are brought to be sincere in their Endeavours, and do as well as they can, they are accepted; and that this must be all that God requires, in order to their being received as the objects of his favour, and must be what God has appointed as the condition of salvation. Concerning this, I would observe, that in such manner of speaking as "men being accepted because they are sincere, and do as well as they can," there is evidently a supposition of some virtue, some degree of that which is truly good; though it does not go so far as were to be wished. For if men *do what they can,* unless their so doing be from some good principle, disposition, or exercise of heart, some virtuous inclination or act of the Will; their so doing what they can, is in some respect not a whit better than if they did nothing at all. In such a case, there is no more positive moral goodness in a man doing what he can, than in a windmill doing what it can; because the action does no more proceed from virtue: and there is nothing in such Sincerity of Endeavour, or doing what we can, that should render it any more a fit recommendation to positive favour and acceptance, or the condition of any reward or actual benefit, than doing nothing; for both the one and the other are alike nothing, as to any true moral weight or value.

Corol. 2. Hence also it follows, there is nothing that appears in the reason and nature of things, which can justly lead us to determine, that God will certainly give the necessary means of salvation, or some way or other bestow true holiness and eternal life on those *heathens,* who are sincere (in the sense above explained) in their Endeavours to find out the Will of the Deity, and to please him, according to their light, that they may escape his future displeasure and wrath, and obtain happiness in the future state, through his favour.

SECT. VI.

Liberty of Indifference, not only not necessary to Virtue, but utterly inconsistent with it; and all, either virtuous or vicious habits or inclinations, inconsistent with Arminian notions of Liberty and moral Agency.

To suppose such a freedom of Will, as *Arminians* talk of, to be requisite to Virtue and Vice, is many ways contrary to common sense.

If Indifference belong to Liberty of Will, as *Arminians* suppose, and it be essential to a virtuous action, that it be performed in a state of Liberty, as they also suppose; it will follow, that it is essential to a virtuous action, that it be performed in a *state* of Indifference: and if it be performed in a *state* of Indifference, then doubtless it must be performed in the *time* of Indifference. And so it will follow, that in order to the Virtue of an act, the heart must be indifferent in the time of the performance of that act, and the more indifferent and cold the heart is with relation to the act performed, so much the better; because the act is performed with so much the greater Liberty. But is this agreeable to the light of nature? Is it agreeable to the notions which mankind in all ages have of Virtue, that it lies in what is contrary to Indifference, even in the *tendency* and *inclination* of the heart to virtuous action; and that the stronger the inclination, and so the further from Indifference, the more virtuous the *heart*, and so much the more praiseworthy the *act* which proceeds from it?

If we should suppose (contrary to what has been before demonstrated) that there may be an act of Will in a state of Indifference; for instance, this act, viz. The Will determining to put itself out of a state of Indifference, and to give itself a preponderation one way; then it would follow, on *Arminian* principles, that this act or determination of the Will is that alone wherein Virtue consists, because this only is performed, while the mind remains in a state of Indifference, and so in a state of Liberty: for when once the mind is put out of its equilibrium, it is no longer in such a state; and therefore all the acts, which follow afterwards, proceeding from bias, can have the nature neither of Virtue nor Vice. Or if the thing which the Will can do, while yet in a state of Indifference, and so of Liberty, be only to suspend acting, and determine to take the matter into consideration; then this determination is that alone wherein Virtue consists, and not proceeding to action after the scale is turned by consideration. So that it will follow, from these principles, that whatever is done after the mind, by any means, is once out of its equilibrium, and arises from an inclination, has nothing of the nature of Virtue or Vice, and is worthy of neither blame nor praise. But how plainly contrary is this to the universal sense of mankind, and to the notion they have of sincerely virtuous actions! Which is, that they proceed from a heart *well disposed* and *well inclined;* and the *stronger*, the more *fixed* and *determined*, the good disposition of the heart, the greater the sincerity of Virtue, and so the more of its truth and reality. But if there be any acts, which are done in a state of equilibrium, or spring immediately from perfect Indifference and coldness of heart, they cannot arise from any good principle or disposition in the heart; and, consequently, according to common sense, have no sincere goodness in them, having no Virtue of heart in them. To have a virtuous heart, is to have a heart that favours Virtue, and is friendly to it, and not one perfectly cold and indifferent about it.

And besides, the actions that are done in a state of Indifference, or that arise immediately out of such a state, cannot be virtuous, because, by the supposition, they are not determined by any preceding choice. For if there be preceding choice, then choice intervenes between the act and the state of Indifference; which is contrary to the supposition of the act arising immediately out of Indifference. But those acts which are not determined by preceding choice, cannot be virtuous or vicious, by *Arminian* principles, because they are not determined by the Will. So that neither one way, nor the other, can any actions be virtuous or vicious, according to those principles. If the action *be determined* by a preceding act of choice, it cannot be virtuous; because the action is not done in a state of Indifference, nor does immediately arise from such a state; and so is not done in a state of Liberty. If the action be *not determined* by a preceding act of choice, then it cannot be virtuous; because then the Will is not self-determined in it. So that it is made certain, that neither Virtue nor Vice can ever find any place in the universe!

Moreover, that it is necessary to a virtuous action that it be performed in a state of Indifference, under a notion of that being a state of Liberty, is contrary to common sense; as it is a dictate of common sense, that Indifference itself, in many cases, is vicious, and so to a high degree. As if when I see my neighbour or near friend, and one who has in the highest degree merited of me, in extreme distress, and ready to perish, I find an Indifference in my heart with respect to any thing proposed to be done, which I can easily do, for his relief. So if it should be proposed to me to blaspheme God, or kill my father, or do numberless other things, which might be mentioned; the being indifferent, for a moment, would be highly vicious and vile.

And it may be further observed, that to suppose this Liberty of Indifference is essential to Virtue and Vice, destroys the great difference of degrees of the guilt of different crimes, and takes away the heinousness of the most flagitious, horrid iniquities; such as adultery, bestiality, murder, perjury, blasphemy, &c. For, according to these principles, there is no harm at all in having the mind in a state of perfect Indifference with respect to these crimes; nay, it is absolutely necessary in order to any Virtue in avoiding them, or Vice in doing them. But for the mind to be in a state of Indifference with respect to them, is to be next door to doing them: it is then infinitely near to choosing, and so committing the fact: for equilibrium is the next step to a degree of preponderation; and one, even the least degree of preponderation (all things considered) is choice. And not only so, but for the Will to be in a state of perfect equilibrium with respect to such crimes, is for the mind to be in such a state, as to be full as likely to choose them as to refuse them, to do them as to omit them. And if our minds must be in such a state, wherein it is as near to choosing as refusing, and wherein it must of necessity, according to the nature of things, be as likely to commit them, as to refrain from them; where is the exceeding heinousness of choosing and committing them? If there be no harm in often being in such a state, wherein the probability of doing and forbearing are exactly equal, there being an equilibrium, and no more tendency to one than the other; then, according to the nature and laws of such a contingence, it may be expected, as an *inevitable* consequence of such a disposition of things, that we should choose them as often as reject them: that it should generally so fall out is necessary, as equality in the effect is the natural consequence of the equal tendency of the cause, or of the antecedent state of things from which the effect arises. Why then should we be so exceedingly to blame, if it does so fall out?

It is many ways apparent, that the *Arminian* scheme of Liberty is utterly inconsistent with the being of any such things as either virtuous or vicious habits or dispositions. If Liberty of *Indifference* be essential to moral Agency, then there can be no Virtue in any habitual inclinations of the heart; which are contrary to Indifference, and imply in their nature the very destruction and exclusion of it. They suppose nothing can be virtuous in which no Liberty is exercised; but how absurd is it to talk of exercising Indifference under bias and preponderation!

And if *self-determining power* in the Will be necessary to moral Agency, praise, blame, &c. then nothing done by the Will can be any further praiseworthy or blameworthy, than so far as the Will is moved, swayed, and determined by itself, and the scales turned by the sovereign power the Will has over itself. And therefore the Will must not be out of its balance, preponderation must not be determined and effected before-hand; and so the self-determining act anticipated. Thus it appears another way, that habitual bias is inconsistent with that Liberty, which *Arminians* suppose to be necessary to Virtue or Vice; and so it follows, that habitual bias itself cannot be either virtuous or vicious.

The same thing follows from their doctrine concerning the Inconsistence of *Necessity* with Liberty, praise, dispraise, &c. None will deny, that bias and inclination may be so strong as to be invincible, and leave no possibility of the Will determining contrary to it; and so be attended with Necessity. This Dr. Whitby allows concerning the Will of God, angels, and glorified saints, with respect to good; and the Will of devils, with respect to evil. Therefore, if Necessity be inconsistent with Liberty; then, when fixed inclination is to such a degree of strength, it utterly excludes all Virtue, Vice, praise, or blame. And, if so, then the nearer habits are to this strength, the more do they impede Liberty, and so diminish praise and blame. If very strong habits destroy Liberty, the lesser ones proportionably hinder it, according to their degree of strength. And therefore it will follow, that then is the act most virtuous or vicious, when performed without any inclination or habitual bias at all; because it is then performed with most Liberty.

Every prepossessing fixed bias on the mind brings a degree of moral inability for the contrary; because so far as the mind is biassed and prepossessed, so much *hinderance* is there of the contrary. And therefore if moral inability be inconsistent with moral Agency, or the nature of Virtue and Vice, then, so far as there is any such thing as evil disposition of heart, or habitual depravity of inclination; whether covetousness, pride, malice, cruelty, or whatever else; so much the more excusable persons are; so much the less have their evil acts of this kind the nature of Vice. And on the contrary, whatever excellent dispositions and inclinations they have. so much are they the less virtuous.

It is evident, that no habitual disposition of heart can be in *any degree* virtuous or vicious, or the actions which proceed from them *at all* praiseworthy or blameworthy. Because, though we should suppose the habit not to be of such strength, as wholly to take away all moral ability and self-determining power; or may be partly from bias, and in part from self-determination; yet in this case, all that is from antecedent bias must be set aside, as of no consideration; and in estimating the degree of Virtue or Vice, no more must be considered than what arises from self-determining power, without any influence of that bias, because Liberty is exercised in no more: so that all that is the exercise of habitual inclination is thrown away, as not belonging to the morality of the action. By which it appears, that no exercise of these habits, let them be stronger or weaker, can ever have any thing of the nature of either Virtue or Vice.

Here if any one should say, that notwithstanding all these things, there may be the nature of Virtue and Vice in the habits of the mind; because these habits may be the effects of those acts, wherein the mind exercised Liberty; that however the forementioned reasons will prove that no habits, which are natural, or that are born or created with us, can be either virtuous or vicious; yet they will not prove this of habits, which have been acquired and established by repeated free acts.

To such an objector I would say, that this evasion will not at all help the matter. For if freedom of Will be essential to the very *nature* of Virtue and Vice, then there is no Virtue or Vice but only in that very thing, wherein this Liberty is exercised. If a man in one or more things, that he does, exercises Liberty, and then by those acts is brought into such circumstances, that his Liberty ceases, and there follows a long series of acts or events that come to pass necessarily; those consequent acts are not virtuous or vicious, rewardable or punishable; but only the free acts that established this necessity; for in them alone was the man free. The following effects, that are necessary, have no more of the nature of Virtue or Vice, than health or sickness of body have properly the nature of Virtue or Vice, being the effects of a course of free acts of temperance or intemperance; or than the good qualities of a clock are of the nature of Virtue, which are the effects of free acts of the artificer; or the goodness and sweetness of the fruits of a garden are moral Virtues, being the effects of the free and faithful acts of the gardener. If Liberty be absolutely requisite to the morality of actions, and necessity wholly inconsistent with it, as *Arminians* greatly insist; then no *necessary effects* whatsoever, let the cause be never so good or bad, can be virtuous or vicious; but the Virtue or Vice must be only in the *free cause.* Agreeably to this, Dr. Whitby supposes, the necessity that attends the good and evil habits of the saints in heaven, and damned in hell, which are the consequence of their free acts in their state of probation, are not rewardable or punishable.

On the whole, it appears, that if the notions of *Arminians* concerning Liberty and moral Agency be true, it will follow, that there is no virtue in any such habits or qualities as humility, meekness, patience, mercy, gratitude, generosity, heavenly-mindedness; nothing at all praiseworthy in loving Christ above father and mother, wife and children, or our own lives; or in delight in holiness, hungering and thirsting after righteousness, love to enemies, universal benevolence to mankind: and, on the other hand, there is nothing at all vicious, or worthy of dispraise, in the most sordid, beastly, malignant, devilish dispositions; in being ungrateful, profane, habitually hating God, and things sacred and holy; or in being most treacherous, envious, and cruel towards men. For all these things are *dispositions* and *inclinations* of the heart. And in short, there is no such thing as any virtuous or vicious *quality of mind;* no such thing as inherent virtue and holiness, or vice and sin: and the stronger those habits or dispositions are, which used to be called virtuous and vicious, the further they are from being so indeed; the more violent men's lusts are, the more fixed their pride, envy, ingratitude, and maliciousness, still the further are they from being blameworthy. If there be a man that by his own repeated acts, or by any other means, is come to be of the most hellish disposition, desperately inclined to treat his neighbours with injuriousness, contempt, and malignity; the further they should be from any disposition to be angry with him, or in the least to blame him. So, on the other hand, if there be a person, who is of a most excellent spirit, strongly inclining him to the most amiable actions, admirably meek, benevolent, &c. so much is he further from any thing rewardable or commendable. On which principles, the man Jesus Christ was very far from being praiseworthy for those acts of holiness and kindness which he performed, these propensities being strong in his heart. And above all, the infinitely holy and gracious God is infinitely remote from any thing commendable, his good inclinations being infinitely strong, and he, therefore, at the utmost possible distance from being at Liberty. And in all cases, the stronger the inclinations of any are to Virtue, and the more they love it, the less virtuous, and the more they love wickedness, the less vicious they are.——Whether these things are agreeable to Scripture, let every Christian, and every man who has read the Bible, judge: and whether they are agreeable to common sense, let every one judge, that has human understanding in exercise.

And, if we pursue these principles, we shall find that Virtue and Vice are wholly excluded out of the world; and that there never was, nor ever can be, any such thing as one or the other; either in God, angels, or men. No propensity, disposition, or habit can be virtuous or vicious, as has been shown; because they, so far as they take place, destroy the freedom of the Will, the foundation of all moral Agency, and exclude all capacity of either Virtue or Vice. —And if habits and dispositions themselves be not virtuous nor vicious, neither can the exercise of these dispositions be so: for the exercise of *bias* is not the exercise of *free self-determining Will,* and so there is no exercise of Liberty in it. Consequently, no man is virtuous or vicious, either in being well or ill disposed, nor in acting from a good or bad disposition. And whether this bias or disposition be habitual or not, if it exists but a moment before the act of Will which is the effect of it, it alters not the case, as to the necessity of the effect. Or if there be no previous disposition at all, either habitual or occasional, that determines the act, then it is not choice that determines it: it is therefore a contingence, that happens to the man, arising from nothing in him; and is necessary, as to any inclination or choice of his; and, therefore, cannot make him either the better or worse; any more than a tree is better than other trees, because it oftener happens to be lighted upon by a nightingale; or a rock more vicious than other rocks, because rattle-snakes have happened oftener to crawl over it. So, that there is no Virtue nor Vice in good or bad dispositions, either fixed or transient; nor any Virtue or Vice in acting from any good or bad previous inclination; nor yet any Virtue or Vice in acting wholly without any previous inclination. Where then shall we find room for Virtue or Vice?

SECT. VII.

Arminian notions of moral Agency inconsistent with all Influence of Motive and Inducement, in either virtuous or vicious actions.

As *Arminian* notions of that liberty which is essential to virtue or vice, are inconsistent with common sense, in their being inconsistent with all virtuous or vicious habits and dispositions; so they are no less inconsistent with all influence of *Motives* in moral actions.—Such influence equally against those notions of liberty, whether there be, previous to the act of choice, a preponderancy of the inclination, or a preponderancy of those circumstances, which have a tendency to move the inclination. And, indeed, it comes to just the same thing: to say, the circumstances of the mind are such as tend to sway and turn its *inclination* one way, is the same thing, as to say, the inclination of the mind, as under such *circumstances*, tends that way.

Or if any think it most proper to say, that Motives do alter the inclination, and give a new bias to the mind, it will not alter the case, as to the present argument. For if Motives operate by giving the mind an inclination, then they operate by destroying the mind's indifference, and laying it under a bias. But to do this, is to destroy the *Arminian* freedom: it is not to leave the Will to its own self-determination, but to bring it into subjection to the power of something extrinsic, which operates upon it, sways and determines it, previous to its own determination. So that what is done from Motive, cannot be either virtuous or vicious. Besides, if the acts of the Will are excited by Motives, those Motives are the *causes* of those acts of the Will; which makes the acts of the Will necessary; as effects necessarily follow the efficiency of the cause. And if the influence and power of the Motive causes the volition, then the influence of the Motive determines volition, and volition does not determine itself; and so is not free, in the sense of *Arminians*, (as has been largely shown already,) and consequently can be neither virtuous nor vicious.

The supposition which has already been taken notice of as an insufficient evasion in other cases, would be, in like manner, impertinently alleged in this case; namely, the supposition that liberty consists in a power of suspending action for the present, in order to deliberation. If it should be said, Though it be true, that the Will is under a necessity of finally following the strongest Motive; yet it may, for the present, forbear to act upon the Motive presented, till there has been opportunity thoroughly to consider it, and compare its real weight with the merit of other Motives. I answer as follows:

Here again, it must be remembered, that if determining thus to suspend and consider, be that act of the Will, wherein alone liberty is exercised, then in this all virtue and vice must consist; and the acts that follow this consideration, and are the effects of it, being necessary, are no more virtuous or vicious than some good or bad events, which happen when they are fast asleep, and are the consequences of what they did when they were awake. Therefore, I would here observe two things:

1. To suppose, that all virtue and vice, in every case, consists in determining, whether to take time for consideration or not, is not agreeable to common sense. For, according to such a supposition, the most horrid crimes, adultery, murder, sodomy, blasphemy, &c. do not at all consist in the horrid nature of the things themselves, but only in the neglect of thorough consideration before they were perpetrated, which brings their viciousness to a small matter, and makes all crimes equal. If it be said, that neglect of consideration, when such heinous evils are proposed to choice, is worse than in other cases: I answer, this is inconsistent, as it supposes the very thing to be, which, at the same time, is supposed not to be; it supposes all moral evil, all viciousness and heinousness, does not consist merely in the want of consideration. It supposes some crimes *in themselves*, in their *own nature*, to be more heinous than others, antecedent to consideration, or inconsideration, which lays the person under a previous obligation to consider in some cases more than others.

2. If it were so, that all virtue and vice, in every case, consisted only in the act of the Will, whereby it determines whether to consider or no, it would not alter the case in the least, as to the present argument. For still in this act of the Will on this determination, it is induced by some Motive, and necessarily follows the strongest Motive; and so is necessarily, even in that act wherein alone it is either virtuous or vicious.

One thing more I would observe, concerning the inconsistence of *Arminian* notions of moral Agency with the Influence of Motives.—I suppose none will deny, that it is possible for such powerful Motives to be set before the mind, exhibited in so strong a light, and under such advantageous circumstances, as to be invincible; and such as the mind cannot but yield to. In this case, *Arminians* will doubtless say, liberty is destroyed. And if so, then if Motives are exhibited with half so much power, they hinder liberty in proportion to their strength, and go halfway towards destroying it. If a thousand degrees of Motive abolish all liberty, then five hundred take it half away. If one degree of the influence of Motive does not at all infringe or diminish liberty, then no more do two degrees; for nothing doubled, is still nothing. And if two degrees do not diminish the Will's liberty, no more do four, eight, sixteen, or six thousand. For nothing however multiplied comes to but nothing. If there be nothing in the nature of Motive or moral suasion, that is at all opposite to liberty, then the greatest degree of it cannot hurt liberty. But if there be somewhat, in the nature of the thing, against liberty, then the *least* degree of it hurts in *some* degree; and consequently diminishes virtue. If invincible Motives to that action which is good, take away all the freedom of the act, and so all the virtue of it; then the more forcible the Motives are, so much the worse, so much the less virtue; and the weaker the Motives are, the better for the cause of virtue; and none is best of all.

Now let it be considered, whether these things are agreeable to common sense. If it should be allowed, that there are some instances wherein the soul chooses without any Motive, what virtue can there be in such a choice? I am sure there is no prudence or wisdom in it. Such a choice is made for no *good* end; being made for no end at all. If it were for any end, the view of the end would be the Motive exciting to the act; and if the act be for no good end, and so from no good aim, then there is no good intention in it: and, therefore, according to all our natural notions of virtue, no more virtue in it than in the motion of the smoke, which is driven to and fro by the wind, without any aim or end in the thing moved, and which knows not whither, nor wherefore, it is moved.

Corol. 1. By these things it appears, that the argument against the *Calvinists*, taken from the use of counsels, exhortations, invitations, expostulations, &c. so much insisted on by *Arminians*, is truly against themselves. For these things can operate no other way to any good effect, than as in them is exhibited Motive and Inducement, tending to excite and determine the acts of the Will.* But it follows, on their principles, that the acts of Will excited by such causes, cannot be virtuous; because, so far as they are

* The *true reason* WHY counsels, exhortations, &c. commonly called motives, are consistent with the doctrine of necessity held by Calvinists, may be here noticed, in addition to some hints before given. In order to this, we must guard against ambiguity in the word "motive," which at one time is intended for the object exhibited, *abstractedly* considered; at another, the object *concretively*, as it stands in the view of the mind. The opposers of that necessity for which our author pleads must in order to make even a show of consistency, understand the word "motive" in the *first* of these acceptations. And if so, it is nothing marvellous that they should maintain the existence of a power in the human mind which can, on the one hand, successfully oppose the *strongest possible motive*; and on the other, be determined by a weaker, and even sometimes by the weakest motive. For how often is the most insignificant bawble preferred to infinite excellence! But consistent Calvinists do not understand the term in any such manner, but rather as an *effect* compounded of the *state of the mind* and the real *object*. And, seeing the object, in itself considered, is not changed by mental perception, the *difference* of the effect, or change of mental view, must arise from the *mind itself*. Hence *one motive*, in the Arminian sense, may produce, in the *other* acceptation of the term, a thousand different motives, according to the different *mental states* to which the object is presented.

Therefore counsels, exhortations, invitations, &c. are most rationally employed by Calvinists; for that which determines the human will to action, is the motive *as it is perceived*, or that which results from an *application* of the object to the mind. According to them, without an *object* presented there can be no *motive*, any more than there can be a *motive* without a *mind* to which it is presented. Without evangelical truth, and an evangelical mind, or disposition, there can be no evangelical *determining* motive. Consequently, if the mind be at all roused from ignorance and apathy, *determining* motives must be produced in it by a representation of *objects*, by counsels, exhortations, invitations, expostulations, &c. These will succeed, or fail of success, morally, according to the state of the mind. But as the agent is free from co-action, constraint, and compulsion, *in the act* of choosing, the true inference is—not that such use of the means is unsuitable or inconsistent, but—that here is clearly implied the great necessity, the rationality, and the perfect consistency of *prayer* to the God of grace, for success on the use of means. Paul may plant, and Apollos may water, but God giveth the increase. To *influence* the mind *without* moral motives, is the prerogative of God. All hearts are in his hand to form them as he pleases. If the tree be good by sovereign influence, or a new birth, the fruit of love to God and hatred to sin, holy fear, unfeigned faith, humble hope, &c. will follow, according to the objects presented. A crop will not follow without the *union* of two things, *seed* and *soil*. If both be good, the crop will be good, but not otherwise. That motive which determines the from these, they are not from the Will's self-determining power. Hence it will follow, that it is not worth while to offer any arguments to persuade men to any virtuous volition or voluntary action; it is in vain to set before them the wisdom and amiableness of ways of virtue, or the odiousness and folly of ways of vice. This notion of liberty and moral Agency frustrates all endeavours to draw men to virtue by instruction or persuasion, precept or example: for though these things may induce them to what is *materially* virtuous, yet at the same time they take away the *form* of virtue, because they destroy liberty; as they, by their own power, put the Will out of its equilibrium, determine and turn the scale, and take the work of self-determining power out of its hands. And the clearer the instructions given, the more powerful the arguments used, and the more moving the persuasions or examples, the more likely they are to frustrate their own design; because they have so much the greater tendency to put the Will out of its balance, to hinder its freedom of self-determination; and so to exclude the very form of virtue, and the essence of whatsoever is praiseworthy.

So it clearly follows, from these principles, that God has no hand in any man's virtue, nor does at all promote it, either by a physical or moral influence; that none of the moral methods he uses with men to promote virtue in the world, have any tendency to the attainment of that end; that all the instructions he has given men, from the beginning of the world to this day, by prophets or apostles, or by his Son Jesus Christ; that all his counsels, invitations, promises, threatenings, warnings, and expostulations; that all means he has used with men, in ordinances, or providences; yea, all influences of his Spirit, ordinary and extraordinary, have had no tendency at all to excite any one virtuous act of the mind, or to promote any thing morally good and commendable, in any respect.—For there is no way that these or any other means can promote virtue, but one of these three. Either, (1.) By a physical operation on the heart. But all effects that are wrought in men in this way, have no virtue in them, by the concurring voice of all *Arminians*. Or, (2.) Morally, by exhibiting Motives to the understanding, to excite good acts in the Will. But it has been demonstrated, that volitions excited by Motives, are necessary, and not excited by a self-moving power; and therefore, by their principles, there is no virtue in them. Or, (3.) By merely giving the Will an opportunity to determine itself concerning the objects proposed, either to choose or reject, by its own uncaused, unmoved, uninfluenced self-determination. And if this be all, then all those means do no more to promote virtue than vice: for they do nothing but give the Will opportunity to determine itself *either way*, either to good or bad, without laying it under any bias to either: and so there is really as much of an opportunity given to determine in favour of evil, as of good.

Thus that horrid blasphemous consequence will certainly follow from the *Arminian* doctrine, which they charge on others; namely, that God acts an inconsistent part in using so many counsels, warnings, invitations, entreaties, &c. with sinners, to induce them to forsake sin, and turn to the ways of virtue; and that all are insincere and fallacious. It will follow, from their doctrine, that God does these things when he knows, at the same time, that they have no manner of tendency to promote the effect he seems to aim at; yea, knows that if they have any influence, this very influence will be inconsistent with such an effect, and will prevent it. But what an imputation of insincerity would this fix on him, who is infinitely holy and true!—So that theirs is the doctrine which, if pursued in its consequences, does horribly reflect on the Most High, and fix on him the charge of hypocrisy; and not the doctrine of the *Calvinist*, according to their frequent and vehement exclamations and invectives.

Corol. 2. From what has been observed in this section, it again appears, that *Arminian* principles and notions, when fairly examined and pursued in their demonstrable consequences, do evidently shut all virtue out of the world, and make it impossible that there should ever be any such thing, in any case; or that any such thing should ever be conceived of. For, by these principles, the very notion of virtue or vice implies absurdity and contradiction. For it is absurd in itself, and contrary to common sense, to suppose a virtuous act of mind without any good intention or aim; and, by their principles, it is absurd to suppose a virtuous act with a good intention or aim; for to act for an end, is to act from a Motive. So that if we rely on these principles, there can be no virtuous act with a good design and end; and it is self-evident, there can be none without: consequently there can be no virtuous act at all.

Corol. 3. It is manifest, that *Arminian* notions of moral Agency, and *the being* of a faculty of Will, cannot consist together; and that if there can be any such thing as either a virtuous or vicious act, it cannot be an act of the Will; no Will can be at all concerned in it. For that act which is performed without inclination, without Motive, without end, must be performed without any concern of the Will. To suppose an act of the Will without these, implies a contradiction. If the soul in its act has no motive or end; then, in that act (as was observed before) it seeks nothing, goes after nothing, exerts no inclination to any thing; and this implies, that in that act it desires nothing, and chooses nothing; so that there is no act of choice in the case: and that is as much as to say, there is no act of Will in the case. Which very effectually shuts all vicious and virtuous acts out of the universe; inasmuch as, according to this, there can be no vicious or virtuous act wherein the Will is concerned: and according to the plainest dictates of reason, and the light of nature, and also the principles of *Arminians* themselves, there can be no virtuous or vicious act wherein the Will is not concerned. And therefore there is no room for any virtuous or vicious acts at all.

Corol. 4. If none of the moral actions of intelligent beings are influenced by either previous inclination or Motive, another strange thing will follow; and this is, that God not only cannot foreknow any of the future moral actions of his creatures, but he can make no conjecture, can give no probable guess concerning them. For all conjecture in things of this nature must depend on some discerning or apprehension of these two things, *previous Disposition* and *Motive*, which, as has been observed, *Arminian* notions of moral Agency, in their real consequence, altogether exclude.

PART IV.

WHEREIN THE CHIEF GROUNDS OF THE REASONINGS OF ARMINIANS, IN SUPPORT AND DEFENCE OF THE FORE-MENTIONED NOTIONS OF LIBERTY, MORAL AGENCY, &c. AND AGAINST THE OPPOSITE DOCTRINE, ARE CONSIDERED.

SECT. I.

*The Essence of the virtue and vice of dispositions of the heart, and acts of the Will, lies not in their Cause, but their Nature.**

ONE main foundation of the reasons, which are brought to establish the forementioned notions of liberty, virtue, vice, &c. is a supposition, that the virtuousness of the dispositions, or acts of the Will, consists not in the nature of these dispositions, or acts of the Will, but wholly in the Origin or Cause of them: so that if the disposition of the mind, or acts of the Will, be never so good, yet if the Cause of the disposition or act be not our virtue, there is nothing virtuous or praiseworthy in it; and, on the contrary, if the

will, cannot arise from any other cause than *the object and the disposition united.* And then only can the *determining* motive be *good,* when it results from a *good object* applied to a *good disposition,* or state of mind. These things duly considered will sufficiently prove *why* Calvinists use counsels, exhortations, invitations, &c.—W.

* This may appear to some to be an identical proposition --" The essence

Will, in its inclination or acts, be never so bad, yet, unless it arises from something that is our vice or fault, there is nothing vicious or blameworthy in it. Hence their grand objection and pretended demonstration, or self-evidence,

of a thing lies in its nature;" but it is not wholly so, and the whole of the proposition is exceedingly important, on account of the *negative* part, or the incidental proposition it contains, viz. The *essence* of virtue and vice lies *not* in their *cause*. A single consideration may be sufficient to show the truth and importance of one part of this last proposition. If the essence of *virtue* lay in its *cause*, how could the *first* cause, or the *uncaused* nature, be virtuous? If therefore the *first* cause be virtuous, or have the essence of virtue, as all atheists will allow, it is plain, *that* essence must lie in the *nature* of that cause itself. Hence, as God is the standard of all moral excellence, created natures are morally excellent in proportion as they resemble him. And as virtue is an *imitable* excellence, and as good reason can be assigned why the resemblance should not hold in this particular, it is highly probable, *a priori*, that, in reference to created natures, the essence of *their* virtue lies not in its cause. To demonstrate this last, is the design of the present section.

Again, as the essence of *virtue* lies not in its cause, so neither does the essence of *vice* lie in its *cause*. But the philosophical ground of this part of the general proposition demands more particular attention. And as this proposition—" the essence of vice lies not in its cause," affects the whole system of morals, and indeed of theology, we beg leave to propose a series of remarks which, it is hoped, will cast some light on the subject.

1. Causes are of two kinds, and of two only, either *positive* or *negative*. Positive causes produce positive effects, from the first cause through all secondary causes: and these positive secondary causes are nothing else but so many decretive antecedents, which act *physically*, and their consequences follow from the nature of things; even as number follows the repetition of units, or happiness results from true virtue.

2. The term " cause " is applied less properly to express a *negative* idea; for it expresses merely an antecedent of a consequent. For instance, if we say that a man cannot read *because* he is blind, or cannot walk *because* he has no legs, or cannot go to heaven *because* he does not love God, and the like; it is manifest that *blindness, want of legs*, and *want of love* to God, are " causes " only as antecedents are causes to their consequents, without positive influence.

3. Negative causes, though they have no positive operation in producing their consequents, are no less the ground of *certainty* than those causes, properly so called, which exist in physical operations. For the consequent follows the antecedent with equal certainty, whether the connexion be formed by decretive will and energy, as in all positive causes, or by the nature of things only, which is essential truth, as in all negative causes.

4. The cause of vicious *acts*, is a vicious disposition; in other words, it is the *want*, or the *absence* of a virtuous disposition. The essence of the vicious *act*, however, is not in the *cause*, or disposition. The vice of the disposition is one thing, and the vice of the act is another. For as the *nature* of the disposition, and the nature of the act, are different; so the vice, or moral badness of the one, is a different badness from that of the other. The one and the other is a *bad thing* whatever be the cause, and irrespective of any. Hence,

5. Evil dispositions or acts should be denominated such, not from their cause, but from their *nature*. Were it otherwise, *personal* fault, or blame, could never exist; for the vicious *act* would transfer the blame to the *disposition*, and the disposition to the *cause* of that; whereby *persons* would be free from blame, and this would attach to *principles* only. But to suppose a moral agent *incapable* of blameworthiness, which on the supposition would be the case, is a gross absurdity. It would be to suppose an accountable being, who at the same time can be accountable for nothing; and it would be to impute blame to principles, or a principle, which is incapable of moral agency.

6. The *cause* of virtuous *acts*, or, if we may so speak, the soil in which they grow, is a previous inclination or disposition to good, before any actual choice takes place. This may be called a *virtuous inclination*, or disposition. But the original and predisposing cause of *that*, is divine energy, influx, or influence; in other words, an assimilating emanation from the holy nature and decretive will of God.

7. Nevertheless, this is not a good, or a virtue, attributable to *man*, until he is actually *possessed* of it, or it becomes *his*, as a quality of his nature. God, the Father of lights, from whom every good and perfect gift proceedeth, is the *cause* of that virtuous disposition; but while the virtue remained in the *cause*, and not in the man, it was no *human* virtue. Nor does the essence of human virtue lie in the *communication* itself, for this was the effect of divine will; but no will can alter the *nature* of virtue: therefore, the essence of virtue consists not in the cause, whether we understand by " cause," the *Will* that communicates the virtuous disposition, or the *communication* itself. Consequently, the *absence* of virtue is so completely confined to the *disposition* of the agent, and the consequent *acts*, as to exclude every thing else that may be termed its *cause*.

8. The cause of vicious acts, whatever it be, is *opposite* to the cause of virtuous acts; for these acts have diametrically opposite effects. That vicious acts have a *cause*, as well as virtuous ones, cannot be denied by any reflecting person, for this plain reason, that there is nothing in the universality of things, beings, qualities, &c. but has a cause, either positive or negative, as before explained. Neither agency, liberty, nor any thing else, considered as an effect, or a consequent, can exist without a cause, or antecedent. The denial of this, and universal scepticism, are the same thing. Then all reasoning, and all common sense, vanish. Then body and spirit, cause and effects, good and evil, &c. are huddled up in endless confusion, without either first or last, great or small, order or proportion.

9. The original, predisposing cause of a vicious disposition, is the very opposite of the original, predisposing cause of a virtuous disposition. This last, it has been shown, is divine energy, which is a positive cause; the other, the opposite of this, is a negative cause. The cause of good, as before observed, is a cause properly so called, in the way of physical influence; but the cause of evil is called " a cause" improperly, as it implies no physical influence, but only stands as an antecedent to a consequent; from which however the consequent may be inferred with as much *certainty* as if the influence were physical and mechanical. Whether you suppose positive quantities, or negative quantities, consequences are equally *certain*, it is no less true that $5-2=3$, than $+3+3=6$. Whether you say, If the sun *were not*, it would cause darkness; or say, If the sun *shine*, it will cause light; the difference is only in the *nature* of the cause, as either positive or negative, not in the certainty of the consequence.

10. It would be very absurd and contradictory to say that the *cause* of vice is *vicious*. For that would be the same as to say, that a thing was before it existed. To be vicious is to *have vice*; and for this to be the *cause* of vice, is for it to be the cause of *itself*, or *self-caused*, which is absurd. It is therefore impossible that the cause of vice should be vicious; consequently the essence of *vice* is no where but in its *own proper nature*, to the exclusion of every cause whatever. And yet, as it is an effect, it must have *a cause*.

11. The principal question to be determined, in this investigation, is, What is precisely the original, predisposing, *negative cause* of a vicious disposition? The answer is plain and short; it is that property of a creature which renders it *absolutely dependent* for its being and well-being. Or, it is that property which is the very *opposite* to independence, self-sufficiency, and immutability: and therefore is a property peculiar to a creature, and cannot belong to God.

12. Nor can this be said to be an *actually existing* property from eternity; since it cannot belong to God, and nothing, the only alternative, has no property. It is not therefore the Manichean eternal evil principle, if by this be meant any thing actually existing, as coeval with a good principle. Good is a principle *positively eternal*; but what we speak of is a mere *negative* principle, and owes its *existence* as a property to a *created* nature; and were every *creature* annihilated, this property would also cease to be.

13. But what shall we call this principle, property, or *predisposing cause* of vice? Shall we call it *defectibility, defect, limitation*, or *imperfection* of existence? Not the first: for the question would return, What *makes* a creature *defectible?* Not the second; for the term is ambiguous, as there are several *kinds* of defect, natural and moral, and therefore, as the word is of common use, and of frequent occurrence, it would require perpetual explanations. Not the third, or the fourth; for the same reason. A term therefore not ambiguous, and sufficiently expressive, should be employed; as we employ technical terms to express a specific object. For this purpose, no term, perhaps, is less exceptionable, or more suitable, than PASSIVE POWER; for it is free from ambiguity, and is sufficiently expressive of the idea already explained. The idea of *passivity* is clearly implied in the name, as in the thing; and the term *power* seems preferable to *property*, or *quality*, because less ambiguous, and yet more expressive to convey the intended idea of *metaphysical influence* of cause and effect.

14. To which we may add, That " passive power " is by no means a new coined expression; but has often been used to express the very idea to which it is here applied. Thus, above a century and a half ago, that eminently pious and profoundly learned divine, Theophilus Gale, in his " Court of the Gentiles," says: " The root and origin of all creatural dependence, is the creature's *passive power*, and God's absolute dominion over it.—Now all limits as to nature and essence speak a mixture of nihility, *passive power* and dependence resulting therefrom; whence Damascene adds, ' Μονον γαρ το θειον απαθες εστι, *The Deity only is impassible*;' namely, because exempt from nihility, *passive power*, and dependence. This *nihility* or *nothingness* of the creature is the same with its *passive power* either physic or metaphysic, natural or obediential: whereby it is limited, and confined to such or such a degree of *entity, existence*, and *operation*." (Court of Gent. Part IV. B. ii. ch. xi. § 4.)

15. Now that the essence of vice consisteth not in this property is plain, in that passive power is essential to a creature, which vice neither is nor can be. It is the soul in which vice grows, and without which it could not grow, or have existence, but is not itself *vicious*; otherwise we should be forced to seek the cause of that cause in perpetual retrogradation, and move from one difficulty to another into endless absurdity. The predisposing *cause* of vice, therefore, is *passive power* which in itself is not vicious, or morally evil. But how moral evil came to *exist*, and what is its true *origin*, will be more conveniently considered in a subsequent part of this work.

16. As the essence of the virtue and vice of dispositions and acts lies not in their cause, so neither does it lie in their *effects*: that is, dispositions and acts are not to be denominated virtuous or vicious on account of their effects or consequences, such as their being productive of happiness or misery. For as the properties of any thing must be different from those of its cause, however similar, so must those properties differ from their effects. The *immediate effect* of virtue is—not *happiness* to the individual, for instance, but—that the agent is *approvable*, or *praiseworthy*. But were the essence of virtue to consist in " its tendency to ultimate happiness," as some have affirmed, *immediate* approbation and praise could not be safely given to any individual act or disposition, as its relation to ultimate happiness could not be ascertained but by the final event. If the essence of the virtue or vice were not in the act or disposition, but to be denominated from its *effects*, many other absurdities would follow. For instance,

17. On that supposition, the supreme excellence of Jehovah would not be *approvable* and *praiseworthy* on its own account, or its intrinsic excellency, but only because of its effects and consequences. On that principle, to *hate* God would be nothing bad, it would have no intrinsic demerit; or to *love* God would be nothing good, nothing in itself praiseworthy, were it not for consequences. Which is not only absurd, but blasphemous also and shocking.

18. That sentiment is evidently founded on the supposition that every thing, property, quality, and event, is the fruit of *divine will*; and therefore that every thing must be equally good *in itself*, though *relatively* good or bad to the individual: even as matter and motion, and their laws, are equally good *in themselves*, but not relatively so to the individuals who suffer from them. But this is a great mistake, as it confounds things totally distinct in their nature, such as positive and negative causes, natural necessity and moral certainty. *Decretive positions* and their consequences are one ground of certainty; *negative causes* and their consequences are another; therefore, from the certainty of result in the divine view we cannot rightly infer that all results are decreed. Decretive positions comprehend neither *negative* causes, nor the *nature of things*. For an intelligent being to *love God*, is agreeable to the *nature of things*; it is what *ought to be* independent of any decretive position, or legal demand in reference to the case. In like manner, for an intelligent being to *hate* God is a voluntary contradiction to the *nature of things*—or the essence of eternal truth which is above all will, or is not founded in will—as well as to constituted law. Again,

19. To deny the " intrinsic merit and demerit of voluntary actions independent on their consequences," as some do,* is to deny the nature of things; and this is nothing less than an attempt to divide eternal unity, to give the lie direct to essential truth, and to convert the first uncaused essence into contradictory contingencies. The nature of things is nothing else, radically, but the nature of God, which is essential truth as well as essential goodness. Decretive positions, or an arbitrary constitution of things by divine will, therefore can no more alter the *intrinsic* merit or demerit of actions, affections, habits, or characters, than divine will can alter the character of essential truth, or choose real contradictions. Moreover,

20. Ultimate happiness is the effect or consequence of virtue as a *reward*. Now to make the merit or *excellence* of virtue to depend on ultimate happiness, while happiness is the *reward* of virtue, is most inconsistent; it is to *reward* for nothing *rewardable*. If virtue be not of *intrinsic* worth, it must be a *mere moral nothing*, as to *rewardableness*, and therefore ultimate happiness would be a *reward* for a mere moral *nothing*; that is, *happiness* would be *no reward*, which is contradictory.

21. As to vice, its consequence is *punishment*. If indeed this consequence were the mere effect of arbitrary positions, or sovereign appointment: if it were the plan of God first to *cause* the existence of vice, and then to *punish* the subject of it, as what the good of the whole required, there would be great plausibility in the sentiment we oppose. But the assumption itself is fundamentally erroneous. It confounds hypothetical antecedents, as the whole of decretive plans may be termed, with that eternal truth which con-

* Belsham's Elements, p. 309.

against any virtue and commendableness, or vice and blameworthiness, of those habits or acts of the Will, which are not from some virtuous or vicious determination of the Will itself.

Now, if this matter be well considered, it will appear to be altogether a mistake, yea, a gross absurdity; and that it is most certain, that if there be any such thing, as a virtuous or vicious disposition, or volition of mind, the virtuousness or viciousness of them consists not in the Origin or Cause of these things, but in the Nature of them.

If the Essence of virtuousness or commendableness, and of viciousness or fault, does not lie in the Nature of the dispositions or acts of mind, which are said to be our virtue or our fault, but in their Cause, then it is certain it lies no where at all. Thus, for instance, if the vice of a *vicious* act of Will, lies not in the Nature of the act, but the Cause; so that its being of a bad Nature will not make it at all our fault, unless it arises from some faulty determination of ours, as its Cause, or something in us that is our fault; then, for the same reason, neither can the viciousness of that Cause lie in the Nature of the thing itself, but in *its* Cause: that evil determination of ours is not our fault, merely because it is of a bad Nature, unless it arises from some Cause in us that is our fault. And when we are come to this higher Cause, still the reason of the thing holds good; though this Cause be of a bad Nature, yet we are not at all to blame on that account, unless it arises from something faulty in us. Nor yet can blameworthiness lie in the Nature of *this Cause*, but in the Cause of *that*. And thus we must drive faultiness back from step to step, from a lower Cause to a higher, *in infinitum:* and that is, thoroughly to banish it from the world, and to allow it no possibility of existence any where in the universality of things. On these principles, vice, or moral evil, cannot consist in any thing that is an *effect;* because *fault* does not consist in the Nature of things, but in their Cause; as well as because effects are necessary, being unavoidably connected with their Cause: therefore the Cause only is to blame. And so it follows, that faultiness can lie *only in that Cause*, which is a *Cause only*, and no effect of any thing. Nor yet can it lie in this; for then it must lie in the Nature of the thing itself; not in its being from any determination of ours, nor any thing faulty in us which is the Cause, nor indeed from any Cause at all; for, by the supposition, it is no effect, and *has no Cause*. And thus, he that will maintain, it is not the Nature of habits or acts of Will that makes them virtuous or faulty, but the Cause, must immediately run himself out of his own assertion; and in maintaining it, will insensibly contradict and deny it.

This is certain, that if effects are vicious and faulty, not from their Nature, or from any thing inherent in them, but because they are from a bad Cause, it must be on account of the *badness* of the Cause: a bad effect in the Will must be bad, because the Cause is *bad*, or *of an evil Nature*, or *has badness* as a quality inherent in it: and a *good* effect in the Will must be *good*, by reason of the *goodness* of the Cause, or its being *of a good Kind and Nature*. And if this be what is meant, the very supposition of fault and praise lying not in the Nature of the thing, but the Cause, contradicts itself, and does at least resolve the Essence of virtue and vice into the Nature of things, and supposes it originally to consist in that.—And if a caviller has a mind to run from the absurdity, by saying, " No, the fault of the thing, which is the Cause, lies not in this, that the Cause itself is *of an evil Nature*, but that the Cause is evil in that sense, that it is from another bad Cause." Still the absurdity will follow him; for, if so, then the Cause before charged is at once acquitted, and all the blame must be laid to the higher Cause, and must consist in that being *evil*, or *of an evil Nature*. So now, we are come again to lay the blame of the thing blameworthy, to the Nature of the thing, and not to the Cause. And if any is so foolish as to go higher still, and ascend from step to step, till he is come to that which is the first Cause concerned in the whole affair, and will say, all the blame lies in that; then, at last, he must be forced to own, that the faultiness of the thing, which he supposes alone blameworthy, lies wholly *in the Nature* of the thing, and not in the Original or Cause of it; for the supposition is, that it has no Original, it is determined by no act of ours, is caused by nothing faulty in us, being absolutely *without any Cause*. And so the race is at an end, but the evader is taken in his flight.

It is agreeable to the natural notions of mankind, that moral evil, with its desert of dislike and abhorrence, and all its other ill deservings, consists in a certain *deformity* in the *Nature* of certain dispositions of the heart, and acts of the Will; and not in the deformity of *something else*, diverse from the very thing itself, which deserves abhorrence, supposed to be the Cause of it. Which would be absurd, because that would be to suppose a thing that is innocent and not evil, is truly evil and faulty, because another thing is evil. It implies a contradiction; for it would be to suppose, the very thing, which is morally evil and blameworthy, is innocent and not blameworthy; but that something else, which is its Cause, is only to blame. To say, that vice does not consist in the thing which is vicious, but in its Cause, is the same as to say, that vice does not consist in vice, but in that which produces it.

It is true, a Cause may be to blame, for being the Cause of vice: it may be wickedness in the Cause, that it produces wickedness. But it would imply a contradiction, to suppose that these two are the same individual wickedness. The wicked act of the Cause in producing wickedness, is one wickedness; and the wickedness produced, if there be any produced, is another. And therefore, the wickedness of the latter does not lie in the former, but is distinct from it; and the wickedness of both lies in the *evil Nature* of the things which are wicked.

The thing, which makes sin hateful, is that by which it deserves punishment; which is but the expression of hatred. And that, which renders virtue lovely, is that on account of which it is fit to receive praise and reward; which are but the expressions of esteem and love. But that which makes vice hateful, is its hateful Nature; and that which renders virtue lovely, is its amiable Nature. It is a certain beauty or deformity that are *inherent* in that good or evil will, which is the *soul* of virtue and vice, (and not in the *occasion* of it,) which is their worthiness of esteem or disesteem, praise or dispraise, according to the common sense of mankind. If the Cause or occasion of the rise of an hateful disposition or act of Will, be also hateful; suppose another antecedent evil will; that is entirely another sin, and deserves punishment by itself, under a distinct consideration. There is worthiness of dispraise in the Nature of an evil volition, and not wholly in some foregoing act, which is its Cause; otherwise the evil volition, which is the effect, is no moral evil, any more than sickness, or some other natural calamity, which arises from a Cause morally evil.

Thus, for instance, ingratitude is hateful and worthy of dispraise, according to common sense; not because something as bad, or worse than ingratitude, was the Cause that produced it; but because it is hateful in itself, by its own inherent deformity. So the love of virtue is amiable, and worthy of praise, not merely because something else went before this love of virtue in our minds, which caused it to take place there—for instance, our own choice; we chose to love virtue, and, by some method or other, wrought ourselves into the love of it—but because of the amiableness and condecency of such a disposition and inclination of heart. If that *was* the case, that we *did* choose to love virtue, and so produced that love in ourselves, this choice itself could be no otherwise amiable or praiseworthy, than as love to virtue, or some other amiable inclination, was exercised and implied in it. If that choice was amiable at all, it must be so on account of some amiable quality in the Nature of the choice. If we choose to love virtue, not in love to virtue, or any thing that was good, and exercised no sort of good disposition in the

nects them with their consequences. To suppose the hatred of God, for instance, to have no *intrinsic* demerit in it, or that it is bad only as dependent on its *consequences;* is the same as to say, it is *agreeable* to the nature of things, *conformable* to eternal truth, that God should be hated, and therefore that he must *approve* of it—only to the agent it is attended with *bad consequences.* That is, on the supposition, God has *appointed misery* as the consequent, for doing nothing that is in itself bad; yea for doing what is perfectly innocent, agreeable to the nature of things, conformable to eternal truth, and acceptable to God, as every thing which he *appoints* must be. Whether such a sentiment be nearest a-kin to " profound philosophy " or to something else, let the competent reader judge.—W.

choice, the choice itself was not virtuous, nor worthy of any praise, according to common sense, because the choice was not of a *good Nature*.

It may not be improper here to take notice of something said by an author, that has lately made a mighty noise in *America*. "A necessary holiness (says he*) is no holiness.—*Adam* could not be originally created in righteousness and true holiness, because he must *choose* to be righteous, *before* he could be righteous. And therefore he must exist, he must be created, yea, he must exercise thought and reflection, before he was righteous." There is much more to the same effect, (p. 437, 438, 439, 440.) If these things are so, it will certainly follow, that the first choosing to be righteous is no righteous choice; there is no righteousness or holiness in it; because no choosing to be righteous goes before it. For he plainly speaks of *choosing to be righteous*, as what *must go before righteousness;* and that which follows the choice, being the effect of the choice, cannot be righteousness or holiness: for an effect is a thing necessary, and cannot prevent the influence or efficacy of its Cause; and therefore is unavoidably dependent upon the Cause: and he says, *a necessary holiness is no holiness.* So that neither can a choice of righteousness be righteousness or holiness, nor can any thing that is consequent on that choice, and the effect of it, be righteousness or holiness; nor can any thing that is without choice, be righteousness or holiness. So that by his scheme, all righteousness and holiness is at once shut out of the world, and no door left open, by which it can ever possibly enter into the world.

I suppose, the way that men came to entertain this absurd notion—with respect to *internal inclinations and volitions* themselves, (or notions that imply it,) *viz.* that the Essence of their moral good or evil lies not in their Nature, but their Cause—was, that it is indeed a very plain dictate of common sense, that it is so with respect to all *outward actions*, and sensible motions of the body; that the moral good or evil of them does not lie at all in the motions themselves; which, taken by themselves, are nothing of a moral nature; and the Essence of all the moral good or evil that concerns them, lies in those internal dispositions and volitions, which are the Cause of them. Now, being always used to determine this, without hesitation or dispute, concerning *external Actions;* which in the common use of language are signified by such phrases, as men's *actions* or their *doings;* hence, when they came to speak of volitions, and *internal exercises* of their inclinations, under the same denomination of their *actions*, or *what they do*, they unwarily determined the case must also be the same with these, as with *external actions;* not considering the vast difference in the Nature of the case.

If any shall still object and say, why is it not necessary that the Cause should be considered, in order to determine whether any thing be worthy of blame or praise? is it agreeable to reason and common sense, that a man is to be praised or blamed for that of which he is not the Cause or author?

I answer, such phrases as *being the Cause*, *being the author*, and the like, are ambiguous. They are most vulgarly understood for being the designing voluntary Cause, or Cause by antecedent choice: and it is most certain, that men are not, in this sense, the Causes or authors of the first act of their Wills, in any case; as certain as any thing is, or ever can be; for nothing can be more certain, than that a thing is not before it is, nor a thing of the same kind before the first thing of that kind; and so no choice before the first choice.—As the phrase, *being the author*, may be understood, not of being the producer by an antecedent act of Will; but as a person may be said to be the author of the act of Will itself, by his being the immediate agent, or the being that *is acting*, or *in exercise* in that act; if the phrase of *being the author*, is used to signify this, then doubtless common sense requires men being the authors of their own acts of Will, in order to their being esteemed worthy of praise or dispraise, on account of them. And common sense teaches, that they must be the authors of *external actions*, in the former sense, namely, their being the Causes of them by an act of Will or choice, in order to their being justly blamed or praised: but it teaches no such thing with respect to the acts of the Will themselves.—But this may appear more manifest by the things which will be observed in the following section.

SECT. II.

The Falseness and Inconsistence of that metaphysical notion of Action, and Agency, which seems to be generally entertained by the defenders of the Arminian Doctrine concerning Liberty, moral Agency, &c.

One thing, that is made very much a ground of argument and supposed demonstration by *Arminians*, in defence of the forementioned principles, concerning moral Agency, virtue, vice, &c. is their metaphysical notion of *Agency* and *Action*. They say, unless the soul has a self-determining power, it has no power of *Action;* if its volitions be not caused by itself, but are excited and determined by some extrinsic cause, they cannot be the soul's own *acts;* and that the soul cannot be *active*, but must be wholly *passive*, in those effects of which it is the subject necessarily, and not from its own free determination.

Mr. Chubb lays the foundation of his scheme of Liberty, and of his arguments to support it, very much in this position, that *man is an Agent, and capable of Action.* Which doubtless is true: but *self-determination* belongs to his notion of *Action*, and is the very essence of it. Whence he infers, that it is impossible for a man to act and be acted upon, in the same thing, at the same time; and that no Action can be the effect of the Action of another: and he insists, that a *necessary Agent*, or an Agent that is necessarily determined to act, is a *plain contradiction.*†

But those are a precarious sort of demonstrations, which men build on the meaning that they arbitrarily affix to a

* Scrip. Doc. of *Original Sin*, p. 180. 3d Edit.

† Were the human mind, indeed, not the subject of either passive power, on the one hand, as the predisposing cause of vice; or of divine holy influence, on the other, as the predisposing cause of real virtue; and were the *determining motive* what some have represented it to be, the *object itself*, irrespective of the changeable state of the mind perceiving it; the objection, that "a necessary agent is a plain contradiction," or, in other words, that man is *no proper agent*, would be unanswerable. For the rank and place of man in creation, and his relative circumstances in the arrangement of providence, being the result of decretive appointment, if he himself were not liable to any change but by the same appointment, it would follow, that if the objects themselves determined him to choose, and to choose always according to the strongest motive, his very volitions in the acts themselves would be *necessitated decretively*, to the exclusion of all *hypothetical* or moral *possibility* of failure; and therefore could never be erroneous, any more than the first cause could act erroneously. On such principles, moral evil, vice or fault, could have no existence. No *effect* could be otherwise than good, amiable, and perfectly innocent; a moral possibility of failure being excluded by natural necessity. For the *volition itself* to be *so* necessitated, and not in a moral or hypothetical manner only, is the same thing as giving it no opportunity of choice or preference, or *constraining* it to choose one way by a *settled purpose*, with a natural impossibility of acting otherwise. But if every act of man be *thus* the result of settled purpose, why should he be *blamed* for any one act whatever? He does nothing but what he is constrained, or decretively necessitated to perform, the contrary being rendered naturally impossible; and if he deserves no *praise*, he can incur no blame, any more than a clock for not keeping time. *Such* a *necessary agent* would be indeed a *plain contradiction*. There is much reason to apprehend that some *philosophical necessarians* have no better notion of *agency* than that which Mr. Chubb charges, and justly charges, with "a plain contradiction." For those who hold the sentiment, that *every act*, even as to its *moral* quality, and every event, are of *decretive* appointment, in subserviency to ultimate good, must allow, in order to be tolerably consistent, that the Supreme Being is "the only proper agent in the universe;"‡ and thus reduce *human agency*, and things else called agency in a creature, to *an appointed necessary choice*, however odious in its nature, mischievous in its tendency, or painful in experience. Thus, according to them, God is the *only proper agent* in all foul crimes and horrid blasphemies, on earth and in hell! They have a right to define their terms, and to say what they mean by *agency* in God, or in a creature, and to state their hypothesis accordingly; but others also have a right to deduce the genuine consequences of that hypothesis, and to show wherein its error lies.—The design of these notes is not to excite a spirit of unprofitable controversy, but to assist the serious inquirer in detecting errors and recognizing truths of radical importance in ethics and theology; and, it is hoped, that to promote these ends the following observations may conduce.

1. It is granted, that in reference to *natural acts*, the Supreme Being is the "only proper agent in the universe," as they all spring from his energy. In this respect he is the first cause of all causes, *efficiently;* and the description of the poet is philosophically just: he

"Warms in the sun, refreshes in the breeze,
Glows in the stars, and blossoms in the trees,
Lives through all life, extends through all extent,
Spreads undivided, operates unspent." Pope.

2. It is also granted, that, in all acts *morally good*, the created agent is the subject of *necessity* several ways. He has an active *nature* from decretive necessity, which it is not in his power to alter. He is also, accordingly, *compelled* to *some* act of choice, from the activity of his nature. He is, moreover, the *subject* of physical influence of a holy and purifying nature, whereby the goodness of his choice is infallibly secured; and with-

‡ Belsham's Elements of the Philosophy of the Mind, p. 254.

word; especially when that meaning is abstruse, inconsistent, and entirely diverse from the original sense of the word in common speech.

That the meaning of the word *Action*, as Mr. Chubb and many others use it, is utterly unintelligible and inconsistent, is manifest, because it belongs to their notion of an Action, that it is something wherein is no passion or passiveness; that is, (according to their sense of passiveness,) it is under the power, influence, or Action of no cause. And this implies, that Action has no cause, and is no effect; for to be an effect implies *passiveness*, or the being subject to the power and Action of its cause. And yet they hold, that the mind's *Action* is the effect of its own determination, yea, the mind's free and voluntary determination; which is the same with free choice. So that Action is the effect of something preceding, even a preceding act of choice: and consequently, in this effect the mind is passive, subject to the power and Action of the preceding cause, which is the foregoing choice, and therefore cannot be active. So that here we have this contradiction, that Action is always the effect of foregoing choice; and therefore cannot be Action; because it is *passive* to the power of that preceding causal choice; and the mind cannot be active and passive in the same thing, at the same time. Again they say, necessity is utterly inconsistent with Action, and a necessary Action is a contradiction; and so their notion of Action implies contingence, and excludes all necessity. And therefore, their notion of Action implies, that it has no necessary dependence on, or connexion with, any thing foregoing; for such a dependence or connexion excludes contingence, and implies necessity. And yet their notion of Action implies necessity, and supposes that it is necessary, and cannot be contingent. For they suppose, that whatever is properly called Action, must be determined by the Will and free choice; and this is as much as to say, that it must be necessary, being dependent upon, and determined by, something foregoing; namely, a foregoing act of choice. Again, it belongs to their notion of Action, that it is the beginning of motion, or of exertion of power; but yet it is implied in their notion of Action, that it is not the beginning of motion or exertion of power, but is consequent and dependent on a preceding exertion of power, *viz.* the power of Will and choice: for they say there is no proper Action but what is freely *chosen*; or, which is the same thing, determined by a foregoing act of free choice. But if any of them shall see cause to deny this, and say they hold no such thing as that every Action is chosen or determined by a foregoing choice; but that the very first exertion of Will only, undetermined by any preceding act, is properly called Action; then I say, such a man's notion of Action implies necessity; for what the mind is the subject of, without the determination of its own previous choice, it is the subject of necessarily, as to any hand that free choice has in the affair; and without any ability the mind has to prevent it, by any will or election of its own; because by the supposition it precludes all previous acts of the Will or choice in the case, which might prevent it. So that it is again, in this other way, implied in their notion of act, that it is both necessary and not necessary. Again it belongs to their notion of an *act*, that it is no effect of a predetermining bias or preponderation, but springs immediately out of indifference; and this implies, that it cannot be from foregoing choice, which is foregoing preponderation: if it be not habitual, but occasional, yet if it causes the act, it is truly previous, efficacious, and determining. And yet, at the same time, it is essential to their notion of the act, that it is what the agent is the author of freely and voluntarily, and that is, by previous choice and design.

So that, according to their notion of the act, considered with regard to its consequences, these following things are all essential to it; *viz.* That it should be necessary, and not necessary; that it should be from a cause, and no cause; that it should be the fruit of choice and design, and not the fruit of choice and design; that it should be the beginning of motion or exertion, and yet consequent on previous exertion; that it should be before it is; that it should spring immediately out of indifference and equilibrium, and yet be the effect of preponderation; that it should be self-originated, and also have its original from

out which there could be no assignable ground of *certainty* that any action would be morally good. There is also a necessity of connexion, arising from the nature of things, or the essence of truth, *first* between the disposition and the act, or that the act will be of the same nature, morally considered, with the disposition from which it proceeds; and, *secondly*, between the act and the end, or consequent, which is happiness.

3. It is moreover allowed, that in all acts *morally evil*, the soul is *passive* in reference to that *necessity* of dependence which is inseparable from a created nature, which may be called *passive power;* without which the existence of moral evil would be impossible. This necessity also arises from the nature of things, not from decree; for no decree can alter its existence, (though it may, and actually does, counteract it,) any more than it can alter the state of a creature from dependence into independence on the first cause. A creature without passive power involves the most palpable absurdities. For its very definition is, "*that* property in a creature whereby it differs essentially from the *independence*, *self-sufficience*, and *indefectibility* of the Creator;" and to deny it, is to suppose that a creature may be independent, self-sufficient, and indefectible—that in these respects the creature and the Creator are on a par—that a necessary and a contingent being are the same, in those very things which constitute their essential difference! Were it not for this property in an agent, he could never *sin;* for all his acts would be *physically necessary*, without any *hypothetical* medium, or moral alternative.

4. *He* is a moral agent, whose volitions might have been otherwise than they are, *if* the motives, and consequently the *state of his mind*, had been otherwise. But to suppose that his volitions might have been otherwise than they are, the motives and state of the mind being the same, would be to make him in his volitions the sport of chance, or a mere non-entity.

5. *He* then is a moral agent who has, in reference to volition, a *moral alternative*, or a hypothetical possibility of a different choice. Where this alternative, or this possibility, is not, there the agent (if he may be so called) is not morally obliged, and therefore is not accountable.

6. But if so, where does the *ground* of such an alternative lie? It lies in the agent's *mind*, or the *disposition* whence the volition springs, and whence its character is derived. *If* God influence the mind so as to make it, in a given degree, to resemble his own moral nature; in that degree would the choice made be morally good. But *if* passive power be not counteracted by such influence, (which being *gracious*, God is not bound in *equity* to do,) in any given degree, the nature of things, the essence of truth; connects, in a corresponding degree, the state of mind with the volition.

7. Hence it is plain, that *moral influence*, as such, effects nothing certain; but always requires a previous state of mind, in order to insure a certainty of *good* effect; and that previous state of mind is effected by no other possible means but a *physical* energy or agency, producing assimilation. There must be a virtuous mind before a virtuous choice; the quality of the act is derived from the agent.

8. One thing, which has been a source of much obscurity and confusion in reference to moral agency, is the supposition that the mind is *equally free*, in *all* respects, when choosing good and when choosing evil; in other words, that the one volition and the other becomes morally certain, from the *same sort* of necessity. But this is not the real case. Indeed the necessity of *connexion* between the previous state of the mind and the corresponding volition, is the same; for it is, in each case, nothing else but the nature of things; but *that necessity* which effects a state of mind previous to good volitions, is as different from the *other necessity* which effects a state of mind previous to volitions morally evil, as light is from darkness. They proceed from opposite quarters, and operate in contrary directions. A holy disposition is generated by decretive holy influence; the other disposition (which ought not however to be called *unholy)* proceeds from the hypothetical nature of things. Such a disposition, though not morally vicious, yet generates vice in union with free agency.

9. It is highly worthy of remark, that though a good volition must proceed from a good heart, morally considered; yet a bad *volition* does not, *originally* and necessarily, proceed from a *morally* bad heart. The reason is, that the one state of heart proceeds from God, from his decretive holy will; the other proceeds from passive power, which is only a *natural* evil, and not a moral. Besides, were the disposition which immediately precedes a bad volition necessarily, or in every case, evil, in a moral sense, either moral evil could have no place at all in the universe, no origin whatever, or else it must be the same as passive power. But passive power is a contrast, not to the *moral* perfections of God, but his *natural;* and has, when alone, no *moral* quality. And, seeing it belongs as a property to every creature, as such, were it any thing morally evil, moral evil would be essential to the very being of every creature; which is absurd.

10. Hence it is plain, that freedom is experienced in a higher sense, or a greater degree, in bad volitions, than in good ones; in such a sense, and to such a degree, as to justify this mode of expression. That man is necessitated to good, but free to evil. This however may need some explanatory qualification; for he is not so necessitated to good, as not to be morally or hypothetically free; nor so free to evil as not to be subject to a necessity of consequence. He who *acts* or *chooses amiss* without constraint, compulsion, or interfering voluntary force in that act, notwithstanding his passive power, is *properly* a *free agent;* for in the moral quality of the act, there is properly and strictly no *will* concerned but his *own.* But he who *acts* or *chooses aright*, is subject to a physical, decretive necessity, as to his disposition and a physical concourse of divine energy in the natural act of the will. He is indeed *morally* free, inasmuch as his volition *might have been of a different*, yea, of an opposite *moral* quality, *if* the state of his mind had been different. Hence it is evident, that in a *good will*, choice, or act, man is an agent in a less proper or secondary sense; but in a *bad will*, choice, or act, man is an *agent*, a *moral* agent, a *free* agent, in the most proper and strict sense. And in the production of an act morally good *two wills* are concerned, that of the agent, and the decretive will of God; in that of evil, only one, the agent's own will.

11. If the Supreme Being is the only proper agent in the universe, either *moral* agency is no *proper* agency, or else man is not a moral agent; and if so, he is not accountable, and has no concern in religion or morals. Besides, if God be the only proper agent in the universe, how come there to exist *evil deeds?* God's agency is *good*, else we have no evidence that he is a good being; but there are in the world *evil deeds* proceeding from *evil minds*, which common sense and universal consent allow, and the nature of the thing proves, to be properly *evil agencies;* consequently man is an *agent*, a *moral agent*, properly so called.

12. If there be no proper agent in the universe but the Supreme Being, there is no evil in the *nature* of bad volitions, but only in their *effects*. Sin, on that supposition, is not bad in its own nature, but only injurious in its effects on the sinner. Sin is not to be *hated*, it seems, on its own account, as odious, but only *shunned* as dangerous. But as this must arise, according to the system of its abettors, from a sovereign *appointment*, it follows, that millions of beings are *by this very appointment*, doomed to the *greatest sufferings* in the universe, for that in which they had no *proper agency*—no *possible* alternative! Where is equity, or benevolence?

13. The only clue out of this labyrinth, and out of many others formed by writers on human agency, is, we are fully persuaded, a right view of *passive power*, in its nature, origin, and tendency, in conjunction with a morally or hypothetically *free choice*. W.

something else; that it is what the mind causes itself, of its own will, and can produce or prevent, according to its choice or pleasure, and yet what the mind has no power to prevent, precluding all previous choice in the affair.

So that an act according to their metaphysical notion of it, is something of which there is no idea; it is nothing but a confusion of the mind, excited by words without any distinct meaning, and is an absolute non-entity; and that in two respects: (1.) There is nothing in the world that ever was, is, or can be, to answer the things which must belong to its description, according to what they suppose to be essential to it. And, (2.) There neither is, nor ever was, nor can be, any notion or idea to answer the word, as they use and explain it. For if we should suppose any such notion, it would many ways destroy itself. But it is impossible any idea or notion should subsist in the mind, whose very nature and essence, which constitutes it, destroys it.—If some learned philosopher, who had been abroad, in giving an account of the curious observations he had made in his travels, should say, "He had been in *Terra del Fuego*, and there had seen an animal, which he calls by a certain name, that begat and brought forth itself, and yet had a sire and dam distinct from itself; that it had an appetite, and was hungry before it had a being; that his master, who led him, and governed him at his pleasure, was always governed by him, and driven by him where he pleased; that when he moved, he always took a step before the first step; that he went with his head first, and yet always went tail foremost; and this, though he had neither head nor tail:" it would be no impudence at all, to tell such a traveller, though a learned man, that he himself had no idea of such an animal as he gave an account of, and never had, nor ever would have.

As the forementioned notion of Action is very inconsistent, so it is wholly diverse from the original meaning of the word. The more usual signification of it, in vulgar speech, seems to be some *motion* or *exertion of power*, that is voluntary, or that is *the effect of the Will;* and is used in the same sense as *doing:* and most commonly it is used to signify *outward Actions.* So *thinking* is often distinguished from *acting;* and *desiring* and *willing*, from *doing.*

Besides this more usual and proper signification of the word *Action*, there are other ways in which the word is used, that are less proper, which yet have place in common speech. Oftentimes it is used to signify some motion or alteration in inanimate things, with relation to some object and effect. So the spring of a watch is said to *act* upon the chain and wheels; the sun-beams, to act upon plants and trees: and the fire, to act upon wood. Sometimes, the word is used to signify motions, alterations, and exertions of power, which are seen in corporeal things, *considered absolutely;* especially when these motions seem to arise from some internal cause which is *hidden;* so that they have a greater resemblance of those motions of our bodies, which are the effects of natural volition, or invisible exertions of Will. So the fermentation of liquor, the operations of the loadstone, and of electrical bodies, are called the *Action* of these things. And sometimes the word *Action* is used to signify the exercise of thought, or of Will and inclination: so meditating, loving, hating, inclining, disinclining, choosing, and refusing, may be sometimes called acting; though more rarely (unless it be by philosophers and metaphysicians) than in any of the other senses.

But the word is never used in vulgar speech for the self-determinate exercise of the Will, or an exertion of the soul that arises without any necessary connexion with any thing foregoing. If a man does something voluntarily, or as the effect of his choice, then in the most proper sense, and as the word is most originally and commonly used, he is said to *act;* but whether that choice or volition be self-determined, or no, whether it be connected with a foregoing habitual bias, whether it be the certain effect of the strongest motive, or some intrinsic cause, never comes into consideration in the meaning of the word.

And if the word *Action* is arbitrarily used by some men otherwise, to suit some scheme of metaphysics or morality, no argument can reasonably be founded on such an use of this term, to prove any thing but their own pleasure. For divines and philosophers strenuously to urge such arguments, as though they were sufficient to support and demonstrate a whole scheme of moral philosophy and divinity, is certainly to erect a mighty edifice on the sand, or rather on a shadow. And though it may now perhaps, through custom, have become natural for them to use the word in this sense, (if that may be called a sense or meaning, which is inconsistent with itself,) yet this does not prove, that it is agreeable to the natural notions men have of things, or that there can be any thing in the creation that should answer such a meaning. And though they appeal to experience, yet the truth is, that men are so far from experiencing any such thing, that it is impossible for them to have any conception of it.

If it should be objected, that *Action* and *Passion* are doubtless words of a contrary signification; but to suppose that the agent, in its Action, is under the power and influence of something intrinsic, is to confound Action and passion, and make them the same thing.

I answer, that Action and Passion are doubtless, as they are sometimes used, words of opposite signification; but not as signifying opposite *existences*, but only opposite *relations.* The words *cause* and *effect* are terms of opposite signification; but, nevertheless, if I assert, that the same thing may, at the same time, in different respects and relations, be both *cause* and *effect*, this will not prove that I confound the terms. The soul may be both *active* and *passive* in the same thing in different respects; *active* with relation to one thing, and *passive* with relation to another.* The word *Passion*, when set in opposition to *Action*, or rather *activeness*, is merely a relative: it signifies no effect or cause, nor any proper existence; but is the same with *Passiveness*, or a being passive, or a being acted upon by some thing. Which is a mere relation of a thing to some power or force exerted by some cause, producing some effect in it, or upon it. And *Action*, when set properly in opposition to *Passion*, or *Passiveness*, is no real existence; it is not the same with *AN Action*, but is a mere relation: it is the *activeness* of something on another thing, being the opposite relation to the other, *viz.* a relation of power, or force, exerted by some cause, towards another thing, which is the subject of the effect of that power. Indeed, the word *Action* is frequently used to signify something not merely *relative*, but more *absolute*, and a real existence; as when we say *an Action;* when the word is not used transitively, but absolutely, for some motion or exercise of body or mind, without any relation to any object or effect: and as used thus, it is not properly the opposite of *Passion;* which ordinarily signifies nothing absolute, but merely the *relation* of *being acted upon.* And therefore if the word *Action* be used in the like relative sense, then Action and Passion are only two contrary relations. And it is no absurdity to suppose, that contrary relations may belong to the same thing at the same time, with respect to different things. So to suppose, that there are acts of the soul by which a man voluntarily moves, and acts upon objects, and produces effects, which yet themselves are effects of something else, and wherein the soul itself is the object of something acting upon, and influencing that, do not at all confound Action and Passion. The words may neverless be properly of opposite signification: there may be as true and real a difference between *acting* and being *caused to act*, though we should suppose the soul to be both in the same volition, as there is between *living* and *being quickened*, or *made to live.* It is no more a contradiction, to suppose that Action may be the effect of some other cause, besides the agent, or being that acts, than to suppose, that life may be the effect of some other cause, besides the being that lives.

What has led men into this inconsistent notion of Action, when applied to volition—as though it were essen-

* This distinction is of considerable moment. The soul is *passive*, for instance, in reference to that *necessity of dependence* which is inseparable from a created nature; and when the subject of ***providential energy*** in natural acts; and also when the subject of that *divine influence* which purifies and enables the mind, and whereby holy effects are secured; and in all these respects it is *passive* at the very time that it is *active* in its choice or preference. In other words, the mind is *necessitated* in some respects; as, to exist, to think, to will, to suffer, or to enjoy; at the same instant that it is *free* in other respects, as, from contingence, (understanding thereby an event without any cause,) and from compulsion, or *physical* necessity in its acts as *moral.*—W.

tial to this internal Action, that the agent should be self-determined in it, and that the Will should be the cause of it—was probably this; that according to the sense of mankind, and the common use of language, it is so, with respect to men's *external* Actions; which originally, and according to the vulgar use and most proper sense of the word, are called *Actions*. Men in these are self-directed, self-determined, and their Wills are the cause of the motions of their bodies, and external things done; so that unless men do them voluntarily, and of choice, and the Action be determined by their antecedent volition, it is no Action or doing of theirs. Hence some metaphysicians have been led unwarily, but exceeding absurdly, to suppose the same concerning volition itself, that *that* also must be determined by the Will; which is to be determined by antecedent volition, as the motion of the body is; not considering the contradiction it implies.

But it is very evident, that in the metaphysical distinction between Action and passion (though long since become common and in general vogue) due care has not been taken to conform language to the nature of things, or to any distinct clear ideas. As it is in innumerable other philosophical metaphysical terms, used in these disputes; which has occasioned inexpressible difficulty, contention, error, and confusion.

And thus probably it came to be thought, that necessity was inconsistent with Action, as these terms are applied to volition. First, these terms *Action* and *necessity* are changed from their original meaning, as signifying external voluntary Action and constraint (in which meaning they are evidently inconsistent) to signify quite other things, *viz. volition* itself, and *certainty* of existence. And when the change of signification is made, care is not taken to make proper allowances and abatements for the difference of sense; but still the same things are unwarily attributed to *Action* and *necessity*, in the new meaning of the words, which plainly belonged to them in their first sense; and on this ground, maxims are established without any real foundation, as though they were the most certain truths, and the most evident dictates of reason.

But however strenuously it is maintained, that what is necessary cannot be properly called Action, and that a necessary Action is a contradiction, yet it is probable there are few *Arminian* divines, who thoroughly tried, would stand to these principles. They will allow, that God is, in the highest sense, an active Being, and the highest Fountain of life and Action; and they would not probably deny, that what are called God's acts of righteousness, holiness, and faithfulness, are truly and properly God's *acts*, and God is really a holy *Agent* in them; and yet, I trust, they will not deny, that God necessarily acts justly and faithfully, and that it is impossible for him to act unrighteously and unholily.

SECT. III.

The reasons why some think it contrary to common Sense, to suppose those things which are necessary to be worthy of either Praise or Blame.

It is abundantly affirmed and urged by *Arminian* writers, that it is contrary to *common Sense*, and the natural notions and apprehensions of mankind, to suppose otherwise than that necessity (making no distinction between natural and moral necessity) is inconsistent with Virtue and Vice, Praise and Blame, Reward and Punishment. And their arguments from hence have been greatly triumphed in; and have been not a little perplexing to many, who have been friendly to the truth, as clearly revealed in the Holy Scriptures: it has seemed to them indeed difficult, to reconcile *Calvinistic* doctrines with the notions men commonly have of justice and equity. The true reasons of it seem to be the following:

I. It is indeed a very plain dictate of common Sense, that *natural* necessity is wholly inconsistent with just Praise or Blame. If men do things which in themselves are very good, fit to be brought to pass, and attended with very happy effects, properly *against* their Wills; or do them from a necessity that is *without* their Wills, or with which their Wills have no concern or connexion; then it is a plain dictate of common Sense, that such doings are none of their virtue, nor have they any moral good in them; and that the persons are not worthy to be rewarded or praised; or at all esteemed, honoured, or loved, on that account. And, on the other hand, that if, from like necessity, they do those things which in themselves are very unhappy and pernicious, and do them because they cannot help it; the necessity is such, that it is all one whether they will them, or no; and the reason why they are done, is from necessity only, and not from their Wills; it is a very plain dictate of common Sense, that they are not at all to blame; there is no vice, fault, or moral evil at all in the effect done; nor are they, who are thus necessitated, in any wise worthy to be punished, hated, or in the least disrespected, on that account.

In like manner, if things in themselves good and desirable are absolutely impossible, with a *natural* impossibility, the universal reason of mankind teaches, that this *wholly and perfectly* excuses persons in their not doing them.

And it is also a plain dictate of common Sense, that if doing things, in themselves good, or avoiding things in themselves evil, is not *absolutely impossible*, with such a natural impossibility, but very *difficult*, with a natural difficulty; that is, a difficulty prior *to*, and not at all consisting *in*, Will and inclination itself, and which would remain the same, let the inclination be what it will; then a person's neglect or omission is excused *in some measure*, though not wholly; his sin is less aggravated, than if the thing to be done were easy. And if instead of difficulty and hinderance, there be a contrary natural propensity in the state of things, to the thing to be done, or effect to be brought to pass, abstracted from any consideration of the inclination of the heart; though the propensity be not so great as to amount to a natural necessity; yet being some approach to it, so that the doing of the good thing be very much from this natural tendency in the state of things, and but little from a good inclination; then it is a dictate of common Sense, that there is so much the less virtue in what is done; and so it is less praiseworthy and rewardable. The reason is easy, *viz.* because such a natural propensity or tendency is an approach to natural necessity; and the greater the propensity, still so much the nearer is the approach to necessity. And, therefore, as natural necessity takes away or shuts out *all* virtue, so this propensity approaches to an abolition of virtue; that is, it *diminishes* it. And on the other hand, natural difficulty, in the state of things, is an approach to natural impossibility. And as the latter, when it is complete and absolute, *wholly* takes away Blame; so such difficulty takes away *some* Blame, or diminishes Blame; and makes the thing done to be less worthy of punishment.

II. Men, in their first use of such phrases as these, *must, cannot, cannot help it, cannot avoid it, necessary, unable, impossible, unavoidable, irresistible, &c.* use them to signify a necessity of constraint or restraint, a natural necessity or impossibility; or some necessity that the Will has nothing to do in; which may be, whether men will or no; and which may be supposed to be just the same, let men's inclinations and desires be what they will. Such kind of terms in their original use, I suppose among all nations, are relative; carrying in their signification (as was before observed) a reference or respect to some contrary Will, desire, or endeavour, which, it is supposed, is, or may be, in the case. All men find, and begin to find in early childhood, that there are innumerable things that cannot be done, which they desire to do; and innumerable things, which they are averse to, that must be, they cannot avoid them, they will be, whether they choose them or no. It is to express this necessity, which men so soon and so often find, and which so greatly and early affects them in innumerable cases, that such terms and phrases are first formed; and it is to signify such a necessity, that they are first used, and that they are most constantly used, in the common affairs of life; and not to signify any such metaphysical, speculative, and abstract notion, as that connexion in the nature or course of things, which is between the subject and predicative of a proposition, and which is the foundation of the certain truth of that proposition; to signify which, they who employ themselves in philosophical inquiries into the first origin and metaphysical relations and dependences of things, have borrowed these terms, for want of others. But we grow up from our cradles in the use of terms and phrases entirely different from this, and carrying a sense exceeding diverse from that in which they are commonly used in the controversy between *Arminians* and *Calvinists*. And it being, as was said before, a dictate of the universal sense of mankind, evident to us as soon as we begin to think, that the necessity signified by these terms, in the sense in which we first learn them, does excuse persons, and free them from all Fault or Blame; hence our ideas of excusableness or faultlessness is tied to these terms and phrases by a strong habit, which is begun in childhood, as soon as we begin to speak, and grows up with us, and is strengthened by constant use and custom, the connexion growing stronger and stronger.

The habitual connexion, which is in men's minds between Blamelessness and those forementioned terms, *must, cannot, unable, necessary, impossible, unavoidable, &c.* becomes very strong, because, as soon as ever men begin to use reason and speech, they have occasion to excuse themselves, from the natural necessity signified by these terms, in numerous instances.—*I cannot do it—I could not help it.*—And all mankind have constant and daily occasion to use such phrases in this sense, to excuse themselves and others, in almost all the concerns of life, with respect to disappointments, and things that happen, which concern and affect ourselves and others, that are hurtful, or disagreeable to us or them, or things desirable, that we or others fail to obtain.

That our being accustomed to an union of different ideas, from early childhood, makes the habitual connexion exceeding strong, as though such connexion were owing to *nature*, is manifest in innumerable instances. It is altogether by such an habitual connexion of ideas, that men judge of the bigness or distance of the objects of sight, from their appearance. Thus it is owing to such a connexion early established, and growing up with a person, that he judges a mountain, which he sees at ten miles distance, to be bigger than his nose, or further off than the end of it. Having been used so long to join a considerable distance and magnitude with such an appearance, men imagine it is by a dictate of natural sense: whereas, it would be quite otherwise with one that had his eyes newly opened, who had been born blind: he would have the same visible appearance, but natural sense would dictate no such thing, concerning the magnitude or distance of what appeared.

III. When men, after they had been so habituated to connect ideas of Innocency or Blamelessness with such terms, that the union seems to be the effect of mere nature, come to hear the same terms used, and learn to use them in the forementioned new and metaphysical sense, to signify quite another sort of necessity, which has no such kind of relation to a contrary supposable Will and endeavour; the notion of plain and manifest Blamelessness, by this means, is, by a strong prejudice, insensibly and unwarily transferred to a case to which it by no means belongs: the change of the use of the terms, to a signification which is very diverse, not being taken notice of, or adverted to. And there are several reasons why it is not.

1. The terms, as used by philosophers, are not very distinct and clear in their meaning: few use them in a fixed determinate sense. On the contrary, their meaning is very vague and confused. Which commonly happens to the words used to signify things intellectual and moral, and to express what Mr. Locke calls *mixt modes*. If men had a clear and distinct understanding of what is intended by these metaphysical terms, they would be able more easily to compare them with their original and common sense; and so would not be easily led into delusion by words of this sort.

2. The change of the signification of terms is the more insensible, because the things signified, though indeed very different, yet do in some generals agree. In *necessity*, that which is *vulgarly* so called, there is a strong connexion between the thing said to be necessary, and something antecedent to it, in the order of nature; so there is also a *philosophical necessity*. And though in both kinds of necessity, the connexion cannot be called by that name, with relation to an opposite Will or endeavour, to which it is *superior;* which is the case in vulgar necessity; yet in both, the connexion is *prior* to Will and endeavour, and so, in some respect, *superior*. In both kinds of necessity, there is a foundation for some certainty of the proposition, that affirms the event.—The terms used being the same, and the things signified agreeing in these and some other general circumstances, and the expressions as used by philosophers being not well defined, and so of obscure and loose signification; hence persons are not aware of the great difference; the notions of innocence or faultiness, which were so strongly associated with them, and were strictly united in their minds, ever since they can remember, remain united with them still, as if the union were altogether natural and necessary; and they that go about to make a separation, seem to them to do great violence even to nature itself.

IV. Another reason why it appears difficult to reconcile it with reason, that men should be blamed for that which is necessary, with a moral necessity, (which, as was observed before, is a species of philosophical necessity) is, that for want of due consideration, men inwardly entertain that apprehension, that this necessity may be against men's Wills and sincere endeavours. They go away with that notion, that men may truly will, and wish, and strive that it may be otherwise; but that invincible necessity stands in the way. And many think thus concerning themselves: some wicked men think they wish that they were good, and that they loved God and holiness; but yet do not find that their wishes produce the effect.—The reasons why men think thus, are as follow:

1. They find what may be called an *indirect willingness* to have a better Will, in the manner before observed. For it is impossible, and a contradiction to suppose the Will to be directly and properly against itself. And they do not consider that this indirect willingness is entirely a different thing from properly willing what is the duty and virtue required; and that there is no virtue in that sort of willingness which they have. They do not consider, that the volitions, which a wicked man may have that he loved God, are no acts of the Will at all against the moral evil of not loving God; but only some disagreeable consequences. But the making of the requisite distinction requires more care of reflection and thought, than most men are used to. And men, through a prejudice in their own favour, are disposed to think well of their own desires and dispositions, and to account them good and virtuous, though their respect to virtue be only *indirect* and *remote*, and it is nothing at all virtuous that truly excites or terminates their inclinations.

2. Another thing that insensibly leads and beguiles men into a supposition that this moral necessity or impossibility is, or may be, against men's Wills and true endeavours, is the derivation of the terms often used to express it. Such words for instance, as *unable, unavoidable, impossible, irresistible;* which carry a plain reference to a supposable power exerted, endeavours used, resistance made, in opposition to the necessity: and the persons that hear them, not considering, nor suspecting, but that they are used in their proper sense: that sense being therefore understood, there does naturally, and as it were necessarily, arise in their minds a supposition, that it may be so indeed, that true desires and endeavours may take place, but that invincible necessity stands in the way, and renders them vain and to no effect.

V. Another thing which makes persons more ready to suppose it to be contrary to reason, that men should be exposed to the punishments threatened to sin, for doing those things which are morally necessary, or not doing those things which are morally impossible, is, that imagination strengthens the argument, and adds greatly to the power and influence of the seeming reasons against it, from the greatness of that punishment. To allow that they may be justly exposed to a small punishment, would not be so difficult. Whereas, if there were any good reason in the case, if it were truly a dictate of reason, that such necessity was inconsistent with faultiness, or just punishment, the demonstration would be equally certain with respect to a small punishment, or any punishment at all, as a very great one: but it is not equally easy to the imagination. They that argue against the justice of *damning* men for those things that are thus necessary, seem to make their argument the stronger, by setting forth the greatness of the punishment in strong expressions:—"That a man should be cast into eternal burnings, that he should be made to fry in hell to all eternity, for those things which he had no power to avoid, and was under a fatal, unfrustrable, invincible necessity of doing," &c.

SECT. IV.

It is agreeable to common sense, and the natural notions of mankind, to suppose moral Necessity to be consistent with Praise and Blame, Reward and Punishment.

WHETHER the reasons, that have been given, why it appears difficult to some persons, to reconcile with common sense the praising or blaming, rewarding or punishing, those things which are morally necessary, are thought satisfactory, or not; yet it most evidently appears, by the following things, that if this matter be rightly understood, setting aside all delusion arising from the impropriety and ambiguity of terms, this is not at all inconsistent with the natural apprehensions of mankind, and that sense of things which is found every where in the common people; who are furthest from having their thoughts perverted from their natural channel, by metaphysical and philosophical subtilties; but, on the contrary, altogether agreeable *to*, and the very voice and dictate *of*, this natural and vulgar sense.

I. This will appear, if we consider what the vulgar notion of *blameworthiness* is. The idea which the common people, through all ages and nations, have of faultiness, I suppose to be plainly this; *a person being or doing wrong, with his own will and pleasure;* containing these two things: 1. *His doing wrong, when he does as he pleases.* 2. *His pleasure being wrong.* Or, in other words, perhaps more intelligibly expressing their notion; *a person having his heart wrong, and doing wrong from his heart.* And this is the sum total of the matter.

The common people do not ascend up in their reflections and abstractions to the metaphysical sources, relations, and dependences of things, in order to form their notion of faultiness or blameworthiness. They do not wait till they have decided by their refinings, what first determines the Will; whether it be determined by something extrinsic, or intrinsic; whether volition determines volition, or whether the understanding determines the Will; whether there be any such thing as metaphysicians mean by contingence (if they have any meaning); whether there be a sort of a strange unaccountable sovereignty in the Will, in the exercise of which, by its own sovereign acts, it brings to pass all its own sovereign acts. They do not take any part of their notion of Fault or Blame from the resolution of any such questions. If this were the case, there are multitudes, yea the far greater part of mankind, nine hundred and ninety-nine out of a thousand, would live and die, without having any such notion, as that of Fault, ever entering into their heads, or without so much as once having any conception that any body was to be either blamed or commended for any thing. If this were the case, it would be a long time before men came to have such notions. Whereas it is manifest, they are in fact some of the first notions that appear in children; who discover, as soon as they can think, or speak, or act at all as rational creatures, a sense of desert. And, certainly, in forming their notion of it, they make no use of metaphysics. All the ground they go upon, consists in these two things: *experience* and a *natural sensation* of a certain fitness or agreeableness, which there is in uniting such moral evil as is above described, *viz. a being or doing wrong with the Will*, and resentment in others, and pain inflicted on the person in whom this moral evil is. Which *natural sense* is what we call by the name of *conscience.*

It is true, the common people and children, in their notion of any faulty act or deed, of any person, do suppose that it is the person's *own act and deed.* But this is all that belongs to what they understand by a thing being a person's *own deed or action;* even that it is something done by him of *choice.* That some exercise or motion should begin of itself, does not belong to their notion of *an action*, or *doing.* If so, it would belong to their notion of it, that it is the cause of its own beginning: and that is as much as to say, that it is before it begins to be. Nor is their notion of *an action* some motion or exercise, that begins accidentally, without any cause or reason; for that is contrary to one of the prime dictates of common sense, namely, that every thing that begins to be, has some cause or reason why it is.

The common people, in their notion of a faulty or praiseworthy work done by any one, do suppose, that the man does it in the exercise of *liberty.* But then their notion of liberty is only a person having opportunity of doing as he pleases. They have no notion of liberty consisting in the Will first acting, and so causing its own acts; determining, and so causing its own determinations; or choosing, and so causing its own choice. Such a notion of liberty is what none have, but those that have darkened their own minds with confused metaphysical speculation, and abstruse and ambiguous terms. If a man is not restrained from acting as his Will determines, or constrained to act otherwise; then he has liberty, according to common notions of liberty, without taking into the idea that grand contradiction of all, the determinations of a man's free Will being the effects of the determinations of his free Will.—Nor have men commonly any notion of freedom consisting in indifference. For if so, then it would be agreeable to their notion, that the greater indifference men act with, the more freedom they act with; whereas, the reverse is true. He that in acting proceeds with the fullest inclination, does what he does with the greatest freedom, according to common sense. And so far is it from being agreeable to common sense, that such liberty as consists in indifference is requisite to Praise or Blame, that, on the contrary, the dictate of every man's natural sense through the world is, that the further he is from being indifferent in his acting good or evil, and the more he does either with full and strong inclination, the more is he esteemed or abhorred, commended or condemned.

II. If it were inconsistent with the common sense of mankind, that men should be either blamed or commended in any volitions, in case of moral Necessity or impossibility; then it would surely also be agreeable to the same sense and reason of mankind, that the nearer the case approaches to such a moral Necessity or impossibility—either through a strong antecedent moral propensity, on the one hand,* or a great antecedent opposition and difficulty, on the other—the nearer does it approach to a person being neither blamable nor commendable; so that acts exerted with such preceding propensity, would be worthy of proportionably less Praise; and when omitted, the act being attended with such difficulty, the omission would be worthy of the less Blame. It is so, as was observed before, with natural Necessity and impossibility, propensity and difficulty: as it is a plain dictate of the sense of all mankind, that natural Necessity and impossibility take away *all* Blame and Praise; and therefore, that the nearer the approach is to these, through previous propensity or difficulty, so Praise and Blame are proportionably *diminished.* And if it were as much a dictate of common sense, that moral Necessity of doing, or impossibility of avoiding, takes away *all* Praise and Blame, as that natural Necessity or impossibility does; then, by a perfect parity of reason, it would be as much the dictate of common sense, that an *approach* of moral Necessity of doing, or impossibility of avoiding, *diminishes* Praise and Blame, as that an approach to natural Necessity and impossibility does so. It is equally the voice of common sense, that persons are *excusable in part*, in neglecting things *difficult* against their Wills, as that they are *excusable wholly* in neglecting things *impossible* against their Wills. And if it made no difference, whether the impossibility were natural and against the Will, or moral, lying in the Will, with regard to excusableness; so neither would it make any difference, whether the difficulty, or approach to Necessity, be natural,

* It is here argued, on supposition that not all propensity implies moral necessity, but only some very high degree; which none will deny.

against the Will, or moral, lying in the propensity of the Will.

But it is apparent, that the reverse of these things is true. If there be an approach to a moral Necessity in a man's exertion of good acts of Will, they being the exercise of a strong propensity to good, and a very powerful love to virtue; it is so far from being the dictate of common sense, that he is less virtuous, and the less to be esteemed, loved, and praised; that it is agreeable to the natural notions of all mankind, that he is so much the better man, worthy of greater respect, and higher commendation. And the stronger the inclination is, and the nearer it approaches to Necessity in that respect; or to impossibility of neglecting the virtuous act, or of doing a vicious one; still the more virtuous, and worthy of higher commendation. And, on the other hand, if a man exerts evil acts of mind; as, for instance, acts of pride or malice from a rooted and strong habit or principle of haughtiness and maliciousness, and a violent propensity of heart to such acts; according to the natural sense of men, he is so far from being the less hateful and blamable on that account, that he is so much the more worthy to be detested and condemned, by all that observe him.

Moreover, it is manifest that it is no part of the notion, which mankind commonly have of a blamable or praiseworthy act of the Will, that it is an act which is not determined by an antecedent bias or motive, but by the sovereign power of the Will itself; because, if so, the greater hand such causes have in determining any acts of the Will, so much the less virtuous or vicious would they be accounted; and the less hand, the more virtuous or vicious. Whereas, the reverse is true; men do not think a good act to be the less praiseworthy, for the agent being much determined in it by a good inclination or a good motive, but the more. And if good inclination, or motive, has but little influence in determining the agent, they do not think his act so much the more virtuous, but the less. And so concerning evil acts, which are determined by evil motives or inclinations.

Yea, if it be supposed, that good or evil dispositions are implanted in the hearts of men, by nature itself, (which, it is certain, is vulgarly supposed in innumerable cases,) yet it is not commonly supposed, that men are worthy of no Praise or Dispraise for such dispositions; although what is natural, is undoubtedly necessary, nature being prior to all acts of the Will whatsoever. Thus, for instance, if a man appears to be of a very haughty or malicious disposition, and is supposed to be so by his natural temper, it is no vulgar notion, no dictate of the common sense and apprehension of men, that such dispositions are no vices or moral evils, or that such persons are not worthy of disesteem, or odium and dishonour; or that the proud or malicious acts which flow from such natural dispositions, are worthy of no resentment. Yea, such vile natural dispositions, and the strength of them, will commonly be mentioned rather as an *aggravation* of the wicked acts, that come from such a fountain, than an extenuation of them. It being natural for men to act thus, is often observed by men in the height of their indignation: they will say, "It is his very nature: he is of a vile natural temper; it is as natural to him to act so, as it is to breathe; he cannot help serving the devil," &c. But it is not thus with regard to hurtful mischievous things, that any are the subjects or occasions of, by *natural necessity*, against their inclinations. In such a case, the necessity, by the common voice of mankind, will be spoken of as a full excuse.—Thus it is very plain, that common sense makes a vast difference between these two kinds of necessity, as to the judgment it makes of their influence on the moral quality and desert of men's actions.

And these dictates are so natural and necessary, that it may be very much doubted whether the *Arminians* themselves have ever got rid of them; yea, their greatest doctors, that have gone furthest in defence of their metaphysical notions of liberty, and have brought their arguments to their greatest strength, and as they suppose, to a demonstration, against the consistence of virtue and vice with any necessity: it is to be questioned, whether there is so much as one of them, but that, if he suffered very much from the injurious acts of a man, under the power of an invincible haughtiness and malignancy of temper, would not, from the forementioned natural sense of mind, resent it far otherwise, than if as great sufferings came upon him from the wind that blows and the fire that burns by natural necessity; and otherwise than he would, if he suffered as much from the conduct of a man perfectly delirious; yea, though he first brought his distraction upon him some way by his own fault.

Some seem to disdain the distinction that we make between *natural* and *moral Necessity*, as though it were altogether impertinent in this controversy; "that which is necessary, say they, is necessary; it is that which must be, and cannot be prevented. And that which is impossible, is impossible, and cannot be done; and, therefore, none can be to blame for not doing it." And such comparisons are made use of, as the commanding of a man to walk, who has lost his legs, and condemning him and punishing him for not obeying; inviting and calling upon a man, who is shut up in a strong prison, to come forth, &c. But in these things *Arminians* are very unreasonable. Let common sense determine whether there be not a great difference between these two cases: the one, that of a man who has offended his prince, and is cast into prison; and after he has lain there a while, the king comes to him, calls him to come forth; and tells him, that if he will do so, and will fall down before him and humbly beg his pardon, he shall be forgiven, and set at liberty, and also be greatly enriched, and advanced to honour: the prisoner heartily repents of the folly and wickedness of his offence against his prince, is thoroughly disposed to abase himself, and accept of the king's offer; but is confined by strong walls, with gates of brass, and bars of iron. The other case is, that of a man who is of a very unreasonable spirit, of a haughty, ungrateful, wilful disposition; and moreover, has been brought up in traitorous principles; and has his heart possessed with an extreme and inveterate enmity to his lawful sovereign; and for his rebellion is cast into prison, and lies long there, loaded with heavy chains, and in miserable circumstances. At length the compassionate prince comes to the prison, orders his chains to be knocked off, and his prison-doors to be set wide open; calls to him, and tells him, if he will come forth to him, and fall down before him, acknowledge that he has treated him unworthily, and ask his forgiveness; he shall be forgiven, set at liberty, and set in a place of great dignity and profit in his court. But he is so stout, and full of haughty malignity, that he cannot be willing to accept the offer; his rooted strong pride and malice have perfect power over him, and as it were bind him, by binding his heart: the opposition of his heart has the mastery over him, having an influence on his mind far superior to the king's grace and condescension, and to all his kind offers and promises. Now, is it agreeable to common sense, to assert and stand to it, that there is no difference between these two cases, as to any worthiness of blame in the prisoners; because, forsooth, there is a necessity in both, and the required act in each case is impossible? It is true, a man's evil dispositions may be as strong and immovable as the bars of a castle. But who cannot see, that when a man, in the latter case, is said to be *unable* to obey the command, the expression is used improperly, and not in the sense it has originally and in common speech? and that it may *properly* be said to be in the rebel's *power* to come out of prison, seeing he can easily do it if he pleases; though by reason of his vile temper of heart, which is fixed and rooted, it is impossible that it should please him?

Upon the whole, I presume there is no person of good understanding, who impartially considers these things, but will allow, that it is not evident, from the dictates of common sense, or natural notions, that moral Necessity is inconsistent with Praise and Blame. And, therefore, if the *Arminians* would prove any such inconsistency, it must be by some philosophical and metaphysical arguments, and not common sense.

There is a grand illusion in the pretended demonstration of *Arminians* from common sense. The main strength of all these demonstrations lies in that prejudice, that arises through the insensible change of the use and meaning of such terms as *liberty, able, unable, necessary, impossible, unavoidable, invincible, action, &c.* from their original and vulgar sense, to a metaphysical sense, entirely diverse; and the strong connexion of the ideas of blamelessness, &c. with some of these terms, by a habit contracted and established, while these terms were used in their first meaning. This prejudice and delusion, is the foundation of all those positions they lay down as maxims, by which most of the scriptures they allege in this controversy, are interpreted, and on which all their pompous demonstrations from Scripture and reason depend. From this secret delusion and prejudice they have almost all their advantages: it is the strength of their bulwarks, and the edge of their weapons. And this is the main ground of all the right they have to treat their neighbours in so assuming a manner, and to insult others, perhaps as wise and good as themselves, as "weak bigots, men that dwell in the dark caves of superstition, perversely set, obstinately shutting their eyes against the noon-day light, enemies to common sense, maintaining the first-born of absurdities," &c. &c. But perhaps, an impartial consideration of the things which have been observed in the preceding parts of this inquiry, may enable the lovers of truth better to judge, whose doctrine is indeed *absurd, abstruse, self-contradictory*, and inconsistent with common sense, and many ways repugnant to the universal dictates of the reason of mankind.

Corol. From the things which have been observed, it will follow, that it is agreeable to common sense to suppose, that the glorified saints have not their freedom at all diminished, in any respect; and that God himself has the highest possible freedom, according to the true and proper meaning of the term; and that he is, in the highest possible respect, an agent, and active in the exercise of his infinite holiness; though he acts therein, in the highest degree, necessarily: and his actions of this kind are in the highest, most absolutely perfect, manner virtuous and praiseworthy; and are so, for that very reason, because they are most perfectly necessary.

SECT. V.

Objections, that this scheme of Necessity renders all Means and Endeavours for avoiding Sin, or obtaining Virtue and Holiness, vain, and to no purpose; and that it makes men no more than mere machines, in affairs of morality and religion, answered.

Arminians say, If sin and virtue come to pass by a Necessity consisting in a sure connexion of causes and effects, antecedents and consequents, it can never be worth while to use any Means or Endeavours to obtain the one, and avoid the other; seeing no Endeavours can alter the futurity of the event, which is become necessary by a connexion already established.

But I desire, that this matter may be fully considered; and that it may be examined with a thorough strictness, whether it will follow that Endeavours and Means, in order to avoid or obtain any future thing, must be more in vain, on the supposition of such a connexion of antecedents and consequents, than if the contrary be supposed.

For Endeavours to be in vain, is for them not to be successful; that is to say, for them not eventually to be the Means of the thing aimed at, which cannot be, but in one of these two ways; either, *first*, That although the Means are used, yet the event aimed at does not follow; or, *secondly*, If the event does follow, it is not because of the Means, or from any connexion or dependence of the event on the Means, the event would have come to pass as well without the Means as with them. If either of these two things are the case, then the Means are not properly successful, and are truly in vain. The success or non-success of Means, in order to an effect, or their being in vain or not in vain, consists in those Means being connected, or not connected, with the effect, in such a manner as this, *viz.* That the effect is *with* the Means, and not *without* them; or, that the being of the effect is, on the one hand, connected with Means, and the want of the effect, on the other hand, is connected with the want of the Means. If there be such a connexion as this between Means and end, the Means are not in vain: the more there is of such a connexion, the further they are from being in vain; and the less of such a connexion, the more they are in vain.

Now, therefore, the question to be answered—in order to determine, whether it follows from this doctrine of the necessary connexion between foregoing things, and consequent ones, that Means used in order to any effect, are more in vain than they would be otherwise—is, whether it follows from it, that there is less of the forementioned connexion between Means and effect; that is, whether on the supposition of there being a real and true connexion between antecedent things and consequent ones, there must be less of a connexion between Means and effect, than on the supposition of there being no fixed connexion between antecedent things and consequent ones: and the very stating of this question is sufficient to answer it. It must appear to every one that will open his eyes, that this question cannot be affirmed, without the grossest absurdity and inconsistence. Means are foregoing things, and effects are following things: And if there were no connexion between foregoing things and following ones, there could be no connexion between Means and end; and so all Means would be wholly vain and fruitless. For it is only by virtue of some connexion, that they become successful: It is some connexion observed, or revealed, or otherwise known, between antecedent things and following ones, that directs in the choice of Means. And if there were no such thing as an established connexion, there could be no choice, as to Means; one thing would have no more tendency to an effect, than another; there would be no such thing as tendency in the case. All those things, which are successful Means of other things, do therein prove connected antecedents of them: and therefore to assert, that a fixed connexion between antecedents and consequents makes Means vain and useless, or stands in the way to hinder the connexion between Means and end, is just so ridiculous, as to say, that a connexion between antecedents and consequents stands in the way to hinder a connexion between antecedents and consequents.

Nor can any supposed connexion of the succession or train of antecedents and consequents, from the very beginning of all things, the connexion being made already sure and necessary, either by established laws of nature, or by these together with a decree of sovereign immediate interpositions of divine power, on such and such occasions, or any other way (if any other there be); I say, no such necessary connexion of a series of antecedents and consequents can in the least tend to hinder, but that the Means we use may belong to the series; and so may be some of those antecedents which are connected with the consequents we aim at, in the established course of things. Endeavours which we use, are things that exist; and, therefore, they belong to the general chain of events; all the parts of which chain are supposed to be connected: and so Endeavours are supposed to be connected with some effects, or some consequent things or other. And certainly this does not hinder but that the events they are connected with, may be those which we aim at, and which we choose, because we judge them most likely to have a connexion with those events, from the established order and course of things which we observe, or from something in divine revelation.

Let us suppose a real and sure connexion between a man having his eyes open in the clear day-light, with good organs of sight, and seeing; so that seeing is connected with his opening his eyes, and not seeing with his not opening his eyes; and also the like connexion between such a man attempting to open his eyes, and his actually doing it: the supposed established connexion between these antecedents and consequents, let the connexion be never so sure and necessary, certainly does not prove that it is in vain, for a man in such circumstances to attempt to open his eyes, in order to seeing: his aiming at that event, and the use of the Means, being the effect of his Will, does not break the connexion, or hinder the success.

So that the objection we are upon does not lie against the doctrine of the Necessity of events by a certainty of connexion and consequence: On the contrary, it is truly forcible against the *Arminian* doctrine of contingence and self-determination; which is inconsistent with such a connexion. If there be no connexion between those events, wherein virtue and vice consist, and any thing antecedent; then, there is no connexion between these events and any Means or Endeavours used in order to them: and if so, then those means must be in vain. The less there is of connexion between foregoing things and following ones, so much the less there is between Means and end, Endeavours and success; and in the same proportion are Means and Endeavours ineffectual and in vain.

It will follow from *Arminian* principles, that there is no degree of connexion between virtue or vice, and any foregoing event or thing: or, in other words, that the determination of the existence of virtue or vice does not in the least depend on the influence of any thing that comes to pass antecedently, as its cause, Means, or ground; because, so far as it is so, it is not from self-determination: and, therefore, so far there is nothing of the nature of virtue or vice. And so it follows, that virtue and vice are not at all, in any degree, dependent upon, or connected with, as, any foregoing event or existence, its cause, ground, or Means. And if so, then all foregoing Means must be totally in vain.

Hence it follows, that there cannot, in any consistence with the *Arminian* scheme, be any reasonable ground of so much as a conjecture concerning the consequence of any Means and Endeavours, in order to escaping vice or obtaining virtue, or any choice or preference of Means, as having a greater probability of success by some than others; either from any natural connexion or dependence of the end on the Means, or through any divine constitution, or revealed way of God, bestowing or bringing to pass these things, in consequence of any Means, Endeavours, Prayers, or Deeds. Conjectures, in this latter case, depend on a supposition, that God himself is the Giver or determining Cause of the events sought: but if they depend on self-determination, then God is not the determining or disposing Author of them: and if these things are not of his disposal, then no conjecture can be made, from any revelation he has given, concerning any method of his disposal of them.

Yea, on these principles, it will not only follow, that men cannot have any reasonable ground of judgment or conjecture, that their Means and Endeavours to obtain virtue or avoid vice will be successful, but they may be sure, they will not; they may be certain, that they will be in vain; and that if ever the thing, which they seek, comes to pass, it will not be at all owing to the Means they use. For Means and Endeavours can have no effect at all, in order to obtain the end, but in one of these two ways: either, (1.) Through a natural tendency and influence, to prepare and dispose the mind more to virtuous acts, either by causing the disposition of the heart to be more in favour of such acts, or by bringing the mind more into the view of powerful motives and inducements; or, (2.) By putting persons more in the way of God's bestowment of the benefit. But neither of these can be the case. *Not the latter;* for, as has been just now observed, it does not consist with the *Arminian* notion of self-determination, which they suppose essential to virtue, that God should be the bestower, or (which is the same thing) the determining, disposing author of virtue. *Not the former;* for natural influence and tendency suppose causality, connexion, and necessity of event, which are inconsistent with *Arminian* liberty. A tendency of Means, by biassing the heart in favour of virtue, or by bringing the Will under the influence and power of motives in its determinations, are both inconsistent with *Arminian* liberty of Will, consisting in indifference, and sovereign self-determination, as has been largely demonstrated.

But for the more full removal of this prejudice against the doctrine of necessity, which has been maintained, as though it tended to encourage a total neglect of all Endeavours as vain, the following things may be considered.

The question is not, Whether men may not thus improve this doctrine: we know that many true and wholesome doctrines are abused: but, whether the doctrine gives any just occasion for such an improvement; or whether, on the supposition of the truth of the doctrine, such a use of it would not be unreasonable? If any shall affirm, that it would not, but that the very nature of the doctrine is such as gives just occasion for it, it must be on this supposition; namely, that such an invariable necessity of all things already settled, must render the interposition of all Means, Endeavours, Conclusions or Actions, of ours, in order to the obtaining any future end whatsoever, perfectly insignificant; because they cannot in the least alter or vary the course and series of things, in any event or circumstance; all being already fixed unalterably by necessity: and that therefore it is folly, for men to use any Means *for any end;* but their wisdom, to save themselves the trouble of Endeavours, and take their ease. No person can draw such an inference from this doctrine, and come to such a conclusion, without contradicting himself, and going counter to the very principles he pretends to act upon: for he comes to a conclusion, and takes a course, *in order to an end,* even *his ease,* or saving himself from trouble; he seeks something future, and uses Means in order to a future thing, even in his drawing up that conclusion, that he will seek nothing, and use no Means in order to any thing in future; he seeks his future ease, and the benefit and comfort of indolence. If prior necessity, that determines all things, makes vain all actions or conclusions of ours, in order to any thing future; then it makes vain all conclusions and conduct of ours, in order to our future ease. The measure of our ease, with the time, manner, and every circumstance of it, is already fixed, by all-determining necessity, as much as any thing else. If he says within himself, "What future happiness or misery I shall have, is already, in effect, determined by the necessary course and connexion of things; therefore, I will save myself the trouble of labour and diligence, which cannot add to my determined degree of happiness, or diminish my misery; but will take my ease, and will enjoy the comfort of sloth and negligence." Such a man contradicts himself: he says, the measure of his future happiness and misery is already fixed, and he will not try to diminish the one, nor add to the other: but yet, in his very conclusion, he contradicts this; for, he takes up this conclusion, *to add to his future happiness,* by the ease and comfort of his negligence; and to diminish his future trouble and misery, by saving himself the trouble of using Means and taking Pains.

Therefore persons cannot reasonably make this improvement of the doctrine of necessity, that they will go into a voluntary negligence of Means for their own happiness. For the principles they must go upon, in order to this, are inconsistent with their making any improvement at all of the doctrine: for to make some improvement of it, is to be influenced by it, to come to some voluntary conclusion, in regard to their own conduct, with some view or aim: but this, as has been shown, is inconsistent with the principles they pretend to act upon. In short, the principles are such as cannot be acted upon at all, or, in any respect, consistently. And, therefore, in every pretence of acting upon them, or making any improvement at all of them, there is a self-contradiction.

As to that objection against the doctrine, which I have endeavoured to prove, that it makes men no more than mere machines; I would say, that notwithstanding this doctrine, man is entirely, perfectly, and unspeakably different from a mere machine, in that he has reason and understanding, with a faculty of Will, and so is capable of volition and choice; in that his Will is guided by the dictates or views of his understanding; and in that his external actions and behaviour, and in many respects also his thoughts, and the exercises of his mind, are subject to his Will; so that he has liberty to act according to his choice, and do what he pleases; and by means of these things, is capable of moral habits and moral acts, such inclinations and actions as, according to the common sense of mankind, are worthy of praise, esteem, love, and reward; or, on the contrary, of disesteem, detestation, indignation, and punishment.

In these things is all the difference from mere machines, as to liberty and agency, that would be any perfection, dignity, or privilege, in any respect: all the difference that can be desired, and all that can be conceived of; and indeed all that the pretensions of the *Arminians* themselves come to, as they are forced often to explain themselves; though their explications overthrow and abolish the things asserted, and pretended to be explained. For they are forced to explain a self-determining power of Will, by a power in the soul, to determine as it chooses or wills; which comes to no more than this, that a man has a power of choosing, and, in many instances, can do as he chooses. Which is quite a different thing from that contradiction, his having power of choosing his first act of choice in the case.

Or, if their scheme make any other difference than this, between men and machines, it is for the worse: it is so far from supposing men to have a dignity and privilege above machines, that it makes the manner of their being determined still more unhappy. Whereas, machines are guided by an intelligent cause, by the skilful hand of the workman or owner; the will of man is left to the guidance of nothing, but absolute blind contingence!

SECT. VI.

Concerning that objection against the doctrine which has been maintained, that it agrees with the Stoical doctrine of Fate, and the opinions of Mr. Hobbes.

When *Calvinists* oppose the *Arminian* notion of the freedom of Will, and contingence of volition, and insist that there are no acts of the Will, nor any other events whatsoever, but what are attended with some kind of necessity; their opposers exclaim against them, as agreeing with the ancient *Stoics* in their doctrine of *Fate*, and with Mr. Hobbes in his opinion of *Necessity*.

It would not be worth while to take notice of so impertinent an objection, had it not been urged by some of the chief *Arminian* writers.—There were many important truths maintained by the ancient *Greek* and *Roman* philosophers, and especially the *Stoics*, that are never the worse for being held by them. The *Stoic* philosophers, by the general agreement of Christian divines, and even *Arminian* divines, were the greatest, wisest, and most virtuous of all the heathen philosophers; and, in their doctrine and practice, came the nearest to Christianity of any of their sects. How frequently are the sayings of these philosophers, in many of the writings and sermons, even of *Arminian* divines, produced, not as arguments for the falseness of the doctrines which they delivered, but as a confirmation of some of the greatest truths of the christian religion, relating to the unity and perfections of the Godhead, a future state, the duty and happiness of mankind, &c. and how the light of nature and reason, in the wisest and best of the heathen, harmonized with and confirms the gospel of Jesus Christ.

And it is very remarkable, concerning Dr. Whitby, that although he alleges the agreement of the *Stoics* with us, wherein he supposes they maintained the like doctrine, as an argument against the truth of ours; yet, this very Dr. Whitby alleges the agreement of the *Stoics* with the *Arminians*, wherein he supposes they taught the same doctrine with them, as an argument for the truth of their doctrine.* So that, when the *Stoics* agree with *them*, it is a confirmation of their doctrine, and a confutation of ours, as showing that our opinions are contrary to the natural sense and common reason of mankind: nevertheless, when the *Stoics* agree with *us*, it argues no such thing in our favour; but, on the contrary, is a great argument against us, and shows our doctrine to be heathenish!

It is observed by some *Calvinistic* writers, that the *Arminians* symbolize with the *Stoics*, in some of those doctrines wherein they are opposed by the *Calvinists*; particularly in their denying an original, innate, total corruption and depravity of heart; and in what they held of man's ability to make himself truly virtuous and conformed to God, and in some other doctrines.

It may be further observed, that certainly it is no better objection against our doctrine, that it agrees, in some respects, with the doctrine of the ancient *Stoic* philosophers; than it is against theirs, wherein they differ from us, that it agrees, in some respects, with the opinion of the very worst of the heathen philosophers, the followers of Epicurus, the father of atheism and licentiousness, and with the doctrine of the *Sadducees* and *Jesuits*.

I am not much concerned to know precisely, what the ancient *Stoic* philosophers held concerning *Fate*, in order to determine what is truth; as though it were a sure way to be in the right, to take good heed to differ from them. It seems, that they differed among themselves; and probably the doctrine of *Fate*, as maintained by most of them, was, in some respects, erroneous. But whatever their doctrine was, if any of them held such a Fate, as is repugnant to any liberty, consisting in our doing as we please, I utterly deny such a Fate. If they held any such Fate, as is not consistent with the common and universal notions that mankind have of liberty, activity, moral agency, virtue and vice; I disclaim any such thing, and think I have demonstrated, that the scheme I maintain is no such scheme. If the *Stoics*, by *Fate*, meant any thing of such a nature, as can be supposed to stand in the way of advantage and benefit of in use of means and endeavours, or would make it less worth while for men to desire and seek after any thing wherein their virtue and happiness consists; I hold no doctrine that is clogged with any such inconvenience, any more than any other scheme whatsoever; and by no means so much as the *Arminian* scheme of contingence; as has been shown. If they held any such doctrine of universal fatality, as is inconsistent with any kind of liberty, that is or can be any perfection, dignity, privilege, or benefit, or any thing desirable, in any respect, for any intelligent creature, or indeed with any liberty that is possible or conceivable; I embrace no such doctrine. If they held any such doctrine of Fate, as is inconsistent with the world being in all things subject to the disposal of an intelligent, wise agent, that presides—not as the *soul* of the world, but—as the Sovereign *Lord* of the Universe, governing all things by proper will, choice, and design, in the exercise of the most perfect liberty conceivable, without subjection to any constraint, or being properly under the power or influence of any thing before, above, or without himself; I wholly renounce any such doctrine.

As to Mr. Hobbes maintaining the same doctrine concerning necessity; I confess, it happens I never read Mr. Hobbes. Let his opinion be what it will, we need not reject all truth which is demonstrated by clear evidence, merely because it was once held by some bad man. This great truth, "that Jesus is the Son of God," was not spoiled because it was once and again proclaimed with a loud voice by the devil. If truth is so defiled, because it is spoken by the mouth, or written by the pen, of some ill minded, mischievous man, that it must never be received, we shall never know, when we hold any of the most precious and evident truths by a sure tenure. And if Mr. Hobbes has made a bad use of this truth, that is to be lamented; but the truth is not to be thought worthy of rejection on that account. It is common for the corrupt hearts of evil men to abuse the best things to vile purposes.

I might also take notice of its having been observed, that the *Arminians* agree with Mr. Hobbes† in many more things than the *Calvinists*. As, in what he is said to hold concerning original sin, in denying the necessity of supernatural illumination, in denying infused grace, in denying the doctrine of justification by faith alone; and other things.

SECT. VII.

Concerning the Necessity of the Divine Will.

Some may, possibly, object against what has been supposed of the absurdity and inconsistence of a self-determining power in the Will, and the impossibility of its being otherwise, than that the Will should be determined in every case by some motive, and by a motive which (as it stands in the view of the understanding) is of superior strength to any appearing on the other side; that if these things are true, it will follow, that not only the Will of created minds, but the Will of *God himself*, is necessary in all its determinations. Concerning which the author

* *Whitby* on the five Points, Edit. 3. p. 325, 326, 327

† Dr. Gill, in his Answer to Dr Whitby. Vol. III. p. 183, &c.

of the *Essay on the Freedom of Will in God and in the Creature*, (pag. 85, 86.) says: "What strange doctrine is this, contrary to all our ideas of the dominion of God? does it not destroy the glory of his liberty of choice, and take away from the Creator and Governor and Benefactor of the world, that most free and Sovereign Agent, all the glory of this sort of freedom? does it not seem to make him a kind of mechanical medium of fate, and introduce Mr. Hobbes's doctrine of fatality and Necessity, into all things that God hath to do with? Does it not seem to represent the blessed God, as a Being of vast understanding, as well as power, and efficiency, but still to leave him without a Will to choose among all the objects within his view? In short, it seems to make the blessed God a sort of Almighty Minister of Fate, under its universal and supreme influence; as it was the professed sentiment of some of the ancients, that Fate was above the gods.

This is declaiming, rather than arguing; and an application to men's imaginations and prejudices, rather than to mere reason. I would now calmly endeavour to consider, whether there be any reason in this frightful representation. But, before I enter upon a particular consideration of the matter, I would observe; that it is reasonable to suppose, it should be much more difficult to express or conceive things according to exact metaphysical truth, relating to the nature and manner of the existence of things in the Divine Understanding and Will, and the operation of these faculties (if I may so call them) of the Divine Mind, than in the human mind; which is infinitely more within our view, more proportionate to the measure of our comprehension, and more commensurate to the use and import of human speech. Language is indeed very deficient, in regard of terms to express precise truth concerning our own minds, and their faculties and operations. Words were first formed to express external things; and those that are applied to express things internal and spiritual, are almost all borrowed, and used in a sort of figurative sense. Whence they are, most of them, attended with a great deal of ambiguity and unfixedness in their signification, occasioning innumerable doubts, difficulties, and confusions, in inquiries and controversies about things of this nature. But language is much less adapted to express things existing in the mind of the incomprehensible Deity, precisely as they are.

We find a great deal of difficulty in conceiving exactly of the nature of our own souls. And notwithstanding all the progress which has been made, in past ages, and the present, in this kind of knowledge, whereby our metaphysics, as it relates to these things, is brought to greater perfection than once it was; yet, here is still work enough left for future inquiries and researches, and room for progress still to be made, for many ages and generations. But we had need to be infinitely able metaphysicians, to conceive with clearness, according to strict, proper, and perfect truth, concerning the nature of the Divine Essence, and the modes of action and operation in the powers of the Divine Mind.

And it may be noted particularly, that though we are obliged to conceive of some things in God as consequent and dependent on others, and of some things pertaining to the Divine Nature and Will as the foundation of others, and so before others in the order of nature: as, we must conceive of the knowledge and holiness of God as prior, in the order of nature, to his happiness; the perfection of his understanding, as the foundation of his wise purposes and decrees; the holiness of his nature, as the cause and reason of his holy determinations. And yet, when we speak of cause and effect, antecedent and consequent, fundamental and dependent, determining and determined, in the first Being, who is self-existent, independent, of perfect and absolute simplicity and immutability, and the first cause of all things: doubtless there must be less propriety in such representations, than when we speak of derived dependent beings, who are compounded, and liable to perpetual mutation and succession.

Having premised this, I proceed to observe concerning the forementioned author's exclamation, about the *necessary determination of God's Will*, in all things, by what he sees to be *fittest* and *best;*

That all the seeming force of such objections and exclamations must arise from an imagination, that there is some sort of privilege or dignity in being without such a moral Necessity, as will make it impossible to do any other, than always choose what is wisest and best; as though there were some disadvantage, meanness, and subjection, in such a Necessity; a thing by which the Will was confined, kept under, and held in servitude by something, which, as it were, maintained a strong and invincible power and dominion over it, by bonds that held him fast, and from which he could, by no means, deliver himself. Whereas, this must be all mere imagination and delusion. It is no disadvantage or dishonour to a being, necessarily to act in the most excellent and happy manner, from the necessary perfection of his own nature. This argues no imperfection, inferiority, or dependence, nor any want of dignity, privilege, or ascendency.* It is not inconsistent with the absolute and most perfect sovereignty of God.

* "It might have been objected, with more plausibleness, that the Supreme Cause cannot be free, because he must needs do always what is best in the whole. But this would not at all serve *Spinoza's* purpose; for this is a necessity, not of nature and of fate, but of fitness and wisdom; a necessity consistent with the greatest freedom, and most perfect choice. For the only foundation of this necessity is such an unalterable rectitude of will, and perfection of wisdom, as makes it impossible for a wise being to act foolishly." *Clark's* Demonstration of the Being and Attributes of God. Edit. 6. p. 64.

"Though God is a most perfect free Agent, yet he cannot but do always what is best and wisest in the whole. The reason is evident; because perfect wisdom and goodness are as steady and certain principles of action, as necessity itself; and an infinitely wise and good Being, indued with the most perfect liberty, can no more choose to act in contradiction to wisdom and goodness, than a necessary agent can act contrary to the necessity by which it is acted; it being as great an absurdity and impossibility in choice, for Infinite Wisdom to choose to act unwisely, or Infinite Goodness to choose what is not good, as it would be in nature, for absolute necessity to fail of producing its necessary effect. There was, indeed, no necessity in nature, that God should at first create such beings as he has created, or indeed any being at all; because he is, in himself, infinitely happy and all-sufficient. There was, also, no necessity in nature, that he should preserve and continue things in being, after they were created; because he would be self-sufficient without their continuance, as he was before their creation. But it was fit and wise and good, that Infinite Wisdom should manifest, and Infinite Goodness communicate itself: and therefore it was necessary, in the sense of necessity I am now speaking of, that things should be made *at such a time*, and continued *so long*, and indeed with various perfections in such degrees, as Infinite Wisdom and Goodness saw it wisest and best that they should." *Ibid.* p. 112, 113.

"It is not a fault, but a perfection of our nature, to desire, will, and act, according to the last result of a fair examination.—This is so far from being a restraint or diminution of freedom, that it is the very improvement and benefit of it: it is not an abridgment, it is the end and use of our liberty; and the further we are removed from such a determination, the nearer we are to misery and slavery. A perfect indifference in the mind, not determinable by its last judgment, of the good or evil that is thought to attend its choice, would be so far from being an advantage and excellency of any intellectual nature, that it would be as great an imperfection, as the want of indifferency to act, or not to act, till determined by the will, would be an imperfection on the other side.—It is as much a perfection, that desire or the power of preferring should be determined by good, as that the power of acting should be determined by the will: and the certainer such determination is, the greater the perfection. Nay, were we determined by any thing but the last result of our own minds, judging of the good or evil of any action, we were not free. This very end of our freedom being, that we might attain the good we choose; and, therefore, every man is brought under a necessity by his constitution, as an intelligent being, to be determined in willing by his own thought and judgment, what is best for him to do; else he would be under the determination of some other than himself, which is want of liberty. And to deny that a man's will, in every determination, follows his own judgment, is to say, that a man wills and acts for an end that he would not have, at the same time that he wills and acts for it. For if he prefers it in his present thoughts, before any other, it is plain he then thinks better of it, and would have it before any other; unless he can have and not have it, will and not will it, at the same time; a contradiction too manifest to be admitted.—If we look upon those superior beings above us, who enjoy perfect happiness, we shall have reason to judge, that they are more steadily determined in their choice of good than we; and yet we have no reason to think they are less happy, or less free, than we are. And if it were fit for such poor finite creatures as we are, to pronounce what Infinite Wisdom and Goodness could do, I think we might say, that God himself cannot choose what is not good. *The freedom of the Almighty hinders not his being determined by what is best.*—But to give a right view of this mistaken part of liberty, let me ask, Would any one be a changeling, because he is less determined by wise determination, than a wise man? Is it worth the name of freedom, to be at liberty to play the fool, and draw shame and misery upon a man's self? If to break loose from the conduct of reason, and to want that restraint of examination and judgment, that keeps us from doing or choosing the worse, be liberty, true liberty, mad men and fools are the only free men. Yet, I think, nobody would choose to be mad, for the sake of such liberty, but he that is mad already." Locke Hum. Und. Vol. I. Edit. 7. p. 215, 216.

"This Being, having all things always necessarily in view, must always and eternally will, according to his infinite comprehension of things; that is, must will all things that are wisest and best to be done. There is no getting free of this consequence. If it can will at all, it must will this way. To be capable of knowing, and not capable of willing, is not to be understood. And to be capable of willing otherwise than what is wisest and best, contradicts that knowledge which is infinite. Infinite Knowledge must direct the will without error. *Here then, is the origin of moral Necessity; and that is, really, of freedom*—Perhaps it may be said, when the Divine Will is determined, from the consideration of the eternal aptitudes of things, it is as necessarily determined, as if it were physically impelled, if that were possible. But it is unskilfulness, to suppose this an objection. The great principle is once established, *viz.* That the Divine Will is determined by the eternal reason and aptitudes of things, instead of being physically impelled; and after that, the more strong and necessary this determination is, the more perfect the Deity must be allowed to be: it is this that makes him an amiable and adorable Being, whose will and power are constantly, immutably determined, by the consideration of what is wisest and best; instead of a surd Being, with power, but without discerning and reason. *It*

The sovereignty of God is his ability and authority to do whatever pleases him; whereby "he doth according to his will in the armies of heaven, and amongst the inhabitants of the earth, and none can stay his hand, or say unto him, what dost thou?"—The following things belong to the *sovereignty* of God; *viz.* (1.) Supreme, universal, and infinite *Power;* whereby he is able to do what he pleases, without control, without any confinement of that power, without any subjection, in the least measure, to any other power; and so without any hinderance or restraint, that it should be either impossible, or at all difficult, for him to accomplish his Will; and without any dependence of his power on any other power, from whence it should be derived, or of which it should stand in any need: so far from this, that all other power is derived from him, and is absolutely dependent on him. (2.) That he has supreme *authority;* absolute and most perfect right to do what he wills, without subjection to any superior authority, or any derivation of authority from any other, or limitation by any distinct independent authority, either superior, equal, or inferior; he being the head of all dominion, and fountain of all authority; and also without restraint by any obligation, implying either subjection, derivation, or dependence, or proper limitation. (3.) That his *Will* is supreme, underived, and independent on any thing without himself; being in every thing determined by his own counsel, having no other rule but his own wisdom; his Will not being subject to or restrained by the Will of any other, and other Wills being perfectly subject to his. (4.) That his *Wisdom*, which determines his Will, is supreme, perfect, underived, self-sufficient, and independent; so that it may be said, as in Isa. xl. 14. "With whom took he counsel? And who instructed him and taught him in the path of judgment, and taught him knowledge, and showed him the way of understanding?" There is no other Divine Sovereignty but this; and this is properly *absolute sovereignty:* no other is desirable; nor would any other be honourable, or happy: and indeed, there is no other conceivable or possible. It is the glory and greatness of the Divine Sovereign, that his Will is determined by his own infinite, all-sufficient wisdom in every thing; and is in nothing at all directed either by inferior wisdom, or by no wisdom; whereby it would become senseless arbitrariness, determining and acting without reason, design, or end.

If God's Will is steadily and surely determined in every thing by *supreme* wisdom, then it is in every thing necessarily determined to that which is *most* wise. And, certainly, it would be a disadvantage and indignity, to be otherwise. For if the Divine Will was not necessarily determined to what in every case is wisest and best, it must be subject to some degree of undesigning contingence; and so in the same degree liable to evil. To suppose the Divine Will liable to be carried hither and thither at random, by the uncertain wind of blind contingence, which is guided by no wisdom, no motive, no intelligent dictate whatsoever, (if any such thing were possible,) would certainly argue a great degree of imperfection and meanness, infinitely unworthy of the Deity. If it be a disadvantage, for the Divine Will to be attended with this moral Necessity, then the more free from it, and the more left at random, the greater dignity and advantage. And, consequently, to be perfectly free from the direction of understanding, and universally and entirely left to senseless unmeaning contingence, to act absolutely at random, would be the supreme glory!

It no more argues any dependence of God's Will, that his supremely wise volition is necessary, than it argues a dependence of his being, that his existence is necessary. If it be something too low, for the Supreme Being to have his Will determined by moral Necessity, so as necessarily, in every case, to Will in the highest degree holily and happily; then why is it not also something too low, for him to have his existence, and the infinite perfection of his nature, and his infinite happiness, determined by Necessity? It is no more to God's dishonour, to be necessarily wise, than to be necessarily holy. And, if neither of them be to his dishonour, then it is not to his dishonour necessarily to act holily and wisely. And if it be not dishonourable to be necessarily holy and wise, in the highest possible degree, no more is it mean and dishonourable, necessarily to act holily and wisely in the highest possible degree; or which is the same thing, to do that, in every case, which, above all other things, is wisest and best.

The reason why it is not dishonourable to be necessarily *most* holy is, because holiness in itself is an excellent and honourable thing. For the same reason, it is no dishonour to be necessarily *most* wise, and, in every case, to act most wisely, or do the thing which is the wisest of all; for wisdom is also in itself excellent and honourable.

The forementioned author of the *Essay on the Freedom of Will, &c.* as has been observed, represents that doctrine of the Divine Will being in every thing necessarily determined by superior fitness, as making the blessed God a kind of Almighty Minister and mechanical medium of fate: he insists, (p. 93, 94.) that this moral Necessity and impossibility is, in effect, the same thing with physical and natural Necessity, and impossibility: and says, (p. 54, 55.) "The scheme which determines the Will always and certainly by the understanding, and the understanding by the appearance of things, seems to take away the true nature of vice and virtue. For the sublimest of virtues, and the vilest of vices, seem rather to be matters of fate and Necessity, flowing naturally and necessarily from the existence, the circumstances, and present situation of persons and things; for this existence and situation necessarily makes such an appearance to the mind; from this appearance flows a necessary perception and judgment, concerning these things; this judgment necessarily determines the Will; and thus, by this chain of necessary causes, virtue and vice would lose their nature, and become natural ideas, and necessary things, instead of moral and free actions."

And yet this same author allows, (p. 30, 31.) That a perfectly wise being will constantly and certainly choose what is most fit; and says, (p. 102, 103.) "I grant, and always have granted, that wheresoever there is such antecedent superior fitness of things, God acts according to it, so as never to contradict it; and, particularly, in all his judicial proceedings as a Governor and Distributer of rewards and punishments." Yea, he says expressly, (p. 42.) "That it is not possible for God to act otherwise, than according to this fitness and goodness in things."

So that, according to this author, putting these several passages of his Essay together, there is *no virtue, nor any thing of a moral nature*, in the most sublime and glorious acts and exercises of God's holiness, justice, and faithfulness; and he never does any thing which is in itself supremely worthy, and, above all other things, fit and excellent, but only as a kind of mechanical medium of fate; and in *what he does as the Judge, and moral Governor of the world*, he exercises no moral excellency; exercising no freedom in these things, because he acts by moral Necessity, which is, in effect, the same with physical or natural Necessity; and therefore, he only acts by an *Hobbistical* fatality; "as a Being indeed of vast understanding, as well as power and efficiency, (as he said before,) but without a will to choose, being a kind of Almighty Minister of fate, acting under its supreme influence." For he allows, that in all these things, God's Will is determined constantly and certainly by a superior fitness, and that it is not possible for him to act otherwise. And if these things are so, what glory or praise belongs to God for doing holily and justly, or taking the most fit, holy, wise, and excellent course, in any one instance? Whereas, according to the Scriptures, and also the common sense of mankind, it does not, in the least, derogate from the honour of any being, that through the moral perfection of his nature, he necessarily acts with supreme wisdom and holiness; but on the contrary, his praise is the greater: herein consists the height of his glory.

The same author (p. 56.) supposes, that herein appears the excellent "character of a wise and good man, that though he can choose contrary to the fitness of things, yet

is the beauty of this Necessity, that it is strong as fate itself, with all the advantage of reason and goodness.—It is strange, to see men contend, that the Deity is not free, because he is necessarily rational, immutably good and wise; when a man is allowed still the perfecter being, the more fixedly and constantly his Will is determined by reason and truth." *Inquiry into the Nature of the Hum. Soul.* Edit. 3. Vol. II. p. 403, 404.

he does not; but suffers himself to be directed by fitness;" and that, in this conduct, "he imitates the blessed God." And yet, he supposes it is contrarywise with the blessed God; not that he suffers himself to be directed by fitness, when "*he can choose, contrary to the fitness of things;*" but that "*he cannot choose contrary to the fitness of things;*" as he says, p. 42. "That it is not possible for God to act otherwise than according to this fitness, where there is any fitness or goodness in things:" Yea, he supposes, (p. 31.) That if a man "were perfectly wise and good, he could not do otherwise than be constantly and certainly determined by the fitness of things."

One thing more I would observe, before I conclude this section; and that is, that if it derogate nothing from the glory of God, to be necessarily determined by superior fitness in some things, then neither does it to be thus determined in all things; from any thing in the nature of such Necessity, as at all detracting from God's freedom, independence, absolute supremacy, or any dignity or glory of his nature, state, or manner of acting; or as implying any infirmity, restraint, or subjection. And if the thing be such as well consists with God's glory, and has nothing tending at all to detract from it; then we need not be afraid of ascribing it to God in too many things, lest thereby we should detract from God's glory too much.

SECT. VIII.

Some further objections against the moral Necessity of God's Volitions considered.

THE author last cited, as has been observed, owns that God, being perfectly wise, will constantly and certainly choose what appears most fit, where there is a superior fitness and goodness in things; and that it is not possible for him to do otherwise. So that it is in effect confessed, that in those things where there is any real preferableness, it is no dishonour, nothing in any respect unworthy of God, for him to act from Necessity; notwithstanding all that can be objected from the agreement of such a Necessity with the fate of the *Stoics*, and the Necessity maintained by Mr. Hobbes. From which it will follow, that if in all the different things, among which God chooses, there were evermore a superior fitness or preferableness on one side, then it would be no dishonour, or any thing unbecoming, for God's Will to be necessarily determined in every thing. And if this be allowed, it is giving up entirely the argument, from the unsuitableness of such a Necessity to the liberty, supremacy, independence, and glory of the Divine Being; and resting the whole weight of the affair on the decision of another point wholly diverse; *viz. Whether it be so indeed*, that in all the various possible things, which are in God's view, and may be considered as capable objects of his choice, there is not evermore a preferableness in one thing above another. This is denied by this author; who supposes, that in many instances, between two or more possible things, which come within the view of the Divine Mind, there is a perfect indifference and inequality, as to fitness or tendency, to attain any good end which God can have in view, or to answer any of his designs. Now, therefore, I would consider whether this be evident.

The arguments brought to prove this, are of two kinds. (1.) It is urged, that, in many instances, we must suppose there is absolutely no difference between various possible objects of choice, which God has in view: and, (2.) that the difference between many things is so inconsiderable, or of such a nature, that it would be unreasonable to suppose it to be of any consequence; or to suppose that any of God's wise designs would not be answered in any one way as well as the other.

Therefore,

I. The first thing to be considered is, whether there are any instances wherein there is a perfect likeness, and absolutely no difference, between different objects of choice, that are proposed to the Divine Understanding?

And here, in the *first* place, it may be worthy to be considered, whether the contradiction there is in the *terms* of the question proposed, does not give reason to suspect, that there is an inconsistence in the *thing* supposed. It is inquired whether *different* objects of choice may not be absolutely *without difference?* If they are absolutely *without difference*, then how are they *different* objects of choice? If there be absolutely *no difference*, in any respect, then there is *no variety* or *distinction*: for distinction is only by some difference. And if there be no *variety* among proposed *objects of choice*, then there is no opportunity for *variety of choice*, or difference of determination. For that determination of a thing, which is not different in any respect, is not a different determination, but the same. That this is no quibble, may appear more fully in a short time.

The arguments, to prove that the Most High, in some instances, chooses to do one thing rather than another, where the things themselves are perfectly without difference, are two.

1. That the various parts of infinite time and space, absolutely considered, are perfectly alike, and do not differ at all one from another: and that therefore, when God determined to create the world in such a part of infinite duration and space, rather than others, he determined and preferred, among various objects, between which there was no preferableness, and absolutely no difference.

Answ. This objection supposes an infinite length of time before the world was created, distinguished by successive parts, properly and truly so; or a succession of limited and unmeasurable periods of time, following one another, in an infinitely long series: which must needs be a groundless imagination. The eternal duration which was before the world, being only the eternity of God's existence; which is nothing else but his immediate, perfect, and invariable possession of the whole of his unlimited life, together and at once; *Vitæ interminabilis, tota, simul et perfecta possessio.* Which is so generally allowed, that I need not stand to demonstrate it.*

So this objection supposes an extent of space beyond the limits of the creation, of an infinite length, breadth, and depth, truly and properly distinguished into different measurable parts, limited at certain stages, one beyond another, in an infinite series. Which notion of absolute and infinite space is doubtless as unreasonable, as that now mentioned, of absolute and infinite duration. It is as improper, to imagine that the immensity and omnipresence of God is distinguished by a series of miles and leagues, one beyond another; as that the infinite duration of God is distinguished by months and years, one after another. A diversity and order of distinct parts, limited by certain periods, is as conceivable, and does as naturally obtrude itself on our imagination, in one case as the other; and there is equal reason in each case, to suppose that our imagination deceives us. It is equally improper to talk of months and years of the Divine Existence, as of square miles of Deity: and we equally deceive ourselves, when we talk of the world being differently fixed, with respect to either of these sorts of measures. I think, we know not what we mean, if we say, the world might have been differently placed from what it is, in the broad expanse of infinity; or, that it might have been differently fixed in the long line

* "If all created beings were taken away, all possibility of any mutation or succession of one thing to another, would appear to be also removed. Abstract succession in eternity is scarce to be understood. What is it that succeeds? One minute to another, perhaps, *velut unda supervenit undam.* But when we imagine this, we fancy that the minutes are things separately existing. This is the common notion; and yet it is a manifest prejudice. Time is nothing but the existence of created successive beings, and eternity the necessary existence of the Deity.—Therefore, if this necessary Being hath no change or succession in his nature, his existence must of course be unsuccessive. We seem to commit a double oversight in this case; *first*, we find succession in the necessary nature and existence of the Deity himself: which is wrong, if the reasoning above be conclusive. And *then* we ascribe this succession to eternity, considered abstractedly from the Eternal Being; and suppose it, one knows not what, a thing subsisting by itself, and flowing, one minute after another. This is the work of pure imagination, and contrary to the reality of things. Hence the common metaphorical expressions: *Time runs apace, let us lay hold on the present minute*, and the like. The philosophers themselves mislead us by their illustration. They compare eternity to the motion of a point running on for ever, and making a traceless infinite line. Here the point is supposed a thing actually subsisting, representing the present minute; and then they ascribe motion or succession to it: that is, they ascribe motion to a mere nonentity, to illustrate to us a successive eternity, made up of finite successive parts. —If once we allow an all-perfect mind, which hath an eternal, immutable, and infinite comprehension of all things, always (and allow it we must) the distinction of past and future vanishes with respect to such a mind.—In a word, if we proceed step by step, as above, the eternity or existence of the Deity will appear to be *Vitæ interminabilis, tota, simul et perfecta possessio*; how much soever this may have been a paradox hitherto." *Inquiry into the Nature of the Human Soul.* Vol. ii. 409, 410, 411. Edit. 3.

of eternity: and all arguments and objections, which are built on the imaginations we are apt to have of infinite extension or duration, are buildings founded on shadows, or castles in the air.

2. The second argument, to prove that the Most High wills one thing rather than another, without any superior fitness or preferableness in the thing preferred, is God's actually placing in different parts of the world, particles, or atoms of matter, that are perfectly equal and alike. The forementioned author says, (p. 78, &c.) "If one would descend to the minute specific particles, of which different bodies are composed, we should see abundant reason to believe, that there are thousands of such little particles, or atoms of matter, which are perfectly equal and alike, and could give no distinct determination to the Will of God, where to place them." He there instances in particles of water, of which there are such immense numbers, which compose the rivers and oceans of this world; and the infinite myriads of the luminous and fiery particles, which compose the body of the sun; so many, that it would be very unreasonable to suppose no two of them should be exactly equal and alike.

Answ. (1.) To this I answer: that as we must suppose matter to be infinitely divisible, it is very unlikely, that any two of all these particles are exactly equal and alike; so unlikely, that it is a thousand to one, yea, an infinite number to one, but it is otherwise: and that although we should allow a great similarity between the different particles of water and fire, as to their general nature and figure; and however small we suppose those particles to be, it is infinitely unlikely, that any two of them should be exactly equal in dimensions and quantity of matter.—If we should suppose a great many globes of the same nature with the globe of the earth, it would be very strange, if there were any two of them that had exactly the same number of particles of dust and water in them. But infinitely less strange, than that two particles of light should have just the same quantity of matter. For a particle of light, according to the doctrine of the infinite divisibility of matter, is composed of infinitely more assignable parts, than there are particles of dust and water in the globe of the earth. And as it is infinitely unlikely, that any two of these particles should be *equal;* so it is, that they should be *alike* in other respects: to instance in the configuration of their surfaces. If there were very many globes, of the nature of the earth, it would be very unlikely that any two should have exactly the same number of particles of dust, water, and stone, in their surfaces, and all posited exactly alike, one with respect to another, without any difference, in any part discernible either by the naked eye or microscope; but infinitely less strange, than that two particles of light should be perfectly of the same figure. For there are infinitely more assignable real parts on the surface of a particle of light, than there are particles of dust, water, and stone, on the surface of the terrestrial globe.

Answ. (2.) But then, supposing that there are two particles, or atoms of matter, perfectly equal and alike, which God has placed in different parts of the creation; as I will not deny it to be possible for God to make two bodies perfectly alike, and put them in different places; yet it will not follow, that two different or distinct acts or effects of the Divine Power have exactly the same fitness for the same ends. For these two different bodies are not different or distinct, in any other respects than those wherein they *differ:* they are two in no other respects than those wherein there is a difference. If they are perfectly equal and alike *in themselves,* then they can be distinguished, or be distinct, only in those things which are called *circumstances;* as place, time, rest, motion, or some other present or past circumstances or relations. For it is difference only that constitutes distinction. If God makes two bodies, *in themselves* every way equal and alike, and agreeing perfectly in all other circumstances and relations, but only *their place;* then in this only is there any distinction or duplicity. The figure is the same, the measure is the same, the solidity and resistance are the same, and every thing the same but only the place. Therefore what the Will of God determines is this, that there should be the same figure, the same extension, the same resistance, &c. in two different places. And for this determination he has some reason. There is some end, for which such a determination and act has a peculiar fitness, above all other acts. Here is no one thing determined without an end, and no one thing without a fitness for that end, superior to any thing else. If it be the pleasure of God to cause the same resistance, and the same figure, to be in two different places and situations, we can no more justly argue from it, that here must be some determination or act of God's Will that is wholly without motive or end, than we can argue, that whenever, in any case, it is a man's Will to speak the same words, or make the same sounds, at two different times, there must be some determination or act of his Will, without any motive or end. The difference of place, in the former case, proves no more than the difference of time does in the other. If any one should say, with regard to the former case, that there must be something determined without an end; *viz.* that of those two similar bodies, this in particular should be made in this place, and the other in the other, and should inquire, why the Creator did not make them in a transposition, when both are alike, and each would equally have suited either place? The inquiry supposes something that is not true; namely, that the two bodies differ and are distinct in other respects besides their place. So that with this distinction *inherent* in them, they might, in their first creation, have been transposed, and each might have begun its existence in the place of the other.

Let us, for clearness sake, suppose, that God had, at the beginning, made two globes, each of an inch diameter, both perfect spheres, and perfectly solid, without pores, and perfectly alike in every respect, and placed them near one to another, one towards the right hand, and the other towards the left, without any difference as to time, motion, or rest, past or present, or any circumstance, but only their place; and the question should be asked, why God in their creation placed them so? why that which is made on the right hand, was not made on the left, and *vice versa?* Let it be well considered, whether there be any sense in such a question; and whether the inquiry does not suppose something false and absurd. Let it be considered, what the Creator must have done otherwise than he did, what different act of Will or power he must have exerted, in order to the thing proposed. All that could have been done, would have been to have made two spheres, perfectly alike, in the same places where he has made them, without any difference of the things made, either in themselves or in any circumstance; so that the whole effect would have been without any difference, and, therefore, just the same. By the supposition, the two spheres are different in no other respect but their place; and therefore in other respects they are the same. Each has the same roundness; it is not a distinct rotundity, in any other respect but its situation. There are, also, the same dimensions, differing in nothing but their place. And so of their resistance, and every thing else that belongs to them.

Here, if any chooses to say, "that there is a difference in another respect, *viz.* that they are not numerically the same: that it is thus with all the qualities that belong to them: that it is confessed, they are, in some respects, the same; that is, they are both exactly alike; but yet *numerically* they differ. Thus the roundness of one is not the same *numerical, individual* roundness with that of the other." Let this be supposed; then the question about the determination of the Divine Will in the affair, is, why did God will, that this *individual* roundness should be at the right hand, and the other *individual* roundness at the left? why did not he make them in a contrary position? Let any rational person consider, whether such questions be not words without a meaning; as much as if God should see fit for some ends, to cause the same sounds to be repeated, or made at two different times; the sounds being perfectly the same in every other respect, but only one was a minute after the other; and it should be asked, upon it, why God caused these sounds, numerically different, to succeed one the other in such a manner? why he did not make that individual sound, which was in the first minute, to be in the second, and the individual sound of the last minute to be in the first? which inquiries would be even ridiculous; as, I think, every person must see, in the case proposed of two sounds, being only the same repeated, absolutely without any difference, but that one circumstance of time. If the Most High sees it will answer some good end, that the same sound be made thunder at two distinct times, and therefore wills that it should be so, must it needs therefore be, that herein there is some act of God's Will without any motive or end? God saw fit often, at distinct times, and on different occasions, to say the very same words to *Moses;* namely, those, *I am Jehovah.* And would it not be unreasonable to infer, as a certain consequence, from this, that here must be some act or acts of the Divine Will, in determining and disposing the words exactly alike, at different times, wholly without aim or inducement? But it would be no more unreasonable than to say, that there must be an act of God without any inducement, if he sees it best, and, for some reasons, determines that there shall be the same resistance, the same dimensions, and the same figure, in several distinct places.

If, in the instance of the two spheres, perfectly alike, it be supposed possible that God might have made them in a contrary position; that which is made at the right hand, being made at the left; then I ask, Whether it is not evidently equally possible, if God had made but one of them, and that in the place of the right hand globe, that he might have made that numerically different from what it is, and numerically different from what he did make it; though perfectly alike, and in the same place; and at the same time, and in every respect, in the same circumstances and relations? Namely, Whether he might not have made it numerically the same with that which he has now made at the left hand; and so have left that which is now created at the right hand, in a state of non-existence? And, if so, whether it would not have been possible to have made one in that place, perfectly like these, and yet numerically differing from both? And let it be considered, whether, from this notion of a numerical difference in bodies, perfectly equal and alike, which numerical difference is something inherent in the bodies themselves, and diverse from the difference of place or time, or any circumstance whatsoever; it will not follow, that there is an infinite number of numerically different possible bodies, perfectly alike, among which God chooses, by a self-determining power, when he goes about to create bodies.

Therefore let us put the case thus: Supposing that God, in the beginning, had created but one perfectly solid sphere, in a certain place: and it should be inquired, Why God created that individual sphere, in that place, at that time? and why he did not create another sphere perfectly like it, but numerically different, in the same place, at the same time? Or why he chose to bring into being there, that very body, rather than any of the infinite number of other bodies, perfectly like it; either of which he could have made there as well, and would have answered his end as well? Why he caused to exist, at that place and time, that individual roundness, rather than any other of the infinite number of individual rotundities, just like it? Why that individual resistance, rather than any other of the infinite number of possible resistances, just like it? And it might as reasonably be asked, Why, when God first caused it to thunder, he caused that individual sound then to be made, and not another just like it? Why did he make choice of this very sound, and reject all the infinite number of other possible sounds just like it, but numerically differing from it, and all differing one from another? I think, every body must be sensible of the absurdity and nonsense of what is supposed in such inquiries. And, if we calmly attend to the matter, we shall be convinced, that all such kind of objections as I am answering, are founded on nothing but the imperfection of our manner of conceiving things, and the obscureness of language, and great want of clearness and precision in the signification of terms.

If any should find fault with this reasoning, that it is going a great length into metaphysical niceties and subtilties; I answer, the objection to which they are a reply, is a metaphysical subtilty, and must be treated according to the nature of it.*

II. Another thing alleged is, that innumerable things which are determined by the Divine Will, and chosen and done by God rather than others, differ from those that are not chosen in so inconsiderable a manner, that it would be unreasonable to suppose the difference to be of any consequence, or that there is any superior fitness or goodness, that God can have respect to in the determination.

To which I answer; it is impossible for us to determine, with any certainty or evidence, that because the difference is very small, and appears to us of no consideration, therefore there is absolutely no superior goodness, and no valuable end, which can be proposed by the Creator and Governor of the world, in ordering such a difference. The forementioned author mentions many instances. One is, there being one atom in the whole universe more, or less. But, I think, it would be unreasonable to suppose, that God made one atom in vain, or without any end or motive. He made not one atom, but what was a work of his Almighty Power, as much as the whole globe of the earth, and requires as much of a constant exertion of Almighty Power to uphold it; and was made and is upheld with understanding and design, as much as if no other had been made but that. And it would be as unreasonable to suppose, that he made it without any thing really aimed at in so doing, as much as to suppose, that he made the planet *Jupiter* without aim or design.

It is possible, that the most minute effects of the Creator's power, the smallest assignable difference between the things which God has made, may be attended, in the whole series of events, and the whole compass and extent of their influence, with very great and important consequences. If the laws of motion, and gravitation, laid down by Sir Isaac Newton, hold universally, there is not one atom, nor the least assignable part of an atom, but what has influence, every moment, throughout the whole material universe, to cause every part to be otherwise than it would be, if it were not for that particular corporeal existence. And however the effect is insensible for the present, yet it may, in length of time, become great and important.

To illustrate this, let us suppose two bodies moving the same way, in straight lines, perfectly parallel one to another; but to be diverted from this parallel course, and drawn one from another, as much as might be, by the attraction of an atom, at the distance of one of the furthest of the fixed stars from the earth; these bodies being turned out of the lines of their parallel motion, will, by degrees, get further and further distant, one from the other; and though the distance may be imperceptible for a long time, yet at length it may become very great. So the revolution of a planet round the sun being retarded or accelerated, and the orbit of its revolution made greater or less, and more or less elliptical, and so its periodical time longer or shorter, no more than may be by the influence of the least atom, might, in length of time, perform a whole revolution sooner or later than otherwise it would have done; which might make a vast alteration with regard to millions of important events. So the influence of the least particle may, for ought we know, have such effect on something in the constitution of some human body, as to cause another thought to arise in the mind at a certain time, than otherwise would have been; which, in length of time, (yea, and that not very great,) might occasion a vast alteration through the whole world of mankind. And so innumerable other ways might be mentioned, wherein the least assignable alteration may possibly be attended with great consequences.*

Another *argument*, which the fore-mentioned author brings against a necessary determination of the Divine Will, by a superior fitness, is, that such doctrine derogates from the *freeness* of God's *grace* and *goodness*, in choosing the objects of his favour and bounty, and from the *obligation* upon men to *thankfulness* for special benefits. (p. 89, &c.) In answer to this objection, I would observe,

1. That it derogates no more from the goodness of God, to suppose the exercise of the benevolence of his nature to be determined by wisdom, than to suppose it determined by chance, and that his favours are bestowed altogether at random, his Will being determined by nothing but perfect accident, without any end or design whatsoever; which

* "For men to have recourse to subtilties, in raising difficulties, and then complain, that they should be taken off by minutely examining these subtilties, is a strange kind of procedure." *Nature of the Human Soul*, vol. 2. p. 331.

must be the case, as has been demonstrated, if Volition be not determined by a prevailing motive. That which is owing to perfect contingence, wherein neither previous inducement nor antecedent choice has any hand, is not owing more to goodness or benevolence, than that which is owing to the influence of a wise end.

2. It is acknowledged, that if the motive that determines the Will of God, in the choice of the objects of his favours, be any moral quality in the object, recommending that object to his benevolence above others, his choosing that object is not so great a manifestation of the freeness and sovereignty of his grace, as if it were otherwise. But there is no necessity for supposing this, in order to our supposing that he has some wise end in view, in determining to bestow his favours on one person rather than another. We are to distinguish between the *merit of the object of God's favour*, or a moral qualification of *the object* attracting that favour and recommending to it, and the *natural fitness* of such a determination *of the act of God's goodness*, to answer some wise design of his own, some end in the view of God's omniscience.—It is God's own act, that is the proper and immediate object of his Volition.

3. I suppose that none will deny, but that, in some instances, God acts from wise design in determining the particular subjects of his favours: none will say, I presume, that when God distinguishes, by his bounty, particular societies or persons, he never, in any instance, exercises any wisdom in so doing, aiming at some happy consequence. And, if it be not denied to be so in some instances, then I would inquire, whether in these instances God's goodness is less manifested, than in those wherein God has no aim or end at all? And whether the subjects have less cause of thankfulness? And if so, who shall be thankful for the bestowment of distinguishing mercy, with that enhancing circumstance of the distinction being made without an end? How shall it be known when God is influenced by some wise aim, and when not? It is very manifest, with respect to the apostle *Paul*, that God had wise ends in choosing him to be a Christian and an apostle, who had been a persecutor, &c. The apostle himself mentions one end. (1 Tim. i. 15, 16.) "Christ Jesus came into the world to save sinners, of whom I am chief. Howbeit, for this cause I obtained mercy, that in me first, Jesus Christ might show forth all long-suffering, for a pattern to them who should hereafter believe on him to life everlasting." But yet the apostle never looked on it as a diminution of the freedom and riches of divine grace in his election, which he so often and so greatly magnifies. This brings me to observe,

4. Our supposing such a moral Necessity in the acts of God's Will, as has been spoken of, is so far from necessarily derogating from the riches of God's grace to such as are the chosen objects of his favour, that, in many instances, this moral necessity may arise from goodness, and from the great degree of it. God may choose this object rather than another, as having a superior fitness to answer the ends, designs, and inclinations of his goodness; being more sinful, and so more miserable and necessitous than others, the inclinations of infinite mercy and benevolence may be more gratified, and the gracious design of God in sending his Son into the world, may be more abundantly answered, in the exercises of mercy towards such an object, rather than another.

One thing more I would observe, before I finish what I have to say on the head of the Necessity of the acts of God's Will; and that is, that something much more like a servile subjection of the Divine Being to fatal Necessity, will follow from *Arminian* principles, than from the doctrines which they oppose. For they (at least most of them) suppose, with respect to all events that happen in the moral world, depending on the Volitions of moral agents, which are the most important events of the universe, to which all others are subordinate; I say, they suppose, with respect to these, that God has a certain foreknowledge of them, antecedent to any purposes or decrees of his about them. And if so, they have a fixed certain futurity, prior to any designs or Volitions of his, and independent on them, and to which his Volitions must be subject, as he would wisely accommodate his affairs to this fixed futurity of the state of things in the moral world. So that here, instead of a moral Necessity of God's Will, arising from, or consisting in, the infinite perfection and blessedness of the Divine Being, we have a fixed unalterable state of things, properly distinct from the perfect nature of the Divine Mind, and the state of the Divine Will and Design, and entirely independent on these things, and which they have no hand in, because they are prior to them; and to which God's Will is truly subject, being obliged to conform or accommodate himself to it, in all his purposes and decrees, and in every thing he does in his disposals and government of the world; the moral world being the end of the natural; so that all is in vain, that is not accommodated to that state of the moral world, which consists in, or depends upon, the acts and state of the Wills of moral agents, which had a fixed futurition from eternity. Such a subjection to Necessity as this, would truly argue an inferiority and servitude, that would be unworthy of the Supreme Being; and is much more agreeable to the notion which many of the heathen had of fate, as above the gods, than that moral Necessity of fitness and wisdom which has been spoken of; and is truly repugnant to the absolute sovereignty of God, and inconsistent with the supremacy of his Will; and really subjects the Will of the Most High to the Will of his creatures, and brings him into dependence upon them.

SECT. IX.

Concerning that objection against the doctrine which has been maintained, that it makes God the Author of Sin.

IT is urged by *Arminians*, that the doctrine of the Necessity of men's Volitions, or their necessary connexion with antecedent events and circumstances, makes the First Cause, and Supreme Orderer of all things, the Author of Sin; in that he has so constituted the state and course of things, that sinful Volitions become necessary, in consequence of his disposal. Dr. Whitby, in his Discourse on the Freedom of the Will,* cites one of the ancients, as on his side, declaring that this opinion of the Necessity of the Will "absolves sinners, as doing nothing of their own accord which was evil, and would cast all the blame of all the wickedness committed in the world, upon God, and upon his providence, if that were admitted by the assertors of this fate; whether he himself did necessitate them to do these things, or ordered matters so, that they should be constrained to do them by some other cause." And the Doctor says, in another place,† "In the nature of the thing, and in the opinion of philosophers, *causa deficiens, in rebus necessariis, ad causam per se efficientem reducenda est.* In things necessary, the deficient cause must be reduced to the efficient. And in this case the reason is evident; because the not doing what is required, or not avoiding what is forbidden, being a defect, must follow from the position of the necessary cause of that deficiency."—Concerning this, I would observe the following things.

I. If there be any difficulty in this matter, it is nothing peculiar to this scheme; it is no difficulty or disadvantage wherein it is distinguished from the scheme of *Arminians*; and, therefore, not reasonably objected by them.

Dr. Whitby supposes that if sin necessarily follows from God withholding assistance, or if that assistance be not given, which is absolutely necessary to the avoiding of evil; then, in the nature of the thing, God must be as properly the author of that evil, as if he were the efficient cause of it. From whence, according to what he himself says of the devils and damned spirits, God must be the proper author of their perfect unrestrained wickedness: he must be the efficient cause of the great pride of the devils, and of their perfect malignity against God, Christ, his saints, and all that is good, and of the insatiable cruelty of their disposition. For he allows, that God has so forsaken them, and does so withhold his assistance from them, that they are incapacitated from doing good, and deter-

* On the five Points, p. 361

† Ibid. p. 486.

mined only to evil.* Our doctrine, in its consequence, makes God the author of men's sin in this world, no more, and in no other sense, than his doctrine, in its consequence, makes God the author of the hellish pride and malice of the devils. And doubtless the latter is as odious an effect as the former.

Again, if it will *follow at all*, that God is the Author of Sin, from what has been supposed of a sure and infallible connexion between antecedents and consequents, it will *follow because of this, viz.* that for God to be the author or orderer of those things which, he knows beforehand, will infallibly be attended with such a consequence, is the same thing, in effect, as for him to be the author of that consequence. But, if this be so, this is a difficulty which equally attends the doctrine of *Arminians* themselves; at least, of those of them who allow God's certain foreknowledge of all events. For, on the supposition of such a foreknowledge, this is the case with respect to every sin that is committed: God knew, that if he ordered and brought to pass such and such events, such sins would infallibly follow. As for instance, God certainly foreknew, long before *Judas* was born, that if he ordered things so, that there should be such a man born, at such a time, and at such a place, and that his life should be preserved, and that he should, in Divine Providence, be led into acquaintance with Jesus; and that his heart should be so influenced by God's Spirit or providence, as to be inclined to be a follower of Christ; and that he should be one of those twelve, which should be chosen constantly to attend him as his family; and that his health should be preserved, so that he should go up to *Jerusalem*, at the last passover in Christ's life; and it should be so ordered, that *Judas* should see Christ's kind treatment of the woman which anointed him at *Bethany*, and have that reproof from Christ which he had at that time, and see and hear other things which excited his enmity against his Master, and other circumstances should be ordered, as they were ordered; it would most certainly and infallibly follow, that *Judas* would betray his Lord, and would soon after hang himself, and die impenitent, and be sent to hell, for his horrid wickedness.

Therefore, this supposed difficulty ought not to be brought as an objection against the scheme which has been maintained, as *disagreeing* with the *Arminian* scheme, seeing it is no difficulty owing to such a *disagreement*, but a difficulty wherein the *Arminians* share with us. That must be unreasonably made an objection against our differing from them, which we should not escape or avoid at all by agreeing with them.—And therefore I would observe,

II. They who object, that this doctrine makes God the Author of Sin, ought distinctly to explain what they mean by that phrase, *The Author of Sin*. I know the phrase, as it is commonly used, signifies something very ill. If by *the Author of Sin*, be meant *the Sinner, the Agent*, or *Actor of Sin*, or *the Doer of a wicked thing;* so it would be a reproach and blasphemy, to suppose God to be the Author of Sin. In this sense, I utterly deny God to be the Author of Sin; rejecting such an imputation on the Most High, as what is infinitely to be abhorred; and deny any such thing to be the consequence of what I have laid down. But if, by *the Author of Sin*, is meant the permitter, or *not a hinderer* of Sin; and, at the same time, a disposer of the state of events, in such a manner, for wise, holy, and most excellent ends and purposes, that Sin, if it be permitted or not hindered, will most certainly and infallibly follow: I say, if this be all that is meant, by being the Author of Sin, I do not deny that God is the Author of Sin, (though I dislike and reject the phrase, as that which by use and custom is apt to carry another sense,) it is no reproach for the Most High to be thus the Author of Sin. This is not to be the *Actor of Sin*, but, on the contrary, *of holiness*. What God doth herein, is holy; and a glorious exercise of the infinite excellency of his nature. And, I do not deny, that God being thus the Author of Sin, follows from what I have laid down; and, I assert, that it equally follows from the doctrine which is maintained by most of the *Arminian* divines.

That it is most certainly so, that God is in such a manner the Disposer and Orderer of Sin, is evident, if any credit is to be given to the Scripture; as well as because it is impossible, in the nature of things, to be otherwise. In such a manner God ordered the obstinacy of *Pharaoh*, in his refusing to obey God's commands, to let the people go. (Exod. iv. 21.) "I will harden his heart, and he shall not let the people go." (Chap. vii. 2—5.) "Aaron thy brother shall speak unto Pharaoh, that he send the children of Israel out of his land. And I will harden Pharaoh's heart, and multiply my signs and my wonders in the land of Egypt. But Pharaoh shall not hearken unto you; that I may lay mine hand upon Egypt, by great judgments," &c. (Chap. ix. 12.) "And the Lord hardened the heart of Pharaoh, and he hearkened not unto them, as the Lord had spoken unto Moses." (Chap. x. 1, 2.) "And the Lord said unto Moses, Go in unto Pharaoh; for I have hardened his heart, and the heart of his servants, that I might show these my signs before him, and that thou mayest tell it in the ears of thy son, and thy son's son, what things I have wrought in Egypt, and my signs which I have done amongst them, that ye may know that I am the Lord." (Chap. xiv. 4.) "And I will harden Pharaoh's heart, that he shall follow after them: and I will be honoured upon Pharaoh, and upon all his host." (Ver. 8.) "And the Lord hardened the heart of Pharaoh king of Egypt, and he pursued after the children of Israel." And it is certain, that in such a manner God, for wise and good ends, ordered that event, *Joseph* being sold into *Egypt* by his brethren. (Gen. xlv. 5.) "Now, therefore, be not grieved, nor angry with yourselves, that ye sold me hither; for God did send me before you to preserve life." (Ver. 7, 8.) "God did send me before you to preserve a posterity in the earth, and to save your lives by a great deliverance: so that now it was not you that sent me hither, but God." (Psal. cvii. 17.) "He sent a man before them, even Joseph, who was sold for a servant." It is certain, that thus God ordered the Sin and folly of *Sihon* king of the *Amorites*, in refusing to let the people of *Israel* pass by him peaceably. (Deut. ii. 30.) "But Sihon king of Heshbon would not let us pass by him; for the Lord thy God hardened his spirit, and made his heart obstinate, that he might deliver him into thine hand." It is certain, that God thus ordered the Sin and folly of the kings of *Canaan*, that they attempted not to make peace with *Israel*, but, with a stupid boldness and obstinacy, set themselves violently to oppose them and their God. (Josh. xi. 20.) "For it was of the Lord, to harden their hearts, that they should come against Israel in battle, that he might destroy them utterly, and that they might have no favour; but that he might destroy them, as the Lord commanded Moses." It is evident, that thus God ordered the treacherous rebellion of *Zedekiah* against the king of *Babylon*. (Jer. lii. 3.) "For through the anger of the Lord it came to pass in Jerusalem, and Judah, until he had cast them out from his presence, that Zedekiah rebelled against the king of Babylon." (So 2 Kings xxiv. 20.) And it is exceeding manifest, that God thus ordered the rapine and unrighteous ravages of *Nebuchadnezzar*, in spoiling and ruining the nations round about. (Jer. xxv. 9.) "Behold, I will send and take all the families of the north, saith the Lord, and Nebuchadnezzar my servant, and will bring them against this land, and against all the nations round about; and will utterly destroy them, and make them an astonishment, and an hissing, and perpetual desolations." (Chap. xliii. 10, 11.) "I will send and take Nebuchadnezzar the king of Babylon, my servant: and I will set his throne upon these stones that I have hid, and he shall spread his royal pavilion over them. And when he cometh, he shall smite the land of Egypt, and deliver such as are for death to death, and such as are for captivity to captivity, and such as are for the sword to the sword." Thus God represents himself as *sending* for *Nebuchadnezzar*, and *taking* him and his armies, and *bringing* him against the nations, which were to be destroyed by him, to that very end, that he might utterly destroy them, and make them desolate; and as appointing the work that he should do so particularly, that the very persons were designed that he should kill with the sword, and those that should be killed with famine and pestilence, and those that should be carried into captivity; and that in doing all these

* On the five Points, p. 302, 305.

things, he should act as his servant; by which, less cannot be intended, than that he should serve his purposes and designs. And in Jer. xxvii. 4—6. God declares, how he would cause him thus to serve his designs, viz. by bringing this to pass in his sovereign disposals, as the great Possessor and Governor of the universe, that disposes all things just as pleases him. "Thus saith the Lord of hosts, the God of Israel; I have made the earth, the man and the beast that are upon the ground, by my great power, and my stretched out arm, and have given it unto whom it seemed meet unto me; and now I have given all these lands into the hands of Nebuchadnezzar MY SERVANT, and the beasts of the field have I given also to serve him." And *Nebuchadnezzar* is spoken of as doing these things, by having his *arms strengthened* by God, and having God's *sword put into his hands, for this end.* (Ezek. xxx. 24, 25, 26.) Yea, God speaks of his terribly ravaging and wasting the nations, and cruelly destroying all sorts, without distinction of sex or age, as the weapon in God's hand, and the instrument of his indignation, which God makes use of to fulfil his own purposes, and execute his own vengeance. (Jer. li. 20, &c.) "Thou art my battle-axe, and weapons of war. For with thee will I break in pieces the nations, and with thee I will destroy kingdoms, and with thee I will break in pieces the horse and his rider, and with thee I will break in pieces the chariot and his rider; with thee also will I break in pieces man and woman; and with thee I will break in pieces old and young; and with thee will I break in pieces the young man and the maid," &c. It is represented, that the designs of *Nebuchadnezzar* and those that destroyed *Jerusalem*, never could have been accomplished, had not God determined them. (Lam. iii. 37.) "Who is he that saith, and it cometh to pass, and the Lord commandeth it not?" And yet the king of *Babylon* thus destroying the nations, and especially the *Jews*, is spoken of as his great wickedness, for which God finally destroyed him. (Isa. xiv. 4—6, 12. Hab. ii. 5—12. and Jer. chap. l. and li.) It is most manifest, that God, to serve his own designs, providentially ordered *Shimei's* cursing of *David.* (2 Sam. xvi. 10, 11.) "The Lord hath said unto him, Curse David.—Let him curse, for the Lord hath bidden him."

It is certain, that God thus, for excellent, holy, gracious ends, ordered the fact which they committed, who were concerned in Christ's death; and that therein they did but fulfil God's designs. As, I trust, no Christian will deny it was the design of God, that Christ should *be crucified*, and that for this end he came into the world. It is very manifest by many scriptures, that the whole affair of Christ's crucifixion, with its circumstances, and the treachery of *Judas*, that made way for it, was ordered in God's providence, in pursuance of his purpose; notwithstanding the violence that is used with those plain scriptures, to obscure and pervert the sense of them. (Acts ii. 23.) "Him being delivered, by the determinate counsel and foreknowledge of God* ye have taken, and with wicked hands have crucified and slain." Luke xxii. 21, 22.† "But behold the hand of him that betrayeth me, is with me on the table: and truly the Son of man goeth, as it was determined." (Acts iv. 27, 28.) "For of a truth, against the holy child Jesus, whom thou hast anointed, both Herod, and Pontius Pilate, with the Gentiles, and the people of Israel, were gathered together, for to do whatsoever thy hand and thy counsel determined before to be done." (Acts iii. 17, 18.) "And now, brethren, I wot that through ignorance ye did it, as did also your rulers; but these things, which God before had showed by the mouth of all his prophets, that Christ should suffer, he hath so fulfilled." So that what these murderers of Christ did, is spoken of as what God brought to pass or ordered, and that by which he fulfilled his own word.

In Rev. xvii. 17. "The agreeing of the kings of the earth to give their kingdom to the beast;" though it was a very wicked thing in them, is spoken of as "fulfilling God's will," and what "God had put into their hearts to do" It is manifest, that God sometimes permits sin to be committed, and at the same time orders things so, that if he permits the fact, it will come to pass, because on some accounts, he sees it needful and of importance, that it should come to pass. (Matt. xviii. 7.) "It must needs be, that offences come; but woe to that man by whom the offence cometh." With 1 Cor. xi. 19.) "For there must also be heresies among you, that they which are approved may be made manifest among you."

Thus it is certain and demonstrable, from the holy Scriptures, as well as the nature of things, and the principles of *Arminians*, that God permits sin; and at the same time, so orders things, in his providence, that it certainly and infallibly will come to pass, in consequence of his permission. I proceed to observe in the next place,

III. That there is a great difference between God being concerned thus, by his *permission*, in an event and act, which, in the inherent subject and agent of it, is sin, (though the event will certainly follow on his permission,) and his being concerned in it by *producing* it and exerting the act of sin; or between his being the *orderer* of its certain existence, by *not hindering* it, under certain circumstances, and his being the proper *actor* or *author* of it, by a *positive agency* or *efficiency*. And this, notwithstanding what Dr. Whitby offers about a saying of philosophers, that *causa deficiens, in rebus necessariis, ad causam per se efficientem reducenda est*. As there is a vast difference between the sun being the cause of the lightsomeness and warmth of the atmosphere, and the brightness of gold and diamonds, by its presence and positive influence; and its being the occasion of darkness and frost, in the night, by its motion, whereby it descends below the horizon. The motion of the sun is the occasion of the latter kind of events; but it is not the proper cause, efficient, or producer of them; though they are necessarily consequent on that motion, under such circumstances: no more is any action of the Divine Being the cause of the evil of men's Wills. If the sun were the proper *cause* of cold and darkness, it would be the *fountain* of these things, as it is the fountain of light and heat: and then something might be argued from the nature of cold and darkness, to a likeness of nature in the sun; and it might be justly inferred, that the sun itself is dark and cold, and that his beams are black and frosty. But from its being the cause no otherwise than by its departure, no such thing can be inferred, but the contrary; it may justly be argued, that the sun is a bright and hot body, if cold and darkness are found to be the consequence of its withdrawment; and the more constantly and necessarily these effects are connected with and confined to its absence, the more strongly does it argue the sun to be the fountain of light and heat. So, inasmuch as sin is not the fruit of any positive agency or influence of the Most High, but, on the contrary, arises from the withholding of his action and energy, and, under certain circumstances, necessarily follows on the want of his influence; this is no argument that he is sinful, or his operation evil, or has any thing of the nature of evil; but, on the contrary, that he, and his agency, are altogether good and holy, and that he is the fountain of all holiness. It would be strange arguing, indeed, because men never commit sin, but only when God leaves them *to themselves*, and necessarily sin when he does so, that therefore their sin is not *from themselves*, but from God; and so, that God must be a sinful being: as strange as it would be to argue, because it is always dark when the sun is gone, and never dark when the sun is present, that therefore all darkness is from the sun, and that his disk and beams must needs be black.

IV. It properly belongs to the supreme and absolute Governor of the universe, to order all important events within his dominion, by his wisdom: but the events in the moral world are of the most important kind; such as the moral actions of intelligent creatures, and their consequences.

These events will be ordered by something. They will

* "*Grotius*, as well as *Beza*, observes, προγνωσις must here signify decree; and *Elsner* has shown that it has that signification in approved Greek writers. And it is certain εκδοτος signifies one given up into the hands of an enemy:"——Dodd. in *Loc.*

† "As this passage is not liable to the ambiguities which some have apprehended in Acts ii. 23. and iv. 28. (which yet seem on the whole to be parallel to it, in their most natural construction,) I look upon it as an evident proof, that these things are, in the language of Scripture, said to be determined or decreed (or exactly bounded and marked out by God, as the word ωριζω most naturally signifies) which he sees in fact will happen, in consequence of his volitions, without any necessitating agency; as well as those events, of which he is properly the author." Dodd. in *Loc.*

either be disposed by wisdom, or they will be disposed by chance; that is, they will be disposed by blind and undesigning causes, if that were possible, and could be called a disposal. Is it not better, that the good and evil which happen in God's world, should be ordered, regulated, bounded, and determined by the good pleasure of an infinitely wise Being, who perfectly comprehends within his understanding and constant view, the universality of things, in all their extent and duration, and sees all the influence of every event, with respect to every individual thing and circumstance, throughout the grand system, and the whole of the eternal series of consequences; than to leave these things to fall out by chance, and to be determined by those causes which have no understanding or aim? Doubtless, in these important events, there is a better and a worse, as to the time, subject, place, manner, and circumstances of their coming to pass, with regard to their influence on the state and course of things. And if there be, it is certainly best that they should be determined to that time, place, &c. which is best. And therefore it is in its own nature fit, that wisdom, and not chance, should order these things. So that it belongs to the Being, who is the possessor of infinite wisdom, and is the creator and owner of the whole system of created existences, and has the care of all; I say, it belongs to him, to take care of this matter; and he would not do what is proper for him, if he should neglect it. And it is so far from being unholy in him, to undertake this affair, that it would rather have been unholy to neglect it; as it would have been a neglecting what fitly appertains to him; and so it would have been a very unfit and unsuitable neglect.

Therefore the sovereignty of God doubtless extends to this matter: especially considering, that if God should leave men's volitions, and all moral events, to the determination and disposition of blind unmeaning causes, or they should be left to happen perfectly without a cause; this would be no more consistent with liberty, in any notion of it, and particularly not in the *Arminian* notion of it, than if these events were subject to the disposal of Divine Providence, and the Will of man were determined by circumstances which are ordered and disposed by Divine Wisdom; as appears by what has been already observed. But it is evident, that such a providential disposing, and determining of men's moral actions, though it infers a moral necessity of those actions, yet it does not in the least infringe the real liberty of mankind; the only liberty that common sense teaches to be necessary to moral agency, which, as has been demonstrated, is not inconsistent with such necessity.

On the whole, it is manifest, that God may be, in the manner which has been described, the Orderer and Disposer of that event, which, in the inherent subject and agent, is moral Evil; and yet his so doing may be no moral Evil. He may will the disposal of such an event, and its coming to pass for good ends, and his Will not be an immoral or sinful Will, but a perfect, holy Will. And he may actually, in his providence, so dispose and permit things, that the event may be certainly and infallibly connected with such disposal and permission, and his act therein not be an immoral or unholy, but a perfectly holy act. Sin may be an evil thing, and yet that there should be such a disposal and permission, as that it should come to pass, may be a good thing. This is no contradiction, or inconsistence. *Joseph's* brethren selling him into *Egypt*, consider it only as it were acted by them, and with respect to their views and aims, which were evil, was a very bad thing; but it was a good thing, as it was an event of God's ordering, and considered with respect to his views and aims, which were good. (Gen. l. 20.) "As for you, ye thought Evil against me; but God meant it unto Good." So the crucifixion of Christ, if we consider only those things which belong to the event as it proceeded from his murderers, and are comprehended within the compass of the affair considered as their act, their principles, dispositions, views, and aims; so it was one of the most heinous things that ever was done; in many respects the most horrid of all acts; but consider it as it was willed and ordered of God, in the extent of his designs and views, it was the most admirable and glorious of all events; and God willing the event was the most holy volition of God, that ever was made known to men; and God's act in ordering it, was a divine act, which, above all others, manifests the moral excellency of the Divine Being.

The consideration of these things may help us to a sufficient answer to the cavils of *Arminians*, concerning what has been supposed by many *Calvinists*, of a distinction between a *secret* and *revealed* Will of God, and their diversity one from the other; supposing that the *Calvinists* herein ascribe inconsistent Wills to the Most High: which is without any foundation. God's *secret* and *revealed* Will, or, in other words, his *disposing* and *preceptive* Will, may be diverse, and exercised in dissimilar acts, the one in disapproving and opposing, the other in willing and determining, without any inconsistence. Because, although these dissimilar exercises of the Divine Will may, in some respects, relate to the same things, yet, in strictness, they have different and contrary objects, the one evil and the other good. Thus, for instance, the crucifixion of Christ was a thing contrary to the revealed or preceptive Will of God; because, as it was viewed and done by his malignant murderers, it was a thing infinitely contrary to the holy nature of God, and so necessarily contrary to the holy inclination of his heart revealed in his law. Yet this does not at all hinder but that the crucifixion of Christ, considered with all those glorious consequences, which were within the view of the Divine Omniscience, might be indeed, and therefore might appear to God to be, a glorious event; and consequently be agreeable to his Will, though this Will may be secret, *i. e.* not revealed in God's law. And thus considered, the crucifixion of Christ was not evil, but good. If the secret exercises of God's Will were of a kind that is dissimilar, and contrary to his revealed Will, respecting the same, or like objects; if the objects of both were good, or both evil; then, indeed, to ascribe contrary kinds of volition or inclination to God, respecting these objects, would be to ascribe an inconsistent Will to God: but to ascribe to Him different and opposite exercises of heart, respecting different objects, and objects contrary one to another, is so far from supposing God's Will to be *inconsistent* with itself, that it cannot be supposed *consistent* with itself any other way. For any being to have a Will of choice respecting good, and, at the same time, a Will of rejection and refusal respecting evil, is to be very consistent: but the contrary, viz. to have the same Will towards these contrary objects, and to choose and love both good and evil, at the same time, is to be very inconsistent.

There is no inconsistence in supposing, that God may hate a thing as it is in itself, and considered simply as evil, and yet that it may be his Will it should come to pass, considering all consequences. I believe, there is no person of good understanding, who will venture to say, he is certain that it is impossible it should be best, taking in the whole compass and extent of existence, and all consequences in the endless series of events, that there should be such a thing as moral evil in the world.* And, if so, it will certainly follow, that an infinitely wise Being, who always chooses what is best, must choose that there should be such a thing. And, if so, then such a choice is not evil,

* Here are worthy to be observed some passages of a late noted writer, of our nation, that nobody who is acquainted with him, will suspect to be very favourable to *Calvinism*. "It is difficult, says he, to handle the *necessity of evil* in such a manner, as not to stumble such as are not above being alarmed at propositions which have an uncommon sound. But if philosophers will but reflect calmly on the matter, they will find, that consistently with the unlimited power of the supreme cause, it may be said, that in the best ordered system, *evils* must have place."—*Turnbull's* Principles *of Moral Philosophy*, p. 327, 328. He is there speaking of *moral* evils, as may be seen.

Again the same author, in his *second vol.* entitled, *Christian Philosophy*, (p. 35.) has these words: "If the Author and Governor of all things be infinitely *perfect*, then whatever is, is *right*; of all possible systems he hath chosen the *best*: and, consequently, there is *no absolute evil* in the universe.—This being the case, all the seeming *imperfections* or *evils* in it are such only in a *partial* view; and, with respect to the *whole* system, they are *goods*."

Ibid. p. 37. "*Whence then comes evil*, is the question that hath, in all ages, been reckoned the *Gordian* knot in philosophy. And, indeed, if we own the existence of evil in the world in an *absolute* sense, we diametrically contradict what hath been just now proved of God. For if there be any *evil* in the system, that is not good with respect to the *whole*, then is the *whole* not good, but evil: or, at best, very imperfect: and an *author* must be as his *workmanship* is; as is the effect, such is the cause. But the solution of this difficulty is at hand; *That there is no evil in the universe*. What! Are there no pains, no imperfections? Is there no misery, no vice in the world? or are not these *evils?* Evils indeed they are; that is, those of one sort are hurtful, and those of the other sort are equally hurtful, and abominable: but they are *not* evil or mischievous with respect to the *whole?*"

Ibid. p. 42. "But he is, at the same time, said to *create* evil, darkness, out a wise and holy choice. And if so, then that Providence which is agreeable to such a choice, is a wise and holy Providence. Men do *will* sin as sin, and so are the authors and actors of it: they love it as sin, and for evil ends and purposes. God does not will sin as sin, or for the sake of any thing evil; though it be his pleasure so to order things, that, he permitting, sin will come to pass, for the sake of the great good that by his disposal shall be the consequence. His willing to order things so that evil should come to pass, for the sake of the contrary good, is no argument that he does not hate evil, as evil: and if so, then it is no reason why he may not reasonably forbid evil as evil, and punish it as such.

The *Arminians* themselves must be obliged, whether they will or no, to allow a distinction of God's Will, amounting to just the same thing that *Calvinists* intend by their distinction of a *secret and revealed Will*. They must allow a distinction of those things which God thinks best should be, considering all circumstances and consequences, and so are agreeable to his disposing Will, and those things which he loves, and are agreeable to his nature, in themselves considered. Who is there that will dare to say, that the hellish pride, malice, and cruelty of devils, are agreeable to God, and what he likes and approves? And yet, I trust, there is no christian divine but will allow, that it is agreeable to God's Will so to order and dispose things concerning them, so to leave them to themselves, and give them up to their own wickedness, that this perfect wickedness should be a necessary consequence. Dr. Whitby's words plainly suppose and allow it.* These following things may be laid down as maxims of plain truth, and indisputable evidence.

1. That God is a *perfectly happy* Being, in the most absolute and highest sense possible.

2. That it will follow from hence, that God is free from every thing that is *contrary to happiness;* and so, that in strict propriety of speech, there is no such thing as any pain, grief, or trouble, in God.

3. When any intelligent being is really crossed and disappointed, and things are contrary to what he truly desires, he is the *less pleased*, or has *less pleasure*, his *pleasure and happiness is diminished*, and he suffers what is disagreeable to him, or is the subject of something that is of a nature contrary to joy and happiness, even pain and grief.†

From this last axiom it follows, that if no distinction is to be admitted between God's hatred of sin, and his Will with respect to the event and the existence of sin, as the all-wise Determiner of all events, under the view of all consequences through the whole compass and series of things; I say, then it certainly follows, that the coming to pass of every individual act of sin is truly, all things considered, contrary to his Will, and that his Will is really crossed in it; and this in proportion as he hates it. And as God's hatred of sin is infinite, by reason of the infinite contrariety of his Holy Nature to sin; so his Will is infinitely crossed, in every act of sin that happens. Which is as much as to say, he endures that which is infinitely disagreeable to him, by means of every act of sin that he sees committed. And, therefore, as appears by the preceding positions, he endures truly and really, infinite grief or pain from every sin. And so he must be infinitely crossed, and suffer infinite pain, every day, in millions of millions of instances: he must continually be the subject of an immense number of *real*, and truly infinitely *great* crosses and vexations. Which would be to make him infinitely the most miserable of all Beings.

If any objector should say; all that these things amount to, is, that *God may do evil that good may come;* which is justly esteemed immoral and sinful in men; and therefore may be justly esteemed inconsistent with the moral perfections of God. I answer, that for God to dispose and permit evil, in the manner that has been spoken of, is not to do evil that good may come; for it is not to do evil at all.—In order to a thing being morally evil, there must be one of these things belonging to it, either it must be a thing *unfit* and *unsuitable* in its own nature; or it must have a *bad tendency;* or it must proceed from an *evil disposition*, and be done for an evil end. But neither of these things can be attributed to God's ordering and permitting such events, as the immoral acts of creatures, for good ends. (1.) It is not *unfit in its own nature*, that he should do so. For it is in its own nature *fit*, that *infinite wisdom*, and not blind chance, should dispose moral good and evil in the world. And it is *fit*, that the Being who has *infinite wisdom*, and is the Maker, Owner, and Supreme Governor of the world, should take care of that matter. And, therefore, there is no *unfitness* or unsuitableness in his doing it. It may be unfit, and so immoral, for any other beings to go about to order this affair; because they are not possessed of a wisdom that in any manner fits them for it; and, in other respects, they are not fit to be trusted with this affair; nor does it belong to them, they not being the owners and lords of the universe.

We need not be afraid to affirm, that if a wise and good man knew with absolute certainty it would be best, all things considered, that there should be such a thing as moral evil in the world, it would not be contrary to his wisdom and goodness, for him to choose that it should be so. It is no evil desire, to desire good, and to desire that which, all things considered, is best. And it is no unwise choice, to choose that that should be, which it is best should be; and to choose the existence of that thing concerning which this is known, *viz.* that it is best it should be, and so is known in the whole to be most worthy to be chosen. On the contrary, it would be a plain defect in wisdom and goodness, for him not to choose it. And the reason why he might not *order* it, if he were able, would not be because he might not desire it, but only the ordering of that matter does not belong to him. But it is no harm for him who is, by right, and in the greatest propriety, the Supreme Orderer of all things, to order every thing in such a manner, as it would be a point of wisdom in him to choose that they should be ordered. If it would be a plain defect of wisdom and goodness in a being, not to choose that that should be, which he certainly knows it would, all things considered, be best should be, (as was but now observed,) then it must be impossible for a Being who has no defect of wisdom and goodness, to do otherwise than choose it should be; and that, for this very reason, because he is perfectly wise and good. And if it be agreeable to perfect wisdom and goodness for him to choose that it should be, and the ordering of all things supremely and perfectly belongs to him, it must be agreeable to infinite wisdom and goodness, to order that it should be. If the choice is good, the ordering and disposing things according to that choice must also be good. It can be no harm in one to whom it belongs "to do his Will in the armies of heaven, and amongst the inhabitants of the earth," to execute a good volition. If this Will be good, and the object of his Will be, all things considered, good and best, then the choosing or willing it is not *willing evil* that good may come. And if so, then his ordering, according to that Will, is not *doing evil* that good may come.

2. It is not of a *bad tendency*, for the Supreme Being thus to order and permit that moral evil to be, which it is best should come to pass. For that it is of good tendency, is the very thing supposed in the point now in question.—Christ's crucifixion, though a most horrid fact in them that perpetrated it, was of a most glorious tendency as permitted and ordered of God.

3. Nor is there any need of supposing, it *proceeds from any evil disposition or aim;* for by the supposition, what is aimed at is good, and good is the actual issue, in the final result of things.‡

confusion; and yet to do no evil, but to be the author of good only. He is called the "Father of lights," the Author of "every perfect and good gift, with whom there is no variableness nor shadow of turning," who "tempteth no man," but "giveth to all men liberally, and upbraideth not." And yet, by the prophet (Isa. xlv. 7.) he is introduced saying of himself, "I form light and create darkness; I make peace, and create evil: I the Lord, do all these things." What is the meaning, the plain language of all this, but that the Lord delighteth in goodness, and (as the scripture speaks) evil is "his strange work?" He intends and pursues the universal *good* of his creation: and the *evil* which happens, is not permitted for its own sake, or through any pleasure in evil, but because it is requisite to the *greater good* pursued."

* *Whitby* on the five Points, Edit. 2. 300, 305, 309.

† Certainly it is not less absurd and unreasonable, to talk of God's Will and Desires being truly and properly crossed, without his suffering any uneasiness, or any thing grievous or disagreeable, than it is to talk of something that may be called a *revealed Will*, which may, in some respect, be different from a *secret* purpose, which purpose may be fulfilled, when the other is opposed.

‡ From the whole strain of our author's defence of his principles, in refer-

SECT. X.

Concerning sin's first Entrance into the world.

THE things which have already been offered, may serve to obviate or clear many of the objections which might be raised concerning sin's first coming into the world; as though it would follow from the doctrine maintained, that God must be the author of the first sin, through his so disposing things, that it should necessarily follow from his permission, that the sinful act should be committed, &c. I need not, therefore, stand to repeat what has been said

ence to the existence of sin in the universe, though there are many excellent remarks interspersed, and sound reasoning as far as his data would admit, yet he is evidently embarrassed; makes concessions which his general principles of moral necessity did not require, and shelters himself under covers that afford him in reality no effectual protection. To say, that the existence of sin is only a *common difficulty*, which belongs to every hypothesis—that though God is the *author of sin*, in some sense, yet he is not the agent, therefore the phrase should be disliked and rejected that though God *wills the event* of sin, yet he wills it not *as* an evil, but for excellent ends—that the events of moral evils are *disposed by wisdom*—that God may be the *orderer* and *disposer* of moral evil, which in the agent is infinitely evil, but in the orderer of it no evil at all—that in order to a thing being morally evil it must be *unfit* and *unsuitable*, or of a *bad tendency*, or from an *evil disposition*; but that in *willing the event* of sin neither can be attributed to God—that if a wise and good man *knew*, with absolute certainty, that it would be *best*, all things considered, there should be moral evil, he might *choose* that it should be so—that the reason why he might not *order* it, if he were able, would not be because he might not *desire*, but only the ordering of that matter does not *belong* to him—and that, in the language of Turnbull, "there is *no evil in the universe*,—no absolute evil; sins are evils only in a *partial* view, but with respect to the *whole* system they are *not* evil or mischievous, but *goods*," *&c.* to say these things, and more of a similar cast, is not calculated to satisfy a mind that wants the best evidence which the nature of the case will admit; and we strongly suspect, from his manner of writing, that our author's own mind was not satisfied with the solution which he has attempted.

In former notes we have had occasion only to *explain* principles adopted; or to point out others either more evident, or more radical, on which those of the author were founded, or with which they stood inseparably connected. But at the close of the present section we feel ourselves obliged to attempt, at least, the *rectification* of his principles; or perhaps more properly, to point out *other principles*, which, we conceive, are attended with no such embarrassment, are exposed to no self-contradiction, and which represent the Great Supreme in a much more amiable light. The task is indeed arduous; but let it not be thought impossible; nor let the imperfection of language be confounded with the inadequacy of principles. And while we solicit the *candour* of the reader—whereby he will be prepared to make such allowances as the nature of the subject requires, be prevented from drawing hasty conclusions of the impracticability of bringing the subject of inquiry to a satisfactory issue, or of presumption in attempting it—we no less demand a *strictness* of examination. The real inquirer after truth, the christian divine, and the moral philosophers, should be solicitous, not to have the "last word," in controversy, but to make all possible advances in ascertaining the genuine grounds of acknowledged truths, in discovering radical principles, and in ascertaining their just bearings and tendencies.

1. The true point of inquiry is—not whether there *be* moral evil, or whether God *be* just? but—how the actual existence of sin, or moral evil, in the universe, is to be *reconciled* with the moral perfections and character of God? Therefore, the thing wanted is a middle term, or argumentative medium, whereby it may be *shown* that this proposition *is true*, viz. There is *no real inconsistence* between the existence of sin and the moral perfections of God.

2. We may therefore consider the following propositions as first principles:

AXIOMS.

There does exist in the universe moral evil.

II. God is infinitely free from injustice, unholiness, and all imperfections. Hence,

COROLLARY.

There is *no real inconsistence* between the existence of moral evil and the moral perfections of God.

3. Now the question returns, What is the *best evidence* that there is no such inconsistency? Those who are satisfied with these plain propositions the axioms, and corollary, may have the evidence of *faith*, that there is no inconsistence between the subject and predicate of the last proposition. They may know so much of God as to be *assured*, that the existence of sin in the world is no impeachment of the moral character of the Most High. For such evidence it behoves us to be thankful. Millions are now in heaven, who enjoyed no other evidence while on earth than that of faith. But this is no sufficient reason why those who have opportunity should make no further inquiries into the subject. Some, indeed, suppose, that no *rational evidence* is in the present state *attainable* by man. But why any should so conclude it is difficult to say, except it be, that they wish to make their own minds the standard of all others, or their own attainments the *ne plus ultra* of moral philosophy. Such persons are not likely to acknowledge or perceive the real evidence, on supposition that it is laid before them, as their minds will be strongly prejudiced against all reasoning on the subject.

4. One thing, however, is incontrovertible, as necessarily connected with the axioms, that the existence of moral evil, and the spotless and infinitely excellent moral character of God, are *perfectly consistent;* and therefore there must be *somewhere good evidence* of it. And another thing is equally plain, that the brighter the evidence we have of the truth of the proposition which asserts the *consistency* of the two axioms, the more will be our acquaintance with God's real character, and the real nature of sin, which all must allow to be advantageous. To which we may add; that increased evidence of such a proposition is far from being injurious, may be further inferred from this consideration, that the higher any beings rise in holiness and happiness, the more *clear* will be that evidence to their view.

5. The *terms* of the question are so plain, and so generally understood, that it is scarcely necessary to notice them; we may, however, briefly observe, that moral evil is what stands in direct opposition to the moral character of God; and that this latter includes *universal rectitude*, or holiness, and *perfect benevolence.* Therefore,

POSTULATE.

Whatever is perfectly consistent with universal rectitude, and perfect benevolence, is consistent with the moral perfections of God. The reader will observe, that what is asserted of rectitude and benevolence, is different; the one is said to be *universal* and the other *perfect* only. Every attribute of Jehovah is in ITSELF both perfect and universal; but not RELATIVELY so. Thus his *rectitude* is both *perfect* in itself, and *universal* with respect to its object: but his *benevolence*, however infinitely perfect, is *restricted* as to its objects, both in *extent* and in *degree.* And this *restriction* is *necessary* two ways:

6. *First*, the objects of benevolence, at least in this world, compose a *system;* and every system, whether natural or moral, implies a *subordination* and *comparative superiority* of parts; therefore the very idea of a *systematic* whole implies a *restriction* of benevolence as to extent and degree.

7. *Secondly*, the exercise of benevolence is an exercise of *will;* and the exercise of will implies *diversity* of objects, and a *preference* of some, rather than others, to occupy the more excellent parts of the whole system; so that perfect universality, or a strict equality of benevolence, without a distinguishing preference, is necessarily excluded by the *very nature* of benevolence in exercise.

8. Divine *benevolence*, therefore, admits of *gradations*, from the smallest degree conceivable to the utmost extent of the system; while *rectitude* admits of no such degree. Were we to attempt an illustration of so abstracted a subject by mental images, we might say, that *rectitude* in its exercise towards the creatures, may be compared to a plain surface as widely extended as the universe, of infinitely perfect polish, and without a flaw in any part. Hence, in its exercise, it is *universal* as its objects; and can no more admit of *degrees*, than a perfect polish can admit of flaws. On the contrary, *benevolence* may be compared to a cone, in an inverted form, the vertex of which is in contact with a point of that plane, and which, from the least possible degree, is capable of rising at sovereign pleasure, in its exercise towards the universe, to such a height, as that the base of it *may* be, or *may* not be, of equal extent with the plane below.

9. From just views of benevolence we may infer, that its exercise is purely free, and undeserved by the creature; being the fruit of will, choice, and sovereign pleasure. The absence of it, with respect to creatures, implies no flaw in perfect rectitude. Every degree of benevolence, from the least to the greatest, must be altogether optional. Perfect rectitude, with respect to created beings, and each individual creature, may subsist, without any more benevolence than what is necessarily included in mere existence.

10. This being the case, the state of the universe, in reference to perfect rectitude, and irrespective of benevolence, may be further compared to a balance in perfect equilibrium. The least weight of benevolence makes it preponderate, proportionally, in favour of virtue and happiness; but without which weight neither could take place.

11. But, according to what has been said in a former note, every created being is the subject of *passive power;* which, with respect to its influence on the creature, is, in some respect, the opposite of benevolence. In *some*, not in *all* respects. Benevolence is an exercise of *will*, and implies an agent; but passive power is a quality or principle inseparable from every creature, and from the universe at large. In reference to a former illustration, this may be compared to another cone exactly opposite, the vertex of which, from below, meets that of the other in the same plane. The intermediate point, and indeed every point in the same plane, may represent the perfect rectitude of God towards every individual; the inverted cone above, divine benevolence; the cone below, passive power, with its base *necessarily* equal to the whole plane, as it respects the created universe.

12. Hence we may say that the *neutral* state of any being is placed in the plane; his degree of influence from passive power, the predisposing cause of vice, is represented by a corresponding given part of the cone below; and his degree of predisposition to virtue from divine benevolence, is represented by a corresponding given part of the cone above. Or, to change the comparison, if a perfectly poised balance be made to represent perfect rectitude, then we may suppose weights at each end in all possible proportions, from the smallest to the greatest. Passive power not being the effect of will, but of the relative nature of things, and inseparably connected with one end of the balance, it is evident, that it can be counteracted in its tendency only by the weight of benevolence, or sovereign pleasure. Therefore, whoever on earth or in heaven, rises to, and is confirmed in virtue, his attainment must be the *effect* of mere benevolence. And whoever on earth, or in hell, falls into, and is confirmed in vice, his deterioration must be the *effect* of passive power, as the predisposing cause of vice, which nothing in the universe can counteract but sovereign, free, unmerited benevolence.

13. Consequently, all the good and happiness in the universe is the effect of benevolence, or sovereign pleasure, and exists above the plane of perfect rectitude; but all the evil and misery in the world is the effect of passive power, in union with free agency, and exists below the plane of rectitude. The one generates virtue, and raises to happiness and heaven; the other generates vice, and sinks to misery and hell.

14. Every thing in the universe planned, decreed, and effected by Jehovah, is a structure of benevolence. All he effects is good, and only good. The *evil* that exists is not his work. Benevolence has decreed an endless chain of *antecedents*, including the natural and moral worlds; and the consequents peculiar to them result therefrom with infallible certainty. But *other* antecedents, in *this* world, and in *hell*, are constantly interposed by free agents under the influence of passive power, whose consequences also follow with equal infallible certainty. To the eye of created intelligence these counter positions, and opposite consequents, appear blended in an inextricable manner, like the different rays of light in the same pencil, different gasses in a given space, and different subtle fluids in the same body. But to the eye of Omniscience they appear perfectly distinct, in their proper nature, in all their directions and bearings, in all their tendencies and effects.

15. Instead, therefore, of saying, "There is *no evil* in the universe," we should say, "There is *much evil* in the universe; there is much on earth, and more in hell; but none of God's *appointment.*" It is demonstrable, that passive power can no more be an object of appointment, than the most direct contradictions; and yet it is equally demonstrable that such a principle is the inseparable concomitant of every creature. It is of prior consideration to moral agency; for whatever is a *property* of a created nature as such, is of prior consideration to the *agency* of that creature. Consequently it is a property neither divinely appointed, nor yet a *moral* evil.

16. Liberty, in one sense, bears the same relation to good and evil, as rectitude does to benevolence and passive power. Liberty in its lf is equally a medium between good and evil, as rectitude is between benevolence and passive power; and the medium is of a nature perfectly distinct from both extremes. To which we may add, that liberty united to, or under the influence of, sovereign benevolence, generates virtue; but liberty united to, or under the influence of, passive power, generates vice.

17. From the premises it may be seen, that the existence of *all evil*, and especially *moral evil*, in the universe, is not inconsistent with the moral perfections of God. It is evident also that *in no sense whatever*, except by a total misapplication of terms, can God be said to be "the author of sin." Nor can it be said that God "wills the event of sin;" but the contrary is plain, that he *does not will* it, either in a decretive, a legislative, or any other sense.

already, about such a necessity not proving God to be the author of sin, in any ill sense, or in any such sense as to infringe any liberty of man, concerned in his moral agency, or capacity of blame, guilt, and punishment.

But, should it nevertheless be said, that if God, when he had made man, might so order his circumstances, that from these, together with his withholding further assistance and divine influence, his sin would infallibly follow, why might not God as well have first made man with a fixed prevailing principle of sin in his heart?

I answer, 1. It was meet, if sin did come into existence, and appear in the world, it should arise from the imperfection which properly belongs to a creature, as such, and should appear so to do, that it might appear not to be from God as the efficient or fountain. But this could not have been, if man had been made at first with sin in his heart; nor unless the abiding principle and habit of sin were first introduced by an evil act of the creature. If sin had not arisen from the imperfection of the creature, it would not have been so visible, that it did not arise from God, as the positive cause, and real source of it.—But it would require room that cannot be here allowed, fully to consider all the difficulties which have been started, concerning the first Entrance of sin into the world.—And therefore,

2. I would observe, that objections against the doctrine that has been laid down, in opposition to the *Arminian* notion of liberty, from these difficulties, are altogether impertinent; because no additional difficulty is incurred, by adhering to a scheme in this manner differing from theirs, and none would be removed or avoided, by agreeing with, and maintaining theirs. Nothing that the *Arminians* say, about the contingence, or self-determining power of man's Will, can serve to explain, with less difficulty, how the first sinful volition of mankind could take place, and man be justly charged with the blame of it. To say, the Will was self-determined, or determined by free choice, in that sinful volition—which is to say, that the first sinful volition was determined by a foregoing sinful volition—is no solution of the difficulty. It is an odd way of solving difficulties, to advance greater, in order to it. To say, two and two make nine, or, that a child begat his father, solves no difficulty: no more does it, to say, the first sinful act of choice was before the first sinful act of choice, and chose and determined it, and brought it to pass. Nor is it any better solution, to say, the first sinful volition chose, determined, and produced itself; which is to say, it was before it was. Nor will it go any further towards helping us over the difficulty, to say, the first sinful volition arose accidentally, without any cause at all; any more than it will solve that difficult question, *How the world could be made out of nothing?* to say, it came into being out of nothing, without any cause; as has been already observed. And if we should allow, that the first evil volition should arise by perfect accident, without any cause; it would relieve no difficulty, about God laying the blame of it to man. For how was man to blame for perfect accident, which had no cause, and which, therefore, he was not the cause of, any more than if it came by some external cause?—Such kind of solutions are no better, than if some person, going about to solve some of the strange mathematical paradoxes, about infinitely great and small quantities—as, that some infinitely great quantities are infinitely greater than some other infinitely great quantities; and also that some infinitely small quantities, are infinitely less than others, which yet are infinitely little—should say, that mankind have been under a mistake, in supposing a greater quantity to exceed a smaller; and that a hundred, multiplied by ten, makes but a single unit.*

18. The great source of confusion into which many authors have plunged themselves, is, that they draw too hasty an inference in attempting to make *not hindering* an event to be ultimately the same as *willing* it. Upon their *data*, indeed, it may be true, while they regard every event alike to be the effect of divine energy, and even the *worst*, in order to answer a *good end.* And this will always be the case, for self-consistency requires it, until we see and acknowledge a metaphysical *negative cause* of moral evil, and an eternal *nature of things* antecedent to all will, with their infallible effects, when not counteracted by sovereign benevolence.

19. Let us now view the subject in the light of terms a little different. Much error often arises through the defect of language; and where there is danger of misapprehension, it may be of use to change expressions. Hereby a difficult subject may be taken by different handles, or a reader may apprehend it by one handle, which he could not by another. Let us then substitute the word *equity* instead of *rectitude*, and undeserved *favour* instead of benevolence.

POSTULATE.

Whatever is perfectly consistent with *equity* is also perfectly consistent with the *moral character* of God.

20. Whatever is the *pure effect* of *equity* and *the nature of things*, or essential truth, united, cannot be inconsistent with the moral perfections of God; the existence of moral evil in the universe is the pure effect of these; therefore the existence of moral evil in the universe cannot be inconsistent with the moral perfections of God.

21. The only ground of hesitation here is, *How* moral evil is the effect of equity and the nature of things? *Liberty* itself is a *natural* good, and therefore is the fruit of divine favour; and the mere *exercise* of liberty must be ascribed to the same cause. But he who is hypothetically free to good, must be in like manner free to evil. For this hypothetical freedom either to good or to evil is what constitutes the *morality* of his acts of choice. Take away this hypothetical freedom, and you take away the essence of moral agency. It is plain, then, that to possess this freedom and consequent moral agency, is not inconsistent with the equity, rectitude, or moral perfections of God. Yet it is demonstrable that freedom *cannot* be influenced in its choice, so as to constitute it virtuous or vicious, holy or sinful, morally right or wrong, good or evil, but from two causes radically; divine favour and passive power. If the agent be under the influence of divine favour, a happy result, in the same proportion, is secured by the same essential truth as renders the choice of the great I AM, infallibly good; which no one will say is inconsistent with the divine perfections. For though favour raises the agent *above* what rigid or pure equity can do, there is no *inconsistence* between them; any more than between paying a just debt, and bestowing also a free gift in addition. But if the agent be not under the influence of undeserved favour, the only alternative is, that he must necessarily be under the influence of passive power. And as nothing can possibly secure a happy result but undeserved favour, or benevolent influence, a negative cause becomes an infallible ground of certainty of an opposite result. Again,

22. When God gives to creatures what is their *due*, he deals with them in *equity*, but when God gives them less grace than is actually sufficient to secure from sin, or will *in fact* do so, he gives them their due. Were it otherwise, it would be impossible for any to sin. If to give them so much favour, or benevolent influence, as would *actually preserve* them from sin, were their *due*, it is plain that the God of equity would give them their due, and preserve them from sin accordingly. But the fact is widely otherwise. They are not all preserved from sin, though all might be, through the interposition of sovereign favour; therefore it is not their due, or equity does not require it.

23. If it be said, It is owing to their *own fault;* it is very true; but how came any creature to be *faulty?* God made angels and men *upright.* And he has always dealt with every creature, however debased by sin, in *equity.* He has also given to every creature capable of sinning, *liberty* unconstrained. He often influences the disposition by benevolence; and the goodness of God, by providential and gracious dispensations, leadeth to repentance. But never has he dealt with any unjustly, or given them less than their due. Not a fallen spirit, however deeply sunk, can verify such a charge. Assuredly, they have *destroyed themselves,* but in God is the only help. A principle, of which God is not the author, as before explained in union with the abuse of their liberty, satisfactorily accounts for the fact. Our *evil* is of *ourselves;* but all our *good* is from God.

24. From what has been said, we may safely draw this inference, that the existence of moral evil in the universe, is not inconsistent with the moral perfections of God. And the proposition would be equally true, had the proportion of moral evil been greater than it is. But some will continue to cavil, it is probable, because *every* objection is not professedly answered, and *some* difficulties, or divine *arcana*, will always remain. They will still be asking, *why* benevolence is not more universal, and thereby moral evil *altogether* prevented? Why the cone (to which benevolence has been compared) is not a cylinder, whose base is commensurate with the plane of creatural existence, and whose top rises *ad infinitum?* They might as well inquire, Why is not every atom a sun? Why not every drop an ocean? Why not every moment an age? Why not every worm an angel? Why not the solar system as large as all material systems united? Why the number of angels and men not a thousand times greater? And, to complete the absurdity of demanding evidence for every thing, as an objection against demonstrable truth, Why is not any given part on the surface of a cone, a cylinder, or a globe, not in the centre? To all such inquiries—and if advanced as objections *impertinent* inquiries—it is sufficient to reply, Infinite Wisdom has planned an universe, in which divine benevolence appears wonderfully conspicuous; and even the evils, whether natural or moral, which are intermixed, and which in their origin are equally remote from divine causation and from chance, are overruled to answer purposes the most benevolent, and the most wonderfully sublime.

COROLLARIES.

1. The only possible way of avoiding the most ruinous consequences—moral evil and misery—is to direct the will, through the instrumentality of its freedom, to a state of union to God, submission to his will, and an imitation of his moral perfections, according to his most merciful appointment.

2. To creatures fallen below the line of rectitude, and yet the subjects of hope, prayer to God for grace, undeserved favour, or benevolent influence, is an exercise the most becoming, a duty the most necessary and important, and a privilege of the first magnitude.—W.

* On the subject of the *origin* of moral evil, our author is more concise than usual. His design in this very short section, is merely to show, that the difficulties which have been started, concerning the first entrance of sin into the world, are such as cannot be discussed in a small compass; and, that the Arminian cause gains nothing by urging them. That cause has been sufficiently examined in several parts of this Inquiry; but the true and precise *origin* of moral evil, requires further notice. It is indeed of infinitely greater importance to be acquainted with that celestial art, and that sacred influence, whereby we may emerge from the gulf of sin to holiness and heaven, than to be accurately versed in the science of its origination. And so it is far more important to see objects, and improve sight, than to be able to demonstrate the theory of vision; to recover health, and to use it aright, than to have skill to ascertain the cause and the symptom of disease; to contribute vigorously in extinguishing a fire that threatens to destroy our dwellings and ourselves, than to know the author of the calamity; to participate the effects of varied seasons, than to understand, astronomically, the precise reason of those variations. The mariner may navigate without knowing *why* his needle points to the north; and the celestial bodies in the solar system were as equally regular in their motions before Sir Isaac Newton had existence, as they have been since he has ascertained those *laws* and *proportions* according to which they move. And yet the science of optics is not useless, the healing art is not to be despised, to discover an incendiary is desirable, and never is that philosopher who attempts to ascertain the *causes* of *natural* phenomena, held up as blameworthy. In like manner, though millions are delivered from the

SECT. XI.

Of a supposed Inconsistence between these principles and God's moral character.

THE things which have been already observed, may be sufficient to answer most of the objections, and silence the great exclamations of *Arminians* against the *Calvinists*, from the supposed inconsistence of *Calvinistic* principles with the moral perfections of God, as exercised in his government of mankind. The consistence of such a doctrine of necessity as has been maintained, with the fitness and reasonableness of God's commands, promises and threatenings, rewards and punishments, has been particularly

influence of sin, and raised to the most exalted eminence of happiness, who never knew, or even sought to know, scientifically, the origination of sin; this is no good reason that such knowledge is useless, or even unimportant. As we do not wish to swell these notes unnecessarily, we beg leave to refer to what we have said elsewhere on the subject, particularly in notes on the former part of this Treatise, on Dr. Doddridge's Lectures, and on a Sermon, concerning "Predestination to Life," second edition, in connexion with what we now add. (See Doddr. Works, vol. iv. p. 363, &c. vol. v. p. 208, &c. *Notes.*)—As the basis of our present demonstration, we begin with proposing a few axioms.

AXIOMS.

1. No effect can exist without an adequate cause. On this truth are founded all reasonings and all metaphysical evidence.

2. Sin is an effect, and has a cause. On this truth are founded all moral means and all religious principles.

3. The origin of moral evil cannot be moral evil; or, the cause of sin cannot be sin itself. Except we admit this, the same thing may be and not be, at the same time, and in the same respect—the same thing may be sin and no sin—cause and no cause—or, contrary to the first axiom, a contingent event may be the cause of itself, or may exist without an adequate cause.

4. There is no *positive* cause but what is ultimately from God. If otherwise, something positive may *begin* to be *without* a positive cause; or, something may exist without an *adequate* cause; which is the same as an effect to exist without a cause, contrary to the first axiom.

5. There may be a *negative*, metaphysical cause, where there is no decretive divine operation to effect it. Were there no negative metaphysical causes, such ideas as absence, ignorance, folly, weakness, and the like, could have no metaphysical effects; contrary to universal experience. And we must renounce all ideas of congruity to suppose that such things are the mere effects of divine decree and operation.

Having premised these positions as axioms not to be disputed, we proceed to make a few observations, which, though equally true, may not be equally obvious.

6. The origin of moral evil cannot be *one* principle. For were it one, it must be either a positive or negative cause. If *positive*, it would be ultimately from God; but this would exclude a *moral alternative*, the very essence of moral agency, and consequently be incompatible with the existence of *moral* evil. But if a *negative* cause, it must ultimately be referred to the *prime* negative cause, which can be no other than passive power, as before explained; which is nothing independent of positive existence; and consequently can have no effect but in *union* with positive existence.

7. It remains, then, that the origin of moral evil is a compound of *two* causes at least. Yet not more than two; because, as we shall see, these are sufficient, and more would be superfluous, in order to produce the effect.

8. Now the question remains, What are these compounded principles? Are they two positive causes, two negative, or one of each? They cannot be *two positive* causes; for then they might be ultimately reduced to *one*, the first cause; as before proved, *gr.* 4, 6. Nor can they be *two negative* ones; for ultimately there is but *one* cause properly negative. Consequently,

9. The first entrance of sin into the world, or the true and precise origin of moral evil, may be found in *two* causes *united:* the one positive and the other negative. But neither of which is morally good or morally evil; if the cause were morally good, the effect could not be morally bad; and if morally evil, it would be contrary to the third axiom, and to common sense. These two causes are, first, *liberty*, a cause *naturally* good; secondly, *passive power*, a cause *naturally* evil. And these two causes are as necessary for the production of moral evil, as two parents for the production of a human being according to the laws of nature.

9. Dr. Clarke, whose brief account has been more implicitly admitted than any other, says, that moral evil "arises *wholly* from the ABUSE of *liberty;* which God gave to his creatures for other purposes, and which it was reasonable and fit to give them for the perfection and order of the whole creation: only they, contrary to God's intention and command, have *abused* what was necessary for the perfection of the whole, to the corruption and depravation of themselves." This extract from Dr. Clarke (in his Demonstration of the Being and Attributes of God, p. 113. 5th edit.) has been advanced by celebrated writers, as "containing all that can be advanced with certainty" on the subject. But surely those minds must be easily satisfied, who can be satisfied with such evidence. Dr. Clarke allows and proves, that liberty is a *perfection*, rather than an evil. How came it then to *produce* evil? He answers, "This arises wholly from the *abuse* of liberty." But what is the *cause* of this *effect* called "the abuse of liberty?" This in fact is the whole of the difficulty, and yet he leaves it *untouched.* The free agent *fails* in the exercise of liberty; this failure is an effect; but there is no effect without a cause; therefore this *failure* must have a *cause;* and *this cause* (not the abuse of liberty) must bring us to the *origin* of moral evil.

10. What Dr. Clarke has left untouched may yet be ascertained. We think it has been fairly excluded, by what has been already advanced, from every thing except *liberty* and *passive power.* Therefore, the *abuse* of liberty can arise *only* from its associate. But *how* can this operate as a *cause* of the *abuse* of liberty? In order to answer this question, we must recollect what liberty itself is, *viz.* a natural power, or instrument of the mind, capable of producing moral effects. Not a *self-determining* power, which would be contrary to the first axiom; and which our author has abundantly demonstrated to be full of contradictions, and an utter impossibility. It must, then, be determined by *motives.* But motives, as before shown, (in a former note,) are the *objects* of choice in union with the *state* of the mind, as a compound effect. Now the *cause* why the real good, suppose the chief good, which is absolutely unchangeable, is not chosen, and an inferior good *appears* at the instant of choice preferable, and is in fact preferred, must arise from that *part* of the motive which is the state of the mind.

11. Now there are only *two* states of the mind conceivable whereby liberty can be influenced; the one, a state naturally evil; the other, a state morally good. Were we to say, that the state was morally evil, at the first entrance of sin, we should contradict the *third* axiom. And were we to say, that the cause was only naturally good, we should contradict the *first* axiom. Therefore the cause of the *abuse* of liberty, is a state naturally evil. No other cause can possibly be assigned, without involving a contradiction. But what is a state naturally evil, and without any mixture of moral evil? It can be no other but a state under the influence of what we call passive power.

12. Let us view the subject in another light. *Perfect liberty*, in reference to virtue and vice, the scale of merit and demerit, and its attendant degrees of happiness or misery, is a MEDIUM, standing between all extremes—between virtue and vice, merit and demerit, happiness and misery. If we regard divine rectitude or equity, according to a former simile, in reference to the moral system, as an universal plane, liberty may be said to coincide with it. And being a natural perfection, or, when exerted, a good which has a positive cause, it is the effect of benevolent energy. If the mind be under unmerited, sovereign, benevolent influence, its liberty attaches itself to *real* good; then the agent rises on the scale of excellence, and therefore of happiness. But if the mind be under passive influence, or the influence of passive power, (a *depraved* nature and confirmed *vicious* habits being now out of the question,) its liberty attaches itself to *apparent* good, in opposition to real; then vice is generated, the agent sinks on the scale of deterioration, and consequently of misery.

13. It appears, then, that the will, in the exercise of its freedom, when producing moral effects, is the instrument of the disposition; and that the character of the effect bears an infallible and exact proportion to that of the predisposing cause. Yet the will in the exercise of choice is so *free*, that all constraint, coaction, and impulse, are entirely excluded from that which constitutes the *morality* of the act. Here lies the essence of moral agency, and the ground of accountableness. The agent has a *moral alternative;* IF he be DIFFERENTLY MINDED he may choose otherwise than he actually does If under benevolent influence, he will, in proportion, infallibly choose aright; if under equitable, passive influence, the *apparent* good will not be the *real* one, and consequently the choice will be morally bad. Means, objects perfectly suitable and sufficient, are exhibited to view; but these of themselves would never determine the will, otherwise the same effect would always follow the same means. Temptations also are presented; these in like manner of themselves never determine the will, otherwise temptation and sin would be infallibly connected. Then the holy Jesus could not have withstood the numerous and powerful solicitations of the tempter. But why did he withstand all? Because objects of temptation did not constitute the whole of motives; because objects operate according to the state of the mind; and because in him benevolent influence counteracted passive power. Hence, when the prince of this world came, he found nothing in him; and hence he rose to the greatest height of glory, having "a name above every name."

14. There is no end of objections and cavils, however demonstrative the proof; for such there have been against all the first principles of religion—the being of God—a revelation of his will to the human race—the doctrine of a future state, &c. &c. Some may say, Why should sin be made to originate in these two things, liberty and passive power? We answer, it has been demonstrated, that all metaphysical, positive and negative, causation, in reference to moral evil, is reducible to these two; and therefore they might as well ask, Why one and one make two, rather than any other number?

15. Others may say, Why not proceed from *God alone?* They might as well ask, Why is not the sun the cause of darkness? Love, the cause of enmity? Wisdom, the cause of folly? Happiness, the cause of misery? Order, the cause of confusion? But the *effect*, it may be said, is the *same.* We reply, the assignation of a *cause*, whether true or false, does not alter the nature of phenomena. It would be, indeed, a strange phenomenon, hitherto unknown, and unknowable, for an *hypothesis*, however demonstrable, to alter the *nature* of the things in question. *The effects are the same.* Very true. But the question is not about the EFFECTS; the inquiry is about the *true cause* of those effects, in opposition to false philosophy. The *effect* of moral evil is misery, or deserved suffering. Now does it make no difference, in justifying the ways of God to men, whether a rational, immortal being suffer *deservedly* or *undeservedly?* To suffer for moral evil, is to suffer *deservedly;* but were sin and suffering from God alone, or the effect of constituted laws, this could not be the case. To say, that this partial suffering may be ultimately counterbalanced by a restoration, is begging the question, that there will be a restoration. And if there were, what is it better than an apology for past injustice? To suffer *undeservedly*, is to suffer *unjustly;* and to punish *at all* is an act of injustice, if undeserved, as well as to punish for ever.

16. It may be again asked, What advantage is there in fixing on this origin of moral evil, rather than another? We reply by putting another question. Why should we put up with a false cause assigned for any thing? Surely, phenomena more interesting, more alarming in their nature, and more awful in their consequences, than moral evils, cannot arrest human observation. And it would be passing strange to suppose, that the ascertaining of their true cause and origin is not an important part of philosophy, and deserving of the closest investigation. What can be more dishonourable to the moral character of Deity, than to make sin originate in his will alone? Or, if *this* be its origin, how preposterous to call it *moral* evil, as distinguished from natural! How cruel and unjust, beyond precedent, to punish it; and how absurd the idea of *threatening* punishment for what was irreversibly *appointed!*

17. Some may say, Why may we not be satisfied with the idea of *permission?* If properly understood, we acknowledge that this goes a considerable way. But we suspect, few seem acquainted with the full implication of the term. *God permits.* True; if by it we mean he *does not hinder.* The free agent acts amiss when *he is not hindered.* This only shows, that God might hinder if he pleased; but it assigns no *cause* why the agent acts amiss. *Permitting* or *not hindering*, IMPLIES a *cause* distinct from divine causation. And the question returns, *what is* the cause of sin taking place when not hindered? In vain do we fix on chance, or a self-determining power; these explain nothing, and in fact are nothing, as our author has demonstrated various ways. In vain do we say, sin arises from the *abuse* of liberty. For the question recurs, What is the *cause* of that abuse? If this be not explained, nothing is effected. In vain shall we say, It proceeds from the cause of causes. For that cause is *good only.* From such a cause only good can proceed; and to ascribe sin to this cause is as proper as to say that *moral evil* is a *good thing*, and ought to be rewarded rather than punished. If this be not a reprovable mode of calling "evil good, and good evil," (Isa. v. 20.) we know not what is.

COROLLARIES.

18. Those who renounce the idea of passive power, as before explained, and its influence on the mind of a free agent, as a negative metaphysical cause; can never find the true, philosophical cause of vice and sin, and consequently of *deserved* suffering. As soon might they ascertain the laws of the planetary motions, while rejecting the principle of gravitation. If it

considered. The cavils of our opponents, as though our doctrine of necessity made God the author of sin, have been answered; and also their objections against these principles, as inconsistent with God's sincerity, in his counsels, invitations and persuasions, has been already obviated, in what has been observed respecting the consistence of what *Calvinists* suppose, concerning the secret and revealed Will of God. By that it appears, there is no repugnance in supposing it may be the secret Will of God, that his ordination and permission of events should be such, that it shall be a certain consequence, that a thing never will come to pass; which yet it is man's duty to do, and so God's preceptive Will, that he should do; and this is the same thing as to say, God may sincerely command and require him to do it. And if he may be sincere in commanding him, he may, for the same reason, be sincere in counselling, inviting, and using persuasions with him to do it. Counsels and invitations are manifestations of God's preceptive Will, or of what God loves, and what is in itself, and as man's act, agreeable to his heart; and not of his disposing Will, and what he chooses as a part of his own infinite scheme of things. It has been particularly shewn, Part III. Sect. IV. that such a necessity as has been maintained, is not inconsistent with the propriety and fitness of divine commands; and for the same reason, not inconsistent with the sincerity of invitations and counsels, in the Corollary at the end of that Section. Yea, it hath been shown, Part III. Sect. VII. Corol. 1. that this objection of *Arminians*, concerning the sincerity and use of divine exhortations, invitations, and counsels, is demonstrably against themselves.

Notwithstanding, I would further observe, that the difficulty of reconciling the sincerity of counsels, invitations, and persuasions with such an antecedent known fixedness of all events, as has been supposed, is not peculiar to this scheme, as distinguished from that of the generality of *Arminians*, which acknowledge the absolute foreknowledge of God: and therefore, it would be unreasonably brought as an objection against my differing from them. The main seeming difficulty in the case is this: that God, in counselling, inviting, and persuading, makes a show of aiming at, seeking, and using endeavours for the thing exhorted and persuaded to; whereas, it is impossible for any intelligent being truly to seek, or use endeavours for a thing, which he at the same time knows, most perfectly, will not come to pass; and that it is absurd to suppose, he makes the obtaining of a thing his end, in his calls and counsels, which he, at the same time, infallibly knows will not be obtained by these means. Now, if God knows this, in the utmost certainty and perfection, the way by which he comes by this knowledge makes no difference. If he knows it is by the necessity which he sees in things, or by some other means; it alters not the case. But it is in effect allowed by *Arminians* themselves, that God's inviting and persuading men to do things, which he, at the same time, certainly knows will not be done, is no evidence of insincerity; because they allow, that God has a certain foreknowledge of all sinful actions and omissions. And as this is implicitly allowed by most *Arminians*, so all that pretend to own the Scriptures to be the word of God, must be constrained to allow it.—God commanded and counselled *Pharaoh* to let his people go, and used arguments and persuasions to induce him to it; he laid before him arguments taken from his infinite greatness and almighty power, (Exod. vii. 16.) and forewarned him of the fatal consequences of his refusal, from time to time; (chap. viii. 1, 2, 20, 21. ix. 1—5, 13—17. and x. 3, 6.) He commanded *Moses*, and the elders of *Israel*, to go and beseech *Pharaoh* to let the people go; and at the same time told them, he knew surely that he would not comply with it. (Exod. iii. 18, 19.) "And thou shalt come, thou and the elders of Israel, unto the king of Egypt, and you shall say unto him, The Lord God of the Hebrews hath met with us; and now let us go, we beseech thee, three days' journey into the wilderness, that we may sacrifice unto the Lord our God:" and, "I am sure, that the king of Egypt will not let you go." So our blessed Saviour, the evening wherein he was betrayed, knew that *Peter* would shamefully deny him, before the morning; for he declares it to him with asseverations, to show the certainty of it; and tells the disciples, that all of them should be offended because of him that night; (Matt. xxvi. 31—35. John xiii. 38. Luke xxii. 31—34. John xvi. 32.) And yet it was their duty to avoid these things; they were very sinful things, which God had forbidden, and which it was their duty to watch and pray against; and they were obliged to do so from the *counsels* and *persuasions* Christ used with them, at that very time, so to do; (Matt. xxvi. 41.) "Watch and pray, that ye enter not into temptation." So that whatever difficulty there can be in this matter, it can be no objection against any principles which have been maintained in opposition to the principles of *Arminians;* nor does it any more concern me to remove the difficulty, than it does them, or indeed all, that call themselves Christians, and acknowledge the divine authority of the Scriptures.—Nevertheless, this matter may possibly (God allowing) be more particularly and largely considered, in some future discourse on the doctrine of *predestination*.*

But I would here observe, that however the defenders of that notion of liberty which I have opposed, exclaim against the doctrine of *Calvinists*, as tending to bring men into doubts concerning the moral perfections of God; it is *their* scheme, and not the scheme of *Calvinists*, that indeed is justly chargeable with this. For it is one of their most fundamental points, that a freedom of Will consisting in self-determination, without all necessity, is essential to *moral agency*. This is the same thing as to say, that such a determination of the Will, without all necessity, must be in all intelligent beings, in those things wherein they are *moral agents*, or in their *moral acts:* and from this it will follow, that God's Will is not necessarily determined, in any thing he does, as a *moral agent*, or in any of his *acts* that are of a *moral nature:* So that in all things, wherein he acts *holily, justly*, and *truly*, he does not act necessarily; or his Will is not necessarily determined to act holily and justly; because, if it were necessarily determined, he would not be a *moral agent* in thus acting: his Will would be attended with necessity; which, they say, is inconsistent with *moral agency:* "He can act no otherwise; he is at no liberty in the affair; he is determined by unavoidable, invincible necessity: therefore such agency is no moral agency; yea, no agency at all, properly speaking: a necessary agent is no agent: he being passive, and subject to necessity, what he does is no act of his, but an effect of a necessity prior to any act of his." This is agreeable to their manner of arguing. Now then, what is become of all our proof of the moral perfections of God? How can we prove, that God certainly will, in any one instance, do that which is just and holy; seeing his Will is determined in the matter by no necessity? We have no other way of proving that any thing *certainly* will be, but only by the necessity of the event. Where we can see no necessity, but that the thing may be, or may not be, there we are unavoidably left at a loss. We have no other way properly and truly to demonstrate the moral perfections of God, but the way that Mr. Chubb proves them, (p. 252, 261—263. of his Tracts,) *viz.* that God must, necessarily, perfectly know what is most worthy and valuable in itself, which, in the nature of things, is best and fittest to be done. And, as this is most eligible in itself, he, being omniscient, must see it to be so; and being both omniscient and self-sufficient, cannot have any temptation to reject it; and so must necessarily will that which is best. And thus, by this necessity of the determination of God's Will to what is good and best, we demonstrably establish God's moral character.

Corol. From what has been observed, it appears, that most of the arguments from Scripture which *Arminians*

be asked, What is the link of connexion between this principle and the event? We reply, Essential truth, the same truth as connects 2+2=4 or 2−1=1.

19. Those who renounce a sovereign, benevolent, physical, holy influence on the mind can never find the true, philosophical origin of virtue and holiness, and consequently happiness.

20. From the premises we infer, that the highest wisdom, the best interest, and the greatest honour of a rational and accountable being, is to employ his liberty, and all his powers, in the way of absolute *submission* to the divine will; in supreme *affection*, fear and love, to the infinite majesty and self-existent excellence of God; and in the way of humble and diligent *obedience*, according to the manifestation which God has made for himself.—W.

* It does not appear that the author did any thing more, towards accomplishing this design, than to pen some thoughts, probably with a view to an elaborate treatise, which are included in his Miscellaneous Remarks and Observations.—W.

make use of to support their scheme, are no other than *begging the question*. For in these they determine in the first place, that without such a freedom of Will as they hold, men cannot be proper moral agents, nor the subjects of command, counsel, persuasion, invitation, promises, threatenings, expostulations, rewards, and punishments; and that without such freedom it is to no purpose for men to take any care, or use any diligence, endeavours, or means, in order to their avoiding sin, or becoming holy, escaping punishment, or obtaining happiness: and having supposed these things, which are grand things in question in the debate, then they heap up scriptures, containing commands, counsels, calls, warnings, persuasions, expostulations, promises, and threatenings; (as doubtless they may find enough such; the Bible being confessedly full of them, from the beginning to the end;) and then they glory, how full the Scripture is on their side, how many more texts there are that evidently favour their scheme, than such as seem to favour the contrary. But let them first make manifest the things in question, which they suppose and take for granted, and show them to be consistent with themselves; and produce clear evidence of their truth; and they have gained their point, as all will confess, without bringing one scripture. For none denies, that there are commands, counsels, promises, threatenings, &c. in the Bible. But unless they do these things, their multiplying such texts of Scripture is insignificant and vain.

It may further be observed, that such scriptures as they bring, are really against them, and not for them. As it has been demonstrated, that it is *their* scheme, and not ours, is inconsistent with the use of motives and persuasives, or any moral means whatsoever, to induce men to the practice of virtue, or abstaining from wickedness. Their principles, and not ours, are repugnant to moral agency, and inconsistent with moral government, with law or precept, with the nature of virtue or vice, reward or punishment, and with every thing whatsoever of a moral nature, either on the part of the moral governor, or in the state, actions, or conduct of the subject.

SECT. XII.

Of a supposed tendency of these principles to Atheism and Licentiousness.

If any object against what has been maintained, that it tends to *Atheism;* I know not on what grounds such an objection can be raised, unless it be, that some Atheists have held a doctrine of necessity which they suppose to be like this. But if it be so, I am persuaded the *Arminians* would not look upon it just, that their notion of freedom and contingence should be charged with a tendency to all the errors that ever any embraced, who have held such opinions. The *Stoic* philosophers, whom the *Calvinists* are charged with agreeing with, were no Atheists, but the greatest Theists, and nearest akin to Christians in their opinions concerning the unity and the perfections of the Godhead, of all the heathen philosophers. And *Epicurus*, that chief father of Atheism, maintained no such doctrine of necessity, but was the greatest maintainer of contingence.

The doctrine of necessity, which supposes a necessary connexion of all events, on some antecedent ground and reason of their existence, is the only medium we have to prove the being of God. And the contrary doctrine of contingence, even as maintained by *Arminians*, (which certainly implies, or infers, that events may come into existence, or begin to be, without dependence on any thing foregoing, as their cause, ground, or reason,) takes away all proof of the being of God; which proof is summarily expressed by the apostle, in Rom. i. 20. And this is a tendency to *Atheism* with a witness. So that, indeed, it is the doctrine of *Arminians*, and not of the *Calvinists*, that is justly charged with a tendency to *Atheism;* it being built on a foundation that is the utter subversion of every demonstrative argument for the proof of a Deity; as has been shown, Part II. Sect. III.

And whereas it has often been said, that the *Calvinistic* doctrine of necessity saps the foundations of all religion and virtue, and tends to the greatest licentiousness of practice: this objection is built on the pretence, that our doctrine renders vain all means and endeavours, in order to be virtuous and religious. Which pretence has been already particularly considered in the 5th Section of this Part; where it has been demonstrated, that this doctrine has no such tendency; but that such a tendency is truly to be charged on the contrary doctrine: inasmuch as the notion of contingence, which their doctrine implies, in its certain consequences, overthrows all connexion in every degree, between endeavour and event, means and end.

And besides, if many other things, which have been observed to belong to the *Arminian* doctrine, or to be plain consequences of it, be considered, there will appear just reason to suppose, that it is *that* which must rather tend to licentiousness. Their doctrine excuses all evil inclinations, which men find to be natural; because, in such inclinations, they are not self-determined, as such inclinations are not owing to any choice or determination of their own Wills. Which leads men wholly to justify themselves in all their wicked actions, so far as natural inclination has had a hand in determining their Wills to the commission of them. Yea, these notions, which suppose moral necessity and inability to be inconsistent with blame or moral obligation, will directly lead men to justify the vilest acts and practices, from the strength of their wicked inclinations of all sorts; strong inclinations inducing a moral necessity; yea, to excuse every degree of evil inclination, so far as this has evidently prevailed, and been the thing which has determined their Wills: because, so far as antecedent inclination determined the Will, so far the Will was without liberty of indifference and self-determination. Which, at last, will come to this, that men will justify themselves in all the wickedness they commit. It has been observed already, that this scheme of things exceedingly diminishes the guilt of sin, and the difference between the greatest and smallest offences;* and if it be pursued in its real consequences, it leaves room for no such thing, as either virtue or vice, blame or praise in the world. † And again, how naturally does this notion of the sovereign self-determining power of the Will, in all things virtuous or vicious, and whatsoever deserves either reward or punishment, tend to encourage men to put off the work of religion and virtue, and turning from sin to God; since they have a sovereign power to determine themselves, just when they please; or if not, they are wholly excusable in going on in sin, because of their inability to do any other.

If it should be said, that the tendency of this doctrine of necessity to licentiousness, appears by the improvement many at this day actually make of it, to justify themselves in their dissolute courses; I will not deny that some men do unreasonably abuse this doctrine, as they do many other things, which are true and excellent in their own nature: but I deny, that this proves the doctrine itself has any tendency to licentiousness. I think, the tendency of doctrines, by what now appears in the world, and in our nation in particular, may much more justly be argued, from the general effect which has been seen to attend the prevailing of the principles of *Arminians*, and the contrary principles; as both have had their turn of general prevalence in our nation. If it be indeed, as is pretended, that *Calvinistic* doctrines undermine the very foundation of all religion and morality, and enervate and disannul all rational motives to holy and virtuous practice; and that the contrary doctrines give the inducements to virtue and goodness their proper force, and exhibit religion in a rational light, tending to recommend it to the reason of mankind, and enforce it in a manner that is agreeable to their natural notions of things: I say, if it be thus, it is remarkable, that virtue and religious practice should prevail most, when the former doctrines, so inconsistent with it, prevailed almost universally: and that ever since the latter doctrines, so happily agreeing with it, and of so proper and excellent a tendency to promote it, have been gradually prevailing, vice, profaneness, luxury, and wickedness of all sorts, and contempt of all religion, and

* Part III. Sect. VI.

† Part III. Sect. VI. Ibid. Sect. VII. Part IV. Sect. I. Part. III. Sect. III. *Corol.* I. after the first head.

of every kind of seriousness and strictness of conversation, should proportionably prevail; and that these things should thus accompany one another, and rise and prevail one with another, now for a whole age together! It is remarkable, that this happy remedy (discovered by the free inquiries and superior sense and wisdom of this age) against the pernicious effects of *Calvinism*, so inconsistent with religion, and tending so much to banish all virtue from the earth, should, on so long a trial, be attended with no good effect; but that the consequence should be the reverse of amendment; that in proportion as the remedy takes place, and is thoroughly applied, so the disease should prevail; and the very same dismal effect take place, to the highest degree, which *Calvinistic* doctrines are supposed to have so great a tendency to; even the banishing of religion and virtue, and the prevailing of unbounded licentiousness of manners! If these things are truly so, they are very remarkable, and matter of very curious speculation.

SECT. XIII.

Concerning that objection against the reasoning, by which the Calvinistic doctrine is supposed, that it is metaphysical and abstruse.

It has often been objected against the defenders of *Calvinistic* principles, that in their reasonings, they run into nice scholastic distinctions, and abstruse metaphysical subtilties, and set these in opposition to common sense. And it is possible, that, after the former manner, it may be alleged against the reasoning by which I have endeavoured to confute the *Arminian* scheme of liberty and moral agency, that it is very abstracted and metaphysical. Concerning this, I would observe the following things:

I. If that be made an objection against the foregoing reasoning, that it is *metaphysical*, or may properly be reduced to the science of *metaphysics*, it is a very impertinent objection; whether it be so or no, is not worthy of any dispute or controversy. If the reasoning be good, it is as frivolous to inquire what science it is properly reduced to, as what language it is delivered in: and for a man to go about to confute the arguments of his opponent, by telling him, his arguments are *metaphysical*, would be as weak as to tell him, his arguments could not be substantial, because they were written in *French* or *Latin*. The question is not, whether what is said be metaphysics, physics, logic, or mathematics, *Latin*, *French*, *English*, or *Mohawk*? But whether the reasoning be good, and the arguments truly conclusive? The foregoing arguments are no more metaphysical, than those which we use against the papists, to disprove their doctrine of transubstantiation; alleging it is inconsistent with the notion of corporeal identity, that it should be in ten thousand places at the same time. It is by metaphysical arguments only we are able to prove, that the rational soul is not corporeal, that lead or sand cannot think; that thoughts are not square or round, or do not weigh a pound. The arguments by which we prove the being of God, if handled closely and distinctly, so as to show their clear and demonstrative evidence, must be metaphysically treated. It is by metaphysics only that we can demonstrate, that God is not limited to a place, or is not mutable; that he is not ignorant, or forgetful; that it is impossible for him to lie, or be unjust; and that there is one God only, and not hundreds or thousands. And, indeed, we have no strict demonstration of any thing, excepting mathematical truths, but by metaphysics. We can have no proof, that is properly demonstrative, of any one proposition, relating to the being and nature of God, his creation of the world, the dependence of all things on him, the nature of bodies or spirits, the nature of our own souls, or any of the great truths of morality and natural religion, but what is metaphysical. I am willing my arguments should be brought to the test of the strictest and justest reason, and that a clear, distinct, and determinate meaning of the terms I use should be insisted on; but let not the whole be rejected, as if all were confuted, by fixing on it the epithet, *metaphysical*.

II. If the reasoning, which has been made use of, be in some sense metaphysical, it will not follow, that therefore it must need be abstruse, unintelligible, and akin to the jargon of the schools. I humbly conceive, the foregoing reasoning at least to those things which are most material belonging to it, depends on no abstruse definitions or distinctions, or terms without a meaning, or of very ambiguous and undetermined signification, or any points of such abstraction and subtilty, as tends to involve the attentive understanding in clouds and darkness. There is no high degree of refinement and abstruse speculation, in determining, that a thing is not before it is, and so cannot be the cause of itself; or that the first act of free choice, has not another act of free choice going before that, to excite or direct it; or in determining, that no choice is made, while the mind remains in a state of absolute indifference; that preference and equilibrium never coexist; and that therefore no choice is made in a state of liberty, consisting in indifference: and that so far as the Will is determined by motives, exhibiting and operating previous to the act of the Will, so far it is not determined by the act of the Will itself; that nothing can begin to be, which before was not, without a cause, or some antecedent ground or reason, why it then begins to be; that effects depend on their causes, and are connected with them; that virtue is not the worse, nor sin the better, for the strength of inclination with which it is practised, and the difficulty which thence arises of doing otherwise; that when it is already infallibly known that the thing will be, it is not contingent whether it will ever be or no; or that it can be truly said, notwithstanding, that it is not necessary it should be, but it either may be, or may not be. And the like might be observed of many other things which belong to the foregoing reasoning.

If any shall still stand to it, that the foregoing reasoning is nothing but mere metaphysical sophistry: and that it must be so, that the seeming force of the arguments all depends on some fallacy and wile that is hid in the obscurity which always attends a great degree of metaphysical abstraction and refinement; and shall be ready to say, "Here is, indeed, something tends to confound the mind, but not to satisfy it: for who can ever be truly satisfied in it, that men are fitly blamed or commended, punished or rewarded, for those volitions which are not from themselves, and of whose existence they are not the causes. Men may refine, as much as they please, and advance the abstract notions, and make out a thousand seeming contradictions, to puzzle our understandings; yet there can be no satisfaction in such doctrine as this: the natural sense of the mind of man will always resist it."* I humbly

* A certain noted author of the present age says, the arguments for *necessity* are nothing but *quibbling, or logomachy, using words without a meaning, or begging the question.*—I do not know what kind of necessity any authors to whom he may have reference are advocates for; or whether they have managed their arguments well or ill. As to the arguments I have made use, if they are *quibbles* they may be shown to be so; such knots are capable of being untied, and the trick and cheat may be detected and plainly laid open. If this be fairly done, with respect to the grounds and reasons I have relied upon. I shall have just occasion, for the future, to be silent, if not to be ashamed of my argumentations. I am willing my proofs should be thoroughly examined; and if there be nothing but *begging the question*, or mere *logomachy*, or dispute of words, let it be made manifest and shown how the seeming strength of the argument depends on my *using words without a meaning*, or arises from the ambiguity of terms, or my making use of words in an indeterminate and unsteady manner; and that the weight of my reasons rest mainly on such a foundation: and then, I shall either be ready to retract what I have urged, and thank the man that has done the kind part, or shall be justly exposed for my obstinacy.

The same author is abundant in appealing, in this affair, from what he calls *logomachy and sophistry*, to *experience.*——A person can experience only what passes in his own mind. But yet, as we may well suppose, that all men have the same human faculties; so a man may well argue from his own experience to that of others, in things that show the nature of these faculties, and the manner of their operation. But then one has as good a right to allege his experience as another. As to my own experience, I find, that in innumerable things I can do as I will; that the motions of my body, in many respects, instantaneously follow the acts of my will concerning those motions; and that my will has some command of my thoughts; and that the acts of my will are my own, *i. e.* that they are acts of my will, the volitions of my own mind; or, in other words, that what I will, I will. Which, I presume, is the sum of what others experience in this affair. But as to finding by experience, that my will is originally determined by itself; or that, my will first choosing what volition there shall be, the chosen volition accordingly follows; and that this is the first rise of the determination of my will in any affair; or that any volition arises in my mind contingently; I declare, I know nothing in myself, by experience, of this nature: and nothing that ever I experienced, carries the least appearance or shadow of any such thing, or gives me any more reason to suppose or suspect any such thing, than to suppose that my volitions existed twenty years before they existed. It is true, I find myself possessed of my volitions, before I can see the effectual power of any cause to produce them, for the power and efficacy of the cause is not seen but by the effect, and this, for ought I know, may make some imagine, that volition has no cause, or that it produces itself. But I have no more reason from hence to determine any such conceive, that such an objector, if he has capacity, and humility, and calmness of spirit sufficient, impartially and thoroughly to examine himself, will find that he knows not really what he would be at; and indeed, his difficulty is nothing but a mere prejudice, from an inadvertent customary use of words, in a meaning that is not clearly understood, nor carefully reflected upon. Let the objector reflect again, if he has candour and patience enough, and does not scorn to be at the trouble of close attention in the affair.—He would have a man's volition be *from himself*. Let it be *from himself*, most primarily and originally of any way conceivable; that is, from its own choice; how will that help the matter, as to his being justly blamed or praised, unless that choice itself be blameworthy or praiseworthy? And how is the choice itself (an ill choice, for instance) blameworthy, according to these principles, unless that be from himself too, in the same manner; that is, from his own choice? But the original and first determining choice in the affair is not from his choice: his choice is not the cause of it. And if it be from himself some other way, and not from his choice, surely that will not help the matter. If it be not from himself of choice, then it is not from himself voluntarily: and if so, he is surely no more to blame, than if it were not from himself at all. It is vanity to pretend, it is a sufficient answer to this, to say, that it is nothing but metaphysical refinement and subtilty, and so attended with obscurity and uncertainty.

If it be the natural sense of our minds, that what is blameworthy in a man must be from himself, then it doubtless is also, that it must be from something *bad* in himself, a *bad choice*, or *bad disposition*. But then our natural sense is, that this bad choice or disposition is evil *in itself*, and the man blameworthy for it, *on its own account*, without taking into our notion of its blameworthiness, another bad choice, or disposition going before this, from whence this arises: for that is a ridiculous absurdity, running us into an immediate contradiction, which our natural sense of blameworthiness has nothing to do with, and never comes into the mind, nor is supposed in the judgment we naturally make of the affair. As was demonstrated before, natural sense does not place the moral evil of volitions and dispositions in the cause of them, but the nature of them. An evil thing being FROM a man, or from something antecedent in him, is not essential to the original notion we have of blameworthiness: but it is its being the choice of the heart; as appears by this, that if a thing be *from* us, and not from our choice, it has not the nature of blameworthiness or ill desert, according to our natural sense. When a thing is *from* a man, in that sense, that it is from his Will or choice, he is to blame for it, because his Will is IN IT: so far as the Will is *in it*, blame is *in it*, and no further. Neither do we go any further in our notion of blame, to inquire whether the bad Will be FROM a bad Will: there is no consideration of the original of that bad Will; because, according to our natural apprehension, blame *originally consists in it*. Therefore a thing being *from* a man, is a secondary consideration, in the notion of blame or ill desert. Because those things, in our *external* actions, are most properly said to be *from* us, which are *from* our choice; and no other *external* actions, but those that are from us in this sense, have the nature of blame; and they indeed, not so properly because they are *from us*, as because we are *in them*, *i. e.* our Wills are in them; not so much because they are from some *property* of ours, as because they are our *properties*.

However, all these external actions being truly *from us* as their cause; and we being so used, in ordinary speech, and in the common affairs of life, to speak of men's actions and conduct which we see, and which affect human society, as deserving ill or well, as worthy of blame or praise; hence it is come to pass, that philosophers have incautiously taken all their measures of good and evil, praise and blame, from the dictates of common sense, about these *overt acts* of men; to the running of every thing into the most lamentable and dreadful confusion. And, therefore, I observe,

III. It is so far from being true, (whatever may be pretended,) that the proof of the doctrine which has been maintained, depends on certain abstruse, unintelligible, metaphysical terms and notions; and that the *Arminian* scheme, without needing such clouds and darkness for its defence, is supported by the plain dictates of common sense; that the very reverse is most certainly true, and that to a great degree. It is fact, that they, and not we, have confounded things with metaphysical, unintelligible notions and phrases, and have drawn them from the light of plain truth, into the gross darkness of abstruse metaphysical propositions, and words without a meaning. Their pretended demonstrations depend very much on such unintelligible, metaphysical phrases, as *self-determination*, and *sovereignty of the Will;* and the metaphysical sense they put on such terms, as *necessity*, *contingency*, *action*, *agency*, *&c.* quite diverse from their meaning as used in common speech; and which, as they use them, are without any consistent meaning, or any manner of distinct consistent ideas; as far from it as any of the abstruse terms and perplexed phrases of the peripatetic philosophers, or the most unintelligible jargon of the schools, or the cant of the wildest fanatics. Yea, we may be bold to say, these metaphysical terms, on which they build so much, are what they use without knowing what they mean themselves; they are pure metaphysical sounds, without any ideas whatsoever in their minds to answer them; inasmuch as it has been demonstrated, that there cannot be any notion in the mind consistent with these expressions, as they pretend to explain them; because their explanations destroy themselves. No such notions as imply self-contradiction, and self-abolition, and this a great many ways, can subsist in the mind; as there can be no idea of a whole which is less than any of its parts, or of solid extension without dimensions, or of an effect which is before its cause.—*Arminians* improve these terms, as terms of art, and in their metaphysical meaning, to advance and establish those things which are contrary to common sense, in a high degree. Thus, instead of the plain vulgar notion of liberty, which all mankind, in every part of the face of the earth and in all ages, have, consisting in opportunity to do as one pleases; they have introduced a new strange liberty, consisting in indifference, contingence, and self-determination; by which they involve themselves and others in great obscurity, and manifold gross inconsistence. So, instead of placing virtue and vice, as common sense places them very much, in fixed bias and inclination, and greater virtue and vice in stronger and more established inclination; these, through their refinings and abstruse notions, suppose a liberty consisting in indifference to be essential to all virtue and vice. So they have reasoned themselves, not by metaphysical distinctions, but metaphysical confusion, into many principles about moral agency, blame, praise, reward, and punishment, which are, as has been shown, exceeding contrary to the common sense of mankind; and perhaps to their own sense, which governs them in common life.

SECT. XIV.

The Conclusion.

WHETHER the things which have been alleged, are liable to any tolerable answer in the way of calm, intelligible, and strict reasoning, I must leave others to judge: but I am sensible they are liable to one sort of answer. It is not unlikely, that some, who value themselves on the supposed rational and generous principles of the modern fashionable divinity, will have their indignation and disdain raised at the sight of this discourse, and on perceiving what things are pretended to be proved in it. And if they think it worthy of being read, or of so much notice as to say much about it, they may probably renew the usual exclamations, with additional vehemence and contempt, about the *fate of the heathen*, Hobbes's *Necessity*, and *making men mere machines;* accumulating the terrible epithets of *fatal*, *unfrustrable*, *inevitable*, *irresistible*, *&c.* and it may be, with addition of *horrid* and *blasphemous;* and perhaps much skill may be used to set forth things, which have been said, in colours which shall be shocking to the

thing, than I have to determine that I gave myself my own being, or that I came into being accidentally without a cause because I first found myself possessed of being, before I had knowledge of a cause of my being.

imaginations, and moving to the passions of those, who have either too little capacity, or too much confidence of the opinions they have imbibed, and contempt of the contrary, to try the matter by any serious and circumspect examination.* Or difficulties may be stated and insisted on, which do not belong to the controversy; because, let them be more or less real, and hard to be resolved, they are not what are owing to any thing distinguishing of this scheme from that of the *Arminians*, and would not be removed nor diminished by renouncing the former, and adhering to the latter. Or some particular things may be picked out, which they may think will sound harshest in the ears of the generality; and these may be glossed and descanted on, with tart and contemptuous words; and from thence, the whole discourse may be treated with triumph and insult.

It is easy to see, how the decision of most of the points in controversy between *Calvinists* and *Arminians*, depends on the determination of this grand article concerning *the Freedom of the Will requisite to moral agency;* and that by clearing and establishing the *Calvinistic* doctrine in this point, the chief arguments are obviated by which *Arminian* doctrines in general are supported, and the contrary doctrines demonstratively confirmed. Hereby it becomes manifest, that God's moral government over mankind, his treating them as moral agents, making them the objects of his commands, counsels, calls, warnings, expostulations, promises, threatenings, rewards, and punishments, is not inconsistent with a *determining disposal* of all events, of every kind, throughout the universe, *in his providence;* either by positive efficiency, or permission. Indeed, such an *universal determining providence*, infers some kind of necessity of all events, such a necessity as implies an infallible previous fixedness of the futurity of the event: but no other necessity of moral events, or volitions of intelligent agents, is needful in order to this, than *moral necessity;* which does as much ascertain the futurity of the event as any other necessity. But, as has been demonstrated, such a necessity is not at all repugnant to moral agency, and a reasonable use of commands, calls, rewards, punishments, &c. Yea, not only are objections of this kind against the doctrine of an universal *determining providence*, removed by what has been said; but the truth of such a doctrine is demonstrated. As it has been demonstrated, that the futurity of all future events is established by previous necessity, either natural or moral; so it is manifest, that the sovereign Creator and Disposer of the world has ordered this necessity, by ordering his own conduct, either in designedly acting, or forbearing to act. For, as the being of the world is from God, so the circumstances in which it had its being at first, both negative and positive, must be ordered by him, in one of these ways; and all the necessary consequences of these circumstances, must be ordered by him. And God's active and positive interpositions, after the world was created, and the consequences of these interpositions; also every instance of his forbearing to interpose, and the sure consequences of this forbearance, must all be determined according to his pleasure. And therefore every event, which is the consequence of any thing whatsoever, or that is connected with any foregoing thing or circumstances, either positive or negative, as the ground or reason of its existence, must be ordered of God; either by a designing efficiency and interposition, or a designed forbearing to operate or interpose. But, as has been proved, all events whatsoever are necessarily connected with something foregoing, either positive or negative, which is the ground of its existence. It follows, therefore, that the whole series of events is thus connected with something in the state of things either positive or negative, which is *original* in the series; *i. e.* something which is connected with nothing preceding that, but God's own immediate conduct, either his acting or forbearing to act. From whence it follows, that as God designedly orders his own conduct, and its connected consequences, it must necessarily be, that he designedly orders all things.

The things which have been said, obviate some of the chief objections of *Arminians* against the *Calvinistic* doctrine of the *total depravity and corruption of man's nature*, whereby his heart is wholly under the power of sin, and he is utterly unable, without the interposition of sovereign grace, savingly to love God, believe in Christ, or do any thing that is truly good and acceptable in God's sight. For the main objection against this doctrine, that it is inconsistent with the freedom of man's Will, consisting in indifference and self-determining power; because it supposes man to be under a necessity of sinning, and that God requires things of him, in order to his avoiding eternal damnation, which he is unable to do; and that this doctrine is wholly inconsistent with the sincerity of counsels, invitations, &c. Now, this doctrine supposes *no other necessity* of sinning, than a moral necessity; which, as has been shown, does not at all excuse sin; and supposes *no other inability* to obey any command, or perform any duty, even the most spiritual and exalted, but a moral inability, which, as has been proved, does not excuse persons in the non-performance of any good thing, or make them not to be the proper objects of commands, counsels, and invitations. And, moreover, it has been shown, that there is not, and never can be, either in existence, or so much as in idea, any such freedom of Will, consisting in indifference and self-determination, for the sake of which, this doctrine of original sin is cast out: and that no such freedom is necessary, in order to the nature of sin, and a just desert of punishment.

The things which have been observed, do also take off the main objections of *Arminians* against the doctrine of *efficacious grace;* and, at the same time, prove the grace of God in a sinner's conversion (if there be any grace or divine influence in the affair) to be *efficacious*, yea, and *irresistible* too, if by irresistible is meant, that which is attended with a moral necessity, which it is impossible should ever be violated by any resistance. The main objection of *Arminians* against this doctrine is, that it is inconsistent with their self-determining freedom of Will; and that it is repugnant to the nature of virtue, that it should be wrought in the heart by the determining efficacy and power of another, instead of its being owing to a self-moving power; that, in that case, the good which is wrought, would not be *our* virtue, but rather *God's* virtue; because not the person in whom it is wrought is the determining author of it, but God that wrought it in him. But the things which are the foundation of these objections, have been considered; and it has been demonstrated, that the liberty of moral agents does not consist in self-determining power; and that there is no need of any such liberty, in order to the nature of virtue; nor does it at all hinder, but that the state or act of the Will may be the virtue of the subject, though it be not from self-determination, but the determination of an intrinsic cause; even so as to cause the event to be morally necessary to the subject of it.—And as it has been proved, that nothing in the state or acts of the Will of man is contingent; but that, on the contrary, every event of this kind is necessary, by a moral necessity; and has also been now demonstrated, that the doctrine of an universal determining Providence, follows from that doctrine of necessity, which was proved before: and so, that God does decisively, in his providence, order all the volitions of moral agents, either by positive influence or permission: and it being allowed, on all hands, that what God does in the affair of man's virtuous volitions, whether it be more or less, is by some positive influence, and not by mere permission, as in the affair of a sinful volition: if we put these things together, it will follow, that God's assistance or influence must be determining and decisive, or must be attended with a moral

* A writer of the present age, whom I have several times had occasion to mention, speaks once and again of those who hold the doctrine of *Necessity*, as scarcely worthy of the name of *philosophers*. I do not know, whether he has respect to any particular notion of necessity, that some may have maintained; and, if so, what doctrine of necessity it is that he means. Whether I am worthy of the name of a philosopher, or not, would be a question little to the present purpose. If any, and ever so many, should deny it, I should not think it worth the while to enter into a dispute on that question: Though at the same time I might expect some better answer should be given to the arguments brought for the truth of the doctrine I maintain; and I might further reasonably desire, that it might be considered, whether it does not become those, who are *truly worthy* of the name of philosophers, to be sensible, that there is a difference between *argument* and *contempt*, yea, and a difference between the contemptibleness of the *person* that argues, and the inconclusiveness of the *arguments* he offers.

necessity of the event; and so, that God gives virtue, holiness, and conversion to sinners, by an influence which determines the effect, in such a manner, that the effect will infallibly follow by a moral necessity; which is what *Calvinists* mean by efficacious and irresistible grace.

The things which have been said, do likewise answer the chief objections against the doctrine of God's *universal* and *absolute decree*, and afford infallible proof of this doctrine; and of the doctrine of *absolute, eternal, personal election* in particular. The main objections against these doctrines are, that they infer a necessity of the volitions of moral agents, and of the future and moral state and acts of men; and so are not consistent with those eternal rewards and punishments, which are connected with conversion and impenitence; nor can be made to agree with the reasonableness and sincerity of the precepts, calls, counsels, warnings, and expostulations of the word of God; or with the various methods and means of grace, which God uses with sinners to bring them to repentance; and the whole of that moral government, which God exercises towards mankind: and that they infer an inconsistence between the *secret* and *revealed Will of God;* and make God the author of sin. But all these things have been obviated in the preceding discourse. And the certain truth of these doctrines, concerning God's eternal purposes, will follow from what was just now observed concerning God's universal providence; how it infallibly follows from what has been proved, that God orders all events, and the volitions of moral agents amongst others, by such a decisive disposal, that the events are infallibly connected with his disposal. For if God disposes all events, so that the infallible existence of the events is decided by his providence, then, doubtless, he thus orders and decides things *knowingly*, and *on design*. God does not do what he does, nor order what he orders, accidentally and unawares; either *without* or *beside* his intention. And if there be a foregoing *design* of doing and ordering as he does, this is the same with a *purpose* or *decree*. And as it has been shown, that nothing is new to God, in any respect, but all things are perfectly and equally in his view from eternity; hence it will follow, that his designs or purposes are not things formed anew, founded on any new views or appearances, but are all eternal purposes. And as it has been now shown, how the doctrine of determining efficacious grace certainly follows from things proved in the foregoing discourse; hence will necessarily follow the doctrine of *particular, eternal, absolute election.* For if men are made true saints, no otherwise than as God makes them so, and distinguishes them from others, by his efficacious power and influence, that decides and fixes the event; and God thus makes some saints, and not others, on design or purpose, and (as has been now observed) no designs of God are new; it follows, that God thus distinguished from others, all that ever become true saints, by his eternal design or decree. I might also show, how God's certain foreknowledge must suppose an absolute decree, and how such a decree can be proved to a demonstration from it: but that this discourse may not be lengthened out too much, that must be omitted for the present.*

From these things it will inevitably follow, that however Christ in some sense may be said to *die for all*, and to redeem all visible Christians, yea, the whole world, by his death; yet there must be something *particular* in the design of his death, with respect to such as he intended should actually be saved thereby. As appears by what has been now shown, God has the actual salvation or redemption of a certain number in his proper absolute design, and of a certain number only; and therefore such a design only can be prosecuted in any thing God does, in order to the salvation of men. God pursues a proper design of the salvation of the elect in giving Christ to die, and prosecutes such a design with respect to no other, most strictly speaking; for it is impossible, that God should prosecute any other design than only such as he has: he certainly does not, in the highest propriety and strictness of speech, pursue a design that he has not. And, indeed, such a particularity and limitation of redemption will as infallibly follow, from the doctrine of God's foreknowledge, as from that of the decree. For it is as impossible, in strictness of speech, that God should prosecute a design, or aim at a thing, which he at the same time most perfectly knows will not be accomplished, as that he should use endeavours for that which is beside his decree.†

By the things which have been proved, are obviated some of the main objections against the doctrine of the infallible and necessary *perseverance* of saints, and some of the main foundations of this doctrine are established. The main prejudices of *Arminians* against this doctrine seem to be these; they suppose such a necessary, infallible perseverance to be repugnant to the freedom of the Will; that it must be owing to man's own self-determining power he *first becomes* virtuous and holy; and so, in like manner, it must be left a thing contingent, to be determined by the same freedom of Will, whether he will *persevere* in virtue and holiness; and that otherwise his continuing stedfast in faith and obedience would not be his virtue, or at all praiseworthy and rewardable; nor could his perseverance be properly the matter of divine commands, counsels, and promises, nor his apostasy be properly threatened, and men warned against it. Whereas, we find all these things in Scripture: there we find stedfastness and perseverance in true Christianity, represented as the virtue of the saints, spoken of as praiseworthy in them, and glorious rewards promised to it; and also find, that God makes it the subject of his commands, counsels, and promises; and the contrary, of threatenings and warnings. But the foundation of these objections has been removed, by showing that moral necessity and infallible certainty of events is not inconsistent with these things; and that, as to freedom of Will, lying in the power of the Will to determine itself, there neither is any such thing, nor is there any need of it, in order to virtue, reward, commands, counsels, &c.

And as the doctrines of efficacious grace and absolute election do certainly follow from the things proved in the preceding discourse; so some of the main foundations of the doctrine of perseverance, are thereby established. If the beginning of true faith and holiness, and a man becoming a true saint at first, does not depend on the self-determining power of the Will, but on the determining efficacious grace of God; it may well be argued, that it is also with respect to men being continued saints, or persevering in faith and holiness. The conversion of a sinner being not owing to a man's self-determination, but to God's determination, and eternal election, which is absolute, and depending on the sovereign Will of God, and not on the free Will of man; as is evident from what has been said: and it being very evident from the Scriptures, that the eternal election of saints to faith and holiness, is also an election of them to eternal salvation; hence their appointment to salvation must also be absolute, and not depending on their contingent, self-determining Will. From all which it follows, that it is absolutely fixed in God's decree, that all true saints shall persevere to actual eternal salvation.

But I must leave all these things to the consideration of the impartial reader; and when he has maturely weighed them, I would propose it to his consideration, whether many of the first reformers, and others that succeeded them, whom God in their day made the chief pillars of his church, and the greatest instruments of their deliverance from error and darkness, and of the support of the cause of piety among them, have not been injured, in the con-

* Certain foreknowledge does imply *some* necessity. But our author is not sufficiently guarded, or else not sufficiently explicit, when he says, that foreknowledge must suppose an absolute decree. For certainty, or hypothetical necessity, may arise from the *nature of things*, and from *negative causes*, as well as from a decree. If, indeed, the remark be limited to the subject immediately preceding, it is an important truth.—W.

† The terms *design* and *endeavours* are not sufficiently discriminating. It is here supposed that it is unworthy of God to use *endeavours* which are *beside his decree*, or to prosecute a *design* which he knows will not be *accomplished*. Is it not a matter of plain fact that he uses *endeavours* which are beside his decree, and prosecutes a *design* which he knows will not be accomplished, through the whole system of legislation and government? Is it not the very *design* of legislation and government to *prevent* crimes as well as to punish them, and to *promote* obedience and conformity to law? *Legislative design*, therefore, is *not accomplished* in the commission of crimes, otherwise the legislator, as such, could not find fault for breach of law. Our Lord used *endeavours* with the inhabitants of Jerusalem, &c. *beside* his decree, yet with perfect propriety. If we keep in mind that the divine *Will* subsists under two relations, according to the two-fold state of man, who is at once a subject of decree and a subject of government, we shall see the propriety of calling it *decretive* and *rectoral*.—W.

tempt with which they have been treated by many late writers, for their teaching and maintaining such doctrines as are commonly called *Calvinistic.* Indeed, some of these new writers, at the same time that they have represented the doctrines of these ancient and eminent divines, as in the highest degree ridiculous, and contrary to common sense, in an ostentation of a very generous charity, have allowed that they were honest well-meaning men: yea, it may be some of them, as though it were in great condescension and compassion to them, have allowed, that they did pretty well for the day in which they lived, and considering the great disadvantages they laboured under: when, at the same time, their manner of speaking has naturally and plainly suggested to the minds of their readers, that they were persons, who—through the lowness of their genius, and the greatness of the bigotry with which their minds were shackled, and their thoughts confined, living in the gloomy caves of superstition—fondly embraced, and demurely and zealously taught, the most absurd, silly, and monstrous opinions, worthy of the greatest contempt of gentlemen possessed of that noble and generous freedom of thought, which happily prevails in this age of light and inquiry. When, indeed, such is the case that we might, if so disposed, speak as big words as they, and on far better grounds. And really all the *Arminians* on earth might be challenged without arrogance or vanity, to make these principles of theirs, wherein they mainly differ from their fathers, whom they so much despise, consistent with common sense; yea, and perhaps to produce any doctrine ever embraced by the blindest bigot of the church of *Rome*, or the most ignorant *Mussulman*, or extravagant enthusiast, that might be reduced to more demonstrable inconsistencies, and repugnancies to common sense, and to themselves; though their inconsistencies indeed may not lie so deep, or be so artfully veiled by a deceitful ambiguity of words, and an indeterminate signification of phrases. I will not deny, that these gentlemen, many of them, are men of great abilities, and have been helped to higher attainments in philosophy, than those ancient divines, and have done great service to the church of God in some respects: but I humbly conceive, that their differing from their fathers, with such magisterial assurance, in these points in divinity, must be owing to some other cause than superior wisdom.

It may also be worthy of consideration, whether the great alteration which has been made in the state of things in our nation, and some other parts of the protestant world, in this and the past age, by exploding so generally *Calvinistic* doctrines—an alteration so often spoken of as worthy to be greatly rejoiced in by the friends of truth, learning, and virtue, as an instance of the great increase of light in the Christian church—be indeed a happy change, owing to any such cause as an increase of true knowledge and understanding in the things of religion; or whether there is not reason to fear, that it may be owing to some worse cause.

And I desire it may be considered, whether the boldness of some writers may not deserve to be reflected on, who have not scrupled to say, that if these and those things are true, (which yet appear to be the demonstrable dictates of reason, as well as the certain dictates of the mouth of the Most High,) then God is unjust, and cruel, and guilty of manifest deceit and double dealing, and the like. Yea, some have gone so far as confidently to assert, that if any book which pretends to be Scripture, teaches such doctrines, that alone is sufficient warrant for mankind to reject it, as what cannot be the word of God. Some, who have not gone so far, have said, that if the Scripture seems to teach any such doctrines, so contrary to reason, we are obliged to find out some other interpretation of those texts, where such doctrines seem to be exhibited. Others express themselves yet more modestly: they express a tenderness and religious fear, lest they should receive and teach any thing that should seem to reflect on God's moral character, or be a disparagement to his methods of administration, in his moral government; and therefore express themselves as not daring to embrace some doctrines, though they seem to be delivered in Scripture, according to the more obvious and natural construction of the words. But indeed it would show a truer modesty and humility, if they would more entirely rely on God's wisdom and discernment, who knows infinitely better than we what is agreeable to his own perfections, and never intended to leave these matters to the decision of the wisdom and discernment of men; but by his own unerring instruction, to determine for us what the truth is; knowing how little our judgment is to be depended on, and how extremely prone vain and blind men are to err in such matters.

The truth of the case is, that if the Scripture plainly taught the opposite doctrines to those that are so much stumbled at, *viz.* the *Arminian* doctrine of free Will, and others depending thereon, it would be the greatest of all difficulties that attend the Scriptures, incomparably greater than its containing any, even the most mysterious, of those doctrines of the first reformers, which our late freethinkers have so superciliously exploded. Indeed, it is a glorious argument of the divinity of the Holy Scriptures, that they teach such doctrines, which in one age and another, through the blindness of men's minds, and strong prejudices of their hearts, are rejected, as most absurd and unreasonable, by the wise and great men of the world; which yet, when they are most carefully and strictly examined, appear to be exactly agreeable to the most demonstrable, certain, and natural dictates of reason. By such things it appears, that "the foolishness of God is wiser than men." (1 Cor. i. 19, 20.) "For it is written, I will destroy the wisdom of the wise; I will bring to nothing the understanding of the prudent. Where is the wise? where is the scribe? where is the disputer of this world? hath not God made foolish the wisdom of this world?" And as it was in time past, so probably it will be in time to come, as it is also written, (ver. 27—29.) "But God hath chosen the foolish things of the world, to confound the wise; and God hath chosen the weak things of the world to confound the things that are mighty; and base things of the world, and things which are despised, hath God chosen, yea, and things which are not, to bring to nought things that are: that no flesh should glory in his presence." Amen.

APPENDIX.

SECT. XV.

*Containing Remarks on the Essays on the Principles of Morality and Natural Religion, in a Letter to a Minister of the Church of Scotland.**

Rev. Sir,

The intimations you have given me of the use which has by some been made of what I have written on the *Freedom of the Will, &c.* to vindicate what is said on the subject of liberty and necessity, by the author of the *Essays on the Principles of Morality and Natural Religion*, has occasioned my reading this author's Essay on that subject with particular care and attention. And I think it must be evident to every one, that has read both his *Essay* and my *Inquiry*, that our schemes are exceedingly different from each other. The wide difference appears particularly in the following things.

This author supposes, that such a necessity takes place with respect to all men's actions, as is inconsistent with liberty,† and plainly denies that men have any liberty in acting. Thus, (p. 168.) after he had been speaking of the necessity of our determinations, as connected with motives, he concludes with saying, "In short, if motives are not under our power or direction, which is confessedly the fact, we can at bottom have—NO LIBERTY." Whereas, I have abundantly expressed it as my mind, that man, in his moral actions, has true liberty; and that the moral necessity which universally takes place, is not in the least inconsistent with any thing that is properly

* The "Essays" to which this Appendix relates, were the production of Lord Kaimes.

† P. 160, 161, 164, 165, and many other places.

called liberty, and with the utmost liberty that can be desired, or that can possibly exist or be conceived of.

I find that some are apt to think, that in that kind of moral necessity of men's volitions, which I suppose to be universal, at least some degree of liberty denied; that though it be true I allow a sort of liberty, yet those who maintain a self-determining power in the Will, and a liberty of contingence and indifference, hold a higher sort of freedom than I do: but I think this is certainly a great mistake.

Liberty, as I have explained it, is *the power, opportunity, or advantage that any one has to do as he pleases, or conducting himself*, IN ANY RESPECT, *according to his pleasure;* without considering how his pleasure comes to be as it is. It is demonstrable, and, I think, has been demonstrated, that no necessity of men's volitions that I maintain, is inconsistent with this liberty: and I think it is impossible for any one to rise higher in his conceptions of liberty than this: If any imagine they desire, and that they conceive of, a higher and greater liberty than this, they are deceived, and delude themselves with confused ambiguous words, instead of ideas. If any one should here say, "Yes, I conceive of a freedom above and beyond the liberty a man has of conducting himself in any respect as he pleases, *viz.* a liberty of *choosing* as he pleases." Such an one, if he reflected, would either blush or laugh at his own proposal. For, is not choosing as he pleases, conducting himself, IN SOME RESPECT, according to his pleasure, and still without determining how he came by that pleasure? If he says, "Yes, I came by that pleasure by my own choice." If he be a man of common sense, by this time he will see his own absurdity: for he must needs see that his notion or conception, even of this liberty, does not contain any judgment or conception how he comes by that choice, which first determines his pleasure, or which originally fixed his own Will respecting the affair. Or if any shall say, "That a man exercises liberty in this, even in determining his own choice, but not as he pleases, or not in consequence of any choice, preference, or inclination of his own, but by a determination arising contingently out of a state of absolute indifference;" this is not rising higher in his conception of liberty: as such a determination of the Will would not be a voluntary determination of it. Surely he that places liberty in a power of doing something not according to his own choice, or from his choice, has not a higher notion of it, than he that places it in doing as he pleases, or acting from his own election. If there were a power in the mind to determine itself, but not by its choice or according to its pleasure, what advantage would it give? and what liberty, worth contending for, would be exercised in it? Therefore no *Arminian*, *Pelagian*, or *Epicurean*, can rise higher in his conceptions of liberty, than the notion of it which I have explained: which notion is perfectly consistent with the whole of that necessity of men's actions, which I suppose takes place. And I scruple not to say, it is beyond all their wits to invent a higher notion, or form a higher imagination of liberty; let them talk of *sovereignty of the Will, self-determining power, self-motion, self-direction, arbitrary decision, liberty ad utrumvis, power of choosing differently in given cases, &c. &c.* as long as they will. It is apparent that these men, in their strenuous dispute about these things, aim at they know not what, fighting for something they have no conception of, substituting a number of confused unmeaning words, instead of things, and instead of thoughts. They may be challenged clearly to explain what they would have; but they never can answer the challenge.

The author of the *Essays*, through his whole Essay on Liberty and Necessity, goes on the supposition, that, in order to the being of real liberty, a man must have a freedom that is opposed to moral necessity: and yet he supposes, (p. 175.) that "*such a liberty must signify a power in the mind of acting without and against motives, a power of acting without any view, purpose, or design, and even of acting in contradiction to our own desires and aversions, and to all our principles of action; and is an absurdity altogether inconsistent with a rational nature.*" Now, who ever imagined such a liberty as this, a higher sort or degree of freedom, than a liberty of following one's own views and purposes, and acting agreeably to his own inclinations and passions? Who will ever reasonably suppose, that a liberty which is an absurdity altogether inconsistent with a rational nature, is above that which is consistent with the nature of a rational, intelligent, designing agent.

The author of the *Essays* seems to suppose such a necessity to take place, as is inconsistent with some supposable POWER OF ARBITRARY CHOICE,* or that there is some liberty conceivable, whereby men's own actions might be more PROPERLY IN THEIR POWER,† and by which events might be more DEPENDENT ON OURSELVES: ‡ contrary to what I suppose to be evident in my *Inquiry*. What way can be imagined, of our actions being more *in our power, from ourselves*, or *dependent on ourselves*, than their being from our power to fulfil our own choice, to act from our own inclination, pursue our own views, and execute our own designs? Certainly, to be able to act thus, is as properly having our actions in our power, and dependent on ourselves, as a being liable to be the subject of acts and events contingently and fortuitously, *without desire, view, purpose, or design, or any principle of action* within ourselves; as we must be, according to this author's own declared sense, if our actions are performed with that liberty that is opposed to moral necessity.

This author seems every where to suppose, that necessity, most properly so called, attends all men's actions; and that the terms, *necessary, unavoidable, impossible, &c.* are equally applicable to the case of moral and natural necessity. In p. 173. he says, *The idea* of necessary *and* unavoidable *equally agrees, both to moral and physical necessity*. And in p. 184. *All things that fall out in the natural and moral world are alike necessary*. P. 174. *This inclination and choice is* unavoidable, *caused or occasioned by the prevailing motive. In this lies the necessity of our actions, that, in such circumstances, it was* impossible *we* could *act otherwise*. He often expresses himself in like manner elsewhere, speaking in strong terms of men's actions as *unavoidable*, what they *cannot* forbear, having *no power* over their own actions, the order of them being *unalterably* fixed, *and inseparably* linked together, &c. §

On the contrary, I have largely declared, that the connexion between antecedent things and consequent ones, which takes place with regard to the acts of men's Wills, which is called moral necessity, is called by the name of *Necessity* improperly; and that all such terms as *must, cannot, impossible, unable, irresistible, unavoidable, invincible, &c.* when applied here, are not applied in their proper signification, and are either used nonsensically, and with perfect insignificance, or in a sense quite diverse from their original and proper meaning, and their use in common speech: and, that such a necessity as attends the acts of men's Will, is more properly called *certainty*, than *necessity;* it being no other than the certain connexion between the subject and predicate of the proposition which affirms their existence.

Agreeably to what is observed in my *Inquiry*, I think it is evidently owing to a strong prejudice, arising from an insensible habitual perversion and misapplication of such like terms, as *necessary, impossible, unable, unavoidable, invincible, &c.* that they are ready to think, that to suppose a certain connexion of men's volitions, without any foregoing motives or inclinations, or any preceding moral influence whatsoever, is truly and properly to suppose a strong irrefragable chain of causes and effects, as stand in the way of, and makes utterly vain, *opposite desires* and endeavours, like immovable and impenetrable mountains of brass; and impedes our liberty like walls of adamant, gates of brass, and bars of iron: whereas, all such representations suggest ideas as far from the truth, as the east is from the west. Nothing that I maintain, supposes that men are at all hindered by any fatal necessity, from doing, and even willing and choosing, as they please, with full freedom; yea, with the highest degree of liberty that ever was thought of, or that ever could possibly enter into the heart of any man to conceive. I know it is in vain to endeavour to make some persons believe this, or at least fully and steadily to believe it: for if it be demonstrated to them, still the old prejudice remains, which has been long fixed by the use of

* P. 169. † P. 191, 195, 197, 206. ‡ P. 183.

§ P. 180, 188, 193, 194, 195, 197, 198, 199, 205, 206

the terms *necessary, must, cannot, impossible, &c.* the association with these terms of certain ideas, inconsistent with liberty, is not broken; and the judgment is powerfully warped by it; as a thing that has been long bent and grown stiff, if it be straightened, will return to its former curvity again and again.

The author of the *Essays* most manifestly supposes, that if men had the truth concerning the real necessity of all their actions clearly in view, they would not appear to themselves, or one another, as at all praiseworthy or culpable, or under any moral obligation, or accountable for their actions:* which supposes, that men are not to be blamed or praised for any of their actions, and are not under any obligations, nor are truly accountable for any thing they do, by reason of this necessity; which is very contrary to what I have endeavoured to prove, throughout the *third part* of my *Inquiry.* I humbly conceive it is there shown, that this is so far from the truth, that the moral necessity of men's actions which truly take place, is requisite to the being of virtue and vice, or any thing praiseworthy or culpable: that the liberty of indifference and contingence, which is advanced in opposition to that necessity, is inconsistent with the being of these; as it would suppose that men are not determined in what they do, by any virtuous or vicious principles, nor act from any motives, intentions, or aims whatsoever; or have any end, either good or bad, in acting. And is it not remarkable, that this author should suppose, that, in order to men's actions truly having any desert, they must be performed *without any view, purpose, design, or desire,* or *any principle of action,* or any thing *agreeable to a rational nature?* as it will appear that he does, if we compare, p. 206, 207, with p. 175.

The author of the *Essays* supposes, that God has deeply implanted in man's nature a strong and invincible apprehension, or feeling, as he calls it, of a liberty, and contingence of his own actions, opposite to that necessity which truly attends them; and which in truth does not agree with real fact,† is not agreeable to strict philosophic truth,‡ is contradictory to the truth of things,§ and which truth contradicts,|| not tallying with the real plan:¶ and that therefore such feelings are deceitful,** and are in reality of the delusive kind.†† He speaks of them as a wise delusion,‡‡ as nice artificial feelings, merely that conscience may have a commanding power:§§ meaning, plainly, that these feelings are a cunning artifice of the Author of nature, to make men believe they are free, when they are not.|||| He supposes that, by these feelings, the moral world has a disguised appearance,¶¶ &c. He supposes that all self-approbation, and all remorse of conscience, all commendation or condemnation of ourselves or others, all sense of desert, and all that is connected with this way of thinking, all the ideas which at present are suggested by the words *ought, should,* arise from this delusion, and would entirely vanish without it.***

All which is very contrary to what I have abundantly insisted on and endeavoured to demonstrate in my *Inquiry;* where I have largely shown, that it is agreeable to the natural sense of mankind, that the moral necessity or certainty that attends men's actions, is consistent with praise and blame, reward and punishment;††† and that it is agreeable to our natural notions, that moral evil, with its desert of dislike and abhorrence, and all its other ill-deservings, consists in a certain deformity in the nature of the dispositions and acts of the heart, and not in the evil of something else, diverse from these supposed to be their cause or occasion.‡‡‡

I might well ask here, whether any one is to be found in the world of mankind, who is conscious to a sense or feeling, naturally and deeply rooted in his mind, that, in order to a man's performing any action that is praiseworthy or blameworthy, he must exercise a liberty that implies and signifies a power of acting without any motive, view, design, desire, or principle of action? For such a liberty, this author supposes, that must be which is opposed to moral necessity, as I have already observed. Supposing a man should actually do good, independent of desire, aim, inducement, principle, or end, is it a dictate of invincible natural sense, that his act is more meritorious or praiseworthy, than if he had performed it for some *good end,* and had been governed in it by *good principles* and *motives?* and so I might ask, on the contrary, with respect to evil actions.§§§

The author of the *Essays* supposes that the liberty without necessity of which we have a natural feeling, implies *contingence;* and, speaking of this contingence, he sometimes calls it by the name of *chance.* And it is evident, that his notion of it, or rather what he says about it, implies things happening *loosely, fortuitously,* by *accident,* and *without a cause.*|||||| Now I conceive the slightest reflection may be sufficient to satisfy any one, that such a contingence of men's actions, according to our natural sense, is so far from being essential to the morality or merit of those actions, that it would destroy it; and that, on the contrary, the dependence of our actions on such causes, as inward inclinations, incitements, and ends, is essential to the being of it. Natural sense teaches men, when they see any thing done by others of a good or evil tendency, to inquire what their *intention* was, what principles and views they were moved by, in order to judge how far they are to be justified or condemned; and not to determine, that, in order to their being approved or blamed at all, the action must be performed altogether *fortuitously,* proceeding from nothing, arising from no cause. Concerning this matter, I have fully expressed my mind in the *Inquiry.*

If the liberty of which we have a natural sense, as necessary to desert, consists in the mind's self-determination, without being determined by previous inclination or motive, then indifference is essential to it, yea absolute indifference; as is observed in my *Inquiry.* But men naturally have no notion of any such liberty as this, as essential to the morality or demerit of their actions; but on the contrary, such a liberty, if it were possible, would be inconsistent with our natural notions of desert, as is largely shown in the *Inquiry.*¶¶¶ If it be agreeable to natural sense, that men must be indifferent in determining their own actions; then, according to the same, the more they are determined by inclination, either good or bad, the less they have of desert: the more good actions are performed from good disposition, the less praiseworthy; and the more evil deeds are from evil dispositions, the less culpable; and, in general, the more men's actions are from their hearts, the less they are to be commended or condemned: which all must know is very contrary to natural sense.

Moral necessity is owing to the power and government of the inclination of the heart, either habitual or occasional, excited by motive: but, according to natural and common sense, the more a man does any thing with full inclination of heart, the more is it to be charged to his account for his condemnation, if it be an ill action, and the more to be ascribed to him for his praise, if it be good.

If the mind were determined to evil actions by contingence, from a state of indifference, then either there would be no fault in them, or else the fault would be in being so perfectly indifferent, that the mind was equally liable to a bad or good determination. And if this indifference be liberty, then the very essence of the blame or fault would lie in the liberty itself, or the wickedness would, primarily and summarily, lie in being a free agent. If there were no fault in being indifferent, then there would be no fault in the determination being agreeable to such a state of indifference: that is, there could be no fault found, that opposite determinations actually happen to take place *indifferently,* sometimes good and sometimes bad, as contingence governs and decides. And if it be a fault to be indifferent to good and evil, then such indifference is no indifference to good and evil, but is a determination to evil, or to a fault; and such an indifferent disposition would be an evil disposition, tendency, or determination of mind. So inconsistent are these notions of liberty, as essential to praise or blame.

* P. 207, 209, and other places. † P. 200. ‡ P. 152. § P. 183. || P. 186. ¶ P. 205. ** P. 203, 204, 211. †† P. 183. ‡‡ P. 209. §§ P. 211. |||| P. 153. ¶¶ P. 214. *** P. 160, 194, 199, 205, 206, 207, 209. ††† *Inquiry,* Part IV. Sect. 4. throughout.

‡‡‡ *Idem,* Part IV. Sect. 1. throughout. §§§ See this matter illustrated in my *Inquiry,* Part IV. Sect. 4. |||||| P. 156–159, 177, 178, 181, 183—185. ¶¶¶ Especially in Part. III Sect. 6, and 7.

The author of the *Essays* supposes men's natural delusive sense of a liberty of contingence, to be, in truth, the foundation of all the labour, care, and industry of mankind;* and that if men's "practical ideas had been formed on the plan of universal necessity, the ignava ratio, the inactive doctrine of the Stoics, would have followed; and that there would have been no ROOM for forethought about futurity, or any sort of industry and care:"† plainly implying, that, in this case, men would see and know that all their industry and care signified nothing, was in vain, and to no purpose, or of no benefit; events being fixed in an irrefragable chain, and not at all DEPENDING on their care and endeavour; as he explains himself, particularly, in the instance of men's use of means to prolong life:‡ not only very contrary to what I largely maintain in my *Inquiry*,§ but also very inconsistently with his own scheme, in what he supposes of the ends for which God has so deeply implanted this deceitful feeling in man's nature; in which he manifestly supposes men's care and industry not to be in vain and of no benefit, but of great use, yea of absolute necessity, in order to their obtaining the most important ends and necessary purposes of human life, and to fulfil the ends of action to the BEST ADVANTAGE; as he largely declares.‖ Now, how shall these things be reconciled? That, if men had *a clear view of real truth*, they would see that there was *no* ROOM for their care and industry, because they would see it to be in vain, and of no benefit; and yet that God, by having a clear view of real truth, sees their being excited to care and industry will be of excellent use to mankind, and greatly for the benefit of the world, yea absolutely necessary in order to it: and that therefore the great wisdom and goodness of God to men appears, in artfully contriving to put them on care and industry for their good, which good could not be obtained without them; and yet both these things are maintained at once, and in the same sentences and words, by this author. The very reason he gives, *why* God has put this deceitful feeling into men, contradicts and destroys itself; that God in his great goodness to men gave them such a deceitful feeling, because it was very useful and necessary for them, and greatly for their benefit, or excites them to care and industry for their own good, which care and industry is useful and necessary to that end; and yet the very thing for which, as a reason, this great benefit of care and industry is given, is God's deceiving men in this very point, in making them think their care and industry to be of great benefit to them, when indeed it is of none at all; and if they saw the real truth, they would see all their endeavours to be wholly useless, that there was NO ROOM for them, and that the event does not at all DEPEND upon them.¶

And besides, what this author says plainly implies, (as appears by what has been already observed,) that it is necessary men should be deceived, by being made to believe that future events are contingent, and their own future actions free, with such a freedom, as signifies that their actions are not the fruit of their own desires, or designs, but altogether contingent, fortuitous, and without a cause. But how should a notion of liberty, consisting in accident or loose chance, encourage care and industry? I should think it would rather entirely discourage every thing of this nature. For surely, if our actions do not depend on our desires and designs, then they do not depend on our endeavours, flowing from our desires and designs. This author himself seems to suppose, that if men had, indeed, such a liberty of contingence, it would render all endeavours to determine or move men's future volitions, in vain: he says, that, in this case, *to exhort, to instruct, to promise, or to threaten*, would be to no purpose.** Why? Because (as he himself gives the reason) "then our Will would be capricious and arbitrary, and we should be thrown loose altogether, and our arbitrary power could do us good or ill only by accident." But if such a loose fortuitous state would render vain others' endeavours upon us, for the same reason would it make useless our endeavours on ourselves: for events that are truly contingent and accidental, and altogether loose from, and independent of, all foregoing causes, are independent on every foregoing cause within ourselves, as well as in others.

I suppose that it is so far from being true, that our minds are naturally possessed with a notion of such liberty as this, so strongly, that it is impossible to root it out, that indeed men have no such notion of liberty at all, and that it is utterly impossible, by any means whatsoever, to implant or introduce such a notion into the mind. As no such notions as imply self-contradiction and self-abolition can subsist in the mind, as I have shown in my *Inquiry;* I think a mature sensible consideration of the matter is sufficient to satisfy any one, that even the greatest and most learned advocates themselves for liberty of indifference and self-determination, have no such notion; and that indeed they mean something wholly inconsistent with, and directly subversive of, what they strenuously affirm, and earnestly contend for. By a man having a power of determining his own Will, they plainly mean a power of determining his Will as he pleases, or as he chooses; which supposes that the mind has a choice, prior to its going about to confirm any action or determination to it. And if they mean that they determine even the original or prime choice, by their own pleasure or choice, as the thing that causes and directs it; I scruple not most boldly to affirm, that they speak they know not what, and that of which they have no manner of idea; because no such contradictory notion can come into, or have a moment's subsistence in, the mind of any man living, as an original or first choice being caused, or brought into being, by choice. After all, they say, they have no higher or other conception of liberty, than that vulgar notion of it, which I contend for, viz. a man's having power or opportunity to do as he chooses: or if they had a notion that every act of choice was determined by choice, yet it would destroy their notion of the contingence of choice; for then no one act of choice would arise contingently, or from a state of indifference, but every individual act, in all the series, would arise from foregoing bias or preference, and from a cause predetermining and fixing its existence, which introduces at once such a chain of causes and effects, each preceding link decisively fixing the following, as they would by all means avoid.

And such kind of delusion and self-contradiction as this, does not arise in men's minds by nature: it is not owing to any natural feeling which God has strongly fixed in the mind and nature of man; but to false philosophy, and strong prejudice, from a deceitful abuse of words. It is *artificial;* not in the sense of the author of the *Essays*, supposing it to be a deceitful artifice of God; but artificial as opposed to natural, and as owing to an artificial deceitful management of terms, to darken and confound the mind. Men have no such thing when they first begin to exercise reason; but must have a great deal of time to blind themselves with metaphysical confusion, before they can embrace, and rest in, such definitions of liberty as are given, and imagine they understand them.

On the whole, I humbly conceive, that whosoever will give himself the trouble of weighing, what I have offered to consideration in my *Inquiry*, must be sensible, that such a moral necessity of men's actions as I maintain, is not at all inconsistent with any liberty that any creature has, or can have, as a free, accountable, moral agent, and subject of moral government; and that this moral necessity is so far from being inconsistent with praise and blame, and the benefit and use of men's own care and labour, that, on the contrary, it implies the very ground and reason, why men's actions are to be ascribed to them as their own, in such a manner as to infer desert, praise and blame, approbation and remorse of conscience, reward and punishment; and that it establishes the moral system of the universe, and God's moral government, in every respect, with the proper use of motives, exhortations, commands, counsels, promises, and threatenings; and the use and benefit of endeavours, care and industry. There is therefore no need that the strict philosophic truth should be at all concealed; nor is there any danger in *contemplation* and *profound discovery* in these things. So far from this, that the truth in this matter is of vast importance, and extremely needful to be known; and the more clearly and perfectly the real fact is known, and the more constantly

* P. 184. † P. 189. ‡ P. 184, 185.
§ Especially Part. IV. Sect. 5.
‖ P. 188—192. and in many other places ¶ P. 188, 189, &c.
** P. 178, 213, 214.

it is in view, the better. More particularly, that the clear and full knowledge of that, which is the true system of the universe, in these respects, would greatly establish the doctrines which teach the true christian scheme of divine administration in the city of God, and the gospel of Jesus Christ, in its most important articles. Indeed these things never can be well established, and the opposite errors—so subversive of the whole gospel, which at this day so greatly and generally prevail—be well confuted, or the arguments by which they are maintained, answered, till these points are settled. While this is not done, it is, to me, beyond doubt, that the friends of those great gospel truths, will but poorly maintain their controversy with the adversaries of those truths: they will be obliged often to shuffle, hide, and turn their backs; and the latter will have a strong fort, from whence they never can be driven, and weapons to use, from which those whom they oppose will find no shield to screen themselves; and they will always puzzle, confound, and keep under the friends of sound doctrine; and glory, and vaunt themselves in their advantage over them; and carry their affairs with a high hand, as they have done already for a long time past.

I conclude, Sir, with asking your pardon for troubling you with so much in vindication of myself from the imputation of advancing a scheme of necessity, like that of the author of the *Essays on the Principles of Morality and Natural Religion.* Considering that what I have said is not only in vindication of myself, but, as I think, of the most important articles of moral philosophy and religion; I trust in what I know of your candour, that you will excuse,

Your obliged friend and brother,

J. EDWARDS.

Stockbridge, July 25th, 1757.

A

DISSERTATION

CONCERNING

THE END FOR WHICH GOD CREATED THE WORLD.

PREFACE BY THE FIRST EDITOR.

The Author had designed these Dissertations* for the public view; and wrote them out as they now appear: though it is probable, that if his life had been spared, he would have revised them, and rendered them in some respects more complete. Some new sentiments, here and there, might probably have been added; and some passages brightened with farther illustrations. This may be conjectured from some brief hints or sentiments minuted down on loose papers, found in the manuscripts.

But those sentiments concisely sketched out, which, it is thought, the author intended to enlarge, and digest into the body of the work, cannot be so amplified by any other hand, as to do justice to the author: it is therefore probably best that nothing of this kind should be attempted.

As these Dissertations were more especially designed for the learned and inquisitive, it is expected that the judicious and candid will not be disposed to object, that the manner in which these subjects are treated is something above the level of common readers. For though a superficial way of discourse and loose harangues may well enough suit some subjects, and answer some valuable purposes; yet other subjects demand more closeness and accuracy. And if an author should neglect to do justice to a subject, for fear that the simpler sort should not fully understand him, he might expect to be deemed a trifler by the more intelligent.

Our author had a rare talent to penetrate deep in search of truth; to take an extensive survey of a subject, and look through it into remote consequences. Hence many theorems, that appeared hard and barren to others, were to him pleasant and fruitful fields, where his mind would expatiate with peculiar ease, profit, and entertainment. Those studies, which to some are too fatiguing to the mind, and wearying to the constitution, were to him but a natural play of genius, and which his mind without labour would freely and spontaneously perform. A close and conclusive way of reasoning upon a controversial point was easy and natural to him.

This may serve, it is conceived, to account for his usual manner of treating abstruse and controverted subjects, which some have thought has been too metaphysical. But the truth is, that his critical method of looking through the nature of his subject,—his accuracy and precision in canvassing truth, comparing ideas, drawing consequences, pointing out and exposing absurdities,—naturally led him to reduce the evidence in favour of truth into the form of demonstration; which, doubtless, where it can be obtained, is the most eligible, and by far the most satisfying to great and noble minds. And though some readers may find the labour hard to keep pace with the writer, in the advances he makes, where the ascent is arduous; yet in general all was easy to him: such was his peculiar love and discernment of truth, and natural propensity to search after it. His own ideas were clear to him, where some readers have thought them obscure. Thus many things in the works of Newton and Locke, which appear either quite unintelligible, or very obscure, to the illiterate, were clear and bright to those illustrious authors, and their learned readers.

The subjects here handled are sublime and important. The *end* which God had in view in creating the world, was doubtless worthy of him; and consequently the most excellent and glorious possible. This therefore must be worthy to be known by all the intelligent creation, as excellent in itself, and worthy of their pursuit. And as true virtue distinguishes the inhabitants of heaven, and all the happy candidates for that world of glory, from all others; there cannot surely be a more interesting subject.

The notions which some men entertain concerning God's end in creating the world, and concerning true virtue, in our late author's opinion, have a natural tendency to corrupt Christianity, and to destroy the gospel of our divine Redeemer. It was therefore, no doubt, in the exercise of a pious concern for the honour and glory of God, and a tender respect to the best interests of his fellow-men, that this devout and learned writer undertook the following work.—May the Father of lights smile upon the pious and benevolent aims and labours of his servant, and crown them with his blessing!

* This preface was originally prefixed to the two following Dissertations, "concerning the End for which God created the World, and the Nature of True Virtue," in one volume.—W.

A

DISSERTATION, &c.

INTRODUCTION.

Containing explanations of terms and general positions.

To avoid all confusion in our inquiries concerning the end for which God created the world, a distinction should be observed between the *chief* end for which an agent performs any work, and the *ultimate* end. These two phrases are not always precisely of the same signification: and though the *chief* end be always an *ultimate* end, yet every ultimate end is not always a chief end. A *chief* end is opposite to an *inferior* end: an *ultimate* end is opposite to a *subordinate* end.

A *subordinate* end is what an agent aims at, not at all upon its own account, but wholly on the account of a *further* end, of which it is considered as a means. Thus when a man goes a journey to obtain a medicine to restore his health, the obtaining of that medicine is his subordinate end; because it is not an end that he values at all upon its own account, but wholly as a means of a further end, *viz.* his health. Separate the medicine from that further end, and it is not at all desired.

An *ultimate* end is that which the agent seeks, in what he does, for its *own* sake; what he loves, values, and takes pleasure in on its own account, and not merely as a means of a further end. As when a man loves the taste of some particular sort of fruit, and is at pains and cost to obtain it, for the sake of the pleasure of that taste which he values upon its own account, as he loves his own pleasure; and not merely for the sake of any other good, which he supposes his enjoying that pleasure will be the means of.

Some ends are subordinate, not only as they are subordinated to an ultimate end; but also to another end that is itself but subordinate. Yea, there may be a succession or chain of many subordinate ends, one dependent on another, one sought for another; before you come to any thing that the agent aims at, and seeks for its *own* sake. As when a man sells a garment to get money—to buy tools—to till his land—to obtain a crop—to supply him with food—to gratify the appetite. And he seeks to gratify his appetite, on its *own* account, as what is grateful in itself. Here the end of his selling his garment to get money, is only a subordinate end; and it is not only subordinate to the *ultimate* end—gratifying his appetite—but to a *nearer* end—buying husbandry tools; and his obtaining these is only a subordinate end, being only for the sake of tilling land. And the tillage of land is an end not sought on its own account, but for the sake of the crop to be produced; and the crop produced is an end sought only for the sake of making bread; and bread is sought for the sake of gratifying the appetite.

Here gratifying the appetite is called the *ultimate* end; because it is the *last* in the chain where a man's aim rests, obtaining in that the thing finally aimed at. So whenever a man comes to that in which his desire terminates and rests, it being something valued on its *own* account, then he comes to an *ultimate* end, let the chain be longer or shorter; yea, if there be but one link or one step that he takes before he comes to this end. As when a man that loves honey puts it into his mouth, for the sake of the pleasure of the taste, without aiming at any thing further. So that an end which an agent has in view, may be both his *immediate* and his *ultimate* end; his *next* and his *last* end. That end which is sought for the sake of itself, and not for the sake of a further end, is an ultimate end; there the aim of the agent stops and rests.

A thing sought may have the nature of an ultimate, and also of a subordinate end; as it may be sought partly on its own account, and partly for the sake of a further end. Thus a man, in what he does, may seek the love and respect of a particular person, partly on its own account, because it is in itself agreeable to men to be the objects of others' esteem and love; and partly, because he hopes, through the friendship of that person, to have his assistance in other affairs; and so to be put under advantage for obtaining further ends.

A *chief* end, which is opposite to an *inferior* end, is something diverse from an ultimate end; it is most valued, and therefore most sought after by the agent in what he does. It is evident, that to be an end *more* valued than another end, is not exactly the same thing as to be an end valued *ultimately*, or for its own sake. This will appear, if it be considered,

1. That two different ends may be both ultimate, and yet not be chief ends. They may be both valued for their *own* sake, and both sought in the same work or acts; and yet one valued more highly, and sought more than another. Thus a man may go a journey to obtain two different benefits or enjoyments, both which may be agreeable to him in *themselves* considered; and yet one may be much more agreeable than the other; and so be what he sets his heart *chiefly* upon. Thus a man may go a journey, partly to obtain the possession and enjoyment of a bride that is very dear to him; and partly to gratify his curiosity in looking in a telescope, or some new-invented and extraordinary optic glass; and the one not properly subordinate to the other; and therefore *both* may be *ultimate* ends. But yet obtaining his beloved bride may be his *chief* end; and the benefit of the optic glass his *inferior* end.

2. An ultimate end is not always the chief end, because some *subordinate* ends may be *more* valued and sought after than some *ultimate* ends. Thus, for instance, a man may aim at two things in his journey; one, to visit his friends, and another, to receive a large sum of money. The latter may be but a *subordinate* end; he may not value the silver and gold on their *own* account, but only for pleasure, gratification, and honour; the money is valued only as a means of the other. But yet, obtaining the money may be *more* valued, and so is a *higher* end of his journey than the pleasure of seeing his friends; though the latter is valued on its *own* account, and so is an *ultimate* end.

But here several things may be noted:

First, When it is said, that some *subordinate* ends may be *more* valued than some *ultimate* ends, it is not supposed that ever a subordinate end is more valued than *that* to which it is subordinate. For that reason it is called a *subordinate* end, because it is valued and sought not for its own sake, but only in subordination to a *further* end. But yet a subordinate end may be valued more than some *other* ultimate end that it is not subordinate to. Thus, for instance, a man goes a journey to receive a sum of money, only for the value of the pleasure and honour that the money may be a means of. In this case it is impossible that the *subordinate* end, *viz.* his having the money, should be *more* valued by him than the pleasure and honour for which he values it. It would be absurd to suppose that he values the means more than the end, when he has no value for the means, but for the sake of the end of which it is the means. But yet he may value the money, though but a subordinate end, *more* than some *other ultimate* end to which it is not subordinate, and with which it has no connexion. For instance, *more* than the comfort of a friendly visit, which was one ultimate end of his journey.

Secondly, The ultimate end is always *superior* to its subordinate end, and more valued by the agent, unless it be when the ultimate end entirely depends on the subordinate. If he has no other means by which to obtain his last end, then the subordinate may be *as much* valued as the last end; because the last end, in such a case, altogether depends upon, and is wholly and certainly conveyed by it. As for instance, if a pregnant woman has a peculiar appetite to a certain rare fruit that is to be found only in the garden of a particular friend of hers, at a distance—and she goes a journey to her friend's house or garden, to obtain that fruit—the *ultimate* end of her journey is to gratify that strong appetite; the obtaining that fruit, is the *subordinate* end of it. If she looks upon it, that the appetite can be gratified by *no other* means than the obtaining of that fruit; and that it will *certainly* be gratified if she obtain it, then she will value the fruit *as much* as she values the gratification of her appetite. But otherwise, it will not be so. If she be *doubtful* whether that fruit will satisfy her craving, then she will not value it *equally* with the gratification of her appetite itself. Or if there be some *other fruit* that she knows of, that will gratify her desire, at least *in part*, which she can obtain without such trouble as shall countervail the gratification—or if her appetite cannot be gratified without this fruit, nor yet with it *alone*, without something else to be compounded with it—then her *value* for her last end will be *divided* between these several ingredients, as so many subordinate ends, and no *one alone* will be equally valued with the last end. Hence it rarely happens, that a subordinate end is *equally* valued with its last end; because the obtaining of a last end rarely depends on *one* single, uncompounded means, and infallibly connected with it. Therefore, men's *last* ends are *commonly* their *highest* ends.

Thirdly, If any being has but *one* ultimate end, in all that he does, and there be a great variety of operations, his *last* end may justly be looked upon as his *supreme* end. For in such a case, *every other* end but that one, is in order to that end; and therefore no other can be superior to it. Because, as was observed before, a subordinate end is never *more* valued than the end to which it is subordinate. Moreover, the subordinate effects, or events, brought to pass, as means of this end, all uniting to contribute their share towards obtaining the one last end, are very various; and therefore, by what has been now observed, the ultimate end of all must be valued more than any one of the particular means. This seems to be the case with the works of God, as may more fully appear in the sequel.

Fourthly, Whatsoever any agent has in view in any thing he does, which is agreeable to him *in itself*, and not merely for the sake of something else, is regarded by that agent as his *last* end. The same may be said of avoiding that which is in itself painful or disagreeable; for the avoiding of what is disagreeable is agreeable. This will be evident to any bearing in mind the meaning of the terms. By *last* end being meant, that which is regarded and sought by an agent, as agreeable or desirable for its *own* sake; a *subordinate*, that which is sought only for the sake of something *else*.

Fifthly, From hence it will follow, that, if an agent has in view *more things than one* that will be brought to pass by what he does, which he loves and delights in on their *own* account, then he must have *more things than one* that he regards as his *last* ends in what he does. But if there be *but one thing* that an agent seeks, on its *own* account, then there can be *but one* last end which he has in all his actions and operations.

But only here a distinction must be observed of things which may be said to be *agreeable* to an agent, in *themselves* considered: (1.) What is in itself grateful to an agent, and valued on its own account, *simply* and *absolutely* considered; antecedent to, and *independent* of all conditions, or any supposition of particular cases and circumstances. And, (2.) What may be said to be in itself agreeable to an agent, *hypothetically* and consequentially; or, on supposition of such and such circumstances, or on the happening of such a particular case.

Thus, for instance, a man may originally love society. An inclination to society may be implanted in his very nature; and society may be agreeable to him *antecedent* to all pre-supposed cases and circumstances; and this may cause him to seek a family. And the comfort of society may be originally his *last* end, in seeking a family. But after he has a family, peace, good order, and mutual justice and friendship in his family, may be agreeable to him, and what he delights in for their *own* sake; and therefore these things may be his *last* end in many things he does in the government and regulation of his family. But they were not his *original* end with respect to his family. The justice and the peace of a family was not properly his last end *before* he had a family, that induced him to seek a family, but consequentially. And the case being put of his having a family, then these things wherein the good order and beauty of a family consist, become his last end in many things he does in such circumstances.

In like manner we must suppose that God, *before* he created the world, had some good in view, as a consequence of the world's existence, that was *originally* agreeable to him in itself considered, that inclined him to bring the universe into existence, in such a manner as he created it. But *after* the world was created, and such and such intelligent creatures actually had existence, in such and such circumstances, then a wise, just regulation of them was agreeable to God, *in itself* considered. And God's love of justice, and hatred of injustice, would be sufficient in such a case to induce God to deal *justly* with his creatures, and to prevent all injustice in him towards them. But yet there is no necessity of supposing, that God's love of doing justly to intelligent beings, and hatred of the contrary, was what *originally* induced God to create the world, and make intelligent beings; and so to order the occasion of doing either justly or unjustly. The justice of God's nature makes a just regulation agreeable, and the contrary disagreeable, as there is occasion; the *subject* being supposed, and the *occasion* given. But we must suppose something else that should incline him to *create* the subjects, or *order* the occasion.

So that perfection of God which we call his faithfulness, or his inclination to fulfil his promises to his creatures, could not properly be what *moved* him to create the world; nor could such a fulfilment of his promises to his creatures be his *last* end in giving the creatures being. But yet *after* the world is created, *after* intelligent creatures are made, and God has bound himself by promise to them, then that disposition, which is called his faithfulness, may move him in his providential disposals towards them; and this may be the *end* of many of God's works of providence, even the exercise of his faithfulness in fulfilling his promises, and may be in the *lower* sense his *last* end; because faithfulness and truth must be supposed to be what is in *itself* amiable to God, and what he delights in for its *own* sake. Thus God may have ends of particular works of *providence*, which are ultimate ends in a lower sense, which were not ultimate ends of the *creation*.

So that here we have two sorts of ultimate ends; one of which may be called, *original* and *independent*, the other, *consequential* and *dependent;* for it is evident, the latter sort are truly of the nature of ultimate ends; because though their being agreeable to the agent, be consequential on the existence, yet the subject and occasion being supposed, they are agreeable and amiable in themselves. We may suppose, that, to a righteous Being, doing justice between two parties, with whom he is concerned, is agreeable in *itself*, and not merely for the sake of some *other* end: And yet we may suppose, that a desire of doing justice between two parties, may be *consequential* on the being of those parties, and the occasion given.—It may be observed, that when I speak of God's ultimate end in the creation of the world, in the following discourse, I commonly mean in that *highest* sense, *viz.* the *original* ultimate end.

Sixthly, It may be further observed, that the *original* ultimate end or ends of the creation of the world is *alone* that which induces God to give the occasion for consequential ends, by the first creation of the world, and the original disposal of it. And the more original the end is, the more extensive and universal it is. That which God had *primarily* in view in creating, and the *original* ordination of the world, must be constantly kept in view, and have a governing influence in all God's works, or with respect to every thing he does towards his creatures. And therefore,

Seventhly, If we use the phrase ultimate end in this highest sense, then the same that is God's ultimate end in creating the world, if we suppose but one such end, must be what he makes his ultimate aim in all his works, in every thing he does either in creation or providence. But we must suppose, that, in the *use* to which God puts his creatures, he must evermore have a regard to the *end* for which he has made them. But if we take *ultimate end* in the other *lower* sense, God may sometimes have regard to those things as ultimate ends, in particular works of providence, which could not in any proper sense be his *last* end in creating the world.

Eighthly, On the other hand, whatever appears to be God's ultimate end, in any sense, of his works of providence *in general*; that must be the ultimate end of the work of *creation* itself. For though God may act for an end that is ultimate in a lower sense, in *some* of his works of providence, which is not the ultimate end of the creation of the world, yet this doth not take place with regard to the works of providence *in general*; for God's works of providence in general, are the *same* with the *general use* to which he puts the world he has made. And we may well argue from what we see of the general *use* which God makes of the world, to the general *end* for which he designed the world. Though there may be some ends of particular works of providence, that were not the *last* end of the creation, which are in themselves grateful to God in such particular emergent circumstances, and so are last ends in an inferior sense; yet this is only in certain cases, or particular occasions. But if they are last ends of God's proceedings in the use of the world *in general*, this shows that his making them last ends does not depend on particular cases and circumstances, but the nature of things in general, and his general design in the being and constitution of the universe.

Ninthly, If there be but *one thing* that is originally, and independent on any future supposed cases, agreeable to God, to be obtained by the creation of the world, then there can be *but one last end* of God's work, in this highest sense. But if there are *various* things, properly diverse one from another, that are absolutely and independently agreeable to the Divine Being, which are actually obtained by the creation of the world, then there were *several* ultimate ends of the creation in that highest sense.

CHAP. I.

WHEREIN IS CONSIDERED, WHAT REASON TEACHES CONCERNING THIS AFFAIR.

Sect. I.

Some things observed in general, which reason dictates.

Having observed these things, to prevent confusion, I now proceed to consider what *may*, and what may *not*, be supposed to be God's ultimate end in the creation of the world.

Indeed this affair seems properly to be an affair of divine revelation. In order to be determined what was designed, in the creating of the astonishing fabric of the universe we behold, it becomes us to attend to, and rely on, what HE has told us, who was the architect. He best knows his own heart, and what his own ends and designs were, in the wonderful works which he has wrought. Nor is it to be supposed that mankind—who, while destitute of revelation, by the utmost improvements of their own reason, and advances in science and philosophy, could come to no clear and established determination who the *author* of the world was—would ever have obtained any tolerable settled judgment of the end which the author of it proposed to himself in so vast, complicated, and wonderful a work of his hands. And though it be true, that the revelation which God has given to men, as a light shining in a dark place, has been the occasion of great improvement of their faculties, and has taught men how to use their reason; and though mankind now, through the long-continued assistance they have had by this divine light, have come to great attainments in the habitual exercise of reason; yet I confess it would be relying too much on reason, to determine the affair of God's last end in the creation of the world, without being herein *principally* guided by divine revelation, since God has given a revelation containing instructions concerning this very matter. Nevertheless, as objections have chiefly been made, against what I think the Scriptures have truly revealed, from the pretended dictates of reason, I would, in the *first* place, soberly consider in a few things, what seems rational to be supposed concerning this affair;—and *then* proceed to consider what light divine revelation gives us in it.

As to the *first* of these, I think the following things appear to be the dictates of reason:

1. That no notion of God's last end in the creation of the world, is agreeable to reason, which would truly imply any indigence, insufficiency, and mutability in God; or any dependence of the Creator on the creature, for any part of his perfection or happiness. Because it is evident, by both Scripture and reason, that God is infinitely, eternally, unchangeably, and independently glorious and happy: that he cannot be profited by, or receive any thing from, the creature; or be the subject of any sufferings, or diminution of his glory and felicity, from any other being. The notion of God creating the world, in order to receive any thing properly from the creature, is not only contrary to the nature of God, but inconsistent with the notion of creation; which implies a being receiving its existence, and all that belongs to it, out of nothing. And this implies the most perfect, absolute, and universal derivation and dependence. Now, if the creature receives its ALL from God, entirely and perfectly, how is it possible that *it* should have any thing to add to God, to make him in any respect more than he was before, and so the Creator become dependent on the creature?

2. Whatsoever is good and valuable *in itself*, is worthy that God should value it with an *ultimate* respect. It is therefore worthy to be made the *last end* of his operation; if it be properly *capable* of being attained. For it may be supposed that some things, valuable and excellent in themselves, are not properly capable of being *attained* in any divine operation; because their existence, in all possible respects, must be conceived of as *prior* to any divine operation. Thus God's existence and infinite perfection, though infinitely valuable in themselves, cannot be supposed to be the *end* of any divine operation; for we cannot conceive of them as, in any respect, *consequent* on any works of God. But whatever is *in itself valuable*, absolutely so, and is *capable* of being sought and *attained*, is worthy to be made a last end of the divine operation.—Therefore,

3. Whatever that be which is *in itself* most valuable, and was so originally, prior to the creation of the world, and which is *attainable* by the creation, if there be any thing which was superior in value to all others, *that* must be worthy to be God's *last* end in the creation; and also worthy to be his *highest* end.—In consequence of this it will follow,

4. That if God *himself* be, in *any respect*, properly *ca-*

pable of being his own end in the creation of the world, then it is reasonable to suppose that he had respect to *himself*, as his last and highest end, in this work; because he is *worthy* in himself to be so, being infinitely the greatest and best of beings. All things else, with regard to worthiness, importance, and excellence, are perfectly as nothing in comparison of him. And therefore, if God has respect to things according to their nature and proportions, he must necessarily have the greatest respect to himself. It would be against the perfection of his nature, his wisdom, holiness, and perfect rectitude, whereby he is disposed to do every thing that is fit to be done, to suppose otherwise. At least, a great part of the moral rectitude of God, whereby he is disposed to every thing that is fit, suitable, and amiable in itself, consists in his having the highest regard to that which is in itself highest and best. The moral rectitude of God must consist in a due respect to things that are objects of moral respect; that is, to intelligent beings capable of moral actions and relations. And therefore it must chiefly consist in giving due respect to that Being to whom most is due; for God is infinitely the most worthy of regard. The worthiness of others is as nothing to his; so that to him belongs all possible respect. To him belongs the *whole* of the respect that any intelligent being is capable of. To him belongs ALL the heart. Therefore, if moral rectitude of heart consists in paying the respect of the heart which is due, or which fitness and suitableness requires, fitness requires infinitely the greatest regard to be paid to God; and the denying of supreme regard here would be a conduct infinitely the most unfit. Hence it will follow, that the moral rectitude of the disposition, inclination, or affection of God CHIEFLY consists in a regard to HIMSELF, infinitely above his regard to all other beings; or, in other words, his holiness consists in this.

And if it be thus fit that God should *have* a supreme regard to himself, then it is fit that this supreme regard should *appear* in those things by which he makes himself known, or by his *word* and *works*, i. e. in what he *says*, and in what he *does*. If it be an infinitely amiable thing in God, that he should have a supreme regard to himself, then it is an amiable thing that he should *act* as having a chief regard to himself; or act in such a manner, as to *show* that he has such a regard: that what is highest in God's *heart*, may be highest in his *actions* and *conduct*. And if it was God's intention, as there is great reason to think it was, that his *works* should exhibit an *image* of himself their author, that it might brightly appear by his works what manner of being he is, and afford a proper representation of his divine excellencies, and especially his *moral* excellence, consisting in the *disposition of his heart;* then it is reasonable to suppose that his works are so wrought as to *show* this supreme respect to himself, wherein his moral excellence primarily consists.

When we are considering what would be most fit for God *chiefly* to respect, with regard to the universality of things, it may help us to judge with greater ease and satisfaction, to consider, what we can *suppose* would be determined by some third being of perfect wisdom and rectitude, that should be perfectly indifferent and disinterested. Or if we make the supposition, that infinitely wise justice and rectitude were a distinct disinterested person, whose office it was to determine how things shall be most properly ordered in the whole kingdom of existence, including king and subjects, God and his creatures; and, upon a view of the whole, to decide what regard should prevail in all proceedings. Now such a judge, in adjusting the proper measures and kinds of regard, would weigh things in an even balance; taking care, that a greater part of the whole should be more respected, than the lesser, in proportion (other things being equal) to the measure of existence. So that the *degree of regard* should always be in a *proportion compounded* of the *proportion* of *existence*, and *proportion* of *excellence*, or according to the degree of *greatness* and *goodness*, considered *conjunctly*. Such an arbiter, in considering the system of *created* intelligent beings by itself, would determine, that the *system in general*, consisting of many millions, was of greater importance, and worthy of a greater share of regard, than only one individual. For, however considerable some of the individuals might be, no one exceeds others so much as to countervail all the system. And if this judge consider not only the system of created beings, but the system of *being in general*, comprehending the *sum total* of universal existence, both Creator and creature; still every part must be considered according to its importance, or the measure it has of *existence* and *excellence*. To determine then, what proportion of regard is to be allotted to the Creator, and all his creatures taken together, both must be as it were put in the balance; the *Supreme Being*, with all in him that is great and excellent, is to be compared with all that is to be found in the *whole creation:* and according as the former is found to outweigh, in such proportion is he to have a greater share of regard. And in this case, as the whole system of created beings, in comparison of the Creator, would be found as the light dust of the balance, or even as nothing and vanity; so the arbiter must determine accordingly with respect to the *degree* in which God should be regarded, by all intelligent existence, in all actions and proceedings, determinations and effects whatever, whether creating, preserving, using, disposing, changing, or destroying. And as the Creator is infinite, and has all possible existence, perfection, and excellence, so he must have all possible regard. As he is every way the first and supreme, and as his excellency is in all respects the supreme beauty and glory, the original good, and fountain of all good; so he must have in all respects the supreme regard. And as he is *God over all*, to whom all are properly subordinate, and on whom all depend, worthy to reign as supreme Head, with absolute and universal dominion; so it is *fit* that he should be so regarded by all, and in all proceedings and effects through the whole system: The universality of things, in their whole compass and series, should look to him, in such a manner, as that respect to him should reign over all respect to other things, and regard to creatures should, universally, be subordinate and subject.

When I speak of *regard* to be thus adjusted in the universal system, I mean the regard of the *sum total;* all intelligent existence, created and uncreated. For it is fit, that the regard of the *Creator* should be proportioned to the worthiness of objects, as well as the regard of creatures. Thus, we must conclude, that such an arbiter as I have supposed, would determine, that the whole universe, in all its actings, proceedings, revolutions, and entire series of events, should proceed with a view to *God*, as the supreme and last end; that every wheel, in all its rotations, should move with a constant invariable regard to him as the ultimate end of all; as perfectly and uniformly, as if the whole system were animated and directed by one common soul. Or, as if such an arbiter as I have before supposed, possessed of perfect wisdom and rectitude, became the common soul of the universe, and actuated and governed it in all its motions.

Thus I have gone upon the supposition of a third disinterested person. The thing supposed is impossible; but the case is, nevertheless, just the same, as to what is most fit and suitable in itself. For it is most certainly proper for God to act, according to the greatest *fitness*, and he knows what the greatest fitness is, as much as if perfect rectitude were a distinct person to direct him. God himself is possessed of that perfect discernment and rectitude which have been supposed. It belongs to him as supreme arbiter, and to his infinite wisdom and rectitude, to state all rules and measures of proceedings. And seeing these attributes of God are infinite, and most absolutely perfect, they are not the less fit to order and dispose, because they are in him, who is a being concerned, and not a third person that is disinterested. For being *interested* unfits a person to be an arbiter or judge, no otherwise, than as interest tends to mislead his judgment, or incline him to act contrary to it. But that God should be in danger of either, is contrary to the supposition of his being absolutely perfect. And as there must be *some* supreme judge of fitness and propriety in the universality of things, or otherwise there could be no order, it therefore belongs to God, whose are all things, who is perfectly fit for this office, and who alone is so, to state all things according to the most perfect fitness and rectitude, as much as if perfect rectitude were a distinct person. We may therefore be sure it is and will be done.

I should think that these things might incline us to suppose, that God has not forgot himself, in the ends which he proposed in the creation of the world; but that he has so stated these ends, (however self-sufficient, immutable, and independent,) as therein plainly to show a supreme regard to himself. Whether this can be, or whether God has done thus, must be considered afterwards, as also what may be objected against this view of things.

5. Whatsoever is good, amiable, and valuable *in itself*, *absolutely* and *originally*, (which facts and events show that God aimed at in the creation of the world,) must be supposed to be regarded or aimed at by God *ultimately*, or as an ultimate end of creation. For we must suppose, from the perfection of God's nature, that whatsoever is valuable and amiable in itself, simply and absolutely considered, God values simply for itself; because God's judgment and esteem are according to truth. But if God values a thing simply and absolutely on its own account, then it is the *ultimate* object of his value. For to suppose that he values it only for some *farther* end, is in direct contradiction to the present supposition, which is, that he values it absolutely, and for itself. Hence it most clearly follows, that if that which God values *for itself*, appears, in fact and experience, to be what he seeks by any thing he does, he must regard it as an *ultimate* end. And, therefore, if he seeks it in creating the world, or any part of the world, it is an ultimate end of the work of creation. Having got thus far, we may now proceed a step farther, and assert,

6. Whatsoever thing is *actually* the *effect* of the creation of the world, which is simply and absolutely valuable in itself, that thing is an ultimate end of God's creating the world. We see that it is a good which God *aimed* at by the creation of the world; because he has *actually attained* it by that means. For we may justly infer what God *intends*, by what he actually *does*; because he does nothing inadvertently, or without design. But whatever God *intends* to attain, from a value for it, in his actions and works, that he *seeks* in those acts and works. Because, for an agent to *intend* to attain something he values by the means he uses, is the same thing as to *seek* it by those means. And this is the same as to make that thing his *end* in those means. Now, it being, by the supposition, what God *values ultimately*, it must therefore, by the preceding position, be *aimed at* by God, as an ultimate end of creating the world.

SECT. II.

Some further observations concerning those things which reason leads us to suppose God aimed at in the creation of the world.

FROM what was last observed, it *seems* to be the most proper way of proceeding—as we would see what light *reason* will give us, respecting the particular end or ends God had ultimately in view in the creation of the world—to consider, what thing or things are *actually* the effect or *consequence* of the creation of the world, that are simply and originally valuable in themselves. And this is what I would directly proceed to, without entering on any tedious metaphysical inquiries, wherein fitness, or amiableness, consists; referring what I say to the dictates of the reader's mind, on sedate and calm reflection.

1. It seems a thing in itself proper and desirable, that the glorious attributes of God, which consist in a *sufficiency* to certain acts and effects, should be *exerted* in the production of such effects as might manifest his infinite power, wisdom, righteousness, goodness, &c. If the world had not been created, these attributes never would have had any *exercise*. The *power* of God, which is a sufficiency in him to produce great effects, must for ever have been dormant and useless as to any effect. The divine *wisdom* and prudence would have had no exercise in any wise contrivance, any prudent proceeding, or disposal of things; for there would have been no objects of contrivance or disposal. The same might be observed of God's *justice*, *goodness*, and *truth*. Indeed God might have *known* as perfectly that he possessed these attributes, if they never had been exerted or expressed in any effect. But then, if the attributes which consist in a *sufficiency* for correspondent effects, are in themselves excellent, the *exercises* of them must likewise be excellent. If it be an excellent thing, that there should be a sufficiency for a certain kind of action or operation, the excellency of such a sufficiency must consist in its *relation* to this kind of operation or effect; but that could not be, unless the *operation itself* were excellent. A sufficiency for any work is no further valuable, than the work itself is valuable.* As God therefore esteems these attributes *themselves* valuable, and delights in them; so it is natural to suppose that he delights in their proper *exercise* and expression. For the same reason that he esteems his own sufficiency wisely to *contrive* and dispose effects, he also will esteem the wise *contrivance* and disposition itself. And for the same reason, as he delights in his own disposition to do justly, and to dispose of things according to truth and just proportion; so he must delight in such a righteous disposal itself.

2. It seems to be a thing in itself fit and desirable, that the glorious perfections of God should be *known*, and the operations and expressions of them seen, by *other beings* besides himself. If it be fit that God's power and wisdom, &c. should be exercised and *expressed* in some effects, and not lie eternally dormant, then it seems proper that these exercises should *appear*, and not be totally hidden and unknown. For if they are, it will be just the same, as to the above purpose, as if they were not. God as perfectly knew himself and his perfections, had as perfect an idea of the exercises and effects they were sufficient for, *antecedently* to any such actual operations of them, and since. If, therefore, it be nevertheless a thing in itself valuable, and worthy to be desired, that these glorious perfections be actually *exhibited* in their correspondent effects; then it seems also, that the *knowledge* of these perfections and discoveries is valuable in itself absolutely considered; and that it is *desirable* that this knowledge should exist. It is a thing infinitely good in itself, that God's glory should be *known* by a glorious society of created beings. And that there should be in them an *increasing* knowledge of God to all eternity, is worthy to be regarded by him, to whom it belongs to order what is fittest and best. If *existence* is more worthy than defect and non-entity, and if any *created* existence is in itself worthy to be, then *knowledge* is; and if any knowledge, then the most *excellent sort* of knowledge, *viz.* that of God and his glory. This knowledge is one of the highest, most real, and substantial parts of all created existence, most remote from non-entity and defect.

3. As it is desirable in itself that God's glory should be known, so when known it seems equally reasonable it should be esteemed and delighted in, answerably to its dignity. There is no more reason to esteem it a suitable thing, that there should be an idea in the *understanding* corresponding unto the glorious object, than that there should be a corresponding *affection* in the will. If the perfection itself be excellent, the knowledge of it is excellent, and so is the esteem and love of it excellent. And as it is fit that God should love and esteem his own *excellence*, it is also fit that he should value and esteem the *love* of his excellency. And if it becomes a being highly to *value* himself, it is fit that he should love to have himself *valued* and esteemed. If the idea of God's perfection in the understanding be valuable, then the love of the heart seems to be more especially valuable, as moral beauty especially consists in the disposition and affection of the heart.

4. As there is an infinite fulness of all possible good in God—a fulness of every perfection, of all excellency and beauty, and of infinite happiness—and as this fulness is capable of communication, or emanation *ad extra;* so it seems a thing amiable and valuable in *itself* that this infinite fountain of good should send forth abundant streams. And as this is in itself excellent, so a *disposition* to this in the Divine Being, must be looked upon as an *excellent* dis-

* "The *end* of wisdom (says Mr. G. Tennent, in his sermon at the opening of the presbyterian church of Philadelphia) is *design;* the *end* of power is *action;* the *end* of goodness is *doing* good. To suppose these perfections not to be *exerted* would be to represent them as insignificant. Of what use would God's *wisdom* be, if it had nothing to design or direct? To what purpose his *almightiness*, if it never brought any thing to pass? And of what avail his *goodness*, if it never did any good?"

position. Such an emanation of good is, in some sense, a *multiplication* of it. So far as the stream may be looked upon as any thing besides the fountain, so far it may be looked on as an *increase* of good. And if the fulness of good that is in the fountain, is in itself excellent, then the emanation, which is as it were an increase, repetition, or multiplication of it, is excellent. Thus it is fit, since there is an infinite fountain of light and knowledge, that this light should shine forth in beams of communicated knowledge and understanding; and, as there is an infinite fountain of holiness, moral excellence, and beauty, that so it should flow out in communicated holiness. And that, as there is an infinite fulness of joy and happiness, so these should have an emanation, and become a fountain flowing out in abundant streams, as beams from the sun.

Thus it appears reasonable to suppose, that it was God's last end, that there might be a glorious and abundant emanation of his infinite fulness of good *ad extra*, or without himself; and that the disposition to communicate himself, or diffuse his own FULNESS,* was what moved him to create the world. But here I observe, that there would be some impropriety in saying, that a disposition in God to communicate himself *to the creature*, moved him to create the world. For an inclination in God to communicate himself to an *object*, seems to presuppose the *existence* of the object, at least in idea. But the diffusive disposition that excited God to give creatures existence, was rather a communicative *disposition* in general, or a disposition in the fulness of the divinity to flow out and diffuse itself. Thus the disposition there is in the root and stock of a tree to diffuse sap and life, is doubtless the reason of their communication to its buds, leaves, and fruits, *after* these exist. But a disposition to communicate of its life and sap to its *fruits*, is not so properly the cause of its *producing* those fruits, as its disposition to diffuse its sap and life in general. Therefore, to speak strictly according to truth, we may suppose, *that a disposition in God, as an original property of his nature, to an emanation of his own infinite fulness, was what excited him to create the world; and so, that the emanation itself was aimed at by him as a last end of the creation.*

SECT. III.

Wherein it is considered how, on the supposition of God's making the forementioned things his last end, he manifests a supreme and ultimate regard to himself in all his works.

IN the last section I observed some things which are actually the consequence of the creation of the world, which seem absolutely valuable in themselves, and so worthy to be made God's last end in his work. I now proceed to inquire, how God's making such things as these his last end, is consistent with his making *himself* his last end, or his manifesting an ultimate respect to himself in his acts and works. Because it is agreeable to the dictates of reason, that in all his proceedings he should set himself highest; therefore, I would endeavour to show, how his infinite love to and delight in himself, will naturally cause him to value and delight in these things: or rather, how a value to these things is implied in his value of that infinite fulness of good that is in himself.

Now, with regard to the first of the particulars mentioned above—God's regard to the *exercise* of those attributes of his nature, in their proper operations and effects, which consist in a *sufficiency* for these operations—it is not hard to conceive that God's regard to *himself*, and value for his own perfections, should cause him to value these exercises and expressions of his perfections; inasmuch as their excellency consists in their relation to use, exercise, and operation. God's love to himself, and his own attributes, will therefore make him delight in that which is the use, end, and operation of these attributes. If one highly esteem and delight in the virtues of a friend, as wisdom, justice, &c. that have relation to action, this will make him delight in the *exercise* and genuine *effects* of these virtues. So if God both esteem and delight in his own perfections and virtues, he cannot but value and delight in the expressions and genuine effects of them. So that in delighting in the *expressions* of his perfections, he manifests a delight in himself; and in making these expressions of his own perfections his end, *he makes himself his end.*

And with respect to the second and third particulars, the matter is no less plain. For he that loves any being, and has a disposition highly to prize and greatly to delight in his virtues and perfections, must from the same disposition be well pleased to have his excellencies known, acknowledged, esteemed, and prized by others. He that loves any thing, naturally loves the *approbation* of that thing, and is opposite to the disapprobation of it. Thus it is when one loves the virtues of a friend. And thus it will necessarily be, if a being loves himself and highly prizes his own excellencies; and thus it is *fit* it should be, if it be fit he should thus love himself, and prize his own valuable qualities; that is, it is fit that he should take delight in his own excellencies being seen, acknowledged, esteemed, and delighted in. This is implied in a love to himself and his own perfections; and in making *this* his end, he makes himself his end.

And with respect to the fourth and last particular, viz. God's being disposed to an abundant communication, and glorious emanation, of that infinite fulness of good which he possesses, as of his own knowledge, excellency, and happiness, in the manner he does; if we thoroughly consider the matter, it will appear, that herein also God makes himself his end, in such a sense, as plainly to manifest and testify a supreme and ultimate regard to himself.

Merely in this *disposition* to cause an emanation of his glory and fulness—which is prior to the existence of any other being, and is to be considered as the inciting cause of giving existence to other beings—God cannot so properly be said to make the *creature* his end, as *himself*. For the creature is not as yet considered as existing. This disposition or desire in God, must be *prior* to the existence of the creature, even in foresight. For it is a disposition that is the original ground even of the future, intended, and foreseen existence of the creature. God's benevolence, as it respects the creature, may be taken either in a larger or stricter sense. In a larger sense, it may signify nothing diverse from that good disposition in his nature to communicate of his own fulness in general; as his knowledge, his holiness, and happiness; and to give creatures existence in order to it. This may be called benevolence, or love, because it is the same good disposition that is exercised in love. It is the very fountain from whence love originally proceeds, when taken in the most proper sense; and it has the same general tendency and effect in the creature's well-being. But yet this cannot have any particular present or future created existence for its object; because it is prior to any such object, and the very source of the futurition of its existence. Nor is it really diverse from God's love to himself; as will more clearly appear afterwards.

But God's love may be taken more strictly, for this general disposition to communicate good, as directed to *particular objects.* Love, in the most strict and proper sense, *presupposes* the existence of the object beloved, at least in idea and expectation, and represented to the mind as future. God did not love angels in the strictest sense, but in consequence of his intending to create them, and so having an idea of future existing angels. Therefore his love to them was not properly what *excited* him to *intend* to create them. Love or benevolence, strictly taken, presupposes an *existing* object, as much as pity a miserable suffering object.

This propensity in God to diffuse himself, may be considered as a propensity to himself diffused; or to his own glory existing in its emanation. A respect to himself, or an infinite propensity to and delight in his own glory, is that which causes him to incline to its being abundantly diffused, and to delight in the emanation of it. Thus, that

* I shall often use the phrase *God's fulness*, as signifying and comprehending all the good which is in God natural and moral, either excellence or happiness: partly, because I know of no better phrase to be used in this general meaning; and partly, because I am led hereto by some of the inspired writers, particularly the apostle Paul, who often useth the phrase in this sense.

nature in a tree, by which it puts forth buds, shoots out branches, and brings forth leaves and fruit, is a disposition that terminates in its own complete self. And so the disposition in the sun to shine, or abundantly to diffuse its fulness, warmth, and brightness, is only a tendency to its own most glorious and complete state. So God looks on the communication of himself, and the emanation of his infinite glory, to belong to the fulness and completeness of himself; as though he were not in his most glorious state without it. Thus the church of Christ, (toward whom and in whom are the emanations of his glory, and the communication of his fulness,) is called the *fulness of Christ;* as though he were not in his complete state without her; like Adam without Eve. And the church is called the glory of Christ, as the woman is the glory of the man, 1 Cor. xi. 7. Isa. xlvi. 13. *I will place salvation in Zion, for Israel* MY GLORY.*—Indeed, after the creatures are *intended* to be created, God may be conceived of as being moved by benevolence to them, in the strictest sense, in his dealings with them. His exercising his goodness, and gratifying his benevolence to them in particular, may be the spring of all God's proceedings through the universe; as being now the determined way of gratifying his general inclination to diffuse himself. Here God acting for *himself,* or making himself his last end, and his acting for *their* sake, are not to be set in opposition; they are rather to be considered as coinciding one with the other, and implied one in the other. But yet God is to be considered as first and original in his regard; and the creature is the object of God's regard, consequently, and by implication, as being as it were comprehended in God; as it shall be more particularly observed presently.

But how God's value for, and delight in, the emanations of his fulness in the work of creation, argues his delight in the infinite fulness of good in himself, and the supreme regard he has for himself; and that in making these emanations, he ultimately makes himself his end in creation; will more clearly appear by considering more particularly the nature and circumstances of these communications of God's fulness.

One part of that divine fulness which is communicated, is the divine *knowledge.* That communicated knowledge, which must be supposed to pertain to God's last end in creating the world, is the creature's knowledge of HIM. For this is the end of all other knowledge; and even the faculty of understanding would be vain without it. And this knowledge is most properly a communication of God's infinite knowledge, which primarily consists in the knowledge of himself. God, in making *this* his end, makes *himself* his end. This knowledge in the creature, is but a conformity to God. It is the image of God's own knowledge of himself. It is a participation of the same; though infinitely less in degree: as particular beams of the sun communicated are the light and glory of the sun itself, in part.

Besides, God's glory is the object of this knowledge, or the thing known; so that God is glorified in it, as hereby his excellency is seen. As therefore God values himself, as he delights in his own knowledge, he must delight in every thing of that nature: as he delights in his own light, he must delight in every beam of that light; and as he highly values his own excellency, he must be well pleased in having it *manifested,* and so *glorified.*

Another emanation of divine fulness, is the communication of virtue and *holiness* to the creature: this is a communication of God's holiness; so that hereby the creature partakes of God's own moral excellency; which is properly the beauty of the divine nature. And as God delights in his own beauty, he must necessarily delight in the creature's holiness; which is a conformity to and participation of it, as truly as a brightness of a jewel, held in the sun's beams, is a participation or derivation of the sun's brightness, though immensely less in degree. And then it must be considered wherein this holiness in the creature consists, viz. in love, which is the comprehension of all true virtue; and primarily in love to God, which is exercised in a high esteem of God, admiration of his perfections, complacency in them, and praise of them. All which things are nothing else but the heart exalting, magnifying, or glorifying God; which, as I showed before, God necessarily approves of, and is pleased with, as he loves himself, and values the glory of his own nature.

Another part of God's fulness which he communicates, is his *happiness.* This happiness consists in enjoying and rejoicing in himself; and so does also the creature's happiness. It is a participation of what is in God; and God and his glory are the objective ground of it. The happiness of the creature consists in rejoicing in God; by which also God is magnified and exalted. Joy, or the exulting of the heart in God's glory, is one thing that belongs to praise. So that God is all in all, with respect to each part of that communication of the divine fulness which is made to the creature. What is communicated is divine, or something of God; and each communication is of that nature, that the creature to whom it is made, is thereby conformed to God, and united to him: and that in proportion as the communication is greater or less. And the communication itself is no other, in the very nature of it, than that wherein the very honour, exaltation, and praise of God consists.

And it is farther to be considered, that what God aimed at in the creation of the world, as the end which he had ultimately in view, was that communication of himself which he intended through all eternity. And if we attend to the nature and circumstances of this eternal emanation of divine good, it will more clearly show HOW, in making this his end, God testifies a supreme respect to himself, and makes himself his end. There are many reasons to think that what God has in view, in an increasing communication of himself through eternity, is an *increasing* knowledge of God, love to him, and joy in him. And it is to be considered, that the more those divine communications *increase* in the creature, the more it becomes one with God: for so much the more is it united to God in love, the heart is drawn nearer and nearer to God, and the union with him becomes more firm and close: and, at the same time, the creature becomes more and more *conformed* to God. The image is more and more perfect, and so the good that is in the creature comes for ever nearer and nearer to an identity with that which is in God. In the view therefore of God, who has a comprehensive prospect of the increasing union and conformity through eternity, it must be an infinitely strict and perfect nearness, conformity, and oneness. For it will for ever come nearer and nearer to that strictness and perfection of union which there is between the Father and the Son. So that in the eyes of God, who perfectly sees the whole of it, in its infinite progress and increase, it must come to an eminent fulfilment of Christ's request, in John xvii. 21, 23. *That they all may be* ONE, *as thou Father art in me, and I in thee, that they also may be* ONE *in us; I in them and thou in me, that they may be made perfect in* ONE. In this view, those elect creatures, which must be looked upon as the end of all the rest of the creation, considered with respect to the whole of their eternal duration, and as such made God's end, must be viewed as being, as it were, one with God. They were respected as brought home to him, united with him, centering most perfectly, as it were swallowed up in him: so that his respect to *them* finally coincides, and becomes one and the same, with respect to himself. The interest of the creature is, as it were, God's own interest, in proportion to the degree of their relation and union to God. Thus the interest of a man's *family* is looked upon as the same with his *own* interest; because of the relation they stand in to him, his propriety in them, and their strict union with him. But God's elect creatures, with respect

* Very remarkable is that place, John xii. 23, 24. *And Jesus answered them, saying, The hour is come, that the Son of man should be glorified. Verily, I say unto you, except a corn of wheat fall into the ground and die, it abideth alone; but if it die, it bringeth forth much fruit.* Christ had respect herein to the blessed fruits of his death, in the conversion, salvation, and eternal happiness of those that should be redeemed by him. This consequence of his death, he calls his glory; and his obtaining this fruit, he calls his being glorified; as the flourishing, beautiful produce of a corn of wheat sown in the ground is its glory. Without this he is alone, as Adam was before Eve was created. But from him, by his death, proceeds a glorious offspring; in which are communicated his fulness and glory: As from Adam, in his deep sleep, proceeds the woman, a beautiful companion to fill his emptiness, and relieve his solitariness; by Christ's death, his fulness is abundantly diffused in many streams; and expressed in the beauty and glory of a great multitude of his spiritual offspring.

to their eternal duration, are infinitely dearer to God, than a man's family is to him. What has been said shows, that as all things are *from* God, as their first cause and fountain; so all things tend *to* him, and in their progress come nearer and nearer to him through all eternity: which argues, that he who is their first cause is their last end.*

SECT. IV.

Some objections considered, which may be made against the reasonableness of what has been said of God making himself his last end.

Object. I. Some may object against what has been said as being inconsistent with God's absolute independence and immutability: particularly, as though God were inclined to a communication of his fulness, and emanations of his own glory, as being his own most glorious and complete state. It may be thought that this does not well consist with God, being self-existent from all eternity; absolutely perfect in himself, in the possession of infinite and independent good. And that, in general, to suppose that God makes himself his end, in the creation of the world, seems to suppose that he aims at some interest or happiness of his own, not easily reconcilable with his being perfectly and infinitely happy in himself. If it could be supposed that God needed any thing; or that the goodness of his creatures could extend to him; or that they could be profitable to him; it might be fit, that God should make himself, and his own interest, his highest and last end in creating the world. But seeing that God is above all need, and all capacity of being made better or happier in any respect; to what purpose should God make himself his end, or seek to advance himself in any respect by any of his works? How absurd is it to suppose that God should do such great things, with a view to obtain what he is already most perfectly possessed of, and was so from all eternity; and therefore cannot now possibly need, nor with any colour of reason be supposed to seek!

Ans. 1. Many have wrong notions of God's happiness, as resulting from his absolute self-sufficience, independence, and immutability. Though it be true, that God's glory and happiness are in and of himself, are infinite and cannot be added to, and unchangeable, for the whole and every part of which he is perfectly independent of the creature; yet it does not hence follow, nor is it true, that God has no real and proper delight, pleasure, or happiness, in any of his acts or communications relative to the creature, or effects he produces in them; or in any thing he sees in the creature's qualifications, dispositions, actions and state.

God may have a real and proper pleasure or happiness in seeing the *happy state* of the creature; yet this may not be different from his delight in himself; being a delight in his own infinite goodness; or the exercise of that glorious propensity of his nature to diffuse and communicate himself, and so gratifying this inclination of his own heart. This delight which God has in his creature's happiness, cannot properly be said to be what God receives from the creature. For it is only the effect of his own work in and communications to the creature; in making it, and admitting it to a participation of his fulness. As the sun receives nothing from the jewel that receives its light, and shines only by a participation of its brightness.

With respect also to the creature's *holiness;* God may have a proper delight and joy in imparting this to the creature, as gratifying hereby his inclination to communicate of his own excellent fulness. God may delight, with true and great pleasure, in beholding that beauty which is an image and communication of his own beauty, an expression and manifestation of his own loveliness. And this is so far from being an instance of his happiness not being in and from himself, that it is an evidence that he is happy in himself, or delights and has pleasure in his own beauty. If he did not take pleasure in the *expression* of his own beauty, it would rather be an evidence that he does not *delight* in his own beauty; that he hath not his happiness and enjoyment in his own beauty and perfection. So that if we suppose God has real pleasure and happiness in the holy love and praise of his saints, as the image and communication of his own holiness, it is not properly any pleasure distinct from the pleasure he has in himself; but it is truly an instance of it.

And with respect to God's being glorified in those perfections wherein his glory consists, expressed in their corresponding effects,—as his wisdom, in wise designs and well-contrived works, his power, in great effects, his justice, in acts of righteousness, his goodness, in communicating happiness,—this does not argue that his pleasure is not in himself, and his own glory; but the contrary. It is the *necessary consequence* of his delighting in the glory of his nature, that he delights in the emanation and effulgence of it.

Nor do these things argue any *dependence* in God on the creature for happiness. Though he has real pleasure in the creature's holiness and happiness, yet this is not properly any pleasure which he receives from the creature. For these things are what he *gives* the creature. They are wholly and entirely from him. His rejoicing therein is rather a rejoicing in his own acts, and his own glory expressed in those acts, than a joy derived from the creature. God's joy is dependent on nothing besides his own act, which he exerts with an absolute and independent power. And yet, in some sense, it can be truly said, that God has the more delight and pleasure for the holiness and happiness of his creatures. Because God would be less happy, if he were less good: or if he had not that perfection of nature which consists in a propensity of nature to diffuse his own fulness. And he would be less happy, if it were possible for him to be hindered in the exercise of his goodness, and his other perfections, in their proper effects. But he has complete happiness, because he has these perfections, and cannot be hindered in exercising and displaying them in their proper effects. And this surely is not, because he is dependent; but because he is independent on any other that should hinder him.

From this view, it appears, that nothing which has been said, is in the least inconsistent with those expressions in Scripture, that signify, "man cannot be profitable to God," &c. For these expressions plainly mean no more, than that God is absolutely independent of us; that we have nothing of our own, no stock from whence we can give to God; and that no part of his happiness originates from man.

From what has been said, it appears, that the pleasure God hath in those things which have been mentioned, is rather a pleasure in diffusing and *communicating* to, than in *receiving* from, the creature. Surely, it is no argument of indigence in God, that he is inclined to communicate of his infinite fulness. It is no argument of the emptiness or deficiency of a fountain, that it is inclined to overflow. Nothing from the creature alters God's happiness, as though it were changeable either by increase or diminution. For though these *communications* of God—these exercises, operations, and expressions of his glorious perfections, which God rejoices in—are in time; yet his *joy* in them is without beginning or change. They were always equally present in the divine mind. He beheld them with equal clearness, certainty, and fulness, in every respect, as he doth now. They were always equally present; as with him there is no variableness or succession. He ever beheld and enjoyed them perfectly in his own independent and immutable power and will.

Ans. 2. If any are not satisfied with the preceding answer, but still insist on the objection, let them consider whether they can devise any other scheme of God's last end in creating the world, but what will be equally obnoxious to this objection in its full force, if there be any force in it. For if God had any last end in creating the world, then there was something in some respect future, that he aimed at, and designed to bring to pass by creating the world; something that was agreeable to his inclination or will; let that be his own glory, or the happiness of his creatures, or what it will. Now, if there be something that God seeks as agreeable, or grateful to him, then, in the accomplish-

*** This remark must be understood with limitation; as expressing the effect of *benevolent* influence, but not the effect of *justice* on a moral system.- W**

ment of it, he is gratified. If the last end which he seeks in the creation of the world be truly a thing grateful to him, (as certainly it is, if it be truly his end, and truly the object of his will,) then it is what he takes a real delight and pleasure in. But then, according to the argument of the objection, how can he have any thing future to desire or seek, who is already perfectly, eternally, and immutably satisfied in himself? What can remain for him to take any delight in, or to be further gratified by, whose eternal and unchangeable delight is in himself, as his own complete object of enjoyment. Thus the objector will be pressed with his own objection, let him embrace what notion he will of God's end in the creation. And I think he has no way left to answer but that which has been taken above.

It may therefore be proper here to observe, that let what will be God's last end, *that* he must have a real and proper pleasure in. Whatever be the proper object of his will, he is gratified in. And the thing is either grateful to him in itself, or for something else for which he wills it; and so is his further end. But whatever is God's last end, that he wills *for its own sake;* as grateful to him in itself, or in which he has some degree of true and proper pleasure. Otherwise we must deny any such thing as will in God with respect to any thing brought to pass in time; and so must deny his work of creation, or any work of his providence, to be truly voluntary. But we have as much reason to suppose, that God's works in creating and governing the world, are properly the fruits of his will, as of his understanding. And if there be any such thing at all, as what we mean by *acts of will* in God; then he is not indifferent whether his will be fulfilled or not. And if he is not indifferent, then he is truly gratified and pleased in the fulfilment of his will. And if he has a real *pleasure* in attaining his end, then the attainment of it belongs to his *happiness;* that in which God's delight or pleasure in any measure consists. To suppose that God has pleasure in things that are brought to pass in time, only figuratively and metaphorically; is to suppose that he exercises will about these things, and makes them his end only metaphorically.

Ans. 3. The doctrine that makes God's *creatures* and not *himself* to be his last end, is a doctrine the furthest from having a favourable aspect on God's absolute self-sufficience and independence. It far less agrees therewith than the doctrine against which this is objected. For we must conceive of the efficient as *depending* on his ultimate end. He depends on this end, in his desires, aims, actions, and pursuits; so that he fails in all his desires, actions, and pursuits, if he fails of his end. Now if God himself be his last end, then in his dependence on his end, he depends on nothing but himself. If all things be of him, and to him, and he the first and the last, this shows him to be all in all. He is all to himself. He goes not out of himself in what he seeks; but his desires and pursuits as they originate from, so they terminate in, himself; and he is dependent on none but himself in the beginning or end of any of his exercises or operations. But if not himself, but the creature, were his last end, then as he depends on his last end, he would be in some sort dependent on the creature.

OBJECT. II. Some may object, that to suppose God makes himself his highest and last end, is dishonourable to him; as it in effect supposes, that God does every thing from a selfish spirit. Selfishness is looked upon as mean and sordid in the creature; unbecoming and even hateful in such a worm of the dust as man. We should look upon a man as of a base and contemptible character, who should in every thing he did, be governed by selfish principles; should make his private interest his governing aim in all his conduct in life. How far then should we be from attributing any such thing to the Supreme Being, the blessed and only Potentate! Does it not become us to ascribe to him the most noble and generous dispositions, and qualities the most remote from every thing private, narrow, and sordid?

Ans. 1. Such an objection must arise from a very ignorant or inconsiderate notion of the vice of selfishness, and the virtue of generosity. If by selfishness be meant, a disposition in any being to regard himself; this is no otherwise vicious or unbecoming, than as one is less than a multitude; and so the public weal is of greater value than his particular interest. Among created beings one single person is inconsiderable in comparison of the generality; and so his interest is of little importance compared with the interest of the whole system. Therefore in them, a disposition to prefer self, as if it were more than all, is exceeding vicious. But it is vicious on no other account, than as it is a disposition that does not agree with the nature of things; and that which is indeed the greatest good. And a disposition in any one to forego his own interest for the sake of others, is no further excellent, no further worthy the name of generosity, than it is treating things according to their true value; prosecuting something most worthy to be prosecuted; an expression of a disposition to prefer something to self-interest, that is indeed preferable in itself. But if God be indeed so great, and so excellent, that all other beings are as nothing to him, and all other excellency be as nothing, and less than nothing and vanity, in comparison of his; and God be omniscient and infallible, and perfectly knows that he is infinitely the most valuable being; then it is fit that his heart should be agreeable to this—which is indeed the true nature and proportion of things, and agreeable to this infallible and all-comprehending understanding which he has of them, and that perfectly clear light in which he views them—and that he should value himself infinitely more than his creatures.

Ans. 2. In created beings, a regard to self-interest may properly be set in *opposition* to the public welfare; because the private interest of one person may be inconsistent with the public good; at least it may be so in the apprehension of that person. That which this person looks upon as his interest, may interfere with or oppose the general good. Hence his private interest may be regarded and pursued in opposition to the public. But this cannot be with respect to the Supreme Being, the author and head of the whole system; on whom all absolutely depend; who is the fountain of being and good to the whole. It is more absurd to suppose that his interest should be opposite to the interest of the universal system, than that the welfare of the head, heart, and vitals of the natural body, should be opposite to the welfare of the body. And it is impossible that God, who is omniscient, should apprehend his interest, as being inconsistent with the good and interest of the whole.

Ans. 3. God seeking himself in the creation of the world, in the manner which has been supposed, is so far from being inconsistent with the good of his creatures, that it is a kind of regard to himself that inclines him to seek the good of his creature. It is a regard to himself that disposes him to diffuse and communicate himself. It is such a delight in his own internal fulness and glory, that disposes him to an abundant effusion and emanation of that glory. The same disposition, that inclines him to delight in his glory, causes him to delight in the exhibitions, expressions, and communications of it. If there were any person of such a taste and disposition of mind, that the brightness and light of the sun seemed unlovely to him, he would be willing that the sun's brightness and light should be retained within itself. But they that delight in it, to whom it appears lovely and glorious, will esteem it an amiable and glorious thing to have it diffused and communicated through the world.

Here, by the way, it may be properly considered, whether some writers are not chargeable with inconsistence in this respect. They speak against the doctrine of GOD making himself his own highest and last end, as though this were an ignoble selfishness—when indeed he only is fit to be made the highest end, by himself and all other beings; inasmuch as he is infinitely greater and more worthy than all others—yet with regard to *creatures,* who are infinitely less worthy of supreme and ultimate regard, they suppose, that they necessarily, at all times, seek their own happiness, and make it their ultimate end in all, even their most virtuous actions; and that this principle, regulated by wisdom and prudence, as leading to that which is their true and highest happiness, is the foundation of all virtue, and every thing that is morally good and excellent in them.

OBJECT. III. To what has been supposed, that God

makes himself his end—in seeking that his glory and excellent perfections should be known, esteemed, loved, and delighted in by his creatures—it may be objected, that this seems unworthy of God. It is considered as below a truly great man, to be much influenced in his conduct by a desire of popular applause. The notice and admiration of a gazing multitude, would be esteemed but a low end, to be aimed at by a prince or philosopher, in any great and noble enterprise. How much more is it unworthy the great God, to perform his magnificent works, e. g. the creation of the vast universe, out of regard to the notice and admiration of worms of the dust, that the displays of his magnificence may be gazed at, and applauded by those who are infinitely more beneath him, than the meanest rabble are beneath the greatest prince or philosopher.

This objection is specious. It hath a show of argument; but it will appear to be nothing but a show, if we consider,

1. Whether it be not worthy of God, to regard and value what is excellent and valuable in itself; and so to take pleasure in its existence.

It seems not liable to any doubt, that there could be no future existence worthy to be desired or sought by God, and so worthy to be made his end, if no future existence was valuable and worthy to be brought to effect. If, when the world was not, there was any possible future thing fit and valuable in itself, I think the knowledge of God's glory, and the esteem and love of it, must be so. Understanding and will are the highest kind of created existence. And if they be valuable, it must be in their exercise. But the highest and most excellent kind of their exercise, is in some actual knowledge, and exercise of will. And, certainly, the most excellent actual knowledge and will that can be in the creature, is the knowledge and the love of God. And the most true excellent knowledge of God, is the knowledge of his glory or moral excellence; and the most excellent exercise of the will consists in esteem and love, and a delight in his glory.—If any created existence is in itself worthy to be, or any thing that ever was future is worthy of existence, such a communication of divine fulness, such an emanation and expression of the divine glory, is worthy of existence. But if nothing that ever was future was worthy to exist, then no future thing was worthy to be aimed at by God in creating the world. And if nothing was worthy to be aimed at in creation, then nothing was worthy to be God's end in creation.

If God's own excellency and glory is worthy to be highly valued and delighted in by him, then the value and esteem hereof by others, is worthy to be regarded by him: for this is a necessary consequence. To make this plain let it be considered, how it is with regard to the excellent qualities of another. If we highly value the virtues and excellencies of a *friend*, in proportion, we shall approve of others' esteem of them; and shall disapprove the contempt of them. If these virtues are truly valuable, they are worthy that we should thus approve others' esteem, and disapprove their contempt of them. And the case is the same with respect to any being's *own* qualities or attributes. If he highly esteems them, and greatly delights in them, he will naturally and necessarily love to see esteem of them in others, and dislike their disesteem. And if the attributes are worthy to be highly esteemed by the being who hath them, so is the esteem of them in others worthy to be proportionably approved and regarded. I desire it may be considered, whether it be unfit that God should be displeased with contempt of himself? If not, but on the contrary it be fit and suitable that he should be displeased with this, there is the same reason that he should be pleased with the proper love, esteem, and honour of himself.

The matter may be also cleared, by considering what it would become us to approve of and value with respect to any public society we belong to, e. g. our nation or country. It becomes us to love our country; and therefore it becomes us to value the just honour of our country. But the same that it becomes us to value and desire for a friend, and the same that it becomes us to desire and seek for the community, the same does it become God to value and seek for himself; that is, on supposition, that it becomes God to love himself as it does men to love a friend or the public; which I think has been before proved.

Here are two things that ought particularly to be adverted to. (1.) That in God, the love of himself and the love of the public are not to be distinguished, as in man: because God's being, as it were, comprehends all. His existence, being infinite, must be equivalent to universal existence. And for the same reason that public affection in the creature is fit and beautiful, God's regard to himself must be so likewise.—(2.) In God, the love of what is fit and decent, cannot be a distinct thing from the love of himself; because the love of God is that wherein all holiness primarily and chiefly consists, and God's own holiness must primarily consist in the love of himself. And if God's holiness consists in love to himself, then it will imply an approbation of the esteem and love of him in others. For a being that loves himself, necessarily loves love to himself. If holiness in God consist chiefly in love to himself, holiness in the creature must chiefly consist in love to him. And if God loves holiness in himself, he must love it in the creature.

Virtue, by such of the late philosophers as seem to be in chief repute, is placed in public affection, or general benevolence. And if the essence of virtue lies primarily in this, then the love of virtue itself is virtuous no otherwise, than as it is implied in, or arises from, this public affection, or extensive benevolence of mind. Because if a man truly loves the public, he necessarily loves love to the public.

Now therefore, for the same reason, if universal benevolence in the highest sense, be the same thing with benevolence to the Divine Being, who is in effect universal Being, it will follow, that love to virtue itself is no otherwise virtuous, than as it is implied in, or arises from, love to the Divine Being. Consequently, God's own love to virtue is implied in love to himself: and is virtuous no otherwise than as it arises from love to himself. So that God's virtuous disposition, appearing in love to holiness in the creature, is to be resolved into the same thing with love to himself. And consequently, whereinsoever he makes *virtue* his end, he makes *himself* his end. In fine, God being as it were an all-comprehending Being, all his moral perfections—his holiness, justice, grace, and benevolence—are some way or other to be resolved into a supreme and infinite regard to himself; and if so, it will be easy to suppose that it becomes him to make himself his supreme and last end in his works.

I would here observe, by the way, that if any insist that it becomes God to love and take delight in the virtue of his creatures for its *own* sake, in such a manner as not to love it from regard to *himself;* this will contradict a former objection against God taking pleasure in communications of himself; *viz.* that inasmuch as God is perfectly independent and self-sufficient, therefore all his happiness and pleasure consists in the enjoyment of himself. So that if the same persons make both objections, they must be inconsistent with themselves.

2. I would observe, that it is not unworthy of God to take pleasure in that which is in itself fit and amiable, even in those that are infinitely below him. If there be infinite grace and condescension in it, yet these are not unworthy of God; but infinitely to his honour and glory.

They who insist, that God's own glory was not an ultimate end of his creation of the world; but the happiness of his creatures; do it under a colour of exalting God's benevolence to his creatures. But if his love to them be so great, and he so highly values them as to look upon them worthy to be his *end* in all his great works, as they suppose; they are not consistent with themselves, in supposing that God has so little value for their love and esteem. For as the nature of love, especially great love, causes him that loves to value the esteem of the person beloved; so, that God should take pleasure in the creature's just love and esteem, will follow from God's love both to himself and to his creatures. If he esteem and love himself, he must approve of esteem and love to himself, and disapprove the contrary. And if he loves and values the creature, he must value and take delight in their *mutual* love and esteem.

3. As to what is alleged, that it is unworthy of great

men to be governed in their conduct and achievements by a regard to the applause of the populace; I would observe, What makes their applause worthy of so little regard, is their ignorance, giddiness, and injustice. The applause of the multitude very frequently is not founded on any just view of things, but on humour, mistake, folly, and unreasonable affections. Such applause deserves to be disregarded.—But it is not beneath a man of the greatest dignity and wisdom, to value the wise and just esteem of others, however inferior to him. The contrary, instead of being an expression of greatness of mind, would show a haughty and mean spirit. It is *such* an esteem in his creatures, that God regards; for, such an esteem only is fit and amiable in itself.

OBJECT. IV. To suppose that God makes himself his ultimate end in the creation of the world, derogates from the freeness of his goodness, in his beneficence to his creatures; and from their obligations to gratitude for the good communicated. For if God, in communicating his fulness, makes himself, and not the creatures, his end; then what good he does, he does for himself, and not for them; for his sake, and not theirs.

Answer. God and the creature, in the emanation of the divine fulness, are not properly set in opposition; or made the opposite parts of a disjunction. Nor ought God's glory and the creature's good, to be viewed as if they were properly and entirely distinct, in the objection. This supposeth, that God having respect to his glory, and the communication of good to his creatures, are things altogether different: that God communicating his fulness for *himself*, and his doing it for *them*, are things standing in a proper disjunction and opposition. Whereas, if we were capable of more perfect views of God and divine things, which are so much above us, it probably would appear very clear, that the matter is quite otherwise: and that these things, instead of appearing entirely distinct, are *implied* one in the other. God in seeking his glory, seeks the good of his creatures; because the emanation of his glory (which he seeks and delights in, as he delights in himself and his own eternal glory) implies the communicated excellency and happiness of his creatures. And in communicating his fulness for them, he does it for himself; because their good, which he seeks, is so much in union and communion with himself. God is their good. Their excellency and happiness is nothing, but the emanation and expression of God's glory: God, in seeking their glory and happiness, seeks himself: and in seeking himself, *i. e.* himself diffused and expressed, (which he delights in, as he delights in his own beauty and fulness,) he seeks their glory and happiness.

This will the better appear, if we consider the degree and manner in which he aimed at the creature's excellency and happiness in creating the world; *viz.* during the whole of its designed eternal duration; in greater and greater nearness, and strictness of union with himself, in his own glory and happiness, in constant progression, through all eternity. As the creature's good was viewed, when God made the world, with respect to its whole duration, and eternally progressive union to, and communion with him: so the creature must be viewed as in infinitely strict union with himself. In this view it appears, that God's respect to the *creature*, in the whole, *unites* with his respect to *himself*. Both regards are like two lines which at the beginning appear separate, but finally meet in one, both being directed to the same centre. And as to the *good* of the creature itself, in its whole duration and infinite progression, it must be viewed as *infinite;* and as coming nearer and nearer to the same thing in its infinite fulness. The nearer any thing comes to infinite, the nearer it comes to an identity with God. And if any *good*, as viewed by God, is beheld as infinite, it cannot be viewed as a distinct thing from God's own infinite glory.

The apostle's discourse of the great love of Christ to men, (Eph. v. 25, &c.) leads us thus to think of the love of Christ to his church; as coinciding with his love to himself, by virtue of the strict union of the church with him. "Husbands, love your wives, as Christ also loved the church, and gave himself for it—that he might present it to himself a glorious church. So ought men to love their wives, as their own bodies. He that loveth his wife loveth himself—even as the Lord the church; for we are members of his body, of his flesh, and of his bones." Now I apprehend, that there is nothing in God's disposition to communicate of his own fulness to the creatures, that at all derogates from the excellence of it, or the creature's obligation.

God's disposition to cause his own infinite fulness to flow forth, is not the less properly called his *goodness*, because the good he communicates is what he delights in, as he delights in his own glory. The creature has no less benefit by it; neither has such a disposition less of a direct tendency to the creature's benefit. Nor is this disposition in God, to diffuse his own good, the less excellent, because it is implied in his love to himself. For his love to himself does not imply it any otherwise, but as it implies a love to whatever is worthy and excellent. The emanation of God's glory is in itself worthy and excellent, and so God delights in it; and this delight is implied in his love to his own fulness; because that is the fountain, the sum and comprehension of every thing that is excellent. Nor does God's inclination to communicate good from regard to himself, or delight in his own glory, at all diminish the freeness of his beneficence. This will appear, if we consider particularly, in what ways doing good to others from self-love, may be inconsistent with the freeness of beneficence. And I conceive there are only these two ways,

1. When any does good to another from confined self-love, which is *opposite* to a general benevolence. This kind of self-love is properly called *selfishness*. In some sense, the most benevolent, generous person in the world, seeks his *own* happiness in doing good to others; because he places his happiness in their good. His mind is so enlarged as to take them, as it were, into himself. Thus when they are happy, he feels it; he partakes with them, and is happy in their happiness. This is so far from being inconsistent with the freeness of beneficence, that, on the contrary, free benevolence and kindness consists in it. The most free beneficence that can be in men, is doing good, not from a confined selfishness, but from a disposition to general benevolence, or love to being in general.

But now, with respect to the Divine Being, there is no such thing as confined selfishness in him, or a love to himself *opposite* to general benevolence. It is impossible, because he comprehends all entity, and all excellence, in his own essence. The eternal and infinite Being, is in effect, *being in general;* and comprehends universal existence. God, in his benevolence to his creatures, cannot have his heart enlarged, in such a manner as to take in beings who are originally out of himself, distinct and independent. This cannot be in an infinite Being, who exists alone from eternity. But he, from his goodness, as it were enlarges himself in a more excellent and divine manner. This is by communicating and diffusing himself; and *so*, instead of *finding*, he *makes* objects of his benevolence—not by taking what he finds distinct from himself, and so partaking of their good, and being happy in them, but—by flowing forth, and expressing himself in them, and making them to partake of him, and then rejoicing in himself expressed in them, and communicated to them.

2. Another thing, in doing good to others from self-love, that derogates from the freeness of the goodness, is acting from *dependence* on them for the good we need or desire. So that, in our beneficence, we are not self-moved, but as it were constrained by something without ourselves. But it has been particularly shown already, that God making himself his end, argues no dependence; but is consistent with absolute independence and self-sufficiency.

And I would here observe, that there is something in that disposition to communicate goodness, that shows God to be independent and self-moved in it, in a manner that is peculiar, and above the beneficence of creatures. Creatures, even the most excellent, are not independent and self-moved in their goodness; but in all its exercises, they are excited by some object they find: something appearing good, or in some respect worthy of regard, presents itself, and moves their kindness. But God, being all, and alone, is absolutely self-moved. The exercises of his communicative disposition are absolutely from within himself; all that is good and worthy in the object, and its very *being*, proceeding from the overflowing of his fulness.

These things show that the supposition of God making himself his ultimate end, does not at all diminish the creature's obligation to gratitude for communications of good received. For if it lessen its obligation, it must be on one of the following accounts. Either, that the creature has not so much benefit by it; or, that the disposition it flows from, is not proper goodness, not having so direct a tendency to the creature's benefit; or, that the disposition is not so virtuous and excellent in its kind; or, that the beneficence is not so free. But it has been observed, that none of these things take place, with regard to that disposition, which has been supposed to have excited God to create the world.

I confess there is a degree of indistinctness and obscurity in the close consideration of such subjects, and a great imperfection in the expressions we use concerning them; arising unavoidably from the infinite sublimity of the subject, and the incomprehensibleness of those things that are divine. Hence revelation is the surest guide in these matters: and what that teaches shall in the next place be considered. Nevertheless, the endeavours used to discover what the voice of reason is, so far as it can go, may serve to prepare the way, by obviating cavils insisted on by many; and to satisfy us, that what the word of God says of the matter is not unreasonable.

CHAP. II.

WHEREIN IT IS INQUIRED, WHAT IS TO BE LEARNED FROM HOLY SCRIPTURES, CONCERNING GOD'S LAST END IN THE CREATION OF THE WORLD.

SECT. I.

The Scriptures represent God as making himself his own last end in the creation of the world.

It is manifest, that the Scriptures speak, on all occasions, as though God made *himself* his end in all his works; and as though the same being, who is the *first cause* of all things, were the supreme and *last end* of all things. Thus in Isa. xliv. 6. "Thus saith the Lord, the king of Israel, and his Redeemer the Lord of hosts, I am the first, I also am the last, and besides me there is no God." Chap. xlviii. 12. "I am the first and I am the last." Rev. i. 8. "I am Alpha and Omega, the beginning and the ending, saith the Lord, which is, and was, and which is to come, the Almighty." Ver. 11. "I am Alpha and Omega, the first and the last." Ver. 17. "I am the first and the last." Chap. xxi. 6. "And he said unto me, it is done; I am Alpha and Omega, the beginning and the end." Chap. xxii. 13. "I am Alpha and Omega, the beginning and the end, the first and the last."

When God is so often spoken of as the *last* as well as the *first*, the *end* as well as the *beginning*, it is implied, that as he is the first, efficient cause and fountain, from whence all things originate; so, he is the last, final cause for which they are made; the final term to which they all tend in their ultimate issue. This seems to be the most natural import of these expressions; and is confirmed by other parallel passages; as Rom. xi. 36. "For of him, and through him, and to him, are all things." Col. i. 16. "For by him were all things created, that are in heaven, and that are in earth, visible and invisible, whether they be thrones, or dominions, or principalities, or powers; all things were created by him, and for him." Heb. ii. 10. "For it became him, by whom are all things, and for whom are all things." And in Prov. xvi. 4. it is said expressly, "The Lord hath made all things for himself."

And the *manner* is observable, in which God is said to be the last, *to* whom, and *for* whom, are all things. It is evidently spoken of as a meet and suitable thing, a branch of his glory; a meet prerogative of the great, infinite, and eternal Being; a thing becoming the dignity of him who is infinitely above all other beings; from whom all things are, and by whom they consist; and in comparison with whom all other things are as nothing.

SECT. II.

Wherein some positions are advanced concerning a just method of arguing in this affair, from what we find in the Holy Scriptures.

We have seen, that the Scriptures speak of the creation of the world as being *for God,* as its end. What remains therefore to be inquired into, is, *which way do the Scriptures represent God as making himself his end?* It is evident, that God does not make his *existence* or being the end of the creation; which cannot be supposed without great absurdity. His existence cannot be conceived of but as *prior* to any of God's designs. Therefore he cannot create the world to the end that he may have existence; or may have certain attributes and perfections. Nor do the Scriptures give the least intimation of any such thing. Therefore, what divine effect, or what in relation to God, is that which the Scripture teacheth us to be the end he aimed at, in his works of creation, and in designing which he makes *himself* his end?

In order to a right understanding of the Scripture doctrine, and drawing just inferences from what we find said in the word of God, relative to this matter; and so to open the way to a true and definite answer to the above inquiry, I would lay down the following positions.

Position 1. That which appears to be God's ultimate end in his works of *providence* in general, we may justly suppose to be his last end in the work of *creation.* This appears from what was observed before, under the fifth particular of the introduction, which I need not now repeat.

Pos. 2. When any thing appears, by the Scripture, to be the last end of *some* of the works of God, that thing appears to be the result of God's works in *general.* And although it be not mentioned as the end of those works, but only of *some* of them; yet as nothing appears *peculiar* in the nature of the case, that renders it a fit, beautiful, and valuable result of those particular works, more than of the rest; we may justly infer that thing to be the last end of those *other* works also. For we must suppose it to be on account of the value of the effect, that it is made the end of those works of which it is *expressly* spoken as the end; and this effect, by the supposition, being equally, and in like manner, the result of the work, and of the same value, it is but reasonable to suppose, that it is the end of the work, of which it is naturally the consequence, in *one* case as well as in *another*.

Pos. 3. The ultimate end of God in creating the world being also the last end of all his works of *providence,* we may well presume that, if there be any *particular* thing, more frequently mentioned in Scripture, as God's ultimate aim in his works of providence, than any thing else, this is the ultimate end of God's works in *general,* and so the end of the work of *creation*

Pos. 4. That which appears, from the word of God, to be his ultimate end with respect to the *moral* world, or the *intelligent* part of the system, that is God's last end in the work of creation in *general.* Because it is evident, from the constitution of the world itself, as well as from the word of God, that the moral part is the end of all the rest of the creation. The inanimate, unintelligent part, is made for the rational, as much as a house is prepared for the inhabitant. And it is evident also from reason and the word of God, that it is for the sake of some *moral good* in them, that moral agents are made, and the world made for them. But it is further evident, that whatsoever is the last end of *that part* of creation, which is the end of all the rest, and for which all the rest of the world was made, must be the last end of the *whole.* If all the other parts of a watch are made for the hand of the watch, in order to move that aright, then it will follow, that the last end of the *hand* is the last end of the *whole* machine.

Pos. 5. That which appears from the Scripture to be God's ultimate end in the *chief* works of his providence, we may well determine is God's last end in creating the *world.* For, as observed, we may justly infer the *end* of a thing from the *use* of it. We must justly infer the end of a clock, a chariot, a ship, or water-engine, from the main *use* to which it is applied. But God's *providence* is his *use* of the *world* he has made. And if there be any works of providence which are evidently God's *main works*, herein appears and consists the *main use* that God makes of the creation.—From these two last positions we may infer the next, *viz.*

Pos. 6. Whatever appears, by the Scriptures, to be God's ultimate end in his main works of *Providence* towards the *moral world*, that we may justly infer to be the last end of the *creation* of the world. Because, as was just now observed, the *moral* world is the *chief* part of the creation, and the end of the rest; and God's last end in creating *that part* of the world, must be his last end in the creation of the *whole*. And it appears, by the last position, that the end of God's main works of Providence towards moral beings, or the *main use* to which he puts them, shews the last end for which he has *made* them; and consequently the main end for which he has made the *whole world*.

Pos. 7. That which divine revelation shows to be God's ultimate end with respect to *that part* of the moral world which are *good*, in their *being*, and in their being *good*, this we must suppose to be the last end of God's *creating* the world. For it has been already shown, that God's last end in the *moral* part of creation must be the end of the *whole*. But his end in that part of the moral world that are *good*, must be the last end for which he has made the moral world in *general*. For therein consists the goodness of a thing, its fitness to answer its end; at least this must be goodness in the eyes of its author. For goodness in his eyes, is its agreeableness to his mind. But an agreeableness to his mind, in what he makes for some end or use, must be an agreeableness or fitness to that end. For his end in this case is his mind. That which he chiefly aims at in that thing, is chiefly his mind with respect to that thing. And therefore, they are good moral agents who are fitted for the end for which God has made moral agents. And consequently, that which is the chief end to which *good* created moral agents, in being good, are fitted, this is the *chief* end of the moral part of the creation; and consequently of the *creation in general*.

Pos. 8. That which the word of God requires the intelligent and moral part of the world to *seek*, as their ultimate and highest end, that we have reason to suppose is the last end for which God has *made them;* and consequently, by position fourth, the last end for which he has made the *whole world*. A main difference between the intelligent and moral parts, and the rest of the world, lies in this, that the former are capable of *knowing* their Creator, and the end for which he made them, and capable of *actively* complying with his design in their creation, and promoting it; while other creatures cannot promote the design of their creation, only *passively* and *eventually*. And seeing they are capable of knowing the end for which their author has made them, it is doubtless their duty to fall in with it. Their wills ought to comply with the will of the Creator in this respect, in *mainly seeking* the same, as *their* last end, which *God* mainly seeks as their last end. This must be the law of nature and reason with respect to them. And we must suppose that God's revealed law, and the law of nature, agree; and that his will, as a *lawgiver*, must agree with his will as a *Creator*. Therefore we justly infer, that the same thing which God's *revealed* law requires intelligent creatures to seek, as their last and greatest end, that God their *Creator* had made their last end, and so the end of the *creation of the world*.

Pos. 9. We may well suppose, that what is in Holy Scripture, stated as the main end of the *goodness* of the moral world—so that the respect and relation their goodness has to that end, is what chiefly makes it valuable and desirable—is God's ultimate end in the *creation* of the moral world; and so, by position the fourth, of the *whole world*. For the end of the *goodness* of a thing, is the end of the *thing*.

Pos. 10. That which persons who are described in Scripture as *approved* saints, and set forth as *examples* of piety, sought as their last and highest end, in the instances of their good and approved behaviour; that, we must suppose, was what they *ought* to seek as their last end: and consequently by the preceding position, was the same with *God's* last end in the *creation of the world*.

Pos. 11. What appears by the word of God to be that end, in the desires of which the souls of the best, and in their best frames, most naturally and directly *exercise* their goodness, and in expressing their desire of this end, they do most properly and directly express their respect to God; we may well suppose that end to be the *chief* and *ultimate* end of a spirit of piety and *goodness*, and God's chief end in making the *moral* world, and so the *whole world*. For, doubtless, the most direct tendency of a spirit of true goodness, in the best part of the moral world, is to the *chief end of goodness*, and so the chief end of the *creation* of the moral world. And in what else can the spirit of the true respect and friendship to God be expressed by way of desire, than in desires of the *same end* which God himself chiefly and ultimately desires in *making them and all other things*.

Pos. 12. Since the Holy Scriptures teach us that Jesus Christ is the Head of the moral world, and especially of all the good part of it; the chief of God's servants, appointed to be the Head of his saints and angels, and set forth as the chief and most perfect pattern and example of goodness; we may well suppose, by the foregoing positions, that what *he* sought as his last end, was God's last end in the *creation of the world*.

SECT. III.

Particular texts of Scripture, that show that God's glory is an ultimate end of the creation.

1. WHAT God says in his word, naturally leads us to suppose, that the way in which he makes himself his end in his work or works, which he does *for his own sake*, is in making *his glory his end*.

Thus Isa. xlviii. 11. "For my own sake, even for my own sake, will I do it. For how should my name be polluted; and I will not give my glory to another." Which is as much as to say, I will obtain my end; I will not forego my glory; another shall not take this prize from me. It is pretty evident here, that God's *name* and his *glory*, which seem to intend the same thing, as shall be observed more particularly afterwards, are spoken of as his *last end* in the great work mentioned; not as an inferior, subordinate end, subservient to the interest of others. The words are emphatical. The emphasis and repetition constrain us to understand, that what God does is ultimately for his *own sake:* "For *my own sake*, even for *my own sake* will I do it."

So the words of the apostle, in Rom. xi. 36. naturally lead us to suppose, that the way in which all things are *to* God, is in being *for his glory*. "For of him, and through him, and to him are all things, to whom be glory for ever and ever. Amen." In the preceding context, the apostle observes the marvellous disposals of divine wisdom, for causing all things to be *to* him, in their final issue and result, as they are *from* him at first, and governed by him. His discourse shows how God contrived this and brought it to pass, by setting up the kingdom of Christ in the world; leaving the Jews, and calling the Gentiles; including what he would hereafter do in bringing in the Jews, with the fulness of the Gentiles; with the circumstances of these wonderful works, so as greatly to show his justice and his goodness, to magnify his grace, and manifest the sovereignty and freeness of it, and the absolute dependence of all on him. And then, in the four last verses, he breaks out into a most pathetic exclamation, expressing his great admiration of the *depth* of divine wisdom, in the steps he takes for attaining his end, and causing all things to be *to* him: and finally, he expresses a joyful consent to God's excellent design in all to *glorify himself*, in saying, "to him be glory for ever;" as much as to say, as all things are so wonderfully *ordered for his glory*, so let him *have the glory* of all, for evermore.

2. The glory of God is spoken of in Holy Scripture as the last end for which those parts of the moral world that are *good* were made.

Thus in Isa. xliii. 6, 7. "I will say to the north, Give up, and to the south, Keep not back; bring my sons from afar, and my daughters from the ends of the earth, even every one that is called by my name; for I have created him *for my glory*, I have formed him, yea I have made him." Again, Isa. lx. 21. "Thy people also shall be all righteous. They shall inherit the land for ever, the branch of my planting, the work of my hand, *that I may be glorified*." Also chap. lxi. 3. "That they may be called trees of righteousness, the planting of the Lord, *that he might be glorified*."

In these places we see, that the *glory of God* is spoken of as the end of God's saints, the end for which he makes them, *i. e.* either gives them being, or gives them a being as saints, or both. It is said, that God has made and formed them to be his sons and daughters, *for his own glory*: That they are trees of his planting, the work of his hands, as trees of righteousness, *that he might be glorified*. And if we consider the words, especially as taken with the context in each of the places, it will appear quite natural to suppose, that God's glory is here spoken of only as an end inferior and subordinate to the happiness of God's people. On the contrary, they will appear rather as promises of making God's people happy, that God therein might be glorified.

So is that in Isa. xliii. as we shall see plainly, if we take the whole that is said from the beginning of the chapter, ver. 1—7. It is wholly a promise of a future, great, and wonderful work of God's power and grace, delivering his people from all misery, and making them exceeding happy; and then the end of all, or the sum of God's design in all, is declared to be *God's own glory*. "I have redeemed thee, I have called thee by thy name, thou art mine.—I will be with thee.—When thou walkest through the fire, thou shalt not be burnt, neither shall the flame kindle upon thee.—Thou art precious and honourable in my sight. I will give men for thee, and people for thy life. Fear not, I am with thee.—I will bring my sons from far, and my daughters from the ends of the earth; every one that is called by my name: *for I have created him for my glory*."

So Isa. lx. 21. The whole chapter is made up of nothing but promises of future, exceeding happiness to God's church; but, for brevity's sake, let us take only the two preceding verses 19, 20. "The sun shall be no more thy light by day, neither for brightness shall the moon give light unto thee: but the Lord shall be unto thee an everlasting light, and thy God thy glory. Thy sun shall no more go down, neither shall thy moon withdraw itself; for the Lord shall be thine everlasting light, and the days of thy mourning shall be ended. Thy people also shall be all righteous; they shall inherit the land for ever, the branch of my planting, the work of my hands;" and then the end of all is added, "*that I might be glorified*." All the preceding promises are plainly mentioned as so many parts, or constituents, of the great and exceeding happiness of God's people; and *God's glory* is mentioned, as the sum of his design in this happiness.

In like manner is the promise in chap. lxi. 3. "To appoint unto them that mourn in Zion, to give unto them beauty for ashes, the oil of joy for mourning, the garment of praise for the spirit of heaviness, that they might be called trees of righteousness, the planting of the Lord, *that he might be glorified*." The work of God promised to be effected, is plainly an accomplishment of the joy, gladness, and happiness of God's people, instead of their mourning and sorrow; and the *end* in which God's design in this work is obtained and summed up, is *his glory*. This proves, by the seventh position, that *God's glory* is the *end of the creation*.

The same thing may be argued from Jer. xiii. 11. "For as a girdle cleaveth to the loins of a man, so have I caused to cleave unto me the whole house of Israel, and the whole house of Judah, saith the Lord: that they might be unto me for a people, and for a name, and for a praise, and *for a glory*: but they would not hear." That is, God sought to make them to be his own holy people; or, as the apostle expresses it, his peculiar people, zealous of good works; that so they might be a *glory* to him; as girdles were used in those days for ornament and beauty, and as badges of dignity and honour.*

Now when God speaks of himself, as seeking a peculiar and holy people for himself, to be for his glory and honour, as a man that seeks an ornament and badge of honour for his glory, it is not natural to understand it merely of a *subordinate* end, as though God had no respect to himself in it; but only the good of others. If so, the comparison would not be natural; for men are commonly wont to seek their *own glory* and honour in adorning themselves, and dignifying themselves with badges of honour.

The same doctrine seems to be taught, Eph. i. 5. "Having predestinated us to the adoption of children by Jesus Christ, unto himself, according to the good pleasure of his will, *to the praise of the glory of his grace*."—And the same may be argued from Isa. xliv. 23. "For the Lord hath redeemed Jacob, he hath *glorified himself* in Israel." And chap. xlix. 3. "Thou art my servant Jacob, in whom *I will be glorified*." John xvii. 10. "And all mine are thine, and thine are mine, and *I am glorified* in them." 2 Thess. i. 10. "When he shall come to be *glorified* in his saints." Ver. 11, 12. "Wherefore also we pray always for you, that our God would count you worthy of his calling, and fulfil all the good pleasure of his goodness, and the work of faith with power: that the name of our Lord Jesus may be *glorified* in you, and ye in him, according to the grace of God and our Lord Jesus Christ."

3. The Scripture speaks of God's glory, as his ultimate end of the *goodness* of the moral part of the creation; and that end, in relation to which chiefly the value of their virtue consists.

As in Phil. i. 10, 11. "That ye may approve things that are excellent, that ye may be sincere, and without offence, till the day of Christ: being filled with the fruits of righteousness, which are by Jesus Christ, *unto the glory and praise of God*." Here the apostle shows how the fruits of righteousness in them are valuable, and how they answer their end, viz. in being "by Jesus Christ *to the praise and glory of God*." John xv. 8. "Herein is my Father *glorified*, that ye bear much fruit." Signifying, that by this means it is that the great *end* of religion is to be answered. And in 1 Pet. iv. 11. the apostle directs the Christians to regulate all their religious performances with reference to that one end. "If any man speak, let him speak as the oracles of God: if any man minister, let him do it as of the ability which God giveth, *that God in all things may be glorified*; to whom be praise and dominion for ever and ever. Amen."

And, from time to time, embracing and practising true religion, and repenting of sin, and turning to holiness, is expressed by *glorifying God*, as though that were the sum and end of the whole matter. Rev. xi. 13. "And in the earthquake were slain of men seven thousand; and the remnant were affrighted, and *gave glory to the God of heaven*." So Rev. xiv. 6, 7. "And I saw another angel fly in the midst of heaven, having the everlasting gospel to preach to them that dwell on the earth; saying with a loud voice, Fear God, and *give glory to him*." As though this were the sum and *end* of that virtue and religion, which was the grand design of preaching the gospel, every where through the world. Rev. xvi. 9. "And repented not to *give him glory*." Which is as much as to say, they did not forsake their sins and turn to true religion, that God might receive that which is the great end he seeks, in the religion he requires of men. (See to the same purpose, Psal. xxii. 21—23. Isa. lxvi. 19. xxiv. 15. xxv. 3. Jer. xiii. 15, 16. Dan. v. 23. Rom. xv. 5, 6.)

And as the *exercise* of true religion and virtue in Christians is summarily expressed by their *glorifying God*, so, when the good influence of this on others is spoken of, it is expressed in the same manner. Matt. v. 16. "Let your light so shine before men, that others seeing your good works, may *glorify your Father* which is in heaven." 1 Pet. ii. 12. "Having your conversation honest among the Gentiles, that whereas they speak evil against you as evildoers, they may, by your good works which they behold, glorify God in the day of visitation."

That the ultimate end of moral goodness, or righteousness, is answered in God's glory being attained, is *supposed* in the *objection* which the apostle makes, or supposes some will make, Rom. iii. 7. "For if the truth of God hath more abounded through my lie unto *his glory*, why am I judged as a sinner?" *i. e.* seeing the great end of righteous-

* See ver. 9. and also Isa. iii. 24. and xxii. 21. and xxiii. 10. 2 Sam. xviii. 11. Exod. xxviii. 8.

ness is answered by my sin, in God being glorified, why is my sin condemned and punished? and why is not my vice equivalent to virtue?

And the glory of God is spoken of as that wherein consists the value and end of particular graces. As of *faith*. Rom. iv. 20. "He staggered not at the promise of God through unbelief: but was strong in faith, *giving glory to God*." Phil. ii. 11. "That every tongue should confess that Jesus is the Lord, *to the glory of God the Father*." Of *repentance*. Josh. vi. 19. "Give, I pray thee, *glory to the Lord God of Israel*, and make confession unto him." Of *charity*. 2 Cor. viii. 19. "With this grace, which is administered by us, *to the glory of the same Lord*, and declaration of your ready mind." Thanksgiving and praise. Luke vii. 18. "There are not found that returned to *give glory to God*, save this stranger." Psal. l. 23. "Whoso offereth praise *glorifieth me*; and to him that ordereth his conversation aright, will I show the salvation of God." Concerning which last place may be observed, that God seems to say this to such as supposed, in their religious performances, that the *end of all religion was to glorify God*. They supposed they did this in the best manner, in offering a multitude of sacrifices; but God corrects their mistake, and informs them, that this grand end of religion is not attained this way, but in offering the more spiritual sacrifices of praise and a holy conversation.

In fine, the words of the apostle in 1 Cor. vi. 20. are worthy of particular notice. "Ye are not your own; for ye are bought with a price: therefore glorify God in your body and in your spirit, which are his." Here, not only is glorifying God spoken of, as what summarily comprehends the end of religion, and of Christ redeeming us; but the apostle urges, that inasmuch as we are not our own, we ought not to act as if we were our own, but as God's; and should not use the members of our bodies, or faculties of our souls, for ourselves, but for God, as making him our end. And he expresses the way in which we are to make God our end, viz. in making his *glory* our end. "Therefore *glorify God* in your body and in your spirit, which are his." Here it cannot be pretended, that though Christians are indeed required to make God's glory their end; yet it is but as a *subordinate* end, as subservient to their own happiness; for then, in acting chiefly and ultimately for their ownselves, they would use themselves more as their *own* than as God's; which is directly contrary to the design of the apostle's exhortation, and the argument he is upon; which is, that we should give ourselves as it were away *from ourselves to God*, and use ourselves as *his*, and not our *own*, acting for his *sake*, and not our *own sakes*. Thus it is evident, by position the ninth, that the *glory of God is the last end for which he created the world*.

4. There are some things in the word of God which lead us to suppose, that it *requires* of men that they should *desire* and *seek* God's glory, as their highest and last end in what they do.

As particularly, from 1 Cor. x. 30. "Whether therefore ye eat or drink, or whatsoever ye do, do all *to the glory of God*." And 1 Pet. iv. 11.—"That God in all things *may be glorified*." And this may be argued, that Christ requires his followers should desire and seek God's glory in the *first place*, and *above all* things else, from that prayer which he gave his disciples, as the pattern and rule for the direction of his followers in their prayers. The first petition of which is, *Hallowed be thy name*. Which in scripture language is the same with *glorified* be thy name; as is manifest from Lev. x. 3. Ezek. xxviii. 22. and many other places. Now our last and highest end is doubtless what should be first in our *desires*, and consequently first in our *prayers*; and therefore, we may argue, that since Christ directs that God's glory should be first in our prayers, that therefore this is our last end. This is further confirmed by the conclusion of the Lord's prayer, *For thine is the kingdom, the power, and the glory*. Which, as it stands in connexion with the rest of the prayer, implies, that we desire and ask all the things mentioned in each petition, with a subordination, and in subservience, to the dominion and glory of God; in which all our desires ultimately terminate, as their last end. God's glory and dominion are the two first things mentioned in the prayer, and are the subject of the first half of the prayer; and they are the two last things mentioned in the same prayer, in its conclusion. God's glory is the Alpha and Omega in the prayer. From these things we may argue, according to position the eighth, that *God's glory is the last end of the creation*.

5. The glory of God appears, by the account given in Scripture, to be that event, in the earnest desires of which, and in their delight in which, the *best part* of the moral world, and when in their *best frames*, most naturally express the direct tendency of the spirit of true goodness, the virtuous and pious affections of their heart.

This is the way in which the holy *apostles*, from time to time, gave vent to the ardent exercises of their piety, and breathed forth their regard to the Supreme Being. Rom. xi. 36. "To whom be glory for ever and ever. Amen." Chap. xvi. 27. "To God only wise, be glory, through Jesus Christ, for ever. Amen." Gal. i. 4, 5. "Who gave himself for our sins, that he might deliver us from this present evil world, according to the will of God and our Father, to whom be glory for ever and ever. Amen." 2 Tim. iv. 18. "And the Lord shall deliver me from every evil work, and will preserve me to his heavenly kingdom: to whom be glory for ever and ever. Amen." Eph. iii. 21. "Unto him be glory in the church by Christ Jesus, throughout all ages, world without end." Heb. xiii. 21.—"Through Jesus Christ, to whom be glory for ever and ever. Amen." Phil. iv. 20. "Now unto God and our Father be glory for ever and ever. Amen." 2 Pet. iii. 18. "To him be glory both now and for ever. Amen." Jude 25. "To the only wise God our Saviour, be glory and majesty, dominion and power, both now and ever. Amen." Rev. i. 5, 6. "Unto him that loved us, &c. —to him be glory and dominion for ever and ever. Amen."

It was in this way that holy *David*, the sweet psalmist of Israel, vented the ardent tendencies and desires of his pious heart. 1 Chron. xvi. 28, 29. "Give unto the Lord, ye kindreds of the people, give unto the Lord *glory* and strength: give unto the Lord the *glory* due unto his name." We have much the same expressions again, Psal. xxix. 1, 2. and lxix. 7, 8. See also, Psal. lvii. 5. lxxii. 18, 19. cxv. 1. So the whole church of God through all parts of the earth, Isa. xlii. 10—12. In like manner the *saints and angels in heaven express* the piety of their hearts, Rev. iv. 9, 11—14. and vii. 12. This is the event that the hearts of the seraphim especially exult in, as appears by Isa. vi. 2, 3. "Above it stood the seraphim—And one cried unto another, and said, Holy, holy, holy is the Lord of hosts, the whole earth is full of his *glory*." So at the birth of Christ, Luke ii. 14. "*Glory* to God in the highest," &c.

It is manifest that these holy persons in earth and heaven, in thus expressing their desires of the glory of God, have respect to it, not merely as a subordinate end, but as that which is in *itself* valuable in the *highest degree*. It would be absurd to say, that in these ardent exclamations, they are only giving vent to their vehement *benevolence to their fellow-creatures*, and expressing their earnest desire that *God might be glorified*, that so his *subjects* may be made happy by *that means*. It is evident, it is not so much their love, either to themselves, or their fellow-creatures, which they express, as their exalted and supreme regard to the most high and infinitely glorious Being. When the church says, *Not unto us, not unto us, O Jehovah, but to thy name give glory*, it would be absurd to say, that she only desires that God may have glory, as a necessary or *convenient means* of their own advancement and felicity. From these things it appears by the eleventh position, that *God's glory is the end of the creation*.

6. The Scripture leads us to suppose, that *Christ* sought God's glory, as his highest and last end.

John vii. 18. "He that speaketh of himself, seeketh his own glory; but he that seeketh *his* glory that sent him, the same is true, and no unrighteousness is in him." When Christ says, he did not seek his own glory, we cannot reasonably understand him, that he had no regard to his own glory, even the glory of the human nature; for the glory of that nature was part of the reward promised him, and of the joy set before him. But we must understand him, that this was not his *ultimate* aim; it was not the end that *chiefly* governed his conduct: and therefore, when in opposition to this, in the latter part of the sentence, he says, "But he that seeketh his glory that sent him, the same is true," &c. It is natural from the antithesis to understand him, that this was his ultimate aim, his supreme governing end.

John xii. 27, 28. "Now is my soul troubled, and what shall I say? Father, save me from this hour: but for this cause came I unto this hour, Father, *glorify thy name.*" Christ was now going to Jerusalem, and expected in a few days there to be crucified: and the prospect of his last sufferings, in this near approach, was very terrible to him. Under this distress of mind, he supports himself with a prospect of what would be the consequence of his sufferings, *viz. God's glory.* Now, it is the *end* that supports the agent in any difficult work that he undertakes, and above all others, his *ultimate* and supreme end; for this is above all others valuable in his eyes; and so, sufficient to countervail the difficulty of the means. That end, which is in itself agreeable and sweet to him, and which ultimately terminates his desires, is the centre of rest and support; and so must be the fountain and sum of all the delight and comfort he has in his prospects, with respect to his work. Now Christ has his soul straitened and distressed with a view of that which was infinitely the most difficult part of his work, and which was just at hand. Now certainly, if his mind seeks support in the conflict from a view of his end, it must most naturally repair to the *highest* end, which is the proper fountain of all support in this case. We may well suppose, that when his soul conflicts with the most extreme difficulties, it would resort to the idea of his supreme and ultimate end, the fountain of all the support and comfort he has in the work.

The same thing, Christ seeking the glory of God as his ultimate end, is manifest by what he says, when he comes yet nearer to the hour of his last sufferings, in that remarkable prayer, the last he ever made with his disciples, on the evening before his crucifixion; wherein he expresses the sum of his aims and desires. His first words are, "Father, the hour is come, glorify thy Son, that thy Son also may glorify thee." As this is his first request, we may suppose it to be his supreme request and desire, and what he ultimately aimed at in all. If we consider what follows to the end, all the rest that is said in the prayer, seems to be but an amplification of this great request.—On the whole, I think it is pretty manifest, that Jesus Christ sought the *glory of God* as his highest and last end; and that therefore, by position twelfth, this was *God's last end in the creation of the world.*

7. It is manifest from Scripture, that God's glory is the last end of that great work of providence, the work of *redemption* by Jesus Christ.

This is manifest from what is just now observed, of its being the end ultimately sought by Jesus Christ the Redeemer. And if we further consider the texts mentioned in the proof of that, and take notice of the context, it will be very evident, that it was what Christ sought as his last end, in that great work which he came into the world upon, *viz.* to procure redemption for his people. It is manifest, that Christ professes in John vii. 18. that he did not seek his own glory in what he did, but the glory of him that sent him. He means, in the work of his ministry; the work he performed, and which he came into the world to perform, which is the work of redemption. And with respect to that text, John xii. 27, 28. it has been already observed, that Christ comforts himself in the view of the extreme difficulty of his work, in the prospect of the highest, ultimate, and most excellent end of that work, which he set his heart most upon, and delighted most in.

And in the answer that the Father made him from heaven at that time, in the latter part of the same verse, John xii. 28. "I have both glorified it, and will glorify it again." The meaning plainly is, that God had glorified his name in what Christ had done, in the work he sent him upon; and would glorify it again, and to a greater degree, in what he should further do, and in the success thereof. Christ shows that he understood it thus, in what he says upon it, when the people took notice of it, wondering at the voice; some saying, that it thundered, others, that an angel spake to him. Christ says, "This voice came not because of me, but for your sakes." And then he says, (exulting in the prospect of this glorious end and success,) "Now is the judgment of this world; now is the prince of this world cast out; and I, if I be lift up from the earth, will draw all men unto me." In the success of the same work of redemption, he places his own glory, as was observed before. John xii. 23, 24. "The hour is come that the Son of man should be glorified. Verily, verily, I say unto you, except a corn of wheat fall into the ground, it abideth alone; but if it die, it bringeth forth much fruit."

So it is manifest, that when he seeks his own and his Father's glory, in that prayer, John xvii. he seeks it as the end of that great work he came into the world upon, and which he is about to finish in his death. What follows through the whole prayer, plainly shows this; particularly the 4th and 5th verses. "I have glorified thee on earth: I have finished the work which thou gavest me to do. And now, O Father, glorify thou me with thine own self." Here it is pretty plain, that declaring to his Father he had glorified him on earth, and finished the work given him to do, meant that he had finished the work which God gave him to do *for this end,* that he might be *glorified.* He had now finished that foundation that he came into the world to lay for his glory. He had laid a foundation for his Father's obtaining his will, and the utmost that he designed. By which it is manifest, that God's glory was the utmost of his design, or his *ultimate* end in this great work.

And it is manifest, by John xiii. 31, 32. that the glory of the Father, and his own glory, are what Christ exulted in, in the prospect of his approaching sufferings, when Judas was gone out to betray him, as the end his heart was mainly set upon, and supremely delighted in. "Therefore, when he was gone out, Jesus said, Now is the Son of man glorified, and God is glorified in him. If God be glorified in him, God shall also glorify him in himself, and shall straightway glorify him."

That the glory of God is the highest and last end of the work of redemption, is confirmed by the song of the angels at Christ's birth. Luke ii. 14. "Glory to God in the highest, and on earth peace, and good will toward men." It must be supposed that they knew what was God's last end in sending Christ into the world: and that in their rejoicing on the occasion, their minds would most rejoice in that which was most valuable and glorious in it; which must consist in its relation to that which was its chief and ultimate end. And we may further suppose, that the thing which chiefly engaged their minds was most glorious and joyful in the affair; and would be first in that song which was to express the sentiments of their minds, and exultation of their hearts.

The glory of the Father and the Son is spoken of as the end of the work of redemption, in Phil. ii. 6—11. (very much in the same manner as in John xii. 23, 28. and xiii. 31, 32, and xvii. 1, 4, 5.) "Who being in the form of God,—made himself of no reputation, and took upon him the form of a servant, and was made in the likeness of men: and being found in fashion as a man, he humbled himself, and became obedient unto death, even the death of the cross: wherefore God also hath highly exalted him, and given him a name, &c. that at the name of Jesus every knee should bow,—and every tongue confess, that Jesus is the Lord, *to the glory of God the Father.*" So God's glory, or the praise of his glory, is spoken of as the end of the work of redemption, in Eph. i. 3, &c. "Blessed be the God and Father of our Lord Jesus Christ, who hath blessed us with all spiritual blessings in heavenly places in Christ: according as he hath chosen us in him. Having predestinated us to the adoption of children, *to the praise of the glory of his grace.*" And in the continuance of the same discourse, concerning the redemption of Christ, God's glory is once and again mentioned as the great end of all.

Several things belonging to that great redemption, are mentioned in the following verses: Such as God's great wisdom in it, ver. 8. The clearness of light granted through Christ, ver. 9. God's gathering together in one, all things in heaven and earth in Christ, ver. 10. God's giving the Christians that were first converted to the Christian faith from among the Jews, an interest in this great redemption, ver. 11. Then the great end is added, ver. 12. "That we should be *to the praise of his glory,* who first trusted in Christ." And then is mentioned the bestowing of the same great salvation on the Gentiles, in its beginning or first fruits in the world, and in completing it in another world, in the two next verses. And then the same great end is added again. "In whom ye also trusted, after that ye heard the word of truth, the gospel of your salvation: In whom also, after that ye believed, ye were sealed with the holy spirit of promise, which is the earnest of our inheritance, until the redemption of the purchased possession, *unto the praise of his glory.*" The same thing is expressed much in the same manner, in 2 Cor. iv. 14, 15.—"He which raised up the Lord Jesus, shall raise us up also by Jesus, and shall present us with you. For all things are for your sakes, that the abundance of grace might, through the thanksgiving of many, redound *to the glory of God.*"

The same is spoken of as the end of the work of redemption in the Old Testament, Psal. lxxix. 9. "Help us, O God of our salvation, *for the glory of thy name;* deliver us and purge away our sins, for thy name's sake." So in the prophecies of the redemption of Jesus Christ. Isa. xliv. 23. "Sing, O ye heavens; for the LORD hath done it: shout, ye lower parts of the earth: break forth into singing, ye mountains: O forest, and every tree therein: for the LORD hath redeemed Jacob, and *glorified himself* in Israel!" Thus the works of creation are called upon to rejoice at the attaining of the same end, by the redemption of God's people, that the angels rejoiced at when Christ was born. See also Isa. xlviii. 10, 11. and xlix. 3.

Thus it is evident, that the glory of God is the ultimate end of the work of redemption; which is the chief work of providence towards the moral world, as is abundantly manifest from Scripture. For the whole universe is put in subjection to Jesus Christ; all heaven and earth, angels and men, are subject to him, as executing this office; and are put under him to that end, that all things may be ordered by him, in subservience to the great designs of his redemption. All power, as he says, is given to him, in heaven and in earth, that he may give eternal life to as many as the Father has given him; and he is exalted far above all principality and power, and might and dominion, and made head over all things to the church. The angels are put in subjection to him, that he may employ them all as ministering spirits, for the good of them that shall be the heirs of salvation: and all things are so governed by their Redeemer, that all things are theirs, whether things present or things to come: and all God's works of providence in the moral government of the world, which we have an account of in scripture history, or that are foretold in scripture prophecy, are evidently subordinate to the great purposes and ends of this great work. And besides, the work of redemption is that, by which good men are, as it were, brought into being, as good men, or as restored to holiness and happiness. The work of redemption is a new creation, according to Scripture, whereby men are brought into a new existence, or are made new creatures.

From these things it follows, according to the 5th, 6th, and 7th positions, that *the glory of God is the last end of the creation of the world.*

8. The Scripture leads us to suppose that God's glory is his last end in his *moral government* of the world in general. This has been already shown concerning several things that belong to God's moral government of the world. As particularly in the work of redemption, the chief of all his dispensations in his moral government of the world. And I have also observed it, with respect to the duty which God requires of the subjects of his moral government, in requiring them to seek his glory as their last end. And this is actually the last end of the moral goodness required of them, the end which gives their moral goodness its chief value. And also, that it is what that person which God has set at the head of the moral world, as its chief governor, even Jesus Christ, seeks as *his* chief end. And it has been shown, that it is the chief end for which that part of the moral world which are good are made, or have their existence as good.

I now further observe, that this is the end of the establishment of the public *worship* and *ordinances* of God among mankind. Hag. i. 8. "Go up to the mountain, and bring wood, and build the house; and I will take pleasure in it, and I will *be glorified,* saith the *Lord.*" This is spoken of as the end of God's promises of rewards, and of their fulfilment. 2 Cor. i. 20. "For all the promises of God in him are yea, and in him Amen, *to the glory of God* by us." And this is spoken of as the end of the execution of God's threatenings, in the punishment of sin. Numb. xiv. 20, 21, 22, 23. "And the Lord said, I have pardoned according to thy word. But, as truly as I live, all the earth shall be filled with *the glory of Jehovah.*" The glory of Jehovah is evidently here spoken of, as that to which he had regard, as his highest and ultimate end, which therefore he could not fail of; but must take place every where, and in every case, through all parts of his dominion, whatever became of men. And whatever abatements might be made, as to judgments deserved; and whatever changes might be made in the course of God's proceedings from compassion to sinners; yet the attaining of God's glory was an end, which, being ultimate and supreme, must in no case whatsoever give place. This is spoken of as the end of God executing judgments on his enemies in this world. Exod. xiv. 17, 18. "And I will get me honour (ואכבדה *I will be glorified)* upon Pharaoh, and upon all his host," &c. Ezek. xxviii. 22. "Thus saith the Lord God, Behold, I am against thee, O Zidon, and I *will be glorified* in the midst of thee: And they shall know that I am the Lord, when I shall have executed judgments in her, and shall be *sanctified* in her." So Ezek. xxxix. 13. "Yea, all the people of the land shall bury them; and it shall be to them a renown, the day *that I shall be glorified,* saith the Lord God." And this is spoken of as the end, both of the executions of wrath, and in the glorious exercises of mercy, in the misery and happiness of another world. Rom. ix. 22, 23. "What if God, willing to show his wrath, and make his power known, endured with much long-suffering, the vessels of wrath fitted to destruction; and that he might make known the *riches of his glory* on the vessels of mercy, which he had afore prepared unto glory." And this is spoken of as the end of the day of judgment, which is the time appointed for the highest exercises of God's authority as moral Governor of the world; and is as it were the day of the consummation of God's moral government, with respect to all his subjects in heaven, earth, and hell. 2 Thess. i. 9, 10. "Who shall be punished with everlasting destruction from the presence of the Lord, and from *the glory of his power;* when he shall come *to be glorified* in his saints, and *to be admired* in all them that believe." Then his glory shall be obtained, with respect both to saints and sinners.—From these things it is manifest, by the fourth position, that God's glory is the ultimate end of the creation of the world.

9. It appears, from what has been already observed, that the glory of God is spoken of in Scripture as the last end of many of his works: and it is plain that this is in fact the result of the works of God's common providence, and of the creation of the world. Let us take God's glory in what sense soever, consistent with its being a good attained by any work of God, certainly it is the consequence of these works: and besides, it is expressly so spoken of in Scripture.

This is implied in the eighth psalm, wherein are celebrated the works of creation: the heavens, the work of God's fingers; the moon and the stars, ordained by him; and man, made a little lower than the angels, &c. The first verse is—"O Lord, our Lord, how excellent is thy name in all the earth! who hast set thy *glory* above the heavens," or upon the heavens. By *name* and *glory,* very much the same thing is intended here, as in many other places, as shall be particularly shown afterwards. The psalm concludes as it began. "O Lord, our Lord, how excellent is thy name in all the earth!" So, in the 148th psalm, after a particular mention of most of the works of creation, enumerating them in order, the psalmist says, ver. 13. "Let them praise the name of the Lord, for his name alone is excellent, *his glory* is above the earth and the heaven." And in the 104th psalm, after a very particular, orderly, and magnificent representation of God's works of creation and common providence, it is said in the 31st verse, "The *glory of the Lord* shall endure for ever: the Lord shall rejoice in his works." Here God's glory is spoken of as the grand result and blessed consequence, on account of which he rejoices in these works. And this is one thing doubtless implied in the song of the seraphim, Isa. vi. 3. "Holy, holy, holy is the Lord of hosts, the whole earth is full of his glory."

The glory of God, in being the result and consequence of those works of providence that have been mentioned, is in fact the consequence of the creation. The good attained in the use of a thing, made for use, is the result of the making of that thing; as signifying the time of day, when actually attained by the use of a watch, is the consequence of making the watch. So it is apparent, that the glory of God is actually the result and consequence of the creation of the world. And from what has been already observed, it appears, that it is what God seeks as good, valuable, and excellent in itself. And I presume none will pretend, that there is any thing peculiar in the nature of the case, rendering it a thing valuable in some of the instances wherein it takes place, and not in others: or that the glory of God, though indeed an effect of all God's works, is an exceeding desirable effect of some of them; but of others, a worthless and insignificant effect. God's glory therefore must be a desirable, valuable consequence of the work of creation. Therefore it is manifest, by position the third, that the glory of God is an ultimate end in the creation of the world.

SECT. IV.

Places of Scripture that lead us to suppose, that God created the world for his name, to make his perfections known; and that he made it for his praise.

1. Here I shall first take notice of some passages of Scripture that speak of God's *name* as being the object of his regard, and the regard of his virtuous and holy intelligent creatures, much in the same manner as has been observed of *God's glory*.

God's *name* is, in like manner, spoken of as the *end* of his acts of goodness towards the good part of the moral world, and of his works of mercy and salvation towards his people. As 1 Sam. xii. 22. "The Lord will not forsake his people, *for his great name's sake.*" Psal. xxiii. 3. "He restoreth my soul, he leadeth me in the paths of righteousness, *for his name's sake.*" Psal. xxxi. 3. "*For thy name's sake*, lead me, and guide me." Psal. cix. 21. "But do thou for me,——*for thy name's sake.*" The forgiveness of sin in particular, is often spoken of as being for God's *name's sake.* 1 John ii. 12. "I write unto you, little children, because your sins are forgiven you *for his name's sake.*" Psal. xxv. 11. "*For thy name's sake*, O Lord, pardon mine iniquity, for it is great." Psal. lxxix. 9. "Help us, O God of our salvation, *for the glory of thy name;* and deliver us, and purge away our sins, *for thy name's sake.*" Jer. xiv. 7. "O Lord, though our iniquities testify against us, do thou it *for thy name's sake.*"

These things seem to show, that the *salvation of Christ* is for God's *name's sake.* Leading and guiding in the way of safety and happiness, restoring the soul, the forgiveness of sin; and that help, deliverance, and salvation, that is consequent therein, is *for God's name.* And here it is observable, that those two great temporal salvations of God's people, the redemption from Egypt, and that from Babylon, often represented as figures and similitudes of the redemption of Christ, are frequently spoken of as being wrought *for God's name's sake.*

Thus that great work of God, in delivering his people from *Egypt*, and conducting them to Canaan. 2 Sam. vii. 23. "And what one nation in the earth is like thy people, even like Israel, whom God went to redeem for a people to himself, and to *make him a name.*" Psal. cvi. 8. "Nevertheless he saved them *for his name's sake.*" Isa. lxiii. 12. "That led them by the right hand of Moses, with his glorious arm, dividing the waters before them, *to make himself an everlasting name.*" In the 20th chap. of Ezekiel, God, rehearsing the various parts of this wonderful work, adds, from time to time, "*I wrought for my name's sake*, that it should not be polluted before the heathen," as in ver. 9, 14, 22. (See also Josh. vii. 8, 9. Dan. ix. 15.)

So is the redemption from the *Babylonish* captivity. Isa. xlviii. 9, 10. "*For my name's sake* will I defer mine anger. For mine own sake, even for mine own sake, will I do it; for how should *my name* be polluted?" In Ezek. xxxvi. 21, 22, 23. the reason is given for God's mercy in restoring Israel. "But I had pity for my holy name. Thus saith the Lord, I do not this for your sakes, O house of Israel, but *for my holy name's sake;*—And I will *sanctify my great name*, which was profaned among the heathen." And chap. xxxix. 25. "Therefore, thus saith the Lord God, now will I bring again the captivity of Jacob, and have mercy upon the whole house of Israel, *and will be jealous for my holy name.*" Daniel prays, that God would forgive his people, and show them mercy *for his own sake.* Dan. ix. 19.

When God, from time to time, speaks of showing *mercy*, and exercising goodness, and promoting his people's happiness for his *name's sake*, we cannot understand it as of a merely subordinate end. How absurd would it be to say, that he promotes their happiness for his name's sake, in subordination to their good; and that his name may be exalted only for their sakes, as a means of promoting their happiness! especially when such expressions as these are used, "For mine own sake, even for mine own sake will I do it; for how should my name be polluted?" and "Not for your sakes do I this, but for my holy name's sake."

Again, it is represented as though God's people had their existence, at least as God's people, for God's name's sake. God's redeeming or purchasing them, that they might be his people, *for his name*, implies this. As in that passage mentioned before, 2 Sam. vii. 23. "Thy people Israel, whom God went to redeem for a people to himself, and *to make him a name.*" So God making them a people for his name, is implied in Jer. xiii. 11. "For as the girdle cleaveth to the loins of a man, so have I caused to cleave unto me the whole house of Israel, &c.—that they may be unto me for a people, *and for a name.*" Acts xv. 14. "Simeon hath declared how God at the first did visit the Gentiles, to take out of them a people *for his name.*"

This also is spoken of as the end of the *virtue*, religion, and holy behaviour of the saints. Rom. i. 5. "By whom we have received grace and apostleship, for obedience to the faith among all nations *for his name.*" Matt. xix. 29. "Every one that forsaketh houses, or brethren, &c.—*for my name's sake*, shall receive an hundred fold, and shall inherit everlasting life." 3 John 7. "Because, that *for his name's sake*, they went forth, taking nothing of the Gentiles." Rev. ii. 3. "And hast borne, and hast patience, and *for my name's sake* hast laboured and hast not fainted."

And we find that holy persons express their *desire* of this, and their *joy* in it, in the same manner as in the glory of God. 2 Sam. vii. 26. "Let thy *name* be magnified for ever." Psal. lxxvi. 1. "In Judah is God known, his *name* is great in Israel." Psal. cxlviii. 13. "Let them praise the *name* of the Lord; for his *name* alone is excellent, his *glory* is above the earth and heaven." Psal. cxxxv. 13. "Thy *name*, O Lord, endureth for ever, and thy memorial throughout all generations." Isa. xii. 4. "Declare his doings among the people, make mention that his *name* is exalted."

The *judgments* God executes on the wicked, are spoken of as being *for the sake of his name*, in like manner as for his glory. Exod. ix. 16. "And in very deed, for this cause have I raised thee up, for to show in thee my power; and that my *name* may be declared throughout all the earth." Neh. ix. 10. "And showedst signs and wonders upon Pharaoh, and on all his servants, and on all the people of his land; for thou knewedst that they dealt proudly against them: so didst thou *get thee a name*, as at this day."

And this is spoken of as a *consequence* of the works of creation, in like manner as God's *glory.* Psal. viii. 1. "O Lord, *how excellent is thy name* in all the earth! who hast set thy glory above the heavens." And then, at the conclusion of the observations on the works of creation, the psalm ends thus, ver. 9. "O Lord our Lord, *how excellent is thy name* in all the earth!" So Psal. cxlviii. 13. after a particular mention of the various works of creation. "Let them praise the name of the Lord, for *his name alone* is excellent in all the earth, his glory is above the earth and the heaven."

2. So we find the manifestation of God's *perfections*, his

greatness, and *excellency*, is spoken of very much in the same manner as God's glory.

There are several scriptures which would lead us to suppose this to be the great thing that God sought of the *moral world*, and the end aimed at in moral agents, wherein they are to be active in answering their end. This seems implied in that argument God's people sometimes made use of, in deprecating a state of death and destruction: that, in such a state, they cannot know, or make known, the glorious excellency of God. Psal. lxxxviii. 18, 19. "Shall thy loving-kindness be declared in the grave, or thy faithfulness in destruction? Shall thy wonders be known in the dark, and thy righteousness in the land of forgetfulness?" So Psal. xxx. 9. Isa. xxxviii. 18, 19. The argument seems to be this: Why should we perish? and how shall thine end, for which thou hast made us, be obtained in a state of destruction, in which thy glory cannot be known or declared?

This is the end of the *good part* of the moral world, or the end of God's people in the same manner as the glory of God. Isa. xliii. 21. "This people have I formed for myself, they shall show forth my *praise*." 1 Pet. ii. 9. "But ye are a chosen generation, a royal priesthood, an holy nation, a peculiar people, *that ye should show forth the praises of him* who hath called you out of darkness into marvellous light."

And this seems to be represented as the thing wherein the *value*, the proper *fruit* and end of their virtue appears. Isa. lx. 6. speaking of the conversion of the Gentile nations to true religion, "They shall come and *show forth the praises* of the Lord." Isa. lxvi. 19. "I will send—— unto the nations——and to the isles afar off, that have not *heard my fame*, neither have seen my glory; and they shall *declare* my *glory* among the Gentiles."—To which we may add, the *proper tendency* and rest of true virtue, and holy dispositions. 1 Chron. xvii. 8. "Make known his deeds among the people." Verse 23, 24. "Show forth from day to day thy salvation. Declare his glory among the heathen."*

This seems to be spoken of as a great end of the acts of God's *moral government;* particularly, the great *judgments* he executes for sin. Exod. ix. 16. "And in very deed, for this cause have I raised thee up, to show in thee my power; and that my name might be declared throughout all the earth." Dan. iv. 17. "This matter is by the decree of the watchers, &c. To the intent, that the living may know that the Most High ruleth in the kingdom of men, and giveth it to whomsoever he will; and setteth up over it the basest of men." But places to this purpose are too numerous to be particularly recited. See them in the margin.†

This is also a great end of God's works of *favour* and *mercy* to his people. 2 Kings xix. 19. "Now, therefore, O Lord our God, I beseech thee, save thou us out of his hand, that all the kingdoms of the earth *may know that thou art the Lord God*, even thou only." 1 Kings viii. 59, 60.—"That he maintain the cause of his servant, and the cause of his people Israel, at all times, as the matter shall require, that all the people of the earth may know that the Lord is God, and that there is none else." See other passages to the same purpose referred to in the margin.‡

This is spoken of as the end of the eternal *damnation* of the wicked, and also the eternal *happiness* of the righteous. Rom. ix. 22, 23. "What if God, willing to show his wrath, and make his power known, endured with much long-suffering the vessels of wrath fitted to destruction: and that he might make known the riches of his glory on the vessels of mercy, which he hath afore prepared unto glory?"

This is spoken of, from time to time, as a great end of the *miracles* which God wrought. (See Exod. vii. 17. and viii. 10. and x. 2. Deut. xxix. 5, 6. Ezek. xxiv. 17.) And of the *ordinances* he has established. Exod. xxix. 44, 45, 46. "And I will sanctify also both Aaron and his sons, to minister to me in the priests' office. And I will dwell among the children of Israel, and will be their God. And they shall know that I am the Lord their God," &c. Chap. xxxi. 13. "Verily, my sabbaths shall ye keep; for it is a sign between me and you, throughout your generations; that ye may know that I am the Lord that doth sanctify you." We have again almost the same words, Ezek. xx. 12. and ver. 20.

This was a great end of the redemption out of *Egypt*. Psal. cvi. 8. "Nevertheless he saved them for his name's sake, that *he might make his mighty power to be known*." (See also Exod. vii. 5. and Deut. iv. 34, 35.) And also of the redemption from the Babylonish captivity. Ezek. xx. 34—38. "And I will bring you out from the people, and will gather you out of the countries whither ye are scattered.——And I will bring you into the wilderness of the people; and there I will plead with you, as I pleaded with your fathers in the wilderness of the land of Egypt.—And I will bring you into the bond of the covenant. And I will purge out the rebels.—*And ye shall know that I am the Lord*." Verse 42. "*And ye shall know that I am the Lord*, when I shall bring you into the land of Israel." Verse 44. "*And ye shall know that I am the Lord*, when I have wrought with you *for my name's sake*." (See also chap. xxviii. 25, 26. and xxxvi. 11. and xxxvii. 6. 13.)

This is also declared to be a great end of the work of *redemption by Jesus Christ*: both of its *purchase*, and its application. Rom. iii. 25, 26. "Whom God hath set forth to be a propitiation, through faith in his blood, *to declare his righteousness.—To declare, I say, at this time, his righteousness:* that he might be just, and the justifier of him that believeth in Jesus." Eph. ii. 4—7. "But God, who is rich in mercy, &c. *That he might show the exceeding riches of his grace*, in his kindness towards us through Jesus Christ." Chap. iii. 8, 9, 10. "To preach among the Gentiles the unsearchable riches of Christ, and to make all men see, what is the fellowship of that mystery which, from the beginning of the world, hath been hid in God, who created all things by Jesus Christ: *To the intent that now unto the principalities and powers* in heavenly places, might *be known by the church the manifold wisdom of God*." Psal. xxii. 21, 22. "Save me from the lion's mouth. *I will declare thy name unto my brethren;* in the midst of the congregation will I praise thee." (Compared with Heb. ii. 12. and John xvii. 26.) Isa. lxiv. 4. "O that thou wouldest rend the heavens—*to make thy name known to thine adversaries*."

And it is pronounced to be the end of that great, *actual salvation*, which should follow Christ's purchase of salvation, both among Jews and Gentiles. Isa. xlix. 22, 23. "I will lift up my hand to the Gentiles,—and they shall bring thy sons in their arms—and kings shall be thy nursing-fathers—*and thou shalt know that I am the Lord*." §

This appears to be the end of God's *common providence*, Job xxxvii. 6, 7. "For he saith to the snow, Be thou on the earth. Likewise to the small rain, and to the great rain of his strength. He sealeth up the hand of every man, that all men may know his work." And of the *day of judgment*, that grand consummation of God's moral government of the world, and the day for bringing all things to their designed ultimate issue. It is called, "The day of the revelation of the righteous judgment of God." Rom. ii. 5.

And the *declaration*, or openly manifesting of God's excellency, is spoken of as the actual, happy consequence and effect of the work of creation. Psal. xix. 1, &c. "The heavens declare the glory of God, and the firmament showeth his handy-work. Day unto day uttereth speech, night unto night showeth knowledge.—In them hath he placed a tabernacle for the sun, which is as a bridegroom coming out of his chamber, and rejoiceth as a strong man to run his race," &c.

3. In like manner, there are many scriptures that speak of God's PRAISE, in many of the forementioned respects, just in the same manner as of his *name* and *glory*.

This is spoken of as the end of the very *being* of God's

* See also, Psal. ix. 1, 11, 14, and xix. 1. and xxvi. 7. and lxxi. 18. and lxxv. 9. and lxxvi. 1. and lxxix. 13. and xcvi. 2, 3. and ci. 1. and cvii. 22. and cxviii. 17. and cxlv. 6, 11, 12. Isa. xlii. 12. and lxiv. 1, 2. Jer. li. 10.

† Exod. xiv. 17, 18. 1 Sam. xvii. 46. Psal. lxxxiii. 18. Isa. xlv. 3. Ezek. vi. 7, 10, 13, 14. and vii. 4, 9, 27. and xi. 10, 11, 12. and xii. 15, 16, 20. and xiii. 9, 14, 21, 23. and xiv. 8. and xv. 7. and xxi. 5. and xxii. 16. and xxv. 7, 11, 17. and xxvi. 6. and xxviii. 22, 23, 24. and xxix. 9, 16. and xxx. 8, 19, 25, 26. and xxxii. 15. and xxxiii. 29. and xxxv. 4, 12, 15. and xxxviii. 23. and xxxix. 6, 7, 21, 22.

‡ Exod. vi. 7. and viii. 22. and xvi. 12. 1 Kings viii. 43. and xx. 28. Psal cii. 21. Ezek. xxiii. 49. and xxiv. 21. and xxv. 5. and xxxv. 9. and xxxix. 21, 22.

§ See also, Ezek. xvi. 62. and xxix. 21. and xxxiv. 27. and xxxvi. 38. and xxxix. 28, 29. Joel iii. 17.

people, in the same manner as before, Jer. xiii. 11. "For as the girdle cleaveth to the loins of a man, so have I caused to cleave unto me the whole house of Israel, and the whole house of Judah, saith the Lord: that they might be unto me for a name, *and for a praise*, and a glory."

It is spoken of as the end of the *moral world*. Matt. xxi. 16. "Out of the mouth of babes and sucklings *hast thou perfected praise*." That is, so hast thou in thy sovereignty and wisdom ordered it, that thou shouldest obtain the *great end* for which intelligent creatures are made, more especially from some of them that are in themselves weak, inferior, and more insufficient. (Compare Psal. viii. 1, 2.)

And the same thing that was observed before concerning the making known God's excellency, may also be observed concerning *God's praise*. That it is made use of as an argument in deprecating a state of destruction; that, in such a state, this end cannot be answered, in such a manner as seems to imply its being an ultimate end, for which God had made man. Psal. lxxxviii. 10. "Shall the dead arise and *praise thee?* Shall thy loving-kindness be declared in the grave?—Shall thy wonders be known in the dark?" Psal. xxx. 9. "What profit is there in my blood? When I go down to the pit, *shall the dust praise thee?* Shall it declare thy truth? Psal. cxv. 17, 18. "The dead *praise not the Lord*, neither any that go down into silence: but we will *bless the Lord*, from this time forth and for evermore. *Praise ye the Lord*." Isa. xxxviii. 18, 19. "For the grave *cannot praise thee*, death cannot celebrate thee; they that go down into the pit cannot hope for thy truth. The living, the living, *he shall praise thee*." And God's praise is spoken of as the end of the *virtue* of God's people, in like manner as his glory. Phil. i. 11. "Being filled with the fruits of righteousness, which are by Jesus Christ *to the praise and glory of God*."

God's praise is the end of the *work of redemption*. In Eph. i. where that work in its various parts is particularly insisted on, and set forth in its exceeding glory, this is mentioned, from time to time, as the great end of all, that it should be "*to the praise of his glory*." As in ver. 6, 12, 14. By which we may doubtless understand much the same thing with what in Phil. i. 11. is expressed, "*his praise and glory*." Agreeably to this, Jacob's fourth son, from whom the great Redeemer was to proceed, by the special direction of God's providence, was called Praise. This happy consequence, and glorious end of that great redemption, Messiah, one of his posterity, was to work out.

In the Old Testament this praise is spoken of as the end of the forgiveness of God's people, and their salvation, in the same manner as God's name and glory. Isa. xlviii. 9, 10, 11. "For my name's sake will I defer mine anger, and for my *praise* will I refrain for thee, that I cut thee not off. Behold I have refined thee—for mine own sake, even for mine own sake will I do it; for how should my name be polluted? and my glory will I not give to another." Jer. xxxiii. 8, 9. "And I will cleanse them from all their iniquity—and I will pardon all their iniquities. And it shall be to me a name of joy, a *praise* and an honour."

And that the *holy* part of the moral world express desires of this, and delight in it, as the end which holy principles in them tend to, reach after, and rest in, in their highest exercises—just in the same manner as the glory of God, is abundantly manifest. It would be endless to enumerate particular places wherein this appears; wherein the saints declare this, by expressing their earnest desires of God's praise; calling on all nations, and all beings in heaven and earth, to praise him; in a rapturous manner calling on one another, crying "Hallelujah; praise ye the Lord, praise him for ever." Expressing their resolutions to praise him as long as they live through all generations, and for ever; declaring how good, how pleasant and comely the *praise* of God is, &c. And it is manifest, that God's *praise* is the desirable and glorious consequence and effect of all the works of creation, by such places as these. Psal. cxlv. 5—10. and cxlviii. throughout, and ciii. 19—22.

SECT. V.

Places of Scripture from whence it may be argued, that communication of good to the creature, was one thing which God had in view, as an ultimate end of the creation of the world.

1. According to the Scripture, *communicating good* to the creatures is what is *in itself* pleasing to God. And this is not merely subordinately agreeable, and esteemed valuable on account of its *relation* to a further end, as it is in executing justice in punishing the sins of men; but what God is inclined to on its own account, and what he delights in simply and ultimately. For though God is sometimes in Scripture spoken of as taking pleasure in punishing men's sins, Deut. xxviii. 63. "The Lord will rejoice over you, to destroy you." Ezek. v. 13. "Then shall mine anger be accomplished, and I will cause my fury to rest upon them, and I will be comforted." Yet God is often spoken of as exercising goodness and showing mercy, with delight, in a manner quite different, and opposite to that of his executing wrath. For the latter is spoken of as what God proceeds to with backwardness and reluctance; the misery of the creature being not agreeable to him *on its own account*. Neh. ix. 17. "Thou art a God ready to pardon, gracious and merciful, slow to anger, and of great kindness." Psal. ciii. 8. "The Lord is merciful and gracious, slow to anger, and plenteous in mercy." Psal. cxlv. 8. "The Lord is gracious and full of compassion, slow to anger, and of great mercy." We have again almost the same words, Jonah iv. 2. Mic. vii. 18. "Who is a God like unto thee, that pardoneth iniquity, &c.—He retaineth not his anger for ever, because he delighteth in mercy." Ezek. xviii. 32. "I have no pleasure in the death of him that dieth, saith the Lord God; wherefore turn yourselves, and live ye." Lam. iii. 33. "He doth not afflict willingly, nor grieve the children of men." Ezek. xxxiii. 11. "As I live, saith the Lord God, I have no pleasure in the death of the wicked, but that the wicked turn from his way and live: turn ye, turn ye from your evil ways; for why will ye die, O house of Israel!" 2 Pet. iii. 9. "Not willing that any should perish, but that all should come to repentance."

2. The work of *redemption* wrought out by Jesus Christ, is spoken of in such a manner as, being from the grace and love of God to men, does not well consist with his seeking a communication of good to them, *only subordinately*. Such expressions as that in John iii. 16. carry another idea. "God so loved the world, that he gave his only-begotten Son, that whosoever believeth in him, should not perish, but have everlasting life." And 1 John iv. 9, 10. "In this was manifested the love of God towards us, because that God sent his only-begotten Son into the world, that we might live through him. Herein is love; not that we loved God, but that he loved us, and sent his Son to be the propitiation for our sins." So Eph. ii. 4. "But God who is rich in mercy, for his great love wherewith he loved us," &c. But if, indeed this was only from a regard to a *further* end, entirely diverse from our good; then all the love is truly terminated in that, its ultimate object, and *therein* is his love manifested, strictly and properly speaking, and not in that he *loved* us, or exercised such high regard towards us. For if our good be not at all regarded ultimately, but only subordinately, then our good or interest is, in itself considered, *nothing* in God's regard.

The Scripture every where represents it, as though the great things Christ did and suffered, were in the most *direct* and proper sense from exceeding *love to us*. Thus the apostle Paul represents the matter, Gal. ii. 20. "Who loved me, and gave himself for me." Eph. v. 25. "Husbands, love your wives, even as Christ loved the church, and gave himself for it." And Christ himself, John xvii. 19. "For their sakes I sanctify myself." And the scripture represents Christ as resting in the salvation and glory of his people, when obtained as in what he *ultimately* sought, as having therein reached the goal, obtained the prize he aimed at, enjoying the travail of his soul in which he is satisfied, as the recompence of his labours and extreme agonies, Isa. liii. 10, 11. "When thou shalt make his soul an offering for sin, he shall see his seed, he shall prolong his days, and the pleasure of the Lord shall prosper in his hand. He shall see of the travail of his soul, and shall be satisfied; by his knowledge shall my righteous servant justify many, for he shall bear their iniquities." He sees the travail of his soul, in seeing his seed, the children brought forth as the result of his travail. This implies, that Christ has his delight, most truly and properly, in obtaining the salvation of his church, not merely as a means, but as what he rejoices and is satisfied in, *most directly* and properly. This is proved by those scriptures which represent him as rejoicing in his obtaining this fruit of his labour and purchase, as the bridegroom, when he obtains his bride, Isa. lxii. 5. "As the bridegroom rejoices over the bride, so shall thy God rejoice over thee." And how emphatical and strong to the purpose, are the expressions in Zeph. iii. 17. "The Lord thy God in the midst of thee is mighty; he will save, he will rejoice over thee with joy; he will rest in his love, he will rejoice over thee with singing." The same thing may be argued from Prov. viii. 30, 31. "Then was I by him, as one brought up with him: and I was daily his delight, rejoicing always before him: rejoicing in the habitable part of his earth, and my delights were with the sons of men." And from those places, that speak of the saints as God's portion, his jewels and peculiar treasure, these things are abundantly confirmed, John xii. 23—32. But the particular consideration of what may be observed to the present purpose, in that passage of Scripture, may be referred to the next section.

3. The communications of divine goodness, particularly forgiveness of sin, and salvation, are spoken of, from time to time, as being for God's *goodness'* sake, and for his *mercies'* sake, just in the same manner as they are spoken of as being for God's *name's* sake, in the places observed before. Psal. xxv. 7. "Remember not the sins of my youth, nor my transgressions: according to thy mercy remember thou me, *for thy goodness' sake*, O Lord." In the 11th verse, the psalmist says, "For thy name's sake, O Lord, pardon mine iniquity." Neh. ix. 31. "Nevertheless, *for thy great mercies' sake*, thou hast not utterly consumed them, nor forsaken them; for thou art a gracious and a merciful God." Psal. vi. 4. "Return, O Lord, deliver my soul: O save me *for thy mercies' sake*." Psal. xxxi. 16. "Make thy face to shine upon thy servant: save me *for thy mercies' sake*." Psal. xliv. 26. "Arise for our help; redeem us *for thy mercies' sake*." And here it may be observed, after what a remarkable manner God speaks of his love to the children of Israel in the wilderness, as though his love were for love's sake, and his goodness were its own end and motive. Deut. vii. 7, 8. "The Lord did not set his love upon you, nor choose you, because ye were more in number than any people, for ye were the fewest of all people: *but because the Lord loved you*."

4. That the government of the world in all its parts, is *for the good* of such as are to be the eternal subjects of God's goodness, is *implied* in what the Scripture teaches us of Christ being set at God's right hand, made king of angels and men; set at the head of the universe, having all power given him in heaven and earth, *to that end* that he may promote their *happiness;* being made head over all things to the church, and having the government of the whole creation for their good.* Christ mentions it, Mark ii. 28. as the *reason* why the Son of man is made Lord of the sabbath, because "the sabbath was made for man." And if so, we may in like manner argue, that *all things* were made for man, because the Son of man is made *Lord of all things.*

5. That God uses the whole creation, in his government of it, for the good of his people, is most elegantly represented in Deut. xxxiii. 26. "There is none like unto the God of Jeshurun, who rideth upon the heaven." The whole universe is a machine, or chariot, which God hath made for his own use, as is represented in Ezekiel's vision. God's seat is heaven, where he sits and governs, Ezek. i. 22, 26—28. The inferior part of the creation, this visible universe, subject to such continual changes and revolutions, are the wheels of the chariot. God's providence, in the constant revolutions, alterations, and successive events, is represented by the motion of the wheels of the chariot, by the spirit of him who sits on his throne on the heavens, or above the firmament. Moses tells us for whose sake it is, that God moves the wheels of this chariot, or rides in it, sitting in his heavenly seat; and to what end he is making his progress, or goes his appointed journey in it, *viz. the salvation of his people.*

6. God's *judgments* on the wicked in this world, and also their eternal damnation in the world to come, are spoken of, as being for the *happiness of God's people.* So are his judgments on them in this world. Isa. xliii. 3, 4. "For I am the Lord thy God, the Holy One of Israel, thy Saviour. I gave Egypt for thy ransom, Ethiopia and Seba for thee. Since thou hast been precious in my sight, thou hast been honourable, and I have loved thee; therefore will I give men for thee, and people for thy life." So the works of God's vindictive justice and wrath are spoken of as works of mercy to his people, Psal. cxxxvi. 10, 15, 17—20. And so is their eternal damnation in another world. Rom. ix. 22, 23. "What if God, willing to show his wrath and make his power known, endured with much long-suffering the vessels of wrath fitted to destruction: and that he might make known the riches of his glory on the vessels of mercy, which he had afore prepared unto glory." Here it is evident the last verse comes in, in connexion with the foregoing, as giving *another* reason of the destruction of the wicked, *viz. showing the riches of his glory on the vessels of mercy: higher degrees* of their glory and happiness, in a relish of their own enjoyments, and a greater sense of their value, and of God's free grace in bestowing them.

7. It seems to argue, that God's goodness to them who are to be the eternal subjects of his goodness, is the end of the creation; since the whole creation, in all its parts, is spoken of as THEIRS. 1 Cor. iii. 22, 23. "*All things are yours*, whether Paul, or Apollos, or Cephas, or the world, or life, or death, or things present, or things to come, *all are yours*." The terms are very universal; and both works of creation and providence are mentioned; and it is manifestly the design of the apostle to be understood of every work of God whatsoever. Now, how can we understand this any otherwise, than that all things are for their benefit; and that God made and uses all for their good?

8. All God's works, both of creation and providence, are represented as works of *goodness* or *mercy* to his people; as in the 136th psalm. His wonderful works *in general.* Ver. 4. "To him who alone doth great wonders; for his mercy endureth for ever." The works of *creation* in all its parts. Ver. 5—9. "To him that by wisdom made the heavens; for his mercy endureth for ever. To him that stretched out the earth above the waters; for his mercy endureth for ever. To him that made great lights; for his mercy endureth for ever. The sun to rule by day; for his mercy endureth for ever. The moon and stars to rule by night; for his mercy endureth for ever." And God's works of *providence*, in the following part of the psalm.

9. That expression in the blessed sentence pronounced on the righteous at the day of judgment, "Inherit the kingdom *prepared for you* from the foundation of the world," seems to hold forth thus much, that the fruits of God's goodness to them, was his end in creating the world, and in his providential disposals: that God in all his works, in laying the foundation of the world, and ever since the foundation of it, had been preparing this kingdom and glory for them.

10. Agreeable to this, the *good of men* is spoken of as an ultimate end of the *virtue of the moral world.* Rom. xiii. 8, 9, 10. "He that loveth another hath fulfilled the law. For this, Thou shalt not commit adultery, Thou shalt not kill, &c.—And if there be any other commandment, it is briefly comprehended in this saying, Thou shalt love thy neighbour as thyself. *Love worketh no ill to his neighbour; therefore love is the fulfilling of the law.*" Gal. v. 14. "All the law is fulfilled in one word, even in this, *Thou shalt love thy neighbour as thyself.*" Jam. ii. 8. "If ye fulfil the royal law, according to the scripture,

* Eph. i. 20—23. John xvii. 2. Matt. xi. 27. and xxviii. 18, 19. John iii. 35.

Thou shalt love thy neighbour as thyself, thou shalt do well."

If the *good of the creature* be one end of God in all he does; and in all he requires moral agents to do; an end by which they should regulate all their conduct; these things may be easily explained: but otherwise, it seems difficult to be accounted for, that the Holy Ghost should thus express himself. The Scripture represents it to be the spirit of all true saints, to prefer the welfare of God's people to their chief joy. This was the spirit of Moses and the *prophets* of old: the good of God's church was an end by which they regulated all their conduct. And so it was with the *apostles.* 2 Cor.iv. 15. "For all things are *for your sakes.*" 2 Tim. ii. 10. "I endured all things *for the elect's sake,* that they may also obtain the salvation which is in Christ Jesus, with eternal glory." And the Scriptures represent it, as though every Christian should, in all he does, be employed for the good of the church, as each particular member is employed for the good of the body; Rom. xii. 4, 5, &c. Eph. iv. 15, 16. 1 Cor. xii. 12, 25, &c. To this end, the Scripture teaches us, the angels are continually employed, Heb. i. 14.

SECT. VI.

Wherein is considered what is meant by the glory of God and the name of God in Scripture, when spoken of as God's end in his works.

HAVING thus considered, what are spoken of in the Holy Scriptures, as the *ends* which God had *ultimately* in view in the creation of the world, I now proceed particularly to inquire what they are, and how the terms are to be understood?

I. Let us begin with the phrase, the GLORY OF GOD—And here I might observe, that it is sometimes used to signify the second person in the Trinity; but it is not necessary, at this time, to prove it from particular passages of Scripture. Omitting this, I proceed to observe some things concerning the Hebrew word (כבוד) which is most commonly used in the Old Testament, where we have the word *glory* in the English Bible. The root it comes from, is either the verb, (כבד) which signifies *to be heavy,* or make heavy, or from the adjective (כבד) which signifies *heavy* or weighty. These, as seems pretty manifest, are the primary signification of these words, though they have also other meanings, which seem to be derivative. The noun (כובד) signifies *gravity,* heaviness, *greatness,* and abundance. Of very many places it will be sufficient to specify a few. Prov. xxvii. 3. 2 Sam. xiv. 26. 1 Kings xii. 11. Psal. xxxviii. 4. Isa. xxx. 27. And as the weight of bodies arises from two things, *density* and *magnitude;* so we find the word used to signify *dense,* Exod. xix. 16. (ענן כבד *nubes gravis,* Vulg. *densissima,*) *a dense cloud;* and is very often used for *great.* Isa. xxxii. 2. Gen. v. 9. 1 Kings x. 2. 2 Kings vi. 14. and xviii. 17. Isa. xxxvi. 2. &c.

The Hebrew word (כבוד) which is commonly translated *glory,* is used in such a manner as might be expected from this signification of the words from whence it comes. Sometimes it is used to signify what is *internal, inherent,* or in the *possession* of the person: and sometimes for *emanation, exhibition,* or *communication* of this internal glory: and sometimes for the *knowledge,* or *sense* of these, in those to whom the exhibition or communication is made; or an *expression* of this knowledge, sense, or effect. And here I would note, that agreeable to the use of this word in the Old Testament, is the Greek word (δοξα) in the New. For as the word (כבוד) is generally translated by the just mentioned Greek word (δοξα) in the Septuagint; so it is apparent, that this word is designed to be used to signify the *same thing* in the New Testament with the other in the Old. This might be abundantly proved, by comparing particular places of the Old Testament; but probably it will not be denied. I therefore proceed particularly to consider these words, with regard to their use in Scripture, in each of the fore-mentioned ways.

1. The word *glory* denotes sometimes what is *internal.* When the word is used to signify what is within, or in the possession of the subject, it very commonly signifies *excellency,* dignity, or worthiness of regard. This, according to the Hebrew *idiom,* is, as it were, the *weight* of a thing, as that by which it is heavy; as to be *light,* is to be worthless, without value, contemptible. Numb. xxi. 5. "This *light* bread." 1 Sam. xviii. 23. "Seemeth it a *light* thing." Judg. ix. 4. "*Light* persons," *i. e.* worthless, vain, vile persons. So Zeph. iii. 4. To set *light* by is to despise, 2 Sam. xix. 43. Belshazzar's vileness in the sight of God, is represented by his being *Tekel,* weighed in the balances and found *light,* Dan. v. 27. And as the weight of a thing arises from its *magnitude,* and its specific *gravity* conjunctly; so the word *glory* is very commonly used to signify the *excellency* of a person or a thing, as consisting either in *greatness,* or in *beauty,* or in both conjunctly; as will abundantly appear by considering the places referred to in the margin.*

Sometimes that internal, great and excellent good, which is called glory, is rather in *possession,* than inherent. Any one may be called *heavy,* that possesses an abundance; and he that is empty and destitute, may be called *light.* Thus we find riches are sometimes called *glory.* Gen. xxxi. 1. "And of that which was our fathers' hath he gotten *all this glory.*" Esth. v. 11. "Haman told them of the *glory of his riches.*" Psal. xlix. 16, 17. "Be not afraid when one is made rich, when the *glory of his house* is increased. For when he dieth, he shall carry nothing away, his *glory* shall not descend after him." Nah. ii. 9. "Take ye the spoil of silver, take the spoil of gold; for there is none end of the store and *glory* out of the pleasant furniture."

And it is often put for a great height of prosperity, and fulness of good in general. Gen. xlv. 13. "You shall tell my father of *all my glory* in Egypt." Job xix. 9. "He hath stripped me of *my glory.*" Isa. x. 3. "Where will you leave your glory." Ver. 16. "Therefore shall the Lord of hosts send among his fat ones leanness, and under his *glory* shall he kindle a burning, like the burning of a fire." Isa. xvii. 3, 4. "The kingdom shall cease from Damascus, and the remnant of Syria; they shall be as the *glory* of the children of Israel. And in that day, it shall come to pass, that the *glory* of Jacob shall be made thin, and the fatness of his flesh shall be made lean." Isa. xxi. 16. "And all the *glory* of Kedar shall fail." Isa. lxi. 6. "Ye shall eat the riches of the Gentiles, and in their *glory* shall ye boast yourselves." Chap. lxvi. 11, 12. "That ye may milk out, and be delighted with the abundance of her *glory.*—I will extend peace to her, like a river, and the glory of the Gentiles like a flowing stream." Hos. ix. 11. "As for Ephraim, their *glory* shall fly away as a bird." Matt. iv. 8. "Showeth him all the kingdoms of the world, and the *glory* of them." Luke xxiv. 26. "Ought not Christ to have suffered these things, and to enter into his *glory?*" John xvii. 22. "And the *glory* which thou gavest me, have I given them." Rom. v. 2. "And rejoice in hope of the *glory* of God." Chap. viii. 18. "The sufferings of this present time, are not worthy to be compared with the *glory* which shall be revealed in us." (See also chap. ii. 7, 10. and iii. 23. and ix. 23.) 1 Cor. ii. 7. "The hidden wisdom which God ordained before the world, unto our *glory.*" 2 Cor. iv. 17. "Worketh out for us a far more exceeding and eternal weight of *glory.*" Eph. i. 18. "And what the riches of the *glory* of his inheritance in the saints." 1 Pet. iv. 13. "But rejoice, inasmuch as ye are made partakers of Christ's sufferings; that when his *glory* shall be revealed, ye may be glad also with exceeding joy." Chap. i. 8. "Ye rejoice, with joy unspeakable and full of *glory.*"†

2. The word *glory* is used in Scripture often to express the *exhibition, emanation,* or *communication* of the internal glory. Hence it often signifies an effulgence, or shining brightness, by an emanation of beams of light. Thus the brightness of the sun, and moon, and stars, is called their

* Exod. xvi. 7. and xxviii. 2, 40. and iii. 8. Numb. xvi. 19. Deut. v. 24. and xxviii. 58. 2 Sam. 6, 20. 1 Chron. xvi. 24. Esth. i. 4. Job xxix. 20. Psal. xix. 1. and xlv. 13. and lxiii. 3. and lxvi. 3. and lxvii. 6. and lxxxvii. 3. and cii. 16. and cxlv. 5, 12, 13. Isa. iv. 2. and x. 18. and xvi. 40. and xxxv. 21. and xl. 5. and lx. 13. and lxii. 2. Ezek. xxxi. 18. Hab. ii. 14. Hag. ii. 3, 9. Matt. vi. 29. and xvi. 27. and xxiv. 30. Luke ix. 31, 32. John i. 14. and ii. 11. and xi. 40. Rom. vi. 4. 1 Cor. ii. 8. and xv. 40. 2 Cor. iii. 10. Eph. iii. 21. Col. i. 11. 2 Thess. i. 9. Tit. ii. 13. 1 Pet. i. 24. 2 Pet. i. 17.

† See also, Colos. i. 27. and iii. 4. 1 Thess. ii. 12. 2 Thess. ii. 14. 1 Tim. iii. 16. 2 Tim. ii. 10. Heb. ii. 10. 1 Pet. i. 11, 21. and v. 10. 2 Pet. i. 3. Rev xxi. 24, 26. Psal. lxxiii. 24. and cxlix. 5. Isa. vi. 10.

glory, in 1 Cor. xv. 41. But in particular, the word is very often thus used, when applied to God and Christ. As in Ezek. i. 28. "As the appearance of the bow that is in the cloud in the day of rain, so was the appearance of the brightness round about. This was the appearance of the likeness of the *glory* of the Lord." And chap. x. 4. "Then the *glory* of the Lord went up from the cherub, and stood over the threshold of the house, and the house was filled with the cloud, and the court was full of the brightness of the Lord's *glory*." Isa. vi. 1, 2, 3. "I saw the Lord sitting upon a throne, high and lifted up, and his train filled the temple. Above it stood the seraphim—And one cried to another and said, Holy, holy, holy is the Lord of hosts, the whole earth is full of his *glory*." Compared with John xii. 41. "These things said Esaias, when he saw his *glory* and spake of him." Ezek. xliii. 2. "And behold the *glory* of the God of Israel came from the way of the east.——And the earth *shined* with his *glory*." Isa. xxiv. 23. "Then the moon shall be confounded, and the sun ashamed, when the Lord of hosts shall reign in mount Zion, and in Jerusalem, and before his ancients *gloriously*." Isa. lx. 1, 2. "Arise, shine, for thy light is come, and the *glory* of the Lord is risen upon thee. For behold the darkness shall cover the earth, and gross darkness the people; but the Lord shall arise upon thee, and his *glory* shall be seen upon thee." Together with verse 19. "The sun shall be no more thy light by day, neither for brightness shall the moon give light unto thee: but the Lord shall be unto thee an everlasting light, and thy God thy *glory*." Luke ii. 9. "The *glory* of the Lord shone round about them." Acts xxii. 11. "And when I could not see for the glory of that *light*." In 2 Cor. iii. 7. The shining of Moses's face is called *the glory of his countenance*. And to this Christ's glory is compared, verse 18. "But we all with open face, beholding as in a glass the *glory* of the Lord, are changed into the same image, *from glory to glory*." And so chap. iv. 4. "Lest the light of the *glorious* gospel of Christ, who is the image of God, should shine unto them." Ver. 6. "For God, who commanded the light to shine out of darkness, hath shined in our hearts, to give the light of the knowledge of the *glory* of God in the face of Jesus Christ." Heb. i. 3. "Who is the *brightness* of his *glory*." The apostle Peter, speaking of that emanation of exceeding brightness, from the bright cloud that overshadowed the disciples in the mount of transfiguration, and of the shining of Christ's face at that time, says, 2 Pet. i. 17. "For he received from God the Father honour and *glory*, when there came such a voice to him from the *excellent glory*, This is my beloved Son, in whom I am well pleased." Rev. xviii. 1. "Another angel came down from heaven, having great power, *and the earth was lightened with his glory*." Rev. xxi. 11. "Having the *glory* of God, and her *light* was like unto a stone most precious, like a jasper stone, clear as crystal." Ver. 23. "And the city had no need of the sun nor of the moon to shine in it; for the *glory* of God did lighten it." See the word for a *visible effulgence* or emanation of light in the places to be seen in the margin.*

The word *glory*, as applied to God or Christ, sometimes evidently signifies the *communications* of God's *fulness*, and means much the same thing with God's abundant goodness and grace. So Eph. iii. 16. "That he would grant you, *according to the riches of his glory*, to be strengthened with might by his Spirit in the inner man." The expression, "According to the riches of his glory," is apparently equivalent to that in the same epistle, chap. i. 7. "According to the riches of his grace." And chap. ii. 7. "The exceeding riches of his grace in his kindness towards us, through Christ Jesus." In like manner is the word *glory* used in Phil. iv. 19. "But my God shall supply all your need, according to his *riches in glory*, by Christ Jesus." And Rom. ix. 23. "And that he might make known the *riches of his glory*, on the vessels of his mercy." In this and the foregoing verse, the apostle speaks of God's making known two things, his *great wrath*, and his *rich grace*. The former on the vessels of wrath, ver. 22. The latter, which he calls *the riches of his glory*, on the vessels of mercy, ver. 23. So when Moses says, "I beseech thee show me thy *glory*;" God granting his request, makes answer, "I will make all my *goodness* to pass before thee." Exod. xxxiii. 18, 19.†

What we find in John xii. 23—32. is worthy of particular notice in this place. The words and behaviour of Christ, of which we have here an account, argue two things.

(1.) That the happiness and salvation of men, was an end that Christ ultimately aimed at in his labours and sufferings. The very same things which were observed before, (chapter second, section third,) concerning God's *glory*, are in the same manner observable, concerning the salvation of men. Christ, in the near approach of the most extreme difficulties which attended his undertaking, comforts himself in a certain prospect of obtaining the *glory of God*, as his great end. And at the same time, and exactly in the same manner, is the *salvation of men* mentioned, as the end of these great labours and sufferings, which satisfied his soul in the prospect of undergoing them. (Compare the 23rd and 24th verses; and also the 28th and 29th verses; ver. 31 and 32.)

(2.) The glory of God, and the emanations and fruits of his grace in man's salvation, are so spoken of by Christ on this occasion in just the same manner, that it would be quite unnatural to understand him as speaking of two distinct things. Such is the connexion, that what he says of the latter, must most naturally be understood as exegetical of the former. He first speaks of his *own glory*, and the *glory of his Father*, as the great end that should be obtained by what he was about to suffer; and then explains and amplifies this, in what he expresses of the *salvation of men* that shall be obtained by it. Thus, in the 23d verse, he says, "The hour is come that the Son of man should be glorified." And in what next follows, he evidently shows how he was to be glorified, or wherein his glory consisted: "Verily, verily, I say unto you, except a corn of wheat fall into the ground, and die, it abideth alone; but if it die, it bringeth forth much fruit." As *much fruit* is the *glory* of the seed, so is the multitude of redeemed ones, which should spring from his death, his glory.‡ So concerning the glory of his Father, in the 27th and following verses. "Now is my soul troubled, and what shall I say? Father, save me from this hour! But for this cause came I unto this hour. Father, *glorify thy name*. Then came there a voice from heaven, saying, *I have both glorified it*, and *will glorify it again*." In an assurance of this, which this voice declared, Christ was *greatly comforted*; and his soul even *exulted* under the view of his approaching sufferings. And what this glory was, in which Christ's soul was so comforted on this occasion, his own words plainly show. When the people said, it thundered; and others said, an angel spake to him; then Christ tells them what this voice meant. Ver. 30—32. "Jesus answered and said, This voice came not because of me, but for your sakes. Now is the judgment of this world; now shall the prince of this world be cast out. And I, if I be lifted up from the earth, will draw all men unto me." By this behaviour and these speeches of our Redeemer, it appears, that the expressions of *divine grace*, in the sanctification and happiness of the redeemed, are especially that *glory* of his, and his Father, which was the *joy that was set before him*, for which he endured the cross, and despised the shame: and that this glory especially was the end of the travail of his soul, in obtaining which end he was satisfied. (Isa. liii. 10, 11.)

This is agreeable to what has been just observed, of God's glory being so often represented by an effulgence, or emanation, or communication of light, from a luminary or fountain of light. What can so naturally and aptly repre-

* Exod. xvi. 12. and xxiv. 16, 17, 23. and xl. 34, 35. Lev. ix. 6. 23. Num. xiv. 10. and xvi. 19. 1 Kings viii. 11. 2 Chron. v. 14. and vii. 1, 2, 3. Isa. lviii. 8. Ezek. iii. 23. and viii. 4. and ix. 3. and x. 18, 19. and xi. 22, 23. and xliii. 4, 5. and xliv. 4. Acts vii. 55. Rev. xv. 8.

† Dr. Goodwin observes, (Vol. I. of his works, part 2d, page 166.) that riches of grace are called *riches of glory* in Scripture. "The Scripture," says he, "speaks of riches of glory in Eph. iii. 6. *That he would grant you according to the riches of his glory*; yet eminently *mercy* is there intended: for it is that which God bestows, and which the apostle there prayeth for. And he calls his *mercy* there his *glory*, as elsewhere he doth, as being the most eminent excellency in God.—That in Rom. ix. 22, 23. compared, is observable. In the 22d verse, where the apostle speaks of God's making known the power of his wrath, saith he, *God willing to show his wrath, and make his power known*. But in verse 3d, when he comes to speak of mercy, he saith, *That he might make known the riches of his glory on the vessels of mercy*."

‡ Here may be remembered what was before observed of the church being so often spoken of as the glory and fulness of Christ.

sent the emanation of the internal glory of God; or the flowing forth and abundant communication of that infinite fulness of good that is in God? Light is very often in Scripture put for comfort, joy, happiness, and for good in general.*

3. Again, the word *glory*, as applied to God in Scripture, implies the *view* or *knowledge* of God's excellency. The exhibition of glory is to the *view* of beholders. The manifestation of glory, the emanation or effulgence of brightness, has relation to the *eye*. Light or brightness is a quality that has relation to the *sense* of seeing; we see the luminary by its light. And *knowledge* is often expressed in Scripture by light. The word *glory* very often in Scripture signifies, or implies, *honour*, as any one may soon see by casting his eye on a concordance.† But *honour* implies the *knowledge* of the dignity and excellency of him who hath the honour; and this is often more especially signified by the word *glory*, when applied to God. Num. xiv. 21. "But as truly as I live, all the earth shall be filled with the *glory* of the Lord," *i. e.* All the inhabitants of the earth shall *see* the manifestations I will make of my perfect holiness and hatred of sin, and so of my infinite excellence. This appears by the context. So Ezek. xxxix. 21, 22, 23. "And I will set my glory among the heathen, and all the heathen *shall see* my judgment that I have executed, and my hand that I have laid upon them. So the house of Israel *shall know* that I am the Lord their God. And the heathen *shall know* that the house of Israel went into captivity for their iniquity." And it is manifest in many places, where we read of God glorifying himself, or of his being glorified, that one thing, directly intended, is *making known* his divine greatness and excellency.

4. Again, *glory*, as the word is used in Scripture, often signifies or implies *praise*. This appears from what was observed before, that glory very often signifies *honour*, which is much the same thing with praise, *viz.* high esteem and the expression of it in words and actions. And it is manifest that the words *glory* and *praise*, are often used as equivalent expressions in Scripture. Psal. l. 23. "Whoso offereth *praise*, *glorifieth* me." Psal. xxii. 23. "Ye that fear the Lord, *praise* him; all ye seed of Israel, *glorify* him." Isa. xlii. 8. "My *glory* I will not give unto another, nor my *praise* to graven images." Ver. 12. "Let them give *glory* unto the *Lord*, and declare his *praise* in the islands." Isa. xlviii. 9—11. "For my *name's* sake will I defer mine anger; for my *praise* will I refrain for thee.—For mine *own sake* will I do it; for——I will not give my *glory* unto another." Jer. xiii. 11. "That they might be unto me for a people, and for a *name*, and for a *praise*, and for a *glory*." Eph. i. 6. "To the *praise* of the *glory* of his grace." Ver. 12. "To the *praise* of his *glory*." So ver. 14. The phrase is apparently equivalent to this, Phil. i. 11. "Which are by Jesus Christ unto the *praise* and *glory* of God." 2 Cor. iv. 15. "That the abundant grace might, through the *thanksgiving* of many, redound to the *glory of God*."

It is manifest the *praise of God*, as the phrase is used in Scripture, implies the high *esteem* and love of the heart, exalting thoughts of God, and complacence in his excellence and perfection. This is manifest to every one acquainted with the Scripture. However, if any need satisfaction, they may, among innumerable other places which might be mentioned, turn to those in the margin.‡

It also implies joy in God, or *rejoicing* in his perfections, as is manifest by Psal. xxxiii. 2. "*Rejoice* in the Lord, O ye righteous, for *praise* is comely for the upright." Other passages to the same purpose, see in the margin.§ How often do we read of *singing praise!* But *singing* is commonly an expression of *joy*. It is called, making a *joyful noise*.‖ And as it is often used, it implies *gratitude* or *love* to God for his benefits to us.¶

II. Having thus considered what is implied in the phrase, *the glory of God*, as we find it used in Scripture; I proceed to inquire what is meant by the NAME of God.

God's *name* and his *glory*, at least very often, signify the same thing in Scripture. As it has been observed concerning the glory of God, that it sometimes signifies the second person in the Trinity; the same might be shown of the *name* of God, if it were needful in this place. But that the name and glory of God are often equipollent expressions, is manifest by Exod. xxxiii. 18, 19. When Moses says, "I beseech thee, show me *thy glory*," and God grants his request, he says, "I will proclaim the *name* of the Lord before thee." Psal. viii. 1. "O Lord, how excellent is thy *name* in all the earth! who hast set thy *glory* above the heavens," Psal. lxxix. 9. "Help us! O God of our salvation, for the *glory* of thy *name;* and deliver us, and purge away our sins for thy *name's* sake." Psal. cii. 15. "So the heathen shall fear the *name* of the Lord; and all the kings of the earth thy *glory*." Psal. cxlviii. 13. "His *name* alone is excellent, and his *glory* is above the earth and heaven." Isa. xlviii. 9. "For my *name's* sake will I defer mine anger, and for my *praise* will I refrain for thee." Ver. 11. "For mine own sake, even for mine own sake will I do it: for how should my *name* be polluted? And I will not give my *glory* unto another." Isa. lix. 19. "They shall fear the *name* of the Lord from the west, and his *glory* from the rising of the sun." Jer. xiii. 11. "That they might be unto me for a *name*, and for a *praise*, and for a *glory*." As *glory* often implies the *manifestation, publication*, and *knowledge* of excellency, and the *honour* that any one has in the world; so does *name*. Gen. xi. 4. "Let us make us a *name*." Deut. xxvi. 19. "And to make thee high above all nations, in *praise*, in *name*, and in *honour*." **

So it is evident, that by *name* is sometimes meant much the same thing as *praise*, by several places which have been just mentioned, (as Isa. xlviii. 9. Jer. xiii. 11. Deut. xxvi. 19.) And also by Jer. xxxiii. 9. "And it shall be unto me for a *name*, a *praise*, and an *honour*, before all the nations of the earth, which shall hear of all the good I do unto them." Zeph. iii. 20. "I will make you a *name* and a *praise* among all people of the earth."

And it seems that the expression or exhibition of God's *goodness* is especially called his *name*, in Exod. xxxiii. 19. "I will make all my goodness pass before thee, and I will proclaim the *name* of the Lord before thee." And chap. xxxiv. 5, 6, 7. "And the Lord descended in the cloud, and stood with him there, and proclaimed the *name* of the Lord. And the Lord passed by before him, and proclaimed, The Lord, the Lord God, *gracious and merciful, long-suffering* and abundant in *goodness and truth;* keeping *mercy* for thousands," &c.

And the same illustrious brightness and *effulgence* in the pillar of cloud that appeared in the wilderness, and dwelt above the mercy-seat in the tabernacle and temple, (or rather the spiritual, divine brightness and effulgence *represented* by it,) so often called *the glory of the Lord*, is also often called *the name of the Lord*. Because God's glory was to dwell in the tabernacle, therefore he promises, Exod. xxix. 43. "There will I meet with the children of Israel, and the tabernacle shall be sanctified by my *glory*." And the temple was called *the house of God's glory*, Isa. lx. 7. In like manner, the *name* of God is said to dwell in the sanctuary. Thus we often read of the place that God chose, *to put his name there:* or, as it is in the Hebrew, *to cause his* NAME *to inhabit there*. So it is sometimes rendered by our translators. As Deut. xii. 11. "Then there shall be a place which the Lord your God shall choose *to cause his name to dwell there*." And the temple is often spoken of as built *for God's name*. And in Psal. lxxiv. 7. the temple is called *the dwelling-place of God's name*. The mercy-seat in the temple was called the throne of God's

* Isa. vi. 3.—"Holy, holy, holy is the Lord of hosts, the whole earth is full of his *glory*." In the original, *His glory is the fulness of the whole earth:* which signifies much more than the words of the translation. God's glory, consisting especially in his holiness, is that, in the sight or communications of which man's fulness, *i. e.* his holiness and happiness, consists. By *God's glory* here, there seems to be respect to those effulgent beams that filled the temple: these beams signifying God's glory shining forth and communicated. This effulgence or communication, is the fulness of all intelligent creatures, who have no fulness of their own.

† See particularly, Heb. iii. 3

‡ Psal cxlv. 1.—12. and xxxiv. 1, 2, 3, and xliv. 8. and xxi. 14, 15. and xcix. 2, 3. and cvii. 31, 32. and cviii. 3, 4, 5. and cxix. 164. and cxlviii. 13. and cl. 2. Rev. xix. 1, 2, 3.——

§ Psal. ix. 1, 2, 14. and xxviii. 7. and xxxv. 27, 28. and xlii. 4. and lxiii. 5. and lxvii. 3, 4, 5. and lxxi. 22, 23. and civ. 33, 34. and cvi. 47. and cxxxv. 3. and cxlvii. 1. and cxlix. 1, 2, 5, 6. Acts ii. 46, 47. and iii. 8. Rev. xix. 6, 7.

‖ Psal. lxvi. 1, 2. and xcvi. 4, 5.

¶ Psal. xxx. 12. and xxxv. 18. and lxiii. 3, 4. and lxvi. 8, 9. and lxxi. 6, 7, 8. and lxxxix. 13. and xcviii. 4, 5. and c. 4. and cvii. 21, 22. and cxxxviii. 2. And many other places.

** See also, 2 Sam. vii. 9. and viii. 13. and xxiii. 18. Neh. ix. 10. Job xxx. 8. Prov. xxii. 1. Many other places import the same thing.

name or glory, Jer. xiv. 21. "Do not abhor us, for thy *name's sake* do not disgrace the *throne of thy glory*." Here God's *name* and his *glory* seem to be spoken of as the same.

SECT. VII

Showing that the ultimate end of the creation of the world is but one, and what that one end is.

FROM what has been observed in the last section, it appears, if the whole of what is said relating to this affair be duly weighed, and one part compared with another, we shall have reason to think, that the design of the Spirit of God is not to represent God's ultimate end as *manifold*, but as ONE. For though it be signified by various names, yet they appear not to be names of *different* things, but various names involving each other in their meaning; either different names of the *same thing*, or names of several parts of *one whole*; or of the same whole viewed in *various lights* or in its *different respects* and relations. For it appears, that all that is ever spoken of in the Scripture as an ultimate end of God's works, is included in that one phrase, *the glory of God*; which is the name by which the ultimate end of God's works is most commonly called in Scripture; and seems most aptly to signify the thing.

The thing signified by that name, *the glory of God*, when spoken of as the supreme and ultimate end of all God's works, is the emanation and true external expression of God's internal glory and fulness; meaning by his *fulness* what has already been explained; or, in other words, God's internal glory, in a true and just exhibition, or external existence of it. It is confessed, that there is a degree of obscurity in these definitions; but perhaps an obscurity which is unavoidable, through the imperfection of language to express things of so sublime a nature. And therefore the thing may possibly be better understood, by using a variety of expressions, by a particular consideration of it, as it were, by parts, than by any short definition.

It includes the *exercise* of God's perfections to produce a proper *effect*, in opposition to their lying eternally dormant and ineffectual: as his power being eternally without any act or fruit of that power; his wisdom eternally ineffectual in any wise production, or prudent disposal of any thing, &c. The *manifestation* of his internal glory to created understandings. The *communication* of the infinite fulness of God to the creature. The creature's high *esteem* of God, love to him, and complacence and joy in him; and the proper *exercises* and *expressions* of these.

These at first view may appear to be entirely distinct things: but if we more closely consider the matter, they will all appear to be ONE thing, in a variety of views and relations. They are all but the *emanation of God's glory*; or the excellent brightness and fulness of the divinity *diffused*, *overflowing*, and as it were *enlarged*; or in one word, *existing ad extra*. God *exercising* his perfection to produce a proper *effect*, is not distinct from the emanation or *communication* of his *fulness*: for this is the effect, *viz.* his *fulness communicated*, and the producing of this effect is the communication of his fulness; and there is nothing in this effectual exerting of God's perfection, but the emanation of God's internal glory.

Now God's *internal* glory, is either in his understanding or will. The glory or fulness of his *understanding*, is his knowledge. The internal glory and fulness of God, having its special seat in his *will*, is his holiness and happiness. The *whole* of God's *internal* good or glory, is in these three things, *viz.* his infinite *knowledge*, his infinite virtue or *holiness*, and his infinite joy and *happiness*. Indeed there are a great many attributes in God, according to our way of conceiving them: but all may be reduced to these; or to their degree, circumstances, and relations. We have no conception of God's *power*, different from the degree of these things, with a certain relation of them to effects. God's *infinity* is not properly a distinct *kind* of good, but only expresses the *degree* of good there is in him. So God's *eternity* is not a distinct good; but is the duration of good. His *immutability* is still the same good, with a negation of change. So that, as I said, the *fulness* of the Godhead is the fulness of his *understanding*, consisting in his knowledge; and the fulness of his will consisting in his virtue and happiness.

And therefore, the *external* glory of God consists in the *communication* of these. The communication of his knowledge is chiefly in giving the *knowledge of himself*: for this is the knowledge in which the fulness of God's understanding chiefly consists. And thus we see how the manifestation of God's glory to created understandings, and their seeing and knowing it, is not distinct from an emanation or communication of God's fulness, but clearly implied in it. Again, the communication of God's virtue or holiness, is principally in communicating the *love of himself*. And thus we see how, not only the creature's seeing and knowing God's excellence, but also supremely esteeming and loving him, belongs to the communication of *God's fulness*. And the communication of God's joy and happiness, consists chiefly in communicating to the creature that happiness and joy which consists in *rejoicing in God*, and in his glorious excellency; for in such joy God's own happiness does principally consist. And in these things, *knowing* God's excellency, *loving* God for it, and *rejoicing* in it, and in the *exercise* and *expression* of these, consists God's honour and praise; so that these are clearly implied in that glory of God, which consists in the *emanation* of his internal glory.

And though all these things, which seem to be so various, are signified by that *glory*, which the Scripture speaks of as the ultimate end of all God's works; yet it is manifest there is no greater, and no other variety in it, than in the internal and essential glory of God itself. God's internal glory is partly in his understanding, and partly in his will. And this internal glory, as seated in the will of God, implies both his holiness and his happiness: both are evidently God's glory, according to the use of the phrase. So that as God's external glory is only the emanation of his internal, this variety necessarily follows. And again, it hence appears that here is no other variety or distinction, but what necessarily arises from the distinct faculties of the creature, to which the communication is made, as created in the image of God: even as having these two faculties of understanding and will. God communicates himself to the *understanding* of the creature, in giving him the *knowledge* of his glory; and to the *will* of the creature, in giving him *holiness*, consisting primarily in the love of God: and in giving the creature *happiness*, chiefly consisting in *joy* in God. These are the sum of that emanation of divine fulness called in Scripture, *the glory of God*. The first part of this glory is called *truth*, the latter, *grace*, John i. 14. "We beheld his *glory*, the glory of the only-begotten of the Father, full of *grace* and *truth*."

Thus we see that the great end of God's works, which is so variously expressed in Scripture, is indeed but ONE; and this *one* end is most properly and comprehensively called, THE GLORY OF GOD; by which name it is most commonly called in Scripture; and is fitly compared to an effulgence or emanation of light from a luminary. Light is the external expression, exhibition, and manifestation of the excellency of the luminary, of the sun for instance: It is the abundant, extensive emanation and communication of the fulness of the sun to innumerable beings that partake of it. It is by this that the sun itself is seen, and his glory beheld, and all other things are discovered: it is by a participation of this communication from the sun, that surrounding objects receive all their lustre, beauty, and brightness. It is by this that all nature receives life, comfort, and joy. Light is abundantly used in Scripture to represent and signify these three things, knowledge, holiness, and happiness.*

What has been said may be sufficient to show, how those things, which are spoken of in Scripture as ultimate

* It is used to signify *knowledge*, or that manifestation and evidence by which knowledge is received. Psal. xix. 8. and cxix. 105, 130. Prov. vi. 23. Isa. viii. 20. and ix. 2. and xxix. 18. Dan. v. 11. Eph. v. 13. "But all things that are reproved, are made manifest by the light; for whatsoever doth make manifest, is light," &c.

It is used to signify *virtue*, or moral good Job xxv. 5. Eccl. viii. 1. Isa. v. 20. and xxiv. 23. and lxii. 1. Ezek. xxviii. 7, 17. Dan. ii. 31. 1 John. i. 5, &c.

And it is abundantly used to signify comfort, joy, and *happiness*. Esth. viii. 16. Job xviii. 8. and xxii. 28. and xxix. 3. and xxx. 26. Psal. xxvii. 1. and xcvii. 11. and cxviii. 27. and cxii. 4. Isa. xliii. 16. and l. 10. and lix. 9. Jer. xiii. 16. Lam. iii. Ezek. xxxii. 8. Amos v. 18. Mic. vii. 8, 9, &c.

ends of God's works, though they may seem at first view to be distinct, are all plainly to be reduced to this *one* thing, *viz. God's internal glory or fulness existing in its emanation.* And though God, in seeking this end, seeks the creature's good; yet therein appears his supreme regard to himself.

The emanation or communication of the divine fulness, consisting in the knowledge of God, love to him, and joy in him, has relation indeed both to *God* and the *creature:* but it has relation to God as its *fountain*, as the thing communicated is something of its internal fulness. The water in the stream is something of the fountain; and the beams of the sun are something of the sun. And again, they have relation to God as their *object*: for the knowledge communicated, is the knowledge of God; and the love communicated, is the love of God; and the happiness communicated, is joy in God. In the creature's knowing, esteeming, loving, rejoicing in, and praising God, the glory of God is both *exhibited* and *acknowledged;* his fulness is *received* and *returned.* Here is both an *emanation* and *remanation.* The refulgence shines upon and into the creature, and is reflected back to the luminary. The beams of glory come from God, are something of God, and are refunded back again to their original. So that the whole is *of* God, and *in* God, and *to* God; and he is the beginning, and the middle, and the end.

And though it be true that God has respect to the *creature* in these things; yet his respect to himself, and to the creature, are not properly a double and divided respect. What has been said, (chap. I. sect. 3, 4.) may be sufficient to show this. Nevertheless, it may not be amiss here briefly to say a few things; though mostly implied in what has been said already.

When God was about to create the world, he had respect to that *emanation of his glory*, which is *actually* the consequence of the creation, both with regard to himself and the creature. He had regard to it as an *emanation* from himself, a *communication* of himself, and, as the *thing communicated*, in its nature *returned* to himself, as its final term. And he had regard to it also as the *emanation* was *to* the creature, and as the *thing communicated* was *in* the creature, as its subject.

And God had regard to it in this manner, as he had a supreme regard to himself, and value for his own infinite, internal glory. It was this value for himself that caused him to value and seek that his internal glory should *flow forth* from himself. It was from his value for his glorious perfections of wisdom, righteousness, &c. that he valued the proper *exercise* and effect of these perfections, in wise and righteous acts and effects. It was from his infinite value for his internal glory and fulness, that he valued the *thing itself* communicated, which is something of the same, extant in the creature. Thus, because he infinitely values his own glory, consisting in the knowledge of himself, love to himself, and complacence and joy in himself; he therefore valued the image, communication, or participation of these in the creature. And it is because he values himself, that he delights in the knowledge, and love, and joy of the creature; as being himself the object of this knowledge, love, and complacence. For it is the necessary consequence of true esteem and love, that we value others' esteem of the same object, and dislike the contrary. For the same reason, God approves of others' esteem and love of himself.

Thus it is easy to conceive, how God should seek the good of the creature, consisting in the creature's knowledge and holiness, and even his happiness, from a supreme regard to *himself;* as his happiness arises from that which is an image and participation of God's own beauty; and consists in the creature's exercising a supreme regard to God, and complacence in him; in beholding God's glory, in esteeming and loving it, and rejoicing in it, and in his exercising and testifying love and supreme respect to God: which is the same thing with the creature's exalting God as his chief good, and making him his supreme end.

And though the emanation of God's fulness, intended in the creation, is to the creature as its *object;* and though the creature is the *subject* of the fulness communicated, which is the creature's good; yet it does not necessarily follow, that even in so doing, God did not make *himself* his end. It comes to the same thing. God's respect to the creature's good, and his respect to himself, is not a divided respect; but both are united in one, as the happiness of the creature aimed at is happiness in union with himself. The creature is no further happy with this happiness which God makes his ultimate end, than he becomes one with God. The more happiness the greater union: when the happiness is perfect, the union is perfect. And as the happiness will be increasing to eternity, the union will become more and more strict and perfect; nearer and more like to that between God the Father and the Son; who are so united, that their interest is perfectly one. If the happiness of the creature be considered in the whole of the creature's eternal duration, with all the infinity of its progress, and infinite increase of nearness and union to God; in this view, the creature must be looked upon as united to God in an infinite strictness.

If God has respect to something in the creature, which he views as of everlasting duration, and as rising higher and higher through that infinite duration, and that not with constantly diminishing (but perhaps an increasing) celerity; then he has respect to it, as, in the whole, of infinite height; though there never will be any particular time when it can be said already to have come to such a height.

Let the most perfect union with God be represented by something at an infinite height above us; and the eternally increasing union of the saints with God, by something that is ascending constantly towards that infinite height, moving upwards with a given velocity; and that is to continue thus to move to all eternity. God, who views the whole of this eternally increasing height, views it as an infinite height. And if he has respect to it, and makes it his end, as in the whole of it, he has respect to it as an infinite height, though the time will never come when it can be said it has already arrived at this infinite height.

God aims at that which the motion or progression which he causes, aims at, or tends to. If there be many things supposed to be so made and appointed, that, by a constant eternal motion, they all tend to a certain centre; then it appears that he who made them, and is the cause of their motion, aimed at that centre; that term of their motion, to which they eternally tend, and are eternally, as it were, striving after. And if God be this centre, then God aimed at himself. And herein it appears, that as he is the first author of their being and motion, so he is the last end, the final term, to which is their ultimate tendency and aim.

We may judge of the end that the Creator aimed at, in the being, nature, and tendency he gives the creature, by the mark or term which they constantly aim at in their tendency and eternal progress; though the time will never come, when it can be said it is attained to, in the most absolutely perfect manner.

But if strictness of union to God be viewed as thus infinitely exalted; then the creature must be regarded as nearly and closely united to God. And viewed thus, their interest must be viewed as one with God's interest; and so is not regarded properly with a disjunct and separate, but an undivided respect. And as to any difficulty of reconciling God's not making the creature his ultimate end, with a respect properly distinct from a respect to himself; with his benevolence and free grace, and the creature's obligation to gratitude, the reader must be referred to chap. I. sect. 4. obj. 4. where this objection has been considered and answered at large.

If by reason of the strictness of the union of a man and his family, their interest may be looked upon as one, how much more so is the interest of Christ and his church,—whose first union in heaven is unspeakably more perfect and exalted, than that of an earthly father and his family ——if they be considered with regard to their eternal and increasing union? Doubtless it may justly be esteemed so much one, that it may be sought, not with a distinct and separate, but an undivided respect. It is certain that what God aimed at in the creation of the world, was the good that would be the consequence of the creation, in the whole continuance of the thing created.

It is no solid objection against God aiming at an infinitely perfect union of the creature with himself, that the particular time will never come when it can be said, the union is now infinitely perfect. God aims at satisfying justice in the eternal damnation of sinners; which will be satisfied by their damnation, considered no otherwise than with regard to its eternal duration. But yet there never will come that particular moment, when it can be said, that now justice is satisfied. But if this does not satisfy our modern free-thinkers who do not like the talk about satisfying justice with an infinite punishment; I suppose it will not be denied by any, that God, in glorifying the saints in heaven with eternal felicity, aims to satisfy his infinite grace or benevolence, by the bestowment of a good infinitely valuable, because eternal: and yet there never will come the moment, when it can be said, that *now* this infinitely valuable good has been actually bestowed.*

* Our author has produced, from the purest principles of reason, and the fountain of revealed truth, abundant evidence, that God's *ultimate* and *chief* END in the creation of the universe, in the operations of providence, and in the methods of salvation, is his OWN GLORY. But we do not think it superfluous to add a few observations on this important subject.

1. A clear and comprehensive view of the universe, or what our author calls "the world," will lead us to observe two grand divisions, which may be termed *physical* and *moral*. And though in *both the glory of God* is the *chief end*, yet this end is not attained by the *same means* in the *moral* as in the *physical* department.

2. By the creation and disposal of the *physical* part of the universe, the GLORY of God's *natural perfections*, as of sovereign wisdom, power, and goodness, is chiefly displayed. But by the creation and government of the *moral* part, the GLORY of the *moral perfections* of Deity, that is, of infinite moral rectitude, or equity, and of sovereign benevolence and mercy, is made to appear.

3. God being an infinite sovereign, controlled by no consideration but infinite rectitude, or a regard to the consistency of his own character; and a created universe being capable of two forms, and it should seem, for ought that appears to the contrary, of *two only*, physical and moral; a *full emanation* and display *ad extra* of the *moral perfections* of Deity could not be made without a *moral system* in all its capabilities of relation.

4. The *physical* part of the universe, even including the *physical operations* of intelligent beings, *may* subsist, it is evident, without requiring any other display of GLORY than what is included in sovereign wisdom, power, and goodness; and it is equally plain, that there would be no *opportunity* of manifesting *strict equity*, much less *mercy*, to existent beings, without a *moral* system. Therefore,

5. If strict or absolute equity, and sovereign mercy, be manifested, a moral system was NECESSARY. To exercise strict, unmixed, or absolute equity, whereby is given to its object what is DUE to it, (a capacity for moral agency being supposed,) and yet to preserve that object, that is, a moral agent, from being *liable* to sin, involves a contradiction. For it is the same as to say, a free agent is not free to sin, though fully permitted to follow his own tendencies. And this is the same thing as to say, an accountable creature is not *liable* to fail; in other words, a moral agent is no moral agent, and a moral system is no moral system. Man would be *impeccable*, and the very existence of sin *impossible*.

6. If it be asked, might not the *whole* of the moral part of the universe have been preserved from sin? We reply, undoubtedly it might; IF sovereign benevolence had thought proper to interpose, in order to counteract the exercise of strict, unmixed, and absolute rectitude or equity; but then it must have been at the expense of ETERNALLY CONCEALING the GLORY of this divine perfection,—ABSOLUTE RECTITUDE.

7. To *permit* the creature to sin, and to *exercise absolute equity*, is the same thing; in other words, to *exercise* this glorious perfection, and *not to permit* the creature to sin, are incompatible ideas. IF this perfection be exercised, there is, there can be, no principle belonging to a moral system, which *preserves* it from being *liable* to sin. Nor is there any principle belonging to it independent of sovereign benevolence, which is adequate to preserve that *liability* to sin from actual defection. But to *appeal*, in the way of objection, to the alternative of sovereign benevolence, which alone can *preserve* from sin, is the same as to concede what the proposition asserts.

8. Equity, in *one view* of it, is indeed *compatible* with the exercise of sovereign benevolence towards the same object, and at the same time. To question this, would be to question God's proper sovereignty, and therefore his right of creating and preserving the universe, and of beatifying any creatures he hath made. For neither of these effects could take place but by sovereign benevolence as a cause. But if sovereign benevolence were not *compatible* with justice, or equity, in one view of it, God could not be benevolent without being unjust, which is absurd.

9. Yet equity, in *another view*, stands as a *contrast* to benevolence. *Strict* or *absolute* equity, is that which excludes all sovereign, benevolent influence; and when *moral agents* are its object, (their *being* and natural capacities, or their *moral capabilities*, being *supposed*,) the exercise of absolute equity must *necessarily exclude* benevolent, sovereign influence. Thus among men we find some resemblance of this abstract but momentous truth. In one view, justice and generosity are *compatible*; while one deals justly with another, he may also be additionally generous. But in another view, these are *incompatible*; for *strict, absolute* justice, is the same as justice and *nothing more*, and therefore must *exclude generosity*.

10. Therefore, equity, in the one view, implies the exclusion of *injustice*; and in the other, the exclusion of *undeserved favour*, or sovereign *benevolent influence*. The exercise of rectitude in the former sense, might have been *without* the permission of sin; but not so in the latter sense. If perfect *absolute* rectitude towards a moral system, be made to emanate *ad extra*, to the full developement of the capabilities of such a system, the *permission* of sin is not only *equitable*, but even *metaphysically necessary*. That is, it involves a contradiction to say, that such a divine perfection may be so displayed, or its *glory* made to appear *ad extra*, and yet *not to permit* the existence of moral defect, or, in other words, to *actually hinder* its existence.

11. The very idea of a moral system, in which the *permission* of defect is excluded by *equity*, is one of the most absurd that can be conceived. For it is the same as to say that God was bound in *equity* not to permit sin, while at the same time he constituted the agent *free*, and *accountable* for the exercise of his freedom; and as he has *in fact permitted* the introduction of sin into the world, such an idea would be the same as to charge *infinite perfection with* want *of equity*.

12. We may therefore safely conclude, that the GLORY of the divine *rectitude*, towards the intelligent and moral part of the universe, considered as accountable, and to the full extent of its moral capabilities, could not be manifested without the *permission* of sin. The *full* exercise of *equity* must *necessarily leave* the moral system to its own tendencies and operations.

13. To *permit* the event of sin, or *not to hinder* it, implies, that the *cause* of defection is not in the *permitter*, but in the *permitted*; not in the *governor*, but the *governed*. There is in the moral part of the universe a *cause*, why an event which *ought not* to take place, *will* take place, IF not hindered. IF there be *no such cause* in the system, how could the event take place on *permission?* If it be said, There is a *chance* it may not ake place, and there is a *chance* of the contrary—it is but fair to ask, Is this chance something which *has* a cause, or has it *no* cause? If the *latter*, the concession itself reduces chance to a *mere nothing*. For a contingent event, as the operation of chance is supposed to be, *without any* cause, is a metaphysical impossibility. If the *former;* what is the cause of what the objector calls chance? Is it something external, or internal? What is its nature and character? To say that *liberty of indifference*, or a *self-determining power*, is the chance which requires no preceding cause to produce the event, is to contradict *absolute demonstration*, if ever there was a metaphysical demonstration of any subject; as our author has abundantly shown in his "Essay on the Freedom of the Will."

14. It is therefore inaccurate and unintelligible language to say, that either *chance, liberty of indifference*, or a *self-determining power*, independent of any antecedent cause, is adequate to account for the event of sin, or a deterioration of a moral system. God, therefore, *permitting*, there is an *inherent* adequate cause of failure, distinct from divine causation. What this cause is, and what is its nature, has been shown and proved in a former note.

15. *Permission* is an act of *equity;* or, it is the *exercise* of *rectitude*, to the exclusion of benevolent influence; whether we regard that influence as *preventing* the event of sin, or as *delivering* from its power. Sovereign benevolence *prevents* the fall of angels; and it *delivers, restores*, and eternally *saves* a goodly number of the human fallen race. Without the *permission* of sin, *restoring* benevolence, or the exercise of *mercy*, would have been impossible; and consequently, the GLORY of that perfection, which can be fully displayed only by its *exercise* towards the *miserable*, would have been eternally *concealed*.

16. IF, therefore, EQUITY be a *glorious* attribute of God, its *emanation* and *exercise* must be *glorious*. But the *exercise* of equity, in the *strict* sense, includes the *permission* of sin, as before proved. And, here we may add, if *not to hinder* be an *exercise* of strict rectitude, the continued existence of sin is not inconsistent with it.

17. It will be allowed by every one, that, as MERCY *itself* is a GLORIOUS attribute, so is the *exercise* of it a glorious thing. But this would have been impossible, IF sin had no *existence;* nor could sin have had existence, IF not *permitted* to exist; and sin could not have been permitted, IF *strict equity* had not been *exercised;* nor could strict equity have been exercised, IF the exercise of *preventing* sovereign benevolence had not been *excluded*, in those instances wherein moral defect actually took place.

COROLLARIES.

18. The *ultimate* and *chief* END of God in the creation and government of the *moral* part of the universe, is the GLORY of his *moral perfections;* which are virtually included in strict *rectitude* and sovereign *benevolence*.

19. IF *strict rectitude* be exercised towards the degenerate part of the system, the *restoration* of those who are the objects of it is not possible; that is, to suppose it possible involves a contradiction. Therefore,

20. IF any *degenerate* moral agent be *restored*, it must necessarily be by the exercise of that sovereign benevolence which we call *mercy*.

21. "Behold therefore the GOODNESS and SEVERITY of God! on them who fell, severity; but toward thee goodness, if thou continue in his goodness; otherwise thou also shalt be cut off." *Goodness* and *severity* are but other words for *sovereign* BENEVOLENCE and *strict* EQUITY, the GLORY of which is abundantly conspicuous in the various divine dispensations towards the children of men, even in *this* life; but will appear still more transcendent in the day when God shall judge the world in righteousness, and in the day of ETERNITY.—W.

A

DISSERTATION

CONCERNING

THE NATURE OF TRUE VIRTUE.

CHAP. I.

Showing wherein the essence of true virtue consists.

Whatever controversies and variety of opinions there are about the *nature* of virtue, yet all excepting, some sceptics, who deny any real difference between virtue and vice, mean by it something *beautiful*, or rather some kind of *beauty*, or excellency. It is not *all* beauty that is called virtue; for instance, not the beauty of a building, of a flower, or of the rainbow; but some beauty belonging to beings that have *perception* and *will*. It is not all beauty of *mankind* that is called virtue; for instance, not the external beauty of the countenance, or shape, gracefulness of motion, or harmony of voice: but it is a beauty that has its original seat in the mind. But yet perhaps not *every* thing that may be called a beauty of *mind*, is properly called virtue. There is a beauty of understanding and speculation; there is something in the ideas and conceptions of great philosophers and statesmen, that may be called beautiful; which is a different thing from what is most commonly meant by virtue.

But virtue is the beauty of those qualities and acts of the mind, that are of a *moral* nature, *i. e.* such as are attended with desert or worthiness of *praise* or *blame*. Things of this sort, it is generally agreed, so far as I know, do not belong merely to speculation; but to the *disposition* and *will*, or (to use a general word, I suppose commonly well understood) to the *heart*. Therefore, I suppose, I shall not depart from the common opinion, when I say, that virtue is the beauty of the qualities and exercises of the heart, or those actions which proceed from them. So that when it is inquired, what is the nature of true *virtue?* this is the same as to inquire, what that is, which renders any habit, disposition, or exercise of the heart truly *beautiful?*

I use the phrase *true* virtue, and speak of things *truly* beautiful, because I suppose it will generally be allowed, that there is a distinction to be made between some things which are truly virtuous, and others which only *seem* to be so, through a partial and imperfect view of things: that some actions and dispositions appear beautiful, if considered partially and superficially, or with regard to some things belonging to them, and in some of their circumstances and tendencies, which would appear otherwise in a more extensive and comprehensive view, wherein they are seen clearly in their whole nature, and the extent of their connexions in the universality of things.

There is a general and particular beauty. By a *particular* beauty, I mean that by which a thing appears beautiful when considered only with regard to its connexion with, and tendency to, some particular things within a limited, and as it were a private, sphere. And a *general* beauty is that by which a thing appears beautiful when viewed most perfectly, comprehensively, and universally, with regard to all its tendencies, and its connexions with every thing to which it stands related. The former may be without and against the latter. As a few notes in a tune, taken only by themselves, and in their relation to one another, may be harmonious; which, when considered with respect to all the notes in the tune, or the entire series of sounds they are connected with, may be very discordant, and disagreeable. *That only*, therefore, is what I mean by *true* virtue, which, belonging to the *heart* of an intelligent being, is beautiful by a *general* beauty, or beautiful in a comprehensive view, as it is in itself, and as related to every thing with which it stands connected. And therefore, when we are inquiring concerning the nature of true virtue—wherein this true and general beauty of the heart does most essentially consist—this is my answer to the inquiry:——

True virtue most essentially consists in BENEVOLENCE TO BEING IN GENERAL. Or perhaps, to speak more accurately, it is that consent, propensity, and union of heart to being in general, which is immediately exercised in a general good will.

The things before observed respecting the nature of true virtue, naturally lead us to such a notion of it. If it has its seat in the heart, and is the general goodness and beauty of the disposition and its exercise, in the most comprehensive view, considered with regard to its universal tendency, and as related to every thing with which it stands connected; what can it consist in, but a consent and good will to being in general? Beauty does not consist in discord and dissent, but in consent and agreement. And if every intelligent being is some way related to being in general, and is a part of the universal system of existence; and so stands in connexion with the whole; what can its general and true beauty be, but its union and consent with the great whole?

If any such thing can be supposed as a union of heart to some particular being, or number of beings, disposing it to benevolence to a private circle or system of beings, which are but a small part of the whole; not implying a tendency to an union with the great system, and not at all inconsistent with enmity towards being in general; this I suppose not to be of the nature of true virtue; although it may in some respects be good, and may appear beautiful in a confined and contracted view of things.—But of this more afterwards.

It is abundantly plain by the Holy Scriptures, and generally allowed, not only by christian divines, but by the more considerable Deists, that virtue most essentially consists in love. And I suppose, it is owned by the most considerable writers, to consist in general love of benevolence, or kind affection: though it seems to me the meaning of some in this affair is not sufficiently explained; which perhaps occasions some error or confusion in discourses on this subject.

When I say, true virtue consists in *love to being in general*, I shall not be likely to be understood, that no one act of the mind or exercise of love is of the nature of true virtue, but what has being in general, or the great system of universal existence, for its *direct* and *immediate* object: so that no exercise of love, or kind affection, to any one particular being, that is but a small part of this whole, has any thing of the nature of true virtue. But, that the nature of true virtue consists in a *disposition* to benevolence towards being in general; though from such a disposition may arise exercises of love to *particular* beings, as objects are presented, and occasions arise. No wonder, that he who is of a *generally* benevolent disposition, should be more disposed than another to have his heart moved with benevolent affection to *particular* persons, with whom he is acquainted and conversant, and from whom arise the greatest and most frequent *occasions* for exciting his benevolent temper. But my meaning is, that no affections towards particular persons or beings are of the nature of true virtue, but such as arise from a generally benevolent temper, or from that habit or frame of mind, wherein consists a disposition to love being in general.

And perhaps it is needless for me to give notice to my readers, that when I speak of an intelligent being having a heart united and benevolently disposed to being in general, I thereby mean *intelligent* being in general. Not inanimate things, or beings that have no perception or will; which are not properly capable objects of benevolence.

Love is commonly distinguished into love of benevolence, and love of complacence. Love of *benevolence* is that affection or propensity of the heart to any being, which causes it to incline to its well-being, or disposes it to desire and take pleasure in its happiness. And if I mistake not, it is agreeable to the common opinion, that beauty in the object is not always the ground of this propensity; but that there may be a disposition to the welfare of those that are *not* considered as beautiful, unless mere existence be accounted a beauty. And benevolence or goodness in the Divine Being is generally supposed, not only to be prior to the beauty of many of its objects, but to their existence; so as to be the ground both of their existence and their beauty, rather than the foundation of God's benevolence; as it is supposed that it is God's goodness which moved him to give them both being and beauty. So that if all virtue primarily consists in that affection of heart to being, which is exercised in benevolence, or an inclination to its good, then God's virtue is so extended as to include a propensity not only to being actually existing, and actually beautiful, but to possible being, so as to incline him to give a being beauty and happiness.

What is commonly called love of *complacence*, presupposes beauty. For it is no other than delight in beauty; or complacence in the person or being beloved for his beauty. If virtue be the beauty of an intelligent being, and virtue consists in love, then it is plain inconsistence, to suppose that virtue primarily consists in any love to its object for its beauty; either in a love of complacence, which is delight in a being for its beauty, or in a love of benevolence, that has the beauty of its object for its foundation. For that would be to suppose, that the beauty of intelligent beings primarily consists in love to beauty; or that their virtue first of all consists in their love to virtue. Which is an inconsistence, and going in a circle. Because it makes virtue, or beauty of mind, the foundation or first motive of that love wherein virtue originally consists, or wherein the very first virtue consists; or, it supposes the first virtue to be the consequence and effect of virtue. Which makes the first virtue both the ground and the consequence, both cause and effect of itself. Doubtless virtue primarily consists in something else besides any effect or consequence of virtue. If virtue consists primarily in love to virtue, then virtue, the thing loved, is the love of virtue: so that virtue must consist in the love of the love of virtue —and so on *in infinitum*. For there is no end of going back in a circle. We never come to any beginning or foundation; it is without beginning, and hangs on nothing. —Therefore, if the essence of *virtue*, or *beauty* of mind, lies in love, or a disposition to love, it must primarily consist in something *different* both from complacence, which is a delight in beauty, and also from any benevolence that has the beauty of its object for its foundation. Because it is absurd to say, that virtue is primarily and first of all the consequence of itself; which makes virtue primarily prior to itself.

Nor can virtue primarily consist in *gratitude;* or one being's benevolence to another for his benevolence to him. Because this implies the same inconsistence. For it supposes a benevolence prior to gratitude, which is the cause of gratitude. The *first* benevolence cannot be gratitude. Therefore there is room left for no other conclusion, than that the primary object of virtuous love is being, simply considered; or that true virtue primarily consists, not in love to any particular beings, because of their virtue or beauty, nor in gratitude, because they love us; but in a propensity and union of heart to being simply considered; exciting *absolute* benevolence, if I may so call it, to being in general. I say, true virtue *primarily* consists in this. For I am far from asserting, that there is no true virtue in any other love than this absolute benevolence. But I would express what appears to me to be the truth, on this subject, in the following particulars.

The *first* object of a virtuous benevolence is *being*, simply considered: and if being, *simply* considered, be its object, then being *in general* is its object; and what it has an ultimate propensity to, is the *highest good* of being in general. And it will seek the good of every *individual* being unless it be conceived as not consistent with the highest good of being in general. In which case the good of a particular being, or some beings, may be given up for the sake of the highest good of being in general. And particularly, if there be any being statedly and irreclaimably opposite, and an enemy to being in general, then consent and adherence to being in general will induce the truly virtuous heart to forsake that enemy, and to oppose it.

Further, if BEING, simply considered, be the first object of a truly virtuous benevolence, then that object who has *most* of being, or has the greatest share of existence, *other things being equal*, so far as such a being is exhibited to our faculties, will have the *greatest* share of the propensity and benevolent affections of the heart. I say, "other things being equal," especially because there is a *secondary* object of virtuous benevolence, that I shall take notice of presently, which must be considered as the ground or motive to a purely virtuous benevolence. Pure benevolence in its *first* exercise is nothing else but being's uniting consent, or propensity to being; and inclining to the general highest good, and to each being, whose welfare is consistent with the highest general good, in proportion to the degree of *existence*,* understand, "other things being equal."

The *second* object of a virtuous propensity of heart is *benevolent* being. A secondary ground of pure benevolence is virtuous benevolence itself in its object. When any one under the influence of general benevolence, sees another being possessed of the like general benevolence, this attaches his heart to him, and draws forth greater love to him, than merely his having existence: because so far as the being beloved has love to the being in general, so far his own being is, as it were, enlarged; extends to, and in some sort comprehends, being in general: and therefore, he that is governed by love to being in general, must of necessity have complacence in him, and the greater degree of benevolence to him, as it were out of gratitude to him for his love to general existence, that his own heart is extended and united to, and so looks on its interest as its own. It is because his heart is thus united to being in general, that he looks on a benevolent propensity to being in general, wherever he sees it, as the beauty of the being in whom it

* I say, "in proportion to the degree of *existence*," because one being may have more *existence* than another, as he may be greater than another. That which is *great*, has more existence, and is further from nothing, than that which is *little*. One being may have every thing positive belonging to it, or every thing which goes to its positive existence (in opposition to defect) in a higher degree than another; or a greater capacity and power, greater understanding, every faculty and every positive quality in a higher degree. An *arch-angel* must be supposed to have more existence, and to be every way further removed from *non-entity*, than a *worm*.

is; an excellency that renders him worthy of esteem, complacence, and the greater good will.—But several things may be noted more particularly concerning this *secondary* ground of a truly virtuous love.

1. That loving a being on *this ground* necessarily arises from pure benevolence to being *in general*, and comes to the same thing. For he that has a simple and pure good will to general existence, must love that temper in others, that agrees and conspires with itself. A spirit of consent to being must agree with consent to being. That which truly and sincerely seeks the good of others, must approve of and love that which joins with him in seeking the good of others.

2. This secondary ground of virtuous love, is the thing wherein true moral or spiritual *beauty* primarily consists. Yea, spiritual beauty consists wholly in this, and in the various qualities and exercises of mind which proceed from it, and the external actions which proceed from these internal qualities and exercises. And in these things consists all true *virtue, viz.* in this love of being, and the qualities and acts which arise from it.

3. As all spiritual beauty lies in these virtuous principles and acts, so it is primarily *on this account* they are beautiful, *viz.* that they imply *consent* and *union* with being *in general.* This is the primary and most essential beauty of every thing that can justly be called by the name of virtue, or is any moral excellency in the eye of one that has a perfect view of things. I say, "the *primary* and *most essential* beauty," because there is a secondary and inferior sort of beauty; which I shall take notice of afterwards.

4. This spiritual beauty, which is but a *secondary* ground of virtuous benevolence, is the ground, not only of benevolence, but *complacence,* and is the *primary* ground of the latter; that is, when the complacence is truly virtuous. Love to us in particular, and kindness received, may be a secondary ground: but this is the primary objective foundation of it.

5. It must be noted, that the *degree* of the *amiableness* of true virtue, primarily consisting in consent, and a benevolent propensity of heart to being in general, is not in the *simple* proportion of the degree of benevolent affection seen, but in a proportion *compounded* of the greatness of the benevolent being, or the degree of *being* and the degree of *benevolence.* One that loves being in general, will necessarily value good will to being in general, wherever he sees it. But if he sees the same benevolence in *two* beings, he will value it *more* in two, than in one only. Because it is a greater thing, more favourable to being in general, to have two beings to favour it, than only one of them. For there is more being that favours being: both together having more being than one alone. So, if one being be as great as two, has as much existence as both together, and has the same degree of general benevolence, it is more favourable to being in general, than if there were general benevolence in a being that had but half that share of existence. As a large quantity of gold, with the same quality, is more valuable than a small quantity of the same metal.

6. It is impossible that any one should truly *relish* this beauty, consisting in general benevolence, who has *not* that temper himself. I have observed, that if any being is possessed of such a temper, he will unavoidably be pleased with the same temper in another. And it may in like manner be demonstrated, that it is such a spirit, and nothing else, which will relish such a spirit. For if a being, destitute of benevolence, should love benevolence to being in general, it would prize and seek that for which it had no value. For how should one love and value a *disposition* to a thing, or a *tendency to promote* it, and for that very reason, when the *thing* itself is what he is regardless of, and has no value for, nor desires to have promoted.*

* In this masterly Dissertation on the *nature* of virtue, our author enters at once on his *own* definition of the term, and explains very clearly what *he means* by *true* virtue. His views, in some respects, are considerably different from those which are most current among ethical writers; and, probably, for want of some explanations, whereby the different definitions adopted by others may be accounted for, his invaluable treatise has not only been underrated, but even, by some, unreasonably opposed. We shall here offer a few remarks, which, perhaps, may tend to cast some light on the subject in general, as well as to relieve our author's definition from unfair imputations.

1. Virtue, if we regard the use of the term (αρετη) among the Greeks, seems to have been appropriated as much to the idea of martial *courage*, as the English term is appropriated to that of female *chastity.* Not that it was used *exclusively* in the former case, any more than in the latter. It often signifies power, energy, efficacy, and excellence. But by moral writers both ancient and modern, it has been unanimously adopted to represent a very general moral idea.—It would be easy to produce a great number of definitions from moralists and divines; but this is neither necessary, nor does it comport with our present purpose.

2. If we mistake not, there is no just definition of virtue, which is not reducible to this general one: VIRTUE IS A LAUDABLE MEAN OF REAL HAPPINESS. Cicero, indeed, says of it, that it is "affectio animi constans, conveniensque, laudabiles efficiens eos, in quibus est, et *ipsa per se, sua sponte, separata etiam utilitate, laudabilis.*" (Tuscul. Quæst. Lib. iv. § 15.) But virtue being *laudable* from its very nature, independently of any advantageous result, does not hinder it from being "a laudable *mean* of real happiness."

3. Now happiness being the uniform and voluntary *end* of intellectual existence, a *desire* of it being inseparable from our nature; we become liable to err, not only by adopting *wrong means* for accomplishing the end we propose to ourselves, but also by forming a false estimate of the nature of happiness, or the *end itself.* If the happiness be not real but imaginery, in the contemplation of the agent, however well adapted the means may be in order to attain it, they deserve not the epithet *virtuous.*

4. To discover the nature of true happiness, the light of wisdom is requisite; and while desire is blind, false estimates will be made. But every one thinks himself wise and prudent enough to prescribe his *own happiness*, till such folly be shown him by the wisdom which is from above; and he who supposes himself adequate to fix the *end*, cannot be very diffident about the *means* to be employed.

5. Hence there is room for as many representations of virtue, as there are *kinds* of happiness which men think to be *real;* in addition to as many *means* employed to accomplish their proposed end, as they judge to be *laudable.*

6. From these preliminary remarks, it appears, that the *nature* and real *character* of virtue, must arise from the nature of the *end proposed*, and of the *means employed* for securing it. We shall now attempt to illustrate the ground of numerous representations of virtue, by comparison.

7. Let the different *kinds of happiness* which we propose to ourselves, whether those which have been classified by moral writers, or any others, be represented by so many *concentric circles.* For instance, let happiness be considered as *personal* and *relative*, *private* and *public*, *domestic* and *national*, *temporal* and *eternal*, or the like; and for every species of happiness let there be a corresponding circle drawn. Let the filling up of that circle express the *virtue* requisite to attain the happiness thus represented.

8. Suppose, for example, that *health*, *friendship*, *domestic unanimity*, *national prosperity*, the *welfare* of the *human race*, and our individual *conformity to God* in his moral excellence through eternal ages, or the *happiness* implied in these respectively, be represented by the concentric circles above mentioned. Then, the happiness implied in *health*, a small circle, will be filled by corresponding *virtues*, when the end is sought by *laudable* means; such as temperance, moderation, chastity, government of the passions, &c. The circle representing the happiness implied in *friendship* will be filled by corresponding *virtues*, when the end is sought, as before, by *laudable* means; such as benevolence, fidelity, prudence, sympathy, &c. The circle of *domestic* happiness is filled with the virtues of kindness, meekness, patience, industry, economy, &c. That of *national prosperity* by diligence in business, honesty, justice, truth, liberality, conscientious submission, fortitude, real patriotism, &c. The circle representing the *welfare* of the *human race*, as the common offspring of one progenitor, and who are regarded by the Supreme Parent as the children of one family, is filled by the virtues of philanthropy, expansive benevolent zeal, self-denial, public spirit, passive courage, &c. And the circle of that happiness which is implied in our individual *conformity to God's moral excellence;* in other words, that happiness which is *ultimate* and *supreme*, is filled by nothing short of *supreme love to God*, or, in language more philosophically accurate, *consent of will to* BEING *in general—benevolent attachment to universal* BEING.

9. Now who can question whether temperance, fidelity, meekness, honesty and liberality, philanthropy and public spirit, should be ranked among the virtues? And who can doubt that they are calculated to secure the happiness implied in health, friendship, national prosperity, and the welfare of the human race, respectively? And yet, if we exclude the *disposition* which is required to fill the *largest* circle—*benevolent attachment to universal being*—which of these virtues may not an *atheist* actually possess? Nay, may not an atheist possess them *all?* For may he not promote his *health* by temperance, moderation, chastity, and the like? May he not exercise *friendly* benevolence, fidelity, prudence, sympathy, and similar virtues? Have not atheists been great *patriots*, if by patriotism we mean a supreme regard for the prosperity and glory of the nation to which they belonged, manifested by severe studies, by the lightning and thunder of their eloquence, the fatigues of war, and a willingness to shed the last drop of their blood in defence of their country? Nay more, may not an atheist possess the virtues of generous philanthropy, and, to a certain extent, of benevolent zeal for the welfare of mankind in general, expressed by an attempt to remove their ignominious chains, to promote the civilization of savage nations whom he has never seen, to alleviate the sufferings and to enhance the comforts of all mankind?

10. Far be it from us to suppose that atheists are *favourable* to virtue, even in these inferior acceptations of the term. The reverse is abundantly evident. But this is what we assert, that such virtues as those above mentioned, when *exclusive* of what our author contends for, are what an atheist *may possess*, without inconsistency; and that they have no *moral* worth, no *direct* connexion, either with the complacency of God in them, or with the ultimate happiness of the agent. However attentive a man may be to practise virtues in subservience to his health, while he repels those of friendship; or however observant of the virtues of friendship, while he repels others which are conducive to domestic, national, and universal happiness; his virtues, if the name be retained, are those of a *bad character.* Some have been conspicuous and zealous patriots, while determined foes to philanthropy and general good will to mankind as such. And how many have fought with the most patriotic zeal and courage in the field of honour, though tyrants at home, and in private life trampling on those virtues which constitute a good husband, a good father, a good master, a good neighbour, a good friend, or a good *any thing.* In short, were a man to "give all his goods to feed the poor, and his body to be burned," out of zeal to promote some public good, yet without *love to God*, without benevolent attachment to *universal being*, he is *morally nothing*, or worse than nothing.

11. What are called *virtues*, without a disposition to embrace *universal being* and *excellence*, are, morally considered, but lifeless images. To compare them to a series of decimal figures, which, however increased, will never amount to an unit of moral worth, is to place them in too favourable a view; they are more like cyphers. But let these unmeaning cyphers be preceded by a figure, let these images have an informing and invigorating principle, let these dry bones have the spirit of life in them, and they

CHAP. II.

Showing how that love, wherein true virtue consists, respects the Divine Being and created beings.

FROM what has been said, it is evident, that true virtue must chiefly consist in LOVE TO GOD; the Being of beings, infinitely the greatest and best. This appears, whether we consider the primary or secondary ground of virtuous love. It was observed, that the *first* objective ground of that love, wherein true virtue consists, is BEING simply considered: and, as a necessary consequence of this, that being who has the greatest share of universal existence has proportionably the greatest share of virtuous benevolence, so far as such a being is exhibited to the faculties of our minds, other things being equal. But God has infinitely the greatest share of existence. So that all other being, even the whole universe, is as nothing in comparison of the Divine Being.

And if we consider the *secondary* ground of love, or moral excellency, the same thing will appear. For as God is infinitely the greatest Being, so he is allowed to be infinitely the most beautiful and excellent: and all the beauty to be found throughout the whole creation, is but the reflection of the diffused beams of that Being who hath an infinite fulness of brightness and glory. God's beauty is infinitely more valuable than that of all other beings upon both those accounts mentioned, *viz.* the degree of his virtue, and the *greatness* of his being, possessed of this virtue. And God has sufficiently exhibited himself, both in his being, and his infinite greatness and excellency: and has given us faculties, whereby we are capable of plainly discovering his immense superiority to all other beings, in these respects. Therefore, he that has true virtue, consisting in benevolence to *being* in general, and in benevolence to *virtuous* being, must necessarily have a supreme love to God, both of benevolence and complacence. And all true virtue must radically and essentially, and, as it were, summarily, consist in this. Because God is not only infinitely greater and more excellent than all other being, but he is the head of the universal system of existence; the foundation and fountain of all being and all beauty; from whom all is perfectly derived, and on whom all is most absolutely and perfectly dependent; *of whom*, and *through whom*, and *to whom* is all being and all perfection; and whose being and beauty are, as it were, the sum and comprehension of all existence and excellence: much more than the sun is the fountain and summary comprehension of all the light and brightness of the day.

If it should be objected, that virtue consists primarily in benevolence, but that our fellow-creatures, and not God, seem to be the most proper objects of our benevolence; inasmuch as *our goodness extendeth not to God*, and *we cannot be profitable to him.*—To this I answer,

1. A benevolent propensity of heart is exercised, not only in *seeking to promote* the happiness of the being towards whom it is exercised, but also in *rejoicing in* his happiness. Even as gratitude for benefits received will not only excite endeavours to requite the kindness we receive, by equally benefiting our benefactor, but also if he be above any need of us, or we have nothing to bestow, and are unable to repay his kindness, it will dispose us to rejoice in his prosperity.

2. Though we are not able to give any thing to God, which we have of our own, independently; yet we may be the instruments of promoting *his glory*, in which he takes a true and proper *delight.**—Whatever influence such an objection may seem to have on the minds of some, yet is there any that owns the being of a God, who will deny that any benevolent affection is due to God, and proper to be exercised towards him? If no *benevolence* is to be exercised towards God, because we cannot profit him, then, for the same reason, neither is *gratitude* to be exercised towards him for his benefits to us; because we cannot requite him. But where is the man, who believes a God and a providence, that will say this?

There seems to be an inconsistence in some writers on morality, in this respect, that they do not wholly exclude a regard to the *Deity* out of their schemes of morality, but yet mention it so slightly, that they leave me room and reason to suspect they esteem it a less important and subordinate part of true morality; and insist on benevolence to the *created system*, in such a manner as would naturally lead one to suppose they look upon that as by far the most important and essential thing in their scheme. But why should this be? If true virtue consists partly in a respect to God, then doubtless it consists *chiefly* in it. If true morality requires that we should have some regard, some benevolent affection to our Creator, as well as to his creatures, then doubtless it requires the first regard to be paid to him; and that he be every way the supreme object of our benevolence. If his being above our reach, and beyond all capacity of being profited by us, does not hinder, but that nevertheless he is the proper object of our love, then it does not hinder that he should be loved according to his *dignity*, or according to the degree in which he has those things wherein worthiness of regard consists, so far as we are capable of it. But this worthiness, none will deny, consists in these two things, *greatness* and moral *goodness*. And those that own a God, do not deny that he

will acquire a moral excellence; they will deserve the name of REAL VIRTUES.

12. Some have defined virtue, by calling it, "a tendency to ultimate happiness." If the meaning of this definition be, "a tendency to God, in whom our ultimate happiness is found," it may be admitted; otherwise, it seems not admissible on many accounts. Tendency may be considered as either *voluntary* or *involuntary*. In the first place, let us suppose it to be *voluntary*. We then observe, that it is not *rational*, nor even compatible with common sense, to say, that virtue is a voluntary tendency to a *quality of our own minds*, as happiness evidently is. For happiness, from its very nature, is a relative state, or quality of mind, which is the result of enjoying an object suited to our wants. And to desire ultimate happiness, without including the *object* of choice from whence happiness results, is the same as to seek happiness in *nothing*. If it be said, that *happiness itself* is the object sought; then virtue consists in a voluntary tendency to seek happiness in happiness, which is absurd.

13. Ultimate happiness has been defined, "the durable possession of perfect good." If this be a just statement, which few or none will question, what is the *perfect good* possessed? If it be answered, The Supreme Being; to this there is no objection. But if it be said, the ultimate happiness *itself* is the perfect good enjoyed; then the happiness to which the choice is directed is both cause and effect at the same time. Both the *thing enjoyed* and the *enjoyment* itself are the same thing. Which is no less absurd than for a man to assert, that the stock of a tree and the fruit on its branches, are the same thing; or that his *relish* of food is the same as the *food itself.* A tendency to happiness resulting from *no object* of that tendency, is the same thing as a tendency to *no happiness.* In other words, according to this definition, supposing the tendency to be *voluntary*, virtue is a *desire* of ultimate happiness. And this will reduce it to another absurdity; for, as a desire of ultimate happiness is an inseparable property of intelligent beings, the *most vicious* being in existence is *virtuous.* These consequences, however just, will not be thought very extraordinary, when compared with the following declarations. "The following seems to be at present the true moral state of the world: In *every* moral agent the number of virtuous actions greatly exceed that of vicious ones.—In by far the greater number of moral agents, and even amongst those who are considered as most vicious and profligate, the number of virtuous affections and habits greatly preponderates over the vicious ones. A character in which there is a preponderance of vice, is very rarely, if ever, to be met with." (Belsham's Elements, p. 400.) And, to advance one step further in this hopeful way, as this *desire* belongs to *all* intelligent beings *alike*, all intelligent beings are *alike virtuous!*

14. In reality, a *mere desire* of ultimate happiness is *no virtue*, has nothing *laudable* in it, but is a mere instinct of intellectual nature, and belongs alike to the best and the worst of intelligent beings. But virtue consists in the *choice* of, or a *disposition* to choose, *laudable means* in order to arrive at this end. A *bad* man in his choice of objects, or a *vicious choice* itself, aims at ultimate happiness; but the *means* are *not laudable*, and this *wrong choice of means* constitutes the very essence of his *vice*.

15. If it be said, that virtue is a tendency to ultimate *self-enjoyment*, as constituting happiness; then it follows that *self* is the *perfect good* desired. And then every one is *himself* all-sufficient to constitute his own happiness. Let any rational person judge, whether this be not a definition of *sordid vice*, rather than of virtue; and whether such a disposition would not be a tendency to insubordination, anarchy, and confusion, rather than to happiness—the very temper of an apostate spirit.

16. If it be said, moreover, that "a *tendency* to ultimate happiness," does not refer to the will, desire, or choice; but expresses *any thing* which *in fact* tends to ultimate happiness. This leads us to suppose secondly, that the tendency is *involuntary*. It seems, then, on this supposition, that the *means* employed to acquire ultimate happiness need not be *laudable*. This is the *genuine result* of that account of virtue which is here animadverted upon; and which the abettors of it are forced to admit. The doctrine of "intrinsic merit or demerit of actions, independent on their consequences," they call an "absurd supposition." (Belsham's Elements, p. 309, 372, 373.)

17. It seems, then, we are all bound to be *virtuous* at our peril, and yet we must wait the *result* of *all* our actions, before we can know what is virtuous and what is not. For if virtue and vice have no intrinsic character of good or evil, but actions, affections, habits, or characters, are either good or bad from their ultimate *consequences;* then we must wait for those *consequences*, as the only expositors of virtue and vice.

18. Can any thing more be necessary, in order to show the absurdity of such a notion of virtue? Happiness, it is allowed, is a *consequent*, of which virtue is the *antecedent*. But what is the *moral nature* of this antecedent? Is it any thing good, beautiful, or laudable *per se?* No, say they; it has no nature beside tendency; which has no intrinsic merit or demerit; and consequently, that which has no moral nature is a *moral nothing;* that is, virtue is a moral nothing, or *nothing moral.* And whether this character of virtue be not totally distinct from the distant of right reason, philosophic accuracy, common sense, and christian piety, let the reader judge.—W.

* As was shown at large in the former treatise, on God's end in creating the world, Chap. I. sect. 4. whither I must refer the reader for a more full answer to this objection.

infinitely exceeds all other beings in these. If the Deity is to be looked upon as within that system of beings which properly terminates our benevolence, or belonging to that whole, certainly he is to be regarded as the *head* of the system, and the *chief* part of it: if it be proper to call him a *part*, who is infinitely more than all the rest, and in comparison of whom, and without whom, all the rest are nothing, either as to beauty or existence. And therefore certainly, unless we will be atheists, we must allow that true virtue does primarily and most essentially consist in a supreme love to God; and that where this is wanting, there can be no true virtue.

But this being a matter of the highest importance, I shall say something further to make it plain, that love to God is most essential to true virtue; and that no benevolence whatsoever to other beings can be of the nature of true virtue without it.

And therefore, let it be supposed, that some beings, by natural instinct, or by some other means, have a determination of mind to union and benevolence to a *particular person*, or *private system*,* which is but a small part of the universal system of being: and that this disposition or determination of mind is independent on, or not subordinate to, benevolence to *being in general*. Such a determination, disposition, or affection of mind is not of the nature of true virtue.

This is allowed by all with regard to *self-love;* in which good will is confined to one single person only. And there are the same reasons why any other private affection or good will, though extending to a society of persons independent of, and unsubordinate to, benevolence to the universality, should not be esteemed truly virtuous. For, notwithstanding it extends to a number of persons, which taken together are more than a single person, yet the whole falls infinitely short of the universality of existence; and if put in the scales with it, has no greater proportion to it than a single person.

However, it may not be amiss more particularly to consider the reasons why *private affections*, or good will limited to a particular circle of beings, falling infinitely short of the whole existence, and not dependent upon it, nor subordinate to general benevolence, cannot be of the nature of true virtue.

1. Such a private affection, detached from general benevolence, and independent on it, as the case may be, will be *against* general benevolence, or of a contrary tendency; and will set a person *against* general existence, and make him an enemy to it. As it is with *selfishness*, or when a man is governed by a regard to his own private interest, independent of regard to the public good, such a temper exposes a man to act the part of an enemy to the public. As, in every case wherein his private interest seems to clash with the public; or in all those cases wherein such things are presented to his view, that suit his personal appetites or private inclinations, but are inconsistent with the good of the public. On which account, a selfish, contracted, narrow spirit is generally abhorred, and is esteemed base and sordid. But if a man's affection takes in half a dozen more, and his regards extend so far beyond his own single person as to take in his children and family; or if it reaches further still to a larger circle, but falls infinitely short of the universal system, and is exclusive of being in general; his private affection exposes him to the same thing, *viz.* to pursue the interest of its particular object in *opposition* to general existence: which is certainly contrary to the tendency of true virtue; yea, directly contrary to the main and most essential thing in its nature, the thing on account of which chiefly its nature and tendency is good. For the chief and most essential good that is in virtue, is its favouring being in general. Now certainly, if private affection to a limited system had in itself the essential nature of virtue, it would be impossible that it should, in any circumstance whatsoever, have a tendency and inclination directly *contrary* to that wherein the essence of virtue chiefly consists.

2. Private affection, if not subordinate to general affection, is not only liable, as the case *may* be, to issue in enmity to being in general, but has a *tendency* to it as the case certainly *is*, and must necessarily be. For he that is influenced by private affection, not subordinate to a regard to being in general, sets up its particular or limited object *above* being in general; and this most naturally tends to enmity against the latter, which is by right the great supreme, ruling, and absolutely sovereign object of our regard. Even as the setting up another prince as supreme in any kingdom, distinct from the lawful sovereign, naturally tends to enmity against the lawful sovereign. Wherever it is sufficiently published, that the supreme, infinite, and all-comprehending Being requires a supreme regard to himself; and insists upon it, that our respect to him should universally rule in our hearts, and every other affection be subordinate to it, and this under the pain of his displeasure, (as we must suppose it is in the world of intelligent creatures, if God maintains a moral kingdom in the world,) then a consciousness of our having chosen and set up another prince to rule over us, and subjected our hearts to him, and continuing in such an act, must unavoidably excite enmity, and fix us in a stated opposition to the Supreme Being. This demonstrates, that affection to a private society or system, independent on general benevolence, cannot be of the nature of true virtue. For this would be absurd, that it has the nature and essence of true virtue, and yet at the same time has a *tendency opposite* to true virtue.

3. Not only would affection to a private system, unsubordinate to a regard to being in general, have a tendency to oppose the supreme object of virtuous affection, as its effect and consequence, but would become *itself* an opposition to that object. Considered by itself in its nature, detached from its effects, it is an instance of great opposition to the rightful supreme object of our respect. For it exalts its private object above the other great and infinite object; and sets that up as supreme, in opposition to this. It puts down being in general, which is infinitely superior in itself, and infinitely more important, in an inferior place; yea, subjects the supreme general object to this private infinitely inferior object: which is to treat it with great contempt, and truly to act in opposition to it, and to act in opposition to the true order of things, and in opposition to that which is infinitely the supreme interest; making this supreme and infinitely important interest, as far as in us lies, to be subject to, and dependent on, an interest infinitely inferior. This is to act the part of an enemy to it. He that takes a subject, and exalts him above his prince, sets him as supreme instead of the prince, and treats his prince wholly as a subject, therein acts the part of an enemy to his prince.

From these things, I think, it is manifest, that no affection limited to any private system, not depending on nor subordinate to being in general, can be of the nature of true virtue; and this, whatever the private system be, let it be more or less extensive, consisting of a greater or smaller number of individuals, so long as it contains an infinitely little part of universal existence, and so bears no proportion to the great all-comprehending system. And consequently, that no affection whatsoever to any creature, or any system of created beings, which is not dependent on, nor subordinate to, a propensity or union of the heart to God, the supreme and infinite Being, can be of the nature of true virtue.

From hence also it is evident, that the *divine virtue*, or the virtue of the divine mind, must consist primarily in *love to himself*, or in the mutual love and friendship which subsists eternally and necessarily between the several persons in the Godhead, or that infinitely strong propensity there is in these divine persons one to another. There is no need of multiplying words, to prove that it must be thus, on a supposition that virtue, in its most essential nature, consists in benevolent affection or propensity of heart towards being in general; and so flowing out to particular beings, in a greater or lesser degree, according to the measure of existence and beauty which they are pos-

* It may be here noted, that when hereafter I use such a phrase as *private system* of being, or others similar, I thereby intend any system or society of beings that contains but a small part of the great system, comprehending the universality of existence. I think *that* may well be called a *private system*, which is but an infinitely small part of this great whole we stand related to. I therefore also call that affection *private affection*, which is limited to so narrow a circle: and that *general* affection or benevolence, which has *being in general* for its object.

sessed of. It will also follow, from the foregoing things, that God's goodness and love to created beings, is derived from and subordinate to his love to himself.*

With respect to the manner in which a virtuous love in *created* beings, *one to another*, is dependent on, and derived from love to *God*, this will appear by a proper consideration of what has been said; that it is sufficient to render love to any created being, virtuous, if it arise from the temper of mind wherein consists a *disposition* to love God supremely. Because it appears from what has been already observed, all that love to *particular beings*, which is the fruit of a benevolent propensity of heart to *being in general*, is virtuous love. But, as has been remarked, a benevolent propensity of heart to being in general, and a temper or disposition to love God supremely, are in effect the same thing. Therefore, if love to a created being comes from that temper, or propensity of the heart, it is virtuous. However, every particular exercise of love to a creature may not *sensibly* arise from any exercise of love to God, or an explicit consideration of any similitude, conformity, union, or relation to God, in the creature beloved.

The most proper *evidence* of love to a created being, arising from that temper of mind wherein consists a supreme propensity of heart to God, seems to be the agreeableness of the kind and degree of our love to *God's end* in our creation, and in the creation of all things, and the coincidence of the exercise of our love, in their manner, order, and measure, with the *manner* in which *God* himself exercises love to the creature in the creation and government of the world, and the way in which God, as the first cause and supreme disposer of all things, has respect to the creature's happiness, in subordination to himself as his own supreme end. For the true virtue of created beings is doubtless their highest excellency, and their true goodness, and that by which they are especially agreeable to the mind of their Creator. But the true goodness of a thing, must be its agreeableness to its *end*, or its fitness to answer the design for which it was made. Therefore, they are good moral agents, whose temper of mind, or propensity of heart, is agreeable to the *end* for which God made moral agents. But, as has been shown, the last end for which God has made moral agents, must be the last end for which God has made all things: it being evident, that the moral world is the end of the rest of the world; the inanimate and unintelligent world being made for the rational and moral world, as much as a house is prepared for the inhabitants.

By these things, it appears, that a truly virtuous mind, being as it were under the sovereign dominion of *love to God*, above all things, seeks the *glory of God*, and makes *this* his supreme, governing, and ultimate end. This consists in the expression of God's perfections in their proper effects,—the manifestation of God's glory to created understandings,—the communications of the infinite fulness of God to the creature,—the creature's highest esteem of God, love to, and joy in him,—and in the proper exercises and expressions of these. And so far as a virtuous mind exercises true virtue in *benevolence* to created beings, it chiefly seeks the *good* of the creature; consisting in its *knowledge* or view of God's glory and beauty, its *union* with God, conformity and love to him, and joy in him. And that disposition of heart, that consent, union, or propensity of mind to being in general, which appears chiefly in such exercises, is VIRTUE, truly so called; or in other words, true GRACE and real HOLINESS. And no other disposition or affection but this is of the nature of true virtue.

Corollary. Hence it appears, that those *schemes* of religion or moral philosophy, which—however well in some respects they may treat of benevolence to *mankind*, and other virtues depending on it, yet—have not a supreme regard to God, and love to him, laid as the *foundation*, and all other virtues handled in a *connexion* with this, and in *subordination* to it, are not true schemes of philosophy, but are fundamentally and essentially defective. And whatever other benevolence or generosity towards mankind, and other virtues, or moral qualifications which go by that name, any are possessed of, that are not attended with a *love to God*, which is altogether above them, and to which they are subordinate, and on which they are dependent, there is nothing of the nature of true virtue or religion in them. And it may be asserted in general, that nothing is of the nature of true virtue, in which God is not the *first* and the *last*; or which, with regard to their exercises in general, have not their first foundation and source in apprehensions of God's supreme dignity and glory, and in answerable esteem and love of him, and have not respect to God as the supreme end.

* In what manner it is so, I have endeavoured in some measure to explain in the preceding discourse of *God's end in creating the world.*

CHAP. III.

Concerning the secondary and inferior kind of beauty.

THOUGH what has been spoken of is, alone, justly esteemed the true beauty of moral agents, or spiritual beings; this alone being what would appear beautiful in them upon a clear and comprehensive view of things; and therefore alone is the moral amiableness of beings that have understanding and will, in the eyes of him that perfectly sees all things as they are; yet there are other qualities, other sensations, propensities, and affections of mind, and principles of action, that often obtain the epithet of *virtuous*, and by many are supposed to have the nature of true virtue; which are entirely of a distinct nature from this, and have nothing of that kind; and therefore are erroneously confounded with real virtue.

That consent, agreement, or union of being to being, which has been spoken of, *viz.* the union or propensity of *minds* to mental or spiritual existence, may be called the highest and primary beauty; being the proper and peculiar beauty of spiritual and moral beings, which are the highest and first part of the universal system, for whose sake all the rest has existence. Yet there is another, inferior, secondary beauty, which is some image of this, and which is not peculiar to spiritual beings, but is found even in inanimate things; which consists in a mutual consent and agreement of different things, in form, manner, quantity, and visible end or design; called by the various names of regularity, order, uniformity, symmetry, proportion, harmony, &c. Such is the mutual agreement of the various sides of a square, or equilateral triangle, or of a regular polygon. Such is, as it were, the mutual consent of the different parts of the periphery of a circle, or surface of a sphere, and of the corresponding parts of an ellipsis. Such is the agreement of the colours, figures, dimensions, and distances of the different spots on a chess board. Such is the beauty of the figures on a piece of chintz or brocade. Such is the beautiful proportion of the various parts of a human body, or countenance. And such is the sweet mutual consent and agreement of the various notes of a melodious tune. This is the same that Mr. Hutchinson, in his Treatise on Beauty, expresses by uniformity in the midst of variety. Which is no other than the consent or agreement of different things, in form, quantity, &c. He observes, that the greater the variety is in equal uniformity the greater the beauty. Which is no more than to say, the more there are of different mutually agreeing things, the greater is the beauty. And the reason of that is, because it is more considerable to have many things consent one with another, than a few only.

The beauty which consists in the visible fitness of a thing to its use, and unity of design, is not a distinct sort of beauty from this. For it is to be observed, that one thing which contributes to the beauty of the agreement and proportion of various things, is their relation one to another; which connects them, and introduces them together into view and consideration, and whereby one suggests the other to the mind, and the mind is led to compare them, and so to expect and desire agreement. Thus the uniformity of two or more pillars, as they may happen to be found in *different* places, is not an equal degree of beauty, as that uniformity in so many pillars in the corresponding parts of the *same* building. So means and an intended effect are related one to another. The answerableness of a thing to its use is only the proportion and fitness of a cause, or means, to a visibly designed effect, and so an effect suggested to the mind by the idea of the means. This kind of beauty is not entirely different from that beauty which there is in fitting a mortise to its tenon. Only when the beauty consists in unity of design, or the adaptedness of a variety of things to promote one intended effect, in which all conspire, as the various parts of an ingenious complicated machine, there is a *double* beauty, as there is a twofold agreement and conformity. First, there is the agreement of the various parts to the designed end. Secondly, through this designed end or effect, all the various particulars agree one with another as the general medium of their union, whereby they, being united in this third, are all united one to another.

The reason, or at least one reason, why God has made this kind of mutual agreement of things beautiful and grateful to those intelligent beings that perceive it, probably is, that there is in it some image of the true, spiritual, original beauty, which has been spoken of; consisting in being's consent to being, or the union of spiritual beings in a mutual propensity and affection of heart. The other is an image of this, because by that uniformity diverse things become as it were one, as it is in this cordial union. And it pleases God to observe analogy in his works, as is manifest in fact, in innumerable instances; and especially to establish inferior things with analogy to superior. Thus, in how many instances has he formed brutes in analogy to the nature of mankind! and plants, in analogy to animals, with respect to the manner of their generation, nutrition, &c. And so he has constituted the external world in analogy to the spiritual world, in numberless instances; as might be shown, if it were necessary, and here were a proper place for it.—Why such analogy in God's works pleases him, it is not needful now to inquire. It is sufficient that he makes an agreement of different things, in their form, manner, measure, &c. to appear beautiful, because here is some image of a higher kind of agreement and consent of spiritual beings. It has pleased him to establish a law of nature, by virtue of which the uniformity and mutual correspondence of a beautiful plant, and the respect which the various parts of a regular building seem to have one to another, and their agreement and union, and the consent or concord of the various notes of a melodious tune, should appear beautiful; because therein is some image of the consent of mind, of the different members of a society or system of intelligent beings, sweetly united in a benevolent agreement of heart.

And here by the way, I would further observe, probably it is with regard to this image or resemblance, which secondary beauty has of true spiritual beauty, that God has so constituted nature, that the presenting of this inferior beauty, especially in those kinds of it which have the greatest resemblance of the primary beauty, as the harmony of sounds, and the beauties of nature, have a tendency to assist those whose hearts are under the influence of a truly virtuous temper, to dispose them to the exercises of divine love, and enliven in them a sense of spiritual beauty.

From what has been said we may see, that there are two sorts of agreement or consent of one thing to another. (1.) There is a *cordial* agreement; that consists in concord and union of mind and heart: which, if not attended (viewing things in general) with more discord than concord, is true virtue, and the original or primary beauty, which is the only true *moral* beauty. (2.) There is a *natural* union or agreement; which, though some image of the other, is entirely a distinct thing; the will, disposition, or affection of the heart having no concern in it, but consisting only in uniformity and consent of nature, form, quantity, &c. (as before described,) wherein lies an inferior secondary sort of beauty, which may in distinction from the other, be called *natural* beauty. This may be sufficient to let the reader know how I shall hereafter use the phrases *cordial* and *natural* agreement; and moral, spiritual, divine, and *primary* original beauty, and *secondary* or natural beauty. Concerning this latter, the inferior kind of beauty, the following things may be observed:

1. The *cause* why secondary beauty is grateful to men, is only a *law of nature*, which God has fixed, or an *instinct* he has given to mankind; and not their perception of the same thing which *God* is pleased to regard as the ground or rule by which he has established such a law of nature. This appears in two things.

(1.) That which God respects, as the *ground* of this law of nature, whereby things having a secondary beauty are made grateful to men, is their mutual *agreement* and proportion, in measure, form, &c. But, in many instances, persons that are gratified and affected with this beauty, do not reflect on that particular agreement and proportion, which, according to the law of nature, is the ground and rule of beauty in the case, yea, are ignorant of it. Thus, a man may be pleased with the harmony of the notes in a tune, and yet know nothing of that proportion or adjustment of the notes, which, by the law of nature, is the ground of the melody. He knows not, that the vibrations in one note regularly coincide with the vibrations in another; that the vibrations of a note coincide in time with two vibrations of its octave; and that two vibrations of a note coincide with three of its fifth, &c.—Yea, he may not know, that there are vibrations of the air in the case, or any corresponding motions in the organs of hearing, in the auditory nerve, or animal spirits.——So a man may be affected and pleased with a beautiful proportion of the features in a face, and yet not know what that proportion is, or in what measures, quantities, and distances it consists. In this, therefore, a sensation of *secondary* beauty differs from a sensation of *primary* and spiritual beauty, consisting in a spiritual union and agreement. What makes the *latter* grateful, is perceiving the *union itself*. It is the immediate view of that wherein the beauty fundamentally lies, that is pleasing to the virtuous mind.

(2.) God, in establishing such a law—that mutual natural agreement of different things, in form, quantity, &c. should appear beautiful or grateful to men—seems to have had regard to the *resemblance* there is in such a natural agreement, to that spiritual, cordial agreement, wherein original beauty consists. But it is not any reflection upon, or perception of, such a resemblance, that is the reason why such a form or state of objects appear beautiful to men: but their sensation of pleasure, on a view of this secondary beauty, is immediately owing to the law God has established, or the instinct he has given.

2. Another thing observable concerning this kind of beauty, is, that it affects the mind more (other things being equal) when taken notice of in objects which are of considerable *importance*, than in little trivial matters. Thus, the symmetry of the parts of a human body, or countenance, affects the mind more than the beauty of a flower. So the beauty of the solar system, more than as great and as manifold an order and uniformity in a tree. And the proportions of the parts of a church, or a palace, more than the same proportions in some little slight compositions, made to please children.

3. Not only uniformity and proportion, &c. of different things, is requisite, in order to this inferior beauty; but also some *relation* or connexion of the things thus agreeing one with another. As the uniformity or likeness of a number of pillars, scattered hither and thither, does not constitute beauty, or at least by no means in an equal degree, as uniformity in pillars connected in the same building, in parts that have *relation* one to another. So, if we see things unlike, and very disproportioned, in *distant* places, which have no relation to each other, this excites no such idea of deformity, as disagreement, inequality, or disproportion in things related and connected; and the nearer the relation, and the stricter the connexion, so much the greater and more disgustful is the deformity, consisting in their disagreement.

4. This secondary kind of beauty, consisting in uniformity and proportion, not only takes place in material and external things, but also in things immaterial; and is, in very many things, plain and sensible in the latter, as well as the former. And when it is so, there is no reason why it should not be grateful to them that behold it, in these as well as the other, by virtue of the same sense, or the same determination of mind, to be gratified with uniformity and proportion. If uniformity and proportion be the things that affect and appear agreeable to this sense of beauty, then why should not uniformity and proportion affect the same sense in immaterial things as well as material, if there be equal capacity of discerning it in both?

and indeed *more* in spiritual things *(cæteris paribus)* as these are more important than things merely external and material?

This is not only reasonable to be supposed, but is evident in fact, in numberless instances. There is a beauty of order in society, besides what consists in benevolence, or can be referred to it, which is of the *secondary* kind. As, when the different members of society have all their appointed office, place, and station, according to their several capacities and talents, and every one keeps his place, and continues in his proper business. In this there is a beauty, not of a different kind from the regularity of a beautiful building, or piece of skilful architecture, where the strong pillars are set in their proper place, the pilasters in a place fit for them, the square pieces of marble in the pavement, the pannels, partitions, and cornices, &c. in places proper for them. As the agreement of a variety of things in one common design,—as of the parts of a building, or complicated machine,—is one instance of that regularity which belongs to the secondary kind of beauty, so there is the same kind of beauty in what is called *wisdom*, consisting in the united tendency of thoughts, ideas, and particular volitions, to one general purpose: which is a distinct thing from the *goodness* of that general purpose, as being useful and benevolent.

There is a beauty in the virtue called *justice*, which consists in the agreement of different things, that have relation to one another, in nature, manner, and measure; and therefore is the very same sort of beauty with that uniformity and proportion, which is observable in those external and material things that are esteemed beautiful. There is a natural agreement and adaptedness of things that have relation one to another, and an harmonious corresponding of one thing with another. He who from his will *does* evil to others, should *receive* evil from the will of him or them whose business it is to take care of the injured, and to act in their behalf, in *proportion* to the evil of his doings. Things are in natural regularity and mutual agreement, in a literal sense, when he whose heart opposes the general system, should have the hearts of that system, or the heart of the ruler of the system, against him; and, in consequence, should receive evil, in proportion to the evil tendency of the opposition of his heart. So, there is an agreement in nature and measure, when he that loves has the proper returns of love; when he that from his heart promotes the good of another, has his good promoted by the other; for there is a kind of justice in becoming gratitude.

Indeed most of the duties incumbent on us, if well considered, will be found to partake of the nature of *justice*. There is some natural agreement of one thing to another; some adaptedness of the agent to the object; some answerableness of the act to the occasion; some equality and proportion in things of a similar nature, and of a direct relation one to another. So it is in relative duties; duties of children to parents, and of parents to children; duties of husbands and wives; duties of rulers and subjects; duties of friendship and good neighbourhood; and all duties that we owe to God, our creator, preserver, and benefactor; and all duties whatsoever, considered as required by God, and as what are to be performed with a regard to Christ.

It is this secondary kind of beauty, which Mr. Wollaston seems to have had in his eye, when he resolved all virtue into an agreement of inclinations, volitions, and actions with *truth*. He evidently has respect to the *justice* there is in virtues and duties; which consists in one being expressing such affections, and using such a conduct, towards another, as hath a natural agreement and proportion to what is in them, and what we receive from them: which is as much a natural conformity of affection and action with its ground, object, and occasion, as that which is between a true proposition and the thing spoken of in it.

But there is another and higher beauty in true virtue, and in all truly virtuous dispositions and exercises, than what consists in any uniformity or similarity of various things; *viz.* the *union of heart* to *being in general*, or to GOD, the Being of beings, which appears in those virtues; and of which those virtues, when true, are the various expressions or effects. Benevolence to being in general, or to being simply considered, is entirely a distinct thing from uniformity in the midst of variety, and is a superior kind of beauty.

It is true, that benevolence to being in general, will naturally incline to justice, or proportion in the exercises of it. He that loves being, simply considered, will naturally, other things being equal, love *particular* beings, in a proportion compounded of the degree of being, and the degree of virtue, or benevolence to being, which they have. And that is to love beings in proportion to their dignity. For the dignity of any being consists in those two things. Respect to being, in this proportion, is the first and most general kind of justice; which will produce all the subordinate kinds. So that, after benevolence to being in general exists, the *proportion* which is observed in objects may be the cause of the *proportion of benevolence* to those objects: but *no proportion* is the *cause* or ground of the existence of such a thing as benevolence to being. The tendency of objects to excite that degree of benevolence, which is proportionable to the degree of being, &c. is the *consequence* of the existence of benevolence, and not the *ground* of it. Even as a tendency of bodies one to another, by mutual attraction, in proportion to the quantity of matter, is the consequence of the being of such a thing as mutual attraction; and not attraction the effect of proportion.

By this it appears, that *just* affections and acts have a *beauty* in them, distinct from and superior to the uniformity and equality there is in them: for which, he that has a truly virtuous temper, relishes and delights in them. And that is the expression and manifestation there is in them of benevolence to being in general. And besides this, there is the agreement of *justice* to the will and command of God; and also something in the tendency and consequences of justice, agreeable to general benevolence, as the glory of God, and the general good. Which tendency also makes it beautiful to a truly virtuous mind. So that the tendency of general benevolence to produce justice, also the tendency of justice to produce effects agreeable to general benevolence, both render justice pleasing to a virtuous mind. And it is on these accounts *chiefly*, that justice is grateful to a virtuous taste, or a truly benevolent heart. But though it be true, that the uniformity and proportion there is in justice, is grateful to a benevolent heart, as this uniformity and proportion tends to the general good; yet that is no argument that there is no *other* beauty in it but its agreeing with benevolence. For so the external regularity and order of the natural world gratifies benevolence, as it is profitable, and tends to the general good; but that is no argument that there is no *other* sort of beauty in external uniformity and proportion, but only its suiting benevolence, by tending to the general good.

5. From all that has been observed concerning this *secondary* kind of beauty, it appears, that the disposition, which consists in a determination of mind to approve and be pleased with this beauty, considered simply and by itself, has nothing of the nature of true virtue, and is entirely a different thing from a truly virtuous taste. For it has been shown, that this kind of *beauty* is entirely diverse from the beauty of true virtue, whether it takes place in material or immaterial things; and therefore it will follow, that a *taste* of this kind of beauty is entirely a different thing from a taste of true virtue. Who will affirm, that a disposition to approve of the harmony of good music, or the beauty of a square, or equilateral triangle, is the same with true holiness, or a truly virtuous disposition of mind? It is a relish of *uniformity* and *proportion* that determines the mind to approve these things. And there is no need of any thing higher, or of any thing in any respect diverse, to determine the mind to approve and be pleased with equal *uniformity* and *proportion* among spiritual things which are equally discerned. It is virtuous to love true virtue, as that denotes an agreement of the heart with virtue. But it argues no virtue for the heart to be pleased with that which is entirely distinct from it.

Though it be true, that there is some *analogy* in it to spiritual and virtuous beauty—as far as material things can have analogy to things spiritual, of which they can have no more than a shadow—yet, as has been observed, men do not approve it *because* of any such analogy perceived. And not only reason but *experience* plainly shows, that men's approbation of this sort of beauty does not spring from any virtuous temper, and has no connexion with virtue. For otherwise their delight in the beauty of squares, and cubes, and regular polygons, in the regularity of buildings, and the beautiful figures in a piece of embroidery, would increase in proportion to men's virtue; and would be raised to a great height in some eminently virtuous or holy men; but would be almost wholly lost in some others that are very vicious and lewd. It is evident in fact, that a relish of these things does not depend on general benevolence, or *any benevolence at all* to any being whatsoever, any more than a man's loving the taste of honey, or his being pleased with the smell of a rose. A taste of this *inferior* beauty in things immaterial, is one thing which has been mistaken by some moralists, for a true virtuous principle, supposed to be implanted naturally in the hearts of all mankind.

CHAP. IV.

Of self-love, and its various influence, to cause love to others, or the contrary.

MANY assert, that all love arises from self-love. In order to determine this point, it should be clearly determined what is meant by self-love. Self-love, I think, is generally defined "a man's love of his own happiness;" which is short, and may be thought very plain: but in reality is an ambiguous definition, as the expression *his own*, is equivocal, and liable to be taken in two very different senses. For a man's *own happiness* may either be taken universally, for all the happiness or pleasure of which the mind is in any regard the subject, or whatever is grateful and pleasing to men; or it may be taken for the pleasure a man takes in his own proper, private, and separate good. And so *self-love* may be taken two ways.

1. It may be taken for the same as his loving whatsoever is pleasing to him. Which comes only to this, that self-love is a man's liking, and being suited and pleased in that which he likes, and which pleases him; or, that it is a man's loving what he loves. For whatever a man loves, that thing is grateful and pleasing to him, whether that be his own peculiar happiness, or the happiness of others. And if this be all that they mean by self-love, no wonder they suppose that all love may be resolved into self-love. For it is undoubtedly true, that whatever a man loves, his love may be resolved into his *loving what he loves.*—— If by self-love is meant nothing else but a man's loving what is grateful or pleasing to him, and being averse to what is disagreeable, this is calling *that* self-love, which is only a general capacity of loving or hating; or a capacity of being either pleased or displeased; which is the same thing as a man's having a faculty of will. For if nothing could be either pleasing or displeasing, agreeable or disagreeable, to a man, then he could incline to nothing, and will nothing. But if he is capable of having inclination, will and choice, then what he inclines to, and chooses, is grateful to him, whatever that be; whether it be his own private good, the good of his neighbours, or the glory of God. And so far as it is grateful or pleasing to him, so far it is a part of his pleasure, good, or happiness.

But if this be what is meant by self-love, there is an impropriety and absurdity even in the putting of the question, Whether all our love, or our love to each particular object of our love, does not arise from self-love? For that would be the same as to inquire, Whether the reason why our love is fixed on such and such particular objects, is not, that we have a capacity of loving some things? This may be a general reason why men love or hate any thing at all; and therein differ from stones and trees, which love nothing, and hate nothing. But it can never be a reason why men's love is placed on such and such objects. That a man in general loves, and is pleased with happiness, or has a capacity of enjoying happiness, cannot be the reason why such and such things become his happiness: as for instance, why the good of his neighbour, or the happiness and glory of God, is grateful and pleasing to him, and so becomes a part of his happiness.

Or if what they mean, who say that all love comes from self-love, be not, that our loving such and such particular persons and things arises from our love to happiness in general, but from a love to *our own happiness*, which consists in these objects; so, the reason why we love benevolence to our friends, or neighbours, is, because we love our happiness, consisting in their happiness, which we take pleasure in:—still the notion is absurd. For here the effect is made the cause of that of which it is the effect: our happiness, consisting in the happiness of the person beloved, is made the cause of our love to that person. Whereas the truth plainly is, that our love to the person is the cause of our delighting or being happy in his happiness. How comes our happiness to consist in the happiness of such as we love, but by our hearts being first united to them in affection, so that we as it were look on them as ourselves, and so on their happiness as our own? Men who have benevolence to others have pleasure when they see others' happiness, because seeing their happiness gratifies some inclination that was in their hearts before. They before inclined to their happiness; which was by benevolence or good-will; and therefore, when they see their happiness, their inclination is suited, and they are pleased. But the being of inclinations and appetites is prior to any pleasure in gratifying these appetites.

2. Self-love, as the phrase is used in common speech, most commonly signifies a man's regard to his confined *private self*, or love to himself with respect to his *private interest.*

By *private* interest I mean that which most immediately consists in those pleasures, or pains, that are *personal.* For there is a comfort, and a grief, that some have in others' pleasures, or pains; which are in *others* originally, but are derived to them, or in some measure become theirs, by virtue of a benevolent union of heart with others. And there are other pleasures and pains that are originally our *own*, and not what we have by such a participation with others. Which consist in perceptions agreeable, or contrary, to certain personal inclinations implanted in our nature; such as the sensitive appetites and aversions. Such also is the disposition or the determination of the mind to be pleased with external beauty, and with all inferior, secondary beauty, consisting in uniformity, proportion, &c. whether in things external or internal, and to dislike the contrary deformity. Such also is the natural disposition in men to be pleased in a perception of their being the objects of the honour and love of others, and displeased with others' hatred and contempt. For pleasures and uneasiness of this kind are doubtless as much owing to an immediate determination of the mind by a fixed law of our nature, as any of the pleasures or pains of external sense. And these pleasures are properly of the private and personal kind; being not by any participation of the happiness or sorrow of others, through benevolence. It is evidently mere self-love that appears in this disposition. It is easy to see, that a man's love to himself will make him love *love* to himself, and hate *hatred* to himself. And as God has constituted our nature, self-love is exercised in no one disposition more than in this. Men, probably, are capable of much more pleasure and pain through this determination of the mind, than by any other personal inclination or aversion whatsoever. Though perhaps we do not so very often see instances of extreme suffering by this means, as by some others, yet we often see evidences of men's dreading the contempt of others more than death; and by such instances may conceive something what men would suffer, if universally hated and despised; and may reasonably infer something of the greatness of the misery, that would arise under a sense of universal abhorrence, in a great view of intelligent being in general, or in a clear view of the Deity, as incomprehensibly and immensely great, so that all other beings are as nothing and vanity—together with a sense of his immediate continual presence, and an infinite concern with him and dependence upon him—and living constantly in the midst of most clear and strong evidences and manifestations of his hatred and contempt. These things may be sufficient to explain what I mean by *private* interest; in regard to which, self-love, most properly so called, is immediately exercised.

And here I would observe, that if we take self-love in

this sense, so love to some *others* may truly be the *effect* of self-love; *i. e.* according to the common method and order which is maintained in the laws of nature. For no created thing has power to produce an effect any otherwise than by virtue of the laws of nature. Thus, that a man should love those who are of his party, and who are warmly engaged on his side, and promote his interest, is the natural consequence of a private self-love. Indeed there is no metaphysical necessity, in the nature of things, that because a man loves himself, and regards his own interest, he therefore should love those that love him, and promote his interest, *i. e.* to suppose it to be otherwise implies no contradiction. It will not follow from any absolute metaphysical necessity, that because bodies have solidity, cohesion, and gravitation towards the centre of the earth, therefore a weight suspended on the beam of a balance should have greater power to counterbalance a weight on the other side, when at a distance from the fulcrum, than when it is near. It implies no contradiction that it should be otherwise; but only as it contradicts that beautiful proportion and harmony, which the Author of nature observes in the laws of nature he has established. Neither is there any absolute necessity, that because there is an internal mutual attraction of the parts of the earth, or any other sphere, whereby the whole becomes one solid coherent body, therefore other bodies that are around it, should also be attracted by it, and those that are nearest, be attracted most. But according to the order and proportion generally observed in the laws of nature, one of these effects is connected with the other, so that it is justly looked upon as the same power of attraction in the globe of the earth, which draws bodies about the earth towards its centre, with that which attracts the parts of the earth themselves one to another; only exerted under different circumstances. By a like order of nature, a man's love to those that love him, is no more than a certain expression or effect of self-love. No other principle is needful in order to the effect, if nothing intervenes to countervail the natural tendency of self-love. Therefore there is no more true virtue in a man thus loving his friends merely from self-love, than there is in self-love itself, the principle from whence it proceeds. So, a man being disposed to hate those that hate him, or to resent injuries done him, arises from self-love, in like manner as loving those that love us, and being thankful for kindness shown us.

But it is said by some, that it is apparent there is some *other* principle concerned in exciting the passions of gratitude and anger besides self-love, *viz. moral sense*, or sense of moral beauty and deformity, determining the minds of all mankind to approve of, and be pleased with virtue, and to disapprove of vice, and behold it with displicence; and that their seeing or supposing this moral beauty or deformity, in the kindness of a benefactor, or opposition of an adversary, is the occasion of these affections of gratitude or anger. Otherwise, why are not these affections excited in us towards inanimate things that do us good or hurt? Why do not we experience gratitude to a garden, or fruitful field? And why are we not angry with a tempest, or blasting mildew, or an overflowing stream? We are very differently affected towards those that do us good from the virtue of generosity, or hurt us from the vice of envy and malice, than towards things that hurt or help us, which are destitute of reason and will. Concerning this, I would make several remarks.

1. Those who thus argue, that gratitude and anger cannot proceed from *self-love*, might argue in the same way, and with equal reason, that neither can these affections arise from love to *others:* which is contrary to their own scheme. They say, that the reason why we are affected with gratitude and anger towards *men*, rather than *things* without life, is moral sense: which they say is the effect of that principle of benevolence or love to others, or love to the public, which is naturally in the hearts of all mankind. But now I might say, according to their own way of arguing, gratitude and anger cannot arise from love to others, or love to the public, or any sense of mind that is the fruit of public affection. For how differently are we affected towards those that do good or hurt to the public from understanding and will, and public motive, from what we are towards such inanimate things as the sun and the clouds, that do good to the public, by enlightening and enlivening beams and refreshing showers; or mildew, and an overflowing stream, that does hurt to the public, by destroying the fruits of the earth! Yea, if such a kind of argument be good, it will prove that gratitude and anger cannot arise from the united influence of self-love, and public love, or moral sense arising from public affection. For, if so, why are we not affected towards inanimate things, that are beneficial or injurious both to us and the public, in the same manner as to them that are profitable or hurtful to both on choice and design, and from benevolence or malice?

2. On the supposition, that men love those who love them, and are angry with those who hate them, from the natural influence of self-love; it is not at all strange that the Author of nature, who observes order, uniformity, and harmony in establishing its laws, should so order, that it should be natural for self-love to cause the mind to be affected differently towards exceedingly different objects; and that it should cause our heart to extend itself in *one* manner towards inanimate things, which gratify self-love, without sense or will, and in *another* manner towards beings which we look upon as having understanding and will, like ourselves, and exerting these faculties in our favour, and promoting our interest from love to us. No wonder, seeing we love ourselves, that it should be natural to us to extend something of that same kind of love which we have for ourselves, to them who are the same kind of beings as ourselves, and comply with the inclinations of our self-love, by expressing the same sort of love towards us.

3. If we should allow that to be universal, that in gratitude and anger there is the exercise of some kind of moral sense—as it is granted there is something that may be so called—all the moral sense that is essential to those affections, is a sense of DESERT; which is to be referred to that sense of *justice*, before spoken of, consisting in an apprehension of that secondary kind of beauty that lies in uniformity and proportion; which solves all the difficulty in the objection. Others' love and kindness to us, or their ill-will and injuriousness, appear to us to *deserve* our love or our resentment. Or, in other words, it seems to us no other than *just*, that as they love us and do us good, we also should love them and do them good. And so it seems *just*, that when others' hearts oppose us, and they from their hearts do us hurt, our hearts should oppose them, and that we should desire themselves may suffer in like manner as we have suffered, *i. e.* there appears to us to be a natural agreement, proportion, and adjustment between these things; which is indeed a kind of *moral sense*, or sense of beauty in moral things. But, as was before shown, it is a moral sense of a *secondary* kind, and is entirely different from a sense or relish of the original essential beauty of true virtue; and may be without any principle of true virtue in the heart. Therefore, doubtless, it is a great *mistake* in any to suppose, that the moral sense which appears and is exercised in a sense of *desert*, is the same thing as a love of virtue, or a disposition and determination of mind to be pleased with true virtuous beauty, consisting in public benevolence. Which may be further confirmed, if it be considered, that even with respect to a sense of *justice* or *desert*, consisting in uniformity, and agreement between others' actions, towards us, and our actions towards them, in a way of well-doing, or of ill-doing, it is not absolutely necessary to the being of these passions of gratitude and anger, that there should be any notion of justice in them, in any public or general view of things: as will appear by what shall be next observed.

4. Those authors who hold, that the moral sense, which is natural to all mankind, consists in a natural relish of the beauty of virtue, and so arises from a principle of true virtue implanted by nature in the hearts of all, hold that true virtue consists in *public benevolence*. Therefore, if the affections of gratitude and anger necessarily imply such a moral sense as they suppose, then these affections imply some delight in the public good, and an aversion of the mind to public evil. And if so, then every time a man feels anger for opposition, or gratitude for any favour, there must be at least a supposition of a tendency to public injury in that opposition, and a tendency to public benefit

in the favour that excites his gratitude. But how far is this from being true! For instance; a ship's crew enter into a conspiracy against the master, to murder him, and run away with the ship, and turn pirates: but before they bring their matters to ripeness for execution, one of them repents, and opens the whole design; whereupon the rest are apprehended and brought to justice. The crew are enraged with him that has betrayed them, and earnestly seek opportunity to *revenge* themselves upon him. And for an instance of *gratitude*; a gang of robbers that have long infested the neighbouring country, have a particular house whither they resort, and where they meet from time to time, to divide their booty, and hold their consultations for carrying on their pernicious designs. The magistrates and officers of the country, after many fruitless endeavours to discover their secret place of resort, at length are well-informed where it is, and are prepared with sufficient force to surprise them, and seize them all, at the place of rendezvous, at an hour appointed, when they understand they will all be there. A little before the arrival of the appointed hour, while the officers with their bands are approaching, some person is so kind to these robbers, as to give them notice of their danger, so as just to give them opportunity to escape. They are *thankful* to him, and give him a handful of money for his kindness. Now, in such instances, I think it is plain, that there is no supposition of a *public injury* in that which is the occasion of their *anger;* yea, they know the contrary. Nor is there any supposition of *public good* in that which excites their *gratitude;* neither has public benevolence, or moral sense, consisting in a determination to approve of what is for the public good, any influence at all in the affair. And though there be some affection, besides a sense of uniformity and proportion, that has influence in such anger and gratitude, it is not *public* affection or benevolence, but *private* affection; yea, that affection which is to the *highest degree* private, consisting in a man's love of his own person.

5. The passion of *anger*, in particular, seems to have been unluckily chosen as a medium to prove a sense and determination to delight in virtue, consisting in benevolence natural to all mankind. For if that moral sense which is exercised in anger, were that which arose from a benevolent temper of heart, being no other than a sense or relish of the beauty of benevolence, one would think, a disposition to anger should *increase*, at least in some proportion, as a man had more of a sweet, benign, and benevolent temper: which seems contrary to experience, which shows that the less men have of benevolence, and the more they have of a contrary temper, the more are they disposed to anger and deep resentment of injuries.

And though *gratitude* be that which many speak of as a certain noble principle of virtue, which God has implanted in the hearts of all mankind; and though it be true there is a gratitude that is *truly virtuous;* and the want of gratitude, or an ungrateful temper, is *truly vicious*, and argues an abominable depravity of heart; yet I think, what has been observed may serve to convince such as impartially consider it, not only that not all anger, or hating those which hate us, but also that not all gratitude, or loving those which love us, arises from a truly virtuous benevolence of heart.

Another sort of affections, which may be properly referred to self-love, as its source, and which might be expected to be the fruit of it, according to the general analogy of nature's laws, is that of affections to such as are near to us by the ties of nature. Such are those of whose beings we have been the occasion, in whom we have a very peculiar propriety, and whose circumstances, even from the beginning of their existence, many ways lead them to a high esteem of us, and to treat us with great dependence, submission, and compliance. These the constitution of the world makes to be united in interest, and accordingly to act as one, in innumerable affairs, with a communion in each other's affections, desires, cares, friendships, enmities, and pursuits. As to the opinion of those who ascribe the natural affection there is between parents and children to a particular *instinct* of nature, I shall take notice of it afterwards.

And as men may love persons and things from self-love, so may their love to *qualities* and *characters* arise from the same source. Some represent this, as though there were need of a great degree of metaphysical refining to make it out, that men approve of others from self-love, whom they hear of at a distance, or read of in history, or see represented on the stage, from whom they expect no profit or advantage. But perhaps it is not considered, that what we approve of in the first place is the *character;* and from the character we approve the *person*. And is it a strange thing, that men should from self-love like a temper or character, which, in its nature and tendency, falls in with the nature and tendency of self-love; and which we know by experience and self-evidence, without metaphysical refining, in the general tends to men's pleasure and benefit? And on the contrary, is it strange that any should dislike what they see tends to men's pain and misery? Is there need of a great degree of subtilty and abstraction, to make it out, that a child, who has heard and seen much of what is calculated strongly to fix an idea of the pernicious, deadly nature of the rattlesnake, should have an aversion to that species from self-love; so as to have a degree of this aversion and disgust excited by seeing even the picture of that animal? And that from the same self-love it should be pleased with a lively representation of some pleasant fruit of which it has often tasted the sweetness? Or, with the image of some bird, which it has always been told is innocent, and with whose pleasant singing it has often been entertained? Yet the child neither fears being bitten by the picture of the snake, nor expects to eat of the painted fruit, or to hear the figure of the bird sing. I suppose none will think it difficult to allow, that such an approbation or disgust of a child may be accounted for from its natural delight in the pleasures of *taste* and *hearing*, and its aversion to *pain* and *death*, through *self-love*, together with the habitual connexion of these agreeable or terrible ideas with the form and qualities of these objects, the ideas of which are impressed on the mind of the child by their images.

And where is the difficulty of allowing, that a person may hate the general character of a spiteful and malicious man, for the like reason as he hates the general nature of a serpent; knowing, from reason, instruction, and experience, that malice in men is pernicious to mankind, as well as spite or poison in a serpent? And if a man may from *self-love* disapprove the vices of malice, envy, and others of that sort, which naturally tend to the *hurt* of mankind, why may he not from the same principle approve the contrary virtues of meekness, peaceableness, benevolence, charity, generosity, justice, and the social virtues in general; which, he as easily and clearly knows, naturally tend to the good of mankind?—It is undoubtedly true, that some have a love to these virtues from a *higher* principle. But yet I think it as certainly true, that there is generally in mankind a sort of approbation of them, which arises from *self-love*.

Besides what has been already said, the same thing further appears from this; that men commonly are most affected towards, and most highly approve, those virtues which agree with their interest most, according to their various conditions in life. We see that persons of low condition are especially enamoured with a condescending, accessible, affable temper in the great; not only in those whose condescension has been exercised towards themselves; but they will be peculiarly taken with such a character when they have accounts of it from others, or when they meet with it in history, or even in romance. The poor will most highly approve and commend liberality. The weaker sex, who especially need assistance and protection, will peculiarly esteem and applaud fortitude and generosity in those of the other sex, of whom they read or hear, or which they have represented to them on a stage.

I think it plain from what has been observed, that as men may approve, and be disposed to commend, a benevolent temper from *self-love;* so the higher the degree of benevolence is, the more may they approve of it. This will account for some kind of approbation, from this principle, even of love to enemies, *viz.* as a man loving his enemies is an evidence of a high degree of benevolence of temper; the degree of it appearing from the obstacles it overcomes. And it may be here observed, that the consideration of the tendency and influence of *self-love* may show, how men in general may approve of *justice* from another ground, besides that approbation of the secondary beauty there is in uniformity and proportion, which is natural to all. Men, from their infancy, see the necessity of it, not only that it is necessary for others, or for human society; but they find the necessity of it for themselves, in instances that continually occur; which tends to prejudice them in its favour, and to fix an habitual approbation of it from self-love.

Again, that forementioned approbation of justice and desert, arising from a sense of the beauty of natural agreement and proportion, will have a kind of reflex and indirect influence to cause men to approve benevolence, and disapprove malice; as men see that he who hates and injures others deserves to be hated and punished, and that he who is benevolent and loves others, and does them good, deserves himself also to be loved and rewarded by others, as they see the natural congruity or agreement, and mutual adaptedness, of these things. And having always seen this, malevolence becomes habitually connected in the mind with the idea of being hated and punished, which is disagreeable to self-love; and the idea of benevolence is habitually connected and associated with the idea of being loved and rewarded by others, which is grateful to self-love. And by virtue of this association of ideas, benevolence itself becomes grateful, and the contrary displeasing.

Some vices may become in a degree odious by the influence of self-love, through an habitual connexion of ideas of contempt with it; contempt being what self-love abhors. So it may often be with drunkenness, gluttony, sottishness, cowardice, sloth, niggardliness. The idea of contempt becomes associated with the idea of such vices, both because we are used to observe, that these things are commonly objects of contempt, and also find, that they excite contempt in ourselves. Some of them appear marks of littleness, *i. e.* of small abilities, and weakness of mind, and insufficiency for any considerable effects among mankind. By others, men's influence is contracted into a narrow sphere, and by such means persons become of less importance, and more insignificant. And things of little importance are naturally little accounted of. And some of these ill qualities are such as mankind find it their interest to treat with contempt, as they are very hurtful to human society.—There are no particular moral virtues whatsoever, but what in some or other of these ways, and most of them in several, come to have some kind of approbation from *self-love*, without the influence of a truly virtuous principle; nor any particular vices, but what, by the same means, meet with some disapprobation.

This kind of approbation and dislike, through the joint influence of *self-love* and *association* of ideas, is in many vastly heightened by *education*. This is the means of a strong, close, and almost irrefragable association, in innumerable instances of ideas, which have no connexion any other way than by education; and is the means of greatly strengthening that association, or connexion, which persons are led into by other means: as any one would be convinced, perhaps more effectually than in most other ways, if they had opportunity of any considerable acquaintance with *American* savages and their children.

CHAP. V.

Of natural conscience, and the moral sense.

THERE is yet another disposition or principle, of great importance, natural to mankind; which, if we consider the consistence and harmony of nature's laws, may also be looked upon as, in some sort, arising from self-love, or self-union; and that is, a disposition in man to be uneasy in a consciousness of being inconsistent with himself, and as it were against himself in his own actions. This appears particularly in the inclination of the mind to be uneasy in the consciousness of doing that to others, which he should be angry with them for doing to him, if they were in his case, and he in theirs; or of forbearing to do that to them, which he would be displeased with them for neglecting to do to him.

I have observed, from time to time, that in *pure love to others, i. e.* love not arising from self-love, there is an union of the heart with others; a kind of enlargement of the mind, whereby it so extends itself as to take others into a man's self: and therefore it implies a disposition to feel, to desire, and to act as though others were one with ourselves. So, *self-love* implies an inclination to feel and act as one with ourselves; which naturally renders a sensible inconsistence with ourselves, and self-opposition in what we ourselves choose and do, to be uneasy to the mind: which will cause uneasiness of mind to be the consequence of a malevolent and unjust behaviour towards others, and a kind of disapprobation of acts of this nature, and an approbation of the contrary. To do that to another, which we should be angry with him for doing to us, and to hate a person for doing that to us, which we should incline to and insist on doing to him, if we were exactly in the same case, is to disagree with ourselves, and contradict ourselves. It would be for ourselves both to choose and adhere to, and yet to refuse and utterly reject, the very same thing. No wonder this is contrary to nature. No wonder, that such a self-opposition, and inward war with a man's self, naturally begets unquietness, and raises disturbance in his mind.

Thus approving of actions, because we therein act as in agreement with ourselves; and thus disapproving, and being uneasy in the consciousness of disagreeing with *ourselves*, in what we do, is quite a different thing from approving or disapproving actions because in them we are united with being in general: which is loving or hating actions from a sense of the primary beauty of true virtue, and of the odiousness of sin. The former of these principles is private; the latter is public, and truly benevolent in the highest sense. The former—an inclination to agree with ourselves—is a natural principle: but the latter—an agreement or union of heart to the great system, and to God the head of it, who is all and all in it—is a divine principle.

In that uneasiness now mentioned, consists very much of that inward trouble men have from reflections of conscience: and when they are free from this uneasiness, and are conscious to themselves, that in what they have acted towards others, they have done the same which they should have expected from them in the same case, then they have what is called peace of conscience, with respect to these actions. And there is also an approbation of conscience, respecting the conduct of others towards ourselves. As when we are blamed, condemned, or punished by them, and are conscious to ourselves that if we were in their case, and they in ours, we should in like manner blame, condemn, and punish them. And thus men's consciences may justify God's anger and condemnation. When they have the ideas of God's greatness, their relation to him, the benefits they have received from him, the manifestations he has made of his will to them, &c. strongly impressed on their minds, a *consciousness* is excited within them of those resentments, which would be occasioned in themselves by an injurious treatment in any wise parallel.

There certainly is such a consciousness as this oftentimes within men, implied in the thoughts and views of the mind, of which, perhaps on reflection, they could hardly give an account. Unless men's consciences are greatly stupified, it is naturally and necessarily suggested; and habitually, spontaneously, instantaneously, and, as it were, insensibly, arises in the mind. And the more so for this reason, that we have no other way to conceive of any thing which other persons act or suffer, but by recalling and exciting the ideas of what we ourselves are conscious we have found in our own minds; and by putting the ideas which we obtain by this means in the place of another; or, as it were, substituting ourselves in their place. Thus we have no conception, what understanding, perception, love, pleasure, pain, or desire are in others; but by putting ourselves as it were in their stead, or transferring the ideas we obtain of such things in our own minds by *consciousness* into their place; making such an alteration, as to degree and circumstances, as what we observe of them requires. It is thus in all *moral* things that we conceive of in others; and indeed in every thing we conceive of, belonging to others, more than shape, size, complexion, situation, and motion of their bodies. And this is the only way that we come to be *capable* of having ideas of any perception or act even of the Godhead. We never could have any notion what understanding or volition, love or hatred are, either in created spirits or in God, if we had never experienced what understanding and volition, love and hatred, are in our own minds. Knowing what they are by *consciousness*, we can deny limits, and remove changeableness and other imperfections, and ascribe them to God.

But though men in thinking of others do as it were put themselves in their place, they do it so habitually, instantaneously, and without set purpose, that they can scarce give any account of it, and many would think it strange if they were told of it. In all a man's thoughts of another person, in whatever he apprehends of his moral conduct to others or to himself, if it be in loving or hating him, approving or condemning him, rewarding or punishing him, he necessarily, as it were, puts himself in his stead; and therefore the more naturally, easily, and quietly sees whether he, being in his place, should approve or condemn, be angry or pleased as he is.

Natural conscience consists in these two things.

1. In that disposition to approve or disapprove the moral treatment which passes between us and others, from a determination of the mind to be easy or uneasy, in a consciousness of our being consistent or inconsistent with ourselves. Hereby we have a disposition to *approve* our own treatment of another, when we are conscious to ourselves that we treat him so as we should expect to be treated by him, were he in our case and we in his; and to *disapprove* of our own treatment of another, when we are conscious that we should be displeased with the like treatment from him, if we were in his case. So we in our consciences approve of another's treatment of us, if we are conscious to ourselves, that if we were in his case, and he in ours, we should think it just to treat him as he treats us; and disapprove his treatment of us, when we are conscious that we should think it unjust, if we were in his case. Thus men's consciences approve or disapprove the sentence of their judge, by which they are acquitted or condemned. But this is not all that is in natural conscience. Besides this approving or disapproving from uneasiness as being inconsistent with ourselves, there is another thing that must precede it, and be the foundation of it. As for instance, when my conscience disapproves my own treatment of another, being conscious to myself, that were I in his case, I should be displeased and angry with him for so treating me; the question might be asked, What would be the ground of that supposed disapprobation, displeasure, and anger, which I am conscious would be in me in that case? Therefore,

2. The other thing which belongs to the approbation or disapprobation of natural conscience, is the sense of *desert* which was spoken of before; consisting, as was observed, in a natural agreement, proportion, and harmony, between malevolence or injury, and resentment and punishment; or between loving and being loved, between showing kindness and being rewarded, &c. Both these kinds of approving or disapproving, concur in the approbation or disapprobation of conscience: the one founded on the other. Thus, when a man's conscience disapproves of his treatment of his neighbour, in the first place, he is conscious, that if he were in his neighbour's stead, he should resent such treatment from a sense of justice, or from a sense of uniformity and equality between such treatment, and resentment, and punishment; as before explained. And then, in the next place, he perceives, that therefore he is not consistent with himself, in doing what he himself should resent in that case; and hence disapproves it, as being naturally averse to opposition to himself.

Approbation and disapprobation of conscience, in the sense now explained, will extend to all virtue and vice; to every thing whatsoever that is morally good or evil, in a mind which does not confine its view to a private sphere, but will take things in general into its consideration, and is free from speculative error. For, as all virtue or moral good may be resolved into love to others, either God or creatures; so, men easily see the uniformity and natural agreement there is between loving others, and being accepted and favoured by others. And all vice, sin, or moral evil summarily consisting in the *want* of this love to others, or in malevolence; so, men easily see the natural agreement there is between hating and doing ill to others, and being hated by them, and suffering ill from them, or from him that acts for all, and has the care of the whole system. And as this sense of equality and natural agreement extends to all moral good and evil; so, this lays a foundation of an equal extent with the other kind of approbation and disapprobation which is grounded upon it, arising from an aversion to self-inconsistence and opposition. For in all cases of benevolence, or the contrary, towards others, we are capable of putting ourselves in the place of others, and are naturally led to do it; and so of being conscious to ourselves, how we should like or dislike such treatment from others. Thus natural conscience, if the understanding be properly enlightened, and stupifying prejudices are removed, concurs with the law of God, is of equal extent with it, and joins its voice with it in every article.

And thus, in particular, we may see in what respect this natural conscience extends to *true virtue*, consisting in union of heart to being in general, and *supreme love to God*. For, although it sees not, or rather does not *taste*, its primary and essential beauty, *i. e.* it tastes no sweetness in benevolence to being in general, simply considered, for nothing but general benevolence itself can do that, yet, this natural conscience, common to mankind, may *approve* of it from that uniformity, equality, and *justice*, which there is in it; and the *demerit* which is seen in the contrary, consisting in the natural agreement between the contrary, and being hated of being in general. Men, by natural conscience, may see the justice, or natural agreement, there is in yielding all to God, as we receive all from him; and the justice there is in being his that made us, and willingly so, which is the same as being dependent on his will, and conformed to it in the *manner* of our being; as we are for our being itself, and in the conformity of our will to his, on whose will we are universally and most perfectly dependent. There is also *justice* in our *supreme love* to God; a natural agreement in our having a supreme respect to him who exercises infinite goodness to us, and from whom we receive all well-being. Besides, disagreement and discord appears worse to natural sense in things nearly related, and of great importance: and therefore it must appear very ill, as it respects the infinite Being, and that infinitely great relation which there is between the Creator and his creatures. And it is easy to conceive how natural conscience should see the desert of punishment, in the contrary of true virtue, *viz.* opposition and enmity to being in general. For, this is only to see the *natural agreement* there is between opposing being in general, and being opposed by being in general; with a consciousness how, if we were infinitely great, we should expect to be regarded according to our greatness, and should proportionably resent contempt. This natural conscience, if well-informed, will *approve* of true virtue, and will disapprove and condemn the want of it, and opposition to it; and yet without seeing the true beauty of it. Yea, if men's consciences were fully enlightened, if they were delivered from being confined to a private sphere, and brought to view, and consider things in general, and delivered from being stupified by sensual objects and appetites, as they will be at the day of judgment, they would approve nothing but true virtue, nothing but general benevolence, and those affections and actions that are consistent with it, and subordinate to it. For they must see, that consent to being in general, and supreme respect to the Being of beings, is most just; and that every thing which is inconsistent with it, and interferes with it, or flows from the want of it, is unjust, and deserves the opposition of universal existence.

Thus has God established and ordered that this principle of *natural conscience*, which, though it implies no such thing as actual benevolence to being in general, nor any delight in such a principle, simply considered, and so implies no truly spiritual sense or virtuous taste, yet should approve and condemn the same things that are approved and condemned by a spiritual sense or virtuous taste. And that *moral sense* which is natural to mankind, so far as it is disinterested, and not founded in association of ideas, is the *same* with this natural conscience.

The sense of moral good and evil, and that disposition

to approve virtue, and disapprove vice, which men have by natural conscience, is that *moral sense* so much insisted on in the writings of many of late. A misunderstanding of this, seems to have misled those moralists who have insisted on a *disinterested* moral sense, universal in the world of mankind, as an evidence of a disposition to true virtue, consisting in a benevolent temper, naturally implanted in the minds of all men. Some of the arguments used by these writers, indeed prove, that there is a moral sense or taste, universal among men, distinct from what arises from *self-love*. Though I humbly conceive, there is some confusion in their discourses on the subject, and not a proper distinction observed in the instances of men's approbation of virtue, which they produce. Some of which are not to their purpose, being instances of that approbation of virtue which arises from self-love. But other instances prove, that there is a moral taste, or sense of moral good and evil, natural to all, which do not properly arise from self-love. Yet I conceive there are no instances of this kind which may not be referred to *natural conscience*, and particularly to that which I have observed to be *primary* in the approbation of natural conscience, *viz.* a sense of *desert*, and approbation of that natural agreement there is, in manner and measure, in *justice*. But I think it is plain from what has been said, that neither this, nor any thing else wherein consists the sense of moral good and evil, which there is in natural conscience, is of the nature of a truly virtuous taste, or determination of mind to relish and delight in the essential beauty of true virtue, arising from a virtuous benevolence of heart.

But it further appears from this; if the approbation of *conscience* were the same with the approbation of the *inclination of the heart*, or the natural disposition and determination of the mind to love and be pleased with virtue, then approbation and condemnation of conscience would always be in *proportion* to the virtuous temper of the mind; or rather, the degree would be just the *same*. In that person who had a high degree of a virtuous temper, therefore, the testimony of conscience in favour of virtue would be equally full: But he who had but little, would have as little a degree of the testimony of conscience for virtue, and against vice. But I think the case is evidently otherwise. Some men, through the strength of vice in their hearts, will go on and sin against clearer light and stronger convictions of conscience than others. If conscience, approving duty and disapproving sin, were the same thing as the exercise of a virtuous principle of the heart, in loving duty and hating sin, then *remorse* of conscience will be the same thing as *repentance;* and just in the same degree as the sinner feels *remorse* of conscience for sin, in the same degree is the heart turned from the love of sin to the *hatred* of it, inasmuch as they are the very same thing.

Christians have the greatest reason to believe, from the Scriptures, that in the future day of the revelation of the righteous judgment of God, when sinners shall be called to answer before their judge, and all their wickedness, in all its aggravations, brought forth, and clearly manifested in the perfect light of that day, and God will reprove them, and set their sins in order before them, their consciences will be greatly awakened and convinced, their mouths will be stopped, all stupidity of conscience will be at an end, and conscience will have its full exercise; and therefore their consciences will *approve* the dreadful sentence of the judge against them; and seeing that they have deserved so great a punishment, will join with the judge in condemning them. And this, according to the notion I am opposing, would be the same thing as their being brought to the fullest *repentance;* their hearts being perfectly changed to hate sin and love holiness; and virtue or holiness of heart in them will be brought to the most full and perfect exercise. But how much otherwise have we reason to suppose it will then be! Then the sin and wickedness of their heart will come to its highest dominion and completest exercise; they shall be wholly left of God, and given up to their wickedness, even as the devils are! When God has done waiting on sinners, and his Spirit done striving with them, he will not restrain their wickedness, as he does now. But sin shall then rage in their hearts, as a fire no longer restrained or kept under. It is proper for a judge when he condemns a criminal, to endeavour so to set his guilt before him as to convince his conscience of the justice of the sentence. This the Almighty will do effectually, and do to perfection, so as most thoroughly to awaken and convince the conscience But if natural conscience, and the disposition of the heart to be pleased with virtue, were the *same*, then at the same time that the conscience was brought to its perfect exercise, the heart would be made perfectly holy; or, would have the exercise of true virtue and holiness in perfect benevolence of temper. But instead of this, their wickedness will then be brought to perfection, and wicked men will become very devils, and accordingly will be sent away as cursed into everlasting fire prepared for the devil and his angels.

But supposing natural conscience to be what has been described, all these difficulties and absurdities are wholly avoided. Sinners when they see the greatness of the Being in contempt of whom they have lived with rebellion and opposition, and have clearly set before them their obligations to him, as their Creator, Preserver, Benefactor, &c. together with the degree in which they have acted as enemies to him, may have a clear sense of the *desert* of their sin, consisting in the *natural agreement* there is between such contempt and opposition of such a Being, and his despising and opposing them; between their *being* and acting as so great enemies to such a God, and their *suffering* the dreadful consequences of his being and acting as their great enemy; and their being conscious within themselves of the degree of anger, which would naturally arise in their own hearts in such a case, if they were in the place and state of their judge. In order to these things, there is no need of a virtuous benevolent temper, relishing and delighting in benevolence, and loathing the contrary. The conscience may *see* the natural agreement between opposing and being opposed, between hating and being hated, without *abhorring* malevolence from a benevolent temper of mind, or without *loving* God from a view of the beauty of his holiness. These things have no necessary dependence one on the other.

CHAP. VI.

Of particular instincts of nature, which in some respects resemble virtue.

THERE are various dispositions and inclinations natural to men, which depend on particular laws of nature, determining their minds to certain affections and actions towards particular objects; which laws seem to be established chiefly for the preservation of mankind, and their comfortably subsisting in the world. These dispositions may be called *instincts.*

Some of these instincts respect only ourselves personally: such are many of our natural appetites and aversions. Some of them are more social, and extend to others: such are the mutual inclinations between the sexes, &c.—Some of these dispositions are more *external* and sensitive: such are those that relate to meat and drink, and the more sensitive inclinations of the sexes towards each other. Others are more *internal* and mental: consisting in affections which mankind naturally exercise towards some of their fellow-creatures, and in come cases towards men in general. Some of these may be called *kind* affections; as having something in them of benevolence, or a resemblance of it: and others are of an *angry* appearance; such as the passion of jealousy between the sexes, especially in the male towards the female.

It is only the former of these two last mentioned sorts that it is to my purpose to consider in this place, *viz.* those natural instincts which have the appearance of benevolence, and so in some respects resemble virtue. These I shall therefore consider; and shall endeavour to show, that none of them can be of the nature of true virtue.

That kind affection which is exercised one towards another in natural relation, particularly the love of parents to their children, called natural affection, is by many referred to instinct. I have already considered this sort of love as an affection that arises from self-love; and in that view, have shown it cannot be of the nature of true virtue.

But if any think, that natural affection is more properly to be referred to a particular instinct of nature than to self-love, as its cause, I shall not think it a point worthy of any controversy or dispute. In my opinion *both* are true; *viz.* that natural affection is owing to natural instinct, and also that it arises from self-love. It may be said to arise from instinct, as it depends on a law of nature. But yet it may be truly reckoned as an affection arising from self-love; because, though it arises from a law of nature, yet that is such a law as according to the order and harmony every where observed among the laws of nature, is connected with and follows from self-love; as was shown before. However, it is not necessary to my present purpose to insist on this. For if natural affection to a man's children, or near relations, is an affection arising from a particular independent instinct of nature—which the Creator in his wisdom has implanted in men for the preservation and well-being of the world of mankind: yet it cannot be of the nature of true virtue. For it has been observed, and, I humbly conceive, proved before, (Chap. II.) that if any being or beings have by natural instinct, or any other means, a determination of mind to benevolence, extending only to some particular persons or *private* system, however large that system may be—or however great a number of individuals it may contain, so long as it contains but an infinitely small part of universal existence, and so bears no proportion to this great and universal system—such limited private benevolence, not *arising* from, not being *subordinate* to, benevolence to being in general, cannot have the nature of true virtue. However, it may not be amiss briefly to observe now, that it is evident to a demonstration, those affections cannot be of the nature of true virtue, from these two things.

First, That they do not arise from a *principle* of virtue. A principle of virtue, I think, is owned by the most considerable of late writers on morality to be general benevolence or public affection: and I think it has been proved to be union of heart to being simply considered; which implies a disposition to benevolence to being in general. Now, by the supposition, the affections we are speaking of do not arise from this principle; and that, whether we suppose they arise from self-love, or from particular instincts: because either of those sources is diverse from a principle of general benevolence. And,

Secondly, These private affections, if they do not arise from general benevolence, and they are not connected with it in their first existence, have no tendency to produce it. This appears from what has been observed: for being not dependent on it, their detached and unsubordinate operation rather implies *opposition* to being in general, than general benevolence; as every one sees and owns with respect to self-love. And there are the very same reasons why any other private affection, confined to limits infinitely short of universal existence, should have that influence, as well as love that is confined to a single person. Now upon the whole, nothing can be plainer than that affections which do not arise from a virtuous principle, and have no tendency to true virtue, as their effect, cannot be of the nature of true virtue.

For the reasons which have been given, it is undeniably true, that if persons have a benevolent affection limited to a party, or to the nation in general, of which they are a part, or the public community to which they belong, though it be as large as the Roman empire was of old; yea, if there could be a cause determining a person to benevolence towards the whole world of mankind, or even all created sensible natures throughout the universe, exclusive of union of heart to general existence and of love to God—not derived from that temper of mind which disposes to a supreme regard to him, nor subordinate to such divine love—it cannot be of the nature of true virtue.

If what is called natural affection, arises from a particular natural instinct, much more indisputably does that mutual affection which naturally arises between the sexes. I agree with Hutchison and Hume in this, that there is a foundation laid in nature for kind affections between the sexes, diverse from all inclinations to sensitive pleasure, and which do not properly arise from any such inclination. There is doubtless a disposition both to a mutual benevolence and mutual complacence, that are not naturally and necessarily connected with any sensitive desires. But yet it is manifest such affections as are limited to opposite sexes, are from a particular instinct thus directing and limiting them; and not arising from a principle of general benevolence; for this has no tendency to any such limitation. And though these affections do not properly arise from the sensitive desires which are between the sexes, yet they are implanted by the Author of nature chiefly for the same purpose, *viz.* the preservation or continuation of the world of mankind. Hereby persons become willing to forsake father and mother, and all their natural relations in the families where they were born and brought up; for the sake of a stated union with a companion of the other sex, in bearing and going through that series of labours, anxieties, and pains, requisite to the being, support, and education of a family of children; and partly also for the comfort of mankind as united in a marriage-relation. But I suppose few, if any, will deny, that the peculiar natural dispositions there are to mutual affection between the sexes, arise from an *instinct* or particular law of nature. And therefore it is manifest, from what has been said already, that those natural dispositions cannot be of the nature of true virtue.

Another affection which is owing to a particular instinct, is that pity which is natural to mankind when they see others in great distress. It is acknowledged, that such an affection is *natural* to mankind. But I think it evident, that the pity which is general and natural, is owing to a particular instinct, and is not of the nature of true virtue. I am far from saying, that there is no such thing as a truly *virtuous pity* among mankind; or, that none is to be found, which arises from that truly virtuous divine principle of general benevolence to sensitive beings. Yet at the same time I think, this is not the case with ALL pity, or with that disposition to pity which is *natural* to mankind in common. I think I may be bold to say, this does not arise from benevolence, nor is it properly called by that name.

If all that uneasiness on the sight of others' extreme distress, which we call pity, were properly of the nature of benevolence, then they who are the subjects of this passion, must needs be in a degree of uneasiness in being sensible of the total want of happiness, of all such as they would be disposed to pity in extreme distress. For that certainly is the most direct tendency and operation of benevolence or good will, to desire the happiness of its object. But now this is not the case universally, where men are disposed to exercise pity. There are many who would not be sensibly affected with any uneasiness to know that others were *dead*—yea men, who are not influenced by the consideration of a future state, but view death as only a cessation of all sensibility, and consequently an end of all happiness—who yet would have been moved with pity towards the same persons, if they had seen them under some very extreme anguish. Some would be moved with pity by seeing a brute-creature under extreme and long torments, who yet suffer no uneasiness in knowing that many thousands of them every day cease to live, and so have an end put to all their pleasure. It is the nature of true benevolence to desire and rejoice in the prosperity and pleasure of its object; and that, in some proportion to its degree of prevalence. But persons may greatly pity those that are in extreme pain, whose positive pleasure they may still be very indifferent about. In this case, a man may be much moved and affected with uneasiness, who yet would be affected with no sensible joy in seeing signs of the same person's enjoyment of very high degrees of pleasure.

Yea, pity may not only be without benevolence, but may consist with true malevolence, or with such ill will as shall cause men not only not to desire the positive happiness of another, but even to desire his calamity. They may pity such an one when his calamity goes beyond their hatred. A man may have true malevolence towards another, desiring no positive good for him, but evil; and yet his hatred not be infinite, but only to a certain degree. And when he sees the person whom he thus hates in misery far beyond his ill will, he may then pity him: because then the natural instinct begins to operate. For malevolence will not overcome the natural instinct, inclining to pity others in extreme calamity, any further than it goes, or to the limits of the degree of misery it wishes to its object. Men may pity others under exquisite torment, when yet they would have been grieved if they had seen their prosperity. And some have such a grudge against another, that they would be far from uneasy at their very death, nay, would even be glad of it. And when this is the case, it is manifest that their heart is void of benevolence towards such persons, and under the power of malevolence. Yet at the same time, they are capable of pitying even these very persons, if they should see them under a degree of misery very much disproportioned to their ill will.

These things may convince us, that *natural pity* is of a nature very different from true virtue, and not arising from a disposition of heart to general benevolence; but is owing to a particular instinct, which the Creator has implanted, chiefly for the preservation of mankind, though not exclusive of their well being. The giving of this instinct is the fruit of God's mercy, and an instance of his love to the world of mankind, and an evidence, that though the world be so sinful, it is not God's design to make it a world of punishment; and therefore has many ways made a merciful provision of relief in extreme calamities. The natural exercises of pity extend beyond those with whom we are nearly connected, especially in cases of great calamity; because, commonly in such cases, men stand in need of the help of *others* besides their near friends, and because commonly those calamities which are extreme, without relief, tend to their *destruction*. This may be given as the reason why men are so made by the Author of nature, that they have no instinct inclining as much to rejoice at the sight of others' great prosperity and pleasure, as to be grieved at their extreme calamity, *viz.* because they do not stand in equal necessity of such an instinct as that in order to their preservation. But if pure benevolence were the source of natural pity, doubtless it would operate to as great a degree in congratulation, in cases of others' great prosperity, as in compassion towards them in great misery.

The instincts which in some respects resemble a virtuous benevolence, are agreeable to the state that God designed mankind for here, where he intends their preservation and comfortable subsistence. But in the world of punishment—where the state of the wicked inhabitants will be exceeding different, and God will have none of these merciful designs to answer—we have great reason to think, there will be no such thing as a disposition to *pity*, in any case; as also no *natural affection* toward near relations, and no mutual affection between opposite sexes.

To conclude, natural instinct, disposing men to pity others in misery, is also a source of a kind of abhorrence in men of some vices, as cruelty and oppression; and so of a sort of approbation of the contrary virtues, humanity, mercy, &c. which aversion and approbation, however, so far as they arise from this cause only, are not from a principle of true virtue.

CHAP. VII.

The reasons why those things that have been mentioned, which have not the essence of virtue, have yet by many been mistaken for true virtue.

THE first reason may be this, that although they have not the specific and distinguishing nature and essence of virtue, yet they have something that *belongs to the general nature* of virtue. The general nature of true virtue is love. It is expressed both in love of benevolence and complacence; but *primarily* in benevolence to persons and beings, and consequently and *secondarily* in complacence in virtue, as has been shown. There is something of the *general nature* of virtue in those natural affections and principles that have been mentioned, in both those respects.

In many of these *natural affections* there appears the *tendency* and *effect* of benevolence, in part. Others have truly a sort of private benevolence, but which in several respects falls short of the extent of true virtuous benevolence, both in its nature and object. *Pity* to others in distress, though not properly of the nature of love, as has been demonstrated, yet has partly the same influence and effect with benevolence. One effect of true benevolence is for persons to be uneasy when the objects of it are in distress, and to desire their relief. And natural pity has the same effect.

Natural *gratitude*, though not properly called love—because persons may be moved with a degree of gratitude towards others on certain occasions for whom they have no real and proper friendship; as in the instance of *Saul* towards *David*, once and again, after *David's* sparing his life, when he had so fair opportunity to kill him—yet has the like operation and effect with friendship, in part, for a season, and with regard to so much of the welfare of its object, as appears a deserved requital of kindness received. And in other instances, it may have a more general and abiding influence, so as more properly to be called by the name of love. So that many times men, from natural gratitude, do really with a sort of benevolence, love those who love them. From this, together with some other natural principles, men may love their near friends, their own party, their country, &c. The natural disposition there is to mutual affection between the sexes, often operates by what may properly be called love. There is oftentimes truly a kind both of benevolence and complacence. As there also is between parents and children.

Thus these things have something of the *general nature* of virtue. What they are essentially defective in, is, that they are *private* in their nature; they do not arise from any temper of benevolence to being in general, nor have they a tendency to any such effect in their operation. But yet agreeing with virtue in its general nature, they are *beautiful* within their own *private sphere, i. e.* they appear beautiful if we confine our views to that private system, and while we shut out all other things to which they stand related from our consideration. If that private system contained the sum of universal existence, their benevolence would have true beauty; or, in other words, would be beautiful, all things considered; but now it is not so. These private systems are so far from containing the sum of universal being, or comprehending all existence to which we stand related, that it contains but an infinitely small part of it. The reason why men are so ready to take these private affections for true virtue, is the narrowness of their views; and above all, that they are so ready to leave the Divine Being out of their view, and to neglect him in their consideration, or to regard him in their thoughts, as though he did not properly belong to the system of real existence, but was a kind of shadowy, imaginary being. And though most men allow that there is a God, yet, in their ordinary view of things, his being is not apt to come into the account, and to have the influence and effect of real existence, as it is with other beings which they see, and are conversant with, by their external senses. In their views of beauty and deformity, and in their inward sensations of displicence and approbation, it is not natural to them to view the Deity as part of the system, and as the head of it, in comparison of whom all other things are to be viewed with corresponding impressions.

Yea, we are apt, through the narrowness of our views, in judging of the beauty of affections and actions, to *limit* our consideration to only a small part of the created system. When private affections extend themselves to a considerable number, we are ready to look upon them as truly virtuous, and accordingly to applaud them highly. Thus it is with respect to a man's love to a large party, or a country. For though his private system contains but a *small part* even of the world of mankind, yet, being a considerable number, they—through the contracted limits of his mind, and the narrowness of his views—are ready to engross his sight, and to seem as if they were *all*. Hence, among the *Romans*, love to their country was the highest virtue; though this affection of theirs, so much extolled, was employed as it were for the destruction of the rest of mankind. The larger the number is, to which that private affection extends, the more apt men are, through the narrowness of their sight, to mistake it for true virtue; because then the private system appears to have more of the image of the universal.

And this is the reason why *self-love* is not mistaken for true virtue. For though there be something of the general nature of virtue in it, as love and good will, yet the object is so private, the limits so narrow, that it by no means engrosses the view; unless it be of the person himself, who through the greatness of his pride may imagine himself as it were *all*. The minds of men are large enough to take in a vastly greater extent. And though self-love is far from being useless in the world, yea, it is exceeding necessary to society; yet every body sees that if it be not *subordinate* to, and regulated by, another more extensive principle, it may make a man a common *enemy* to the general system. And this is as true of *any other private affection*, notwithstanding its extent may be to a system that contains millions of individuals. And though *private* systems bear no greater proportion to the *whole* of universal existence, than one alone; yet, they bear a greater proportion to the view and comprehension of men's minds, and are more apt to be regarded as if they were *all*, or at least as some resemblance of the universal system.

Thus I have observed how many of these natural principles resemble virtue in its *primary* operation, which is *benevolence*. Many of them also have a resemblance of it in its *secondary* operation, which is its *approbation* of and complacence in virtue itself. Several kinds of approbation of virtue, are not of the nature of a truly *virtuous* approbation, consisting in a sense and relish of the essential beauty of virtue. As particularly, the approbation of conscience, from a sense of the inferior and *secondary* beauty which there is in virtue, consisting in *uniformity;* and from a sense of *desert*, consisting in a sense of the *natural agreement* of loving and being beloved, showing kindness and receiving kindness. So, from the same principle, there is a disapprobation of vice, from a natural opposition to deformity and disproportion; and a sense of evil desert, or the natural agreement there is between hating and being hated, opposing and being opposed, &c. together with a painful sensation naturally arising from a sense of self-opposition and inconsistence. Approbation of conscience is the more readily mistaken for a truly virtuous approbation, because by the wise constitution of the great Governor of the world, when conscience is well informed, and thoroughly awakened, it agrees with him fully and exactly, as to the object approved, though not as to the ground and reason of approving. It approves all virtue, and condemns all vice. It approves true virtue, and indeed approves nothing that is against it, or that falls short of it; as was shown before. Natural conscience is implanted in all mankind, to be as it were in God's stead, as an internal judge or rule, whereby to distinguish right and wrong.

It has also been observed, how that virtue, consisting in benevolence, is approved; and vice, consisting in ill will, is disliked; from the influence of *self-love*, together with the association of ideas. In the same manner, men *dislike* those qualities in things without life or reason, with which they have always connected the ideas of hurtfulness, malignancy, perniciousness; but *approve* those things with which they habitually connect the ideas of profit, pleasantness, &c. This approbation of virtue, and dislike of vice, is easily mistaken for true virtue, not only because those things are approved by it that have the nature of virtue, and the things disliked have the nature of vice; but because here is a great resemblance of virtuous approbation, it being complacence from love; the difference only lying in this, that it is not from love to being in general, but from self-love.

There is also, as before shown, a liking of some virtues, and a dislike of some vices, from the influence of the natural instinct of *pity*. This we are apt to mistake for the exercise of true virtue on many accounts. Here is not only a kind of complacence, and the objects of complacence have the nature of virtue, and the virtues themselves are very amiable, such as humanity, mercy, tenderness of heart, &c. and the contrary very odious; but besides, the approbation is not merely from self-love, but from *compassion;* an affection that respects others, and resembles benevolence, as before explained.

Another reason why the things mentioned are mistaken for true virtue, is, that there is indeed a true *negative* moral goodness in them. By a negative moral goodness, I mean the negation or absence of true moral evil. They have this negative moral goodness, because being without them would be an evidence of a much greater moral evil. Thus the exercise of natural conscience in such and such degrees, wherein appears such a measure of sensibility, though it be not of the nature of real positive virtue, or true moral goodness, yet has a *negative* moral goodness; because in the present state of things, it is an evidence of the absence of that higher degree of wickedness, which causes great insensibility, or stupidity of conscience. For sin is not only against a spiritual and divine sense of virtue, but is also against the dictates of that moral sense which is in natural conscience. No wonder, that this sense, being long opposed and often conquered, grows weaker. All sin has its source from *selfishness*, or from self-love, not subordinate to a regard to being in general. And natural conscience chiefly consists in a sense of *desert*, or the natural agreement between sin and misery. But if *self* were indeed *all*, and so more considerable than all the world besides, there would be no ill desert in a man regarding himself *above* all, and making all other interests give place to private interest. And no wonder that men, by long acting from the selfish principle, and by being habituated to treat themselves as if they were *all*, increase in pride, and come to look on themselves as *all*, and so to lose entirely the sense of ill desert in their making all other interests give place to their own. And no wonder that any, by often repeating acts of sin without punishment, or visible appearance of approaching punishment, have less and less present sense of the connexion of sin with punishment.

That sense which an awakened conscience has of the desert of sin, consists chiefly in a sense of its desert of resentment from the Deity, the fountain and head of universal existence. But no wonder that, by a long continued worldly and sensual life, men more and more lose all sense of the Deity, who is a spiritual and invisible Being. The mind being long involved in, and engrossed by, sensitive objects, becomes *sensual* in all its operations, and excludes all views and impressions of spiritual objects, and is unfit for their contemplation. Thus conscience and general benevolence, are entirely different principles; and thus a sense of conscience differs from the holy complacence of a benevolent and truly virtuous heart. Yet wickedness may by long habitual exercise greatly diminish a sense of conscience. So that there may be *negative* moral goodness, in sensibility of conscience, as it may be an argument of the absence of that higher degree of wickedness, which causeth stupidity of conscience.

So with respect to natural *gratitude;* though there may be no virtue merely in loving them that love us, yet the contrary may be an evidence of a great degree of depravity, as it may argue a higher degree of selfishness, so that a man is come to look upon himself as all, and others as nothing, and so their respect and kindness as nothing. Thus an increase of pride diminishes gratitude. So doth sensuality, or the increase of sensual appetites; which, coming more and more under the power and impression of sensible objects, tends by degrees to make the mind insensible to any thing else. Those appetites take up the whole soul; and, through habit and custom, the water is all drawn out of *other* channels, in which it naturally flows, and is all carried as it were into *one* channel.

In like manner, natural affection, and natural pity, though not of the nature of virtue, may be diminished greatly by the increase of pride and sensuality; and, as the consequence of this, be habitually disposed to envy, malice, &c. These lusts, when they prevail to a high degree, may overcome and diminish the exercise of those natural principles; even as they often overcome and diminish common prudence in a man, who seeks his own private interest in point of health, wealth, or honour; and yet no one will think it proves that a man being cunning in seeking his own personal and temporal interest, has any thing of the nature and essence of true virtue.

Another reason why these natural principles and affections are mistaken for true virtue, is, that in several respects they have the same *effect* which true virtue tends to; especially in these two ways:

1. The present state of the world is so constituted by the wisdom and goodness of its supreme Ruler, that these natural principles, for the most part, tend to the *good* of mankind. So do natural pity, gratitude, parental affec-

tion, &c. Herein they agree with the *tendency* of general benevolence, which seeks and tends to the general good. But this is no proof that these natural principles have the *nature* of true virtue. For self-love is exceeding useful and necessary; and so are the natural appetites of hunger, thirst, &c. Yet nobody will assert that *these* have the nature of true virtue.

2. These principles have a like effect with true virtue in this respect, that they tend several ways to *restrain vice*, and prevent many acts of wickedness. So natural affection, love to our party, or to particular friends, tends to keep us from acts of injustice towards these persons; which would be real wickedness. Pity preserves from cruelty, which would be real and great moral evil. Natural conscience tends to restrain sin in general. But this cannot prove these principles themselves to be of the nature of true virtue. For so is this present state ordered by a merciful God, that even *self-love* often restrains from acts of true wickedness; and not only so, but puts men upon seeking true virtue; yet is not itself true virtue, but is the source of all the wickedness that is in the world.

Another reason why these inferior affections, especially some of them, are accounted virtuous, is, that there are affections of the *same denomination* which are *truly* virtuous. Thus, for instance, there is a truly virtuous *pity*, or a compassion to others, under affliction or misery, from general benevolence. Pure benevolence would be sufficient to excite pity to another in calamity, if there were no particular instinct, or any other principle determining the mind thereto. It is easy to see how benevolence, which seeks another's *good*, should cause us to desire his deliverance from *evil*. And this is a source of pity far more extensive than the other. It excites compassion in cases that are overlooked by natural instinct; and even in those cases to which instinct extends, it *mixes its influence* with the natural principle, and *guides* and *regulates its operations*. And when this is the case, the pity which is exercised, may be called a *virtuous* compassion. So there is a virtuous *gratitude;* or a gratitude that arises not only from self-love, but from a superior principle of disinterested general benevolence. As, when we receive kindness from such as we love already, we are *more* disposed to gratitude, and disposed to greater *degrees* of it, than when the mind is destitute of any such friendly prepossession. Therefore, when the superior principle of virtuous love has a governing hand, and regulates the affair, it may be called a virtuous gratitude. There is also a virtuous love of *justice*, arising from pure benevolence to being in general; as that naturally and necessarily inclines the heart, that every particular being should have such a share of benevolence as is proportioned to its dignity, consisting in the degree of its being, and the degree of its virtue. And thus it is easy to see, how there may be a *virtuous* sense of *desert* different from what is natural and common; and a virtuous *conscientiousness*, or a sanctified conscience. And as, when *natural affections* have their operations *mixed* with the influence of virtuous benevolence, and are *directed* and *determined* thereby, they may be called *virtuous;* so there may be a *virtuous* love of parents to children, and between other near relatives; a *virtuous* love of our town, or country, or nation. Yea, and a *virtuous* love between the sexes, as there may be the influence of virtue *mingled* with instinct; and virtue may govern with regard to the particular manner of its operation, and may guide it to such *ends* as are agreeable to the great purposes of true virtue.

Genuine virtue prevents that increase of the habits of pride and sensuality, which tend to diminish the exercises of the useful and necessary principles of nature. And a principle of general benevolence softens and sweetens the mind, makes it more susceptible of the proper influence of the gentler natural instincts, directs every one into its proper channel, determines the exercise to the proper manner and measure, and guides all to the best purposes.*

* In this chapter our very ingenious and judicious author has assigned several reasons why many things are commonly thought to be *virtuous* which in reality are not so, or have no claim to *moral goodness* in the proper acceptation of these words.

It is with some reluctance that we notice in this place a writer, who by his masterly attack on modern infidelity and atheism, has rendered such important service to the cause of truth and virtue; but who seems either to have been dissatisfied with these reasons, or to have omitted a strict examination of them when duty required it. We shall not here inquire into the *candour* of Mr. Robert Hall's remarks, in associating President Edwards with modern infidels on the subject of virtue; nor on the *congruity* of the business, whereby a definition implying, and an explication declaring, the *love of God* to be essential to true virtue, is made to coincide with a definition adopted by *infidels*, and consistent with *atheism* itself. These are his words:

"It is somewhat singular, that many of the fashionable infidels have hit upon a definition of virtue which perfectly coincides with that of certain metaphysical divines in America, first invented and defended by that most acute reasoner, Jonathan Edwards. They both place virtue exclusively in a passion for the general good; or, as Mr. Edwards expresses it, *love to being in general:* so that our love is always to be proportioned to the magnitude of its object in the scale of being; which is liable to the objections I have already stated, as well as to many others which the limits of this note will not permit me to enumerate. Let it suffice to remark, (1) That virtue, on these principles, is an utter impossibility: for the system of being, comprehending the great Supreme, is *infinite;* and therefore, to maintain the proper proportion, the force of particular attachment must be infinitely less than the passion for the general good: but the limits of the human mind are not capable of any emotions so infinitely different *in degree*. (2) Since *our views* of the extent of the universe are capable of perpetual enlargement, admitting the sum of existence is ever the same, we must return back at each step to diminish the strength of particular affections, or they will become disproportionate; and consequently, on these principles, vicious: so that the balance must be continually fluctuating, by the weights being taken out of one scale and put one into the other. (3) If virtue consist *exclusively* in love to being in general, or attachment to the general good, the particular affections are, to every purpose of virtue, useless, and even pernicious; for their immediate, nay, their necessary tendency is to attract to their objects a proportion of attention which far exceeds their comparative value in the general scale. To allege that the *general good* is promoted by them, will be of no advantage to the defence of this system, but the contrary, by confessing that a greater sum of happiness is attained by a deviation from, than an adherence to, its principles; unless its advocates mean by the love of being in general, the same thing as the private affections, which is to confound all the distinctions of language, as well as all the operations of mind. Let it be remembered we have no dispute respecting what is the ultimate end of virtue, which is allowed on both sides to be the greatest sum of happiness in the universe. The question is merely what is *virtue itself;* or, in other words, what are the means appointed for the attainment of that end?

There is little doubt, from some parts of Mr. Godwin's work, entitled '*Political Justice*,' as well as from his early habits of reading, that he was indebted to Mr. Edwards for his principal arguments against the private affections; though, with a daring consistence, he has pursued his principles to an extreme from which that most excellent man would have revolted with horror.—The fundamental error of the whole system arose, as I conceive, from a mistaken pursuit of simplicity; from a wish to construct a moral system, without leaving sufficient scope for the infinite variety of moral phenomena and mental combination; in consequence of which its advocates were induced to place virtue *exclusively* in some *one disposition* of mind: and, since the passion for the general good is undeniably the *noblest* and most extensive of all others, when it was once resolved to place virtue in any *one thing*, there remained little room to hesitate which should be preferred. It might have been worth while to reflect, that in the natural world there are two kinds of attraction; one, which holds several *parts* of individual bodies in contact; another, which maintains the union of bodies themselves with the general system: and that, though the union in the former case is much more *intimate* than in the latter, each is equally essential to the order of the world. Similar to this is the relation which the public and private affections bear to each other, and their use in the moral system." (Modern Infidelity considered, p. 62, &c. Note, sixth edition.)

On this note, so very uncongenial with the body of the work; we were going to say, as unseemly, when connected with the discourse, as a deforming wart on a fair countenance, justice constrains us to make a few remarks.

1. "Singular" indeed would it be to find an Atheist, or an *infidel*, who should even *approve* of Edwards's definition, and still more "singular" to find them *maintaining*, in conformity with his explanation of that definition, that *supreme love to God* is of the essence of true virtue. But so far are their definitions from "coinciding," that they differ *toto cœlo*. A passionate attachment for the welfare of a country, or "a passion for the general good," in any sense wherein this expression can be ascribed to infidels, is a representation not more different from that of President Edwards, than Mr. Hall is different from Voltaire or D'Alembert. Our author's meaning, as explained by himself, is as truly sublime as theirs is truly selfish and contracted. For their definition had no regard to the Being of beings; but this adorable Being is necessarily *included* in Mr. E's definition, and essential to it. We say, is "included," because the Supreme Being, together with every derived existence, is *contained* in "being in general."

2. If by "a metaphysical divine" be meant "a most acute reasoner," we feel no objection in having the term "metaphysical" applied to our author, for few, if any, have deserved it better. If error and absurdity appeal to metaphysical discussions, and involve the truth in a labyrinth of sophisms, surely hard would be the case of a man who should be called by an opprobrious name, for venturing into that labyrinth by the light of essential principles, in order to detect and expose false reasoning.

3. Mr. H. objects to the sentiment, "that our love is always to be proportioned to the magnitude of its object in the scale of being." We presume, however, he will allow, that the whole system of being is *in itself* the most worthy of being prized, *other things being equal*. But if so, the nature of true virtue requires this regard to the whole system of being, compared with its parts. Nor does it follow from this, that the same principle, in the progress of its operations, disregards the smaller circle of attachments. Surely a virtuous person, loving God supremely, is not, on that account, less qualified for personal and domestic duties. Besides, Mr. E. does not maintain that our love is always to be proportioned to the magnitude of its object in the scale of being, except where *other things are equal*. This he expressly and repeatedly mentions—"other things being equal." To this important distinction Mr. H. does not appear to have adverted; his representation of the case, therefore, is defective, and calculated to mislead the unwary.

4. Mr. H's statement in the *first* objection, does not distinguish between the *nature* of the attachment and its *force* or *degree*. A little reflection will fully show, that these are entirely distinct considerations. The greatest *force*, or the highest *degree* of attachment, may exist, when the *nature* of it is not at all virtuous. If, indeed, attachment be made to include accurate knowledge, a divine relish, and *deliberate esteem* in appreciating the worth of any object, then the degree of attachment may be justly considered as proportionate to the "magnitude of the object in the scale of being," but not otherwise. A truly virtuous mother, for instance, may have a great *force* of affection for her child, or husband, and be more conscious of

CHAP. VIII.

In what respects virtue or moral good is founded in sentiment; and how far it is founded in the reason and nature of things.

VIRTUE is a certain kind of beautiful nature, form or quality. That form or quality is called *beautiful*, which appears in itself agreeable or comely, or the view of which is immediately pleasant to the mind. I say, agreeable *in itself*, and *immediately* pleasant, to distinguish it from things which in *themselves* are not so, but either indifferent or disagreeable; which yet appear eligible, and agreeable *indirectly*, for something else with which they are connected. Such indirect agreeableness, or eligibleness in things not for themselves, but for something else, is not beauty. But when a form or quality appears lovely, pleasing, and delightful *in itself*, then it is called *beautiful*; and this agree-

it than of her love to God; but let her be put to the test of *deliberate esteem*, and she would sooner part with child, husband, or life itself, than renounce her supreme love to God.

5. Our author's representation of true virtue, by no means implies, as Mr. H. supposes, that the *degree* or *force* of attachment, *in its operation*, should bear an *exact proportion* to the magnitude of its object. The *nature* of virtue indeed is to be denominated according to its object, but its *degree* must necessarily be measured *pro captu agentis*. The *nature* of love to God may be the same in the heart of a child, as in that of an angel, because the *object* of it is the same; but the *degree* of it will be as differently varied as the views and capacities of the subjects. It is not a little surprising how Mr. H. came to imagine, that our author held the sentiment he is pleased to ascribe to him, a sentiment so absurd as to be held, we apprehend, by no person in the world; a sentiment which requires an *infinite* force of affection from a *finite* being, an affection equal in degree to that of his Maker.

6. So far is the exercise of virtue, according to Mr. E's definition, from being an impossibility, that we think he has fully proved, there can be no true virtue on any other principle. To illustrate this, suppose a man has a *strong* attachment to *himself*, but none to his family; will that force of affection constitute him virtuous? Again, suppose his affection, with any assignable force, be extended to his *family*, but repels the well-founded claims of a whole *nation*, can that be virtuous? Or if he extend his force of affection to a whole *nation*, if it repels all the human race beside, can it be virtuous? Moreover, suppose his ardent affection embrace the whole human kind, can it be virtuous while it repels all other created beings? Or if, together with himself, he feels an affectionate attachment, in different and proportionate degrees, to *every created being*, but repels the Creator of all, can that forcible and orderly affection be denominated truly virtuous? If the reply be in the affirmative, then an *atheist* may be virtuous, which is absurd. Therefore, attachment to the *Supreme Being*, or to *being in general*, is essential to the *very nature* of true virtue.

7. No one yet denied, except those who deny the being of a God, that *supreme love to him* is virtuous, if any thing be so. The great Supreme is *infinite*, and if he ought not to be loved *according* to his greatness, what constitutes the crime of Idolatry? And if supreme love to an infinite being were *inconsistent* with subordinate attachments, we ought to extinguish the supremacy of our love to God, before we could discharge our duty to our fellow-creatures, which every one must allow to be preposterous.

8. As the *second* objection is founded on the same principle which was assumed in the first, it has been already virtually answered. But it may be controverted on another account. That "extended views" diminish the strength of particular affections, does not appear consonant with experience. Is it consistent with experience, that the acquisition of a *second* friend must rob the first of a moiety of his friendly affection? Does a parent experience any diminution of affection to a first child, in proportion to a subsequent increase of number? Has a tenth child but a tenth part of a mother's former affection to her first? Does a man love his neighbour the *less* because his views are extended to an *infinite* object? Or when the heart, or supremacy of affection, is fixed on God, is virtuous affection to man diminished?

9. Besides, this objection proceeds on another gratuitous principle, viz. that there may be true virtue, or virtuous affection, when our *views* of existence do not include God. For if we *view him*, we view an object *infinite* and *unchangeable*, who is *all in all*, and the sum of existence. That our *views* of the *extent* of the created universe are capable of perpetual enlargement, is no good reason why "particular affections" should fluctuate, become disproportionate, or vicious; any more than the love of God should constitute the love of our neighbour criminal. So that there is no necessity for "the balance to be continually fluctuating by the weights being taken out of one scale and put into the other;" except it be by correcting past mistakes, as those do, who, when grown up to manhood, put away childish things.

10. Virtuous love, however forcible to oneself, to relatives, to a nation, to mankind, or to the whole created universe, is not *virtuous* because of this particular, private, or limited attachment, but because of its *tendency to God*, except we prostitute the term virtue to signify something claimed equally by the worst and the best of men. And this general attachment, or love to God and universal being, does not at all counteract, or even lessen, the commendable force of private ones, any more than the force of general *gravity* tends to destroy the force of *cohesion*.

11. Mr. H's *third* and last objection, like the preceding ones, rests on a mistaken apprehension of Mr. E's real sentiment. Mr. H. still confounds the *nature* of attachment with its *degree*. If virtue, according to Mr. E. consists *exclusively* in love to being in general, his meaning is, that no *force* of affection which has not *universal being* for its ultimate *object*, can be *virtuous*, in the most proper sense of the word. He cannot mean that there is no virtuous love to *particular* beings; for, in perfect consistency with his views, even a love of *ourselves* may be virtuous, as well as a love of our *neighbour*. What he maintains, then, is, that the love of ourselves, of our neighbour, our nation, or any private system whatever, if *detached* from a *tendency* of affection to *universal* being, is not truly virtuous. And what is this, more or less, than what all judicious divines have maintained, that he who does not *really* love God, does not *truly* love his neighbour? If Mr. E. uses language more philosophically exact, and investigates the principle on which a commonly received truth is founded, he certainly deserves commendation, rather than blame.

12. On Mr. E's principles, the particular affections are so far from being "useless," that their operations are not at all affected by those principles, except in being more exalted and refined. When the heart is enlarged to the love of being in general, it *includes* all *particular* objects; and then the attachment to them is *for the sake* of the whole system of being. Thus a truly virtuous love of our neighbour, *springs from* our love to God: or without a supreme regard to God, there is no genuine, or, in the highest sense, praiseworthy, love to our neighbour. And so far are particular affections from being "pernicious," on Mr. E's principles, that they are highly *useful*. Those objects which contain, or are apprehended to contain, only a *secondary* beauty, attract a particular affection which is useful in various respects, as explained by our author; and those which contain the *primary* beauty, attract affections still more useful. For governors, and subjects, and friends, and relatives to feel attachment to their subjects, governors, friends, and relatives, must be *useful*, even when not virtuous; but when these attachments are animated, regulated, and ennobled by the love of God, or benevolence to universal being, they must be still *more* so. Benevolent affections are like a pleasant flame; a flame which is not *lessened* by an addition of fuel. Zeal at *home* is not found in fact to be weakened by the extension of zealous and benevolent affections *abroad*. National reform, and religious revival, will not be impeded by a truly benevolent missionary spirit. Neither will the love of God, or of universal being, prove detrimental to "particular affections."

13. Respecting the "particular affections," Mr. H. remarks, that "their immediate, nay their necessary tendency is, to attract to their object a proportion of attention, which far exceeds their comparative value in the general scale." But surely "attention" is a very different thing from "attachment." A man who is about to buy a horse, has his *attention* attracted very forcibly to the size, the shape, the age, and the action of the animal; but does this imply *attachment*. The word *Satan* may attract our "attention" to the malevolent being signified by it; but does this prove that the "immediate, nay the necessary tendency" of the word is to attract to this object any degree of "attachment?" It would be difficult to find either man, woman, or child, but has much "attention attracted" to what he does not esteem, and to which he feels no attachment. If a person feels an attachment to any object not founded on the "comparative value" of that object, let the "particular affection" be denominated as we please, but let us not attach to it the idea of *true virtue*. For why should we be tempted to call that *truly virtuous* which has no relation to God, the object and fountain of all excellence?

14. It is but justice to our author to say, that his definition of virtue, against which Mr. H. objects, by no means countenances that perversion of our powers which is but too justly ascribed to modern infidels. No one acting on the principles of this Dissertation, will be less amiable in private life, than when acting on any others which Mr. H. might point out. This hypothesis, which we believe is the *scriptural* one, and which, in substance, has been maintained by theological writers and holy men of every age, pours no chilling influence on the affections, encourages no unscriptural disregards or antipathies in society, nor does it countenance any neglect of private duties under pretence of public utility. We are assured, by an authority from which, in the views of Christians, there lies no appeal, that "*to love God with all our heart*," is the first and great commandment. We would fain know, if knowable, wherein this requisition differs from that which is implied in Mr. E's notion of true virtue? Moreover, whether loving God *with* ALL *our heart* is calculated to render "the particular affections, to every purpose of virtue, useless, and even pernicious?" And, once more, whether that act of the mind which is compatible with a rejection of what the divine oracle thus requires, can in any propriety of language, among Christians, be termed virtuous?

15. "To allege," Mr. H. observes, "that the *general good* is promoted by them will be no advantage to the defence of this system." We apprehend he means, that some may be disposed to allow, that the private affections, *though not virtuous*, may yet promote the general good, on some other account. But the objector is under a mistake, if he suppose, as he apparently does, that Mr. E. held any notion of true virtue which will admit no private or "particular affections" to be virtuous. In fact, the system explained in this Dissertation excludes *no* particular affection; but fully admits that *any*, yea, that *all* of them *may* be virtuous, by a proper direction. Supreme love to God, or attachment to universal being, is virtue *per se*; but any other affection, however public or private, particular or general, is a virtue only *relatively*; that is, only so far as it is a *tendency* to universal being. When the affection *terminates* on any *particular* object, without any *relation in its tendency* to universal existence, it is not a mean of ultimate happiness in itself commendable, and therefore is not virtuous.

16. "We have no dispute," says Mr. H. "respecting what is the ultimate end of virtue—the question is, What is *virtue itself?*" Very true; what is it? We say, a love, an attachment, or a *tendency* of mind, to general or universal existence; whatever be the *immediate* object of the will or affections. If the affection be, for instance, that of parent to a child, however strong in its operation, it is no further truly virtuous, than there is a regard to God in it; or, a tendency to general being. But what is *virtue itself*, according to Mr H.? The answer is not given. Had Mr. H. thought proper to give us a definition of virtue, we might compare notes, and form an estimate. It is much easier to find fault than to amend it; but this we feel disposed to promise, that if the objector produce what he thinks a better definition than what he opposes, we will endeavour to examine it with impartiality.

17. Mr. H. supposes that the author of the work entitled "Political Justice" was "indebted to Mr. Edwards for his principal arguments against the private affections." Surely that author must possess a most perverse kind of ingenuity, who could deduce any thing from the works of President Edwards *against* the private affections. Such ingenuity as an infidel some times employs, when he is indebted to the writers of the Old or New Testament for his principal arguments *against* religion, and in favour of infidelity.

18. "A mistaken pursuit of simplicity," Mr. H. supposes, attaches to this system, whereby its advocates "place virtue *exclusively* in some one disposition of mind." We conceive, there is just as much propriety in this remark, as in the following: A mistaken pursuit of simplicity led a certain writer to place *conformity to law* "exclusively" in some *one disposition* of mind, where he says, that the law is fulfilled in one word, LOVE. We are not aware that it is a matter of doubt, whether moral acts, and consequently virtue, proceed from the *will*, or the *heart?* and, as *every* exercise of will or affection is not virtuous, it requires no long "pursuit of simplicity" to determine that the virtuous character of the affection must arise from its *nature*, rather than its *degree*; and from its being directed to a *worthy*, rather than an *unworthy* object.

19. Mr. H. illustrates his meaning by two kinds of attraction; and so does Mr. E. illustrate his. Private affections, or instincts, irrespective of their virtuous quality, may be represented by the attraction of *cohesion*, whereby the several parts of individual bodies are held in contact. A truly virtuous affection may be represented by the attraction of *gravitation*, which maintains the union of bodies themselves with the general system. And, "though the union in the former case is much more *intimate*, than in the latter," and "each is equally essential to the order of the world:" yet, *private affections*, irrespective of their tendency to God, can with no more propriety be respected as *virtues*, than *cohesion* can be termed *gravitation*.—W.

ableness or gratefulness of the idea is BEAUTY. It is evident, that the way we come by the idea of beauty, is by immediate sensation of the gratefulness of the idea called *beautiful;* and not by finding out by argumentation any consequences, or other things with which it stands connected; any more than tasting the sweetness of honey, or perceiving the harmony of a tune, is by argumentation on connexions and consequences. The *manner* of being affected with the immediate presence of the beautiful idea, depends not on any reasonings about the idea, after we have it, before we can find out whether it be beautiful or not; but on the *frame of our minds*, whereby they are so made, that such an idea, as soon as we have it, is grateful, or appears beautiful.

Therefore, if this be all that is meant by them who affirm that virtue is founded in *sentiment*, and not in *reason*, that they who see the beauty of true virtue do not perceive it by argumentation on its connexions and consequences, but by the *frame of their own minds*, or a certain *spiritual sense* given them of God—whereby they *immediately* perceive pleasure in the presence of the idea of true virtue in their minds, or are *directly* gratified in the view or contemplation of this object—this is certainly true. But if thereby be meant, that the frame of mind, or inward sense given them by God, whereby the mind is disposed to delight in the idea of true virtue, is given *arbitrarily*, so that if he had pleased he might have given a contrary sense and determination of mind, which would have agreed as well with the necessary nature of things, this I think is not true.

Virtue, as I have observed, consists in the cordial consent or union of being to being in general. And that frame of mind, whereby it is disposed to *relish* and be *pleased* with the view of this, is benevolence, or union of heart, to being in general; or it is an universally benevolent frame of mind. Because, he whose temper is to love being in general, must therein have a disposition to approve and be pleased with love to being in general. Therefore, now the question is, whether God, in giving this temper to a created mind, acts so arbitrarily, that there is nothing in the necessary nature of things to hinder, but that a *contrary* temper might have agreed or consisted as well with that nature of things as this?

And in the *first* place, to assert this would be a plain absurdity, and contrary to the very supposition. For here it is supposed, that virtue in its very essence consists in agreement or consent of being to being. Now certainly agreement itself to being in general must necessarily agree better with general existence, than opposition and contrariety to it.

I observe, *secondly*, that God in giving to the creature such a temper of mind, gives that which is agreeable to what is by absolute necessity his *own* temper and nature. For, as observed, God himself is in effect being in general; and without all doubt it is in itself necessary, that God should agree with himself, be united with himself, or love himself: and therefore, when he gives the same temper to his creatures, this is more agreeable to his necessary nature, than the opposite temper: yea, the latter would be infinitely contrary to his nature.

Let it be noted, *thirdly*, that by this temper only can created beings be united to and agree with one another. This appears, because it consists in consent and union to being in general; which implies agreement and union with every particular being, except in such cases wherein union with them is by some means inconsistent with union to general existence. But certainly, if any particular created being were of a temper to oppose being in general, that would infer the most universal and greatest possible discord, not only of creatures with their Creator, but of created beings one with another.

Fourthly, There is no other temper but this, whereby a man can agree with himself, or be without self-inconsistence, *i. e.* without having some inclinations and relishes repugnant to others; and that for these reasons. Every being that has understanding and will necessarily loves happiness. For, to suppose any being not to love happiness, would be to suppose he did not love what was agreeable to him; which is a contradiction: or at least would imply, that nothing was agreeable or eligible to him, which is the same as to say that he has no such thing as choice, or any faculty of will. So that every being who has a faculty of will, must of necessity have an inclination to happiness. And therefore, if he be consistent with himself, and has not some inclinations repugnant to others, he must approve of those inclinations whereby beings desire the happiness of being in general, and must be against a disposition to the misery of being in general: because otherwise he would approve of opposition to his own happiness. For if a temper inclined to the misery of being in general prevailed universally, it is apparent, it would tend to universal misery. But he that loves a tendency to *universal* misery, in effect loves a tendency to his *own* misery: and as he necessarily hates his own misery, he has then one inclination repugnant to another. And besides, it necessarily follows from self-love, that men love to be loved by others; because in this others' love agrees with their own love. But if men loved hatred to being in general, they would in effect love the hatred of *themselves;* and so would be inconsistent with themselves, having one natural inclination contrary to another.

These things may help us to understand *why* that spiritual and divine sense, by which those who are truly virtuous and holy perceive the excellency of true virtue, is in the sacred Scriptures called by the name of light, knowledge, understanding, &c. If this divine sense were a thing arbitrarily given, without any foundation in the nature of things, it would not properly be called by such names. For if there were no correspondence, or agreement, in such a sense with the nature of things, any more than there would have been in a contrary sense, the idea we obtain by this spiritual sense could in no respect be said to be a *knowledge* or perception of any thing besides what was in our own minds. For this idea would be no representation of any thing without. But since it is agreeable, in the respects above mentioned, to the nature of things; and especially since it is the representation of the moral perfection and excellency of the Divine Being; hereby we have a perception of that moral excellency, of which we could have no true idea without it. And hereby persons have that true *knowledge of God*, which greatly enlightens the mind in the knowledge of divine things in general, and which, as might be shown, if it were necessary to the main purpose of this discourse, in many respects, assists persons to a right understanding of *things in general; viz.* to see the nature and truth of them, in their proper evidence. Whereas, the want of this spiritual sense, and the prevalence of those dispositions which are contrary to it, tends to darken and distract the mind, and dreadfully to delude and confound men's understandings.

Nor can that *moral sense*, common to mankind, which there is in *natural conscience*, be truly said to be no more than a *sentiment arbitrarily* given by the Creator, without any relation to the necessary nature of things: but rather, this is established in *agreement* with the nature of things; so established, as no sense of mind that can be supposed of a *contrary* nature and tendency could be. This will appear by these two things:

1. This moral sense—if the understanding be well informed, exercised at liberty, and in an extensive manner, without being restrained to a private sphere—approves the very *same* things which a spiritual and divine sense approves; and those things only; though not on the same *grounds*, nor with the same kind of approbation. Therefore, as that *divine* sense is agreeable to the necessary nature of things, as already shown; so this *inferior moral* sense, being so far correspondent to that, must also so far agree with the nature of things.

2. It has been shown, that this moral sense consists in approving the uniformity and natural agreement there is between one thing and another. So that, by the supposition, it is agreeable to the nature of things. For therein it consists, *viz.* a disposition of mind to consent to, or like, the agreement of the nature of things, or the agreement of the nature and form of one thing with another. And certainly, such a temper of mind is more agreeable to the nature of things than an opposite temper.

The use of *language* is to express our SENTIMENTS, or ideas, to each other; so that those terms by which things of a moral nature are signified, express those moral *sentiments* which are common to mankind. Therefore, that

MORAL SENSE which is in natural conscience, chiefly *governs* the use of language, and is the mind's *rule* of language in these matters. It is indeed the *general natural rule* which God has given to all men, whereby to judge of moral good and evil. By such words, *right* and *wrong*, *good* and *evil*, when used in a moral sense, is meant in common speech, that which deserves *praise* or *blame*, *respect* or *resentment;* and mankind in general have a sense of *desert*, by this natural *moral sense*.

Therefore, here is a question which may deserve to be considered: seeing *sentiment* is the *rule* of language, as to what is called *good* and *evil*, *worthy* and *unworthy;* and it is apparent that sentiment, at least as to many particulars, is different, in different persons, especially in different nations—that being thought to deserve praise by *one*, which by others is thought to be worthy of blame—how therefore can virtue and vice be any other than *arbitrary;* not at all determined by the *nature* of things, but by the *sentiments* of men with relation to the nature of things?

In order to the answering of this question with clearness, it may be divided into two: *viz.* Whether men's sentiments of moral good and evil are casual and accidental? And, whether their way of using words in what they call good and evil, is not *arbitrary*, without respect to any common sentiment conformed to the nature of things?

As to the *first*, I would observe, that the *general* disposition or sense of mind, exercised in a sense of desert of esteem or resentment, may be the same in all: though as to *particular* objects and occasions with regard to which it is exercised, it may be very various in different men, or bodies of men, through the partiality or error that may attend the view or attention of the mind. In all, a notion of *desert* of love or resentment, may consist in the same thing, in general—a suitableness, or natural uniformity and agreement, between the affections and acts of the agent, and the affections and treatment of others some way concerned—and yet *occasions* and *objects*, through a variety of apprehensions about them, and the various *manner* in which they are viewed, by reason of the partial attention of the mind, may be extremely various. Besides, example, custom, education, and association, may contribute to this, in ways innumerable. But it is needless to enlarge here, since what has been said by others, Mr. Hutchison in particular, may abundantly show, that the differences which are to be found among different persons and nations, concerning moral good and evil, are not inconsistent with a general *moral sense*, common to all mankind.

Nor, *secondly*, is the use of the words, *good* and *evil*, *right* and *wrong*, when used in a moral sense, altogether unfixed and arbitrary, according to the variety of notions, opinions, and views, that occasion the forementioned variety of sentiment. For though the signification of words is determined by particular use, yet that which *governs* in the use of terms, is *general* or common use. And mankind, in what they would signify by terms, are obliged to aim at a *consistent* use: because it is easily found that the end of language, which is to be a common medium of manifesting ideas and sentiments, cannot be obtained any other way than by a consistent use of words; both that men should be consistent with themselves, and one with another, in the use of them. But men cannot call any thing right or wrong, worthy or ill-deserving, consistently, any other way than by calling things so, which truly deserve praise or blame, *i. e.* things, wherein all things considered there is most uniformity in connecting with them praise or blame. There is no other way in which they can use these terms consistently with themselves. Thus if thieves or traitors may be angry with informers that bring them to justice, and call their behaviour by odious names; yet herein they are inconsistent with themselves; because, when they put themselves in the place of those who have injured them, they approve the same things they condemn. And therefore, such are capable of being convinced, that they apply these odious terms in an abusive manner. So, a nation that prosecutes an ambitious design of universal empire, by subduing other nations with fire and sword, may affix terms, that signify the highest degrees of virtue, to the conduct of such as show the most engaged, stable, resolute spirit in this affair, and do most of this bloody work. But yet they are capable of being convinced, that they use these terms inconsistently, and abuse language in it, and so having their mouths stopped. And not only will men use such words inconsistently with themselves, but also with one another, by using them any otherwise than to signify true merit or ill deserving, as before explained. For there is no way else wherein men have any notion of good or ill desert, in which mankind in general can agree. Mankind in general seem to suppose some *general standard*, or foundation in *nature*, for an universal consistence in the use of the terms whereby they express moral good and evil; which none can depart from but through error and mistake. This is evidently supposed in all their *disputes* about *right* and *wrong;* and in all *endeavours* used to prove *that any* thing is either *good* or *evil*, in a moral sense.

THE

GREAT CHRISTIAN DOCTRINE

OF

ORIGINAL SIN

DEFENDED;

EVIDENCES OF ITS TRUTH PRODUCED,

AND

ARGUMENTS TO THE CONTRARY ANSWERED,

CONTAINING, IN PARTICULAR,

A REPLY TO THE OBJECTIONS OF DR. JOHN TAYLOR,

IN HIS BOOK, ENTITLED,

"THE SCRIPTURE-DOCTRINE OF ORIGINAL SIN PROPOSED TO FREE AND CANDID EXAMINATION, &c."

Matt. ix. 12. They that be whole, need not a physician; but they that are sick.

—Et hæc non tantum ad peccatores referenda est; quia in omnibus maledictionibus primi hominis, omnes ejus generationes conveniunt.— *R. Sal. Jarchi.*

Propter concupiscentiam, innatam cordi humano, dicitur, In iniquitate genitus sum; atque sensu est, quod à nativitate implantatum cordi sit humano *Jetzer harang*, figmentum malum.— *Aben-Ezra.*

—Ad mores natura recurrit
Damnatos, fixa et mutari nescia.—
—Dociles imitandis
Turpibus et pravis omnes sumus. *Juv.*

ADVERTISEMENT,

CONTAINING A

BRIEF ACCOUNT OF THIS BOOK AND ITS AUTHOR,

BY THE FIRST EDITOR.

The Reverend Author of the following piece, was removed by death before its publication. But, ere his decease, the copy was finished and brought to the press; and a number of sheets passed his own review. They who were acquainted with the author, or know his just character, and have any taste for the serious theme, will want nothing to be said in recommendation of the ensuing tract, but only that Mr. Edwards wrote it.

Several valuable pieces on this subject have lately been published, upon the same side of the question. But he had no notice of so much as the very first of them, till he had wholly concluded what he had in view: nor has it been thought, that any thing already printed should supersede this work; being designed on a more extensive plan—comprising a variety of arguments, and answers to many objections, that fell not in the way of the other worthy writers—and the whole done with a care of familiar method and language, as well as clear reasoning, accommodated very much to common capacities. It must be a sensible pleasure to every friend of truth, that so masterly a hand undertook a reply to Dr. Taylor; notwithstanding the various answers already given him, both at home and abroad.

Since it has been thought unfit, that this posthumous book should go unattended with a respectful memorial of the author, it is hoped, the reader will candidly accept the following:*

As he lived cheerfully resigned in all things to the will of Heaven, so he died, or rather, as the Scripture emphatically expresses it, in relation to the saint in Christ Jesus, he *fell asleep*, without the least appearance of pain, and with great calm of mind. Indeed, when he first perceived the symptoms upon him to be mortal, he is said to have been a little perplexed for a while, about the meaning of this mysterious conduct of Providence, in calling him out from his beloved privacy, to a public scene of action and influence; and then so suddenly, just upon his entrance into it, translating him from thence, in such a way, by mortality! However, he quickly got believing and composing views of the wisdom and goodness of God in this surprising event: and readily yielded to the sovereign disposal of Heaven, with

* As we have given a full Memoir in the first volume, those particulars which were contained in this brief account, and which are more fully and accurately narrated there, are omitted, in order to avoid needless repetitions.

the most placid submission. Amidst the joy of faith, he departed this world, to go and see Jesus, whom his soul loved; to be with him, to behold his glory, and rejoice in his kingdom.

In person, he was tall of stature, and of a slender make. There was something extremely delicate in his constitution; which always obliged him to observe the exactest rules of temperance, and every method of cautious and prudent living. By such means he was helped to go through incessant labours, and to bear up under much study, which, Solomon observes, is a weariness to the flesh. Perhaps, never was a man more constantly retired from the world; giving himself to reading, and contemplation. And a wonder it was, that his feeble frame could subsist under such fatigues, daily repeated and so long continued. Yet upon occasion of some remark upon it by a friend, which was only a few months before his death, he told him, "He did not find but he was then as well able to bear the closest study, as he was thirty years before; and could go through the exercises of the pulpit with as little weariness or difficulty." In his youth he appeared healthy, and with a good degree of vivacity; but was never robust. In middle life, he appeared very much emaciated (I had almost said, mortified) by severe studies, and intense applications of thought. Hence his voice was a little languid, and too low for a large assembly; though much relieved and advantaged by a proper emphasis, just cadence, well-placed pauses, and great distinctness in pronunciation.

He had a piercing eye, the truest index of the mind. His aspect and mien had a mixture of severity and pleasantry. He had a natural turn for gravity and sedateness; ever contemplative; and in conversation usually reserved, but always observant of a genuine decorum in his deportment; free from sullen, supercilious, and contemptuous airs, and without any appearance of ostentation, levity, or vanity. As to imagination, he had enough of it for a great and good man: but the gaieties of a luxuriant fancy, so captivating to many, were what he neither affected himself, nor was much delighted with in others. He had a natural steadiness of temper, and fortitude of mind; which being sanctified by the Spirit of God, was ever of vast advantage to him, to carry him through difficult services, and support him under trying afflictions, in the course of his life. Personal injuries he bore with a becoming meekness and patience, and a disposition to forgiveness. The humility, modesty, and serenity of his behaviour, much endeared him to his acquaintance; and made him appear amiable in the eyes of such as had the privilege of conversing with him. He was a true and faithful friend; and showed much of a disinterested benevolence to his neighbour. The several relations sustained by him, he adorned with an exemplary conduct; and was solicitous to fill every station with its proper duty. He kept up an extensive correspondence, with ministers and others, in various parts; and his letters always contained some significant and valuable communications. In his private walk, as a Christian, he appeared an example of truly rational, consistent, uniform religion and virtue: a shining instance of the power and efficacy of that holy faith, to which he was so firmly attached, and of which he was so strenuous a defender. He exhibited much of spirituality, and a heavenly bent of soul. In him one saw the loveliest appearance, a rare assemblage of christian graces, united with the richest gifts, and mutually subserving and recommending one another.

As a scholar, his intellectual furniture exceeded what is common, considering the disadvantages we labour under in this remote corner of the world. He very early discovered a genius above the ordinary size; which gradually ripened and expanded, by daily exertion and application. He was remarkable for the penetration and extent of his understanding, for his powers of criticism and accurate distinction, quickness of thought, solidity of judgment, and force of reasoning; which made him an acute and strong disputant. By nature he was formed for a logician, and a metaphysician; but by speculation, observation, and converse, greatly improved. He had a good insight into the whole circle of liberal arts and sciences; possessed a very valuable stock of classic learning, philosophy, mathematics, history, chronology, &c. By the blessing of God on his indefatigable studiousness, to the last, he was constantly treasuring up useful knowledge, both human and divine.

Thus he appears uncommonly accomplished for the arduous and momentous province to which he was finally called. And had Heaven indulged us with the continuance of his precious life, we have reason to think, he would have graced his new station, and been a signal blessing to the college, and therein extensively served his generation, according to the will of God.

After all, it must be owned, divinity was his favourite study; and the ministry, his most delightful employment. Among the luminaries of the church, in these American regions, he was justly reputed a star of the first magnitude; thoroughly versed in all the branches of theology, didactic, polemic, casuistic, experimental, and practical. In point of divine knowledge and skill, he had few equals, and perhaps no superior, at least in these parts. On the maturest examination of the different schemes of principles, obtaining in the world, and on comparing them with the sacred Scriptures, the oracles of God and the great standard of truth, he was a Protestant and a Calvinist in judgment; adhering to the main articles of the reformed religion with an unshaken firmness, and with a fervent zeal, but tempered with charity and candour, and governed by discretion. He seemed as little as most men under the bias of education, or the influence of bigotry. As to practical and vital Christianity, no man appeared to have a better acquaintance with its nature and importance; or to understand true religion, and feel its power, more than he; which made him an excellently fit guide to inquiring souls, and qualified him to guard them against all false religion. His internal sense of the intercourse between God and souls, being brought by him to the severe test of reason and revelation, preserved him, both in sentiment and conduct, from the least tincture of enthusiasm. The accomplished divine enters deep into his character.

As a preacher, he was judicious, solid, and instructive. Seldom was he known to bring controversy into the pulpit; or to handle any subject in the nicer modes and forms of scholastic dissertation. His sermons, in general, seemed to vary exceedingly from his controversial compositions. In his preaching, usually, all was plain, familiar, sententious, practical; and very distant from any affectation of appearing the great man, or displaying his extraordinary abilities as a scholar. But still he ever preserved the character of a skilful and thorough divine. The common themes of his ministry were the most weighty and profitable; and especially, the great truths of the gospel of Christ, in which he himself lived by faith. His method in preaching was, first to apply to the understanding and judgment, labouring to enlighten and convince them; and then to persuade the will, engage the affections, and excite the active powers of the soul. His language was with propriety and purity, but with a noble negligence; nothing ornamented. Florid diction was not the beauty he preferred. His talents were of a superior kind. He regarded thoughts, rather than words. Precision of sentiment and clearness of expression are the principal characteristics of his pulpit style. Neither quick nor slow of speech, there was a certain *pathos* in his utterance, and such skill of address, as seldom failed to draw the attention, warm the hearts, and stimulate the consciences of the auditory. He studied to show himself approved unto God, a workman that needed not to be ashamed, rightly dividing the word of truth. And he was one who gave himself to prayer, as well as to the ministry of the word. Agreeably it pleased God to put great honour upon him, by crowning his labours with surprising successes, in the conversion of sinners, and the edification of saints, to the advancement of the kingdom and glory of God our Saviour Jesus Christ.

As a writer, Mr. Edwards distinguished himself in controversy, to which he was called on a variety of occasions. Here the superiority of his genius eminently appeared. He knew to arrange his ideas in an exact method: and close application of mind, with the uncommon strength of his intellectual powers, enabled him in a manner to exhaust every subject he took under consideration. He diligently employed the latter part of his life in defending Christianity, both in its doctrinal and practical views, against the errors of the times. Besides his excellent writings in behalf of the power of godliness, which some years ago happily prevailed in many parts of the British *America*, he made a noble stand against enthusiasm and false religion, when it threatened to spread, by his incomparable treatise upon religious affections. And more lately in opposition to Pelagian, Arminian, and other false principles, he published a very elaborate Treatise upon the Liberty of the human Will. A volume, that has procured him the elogy of eminent divines abroad. Several professors of divinity in the Dutch universities very lately sent him their thanks, for the assistance he had given them in their inquiry into some controverted points; having carried his own further than any author they had ever seen. And now this volume of his, on the great christian doctrine of original sin, is presented to public view; which, though studiously adapted to lower capacities, yet carries in it the evident traces of his great genius, and seems with superior force of argument to have entirely baffled the opponent.

His writings will perpetuate his memory, and make his name blossom in the dust. The blessing of Heaven attending the perusal of them, will make them effectually conducive to the glory of God, and the good of souls; which will brighten the author's crown, and add to his joy, in the day of future retribution.

THE

AUTHOR'S PREFACE.

THE following Discourse is intended, not merely as an answer to any *particular book* written against the doctrine of *Original Sin*, but as a *general defence* of that great important doctrine. Nevertheless, I have in this defence taken notice of the main things said against this doctine, by such of the more noted opposers of it as I have had opportunity to read: particularly those two late writers, Dr. Turnbull and Dr. Taylor, of *Norwich;* but especially the latter, in what he has published in those two books of his, the first entitled, *The Scripture-Doctrine of Original Sin proposed to free and candid Examination;* the other, his *Key to the Apostolic Writings*, with *a Paraphrase and Notes on the Epistle to the* Romans. I have closely attended to Dr. Taylor's *Piece on Original Sin*, in all its parts, and have endeavoured that no one thing there said, of any consequence in this controversy, should pass unnoticed, or that any thing which has the appearance of an argument, in opposition to this doctrine, should be left unanswered. I look on the doctrine as of *great importance;* which every body will doubtless own it is, if it be *true*. For, if the case be such indeed, that all mankind are by *nature* in a state of *total ruin*, both with respect to the *moral evil* of which they are the subjects, and the *afflictive evil* to which they are exposed, the one as the consequence and punishment of the other; then, doubtless, the great *salvation* by CHRIST stands in direct relation to this *ruin*, as the remedy to the disease; and the whole *gospel*, or doctrine of salvation, must *suppose* it; and all real belief, or true notion of that gospel, must be built upon it. Therefore, as I think the doctrine is most certainly both true and important, I hope, my attempting a *vindication* of it, will be *candidly* interpreted; and that what I have done towards its defence, will be *impartially* considered, by all that will give themselves the trouble to read the ensuing discourse: in which it is designed to examine every thing material throughout the Doctor's *whole* book, and many things in that other book, containing his *Key* and Exposition on *Romans;* as also many things written in opposition to this doctrine by some *other* modern authors. Moreover, my discourse being not only intended for an *answer* to Dr. Taylor, and other opposers of the doctrine of original sin, but for a *general defence* of that doctrine; producing the *evidence* of the truth of the doctrine, as well as answering *objections* made against it; I hope this attempt of mine will not be thought needless, nor be altogether useless, notwithstanding other publications on the subject.

I would also hope, that the *extensiveness* of the plan of the following treatise will excuse the *length* of it. And that when it is considered, how *much* was absolutely requisite to the full executing of a design formed on such a plan; how much has been written *against* the doctrine of original sin, and with what plausibility; how strong the *prejudices* of many are in favour of what is said in *opposition* to this doctrine—and that it cannot be expected, any thing short of a *full* consideration of almost *every* argument advanced by the main opposers, especially by this late and specious writer, Dr. Taylor, will satisfy many readers—how much must unavoidably be said in order to a full handling of the arguments in *defence* of the doctrine; and how *important* the doctrine must be, if true; I trust, the length of the following discourse will not be thought to exceed what the case really required. However, this must be left to the judgment of the intelligent and candid reader.

Stockbridge, May 26, 1757.

NOTE.—When the *page* is referred to in this manner, p. 40. p. 50. without mentioning the *book*, thereby is to be understood such a page in Dr. Taylor's *Scripture-Doctrine of Original Sin*. S. intends the Supplement. When the word *Key* is used to signify the book referred to, thereby is to be understood Dr. *Taylor's* KEY *to the Apostolic Writings*. This mark [§] with figures or a number annexed, signifies such a section or paragraph in his *Key*. When after mentioning *Preface to Par. on Epist. to Romans*, there is subjoined p. 145. 47. or the like, thereby is intended page and paragraph, page 145. paragraph 47. The letter T. alone, is used to signify Dr. Taylor's name, and no other.

THE

GREAT CHRISTIAN DOCTRINE

OF

ORIGINAL SIN DEFENDED.

PART I.

WHEREIN ARE CONSIDERED SOME EVIDENCES OF ORIGINAL SIN FROM FACTS AND EVENTS, AS FOUNDED BY OBSERVATION AND EXPERIENCE, TOGETHER WITH REPRESENTATIONS AND TESTIMONIES OF HOLY SCRIPTURE, AND THE CONFESSION AND ASSERTION OF OPPOSERS.

CHAP. I.

THE EVIDENCE OF ORIGINAL SIN FROM WHAT APPEARS IN FACT OF THE SINFULNESS OF MANKIND.

Sect. I.

All mankind constantly, in all ages, without fail in any one instance, run into that moral evil, which is in effect their own utter and eternal perdition in a total privation of GOD'S favour, and suffering of his vengeance and wrath.

By *Original Sin*, as the phrase has been most commonly used by divines, is meant the *innate sinful depravity of the heart*. But yet when the *doctrine* of original sin is spoken of, it is vulgarly understood in that latitude, which includes not only the *depravity of nature*, but the *imputation* of Adam's first sin; or, in other words, the liableness or exposedness of Adam's posterity, in the divine judgment, to partake of the punishment of that sin. So far as I know, most of those who have held one of these, have maintained the other; and most of those who have opposed one, have opposed the other; both are opposed by the author chiefly attended to in the following discourse, in his book against original sin: and it may perhaps appear in our future consideration of the subject, that they are closely connected; that the arguments which prove the one establish the other, and that there are no more difficulties attending the allowing of one, than the other.

I shall, in the first place, consider this doctrine more especially with regard to the *corruption of nature;* and as we treat of this, the other will naturally come into consideration, in the prosecution of the discourse, as connected with it. As all moral qualities, all principles either of virtue or vice, lie in the disposition of the heart, I shall consider whether we have any evidence, that the heart of man is naturally of a corrupt and evil disposition. This is strenuously denied by many late writers, who are enemies to the doctrine of original sin; and particularly by Dr. Taylor.

The way we come by the idea of any such thing as disposition or *tendency*, is by observing what is constant or general in *event;* especially under a great variety of circumstances; and above all, when the effect or event continues the same through great and various opposition, much and manifold force and means used to the contrary not prevailing to hinder the effect. I do not know, that such a prevalence of effects is denied to be an evidence of prevailing tendency in causes and agents; or that it is expressly denied by the opposers of the doctrine of original sin, that if, in the course of events, it universally or generally proves that mankind are actually corrupt, this would be an evidence of a prior corrupt propensity in the world of mankind; whatever may be said by some, which, if taken with its plain consequences, may seem to imply a denial of this; which may be considered afterwards. But by many the fact is denied; that is, it is denied, that corruption and moral evil are commonly prevalent in the world: on the contrary, it is insisted on, that good preponderates, and that virtue has the ascendant.

To this purpose, Dr. Turnbull says,* "With regard to the prevalence of vice in the world, men are apt to let their imagination run out upon all the robberies, piracies, murders, perjuries, frauds, massacres, assassinations they have either heard of, or read in history; thence concluding all mankind to be very wicked. As if a court of justice were a proper place to make an estimate of the morals of mankind, or an hospital of the healthfulness of a climate. But ought they not to consider, that the number of honest citizens and farmers far surpasses that of all sorts of criminals in any state, and that the innocent and kind actions of even criminals themselves surpass their crimes in numbers; that it is the rarity of crimes, in comparison of innocent or good actions, which engages our attention to them, and makes them to be recorded in history, while honest, generous domestic actions are overlooked, only because they are so common? as one great danger, or one month's sickness, shall become a frequently repeated story during a long life of health and safety.—Let not the vices of mankind be multiplied or magnified. Let us make a fair estimate of human life, and set over against the shocking, the astonishing instances of barbarity and wickedness that have been perpetrated in any age, not only the exceeding generous and brave actions with which history shines, but the prevailing innocency, good-nature, industry, felicity, and cheerfulness of the greater part of mankind at all times; and we shall not find reason to cry out, as objectors against Providence do on this occasion, that all men are vastly corrupt, and that there is hardly any such thing as virtue in the world. Upon a fair computation, the fact does indeed come out, that very great villanies have been very uncommon in all ages, and looked upon as monstrous; so general is the sense and esteem of virtue."—It seems to be with a like view that Dr. Taylor says, "We must not take the measure of our health and enjoyments from a lazar-house, nor of our understanding from *Bedlam*, nor of our morals from a gaol." (P. 77. S.)

With respect to the propriety and pertinence of such a representation of things, and its force as to the consequence

* Moral Philos. p. 289, 290.

designed, I hope we shall be better able to judge, and in some measure to determine, whether the natural disposition of the hearts of mankind be corrupt or not, when the things which follow have been considered. But for the greater clearness, it may be proper here to premise one consideration, that is of great importance in this controversy, and is very much overlooked by the opposers of the doctrine of original sin in their disputing against it.

That it is to be looked upon as the *true* tendency of the innate disposition of man's heart, which appears to be its tendency, when we consider things as they are in themselves, or in their own nature, without the *interposition of divine grace.* Thus, that state of man's nature, that disposition of the mind, is to be looked upon as evil and pernicious, which, as it is in itself, tends to extremely pernicious consequences, and would certainly end therein, were it not that the free mercy and kindness of God interposes to prevent that issue. It would be very strange if any should argue, that there is no evil tendency in the case, because the mere favour and compassion of the Most High may step in and oppose the tendency, and prevent the sad effect. Particularly, if there be any thing in the nature of man, whereby he has an universal unfailing tendency to that moral evil, which, according to the real nature and true demerit of things, as they are in themselves, implies his utter ruin, that must be looked upon as an evil tendency or propensity; however divine grace may interpose, to save him from deserved ruin, and to overrule things to an issue contrary to that which they tend to of themselves. Grace is sovereign, exercised according to the good pleasure of God, bringing good out of evil. The effect of it belongs not to the nature of things themselves, that otherwise have an ill tendency, any more than the remedy belongs to the disease; but is something altogether independent on it, introduced to oppose the natural tendency, and reverse the course of things. But the event to which things tend, according to their own *demerit*, and according to divine *justice*, is the event to which they tend in their own nature; as Dr. T.'s own words fully imply, *(Pref. to Par. on Rom.* p. 131.) "God alone (says he) can declare whether he will pardon or punish the ungodliness and unrighteousness of mankind, which is in ITS OWN NATURE punishable." Nothing is more precisely according to the truth of things, than divine justice: it weighs things in an even balance; it views and estimates things no otherwise than they are truly in their own nature. Therefore undoubtedly that which implies a tendency to ruin, according to the estimate of divine *justice*, does indeed imply such a tendency in its *own nature*.

And then it must be remembered, that it is a *moral depravity* we are speaking of; and therefore when we are considering whether such depravity do not appear by a tendency to a bad effect or issue, it is a *moral tendency* to such an issue, that is the thing to be taken into the account. A moral tendency or influence is by *desert*. Then may it be said, man's nature or state is attended with a pernicious or destructive tendency, in a *moral* sense, when it tends to that which *deserves* misery and destruction. And therefore it *equally* shows the moral depravity of the nature of mankind in their present state, whether that nature be universally attended with an effectual tendency to destructive vengeance *actually executed*, or to their *deserving* misery and ruin, or their just *exposedness*, to destruction, however that fatal consequence may be prevented by grace or whatever the actual event be.

One thing more is to be observed here, that the topic mainly insisted on by the opposers of the doctrine of original sin, is the *justice* of God; both in their objections against the *imputation* of *Adam's* sin, and also against its being so ordered, that men should come into the world with a *corrupt* and ruined nature, without having merited the displeasure of their Creator by any personal fault. But the latter is not repugnant to God's justice, if men *actually are* born into the world with a tendency to sin, and to misery and ruin for their sin, which actually will be the consequence, unless *mere grace* steps in and prevents it. If this be allowed, the argument from *justice* is given up: For it is to suppose, that their liableness to misery and ruin comes in a way of justice; otherwise there would be no need of the interposition of divine grace to save them. Justice alone would be sufficient security, if exercised, without grace. It is all one in this dispute about what is just and righteous, whether men are born in a miserable state, by a tendency to ruin, which *actually follows*, and that *justly*; or whether they are born in such a state as tends to a *desert* of ruin, which *might justly* follow, and *would actually follow*, did not grace prevent. For the controversy is not, what grace *will* do, but what justice *might* do.

I have been the more particular on this head, because it enervates many of the reasonings and conclusions by which Dr. T. makes out his scheme; in which he argues from that state which mankind are in *by divine grace*, yea, which he himself supposes to be by divine grace; and yet not making any allowance for this, he from hence draws conclusions against what others suppose of the deplorable and ruined state mankind are in by the fall.* Some of his arguments and conclusions to this effect, in order to be made good, must depend on such a supposition as this;—that God's dispensations of grace, are rectifications or amendments of his foregoing constitutions and proceedings, which were merely legal; as though the dispensations of grace, which succeed those of mere law, implied an acknowledgment, that the preceding legal constitution would be unjust, if left as it was, or at least very hard dealing with mankind; and that the other were of the nature of a satisfaction to his creatures, for former injuries, or hard treatment. So that, put together the injury with the satisfaction, the legal and injurious dispensation, taken with the following good dispensation, which our author calls grace, and the unfairness or improper severity of the former, amended by the goodness of the latter, both together made up one righteous dispensation.

The reader is desired to bear in mind what I have said concerning the interposition of divine grace not altering the nature of things, as they are in themselves. Accordingly, when I speak of such and such an evil *tendency* of things, belonging to the present nature and state of mankind, understand me to mean their tendency *as they are in them-*

* He often speaks of death and affliction as coming on Adam's posterity in consequence of his sin; and in p. 20, 21. and many other places, he supposes, that these things come in consequence of his sin, not as a punishment or a calamity, but as a *benefit.* But in p. 23. he supposes, those things would be a great calamity and misery, if it were not for the resurrection; which resurrection he there, and in the following pages, and in many other places, speaks of as being by Christ; and often speaks of it as being *by the grace* of God in Christ.

P. 63, 64. Speaking of our being subjected to sorrow, labour, and death, in consequence of *Adam's* sin, he represents these as evils that are reversed and turned into advantages, and from which we are delivered *through grace* in Christ. And p. 65, 66, 67. he speaks of God thus turning death into an advantage *through grace* in Christ, as what vindicates the justice of God in bringing death by Adam.

P. 152, 156. One thing he alleges against this proposition of the Assembly of Divines—That we are by nature bond-slaves to Satan—*That God hath been providing, from the beginning of the world to this day, various means and dispensations, to preserve and rescue mankind from the devil.*

P. 168, 169, 170. In answer to that objection against his doctrine, That we are in worse circumstances than Adam, he alleges the happy circumstances we are under by the provision and means furnished through *free grace in Christ.*

P. 228. In answering that argument against his doctrine—That there is a law in our members, bringing us into captivity to the law of sin and death, Rom. vii—He allows, that the case of those who are under a law threatening death for every sin, (which law he elsewhere says, *shows us the natural and proper demerit of sin, and is perfectly consonant to everlasting truth and righteousness,) must be quite deplorable, if they have no relief from the mercy of the lawgiver.*

P. 90—93. S. In opposition to what is supposed of the miserable state mankind are brought into by Adam's sin, he alleges, *The noble designs of love, manifested by advancing a new and happy dispensation, founded on the obedience and righteousness of the Son of God;* and that, although by Adam we are subjected to death, yet in this dispensation a resurrection is provided; and that Adam's posterity are under a mild dispensation of *Grace, &c.*

P. 112. S. He vindicates God's dealings with *Adam*, in placing him at first under the rigour of law, transgress and die, (which, as he expresses it, *was putting his happiness on a foot extremely dangerous,)* by saying, *that as God had before determined in his own breast, so he immediately established his covenant upon a quite different bottom, namely, upon grace.*

P. 122, 123. S. Against what *R. R.* says, That God forsook man when he fell, and that mankind after Adam's sin were born without the divine favour, &c. he alleges, among other things, *Christ's coming to be the propitiation for the sins of the whole world—And the riches of God's mercy in giving the promise of a Redeemer to destroy the works of the devil—That he caught his sinning falling creature in the arms of his grace.*

In his note on Rom. v. 20. p. 297, 298. he says as follows: "The law I conceive, is not a dispensation suitable to the infirmity of the human nature in our present state; or it doth not seem congruous to the goodness of God, to afford us no other way of salvation but by a law, which, if we once transgress, we are ruined for ever. For who then from the beginning of the world could be saved? And therefore it seems to me, that the law was not absolutely intended to be a rule for obtaining life, even to Adam in paradise: *Grace* was the dispensation God intended mankind should be under; and therefore Christ was fore-ordained before the foundation of the world." —There are various other passages in this author's writings of the like kind.

selves, abstracted from any consideration of that remedy the sovereign and infinite grace of God has provided.—Having premised these things, I now assert, that mankind are all naturally in such a state, as is attended, without fail, with this consequence or issue; that THEY UNIVERSALLY RUN THEMSELVES INTO THAT WHICH IS, IN EFFECT, THEIR OWN UTTER ETERNAL PERDITION, as being finally accursed of God, and the subjects of his remediless wrath through sin.—From which I infer, that the natural state of the mind of man is attended with a *propensity of nature,* which is prevalent and effectual, to such an issue; and that therefore their nature is corrupt and depraved with a moral depravity, that amounts to and implies their utter undoing.

Here I would first consider the *truth* of the proposition; and then would show the certainty of the *consequences* which I infer from it. If both can be clearly and certainly proved, then I trust, none will deny but that the doctrine of original depravity is evident, and so the falseness of Dr. T.'s scheme demonstrated; the greatest part of whose book, called *the Scripture Doctrine of Original Sin, &c.* is against the doctrine of *innate depravity.* In p. 107. S. he speaks of the conveyance of a corrupt and sinful nature to *Adam's* posterity as *the grand point* to be proved by the maintainers of the doctrine of original sin.

In order to demonstrate what is asserted in the proposition laid down, there is need only that these two things should be made manifest: *one* is this fact, that all mankind come into the world in such a state, as without fail comes to this issue, namely, the universal commission of sin; or that every one who comes to act in the world as a moral agent, is, in a greater or less degree, guilty of sin. The *other* is, that all sin deserves and exposes to utter and eternal destruction, unto God's wrath and curse; and would end in it, were it not for the interposition of divine grace to prevent the effect. Both which can be abundantly demonstrated to be agreeable to the word of God, and to Dr. T's own doctrine.

That every one of mankind, at least such as are capable of acting as moral agents, are guilty of sin, (not now taking it for granted that they come guilty into the world,) is most clearly and abundantly evident from the Holy Scriptures: 1 Kings viii. 46. "If any man sin against thee; for there is no man that sinneth not." Eccl. vii. 20. "There is not a just man upon earth that doeth good, and sinneth not." Job ix. 2, 3. "I know it is so of a truth, (i. e. as *Bildad* had just before said, that God would not cast away a perfect man, &c.) but how should man be just with God? If he will contend with him, he cannot answer him one of a thousand." To the like purpose, Psal. cxliii. 2. "Enter not into judgment with thy servant; for in thy sight shall no man living be justified." So the words of the apostle, (in which he has apparent reference to those of the Psalmist,) Rom. iii. 19, 20. "That every mouth may be stopped, and all the world become guilty before God. Therefore by the deeds of the law there shall no flesh be justified in his sight: for by the law is the knowledge of sin." So, Gal. ii. 16. 1 John i. 7—10. "If we walk in the light, the blood of Christ cleanseth us from all sin. If we say that we have no sin, we deceive ourselves, and the truth is not in us. If we confess our sins, he is faithful and just to forgive us our sins, and to cleanse us from all unrighteousness. If we say that we have not sinned, we make him a liar, and his word is not in us." In this and innumerable other places, confession and repentance of sin are spoken of as duties proper for ALL; as also prayer to God for pardon of sin; also forgiveness of those that injure us, from that motive, that we hope to be *forgiven* of God. Universal guilt of sin might also be demonstrated from the appointment, and the declared use and end of the ancient sacrifices; and also from the ransom, which every one that was numbered in *Israel,* was directed to pay, to make atonement for his soul. (Exod. xxx. 11—16.) All are represented, not only as being sinful, but as having great and manifold iniquity. (Job ix. 2, 3. James iii. 1, 2.)

There are many scriptures which both declare the *universal sinfulness* of mankind, and also that all sin *deserves* and justly exposes to *everlasting destruction,* under the wrath and curse of God; and so demonstrate both parts of the proposition I have laid down. To which purpose that passage in Gal. iii. 10. is exceeding full: "For as many as are of the works of the law are under the curse; for it is written, Cursed is every one that continueth not in all things which are written in the book of the law, to do them." How manifestly is it implied in the apostle's meaning here, that there is no man but what fails in some instances of doing all things that are written in the book of the law, and therefore as many as have their dependence on their fulfilling the law, are under that curse which is pronounced on them that fail of it! And hence the apostle infers in the next verse, "that *no man* is justified by the law in the sight of God:" as he had said before in the preceding chapter, ver. 16. "By the works of the law shall no flesh be justified." The apostle shows us he understands, that by this place which he cites from Deuteronomy, "the Scripture hath concluded, or shut up, all under sin." (Gal. iii. 22.) So that here we are plainly taught, both that every one of mankind is a *sinner,* and that every sinner is under the *curse* of God.

To the like purpose is Rom. iv. 14. also 2 Cor. iii. 6, 7, 9. where the law is called "the letter that kills, the ministration of death, and the ministration of condemnation." The wrath, condemnation, and death, which is threatened in the law to all its transgressors, is final perdition, the second death, eternal ruin; as is very plain, and indeed is confessed. And this punishment which the law threatens for every sin, is a *just* punishment; being what every sin truly *deserves;* God's law being a righteous law, and the sentence of it a righteous sentence.

All these things are what Dr. Taylor himself confesses and asserts. He says, that the law of God requires *perfect* obedience. (*Note* on Rom. vii. 6. p. 308.) "God can never require imperfect obedience, or by his holy law allow us to be guilty of any one sin, how small soever. And if the law, as a rule of duty, were in any respect abolished, then we might in some respects transgress the law, and yet not be guilty of sin. The moral law, or law of nature, is the truth, everlasting, unchangeable; and therefore, as such, can never be abrogated. On the contrary, our Lord Jesus Christ has promulgated it anew under the gospel, fuller and clearer than it was in the mosaical constitution, or any where else:—having added to its precepts the sanction of his own divine authority." And many things which he says imply, that all mankind do in some degree transgress the law. In p. 228. speaking of what may be gathered from Rom. vii. and viii. he says, "We are very apt, in a world full of temptation, to be deceived, and drawn into sin by bodily appetites, &c. And the case of those who are under a law threatening death to every sin, must be quite deplorable, if they have no relief from the mercy of the lawgiver."

But this is very fully declared in what he says in his note on Rom. v. 20. p. 297. His words are as follows: "Indeed, as a rule of action prescribing our duty, it (the law) always was and always must be a rule ordained for obtaining life; but not as a rule of justification, not as it subjects to death for every transgression. For if it COULD in its utmost rigour have given us life, then, as the apostle argues, it would have been against the promises of God. For if there had been a law, in the strict and rigorous sense of law, WHICH COULD HAVE MADE US LIVE, verily justification should have been by the law. But he supposes, no such law was ever given: and therefore there is need and room enough for the promises of grace; or as he argues, Gal. ii. 21. it would have frustrated, or rendered useless, the grace of God. For if justification came by the law, then truly Christ is dead in vain, then he died to accomplish what was, or MIGHT HAVE BEEN, EFFECTED by law itself without his death. Certainly the law was not brought in among the *Jews* to be a rule of justification, or to recover them out of a state of death, and to procure life by their sinless obedience to it: For in this, as well as in another respect, it was WEAK; not in itself, but through the WEAKNESS of our flesh, Rom. viii. 3. The law, I conceive, is not a dispensation *suitable to the infirmity of the human nature* in our present state; or it doth not seem congruous to the goodness of God to afford us no other way of salvation, but by LAW; WHICH IF WE ONCE TRANSGRESS, WE ARE RUINED FOR EVER. FOR WHO THEN, FROM THE BEGINNING OF THE WORLD, COULD BE SAVED?"

How clear and express are these things, that no one of mankind, from the beginning of the world, can ever be justified by law, because every one transgresses it!*

And here also we see, Dr. T. declares, that by the law men are sentenced to *everlasting ruin* for one transgression. To the like purpose he often expresses himself. So p. 207. "The law requireth the most extensive obedience, discovering sin in all its branches.—It gives sin a deadly force, subjecting every transgression to the penalty of death; and yet supplieth neither help nor hope to the sinner, but leaving him under the power of sin and sentence of death." In p. 213. he speaks of the law as *extending to lust and irregular desires, and to every branch and principle of sin; and even to its latent principles, and minutest branches;* again (*Note* on Rom. vii. 6. p. 308.) *to every sin, how small soever.* And when he speaks of the law subjecting every transgression to the penalty of death, he means eternal death, as he from time to time explains the matter. In p. 212. he speaks of the law *in the condemning power of it, as binding us in everlasting chains.* In p. 120. S. he says, that death which is the wages of sin, is the *second death;* and this, p. 78. he explains of *final perdition.* In his *Key*, p. 107. § 296. he says, "The curse of the law subjected men for every transgression to *eternal death.*" So in *Note* on Rom. v. 20. p. 291. "The law of *Moses* subjected those who were under it to death, meaning by death, eternal death." These are his words.

He also supposes, that this sentence of the law, thus subjecting men for *every*, even the *least, sin*, and *every minutest branch* and *latent principle of sin*, to so dreadful a punishment, is *just and righteous, agreeable to truth* and the *nature of things*, or to the *natural* and *proper demerits of sin.* In this he is very full. Thus in p. 186. P. "It was sin (says he) which subjected us to death by the law, JUSTLY threatening sin with death. Which law was given us, that sin might appear; might be set forth IN ITS PROPER COLOURS; when we saw it subjected us to death by a law PERFECTLY HOLY, JUST, and GOOD; that sin by the commandment, by the law, might be represented WHAT IT REALLY IS, an exceeding great and deadly evil." So in note on Rom. v. 20. p. 299.. "The law or ministration of death, as it subjects to death for every transgression, is still of use to show the NATURAL AND PROPER DEMERIT OF SIN." *Ibid.* p. 292. "The language of the law, dying thou shalt die, is to be understood of the *demerit* of the transgression, that which it *deserves.*" *Ibid.* p. 298. "The law was added, saith Mr. Locke on the place, because the *Israelites*, the posterity of *Abraham*, were transgressors as well as other men, to show them their sins, and the punishment and death, which in STRICT JUSTICE they incurred by them. And this appears to be a true comment on Rom. vii. 13.—Sin, by virtue of the law, subjected you to death for this end, that sin, working death in us, by that which is *holy, just, and good*, PERFECTLY CONSONANT TO EVERLASTING TRUTH AND RIGHTEOUSNESS.—Consequently every sin is *in strict justice deserving* of wrath and punishment; and the law in its rigour was given to the *Jews*, to set home this awful truth upon their consciences, to show them the evil and pernicious NATURE of sin; and that being conscious they had broke the law of God, this might convince them of the great need they had of the FAVOUR of the lawgiver, and oblige them, by faith in his GOODNESS, to fly to his MERCY, for pardon and salvation."

If the law be holy, just, and good, a constitution perfectly agreeable to God's holiness, justice, and goodness; then he might have put it exactly in execution, agreeably to all these his perfections. Our author himself says, p. 133. S. "How that constitution, which establishes a law, the making of which is inconsistent with the justice and goodness of God, and the executing of it inconsistent with his holiness, can be a righteous constitution, I confess, is quite beyond my comprehension."

Now the reader is left to judge, whether it be not most plainly and fully agreeable to Dr. T.'s own doctrine, that there never was any one person from the beginning of the world, who came to act in the world as a moral agent, and that it is not to be hoped there ever will be any, but what is a sinner or transgressor of the law of God; and that therefore this proves to be the issue and event of things, with respect to all mankind in all ages, that, by the natural and proper demerit of their own sinfulness, and in the judgment of the law of God, which is perfectly consonant to truth, and exhibits things in their true colours, they are the proper subjects of the curse of God, eternal death, and everlasting ruin; which must be the actual consequence, unless the grace or favour of the lawgiver interpose, and mercy prevail for their pardon and salvation. The reader has seen also how agreeable this is to the doctrine of the Holy Scripture. If so, and if the interposition of divine grace alters not the nature of things as they are *in themselves*, and that it does not in the least affect the state of the controversy we are upon—concerning the true nature and tendency of the state in which mankind come into the world—whether grace prevents the fatal effect or no; I trust, none will deny, that the proposition laid down, is fully proved, as agreeable to the word of God, and Dr. T.'s own words; viz. That mankind are all naturally in such a state, as is attended, without fail, with this consequence or issue, that they *universally are the subjects of that guilt and sinfulness, which is, in effect, their utter and eternal ruin*, being cast wholly out of the favour of God, and subjected to his everlasting wrath and curse.

SECT. II.

It follows from the proposition proved in the foregoing section, that all mankind are under the influence of a prevailing effectual tendency in their nature, to that sin and wickedness, which implies their utter and eternal ruin.

THE proposition laid down being proved, the *consequence* of it remains to be made out, *viz.* That the mind of man has a *natural tendency* or *propensity* to that event, which has been shown universally and infallibly to take place; and that this is a *corrupt* or *depraved* propensity.—I shall here consider the former part of this consequence, namely, Whether such an universal, constant, infallible event is truly a proof of any *tendency* or *propensity* to that event; leaving the *evil* and *corrupt nature* of such a propensity to be considered afterwards.

If any should say, they do not think that its being a thing universal and infallible in *event*, that mankind commit some sin, is a proof of a prevailing *tendency* to sin; because they do good, and perhaps more good than evil: Let them remember, that the question at present is not, *How much* sin there is a tendency to; but whether there be a prevailing propensity to that issue, which it is allowed all men do actually come to—that all fail of keeping the law perfectly—whether there be not a tendency to such imperfection of obedience, as always without fail comes to pass; to that degree of sinfulness, at least, which all fall into; and so to that utter ruin, which that sinfulness implies and infers. Whether an effectual propensity to this be worth the name of depravity, because the good that may be supposed to balance it, shall be considered by and by. If all mankind in all nations and ages, were at least one day in their lives deprived of the use of their reason, and raving mad; or that all, even every individual person, once cut their own throats, or put out their own eyes; it might be an evidence of some tendency in the nature or natural state of mankind to such an event; though they might exercise reason many more days than they were distracted, and were kind to and tender of themselves oftener than they mortally and cruelly wounded themselves.

To determine whether the unfailing constancy of the above-named event be an evidence of tendency, let it be considered, What can be meant by *tendency*, but a prevailing liableness or exposedness to such or such an event? Wherein consists the notion of any such thing, but some stated prevalence or preponderation in the nature or state of causes or occasions, that is followed *by*, and so proves to be effectual *to*, a stated prevalence or commonness of any particular kind of effect? Or something in the per-

* I am sensible, these things are quite inconsistent with what he says elsewhere, of *sufficient power in all mankind constantly to do the whole duty which God requires of them* without a necessity of breaking God's law *in any degree*, (p. 63—68. S.) But, I hope, the reader will not think me accountable for his inconsistences.

manent state of things, concerned in bringing a certain sort of event to pass, which is a foundation for the constancy, or strongly prevailing probability, of such an event? If we mean this by tendency, (and I know not what else can be meant by it, but this, or something like,) then it is manifest, that where we see a stated prevalence of any effect there is a tendency to that effect in the nature and state of its causes. A common and steady effect shows, that there is somewhere a preponderation, a prevailing exposedness or liableness in the state of things, to what comes so steadily to pass. The natural dictate of reason shows, that where there is an effect, there is a cause, and a cause sufficient for the effect; because, if it were not sufficient, it would not be effectual; and that therefore, where there is a stated prevalence of the effect, there is a stated prevalence in the cause. A steady effect argues a steady cause. We obtain a notion of tendency, no other way than by observation: and we can observe nothing but events: and it is the commonness or constancy of events, that gives us a notion of tendency in all cases. Thus we judge of tendencies in the natural world. Thus we judge of the tendencies or propensities of nature in minerals, vegetables, animals, rational and irrational creatures. A notion of a stated tendency, or fixed propensity, is not obtained by observing only a single event. A stated preponderation in the cause or occasion, is argued only by a stated prevalence of the effect. If a die be once thrown, and it falls on a particular side, we do not argue from hence, that *that* side is the heaviest; but if it be thrown without skill or care, many thousands or millions of times, and it constantly falls on the same side, we have not the least doubt in our minds, but that there is something of propensity in the case, by superior weight of that side, or in some other respect. How ridiculous would he make himself, who should earnestly dispute against any tendency in the state of things to cold in the winter, or heat in the summer; or should stand to it, that although it often happened that water quenched fire, yet there was no tendency in it to such an effect!

In the case we are upon, human nature, as existing in such an immense diversity of persons and circumstances, and never failing in any one instance of coming to that issue—that sinfulness, which implies extreme misery and eternal ruin—is as the die often cast. For it alters not the case in the least, as to the evidence of tendency, whether the subject of the constant event be an individual, or a nature and kind. Thus, if there be a succession of trees of the same sort, proceeding one from another, from the beginning of the world, growing in all countries, soils, and climates, all bearing ill fruit; it as much proves the nature and tendency of the *kind*, as if it were only one individual tree, that had remained from the beginning of the world, often transplanted into different soils, and had continued to bear only bad fruit. So, if there were a particular family, which, from generation to generation, and through every remove to innumerable different countries, and places of abode, all died of a consumption, or all run distracted, or all murdered themselves, it would be as much an evidence of the *tendency* of something in the nature or constitution of that *race*, as it would be of the tendency of something in the nature or state of an individual, if some one person had lived all that time, and some remarkable event had often appeared in him, which he had been the agent or subject of from year to year, and from age to age, continually and without fail.*

Thus a propensity, attending the present nature or natural state of mankind, eternally to ruin themselves by sin, may certainly be inferred from apparent and acknowledged fact.—And I would now observe further, that not only does this follow from facts acknowledged by Dr. T. but the things he *asserts*, and the expressions which he *uses*, plainly imply that all mankind have such a propensity; yea, one of the highest kind, a propensity that is *invincible*, or a tendency which really amounts to a fixed, constant, unfailing *necessity*. There is a plain confession of a propensity or proneness to sin, p. 143.—"Man, who drinketh in iniquity like water; who is attended with so many sensual appetites, and so APT to indulge them."—And again, p. 228. "WE ARE VERY APT, in a world full of temptation, to be deceived, and drawn into sin by bodily appetites."—If we are *very apt* or prone to be drawn into sin by bodily appetites, and *sinfully to indulge them*, and very apt or prone *to yield to temptation to sin*, then we are *prone to sin*; for to yield to temptation to sin *is sinful*.—In the same page he shows, that on this account, and its consequences, *the case of those who are under a law, threatening death for every sin, must be quite deplorable, if they have no relief from the mercy of the lawgiver.* Which implies, that their case is hopeless, as to an escape from death, the punishment of sin, by any other means than God's mercy. And that implies such an *aptness* to yield to temptation, as renders it hopeless that any of mankind should wholly avoid it. But he speaks of it elsewhere, over and over, as truly *impossible*, or what *cannot be;* as in the words before cited in the last *section*, from his note on Rom. v. 20. where he repeatedly speaks of the law, which subjects us to death for every transgression, as what CANNOT GIVE LIFE; and states, that if God offered us no other way of salvation, *no man from the beginning of the world* COULD *be saved*. In the same place he cites with approbation Mr. Locke's words, in which, speaking of the *Israelites*, he says, "All endeavours after righteousness was LOST LABOUR, since any one slip forfeited life, and it was IMPOSSIBLE for them to expect ought but death." Our author speaks of it as impossible for the law requiring sinless obedience to give life, *not that the law was weak in itself, but through the weakness of our flesh.* Therefore he says, *he conceives the law not to be a dispensation suitable to the infirmity of the human nature in its present state.* These things amount to a full confession, that the *proneness* in men to sin, and to a *demerit* of and just exposedness to eternal ruin, is universally invincible; or, which is the same thing, amounts to invincible necessity; which surely is the highest kind of tendency, or propensity: and that not the less, for his laying this propensity to our *infirmity* or weakness, which may seem to intimate some defect, rather than any thing positive: and it is agreeable to the sentiments of the *best divines*, that *all sin originally comes from a* DEFECTIVE *or* PRIVATIVE *cause*. But sin does not cease to be sin, justly exposing to eternal ruin, (as implied in Dr. T.'s own words,) for arising from infirmity or defect; nor does an invincible propensity to sin cease to be a propensity to such demerit of eternal ruin, because the proneness arises from such a cause.

It is manifest, that this tendency, which has been proved, does not consist in any particular *external* circumstances that persons are in, peculiarly influencing their minds; but is *inherent*, and is seated in that *nature* which is common to all mankind, which they carry with them wherever they go, and still remains the same, however circumstances may differ. For it is implied in what has been proved, and shown to be confessed, that the same event comes to pass in *all* circumstances. *In God's sight no man living can be justified;* but all are sinners, and exposed to condemnation. This is true of persons of all constitutions, capacities, conditions, manners, opinions, and educations; in all countries, climates, nations, and ages; and through all the mighty changes and revolutions, which have come to pass in the habitable world.

We have the same evidence, that the propensity in this case lies in the *nature* of the subject—and does not arise from any particular circumstances—as we have in any case whatsoever; which is only by the *effects* appearing to be the same in all changes of time and place, and under all varieties of circumstances. It is in this way only we judge, that any propensities, which we observe in man-

* Here may be observed the weakness of that objection, made against the validity of the argument for a fixed propensity to sin, from the constancy and universality of the event, that Adam sinned in one instance, without a fixed propensity. Without doubt a single event is an evidence, that there was *some cause* or occasion of that event. But the thing we are speaking of, is a *fixed cause:* propensity is a *stated* continued thing. We justly agree, that a *stated effect* must have a *stated cause*, and truly observe, that we obtain the notion of tendency, or *stated preponderation* in causes, no other way than by observing a stated prevalence of a particular kind of effect. But who ever argues a fixed propensity from a single event? And is it not strange arguing, that because an event which once comes to pass, does not prove any stated tendency, therefore the unfailing constancy of an event is an evidence of no such thing? But because Dr. T. makes so much of this objection from Adam sinning without a propensity, I shall hereafter consider it more particularly, in the beginning of the 9th *section* of this chapter; where will also be considered what is objected from the fall of the angels.

kind, are seated in their nature, in all other cases. It is thus we judge of the mutual propensity betwixt the sexes, or of the dispositions which are exercised in any of the natural passions or appetites, that they truly belong to the nature of man; because they are observed in mankind in general, through all countries, nations, and ages, and in all conditions.

If any should say, Though it be evident that there is a tendency in the state of things to this general event—that all mankind should fail of perfect obedience, and should sin, and incur a demerit of eternal ruin; and also that this tendency does not lie in any distinguishing circumstances of any particular people, person, or age—yet it may not lie in *man's nature*, but in the general constitution and frame of *this world*. Though the nature of man may be good, without any evil propensity inherent in it; yet the nature and universal state of this world may be full of so many and strong temptations, and of such powerful influence on such a creature as man, dwelling in so infirm a body, &c. that the result of the whole may be a strong and infallible tendency *in such a state of things*, to the sin and eternal ruin of every one of mankind.

To this I would reply, that such an evasion will not at all avail to the purpose of those whom I oppose in this controversy. It alters not the case as to this question, Whether man, in his present state, is depraved and ruined by propensities to sin. If any creature be of such a nature that it proves evil in its proper place, or in the situation which God has assigned it in the universe, it is of an evil nature. That part of the system is not good, which is not good in its place in the system; and those inherent qualities of that part of the system, which are not good, but corrupt, in that place, are justly looked upon as evil inherent qualities. That propensity is truly esteemed to belong to the *nature* of any being, or to be inherent in it, that is the necessary consequence of its nature, considered together with its proper situation in the universal system of existence, whether that propensity be good or bad. It is the *nature* of a stone to be heavy; but yet, if it were placed, as it might be, at a distance from this world, it would have no such quality. But being a stone, is of such a nature, that it will have this quality or tendency, in its proper place, in this world, where God has made it, it is properly looked upon as a propensity belonging to its nature. And if it be a good propensity here, in its proper place, then it is a good quality of its nature; but if it be contrariwise, it is an evil natural quality. So, if mankind are of such a nature, that they have an universal effectual tendency to sin and ruin in this world, where God has made and placed them, this is to be looked upon as a pernicious tendency belonging to their nature. There is, perhaps, scarce any such thing, in beings not independent and self-existent, as any power or tendency, but what has some dependence on other beings, with which they stand connected in the universal system of existence. Propensities are no propensities, any otherwise, than as taken with their objects. Thus it is with the tendencies observed in natural bodies, such as gravity, magnetism, electricity, &c. And thus it is with the propensities observed in the various kinds of animals; and thus it is with most of the propensities in created spirits.

It may further be observed, that it is exactly the same thing, as to the controversy concerning an agreeableness with God's moral perfections of such a disposal of things—that man should come into the world in a depraved and ruined state, by a propensity to sin and ruin—whether God has so ordered it, that this propensity should lie in his nature considered *alone*, or with relation to its situation in the universe, and its *connexion* with other parts of the system to which the Creator has united it; which is as much of God's ordering, as man's nature itself, most simply considered.

Dr. T. (p. 188, 189.) speaking of the attempt of some to solve the difficulty of God being the author of our nature, and yet that our nature is polluted, by supposing that God makes the soul pure, but unites it to a polluted body, (or a body so made, as tends to pollute the soul,) he cries out of it as weak and insufficient, and *too gross to be admitted*: For, says he, *who infused the soul into the body? And if it is polluted by being infused into the body, who is the author and cause of its pollution? And who created the body? &c.*—But is not the case just the same, as to those who suppose that God made the soul pure, and places it in a polluted world, or a world tending, by its natural state in which it is made, to pollute the soul, or to have such an influence upon it, that it shall without fail be polluted with sin, and eternally ruined? Here may not I also cry out, on as good grounds as Dr. T.—Who placed the soul here in this world? And if the world be polluted, or so constituted as naturally and infallibly to pollute the soul with sin, who is the cause of this pollution? And, who created the world?

Though in the place now cited, Dr. T. so insists upon it, that God must be answerable for the pollution of the soul, if he has infused or put the soul into a body that tends to pollute it; yet this is the very thing which he himself supposes to be fact, with respect to the soul being created by God, in such a body, and in such a world; where he says, "We are *apt*, in a world full of temptation, to be drawn into sin by bodily appetites." And if so, according to his way of reasoning, God must be the author and cause of this aptness to be drawn into sin. Again, p. 143. we have these words, "*Who drinketh in iniquity like water? Who is attended with so many sensual appetites, and so apt to indulge them?*" In these words our author in effect says the individual things that he exclaims against as so *gross*, *viz.* The tendency of the body, as God has made it, to pollute the soul, which he has infused into it. These sensual appetites, which incline the soul, or make it *apt*, to a sinful *indulgence*, are either from the body which God hath made, or otherwise a proneness to sinful indulgence is immediately and originally seated in the soul itself, which will not mend the matter.

I would lastly observe, that our author insists upon it, p. 42. S. That this lower world, in its present state, "Is as it was, when, upon a review, God pronounced it, and all its furniture, *very good.*—And that the present form and furniture of the earth is full of God's riches, mercy, and goodness, and of the most evident tokens of his love and bounty to the inhabitants." If so, there can be no room for evading the evidences from fact, of the universal infallible tendency of *man's nature* to sin and eternal perdition; since, on the supposition, the tendency to this issue does not lie in the general constitution and frame of this world, which God hath made to be the habitation of mankind.

SECT. III.

That propensity, which has been proved to be in the nature of all mankind, must be a very evil, depraved, and pernicious propensity; making it manifest, that the soul of man, as it is by nature, is in a corrupt, fallen, and ruined state; which is the other part of the consequence, drawn from the proposition laid down in the first section.

THE question to be considered, in order to determine whether man's nature be *depraved and ruined*, is not, Whether he is inclined to perform as many *good deeds as bad ones?* But, to which of these two he preponderates, in the frame of his heart, and the state of his nature, *a state of innocence and righteousness, and favour with God; or a state of sin, guiltiness, and abhorrence in the sight of God?*—Persevering sinless righteousness, or else the guilt of sin, is the alternative, on the decision of which depends—according to the nature and truth of things, as they are in themselves, and according to the rule of right, and of perfect justice—man being approved and accepted of his Maker, and eternally blessed as good; or his being rejected, and cursed as bad. And therefore the determination of the tendency of man's heart and nature, with respect to these terms, is that which is to be looked at, in order to determine whether his nature is good or evil, pure or corrupt, sound or ruined. If such be man's nature, and the state of his heart, that he has an infallibly effectual propensity to the latter of those terms; then it is wholly impertinent to talk of *the innocent and kind actions, even of criminals themselves, surpassing their crimes in numbers, and of the prevailing innocence, good nature, industry, felicity, and cheerfulness of the greater part of mankind.* Let never so many thousands or millions of acts of honesty, good nature, &c. be supposed; yet, by the supposition, there is an unfailing propensity to such moral evil, as in its dreadful consequences infinitely outweighs all effects or consequences of any supposed good. Surely that tendency, which, in effect, is an infallible tendency to eternal destruction, is an infinitely dreadful and pernicious tendency: and that nature and frame of mind, which implies such a tendency, must be an infinitely dreadful and pernicious frame of mind. It would be much more absurd to suppose, that such a state of nature is not bad, under a notion of men doing more honest and kind things than evil ones; than to say, the state of that ship is *good*, for crossing the *Atlantic* ocean, though such as cannot hold together through the voyage, but will infallibly founder and sink, under a notion that it may probably go *great part* of the way before it sinks, or that it will proceed and sail above water more hours than it will be in sinking: or, to pronounce that road a good road to go to such a place, the greater part of which is plain and safe, though some parts of it are dangerous, and certainly fatal, to them that travel in it; or to call that a good propensity, which is an inflexible inclination to travel in such a way.

A propensity to that sin which brings God's eternal wrath and curse (which has been proved to belong to the nature of man) is evil, not only as it is *calamitous* and *sorrowful*, ending in great *natural evil;* but as it is *odious* and *detestable;* for by the supposition, it tends to that *moral evil*, by which the subject becomes odious in the sight of God, and liable, as such, to be condemned, and utterly rejected, and cursed by him. This also makes it evident, that the state which it has been proved mankind are in, is a *corrupt* state in a *moral sense*, that it is inconsistent with the fulfilment of the law of God, which is the rule of moral rectitude and goodness. That tendency, which is opposite to what the moral law requires, and prone to that which the moral law utterly forbids, and eternally condemns, is doubtless a corrupt tendency, in a moral sense.

So that this depravity is both *odious*, and also *pernicious*, fatal and destructive, in the highest sense; as inevitably tending to that which implies man's eternal ruin. It shows, that man, as he is by nature, is in a deplorable state, in the highest sense. And this proves that men do not come into the world perfectly innocent in the sight of God, and without any just exposedness to his displeasure. For the being by nature in a lost and ruined state, in the highest sense, is not consistent with being by nature in a state of favour with God.

But if any should still insist on a notion of men's good deeds exceeding their bad ones, and that, seeing the good more than countervails the evil, they cannot be properly denominated evil; all persons and things being most properly denominated from that which prevails, and has the ascendant in them; I would say further, That if there is in man's nature a tendency to guilt and ill desert, in a vast overbalance to virtue and merit; or a propensity to sin, the demerit of which is so great, that the value and merit of all the virtuous acts that ever he performs, are as nothing to it; then truly the nature of man may be said to be corrupt and evil.

That this is the true case, may be demonstrated by what is evident of the infinite heinousness of sin against God, from the nature of things. The heinousness of this must rise in some proportion to the obligation we are under to regard the Divine Being; and that must be in some proportion to his worthiness of regard; which doubtless is infinitely beyond the worthiness of any of our fellow-creatures. But the merit of our respect or obedience to God is not infinite. The merit of respect to any being does not increase, but is rather diminished, in proportion to the obligations we are under in strict justice to pay him that respect. There is no great merit in paying a debt we owe, and by the highest possible obligations in strict justice are obliged to pay; but there is great demerit in refusing to pay it. That on such accounts as these, there is an infinite demerit in all sin against God, which must therefore immensely outweigh all the merit which can be supposed to be in our virtue, I think, is capable of full demonstration; and that the futility of the objections which some have made against the argument, might most plainly be demonstrated. But I shall omit a particular consideration of the evidence of this matter from the nature of things, as I study brevity, and lest any should cry out, *metaphysics!* as the manner of some is, when any argument is handled against a tenet they are fond of, with a close and exact consideration of the nature of things. And this is not so necessary in the present case, inasmuch as the point asserted—that he who commits any one sin, has guilt and ill desert so great, that the value and merit of all the good which it is possible he should do in his whole life, is as nothing to it—is not only evident by *metaphysics*, but is plainly demonstrated by what has been shown to be *fact*, with respect to God's own constitutions and dispensations towards mankind. Thus, whatever acts of virtue and obedience a man performs, yet if he trespasses in one point, is guilty of any the least sin, he—according to the law of God, and so according to the exact truth of things, and the proper demerit of sin—is exposed to be wholly cast out of favour with God, and subjected to his curse, to be utterly and eternally destroyed. This has been proved; and shown to be the doctrine which Dr. T. abundantly teaches.

But how can it be agreeable to the nature of things, and exactly consonant to everlasting truth and righteousness, thus to deal with a creature for the least sinful act, though he should perform ever so many thousands of honest and virtuous acts, to countervail the evil of that sin? Or how can it be agreeable to the exact truth and real demerit of things, thus wholly to cast off the deficient creature, without any regard to the merit of all his good deeds, unless that be in truth the case, that the value and merit of all those good actions, bear no proportion to the heinousness of the least sin? If it were not so, one would think, that however the offending person might have some proper punishment, yet seeing there is so much virtue to lay in the balance against the guilt, it would be agreeable to the nature of things, that he should find some favour, and not be altogether rejected, and made the subject of perfect and eternal destruction; and thus no account at all be made of all his virtue, so much as to procure him the least relief or hope. How can such a constitution *represent sin in its proper colours*, and *according to its true nature and desert*, (as Dr. T. says it does,) unless this be its true nature, that it is so bad, that even in the least instance it perfectly swallows up all the value of the sinner's supposed good deeds, let them be ever so many. So that this matter is not left to our metaphysics, or philosophy; the great lawgiver, and infallible judge of the universe, has clearly decided it, in the revelation he has made of what is agreeable to exact truth, justice, and the nature of things, in his revealed law, or rule of righteousness.

He that in any respect or degree is a transgressor of God's law, is a wicked man, yea, wholly wicked in the eye of the law; all his goodness being esteemed nothing, having no account made of it, when taken together with his wickedness. And therefore, without any regard to his righteousness, he is, by the sentence of the law, and so by the voice of truth and justice, to be treated as worthy to be rejected, abhorred, and cursed for ever; and must be so, *unless grace interpose*, to cover his transgression. But men are really, in themselves, what they are in the eye of the law, and by the voice of strict equity and justice; however they may be looked upon, and treated by infinite and unmerited mercy.

So that, on the whole, it appears, all mankind have an infallibly effectual propensity to that moral evil, which infinitely outweighs the value of all the good that can be in them; and have such a disposition of heart, that the certain consequence of it is, their being, in the eye of perfect truth and righteousness, wicked men. And I leave all to judge, whether such a disposition be not in the eye of truth a *depraved* disposition?

Agreeable to these things, the Scripture represents all mankind, not only as having guilt, but immense guilt, which they can have no merit or worthiness to countervail. Such is the representation we have in Matt. xviii. 21, to the end. There, on *Peter's* inquiring, *How often his brother should trespass against him, and he forgive him, whether until seven times?* Christ replies, *I say not unto thee, until seven times, but until seventy times seven*; apparently meaning, that he should esteem no number of offences too many, and no degree of injury it is possible our neighbour should be guilty of towards us too great, to be forgiven. For which this reason is given in the parable following, that if ever we obtain forgiveness and favour with God, he must pardon that guilt and injury towards his majesty, which is immensely greater than the greatest injuries that ever men are guilty of one towards another; yea, than the sum of all their injuries put together, let them be ever so many, and ever so great; so that the latter would be but as an hundred pence to ten thousand talents, which immense debt we owe to God, and have nothing to pay; which implies, that we have no merit to countervail any part of our guilt. And this must be, because if all that may be called virtue in us, be compared with our ill desert, it is in the sight of God as nothing to it. The parable is not to represent *Peter's* case in particular, but that of all who then were, or ever should be, Christ's disciples; as appears by the conclusion of the discourse, (ver. 35.) "So likewise shall my heavenly Father do, if ye, from your hearts, forgive not every one his brother their trespasses."

Therefore how absurd must it be for Christians to object, against the depravity of man's nature, a greater number of innocent and kind actions, than of crimes; and to talk of a prevailing innocency, good nature, industry, and cheerfulness of the greater part of mankind! Infinitely more absurd, than it would be to insist, that the domestic of a prince was not a bad servant, because though sometimes he contemned and affronted his master to a great degree, yet he did not spit in his master's face so often as he performed acts of service. More absurd, than it would be to affirm, that his spouse was a good wife to him, because, although she committed adultery, and that with the slaves and scoundrels sometimes, yet she did not do this so often as she did the duties of a wife. These notions would be absurd, because the crimes are too heinous to be atoned for, by many honest actions of the servant or spouse of the prince; there being a vast disproportion between the merit of the one, and the ill desert of the other: but infinitely less, than that between the demerit of our offences against God, and the value of our acts of obedience.

Thus I have gone through with my first argument; having shown the evidence of the truth of the proposition laid down at first, and proved its consequence. But there are many other things, that manifest a very corrupt tendency or disposition in man's nature, in his present state, which I shall take notice of in the following *sections*.

SECT. IV.

The depravity of nature appears by a propensity in all to sin immediately, as soon as they are capable of it, and to sin continually and progressively; and also by the remains of sin in the best of men.

THE great depravity of man's nature appears, not only in that they universally commit sin, who spend any long time in the world; but in that men are naturally so prone to sin, that none ever fail of *immediately* transgressing God's law, and so of bringing infinite guilt on themselves, and exposing themselves to eternal perdition, as soon as they are capable of it.

The Scriptures are so very express upon it, that all mankind, *all flesh, all the world*, every man *living*, are guilty of sin; that it must at least be understood, every one capable of active duty to God, or of sin against him. There are multitudes in the world, who have but very lately begun to exert their faculties, as moral agents; and so have but just entered on their state trial, as acting for themselves: *many thousands constantly*, who have not lived one month, or week, or day, since they have arrived at any period that can be assigned (for the commencement of their agency) from their birth to twenty years of age. Now—if there be not a strong *propensity* in men's nature to sin, that should, as it were, hurry them on to speedy transgression, and if they have no guilt previous to their personal sinning—what should hinder, but that there might always be a *great number*, who have hitherto kept themselves free from sin, and have perfectly obeyed God's law, and so are righteous in his sight, with the righteousness of the law? And who, if they should be called out of the world without any longer trial, as great numbers die at all periods of life, would be justified by the deeds of the law? And how then can it be true, that *in God's sight no man living can be justified*, that *no man can be just with God*, and that *by the deeds of the law no flesh can be justified, because by the law is the knowledge of sin?* And what should hinder but that there may *always be many* in the world—who are capable subjects of instruction and counsel, and of prayer to God—for whom the calls of God's word to *repentance*, to seek *pardon* through the blood of Christ, and to forgive others their injuries *because* they need that God should forgive them, *would not be proper*; and for whom the Lord's prayer is not *suitable*, wherein Christ directs all his followers to pray, that God would *forgive their sins*, as they forgive those that trespass against them?

If there are *any* in the world—though but lately become capable of acting for themselves, as subjects of God's law—who are perfectly free from sin; such are most likely to be found among the children of Christian parents, who give them the most pious education, and set them the best examples. And therefore, such would never be so likely to be found in any part or age of the world, as in the primitive Christian church, in the first age of Christianity, (the age of the church's greatest purity,) so long after Christianity had been established, that there had been time for great numbers of children to be born, and educated by those primitive Christians. It was in that age, and in such a part of that age, that the apostle *John* wrote his first epistle to the Christians. But if there was then a number of them come to understanding, who were perfectly free from sin, why should he write as he does? 1 John i. 8, 9, 10. "If we say that we have no sin, we deceive ourselves, and the truth is not in us. If we confess our sins, he is faithful and just to forgive us our sins, and to cleanse us from all unrighteousness. If we say that we have not sinned, we make him a liar, and the truth is not in us."*

Again, the reality and greatness of the depravity of man's nature appears in this, That he has a prevailing propensity to be *continually* sinning against God. What has been observed above, will clearly prove this. That same disposition of nature, which is an effectual propensity to *immediate* sin, amounts to a propensity to *continual* sin. For a being prone to *continual* sinning, is nothing but a proneness to immediate sin *continued*. Such appears to be the tendency of nature to sin, that as soon as ever man is capable, it causes him immediately to sin, without suffering any considerable time to pass without sin. And therefore, if the same propensity be continued undiminished, there will be an equal tendency to immediate sinning again, without any considerable time passing. And so the same will always be a disposition still immediately to sin, with as little time passing without sin afterwards, as at first. The only reason that can be given why sinning must be

* If any should object, that this is an overstraining of things; and that it supposes a greater niceness and exactness than is observed in scripture representations, to infer from these expressions, that all men sin *immediately* as soon as ever they are capable of it. To this I would say, that I think the arguments used are truly solid, and do really and justly conclude, either that men are born guilty, and so are chargeable with sin before they come to act for themselves, or else commit sin immediately, without the least time intervening, after they are capable of understanding their obligations to God, and reflecting on themselves; and that the Scripture clearly determines, there is not one such person in the world, free from sin. But whether this be straining things to too great an exactness, or not; yet I suppose, none that do not entirely set aside the sense of such scriptures as have been mentioned, and deny those propositions which Dr. T. himself allows to be contained in some of them, will deny they prove, that no *considerable time* passes after men are capable of acting for themselves, as the subjects of God's law, before they are guilty of sin; because if the time were considerable, it would be great enough to deserve to be taken notice of, as an exception to such universal propositions, as, *in thy sight shall no man living be justified*, &c. And if this be allowed, that men are so prone to sin, that in fact all mankind do sin, *as it were*, immediately after they come to be capable of it, or fail not to sin so soon, that *no considerable time* passes before they run into transgression against God; it does not much alter the case, as to the present argument. If the time of freedom from sin be so small, as not to be worthy of notice in the forementioned universal propositions of Scripture, it is also so small, as not to be worthy of notice in the present argument.

immediate at first, is that the disposition is so great, that it will not suffer any considerable time to pass without sin: and therefore, the same disposition being continued in equal degree, without some new restraint, or contrary tendency, it will still equally tend to the same effect. And though it is true, the propensity may be diminished, or have restraints laid upon it, by the gracious disposals of Providence, or the merciful influences of God's Spirit; yet this is not owing to nature. That strong propensity of nature, by which men are so prone to immediate sinning at first, has no tendency in itself to a diminution; but rather to an *increase;* as the continued exercise of an evil disposition, in repeated actual sins, tends to strengthen it more and more: agreeable to that observation of Dr. T.'s, p. 228. "We are apt to be drawn into sin by bodily appetites, and when once we are under the government of these appetites, it is at least exceeding difficult, if not impracticable, to recover ourselves, by the mere force of reason." The increase of strength of disposition in such a case, is as in a falling body, the strength of its tendency to descend is continually increased, so long as its motion is continued. Not only a constant commission of sin, but a constant increase in the habits and practice of wickedness, is the true tendency of man's depraved nature, if unrestrained by divine grace; as the true tendency of the nature of a heavy body, if obstacles are removed, is not only to fall with a continual motion, but with a constantly increasing motion. And we see, that increasing iniquity is actually the consequence of natural depravity, in most men, notwithstanding all the restraints they have. Dispositions to evil are commonly much stronger in adult persons, than in children, when they first begin to act in the world as rational creatures.

If sin be such a thing as Dr. T. himself represents it, p. 69. "a thing of an odious and destructive nature, the corruption and ruin of our nature, and infinitely hateful to God;" then such a propensity to continual and increasing sin, must be a very evil disposition. And if we may judge of the perniciousness of an inclination of nature, by the evil of the effect it naturally tends to, the propensity of man's nature must be evil indeed: for the soul being immortal, as Dr. T. acknowledges, p. 94. S. it will follow from what has been observed above, that man has a natural disposition to one of these two things; either to an increase of wickedness without end, or till wickedness comes to be so great, that the capacity of his nature will not allow it to be greater. This being what his wickedness will come to by its natural tendency, if divine grace does not prevent, it may as truly be said to be the effect which man's natural corruption tends to, as that an acorn in a proper soil, truly tends by its nature to become a great tree.

Again, That sin which is remaining in the hearts of the *best* men on earth, makes it evident, that man's nature is corrupt, as he comes into the world. A remaining depravity of heart in the greatest saints, may be argued from the sins of most of those who are set forth in Scripture as the most eminent instances and examples of virtue and piety: and is also manifest from this, that the Scripture represents all God's children as standing in need of chastisement. Heb. xii. 6, 7, 8. "For whom the Lord loveth, he chasteneth; and scourgeth every son whom he receiveth.—What son is he, whom the father chasteneth not?—If ye are without chastisement, then are ye bastards, and not sons." But this is directly and fully asserted in some places; as in Eccles. vii. 20. "There is not a just man upon earth, that doeth good, and sinneth not." Which is as much as to say, there is no man on earth, that is so just, as to have attained to such a degree of righteousness, as not to commit any sin. Yea, the apostle *James* speaks of all Christians as often sinning, or committing many sins; even in that primitive age of the christian church, an age distinguished from all others by eminent attainments in holiness: Jam. iii. 2. "In many things we all offend." And that there is pollution in the hearts of all antecedent to all means for purification, is very plainly declared in Prov. xx. 9. "Who can say, I have made my heart clean, I am pure from my sin?"

According to Dr. T. men come into the world wholly free from sinful propensities. And if so, it appears from what has been already said, there would be nothing to hinder, but that many, without being better than they are by nature, might perfectly avoid the commission of sin But much more might this be the case with men after they had, by care, diligence, and good practice, attained those positive habits of virtue, whereby they are at a much greater distance from sin, than they were naturally:—which this writer supposes to be the case with many good men. But since the Scripture teaches us, that the best men in the world do often commit sin, and have remaining pollution of heart, this makes it abundantly evident, that men, when they are no otherwise than they were by nature, without any of those virtuous attainments, have a sinful depravity; yea, must have great corruption of nature.

SECT. V.

The depravity of nature appears, in that the general consequence of the state and tendency of man's nature is a much greater degree of sin, than righteousness; not only with respect to value and demerit, but matter and quantity.

I HAVE before shown, that there is a propensity in man's nature to that sin, which in heinousness and ill desert immensely outweighs all the value and merit of any supposed good, that may be in him, or that he can do. I now proceed to say further, that such is man's nature, in his present state, that it tends to this lamentable effect, that there should at all times, through the course of his life, be at least much more sin, than righteousness; not only as to *weight* and *value,* but as to *matter* and *measure;* more disagreement of heart and practice from the law of God, and from the law of nature and reason, than agreement and conformity. The law of God is the rule of right, as Dr. T. often calls it: It is the measure of virtue and sin: so much agreement as there is with this rule, so much is there of rectitude, righteousness, or true virtue, and no more; and so much disagreement as there is with this rule, so much sin is there. Having premised this, the following things may be here observed.

I. The degree of disagreement from this rule of right is to be determined, not only by the degree of distance from it in *excess,* but also in *defect;* or in other words, not only in positive transgression, or doing what is *forbidden,* but also in withholding what is *required.* The divine Lawgiver does as much prohibit the one as the other, and does as much charge the latter as a sinful breach of his law, exposing to his eternal wrath and curse, as the former. Thus at the day of judgment, as described Matt. xxv. The wicked are condemned as *cursed,* to *everlasting fire,* for their sin in defect and omission: *I was an hungred, and ye gave me no meat, &c.* And the case is thus, not only when the defect is in word or behaviour, but in the inward temper and exercise of the mind. 1 Cor. xvi. 22. "If any man love not the Lord Jesus Christ, let him be Anathema Maranatha." Dr. T. speaking of the sentence and punishment of the wicked, (Matt. xxv. 41, 46.) says, p. 159. "It was manifestly for WANT of benevolence, love, and compassion to their fellow-creatures, that they were condemned." And elsewhere, as was observed before, he says, that the law of God extends to the *latent principles* of sin to *forbid* them, and to condemn to eternal destruction for them. And if so, it doubtless also extends to the inward principles of holiness, to *require* them, and in like manner to condemn for the want of them.

II. The sum of our duty to God, required in his law, is LOVE; taking love in a large sense, for the true regard of our hearts to GOD, implying esteem, honour, benevolence, gratitude, complacence, &c. This is not only very plain by the Scripture, but it is evident in itself. The sum of what the law of God requires, is doubtless obedience to that law: no law can require more than that it be obeyed. But it is manifest, that obedience is nothing, any otherwise than as a testimony of the respect of our hearts to God: without the heart, man's external acts are no more than the motions of the limbs of a wooden image; have no more of the nature of either sin or righteousness. It must therefore needs be, that *love to God,* the respect of the heart, must be the sum of the duty required in his law.

III. It therefore appears from the premises, that whosoever withholds more of that love or respect of heart from God, which his law requires, than he affords, has more sin than righteousness. Not only he that has less divine love, than passions and affections which are opposite; but also he that does not love God half so much as he ought, or has reason to do, has justly more wrong than right imputed to him, according to the law of God, and the law of reason; he has more irregularity than rectitude, with regard to the law of love. The sinful disrespect of his heart towards God, is greater than his respect to him.

But what considerate person is there, even among the more virtuous part of mankind, but would be ashamed to say, and profess before God or men, that he loves God half so much as he ought to do; or that he exercises one half of that esteem, honour, and gratitude towards God, which would be altogether becoming him; considering what God is, and what great manifestations he has made of his transcendent excellency and goodness, and what benefits he receives from him? And if few or none of the best of men can with reason and truth make even such a profession, how far from it must the generality of mankind be?

The chief and most fundamental of all the commands of the moral law, requires us *to love the Lord our God with all our hearts, and with all our souls, with all our strength, and all our mind*: that is, plainly, with all that is within us, or to the utmost capacity of our nature. God is in himself *worthy* of infinitely greater love, than any creature can exercise towards him; love equal to his perfections, which are infinite. God loves himself with no greater love than he is worthy of, when he loves himself *infinitely;* but we can give God no more than we *have*. Therefore, if we give him *so much*, if we love him to the *utmost extent* of the faculties of our nature, we are excused. But when what is proposed, is only that we should love him *as much as our capacity will allow*, all excuse of *want of capacity* ceases, and obligation takes hold of us; and we are doubtless *obliged* to love God to the *utmost* of what is *possible* for us, with such faculties, and such opportunities and advantages to know God, as we have. And it is evidently implied in this great commandment of the law, that our love to God should be so great, as to have the most absolute possession of all the soul, and the perfect government of all the principles and springs of action that are in our nature.

Though it is not easy, precisely to fix the limits of man's capacity, as to love to God; yet in general we may determine, that his capacity of love is coextended with his capacity of knowledge: the exercise of the understanding opens the way for the exercise of the other faculty. Now, though we cannot have any proper positive understanding of God's infinite excellency; yet the capacity of the human understanding is very great, and may be extended far. It is needless to dispute, how far man's knowledge may be said to be strictly comprehensive of things that are very great, as of the extent of the expanse of the heavens, &c. The word *comprehensive*, seems to be ambiguous. But doubtless we are capable of some proper *positive* understanding of the greatness of these things, in comparison of other things that we know. We are capable of some clear understanding of the greatness or considerableness of a whole nation; or of the whole world of mankind, as vastly exceeding that of a particular person or family. We can positively understand, that the whole globe of the earth is vastly greater than a particular hill or mountain. And can have some good positive apprehension of the starry heavens, as so greatly exceeding the globe of the earth, that the latter is as it were nothing to it. So the human faculties are capable of a real and clear understanding of the greatness, glory, and goodness of God, and of our dependence upon him, from the manifestations which God has made of himself to mankind, as being beyond all expression above that of the most excellent human friend, or earthly object. And so we are capable of esteem and *love* to God, which shall be proportionable, much exceeding that which we have to any creature.

These things may help us to form some judgment, how vastly the generality of mankind fall below their duty, with respect to love to God; yea, how far they are from coming half way to that height of love, which is agreeable to the rule of right. Surely if our esteem of God, desires after him, and delight in him, were such as become us, considering the things forementioned, they would exceed our regard to other things, as the heavens are high above the earth, and would swallow up all other affections like a deluge. But how far, how exceeding far, are the generality of the world from any appearance of being influenced and governed by such a degree of divine love as this!

If we consider the love of God, with respect to one exercise of it, *gratitude*, how far indeed do the generality of mankind come short of the rule of right and reason in this! If we consider how various, innumerable, and vast the benefits we receive from God, how infinitely great and wonderful that grace, which is revealed and offered to them who live under the gospel—in that eternal salvation which is procured by God giving his only-begotten Son to die for sinners—and also how unworthy we are all, deserving (as Dr. T. confesses) eternal perdition under God's wrath and curse—how great is the *gratitude* that would become us, who are the subjects of so many and great benefits! What grace is this towards poor sinful lost mankind, set before us in so affecting a manner, as in the extreme sufferings of the Son of God; who was carried through those pains by a love stronger than death, a love that conquered those mighty agonies, a love whose length and breadth, and depth and height, passes knowledge? But oh! what poor returns!—How little the gratitude! How low, how cold and inconstant, the affection in the best, compared with the obligation! And what then shall be said of the gratitude of the generality? Or rather, who can express the ingratitude?

If the greater part of them who are called Christians, were no enemies to Christ in heart and practice, were not governed by principles opposite to him and his gospel, but had some real love and gratitude; yet if their love falls vastly short of the obligation, or occasion given, they are guilty of shameful and odious ingratitude. As, when a man has been the subject of some instance of transcendent generosity, whereby he has been relieved from the most extreme calamity, and brought into very opulent, honourable, and happy circumstances, by a benefactor of excellent character; and yet expresses no more gratitude on such an occasion, than would be requisite for some kindness comparatively infinitely small, he may justly fall under the imputation of vile unthankfulness, and of much more ingratitude than gratitude; though he may have no ill will to his benefactor, or no positive affection of mind contrary to thankfulness and benevolence. What is odious in him is his *defect*, whereby he falls so vastly below his duty.

Dr. Turnbull abundantly insists, that the forces of the affections naturally in man are well proportioned; and often puts a question to this purpose,—How man's nature could have been better constituted in this respect? How the affections of his heart could have been better proportioned?—I will now mention one instance, out of many that might be mentioned. Man, if his heart were not depraved, might have had a disposition to *gratitude to God for his goodness*, in proportion to his disposition to *anger towards men for their injuries*. When I say, in proportion, I mean considering the greatness and number of favours and injuries, and the degree in which the one and the other are unmerited, and the benefit received by the former, and the damage sustained by the latter. Is there not an apparent and vast difference and inequality in the dispositions to these two kinds of affection, in the generality of both old and young, adult persons and little children? How ready is resentment for injuries received from men! And how easily is it raised in most, at least to an equality with the desert! And is it so with respect to gratitude for benefits received from God, in any degree of comparison? Dr. Turnbull pleads for the natural disposition to anger for injuries, as being good and useful: but surely gratitude to God, if we were inclined to it, would be at least as good and useful as the other.

How far the generality of mankind are from their duty, with respect to love to God, will further appear, if we consider that we are obliged not only to love him with a love of gratitude for benefits received; but true love to God primarily consists in a supreme regard to him for what he is in *himself*. The tendency of true virtue is to treat every thing as it is, and according to its nature. And if we regard the Most High according to the infinite dignity and glory of his nature, we shall esteem and love him with all our heart and soul, and to the utmost of the capacity of our nature, on this account; and not primarily because he has promoted our interest. If God be infinitely excellent in himself, then he is infinitely lovely on that account; or in other words, infinitely worthy to be loved. And doubtless, if he be *worthy* to be loved for this, then he *ought* to be loved for it. And it is manifest, there can be no *true* love to him, if he be not loved for what he is in *himself*. For if we love him not for his own sake, but for something else, then our love is not terminated on *him*, but on something else, as its ultimate object. That is no true value for infinite worth, which implies no value for that worthiness in itself considered, but only on the account of something foreign. Our esteem of God is fundamentally defective, if it be not primarily for the excellency of his nature, which is the foundation of all that is valuable in him in any respect. If we love not God because he is what he is, but only because he is *profitable* to us, in truth we love him not at all: if we seem to love him, our love is not to him, but to something else.

And now I must leave it to every one to judge for himself, from his own opportunities of observation and information concerning mankind, how little there is of this disinterested love to God, this pure divine affection, in the world. How very little indeed in comparison of other affections altogether diverse, which perpetually urge, actuate, and govern mankind, and keep the world, through all nations and ages, in a continual agitation and commotion! This is an evidence of a horrid contempt of God. It would justly be esteemed a great instance of disrespect and contempt of a prince, if one of his subjects, when he came into his house, should set him below his meanest slave. But in setting the infinite Jehovah below earthly objects and enjoyments, men degrade him below those things, between which and him there is an infinitely greater distance, than between the highest earthly potentate and the most abject of mortals. Such a conduct as the generality of men are guilty of towards God, continually and through all ages, in innumerable respects, would be accounted the most vile contemptuous treatment of a fellow-creature, of distinguished dignity. Particularly men's treatment of the offers God makes of himself to them as their friend, their father, their God, and everlasting portion; their treatment of the exhibitions he has made of his unmeasurable love, and the boundless riches of his grace in Christ, attended with earnest repeated calls, counsels, expostulations, and entreaties; as also of the most dreadful threatenings of his eternal displeasure and vengeance.

Before I finish this *section*, it may be proper to say something in reply to an objection, some may be *ready* to make, against the force of this argument—that men do not come half-way to that degree of love to God, which becomes them, and is their duty. The *objection* is this: That the argument seems to prove too much, in that it will prove, that even good men themselves have more sin than holiness; which also has been supposed. But if this were true, it would follow, that sin is the prevalent principle even in good men, and that it is the principle which has the predominancy in the heart and practice of the truly pious; which is plainly contrary to the word of God.

I answer, If it be indeed so, that there is more sin, consisting in defect of required holiness, than there is of holiness, in good men in this world; yet it will not follow, that sin has the chief government of their heart and practice, for two reasons.

1. They may love God more than other things, and yet there may not be so much love, as there is want of due love; or in other words, they may love God more than the world, and therefore the love of God may be predominant, and yet may not love God near half so much as they ought to do. This need not be esteemed a paradox: A person may love a father, or some great friend and benefactor, of a very excellent character, more than some other object, a thousand times less worthy of his esteem and affection, and yet love him ten times less than he ought; and so be chargeable, all things considered, with a deficiency in respect and gratitude, that is very unbecoming and hateful. If love to God prevails above the love of other things, then virtue will prevail above evil affections, or positive principles of sin; by which principles it is, that sin has a positive power and influence. For evil affections radically consist in inordinate love to other things besides God: and therefore, virtue prevailing beyond these, will have the governing influence. The *predominance* of the love of God in the hearts of good men, is more from the *nature* of the object loved, and the nature of the principle of true love, than the *degree* of the principle. The object is one of supreme loveliness; immensely above all other objects in worthiness of regard; and it is by such a transcendent excellency, that he is God, and *worthy* to be regarded and adored as God: and he that truly loves God, loves him *as* God. True love acknowledges him to be divinely and supremely excellent; and must arise from some knowledge, sense, and conviction of his worthiness of supreme respect: and though the sense and view of it may be very imperfect, and the love that arises from it in like manner imperfect; yet if there be any realizing view of such divine excellency, it must cause the heart to respect God *above all*.

2. Another reason, why a principle of holiness maintains the dominion in the hearts of good men, is the nature of the covenant of grace, and the promises of that covenant, on which true christian virtue relies, and which engage God's strength and assistance to be on its side, and to help it against its enemy, that it may not be overcome. The just live by faith. Holiness in the Christian, or his spiritual life, is maintained, as it has respect by faith to its author and finisher, and derives strength and efficacy from the divine fountain, and by this means overcomes. For, as the apostle says, *This is the victory that overcomes the world, even our faith*. It is our faith in him who has promised never to leave nor forsake his people; not to forsake the works of his own hands, nor suffer his people to be tempted above their ability; that his grace shall be sufficient for them, his strength be made perfect in weakness; and that where he has begun a good work he will carry it on to the day of Christ.

SECT. VI.

The corruption of man's nature appears by its tendency, in its present state, to an extreme degree of folly and stupidity in matters of religion.

It appears, that man's nature is greatly depraved, by an apparent proneness to an exceeding *stupidity* and sottishness in those things wherein his duty and main interest are chiefly concerned. I shall instance in two things, *viz.* men's proneness to *idolatry;* and a general, great *disregard of eternal things*, in them who live under the light of the gospel.

It is manifest, in the *first* instance, that man's nature in its present state is attended with a great propensity to forsake the acknowledgment and worship of the true God, and to fall into the most stupid *idolatry*. This has been sufficiently proved by known fact, on abundant trial: insomuch as the world of mankind in general (excepting one small people, miraculously delivered and preserved) through all nations, in all parts of the world, ages after ages, continued without the knowledge and worship of the true God, and overwhelmed in gross idolatry, without the least appearance or prospect of its recovering itself from so great blindness, or returning from its brutish principles and customs, till delivered by divine grace.

In order to the most just arguing from fact, concerning the tendency of man's nature, as that is in itself, it should be inquired what the event has been, where nature has been left to itself, to operate according to its own tendency, with least opposition made to it by any thing supernatural; rather than in exempt places, where the infinite power and grace of God have interposed, and extraordinary means have been used to stem the current, and bring men to true religion and virtue. As to the means by which God's people of old, in the line of *Abraham*, were delivered and preserved from idolatry, they were miraculous, and of mere grace. Notwithstanding which, they were often relapsing into the notions and ways of the heathen; and when they had backslidden, never were recovered, but by divine gracious interposition. And as to the means by which many gentile nations have been delivered since the days of the gospel, they are such as have been wholly owing to the most wonderful, miraculous, and infinite grace. God was under no obligation to bestow on the heathen world greater advantages than they had in the ages of their gross darkness; as appears by the fact, that God actually did not, for so long a time, bestow greater advantages.

Dr. T. himself observes, (*Key*, p. 1.) *That in about four hundred years after the flood, the generality of mankind were fallen into idolatry.* And thus it was every where through the world, excepting among that people that was saved and preserved by a constant series of miracles, through a variety of countries, nations, and climates, *great enough*—and through successive changes, revolutions, and ages, *numerous enough*—to be a sufficient trial of what mankind are prone to, if there be any such thing as a sufficient trial.

That men should forsake the true God for idols, is an evidence of the most astonishing folly and stupidity, by God's own testimony, Jer. ii. 12, 13. " Be astonished, O ye heavens, at this, and be ye horribly afraid, be ye very desolate, saith the Lord: for my people have committed two evils; they have forsaken me, the fountain of living waters, and have hewed out to themselves cisterns, broken cisterns, that can hold no water." And that mankind in general did thus, so soon after the flood, was from the evil propensity of their hearts, and *because they did not like to retain God in their knowledge;* as is evident by Rom. i. 28. And the universality of the effect shows that the cause was universal, and not any thing belonging to the particular circumstances of one, or only some nations or ages, but something belonging to that nature, which is common to all nations, and which remains the same through all ages. And what other cause could this great effect possibly arise from, but a depraved disposition, natural to all mankind? It could not arise from want of a sufficient capacity or means of knowledge. This is in effect confessed on all hands. Dr. Turnbull (*Chris. Phil.* p. 21.) says: " The existence of one infinitely powerful, wise, and good mind, the Author, Creator, Upholder, and Governor of all things, is a truth that lies plain and obvious to all that will but think." And (ibid. p. 245.) " Moral knowledge, which is the most important of all knowledge, may easily be acquired by all men." And again, (ibid. p. 292.) " Every man by himself, if he would duly employ his mind in the contemplation of the works of God about him, or in the examination of his own frame,—might make very great progress in the knowledge of the wisdom and goodness of God. This all men, generally speaking, might do, with very little assistance; for they have all sufficient abilities for thus employing their minds, and have all sufficient time for it." Mr. Locke says, (*Hum. Und.* p. iv. chap. iv. p. 242. edit. 11.) " Our own existence, and the sensible parts of the universe, offer the proofs of a Deity so clearly and cogently to our thoughts, that I deem it impossible for a considerate man to withstand them. For I judge it as certain and clear a truth, as can any where be delivered, that the invisible things of God are clearly seen from the creation of the world, being understood by the things that are made, even his eternal power and godhead." And Dr. T. himself (in p. 78.) says, " The light given to all ages and nations of the world, is sufficient for the knowledge and practice of their duty." And (p. 111, 112.) citing those words of the apostle, Rom. ii. 14, 15. he says, " This clearly supposes that the Gentiles, who were then in the world, might have done the things contained in the law by nature, or their natural power." And in one of the next sentences he says, " The apostle, in Rom. i. 19, 20, 21. affirms that the Gentiles had light sufficient to have seen God's eternal power and godhead, in the works of creation; and that the reason why they did not glorify him as God, was because they became vain in their imaginations, and had darkened their foolish heart; so that they were without excuse. And in his paraphrase on those verses in the 1st of Rom. he speaks of the very heathens, that were without a written revelation, as having that clear and evident discovery of God's being and perfections, that they are inexcusable in not glorifying him suitably to his excellent nature, and as the author of their being and enjoyments." And (p. 146. S.) he says, " God affords every man sufficient light to know his duty." If all ages and nations of the world have sufficient light for the knowledge of God, and their duty to him, then even such nations and ages, in which the most brutish ignorance and barbarity prevailed, had sufficient light, if they had but a disposition to improve it; and then much more those of the heathen, which were more knowing and polished, and in ages wherein arts and learning had made greatest advances. But even in such nations and ages, there was no advance made towards true religion; as Dr. Winder observes, (*Hist. of Knowl.* vol. ii. p. 336.) in the following words; " The pagan religion degenerated into greater absurdity, the further it proceeded; and it prevailed in all its height of absurdity, when the pagan nations were polished to the height. Though they set out with the talents of reason, and had solid foundations of information to build upon, it in fact proved, that with all their strengthened faculties, and growing powers of reason, the edifice of religion rose in the most absurd deformities and disproportions, and gradually went on in the most irrational, disproportioned, incongruous systems, of which the most easy dictates of reason would have demonstrated the absurdity. They were contrary to all just calculations in moral mathematics." He observes, " that their grossest abominations first began in *Egypt*, where was an ostentation of the greatest progress in learning and science: and they never renounced clearly any of their abominations, or openly returned to the worship of the one true God, the Creator of all things, and to the original, genuine sentiments of the highest and most venerable antiquity. The pagan religion continued in this deep state of corruption to the last. The pagan philosophers, and inquisitive men, made great improvements in many sciences, and even in morality itself; yet the inveterate absurdities of pagan idolatry remained without remedy. Every temple smoked with incense to the sun and moon, and other inanimate material luminaries, and earthly elements, to Jupiter, Juno, Mars, and Venus, &c. the patrons and examples of almost every vice. Hecatombs bled on the altars of a thousand gods; as mad superstition inspired. And this was not the disgrace of our ignorant untaught northern countries only; but even at *Athens* itself, the infamy reigned, and circulated through all *Greece;* and finally prevailed, amidst all their learning and politeness, under the *Ptolemies* in *Egypt*, and the *Cæsars* at *Rome*. Now if the knowledge of the pagan world, in religion, proceeded no further than this; if they retained all their deities, even the most absurd of them all, their deified beasts, and deified men, even to the last breath of pagan power: we may justly ascribe the great improvements in the world, on the subject of religion, to divine revelation, either vouchsafed in the beginning, when this knowledge was competently clear and copious; or at the death of paganism, when this light shone forth in its consummate lustre at the coming of Christ."

Dr. T. often speaks of the idolatry of the heathen world, as *great wickedness*, in which they were wholly inexcusable; and yet often speaks of their case as remediless, and of them as being dead in sin, and unable to recover themselves. If so, and yet, according to his own doctrine, every age, every nation, and every man, had sufficient light afforded, to know God, and their whole duty to him; then their inability to deliver themselves must be a moral inability, consisting in a desperate depravity, and most evil disposition of heart.

And if there had not been sufficient trial of the propensity of the hearts of mankind, through all those ages that passed from *Abraham* to Christ, the trial has been continued down to this day, in all those vast regions of the face of the earth, that have remained without any effects of the light of the gospel; and the dismal effect continues every where unvaried. How was it with that multitude of nations inhabiting *South* and *North America?*

What appearance was there, when the *Europeans* first came hither, of their being recovered, or recovering, in any degree, from the grossest ignorance, delusions, and most stupid paganism? And how is it at this day, in those parts of Africa and Asia, into which the light of the gospel has not penetrated?

This strong and universally prevalent disposition of mankind to idolatry, of which there has been such great trial, and so notorious and vast proof, in fact, is a most glaring evidence of the exceeding depravity of the human nature; as it is a propensity, in the utmost degree, contrary to the highest end, the main business, and chief happiness of mankind—consisting in the knowledge, service, and enjoyment of the living God, the Creator and Governor of the world—in the highest degree contrary to that for which mainly God gave mankind more understanding than the beasts of the earth, and made them wiser than the fowls of heaven; which was, that they might be capable of the knowledge of God. It is also in the highest degree contrary to the first and greatest commandment of the moral law, That *we should have no other gods before* Jehovah, and that we should love and adore him with all our heart, soul, mind, and strength. The Scriptures are abundant in representing the idolatry of the heathen world, as their exceeding wickedness, and their most brutish stupidity. They who worship and trust in idols, are said themselves to be like the lifeless statues they worship, like mere senseless stocks and stones. (Psalm cxv. 4—8. and cxxxv. 15—18.)

A *second* instance of the natural *stupidity* of mankind, is that great *disregard of their own eternal interest*, which appears so remarkably, so generally among them who live under the gospel.

Mr. Locke observes, (*Hum. Und.* vol. i. p. 207.) "Were the will determined by the views of good, as it appears in contemplation, greater or less to the understanding, it could never get loose from the infinite eternal joys of heaven, once proposed, and considered as possible; the eternal condition of a future state infinitely outweighing the expectation of riches or honour, or any other worldly pleasure, which we can propose to ourselves; though we should grant these the more probable to be obtained." Again, (p. 228, 229.) "He that will not be so far a rational creature, as to reflect seriously upon infinite happiness and misery, must needs condemn himself, as not making that use of his understanding he should. The rewards and punishments of another life, which the Almighty has established, as the enforcements of his laws, are of weight enough to determine the choice, against whatsoever pleasure or pain this life can show. When the eternal state is considered but in its bare possibility, which nobody can make any doubt of, he that will allow exquisite and endless happiness to be but the possible consequence of a good life here, and the contrary state the possible reward of a bad one, must own himself to judge very much amiss, if he does not conclude that a virtuous life, with the certain expectation of everlasting bliss, which may come, is to be preferred to a vicious one, with the fear of that dreadful state of misery, which it is very possible may overtake the guilty, or at least the terrible uncertain hope of annihilation. This is evidently so; though the virtuous life here had nothing but pain, and the vicious continual pleasure; which yet is for the most part quite otherwise, and wicked men have not much the odds to brag of, even in their present possession: nay, all things rightly considered, have I think even the worst part here. But when infinite happiness is put in one scale, against infinite misery in the other; if the worst that comes to the pious man, if he mistakes, be the best that the wicked man can attain to, if he be in the right; who can, without madness, run the venture? Who in his wits would choose to come within a possibility of infinite misery? which if he miss, there is yet nothing to be got by that hazard: whereas, on the other side, the sober man ventures nothing, against infinite happiness to be got, if his expectation comes to pass."

That disposition of mind which is a propensity to act contrary to reason, is a depraved disposition. It is not because the faculty of reason, which God has given to mankind, is not sufficient fully to discover to them, that forty, sixty, or an hundred years, is as nothing in comparison of eternity—infinitely less than a second of time to an hundred years—that the greatest worldly prosperity is not treated with the most perfect disregard, in all cases where there is any degree of competition of earthly things, with salvation from exquisite, eternal misery, and the enjoyment of everlasting glory and felicity. But is it a matter of controversy, whether men in general show a strong disposition to act far otherwise, from their infancy, till death sensibly approaches? In things that concern their temporal interest, they easily discern the difference between things of a long and short continuance. It is no hard matter to convince men of the difference between being admitted to the accommodations and entertainments of a convenient, beautiful, well-furnished habitation, and to partake of the provisions and produce of a plentiful estate for a day, or a night; and having all given them, and settled upon them, as their own, to possess as long as they live, and to be theirs and their heirs' for ever. There would be no need of preaching sermons, and spending strength and life, to convince them of the difference. Men know how to adjust things in their dealings and contracts one with another, according to the length of time in which anything agreed for is to be used or enjoyed. In temporal affairs, they are sensible, that it concerns them to provide for *future* time, as well as for the *present*. Thus common prudence teaches them to take care in summer to lay up for winter; yea, to provide a fund, or an estate, whence they may be supplied for a long time to come. And not only so, but they are forward to spend and be spent, in order to provide for their children after they are dead; though it be quite uncertain, who shall enjoy what they lay up, after they have left the world. And if their *children* should have the comfort of it, as they desire, they will not partake with them in that comfort, or have any portion in any thing under the sun. In things which relate to men's temporal interest, they seem very sensible of the uncertainty of life, especially of the lives of others; and to make answerable provision for the security of their worldly interest, that no considerable part of it may rest only on so uncertain a foundation, as the life of a neighbour or friend. Common discretion leads them to take good care, that their outward possessions be well secured, by a good and firm title. In worldly concerns, men discern their opportunities, and are careful to improve them before they are past. The husbandman is careful to plough his ground, and sow his seed, in the proper season; otherwise he knows he cannot expect a crop: and when the harvest is come, he will not sleep away the time; for he knows, if he does so, the crop will soon be lost. How careful and eagle-eyed is the merchant to improve opportunities to enrich himself! How apt are men to be alarmed at the appearance of danger to their worldly estate, or any thing that remarkably threatens great damage to their outward interest! And how will they bestir themselves in such a case, if possible, to avoid the threatened calamity! In things purely secular, and not of a moral or spiritual nature, they easily receive conviction by past experience, when any thing, on repeated trial, proves unprofitable or prejudicial; and are ready to take warning by what they have found themselves, and also by the experience of their neighbours and forefathers.

But if we consider how men generally conduct themselves in things on which their well-being infinitely more depends, how vast is the diversity! In these things how cold, lifeless, and dilatory! With what difficulty are a few, out of multitudes, excited to any tolerable degree of care and diligence, by the innumerable means used, in order to make them wise for themselves! And when some vigilance and activity is excited, how apt is it to die away, like a mere force against a natural tendency! What need of a constant repetition of admonitions and counsels, to keep the heart from falling asleep! How many objections are made! How are difficulties magnified! And how soon is the mind discouraged! How many arguments, often renewed, variously and elaborately enforced, do men stand in need of, to convince them of things that are almost self-evident! As that things which are eternal, are infinitely more important than things temporal, and the like. And after all, how very few are convinced effectually, or in such a manner as to induce them to a practical preference of eternal things! How senseless are men of the necessity of improving their time, as to their spiritual interest, and their welfare in another world! Though it be an *endless* futurity, and though it be their own *personal*, infinitely important good, that is to be cared for. Though men are so sensible of the uncertainty of their neighbours' lives, when any considerable part of their own estates depends on the continuance of them; how stupidly senseless do they seem to be of the uncertainty of their own lives, when their preservation from immensely great, remediless, and endless misery, is risked by a present delay, through a dependence on future opportunity! What a dreadful venture will men carelessly and boldly run, repeat, and multiply, with regard to their eternal salvation; who yet are very careful to have every thing in a deed or bond, firm, and without a flaw! How negligent are they of their special advantages and opportunities for their soul's good! How hardly awakened by the most evident and imminent dangers, threatening eternal destruction, yea, though put in mind of them, and much pains taken to point them forth, show them plainly, and fully to represent them, if possible to engage their attention! How are they like the horse, that boldly rushes into the battle! How hardly are men convinced by their own frequent and abundant experience, of the unsatisfactory nature of earthly things, and the instability of their own hearts in their good frames and intentions! And how hardly convinced by their own observation, and the experience of all past generations, of the uncertainty of life and its enjoyments! Psal. xlix. 11, &c. "Their inward thought is, that their houses shall continue for ever.—Nevertheless, man being in honour, abideth not; he is like the beasts that perish. This their way is their folly; yet their posterity approve their sayings. Like sheep are they laid in the grave."

In these things, men who are prudent for their temporal interest, act as if they were bereft of reason: "They have eyes, and see not; ears, and hear not; neither do they understand: they are like the horse and mule, that have no understanding."—Jer. viii. 7. "The stork in the heaven knoweth her appointed times; and the turtle, and the crane, and the swallow, observe the time of their coming: but my people know not the judgment of the Lord."

These things are often mentioned in Scripture, as evidences of extreme folly and stupidity, wherein men act as great enemies to themselves, as though they loved their own ruin; Prov. viii. 36. Laying wait for their own blood, Prov. i. 18. And how can these things be accounted for, but by supposing a most wretched depravity of nature? Why otherwise should not men be as wise for themselves in spiritual and eternal things, as in temporal? All Christians will confess, that man's faculty of reason was given him chiefly to enable him to understand the former, wherein his main interest and true happiness consist. This faculty would therefore undoubtedly be every way as fit for understanding them, as the latter, if not depraved. The reason why these are understood, and not the other, is not that such things as have been mentioned, belonging to men's spiritual and eternal interest, are more obscure and abstruse in their own nature. For instance, the difference between long and short, the need of providing for futurity, the importance of improving proper opportunities, and of having good security, and a sure foundation, in affairs wherein our interest is greatly concerned, &c. these things are as plain in themselves in religious, as in other matters. And we have far greater means to assist us to be wise for ourselves in eternal than in temporal things. We have the abundant instruction of perfect and infinite wisdom itself, to lead and conduct us in the paths of righteousness, so that we may not err. And the reasons of things are most clearly, variously, and abundantly set before us in the word of God; which is adapted to the faculties of mankind, tending greatly to enlighten and convince the mind: whereas, we have no such excellent and perfect rules to instruct and direct us in things pertaining to our temporal interest, nor any thing to be compared to it.

If any should say, It is true, if men gave full credit to what they are told concerning eternal things, and these appeared to them as real and certain things, it would be an evidence of a sort of madness in them, that they show no greater regard to them in practice: but there is reason to think, this is not the case; the things of another world being unseen, appear to men as things of a very doubtful nature, and attended with great uncertainty.—In answer, I would observe, agreeable to what has been cited from Mr. Locke, though eternal things were considered in their bare *possibility*, if men acted rationally, they would infinitely outweigh all temporal things in their influence on their hearts. And I would also observe, that to suppose eternal things not to be fully believed, at least by them who enjoy the light of the gospel, does not weaken, but rather strengthen, the argument for the depravity of nature. For the eternal world being what God had chiefly in view in the creation of men, this world was made wholly subordinate to the other, man's state here being only a state of probation, preparation, and progression, with respect to the future state. Eternal things are in effect their all, their whole concern; to understand and know which, it chiefly was, that they had understanding given them; therefore we may undoubtedly conclude, that if men have not respect to them as real and certain things, it cannot be for want of sufficient evidence of their truth: but it must be from a dreadful stupidity of mind, occasioning a sottish insensibility of their truth and importance, when manifested by the clearest evidence.

SECT. VII.

That man's nature is corrupt, appears, in that by far the greater part of mankind, in all ages, have been wicked men.

THE depravity of man's nature appears, not only in its propensity to sin in *some degree*, which renders a man an evil or wicked man in the *eye of the law*, and strict justice, as was before shown; but it is so corrupt, that its depravity either shows that men *are*, or tends to make them *to be*, of such an evil character, as shall denominate them wicked men, according to the tenor of the covenant of grace.

This may be argued from several things which have been already observed: as from a tendency to continual sin; a tendency to much greater degrees of sin than righteousness, and from the general extreme stupidity of mankind. But yet the present state of man's nature, as implying, or tending to, a *wicked character*, may deserve to be more particularly considered, and directly proved. And in general, this appears, in that there have been so very few in the world, from age to age, ever since the world has stood, that have been of any other character.

It is abundantly evident in Scripture, and is what I suppose none that call themselves Christians will deny, that the whole world is divided into good and bad, and that all mankind at the day of judgment will either be approved as righteous, or condemned as wicked: either glorified, as *children of the kingdom*, or cast into a furnace of fire, as *children of the wicked one*.

I need not stand to show what things belong to the character of such as shall hereafter be accepted as righteous, according to the word of God. It may be sufficient for my present purpose, to observe what Dr. T. himself speaks of, as belonging essentially to the character of such. In p. 203. he says, "This is infallibly the character of true Christians, and what is essential to such, that they have really mortified the flesh with its lusts;—they are dead to sin, and live no longer therein; the old man is crucified, and the body of sin destroyed: they yield themselves to God, as those that are alive from the dead, and their members as instruments of righteousness to God, and as servants of righteousness to holiness."—There is more to the like purpose in the two next pages. In p. 228. he says, "Whatsoever is evil and corrupt in us, we ought to condemn; not so, as it shall still remain in us, that we may always be condemning it, but that we may speedily reform, and be effectually delivered from it; otherwise certainly we do not come up to the character of the true disciples of Christ."

In p. 248. he says, "Unless God's favour be preferred

before all other enjoyments whatsoever, unless there be a delight in the worship of God, and in converse with him, unless every appetite be brought into subjection to reason and truth, and unless there be a kind and benevolent disposition towards our fellow-creatures, how can the mind be fit to dwell with God, in his house and family, to do him service in his kingdom, and to promote the happiness of any part of his creation."—And in his Key, § 286. p. 101, 102, &c. showing there, *what it is to be a true Christian*, he says, among other things, " That he is one who has such a sense and persuasion of the love of God in Christ, that he devotes his life to the honour and service of God, in hope of eternal glory. And that to the character of a true Christian, it is absolutely necessary, that he diligently study the things that are freely given him of God, *viz.* his election, regeneration, &c. that he may gain a just knowledge of those inestimable privileges, may taste that the Lord is gracious, and rejoice in the gospel-salvation, as his greatest happiness and glory.—It is necessary, that he work these blessings on his heart, till they become a vital principle, producing in him the love of God, engaging him to all cheerful obedience to his will, giving him a proper dignity and elevation of soul, raising him above the best and worst of this world, carrying his heart into heaven, and fixing his affections and regards upon his everlasting inheritance, and the crown of glory laid up for him there.—Thus he is armed against all the temptations and trials resulting from any pleasure or pain, hopes or fears, gain or loss, in the present world. None of these things move him from a faithful discharge of any part of his duty, or from a firm attachment to truth and righteousness; neither counts he his very life dear to him, that he may do the will of God, and finish his course with joy. In a sense of the love of God in Christ, he maintains daily communion with God, by reading and meditating on his word. In a sense of his own infirmity, and the readiness of the divine favour to succour him, he daily addresses the throne of grace, for the renewal of spiritual strength, in assurance of obtaining it, through the one Mediator Christ Jesus. Enlightened and directed by the heavenly doctrine of the gospel," &c.*

Now I leave every one that has any degree of impartiality, to judge, whether there be not sufficient grounds to think, that it is but a very small part indeed, of the many myriads and millions which overspread this globe, who are of a character that in any wise answers these descriptions. However Dr. T. insists, that all nations, and every man on the face of the earth, have light and means sufficient to do the whole will of God, even they that live in the grossest darkness of paganism.

Dr. T. in answer to arguments of this kind, very impertinently from time to time objects, that we are no judges of the viciousness of men's characters, nor are able to decide in what degree they are virtuous or vicious. As though we could have no good grounds to judge, that any thing appertaining to the qualities or properties of the mind, which is invisible, is general or prevailing among a multitude or collective body, unless we can determine how it is with each individual. I think I have sufficient reason, from what I know and have heard of the *American Indians*, to judge, that there are not many good philosophers among them; though the thoughts of their hearts, and the ideas and knowledge they have in their minds, are things invisible; and though I have never seen so much as a thousandth part of the *Indians;* and with respect to most of them, should not be able to pronounce peremptorily concerning any one, that he was not very knowing in the nature of things, if all should singly pass before me. And Dr. T. himself seems to be sensible of the falseness of his own conclusions, that he so often urges against others; if we may judge by his practice, and the liberties he takes, in judging of a multitude himself. He, it seems, is sensible that a man may have good grounds to judge, that wickedness of character is general in a collective body; because he openly does it himself. (*Key*, p. 102.) After declaring the things which belong to the character of a true Christian, he judges of the generality of Christians, that they have cast off these things, that *they are a people that do err in their hearts, and have not known God's ways*, p. 259. he judges, that *the generality of Christians are the most wicked of all mankind*, when he thinks it will throw some disgrace on the opinion of such as he opposes. The like we have from time to time in other places, (as p. 168. p. 258. Key, p. 127, 128.)

But if men are not sufficient judges, whether there are few of the world of mankind but what are wicked, yet doubtless God is sufficient, and his judgment, often declared in his word, determines the matter. Matt. vii. 13, 14. " Enter ye in at the strait gate: for wide is the gate and broad is the way that leadeth to destruction, and many there be that go in thereat: because strait is the gate and narrow is the way that leadeth to life, and few there be that find it." It is manifest, that here Christ is not only describing the state of things, as it was at that day, and does not mention the comparative smallness of the number of them that are saved, as a consequence of the peculiar perverseness of that people, and of that generation; but as a consequence of the general circumstances of the way to life, and the way to destruction, the broadness of the one, and the narrowness of the other. In the straitness of the gate, &c. I suppose none will deny, that Christ has respect to the strictness of those rules, which he had insisted on in the preceding sermon, and which render the way to life very difficult. But certainly these amiable rules would not be difficult, were they not contrary to the natural inclinations of men's hearts; and they would not be contrary to those inclinations, were these not depraved. Consequently the wideness of the gate, and broadness of the way, that leads to destruction, in consequence of which many go in thereat, must imply the agreeableness of this way to men's natural inclinations. The like reason is given by Christ, why few are saved. Luke xiii. 23, 24. " Then said one unto him, Lord, are there few saved? And he said unto them, Strive to enter in at the strait gate: for many I say unto you, shall seek to enter in, and shall not be able." That there are generally but few good men in the world, even among them who have the most distinguishing and glorious advantages for it, is evident by that saying of our Lord, " Many are called, but few are chosen." And if there are but few among these, how few, how very few indeed, must persons of this character be, compared with the whole world of mankind! The exceeding smallness of the number of the saints, compared with the whole world, appears by the representations often made of them as distinguished from the world; in which they are spoken of as called and chosen *out of the world*, redeemed *from the earth*, redeemed *from among men;* as being those that *are of God*, while the *whole world* lieth in wickedness, and the like.

And if we look into the Old Testament, we shall find the same testimony given. Prov. xx. 6. " Most men will proclaim every man his own goodness: but a faithful man who can find?" By the faithful man, as the phrase is used in Scripture, is intended much the same as a sincere, upright, or truly good man; as in Psal. xii. 1. and xxxi. 23. and ci. 6. and other places. Again, Eccl. vii. 25—29. " I applied mine heart to know, and to search, and to find out wisdom, and the reason of things, and to know the wickedness of folly, even of foolishness and madness: and I find more bitter than death, the woman whose heart is snares, &c. Behold, this have I found, saith the preacher, counting one by one, to find out the account, which yet my soul seeketh, but I find not: one man among a thousand have I found: but a woman among all these have I not found. Lo, this only have I found, that God made man upright; but they have sought out many inventions." Solomon here signifies, that when he set himself diligently to find out the account or proportion of true wisdom, or thorough uprightness among men, the result was, that he found it to be but as one to a thousand, &c. Dr. T. on this place, p. 184. says, " The wise man in the context, is inquiring into the corruption and depravity of mankind, of the men and women, THAT LIVED IN HIS TIME." As though what he said represented nothing of the state of things in the world in general, but only *in his time*. But does Dr. T. or any body else, suppose this only to be the

* What Dr. Turnbull says of the character of a good man, is also worthy to be observed, *Chris. Phil.* p. 86, 258. 259, 288, 375, 376, 409, 410.

design of that book, to represent the vanity and evil of the world in that time, and to show that all was vanity and vexation of spirit in *Solomon's* day? That day truly, we have reason to think, was a day of the greatest smiles of Heaven on that nation, that ever had been on any nation from the foundation of the world. Not only does the subject and argument of the whole book show it to be otherwise; but also the declared design of the book in the first chapter; where the world is represented as very much the same, as to its vanity and evil, from age to age. It makes little or no progress, after all its revolutions and restless motions, labours, and pursuits; like the sea, that has all the rivers constantly emptying themselves into it, from age to age, and yet is never the fuller. As to that place, Prov. xx. 6. "A faithful man who can find?" there is no more reason to suppose that the wise man has respect only to *his* time, in these words, than in those immediately preceding, "Counsel in the heart of a man is like deep waters; but a man of understanding will draw it out." Or in the words next following, "The just man walketh in his integrity: his children are blessed after him." Or in any other proverb in the whole book. And if it were so, that *Solomon* in these things meant only to describe his own times, it would not at all weaken the argument. For, if we observe the history of the Old Testament, there is reason to think there never was any time from *Joshua* to the captivity, wherein wickedness was more restrained, and virtue and religion more encouraged and promoted, than in *David's* and *Solomon's* times. And if there was so little true piety in that nation, the only people of God under heaven, even in their best times, what may we suppose, concerning the world in general, take one time with another?

Notwithstanding what some authors advance concerning the prevalence of virtue, honesty, good neighbourhood, cheerfulness, &c. in the world; *Solomon,* whom we may justly esteem as wise and just an observer of human nature, and the state of the world of mankind, as most in these days (besides, Christians ought to remember, that he wrote by divine inspiration)—judged the world to be so full of wickedness, that it was better never to be born, than to be born to live only in such a world. Eccl. iv. 1—3. "So I returned and considered all the oppressions that are done under the sun; and behold, the tears of such as were oppressed, and they had no comforter: and on the side of their oppressors there was power; but they had no comforter. Wherefore, I praised the dead, which were already dead, more than the living, which are yet alive. Yea, better is he than both they, which hath not yet been; *who hath not seen the evil work that is done under the sun.*" Surely it will not be said that Solomon has only respect to *his* time here too, when he speaks of the oppressions of them that were in power; since he himself, and others appointed by him, and wholly under his control, were the men that were in power in that land, and in almost all the neighbouring countries.

The same inspired writer says, Eccles. ix. 3. "The heart of the sons of men is full of evil; and madness is in their heart while they live; and after that they go to the dead." If these general expressions are to be understood only of some, and those the smaller part, when in general, *truth, honesty, good-nature, &c.* govern the world, why are such general expressions from time to time used? Why does not this wise and noble prince express himself in a more generous and benevolent strain, and say, *wisdom is in the hearts of the sons of men while they live, &c.*—instead of leaving in his writings so many sly, ill-natured suggestions, which pour such contempt on human nature, and tend so much to excite mutual jealousy and malevolence, to taint the minds of mankind through all generations after him?

If we consider the various successive parts and periods of the duration of the world, it will, if possible, be yet more evident, that by far the greater part of mankind have, in all ages, been of a wicked character. The short accounts we have of *Adam* and his family are such as lead us to suppose, that the greater part of his posterity in his life-time, yea, in the former part of his life, were wicked. It appears, that his eldest son *Cain,* was a very wicked man, who slew his righteous brother *Abel.* And *Adam* lived an hundred and thirty years before *Seth* was born: and by that time, we may suppose, his posterity began to be considerably numerous: when he was born, his mother *called his name* Seth; *for God, said she, hath appointed me another seed instead of* Abel. Which naturally suggests this to our thoughts; that of all her seed then existing, none were of any such note for religion and virtue, as that their parents could have any great comfort in them, or expectation from them, on that account. And by the brief history we have, it looks as if—however there might be some intervals of a revival of religion, yet—in the general, mankind grew more and more corrupt till the flood. It is signified that *when men began to multiply on the face of the earth,* wickedness prevailed exceedingly, Gen. vi. 1, &c. And that before God appeared to *Noah,* to command him to build the ark, one hundred and twenty years before the flood, the world had long continued obstinate in great and general wickedness, and the disease was become inveterate. The expressions (ver. 3, 5, 6.) suggest as much: "And the Lord said, my spirit shall not *always* strive with man.—And God saw that the wickedness of man was great on the earth, and that every imagination of the thought of his heart was evil, only evil *continually;* and it repented the Lord that he had made man on the earth, and it grieved him at his heart." And by that time, "all flesh had corrupted his way upon the earth," (v. 12.) And as Dr. T. himself observes, (p. 122.) "Mankind were universally debauched into lust, sensuality, rapine, and injustice."

And with respect to the period *after* the flood, to the calling of *Abraham;* Dr. T. says, as already observed, that in about four hundred years after the flood, the generality of mankind were fallen into idolatry; which was before all they were dead who came out of the ark. And it cannot be thought, the world went suddenly into that general and extreme degree of corruption, but that they had been gradually growing more and more corrupt; though it is true, it must be by very swift degrees—however soon we may suppose they began—to get to that pass in one age.

And as to the period from the calling of *Abraham* to the coming of Christ, Dr. T. justly observes as follows: (*Key,* p. 133.) "If we reckon from the call of *Abraham* to the coming of Christ, the *Jewish* dispensation continued one thousand nine hundred and twenty-one years; during which period, the other families and nations of the earth, not only lay out of God's peculiar kingdom, but also lived in idolatry, great ignorance, and wickedness." And with regard to the *Israelites,* it is evident that wickedness was the generally prevailing character among them, from age to age. If we consider how it was with *Jacob's* family, the behaviour of *Reuben* with his father's concubine, the behaviour of *Judah* with *Tamar,* the conduct of *Jacob's* sons towards the *Shechemites,* and the behaviour of *Joseph's* ten brethren in their cruel treatment of him; we cannot think, that the character of true piety belonged to many of them, according to Dr. T.'s own notion of such a character; though it be true, they might afterwards repent. And with respect to the time the children of *Israel* were in *Egypt;* the Scripture, speaking of them in general, or as a collective body, often represents them as complying with the abominable idolatries of the country.* And as to that generation which went out of *Egypt,* and wandered in the wilderness, they are abundantly represented as extremely and almost universally wicked, perverse, and children of divine wrath. And after *Joshua's* death, the Scripture is very express, that wickedness was the prevailing character in the nation, from age to age. So it was till *Samuel's* time. (1 Sam. viii. 7, 8.) "They have rejected me, that I should not reign over them; according to all their works which they have done, since the day that I brought them out of Egypt, unto this day." Yea, so it was till *Jeremiah's* and *Ezekiel's* time. (Jer. xxxii. 30, 31.) "For the children of *Israel,* and the children of *Judah,* have *only* done evil before me *from their youth;* for the children of *Israel have only* provoked me to anger with the work of their hands, saith the Lord: for this city hath been to me a provocation of mine anger, and of my fury, *from the day*

* Levit. xvii. 7. Josh. v. 9. and xxiv. 14. Ezek. xx. 7. 8. and xxii. 3.

they built it, even unto this day." (Compare chap. v. 21, 23. and chap. vii. 25, 26, 27.) So Ezek. ii. 3, 4. "I send thee to the children of *Israel*, to a rebellious nation, that hath rebelled against me, they and their fathers have transgressed against me, *even unto this very day*: for they are impudent children, and stiff-hearted." And it appears by the discourse of *Stephen*, (Acts vii.) that this was generally the case with that nation, from their first rise, even to the days of the apostles. After this summary rehearsal of the instances of their perverseness from the very time of their selling *Joseph* into *Egypt*, he concludes, (ver. 51—53.) "Ye stiff-necked, and uncircumcised in heart and ears, ye do *always* resist the Holy Ghost. As your fathers did, so do ye. Which of the prophets have not your fathers persecuted? And they have slain them which showed before of the coming of that just One, of whom ye have been now the betrayers and murderers: who have received the law by the disposition of angels, and have not kept it."

Thus it appears, that wickedness was the generally prevailing character in all nations, till Christ came. And so also it appears to have been since his coming to this day. So in the age of apostles. There was a great number of persons of a truly pious character in the latter part of the apostolic age, when multitudes of converts had been made, and Christianity was as yet in its primitive purity; but what says the apostle *John* of the church of God at that time, as compared with the rest of the world? (1 John v. 19.) "We know that we are of God, and the *whole world* lieth in wickedness." And after that Christianity came to prevail to that degree, that Christians had the upper hand in nations and civil communities, still the greater part of mankind remained in their old heathen state; which Dr. T. speaks of as a state of great ignorance and wickedness. And besides, this is noted in all ecclesiastical history, that as the Christians gained in power and secular advantages, true piety declined, and corruption and wickedness prevailed among them.—And as to the state of the Christian world, since Christianity began to be established by human laws, wickedness for the most part has greatly prevailed; as is very notorious, and is implied in what Dr. T. himself says: In giving an account how the doctrine of original sin came to prevail among Christians, he observes, (p. 167. S.) "That the christian religion was very early and grievously corrupted, by dreaming, ignorant, superstitious monks." In p. 259. he says, "The generality of Christians have embraced this persuasion concerning original sin; and the consequence has been, that the generality of Christians have been the most wicked, lewd, bloody, and treacherous of all mankind."

Thus, a view of the several successive periods of the past duration of the world, from the beginning to this day, shows, that wickedness has ever been exceeding prevalent, and has had vastly the superiority in the world. And Dr. T. himself in effect owns, that it has been so ever since *Adam* first turned into the way of transgression. "It is certain (says he, p. 168.) the moral circumstances of mankind, since the time *Adam* first turned into the way of transgression, have been very different from a state of innocence. So far as we can judge from history, or what we know at present, the greatest part of mankind have been, and still are, very corrupt; though not equally so in every age and place." And lower in the same page, he speaks of *Adam's posterity, as having sunk themselves into the most lamentable degrees of ignorance, superstition, idolatry, injustice, debauchery, &c.*

These things clearly determine the point, concerning the tendency of man's nature to wickedness, if we may be allowed to proceed according to such rules and methods of reasoning, as are never denied or doubted to be good and sure, in experimental philosophy;* or may reason from experience and facts, in that manner which common sense leads all mankind to in other cases. If experience and trial will evince any thing at all concerning the natural disposition of the human heart, one would think the experience of so many ages, as have elapsed since the beginning of the world, and the trial made by hundreds of different nations together, for so long a time, should be sufficient to convince all, that wickedness is agreeable to the nature of mankind in its present state.

Here, to strengthen the argument, if there were any need of it, I might observe, not only the *extent* and *generality* of the prevalence of wickedness in the world, but the *height* to which it has risen, and the *degree* in which it has reigned. Among innumerable things which confirm this, I shall now only observe, The *degree* in which mankind have from age to age been *hurtful* one to another. Many kinds of brute animals are esteemed very noxious and destructive, many of them very fierce, voracious, and many very poisonous, and the destroying of them has always been looked upon as a public benefit: but have not mankind been a thousand times as hurtful and destructive as any one of them, yea, as all the noxious beasts, birds, fishes, and reptiles in the earth, air, and water, put together, at least of all kinds of animals that are visible? And no creature can be found any where so destructive of its own kind as man is. All others, for the most part, are harmless and peaceable, with regard to their own species. Where one wolf is destroyed by another wolf, one viper by another, probably a thousand men are destroyed by those of their own species. Well therefore might our blessed Lord say, when sending forth his disciples into the world, (Matt. x. 16, 17.) "Behold, I send you forth as sheep in the midst of wolves;—*but, beware of men.*" Why do I say wolves? I send you forth into the wide world of *men*, that are far more hurtful and pernicious, and of whom you had much more need to beware, than of wolves.

It would be strange indeed, that this should be the state of mankind, distinguished by reason, for that very end, that they might be capable of *religion*, which summarily consists in *love*, if men, as they come into the world, are in their nature innocent and harmless, undepraved, and perfectly free from all evil propensities.

SECT. VIII.

The native depravity of mankind appears, in that there has been so little good effect of so manifold and great means, used to promote virtue in the world.

The evidence of the native corruption of mankind, appears much more glaring, when it is considered that the world has been so generally, so constantly, and so exceedingly corrupt, notwithstanding the *various, great*, and *continual means* that have been used to restrain men from sin, and promote virtue and true religion among them.

Dr. T. supposes, that sorrow and death, which come on mankind in consequence of *Adam's* sin, was brought on them in *great favour;* as a *benevolent father*, exercising *an wholesome discipline* towards his children; to restrain them from sin, by *increasing the vanity of all earthly things, to abate their force to tempt and delude;* to induce them to be *moderate in gratifying the appetites of the body;* to *mortify pride and ambition;* and that men might *always have before their eyes a striking demonstration that sin is infinitely hateful to God*, by a sight of that, *than which nothing is more proper to give them the utmost abhorrence of iniquity, and to fix in their minds a sense of the dreadful consequences of sin, &c. &c.* And in general, that they do not come as *punishments*, but purely as means to keep men from vice, and to make them better.—If it be so, surely they are *great* means. Here is a mighty alteration: mankind, once so easy and happy, healthful, vigorous, and beautiful, rich in all the pleasant and abundant blessings of paradise, now turned out, destitute, weak, and decaying, into a wide barren world, yielding briers and thorns, instead of the delightful growth and sweet fruit of the garden of *Eden*, to wear out life in sorrow and toil, on the ground cursed for his sake; and at last, either through long and lingering decay, or severe pain and acute disease, to expire and turn into putrefaction and dust. If these are only used as *medicines*, to prevent and to cure the diseases of the mind, they are sharp medicines indeed; especially death; which, to use *Hezekiah's* representation, is as it

* Dr. Turnbull, though so great an enemy to the doctrine of the depravity of nature, yet greatly insists upon it, that the experimental method of reasoning ought to be adopted in moral matters, and things pertaining to the human nature; and should chiefly be relied upon, in moral as well as natural philosophy. See *Introduc. to Mor. Phil.*

were *breaking all his bones*. And, one would think, should be very effectual, if the subject had no depravity—no evil and contrary bias, to resist, and hinder a proper effect—especially in the old world, when the first occasion of this terrible alteration, this severity of means, was fresh in memory. *Adam* continued alive near two-thirds of the time before the flood; so that a very great part of those who were alive till the flood, might have opportunity of seeing and conversing with him, and hearing from his mouth, not only an account of his fall, and the introduction of the awful consequences of it, but also of his first finding himself in existence in the new-created world, of the creation of *Eve*, and what passed between him and his Creator in paradise.

But what was the success of these great means, to restrain men from sin, and to induce them to virtue? Did they prove sufficient?—instead of this, the world soon grew exceeding corrupt; till, to use our author's own words, *mankind were universally debauched into lust, sensuality, rapine, and injustice*.

Then God used further means: he sent *Noah*, a preacher of righteousness, to warn the world of the universal destruction which would come upon them by a flood of waters, if they went on in sin. This warning he delivered with circumstances tending to strike their minds, and command their attention. He immediately went about building that vast structure, the ark, in which he must employ a great number of hands, and probably spent all he had in the world to save himself and his family. And under these uncommon means God waited upon them *one hundred and twenty years*—But all to no effect. The whole world, for ought appears, continued obstinate, and absolutely incorrigible: so that nothing remained to be done with them, but utterly to destroy the inhabitants of the earth; and to begin a new world, from that single family who had distinguished themselves by their virtue, that from them might be propagated a new and purer race. Accordingly, this was done: and the inhabitants of this new world, *Noah's* posterity, had these new and extraordinary means to restrain sin, and excite to virtue, in addition to the toil, sorrow, and common mortality, which the world had been subjected to before, in consequence of *Adam's* sin; *viz.* that God had newly testified his dreadful displeasure for sin, in destroying the many millions of mankind, all at one blow, old and young, men, women, and children, without pity on any for all the dismal shrieks and cries with which the world was filled. They themselves, the remaining family, were wonderfully distinguished by God's preserving goodness, that they might be a holy seed, being delivered from the corrupting examples of the old world; and being all the offspring of a living parent, whose pious instructions and counsels they had, to enforce these things upon them, to prevent sin, and engage them to their duty. These inhabitants of the new earth, must, for a long time, have before their eyes many evident and striking effects of that universal destruction, to be a continual affecting admonition to them. And besides all this, God now shortened the life of man to about one half of what it used to be. The shortening man's life, Dr. T. says, (p. 68.) "Was that the wild range of ambition and lust might be brought into narrower bounds, and have less opportunity of doing mischief; and that death, being still nearer to our view, might be a more powerful motive to regard less the things of a transitory world, and to attend more to the rules of truth and wisdom."

And now let us observe the consequence.—These new and extraordinary means, in addition to the former, were so far from proving sufficient, that the new world degenerated, and became corrupt, by such swift degrees, that as Dr. T. observes, mankind in general were sunk into idolatry, in about four hundred years after the flood, and so in about fifty years after *Noah's* death, they became so wicked and brutish, as to forsake the true God, and turn to the worship of inanimate creatures.

When things were come to this dreadful pass, God was pleased, for a remedy, to introduce a new and wonderful dispensation—separating a particular family, and people, from all the rest of the world, by a series of most astonishing miracles, done in the open view of the world; and fixing their dwelling, as it were, in the midst of the earth, between *Asia*, *Europe*, and *Africa*, and in the midst of those nations which were most considerable for power, knowledge, and arts—that might, in an extraordinary manner, dwell among that people, in visible tokens of his presence. There he manifested himself, and thence to the world, by a course of miraculous operations and effects, for many ages; that the people might be holy to God, as a kingdom of priests, and might stand as a city on a hill, to be a light to the world. He also gradually shortened man's life, till it was brought to about one-twelfth part of what it used to be before the flood; and so, according to Dr. T. greatly diminishing his temptations to sin, and increasing his excitements to holiness.——And now let us consider what the success of these means was, both as to the *Gentile* world, and the nation of *Israel*.

Dr. T. justly observes, (*Key*, p. 24. § 75.) "The Jewish dispensation had respect to the nations of the world, to spread the knowledge and obedience of God in the earth; and was established for the benefit of all mankind."—But how unsuccessful were these means, and all other means used with the *heathen* nations, so long as this dispensation lasted! *Abraham* was a person noted in all the principal nations then in the world; as in *Egypt*, and the eastern monarchies. God made his name famous by his wonderful, distinguishing dispensations towards him, particularly by so miraculously subduing, before him and his trained servants, those armies of the four eastern kings. This great work of the most high God, possessor of heaven and earth, was greatly noticed by *Melchizedeck;* and one would think, should have been sufficient to awaken the attention of all the nations in that part of the world, and to lead them to the knowledge and worship of the only true God; especially if considered in conjunction with that miraculous and most terrible destruction of *Sodom*, and all the cities of the plain, for their wickedness, with *Lot's* miraculous deliverance; facts which doubtless in their day were much famed abroad in the world. But there is not the least appearance, in any accounts we have, of any considerable good effect. On the contrary, those nations which were most in the way of observing and being affected with these things, even the nations of *Canaan*, grew worse and worse, till their iniquity came to the full, in *Joshua's* time. And the posterity of *Lot*, that saint so wonderfully distinguished, soon became some of the most gross idolaters; as they appear to have been in *Moses's* time. (See Num. xxv.) Yea, and the far greater part even of *Abraham's* posterity, the children of *Ishmael*, *Ziman*, *Jokshan*, *Medan*, *Midian*, *Ishbak* and *Shuah*, and *Esau*, soon forgot the true God, and fell off to heathenism.

Great things were done in the sight of the nations, tending to awaken them, and lead them to the knowledge and obedience of the true God, in *Jacob's* and *Joseph's* time; in that God did miraculously, by the hand of *Joseph*, preserve from perishing by famine, as it were the whole world; as appears by Gen. xli. 56, 57. Agreeably to which, the name that *Pharaoh* gave to *Joseph*, *Zaphnath-Paaneah*, as is said, in the *Egyptian* language, signifies *saviour of the world*. But there does not appear to have been any good abiding effect of this; no, not so much as among the *Egyptians*, the chief of all the heathen nations at that day, who had these great works of *Jehovah* in their most immediate view. On the contrary, they grew worse and worse, and seem to be far more gross in their idolatries and ignorance of the true God, and every way more wicked, and ripe for ruin, when *Moses* was sent to *Pharaoh*, than they were in *Joseph's* time.

After this, in *Moses* and *Joshua's* time, the great God was pleased to manifest himself in a series of the most astonishing miracles, for about fifty years together, wrought in the most public manner, in *Egypt*, in the wilderness, and in *Canaan*, in the view as it were of the whole world; miracles by which the world was shaken, the whole frame of the visible creation, earth, seas, and rivers, the atmosphere, the clouds, sun, moon, and stars were affected; miracles, greatly tending to convince the nations of the world, of the vanity of their false gods, showing Jehovah to be infinitely above them, in the thing wherein they dealt most proudly, and exhibiting God's awful displeasure at the wickedness of the heathen world. And these things are expressly spoken of as one end of these great miracles. (Exod. ix. 14. Numb. xiv. 21. Josh. iv. 23, 24.) However, no reformation followed, but by the scripture account, the nations which had them most in view, were dreadfully hardened, stupidly refusing all conviction and reformation, and obstinately went on in opposition to the living God, to their own destruction.

After this, God from time to time very publicly manifested himself to the nations of the world, by wonderful works wrought in the time of the *Judges*, of a like tendency with those already mentioned. Particularly in so miraculously destroying, by the hand of *Gideon*, almost the whole of that vast army of the *Midianites*, *Amalekites*, and *all the children of the east*, consisting of about 135,000 men. (Judg. vii. 12. and viii. 10.) But no reformation followed this, or the other great works of God, wrought in the times of *Deborah* and *Barak*, *Jeptha* and *Samson*.

After these things, God used new, and in some respects, much greater means with the heathen world, to bring them to the knowledge and service of the true God, in the days of *David* and *Solomon*. He raised up *David*, a man after his own heart, a most fervent worshipper of the true God, and zealous hater of idols, and subdued before him almost all the nations between *Egypt* and *Euphrates;* often miraculously assisting him in his battles with his enemies. And he confirmed *Solomon* his son in the full and quiet possession of that great empire, for about forty years; and made him the wisest, richest, most magnificent, and every way the greatest monarch that ever had been in the world; and by far the most famous, and of greatest name among the nations; especially for his wisdom, and things *concerning the name of his God;* particularly the temple he built, which was *exceeding magnificent, that it might be of fame and glory throughout all lands;* 1 Chron. xxii. 5. And we are told, that there came of all people to hear the wisdom of *Solomon*, from all kings of the earth. (1 Kings iv. 34. and x. 24.) And the Scripture informs us, that these great things were done, that the *nations in far countries might hear of God's great name, and of his out-stretched arm; that all the people of the earth might fear him, as well as his people* Israel: *and that all the people of the earth might know, that the Lord was God, and that there was none else.* (1 Kings viii. 41—43, 60.) But still there is no appearance of any considerable abiding effect, with regard to any one heathen nation.

After this, before the captivity in *Babylon*, many great things were done in the sight of the gentile nations, very much tending to enlighten, affect, and persuade them. As God destroying the army of the *Ethiopians* of a thousand thousand, before *Asa; Elijah's* and *Elisha's* miracles; especially *Elijah* miraculously confounding *Baal's* prophets and worshippers; *Elisha* healing *Naaman*, the king of *Syria's* prime minister, and the miraculous victories obtained, through *Elisha's* prayers, over the *Syrians*, *Moabites*, and *Edomites;* the miraculous destruction of the vast united army of the children of *Moab*, *Ammon*, and *Edom*, at *Jehoshaphat's* prayer. (2 Chron. xx.) *Jonah's* preaching at *Nineveh*, together with the miracle of his deliverance from the whale's belly; which was published, and well attested, as a sign to confirm his preaching: but more especially that great work of God, in destroying *Sennacherib's* army by an angel, for his contempt of the God of *Israel*, as if he had been no more than the gods of the heathen.

When all these things proved ineffectual, God took a new method with the heathen world, and used, in some respects, much greater means to convince and reclaim them, than ever before. In the first place, his people, the *Jews*, were removed to *Babylon*, the head and heart of the heathen world, (*Chaldea* having been very much the fountain of idolatry,) to carry thither the revelations which God had made of himself, contained in the sacred writings; and there to bear their testimony against idolatry; as some of them, particularly *Daniel*, *Shadrach*, *Meshach*, and *Abed-nego*, did, in a very open manner before the king, and the greatest men of the empire, with such circumstances as made their testimony very famous in the world. And God confirmed it with great miracles; which were published through the empire, by order of its monarch, as the mighty works of the God of *Israel*, showing him to be above all gods: *Daniel*, that great prophet, at the same time being exalted to be governor of all the wise men of *Babylon*, and one of the chief officers of *Nebuchadnezzar's* court.

After this, God raised up *Cyrus* to destroy *Babylon*, for its obstinate contempt of the true God, and injuriousness towards his people; according to the prophecies of *Isaiah*, speaking of him by name, instructing him concerning the nature and dominion of the true God. (Isa. xlv.) Which prophecies were probably shown to him, whereby he was induced to publish his testimony concerning the God of *Israel*, as THE GOD. (Ezra i. 2, 3.) *Daniel*, about the same time, being advanced to be prime minister of state in the new empire, erected under *Darius*, did in that place appear openly as a worshipper of the God of *Israel*, and him alone; God confirming his testimony for him, before the king and all the grandees of his kingdom, by preserving him in the den of lions; whereby *Darius* was induced to publish to all people, nations, and languages, that dwelt in all the earth, his testimony, that *the God of* Israel *was the living God, and stedfast for ever*, &c.

When, after the destruction of *Babylon*, some of the *Jews* returned to their own land, multitudes never returned, but were dispersed abroad through many parts of the vast *Persian* empire; as appears by the book of *Esther*. And many of them afterwards, as good histories inform us, were removed into the more western parts of the world; and so were dispersed as it were all over the heathen world, having the Holy Scriptures with them, and synagogues every where, for the worship of the true God. And so it continued to be, to the days of Christ and his apostles; as appears by the *Acts of the Apostles*. Thus that light, which God had given them, was carried abroad into all parts of the world: so that now they had far greater advantages to come to the knowledge of the truth, in matters of religion, if they had been disposed to improve their advantages.

And besides all these things, from about *Cyrus's* time, learning and philosophy increased, and was carried to a great height. God raised up a number of men of prodigious genius, to instruct others, and improve their reason and understanding, in the nature of things: and philosophic knowledge having gone on to increase for several ages, seemed to be got to its height before Christ came, or about that time.

And now let it be considered what was the effect of all these things.—Instead of a reformation, or any appearance or prospect of it, the heathen world in general rather grew worse. As Dr. Winder observes, "The inveterate absurdities of pagan idolatry continued without remedy, and increased as arts and learning increased; and paganism prevailed in all its height of absurdity, when pagan nations were polished to the height, and in the most polite cities and countries; and thus continued to the last breath of pagan power." And so it was with respect to wickedness in general, as well as idolatry; as appears by what the apostle *Paul* observes in Rom. i.—Dr. T. speaking of the time when the gospel-scheme was introduced, (*Key*, § 289.) says, "The moral and religious state of the heathen was very deplorable, being generally sunk into great ignorance, gross idolatry, and abominable vice." Abominable vices prevailed, not only among the common people, but even among their philosophers themselves, yea, some of the chief of them, and of greatest genius; so Dr. T. himself observes, as to that detestable vice of sodomy, which they commonly and openly allowed and practised without shame. (See Dr. T.'s note on Rom. i. 27.)

Having thus considered the state of the heathen world, with regard to the effect of means used for its reformation, during the *Jewish* dispensation, from the first foundation of it in *Abraham's* time; let us now consider how it was with that people themselves, who were distinguished with the peculiar privileges of that dispensation. The means used with the heathen nations were great; but they were small, if compared with those used with the *Israelites*. The advantages by which that people were distinguished, are represented in Scripture as vastly above all parallel, in passages which Dr. T. takes notice of. (*Key*, § 54.) And he reckons these privileges among those which he calls *antecedent blessings,* consisting in motives to virtue and obedience; and says, (*Key,* § 66.) "That this was the very end and design of the dispensation of God's extraordinary favours to the *Jews, viz.* to engage them to duty and obedience, or that it was a scheme for promoting virtue, is clear beyond dispute, from every part of the Old Testament." Nevertheless, the generality of that people, through all the successive periods of that dispensation, were men of a wicked character. But it will be more abundantly manifest, how strong the natural bias to iniquity appeared to be among that people, by considering more particularly their condition from time to time.

Notwithstanding the great things God had done in the times of *Abraham, Isaac,* and *Jacob,* to separate them and their posterity from the idolatrous world, that they might be a holy people to himself; yet in about two hundred years after *Jacob's* death, and in less than one hundred and fifty years after the death of *Joseph,* and while some were alive who had seen *Joseph,* the people had in a great measure lost the true religion, and were apace conforming to the heathen world. For a remedy, and the more effectually to alienate them from idols, and engage them to the God of their fathers, God appeared, in order to bring them out from among the *Egyptians,* and separate them from the heathen world, and to reveal himself in his glory and majesty, in so affecting and astonishing a manner, as tended most deeply and durably to impress their minds; that they might never forsake him any more. But so perverse were they, that they murmured even in the midst of the miracles that God wrought for them in *Egypt,* and murmured at the *Red sea,* in a few days after God had brought them out with such a mighty hand. When he had led them through the sea, *they sang his praise, but soon forgat his works.* Before they got to mount *Sinai,* they openly manifested their perverseness from time to time; so that God says of them, Exod. xvi. 28. "How long refuse ye to keep my commandments, and my laws?" Afterwards they murmured again at *Rephidim.*

In about two months after they came out of *Egypt,* they came to mount *Sinai;* where God entered into a most solemn covenant with the people, that they should be an holy people unto him, with such astonishing manifestations of his power, majesty, and holiness, as were altogether unparalleled. God puts the people in mind, (Deut. iv. 32—34.) "For ask now of the days that are past, which were before thee, since the day that God created man upon the earth; and ask from one side of heaven unto the other, whether there has been any such thing as this great thing is, or hath been heard like it. Did ever people hear the voice of God speaking out of the midst of the fire, as thou hast heard, and live? Or hath God assayed to take him a nation from the midst of another nation?" &c. And these great things were in order to impress their minds with such a conviction and sense of divine truth, and their obligations, that they might never forget them; as God says, (Exod. xix. 9.) "Lo, I come unto thee in a thick cloud, that the people may hear when I speak with thee, and believe thee for ever." But what was the effect of all? It was not more than two or three months, before that people, under that very mountain, returned to their old *Egyptian* idolatry, and were singing and dancing before a golden calf, which they had set up to worship. And after awful manifestations of God's displeasure for that sin, and so much done to bring them to repentance, and confirm them in obedience, it was but a few months before they came to that violence of spirit, in open rebellion against God, that with the utmost vehemence they declared their resolution to follow God no longer, but to make them a captain to return into *Egypt.* And thus they went on in perverse opposition to the Most High, from time to time repeating their open acts of rebellion, in the midst of continued astonishing miracles, till that generation was destroyed. And though the following generation seems to have been the best that ever was in *Israel,* yet notwithstanding their good example, and notwithstanding all the wonders of God's power and love to that people in *Joshua's* time, how soon did that people degenerate, and begin to forsake God, and join with the heathen in their idolatries, till God by severe means, and by sending prophets and judges, extraordinarily influenced from above, reclaimed them! But when they were brought to some reformation by such means, they soon fell away again into the practice of idolatry; and so from one age to another; and nothing proved effectual for any abiding reformation.

After things had gone on thus for several hundred years, God used new methods with his people, in two respects: *First,* he raised up a great prophet, under whom a number of young men were trained up in schools, that from among them there might be a constant succession of great prophets in *Israel,* of such as God should choose; which seems to have been continued for more than five hundred years. *Secondly,* God raised up a great king, *David,* one eminent for wisdom, piety, and fortitude, to subdue all their heathen neighbours, who used to be such a snare to them; and to confirm, adorn, and perfect the institutions of his public worship; and by him to reveal more fully the great salvation, and future glorious kingdom of the Messiah. And after him was raised up his son, *Solomon,* the wisest and greatest prince that ever was on earth, more fully to settle and establish those things which his father *David* had begun, concerning the public worship of God in *Israel,* and to build a glorious temple for the honour of JEHOVAH, and the institutions of his worship, and to instruct the neighbour nations in true wisdom and religion. But what was the success of these new and extraordinary means? If we take Dr. T. for our expositor of Scripture, the nation must be extremely corrupt in *David's* time; for he supposes he has respect to his own times, in those words, Psal. xiv. 2, 3. "The Lord looked down from heaven, to see if there were any that did understand, and seek God; they are all gone aside: they are together become filthy; there is none that doeth good; no, not one." But, whether Dr. T. be in the right in this, or not, yet if we consider what appeared in *Israel,* in *Absalom's* and *Sheba's* rebellion, we shall not see cause to think, that the greater part of the nation at that day were men of true wisdom and piety. As to *Solomon's* time, Dr. T. supposes, as has been already observed, that *Solomon* speaks of his own times, when he says, he had found but one in a thousand that was a thoroughly upright man.

However, it appears, that all those great means used to promote and establish virtue and true religion, in *Samuel's, David's, and Solomon's* times, were so far from having any general abiding good effect in *Israel,* that *Solomon* himself, with all his wisdom, and notwithstanding the unparalleled favours of God to him, had his mind corrupted, so as openly to tolerate idolatry in the land, and greatly to provoke God against him. And as soon as he was dead, ten tribes of the twelve forsook the true worship of God, and instead of it, openly established the like idolatry that the people fell into at mount *Sinai,* when they made the golden calf; and continued fully obstinate in this apostacy, notwithstanding all means that could be used with them by the prophets, whom God sent, one after another, to reprove, counsel, and warn them, for about two hundred and fifty years; especially those two great prophets, *Elijah* and *Elisha.* Of all the kings that reigned over them, there was not so much as one but what was of a wicked character. And at last their case seemed utterly desperate; so that nothing remained to be done with them, but to remove them out of God's sight. Thus the scripture represents the matter, 2 Kings xvii.

And as to the other two tribes; though their kings were always of the family of *David,* and they were favoured in many respects far beyond their brethren, yet they were generally exceeding corrupt. Their kings were, most of them, wicked men, and their other magistrates, and priests, and people, were generally agreed in the corruption. Thus the matter is represented in the scripture history, and the books of the prophets. And when they had seen how God had cast off the ten tribes, instead of taking warning, they made themselves vastly more vile than ever the others had done. 2 Kings xvii. 18, 19. Ezek. xvi. 46, 47, 51. God indeed waited longer upon them, for his servant *David's* sake, and for *Jerusalem's* sake, that he had chosen; and used more extraordinary means with them; especially by those great prophets, *Isaiah* and *Jeremiah,* but to no effect: so that at last, as the prophets represent the matter, they were like a body universally and desperately diseased and corrupted, that would admit of no cure, the whole head sick, and the whole heart faint, &c.

Things being come to that pass, God took this method with them; he utterly destroyed their city and land, and the temple which he had among them, made thorough work in purging the land of them; as when a man *empties a dish, wipes it, and turns it upside down; or when a vessel is cast into a fierce fire, till its filthiness is thoroughly burnt out.* (2 Kings xxi. 13. Ezek. chap. xxiv.) They were carried into captivity, and there left, till that wicked generation was dead, and those old rebels were purged out; that afterwards the land might be resettled with a more pure generation.

After the return from the captivity, and God had built the Jewish church again in their own land, by a series of wonderful providences; yet they corrupted themselves again, to so great a degree, that the transgressors were come to the full again in the days of *Antiochus Epiphanes;* as the matter is represented in the prophecy of *Daniel.* (Dan. viii. 23.) And then God made them the subjects of a dispensation, little, if any thing, less terrible, than that which had been in *Nebuchadnezzar's* days. And after God had again delivered them, and restored the state of religion among them, by the instrumentality of the *Maccabees,* they degenerated again: so that when Christ came, they were arrived to that extreme degree of corruption, which is represented in the accounts given by the evangelists.

It may be observed here in general, that the *Jews,* though so vastly distinguished with advantages, means, and motives to holiness, yet are represented, from time to time, as more wicked in the sight of God, than the very worst of the heathen. As, of old, God sware by his life, that the wickedness of *Sodom* was small, compared with that of the *Jews;* (Ezek. xvi. 47, 48, &c. also chap. v. 5—10.) So, Christ speaking of the *Jews,* in his time, represents them as having much greater guilt than the inhabitants of *Tyre* and *Sydon,* or even *Sodom* and *Gomorrah.*

But we are now come to the time when the grandest scene was displayed that ever was opened on earth. After all other schemes had been so long and so thoroughly tried, and had so greatly failed of success, both among *Jews* and *Gentiles;* that wonderful dispensation was at length introduced—the greatest scheme for suppressing and restraining iniquity among mankind, that ever infinite wisdom and mercy contrived—even the glorious gospel of Jesus Christ. "A new dispensation of grace was erected (to use Dr. T.'s own words, p. 239, 240.) for the more certain and effectual sanctification of mankind, into the image of God; delivering them from the sin and wickedness, into which they might fall, or were already fallen; to redeem them from all iniquity, and bring them to the knowledge and obedience of God." In whatever high and exalted terms the Scripture speaks of the means and motives which the *Jews* enjoyed of old; yet their privileges are represented as having no glory, in comparison of the advantages of the gospel. Dr. T.'s words (p. 233.) are worthy to be here repeated. "Even the heathen (says he) knew God, and might have glorified him as God; but under the glorious light of the gospel, we have very clear ideas of the divine perfections, and particularly of the love of God as our Father, and as the God and Father of our Lord and Saviour Jesus Christ. We see our duty in the utmost extent, and the most cogent reasons to perform it: we have eternity opened to us, even an endless state of honour and felicity, the reward of virtuous actions; and the Spirit of God promised for our direction and assistance. And all this may and ought to be applied to the purifying of our minds, and the perfecting of holiness. And to these happy advantages we are born; for which we are bound for ever to praise and magnify the rich grace of God in the Redeemer." And he elsewhere says,* "The gospel-constitution is a scheme the most perfect and effectual for restoring true religion, and promoting virtue and happiness, that ever the world has yet seen." And † *admirably adapted to enlighten our minds, and sanctify our hearts.* And ‡ *never were motives so divine and powerful proposed, to induce us to the practice of all virtue and goodness.*

And yet even these means have been ineffectual upon the far greater part of them with whom they have been used; of the *many that have been called, few have been chosen.*

As to the *Jews,* God's ancient people, with whom they were used in the first place, and used long by Christ and his apostles, the generality of them rejected Christ and his gospel, with extreme pertinacity of spirit. They not only went on still in that career of corruption which had been increasing from the time of the *Maccabees;* but Christ's coming, his doctrine and miracles, the preaching of his followers, and the glorious things that attended the same, were the occasion, through their perverse misimprovement, of an infinite increase of their wickedness. They crucified the Lord of glory, with the utmost malice and cruelty, and persecuted his followers; they pleased not God, and were contrary to all men; they went on to grow worse and worse, till they filled up the measure of their sin, and wrath came upon them to the uttermost; and they were destroyed, and cast out of God's sight, with unspeakably greater tokens of the divine abhorrence and indignation, than in the days of *Nebuchadnezzar.* The greater part of the whole nation were slain, and the rest were scattered abroad through the earth in the most abject and forlorn circumstances. And in the same spirit of unbelief and malice against Christ and the gospel, and in their miserable dispersed circumstances, do they remain to this day.

And as to the *gentile* nations, though there was a glorious success of the gospel amongst them, in the apostles' days; yet probably not one in ten of those that had the gospel preached to them embraced it. The powers of the world were set against it, and persecuted it with insatiable malignity. And among the professors of Christianity, there presently appeared in many a disposition to abuse the gospel to the service of pride and licentiousness. The apostles foretold a grand apostacy of the christian world, which should continue many ages; and observed, that there appeared a disposition to such an apostacy, among professing Christians, even in that day. (2 Thess. ii. 7.) The greater part of the ages now elapsed, have been spent in that grand and general apostacy, under which the christian world, as it is called, has been transformed into what has been vastly more dishonourable and hateful to God, and repugnant to true virtue, than the state of the heathen world before: which is agreeable to the prophetical descriptions given of it by the Holy Spirit.

In these latter ages of the christian church, God has raised up a number of great and good men, to bear testimony against the corruptions of the church of *Rome,* and by their means introduced that light into the world, by which, in a short time, at least one-third part of *Europe* was delivered from the more gross enormities of *Antichrist:* which was attended at first with a great reformation, as to vital and practical religion. But how is the gold become dim! To what a pass are things come in protestant countries at this day, and in our nation in particular! To what a prodigious height has a deluge of infidelity, profaneness, luxury, debauchery, and wickedness of every kind, arisen! The poor savage *Americans* are mere babes, if I may so speak, as to proficiency in wickedness, in comparison of multitudes in the christian world. Dr. T. himself, as before observed, represents, that the *generality of Christians have been the most wicked, lewd, bloody, and treacherous of all mankind;* and (*Key,* § 388.) that "The wickedness of the christian world renders it so much like the heathen, that the good effects of our change to Christianity are but little seen."

With respect to the dreadful corruption of the present day, it is to be considered, besides the advantages already mentioned, that great advances in learning and philosophic knowledge have been made in the present and past century; affording great advantage for a proper and enlarged exercise of our rational powers, and for our seeing the bright manifestation of God's perfections in his works. And it is to be observed, that the means and inducements to virtue, which this age enjoys, are in *addition* to most of

* *Key,* § 167.

† *Note on* Rom. i. 16.

‡ *Pref. to Par. on* Rom. p. 145, 47

those which were mentioned before, as given of old; and among other things, in addition to the shortening of man's life to 70 or 80 years, from near a thousand. And, with regard to this, I would observe, that as the case now stands in christendom, take one with another of those who ever come to years of discretion, their life is not more than forty or forty-five years; which is but about the twentieth part of what it once was: and not so much in great cities, places where profaneness, sensuality, and debauchery, commonly prevail to the greatest degree.

Dr. T. (Key, § 1.) truly observes, That God has from the beginning exercised wonderful and infinite wisdom, in the methods he has, from age to age, made use of to oppose vice, cure corruption, and promote virtue in the world; and introduced several schemes to that end. It is indeed remarkable, how many schemes and methods were tried of old, both before and after the flood; how many were used in the times of the Old Testament, both with Jews and heathens, and how ineffectual all these ancient methods proved, for 4000 years together, till God introduced that grand dispensation, for redeeming men from all iniquity, and purifying them to himself, a people zealous of good works; which the Scripture represents as the subject of the admiration of angels. But even this has now so long proved ineffectual, with respect to the generality, that Dr. T. thinks *there is need of a new dispensation; the present light of the gospel being insufficient for the full reformation of the christian world, by reason of its corruptions:* (Note on Rom. i. 27.)—And yet all these things, according to him, without any natural bias to the contrary; no stream of natural inclination or propensity at all, to oppose inducements to goodness; no native opposition of heart, to withstand those gracious means, which God has ever used with mankind, from the beginning of the world to this day; any more than there was in the heart of *Adam,* the moment God created him in perfect innocence.

Surely Dr. T.'s scheme is attended with strange paradoxes. And that his mysterious tenets may appear in a true light, it must be observed that—at the same time he supposes these means, even the very greatest and best of them, to have proved so ineffectual, that help from them, as to any general reformation, is to be despaired of—that he maintains all mankind, even the heathen in all parts of the world, yea, every single person in it, (which must include every *Indian* in *America,* before the *Europeans* came hither; and every inhabitant of the unknown parts of *Africa* and *Terra Australis,*) has ability, light, and means sufficient to do their whole duty; yea, many passages in his writings plainly suppose, to perform perfect obedience to God's law, without the least degree of vice or iniquity.*

But I must not omit to observe, that Dr. T. supposes, the reason why the gospel-dispensation has been so ineffectual, is, that it has been greatly misunderstood and perverted. In his Key, (§ 389.) he says, "Wrong representations of the scheme of the gospel have greatly obscured the glory of divine grace, and contributed much to the corruption of its professors.—Such doctrines have been almost universally taught and received, as quite subvert it. Mistaken notions about nature, grace, election and reprobation, justification, regeneration, redemption, calling, adoption, &c. have quite taken away the very ground of the christian life."

But how came the gospel to be so universally and exceedingly misunderstood? Is it because it is in itself so very dark and unintelligible, and not adapted to the apprehension of the human faculties? If so, how is the possession of such an obscure and unintelligible thing, so glorious an advantage?—Or is it because of the native blindness, corruption, and superstition of mankind? But this is giving up the thing in question, and allowing a great depravity of nature. Dr. T. speaks of the gospel as far otherwise than dark and unintelligible; he represents it as exhibiting the clearest and most glorious light, calculated to deliver the world from darkness, and to bring them into marvellous light. He speaks of the light which the *Jews* had, under the *Mosaic* dispensation, as vastly exceeding the light of nature, which the heathen enjoyed; and yet he supposes that even the latter was so clear, as to be sufficient to lead men to the knowledge of God, and their whole duty to him. He speaks of the light of the gospel as vastly exceeding the light of the Old Testament; and says of the apostle *Paul* in particular, "That he wrote with great perspicuity; that he takes great care to explain every part of his subject; that he has left no part of it unexplained and unguarded; and that never was an author more exact and cautious in this."† Is it not strange, therefore, that the *Christian* world, without any native depravity, should be so blind in the midst of such glaring light, as to be all, or the generality, agreed, from age to age, so essentially to *misunderstand* that which is made so very plain?

Dr. T. says, (p. 167. S.) "It is my persuasion, that the christian religion was very early and grievously corrupted, by dreaming, ignorant, superstitious *monks,* too conceited to be satisfied with the plain gospel; and has long remained in that deplorable state."——But how came the whole christian world, without any blinding depravity, to hearken to these ignorant foolish men, rather than unto wiser and better teachers? especially, when the latter had *plain gospel* on their side, and the doctrines of the other were (as our author supposes) so very contrary not only to the plain gospel, but to men's reason and common sense? or were all the teachers of the Christian church nothing but a parcel of *ignorant dreamers?* If so, this is very strange indeed, unless mankind naturally *love darkness* rather than light; seeing in all parts of the christian world, there was a great multitude in the work of the ministry, who had the gospel in their hands, and whose whole business it was to study and teach it; and therefore had infinitely greater advantages to become truly wise, than the heathen philosophers. But if, by some strange and inconceivable means, notwithstanding all these glorious advantages, all the teachers of the christian church through the world, without any native evil propensity, very early became silly *dreamers*—and also in their *dreaming,* generally stumbled on the *same* individual monstrous opinions, and so the world might be blinded for a while—yet, why did not they hearken to that wise and great man, *Pelagius,* and others like him, when he plainly held forth the truth to the christian world? Especially seeing his instructions were so agreeable to the plain doctrines, and the bright and clear light of the gospel of Christ, and also so agreeable to the plainest dictates of the common sense and understanding of all mankind; but the other so repugnant to it, that (according to our author) if they were true, it would prove *understanding* to be *no understanding,* and *the word of God to be no rule of truth, nor at all to be relied upon, and God to be a Being worthy of no regard?*

Besides, if the inefficacy of the gospel to restrain sin and promote virtue, be owing to the general prevalence of these doctrines, which are supposed to be so absurd and contrary to the gospel, here is this further to be accounted for; namely, Why, since there has been so great an increase of light in religious matters (as must be supposed on Dr. T.'s scheme) in this and the last age, and these monstrous doctrines of original sin, election, reprobation, justification, regeneration, &c. have been so much exploded, especially in our nation, there has been no reformation attending this great advancement of light and truth: but on the contrary, vice, and every thing opposite to practical Christianity, has gone on to increase, with such a prodigious celerity, as to become like an overflowing deluge; threatening, unless God mercifully interposes, speedily to swallow up all that is virtuous and praiseworthy.

Many other things might have been mentioned under this head—the *means* which mankind have had to restrain vice, and promote virtue—such as wickedness being many ways contrary to men's temporal interest and comfort, and their having continually before their eyes so many instances of persons made miserable by their vices; the restraints of human laws, without which men cannot live in society; the judgments of God brought on men for their wickedness, with which history abounds, and the providential rewards of virtue; and innumerable particular means.

* See p. 259. 63, 64, 72. S.

† Pref. to Par. on Rom. p. 146. 48.

that God has used from age to age to curb the wickedness of mankind, which I have omitted. But there would be no end of a particular enumeration of such things. They that will not be convinced by the instances which have been mentioned, probably would not be convinced, if the world had stood a thousand times so long, and we had the most authentic and certain accounts of means having been used from the beginning, in a thousand times greater variety; and new dispensations had been introduced, after others had been tried in vain, ever so often, and still to little effect. He that will not be convinced by a thousand good witnesses, it is not likely that he would be convinced by a thousand thousand.

The proofs that have been extant in the world, from trial and fact, of the depravity of man's nature, are inexpressible, and as it were infinite, beyond the representation of all similitude. If there were a piece of ground which abounded with briers and thorns, or some poisonous plant, and all mankind had used their endeavours, for a thousand years together, to suppress that evil growth—and to bring that ground by manure and cultivation, planting and sowing, to produce better fruit, all in vain; it would still be overrun with the same noxious growth—it would not be a proof, that such a produce was agreeable to the nature of that soil, in any wise to be compared to that which is given in divine providence, that wickedness is a produce agreeable to the nature of the field of the world of mankind. For the means used with it have been various, great, and wonderful, contrived by the unsearchable and boundless wisdom of God; medicines procured with infinite expense, exhibited with a vast apparatus; a marvellous succession of dispensations, introduced one after another, displaying an incomprehensible length and breadth, depth and height, of divine wisdom, love, and power, and every perfection of the godhead, to the eternal admiration of principalities and powers in heavenly places.

SECT. IX.

Several evasions of the arguments for the depravity of nature, from trial and events considered.

Evasion I. Dr. T. says, (p. 231, 232.) " *Adam's* nature, it is allowed, was very far from being sinful; yet he sinned. And therefore, the common doctrine of Original Sin, is no more necessary to account for the sin that has been or is in the world, than it is to account for *Adam's* sin."* Again, (p. 52—54. S. &c.) " If we allow mankind to be as wicked as R. R. has represented them to be; and suppose that there is not one upon earth that is truly righteous, and without sin, and that some are very enormous sinners, yet it will not thence follow, that they are naturally corrupt.—For, if sinful action infers a nature originally corrupt, then, whereas *Adam* (according to them that hold the doctrine of Original Sin) committed the most heinous and aggravated sin, that ever was committed in the world; for, according to them, he had greater light than any other man in the world, to know his duty, and greater power than any other man to fulfil it, and was under greater obligations than any other man to obedience; he sinned, when he knew he was the representative of millions, and that the happy or miserable state of all mankind, depended on his conduct; which never was, nor can be, the case of any other man in the world:—then, I say, it will follow, that *his* nature was originally *corrupt*, &c.—Thus their argument from the wickedness of mankind, to prove a sinful and corrupt nature, must inevitably and irrecoverably fall to the ground.—Which will appear more abundantly, if we take in the case of the angels, who in numbers sinned, and kept not their first estate, though created with a nature superior to *Adam's*." Again, (p. 145. S.) " When it is inquired, how it comes to pass that our appetites and passions are now so irregular and strong, as that not one person has resisted them, so as to keep himself pure and innocent? If this be the case, if such as make the inquiry will tell the world, how it came to pass that *Adam's* appetites and passions were so irregular and strong, that he did not resist them, so as to keep himself pure and innocent, when upon their principles he was far more able to have resisted them; I also will tell them how it comes to pass, that his posterity does not resist them.† Sin doth not alter its nature, by its being general; and therefore how far soever it spreads, it must come upon all just as it came upon *Adam*."

These things are delivered with much assurance. But is there any reason in such a way of talking? One thing implied in it, and the main thing, if any at all to the purpose, is, that because an effect being general, does not alter the *nature* of the effect, therefore nothing more can be argued concerning the cause, from its happening constantly, and in the most steady manner, than from its happening but once. But how contrary is this to reason! Suppose a person, through the deceitful persuasions of a pretended friend, once takes a poisonous draught of a liquor to which he had before no inclination; but after he has once taken of it, he is observed to act as one that has an insatiable, incurable thirst after more of the same, in his constant practice, obstinately continued in as long as he lives, against all possible arguments and endeavours used to dissuade him from it. And suppose we should from hence argue a fixed inclination, and begin to suspect that this is the nature and operation of the poison, to produce such an inclination, or that this strong propensity is some way the consequence of the first draught. In such a case, could it be said with good reason, that a fixed propensity can no more be argued from his consequent *constant* practice, than from his *first* draught? Or, suppose a young man, soberly inclined, enticed by wicked companions, should drink to excess, until he had got a habit of excessive drinking, and should come under the power of a greedy appetite after strong drink, so that drunkenness should become a common and constant practice with him: and suppose an observer, arguing from this general practice, should say, " It must needs be that this young man has a fixed inclination to that sin; otherwise, how should it come to pass that he should make such a trade of it?" And another, ridiculing the weakness of his arguing, should reply, " Do you tell me how it came to pass, that he was guilty of that sin the first time, without a fixed inclination, and I will tell you how he is guilty of it so generally without a fixed inclination. Sin does not alter its nature by being general: and therefore, how common soever it becomes, it must come at all times by the same means that it came at first." I leave it to every one to judge, *who* would be chargeable with weak arguing in such a case.

It is true, there is no effect without some cause, ground, or reason of that effect, and some cause answerable to the effect. But certainly it will not follow, that a *transient* effect requires a *permanent* cause, or a fixed propensity. An effect happening once, though great, yea, though it may come to pass on the same occasion in many subjects at the same time, will not prove any fixed propensity, or permanent influence. It is true, it proves an influence great and extensive, answerable to the effect, *once* exerted, or once effectual; but it proves nothing in the cause *fixed* or constant. If a particular tree, or a great number of trees standing together, have blasted fruit on their branches at a particular season—or if the fruit be very much blasted, and entirely spoiled—it is evident that something was the occasion of such an effect at that time; but this alone does not prove the *nature* of the tree to be bad. But if it be observed, that those trees, and all other trees of the kind, wherever planted, and in all soils, countries, climates, and seasons, and however cultivated and managed, still bear ill fruit, from year to year, and in all ages, it is a good evidence of the evil nature of the tree. And if the fruit, at all these times, and in all these cases, be very bad, it proves the nature of the tree to be very bad. If we argue, in like manner, from what appears among men, it is easy to determine, whether the universal sinfulness of mankind—all sinning immediately, as soon as capable of it, and continually and generally being of a wicked character, at all times, in all ages, in all places, and under all possible circumstances, against means and motives inexpressibly mani-

* Belsham.

† See p. 81. *note*.

fold and great, and in the utmost conceivable variety—be from a *permanent* internal great cause.

If the voice of common sense were heard, there would be no occasion for labour in multiplying arguments to show, that one act does not prove a fixed inclination; but that constant pursuit does. We see that, in fact, it is agreeable to the reason of all mankind, to argue fixed principles, tempers, and prevailing inclinations, from repeated and continued actions—though the actions are voluntary, and performed of choice—and thus to judge of the tempers and inclinations of persons, ages, sexes, tribes, and nations. But is it the manner of men to conclude, that whatever they see others *once* do, they have a fixed abiding inclination to do? Yea, there may be *several* acts seen, and yet not be taken as good evidence of an established propensity; even though that one act, or those several acts, are followed by such constant practice, as afterwards evidences fixed disposition. As for example; there may be several instances of a man drinking some spirituous liquor, and those instances be no sign of a fixed inclination to that liquor: but these acts may be introductory to a settled habit or propensity, which may be made very manifest afterwards by constant practice.

From these things it is plain, that what is alleged concerning the first sin of *Adam*, and of the angels, without a previous fixed disposition to sin, cannot in the least weaken the arguments brought to prove a fixed propensity to sin in mankind, in their present state. From the permanence of the cause has been argued, the permanence of the effect. And that the permanent cause consists in an internal fixed propensity, and not in any particular external circumstances, has been argued from the effects being the same, through a vast variety and change of circumstances. But the first acts of sin in *Adam* or the angels, considered in themselves, were no permanent, continued effects. And though a great number of the angels sinned, and the effect on that account was the greater, and more extensive; yet this *extent* of the effect is a very different thing from that *permanence*, or settled continuance of effect, which is supposed to show a permanent cause, or fixed propensity. Neither was there any trial of a vast variety of circumstances attending a permanent effect, to show the fixed cause to be internal, consisting in a settled disposition of nature, in the instances objected. And however great the sin of *Adam*, or of the *angels*, was, and however great the means, motives, and obligations were against which they sinned—and whatever may be thence argued concerning the transient cause, occasion, or temptation, as being very subtle, remarkably tending to deceive and seduce, &c.—yet it argues nothing of any *settled* disposition, or *fixed* cause, either great or small; the effect both in the angels and our first parents, being in itself *transient*, and, for ought appears, happening in each of them under one system or coincidence of influential circumstances.*

The general continued wickedness of mankind, against such means and motives, proves each of these things, *viz.* that the cause is *fixed*, and that the fixed cause is *internal* in man's nature, and also that it is very *powerful.* It proves, that the cause is *fixed*, because the effect is so abiding, through so many changes. It proves that the fixed cause is *internal*, because the circumstances are so various—including a variety of means and motives—and they are such circumstances as cannot possibly cause the effect, being most opposite to it in their tendency. And it proves the *greatness* of the internal cause; or that the propensity is powerful; because the means which have opposed its influence, have been so great, and yet have been statedly overcome.

But here I may observe, by the way, that with regard to the motives and obligations against which our first father sinned, it is not reasonably alleged, that he sinned when he *knew* his sin would have destructive consequences to all his posterity, *and might in process of time, pave the whole globe with skulls*, &c. It is evident, by the plain account the scripture gives us of the temptation which prevailed with our first parents to commit that sin, that it was so contrived by the subtlety of the tempter, as first to blind and deceive them as to that matter, and to make them believe that their disobedience should be followed with *no destruction or calamity at all* to themselves, (and therefore not to their posterity,) but on the contrary, with a great increase and advancement of dignity and happiness.

Evasion II. Let the wickedness of the world be ever so general and great, there is no necessity of supposing any depravity of nature to be the cause: man's own *free will* is cause sufficient. Let mankind be more or less corrupt, they make themselves corrupt by their own free choice. This Dr. T. abundantly insists upon, in many parts of his book.†

But I would ask, how it comes to pass that mankind so universally agree in this evil exercise of their free will? If their wills are in the first place as free to good as to evil, what is it to be ascribed to, that the world of mankind, consisting of so many millions, in so many successive generations, without consultation, all agree to exercise their freedom in favour of evil? If there be no natural tendency or preponderation in the case, then there is as good a chance for the will being determined to good as to evil. If the *cause* be indifferent, why is not the effect in some measure indifferent? If the balance be no heavier at one end than the other, why does it perpetually preponderate one way? How comes it to pass, that the free will of mankind has been determined to evil, in like manner before the flood and after the flood; under the law and under the gospel; among both *Jews* and *Gentiles*, under the Old Testament, and since then, among *Christians, Jews, Mahometans;* among papists and protestants; in those nations where civility, politeness, arts, and learning most prevail, and among the *Negroes* and *Hottentots* in *Africa*, the *Tartars* in *Asia*, and *Indians* in *America*, towards both the poles, and on every side of the globe; in greatest cities and obscurest villages; in palaces and in huts, wigwams, and cells under ground? Is it enough to reply, It happens so, that men every where, and in all times, choose thus to determine their own wills, and so to make themselves sinful, as soon as ever they are capable of it, and to sin constantly as long as they live, and universally to choose never to come up half way to their duty?

A steady effect requires a steady cause; but free will, without any previous propensity to influence its determinations, is no *permanent* cause; nothing can be conceived of, farther from it: for the very notion of freedom of will, consisting in self-determining power, implies contingence; and if the will is perfectly free from any government of previous inclination, its freedom must imply the most *absolute* and *perfect* contingence: and surely nothing can be conceived of, more unfixed than that. The notion of liberty of will, in this sense, implies perfect freedom from every thing that should previously fix, bind, or determine it; that it may be left to be fixed and determined wholly by itself: therefore its determinations must be previously altogether unfixed. And can that which is so unfixed, so contingent, be a cause sufficient to account for an effect, in such a manner, and to such a degree, permanent, fixed, and constant?

When we see any person going on in a certain course with great constancy, against all manner of means to dissuade him, do we judge this to be no argument of a *fixed* disposition of mind, because, being free, he may determine to do so, if he will, without any such disposition? Or if we see a nation, or people, that differ greatly from other nations, in such and such instances of their constant conduct—as though their tempers and inclinations were very diverse—and any should say, We cannot judge at all of the temper or disposition of people, by any thing observable in their constant practice or behaviour, because they have all free will, and therefore may all choose to act so, if they please, without any thing in their temper or inclination to bias them. Would such an account of such effects be satisfying to the reason of mankind? But infinitely further would it be from satisfying a considerate mind, to account for the constant and universal sinfulness of mankind, by saying, that their will is free, and therefore all may, if they please, make themselves wicked: they are free when they first begin to act as moral agents, and therefore all may, if they please, begin to sin as soon as they begin to act: they are

* See p. 81. *note.*

† Page 257, 258. 52, 53. S. and many other places.

free as long as they continue to act in the world, and therefore they may all commit sin continually, if they will: men of all nations are free, and therefore all nations may act alike in these respects, if they please, though some do not know how other nations do act. Men of high and low condition, learned and ignorant, are free, and therefore they may agree in acting wickedly, if they please, though they do not consult together. Men in all ages are free, and therefore men in one age may all agree with men in every other age in wickedness, if they please, though they do not know how men in other ages have acted, &c. Let every one judge whether such an account of things can satisfy reason.

Evasion III. It is said by many opposers of the doctrine of original sin, that the corruption of mankind may be owing not to a depraved nature, but to bad *example*. And I think we must understand Dr. T. as having respect to the powerful influence of bad instruction and example, when he says, (p. 118.) "The Gentiles in their heathen state, when incorporated into the body of the gentile world, were without strength, unable to help or recover themselves." And in several other places to the like purpose. If there was no depravity of nature, what else could there be but bad instruction and example, to hinder the heathen world, as a collective body, (for as such Dr. T. speaks of them, as may be seen p. 117, 118.) from emerging out of their corruption, on the rise of each new generation? As to their bad instruction, our author insists upon it, that the heathen, notwithstanding all their disadvantages, had sufficient light to know God, and do their whole duty. Therefore it must be chiefly bad example, according to him, that rendered their case helpless.

Now concerning this way of accounting for the corruption of the world, by the influence of bad example, I would observe,

1. It is accounting for the thing by the thing itself. It is accounting for the corruption of the world by the corruption of the world. For, that bad examples are general all over the world to be followed by others, and have been so from the beginning, is only an instance, or rather a description, of that corruption of the world which is to be accounted for. If mankind are naturally no more inclined to evil than good, then how come there to be so many more bad examples than good ones, in all ages? And if there are not, how come the bad examples that are set, to be so much more followed than the good? If the propensity of man's nature be not to evil, how comes the current of general example, every where, and at all times, to be so much to evil? And when opposition has been made by good examples, how comes it to pass that it has had so little effect to stem the stream of general wicked practice?

I think from the brief account the Scripture gives us of the behaviour of our first parents, and of the expressions of their faith and hope in God's revealed mercy, we have reason to suppose, that before ever they had any children, they repented, were pardoned, and became truly pious. So that God planted the world at first with a *noble vine;* and at the beginning of their generations, he set the stream of example the right way. And we see, that children are more apt to follow the example of their parents, than of any others; especially in early youth, their forming time, when those habits are generally contracted, which abide by them all their days. Besides, *Adam's* children had *no other* examples to follow, but those of their parents. How therefore came the stream so soon to turn, and to proceed the contrary way, with so violent a current? When mankind became so universally and desperately corrupt, as not to be fit to live on earth any longer, and the world was every where full of bad examples, God destroyed them all at once—except righteous *Noah* and his family—in order to remove those bad examples, and that the world might be planted again with good example, and the stream again turned the right way. How therefore came it to pass, that *Noah's* posterity did not follow his good example, especially when they had such extraordinary things to enforce it, but so generally, even in his life-time, became exceeding corrupt? One would think, the first generations at least, while all lived together as one family, under *Noah*, their venerable father, might have followed his good example. And if they had done so, then, when the earth came to be divided in *Peleg's* time, the heads of the several families would have set out their particular colonies with good examples, and the stream would have been turned the right way in all the various divisions, colonies, and nations of the world. But we see, in fact, that in about fifty years after *Noah's* death, the world in general was overrun with dreadful corruption; so that all virtue and goodness was like soon to perish from among mankind, unless something extraordinary should be done to prevent it.

Then, for a remedy, God separated *Abraham* and his family from all the rest of the world, that they might be delivered from the influence of bad example, and that in his posterity he might have an holy seed. Thus God again planted a *noble vine; Abraham, Isaac,* and *Jacob* being eminently pious. But how soon did their posterity degenerate, till true religion was like to be swallowed up! We see how desperately and almost universally corrupt they were, when God brought them out of Egypt, and led them in the wilderness.

Then God was pleased, before he planted his people in *Canaan*, to destroy that perverse generation in the wilderness, that he might plant them there a *noble vine, wholly a right seed,* and set them out with good example, in the land where they were to have their settled abode. Jer. ii. 21. It is evident, that the generation which came with *Joshua* into *Canaan* was an excellent generation, by innumerable things said of them.* But how soon did that people, nevertheless, become *the degenerate plant of a strange vine!*

And when the nation had a long time proved desperately and incurably corrupt, God destroyed them, and sent them into captivity—till the old rebels were dead and purged out, in order to deliver their children from their evil example. And when the following generation was purified as in a furnace, God planted them again in the land of *Israel*, a *noble vine*, and set them out with good example; which yet was not followed by their posterity.

When again the corruption was become inveterate, the christian church was planted; and a glorious out-pouring of the Spirit of God caused true virtue and piety to be exemplified far beyond whatever had been on earth before; and thus the christian church was planted a *noble vine.* But that primitive good example has not prevailed, to cause virtue to be generally and stedfastly maintained in the christian world. To how great a degree it has been *otherwise*, has already been observed.

After many ages of general and dreadful apostacy, God was pleased to erect the protestant church, as separated from the more corrupt part of christendom; and true piety flourished in it very much at first; God planted it a *noble vine:* but notwithstanding the good examples of the first reformers, what a melancholy pass is the protestant world come to at this day!

When *England* grew very corrupt, God brought over a number of pious persons, and planted them in *New England*, and this land was planted a *noble vine.* But how is the gold become dim! How greatly have we forsaken the pious examples of our fathers!

So prone have mankind always proved themselves to degeneracy and backsliding, that it shows plainly their natural propensity. And when good has revived, and been promoted among men, it has been by some divine interposition, opposing the natural current; the fruit of some extraordinary means. And the efficacy of such means has soon been overcome by constant natural bias, the effect of good example presently lost, and evil has regained the dominion. Like a heavy body, which may by some great power be caused to ascend, against its nature, a little while, but soon goes back again towards the centre, to which it naturally and constantly tends.

So that evil example will in no wise account for the corruption of mankind, without supposing a natural proneness to sin. The tendency of example alone will not account for general wicked practice, as consequent on good example. And if the influence of bad example is a reason of *some* of the wickedness, that alone will not account for

* See Jer. ii. 2, 3. Psal. lxviii. 14. Josh. xxii. 2. and xxiii. 8. Deut. iv. 3, 4. Hos. xi. 1. and ix. 10. Judg. ii. 7, 17, 22. and many other places.

men becoming worse than the example set, degenerating more and more, and growing worse and worse, which has been their manner.

2. There has been given to the world an example of virtue, which, were it not for a dreadful depravity of nature, would have influence on them who live under the gospel, far beyond all other examples; that is, the example of Jesus Christ.

God, who knew the human nature, and how apt men are to be influenced by example, has made answerable provision. His infinite wisdom has contrived that we should have set before us the most amiable and perfect example, in such circumstances, as should have the greatest tendency to influence all the principles of man's nature, but his corruption. Men are apt to be moved by the example of others *like themselves*, or in their own nature: therefore this example was given in our nature. Men are ready to follow the example of the *great* and honourable; and this—though that of one in our nature, yet—was the example of one infinitely higher and more honourable than kings or angels. A people are apt to follow the example of their *prince*. This is the example of that glorious person, who stands in a peculiar relation to Christians as their Lord and King, the supreme head of the church; and not only so, but the King of kings, supreme head of the universe, and head over all things to the church. Children are apt to follow the example of their *parents;* this is the example of the Author of our being, and of our holy and happy being; the Creator of the world, and everlasting Father of the universe. Men are very apt to follow the example of their *friends:* the example of Christ is that of one who is infinitely our greatest friend, standing in the most endearing relations of brother, redeemer, spiritual head and husband; whose grace and love expressed to us, transcends all other love and friendship, as much as heaven is higher than the earth. The virtues and acts of his example were exhibited to us in the most endearing and engaging circumstances that can possibly be conceived of.—His obedience and submission to God, his humility, meekness, patience, charity, self-denial, &c. being exercised and expressed in a work of infinite grace, love, condescension, and beneficence to us—and had all their highest expressions in his laying down his life, and meekly, patiently, and cheerfully undergoing unutterable suffering for our eternal salvation. Men are peculiarly apt to follow the example of those from whom they have great *benefits:* but it is utterly impossible to conceive of greater benefits, that we could have by the virtues of any person, than we have by the virtuous acts of Christ; we, who depend upon being thereby saved from eternal destruction, and brought to inconceivable, immortal glory at God's right hand. Surely if it were not for an extreme corruption of the human heart, such an example would have that strong influence on it, which would as it were swallow up the power of all the evil and hateful examples of a generation of vipers.

3. The influence of bad example, without corruption of nature, will not account for children universally committing sin as soon as capable of it; which, I think, is a fact that has been made evident by the Scripture. It will not account for it in the children of eminently pious parents; the first example set in their view being very good; which was especially the case of many children in christian families in the apostolic days, when the apostle *John* supposes that every individual person had sin to repent of, and confess to God.

4. What Dr. T. supposes to have been fact, with respect to a great part of mankind—the state of the heathen world, which he supposes, considered as a collective body, was helpless, dead in sin, and unable to recover itself—cannot consistently be accounted for from the influence of bad example. Not evil example alone, no, nor as united with evil instruction, can be supposed a sufficient reason why every new generation that arose among them, should not be able to emerge from the idolatry and wickedness of their ancestors, in any consistence with his scheme. The ill example of ancestors could have no power to oblige them to sin, any other way than as a strong temptation. But Dr. T. himself says, (p. 72. S.) "To suppose men's temptations to be superior to their powers, will impeach the goodness and justice of God, who appoints every man's trial." And as to bad instructions, as he supposes that they all, yea every individual person, had light sufficient to know God, and do their whole duty. And if each one could do this for himself, then surely they might all be agreed in it through the power of free will, as well as the whole world be agreed in corruption by the same power.

Evasion IV. Some modern opposers of the doctrine of original sin, thus account for the general prevalence of wickedness, *viz.* that in the course of nature our senses grow up first, and the animal passions get the start of reason. So Dr. Turnbull,* "Sensitive objects first affect us, and inasmuch as reason is a principle, which, in the nature of things, must be advanced to strength and vigour, by gradual cultivation, and these objects are continually assailing and soliciting us; so, unless a very happy education prevents, our sensitive appetites must have become very strong, before reason can have force enough to call them to an account, and assume authority over them." From hence Dr. Turnbull supposes it comes to pass,† "That though some few may, through the influence of virtuous example, be said to be sanctified from the womb, so liberal, so generous, so virtuous, so truly noble is their cast of mind; yet generally speaking, the whole world lieth in such wickedness, that, with respect to the far greater part of mankind, the *study of virtue is beginning to reform,* and is a severe struggle against bad habits, early contracted, and deeply rooted; it is therefore putting off an old inveterate corrupt nature, and putting on a new form and temper; it is moulding ourselves anew; it is a being born again, and becoming as children.—And how few are there in the world who escape its pollutions, so as not to be early in that class, or to be among the righteous that need no repentance!"

Dr. Taylor, though not so explicit, seems to hint at the same thing, (p. 192.) "It is by slow degrees that children come to the use of understanding; the animal passions being for some years the governing part of their constitution. And therefore, though they may be froward and apt to displease us, yet how far this is sin in them, we are not capable of judging. But it may suffice to say, that it is the will of God that children should have appetites and passions to regulate and restrain, that he hath given parents instructions and commands to discipline and inform their minds, that if parents first learned true wisdom for themselves, and then endeavoured to bring up their children in the way of virtue, there would be less wickedness in the world."

Concerning these things I would observe, that such a scheme is attended with the very same difficulties, which they who advance it would avoid by it; liable to the same objections, which they make against God's ordering it so, that men should be brought into being with a prevailing propensity to sin. For this scheme supposes, the Author of nature has so ordered things, that men should come into being as moral agents, that is, should first have existence in a state and capacity of moral agency, under a prevailing propensity to sin. For that strength, which sensitive appetites and animal passions come to by their habitual exercise, before persons come to the exercise of their rational powers, amounts to a strong propensity to sin, when they first come to the exercise of those rational powers, by the supposition: because this is given as a reason why the scale is turned for sin, and why, *generally speaking, the whole world lies in wickedness, and the study of virtue is a severe struggle against bad habits, early contracted, and deeply rooted.* These deeply rooted habits must imply a tendency to sin; otherwise they could not account for that which they are brought to account for, namely, prevailing wickedness in the world: for that cause cannot account for an effect, which is supposed to have no *tendency* to that effect. And this *tendency* which is supposed, is altogether equivalent to a *natural tendency*, being as necessary to the subject. For it is supposed to be brought on the person, who is the subject of it, when he has no power to oppose it; the habit, as Dr. Turnbull says, becoming very

* See *Mor. Phil.* p. 279. and *Chris. Phil.* p. 274.

† *Chris. Phil.* p. 282, 283.

strong, before reason can have force enough to call the passions to account, or assume authority over them. And it is supposed, that this necessity, by which men become subject to this propensity to sin, is from the ordering and disposal of the Author of nature; and therefore must be as much from his hand, and as much without the hand of the person himself, as if he were first brought into being with such a propensity. Moreover, it is supposed that the effect is truly *wickedness*. For it is alleged as a cause why the whole world lies in *wickedness*, and why all but a very few are first in the class of the *wicked*, and not among the righteous, that need no repentance. If they need *repentance*, what they are guilty of is truly and properly wickedness, or moral evil; for certainly men need no repentance for that which is no sin, or blamable evil. If, as a consequence of this propensity, the world lies in wickedness, and the far greater part are of a wicked character, without doubt the far greater part go to eternal perdition: for death does not pick and choose, only for men of a righteous character. And certainly that is an evil, corrupt state of things, which naturally tends to and issues in this consequence, that as it were the whole world lies and lives in wickedness, dies in wickedness, and perishes eternally. And this by the supposition, is a state of things, wholly ordered by the Author of nature, before mankind are capable of having any hand in the affair. And is this any relief to the difficulties, which these writers object against the doctrine of natural depravity?

And I might here also observe, that this way of accounting for the wickedness of the world amounts to just the same thing with that solution of man's depravity, mentioned before, against which Dr. T. cries out, as too gross to be admitted, (p. 188, 189.) *viz.* God creating the soul pure, and putting it into such a body, as naturally tends to pollute it. For this scheme supposes, that God creates the soul pure, and puts it into a body, and into such a state in that body, that the natural consequence is a strong propensity to sin, as soon as the soul is capable of sinning.

Dr. Turnbull seems to suppose, that the matter could not have been ordered otherwise, consistent with the nature of things, than that animal passions should be so aforehand with reason, as that the consequence should be that which has been mentioned; because reason is a faculty of such a nature, that it can have strength and vigour no otherwise than by exercise and culture.* But can there be any force in this? Is there any thing in nature, to make it impossible, but that the superior principles of man's nature should be so proportioned to the inferior, as to prevent such a dreadful consequence, as the moral and natural ruin, and eternal perdition of the far greater part of mankind? Could not those superior principles be in much greater strength at first, and yet be capable of endless improvement? And what should hinder its being so ordered by the Creator, that they should improve by vastly swifter degrees than they do? If we are Christians, we must be forced to allow it to be *possible* in the nature of things, that the principles of human nature should be so balanced, that the consequence should be no propensity to sin, in the very beginning of a capacity for moral agency; because we must own, that it was so in fact in *Adam*, when first created, and also in the man Christ Jesus; though the faculties of the latter were such as grew by culture and improvement, so that he increased in wisdom as he grew in stature.

Evasion V. Seeing men in this world are in a state of trial, it is fit that their virtue should meet with trials, and consequently that it should have opposition and temptation to overcome; not only from without, but from within, in the animal passions and appetites; that by the conflict and victory our virtue may be refined and established.† Agreeably to this Dr. T. (p. 253.) says, "Without a right use and application of our powers, were they naturally ever so perfect, we could not be judged fit to enter into the kingdom of God.—This gives a good reason why we are now in a state of trial and temptation, *viz.* to prove and discipline our minds, to season our virtue, and to fit us for the kingdom of God; for which, in the judgment of infinite wisdom, we cannot be qualified, but by overcoming our present temptations." And, (p. 78. S.) "We are upon trial, and it is the will of our Father that our constitution should be attended with various passions and appetites, as well as our outward condition with various temptations." He says the like in several other places. To the same purpose very often Dr. Turnbull, particularly *Chris. Phil.* p. 310. "What merit (he says) except from combat? What virtue without the encounter of such enemies, such temptations, as arise both from within and from abroad? To be virtuous, is to prefer the pleasures of virtue to those which come into competition with it, and vice holds forth to tempt us; and to dare to adhere to truth and goodness, whatever pains and hardships it may cost. There must therefore, in order to the formation and trial, in order to the very being of virtue, be pleasures of a certain kind to make temptations to vice."

In reply to these things I would say, either the state of temptation, which is supposed to be ordered for men's trial, amounts on the whole to a prevailing tendency to that state of general wickedness and ruin, which has been proved to take place, or it does not. If it does not amount to a tendency to such an effect, then how does it account for it? When it is inquired, by what cause such an effect should come to pass, is it not absurd to allege a cause, which is owned at the same time to have no tendency to such an effect? Which is as much as to confess, that it will not account for it. I think it has been demonstrated, that this effect must be owing to some prevailing tendency.—But if the other part of the dilemma be taken, and it be said, that this state of things does imply a prevailing tendency to that effect, which has been proved, *viz.* that all mankind, without one exception, sin against God, to their own deserved eternal ruin—and not only so, but sin thus immediately, as soon as capable of it, and continually, have more sin than virtue, and have guilt that infinitely outweighs the value of all the goodness any ever have, and that the generality of the world in all ages are extremely stupid and foolish, of a wicked character, and actually perish for ever—then I say, if the state of temptation implies a natural tendency to such an effect as this, it is a very evil, corrupt, and dreadful state of things, as has been already largely shown.

Besides, such a state has a tendency to defeat its own supposed end, which is to refine, ripen, and perfect virtue, and so to fit men for the greater eternal happiness and glory: whereas, the effect it tends to, is the reverse of this, *viz.* general, eternal infamy and ruin, in all generations. It is supposed, that men's virtue must have passions and appetites to struggle with, in order to have the glory and reward of victory: but the consequence is, a prevailing, continual, and generally effectual tendency—not to men's victory *over evil appetites and passions*, and the glorious reward of that victory, but—to the victory of evil appetites and lusts *over men*, utterly and eternally destroying them. If a trial of virtue be requisite, yet the question is, Whence comes so general a failing in the trial, if there be no depravity of nature? If conflict and war be necessary, whence the necessity that there should be more cowards than good soldiers? and whence is it necessary that the whole world as it were should lie in wickedness, and die in cowardice?

I might also here observe, that Dr. Turnbull is not very consistent, in supposing, that combat with temptation is requisite to the *very being* of virtue. For I think it clearly follows from his own notion of virtue, that it must have a being prior to any virtuous or praiseworthy combat with temptation. For by his principles, all virtue lies in good affection, and no actions can be virtuous, but what proceed from good affection.‡ Therefore, surely the combat itself can have no virtue in it, unless it proceeds from virtuous affection: and therefore virtue must have an existence before the combat, and be the cause of it.

* *Mor. Phil.* p. 311.

† Belsham.

‡ *Chris. Phil.* p. 113, 114, 115.

CHAP. II.

UNIVERSAL MORTALITY PROVES ORIGINAL SIN; PARTICULARLY THE DEATH OF INFANTS, WITH ITS VARIOUS CIRCUMSTANCES.

The universal reign of *death* over persons of all ages indiscriminately, with the awful circumstances and attendants of death, prove that men come sinful into the world.—It is needless here particularly to inquire, Whether God has not a sovereign right to set bounds to the lives of his own creatures, be they sinful or not; and as he gives life, so to take it away when he pleases? Or how far God has a right to bring extreme suffering and calamity on an innocent moral agent? For death, with the pains and agonies with which it is usually brought on, is not merely a limiting of existence, but is a most terrible calamity; and to such a creature as man—capable of conceiving of immortality, made with an earnest desire after it, capable of foresight and reflection on approaching death, and having an extreme dread of it—is a calamity above all others terrible. I say, it is needless elaborately to consider, whether God may not, consistent with his perfections by absolute sovereignty, bring so great a calamity on mankind when perfectly innocent. It is sufficient, if we have good evidence from Scripture, that it is not agreeable to God's manner of dealing with mankind so to do.

It is manifest, that mankind were not originally subjected to this calamity: God brought it on them afterwards, on occasion of man's sin, when manifesting his great displeasure, and by a sentence pronounced by him as a judge; which Dr. T. often confesses. Sin entered into the world, as the apostle says, and death by sin. Which certainly leads us to suppose, that this affair was ordered, not merely by the sovereignty of a creator, but by the righteousness of a judge. And the Scripture every where speaks of all great afflictions and calamities, which God in his providence brings on mankind, as testimonies of his displeasure for sin, in the subjects of those calamities; excepting those sufferings which are to atone for the sins of others. He ever taught his people to look on such calamities as his *rod, the rod of* his *anger*, his *frown*, the *hidings of his face* in displeasure. Hence such calamities are in Scripture so often called by the name of *judgments*, being what God brings on men as a *judge*, executing a righteous sentence for transgression. Yea, they are often called by the name of *wrath*, especially calamities consisting or issuing in death.* And hence also is that which Dr. T. would have us take so much notice of, that sometimes, in the Scripture, calamity and suffering is called by such names as *sin, iniquity, being guilty, &c.* which is evidently by a metonymy of the cause for the effect. It is not likely that, in the language used of old among God's people, calamity or suffering would have been called by the names of sin and guilt, if it had been so far from having any connexion with sin, that even death itself, which is always spoken of as the most terrible of calamities, is not so much as any sign of the sinfulness of the subject, or any testimony of God's displeasure for his guilt, as Dr. T. supposes.

Death is spoken of in Scripture as the *chief* of calamities, the most extreme and terrible of all natural evils in this world. *Deadly destruction* is spoken of as the most terrible destruction. (1 Sam. v. 11.) *Deadly sorrow*, as the most extreme sorrow. (Isa. xvii. 11. Matt. xxvi. 38.) And *deadly enemies*, as the most bitter and terrible enemies. (Psal. xvii. 9.) The extremity of Christ's sufferings is represented by his suffering *unto death*. (Philip. ii. 8. and other places.) Hence the greatest testimonies of God's anger for the sins of men in this world, have been by inflicting *death;* as on the sinners of the old world; on the inhabitants of *Sodom* and *Gomorrah;* on *Onan, Pharaoh*, and the *Egyptians;* on *Nadab* and *Abihu, Korah* and his company, and the rest of the rebels in the wilderness; on the wicked inhabitants of *Canaan;* on *Hophni* and *Phinehas, Ananias* and *Sapphira*, and the unbelieving *Jews*, upon whom wrath came to the uttermost, in the time of the last destruction of *Jerusalem*. This calamity is often spoken of as in a peculiar manner the fruit of guilt. Exod. xxviii. 43. "That they bear not iniquity and *die*." Levit. xxii. 9. "Lest they bear sin for it and *die*." (So Num. xviii. 22. compared with Levit. x. 1, 2.) The very light of nature, or tradition from ancient revelation, led the heathen to conceive of death as in a peculiar manner an evidence of divine vengeance. Thus we have an account, (Acts xxviii. 4.) That "when the barbarians saw the venomous beast hang on Paul's hand, they said among themselves, no doubt this man is a murderer, whom though he hath escaped the seas, yet *vengeance suffereth not to live*."

Calamities, very small in comparison of the universal temporal destruction of mankind by death, are spoken of as manifest indications of God's great displeasure for the sinfulness of the subject; such as the destruction of particular cities, countries, or numbers of men, by war or pestilence. Deut. xxix. 24. "All nations shall say, Wherefore hath the Lord done thus unto this land? what meaneth the heat of this great anger?" (Compare Deut. xxxii. 30. 1 Kings ix. 8. and Jer. xxii. 8, 9.) These calamities, thus spoken of as plain testimonies of God's great anger, consisted only in *hastening* on that death, which otherwise, by God's disposal, would most certainly have come in a short time. Now to take off thirty or forty years from seventy or eighty, supposing it to be so much, one with another, in the time of these extraordinary judgments, is but a small matter, in comparison of God first making man mortal, cutting off his hope of immortality, subjecting him to inevitable death, which his nature so exceedingly dreads; and afterwards shortening his life further, by cutting off more than eight hundred years of it: so bringing it to be less than a twelfth part of what it was in the first ages of the world. Besides that innumerable multitudes in the common course of things, without any extraordinary judgment, die in youth, in childhood, and infancy. Therefore how inconsiderable a thing is the additional or hastened destruction, that is sometimes brought on a particular city or country by war, compared with that universal havoc which death makes of the whole human race, from generation to generation, without distinction of sex, age, quality, or condition; with all the infinitely various dismal circumstances, torments, and agonies, which attend the death of old and young, adult persons and little infants! If those particular and comparatively trivial calamities, extending perhaps not to more than the thousandth part of one generation, are clear evidences of God's great anger; certainly this universal destruction—by which the whole world, in all generations, is swallowed up, as by a flood that nothing can resist—must be a most glaring manifestation of God's anger for the sinfulness of mankind. Yea, the Scripture is express, that it is so: (Psal. xc. 3, &c.) "Thou turnest man to destruction, and sayest, Return, ye children of men.—Thou carriest them away as with a flood: they are as a sleep: in the morning they are like grass, which groweth up; in the morning it flourisheth and groweth up; in the evening it is cut down and withereth. For we are consumed by thine anger, and by thy wrath are we troubled. Thou hast set our iniquities before thee, our secret sins in the light of thy countenance. For all our days are passed away in thy wrath: we spend our years as a tale that is told. The days of our years are threescore years and ten: and if by reason of strength they be fourscore years, yet is their strength labour and sorrow; for it is soon cut off, and we fly away. Who knoweth the power of thine anger? According to thy fear, so is thy wrath. So teach us to number our days that we may apply our hearts unto wisdom." How plain and full is this testimony, that the general mortality of mankind is an evidence of God's anger for the sin of those who are the subjects of such a dispensation!

Abimelech speaks of it as what he had reason to conclude from God's nature and perfection, *that he would not slay a righteous nation*. Gen. xx. 4. By *righteous* evidently meaning *innocent*. And if so, much less *will God slay a righteous world*—consisting of so many nations, repeating

* See Lev. x. 6. Num. i. 53. and xviii. 5. Josh. ix. 20. 2 Chron. xxiv. 18. and xix. 2, 10. and xxviii. 13. and xxxii. 25 Ezra vii. 23. Neh. xiii. 18. Zech. vii. 12. and many other places.

the great slaughter in every generation—or subject the whole world of mankind to death, when they are considered as innocent, as Dr. T. supposes. We have from time to time in Scripture such phrases as—*worthy of death*, and *guilty of death*: but certainly the righteous Judge of all the earth will not bring death on thousands of millions, not only that are not worthy of death, but are worthy of no punishment at all.

Dr. T. from time to time speaks of affliction and death as a great *benefit*, as they increase the vanity of all earthly things, and tend to excite sober reflections, and to induce us to be moderate in gratifying the appetites of the body, and to mortify pride and ambition, &c.* To this I would say,

1. It is not denied but God may see it needful for mankind in their present state, that they should be mortal, and subject to outward afflictions, to restrain their lusts, mortify their pride, &c. But then is it not an evidence of man's *depravity*, that it is so? Is it not an evidence of distemper of mind, yea, strong disease, when man stands in need of such sharp medicines, such severe and terrible means to restrain his lusts, keep down his pride, and to make him willing, and obedient to God? It must be owing to a corrupt and ungrateful heart, if the riches of divine bounty, in bestowing life and prosperity, things comfortable and pleasant, will not engage the heart to God and virtue, love and obedience. Whereas he must always have the *rod* held over him, be often *chastised*, and held under the apprehensions of death, to keep him from running wild in pride, contempt, and rebellion; ungratefully using the blessings dealt forth from God's hand, in sinning against him, and serving his enemies. If man has no natural disingenuity of heart, it must be a mysterious thing indeed, that the sweet blessings of God's bounty have not as powerful an influence to restrain him from sinning against God, as terrible afflictions. If any thing can be a proof of a perverse and vile disposition, this must be a proof of it, that men should be most apt to forget and despise God, when his providence is most kind; and that they should need to have God chastising them with great severity, and even killing them, to keep them in order. If we were as much disposed to gratitude to God for his benefits, as we are to anger at our fellow-creatures for injuries, as we must be (so far as I can see) if we are not of a depraved heart; then the sweetness of divine bounty, and the height of every enjoyment pleasing to innocent human nature, would be as powerful incentives to a proper regard for God—tending as much to promote religion and virtue—as to have the world filled with calamities, and to have God (to use the language of *Hezekiah*, Isaiah xxviii. 13. describing death and its agonies) *as a lion, breaking all our bones, and from day even to night, making an end of us.*

Dr. T. himself (p. 252.) says, "that our first parents before the fall were placed in a condition proper to engage their gratitude, love, and obedience." Which is as much as to say, a condition proper to engage them to the exercise and practice of all religion. And if the paradisaical state was proper to engage to all religion and duty, and men still come into the world with hearts as good as the two first of the species, why is it not proper to engage them to it still? What need of so vastly changing man's state, depriving him of all those blessings, and instead of them allotting to him a world full of briers and thorns, affliction, calamity, and death, to engage him to it? The taking away of life, and all those pleasant enjoyments man had at first, by a permanent constitution, would be no stated benefit to mankind, unless there was in them a stated disposition to abuse such blessings. The taking of them away, is supposed to be a benefit, under the notion of their tending to lead men to sin: but they would have no such tendency, at least in a *stated* manner, unless there was in men a *fixed* tendency to make that unreasonable misimprovement of them. Such a temper of mind, as amounts to a disposition to make such a misimprovement of blessings, is often spoken of in Scripture as most astonishingly vile and perverse. So concerning *Israel* abusing the blessings of *Canaan*, that land flowing with milk and honey; their ingratitude in it is spoken of by the prophets, as enough to astonish all heaven and earth, and as more than brutish stupidity and vileness. Jer. ii. 7. "I brought them into a plentiful country, to eat the fruit thereof, and the goodness thereof. But when ye entered, ye defiled my land," &c. See the following verses, especially ver. 12. "Be astonished, O ye heavens, at this." So Isa. i. 2—4. "Hear, O heavens, and give ear, O earth; I have nourished and brought up children, and they have rebelled against me. The ox knoweth his owner, and the ass his master's crib; but my people doth not know, Israel doth not consider. Ah, sinful nation! a people laden with iniquity, a seed of evil-doers, children that are corrupters." (Compare Deut. xxxii. 6—19.) If to be disposed thus to abuse the blessings of so fruitful and pleasant a land as *Canaan*, showed so great depravity, surely it would be an evidence of a corruption no less astonishing, to be inclined to abuse the blessings of *Eden*, and the garden of God.

2. If death be brought on mankind only as a benefit, and in that manner which Dr. T. mentions,—to mortify or moderate their carnal appetites and affections, wean them from the world, excite them to sober reflections, and lead them to the fear and obedience of God, &c.—is it not strange that it should fall so heavily on infants, who are not capable of making any such improvement of it; so that many more of mankind suffer death in infancy, than in any other equal part of the age of man? Our author sometimes hints, that the death of infants may be for the correction and punishment of parents. But hath God any need of such methods to add to parents' afflictions? Are there not other ways for increasing their trouble, without destroying the lives of such multitudes of those who are perfectly innocent, and who, on the supposition, have in no respect any sin belonging to them? On whom death comes at an age, when not only the subjects are not capable of reflection, or making any improvement of it, either in suffering, or the expectation of it: but also at an age, when parents and friends—who alone can improve, and whom Dr. T. supposes alone to be punished by it—suffer least by being bereaved of them; though the infants themselves sometimes suffer to great extremity?

3. To suppose, as Dr. T. does, that death is brought on mankind in consequence of *Adam's* sin, not at all as a calamity but only as a *favour* and benefit, is contrary to the gospel; which teaches, that when Christ, as the second *Adam*, comes to remove and destroy that death, which came by the first *Adam*, he finds it not as a friend, but an enemy. 1 Cor. xv. 22. "For as in Adam all die, so in Christ shall all be made alive;" (with ver. 25, and 26.) "For he must reign, till he hath put all enemies under his feet. The last ENEMY that shall be destroyed, is DEATH."

Dr. T. urges, that the afflictions to which mankind are subjected, and particularly their common mortality, are represented in Scripture as the chastisements of our heavenly Father; and therefore are designed for our spiritual good, and consequently are not of the nature of punishments. (So in p. 68, 69. 38, 39. S.)

Though I think the thing asserted far from being true, *viz.* that the Scripture represents the afflictions of mankind in general, and particularly their common mortality, as the chastisement of a heavenly Father; yet it is needless to stand to dispute that matter. For if it be so, it will be no argument that the afflictions and death of mankind are not evidences of their sinfulness. Those would be strange chastisements from the hand of a wise and good Father, which are wholly for nothing; especially such severe chastisements, as to break the child's bones, when at the same time the father does not suppose any guilt, fault, or offence, in any respect, belonging to the child; but it is chastised in this terrible manner, only for fear that it will be faulty hereafter. I say, these would be a strange sort of chastisements; yea, though he should be able to make it up to the child afterwards. Dr. T. speaks of representations made by the whole current of Scripture; I am certain, it is not agreeable to the current of Scripture, to represent divine fatherly chastisements after this manner. It is true, the Scripture supposes such chastenings to be the fruit of God's goodness; yet at the

* P 21, 67, and other places.

same time it evermore represents them as being for the *sin* of the subject, and as evidences of the divine displeasure for its *sinfulness*. Thus the apostle (1 Cor. xi. 30—32.) speaks of God chastening his people by mortal sickness, for their good, *that they might not be condemned with the world*, and yet signifies that it was *for their sin;* FOR THIS CAUSE *many are weak and sickly among you, and many sleep*: that is, for the profaneness and sinful disorder before mentioned. So *Elihu*, (Job xxxiii. 16, &c.) speaks of the same *chastening* by sickness, as for men's good; *to withdraw man from his* sinful *purpose, and to hide pride from man, and keep back his soul from the pit; that therefore God chastens man with pain on his bed, and the multitude of his bones with strong pain*. But these chastenings are for his SINS, as appears by what follows; (ver. 28.) Where it is observed, that when God by this means has brought men to *repent*, and humbly *confess their sins*, he delivers them. Again, the same *Elihu*, speaking of the unfailing love of God to the righteous, even when he *chastens them*, and *they are bound in fetters, and holden in cords of affliction*, (chap. xxxvi. 7, &c.) yet speaks of these chastenings as being for their SINS, (ver. 9.) "Then he showeth them their work, and their transgressions, that they have exceeded." So *David* (Psal. xxx.) speaks of God's *chastening* by some afflictions, as being for his good, and issuing joyfully; and yet being the fruit of God's anger for his sin, (ver. 5.) *God's* ANGER *endureth but for a moment*, &c. (compare Psal. cxix. 67, 71, 75.) God's fatherly chastisements are spoken of as being for sin. (2 Sam. vii. 14, 15.) "I will be his father, and he shall be my son. If he commit *iniquity*, I will chasten him with the rod of men, and with the stripes of the children of men; but my mercy shall not depart away from him." So the prophet *Jeremiah* speaks of the great affliction that God's people suffered in the time of the captivity, as being for their *good*. (Lam. iii. 25, &c.) But yet these chastisements are spoken of as being for their SIN, (see especially ver. 39, 40.) So Christ says, Rev. iii. 19. "As many as I love, I rebuke and chasten." But the words following show, that these chastenings from love are for sin that should be repented of: "Be zealous therefore, and repent." And though Christ tells us, they are blessed that are persecuted for righteousness' sake, and have reason to rejoice and be exceeding glad; yet even the persecutions of God's people, as ordered in divine providence, are spoken of as divine chastenings for sin, like the just corrections of a father, when the children deserve them, Heb. xii. The apostle there speaking to the Christians concerning the persecutions which they suffered, calls their sufferings by the name of divine *rebukes;* which implies testifying *against a fault:* and that they may not be discouraged, puts them in mind, that whom the Lord loves he chastens, and scourgeth every son that he receiveth. It is also very plain, that the persecutions of God's people, as they are from the disposing hand of God, are chastisements for SIN.*

If divine chastisements in general are certain evidences that the subjects are not wholly without sin, some way belonging to them, then in a peculiar manner is death so; for these reasons:

(1.) Because slaying, or delivering to death, is often spoken of as, in general, a more awful thing than the chastisements which are endured in this life. Thus, Psal. cxviii. 17, 18. "I shall not die, but live, and declare the works of the Lord. The Lord hath chastened me sore; but he hath not given me over unto death." So the Psalmist, (Psal. lxxxviii. 15.) setting forth the extremity of his affliction, represents it as what was next to death. "I am afflicted, and ready to die,—while I suffer thy terrors, I am distracted." (See 1 Sam. xx. 3.) And so God's tenderness towards persons under chastisement, is, from time to time, set forth, that he did not proceed so far, as to make an end of them by death.† God's people often pray, when under great affliction, that God would not proceed to this, as the greatest extremity. Psal. xiii. 3. "Consider, and hear me, O Lord, my God; lighten mine eyes, lest I sleep the sleep of death."‡

Especially may death be looked upon as the most extreme of all temporal sufferings, when attended with such dreadful circumstances, and extreme pains, as those with which Providence sometimes brings it on *infants;* as on the children that were offered up to *Moloch*, and some other idols, who were tormented to death in burning brass. Dr. T. says, (p. 83, 128. S.) "The Lord of all being can never want time, and place, and power, to compensate abundantly any sufferings infants now undergo in subserviency to his good providence." But there are no bounds to such a licence, in evading evidences from fact. It might as well be said, that there is not and cannot be any such thing as evidence, from events of God's displeasure; which is most contrary to the whole current of Scripture, as may appear in part from what has been observed. This gentleman might as well go further still, and say, that God may cast guiltless persons into hell fire, to remain there in the most unutterable torments for ages of ages, (which bear no greater proportion to eternity than a quarter of an hour,) and if he does so, it is no evidence of God's displeasure; because he can never want time, place, and power, abundantly to compensate their sufferings afterwards. If it be so, it is not to the purpose, as long as the Scripture so abundantly teaches us to look on great calamities and sufferings which God brings on men, especially death, as marks of his displeasure for sin, and for sin belonging to them who suffer.

(2.) Another thing—which may well lead us to suppose death, in a peculiar manner, above other temporal sufferings, to be intended as a testimony of God's displeasure for sin—is, that death is attended with that awful appearance, that gloomy and terrible aspect, which naturally suggests to our minds God's awful displeasure. Of this Dr. T. himself takes particular notice, when (p. 69.) speaking of death; "Herein (says he) have we before our eyes a striking demonstration, that sin is infinitely hateful to God, and the corruption and ruin of our nature. Nothing is more proper than such a sight to give us the utmost abhorrence of all iniquity," &c. Now, if death be no testimony of God's displeasure for sin—no evidence that the subject is looked upon, by him who inflicts it, as any other than perfectly innocent, free from all imputation of guilt, and treated only as an object of favour—is it not strange, that God should annex to it such affecting appearances of his hatred and anger for sin, more than to other chastisements? Which yet the Scripture teaches us are always for sin. These gloomy and striking manifestations of God's hatred of sin attending death, are equivalent to the awful frowns of God attending the stroke of his hand. If we should see a wise and just father chastising his child, mixing terrible frowns with severe strokes, we should justly argue, that the father considered his child as having in him something displeasing, and that he did not thus treat his child *only* under a notion of *mortifying* him, and preventing his being faulty *hereafter*, and making it up to him afterwards, when he had been perfectly innocent, and without fault, either of action or disposition.

We may well argue from these things, that infants are not sinless, but are by nature children of wrath, seeing this terrible evil comes so heavily on mankind at this early period. But, besides the mortality of infants in general, there are some *particular cases* of their death attended with circumstances, which, in a peculiar manner, give evidence of their sinfulness, and of their just exposedness to divine wrath. Particularly,

The destroying of the infants in *Sodom* and the neighbouring cities, may be pleaded in evidence; for these cities destroyed in so miraculous and awful a manner, are set forth as a signal example of God's dreadful vengeance for sin. (Jude, ver. 7.) God did not reprove, but manifestly countenanced, *Abraham*, when he said, with respect to the destruction of *Sodom*, (Gen. xviii. 23, 25.) "Wilt thou destroy the righteous with the wicked? That be far from thee to do after this manner, to slay the righteous with the wicked, and that the righteous should be as the wicked, that be far from thee. Shall not the Judge of all the earth do right?" *Abraham's* words imply that God

* See 1 Pet. iv. 17, 18, compared with Prov. xi. 31. See also Psal. lxix. 4—9.

† As in Psal. lxxviii. 38, 39. Psal. ciii. 9, with ver. 14, 15. Psal. xxx. 2, 3, 9. and Job xxxiii. 22—24.

‡ So Job x. 9. Psal. vi. 1—5. lxxxviii 9, 10, 11. and cxliii. 7.

would not destroy the *innocent* with the *guilty*. We may well understand *innocent* as included in the word *righteous*, according to the language usual in Scripture, in speaking of such cases of judgment and punishment.* Eliphaz says, Job iv. 7. "Who ever perished, being *innocent?* or where were the *righteous* cut off?" We see what great care God took that *Lot* should not be involved in that destruction. He was miraculously rescued by angels, sent on purpose; who laid hold on him, brought him, set him without the gates of the city, and told him that they could do nothing till he was out of the way. (Gen. xix. 22.) And not only was he thus miraculously delivered, but his two wicked daughters for his sake. The whole affair, both the destruction and the rescue, was miraculous; and God could as easily have delivered the infants which were in those cities. And if they had been without sin, their perfect innocency, one should think, would have pleaded much more strongly for them, than those lewd women's relation to *Lot* pleaded for them. When in such a case, we must suppose these infants much further from deserving to be involved in that destruction, than even *Lot* himself. To say, that God could make it up to those infants in another world, must be an insufficient reply. For so he could as easily have made it up to *Lot*, or to *ten* or *fifty righteous*, if they had been destroyed in the same fire. Nevertheless, it is plainly signified, that this would not have been agreeable to the wise and holy proceedings of *the judge of all the earth*.

Since God declared, that if there had been found but ten righteous in *Sodom*, he would have spared the whole city for their sakes, may we not well suppose, if infants are perfectly innocent, that he would have spared the *old world*, in which there were, without doubt, many hundred thousand infants, and in general, one in every family, whose perfect innocence pleaded for its preservation? Especially when such vast care was taken to save *Noah* and his family, (some of whom, one at least, seem to have been none of the best,) that they might not be involved in that destruction. If the perfect sinlessness of infants had been a notion entertained among the people of God, in the ages next following the flood—handed down from *Noah* and his children, who well knew that vast multitudes of infants perished in the flood—is it likely that *Eliphaz*, who lived within a few generations of *Shem* and *Noah*, would have said to *Job*, (Job iv. 7.) "Who ever perished, being innocent? and when were the righteous cut off? Especially, since in the same discourse (chap. v. 1.) he appeals to the tradition of the ancients for a confirmation of this very point, (also in chap. xv. 7—10. and xxii. 15, 16.) and he mentions the destruction of the wicked by the flood, as an instance of that perishing of the wicked, which he supposes to be peculiar to them, for *Job's* conviction; in which *the wicked were cut down out of time, their foundation being overflown with a flood.* Where it is also observable, that he speaks of such an *untimeliness* of death as they suffered by the flood, as one evidence of guilt; as he also does, chap. xv. 32, 33. "It shall be accomplished before his time; and his branch shall not be green." But those who were destroyed by the flood in infancy, above all the rest, were *cut down out of time;* when instead of living above nine hundred years, according to the common period of man's life, at that time, many were cut down before they were one year old.

When God executed vengeance on the ancient inhabitants of *Canaan,* he not only did not spare their cities and families for the sake of their infants, nor took care that they should not be involved in the destruction; but he often repeated his express commands, that their infants should not be spared, but should be utterly destroyed, without any pity; while *Rahab* the *harlot* (who had been far from innocence, though she expressed her faith in entertaining and safely dismissing the spies) was preserved, and all her friends for her sake. And when God executed his wrath on the *Egyptians*, by slaying their first-born—though the children of *Israel*, who were most of them wicked men, as was before shown, were wonderfully spared by the destroying angel, yet—the *Egyptian* infants were not spared. They not only were not rescued by the angel, and no miracle wrought to save them, (as was observed in the case of the infants of *Sodom*,) but the angel destroyed them by his own immediate hand, and a miracle was wrought to kill them.

Not to be particular, concerning the command by *Moses*, respecting the destruction of the infants of the *Midianites;* (Numb. xxxi. 17.) and that given to *Saul* to destroy all the infants of the *Amalekites;* (1 Sam. xv. 3.) and what is said concerning *Edom*, (Psal. cxxxvii. 9.) "Happy shall he be, that taketh and dasheth thy little ones against the stones;" I proceed to take notice of something remarkable concerning the destruction of *Jerusalem*, represented in Ezek. ix. when command was given to destroy the inhabitants, ver. 1—8. And this reason is given for it, that their iniquity required it, and it was a just recompence of their sin, (ver. 9, 10.) God, at the same time, was most particular and exact in his care, that such as had proved by their behaviour, that they were not partakers in the abominations of the city, should by no means be involved in the slaughter. Command was given to the angel to go through the city, and set a mark upon their foreheads, and the destroying angel had a strict charge not to come near any man, on whom was the mark; yet the infants were not marked, nor a word said of sparing them: on the contrary, infants were expressly mentioned as those that should be utterly destroyed, without pity, (ver. 5, 6.) "Go through the city and smite: let not your eye spare, neither have ye pity. Slay utterly old and *young*, both maids and *little children:* but come not near any man upon whom is the mark."

And if any should suspect, that such instances as these were peculiar to a more severe dispensation, under the Old Testament, let us consider a remarkable instance in the days of the glorious gospel of the grace of God; even the last destruction of *Jerusalem*. This was far more terrible, and with greater testimonies of God's wrath and indignation, than the destruction of *Sodom*, or of *Jerusalem* in *Nebuchadnezzar's* time, or any thing that ever had happened to any city, or people, from the beginning of the world to that time. (Agreeable to Matt. xxiv. 21. and Luke xxi. 22, 23.) At that time particular care was taken to distinguish and to deliver God's people; as foretold, Dan. xii. 1. And we have in the New Testament a particular account of the care Christ took for the preservation of his followers: he gave them a sign, by which they might know when the desolation of the city was nigh, that they who were in *Jerusalem* might flee to the mountains, and escape. And, as history relates, the Christians followed the directions given, and escaped to a place in the mountains called *Pella*, and were preserved. Yet no care was taken to preserve the infants of the city, in general; but according to the predictions of that event, they were involved with others in that great destruction. So heavily did the calamity fall upon them, that those words were verified, Luke xxiii. 29. "Behold the days are coming, in which they shall say, Blessed are the barren, and the womb that never bare, and the paps which never gave suck:" and that prophecy in Deut. xxxii. 21—25. which has undoubtedly a special respect to this very time, and is so applied by the best commentators;—"I will provoke them to jealousy with those that are not a people: for a fire is kindled in mine anger,—and it shall burn to the lowest hell. I will heap mischiefs upon them: I will spend mine arrows upon them. They shall be burnt with hunger, and devoured with burning heat, and bitter destruction. The sword without, and terror within, shall destroy both the young man, and the virgin, the *suckling* also, with the man of grey hairs." And, by the history of that destruction appears, that then it was a remarkable fulfilment of Deut. xxviii. 53—57. concerning *parents eating their children in the siege,—and the tender and delicate woman eating her new-born child.* And here it must be remembered, that these very destructions of that city and land are spoken of as clear evidences of God's wrath, to all nations who shall behold them. And if so, they were evidences of God's wrath towards *infants;* who, equally with the rest, were the subject of the destruction. If a particular kind or rank of persons, which made

* Gen. xx. 4. Exod. xxiii. 7. Deut. xxv. 1. 2 Sam. iv. 11. 2 Chron. vi. 23. and Prov. xviii. 5.

made a very considerable part of the inhabitants, were from time to time partakers of the overthrow, without any distinction made in Divine Providence, and yet this was no evidence at all of God's displeasure with any of them; then being the subjects of such a calamity could not be an evidence of God's wrath against *any* of the inhabitants, to the reason of *all nations*, or any nation, or so much as one person.

PART II.

CONTAINING OBSERVATIONS ON PARTICULAR PARTS OF THE HOLY SCRIPTURE, WHICH PROVE THE DOCTRINE OF ORIGINAL SIN.

CHAP. I.

OBSERVATIONS RELATING TO THINGS CONTAINED IN THE THREE FIRST CHAPTERS OF GENESIS, WITH REFERENCE TO THE DOCTRINE OF ORIGINAL SIN.

SECT. I.

Concerning original righteousness; and whether our first parents were created with righteousness, or moral rectitude of heart?

THE doctrine of *Original Righteousness*, or the creation of our first parents with holy principles and dispositions, has a close connexion, in several respects, with the doctrine of original sin. Dr. T. was sensible of this; and accordingly he strenuously opposes this doctrine, in his book against original sin. And therefore in handling the subject, I would in the first place remove this author's main objection against this doctrine, and then show how it may be inferred from the account which *Moses* gives us, in *the three first chapters of Genesis*.

Dr. T.'s grand objection against this doctrine, which he abundantly insists on, is this: that it is utterly inconsistent with the nature of virtue, that it should be concreated with any person; because, if so, it must be by an act of God's absolute power, without our knowledge or concurrence; and that moral virtue, in its very nature, implieth the choice and consent of the moral agent, without which it cannot be virtue and holiness: that a *necessary* holiness is *no* holiness. So p. 180. where he observes, "That *Adam* must exist, he must be created, yea he must exercise thought and reflection, before he was righteous." (See also p. 250, 251.) In p. 161. S. he says, "To say, that God not only endowed *Adam* with a capacity of being righteous, but moreover that righteousness and true holiness were created with him, or wrought into his nature, at the same time he was made, is to affirm a contradiction, or what is inconsistent with the very nature of righteousness." And in like manner Dr. Turnbull in many places insists upon it, that it is necessary to the very being of virtue, that it be owing to our own choice, and diligent culture.

With respect to this, I would observe, that it consists in a notion of virtue quite inconsistent with the nature of things, and the common notions of mankind; and also inconsistent with Dr. T.'s own notions of virtue. Therefore, if to affirm that to be virtue or holiness, which is not the fruit of preceding thought, reflection, and choice, is to affirm a contradiction, I shall show plainly, that for him to affirm otherwise, is a contradiction to himself.

In the first place, I think it a contradiction to the nature of things, as judged of by the common sense of mankind. It is agreeable to the sense of men, in all nations and ages, not only that the fruit or effect of a good choice is virtuous, but that the good choice itself, from whence that effect proceeds, is so; yea, also the antecedent good disposition, temper, or affection of mind, from whence proceeds that *good* choice, is virtuous. This is the general notion—not that principles derive their goodness from actions, but—that actions derive their goodness from the principles whence they proceed; so that the act of choosing what is good, is no further virtuous, than it proceeds from a good principle, or virtuous disposition of mind. Which supposes, that a virtuous disposition of mind may be before a virtuous act of choice; and that, therefore, it is not necessary there should first be thought, reflection, and choice, before there can be any virtuous disposition. If the choice be first, before the existence of a good disposition of heart, what is the character of that choice? There can, according to our natural notions, be no virtue in a choice which proceeds from no virtuous principle, but from mere self-love, ambition, or some animal appetites; therefore, a virtuous temper of mind may be before a good act of choice, as a tree may be before the fruit, and the fountain before the stream which proceeds from it.

The following things, in Mr. Hutcheson's inquiry concerning moral good and evil, are evidently agreeable to the nature of things, and the voice of human sense and reason. (Sect. II. p. 132, 133.) "Every action which we apprehend as either morally good or evil, is always supposed to FLOW FROM some affections towards sensitive natures. And whatever we call virtue or vice, is either some such affection, or some action CONSEQUENT UPON IT.—All the actions counted religious in any country, are supposed by those who count them so, to FLOW FROM some affections towards the Deity: and whatever we call social virtue, we still suppose to FLOW FROM affections towards our fellow-creatures.—Prudence, if it is only employed in promoting private interest, is never imagined to be a virtue." In these things Dr. Turnbull expressly agrees with Mr. Hutcheson, his admired author.*

If a virtuous disposition or affection is before its acts, then they are before those virtuous acts of choice which proceed from it. Therefore, there is no necessity that all virtuous dispositions or affections should be the effect of choice: and so, no such supposed necessity can be a good objection against such a disposition being natural, or from a kind of instinct, implanted in the mind in its creation. Agreeably to this Mr. Hutcheson says, (*Ibid.* sect. III. p. 196, 197.) "I know not for what reason some will not allow that to be virtue, which flows from instinct or passions. But how do they help themselves? They say, virtue arises from reason. What is reason, but the sagacity we have in prosecuting any end? The ultimate end proposed by common moralists, is the happiness of the agent himself. And this certainly he is determined to pursue from instinct. Now may not another instinct towards the public, or the good of others, be as proper a principle of virtue as the instinct towards private happiness? If it be said, that actions from instinct are not the effect of prudence and choice, this objection will hold full as strongly against the actions which flow from self-love."

And if we consider what Dr. T. declares, as his own notion of the essence of virtue, and which he so confidently and often affirms, that it should follow choice, and proceed from it, we shall find it is no less repugnant to that sentiment, than it is to the nature of things, and the general notions of mankind. For it is his notion, as well as Mr. Hutcheson's, that the essence of virtue lies in *good affection*, and particularly in benevolence or *love*: as he very fully declares in these words in his Key,† "That the word that signifies goodness and mercy should also signify moral rectitude in general, will not seem strange, if we consider that *love* is the fulfilling of the law. Goodness, according to the sense of Scripture, and the nature of things, includes all *moral rectitude*; which, I reckon,

* *Mor. Phil.* p. 112—115. p. 142. *et alibi passim.*

† Marginal Note, annexed to § 358.

may every part of it, where it is true and genuine, be resolved into this *single principle.*" If it be so indeed, then certainly no act whatsoever can have *moral rectitude,* but what proceeds from *this principle.* And consequently no act of volition or choice can have any moral rectitude, that takes place before this principle exists. And yet he most confidently affirms, that thought, reflection, and choice must go before virtue, and that all virtue or righteousness must be the fruit of preceding choice. This brings his scheme to an evident contradiction. For no act of choice can be virtuous but what proceeds from a principle of benevolence, or *love;* for he insists that all genuine moral rectitude, in every part of it, is resolved into this single principle. And yet the principle of benevolence itself cannot be virtuous, unless it proceeds from choice; for he affirms, that nothing can have the nature of virtue but what comes from choice. So that virtuous love as the principle of all virtue, must go before virtuous choice, and be the principle or spring of it; and yet virtuous choice must go before virtuous benevolence, and be the spring of that. If a virtuous act of choice goes before a principle of benevolence, and produces it, then this virtuous act is something distinct from that principle which follows it, and is its effect. So that here is at least one part of virtue, yea the spring and source of all virtue, *viz.* a virtuous choice, that cannot be resolved into that single principle of *love.*

Here also it is worthy to be observed, that Dr. T. (p. 128.) says, *the cause of every effect is alone chargeable with the effect it produceth or which proceedeth from it*. and so he argues, that if the effect be *bad,* the cause *alone* is sinful. According to which reasoning, when the effect is *good,* the cause *alone* is righteous or virtuous. To the cause is to be ascribed all the praise of the good effect it produceth. And by the same reasoning it will follow, that if, as Dr. Taylor says, Adam must *choose* to be righteous, before he was righteous, and if it be essential to the nature of righteousness, or moral rectitude, that it be the effect of choice, and hence a principle of benevolence cannot have moral rectitude, unless it proceeds from choice; then not the principle of benevolence, which is the effect, but to the foregoing choice alone is to be ascribed all the virtue or righteousness that is in the case. And so, instead of all moral rectitude, in every part of it, being resolved into that single principle of benevolence, no moral rectitude, in any part of it, is to be resolved into that principle; but all is to be resolved into the foregoing choice, which is the cause.

But yet it follows from these inconsistent principles, that there is no moral rectitude or virtue in that first act of choice, that is the cause of all consequent virtue. This follows two ways; 1. Because every part of virtue lies in the benevolent principle, which is the effect; and therefore no part of it can lie in the cause. 2. The choice of virtue, as to the first act at least, can have no virtue or righteousness at all; because it does not proceed from any foregoing choice. For Dr. T. insists, that a man must first have reflection and choice, before he can have righteousness; and that it is essential to holiness that it proceed from choice. So that the first choice from which holiness proceeds, can have no virtue at all, because, by the supposition, it does not proceed from choice, being the first choice. Hence, if it be essential to holiness that it proceeds from choice, it must proceed from an unholy choice; unless the first holy choice can be *before itself.*

And with respect to Adam, let us consider how upon Dr. T.'s principles, it was possible he ever should have any such thing as righteousness, by any means at all. In the state wherein God created him, he could have no such thing as love to God, or any benevolence in his heart. For if so, there would have been original righteousness; there would have been *genuine moral rectitude;* nothing would have been wanting: for our author says, *True genuine moral rectitude, in every part of it, is to be resolved into this single principle.* But if he were wholly without any such thing as love to God, or any virtuous love, how should he come by virtue? The answer doubtless will be, by act of choice: he must first choose to be virtuous. But what if he did choose to be virtuous? It could not be from love to God, or any virtuous principle, that he chose it; for, by the supposition, he has no such principle in his heart. And if he chooses it without such a principle, still, according to this author, there is no virtue in his choice; for all virtue, he says, is to be resolved into that single principle of love. Or will he say, there may be produced in the heart a virtuous benevolence by an act or acts of choice, that are not virtuous? But this does not consist with what he implicitly asserts, that to the cause alone is to be ascribed what is in the effect. So that there is no way that can possibly be devised, in consistence with Dr. T.'s scheme, in which Adam ever could have any righteousness, or could ever either obtain any principle of virtue, or perform any one virtuous act.

These confused inconsistent assertions, concerning virtue and moral rectitude, arise from the absurd notions in vogue, concerning *freedom of will,* as if it consisted in the will's *self-determining power,* supposed to be necessary to moral agency, virtue, and vice. The absurdities of which, with the grounds of these errors, and what the truth is respecting these matters, with its evidences, I have, according to my ability, fully and largely considered, in my "*Inquiry*" on that subject; to which I must refer the reader, who desires further satisfaction, and is willing to give himself the trouble of reading that discourse.

Having considered this great argument, and pretended demonstration of Dr. T. against original righteousness; I proceed to the *proofs* of the doctrine. And, in the first place, I would consider, whether there be not evidence of it in the *three first* chapters of *Genesis:* or, whether the history there delivered does not lead us to suppose, that our *first parents* were created in a state of moral rectitude and holiness.

I. This history leads us to suppose, that Adam's sin, with relation to the forbidden fruit, was the *first* sin he committed. Which could not have been, had he not always, till then, been perfectly righteous, righteous from the first moment of his existence; and consequently, created or brought into existence righteous. In a moral agent, subject to moral obligations, it is the same thing, to be perfectly *innocent,* as to be perfectly *righteous.* It must be the same, because there can no more be any *medium* between sin and righteousness, or between being right and being wrong, in a moral sense, than there can be a medium between straight and crooked, in a natural sense. Adam was brought into existence capable of acting immediately, as a moral agent; and therefore he was immediately under a rule of *right* action. He was obliged as soon as he existed to *act aright.* And if he was obliged to act aright as soon as he existed, he was obliged even then to be *inclined* to act right. Dr. T. says, (p. 166. S.) "Adam could not *sin* without a sinful *inclination*:"* and, just for the same reason, he could not do *aright,* without an *inclination* to right action. And as he was obliged to act rightly from the first moment of his existence, and did so, till he sinned in reference to the forbidden fruit, he must have had a disposition of heart to do rightly the first moment of his existence; and that is the same as to be created, or brought into existence, with an inclination to right action, or, which is the same thing, a virtuous and holy disposition of heart.

Here it will be in vain to say, "It is true, that it was *Adam's* duty to have a good disposition or inclination, as soon as it was possible to be obtained, in the nature of things; but as it could not be without *time* to establish such a habit, which requires antecedent thought, reflection, and repeated right action; therefore all that *Adam* could be obliged to, in the first place, was to reflect, and consider things in a right manner, and apply himself to right action, in order to obtain a right disposition:" for this supposes, that even the reflection and consideration to which he was obliged, was *right action.* Surely he was obliged to it no otherwise than as a thing that was *right:* and therefore he must have an *inclination* to this right action immediately, before he could perform those first right actions. And as the inclination to them should be right, the principle, or disposition from which he performed even those actions, must be good: otherwise the actions would

† This is doubtless true: for although there was no natural *sinful* inclination in *Adam,* yet an inclination to that sin of eating the forbidden fruit, was begotten in him by the delusion and error he was led into; and this inclination to eat the forbidden fruit, must precede his actual eating.

not be right in the sight of him who looks at the heart; nor would they answer his obligations, if he had done them for some sinister end, and not from a regard to God and his duty. Therefore there must have been a regard to God and his duty implanted in him at his first existence: otherwise it is certain, he would have done nothing from a regard to God and his duty; no, not so much as to reflect and consider, and try to obtain such a disposition. The very supposition of a *disposition* to right action being first obtained by repeated right *action*, is grossly inconsistent with itself: for it supposes a course of right action, *before* there is a disposition to perform any right action.

These are no invented quibbles or sophisms. If God expected from *Adam* any obedience, or duty to him at all, when he first made him—whether it was in reflecting, considering, or any way exerting his faculties—then he was expected immediately to exercise love to God. For how could it be expected, that Adam should have a strict and perfect regard to God's commands and authority, and his duty to him, when he had no love nor regard to him in his heart, nor could it be expected he should have any? If Adam from the beginning did his duty to God, and had more respect to the will of his Creator, than to other things, and as much respect to him as he ought to have; then from the beginning he had a supreme and perfect respect and love to God: and if so, he was created with such a principle. There is no avoiding the consequence. Not only external duties, but internal ones, such as summarily consist in love, must be immediately required of Adam, as soon as he existed, if any duty at all was required. For it is most apparently absurd, to talk of a spiritual being, with the faculties of understanding and will, being required to perform external duties, without internal. Dr. T. himself observes, that love is the fulfilling of the law, and that *all moral rectitude, even every part of it, must be resolved into that single principle*. Therefore, if any morally right act at all, reflection, consideration, or any thing else, was required of Adam immediately, on his first existence, and was performed as required; then he must, the first moment of his existence, have his heart possessed of that principle of divine *love;* which implies the whole of moral rectitude in every part of it, according to our author's own doctrine; and so the whole of moral rectitude or righteousness must begin with his existence: which is the thing taught in the doctrine of original righteousness.

Let us consider how it could be otherwise, than that Adam was always, in every moment of his existence, obliged to exercise such respect of heart towards every object, as was agreeable to the apparent merit of that object. For instance, would it not at any time have become Adam, on the exhibition of God's infinite goodness to him, to have exercised answerable gratitude; and would not the contrary have been unbecoming and odious? And if something had been presented to Adam's view, transcendently amiable in itself, for instance, the glorious perfection of the divine nature, would it not have become him to love, relish, and delight in it? Would not such an object have merited this? And if the view of an object so amiable in itself did not affect his mind with complacence, would it not, according to the plain dictates of our understanding, have shown an unbecoming temper of mind? Time, by culture, to form and establish a good disposition, would not have taken off the odiousness of the temper. And if there had been never so much time, I do not see how it could be expected he should improve it aright, in order to obtain a good disposition, if he had not already some good disposition to engage him to it.

That belonging to the will, and disposition of the heart, which is in *itself* either odious or amiable, unbecoming or decent, always would have been Adam's virtue or sin, in any moment of his existence; if there be any such thing as virtue or vice; by which terms nothing can be meant, but something in our moral disposition and behaviour, which is becoming or unbecoming, amiable or odious.

Human nature must be created with some dispositions; a disposition to relish some things as good and amiable, and to be averse to other things as odious and disagreeable: otherwise, it must be without any such thing as inclination or will; perfectly indifferent, without preference, without choice, or aversion, towards any thing as agreeable or disagreeable. But if it had any concreated dispositions at all, they must be either right or wrong, either agreeable or disagreeable to the nature of things. If man had at first the highest relish of things excellent and beautiful, a disposition to have the quickest and highest delight in those things which were most worthy of it, then his dispositions were morally right and amiable, and never can be excellent in a higher sense. But if he had a disposition to love most those things that were inferior and less worthy, then his dispositions were vicious. And it is evident there can be no medium between these.

II. This notion of Adam being created without a principle of holiness in his heart, taken with the rest of Dr. T.'s scheme, is inconsistent with what the history in the beginning of *Genesis* leads us to suppose of the great favours and smiles of Heaven, which Adam enjoyed while he remained in innocency. The *Mosaic* account suggests to us, that till Adam sinned, he was in happy circumstances, surrounded with testimonies and fruits of God's favour. This is implicitly owned by Dr. T. when he says, (p. 252.) "That in the dispensation our first parents were under before the fall, they were placed in a condition proper to engage their gratitude, love, and obedience." But it will follow, on our author's principles, that Adam, while in innocency, was placed in far worse circumstances, than he was in after his disobedience, and infinitely worse than his posterity are in; under unspeakably greater disadvantages for avoiding sin, and the performance of duty. For by this doctrine, Adam's posterity come into the world with their hearts as free from any propensity to sin as he, and he was made as destitute of any propensity to righteousness as they: and yet God, in favour to them, does great things to restrain them from sin, and excite them to virtue, which he never did for Adam in innocency, but laid him, in the highest degree, under contrary disadvantages. God, as an instance of his great favour, and fatherly love to man, since the fall, has denied him the ease and pleasures of paradise, which gratified and allured his senses, and bodily appetites; that he might diminish his temptations to sin. And as a still greater means to restrain from sin, and promote virtue, has subjected him to labour, toil, and sorrow in the world: and not only so, but as a means to promote his spiritual and eternal good far beyond this, has doomed him to death. When all this was found insufficient, he, in further prosecution of the designs of his love, shortened men's lives exceedingly, made them twelve or thirteen times shorter than in the first ages. And yet this, with all the innumerable calamities which God, in great favour to mankind, has brought on the world—whereby their temptations are so vastly cut short, and the inducements to virtue heaped one upon another to so great a degree—have proved insufficient, now for so many thousand years together, to restrain from wickedness in any considerable degree; while innocent human nature, all along, comes into the world with the same purity and harmless dispositions that our first parents had in paradise. What vast disadvantages indeed then must Adam and Eve be in, who had no more in their nature to keep them from sin, or incline them to virtue, than their posterity, and yet were without all those additional and extraordinary means! They were not only without such exceeding great means as we now have, when our lives are made so very short, but had vastly less advantages than their antediluvian posterity, who to prevent their being wicked, and to make them good, had so much labour and toil, sweat and sorrow, briers and thorns, with a body gradually decaying and returning to the dust. Our first parents had the extreme disadvantage of being placed amongst many and exceeding great temptations—not only without toil or sorrow, pain or disease, to humble and mortify them, and a sentence of death to wean them from the world, but—in the midst of the most exquisite and alluring sensitive delights; the reverse in every respect, and the highest degree, of that most gracious state of requisite means, and great advantages, which mankind now enjoy! If mankind now, under these vast restraints, and great advantages, are not restrained from general, and as it were universal wickedness, how could it be expected that Adam and Eve, created with no better hearts than men bring into the world now, and destitute of all these advantages, and in the midst of all contrary disadvantages, should escape it?

These things are not agreeable to *Moses's* account. That represents a happy state of peculiar favours and blessings before the fall, and the curse coming afterwards; but according to this scheme, the curse was before the fall, and the great favours and testimonies of love followed the apostacy. And the curse before the fall must be a curse with a witness, being to so high a degree the reverse of such means, means so necessary for such a creature as innocent man, and in all their multitude and fulness proving too little. Paradise therefore must be a mere delusion! There was indeed a great show of favour, in placing man in the midst of such delights. But this delightful garden, it seems, with all its beauty and sweetness, was in its real tendency worse than the apples of *Sodom*. It was but a mere bait, (God forbid the blasphemy,) the more effectually enticing by its beauty and deliciousness, to Adam's eternal ruin. Which might be the more expected to be fatal to him, seeing he was the first man, having no capacity superior to his posterity, and wholly without the advantage of their observations, experiences, and improvements.

I proceed now to take notice of an additional proof of the doctrine we are upon, from another part of the Holy Scripture. A very clear text for *original righteousness* we have in Eccles. vii. 29. " Lo, this only have I found, that God made man upright; but they have sought out many inventions."

It is an observation of no weight which Dr. T. makes on this text, that the word *man* is commonly used to signify mankind in general, or mankind collectively taken. It is true, it often signifies the species of mankind; but then it is used to signify the species, with regard to its duration and *succession* from its beginning, as well as with regard to its *extent*. The English word *mankind* is used to signify the species: but what then? Would it be an improper way of speaking, to say, that when God first made *mankind*, he placed them in a pleasant paradise, (meaning in their first parents,) but now they live in the midst of briers and thorns? And it is certain, that to speak thus of God making mankind—his giving the species an existence in their first parents, at the creation—is agreeable to the scripture use of such an expression. As in Deut. iv. 32. " Since the day that God *created man* upon the earth." Job xx. 4. " Knowest thou not this of old, since *man* was placed upon the earth." Isa. xlv. 12. " I have made the earth, and *created man* upon it: I, even my hands, have stretched out the heavens." Jer. xxvii. 5. " I *have made* the earth, the *man* and the beast that are upon the ground, by my great power." All these texts speak of God *making man*, signifying the *species* of mankind; and yet they all plainly have respect to God making man *at first*, when he *made the earth, and stretched out the heavens*. In all these places the same word, Adam, is used as in Ecclesiastes; and in the last of them, used with (he *emphaticum*) *the emphatic sign*, as here; though Dr. T. omits it, when he tells us he gives us a catalogue of *all* the places in Scripture where the word is used. And it argues nothing to the Doctor's purpose, that the pronoun they is used;—THEY *have sought out many inventions*. This is properly applied to the species, which God made at first upright; the species begun with more than one, and continued in a multitude. As Christ speaks of the two sexes, in the relation of man and wife, continued in successive generations; Matt. xix. 4. " He that *made them* at the beginning, made them male and female;" having reference to Adam and Eve.

No less impertinent, and also very unfair, is his criticism on the word (ישר) translated *upright*. Because the word sometimes signifies *right*, he would from thence infer, that it does not properly signify moral rectitude, even when used to express the character of moral agents. He might as well insist, that the English word *upright*, sometimes, and in its most original meaning, signifies *right up*, or in an erect posture, therefore it does not properly signify any moral character, when applied to moral agents. And indeed less unreasonably; for it is known, that in the *Hebrew* language, in a peculiar manner, most words used to signify moral and spiritual things, are taken from external and natural objects. The word (ישר *Jashar*) is used, as applied to moral agents, or to the words and actions of such, (if I have not misreckoned,*) about an hundred and ten times in Scripture; and about an hundred of them, without all dispute, to signify virtue, or moral rectitude, (though Dr. T. is pleased to say, the word does not generally signify a moral character,) and for the most part it signifies *true virtue*, or virtue in such a sense, as distinguishes it from all false appearances of virtue, or what is only virtue in some respects, but not truly so in the sight of God. It is used at least eighty times in this sense: and scarce any word can be found in the *Hebrew* language more significant of this. It is thus used constantly in *Solomon's* writings, (where it is often found) when used to express a character or property of moral agents. And it is beyond all controversy, that he uses it in this place, (the 7th of Eccles.) to signify moral rectitude, or a character of real virtue and integrity. For the wise man is speaking of persons with respect to their *moral* character, inquiring into the corruption and depravity of mankind, (as is confessed, p. 184.) and he here declares, he had not found more than one among a thousand of the right stamp, truly and thoroughly virtuous and upright: which appeared a strange thing! But in this text he clears God, and lays the blame on man: man was not made thus at first. He was made of the right stamp, altogether good in his kind, (as all other things were,) truly and thoroughly virtuous, as he ought to be; *but they have sought out many inventions*. Which last expression signifies things sinful, or morally evil; (as is confessed, p. 185.) And this expression, used to signify those moral evils he found in man, which he sets in opposition to the uprightness man was made in, shows, that by uprightness he means the most true and sincere goodness. The word rendered *inventions*, most naturally and aptly signifies the subtile devices, and crooked deceitful ways, of hypocrites, wherein they are of a character contrary to men of simplicity and godly sincerity; who, though wise in that which is good, are simple concerning evil. Thus the same wise man, in Prov. xii. 2. sets a truly good man in opposition to a man of *wicked devices*, whom God will condemn. *Solomon* had occasion to observe many who put on an artful disguise and fair show of goodness; but on searching thoroughly, he found very few truly upright. As he says, Prov. xx. 6. " Most men will proclaim every one his own goodness: but a faithful man who can find?" So that it is exceeding plain, that by uprightness, in this place, (Eccles. vii.) *Solomon* means true moral goodness.

What our author urges concerning *many inventions*, whereas Adam's eating of the forbidden fruit was but *one invention*, is of as little weight as the rest of what he says on this text. For the many lusts and corruptions of mankind, appearing in innumerable ways of sinning, are all the consequence of that sin. The great corruption men are fallen into by the original apostacy, appears in the multitude of the wicked ways to which they are inclined. And therefore these are properly mentioned as the fruits and evidences of the greatness of that apostacy and corruption.

SECT. II.

Concerning the kind of death, threatened to our first parents, if they should eat of the forbidden fruit.

Dr. T. in his observations on the three first chapters of *Genesis* says, (p. 7.) " The threatening to man in case of transgression was, that he should surely die.—Death is the losing of life. Death is opposed to life, and must be understood according to the nature of that life, to which it is opposed. Now the death here threatened can, with any certainty, be opposed only to the life God gave Adam, when he created him, (ver. 7.) Any thing besides this must be pure conjecture, without solid foundation."

To this I would say; it is true, *Death is opposed to life, and must be understood according to the nature of that life, to which it is opposed.* But does it therefore follow, that nothing can be meant by it but the *loss* of life? Misery is opposed to happiness, and sorrow is in Scripture often opposed to joy; but can we conclude from thence, that nothing is meant in Scripture by sorrow, but the *loss of joy?* or that there is no more in misery, than the *loss* or

* Making use of Buxtorf's Concordance, which, according to the author's professed design, directs to all the places where the word is used.

absence of happiness? And if the death threatened to Adam can, with certainty, be opposed only to the life *given to Adam, when God created him;* I think, a state of perfect, perpetual, and hopeless misery is properly opposed to that state *Adam was in, when God created him.* For I suppose it will not be denied, that the life Adam had, was truly a *happy* life; happy in perfect innocency, in the favour of his Maker, surrounded with the happy fruits and testimonies of his love. And I think it has been proved, that he also was happy in a state of perfect righteousness. Nothing is more manifest, than that it is agreeable to a very common acceptation of the word *life*, in Scripture, that it be understood as signifying a state of excellent and happy existence. Now that which is most opposite to *that life* and state *in which Adam was created*, is a state of total, confirmed wickedness, and perfect hopeless misery, under the divine displeasure and curse; not excluding temporal death, or the destruction of the body, as an introduction to it.

Besides, that which is much more evident, than any thing Dr. T. says on this head, is, that the *death* which was to come on Adam, as the *punishment of his disobedience*, was opposed to that *life*, which he would have had as the *reward* of his *obedience* in case he had not sinned. *Obedience* and *disobedience* are contraries; the *threatenings* and *promises* which are sanctions of a law, are set in direct opposition; and the *promises, rewards*, and *threatened punishments*, are most properly taken as each others' opposites. But none will deny, that the life which would have been *Adam's reward*, if he had persisted in obedience, was *eternal life*. And therefore we argue justly that the death which *stands opposed to that life*, (Dr. T. himself being judge, p. 120. S.) *is manifestly eternal death, a death widely different from the death we now die*—to use his own words. If Adam, for his persevering *obedience*, was to have had *everlasting life and happiness, in perfect holiness, union* with his Maker, and *enjoyment of his favour*, and this was the life which was to be confirmed by the tree of life; then, doubtless, the death threatened in case of disobedience, which stands in direct opposition to this, was an exposure to *everlasting wickedness and misery, in separation* from God, and in *enduring his wrath*.

When God first made mankind, and made known to them the methods of his moral government towards them, in the revelation he made of himself to the natural head of the whole species—and letting him know, that obedience to him was expected, and enforcing his duty with the sanction of a threatened punishment, called by the name of *death*—we may with the greatest reason suppose, in such a case, that by *death* was meant the most proper punishment of the sin of mankind, and which he speaks of under that name throughout the Scripture, as the proper wages of sin; and this was always, from the beginning, understood to be so in the church of God. It would be strange indeed, if it should be otherwise. It would have been strange, if, when the law of God was first given, and enforced by the threatening of a punishment, nothing at all had been mentioned of that *great punishment*, ever spoken of under the name of *death*—in the revelations which he has given to mankind from age to age—as the proper punishment of the sin of mankind. And it would be no less strange, if when the punishment which was mentioned and threatened on that occasion, was called by the same name, even death, yet we must not understand it to mean the same thing, but something infinitely diverse, and infinitely more inconsiderable.

But now let us consider what that death is, which the Scripture ever speaks of as the proper wages of sin, and is spoken of as such by God's saints in all ages of the church. I will begin with the New Testament. When the apostle *Paul* says, (Rom. vi. 23.) "The wages of sin is *death*," Dr. T. tells us, (p. 120. S.) that *this means eternal death, the second death, a death widely different from the death we now die.* The same apostle speaks of death as the proper punishment due for sin, Rom. vii. 5. and chap. viii. 13. 2 Cor. iii. 7. 1 Cor. xv. 56. In all which places, Dr. T. himself supposes the apostle to intend *eternal* death.* And when the apostle James speaks of death, as the proper reward, fruit, and end of sin, (James i. 15.) "Sin, when it is finished, bringeth forth death;" it is manifest, that our author supposes eternal destruction to be meant.† And the apostle John, agreeably to Dr. T.'s sense, speaks of the second death as that which sin unrepented of will bring all men to at last. Rev. ii. 11. xx. 6, 14. and xxi. 8. In the same sense the apostle John uses the word in his first epistle, chap. iii. 14. "We know that we have passed from death to life, because we love the brethren. He that hateth his brother, abideth in death." In the same manner Christ used the word from time to time, when he was on earth, and spake concerning the punishment of sin. John v. 24. "He that heareth my word, and believeth, &c. hath everlasting life; and shall not come into condemnation; but is passed from *death* to life." Where, according to Dr. T.'s own way of arguing, it cannot be the death which we now die, that Christ speaks of, but *eternal* death, because it is set in opposition to everlasting life. John vi. 50. "This is the bread which cometh down from heaven, that a man may eat thereof, and not *die*." Chap. viii. 51. "Verily, verily, I say unto you, if a man keep my saying, he shall never see *death*." Chap. xi. 26. "And whosoever liveth and believeth in me, shall never *die*." In which places it is plain Christ does not mean that believers shall never see *temporal* death. (See also Matt. x. 28. and Luke x. 28.) In like manner, the word was commonly used by the prophets of old, when they spake of death as the proper end and recompence of sin. So, abundantly by the prophet Ezekiel. Ezek. iii. 18. "When I say unto the wicked man, thou shalt surely *die*." In the original it is, *Dying thou shalt die:* the same form of expression, which God used in the threatening to Adam. We have the same words again, chap. xxxiii. 18.—In chap. xviii. 4. it is said, "The soul that sinneth it shall *die*."‡ And that temporal death is not meant in these places is plain, because it is promised most absolutely, that the righteous shall not die the death spoken of. Chap. xviii. 21. "He shall surely live, he shall not *die*." (So ver. 9, 17, 19, and 22. and chap. iii. 21.) And it is evident the prophet Jeremiah uses the word in the same sense. Jer. xxxi. 30. "Every one shall *die* for his own iniquity." And the same death is spoken of by the prophet Isaiah. Isa. xi. 4. "With the breath of his lips shall he *slay* the wicked." (See also chap. lxvi. 16. with ver. 24.) Solomon, who we must suppose was thoroughly acquainted with the sense in which the word was used by the wise, and by the ancients, continually speaks of *death* as the proper fruit, issue, and recompence of sin, using the world only in this sense. Prov. xi. 19. "As righteousness tendeth to *life*, so he that pursueth evil pursueth it to his own *death*."§ He cannot mean *temporal* death, for he often speaks of it as a punishment of the wicked, wherein the righteous shall certainly be distinguished from them: as in Prov. xii. 28. "In the way of righteousness is life, and in the path-way thereof is no *death*." (So in chap. x. 2. xi. 4. xiii. 14. xiv. 27. and many other places.) But we find this same wise man observes, that as to temporal death, and temporal events in general, there is no distinction, but that they happen alike to good and bad. (Eccl. ii. 4—16. viii. 14. and ix. 2, 3.) His words are remarkable in Eccl. vii. 15. "There is a just man that *perisheth* in his righteousness; and there is a wicked man that prolongeth his life, in his wickedness." So we find, David in the book of Psalms uses the word *death* in the same sense, when he speaks of it as the proper wages and issue of sin, Psal. xxxiv. 21. "Evil shall *slay* the wicked." He speaks of it as a certain thing, Psal. cxxxix. 19. "Surely thou wilt *slay* the wicked, O God." And he speaks of it as a thing wherein the wicked are distinguished from the righteous, Psal. lxix. 28. "Let them be blotted out of the book of the *living*, and not be written with the righteous."—And thus we find the word *death* used in the *Pentateuch*, where we have the account of the threatening of death to Adam. When, in these

* See p. 78. note on Rom. vii. 5. and note on ver. 6. Note on Rom. v. 20. Note on Rom. vii. 8.

† By comparing what he says, p. 126. with what he often says of that death and destruction which is the demerit and end of personal sin, which he says is the *second death or eternal destruction*.

‡ To the like purpose are chap. iii. 19, 20. and xviii. 4, 9, 13, 17—21, 24, 26, 28. chap. xxxiii. 8, 9, 12—14, 19.

§ So chap. v. 5, 6, 23. vii. 27. viii. 36. ix. 18. x. 21. xi. 19. xiv. 12. xv. 10. xviii. 21. xix. 16, 21. and xxiii. 13, 14.

books, it is spoken of as the proper fruit, and appointed reward of sin, it is to be understood of *eternal* death. Thus, Deut. xxx. 15. " See, I have set before thee this day *life*, and good, and *death* and evil." Ver. 19. " I call heaven and earth to record this day against you, that I have set before you *life* and *death*, blessing and cursing." The life that is spoken of here, is doubtless the same that is spoken of in Lev. xviii. 5. " Ye shall therefore keep my statutes and my judgments, which if a man do, he shall *live* in them." This the apostle understands of *eternal* life; as is plain by Rom. x. 5. and Gal. iii. 12. But that the death threatened for sin in the law of *Moses* meant *eternal* death, is what Dr. T. abundantly declares. So in his note on Rom. v. 20. (Par. p. 291.) " *Such a constitution the law of Moses was, subjecting those who were under it to death for every transgression: meaning by death* ETERNAL DEATH." These are his words. The like he asserts in many other places. When it is said, in the place now mentioned, *I have set before thee* LIFE *and* DEATH, *blessing and cursing*, without doubt, the same *blessing and cursing* is meant which God had already set before them with such solemnity, in the 27th and 28th chapters; where we have the sum of the curses in those last words of the 27th chapter, *Cursed is every one, which confirmeth not all the words of this law to do them.* Which the apostle speaks of as a threatening of *eternal* death; and with him Dr. T. himself:* In this sense also *Job* and his friends spake of *death*, as the wages and end of sin, who lived before any written revelation, and had their religion, and their phraseology about religion, from the ancients.

If any should insist upon it as an objection—against supposing that death was intended to signify *eternal* death in the threatening to Adam—that this use of the word is figurative: I reply, that though this should be allowed, yet it is by no means so figurative as many other phrases used in the history contained in these three chapters: as when it is said, *God said, Let there be light; God said, Let there be a firmament, &c.* as though God spake such words with a voice. So when it is said, *God* called *the light, day: God* called *the firmament, heaven, &c. God* rested *on the seventh day;* as though he had been weary, and then rested. *And when it is said, They heard the* voice of God walking; as though the Deity had feet, and took steps on the ground. Dr. T. supposes, that when it is said of *Adam* and *Eve*, *Their eyes were opened, and they saw that they were naked;* by the word *naked* is meant a *state of guilt.* (P. 12.) Which sense of the word, *naked*, is much further from the *common* use of the word, than the supposed sense of the word *death.* So this author supposes the promise concerning the seed of the woman *bruising the serpent's head*, while the serpent should *bruise his heel*, is to be understood of *the Messiah destroying the power and sovereignty of the devil, and receiving some slight hurt from him.* (P. 15, 16.) Which makes the sentence full of figures. And why might not God deliver *threatenings* to our first parents in figurative expressions, as well as *promises?*

But indeed, there is no necessity of supposing the word *death*, or the *Hebrew* word so translated, if used in the manner that has been supposed, to have been figurative at all. It does not appear but that this word, in its true and proper meaning, might signify perfect misery, and sensible destruction; though the word was also applied to signify something more external and visible. There are many words in our language, such as *heart, sense, view, discovery, conception, light,* and many others, which are applied to signify *external* things; as that muscular part of the body called *heart;* external feeling, called *sense;* the sight of the bodily eye, called *view;* the finding of a thing by its being uncovered, called *discovery;* the first beginning of the fœtus in the womb, called *conception;* and the rays of the sun, called *light.* Yet these words do as truly and properly signify other things of a more spiritual *internal* nature; such as the disposition, affection, perception, and thought of the mind, and manifestation and evidence to the soul. Common use, which governs the propriety of language, makes the latter things to be as much signified by those words, in their proper meaning, as the former. It is especially common in the *Hebrew*, and I suppose, other Oriental languages, that the same word that signifies something external, does no less properly and usually signify something more spiritual. So the *Hebrew* words used for breath, have such a double signification; (נשמה) *Neshama* signifies both *breath* and the *soul;* and the latter as commonly as the former: (רוח) *Ruach* is used for *breath* or *wind*, but yet more commonly signifies *spirit.* (נפש) *Nephesh* is used for *breath*, but yet more commonly signifies *soul.* So the word (לבב or לב) *Lébh, heart,* no less properly signifies the *soul*, especially with regard to the will and affections, than that part of the body so called. The word (שלום) *Shalom*, which we render peace, no less properly signifies prosperity and happiness, than mutual agreement. The word translated *life*, signifies the natural life of the body, and also the perfect and happy state of sensible active being; and the latter as properly as the former. So the word *death*, signifies destruction, as to outward *sensibility*, activity, and enjoyment: but it has most evidently another signification, which in the *Hebrew* tongue is no less proper, viz. *perfect, sensible, hopeless ruin and misery.*

It is therefore wholly without reason urged, that death properly signifies only the *loss* of this *present* life; and that therefore nothing else was meant by that death which was threatened for eating the forbidden fruit. Nor does it at all appear but that Adam—who, from what God said concerning the seed of the woman, could understand that *relief* was promised as to the death which was threatened, as Dr. T. himself supposes—understood the death which was threatened, in the *more important* sense. Especially seeing temporal death, considered originally and in itself, is evermore, excepting as changed by divine grace, an entrance into that dismal state of misery which is shadowed forth by the awful circumstances of this death; circumstances naturally suggesting to the mind the most dreadful state of hopeless, sensible ruin.

As to the objection, that the phrase, *Dying thou shalt die*, is several times used in the books of *Moses*, to signify *temporal* death, it can be of no force. For it has been shown already, that the same phrase is sometimes used in Scripture to signify *eternal* death, in instances much more parallel with this. But indeed nothing can be certainly argued concerning the nature of the thing intended, from its being expressed in such a manner. For it is evident, that such repetitions of a word in the *Hebrew* language, are no more than an emphasis upon a word in the more modern languages, to signify the great degree of a thing, the importance or certainty of it, &c. When we would signify and impress these, we commonly put an *emphasis* on our words. Instead of this, the *Hebrews*, when they would express a thing strongly, *repeated* or doubled the word, the more to impress the mind of the hearer; as may be plain to every one in the least conversant with the *Hebrew* Bible. The repetition in the threatening to *Adam*, therefore, only implies the solemnity and importance of the threatening. But God may denounce either eternal or temporal death with peremptoriness and solemnity, and nothing can certainly be inferred concerning the nature of the thing threatened, because it is threatened with *emphasis*, more than this, that the threatening is *much to be regarded.* Though it be true, that it might in an especial manner be expected that a threatening of eternal death would be denounced with great emphasis, such a threatening being infinitely important, and to be regarded above all others.

SECT. III.

Wherein it is inquired, whether there be any thing in the history of the three first chapters of Genesis, which should lead us to suppose, that God, in his constitution with Adam, dealt with mankind in general, as included in their first father, and that the threatening of death, in case he should eat the forbidden fruit, had respect not only to him, but his posterity?

Dr. T. rehearsing that threatening to *Adam*, *Thou shalt surely die*, and giving us his paraphrase of it, (p. 7, 8.)

* Note on Rom. v. 20. Par. p. 291—299.

concludes thus; "Observe, here is not *one word* relating to *Adam's* posterity." But it may be observed, in opposition to this, that there is scarcely *one word* that we have an account of, which God ever said to Adam or Eve, but what *does* manifestly include their posterity in the meaning and design of it. There is as much of *a word* said about *Adam's* posterity in that threatening, as there is in those words of God to Adam and Eve, Gen. i. 28. "Be fruitful, and multiply, and replenish the earth, and subdue it;" and as much in events, to lead us to suppose Adam's posterity to be included. There is as much of *a word* of his posterity in that threatening, as in those words, (ver. 29.) "Behold, I have given you every herb bearing seed,—and every tree in which is the fruit of a tree yielding seed," &c. Even when God was about to create Adam, what he said on that occasion, had not respect only to Adam, but to his posterity. Gen. i. 26. "Let us make man in our image, and let them have dominion over the fish of the sea," &c. And, what is more remarkable, there is as much of *a word* said about Adam's posterity in the threatening of death, as there is in that sentence, (Gen. iii. 19.) "Unto dust shalt thou return." Which Dr. T. himself supposes to be a sentence pronounced for the execution of that very threatening, *Thou shalt surely die.* This sentence he himself also often speaks of as including Adam's posterity: and, what is much more remarkable still, is a sentence which Dr. T. himself often speaks of, as *including his posterity, as a* SENTENCE OF CONDEMNATION, as a JUDICIAL sentence, and a sentence which God pronounced with regard to Adam's POSTERITY, ACTING THE PART OF A JUDGE, and as such condemning them to temporal death.—Though he is therein utterly inconsistent with himself, inasmuch as he at the same time abundantly insists, that death is not brought on Adam's posterity in consequence of his sin, at all as a punishment; but merely by the gracious disposal of a father, bestowing a *benefit of the highest nature* upon him.*

But I shall show, that I do not in any of these things falsely charge or misrepresent Dr. T.—He speaks of the sentence in chap. iii. 19. as pronounced in pursuance of the threatening in the former chapter, in these words, (p. 17, 18.) "The sentence upon the man, ver. 17, 18, 19. first affects the earth, upon which he was to subsist: the ground should be encumbered with many noxious weeds, and the tillage of it more toilsome: which would oblige the man to procure a sustenance by hard labour, till he should die, and drop into the ground, from whence he was taken. Thus death entered by sin into the world, and man became mortal,† ACCORDING TO THE THREATENING IN THE FORMER CHAPTER." Now, if mankind became mortal, and must die, according to the threatening in the former chapter, then doubtless the threatening in the former chapter, *Thou shalt die*, had respect not only to Adam, but to mankind, and included Adam's posterity. Yea, and Dr. T. is express in it, and very often so, that the sentence concerning dropping into the ground, or returning to the dust, did include Adam's posterity. So, p. 20. speaking there of that sentence, "Observe (says he) that we their posterity are in fact subjected to the same affliction and mortality, here by sentence inflicted upon our first parents."—P. 42. Note. "But yet men through that long tract, were all subject to death, therefore they must be included in the sentence." The same he affirms in innumerable other places, some of which I shall have occasion to mention presently.

The sentence which is founded on the threatening, and (as Dr. T. says) *according to the threatening*, extends to as many as were included in the threatening, and to no more. If the sentence be upon a collective subject, indefinitely, the greatest part of which were not included in the threatening, nor were ever threatened at all, then certainly this sentence is not *according to the threatening*, nor built upon it. If the sentence be according to the threatening, then we may justly explain the threatening by the sentence. And if we find the *sentence* spoken to the *same* person whom the *threatening* was spoken, and spoken in the second person singular in like manner with the threatening, *founded on* the threatening, and *according to* it; and if we find the *sentence* includes Adam's posterity, then we may certainly infer, that so did the *threatening*. And hence, that both the threatening and sentence were delivered to Adam as the *public head* and representative of his posterity.

And we may also further infer from it, in another respect, directly contrary to Dr. T.'s doctrine, that the sentence which included *Adam's* posterity, was to death, *as a punishment* to that posterity, as well as to Adam himself. For a sentence pronounced in execution of a threatening, is for a punishment. *Threatenings* are of *punishments.* Neither God nor man are wont to *threaten* others with *favours* and benefits.

But lest any of this author's admirers should stand to it, that it may very properly be said, God *threatened* mankind with bestowing great kindness upon them, I would observe, that Dr. T. himself often speaks of this sentence as pronounced by God on *all mankind*, as *condemning them; as a sentence of condemnation judicially pronounced*, or a sentence which God pronounced on all mankind *acting as their judge*, and *in a judicial proceeding.* This he affirms in multitudes of places. In p. 20. speaking of this sentence, which, he there says, subjects us, *Adam's* and *Eve's* posterity, to affliction and mortality, he calls it a *judicial* act of condemnation. "The *judicial act of condemnation* (says he) clearly implies, a taking him to pieces, and turning him to the ground from whence he was taken." And (p. 28, 29. Note.) 'In all the Scripture from one end to the other, there is recorded but one *judgment to condemnation*, which came upon *all men*, and that is, Gen. iii. 17—19. *Dust thou art*," &c. P. 40. speaking of the same, he says, "*All men* are brought under *condemnation.*" In p. 27, 28. "By judgment, *judgment to condemnation*, it appeareth evidently to me, he *(Paul)* means the being *adjudged* to the forementioned death; he means the *sentence of death*, of a general mortality, *pronounced upon mankind*, in consequence of *Adam's* first transgression. And the *condemnation* inflicted by the *judgment of God*, answereth to, and is in effect the same thing with, being dead." P. 30. "The many, that is mankind, were subject to death by the *judicial act* of God." P. 31. "Being made sinners, may very well signify, being *adjudged*, or *condemned* to death.—For the *Hebrew* word, &c. signifies to make one a sinner by a *judicial sentence*, or to *condemn*."—P. 178. Par. on Rom. v. 19. "Upon the account of one man's disobedience, *mankind* were *judicially constituted sinners;* that is, subjected to death, by the *sentence* of God the *Judge*."—And there are many other places where he repeats the same thing. And it is pretty remarkable, that (page 48, 49.) immediately after citing Prov. xvii. 15. "He that justifieth the wicked, and he that condemneth the just, are both an abomination to the Lord"—and when he is careful in citing these words, to put us in mind, that it is meant of a *judicial act*—yet, in the very next words, he supposes that God himself does so, since he constantly supposes that *Adam's* posterity, whom God condemns, are innocent. His words are these, "From all this it followeth, that as the judgment, that passed upon all men to *condemnation*, is death's coming upon *all men*, by the *judicial act of God*, upon occasion of Adam's transgression: so," &c.—And it is very remarkable, that (p. 3, 4, 7. S.) he insists, "That in Scripture no action is said to be imputed, reckoned, or accounted to any person for righteousness or CONDEMNATION, but the proper act and deed of that person."—And yet he thus continually affirms, that all mankind are made sinners by a *judicial act of God the Judge*, even to *condemnation*, and *judicially constituted sinners*, and so subjected to a *judicial sentence of condemnation*, on occasion of *Adam's* sin; and all *according to the threatening* denounced to *Adam*, "Thou shalt surely die:" though he supposes Adam's posterity were not included in the threatening, and are looked upon as perfectly innocent, and treated wholly as such.

I am sensible Dr. T. does not run into all this inconsistence, only through oversight and blundering; but that he is driven to it, to make out his matters in his evasion of that noted paragraph in the fifth chapter of Romans; especially those three sentences; (ver. 16.) "The judgment was by one to condemnation." (ver. 18.) "By the offence of one, judgment came upon all men to condemnation;" and (ver. 19.) "By one man's disobedience

* Page 27. S.

† The subsequent part of the quotation the reader will not meet with in the third edition of Dr. T. but the second, of 1741.

many were made sinners." And I am also sensible of what he offers to salve the inconvenience, *viz.* "That if the threatening had immediately been executed on Adam, he would have had no posterity; and that so far the possible existence of Adam's posterity fell under the threatening of the law, and into the hands of the judge, to be disposed of as he should think fit: and that this is the ground of the judgment to condemnation, coming upon all men."* But this is trifling, to a great degree: for,

1. Suffering *death*, and failing of possible *existence*, are entirely different things. If there had never been any such thing as sin committed, there would have been infinite numbers of possible beings, which would have failed of existence, by God's appointment. God has appointed (if the phrase be allowable) not to bring into existence numberless possible worlds, each replenished with innumerable possible inhabitants. But is this equivalent to God's appointing them all to suffer death?

2. Our author represents, that *by Adam's sin, the possible existence of his posterity fell into the hands of the Judge, to be disposed of as he should think fit.* But there was no need of any sin of Adam, or of any body else, in order to their being brought into God's hands, in this respect. The future possible existence of all created beings is in God's hands, antecedently to the existence of any sin. And therefore, infinite numbers of possible beings, without any relation to Adam, or any other sinning being, fail of their possible existence. And if Adam had never sinned, yet it would be unreasonable to suppose, but that innumerable multitudes of his possible posterity would have failed of existence by God's disposal. For will any be so unreasonable as to imagine, that God would and must have brought into existence as many of his posterity as it was possible should be, if he had not sinned? Or, that then it would not have been possible, that any other persons of his posterity should ever have existed, than those individual persons who now actually suffer death, and return to the dust?

3. We have many accounts in Scripture, which imply the actual failing of the possible existence of innumerable multitudes of Adam's posterity, yea, of many more than ever come into existence. As, of the possible posterity of *Abel*, the possible posterity of all them that were destroyed by the flood, and the possible posterity of the innumerable multitudes, which we read of in Scripture, destroyed by sword, pestilence, &c. And if the threatening to *Adam* reached his posterity, in no other respect than this, that they were liable to be deprived by it of their possible existence, then *these* instances are much more properly a fulfilment of that threatening, than the suffering of death by such as *actually* come into existence; and so is that which is most properly the judgment to condemnation, executed by the sentence of the Judge, proceeding on the ground of that threatening. But where do we ever find this so represented in Scripture? We read of multitudes cut off for their personal sins, who thereby failed of their possible posterity. And these are mentioned as God's judgments on them, and effects of God's condemnation of them: but when are they ever spoken of as God judicially proceeding against, and condemning their possible posterity?

4. Dr. T. in what he says concerning this matter, speaks of the threatening of the law delivered to Adam, which the possible existence of his posterity fell under, *as the ground of the judgment to condemnation coming upon all men.* But herein he is exceeding inconsistent with himself: for he affirms in a place forecited, that the Scripture never speaks of any sentence of condemnation coming upon all men, but that sentence in the third of *Genesis*, concerning man turning to dust. But, according to him, the threatening of the law delivered to Adam, could not be the ground of that sentence; for he greatly insists upon it, that that law was entirely abrogated before that sentence was pronounced, *had no existence* to have any such influence as might procure a sentence of death; and therefore this sentence was introduced entirely on another footing, a new dispensation of grace. The reader may see this matter strenuously urged, and particularly argued by him, p. 113—120. S. So that this sentence could not, according to him, have the threatening of that law for its ground, as he supposes; for it never stood upon that ground. It could not be called a judgment of condemnation, *under any such view;* for it could not be viewed in circumstances where it never existed.

5. If, as our author supposes, that the sentence of death on all men comes under the notion of a judgment to condemnation by this means, *viz.* that the threatening to *Adam* was in some respect the ground of it; then it also comes under the notion of a punishment: for threatenings annexed to breaches of laws, are to punishments; and a judgment of condemnation to the thing threatened, must be to punishment; and the thing condemned to, must have as much the notion of a punishment, as the sentence has the notion of a judgment to condemnation. But this Dr. T. wholly denies: he denies that death comes as any punishment at all; but insists that it comes only as a favour and benefit, and a fruit of fatherly love to Adam's posterity, respected not as guilty, but wholly innocent. So that his scheme will not admit of its coming under the notion of a sentence to condemnation in any respect whatsoever. Our author's supposition, that the possible existence of Adam's posterity comes under the threatening of the law, and into the hands of the Judge, and is the ground of the condemnation of all men to death, implies, that death by this sentence is appointed to mankind as an evil, at least negatively so; as it is a privation of good: for he manifestly speaks of a non-existence as a negative evil. But herein he is inconsistent with himself: for he continually insists, that mankind are subjected to death *only as a benefit*, as has been before shown. According to him, death is not appointed to mankind, as a negative evil, as any cessation of existence, or even diminution of good; but on the contrary, as a means of *a more happy existence*, and a great *increase of good.*

So that this evasion of Dr. T. is so far from helping the matter, that it increases and multiplies the inconsistence. And that the law, with the threatening of death annexed, was given to Adam, as the head of mankind, and to his posterity as included in him, not only follow from some of our author's own assertions—and the plain, full declarations of the apostle in the fifth of *Romans*, which drove Dr. T. into such gross inconsistencies—but the account given in the three first chapters of *Genesis*, directly and inevitably lead us to such a conclusion.

Though the sentence, Gen. iii. 19. "Unto dust thou shalt return," be not of equal extent with the threatening in the foregoing chapter, or an execution of the main curse of the law therein denounced—for, that it should have been so, would have been inconsistent with the intimations of mercy just before given—yet it is plain, this sentence is in pursuance of that threatening, being to something that was included in it. The words of the *sentence* were delivered to the same person with the words of the *threatening*, and in the same manner, in like singular terms, and as much without any express mention of his posterity. Yet it manifestly appears by the consequence, as well as all circumstances, that his posterity were included in the words of the sentence; as is confessed on all hands. And as the words were apparently delivered in the form of the sentence of a judge, condemning for something that he was displeased with, and ought to be condemned, *viz.* sin; and as the sentence to him and his posterity was but one, dooming to the same suffering, under the same circumstances, both the one and the other sentenced in the same words, spoken but once, and immediately to but one person, we hence justly infer, that it was the same thing to both; and not as Dr. T. suggests, (p. 67.) a sentence to a proper punishment to Adam, but a mere promise of favour to his posterity.

Indeed, sometimes our author seems to suppose, that God meant the thing denounced in this sentence, as a favour both to Adam and his posterity.† But to his posterity, or mankind in general, who are the main subject, he ever insists, that it was purely intended as a favour. And therefore, one would have thought, the sentence should have been delivered, with manifestations and appearances

* Page 95, 90, 91. S.

† Page 25, 45, 46. S.

of favour, and not of anger. How could Adam understand it as a promise of great favour, considering the manner and circumstances of the denunciation? How could he think, that God would go about to delude him, by clothing himself with garments of vengeance, using words of displeasure and rebuke, setting forth the heinousness of his crime, attended with cherubims and a flaming sword; when all that he meant was only higher testimonies of favour than he had before in a state of innocence, and to manifest fatherly love and kindness, in promises of great blessings? If this was the case, God's words to Adam must be understood thus: "Because thou hast done so wickedly, hast hearkened unto the voice of thy wife, and hast eaten of the tree of which I commanded thee, saying, thou shalt not eat of it; therefore I will be more kind to thee than I was in thy state of innocence, and do now appoint for thee the following great favours: *Cursed be the ground for thy sake,*" *&c.* And thus *Adam* must understand what was said, unless any will say, (and God forbid that any should be so blasphemous,) that God clothed himself with appearances of displeasure, to deceive Adam, and make him believe the contrary of what he intended, and lead him to expect a dismal train of evils on his posterity, contrary to all reason and justice, implying the most horribly unrighteous treatment of millions of perfectly innocent creatures. It is certain, there is not the least appearance in what God said, or the manner of it, as *Moses* gives us the account, of any other, than that God was now testifying displeasure, condemning the subject of the sentence he was pronouncing, as justly exposed to punishment for sin, and for that sin which he mentions.

When God was pronouncing this sentence, *Adam* doubtless understood, that God had respect to his posterity, as well as himself; though God spake wholly in the second person singular, *Because thou hast eaten,—In sorrow thou shalt eat,—Unto the dust shalt thou return.* But he had as much reason to understand God as having respect to his posterity, when he directed his speech to him in like manner in the threatening, *Thou shalt surely die.* The sentence plainly refers to the threatening, and results from it. The threatening says, *If thou eat, thou shalt die:* the sentence says, *Because thou hast eaten thou shalt die.* And Moses, who wrote the account, had no reason to doubt but that the affair would be thus understood by his readers; for such a way of speaking was well understood in those days: the history he gives us of the origin of things, abounds with it. Such a manner of speaking to the heads of the race, having respect to the progeny, is not only used in almost every thing that God said to Adam and Eve, but even in what he said to the very *birds* and *fishes*, Gen. i. 22. And also in what he said afterwards to Noah, Gen. ix. to Shem, Ham, and Japheth, and Canaan, Gen. ix. 25—27. So in promises made to Abraham, God directed his speech to him, and spake in the second person singular, from time to time, but meant chiefly his posterity: *To thee will I give this land. In thee shall all the families of the earth be blessed*, &c. &c. And in what is said of Ishmael, as of his person, but meant chiefly of his posterity, Gen. xvi. 12. and xvii. 20. Thus in what Isaac said to Esau and Jacob, in his blessing he spake to them in the second person singular; but meant chiefly their posterity. And so for the most part in the promises made to Isaac and Jacob; and in Jacob blessing Ephraim and Manasseh, and his twelve sons.

But I shall take notice of one or two things further, showing that Adam's posterity were included in God's establishment with him, and the threatening denounced for his sin; and that the calamities which come upon them in consequence of his sin, are brought on them as punishments.

This is evident from the *curse on the ground;* which if it be any curse at all, comes equally on Adam's posterity with himself. And if it be a curse, then against whomsoever it is designed, and on whomsoever it terminates, it comes as a punishment, and not as a blessing, so far as it comes in consequence of that sentence.

Dr. T. (p. 19.) says, "A curse is pronounced upon the ground, but no curse upon the woman and the man." And (p. 45, 46. S.) he insists, that the *ground* only was cursed, and not the man: as though a curse could terminate on lifeless, senseless earth! To understand this curse otherwise than as terminating upon man through the ground, would be as senseless as to suppose the meaning to be, *The ground shall be punished and shall be miserable for thy sake.* Our author interprets the curse on the ground, of its being encumbered with noxious weeds: but would these weeds have been any curse on the ground, if there had been no inhabitants, or if the inhabitants had been of such a nature, that these weeds should not have been noxious, but useful to them? It is said, Deut. xxviii. 17. "Cursed shall be thy basket, and thy store:" and would he not be thought to talk very ridiculously, who should say, "Here is a curse upon the basket; but not a word of any curse upon the owner: and therefore we have no reason at all to look upon it as any punishment upon him, or any testimony of God's displeasure towards him." How plain is it, that when *lifeless* things, not capable either of benefit or suffering, are said to be cursed or blessed with regard to *sensible* beings—who use or possess these things, or have connexion with them—the meaning must be, that these *sensible* beings are cursed or blessed *in the other*, or with respect to them! In Exod. xxiii. 25. it is said, "He shall bless thy bread and thy water." And I suppose, never any body yet proceeded to such a degree of subtilty in distinguishing, as to say, "Here is a blessing on the *bread* and the *water*, which went into the possessor's mouth, but no blessing on him." To make such a distinction, with regard to the curse God pronounced on the ground, would in some respects be more unreasonable; because God is express in *explaining* the matter, declaring that it was *for man's sake*, expressly referring this curse to *him*, as being for the sake of his guilt; and as consisting in the sorrow and suffering he should have from it: "In sorrow shalt *thou* eat of it.—Thorns and thistles shall it bring forth *to thee.*" So that God's own words tell us where the curse terminates. The words are parallel with those in Deut. xxviii. 16. but only more plain and explicit, "Cursed shalt *thou* be in the field, or in the ground."

If this part of the sentence was pronounced under no notion of any curse or punishment at all upon mankind, but, on the contrary, as making an alteration for the *better*, as to *them*—that instead of the sweet, but tempting, pernicious fruit of paradise, it might produce wholesome fruits, more for the health of the soul; that it might bring forth thorns and thistles, as excellent medicines, to prevent or cure moral distempers, diseases which would issue in eternal death—then it was a *blessing* on the ground, and not a curse; and it might more properly have been said, "BLESSED *shall the ground be for thy sake.*—I will make a happy change in it, that it may be a habitation more fit for a creature so infirm, and so apt to be overcome with temptation, as thou art."

The *event* makes it evident, that in pronouncing this curse, God had as much respect to Adam's *posterity*, as to himself. And so it was understood by his pious posterity before the flood; as appears by what Lamech, the father of Noah, says, Gen. v. 29. "And he called his name Noah; saying, This same shall comfort us concerning our work, and the toil of our hands, *because of the ground which the Lord hath cursed.*"

Another thing which argues, that Adam's posterity were included in the threatening of death—and that our first parents understood, when fallen, that the tempter, in persuading them to eat the forbidden fruit, had aimed at the punishment and ruin of both them and their posterity, and had procured it—is Adam immediately giving his wife that new name, *Eve* or *Life*, on the promise or intimation of the disappointment and overthrow of the tempter in that matter, by her seed. This Adam understood to be by his procuring LIFE; not only for themselves, but for many of their posterity; and thereby delivering them from that death and ruin which the serpent had brought upon them. Those that should be thus delivered, and obtain life, Adam calls *the living.* And because he observed, by what God had said, that deliverance, or life, was to be by the seed of the woman, he therefore remarks, that *she is the mother of all living*, and thereupon gives her a new name, חוה LIFE, Gen. iii. 20.

There is a great deal of evidence, that this is the occasion of Adam giving his wife her new name. This was her new honour, and the greatest honour, at least in her present state, that the Redeemer was to be of her seed. New names were wont to be given for something that was the person's peculiar honour. So it was with regard to the new names of *Abraham, Sarah,* and *Israel.* Dr. T. himself observes,* that they who are saved by Christ, are called, (οἱ ζωντες, 2 Cor. iv. 11.) *the living* or *they that live.* Thus we find in the Old Testament, the *righteous* are called by the name of *the living,* Psal. lxix. 28. "Let them be blotted out of the book of the *living,* and not be written with the righteous." If what Adam meant by her being the *mother of all living,* was only her being the mother of mankind; and gave her the name *life* upon that account; it were much the most likely that he would have given her this name at first; when God first united them, under that blessing, *be fruitful and multiply,* and when he had a prospect of her being the mother of mankind *in a state of immortality, living indeed, living* and never *dying.* But that Adam should at that time give her only the name of (אשה) *Isha,* and then immediately on that melancholy change, by their coming under the *sentence of death,* with all their posterity—having now a new awful prospect of her being the mother of nothing but a *dying race,* all from generation to generation turning to dust, through her folly—he should change her name into *life,* calling her now the mother of *all living,* is (on that supposition) perfectly unaccountable. Besides, it is manifest, that it was not her being the mother of all *mankind*—or *her relation,* as a mother, to her posterity—but the *quality of those* of whom she was to be the mother, Adam had in view, in giving his wife this new name; as appears by the name itself, which signifies *life.* And if it had been only a *natural* and mortal life he had in view, this was nothing to distinguish her posterity from the brutes; for the very same name of *living* ones, or *living* things, is given from time to time to *them.*† Besides, if by *life* the *quality* of her posterity was not meant, there was nothing in it to distinguish her from Adam; for thus she was no more the mother of all living, than he was the father of all living; and she could no more properly be called by the name of *life* on any such account, than he: but names are given for distinction. Doubtless Adam took notice of something distinguishing concerning her, that occasioned his giving her this new name. And I think it is exceeding natural to suppose, that as Adam had given her the *first name* from the manner of her *creation,* so he gave her the *new name* from *redemption,* and as it were *new creation,* through a Redeemer, of her seed. And, it is equally probable, that he should give her this name from that which comforted him, with respect to the curse that God had pronounced on him and the earth, as *Lamech* named *Noah,* Gen. v. 29. "Saying, this same shall comfort us concerning our work, and toil of our hands, because of the ground which the Lord hath cursed." Accordingly he gave her this new name, not at her first creation, but immediately after the promise of a Redeemer. (See Gen. iii. 15—20.)

Now, as to the consequence which I infer from *Adam* giving his wife this name, on the intimation which God had given—that *Satan* should by her seed be overthrown and disappointed, as to his malicious design in tempting the woman—it is, that great numbers of mankind should be saved, whom he calls *the living;* they should be saved from the effects of this malicious design of the old serpent, and from that ruin which he had brought upon them by tempting their first parents to sin; and so the serpent would be, with respect to them, disappointed and overthrown in his design. But how is any death, or indeed any calamity at all, brought upon their posterity by *Satan's* malice in that temptation, if instead of that, all the consequent death and sorrow was the fruit of God's fatherly love? an instance of his free and sovereign favour? And if multitudes of *Eve's* posterity are saved from either spiritual or temporal death, by a Redeemer, one of her seed, how is that any disappointment of *Satan's* design, in tempting our first parents? How came he to have any such thing in view, as the death of *Adam's* and *Eve's* posterity, by tempting them to sin, or any expectation that their death would be the consequence, *unless he knew that they were included in the* THREATENING?

* Note annexed to § 287.

Some have objected, against his *posterity* being included in the threatening delivered to Adam, that the threatening itself was inconsistent with his *having any posterity*: it being that he should die *on the day that he sinned.* To this I answer, that the threatening was not inconsistent with his having posterity, on two accounts:

I. Those words, *In the day thou eatest thereof thou shalt surely die,* according to the use of such like expressions among the *Hebrews,* do not signify *immediate* death, or that the execution shall be within twenty-four hours from the commission of the fact; nor did God by those words limit himself as to the *time* of executing the threatened punishment; but that was still left to God's pleasure. Such a phrase, according to the idiom of the *Hebrew* tongue, signifies no more than these two things:

1. A *real connexion* between the sin and the punishment. So Ezek. xxxiii. 12, 13. "The righteousness of the righteous shall not deliver him *in the day* of his transgression. As for the wickedness of the wicked, he shall not fall thereby *in the day* that he turneth from his wickedness: neither shall the righteous be able to live *in the day that he sinneth:* but for his iniquity that he hath committed, *he shall die* for it." Here it is said, that *in the day* he sinneth, he shall not be able to live, but he shall die; not signifying the time when death shall be executed upon him, but the connexion between his sin and death; such a connexion as in our present common use of language is signified by the adverb of time, *when;* as if one should say, "According to the laws of our nation, so long as a man behaves himself as a good subject, he may live; but *when* he turns rebel, he must die:" not signifying the hour, day, or month, in which he must be executed, but only the connexion between his crime and death.

2. Another thing which seems to be signified by such an expression, is, that Adam should be exposed to *death by one transgression,* without waiting to try him the second time. If he eat of that tree, he should immediately fall under condemnation, though afterwards he might abstain ever so strictly. In this respect the words are much of the same force with those words of *Solomon to Shimei;* 1 Kings ii. 37. "For it shall be that *on the day* that thou goest out, and passest over the brook Kidron, thou shalt know for *certain, that thou shalt surely die.*" Not meaning, that he should certainly be *executed* on that day, but that he should be assuredly *liable* to death for the first offence, and that he should not have another trial to see whether he would go over the brook *Kidron* a second time.—Besides,

II. If the words had implied, that Adam should die that very *day* (within twenty-four or twelve hours) or that *moment* in which he transgressed, yet it will by no means follow, that God obliged himself to execute the punishment *in its utmost extent* on that day. The sentence was in great *part* executed immediately; he then died *spiritually;* he lost his innocence and original righteousness, and the favour of God; a dismal alteration was made in his soul, by the loss of that holy divine principle, which was in the highest sense the life of the soul. In this he was truly ruined and undone *that very day;* becoming corrupt, miserable, and helpless. And I think it has been shown, that such a spiritual death was one great thing implied in the threatening. And the alteration then made in his body and external state, was the beginning of temporal death. Grievous external calamity is called by the name of *death* in Scripture, Exod. x. 17.—"Entreat the Lord that he may take away this *death.*" Not only was Adam's soul ruined that day, but his BODY was ruined; it lost its beauty and vigour, and became a poor, dull, decaying, dying thing.

And besides all this, Adam was that day undone in a more dreadful sense; he immediately fell under the curse of the law, and condemnation to eternal perdition. In the language of Scripture, he is *dead,* that is, in a state of condemnation to death; even as our author often explains this language in his exposition upon *Romans.* In scripture language, he that believes in Christ, immediately receives *life.* He passes at that time from death to life, and thenceforward (to use the apostle *John's* phrase) "has

† As in Gen. i. 21, 24, 28. Chap. ii. 19. Chap. vi. 19. vii. 23. and viii. 1. and many other places in the Bible.

eternal life abiding in him." But yet, he does not then receive eternal life in its highest completion; he has but the *beginning* of it; and receives it in a vastly greater degree at death. The proper time for the complete fulness, is not till the day of judgment. When the angels sinned, their punishment was *immediately* executed in a degree; but their full punishment is not till the end of the world. And there is nothing in God's threatening to Adam that bound him to execute his full punishment at once; nor any thing which determines, that he should have no posterity. The constitution which God established and declared, determined, that IF he sinned, and had posterity, he and they should die. But there was no constitution determining the actual being of his posterity in this case; what posterity he should have, how many, or whether any at all. All these things God had reserved in his own power: the law and its sanction intermeddled not with the matter.

It may be proper in this place also to take some notice of that objection of Dr. T. against Adam being supposed to be a federal head for his posterity, that it gives him greater honour than Christ, as it supposes that all his posterity would have had eternal life by his obedience, if he had stood; and so a greater number would have had the benefit of his obedience, than are saved by Christ.*—I think, a very little consideration is sufficient to show, that there is no weight in this objection. For the benefit of Christ's merit may nevertheless be vastly beyond that which would have been by the obedience of Adam. For those that are saved by Christ, are not merely advanced to happiness by his merits, but saved from the infinitely dreadful effects of Adam's sin, and many from immense guilt, pollution, and misery, by personal sins. They are also brought to a holy and happy state through infinite obstacles; and exalted to a far greater degree of dignity, felicity, and glory, than would have been due for *Adam's* obedience; for aught I know, many thousand times so great. And there is enough in the gospel-dispensation, clearly to manifest the sufficiency of Christ's merits for such effects in all *mankind*. And how great the number will be, that shall *actually* be the subjects of them, or how great a proportion of the whole race, considering the vast success of the gospel that shall be in that future, extraordinary, and glorious season, often spoken of, none can tell. And the honour of these two federal heads arises not so much from what was proposed to each for his trial, as from their success, and the good actually obtained; and also the manner of obtaining. Christ obtains the benefits men have through him by proper merit of condignity, and a true purchase by an equivalent; which would not have been the case with Adam if he had obeyed.

I have now particularly considered the account which Moses gives us, in the beginning of the Bible, of our first parents, and God's dealings with them; the constitution he established with them, their transgression, and what followed. And on the whole, if we consider the *manner* in which God apparently speaks to Adam from time to time; and particularly, if we consider how plainly and undeniably his *posterity* are included in the sentence of death pronounced on him after his fall, founded on the foregoing threatening; and consider the *curse* denounced on the ground for his sake, for his sorrow, and that of his posterity; and also consider, what is evidently the *occasion* of his giving his *wife* the new name of *Eve*, and his meaning in it—and withal consider apparent fact in constant and universal events, with relation to the state of our first parents and their posterity from that time forward, through all ages of the world—I cannot but think, it must appear to every impartial person, that Moses's account does, with sufficient evidence, lead all mankind, to whom his account is communicated, to understand, that God, in his constitution with Adam, dealt with him as a *public* person—as the head of the human species—and had respect to his posterity, as included in him. And it must appear, that this history is given by divine direction, in the beginning of the first written revelation, in order to exhibit to our view the origin of the present sinful, miserable state of mankind, that we might see what that was, which first gave occasion for all those consequent wonderful dispensations of divine mercy and grace towards mankind, which are the great subject of the Scriptures, both of the Old and New Testament; and that these things are not obscurely and doubtfully pointed forth, but delivered in a plain account of things, which easily and naturally exhibits them to our understandings.

* Page 120, &c. S.

CHAP. II.

OBSERVATIONS ON OTHER PARTS OF THE HOLY SCRIPTURES, CHIEFLY IN THE OLD TESTAMENT, THAT PROVE THE DOCTRINE OF ORIGINAL SIN.

ORIGINAL depravity may well be argued, from wickedness being often spoken of in Scripture, as a thing *belonging to the race of mankind, and as if it were a property of the species*. So in Psal. xiv. 2, 3. "The Lord looked down from heaven upon the *children of men*, to see if there were any that did understand, and seek God. They are all gone aside; they are altogether become filthy: there is none that doeth good; no, not one." The like we have again, Psal. liii. 2, 3.—Dr. T. says, (p. 104, 105.) "The Holy Spirit does not mean this of every individual; because in the very same psalm, he speaks of some that were righteous, ver. 5. *God is in the generation of the righteous.*" But how little is this observation to the purpose? For who ever supposed, that no unrighteous men were ever changed by divine grace, and afterwards made righteous? The psalmist is speaking of what men are as they are the *children of men*, born of the corrupt human race; and not as born of God, whereby they come to be the children of God, and of the *generation of the righteous*. The apostle *Paul* cites this place in Rom. iii. 10—12. to prove the universal corruption of mankind; but yet in the same chapter he supposes the same persons spoken of as wicked, may become righteous, through the righteousness and grace of God.

Wickedness is spoken of in other places in the book of Psalms, as a thing that *belongs to men, as of the human race, as sons of men*. Thus, in Psal. iv. 2. "O ye *sons of men*, how long will ye turn my glory into shame? How long will ye love vanity?" &c. Psal. lvii. 4. "I lie among them that are set on fire, *even the sons of men*, whose teeth are spears and arrows, and their tongue a sharp sword." Psal. lviii. 1, 2. "Do ye indeed speak righteousness, O congregation? Do ye judge uprightly, *O ye sons of men?* Yea, in heart ye work wickedness; ye weigh out the violence of your hands in the earth." Our author mentioning these places, says, (p. 105. note,) "There was a strong party in Israel disaffected to David's person and government, and sometimes he chooseth to denote them by the sons or children of men." But it would have been worth his while to have inquired, *Why* the psalmist *should choose to denote* the worst men in Israel by this name? Why he should choose thus to disgrace mankind, as if the compellation of sons of men most properly belonged to such as were of the vilest character, and as if all the sons of men, even every one of them, were of such a character, and none of them did good; no, not one? Is it not strange, that the righteous should not be thought worthy to be called *sons of men*, and ranked with that noble race of beings, who are born into the world wholly right and innocent? It is a good, easy, and natural reason, why he chooseth to call the wicked, *sons of men*, as a proper name for them, That by being of the sons of men, or of the corrupt, ruined race of mankind, they come by their depravity. And the psalmist himself leads us to this very reason, Psal. lviii. "Do ye judge uprightly, *O ye sons of men?* yea, in heart ye work wickedness, ye weigh out the violence of your hands. The wicked are *estranged from the womb*," &c. Of which I shall speak more by and by.

Agreeable to these places is Prov. xxi. 8. "The way of *man* is froward and strange; but as for the *pure*, his work is right." He that is perverse in his walk, is here called by the name of *man*, as distinguished from the pure:

which I think is absolutely unaccountable, if all mankind by nature are *pure*, and perfectly innocent, and all such as are froward and strange in their ways, therein depart from the native purity of all mankind. The words naturally lead us to suppose the contrary; that depravity and perverseness properly belong to mankind as they are naturally, and that a being made pure, is by an after-work, by which some are delivered from native pollution, and distinguished from mankind in general: which is perfectly agreeable to the representation in Rev. xiv. 4. where we have an account of a number that *were not defiled*, but were pure, and *followed the Lamb;* of whom it is said, "These were *redeemed from among men.*"

To these things agree Jer. xvii. 5, 9. In ver. 5. it is said, "Cursed is he that trusteth in *man.*" And in ver. 9. this reason is given, "The heart is deceitful above all things, and desperately wicked; who can know it?" What heart is this so wicked and deceitful? Why, *evidently the heart of him, who, it was said before, we must not trust;* and that is MAN. It alters not the case as to the present argument, whether the deceitfulness of the heart here spoken of, be its deceitfulness to the man himself, or to others. So Eccl. ix. 3. "Madness is in the heart of the *sons of men*, while they live." And those words of Christ to *Peter*, Matt. xvi. 23. "Get thee behind me, Satan—for thou savourest not the things that be of God, but the things that be of *men*. Signifying plainly, that to be carnal and vain, and opposite to what is spiritual and divine, is what properly belongs to *men* in their present state. The same thing is supposed in that of the apostle, 1 Cor. iii. 3. "For ye are yet carnal. For whereas there is among you envying and strife, are ye not carnal, and walk as *men?*" And that in Hos. vi. 7. "But they, like *men*, have transgressed the covenant." To these places may be added Matt. vii. 11. "If *ye being evil*, know how to give good gifts." Jam. iv. 5. "Do ye think that the scripture saith in vain, the spirit that *dwelleth in us, lusteth to envy?*"—1 Pet. iv. 2. "That he no longer should live the rest of his time in the lusts of *men*, but to the will of God."—Yet above all, that in Job xv. 16. "How much more abominable and filthy is *man, who drinketh iniquity like water?*" Of which more presently.

Now what account can be given of these things, on Dr. T.'s scheme? How strange is it, that we should have such descriptions, all over the Bible, of MAN, and the SONS OF MEN! Why should man be so continually spoken of as evil, carnal, perverse, deceitful, and desperately wicked, if all men are by nature as perfectly innocent, and free from any propensity to evil, as Adam was the first moment of his creation, all *made right*, as our author would have us understand Eccl. vii. 29.? Why, on the contrary, is it not said, at least as often, and with equal reason, that *the heart of man is right and pure;* that *the way of man is innocent and holy;* and that *he who savours true virtue and wisdom, savours the things that be of men?* Yea, and why might it not as well have been said, *the Lord looked down from heaven on the sons of men, to see if there were any that did understand, and did seek after God; and they were all right, altogether pure, there was none inclined to do wickedness, no, not one?*

Of the like import with the texts mentioned are those which represent wickedness as what properly belongs to the WORLD; and that they who are otherwise, are *saved from the world*, and *called out of it*. As John vii. 7. "The *world* cannot hate you; but me it hateth; because I testify of it, that the works thereof are evil." Chap. viii. 23. "Ye are of this *world:* I am not of this *world.*" Chap. xiv. 17. "The spirit of truth, whom the *world* cannot receive; because it seeth him not, neither knoweth him: but ye know him." Chap. xv. 18, 19. "If the *world* hate you, ye know that it hated me before it hated you. If ye were of the *world*, the *world* would love its own: but because ye are not of the *world*, but I have chosen you out of the *world*, therefore the *world* hateth you." Rev. xiv. 3, 4. "These are they which were redeemed from the *earth*,—redeemed from among men." John xvii. 9. "I pray not for the *world*, but for them which thou hast given me." Ver. 14. "I have given them thy word; and the *world* hath hated them, because they are not of the *world*, even as I am not of the *world*." 1 John iii. 13 "Marvel not, my brethren, if the *world* hate you." Chap. iv. 5. "They are of the *world*, therefore speak they of the *world*, and the *world* heareth them." Chap. v. 19. "We are of God, and the whole *world* lieth in wickedness." It is evident, that in these places, by the world is meant the world of mankind; not the habitation, but the inhabitants: for, it is the world spoken of as *loving, hating, doing evil works, speaking, hearing*, &c.

The same thing is shown, when wickedness is often spoken of as being man's OWN, in contradistinction from virtue and holiness. So men's lusts are often called their OWN hearts' lusts, and their practising wickedness is called walking in their OWN ways, walking in their OWN counsels, in the imagination of their OWN heart, and in the sight of their OWN eyes, according to their OWN devices, &c. These things denote wickedness to be a quality belonging properly to the character and nature of mankind in their present state: as, when Christ would represent that lying is remarkably the character and the very nature of the devil in his present state, he expresses it thus, John viii. 44. "When he speaketh a lie, he speaketh of his *own:* for he is a liar, and the father of it."

And that wickedness belongs to the very *nature* of men in their present state, may be argued from those places which speak of mankind as being wicked *in their childhood*, or *from their childhood*. So Prov. xxii. 15. "Foolishness is bound in the heart of a child; but the rod of correction shall drive it far from him." Nothing is more manifest, than that the wise man in this book continually uses the word folly, or foolishness, for wickedness; and that this is what he means in this place, the words themselves explain. For the rod of correction is proper to drive away no other foolishness, but that which is of a moral nature. The word rendered *bound*, signifies (as observed in *Pool's Synopsis*) a close and firm union. The same word is used in chap. vi. 21. "*Bind* them continually upon thine heart." And chap. vii. 3. "*Bind* them upon thy fingers. write them upon the table of thine heart."* The same verb is used, 1 Sam. xviii. 1. "The soul of Jonathan was knit, or *bound*, to the soul of David, and Jonathan loved him as his own soul."—But how comes wickedness to be so firmly bound, and strongly fixed, in the hearts of children, if it be not there naturally? They have had no time firmly to fix habits of sin, by long custom in actual wickedness, as those who have lived many years in the world.

The same thing is signified in that noted place, Gen. viii. 21. "For the imagination of man's heart is evil, *from his youth.*" It alters not the case, whether it be translated *for* or *though* the imagination of man's heart is evil from his youth, as Dr. T. would have it. The word translated *youth*, signifies the whole of the former part of the age of man, which commences from the beginning of life. The word in its derivation, has reference to the birth or beginning of existence. It comes from (נער) a word *to shake off*, as a tree shakes off its ripe fruit, or a plant its seed; the birth of children being commonly represented by a tree yielding fruit, or a plant yielding seed. So that the word here translated *youth*, comprehends not only what we in *English* most commonly call the time of youth, but also childhood and infancy, and is very often used to signify these latter.†

Dr. T. says, (p. 124. note,) that he "conceives, *from the youth*, is a phrase signifying the greatness or long duration of a thing." But if by long duration he means any thing else than what is literally expressed, *viz.* from the beginning of life, he has no reason to conceive so, neither has what he offers so much as the shadow of a reason for his conception. There is no appearance in the words of the two or three texts he mentions, of their meaning any thing else than what is most literally signified. And it is certain, that what he suggests is not the *ordinary* import of

* To the like purpose is chap. iii. 3. and Deut. xi. 18. where this word is used.

† A word of the same root is used to signify a *young child*, or a *little child*, in the following places; 1 Sam. i. 24, 25, 27. 1 Kings iii. 7. and xi. 17. 2 Kings ii. 23. Job xxxiii. 25. Prov. xxii. 6. xxiii. 13. and xxix. 21. Isa. x. 19. xi. 6. and lxv. 20. Hos. xi. 1. The same word is used to signify an *infant*, in Exod. ii. 6. and x. 9. Judg. xiii. 5, 7, 8, 24. 1 Sam. i. 22. and iv. 21. 2 Kings v. 14. Isa. vii. 16. and viii. 4.

such a phrase among the *Hebrews;* but that thereby is meant *from the beginning*, or *the early time of life*, or existence; as may be seen in the places following, where the same word in the *Hebrew* is used, as in the eighth of *Genesis.* 1 Sam. xii. 2. "I am old and grey-headed—and I have walked before you from my *childhood* unto this day." Ps. lxxi. 5, 6. "Thou art my trust *from my youth:* by thee have I been holden up from the womb. Thou art he that took me out of my mother's bowels." (Ver. 17, 18.) "O God, thou hast taught me *from my youth;* and hitherto have I declared thy wondrous works: now also, when I am old and grey-headed, forsake me not." Ps. cxxix. 1, 2. "Many a time have they afflicted me *from my youth*, may Israel now say: many a time have they afflicted me *from my youth;* yet have they not prevailed against me." Isa. xlvii. 12. "Stand now with the multitude of thy sorceries, wherein thou hast laboured *from thy youth.*" (So also ver. 15.) 2 Sam. xix. 7. "That will be worse unto thee, than all the evil that befell thee *from thy youth* until now." Jer. iii. 24, 25. "Shame hath devoured the labour of our fathers, *from our youth.*—We have sinned against the Lord our God *from our youth*, even to this day."*

And it is to be observed, that according to the manner of the *Hebrew* language, when it is said, such a thing has been *from youth*, or the first part of existence, the phrase is to be understood as *including* that first time of existence. So Josh. vi. 21. "They utterly destroyed all, from the young to the old," (so in the *Hebrew,) i. e.* including both. (So Gen. xix. 4. and Esther iii. 13.)

And as mankind are represented in Scripture, as being of a wicked heart *from their youth*, so in other places they are spoken of as being thus *from the womb.* Psal. lviii. 3. "The wicked are estranged *from the womb:* they go astray as soon as they be born, speaking lies." It is observable, that the psalmist mentions this as what belongs to the wicked, as the SONS OF MEN: for, these are the preceding words; "Do ye judge uprightly, O ye sons of men? Yea, in heart ye work wickedness."† Then it follows, *the wicked are estranged* FROM THE WOMB, &c. The next verse is, *their poison is like the poison of a serpent.* Serpents are poisonous as soon as they come into the world; they derive a poisonous nature by their generation. Dr. T. (p. 134, 135.) says, "It is evident that this is a scriptural figurative way of aggravating wickedness on the one hand, and of signifying early and settled habits of virtue on the other, to speak of it as being *from the womb.*" And as a probable instance of the latter, he cites that in Isa. xlix. 1. "The Lord hath called me from the womb; from the bowels of my mother hath he made mention of my name." But I apprehend, that in order to seeing this to be either *evident* or *probable*, a man must have eyes peculiarly affected. I humbly conceive that such phrases as that in the 49th of *Isaiah*, of God's calling the prophet *from the womb*, are *evidently* not of the import which he supposes; but mean truly from the beginning of existence, and are manifestly of like signification with that which is said of the prophet *Jeremiah*, Jer. i. 5. "Before I formed thee in the belly, I knew thee: before thou camest out of the womb, I sanctified thee, and ordained thee a prophet unto the nations." Which surely means something else besides a high degree of virtue: it plainly signifies that he was, from his first existence, set apart by God for a prophet. And it would be as unreasonable to understand it otherwise, as to suppose the angel meant any other than that *Samson* was set apart to be a Nazarite from the beginning of his life, when he says to his mother, "Behold, thou shalt conceive and bear a son: and now drink no wine, nor strong drink, &c. For the child shall be a Nazarite to God, *from the womb*, to the day of his death." By these instances it is plain, that the phrase, *from the womb*, as the other, *from the youth*, as used in Scripture, properly signifies from the beginning of life.

Very remarkable is that place, Job xv. 14—16. "What is man, that he should be clean? And he that is *born of a woman*, that he should be righteous? Behold, he putteth no trust in his saints; yea, the heavens are not clean in his sight: how much more abominable and filthy is man, which drinketh iniquity like water!" And no less remarkable is our author's method of managing it. The 16th verse expresses an exceeding degree of wickedness, in as plain and emphatical terms, almost, as can be invented; every word representing this in the strongest manner: "How much more abominable and filthy is man, that drinketh iniquity like water!" I cannot now recollect, where we have a sentence equal to it in the whole Bible, for an emphatical, lively, and strong representation of great wickedness of heart. Any one of the words, as such words are used in Scripture, would represent great wickedness: if it had been only said, "How much more abominable is man! Or, how much more filthy is man! Or, man that drinketh iniquity." But all these are accumulated with the addition of—*like water*,—the further to represent the boldness or greediness of men in wickedness. Though iniquity be the most deadly poison, yet men drink it as boldly as they drink water, are as familiar with it as with their common drink, and drink it with like greediness, as he that is thirsty drinks water. That boldness and eagerness in persecuting the saints, by which the great degree of the depravity of man's heart often appears, as thus represented, Psal. xiv. 4. "Have the workers of iniquity no knowledge, who eat up my people as they eat bread?" And the greatest eagerness of thirst is represented by thirsting as an animal thirsts after water, Psal. xlii. 1.

Now let us see the soft, easy, light manner, in which Dr. T. treats this place. (p. 143.) "*How much more abominable and filthy is man*, IN COMPARISON OF THE DIVINE PURITY, who drinketh iniquity like water! who is attended with so many sensual appetites, and so apt to indulge them. You see the argument, man in his present weak and fleshly state, cannot be clean before God. Why so? Because he is conceived and born in sin, by reason of *Adam's* sin? No such thing. But because, if the purest creatures are not pure, *in comparison of God*, much less a being subject to so many INFIRMITIES as a MORTAL man. Which is a demonstration to me, not only that *Job* and his friends did not intend to establish the doctrine we are now examining, but that they were wholly strangers to it." Thus he endeavours to reconcile this text with his doctrine of the perfect native innocence of mankind; in which we have a notable specimen of his *demonstrations*, as well as of that great *impartiality* and fairness in examining and expounding the Scripture, of which he so often makes a profession!

In this place we are not only told, how wicked man's heart is, but also how men come by such wickedness; even by being of the race of mankind, by ordinary generation: *What is man, that he should be clean? and he that is born of a woman, that he should be righteous?* Our author (p. 141, 142.) represents man being born of a woman, as a *periphrasis*, to signify man; and that there is no design in the words to give a reason, why man is not clean and righteous. But the case is most evidently otherwise, if we may interpret the book of *Job* by itself. It is most plain, that man's being *born of a woman* is given as a reason of his not being clean; chap. xiv. 4. "Who can bring a clean thing out of an unclean?" *Job* is speaking there expressly of man's being born of a woman, as appears in ver. 1. And here how plain is it, that this is given as a reason of man's not being clean! Concerning this Dr. T. says, *That this has no respect to any moral uncleanness, but only common frailty, &c.* But how evidently is this also otherwise! when that uncleanness, which a man has by being born of a woman, is expressly explained of *unrighteousness*, in the next chapter at the 14th verse, "What is man that he should be clean? and he that is born of a woman, that he should be righteous?" Also in chap. xxv. 4. "How then can man be justified with God? And how can he be clean that is born of a woman?" It is a moral cleanness *Bildad* is speaking of, which a man needs in order to his being *justified.* His design is, to convince *Job* of his *moral impurity*, and from thence of God's righteousness in his severe judgments upon him; and not of his *natural frailty.*

And, without doubt, David has respect to this way of derived wickedness of heart, when he says, Psal. li. 5. "Behold, I was shapen in iniquity, and in sin did my

* So Gen. xlvi. 34. Job xxxi. 18. Jer. xxxii. 30. and xlviii. 11. Ezek. iv. 14. Zech. xiii. 5.

† A phrase of the like import with that in Gen. viii. 21. The *imagination*, or, as it might have been rendered, the *operation*, of his heart is evil.

mother conceive me." It alters not the case, as to the argument we are upon, whether the word (יחמתני) *conceive me*, signifies to *conceive*, or to *nurse;* which latter, our author takes so much pains to prove: for, when he has done all, he speaks of it as a just translation of the words to render them thus, *I was* BORN *in iniquity, and in sin did my mother nurse me.* (p. 135.) If it is owned that man is *born in sin*, it is not worth the while to dispute, whether it is expressly asserted, that he is *conceived in sin.* But Dr. T. after his manner, insists, that such expressions, as being *born in sin*, being *transgressors from the womb*, and the like, are only phrases *figuratively* to denote aggravation, and a high degree of wickedness. But the contrary has been already demonstrated, from many plain scripture instances. Nor is one instance produced, in which there is any evidence that such a phrase is used in such a manner. A poetical sentence out of Virgil's *Æneid*, has here been produced, and made much of by some, as parallel with this, in what *Dido* says to *Æneas*, in these lines:

> Nec tibi diva parens, generis nec dardanus auctor,
> Perfide: Sed duris genuit te cautibus horrens
> Caucasus, hyrcanæque admôrunt ubera tygres.

In which she tells *Æneas*, that not a goddess was his mother, nor *Anchises* his father; but that he had been brought forth by a horrid rocky mountain, and nursed at the dugs of tigers, to represent the greatness of his cruelty to her. But how unlike and unparallel is this! Nothing could be more natural, than for a woman overpowered with the passion of love, and distracted with raging jealousy and disappointment, thinking herself treated with brutish perfidy and cruelty, by a lover whose highest fame had been his being the son of a goddess, to aggravate his inhumanity and hard-heartedness with this, that his behaviour was not worthy the son of a goddess, nor becoming one whose father was an illustrious prince: and that he acted more as if he had been brought forth by hard unrelenting rocks, and had sucked the dugs of tigers. But what is there in the case of David parallel, or at all in like manner leading him to speak of himself as born in sin, in any such figurative sense? He is not speaking himself, nor any one speaking to him, of any excellent and divine father and mother, of whom he was born: nor is there any appearance of his aggravating his sin, by its being unworthy of his high birth. There is nothing else visible in David's case to lead him to take notice of his being *born in sin*, but only his having such experience of the continuance and power of indwelling sin, after so long a time, and so many and great means to engage him to holiness; which showed that sin was inbred, and in his very nature.

Dr. T. often objects to these and other texts, brought by divines to prove original sin, that there is no mention made in them of *Adam*, nor of his sin. He cries out, *Here is not the least mention, or intimation of* Adam, *or any ill effects of his sin upon us.—Here is not one word, nor the least hint of* Adam, *or any consequences of his sin, &c. &c.** He says,† "If *Job* and his friends had known and believed the doctrine of a corrupt nature, derived from Adam's sin only, they ought in reason and truth to have given this as the true and only reason of the human imperfection and uncleanness they mention." But these objections and exclamations are made no less impertinently, than frequently. It is no more a proof, that *corruption of nature* did not come by Adam's sin, because many times when it is mentioned, his sin is not expressly mentioned as the cause of it; than that *death* did not come by Adam's sin, as Dr. T. says it did. For though death, as incident to mankind, is mentioned so often in the Old Testament, and by our Saviour in his discourses, yet Adam's sin is not once expressly mentioned, after the three first chapters of *Genesis*, any where in all the Old Testament, or the four Evangelists, as the occasion of it.

What Christian has there ever been, that believed the moral corruption of human nature, who ever doubted that it came in the way, of which the apostle speaks, when he says, "*By one man* sin entered into the world, and death by sin?" Nor indeed have they any more reason to doubt of it, than to doubt of the whole history of our first parents, because Adam's name is so rarely mentioned, on any occasion in Scripture, after that first account of him, and Eve's never at all; and because we have no more any express mention of the particular manner, in which mankind were first brought into being, either with respect to the creation of Adam or Eve. It is sufficient, that the abiding, most visible effects of these things, remain in the view of mankind in all ages, and are often spoken of in Scripture; and that the particular manner of their being introduced, is once plainly set forth in the beginning of the Bible, in that history which gives us an account of the origin of all things. And doubtless it was expected, by the great author of the Bible, that the account in the three first chapters of Genesis should be taken as a plain account of the introduction of both natural and moral evil into the world. The history of Adam's sin, with its circumstances, God's threatening, the sentence pronounced upon him after his transgression and the immediate consequences, consisting in so vast an alteration in his state—and the state of the world, with respect to all his posterity—most directly and sufficiently lead us to understand the rise of calamity, sin, and death, in this sinful, miserable world.

It is fit we all should know, that it does not become us to tell the Most High, how often he shall particularly explain and give the reason of any doctrine which he teaches, in order to our believing what he says. If he has at all given us evidence that it is a doctrine agreeable to his mind, it becomes us to receive it with full credit and submission; and not sullenly to reject it, because our notions and humours are not suited in the manner, and number of times, of his particularly explaining it. How often is pardon of sins promised in the Old Testament to repenting and returning sinners! How many hundred times is God's special favour there promised to the sincerely righteous, without any express mention of these benefits being through Christ! Would it therefore become us to say, that inasmuch as our dependence on Christ for these benefits is a doctrine, which, if true, is of such importance, God ought expressly to have mentioned Christ's merits as the reason and ground of the benefits, if he knew they were the ground of them; and should have plainly declared it sooner, and more frequently, if ever he expected we should believe him, when he did tell us of it? How oft is vengeance and misery threatened in the Old Testament to the wicked, without any clear and express signification of any such thing intended, as that everlasting fire, where there is wailing and gnashing of teeth, in another world, which Christ so often speaks of as the punishment appointed for all the wicked! Would it now become a Christian, to object and say, that if God really meant any such thing, he ought in *reason and truth* to have declared it plainly and fully; and not to have been so silent about a matter of such vast importance to all mankind, for four thousand years together?

CHAP. III.

OBSERVATIONS ON VARIOUS OTHER PLACES OF SCRIPTURE, PRINCIPALLY OF THE NEW TESTAMENT, PROVING THE DOCTRINE OF ORIGINAL SIN.

Sect. I.

Observations on John iii. 6. in connexion with some other passages in the New Testament.

Those words of Christ, giving a reason to Nicodemus, why we must be born again, John iii. 6. "That which is born of the flesh, is flesh, and that which is born of the Spirit is spirit," have not without good reason been produced by divines, as a proof of the doctrine of original sin: supposing, that by *flesh* here is meant *the human nature in a debased and corrupt state.* Yet Dr. T. (p. 144.) thus explains these words, *that which is born of the flesh, is flesh;* "that which is born by natural descent and propagation, is a man consisting of body and soul, or the mere constitution and powers of a man in their natural state." But the constant use of these terms, *flesh* and *spirit*, in

* Page 5, 64, 96, 97, 98, 102, 108, 112, 118, 120, 122, 127, 128, 136, 142, 143, 149, 152, 155, 229.

† 142.

other parts of the New Testament, when thus set in opposition, and the latter said to be produced by the Spirit of God, as here—and when expressive of the same thing, which Christ is here speaking of to Nicodemus, *viz.* the requisite qualifications to salvation—will fully vindicate the sense, of our divines. Thus in the 7th and 8th chapters of Romans, where these terms *flesh* and *spirit* (σαρξ and πνευμα) are abundantly repeated, and set in opposition, as here. So chap. vii. 14. *The law is* (πνευματικος) *spiritual*, but I am (σαρκικος) *carnal*, sold under sin. He cannot only mean, " I am *a man consisting of body and soul, and having the powers of a man*." Ver. 18. " I know that in me, that is, in my *flesh*, dwelleth no good thing." He does not mean to condemn his frame, *as consisting of body and soul;* and to assert, that in his *human constitution, with the powers of a man*, dwells no good thing. And when he says in the last verse of the chapter, " With the mind, I myself serve the law of God, but with the *flesh*, the law of sin ;" he cannot mean, " *I myself serve the law of God;* but with my innocent *human constitution, as having the powers of a man*, I serve the law of sin." And when he says in the next words, the beginning of the 8th chapter, " there is no condemnation to them,—that walk not after the *flesh*, but after the spirit ;" and ver. 4. "The righteousness of the law is fulfilled in us, who walk not after the flesh ;" he cannot mean, "there is no condemnation to them that walk not according to *the powers of a man*," &c. And when he says, (ver. 5 and 6.) "They that are after the *flesh*, do mind the things of the *flesh ; and* to be *carnally* minded is death ;" he does not intend, "they that are according to *the human constitution, and the powers of a man*, do mind the things of the *human constitution and powers ;* and to mind these is death." And when he says, (ver. 7 and 8.) "The carnal (or fleshly) mind is enmity against God, and is not subject to the law of God, neither indeed can be : so that they that are in the *flesh*, cannot please God ;" he cannot mean, that to mind the things which are agreeable to "the *powers and constitution of a man*," who as our author says, is constituted or made right, is enmity against God ; and that a mind which is agreeable to this right human constitution, as God hath made it, is not subject to the law of God, nor indeed can be ; and that they who are according to such a constitution, cannot please God. And when it is said, (ver. 9.) "Ye are not in the flesh, but in the spirit ;" the apostle cannot mean, "ye are not in the *human nature, as constituted of body and soul, and with the powers of a man*." It is most manifest, that by the *flesh* here the apostle means a nature that is *corrupt*, of an evil tendency, and directly opposite to the law and holy nature of God ; so that to walk according to it, and to have a mind so conformed, is to be an utter enemy to God and his law ; in a state of perfect inconsistence with subjection to God, and of being pleasing to him ; and in a sure and infallible tendency to death, and utter destruction. And it is plain, that here by *walking after*, or according to, *the flesh*, is meant the same thing as walking according to a corrupt and sinful nature ; and to walk according to the *spirit*, is to walk according to a holy and divine nature, or principle : and to be *carnally* minded, is the same as being viciously and corruptly minded ; and to be *spiritually* minded, is to be of a virtuous and holy disposition.

When Christ says, John iii. 6. "That which is born of the *flesh*, is *flesh*," he represents the *flesh* not merely as a quality ; for it would be incongruous to speak of a quality as a thing born. Therefore man, as in his whole nature corrupt, is called *flesh ;* which is agreeable to other scripture representations, where the corrupt nature is called the *old man*, the *body of sin*, and the *body of death*. Agreeable to this are those representations in the 7th and 8th chapters of *Romans*. There, *flesh* is figuratively represented as a person, according to the apostle's manner. This is observed by Mr. Locke, and after him by Dr. T. who takes notice, that the apostle, in the 6th and 7th of *Romans*, represents sin as a person ; and that he figuratively distinguishes in himself two persons, speaking of flesh as his person. *For I know that in* ME, *that is, in my* FLESH, *dwelleth no good thing*. And it may be observed, that in the 8th chapter he still continues this representation, speaking of the *flesh* as a person. Accordingly, in the 6th and 7th verses, he speaks of *the mind of the flesh*, (φρονημα σαρκος,) and of the *mind of the spirit*, (φρονημα πνευματος,) as if the *flesh* and *spirit* were two opposite persons, each having a mind contrary to that of the other. Dr. T. interprets this *mind of the flesh, and mind of the spirit*, as though the *flesh and the spirit* were the different *objects*, about which the mind is conversant. But this is plainly beside the apostle's meaning ; who speaks of the flesh and spirit as the *subjects* in which the mind is ; and in a sense the agents, but not the *objects*, about which it acts. We have the same phrase again, ver. 27. " He that searcheth the hearts, knoweth what is the *mind of the spirit*" (φρονημα πνευματος). The mind of the spiritual nature in the saints is the same with the mind of the Spirit of God himself, who imparts and actuates that spiritual nature ; and here the spirit is the subject and agent ; but not the object. The same apostle, in a similar manner, uses the word, (νυς,) *mind*. Col. ii. 18. " Vainly puffed up by his *fleshly mind*, (απο τη νοα της σαρκος αυτυ,) by the mind of his flesh." And this agent so often called *flesh*, represented by the apostle as altogether evil, without any good thing dwelling in it, or belonging to it—yea perfectly contrary to God and his law, and tending only to death and ruin, and directly opposite to the spirit—is what Christ speaks of to Nicodemus as born in the first birth, and furnishing a reason why there is a necessity of a new birth, in order to a better production.

One thing is particularly observable in that discourse of the apostle—in which he so often uses the term *flesh*, as opposite to *spirit*—that he expressly calls it *sinful flesh*, Rom. viii. 3. It is manifest, that by *sinful flesh* he means the same thing with that *flesh* spoken of in all the context : and that when it is said, Christ was made in the likeness of *sinful flesh*, the expression is equipollent with those that speak of Christ as *made sin*, and *made a curse for us*.

Flesh and *spirit* are opposed to one another in Gal. v. in the same manner as in the 8th of Romans. And there, assuredly, by *flesh* cannot be meant only the *human nature of body and soul*, or *the mere constitution and powers of a man*, as in its natural state, innocent and right. In the 16th ver. the apostle says, " Walk in the *spirit*, and ye shall not fulfil the lusts of the *flesh* :" the *flesh*, is something of an evil inclination, desire, or lust. But this is more strongly signified in the next words ; " For the *flesh* lusteth against the *spirit* and the *spirit* against the *flesh ;* and these are contrary the one to the other." What could have been said more plainly, to show that what the apostle means by *flesh*, is something very evil in its nature, and an irreconcilable enemy to all goodness ? And it may be observed, that in these words, and those that follow, the apostle still figuratively represents the *flesh* as a person or agent, desiring, acting, having lusts, and performing works. And by works of the *flesh*, and fruits of the *spirit*, which are opposed to each other, (from ver. 19, to the end,) are plainly meant the same as works of a sinful nature, and fruits of a holy renewed nature. " Now the works of the *flesh* are manifest, which are these : adultery, fornication, uncleanness, lasciviousness, idolatry, witchcraft, hatred, variance, wrath, strife, seditions, heresies," &c. " But the fruit of the *spirit* is love, joy, peace, long-suffering, gentleness, goodness," &c. The apostle, by *flesh*, does not mean any thing that is innocent and good in itself, which only needs to be restrained, and kept in proper bounds ; but something altogether evil, which is to be destroyed. 1 Cor. v. 5. " To deliver such an one to Satan, for the *destruction of the flesh*." We must have *no mercy on it ;* we cannot be *too cruel to it ;* it must even *be crucified*. Gal. v. 24. "They that are Christ's, have *crucified* the *flesh* with the affections and lusts."

The apostle John—the same apostle that writes the account of what Christ said to Nicodemus—by the *spirit* means the same thing as a new, divine, and holy nature, exerting itself in a principle of divine love, which is the sum of all christian holiness. 1 John iii. 23, 24. " And that we should love one another, as he gave us commandment ; and he that keepeth his commandments, dwelleth in him, and he in him : and hereby we know that he abideth in us, by the *spirit* that he hath given us. Chap. iv. 12, 13. " If we love one another, God dwelleth in us, and his love is perfected in us : hereby know we, that we dwell in him, because he hath given us of his *Spirit*."

The spiritual principle in us being as it were a communication of the Spirit of God to us.

And as by (πνευμα) *spirit*, is meant a holy nature, so by the epithet, (πνευματικος,) *spiritual*, is meant the same as truly virtuous and holy. Gal. vi. 1. "Ye that are *spiritual*, restore such an one in the spirit of meekness." The apostle refers to what he had just said at the end of the foregoing chapter, where he had mentioned *meekness* as a fruit of the *spirit*. And so by *carnal*, or *fleshly*, (σαρκικος,) is meant the same as sinful. Rom. vii. 14. "The law is *spiritual*, (i. e. holy,) but I am *carnal*, sold under sin.".

And it is evident, that by *flesh*, as the word is used in the New Testament, and opposed to *spirit*, when speaking of the qualifications for eternal salvation, is meant—not only what is now vulgarly called *the sins of the flesh*, consisting in inordinate appetites of the body, and their indulgence; but—the whole body of sin, implying those lusts that are most subtle, and farthest from any relation to the body; such as pride, malice, envy, &c. When the *works of the flesh* are enumerated, Gal. v. 19—21. they are vices of the latter kind chiefly that are mentioned; "idolatry, witchcraft, hatred, variance, emulations, wrath, strife, seditions, heresies, envyings." So, pride of heart is the effect or operation of the *flesh*. Col. ii. 18. "Vainly puffed up by his fleshly mind:" in the Greek, (as before observed,) *by the mind of the flesh*. So, *pride*, *envying*, and *strife*, and *division*, are spoken of as works of the *flesh*, 1 Cor. iii. 3, 4. "For ye are yet carnal (σαρκικοι, *fleshly*). For whereas there is envying, and strife, and division, are ye not *carnal*, and walk as men? For while one saith, I am of Paul, and another, I am of Apollos, are ye not carnal?" Such kind of lusts do not depend on the body, or external senses; for the devil himself has them in the highest degree, who has not, nor ever had, any body or external senses to gratify.

Here, if it should be inquired, how corruption or depravity in general, or the nature of man as corrupt and sinful, came to be called *flesh*, and not only that corruption which consists in inordinate bodily appetites? I think, what the apostle says in the last cited place, "Are ye not carnal, and walk *as men?*" leads us to the true reason. It is because a corrupt and sinful nature is what properly belongs to *mankind*, or the race of Adam, as they are in themselves, and as they are *by nature*. the word *flesh* is often used in both the Old and the New Testament to signify *mankind* in their present state. To enumerate all the places, would be very tedious; I shall therefore only mention a few in the New Testament. Matt. xxiv. 22. "Except those days should be shortened, no *flesh* should be saved." Luke iii. 6. "All *flesh* shall see the salvation of God." John xvii. 2. "Thou hast given him power over all *flesh*."* Man's nature, being left *to itself*, forsaken of the Spirit of God, as it was when man fell, and consequently forsaken of divine and holy principles, *of itself* became exceeding corrupt, utterly depraved and ruined: and so the word *flesh*, which signifies *man*, came to be used to signify man as he is in himself, in his natural state, debased, corrupt, and ruined. On the other hand, the word *spirit* came to be used to signify a divine and holy principle, or new nature; because that is not *of man*, but *of God*, by the indwelling and vital influence of his *Spirit*. And thus to be *corrupt*, and to be *carnal*, or *fleshly*, and to *walk as men*, are the same thing. And so in other parts of Scripture, to *savour the things that be of man*, and to *savour things which are corrupt*, are the same; and, *sons of men*, and *wicked men*, also are the same, as observed before. And on the other hand, to *savour the things that be of God*, and to *receive the things of the Spirit of God*, are phrases that signify as much as relishing and embracing true holiness or divine virtue.

All these things confirm what we have supposed to be Christ's meaning, in saying, "That which is born of the flesh, is flesh; and that which is born of the Spirit, is spirit." His speech implies, that what is born in the first birth of man, is nothing but man as he is *of himself*, without any thing divine in him; depraved, debased, sinful, ruined man, utterly unfit to enter into the kingdom of God, and incapable of the spiritual divine happiness of that kingdom. But that which is born, in the new birth, of the Spirit of God, is a spiritual principle, a holy and divine nature, meet for the heavenly kingdom. It is no small confirmation of this being the true meaning, that the words understood in this sense, contain the proper and true reason, why a man must be born again, in order to enter into the kingdom of God; the reason given every where in other parts of Scripture for the necessity of a renovation, a change of mind, a new heart, &c. in order to salvation: to give a reason of which to *Nicodemus*, is plainly Christ's design in the words which have been insisted on.——Before I proceed, I would observe one thing as a corollary from what has been said.

Corol. If by flesh and spirit, when spoken of in the New Testament, and opposed to each other, in discourses on the necessary qualifications for salvation, we are to understand what has been now supposed, it will not only follow, that men by nature are corrupt, but *wholly corrupt*, without any good thing. If by flesh is meant man's nature, as he receives it in his first birth, then *therein dwelleth no good thing;* as appears by Rom. vii. 18. It is wholly opposite to God, and to subjection to his law, as appears by Rom. viii. 7, 8. It is directly contrary to true holiness, and wholly opposes it, as appears by Gal. v. 17 So long as men are in their natural state, they not only have no good thing, but it is impossible they should have or do any good thing; as appears by Rom. viii. 8. There is nothing in their nature, as they have it by the first birth, whence should arise any true subjection to God; as appears by Rom. viii. 7. If there were any thing truly good in the *flesh*, or in *man's nature*, or natural disposition, under a moral view, then it should only be amended; but the Scripture represents as though we were to be enemies to it, and were to seek nothing short of its entire destruction, as before observed. And elsewhere the apostle directs not to the amending of the *old man*, but *putting it off*, and putting on the *new man;* and seeks not to have the *body of death* made better, but to be *delivered* from it; and says, "that if any man be in Christ, he is a new creature, (which doubtless means the same as a man *new born*,) old things are (not amended, but) passed away, and *all* things are become new."

But this will be further evident, if we particularly consider the apostle's discourse in 1 Cor. the latter part of the second chapter and the beginning of the third. There the apostle speaks of the *natural man*, and the *spiritual man;* where *natural* and *spiritual* are opposed just in the same manner as *carnal* and *spiritual* often are. In chap. ii. 14, 15. he says, "the natural man receiveth not the things of the Spirit of God: for they are foolishness unto him; neither can he know them, because they are spiritually discerned. But he that is spiritual, judgeth all things." And not only does the apostle here oppose *natural* and *spiritual*, just as he elsewhere does *carnal* and *spiritual*, but his following discourse evidently shows, that he means the very same distinction, the same two distinct and opposite things. For immediately on his thus speaking of the difference between the *natural* and the *spiritual* man, he says, "And I, brethren, could not speak unto you as unto *spiritual*, but as unto *carnal*." Referring manifestly to what he had been saying, in the immediately preceding discourse, about *spiritual* and *natural men*, and evidently using the word, *carnal*, as synonymous with *natural*. By which it is put out of all reasonable dispute, that the apostle by *natural men* means the same as men in that *carnal*, sinful state, that they are in by their first birth;—notwithstanding all the glosses and criticisms, by which modern writers have endeavoured to palm upon us another sense of this phrase; and so to deprive us of the clear instruction the apostle gives in that 14th verse, concerning the sinful miserable state of man by nature. Dr. T. says, by ψυχικος, is meant the *animal man*, the man who maketh sense and appetite the law of his action. If he aims to limit the meaning of the word to external sense, and bodily appetite, his meaning is certainly not the apostle's. For the apostle in his sense includes the more spiritual vices of envy, strife, &c. as appears by the four first verses of the next chapter; where, as I have observed, he substitutes the word *carnal* in the place of ψυχικος. So the

* See also Acts ii. 17. Rom. iii. 20. 1 Cor. i. 29. Gal. ii. 16.

apostle *Jude* used the word in like manner, opposing it to *spiritual*, or *having the Spirit*, ver. 19. "These are they that separate themselves, sensual, (ψυχικοι,) *not having the Spirit.*" The vices he had been just speaking of, were chiefly of the more spiritual kind, ver. 16. "These are murmurers, complainers, walking after their own lusts; and their mouth speaketh great swelling words, having men's persons in admiration, because of advantage." The vices mentioned are much of the same kind with those of the *Corinthians*, for which he calls them *carnal; envy, strife, divisions*, saying, *I am of Paul*, and *I of Apollos;* and being *puffed up for one against another*. We have the same word again, James iii. 14, 15. "If ye have bitter envying and strife, glory not, and lie not against the truth: this wisdom descendeth not from above, but is earthly, *sensual*, (ψυχικη,) and devilish;" where also the vices the apostle speaks of are of the more spiritual kind.

So that on the whole, there is sufficient reason to understand the apostle, when he speaks of the *natural man*, in 1 Cor. ii. 14. as meaning man in his native corrupt state. And his words represent him as totally corrupt, wholly a stranger and enemy to true virtue or holiness, and things appertaining to it, which it appears are commonly intended in the New Testament by things *spiritual*, and are doubtless here meant by *things of the Spirit of God*. These words also represent, that it is impossible man should be otherwise, while in his natural state. The expressions are very strong: *The natural man receiveth not the things of the Spirit of God*, is not susceptible of things of that kind, *neither can he know them*, can have no true sense or relish of them, or notion of their real nature and true excellency; *because they are spiritually discerned;* they are not discerned by means of any principle in nature, but altogether by a principle that is divine, something introduced by the grace of God's Holy Spirit, which is above all that is natural. The words are in a considerable degree parallel with those of our Saviour, John xiv. 16, 17. "He shall give you the Spirit of truth, whom the world cannot receive, because it seeth him not, neither knoweth him: but ye know him; for he dwelleth with you, and shall be in you."

SECT. II.

Observations on Rom. iii. 9—24.

If the Scriptures represent all mankind as wicked in their first state, before they are made partakers of the benefits of Christ's redemption, then they are wicked by nature: for doubtless men's *first* state is their *native* state, or that in which they come into the world. But the Scriptures do thus represent all mankind.

Before I mention particular texts to this purpose, I would observe, that it alters not the case, as to the argument in hand, whether we suppose these texts speak directly of infants, or only of such as understand something of their duty and state. For if all mankind, as soon as ever they are capable of reflecting, and knowing their own moral state, find themselves wicked, this proves that they are wicked *by nature;* either born so, or born with an infallible disposition to be wicked as soon as possible, if there be any difference between these; and either of them will prove men to be born exceedingly *depraved*. I have before proved, that a native propensity to sin certainly follows from many things said of mankind in the Scripture; but what I intend now, is to prove by direct scripture testimony, that all mankind, in their first state, are really of a wicked character.

To this purpose, exceeding full, express, and abundant is that passage of the apostle, in Rom. iii. 9—24. which I shall set down at large, distinguishing the universal terms which are here so often repeated, by a distinct character. The apostle having in the first chapter (ver. 16, 17.) laid down his proposition, that none can be saved in any other way than through the righteousness of God, by faith in Jesus Christ, he proceeds to prove this point, by showing particularly that all are in themselves wicked, and without any righteousness of their own. First, he insists on the wickedness of the *Gentiles*, in the first chapter; next, on the wickedness of the *Jews*, in the second chapter. And then, in this place, he comes to sum up the matter, and draw the conclusion in the words following: "What then, are we better than they? No, in no wise; for we have before proved both *Jews* and *Gentiles*, that they are ALL under sin: as it is written, there is NONE righteous, NO, NOT ONE; there is NONE that understandeth; there is NONE that seeketh after God; they are ALL gone out of the way; they are TOGETHER become unprofitable; there is NONE that doeth good, NO, NOT ONE. Their throat is an open sepulchre; with their tongues they have used deceit; the poison of asps is under their lips; whose mouth is full of cursing and bitterness; their feet are swift to shed blood; destruction and misery are in their ways, and the way of peace they have not known; there is no fear of God before their eyes. Now we know, that whatsoever things the law saith, it saith to them that are under the law, that EVERY mouth may be stopped, and ALL THE WORLD may become guilty before God. Therefore by the deeds of the law, there shall NO FLESH be justified in his sight; for by the law is the knowledge of sin. But now the righteousness of God without the law, is manifest, being witnessed by the law and the prophets; even the righteousness of God, which is by faith of Jesus Christ, unto ALL, and upon ALL them that believe; for there is NO DIFFERENCE. For ALL have sinned, and come short of the glory of God. Being justified freely by his grace, through the redemption which is in Jesus Christ."

Here the thing which I would prove, *viz.* that mankind in their first state, before they are interested in the benefits of Christ's redemption, are universally wicked, is declared with the utmost possible fulness and precision. So that if here this matter be not set forth plainly, expressly, and fully, it must be because no words can do it, and it is not in the power of language, or any manner of terms and phrases, however contrived and heaped up one upon another, determinately to signify any such thing.

Dr. T. to take off the force of the whole, would have us to understand, (p. 104—107.) that these passages quoted from the Psalms, and other parts of the Old Testament, do not speak of *all mankind, nor of all the Jews; but only of them of whom they were true*. He observes, there were many that were innocent and righteous; though there were also many, a strong party, that were wicked, corrupt, &c. of whom these texts were to be understood. Concerning which I would observe the following things:

1. According to this, the *universality* of the terms in these places, which the apostle cites from the Old Testament, to prove that *all the world, both Jews and Gentiles, are under sin*, is nothing to his purpose. The apostle uses universal terms in his proposition, and in his conclusion, that ALL are under sin, that EVERY MOUTH is stopped, ALL THE WORLD guilty,—that by the deeds of the law NO FLESH can be justified. And he chooses out a number of universal sayings or clauses out of the Old Testament, to confirm this universality; as, *There is none righteous; no, not one: they are all gone out of the way; there is none that understandeth, &c.* But yet the universal terms found in them have no reference to any such universality, either in the collective, or personal sense; no universality of the nations of the world, or of particular persons in those nations, or in any one nation in the world: "*but only of those of whom they are true!*" That is, *there is none of them righteous*, of whom it is *true*, that they are not *righteous: no, not one; there is none that understand*, of whom it is *true*, that *they* understand not: *they are all gone out of the way*, of whom it is *true*, that they are gone out of the way, &c. Or these expressions are to be understood concerning that strong party in Israel, in David and Solomon's days, and in the prophets' days; they are to be understood of *them* universally. And what is that to the apostle's purpose? How does *such* an universality of wickedness—that all were wicked in Israel, who were wicked; or, that there was a particular evil party, all of which were wicked—confirm that universality which the apostle would prove, *viz.* That *all Jews and Gentiles, and the whole world*, were wicked, and *every mouth stopped*, and that *no flesh* could be justified by their own righteousness.

Here nothing can be said to abate the nonsense, but this, that the apostle would convince the Jews, that they were capable of being wicked, as well as other nations;

and to prove it, he mentions some texts, which show that there was a wicked party in Israel a thousand years ago. And as to the universal terms which happened to be in these texts, the apostle had no respect to them; but his reciting them is as it were accidental, they *happened* to be in some texts which speak of an evil party in Israel, and the apostle cites them as they are, not because they are any more to his purpose for the universal terms, which happen to be in them. But let the reader look on the words of the apostle, and observe the violence of such a supposition. Particularly let the words of the 9th and 10th verses, and their connexion, be observed. *All are under sin: as it is written, There is none righteous; no, not one.* How plain it is, that the apostle cites that latter universal clause out of the 14th Psalm, to confound the preceding universal words of his own proposition! And yet it will follow from what Dr. T. supposes, that the universality of the terms in the last words, *there is none righteous; no, not one,* hath no relation at all to that universality he speaks of in the preceding clause, to which they are joined, *all are under sin:* and is no more a confirmation of it, than if the words were thus, "There are *some* or there are *many* in Israel, that are not righteous."

2. To suppose, the apostle's design in citing these passages, was only to prove to the Jews, that of old there was a considerable number of their nation that were wicked men, is to suppose him to have gone about to prove what none of the Jews denied, or made the least doubt of, even the Pharisees, the most self-righteous sect of them, who went furthest in glorying in the distinction of their nation from other nations, as a holy people, knew it, and owned it; they openly confessed that their *forefathers killed the prophets,* Matt. xxiii. 29—31. And if the apostle's design had been only to refresh their memories, to put them in mind of the ancient wickedness of their nation, to lead to reflection on themselves as guilty of the like wickedness, as Stephen does, (Acts vii.) what need had he to go so far about to prove this—gathering up many sentences here and there which prove, that their scriptures speak of *some* as wicked men—and then to prove, that the wicked men spoken of must be Jews, by this argument, that *what things soever the law saith, it saith to them that are under the law,* or that whatsoever the books of the Old Testament said, it must be understood of that people who had the Old Testament? What need had the apostle of such an ambages as this, to prove to the Jews, that there had been many of their nation in past ages, which were wicked men; when the Old Testament was full of passages that asserted this *expressly,* not only of a strong party, but of the nation in general? How much more would it have been to such a purpose, to have put them in mind of the wickedness of the people in general in worshipping the golden calf; of the unbelief, murmuring, and perverseness of the whole congregation in the wilderness, for forty years, as *Stephen* does! Which things he had no need to prove to be spoken of their nation, by any such indirect argument as this, *Whatsoever things the law saith, it saith to them that are under the law.*

3. It would have been impertinent to the apostle's purpose, even as our author understands his purpose, for him to have gone about to convince the *Jews,* that there had been a strong *party* of bad men in the time of *David* and *Solomon,* and the prophets. For Dr. T. supposes, the apostle's aim is to prove the great corruption of both *Jews* and *Gentiles* when *Christ* came into the world.*

In order the more fully to evade the clear and abundant testimonies to the doctrine of original sin, contained in this part of the Holy Scripture, our author says, the apostle is here speaking of *bodies* of people, of *Jews* and *Gentiles* in a *collective* sense, as two great bodies into which mankind are divided; speaking of them in their collective capacity, and not with respect to particular persons; that the apostle's design is to prove, that neither of these two great bodies, in their collective sense, can be justified by law, because both were corrupt; and so that no more is implied, than that the *generality* of both were wicked.† On this I observe,

(1.) That this supposed sense disagrees extremely with the *terms* and language which the apostle here makes use of. For according to this, we must understand, either,

First, That the apostle means *no universality* at all, but only the far greater part. But if the words which the apostle uses, do not most fully and determinately signify an universality, no words ever used in the Bible are sufficient to do it. I might challenge any man to produce any one paragraph in the Scripture, from the beginning to the end, where there is such a repetition and accumulation of terms, so strongly, and emphatically, and carefully, to express the most perfect and absolute universality; or any place to be compared to it. What instance is there in the Scripture, or indeed in any other writing, where the meaning is only the *much greater part,* where this meaning is signified in such a manner, *They are all,—They are all,—They are all—together,—every one,— all the world;* joined to multiplied negative terms, to show the universality to be without exception; saying, *There is no flesh,—there is none,—there is none,—there is none,—there is none,* four times *over;* besides the addition of *No, not one,—no, not one,*—once and again! Or,

Secondly, If any universality at all be allowed, it is only of the *collective bodies* spoken of: and these collective bodies but two, as Dr. T. reckons them, viz. the *Jewish* nation, and the *Gentile* world; supposing the apostle is here representing each of these parts of mankind as being wicked. But is this the way of men using language, when speaking of but *two* things, to express themselves in such *universal* terms, when they mean no more than that the thing affirmed is predicated of *both* of them? If a man speaking of his two *feet* as both lame, should say, *All my feet are lame—They are all lame—All together are become weak—None of my feet are strong—None of them are sound—No, not one;* would not he be thought to be lame in his understanding, as well as his feet? When the apostle says, *That every mouth may be stopped,* must we suppose, that he speaks only of these two great collective bodies, figuratively ascribing to each of them a mouth, and means that these two mouths are stopped? Besides, according to our author's own interpretation, the universal terms used in these texts, cited from the Old Testament, have no respect to those two great collective bodies, nor indeed to either of them; but to *some* in *Israel,* a particular disaffected party in that one nation, which was made up of wicked men. So that his interpretation is every way absurd and inconsistent.

(2.) If the apostle is speaking only of the wickedness or guilt of great collective bodies, then it will follow, that also the *justification* he here treats of, is no other than the justification of such collective bodies. For, they are the *same* of whom he speaks as guilty and wicked, and who cannot be *justified* by the works of the law, by reason of their being *wicked.* Otherwise his argument is wholly disannulled. If the guilt he speaks of be only of collective bodies, then what he argues from that guilt, must be only, that collective bodies cannot be justified by the works of the law, having no respect to the justification of particular persons. And indeed this is Dr. T.'s declared opinion. He supposes the apostle here, and in other parts of this epistle, is speaking of men's justification *considered only as in their collective capacity.*‡ But the contrary is most manifest. The 26th and 28th verses of this third chapter, cannot, without the utmost violence, be understood otherwise than of the justification of particular persons. "That he might be just, and the justifier of *him* that believeth in Jesus.—Therefore we conclude that *a man* is justified by faith, without the deeds of the law." So in chap. iv. 5. "But to *him* that worketh not, but believeth on him that justifieth the ungodly, *his* faith is counted for righteousness." And what the apostle cites in the 6th, 7th, and 8th verses from the book of Psalms, evidently shows, that he is speaking of the justification of particular persons. "Even as David also describeth the blessedness of *the man* unto whom God imputeth righteousness without works, saying, Blessed are they whose iniquities are forgiven, and whose sins are covered." *David* says these things in the 32d Psalm, with a special respect to his own particular case; here expressing the great distress he was

* See Key, § 307, 310.

† Page 102, 104, 117, 119, 120, and note on Rom. iii. 10—19.

‡ See note on Rom. iii. 10—19. chap. v. 11. and chap. ix. 30, 31

in, while under a sense of personal sin and guilt, and the great joy he had when God forgave him.

And what can be plainer, that in the paragraph we have been upon, (Rom. iii. 20.) it is the justification of *particular persons* of which the apostle speaks. "Therefore by the deeds of the law, there shall no flesh be justified in his sight." He refers to Psal. cxliii. 2. "Enter not into judgment with thy servant; for in thy sight shall *no man living* be justified." Here the psalmist is not speaking of the justification of a nation, as a collective body, or of one of the two parts of the world, but of a particular man. And it is further manifest, that the apostle is here speaking of personal justification, inasmuch as this place is evidently parallel with Gal. iii. 10, 11. "For as many as are of the works of the law, are under the curse: for it is written, Cursed is *every one* that continueth not in all things that are written in the book of the law to do them. But that *no man* is justified by the works of the law, is evident; for, The just shall live by faith." It is plain, that this place is parallel with that in the 3d of *Romans*, not only as the thing asserted is the same, and the argument by which it is proved—that all are guilty, and exposed to condemnation by the law.—But the same saying of the Old Testament is cited, (Gal. ii. 16.) Many other things demonstrate, that the apostle is speaking of the same justification in both places, which I omit for brevity's sake.

And besides all these things, our author's interpretation makes the apostle's argument wholly void another way. The apostle is speaking of a certain subject which cannot be justified by the works of the law; and his argument is, that the same subject is guilty, and is condemned by the law. If he means, that one subject, suppose a collective body or bodies, cannot be justified by the law, because another subject, another collective body, is condemned by the law, it is plain, the argument would be quite vain and impertinent. Yet thus the argument must stand according to Dr. T.'s interpretation. The collective bodies which he supposes are spoken of as wicked, and condemned by the law, considered as in their collective capacity, are those two, the *Jewish* nation, and the heathen world: but the collective body which he supposes the apostle speaks of as justified without the deeds of the law, is neither of these, but the christian church, or body of believers; which is a new collective body, a new creature, and a new man, (according to our author's understanding of such phrases,) which never had any existence before it was justified, and therefore never was wicked or condemned, unless it was with regard to the *individuals* of which it was constituted; and it does not appear, according to our author's scheme, that these individuals had before been generally wicked. For according to him, there was a number both among the *Jews* and *Gentiles*, that were righteous before. And how does it appear, but that the comparatively few *Jews* and *Gentiles*, of which this new-created collective body was constituted, were chiefly of the best of each?

So that in every view, this author's way of explaining the passage appears vain and absurd. And so clearly and fully has the apostle expressed himself, that it is doubtless impossible to invent any other sense to put upon his words, than that which will imply, that all mankind, even every individual of the whole race, but their Redeemer himself, are in their first original state corrupt and wicked.

Before I leave this passage, (Rom. iii. 9—24.) it may be proper to observe, that it not only is a most clear and full testimony to the native depravity of mankind, but also plainly declares that natural depravity to be total and exceeding great. It is the apostle's manifest design in these citations from the Old Testament, to show these three things. 1. That *all mankind* are by nature *corrupt*. 2. That every one is *altogether corrupt*, and, as it were, depraved in every part. 3. That they are in every part *corrupt in an exceeding degree*. With respect to the second of these, it is plain the apostle puts together those particular passages of the Old Testament, wherein most of those members of the body are mentioned, that are the soul's chief instruments or organs of external action. The hands (implicitly) in those expressions, "They are together become unprofitable, There is none that doth good." The throat, tongue, lips, and mouth, the organs of speech, in those words; "Their *throat* is an open sepulchre; with their *tongues* they have used deceit; the poison of asps is under their *lips;* whose *mouth* is full of cursing and bitterness." The feet in those words, ver. 15. "Their *feet* are swift to shed blood." These things together signify, that man is as it were *all over corrupt* in every part. And not only is the total corruption thus intimated, by enumerating the several parts, but also by denying all good; any true understanding or spiritual knowledge, any virtuous action, or so much as a truly virtuous desire, or seeking after God. "There is none that *understandeth;* there is none that *seeketh* after God; there is none that *doth good;* the way of peace have they *not known.*" And in general, by denying all true piety or religion in men in their first state, ver. 18. "There is *no fear* of God before their eyes."—The expressions also are evidently chosen to denote a most extreme and desperate wickedness of heart. An exceeding depravity is ascribed to every part: to the throat, the scent of an *open sepulchre;* to the tongue and lips, *deceit,* and *the poison of asps;* to the mouth, *cursing* and *bitterness;* of their feet it is said, *they are swift to shed blood:* and with regard to the whole man, it is said, *destruction* and *misery* are in their ways. The representation is very strong of each of these things, *viz.* That *all* mankind are corrupt; that every one is *wholly* and altogether corrupt; and also *extremely* and desperately corrupt. And it is plain, it is not accidental, that we have here such a collection of such strong expressions, so emphatically signifying these things; but that they are chosen of the apostle on design, as being directly and fully to his purpose; which purpose appears in all his discourse in the whole of this chapter, and indeed from the beginning of the epistle.

SECT. III.

Observations on Rom. v. 6—10. *and Eph.* ii. 3. *with the context, and Rom.* vii.

ANOTHER passage of this apostle, which shows that all who are made partakers of the benefits of Christ's redemption, are in their first state wicked, desperately wicked, is Rom. v. 6—10. "For when we were yet *without strength,* in due time Christ died for the *ungodly.* For scarcely for a righteous man will one die; yet peradventure for a good man some would even dare to die. But God commendeth his love towards us, in that while we were yet *sinners,* Christ died for us. Much more then, being now justified by his blood, we shall be saved from *wrath* through him. For if while we were *enemies* we were reconciled to God through the death of his Son; much more, being reconciled, we shall be saved by his life."—Here all for whom Christ died, and who are saved by him, are spoken of as being in their first state *sinners, ungodly, enemies* to God, exposed to divine *wrath,* and *without strength,* without ability to help themselves, or deliver their souls from this miserable state.

Dr. T. says, the apostle here speaks of the *Gentiles only in their heathen state,* in contradistinction to the *Jews;* and that not of particular persons among the heathen Gentiles, or as to the state they were in personally; but only of the Gentiles *collectively taken,* or of the miserable state of that great collective body, the heathen world: and that these appellations, *sinners, ungodly, enemies,* &c. were names by which the apostles in their writings were wont to signify and distinguish the heathen world, in opposition to the *Jews;* and that in this sense these appellations are to be taken in their epistles, and in this place in particular.* And it is observable, that this way of interpreting these phrases in the apostolic writings is become fashionable with many late writers; whereby they not only evade several clear testimonies to the doctrine of original sin, but make void great part of the New Testament; on which account it deserves the more particular consideration.

It is allowed to have been long common and customary among the *Jews,* especially the sect of the *Pharisees,* in

* Page 114—120. See also Dr. T.'s Paraph. and notes on the place.

their pride, and confidence in their privileges as the peculiar people of God, to exalt themselves exceedingly above other nations, and greatly to despise the Gentiles, calling them by such names as *sinners, enemies, dogs,* &c. Themselves they accounted, in general, (excepting the *publicans,* and the notoriously profligate,) as the *friends,* the special *favourites* and *children,* of God; because they were the children of *Abraham,* were circumcised, and had the law of *Moses,* as their peculiar privilege, and as a wall of partition between them and the Gentiles.

But it is very remarkable, that a christian divine, who has studied the New Testament, and the epistle to the *Romans* in particular, so diligently as Dr. T. has done, should so strongly imagine that the apostles of Jesus Christ countenance and cherish these self-exalting, uncharitable dispositions and notions of the *Jews* which gave rise to such a custom, so far as to fall in with that custom, and adopt that language of their pride and contempt; and especially that the apostle *Paul* should do it. It is a most unreasonable imagination on many accounts.

1. The whole gospel dispensation is calculated entirely to overthrow and abolish every thing to which this self-distinguishing, self-exalting language of the *Jews* was owing. It was calculated wholly to exclude such boasting, and to destroy the pride and self-righteousness which were the causes of it. It was calculated to abolish the enmity, and break down the partition-wall between *Jews* and *Gentiles,* and *of twain,* to *make one new man, so making peace:* to destroy all dispositions in nations and particular persons to despise one another, or to say one to another, *Stand by thyself, come not near to me; for I am holier than thou;* and to establish the contrary principles of humility, mutual esteem, honour and love, and universal union, in the most firm and perfect manner.

2. Christ, when on earth, set himself, through the whole course of his ministry, to militate against this pharisaical spirit, practice, and language of the *Jews;* by which they showed so much contempt of the *Gentiles, publicans,* and such as were openly lewd and vicious, and thus exalted themselves above them; calling them *sinners* and *enemies,* and themselves *holy,* and *God's children;* not allowing the Gentile to be their neighbour, &c. He condemned the *Pharisees* for not esteeming themselves *sinners,* as well as the *publicans;* trusting in themselves that they were righteous, and despising others. He militated against these things in his own treatment of some Gentiles, publicans, and others, whom they called *sinners,* and in what he said on those occasions.*

He opposed these notions and manners of the Jews in his parables,† and in his instructions to his disciples how to treat the unbelieving Jews;‡ and in what he says to Nicodemus about the necessity of a new birth, even for the Jews, as well as the unclean Gentiles with regard to their proselytism, which some of the Jews looked upon as a *new birth.* And in opposition to their notions of their being the children of God, because the children of Abraham, but the Gentiles by nature sinners and children of wrath, he tells them that even they were *children of the devil.*§

3. Though we should suppose the apostles not to have been thoroughly brought off from such notions, manners, and language of the Jews, till after Christ's ascension; yet after the pouring out of the Spirit on the day of Pentecost, or at least, after the calling of the Gentiles, begun in the conversion of Cornelius, they were fully instructed in this matter, and effectually taught no longer to call the Gentiles *unclean,* as a note of distinction from the Jews, Acts x. 28. which was before any of the apostolic epistles were written.

4. Of all the apostles, none were more perfectly instructed in this matter, than Paul, and none so abundant in instructing others in it, as this great apostle of the Gentiles. None of the apostles had so much occasion to exert themselves against the forementioned notions and language of the Jews, in opposition to Jewish teachers and judaizing Christians who strove to keep up the separation-wall between Jews and Gentiles, and to exalt the former, and set at nought the latter.

5. This apostle, in his epistle to the Romans, above all his other writings, exerts himself in a most elaborate manner, and with his utmost skill and power, to bring the Jewish Christians off from every thing of this kind. He endeavours by all means that there might no longer be in them any remains of these old notions, in which they had been educated, of such a great distinction between Jews and Gentiles, as were expressed in the names they used to distinguish them by; the Jews, *holy children of* Abraham, *friends and children of God;* but the Gentiles, *sinners, unclean, enemies,* and the like. He makes it almost his whole business, from the beginning of the epistle, Rom. v. 6, &c. to convince them that there was no ground for any such distinction, and to prove that in common, both Jews and Gentiles, all were desperately wicked, and none righteous, no not one. He tells them, chap. iii. 9. that the Jews were by no means better than the Gentiles; and (in what follows in that chapter) that there was no difference between Jews and Gentiles; and represents all as without strength, or any sufficiency of their own in the affair of justification and redemption. And in the continuation of the same discourse, in the 4th chapter, he teaches that all who were justified by Christ, were in themselves *ungodly;* and that being the children of Abraham was not peculiar to the Jews. In this 5th chap. still in continuation of the same discourse—on the same subject and argument of justification through Christ, and by faith in him—he speaks of Christ dying for the *ungodly* and *sinners,* and those who were without *strength* or sufficiency for their own salvation, as he had done all along before. But now, it seems, the apostle by *sinners and ungodly,* must not be understood according as he used these words before; but must be supposed to mean only the Gentiles as distinguished from the Jews; adopting the language of those self-righteous, self-exalting, disdainful judaizing teachers, whom he was with all his might opposing: countenancing the very same thing in them, which he had been from the beginning of the epistle discountenancing, and endeavouring to discourage, and utterly to abolish, with all his art and strength.

One reason why the Jews looked on themselves better than the Gentiles, and called themselves *holy,* and the Gentiles *sinners,* was, that they had the *law of Moses.* They *made their boast of the law.* But the apostle shows them, that this was so far from making them better, that it condemned them, and was an occasion of their being *sinners,* in a higher degree, and more aggravated manner, and more effectually and dreadfully *dead* in sin.‖

It cannot be justly objected here, that this apostle did, in fact, use this language, and call the gentiles sinners, in contradistinction to the Jews, in what he said to Peter, Gal. ii. 15, 16. "We who are *Jews* by nature, and not *sinners* of the *Gentiles,* knowing that a man is not justified by the works of the law, but by faith in Jesus Christ." It is true, that the apostle here refers to this distinction, as what was usually made by the self-righteous *Jews,* between themselves and the *Gentiles;* but not in such a manner as to adopt, or favour it; but on the contrary, so as plainly to show his disapprobation of it; *q.d.* "Though we were born *Jews,* and by nature are of that people which are wont to make their boast of the law, expecting to be justified by it, and trust in themselves that they are righteous, despising others, calling the Gentiles *sinners,* in distinction from themselves; yet we being now instructed in the gospel of Christ, know better; we now know that a man is not justified by the works of the law; that we are all justified only by faith in Christ, in whom there is no difference, no distinction of *Greek* or *Gentile,* and *Jew,*

* Matt. viii. 5—13. Chap. ix. 9—13. Chap. xi. 19—24. Chap. xv. 21—28. Luke vii. 37, to the end. Chap. xvii 12—19. Chap. xix. 1—10. John iv. 9, &c. ver. 39, &c. Compare Luke x. 29, &c.

† Matt. xxi 28—32. Chap. xxii. 1—10. Luke xiv. 16—24. Compare Luke xiii. 28, 29, 30.

‡ Matt. x. 14, 15.

§ John viii. 33—44. It may also be observed, that *John the Baptist* greatly contradicted the *Jews'* opinion of themselves, as being a holy people, and accepted of God, because they were the children of *Abraham*—and on that account better than the heathen whom they called sinners, enemies, unclean, &c.—in baptizing the *Jews* as a *polluted* people, and *sinners,* as the *Jews* used to baptize proselytes from among the heathen; calling them to repentance as *sinners,* saying, *Think not to say within yourselves, We have* Abraham *to our father; for I say unto you, that God is able, of these stones, to raise up children unto* Abraham; and teaching the *Pharisees,* that instead of their being a holy generation, and children of God, as they called themselves, they were a *generation of vipers.*

‖ See chap. vii. 4--13. agreeably to those words of Christ, John v. 45.

but all are one in Christ Jesus." And this is the very thing he there speaks of, which he blamed *Peter* for; that by his withdrawing and separating himself from the *Gentiles*, refusing to eat with them, &c. he had countenanced this self-exalting, self-distinguishing, separating spirit and custom of the *Jews*, whereby they treated the *Gentiles*, as in a distinguishing manner *sinners* and *unclean*, and not fit to come near them who were a holy people.

6. The very words of the apostle in this place, show plainly, that he uses the term *sinners*, not as signifying *Gentiles*, in opposition to *Jews*, but as denoting the *morally evil*, in opposition to such as are *righteous* or *good*. This latter distinction between *sinners* and *righteous* is here expressed in plain terms. "Scarcely for a *righteous man* will one die; yet peradventure for a *good man* some would even dare to die; but God commended his love towards us, in that while we were yet *sinners*, Christ died for us." By *righteous men* are doubtless meant the same that are meant by such a phrase, throughout this apostle's writings, throughout the New Testament, and throughout the Bible. Will any one pretend, that by the righteous man, for whom men would scarcely die, and by the good man, for whom perhaps some might even dare to die, is meant a *Jew?* Dr. T. himself does not explain it so, in his exposition of this epistle; and therefore is not very consistent with himself, in supposing, that in the other part of the distinction the apostle means *Gentiles*, as distinguished from the *Jews*. The apostle himself had been labouring abundantly, in the preceding part of the epistle, to prove, that the *Jews* were *sinners* in opposition to *righteous;* that all *had sinned*, that all were *under sin*, and therefore could not be justified, could not be accepted as *righteous*, by their own righteousness.

7. Another thing which makes it evident that the apostle, when he speaks in this place of the *sinners* and *enemies* for whom Christ died, does not mean only the *Gentiles*, is, that he includes *himself* among them, saying, *while* WE *were sinners*, and *when* WE *were enemies*.

Our author from time to time says, the apostle, though he speaks only of the Gentiles in their heathen state, yet *puts himself with them, because he was the apostle of the Gentiles*. But this is very unreasonable. There is no more sense in it, than there would be in a father ranking himself among his children, when speaking to his children of the benefits they have by being begotten by himself; and saying, *We children*. Or in a physician ranking himself with his patients, when talking to them of their diseases and cure; saying, *We sick folks*. *Paul* being the apostle of the *Gentiles* to save them from their heathenism, is so far from being a reason for him to reckon himself among the heathen, that on the contrary, it is the very thing that would render it in a peculiar manner unnatural and absurd for him so to do. Because, as the apostle of the *Gentiles*, he appears as their healer and deliverer from heathenism; and therefore in that capacity, in a peculiar manner, appears in his distinction from the heathen, and in opposition to the state of heathenism. For it is by the most opposite qualities only, that he is fitted to be an apostle of the heathen, and recoverer from heathenism. As the clear light of the sun is what makes it a proper restorative from darkness; and, therefore, the sun being spoken of as such a remedy, none would suppose to be a good reason why it should be ranked among dark things. Besides, the apostle, in this epistle, expressly ranks himself with the *Jews* when he speaks of them as distinguished from the *Gentiles;* as in chap. iii. 9. "What then? are *we* better than they?" That is, are we *Jews* better than the *Gentiles?*

It cannot justly be alleged in opposition to this, that the apostle *Peter* puts himself with the heathen, 1 Pet. iv. 3. "For the time past of *our* life may suffice *us* to have wrought the will of the *Gentiles;* when *we* walked in lasciviousness, lusts, excess of wine, revellings, banquetings, and abominable idolatries." For the apostle *Peter* (who by the way was not an apostle of the Gentiles) here does not speak of himself as one of the heathen, but as one of the church of Christ in general, made up of those who had been *Jews*, *proselytes*, and *heathens*, who were now all one body, of which body he was a member. It is *this* society, therefore, and not the *Gentiles*, that he refers to in the pronoun us. He is speaking of the wickedness that the members of this *body* or *society* had lived in before their conversion; not that every member had lived in all those vices here mentioned, but some in one, others in another. Very parallel is the passage with that of the apostle *Paul* to *Titus*, chap. iii. 3. "For *we* ourselves also" (*i. e.* we of the christian church) "were sometimes foolish, disobedient, deceived, serving divers lusts and pleasures," (some one lust and pleasure, others another,) "living in malice, envy, hateful, and hating one another," &c. There is nothing in this, but what is very natural. That the apostle, speaking *to* the christian church, and *of* that church, confessing its former sins, should speak of *himself* as one of that society, and yet mention some sins that he personally had not been guilty of, and among others, heathenish idolatry, is quite a different thing from what it would have been for the apostle, expressly distinguishing those of the Christians, which had been heathen, from those which had been *Jews*, to have ranked himself with the former, though he was truly of the latter.

If a minister in some congregation in *England*, speaking in a sermon of the sins of the nation, being himself of the nation, should say, "*We* have greatly corrupted ourselves, and provoked God by our deism, blasphemy, profane swearing, lasciviousness, venality," &c. speaking in the first person plural, though he himself never had been a deist, and perhaps none of his hearers, and they might also have been generally free from other sins he mentioned; yet there would be nothing unnatural in his thus expressing himself. But it would be quite a different thing, if one part of the *British* dominions, suppose our king's *American* dominions, had universally apostatized from Christianity to deism, and had long been in such a state, and if one who had been born and brought up in *England* among Christians, the country being universally Christian, should be sent among them to show them the folly and great evil of deism, and convert them to Christianity; and this missionary, when making a distinction between *English* Christians, and these deists, should rank himself with the latter, and say, WE American *deists*, WE *foolish blind infidels, &c.* This indeed would be very unnatural and absurd.

Another passage of the apostle, to the like purpose with that which we have been considering in the 5th of Romans, is that in Eph. ii. 3.—"And were by nature children of wrath, even as others." This remains a plain testimony to the doctrine of original sin, as held by those who used to be called orthodox Christians, after all the pains and art used to torture and pervert it. This doctrine is here not only plainly and fully taught, but abundantly so, if we take the words with the context; where Christians are once and again represented as being, in their first state, *dead in sin*, and as *quickened* and *raised up* from such a state of death, in a most marvellous display of free *rich grace and love*, and *exceeding greatness of God's power, &c.*

With respect to those words, (ημεν τεκνα φυσει οργης,) *We were by nature children of wrath*, Dr. T. says, p. 112—114.) "The apostle means no more by this, than *truly* or *really children of wrath;* using a metaphorical expression, borrowed from the word that is used to signify a true and genuine child of a family, in distinction from one that is a child only by adoption." In which it is owned, that the proper sense of the phrase is, being a child by *nature*, in the same sense as a child by birth or natural generation; but only he supposes, that here the word is used *metaphorically*. The instance he produces as parellel, to confirm his supposed metaphorical sense of the phrase, as meaning only *truly*, *really*, or *properly* children of wrath, *viz.* the apostle *Paul's* calling *Timothy* his *own son in faith*, (γνησιον τεκνον,) is so far from confirming his sense, that it is rather directly against it. For doubtless the apostle uses the word here (γνησιον) in its original signification, meaning his *begotten son;* γνησιος being the adjective from γονη, offspring, or the verb, γενναω, to beget; as much as to say, *Timothy my begotten son in the faith*. For as there are two ways of being begotten, one natural, and the other spiritual; the first generation, and regeneration; so the apostle expressly signifies which of these he means in this place, *Timothy my begotten son* IN THE FAITH, in the same manner as he says to the *Corinthians*, 1 Cor. iv. 15. "In Christ Jesus I have begotten you through the gospel." To say, the apostle uses the word, φυσει, in Eph. ii. 3. only as signifying *real*, true, and proper, is a most arbitrary interpretation, having nothing to warrant it in the whole Bible. The word φυσις is no where used in this sense in the New Testament.*

Another thing which our author alleges to evade the force of this, is, that the word rendered *nature*, sometimes signifies habit contracted by *custom*, or an acquired nature. But this is not its proper meaning. And it is plain, the word in its common use, in the New Testament, signifies what we properly express in *English* by the word *nature*. There is but one place where there can be the least pretext for supposing it to be used otherwise; and that is 1 Cor. xi. 14. "Doth not even *nature* itself teach you, that if a man have long hair, it is a shame unto him?" And even here there is, I think, no manner of reason for understanding *nature* otherwise than in the proper sense. The emphasis used, (αυτη η φυσις,) *nature* ITSELF, shows that the apostle does not mean *custom*, but nature in the proper sense. It is true, it was long custom which made having the head covered a token of subjection, and a feminine appearance; as it is custom that makes any outward action or word a sign or signification of any thing. But nature *itself*, nature in its proper sense, teaches, that it is a shame for a man to appear with the established signs of the female sex, and with significations of inferiority, &c. As nature itself shows it to be a shame for a father to bow down or kneel to his own child or servant, or for men to bow to an idol, because bowing down is by custom an established token or sign of subjection and submission. Such a sight therefore would be *unnatural*, shocking to a man's *very nature*. So nature would teach, that it is a shame for a woman to use such and such lascivious words or gestures, though it be custom that establishes the unclean signification of those gestures and sounds.

It is particularly unnatural and unreasonable, to understand the phrase, (τεκνα φυσει,) in this place, any otherwise than in the proper sense, on the following accounts. 1. It may be observed, that both the words, τεκνα and φυσις, in their original signification, have reference to birth or generation. So the word φυσις, from φυω, which signifies to beget or bring forth young, or to bud forth, as a plant, that brings forth young buds and branches. And so the word τεκνον comes from τικτω, which signifies to bring forth children.—2. As though the apostle took care by the word used here, to signify what we are by birth, he changes the word he used before for children. In the preceding verse he used υιοι, speaking of the *children* of disobedience; but here τεκνα, which is a word derived, as observed, from τικτω, to bring forth a child, and more properly signifies a *begotten* or *born child*.—3. It is natural to suppose that the apostle here speaks in opposition to the pride of some, especially the *Jews*, (for the church in *Ephesus* was made up partly of *Jews*, as well as the church in *Rome*,) who exalted themselves in the privileges they had by *birth*, because they were *born* the children of *Abraham*, and were *Jews by nature*, φυσει Ιȣδαιοι, as the phrase is, Gal. ii. 15. In opposition to this proud conceit, he teaches the *Jews*, that notwithstanding this they were *by nature* children of wrath, *even as others, i. e.* as well as the *Gentiles*, which the *Jews* had been taught to look upon as *sinners*, and out of favour with God by *nature*, and *born children of wrath*.—4. It is more plain, that the apostle uses the word *nature* in its proper sense here, because he sets what they were *by nature* in opposition to what they are *by grace*. In this verse, the apostle shows what they are *by nature*, *viz.* children of wrath; and in the following verses he shows, how very different their state is *by grace*; saying, ver. 5. "By grace ye are saved;" repeating it again, ver. 8. "By grace ye are saved." But if, by being children of wrath by nature, were meant no more than only their being *really* and *truly* children of wrath, as Dr. T. supposes, there would be no opposition in the signification of these phrases; for in this sense they were *by nature* in a state *of salvation*, as much as *by nature children of wrath*; for they were *truly*, *really*, and *properly* in a state of salvation.

If we take these words with the context, the whole abundantly proves, that by nature we are *totally corrupt*, without any good thing in us. For if we allow the plain scope of the place, without attempting to hide it by doing extreme violence to the apostle's words, the design here is strongly to establish this point; that what Christians have that is good in them, or in their state, is *in no part* of it naturally in themselves, or from themselves, but is *wholly from divine grace*, all *the gift of God*, and *his workmanship*, the effect of his power, his free and wonderful love. None of our *good works* are primarily from ourselves, but with respect to them all, *we are God's workmanship, created unto good works*, as it were out of nothing. Not so much as *faith itself*, the first principle of good works in Christians, is of themselves, but that *is the gift of God*. Therefore the apostle compares the work of God, in forming Christians to true virtue and holiness, not only to a *new creation*, but a *resurrection*, or raising from the dead. Ver. 1. "You hath he quickened, who were dead in trespasses and sins." And again, ver. 5. "Even when we were dead in sins, hath quickened us together with Christ." In speaking of Christians being quickened with Christ, the apostle has reference to what he had said before, in the latter part of the foregoing chapter, of God manifesting *the exceeding greatness of his power* towards christian converts in their conversion, *agreeable to the operation of his mighty power, when he raised Christ from the dead*. So that it is plain by every thing in this discourse, the apostle would signify, that *by nature* we have *no goodness;* but are as destitute of it as a dead corpse is of life. And that all goodness, all good works, and faith the principle of all, are perfectly the gift of God's grace, and the work of his great, almighty, and exceeding excellent power. I think, there can be need of nothing but reading the chapter, and minding what is read, to convince all who have common understanding, of this; whatever any of the most subtle critics have done, or ever can do, to twist, rack, perplex, and pervert the words and phrases here used.

Dr. T. here again insists, that the apostle speaks only of the Gentiles in their heathen state, when he speaks of those that were *dead in sin*, and *by nature children of wrath;* and that though he seems to include himself among those, saying, WE *were by nature children of wrath*, WE *were dead in sins;* yet he only puts himself among them because he was the apostle of the *Gentiles*. The gross absurdity of this may appear from what was said before. But besides the things which have been already observed, there are some things which make it peculiarly unreasonable to understand it so here. It is true, the greater part of the church of *Ephesus* had been heathens, and therefore the apostle often has reference to their heathen state, in this epistle. But the words in this chap. ii. 3. plainly show, that he means himself and other *Jews* in distinction from the *Gentiles;* for the distinction is fully expressed. After he had told the *Ephesians*, who had been generally heathen, that they had been dead in sin, and had walked according to the course of this world, &c. (ver. 1, and 2.) he makes a *distinction*, and says, "among whom *we also* had our conversation, &c. and were by nature children of wrath, *even as others*." Here first he changes the person; whereas, before he had spoken in the second person, "*ye* were dead,—*ye* in time past walked," &c. now he changes style, and uses the first person, in a most manifest distinction, *among whom* WE ALSO, that is, *we Jews*, as well as *ye Gentiles:* not only changing the person, but adding a particle of distinction, *also;* which would be nonsense, if he meant the same without distinction. And besides all this, more fully to express the distinction, the apostle further adds a pronoun of distinction; WE *also, even as* OTHERS, or we as well as others: most evidently having respect to the notions, so generally entertained by the *Jews*, of their being much better than the *Gentiles*, in being *Jews by nature*, children of *Abraham*, and children of God; when they supposed the Gentiles to be utterly cast off, as *born aliens*, and *by nature children of wrath:* in opposition to this, the apostle says, "We Jews, after all our glorying in our distinction, *were by nature children of wrath, as well as the rest of the world*." And a yet further evidence, that the apostle here means to include the Jews, and even him-

* The following are all the other places where the word is used, Rom. i. 26. and ii. 14. and ver. 27. and xi. 21. and ver. 24. thrice in that verse. 1 Cor. xi. 14. Gal. ii. 15. and iv. 8. Jam. iii. 7. twice in that verse, and 2 Pet. i. 4.

self, is the universal term he uses, *Among whom also we* ALL *had our conversation*, &c. Though wickedness was supposed by the Jews to be the *course of this world*, as to the generality of mankind, yet they supposed themselves an exempt people, at least the Pharisees, and the devout observers of the law of Moses and traditions of the elders; whatever might be thought of *publicans* and *harlots*. But in opposition to this, the apostle asserts, that *they all* were no better by nature than others, but were to be reckoned among the *children of disobedience, and children of wrath.*

Besides, if the apostle chooses to put himself among the Gentiles, because he was the apostle of the Gentiles, I would ask, why does he not do so in the 11th verse of the same chapter, where he speaks of the Gentile state expressly? "Remember that *ye* being in time past Gentiles in the flesh." Why does he here make a distinction between the Gentiles and himself? Why did he not say, Let *us* remember, that *we* being in time past Gentiles? And why does the same apostle, even universally, make the same distinction, speaking either in the second or third person, and never in the first, where he expressly speaks of the Gentilism of those to whom he wrote, or of whom he speaks, with reference to their distinction from the Jews? So every where in this same epistle; as in chap. i. 12, 13. where the distinction is made just in the same manner as here, by the change of the person, and by the distinguishing particle, also: "That *we* should be to the praise of his glory who first trusted in Christ, (the first believers in Christ being of the Jews, before the Gentiles were called,) in whom *ye also* trusted, after that ye heard the word of truth, the gospel of your salvation." And in all the following part of this second chapter, as ver. 11, 17, 19, and 22. in which last verse the same distinguishing particle again is used; "In whom *ye also* are builded together for an habitation of God through the Spirit."*

Though I am far from thinking our author's exposition of the 7th chap. of Romans to be in any wise agreeable to the true sense of the apostle, yet it is needless here to stand particularly to examine it; because the doctrine of original sin may be argued not the less strongly, though we should allow the thing wherein he mainly differs from such as he opposes in his interpretation, *viz.* That the apostle does not speak in his own name, or to represent the state of a true Christian, but as representing the state of the Jews under the law. For even on this supposition, the drift of the place will prove, that every one who is under the law, and with equal reason every one of mankind, *is carnal, sold under sin*, in his first state, and till delivered by Christ. For it is plain, that the apostle's design is to show the insufficiency of the law to give life to any one whatsoever. This appears by what he says when he comes to draw his conclusion, in the continuation of this discourse; chap. viii. 3.† "For what the law could not do in that it was weak through the flesh, God sending his own Son," &c. Our author supposes what is here spoken of, viz. "that the law cannot give life, because it is weak through the flesh," is true with respect to *every one of mankind*.‡ And when the apostle gives this reason, *in that it is weak through the flesh*, it is plain, that by the *flesh*, which here he opposes to the *spirit*, he means the same thing which in the preceding part of the same discourse, in the foregoing chapter, he had called by the name *flesh*, ver. 5, 14, 18. and *the law of the members*, ver. 23. and *the body of death*, ver. 24. This is what, through this chapter, he insists on as the grand hinderance why the law could not give life; just as he does in his conclusion, chap. viii. 3. Which, in his last place, is given as a reason why the law cannot give life *to any of mankind*. And it being the *same reason* of the *same thing*, spoken of in the *same discourse*, in the former part of it—this last place being the conclusion, of which that former part is the premises—and inasmuch as the reason there given is *being in the flesh, and being carnal, sold under sin*: therefore, taking the whole of the apostle's discourse, this is justly understood to be a *reason* why the law cannot give life to *any* of mankind; and consequently, that *all* mankind are *in the flesh*, and are *carnal, sold under sin*, and so remain till delivered by Christ: and consequently, all mankind in their first original state are very sinful; which was the thing to be proved.

CHAP. IV.

CONTAINING OBSERVATIONS ON ROM. V. 12, TO THE END.

SECT. I.

Remarks on Dr. T.'s way of explaining this text.

THE following things are worthy of notice, concerning our author's exposition of this remarkable passage.

I. He greatly insists, that by *death* in this place no more is meant, than that death which we all die, when this present life is extinguished, and the body returns to the dust. That no more is meant in the 12, 14, 15, and 17th verses, (p. 27.) he declares as *evidently, clearly, and infallibly so*, because the apostle is still discoursing on the same subject; plainly implying, that *infallibly* the apostle means no more by death, throughout this paragraph on the subject. But as infallible as this is, if we believe what Dr. T. says elsewhere, it must needs be otherwise: for (p. 120. S.) speaking of those words in Rom. vi. 23. "The wages of sin is *death*, but the gift of God is *eternal life*, through Jesus Christ our Lord," he says, "Death in this place is widely different from the death we *now die*; as it stands there *opposed to eternal life*, which is the gift of God through Jesus Christ, it manifestly signifies *eternal death*, the *second death*, or that death which they shall *hereafter die*, who live after the flesh." But the death (in the conclusion of the paragraph we are upon) that comes by Adam, and the life that comes by Christ, (in the last verse of the chapter,) is *opposed to eternal life* just in the same manner as in the last verse of the next chapter: "That as sin has reigned unto *death*, even so might grace reign through righteousness, unto *eternal life*, by Jesus Christ our Lord." So that by our author's own argument, death in *this* place also, is *manifestly widely different from the death we now die, as it stands here opposed to eternal life, through Jesus Christ; and signifies eternal death, the second death*. And yet this is a part of the *same discourse*, begun in the 12th verse; as reckoned by Dr. T. himself in his division of paragraphs, in his paraphrase and notes on the epistle. So that if we will follow him, and admit his reasonings in the various parts of his book, here is *manifest* proof, against *infallible* evidence! So that it is true, the apostle throughout this whole passage on the same subject, by death, *evidently, clearly*, and *infallibly means no more than that death we now die, when this life is extinguished;* and yet by death, in some part of this passage, is meant something *widely different from the death we now die*—MANIFESTLY *eternal death, the second death*.

But had our author been more consistent with *himself*, in laying it down as certain and *infallible*, that because the apostle has a special respect to temporal death, in the 14th verse, "*Death reigned from* Adam *to* Moses," therefore he means no more in the several consequent parts of this passage, yet he is doubtless too confident and positive in this matter. This is no more *evident, clear*, and *infallible*, than that Christ meant by *perishing*—in Luke xiii. 5. when he says, *I tell you, Nay, but except ye repent, ye shall all likewise perish*—no more than such a temporal death, as came on those who died by the fall of the tower of *Siloam*, spoken of in the preceding words of the same speech; and no more infallible, than that by *life*, Christ means no more than this temporal life, in each part of that one sentence—Matt. x. 39. "He that findeth his *life* shall lose *it;* and he that loseth his *life* for my sake, shall find *it*"—because in the first part of each clause he has respect especially to temporal life. §

* See also the following chapters, chap. iii. 6. and iv. 17. And not only in this epistle, but constantly in other epistles; as Rom. i. 12, 13. chap. xi. 13, 14, 17, 18, 19, 20, 21, 22, 23, 24, 25, 28, 30, 31. chap. xv. 15, 16. 1 Cor. xii. 2. Gal. iv. 8. Col. i. 27. chap. ii. 13. 1 Thess. i. 5, 6, 9. chap. ii. 13, 14, 15, 16.

† Dr. T. himself reckons this a part of the same discourse or paragraph, in the division he makes of the epistle, in his *paraphrase*, and *notes* upon it.

‡ See note on Rom. v. 20.

§ There are many places parallel with these, as John xi. 25, 26. "I am the resurrection and the life: he that believeth in me, though he were dead, yet shall he live: and whosoever liveth, and believeth in me, shall never die." Here both the words, *life* and *death*, are used with this variation; "I am the resurrection and the life," meaning spiritual and eternal life; "He that

The truth of the case, with respect to what the apostle here intends by the word *death*, is this, *viz.* The whole of that death which he, and the Scripture every where, speaks of as the proper wages and punishment of sin, including death *temporal*, *spiritual*, and *eternal;* though in some parts of this discourse he has a more special respect to one part of this whole, in others to another, as his argument leads him; without any more variation than is quite common in the same discourse. That life, which the Scripture speaks of as the reward of righteousness, is a whole containing several parts, *viz.* The life of the body, union of soul and body, and the most perfect sensibility, activity, and felicity of both, which is the chief thing. In like manner the death, which the Scripture speaks of as the punishment of sin, is a whole including the death of the body and the death of the soul, and the eternal, sensible, perfect destruction and misery of both. It is this latter whole, that the apostle speaks of by the name of death in this discourse, in Rom. v. though in some sentences he has a more special respect to one part, in others to another: and this, without changing the signification of the word. For having respect to several things included in the extensive signification of the word, is not the same thing as using the word in several distinct significations. As for instance, the appellative, *man*, or the proper name of any particular man, is the name of a whole, including the different parts of soul and body. And if any one in speaking of *James* or *John*, should say, he was a wise *man*, and a beautiful *man;* in the former part of the sentence, respect would be had more especially to his soul, in the latter to his body, in the word *man:* but yet without any proper change of the signification of the name to distinct senses. In John xxi. 7. it is said, *Peter was naked*, and in the following part of the same story it is said, *Peter was grieved.* In the former proposition, respect is had especially to his body, in the latter to his soul: but yet here is no proper change of the meaning of the name, *Peter*. And as to the apostle's use of the word *death* in the passage now under consideration, on the supposition that he in general means the whole of that death which is the wages of sin, there is nothing but what is perfectly natural in supposing that—in order to evince that death, the proper punishment of sin, comes on all mankind in consequence of *Adam's* sin—he should take notice of that part of this punishment which is visible in this world, and which every body therefore sees does in fact come on all mankind, (as in ver. 14.) And is it not equally natural from thence to infer, that all mankind are exposed to the whole of that death which is the proper punishment of sin, whereof temporal death is a part, and a visible image of the whole, and (unless changed by divine grace) an introduction to the principal, and infinitely the most dreadful, part?

II. Dr. T.'s explanation of this passage makes wholly insignificant those first words, *By one man sin entered into the world*, and leaves this proposition without any sense at all. The apostle had been largely and elaborately representing, how the whole world was full of sin, both among *Jews* and *Gentiles*, and all exposed to death and condemnation. It is plain, that in these words he would tell us how this came to pass, namely, that the sorrowful event came *by one man*, even the first man. That the world was full of sin, and full of death, were two great and notorious facts, deeply affecting the interests of mankind; and they seemed very wonderful facts, drawing the attention of the more thinking part of mankind every where, who often asked this question, *Whence comes evil*, moral and natural evil? It is manifest, the apostle here means to tell us, how these came into the world, and came to prevail in it as they do. But all that is meant, according to Dr. T.'s interpretation, is, "*He begun transgression.*"* As if all that the apostle meant, was, to tell us who happened to sin first; not how such a malady came upon the world, or how any one in the world, besides *Adam* himself, came by such a distemper. The words of the apostle, "By one man sin entered *into the world*, and death by sin," show the design to be, to tell us how these evils came, as affecting the state of *the world;* and not only as reaching one man in the world. If this were not plain enough in itself, the words immediately following demonstrate it; "And so death passed upon *all men*, for that all have sinned." By *sin being in the world*, the apostle does not mean being in the world only in that *one instance* of *Adam's* first transgression, but being *abroad in the world*, among the inhabitants of the earth, in a wide extent, and continued series of wickedness; as is plain in the first words of the next verse, "For until the law, sin was *in the world*." And therefore when he gives us an account how it came to be *in the world*, or, which is the same thing, how it *entered into the world*, he does not mean only coming in one instance.

If the case were as Dr. T represents, that the sin of *Adam*, either in its pollution or punishment, reached none but himself, any more than the sin of any other man, it would be no more proper to say, that *by one man sin entered into the world*, than if—were it inquired, how mankind came into *America*, and there had anciently been a ship of the *Phenicians* wrecked at sea, and a single man of the crew was driven on this continent, and here died as soon as he reached the shore—it should be said, *By that one man mankind came into America.*

Besides, it is not true, that by *one man*, or by *Adam*, sin entered into the world, in Dr. T.'s sense: for it was not he but *Eve* that *began transgression*. By one man Dr. T. understands *Adam*, as the figure of Christ. And it is plain, that it was for *his* transgression, and not *Eve's*, that the sentence of death was pronounced on mankind after the fall, Gen. iii. 19. It appears unreasonable to suppose the apostle means to include *Eve*, when he speaks of *Adam;* for he lays great stress on it, that it was BY ONE, repeating it several times.

III. In like manner this author brings to nothing the sense of the causal particles, in such phrases as these, so often repeated, "Death *by* sin," ver. 12. "If *through* the offence of one, many be dead," ver. 15. "*by* one that sinned,—judgment was *by* one to condemnation," ver. 16. "*By* one man's offence, death reigned *by* one," ver. 17. "*By* the offence of one, judgment came upon all," &c. ver. 18. "*By* one man's disobedience," ver. 19. These *causal* particles, so variously repeated, unless we make mere nonsense of the discourse, signify some connexion and dependence, by some sort of influence of that sin of one man, or some tendency to that effect, which is so often said to come BY it. But according to Dr. T. there can be no *real* dependence or influence in the case, of any sort whatsoever. There is no connexion by any *natural* influence of that one act to make all mankind mortal. Our author does not pretend to account for this effect in any such manner, but in another most diverse, *viz.* A gracious act of God, laying mankind under affliction, toil, and death, from special favour and kindness. Nor can there be any dependence of this effect on that transgression of *Adam*, by any *moral* influence, as deserving such a consequence, or exposing to it on any *moral account:* for he supposes, that mankind are not in this way exposed to the least degree of evil. Nor has this effect any *legal* dependence on that sin, or any connexion by virtue of any antecedent constitution, which God had established with *Adam:* for he insists, that in that threatening, "In the day thou eatest thou shalt die," there is not a word said of his posterity, (p. 8.) And death on mankind, according to him, cannot come by virtue of that legal constitution with *Adam;* because the sentence by which it came was after the annulling and abolishing that constitution, (p. 113. S.) And it is manifest, that this consequence cannot be through any kind of *tendency* of that sin to such an effect; because the effect comes only as a benefit, and is the fruit of mere favour: but sin has no tendency, either *natural or moral*, to *benefits*, and divine favours. And thus that sin of *Adam* could neither be *the efficient* cause, nor the *procuring* cause; neither the *natural, moral, nor legal* cause; nor an *exciting and moving* cause, any more than Adam's eating of

believeth in me, though he were dead," having respect to temporal death, "yet shall he live," with respect to spiritual life, and the restoration of the life of the body. "And whosoever liveth and believeth in me, shall never die," meaning a spiritual and eternal death. So in John vi. 49, 50. "Your fathers did eat manna in the wilderness, and are dead," having respect chiefly to temporal death. "This is the bread which cometh down from heaven, that a man may eat thereof, and not die," *i. e.* by the loss of spiritual life, and by eternal death. (See also ver. 58.) And in the next verse, "If any man eat of this bread, he shall live for ever," have eternal life. So ver. 54. See another like instance, John v. 24—29.

* Page 56.

any other tree of the garden. And the only real relation that the effect can have to that sin, is a relation as to time, *viz.* that it is *after* it. And when the matter is closely examined, the whole amounts to no more than this, that God is pleased, of his mere good will and pleasure, to bestow a greater favour upon us, than he did upon Adam in innocency, *after that sin* of his eating the forbidden fruit; which sin we are no more concerned in, than in the sin of the king of *Pegu*, or the emperor of *China*.

IV. It is altogether inconsistent with the apostle's scope, and the import of what he says, to suppose that the death of which he here speaks, as coming on mankind by Adam's sin, comes not as a *punishment*, but only as a *favour*. It quite makes void the *opposition*, in which the apostle sets the consequences of *Adam's sin*, and the consequences of the *grace and righteousness of Christ*. They are set in opposition to each other, as opposite effects, arising from opposite causes, throughout the paragraph: one, *as the just consequence of an offence;* the other, *a free gift*, ver. 15—18. Whereas, according to this scheme, there is no such opposition in the case; both are benefits, and both are free gifts. A very wholesome medicine to save from perishing, ordered by a kind father, or a shield to preserve from an enemy, bestowed by a friend, is as much a free gift as pleasant food. The death that comes by Adam, is set in opposition to the life and happiness that comes by Christ, as being the fruit of *sin, and judgment for sin:* when the latter is the fruit of *divine grace*, ver. 15, 17, 20, 21. Whereas, according to our author, both came by grace. Death comes on mankind by the free kindness and love of God, much more truly and properly than by *Adam's sin*. Dr. T. speaks of it as coming *by* OCCASION *of Adam's sin:* but, as I have observed, it is an occasion without any influence. Yet the proper CAUSE *is God's grace*. So that the true cause is wholly good. Which, by the way, is directly repugnant to the apostle's doctrine in Rom. vii. 13. "Was then that which is good made death unto me? God forbid. But sin, that it might appear sin, working death in me by that which is good." Where the apostle utterly rejects any such suggestion, as though that which is good were *the proper cause of death;* and signifies that *sin* is the proper *cause*, and that which is *good*, only the *occasion*. But according to this author, the reverse is true: that which is good in the highest sense, even the love of God, and a divine gracious constitution, is the proper *cause* of death, and sin only the *occasion*.

But to return, it is plain, that death by Adam, and life and happiness *by Christ*, are here set in opposition: the latter being spoken of as *good*, the other as *evil;* one as the effect *of righteousness*, the other of an *offence;* one of the fruit *of obedience*, the other *of disobedience;* one as the fruit of *God's favour*, in consequence of what *was pleasing and acceptable to him*, but the other the fruit of *his displeasure*, in consequence of what was *displeasing and hateful* to him; the latter coming by *justification*, the former by the *condemnation* of the subject. But according to the scheme of our author, there can be no opposition in any of these respects: the death here spoken of, neither comes as an *evil*, nor from an *evil cause;* either an evil *efficient* cause, *or procuring* cause, nor at all as any testimony of God's *displeasure* to the subject, but as properly the effect of *his favour*, no less than that which is spoken of as coming by Christ; yea, as much as an act of JUSTIFICATION of the subject; as he understands and explains the word *justification;* for both are *by a grant of favour*, and are instances of mercy and goodness. And he abundantly insists upon it, that "ANY grant of favour, ANY instance of mercy and goodness, whereby God delivers and exempts from any kind of danger, suffering, or calamity, or confers ANY favour, blessing, or privilege, is called *justification* in the scripture-sense and use of the word."*

Moreover, our author makes void the grand and fundamental opposition—to illustrate which is the chief scope of this whole passage—between *the first and second Adam;* in the *death* that comes by *one*, and the *life* and happiness by the *other*. For, according to his doctrine, *both come by Christ the second Adam;* both by his grace, righteousness, and obedience: the death to which God sentenced mankind (Gen. iii. 19.) being a great deal more properly and truly by Christ, than by *Adam*. For, according to him, that sentence was not pronounced on the basis of the covenant with *Adam;* because that was abrogated, and entirely set aside, as he largely insists for many pages together, (p. 113—120. S.) "This covenant with *Adam* was disannulled immediately after *Adam sinned*. Even before God passed sentence upon *Adam*, grace was introduced." "The death that mankind are the subjects of now, stands under the covenant of grace.—In the counsel and appointment of God, it stood in this very light, even before the sentence of death was pronounced upon *Adam:* and consequently, death is no proper and legal punishment of sin." And he often insists, that it comes only as a favour and benefit; and standing, as he says, under the covenant of grace, which is by Christ, therefore is truly one of the benefits of the new covenant, which comes by Christ, the second *Adam*. For he himself is decided, to use his own words,† "That all the grace of the gospel is dispensed to us, IN, BY, or THROUGH the Son of God." "Nothing is clearer (says he‡) from the whole current of Scripture, than that all the mercy and love of God, and all the blessings of the gospel, from first to last, are IN, BY, and THROUGH Christ, and particularly by his blood, by the redemption that is in him. This can bear no dispute among Christians." What then becomes of all this discourse of the apostle's, about the great difference and opposition between *Adam and Christ;* as death is by one, and eternal life and happiness by the other? This grand distinction between the two Adams, it seems, and the other instances of opposition and difference here insisted on—as between the effects of *sin and righteousness*, the consequences of *obedience* and *disobedience*, of the *offence* and the *free gift*, *judgment and grace*, *condemnation and justification*—all come to nothing. And this whole discourse of the apostle, wherein he seems to labour much, as if it were to set forth some very grand and most important *distinction and oppositions* in the state of things, as derived from the two great *heads* of mankind, proves nothing but a multitude of words without meaning, or rather a heap of inconsistencies.

V. Our author's own doctrine entirely *makes void* what he supposes to be the apostle's *argument*, in the 13th and 14th verses, in these words; "For until the law, sin was in the world: but sin is not imputed where there is no law. Nevertheless death reigned from *Adam* to *Moses*, even over them that had not sinned after the similitude of *Adam's* transgression."

What he supposes the apostle would prove here, is, that the mortality of mankind comes only by *Adam's* sin, and not by men's *personal* sins, because there was *no law* threatening death to *Adam's* posterity for *personal* sins, before the law of *Moses;* but death, or the mortality of *Adam's* posterity, took place many ages before the law was given; therefore death could not be by any law threatening death for *personal* sins, and consequently could be by nothing but *Adam's* sin.§ On this I would observe,

1. That which he supposes the apostle to take for a truth in this argument, *viz.* That there was *no law of God* in being, by which men were exposed to death for *personal sin*, during the time from *Adam* to *Moses*, is neither true, nor agreeable to this apostle's own doctrine.

First, The assertion is *not true*. For the law of *nature*, written in men's hearts, was then in being, and was a law by which men were exposed to death for *personal* sin. That there was a divine establishment, fixing the death and destruction of the sinner as the consequence of personal sin, which was well known before the giving of the law by Moses, is plain by many passages in the book of *Job*, as fully and clearly implying a connexion between such sin and such a punishment, as any passage in the law of *Moses:* such as that in Job xxiv. 19. "Drought and heat consume the snow-waters; so doth the grave them that have sinned." (Compare ver. 20, and 24.) Also chap. xxxvi. 6. "He preserveth not the life of the wicked."

* *Key*, § 374. where it is to be observed, that he himself puts the word ANY in capital letters. The same thing in substance is often asserted elsewhere. And this indeed is his main point in what he calls *the true gospel-scheme*.

† *Key*, chap. viii. title, p. 44.

‡ *Key*, § 145.

§ Page 40, 41, 42, 57. and often elsewhere.

Chap. xxi. 29—32. "Have ye not asked them that go by the way? and do ye not know their tokens? That the wicked is reserved to the day of destruction; they shall be brought forth to the day of wrath." Ver. 32. "He shall be brought to the grave."*

Secondly. To suppose that there is no law in being, by which men are exposed to death for *personal sins*, when a revealed law of God is not in being, *is contrary to our apostle's own doctrine* in this epistle. Rom. ii. 12, 14, 15. "For as many as have sinned without law (*i. e.* the revealed law) shall perish without law." But how they can be exposed to die and perish, who have not the law of *Moses*, nor any revealed *law*, the apostle shows us in the 14th and 15th verses; *viz.* in that they have the law of nature, by which they fall under sentence to this punishment. "For when the *Gentiles*, which have not the law, do by nature the things contained in the law, these having not the law, are a law to themselves; which show the work of the law written in their hearts; their conscience also bearing witness."—Their conscience not only bore witness to the duty prescribed by this law, but also to the *punishment* before spoken of, as that which they who sinned without law, were liable to suffer, *viz.* that they should *perish*. In which the apostle is yet more express, chap. i. 32. speaking more especially of the heathen, "Who knowing the judgment of God, that they which commit such things are worthy of death." Dr. T. often calls the law the *rule of right;* and this rule of right sentenced those sinners to death, who were not under the law of *Moses*, according to this author's own paraphrase of this verse, in these words, "The heathen were not ignorant of the *rule of right*, which God had implanted in the human nature; and which shows that they which commit such crimes, are deserving of death." And he himself supposes *Abraham*, who lived between *Adam* and *Moses*, to be *under law*, by which he would have been *exposed to punishment without hope*, were it not for the promise of grace.—(Paraph. on Rom. iv. 15.)

So that in our author's way of explaining the passage before us, the grand argument which the apostle insists upon here to prove his main point, *viz.* that death does not come by men's *personal sins*, but by *Adam's* sin, because it came *before* the law was given, that threatened death for personal sin; I say, this argument which Dr. T. supposes so clear and strong,† is brought to nothing more than a mere shadow without substance; the very foundation of the argument having no truth. To say, there was no such law actually expressed in any standing revelation, would be mere trifling. For it no more appears, that God would not bring *temporal* death for personal sins without a standing revealed law threatening it, than that he would not bring *eternal* death before there was a revealed law threatening that: which yet wicked men that lived in *Noah's* time, were exposed to, as appears by 1 Pet. iii. 19, 20. and which Dr. T. supposes all mankind are exposed to by their personal sins; and he himself says,‡ "Sin in its own unalterable nature leads to death." Yea, it might be argued with as much strength of reason, that God could bring on men *no punishment at all* for any sin, that was committed from *Adam* to *Moses*, because there was no standing revealed law then extant threatening any punishment. It may here be properly observed, that our author supposes, the shortening of man's days, and hastening of death, *entered into the world by the sin of the antediluvians*, in the same sense as death and mortality entered into the world by *Adam's* sin.§ But where was there any standing revealed law for that, though the event was so universal? If God might bring this on all mankind, on occasion of *other* men's sins, for which they deserved nothing, without a revealed law, what could there be to hinder God bringing death on men for their *personal* sins, for which their own consciences tell them they deserve death without a revealed law?

2. If from *Adam* to *Moses* there had been no law in being, of any kind, revealed or natural, by which men could be properly exposed to temporal death for personal sin, yet the mention of *Moses's* law would have been wholly impertinent, and of no signification in the argument, according to our author. He supposes that what the apostle would prove, is, that *temporal* death comes by *Adam;* and not by *any law* threatening such a punishment for personal sin; because this death prevailed before the law of *Moses* was in being, which is the only law threatening death for personal sin. And yet he himself supposes, that the law of *Moses, when it was in being*, threatened *no such death* for personal sin. For he abundantly asserts, that the death which the law of *Moses* threatened for personal sin, *was eternal death*, as has been already noted: and he says in express terms, that eternal death is of a nature *widely different from the death we now die;*‖ as was also observed before.

How impertinently therefore does Dr. T. make an inspired writer argue, when, according to him, the apostle would prove, that *this kind of death* did not come by any law threatening *this kind of death*, because it came before the existence of a law threatening *another kind of death*, of a nature *widely different!* How is it to the apostle's purpose, to fix on that period, the time of giving *Moses's* law, as if that had been the period wherein men began to be threatened with *this punishment* for their personal sins, when in truth it was no such thing? And therefore it was no more to this purpose to fix on that period, from *Adam* to *Moses*, than from *Adam* to *David*, or any other period whatsoever. Dr. T. holds, that even now, since the law of *Moses* has been given, the mortality of mankind, or the death we now die, does not come by that law; but that it always comes only by *Adam.*¶ And if it *never comes* by that law, we may be sure it *never was threatened* in that law.

3. If we should allow the argument in Dr. T.'s sense of it, to prove that death does not come by *personal sin*, yet it will be wholly without force to prove the main point, even that it must come by *Adam's sin:* for it might come by God's sovereign and gracious pleasure; as innumerable other divine benefits do. If it be ordered, agreeable to our author's supposition, not as a punishment, nor as a calamity, but only as a *favour*, what necessity of any settled constitution, or revealed sentence, in order to bestow *such* a favour, more than *other* favours; and particularly more than that *great benefit*, which he says entered into the world by the sin of the *antediluvians*, the shortening men's lives so much after the flood? Thus the apostle's arguing, by Dr. T.'s explanation of it, is turned into mere trifling, a vain and impertinent use of words, without any real force or significance.

VI. The apostle here speaks of that great benefit which we have by Christ, as the antitype of *Adam*, under the notion of the fruit of GRACE. I do not mean only that *superabounding* of grace wherein the benefit we have by Christ goes beyond the damage sustained by *Adam;* but that benefit, with regard to which *Adam was the figure of him that was to come*, and which is as it were the counterpart of the suffering by Adam, and which repairs the loss we have by him. This is here spoken of as the fruit of the *free grace of God;* (as appears by ver. 15—18, 20, 21.) which according to our author, is the restoring of mankind to that life which they lost in *Adam:* and he himself supposes this restoration of life by Christ to be what *grace* does for us, and calls it the *free gift of God*, and *the grace and favour of the lawgiver.*** And speaking of this restoration, he breaks out in admiration of the *unspeakable riches of this grace.*††

But it follows from his doctrine, that there is no *grace at all* in this benefit, and it is no more than a mere act of *justice*, being only a removing of what mankind suffer, being *innocent*. Death, as it commonly comes on mankind, and even on infants, (as has been observed,) is an extreme, positive calamity; to bring which on the perfectly *innocent*, unremedied, and without any thing to countervail it, we are sufficiently taught, is not consistent with the *righteousness of the judge of all the earth.* What *grace* therefore, worthy of being so celebrated, would there be in affording remedy and relief, after there had been brought on

* See also Job iv. 7, 8, 9. Chap. xv. 17—35. Chap. xviii. 5—21. xix. 29. and xx. 4—8. and ver. 23—29. Chap. xxi. 16—18. 20—26. xxii. 13—20. and xxvii. 11, to the end. Chap. xxxi. 3, 23. xxxiii. 18, 22, 23, 24, 28, 30. xxxiv. 11. 21—26. xxxvii 12. 18, 19, 20. and xxxviii. 13.

† Page 117. S. ‡ Page 77, 78. § Page 68.

‖ Page 120. S. He says to the like purpose in his note on Rom. v. 17.

¶ This is plain by what he says, p. 38, 40, 53, 117. S.

** Page 39, 70, 148. 27. S. See also contents of this paragraph in Rom v. in his notes on the epistle, and his note on ver. 15, 16, 17.

†† Page 119. S.

innocent mankind that which is (as Dr. T. himself represents*) the dreadful and universal destruction of their nature; being a striking demonstration how infinitely hateful sin is to God! What *grace* in delivering from such shocking ruin, them who did not deserve the least calamity! Our author says, "We could not *justly* lose communion with God by *Adam's* sin."† If so, then we could not justly lose our lives, and be annihilated, after a course of extreme pains and agonies of body and mind, without any restoration; which would be an eternal loss of communion with God, and all other good, besides the positive suffering. The apostle, throughout this passage, represents the *death* which is the consequence of *Adam's* transgression, as coming in a way of *judgment* and *condemnation* for sin; but deliverance and life through Christ, as by *grace*, and the *free gift* of God. Whereas, on the contrary, by Dr. T.'s scheme, the death that comes by *Adam*, comes by *grace, great grace*; it being a great benefit, ordered in fatherly love and kindness, and on the basis of a covenant of grace: but in the deliverance and restoration by Christ, there is *no grace at all*. So things are turned *topsy-turvy*, the apostle's scope and scheme entirely inverted and confounded.

VII. Dr. T. explains the words, *judgment, condemnation, justification*, and *righteousness*, as used in this place in a very unreasonable manner.

I will first consider the sense he puts upon the two former, *judgment* and *condemnation*. He often calls this condemnation a *judicial act*, and a *sentence of condemnation*. But, according to his scheme, it is a judicial sentence of condemnation passed upon them who are perfectly *innocent*—and viewed by the judge, even in passing the condemnatory sentence, as having no guilt of sin, or any fault at all chargeable upon them—and a *judicial proceeding, passing sentence* arbitrarily, without any law or rule of right before established. For there was no preceding law threatening death, that he or any one else ever pretended to have been established, but only this, "In the day that thou eatest thereof, thou shalt surely die." And concerning this he insists, that there is not a word said in it of Adam's posterity. So that the condemnation spoken of, is a sentence of condemnation to death, for, or in consequence of, the sin of *Adam*, without any law by which that sin could be imputed to bring any such consequence; contrary to the apostle's plain scope. And not only so, but, over and above all this, it is a *judicial sentence* of *condemnation* to that which is no calamity, nor is considered as such in the sentence; but a condemnation to a great favour!

The apostle uses the words *judgment* and *condemnation* in other places; they are no strange and unusual terms with him: but never are they used by him in this sense, or any like it; nor are they ever used thus any where else in the New Testament. This apostle, in this epistle to the *Romans*, often speaks of *condemnation*, using the same or similar terms and phrases as here, but never in the abovesaid sense.‡ This will be plain to every one who casts his eye on those places. And if we look into the former part of this chapter, the apostle's discourse makes it evident, that he is speaking of a condemnation, which is no testimony of *favour* to the innocent; but of God's *displeasure* towards those to whom he is not reconciled, but looks on as offenders and enemies, and holds as the objects of his *wrath*, from which we are delivered by Christ. (See ver. 6—11.)

And even viewing this discourse itself, in the very paragraph we are upon, if we may judge any thing by language, there is every thing to lead us to suppose, that the apostle uses words here, as he does elsewhere, *properly*, and as implying a supposition of sin, chargeable on the subject, and exposing to punishment. He speaks of *condemnation* as what *comes by sin*, a condemnation to *death*, which seems to be a most terrible evil, and capital punishment, even in what is temporal and visible; and this in the way of *judgment* and execution of justice, in opposition to *grace* or *favour*, and *gift* or a benefit coming by favour. And sin, offence, transgression, and disobedience are, over and over again, spoken of as the *ground* of the condemnation, and of the capital suffering, for ten verses successively; that is, in every verse in the whole paragraph.

The words, *justification* and *righteousness*, are explained by Dr. T. in a manner no less unreasonable. He understands *justification*, in ver. 18. and *righteousness*, in ver. 19. in such a sense, as to suppose they belong to all, and are actually to be applied to all mankind, good and bad, believers and unbelievers; to the worst enemies of God, remaining such, as well as his peculiar favourites, and many that never had any sin imputed to them; meaning thereby no more than what is fulfilled in an universal resurrection from the dead, at the last day.§ Now this is a most arbitrary, forced sense. Though these terms are used all over the New Testament, yet nothing like such an use of them is to be found in any one instance. The words *justify, justification*, and *righteousness*, as from God to men, are never used but to signify a *privilege* belonging only to *some*, and that which is peculiar to *distinguished favourites*. This apostle in particular, above all the other writers of the New Testament, abounds in the use of these terms; so that we have all imaginable opportunity to understand his language, and know the sense in which he uses these words: but he never elsewhere uses them in the sense supposed here, nor is there any *pretence* that he does. Above all, this apostle abounds in the use of these terms in this epistle. JUSTIFICATION is the subject he had been upon through all the preceding part of the epistle. It was the grand subject of all the foregoing chapters, and the preceding part of this chapter, where these terms are continually repeated. And the word, *justification*, is constantly used to signify something peculiar to believers, who had been sinners; implying some reconciliation and forgiveness of sin, and special privilege in nearness to God, above the rest of the world. Yea, the word is constantly used thus, according to Dr. T's own explanations, in his paraphrase and notes on this epistle. And there is not the least reason to suppose but that he is *still* speaking of the *same justification*, which he had dwelt upon from the beginning to this place. He speaks of *justification* and *righteousness* here, just in the same manner as he had done in the preceding part of the epistle. He had all along spoken of justification as standing in relation to *sin*, disobedience to God, and offence against him, and so he does here. He had before been speaking of justification through free *grace*, and so he does here. He before had been speaking of justification through *righteousness, as in Christ Jesus*, and so he does here.

And if we look into the former part of this very chapter, we shall find *justification* spoken of just in the same sense as in the rest of the epistle; which is also supposed by our author in his exposition. It is still *justification by faith, justification* of them who had been *sinners, justification* attended with *reconciliation, justification* peculiar to them who had *the love of God shed abroad in their hearts*. The apostle's foregoing discourse on justification by grace through faith—and what he had so greatly insisted on as the evidence of the truth of this doctrine, even the universal sinfulness of mankind in their original state—is plainly what introduces this discourse in the latter part of this 5th chapter; where he shows how all mankind came to be sinful and miserable, and so to need this grace of God, and righteousness of Christ. And therefore we cannot, without the most absurd violence, suppose any other than that he is still speaking of the same *justification*.

And as to the universal expression used in the 18th verse, "by the righteousness of one, the free gift came upon *all men* to justification of life;" it is needless here to go into the controversy between *the remonstrants and anti-remonstrants*, concerning universal redemption, and their different interpretations of this place. If we take the words even as the *Arminians* do; yet, in their sense of them, the free gift comes on all men to justification only *conditionally, i. e. provided* they believe, repent, &c. But in our author's sense, it *actually* comes on all, whether they believe and repent, or not; which certainly cannot be inferred from the universal expression, as here used. Dr. T. himself supposes, the main design of the apostle in this universal phrase, *all men*, is to signify that the benefits

* Page 69. † Page 148.

‡ See chap. ii. 1, 2, 3. six times in these verses; also ver. 12 and 27. and chap. iii. 7. chap. viii. 1 and 3. chap. xiv. 3, 4. and ver. 10, 13, 22, and 23.

§ So page 47, 49, 60, 61, 62, and other places.

of Christ shall come on *Gentiles* as well as *Jews*.* And he supposes *that the Many and the All*, here signify the same; but it is quite certain, that all the benefits here spoken of, which the apostle says are to *the many*, does not *actually* come upon all mankind; as particularly *the abounding of grace*, ver. 15. "The grace of God, and the gift by grace, hath abounded unto the many (εις τȣς πολλȣς)."

This abounding of grace our author explains thus; "a rich overplus of grace, in erecting a new dispensation, furnished with a glorious fund of light, means, and motives," (p. 44.) But will any pretend, that all mankind have actually been partakers of this new fund of light, &c. How were the many millions of *Indians*, on the *American* side of the globe, partakers of it, before the *Europeans* came hither? Yea, Dr. T. himself supposes, *that it is only free for all that are willing to accept of it*.† The agreement between *Adam* as the type or figure of him that was to come, and *Christ* as the anti-type, appears full and clear, if we suppose that ALL who are IN CHRIST (to use the common scripture phrase) have the benefit of his obedience, even as ALL who are IN ADAM have the sorrowful fruit of his disobedience. The Scripture speaks of believers as the seed or posterity of Christ. (Gal. iii. 29.) They are *in Christ by grace*, as *Adam's* posterity *are in him by nature*. See also 1 Cor. xv. 45—49. The spiritual seed are those which this apostle often represents as *Christ's body*: and the οι πολλοι here spoken of as made righteous by Christ's obedience, are doubtless the same with the οι πολλοι which he speaks of in chap. xii. 5. *We, being many, are one body*; or, *we*, the many, οι πολλοι εν σωμα εσμεν. And again, 1 Cor. x. 17. εν σωμα οι πολλοι εσμεν. And the same which the apostle had spoken of in the preceding chapter. (Rom. iv. 18. compared with Gen. xv. 5.)

Dr. T. insists much on 1 Cor. xv. 21, 22. "For since by man came death, by man came also the resurrection of the dead; for as in Adam all die, so in Christ shall all be made alive;" to confirm his suppositions, that the apostle in the 5th of *Romans*, speaking of the death and condemnation which come by *Adam*, has respect only to the death *we all die*, when this life ends: and that by the justification and life which come by Christ, he has respect only to the general *resurrection* at the last day. But it is observable, that his argument is wholly built on these two suppositions, *viz. First*, that the resurrection meant by the apostle, 1 Cor. xv. is the resurrection of *all* mankind, both just and unjust. *Secondly*, That the opposite consequences of *Adam's sin*, and Christ's obedience, in Rom. v. are the very same, neither more nor less, than are spoken of there. But there are no grounds for supposing either of these things to be true.

1. There is no evidence, that the *resurrection* there spoken of, relates both to the *just and unjust*; but abundant evidence of the contrary. The resurrection of the wicked is seldom mentioned in the New Testament, and rarely included in the meaning of the word; it being esteemed not worthy to be called a rising to life, being only for a great increase of the misery and darkness of eternal death: and therefore by the *resurrection* is most commonly meant a rising to life and happiness.‡ The saints are called *the children of the resurrection*, as Dr. T. observes in his note on Rom. viii. 11. And it is exceeding evident, that it is the resurrection to life and happiness, which the apostle is speaking of in 1 Cor. xv. 21, 22. As appears by each of the three foregoing verses. Ver. 18. "Then they which are fallen asleep *in Christ* (*i. e.* the saints) are perished." Ver. 19. "If in this life only *we* (Christians or apostles) have hope in Christ, (and have no resurrection and eternal life to hope for,) we are of all men most miserable." Ver. 20. "But now is Christ risen from the dead, and is become the *first-fruits* of them that slept." He is the forerunner and first-fruits only with respect to them that are his; who are to follow him, and partake with him in the glory and happiness of his resurrection: but he is not the first-fruits of them that shall come forth to the resurrection of *damnation*. It also appears by the verse immediately following, ver. 23. "But every man in his own order; Christ the first-fruits, and afterwards they that are Christ's, at his coming." The same is plain by what is said in verse 29—32. and by all that is said from the 35th verse to the end of the chapter, for twenty-three verses together: it there expressly appears, that the apostle is speaking only of a rising *to glory, with a glorious body*, as the little grain that is sown, being quickened, rises a beautiful flourishing plant. He there speaks of the different degrees of glory among them that shall rise, and compares it to the different degrees of glory among the celestial luminaries. The resurrection he treats of, is expressly, *being raised in incorruption, in glory, in power, with a spiritual body, having the image of the second man*, the spiritual and heavenly *Adam*: a resurrection wherein this *corruptible shall put on incorruption, and this mortal put on immortality, and death be swallowed up in victory*, and the saints gloriously triumph over that last enemy. Dr. T. himself says what is in effect owning that the resurrection here spoken of is only of the righteous; for it is expressly a resurrection εν αθανασια, and αφθαρσια, (ver 53, and 42.) But Dr. T. says, *These are never attributed to the wicked in Scripture*.§ So that when the apostle says here, "As in Adam all die, so in Christ shall all be made alive;" it is as much as if he had said, *As in Adam we all die*, and our bodies *are sown in corruption, in dishonour, and in weakness: so in Christ we all* (we Christians, whom I have been all along speaking of) *shall be raised in power, glory, and incorruption, spiritual and heavenly*, conformed to the second Adam. *For as we have borne the image of the earthy, we shall also bear the image of the heavenly*, ver. 49. Which clearly explains and determines his meaning in ver. 21, 22.

2. There is no evidence, that the benefit by the second *Adam*, spoken of in Rom. v. is the very same (containing neither more nor less) as the resurrection spoken of in 1 Cor. xv. It is no evidence of it, that the benefit is opposed to the death that comes by the first *Adam*, in like manner in both places. The resurrection to eternal life, though it be not the whole of that salvation and happiness which comes by the second *Adam*, yet is it that wherein this salvation is principally obtained. The time of the saints' glorious resurrection is often spoken of as the proper time of their salvation, *The day of their redemption*, the time of their adoption, glory, and recompence.|| All that happiness which is given before, is only a prelibation and earnest of their great reward. Well therefore may that consummate salvation bestowed on them, be set in opposition to the death and ruin which comes by the first *Adam*, in like manner as the whole of their salvation is opposed to the same in Rom. v. Dr. T. himself observes,¶ *That the revival and resurrection of the body, is frequently put for our advancement to eternal life*. It being the highest part, it is often put for the whole.

This notion, as if the justification, righteousness, and life spoken of in Rom. v. implied the resurrection of damnation, is not only without ground from Scripture, but contrary to *reason*. For those are there spoken of as great benefits, by the grace and free gift of God: but this is the contrary, in the highest degree possible; the most consummate calamity. To obviate this, our author supposes the resurrection of all to be a great benefit *in itself*, though turned into a calamity by the sin and folly of obstinate sinners, who abuse God's goodness. But the far greater part of mankind, since *Adam*, have never had opportunity to abuse this goodness, it having never been made known to them. Men cannot abuse a kindness, which they never had either in possession, promise, offer, or some intimation: but a resurrection is made known only by divine revelation which few comparatively have enjoyed. So that as to such wicked men as die in lands of darkness, if their resurrection comes at all by Christ, it comes *from* him, and *to* them, only as a curse, and not a blessing; for it never comes to them at all by any *conveyance, grant, promise*, or *offer*, or any thing by which they can claim it, or know any thing of it, till it comes as an infinite calamity, past all remedy.

* Page 60, 61. See also contents of this paragraph, in his notes on the epistle.

† Notes on the epistle, page 284.

‡ As may be observed in Matt. xxii. 30. Luke xx. 35, 36. John vi. 39, 40, 54. Philip. iii. 11. and other places.

§ Note on Rom. viii. 27.

|| As in Luke xiv. 14. and xxi. 28. Rom. viii. 23. Eph. iv. 30. Colos. iii. 4. 2 Thess. i. 7. 2 Tim. iv. 8. 1 Pet. i. 13. and v. 4. 1 John iii. 2. and other places.

¶ Note on Rom. viii. 11.

VIII. In a peculiar manner is there an unreasonable violence used in our author's explanation of the words *sinners* and *sinned*, in the paragraph before us. He says, "These words, *By one man's disobedience many were made sinners*, mean neither more nor less, than that by one man's disobedience, the many were made subject to death, by the judicial act of God."* And he says in the same place, "By death, most certainly, is meant no other than the death and mortality common to all mankind." And those words, ver. 12. "For that all have sinned," he thus explains, "All men became *sinners*, as all mankind are brought into a state of suffering."† Here I observe,

1. The main thing, by which he justifies such interpretations, is, that *sin*, in various instances, is used for *suffering*, in the Old Testament.‡ To which I reply; though it be true, that the original word (חטא) signifies both *sin*, and a *sin-offering*—and though this, and some other *Hebrew* words which signify sin, iniquity, and wickedness, are sometimes put for the effect or punishment of iniquity, by a metonymy of the cause for the effect—yet it does not appear, that these words are ever used for suffering, where that suffering is not a *punishment*, or a fruit of God's anger for sin. And therefore none of the instances he mentions, come up to his purpose. When *Lot* is commanded to leave *Sodom*, that he might not be consumed *in the iniquity* of the city, meaning in that fire which was the *effect* and *punishment* of the iniquity of the city; this is quite *another* thing, than if that fire came on the city in general, as no punishment at all, nor as any fruit of a charge of iniquity, but as a token of God's *favour* to the inhabitants. For according to Dr. T. the death of mankind is introduced only as a *benefit*, from a covenant of grace. And especially is this quite another thing, than if, in the expression used, the iniquity had been ascribed to *Lot;* and God, instead of saying, Lest thou be consumed in *the iniquity of the city*, had said, Lest thou be consumed *in thine iniquity*, or, Lest *thou sin*, or *be made a sinner*. Whereas the expression is such, as expressly removes the iniquity spoken of from *Lot*, and fixes it on the city. The place cited by our author in Jer. li. is exactly parallel. And as to what *Abimelech* says to *Abraham*, "What have I offended thee, that thou hast brought on me, and on my kingdom, a great *sin?*" It is manifest, *Abimelech* was afraid that God was angry for what he had done to *Sarah;* or would have been angry with him, if he had done what he was about to do, as imputing *sin* to him for it. Which is a quite different thing from calling some calamity, *sin*, under no notion of its being any punishment of sin, nor in the least degree from God's displeasure. And so with regard to every place our author cites in the margin, it is plain, that what is meant in each of them, is *the punishment of sin*, and not some suffering which is no punishment at all. And as to the instances he mentions in his *Supplement*, (p. 8.) the two that look most favourable to his design are those in Gen. xxxi. 39. and 2 Kings vii. 9. With respect to the former, where *Jacob* says, *that which was torn of beasts*, (אנכי אחטנה,) *I bare the loss of it*. Dr. T. is pleased to translate it, *I was the sinner;* but properly rendered, it is, *I expiated it;* the verb in *Pihel* properly signifying to *expiate;* and the plain meaning is, *I bore the blame of it, and was obliged to pay for it*, as being supposed to be lost through my *fault* or neglect: which is a quite different thing from suffering without any supposition of fault. And as to the latter place, where the lepers say, *this day is a day of good tidings, and we hold our peace: if we tarry till morning some mischief will befall us:* in the *Hebrew* it is (ומצאנו עוון) *iniquity will find us*, that is, some punishment of our fault will come upon us. Elsewhere such phrases are used, as *your iniquity will find you out*, and the like. But certainly this is a different thing from suffering without fault, or supposition of fault. And it does not appear, that the verb in Hiphil, (הרשיע) rendered *to condemn*, is ever put for *condemn*, in any other sense than for sin, or guilt, or supposed guilt belonging to the subject condemned. This word is used in the participle of Hiphil, to signify CONDEMNING, in Prov. xvii. 15. "He that justifieth the wicked, and he that *condemneth* the just, even both are an abomination to the Lord." This Dr. T. observes, as if it were to his purpose, when he is endeavouring to show, that in this place (Rom. v.) the apostle speaks of God himself as *condemning the just*, or perfectly innocent, in a parallel signification of terms. Nor is any instance produced, wherein the verb *sin*, which is used by the apostle when he says, *all have sinned*, is any where used in our author's sense, for being brought into a state of suffering, and that not as a punishment for sin, or as any thing arising from God's displeasure; much less for being the subject of what comes only as the fruit of divine love, and as a benefit of the HIGHEST NATURE.§ Nor can any thing like this sense of the verb be found in the whole Bible.

2. If there had been any thing like such an use of the words *sin* and *sinner*, as our author supposes, in the *Old Testament*, it is evident that such an use of them is quite alien from the language of the *New Testament*. Where can an instance be produced of any thing like it, in any one place, besides what is pretended in this? and particularly in any of this apostle's writings? We have enough of his writings, by which to learn his way of speaking about *sin, condemnation, punishment, death*, and *suffering*. He wrote much more of the New Testament than any other person. He very often has occasion to speak of *condemnation:* but where does he express it by such a phrase as *being made sinners?* Especially how far is he elsewhere from using such a phrase, to signify being condemned without guilt, or any imputation or supposition of guilt? Vastly more still is it remote from his language, so to use the verb *sin*, and to say, man *sinneth*, or *has sinned*, though hereby meaning nothing more nor less, than that he, by a *judicial act*, is *condemned*, according to a dispensation of *grace*, to receive a *great favour!* He abundantly uses the words *sin* and *sinner;* his writings are full of such terms; but where else does he use them in such a sense? He has much occasion in his epistles to speak of *death*, temporal and eternal; to speak of *suffering* of all kinds, in this world, and the world to come: but where does he call these things *sin?* or denominate innocent men *sinners*, meaning, that they are brought into a state of *suffering?* If the apostle, because he was a *Jew*, was so addicted to the *Hebrew* idiom, as thus in *one* paragraph to repeat this particular *Hebraism*, which, at most, is comparatively rare even in the Old Testament; is it not strange, that never any thing like it should appear any where else in his writings? and especially, that he should never fall into such a way of speaking in his epistle to the *Hebrews*, written to *Jews* only, who were most used to the *Hebrew* idiom? And why does *Christ* never use such language in any of his speeches, though he was born and brought up among the *Jews*, and delivered almost all his speeches to *Jews* only? And why do none of the other New-Testament writers ever use it, who were all born and educated *Jews*, (excepting perhaps *Luke*,) and some of them wrote especially for the benefit of the *Jews?*

It is worthy to be observed, what liberty is taken and boldness is used with this apostle. Such words as αμαρτολος, αμαρτανω, κριμα, κατακριμα, δικαιοω, δικαιωσις, are abundantly used by him elsewhere in this and other epistles, when speaking, as here, of Christ's redemption and atonement, the general sinfulness of mankind, the condemnation of sinners, the justification by Christ, death as the consequence of sin, and restoration to life by Christ; yet no where are any of these words used, but in a sense very remote from what is supposed by Dr. T. however, in this place, it seems, these terms must have a *distinguished singular* sense annexed to them! A *new* language must be coined for the apostle, to which he is evidently quite unused, for the sake of evading this clear, precise, and abundant testimony of his, to the doctrine of original sin.

3. To put such a sense on the word *sin*, in this place, is not only to make the apostle greatly disagree with himself in the language he uses *every where else*, but also *in this very passage*. He often here uses the word *sin*, and other words plainly of the same import, such as *transgression, disobedience, offence*. Nothing can be more evident, than that these are used as several names of the same

* Page 30. † Page 54, and elsewhere. ‡ Page 34. § Page 27. S.

thing; for they are used interchangeably, and put one for another. And these words are used no less than *seventeen* times in this one paragraph. Perhaps we shall find no place in the whole Bible, in which the word *sin*, and other words plainly synonymous, are used so often in so little compass: and in all these instances, in the *proper* sense, as signifying *moral evil*, and even so understood by Dr. T. himself, (as appears by his own exposition,) but only in these two places, (ver. 12, 19.) where, in the midst of all, to evade a clear evidence of the doctrine of original sin, another meaning must be found out, and it must be supposed that the apostle uses the word in a sense entirely different, signifying something that neither *implies* nor *supposes* any moral evil at all in the subject.

Here it is very remarkable, how the gentleman who so greatly insisted upon it, that the word *death* must needs be understood in the *same* sense throughout this paragraph; yea, that it is *evidently*, *clearly*, and *infallibly* so, inasmuch as the apostle is still discoursing on the same subject; yet can, without the least difficulty, suppose the word *sin*, to be used so differently in the very same passage, wherein the apostle is discoursing on the same thing. Let us take that one instance in ver. 12. "Wherefore as by one man *sin* entered into the world, and death by *sin*, and so death passed upon all men, for that all have *sinned*." Here, by *sin*, implied in the word *sinned*, in the end of the sentence, our author understands something perfectly and altogether *diverse* from what is meant by the word *sin*, twice in the former part of the very same sentence, of which this latter part is the explication. And a sense entirely *different* from the use of the word twice in the *next* sentence, wherein the apostle is still most plainly discoursing on the same subject, as is not denied. And so our author himself understands ver. 14. Afterwards (ver. 19.) the apostle uses the word *sinners*, which our author supposes to be in a somewhat different sense still. So that here is the utmost violence of the kind that can be conceived of, to make out a scheme against the plainest evidence, in changing the meaning of a word backward and forward in one paragraph, all about one thing, and in different parts of the same sentence, occurring in quick repetitions, with a variety of other synonymous words to fix its signification. To which we may add, the continued use of the word in all the preceding and subsequent parts of this epistle; in none of which places is it pretended, but that the word is used in the proper sense, by our author in his paraphrase and notes on the whole epistle.*

But indeed we need go no further than ver. 12. What the apostle means by *sin*, in the latter part of the verse, is evident, by comparing it with the former part; the last clause being exegetical of the first. "Wherefore, as by one man sin entered into the world, and death by sin; and so death passed upon all men, for that (or unto which) all have sinned." Here *sin* and *death* are so spoken of in the former and in the latter part that the same things are clearly meant by the terms in both parts. Besides, to interpret *sinning*, here, by falling under the suffering of *death*, is yet the more violent and unreasonable, because the apostle in this very place once and again *distinguishes* between *sin* and *death*; plainly speaking of one as the effect, and the other the cause. So in the 21st verse, "that as *sin* hath reigned unto *death*;" and in the 12th verse, "*sin* entered into the world, and *death* by sin." And this plain distinction holds through all the discourse, as between *death* and the *offence*, ver. 15. and ver. 17. and between the *offence* and *condemnation*, ver. 18.

4. Though we should omit the consideration of the manner in which the apostle uses the words, *sin*, *sinned*, &c. in other places, and in other parts of this discourse, yet Dr. T.'s interpretation of them would be very absurd.

The case stands thus: according to *his* exposition, we are said to have *sinned* by an *active* verb, as though we had actively sinned; yet this is not spoken truly and properly, but it is put figuratively for our becoming sinners *passively*, our being *made* or *constituted* sinners. Yet again, not that we do truly become sinners *passively*, or are really *made sinners*, by any thing that God does; this also is only a figurative or tropical representation; and the meaning is only, we are *condemned*, and treated AS IF we were *sinners*. Not indeed that we are properly *condemned*, for God never truly condemns the innocent; but this also is only a figurative representation of the thing. It is but *as it were* condemning; because it is appointing to *death*, a terrible evil, *as if it were* a punishment. But then, in reality, here is no appointment to a terrible *evil*, or any evil at all; but truly to a *benefit*, a *great* benefit; and so in representing death as a punishment, another figure is used, and an exceeding bold one; for, as we are appointed to it, it is so far from being an evil or punishment, that it is really a *favour*, and that of the highest nature, appointed by mere grace and love, though it *seems* to be a calamity.

Thus we have tropes and figures multiplied, one upon another; and all in that one word, *sinned;* according to the manner, as it is supposed, in which the apostle uses it. We have a *figurative representation*, not of a reality, but of a *figurative representation*. Neither is this a representation of a reality, but of another thing that still is but a *figurative representation* of something else: yea, even this *something else* is still but a *figure*, and one that is very harsh and far-fetched. So that here we have a *figure* to represent a *figure*, even a *figure* of a *figure*, representing some very remote *figure*, which most obscurely represents the thing intended; if the most *terrible evil* can indeed be said at all to *represent* the contrary *good* of the highest kind. And now, what cannot be made of *any* place of Scripture, in such a way as this? And is there any hope of ever deciding any controversy by the Scripture, in the way of using such a licence in order to force it to a compliance with our own schemes? If the apostle indeed uses language after so strange a manner in this place, it is perhaps such an instance, as not only there is not the like in all the Bible besides, but perhaps in no writing whatsoever. And this, not in any parabolical, visionary, or prophetic description, in which difficult and obscure representations are wont to be made; nor in a dramatic or poetical representation, in which a great licence is often taken, and bold figures are commonly to be expected. But it is in a familiar letter, wherein the apostle is delivering gospel-instruction, as a minister of the New Testament: and wherein, as he professes, he delivers divine truth without the vail of ancient figures and similitudes, and uses great plainness of speech. And in a discourse that is wholly didactic, narrative, and argumentative; evidently setting himself to explain the doctrine he is upon, in the reason and nature of it, with a great variety of expressions, turning it as it were on every side, to make his meaning plain, and to fix in his readers the exact notion of what he intends. Dr. T. himself observes,† "This apostle takes great care to guard and explain every part of his subject: and I may venture to say, he has left no part of it unexplained or unguarded. Never was an author more exact and cautious in this than he. Sometimes he writes notes on a sentence liable to exception, and wanting explanation." Now I think, this care and exactness of the apostle no where appears more than in the place we are upon. Nay, I scarcely know another instance equal to this, of the apostle's care to be well understood, by being very particular, explicit, and precise, setting the matter forth in every light, going over and over again with his doctrine, clearly to exhibit, and fully to settle and determine the thing at which he aims.

* Agreeably to his manner, our author, in explaining the 7th chap. of Romans, understands the pronoun *I*, or *me*, used by the apostle in that one continued discourse, in no less than *six* different senses. He takes it in the 1st ver. to signify the apostle Paul himself. In the 8, 9, 10, and 11th verses, for the people of the *Jews*, through all ages, both before and after *Moses*, especially the carnal ungodly part of them. In the 13th ver. for an objecting *Jew*, entering into a dialogue with the apostle. In the 15, 16, 17, 20, and latter part of the 25th ver. it is understood in two different senses, for two I's in the same person; one, a man's reason; and the other, his passions and carnal appetites. And in the 7th and former part of the last verse, for us Christians in general; or, for all that enjoy the word of God, the law and the gospel: and these different senses, the most of them strangely inter mixed and interchanged backwards and forwards.

† Pref. to Paraph. on Rom. p. 146. 48.

SECT. II.

Some observations on the connexions, scope, and sense of this remarkable paragraph, Rom. v. 12, &c. With some reflections on the evidence which we here have of the doctrine of original sin.

THE connexion of this remarkable paragraph with the foregoing discourse in this epistle, is not obscure and difficult, nor to be sought for at a distance. It may be plainly seen, only by a general glance on what goes before, from the beginning of the epistle: and indeed what is said immediately before in the same chapter, leads directly to it. The apostle in the preceding part of this epistle had largely treated of the *sinfulness* and *misery* of all mankind, *Jews* as well as *Gentiles*. He had particularly spoken of the depravity and ruin of mankind in their natural state, in the foregoing part of this chapter; representing them as being *sinners, ungodly, enemies*, exposed to divine *wrath*, and *without strength*. This naturally leads him to observe, *how* this so great and deplorable an event came to pass; *how* this universal sin and ruin came into the world. And with regard to the *Jews* in particular, though they might allow the doctrine of original sin in profession, they were strongly prejudiced against what was implied in it, or evidently followed from it, with regard to themselves. In this respect they were prejudiced against the doctrine of universal sinfulness, and exposedness to wrath by nature, looking on themselves as by nature holy, and favourites of God, because they were the children of *Abraham*; and with them the apostle had laboured most in the foregoing part of the epistle, to convince them of their being by nature as sinful, and as much the children of wrath, as the *Gentiles*: it was therefore exceeding proper, and what the apostle's design most naturally led him to, that they should take off their eyes from their father *Abraham*, their father in distinction from other nations, and direct them to their father *Adam*, who was the common father of mankind, equally of *Jews* and *Gentiles*. And when he had entered on this doctrine of the derivation of sin and death, to all mankind from *Adam*, no wonder if he thought it needful to be somewhat particular in it, seeing he wrote to *Jews* and *Gentiles;* the former of which had been brought up under the prejudices of a proud opinion of themselves, as a holy people by nature, and the latter had been educated in total ignorance.

Again, the apostle had, from the beginning of the epistle, been endeavouring to evince the absolute dependence of all mankind on the free *grace* of GOD for salvation, and the greatness of this grace; and particularly in the former part of this chapter. The greatness of this grace he shows especially by two things. (1.) The universal corruption and misery of mankind; as in all the foregoing chapters, and in several preceding verses of this chapter, (ver. 6—10.) (2.) The greatness of the benefits which believers receive, and the greatness of the glory for which they hope. So especially in ver. 1—5, and 11th of this chapter. And here, ver. 12, to the end, he still pursues the same design of magnifying the grace of God, in the favour, life, and happiness which believers in Christ receive; speaking here of *the grace of God, the gift by grace, the abounding of grace, and the reign of grace*. And he still sets forth the freedom and riches of grace by the same two arguments, *viz.* The universal *sinfulness* and *ruin* of mankind, all having sinned, all being naturally exposed to death, judgment, and condemnation; and the exceeding greatness of the benefit received, being far greater than the misery which comes by the first Adam, and abounding beyond it. And it is by no means consistent with the apostle's scope, to suppose, that the benefit which we have by Christ, as the antitype of Adam, here mainly insisted on, is without any grace at all, being only a restoration to life of such as never deserved death.

Another thing observable in the apostle's grand scope from the beginning of the epistle, is, that he endeavours to show the greatness and absoluteness of dependence on the *redemption* and *righteousness* of CHRIST, for justification and life, that he might *magnify* and *exalt* the *Redeemer;* in which design his whole heart was swallowed up, and may be looked upon as the main design of the whole epistle. And this is what he had been upon in the preceding part of this chapter, inferring it from the same argument, even the utter sinfulness and ruin of all men. And he is evidently still on the same thing from the 12th verse to the end; speaking of the *same* justification and righteousness, which he had dwelt on before, and not another totally diverse. No wonder, when the apostle is treating so fully and largely of our restoration, righteousness, and life by Christ, that he is led by it to consider our fall, sin, death, and ruin by *Adam;* and to observe wherein these two opposite heads of mankind agree, and wherein they differ, in the manner of conveyance of opposite influences and communications from each.

Thus, if the place be understood, as it used to be understood by orthodox divines, the whole stands in a natural, easy, and clear connexion with the preceding part of the chapter, and all the former part of the epistle; and in a plain agreement with the express design of all that the apostle had been saying; and also in connexion with the words last before spoken, as introduced by the two immediately preceding verses, where he is speaking of our justification, reconciliation, and salvation by Christ; which leads the apostle directly to observe, how, on the contrary, we have sin and death by *Adam*. Taking this discourse of the apostle in its true and plain sense, there is no need of great extent of learning, or depth of criticism, to find out the connexion. But if it be understood in Dr. T.'s sense, the plain scope and connexion are wholly lost, and there was truly need of skill in criticism, and the art of discerning, beyond or at least different from that of former divines, and a faculty of seeing what other men's sight could not reach, in order to find out the connexion.

What has been already observed, may suffice to show the apostle's general scope in this place. But yet there seem to be some *other* things to which he alludes in several expressions. As particularly the *Jews* had a very superstitious and extravagant notion of their law, delivered by *Moses;* as if it were the prime, grand, and indeed only rule of God's proceeding with mankind as their judge, both in their justification and condemnation, or from whence all, both sin and righteousness, was imputed; and had no consideration of the law of nature, written in the hearts of the *Gentiles*, and of all mankind. Herein they ascribed infinitely too much to their particular law, beyond the true design of it. They *made their boast of the law;* as if their being distinguished from all other nations by that great privilege, *the giving of the law*, sufficiently made them a holy people, and God's children. This notion of theirs the apostle evidently refers to, chap. ii. 13, 17—19. and indeed through that whole chapter. They looked on the law of *Moses* as intended to be the only rule and means of justification; and as such, trusted in the works of the law, especially circumcision; which appears by the third chapter. But as for the *Gentiles*, they looked on them as by nature sinners, and children of wrath; because born of uncircumcised parents, and aliens from their law, and who themselves did not know, profess, and submit to the law of *Moses*, become proselytes, and receive circumcision. What they esteemed the sum of *their* wickedness, and condemnation, was, that they did not turn *Jews*, and act as *Jews*.* To this notion the apostle has a plain respect, and endeavours to convince them of its falseness, in chap. ii. 12—16. And he has a manifest regard again to the same thing here. (Chap. v. 12—14.) Which may lead us the more clearly to see the true sense of those verses; about the sense of which is the main controversy, and the meaning of which being determined, it will settle the meaning of every other controverted expression through the whole discourse.

Dr. T. misrepresents the apostle's argument in these verses; which, as has been demonstrated, is in his sense altogether vain and impertinent. He supposes, the thing which the apostle mainly intends to prove, is, that *death* or mortality does not come on mankind by *personal* sin; and that he would prove it by this medium, that *death reigned* when there was *no law* in being which threatened personal sin with death. It is acknowledged, that this is

* Here are worthy to be observed the things which Dr. T. himself says to the same purpose, *Key*, § 302, 303. and *Pref. to Par. on Ep. to* Rom. p. 144. 43.

implied, even that death came into the world by *Adam's* sin: yet this is not the *main* thing the apostle designs to prove. But his main point evidently is, that *sin* and *guilt*, and *just exposedness to death and ruin*, came into the world by *Adam's* sin; as *righteousness, justification*, and a *title to eternal life* come by Christ. Which point he confirms by this consideration, that from the very time when *Adam* sinned, sin, guilt, and desert of ruin, became *universal* in the world, long before the law given by *Moses* to the *Jewish* nation had any being.

The apostle's remark, that sin entered into the world by *one man*, who was the father of the whole human race, was an observation which afforded proper instruction for the *Jews*, who looked on themselves as an holy people, because they had the law of *Moses*, and were the children of *Abraham*, an holy father; while they looked on other nations as by nature unholy and sinners, because they were not Abraham's children. He leads them up to a higher ancestor than this patriarch, even to Adam, who being equally the father of *Jews* and *Gentiles*, both alike come from a sinful father; from whom guilt and pollution were derived alike to all mankind. And this the apostle proves by an argument, which of all that could possibly be invented, tended the most briefly and directly to convince the *Jews;* even by this reflection, that death had come equally on all mankind from *Adam's* time, and that the posterity of *Abraham* were equally subject to it with the rest of the world. This was apparent in *fact*, a thing they all knew. And the Jews had always been taught, that *death* (which began in the destruction of the body, and of this present life) was the proper punishment of *sin*. This they were taught in *Moses's* history of *Adam*, and God's first threatening of punishment for sin, and by the constant doctrine of the law and the prophets; as already observed.

And the apostle's observation—that *sin was in the world* long before the *law* was given, and was as *universal* in the world from the times of Adam, as it had been among the heathen since the law of Moses—showed plainly, that the *Jews* were quite mistaken in their notion of their particular law; and that the *law* which is the original and universal rule of righteousness and judgment for all mankind, was another law, of far more ancient date, even the law of nature. This began as early as the human nature began, and was established with the first father of mankind, and in him with the whole race. The positive precept of abstaining from the forbidden fruit, was given for the trial of his compliance with this law of nature; of which the main rule is supreme regard to God and his will. And the apostle proves that it must be thus, because if the law of *Moses* had been the highest rule of judgment, and if there had not been a superior, prior, divine rule established, mankind in general would not have been judged and condemned as sinners, *before* that was given, (for "sin is not imputed, when there is no law,") as it is apparent in fact they were, because *death reigned* before that time, even from the time of *Adam*.

It may be observed, that the apostle, both in this epistle, and in that to the *Galatians*, endeavours to convince the *Jews* of these two things, in opposition to the notions and prejudices they had entertained concerning *their law*. (1.) That it never was intended to be the *covenant*, or method by which they should actually be *justified*. (2.) That it was not the *highest* and *universal* rule or law, by which mankind in general, and particularly the heathen world, were *condemned*. And he proves both by similar arguments.—He proves, that the law of *Moses* was not the *covenant*, by which any of mankind were to obtain *justification*, because that covenant was of older date, being expressly established in the time of *Abraham*, and Abraham himself was *justified* by it. This argument the apostle particularly handles in the third chapter of *Galatians*, particularly in ver. 17—19. and especially in Rom. iv. 13—15. He proves also, that the law of *Moses* was not the *prime* rule of judgment, by which mankind in general, and particularly the heathen world, were *condemned*. And this he proves also the same way, *viz.* by showing this to be of *older date* than that law, and that it was established with *Adam*. Now, these things tended to lead the *Jews* to right notions of their law, not as the intended method of *justification*, nor as the original and universal rule of *condemnation*, but something *superadded* to both; superadded to the *latter*, to illustrate and confirm it, that the *offence might abound;* and superadded to the *former*, to be as a schoolmaster, to prepare men for its benefits, and to magnify divine *grace* in it, that this might *much more abound*.

The chief occasion of obscurity and difficulty, attending the scope and connexion of the various clauses of this discourse, particularly in the 13th and 14th verses, is that there are *two* things (although closely connected) which the apostle has in view *at once*. He would illustrate the grand point he had been upon from the beginning, even *justification through Christ's righteousness alone*, by showing how we are originally in a sinful miserable state, how we derive this sin and misery from *Adam*, and how we are delivered and justified by Christ as a second *Adam*. At the same time he would confute those foolish and corrupt notions of the *Jews*, about their *nation*, and their *law*, which were very inconsistent with these doctrines. And he here endeavours to establish, at once, these two things in opposition to those *Jewish* notions.

(1.) That it is our natural relation to *Adam*, and not to *Abraham*, which determines our native moral state; and that, therefore, being natural children of *Abraham*, will not make us by nature holy in the sight of God, since we are the natural seed of sinful *Adam*. Nor does the *Gentiles* being not descended from *Abraham*, denominate them *sinners*, any more than the *Jews*, seeing both alike are descended from *Adam*.

(2.) That the law of *Moses* is not the prime and general law and rule of judgment for mankind, to *condemn* them, and denominate them *sinners;* but that the state they are in with regard to a higher, more ancient, and universal law, determines them in general to be *sinners* in the sight of God, and liable to be *condemned* as such. Which observation is, in many respects, to the apostle's purpose; particularly in this respect, that if the *Jews* were convinced, that the law, which was the prime rule of *condemnation*, was given to *all*, was common to all mankind, and that all fell under condemnation through the violation of that law by the common father of all, both *Jews* and *Gentiles*, then they would be led more easily and naturally to believe, that the method of *justification*, which God had established, also extended equally to *all* mankind: and that the *Messiah*, by whom we have this justification, is appointed, as *Adam* was, for a common head to all, both *Jews and Gentiles*.—The apostle aiming to confute the *Jewish* notion, is the principal occasion of those words in the 13th verse, "for until the law, sin was in the world; but sin is not imputed, when there is no law."

As to the import of that expression, "even over them that had not sinned after the similitude of Adam's transgression," not only is the thing signified, in Dr. T.'s sense of it, *not true;* or if it had been true, would have been impertinent, as has been shown: but his interpretation is, otherwise, very much *strained* and unnatural. According to him, "by sinning after the similitude of Adam's transgression," is not meant any similitude of the act of sinning, nor of the command sinned against, nor properly any circumstance of the *sin;* but only the similitude of a circumstance of the *command, viz. the threatening* with which it is attended. A far-fetched thing, truly, to be called a *similitude of sinning!* Besides, this expression in such a meaning, is only a needless, impertinent, and awkward *repetition* of the same thing, which it is supposed the apostle had observed in the foregoing verse, even after he had proceeded another step in the series of his discourse. As thus, in the foregoing verse the apostle had plainly laid down his argument, (as our author understands it,) by which he would prove, that *death* did not come by *personal sin, viz.* because death reigned before any *law, threatening* death for personal sin, was in being: so that the sin then committed was against *no law*, threatening death for personal sin. Having laid this down, the apostle leaves this part of his argument, and proceeds another step, *nevertheless death reigned from Adam to Moses:* and then returns, in a strange unnatural manner, and *repeats* that argument or assertion again, but only more obscurely than before, in these words, *even over them that had not sinned after the similitude of Adam's transgression; i. e.* over them that had not sinned against a law threatening death for personal sin. Which is just the same thing as if the apostle had said, "they that sinned *before the law*, did not sin against a law threatening death for personal sin; for there was *no such law* for any to sin against at that time: *nevertheless* death reigned at that time, *even over such as did not sin* against a law threatening death for personal sin." Which latter clause *adds* nothing to the premises, and tends nothing to illustrate what was said before, but rather to obscure and darken it. The particle (και) *even*, when prefixed in this manner, is used to signify something additional, some advance in the sense or argument; implying, that the words following express something more, or express the same thing more fully, plainly, or forcibly. But to unite two clauses by such a particle, in such a manner, when there is nothing besides a flat repetition, with no superadded sense or force, but rather a greater uncertainty and obscurity, would be very unusual, and indeed very absurd.

I can see no reason why we should be dissatisfied with that explanation of this clause, which has more commonly been given, *viz.* That by *them who have not sinned after the similitude of Adam's transgression*, are meant *infants;* who, though they have indeed sinned in Adam, yet never sinned as *Adam* did, by actually transgressing in their own persons; unless it be, that this interpretation is too *old*, and too *common*. It was well understood by those to whom the apostle wrote, that vast numbers had *died* in infancy, within that period of which he speaks, particularly in the time of the deluge. And it would be strange, that the apostle should not have the case of such infants in his mind; even supposing his scope were what our author supposes, and he had only intended to prove that death did not come on mankind for their *personal* sin. How directly would it have served the purpose of proving this, to have mentioned so great a part of mankind who are subject to death, and who, all know, never committed any sin *in their own persons!* How much more plain and easy the proof of the point by that, than to go round about, as Dr. T. supposes, and bring in a thing so dark and uncertain as this, that God never would bring death on all mankind for *personal* sin (though they had personal sin) without an express revealed *constitution;* and then to observe, that there was *no* revealed constitution of this nature from *Adam* to *Moses*—which also seems to be an assertion without any plain evidence—and then to infer, that it must needs be so, that it could come only on *occasion of Adam's sin*, though not *for* his sin, or as any punishment of it; which inference also is very dark and unintelligible.

If the apostle in this place meant those who never sinned by their personal act, it is not strange that he should express this by their *not sinning after the similitude of Adam's transgression*. We read of two ways of men being like *Adam*, or in which a similitude to him is ascribed to men: one is, being begotten or born in his *image* or *likeness*, Gen. v. 3. Another is, transgressing God's covenant or law, *like him*, Hos. vi. 7. *They, like Adam*, (so, in the *Heb.* and *Vulg. Lat.*) *have transgressed the covenant*. Infants have the former similitude, but not the latter. And it was very natural, when the apostle would infer that infants become sinners by that one act and offence of Adam, to observe, that they had not renewed the act of sin themselves, by any second instance of a like sort. And such might be the state of language among *Jews* and Christians at that day, that the apostle might have no phrase more aptly to express this meaning. The manner in which the epithets, *personal* and *actual*, are used and applied now in this case, is probably of later date, and more modern use.

And the apostle having the case of *infants* in view, in this expression, makes it more to his purpose to mention death reigning before the law of Moses was given. For the Jews looked on all nations besides themselves, as *sinners*, by virtue of *their law;* being made so especially by the *law of circumcision*, given first to *Abraham*, and completed by *Moses*, making the want of circumcision a legal *pollution*, utterly disqualifying for the privileges of the sanctuary. This law, the *Jews* supposed, made the very infants of the *Gentiles* to be sinners, polluted and hateful to God; they being uncircumcised, and born of uncircumcised parents. But the apostle proves, against these notions of the Jews, that the nations of the world do not become sinners by nature, and sinners from infancy, by virtue of *their law*, in this manner, but by *Adam's* sin: inasmuch as infants were treated as sinners long *before* the law of circumcision was given, as well as before they had committed actual sin.

What has been said, may, as I humbly conceive, lead us to that which is the *true* scope and sense of the apostle in these three verses; which I will endeavour more briefly to represent in the following *paraphrase*.

"The things which I have largely insisted on, viz. the evil that is in the world, the general wickedness, guilt, and ruin of mankind, and the opposite good, even justification and life, as only by Christ, lead me to observe the *likeness* of the manner in which they are each of them *introduced*. For it was by *one man* that the general corruption and guilt which I have spoken of, came into the world, and condemnation and death by sin: and this dreadful punishment and ruin came on all mankind by the great *law of works*, originally established with mankind in their first father, and by his *one offence*, or breach of that law; *all* thereby becoming *sinners* in God's sight, and exposed to final destruction.

12. *Wherefore, as by one man sin entered into the world, and death by sin; and so death passed upon all men, for that all have sinned.*

"It is manifest that it was in this way the world became sinful and guilty; and not in that way which the *Jews* suppose, viz. That their law, given by *Moses*, is the grand universal rule of righteousness and judgment for mankind, and that it is by being *Gentiles*, uncircumcised, and aliens from that law, that the nations of the world are *constituted sinners*, and unclean. For *before* the law of *Moses* was given, mankind were all looked upon by the great Judge as sinners, by corruption and guilt derived from *Adam's* violation of the original law of works; which shows, that the original universal rule of righteousness is not the law of *Moses;* for if so, there would have been no sin imputed *before* that was given; because sin is not imputed, when there is no law.

13. *For until the law sin was in the world: but sin is not imputed, when there is no law.*

"But that at that time sin was *imputed*, and men were by their judge reckoned as *sinners*, through guilt and corruption derived from *Adam*, and condemned for sin to *death*, the proper punishment of sin, we have a plain proof; in that it appears in fact, all mankind, during that whole time which preceded the law of *Moses*, were subjected to that temporal death, which is the visible introduction and image of that utter destruction which sin deserves, not excepting even *infants*, who could be sinners no other way than by virtue of *Adam's* transgression, having never in their own persons actually sinned as *Adam* did; nor could at that time be made polluted by the law of *Moses*, as being uncircumcised, or born of uncircumcised parents."

14. *Nevertheless, death reigned from* Adam *to* Moses, *even over them that had not sinned after the similitude of* Adam's *transgression.*

Now, by way of reflection on the whole, I would observe, that though there are two or three expressions in this paragraph, Rom. v. 12, &c. the design of which is attended with some difficulty and obscurity, as particularly in the 13th and 14th verses, yet the scope and sense of the discourse in general is not obscure, but on the contrary very clear and manifest; and so is the particular doctrine mainly taught in it. The apostle sets himself with great care to make it plain, and precisely to fix and settle the point he is upon. And the discourse is so framed, that one part of it greatly clears and fixes the meaning of other parts; and the whole is determined by the clear connexion it stands in with other parts of the epistle, and by the manifest drift of all the preceding part of it.

The doctrine of *original* sin is not only here taught, but most plainly, explicitly, and abundantly taught. This doctrine is asserted, expressly or implicitly, in almost every verse, and in some of the verses several times. It is fully implied in that first expression in the 12th ver. "By one man sin entered into the world." The passage implies, that sin became *universal* in the world; as the apostle had before largely shown it was; and not merely (which would be a trifling observation) that one man, who was made first, sinned first, before other men sinned; or, that it did not so happen that many men began to sin just together at the same moment. The latter part of the verse, "and death by sin, and so death passed upon all men, for that (or, if you will, *unto which*) all have sinned," shows, that in the eye of the Judge of the world, in *Adam's* first sin, *all* sinned; not only *in some sort*, but all sinned *so* as to be exposed to that *death*, and final destruction, which is the proper *wages of sin*. The same doctrine is taught again twice over in the 14th verse. It is there observed, as a proof of this doctrine, that "death reigned over them which had not sinned after the similitude of Adam's transgression," *i. e.* by their personal act; and therefore could be exposed to death, only by deriving guilt and pollution from *Adam*, in consequence of his sin. And it is taught again in those words, *who is the figure of him that was to come*. The resemblance lies very much in this circumstance, viz. our deriving sin, guilt, and punishment by Adam's sin, as we do righteousness, justification, and the reward of life, by Christ's obedience; for so the apostle explains himself. The same doctrine is expressly taught again, ver. 15. "Through the offence of one, many be dead." And again twice in the 16th verse, "it was by one that sinned:" *i. e.* It was by Adam, that guilt and punishment (before spoken of) came on mankind: and in these words, "judgment was by one to condemnation." It is again plainly and fully laid down in the 17th verse, "By one man's offence, death reigned by one." So again in the 18th verse, "By the offence of one, judgment came upon all men to condemnation." Again very plainly in the 19th verse, "By one man's disobedience, many were made sinners."

Here is every thing to determine and fix the *meaning* of all the important *terms* used; as, the *abundant use* of them in all parts of the New Testament; and especially in this apostle's writings, which make up a very great part of the New Testament; and his repeated use of them in this epistle in particular; and in the former part of this very chapter; and also the *light that* one sentence in this paragraph casts on another, which fully settles their meaning: as, with respect to the words *justification, righteousness*, and *condemnation;* and above all, in regard of the word *sin*, which is the most important of all, with relation to the doctrine and controversy we are upon. Besides the constant use of this term every where else through the New Testament, through the epistles of this apostle, this epistle in particular, and even the former part of this chapter, it is often repeated in this very paragraph, and evidently used in the very sense that is denied to belong to it in the end of ver. 12. and ver. 19. though owned every where else: and its meaning is fully determined by the apostle varying the term; using together with it, to signify the same thing, such a variety of other synonymous words, such as *offence, transgression, disobedience*. And further, to put the matter out of all controversy, it is particularly, expressly, and repeatedly distinguished from that which our opposers would *explain* it by, *viz. condemnation* and *death*. And what is meant by *sin entering into the world*, in ver. 12. is determined by a like phrase of *sin being in the world*, in the next verse.—And that by the *offence of one*, so often spoken of here, as bringing death and condemnation on all, the apostle means the *sin of one*, derived in its guilt and pollution to mankind in general, (over and above all that has been already observed,) is determined by those words in the conclusion of this discourse, ver. 20. "Moreover, the law entered, that the offence might abound: but where sin abounded, grace did much more abound." These words plainly show, that the OFFENCE spoken of so often, the offence of *one* man, became the sin of *all*. For when he says, "The law entered, that the offence might abound," his meaning cannot be, that the offence of Adam, merely as *his* personally, should *abound;* but, as it exists in its *derived* guilt, corrupt influence, and evil fruits, in the sin of mankind in general, even as a tree in its root and branches.*

What further confirms the certainty of the *proof* of *original sin*, which this place affords, is this, that the utmost art *cannot* pervert it to *another* sense. What a variety of the most artful methods have been used by the *enemies* of this doctrine, to *wrest* and *darken* this paragraph of Holy Writ, which stands so much in their way, as it were to *force* the Bible to speak a language agreeable to their mind! How have expressions been strained, words and phrases racked! What strange figures of speech have been invented, and with violent hands thrust into the apostle's mouth; and then with a bold countenance and magisterial airs obtruded on the world, as from him!—But blessed be God, we have his words as he delivered them, and the rest of the same epistle, and his other writings to compare with them; by which his meaning stands in too strong and glaring a light to be hid by any of the artificial mists which they labour to throw upon it.

It is really no less than *abusing* the Scripture and its readers, to represent this paragraph as the most *obscure* of all the places of Scripture, that speak of the consequences of *Adam's* sin; and to treat it as if there was need first to consider other places as more *plain*. Whereas, it is most manifestly a place in which these things are declared, the most plainly, particularly, precisely, and of set purpose, by that great apostle, who has most fully explained to us those doctrines in general, which relate to the redemption by Christ, and the sin and misery we are redeemed from. And it must be now left to the reader's judgment, whether the christian church has not proceeded reasonably, in looking on this as a place of Scripture most clearly and fully treating of these things, and in using its determinate sense as a help to settle the meaning of many other passages of Sacred Writ.

As this place in general is very full and plain, so the doctrine of the corruption of nature, as derived from Adam, and also the imputation of his first sin, are *both* clearly taught in it. The *imputation* of *Adam's* one transgression, is indeed most directly and frequently asserted. We are here assured, that *by one man's sin, death passed on all;* all being adjudged to this punishment, as having *sinned* (so it is implied) in that one man's sin. And it is repeated, over and over, that *all are condemned, many are dead, many made sinners*, &c. by *one man's offence, by the disobedience of one*, and *by one offence*. And the doctrine of original *depravity* is also here taught, when the apostle says, "By one man sin entered into the world;" having a plain respect (as hath been shown) to that universal corruption and wickedness, as well as guilt, of which he had before largely treated.

* The *offence*, according to Dr. T.'s explanation, does not *abound* by the *law* at all really and truly, in any sense; neither the *sin*, nor the *punishment*. For he says, "The meaning is not, that men should be made more wicked; but, that men should be liable to death for every transgression." But after all, they are liable to no more deaths, nor to any worse deaths, if they are not more sinful: for they were to have punishments according to their desert, *before*. Such as died, and went into another world, before the law of *Moses* was given, were punished according to their *deserts;* and the law, when it came, threatened no more.

PART III.

THE EVIDENCE GIVEN US, RELATIVE TO THE DOCTRINE OF ORIGINAL SIN, IN WHAT THE SCRIPTURES REVEAL CONCERNING THE REDEMPTION BY CHRIST.

CHAP. I.

THE EVIDENCE OF ORIGINAL SIN, FROM THE NATURE OF REDEMPTION, IN THE PROCUREMENT OF IT.

ACCORDING to Dr. T.'s scheme, a very great part of mankind are the subjects of Christ's *redemption*, who live and die perfectly *innocent*, who never have had, and never will have, any *sin* charged to their account, and never are exposed to any *punishment* whatsoever, *viz.* all that die in *infancy*. They are the subjects of *Christ's redemption*, as he redeems them from *death*, or as they by his righteousness have *justification*, and by his obedience are *made righteous*, in the *resurrection* of the body, in the sense of Rom. v. 18, 19. And *all* mankind are thus the subjects of Christ's redemption, while they are perfectly guiltless, and exposed to no punishment, as by Christ they are entitled to a *resurrection*. Though, with respect to such persons as have *sinned*, he allows it is *in some sort* by Christ and his death, that they are saved from sin, and the punishment of it.

Now let us see whether such a scheme well consists with the scripture-account of the redemption by Jesus Christ.

I. The representations of the redemption by Christ, every where in Scripture, lead us to suppose, that *all* whom he came to redeem are *sinners;* that his salvation, as to the term *from which*, (or the evil to be redeemed from,) in *all*, is *sin*, and the deserved *punishment* of sin. It is natural to suppose, that when he had his name *Jesus*, or *Saviour*, given him by God's special and immediate appointment, the salvation meant by that name should be his salvation in general; and not only a *part* of his salvation, and with regard only to *some* of them whom he came to save. But this name was given him to signify "his saving his people from their *sins*," Matt. i. 21. And the great doctrine of Christ's salvation is, that "he came into the world to save *sinners*," 1 Tim. i. 15. And that "Christ hath once suffered, the just for the *unjust*," 1 Pet. iii. 18. "In this was manifested the love of God towards us, (towards such in general as have the benefit of God's love in giving Christ,) that God sent his only-begotten Son into the world, that we might live through him. Herein is love, that he sent his Son to be the propitiation for our *sins*," 1 John iv. 9, 10. Many other texts might be mentioned, which seem evidently to suppose, that all who are redeemed by Christ are saved from SIN. We are led by what Christ himself said, to suppose, that if any are not *sinners*, they have *no need* of him as a Redeemer, any more than a man in health of a physician, Mark ii. 17. And that, in order to our being the proper subjects of the mercy of God through Christ, we must first be in a state of *sin*, is implied in Gal. iii. 22. "But the Scripture hath concluded all under *sin*, that the promise by faith of Jesus Christ might be given to them that believe." To the same effect is Rom. xi. 32.

These things are greatly confirmed by the scripture doctrine of *sacrifices*. It is abundantly plain, both from the Old and New Testament, that these were types of Christ's death, and were for *sin*, and supposed *sin* in those for whom they were offered. The apostle supposes, that in order to any having the benefit of *the eternal inheritance* by Christ, *there must of necessity be the death of the testator;* and gives that reason for it, "That without shedding of blood there is no remission," Heb. ix. 15, &c. And Christ himself, in representing the benefit of his blood, in the institution of the Lord's supper, under the notion of the blood of a *testament*, calls it, "The blood of the New Testament shed for the *remission of sins*," Matt. xxvi. 28. But according to the scheme of our author, many have the eternal inheritance by the death of the testator, who never had any need of remission.

II. The Scripture represents the redemption by Christ, as a redemption from *deserved* destruction; and that, not merely as it respects some particulars, but as the fruit of God's love to mankind. John iii. 16. "God so loved the *world*, that he gave his only-begotten Son, that whosoever believeth in him *should not perish*, but have everlasting life;" implying, that otherwise they must perish, or be destroyed. But what necessity of this, if they did not *deserve* to be destroyed? Now, that the destruction here spoken of, is deserved destruction, is manifest, because it is there compared to the perishing of such of the children of *Israel* as died by the bite of the fiery *serpents*, which God in his wrath, for their *rebellion*, sent amongst them. And the same thing clearly appears by the last verse of the same chapter, "He that believeth on the Son, hath everlasting life; and he that believeth not the Son, shall not see life, but the wrath of God abideth on him," or, is left remaining on him: implying, that all in general *are found* under the *wrath* of God, and that they only of all mankind who are interested in Christ, have this wrath *removed*, and eternal life bestowed; the rest are *left* with the *wrath of God still remaining on them.* The same is clearly illustrated and confirmed by John v. 24. "He that believeth, hath everlasting life, and shall not come into condemnation, but is passed from death to life." In being passed from death to life is implied, that *before*, they were all in a state of death; and they are spoken of as being so by a sentence of *condemnation;* and if it be a *just* condemnation, it is a *deserved* condemnation.

III. It will follow on Dr. T.'s scheme, that Christ's redemption, with regard to a great part of them who are the subjects of it, is not only a redemption from *no sin*, but from *no calamity*, and so from *no evil* of any kind. For as to *death*, which *infants* are redeemed from, they never were subjected to it as a calamity, but purely as a *benefit*. It came by no threatening or curse denounced upon or through Adam; the covenant with him being utterly *abolished*, as to all its force and power on mankind, (according to our author,) before the sentence of mortality. Therefore trouble and death could be appointed to innocent mankind no other way than on account of another covenant, the covenant of *grace;* and in this channel they come only as *favours*, not as evils. Therefore they could need no remedy, for they had no disease. Even death itself, which it is supposed Christ saves them from, is only a medicine; and one of the greatest of benefits. It is ridiculous to talk of persons' needing a medicine, or a physician, to save them from an excellent medicine; or of a remedy from a happy remedy! If it be said, though death be a benefit, yet it is so because Christ *changes* it, and turns it into a benefit, by procuring a *resurrection:* I would ask, what can be meant by *turning* or *changing* it into a benefit, when it never *was* otherwise, nor could ever *justly be* otherwise? *Infants* could not at all be brought under death as a calamity; for they never *deserved* it. And it would be only an abuse (be it far from us, to ascribe such a thing to God) in any being, to offer any poor sufferers a Redeemer from a calamity which *he* had brought upon them, without the least *desert* of it on their part.

But it is plain, that mortality was not at first brought on mankind as a blessing, by the covenant of grace through Christ; and that Christ and grace do not *bring* mankind under death, but *find* them under it. 2 Cor. v. 14. "We thus judge, that if one died for all, then were *all dead.*" Luke xix. 10. "The Son of man is come to seek and save that which was *lost.*" The grace which appears in providing a deliverer *from* any state, supposes the subject to be in that state *prior* to his deliverance. In our author's scheme, there never could be any sentence of death or condemnation, that requires a Saviour from it; because the very sentence itself, according to the true meaning of it, implies and makes sure all that good, which is requisite to abolish and make void the seeming evil to the innocent subject. So that the sentence itself is in effect the deliverer; and there is no need of another to deliver from that sentence. Dr. T. insists upon it, that "nothing comes upon us in consequence of *Adam's* sin, in any SENSE, KIND, or DEGREE, inconsistent with the *original blessing* pronounced on Adam at his creation; and nothing but what is perfectly consistent with God's blessing, love, and goodness, declared to Adam as soon as he came out of his Maker's hands."* If the case be so, it is certain there is no evil or calamity at all for Christ to redeem us from; *unless things agreeable to the divine goodness, love, and blessing*, are things from which we need redemption.†

IV. It will follow, on our author's principles, not only with respect to infants, but even *adult* persons, that redemption is *needless*, and Christ is dead in vain. Not only is there no need of Christ's redemption in order to deliverance from any consequences of *Adam's* sin, but also in order to perfect freedom from *personal* sin, and all its evil consequences. For God has made other sufficient provision for that, *viz. a sufficient power and ability, in all mankind, to do all their duty, and wholly to avoid sin.* Yea, he insists upon it, that "when men have not sufficient *power* to do their duty, they have *no* duty to do. We may safely and assuredly conclude, (says he,) that mankind in all parts of the world have SUFFICIENT power to do the duty which God requires of them; and that he requires of them NO MORE than they have SUFFICIENT powers to do."‡ And in another place,§ "God has given powers EQUAL to the duty which he expects." And he expresses a great dislike at R. R.'s supposing, that our propensities to evil, and temptations, are too strong to be EFFECTUALLY and CONSTANTLY resisted; or that we are unavoidably sinful IN A DEGREE; that our appetites and passions will be breaking out, notwithstanding our everlasting watchfulness."|| These things fully imply, that men have in their own natural ability sufficient means to avoid sin, and to be perfectly free from it; and so, from all the bad consequences of it. And if the means are *sufficient*, then there is no need of *more;* and therefore there is no need of Christ dying, in order to it. What Dr. T. says, (p. 72. S.) fully implies, that it would be unjust in God to give mankind being in such circumstances, as that they would be more likely to sin, so as to be exposed to final misery, than otherwise. Hence then, without Christ and his redemption, and without any grace at all, MERE JUSTICE makes *sufficient provision* for our being free from sin and misery, by our own power.¶

If all mankind, in all parts of the world, have such sufficient power to do their whole duty, without being sinful *in any degree*, then they have sufficient power to obtain righteousness by the law: and then, according to the apostle Paul, *Christ is dead in vain.* Gal. ii. 21. "If righteousness come by law, Christ is dead in vain;"—δια νομυ, without the article, *by law*, or the rule of right action, as our author explains the phrase.** And according to the sense in which he explains this very place, "it would have frustrated, or rendered useless, the grace of God, if Christ died to accomplish what was or MIGHT have been effected by law itself, without his death."†† So that it most clearly follows from his own doctrine, *that Christ is dead in vain*, and the grace of God is *useless*. The same apostle says, *if there had been a law* which COULD *have given life, verily righteousness should have been by the law*, Gal. iii. 21. *i. e.* (still according to Dr. T.'s own sense,) if there was a law, that man, in his present state, had sufficient power perfectly to fulfil. For Dr. T. supposes the reason why the law could not give life, to be "not because it was weak in itself, but through the weakness of our flesh, and the infirmity of the human nature in the present state."‡‡ But he says, "We are under a mild dispensation of GRACE, making allowance for our infirmities."§§ By *our infirmities*, we may upon good grounds suppose he means that infirmity of human nature, which he gives as the reason why the law cannot give life. But what *grace* is there in making that allowance for our infirmities, which *justice* itself (according to his doctrine) most absolutely requires, as he supposes divine justice exactly proportions our duty to our ability?

Again, if it be said, that although Christ's redemption was not necessary to preserve men from *beginning to sin*, and getting into a course of sin, because they have sufficient power in themselves to avoid it; yet it may be necessary to deliver men, *after* they have by their own folly brought themselves under the *dominion* of evil appetites and passions.|||| I answer, if it be so, that men need deliverance from those habits and passions, which are become too strong for them, yet that deliverance, on our author's principles, would be no salvation from *sin*. For the exercise of passions which are too strong for us, and which we cannot overcome, is *necessary:* and he strongly urges, that a necessary evil can be no *moral* evil. It is true, it is the *effect* of evil, as it is the *effect* of a bad practice, while the man had power to have avoided it. But then according to Dr. T. that evil *cause* alone is sin; for he says expressly, "*The cause of* every effect is alone chargeable with the effect it produceth, or which proceedeth from it."¶¶ And as to that sin which was the *cause*, the man needed no Saviour from *that*, having had *sufficient power* in himself to have avoided it. So that it follows by our author's scheme, that *none* of mankind, neither infants nor adult persons, neither the more nor less vicious, neither *Jews* nor *Gentiles*, neither *heathens* nor *Christians*, ever did or ever could stand in any *need* of a Saviour; and that, with respect to *all*, the truth is, *Christ is dead in vain.*

If any should say, although all mankind in all ages have sufficient ability to do their whole duty, and so may by their own power enjoy perfect freedom from sin, yet God *foresaw* that they *would sin*, and that *after* they had sinned, they would need Christ's death. I answer, it is plain, by what the apostle says in those places which were just now mentioned, (Gal. ii. 21. and iii. 21.) that God would have esteemed it needless to give his Son to die for men, unless there had been a prior impossibility of their having righteousness by any law; and that, *if there had been a law which* COULD *have given life*, this other way by the death of Christ would not have been provided. And this appears to be agreeable to our author's own sense of things, by his words which have been cited, wherein he says, "It would have FRUSTRATED or rendered USELESS the grace of God, if Christ died to accomplish what was or MIGHT HAVE BEEN effected by law itself, without his death."

V. It will follow on Dr. T.'s scheme, not only that Christ's redemption is *needless* for saving from sin, or its consequences, but also that it does *no good* that way, has no tendency to any *diminution* of *sin* in the world. For as to any *infusion* of virtue or holiness into the heart, by divine power through Christ or his redemption, it is altogether inconsistent with this author's notions. With him, *inwrought* virtue, if there were any such thing, would be *no* virtue; not being the effect of our own will, choice, and design, but only of a sovereign act of God's power.*** And therefore, all that Christ does to increase virtue, is only increasing our talents, our light, advantages, means, and motives; as he often explains the matter.††† But *sin* is not at all diminished. For he says, *our duty must be measured by our talents;* as, a child that has less talents, has less duty; and therefore must be no more exposed to commit sin, than he that has greater talents; because he that has greater talents, has more duty required, in exact proportion.‡‡‡ If so, he that has but *one* talent, has as much *advantage* to perform that *one* degree of duty which is required of him, as he that has *five* talents, to perform his *five* degrees of duty, and is no more exposed to fail of it. And that man's *guilt*, who sins against *greater* advan-

* Page 88, 89. S.

† In this inferential short reply, our author is not quite so guarded as usual. It seems applicable only to *infants;* since adults have *actual* or *personal* sin and guilt from which to be redeemed. But what immediately follows anticipates the objection.—W.

‡ Page 111. 63, 64. S. § Page 67. S. || Page 68. S.

¶ Here, also, our author will be thought not quite accurate, in the inference he draws against Dr. T. for the "sufficient power," for which Dr. T. pleads, relates only to the *prevention* of sin, but not to its *remission*, or the removal of its *effects*. But this also will be soon answered.—W.

** Pref. to Par. on Rom. p. 143. 38. †† Note on Rom. v. 20. p. 297.

‡‡ Ibid. §§ Page 92. S.

|||| See p. 228. and also what he says of the helpless state of the heathen, in paraph. and notes on Rom. vii. and beginning of chap. viii. ¶¶ Page 128.

*** See p. 180, 245, 250. ††† In p. 44, 50. and innumerable other places

‡‡‡ See page 234. 61, 64—72. S.

tages, means, and motives, is *greater* in proportion to his talents.* And therefore it will follow, on Dr. T.'s principles, that men stand no better chance, have no more eligible or valuable probability of freedom from sin and punishment, or of contracting but little guilt, or of performing required duty, with the great advantages and talents implied in Christ's redemption, than without them; when all things are computed, and put into the balances together, the numbers, degrees, and aggravations of sin exposed to, degrees of duty required, &c. So that men have no redemption from sin, and no new means of performing duty, that are valuable or worth any thing at all. And thus the great redemption by Christ in every respect comes to nothing, with regard both to infants and adult persons.

CHAP. II.

THE EVIDENCE OF THE DOCTRINE OF ORIGINAL SIN FROM WHAT THE SCRIPTURE TEACHES OF THE APPLICATION OF REDEMPTION.

THE truth of the doctrine of original sin is very clearly manifest from what the Scripture says of that *change of state*, which it represents as necessary to an actual interest in the spiritual and eternal blessings of the Redeemer's kingdom.

In order to this, it speaks of it as absolutely necessary for every one, that he be regenerated, or *born again*. John iii. 3. "Verily, verily, I say unto thee, except a man (γεννηθη ανωθεν) be begotten again, or born again, he cannot see the kingdom of God." Dr. T. though he will not allow that this signifies any change from a state of *natural propensity* to sin, yet supposes that the new birth here spoken of, means a man's being brought to *a divine life, in a right use and application of the natural powers, in a life of true holiness:*† and that it is the attainment of *those habits of virtue and religion, which gives us the real character of true Christians, and the children of God;*‡ and that it is *putting on the new nature of right action.*§

But in order to proceed in the most sure and safe manner, in understanding what is meant in Scripture by *being born again*, and so in the inferences we draw from what is said of the necessity of it, let us compare scripture with scripture, and consider what *other* terms or phrases are used, where respect is evidently had to the same change. And here I would observe the following things.

I. If we compare one scripture with another, it will be sufficiently manifest, that by regeneration, or being *begotten*, or *born again*, the same change in the state of the mind is signified with that which the scripture speaks of as affected in true REPENTANCE and CONVERSION. I put repentance and conversion together, because the scripture puts them together, Acts iii. 19. and because they plainly signify much the same thing. The word (μετανοια) *repentance*, signifies a *change of the mind;* as the word *conversion*, means a *change* or *turning* from sin to God. And that this is the same change with that which is called *regeneration* (excepting that this latter term especially signifies the change, as the mind is *passive* in it) the following things may show.

In the *change* which the mind undergoes in *repentance* and *conversion*, is attained that *character* of true Christians which is necessary to the eternal privileges of such. Acts iii. 19. "*Repent* ye therefore, and be *converted*, that your sins may be blotted out, when the times of refreshing shall come from the presence of the Lord." And thus it is in *regeneration;* as is evident from what Christ says to Nicodemus, and as is allowed by Dr. T.

The *change* of the mind in *repentance* is that in which *saving faith* is attained. Mark i. 15. "The kingdom of God is at hand, *repent* ye, and *believe* the gospel." And so it is in being born *again*, or born of *God;* as appears by John i. 12, 13. "But as many as received him, to them he gave power to become the sons of God, even to them that *believe* on his name, which were *born* not of blood, &c. but *of God*." Just as Christ says concerning *conversion*, Matt. xviii. 3. "Verily, verily, I say unto you, except ye be *converted*, and become as little children, ye shall not enter the kingdom of heaven:" so does he say concerning being *born again*, in what he spake to *Nicodemus*.

By the change men undergo in *conversion*, they become *as little children;* which appears in the place last cited: and so they do by *regeneration*. (1 Pet. i. 23. and ii. 2.) "Being born again.—Wherefore as new-born babes, desire," &c. It is no objection, that the disciples, to whom Christ spake in Matt. xviii. 3. were converted already: this makes it not less proper for Christ to declare the necessity of conversion to them, leaving it with them to try themselves, and to make sure their conversion: in like manner as he declared to them the necessity of *repentance*, in Luke xiii. 3, 5. "Except ye repent, ye shall all likewise perish."

The change effected by *repentance*, is expressed and exhibited by *baptism*. Hence it is called the *baptism of repentance*. (Matt. iii. 11. Luke iii. 3. Acts xiii. 24. and xix. 4.) And so is *regeneration*, or being born again, expressed by *baptism;* as is evident by such representations of regeneration as those: John iii. 5. "Except a man be born of water, and of the Spirit."—Tit. iii. 5. "He saved us by the washing of regeneration."—Many other things might be observed, to show that the change men pass under in their *repentance* and *conversion*, is the *same* with that of which they are the subjects in regeneration.—But these observations may be sufficient.

II. The change which a man undergoes when born again, and in his repentance and conversion, is the same that the scripture calls the CIRCUMCISION OF THE HEART.—This may easily appear by considering, that as *regeneration* is that in which are attained the habits of true *virtue* and *holiness*, as has been shown, and as is confessed; so is *circumcision of heart*. Deut. xxx. 6. "And the Lord thy God will *circumcise thine heart*, and the *heart* of thy seed, to love the Lord thy God with all thine heart, and with all thy soul."

Regeneration is that whereby men come to have the character of *true Christians;* as is evident, and as is confessed; and so is *circumcision of heart:* for by this men become *Jews inwardly*, or *Jews* in the spiritual and *christian sense*, (and that is the same as being *true Christians*,) as of old, *proselytes* were made *Jews* by circumcision of the flesh. Rom. ii. 28, 29. "For he is not a *Jew* which is one outwardly; neither is that *circumcision* which is outward in the flesh: but he is a *Jew*, which is one inwardly; and *circumcision* is that *of the heart*, in the spirit and not in the letter, whose praise is not of men, but of God."

That *circumcision of the heart*, is the same with *conversion*, or *turning* from sin to God, is evident by Jer. iv. 1—4. "If thou wilt *return*, O Israel, *return unto me*. *Circumcise* yourselves to the Lord, and put away the foreskins *of your heart*." And Deut. x. 16. "*Circumcise* therefore the foreskin of your *heart*, and be no more stiffnecked." *Circumcision of the heart* is the same change of the heart that men experience in *repentance;* as is evident by Lev. xxvi. 41. "If their *uncircumcised hearts* be humbled, and they accept the punishment of their iniquity.

The change effected in *regeneration*, *repentance*, and *conversion*, is signified by *baptism*, as has been shown; and so is *circumcision of the heart* signified by the same thing. None will deny, that it was this internal circumcision, which of old was signified by external circumcision; nor will any deny, now under the New Testament, that inward and spiritual baptism, or the cleansing of the heart, is signified by external washing or baptism. But spiritual circumcision and spiritual baptism are the same thing; both being *putting off the body of the sins of the flesh;* as is very plain by Colos. ii. 11—13. "In whom also ye are circumcised, with the *circumcision* made without hands, in putting off the body of the sins of the flesh, by the circumcision of Christ, buried with him in *baptism*, wherein also ye are risen with him," &c.

III. This inward change, called *regeneration*, and *circumcision of the heart*, which is wrought in *repentance* and *conversion*, is the same with that spiritual RESURRECTION so often spoken of, and represented as *a dying unto sin, and a living unto righteousness*.—This appears with great plain-

* See Paraph. on Rom. ii. 9. also on ver. 12.

† Page 144.

‡ Page 246, 248.

§ Page 251.

ness in that last cited place, Col. ii. "In whom also ye are circumcised, with the circumcision made without hands,—buried with him in baptism, wherein also ye are *risen with him*, through the faith of the operation of God, &c. And you, being dead in your sins, and the uncircumcision of your flesh, hath he *quickened together with him;* having forgiven you all trespasses."

The same appears by Rom. vi. 3—5. "Know ye not, that so many of us as were baptized into Jesus Christ, were baptized into his death? Therefore we are buried with him by baptism into death; that like as Christ was *raised up from the dead*, by the glory of the Father, even so we also should walk in newness of life," &c. ver. 11. "Likewise reckon ye also yourselves to be dead unto sin, but *alive unto God*, through Jesus Christ our Lord." In which place also it is evident, and by the whole context, that this spiritual *resurrection* is that change, in which persons are brought to habits of holiness and to the divine life, by which Dr. T. describes the thing obtained in being *born again*.

That a *spiritual resurrection* to a new, divine life, should be called a being *born again*, is agreeable to the language of Scripture. So those words in the 2d Psalm, "Thou art my Son, this day have I begotten thee," are applied to Christ's *resurrection*, Acts xiii. 33. So in Colos. i. 18. Christ is called the *first* BORN *from the dead;* and in Rev. i. 5. *The first* BEGOTTEN *of the dead.* The saints, in their *conversion or spiritual resurrection, are risen with Christ, and are begotten and born with him.* 1 Pet. i. 3. "Who hath *begotten us again* to a lively hope, by the resurrection of Jesus Christ from the dead, to an inheritance incorruptible." This inheritance is the same thing with that KINGDOM of HEAVEN, which men obtain by being *born again*, according to Christ's words to *Nicodemus;* and that same *inheritance of them that are sanctified*, spoken of as what is obtained in true CONVERSION. Acts xxvi. 18. "To turn them (or convert them) from darkness to light, and from the power of Satan unto God, that they may receive forgiveness of sin, and inheritance among them that are sanctified, through faith that is in me." Dr. T.'s own words, in his note on Rom. i. 4. speaking of that place in the 2d Psalm, are very worthy to be here recited. He observes how this is applied to Christ's *resurrection* and exaltation, in the New Testament, and then has this remark, "note, begetting is conferring a new and happy state: a son is a person put into it. Agreeably to this, good men are said to be the sons of God, as they are the sons of the *resurrection to eternal life*, which is represented as a παλιγγενεσια, a being BEGOTTEN, OR BORN AGAIN, REGENERATED." So that I think it is abundantly plain, that the *spiritual resurrection* spoken of in Scripture, by which the saints are brought to a new divine life, is the same with that being *born again*, which Christ says is *necessary* for every one, in order to his seeing the kingdom of God.

IV. This change, of which men are the subjects, when they are *born again, and circumcised in heart*, when they *repent*, and are *converted*, and spiritually *raised from the dead*, is the same change which is meant when the Scripture speaks of making the HEART and SPIRIT NEW, or giving a *new heart and spirit*.

It is almost needless to observe, how evidently this is spoken of as *necessary* to salvation, and as the change in which are attained the habits of true virtue and holiness, and the character of a true saint; as has been observed of *regeneration, conversion, &c.* and how apparent it is, that the change is the *same.* Thus repentance, (μετανοια,) *the change of the mind*, is the same as being changed to a NEW mind, or a NEW heart and spirit. *Conversion* is the turning of the heart; which is the same thing as changing it so, that there shall be another heart, or a *new heart*, or a new spirit. To be *born again*, is to be born *anew;* which implies a becoming NEW, and is represented as becoming *new-born babes.* But none supposes it is the *body*, that is immediately and properly new, but the *mind, heart,* or *spirit.* And so a *spiritual resurrection* is the resurrection of the spirit, or rising to begin a NEW existence and life, as to the *mind, heart,* or *spirit.* So that all these phrases imply, having a *new heart*, and being *renewed in the spirit*, according to their plain signification.

When *Nicodemus* expressed his wonder at Christ declaring it necessary, that a man should be *born again* in order to see the kingdom of God, or enjoy the privileges of the kingdom of the Messiah, Christ says to him, *Art thou a master of Israel, and knowest not these things? i. e.* "Art thou one who is set to teach others the things written in the law and the prophets, and knowest not a doctrine so plainly taught in your Scriptures, that such a change is necessary to a partaking of the blessings of the Messiah's kingdom?" But what can Christ refer to, unless such prophecies as that in Ezek. xxxvi. 25—27.? Where God, by the prophet, speaking of the days of the Messiah's kingdom, says, "Then will I sprinkle clean water upon you, and ye shall be clean.—A *new heart* also will I give you, and a *new spirit* will I put within you—and I will put my Spirit within you." Here God speaks of having a *new heart and spirit*, by being *washed with water*, and receiving *the Spirit of God*, as the qualification of God's people, that shall enjoy the privileges of the Messiah's kingdom. How much is this like the doctrine of Christ to *Nicodemus*, of being *born again of water, and of the Spirit!* We have another like prophecy in Ezek. xi. 19.—Add to this, that regeneration, or a *being born again*, and the *renewing* (or making new) by the Holy Ghost, are spoken of as the same thing, Tit. iii. 5. "By the washing of *regeneration* and *renewing* of the Holy Ghost."

V. It is abundantly manifest, that being *born again*, spiritually *rising from the dead to newness of life*, receiving a *new heart*, and being *renewed in the spirit of the mind*, are the same thing with that which is called *putting off the* OLD MAN, *and putting on the* NEW MAN.

The expressions are equivalent; and the representations are plainly of the same thing. When Christ speaks of being *born again*, two births are supposed: a *first and a second, an* OLD *birth and a* NEW *one:* and the thing born is called *man.* So what is born in the first birth is the *old man;* and what is brought forth in the *second birth*, is the *new man.* That which is born in the first birth (says Christ) is *flesh:* it is the *carnal man*, wherein we have borne the image of the *earthly Adam*, whom the apostle calls the *first man.* That which is born in the new birth, is *spirit*, or the spiritual and heavenly man: wherein we proceed from Christ the *second man*, the *new man*, who is made a quickening Spirit, and is the Lord from heaven, and the Head of the *new creation.*—In the new birth, men are represented as becoming *new-born babes*, which is the same thing as becoming *new men.*

And how apparently is what the Scripture says of the spiritual *resurrection* of the Christian convert, equivalent and of the very same import with putting off the *old man*, and putting on the *new man.* So in Rom. vi. the convert is represented as *dying*, and being *buried with Christ;* which is explained in the 6th verse, by this, that *the old man is crucified, that the body of sin might be destroyed.* And in the 4th verse, converts in this change are spoken of as *rising to newness of life.* Are not these things plain enough? The apostle in effect tells us, that when he speaks of spiritual death and resurrection, he means the same thing as *crucifying and burying the old man*, and rising as a *new man.*

And it is most apparent, that spiritual *circumcision*, and spiritual *baptism*, and the spiritual *resurrection*, are all the same with *putting off the old man, and putting on the new man.* This appears by Colos. ii. 11, 12. "In whom also ye are circumcised with the circumcision made without hands, *in putting off* the body of the sins of the flesh, by the circumcision of Christ, buried with him in *baptism;* wherein also ye are risen with him." Here it is manifest, that the spiritual circumcision, baptism, and resurrection, all signify that change wherein men *put off the body of the sins of the flesh:* but that is the same thing, in this apostle's language, *as putting off the old man;* as appears by Rom. vi. 6. "Our old man is crucified, that the body of sin may be destroyed." And that putting off the *old man* is the same with putting off the *body of sin*, appears further by Ephes. iv. 22—24. and Colos. iii. 8—10. As Dr. T. confesses, "that to be *born again*, is that wherein are obtained the habits of virtue, religion, and true holiness;" so how evidently is the same thing predicated of that change, which is called *putting off the old man, and putting on the new man!* Eph. iv. 22—24. "That ye put off the old man, which is corrupt, &c. and put on the new man, which after God is created in righteousness and true holiness."

And it is most plain, that this putting off the old man, &c. is the very same thing with making the *heart and spirit new*. It is apparent in itself; the spirit is called *the man*, in the language of the apostle; it is called the *inward man*, and the *hidden man*. (Rom. vii. 22. 2 Cor. iv. 16. 1 Pet. iii. 4.) And therefore, putting off the *old man*, is the same thing with the removal of the *old heart;* and the putting on of the *new man*, is the receiving of *a new heart, and a new spirit*. Yea, putting on the *new man* is expressly spoken of as the same thing with receiving a *new spirit, or being renewed in spirit*, Eph. iv. 22—24. "That ye put off the old man—and be renewed in the spirit of your mind, and that ye put on the new man."

From these things it appears, how unreasonable, and contrary to the utmost degree of scriptural evidence, is Dr. T.'s way of explaining the *old man*, and the *new man*,* as though thereby was meant nothing *personal;* but that by the *old man* was meant the *heathen state*, and by the *new man the christian dispensation*, or state of professing Christians, or the whole *collective body of professors of* Christianity, made up of *Jews* and *Gentiles;* when all the colour he has for it is, that the apostle once calls the christian church a *new man*. (Eph. ii. 15.) It is very true, in the Scriptures often, both in the Old Testament and the New, *collective bodies*, nations, peoples, and cities, are figuratively represented by *persons:* particularly the *church* of Christ is represented as *one* holy person, and has the same appellatives as a particular saint or believer; and so is called a *child, a son of God*, (Exod. iv. 22. Gal. iv. 1, 2.) *a servant of God*, (Isa. xli. 8, 9. and xliv. 1.) *The daughter of God, and spouse of Christ*, (Psal. xlv. 10, 13, 14. Rev. xix. 7.) Nevertheless, would it be reasonable to argue, that such appellations, as a *servant of God, child of God*, &c. are *always* or *commonly* to be taken as signifying only the *church* of God in general, or great collective bodies; and not to be understood in a *personal* sense? But certainly this would not be more unreasonable than to urge, that by the *old* and the *new man*, as the phrases are mostly used in Scripture, is to be understood nothing but the great collective bodies of pagans and of Christians, or the heathen and the christian world, as to their *outward* profession, and the dispensation they are under. It might have been proper, in this case, to have considered the unreasonableness of that practice which our author charges on others, and finds so much fault with in them,† "That they content themselves with a *few scraps* of Scripture, which though wrong understood, they make the test of truth, and the ground of their principles, in contradiction to the *whole tenor of revelation*."

VI. I observe once more, it is very apparent, that *being born again*, and *spiritually raised* from death to a state of new existence and life, having a *new heart created in us, being renewed in the spirit of our mind*, and being the subjects of that change by which we *put off the old man, and put on the new man*, is the same thing with that which in Scripture is called *being* CREATED ANEW, or made NEW CREATURES.

Here, to pass over many other evidences which might be mentioned, I would only observe, that the representations are exactly equivalent. These several phrases naturally and most plainly signify the same effect. In the first *birth*, or generation, we are *created*, or brought into existence; it is then the *whole man* first *receives being:* the soul is then *formed*, and then our bodies are *fearfully and wonderfully made, being curiously wrought by our Creator*. So that a new-born child is a *new creature*. So, when a man is *born again, he is created again;* in that *new birth*, there is a *new creation;* and therein he becomes as a *new-born babe*, or a NEW CREATURE. So, in a *resurrection*, there is a *new creation*. When a man is *dead*, that which was made in the first creation is destroyed: when that which was dead is *raised* to life, the mighty power of the author of life is exerted the second time, and the subject restored to a new existence, and a new life, as by a *new creation*. So giving a new heart is called CREATING *a clean heart*, Psal. li. 10. where the word, translated *create*, is the same that is used in the first verse, in *Genesis*. And when we read in Scripture of the *new creature*, the creature that is called NEW is MAN; and therefore the phrase, *new man*, is evidently equipollent with *new creature;* and putting off the *old man*, and putting on the *new man*, is spoken of expressly as brought to pass by a work of *creation*. Col. iii. 9, 10. "Ye have put off the old man—and have put on the new man, which is renewed in knowledge, after the image of him that *created* him." So Eph. iv. 22—24. "That ye put off the old man, which is corrupt, &c. and be renewed in the spirit of your mind, and that ye put on the new man, which after God is *created* in righteousness and true holiness." These things absolutely fix the meaning of 2 Cor. v. 17. "If any man be in Christ, he is a *new creature:* old things are passed away; behold, all things are become new."

On the whole, the following reflections may be made:

1. That it is a truth of the utmost certainty, with respect to *every* man born of the race of Adam, by ordinary generation, *that unless he be born again, he cannot see the kingdom of God*. This is true, not only of the heathen, but of them that are born of the professing people of God, as *Nicodemus*, and the *Jews*, and every man *born of the flesh*. This is most manifest by Christ's discourse in John iii. 3—11. So it is plain by 2 Cor. v. 17. *That every man who is in Christ, is a* NEW CREATURE.

2. It appears from this, together with what has been proved above, that it is most certain with respect to *every* one of the human race, that he can never have any interest in Christ, or see the kingdom of God, unless he be the subject of that CHANGE in the temper and disposition of his heart, which is made in *repentance and conversion, circumcision of heart, spiritual baptism, dying to sin, and rising to a new and holy life;* and unless he has the *old heart taken away, and a new heart and spirit given, and puts off the old man, and puts on the new man, and old things are passed away, and all things made new*.

3. From what is plainly implied in these things, and from what the Scripture most clearly teaches of the nature of them, it is certain, that *every* man is *born* into the world in a state of *moral pollution*. For SPIRITUAL BAPTISM is a cleansing from moral filthiness. (Ezek. xxxvi. 25. compared with Acts ii. 16. and John iii. 5.) So the washing of regeneration, or the NEW BIRTH, is a change from a state of wickedness. (Tit. iii. 3—5.) Men are spoken of as purified in their regeneration. (1 Pet. i. 22, 23. See also 1 John ii. 29. and iii. 1, 3.) And it appears, that every man in his first or natural state is a *sinner;* for otherwise he would then need no REPENTANCE, no CONVERSION, no turning from sin to God. And it appears, that every man in his original state has a *heart of stone;* for thus the Scripture calls that *old heart*, which is taken away, when a NEW HEART and NEW SPIRIT is given. (Ezek. xi. 19. and xxxvi. 26.) And it appears, that man's nature, as in his native state, is *corrupt according to the deceitful lusts*, and of its own motion exerts itself in nothing but *wicked deeds*. For thus the Scripture characterizes the OLD MAN, which is put off, when men are renewed in the spirit of their minds, and put on the NEW MAN. (Eph. iv. 22—24. Col. iii. 8—10.) In a word, it appears, that man's nature, as in its native state, is a *body of sin*, which must *be destroyed*, must *die, be buried, and never rise more*. For thus the OLD MAN is represented, which is *crucified*, when men are the subjects of a spiritual RESURRECTION. Rom. vi. 4—6. Such a nature, such a body of sin as this, is put off in the spiritual RENOVATION, wherein we put on the NEW MAN, and are the subjects of the spiritual CIRCUMCISION. Eph. iv. 21—23.

It must now be left with the reader to judge for himself, whether what the Scripture teaches of the APPLICATION of Christ's redemption, and the *change* of state and nature necessary to true and final happiness, does not afford clear and abundant evidence to the truth of the doctrine of *original sin*.

* Page 149—153. S.

† Page 224.

PART IV.

CONTAINING ANSWERS TO OBJECTIONS.

CHAP. I.

CONCERNING THE OBJECTION, THAT TO SUPPOSE MEN BORN IN SIN, WITHOUT THEIR CHOICE, OR ANY PREVIOUS ACT OF THEIR OWN, IS TO SUPPOSE WHAT IS INCONSISTENT WITH THE NATURE OF SIN.

SOME of the objections made against the doctrine of original sin, which have reference to particular arguments used in defence of it, have been already considered in the handling of those arguments. What I shall therefore now consider, are such objections as I have not yet had occasion to notice.

There is no argument Dr. T. insists more upon, than that which is taken from the *Arminian* and *Pelagian* notion of freedom of will, consisting in the will's *self-determination*, as necessary to the being of moral good or evil. He often urges, that if we come into the world infected with sinful and depraved dispositions, then *sin* must be *natural* to us; and if natural, then *necessary;* and if necessary, then *no* sin, nor any thing we are blamable for, or that can in any respect be our fault, being what we cannot help: and he urges, that sin must proceed from our own *choice*, &c.*

Here I would observe in general, that the forementioned notion of freedom of will, as essential to moral agency, and necessary to the very existence of virtue and sin, seems to be a grand favourite point with *Pelagians* and *Arminians*, and all divines of such characters, in their controversies with the orthodox. There is no one thing more fundamental in their schemes of religion: on the determination of this one leading point depends the issue of almost all controversies we have with such divines. Nevertheless, it seems a *needless* task for me particularly to consider that matter in this place; having already largely discussed it, with all the main grounds of this notion, and the arguments used to defend it, in a late book on this subject, to which I ask leave to refer the reader. It is very necessary, that the modern prevailing doctrine concerning this point, should be well understood, and therefore thoroughly considered and examined: for without it there is no hope of putting an end to the controversy about original sin, and innumerable other controversies that subsist, about many of the main points of religion. I stand ready to confess to the forementioned modern divines, if they can maintain their pecular notion of *freedom*, consisting in the *self-determining power of the will*, as necessary to *moral agency*, and can thoroughly establish it in opposition to the arguments lying against it, then they have an impregnable castle, to which they may repair, and remain invincible, in all the controversies they have with the reformed divines, concerning *original sin*, the *sovereignty* of grace, *election*, *redemption*, *conversion*, the *efficacious operation* of the Holy Spirit, the nature of saving *faith*, *perseverance* of the saints, and other principles of the like kind. However, at the same time, I think this will be as strong a fortress for the *Deists*, in common with them; as the great doctrines, subverted by their notion of *freedom*, are so plainly and abundantly taught in the Scripture. But I am under no apprehensions of any danger, which the cause of Christianity, or the religion of the reformed, is in, from any possibility of *that notion* being ever established, or of its being ever evinced that there is not proper, perfect, and manifold *demonstration* lying against it. But as I said, it would be needless for me to enter into a particular disquisition of this point here; from which I shall easily be excused by any reader who is willing to give himself the trouble of consulting what I have already written. And as to others, probably they will scarce be at the pains of reading the present discourse; or at least would not, if it should be enlarged by a full consideration of that controversy.

I shall at this time therefore only take notice of some gross *inconsistencies* that Dr. T. has been guilty of, in his handling this objection against the doctrine of original sin. In places which have been cited, he says, that *sin must proceed from our own choice:* and that *if it does not, it being necessary to us, it cannot be sin, it cannot be our fault, or what we are to blame for: and therefore all our sin must be chargeable on our choice*, which is the *cause* of sin: for he says, *the cause of every effect is alone chargeable with the effect it produceth, and which proceedeth from it.*† Now here are implied several gross contradictions. He greatly insists, that nothing can be *sinful*, or have the nature of sin, but what proceeds from our *choice*. Nevertheless he says, "Not the *effect*, but the *cause* alone is chargeable with *blame*." Therefore the *choice*, which is the *cause*, is *alone* blamable, or has the nature of sin; and not the *effect* of that choice. Thus nothing can be sinful, but the effect of choice; and yet the effect of choice never can be sinful, but only the *cause*, which alone is chargeable with all the blame.

Again, the *choice*, from which sin proceeds, is *itself* sinful. Not only is this implied in his saying, "The *cause* alone is chargeable with all the *blame;*" but he expressly speaks of the choice as *faulty*,‡ and calls that choice *wicked*, from which depravity and *corruption proceeds*.§ Now if the choice itself be *sin*, and there be no sin but what proceeds from a sinful choice, then the sinful choice must proceed from another *antecedent* choice; it must be chosen by a foregoing act of will, determining itself to that sinful choice, that so it may have that which he speaks of as absolutely essential to the nature of *sin*, namely, *that it proceeds from our choice*, and does not happen to us necessarily. But if the sinful choice itself proceeds from a foregoing choice, then also that foregoing choice must be sinful; it being the *cause of sin*, and so alone chargeable with the *blame*. Yet if that foregoing choice be sinful, then neither must *that* happen to us necessarily, but must likewise proceed from choice, another act of choice preceding that: for we must remember, that "Nothing is sinful but what proceeds from our *choice*." And then, for the same reason, even this prior choice, last mentioned, must also be sinful, being chargeable with all the blame of that consequent evil choice, which was its effect. And so we must go back till we come to the very *first* volition, the prime or original act of choice in the whole chain. And *this* to be sure must be a *sinful* choice, because this is the *origin* or primitive *cause* of all the train of evils which follow; and according to our author, must therefore be "alone chargeable with all the blame." And yet so it is, according to him, *this* "cannot be sinful," because it does not "proceed from our own choice," or any foregoing act of our will; it being, by the supposition, the very *first* act of will in the case. And therefore it must be *necessary*, as to us, having no choice of ours to be the cause of it.

In p. 232. he says, "*Adam's* sin was from his own *disobedient will;* and so must every man's sin, and all the sin in the world be, as well as his." By this, it seems, he must have a "disobedient will" *before* he sins; for the cause must be before the effect: and yet that disobedient will itself is *sinful;* otherwise it could not be called *disobedient*. But the question is, How do men come by the *disobedient will*, this cause of all the sin in the world? It must not come *necessarily*, without men's choice; for if so, it is *not* sin, nor is there any *disobedience* in it. Therefore that disobedient will must also come from a *disobedient will;* and so on, *in infinitum*. Otherwise it must be supposed, that there is some *sin* in the world, which does not

* Page 125, 128—130, 186—188, 190, 200, 245, 246, 253, 258. 63, 64, 161. S. and other places.

† Page 128.

‡ Page 190.

§ Page 200. See also p. 216.

come from a *disobedient will*: contrary to our author's dogmatical assertions.

In p. 166. S. he says, "Adam *could not sin without a sinful inclination.*" Here he calls that inclination itself *sinful*, which is the principle from whence sinful acts proceed; as elsewhere he speaks of the *disobedient will* from whence all sin comes: and he allows,* that "the *law* reaches to all the *latent principles of sin*;" meaning plainly, that it *forbids*, and *threatens punishment* for, those latent principles. Now these latent principles of sin, these sinful inclinations, without which, according to our author, there can be no sinful act, cannot all proceed from a *sinful choice*; because that would imply great contradiction. For, by the supposition, they are the principles from whence a sinful choice comes, and whence all sinful acts of will proceed; and there can be no sinful act without them. So that the *first* latent principles and inclinations, from whence all sinful acts proceed, are *sinful*; and yet they are *not sinful*, because they do not proceed from a *wicked choice*, without which, according to him, "nothing can be sinful."

Dr. T. speaking of that proposition of the *Assembly of Divines*, wherein they assert, that *man is by nature utterly corrupt*, &c.† thinks himself well warranted, by the supposed great evidence of these his contradictory notions, to say, "Therefore sin is not natural to us; and therefore I shall not scruple to say, this proposition in the *Assembly of Divines* is FALSE." But it may be worthy of consideration, whether it would not have greatly become him, before he had clothed himself with so much assurance, and proceeded, on the foundation of these his notions, so magisterially to charge the *Assembly's* proposition with *falsehood*, to have taken care that his own propositions, which he has set in opposition to them, should be a little more *consistent*; that he might not have contradicted *himself*, while contradicting them; lest some impartial judges, observing his inconsistence, should think they had warrant to declare with equal assurance, that "they should not scruple to say, Dr. T.'s doctrine is FALSE."

CHAP. II.

CONCERNING THE OBJECTION, AGAINST THE DOCTRINE OF NATIVE CORRUPTION, THAT TO SUPPOSE MEN RECEIVE THEIR FIRST EXISTENCE IN SIN, IS TO MAKE HIM WHO IS THE AUTHOR OF THEIR BEING, THE AUTHOR OF THEIR DEPRAVITY.

ONE argument against a supposed native, sinful depravity, which Dr. T. greatly insists upon, is, "that this does in effect charge him, who is *the author of our nature, who formed us in the womb, with being the author of a sinful corruption of nature*; and that it is *highly injurious* to the God of our nature, *whose hands have formed and fashioned us*, to believe *our nature* to be *originally corrupted*, and *that in the worst sense of corruption.*‡

With respect to this, I would observe, in the first place, that this writer, in handling this grand objection, supposes something to *belong* to the doctrine objected against, as maintained by the divines whom he is opposing, which does *not* belong to it, nor follow from it. As particularly, he supposes the doctrine of original sin to imply, that nature must be corrupted by some *positive influence*; "something, by some means or other, *infused* into the human nature; some *quality* or other, not from the *choice* of our minds, but like a *taint, tincture,* or *infection*, altering the natural constitution, faculties, and dispositions of our souls.§ That sin and evil dispositions are IMPLANTED in the fœtus in the womb."‖ Whereas truly our doctrine neither implies nor infers any such thing. In order to account for a sinful corruption of nature, yea, a total native depravity of the heart of man, there is not the least need of supposing any evil quality, *infused, implanted,* or *wrought* into the nature of man, by any *positive* cause, or influence whatsoever, either from God, or the creature; or of supposing, that man is conceived and born with a *fountain of evil* in his heart, such as is any thing properly *positive*. I think, a little attention to the nature of things will be sufficient to satisfy any impartial considerate inquirer, that the absence of positive good principles, and so the withholding of a special divine influence to impart and maintain those good principles—leaving the common natural principles of self-love, natural appetite, &c. to themselves, without the government of superior divine principles—will certainly be followed with the corruption; yea, the total corruption of the heart, without occasion for any *positive* influence at all: and that it was thus in fact that corruption of nature came on Adam, immediately on his fall, and comes on all his posterity, as sinning in him, and falling with him.¶

The case with man was plainly this: When God made man at first, he implanted in him two kinds of principles. There was an *inferior* kind, which may be called NATURAL, being the principles of mere human nature; such as self-love, with those natural appetites and passions, which belong to the *nature of man*, in which his love to his own liberty, honour, and pleasure, were exercised: these, when alone, and left to themselves, are what the Scriptures sometimes call FLESH. Besides these, there were *superior* principles, that were spiritual, holy, and divine, summarily comprehended in divine love; wherein consisted the spiritual image of God, and man's righteousness and true holiness; which are called in Scripture the *divine na-*

* Contents of Rom. chap. vii. in Notes on the epistle.

† Page 125.

‡ P. 137, 187—189, 256, 258, 260. 143. S. and other places.

§ Page 187.

‖ Page 146, 148, 149. S. and the like in many other places.

¶ The sentiment contained in this paragraph, and illustrated in the following part of this chapter, is of the utmost importance, in order not only to remove Pelagian prejudices, and the cavils of modern philosophers, but also to give a just and consistent view of the nature and cause of sin; the cause of all sin in general, and original sin in particular. Our author's explanation, which immediately follows, both in the text and in the note, is ingenious, and in some respects quite satisfactory. But a brief representation of the same result in another way, may demand some attention.

1. It is probably more philosophical, as well as more intelligible, in describing the two kinds of principles, as the author calls them, possessed by Adam, to say, that the *inferior* ones were, THOSE FACULTIES IN MAN WHICH CONSTITUTED HIM A MORAL AGENT; rather than calling them "the principles of *mere human nature.*" The *superior* ones are very accurately described; but instead of calling them "*supernatural principles*;" they may more properly be termed, DIVINE, BENEVOLENT, SOVEREIGN INFLUENCE, SUPERADDED TO THOSE FACULTIES WHICH CONSTITUTED ADAM A MORAL AGENT. This representation leads to the essential relations that subsist between God and his creature man. "Mere human nature," and "supernatural principles" convey no distinctive character of relation. "Faculties which constitute a moral agent," express the *ground of relation* between *equity* in God and *accountableness* in man; and "benevolent influences," express the *ground of relation* between *sovereignty* in God and *passiveness* in man.

2. That Adam had such qualifications, or faculties, as rendered him a *moral agent*, independently of his spiritual knowledge, righteousness, holiness, dominion, honour, and glory—in other words, his divine light, holy life, and supreme love to God—is self-evident. For, *after* he had lost these excellencies, he was confessedly no less a moral agent, and accountable to his divine Governor and Judge for his temper, thoughts, desires, words, and works, than he was *before* he lost them.

3. The *philosophical cause*, or the *true origin*, of Adam's defection, was his *liberty* in union with his *passive power*. For an explanation of these terms, and the proof of the proposition just laid down, we must refer the reader to our *notes* on the first volume of this work, where the subject is professedly discussed.

4. The true and ultimate *cause* of the first sin of Adam, of all his subsequent sins, and those of his posterity, whether infants or adults, is not essentially different. If the principles, as our author calls them, or the faculties and qualifications, which constitute moral agency and accountability, be left to themselves—whereby they become influenced by passive power, not counteracted by sovereign, benevolent, or holy divine influence—the effect will be the same, though attended with different circumstances.

5. When the cause of Adam's integrity, perfection, spirituality, and happiness, or his paradisiacal life, was no longer operative for his preservation, defection ensued; which consisted in the loss of the chief good, together with that disorder, confusion, and a conscious exposedness to a continuance in that state, whereby happiness was necessarily exchanged for a restless uneasiness, called misery.

6. This was the case of Adam in his own person. But our author, in the next chapter, excellently shows, that Adam and all his posterity were strictly *one*. This union we may call a *systematic whole*. For mankind, or the whole race of man, has a *constituted connexion*, no less than a seed with its plant; for instance, the acorn with the oak-plant, and that with its future branches. We justly called it the *same tree* from the time it was planted to its utmost longevity, though some of its branches came into existence a hundred years or more after the first shoot. This union of Adam with his posterity, is no less a *constituted union*, than that which connects the solar system; or any other inferior systematic whole, as an animal body, which is regarded as *one* from its birth till its death. For instance, nothing but a *constitution* founded in the sovereign pleasure of God, caused the body of Methuselah to be the *same*, or *regarded* as the same, when in infancy, and above nine hundred years after. The parts of his body, at least most of them, were as different in old age, compared with his infancy, as any of his posterity are different from Adam. In each case alike, the *appointment* of God in forming a *course of nature*, or his operations according to a constituted plan, could make the body of Methuselah to be the *same body* from the first to the last; and the posterity of Adam the same with himself.

7. In every *vital system* there is a *vital part*, and in every other *system*, as such, one part is more essential than another. Adam was the *vital* part of the system of mankind.—The *root* of the tree, the *foundation* of the building, the *main spring* of the machine, the *sun* of the system. We his posterity are but so many members of a body, and are all dependent on him as on our head or heart; but not so on one another. There may be the amputation of a limb, while the other limbs are not injured; but if the head or heart be deprived of life, all the members are deprived at the same time.

ture. These principles may, in some sense, be called SUPERNATURAL,* being (however concreated or connate, yet) such as are *above* those principles that are essentially implied in, or necessarily resulting from, and inseparably connected with, *mere human nature ;* and being such as immediately depend on man's union and communion with God, or divine communications and influences of God's Spirit: which though withdrawn, and man's nature forsaken of these principles, human nature would be human nature still; man's nature, as such, being entire without these divine *principles*, which the Scripture sometimes calls SPIRIT, in contradistinction to *flesh.* These superior principles were given to possess the throne, and maintain an absolute dominion in the heart; the other to be wholly subordinate and subservient. And while things continued thus, all was in excellent order, peace, and beautiful harmony, and in a proper and perfect state. These divine principles thus reigning, were the dignity, life, happiness, and glory of man's nature. When man sinned and broke God's covenant, and fell under his curse, these superior principles left his heart: for indeed God then left him; that communion with God on which these principles depended, entirely ceased; the Holy Spirit, that divine inhabitant, forsook the house. Because it would have been utterly improper in itself, and inconsistent with the constitution God had established, that he should still maintain communion with man, and continue by his friendly, gracious, vital influences, to dwell with him and in him, after he was become a rebel, and had incurred God's wrath and curse. Therefore immediately the superior divine principles wholly ceased; so light ceases in a room when the candle is withdrawn; and thus man was left in a state of darkness, woful corruption, and ruin; nothing but *flesh* without *spirit.* The inferior principles of self-love, and natural appetite, which were given only to serve, being alone, and left to themselves, *of course* became reigning principles; having no superior principles to regulate or control them, they became absolute masters of the heart. The immediate consequence of which was a *fatal catastrophe*, a turning of all things upside down, and the succession of a state of the most odious and dreadful confusion. Man immediately set up *himself*, and the objects of his private affections and appetites, as supreme; and so they took the place of GOD. These inferior principles are like *fire* in a house; which, we say, is a good servant, but a bad master; very useful while kept in its

A branch of a tree may be lopped off without injury to the other part; but if the root, the *vital* part, be affected, all the branches are also affected as the necessary consequence. A dead root and a living tree are incompatible; though a dead branch and a living branch of the same tree are not. A watch is a system formed on principles of mechanism, the index may be mutilated, or the cog of a wheel may be broken and detached, without affecting the more essential parts; but if the main spring be broken, the whole system, as to its designed use, is destroyed. A building is a system; a slate or a chimney may be blown down, without affecting the foundation, but if the whole foundation be undermined, the whole fabric must fall to ruin. The solar system might subsist, for ought that appears to the contrary, though a comet, a satellite, or a planet, were annihilated; but if the *sun* were annihilated, ruin and confusion must ensue.

8. Whatever Adam lost by transgression, he could have no claim either in equity or by promise, that is, he could have no claim at all, for a *restoration* of it. And what he could have no claim for himself, could not be claimable by or for his posterity; any more than a branch or a member could obtain life, when the root of that branch or the head of that member had ceased to live; or any more than the subordinate parts of any system when the radical, vital, fundamental, and essential parts had failed.

9. What Adam lost was the divine *life*, and the happiness implied in it, as a *favour* granted on a condition. Observing this condition, he was to have it continued; but on breaking the condition, it was to be forfeited. Adam may be compared to a lord in waiting, who should have free access to every room in the king's palace one excepted. By abstaining from this intrusion, he should have his honour and dignity preserved, and confirmed to his heirs for ever; but by offending as to the condition prescribed, he must sink to the rank of a common subject, stripped of all his former dignity. How absurd would it be for the heirs of such a lord to step forward and claim what he had forfeited! Equally absurd is it to say, that Adam's posterity are no sufferers by his transgression.

10. If we would form accurate notions of Adam's transgression, original sin, and the imputation of guilt, it will be of the utmost importance to consider the divine law, by which is the knowledge of sin, under a twofold consideration. As a *rule* requiring conformity and obedience in every period of our existence, or the measure of moral obligation; and as a *covenant*, the condition of which was *perfect* conformity and obedience, under a forfeiture of a special favour. The law as a *rule* may be transgressed times and methods innumerable; but as a *covenant* it could be transgressed only once. For the very *first* offence was a breach of the condition, and a forfeiture of that favour which depended on the performance of that condition. It is *possible* for the transgressor of the law as a *rule* to become, through grace, a *perfect* character, and therefore *perfectly* conformable to that law. But to be perfectly conformable to the required condition, once broken, is *impossible ;* as impossible as to recall time once past, or to make transgression to be no transgression.

11. Our author very justly remarks that "there is not the least, need of supposing any evil quality *infused, implanted*, or *wrought* into the nature of man, by any *positive* cause or influence whatsoever, either from God, or the creature; or of supposing, that man is conceived and born with a *fountain of evil* in his heart, such as is any thing properly *positive.*" But however just this remark, there is reason to fear that many beside Dr. Taylor have imbibed a notion of original sin considerably different from what is here asserted. It is not improbable that the *terms* by which the evil has been commonly expressed without a due examination of the idea intended, have had no small influence to effect this. The frequent use of such analogical and allusive terms as *pollution, defilement, corruption, contamination*, and the like, seems to intimate something positive; as these expressions in their original meaning convey an idea of something *superadded* to the subject. Whereas other terms, though equally analogical and allusive, imply no such thing; such as, *disorder, discord, confusion*, and the like. We do not mean to condemn the use of the former, or to recommend the latter to their exclusion; but only design to caution against a *wrong inference* from a frequent use of them.

12. On the subject of the *imputation* of Adam's offence to his posterity, our author, in the next chapter, has treated very ably and fully. But we may here observe, that it is of the greatest importance to have just views of what is called *original guilt.* It is to be feared that many form very confused notions of the subject, when it is said, "we are all *guilty* when born," or "we are all *guilty* of Adam's transgression," or "the *guilt* of Adam's offence is ours." Though we conceive these, and similar propositions, to be expressive of an important truth; yet we are no less liable to be led astray from the true idea referred to by these expressions, than by others employed to represent moral depravity.

13. It may contribute to a clearness of conception on the subject, if we keep in mind, that Adam was *guilty* by his first offence, under a twofold consideration. He was *guilty* of a breach of law considered as a *rule* of rectitude, and of the same law as a *covenant* enjoining the observance of a special duty, which was the avowed and express *condition* of it. The performance of the condition was to secure not merely moral purity and innocence, but also the favour, or gracious benefit, which he possessed on the footing of a sovereign grant. This was his *federal privilege.* How by the transgression of the law, considered as a *covenant*, this *favour* was forfeited; and for God to treat him as one deprived of this favour, is the *same thing* as to treat him as *guilty.* For how could he be treated otherwise, when the very condition on which he retained the favour was broken?

14. Whatever Adam possessed, beyond those considerations which constituted him a moral agent, was the fruit of *sovereign benevolence.* Hence arises the propriety of regarding the possession of his privilege, on the observance of a specified condition, under the term *covenant.* For, if Adam possessed some *spiritual principles*, or *benevolent influences*, as a person possesses immunities and privileges by *charter* for himself and his heirs; and if these chartered benefits be retained on *condition* of not offending in a specified manner; it follows, that a *privation* of such benefits belongs as much to the heirs as to the individual offending. But if they are treated for breach of such covenant, or charter held on condition, as persons included in the forfeiture, it is manifest they are regarded *so far guilty* or *worthy to suffer* such loss.

15. From these considerations it follows that Adam's breach of law as a *rule* which brought *guilt* upon him as an *individual*, is not the guilt imputable to his posterity. During his long life, no doubt, he was guilty of innumerable offences after the first transgression, but not one of these is imputed to us; the reason is, that after he broke the condition of the charter, he stood upon the bare ground of personal moral obligation. But personal guilt, on such ground, cannot in *equity* be transferred from one to another. The sins of the father, whether the first father or any other, considered merely as a *personal* deviation from rectitude, or a breach of moral obligation, cannot be imputed to the children.

16. What Adam, therefore, suffered for breach of covenant, was a privation of chartered benefits. The unavoidable effect of this was, DEATH; a privation of spiritual life—which continued is death eternal—and a privation of that protection and care which would have preserved from temporal death. There seems little room to doubt that even the corporeal, or elementary part of Adam underwent a great change by the fall. However, having forfeited his charter of preservation by transgression, he and all his posterity became exposed to the natural operations of this world and its elements. Matter and motion, in animals and vegetables, in the natural state of things, insure a dissolution.

17. Much has been said by some divines, about the probability of Adam, had he kept the condition, being *promoted* to some situation still more exalted. But there is reason to suspect, that such a sentiment proceeds on the supposition of Adam possessing a less exalted situation than he really did possess. The idea seems to be founded on a probable promotion for continued obedience. But what could be a greater reward than a continuance of his chartered privileges? And what a greater loss than their forfeiture?

18. It would not be difficult to demonstrate, were not this note too far extended to admit of it, that Adam, dealt with on the ground of *strict equity*, would have been not less liable to defection than his posterity are, when they begin to exercise moral agency. Therefore, the objection against the constitution of Adam and his posterity being regarded as one, is deprived of all force. For, whatever creature, in whatever world, were dealt with in *strict equity*, without *benevolent influence* to counteract *passive power*, he would have no advantage against a *liability* to defection above the race of man after the fall. The only difference is, that Adam *once actually possessed* an exalted privilege, and fell from it. And if his posterity, rendered so far *guilty* as to be deprived of chartered benefits with him, cannot be *raised* to happiness from their fallen state without the exercise of *benevolent sovereign influence* in the plan of salvation; it should be recollected, that Adam *himself* could not have *maintained* his standing but by the same *benevolent sovereign influence*, though exercised in a different way.

COROLLARY.

19. Hence the *propriety* and the *true ground* of the well known distinction of a believer in the second Adam not being under the law (*i. e.* the condemnation of the law) as a *covenant*, though under the law as a *rule.* It is found, as to its true reason, in the state of Adam, as above explained.—W

* To prevent all cavils, the reader is desired particularly to observe, in what sense I here use the words *natural* and *supernatural :*—Not as epithets of distinction between that which is concreated or connate, and that which is extraordinarily introduced afterwards, besides the first state of things, or the order established originally, beginning when man's nature began; but as distinguishing between what belongs *to*, or flows *from*, that nature which man has, merely *as* man, and those things which are *above* this, by which one is denominated, not only a *man*, but a truly *virtuous, holy*, and *spiritual* man; which, though they began in *Adam* as soon as humanity began, and are necessary to the perfection and well-being of the human nature, yet are not essential to the constitution of it, or necessary to its being: inasmuch as one may have every thing needful to his being *man*, exclusively of them. If in thus using the words, *natural* and *supernatural*, I use them in an uncommon sense, it is not from any affectation of singularity, but for want of other terms more aptly to express my meaning.

place, but if left to take possession of the whole house, soon brings all to destruction. Man's love to his own honour, separate interest, and private pleasure, which before was *wholly subordinate* unto love to God, and regard to his authority and glory, now disposes and impels him to pursue those objects, without regard to God's honour, or law; because there is no true regard to these divine things left in him. In consequence of which, he seeks those objects as much when *against* God's honour and law, as when *agreeable* to them. God still continuing strictly to require *supreme* regard to himself, and forbidding all undue gratifications of these inferior passions—but only in perfect subordination to the ends, and agreeableness to the rules and limits, which his holiness, honour, and law prescribe—hence immediately arises *enmity* in the heart, now wholly under the power of self-love; and nothing but *war* ensues, in a constant course, against God. As, when a subject has once renounced his lawful sovereign, and set up a pretender in his stead, a state of enmity and war against his rightful king necessarily ensues. It were easy to show, how every lust, and depraved disposition of man's heart, would naturally arise from this *private* original, if here were room for it. Thus it is easy to give an account, how total corruption of heart should follow on man's eating the forbidden fruit, though that was but one act of sin, *without God putting* any evil into his heart, or *implanting* any bad principle, or *infusing* any corrupt taint, and so becoming the *author* of depravity. Only God's *withdrawing*, as it was highly proper and necessary that he should, from rebel-man, and his *natural* principles being *left to themselves*, is sufficient to account for his becoming entirely corrupt, and bent on sinning against God.

And as *Adam's* nature became corrupt, without God's implanting or infusing of any evil thing into it; so does the nature of his *posterity*. God dealing with Adam as the head of his posterity, (as has been shown,) and treating them as one, he deals with his posterity as having *all sinned in him*. And therefore, as God withdrew spiritual communion, and his vital gracious influence, from the common head, so he withholds the same from all the members, as they come into existence; whereby they come into the world mere *flesh*, and entirely under the government of natural and inferior principles; and so become wholly corrupt, as Adam did.

Now, for God so far to have the disposal of this affair, as to *withhold* those influences, without which, *nature* will be *corrupt*, is not to be the *author of sin*. But, concerning this, I must refer the reader to what I have said of it in my discourse on the *Freedom of the Will.** Though, besides what I have there said, I may here observe, that if for God so far to order and dispose the being of sin, as to *permit* it, by withholding the gracious influences necessary to prevent it, is for him to be the author of sin, then some things which Dr. T. himself lays down, will equally be attended with this very consequence. For, from time to time he speaks of God giving men up to the vilest lusts and affections, by *permitting*, or *leaving* them.† Now, if the *continuance of sin*, and its increase and prevalence, may be in consequence of God's disposal, in withholding needful grace, without God being the author of that *continuance* and prevalence of sin; then, by parity of reason, may the *being of sin*, in the race of *Adam*, be in consequence of God's disposal, by his withholding that grace which is needful to prevent it, without his being the author of *sin*.

If here it should be said, that God is not the author of sin, in giving up to sin those who have already made themselves sinful, because when men have once made themselves sinful, their continuing so, and sin prevailing in them, and becoming more and more habitual, will follow *in a course of nature*: I answer, let that be remembered which this writer so greatly urges, in opposition to them who suppose original corruption comes in a course of nature, *viz. That the course of nature is nothing without God.* He utterly rejects the notion of the "*course of nature's* being a proper active cause, which will work, and go on by itself, *without God*, if he lets or permits it." ‡ But affirms, "That the course of nature, separate from the agency of God, is *no cause* or *nothing;* and that the course of nature should continue itself, or go on to operate by itself, any more than at first produce itself, is *absolutely impossible.*" These strong expressions are his. Therefore, to explain the continuance of the habits of sin in the same person, when once introduced, yea, to explain the very being of any such habits, in consequence of repeated acts, our author must have recourse to those same principles, which he rejects as absurd to the utmost degree, when alleged to explain the corruption of nature in the posterity of *Adam*. For, that habits, either good or bad, should *continue*, after being once established, or that habits should be settled and have existence in consequence of repeated acts, can be owing only to *a course of nature*, and those *laws of nature* which God has established.

That the posterity of *Adam* should be born without holiness, and so with a depraved nature, comes to pass as much by the *established course of nature*, as the continuance of a corrupt disposition in a particular person, after he once has it; or as much as *Adam's* continuing unholy and corrupt, after he had once lost his holiness. For *Adam's* posterity are from him, and as it were in him, and belonging to him, according to an *established course of nature*, as much as the branches of a tree are, according to a *course of nature*, from the tree, in the tree, and belonging to the tree; or, (to make use of the comparison which Dr. T. himself chooses from time to time, as proper to illustrate the matter,§) *just as the acorn is derived from the oak.* And I think, the acorn is as much derived from the oak, according to the *course of nature*, as the buds and branches. It is true, that God, by his own almighty power, creates the *soul* of the infant; and it is also true, as Dr. T. often insists, that God, by his immediate power, forms and fashions the *body* of the infant in the womb; yet he does both according to that *course of nature*, which he has been pleased to establish. The course of nature is demonstrated, by late improvements in philosophy, to be indeed what our author himself says it is, *viz.* Nothing but the established order of the agency and operation of the author of nature. And though there be the immediate agency of God in bringing the soul into existence in generation, yet it is done according to the method and order established by the author of nature, as much as his producing the bud, or the acorn of the oak; and as much as his continuing a particular person in being, after he once has existence. God's immediate agency in bringing the soul of a child into being, is as much according to an *established order*, as his immediate agency in any of the works of nature whatsoever. It is agreeable to the established order of nature, that the good qualities wanting in the *tree*, should also be wanting in the *branches* and *fruit*. It is agreeable to the order of nature, that when a particular person is without good moral qualities in his heart, he should continue without them, till some new cause or efficiency produces them. And it is as much agreeable to an established course and order of nature, that since Adam, the head of mankind, the root of that great tree with many branches springing from it, was deprived of original righteousness, the branches should come forth without it. Or, if any dislike the word *nature*, as used in this last case, and instead of it choose to call it a *constitution*, or *established order* of successive events, the alteration of the name will not in the least alter the state of the present argument. Where the name, *nature*, is allowed without dispute, no more is meant than an established method and order of events, settled and limited by divine wisdom.

If any should object to this, that if the want of original righteousness be thus according to an established course of *nature*, then why are not principles of holiness, when restored by divine *grace*, also communicated to *posterity;* I answer, The divine law and establishments of the author of *nature*, are precisely settled by him as he pleaseth, and limited by his wisdom. *Grace* is introduced among the race of man by a *new establishment;* not on the ground of God's original establishment, as the head of the natural world, and author of the first creation; but by a constitution of a vastly higher kind; wherein *Christ* is made the *root* of the tree, whose branches are his spiritual *seed*, and

* Part iv. § 9.
† Key, § 388, note: and Par. on Rom. i. 24, 36.

‡ Page 134. S. See also with what vehemence this is urged in p. 137. S.
§ Page 146, 187.

he is the *head* of the *new creation;* of which I need not stand now to speak particularly.

But here I desire it may be noted, that I do not suppose the natural depravity of the posterity of Adam is owing to the course of nature only; it is also owing to the just *judgment* of God. But yet I think, it is as truly and in the same manner owing to the course of *nature*, that Adam's posterity come into the world without original righteousness, as that Adam himself continued without it, after he had once lost it. That Adam continued destitute of holiness, when he had lost it, and would always have so continued, had it not been restored by a Redeemer, was not only a *natural* consequence, according to the course of things established by God, as the author of nature; but it was also a *penal* consequence, or a punishment of his sin. God, in righteous *judgment*, continued to absent himself from Adam after he became a rebel; and withheld from him now those influences of the Holy Spirit, which he before had. And just thus I suppose it to be with every natural branch of mankind: all are looked upon as *sinning* in and with their common root; and God righteously withholds special influences and spiritual communications from all, for this sin. But of the manner and order of these things, more may be said in the next chapter.

On the whole, this grand objection against the doctrine of men being born corrupt, that it makes him who *gave us our being*, to be the cause of the *being of corruption*, can have no more force in it, than a like argument has to prove, that if men by a course of nature *continue* wicked, or remain without goodness, after they have by vicious acts contracted vicious habits, and so made themselves wicked, it makes him, who is *the cause of their* CONTINUANCE *in being*, and *the cause of the* CONTINUANCE *of the course of nature*, to be *the cause of their* CONTINUED *wickedness*. Dr. T. says,* "God would not *make* any thing that is *hateful* to him; because, by the very terms, he would *hate to make* such a thing." But if this be good arguing in the case to which it is applied, may I not as well say, *God would not* CONTINUE *a thing in being that is* HATEFUL *to him; because, by the very terms, he would* HATE TO CONTINUE *such a thing in being?* I think, the very terms do as much (and no more) infer one of these propositions, as the other. In like manner, the rest that he says on that head may be shown to be unreasonable, by only substituting the word *continue*, in the place of *make* and *propagate*. I may fairly imitate his way of reasoning thus: to say, God *continues* us according to his own original decree, or law of *continuation*, which obliges him to *continue* us in a manner he abhors, is really to make bad worse: for it is supposing him to be defective in wisdom, or by his own decree or law to lay such a constraint upon his own actions, that he cannot do what he would, but is continually doing what he would not, what he hates to do, and what he condemns in *us;* viz. *continuing* us sinful when he condemns us for *continuing* ourselves sinful." If the reasoning be *weak* in the one case, it is no less so in the other.

If any shall still insist, that there is a *difference* between God so disposing things, as that depravity of heart shall be *continued*, according to the settled course of nature, in the same person, who has by his own fault introduced it; and his so disposing as that men, according to a course of nature, should be *born* with depravity, in consequence of Adam's introducing of sin, by his act which we had no concern in, and cannot be justly charged with: on this I would observe, that it is quite going off the objection, which we have been upon, from God's agency, and flying to another. It is then no longer insisted on, that *simply* for him, from whose agency the course of nature and our existence derive, so to dispose things as that we should have existence in a corrupt state, is for him to be the author of sin: but the plea now advanced is, that it is not proper and just for such an agent so to dispose, *in this case*, and only in consequence of Adam's sin; it not being just to charge Adam's sin to his posterity. And this matter shall be particularly considered, in answer to the next objection; to which I now proceed.

* Page 136. S.

CHAP. III.

THAT GREAT OBJECTION AGAINST THE IMPUTATION OF ADAM'S SIN TO HIS POSTERITY, CONSIDERED, THAT SUCH IMPUTATION IS UNJUST AND UNREASONABLE, INASMUCH AS ADAM AND HIS POSTERITY ARE NOT ONE AND THE SAME. WITH A BRIEF REFLECTION SUBJOINED OF WHAT SOME HAVE SUPPOSED, OF GOD IMPUTING THE GUILT OF ADAM'S SIN TO HIS POSTERITY, BUT IN AN INFINITELY LESS DEGREE THAN TO ADAM HIMSELF.

That we may proceed with the greater clearness in considering the main objections against supposing the guilt of Adam's sin to be imputed to his posterity; I would premise some observations with a view to the right *stating* of the doctrine; and then show its *reasonableness*, in opposition to the great clamour raised against it on this head.

I think, it would go far towards directing us to the more clear conception and right statement of this affair, were we steadily to bear this in mind: that God, in every step of his proceeding with Adam, in relation to the covenant or constitution established with him, looked on his posterity as being *one with him*. And though he dealt more immediately with Adam, it yet was as the *head* of the whole body, and the *root* of the whole tree; and in his proceedings with him, he dealt with all the branches, as if they had been then existing in their root.

From which it will follow, that both guilt, or exposedness to punishment, and also depravity of heart, came upon Adam's posterity just as they came upon him, as much as if he and they had all co-existed, like a tree with many branches; allowing only for the difference necessarily resulting from the place Adam stood in, as head or root of the whole. Otherwise, it is as if, in every step of proceeding, every alteration in the root had been attended, at the same instant, with the same alterations throughout the whole tree, in each individual branch. I think, this will naturally follow on the supposition of there being a *constituted oneness* or *identity* of Adam and his posterity in this affair.

Therefore I am humbly of opinion, that if any have supposed the children of Adam to come into the world with a *double guilt*, one the guilt of Adam's sin, another the guilt arising from their having a corrupt heart, they have not so well conceived of the matter. The *guilt* a man has upon his soul at first existence, is one and simple, *viz.* the guilt of the original apostacy, the guilt of the sin by which the species first rebelled against God. This, and the guilt arising from the depraved disposition of the heart, are not to be looked upon as *two* things, *distinctly* imputed and charged upon men in the sight of God. Indeed the guilt that arises from the corruption of the heart, as it remains a confirmed principle, and appears in its consequent operations, is a *distinct and additional* guilt: but the guilt arising from the first existing of a depraved disposition in Adam's posterity, I apprehend, is *not* distinct from their guilt of Adam's first sin. For so it was not in Adam himself. The first evil disposition or inclination of Adam to sin, was not properly distinct from his first act of sin, but was included in it. The external act he committed was no otherwise his, than as his heart was in it, or as that action proceeded from the wicked inclination of his heart. Nor was the guilt he had *double*, as for two distinct sins: one, the wickedness of his will in that affair; another, the wickedness of the external act, caused by it. His guilt was all truly from the act of his inward man; exclusive of which the motions of his body were no more than the motions of any lifeless instrument. His sin consisted in wickedness of heart, fully sufficient *for*, and entirely amounting *to*, all that appeared in the act he committed.

The depraved disposition of *Adam's* heart is to be considered two ways. (1.) As the *first rising* of an evil inclination in his heart, exerted in his first act of sin, and the ground of the complete transgression. (2.) An evil disposition of heart *continuing* afterwards, as a confirmed principle that came by God's forsaking of him; which was a *punishment* of his first transgression. This confirmed corruption, by its remaining and continued operation, brought additional guilt on his soul.

In like manner, depravity of heart is to be considered two ways in Adam's posterity. The *first existing* of a corrupt disposition, is not to be looked upon as sin *distinct* from their participation of Adam's first sin. It is as it were the *extended pollution* of that sin, through the whole tree, by virtue of the constituted *union* of the branches with the root; or the *inherence* of the sin of that head of the species in the members, in their consent and concurrence with the head in that first act. But the depravity of nature remaining as an *established principle* in a child of Adam, and as exhibited in after-operations, is a *consequence* and *punishment* of the first apostacy thus participated, and brings new guilt. The *first being* of an evil disposition in a child of Adam, whereby he is disposed to *approve* the sin of his first father, so far as to imply a full and perfect *consent* of heart to it, I think, is not to be looked upon as a consequence of the imputation of that first sin, any more than the full consent of Adam's own heart in the act of sinning; which was not consequent on the imputation, but rather *prior* to it in the order of nature. Indeed the derivation of the evil disposition to Adam's posterity, or rather, the *co-existence* of the evil disposition, implied in *Adam's* first rebellion, in the *root* and *branches*, is a consequence of the *union* that the wise Author of the world has established between *Adam* and his posterity; but not properly a *consequence* of the *imputation* of his sin; nay, is rather *antecedent* to it, as it was in *Adam* himself. The first depravity of heart, and the imputation of that sin, are both the consequences of that established union; but yet in such order, that the evil disposition is *first*, and the charge of guilt *consequent*, as it was in the case of *Adam* himself.*

The first existence of an evil disposition, amounting to a full consent to *Adam's* sin, no more infers God being the author of that evil disposition in the *child*, than in the *father*. The first arising or existing of that evil disposition in the heart of *Adam*, was by God's *permission;* who could have prevented it, if he had pleased, by *giving* such influences of his Spirit, as would have been absolutely effectual to hinder it; which, it is plain in fact, he did *withhold:* and whatever mystery may be supposed in the affair, yet no Christian will presume to say, it was not in perfect consistence with God's *holiness* and *righteousness*, notwithstanding Adam had been guilty of no offence before. So root and branches being one, according to God's wise constitution, the case in fact is, that by virtue of this oneness answerable changes or effects through all the *branches* co-exist with the changes in the *root:* consequently an evil disposition exists in the hearts of Adam's posterity, equivalent to that which was exerted in his own heart, when he eat the forbidden fruit. Which God has no hand in, any otherwise, than in not exerting such an influence, as might be effectual to prevent it; as appears by what was observed in the former chapter.†

But now the grand objection is against the *reasonableness* of such a *constitution*, by which *Adam* and his posterity should be looked upon as *one*, and dealt with accordingly, in an affair of such infinite consequence; so that if *Adam* sinned, they must necessarily be made *sinners* by his disobedience, and come into existence with the same *depravity* of disposition, and be looked upon and treated as though they were partakers with him in his act of sin. I have not room here to rehearse all Dr. T.'s vehement exclamations against the reasonableness and justice of this. The reader may at his leisure consult his book, and see them in the places referred to below.‡ Whatever black colours and frightful representations are employed on this occasion, all may be summed up in this, That *Adam* and his posterity are *not one*, but entirely *distinct agents*. But with respect to this mighty outcry made against the *reasonableness* of any such *constitution*, by which God is supposed to treat Adam and his posterity as *one*, I would make the following observations.

I. It signifies nothing to exclaim against plain *fact*. Such is the *fact*, the most evident and acknowledged *fact*, with respect to the state of all mankind, without exception of one individual among all the natural descendants of *Adam*, as makes it apparent, that God actually deals with Adam and his posterity as *one*, in reference to his apostacy, and its infinitely terrible consequences. It has been demonstrated, and shewn to be in effect plainly acknowledged, that every individual of mankind comes into the world in such circumstances, as that there is no hope or possibility of any other than their violating God's holy law, (if they ever live to act at all as moral agents,) and being thereby justly exposed to eternal ruin.§ And God either thus deals with mankind, because he looks upon

* My meaning, in the whole of what has been here said, may be illustrated thus: Let us suppose that *Adam* and all his posterity had *co-existed*, and that his posterity had been, through a law of nature established by the Creator, *united* to him, something as the branches of a tree are united to the root, or the members of the body to the head, so as to constitute as it were *one* complex person, or *one* moral whole: so that by the law of union there should have been a *communion* and *co-existence* in acts and affections; all jointly participating, and all concurring, as *one whole*, in the disposition and action of the head: as we see in the body natural, the whole body is affected as the head is affected; and the whole body concurs when the head acts. Now, in this case, all the branches of mankind, by the constitution of nature and law of union, would have been affected just as *Adam*, their common root, was affected. When the heart of the root, by a full disposition, committed the first sin, the hearts of all the branches would have concurred; and when the root, in consequence of this, became guilty, so would all the branches; and when the root, as a punishment of the sin committed, was forsaken of God, in like manner would it have fared with all the branches; and when the root, in consequence of this, was confirmed in permanent depravity, the case would have been the same with all the branches; and as new guilt on the soul of *Adam* would have been consequent on this, so also would it have been with his moral branches. And thus all things, with relation to evil disposition, guilt, pollution, and depravity, would exist, in the same order and dependence, in each branch, as in the root. Now, difference of the *time* of existence does not at all hinder things succeeding in the same order, any more than difference of *place* in a co-existence of time.

Here may be observed, as in several respects to the present purpose, some things that are said by Stapferus, an eminent divine of *Zurich*, in *Switzerland*, in his *Theologia Polemica*, published about fourteen years ago;—in *English* as follows. "Seeing all Adam's posterity are derived from their first parent, as their root, the whole of the human kind, with its root, may be considered as constituting but one whole, or one mass; so as not to be properly distinct from its root; the posterity not differing from it, any otherwise than the branches from the tree. From which it easily appears, how that when the root sinned, all that which is derived from it, and with it constitutes but one whole, may be looked upon as also sinning; seeing it is not distinct from the root, but one with it."—*Tom.* i. cap. 3. § 856. 57.

"It is objected, against the imputation of *Adam's* sin, that we never committed the same sin with *Adam*, neither in number nor in kind. I answer, we should distinguish here between the *physical act* itself, which Adam committed, and the *morality* of the action, and *consent* to it. If we have respect only to the external act, to be sure it must be confessed, that Adam's posterity did not put forth their hands to the forbidden fruit: in which sense, that act of transgression, and that fall of *Adam*, cannot be *physically* one with the sin of his posterity. But if we consider the *morality* of the action, and what *consent* there is to it, it is altogether to be maintained, that his posterity committed the *same* sin, both in number and in kind, inasmuch as they are to be looked upon as consenting to it. For where there is consent to a sin, there the same sin is committed. Seeing therefore that Adam with all his posterity constitute but *one moral person*, and are united in the same covenant, and are transgressors of the same law, they are also to be looked upon as having, in a moral estimation, committed the same transgression of the law, both in number and in kind. Therefore this reasoning avails nothing against the righteous imputation of the sin of Adam to all mankind or to the whole moral person that is consenting to it. And for the reason mentioned, we may rather argue thus: the sin of the posterity, on account of their consent, and the moral view in which they are to be taken, is the same with the sin of Adam, not only in kind, but in number; therefore the sin of Adam is rightfully imputed to his posterity."—*Id.* Tom. iv. cap. 16. § 60, 61.

The imputation of Adam's first sin consists in nothing else than this, that his posterity are viewed as in the same place with their father, and are like him. But seeing, agreeable to what we have already proved, God might, according to his own righteous judgment, which was founded on his most righteous law, give Adam a posterity that were *like himself;* and indeed it could not be otherwise, according to the very laws of nature; therefore he might also in righteous judgment impute Adam's sin to them, inasmuch as to give Adam a posterity *like himself*, and to *impute* his sin to them, is one and the same thing. And therefore if the former be not contrary to the divine perfections, so neither is the latter. Our *adversaries* contend with us chiefly on this account, that according to our doctrine of original sin, such an *imputation* of the first sin is maintained, whereby God, without any regard to universal native *corruption*, esteems all Adam's posterity as *guilty*, and holds them as liable to condemnation, *purely* on account of that sinful act of their first parent; so that they without any respect had to *their own sin*, and so, as *innocent* in themselves, are destined to eternal punishment.—I have therefore ever been careful to show, that they do *injuriously* suppose those things to be *separated* in our doctrine which are *by no means* to be separated. The whole of the controversy they have with us about this matter, evidently arises from this, that they suppose the *mediate* and the *immediate* imputation are distinguished one from the other, not only in the manner of conception, but in reality. And so indeed they consider imputation only as *immediate* and abstractly from the *mediate;* when yet our divines suppose, that neither ought to be considered *separately* from the other. Therefore I chose not to use any such distinction, or to suppose any such thing, in what I have said on the subject; but only have endeavoured to explain the thing itself, and to reconcile it with the divine attributes. And therefore I have every where *conjoined* both these conceptions concerning the imputation of the first sin, as inseparable; and judged, that one ought never to be considered without the other.—While I have been writing this note, I consulted all the systems of divinity, which I have by me, that I might see what was the true and genuine opinion of our chief divines in this affair; and I found that they were of the same mind with me; namely, that these two kinds of imputation are by no means to be separated, or to be considered abstractly one from the other, but that one does involve the other." He there particularly cites those two famous reformed divines, *Vitringa* and *Lampius*. Tom. iv. cap. 17. § 78.

† See also p. 39. note, § 8, &c. 48. § 12, &c. 80. § 9, &c. 82. § 17, &c. 121 § 7, &c.

‡ Page 13. 150, 151, 156, 261. 108, 109, 111 S.

§ Part I. Chap. I. the three first sections.

them as *one* with their first father, and so treats them as *sinful* and *guilty* by his apostacy; or (which will not mend the matter) he, *without* viewing them as at all concerned in that affair, but as in every respect perfectly *innocent*, subjects them nevertheless to this infinitely dreadful calamity. Adam by his sin was exposed to the *calamities and sorrows of this life*, to *temporal death and eternal ruin;* as is confessed. And it is also in effect confessed, that all his posterity come into the world in such a state, as that the certain consequence is their being *exposed*, and *justly* so, to the *sorrows of this life*, to *temporal death, and eternal ruin*, unless saved by grace. So that we see, God *in fact* deals with them together, or as *one*. If God orders the consequences of Adam's sin, with regard to his posterity's welfare—even in those things which are most important, and which in the highest degree concern their eternal interest—to be the *same* with the consequences to Adam himself, then he treats Adam and his posterity as *one* in that affair. Hence, however the matter be attended with difficulty, *fact* obliges us to *get over* it, either by finding out some solution, or by shutting our mouths, and acknowledging the weakness and scantiness of our understandings; as we must in other innumerable cases, where apparent and undeniable *fact*, in God's works of creation and providence, is attended with events and circumstances, the *manner* and *reason* of which are difficult to our understandings.—But to proceed.

II. We will consider the *difficulties* themselves, insisted on in the objections of our opposers. They may be reduced to these two: *First*, That such a constitution is *injurious* to Adam's posterity. *Secondly*, That it is altogether *improper*, as it implies *falsehood*, viewing and treating those as one, which indeed are not one, but entirely *distinct*.

First *difficulty*, That appointing *Adam* to stand, in this great affair, as the moral *head* of his posterity, and so treating them as *one* with him, as standing or falling with him, is *injurious* to them. To which I answer, it is demonstrably *otherwise;* that such a constitution was so far from being *injurious* to Adam's posterity, any more than if every one had been appointed to stand for himself personally, that it was, in itself considered, attended with a more eligible *probability* of a *happy* issue than the latter would have been: and so a constitution that truly expresses the *goodness* of its Author. For,

1. It is reasonable to suppose, that *Adam* was *as likely*, on account of his capacity and natural talents, to *persevere* in obedience, as his posterity, (taking one with another,) if they had all been put on the trial singly for themselves. And supposing that there was a constituted union or oneness of him and his posterity, and that he stood as a public person, or common head, all by this constitution would have been as sure to partake of the benefit of his obedience, as of the ill consequence of his disobedience, in case of his fall.

2. There was a *greater tendency* to a happy issue, in such an appointment, than if every one had been appointed to stand for himself; especially on two accounts. (1.) That *Adam* had *stronger motives to watchfulness* than his posterity would have had; in that not only his own eternal welfare lay at stake, but also that of all his posterity: (2.) *Adam* was in a state of complete *manhood*, when his trial began. It was a constitution very agreeable to the *goodness* of God, considering the state of mankind, which was to be propagated in the way of generation, that their *first father* should be appointed to stand for all. For by reason of the manner of their coming into existence in a state of *infancy*, and their coming so gradually to *mature* state, and so remaining for a great while in a state of childhood and comparative imperfection, after they were become moral agents, they would be *less fit* to stand for themselves, than their first father to stand for them.

If any man, notwithstanding these things, shall say, that for his own part, if the affair had been proposed to him, *he* should have *chosen* to have had his eternal interest trusted in *his own* hands: it is sufficient to answer, that no man's vain opinion of himself, as *more fit* to be trusted than others, alters the true nature and tendency of things, as they demonstrably are in themselves. Nor is it a just objection, that this constitution has in *event* proved for the *hurt* of mankind. For it does not follow, that no advantage was given for a *happy* event, in such an establishment, because it was not such as to make it utterly impossible there should be any other event.

3. The *goodness* of God in such a constitution with *Adam* appears in this: that if there had been no *sovereign gracious* establishment at all, but God had proceeded only on the basis of mere *justice*, and had gone no further than this required, he might have demanded of *Adam* and all his posterity, that they should perform *perfect perpetual obedience*, without ever failing in the least instance, on pain of *eternal death;* and might have made this demand *without* the *promise* of any positive *reward* for their obedience. For perfect obedience is a *debt*, that every one owes to his Creator; and therefore is what his Creator was not obliged to pay him for. None is obliged to pay his debtor for discharging his just debt.—But such was evidently the constitution with Adam, that an eternal happy life was to be the consequence of his persevering fidelity, to all such as were included within that constitution, (of which the *tree of life* was a sign,) as well as eternal death to be the consequence of his disobedience.—I come now to consider the

Second *difficulty*.—It being thus manifest, that this constitution, by which *Adam* and his posterity are dealt with as *one*, is not unreasonable on account of its being *injurious* and *hurtful* to the interest of mankind, the only thing remaining in the objection, against such a constitution, is the *impropriety* of it, as implying *falsehood*, and contradiction to the true nature of things; as hereby they are viewed and treated *as one*, who are *not* one, but wholly distinct; and no arbitrary constitution can ever make that to be true, which in itself considered is not true.

This objection, however specious, is really founded on a false hypothesis, and wrong notion of what we call *sameness* or *oneness*, among created things; and the seeming force of the objection arises from ignorance or inconsideration of the *degree*, in which created identity or oneness with past existence, in general, depends on the sovereign constitution and law of the supreme Author and Disposer of the universe.

Some things are *entirely distinct*, and *very diverse*, which yet are so united by the established law of the Creator, that by virtue of that establishment, they are in a sense *one*. Thus a *tree*, grown great, and a hundred years old, is *one* plant with the little *sprout*, that first came out of the ground from whence it grew, and has been continued in constant succession; though it is now so exceeding *diverse*, many thousand times bigger, and of a very different form, and perhaps not one atom the very same: yet God, according to an established law of nature, has in a constant succession communicated to it many of the same qualities, and most important properties, as if it were *one*. It has been his pleasure, to constitute an union in these respects, and for these purposes, naturally leading us to look upon all as *one*.—So the *body* of *man* at forty years of age, is *one* with the *infant body* which first came into the world, from whence it grew; though now constituted of different substance, and the greater part of the substance probably changed scores (if not hundreds) of times: and though it be now in so many respects exceeding diverse, yet God, according to the course of nature, which he has been pleased to establish, has caused, that in a certain method it should communicate with that *infantile* body, in the same life, the same senses, the same features, and many the same qualities, and in union with the same soul; and so, with regard to these purposes, it is dealt with by him as *one* body. Again, the *body* and *soul* of a man are *one*, in a very different manner, and for different purposes. Considered in themselves, they are exceeding different beings, of a nature as diverse as can be conceived; and yet, by a very peculiar divine constitution, or law of nature, which God has been pleased to establish, they are strongly united, and become *one*, in most important respects; a wonderful mutual communication is established; so that both become different parts of the *same man*. But the union and mutual communication they have, has existence, and is entirely regulated and limited, according to the sovereign pleasure of God, and the constitution he has been pleased to establish.

And if we come even to the *personal identity* of created intelligent beings, though this be not allowed to consist *wholly* in what Mr. Locke supposes, *i. e. Same consciousness;* yet I think it cannot be denied, that this is one thing essential to it. But it is evident, that the communication or continuance of the same consciousness and memory to any subject, through successive parts of duration, depends wholly on a divine establishment. There would be no necessity, that the remembrance and ideas of what is past should continue to exist, but by an arbitrary constitution of the Creator.—If any should here insist, that there is no need of having recourse to any such *constitution*, in order to account for the continuance of the *same consciousness;* and should say, that the very *nature* of the soul is such as will sufficiently account for it, its ideas and consciousness being retained, according to the *course of nature:* then let it be remembered, who it is that gives the soul this nature; and let that be remembered, which Dr. T. says of the course of nature, before observed; denying, that *the course of nature is a proper active cause, which will work and go on by itself without God, if he lets and permits it;* saying, *that the course of nature, separate from the agency of God, is no cause, or nothing;* and affirming, that *it is absolutely impossible, the course of nature should continue itself, or go on to operate by itself, any more than produce itself;** *and that God, the original of all being, is the* ONLY CAUSE *of all natural effects.*† Here it is worthy also to be observed, what Dr. Turnbull says of the *laws of nature*, as cited from Sir Isaac Newton.‡ "It is the will of the mind that is the *first cause*, that gives subsistence and efficacy to all those *laws*, who is the *efficient cause* that produces the *phænomena*, which appear in analogy, harmony, and agreement, according to these *laws*." And, "the same principles must take place in things pertaining to *moral* as well as natural philosophy."§

From these things it will clearly follow, that identity of *consciousness* depends wholly on a law of *nature;* and so, on the sovereign *will* and *agency of* GOD. And therefore, that personal identity, and so the derivation of the pollution and guilt of past sins in the same person, depends on an arbitrary divine *constitution;* and this, even though we should allow the same consciousness not to be the only thing which constitutes oneness of person, but should, besides that, suppose sameness of substance requisite. For, if same consciousness be *one thing* necessary to personal identity, and this depends on God's sovereign *constitution*, it will still follow that personal identity depends on God's sovereign *constitution*.

And with respect to the identity of created substance itself, in the different moments of its duration, I think we shall greatly mistake, if we imagine it to be like that absolute, independent identity of the FIRST BEING, whereby he is *the same yesterday, to-day, and for ever.* Nay, on the contrary, it may be demonstrated, that even this oneness of created substance, existing at different times, is a merely *dependent* identity; dependent on the pleasure and sovereign constitution of him who *worketh all in all.* This will follow from what is generally allowed, and is certainly true, that God not only created all things, and gave them being at first, but continually preserves them, and upholds them in being. This being a matter of considerable importance, it may be worthy here to be considered with a little attention. Let us inquire therefore, in the first place, whether it be not evident, that God does continually, by his immediate power, *uphold* every created substance in being; and then let us see the *consequence*.

That God does, by his immediate power, *uphold* every created substance in being, will be manifest, if we consider that their present existence is a *dependent* existence, and therefore is an *effect* and must have some *cause;* and the cause must be one of these two; either the *antecedent existence* of the same substance, or else the *power* of the *Creator*. But it cannot be the *antecedent existence* of the same substance. For instance, the existence of the body of the *moon*, at this present moment, cannot be the *effect* of its existence at the last foregoing moment. For not only was what existed the last moment, no active cause, but wholly a passive thing; but this also is to be considered, that no cause can produce effects in a *time and place* in which itself is *not*. It is plain, nothing can exert itself, or operate, *when* and *where* it is not existing. But the moon's past existence was neither *where* nor *when* its present existence is. In point of *time*, what is *past* entirely ceases, when *present* existence begins; otherwise it would not be *past*. The past moment has ceased, and is gone, when the present moment takes place; and no more *co-exists* with it, than any other moment that had ceased, twenty years ago. Nor could the past existence of the particles of this *moving body* produce effects in any *other place*, than where it then was. But its existence at the present moment, in every point of it, is in a different *place*, from where its existence was at the last preceding moment. From these things, I suppose, it will certainly follow, that the present existence, either of this, or any other created substance, cannot be an effect of its past existence. The existences (so to speak) of an effect, or thing dependent, in different parts of space or duration, though ever so *near* one to another, do not at all *co-exist* one with the other; and therefore are as truly different effects, as if those parts of space and duration were ever so far asunder. And the prior existence can no more be the proper cause of the new existence, in the next moment, or next part of space, than if it had been in an age before, or at a thousand miles' distance, without any existence to fill up the intermediate time or space. Therefore the existence of created substances, in each successive moment, must be the effect of the *immediate* agency, will, and power of GOD.

If any shall insist upon it, that their present existence is the effect or consequence of past existence, according to the *nature* of things; that the established *course of nature* is sufficient to *continue* existence once given; I allow it. But then it should be remembered, *what* nature is in created things; and *what* the established *course* of nature is; that, as has been observed already, *it is nothing, separate from the agency of God;* and that, as Dr. T. says, GOD, *the original of all being, is the* ONLY *cause of all natural effects.* A father, according to the course of nature, begets a child; an oak, according to the course of nature, produces an acorn, or a bud; so according to the course of nature, the former existence of the trunk of the tree is followed by its new or present existence. In one case, and the other, the new effect is consequent on the former, only by the *established laws* and *settled course of nature;* which is allowed to be nothing but the continued immediate efficiency of GOD, according to a *constitution* that he has been pleased to establish. Therefore, according to what our author urges; as the child and the acorn which come into existence according to the *course of nature*, in consequence of the prior existence and state of the parent and the oak, are truly *immediately* created by God; so must the existence of each created person and thing, at each moment, be from the immediate *continued* creation of God. It will certainly follow from these things, that God's *preserving* of created things in being, is perfectly equivalent to a *continued creation*, or to his creating those things out of nothing at *each moment* of their existence. If the continued existence of created things be wholly dependent on God's preservation, then those things would drop into *nothing* upon the ceasing of the present moment, without a new exertion of the divine power to cause them to exist in the following moment.|| If there be any who own, that God *preserves* things in being, and yet hold that they would continue in

* Page 134. S. † Page 140. S. ‡ Mor. Phil. p. 7. § Ibid. p. 9.

|| The CHRISTIAN OBSERVER, (vol. v. p. 177.) in reviewing a sermon, entitled, "Predestination to Life," remarks: "It may be allowed, (though even this is not to us in the sense formerly explained, a *self-evident* proposition,) that all created nature, as such, tends to nihility. Since it sprung out of nothing, only through the intervention of Almighty Power, it must certainly relapse into nothing when the intervening power is removed. Since it became something only during the pleasure of another, it will cease to be something when left to itself. But it is not so apparent, why that which never subsisted but in a state of virtue and purity, should of itself have a tendency to subsist in any other state; or why, when left to itself, if it continue at all, it should not continue in that state in which it was left."—But, in p. 186. he *retracts* what he first said, in the following very singular *note:* "The preceding sheet was printed off before we perceived that we had expressed ourselves at p. 177. col. 2. in language which may be construed into an admission of the truth of the doctrine maintained by Dr. Williams, as it respects the necessary tendency of all created nature to *nihility*. In a *popular* sense, indeed, it may perhaps be said, (though the proposition will be found "to fill the ear rather than the mind,") that what sprung out of nothing at the pleasure of another, must again become nothing when left to itself; and, for the sake of shortening the discussion, we were willing to concede thus much. We must at the same time confess that *we do not quite understand* the position, that *created beings tend to nihility:* and we leave it to our readers to judge whether there be much more meaning in saying that 'what *is* tends

being without any further help from him, after they once have existence; I think, it is hard to know what they mean. To what purpose can it be, to talk of God *preserving* things in being, when there is *no need* of his preserving them? Or to talk of their being *dependent* on God for continued existence, when they would of themselves continue to exist, without his help; nay, though he should wholly withdraw his sustaining power and influence?

It will follow from what has been observed, that God's upholding of created substance, or causing of its existence in each successive moment, is altogether equivalent to an *immediate production out of nothing*, at each moment. Because its existence at this moment is not merely in part from *God*, but wholly from him; and not in any part, or degree, from its *antecedent existence*. For, to suppose that its antecedent existence *concurs* with God in *efficiency*, to produce some *part* of the effect, is attended with all the very same absurdities, which have been shown to attend the supposition of its producing it *wholly*. Therefore the antecedent existence is nothing, as to any proper influence or assistance in the affair: and consequently *God* produces the effect as much from *nothing*, as if there had been nothing *before*. So that this effect differs not at all from the first creation, but only *circumstantially*; as, in the *first* creation there had been no such act and effect of God's power *before*: whereas, his giving existence afterwards, *follows* preceding acts and effects of the same kind, in an established order.

Now, in the next place, let us see how the *consequence* of these things is to my present purpose. If the existence of created *substance*, in each successive moment, be wholly the effect of God's immediate power, in *that* moment, without any dependence on prior existence, as much as the first creation out of *nothing*, then what exists at this moment, by this power, is a *new effect*; and simply and absolutely considered, not the same with any past existence, though it be like it, and follows it according to a certain established method.* And there is no identity or oneness in the case, but what depends on the *arbitrary* constitution of the Creator; who by his wise sovereign establishment so unites these successive new effects, that he *treats them as one*, by communicating to them like properties, relations, and circumstances; and so, leads *us* to regard and treat them as *one*. When I call this an *arbitrary constitution*, I mean, that it is a constitution which depends on nothing but the *divine will*; which divine will depends on nothing but the *divine wisdom*. In this sense, the whole *course of nature*, with all that belongs to it, all its laws and methods, constancy and regularity, continuance and proceeding, is an *arbitrary constitution*. In this sense, the continuance of the very being of the world and all its parts, as well as the manner of continued being, depends entirely on an *arbitrary constitution*. For it does not at all *necessarily* follow, that because there was sound, or light, or colour, or resistance, or gravity, or thought, or consciousness, or any other dependent thing the last moment, that therefore there shall be the like at the next. All dependent existence whatsoever is in a constant flux, ever passing and returning; renewed every moment, as the colours of bodies are every moment renewed by the light that shines upon them; and all is constantly proceeding from GOD, as light from the sun. *In him we live, and move, and have our being.*

Thus it appears, if we consider matters strictly, there is no such thing as any identity or oneness in created objects, existing at different times, but what depends on *God's sovereign constitution*. And so it appears, that the *objection* we are upon, made against a supposed divine constitution, whereby *Adam* and his *posterity* are viewed and treated as *one*, in the manner and for the purposes supposed—as if it were *not consistent with truth*, because no constitution can make those to be *one*, which are *not* one—is built on a false hypothesis: for it appears, that a *divine constitution* is what *makes truth*, in affairs of this nature. The objection supposes, there is a oneness in created beings, whence qualities and relations are derived down from past existence, *distinct* from, and *prior* to, any oneness that can be supposed to be founded on divine *constitution*. Which is demonstrably false; and sufficiently appears so from things conceded by the adversaries themselves: and therefore the objection wholly falls to the ground.

There are *various kinds* of identity and oneness, found among created things, by which they become one in *different manners*, *respects*, and *degrees*, and to *various pur-*

not to be,' than in saying that 'what *is not* tends to *be*;' or, in other words, whether a tendency to *annihilation* in that which *exists*, be at all more conceivable, than a tendency to *become existent* in that which *exists not*."

How far the writer had any good reason for *retracting* what he first asserted, and thereby *opposing* the sentiments, not only of the author he reviews, but of *nearly all* the divines that ever have written upon providence, let the reader judge by a careful perusal of this chapter. We are ignorant of what Bishop Burnet says on this head, (Art. 1. p. 30. 3d Ed.) but are well satisfied his notion is as incapable of being supported by sound reason, as it was *novel*; and as little calculated to support the cause of *piety* as any one opinion he advances, in his undecisive and latitudinarian exposition of the Thirty-nine Articles. (See particularly Art. ix. on Original Sin.) For what can be a more heterodox opinion, or more full of horrid *impiety*, if traced to its just consequences, that the sentiment advanced by that Bishop and by the CHRISTIAN OBSERVER! though we are far from supposing that either the one or the other *foresaw* those consequences. The best excuse we can form for this writer is, that "he *does not quite understand the position*" against which he writes. *This record*, we believe, *is true*; and is equally applicable to *several other* positions in that article. But then, the public expects from a *Reviewer* a comprehensive acquaintance with the subject which he criticises, instead of "a wood of words" and inconclusive declamations. However, he seems to be *notoriously deficient* in comprehending the *true state of the question*. A great part of that long article consists in *proving* what was *not denied*, and in *disproving* what was *never asserted*; with a goodly portion of *contradictory propositions*.

We might have expected, that an author who *studiously shuns* the *intricacies* of a subject which will, in his apprehension, "descend to posterity with all its difficulties on its head"—a subject, the *depth* of which "the sounding line of metaphysics will *never fathom*"—would have kept himself more free from embarrassments and *self-contradictions*. And it was also to be expected from one who professes to advocate the cause of *piety* and *practical* religion, that he should keep aloof from the *horrible* sentiment suggested by Burnet, in opposition to the *almost unanimous* verdict of all the pious and learned divines that ever lived. We almost shudder to draw the inference demonstrably implied in the sentiment.—*That the world would continue in being, were there no God to uphold it!* When we say, that this is the just inference drawn from the sentiment held by the CHRISTIAN OBSERVER, we mean, by the individual *Reviewer* in question, whose critique disgraces that excellent work.

Aware, perhaps, that the author whose works we now publish was of the *same way of thinking*; or at least, that his works have *the same tendency* with what he opposes, he observes: "We are apt to think that the metaphysical cast which the celebrated Mr. Edwards gave to his writings in divinity, has to a certain degree produced an unfavourable effect on the minds of his followers." It would have been extremely difficult for this writer to point out any *preacher* who came closer to men's consciences, or any *writer* who more effectually promotes the interest of genuine, humble, holy, practical religion, than President Edwards; and the editors of his works are *fully conscious*, that what they publish tends, in the *most direct manner*, when duly considered and understood, to *essential truth*—to GOD; *of whom, and through whom, and to whom are all things: to whom be glory for ever. Amen.*—W.

* When I suppose, that an effect which is produced every moment by a new action or exertion of power, must be a *new* effect in each moment, and not absolutely and numerically the same with that which existed in preceding moments, what I intend, may be illustrated by this example. The lucid colour or brightness of the *moon*, as we look stedfastly upon it, seems to be a *permanent* thing, as though it were perfectly the same brightness continued. But indeed it is an effect produced every moment. It ceases, and is renewed, in each successive point of time; and so becomes altogether a *new* effect at each instant; and no one thing that belongs to it, is numerically the same that existed in the preceding moment. The rays of the sun, impressed on that body, and reflected from it, which cause the effect, are none of them the same: the impression, made in each moment on our sensory, is by the stroke of *new* rays: and the sensation excited by the stroke, is a new effect, an effect of a *new* impulse. Therefore the brightness or lucid whiteness of this body is no more numerically the same thing with that which existed in the preceding moment, than the *sound* of the wind that blows now, is individually the same with the sound of the wind that blew just before; which, though it be like it, is not the same, any more than the agitated *air*, that makes the sound, is the same; or than the *water*, flowing in a river, that now passes by, is individually the same with that which passed a little before. And if it be thus with the brightness or colour of the moon, so it must be with its *solidity*, and every thing else belonging to its substance, if all be, each moment, as much the immediate effect of a *new* exertion or application of power.

The matter may perhaps be in some respects still more clearly illustrated thus.—The *images* of things in a *glass*, as we keep our eye upon them, seem to remain precisely the same, with a continuing perfect identity. But it is known to be otherwise. Philosophers well know, that these images are constantly *renewed*, by the impression and reflection of *new* rays of light; so that the image impressed by the former rays is constantly vanishing, and a *new* image impressed by *new* rays every moment, both on the glass and on the eye. The image constantly renewed, by new successive rays, is no more numerically the same, than if it were by some artist put on anew with a pencil, and the colours constantly vanishing as fast as put on. And the new images being put on *immediately* or instantly, do not make them the same, any more than if it were done with the intermission of an *hour* or a *day*. The image that exists this moment, is not at all *derived* from the image which existed the last preceding moment: for, if the succession of new *rays* be intercepted, by something interposed between the object and the glass, the image immediately ceases; the *past existence* of the image has no influence to uphold it, so much as for one moment. Which shows, that the image is altogether new-made every moment; and strictly speaking, is in no part numerically the same with that which existed the moment preceding. And truly so the matter must be with the *bodies* themselves, as well as their images: they also cannot be the same, with an absolute identity, but must be wholly renewed every moment, if the case be as has been proved, that their present existence is not, strictly speaking, at all the effect of their past existence; but is wholly, every instant, the effect of a new agency, or exertion of the powerful cause of their existence. If so, the existence caused is every instant a new effect, whether the cause be *light*, or immediate *divine power*, or whatever it be.

poses; several of which differences have been observed; and every kind is ordered, regulated, and limited, in every respect, by *divine constitution.* Some things, existing in different times and places, are treated by their Creator as one in *one respect*, and others in *another;* some are united for *this communication*, and others for *that;* but all according to the *sovereign pleasure* of the fountain of all being and operation.

It appears, particularly, from what has been said, that all oneness, by virtue whereof *pollution* and *guilt* from *past* wickedness are derived, depends entirely on a *divine establishment.* It is this, and this only, that must account for guilt and an evil taint on any individual soul, in consequence of a crime committed twenty or forty years ago, remaining still, and even to the end of the world, and for ever. It is this that must account for the continuance of any such thing, and where, as *consciousness* of acts that are past; and for the continuance of all *habits*, either good or bad: and on this depends every thing that can belong to *personal identity.* And all communications, derivations, or continuation of qualities, properties, or relations, natural or moral, from what is *past*, as if the subject were *one*, depends on no other foundation.

And I am persuaded, that no solid reason can be given, why God—who constitutes all other created union or oneness according to his pleasure, and for what purposes, communications, and effects he pleases—may not establish a constitution whereby the natural *posterity* of *Adam*, proceeding from him, much as the buds and branches from the stock or root of a tree, should be treated as *one* with him, for the derivation, either of righteousness, and communion in rewards, or of the loss of righteousness, and consequent corruption and guilt.*

As I said before, all oneness in created things, whence qualities and relations are derived, depends on a divine constitution that is *arbitrary*, in every other respect, excepting that it is regulated by divine wisdom. The wisdom which is exercised in these constitutions, appears in these two things. *First*, in a beautiful *analogy* and *harmony* with *other* laws or constitutions, especially, relating to the same subject; and *secondly*, in the good *ends* obtained, or useful *consequences* of such a constitution. If therefore there be any objection still lying against this constitution with Adam and his posterity, it must be, that it is not sufficiently *wise* in these respects. But what extreme *arrogance* would it be in us, to take upon us to act as judges of the beauty and wisdom of the laws and established constitutions of the supreme Lord and Creator of the universe! And not only so, but if this constitution, in particular, be well considered, its wisdom, in the two forementioned respects, may easily be made evident. There is an apparent manifold *analogy* to other constitutions and laws, established and maintained through the whole system of vital nature in this lower world; all parts of which, in all successions, are derived from the *first of the kind*, as from their root, or fountain; each deriving from thence all properties and qualities, that are proper to the nature and capacity of the species: no *derivative* having any one perfection, unless it be what is merely circumstantial, but what was in its *primitive.* And that Adam's posterity should be without that *original righteousness*, which Adam had lost, is also *analogous* to other laws and establishments, relating to the nature of mankind; according to which, Adam's posterity have no one perfection of nature, in any kind, superior to what was in him, when the human race began to be propagated from him.

And as such a constitution was *fit and wise* in other respects, so it was in this that follows. Seeing the divine constitution concerning the *manner* of mankind coming into existence, was such as did so naturally *unite* them, and make them in so many respects *one*, naturally leading them to a close union in society, and manifold intercourse, and mutual dependence—things were wisely so established, that all should naturally be in one and the same *moral state;* and not in such exceeding different states, as that some should be perfectly *innocent* and holy, but others *corrupt* and wicked; some needing a *Saviour*, but others needing none; some in a confirmed state of perfect *happiness*, but others in a state of public condemnation to perfect and eternal *misery;* some justly exposed to great calamities in this world, but others by their innocence raised above all suffering. Such a vast diversity of state would by no means have agreed with the natural and necessary constitution and unavoidable situation and circumstances of the world of mankind; *all made of one blood, to dwell on all the face of the earth*, to be united and blended in society, and to partake together in the natural and common goods and evils of this lower world.

Dr. T. urges,† that *sorrow and shame* are only for *personal* sin; and it has often been urged, that *repentance* can be for no other sin. To which I would say, that the use of *words* is very arbitrary: but that men's *hearts* should be deeply affected with grief and humiliation before God, for the pollution and guilt which they bring into the world with them, I think, is not in the least *unreasonable.* Nor is it a thing strange and unheard of, that men should be *ashamed* of things done by *others*, in whom they are nearly concerned. I am sure, it is not *unscriptural;* especially when they are justly looked upon in the sight of God, who sees the disposition of their hearts, as fully *consenting* and *concurring.*

From what has been observed it may appear, there is no sure ground to conclude, that it must be an absurd and impossible thing, for the race of mankind truly to partake of the *sin* of the first apostacy, so as that this, in reality and propriety, shall become *their* sin; by virtue of a real *union* between the root and branches of mankind, (truly and properly availing to such a consequence,) established by the author of the whole system of the universe; to whose establishments are owing all propriety and reality of *union*, in any part of that system; and by virtue of the full *consent* of the hearts of Adam's posterity to that first apostacy. And therefore the sin of the apostacy is not theirs, merely because God *imputes* it to them; but it is *truly* and *properly* theirs, and on that *ground* God imputes it to them.

By reason of the established *union* between Adam and his posterity, the case is far otherwise between him and them, than it is between distinct parts or individuals of Adam's race; betwixt whom is no such constituted *union:* as, between children and other ancestors. Concerning whom is apparently to be understood that place, Ezek. xviii. 1—20.‡ Where God reproves the *Jews* for the use they made of that proverb, "The fathers have eaten sour grapes, and the children's teeth are set on edge;" and tells them, that hereafter they shall no more have *occasion* to use this proverb; and that if a *son* sees the wickedness of his *father*, and sincerely *disapproves* it and *avoids* it, and he himself is righteous, *he shall not die for the iniquity of his father; that all souls, both the soul of the father and the son are his, and that therefore the son shall not bear the iniquity of his father, nor the father bear the iniquity of the son; but the soul that sinneth, it shall die; that the righteousness of the righteous shall be upon him, and the wickedness of the wicked shall be upon him.* The thing *denied*, is

* I appeal to such as are not wont to content themselves with judging by a superficial appearance and view of things, but are habituated to examine things strictly and closely, that they may judge righteous judgment, whether on supposition that all mankind had *co-existed*, in the manner mentioned before, any good reason can be given, why their Creator might not, if he had pleased, have established such an *union* between Adam and the rest of mankind, as was in that case supposed. Particularly, if it had been the case, that Adam's posterity had actually, according to the law of nature, some how *grown out of him*, and yet remained *contiguous* and literally *united to him*, as the branches to a tree, or the members of the body to the head; and had all, before the fall, existed together at the *same time*, though in *different places*, as the head and members are in different places: in this case who can determine, that the Author of nature might not, if it had pleased him, have established such an *union* between the root and branches of this complex being, as that all should constitute *one* moral whole; so that by the law of union, there should be a communion in each *moral alteration*, and that the heart of every *branch* should at the same moment participate with the heart of the *root*, be conformed to it and concurring with it in all its affections and acts, and so jointly partaking in its state, as a *part of the same thing?* Why might not God, if he had pleased, have fixed such a kind of union as this, an union of the various parts of such a *moral whole*, as well as many other unions, which he has actually fixed, according to his sovereign pleasure? And if he might, by his sovereign constitution, have established such an union of the various branches of mankind, when existing in different *places*, I do not see why he might not also do the same, though they exist in different *times.* I know not why succession, or diversity of *time*, should make any such constituted union more unreasonable, than diversity of *place.* The only reason, why diversity of *time* can seem to make it unreasonable, is that difference of time shows, there is no absolute identity of the things existing in those different times: but it shows this, I think, not at all more than the difference of the *place* of existence.

† Page 14.

‡ Which Dr. T. alleges, p. 10, 11. S.

communion in the guilt and punishment of the sins of others, that are distinct parts of Adam's race; and expressly, in that case, where there is *no consent and concurrence*, but a sincere disapprobation of the wickedness of ancestors. It is declared, that *children* who are *adult* and come to act for themselves, who are *righteous*, and do not approve of, but sincerely condemn, the wickedness of their *fathers*, shall not be punished for their disapproved and avoided iniquities. The *occasion* of what is here said, as well as the *design* and plain sense, shows, that nothing is intended in the least degree *inconsistent* with what has been supposed concerning Adam's posterity sinning and falling in *his apostacy*. The *occasion* is, the people's murmuring at God's methods under the *Mosaic* dispensation; agreeable to that in Levit. xxvi. 39. "And they that are left of you, shall pine away in their iniquity in their enemies' land, and also in the iniquities of their fathers shall they pine away with them:" and other parallel places, respecting external judgments, which were the punishments most plainly threatened, and chiefly insisted on, under that dispensation, (which was, as it were, an *external* and *carnal* covenant,) and particularly the people suffering such terrible judgments in *Ezekiel's* time, for the sins of *Manasseh;* according to what God says by *Jeremiah*, (Jer. xv. 4.) and agreeable to what is said in that confession, Lam. v. 7. "Our fathers have sinned and are not, and we have borne their iniquities."

In what is said here, there is a special respect to the gospel-dispensation; as is greatly confirmed by comparing this place with Jer. xxxi. 29—31. Under which dispensation, the righteousness of God's dealings with mankind would be more fully manifested, in the clear revelation then to be made of the method of God's *judgment*, by which the *final state* of wicked men is determined; which is not according to the behaviour of their particular *ancestors;* but every one is dealt with according to the sin of *his own* wicked heart, or sinful nature and practice. The affair of *derivation* of the natural corruption of mankind in general, and of their consent *to*, and participation *of*, the *primitive* and *common* apostacy, is not in the least intermeddled with, by any thing meant in the true scope and design of this place in *Ezekiel*.

On the whole, if any do not like the *philosophy* or the *metaphysics* (as some perhaps may choose to call it) made use of in the foregoing reasonings; yet I cannot doubt, but that a proper consideration of what is apparent and undeniable in *fact*, with respect to the *dependence* of the state and course of things in the universe on the sovereign *constitutions* of the supreme Author and Lord of all—who *gives account* to none *of any of his matters*, and *whose ways are past finding out*—will be sufficient, with persons of common modesty and sobriety, to stop their mouths from making peremptory decisions against the *justice* of God, respecting what is so plainly and fully taught in *his holy word*, concerning the *derivation* of depravity and guilt from Adam to his posterity.

This is enough, one would think, for ever to silence such bold expressions as these—"If this be *just*,—if the *Scriptures* teach such doctrine, &c. then the Scriptures are of *no use*—understanding is *no* understanding,—and, *what* a God must *he* be, that can thus *curse* innocent creatures!—Is *this* thy God, O *Christian!*"—&c. &c.

It may not be improper here to add something (by way of supplement to this chapter, in which we have had occasion to say so much about the *imputation* of *Adam's* sin) concerning the opinions of *two divines*, of no inconsiderable note among the *dissenters* in *England*, relating to a *partial imputation* of *Adam's* first sin.

One of them supposes, that this sin, though truly *imputed* to INFANTS, so that thereby they are exposed to a proper *punishment*, yet is not imputed to them in such a *degree*, as that upon this account they should be liable to *eternal* punishment, as *Adam* himself was, but only to *temporal death*, or *annihilation; Adam* himself, the immediate actor, being made infinitely *more guilty* by it, than his posterity. On which I would observe; that to suppose, God imputes not *all* the guilt of *Adam's* sin, but only some *little part* of it, relieves nothing but one's *imagination*. To think of poor little *infants* bearing such torments for *Adam's* sin, as they sometimes do in this world, and these torments ending in death and annihilation, may sit easier on the imagination, than to conceive of their suffering eternal misery for it. But it does not at all relieve one's *reason*. There is no rule of reason, that can be supposed to lie against imputing a sin in the *whole* of it, which was committed by one, to another who did not personally commit it, but what will also lie against its being so imputed and punished in *part*. For all the reasons (if there be any) lie against the *imputation;* not the *quantity* or *degree of what is imputed*. If there be any rule of reason, that is strong and good, lying against a proper derivation or communication of guilt, from one that acted, to another that did not act; then it lies against *all* that is of this nature. The force of the reasons brought against imputing Adam's sin to his posterity (if there be any force in them) lies in this, That Adam and his posterity are not *one*. But this lies as properly against charging a *part* of the guilt, as the whole. For Adam's posterity, by not being the same with him, had no more hand in a *little* of what was done, than the whole. They were as absolutely free from being concerned in that act *partly*, as they were *wholly*. And there is no reason to be brought, why one man's sin cannot be justly reckoned to another's account, who was not then in being, in the *whole* of it; but what will as properly lie against its being reckoned to him in any *part*, so as that he should be subject to any condemnation or punishment on that account. If those reasons are good, all the *difference* is this; that to bring a *great* punishment on infants for Adam's sin, is a *great* act of injustice, and to bring a comparatively *smaller* punishment, is a *smaller* act of injustice; but not, that this is not *as truly and demonstrably* an act of injustice, as the other.

To illustrate this by an instance something parallel. It is used as an argument why I may not exact from one of my neighbours, what was due to me from *another*, that *he* and *my debtor* are *not the same;* and that their concerns, interests, and properties are entirely distinct. Now if this argument be good, it lies as truly against my demanding from him a *part* of the debt, as the whole. Indeed it is a *greater* act of injustice for me to take from him the *whole* of it, than a part; but not *more truly* and *certainly* an act of injustice.

The *other* divine thinks, there is truly an imputation of Adam's sin, so that infants cannot be looked upon as *innocent* creatures; yet seems to think it *not agreeable to the perfections of God*, to make the state of infants in another world *worse* than a state of *non-existence*. But this to me appears plainly a *giving up* of that grand point of *imputation*, both in whole and in part. For it supposes it to be not right, for God to bring any *evil* on a child of *Adam*, which is innocent as to personal sin, without *paying for it*, or balancing it with *good;* so that still the state of the child shall be as *good* as could be demanded in *justice*, in case of mere *innocence*. Which plainly supposes, that the child is not exposed to any proper *punishment* at all, or is not at all in *debt* to divine justice, on account of *Adam's* sin. For if the child were truly in *debt*, then surely *justice* might *take* something from him, *without paying for it*, or without *giving* that which makes its state as *good*, as mere *innocence* could in justice require. If he owes the suffering of some *punishment*, then there is no need that justice should *requite* the infant for suffering that punishment; or *make up for it*, by conferring some *good*, that shall countervail it, and in effect remove and disannul it; so that, on the whole, *good* and *evil* shall be at even *balance*, yea, so that the scale of *good* shall *preponderate*. If it is *unjust* in a judge, to order any quantity of money to be taken from another, without paying him again, and fully making it up to him, it must be because he had justly *forfeited none* at all.

It seems to me pretty manifest, that none can, in good consistence with themselves, own a real *imputation* of the guilt of Adam's first sin to his posterity, without owning that they are *justly* treated as *sinners*, truly guilty, and *children of wrath*, on that account; nor unless they allow a just imputation of the *whole* of the *evil* of that transgression; at least, all that pertains to the essence of that act, as a full and complete violation of the *covenant*, which God had established; even as much as if each one of mankind had the like covenant established with him singly, and had by the like direct and full act of rebellion, violated it for himself.

CHAP. IV.

WHEREIN SEVERAL OTHER OBJECTIONS ARE CONSIDERED.

DR. T. objects against Adam's posterity being supposed to come into the world under a *forfeiture* of God's *blessing*, and subject to his curse through his sin,---That at the RESTORATION of the world after the flood, *God pronounced equivalent or greater* BLESSINGS on Noah and his sons, than he did on Adam at his creation, when he said, *be fruitful, and multiply, and replenish the earth, and have dominion over the fish of the sea, &c.**---To this I answer, in the following remarks.

1. As has been already shown, that in the *threatening* denounced for Adam's sin, there was nothing which appears *inconsistent* with the *continuance* of this *present* life for a season, or with *propagating* his kind; so for the like reason, there appears nothing in that threatening, upon the supposition that it reached Adam's posterity, *inconsistent* with enjoying the *temporal blessings* of the present life, as long as this is continued; even those temporal blessings which God pronounced on Adam at his first creation. For it must be observed, that the blessings which God pronounced on Adam when he created him, and *before the trial of his obedience*, were not the same with the blessings which were *suspended on his obedience.* The blessings thus suspended, were the blessings of *eternal life;* which, if he had maintained his integrity through his trial, would have been pronounced upon him *afterwards;* when God, as his judge, should have given him his reward. God might indeed, if he had pleased, *immediately* have deprived him of *life*, and of all *temporal blessings*, given him before. But those blessings pronounced on him before-hand, were not the things for the obtaining of which his *trial* was appointed. These were *reserved* till the *issue* of his trial should be seen, and *then* to be pronounced in the blessed sentence, which would have been passed upon him by his judge, when God came to decree to him his reward for his approved fidelity. The pronouncing of these latter blessings on a degenerate race, that had fallen under the *threatening* denounced, would indeed (without a redemption) have been inconsistent with the *constitution* which had been established. But giving them the *former* kind of blessings, which were not the things suspended on the trial, or dependent on his fidelity, (and these to be continued for a season,) was not at all inconsistent therewith.

2. It is no more an evidence of *Adam's* posterity being not included in the threatening denounced for his eating the forbidden fruit, That they still have the *temporal* blessings of fruitfulness, and a dominion over the creatures, *continued* to them; than it is an evidence of Adam being not included in that threatening himself, That *he* had these blessings *continued* to him, was fruitful, and had dominion over the creatures, *after his fall*, equally with his posterity.

3. There is good evidence, that the benedictions God pronounced on Noah and his posterity, were granted on a *new foundation;* a dispensation *diverse* from any grant, promise, or revelation, which God gave to *Adam*, antecedently to his fall; even on the foundation of the *covenant of grace*, established in *Christ Jesus;* a dispensation, the design of which is to deliver men from the *curse* that came upon them by Adam's sin, and to bring them to *greater* blessings than ever *he* had. These blessings were pronounced on Noah and his seed, on the same foundation whereon afterwards the blessing was pronounced on *Abraham* and his seed, which included both spiritual and temporal benefits.—*Noah* had his name prophetically given him by his father *Lamech*, because by him and his seed deliverance should be obtained from the *curse*, which came by *Adam's* fall. Gen. v. 29. "And he called his name *Noah, (i. e. rest,)* saying, This same shall comfort us concerning our work, and toil of our hands, because of the ground which the Lord hath cursed." Pursuant to the scope and intent of this *prophecy* (which indeed seems to respect the same thing with the prophecy in Gen. iii. 15.) are the blessings pronounced on *Noah* after the flood. There is this evidence of these blessings being conveyed through the channel of the covenant of grace, and by the redemption through Jesus Christ, that they were obtained by *sacrifice;* or were bestowed as the effect of *God's favour* to mankind, which was in consequence of *smelling a sweet savour* in the sacrifice which Noah offered. And it is very evident by the epistle to the *Hebrews*, that the ancient sacrifices never obtained the favour of God, but only by virtue of the *relation* they had to the sacrifice of *Christ.*—Now that *Noah* and his family had been so wonderfully saved from the wrath of God, which had destroyed the rest of the world, and the world was as it were restored from a ruined state, there was a proper occasion to point to the *great salvation* to come by Christ: as it was a common thing for God, on occasion of some great *temporal* salvation of his people, or restoration from a low and miserable state, to renew the intimations of the great *spiritual* restoration of the world by *Christ's redemption.* † God deals with the generality of mankind, in their present state, far differently, on occasion of the redemption by Jesus Christ, from what he otherwise would do; for, being capable subjects of saving mercy, they have a day of patience and grace, and innumerable temporal blessings bestowed on them; which, as the apostle signifies, (Acts xiv. 17.) are testimonies of God's reconcilableness to sinful men, to put them upon *seeking after God.*

But beside the sense in which the posterity of *Noah* in general partake of these blessings of *dominion over the creatures*, &c. *Noah* himself, and all such of his posterity as have obtained like precious *faith* with that exercised by him in offering his *sacrifice*, which made it a *sweet savour*, and by which it procured these blessings, have *dominion* over the creatures, through Christ, in a more excellent sense than Adam in innocency; as they are *made kings and priests unto God, and reign with Christ*, and *all things are theirs*, by a covenant of *grace.* They partake with Christ in that *dominion over the beasts of the earth, the fowls of the air, and fishes of the sea*, spoken of in the 8th *Psalm;* which is by the apostle interpreted of *Christ's* dominion over the world, (1 Cor. xv. 27. and Heb. ii. 7.) And the time is coming, when the greater part of the posterity of *Noah*, and each of his sons, shall partake of this more honourable and excellent dominion over the creatures, through him *in whom all the families of the earth shall be blessed.* Neither is there any need of supposing that these blessings have their most complete accomplishment, till many ages after they were granted, any more than the blessing on Japhet, expressed in those words, *God shall enlarge Japhet, and he shall dwell in the tents of Shem.*

But that Noah's posterity have such *blessings* given them through the great *Redeemer*, who suspends and removes the *curse* which came through Adam's sin, surely is no argument, that they originally, as in their natural state, are not under the *curse.* That men have blessings *through grace*, is no evidence of their being not justly exposed to the curse *by nature;* but it rather argues the contrary. For if they did not deserve the *curse*, they would not depend on *grace and redemption* for the removal of it, and for bringing them into a state of favour with God.

Another *objection*, which our author strenuously urges against the doctrine of original sin, is, that it *disparages* the divine *goodness* in giving us our *being;* which we ought to receive with *thankfulness*, as a great gift of God's beneficence, and look upon as the first, original, and fundamental fruit of the divine liberality.‡

To this I answer, in the following observations:

1. This argument is built on the supposed *truth* of a thing in *dispute;* and so is a *begging of the question.* It is built on this supposition, that we are not properly looked upon as *one* with our *first father*, in the state wherein God at first created him, and in his fall from that state. If we *are* so, it becomes the whole race to acknowledge God's great *goodness* to them, in the state wherein mankind was made *at first;* in the *happy* state they were then in, and the fair

* See page 82, &c. S.

† It may be noted, that Dr. T. himself signifies it as his mind, that these blessings on *Noah* were on account of the *covenant of grace*, p. 84, 90, 91, 92. S.

‡ Page 256, 357, 260. 71–74. S.

opportunity they then had of obtaining *confirmed and eternal happiness;* and to acknowledge it as an aggravation of their apostacy; and to humble themselves, that they were so ungrateful as to rebel against their good Creator. Certainly, we may all do this with as much reason, as the people of Israel in Daniel's and Nehemiah's times who did with thankfulness acknowledge God's great goodness to *their fathers,* many ages before; and in their confessions they bewailed, and took shame to themselves, for the sins committed by their *fathers,* notwithstanding such great goodness. (See the 9th chapter of Daniel, and the 9th of Nehemiah.)

2. If Dr. T. would imply in his objection, that it doth not consist with the *goodness* of God, to give mankind being in a state of *misery,* what ever was done before by Adam, whether he sinned or did not sin. I reply, if it be justly so ordered, that there should be a posterity of Adam, which must be looked upon as *one with him;* then it is no more contrary to God's attribute of goodness to give being to his posterity in a state of punishment, than to *continue* the being of the *same* wicked and guilty person, who has made himself guilty, in a state of punishment. The *giving* of being, and the continuing of being, are both *alike* the work of God's power and will, and both are alike fundamental to all blessings of man's present and future existence. And if it be said, it cannot be justly so ordered, that there should be a posterity of Adam, which should be looked upon as *one* with him, this is *begging the question.*

3. If our author would have us to suppose, that it is contrary to the attribute of goodness for God, in *any case,* by an immediate act of his power, to cause *existence,* and to cause *new* existence, which shall be an exceeding *miserable* existence, by reason of exposedness to eternal ruin; then *his own* scheme must be supposed *contrary* to the attribute of God's goodness: for he supposes that God will raise multitudes from the dead at the last day (which will be giving new existence to their bodies, and to bodily life and sense) in order only to their suffering eternal destruction.

4. Notwithstanding we are so sinful and miserable, as we are by nature, yet we may have great reason to bless God, that he has given us our being under so glorious a dispensation of *grace* through Jesus Christ: by which we have a happy opportunity to be *delivered* from this sin and misery, and to obtain unspeakable eternal *happiness.* And because, through our own wicked inclinations, we are disposed so to neglect and abuse this mercy, as to fail of final benefit by it, this is no reason why we ought not to be *thankful* for it, even according to our author's own sentiments. What (says he*) if *the whole world lies in wickedness,* and few therefore shall be saved? Have men no *reason* to be *thankful,* because they are wicked and ungrateful, and abuse their being and God's bounty? Suppose our own *evil inclinations* do withhold us, *viz.* from seeking after happiness, of which under the light of the gospel we are placed within the nearer and easier reach, "suppose, the whole Christian world should lie in wickedness, and but few Christians should be saved, is it therefore certainly true, that we cannot reasonably *thank* God for the gospel?" Well, and though the *evil inclinations,* which hinder our seeking and obtaining happiness by so glorious an advantage, are what we are *born* with, yet if those inclinations are *our fault or sin,* that alters not the case: and to say, they are *not* our sin, is still begging the question. Yea, it will follow from several things asserted by our author, that notwithstanding men are *born* in such circumstances, as that they are under a very great *improbability* of ever becoming *righteous,* yet they may have *reason to be thankful* for their being. Thus particularly, Dr. T. asserts, that all men have reason of thankfulness for their being; and yet he supposes, that the *heathen* world, taken as a collective body, were *dead in sin,* and could not deliver or help themselves, and therefore stood in necessity of the christian dispensation. And not only so, but he supposes, that the *christian* world is now at length brought to the *like* deplorable and helpless circumstances, and needs a *new* dispensation for its relief. According to these things, the world in general, not only formerly but even at this day, are *dead in sin,* and helpless as to their salvation; and therefore the generality of them that are born into it, are much more *likely* to perish, than otherwise, till the *new* dispensation comes: and yet he supposes, we all have reason to be thankful for our being. Yea, further still, I think, according to our author's doctrine, men may have great reason to be *thankful* to God for bringing them into a state, which yet, as the case is, is attended with *misery,* as its *certain* consequence. As, with respect to God's *raising* the wicked to life, at the last day; which, he supposes, is in itself a great *benefit,* procured by Christ, and the wonderful *grace* of God through him: and if it be the fruit of God's wonderful grace, surely men ought to be *thankful* for that grace, and praise God for it. Our doctrine of original sin, therefore, no more disparages God's goodness in man's *formation* in the womb, than *his* doctrine disparages God's goodness in their *resurrection* from the grave.

Another argument, which Dr. T. makes use of, against the doctrine of original sin, is what the Scripture reveals of the process of the day of *judgment;* which represents the judge as dealing with men *singly and separately,* rendering to *every* man according to *his* deeds, and according to the improvement he has made of the particular powers and talents God has given *him* personally.†

But this objection will vanish, if we consider what is the *end* or *design* of that public judgment. Now this will not be, that God may *find out* what men are, or what punishment or reward is proper for them, or in order to the passing of a right judgment of these things within himself, which is the end of human trials; but it is to *manifest* what men are to their own consciences, and to the world. As the day of judgment is called *the day of the* revelation *of the righteous judgment of God;* in order to this, God will make use of *evidences,* or *proofs.* But the proper evidences of the wickedness of men's *hearts* (the true seat of all wickedness) both as to corruption of nature, and additional pollution and guilt, are men's *works.*

The special end of God's public judgment will be, to make a proper, perfect, open *distinction* among men, rightly to state and manifest their *difference* one from another, in order to that separation and difference in the eternal retribution that is to follow: and this difference will be made to appear, by their *personal works.*

There are two things, with regard to which men will be tried, and openly *distinguished,* by the perfect judgment of God at the last day; according to the twofold *real distinction* subsisting among mankind: *viz.* (1.) The *difference of* STATE; that *primary* and grand distinction, whereby all mankind are divided into two sorts, the righteous and the wicked. (2.) That *secondary distinction,* whereby both sorts differ from others in the *same* general state, in DEGREES of additional fruits of righteousness and wickedness. Now the Judge, in order to *manifest* both these, will judge men *according to their* personal *works.* But to inquire at the day of judgment, whether *Adam* sinned or no, or whether men are to be looked upon as one with him, and so partakers in his sin, is what in no respect tends to manifest either of these distinctions.

1. The *first* thing to be manifest, will be the *state,* that each man is in, with respect to the *grand distinction* of the whole world of mankind into *righteous* and *wicked;* or, in metaphorical language, *wheat* and *tares;* or, the *children of the kingdom* of Christ, and the *children of the wicked one;* the latter, the head of the apostacy; but the former, the head of the restoration and recovery. The Judge, in manifesting this, will prove men's hearts by *their works,* in such as have had opportunity to perform any works in the body. The *evil works* of the children of the *wicked one* will be the proper *manifestation* and evidence or proof of whatever belongs to the general state of such; and particularly they will prove, that they belong to the kingdom of the great deceiver, and head of the apostacy, as they will demonstrate the exceeding corruption of their nature, and full consent of their hearts to the common apostacy; and also that their hearts never relinquished the apostacy, by a cordial adherence to Christ, the great re-

* Page 72, 73. S.

† Page 65, 66, 111. S.

storer. The Judge will also make use of the *good works* of the *righteous* to show their interest in the redemption of Christ; as thereby will be manifested the sincerity of their hearts in their acceptance of, and adherence to, the Redeemer and his righteousness. And in thus proving the state of men's hearts by their actions, the *circumstances* of those actions must necessarily come into consideration, to manifest the true *quality* of their actions; as, each one's talents, opportunities, advantages, light, motives, &c.

2. The other thing to be manifested, will be that *secondary distinction*, wherein particular persons, both righteous and wicked, differ from one another, in the *degree* of secondary good or evil; the *degree* of evil fruit, which is additional to the guilt and corruption of the whole body of apostates and enemies; and the *degree* of personal goodness and good fruit, which is a secondary goodness, with respect to the righteousness and merits of Christ, which belong to all by that sincere faith manifested in all. Of this also each one's *works*, with their circumstances, opportunities, talents, &c. will be the proper evidence.

As to the nature and aggravations of the general apostacy by *Adam's* sin, and also the nature and sufficiency of the redemption by *Jesus Christ*, the great restorer, though both these will have vast *influence* on the eternal state, which men shall be adjudged to, yet neither of them will properly belong to the *trial* men will be the subjects of at that day, in order to the *manifestation* of their *state*, wherein they are *distinguished one from another*. They will belong to the business of that day no otherwise, than the manifestation of the great *truths* of religion in general; as the nature and perfections of God, the dependence of mankind on God, as their creator and preserver, &c. Such truths as these will also have great influence on the eternal state, to which men will then be adjudged, as they aggravate the guilt of man's wickedness, and must be considered in order to a due estimate of Christ's righteousness, and men's personal virtue; yet being of general and equal concernment, will not properly belong to the trial of particular persons.

Another thing urged by our author particularly against the *imputation* of Adam's sin, is this: "Though, in Scripture, action is frequently said to be *imputed, reckoned, accounted* to a person, it is no other than *his own* act and deed."* In the same place he cites a number of places of Scripture, where these words are used, which he says are all that he can find in the Bible.

But we are no way concerned with this argument at present, any further than it relates to *imputation of sin*, or *sinful action*. Therefore all that is in the argument, which relates to the present purpose, is this: that the word is *so often* applied in Scripture to signify God's imputing of personal sin, but never once to his imputing of *Adam's* sin.—*So often!*—How often?—But *twice*. There are but two of all those places which he reckons up, that have any reference to God *imputing* sin to any person, where there is any evidence that only *personal* sin is meant; (Levit. xvii. 3, 4. and 2 Tim. iv. 16.) All therefore that the argument comes to, is this: that the word *impute*, is applied *twice* in Scripture to the case of God imputing sin, and neither of those times to signify the imputing of Adam's sin, but both times it has reference to *personal* sin; therefore Adam's sin is not imputed to his posterity. And this is to be noted, that one of these two places, even that in Levit. xvii. 3, 4. does not speak of imputing the *act* committed, but another *not* committed. The words are, "what man soever there be of the house of Israel, that killeth an ox or lamb or goat in the camp, or that killeth it out of the camp, and bringeth it not unto the door of the tabernacle of the congregation, to offer an offering unto the Lord, before the tabernacle of the Lord, blood shall be *imputed* unto that man; he hath shed blood; that man shall be cut off from among his people," *i. e.* plainly, *murder* shall be imputed to him: he shall be put to death for it, and therein punished with the same severity as if he had *slain a man*. It is plain by Isa. lxvi. 3. that, in some cases, shedding the blood of *beasts*, in an unlawful manner, was *imputed* to them, *as if they slew a man*.

But whether it be so or not, although in both these places the word *impute*, be applied to personal sin, and to the very act, or although this could be said of all the places which our author reckons up; yet that the word *impute*, is never expressly applied to Adam's sin, does no more argue, that it is not imputed to his posterity, than it argues, that pride, unbelief, lying, theft, oppression, persecution, fornication, adultery, sodomy, perjury, idolatry, and innumerable other particular moral evils, are never *imputed* to the persons that committed them, or in whom they are; because the word *impute*, though so often used in Scripture, is never applied to any of these kinds of wickedness.

I know not what can be said here, except one of these two things: that though these sins are not expressly said to be *imputed*, yet *other* words are used that do as plainly and certainly *imply* that they are imputed, as if it were said so expressly. Very well, and so I say with respect to the imputation of Adam's sin. The thing meant by the word *impute*, may be as plainly and certainly expressed by using other words, as if *that* word were expressly used; and *more certainly*, because the words used instead of it, may amount to an *explanation* of this word. And this, I think, is the very case here. Though the word, *impute*, is not used with respect to Adam's sin, yet it is said, *all have sinned;* which, respecting infants, can be true only of their sinning by his sin. And, it is said, *by his disobedience many were made sinners;* and, *judgment and condemnation came upon all by that sin;* and that by this means *death*, the wages of sin, *passed on all men, &c.* Which phrases amount to full and precise explanations of the word, *impute;* and therefore do more certainly determine the point really insisted on.

Or, perhaps it will be said, with respect to those personal sins before-mentioned, *pride, unbelief*, &c. it is no argument they are not *imputed* to those who are guilty of them, that the very word *impute*, is not applied to them; for the *word* itself is *rarely* used; not one time in a hundred, and perhaps five hundred, of those wherein the *thing* meant is plainly implied, or may be certainly inferred. Well, and the same also may be applied likewise, with respect to *Adam's* sin.

It is probable, Dr. T. intends an argument against original sin, by that which he says in opposition to what R. R. suggests of *children discovering the principles of iniquity, and seeds of sin, before they are capable of moral action*,† viz. That *little children are made* PATTERNS *of humility, meekness, and innocence*, (Matt. xviii. 3. 1 Cor. xiv. 20. and Psal. cxxxi. 2.)

But when the utmost is made of this, there can be no shadow of reason, to understand more by these texts, than that little children are recommended as patterns in regard of a *negative* virtue, innocence with respect to the *exercises* and *fruits* of sin, *harmlessness* as to the hurtful effects of it; and that *image* of meekness and humility arising from this, in conjunction with a natural tenderness of mind, fear, self-diffidence, yieldableness, and confidence in parents and others older than themselves. And so, they are recommended as patterns of virtue no more than *doves*, which are an harmless sort of creatures, and have an *image* of the virtues of meekness and love. Even according to Dr. T.'s own doctrine, no more can be made of it than this: for *his scheme* will not admit of any such thing as *positive* virtue, or virtuous disposition, in infants; he insisting (as was observed before) that virtue must be the fruit of *thought* and *reflection*. But there can be no thought and reflection, that produces positive virtue, in children not yet capable of *moral action;* and it is *such* children he speaks of. And that little children have a *negative* virtue or innocence, in relation to the *positive* acts and hurtful effects of vice, is no argument that they have not a *corrupt nature* within them: for let their nature be ever so corrupt, yet surely it is no wonder that they be not guilty of *positive* wicked action, before they are capable of any *moral* action at all. A young viper has a malignant *nature*, though incapable of doing a malignant action, and at present appearing a harmless creature.

Another objection, which Dr. T. and some others offer against this doctrine, is, *That it pours contempt upon the human nature.*‡

* Page 3, &c 105.

† Page 77, 78. S.

‡ Page 74, 75. S.

But their declaiming on this topic is like addressing the affections and conceits of *children*, rather than rational arguing with *men*. It seems this doctrine is not *complaisant* enough. I am sensible, it is not suited to the taste of some, who are so very *delicate* (to say no worse) that they can bear nothing but compliment and flattery. No *contempt* is by this doctrine cast upon the noble faculties and capacities of *man's nature*, or the exalted business, and divine and immortal happiness, of which he is made capable. And as to speaking ill of man's present *moral state*, I presume, it will not be denied, that *shame* belongs to them who are truly *sinful;* and to suppose, that this is not the *native* character of mankind, is still but meanly begging the question. If we, as we come into the world, are truly sinful, and consequently miserable, he acts but a *friendly* part to us, who endeavours fully to discover and manifest our disease. Whereas, on the contrary, he acts an *unfriendly* part, who to his utmost hides it from us: and so, in effect, does what in him lies to prevent our seeking a remedy from that, which if not remedied in time, must bring us finally to shame and *everlasting contempt*, and end in perfect and remediless destruction hereafter.

Another *objection*, which some have made against this doctrine, much like the former, is, that it tends to *beget in us an ill opinion of our fellow-creatures, and so to promote ill-nature and mutual hatred*.

To which I would say, if it be truly so, that we all come *sinful* into the world, then our heartily *acknowledging* it, tends to promote *humility:* but our *disowning* that sin and guilt which truly belongs to us, and endeavouring to persuade ourselves that we are vastly *better* than in truth we are, tends to a foolish *self-exaltation* and *pride*. And it is manifest, by reason, experience, and the word of God, that *pride* is the chief source of all the *contention*, mutual *hatred*, and *ill-will* which are so prevalent in the world; and that nothing so effectually promotes the *contrary* tempers and deportments, as *humility*. This doctrine teaches us to think no worse of others, than of ourselves: it teaches us, that we are *all*, as we are by nature, *companions* in a miserable helpless condition; which under a revelation of the divine mercy, tends to promote mutual *compassion*. And nothing has a greater tendency to promote those amiable dispositions of mercy, forbearance, long-suffering, gentleness, and forgiveness, than a sense of our own extreme unworthiness and misery, and the infinite need we have of the divine pity, forbearance, and forgiveness, together with a hope of obtaining mercy. If the doctrine which teaches that mankind are corrupt by nature, tends to promote *ill-will*, why should not Dr. T.'s doctrine tend to it as much? For he teaches us, that the generality of mankind are *very wicked*, having *made themselves so* by their own free choice, without any necessity: which is a way of becoming wicked, that renders men truly *worthy of resentment;* but the other, *not at all*, even according to his own doctrine.

Another *exclamation* against this doctrine is, that it tends to *hinder comfort and joy*, and to *promote melancholy* and *gloominess* of mind.*

To which I shall briefly say, doubtless, supposing men are really become sinful, and so exposed to the displeasure of God, *by whatever means*, if they once come to have their eyes opened, and are not very stupid, the reflection on their case will tend to make them *sorrowful;* and it is *fit* it should. Men, with whom this is the case, may well be filled with sorrow, till they are sincerely willing to forsake their sins, and turn to God. But there is nothing in this doctrine, that in the least stands in the way of comfort and exceeding joy, to such as find in their hearts a sincere willingness wholly to forsake all sin, and give their hearts and whole selves to Christ, and comply with the gospel-method of salvation by him.

Another thing *objected*, is, that to make men believe that wickedness belongs to their very *nature*, tends to *encourage* them in *sin*, and plainly to *lead* them to all manner of iniquity; because they are taught, that sin is *natural*, and therefore *necessary and unavoidable*.†

But if this doctrine, which teaches that *sin* is natural to us, does also at the same time teach us, that it is *never the better, or less to be condemned*, for its being natural, then it does not at all encourage sin, any more than Dr. T.'s doctrine encourages wickedness when it is become *inveterate;* who teaches that such as by custom have contracted strong habits of sin, are *unable to help themselves*.‡ And is it reasonable, to represent it as encouraging a man in boldly neglecting and wilfully continuing in his *disease*, without seeking a *cure*, to tell him of his disease, to show him that it is real and very fatal, and what *he* can never cure himself of; yet withal directing him to a great *Physician*, who is sufficient for his restoration? But for a more particular answer to what is objected against the doctrine of our natural *impotence and inability*, as being an encouragement to go on in sin, and a discouragement to the use of all means for our help, I must for brevity refer the reader to what has been largely written on this head in my discourse on the *Freedom of the Will*.

Our author is pleased to advance another notion, among others, by way of *objection* against the doctrine of original sin: that if this doctrine be true, *it would be unlawful to beget children*. He says,§ "If natural *generation* be the means of unavoidably *conveying* all sin and wickedness into the world, it must *itself* be a *sinful and unlawful* thing." Now, if there be any force of argument here, it lies in this proposition, *whatsoever is a means or occasion of the certain infallible existence of sin and wickedness, must itself be sinful*. But I imagine Dr. T. had not thoroughly weighed this proposition, nor considered where it would carry him. For, God *continuing in being* the devil, and others that are finally given up to wickedness, will be attended, most certainly and infallibly, with an eternal series of the most hateful and horrid wickedness. But will any be guilty of such vile blasphemy, as to say, therefore God's upholding of them in being is itself a *sinful* thing? In the same place our author says, "so far as we are *generated in sin*, it must be a *sin* to generate." But there is no appearance of evidence in that position, any more than in this: "So far as any is *upheld in existence* in sin, it is a *sin* to uphold them in existence." Yea, if there were any reason in the case, it would be strongest in the latter position: for parents, as Dr. T. himself observes, are not the *authors* of the *beginning* of existence: whereas, God is truly the author of the *continuance* of existence. As it is the known will of God, to continue *Satan* and millions of others *in being*, though the most sure *consequence* is the continuance of a vast infernal world, full of everlasting hellish *wickedness:* so it is part of the revealed will of God, that this world of mankind should be *continued*, and the species *propagated*, for his own wise and holy purposes; which *will is complied with* by the parents joined in lawful *marriage*. Their children, though they come into the world in sin, yet are capable subjects of eternal holiness and happiness: which infinite benefits for their children, parents have great reason to expect, in the way of giving up their children to God in faith, through a Redeemer, and bringing them up in the nurture and admonition of the Lord. I think, this may be answer enough to such a cavil.

Another *objection* is, That the doctrine of original sin is no *oftener*, and no more *plainly*, spoken of in *Scripture;* it being, if true, a very *important* doctrine. Dr. T. in many parts of his book suggests to his readers, that there are very *few texts*, in the whole Bible, wherein there is the least appearance of their teaching any such doctrine.

Of this I took notice before, but would here say further: That the reader who has perused the preceding defence of this doctrine, must now be left to judge for himself, whether there be any *ground* for such an allegation; whether there be not texts in *sufficient* number, both in the Old Testament and New, that exhibit undeniable *evidence* of this great article of christian divinity; and whether it be not a doctrine taught in the Scripture with great *plainness*. I think, there are few, if any, doctrines of revelation, taught more plainly and expressly. Indeed it is taught in an explicit manner more in the *New Testament* than in the *Old*. Which is not to be wondered at; it being thus with respect to all the most important doctrines of revealed religion.

* Page 231, and some other places.
† Page 139, and 259.

‡ See his exposition on Rom. vii. p. 205–220. But especially in his *paraphrase and notes* on the epistle.
§ Page 145.

But if it had been so, that this doctrine were but *rarely* taught in Scripture; yet if we find that it is *indeed* declared to us by God, if held forth to us by *any* word of his; then what belongs to us, is, to *believe* his word, and *receive* the doctrine which he teaches us; and not to prescribe to him how *often* he shall speak of it, and to insist upon knowing what *reasons* he has for speaking of it *no oftener*, before we will receive what he teaches us; or to pretend that he should give us an account, why he did not speak of it so *plainly* as we think he ought to have done, *sooner* than he did. In this way of proceeding, if it be reasonable, the *Sadducees* of old, who denied any resurrection or future state, might have maintained their cause against Christ, when he blamed them for *not knowing the Scriptures, nor the power of God;* and for not understanding by the Scripture, that there would be a resurrection to spiritual enjoyment, and not to animal life, and sensual gratifications; and they might have insisted, that these doctrines, if true, were very *important*, and therefore ought to have been spoken of in the Scriptures *oftener* and more *explicitly*, and not that the church of God should be left, till that time, with only a *few obscure* intimations of that which so infinitely concerned them. And they might with disdain have rejected Christ's argument, by way of *inference* from God calling himself in the books of *Moses*, the God of *Abraham, Isaac*, and *Jacob*. For answer, they might have said, that *Moses* was sent on purpose to teach the people the mind and will of God; and therefore, if these doctrines were true, he *ought in reason and in truth* to have taught them plainly and frequently, and not have left the people to spell out so important a doctrine, only from God's saying, that he was the God of *Abraham*, &c.

One great *end* of the *Scripture* is, to teach the world *what manner of being* God is; about which the world, without revelation, has been so wofully in the dark: and that *God is an infinite being*, is a doctrine of great *importance*, and a doctrine sufficiently taught in the Scripture. But yet, it appears to me, this doctrine is not taught there, in any measure, with such *explicitness* and *precision*, as the doctrine of original sin: and the *Socinians*, who denied God's omnipresence and omniscience, had as much room left them for cavil, as the *Pelagians* who deny original sin.

Dr. T. particularly urges, that *Christ* says *not one word* of this doctrine throughout the *four Gospels;* which doctrine, if true, being so important, and what so nearly concerned the great work of redemption, which he came to work out, (as is supposed,) one would think, *it should have been emphatically spoken of in every page of the Gospels.**

In reply to this, it may be observed, that by the account given in the four Gospels, Christ was continually saying, *those things* which plainly *implied*, that all men in their original state are sinful and miserable. As, when he declared, that *they which are whole, need not a physician, but they which are sick;*† That *he came to seek and to save that which was lost.*‡ That it was necessary for all to be *born again*, and to be *converted*, and that otherwise they could not *enter into the kingdom of heaven;*§—and, that all were *sinners*, as well as those whose blood *Pilate* mingled with their sacrifices, &c. and that *every one who did not repent, should perish;*||—Withal directing every one to *pray* to God for *forgiveness of sin;*¶—Using our necessity of forgiveness from God, as an argument with all to forgive the injuries of their neighbours;**—Teaching, that earthly *parents*, though kind to their children, are in themselves *evil;*††—And signifying, that things *carnal* and *corrupt* are properly *the things of men;*‡‡—Warning his disciples rather to beware of *men*, than of wild beasts;§§—Often representing the world as *evil*, as *wicked* in its works, at *enmity* with *truth* and *holiness*, and *hating him;*||||—Yea, and teaching plainly, that all men are extremely and inexpressibly sinful, owing *ten thousand talents* to their divine creditor.¶¶

And whether Christ did not plainly teach *Nicodemus* the doctrine of original total depravity, when he came to him to know what his doctrine was, must be left to the reader to judge, from what has been already observed on John iii. 1—11. And besides, Christ in the course of his preaching took the most proper method to convince men of the corruption of their nature, and to give them an effectual and practical knowledge of it, in application to themselves in particular, by teaching and urging the holy and strict *law* of God, in its extent, and spirituality, and dreadful threatenings: which, above all things, tends to search the hearts of men, and to teach them their inbred exceeding depravity; not merely as a matter of speculation, but by proper conviction of conscience; which is the only knowledge of original sin, that can avail to prepare the mind for receiving Christ's redemption; as a man's sense of his own sickness prepares him to apply in good earnest to the physician.

And as to Christ being no more frequent and particular in mentioning and inculcating this point in a *doctrinal* manner, it is probable, one reason to be given for it, is the same that is to be given for his speaking no oftener of God's *creating of the world:* which, though so important a doctrine, is scarce ever spoken of in any of Christ's discourses; and no wonder, seeing this was a matter which the *Jews*, to whom he confined his personal ministry, had all been instructed in from their forefathers, and never was called in question among them. And there is a great deal of reason, from the ancient *Jewish* writers, to suppose, that the doctrine of original sin had ever been allowed in the open profession of that people:*** though they were generally, in that corrupt time, very far from a practical

* Page 242, 243. † Matt. ix. 12. ‡ Matt. xviii. 11. Luke xix. 10.
§ Matt. xviii. 3. || Luke xiii. 1—5. ¶ Matt. vi. 12. Luke xi. 4.
** Matt. vi. 14, 15. and xviii. 35. †† Matt. vii. 11.
‡‡ Matt. xvi. 23. §§ Matt. x. 16, 17.
|||| John vii. 7. and viii. 23. and xiv. 17. and xv. 18, 19.
¶¶ Matt. xviii. 21, to the end.

*** What is found in the more ancient of the *Jewish* rabbies, who have written since the coming of Christ, is an argument of this. Many things of this sort are taken notice of by *Stapferus*, in his *Theologia Polemica* before mentioned. Some of these things which are there cited by him in *Latin*, I shall here faithfully give in *English*, for the sake of the *English* reader.

"—So *Manasseh*, concerning Human Frailty, p. 129.—Gen. viii. 21. *I will not any more curse the earth for man's sake; for the appetite of man is evil from his youth;* that is, from the time when he comes forth *from his mother's womb*. For at the same time that he sucks the breasts, he follows his *lust;* and while he is yet an infant, he is under the dominion of anger, envy, hatred, and other vices to which that tender age is obnoxious,"—"Prov. xxii. 15. *Solomon* says, *Foolishness is bound to the mind of a child.*" Concerning which place *R. Levi Ben Gersom* observes thus, "*Foolishness as it were grows to him in his very beginning.*" Concerning this sin, which is common and original to all men, *David* said, Psal. li. 5. *Behold I was begotten in iniquity, and in sin did my mother warm me.* Upon which place *Eben-Ezra* says thus: "Behold, because of the concupiscence which is *innate* in the heart of man, it is said, *I am begotten in iniquity.* And the sense is, that there is implanted in the heart of man, *jetzer harang*, an evil figment, from his nativity."

And *Manasseh Ben Israel*, de Fragil. pag. 2. "*Behold, I was formed in iniquity, and in sin hath my mother warmed me.* But whether this be understood concerning the common mother, which was *Eve*, or whether *David* spake only of his own mother, he would signify, that sin is as it were *natural*, and *inseparable* in this life. For it is to be observed, that *Eve* conceived after the transgression was committed: and as many as were begotten afterwards, were not brought forth in a conformity to the rule of right reason, but in conformity to disorderly and lustful affections." He adds, "One of the wise men of the *Jews*, namely, *R. Aha*, rightly observed, *David* would signify that it is impossible, even for pious men who excel in virtue, never to commit any sin." "*Job* also asserts the same thing with *David*, chap. xiv. 4. saying, *Who will give a clean thing for an unclean? Truly not one.*" Concerning which words *Aben-Ezra* says thus: "The sense is the same with that, *I was begotten in iniquity*, because man is made out of an unclean thing." *Stapferus*, Theolog. Polem. *tom.* iii. p. 36, 37.

Id. Ibid. p. 132, &c. So *Sal. Jarchi ad Gemaram, Cod. Schabbath*, fol. 142. p. 2. "And this is not only to be referred to *sinners;* because *all* the posterity of the *first man* are in like manner subjected to all the *curses* pronounced on him." And *Manasseh Ben Israel*, in his preface to *Human Frailty*, says, "I had a mind to show by what means it came to pass, that when the *first father* of all had *lost his righteousness*, his posterity are begotten liable to the *same punishment* with him." And *Munsterus* on the Gospel of *Matthew* cites the following words, from the book called *The Bundle of Myrrh:* "The blessed Lord said to the *first man*, when he cursed him, *Thorns and thistles shall it bring forth to thee; and thou shalt eat the herb of the field.* The thing which he means is, that because of *his* sin *all who should descend from him*, should be wicked and perverse, like *thorns and thistles*, according to that word of the Lord, speaking to the prophet: *Thorns and irritators are with thee, and thou dwellest among scorpions.* And all this is from the *serpent*, who was the devil, *Sammael*, who emitted a mortiferous and corruptive poison into *Eve*, and became the cause of death to *Adam* himself, when he eat the fruit." Remarkable is the place quoted in *Joseph de Voisin*, against *Martin Raymund*, p. 471. of Master *Menachem Rakanatensis*, sect. *Bereschit*, from *Midrasch Tehillim:* which is cited by *Hoorndekius*, against the *Jews*, in these words: "It is no wonder, that the sin of *Adam* and *Eve* is written and sealed with the king's ring, and to be propagated to all following generations; because on the day that *Adam* was created, all things were finished; so that he stood forth the perfection and completion of the whole workmanship of the world: so when *he* sinned, the *whole world* sinned; whose sin we bear and suffer. But the matter is not thus with respect to the sins of his posterity."—Thus far *Stapferus*.

Besides these, as *Ainsworth* on Gen. viii. 21. observes, "In *Bereshith Rabba*, a Hebrew commentary on this place, a rabbin is said to be asked, *When is the evil imagination put into man?* And he answered, *From the hour that he is formed.*" And in *Pool's* Synopsis it is added, from *Grotius*, "So *Rabbi Salomon* interprets Gen. viii. 21. *The imagination of man's heart*, is *evil from his youth*, of its being evil from the time that he is taken out of his mother's bowels." *Aben-Ezra* thus interprets Psal. li. 5. "*I was shapen in iniquity, and in sin did my mother conceive me;* that evil concupiscence is implanted in the heart from *childhood*, as if he were conviction of it; and many notions were then prevalent, especially among the *Pharisees*, which were indeed inconsistent with it. And though on account of these prejudices they might need to have this doctrine explained and applied to them, yet it is well known, by all acquainted with their Bibles, that Christ, for wise reasons, spake more sparingly and obscurely of several of the most important doctrines of revealed religion, relating to the necessity, grounds, nature, and way of his redemption, and the method of the justification of sinners, while he lived here in the flesh; and left these doctrines to be more plainly and fully opened and inculcated by the Holy Spirit after his ascension.

But if, after all, Christ did not speak of this doctrine often enough to suit Dr. T. he might be asked, Why he supposes Christ did no *oftener* and no more *plainly* teach some of *his*, Dr. T.'s, doctrines, which he so much insists on? As, that temporal *death* comes on all mankind by Adam; and that it comes on them by him, not as a punishment or calamity, but as a great *favour*, being made a rich benefit, and a fruit of God's abundant grace, by Christ's *redemption*, who came into the world as a second Adam for this end. Surely, if this were so, it was of vast *importance*, that it should be *known* to the church of God in all ages, who saw *death* reigning over *infants*, as well as others. If infants were indeed perfectly *innocent*, was it not needful, that the *design* of that which was such a melancholy and awful dispensation towards so many millions of innocent creatures, should be *known*, in order to prevent the worst thoughts of God from arising in the minds of the constant spectators of so mysterious and gloomy a dispensation? But why then such a *total silence* about it, for four thousand years together, and not one word of it in all the *Old Testament;* nor one word of it in all the *four Gospels:* and indeed not one word of it in the *whole Bible*, but only as forced and wrung out by Dr. T.'s arts of criticism and deduction, against the plainest and strongest evidence?

As to the arguments, made use of by many late writers, from the universal *moral sense*, and the reasons they offer from experience, and observation of the *nature* of mankind, to show that we are *born* into the world with principles of *virtue;* with a natural prevailing relish, approbation, and love of righteousness, truth, and goodness, and of whatever tends to the public welfare; with a prevailing natural disposition to dislike, to resent, and condemn what is selfish, unjust, and immoral; and a native bent in mankind to mutual benevolence, tender compassion, &c. those who have had such objections against the doctrine of original sin thrown in their way, and desire to see them particularly considered, I ask leave to refer them to a *treatise on the* nature *of true* VIRTUE, lying by me prepared for the press, which may ere long be exhibited to public view.*

CONCLUSION.

ON the whole, I observe, there are some *other* things, besides arguments, in Dr. T.'s book, which are calculated to influence the minds, and bias the judgment, of some sorts of readers. Here, not to insist on the profession he makes, in many places, of *sincerity, humility, meekness, modesty, charity*, &c. in searching after truth; and freely proposing his thoughts, with the *reasons* of them, to others;† nor on his magisterial *assurance*, appearing on many occasions, and the high *contempt* he sometimes expresses of the opinions and arguments of very excellent divines and fathers in the church of God, who have thought *differently* from him‡—*both* of which, it is not unlikely, may have a degree of influence on some of his readers—I would take some notice of another thing, observable in the writings of Dr. T. and many of the late opposers of the more peculiar doctrines of Christianity, tending (especially with *juvenile* and *unwary* readers) not a little to abate the force, and prevent the due effect, of the clearest *scripture-evidences* in favour of those important doctrines; and particularly to make void the arguments taken from the writings of the apostle *Paul*, in which those doctrines are more plainly and fully revealed, than in any other part of the Bible. What I mean, is this: These gentlemen express a *high opinion* of this apostle, and that very justly, for his eminent genius, his admirable sagacity, strong powers of reasoning, acquired learning, &c. They speak of him as a writer of masterly address, of extensive reach, and deep design, every where in his epistles, almost in every word he says. This looks exceedingly *specious:* it carries a plausible appearance of *christian zeal* and attachment to the *Holy Scriptures*, to bear such a testimony of high veneration for that great apostle, who was not only the principal instrument of propagating Christianity, but with his own hand wrote so considerable a part of the New Testament. And I am far from determining, with respect at least to some of these writers, that they are *not sincere* in their declarations; or, that all is mere *artifice*, only to make way for the reception of *their own* peculiar sentiments. However, it tends

formed in it; and by *my mother*, he understands *Eve*, who did not bear children till she had sinned. And so Kafvenaki says, *How shall I avoid sinning? My* ORIGINAL *is corrupt, and from thence are those sins.* So *Manasseh Ben Israel*, from this place (Psal. li. 5.) concludes, that not only David, but *all* mankind, ever since sin was introduced into the world, do sin from their *original.* To this purpose is the answer of Rabbi Hakkadosch which there is an account of in the Talmud. *From what time does concupiscence rule over man? From the very moment of his first formation, or from his nativity?* Ans. *From his formation.*"—Pool's Synops. in Loc.

On these things I observe, there is the greatest reason to suppose, that these old rabbies of the Jewish nation, who gave such heed to the *tradition of the elders*, would never have *received* this doctrine of *original sin*, had it not been delivered down to them from their *forefathers.* For it is a doctrine very disagreeable to those practical principles and notions, wherein the religion of the unbelieving Jews most fundamentally *differs* from the religion maintained among *Christians:* particularly their notion of *justification* by their own righteousness, and privileges as the children of Abraham, &c. without standing in need of any satisfaction, by the sufferings of the Messiah. On which account the modern Jews do now universally reject the doctrine of original sin, and corruption of nature; as Stapferus observes. And it is not at all likely, that the ancient Jews, if no such doctrine had been received by *tradition* from the fathers would have taken it up from the *Christians*, whom they had in such great contempt and enmity; especially as it is a doctrine so peculiarly agreeable to the christian notion of the *spiritual* salvation of Jesus, and so contrary to their *carnal* notions of the Messiah, and of his salvation and kingdom, and so contrary to their opinion of themselves; and a doctrine, which men in general are so apt to be prejudiced against. And besides, these rabbies do expressly refer to the opinion of their *forefathers;* as R. Manasseh says, "according to the opinion of the *ancients*, none are subject to *death*, but those which have *sinned;* for where there is *no sin*, there is *no death.*" Stapfer. tom. iii. p. 37, 38.

But we have more direct evidence, that the doctrine of original sin was truly a *received* doctrine among the ancient Jews, even before the coming of Christ. This appears by ancient Jewish writings, which were written before Christ; as, in the apocrypha, 2 Esdras iii. 21. "For the first Adam, bearing a wicked heart, transgressed, and was overcome; and so be *all* they that are *born of him.* Thus *infirmity* was made permanent; and the law also in the heart of the people, with the *malignity* of the root; so that the *good* departed away, and the *evil* abode still."—2 Esdras iv. 30. "For the grain of *evil seed* hath been sown in the heart of Adam, from the beginning; and how much ungodliness hath it brought up unto this time? And how much shall it yet bring forth, till the time of threshing shall come?" And chap. vii. 46. "It had been better, not to have given the earth unto Adam; or else, when it was given him, to have restrained him from sinning; for what profit is it, for men now in this present time, to live in heaviness, and after death to look for punishment? O thou Adam, what hast thou done? For though it was thou that sinned, *thou art not fallen alone, but we all that come of thee.*" And we read, Eccl. xxv. 24. "Of the woman came the *beginning of sin, and through her we all die.*"

As this doctrine of *original corruption* was constantly maintained in the church of God from the beginning; so from thence, in all probability, as well as from the evidence of it in universal experience, it was, that the wiser *heathens* maintained the like doctrine. Particularly Plato, that great philosopher, so distinguished for his veneration of ancient traditions, and diligent inquiries after them. Gale, in his *Court of the Gentiles*, observes as follows: "PLATO says, (Gorg. fol. 493.) *I have heard from the wise men, that we are now dead, and that the body is but our sepulchre.* And in his Timæus Locrus (fol. 103.) he says, *The cause of vitiosity is from our parents, and first principles, rather than from ourselves. So that we never relinquish those actions, which lead us to follow these primitive blemishes of our first parents.* Plato mentions the corruption of the *will*, and seems to disown any *free will* to *true* good; albeit he allows some ευφυια, or natural dispositions, to *civil* good, in some great heroes. Socrates asserted the corruption of human nature, or κακον εμφυτον.—Grotius affirms, that the philosophers acknowledged, it was *con-natural* to men to *sin.*

Seneca (Benef. 5. 14.) says, *wickedness has not its first beginning in wicked practice; though by that it is first exercised and made manifest.* And Plutarch (de sera vindicta) says *man does not first become wicked, when he first* manifests himself so: *but he hath wickedness* from the beginning; *and he shows it as soon as he finds opportunity and ability. As men rightly judge, that the sting is not first engendered in scorpions when they strike, or the poison in vipers when they bite.*—Pool's Synopsis on Gen. viii. 21.

To which may be subjoined what Juvenal says,

—Admores natura *recurrit.*
Damnatos fixa et mutari nescia.

Englished thus, in prose;

Nature, a thing fixed and not knowing how to change, returns to its wicked manners.——WATTS, *Ruin and Recovery.*

* See Dissertation concerning the Nature of True Virtue, p. 122.

† See his Preface, and p. 6. 237, 265, 267, 175. S.

‡ Page 110, 125, 150, 151, 159, 161, 183, 188. 77. S.

greatly to subserve such a purpose; as much as if it were designedly contrived, with the utmost subtilty, for that end. Hereby their incautious readers are prepared the more easily to be drawn into a belief, that they, and others in their way of thinking, have not *rightly understood* many of those things in this apostle's writings, which before seemed very *plain* to them. Thus they are prepared, by a prepossession in *favour* of these *new writers*, to entertain a favourable thought of the *interpretations* put by them upon the words and phrases of this apostle; and to admit in many passages a meaning which before lay entirely out of sight; quite foreign to all that in the view of a common reader seems to be their obvious sense; and most remote from the expositions agreed in by those who used to be esteemed the greatest divines, and best commentators. As to this apostle, being a man of no *vulgar* understanding, it is nothing strange if his meaning lies very *deep;* and no wonder then, if the superficial observation of vulgar Christians, or indeed of the herd of common divines, such as the *Westminster Assembly*, &c. falls vastly short of the apostle's reach, and frequently does not enter into the true spirit and design of his epistles. They must understand, that the *first reformers*, and indeed preachers and expositors in general, for fifteen or sixteen hundred years past, were too *unlearned* and *short-sighted*, to be capable of penetrating into the sense, or fit to make comments on the writings, of so great a man as this apostle; or else had dwelt in a cave of *bigotry* and *superstition*, too gloomy to allow them to use their own understandings with freedom, in reading the Scripture. But, at the same time, it must be understood, that there is risen up now at length, in this happy age of light and liberty, a set of men, of a more free and generous turn of mind, of a more inquisitive genius, and of better discernment. By such insinuations, they seek advantage to their cause; and thus the most unreasonable and extravagant interpretations of Scripture are palliated and recommended: so that, if the simple reader is not very much on his guard, if he does not clearly see with his own eyes, or has too much indolence, or too little leisure, thoroughly to examine for himself, he is in danger of being imposed on with delusive appearances.

But I humbly conceive, that their interpretations—particularly of the apostle Paul's writings, though in some things ingenious—are in many things extremely absurd, and demonstrably disagreeable, in the highest degree, to *his* real design, to the language he commonly uses, and to the doctrines currently taught in his epistles. Their *criticisms*, when examined, appear far more subtile, than solid; and it seems as if nothing can possibly be strong enough, nothing perspicuous enough, in any composure whatever, to stand before such *liberties* as these writers indulge. The plainest and most nervous discourse is analyzed and criticized, till it either dissolves into nothing, or becomes a thing of little significance. The Holy Scripture is subtilized into a mere mist; or made to evaporate into a thin cloud, that easily puts on any shape, and is moved in any direction, with a puff of wind, just as the manager pleases. It is not in the nature and power of language, to afford sufficient defence against such an art, so abused; as, I imagine, a due consideration of some things I have had occasion in the preceding discourse to observe, may abundantly convince us.

But this, with the rest of what I have offered on the subject, must be left with every candid reader's judgment; and the *success* of the whole must now be left with God, who knows what is agreeable to his own mind, and is able to make his own truths prevail; however mysterious they may seem to the poor, partial, narrow, and extremely imperfect views of mortals, while looking through a cloudy and delusory medium; and however disagreeable they may be to the innumerable prejudices of men's hearts:—and who has promised, that the gospel of CHRIST, such as is really *his*, shall finally be victorious; and has assured us, that the *word* which goes out of his mouth, *shall not return to him void, but shall accomplish that which he pleaseth, and shall prosper in the thing whereto he sends it.*—Let GOD arise, and plead his own cause, and glorify his own great name. AMEN.

A

TREATISE

CONCERNING

RELIGIOUS AFFECTIONS:

IN THREE PARTS.

PART I. CONCERNING THE NATURE OF THE AFFECTIONS, AND THEIR IMPORTANCE IN RELIGION.

PART II. SHOWING WHAT ARE NO CERTAIN SIGNS THAT RELIGIOUS AFFECTIONS ARE GRACIOUS, OR THAT THEY ARE NOT.

PART III. SHOWING WHAT ARE DISTINGUISHING SIGNS OF TRULY GRACIOUS AND HOLY AFFECTIONS.

Lev. ix. ult. and x. 1, 2.—And there came a fire out from before the Lord,—upon the altar;—which when all the people saw, they shouted, and fell on their faces. And Nadab and Abihu—offered strange fire before the Lord, which he commanded them not: and there went out fire from the Lord, and devoured them, and they died before the Lord.

Cant. ii. 12, 13.—The flowers appear on the earth, the time of the singing of birds is come, and the voice of the turtle is heard in our land. The fig-tree putteth forth her green figs, and the vines with the tender grape give a good smell.—Ver. 15. Take us the foxes, the little foxes which spoil the vines: for our vines have tender grapes.

PREFACE.

There is no question of greater importance to mankind, and that it more concerns every individual person to be well resolved in, than this: *What are the distinguishing qualifications of those that are in favour with God, and entitled to his eternal rewards?* Or, which comes to the same thing, *What is the nature of true religion? and wherein lie the distinguishing notes of that virtue which is acceptable in the sight of God?* But though it be of such importance, and though we have clear and abundant light in the word of God to direct us in this matter, yet there is no one point wherein professing Christians differ more one from another. It would be endless to reckon up the variety of opinions, in this point, that divide the Christian world; making manifest the truth of that declaration of our Saviour, " Strait is the gate, and narrow is the way, that leads to life, and few there be that find it.

The consideration of these things has long engaged me to attend to this matter with the utmost diligence and care, and all the exactness of search and inquiry of which I have been capable. It is a subject on which my mind has been peculiarly intent, ever since I first entered on the study of divinity.—But as to the *success* of my inquiries, it must be left to the judgment of the reader of the following treatise.

I am sensible it is difficult to judge impartially of the subject of this discourse, in the midst of the dust and smoke of present controversy, about things of this nature. As it is more difficult to *write* impartially, so it is more difficult to *read* impartially.—Many will probably be hurt, to find so much that appertains to religious affection here condemned: and perhaps indignation and contempt will be excited in others, by finding so much justified and approved. And it may be, some will be ready to charge me with inconsistence with myself, in so much approving some things, and so much condemning others; as I have found that this has always been objected to me by some, ever since the beginning of our late controversies about religion. It is a difficult thing to be a hearty zealous friend of what has been *good* and glorious in the late extraordinary appearances, and to rejoice much in it; and, at the same time, to see the evil and pernicious tendency of what has been *bad*, and earnestly to oppose that. Yet, I am *humbly* but *fully* persuaded, we shall never be in the way of truth, a way acceptable to God, and tending to the advancement of Christ's kingdom, till we do so. There is indeed something very mysterious in it, that so much good, and so much bad, should be mixed together in the *church of God*: as it is a mysterious thing, and what has puzzled and amazed many a good Christian, that there should be that which is so divine and precious, as the saving grace of God, dwelling in the same heart, with so much corruption, hypocrisy, and iniquity, in *a particular saint*. Yet neither of these is more mysterious than real. And neither of them is a new thing. It is no new thing, that much false religion should prevail, at a time of great revival; and that, at such a time, multitudes of hypocrites should spring up among true saints. It was so in that great reformation, and revival of religion, in Josiah's time; as appears by Jer. iii. 10. and iv. 3, 4. and also by the great apostacy there was in the land, so soon after his reign. So it was in that great outpouring of the Spirit upon the Jews, in the days of John the Baptist; as appears by the great apostacy of that people, so soon after so general an awakening, and the temporary religious comforts and joys of many; John v. 35. " Ye were willing for a season to rejoice in his light." So it was in those great commotions among the multitude, occasioned by the preaching of Jesus Christ. *Of the many that were then called, but few were chosen;* of the multitude that were roused and affected by his preaching—and at one time or other appeared mightily engaged, full of admiration of Christ, and elevated with joy—but few were true disciples, that stood the shock of trials, and endured to the end. Many were like the *stony* or *thorny* ground; and but few, comparatively, like the *good* ground. Of the whole heap that was gathered, great part was chaff, that the wind afterwards drove away; and the heap of wheat that was left, was comparatively small; as appears abundantly by the history of the New Testament. So it was in that great outpouring of the Spirit in the apostles' days; as appears by Matt. xxiv. 10—13. Gal. iii. 1. and iv. 11, 15. Phil. ii. 21. and iii. 18, 19. the two Epistles to the Corinthians, and many other parts of the New Testament. And so it was in the great *reformation* from popery.—It appears plainly to have been in the visible church of God, in times of great revivals, as it is with the fruit-trees in the spring; there are multitudes of blossoms, which appear fair and beautiful, and there is a promising appearance of young fruits: but many of them are of short continuance; they soon fall off, and never come to maturity.

It is not, however, to be supposed, that it will *always* be so; for, though there never will, in this world, be an entire purity, either in particular saints, by a perfect freedom from mixture of corruption; or in the church of God, without any mixture of hypocrites with saints—or counterfeit religion and false appearances of grace with true religion and real holiness—yet, it is evident, there will come a time of much greater purity in the church, than has been in ages past.* And one great reason of it will be, that at that time, God will give much greater light to his people, to distinguish between true religion and counterfeits; Mal. iii. 3. " And he shall sit as a refiner and purifier of silver: and he shall purify the sons of Levi, and purge them as gold and silver, that they may offer to the Lord an offering in righteousness." With ver. 18. which is a continuation of the prophecy of the same happy times, " Then shall ye return, and discern between the righteous and the wicked; between him that serveth God, and him that serveth him not."

It is by the mixture of counterfeit religion with true, not discerned and distinguished, that the devil has had his greatest advantage against the cause and kingdom of Christ. It is plainly by this means, principally, that he has prevailed against all revivals of religion, since the first founding of the christian church. By this he hurt the cause of Christianity, in and after the apostolic age, much more than by all the persecutions of both Jews and heathens. The apostles, in all their epistles, show themselves much more concerned at the former mischief, than the latter. By this, Satan prevailed against the reformation, begun by Luther, Zuinglius, &c. to put a stop to its progress, and bring it into disgrace, ten times more than by all the bloody and cruel persecutions of the church of Rome. By this, principally, has he prevailed against revivals of religion in our nation. By this he prevailed against New England, to quench the love and spoil the joy of her espousals, about a hundred years ago. And, I think, I have had opportunity enough to see plainly, that by this the devil has prevailed against the late great revival of religion in New England, so happy and promising in its beginning. Here, most evidently, has been the main advantage Satan has had against us; by this he has foiled us. It is by this means that the daughter of Zion in this land now lies on the ground, in such piteous circumstances, with her garments rent, her face disfigured, her nakedness exposed, her limbs broken, and weltering in the blood of her own wounds, and in no wise able to arise; and this, so quickly after her late great joys and hopes: Lam. i. 17. " Zion spreadeth forth her hands, and there is none to comfort her: the Lord hath commanded concerning Jacob, that his adversaries shall be round about him: Jerusalem is as a menstruous woman among them." I have seen the devil prevail the same way, against two great revivals of religion in this country.—Satan goes on with mankind as he began with them. He prevailed against our first parents, cast them out of paradise, and suddenly brought all their happiness and glory to an end, by appearing to be a friend to their happy state, and pretending to advance it to higher degrees. So the same cunning serpent that beguiled Eve through his subtilty, by perverting us from the simplicity that is in Christ, hath suddenly prevailed to deprive us of that fair prospect we had, a little while ago, of a kind of paradisiacal state of the church of God in New England.

After religion has revived in the church of God, and enemies appear, people that are engaged to defend its cause are commonly most exposed, where they are least sensible of danger. While they are wholly intent upon the opposition that appears *openly* before them, in order to make head against that, and while they neglect carefully to look around, the devil comes behind them, and gives a fatal stab unseen; and he has opportunity to give a more home stroke, and to wound the deeper, because he strikes at his leisure, being obstructed by no resistance or guard.

And so it is likely ever to be in the church, whenever religion revives remarkably, till we have learned well to distinguish between true and false religion, between saving affections and experiences, and those manifold fair shows, and glistering appearances, by which they are counterfeited; the consequences of which, when they are not distinguished, are often inexpressibly dreadful. *By this means*, the devil gratifies himself, that multitudes should offer to God, under the notion of acceptable service, what is indeed above all things abominable to him. *By this means*, he deceives great multitudes about the state of their souls; making them think they are something, when they are nothing; and so eternally undoes them: and not only so, but establishes many in a strong confidence of their eminent holiness, who, in God's sight, are some of the vilest hypocrites. *By this means*, he many ways damps religion in the hearts of the saints, obscures and deforms it by corrupt mixtures, causes their religious affections wofully to degenerate, and sometimes, for a considerable time, to be like the *manna* that bred worms and stank; and dreadfully insnares and confounds the minds of others, brings them into great difficulties and temptations, and entangles them in a wilderness, out of which they can by no means extricate themselves. *By this means*, Satan mightily encourages the hearts of open enemies, strengthens their hands, fills them with weapons, and makes strong their fortresses; when at the same time, religion and the church of God lie exposed to them, as a city without walls. *By this means*, he brings it to pass, that men work wickedness under a notion of doing God service, and so sin without restraint, yea with earnest forwardness and zeal, and with all their might. *By this means*, he brings in even the friends of religion, insensibly, to do the work of enemies, by destroying religion in a far more effectual manner than open enemies can do, under a notion of advancing it. *By this means*, the devil scatters the flock of Christ, and sets them one against another with great heat of spirit, under a notion of zeal for God; and religion, by degrees, degenerates into vain jangling. During the strife, Satan leads both parties far out of the right way, driving each to great extremes, one on the right hand, and the other on the left, according as he finds they are most inclined, or most easily moved and swayed, till the right path in the middle is almost wholly neglected. In the midst of this confusion, the devil has great opportunity to advance his own interest, to make it strong in ways innumerable, to get the government of all into his own hands, and to work his own will. And by what is seen of the terrible consequences of this counterfeit, when not distinguished from true religion, God's people in general have their minds unsettled in religion, and know not where to set their foot, or what to think, and many are brought into doubts, whether there be any thing at all in religion; and heresy, infidelity, and atheism greatly prevail.

Therefore, it greatly concerns us to use our utmost endeavours, clearly to discern, and have it well settled and established, wherein true religion does consist. Till this be done, it may be expected that great revivals of religion will be but of short continuance; till this be done, there is but little good to be expected of all our warm debates, in conversation and from the press, not knowing clearly and distinctly what we ought to contend for.

My design is to contribute my mite, and use my best (however feeble) endeavours to this end, in the ensuing treatise: wherein it must be noted, that it is somewhat diverse from the design of what I formerly published, which was to show *The distinguishing marks of a work of the Spirit of God*, including both his common and saving operations. What I aim at now, is to show the nature and signs of the *gracious operations* of God's Spirit, by which they are to be distinguished from all things whatsoever which are not of a saving nature. If I have succeeded in this my aim, in any tolerable measure, I hope it will tend to promote the interest of religion. And whether I have succeeded to bring any light to this subject, or not, and however my attempt may be reproached, in these captious, censorious times, I hope in the mercy of a gracious and righteous God, for the acceptance of the sincerity of my endeavours; and hope also, for the candour and prayers of the true followers of the meek and charitable Lamb of God.

* This appears plain by these texts of Scripture, Isa. lii. 1. Ezek. xliv. 6, 7, 9. Joel iii. 17. Zech. xiv. 21. Psal. lxix. 32, 35, 36. Isa. xxxv. 8, 10. chap. iv. 3, 4. Ezek. xx. 38. Ps. xxxvii. 9, 10, 11, 29.

A TREATISE

CONCERNING RELIGIOUS AFFECTIONS.

PART I.

CONCERNING THE NATURE OF THE AFFECTIONS AND THEIR IMPORTANCE IN RELIGION.

1 Peter i. 8.

Whom having not seen, ye love; in whom, though now ye see him not, yet believing, ye rejoice with joy unspeakable and full of glory.

SECT. I.

Introductory remarks respecting the affections.

In these words, the apostle represents the state of the Christians to whom he wrote, under persecutions. To these persecutions he has respect, in the two preceding verses, when he speaks of *the trial of their faith*, and of *their being in heaviness through manifold temptations.*

Such *trials* are of threefold benefit to true religion.—Hereby the *truth* of it is manifested, it appears to be indeed *true religion.* Trials, above all other things, have a tendency to distinguish true religion and false, and to cause the difference between them evidently to appear. Hence they are called by the name of *trials,* in the verse preceding the text, and innumerable other places. They try the faith and religion of professors, of what sort it is, as apparent gold is tried in the fire, and manifested, whether it be true gold or not. And the faith of true Christians, being thus tried and proved to be true, is *found to praise, and honour, and glory.*

And then, these trials not only manifest the *truth* of true religion, but they make its genuine *beauty* and *amiableness* remarkably to appear. True virtue never appears so lovely, as when it is most oppressed: and the divine excellency of real Christianity is never exhibited with such advantage, as when under the greatest trials. Then it is that true faith appears much more precious than gold; and upon this account, is *found to praise, and honour, and glory.*

Again, another benefit of such trials to true religion, is that they *purify* and *increase* it. They not only manifest it to be *true*, but also tend to *refine* it, and deliver it from those mixtures of what is false, which encumber and impede it; that nothing may be left but that which is true. They not only show the amiableness of true religion to the best advantage, but they tend to increase its beauty by establishing and confirming it; making it more lively and vigorous, and purifying it from those things that obscured its lustre and glory. As gold that is tried in the fire is purged from its alloy, and all remainders of dross, and comes forth more beautiful; so true faith being tried as gold is tried in the fire, becomes more precious; and thus also is *found unto praise, and honour, and glory.* The apostle seems to have respect to each of these benefits in the verse preceding the text.

And, in the text, the apostle observes how true religion *operated* in these Christians under their persecutions, whereby these benefits appeared in them; or what manner of operation it was, whereby their religion, under persecution, was manifested to be *true* religion in its genuine *beauty* and *amiableness*, and also appeared to be *increased* and *purified*, and so was like to be *found unto praise, and honour, and glory, at the appearing of Jesus Christ.* And there were two kinds of operation, or exercise of true religion, in them, under sufferings, that the apostle takes notice of in the text, wherein these benefits appeared.

1. *Love to Christ. Whom having not seen, ye love.* The world was ready to wonder, what strange principle it was, that influenced them to expose themselves to so great sufferings, to forsake the things that were seen, and renounce all that was dear and pleasant, which was the object of sense. They seemed to the men of the world as if they were beside themselves, and to act as though they hated themselves; there was nothing in *their* view, that could induce them thus to suffer, or to support them under and carry them through such trials. But although there was nothing that the world saw, or that the Christians themselves ever saw with their bodily eyes, that thus influenced and supported them, yet they had a supernatural principle of love to something *unseen;* they loved Jesus Christ, for they saw him spiritually, whom the world saw not, and whom they themselves had never seen with bodily eyes.

2. *Joy in Christ.* Though their outward sufferings were very grievous, yet their inward spiritual joys were greater than their sufferings; and these supported them, and enabled them to suffer with cheerfulness.

There are two things which the apostle takes notice of in the text concerning this joy. 1. The *manner* in which it rises, the way in which Christ, though unseen, is the foundation of it, *viz.* by *faith;* which is the evidence of things not seen; *In whom, though now ye see him not, yet* BELIEVING, *ye rejoice.* 2. The *nature* of this joy; *unspeakable, and full of glory. Unspeakable* in the *kind* of it; very different from worldly joys, and carnal delights; of a vastly more pure, sublime, and heavenly nature, being something supernatural, and truly divine, and so ineffably excellent! the sublimity and exquisite sweetness of which, there were no words to set forth. Unspeakable also in *degree;* it having pleased God to give them this holy joy with a liberal hand, in their state of persecution.

Their joy was *full of glory.* Although the joy was unspeakable, and no words were sufficient to describe it; yet something might be said of it, and no words more fit to represent its excellency than these, that it was *full of glory;* or, as it is in the original, *glorified joy.* In rejoicing with this joy, their minds were filled, as it were, with a glorious brightness, and their natures exalted and perfected. It was a most worthy, noble rejoicing, that did not corrupt and debase the mind, as many carnal joys do; but did greatly beautify and dignify it. It was a prelibation of the joy of heaven, that raised their minds to a degree of heavenly blessedness; it filled their minds with the light of God's glory, and made themselves to shine with some communication of that glory.

Hence the proposition or doctrine, that I would raise from these words is this, TRUE RELIGION, IN GREAT PART, CONSISTS IN HOLY AFFECTIONS.

We see that the apostle, in remarking the operations and

exercises of religion in these Christians, when it had its greatest trial by persecution, as gold is tried in the fire—and when it not only proved true, but was most pure from dross and mixtures—and when it appeared in them most in its genuine excellency and native beauty, and was found to praise, and honour, and glory—he singles out the religious affections of *love* and *joy*, as those exercises, wherein their religion did thus appear *true, pure,* and *glorious.*

Here it may be inquired, what the *affections* of the mind are?—I answer, The affections are no other, than the more vigorous and *sensible exercises of the inclination and will* of the soul.

God has endued the soul with two principal faculties: The one, that by which it is capable of *perception* and speculation, or by which it discerns and judges of things; which is called the *understanding.* The other, that by which the soul is some way *inclined* with respect to the things it views or considers: or it is the faculty by which the soul beholds things—not as an indifferent unaffected spectator, but—either as liking or disliking, pleased or displeased, approving or rejecting. This faculty is called by various names: it is sometimes called the *inclination;* and, as it respects the actions determined and governed by it, the *will:* and the *mind,* with regard to the exercises of this faculty, is often called the *heart.*

The *exercises* of this last faculty are of two sorts; either, those by which the soul is carried out towards the things in view in *approving* them, being pleased with and inclined to them; or, those in which the soul opposes the things in view, in *disapproving* them; and in being displeased with, averse from, and rejecting them.—And as the exercises of the inclination are various in their *kinds,* so they are much more various in their *degrees.* There are some exercises of pleasedness or displeasedness, inclination or disinclination, wherein the soul is carried but a little beyond a state of perfect indifference. And there are other degrees, wherein the approbation or dislike, pleasedness or aversion, are stronger; wherein we may rise higher and higher, till the soul comes to act vigorously and sensibly, and its actings are with that strength, that (through the laws of union which the Creator has fixed between soul and body) the motion of the blood and animal spirits begins to be sensibly altered: whence oftentimes arises some bodily sensation, especially about the *heart* and vitals, which are the fountain of the fluids of the body. Whence it comes to pass, that the *mind,* with regard to the exercises of this faculty, perhaps in all nations and ages, is called *the heart.* And it is to be noted, that they are these more vigorous and sensible exercises of this faculty, which are called the *affections.*

The *will,* and the *affections* of the soul, are not two faculties; the affections are not essentially distinct from the will, nor do they differ from the mere *actings* of the will and inclination, but only in the liveliness and sensibility of exercise.—It must be confessed, that language is here somewhat imperfect, the meaning of words in a considerable measure loose and unfixed, and not precisely limited by custom which governs the use of language. In some sense, the affection of the soul differs nothing at all from the will and inclination, and the will never is in any exercise further than it is *affected;* it is not moved out of a state of perfect indifference, any otherwise than as it is *affected* one way or other. But yet there are many actings of the will and inclination, that are not so commonly called *affections.* In every thing we do, wherein we act voluntarily, there is an exercise of the will and inclination. It is our inclination that governs us in our actions; but *all the actings* of the inclination and will, are not ordinarily called affections. Yet, what are commonly called affections are not essentially different from them, but only in the *degree* and *manner* of exercise. In every act of the will whatsoever, the soul either likes or dislikes, is either inclined or disinclined to what is in view. These are not *essentially* different from the affections of *love* and *hatred.* A liking or inclination of the soul to a thing, if it be in a high degree vigorous and lively, is the very same thing with the affection of *love:* and a disliking and disinclining, if in a great degree, is the very same with *hatred.* In every act of the will *for* or *towards* something not present, the soul is in some degree *inclined* to that thing; and that inclination, if in a considerable degree, is the very same with the affection of *desire.* And in every degree of an act of the will, wherein the soul approves of something present, there is a degree of pleasedness; and that pleasedness, if it be in a considerable degree, is the very same with the affection of *joy* or *delight.* And if the will disapproves of what is present, the soul is in some degree displeased, and if that displeasedness be great, it is the very same with the affection of *grief* or *sorrow.*

Such seems to be our nature, and such the laws of the union of soul and body, that there never is in any case whatsoever, any lively and vigorous exercise of the inclination, without some effect upon the body, in some alteration of the motion of its fluids, and especially of the animal spirits.—And, on the other hand, from the same laws of union, over the constitution of the body, and the motion of its fluids, may promote the exercise of the affections. But yet, it is not the body, but the mind only, that is the proper seat of the affections. The body of man is no more capable of being really the subject of love or hatred, joy or sorrow, fear or hope, than the body of a tree, or than the same body of man is capable of thinking and understanding. As it is the soul only that has ideas, so it is the soul only that is pleased or displeased with its ideas. As it is the soul only that thinks, so it is the soul only that loves or hates, rejoices or is grieved at, what it thinks of. Nor are these motions of the animal spirits, and fluids of the body, any thing properly belonging to the *nature* of the affections; though they always *accompany* them, in the present state; but are only effects or concomitants of the affections, which are entirely distinct from the affections themselves, and no way essential to them; so that an unbodied spirit may be as capable of love and hatred, joy or sorrow, hope or fear, or other affections, as one that is united to a body.

The *affections* and *passions* are frequently spoken of as the same; and yet, in the more common use of speech, there is in some respect a difference. *Affection* is a word, that, in its ordinary signification, seems to be something more extensive than *passion,* being used for all vigorous lively actings of the will or inclination; but *passion* is used for those that are more sudden, and whose effects on the animal spirits are more violent, the mind being more overpowered, and less in its own command.

As all the exercises of inclination and will, are concerned either in approving and liking, or disapproving and rejecting; so the affections are of two sorts; they are those by which the soul is carried out to what is in view, cleaving *to* it, or *seeking* it; or those by which it is averse *from* it, and *opposes* it. Of the former sort are *love, desire, hope, joy, gratitude, complacence.* Of the latter kind are *hatred, fear, anger, grief,* and such like; which it is needless now to stand particularly to define.

And there are some affections wherein there is a *composition* of each of the aforementioned kinds of actings of the will; as in the affection of *pity,* there is something of the *former kind,* towards the person suffering, and something of the *latter,* towards what he suffers. And so in *zeal,* there is in it high *approbation* of some person or thing, together with vigorous *opposition* to what is conceived to be contrary to it.

SECT. II.

True religion, in great part, consists in the affections.

1. WHAT has been said of the *nature* of the affections makes this evident; and may be sufficient, without adding any thing further, to put this matter out of doubt: for who will deny that true religion consists, in a great measure, in vigorous and lively actings of the *inclination* and *will* of the soul, or the fervent exercises of the *heart?* That religion which God requires, and will accept, does not consist in weak, dull, and lifeless wishes, raising us but a little above a state of indifference. God, in his word, greatly insists upon it, that we be in good earnest, *fervent in spirit,* and our hearts vigorously engaged in religion: Rom. xii. 11. "Be ye fervent in spirit, serving the Lord." Deut. x. 12. "And now Israel, what doth the

Lord thy God require of thee, but to fear the Lord thy God, to walk in all his ways, and to love him, and to serve the Lord thy God with all thy heart, and with all thy soul?" And chap. vi. 4, 5. "Hear, O Israel, the Lord our God is one Lord: and thou shalt love the Lord thy God with all thy heart, and with all thy soul, and with all thy might." It is such a fervent, vigorous engagedness of the heart in religion, that is the fruit of a real circumcision of the heart, or true regeneration, and that has the promises of life: Deut. xxx. 6. "And the Lord thy God will circumcise thine heart, and the heart of thy seed, to love the Lord thy God with all thy heart, and with all thy soul, that thou mayest live."

If we be not in good earnest in religion, and our wills and inclinations be not strongly exercised, we are nothing. The things of religion are so great, that there can be no suitableness in the exercises of our hearts, to their nature and importance, unless they be lively and powerful. In nothing is vigour in the actings of our inclinations so requisite, as in religion; and in nothing is lukewarmness so odious. True religion is evermore a powerful thing; and the power of it appears, in the first place, in its exercises in the heart, its principal and original seat. Hence true religion is called the *power of godliness*, in distinction from external appearances, which are *the form* of it, 2 Tim. iii. 5. "Having a form of godliness, but denying the power of it." The Spirit of God, in those who have sound and solid religion, is a Spirit of powerful holy affection; and therefore, God is said "to have given them the Spirit of power, and of love, and of a sound mind," (2 Tim. i. 7.) And such, when they receive the Spirit of God in his sanctifying and saving influences, are said to be "baptized with the Holy Ghost, and with fire;" by reason of the power and fervour of those exercises which the Spirit of God excites in them, and whereby *their hearts*, when grace is in exercise, may be said to *burn within them.* (Luke xxiv. 32.)

The business of *religion* is, from time to time, compared to those *exercises*, wherein men are wont to have their hearts and strength greatly exercised and engaged; such as running, wrestling, or agonizing for a great prize or crown, and fighting with strong enemies that seek our lives, and warring as those that by violence take a city or kingdom. Though true grace has various degrees, and there are some who are but babes in Christ, in whom the exercise of the inclination and will towards divine and heavenly things, is comparatively weak; yet every one that has the power of godliness, has his inclinations and heart exercised towards God and divine things with such strength and vigour, that these holy exercises prevail in him above all carnal or natural affections, and are effectual to overcome them: for every true disciple of Christ "loves him above father or mother, wife and children, brethren and sisters, houses and lands; yea more than his own life." Hence it follows, that wherever true religion is, there are vigorous exercises of the inclination and will towards divine objects: but by what was said before, the vigorous, lively, and sensible exercises of the will, are no other than the *affections* of the soul.

2. The Author of our nature has not only given us affections, but has made them very much the spring of actions. As the *affections* not only necessarily belong to the *human nature*, but are a very *great part* of it; so (inasmuch as by regeneration persons are renewed in the whole man) *holy affections* not only necessarily belong to *true religion*, but are a very great part of such religion. And as true religion is practical, and God hath so constituted the human nature, that the affections are very much the spring of men's actions, this also shows, that true religion must consist very much in the affections.

Such is man's nature, that he is very inactive, any otherwise than he is influenced by either *love* or *hatred, desire, hope, fear*, or some other affection. These affections we see to be the moving springs in all the affairs of life, which engage men in all their pursuits; and especially in all affairs wherein they are earnestly engaged, and which they pursue with vigour. We see the world of mankind exceedingly busy and active; and their affections are the springs of motion: take away all *love* and *hatred*, all *hope* and *fear*, all *anger, zeal,* and affectionate *desire*, and the world would be, in a great measure, motionless and dead: there would be no such thing as activity amongst mankind, or any earnest pursuit whatsoever. It is affection that engages the covetous man, and him that is greedy of worldly profits; it is by the affections that the ambitious man is put forward in his pursuit of worldly glory; and the affections also actuate the voluptuous man, in his pleasure and sensual delights. The world continues from age to age, in a continual commotion and agitation, in pursuit of these things; but take away affection, and the *spring* of all this motion would be gone; the motion itself would cease. And as in worldly things, worldly affections are very much the spring of men's motion and action; so in religious matters, the spring of their actions are very much religious affections: he that has doctrinal knowledge and speculation only, without affection, never is *engaged* in the business of religion.

3. Nothing is more manifest *in fact*, than that the things of religion take hold of men's souls no further than they *affect* them. There are multitudes who often hear the word of God, of things infinitely great and important, and which most nearly concern them, yet all seems to be wholly ineffectual upon them, and to make no alteration in their disposition or behaviour; the reason is, they are not *affected* with what they hear. There are many who often hear of the glorious perfections of God, his almighty power, boundless wisdom, infinite majesty, and that holiness by which he is of purer eyes than to behold evil, and cannot look on iniquity; together with his infinite goodness and mercy. They hear of the great works of God's wisdom, power, and goodness, wherein there appear the admirable manifestations of these perfections. They hear particularly of the unspeakable love of God and Christ, and what Christ has done and suffered. They hear of the great things of another world, of eternal misery, in bearing the fierceness and wrath of almighty God; and of endless blessedness and glory in the presence of God, and the enjoyment of his love. They also hear the peremptory commands of God, his gracious counsels and warnings, and the sweet invitations of the gospel. Yet they remain as before, with no sensible alteration, either in heart or practice, because they are not *affected* with what they hear. I am bold to assert, that there never was any considerable change wrought in the mind or conversation of any person, by any thing of a religious nature that ever he read, heard, or saw, who had not his affections moved. Never was a natural man engaged earnestly to seek his salvation; never were any such brought to cry after wisdom, and lift up their voice for understanding, and to wrestle with God in prayer for mercy; and never was one humbled, and brought to the foot of God, from any thing that ever he heard or imagined of his own unworthiness and deservings of God's displeasure; nor was ever one induced to fly for refuge unto Christ, while his heart remained *unaffected.* Nor was there ever a saint awakened out of a cold, lifeless frame, or recovered from a declining state in religion, and brought back from a lamentable departure from God, without having his heart *affected.* And, in a word, there never was any thing *considerable* brought to pass in the heart or life of any man living, by the things of religion, that had not his heart *deeply affected* by those things.

4. The Holy Scriptures every where place religion very much in the affections; such as fear, hope, love, hatred, desire, joy, sorrow, gratitude, compassion, and zeal.

The Scriptures place much of religion in godly *fear;* insomuch that an experience of it is often spoken of as the character of those who are truly religious persons. *They tremble at God's word,* they *fear before him, their flesh trembles for fear of him, they are afraid of his judgments, his excellency makes them afraid, and his dread falls upon them,* &c. An appellation commonly given the saints in Scripture, is, *fearers of God*, or they *that fear the Lord.* And because this is a great part of true godliness, hence true godliness in general is very commonly called *the fear of God.*

So *hope* in God, and in the promises of his word, is often spoken of in the Scripture, as a very considerable *part of true religion.* It is mentioned as one of the three great things of which religion consists, 1 Cor. xiii. 13. Hope in the Lord is also frequently mentioned as the *character of the saints*: Psal. cxlvi. 5. "Happy is he that hath the God of Jacob for his help, whose *hope* is in the Lord his God." Jer. xvii. 7. "Blessed is the man that trusteth in the Lord, and whose *hope* the Lord is." Psal. xxxi. 24. "Be of good courage, and he shall strengthen your heart, all ye that *hope* in the Lord." And the like in many other places. Religious fear and hope are, once and again, joined together, as jointly constituting the character of the true saints: Psal. xxxiii. 18. "Behold, the eye of the Lord is upon them that *fear* him, upon them that *hope* in his mercy." Psal. cxlvii. 11. "The Lord taketh pleasure in them that *fear* him, in those that *hope* in his mercy." Hope is so great a part of true religion, that the apostle says *we are saved by* HOPE, Rom. viii. 24. And this is spoken of as the *helmet* of the Christian soldier, 1 Thess. v. 8. "And for an helmet, the *hope* of salvation;" and the sure and stedfast *anchor* of the soul, which preserves it from being cast away by the storms of this evil world, Heb. vi. 19. "Which *hope* we have as an anchor of the soul, both sure and stedfast, and which entereth into that within the vail." It is spoken of as a great benefit which true saints receive by Christ's resurrection, 1 Pet. i. 3. "Blessed be the God and Father of our Lord Jesus Christ, which, according to his abundant mercy, hath begotten us again unto a lively *hope*, by the resurrection of Jesus Christ from the dead."

The Scriptures place religion very much in the affection of *love;* love to God, and the Lord Jesus Christ; love to the people of God, and to mankind. The texts in which this is manifest, both in the Old Testament and New, are innumerable. But of this more afterwards. The contrary affection of *hatred* also, as having sin for its object, is spoken of in Scripture as no inconsiderable part of true religion. It is spoken of as that by which true religion may be known and distinguished. Prov. viii. 13. "The fear of the Lord is to *hate* evil." Accordingly, the saints are called upon to give evidence of their sincerity by this, Psal. xcvii. 10. "Ye that love the Lord, *hate* evil." And the psalmist often mentions it as an evidence of his sincerity; Psal. ci. 2, 3. "I will walk within my house with a perfect heart. I will set no wicked thing before mine eyes: I *hate* the work of them that turn aside." Psal. cxix. 104. "I *hate* every false way." So ver. 128. Again, Psal. cxxxix. 21. "Do I not *hate* them, O Lord, that hate thee?"

So holy *desire*, exercised in longings, hungerings, and thirstings after God and holiness, is often mentioned in Scripture as an important part of true religion: Isa. xxvi. 8. "The *desire* of our soul is to thy name, and to the remembrance of thee." Psal. xxvii. 4. "One thing have I *desired* of the Lord, and that will I seek after, that I may dwell in the house of the Lord all the days of my life; to behold the beauty of the Lord, and to inquire in his temple." Psal. xlii. 1, 2. "As the hart panteth after the water-brooks, so panteth my soul after thee, O God. My soul *thirsteth* for God, for the living God: when shall I come and appear before God?" Psal. lxiii. 1, 2. "My soul *thirsteth* for thee, my flesh *longeth* for thee, in a dry and thirsty land where no water is: to see thy power and thy glory, so as I have seen thee in the sanctuary." Psal. lxxxiv. 1, 2. "How amiable are thy tabernacles, O Lord of hosts! My soul *longeth*, yea, even fainteth for the courts of the Lord: my heart and my flesh crieth out for the living God." Psal. cxix. 20. "My soul breaketh for the *longing* that it hath unto thy judgments at all times."* Such a holy desire, or thirst of soul, denotes a man *truly blessed:* Matt. v. 6. "Blessed are they that do hunger and thirst after righteousness: for they shall be filled." And this holy thirst is connected with the blessings of *eternal life:* Rev. xxi. 6. "I will give unto him that is *athirst*, of the fountain of the water of life freely."

The Scriptures speak of holy *joy*, as a great part of true religion. So it is represented in the text. And as an important part of religion, it is often pressed with great earnestness; Psal. xxxvii. 4. "*Delight* thyself in the Lord; and he shall give thee the desires of thine heart." Psal. xcvii. 12. "*Rejoice* in the Lord, ye righteous." So Psal. xxxiii. 1. "*Rejoice* in the Lord, O ye righteous." Matt. v. 12. "*Rejoice*, and be exceeding glad." Phil. iii. 1. "Finally, brethren, *rejoice* in the Lord." And chap. iv. 4. "*Rejoice* in the Lord alway: and again I say, *rejoice*." 1 Thess. v. 16. "*Rejoice* evermore." Psal. cxlix. 2. "Let Israel *rejoice* in him that made him: let the children of Zion be *joyful* in their King." This is mentioned among the principal fruits of the Spirit of grace, Gal. v. 22. "The fruit of the Spirit is love, *joy*," &c.—The psalmist mentions his holy joy, as an evidence of his sincerity, Psal. cxix. 14. "I have *rejoiced* in the way of thy testimonies, as much as in all riches."

Religious *sorrow*, mourning, and brokenness of heart, are also frequently spoken of as a great part of true religion. These things are often mentioned as distinguishing qualities of the true saints, and a great part of their character: Matt. v. 4. "Blessed are they that *mourn:* for they shall be comforted." Psal. xxxiv. 18. "The Lord is nigh unto them that are of a *broken heart;* and saveth such as be of a *contrite* spirit." Isa. lxi. 1, 2. "The Lord hath anointed me—to bind up the *broken hearted*,—to comfort all that *mourn*." This godly sorrow and brokenness of heart is often spoken of, not only as a distinguishing character of the saints, but as that in them, which is peculiarly acceptable and pleasing to God: Psal. li. 17. "The sacrifices of God are a broken spirit: a broken and a contrite heart, O God, thou wilt not despise." Isa. lvii. 15. "Thus saith the high and lofty One that inhabiteth eternity, whose name is holy, I dwell in the high and holy place; with him also that is of a contrite and humble spirit, to revive the spirit of the humble, and to revive the heart of the contrite ones." Chap. lxvi. 2. "To this man will I look, even to him that is poor and of a contrite spirit."

Another affection often mentioned, as that in the exercise of which much of true religion appears, is *gratitude;* especially as exercised in thankfulness and praise to God. This being so much spoken of in the book of Psalms, and other parts of the Holy Scriptures, I need not mention particular texts.

Again, the Holy Scriptures frequently speak of *compassion* or *mercy*, as a very great and essential thing in true religion; insomuch that a *merciful* man, and a *good* man, are equivalent terms in Scripture: Isa. lvii. 1. "The righteous perisheth, and no man layeth it to heart; and *merciful men* are taken away." And the Scripture chooses out this quality, as that by which, in a peculiar manner, a righteous man is deciphered: Psal. xxxvii. 21. "The *righteous* showeth *mercy*, and giveth; and ver. 26. "He is ever *merciful*, and lendeth." And Prov. xiv. 31. "He that honoureth the Lord, hath *mercy* on the poor." And Col. iii. 12. "Put ye on, as the elect of God, holy and beloved, *bowels* OF *mercies*," &c. This is one of those great things, by which the truly blessed are described by our Saviour, Matt. v. 7. "Blessed are the merciful: for they shall obtain mercy." And this Christ also speaks of, as one of the weightier matters of the law, Matt. xxiii. 23. "Woe unto you, scribes and Pharisees, hypocrites! for ye pay tithe of mint, and anise, and cummin, and have omitted the weightier matters of the law, judgment, *mercy*, and faith." To the like purpose is Mic. vi. 8. "He hath showed thee, O man, what is good: and what doth the Lord require of thee, but to do justice, and love *mercy*, and walk humbly with thy God?" And also Hos. vi. 6. "For I desired *mercy*, and not sacrifice;" a text much delighted in by our Saviour, it seems, by his manner of citing it once and again. (Matt. ix. 13. and xii. 7.)

Zeal is also spoken of, as a very essential part of the religion of true saints. This was a great thing which Christ had in view, in giving himself for our redemption: Tit. ii. 14. "Who gave himself for us, that he might redeem us from all iniquity, and purify unto himself a peculiar people, *zealous* of good works." And this was the great thing wanting in the luke-warm Laodiceans. (Rev. iii. 15, 16, 19.)

I have mentioned but a few texts, out of an innumerable multitude, which place religion very much in the affections. But what has been observed may be sufficient to show, that they who maintain the contrary, must throw away what we have been wont to own for our Bible, and

* So Psal. lxxiii. 25. and cxliii. 6, 7. and cxxx. 6. Cant. iii. 1, 2, and vi. 8.

get some other rule by which to judge of the nature of religion.

5. The Scriptures represent true religion, as being summarily comprehended in *love*, the chief of the affections, and the fountain of all others. So our blessed Saviour represents the matter, in answer to the lawyer who asked him, Which was the great commandment of the law? (Matt. xxii. 37—40.) " Jesus said unto him, Thou shalt love the Lord thy God with all thy heart, and with all thy soul, and with all thy mind. This is the first and great commandment. And the second is like unto it, Thou shalt love thy neighbour as thyself. On these two commandments hang all the law and the prophets." These two commandments comprehend all the duty prescribed in the law and the prophets. And the apostle Paul makes the same representation of the matter; as in Rom. xiii. 8. " He that loveth another, hath fulfilled the law." And verse 10. " Love is the fulfilling of the law." And Gal. v. 14. " For all the law is fulfilled in one word, even in this, Thou shalt love thy neighbour as thyself." So likewise in 1 Tim. i. 5. " Now the end of the commandment is charity, out of a pure heart," &c. The same apostle speaks of *love*, as the greatest thing in religion, as the essence and soul of it; without which, the greatest knowledge and gifts, the most glaring profession, and every thing else which appertains to religion, are vain and worthless. He also represents it as the *fountain* from whence proceeds all that is good, in 1 Cor. xiii. throughout; for that which is there rendered *charity*, is in the original αγαπη, the proper English of which is *love*.

Now, although it be true, that the love thus spoken of, includes the whole of a sincerely benevolent propensity of the soul towards God and man; yet, it is evident from what has been before observed, that this propensity or inclination of the soul, when in sensible and vigorous exercise, becomes *affection*, and is no other than affectionate love. And surely it is such vigorous and fervent love, which Christ represents as the sum of all religion, when he speaks of loving God with *all our hearts*, with *all our souls*, and with *all our minds*, and our neighbour as ourselves.

Indeed it cannot be supposed, when this affection of love is spoken of as the sum of all religion, that hereby is meant the act, exclusively of the habit, or that the exercise of the understanding is excluded, which is implied in all reasonable affection. But it is doubtless true, and evident from the Scriptures, that the *essence* of all true religion lies in holy love; and that in this divine affection —and habitual disposition to it, that light which is the foundation to it, and those things which are its fruits— consists the *whole* of religion.

From hence it clearly and certainly appears, that great part of true religion consists in the affections. For love is not only one of the affections, but it is the first and chief of them, and the fountain of all the others. From *love* arises *hatred* of those things which are contrary to what we love, or which oppose and thwart us in those things that we delight in: and from the various exercises of love and hatred, according to the circumstances of the objects of these affections, as present or absent, certain or uncertain, probable or improbable, arise all those other affections of *desire, hope, fear, joy, grief, gratitude, anger*, &c. From a vigorous, affectionate, and fervent *love to God*, will necessarily arise other *religious* affections; hence will arise an intense *hatred* and a *fear* of sin; a *dread* of God's displeasure; *gratitude* to God for his goodness; *complacence* and *joy* in God when he is graciously and sensibly present; *grief* when he is absent; a joyful *hope* when a future enjoyment of God is expected; and fervent *zeal* for the divine glory. In like manner, from a fervent *love to men*, will arise all other virtuous affections towards them.

6. The religion of the most eminent saints of whom we have an account in the Scripture, consisted much in holy *affections*.—I shall take particular notice of three eminent saints, who have expressed the frame and sentiments of their own hearts, described their own religion, and the manner of their intercourse with God, in the writings which they have left us, and which are a part of the sacred canon.

The *first* instance is *David*, that *man after God's own heart;* who has given us a lively portraiture of his religion in the book of Psalms. Those holy songs are nothing else but the expressions and breathings of devout and holy *affections;* such as an humble and fervent *love* to God, *admiration* of his glorious perfections and wonderful works, earnest *desires*, thirstings, and pantings of soul after him; *delight* and *joy* in God, a sweet and melting *gratitude* for his great goodness, a holy *exultation* and triumph of soul in his favour, sufficiency, and faithfulness; his *love* to, and *delight* in, the saints, the excellent of the earth, his great *delight* in the word and ordinances of God, his *grief* for his own and others' sins, and his fervent *zeal* for God, and against the enemies of God and his church. And these expressions of holy affection of which the Psalms of David are every where full, are the more to our present purpose, because those psalms are not only the expressions of the religion of so eminent a saint, but were also, by the direction of the Holy Ghost, penned for the use of the church of God in its public worship, not only in that age, but in after ages; as being fitted to express the religion of all saints, in all ages, as well as the religion of the psalmist. And it is moreover to be observed, that David, in the book of Psalms, speaks not as a private person, but as the *Psalmist of Israel*, as the subordinate head of the church of God, and leader in their worship and praises; and in many of the psalms, he speaks in the name of Christ, as personating him in these breathings forth of holy affections; and in many others he speaks in the name of the church.

Another instance I shall observe, is the apostle *Paul;* who was, in many respects, the chief of all the ministers of the New Testament; being above all others a chosen vessel unto Christ, to bear his name before the Gentiles. He was made the chief instrument of propagating and establishing the christian church in the world, and of distinctly revealing the glorious mysteries of the gospel, for the instruction of the church in all ages; and (as not improbably thought by some) was the most eminent servant of Christ that ever lived, and received the highest rewards in the heavenly kingdom of his Master. By what is said of him in the Scripture, he appears to have been a person full of affection; and it is very manifest, that the religion he expresses in his epistles, consisted very much in holy affections. It appears by all his expressions of himself, that he was, in the course of his life, inflamed, actuated, and entirely swallowed up, by a most ardent *love* to his glorious Lord, esteeming all things as loss, for the excellency of the knowledge of him, and esteeming them but dung that he might win him. He represents himself as overpowered by this holy affection, and as it were compelled by it to go forward in his service, through all difficulties and sufferings, 2 Cor. v. 14, 15. And his epistles are full of expressions of an overflowing affection towards the people of Christ: he speaks of his *dear love* to them, 2 Cor. xii. 19. Phil. iv. 1. 2 Tim. i. 2. of his *abundant love*, 2 Cor. ii. 4. and of his *affectionate and tender love*, as of a nurse towards her children, 1 Thess. ii. 7, 8. " But we were gentle among you, even as a nurse cherisheth her children: so, being affectionately desirous of you, we were willing to have imparted unto you, not the gospel of God only, but also our own souls, because ye were dear unto us." So also he speaks of his *bowels of love*, Phil. i. 8. Philem. 5, 12, and 20. of his *earnest care* for others, 2 Cor. viii. 16. of his *bowels of pity* or *mercy* towards them, Phil. ii. 1. and of his concern for others, even to *anguish of heart*, 2 Cor. ii. 4. " For out of much affliction and anguish of heart, I wrote unto you with many tears; not that you should be grieved, but that ye might know the love which I have more abundantly unto you." He speaks of the *great conflict* of his soul for them, Col. ii. 1. and of *great and continual grief* he had *in his heart* from *compassion* to the Jews, Rom. ix. 2. He speaks of *his mouth being opened, and his heart enlarged* towards Christians, 2 Cor. vi. 11. "O ye Corinthians, our mouth is open unto you, our heart is enlarged." He often speaks of his *affectionate and longing desires*, (1 Thess. ii. 8. Rom. i. 11. Phil. i. 8. and chap. iv. 1. 2 Tim. i. 4.)

The same apostle very often, in his epistles, expresses the affection of *joy*, (2 Cor. i. 12. and chap. vii. 7, and ver. 9, 16. Phil. i. 4. and chap. ii. 1, 2. and chap. iii. 3.

Col. i. 24. 1 Thess. iii. 9.) He speaks of his *rejoicing with great joy*, (Phil. iv. 10. Philem. 1, 7.) of his *joying and rejoicing*, (Phil. ii. 1, 7.) of his *rejoicing exceedingly*, (2 Cor. vii. 13.) being *filled with comfort, exceeding joyful*, (2 Cor. vii. 4.) and *always rejoicing*, (2 Cor. vi. 10.) So he speaks of the *triumphs* of his soul, (2 Cor. ii. 14.) and of *his glorying in tribulation*, (2 Thess. i. 4. and Rom. v. 3.) In Phil. i. 20. he speaks of his *earnest expectation*, and *his hope*. He likewise expresses an affection of *godly jealousy*, 2 Cor. xi. 2, 3. And it appears by his whole history, after his conversion, that the affection of *zeal*, as having the cause of his Master and the interest and prosperity of his church for its object, was mighty in him, continually inflaming his heart, strongly engaging to great and constant labours, in instructing, exhorting, warning, and reproving others, *travailing in birth with them*; conflicting with those powerful and innumerable enemies who continually opposed him, wrestling with principalities and powers, not fighting as one who beats the air, running the race set before him, continually pressing forwards through all manner of difficulties and sufferings; so that others thought him quite beside himself. And how full he was of affection further appears by his being so full of tears: in 2 Cor. ii. 4. he speaks of his *many tears;* and so Acts xx. 19. and of his *tears* that he shed *continually, night and day*, ver. 31.

Now if any one can consider these accounts given in the Scripture of this great apostle, and which he gives of himself, and yet not see that his religion consisted much in *affection*, he must have a strange faculty of managing his eyes in order to shut out the light which shines most full in his face.

The other instance I shall mention, is that of the apostle *John*, the beloved disciple, who was the nearest and dearest to his Master of any of the twelve, and who was by him admitted to the greatest privileges of any of them. He was not only one of the three who were admitted to be present with him in the mount at his transfiguration, and at the raising of Jairus's daughter, and whom he took with him when he was in his agony, and one of three spoken of by the apostle Paul, as the three main pillars of the christian church; but he was favoured above all, in being admitted to lean on his Master's bosom at his last supper, and in being chosen by Christ as the disciple to whom he would reveal his wonderful dispensations towards his church, to the end of time. By him was shut up the canon of the New Testament, and of the whole Scripture; and he was preserved much longer than all the rest of the apostles, to set all things in order in the christian church after their death.

It is evident by all his writings, that he was a person remarkably full of affection: his addresses to those whom he wrote to, being inexpressibly tender and pathetic, breathing nothing but the most fervent *love;* as though he were all made up of sweet and holy affection. The proofs of which cannot be given without disadvantage, unless we should transcribe his whole writings.

7. He whom God sent into the world, to be the light of the world and the head of the whole church, and the perfect example of true religion and virtue for the imitation of all, the Shepherd whom the whole flock should follow wherever he goes, even the *Lord Jesus Christ*, was of a remarkably tender and affectionate heart; and his virtue was expressed very much in the exercise of holy affections. He was the greatest instance of ardency, vigour, and strength of *love*, to both God and man, that ever was. It was these affections which got the victory, in that mighty struggle and conflict of his affections, in his agonies, when *he prayed more earnestly, and offered strong crying and tears*, and wrestled in tears and in blood. Such was the power of the exercises of his holy love, that they were stronger than death, and in that great struggle, overcame those strong exercises of the natural affections of fear and grief, when he was sore amazed, and his soul was exceeding sorrowful, even unto death.

He also appeared to be full of affection, in the course of his life. We read of his great *zeal*, fulfilling that expression in the 69th Psalm, "The zeal of thine house hath eaten me up," John ii. 17. We read of his *grief* for the sins of men, Mark iii. 5. "He looked round about on them with anger, being grieved for the hardness of their hearts;" and his breaking forth in tears and exclamations, from the consideration of the sin and misery of ungodly men, and on the sight of the city of Jerusalem, which was full of such inhabitants, Luke xix. 41, 42. "And when he was come near, he beheld the city, and wept over it, saying, If thou hadst known, even thou, at least in this thy day, the things which belong unto thy peace! but now they are hid from thine eyes." With chap. xiii. 34. "O Jerusalem, Jerusalem, which killest the prophets, and stonest them that are sent unto thee: how often would I have gathered thy children together, as a hen doth gather her brood under her wings, and ye would not!" We read of Christ's earnest *desire*, Luke xxii. 15. "With desire have I desired to eat this passover with you before I suffer." We often read of the affection of *pity* or *compassion* in Christ, (Matt. xv. 32. and xviii. 34. Luke vii. 13.) and of his *being moved with compassion*, (Matt. ix. 36. and xiv. 14. and Mark vi. 34.) And how tender did his heart appear to be, on occasion of Mary's and Martha's mourning for their brother, and coming to him with their complaints and tears! Their tears soon drew tears from his eyes; he was affected with their grief, and *wept* with them; though he knew their sorrow should so soon be turned into joy, by their brother being raised from the dead: see John xi. And how ineffably affectionate was that last and dying discourse, which Jesus had with his eleven disciples the evening before he was crucified; when he told them he was going away, and foretold them the great difficulties and sufferings they should meet with in the world, when he was gone; and comforted and counselled them, as his dear little children; and bequeathed to them his Holy Spirit, and therein his peace, his comfort and joy, as it were in his last will and testament, in the 13th, 14th, 15th, and 16th chapters of John; and concluded the whole with that affectionate intercessory prayer for them, and his whole church, in chap. xvii. Of all the discourses ever penned or uttered by the mouth of any man, this seems to be the most affectionate and affecting.

8. The religion of *heaven* consists very much in affection.—There is doubtless true religion in heaven, and true religion in its utmost purity and perfection. But according to the scripture representation of the heavenly state, the religion of heaven consists chiefly in holy and mighty *love* and *joy*, and the expression of these in most fervent and exalted praises. So that the religion of the saints in heaven, consists in the same things with that religion of the saints on earth, which is spoken of in our text, *viz. love*, and *joy unspeakable, and full of glory*. Now, it would be very foolish to pretend, that because the saints in heaven are not united to flesh and blood, and have no animal fluids to be moved (through the laws of union of soul and body) with those great emotions of their souls, that therefore their exceeding love and joy are no affections. We are not speaking of the affections of the body, but those of the soul, the chief of which are *love and joy*. When these are in the soul, whether that be in the body or out of it, the soul is affected and moved. And when they are in the soul, in that strength in which they are in the saints in heaven, it is mightily affected and moved, or, which is the same thing, has great affections. It is true, we do not experimentally know what love and joy are in a soul out of a body, or in a glorified body; *i. e.* we have not had experience of love and joy in a soul in these circumstances; but the saints on earth do know what divine love and joy in the soul are, and they know that love and joy are of the same kind with the love and joy which are in heaven, in separate souls there. The love and joy of the saints on earth, is the beginning and dawning of the light, life, and blessedness of heaven, and is like their love and joy there; or rather, the same in nature, though not the same in degree and circumstances.* It is unreasonable therefore to suppose, that the love and joy of the saints in heaven differ not only in degree and circumstances, from the holy love and joy of the saints on earth,

* This is evident by many scriptures, as Prov. iv. 18. John iv. 14. and chap. vi. 40, 47, 50, 51, 54, 58. 1 John iii. 15. 1 Cor. xiii. 8—12.

but also in nature, so that they are no affections; and merely because they have no blood and animal spirits to be set in motion by them. The motion of the blood and animal spirits is not of the *essence* of these affections, in men on the earth, but the *effect* of them; although by their reaction they may make some circumstantial difference in the sensation of the mind. There is a sensation of the *mind* which loves and rejoices, *antecedent* to any effects on the fluids of the body; and therefore, does not depend on these motions in the body, and so may be in the soul without the body. And wherever there are the exercises of love and joy, there is that sensation of the mind, whether it be in the body or out; and that inward sensation, or kind of spiritual feeling, is what is called affection. The soul, when it is thus moved, is said to be *affected*, and especially when this inward sensation and motion are to a very high degree, as they are in the saints in heaven. If we can learn any thing of the state of heaven from the Scripture, the love and joy that the saints have there, is exceeding great and vigorous; impressing the heart with the strongest and most lively sensation of inexpressible sweetness, mightily moving, animating, and engaging them, making them like to a flame of fire. And if such love and joy be not affections, then the word *affection* is of no use in language.—Will any say, that the saints in heaven, in beholding the face of their Father and the glory of their Redeemer, in contemplating his wonderful works, and particularly his laying down his life for them, have their hearts nothing moved and affected by all which they behold or consider?

Hence, therefore, the *religion of heaven*, being full of holy love and joy, consists very much in affection: and therefore, undoubtedly, *true religion* consists very much in affection. The way to learn the true nature of any thing, is to go where that thing is to be found in its purity and perfection. If we would know the nature of true gold, we must view it, not in the ore, but when it is refined. If we would learn what true religion is, we must go where there is true religion, and nothing but true religion, and in its highest perfection, without any defect or mixture. All who are truly religious are not of this world, they are strangers here, and belong to heaven; they are born from above, heaven is their native country, and the nature which they receive by this heavenly birth, is a heavenly nature, they receive *an anointing from above;* that principle of true religion which is in them, is a communication of the religion of heaven; their grace is the dawn of glory; and God fits them for that world by conforming them to it.

9. This appears from the nature and design of the ordinances and duties, which God hath appointed, as means and expressions of true religion.

To instance in the duty of *prayer:* it is manifest, we are not appointed, in this duty, to declare God's perfections, his majesty, holiness, goodness, and all-sufficiency; our own meanness, emptiness, dependence, and unworthiness, our wants and desires, in order to inform God of these things, or to incline his heart, and prevail with him to be willing to show us mercy; but rather suitably to affect our own hearts with the things we express, and so to prepare us to receive the blessings we ask. And such gestures and manner of external behaviour in the worship of God, which custom has made to be significations of humility and reverence, can be of no further use, than as they have some tendency to *affect* our own hearts, or the hearts of others.

And the duty of *singing* praises to God, seems to be appointed wholly to excite and express religious affections. No other reason can be assigned, why we should express ourselves to God in verse, rather than in prose, and do it with music, but only, that such is our nature and frame, that these things have a tendency to move our affections.

The same thing appears in the nature and design of the *sacraments*, which God hath appointed. God, considering our frame, hath not only appointed that we should be told of the great things of the gospel and the redemption of Christ, and be instructed in them by his word; but also that they should be, as it were, exhibited to our view in sensible representations, the more to affect us with them.

And the impressing of divine things on the hearts and affections of men, is evidently one great end for which God has ordained, that his word delivered in the Holy Scriptures, should be opened, applied, and set home upon men, in *preaching*. And therefore it does not answer the aim which God had in this institution, merely for men to have good commentaries and expositions on the Scripture, and other good books of divinity; because, although these may tend, as well as preaching, to give a good doctrinal or speculative understanding of the word of God, yet they have not an equal tendency to impress them on men's hearts and affections. God hath appointed a particular and lively application of his word, in the preaching of it, as a fit means to affect sinners with the importance of religion, their own misery, the necessity of a remedy, and the glory and sufficiency of a remedy provided; to stir up the pure minds of the saints, quicken their affections by often bringing the great things of religion to their remembrance, and setting them in their proper colours, though they know them, and have been fully instructed in them already, 2 Pet. i. 12, 13. And particularly, to promote those two affections in them, which are spoken of in the text, *love* and *joy:* "Christ gave some, apostles; and some, prophets; and some, evangelists; and some, pastors and teachers; that the body of Christ might be edified in love," Eph. iv. 11, 12, 16. The apostle, in instructing and counselling Timothy, concerning the work of the ministry, informs him, that the great end of that word which a minister is to preach, is *love* or *charity*, 1 Tim. i. 3—5. And God has appointed preaching as a means to promote in the saints *joy:* therefore ministers are called *helpers of their joy*, 2 Cor. i. 24.

10. It is an evidence that true religion lies very much in the affections, that the Scriptures place the sin of the heart very much in *hardness of heart*. It was hardness of heart which excited grief and displeasure in Christ towards the Jews, Mark iii. 5. "He looked round about on them with anger, being grieved for the hardness of their hearts." It is from men's having such a heart as this, that they treasure up wrath for themselves; Rom. ii. 5. "After thy hardness and impenitent heart, treasurest up unto thyself wrath against the day of wrath, and revelation of the righteous judgment of God." The reason given why the house of Israel would not obey God, was, that they were hard-hearted; Ezek. iii. 7. "But the house of Israel will not hearken unto thee; for they will not hearken unto me; for all the house of Israel are impudent and hard-hearted." The wickedness of that perverse rebellious generation in the wilderness, is ascribed to the hardness of their hearts; Psal. xcv. 7—10. "To-day if ye will hear my voice, harden not your heart, as in the provocation, and as in the day of temptation in the wilderness; when your fathers tempted me, proved me, and saw my work: forty years long was I grieved with this generation, and said, It is a people that do err in their heart," &c.—This is spoken of as what prevented Zedekiah's turning to the Lord, 2 Chron. xxxvi. 13. "He stiffened his neck, and hardened his heart from turning to the Lord God of Israel." This principle is that from whence men are without the fear of God, and depart from his ways: Isa. lxiii. 17. "O Lord, why hast thou made us to err from thy ways? and hardened our heart from thy fear?" And men rejecting Christ, and opposing Christianity, are charged with this principle; Acts xix. 9. "But divers were hardened, and believed not, but spake evil of that way before the multitude."—God's leaving men to the power of the sin and corruption of the heart, is often expressed by his hardening their hearts; Rom. ix. 18. "Therefore hath he mercy on whom he will have mercy, and whom he will he hardeneth. John xii. 40. "He hath blinded their minds, and hardened their hearts." And the apostle seems to speak of *an evil heart, that departs from the living God*, and *a hard heart*, as the same thing, Heb. iii. 8. "Harden not your heart, as in the provocation," &c. verse 12, 13. "Take heed, brethren, lest there be in any of you an evil heart of unbelief, in departing from the living God: but exhort one another daily while it is called to-day; lest any of you be hardened through the deceitfulness of sin." And that great work of God in conversion, which consists in delivering a person from the power of sin, and mortifying corruption, is expressed, once and again, by God's "taking away the heart of stone,

and giving a heart of flesh, (Ezek. xi. 19. and chap. xxxvi. 26.)

Now, by a *hard* heart is plainly meant an *unaffected* heart, or a heart not easy to be moved with virtuous affections, like a stone, insensible, stupid, unmoved, and hard to be impressed. Hence the hard heart is called a *stony heart*, and is opposed to a *heart of flesh*, that has feeling, and is sensibly touched and moved. We read in Scripture of a *hard heart*, and a *tender heart*: and doubtless we are to understand these, as contrary the one to the other. But what is a tender heart, but a heart which is easily impressed with what ought to affect it? God commends Josiah, because his heart was tender: and it is evident by those things which are mentioned as expressions and evidences of this tenderness of heart, that by it is meant, his heart being easily moved with religious and pious affections: 2 Kings xxii. 19. "Because thine heart was tender, and thou hast humbled thyself before the Lord, when thou heardst what I spake against this place, and against the inhabitants thereof, that they should become a desolation and a curse, and hast rent thy clothes, and went before me, I also have heard thee, saith the Lord." And this is one thing, wherein it is necessary we should *become as little children, in order to our entering into the kingdom of God*, even that we should have our hearts tender, and easily affected and moved in spiritual and divine things, as little children have in other things.

It is very plain in some places, that by hardness of heart is meant a heart void of affection. So, to signify the ostrich's being without natural affection to her young, it is said, Job xxxix. 16. "She hardeneth her heart against her young ones, as though they were not hers." So a person having a heart unaffected in time of danger, is expressed by his hardening his heart, Prov. xxviii. 14. "Happy is the man that feareth alway; but he that hardeneth his heart, shall fall into mischief."

Now, therefore, since it is so plain, that by a hard heart in Scripture, is meant a heart destitute of pious affections; and since also the Scriptures so frequently place the sin and corruption of the heart in its hardness; it is evident, that the grace and holiness of the heart, on the contrary, must in a great measure consist in its having pious affections, and being easily susceptive of such affections. Divines are generally agreed, that sin radically and fundamentally consists in what is negative, or privative, having its root and foundation in a privation or want of holiness. And therefore undoubtedly, if sin very much consist in hardness of heart, and so in the want of pious affections, holiness does consist very much *in those pious affections.*

I am far from supposing that all affections manifest a tender heart; hatred, anger, vain-glory, and other selfish and self-exalting affections, may greatly prevail in the hardest heart. But yet it is evident, that *hardness of heart*, and *tenderness of heart*, are expressions that relate to the affections of the heart, and denote its being susceptible of, or shut up against, *certain affections;* of which I shall have occasion to speak more afterwards.

Upon the whole, I think it clearly and abundantly evident, that true religion *lies very much in the affections.* Not that I think these arguments prove, that religion in the hearts of the truly godly, is ever in exact proportion to the degree of affection and present emotion of the mind: for, undoubtedly, there is much affection in the true saints which is not spiritual; their religious affections are often mixed; all is not from grace, but much from nature. And though the affections have not their seat in the body, yet the constitution of the body may very much contribute to the present emotion of the mind. The degree of religion is to be estimated by the fixedness and strength of habit exercised in affection, whereby holy affection is habitual, rather than by the degree of the present exercise: and the strength of that habit is not always in proportion to outward effects and manifestations, or indeed inward ones, in the hurry, vehemence, and sudden changes of the course of the thoughts. But yet it is evident, that religion consists so much in the affections, as that without holy affection there is no true religion. No light in the understanding is good, which does not produce holy affection in the heart; no habit or principle in the heart is good, which has no such exercise; and no external fruit is good, which does not proceed from such exercises.

SECT. III.

Some inferences deduced from the doctrine.

1. WE may hence learn how great their error is, who are for discarding all religious affections, as having nothing solid or substantial in them. There seems to be too much of a disposition this way prevailing at this time. Because many who, in the late extraordinary season, appeared to have great religious affections, did not manifest a right temper of mind, and run into many errors, in the heat of their zeal; and because the high affections of many seem to be so soon come to nothing, and some who seemed to be mightily raised and swallowed with joy and zeal for a while, seem to have returned like the dog to his vomit: hence religious affections in general are grown out of credit with great numbers, as though true religion did not at all consist in them. Thus we easily and naturally run from one extreme to another. A little while ago we were in the other extreme; there was a prevalent disposition to look upon all high religious affections as eminent exercises of true grace, without much inquiry into the nature and source of those affections, and the manner in which they arose. If persons did but appear to be indeed very much moved and raised, so as to be full of religious talk, and express themselves with great warmth and earnestness, and to be *filled*, or to be *very full*, as the phrases were; it was too much the manner, without further examination, to conclude such persons were full of the Spirit of God, and had eminent experience of his gracious influences. This was the extreme which was prevailing three or four years ago. But of late, instead of *esteeming* and *admiring* all religious *affections, without distinction*, it is much more prevalent to *reject* and *discard* all *without distinction*. Herein appears the subtilty of Satan. While he saw that *affections* were much in vogue, knowing the greater part were not versed in such things, and had not had much experience of great *religious affections*, enabling them to judge well, and to distinguish between true and false; then he knew he could best play his game, by sowing tares amongst the wheat, and mingling *false affections* with the works of God's Spirit. He knew this to be a likely way to delude and eternally ruin many souls, and greatly to wound religion in the saints, and entangle them in a dreadful wilderness, and by and by to bring all religion into disrepute.

But now, when the ill consequences of these *false affections* appear, and it is become very apparent, that some of those emotions which made a glaring show, and were by many greatly admired, were in reality nothing; the devil sees it to be for his interest to go another way to work, and to endeavour to his utmost to propagate and establish a persuasion, that all affections and sensible emotions of the mind in religion, are nothing at all to be regarded, but are rather to be avoided, and carefully guarded against, as things of a pernicious tendency. This he knows is the way to bring all religion to a mere lifeless formality, and effectually to shut out the power of godliness and every thing spiritual. For although to true religion there must indeed be something else besides affection; yet true religion consists so much in the affections, that there can be no true religion without them. He who has no religious affection, is in a state of spiritual death, and is wholly destitute of the powerful, quickening, saving influences of the Spirit of God upon his heart. As there is no true religion where there is nothing else but affection, so there is no true religion where there is no *religious affection.* As on the one hand, there must be light in the understanding, as well as an *affected* fervent heart; or where there is heat without light, there can be nothing divine or heavenly in that heart: so, on the other hand, where there is a kind of light without heat, a head stored with notions and speculations with a cold and unaffected heart, there can be nothing divine in that light, that knowledge is no true spiritual knowledge of divine things. If the great things of religion are rightly understood, they will affect the heart. The reason why men are not affected by such infinitely great, important, glorious, and wonderful things, as they often hear and read of in the word of God, is, undoubtedly, because they are blind; if they were not so, it would be impossible, and utterly inconsistent with human nature, that their hearts should be otherwise than strongly impressed, and greatly moved by such things.

This manner of slighting all religious *affections*, is the way exceedingly to harden the hearts of men, to encourage them in their stupidity and senselessness, to keep them in a state of spiritual death as long as they live, and bring them at last to death eternal. The prevailing prejudice against *religious affections* at this day, is apparently of awful effect to harden the hearts of sinners, to damp the graces of the saints, to preclude the effect of ordinances, and hold us down in a state of dulness and apathy; and this undoubtedly causes many persons greatly to offend God, in entertaining mean and low thoughts of the extraordinary work he has lately wrought in this land. For persons to despise and cry down all religious *affections*, is the way to shut all religion out of their own hearts, and to make thorough work in ruining their souls.

They who condemn high affections in others, are certainly not likely to have high affections themselves. And let it be considered, that they who have but little religious affection, have certainly but little religion. And they who condemn others for their *religious affections*, and have none themselves, have no religion. There are false *affections*, and there are true. A man's having *much affection*, does not prove that he has any true religion: but if he has *no affection*, it proves that he has no true religion. The right way, is not to reject all affections, nor to approve all: but to distinguish between them, approving some and rejecting others; separating between the wheat and the chaff, the gold and the dross, the precious and the vile.

2. If true religion lies much in the *affections*, we may infer, that such means are to be desired, as have much tendency to move the affections. Such books, and such a way of preaching the word and the administration of ordinances, and such a way of worshipping God in prayer and praises, as has a tendency deeply to affect the hearts of those who attend these means, is much to be desired.

Such kind of means would formerly have been highly approved, and applauded by the generality of people, as the most excellent and profitable, and having the greatest tendency to promote the ends of the means of grace. But the prevailing taste seems of late strangely to be altered: that pathetic manner of praying and preaching which would formerly have been admired and extolled, and for this reason, because it had such a tendency to move the affections, now, in great multitudes, immediately excites disgust, and moves no other affections, than those of displeasure and contempt.

Perhaps, formerly, the generality (at least of the common people) were in the extreme of looking too much to an affectionate address in public performances: but now, a very great part of the people seem to have gone far into a contrary extreme. Indeed there *may* be such means, as have a great tendency to stir up the passions of weak and ignorant persons, and yet have none to benefit their souls: for though they may have a tendency to excite *affections*, they have little or none to excite *gracious* affections. But, undoubtedly, if the things of religion in the means used, are treated according to their nature, and exhibited truly, so as tends to convey just apprehensions and a right judgment of them; the more they have a tendency to move the affections, the better.

3. If true religion lies much in the affections, hence we may learn, what great cause we have to be ashamed and confounded before God, that we are no more *affected* with the great things of religion. It appears from what has been said, that this arises from our having so little true religion.

God has given to mankind affections, for the same purpose as that for which he has given all the faculties and principles of the human soul, *viz.* that they might be subservient to man's chief end, and the great business for which God has created him, that is, the business of religion. And yet how common is it among mankind, that their affections are much more exercised and engaged in other matters, than in religion! In matters which concern men's worldly interest, their outward delights, their honour and reputation, and their natural relations, they have their desires eager, their appetites vehement, their love warm and affectionate, their zeal ardent; in these things their hearts are tender and sensible, easily moved, deeply impressed, much concerned, very sensibly affected, and greatly engaged; much depressed with grief at worldly losses, and highly raised with joy at worldly successes and prosperity. But how insensible and unmoved are most men, about the great things of another world! how dull are their affections! how heavy and hard their hearts in these matters! here their love is cold, their desires languid, their zeal low, and their gratitude small. How they can sit and hear of the infinite height, and depth, and length, and breadth of the love of God in Christ Jesus; of his giving his infinitely dear Son to be offered up a sacrifice for the sins of men, and of the unparalleled love of the innocent, holy Lamb of God manifested in his dying agonies, his bloody sweat, his loud and bitter cries and bleeding heart; and all this for enemies, to redeem them from deserved, eternal burnings, and to bring to unspeakable and everlasting joy and glory; and yet be cold, heavy, insensible, and regardless! Where are the exercises of our affections proper, if not here? what is it that more requires them? and what can be a fit occasion of their lively and vigorous exercise, if not such as this? Can any thing be set in our view, greater and more important? any thing more wonderful and surprising? or that more nearly concerns our interest? Can we suppose that the wise Creator implanted such principles in our nature as the affections, to lie still on such an occasion as this? Can any Christian, who believes the truth of these things, entertain such thoughts?

If we ought ever to exercise our affections at all, and if the Creator has not unwisely constituted the human nature in making these principles a part of it, then they ought to be exercised about those objects which are most worthy of them. But is there any thing in heaven or earth, so worthy to be the objects of our admiration and love, our earnest and longing desires, hope, rejoicing, and fervent zeal, as those things which are held forth to us in the gospel of Jesus Christ? There not only are things declared most worthy to affect us, but they are exhibited in the most affecting manner. The glory and beauty of the blessed Jehovah, which is most worthy in itself to be the object of our admiration and love, is there exhibited in the most *affecting* manner that can be conceived of; as it appears shining in all its lustre, in the face of an incarnate, infinitely loving, meek, compassionate, dying Redeemer. All the *virtues* of the Lamb of God, his humility, patience, meekness, submission, obedience, love, and compassion, are exhibited to our view, in a manner the most tending to move our affections of any that can be imagined; for they all had their greatest trial, their highest exercise, and brightest manifestation, when he was in the most affecting circumstances; even when he was under his last sufferings, those unutterable and unparalleled sufferings which he endured from his tender love and pity to us. There, also, the hateful *nature* of our *sins* is manifested in the most affecting manner possible; as we see the dreadful effects of them, in what our Redeemer who undertook to answer for us, suffered for them. And there we have the most affecting manifestations of God's *hatred* of sin, and his wrath and justice in punishing it; as we see his justice in the strictness and inflexibleness of it, and his wrath in its terribleness, in so dreadfully punishing our sins, in one who was infinitely dear to him, and loving to us. So has God disposed things in the affair of our redemption, and in his glorious dispensations revealed to us in the gospel, as though every thing were purposely contrived in such a manner, as to have the greatest possible tendency to reach our hearts in the most tender part, and move our affections most sensibly and strongly. How great cause have we therefore to be humbled to the dust, that we are no more affected!

PART II.

SHOWING WHAT ARE NO CERTAIN SIGNS THAT RELIGIOUS AFFECTIONS ARE TRULY GRACIOUS, OR THAT THEY ARE NOT.

IF any one, on reading what has been just now said, is ready to acquit himself, and say, "I am not one of those who have no religious affections; I am often greatly moved with the consideration of the great things of religion; let him not content himself with this: for, as we ought not to reject and condemn all affections, as though true religion did not at all consist in them; so, on the other hand, we ought not to approve of all, as though every one that was religiously affected had true grace, and was therein the subject of the saving influences of the Spirit of God. Therefore, the right way is to distinguish, among religious affections, between one sort and another. Let us now endeavour to do this, by noticing, in the first place, some *things, which are no signs that affections are gracious, or that they are not.*

SECT. I.

It is no sign, one way or other, that religious affections are very great, or raised very high.

SOME are ready to condemn all high affection: if persons appear to have their religious affections raised to an extraordinary pitch, they are prejudiced against them, and determine that they are delusions, without further inquiry. But if, as before proved, true religion lies very much in religious affections, then it follows, that if there be a great deal of true religion, there will be great religious affections; if true religion in the hearts of men be raised to a great height, divine and holy affections will be raised to a great height.

Love is an affection; but will any Christian say, men ought not to love God and Jesus Christ in a high degree? and will any say, we ought not to have a very great hatred of sin, and a very deep sorrow for it? or that we ought not to exercise a high degree of gratitude to God, for the mercies we receive of him, and the great things he has done for the salvation of fallen men? or that we should not have very great and strong desires after God and holiness? Is there any who will profess, that his affections in religion are great enough; and will say, "I have no cause to be humbled, that I am no more affected with the things of religion than I am; I have no reason to be ashamed, that I have no greater exercises of love to God, and sorrow for sin, and gratitude for the mercies which I have received?" Who is there that will go and bless God, that he is affected *enough* with what he has read and heard of the wonderful love of God to worms and rebels in giving his only-begotten Son to die for them, and of the dying love of Christ; and will pray that he may not be affected with them in any higher degree, because high affections are improper, and very unlovely in Christians, being enthusiastical, and ruinous to true religion?

Our text plainly speaks of great and high affections, when it speaks of *rejoicing with joy unspeakable, and full of glory.* Here the most superlative expressions are used, which language will afford. The Scriptures often require us to exercise *very high* affections: thus in the first and great commandment of the law, there is an accumulation of expressions, as though words were wanting to express the *degree* in which we ought to *love* God; "Thou shalt love the Lord thy God with *all* thy *heart*, with *all* thy *soul*, with *all* thy *mind*, and with *all* thy *strength.*" So the saints are called upon to exercise high degrees of *joy: Rejoice*, says Christ to his disciples, *and be exceeding glad*, Matt. v. 12. So, Psal. lxviii. 3. "Let the righteous be glad: let them rejoice before God; yea, let them exceedingly rejoice." In the book of Psalms, the saints are often called upon to *shout for joy;* and in Luke vi. 23. to *leap for joy.* So they are abundantly called upon to exercise high degrees of *gratitude* for mercies, to *praise God with all their hearts, with hearts lifted up in the ways of the Lord, their souls magnifying the Lord, singing his praises, talking of his wondrous works, declaring his doings, &c.*

We find the most eminent saints in Scripture often *professing* high affections. Thus the *psalmist* mentions his *love* as if it were *unspeakable;* Psal. cxix. 97. "Oh how love I thy law!" So he expresses a great degree of *hatred of sin*; Psal. cxxxix. 21, 22. "Do not I hate them, O Lord, that hate thee? and am not I grieved with them that rise up against thee? I hate them with perfect hatred." He also expresses a high degree of *sorrow for sin:* he speaks of his sins *going over his head, as a heavy burden, that was too heavy for him;* of *his roaring all the day, his moisture being turned into the drought of summer*, and *his bones being* as it were *broken* with sorrow. So he often expresses great degrees of spiritual *desires*, in a multitude of the strongest expressions which can be conceived of; such as *his longing, his soul thirsting as a dry and thirsty land where no water is, his panting, his flesh and heart crying out, his soul breaking for the longing it hath, &c.* He expresses the exercises of great and extreme *grief* for the sins of others, Psal. cxix. 136. "Rivers of water run down mine eyes, because they keep not thy law." And verse 53. "Horror hath taken hold upon me, because of the wicked that forsake thy law." He expresses high exercises of *joy*, Psal. xxi. 1. "The king shall joy in thy strength, and in thy salvation how greatly shall he rejoice!" Psal. lxxi. 23. "My lips shall greatly rejoice, when I sing unto thee." Psal. lxiii. 3—7. "Because thy loving-kindness is better than life: my lips shall praise thee. Thus will I bless thee, while I live: I will lift up my hands in thy name. My soul shall be satisfied as with marrow and fatness; and my mouth shall praise thee with joyful lips: when I remember thee upon my bed, and meditate on thee in the night-watches. Because thou hast been my help; therefore in the shadow of thy wings will I rejoice."

The *apostle Paul* expresses high exercises of affection. Thus he expresses the exercises of pity and concern for others' good, even to *anguish of heart;* a *great, fervent*, and *abundant love, earnest* and *longing desires*, and *exceeding joy.* He speaks of the *exultation* and *triumphs* of his soul, his *earnest expectation* and *hope*, his *abundant tears*, and the *travails of his soul*, in pity, grief, earnest desires, godly jealousy, and fervent zeal, in many places that have been cited already, and which therefore I need not repeat. *John* the *Baptist* expressed *great joy*, John iii. 39. Those blessed women who anointed the body of Jesus, are represented as in a very high exercise of religious affection, at the resurrection of Christ. Matt. xxviii. 8. "And they departed from the sepulchre, with fear and great joy."

It is often foretold of the *church* of God, in her future happy seasons on earth, that they shall exceedingly rejoice: Psal. lxxxix. 15, 16. "They shall walk, O Lord, in the light of thy countenance. In thy name shall they rejoice all the day: and in thy righteousness shall they be exalted." Zech. ix. 9. "Rejoice greatly, O daughter of Zion; shout, O daughter of Jerusalem: behold, thy King cometh," &c. The same is represented in other places innumerable. And because high degrees of joy are the proper and genuine fruits of the gospel of Christ, therefore the angel calls this gospel, *good tidings of great joy, that should be to all people.*

The *saints* and *angels* in *heaven*, who have religion in its highest perfection, are exceedingly affected with what they behold and contemplate of God's perfections and works. They are all as a pure heavenly flame of fire, in their love, and in the greatness and strength of their joy and gratitude. Their praises are represented, *as the voice of many waters, and as the voice of a great thunder.* Now the only reason why their affections are so much higher than the holy affections of saints on earth, is, they see things more according to their truth, and have their affections more conformed to the nature of things. And therefore, if religious affections in men here below, are but of the same nature and kind with theirs, the higher they are, and the nearer they are to theirs in degree, the better; because therein they will be so much the more conformed to truth, as theirs are.

From these things it certainly appears, that the existence of religious affections, in a very high degree, is no evidence that they are not such as have the nature of true religion. Therefore, they greatly err, who condemn persons as enthusiasts, merely because their affections are very high.

On the other hand, it is no evidence that religious affections are of a spiritual and gracious nature, because they are great. It is very manifest by the Holy Scripture, our sure and infallible rule in things of this nature, that there are very high religious affections which are not spiritual and saving. The apostle Paul speaks of affections in the Galatians which had been exceedingly elevated, but yet he feared that they were vain, and had come to nothing, Gal. iv. 15. "Where is the blessedness ye spake of? for I bear you record, that if it had been possible, you would have plucked out your own eyes, and have given them to me." And in the 11th verse he tells them, *he was afraid of them, lest he had bestowed upon them labour in vain.* So the children of Israel were greatly affected with God's mercy to them, when they had seen how wonderfully he wrought for them at the Red sea, where they *sang God's praise;* though they soon forgat his works. They were greatly affected again at mount Sinai, when they saw the marvellous manifestations God made of himself there; and seemed mightily engaged in their minds, and with great forwardness made answer, when God proposed his holy covenant to them, saying, *All that the Lord hath spoken will we do, and be obedient.* But how soon was there an end to all this mighty forwardness and engagedness of affection! How quickly were they turned aside after other gods, rejoicing and shouting around their golden calf! Great multitudes who were affected with the miracle of raising Lazarus from the dead, were elevated to a high degree, and made a mighty stir when Jesus very soon after entered into Jerusalem, exceedingly magnifying Christ, as though the ground were not good enough for the ass he rode to tread upon; and therefore cut down branches of palm trees, and strewed them in the way; yea, they pulled off their garments, and spread them; and cried with loud voices, *Hosanna to the son of David, blessed is he that cometh in the name of the Lord, hosanna in the highest;* so as to make the whole city ring again, and put all into an uproar. We learn by the evangelist John, that the reason why the people made this ado, was because they were affected with the miracle of raising Lazarus, John xii. 18. This vast multitude crying *Hosanna*, gave occasion to the Pharisees to say, *Behold, the world is gone after him,* John xii. 19.—but Christ had at that time but few true disciples. And how quickly was this fervour at an end! All is extinct when this Jesus stands bound, with a mock robe and a crown of thorns, to be derided, spit upon, scourged, condemned, and executed. Indeed there was a great and loud outcry concerning him, among the multitude then, as well as before; but of a very different kind: it is not then *Hosanna, hosanna,* but, *Crucify, crucify.*—In a word, it is the concurring voice of all orthodox divines, that there may be religious affections raised to a very high degree, and yet nothing of true religion.*

SECT. II.

It is no sign that affections have the nature of true religion, or that they have not, that they have great effects on the body.

ALL affections whatsoever have in some respect or degree, an effect on the body. As was observed before, such is our nature, and such are the laws of union of soul and body, that the mind can have no lively or vigorous exercise, without some effect upon the body. So subject is the body to the mind, and so much do its fluids, especially the animal spirits, attend the motions and exercises of the mind, that there cannot be so much as an intense thought, without an effect upon them. Yea it is questionable, whether an embodied soul ever so much as thinks one thought, or has any exercise at all, but that there is some corresponding motion or alteration of the fluids, in some part of the body. But universal experience shows, that the exercise of the affections have, in a special manner, a tendency to some sensible effect upon the body. And if all affections have some effect on the body, we may then well suppose, the greater those affections, and the more vigorous their exercises are, (other circumstances being equal,) the greater will be the effect on the body. Hence it is not to be wondered at, that very *great* and strong exercises of the affections should have *great* effects on the body. And therefore, seeing there are very great affections, both common and spiritual; hence it is not to be wondered at, that great effects on the body should arise from both these kinds of affections. And consequently these effects are no signs, that the affections they arise from are of one kind or the other.

Great effects on the body certainly are no sure evidences that affections are spiritual; for we see them oftentimes arise from great affections about temporal things, and when religion is no way concerned in them. And if great affections about things *purely natural* may have these effects, I know not by what rule we should determine, that high affections about *religious things,* which arise in like manner from nature, cannot have the like effect.

Nor, on the other hand, do I know of any rule to determine, that gracious affections, when raised as high as any natural affections, with equally strong and vigorous exercises, cannot have a great effect on the body. No such rule can be drawn from *reason:* I know of no reason, why a being affected with a view of God's glory should not cause the body to faint, as well as being affected with a view of Solomon's glory. And no such rule has as yet been produced from the *Scripture:* none has ever been found in all the late controversies about things of this nature. There is a great power in spiritual affections; we read of the *power which worketh in Christians,*† and of the Spirit of God being in them as the *Spirit of power,*‡ and of the effectual *working of his power* in them,§ yea, of the working of God's *mighty power* in them.‖ But man's nature is weak: flesh and blood are represented in Scripture as exceeding weak; and particularly with respect to its unfitness for great, spiritual, and heavenly operations and exercises. (Matt. xxvi. 41. 1 Cor. xv. 43, and 50.) The text prefixed to this discourse speaks of *joy unspeakable, and full of glory.* And who that considers what man's nature is, and what the nature of the affections are, can reasonably doubt, but that such unutterable and glorious joys, may be too great and mighty for weak dust and ashes, so as to be considerably overbearing to it? It is evident by the Scripture, that discoveries of God's glory, when given in a great degree, have a tendency, by affecting the mind, to overbear the body. The Scripture teaches us, that if these views should be given to such a degree, as they are given in heaven, the weak frame of the body could not subsist under it, and that no man can, in that manner, see God and live. The knowledge which the saints have of God's beauty and glory in this world, and those holy affections that arise from it, are of the same nature and kind with what the saints are the subjects of in heaven, differing only in degree and circumstances. What God gives them here, is a *foretaste* of heavenly happiness, and an *earnest* of their future inheritance. And who shall limit God in his giving this earnest, or say he shall give so much of the inheritance, such a part of the future reward, as an earnest of the whole, and no more? And seeing God has taught us in his word, that the whole reward is such, that it would at once destroy the body, is it not too bold a thing for us to set bounds to the sovereign God; or to say, that in giving the earnest of this reward, he shall never

* Mr. STODDARD observes, "That common affections are sometimes stronger than saving." *Guide to Christ,* p. 21.

† Eph. ii. 7. ‡ 2 Tim. i. 7. § Eph. iii. 7, 20. ‖ Eph. i. 19.

give so much of it, as in the least to diminish the strength of the body, when God has no where thus limited himself?

The psalmist speaking of his vehement religious affections, and of an effect in his flesh or body, besides what was in his soul, expressly distinguishes one from the other, Psal. lxxxiv. 2. "My soul longeth, yea, even fainteth for the courts of the Lord: my *heart* and my *flesh* crieth out for the living God." Here is a plain distinction between the *heart* and the *flesh*, as being each affected. So Psal. lxiii. 1. "My *soul* thirsteth for thee, my *flesh* longeth for thee in a dry and thirsty land, where no water is." Here also is an evident, designed distinction between the soul and the flesh.

The prophet Habakkuk speaks of his body being overborne by a sense of the majesty of God, Hab. iii. 16. "When I heard my belly trembled: my lips quivered at the voice: rottenness entered into my bones, and I trembled in myself." So the psalmist, Psal. cxix. 120 "My flesh trembleth for fear of thee."

That such ideas of God's glory as are given sometimes even in this world, have a tendency to overbear the body, is evident, because the Scripture gives us an account, that this has actually been the effect of those external manifestations which God made of himself to some of the saints, in order to give them an idea of his majesty and glory. Daniel giving an account of an external representation of the glory of Christ, says, Dan. x. 8. "And there remained no strength in me; for my comeliness was turned into corruption, and I retained no strength." And the apostle John, giving an account of a similar manifestation made to him, says, Rev. i. 17. "And when I saw him, I fell at his feet as dead." It is in vain to say here, that these were only external manifestations of the glory of Christ; for though this be true, yet the use of these representations, was to give an idea of the thing represented, the true divine glory and majesty of Christ. They were made use of only as significations of this spiritual glory, and thus undoubtedly they received and improved them, and were affected by them. According to the end for which God intended these outward signs, they received by them a great and lively apprehension of the real glory and majesty of God's nature, of which they were signs; and thus were greatly affected, their souls swallowed up, and their bodies overborne. And, I think, they are very bold and daring, who will say that God cannot, or shall not, give the like affecting apprehensions of the same real glory of his nature to none of his saints, without the intervention of such external shadows.

Before I leave this head, I would further observe, that it is plain the Scripture often makes use of bodily effects to express the strength of holy and spiritual affections; such as *trembling*,* *groaning*, † *being sick*, ‡ *crying out*, § *panting*, || and *fainting*.¶ Now if it be supposed, that these are only figurative expressions to represent the degree of affection; yet I hope all will allow, that they are *suitable* figures to represent the high degree of those spiritual affections; which I see not how they would be, if those spiritual affections are the proper effects and sad tokens of false affections, and the delusion of the devil. I cannot think, God would commonly make use of things which are very alien from spiritual affections, and are shrewd marks of the hand of Satan, and smell strong of the bottomless pit, as beautiful figures, to represent the high degree of holy and heavenly affections.

SECT. III.

It is no sign that affections are truly gracious, or that they are not, that they cause those who have them, to be fluent, fervent, and abundant in talking of religious things.

THERE are many persons, who, if they see this in others, are greatly prejudiced against them. Their being so full of talk, is with them a sufficient ground to condemn them as Pharisees, and ostentatious hypocrites. On the other hand, there are many who, if they see this effect in any, are very ignorantly and imprudently forward, at once to determine that they are the true children of God, under the saving influences of his Spirit, and speak of it as a great evidence of a new creature. *Such an one's mouth, say they, is now opened: he used to be slow to speak; but now he is full and free: he is free now to open his heart, and tell his experiences, and declare the praises of God; it comes from him, as free as water from a fountain;* and the like. And especially are they captivated into a confident persuasion that they are savingly wrought upon, if they are not only free and abundant, but very affectionate and earnest in their talk.

But this is the fruit of little judgment, and short experience; as events abundantly show: and is a mistake into which persons often run, through their trusting their own wisdom, and making their own notions their rule, instead of the Holy Scripture. Though the Scripture be full of rules, both how we should judge of our own state, and also how we should be conducted in our own opinion of others; yet we have no where any rule, by which to judge ourselves or others to be in a good estate, from any such effect: for this is but the religion of the tongue, and what is in the Scripture represented by the leaves of a tree, which—though the tree ought not to be without them, yet—are no where given as an evidence of the goodness of the tree.

That persons are disposed to be abundant in talking of religious things, may be from a good cause, and it may be from a bad one. It may be because their hearts are very full of holy affections; for *out of the abundance of the heart, the mouth speaketh*: and it may be because persons' hearts are very full of affection which is not holy; for still out of the abundance of the heart the mouth speaketh. It is very much the nature of the affections, of whatever kind, and whatever objects they are exercised about, if they are strong, to dispose persons to be very much in speaking of that with which they are affected; and not only to speak much, but to speak very earnestly and fervently. And therefore persons talking abundantly and very fervently about the things of religion, can be an evidence of no more than this, that they are very much *affected* with the things of religion; but this may be (as has been already shown) without any grace. That which men are greatly affected with, while the high affection lasts, they will be earnestly engaged about, and will be likely to show that earnestness in their talk and behaviour; as the greater part of the Jews, in all Judah and Galilee, did for a while, about John the Baptist's preaching and baptism, when they were willing for a season to rejoice in his light: a mighty stir was made all over the land, and among all sorts of persons, about this great prophet and his ministry. And so the multitude, in like manner, often manifested a great earnestness, a mighty engagedness of spirit, in every thing that was external, about Christ, his preaching and miracles, *being astonished at his doctrine, anon with joy receiving the word.* They followed him sometimes night and day, leaving meat, drink, and sleep to hear him; once they followed him into the wilderness, fasting three days going to hear him; sometimes extolling him to the clouds, saying, *Never man spake like this man!* being fervent and earnest in what they said. But what did these things come to, in the greater part of them?

A person may be over full of talk of his own experiences; falling upon it every where, and in all companies; and when so, it is rather a dark sign than a good one. A tree that is over full of leaves, seldom bears much fruit. And a cloud, though to appearance very pregnant and full of water, if it brings with it over much wind, seldom affords much rain to the dry and thirsty earth: which very thing the Holy Spirit is pleased several times to make use of, to represent a great show of religion with the mouth, without answerable fruit in the life, Prov. xxv. 14. "Whoso boasteth himself of a false gift, is like clouds and wind without rain." And the apostle Jude, speaking of some in the primitive times, that *crept in unawares* among the saints, and having a great show of religion, were for a while not suspected, *These are clouds* (says he) *without water, carried about of winds,* Jude ver. 4. and 12. And the apostle

* Psal. cxix. 120. Ezra ix. 4. Isa. lxvi. 2. 5, Hab. iii. 16.
† Rom. viii. 26. ‡ Cant. ii. 5. and v. 8. § Psal. lxxxiv. 2.
|| Psal. xxxviii. 10. and xlii. 1. and cxix 131.
¶ Psal lxxxiv. 2. and cxix. 81.

Peter, speaking of the same, says, 2 Pet. ii. 17. "These are clouds without water, carried with a tempest." False affections, if they are equally strong, are much more forward to declare themselves, than true: because it is the nature of false religion to affect show and observation; as it was with the Pharisees.*

SECT. IV.

It is no sign that affections are gracious, or that they are otherwise, that persons did not excite them by their own endeavours.

THERE are many in these days, who condemn all affections which are excited in a way that seems not to be the natural consequence of the faculties and principles of human nature, in such circumstances, and under such means; but to be from the influence of some extrinsic and supernatural power upon their minds. How greatly has the doctrine of the inward experience or sensible perceiving of the immediate power and operation of the Spirit of God, been reproached and ridiculed by many of late! They say, the manner of the Spirit of God, is to co-operate in a silent, secret, and undiscernible way with the use of means, and our own endeavours; so that there is no distinguishing by sense, between the influences of the Spirit of God, and the natural operations of the faculties of our own minds.

And it is true, that for any to expect to receive the saving influences of the Spirit of God, while they neglect a diligent improvement of the appointed means of grace, is unreasonable presumption. And to expect that the Spirit of God will savingly operate upon their minds, without the use of means, as subservient to the effect, is enthusiastical. It is also undoubtedly true, that the Spirit of God is very various in the manner and circumstances of his operations, and that sometimes he operates in a way more secret and gradual, and from smaller beginnings, than at others.

But if there be indeed a power, entirely different from and beyond our power—or the power of all means and instruments, and above the power of nature—which is requisite in order to the production of saving grace in the heart, according to the general profession of the country; then certainly, it is in no wise unreasonable to suppose, that this effect should very frequently be produced after such a manner, as to make it very manifest and sensible, that it is so. If grace be indeed owing to the powerful and efficacious operation of an extrinsic agent, or divine efficient out of ourselves, why is it unreasonable to suppose, it should seem to be so, to them who are the subjects of it? Is it a strange thing, that it should seem to be as it is? When grace in the heart indeed is not produced by our strength, nor is the effect of the natural power of our own faculties, or any means or instruments, but is properly the workmanship and production of the Spirit of the Almighty, is it a strange thing, that it should seem to them who are subjects of it, agreeable to truth, and not contrary to truth? If persons tell of effects that seem to them not to be from the natural power or operation of their minds, but from the supernatural power of some other agent, should it at once be looked upon as a sure evidence of their being under a delusion, because things seem to them to be as they are? For this is the objection which is made: it is looked upon as a clear evidence, that the apprehensions and affections that many persons have, are not really from such a cause, because they *seem* to them to be from that cause. They declare that what they are conscious of, seems to them evidently not to be from themselves, but from the mighty power of the Spirit of God; and others from hence condemn them, and determine that what they experience is not from the Spirit of God, but from themselves, or from the devil. Thus unreasonably are multitudes treated at this day, by their neighbours.

If it be indeed so, as the Scripture abundantly teaches, that grace in the soul is so the effect of God's power, that it is fitly compared to those effects, which are farthest from being owing to any strength in the subject, such as *generation*, or *a being begotten*, and *resurrection*, or *a being raised from the dead*, and *creation*, or *a being brought out of nothing into being*, and that is an effect wherein the mighty power of God is greatly glorified, and the exceeding greatness of his power manifested;† then what account can be given of it, that the Almighty, in so great a work of his power, should so carefully hide his power, that the subjects of it should be able to discern nothing of it? or what reason or revelation have any to determine that he does so? If we may judge by the Scripture, this is not agreeable to God's manner, in his operations and dispensations; but on the contrary, it is God's manner, in the great works of his power and mercy, to make his hand visible, and his power conspicuous, and men's dependence on him most evident, that no flesh should glory in his presence,‡ that God alone might be exalted,§ and that the excellency of the power might be of God and not of man,|| and that Christ's power might be manifested in our weakness,¶ and none might say, mine own hand hath saved me.** So it was in most of those temporal salvations which God wrought for Israel of old, which were types of the salvation of his people from their spiritual enemies. So, in the redemption of Israel from their Egyptian bondage; he redeemed them with a strong hand, and an outstretched arm; and that his power might be the more conspicuous, he suffered Israel first to be brought into the most helpless and forlorn circumstances. So, in the great redemption by Gideon; God would have his army diminished to a handful, and they without any other arms, than trumpets, and lamps, and earthen pitchers. So in the deliverance of Israel from Goliath, by a stripling, with a sling and a stone. So it was in that great work of God, his calling the Gentiles, after that the world by wisdom knew not God, and all the endeavours of philosophers to reform the world had failed, and it was become abundantly evident that the world had no effectual help but the mighty power of God. And so it was in most of the conversions of particular persons recorded in the history of the New Testament: they were not affected in that silent, secret, gradual, and insensible manner, which is now insisted on; but with those manifest evidences of a supernatural power, wonderfully and suddenly causing a great change, which in these days are looked upon as certain signs of delusion and enthusiasm.

The apostle in Eph. i. 18, 19. speaks of God enlightening the minds of Christians, and so bringing them to believe in Christ, to the end that they *might know* the exceeding greatness of his power to them who believe. The words are, "The eyes of your understanding being enlightened: that ye may know what is the hope of his calling, and what the riches of the glory of his inheritance in the saints, and what is the exceeding greatness of his power to us-ward who believe, according to the working of his mighty power," &c. Now when the apostle speaks of their being thus the subjects of his power, in their enlightening and effectual calling, to the end that they might *know* what his mighty power was to them who believe, he can mean nothing else, than *that they might know by experience*. But if the saints know this power by *experience*, then they feel it, discern it, and are conscious of it; as sensibly distinguishable from the natural operations of their own minds. But this is not agreeable to a notion of God operating so secretly, and undiscernibly, that it cannot be known they are the subjects of any extrinsic in-

* That famous experimental divine Mr. Shephard, says, "A Pharisee's trumpet shall be heard to the town's end; when simplicity walks through the town unseen. Hence a man will sometimes covertly commend himself, (and *myself* ever comes in,) and tells you a long story of conversion: and an hundred to one if some lie or other slip not out with it. Why, the secret meaning is, *I pray admire me*. Hence complain of wants and weaknesses; *pray think what a broken-hearted Christian I am*."—*Parab. of the Ten Virgins*, Part I. page 179, 180.

And holy Mr. Flavel says thus, "O reader, if thy heart were right with God, and thou didst not cheat thyself with a vain profession, thou wouldst have frequent business with God, which thou wouldst be loth thy dearest friend, or the wife of thy bosom, should be privy to. *Non est religio, ubi omnia patent*. Religion doth not lie open to all, to the eyes of men. Observed duties maintain our credit, but secret duties maintain our life. It was the saying of a heathen, about his secret correspondency with his friend, *What need the world to be acquainted with it? Thou and I are theatre enough to each other*. There are inclosed pleasures in religion, which none but renewed spiritual souls do feelingly understand." Flavel's *Touchstone of Sincerity*, chap. II. sect. 2.

† Eph. i. 17—20. ‡ 1 Cor. i. 27, 28, 29. § Isa. i. 11—17. || 2 Cor. iv. 7. ¶ 2 Cor. xii. 9. ** Judg. vii. 2.

fluence at all, otherwise than as they may argue it from scripture *assertions;* which is a different thing from knowing it by experience. So that it is very unreasonable and unscriptural, to determine that affections are not from the gracious operations of God's Spirit, because they are sensibly not from the persons themselves who are the subjects of them.

On the other hand, it is no evidence that affections are gracious, that they are not purposely produced by those who are the subjects of them, or that they arise in their minds in a manner which they cannot account for.

There are some who make this an argument in their own favour, when speaking of what they have experienced: "I am sure I did not make it myself: it was a fruit of no contrivance or endeavour of mine; it came when I thought nothing of it; if I might have the world for it, I cannot make it again when I please." And hence they determine, that what they have experienced, must be from the mighty influence of the Spirit of God, and is of a saving nature; but very ignorantly, and without grounds. What they have experienced may indeed not be from themselves directly, but may be from the operation of an invisible agent, some spirit besides their own: but it does not thence follow, that it was from the Spirit of God. There are other spirits who have influence on the minds of men, besides the Holy Ghost. We are directed not to believe every spirit, but to try the spirits, whether they be of God. There are many false spirits, exceeding busy with men, who often transform themselves into angels of light, and in many wonderful ways, with great subtlety and power, mimic the operations of the Spirit of God. And there are many of Satan's operations, which are very distinguishable from the voluntary exercises of men's own minds. They are so, in those dreadful and horrid suggestions, and blasphemous injections, with which he follows many persons; also in vain and fruitless frights and terrors, of which he is the author. And the power of Satan may be as immediate and as evident in false comforts and joys, as in terrors and horrid suggestions; and oftentimes is so in fact. It is not in men's power to put themselves into such raptures as those of the Anabaptists in Germany, and many other raving enthusiasts like them.

Besides, it is to be considered, that persons may have impressions on their minds, which may not be of their own producing, nor from an evil spirit, but from a common influence of the Spirit of God: and the subjects of such impressions, may be of the number of those we read of, Heb. vi. 4, 5. "that are once enlightened, and taste of the heavenly gift, and are made partakers of the Holy Ghost, and taste the good word of God, and the powers of the world to come;" and yet may be wholly unacquainted with those "better things that accompany salvation." And where neither a good nor evil spirit have any immediate hand, persons, especially such as are of a weak and vapoury habit of body, and the brain easily susceptive of impressions, may have strange apprehensions and imaginations, and strong affections attending them, unaccountably arising, which are not voluntarily produced by themselves. We see that such persons are liable to such impressions, about temporal things; and there is equal reason, why they should about spiritual things. As a person asleep has dreams, of which he is not the voluntary author; so may such persons, in like manner, be the subjects of involuntary impressions, when they are awake.

SECT. V.

It is no sign that religious affections are truly holy and spiritual, or that they are not, that they come to the mind in a remarkable manner with texts of Scripture.

IT is no sign that affections are *not* gracious, that they are occasioned by scriptures *so* coming to mind; provided it be the *Scripture* itself—or the truth which the Scripture so brought contains and teaches—that is the foundation of the affection, and not merely or mainly the sudden and unusual *manner* of its coming to the mind.

But on the other hand, neither is it any sign that affections *are* gracious, that they arise on occasion of scriptures brought suddenly and wonderfully to the mind; whether those affections be fear or hope, joy or sorrow, or any other. Some seem to look upon *this* as a good evidence that their affections are saving, especially if the affections excited are hope or joy, or any other which are pleasing and delightful. They will mention it as an evidence that all is right, that their experience *came with the word,* and will say, "There were such and such sweet promises brought to my mind: they came suddenly, as if they were spoke to me: I had no hand in bringing such a text to my own mind; I was not thinking of any thing leading to it; it came all at once, so that I was surprised. I had not thought of it a long time before; I did not know at first that it was Scripture; I did not remember that ever I had read it." And it may be they will add, "One scripture came flowing in after another, and so texts all over the Bible, the most sweet and pleasant, and the most apt and suitable, which could be devised; and filled me full as I could hold: I could not but stand and admire: the tears flowed; I was full of joy, and could not doubt any longer." And thus they think they have undoubted evidence, that their affections must be from God, and of the right kind, and their state good: but without any good grounds. How come they by any such *rule,* as that if any affections or experiences arise with promises, and comfortable texts of Scripture, unaccountably brought to mind, without their recollection, or if a great number of sweet texts follow one another in a chain, that this is a certain evidence their experiences are saving? Where is any such rule to be found in the Bible, the great and only sure directory in things of this nature?

What deceives many of the less knowing and considerate sort of people, in this matter, seems to be this; that the Scripture is the word of God, and has nothing in it which is wrong, but is pure and perfect: and therefore, those experiences which come from the Scripture must be right But then it should be considered, affections may arise on *occasion* of the Scripture, and not properly come *from,* as the genuine fruit of the Scripture; but from an abuse of it. All that can be argued from the purity and perfection of the word of God, with respect to experiences, is this, that those experiences which are *agreeable* to the word of God, are right, and cannot be otherwise: and not that those affections must be right, which arise *on occasion* of the word of God coming to the mind.

What evidence is there that the devil cannot bring texts of Scripture to the mind, and misapply them, to deceive persons? There seems to be nothing in this which exceeds the power of Satan. It is no work of such mighty power, to bring sounds or letters to persons' minds. If Satan has power to bring *any* words or sounds at all to persons' minds, he may have power to bring words contained in the Bible. There is no higher sort of power required in men, to make the sounds which express the words of a text of Scripture, than to make the sounds which express the words of an idle story or song. And so the same power in Satan which is sufficient to renew one of those in the mind, is sufficient to renew the other: the different signification, which depends wholly on custom, alters not the case, as to ability to make or revive the sounds or letters. Or will any suppose, that texts of Scripture are such sacred things, that the devil durst not abuse them, nor touch them? In this also they are mistaken. He who was bold enough to lay hold on Christ himself, and carry him hither and thither, into the wilderness, into a high mountain, and to a pinnacle of the temple, is not afraid to touch the Scripture, and abuse that for his own purposes. For, at the same time that he was so bold with Christ, he brought one scripture and another to deceive and tempt him. And if Satan did presume, and was permitted to put Christ himself in mind of texts of Scripture to tempt *him,* what reason have we to determine, that he dare not, or will not be permitted, to put wicked men in mind of texts of Scripture, to tempt and deceive *them?* And if Satan may thus abuse one text of Scripture, so he may another. Its being a very excellent place of Scripture, a comfortable and precious promise, alters not the case, as to his courage or ability. And if he can bring one comfortable text to the mind, so he may a thousand; and may choose out such scriptures as tend most to serve his purpose. He may heap up scripture promises, tending, according to the perverse application he makes of them, wonderfully to remove the rising doubts, and to confirm the false joy and confidence, of a poor deluded sinner.

We know the devil's instruments, corrupt and heretical teachers, can and do pervert the Scripture, to their own and other's damnation, 2 Pet. iii. 16. We see they have the free use of Scripture, in every part of it; there is no text so precious and sacred, but they are permitted to abuse it, to the eternal ruin of souls; and there are no weapons they use, with which they do more execution. There is no manner of reason to determine, that the devil is not permitted thus to abuse the Scripture, as well as his instruments. For when the latter do it, they do it as his instruments, through his instigation and influence: and doubtless the devil's servants do but follow their master, and do the same work that he does himself.

And as the devil can abuse the Scripture, to deceive and destroy men, so may men's own folly and corruptions. Men's own hearts are deceitful like the devil, and use the same means to deceive. So that it is evident, that persons may have high affections of hope and joy, arising on occasion of texts of Scripture, yea precious promises coming suddenly and remarkably to their minds, as though they were spoken to them, yea a great multitude of such texts following one another in a wonderful manner; and yet all this be no argument that these affections are divine, or that they are any other than the effects of Satan's delusions.

I would further observe, that persons may have raised and joyful affections, which may come *with* the word of God, and not only so, but *from* the word, and those affections not be from Satan, nor yet properly from the corruptions of their own hearts, but from some influence of the Spirit of God with the word, and yet have nothing of the nature of *true* and *saving* religion in them. Thus the stony-ground hearers had great joy from the word; yea, arising from the word, as growth from a seed; and their affections had, in their appearance, a very great and exact resemblance with those represented by the growth on the good ground—the difference not appearing, until it was discovered by the consequences in a time of trial—and yet there was no *saving* religion in these affections.*

SECT. VI.

It is no evidence that religious affections are saving, or that they are otherwise, that there is an appearance of love in them.

THERE are no professing Christians who pretend, that this is an argument against the truth and saving nature of religious affections. But on the other hand, there are some who suppose, it is a good evidence that affections are from the sanctifying and saving influences of the Holy Ghost. Their argument is, that *Satan cannot love;* this affection being directly contrary to the devil, whose very nature is enmity and malice. And it is true, that nothing is more excellent, heavenly, and divine, than a spirit of true christian love to God and men: it is more excellent than *knowledge*, or *prophecy*, or *miracles*, or *speaking with the tongue of men and angels*. It is the chief of the graces of God's Spirit, and the life, essence, and sum of all true religion; and that by which we are most conformed to heaven, and most contrary to hell and the devil. But yet it is ill arguing from hence, that there are no counterfeits of it. It may be observed, that the more excellent any thing is, the more will be the counterfeits of it. Thus there are many more counterfeits of silver and gold, than of iron and copper: there are many false diamonds and rubies, but who goes about to counterfeit common stones? Though the more excellent things are, the more difficult it is to make any thing like them, in their essential nature and internal virtue; yet the more manifold will the counterfeits be, and the more will art and subtlety be exercised and displayed, in an exact imitation of the outward appearance. Thus there is the greatest danger of being cheated in buying medicines that are most excellent and sovereign, though it be most difficult to imitate them, with any thing of the like value and virtue, and their counterfeits are good for nothing when we have them. So it is with christian virtues and graces; the subtlety of Satan, and men's deceitful hearts, are wont chiefly to be exercised in counterfeiting those that are in highest repute. So there are perhaps no graces that have more counterfeits than love and humility; these being virtues wherein the beauty of a true Christian especially appears.

But with respect to love, it is plain by the Scripture, that persons may have a kind of religious love, and yet have no saving grace. Christ speaks of many professing Christians whose love will not continue, and so shall fail of salvation, Matt. xxiv. 12, 13. "And because iniquity shall abound, the love of many shall wax cold. But he that shall endure unto the end, the same shall be saved." Which latter words plainly show, that those spoken of before, whose love shall not *endure to the end*, but *wax cold*, should not be saved. Persons may seem to have love to God and Christ, yea, to have very strong and violent affections of this nature, and yet have no grace. This was evidently the case with many graceless Jews, such as cried Jesus up so high, following him day and night, without meat, drink, or sleep; such as said, *Lord, I will follow thee whithersoever thou goest*, and cried, *Hosanna to the son of David.*†—The apostle seems to intimate, that there were many in his days, who had a counterfeit love to Christ, in Eph. vi. 24. "Grace be with all them that love our Lord Jesus Christ *in sincerity*." The last word, in the original, signifies *in incorruption;* which shows, that the apostle was sensible there were many who had a kind of love to Christ, which was not pure and spiritual.

So also christian love to the people of God may be counterfeited. It is evident by the Scripture, that there may be strong affections of this kind, without saving grace; as there were in the Galatians towards the apostle Paul, when they were ready to pluck out their eyes and give them to him; although the apostle expresses his fear that their affections were come to nothing, and that he had bestowed upon them labour in vain. Gal. iv. 11, 15.

SECT. VII.

Persons having religious affections of many kinds, accompanying one another, is not sufficient to determine whether they have any gracious affections or no.

THOUGH false religion is wont to be maimed and monstrous, and not to have that entireness and symmetry of parts, which is to be seen in true religion; yet there may be a great variety of false affections together, that may resemble gracious affections.

It is evident that there are counterfeits of all kinds of gracious affections; as of *love to God*, and *love to the brethren*, as just now observed; so of *godly sorrow for sin*, as in Pharaoh, Saul, Ahab, and the children of Israel in the wilderness;‡ and of the *fear of God*, as in the Samaritans, *who feared the Lord, and served their own gods* at the same time, (2 Kings xvii. 32, 33.) and those enemies of God we read of, Psal. lxvi. 3. who *through the greatness of God's power, submit themselves to him*, or, as it is in the Hebrew, *lie unto him, i. e.* yield a counterfeit reverence and submission: so of a *gracious gratitude*, as in the children of Israel, who sang God's praise at the Red sea, (Psal. cvi. 12.) and Naaman the Syrian, after his miraculous cure of his leprosy, (2 Kings v. 15, &c.)

* Mr. Stoddard, in his *Guide to Christ*, speaks of it as a *common thing*, for persons while in a natural condition, and before they have ever truly *accepted of Christ*, to have scripture *promises* come to them, with *a great deal of refreshing;* which they *take as tokens of God's love, and hope that God has accepted them;* and so are confident of their good estate, page 8, 9. Impression *anno* 1735.

† Agreeable to this Mr. Stoddard observes, in his *Guide to Christ*, that some sinners have pangs of affection, and give an account that they find a spirit of love to God, and of their aiming at the glory of God, having that which has a great resemblance of saving grace; and that sometimes their common affections are stronger than saving. And supposes, that sometimes natural men may have such violent pangs of false affection to God, that they may think themselves willing to be damned. Page 21, and 65.

‡ Exod. ix. 27. 1 Sam. xxiv. 16, 17. and xxvi. 21. 1 Kings xxi. 27. Num. xiv 39, 40.

So of *spiritual joy*, as in the stony-ground hearers, (Matt. xiii. 20.) and particularly many of John the Baptist's hearers, (John v. 35.) So of *zeal*, as in Jehu, (2 Kings x. 6.) and in Paul before his conversion, (Gal. i. 14. Phil. iii. 6.) and the unbelieving Jews, (Acts xxii. 3. Rom. x. 2.) So graceless persons may have earnest religious *desires*, which may be like Balaam's desires, which he expresses under an extraordinary view of the happy state of God's people, as distinguished from all the rest of the world, (Num. xxiii. 9, 10.) They may also have a strong *hope* of eternal life, as the Pharisees had.

And as men, while in a state of nature, are capable of a resemblance of all kinds of religious affection, so nothing hinders but that they may have many of them together. And what appears in fact, abundantly evinces that it is thus very often. Commonly, when false affections are raised high, many of them attend each other. The multitude that attended Christ into Jerusalem, after that great miracle of raising Lazarus, seem to be moved with many religious affections at once, and all in a high degree. They seem to be filled with *admiration;* and there was a show of high affection of *love;* also a great degree of *reverence*, in their laying their garments on the ground for Christ to tread upon. They express great *gratitude* to him, for the great and good works he had wrought, praising him with loud voices for his salvation; and earnest *desires* of the coming of God's kingdom, which they supposed Jesus was now about to set up; and they showed great *hopes* and raised expectations of it, *expecting it would immediately appear*. Hence they were filled with *joy*, by which they were so animated in their acclamations, as to make the whole city ring again with the noise of them; and they appeared great in their *zeal* and forwardness to attend Jesus, and assist him without further delay, now in the time of the great feast of the *passover*, to set up his kingdom.

It is easy from the nature of the affections, to give an account why, when one affection is raised very high, that it should excite others; especially if the affection which is raised high, be that of counterfeit *love*, as it was in the multitude who cried *Hosanna*. This will naturally draw many other affections after it. For, as was observed before, love is the chief of the affections, and as it were, the fountain of them. Let us suppose a person, who has been for some time in great exercise and terror through fear of hell; his heart weakened with distress and dreadful apprehensions, upon the brink of despair; and who is all at once delivered, by being firmly made to believe, through some delusion of Satan, that God has pardoned him, and accepts him as the object of his dear love, and promises him eternal life. Suppose also, that this is done through some vision, or strong imagination suddenly excited in him, of a person with a beautiful countenance smiling on him—with arms open, and with blood dropping down—which the person conceives to be Christ, without any other enlightening of the understanding to give a view of the spiritual, divine excellency of Christ and his fulness, and of the way of salvation revealed in the gospel. Or, suppose some voice or words coming as if they were spoken to him, such as these, "Son, be of good cheer, thy sins be forgiven thee;" or, "Fear not, it is the Father's good pleasure to give you the kingdom," which he takes to be immediately spoken by God to him, though there was no preceding acceptance of Christ, or closing of the heart with him: I say, if we should suppose such a case, what various passions would naturally crowd at once, or one after another, into such a person's mind! It is easy to be accounted for, from the mere principles of nature, that a person's heart, on such an occasion, should be raised up to the skies with transports of joy, and be filled with fervent affection to that imaginary God or Redeemer, who, he supposes, has thus rescued him from the jaws of such dreadful destruction, and received him with such endearment, as a peculiar favourite. Is it any wonder that now he should be filled with admiration and gratitude, his mouth should be opened, and be full of talk about what he has experienced? That, for a while, he should think and speak of scarce any thing else, should seem to magnify that God who has done so much for him, call upon others to rejoice with him, appear with a cheerful countenance, and talk with a loud voice? That however, before his deliverance, he was full of quarrellings against the justice of God, now it should be easy for him to submit to God, own his unworthiness, cry out against himself, appear to be very humble before God, and lie at his feet as tame as a lamb; now confessing his unworthiness, and crying out, *Why me? why me?* Thus Saul, who, when Samuel told him that God had appointed him to be king, makes answer, "Am not I a Benjamite, of the smallest of the tribes of Israel, and my family the least of all the families of the tribe of Benjamin? wherefore then speakest thou so to me?" Much in the language of David, the true saint, 2 Sam. vii. 18. "Who am I, and what is my father's house, that thou hast brought me hitherto?" Is it to be wondered at, that now he should delight to be with them who acknowledge and applaud his happy circumstances, and that he should love all such as esteem and admire him and what he has experienced? That he should have violent zeal against all who make nothing of such things, be disposed openly to separate, and as it were to proclaim war with all who are not of his party? That he should now glory in his sufferings, and be very much for condemning and censuring all who seem to doubt, or make any difficulty of these things? And, while the warmth of his affections last, that he should be mighty forward to take pains, and to deny himself, and to promote the interest of a party favouring such things? Or that he should seem earnestly desirous to increase the number of them, as the Pharisees compassed sea and land to make one *proselyte?** I might mention many other things, which will naturally arise in such circumstances. He must have but slightly considered human nature, who thinks that such things as these cannot arise in this manner, without any supernatural interposition of divine power.

As from true divine love flow all Christian affections, so from counterfeit love naturally flow other false affections. In both cases, love is the fountain, and the other affections are the streams. The various faculties, principles, and affections of the human nature, are as it were many channels from one fountain. If there be sweet water in the fountain, sweet water will flow out into those various channels; but if the water in the fountain be poisonous, then poisonous streams will also flow into all those channels. So that the channels and streams will be alike, corresponding one with another; but the great difference will lie in the nature of the water. Or man's nature may be compared to a tree with many branches, coming from one root: if the sap in the root be good, there will also be good sap distributed throughout the branches, and the fruit brought forth will be good and wholesome; but if the sap in the root and stock be poisonous, so it will be in many branches, and the fruit will be deadly. The tree in both cases may be alike; there may be an exact resemblance in shape; but the difference is found only in eating the fruit. It is thus, in some measure at least, oftentimes between saints and hypocrites. There is sometimes a very great similitude between true and false experiences in their appearance, and in what is expressed by the subjects of them; the difference between them is much like the difference between the dreams of Pharaoh's chief butler and baker. They seemed to be much alike, insomuch that when Joseph interpreted the chief butler's dream, that he should be delivered from his imprisonment, and restored to the king's favour, and his honourable office in the palace, the chief baker had raised hopes and expectations, and told his dream also. But he was wofully disappointed; for though his dream was so much like the happy and well-boding dream of his companion, yet it was quite contrary in its issue.

* "Associating with godly men does not prove that a man has grace: Ahithophel was David's companion. Sorrows for the afflictions of the church, and desires for the conversion of souls, do not prove it. These things may be found in carnal men, and so can be no evidences of grace." Stoddard's *Nature of Saving Conversion*, p. 82.

SECT. VIII.

Nothing can certainly be determined concerning the nature of the affections, that comforts and joys seem to follow in a certain order.

Many persons seem to be prejudiced against affections and experiences that come in such a method as has been much insisted on by many divines; first, such awakenings, fears, and awful apprehensions, followed with such legal humblings, in a sense of total sinfulness and helplessness, and then, such and such light and comfort. They look upon all such schemes, laying down such methods and steps, to be of men's devising: and particularly if high affections of joy follow great distress and terror, it is made by many an argument against those affections. But such prejudices and objections are without reason or Scripture. Surely it cannot be unreasonable to suppose, that before God delivers persons from a state of sin and exposedness to eternal destruction, he should give them some considerable sense of the evil from which he delivers; that they may be delivered sensibly, and understand their own salvation, and know something of what God does for them. As men that are saved are in two exceeding different states, first a state of condemnation, and then in a state of justification and blessedness; and as God, in the work of salvation, deals with them suitably to their intelligent nature; so it seems reasonable, and agreeable to God's wisdom, that men who are saved, should be in these two states *sensibly;* that they should be first sensible of their absolute extreme necessity, and afterwards of Christ's sufficiency and God's mercy through him.

And that it is God's manner of dealing with men, to *lead them into a wilderness, before he speaks comfortably to them*, and so to order it, that they shall be brought into distress, and made to see their own helplessness, and absolute dependence on his power and grace, before he appears to work any great deliverance for them, is abundantly manifest by the Scripture. Then is God wont to *repent himself for his professing people, when their strength is gone, and there is none shut up or left:* and when they are brought to see that their false gods cannot help them, and that the rock in whom they trusted is vain, Deut. xxxii. 36, 37. Before God delivered the children of Israel out of Egypt, they were prepared for it, by being made to *see that they were in an evil case, and to cry unto God, because of their hard bondage*, Exod. ii. 23. and v. 19. And before God wrought that great deliverance for them at the Red sea, they were brought into great distress, *the wilderness had shut them in*, they could not turn to the right hand nor the left. The Red sea was before them, the great Egyptian host behind, and they were brought to see that they could do nothing to help themselves, and that if God did not help them, they should be immediately swallowed up. Then God appeared, and turned their cries into songs. So before they were brought to their rest, and to enjoy the milk and honey of Canaan, God "led them through a great and terrible wilderness, that he might humble them, and teach them what was in their heart, and so do them good in their latter end," Deut. viii. 2, 16. The woman that had the issue of blood twelve years, was not delivered, until she had first *spent all her living on earthly physicians, and could not be healed of any*, and so was left helpless, having no more money to spend. Then she came to the great Physician, without money or price, and was healed by him, Luke viii. 43, 44. Before Christ would answer the request of the woman of Canaan, he first seemed utterly to deny her, and humbled her, and brought her to own herself worthy to be called a dog; and then he showed her mercy, and received her as a dear child, Matt. xv. 22, &c. The apostle Paul, before a remarkable deliverance, was "pressed out of measure above strength, insomuch that he despaired even of life; but had the sentence of death in himself, that he might not trust in himself, but in God that raiseth the dead," 2 Cor. i. 8, 9, 10. There was first a great tempest, and the ship was covered with the waves, and just ready to sink, and the disciples were brought to cry to Jesus, *Lord, save us, we perish;* then the winds and seas were rebuked, and there was a great calm, Matt. viii. 24—26. The leper, before he was cleansed, must have his mouth stopped, by a covering on his upper lip, and was to acknowledge his great misery and utter uncleanness, by rending his clothes, and crying, *Unclean, unclean*, Lev. xiii. 45. And backsliding Israel, before God heals them, are brought to "acknowledge that they have sinned, and have not obeyed the voice of the Lord; to see that they lie down in their shame, and that confusion covers them; that in vain is salvation hoped for from the hills, and from the multitude of mountains," and that God only can save them, Jer. iii. 23, 24, 25. Joseph, who was sold by his brethren, and therein was a type of Christ, brings his brethren into great perplexity and distress, to reflect on their sin, and to say, *we are verily guilty*, and at last to resign up themselves entirely into his hands for bondmen. Then he reveals himself to them, as their brother and their saviour.

If we consider those extraordinary manifestations which God made of himself to saints of old, we shall find that he commonly first manifested himself in a way which was *terrible*, and then by those things that were *comfortable*. So it was with Abraham; first, *a horror of great darkness fell upon him*, and then God revealed himself to him in sweet promises, Gen. xv. 12, 13. So it was with Moses at mount Sinai; first, God appeared to him in all the terrors of his dreadful majesty, so that Moses said, *I exceedingly fear and quake;* and then he made all his goodness to pass before him, and proclaimed his name, *The Lord God gracious and merciful*, &c. So it was with Elijah; first, there is a stormy wind, and earthquake, and devouring fire, and then a still, small, sweet voice, 1 Kings xix. So it was with Daniel; he first saw Christ's countenance as lightning, that terrified him, and caused him to faint away; and then he is strengthened and refreshed with such comfortable words as these, "O Daniel, a man greatly beloved," Dan. x. So it was with the apostle John, Rev. i. There is an analogy observable in God's dispensations and deliverances which he works for his people, and the manifestation which he makes of himself to them, both ordinary and extraordinary.

But there are many things in Scripture which more directly show, that this is God's ordinary manner in working salvation for the souls of men; and in the manifestations he makes of himself and of his mercy in Christ, in the ordinary works of his grace on the hearts of sinners. The servant that owed his prince ten thousand talents, is first held to his debt. The king pronounces sentence of condemnation upon him, and commands him to be sold, and his wife and children, that payment be made. Thus he humbles him, and brings him to own the whole debt to be just; and then forgives him all. The prodigal son spends all he has, is brought to see himself in extreme circumstances, to humble himself, and own his unworthiness, before he is relieved and feasted by his father, Luke xv. Old inveterate wounds must be searched to the bottom, in order to healing: and to this the Scripture compares sin, the wound of the soul, and speaks of healing this wound without thus searching it, as vain and deceitful, Jer. viii. 11. Christ, in the work of his grace on the hearts of men, is compared to rain on the mown grass, grass that is cut down with a scythe, Psal. lxxii. 6. representing his refreshing, comforting influences on the wounded spirit. Our first parents, after they had sinned, were first terrified with God's majesty and justice, and had their sin, with its aggravations, set before them by their Judge, before they were relieved by the promise of the seed of the woman. Christians are spoken of as those "that have fled for refuge, to lay hold on the hope set before them," Heb. vi. 18. which representation implies great fear, and sense of danger preceding. To the like purpose, Christ is called "a hiding-place from the wind, and a covert from the tempest, and as rivers of water in a dry place, and as the shadow of a great rock in a weary land," Isa. xxxii. And it seems to be the natural import of the word *gospel*, glad tidings, that it is news of deliverance and salvation, after great fear and distress. There is all reason to suppose, that God deals with particular believers, as he dealt with his church, which he first made to hear his voice in the law, with terrible thunders and lightnings, and kept her under that schoolmaster, to prepare her for Christ; and then comforted her with the joyful sound of the gospel from mount Sion. So likewise John the Baptist came to prepare the way for Christ, and prepare men's hearts for his reception, by showing them their sins, and by bringing the self-righteous Jews off from their own righteousness, telling them that they were a *generation of vipers*, and showing them their danger of *the wrath to come*, telling them that *the axe was laid at the root of the trees*, &c.

If it be indeed God's manner, (and I think the foregoing considerations show that it undoubtedly is,) before he gives men the comfort of a deliverance from their sin and misery, to give them a considerable sense of the greatness and dreadfulness of those evils, and their extreme wretchedness by reason of them; surely it is not unreasonable to suppose, that persons, at least oftentimes, while under these views, should have great distresses and terrible apprehensions of mind. For let it be considered what these evils are, of which they have a view; *viz.* great and manifold sins, against the infinite majesty of the great JEHOVAH, and the suffering of the fierceness of his wrath to all eternity. And we have many plain instances in Scripture, of persons that have actually been brought into extreme distress by such convictions, before they have received saving consolations: as the multitude at Jerusalem, who were "pricked in their heart, and said unto Peter, and the rest of the apostles, Men and brethren, what shall we do?" The apostle Paul *trembled, and was astonished*, before he was comforted; and the jailor "called for a light, sprang in, and came trembling, and fell down before Paul and Silas, and said, Sirs, what must I do to be saved?"

From these things it appears to be very unreasonable in professing Christians, to make this an objection against the truth and spiritual nature of their comfortable and joyful affections, *viz.* that they follow such awful apprehensions and distresses as have been mentioned.

On the other hand, it is no evidence that comforts and joys are right, because they succeed great terrors, and amazing fears of hell.* This seems to be what some persons lay great weight upon; esteeming great terrors an evidence of a great work of the law wrought on the heart, well preparing the way for solid comfort: not considering that terror, and a conviction of conscience, are different things. For though convictions of conscience often *cause* terror; yet they do not *consist* in it; and terrors often arise from other causes. Convictions of conscience, through the influences of God's Spirit, consist in conviction of sinfulness in heart and practice, and of the dreadfulness of sin, as committed against a God of terrible majesty, infinite holiness and hatred of sin, and strict justice in punishing of it. But some persons have frightful apprehensions of hell—a dreadful pit ready to swallow them up, flames just ready to lay hold of them, and devils all around ready to seize them—who at the same time seem to have very little proper light of conscience, really convincing them of their sinfulness of heart and life. The devil, if permitted, can terrify men as well as the Spirit of God. It is a work natural to him, and he has many ways of doing it in a manner tending to no good. He may exceedingly affright persons by impressing on them many external images and doleful ideas; as of a countenance frowning, a sword drawn, black clouds of vengeance, words of an awful doom pronounced,† hell gaping, devils coming, and the like—not in order to convince persons of things that are true, and revealed in the word of God, but—to lead them to vain and groundless determinations; as that their day is past, that they are reprobated, that God is implacable, that he has come to a resolution immediately to cut them off, &c.

And the terrors of some persons are very much owing to their particular constitution and temper. Nothing is more manifest, than that some persons are of such a temper and frame, that their imaginations are strongly impressed with every thing they are affected with; and the impression on the imagination re-acts on the affection, and raises that still higher. Affection and imagination act reciprocally one on another, till their affection is raised to a vast height; so the person is swallowed up, and loses all possession of himself.‡

Some speak of a great sight they have of their wickedness, who really, when the matter comes to be well examined, are found to have little or no convictions of conscience. They speak of a dreadful hard heart, and how it lies like a stone; when truly they have none of those things in their minds or thoughts, wherein the hardness of their heart really consists. They speak of a dreadful load and sink of sin, a heap of black and loathsome filthiness within them; when, if the matter be carefully inquired into, they have not in view any thing wherein the corruption of nature does truly consist. Nor have they any thought of particular things wherein their hearts are sinfully defective, or fall short of what ought to be in them. And many think they have great convictions of their actual sins, who truly have none. They tell you that their sins are set in order before them, they see them stand encompassing them round, with a frightful appearance; when really they are not affected with the aggravations of any one of their sins.

And if persons have had great terrors which really have been from the awakening and convincing influences of the Spirit of God, it doth not thence follow that their terrors must needs issue in true comfort. The unmortified corruption of the heart may quench the Spirit of God, (after he has been striving,) by leading men to presumptuous and self-exalting hopes and joys, as well as otherwise. It is not every woman who is really in travail, that brings forth a real child; but it may be a monstrous production, without the form or properties of human nature. Pharaoh's chief baker, after he had lain in the dungeon with Joseph, had a vision that raised his hopes, and he was lifted up out of the dungeon, as well as the chief butler; but it was to be hanged.

But if comforts and joys not only come after great terrors and awakenings, but with an appearance of *such* preparatory convictions and humiliations, and brought about very distinctly, by *such* steps, and in *such* a method, as has frequently been observable in true converts; this is no certain sign that the light and comforts which follow are true and saving; for these following reasons:

First, As the devil can counterfeit all the saving operations and graces of the Spirit of God, so he can counterfeit those operations that are preparatory to grace. If Satan can counterfeit those effects of God's Spirit which are special, divine, and sanctifying; so that there shall be a very great resemblance, in all that can be observed by others; much more easily may he imitate those works of God's Spirit which are common, and of which men, while they are yet his own children, are the subjects. These works are in no wise so much above him as the other. There are no works of God that are so high and divine, above the powers of nature, and out of the reach of the power of all creatures, as those works of his Spirit whereby he forms the creature in his own image, and makes it to be a partaker of the divine nature. But if the devil can be the author of such resemblances of these as have been spoken of, without doubt he may of those that are of an infinitely inferior kind. And it is abundantly evident in fact, that there are false humiliations, and false submissions, as well as false comforts.§ How far was Saul brought, though a very wicked man, and of a haughty spirit, when he (though a great king) was brought, in conviction of his sin,

* Mr. Shepard speaks of "men's being cast down as low as hell by sorrow, and lying under chains, quaking in apprehension of terror to come, and then raised up to heaven in joy, not able to live; and yet not rent from lust; and such are objects of pity now, and are like to be the objects of terror at the great day."—*Parable of the Ten Virgins* P. i. p. 125.

† "The way of the Spirit's working, when it does convince men, is by enlightening natural conscience. The Spirit does not work by giving a testimony, but by assisting natural conscience to do its work. Natural conscience is the instrument in the hand of God, to accuse, condemn, terrify, and to urge to duty. The Spirit of God leads men into the consideration of their danger, and makes them to be affected therewith, Prov. xx. 27. 'The spirit of man is the candle of the Lord, searching all the inward parts of the belly.'" Stoddard's *Guide to Christ*, p. 44.

‡ The famous Mr. Perkins distinguishes between "those sorrows that come through convictions of conscience, and melancholic passions arising only from mere imaginations, strongly conceived in the brain; which he says, usually come on a sudden, like lightning into a house." Vol. i. of his works, p. 385.

§ The venerable Stoddard observes, "A man may say, that now he can *justify God however he deals with him*, and not be brought off from his own righteousness; and that some men do justify God, from a partial conviction of the righteousness of their condemnation; conscience takes notice of their sinfulness, and tells them that they may be righteously damned; as Pharaoh, who justified God, Exod. ix. 27. And they give some kind of consent to it, but many times it does not continue, they have only a pang upon them, that usually dies away after a little time."—*Guide to Christ*, p. 11.

all in tears, weeping aloud, before David his own subject—one whom he had for a long time mortally hated, and openly treated as an enemy—crying out, "Thou art more righteous than I: for thou hast rewarded me good, whereas I have rewarded thee evil!" And at another time, "I have sinned, I have played the fool, I have erred exceedingly," 1 Sam. xxiv. 16, 17. and chap. xxvi. 21. And yet Saul seems then to have had very little of the influences of the Spirit of God, it being after God's Spirit had departed from him, and an evil spirit from the Lord troubled him. And if this proud monarch, in a pang of affection, was brought to humble himself so low, before a subject that he hated; there doubtless may be appearances of great conviction and humiliation in men, before God, while they yet remain enemies to him, and though they finally continue so. There is oftentimes in men, who are terrified through fears of hell, a great appearance of their being brought off from their own righteousness, when they are not brought off from it in *all* ways. They have only exchanged *some* ways of trusting in their own righteousness, for others that are more secret and subtle. Oftentimes a great degree of discouragement, as to many things they used to depend upon, is taken for humiliation: and that is called a submission to God, which is no absolute submission, but has some secret bargain in it, that it is hard to discover.

Secondly, If the operations and effects of the Spirit of God, in the convictions and comforts of true converts, may be sophisticated, then the order of them may be imitated. If Satan can imitate the things themselves, he may easily put them one after another, in such a certain order. If the devil can make A, B, and C, it is as easy for him to put A first, and B next, and C next, as to range them in a contrary order. The nature of divine things is harder for the devil to imitate, than their order. He cannot *exactly* imitate divine operations in their *nature,* though his counterfeits may be very much like them in external appearance; but he can exactly imitate their *order.* When counterfeits are made, there is no divine power needful in order to the placing one of them first, and another last. And therefore no order or method of operations and experiences, is any certain sign of their divinity. That only is to be trusted to, as a certain evidence of grace, which Satan cannot do, and which it is impossible should be brought to pass by any power short of divine.

Thirdly, We have no certain rule to determine how far God's own Spirit may go in those operations and convictions which in themselves are not spiritual and saving. There is no necessary connexion, in the nature of things, between any thing that a natural man may experience, while in a state of nature, and the saving grace of God's Spirit. And if there be no connexion in the nature of things, then there can be no known and certain connexion at all, unless it be by divine revelation. But there is no revealed certain connexion between a state of salvation, and any thing that a natural man can be the subject of, before he believes in Christ. God has revealed no certain connexion between salvation and any qualifications in men, but only grace and its fruits. And therefore we do not find any legal convictions, or comforts following these legal convictions, in any certain method or order, ever once mentioned in the Scripture, as certain signs of grace, or things peculiar to the saints; although we do find gracious operations and effects themselves so mentioned thousands of times. Which should be enough with Christians, who are willing to have the word of God, rather than their own philosophy, and experiences, and conjectures, as their sufficient and sure guide in things of this nature.

Fourthly, Experience confirms that persons seeming to have convictions and comforts following one another in such a method and order, as is frequently observable in true converts, is no certain sign of grace.* I appeal to all those ministers in this land, who have had much occasion of dealing with souls, in the late extraordinary season, whether there have not been many who do not prove well, that have given a fair account of their experiences, and have seemed to be converted according to rule, *i. e.* with convictions and affections, succeeding distinctly and exactly, in that order and method, which has been ordinarily insisted on, as the order of the operations of the Spirit of God in conversion.

But as this distinctness, as to method, is no certain sign that a person is converted; so, being without it is no evidence that a person is not converted. For, though it might be made evident to a demonstration, on scripture principles, that a sinner cannot be brought heartily to receive Christ as his Saviour, who is not convinced of his sin and misery, his own emptiness and helplessness, and his just desert of eternal condemnation—and therefore such convictions must be some way *implied* in what is wrought in his soul—yet nothing proves it to be necessary, that all those things which are implied or presupposed in an act of faith in Christ, must be plainly and distinctly wrought in the soul, in so many successive and separate works of the Spirit, that shall be each one manifest, in all who are truly converted. On the contrary, (as Mr. Shepard observes,) sometimes the change made in a saint, at first work, is like a confused chaos; so that the saints know not what to make of it. The manner of the Spirit's proceeding in them that are born of the Spirit, is very often exceeding mysterious and unsearchable: we, as it were, *hear the sound* of it, the *effect* is discernible; but no man can tell *whence it came,* or *whither it went.* And it is oftentimes as difficult to know the way of the Spirit in the new birth, as in the first birth: Eccl. xi. 5. "Thou knowest not what is the way of the Spirit, or how the bones do grow in the womb of her that is with child: even so thou knowest not the works of God, that worketh all." The ingenerating of a principle of grace in the soul, seems in Scripture to be compared to the conceiving of Christ in the womb, Gal. iv. 19. And therefore the church is called Christ's mother, Cant. iii. 11. And so is every particular believer, Matt. xii. 49, 50. And the conception of Christ in the womb of the blessed virgin, by the power of the Holy Ghost, seems to be a designed resemblance of the conception of Christ in the soul of a believer, by the power of the same Holy Ghost. And we know not what is the way of the Spirit, in the heart that conceives this holy child. The new creature may use that language in Psal. cxxxix. 14, 15. "I am fearfully and wonderfully made; marvellous are thy works, and that my soul knoweth right well. My substance was not hid from thee, when I was made in secret." Concerning the generation of Christ, both in his person, and also in the hearts of his people. it may be said, as in Isa. liii. 8. "Who can declare his generation?" We know not the works of God, that worketh all. It is the glory of God to conceal a thing, (Prov. xxv. 2.) and to have *his path as it were in the mighty waters, that his footsteps may not be known*: and especially in the works of his Spirit on the hearts of men, which are the highest and chief of his works. And therefore it is said, Isa. xl. 13. "Who hath directed the Spirit of the Lord, or being his counsellor hath taught him?" It is to be feared that some have gone too far towards directing the Spirit of the Lord, and marking out his footsteps for him, and limiting him to certain steps and methods. Experience plainly shows that God's Spirit is unsearchable and untraceable, in some of the best of Christians, as to the method of his operations in their conversion. Nor does the Spirit of God proceed discernibly in the steps of a particular established scheme, one half so often as is imagined. A scheme of what is necessary, and according to a rule already received and established by common opinion, has a vast, though to many a very insensible, influence in forming men's notions of the steps and method of their own experiences. I know very well what their way is; for I have had much opportunity to observe it. Very often, at first, their experiences appear like a confused chaos, as Mr. Shepard expresses it: but then, those passages of their experience are picked out, that have most of the appearance of such particular steps that are insisted on; and these are dwelt upon in the thoughts, and from time to time, in the relation

* Mr. Stoddard, who had much experience of things of this nature, long ago observed, that converted and unconverted men cannot be certainly distinguished by the account they give of their experience; the same relation of experiences being common to both. And that many persons have given a fair account of a work of conversion, that have carried well in the eye of the world for several years, but have not proved well at last. *Appeal to the Learned*, p. 75, 76.

they give. These parts grow and brighten in their view; and others, being neglected, grow more and more obscure. What they have experienced is insensibly strained to bring all to an exact conformity to the scheme established. And it becomes natural for ministers, who have to deal with and direct them while insisting upon distinctness and clearness of method, to do so too. But yet there has been so much to be seen of the operations of the Spirit of God, of late, that they who have had much to do with souls, and are not blinded with a sevenfold vail of prejudice, must know that the Spirit is so exceeding various in his manner of operating, that in many cases it is impossible to trace him, or find out his way.

What we have principally to do with, in our inquiries into our own state, or the directions we give to others, is the *nature* of that effect which God has brought to pass in the soul. As to the *steps* which the Spirit took to bring that effect to pass, we may leave them to him. We are often in Scripture expressly directed to try ourselves by the *nature* of the fruits; but no where by the Spirit's *method* of producing them.* Many greatly err in their notions of a clear work of conversion; calling that a clear work, where the successive steps of influence and method of experience is clear: whereas that indeed is the clearest work, (not where the order of *doing* is clearest, but,) where the spiritual and divine nature of the work *done*, and effect *wrought*, is most clear.

SECT. IX.

It is no certain sign that affections have in them the nature of true religion, or that they have not, that they dispose persons to spend much time in religion, and to be zealously engaged in the external duties of worship.

THIS has, very unreasonably, of late been looked upon as an argument against the religious affections of some, that they spend so much time in reading, praying, singing, hearing sermons, and the like. It is plain from the Scripture, that it is the tendency of true grace to cause persons very much to delight in such religious exercises. True grace had this effect on Anna the prophetess; Luke ii. 37. "She departed not from the temple, but served God with fastings and prayers night and day." And grace had this effect upon the primitive Christians in Jerusalem; Acts ii. 46, 47. "And they continuing daily with one accord in the temple, and breaking bread from house to house, did eat their meat with gladness and singleness of heart, praising God." Grace made Daniel delight in the duty of prayer, and solemnly to attend it three times a day: as it also did David, Psal. lv. 17. "Evening, morning, and at noon, will I pray." Grace makes the saints delight in singing praises to God: Psal. cxxxv. 3. "Sing praises unto his name, for it is pleasant." And cxlvii. 1. "Praise ye the Lord: for it is good to sing praises unto our God; for it is pleasant, and praise is comely." It also causes them to delight to hear the word of God preached: it makes the gospel a joyful sound to them, Psal. lxxxix. 15. and makes the feet of those who publish these good tidings, to be beautiful; Isa. lii. 7. "How beautiful upon the mountains are the feet of him that bringeth good tidings!" &c. It makes them love God's public worship; Psal. xxvi. 8. "Lord, I have loved the habitation of thy house, and the place where thine honour dwelleth." And Psal. xxvii. 4. "One thing have I desired of the Lord, that will I seek after, that I may dwell in the house of the Lord all the days of my life, to behold the beauty of the Lord, and to inquire in his temple." Psal. lxxxiv. 1, 2. &c. "How amiable are thy tabernacles, O Lord of hosts! my soul longeth, yea, even fainteth for the courts of the Lord.—Yea, the sparrow hath found an house, and the swallow a nest for herself, where she may lay her young, even thine altars, O Lord of hosts, my King and my God. Blessed are they that dwell in thy house: they will be still praising thee. Blessed is the man in whose heart are the ways of them, who passing through the valley of Baca, —go from strength to strength, every one of them in Zion appeareth before God."—Ver 10. "A day in thy courts is better than a thousand."

This is the nature of true grace. But yet, on the other hand, persons being disposed to abound and to be zealously engaged in the external exercises of religion, and to spend much time in them, is no sure evidence of grace; because such a disposition is found in many who have no grace. So it was with the Israelites of old, whose services were abominable to God; they attended the *new moons, and sabbaths, and calling of assemblies; and spread forth their hands, and made many prayers*, Isa. i. 12—15. So it was with the Pharisees; they *made long prayers, and fasted twice a week*. False religion may cause persons to be loud and earnest in prayer: Isa. lviii. 4. "Ye shall not fast as ye do this day, to cause your voice to be heard on high." That religion which is not spiritual and saving, may cause men to delight in religious duties and ordinances: Isa. lviii. 2. "Yet they seek me daily, and delight to know my ways, as a nation that did righteousness, and forsook not the ordinance of their God: they ask of me the ordinances of justice: they take delight in approaching to God." It may cause them to take delight in hearing the word of God preached; as it was with Ezekiel's hearers, Ezek. xxxiii. 31, 32. "And they come unto thee as the people cometh, and they sit before thee as my people, and they hear thy words, but they will not do them: for with their mouth they show much love, but their heart goeth after their covetousness. And lo, thou art unto them as a very lovely song of one that hath a pleasant voice, and can play well on an instrument: for they hear thy words, but they do them not." Herod *heard* John the Baptist *gladly*, Mark vi. 20. and others of his hearers, *for a season, rejoiced in his light*, John v. 35. So the stony-ground hearers *heard the word with joy*.

Experience shows, that persons, from false religion, may be abundant in the external exercises of religion; yea, to give themselves up to them, and devote almost their whole time to them. Formerly, a sort of people were very numerous in the Romish church, called *recluses*, who forsook the world, and utterly abandoned the society of mankind. They shut themselves up close in a narrow cell, with a vow never to stir out of it, nor to see the face of any, (unless that they might be visited in case of sickness,) but to spend all their days in the exercises of devotion and converse with God. There were also in old time, great multitudes called Hermites and Anchorites, who left the world in order to spend all their days in lonesome deserts, and to give themselves up to religious contemplations and exercises of devotion. Some sorts of them had no dwellings, but the caves and vaults of the mountains, and no food, but the spontaneous productions of the earth.—I once lived, for many months, next door to a Jew, (the houses adjoining one to another,) and had much opportunity daily to observe him; who appeared to me the devoutest person that ever I saw in my life; great part of his time being spent in acts of devotion, at his eastern window, which opened next to mine, seeming to be most earnestly engaged, not only in the day-time, but sometimes whole nights.

SECT. X.

Nothing can be certainly known of the nature of religious affections, that they much dispose persons with their mouths to praise and glorify God.

THIS indeed is implied in what has been just now observed, of abounding and spending much time in the external exercises of religion, and was also hinted before;

* Mr. Shepard, speaking of the soul's closing with Christ, says, "As a child cannot tell how his soul comes into it, nor it may be when; but afterwards it sees and feels that life; so that he were as bad as a beast, that should deny an immortal soul; so here." *Parable of the Ten Virgins*, Part II. p. 171.

"If the man do not know the time of his conversion, or first closing with Christ; the minister may not draw any peremptory conclusion from thence, that he is not godly."—Stoddard's *Guide to Christ*, p. 83.

"Do not think there is no compunction, or sense of sin, wrought in the soul because you cannot so clearly discern and feel it; nor the time of the working, and first beginning of it. I have known many that have come with their complaints, that they *were never humbled, they never felt it so*; yet there it hath been, and many times they have seen it, by the other spectacles, and blessed God for it." Shepard's *Sound Believer*, page 38. The late impression in Boston.

but because many seem to look upon it as a bright evidence of gracious affection, when persons appear greatly disposed to praise and magnify God, to have their mouths full of his praises, and affectionately to be calling on others to praise and extol him, I thought it deserved a more particular consideration.

No Christian will make it an argument against a person that he seems to have such a disposition. Nor can it reasonably be looked upon as an evidence *for* a person, if those things which have been already observed and proved be duly considered: viz. that persons, without grace, may have high affections towards God and Christ, and that there may be counterfeits of all kinds of gracious affection. But it will appear more evidently and directly, that this is no certain sign of grace, if we consider what instances the Scripture gives us of it in those that were graceless. We often have an account of this, in the multitude that were present when Christ preached and wrought miracles; Mark ii. 12. "And immediately he arose, took up his bed, and went forth before them all, insomuch that they were all amazed, and glorified God, saying, We never saw it on this fashion." So Matt. ix. 8. and Luke v. 26. Also Matt. xv. 31. "Insomuch that the multitude wondered when they saw the dumb to speak, the maimed to be whole, the lame to walk, and the blind to see: and they glorified the God of Israel." So we are told, that on occasion of Christ raising the son of the widow of Nain, Luke vii. 16. "There came a fear on all: and they glorified God, saying, That a great prophet is risen up among us; and, That God hath visited his people." So we read of their glorifying Christ, or speaking exceeding highly of him, Luke iv. 15. "And he taught in their synagogues, being glorified of all." And how did they praise him with loud voices, crying, "Hosanna to the Son of David, Hosanna in the highest; blessed is he that cometh in the name of the Lord," a little before he was crucified! And after Christ's ascension, when the apostles had healed the impotent man, we are told, that *all man glorified God for that which was done*, Acts iv. 21. When the Gentiles in Antioch of Pisidia, heard from Paul and Barnabas, that God would reject the Jews, and take the Gentiles to be his people in their room, they were affected with this goodness of God to the Gentiles, *and glorified the word of the Lord*. Yet, all that did so were not true believers; but only a certain elect number of them; as is intimated, Acts xiii. 48. "And when the Gentiles heard this, they were glad, and glorified the word of the Lord: and as many as were ordained to eternal life, believed." Israel, at the Red sea, *sang God's praise; but soon forgat his works*. And the Jews in Ezekiel's time, *with their mouth showed much love, while their heart went after their covetousness*. And it is foretold of false professors, and real enemies of religion, that they should show a forwardness to glorify God; Isa. lxvi. 5. "Hear the word of the Lord, ye that tremble at his word; Your brethren that hated you, that cast you out for my name's sake, said, Let the Lord be glorified."

It is no certain sign that a person is graciously affected, if in the midst of hopes and comforts he is greatly affected with God's unmerited mercy to him that is so unworthy, and seems greatly to extol and magnify free grace. Those that yet remain with unmortified pride and enmity against God, may—when they imagine that they have received extraordinary kindness from God—deplore their unworthiness, and magnify God's undeserved goodness to them. Yet this may arise from no other conviction of their ill-deservings, and from no higher principle, than Saul had, who—while he remained with unsubdued pride and enmity against David—was brought, though a king, to acknowledge his unworthiness, and cry out, *I have played the fool, I have erred exceedingly*. And with what great affection and admiration does he magnify and extol David's unmerited and unexampled kindness to him, 1 Sam. xxv. 16—19. and xxvi. 21. Nebuchadnezzar is affected with God's dispensations, and praises, extols, and honours the King of heaven; and both he, and Darius, in their high affections, call upon all nations to praise God, Dan. iii. 28—30. and iv. 1—3. 34, 35, 37. and vi. 25—27.

SECT. XI.

It is no sign that affections are right, or that they are wrong, that they make persons exceeding confident.

It is an argument with some, that persons are deluded if they pretend to be assured of their good estate, and to be carried beyond all doubting of the favour of God, supposing that there is no such thing to be expected, as a full and absolute assurance of hope; unless it be in some very extraordinary circumstances; as in the case of martyrdom. But this is contrary to the doctrine of protestants, which has been maintained by their most celebrated writers against the papists; and contrary to the plainest scripture evidence. It is manifest, that it was a common thing for the saints of whom we have a particular account in Scripture, to be *assured*. God, in the plainest and most positive manner, revealed and testified his special favour to Noah, Abraham, Isaac, Jacob, Moses, Daniel, and others. Job often speaks of his sincerity and uprightness with the greatest imaginable confidence and assurance, often calling God to witness it; and says plainly, "I know that my Redeemer liveth, and that I shall see him for myself, and not another," Job xix. 25, &c. David throughout the book of Psalms, speaks without hesitancy, and in the most positive manner, of God as *his* God; glorying in him as his portion and heritage, his rock and confidence, his shield, salvation, high tower, and the like. Hezekiah appeals to God, as one that knew he had walked before him in truth, and with a perfect heart, 2 Kings xx. 3. Jesus Christ, in his dying discourse with his eleven disciples, John xiv—xvi. (which was as it were Christ's last will and testament to his disciples and to his whole church,) often declares his special and everlasting love to them, in the plainest and most positive terms; and promises them a future participation with him in his glory, in the most absolute manner. And he tells them, at the same time, that he does so to this end, that their joy might be *full*; John xv. 11. "These things have I spoken unto you, that my joy might remain in you, and that your joy might be full." See also at the conclusion of his whole discourse, chap. xvi. 33. "These things have I spoken unto you, that in me ye might have peace. In the world ye shall have tribulation: but be of good cheer, I have overcome the world." Christ was not afraid of speaking too plainly and positively to them; he did not desire to hold them in the least suspense. And he concluded that last discourse, with a prayer in their presence; wherein he speaks positively to his Father of those eleven disciples, as having savingly *known* him, believed in him, and received and kept his word. He declares, that they were not of the world; that for their sakes he sanctified himself; and that his will was, that they should be with him in his glory. And tells his Father, that he spake these things in his prayer, to the end, that his joy might be fulfilled in them, ver. 13. By these things it is evident, that it is agreeable to Christ's designs, that there should be sufficient provision made, for his saints to have full assurance of their future glory.

The apostle Paul, through all his epistles, speaks in an assured strain; ever asserting his special relation to Christ, his Lord, Master, and Redeemer, with his interest in, and expectation of, the future reward. It would be endless to take notice of all places that might be enumerated; I shall mention but three or four: Gal. ii. 20. "Christ liveth in me: and the life which I now live in the flesh, I live by the faith of the Son of God, who loved me, and gave himself for me." Phil. i. 21. "For me to live is Christ, and to die is gain." 2 Tim. i. 12. "I know whom I have believed, and I am persuaded that he is able to keep that which I have committed unto him against that day." 2 Tim. iv. 7, 8. "I have fought a good fight, I have finished my course, I have kept the faith. Henceforth there is laid up for me a crown of righteousness, which the Lord, the righteous Judge, will give me at that day."

The nature of the covenant of grace, and God's declared ends in the appointment and constitution of things in that covenant, plainly show it to be God's design to make ample provision for the saints having an assured hope of eternal life, while living here upon earth. For so are all things ordered in that covenant, that every thing might be made sure on God's part. *The covenant is ordered in all things and sure*: the promises are most full, very often repeated, and various ways exhibited; there are many witnesses, and many seals; and God has confirmed his promises with an oath. God's declared design in all this is, that the heirs of the promises might have an undoubting hope, and full joy, in an assurance of their future glory. Heb. vi. 17, 18. "Wherein God willing more abundantly to show unto the heirs of promise the immutability of his counsel, confirmed it by an oath: that by two immutable things, in which it was impossible for God to lie, we might have a strong consolation, who have fled for refuge to lay hold upon the hope set before us." But all this would be in vain, for any such purpose as the saints' strong consolation, and their hope of obtaining future glory, if their interest in those sure promises in ordinary cases were not attainable. For God's promises and oaths, let them be as sure as they will, cannot give strong hope and comfort to any particular person, any further than he can *know* that those promises are made to him. And in vain is provision made in Jesus Christ, that believers might be perfect, as pertaining to the conscience, Heb. ix. 9. if *assurance* of freedom from the guilt of sin is not attainable.

It further appears, that *assurance* is attainable in ordinary cases, in that *all* Christians are directed to give all diligence to make their calling and election sure, and are told how they may do it, 2 Pet. i. 5—8. And it is spoken of as a thing very unbecoming Christians, and an argument of something very blamable in them, not to *know* whether Christ be in them or no, 2 Cor. xiii. 5. "Know ye not your ownselves, how that Jesus Christ is in you, except ye be reprobates?" And it is implied, that it is a very blamable negligence in christians, if they practise Christianity after such a manner as to remain uncertain of the reward, 1 Cor. ix. 26. "I therefore so run, as not uncertainly." And, to add no more, it is manifest, that Christians knowing their interest in the saving benefits of Christianity, is a thing ordinarily attainable, because the apostles tell us by what means *Christians* (and not only *apostles* and *martyrs*) were wont to know this; 1 Cor. ii. 12. "Now we have received, not the spirit of the world, but the Spirit which is of God; that we might know the things that are freely given to us of God." And 1 John ii. 3. "And hereby we do know that we know him, if we keep his commandments." And ver. 5. "Hereby know we that we are in him." Chap. iii. 14. "We know that we have passed from death unto life, because we love the brethren." Verse 19. "Hereby we know that we are of the truth, and shall assure our hearts before him." Verse 24. "Hereby we know that he abideth in us, by the Spirit which he hath given us." (So chap. iv. 13. and chap. v. 2, 19.)

Therefore it must needs be very unreasonable to determine, that persons are hypocrites, and their affections wrong, because they seem to be out of doubt respecting their own salvation, and their affections seem to banish all fears of hell.

On the other hand, it is no sufficient reason to determine that men are saints, and their affections gracious, because they are attended with confidence that their state is good, and their affections divine.* Nothing can be certainly argued from their confidence, how great and strong soever it be. A man may boldly call God his Father, and commonly speak in the most bold, familiar, and appropriating language in prayer, *My Father, my dear Redeemer, my sweet Saviour, my beloved*, and the like. He may use the most confident expressions before men, about the goodness of his state; such as, "I know certainly that God is my Father: I know so surely as there is a God in heaven, that he is my God; I know I shall go to heaven, as well as if I were there; I know that God is now manifesting himself to my soul, and is now smiling upon me." He may seem to have done for ever with any inquiry or examination into his state, as a thing sufficiently known, and out of doubt, and to contemn all that so much as intimate that there is reason to doubt whether all is right. Yet such things are no signs at all that it is indeed what he is confident it is.†—Such an over-bearing, high-handed, and violent sort of confidence as this, affecting to declare itself with a most glaring show in the sight of men, has not the countenance of a true christian assurance. It savours more of the spirit of the Pharisees, who never doubted but that they were saints, the most eminent of saints, and were bold to thank God for the great distinction he had made between them and other men. And when Christ intimated that they were blind and graceless, they despised the suggestion; John ix. 40. "And some of the Pharisees which were with him, heard these words, and said unto him, Are we blind also?" If they had more of the spirit of the publican—who, in a sense of his exceeding unworthiness, stood afar off, and durst not so much as lift up his eyes to heaven, but smote on his breast, condemning himself as a sinner—their confidence would have more resembled one who humbly trusts and hopes in Christ, and has no confidence in himself.

If we do but consider what the hearts of natural men are, what principles they are under, what blindness and deceit, what self-flattery, self-exaltation, and self-confidence reigns there, we need not at all wonder that their high opinion of themselves, and confidence of their happy circumstances, are as high and strong as mountains, and as violent as a tempest. For what should hinder, when once conscience is blinded, convictions are killed, false affections high, and those forementioned principles let loose? When, moreover, these principles are prompted by false joys and comforts, excited by some pleasing imaginations impressed by Satan, transforming himself into an angel of light?

When once a hypocrite is thus established in a false hope, he has not those things to cause him to call his hope in question, that oftentimes are the occasion of doubting to true saints; as, *first*, he has not that cautious spirit, that great sense of the vast importance of a sure foundation, and that dread of being deceived. The comforts of the true saints increase awakening and caution, and a lively sense how great a thing it is to appear before an infinitely holy, just, and omniscient Judge. But false comforts put an end to these things, and dreadfully stupify the mind. *Secondly*, The hypocrite has not the knowledge of his own blindness, and the deceitfulness of his own heart, and that mean opinion of his own understanding, that the true saint has. Those that are deluded with false discoveries and affections, are evermore highly conceited of their light and understanding. *Thirdly*, The devil does not assault the hope of the hypocrite, as he does the hope of a true saint. The devil is a great enemy to a true Christian's hope, not only because it tends greatly to his comfort, but also because it is of a holy, heavenly nature, greatly tending to promote and cherish grace in the heart, and a great incentive to strictness and diligence in the Christian life. But he is no enemy to the hope of a hypocrite, which above all things establishes his interest in him. A hypocrite may retain his hope without opposition, as long as he lives, the devil never attempting to disturb it. But there is perhaps no true Christian but what has his hope assaulted by him. Satan assaulted Christ himself, upon this, whether he were the Son of God or no: and the servant is not above his Master, nor

* "O professor, look carefully to your foundation: *be not high-minded, but fear.* You have, it may be, done and suffered many things in and for religion; you have excellent gifts and sweet comforts; a warm zeal for God, and high confidence of your integrity: all this may be right, for ought that I, or (it may be) you know: but yet, it is possible it may be false also. You have sometimes judged yourselves, and pronounced yourselves upright; but remember your final sentence is not yet pronounced by your Judge. And what if God weigh you over again, in his more equal balance, and should say, *Mene, Tekel, Thou art weighed in the balance, and art found wanting?* What a confounded man wilt thou be, under such a sentence! *Quæ resplendent in conspectu hominis, sordent in conspectu Judicis;* Things that are highly esteemed of men, are an abomination in the sight of God: he seeth not as men seeth. Thy heart may be false, and thou not know it: yea, it may be false, and thou strongly confident of its integrity."—Flavel's *Touchstone of Sincerity*, chap. ii. sect. 5.

"Some hypocrites are a great deal more confident than many saints."—Stoddard's *Discourse on the way to know Sincerity and Hypocrisy*, p. 128.

† "Doth the work of faith in some believers, bear upon its top-branches, the full ripe fruits of a blessed assurance? Lo, what strong confidence, and high-built persuasions of an interest in God, have sometimes been found in unsanctified ones! Yea, so strong may this false assurance be, that they dare boldly venture to go to the judgment-seat of God, and there defend it. Doth the Spirit of God fill the heart of the assured believer with joy unspeakable, and full of glory, giving them, through faith, a prelibation or foretaste of heaven itself, in those first-fruits of it? How near to this comes what the apostle supposes may be found in apostates!" Flavel's *Husbandry Spiritualized*, chap. xii.

the disciple above his Lord. It is enough for the disciple, who is most privileged in this world, to be as his Master. *Fourthly*, He who has a false hope, has not that sight of his own corruptions which the saint has. A true Christian has ten times so much to do with his heart and its corruptions, as a hypocrite. The sins of his heart and practice appear to him in their awful blackness; they look dreadful: and it often appears a very mysterious thing, that any grace can be consistent with such corruption, or should be in such a heart. But a false hope hides corruption, covers it all over, and the hypocrite looks clean and bright in his own eyes.

There are two sorts of hypocrites: one such as are deceived with their outward morality and external religion; many of whom are professed Arminians, in the doctrine of justification: and the other, such as are deceived with false discoveries and elevations. These last often cry down works and men's own righteousness, and talk much of free grace; but at the same time make a righteousness of their discoveries and humiliation, and exalt themselves to heaven with them. These two kinds of hypocrites Mr. Shepard, in his exposition of the Parable of the Ten Virgins, distinguishes by the names of *legal* and *evangelical* hypocrites; and often speaks of the latter as the worst. And it is evident, that the latter are commonly by far the most confident in their hope, and are with the most difficulty brought off from it. I have scarcely known an instance of such an one that has been undeceived. The chief grounds of the confidence of many of them, are impulses and supposed revelations, (sometimes with texts of Scripture, and sometimes without,) like what many of late have had concerning future events. These impulses about their good estate they call the witness of the Spirit; entirely misunderstanding the nature of the witness of the Spirit, as I shall show hereafter. Those who have had visions and impulses about other things, have generally had such things as they are desirous and fond of, revealed to them: and no wonder that persons who give heed to such things, have the same sort of visions or impressions about their own eternal salvation. Why may they not suppose a revelation made to them, that their sins are forgiven them, that their names are written in the book of life, that they are in high favour with God, &c. and especially when they earnestly seek, expect, and wait for evidence of their election and salvation this way, as the surest and most glorious evidence of it? Neither is it any wonder, that when they have such a supposed revelation of their good estate, it raises in them the highest degree of confidence of it. It is found by abundant experience, that those who are led away by impulses and imagined revelations, are extremely confident. They suppose, that the great Jehovah has declared these and those things to them; and having his immediate testimony, a strong confidence is the highest virtue. Hence they are bold to say, *I know this or that; —I know certainly;—I am as sure as that I have a being*, and the like: and they despise all argument and inquiry into the case. And it is easy to be accounted for, that impressions and impulses about that which is so pleasing, so suiting their self-love and pride, as their being the dear children of God, should make them strongly confident: especially when, with their impulses and revelations, they have high affections, which they take to be the most eminent exercises of grace. I have known several persons, who have had a fond desire of something of a temporal nature, through a violent passion that has possessed them; they have earnestly wished it should come to pass, and have met with many discouragements in it; but at last have had an impression, or supposed revelation, that they should obtain what they sought. They have looked upon this as a sure promise from the Most High, which has made them most ridiculously confident, against all manner of reason to convince them to the contrary, and all events working against them. And nothing hinders, but that persons who are seeking their salvation may be deceived by the like delusive impressions, and be made confident the same way.

The confidence of many of this sort, whom that Mr. Shepard calls *evangelical hypocrites*, is like the confidence of some mad men, who think they are kings: they will maintain it against all manner of reason and evidence. And in one sense, it is much more immovable than a truly gracious assurance; a true assurance is not upheld, but by the soul being kept in a holy frame, and grace maintained in lively exercise. If the actings of grace do much decay in the Christian, and he falls into a lifeless frame, he loses his assurance: but this confidence of hypocrites will not be shaken by sin; they (at least some of them) will maintain their boldness in their hope, in the most corrupt frames and wicked ways; which is a sure evidence of their delusion.*

And here I cannot but observe, that there are certain doctrines often preached to the people, which need to be delivered with more caution and explanation than they frequently are; for as they are by many understood, they tend greatly to establish this delusion and false confidence of hypocrites. The doctrines I speak of are those of *Christians living by faith, not by sight: their giving glory to God, by trusting him in the dark; living upon Christ, and not upon experiences; not making their good frames the foundation of their faith.* These are excellent and important doctrines indeed, rightly understood, but corrupt and destructive, as many understand them. The Scripture speaks of our living or walking by faith, and not by sight, in no other way than these, viz. When we are governed by a respect to eternal things, which are the objects of faith, and are not seen, and not by a respect to temporal things, which are seen; when we believe things revealed, that we never saw with bodily eyes; and also exercise faith in the promise of future things, without yet seeing or enjoying the things promised, or knowing the way how they can be fulfilled. This will be easily evident to any one that looks over the Scriptures, which speak of *faith* in opposition to *sight*.† But this doctrine, as it is understood by many, is, that Christians ought firmly to believe and trust in Christ, without spiritual light; even although they are in a dark, dead frame, and for the present, have no spiritual experiences or discoveries. It is truly the *duty* of those who are thus in darkness to *come out* of darkness into light, and to *believe*. But that they should confidently believe and trust, while they yet remain without spiritual light or sight, is an antiscriptural and absurd doctrine.

The Scripture is ignorant of any such faith in Christ of the operation of God, that is not founded in a spiritual sight of Christ. That believing on Christ, which accompanies a title to everlasting life, is a *seeing the Son, and believing on him*, John vi. 40. True faith in Christ is never exercised, any further than persons *behold as in a glass the glory of the Lord*, and have *the knowledge of the glory of God in the face of Jesus Christ*, 2 Cor. iii. 18. and iv. 6. They into whose minds *the light of the glorious gospel of Christ, who is the image of God, does not shine, they believe not*, 2 Cor. iv. 4. That faith, which is without spiritual light, is not the faith of the children of the light and of the day; but the presumption of the children of darkness. And therefore to press and urge them to believe, without any spiritual light or sight, tends greatly to help forward the delusions of the prince of darkness. Men not only cannot exercise faith without some spiritual light, but they can exercise faith only just in *such proportion* as they have spiritual light. Men will trust in God no further than they know him: and they cannot be in the exercise of faith in him, further than they have a sight of his fulness and faithfulness *in exercise*. Nor can they have the exercise of trust in God, any further than they are in a *gracious frame*. They that are in a dead carnal frame, doubtless *ought* to trust in God; because that would be the same thing as coming out of their bad frame, and turning to God: but to exhort men confidently to trust in God, and so hold up their hope and

* Mr. Shepard speaks of it, "as a presumptuous peace, that is not interrupted and broke by evil works." And says, that "the spirit will sigh, and not sing, in that bosom, whence corrupt dispositions and passions break out." And that, "though men in such frames may seem to maintain the consolation of the Spirit, and not suspect their hypocrisy, under pretence of trusting the Lord's mercy; yet they cannot avoid the 'condemnation of the world.'" *Parable of the Ten Virgins*, Part I. p. 139.

Dr. Ames speaks of it as a thing, by which the peace of a wicked man may be distinguished from the peace of a godly man, "that the peace of a wicked man continues, whether he performs the duties of piety and righteousness or no; provided those crimes are avoided that appear horrid to nature itself." *Cases of Conscience, lib.* III. chap. vii.

† As 2 Cor. iv. 18. and v. 7. Heb. xi. 1, 8, 13, 17, 27, 29. Rom. viii. 24 John xx. 29.

peace, though they are not in a gracious frame, and continue still to be so, is the same thing, in effect, as to exhort them confidently to trust in God, but not with a gracious trust: and what is that but a wicked presumption? It is just as impossible for men to have a strong or lively trust in God, when they have no lively exercises of grace, or sensible christian experiences, as it is for them to be *in* the lively exercises of grace, *without* the exercises of grace!

It is true, that it is the *duty* of God's people to trust in him when in darkness, even though they remain still in darkness, in one sense, viz. when the aspects of his providence are dark, and look as though God had forsaken them, and did not hear their prayers. Many clouds gather, many enemies surround them with a formidable aspect, threatening to swallow them up, and all events of providence seem to be against them. All circumstances seem to render the promise of God difficult to be fulfilled, but he must be trusted out of sight, *i. e.* when we cannot see which way it is possible for him to fulfil his word. Every thing but God's mere word makes it look unlikely, so that if persons believe, they must hope against hope. Thus the ancient patriarchs, and thus the psalmist, Jeremiah, Daniel, Shadrach, Meshech, and Abednego, and the apostle Paul, gave glory to God by trusting him in darkness. We have many instances of such a glorious, victorious faith in the eleventh of the Hebrews. But how different a thing is this, from trusting in God, without spiritual sight, and being at the same time in a dead and carnal frame!

Spiritual light may be let into the soul in one way, when it is not in another; and so there is such a thing as the saints trusting in God, and also knowing their good estate, when they are destitute of some kinds of experience. For instance, they may have clear views of God's all-sufficiency and faithfulness, and so may confidently trust in him, and know that they are his children; and yet not have those clear and sweet ideas of his love, as at other times. Thus it was with Christ himself in his last passion. They may also have views of God's sovereignty, holiness, and all-sufficiency, enabling them quietly to submit to him, and to exercise a sweet and most encouraging hope in his fulness, when they are not satisfied of their own good estate. But how different things are these, from confidently trusting in God, without spiritual light or experience!

Those who thus insist on persons' living by faith, when they have no experience, and are in very bad frames, are also very *absurd* in their notions of *faith*. What they mean by faith is, believing that they *are in a good estate*. Hence they count it a dreadful sin for them to doubt of their state, whatever frames they are in, and whatever wicked things they do, because it is the great and heinous sin of unbelief; and he is the best man, and puts most honour upon God, that maintains his hope of his *good estate* the most confidently and immovably, when he has the least light or experience; that is to say, when he is in the worst frame and way; because forsooth, that it is a sign that he is strong in faith, giving glory to God, and against hope believes in hope. But from what Bible do they learn this notion of faith, that it is a man's confidently believing that he is in a good estate?* If this be faith, the Pharisees had faith in an eminent degree; some of whom Christ teaches, committed the unpardonable sin against the Holy Ghost. The Scripture represents faith, as that by which men are *brought into* a good estate; and therefore it cannot be the same thing, as believing that they *are already* in a good estate. To suppose that faith consists in persons' believing that they are in a good estate, is in effect the same thing, as to suppose that faith consists in a person's believing that he has faith, or in *believing that he believes!*

Indeed persons' doubting of their good estate, may in several respects *arise from* unbelief. It may be from unbelief, or because they have so little faith, that they have so little *evidence* of their good estate. If they had more experience of the actings of faith, and so more experience of the exercise of grace, they would have clearer evidence that their state was good; and so their doubts would be removed. And their doubting of their state may be from unbelief thus, when though there be many things that are good evidences of a work of grace in them, yet they doubt very much whether they are really in a state of favour with God, because it is *they*, those that are so unworthy, and have done so much to provoke God to anger against them. Their doubts in such a case arise from unbelief, as they arise from want of a sufficient sense *of*, and reliance *on*, the infinite riches of God's grace, and the sufficiency of Christ for the chief of sinners. They may also be from unbelief, when they doubt of their state, because of the *mystery* of God's dealings with them. They are not able to reconcile such dispensations with God's favour to them. Some doubt whether they have any interest in the promises, because from the aspect of providence, they appear so unlikely to be fulfilled; the difficulties in the way are so many and great. Such doubting arises from want of dependence upon God's almighty power, and his knowledge and wisdom, as infinitely above theirs. But yet, in such persons their *unbelief*, and their *doubting of their state*, are not the same thing; though one arises from the other.

Persons may be greatly to blame for doubting of their state, on such grounds as these; and they may be to blame, that they have no more grace, and no more of its present exercises, to be an evidence to them of the goodness of their state. Men are doubtless to blame for being in a dead, carnal frame; but when they are in such a frame, and have no sensible experience of the exercises of grace, but on the contrary, are very much under the prevalence of their lusts, and an unchristian spirit, *they are not to blame for doubting of their state.* It is as impossible, in the nature of things, that a holy and christian hope should be kept alive in its clearness and strength, in such circumstances, as it is to keep the light in the room, when the candle that gives it is put out; or to maintain the bright sunshine in the air, when the sun is gone down. Distant experiences, when darkened by present prevailing lust and corruption, will never keep alive a gracious confidence and assurance. If the one prevail, the other sickens and decays upon it. Does any one attempt to nourish and strengthen a little child by repeated blows on the head with a hammer? Nor is it at all to be lamented, that persons doubt of their state in such circumstances; but on the contrary, it is desirable and every way best that they should. It is agreeable to that wise and merciful constitution of things which God hath established. For so hath God constituted things, in his dispensations towards his own people, that when their *love* decays, and the exercises of it become weak, *fear* should arise. They need *fear* then to restrain them from sin, to excite them to care for the good of their souls, and so to stir them up to watchfulness and diligence in religion. But God hath so ordered, that when *love* rises, and is in vigorous exercise, then fear should vanish, and be driven away; for then they need it not, having a higher and more excellent principle in exercise, to restrain them from sin, and stir them up to duty. No other principles will ever make men conscientious, but one of these two, *fear* or *love:* and therefore, if one of these should not prevail as the other decayed, God's people when fallen into dead and carnal frames, when love is asleep, would be lamentably exposed indeed. Hence, God has wisely ordained, that these two opposite principles of love and fear, should rise and fall, like the two opposite scales of a balance; when one rises the other sinks. Light and darkness unavoidably succeed each other; if light prevail so much does darkness cease, and no more; and if light *decay*, so much does darkness prevail. So it is in the heart of a child of God; if divine *love decay* and fall asleep, and lust prevail, the light and joy of hope goes out, and dark fear arises; and if, on the contrary, divine *love prevail*, and come into lively exercise,

* "Men do not know that they are godly, by believing that they are godly. We know many things by faith, Heb. xi. 3. *By faith we understand that the worlds were made by the word of God.* Faith *is the evidence of things not seen,* Heb. xi. 1. Thus men know the Trinity of persons of the Godhead; that Jesus Christ is the Son of God; that he that believes in him will have eternal life; the resurrection of the dead. And if God should tell a saint that he has grace, he might know it by believing the word of God. But it is not this way, that godly men do know that they have grace. It is not revealed in the word, and the Spirit of God doth not testify it to particular persons." Stoddart's *Nature of Saving Conversion*, p. 83, 84.

this brings in the brightness of hope, and drives away black lust and fear with it. Love is the *spirit of adoption*, or the childlike principle; if that slumbers, men fall under fear, which is the *spirit of bondage*, or the servile principle: and so on the contrary. And if love, or the spirit of adoption, be carried to a great height, it quite drives away all fear, and gives full assurance; 1 John iv. 18. "There is no fear in love, but perfect love casteth out fear." These two opposite principles of lust and holy love, bring fear or hope into the hearts of God's children, just in proportion as they prevail; that is, when left to their own natural influence, without something adventitious or accidental intervening; as the distemper of melancholy, doctrinal ignorance, prejudices of education, wrong instruction, false principles, peculiar temptations, &c.

Fear is cast out by the Spirit of God, no other way than by the prevailing of love: nor is it ever maintained by his Spirit, but when love is asleep. At such a time, in vain is all the saint's self-examinations, and poring on past experience, in order to establish his peace, and get assurance. For it is contrary to the nature of things, as God hath constituted them, that he should have assurance at such a time.

They therefore directly thwart God's wise and gracious constitution of things, who exhort others to be confident in their hope, when in dead frames; under a notion of *living by faith*, and *not by sight*, and *trusting God in the dark*, and *living upon Christ, and not upon experiences;* and who warn them not to doubt of their good estate, lest they should be guilty of the dreadful sin of unbelief. It has a direct tendency to establish the most presumptuous hypocrites, and to prevent their ever calling their state in question, how much soever wickedness rages—reigns in their hearts, and prevails in their lives—under a notion of honouring God, by *hoping against hope*, and confidently trusting in God, when things look very dark. And, doubtless, vast has been the mischief that has been done this way.

Persons cannot be said to forsake Christ, and live on their experiences, merely because they use them as evidences of grace; for there are no other evidences that they can take. But then may persons be said to live upon their experiences, when they make a *righteousness* of them; and when, instead of keeping their eye on God's glory, and Christ's excellency, they turn it on themselves. They entertain their minds by viewing their own attainments, their high experiences, and the great things they have met with, which are bright and beautiful in their own eyes. They are rich and increased with goods in their own apprehensions, and think that God has as admiring an esteem of them, on the same account, as they have of themselves. This is living on experiences, and not on Christ; and is more abominable in the sight of God, than the gross immoralities of those who make no pretences to religion. But this is a far different thing from improving experiences as *evidences* of an interest in a glorious Redeemer.

SECT. XII.

Nothing can be certainly concluded concerning the nature of religious affections, that the relations persons give of them, are very affecting.

THE true saints have not such a spirit of discerning, that they can certainly determine who are godly, and who are not. For though they know experimentally what true religion is, in the internal exercises of it; yet these are what they can neither feel nor see, in the heart of another.* There is nothing in others, that comes within their view, but outward manifestations and appearances; but the Scripture plainly intimates, that this way of judging what is in men by outward appearances is at best uncertain, and liable to deceit: 1 Sam. xvi. 7. "The Lord seeth not as man seeth; for man looketh on the outward appearance, but the Lord looketh on the heart." Isa. xi. 3. "He shall not judge after the sight of his eyes, neither reprove after the hearing of his ears."† They commonly are but poor judges and dangerous counsellors in soul cases, who are quick and peremptory in determining persons' states, vaunting themselves in their extraordinary faculty of discerning and distinguishing, in these great affairs; as though all was open and clear to them. They betray one of these three things; either that they have had but little experience; or are persons of a weak judgment; or that they have a great degree of pride and self-confidence, and so ignorance of themselves. Wise and experienced men will proceed with great caution in such an affair.

When there are many probable appearances of piety in others, it is the duty of the saints to receive them cordially into their charity, to love, and rejoice in them, as their brethren in Christ Jesus. But yet the best of men may be deceived, when the appearances seem to them exceeding fair and bright, even so as entirely to gain their charity, and conquer their hearts. It has been a common thing in the church of God, for bright professors, received as eminent among the saints, to fall away and come to nothing.‡ And this we need not wonder at, if we consider the things already observed; things which may appear in men who are altogether graceless. Nothing hinders but that *all* these things may meet together in men, and yet they be without a spark of grace in their hearts. They may have religious affections of many kinds together; they may have a sort of affection towards God, that bears a great resemblance of real love to him. They may have a kind of love to the brethren, great appearances of admiration of God's perfections and works, sorrow for sin, reverence, submission, self-abasement, gratitude, joy, religious longings, and zeal for the interest of religion and the good of souls. These affections may come after great awakenings and convictions of conscience; and there may be great appearances of a work of humiliation. Counterfeit love and joy, and other affections, may seem to follow one another, just in the same order that is commonly observable in the holy affections of true converts. And these religious affections may be carried to a great height, may cause abundance of tears, yea, may overcome the nature of those who are the subjects of them, and may make them affectionate, fervent, and fluent in speaking of the things of God, and dispose them to be abundant in it. They may have many sweet texts of Scripture, and precious promises, brought with great impression on their minds; and their affections may dispose them, with their mouths, to praise and glorify God in a very ardent manner, and fervently to call upon others to praise him, exclaiming against their unworthiness, and extolling free grace. They may, moreover, dispose them to abound in the external duties of religion, such as prayer, hearing the word preached, singing, and religious conference; and these things attended with a great resemblance of christian assurance in its greatest height, when the saints mount on eagles' wings, above all darkness and doubting. I think it has been made plain, that there may be all these things, and yet nothing more than the common influences of the Spirit of God, joined with the delusions of Satan, and a wicked,

* "Men may have the knowledge of their own conversion; the knowledge that other men have of it is uncertain; because no man can look into the heart of another, and see the workings of grace there." Stoddard's *Nature of Saving Conversion*, chap. xv. at the beginning.

† Mr. Stoddard observes, That "all visible signs are common to converted and unconverted men; and a relation of experiences, among the rest." *Appeal to the Learned*, p. 75.

"O how hard is it for the eye of man to discern betwixt chaff and wheat! and how many upright hearts are now censured, whom God will clear! how many false hearts are now approved, whom God will condemn! Men ordinarily have no convictive proofs, but only probable symptoms; which at most beget but a conjectural knowledge of another's state. And they that shall peremptorily judge either way, may possibly wrong the generation of the upright, or on the other side, absolve and justify the wicked. And truly, considering what hath been said, it is no wonder that dangerous mistakes are so frequently made in this matter." Flavel's *Husbandry Spiritualized*, chap. xii.

‡ "Be not offended, if you see great cedars fall, stars fall from heaven, great professors die and decay: do not think they be all such: do not think that the elect shall fall. Truly, some are such that when they fall, one would think a man truly sanctified might fall away, as the Arminians think; 1 John ii. 19. *They were not of us.* I speak this, because the Lord is shaking; and I look for great apostacies: for God is trying all his friends, through all the christian world. In Germany what profession was there! who would have thought it? The Lord who delights to manifest that openly, which was hid secretly, sends a sword and they fall." Shepard's *Parab.* Part I. p. 118, 119.

"The saints may approve thee, and God condemns thee; Rev. iii. 1. *Thou hast a name that thou livest, and art dead.* Men may say, There is a true Nathaniel; and God may say, There is a self-cozening Pharisee. Reader, thou hast heard of Judas and Demas, of Ananias and Sapphira, of Hymeneus and Philetus, once renowned and famous professors, and thou hast heard how they proved at last." Flavel's *Touchstone of Sincerity*, chap. ii. sect. 5.

deceitful heart. To which I may add, that all these things may be attended with a sweet natural temper, a good doctrinal knowledge of religion, a long acquaintance with the saints' way of expressing their affections and experiences, and a natural ability and subtlety in accommodating their expressions and manner of speaking to the dispositions and notions of the hearers, with a taking decency of expression and behaviour, formed by a good education. How great therefore may the resemblance be, as to all outward expressions and appearances, between a hypocrite and a true saint! Doubtless, it is the glorious prerogative of the omniscient God, as the great searcher of hearts, to be able well to separate between these sheep and goats. And what an indecent self-exaltation and arrogance is it, in poor fallible dark mortals, to pretend, that they can determine and know, who are really sincere and upright before God, and who are not.

Many seem to lay great weight on that, and to suppose it to be what may determine them with respect to others' real piety, when they not only tell a plausible story, but when, in giving an account of their experiences, they make such a representation, and speak after such a manner, that they *feel* their talk; that is to say, when their talk seems to harmonize with their own experience, and their hearts are touched, affected, and delighted, by what they hear them say, and drawn out by it in dear love to them. But there is not that certainty in such things, and that full dependence to be laid upon them which many imagine. A true saint greatly delights in holiness; it is a most beautiful thing in his eyes; and God's work, in savingly renewing and making holy and happy a poor perishing soul, appears to him a most glorious work. No wonder, therefore, that his heart is touched, and greatly affected, when he hears another give a probable account of this work, wrought on his own heart, and when he sees in him probable appearances of holiness; whether those pleasing appearances have any thing real to answer them, or no. And if he use the same words, which are commonly used to express the affections of true saints, and tell of many things following one another in an order agreeable to the method of another's experience, and also speak freely and boldly, and with an air of assurance; no wonder that the other thinks his experiences harmonize with his own. And if besides all this, in giving his relation, he speak with much affection; and above all, if in speaking he show much affection, such affection as the Galatians did to the apostle Paul; these things will naturally have a powerful influence to affect and draw his hearer's heart, and open wide the doors of his charity towards him. David speaks as one who had felt Ahithophel's talk, and had once a sweet savour and relish of it. And therefore exceeding great was his surprise and disappointment, when he fell; it was almost too much for him. Psal. lv. 12—14. "It was not an enemy—then I could have borne it;—but it was thou, a man, mine equal, my guide, and mine acquaintance: we took sweet counsel together, and walked unto the house of God in company."

It is with professors of religion, especially such as become so in a time of an outpouring of the Spirit of God, as it is with the blossoms in the spring;* there are vast numbers of blossoms upon the trees, which all look fair and promising; but yet very many of them never come to any thing. Many, in a little time, wither, drop off, and rot under the trees. Indeed, for a while, they look as beautiful and gay as others; and not only so, but smell sweet, and send forth a pleasant odour; so that we cannot certainly distinguish those blossoms which have in them that secret virtue which will afterwards appear in the fruit. We cannot tell which of them have that inward solidity and strength which shall enable them to bear, and cause them to be perfected by the hot summer sun that will dry up the others. It is the mature fruit, which comes afterwards, and not the beautiful colours and smell of the blossom, that we must judge by. So new converts, professedly so, in their talk about religious things, may appear fair, and be very savoury, and the saints may think they talk feelingly. They may *relish* their talk, and imagine they perceive a *divine* savour in it; and yet all may come to nothing.

It is strange how hardly men are brought to be contented with the rules and directions Christ has given them, but they must needs go by other rules of their own inventing that seem to them wiser and better. I know of no directions or counsels which Christ ever delivered more plainly, than the rules he has given to guide us in our judging of others' sincerity; *viz. that we should judge of the tree chiefly by the fruit.* Yet this, it seems, will not do; but other ways are found out, which are imagined to be more distinguishing and certain. And woful have been the mischievous consequences of this arrogant setting up of men's wisdom, above the wisdom of Christ. I believe many *saints* have gone much out of the way of Christ's word, in this respect: and some of them have been chastised with whips, and (I had almost said) scorpions, to bring them back again. But many things which have lately appeared, and do now appear, may convince us, that ordinarily those who have gone farthest this way—that have been most highly conceited of their faculty of discerning, and have appeared most forward, peremptorily and suddenly to determine the state of men's souls—have been hypocrites, who have known nothing of true religion.

In the parable of the wheat and tares, it is said, Matt. xiii. 26. "When the blade was sprung up, and brought forth fruit, then appeared the tares also." As though the tares were not discerned, nor distinguishable from the wheat, *until then*, as Mr. Flavel observes;† who mentions it as an observation of Jerome's, that *wheat and tares are so much alike, until the blade of the wheat comes to bring forth the ear, that it is next to impossible to distinguish them.* And then, Mr. Flavel adds, "How difficult soever it be to discern the difference between wheat and tares; yet doubtless the eye of sense can much easier discriminate them, than the most quick and piercing eye of man can discern the difference between special and common grace. For all saving graces in the saints, have their counterfeits in hypocrites; there are similar works in those, which a spiritual and very judicious eye may easily mistake for the saving and genuine effects of a sanctifying spirit."

As it is the ear or the fruit which distinguishes the wheat from the tares, so this is the true *Shibboleth*, that he who stands as judge at the passages of Jordan, makes use of to distinguish those that shall pass over Jordan into the true Canaan, from those that should be slain at the passages. For the Hebrew word *Shibboleth*, signifies an ear of corn. And perhaps the more full pronunciation of Jephthah's friends, *Shibboleth*, may represent a full ear with fruit in it, typifying the fruits of the friends of Christ, the anti-type of Jephthah; and the more lean pronunciation of the Ephraimites, his enemies, may represent their empty ears, typifying the show of religion in hypocrites, without substance and fruit. This is agreeable to the doctrine we are abundantly taught in Scripture, viz. That he who is set to judge those that pass through death, whether they have a right to enter into the heavenly Canaan or no, or whether they should not be slain, will judge every man according to his works.

We seem to be taught the same things, by the rules given for the priest's discerning of the leprosy. In many cases it was impossible for the priest to determine whether a man had the leprosy, or whether he were clean, by the most narrow inspection of the appearances upon him, until he had waited to see what the appearances would come to, and had shut up the person who showed himself, one seven days after another; and when he judged, he was to determine by the hair, which grew out of the spot that was showed him, which was as it were the fruit that it brought forth.

And here, before I finish what I have to say under this head, I would say something to a strange notion some have of late been led away with, of certainly knowing the good estate that others are in—as though it were immediately revealed to them from heaven—by their love flowing out to them in an extraordinary manner. They argue thus,

* A time of outpouring of the Spirit of God, reviving religion, and producing the pleasant appearances of it, in new converts, is in Scripture compared to this very thing, *viz.* the spring-season, when the benign influences of the heavens cause the blossoms to put forth. Cant. ii. 11, 12.

† Husbandry Spiritualized, chap. xii.

that their love, being very sensible and great, may be certainly known by them who feel it, to be a true christian love: and if it be a true christian love, the Spirit of God must be the author of it: and inasmuch as the Spirit of God—who knows certainly whether others are the children of God or no, and is a Spirit of truth—is pleased, by an uncommon influence upon them, to cause their love to flow out, in an extraordinary manner, towards such a person, as a child of God; it must needs be, that this infallible Spirit, who deceives none, knows that that person is a child of God. But such persons might be convinced of the falseness of their reasoning, if they would consider whether or no it be not their duty, and what God expressly requires of them, to love those as the children of God, who they think are the children of God, and of whom they have no reason to think otherwise, from all that they can see in them, though God, who searches the hearts, knows them not to be his children. If it be their duty, then it is good, and the want of it sin; and therefore, the Spirit of God may be the author of it. Surely, the Spirit of God, without being a spirit of falsehood, may in such a case assist a person to do his duty, and keep him from sin. But then, they argue from the uncommon *degree* and special *manner*, in which their love flows out to the person; which they think the Spirit of God never would cause, if he did not know the object to be a child of God. But then I would ask them, whether or no it is not their duty to love all such as they are bound to think are the children of God, from all that they can see in them, to a *very great degree*, though God, from other things which he sees, knows them not to be so. It is men's duty to love all whom they are bound in charity to look upon as the children of God, with a vastly dearer affection than they commonly do. As we ought to love Christ to the utmost capacity of our nature, so it is our duty to love those who we think are so near and dear to him as his members, with an exceeding dear affection, as Christ has loved us; and therefore it is sin in us not to love them so. We ought to pray to God that he would by his Spirit keep us from sin, and enable us to do our duty: and may not his Spirit answer our prayers, and enable us to do our duty, in a particular instance, without lying? If he cannot, then the Spirit of God is bound not to help his people to do their duty in some instances, because he cannot do it without being a spirit of falsehood. But surely God is so far a sovereign, that he may enable us to do our duty when he pleases, and on what occasion he pleases. When persons think others are his children, God may have other ends in causing their exceedingly endeared love to flow out to them, besides revealing to them whether their opinion of them be right or no. May he not have that merciful end in it, to enable them to do their duty, and to keep them from that dreadful, infinite evil, sin? And will they say, God shall not show them that mercy in such a case? If I am at a distance from home, and hear, that in my absence my house is burnt, but my family have, in some extraordinary manner, all escaped the flames; and every thing in the circumstances of the story, as I hear it, makes it appear very credible; would it not be sin in me, in such a case, not to feel a very great degree of gratitude to God, though the story in fact be not true? And is not God so sovereign, that he may, if he please, on that occasion, enable me to do my duty in a much further degree than I used to do it, and yet not incur the charge of deceitfulness, in confirming a falsehood?

It is exceeding manifest, that a *mistake* may be the *occasion* of a gracious exercise, and consequently a gracious influence of the Spirit of God, by Rom. xiv. 6. "He that eateth to the Lord, he eateth, and giveth God thanks; and he that eateth not to the Lord, he eateth not, and giveth God thanks." The apostle is speaking of those who, through erroneous and needless scruples, avoided eating legally unclean meats. By this it is very evident, that there may be true exercises of grace, a true respect *to the Lord*, and particularly a true thankfulness, which may be occasioned by an erroneous judgment and practice. And consequently, an error may be the occasion of those truly holy exercises that are from the infallible Spirit of God. And if so, it is certainly too much for us to determine, to how great a degree the Spirit of God may give this holy exercise on such an occasion.

This notion, of certainly discerning another's state by love flowing out, is not only *not founded* on reason or Scripture, but it is *anti-scriptural, against* the rules of Scripture; which—without saying a word of any such way of judging the state of others as this—direct us to judge chiefly by the *fruits* that are seen in them. The doctrines of Scripture plainly teach us, that the state of others, towards God, cannot be known by us, as in Rev. ii. 17. "To him that overcometh will I give to eat of the *hidden manna*, and I will give him a white stone, and in the stone a new name written, which *no man knoweth, saving he that receiveth it*." And Rom. ii. 29. "He is a Jew, which is one inwardly; and circumcision is that of the heart, in the spirit, and not in the letter, whose praise is not of men, but of God." By this last expression, *whose praise is not of men, but of God*, the apostle has respect to the insufficiency of men to judge concerning him, whether he be *inwardly* a Jew or no. They could easily see by *outward* marks, whether men were outwardly Jews, but it belongs to God alone to give a determining voice, respecting their inward state. This is confirmed by the same apostle's use of the phrase in 1 Cor. iv. 5. "Therefore judge nothing before the time, until the Lord come, who both will bring to light the hidden things of darkness, and will make manifest the counsels of the hearts: and then shall every man have praise of God." The apostle, in the two foregoing verses, says, "But with me it is a very small thing that I should be judged of you, or of man's judgment: yea, I judge not mine own self. For I know nothing by myself, yet am I not hereby justified: but he that judgeth me is the Lord." It is further confirmed, because the apostle, in this second chapter to the Romans, directs his speech especially to those who had a high conceit of their own holiness, made their boast of God, were confident of their own power of discerning, that they knew God's will, and approved the things which were excellent, or tried the things that differ, (as in the margin, v. 18.) "They were confident that they were guides of the blind, and a light to them which are in darkness, instructors of the foolish, teachers of babes:" and so took upon them to judge others. (See ver. 1 and 17—20.)

And how arrogant must their notion be, who imagine they can certainly know others' godliness, when that great apostle Peter pretends not to say any more concerning Sylvanus, than that he was *a faithful brother, as he supposed!* 1 Pet. v. 12. Though this Sylvanus appears to have been a very eminent minister of Christ, an evangelist, a famous light in God's church at that day, and an intimate companion of the apostles. (See 2 Cor. i. 19. 1 Thess. i. 1. and 2 Thess. i. 1.)

PART III.

SHOWING WHAT ARE DISTINGUISHING SIGNS OF TRULY GRACIOUS AND HOLY AFFECTIONS.

INTRODUCTORY REMARKS.

I come now to take notice of some things, wherein those affections that are spiritual and gracious, differ from those that are not so.—But before I proceed directly to the distinguishing characters, I would previously mention some things which I desire may be observed, concerning the marks I shall lay down.

1. I am far from undertaking to give such signs of gracious affections, as shall be sufficient to enable any

certainly to distinguish true affections from false in others; or to determine positively which of their neighbours are true professors, and which are hypocrites. In so doing, I should be guilty of that arrogance which I have been condemning. It is plain that Christ has given rules to all Christians, to enable them to judge of those professors of religion, with whom they are concerned, so far as is necessary for their own safety, and to prevent their being led into a snare by false teachers, and false pretenders to religion. It is also beyond doubt, that the Scriptures abound with rules, which may be very serviceable to ministers, in counselling and conducting souls committed to their care, in things appertaining to their spiritual and eternal state. Yet it is also evident, that it was never God's design to give us any rules, by which we may certainly know, who of our fellow-professors are his, and to make a full and clear separation between sheep and goats. On the contrary, it was God's design to reserve this to himself, as his prerogative. And therefore no such distinguishing signs as shall enable Christians or ministers to do this, are ever to be expected to the world's end: for no more is ever to be expected from any signs found in the word of God, or gathered from it, than Christ designed them for.

2. No such signs are to be expected, that shall be sufficient to enable those saints certainly to discern their own good estate, who are very low in grace, or are such as have much departed from God, and are fallen into a dead, carnal, and unchristian frame. It is not agreeable to God's design, (as already observed,) that such should know their good estate: nor is it desirable that they should; but on the contrary, it is every way best that they should not. We have reason to bless God, that he has made no provision that such should certainly know the state they are in, any other way, than by first coming out of their ill frame and way.

Indeed it is not properly through the defect of the *signs* given in the word of God, that every saint living, whether strong or weak, and those who are in a bad frame, as well as others, cannot certainly know their good estate by them. For the rules *in themselves* are certain and infallible, and every saint has, or has had, those things in himself, which are sure evidences of grace; for *every*, even the *least*, act of grace is so. But the difficulty comes through his defect to whom the signs are given. There is a twofold defect in that saint who is very low in grace, or in an ill frame, which makes it impossible for him to know certainly that he has true grace, by the best signs and rules which can be given him.

First, A defect in the *object*, or the qualification to be viewed and examined. I do not mean an essential defect; because I suppose the person to be a real saint: but a defect in degree: grace being very small, cannot be clearly and certainly discerned and distinguished. Things that are very small we cannot clearly discern, as to their form, or distinguish them one from another; though as they are in themselves, their form may be very different. There is doubtless a great difference between the body of man, and the bodies of other animals, in the first conception in the womb: but yet, if we should view the different embryos, it might not be possible for us to discern the difference, by reason of the imperfect state of the object: but as it comes to greater perfection, the difference becomes very plain. The difference between creatures of very *contrary qualities*, is not so plainly to be seen while they are very young, even after they are actually brought forth, as in their more perfect state. The difference between doves and ravens, or doves and vultures, when they first come out of the egg, is not so evident; but as they grow to their perfection, it is exceeding great and manifest. The grace of those I am speaking of is mingled with so much corruption, which clouds and hides it, as makes it impossible to be known with certainty. Though different things before us, may have in themselves many marks thoroughly distinguishing them one from another; yet if we see them only in a thick smoke, it may nevertheless be impossible to distinguish them. A fixed star is easily distinguishable from a comet, in a clear sky; but if we view them through a cloud, it may be impossible to see the difference. When true Christians are in an ill frame, guilt lies on the conscience; which will bring fear, and so prevent the peace and joy of an assured hope.

Secondly, There is in such a case a defect in the *eye*. As the feebleness of grace, and the prevalence of corruption, obscures the object; so it enfeebles the sight. Corruption in the soul darkens the sight as to all spiritual objects, of which grace is one. Sin is like some distempers of the eyes, that make things to appear of different colours from those which properly belong to them; or, like other distempers that put the mouth out of taste, so as to disable it from distinguishing good and wholesome food from bad, but every thing tastes bitter. Men in a corrupt and carnal frame, have their spiritual senses in but a poor plight for judging and distinguishing spiritual things.

For these reasons, no signs that can be given will actually satisfy persons in such a case. Let the signs given be never so good and infallible, and clearly laid down, they will not serve them. It is like giving a man rules how to distinguish visible objects in the dark: the things themselves may be very different, and their difference may be very well and distinctly described to him; yet all is insufficient to enable him to distinguish them, because he is in the dark. And therefore many persons in such a case spend time in a fruitless labour, in poring on past experiences, and examining themselves by signs which they hear laid down from the pulpit, or read in books. There is other work for them to do, which, while they neglect, all their self-examinations are like to be in vain, if they should spend never so much time in them. The accursed thing is to be destroyed from their camp, and Achan to be slain; and until this be done they will be in trouble. It is not God's design that men should obtain assurance in any other way, than by mortifying corruption, increasing in grace, and obtaining the lively exercises of it. And although self-examination be a duty of great use and importance, and by no means to be neglected; yet it is not the *principal* means, by which the saints do get satisfaction of their good estate. Assurance is not to be obtained so much by *self-examination*, as by *action*. The apostle Paul sought assurance chiefly this way, even by *forgetting the things that were behind, and reaching forth unto those things that were before, pressing towards the mark for the prize of the high calling of God in Christ Jesus; if by any means he might attain unto the resurrection of the dead.* And it was by this means chiefly that he obtained assurance, 1 Cor. ix. 26. " I therefore so run, as not uncertainly." He obtained assurance of winning the prize more by *running* than by *considering*. The *swiftness of his pace*, did more towards his assurance of a conquest, than the *strictness of his examination*. Giving all diligence to grow in grace, by adding to faith, virtue, &c. is the direction that the apostle Peter gives us, for *making our calling and election sure*, and having *an entrance ministered to us abundantly into Christ's everlasting kingdom*. Without this, our eyes will be dim, and we shall be as men in the dark; we cannot plainly see either the forgiveness of our sins past, or our heavenly inheritance that is future, and *far off*, 2 Pet. i. 5—11.*

Therefore, though good rules to distinguish true grace from counterfeit, may tend to convince hypocrites, and be of great use to the saints, in many respects; and among other benefits, they may be very useful to them in order to remove many needless scruples, and establish their hope; yet I am far from pretending to lay down any such rules as shall be sufficient of themselves, without other means, to enable all true saints to see their good estate, or from supposing that they should be the principal means of their satisfaction.

3. Nor is there much encouragement, from the experience of present or past times, to lay down rules or marks to distinguish between true and false affections, in hopes of convincing any considerable number of that sort of hy-

* "The way to know your godliness, is to renew the visible exercises of grace."—" The more visible exercises of grace are renewed, the more certain you will be. The more frequently these actings are renewed, the more abiding and confirmed your assurance will be."—" The more men's grace is multiplied, the more their peace is multiplied; 2 Pet. i. 2. 'Grace and peace be multiplied unto you, through the knowledge of God and Jesus Christ our Lord.'" Stoddard's *Way to know Sincerity and Hypocrisy*, p. 139, and 142.

pocrites, who have been deceived with great false discoveries and affections, and are once settled in false confidence. Such hypocrites are so conceited of their own wisdom, so blinded and hardened with self-righteousness, (but very subtle and secret, under the disguise of great humility,) and so invincible a fondness of their pleasing conceit, their great exaltation, that it usually signifies nothing at all to lay before them the most convincing evidences of their hypocrisy. Their state is indeed deplorable, and next to those that have committed the unpardonable sin. Some of this sort seem to be most out of the reach of means of conviction and repentance. But yet the laying down of good rules may be a means of convincing other kinds of hypocrites; and God is able to convince even this kind, and his grace is not to be limited, nor means to be neglected. Besides, such rules may be of use to the true saints, in order to detect false affections, which they may have mingled with true; and be a means of their religion becoming more pure, and like gold tried in the fire.

Having premised these things, I now proceed directly to take notice of those things in which true religious affections are distinguished from false.

SECT. I.

Affections that are truly spiritual and gracious, arise from those influences and operations on the heart, which are spiritual, supernatural, and divine.

I WILL explain what I mean by these terms, whence will appear their use to distinguish between those affections which are spiritual, and those which are not so.—We find that true saints, or those persons who are sanctified by the Spirit of God, are in the New Testament called *spiritual* persons. And their being *spiritual* is spoken of as their peculiar character, and that wherein they are distinguished from those who are not sanctified. This is evident, because those who are spiritual are set in opposition to natural men, and carnal men. Thus the spiritual man and the natural man are set in opposition one to another, 1 Cor. ii. 14, 15. "The natural man receiveth not the things of the Spirit of God: for they are foolishness unto him: neither can he know them, because they are spiritually discerned. But he that is *spiritual*, judgeth all things." The Scripture explains itself to mean an ungodly man, or one that has no grace, by a natural man: thus the apostle Jude, speaking of certain *ungodly men*, that had crept in unawares among the saints, (ver. 4. of his epistle,) says, ver. 19. "There are sensual, having not the Spirit." This the apostle gives as a reason why they behaved themselves in such a wicked manner as he had described. Here the word ψυχικοι translated *sensual*, is the very same, which in 1 Cor. ii. 14, 15. is translated *natural*. In like manner, in the continuation of the same discourse, *spiritual men* are opposed to *carnal men;* which the connexion plainly shows mean the same, as *spiritual men* and *natural men*, in the foregoing verses; "And I, brethren, could not speak unto you as unto *spiritual*, but as unto *carnal;*" *i. e.* as in a great measure unsanctified.* Now therefore, if by natural and carnal, in these texts, be intended *unsanctified*, then doubtless by spiritual, which is opposed thereto, is meant sanctified and gracious. And as the saints are called spiritual in Scripture, so we also find that there are certain properties, qualities, and principles, that have the same epithet given them. So we read of a *spiritual mind*, Rom. viii. 6, 7. of *spiritual wisdom*, Col. i. 9. and of *spiritual blessings*, Eph. i. 3.

Now it may be observed, that the epithet *spiritual*, in these and other parallel texts of the New Testament, is not used to signify any relation of persons or things to the spirit or soul of man, as the spiritual part of man, in opposition to the body, or material part. Qualities are not said to be spiritual, because they have their seat in the soul, and not in the body: for there are some properties that the Scripture calls *carnal* or *fleshly*, which have their seat as much in the soul, as those properties that are called *spiritual*. Thus pride and self-righteousness, and a man's trusting to his own wisdom, the apostle calls *fleshly*, Col. ii. 18. Nor are things called spiritual, because they are conversant about those things that are immaterial, and not corporeal. For so was the wisdom of the wise men, and princes of this world, conversant about spirits, and immaterial beings; yet the apostle speaks of them as *natural men*, totally ignorant of those things that are *spiritual*, 1 Cor. chap. ii. But it is with relation to the *Holy Ghost*, or *Spirit of God*, that persons or things are termed *spiritual*, in the New Testament. *Spirit*, as the word is used to signify the third person in the Trinity, is the substantive, of which is formed the adjective *spiritual* in the Holy Scriptures. Thus Christians are called spiritual persons, because they are born of the Spirit, and because of the indwelling and holy influences of the Spirit of God in them. And things are called spiritual as related to the Spirit of God; 1 Cor. ii. 13, 14. "Which things also we speak, not in the words man's wisdom teacheth, but which the Holy Ghost teacheth; comparing spiritual things with spiritual. But the natural man receiveth not the things of the Spirit of God." Here the apostle himself expressly signifies, that by *spiritual things*, he means *the things of the Spirit of God*, and *things which the Holy Ghost teacheth*. The same is yet more abundantly apparent by viewing the whole context. Again, Rom. viii. 6. *To be* carnally minded, *is death; but to be* SPIRITUALLY MINDED, *is life and peace.* The apostle explains what he means by being carnally and spiritually minded, in what follows in the 9th verse, and shows that by being spiritually minded he means, having the indwelling and holy influences of the Spirit of God in the heart. *But ye are not in the flesh, but* IN THE SPIRIT, *if so be the Spirit of God dwell in you. Now if any man* have not the *Spirit of Christ, he is none of his.* The same is evident by all the context. But time would fail to produce all the evidence of this in the New Testament.

And it must be here observed, that although it is with relation to the Spirit of God and his influences, that persons and things are called *spiritual;* yet not all those persons who are subject to any kind of influence of the Spirit of God, are ordinarily called so in the New Testament. They who have only the *common* influences of God's Spirit, are not so called, in the places cited above. It has been already proved, that by *spiritual* men is meant *godly* men, in opposition to natural, carnal, and unsanctified men. And it is most plain, that the apostle by *spiritually minded*, Rom. viii. 6. means *graciously* minded. And though the extraordinary gifts of the Spirit, which natural men might have, are sometimes called spiritual, because they are from the Spirit; yet natural men, whatever gifts of the Spirit they had, were not, in the usual language of the New Testament, called spiritual persons. For it was not by men's having the *gifts*, but the *virtues* of the Spirit, that they are called spiritual; as is apparent, by Gal. vi. 1. "Brethren, if any man be overtaken in a fault, ye which are spiritual, restore such an one in the spirit of meekness." Meekness is one of those virtues which the apostle had just spoken of in the verses next preceding, showing what are the *fruits of the Spirit*. Those qualifications, therefore, are said to be *spiritual* in the language of the New Testament, which are truly *gracious*, and peculiar to the saints.

Thus when we read of spiritual wisdom and understanding—as in Col. i. 9. "We desire that ye may be filled with the knowledge of his will, in all wisdom and spiritual understanding"—hereby is intended that wisdom which is gracious, and from the sanctifying influences of the Spirit of God. For, doubtless, by *spiritual wisdom*, is meant that which is opposite to what the Scripture calls *natural wisdom;* as the *spiritual man* is opposed to the *natural man*. And therefore spiritual wisdom is doubtless the same with that wisdom which is from above, James iii. 17. "The wisdom that is from above, is first pure, then peaceable, gentle," &c. for this the apostle opposes to *natural* wisdom, ver. 15. "This wisdom descendeth not from above, but is earthly, sensual"—the last word in the original is the same that is translated *natural*, in 1 Cor. ii. 14.

So that although natural men may be the subjects of many influences of the Spirit of God, as is evident by many scriptures,† yet they are not in the sense the Scrip-

* That by *carnal* the apostle means corrupt and unsanctified, is abundantly evident, by Rom. vii. 25. & viii. 1, 4—12, 13. Gal. v. 16. to the end. Col. ii. 18.

† As Num. xxiv. 2. 1 Sam. x. 10. and xi. 6. and xvi. 14. 1 Cor. xiii. 1, 2, 3. Heb. vi. 4, 5, 6. and many others.

ture, spiritual persons; neither are any of those effects, common gifts, qualities, or affections, that are from the influence of the Spirit of God upon them, called spiritual things. The great difference lies in these two things.

1. The Spirit of God is given to the true saints to dwell in them, as his proper lasting abode; and to influence their hearts, as a principle of new nature, or as a divine supernatural spring of life and action. The Scriptures represent the Holy Spirit, not only as moving, and occasionally influencing, the saints, but as dwelling in them as his temple, his proper abode, and everlasting dwelling-place, (1 Cor. iii. 16. 2 Cor. vi. 16. John xiv. 16, 17.) And he is represented as being there so united to the faculties of the soul, that he becomes there a principle or spring of a new nature and life.

So the saints are said to live by Christ living in them, Gal. ii. 20. Christ by his Spirit not only *is* in them, but *lives* in them; they live by his life. His Spirit is united to them, as a principle of life in them. They not only drink living water, but this *living water becomes a well* or *fountain of water*, in the soul, *springing up into* spiritual and *everlasting life*, John iv. 14. and thus becomes a principle of life in them—this living water the evangelist himself explains to intend the Spirit of God, (chap. vii. 38, 39.) The light of the Sun of righteousness does not only shine *upon them*, but is so communicated to them that *they shine* also, and become little images of that sun which shines upon them. The sap of the true vine is not only conveyed into them, as the sap of a tree may be conveyed into a vessel, but is conveyed as sap is from a tree into one of its living branches, where it becomes a principle of life. The Spirit of God being thus communicated and united to the saints, they are from thence properly denominated from it, and are called *spiritual*.

On the other hand, though the Spirit of God may many ways influence natural men; yet because it is not thus communicated to them, as an indwelling principle, they do not derive any denomination or character from it; for there being no *union*, it is not their *own*. The light may shine upon a body that is very dark or black; and though that body be the subject of the light, yet, because the light becomes no principle of light to it, so as to cause the body to shine, hence that body does not properly receive its denomination from it, so as to be called a *lightsome body*. So the Spirit of God acting *upon* the soul only, without communicating itself to be an active principle *in* it, cannot denominate it *spiritual*. A body that continues black, may be said *not to have light*, though the light shines upon it: so natural men are said *not to have the Spirit*, Jude 19. *sensual* or *natural*, as the word is elsewhere rendered, *having not the Spirit*.

2. Another reason why the saints and their virtues are called spiritual, (and which is the principal thing,) is, that the Spirit of God, dwelling as a vital principle in the souls, produces there those effects wherein he exerts and communicates himself in his own *proper nature*. Holiness is the nature of the Spirit of God, therefore he is called in Scripture the *Holy Ghost*. Holiness, which is as it were the beauty and sweetness of the divine nature, is as much the proper nature of the Holy Spirit, as heat is the nature of fire, or sweetness was the nature of that holy anointing oil, which was the principal type of the Holy Ghost in the Mosaic dispensation. Yea, I may rather say, that holiness is as much the proper nature of the Holy Ghost, as sweetness was the nature of the sweet odour of that ointment. The Spirit of God so dwells in the hearts of the saints, that he there, as a seed or spring of life, exerts and communicates himself, in this his sweet and divine nature. He makes the soul a partaker of God's beauty and Christ's joy, so that the saint has truly fellowship *with* the Father, and *with* his Son Jesus Christ, in thus having the communion or participation *of* the Holy Ghost. The grace which is in the hearts of the saints, is of the *same nature* with the divine holiness, though infinitely less in degree; as the brightness in a diamond which the sun shines upon, is of the same nature with the brightness of the sun, but only that it is as nothing to it in degree. Therefore Christ says, John iii. 6. "That which is born of the Spirit, is spirit," *i. e.* the grace that is begotten in the hearts of the saints, is something of the same nature with that Spirit, and so is properly called a *spiritual nature;* after the same manner as that which is born of the flesh is flesh, or that which is born of corrupt nature is corrupt nature.

But the Spirit of God never influences the minds of natural men after this manner. Though he may influence them many ways, yet he never, in any of his influences, communicates himself to them in his own proper nature. Indeed he never acts *disagreeably* to his nature, either on the minds of saints or sinners: but the Spirit of God may act upon men *agreeably* to his own nature, and not exert his *proper nature* in the acts and exercises of their minds. The Spirit of God may act so, that his *actions* may be agreeable to his nature, and yet may not at all *communicate* himself in his proper nature, in the *effect* of that action. Thus, for instance, the Spirit of God *moved* upon the face of the waters, and there was nothing disagreeable to his nature in that action; but yet he did not at all *communicate himself* in that action, there was nothing of the *proper nature* of the Holy Spirit in that *motion* of the waters. And so he may act upon the minds of men many ways, and not communicate himself any more than when he acts on inanimate things.

Thus, not only the manner of the Spirit's *relation* to the subject of his operations, is different; but the influence and *operation itself*, and the *effect wrought*, exceeding different. So that not only the persons are called *spiritual*, as having the Spirit of God dwelling in them; but those qualifications, affections, and experiences that are wrought in them by the Spirit, are also *spiritual*. Therein they differ vastly in their nature and kind from all that a natural man can be the subject of, while he remains in a natural state; and also from all that of which men or devils can be the authors. It is a spiritual work in this high sense; and therefore above all other works is peculiar to the Spirit of God. There is no work so high and excellent; for there is no work wherein God doth so much communicate himself, and wherein the mere creature hath, in so high a sense, a participation of God; so that it is expressed in Scripture by the saints *being made partakers of the divine nature*, 2 Pet. i. 4. and *having God dwelling in them, and they in God*, 1 John iv. 12, 15, 16. and chap. iii. 21. *and having Christ in them*, John xvii. 21. Rom. viii. 10. *being the temples of the living God*, 2 Cor. vi. 16. *living by Christ's life*, Gal. ii. 20. *being made partakers of God's holiness*, Heb. xii. 10. *having Christ's love dwelling in them*, John xvii. 26. *having his joy fulfilled in them*, John xvii. 13. *seeing light in God's light*, and *being made to drink of the river of God's pleasures*, Ps. xxxvi. 8, 9. *having fellowship with God*, or *communicating and partaking with him*, (as the word signifies,) 1 John i. 3. Not that the saints are made partakers of the *essence* of God—or *godded* with God, and *christed* with Christ, according to the blasphemous language of some heretics—but, to use the scripture phrase, they are made partakers of God's *fulness*, (Eph. iii. 17—19. John i. 16.) that is, of God's spiritual beauty and happiness, according to the measure and capacity of a creature. So the word *fulness* signifies in scripture language. Grace in the hearts of the saints being therefore the most glorious work of God, wherein he communicates of the goodness of his nature, it is doubtless his *peculiar* work, and in an eminent manner above the power of all creatures. And this is what I mean by those influences that are *divine*, when I say, that *truly gracious affections arise from those influences that are spiritual and divine*.

True saints *only* have that which is spiritual; others not only have not these communications of the Spirit in so high a *degree* as the saints, but have nothing of that *nature* or *kind*. For the apostle James tells us, that *natural* men *have not the Spirit;* and Christ teaches the necessity of a new birth, or a being born of the Spirit, from this, that *he that is born of the flesh, has* only *flesh*, and no *spirit*, John iii. 6. They have not the Spirit of God dwelling in them in any degree; for the apostle teaches, that all who have the Spirit of God dwelling in them are his, Rom. viii. 9—11. And, having the Spirit of God is spoken of as a certain sign, that persons shall have the eternal inheritance; for it is the earnest of it, (2 Cor. i. 22. and v. 5. Eph. i. 14.) and having any thing *of the Spirit* is mentioned as a sure sign of being in Christ, 1 John iv. 13. "Hereby know we that we dwell in him, because he hath given us *of* his Spirit." Ungodly men not only have not so much of the divine nature as the saints, but they are not *partakers of it;* which implies that they have nothing of it; for a being *partaker* of the divine nature is spoken of as the peculiar privilege of the true saints, 2 Pet. i. 4. Ungodly men are not *partakers of God's holiness,* Heb. xii. 10. A natural man has no experience of those things that are spiritual: he is so far from it, that he knows nothing about them, and is a perfect stranger to them. To talk about such things is all foolishness to him, he knows not what it means, 1 Cor. ii. 14. "The natural man receiveth not the things of the Spirit of God; for they are foolishness to him: neither can he know them, because they are spiritually discerned." And to the like purpose Christ teaches us that the world is wholly unacquainted with the Spirit of God, John xiv. 17. "Even the Spirit of truth, whom the world cannot receive, because it seeth him not, neither knoweth him." And it is further evident, that natural men have nothing in them of the same nature with the true grace of the saints, because the apostle teaches us, that those of them who go farthest in religion, have *no charity,* or true christian love, (1 Cor. chap. xiii.) So Christ elsewhere reproves the Pharisees, those high pretenders to religion, that they *had not the love of God in them,* John v. 42. Hence natural men have no communion or fellowship with Christ, or *participation with him,* as these words signify, for this is spoken of as the peculiar privilege of the saints, (1 John i. 3, 6, 7. and 1 Cor. i. 8, 9.) And the Scripture speaks of the actual existence of a gracious principle in the soul, though in its first beginning, like a seed planted there, as inconsistent with a man's being a sinner, 1 John iii. 9. And natural men are represented in Scripture, as having no spiritual *light,* no spiritual *life,* and no spiritual *being;* and therefore conversion is often compared to opening the eyes of the *blind,* raising the *dead,* and a work of *creation,* wherein creatures are made entirely new, and becoming new-born children.

From these things it is evident, that those gracious influences of the saints, and the effects of God's Spirit which they experience, are entirely above nature, and altogether of a different kind from any thing that men find in themselves by the exercise of natural principles. No improvement of those principles that are natural, no advancing or exalting of them to higher degrees, and no kind of composition, will ever bring men to them; because they not only differ from what is natural, and from every thing that natural men experience, in degree and circumstances, but also in *kind;* and are of a nature vastly more excellent. And this is what I mean by *supernatural,* when I say, that *gracious affections are from those influences that are supernatural.*

From hence it follows, that in those gracious exercises and affections which are wrought in the saints, through the saving influences of the Spirit of God, there is a new inward *perception* or *sensation* of their minds, entirely different in its nature and kind from any thing that ever their minds were the subjects of before they were sanctified. For, if God by his mighty power produces something that is new, not only in degree and circumstances, but in its whole nature—all that which could be produced by no exalting, varying, or compounding of what was there before, or by adding any thing of the like kind—then, doubtless, something entirely new is felt, or perceived. There is what some metaphysicians call a new *simple idea.* If grace be, in the sense above described, an entirely new kind of principle; then the *exercises* of it are also new. And if there be in the soul a new sort of conscious exercises, which the soul knew nothing of before, and which no improvement, composition, or management of what it was before could produce; then it follows that the mind has an entirely new kind of perception or sensation. Here is, as it were, a new *spiritual sense,* or a principle of new kind of perception or spiritual sensation, which is in its whole nature different from any former kinds of sensation of the mind, as tasting is diverse from any of the other senses. And something is perceived by a true saint, in the exercise of this new sense of mind in spiritual and divine things, as entirely diverse from any thing that is perceived in them by natural men, as the sweet taste of honey is diverse from the ideas men get of honey by only looking on and feeling it. So that the spiritual perceptions which a sanctified and spiritual person has, are not only diverse from all that natural men have as the perceptions of the same sense may differ one from another, but rather as the ideas and sensations of different senses differ. Hence the work of the Spirit of God in regeneration is often in Scripture compared to the giving of a new sense, eyes to see, ears to hear, unstopping the ears of the deaf, opening the eyes of them that were born blind, and turning from darkness unto light. And because this spiritual sense is immensely the most noble and excellent, and that without which all other principles of perception, and all our faculties, are useless and vain; therefore the giving of this new sense, with the blessed fruits and effects of it in the soul, is compared to raising the dead, and to a new creation.

This new spiritual sense, and the new dispositions that attend it, are no new *faculties,* but new *principles* of nature: I use the word *principles,* for want of a word of a more determinate signification. By a *principle of nature* in this place, I mean that foundation which is laid in nature, either old or new, for any particular manner or kind of exercise of the faculties of the soul; or a natural habit, or foundation for action, giving a person ability and disposition to exert the faculties in exercises of such a certain kind; so that to exert the faculties in that kind of exercises, may be said to be his nature. So this new spiritual sense is not a new faculty of understanding, but it is a new foundation laid in the nature of the soul, for a new kind of exercises of the same faculty of understanding. So that the new holy disposition of heart that attends this new sense, is not a new faculty of will, but a foundation laid in the nature of the soul, for a new kind of exercises of the same faculty of will.

The Spirit of God, in all his operations upon the minds of natural men, only moves, impresses, assists, improves, or some way acts upon *natural principles;* but gives no new *spiritual principle.* Thus when the Spirit of God gives a natural man visions, as he did Balaam, he only impresses a natural principle—the sense of seeing, immediately exciting ideas of that sense—but gives no new sense; neither is there any thing supernatural, spiritual, or divine in it. If the Spirit of God impresses on a man's imagination, either in a dream, or when he is awake, any outward ideas of any of the senses, either voices or shapes and colours, it is only exciting ideas of the same kind that he has by natural principles and senses. So if God reveals to a natural man any secret fact; for instance, something that he shall hereafter see or hear; this is not infusing or exercising any new spiritual principle, or giving the ideas of any new spiritual sense; it is only impressing, in an extraordinary manner, the ideas that will hereafter be received by sight and hearing. So in the more ordinary influences of the Spirit of God on the hearts of sinners, he only assists natural principles to do the same work to a greater degree, which they do of themselves by nature. Thus the Spirit of God by his common influences may assist men's natural ingenuity, as he assisted Bezaleel and Aholiab in the curious works of the tabernacle. He may assist men's natural abilities in political affairs, and improve their courage and other natural qualifications; as he is said to have put his Spirit on the seventy elders, and on Saul, so as to *give him another heart.* God may greatly assist natural men's reason, in their reasoning about secular things, or about the doctrines of religion, and may greatly advance the clearness of their apprehensions and notions in many respects, without giving any spiritual sense. So in those awakenings and convictions that natural men may have, God only assists conscience, which is a natural principle, to do that work in a further degree, which it naturally does. Conscience naturally gives men an apprehension of right and wrong, and suggests the relation there is between them and a retribution. The Spirit of God assists men's consciences to do this in a greater degree, and against the stupifying influence of worldly objects and their lusts. Many other ways might be mentioned, wherein the Spirit acts upon, assists, and moves natural principles; but after all, it is no more than nature moved, acted, and improved; here is nothing supernatural and divine. But the Spirit of God in his spiritual influences on the hearts of his saints, operates by infusing or exercising new, divine, and supernatural principles; principles which are indeed a new and spiritual nature, and principles vastly more noble and excellent than all that is in natural men.

From what has been said it follows, that all spiritual and gracious affections are attended with, and arise from, some apprehension, idea, or sensation of mind, which is in its whole nature different, yea exceeding different, from all that is or can be in the mind of a natural man. The natural man discerns nothing of it, (1 Cor. ii. 14.) any more than a man without the sense of tasting can conceive of the sweet taste of honey; or a man without the sense of hearing can conceive of the melody of a tune; or a man born blind can have a notion of the beauty of the rainbow.

But here two things must be observed, in order to the right understanding of this.

1. On the one hand it must be observed, that not every thing which appertains to spiritual affections, is new and entirely different from what natural men experience; some things are common to gracious affections with other affections; many circumstances, appendages, and effects are common. Thus a saint's love to God has a great many things appertaining to it, which are common with a man's natural love to a near relation. Love to God makes a man seek the honour of God, and desire to please him; so does a natural man's love to his friend make him desire his honour, and to please him. Love to God causes a man to delight in the thoughts of him, in his presence; to desire conformity to God, and the enjoyment of him; and so it is with a man's love to his friend. Many other things might be mentioned which are common to both. But yet, that idea which the saint has of the loveliness of God, and the kind of delight he has in that view which is as it were the marrow and quintessence of his love, is peculiar, and entirely diverse from any thing that a natural man has, or can have any notion of. And even in those things that seem to be common, there is something peculiar. Both spiritual love and natural, cause *desires* after the object beloved; but they are not the same sort of desires; there is a sensation of soul in the spiritual desires of one that loves God, which is entirely different from all natural desires. Both spiritual and natural love are attended with *delight* in the object beloved; but the sensations of delight are not the same, but entirely and exceedingly diverse. Natural men may have conceptions of many things *about* spiritual affections; but there is something in them which is as it were the *nucleus*, or kernel, of which they have no more conceptions, than one born blind has of colours.

It may be clearly illustrated thus: we will suppose two men; one, born without the sense of tasting, the other with it. The latter loves honey, because he knows the sweet taste of it; the other loves certain sounds and colours. The *love* of each has many things in *common;* it causes *both* to desire and delight in the object beloved, causes grief when it is absent, &c. but yet that sensation which he, who knows the taste of honey, has of its excellency and sweetness, as the foundation of his love, is entirely different from any thing the other has or can have. So both these persons may in some respects *love the same object*. The one may love a delicious kind of fruit, not only because he has seen its pleasant colours, but knows its sweet taste; the other, perfectly ignorant of the latter, loves it only for its beautiful colours. Many things seem, in some respect, to be common to both; both love, both desire, and both delight; but the love, desire, and delight of the one, is altogether diverse from that of the other. The difference between the love of a natural and spiritual man resembles this; but only it must be observed, that the kinds of excellency perceived in spiritual objects, by these different kinds of persons, are in themselves vastly more diverse than the different kinds of excellency perceived in delicious fruit by a *tasting* and a *tasteless* man. In another respect, it may not be so great, viz. as the spiritual man may have a sense to perceive that divine and most peculiar excellency but in small beginnings, and in a very imperfect degree.

2. On the other hand, it must be observed, that a natural man may have religious apprehensions and affections, which may be, in many respects, very new and surprising to him; and yet what he experiences, be nothing like the exercises of a new nature. His affections may be very new, in a very new degree, with a great many new circumstances, a new co-operation of natural affections, and a new composition of ideas. This may be from some extraordinary powerful influence of Satan, and some great delusion. There is nothing, however, but nature extraordinarily acted. As if a poor man who had always dwelt in a cottage, and had never looked beyond the obscure village where he was born, should, in a jest, be taken to a magnificent city and prince's court, and be there arrayed in princely robes, and set in the throne, with the crown royal on his head, peers and nobles bowing before him—and should be made to believe that he was now a glorious monarch—his ideas, and the affections he would experience, would in many respects be very new, and such as he had no imagination of before. Yet who would suppose, that what was done to him was any thing more than extraordinarily raising and exciting natural principles, and newly exalting, varying, and compounding such sort of ideas as he had by nature? Who would infer, that this was giving him a *new sense?*

Upon the whole, I think it is clearly manifest, that all truly gracious affections arise from special and peculiar influences of the Spirit, working that *sensible effect* or *sensation* in the souls of the saints, which are entirely different from all that is possible a natural man should experience; different, not only in degree and circumstances, but in its whole nature. So that a natural man not only cannot experience that which is *individually* the same, but cannot experience any thing but what is exceedingly diverse, and immensely below it, in its *kind;* and that which the power of men or devils is not sufficient to produce, or any thing of the same nature.

I have insisted the more largely on this matter, because this view of the subject is evidently of great importance and use, in order to discover the delusions of Satan, in many kinds of false religious affections, by which multitudes are deluded, and probably have been in all ages of the christian church; also in order to settle and determine many articles of doctrine, concerning the operations of the Spirit of God, and the nature of true grace.—Let us now, therefore, apply these things to the purpose of this discourse.

From hence it appears, that impressions which some have on their imagination—their imaginary ideas of God, or Christ, or heaven, or any thing appertaining to religion—have nothing in them that is spiritual, or of the nature of true grace. Though such things may attend what is spiritual, and be mixed with it, yet in themselves they are not any part of gracious experience.

Here, for the sake of the less informed, I will explain what is intended by *impressions on the imagination*, and *imaginary ideas*. The imagination is that power of the mind, whereby it can have a conception, or idea, of external things, or objects of the outward senses, when those things are not present, and therefore not perceived by the senses. It is called *imagination*, from the word *image;* because thereby a person can have an image of some external thing in his mind, when that thing is not present in reality, nor any thing like it. What we perceive by our five senses, *seeing*, *hearing*, *smelling*, *tasting*, and *feeling*, are external things: and when a person has an image of these things in his mind, but does not really see, hear, smell, taste, nor feel them; that is to have an *imagination* of them, and these ideas are *imaginary ideas*. When such ideas are strongly impressed upon the mind, and the image is very lively, almost as if one saw, or heard them, &c. that is called an *impression on the imagination*. Thus colours and shapes are outward things, objects of the outward sense of *seeing:* therefore, when any person has in his mind a lively idea of any shape, or colour, or form of countenance; of light or darkness, such as he perceives by the sense of seeing; of any marks made on paper, suppose letters and words written in a book: that is to have an *imagination*, or an external and imaginary idea of such things as we sometimes perceive by our bodily eyes. And when we have the ideas of sounds, voices, or words spoken; this is only to have ideas of outward things, perceived by the external sense of *hearing*, and so that also is *imagination*. When these ideas are impressed with liveliness, almost as if they were really heard with the ears, this is to have an *impression on the imagination*. And so I might instance in the ideas of things appertaining to the other three senses of *smelling*, *tasting*, and *feeling*.

Many who have had such things, have ignorantly supposed them to be of the nature of spiritual discoveries. They have had lively ideas of some external shape, and beautiful form of countenance; and this they call spiritually seeing Christ. Some have had impressed upon them ideas of a great outward light; and this they call a spiritual discovery of God's or Christ's glory. Some have had ideas of Christ hanging on the cross, and his blood running from his wounds; and this they call a spiritual sight of Christ crucified, and the way of salvation by his blood. Some have seen him with his arms open ready to embrace them; and this they call a discovery of the sufficiency of Christ's grace and love. Some have had lively ideas of heaven, and of Christ on his throne there, and shining ranks of saints and angels; and this they call seeing heaven opened to them. Some from time to time have had a lively idea of a person of a beautiful countenance smiling upon them; and this they call a spiritual discovery of the love of Christ to their souls, and tasting the love of Christ. And they look upon it a sufficient evidence that these things are spiritual discoveries, and that they see them spiritually, because they say they do not see these things with their bodily eyes, but in their hearts; for they can see them when their eyes are shut. And in like manner, the imaginations of some have been impressed with ideas of the sense of hearing; they have had ideas of words, as if they were spoken to them, sometimes the words of Scripture, and sometimes other words. They have had ideas of *Christ speaking comfortable words* to them. These things they have called having the inward call of Christ, hearing the voice of Christ spiritually in their hearts, having the witness of the Spirit, the inward testimony of the love of Christ, &c.

The common and less considerate sort of people, are the more easily led into apprehensions that these are spiritual things, because, spiritual things being invisible, we are forced to use figurative expressions in speaking of them, and to borrow names from sensible objects by which to signify them. Thus we call a clear apprehension of things spiritual by the name of *light;* and having an apprehension of things, by the name of *seeing* such things. The conviction of the judgment, and the persuasion of the will, by the word of Christ in the gospel, we signify by *spiritually hearing the call of Christ.* The Scripture itself abounds with such like figurative expressions. Persons hearing these often used, and having pressed upon them the necessity of having their eyes opened, of having a discovery of spiritual things, seeing Christ in his glory, having the inward call, and the like, they ignorantly look and wait for some external discoveries, and imaginary views. And when they have them, they are confident that now their eyes are opened, now Christ has discovered himself to them, and they are his children; and hence they are exceedingly affected and elevated with their deliverance, and many kinds of affections are at once set in a violent motion.

But it is exceedingly apparent that such ideas have nothing in them which is spiritual and divine, in the sense wherein it has been demonstrated that all gracious experiences are spiritual and divine. These external ideas are in no wise entirely, and in their whole nature, diverse from all that men have by nature: so far from this, they are of the same sort which we have by the external senses, among the inferior powers of human nature. They are merely ideas of external objects, of the outward sensitive kind; the same sort of sensations of mind (differing not in degree, but only in circumstances) that we have by those natural principles which are common to us with the beasts. This is a low, miserable notion of spiritual sense, to suppose that it is only a conceiving or imagining that sort of ideas which we have by our animal senses, which senses the beasts have in as great perfection as we. Is this any thing better than, as it were, a turning of Christ, or the divine nature in the soul, into a mere animal? Is there any thing wanting in the soul, as it is by nature, to render it capable of being the subject of all these external ideas, without any new principles? A natural man is capable of having an idea, and a lively idea, of shapes, and colours, and sounds, when they are absent, even as capable as a regenerate man is: so there is nothing supernatural in them. And it is known by abundant experience, that it is not the advancing or perfecting of human nature, which makes persons more capable of having such lively and strong imaginary ideas; but on the contrary, the weakness of body and mind, makes persons abundantly more susceptive of such impressions.*

As to a truly *spiritual* sensation, not only is the manner of its coming into the mind extraordinary, but the sensation itself is totally diverse from all that men have, or can have, in a state of nature, as has been shown. But as to these *external* ideas, though the way of their coming into the mind is sometimes unusual, yet the ideas in themselves are not the better for that; they are still of no different sort from what men have by their senses; they are of no higher kind, nor a whit better. For instance, the external idea a man has now of Christ hanging on the cross, and shedding his blood, is no better in itself, than the external idea that the Jews his enemies had, who stood round his cross, and saw this with their bodily eyes. The imaginary idea which men have now of an external brightness and glory of God, is no better than the idea the wicked congregation in the wilderness had of the external glory of the Lord at mount Sinai, when they saw it with bodily eyes; or any better than that idea which millions of cursed reprobates will have of the external glory of Christ at the day of judgment, who shall see and have a very lively idea of ten thousand times greater external glory of Christ, than ever yet was conceived in any man's imagination.† Is the image of Christ which men conceive in their imaginations, in its own nature, of any superior kind to the idea the papists conceive of Christ, by the beautiful and affecting images of him which they see in their churches? Are the affections they have, if built primarily on such imaginations, any better than the affections raised in ignorant people, by the sight of those images, which oftentimes are very great; especially when these images, through the craft of the priests, are made to move, speak, weep, and the like?‡ Merely the way of persons receiving these imaginary ideas, does not alter the nature of the ideas themselves that are received: let them be received in what way they will, they are still but external ideas, or ideas of outward appearances, and so are not spiritual. Yea, if men should actually receive such external ideas by the immediate power of the most high God upon their minds, they would not be spiritual, they should be no more than a common work of the Spirit of God; as is evident in fact, in the instance of Balaam, who had impressed on his mind, by God himself, a clear and lively outward representation or idea of Jesus Christ, as *the Star rising out of Jacob*, when *he heard the words of God, and knew the knowledge of the Most High, and saw the vision of the Almighty, falling into a trance*, Numb. xxiv. 16, 17. But Balaam had no spiritual discovery of Christ; that day-star never spiritually rose in his heart, he being but a natural man.

And as these external ideas have nothing divine or

* "Conceits and whimsies abound most in men of weak reason; children, and such as are cracked in their understanding, have most of them; strength of reason banishes them, as the sun does mists and vapours. But now the more rational any gracious person is, by so much more is he fixed and settled, and satisfied in the grounds of religion: yea, there is the highest and purest reason in religion; and when this change is wrought upon men, it is carried on in a rational way, Isa. i. 18. John xix. 9." Flavel's *Preparation for Sufferings*, chap. vi.

† "If any man should see and behold Christ really, immediately, this is not the saving knowledge of him. I know the saints do know Christ as if immediately present: they are not strangers by their distance: if others have seen them more immediately, I will not dispute it. But if they have seen the Lord Jesus as immediately as if here on earth, yet Capernaum saw him so; nay some of them were disciples for a time, and followed him, John vi. And yet the Lord was hid from their eyes. Nay, all the world shall see him in his glory, which shall amaze them; and yet this is far short of having the saving knowledge of him, which the Lord doth communicate to the elect. So that though you see the Lord so really, as that you become familiar with him, yet, Luke xiii. 26. *Lord, have we not eat and drank, &c.* —and so perish." Shepard's *Parable of the Ten Virgins*, P. I. p. 197, 198.

‡ "Satan is transformed into an angel of light: and hence we have heard that some have heard voices; some have seen the very blood of Christ dropping on them, and his wounds in his side; some have seen a great light shining in the chamber; some wonderfully affected with their dreams; some in great distress have had inward witness, *Thy sins are forgiven;* and hence such liberty and joy, that they are ready to leap up and down the chamber. O adulterous generation! this is natural and usual with men, they would fain see Jesus, and have him present to give them peace; and hence papists have his images —Woe to them that have no other manifested Christ, but such an one." Shepard's *Parable of the Ten Virgins*, P. I. p. 198.

spiritual in their nature, and nothing but what natural men, without any new principles, are capable of; so there is nothing in their nature which requires that peculiar inimitable and unparalleled exercise of the glorious power of God, in order to their production, which it has been shown there is in the production of true grace. There appears to be nothing in their nature above the power of the devil. It is certainly not above the power of Satan to suggest thoughts to men; because otherwise he could not tempt them to sin. And if he can suggest any thoughts or ideas at all, doubtless imaginary ones, or ideas of things external, are not above his power;* for these are the lowest sort of ideas. These ideas may be raised only by impressions made on the body, by moving the animal spirits, and impressing the brain. Abundant experience certainly shows, that alterations in the body will excite imaginary ideas in the mind; as in a high fever, melancholy, &c. These external ideas are as much below the more intellectual exercises of the soul, as the body is a less noble part of man than the soul.

Again, there is not only nothing in the nature of these imaginations of outward appearances, from whence we can infer that they are above the power of the devil; but it is certain also that the devil can excite, and often hath excited, such ideas. They were external ideas which he excited in the dreams and visions of the false prophets of old, who were under the influence of lying spirits.† And they were *external ideas* that he often excited in the minds of the heathen priests, magicians, and sorcerers, in their visions and ecstasies; and they were *external ideas* that he excited in the mind of the man Christ Jesus, when he showed him all the kingdoms of the world, with the glory of them, when those kingdoms were not really in sight.

And if Satan, or any created being, has power to impress the mind with outward representations, then no particular sort of outward representations can be any evidence of a divine power. Is almighty power any more requisite to represent the shape of man to the imagination, than the shape of any thing else? Is there any higher kind of power necessary to form in the brain one bodily shape or colour than another? Does it need a power any more glorious to represent the form of the body of man, than the form of a chip or block; though it be of a very beautiful human body, with a sweet smile in his countenance, or arms open, or blood running from hands, feet, and side? May not that sort of power which can represent blackness or darkness to the imagination, also represent white and shining brightness? May not the power and skill which can well and exactly paint a straw, or a stick, on a piece of paper or canvass, only perhaps further improved, be sufficient to paint the body of a man, with great beauty and in royal majesty, or a magnificent city, paved with gold, full of brightness, and a glorious throne? So it is no more than the same sort of power, that is requisite to paint one as the other of these on the brain. The same sort of power that can put ink upon paper, can put on leaf-gold. So that it is evident to a demonstration, if we suppose it to be in the devil's power to make any sort of external representation at all on the fancy—and never any one questioned it who believed there was a devil, that had any agency with mankind—that a created power may extend to all kinds of external appearances and ideas in the mind.

From hence it again clearly appears, that no such things have any thing in them that is spiritual, supernatural, and divine, in the sense in which it has been proved that all truly gracious experiences have. And though external ideas, through man's make and frame, ordinarily in some degree *attend* spiritual experiences; yet these ideas are no *part* of their *spiritual* experience, any more than the motion of the blood, and beating of the pulse. And though, undoubtedly, through men's infirmity in the present state, and especially through the weak constitution of some persons, gracious affections which are very strong, do excite lively ideas in the imagination; yet it is also undoubted, that when affections are *founded on* imaginations, which is often the case, those affections are merely natural and common, because they are built on a foundation that is not spiritual; and so are entirely different from gracious affections, which, as has been proved, do evermore arise from those operations that are spiritual and divine.

These imaginations oftentimes raise the carnal affections of men to an exceeding great height:‡ and no wonder, when the subjects of them have an ignorant but undoubting persuasion, that they are divine manifestations, which the great JEHOVAH immediately makes to their souls, therein giving them testimonies, in an extraordinary manner, of his high and peculiar favour.

Again, it is evident from what has been observed and proved of the manner in which gracious operations and effects in the heart are spiritual, supernatural, and divine, that *the immediate suggesting of the words of Scripture* to the mind, has nothing in it which is spiritual.—I have had occasion to say something of this already; and what has been said may be sufficient to evince it: but if the reader bears in mind what has been said concerning the nature of spiritual influences and effects, it will be more abundantly manifest that this is no *spiritual* effect. For I suppose there is no person of common understanding, who will say, that the bringing of any words to the mind, is an effect of that nature, that it requires any new divine sense in the soul; or that the bringing of sounds or letters to the mind, is an effect of so high, holy, and excellent a nature, that it is impossible any created power should be the cause of it.

As the suggesting of scripture words to the mind, is only exciting in the mind ideas of certain sounds or letters; so it is only one way of exciting ideas in the imagination; for sounds and letters are external things, the objects of the external senses of seeing and hearing; therefore, by

* "Consider how difficult, yea and impossible, it is to determine that such a voice, vision, or revelation is of God, and that Satan cannot feign or counterfeit it; seeing he hath left no certain marks by which we may distinguish one spirit from another." Flavel's *Causes and Cures of Mental Errors*, Cause 14.

† See Deut. xiii. 1. 1 Kings xxii. 22. Isa. xxviii. 7. Ezek. xiii. 7. Zech. xiii. 4.

‡ There is a remarkable passage of Mr. John Smith, in his discourse on the shortness of a pharisaic righteousness, p. 370, 371. of his select discourses, describing that sort of religion which is built on such a foundation as I am here speaking of. I cannot forbear transcribing the whole of it. Speaking of a sort of Christians, whose life is nothing but a strong energy of fancy, he says, "Lest their religion might too grossly discover itself to be nothing else but a piece of art, there may be sometimes such extraordinary motions stirred up within them, which may prevent all their own thoughts, that they may seem to be a true operation of the divine life; when yet all this is nothing else but the energy of their own self-love, touched with some fleshly apprehensions of divine things, and excited by them. There are such things in our christian religion, when a carnal, unhallowed mind takes the chair, and gets the expounding of them, may seem very delicious to the fleshly appetites of men; some doctrines and notions of free grace and justification, the magnificent titles of sons of God and heirs of heaven, ever-flowing streams of joy and pleasure that blessed souls shall swim in to all eternity, a glorious paradise in the world to come, always springing up with well-scented and fragrant beauties, a new Jerusalem paved with gold, and bespangled with stars, comprehending in its vast circuit such numberless varieties, that a busy curiosity may spend itself about to all eternity. I doubt not but that sometimes the most fleshly and earthly men, that fly in their ambition to the pomp of this world, may be so ravished with the conceits of such things as these, that they may seem to be made partakers of the powers of the world to come. I doubt not but that they might be much exalted with them, as the souls of crazed or distracted persons seem to be sometimes, when their fancies play with those quick and nimble spirits, which a distempered frame of body, and unnatural heat in their heads, beget within them. Thus may these blazing comets rise up above the moon, and climb higher than the sun; which yet, because they have no solid consistence of their own, and are of a base and earthly alloy, will soon vanish and fall down again, being only borne up by an external force. They may seem to themselves to have attained higher than those noble Christians, that are gently moved by the natural force of true goodness: they seem to be *pleniores Deo, (i. e.* more full of God,) than those that are really informed and actuated by the divine Spirit, and do move on steadily and constantly in the way towards heaven. As the seed that was sown in stony ground, grew up and lengthened out its blade faster, than that which was sown in the good and fruitful soil. And as the motions of our sense, and fancy, and passions, while our souls are in this mortal condition, sunk down deeply into the body, are many times more vigorous, and make stronger impressions upon us, than those of the higher powers of the soul, which are more subtle, and remote from these mixt animal perceptions: that devotion which is there seated, may seem to have more energy and life in it, than that which gently, and with a more delicate kind of touch, spreads itself upon the understanding, and from thence mildly derives itself through our wills and affections. But however the former may be more boisterous for a time, yet this is of a more consistent, spermatical, and thriving nature. For that proceeding indeed from nothing but a sensual and fleshly apprehension of God and true happiness, is but of a flitting and fading nature; and as the sensible powers and faculties grow more languid, or the sun of divine light shines more brightly upon us, these earthly devotions, like our culinary fires, will abate their heat and fervour. But a true celestial warmth will never be extinguished, because it is of an immortal nature; and being once seated vitally in the souls of men, it will regulate and order all the motions of it in a due manner; as the natural heat, radicated in the hearts of living creatures, hath the dominion and economy of the whole body under it. True religion is no piece of artifice; it is no boiling up of our imaginative powers, nor the glowing heats of passion; though these are too often mistaken for it, when in our jugglings in religion we cast a mist before our own eyes; but it is a new nature, informing the souls of men; it is a God-like frame of spirit, discovering itself most of all in serene and clear minds, in deep humility, meekness, self-denial, universal love to God and all true goodness, without partiality, and without hypocrisy, whereby we are taught to know God, and knowing him, to love him, and conform ourselves as much as may be to all that perfection which shines in him"

what has been already said concerning these external ideas, it is evident they are nothing spiritual; and if at any time the Spirit of God suggests these letters or sounds to the mind, this is a *common*, and not any *special* or *gracious*, influence of that Spirit. And therefore it follows from what has been already proved, that those affections which have this effect for their foundation, are no spiritual or gracious affections.—But let it be remembered, that what I maintain is briefly this: when the immediate and extraordinary *manner of words of Scripture coming to the mind*, is that which excites the affections, and is properly the foundation of them, then these affections are not spiritual. Indeed persons may have gracious affections going with scriptures which come to their minds, and the Spirit of God may make use of those scriptures to excite them; when it is a spiritual sense or taste they have of the divine things contained in those scriptures, which excites their affections, and not the extraordinary and sudden manner of their entrance. They are affected with the instruction they receive from the words, and the view of the glorious things of God or Christ, which they contain; and not because the words came suddenly, as though God did as it were immediately speak to them. Persons oftentimes are exceedingly affected on this foundation; the words of some great promises of Scripture come suddenly to their minds, as though that moment they proceeded out of the mouth of God as spoken to them. Thus they take it as a voice from God, immediately revealing to them their happy circumstances, and promising them such and such great things: and this it is that affects and elevates them. There is no new or spiritual understanding of the divine *things contained in the Scripture*, or new spiritual sense of the glorious things taught in that part of the Bible, going before their affection, and as the foundation of it: all the new understanding they have, or think they have, as the foundation of their affection, is this, that the words *are spoken to them*, because they come so suddenly and in so extraordinary a manner. And so this affection is built wholly on the sand; because it is built on a conclusion for which they have no foundation. And if it was true that God brought the words to their minds, and they certainly knew it, even that would not be *spiritual* knowledge; it may be without any spiritual sense. Balaam might *know* that the words which God suggested to him, were indeed suggested to him by *God*, and yet have no *spiritual* knowledge. So that *affections* built on that notion, that texts of Scripture are sent immediately from God, are built on no spiritual foundation, and are vain and delusive. Persons who have their affections thus raised, if they should be asked, whether they have any new sense of the excellency of the things contained in those scriptures, would probably say, *Yes*, without hesitation: but it is true no otherwise than because they have taken up that notion, that the words are spoken immediately to them. That it is which makes them appear sweet, excellent, and wonderful. As for instance, supposing these were the words brought suddenly to their minds, *Fear not,—it is your Father's good pleasure to give you the kingdom.* Having confidently taken up a notion that the words were immediately spoken from heaven to them, as an immediate revelation, that God was their Father, and had given the kingdom to them, they are greatly affected by it, and the words seem sweet to them. Oh, say they, *what excellent things are contained in those words!* But the reason why the promise seems excellent to them, is only because they think it is made to them immediately: all the sense they have of any glory in them, is only from self-love, and from their own imagined interest in the words. They had not any sense of the holy nature of the kingdom of heaven, the spiritual glory of that God who gives it, and of his excellent grace to sinful men, in giving them this kingdom of his own good pleasure, preceding their imagined interest in these things, and their being affected by them. On the contrary, they first imagine they are interested in these things, then are highly affected with that consideration, and then can own these things to be excellent. So that the sudden and extraordinary way of the scripture's coming to their mind, is plainly the foundation of the whole; which is a clear evidence of the wretched delusion they are under.

The first comfort of many persons, and what they call their *conversion*, is after this manner: after awakening and terrors, some comfortable promise comes suddenly and wonderfully to their minds; and the manner of its coming makes them conclude it comes from God *to them*. This is the very foundation of their faith, hope, and comfort: from hence they take their first encouragement to trust in God and in Christ, because they think that God, by some scripture so brought, has now already revealed to them that he loves them, and has already promised them eternal life. But this is very absurd; for every one of common knowledge of religious principles, knows that it is God's manner to reveal his love to men, and their interest in the promises, *after* they have believed, and not *before*. They must first *believe*, before they have any *personal* and *possessive* * interest in the promises to be revealed. The Spirit of God is a Spirit of truth, and not of lies: he does not bring scriptures to men's minds in order to reveal to them that they have a personal and possessive interest in God's promises, when they have none, having not yet believed. For this would be the case, if God bringing texts of scripture to men's minds, in order to show them *that their sins were forgiven*, or that it was God's pleasure to give them the kingdom, or any thing of that nature, went *before* and was the *foundation* of their first faith. No promise of the covenant of grace belongs *possessively* to any man, until he has first believed in Christ; for it is by faith alone that we become *thus* interested in Christ, and the promises of the new covenant made in him. Therefore, whatever spirit applies the promises of that covenant to a person who has not first believed, as being *already* his, (in the sense already mentioned,) must be a lying spirit; and that faith which is first built on such an application of promises, is built upon a lie. God's manner is not to bring comfortable texts of scripture to give men *assurance* of his *peculiar* love, and that they shall be happy, before they have had a faith of *dependence*.† And if the scripture which comes to a person's mind, be not so properly a promise, as an invitation; yet if he makes the sudden or unusual manner of its coming to his mind, the ground on which he believes that he is invited, it is not true faith; because it is built on that which is not the true ground of faith. True faith is built on no precarious foundation. But a determination that the words of such a particular text were, by the immediate power of God, suggested to the mind, at such a time, as though then spoken and directed by God to him, because they came after such a manner, is wholly an uncertain and

* *Personal and possessive.*—These words are added for the sake of perspicuity; for this *must* be the author's meaning. The promises, it is plain, must needs be *ours* by grant, exhibitory gift, or overture, and in that sense we have an interest in them, *before* we believe; and this is the very foundation of our *warrant* for believing. —W.

† Mr. Stoddard in his *Guide to Christ*, p. 8. says, that "sometimes men, after they have been in trouble awhile, have some promises come to them, with a great deal of refreshing; and they hope God has accepted them:" And says, that "In this case, the minister may tell them, that God never gives a faith of assurance, before he gives a faith of dependence; for he never manifests his love, until men are in a state of favour and reconciliation, which is by faith of dependence. When men have comfortable scriptures come to them, they are apt to take them as tokens of God's love; but men must be brought into Christ, by accepting the offer of the gospel, before they are fit for such manifestations. God's method is, first to make the soul accept of the offers of grace, and then to manifest his good estate unto him." And p. 76. speaking of them "that seem to be brought to lie at God's foot, and give an account of their closing with Christ, and that God has revealed Christ to them, and drawn their hearts to him, and that they do accept of Christ," he says, "In this case, it is best to examine whether by that light that was given him, he saw Christ and salvation offered to him, or whether he saw that God loved him, or pardoned him: for the offer of grace and our acceptance goes before pardon, and therefore, much more, before the knowledge of it."

Mr. Shepard, in his *Parable of the Ten Virgins*, Part II. p. 15. says, that "Grace and the love of Christ (the fairest colours under the sun) may be pretended; but if you shall receive, under this appearance, that God witnesseth his love, first by an absolute promise, take heed there; for under this appearance you may as well bring in immediate revelations, and from thence come to forsake the Scriptures."

And in Part I. p. 86. he says, "Is Christ yours? Yes, I see it. How? By any word or promise? No: this is delusion." And p. 136. speaking of them that have no solid ground of peace, he reckons, "Those that content themselves with the revelation of the Lord's love, without the sight of any work, or not looking to it." And says presently after, "The testimony of the Spirit does not make a man more a Christian, but only evidenceth it; as it is the nature of a witness, not to make a thing to be true, but to clear and evidence it." And p. 140. speaking of them that say they have the witness of the Spirit, that makes a difference between them and hypocrites, he says, "The witness of the Spirit makes not the first difference: for first a man is a believer, and in Christ, and justified, called, and sanctified, before the Spirit does witness it; else the Spirit should witness to an untruth and lie."

precarious determination; and therefore is a false and sandy foundation for faith; and accordingly the faith which is built upon it is also false. The only certain foundation which any person has to believe that he is *invited* to partake of the blessings of the gospel, is, that the word of God declares that persons so qualified as he is, are invited, and God who declares it, is true and cannot lie. If a sinner be once convinced of the veracity of God, and that the Scriptures are his word, he will need no more to convince and satisfy him that he is invited; for the Scriptures are full of invitations to sinners, to the chief of sinners, to come and partake of the benefits of the gospel. He will not want of God any thing new; what he hath spoken already will be enough with him.

As the first comfort of many persons, and their affections at the time of their supposed conversion, are built on such grounds as these mentioned; so are their joys, hopes, and other affections afterwards. They have often particular words of scriptures, sweet declarations and promises, suggested to them, which, by reason of the manner of their coming, they think are *immediately* sent from God to them, *at that time*. This they look upon as their *warrant*, the main *ground* of appropriating them to themselves, of their comfort, and the confidence they receive from them. Thus they imagine a kind of conversation is carried on between God and them; and that God, from time to time, as it were, immediately speaks to them, and satisfies their doubts, testifies his love to them, promises them supports and supplies, and reveals to them clearly their interest in eternal blessings. And thus they are often elevated, and have a sudden and tumultuous kind of joys, mingled with strong confidence, and a high opinion of themselves; when indeed the main ground of these joys, and this confidence, is not any thing *contained in* or *taught by these* scriptures, but the *manner of their coming to them;* which is a certain evidence of their delusion. There is no *particular* promise in the word of God made to the saint, or spoken to him, otherwise than *all* the promises of the covenant of grace are his, and are spoken to him.* Some indeed of these promises may be more peculiarly adapted to his case than others; and God by his Spirit may enable him better to understand some than others, and to have a greater sense of the preciousness, glory, and suitableness of the blessings contained in them.

But here, some may be ready to say, What, is there no such thing as any *particular* spiritual application of the promises of Scripture by the Spirit of God? I answer, there is doubtless such a thing as a spiritual and saving application of the invitations and promises of Scripture to the souls of men. But it is also certain, that the nature of it is wholly misunderstood by many persons, to the great insnaring of their own souls. Hereby Satan acquires a vast advantage against them, against the interest of religion, and the church of God. The spiritual application of a scripture promise does not consist in its being immediately suggested to the thoughts by some extrinsic agent, and being borne into the mind with this strong apprehension, that it is particularly spoken and directed to them at that time. There is nothing of the hand of God evidenced in this effect, as events have proved in many notorious instances. It is a mean notion of a spiritual application of Scripture; there is nothing in the nature of it at all beyond the power of the devil; for there is nothing in the nature of the effect implying any vital communication of God. A truly spiritual application of the word of God is of a vastly higher nature; as much above the devil's power, as it is for him to apply the word of God to a dead corpse so as to raise it to life; or to a stone, to turn it into an angel. A spiritual application of the word of God consists in *applying it to the heart;* in spiritual, enlightening, sanctifying influences. A *spiritual application* of an invitation, or offer of the gospel, consists in *giving the soul a spiritual sense,* or relish, of the holy and divine blessings offered, and also the sweet and wonderful grace of the offerer, in making so gracious an overture, and of his holy excellency and faithfulness to fulfil what he offers, and his glorious sufficiency for it; so leading and drawing forth the heart to embrace the offer; and thus giving the man evidence of his title to, and *personal interest* in, the thing offered. And so a *spiritual application* of the promises of Scripture, for the comfort of the saints, consists in *enlightening their minds* to see the holy excellency and sweetness of the blessings promised, also the holy excellency of the promiser, his faithfulness and sufficiency; thus drawing forth their hearts to embrace the promiser, and thing promised; and by this means, giving the sensible actings of grace, enabling them to see their grace, and so their *possessive* title to the promise. An application not consisting in this divine sense and enlightening of the mind, but consisting only in the words being borne into the thoughts, as if immediately then spoken, so making persons believe, on no other foundation, that the promise is theirs; is a blind application, and belongs to the spirit of darkness, and not of light.

When persons have their affections raised after this manner, those affections are really not raised by the word of God; the Scripture is not the foundation of them; it is not any thing contained in those scriptures which come to their minds, that raise their affections; but truly that effect, *viz.* the *strange manner* of the word being suggested to their minds, and a proposition from thence taken up by them, which indeed is not contained in that scripture, nor in any other; as that *his* sins are forgiven him, or that it is the Father's good pleasure to give *him in particular* the kingdom, or the like. There are propositions to be found in the Bible, declaring that persons of such and such qualifications are forgiven and beloved of God: but there are none declaring that such and such *particular* persons, independent on any previous knowledge of qualifications, are forgiven and beloved of God. Therefore, when any person is comforted, and affected by any such proposition, it is by another word, a word newly coined, and not any word of God contained in the Bible.† And thus many persons are vainly affected and deluded.

Again, it plainly appears from what has been demonstrated, *that no revelation of secret facts by immediated suggestion*, is any thing spiritual and divine, in that sense wherein gracious effects and operations are so. By *secret facts,* I mean things that have been done, or are come to pass, or shall hereafter come to pass, which do not appear to the senses, nor are known by any argumentation, nor any other way, but only by immediate suggestion of ideas to the mind. Thus for instance, if it should be revealed to me, that the next year this land would be invaded by a fleet from France, or that such and such persons would then be converted, or that I myself should then be converted—not by enabling me to argue these events from any thing which now appears in providence; but—immediately suggesting, in an extraordinary manner, that these things would come to pass: or if it should be revealed to me, that this day there is a battle fought between the armies of such and such powers in Europe, or that such a prince in Europe was this day converted, or is now in a converted state, or that one of my neighbours is converted, or that I myself am converted; not by having any other evidence of these facts, but an immediate extraordinary suggestion or excitation of these ideas, and a strong impression of them upon my mind: this is a revelation of secret facts by immediate suggestion, as much as if the facts were future; for the facts being past, present, or future, alters

* Mr. Shepard, in his *Sound Believer*, p. 159. of the late impression at Boston, says, "Embrace in thy bosom, not only some few promises, but all." And then he asks the question, "When may a Christian take a promise without presumption, as spoken to him?" He answers, "The rule is very sweet, but certain; when he takes all the Scripture, and embraces it as spoken unto him, he may then take any particular promise boldly. My meaning is, when a Christian takes hold and wrestles with God for the accomplishment of all the promises of the New Testament, when he sets all the commands before him, as a compass and guide to walk after, when he applies all the threatenings to drive him nearer unto Christ the end of them. This no hypocrite can do; this the saints shall do; and by this they may know when the Lord speaks in particular unto them."

† "Some Christians have rested with a work without Christ, which is abominable: but after a man is in Christ, not to judge by the work, is first not to judge from the word. For though there is a word, which may give a man a *dependence* on Christ, without feeling any work, nay when he feels none, as absolute promises; yet no word giving *assurance*, but that which is made to some work, *He that believeth, or is poor in spirit*, &c. until that work is seen, has no assurance from that promise." Shepard's *Parable of the Ten Virgins*, Part I. p. 86.

"If God should tell a saint that he has grace, he might know it by believing the word of God: but it is not in this way that godly men do know that they have grace: it is not revealed in the word, and the Spirit of God doth not testify it to particular persons." Stoddard's *Nature of saving Conversion*, p. 84, 85.

not the case, as long as they are *secret*, hidden from my senses and reason, and not spoken of in Scripture, nor known by me any other way than by *immediate suggestion*. If I have it revealed to me, that such a revolution is come to pass this day in the Ottoman empire, it is the very same sort of revelation, as if it were revealed to me that such a revolution would come to pass there this day come twelvemonth; because, though one is present and the other future, yet both are equally *hidden* from me, any other way than by immediate revelation. When Samuel told Saul that the asses which he went to seek were found, and that his father had left caring for the asses, and sorrowed for him; this was by the same kind of revelation, as that by which he told Saul, that in the plain of Tabor there should meet him three men going up to God to Bethel, (1 Sam. x. 2, 3.) though one of these things was future, and the other was not. So when Elisha told the king of Israel the words that the king of Syria spake in his bed-chamber, it was by the same kind of revelation with that by which he foretold many things to come.

It is evident that this revelation of secret facts by immediate suggestion, has nothing of the nature of a spiritual and divine operation, in the sense fore-mentioned. There is nothing at all in the nature of the ideas themselves, excited in the mind, that is divinely excellent, above the ideas of natural men; though the *manner* of exciting the ideas be extraordinary. In those things which are spiritual, as has been shown, not only *the manner of producing the effect*, but *the effect wrought* is divine, and so vastly above all that can be in an unsanctified mind. Now simply the having an idea of facts, setting aside the manner of producing those ideas, is nothing beyond what the minds of wicked men are susceptible of, without any goodness in them; and they all either have or will have, the knowledge of the greatest and most important facts, that have been, are, or shall be.

And as to the extraordinary *manner* of producing the perception of facts, even by immediate suggestion, there is nothing in it, but what the minds of natural men are capable of; as is manifest in Balaam, and others spoken of in the Scripture. And therefore it appears that there is nothing appertaining to this immediate suggestion of secret facts that is spiritual, in the sense in which it has been proved that gracious operations are so. If there be nothing in the ideas themselves, which is holy and divine, and so nothing but what may be in a mind not sanctified, then God can put them into the mind *by immediate power*, without sanctifying it. As there is nothing in the idea of a *rainbow* of a holy and divine nature; so God, if he pleases, and when he pleases, *immediately, and in an extraordinary manner*, may excite that idea in an unsanctified mind. So also, as there is nothing in the idea or knowledge that such particular persons are forgiven and accepted of God, and entitled to heaven, but what *unsanctified* minds may have, and will have, concerning many at the day of judgment; so God can, if he pleases, extraordinarily and immediately suggest this to, and impress it upon, an unsanctified mind now. There is no principle wanting in an unsanctified mind in order to make it capable of such an impression; nor is there any thing in them necessarily to prevent such a suggestion.

And if these suggestions of secret facts be attended with *texts of Scripture*, immediately and extraordinarily brought to mind, about other facts that seem in some respects similar; that does not make the operation to be of a spiritual and divine nature. For that suggestion of words of Scripture is no more divine, than the suggestion of the facts themselves; as has been just now demonstrated; and two effects together, which are neither of them spiritual, cannot make up one complex effect spiritual.

Hence it follows, from what has been already shown, that those affections which are properly founded on such immediate suggestions of secret facts, are not gracious affections. Not but that it is possible that such suggestions may *be the occasion* or *accidental cause* of gracious affections; for so may a mistake and delusion; but it is never properly the *foundation* of gracious affections: for gracious affections, as has been shown, are all the effects of an influence and operation which is spiritual, supernatural, and divine. But there are many affections, and high affections, which have such revelations for their very foundation. They look upon these as spiritual discoveries; but they are a gross delusion; and this delusion is truly the spring whence their affections flow.

Here it may be proper to observe, from what has been said, that what many persons call the *witness of the Spirit*, that they are the children of God, has nothing in it spiritual and divine; and consequently, that the affections built upon it, are vain and delusive. That which many call the witness of the Spirit, is no other than an immediate suggestion and impression of that fact, otherwise secret, that they are made the children of God, and so that their sins are pardoned, and that God has given them a title to heaven. This kind of knowledge, *viz.* knowing that a certain person is converted, and delivered from hell, and entitled to heaven, is no divine sort of knowledge in itself. This sort of fact requires no more divine suggestion, in order to impress it on the mind, than what Balaam had impressed on his mind. It requires no higher sort of idea for a man to have the apprehension of his *own* conversion impressed upon him, than to have the apprehension of his *neighbour's* conversion, in like manner. God, if he pleased, might impress the knowledge of this fact, that he had forgiven his neighbour's sins, and given him a title to heaven, as well as any other fact, without any communication of his holiness. The excellency and importance of the fact, does not at all hinder a natural man's mind being susceptible of an immediate suggestion and impression of it. Balaam had as important facts as this immediately impressed on his mind, without any gracious influence; particularly, the coming of Christ, his setting up his glorious kingdom, the blessedness of the spiritual Israel in his peculiar favour, and their happiness living and dying. Yea, Abimelech king of the Philistines had God's special favour to Abraham revealed to him, Gen. xx. 6, 7. He revealed to Laban his special favour to Jacob, see Gen. xxxi. 24. and Psal. cv. 15. And if a truly good man should have an immediate revelation from God, in like manner, concerning his favour to his neighbour, or himself; would it be any higher kind of influence? Would it be any more than a common influence of God's Spirit, as the gift of prophecy, and all revelation by immediate suggestion is? See 1 Cor. xiii. 2. And though it be true, that a natural man cannot have an individual suggestion from the Spirit of God, that he is converted, because it is not true; yet that does not arise from the nature of the influence, as too high for him. The influence which immediately suggests this fact, when it is true, is of no different kind from that which immediately suggests other true facts: and so the kind and nature of the influence is not above what is common to natural men.

But this is a mean ignoble notion of the witness of the Spirit of God given to his dear children, to suppose that there is nothing in the *nature* of that influence, but what is common to natural men, altogether unsanctified, and the children of hell; and that therefore the gift itself has nothing of the holy nature or vital communication of that Spirit. This notion greatly debases that most exalted kind of operation which there is in the true witness of the Spirit.* That which is called *the witness of the Spirit*, Rom. viii. is elsewhere in the New Testament called *the seal of the Spirit*, 2 Cor. i. 22. Eph. i. 13. and iv. 13. alluding to the seal of princes, annexed to the instrument, by which they advanced any of their subjects to some

* The late venerable Stoddard in his younger time, falling in with the opinion of some others, received this notion of the witness of the Spirit, by way of immediate suggestion: but in the latter part of his life, when he had more thoroughly weighed things, and had more experience, he entirely rejected it; as appears by his treatise of the nature of saving conversion, p. 84. "The Spirit of God doth not testify to particular persons, that they are godly. Some think that the Spirit of God doth testify it to some; and they ground it on Rom. viii. 16. *The Spirit itself beareth witness with our spirit, that we are the children of God.* They think the Spirit reveals it by giving an inward testimony to it; and some godly men think they have had experience of it: but they may easily mistake; when the Spirit of God doth eminently stir up a spirit of faith, and sheds abroad the love of God in the heart, it is easy to mistake it for a testimony. And that is not the meaning of Paul's words. The Spirit reveals things to us, by opening our eyes to see what is revealed in the word; but the Spirit doth not reveal new truths, not revealed in the word. The Spirit discovers the grace of God in Christ, and thereby draws forth special actings of faith and love, which are evidential; but it doth not work in way of testimony. If God do but help us to receive the revelations in the word, we shall have comfort enough without new revelations."

high honour and dignity, as a token of their special favour. Which is an evidence that the influence of the Spirit of the Prince of princes, in sealing his favourites, is far from being of a common kind; and that there is no effect of God's Spirit whatsoever, which is in its nature more divine; nothing more holy, peculiar, inimitable, and distinguishing of divinity. Nothing is more royal than the royal seal; nothing more sacred to a prince, and more peculiarly denoting what belongs to him; it being the very design of it, to be the most peculiar stamp and confirmation of the royal authority. It is the great note of distinction, whereby that which proceeds from the king, or belongs to him, may be known from every thing else. And therefore undoubtedly the seal of the great King of heaven and earth enstamped on the heart, is something high and holy in its own nature, some excellent communication from the infinite fountain of divine beauty and glory; and not merely making known a secret fact by revelation or suggestion; which is a sort of influence of the Spirit of God of which the children of the devil have often been the subjects. The seal of the Spirit is an effect of the Spirit of God on the heart, of which natural men while such, can form no manner of notion. Rev. ii. 17. "To him that overcometh will I give to eat of the hidden manna, and I will give him a white stone, and in the stone a new name written, which no man knoweth, saving he that receiveth it." There is all reason to suppose that what is here spoken of, is the same evidence, or blessed token of special favour, which is elsewhere called the *seal of the Spirit*.

What has misled many in their notion of that influence of the Spirit of God of which we are speaking, is the word WITNESS, its being called *the witness* of the Spirit. Hence they have taken it to be not any work of the Spirit upon the heart, giving evidence from whence men may argue that they are the children of God, but an inward immediate suggestion, as though God inwardly spoke to the man, and told him that he was his child, by a kind of secret voice, or impression. The manner in which the word *witness*, or *testimony*, is often used in the New Testament, viz. holding forth evidence from whence a thing may be argued and proved to be true. Thus, Heb. ii. 4. God is said to *bear witness, with signs and wonders, and divers miracles, and gifts of the Holy Ghost*. Now these miracles are called God's witness, not because they are of the nature of *assertions*, but *evidences* and proofs. So Acts xiv. 3. "Long time therefore abode they speaking boldly in the Lord, which gave testimony unto the word of his grace, and granted signs and wonders to be done by their hands." And John v. 36. "But I have greater witness than that of John; for the works which the Father hath given me to finish, the same works that I do, bear witness of me, that the Father hath sent me." Again, chap. x. 25. "The works that I do in my Father's name, they bear witness of me." So the water and the blood are said to bear witness, 1 John v. 8. not that they *asserted* any thing, but they were evidences. So God's works of providence, in rain and fruitful seasons, are *witnesses* of God's being and goodness, *i. e.* they were *evidences* of these things. And when the Scripture speaks of the *seal* of the Spirit, it is an expression which properly denotes—not an immediate voice or suggestion, but—some work or effect of the Spirit left as a divine mark upon the soul, to be an evidence, by which God's children might be known. The seals of princes were their distinguishing marks; and thus the seal of God is his mark, Rev. vii. 3. "Hurt not the earth, neither the sea, nor the trees, till we have sealed the servants of our God in their foreheads;" Ezek. ix. 4. "Set a mark upon the foreheads of the men that sigh, and that cry for all the abominations that are done in the midst thereof." When God sets his seal on a man's heart by his Spirit, there is some holy stamp, some image impressed, and left upon the heart by the Spirit, as by the seal upon the wax. And this holy stamp, or impressed image, exhibiting clear evidence to the conscience, that the subject of it is the child of God, is the very thing which in Scripture is called *the seal of the Spirit*, and *the witness* or *evidence of the Spirit*. And this mark enstamped by the Spirit on God's children, is his own image. That is the evidence by which they are known to be God's children; they have the image of their Father stamped upon their hearts by the Spirit of adoption. Seals anciently had engraven on them two things, *viz.* the *image* and the *name* of the person whose seal it was. Therefore when Christ says to his spouse, Cant. viii. 6. "Set me as a seal upon thine heart, as a seal upon thine arm:" it is as much as to say, let my name and image remain impressed there. The seals of princes, moreover, were wont to bear their *image;* so that what they set their seal and royal mark upon, had their image left on it. It was their manner also to have their image engraven on their jewels and precious stones; the image of Augustus engraven on a precious stone, was used as the seal of the Roman emperors, in the times of Christ and the apostles.* The saints are the jewels of Jesus Christ, the great potentate, who possesses the empire of the universe: and these jewels have his image enstamped upon them by his royal signet, which is the Holy Spirit. And this is undoubtedly what the Scripture means by the seal of the Spirit; especially when it is fair and plain to the eye of conscience; which is what the Scripture calls *our spirit*. This is truly an effect that is *spiritual, supernatural*, and *divine*. This is in itself of a holy nature, being a communication of the divine nature and beauty. That kind of influence of the Spirit which gives and leaves this stamp upon the heart, is such as no natural man can have. If there were any such thing as a witness of the Spirit by immediate suggestion or revelation, this would be vastly more noble and excellent, and as much above it as the heaven is above the earth. This the devil cannot imitate.†

The *seal of the Spirit* is called the *earnest of the Spirit*, in the Scripture. 2 Cor. i. 22. "Who hath also sealed us, and given the earnest of the Spirit in our hearts." And Eph. i. 13, 14. "In whom, after that ye believed, ye were sealed with that holy Spirit of promise, which is the earnest of our inheritance, until the redemption of the purchased possession, unto the praise of his glory." Now the earnest is part of the money agreed for given in hand, as a token of the whole to be paid in due time; a part of the promised inheritance granted now, in token of full possession of the whole hereafter. But surely that kind of communication of the Spirit of God, which is of the nature of eternal glory, is the highest and most excellent kind of communication, It is something in its own nature spiritual, holy, and divine; and therefore high above any thing of the nature of inspiration, or revelation of hidden

* See Chambers's Dictionary, under the word ENGRAVING.

† Mr. Shepard is abundant in militating against the notion of men's knowing their good estate by an immediate witness of the Spirit, without judging by any effect or work of the Spirit wrought on the heart, as an evidence and proof that persons are the children of God. *Parab.* P. I. p. 134, 135, 137, 176, 177, 215, 216. P. II. 168, 169.

Again, in his *Sound Believer*, there is a long discourse of sanctification as the chief evidence of justification, from p. 221, for many pages following; I shall transcribe but a very small part of it. "Tell me, how you will know that you are justified. You will say, by the testimony of the Spirit. And cannot the same Spirit shine upon your graces, and witness that you are sanctified, as well? 1 John iv. 13, 24. 1 Cor. ii. 12. Can the Spirit make the one clear to you, and not the other? Oh beloved, it is a sad thing, to hear such questions, and such cold answers also, that sanctification *possibly may be* an evidence. May be! Is it not certain?"

Mr. Flavel also much opposes this notion of the witness of the Spirit by immediate revelation. *Sacramental Meditations, med.* 4. speaking of the sealing of the Spirit, he says, "In sealing the believer, he doth not make use of an audible voice, nor the ministry of angels, nor immediate and extraordinary revelations; but he makes use of his own graces, implanted in our hearts, and his own promises, written in the Scripture: and in this method, he usually brings the doubting, trembling heart of a believer to rest and comfort." Again, *ibid.* "Assurance is produced in our souls by the reflexive acts of faith: the Spirit helps us to reflect upon what hath been done by him formerly upon our hearts; *hereby we know that we know him*, 1 John ii. 3. To know that we know, is a reflex act. Now it is impossible there should be a reflex, before there hath been a direct act. No man can have the evidence of his faith, before the habit is infused, and the vital act performed. The object matter, to which the Spirit seals, is his own sanctifying operation." Afterwards, *ibid.* he says, "Immediate ways of the Spirit's sealing are ceased. No man may now expect, by any new revelation, or sign from heaven, by any voice, or extraordinary inspiration, to have his salvation sealed; but must expect that mercy in God's ordinary way and method, searching the Scriptures, examining our own hearts, and waiting on the Lord in prayer. The learned Gerson gives an instance of one that had been long upon the borders of despair, and at last sweetly assured and settled: he answered, *Non ex nova aliqua revelatione; not by any new revelation*, but by subjecting my understanding to, and comparing my heart with, the written word. And Mr. Roberts, in his treatise of *the covenants*, speaks of another, that so vehemently panted after the sealings and assurance of the love of God to his soul, that for a long time he earnestly desired some voice from heaven; and sometimes, walking in the solitary fields, earnestly desired some miraculous voice from the trees or stones there. This was denied him; but in time, a better was afforded, in a scriptural way." Again, *ibid.* "This method of sealing, is beyond all other methods in the world. For in miraculous voices and inspirations, it is impossible there may *subesse falsum, be found some cheat*, or impostures of the devil: but the Spirit's witness in the heart, suitable to the revelation in the Scripture, cannot deceive us."

facts by suggestion of the Spirit of God, which many natural men have had. What is the earnest and beginning of glory, but grace itself, especially in the more lively and clear exercises of it? It is not prophecy, nor tongues, nor knowledge, but that more excellent thing, *charity that never faileth*, which is a beginning of the light, sweetness, and blessedness of heaven, that world of love or charity. Grace is the seed of glory; the earnest of the future inheritance. What is the beginning or earnest of eternal life in the soul, but spiritual life? and what is that but grace? The inheritance that Christ has purchased for the elect, is the Spirit of God; not in any extraordinary gifts, but in his vital indwelling in the heart, exerting and communicating himself there, in his own proper, holy, or divine nature. The Father provides the Saviour, and the purchase is made of him; the Son is the purchaser and the price; and the Holy Spirit is the great blessing or inheritance purchased, as is intimated Gal. iii. 13, 14. and hence the Spirit is often spoken of as the sum of the blessings promised in the gospel.* This inheritance was the grand legacy which Christ left his disciples and church, in his last will and testament, John chap. xiv. xv. xvi. This is the sum of the blessings of eternal life, which shall be given in heaven.† It is through the vital communications and indwelling of the Spirit, that the saints have all their light, life, holiness, beauty, and joy in heaven: and it is through the vital communications and indwelling of the same Spirit, that the saints have all light, life, holiness, beauty, and comfort on earth; but only communicated in less measure. And this vital indwelling of the Spirit in the Saints, in this less measure, is *the earnest of the Spirit, the earnest of the future inheritance, and the first-fruits of the Spirit*, as the apostle calls it, Rom. viii. 22. where, by *the first-fruits of the Spirit*, the apostle undoubtedly means the same vital gracious principle, that he speaks of in all the preceding part of the chapter, which he calls Spirit, and sets in opposition to flesh or corruption. Therefore this *earnest* of the Spirit, and *first-fruits*, which has been shown to be the same with the *seal* of the Spirit, is his vital, gracious, sanctifying influence, and not any immediate suggestion or revelation of facts.‡

And indeed the apostle, when (Rom. viii. 16.) he speaks of the Spirit bearing witness with our spirit, that we are the children of God, sufficiently explains himself. "For as many as are led by the Spirit of God, they are the sons of God: for ye have not received the spirit of bondage again to fear: but ye have received the Spirit of adoption, whereby we cry, Abba, Father: the Spirit itself beareth witness with our spirits, that we are the children of God." Here, what the apostle says, if we take it together, plainly shows, that what he has respect to, when he speaks of the Spirit's giving us *witness* or *evidence* that we are God's children, is his dwelling in us, and leading us, as a spirit of adoption, or of a child, disposing us to behave towards God as to a father. And what is that, but the spirit of love? There are two kinds of spirits of which the apostle speaks, *the spirit of bondage*, that is *fear*; and *the spirit of adoption*, and that is *love*. The apostle says, we have not received the spirit of bondage, or of slaves, which is a spirit of fear; but we have received the more ingenuous, noble spirit of children, a spirit of love, which naturally disposes us to go to God, as children to a father. And this is the witness which the Spirit of God gives us that we are children. This is the plain sense of the apostle. The spirit of bondage works by fear, the slave fears the rod; but love cries, *Abba, Father*; it disposes us to go to God, and behave ourselves as children. So that the witness of the Spirit of which the apostle speaks, is far from being any whisper, or immediate suggestion; but is that gracious, holy effect of the Spirit of God in the hearts of the saints, the disposition and temper of children, appearing in sweet child-like love to God, which casts out fear. It is plain the apostle speaks of the Spirit, over and over again, as dwelling in the hearts of the saints, as a gracious principle, in opposition to the flesh or corruption; as in the words that immediately introduce this passage, ver. 13. "For if ye live after the flesh, ye shall die: but if ye through the Spirit do mortify the deeds of the flesh, ye shall live."

Indeed it is past doubt with me, that the apostle has a more special respect to the spirit of grace, or of love, or the spirit of a child, in its more lively actings; for it is *perfect love* or *strong love* only, which so witnesses or evidences that we are children, as to cast out fear, and wholly deliver from the spirit of bondage. The strong and lively exercises of evangelical, humble love to God, give clear evidence of the soul's relation to God, as his child; which very greatly and directly satisfies the soul. And though it be far from true, that the soul in this case judges only by an immediate witness, without any sign or evidence; yet the saint stands in no need of multiplied signs, or any long reasoning upon them. And though the sight of his *relative union* with God, and being in his favour, is not without a medium, *viz.* his love; yet his sight of the *union of his heart* to God is immediate. Love, the bond of union, is seen intuitively; the saint sees and feels plainly the union between his soul and God; it is so strong and lively, that he cannot doubt of it. And hence he is assured that he is a child. How can he doubt whether he stands in a child-like relation to God, when he plainly sees a child-like union between God and his soul, and hence cries, *Abba, Father*.

And whereas the apostle says, the Spirit bears witness *with our spirits*; by *our spirit* here, is meant our *conscience*, which is called the spirit of man; Prov. xx. 27. "The spirit of man is the candle of the Lord, searching all the inward parts of the belly." We elsewhere read of the witness of this spirit, or of conscience, 2 Cor. i. 12. "For our rejoicing is this, the testimony of our conscience." And 1 John iii. 19—21. "And hereby do we know that we are of the truth, and shall assure our hearts before him. For if our heart condemn us, God is greater than our heart, and knoweth all things. Beloved, if our heart condemn us not, then have we confidence towards God." When the apostle Paul speaks of the Spirit of God bearing *witness with our spirit*, he does not mean two separate, collateral, independent witnesses; but that by one, we receive the witness of the other. The Spirit of God gives the evidence, by infusing and shedding abroad the love of God, the spirit of a child, in the heart; and our spirit, or our conscience, receives and declares this evidence for our rejoicing.

Many mischiefs have arisen from that false and delusive notion of the witness of the Spirit, that it is a kind of inward voice, suggestion, or declaration from God to a man, that he is beloved, pardoned, elected, or the like, sometimes with and sometimes without a text of Scripture; for many have been the false and vain (though very high) affections that have arisen from hence. It is to be feared that multitudes of souls have been eternally undone by it; I have therefore insisted the longer on this head.—But I proceed now to a second characteristic of gracious affections.

SECT. II.

The first objective ground of gracious affections, is the transcendently excellent and amiable nature of divine things, as they are in themselves; and not any conceived relation they bear to self, or self-interest.

I say, that the supremely excellent nature of divine things is the *first*, or *primary and original*, objective foundation of the spiritual affections of true saints; for I do not suppose that all relation which divine things bear to themselves, and their own particular interest, are wholly excluded from all influence in their gracious affections. For this may have, and indeed has, a secondary and consequential influence in those affections that are truly holy and spiritual; as I shall show by and by.

* Luke xxiv. 49. Acts i. 4. and chap. ii. 38, 39. Gal. iii. 14. Eph. i. 13.

† Compare John vii. 37, 38, 39. and John iv. 14. with Rev. xxi. 6. and xxii. 1, 17.

‡ "After a man is in Christ, not to judge by the work, is not to judge by the Spirit. For the apostle makes the *earnest* of the Spirit to be the *seal*. Now, earnest is part of the money bargained for; the beginning of heaven, of the light and life of it. He that sees not that the Lord is his by that, sees no God his at all. Oh therefore, do not look for a spirit, without a word to reveal, nor a word to reveal, without seeing and feeling of some work first. I thank the Lord, I do but pity those that think otherwise. If a sheep of Christ, oh, wander not." Shepard's *Par.* P. I. p. 86.

It was before observed, that the affection of love is as it were the fountain of all affection; and particularly, that Christian love is the fountain of all gracious affections. Now the divine *excellency* of God, and of Jesus Christ, the word of God, his works, ways, &c. is the primary reason, why a true saint loves these things; and not any supposed *interest* that he has in them, or any conceived benefit that he has received or shall receive from them.

Some say that all love arises from *self-love;* and that it is impossible in the nature of things, for any man to love God, or any other being, but that love to *himself* must be the foundation of it. But I humbly suppose, it is for want of consideration they say so. They argue, that whoever loves God, and so desires his glory, or the enjoyment of him, desires these things as his own happiness; the glory of God, and the beholding and the enjoying of his perfections, are considered as things *agreeable to him,* tending to make him happy; he places his happiness in them, and desires them as objects which, if obtained, would fill him with delight and joy, and so make him happy. And so, they say, it is from self-love, or a desire of his own happiness, that he desires God should be glorified, and desires to behold and enjoy his glorious perfections. But then they ought to consider a little further, and inquire how the man came *to place his happiness* in God's being glorified, and in contemplating and enjoying God's perfections. There is no doubt, but that after God's glory, and beholding his perfections, are become *agreeable* to him, he will desire them, as he desires his own happiness. But how came these things to be so *agreeable* to him, that he esteems it his highest happiness to glorify God, &c.? is not this the fruit of love? Must not a man first *love* God, or have his heart united to him, before he will esteem God's good his own, and before he will desire the glorifying and enjoying of God, as his happiness. It is not strong arguing, because *after* a man has his heart united to God in love, and, *as a fruit of this,* he desires his glory and enjoyment as his own happiness, that therefore a desire of this happiness must needs be the *cause and foundation* of his love; unless it be strong arguing, that because a father begat a son, therefore his son certainly begat him. If *after* a man loves God, it will be a *consequence and fruit of this,* that even love to his own happiness will cause him to desire the glorifying and enjoying of God; it will not thence follow, that this very exercise of self-love went *before* his love to God, and that his love to God was a *consequence and fruit of that.* Something else, entirely distinct from self-love, might be the cause of this, *viz.* a change made in the views of his mind, and relish of his heart; whereby he apprehends a beauty, glory, and supreme good, in God's nature, as it is in itself. This may be the thing that first draws his heart to him, and causes his heart to be united to him, prior to all considerations of his own interest or happiness, although after this, and as a fruit of it, he necessarily seeks his interest and happiness in God.

There is a kind of love or affection towards persons or things, which *does properly arise* from self-love. A preconceived relation to himself, or some respect already manifested by another to him, or some benefit already received or depended on, *is truly the first foundation* of his love; what precedes any relish of, or delight in, the nature and qualities inherent in the being beloved, as beautiful and amiable. When the first thing that draws a man's benevolence to another, is the beholding of those qualifications and properties in him, which appear to him lovely in themselves, love arises in a very different manner, than when it first arises from some *gift* bestowed by another, as a judge loves and favours a man that has bribed him; or from the *relation* he supposes another has to him, as a man who loves his child. When love to another arises thus, it arises truly and properly from self-love.

That kind of affection to God or Jesus Christ, which thus properly arises from self-love, cannot be a truly gracious and spiritual love; as appears from what has been said already. For self-love is a principle entirely natural, and as much in the hearts of devils as angels; and therefore surely nothing that is the mere result of it, can be supernatural and divine, in the manner before described.* Christ plainly speaks of this kind of love, as what is nothing beyond the love of wicked men, Luke vi. 32. "If ye love them that love you, what thank have ye? for sinners also love those that love them." And the devil himself knew that a mercenary respect to God, only for benefits received or depended on, (which is all one,) is worthless in the sight of God; Job i. 9, 10. "Doth Job serve God for nought? hast not thou made an hedge about him, and about his house," &c. God would never have implicitly allowed the objection to have been good, in case the accusation had been true, by allowing that matter to be tried, and Job to be so dealt with, that it might appear in the event, whether Job's respect to God was thus mercenary or no. Whereas the proof of the goodness of his respect was put upon that issue.

It is unreasonable to think otherwise, than that the first foundation of a true love to God, is that whereby he is in himself lovely, or worthy to be loved, or the supreme loveliness of his nature. This is certainly what makes him chiefly amiable. What chiefly makes a man or any creature lovely, is his excellency; and so what chiefly renders God lovely, and must undoubtedly be the chief ground of true love, is his excellency. God's nature, or the divinity, is infinitely excellent; yea it is infinite beauty, brightness, and glory itself. But how can that be *true love* of this excellent and lovely nature, which is not built on the foundation of *its true loveliness?* how can that be true love of beauty and brightness, which is not for beauty and brightness' sake? how can that be a true prizing of that which is in itself infinitely worthy and precious, which is not for the sake of its worthiness and preciousness? This infinite excellency of the divine nature, as it is in itself, is the true ground of all that is good in God in any respect; but how can a man truly love God, without loving him for that excellency, which is the foundation of all that is good or desirable in him? They whose affection to God is founded first on his *profitableness* to them, begin at the wrong end; they regard God only for the utmost limit of the stream of divine good, where it touches them, and reaches their interest. They have no respect to that infinite glory of God's nature, which is the original good, and the true fountain of all good, and of loveliness of every kind.

A natural principle of self-love may be the foundation of great affections towards God and Christ, without seeing any thing of the beauty and glory of the divine nature. There is a certain gratitude that is a mere natural thing. Gratitude is one of the natural affections, as well as anger; and there is a gratitude that arises from self-love, very much in the same manner that anger does. Anger in men is an affection excited *against,* or in opposition to, another, for something in him that crosses self-love: gratitude is an affection one has *towards* another, for loving or gratifying him, or for something in him that suits self-love. And there may be a kind of gratitude, without any true or proper love; as there may be anger without hatred; as in parents towards their children, with whom they may be angry, and yet at the same time have a strong habitual love to them. Of this gratitude Christ declares, (Luke vi.) *Sinners love those that love them;* even the publicans, who were some of the most carnal and profligate sort of men, (Matt. v. 46.) This is the principle wrought upon by bribery, in unjust judges; and which even the brute beasts exercise; a dog will love his master that is kind to him. And we see in innumerable instances, that mere nature is sufficient to excite gratitude in men, or to affect their hearts with thankfulness to others for kindnesses received; and sometimes towards them against whom at the same time they have an habitual enmity. Thus Saul was once and again greatly affected, and even dissolved with gratitude towards David, for sparing his life; and yet remained an habitual enemy to him. And as men, from mere nature, may be thus affected towards men; so they may towards God. Nothing hinders, but that the same self-love may work after the same manner towards God, as towards men. And we have manifest instances of it in Scripture; as indeed the children of Israel, *who sang*

* "There is a natural love to Christ, as to one that doth thee good, and for thine own ends; and spiritual, for himself, whereby the Lord only is exalted." Shepard's *Par. of the Ten Virgins,* P. I. p. 25

God's praises at the Red sea, ***but soon forgat his works.*** Naaman the Syrian was greatly affected with the miraculous cure of his leprosy. His heart was engaged thenceforward to worship the God who had healed him, excepting when it would expose him to be ruined in his temporal interest. So was Nebuchadnezzar greatly affected with God's goodness to him, in restoring him to his reason and kingdom, after his dwelling with the beasts.

Gratitude being thus a natural principle, ingratitude is so much the more vile and heinous; because it shows a dreadful prevalence of wickedness, when it even overbears and suppresses the better principles of human nature. It is mentioned as an evidence of the high degree of wickedness in many of the heathen, that they were *without natural affection*, Rom. ii. 31. But that the want of gratitude, or natural affection, are evidences of a high degree of *vice*, is no argument that all gratitude and natural affection has the nature of *virtue*, or *saving grace*.

Self-love, through the exercise of a mere natural gratitude, may be the foundation of a sort of love to God many ways. A kind of love may arise from a false notion of God, that men have some way imbibed; as though he were *only* goodness and mercy, and no revenging justice; or as though the exercises of his goodness were *necessary*, and not free and sovereign; or as though his goodness were *dependent* on what is in them, and as it were constrained by them. Men on such grounds as these, may love a God of their own forming in their imaginations, when they are far from loving such a God as reigns in heaven.

Again, self-love may be the foundation of an affection in men towards God, through a great *insensibility* of their state with regard to God, and for want of conviction of conscience to make them sensible how dreadfully they have provoked him to anger. They have no sense of the heinousness of sin, as against God, and of the infinite and terrible opposition of the holy nature of God against it. Having formed in their minds such a God as suits them, and thinking him to be such an one as themselves, who favours and agrees with them, they may like him very well, and feel a sort of love to him, when they are far from loving the true God. And men's affections may be much moved towards God from self-love, by some remarkable outward benefits received from him; as it was with Naaman, Nebuchadnezzar, and the children of Israel at the Red sea.

Again, a very high affection towards God may, and often does, arise in men, from an opinion of the favour and love of God *to them*, as the first foundation of their love to him. After awakenings and distress, through fears of hell, they may suddenly get a notion, through some impression on their imagination, or immediate suggestion with or without texts of Scripture, or by some other means that God loves *them*, has forgiven their sins, and made them his children; and this is the first thing that causes their affections to flow towards God and Jesus Christ: and then, upon this foundation, many things in God may appear lovely to them, and Christ may seem excellent. And if such persons are asked, whether God appears lovely and amiable in himself? they would perhaps readily answer, Yes; when indeed, if the matter be strictly examined, this good opinion of God was purchased, and paid for, in the distinguishing and infinite benefits they imagined they received from God. They allow God to be lovely in himself no otherwise, than that he has forgiven and accepted them, loves them above most in the world, and has engaged to improve all his infinite power and wisdom in preferring, dignifying, and exalting them, and will do for them just as they would have him. When once they are firm in this apprehension, it is easy to own God and Christ to be lovely and glorious, and to admire and extol them. It is easy for them to own Christ to be a lovely person, and the best in the world, when they are first firm in the notion, that he, though Lord of the universe, is captivated with love to them, has his heart swallowed up in them, prizes them far beyond most of their neighbours, has loved them from eternity, and died for them, and will make them reign in eternal glory with him in heaven. When this is the case with carnal men, their very lusts will make him seem lovely; pride itself will prejudice them in favour of that which they call Christ. Selfish, proud man naturally calls that lovely which greatly contributes to his interest, and gratifies his ambition.

And as this sort of persons begin, so they go on. Their affections are raised, from time to time, primarily on this foundation of self-love, and a conceit of God's love to them. Many have a false notion of communion with God, as though it were carried on by impulses, and whispers, and external representations, immediately made to their imagination. These things they take to be manifestations of God's great love to them, and evidences of their high exaltation above others; and so their affections are often renewedly set a-going.

Whereas the exercises of true and holy love in the saints arise in another way. They do not first see that God loves *them*, and then see that he is lovely; but they first see that God is lovely, and that Christ is excellent and glorious; their hearts are first captivated with this view, and the exercises of their love are wont, from time to time, to begin here, and to arise primarily from these views; and then, consequentially, they see God's love, and great favour to them.* The saints' affections begin with *God;* and self-love has a hand in these affections consequentially and secondarily only. On the contrary, false affections begin with *self*, and an acknowledgment of an excellency in God, and an affectedness with it, is only consequential and dependent. In the love of the true saint, God is the lowest foundation; the love of the excellency of his nature is the foundation of all the affections which come afterwards, wherein self-love is concerned as an handmaid. On the contrary, the hypocrite lays *himself* at the bottom of all, as the first foundation, and lays on God as the superstructure; and even his acknowledgment of God's glory itself, depends on his regard to his private interest.

Self-love may not only influence men, so as to cause them to be affected with God's kindness to them separately; but also with God's kindness to them, as parts of a community. A natural principle of self-love, without any other, may be sufficient to make a man concerned for the interest of the *nation* to which he belongs: as for instance, in the present *war*, self-love may make natural men rejoice at the successes of our nation, and sorry for their disadvantages, they being concerned as members of the body. The same natural principles may extend even to the world of mankind, and might be affected with the benefits the inhabitants of the earth have, beyond those of the inhabitants of other planets; if we knew that such there were, and knew how it was with them. So this principle may cause men to be affected with the benefits mankind have received beyond the fallen angels; with the wonderful goodness of God in giving his Son to die for fallen man, with the marvellous love of Christ in suffering such great things for us, and with the great glory they hear God has provided in heaven for us. Looking on themselves as persons concerned, interested, and so highly favoured; the same principle of natural gratitude may influence men here, as in the case of personal benefits.

But these things by no means imply, that all gratitude to God is a mere natural thing, and that there is no such thing as a spiritual gratitude, which is a holy and divine affection. They imply no more, than that there is a gratitude which is *merely natural*, and that when persons have affections towards God only, or primarily, for *benefits* received, their affection is only the exercise of natural gratitude. There is doubtless such a thing as a gracious gratitude, which greatly differs from all that gratitude which natural men experience. It differs in the following respects.

1. True gratitude, or thankfulness to God for his kindness to us, arises from a foundation, laid before, of love to God for what he is in *himself;* whereas a natural gratitude has no such antecedent foundation. The gracious stirrings of grateful affection to God, for kindness received, always are from a stock of love already in the heart, established in the first place on other grounds, *viz.* God's own excellency; and hence the affections are disposed to flow out, on oc-

* "There is a seeing of Christ after a man believes, which is Christ in his love, &c. But I speak of that first sight of him that precedes the second act of faith: and it is an intuitive, or real sight of him, as he is in his glory." Shepard's *Par. of the Ten Virgins*, Part I. p. 74.

casions of God's kindness. The saint having seen the glory of God, and his heart overcome by it, and captivated into a supreme love to him on that account, his heart hereby becomes tender, and easily affected with kindness received. If a man has no love to another, yet gratitude may be moved by some extraordinary kindness; as in Saul towards David: but this is not the same in kind, as a man's gratitude to a dear friend, for whom his heart had before a high esteem and love. Self-love is not excluded from a gracious gratitude; the saints love God *for his kindness to them,* Psal. cxvi. 1. "I love the Lord, because he hath heard the voice of my supplication." But something else is *included;* another love prepares the way, and lays the foundation for these grateful affections.

2. In a gracious gratitude, men are affected with the attribute of God's goodness and free grace, not only as they are concerned in it, or as it affects their interest, but as a part of the glory and beauty of God's nature. That wonderful and unparalleled grace of God which is manifested in the work of redemption, and shines forth in the face of Jesus Christ, is infinitely glorious in itself, and appears so to the angels; it is a great part of the moral perfection and beauty of God's nature. This would be glorious, whether it were exercised towards us or no; and the saint who exercises a gracious thankfulness for it, sees it to be so, and delights in it as such. Yea, his concern in it serves the more to engage his mind, and raise his attention and affection. Self-love here assists as an handmaid, being subservient to higher principles, to lead forth the mind to contemplation, and to heighten joy and love. God's kindness to them is a glass set before them, wherein to behold the beautiful attribute of God's goodness: the exercises and displays of this attribute, by this means, are brought near to them, and set right before them. So that in a holy thankfulness to God, the concern our interest has in God's goodness, is not the first foundation of our being affected with it; that was laid in the heart before, in love to God for his excellency in himself; that makes the heart tender, and suceptive of such impressions from his goodness to us. Nor is our own interest, or the benefits we have received, the only, or the chief objective ground of the present exercises of the affection, but rather God's goodness, as part of the beauty of his nature. The *manifestations* of that lovely attribute, however, set immediately before our eyes, in the exercise of it for us, are a special *occasion* of the mind's attention to that beauty, at that time; and this may serve to heighten the affection.

Some may perhaps be ready to object, against the whole that has been said, that text, (1 John iv. 19.) "We love him, because he first loved us;" as though this implied that God's love to the true saints were the *first foundation* of their love to him. In answer to this I would observe, that the apostle's drift in these words, is to magnify the love of God to us from hence, that he loved us, while we had no love to him; as will be manifest to any one who compares this verse and the two following, with the 9th, 10th, and 11th verses. And that God loved us, when we had no love to him, the apostle proves by this argument, that God's love to the elect, is the ground of their love to him. And it is so three ways: 1. The saints' love to God is the *fruit* of God's love to them, as it is the *gift* of that love. God gave them a spirit of love to him, because he loved them from eternity; his love to his elect is the foundation of their regeneration, and the whole of their redemption. 2. The exercises and discoveries God has made of his wonderful love to sinful men by Jesus Christ, in the work of redemption, are among the chief *manifestations* of his glorious moral perfections to both angels and men; and so is one main objective ground of the love of both to God, in a good consistence with what was said before. 3. God's love to a particular elect person, discovered by his conversion, is a great manifestation of God's moral perfection and glory to him; and thus is a proper *occasion* of exciting holy gratitude, agreeable to what was before said. And that the saints, in these respects, love God, because he first loved them, fully answers the design of the apostle's argument in that place. So that no good argument can be drawn from hence, against a spiritual and gracious love in the saints, arising *primarily* from the excellency of divine things as they are in themselves, and not from any conceived relation they bear to their interest.

And as it is with the *love* of the saints, so it is with their *joy,* and spiritual *delight:* the first foundation of it is not any consideration of their interest in divine things; but it primarily consists in the sweet entertainment their minds have in the contemplation of the divine and holy beauty of these things, as they are in themselves. And this is indeed the very main difference between the joy of the hypocrite, and the joy of the true saint. The former rejoices in *himself;* self is the first foundation of his joy: the latter rejoices in *God.* The hypocrite has his mind pleased and delighted, in the first place, with his own privilege, and happiness to which he supposes he has attained, or shall attain. True saints have their minds, in the first place, inexpressibly pleased and delighted with the sweet ideas of the glorious and amiable *nature* of the things of God. This is the spring of all their delights, and the cream of all their pleasures; it is the joy of their joy. This sweet and ravishing entertainment they have in viewing the beautiful and delightful *nature* of divine things, is the *foundation* of the joy they have afterward in the consideration of their being *theirs.* But the dependence of the affections of hypocrites is in a *contrary order:* they first rejoice and are elevated, that they are the favourites of God; and then, *on that ground,* he seems in a sort lovely to them.

The first foundation of the delight a true saint has in God, is his own perfection; and the first foundation of the delight he has in Christ, in his own beauty; he appears in himself the chief among ten thousand, and altogether lovely. The way of salvation by Christ is a delightful way to him, for the sweet and admirable manifestations of the divine perfections in it. The holy doctrines of the gospel, by which God is exalted and man abased, holiness honoured and promoted, sin greatly disgraced and discouraged, and free, sovereign love manifested, are *glorious* doctrines in his eyes, and sweet to his taste, *prior* to any conception of his *interest* in these things. Indeed the saints rejoice in their interest in God, and that Christ is theirs; and so they have great reason: but this is not the first spring of their joy. They first rejoice in God as glorious and excellent in himself, and then secondarily rejoice in it, that so glorious a God is theirs. They *first* have their hearts filled with sweetness, from the view of Christ's excellency, the excellency of his grace, and the beauty of salvation by him; and then, they have a *secondary* joy, in that so excellent a Saviour and such excellent grace, is *theirs.** But that which is the true *saint's superstructure* is the *hypocrite's foundation.* When they hear of the wonderful things of the gospel, of God's great love in sending his Son, of Christ's dying love to sinners, the great things Christ has purchased and promised to the saints, and hear these things eloquently set forth; they may hear with a great deal of pleasure, and be lifted up with what they hear. But if their joy be examined, it will be found to have no other foundation than this, that they look upon these things as *theirs,* all this exalts *them,* they love to hear of the great love of Christ vastly distinguishing some from others; for self-love makes them affect great distinction from others. No wonder, in this confident opinion of their own good estate, that they feel well under such doctrine, and are pleased in the highest degree, in hearing how much God and Christ makes of them. So that their joy is really a joy *in themselves,* and not *in God.*

And hence it comes to pass, that in their rejoicings and

* Dr. Owen *on the Spirit,* p. 199, speaking of a common work of the Spirit, says, "The effects of this work on the mind, which is the first subject affected with it, proceeds not so far as to give it delight, complacency, and satisfaction, in the lovely spiritual nature and excellencies of the things revealed unto it. The true nature of saving illumination consists in this, that it gives the mind such a direct intuitive insight and prospect into spiritual things, as that in their own spiritual nature they suit, please, and satisfy it; so that it is transformed into them, cast into the mould of them, and rests in them; Rom. vi. 17. chap. xii. 2. 1 Cor. ii. 13, 14. 2 Cor. iii. 18. chap. iv. 6. This the work we have insisted on, reacheth not unto. For notwithstanding any discovery that is made therein of spiritual things unto the mind, it finds not an immediate, direct, spiritual excellency in them; but only with respect unto some benefit or advantage, which is to be attained by means thereof. It will not give such a spiritual insight into the mystery of God's grace by Jesus Christ, called his glory shining in the face of Christ, 2 Cor. iv. 6. as that the soul, in its first direct view of it, should, for what it is in itself, admire it, delight in it, approve it, and find spiritual solace, with refreshment, in it. But such a light, such a knowledge, it communicates, as that a man may like it well in its *effects,* as a way of mercy and salvation."

elevations, hypocrites are wont to keep their eye upon themselves; having received what they call spiritual discoveries, their minds are taken up about their own experiences; and not the glory of God, or the beauty of Christ. They keep thinking with themselves, what a good experience is this! what a great discovery is this! what wonderful things have I met with! and so they put their experiences in the place of Christ, his beauty and fulness. Instead of rejoicing in Christ Jesus, they rejoice in their admirable experiences. Instead of feeding and feasting their souls in viewing the innate, sweet, refreshing amiableness of the things exhibited in the gospel, they view them only as it were side-ways. The object that fixes their contemplation, is their experience; and they are ever feeding their souls, and feasting a selfish principle, with a view of their discoveries. They take more comfort in their *discoveries* than in *Christ* discovered. This is the true notion of *living upon experiences and frames;* and not our using them as an *evidence* of our good estate. It is very observable, that some who reject *evidences* are most notorious for living upon *experience*, according to the true notion of it.

The affections of hypocrites are very often after this manner; they are first much affected with some impression on their imagination, or some impulse, which they take to be an immediate suggestion, or testimony from God, of his love and their happiness. They fancy a high privilege in some respect, either with or without a text of Scripture; they are mightily taken with this, as a great discovery; and hence arise high affections. When their affections are raised, they view those high affections, and call them great and wonderful experiences; and they have a notion that God is greatly pleased with those affections. This affects them still more; and so they are affected with their affections. Thus their affections rise higher and higher, until they sometimes are perfectly swallowed up; also self-conceit, and a fierce zeal rises; and all is built, like a castle in the air, on nothing but imagination, self-love, and pride.

And as are the thoughts of such persons, so is their talk; for out of the abundance of their heart their mouth speaketh. As in their high affections they keep their eye upon the beauty of their experiences, and greatness of their attainments; so they are great talkers about themselves. The true saint, when under great spiritual affections, from the fulness of his heart is ready to speak much of God, his glorious perfections and works, the beauty and amiableness of Christ, and the glorious things of the gospel; but hypocrites, in their high affections, talk more of the *discovery*, than of the thing discovered. They are full of talk about the wonderful discoveries they have had, how sure they are of the love of God to them, how safe their condition is, how they know they shall go to heaven, &c.

A true saint, when in the enjoyment of true discoveries of the sweet glory of God and Christ, has his mind too much captivated and engaged by what he views without himself, to stand at that time to view himself, and his own attainments. It would be a loss which he could not bear, to have his eye taken off from the ravishing object of his contemplation, in order to survey his own experience, and to spend time in thinking with himself, What a high attainment this is, and what a good story I now have to tell others! Nor does the pleasure and sweetness of his mind at that time, chiefly arise from the consideration of the safety of his state, or any thing he has in view of his own qualifications, experiences, or circumstances; but from the divine and supreme beauty of what is the object of his direct view, without himself; which sweetly entertains, and strongly holds his mind.

As the love and joy of hypocrites are all from the source of self-love, so it is with their other affections, their sorrow for sin, their humiliation and submission, their religious desires and zeal. Every thing is as it were paid for beforehand, in God's highly gratifying their self-love, by making so much of them, and exalting them so highly, as things are in their imagination. It is easy for nature, corrupt as it is, under a notion of being already some of the highest favourites of heaven, and having a God who so protects and favours them in their sins, to love this imaginary God that suits them so well; and equally easy to extol him, submit to him, and to be fierce and zealous for him. The high affections of many are all built on the supposition of their being eminent saints. If that opinion which they have of themselves were taken away, if they thought they were some of the lower form of saints, (though they should yet suppose themselves to be real saints,) their high affections would fall to the ground. If they only saw a little of the sinfulness and vileness of their own hearts, and their deformity in the midst of their best duties and their best affections, it would destroy their affections; because they are built upon *self*, self-knowledge would destroy them. But as to truly gracious affections, they have their foundation in God and Jesus Christ; and therefore a discovery of themselves, of their own deformity, and the meanness of their experiences, though it will purify their affections, yet it will not destroy them, but in some respects sweeten and heighten them.

SECT. III.

Those affections that are truly holy, are primarily founded on the moral excellency of divine things. Or, a love to divine things for the beauty and sweetness of their moral excellency, is the spring of all holy affections.

HERE, for the sake of the more illiterate reader, I will explain what I mean by the moral excellency of divine things.—The word *moral* is not to be understood here, according to the common acceptation, when men speak of *morality*, and a *moral* behaviour; meaning an outward conformity to the duties of the moral law, and especially the duties of the second table. Nor is it taken for mere seeming virtues, proceeding from natural principles, in opposition to those that are more inward, spiritual, and divine. The honesty, justice, generosity, good-nature, and public spirit of many of the heathen, are called *moral* virtues, in distinction from the holy faith, love, humility, and heavenly-mindedness of true Christians; but the word *moral* is not to be understood so in this place.

In order to a right understanding of what is meant, it must be observed, that divines commonly make a distinction between *moral* good and evil, and *natural* good and evil. By *moral* evil, they mean the evil of sin, or that evil which is against *duty*, and contrary to what is right and *ought* to be. By *natural* evil, they do not mean that evil which is properly opposed to duty; but that which is contrary to mere nature, without any respect to a rule of duty. So the evil of *suffering* is called *natural* evil, such as pain and torment, disgrace, and the like: these things are contrary to mere nature, hateful to wicked men and devils, as well as good men and angels. If a child be monstrous, or a natural fool, these are *natural*, but not *moral* evils, because they have not properly the nature of the evil of *sin*. On the other hand, as by *moral evil* divines mean sin, or that which is contrary to what is right; so by *moral good*, they mean that which is contrary to sin: or, in other words, that good in beings who have will and choice, whereby, as voluntary agents, they are, and act, as it *becomes* them to be and to act. And, it is obvious, that is *becoming*, which is most *fit*, *suitable*, and *lovely*. By *natural* good, they mean that good which is entirely of a different kind from holiness or virtue, *viz.* that which perfects or suits nature, considering nature abstractly from any holy or unholy qualifications, and without any relation to any rule or measure of right and wrong.

Thus *pleasure* is a natural good; so is *honour;* so is strength; and so is speculative knowledge, human learning, and policy. Thus there is a distinction to be made between men's natural and their moral good; and also between the natural and moral good of the angels in heaven. The great capacity of angelic understandings, their great strength, and the honourable circumstances they are in as the great ministers of God's kingdom, whence they are called thrones, dominions, principalities, and powers, is their *natural* good. But their perfect holiness and glorious goodness, their pure and flaming love to God, to the saints and one another, is their *moral* good. So divines make a distinction between the natural and moral perfections of God: by the *moral* perfections of God, they mean those attributes which God exercises as a moral agent, or whereby the heart and will of God, are good, right, infinitely becoming, and lovely; such as his righteousness, truth, faithfulness, and goodness; or, in one word, his holiness. By God's *natural* perfections, they mean those attributes wherein his *greatness* consists; such as his power, his knowledge, his being from everlasting to everlasting, his omnipresence, his awful and terrible majesty.

The moral excellency of an intelligent voluntary being, is more immediately seated in the *heart* or *will*. That intelligent being whose will is truly right and lovely, he is morally good or excellent.—This moral excellency, when it is true and real, is *holiness*. Therefore *holiness* comprehends all the true moral excellency of intelligent beings: there is no other *true virtue*, but *real holiness*. Holiness comprehends all the true virtue of a good man; his love to God, his gracious love to men, his justice, his charity, his bowels of mercies, his gracious meekness and gentleness, and all other christian virtues, belong to his holiness. So the holiness of God, in the more extensive sense of the word—the sense in which the word is commonly, if not universally, used concerning God in Scripture—is the same with the moral excellency of the divine nature; comprehending all his moral perfections, his righteousness, faithfulness, and goodness. As in holy men, their christian kindness and mercy belong to their holiness; so the kindness and mercy of God belong to his holiness. Holiness in man, is but the *image* of God's holiness; and surely there are not more virtues belonging to the image, than are in the original. Has derived holiness more in it, than is in that underived holiness, which is its fountain?

As there are two kinds of attributes in God, according to our way of conceiving of him, his moral attributes, which are summed up in his *holiness*, and his natural attributes—strength, knowledge, &c.—that constitute his *greatness;* so there is a twofold image of God in man, his *moral* or *spiritual* image, which is his holiness, that is the image of God's moral excellency; (which image was lost by the fall;) and God's *natural* image, consisting in man's reason and understanding, his natural ability, and dominion over the creatures, which is the image of God's natural attributes. From what has been said, it may easily be understood what I intend, when I say that love to divine things for the beauty of their *moral excellency*, is the spring of all holy affections.

It has been already shown, under the former head, that the first objective ground of all holy affections is the supreme excellency of divine things as they are in their own nature. I now proceed further, and say more particularly, that the *kind* of excellency which is the first objective ground of all holy affections, is their *holiness*. *Holy persons*, in the exercise of *holy affections*, love divine things primarily for their *holiness;* they love God, in the first place, for the beauty of his *holiness*, or *moral* perfection, as being supremely amiable *in itself*. Not that the saints, in the exercise of gracious affections, love God *only* for his holiness; all his attributes are amiable and glorious in their eyes; they delight in every divine perfection; the contemplation of the infinite greatness, power, knowledge, and terrible majesty of God, is pleasant to them. But their love to God for his holiness is what is most *fundamental* and *essential* in their love. Here it is that true love to God *begins;* all other holy love to divine things flows from hence. Love to God for the beauty of his *moral* attributes, necessarily causes a delight in God for *all* his attributes; for his moral attributes cannot be without his natural attributes. Infinite holiness supposes infinite wisdom, and infinite greatness; and all the attributes of God as it were imply one another.

The true beauty and loveliness of all intelligent beings primarily and most essentially consist in their moral excellency or holiness. Herein consists the loveliness of angels, without which, notwithstanding all their natural perfections, they would have no more loveliness than devils. It is moral excellency alone, that is in itself, and on its own account, the excellency of intelligent beings: it is this that gives beauty to, or rather is the beauty of, their natural perfections and qualifications. Moral excellency, if I may so speak, is the excellency of natural excellencies. Natural qualifications are either excellent or otherwise, according as they are joined with moral excellency or not. Strength and knowledge do not render any being lovely without holiness, but more hateful; though they render them more lovely when joined with holiness. Thus the elect angels are the more glorious for their strength and knowledge, because these natural perfections of theirs are sanctified by their moral perfection. But though the devils are very strong, and of great natural understanding, yet they are not the more lovely. They are more *terrible*, indeed, not more *amiable;* but on the contrary, the more hateful. The holiness of an intelligent creature, is the *beauty* of all his natural perfections. And so it is in God, according to our way of conceiving of the Divine Being: holiness is in a peculiar manner the beauty of the divine nature. Hence we often read of the *beauty of holiness*, (Psal. xxix. 2. Psal. xcvi. 9. and cx. 3.) This renders all his other attributes glorious and lovely. It is the glory of God's wisdom, that it is a *holy* wisdom, and not a wicked subtlety. This makes his majesty lovely, and not merely dreadful and horrible, that it is a *holy* majesty. It is the glory of God's immutability, that it is a *holy* immutability, and not an inflexible obstinacy in wickedness.

And therefore it must needs be, that a sight of God's loveliness must begin here. A true love to God must begin with a delight in his holiness, and not with a delight in any other attribute; for no other attribute is truly lovely without this, and no otherwise than as (according to our way of conceiving God) it derives its loveliness from this. Therefore, it is impossible that other attributes should appear lovely, in their true loveliness, until this is seen: and it is impossible that any perfection of the divine nature should be loved with true love until this is loved. If the true *loveliness* of all God's perfections, arises from the loveliness of his holiness; then the true love of all his perfections, arises from the love of his holiness. They that do not see the glory of God's holiness, cannot see any thing of the true glory of his mercy and grace. They see nothing of the glory of those attributes, as any excellency of God's nature, as it is in itself; though they may be affected with them, and love them, as they concern their interest. For these attributes are no part of the excellency of God's nature, as that is excellent in itself, any otherwise than as they are included in his holiness, more largely taken; or as they are a part of his moral perfection.

As the beauty of the divine nature primarily consists in God's holiness, so does the beauty of all divine things. Herein consists the beauty of the saints, that they are *saints*, or holy ones: it is the moral image of God in them, which is their beauty; and that is their holiness. Herein consists the beauty and brightness of the angels of heaven, that they are *holy* angels, and so not devils; (Dan. iv. 13, 17, 23. Matt. xxv. 31. Mark viii. 38. Acts x. 22. Rev. xiv. 10.) Herein consists the beauty of the christian religion, above all other religions, that it is so *holy* a religion. Herein consists the excellency of the word of God, that it is so *holy;* Psal. cxix. 140. "Thy word is very pure, therefore thy servant loveth it. Ver. 128. I esteem all thy precepts concerning all things to be right; and I hate every false way. Ver. 138. Thy testimonies that thou hast commanded, are righteous, and very faithful. And 172. My tongue shall speak of thy word; for all thy commandments are righteousness." And Psal. xix. 7—10. "The law of the Lord is perfect, converting the soul: the testimony of the Lord is sure, making wise the simple. The statutes of the Lord are right, rejoicing the heart: the commandment of the Lord is pure, enlightening the eyes. The fear of the Lord is clean, enduring for ever: the judgments of the Lord are true, and righteous altogether: more to be desired are they than gold, yea, than much fine gold; sweeter also than honey, and the honey-comb." Herein primarily consists the amiableness and beauty of the Lord Jesus, whereby he is the chief among ten thousands, and altogether lovely; even in that he is *the holy One of God*, Acts iii. 14. and *God's holy Child*, Acts iv. 27. and *he that is holy, he that is true*, Rev. iii. 7. All the spiritual beauty of his human nature, his meekness, lowliness, patience, heavenliness, love to God, love to men, condescension to the mean and vile, compassion to the miserable, &c. all is summed up in his *holiness*. And the beauty of his divine nature, of which the beauty of his human nature is the image and reflection, also primarily consists in his holiness.

Herein primarily consists the glory of the gospel, that it is a *holy* gospel, and so bright an emanation of the holy beauty of God and Jesus Christ. Herein consists the spiritual beauty of its doctrines, that they are *holy* doctrines, or doctrines *according to godliness.* Herein consists the spiritual beauty of the way of salvation by Jesus Christ, that it is so *holy* a way. And herein chiefly consists the glory of heaven, that it is the *holy city*, the *holy Jerusalem, the habitation of God's holiness*, and so *of his glory*, Isa. lxiii. 15. All the beauties of the new Jerusalem, as it is described in the two last chapters of Revelation, are but various representations of this. (See chap. xxi. 2, 10, 11, 18, 21, 27. chap. xxii. 1, 3.)

And therefore it is primarily on account of this kind of excellency, that the saints love all these things. Thus they love the word of God, *because it is very pure.* It is on this account they love the saints; and on this account chiefly it is, that heaven is lovely to them, and those holy tabernacles of God amiable in their eyes. It is on this account that they love God; and on this account primarily it is, that they love Christ, and that their hearts delight in the doctrines of the gospel, and sweetly acquiesce in the way of salvation therein revealed.*

Under the head of the first distinguishing characteristic of gracious affection, I observed, that there is given to the regenerated a new supernatural sense, a certain divine spiritual taste. This is in its whole nature diverse from any former kinds of sensation of the mind, as tasting is diverse from any of the other five senses, and something is perceived by a true saint in the exercise of this new sense of mind, in spiritual and divine things, as entirely different from any thing that is perceived in them by natural men, as the sweet taste of honey is diverse from the ideas men get of honey by looking on it or feeling of it. Now the beauty of holiness, is that which is perceived by this spiritual sense, so diverse from all that natural men perceive in them; or, this kind of beauty is the quality that is the immediate object of this spiritual sense; this is the sweetness that is the proper object of this spiritual taste. The Scripture often represents the beauty and sweetness of holiness as the grand object of a spiritual taste and spiritual appetite. This was the sweet food of the holy soul of Jesus Christ, John iv. 32, 34. "I have meat to eat, that ye know not of.———My meat is to do the will of him that sent me, and to finish his work." I know of no part of the Holy Scriptures, where the nature and evidences of true and sincere godliness are so fully and largely insisted on and delineated, as in the 119th Psalm. The psalmist declares his design in the first verses of the psalm, keeps his eye on it all along, and pursues it to the end. The excellency of holiness is represented as the immediate object of a spiritual taste and delight. *God's law*, that grand expression and emanation of the holiness of God's nature, and prescription of holiness to the creature, is all along represented as the great object of the love, the complacence, and rejoicing of the gracious nature, which prizes God's commandments *above gold, yea, the finest gold*, and to which they are *sweeter than the honey, and the honey-comb*; and that upon account of their holiness, as I observed before. The same psalmist declares, that this is the sweetness that a spiritual taste relishes in God's law, Psal. xix. 7—10. "The law of the Lord is perfect:——the commandment of the Lord is pure; the fear of the Lord is clean; the statutes of the Lord are right, rejoicing the heart:——the judgments of the Lord are true, and righteous altogether; more to be desired are they than gold, yea, than much fine gold: sweeter also than honey, and the honey-comb."

A holy love has a holy object: the holiness of love consists especially in this, that it is the love of that which is *holy*, for its holiness; so that the holiness of the object, is the quality whereon it fixes and terminates. A holy nature must needs love that chiefly, which is most agreeable to itself; but surely that which above all others is agreeable to a holy nature, is holiness; for nothing can be more agreeable to any nature than itself. And so the holy nature of God and Christ, the word of God, and other divine things, must be above all agreeable to the holy nature of the saints.

Again, a holy nature doubtless loves holy things *especially* on account of that for which sinful nature has enmity against them: but that for which chiefly sinful nature is at enmity against holy things, is their *holiness;* it is for this, that the carnal mind is enmity against God, against the law, and the people of God. Now, it is just arguing from *contraries;* from contrary causes, to contrary effects; from opposite natures, to opposite tendencies. We know that holiness is of a directly contrary nature to wickedness: as therefore it is the nature of wickedness chiefly to oppose and hate holiness; so it must be the nature of holiness chiefly to tend to and delight in holiness.

The holy nature of saints and angels in heaven (where the true tendency of it best appears) is principally engaged by the holiness of divine things. This is the divine beauty which chiefly engages the attention, admiration, and constant praise of the bright and burning seraphim; Isa. vi. 3. "One cried unto another, and said, Holy, holy, holy is the Lord of hosts, the whole earth is full of his glory." Rev. iv. 8. "They rest not day and night, saying, Holy, holy, holy, Lord God Almighty, which was, and is, and is to come." So the glorified saints, chap. xv. 4. "Who shall not fear thee, O Lord, and glorify thy name? for thou only art holy."

And the Scriptures represent the saints on earth as adoring God *primarily* on this account; they admire and extol all God's attributes, either as deriving loveliness from his holiness, or as being a part of it. Thus when they praise God for his power, his *holiness* is the beauty that engages them; Psal. xcviii. 1. "O sing unto the Lord a new song, for he hath done marvellous things: his right hand and his *holy* arm hath gotten him the victory." So when they praise him for his justice and terrible majesty; Psal. xcix. 2, 3. "The Lord is great in Zion, and he is high above all people. Let them praise thy great and terrible name, for it is *holy*." Verse 5. "Exalt ye the Lord our God, and worship at his footstool: for he is *holy*." Ver. 8, 9. "Thou wast a God that forgavest them, though thou tookest vengeance of their inventions. Exalt ye the Lord our God, and worship at his holy hill: for the Lord our God is *holy*." So when they praise God for his mercy and faithfulness; Psal. xcvii. 11, 12. "Light is sown for the righteous, and gladness for the upright in heart. Rejoice in the Lord, ye righteous: and give thanks at the remembrance of his *holiness*." 1 Sam. ii. 2. "There is none *holy* as the Lord: for there is none beside thee: neither is there any rock like our God."

By this therefore all may try their affections, and particularly their love and joy. Various creatures show the difference of their natures, very much, in the things they relish as their proper good, one delighting in that which another abhors. Such a difference is there between true saints and natural men: natural men have no sense of the goodness and excellency of holy things, at least *for* their holiness. They have no taste for that kind of good, and so may be said not to know it; it is wholly hid from them. But the saints, by the mighty power of God, have it discovered to them; they have that supernatural sense given them, by which they perceive it. It is this that captivates their hearts, and delights them above all things; it is the most amiable and sweet thing, to the heart of a true saint in heaven or earth; that which above all others attracts and engages his soul; and that wherein, above all things, he places his happiness, both in this world, and in another. By this you may examine your love to God, to Jesus Christ, to the word of God, and to his people. By this you may examine your desires after heaven; whether they be from a supreme delight in this sort of beauty, without being primarily moved by your imagined interest in them, or expectations from them. There are many high

* "To the right closing with Christ's person, this is also required, to taste the bitterness of sin, as the greatest evil; else a man will never close with Christ, for his holiness in him, and from him, as the greatest good. For we told you, that that is the right closing with Christ for himself, when it is for his holiness. For ask a whorish heart, what beauty he sees in the person of Christ: he will, after he has looked over his kingdom, his righteousness, all his works, see a beauty in them, because they do serve his turn, to comfort him only. Ask a virgin, he will see his happiness in all; but that which makes the Lord amiable is his holiness, which is in him to make him holy too. As in marriage, it is the personal beauty draws the heart. And hence I have thought it reason, that he that loves the brethren for a little grace, will love Christ much more." Shepard's *Parable*, Part I. p. 84.

affections, great seeming love and rapturous joys, which have nothing of this holy relish belonging to them.

Particularly, you may try your discoveries of the glory of God's grace and love, and your affections arising from them. The grace of God may appear lovely two ways; either as *bonum utile*, a *profitable good* to me, what greatly serves my interest, and so suits my self-love; or as *bonum formosum*, a *beautiful good* in itself, and part of the moral and spiritual excellency of the divine nature. In this latter respect it is that true saints have their hearts affected, and love captivated, by the free grace of God.

Thus it appears, that though persons may have a great sense of the *natural* perfections of God, and are greatly affected with them, or have any other sight or sense of God than that which consists in the beauty of his *moral* perfections, it is no certain sign of grace. What though men have a great sense of the *awful greatness and terrible majesty of God;* this is only his *natural* perfection, which men may see, and yet be entirely blind to the beauty of his moral perfection, and have nothing of that spiritual taste which relishes this divine sweetness.

It has been shown already, in what was said upon the first distinguishing mark of gracious affections, that what is spiritual, is entirely different in its nature, from all that it is possible for any graceless person to have, while he continues graceless. But it is possible that those who are wholly without grace, should have a clear sight, and very great and affecting sense, of God's greatness, his mighty power, and awful majesty; for this is what the devils have, though they have lost the *spiritual* knowledge of God, consisting in a sense of the amiableness of his moral perfections. They are perfectly destitute of any relish of that kind of beauty, yet they have a very great knowledge of the natural glory of God, his awful greatness and majesty; this they behold, and therefore tremble before him. This glory of God all shall behold at the day of judgment; God will make all rational beings to behold it, angels and devils, saints and sinners. Christ will manifest his infinite greatness and awful majesty to every one, in a light that none can resist, when *he shall come in the glory of his Father, and every eye shall see him.* Then they shall cry to the mountains to fall upon them, to hide them from the face of him that sits upon the throne. God will make all his enemies to behold this, and to live in a most clear and affecting view of it, to all eternity. God hath often declared his immutable purpose to make all his enemies to know him in this respect, in so often annexing these words to the threatenings he denounces against them, *And they shall know that I am the Lord;* yea, he hath sworn that all men shall see his glory in this respect, Num. xiv. 21. "As truly as I live, all the earth shall be filled with the glory of the Lord." And this kind of manifestation of God is very often spoken of in Scripture, as made, or to be made, in the sight of God's enemies in this world.* This was a manifestation which God made of himself in the sight of that wicked congregation at mount Sinai; deeply affecting them with it; so that all the people in the camp trembled. Wicked men and devils will see, and have a great sense, of every thing that appertains to the glory of God, except the beauty of his moral perfection. They will see his infinite greatness, majesty, and power, and will be fully convinced of his omniscience, eternity, and immutability; and even will see every thing appertaining to his moral attributes themselves, except their beauty and amiableness. They will see and know that he is perfectly just, righteous, and true; and that he is a holy God, of purer eyes than to behold evil, who cannot look on iniquity; and they will see the wonderful manifestations of his infinite goodness and free grace to the saints. Nothing will be hid from their eyes, but the *beauty* of these moral attributes, and that beauty of the other attributes, which arises from it. And so natural men while in this world are capable of having a very affecting sense of every thing that appertains to God, but this only. Nebuchadnezzar had a great and very affecting sense of the infinite greatness and awful majesty of God; of his supreme and absolute dominion, his irresistible power, and high sovereignty. He saw that he, and all the inhabitants of the earth, were as nothing before him, had a great conviction in his conscience of his justice, and an affecting sense of his great goodness, Dan. iv. 1—3, 34, 35, 37. And the sense that Darius had of God's perfections, seems to be very much like his, Dan. vi. 25, &c. But saints and angels behold the *beauty of God's holiness:* and this sight only, will melt and humble the hearts of men, wean them from the world, draw them to God, and effectually change them. A sight of the awful greatness of God may overpower men's *strength*, and be more than they can endure; but if the *moral* beauty of God be hid, the enmity of the *heart* will remain in its full strength. No love will be kindled, the will, instead of being effectually gained, will remain inflexible; whereas the first glimpse of the moral and spiritual glory of God shining into the heart, produces all these effects with a power which nothing can withstand.

The sense that natural men may have of the awful greatness of God, may affect them various ways; it may not only terrify, but elevate them, and raise their joy and praise. This will be the natural effect of it, under the real or supposed receipt of some extraordinary mercy from God, by the influence of mere principles of nature. It has been shown already, that the receipt of kindness may, by the influence of natural principles, affect the heart with gratitude and praise to God; but if a person, at the same time, has a sense of his infinite greatness, and that he is as nothing in comparison of him, surely this will naturally raise his gratitude and praise the higher, for kindness to one so much inferior. A sense of God's greatness had this effect upon Nebuchadnezzar, on that extraordinary favour of his restoration, after he had been driven from men, and had his dwelling with the beasts. A sense of God's exceeding greatness raises his gratitude very high; so that he does, in the most lofty terms, extol and magnify God, and calls upon all the world to do it with him. If a natural man, at the same time that he is greatly affected with God's infinite greatness and majesty, entertains a strong conceit that this great God has made him his child and special favourite, and promised him eternal glory in his highest love, will not this have a tendency, according to the course of nature, to raise his joy and praise to a great height.

Therefore, it is beyond doubt, that too much weight has been laid on the discoveries of God's greatness, awful majesty, and natural perfection, operating after this manner, without any real view of the holy, lovely majesty of God. And experience does abundantly confirm what reason and Scripture declare as to this matter; there having been very many persons, who have seemed to be overpowered with the greatness and awful majesty of God, but have been very far from a christian spirit and temper, in any proportion, or fruits in practice in any wise agreeable; nay, their discoveries have worked in a way *contrary* to the operation of truly spiritual discoveries.

Not that a sense of God's greatness and natural attributes is not useful and necessary. For, as I observed before, this is implied in a manifestation of the beauty of God's holiness. Though that be something beyond it, it *supposes* it, as the greater supposes the less. And though natural men may have a sense of the natural perfections of God; yet undoubtedly this is more frequent and common with the saints, than with them. Grace enables men to see these things in a better manner, than natural men do; and not only enables them to see God's natural attributes, but that *beauty* of those attributes, which (according to our way of conceiving of God) is derived from his holiness.

SECT. IV.

Gracious affections arise from the mind being enlightened rightly and spiritually to apprehend divine things.

HOLY affections are not heat without light; but evermore arise from some information of the understanding, some spiritual instruction that the mind receives, some light or actual knowledge. The child of God is graciously

* See Exod. ix. 16. and chap. xiv. 18. and xv. 16. Psal. lxvi. 3. and xlvi. 10. and other places innumerable.

affected, because he sees and understands something more of divine things than he did before, more of God or Christ, and of the glorious things exhibited in the gospel. He has a clearer and better view than he had before, when he was not affected; either he receives some new understanding of divine things, or has his former knowledge renewed after the view was decayed; 1 John iv. 7. "Every one that loveth, knoweth God." Phil. i. 9. "I pray that your love may abound more and more in knowledge, and in all judgment." Rom. x. 2. "They have a zeal of God, but not according to knowledge." Col. iii. 10. "The new man, which is renewed in knowledge." Psal. xliii. 3, 4. "O send out thy light and thy truth; let them lead me, let them bring me unto thy holy hill." John vi. 45. "It is written in the prophets, And they shall be all taught of God. Every man therefore that hath heard, and learned of the Father, cometh unto me." Knowledge is the key that first opens the hard heart, enlarges the affections, and opens the way for men into the kingdom of heaven; Luke xi. 52. "Ye have taken away the key of knowledge."

Now there are many affections which do not arise from any light in the understanding; which is a sure evidence that these affections are not spiritual, let them be ever so high.* Indeed they have some new apprehensions which they had not before. Such is the nature of man, that it is impossible his mind should be affected, unless it be by something that he apprehends, or that his mind conceives. But in many persons those apprehensions or conceptions wherewith they are affected, have nothing of the nature of knowledge or instruction in them. For instance; when a person is affected with a lively idea, suddenly excited in his mind, of some shape, or beautiful pleasant form of countenance, a shining light, or other glorious outward appearance: here is something conceived by the mind; but nothing of the nature of instruction. Persons become never the wiser by such things, more knowing about God, a Mediator between God and man, the way of salvation by Christ, or any thing contained in the doctrines of the gospel. Persons by these external ideas have no further acquaintance with God, as to any of the attributes or perfections of his nature; nor have they any further understanding of his word, his ways, or works. Truly spiritual and gracious affections are not raised after this manner; these arise from the enlightening of the understanding, to understand the things taught of God and Christ, in a new manner. There is a new understanding of the excellent nature of God and his wonderful perfections, some new view of Christ in his spiritual excellencies and fulness; or things are opened to him in a new manner, whereby he now understands those divine and spiritual doctrines which once were foolishness to him. Such enlightenings of the understanding as these, are entirely different in their nature, from strong ideas of shapes and colours, outward brightness and glory, or sounds and voices. That all gracious affections arise from some instruction, or enlightening of the understanding, is therefore a further proof, that affections which arise from such an impression on the imagination, are not gracious.

Hence also it appears, that affections arising from texts of Scripture coming to the mind, are vain, when no *instruction* received in the understanding from those texts, or any thing taught in them, is the ground of the affection, but the *manner* of their coming to the mind. When Christ makes the Scripture a means of the heart's burning with gracious affection, it is *by opening the Scriptures to their understandings;* Luke xxiv. 32. "Did not our heart burn within us, while he talked with us by the way, and while he opened to us the Scriptures?" It appears also that the affection which is occasioned by the coming of a text of Scripture must be vain, when the affection is founded on something supposed to be taught by it, which really is not contained in it, nor in any other Scripture; because such supposed instruction is not real instruction, but a misapprehension of the mind. For instance, when persons suppose that they are expressly taught by some scripture coming to their minds, that they in particular are beloved of God, that their sins are forgiven, that God is their Father, and the like; this is a misapprehension; for the Scripture no where reveals the individual persons who are beloved, expressly, but only by revealing the qualifications of persons beloved of God.——There-fore this matter is not to be learned from Scripture any other way than by consequence, from these qualifications; for things are not to be *learned from* the Scripture any other way than they are *taught in* the Scripture.

Affections really arise from ignorance, rather than instruction, in the instances which have been mentioned; as likewise in some others that might be mentioned. Some, when they find themselves free of speech in prayer, call it God's being with them; this affects them, and their affections are increased; when they look not into the cause of this freedom of speech, which may arise many other ways besides God's spiritual presence. So some are much affected with apt thoughts that come into their minds about the Scripture, and call it the Spirit of God teaching them. They ascribe many of the workings of their own minds, of which they have a high opinion, to the special, immediate influences of God's Spirit; and so are mightily affected with their privilege. And there are some instances of persons, in whom it seems manifest, that the first ground of their affection is some bodily sensation. The animal spirits, by some cause, (and probably sometimes by the devil,) are suddenly and unaccountably put into a very agreeable motion, causing persons to feel pleasantly in their bodies; the spirits being put into such a motion as is wont to be connected with the exhilaration of the mind; and the soul, by the laws of its union with the body, hence feels pleasure. This motion of the animal spirits does not first arise from any apprehension of the mind whatsoever; but the very first thing felt, is an exhilaration and a pleasant external sensation, it may be, in their breasts. Hence through ignorance, the person being surprised, begins to think, surely this is the Holy Ghost coming into him. And then the mind begins to be affected and raised: there is first great joy; and then many other affections, in a very tumultuous manner, putting all nature, both body and mind, into a mighty ruffle. For though, as I observed before, it is the soul only that is *the seat of the affections;* yet this hinders not but that bodily sensations may, in this manner, be *an occasion of affections* in the mind.

And though men's religious affections truly arise from some instruction, or light in the understanding; yet the affection is not *gracious*, unless the *light* which is the ground of it be *spiritual.* Affections may be excited by what they obtain merely by human teaching, with the common improvement of their faculties. Men may be much affected by knowledge of religious things obtained this way; as some philosophers have been mightily affected, and almost carried beyond themselves, by the discoveries they have made in mathematics and natural philosophy. So men may be much affected from common illuminations of the Spirit of God, in which he assists their faculties to a greater degree of that kind of understanding of religious matters, which they have by the ordinary exercise and improvement of their own faculties. Such illuminations may much affect the mind; as in many whom we read of in Scripture, *that were once enlightened:* but these affections are not spiritual.

There is, if the Scriptures are of any use to teach us any thing, a spiritual, supernatural understanding of divine things, *peculiar* to the saints. 1 Cor. ii. 14. "But the natural man receiveth not the things of the Spirit of God; for

* "Many that have had mighty strong affections at first conversion, afterwards become dry, and wither, and consume, and pine, and die away: and now their hypocrisy is manifest; if not to all the world by open profaneness, yet to the discerning eye of living Christians, by a formal, barren, unsavoury, unfruitful heart, and course; because they never had light to conviction enough as yet.—It is strange to see some people carried with mighty affection against sin and hell, and after Christ. And what is the hell you fear? A dreadful place. What is Christ? They scarce know so much as devils do; but that is all. Oh trust them not! Many *have*, and these *will* fall away to some lust, or opinion, or pride, or world; and the reason is, they never had light enough, John v. 35. *John was a burning and shining light, and they did joy in him for a season;* yet glorious as it was, they saw not Christ by it, especially not with divine light. It is rare to see Christians full both of light and affection. And therefore consider of this; many a man has been well brought up, and is of a sweet loving nature, mild, and gentle, and harmless, likes and loves the best things, and his meaning, and mind, and heart is good, and has more in heart than in show; and so hopes all shall go well with him. I say, there may lie greatest hypocrisy under greatest affections; especially if they want light. You shall be hardened in your hypocrisy by them. I never liked violent affections and pangs, but only such as were dropped in by light: because those come from an external principle, and last not, but these do.—Men are not affrighted by the light of the sun, though clearer than the lightning."—Shepard's *Parable*, Part I. p. 146.

they are foolishness unto him; neither can he know them, because they are spiritually discerned." It is certainly a kind of seeing spiritual things peculiar to the saints, which is spoken of in 1 John iii. 6. "Whosoever sinneth, hath not seen him, neither known him." 3 John 11. "He that doth evil, hath not seen God." And John vi. 40. "This is the will of him that sent me, that every one that seeth the Son, and believeth on him, may have everlasting life." Chap. xiv. 19. "The world seeth me no more; but ye see me." Chap. xvii. 3. "This is eternal life, that they might know thee the only true God, and Jesus Christ whom thou hast sent." Matt. xi. 27. "No man knoweth the Son, but the Father; neither knoweth any man the Father, but the Son, and he to whomsoever the Son will reveal him." John xii. 45. "He that seeth me, seeth him that sent me." Psal. ix. 10. "They that know thy name, will put their trust in thee." Phil. iii. 8. "I count all things but loss, for the excellency of the knowledge of Christ Jesus my Lord:—ver. 10. That I may know him."—Innumerable other places there are, all over the Bible, which show the same. And that there is an understanding of divine things, which in its nature and kind is wholly different from all knowledge that natural men have, is evident from this, that there is what the Scripture calls spiritual understanding; Col. i. 9. "We do not cease to pray for you, and to desire that you may be filled with the knowledge of his will, in all wisdom and spiritual understanding." It has been already shown, that what is *spiritual*, in the ordinary use of the word in the New Testament, is entirely different in nature and kind, from all which natural men are or can be the subjects of.

From hence it may be surely inferred, wherein spiritual understanding consists. For if there be in the saints a kind of perception, which is in its nature perfectly diverse from all that natural men can have, it must consist in their having a certain kind of ideas, or sensations of mind, which are simply diverse from all that can be in the minds of natural men. And that is the same thing as to say, that it consists in the sensations of a new spiritual sense, which the souls of natural men have not; as is evident by what has been repeatedly observed. But I have already shown what that new spiritual sense is, which the saints have given them in regeneration, and what is the object of it. I have shown that the immediate object of it is the supreme beauty and excellency of the nature of divine things, as they are in themselves. And this is agreeable to the Scripture: the apostle very plainly teaches, that the great thing discovered by spiritual light, and understood by spiritual knowledge, is the glory of divine things, 2 Cor. iv. 3, 4. "But if our gospel be hid, it is hid to them that are lost: in whom the god of this world hath blinded the minds of them that believe not, lest the light of the glorious gospel of Christ, who is the image of God, should shine unto them:" together with ver. 6. "For God, who commanded the light to shine out of darkness, hath shined into our hearts, to give the light of the knowledge of the glory of God, in the face of Jesus Christ." And chap. iii. 18. preceding, "But we all with open face, beholding as in a glass the glory of the Lord, are changed into the same image, from glory to glory, even as by the Spirit of the Lord." And it must needs be so, for the Scripture often teaches, that all true religion summarily consists in the *love* of divine things. And therefore that kind of understanding or knowledge, which is the proper foundation of true religion, must be the knowledge of the *loveliness of divine things*. For doubtless, that knowledge which is the proper foundation of *love*, is the knowledge of *loveliness*. What that beauty or loveliness of divine things is, which is the proper and immediate object of a spiritual sense of mind, was showed under the last head insisted on, *viz*. That it is the beauty of their *moral perfection*. Therefore it is in the view or sense of this, that spiritual understanding does more immediately and primarily consist. And indeed it is plain it can be nothing else; for, (as has been shown,) there is nothing pertaining to divine things, besides the beauty of their moral excellency—and those properties and qualities of divine things of which this beauty is the foundation—but what natural men and devils can see and know, and will know fully and clearly to all eternity.

From what has been said, therefore, we come necessarily to this conclusion, that spiritual understanding consists in a *cordial sense of the supreme beauty and sweetness of the holiness or moral perfection of divine things, together with all that discerning and knowledge of things of religion, that depends upon and flows from such a sense.*

Spiritual understanding consists primarily in a cordial sense, or *a sense of heart, of that spiritual beauty*. I say, a *sense of heart*; for it is not speculation merely that is concerned in this kind of understanding: nor can there be a clear distinction made between the two faculties of understanding and will, as acting distinctly and separately, in this matter. When the mind is sensible of the beauty and amiableness of a thing, that implies a sensibleness of delight in the presence of its idea: and this carries in the very nature of it, *the sense of the heart*; or an effect and impression of the soul of a substance possessed of taste, inclination, and will.

There is a distinction to be made between a mere *notional understanding*, wherein the mind only beholds things in the exercise of a speculative faculty; and *the sense of the heart*, wherein the mind not only *speculates* and *beholds*, but *relishes* and *feels*. That sort of knowledge, by which a man has a sensible perception of amiableness and loathsomeness, or of sweetness and nauseousness, is not the same sort of knowledge with that, by which he knows what a triangle or a square is. The one is mere *speculative* knowledge; the other *sensible* knowledge, in which more than the mere intellect is concerned. The *heart* is the proper subject of it, or the soul, as a being that not only beholds, but has *inclination*, and is pleased or displeased. And yet there is the nature of *instruction* in it; as he that has perceived the sweet taste of honey, knows much more about it, than he who has only looked upon and felt it.

The apostle seems to make a distinction between mere speculative and spiritual knowledge, in calling the former *the form of knowledge, and of the truth*; Rom. ii. 20. "Which hast the form of knowledge, and of the truth in the law." The latter is often represented by relishing, smelling, or tasting; 2 Cor. ii. 14. "Now thanks be to God, which always causeth us to triumph in Christ Jesus, and maketh manifest the savour of his knowledge in every place." Matt. xvi. 23. "Thou savourest not the things that be of God, but those things that be of men." 1 Pet. ii. 2, 3. "As new-born babes desire the sincere milk of the word, that ye may grow thereby; if so be ye have tasted that the Lord is gracious." Cant. i. 3. "Because of the savour of thy good ointments, thy name is as ointment poured forth, therefore do the virgins love thee:" compared with 1 John ii. 20. "But ye have an unction from the Holy One, and ye know all things."

Spiritual understanding *primarily* consists in this *sense or taste of the moral beauty of divine things*; so that no knowledge can be called spiritual, any further than it arises from, and has this in it. But *secondarily*, it includes *all that discerning and knowledge of religious things, which depends upon and flows from such a sense*. When the true beauty and amiableness in divine things, is discovered to the soul, it opens as it were a new world to its view. This shows the glory of all God's perfections, and of every thing appertaining to the Divine Being. For, as was observed before, the beauty of all arises from God's moral perfection. This shows the glory of all God's works, both of creation and providence. For it is their special glory, that God's holiness, righteousness, faithfulness, and goodness, are so manifested in them; and without these moral perfections, there would be no glory in that power and skill with which they are wrought. The glorifying of God's moral perfections, is the special end of all the works of God's hands. By this sense of the moral beauty of divine things, is known the sufficiency of Christ as a Mediator: for it is only by the discovery of beauty in the moral perfection of Christ, that the believer is let into the knowledge of the excellency of his person, so as to know any thing more of it than the devils do: and it is only by the knowledge of the excellency of Christ's person, that any know his sufficiency as a Mediator; for the latter depends upon and arises from the former. It is by seeing the excellency of Christ's person, that the saints are made sensible of the preciousness of his blood, and its sufficiency to atone for sin: for therein consists the preciousness of Christ's blood, that it is the blood of so excellent and amiable a person. And on this depends the meritoriousness of his obedience, the sufficiency and prevalence of his intercession. By this sight of moral beauty, is seen the beauty of salvation by Christ; for that consists in the beauty of God's moral perfections, which wonderfully shines forth in every step of this method of salvation. By this is seen the fitness and suitableness of this way; which consists in its tendency to deliver us from sin and hell, and to bring us to happiness. For true happiness consists in the possession and enjoyment of moral good, in a way sweetly agreeing with God's moral perfections. And in the way being so contrived as to attain these ends, consists the excellent wisdom of that way. By this is seen the excellency of the word of God. Take away all the moral beauty and sweetness in the word, and the Bible is left wholly a dead letter, a dry, lifeless, tasteless thing. By this is seen the true foundation of our duty, the worthiness of God to be so esteemed, honoured, loved, submitted to, and served, as he requires of us, and the amiableness of the duties themselves required. And by this is seen the true evil of sin: for he who sees the beauty of holiness, must necessarily see the hatefulness of sin, its contrary. By this men understand the true glory of heaven, which consists in the beauty and happiness contained in holiness. By this is seen the amiableness and happiness of saints and angels. He that sees the beauty of holiness, or true moral good, sees the greatest and most important thing in the world, which is the fulness of all things, without which all the world is empty, yea, worse than nothing. Unless this is seen, nothing is seen that is worth the seeing; for there is no other true excellency or beauty. Unless this be understood, nothing is understood worthy the exercise of the noble faculty of understanding. This is the beauty of the Godhead, the divinity of divinity, (if I may so speak,) the good of the infinite fountain of good. Without this, God himself (if that were possible) would be an infinite evil, we ourselves had better never have been; and there had better have been no being. He therefore in effect knows nothing, that knows not this; his knowledge is but the shadow of knowledge, or the *form of knowledge*, as the apostle calls it. Well therefore may the Scripture represent those who are destitute of that spiritual sense, by which is perceived the beauty of holiness, as totally *blind, deaf*, and *senseless*, yea, *dead*. And well may regeneration, in which this divine sense is given to the soul by its Creator, be represented as opening the blind eyes, raising the dead, and bringing a person into a new world. For if what has been said be considered, it will be manifest, that when a person has this sense and knowledge given him, he will view nothing as he did before; though before he *knew* all things "after the flesh, yet henceforth he will know them so no more; and he is become a new creature, old things are passed away, behold all things are become new," (2 Cor. v. 16, 17.)

Besides, there arises from this sense of spiritual beauty, all true experimental knowledge of religion, which is of itself as it were a new world of knowledge. He that sees not the beauty of holiness, knows not what one of the graces of God's Spirit is, he is destitute of any conception of gracious exercises of soul, holy comforts and delights, and effects of the saving influences of the Spirit of God on the heart. He is ignorant of the greatest works of God, the most important and glorious effects of his power upon the creature; he is wholly ignorant of the saints as saints, and knows not what they are; and in effect is wholly ignorant of the spiritual world. Thus, it plainly appears, that God implanting a spiritual, supernatural sense, makes a great change in a man. And were it not for the very imperfect degree in which this sense is commonly given at first, or the small degree of this glorious light that first dawns upon the soul; the change made by this spiritual opening of the eyes in conversion, would be much greater, and more remarkable every way, than if a man born blind should have the sense of seeing imparted to him at once, in the midst of the clear light of the sun, discovering a world of visible objects. For though sight be more noble than any of the other external senses, yet this spiritual sense is infinitely more noble, and the object infinitely more important.—This is that knowledge of divine things from whence all truly gracious affections proceed; by which therefore all affections are to be tried. Those affections that arise wholly from any other kind of knowledge, or do result from any other kind of apprehensions, are vain.*

From what has been said may be learned, wherein the most essential difference lies between that light or understanding which is given by the *common influences* of the Spirit of God, on the hearts of natural men, and that *saving instruction* which is given to the saints. The *latter* primarily and most essentially lies in beholding the *holy beauty* of divine things; which is the only *true* moral good, and to which the soul of fallen man is by nature totally blind. The *former* consists only in a further understanding, through the assistance of natural principles, of those things which men may know, in some measure, by the ordinary exercise of their faculties; it is only the knowledge of those things pertaining to religion, which are *natural*. Thus for instance, in awakenings and convictions of conscience in natural men, the Spirit of God gives no knowledge of true *moral* beauty, but only assists the mind to a clearer idea of the guilt of sin, or its relation to punishment, and its connexion with the *evil of suffering*, (without any sight of its true *moral* evil, or odiousness as sin,) and a clearer idea of the *natural* perfections of God, wherein consists, not his holy beauty and glory, but his awful and terrible greatness. It is a clear sight of this, that will fully awaken the consciences of wicked men at the day of judgment, *without any spiritual light*. And it is a lesser degree of the same, that awakens the consciences of natural men, *without spiritual light*, in this world. The same discoveries are in some measure given in the conscience of an awakened sinner in this world, which will be given more fully at the day of judgment. The same kind of apprehension, in a lesser degree, makes awakened sinners in this world sensible of the dreadful guilt of sin against so great and terrible a God, and of its amazing punishment—and fills them with fearful apprehensions of divine wrath—that will thoroughly convince all wicked men, of the infinitely dreadful nature and guilt of sin, and astonish them with apprehensions of wrath, when Christ shall come in the glory of his power and majesty, and every eye shall see him, and all the kindreds of the earth shall wail because of him. And in those common illuminations which are sometimes given to natural men, exciting in them some kind of religious desire, love, and joy, the mind is only assisted to a clearer apprehension of the *natural good* that is in divine things. Thus sometimes, under common illuminations, men are raised with the ideas of the *natural* good that is in heaven; as its outward glory, its ease, its honour and advancement, being there the objects of the high favour of God, and the great respect of men and angels, &c. So there are many things exhibited in the gospel, concerning God and Christ, and the way of salvation, that have a *natural* good in them, which suits the natural principle of self-love. Thus in that great goodness of God to sinners, and the wonderful dying love of Christ, there is a *natural* good, which all men love, as they love *themselves;* as well as a spiritual and holy beauty, which is seen only by the regenerate.

* "Take heed of contenting yourselves with every kind of knowledge. Do not worship every image of your own heads; especially you that fall short of truth, or the knowledge of it. For when you have some, there may be yet that wanting, which may make you sincere. There are many men of great knowledge, able to teach themselves, and others too: and yet their hearts are unsound. How comes this to pass? Is it because they have so much light? No; but because they want much. And therefore content not yourselves with every knowledge. There is some knowledge which men have by the light of nature, (which leaves them without excuse,) from the book of creation; some by power of education; some by the light of the law, whereby men know their sin and evils; some by the letter of the gospel; and so men may know much, and speak well; and so in seeing, see not: some by the Spirit, and may see much, so as to prophesy in Christ's name, and yet bid depart, Matt. vii. Now there is *a light of glory*, whereby the elect see things in another manner: to tell you how, they cannot: it is the beginning of light in heaven: and the same Spirit that fills Christ, filling their minds, that they know, by this anointing, all things: which if ever you have you must become babes and fools in your own eyes. God will never write his law in your minds, until all the scribblings of it are blotted out. Account all your knowledge loss for the gaining of this. It is sad to see many a man pleasing himself in his own dreaming delusions; yet the poor creature in seeing, sees not: which is God's heavy curse upon men under greatest means, and which lays all waste and desolate." Shepard's *Parable*, Part I. p. 147.

Therefore there are many things appertaining to the word of God's grace delivered in the gospel, which may cause natural men, when they hear it, *anon with joy to receive it.* All that love which natural men have to God and Christ, Christian virtues, and good men, is not from any sight of the amiableness, or true *moral* excellency of these things; but only for the sake of the *natural* good there is in them. All natural men's hatred of sin, is as much from principles of nature, as their hatred of a tiger for his rapaciousness, or their aversion to a serpent for his poison and hurtfulness. Their love of Christian virtue, is from no higher principle than their love of a man's good nature, which appears amiable to natural men; but no otherwise than silver and gold appears amiable in the eyes of a merchant, or than the blackness of the soil is beautiful in the eyes of the farmer.

From what has been said it appears, that spiritual understanding does not consist in any new *doctrinal* knowledge, or in having suggested to the mind any new *proposition*, not before read or heard of: for it is plain, that this suggesting of new propositions, is a thing entirely diverse from giving the mind a new taste or relish of beauty and sweetness.* It is also evident, that spiritual knowledge does not consist in any new *doctrinal explanation* of any part of the Scripture; for still, this is but doctrinal knowledge, or the knowledge of propositions; the doctrinal explaining of any part of Scripture, is only giving us to understand, what are the propositions contained or taught in that part of Scripture.

Hence it appears, that the *spiritual understanding* of the Scripture, does not consist in opening to the mind the *mystical meaning* of the Scripture, in its parables, types, and allegories; for this is only a doctrinal explication of the Scripture. He that explains what is meant by the stony ground; and the seed springing up suddenly, and quickly withering away, only explains what *propositions* or *doctrines* are taught in it. So he that explains what is typified by Jacob's ladder, and the angels of God ascending and descending on it, or what was typified by Joshua's leading Israel through Jordan, only shows what propositions are hid in these passages. And many men can explain these types, who have no spiritual knowledge. It is possible that a man might know how to interpret *all* the types, parables, enigmas, and allegories in the Bible, and not have *one beam of spiritual light* in his mind; because he may not have any spiritual sense of the holy beauty of divine things, and may see nothing of this kind of glory in any of these mysteries, or any other part of the Scripture. It is plain, by what the apostle says, that a man might understand all such mysteries, and have no saving grace; 1 Cor. xiii. 2. "And though I have the gift of prophecy, and understand all mysteries, and all knowledge, and have not charity, it profiteth me nothing." They therefore are very foolish, who are exalted in an opinion of their own spiritual attainments, from their notions of the mystical meaning of scripture passages, as though it was a *spiritual* understanding, immediately given them by the Spirit of God. Their affections may be highly raised; but what has been said, shows the vanity of such affections.

From what has been said, it is also evident, that it is not *spiritual* knowledge, for persons to be informed of their duty, by having it immediately suggested to their minds, that such and such outward actions or deeds are the will of God. If we suppose that it is truly God's manner thus to signify his will to his people, by immediate inward suggestions, such suggestions have nothing of the nature of *spiritual* light. Such knowledge would only be *doctrinal;* for a proposition concerning the *will* of God, is as properly a doctrine of religion, as a proposition concerning the nature or a work of God. Having any proposition declared to a man, either by speech, or inward suggestion, differs vastly from having the holy beauty of divine things manifested to the soul, wherein spiritual knowledge most essentially consists. Thus there was no spiritual light in Balaam; though he had the will of God immediately suggested to him by the Spirit, concerning the way that he should go, and what he should do and say.

It is manifest therefore, that being led and directed in this manner, is not that holy and spiritual *leading of the Spirit of God,* which is peculiar to the saints, and a distinguishing mark of the sons of God, spoken of Rom. viii. 14. "For as many as are led by the Spirit of God, are the sons of God." Gal. v. 18. "But if ye be led by the Spirit, ye are not under the law."

And if persons have the will of God concerning their actions, suggested to them by some text of Scripture suddenly brought to their minds—which text, as the words lay in the Bible before they came to their minds, related to the action and behaviour of some other person—it alters not the case. The suggestion being accompanied with an apt text of Scripture, does not make it to be of the nature of spiritual instruction. For instance, suppose a person in New England, on some occasion, were at a loss whether it was his duty to go into some popish or heathenish land, where he was like to be exposed to many difficulties and dangers, and should pray to God that he would show him the way of his duty; and after earnest prayer, should have those words which God spake to Jacob, Gen. xlvi. suddenly and extraordinarily brought to his mind, as if they were spoken to him; "Fear not to go down into Egypt; and I will go with thee; and I will also surely bring thee up again." In which words, though as they lay in the Bible before they came to his mind, they related only to Jacob and his behaviour; yet he supposes that God has a further meaning, as they were brought and applied to him; that by Egypt is to be understood this particular country he has in his mind, and that the action intended is his going thither, and the meaning of the promise is, that God would bring him back into New England again. There is nothing of the nature of a spiritual or gracious leading of the Spirit in this; for there is nothing of the nature of spiritual understanding in it. Spiritually to understand the Scripture, is rightly to understand what *is in* the Scripture, and what *was in* it before it was understood: it is to understand rightly, what *used to be contained in* the meaning of it, and not the *making* a new meaning. When the mind is enlightened spiritually and rightly to understand the Scripture, it is enabled to see that which before was not seen, *by reason of blindness.* But if it was by reason of blindness, that is an evidence that the same meaning was in it *before*, otherwise it would have been no blindness not to see it: it is no blindness not to see a meaning which is not there. Spiritually enlightening the eyes to understand the Scripture, is *to open the eyes,* Psal. cxix. 18. "Open thou mine eyes, that I may behold wondrous things out of thy law;" which argues, that the reason why the same was not seen in the Scripture before, was, that the eyes were *shut;* which would not be the case, if the meaning now understood was not there before, but is now newly added to the Scripture by the *manner* of the Scripture coming to the mind. This making of a *new meaning* to the Scripture, is the same thing as making a *new scripture:* it is properly *adding* to the word, which is threatened with so dreadful a curse. Spiritually to *understand* the Scripture, is to have the eyes of the mind opened to behold the wonderful, spiritual excellency of the glorious things contained in the true meaning of it, and that always were contained in it, ever since it was written; to behold the amiable and bright manifestations of the divine perfections, the excellency and sufficiency of Christ, the suitableness of the way of salvation by him, and the spiritual glory of the precepts and promises of the Scripture, &c. These things are, and always were in the Bible, and would have been seen before, if it had not been for blindness, without having any new sense added.

And as to a gracious *leading of the Spirit,* it consists in two things; partly in *instructing* a person in his duty by the Spirit, and partly in powerfully *inducing* him to comply with that instruction. But so far as the gracious leading of the Spirit lies in instruction, it consists in a person's

* Calvin, in his Institutions, Book I. chap. ix. § 1. says, "It is not the office of the Spirit that is promised us, to make new and before unheard of revelations, or to coin some new kind of doctrine, which tends to draw us away from the received doctrine of the gospel; but to seal and confirm to us that very doctrine which is by the gospel." And in the same place he speaks of some, that in those days maintained the contrary notion, *pretending to be immediately led by the Spirit, as persons that were governed by a most haughty self-conceit; and not so properly to be looked upon as only labouring under a mistake, as driven by a sort of raving madness.*

being guided by a spiritual and distinguishing taste of that which has in it true moral beauty. I have shown that spiritual knowledge primarily consists in a taste or relish of the amiableness and beauty of that which is truly good and holy: this holy relish discerns and distinguishes between good and evil, between holy and unholy, without being at the trouble of a train of reasoning. As he who has a true relish of external beauty, knows what is beautiful by looking upon it; he stands in no need of a train of reasoning about the proportion of the features, in order to determine whether that which he sees be a beautiful countenance or no; he needs nothing, but only the glance of his eye. He who has a rectified musical ear, knows whether the sound he hears be true harmony; he does not need first to be at the trouble of the reasonings of a mathematician, about the proportion of the notes. He that has a rectified palate, knows what is good food, as soon as he tastes it, without the reasoning of a physician about it. There is a holy beauty and sweetness in words and actions, as well as a natural beauty in countenances and sounds, and sweetness in food; Job xii. 11. "Doth not the ear try words, and the mouth taste his meat?" When a holy and amiable action is suggested to the thoughts of a holy soul; that soul, if in the lively exercise of its spiritual taste, at once sees a beauty in it, and so inclines to it, and closes with it. On the contrary, if an unworthy, unholy action be suggested, its sanctified eye sees no beauty in it, and is not pleased with it; its sanctified taste relishes no sweetness in it, but on the contrary, it is nauseous. Yea, its holy taste and appetite leads it to think of that which is truly lovely, and naturally suggests it; as a healthy taste and appetite naturally suggests the idea of its proper object. Thus a holy person is led by the Spirit, as he is instructed and led by his holy taste, and disposition of heart; whereby, in the lively exercise of grace, he easily distinguishes good and evil, and knows at once what is a suitable, amiable behaviour towards God, and towards man, in this case and the other; and judges what is right, as it were spontaneously, without a particular deduction, by any other arguments than the beauty that is seen, and goodness that is tasted. Thus Christ blames the Pharisees, that they *did not, even of their ownselves, judge what was right*, without needing miracles to prove it. Luke xii. 57. The apostle seems plainly to have respect to this way of judging of spiritual beauty, in Rom. xii. 2. "Be ye transformed by the renewing of your mind, that ye may prove what is that good, and perfect, and acceptable will of God."

There is such a thing as *good taste* of *natural* beauty, (of which learned men often speak,) exercised about *temporal* things, in judging of them; as about the justness of a speech, the goodness of style, the beauty of a poem, the gracefulness of deportment, &c. A late great philosopher of our nation, writes thus upon it;* "To have *a taste*, is to give things their real value, to be touched with the good, to be shocked with the ill; not to be dazzled with false lustres, but in spite of all colours, and every thing that might deceive or amuse, to judge soundly. *Taste* and *judgment* then, should be the same thing; and yet it is easy to discern a difference. The *judgment* forms its opinions from reflection: the reason on this occasion fetches a kind of circuit, to arrive at its end; it supposes principles, it draws consequences, and it judges; but not without a thorough knowledge of the case; so that after it has pronounced, it is ready to render a reason of its decrees. *Good taste* observes none of these formalities; ere it has time to consult, it has taken its side; as soon as ever the object is presented it, the impression is made, the sentiment formed, ask no more of it. As the ear is wounded with a harsh sound, as the smell is soothed with an agreeable odour, before ever the reason have meddled with those objects to judge of them, so the *taste* opens itself at once, and prevents all reflection. They may come afterwards to confirm it, and discover the secret reasons of its conduct; but it was not in its power to wait for them. Frequently it happens not to know them at all, and what pains soever it uses, cannot discover what it was determined it to think as it did. This conduct is very different from that the *judgment* observes in its decisions: unless we choose to say, that *good taste* is as it were a first motion, or a kind of instinct of right reason, which hurries on with rapidity, and conducts more securely, than all the reasonings she could make; it is a first glance of the eye, which discovers to us the nature and relations of things in a moment."

Now as there is a *taste* of the mind, whereby persons are guided in their judgment concerning the natural beauty, gracefulness, propriety, nobleness, and sublimity of speeches and actions—whereby they judge as it were by the glance of the eye, or by inward sensation, and the first impression of the object—so there is likewise a *divine taste*, given and maintained by the Spirit of God, in the hearts of the saints, whereby they are in like manner led and guided in discerning and distinguishing the true spiritual and holy beauty of actions; and that more easily, readily, and accurately, as they have more or less of the Spirit of God dwelling in them. And thus *the sons of God are led by the Spirit of God, in their behaviour in the world.*

A holy disposition and spiritual taste, where grace is strong and lively, will enable a soul to determine what actions are right and becoming Christians, not only more speedily, but far more exactly, than the greatest abilities without it. This may be illustrated by the manner in which some habits of mind, and dispositions of heart, of a nature inferior to true grace, will teach and guide a man in his actions. As for instance, if a man be a very good natured man, his good nature will teach him better how to act benevolently amongst mankind, and will direct him, on every occasion, to those speeches and actions, which are agreeable to rules of goodness, than the strongest reason will a man of a morose temper. So if a man's heart be under the influence of an entire friendship, and most endeared affection to another; though he be a man of an indifferent capacity, yet this habit of his mind will direct him, far more readily and exactly, to a speech and deportment, or manner of behaviour, which shall in all respects be sweet and kind, and agreeable to a benevolent disposition of heart, than the greatest capacity without it. He has as it were a spirit within that guides him; the habit of his mind is attended with a taste, by which he immediately relishes that air and mien which is benevolent, and disrelishes the contrary. It causes him to distinguish between the one and the other *in a moment*, more precisely, than the most accurate reasonings can find out *in many hours*. The nature and inward tendency of a heavy body that is let fall from a height, shows the way to the centre of the earth more exactly in an instant, than the ablest mathematician without it could determine, by his most accurate observations, in a whole day. Thus it is that a spiritual disposition and taste teaches and guides a man in his behaviour in the world. So an eminently humble, or meek, or charitable disposition, will direct a person of mean capacity to such a behaviour, as is agreeable to christian rules of humility, meekness, and charity, far more readily and precisely, than the most diligent study, and elaborate reasonings, of a man of the strongest faculties, who has not a christian spirit within him. So also will a spirit of love to God, holy fear and reverence towards God, and filial confidence in him, and a heavenly disposition, teach and guide a man in his behaviour.

It is an exceeding difficult thing for a wicked man, destitute of christian principles in his heart to guide him, to know how to demean himself like a Christian, with the life, beauty, and heavenly sweetness of a truly holy, humble, Christ-like behaviour. He knows not how to put on these garments; neither do they fit him; Eccl. x. 2, 3. "A wise man's heart is at his right hand; but a fool's heart is at his left. Yea also, when he that is a fool walketh by the way, his wisdom faileth him, and he saith to every one that he is a fool;" with verse 15. "The labour of the foolish wearieth every one of them, because he knoweth not how to go to the city." Prov. x. 32. "The lips of the righteous know what is acceptable." Chap. xv. 2. "The tongue of the wise useth knowledge aright: but the mouth of fools poureth out foolishness." And chap.

* Chambers's Dictionary, under the word TASTE.

xvi. 23. "The heart of the righteous teacheth his mouth, and addeth learning to his lips."

The saints in thus judging of actions by a spiritual taste, have not a particular recourse to the express rules of God's word, with respect to every word and action that is before them: but yet their taste itself in general, is subject to the rule of God's word, and must be tried by that, and a right reasoning upon it. A man of a rectified palate judges of particular morsels by his taste; but yet his palate itself must be judged of, whether it be right or no, by certain rules and reasons. But a spiritual taste mightily helps the soul in its reasonings on the word of God, and in judging of the true meaning of its rules; as it removes the prejudices of a depraved appetite, naturally leads the thoughts in the right channel, casts a light on the word, and causes the true meaning most naturally to come to mind, through the harmony there is between the disposition and relish of a sanctified soul, and the true meaning of the rules of God's word. Yea, this harmony tends to bring the texts themselves to mind on proper occasions; as the particular state of the stomach and palate, tends to bring such particular meats and drinks to mind, as are agreeable to that state. Thus *the children of God are led by the Spirit of God* in judging of actions themselves, and in their meditations upon the rules of God's holy word: and so God *teaches them his statutes, and causes them to understand the way of his precepts;* which the psalmist so often prays for.

But this leading of the Spirit is exceedingly diverse from what some call so; which consists, according to them —not in teaching them God's statutes and precepts already given, but—in giving them new precepts, by immediate inward speech or suggestion. They do not determine what is the will of God by any taste, relish, or judgment of the nature of things, but by an immediate dictate concerning the thing to be done; indeed there is no such thing as any judgment or wisdom in the case. Whereas in that leading of the Spirit which is peculiar to God's children, there is imparted that true wisdom, and holy discretion, so often spoken of in the word of God; which is high above the other way, as the stars are higher than a glow-worm; and that which Balaam and Saul (who sometimes were led by the Spirit in that other way) never had, and no natural man can have, without a change of nature.

What has been said of the nature of spiritual understanding, as consisting most essentially in a *supernatural sense* and relish of the heart, not only shows that there is nothing of it in this falsely supposed *leading of the Spirit;* but also shows the *difference* between *spiritual understanding*, and all kinds and forms of *enthusiasm*, all imaginary sights of God, and Christ, and heaven; all supposed *witnessing* of the Spirit and testimonies of the love of God by immediate inward suggestion; all *impressions* of future events, and immediate revelations of any secret facts whatsoever. Hereby we see how different is true spiritual religion, and all enthusiastical impressions and applications of Scripture, as though they were words now immediately spoken by God to a particular person, in a new meaning, and carrying something more in them, than the words contain as they lie in the Bible; and all interpretations of the mystical meaning of the Scripture, by supposed immediate revelation. None of these things consist in a divine sense and relish of the *heart*, of the holy beauty and excellency of divine things; nor have they any thing to do with such a sense; but all consist in impressions in the *head;* all are to be referred to the head of *impressions on the imagination*, and consist in exciting external ideas in the mind, either of outward shapes and colours, or words spoken, or letters written, or ideas of things external and sensible, belonging to actions done, or events accomplished or to be accomplished. An enthusiastical supposed manifestation of the love of God, is made by exciting an idea of a smiling countenance, or some other pleasant outward appearance, or by the idea of pleasant words spoken, or written, excited in the imagination, or some pleasant bodily sensation. So when persons have an imaginary revelation of some secret fact, it is by exciting external ideas; either of some words, implying a declaration of that fact, or some visible or sensible circumstances of such a fact. So the supposed leading of the Spirit, to do the will of God, in outward behaviour, is either by exciting the idea of words (which are outward things) in their minds, either the words of Scripture, or other words, which they look upon as an immediate command of God; or else by exciting and impressing strongly the ideas of the outward actions themselves. So when an interpretation of a scripture type or allegory is immediately, in an extraordinary way, strongly suggested, it is by suggesting words, as though one secretly whispered and told the meaning; or by exciting other ideas in the imagination.

Such sort of experiences and discoveries as these commonly raise the affections of such as are deluded by them, to a great height, and make a mighty uproar in both soul and body. And a very great part of the false religion that has been in the world, from one age to another, consists in such discoveries as these, and in the affections that flow from them. In such things consisted the experiences of the ancient Pythagoreans among the heathen, and many others among them, who had strange ecstasies and raptures, and pretended to a divine *afflatus*, and immediate revelations from heaven. In such things as these seem to have consisted the experiences of the Essenes, an ancient sect among the Jews, at and after the times of the apostles. In such things consisted the experiences of many of the ancient Gnostics, the Montanists, and many other sects of ancient heretics, in the primitive ages of the christian church. And in such things as these consisted the pretended immediate converse with God and Christ, saints and angels, of the Monks, Anchorites, and Recluses, that formerly abounded in the church of Rome. In such things consisted the pretended high experiences and great spirituality of many sects of enthusiasts, that swarmed in the world after the reformation.* And in these things seems to lie the religion of the many kinds of enthusiasts of the present day. It is by such sort of religion as this chiefly that Satan transforms himself into an angel of light: and it is that which he has ever most successfully employed to confound hopeful and happy revivals of religion, from the beginning of the christian church to this day. When the Spirit of God is poured out to begin a glorious work, then the old serpent, as fast as possible, and by all means, introduces this bastard religion, and mingles it with the true; which has from time to time soon brought all things into confusion. The pernicious consequence of it is not easily imagined, until we see and are amazed with the awful effects of it, and the dismal desolation it has made. If the revival of true religion be very great in its beginning, yet if this bastard comes in, there is danger of its doing as Gideon's bastard Ahimelech did, who never left until he had slain all his threescore and ten true-born sons, excepting one that was forced to flee. Great and strict therefore should be the watch and guard that ministers maintain against such things, especially at a time of great awakening: for men, especially the common people, are easily bewitched with such things; they having such a glaring and glistering show of high religion. The devil hiding his own shape, and appearing as an angel of light, men may not be afraid of him.

The imagination, or phantasy, seems to be that wherein are formed all these delusions of Satan, false religion, and counterfeit graces and affections. Here is the devil's grand lurking-place, the very nest of foul and delusive spirits. It is very much to be doubted, whether the devil can come at the *soul* of man to affect it, or to produce any effect whatsoever in it, any other way, than by the phantasy; that power of the soul by which it receives, and is the subject of the species, or ideas of outward and sensible things. As to the laws and means which the Creator has established, for the intercourse and communication of unbodied spirits, we know nothing about them; we do not know by what medium they manifest their thoughts to, or excite thoughts in, each other. But as to spirits united to

* Such as the Anabaptists, Antinomians, and Familists, the followers of N. Stork, Th. Muncer, Jo. Becold, Henry Pleifer, David George, Casper Swenckfield, Henry Nicolas, Johannes Agricola Eislebius; and the many wild enthusiasts that were in England in the days of Oliver Cromwell; and the followers of Mrs. Hutchinson, in New England; as appears by the particular and large accounts given of all these sects, by that eminently holy man, Mr. Samuel Rutherford, in his *Display of the Spiritual Antichrist* And in such things as these consisted the experiences of the late French prophets, and their followers.

bodies, those bodies are their medium of communication. They have no other medium of acting on other creatures, or being acted on by them, than the body. Therefore it is not to be supposed that Satan can excite any thought, or produce any effect in the soul of man, any otherwise, than by some motion of the animal spirits, or by causing some motion or alteration in something which appertains to the body. There is this reason to think that the devil cannot produce thoughts in the soul any other way than by the medium of the body, viz. that he cannot immediately know the thoughts of the soul. This is abundantly declared in the Scripture, to be peculiar to the omniscient God. But it is not likely that the devil can *immediately produce* an effect, which is out of the reach of his *immediate view*. It seems unreasonable to suppose, that his immediate agency should be out of his own sight, or that it should be impossible for him to see what he himself immediately does. Is it not unreasonable to suppose, that any intelligent agent should by the act of his will produce effects, according to his understanding, or agreeable to his own thoughts, and that immediately, and yet the effects produced be beyond the reach of his understanding, or where he can have no immediate perception? But if the devil cannot produce thoughts in the soul immediately, or any other way than by the animal spirits, or by the body, then it follows, that he never brings to pass any thing in the soul, but by the imagination or phantasy, or by exciting external ideas. For we know that alterations in the body do immediately excite no other sort of ideas in the mind, but external ones, or those of the outward senses. As to reflection, abstraction, reasoning, &c. and those thoughts and inward motions which are the *fruits* of these acts of the mind, they are not the nearest effects of impressions on the body. So that it must be only by the imagination that Satan has access to the soul, to tempt and delude it, or suggest any thing to it.* And this seems to be the reason why persons that are under the disease of melancholy, are commonly so visibly and remarkably subject to the suggestions and temptations of Satan; that being a disease which peculiarly affects the animal spirits, and is attended with weakness of that part of the body which is their fountain, even the brain, which is, as it were, the seat of the phantasy. It is by impressions made on the brain, that any ideas are excited in the mind, by the motion of the animal spirits, or any changes made in the body. The brain being thus weakened and diseased, it is less under the command of the higher faculties of the soul, and yields the more easily to extrinsic impressions, and is overpowered by the disordered motions of the animal spirits; and so the devil has greater advantage to affect the mind, by working on the imagination. And thus Satan, when he casts in those horrid suggestions into the minds of many melancholy persons, in which they have no hand themselves, does it by exciting imaginary ideas, either of some dreadful words or sentences, or other horrid outward ideas. And when he tempts other persons who are not melancholy, he does it by presenting to the imagination, in a lively and alluring manner, the objects of their lusts, or by exciting ideas of words, and so by them exciting thoughts; or by promoting an imagination of outward actions, events, circumstances, &c. Innumerable are the ways by which the mind might be led on to all kind of evil thoughts, by exciting external ideas in the imagination.

If persons keep no guard at these avenues of Satan, by which he has access to the soul to tempt and delude it, they will be likely to have enough of him. And especially, if instead of guarding against him, they lay themselves open to him, and seek and invite him, because he appears as an angel of light, and counterfeits the illuminations and graces of the Spirit of God, by inward whispers, and immediate suggestions of facts and events, pleasant voices, beautiful images, and other impressions on the imagination. There are many who are deluded by such things, are lifted up with them, and seek after them. They have a continued course of them, and can have them almost when they will; and especially when their pride and vain-glory has most occasion for them, to make a show of them before company. It is with them, something as it is with those who are professors of the art of telling where lost things are to be found, by impressions made on their imaginations; they laying themselves open to the devil, he is always at hand to give them the desired impression.

Before I finish what I would say on this head of imaginations, counterfeiting spiritual light, and affections arising from them, I would renewedly (to prevent misunderstanding of what has been said) desire it may be observed, that I am far from determining, that no affections are spiritual which are attended with imaginary ideas. Such is the nature of man, that he can scarcely think of any thing intensely, without some kind of outward ideas. They arise and interpose themselves unavoidably, in the course of a man's thoughts; though oftentimes they are very confused, and are not what the mind regards. When the mind is much engaged, and the thoughts intense, oftentimes the imagination is more strong, and the outward idea more lively, especially in persons of some constitutions of body. But there is a great difference between these two things, *viz. lively imaginations arising from strong affections*, and *strong affections arising from lively imaginations.* The former may be, and doubtless often is, in case of truly gracious affections. The affections do not arise from the imagination, nor have any dependence upon it; but on the contrary, the imagination is only the accidental effect, or consequent of the affection, through the infirmity of human nature. But when the latter is the case, as it often is, that the affection arises from the imagination, and is built upon it as its foundation, instead of a spiritual illumination or discovery, then is the affection, however elevated, worthless and vain. And this is the drift of what has been now said, of impressions on the imagination. Having observed this, I proceed to another mark of gracious affections.

SECT. V.

Truly gracious affections are attended with a conviction of the reality and certainty of divine things.

This seems to be implied in the text that was laid as the foundation of this discourse, *Whom having not seen, ye love; in whom though now ye see him not, yet* BELIEVING, *ye rejoice with joy unspeakable, and full of glory.* All gracious persons have a solid, full, thorough, and effectual conviction of the truth of the great things of the gospel. They no longer halt between two opinions; the great doctrines of the gospel cease to be any longer doubtful things, or matters of opinion, which, though probable, are yet disputable; but with them, they are points settled and determined, as undoubted and indisputable; so that they are not afraid to venture their all upon their truth. Their conviction is an *effectual* conviction; so that the great, spiritual, mysterious, and invisible things of the gospel, have the *influence* of real and certain things upon them; they have the *weight* and *power* of real things in their hearts; and accordingly rule in their affections, and govern them through the course of their lives. With respect to Christ's being the Son of God, and Saviour of the world,

* "The imagination is that room of the soul, wherein the devil doth often appear. Indeed (to speak exactly) the devil hath no efficient power over the rational part of a man: he cannot change the will, he cannot alter the heart of a man. So that the utmost he can do, in tempting a man to sin, is by suasion and suggestion only. But then how doth the devil do this? Even by working upon the imagination. He observeth the temper and bodily constitution of a man; and thereupon suggests to his fancy, and injects his fiery darts thereinto, by which the mind and will come to be wrought upon. The devil then, though he hath no imperious efficacy over thy will, yet because he can thus stir and move thy imagination, and thou being naturally destitute of grace, canst not withstand these suggestions; hence it is that any sin in thy imagination, though but in the outward works of the soul, yet doth quickly lay hold on all. And indeed, by this means do arise those horrible delusions, that are in many erroneous ways of religion: all is because their imaginations are corrupted. Yea, how often are these diabolical delusions of the imagination taken for the gracious operations of God's Spirit!—It is from hence that many have pretended to enthusiasms—they leave the Scriptures, and wholly attend to what they perceive and feel within them." Burgess *On Original Sin*, p. 369.

The great Turretine, speaking on that question, *What is the power of angels?* says, "As to bodies there is no doubt, but that they can do a great deal upon all sorts of elementary and sublunary bodies, to move them locally, and variously to agitate them. It is also certain, that they can act upon the external and internal senses, to excite them, or to bind them. But as to the rational soul itself, they can do nothing immediately upon that; for to God alone, who knows and searches the hearts, and who has them in his hands, does it also appertain to bow and move them whithersoever he will. But angels can act upon the rational soul, only mediately, by imaginations." *Theolog. Elench. Loc.* VII. *Quest.* 7.

and the great things he has revealed concerning himself, and his Father, and another world, they have not only a predominating opinion that these things are true, and so yield their assent, as they do in many other matters of doubtful speculation; but they *see that it is really so:* their eyes are opened, so that they see that really Jesus is the Christ, the Son of the living God. And as to the things which Christ has revealed, of God's eternal purposes and designs, concerning fallen man, and the glorious and everlasting things prepared for the saints in another world, they see that they are so indeed: and therefore these things are of great weight with them, and have a mighty power upon their hearts, and influence over their practice, in some measure answerable to their infinite importance.

That all true Christians have such a kind of conviction, is abundantly manifest from the Holy Scriptures. I will mention a few places out of many: Matt. xvi. 15—17. "But whom say ye that I am? Simon Peter answered and said, Thou art Christ, the Son of the living God. And Jesus answered and said unto him, Blessed art thou, Simon Barjona:—my Father which is in heaven hath revealed it unto thee." John vi. 68, 69. "Thou hast the words of eternal life. And we believe, and are sure that thou art that Christ, the Son of the living God." John xvii. 6—8. "I have manifested thy name unto the men which thou gavest me out of the world.—Now they have known that all things whatsoever thou hast given me, are of thee. For I have given unto them the words which thou gavest me; and they have received them, and have known surely that I came out from thee, and they have believed that thou didst send me." Acts viii. 37. "If thou believest with all thy heart thou mayest." 2 Cor. iv. 11—14. "We which live, are always delivered unto death for Jesus' sake.—Death worketh in us.—We having the spirit of faith, according as it is written, I believed and therefore have I spoken: we also believe, and therefore speak; knowing, that he which raised up the Lord Jesus, shall raise up us also by Jesus, and shall present us with you." Together with verse 16. "For which cause we faint not." And verse 18. "While we look not at the things which are seen," &c. And chap. v. 1. "For we know, that if our earthly house of this tabernacle were dissolved, we have a building of God."—And ver. 6—8. "Therefore we are always confident, knowing that whilst we are at home in the body, we are absent from the Lord: for we walk by faith, not by sight. We are confident, I say, and willing rather to be absent from the body, and present with the Lord. 2 Tim. i. 12. "For the which cause I also suffer these things; nevertheless I am not ashamed: for I know whom I have believed, and I am persuaded that he is able to keep that which I have committed unto him against that day." Heb. iii. 6. "Whose house are we, if we hold fast the confidence, and the rejoicing of the hope firm unto the end." Heb. xi. 1. "Now faith is the substance of things hoped for, and the evidence of things not seen:" together with that whole chapter. 1 John iv. 13—16. "Hereby know we that we dwell in him, and he in us, because he hath given us of his Spirit. And we have seen and do testify, that the Father sent the Son to be the Saviour of the world. Whosoever shall confess that Jesus is the Son of God, God dwelleth in him, and he in God. And we have known and believed the love that God hath to us." Chap. v. 4, 5. "For whatsoever is born of God, overcometh the world: and this is the victory that overcometh the world, even our faith. Who is he that overcometh the world, but he that believeth that Jesus is the Son of God?" Therefore truly gracious affections are attended with a conviction and persuasion of the truth of gospel declarations, and a sight of their evidence and reality.

There are many religious affections, which are not attended with such a conviction of the judgment. Many apprehensions and ideas which some call *divine discoveries*, are *affecting*, but not *convincing*. Though for a little while, they may seem to be more persuaded of the truth of religion, than they used to be, and may yield a forward assent, like many of Christ's hearers who believed for a while; yet they have no thorough and effectual conviction. There is no great abiding change in them in this respect, that whereas formerly they did not realize the great things of the gospel, now these things, with regard to reality and certainty, appear new to them, and they behold them quite in another view than they used to do. There are many persons who have been exceedingly raised with religious affections, and think they have been converted, but they do not seem any more convinced of the truth of the gospel, than they used to be; or at least, there is no remarkable alteration. They do not live under the influence and power of a realizing conviction of the infinite and eternal things which the gospel reveals; if they were, it would be impossible for them to live as they do. Because their affections are not attended with a thorough conviction of the mind, they are not at all to be depended on; however great a show and noise they make, it is like the blaze of tow, or crackling of thorns, or like the forward flourishing blade on stony ground, that has no root, nor deepness of earth, to maintain its life.

Some persons, under high affections and a confident persuasion of their good estate, have what they very ignorantly call *seeing the truth* of the word of God, but which is very far from it. They have some text of Scripture coming to their minds, in a sudden and extraordinary manner, immediately declaring unto them (as they suppose) that their sins are forgiven, or that God loves them, and will save them; and it may be have a chain of scriptures coming one after another, to the same purpose; and they are convinced that it is truth; *i. e.* they are confident that it is certainly so, that their sins are forgiven, and God does love them, &c.—they say they know it is so; and when the words of Scripture are suggested to them, and as they suppose immediately spoken to them by God, in this meaning, they are ready to cry out, *Truth, truth! it is certainly so! the word of God is true!* And this they call "seeing the truth of the word of God." Whereas the whole of their faith amounts to no more, than only a strong confidence of their own good estate, and so a confidence that those words are true, which they suppose tell them they are in a good estate: when indeed (as was shown before) there is no scripture which declares that any person is in a good estate directly, or any other way than by consequence. So that this, instead of being a real sight of the truth of the word of God, is a sight of nothing but a phantom, and is all over a delusion. Truly to see the truth of the word of God, is to see the truth of the gospel; which is the glorious doctrine the word of God contains, concerning God, Jesus Christ, the way of salvation by him, and the world of glory that he is entered into, and purchased for all them who believe; and not a revelation that such and such particular persons are true Christians, and shall go to heaven. Therefore those affections which arise from no other persuasion of the truth of the word of God than this, arise from delusion, and not true conviction; and consequently are themselves delusive and vain.

But suppose the religious affections of persons indeed arise from a strong *persuasion* of the truth of the christian religion; their affections are not the better, unless it be a *reasonable* persuasion or conviction. By a reasonable conviction, I mean a conviction founded on *real evidence*, or upon that which is a good reason, or just ground of conviction. Men may have a *strong* persuasion that the christian religion is true, when their persuasion is not at all built on evidence, but altogether on education, and the opinion of others; as many Mahometans are strongly persuaded of the truth of the Mahometan religion, because their fathers, and neighbours, and nation believe it. That belief of the truth of the christian religion, which is built on the very *same grounds* with that of Mahometans who believe in the Mahometan religion, is the same sort of belief. And though the thing believed happens to be better; yet that does not make the belief itself to be of a better sort, for though the thing believed happens to be true, yet the belief of it is not owing to this truth, but to education. So that as the conviction is no better than the Mahometans' conviction; so the affections that flow from it, are no better, in themselves, than the religious affections of Mahometans.

But suppose the belief of christian doctrines be not merely from education, but indeed from reasons and arguments, it will not from thence necessarily follow, that their affections are truly gracious: for in order to that, it is requisite, not only that the belief which their affections arise from, should be a *reasonable*, but also a *spiritual* belief, or conviction. I suppose none will doubt but that some natural men yield a kind of assent of their judgments to the truth of the christian religion, from the rational proofs or arguments that are offered to evince it. Judas, without doubt, thought Jesus to be the Messiah, from the things which he saw and heard; but yet all along was a devil. So in John ii. 23—25. we read of "many that believed in Christ's name, when they saw the miracles that he did;" whom yet Christ knew had not that within them, which was to be depended on. So Simon the sorcerer believed, when he beheld the miracles and signs which were done; but yet remained "in the gall of bitterness, and bond of iniquity," Acts viii. 13, 23. And if there is such a belief or assent of the judgment in some natural men, none can doubt but that religious affections may arise from that assent or belief; as we read of some who *believed for a while* that were greatly affected, and *anon with joy received the word*.

It is evident that there is a *spiritual* conviction of the truth, or a belief peculiar to those who are spiritual, who are regenerated, and who have the Spirit of God, in his holy communications, dwelling in them as a vital principle. So that their conviction does not only differ from that which natural men have, in that it is accompanied with good works; but the *belief itself* is diverse, the assent and conviction of the judgment is of a kind peculiar to those who are spiritual, and of which natural men are wholly destitute. This is evident by the Scripture, if any thing at all is so: John xvii. 8. "They have believed that thou didst send me." Tit. i. 1. "According to the faith of God's elect, and the acknowledging of the truth which is after godliness." John xvi. 27. "The Father himself loveth you, because ye have loved me, and have believed that I came out from God." 1 John iv. 15. "Whosoever shall confess that Jesus is the Son of God, God dwelleth in him, and he in God." Chap. v. 1. "Whosoever believeth that Jesus is the Christ, is born of God. Verse 10. He that believeth on the Son of God, hath the witness in himself."

What a *spiritual conviction* of the judgment is, we are naturally led to determine from what has been said already, under the former head of a *spiritual understanding*. The conviction of the judgment arises from the illumination of the understanding: the passing of a right judgment on things, depends on a right apprehension. And therefore it follows, that a *spiritual* conviction of the truth of the great things of the gospel, is such a conviction as arises from having a spiritual apprehension of those things in the mind. And this is also evident from the Scripture, which often represents a saving belief of the reality and divinity of the things proposed and exhibited to us in the gospel, as what proceeds from the Spirit of God enlightening the mind. Hence right apprehensions of the nature of those things; the Spirit as it were unveiling, or revealing them, and enabling the mind to view them as they are. Luke x. 21, 22. "I thank thee, O Father, Lord of heaven and earth, that thou hast *hid* these things from the wise and prudent, and hast *revealed* them unto babes: even so, Father, for so it seemed good in thy sight. All things are delivered unto me of my Father: and no man knoweth who the Son is, but the Father; and who the Father is, but the Son, and he to whom the Son will *reveal* him." John vi. 40. "And this is the will of him that sent me, that every one which *seeth* the Son, and *believeth* on him, may have everlasting life." Where it is plain, that true faith arises from a spiritual sight of Christ. And John xvii. 6—8. "I have *manifested* thy name unto the men which thou gavest me out of the world.—Now they have known that all things whatsoever thou hast given me, are of thee. For I have given unto them the words which thou gavest me; and they have received them, and have known surely that I came out from thee, and they have believed that thou didst send me." Christ's manifesting God's name to the disciples, or giving them a true apprehension of divine things, was that whereby they knew that Christ's doctrine was of God, and that Christ himself was sent by him. Matt. xvi. 16, 17. "Simon Peter said, Thou art Christ, the Son of the living God. And Jesus answered and said unto him, Blessed art thou Simon Barjona: for flesh and blood hath not *revealed* it unto thee, but my Father which is in heaven." 1 John v. 10. "He that believeth on the Son of God, hath the witness in himself." Gal. i. 14—16. "Being more exceedingly zealous of the traditions of my fathers. But when it pleased God, who separated me from my mother's womb, and called me by his grace, to *reveal* his Son in me, that I might preach him among the heathen; immediately I conferred not with flesh and blood."

If *that* is a spiritual conviction of the divinity and reality of the things exhibited in the gospel, which arises from a *spiritual understanding* of those things; I have shown already what that is. In short, it consists in a sense and taste of the divine, supreme, and holy excellency and beauty of those things. So that then is the mind *spiritually convinced* of the divinity and truth of the great things of the gospel, when that conviction arises, either directly or remotely, from such a sense or view of their divine excellency and glory as is there exhibited. This clearly follows from what has been already said; and for this the Scripture is very plain and express: 2 Cor. iv. 3—6. "But if our gospel be hid, it is hid to them that are lost: in whom the god of this world hath blinded the minds of them that *believe* not, lest the light of the *glorious gospel* of Christ, who is the image of God, should shine unto them. For we preach not ourselves, but Christ Jesus the Lord; and ourselves your servants for Jesus' sake. For God who commanded the light to shine out of darkness, hath shined in our hearts, to give the *light of the knowledge of the glory of God*, in the face of Jesus Christ." Together with the last verse of the foregoing chapter, which introduces this, "But we all with open face, beholding as in a glass the *glory of the Lord*, are changed into the same image, from glory to glory, even as by the Spirit of the Lord." Nothing can be more evident, than that a saving belief of the gospel is here spoken of by the apostle, as arising from the mind being enlightened to behold the divine glory of the things it exhibits. This view or sense of the divine glory, and unparalleled beauty of the things exhibited to us in the gospel, has a tendency to convince the mind of their divinity two ways; first, *directly*, and secondly, more *indirectly* and *remotely*.

I. A view of this divine glory *directly* convinces the mind of the divinity of these things, as this glory is in itself a direct, clear, and all-conquering evidence of it; especially when clearly discovered, or when this supernatural sense is given in a good degree.

He that has his judgment thus *directly* convinced and assured of the divinity of gospel truths by a clear view of their divine glory, has a *reasonable* conviction. His assurance is altogether agreeable to reason; because the divine glory and beauty of divine things is *in itself* a real evidence of their divinity, and the most direct and strong. He that truly sees the divine, transcendent, supreme glory of those things which are divine, does as it were know their divinity *intuitively;* he not only *argues*, but *sees* that they are divine. He sees that in them wherein divinity chiefly consists; for in this glory, which is so vastly and inexpressibly distinguished from the glory of artificial things, and all other glory, mainly consists the true notion of divinity. God is God, and distinguished from all other beings, and exalted above them, chiefly by his divine beauty, which is infinitely diverse from all other beauty. They therefore that see the stamp of this glory in divine things, they see divinity in them, they see God in them, and see them to be divine; because they see *that* in them wherein the truest idea of divinity consists. Thus a soul may have a kind of intuitive knowledge of the divinity of the things exhibited in the gospel; not that he judges the doctrines of the gospel to be from God, without any argument or deduction at all; but it is without any long chain of arguments; the argument is but one, and the evidence direct; the mind ascends to the truth of the gospel but by one step, and that is its divine glory.

It would be very strange, if any professing Christian should deny it to be possible, that there should be an excellency in divine things, which is so transcendent, and exceedingly different from what is in other things, that if it were seen, would evidently distinguish them. We cannot rationally doubt, but that things which are *divine*, that appertain to the supreme Being, are vastly different from things that are *human*. There is God-like, high, and glorious excellency in them, so distinguishing them from the things which are of men, that the difference is ineffable; and therefore such as if seen, will have a most convincing, satisfying influence upon any one, that they are *what they are, viz.* divine. Doubtless there is that glory and excellency in the Divine Being, by which he is so infinitely distinguished from all other beings, that if it were seen, he might be known by it. It would therefore be very unreasonable to deny, that it is possible for God to give manifestations of this distinguishing excellency, in things by which he is pleased to make himself known; and that this distinguishing excellency may be clearly seen in them. There are *natural* excellencies that are very evidently distinguishing of the subjects or authors, to any one who behold them. How vastly is the speech of an intelligent man different from that of a little child! And how greatly distinguished is the speech of some men of great genius, as Homer, Cicero, Milton, Locke, Addison, and others, from that of many other intelligent men! There are no limits to be set to the degrees of manifestation of mental excellency, that there may be in speech. But the appearances of the *natural* perfections of God, in the manifestations he makes of himself, may doubtless be unspeakably more evidently distinguishing, than the appearances of those excellencies of worms of the dust, in which they differ one from another. He that is well acquainted with mankind, and their works, by viewing the sun, may know it is no human work. And it is reasonable to suppose, that when Christ comes at the end of the world, in the glory of his Father, it will be with such ineffable appearances of divinity, as will leave no doubt to the inhabitants of the world, even the most obstinate infidels, that he who appears is a divine person. But above all, do the manifestations of the *moral* and *spiritual* glory of the Divine Being (which is the proper beauty of the divinity) bring their own evidence, and tend to assure the heart. Thus the disciples were assured that Jesus was the Son of God, for "they beheld his glory, as the glory of the only begotten of the Father, full of grace and truth," John i. 14. When Christ appeared in his transfiguration to his disciples, as an outward glory to their bodily eyes—which was a sweet and admirable symbol and semblance of his spiritual glory—together with his spiritual glory itself, manifested to their minds; the manifestation was such as did perfectly, and with good reason, *assure* them of his divinity; as appears by what one of them says concerning it, 2 Pet. i. 16—18. "For we have not followed cunningly devised fables, when we made known unto you the power and coming of our Lord Jesus Christ, but were eye-witnesses of his majesty: for he received from God the Father, honour and glory, when there came such a voice to him from the excellent glory, This is my beloved Son, in whom I am well pleased. And this voice which came from heaven we heard, when we were with him in the holy mount." The apostle calls that mount, *the holy mount*, because the manifestations of Christ there made to their minds, and with which they were especially impressed and ravished, was the glory of his *holiness*, or the beauty of his *moral excellency*: or, as another of these disciples, who saw it, expresses it, "His glory, as full of grace and truth."

Now this distinguishing glory of the Divine Being has its brightest manifestation in the things exhibited to us in the *gospel;* the doctrines there taught, the word there spoken, and the divine counsels, acts, and works there revealed. These things have the clearest, most admirable, and distinguishing representations and exhibitions of the glory of God's moral perfections, that ever were made to the world. And if there be such a distinguishing, evidential manifestation of divine glory in the gospel, it is reasonable to suppose that there may be such a thing as *seeing* it: what should hinder but that it *may* be seen? It is no argument that it *cannot* be seen, because some *do not* see it; though they may be discerning men in temporal matters. If there be such ineffable, distinguishing, evidential excellencies in the gospel, it is reasonable to suppose, that they are such as are not to be discerned, but by the special influence and enlightenings of the Spirit of God. There is need of uncommon force of mind to discern the distinguishing excellencies of the works of authors of great genius. Those things in Milton, which to mean judges appear tasteless and imperfections, are his inimitable excellencies in the eyes of those who are of greater discerning, and better taste. And if there be a book of which God is the author, it is most reasonable to suppose, that the distinguishing glories of his word are of such a kind, as that the sin and corruption of men's hearts—which above all things alienate them from the Deity, and make the heart dull and stupid to any sense or taste of those things wherein the moral glory of the divine perfections consists—would blind them from discerning the beauties of such a book; and that therefore they will not see them, but as God is pleased to enlighten them, and restore a holy taste, to discern and relish divine beauties.

This sense of the spiritual excellency and beauty of divine things, also tends *directly* to convince the mind of the truth of the gospel. Very many of the most important things declared in the gospel are hid from the eyes of natural men, the truth of which in effect consists in this excellency, or so immediately depends upon it, and results from it, that in this excellency being *seen*, the *truth* of those things is seen. As soon as ever the eyes are opened to behold a holy beauty and amiableness in divine things, a multitude of most important doctrines of the gospel that depend upon it, (which all appear strange and dark to natural men,) are at once seen to be true. As for instance, hereby appears the truth of what the word of God declares concerning the exceeding *evil of sin;* for the same eye that discerns the transcendent beauty of holiness, necessarily therein sees the exceeding odiousness of sin: the same taste which relishes the sweetness of true moral good, tastes the bitterness of moral evil. And by this means a man sees his *own sinfulness* and loathsomeness; for he has now a sense to discern objects of this nature; and so sees the truth of what the word of God declares concerning the exceeding sinfulness of mankind, which before he did not see. He now sees the dreadful pollution of his heart, and the desperate depravity of his nature, in a new manner; for his soul has now a sense given it to feel the pain of such a disease. This shows him the truth of what the Scripture reveals concerning the corruption of man's nature, his *original sin*, his ruinous condition, his *need* of a Saviour, and of the mighty *power of God* to renew his heart, and change his nature. Men by seeing the true excellency of holiness, see the glory of all those things which both reason and Scripture show to be in the *Divine Being;* for it has been shown, that the glory of them depends on this. And hereby they see the truth of all that the Scripture declares concerning God's glorious excellency and majesty, his being the fountain of all good, the only happiness of the creature, &c. This again shows the mind the truth of what the Scripture teaches concerning the evil of sin against so glorious a God; also the truth of what it teaches concerning *sin's just desert* of that dreadful punishment which it reveals; and concerning the impossibility of our offering any satisfaction, or sufficient atonement for that which is so infinitely evil and heinous. And this again shows the truth of what the Scripture reveals concerning the necessity of a Saviour, to offer an atonement of infinite value for sin. This sense of spiritual beauty enables the soul to see the glory of those things which the gospel reveals concerning the *person of Christ;* and so enables to see the exceeding beauty and dignity of his person, appearing in what the gospel exhibits of his word, works, acts, and life; and this apprehension of the superlative dignity of his person, shows the truth of what the gospel declares concerning the value of his *blood and righteousness;* the infinite excellency of that offering he has made to God for us, its sufficiency to atone for our sins, and recommend us to God. And thus the Spirit of God discovers the *way of salvation* by Christ; the soul sees the fitness and suitableness of this way, the admirable wisdom of the contrivance, and the perfect answerableness to our necessities of the provision that the gospel exhibits. A sense of true divine beauty being given, the soul discerns the beauty of every part of the gospel-scheme. This also shows the soul the truth of what the word of God declares concerning man's *chief happiness*, as consisting in holy exercises and enjoyments, and the unspeakable glory of the heavenly state. What the prophecies of the Old Testament and the writings of the apostles declare concerning the glory of the Messiah's kingdom, is now all plain; and also what the Scripture teaches concerning the reasons and grounds of our duty. The truth of all these things revealed in the Scripture, and many more that might be mentioned, appear to the soul, only by that spiritual taste of divine beauty, which has been spoken of; they being hidden things before.

And besides all this, the truth of all those things which the Scripture says about *experimental religion*, is hereby known; for they are now experienced. And this convinces the soul, that one who knew the heart of man, better than we know our own hearts, and perfectly knew the nature of virtue and holiness, was the author of the Scriptures. And the opening to view, with such clearness, such a world of wonderful and glorious truth in the gospel, that before was unknown, being quite above the view of a natural eye, but now appearing so clear and bright, has a powerful and invincible influence on the soul, to persuade it of the divinity of the gospel.

Unless men may come to a reasonable solid persuasion and conviction of the truth of the gospel, by internal evidences in the way that has been spoken, viz. by a sight of its glory; it is impossible that those who are illiterate, and unacquainted with history, should have any thorough and effectual conviction of it at all. They may without this see a great deal of probability of it; it may be reasonable for them to give much credit to what learned men and historians tell them; and they may tell them so much, that it may look very probable and rational to them, that the Christian religion is true; and so much that they would be very unreasonable not to entertain this opinion. But to have a conviction, so clear, and evident, and assuring, as to be sufficient to induce them, with boldness to sell all, confidently and fearlessly to run the venture of the loss of all things, and of enduring the most exquisite and long continued torments, and to trample the world under foot, and count all things but dung for Christ; the evidence they can have from history, cannot be sufficient. It is impossible that men, who have not something of a general view of the historical world, or the series of history from age to age, should come at the force of arguments for the truth of Christianity, drawn from history, to that degree, as effectually to induce them to venture their all upon it. After all that learned men have said to them, there will remain innumerable doubts on their minds; they will be ready, when pinched with some great trial of their faith, to say, "How do I know this, or that? How do I know when these histories were written? Learned men tell me these histories were so and so attested in their day; but how do I know that there were such attestations then? They tell me there is equal reason to believe these facts, as any whatsoever that are related at such a distance; but how do I know that other facts which are related of those ages, ever were?" Those who have not something of a general view of the series of historical events, and of the state of mankind from age to age, cannot see the clear evidence from history of the truth of facts in distant ages; but there will remain endless doubts and scruples.

But the gospel was not given only for learned men. There are at least nineteen in twenty, if not ninety-nine in a hundred, of those for whom the Scriptures were written, who are not capable of any certain or effectual conviction of the divine authority of the Scriptures, by such arguments as learned men use. If men who have been brought up in heathenism, must wait for a clear and certain conviction of the truth of Christianity, until they have learning and acquaintance with the histories of politer nations, enough to see clearly the force of such kind of arguments; it will make the evidence of the gospel, to them, immensely cumbersome, and will render the propagation of the gospel among them infinitely difficult. Miserable is the condition of the Houssatunnuck Indians and others, who have lately manifested a desire to be instructed in Christianity, if they can come at no evidence of the truth of Christianity, sufficient to induce them to sell all for Christ, in any other way but this.

It is unreasonable to suppose, that God has provided for his people, no more than *probable* evidences of the truth of the gospel. He has with great care abundantly provided, and given them the most convincing, assuring, satisfying, and manifold evidence of his faithfulness in the covenant of grace; and as David says, *made a covenant, ordered in all things and sure*. Therefore it is rational to suppose, that at the same time, he would not fail of ordering the matter so, that there should not be wanting as great and clear evidence, *that this is his covenant*, and that these promises are his promises; or, which is the same thing, that the christian religion is true, and that the gospel is his word. Otherwise in vain are those great assurances he has given of his faithfulness in his covenant, by confirming it with his oath, and so variously establishing it by seals and pledges. For the evidence that it is his covenant, is properly the foundation on which all the force and effect of those other assurances do stand. We may therefore undoubtedly suppose and conclude, that there is some sort of evidence which God has given, that this covenant and these promises are his, beyond all mere probability; that there are some grounds of *assurance* of it held forth, which, if we are not blind to them, tend to give a higher persuasion, than any arguing from history, human tradition, &c. which the illiterate, and unacquainted with history, are capable of; yea, that which is good ground of the highest and most perfect assurance, that mankind have in any case whatsoever; agreeable to those high expressions which the apostle uses, Heb. x. 22. "Let us draw near in *full assurance of faith*." And Col. ii. 2. "That their hearts might be comforted, being knit together in love, and unto *all riches of the full assurance of understanding*, to the acknowledgment of the mystery of God, and of the Father, and of Christ." It is reasonable to suppose, that God would give the greatest evidence of those things which are greatest, and the truth of which is of greatest importance to us: and that we therefore, if we are wise, and act rationally, shall have the greatest desire of having full, undoubting, and perfect assurance thereof. But it is certain, that such an assurance is not to be attained by the greater part of them who live under the gospel, by arguments fetched from ancient traditions, histories, and monuments.

And if we come to fact and experience, there is not the least reason to suppose, that one in a hundred of those who have been sincere Christians, and have had a heart to sell all for Christ, have come by their conviction of the truth of the gospel this way. If we read over the histories of the many thousands that died martyrs for Christ, since the beginning of the reformation, and have cheerfully undergone extreme tortures, in a confidence of the truth of the gospel, and consider their circumstances and advantages; how few of them were there, that we can reasonably suppose ever came by their assured persuasion this way; or indeed for whom it was possible, reasonably to receive so full and strong an assurance, from such arguments! Many of them were weak women and children, and the greater part of them illiterate persons; many of whom had been brought up in popish ignorance and darkness, were but newly come out of it, and lived and died in times, wherein those arguments for the truth of Christianity from antiquity and history, had been but very imperfectly handled. And indeed, it is but very lately that these arguments have been set in a clear and convincing light, even by learned men themselves: and since it has been done, there never were fewer thorough believers, among those who have been educated in the true religion; infidelity never prevailed so much, in any age, as in this, wherein these arguments are handled to the greatest advantage.

The true martyrs of Jesus Christ, are not those who have only been strong in *opinion* that the gospel of Christ is true, but *those that have seen the truth of it;* as the very name of martyrs or witnesses (by which they are called in Scripture) implies. Those are very improperly called witnesses of the truth of any thing, who only declare they are very much of opinion that such a thing is true. Those only are proper witnesses, who can and do testify that they have seen the truth of the thing they assert; John iii. 11. "We speak that we do know, and *testify* that we have seen." John i. 34. "And I *saw*, and *bare record*, that this is the Son of God." 1 John iv. 14. "And we have *seen* and do *testify*, that the Father sent the Son to be the Saviour of the world." Acts xxii. 14, 15. "The God of our fathers hath chosen thee, that thou shouldst *know* his will, and *see* that just One, and shouldst *hear* the voice of his mouth: for thou shalt be his *witness* unto all men, of what thou hast *seen* and *heard*." But the true martyrs of Jesus Christ are called his witnesses: and all the saints, who by their holy practice under great trials declare that faith *which is the* SUBSTANCE *of things hoped for, and the* EVIDENCE *of things not seen*, are called witnesses, (Heb. xi. 1. and xii. 1.) By their profession and practice they declare their assurance of the truth and divinity of the gospel, having had the eyes of their minds enlightened to see divinity in the gospel, or to behold that unparalleled, ineffably excellent, and truly divine glory shining in it, which is altogether distinguishing, evidential, and convincing: so that they may truly be said to have seen God in it, to have seen that it is indeed divine; and so can speak in the style of witnesses. They can not only say, that *they think* the gospel is divine, but that *it is divine*, giving it in as their testimony, because they have seen it to be so. Doubtless Peter, James, and John, after they had seen that excellent glory of Christ in the mount, would have been ready, when they came down, to speak in the language of witnesses, and to say positively that *Jesus is the Son of God;* as Peter says, *they were eye-witnesses*, 2 Pet. i. 16. And so all nations will be ready positively to say this, when they shall behold his glory at the day of judgment; though that will be universally seen, will be only his natural glory, and not his moral and spiritual glory, which is much more distinguishing.

But yet, it must be noted, that among those who have a spiritual sight of the divine glory of the gospel; there is a great variety in degrees of strength of faith, as there is a vast variety of the degrees of clearness of views of this glory: but there is no true and saving faith, or spiritual conviction of the judgment, of the truth of the gospel, that has nothing in it, of this manifestation of its internal evidence, in some degree. The gospel of the blessed God does not go abroad a begging for its evidence, so much as some think: it has its highest and most proper evidence in itself. Though great use may be made of external arguments, they are not to be neglected, but highly prized and valued; for they may be greatly serviceable to awaken unbelievers, and bring them to serious consideration, and to confirm the faith of true saints; yea, they may be in some respects subservient *to the begetting* of a saving faith in men. Though what was said before remains true, that there is no spiritual conviction of the judgment, but what arises from an apprehension of the spiritual beauty and glory of divine things: for, as has been observed, this apprehension or view has a tendency to convince the mind of the truth of the gospel, two ways; either directly or indirectly.—Having therefore already observed how it does this directly, I proceed now,

II. To observe how a view of this divine glory convinces the mind of the truth of Christianity, more *indirectly*.

First, It doth so, as the *prejudices* of the heart against the truth of divine things are hereby removed, so that the mind thereby lies open to the force of the reasons which are offered. The mind of man is naturally full of enmity against the doctrines of the gospel; which is a disadvantage to those arguments that prove their truth, and causes them to lose their force upon the mind: but when a person has discovered to him the divine excellency of christian doctrines, this destroys that enmity, and removes the prejudices, and sanctifies the reason, and causes it to be open and free. Hence is a vast difference, as to the force that arguments have to convince the mind. Hence was the very different effect which Christ's miracles had to convince the disciples from what they had to convince the scribes and Pharisees: not that they had a stronger reason, or had their reason more improved; but their reason was sanctified, and those blinding prejudices, which the scribes and Pharisees were under, were removed, by the sense they had of the excellency of Christ and his doctrine.

Secondly, It not only removes the hinderances of reason, but positively *helps* reason. It makes even the speculative notions more lively. It assists and engages the attention of the mind to that kind of objects; which causes it to have a clearer view of them, and more clearly to see their mutual relations. The ideas themselves, which otherwise are dim and obscure, by this means have light cast upon them, and are impressed with greater strength, so that the mind can better judge of them; as he that beholds the objects on the face of the earth, when the light of the sun is cast upon them, is under greater advantage to discern them in their true forms and mutual relations, and to see the evidences of divine wisdom and skill in their contrivance, than he that sees them in a dim star-light, or twilight.

What has been said, may serve in some measure to show the nature of a spiritual conviction of the truth and reality of divine things; and so to distinguish truly gracious affections from others; for gracious affections are evermore attended with such a conviction of the judgment. But before I dismiss this head, it will be needful to observe the ways whereby some are deceived, with respect to this matter; and take notice of several things that are sometimes taken for a spiritual and saving belief of the truth, which are indeed very diverse from it.

1. There is a degree of conviction of the truth of the great things of religion, that arises from the common enlightenings of the Spirit of God. The more lively and sensible apprehension of the things of religion, with respect to what is *natural* in them—such as natural men have who are under awakenings and common illuminations—will give some degree of conviction of the truth, beyond what they had before they were thus enlightened. For hereby they see the manifestations made in the Holy Scriptures, of the natural perfections of God; such as his greatness, power, and awful majesty; which tends to convince the mind, that this is the word of a great and terrible God. From the tokens there are of God's greatness and majesty in his word and works, of which they have a great sense, from the common influence of the Spirit of God, they may have a much greater conviction that these are indeed the word and works of a very great invisible Being. And the lively apprehension of the greatness of God, which natural men may have, tends to make them sensible of the great guilt, which sin against such a God brings, and the dreadfulness of his wrath for sin. And this tends to cause them more easily and fully to believe the revelation the Scripture makes of another world, and of the extreme misery it threatens, there to be inflicted on sinners. And so from that sense of the great natural good there is in the things of religion, which is sometimes given in common illuminations, men may be the more induced to believe the truth of religion. These things persons may have, and yet have no sense of the beauty and amiableness of the moral and holy excellency of religion; and therefore no spiritual conviction of their truth. But yet such convictions are sometimes mistaken for saving convictions, and the affections flowing from them, for saving affections.

2. The extraordinary impressions which are made on the imaginations of some persons, in visions, and immediate strong impulses and suggestions, as though they saw sights, and had words spoken to them, may, and often do beget a strong persuasion of the truth of invisible things. Though the general tendency of such things, in their final issue, is to draw men off from the word of God, and to cause them to reject the gospel, and to establish unbelief and atheism; yet for the present, they may, and often do beget a confident persuasion of the truth of some things that are revealed in the Scriptures; however their confidence is founded in delusion, and so nothing worth. As for instance, if a person has by some invisible agent, immediately and strongly impressed on his imagination, the appearance of a bright light, and glorious form of a person seated on a throne, with great external majesty and beauty, uttering some remarkable words, with great force and energy; the person who is the subject of such an operation, may be from hence confident, that there are invisible agents, spiritual beings, from what he has experienced, knowing that he had no hand himself in this extraordinary effect, which he has experienced. He may also be confident, that this is Christ whom he saw and heard speaking; and this may make him confident that there is a Christ, and that Christ reigns on a throne in heaven, as he saw him; and may be confident that the words which he heard him

speak are true, &c. in the same manner as the lying miracles of the papists, may for the present beget in the minds of the ignorant, deluded people, a strong persuasion of the truth of many things declared in the New Testament. Thus when the images of Christ, in popish churches, are on some extraordinary occasions, made by priestcraft to appear to the people as if they wept, and shed fresh blood, and moved, and uttered such and such words; the people may be verily persuaded that it is a miracle wrought by Christ himself; and from thence may be confident there is a Christ, and that what they are told of his death and sufferings, resurrection and ascension, and present government of the world, is true; for they may look upon this miracle, as a certain evidence of all these things, and a kind of ocular demonstration of them. This may be the influence of these lying wonders for the present; though the general tendency of them is not to convince that Jesus Christ is come in the flesh, but finally to promote atheism. Even the intercourse which Satan has with witches, and their often experiencing his immediate power, has a tendency to convince them of the truth of some of the doctrines of religion; as particularly the reality of an invisible world, or world of spirits, contrary to the doctrine of the Sadducees. The general tendency of Satan's influences is delusion; but yet he may mix some truth with his lies, that his lies may not be so easily discovered.

Multitudes are deluded with a counterfeit faith, from impressions on their imagination, in the manner now mentioned. They say they know that there is a God, for they have seen him; they know that Christ is the Son of God, for they have seen him in his glory; they know that Christ died for sinners, for they have seen him hanging on the cross, and his blood running from his wounds; they know there is a heaven and hell, for they have seen the misery of the damned souls in hell, and the glory of saints and angels in heaven; (meaning some external representations, strongly impressed on their imagination;) they know that the Scriptures are the word of God, and that such and such promises in particular are his word, for they have heard him speak them to *them*, they came to their minds suddenly and immediately from God, without their having any hand in it.

3. Persons may seem to have their belief of the truth greatly increased, when the foundation of it is only a persuasion of their interest in them. They first, by some means or other, take up a confidence, that if there be a Christ and a heaven, they are *theirs;* and this prejudices them more in favour of their truth. When they hear of the great and glorious things of religion, it is with this notion, that all these things belong to them; and hence easily become confident that they are true; they look upon it to be greatly for their interest that they should be true. It is very obvious what a strong influence men's interest and inclinations have on their judgments. While a natural man thinks, that if there be a heaven and a hell, the latter and not the former belongs to him; then he will be hardly persuaded that there is a heaven or hell. But when he comes to be persuaded, that hell belongs only to others and not to him; then he can easily allow the reality of hell, and exclaim against the senselessness and sottishness of others in neglecting means of escape from it: and being confident that he is a child of God, and that God has promised heaven to him, he may seem strong in the faith of its reality, and may have a great zeal against that infidelity which denies it. But I proceed to another distinguishing sign of gracious affections.

SECT. VI.

Gracious affections are attended with evangelical humiliation.

Evangelical humiliation is a sense that a Christian has of his own utter insufficiency, despicableness, and odiousness, with an answerable frame of heart. There is a distinction to be made between a *legal* and *evangelical* humiliation. The former is what men may have while in a state of nature, and have no gracious affection; the latter is peculiar to true saints. The former is from the common influence of the Spirit of God, assisting natural principles, and especially natural conscience; the latter is from the special influences of the Spirit of God, implanting and exercising supernatural and divine principles. The former is from the mind being assisted to a greater sense of religious things, as to their natural properties and qualities, and particularly of the natural perfections of God, such as his greatness, terrible majesty, &c.—which were manifested to the congregation of Israel, in giving the law at mount Sinai—the latter is from a sense of the transcendent beauty of divine things in their moral qualities. In the former, a sense of the awful greatness and natural perfections of God, and of the strictness of his law, convinces men that they are exceeding sinful and guilty, and exposed to the wrath of God, as it will convince wicked men and devils at the day of judgment; but they do not see their own *odiousness* on account of sin; they do not see the hateful nature of sin; a sense of this is given in *evangelical humiliation*, by a discovery of the beauty of God's holiness and moral perfection. In a *legal humiliation* men are made sensible that they are nothing before the great and terrible God, and that they are undone, and wholly insufficient to help themselves; as wicked men will be at the day of judgment: but they have not *an answerable frame of heart*, consisting in a disposition to abase themselves, and exalt God alone. This disposition is given only in *evangelical* humiliation, by overcoming the heart, and changing its inclination, by a discovery of God's holy beauty. In a legal humiliation, the conscience is convinced; as the consciences of all will be most perfectly at the day of judgment; but because there is no spiritual understanding, the will is not bowed, nor the inclination altered. In legal humiliation, men are brought to despair of helping themselves; in evangelical, they are brought voluntarily to deny and renounce themselves: in the former, they are subdued and forced to the ground; in the latter, they are brought sweetly to yield, and freely and with delight to prostrate themselves at the feet of God.

Legal humiliation has in it no spiritual good, nothing of the nature of true virtue; whereas evangelical humiliation is that wherein the excellent beauty of christian grace does very much consist. Legal humiliation is useful, as a means in order to evangelical; as a common knowledge of the things of religion is a means requisite in order to spiritual knowledge. Men may be legally humbled and have no *humility;* as the wicked at the day of judgment will be thoroughly convinced that they have no righteousness, but are altogether sinful, exceeding guilty, and justly exposed to eternal damnation—and be fully sensible of their own helplessness—without the least mortification of the pride of their hearts. But the essence of evangelical humiliation consists in such *humility* as becomes a creature in itself exceeding sinful, under a dispensation of grace; consisting in a mean esteem of himself, as in himself nothing, and altogether contemptible and odious; attended with a mortification of a disposition to exalt himself, and a free renunciation of his own glory.

This is a great and most essential thing in true religion. The whole frame of the gospel, every thing appertaining to the new covenant, and all God's dispensations towards fallen man, are calculated to bring to pass this effect. They that are destitute of this, have no true religion, whatever profession they may make, and how high soever their religious affections may be; Hab. ii. 4. "Behold, his soul which is lifted up, is not upright in him; but the just shall live by his faith;" *i.e.* he shall live by his faith on God's righteousness and grace, and not his own goodness and excellency. God has abundantly manifested in his word, that this is what he has a peculiar respect to in his saints, and that nothing is acceptable to him without it; Ps. xxxiv. 18. "The Lord is nigh unto them that are of a broken heart, and saveth such as be of a contrite spirit." Ps. li. 17. "The sacrifices of God are a broken spirit: a broken and a contrite heart, O God, thou wilt not despise." Ps. cxxxviii. 6. "Though the Lord be high, yet hath he respect unto the lowly." Prov. iii. 34. "He giveth grace unto the lowly." Isa. lvii. 15. "Thus saith the high and lofty One who inhabiteth eternity, whose name is Holy, I dwell in the high and holy place; with him also that is of a contrite and humble spirit, to revive the spirit of the humble, and to revive the heart of the contrite ones." Isa. lxvi. 1, 2. "Thus saith the Lord, The heaven is my throne, and the earth is my footstool:—but to this man will I look, even to him that is poor and of a contrite spirit, and trembleth at my word." Micah vi. 8. "He hath showed thee, O man, what is good; and what doth the Lord thy God require of thee, but to do justly, and to love mercy, and to walk humbly with thy God?" Matt. v. 3. "Blessed are the poor in spirit: for theirs is the kingdom of God." Matt. xviii. 3, 4. "Verily I say unto you, Except ye be converted, and become as little children, ye shall not enter into the kingdom of heaven. Whosoever therefore shall humble himself as this little child, the same is greatest in the kingdom of heaven." Mark x. 15. "Verily I say unto you, Whosoever shall not receive the kingdom of God as a little child, he shall not enter therein." The centurion (Luke vii.) acknowledged that *he was not worthy that Christ should enter under his roof*, and that *he was not worthy to come to him*. See the manner of a sinner coming to Christ, Luke vii. 37, &c. "And behold, a woman in the city, which was a sinner, when she knew that Jesus sat at meat in the Pharisee's house, brought an alabaster box of ointment, and stood at his feet behind him weeping, and began to wash his feet with tears, and did wipe them with the hairs of her head." She did not think the hair of her head, which is the natural crown and glory of a woman, (1 Cor. xi. 15.) too good to wipe the feet of Christ. Jesus most graciously accepted her, and says, "Thy faith hath saved thee, go in peace." The woman of Canaan submitted to Christ, in his saying, "It is not meet to take the children's bread, and to cast it to the dogs," and did as it were own that she was worthy to be called a dog; whereupon Christ says unto her, "O woman, great is thy faith: be it unto thee, even as thou wilt," Matt. xv. 26—28. The prodigal son said, "I will arise, and go to my father, and I will say unto him, Father, I have sinned against heaven, and before thee, and am no more worthy to be called thy son: make me as one of thy hired servants," Luke xv. 18, &c. See also Luke xviii. 9, &c. "And he spake this parable unto certain which trusted in themselves that they were righteous, and despised others, &c.—The publican standing afar off, would not so much as lift up his eyes to heaven, but smote upon his breast, saying, God be merciful to me a sinner. I tell you, this man went down to his house justified rather than the other: for every one that exalteth himself shall be abased: and he that humbleth himself, shall be exalted." Matt. xxviii. 9. "And they came, and held him by the feet, and worshipped him." Col. iii. 12. "Put ye on, as the elect of God,—humbleness of mind." Ezek. xx. 41, 43. "I will accept you with your sweet savour, when I bring you out from the people, &c.—And there shall ye remember your ways, and all your doings, wherein ye have been defiled, and ye shall loathe yourselves in your own sight, for all your evils that ye have committed." Chap. xxxvi. 26, 27, 31. "A new heart also will I give unto you,—and I will put my Spirit within you, and cause you to walk in my statutes, &c.—Then shall ye remember your own evil ways, and your doings that were not good, and shall loathe yourselves in your own sight, for your iniquities, and for your abominations." Chap. xvi. 63. "That thou mayst remember and be confounded, and never open thy mouth any more because of thy shame, when I am pacified toward thee for all that thou hast done, saith the Lord." Job xlii. 6. "I abhor myself, and repent in dust and ashes."

As we would therefore make the Holy Scriptures our rule, in judging of the nature of true religion, and judging of our own religious qualifications and state; it concerns us greatly to look at this humiliation, as one of the most essential things pertaining to true Christianity.* This is the principal part of the great christian duty of *self-denial*. That duty consists in two things, *viz. first*, In a man's denying his worldly inclinations, and in forsaking and renouncing all worldly objects and enjoyments; and, *secondly*, In denying his natural self-exaltation, and renouncing his own dignity and glory, and in being emptied of himself; so that he does freely, and from his very heart, as it were renounce, and annihilate himself. Thus the Christian doth in evangelical humiliation. The *latter* is the greatest and most difficult part of self-denial: although they always go together, and one never truly is, where the other is not; yet natural men can come much nearer to the *former* than the latter. Many Anchorites and Recluses have abandoned (though without any true mortification) the wealth, and pleasures, and common enjoyments of the world, who were far from renouncing their own dignity and righteousness. They never denied themselves for Christ, but only sold one lust to feed another, sold a beastly lust to pamper a devilish one; and so were never the better, but their latter end was worse than their beginning. They turned out one black devil to let in seven white ones worse than the first, though of a fairer countenance. It is inexpressible, and almost inconceivable, how strong a self-righteous, self-exalting disposition is naturally in man. What will he not do and suffer, to feed and gratify it? What lengths have been gone in a seeming self-denial in other respects, by Essenes and Pharisees, among the Jews; by papists, many sects of heretics, and enthusiasts, among professing Christians; by many Mahometans; by Pythagorean philosophers, and others, among the heathen; and all to do sacrifice to this Moloch of spiritual pride or self-righteousness; and that they may have something wherein to exalt themselves before God, and above their fellow-creatures?

Real humiliation is what all the most glorious hypocrites, who make the most splendid show of mortification to the world, and high religious affection, grossly fail in. Were it not that this is so much insisted on in Scripture, as a most essential thing in true grace; one would be tempted to think that many of the heathen philosophers were truly gracious, in whom was so bright an appearance of many virtues, and also great illuminations, and inward fervours and elevations of mind, as though they were truly the subjects of divine illapses and heavenly communications.† It is true, that many hypocrites make great pretences to humility, as well as other graces; and very often there is nothing whatsoever of which they make a higher profession. They endeavour to make a great show of humility in speech and behaviour; but they commonly make bungling work of it, though glorious work in their own eyes. They cannot find out what a humble speech and behaviour is, or how to speak and act so that there may indeed be a savour of christian humility in what they say and do: that sweet humble air and mien is beyond their art, being not *led by the Spirit*, or naturally guided to a behaviour becoming holy humility, by the vigour of a lowly spirit within them. And therefore they have no other way, many of them, but to be much in declaring that they are humble, and telling how they were humbled to the dust at such and such times, and abounding in very bad expressions about themselves; such as, *I am the least of all saints, I am a poor vile creature, I am not worthy of the least mercy, or that God should look upon me! Oh, I have a dreadful wicked heart! my heart is worse than the devil!*

* Calvin, in his Institutions, Book II. chap. 2. § 11. says, "I was always exceedingly pleased with that saying of Chrysostom, 'The foundation of our philosophy is humility;' and yet more pleased with that of Augustine, 'As,' says he, 'the rhetorician being asked, what was the first thing in the rules of eloquence, he answered, Pronunciation: what was the second, pronunciation; what was the third, still he answered, pronunciation. So if you should ask me concerning the precepts of the christian religion, I would answer, firstly, secondly, and thirdly, and for ever, Humility.'"

† "Albeit the Pythagoreans were thus famous for Judaic mysterious wisdom, and many moral as well as natural accomplishments; yet were they not exempted from boasting and pride; which was indeed a vice most epidemic, and as it were congenial, among all the philosophers; but in a more particular manner, among the Pythagoreans. So Hornius Hist. Philosoph. L. 3. chap. II. *The manners of the Pythagoreans were not free from boasting. They were all* ΠΕΡΙΑΥΤΟΛΟΓΟΙ, *such as abounded in the sense and commendation of their own excellencies, and boasting even almost to the degree of immodesty and impudence, as great* Heinsius *ad Horat. has rightly observed.* Thus indeed does proud nature delight to walk in the sparks of its own fire. And although many of these old philosophers could, by the strength of their own lights and heats, together with some common elevations and raisures of spirit, (peradventure from a more than ordinary, though not special and saving, assistance of the Spirit.) abandon many grosser vices; yet they were all deeply immersed in that miserable cursed abyss of spiritual pride: so that all their natural, and moral, and philosophic attainments, did feed, nourish, strengthen, and render most inveterate, this hell-bred pest of their hearts. Yea, those of them that seemed most modest, as the Academics, who professed they knew nothing, and the Cynics, who greatly decried, both in words and habits, the pride of others, yet even they abounded in the most notorious and visible pride. So connatural and morally essential to corrupt nature, is this envenomed root, fountain, and plague of spiritual pride; especially where there is any natural, moral, or philosophic excellence to feed the same. Whence Austin rightly judged all these philosophic virtues to be but splendid sins." Gales's *Court of the Gentiles*, Part II. B. ii. chap. x. § 17.

Oh, this cursed heart of mine, &c. Such expressions are very often used, not with a heart broken, not with spiritual mourning, not with the tears of her that washed Jesus's feet with her tears, not as *remembering and being confounded, and never opening their mouth more because of their shame, when God is pacified*, (Ezek. xvi. 63.) but with a light air, with smiles in the countenance, or with a pharisaical affectation. We must believe that they are thus humble, and see themselves so vile, upon the credit of their *say so;* for nothing appears in them of any savour of humility, in the manner of their deportment and deeds. There are many full of expressions of their own vileness, who yet expect to be looked upon as eminent and bright saints by others, as their due; and it is dangerous for any, so much as to hint the contrary, or to carry it towards them any otherwise, than as if we looked upon them some of the chief of Christians. Many are much in exclaiming against their wicked hearts, their great short-comings, and unprofitableness, and in speaking as though they looked on themselves as the meanest of the saints; who yet, if a minister should seriously tell them the same things in private, and should signify, that he feared they were very low and weak Christians—and thought they had reason solemnly to consider of their great barrenness and unprofitableness, and falling so much short of many others—it would be more than they could digest; they would think themselves highly injured; and there would be danger of a rooted prejudice in them against such a minister.

Some are abundant in talking against *legal doctrines, legal preaching*, and a *legal spirit*, who do but little understand the thing they talk against. A *legal spirit* is a more subtle thing than they imagine, it is too subtle for them. It lurks, and operates, and prevails in their hearts, and they are most notoriously guilty of it, at the same time, when they are inveighing against it. So far as a man is not emptied of himself, and of his own righteousness and goodness, in whatever form or shape, so far he is of a *legal spirit*. A spirit of pride of a man's own righteousness, morality, holiness, affection, experience, faith, humiliation, or any goodness whatsoever, is a legal spirit. It was no pride in Adam before the fall, to be of a legal spirit; because of his circumstances, he might seek acceptance by his own righteousness. But a legal spirit in a fallen sinful creature, can be nothing but spiritual pride; and reciprocally, a spiritually proud spirit is a legal spirit. There is no man living lifted up with a conceit of his own experiences and discoveries, and upon the account of them glisters in his own eyes, but what trusts in his experiences, and makes a righteousness of them. However he may use humble terms, and speak of his experiences as of the *great things God has done for him*, and it may be calls upon others to glorify God for them; yet he that is proud of his experiences, arrogates something to himself, as though his experiences were some dignity of his. And if he looks on them as his own dignity, he necessarily thinks that God looks on them so too; for he necessarily thinks his own opinion of them to be true; and consequently judges that God looks on them as he does; and so unavoidably imagines that God looks on his experiences as a dignity in him, as he looks on them himself; and that he glisters as much in God's eyes, as he does in his own. And thus he trusts in what is inherent in him, to make him shine in God's sight, and recommend him to God With this encouragement he goes before God in prayer; this makes him to expect much; to think that Christ loves him, and that he is willing to clothe him with his righteousness; because he supposes that he is taken with his experiences and graces. And this is a high degree of living on his own righteousness; and such persons are in the high road to hell. Poor deluded wretches, who think they look so glistering in God's eyes, when they are a smoke in his nose, and are many of them more odious to him, than the most impure beast in Sodom, that makes no pretence to religion! To do as these do, is to *live upon experiences*, according to the true notion of it; and not to do as those who only make use of spiritual experiences as evidences of a state of grace, and in that way receive hope and comfort from them.

There is a sort of men, who indeed abundantly cry down works, and cry up faith in opposition to works, and set up themselves very much as evangelical persons, in opposition to those that are of a legal spirit, and make a fair show of advancing Christ and the gospel, and the way of free grace; who are indeed some of the greatest enemies to the gospel-way of free grace, and the most dangerous opposers of pure humble Christianity.*

There is a pretended great humiliation, being dead to the law, and emptied of self, which is one of the most elated things in the world. Some there are, who have made great profession of experience of a thorough work of the law on their own hearts, and of being brought fully off from works whose conversation has savoured most of a self-righteous spirit, of any that ever I had opportunity to observe. Some, who think themselves quite emptied of themselves, confident that they are abased in the dust, are full as they can hold with the glory of their own humility, and lifted up to heaven with a high opinion of their abasement. Their humility is a swelling, self-conceited, confident, showy, noisy, assuming humility. It seems to be the nature of spiritual pride to make men conceited and ostentatious of their humility.—This appears in that first-born of pride, among the children of men, that would be called *his holiness*, even the man of sin, that exalts himself above all that is called God or is worshipped; he styles himself *servant of servants;* and to make a show of humility, washes the feet of a number of poor men at his inauguration.

For persons to be truly emptied of themselves, poor in spirit, and broken in heart, is quite another thing, and has other effects, than many imagine. It is astonishing how greatly many are deceived about themselves as to this matter, imagining themselves most humble, when they are most proud, and their behaviour is really the most haughty. The deceitfulness of the heart of man appears in no one thing so much, as this of spiritual pride and self-righteousness. The subtlety of Satan appears in its height, in his managing of persons with respect to this sin. And perhaps one reason may be, that here he has most experience: he knows the way of its coming in; he is acquainted with the secret springs of it; it was his own sin.—Experience gives vast advantage in leading souls, either to good or evil.

But though spiritual pride be so subtle and secret an iniquity, and commonly appears under a pretext of great humility; yet there are two things by which it may (perhaps universally and surely) be discovered and distinguished.

The *first* is this; he that is under the prevalence of this distemper, is apt to think highly of his attainments in religion, as comparing himself with others. It is natural for him to fall into that thought of himself, that he is an eminent saint, that he is very high amongst the saints, and has distinguishingly good and great experiences. That is the secret language of his heart, Luke xviii. 11. "God, I thank thee that I am not as other men." And Isa. lxv. 5. "I am holier than thou." Hence such are apt to put themselves forward among God's people, and as it were to take a high seat among them, as if there was no doubt of it but it belonged to them. They, as it were, naturally do that which Christ condemns, Luke xiv. 7, &c. "Take the highest room." This they do, by being forward to take upon them the place and business of the chief; to guide, teach, direct, and manage: "They are confident that they are guides to the blind, a light of them which are in dark-

* "Take not every opinion and doctrine from men or angels, that bears a fair show of advancing Christ; for they may be but the fruits of evangelical hypocrisy and deceit; that being deceived themselves, may deceive others too; Matt. vii. 15. *Beware of them that come in sheep's clothing;* in the innocency, purity, and meekness of Christ and his people: *but inwardly are wolves*, proud, cruel, censorious, *speaking evil of what they know not. By their fruits ye shall know them.* Do not think, beloved, that Satan will not seek to send delusions among us. And do you think these delusions will come out of the popish pack, whose inventions smell above-ground here? No, he must come, and will come, with more evangelical, fine-spun devices. It is a rule observed amongst Jesuits, at this day, if they would conquer religion by subtlety, never oppose religion with a cross religion; but set it against itself. So oppose the gospel by the gospel. And look, as churches pleading for works, had new invented devised works; so when faith is preached, men will have their new inventions of faith. I speak not this against the doctrine of faith, where it is preached; but am glad of it: not that I would have men content themselves with every form of faith; for I believe that most men's faith needs confirming or trying. But I speak to prevent danger on that hand." Shepard's *Parable*, Part I. p. 122.

ness, instructors of the foolish, teachers of babes," Rom. ii. 19, 20. It is natural for them to take it for granted, that it belongs to them to do the part of dictators and masters in matters of religion; and so they implicitly affect to be called of men Rabbi, which is by interpretation Master, as the Pharisees did, Matt. xxiii. 6, 7. *i. e.* they are apt to expect that others should regard them, and yield to them, as masters, in matters of religion.*

But he whose heart is under the power of christian humility, is of a contrary disposition. If the Scriptures are at all to be relied on, such an one is apt to think his attainments in religion to be comparatively mean, and to esteem himself low among the saints, and one of the least of saints. Humility, or true lowliness of mind, disposes persons to think others better than themselves; Phil. ii. 3. "In lowliness of mind, let each esteem others better than themselves." Hence they are apt to think the lowest room belongs to them; and their inward disposition naturally leads them to obey that precept of our Saviour, Luke xiv. 10. It is not natural to them to take it upon them to do the part of teachers; but on the contrary, they are disposed to think that they are not the persons, that others are fitter for it than they; as it was with Moses and Jeremiah, (Exod. iii. 11. Jer. i. 6.) though they were such eminent saints, and of great knowledge. It is not natural to them to think that it belongs to them to teach, but to be taught: they are much more eager to hear, and to receive instruction from others, than to dictate; Jam. i. 19. "Be ye swift to hear, slow to speak." And when they do speak, it is not natural to them to speak with a bold, masterly air; but humility disposes them rather to speak trembling. Hos. xiii. 1. "When Ephraim spake trembling, he exalted himself in Israel; but when he offended in Baal, he died." They are not apt to assume authority, and to take upon them to be chief managers and masters; but rather to be subject to others; Jam. iii. 1, 2. "Be not many masters." 1 Pet. v. 5. "All of you be subject one to another, and be clothed with humility." Eph. v. 21. "Submitting yourselves one to another in the fear of God."

Some persons' experiences naturally make them think highly of their experiences; and they often speak of them as very great and extraordinary; they freely speak of the *great things they have met with.* This *may* be spoken and meant in a *good* sense. In one sense, every degree of saving mercy is a *great thing:* it is indeed a thing *great,* yea, *infinitely great,* for God to bestow the least crumb of children's bread on such dogs as we are in ourselves; and the more humble a person is that hopes that God has bestowed such mercy on him, the more apt will he be to call it a *great thing that he has met with,* in this sense. But if by *great things which they have experienced,* they mean comparatively great spiritual experiences, or great compared with others' experiences, or beyond what is ordinary, which is evidently oftentimes the case; then for a person to say, *I have met with great things,* is the very same thing as to say, *I am an eminent saint,* and have more grace than ordinary. To have great experiences, if the experiences be true and worth telling, is the same thing as to have great grace: there is no true experience, but the exercise of grace; and exactly according to the degree of true experience, is the degree of grace and holiness. The persons that talk thus about their experiences, when they give an account of them, expect that others should admire them. Indeed they do not call it *boasting* to talk after this manner about their experiences, nor do they look upon it as any sign of pride; because they say, *they know that it was not they that did it, it was free grace, they are the great things that God has done for them, they would acknowledge the great mercy God has shown them, and not make light of it.* But so it was with the Pharisee, Luke xviii. He in words gave God the glory of making him to differ from other men; "God, I thank thee," says he, "that I am not as other men."† Their verbally ascribing it to the grace of God, that they are holier than other saints, does not hinder their forwardness to think so highly of their holiness, being a sure evidence of the pride and vanity of their minds. If they were under the influence of an humble spirit, their attainments in religion would not be so apt to shine in their own eyes, nor would they be so much in admiring their own beauty. The Christians that are really the most eminent saints, and therefore have the most excellent experiences, "and are greatest in the kingdom of heaven, humble themselves as a little child," Matt. xviii. 4. because they look on themselves as but little children in grace, and their attainments to be but the attainments of babes in Christ. They are astonished at, and ashamed of, the low degrees of their love, their thankfulness, and their little knowledge of God.—Moses, when he had been conversing with God in the mount, and his face shone so bright in the eyes of others as to dazzle their eyes, *wist not that his face shone.* Some persons go by the *name* of high professors, and some will *own* themselves to be high professors; but eminently humble saints that will shine brightest in heaven, are not at all apt to profess high. I do not believe there is an eminent saint in the world that is a high professor. Such will be much more likely to profess themselves to be the least of all saints, and to think that every saint's attainments and experiences are higher than his.‡

Such is the nature of grace, and of true spiritual light, that they naturally dispose the saints in the present state, to look upon their grace and goodness little, and their deformity great. And they that have the most grace and spiritual light, of any in this world, have most of this disposition. This will appear most clear and evident to any one that soberly and thoroughly weighs the nature and reason of things, and considers the things following.

That grace and holiness is worthy to be called *little,* which is little in *comparison* of what it ought to be; and so it seems to one that is truly gracious. Such an one has his eye upon the rule of his duty; a conformity to that is what he aims at; it is what his soul reaches after; and it is by that he estimates and judges of what he does, and what he has. To a gracious soul, and especially to one eminently gracious, *that* holiness appears little, which is little compared with what it should be; little in comparison of that for which he sees infinite reason and obligation. If his holiness appears to him to be at a vast distance from this, it naturally appears despicable in his eyes, and not worthy to be mentioned as any beauty or amiableness in him. For the like reason as a hungry man naturally accounts that which is set before him, but a little food, a small matter, not worth mentioning, in comparison of his appetite. Or as the child of a great prince, who is jealous for the honour of his father, and beholds the respect which men show him, naturally looks on that honour and respect very little, and not worthy to be regarded, which is nothing in comparison of that which the dignity of his father requires.

The nature of true grace and spiritual light, opens to a person's view the infinite reason there is that he should be holy in a high degree. The more grace he has, the greater sense he has of the infinite excellency and glory of the Divine Being, the infinite dignity of the person of Christ, and the boundless length and breadth, and depth and height, of the love of Christ to sinners. And as grace increases, the field opens more and more to a distant view,

* "There be two things wherein it appears that a man has only common gifts, and no inward principle; 1. These gifts ever puff up, and make a man something in his own eyes, as the Corinthian knowledge did; and many a private man thinks himself fit to be a minister." Shepard's *Parable,* Part I. p. 181, 182.

† Calvin, in his Institutions, B. III. chap. xii. § 7. speaking of this Pharisee, observes, "That in his outward confession, he acknowledges that the righteousness that he has is the gift of God: but (says he) because he trusts *that he is righteous,* he goes away out of the presence of God, unacceptable and odious."

‡ Luther, as his words are cited by Rutherford, in his *Display of the spiritual Antichrist,* p. 143, 144. says thus, "So is the life of a Christian, that he that has begun seems to himself to have nothing; but strives and presses forward, that he may apprehend. Whence Paul says, *I count not myself to have apprehended.* For indeed nothing is more pernicious to a believer, than that presumption, that he has already apprehended, and has no further need of seeking. Hence also many fall back, and pine away in spiritual security and slothfulness. So Bernard says, *To stand still in God's way, is to go back.* Wherefore this remains to him that has begun to be a Christian, to think that he is not yet a Christian, but to seek that he may be a Christian, that he may glory with Paul, *I am not, but I desire to be;* a Christian not yet finished, but only in his beginnings. Therefore he is not a Christian, that is, he that thinks himself a finished Christian, and is not sensible how he falls short. We reach after heaven, but are not in heaven. Woe to him that is wholly renewed, that is, that thinks himself to be so. That man, without doubt, has never so much as begun to be renewed, nor did he ever taste what it is to be a Christian."

until the soul is swallowed up with the vastness of the object; the person is astonished to think how much it becomes him to love this God, and this glorious Redeemer who has so loved man, and how little he does love. And so the more he apprehends, the more the smallness of his grace and love appears strange and wonderful: and therefore is more ready to think that others are beyond him. Wondering at the littleness of his own grace, he can scarcely believe that so strange a thing happens to other saints. It is amazing to him, that one who is really a child of God, and who has actually received the saving benefits of the unspeakable love of Christ, should love no more. He is apt to look upon it as a thing peculiar to himself, a strange instance; for he sees only the outside of other Christians, but he sees his own inside.

Here the reader may possibly object, that love to God is really increased in proportion as the knowledge of God is increased; and therefore how should an increase of knowledge in a saint, make his love appear less, in comparison of what is known? To which I answer, that although the love of God in the saints, be answerable to the degree of knowledge or sight of God; yet it is not in proportion to the object seen and known. The soul of a saint, by having something of God opened to sight, is convinced of much more than is seen. There is something seen, that is wonderful; and that sight brings with it a strong conviction of something vastly beyond, that is not immediately seen. So that the soul, at the same time, is astonished at its ignorance, and that it knows so little, as well as that it loves so little. And as the soul, in a spiritual view, is convinced of infinitely more in the object, yet beyond sight; so it is convinced of the capacity of the soul, of knowing vastly more, if clouds and darkness were but removed. Which causes the soul, in the enjoyment of a spiritual view, to complain greatly of spiritual ignorance and want of love, and long after more knowledge, and more love.

The love of God in the most eminent saints in this world, is truly very little in comparison of what it ought to be. Because the highest love that ever any attain to in this life, is poor, cold, exceeding low, and not worthy to be named in comparison of what our obligations appear to be, from the joint consideration of these two things; *viz.* 1. The reason God has given us to love him, in the manifestations he has made of his infinite glory, in his word and works; and particularly in the gospel of his Son, and what he has done for sinful man by him. And, 2. The capacity there is in the soul of man, by those intellectual faculties which God has given it, of seeing and understanding these reasons, which God has given us to love him. How small indeed is the love of the most eminent saint on earth, in comparison of what these things jointly considered do require! And of this, grace tends to convince men; and especially eminent grace: for grace is of the nature of light, and brings truth to view. And therefore he that has much grace, apprehends much more than others, that great height to which his love ought to ascend; and he sees better than others, how little a way he has risen towards that height. And therefore, estimating his love by the whole height of his duty, hence it appears astonishingly little and low in his eyes.

And the eminent saint, having such a conviction of the high degree in which he ought to love God, is shown, not only the littleness of his grace, but the greatness of his remaining corruption. In order to judge how much corruption or sin we have remaining in us, we must take our measure from that height to which the rule of our duty extends. The whole of the distance we are at from that height, is sin: for failing of duty is sin; otherwise our duty is not our duty; and by how much the more we fall short of our duty, so much the more sin have we. Sin is no other than disagreeableness, in a moral agent, to the law, or rule of his duty. And therefore the degree of sin is to be judged of by the rule; so much disagreeableness to the rule, so much sin, whether it be in *defect* or *excess.* Therefore if men, in their love to God, do not come up half way to that height which duty requires, then they have more corruption in their hearts than grace; because there is more goodness wanting, than is there; and all that is wanting is sin. Sin is an abominable defect; and appears so to the saints, especially those that are eminent; it appears exceeding abominable to them, that Christ should be loved so little, and thanked so little for his dying love; it is in their eyes hateful ingratitude.

And then the increase of grace has a tendency another way, to cause the saints to think their deformity vastly more than their goodness. It not only tends to convince them that their corruption is much greater than their goodness, which is indeed the case; but it also tends to cause the deformity that there is in the least sin, or the least degree of corruption, to appear so great, as vastly to outweigh all the beauty there is in their greatest holiness; for this also is indeed the case. For the least sin against an infinite God, has an infinite hatefulness or deformity in it; but the highest degree of holiness in a creature, has not an infinite loveliness in it: and therefore the loveliness of it is as nothing, in comparison of the deformity of the least sin. That every sin has infinite deformity and hatefulness in it, is most demonstrably evident; because what the evil, or iniquity, or hatefulness of sin consists in, is the violating of an obligation, or the being or doing contrary to what we should be or do, or are obliged to. And therefore by how much the greater the obligation is that is violated, so much the greater is the iniquity and hatefulness of the violation. But certainly our obligation to love and honour any being, is in some proportion to his loveliness and honourableness, or to his worthiness to be loved and honoured by us; which is the same thing. We are surely under greater obligation to love a more lovely being, than a less lovely: and if a Being be infinitely lovely or worthy to be loved by us, then our obligations to love him, are infinitely great: and therefore, whatever is contrary to this love, has in it infinite iniquity, deformity, and unworthiness. But on the other hand, with respect to our holiness or love to God, there is not an infinite worthiness in that. The sin of the creature against God, is ill-deserving and hateful in proportion to the distance there is between God and the creature: the greatness of the object, and the meanness and inferiority of the subject, aggravate it. But it is the reverse with regard to the worthiness of the respect of the creature to God; it is *worthless,* and not worthy, in proportion to the meanness of the subject. So much the greater the distance between God and the creature, so much the less is the creature's respect worthy of God's notice or regard. The great degree of superiority increases the obligation on the inferior to regard the superior; and so makes the want of regard more hateful: but the great degree of inferiority diminishes the worth of the regard of the inferior; because the more he is inferior—the less is he worthy of notice; the less he is—the less is what he can offer worth; for he can offer no more than himself, in offering his best respect; and therefore as he is little, and little worth, so is his respect little worth. And the more a person has of true grace and spiritual light, the more will it appear thus to him; the more will he appear to himself infinitely deformed by reason of sin, and the less will the goodness that is in his grace, or good experience, appear in proportion to it. For indeed it is nothing to it; it is less than a drop to the ocean; for finite bears no proportion at all to that which is infinite. But the more a person has of spiritual light, the more do things appear to him, in this respect, as they are indeed. Hence it most demonstrably appears, that true grace is of that nature, that the more a person has of it, with remaining corruption, the less does his goodness and holiness appear, in proportion to his deformity; and not only to his past, but to his present deformity, in the sin that now appears in his heart, and in the abominable defects of his highest and best affections, and brightest experiences.

The nature of many high religious affections, and great discoveries (as they are called) in many persons I have been acquainted with, is to hide the corruption of their hearts, and to make it seem to them as if all their sin was gone, and to leave them without complaints of any hateful evil left in them; (though it may be they cry out much of their past unworthiness;) a sure and certain evidence that their discoveries are darkness and not light. It is darkness that hides men's pollution and deformity; but light let into the heart discovers it, searches it out in its secret corners, and makes it plainly to appear; especially that penetrating, all-searching light of God's holiness and glory. It is true, that saving discoveries may for the present hide corruption in one sense; they restrain the *positive exercises* of it, such as malice, envy, covetousness, lasciviousness, murmuring, &c. but they bring corruption to light, in that which is *privative, viz.* that there is no more love, no more humility, no more thankfulness. Which defects appear most hateful, in the eyes of those who have the most eminent exercises of grace; and are very burdensome, and cause the saints to complain of their leanness, odious pride and ingratitude. And whatever positive exercises of corruption at any time arise, and mingle themselves with eminent actings of grace, grace will exceedingly magnify the view of them, and render their appearance far more heinous and horrible.

The more eminent saints are, and the more they have of the light *of heaven* in their souls, the more do they appear to *themselves,* as the most eminent saints in this world do to the saints and *angels in heaven.* How can we rationally suppose the most eminent saints on earth appear to them, if beheld any otherwise than covered with the righteousness of Christ, and their deformities swallowed up and hid in the coruscation of the beams of his abundant glory and love? how can we suppose our most ardent love and praises appear to them, who behold the beauty and glory of God without a veil? how does our highest thankfulness for the dying love of Christ appear to them, who see Christ as he is, who know as they are known, and see the glory of the person of him that died, and the wonders of his dying love, without cloud or darkness? and how do they look on the deepest reverence and humility, with which worms of the dust on earth approach that infinite Majesty, which they behold? do they appear *great* to them, or so much as worthy of the name of reverence and humility, in those whom they behold at such an infinite distance from that great and holy God, in whose glorious presence they are? The reason why the *highest* attainments of the saints on earth appear so mean to them, is that they dwell in the light of God's glory, and *see him as he is.* And it is in this respect with the saints on earth, as it is with those in heaven, in proportion as they are more eminent in grace.

I would not be understood, that the saints on earth have, in all respects, the worst opinion of themselves, when they have most of the exercise of grace. In many respects it is otherwise. With respect to the *positive exercises* of corruption, they may appear to themselves freest and best when grace is most in exercise, and worst when the actings of grace are lowest. And when they compare themselves with themselves, at different times, they may know, when grace is in lively exercise, that it is better with them than it was before; (though before, at the time, they did not see so much evil as they see now;) and when afterwards they sink again in the frame of their minds, they may *know* that they sink, and have a new argument of their great remaining corruption, and a *rational* conviction of a greater vileness than they saw before; and may have a sense of guilt, and a *legal* sense of their sinfulness, far greater than when in the lively exercise of grace. But yet it is true, and demonstrable from the forementioned considerations, that the children of God never have such a *sensible* and *spiritual* conviction of their deformity, and so great, quick, and abasing sense of their present vileness and odiousness, as when they are highest in the exercise of true grace; and never are they so much disposed to set themselves low among Christians as then. And thus *he that is the greatest in the kingdom,* or most eminent in the church of Christ, is he *that humbles himself,* as the least infant among them; Matt. xviii. 4.

A true saint may know that he has some true grace: and the more grace there is, the more easily is it known; as was observed and proved before. But yet it does not follow, that an *eminent* saint is *easily sensible* that he is an eminent saint, when compared with others.—I will not deny that it is possible, that he who has much grace, and is an eminent saint, may know it. But he will not be *apt* to know it; it will not be *obvious* to him. That he is better than others, and has higher experiences and attainments, is not a *foremost* thought, nor does it readily offer itself. It is not in his way, but lies far out of sight; he must take pains to convince himself of it; there will be need of a great command of reason, and a high degree of strictness and care in arguing, to convince himself. And if he be rationally convinced, by a very strict consideration of his own experiences, compared with the great appearances of low degrees of grace in some other saints, it will hardly seem real to him, that he has more grace than they. He will be apt even to lose the conviction he has by pains obtained; nor will it seem at all natural to him to act upon that supposition. And this may be laid down as an infallible thing, *That the person who is apt to think that he, as compared with others, is a very eminent saint, much distinguished in christian experience, in whom this is a first thought, that rises of itself, and naturally offers itself; he is certainly mistaken; he is no eminent saint; but under the great prevailings of a proud and self-righteous spirit.* And if this be *habitual* with the man, and is statedly the prevailing temper of his mind, he is no saint at all; he has not the least degree of any true christian experience; so surely as the word of God is true.

Experiences of that tendency, and found to have this effect, *viz.* to elevate the subject of them with a great conceit of those experiences, are certainly vain and delusive. Those supposed discoveries that naturally blow up the person with an admiration of the eminency of his discoveries, and fill him with conceit, that now he has seen, and knows more than most other Christians, have nothing of the nature of true spiritual light in them. All true spiritual knowledge is of that nature, that the more a person has of it, the more is he sensible of his own ignorance; 1 Cor. viii. 2. "He that thinketh he knoweth any thing, knoweth nothing yet as he ought to know." Agur, when he had a great discovery of God, the wonderful height of his glory and his marvellous works, acknowledging his greatness and incomprehensibleness; had, at the same time, the deepest sense of his brutish ignorance. He looked upon himself as the *most ignorant* of all the saints; Prov. xxx. 2, 3, 4. "Surely I am more brutish than any man, and have not the understanding of a man. I neither learned wisdom, nor have the knowledge of the holy. Who hath ascended up into heaven, or descended? who hath gathered the wind in his fist? who hath bound the waters in a garment? who hath established all the ends of the earth? *what is his name,* and what is his Son's name, *if thou canst tell?*"

For a man to be *highly conceited* of his spiritual knowledge, is for him to be *wise in his own eyes,* if any thing is. And therefore it comes under those prohibitions, Prov. iii. 7. "Be not wise in thine own eyes:" Rom. xii. 16. "Be not wise in your own conceits:" and brings men under that woe, Isa. v. 21. "Woe unto them that are wise in their own eyes, and prudent in their own sight." Those who are *thus* wise, are some of the least likely to get good of any in the world. Experience shows this truth, Prov. xxvi. 12. "Seest thou a man wise in his own conceit? there is more hope of a fool than of him."

To this some may object, that the psalmist, when we must suppose that he was in a holy frame, speaks of his knowledge as eminently great, and far greater than that of other saints, Psal. cxix. 99, 100. "I have more understanding than all my teachers: for thy testimonies are my meditation. I understand more than the ancients: because I keep thy precepts." To this I answer two things:

(1.) There is no restraint to be laid upon the Spirit of God, as to what he shall reveal to a prophet, for the benefit of his church, who is speaking or writing under *immediate inspiration.* The Spirit of God may reveal to such an one, and dictate to him to declare to others, secret things, that otherwise would be hard, yea impossible for him to find out. As he may reveal to him mysteries, which otherwise would be above his reason; or things in a distant place, that he cannot see; or future events, which it would be impossible for him to know and declare, if they were not extraordinarily revealed to him: so the Spirit of God might reveal to David this distinguishing benefit, which he had received by conversing much with God's testimonies; and use him as his instrument to record it for the benefit of others, to excite them to the like duty, and to use the same means to gain knowledge. Nothing can be gathered concerning the natural tendency of the *ordinary* gracious influences of the Spirit of God, from what David declares of his distinguishing knowledge under the *extraordinary* influences of God's Spirit, immediately dictating to him what he pleased for the benefit of his church; any more than we can reasonably argue, that it is the natural tendency of grace to incline men to wish the most dreadful misery to others, because David under inspiration, often prays that such misery may come upon them.

(2.) It is not certain that the knowledge David here speaks of, is *spiritual* knowledge, wherein holiness fundamentally consists. But it may be that greater *revelation* which God made to him of the Messiah and his future kingdom, and the far more clear and extensive knowledge of the mysteries and doctrines of the gospel, than others; as a reward for his keeping God's testimonies. In this, it is apparent by the book of Psalms, that David far exceeded all who had gone before him.

Secondly, Another infallible sign of spiritual pride, is persons being apt to think highly of their humility. False experiences are commonly attended with a counterfeit humility. And it is the very nature of a counterfeit humility, to be highly conceited of itself. False religious affections have generally a tendency, especially when raised to a great height, to make persons think that their humility is great, and accordingly to take much notice of their great attainments in this respect, and admire them. But eminently gracious affections (I scruple not to say it) are evermore of a contrary tendency, and have universally a contrary effect. They indeed make their possessors very sensible that they should be deeply humbled, and cause them earnestly to thirst and long after it; but they make their present humility, or that which they have already attained, to appear small; and their remaining pride great, and exceedingly abominable.

The reason why a proud person is apt to think his humility great, and a very humble person his humility small, may be easily seen, if it be considered, that it is natural for persons, in judging of the degree of their own humiliation, to take their measure from that which they esteem their proper height, or the dignity wherein they properly stand. That may be great humiliation in one, which is no humiliation at all in another; because the degree of honourableness or considerableness, wherein each properly stands, is very different. For some great man to stoop to loose the latchet of the shoes of another great man, his equal, or to wash his feet, would be taken notice of as an act of abasement in him; and he being sensible of his own dignity, would look upon it so himself. But if a poor slave is seen stooping to unloose the shoes of a great prince, nobody will take notice of this, as an act of humiliation in him, or token of any great degree of humility: nor would the slave himself, unless he be horribly proud, and ridiculously conceited: and if after he had done it, he should, in his talk and behaviour, show that he thought his abasement *great* in it, and had his mind much upon it, as an evidence of his being very humble; would not every body cry out, "Who do you think yourself to be, that you should think this a mark of deep humiliation?" This would make it plain to a demonstration, that the slave was swollen with a high degree of pride and vanity of mind, as much as if he declared in plain terms, *I think myself to be some great one.* And the matter is no less plain and certain, when worthless, vile, and loathsome worms of the dust, are apt to put such a construction on their acts of abasement before God; and to think it a token of great humility in them, that they acknowledge themselves to be mean and unworthy, and behave themselves as those who are so inferior. The very reason why such outward acts, and such inward exercises, look like great abasement in such a person is, that he has a high conceit of himself. Whereas if he thought of himself more justly, these things would appear nothing to him, and his humility in them worthy of no regard; but he would rather be astonished at his pride, that one so infinitely despicable and vile, is brought no lower before God. When he says in his heart, "This is a great act of humiliation; it is certainly a sign of great humility in me, that I should feel thus, and do so:" his meaning is, "This is great humility for me, for such a one as I, who am so considerable and worthy." He considers how low he is now brought, and compares this with the height of dignity, on which he thinks he stands, and the distance appears very great; he calls it *humility*, and as such admires it. Whereas, in him who is truly humble, and really sees his own vileness and loathsomeness before God, the distance appears the other way. When he is brought lowest of all, it does not appear to him that he is brought below his proper station, but that he is not come to it; he appears to himself yet vastly above it; he longs to get lower, that he may come to it; but appears at a great distance from it. And this distance he calls pride. And therefore his pride appears great to him, and not his humility. For although he is brought much lower than he used to be; yet it does not appear to him worthy of the name of humiliation, for him that is so infinitely mean and detestable, to come down to a place, which though it be lower than what he used to assume, is yet vastly higher than what is proper for him. Men would hardly count it worthy of the name of humility, in a contemptible slave, that formerly affected to be a prince, to have his spirit so far brought down, as to take the place of a nobleman; when this is still so far above his proper station.

All men, in judging of the degree of their own and others' humility, as appearing in any act of theirs, consider two things; viz. the real degree of dignity they stand in; and the degree of abasement, with the relation it bears to that real dignity. Thus, what may be an evidence of great humility in one, evidences but little or no humility in another. But truly humble Christians have so mean an opinion of their own real dignity, that all their self-abasement, when considered with relation to, and compared with that, appears very small to them. It does not seem to them to be any great humility, for such poor, vile, abject creatures as they are, to lie at the foot of God.

The degree of humility is to be judged of by the degree of *abasement*, and the degree of the *cause for abasement*: but he that is truly and eminently humble, never thinks his humility great. The cause why he should be abased appears so great, and the abasement of the frame of his heart so greatly short of it, that he takes much more notice of his pride than his humility.

Every one that has been conversant with souls under convictions of sin, knows that they are not apt to think themselves greatly convinced. And the reason is, men judge of the degree of their own convictions by two things jointly considered; viz. the degree of *sense* which they have of guilt and pollution, and the degree of *cause* they have for such a sense, in the degree of their real sinfulness. It is really no argument of any *great* conviction of sin, for some men to think themselves sinful, beyond most others in the world; because they are so indeed, very plainly and notoriously: he must be very blind indeed not to be sensible of it. But he that is truly under great convictions of sin, naturally thinks, that the *cause* he has to be sensible of guilt and pollution, is greater than others have; and therefore he ascribes his sensibleness of this, to the greatness of his sin, and not to the greatness of his sensibility. It is natural for one under great convictions, to think himself one of the greatest of sinners. *That* man is under great convictions, whose conviction is great in proportion to his sin. But no man that is truly under great convictions, thinks his conviction great in proportion to his sin. For if he does, it is a certain sign that he inwardly thinks his sins small. And if that be the case, *that* is a certain evidence that his conviction is small. And this, by the way, is the main reason, that persons, when under a work of humiliation, are not sensible of it, in the time of it.

And as it is with conviction of sin, just so it is, by parity of reason, with respect to persons' conviction of their own meanness and vileness, their blindness, their impotence, and all that low sense a Christian has of himself, in the exercise of *evangelical humiliation*. So that in a high degree of this, the saints are never disposed to think their sense of their own meanness, filthiness, impotence, &c. to be great; because it never appears great to them, considering the cause.

An eminent saint is not apt to think himself eminent in any thing; all his graces and experiences appear to him to be comparatively small; but especially his humility.

Nothing that appertains to christian experience, and true piety, is so much out of his sight. He is a thousand times more quick-sighted to discern his pride, than his humility. On the contrary, the deluded hypocrite, who is under the power of spiritual pride, is so blind to nothing as his pride; and so quick-sighted to nothing, as the shows of humility.

The humble Christian is more apt to find fault with his own pride than with that of other men. He is apt to put the best construction on others' words and behaviour, and to think that none are so proud as himself. But the proud hypocrite is quick to discern the mote in his brother's eye, in this respect; while he sees nothing of the beam in his own. He is very often crying out of others' pride, finding fault with others' apparel, and way of living; and is affected ten times as much with his neighbour's ring or riband, as with all the filthiness of his own heart.

From the disposition there is in hypocrites to think highly of their humility, it comes to pass that counterfeit humility is forward to put forth itself to view. Those who have it, are apt to be much in speaking of their humiliations, setting them forth in high terms, and making a great outward show of humility, in affected looks, gestures, manner of speech, meanness of apparel, or some affected singularity. So it was of old with the false prophets, Zech. xiii. 4. so it was with the hypocritical Jews, Isa. lvii. 5. and so Christ tells us it was with the Pharisees, Matt. vi. 16. But it is contrariwise with true humility; they who have it, are not apt to display their eloquence in setting it forth, or to speak of the *degree* of their abasement in strong terms.* It does not affect to show itself in any singular meanness either of apparel, or way of living; agreeable to what is implied in Matt. vi. 17. "But thou, when thou fastest, anoint thine head, and wash thy face." Col. ii. 23. "Which things have indeed a show of wisdom in will-worship and humility, and neglecting of the body." Nor is true humility a *noisy* thing; it is not loud and boisterous. The Scripture represents it as of a contrary nature. Ahab, when he had a visible humility, a resemblance of true humility, *went softly*, 1 Kings xxi. 27. A penitent, in the exercise of true humiliation, is represented as still and *silent*, Lam. iii. 28. "He sitteth alone and keepeth silence, because he hath borne it upon him." And silence is mentioned as what attends humility, Prov. xxx. 32. "If thou hast done foolishly in lifting up thyself, or if thou hast thought evil, lay thine hand upon thy mouth."

Thus I have particularly and largely shown the nature of that true humility which attends holy affections, as it appears in its tendency to cause persons to think meanly of their attainments in religion, compared with the attainments of others, and particularly, of their attainments in humility: and have shown the contrary tendency of spiritual pride, to dispose persons to think their attainments in these respects to be great. I have insisted the longer on this, because I think it a matter of great importance, as it affords a certain distinction between true and counterfeit humility; and also as this disposition of hypocrites—whereby they look on themselves as better than others—is what God has declared to be very hateful to him, *a smoke in his nose, and a fire that burneth all the day*, Isa. lxv. 5. It is mentioned as an instance of pride in the inhabitants of that holy city (as it was called) Jerusalem, that they esteemed themselves far better than the people of Sodom; Ezek. xvi. 56. "For thy sister Sodom was not mentioned by thy mouth in the day of thy pride."

Let not the reader slightly pass over these things in application to himself. When you imagine, reader, that it is a bad sign for a person to be apt to think himself a better saint than others, take heed lest there arise a blinding prejudice in your own favour. There will probably be need of great strictness of self-examination, in order to determine whether it be so with you. If you conclude thus, *It seems to me, none are so bad as I.* Do not let the matter pass off so; but examine again, whether or no you do not think yourself better than others on this very account, because you imagine you think so meanly of yourself. Have not you a high opinion of this humility? If you answer, *No; I have not a high opinion of my humility; it seems to me I am as proud as the devil:* examine again, whether self-conceit do not rise up under this cover; whether on this very account—that you think yourself as proud as the devil—you do not think yourself to be very humble.

From this opposition between the nature of a true and of a counterfeit humility, as to the esteem that the subjects of them have of themselves, arises a manifold contrariety of temper and behaviour. A truly humble person, having such a mean opinion of his righteousness and holiness, is *poor in spirit*. For a person to be poor in spirit, is to be in his own sense and apprehension poor, as to what is in him, and to be of an answerable disposition. Therefore a truly humble person, especially one eminently humble, naturally behaves himself in many respects as a poor man. *The poor useth entreaties, but the rich answereth roughly*. A poor man is not disposed to quick and high resentment when he is among the rich. He is apt to yield to others, for he knows others are above him; nor is he stiff and self-willed. He is patient with hard fare, expects no other than to be despised, and takes it patiently. He does not take it heinously that he is overlooked, and but little regarded; but is prepared to be in a low place; readily honours his superiors, and takes reproofs quietly. He easily yields to be taught, and does not claim much to his understanding and judgment; he is not over nice or humoursome, and has his spirit subdued to hard things; he is not assuming, nor apt to take much upon him, but it is natural for him to be subject to others. Thus it is with the humble Christian. Humility is (as the great Mastricht expresses it) *a kind of holy pusillanimity*. A man that is very poor is a beggar; so is he that is poor in spirit. This constitutes a great difference between those affections that are gracious, and those that are false: under the former, the person continues still a poor beggar at God's gates, exceeding empty and needy; but the latter make men appear to themselves rich, and increased with goods, and not very necessitous; they have a great stock in their own imagination for their subsistence.†

A poor man is modest in his speech and behaviour; much more, and more certainly and universally, is one that is poor in spirit, humble and modest in his behaviour amongst men. It is in vain for any to pretend that they are humble, and as little children before God, when they are haughty, assuming, and impudent in their behaviour amongst men. The apostle informs us, that the design of the gospel is to cut off all glorying, not only before God, but also before men, Rom. iv. 1, 2. Some pretend to great humiliation, while yet they are very haughty, audacious, and assuming in their external appearance and behaviour: but they ought to consider those scriptures, Psal. cxxxi. 1. "Lord, my heart is not haughty, nor mine eyes lofty: neither do I exercise myself in great matters, or in things too high for me." Prov. vi. 16, 17. "These six things doth the Lord hate: yea, seven are an abomination unto him: a proud look," &c.—Chap. xxi. 4. "An high look, and a proud heart, are sin." Psal. xviii. 27. "Thou wilt bring down high looks." And Psal. ci. 5. "Him that hath an high look, and a proud heart, I will not suffer." 1 Cor. xiii. 4. "Charity vaunteth not itself, doth not behave itself unseemly." There is a certain amiable modesty

* It is an observation of Mr. Jones, in his excellent treatise of the canon of the New Testament, that the evangelist Mark—who was the companion of St. Peter, and is supposed to have written his gospel under the direction of that apostle—when he mentions Peter's repentance after his denying his Master, does not use such strong terms to set it forth as the other evangelists; he only uses these words, *When he thought thereon, he wept*, Mark xiv. 72. whereas the other evangelists say thus, *He went out and wept bitterly*, Matt. xxvi. 75. Luke xxii. 62.

† "This spirit ever keeps a man poor and vile in his own eyes, and empty—When the man hath got some knowledge, and can discourse pretty well, and hath some tastes of the heavenly gift, some sweet illapses of grace, and so his conscience is pretty well quieted: and if he hath got some answer to his prayers, and hath sweet affections, he grows full: and having ease to his conscience, casts off sense, and daily groaning under sin. And hence the spirit of prayer dies: he loses his esteem of God's ordinances; feels not such need of them; or gets no good, feels no life or power by them. This is the woful condition of some; but yet they know it not. But now he that is filled with the Spirit, the Lord empties him; and the more, the longer he lives. So that though others think he needs not much grace; yet he accounts himself the poorest." Sheperd's *Parable of the Ten Virgins*, Part II. p. 132.

"After all fillings, be ever empty, hungry, and feeling need, and praying for more." *Ibid.* p. 151.

"Truly, brethren, when I see the curse of God upon many Christians, that are now grown full of their parts, gifts, peace, comforts, abilities, duties, I stand adoring the riches of the Lord's mercy, to a little handful of poor believers; not only in making them empty, but in keeping them so all their days." Shepard's *Sound Believer*, the late edition in Boston, p. 158, 159.

and fear that belongs to a christian behaviour among men, arising from humility, of which the Scripture often speaks; 1 Pet. iii. 15. "Be ready to give an answer to every man that asketh you, with meekness and fear." Rom. xiii. 7. "Fear, to whom fear." 2 Cor. vii. 15. "Whilst he remembereth the obedience of you all, how with fear and trembling you received him." Eph. vi. 5. "Servants, be obedient to them that are your masters according to the flesh, with fear and trembling." 1 Pet. ii. 18. "Servants, be subject to your masters with all fear." 1 Pet. iii. 2. "While they behold your chaste conversation coupled with fear." 1 Tim. ii. 9. "That women adorn themselves in modest apparel, with shamefacedness and sobriety." In this respect a Christian is like a little child; a little child is modest before men, and his heart is apt to be possessed with fear and awe amongst them.

The same spirit will dispose a Christian to honour all men; 1 Pet. ii. 17. "Honour all men." An humble Christian is not only disposed to honour the saints in his behaviour; but others also, in all those ways that do not imply a visible approbation of their sins. Thus Abraham, the great pattern of believers, honoured the children of Heth; Gen. xxiii. 11, 12. "Abraham stood up, and bowed himself to the people of the land." This was a remarkable instance of an humble behaviour towards them whom Abraham knew to be accursed; for which cause he would by no means suffer his servant to take a wife to his son from among them; and for which cause also Esau's wives, being of these children of Heth, were a grief of mind to Isaac and Rebekah. So Paul honoured Festus, Acts xxvi. 25. "I am not mad, most noble Festus." Not only will christian humility dispose persons to honour wicked men out of the visible church, but also false brethren and persecutors. Jacob, when he was in an excellent frame—having just been wrestling all night with God, and received the blessing—honoured Esau, his false and persecuting brother; Gen. xxxiii. 3. "Jacob bowed himself to the ground seven times, until he came near to his brother Esau." So he called him *lord*: and commanded all his family to honour him in like manner.

Thus I have endeavoured to describe the heart and behaviour of one who is governed by a truly gracious humility as exactly agreeable to the Scriptures as I am able. Now, it is out of such a heart as this, that all truly holy affections flow. Christian affections are like Mary's precious ointment poured on Christ's head, that filled the whole house with a sweet odour. *That* was poured out of an *alabaster box;* so gracious affections flow out to Christ out of a *pure heart*. That was poured out of a *broken box;* (until the box was broken, the ointment could not flow, nor diffuse its odour;) so gracious affections flow out of a *broken heart*. Gracious affections are also like those of Mary Magdalene, (Luke vii. at the latter end,) who in like manner pours precious ointment on Christ, out of an alabaster broken box, anointing therewith the feet of Jesus, when she had washed them with her tears, and wiped them with the hair of her head. All gracious affections, which are a sweet odour to Christ, filling the soul of a Christian with a heavenly sweetness and fragrancy, are broken-hearted affections. A truly Christian love, either to God or men, is an humble broken-hearted love. The desires of the saints, however earnest, are humble desires; their hope is an humble hope; and their joy, even when it is *unspeakable and full of glory*, is an humble, broken-hearted joy, leaving the Christian more poor in spirit, more like a little child, and more disposed to an universal lowliness of behaviour.

SECT. VII.

Another thing, wherein gracious affections are distinguished from others, is, that they are attended with a change of nature.

All gracious affections arise from a spiritual understanding, in which the soul has the excellency and glory of divine things discovered to it, as was shown before. But all spiritual discoveries are also transforming. They not only make an alteration of the present exercise, sensation, and frame of the soul; but such is their power and efficacy, that they alter its very nature; 2 Cor. iii. 18. "But we all with open face, beholding as in a glass the glory of the Lord, are changed into the same image, from glory to glory, even as by the Spirit of the Lord." Such power as this, is properly divine, and is peculiar to *the Spirit of the Lord.* Other power may make a great alteration in men's present frames and feelings; but it is the power of a Creator only that can change the nature. And no discoveries or illuminations, but those that are divine and supernatural, will have this supernatural effect. But this effect all those discoveries have, that are truly divine. The soul is deeply affected by these discoveries; so affected, as to be transformed.

Thus it is with those affections of which the soul is the subject in its conversion. The scriptural representations of conversion, strongly imply and signify a change of nature: such as *being born again; becoming new creatures; rising from the dead; being renewed in the spirit of the mind; dying to sin, and living to righteousness; putting off the old man, and putting on the new man; being ingrafted into a new stock; having a divine seed implanted in the heart; being made partakers of the divine nature, &c.*

Therefore if there be no great and remarkable abiding change in persons, who think they have experienced a work of conversion, vain are all their imaginations and pretences, however they may have been affected.* Conversion (if we may give any credit to the Scripture) is a great and universal change of the man, turning him from sin to God. A man may be restrained from sin, before he is converted; but when he is converted, his very heart and nature is turned from it unto holiness: so that thenceforward he becomes a holy person, and an enemy to sin. If, therefore, after a person's high affections at his supposed first conversion, it happens that in a little time there is no very remarkable alteration in him, as to those bad qualities and evil habits which before were visible in him—and he is ordinarily under the prevalence of the same kind of dispositions as heretofore, and the same things seem to belong to his character, he appearing as selfish, carnal, stupid, and perverse, unchristian, and unsavoury as ever—it is greater evidence against him, than the brightest story of experiences that ever was told can be for him. For in Christ Jesus neither circumcision nor uncircumcision, neither high profession nor low profession, neither a fair story nor a broken one, avails any thing; but a new creature. If there be a very great alteration visible in a person for a while; yet if it be not abiding, but he afterwards return, in a stated manner, to his former habits; it appears to be no change of nature; for nature is an abiding thing. A swine may be washed, but the swinish nature remains; a dove may be defiled, but its cleanly nature remains.†

Allowances, indeed, must be made for the natural temper, which conversion does not entirely eradicate: those sins which a man by his natural constitution was most inclined to before his conversion, he may be most apt to fall into still. But yet conversion will make a great alteration even with respect to these sins. Though grace, while imperfect, does not root out an evil natural temper, yet it is of great power and efficacy to correct it. The change wrought in conversion, is an universal change: grace changes a man with respect to whatever is sinful in him; the *old man* is put off, and the *new man* put on; he is sanctified throughout. He is become a new creature, old things are passed away, and *all things* are become new; all sin is mortified, constitutional sins, as well as others. If a man before his conversion was, by his natural constitution, prone to lasciviousness, or drunkenness, or maliciousness; converting grace will make a great alteration in him, with respect to these evil dispositions; so that however he may be still most in danger of these sins, they shall no longer have dominion over him; nor will they any more be pro-

* "I would not judge of the whole soul's coming to Christ, so much by sudden pangs, as by an inward bent. For the whole soul, in affectionate expressions and actions, may be carried to Christ; but being without this bent, and change of affections, is unsound."—Shepard's *Parable*, Part I. p. 203.

† "It is with the soul, as with water; all the cold may be gone, but the native principle of cold remains still. You may remove the burning of lusts, not the blackness of nature. Where the power of sin lies, change of conscience from security to terror, change of life from profaneness to civility, and fashions of the world, to escape the pollutions thereof, change of lusts, nay quenching them for a time: but the nature is never changed, in the best hypocrite that ever was."—Shepard's *Parable*, Part I. p. 194.

perly his character. Yes, true repentance, in some respects especially, turns a man against his *own* iniquity; *that* wherein he has been most guilty, and has chiefly dishonoured God. He that forsakes other sins, but preserves the iniquity to which he is chiefly inclined, is like Saul, who, when sent against God's enemies the Amalekites, with a strict charge to save none of them alive, but utterly to destroy them, small and great; slew the people, but saved the king.

Some foolishly make it an argument in favour of their discoveries and affections, that when they are gone, they are left wholly without any life or sense, or any thing beyond what they had before. They think it an evidence that what they experienced was wholly of God, and not of themselves, because (say they) when God is departed, all is gone; they can see and feel nothing, and are no better than they used to be. It is very true, that all grace and goodness in the hearts of the saints is entirely from God; and they are universally and immediately dependent on him for it. But yet these persons are mistaken, as to the manner of God's communicating himself and his Holy Spirit, in imparting saving grace to the soul. He gives his Spirit to be united to the faculties of the soul, and to dwell there *after the manner of a principle of nature*: so that the soul, in being endued with grace, is endued with a *new nature*: but nature is an *abiding* thing. All the exercises of grace are entirely from Christ: but are not from him as a living agent moves and stirs what is without life, and which yet remains lifeless. The soul has life communicated to it, so as through Christ's power to have inherent in itself a *vital nature*. In the soul where Christ savingly *is*, there he *lives*. He does not merely live *without* it, so as violently to actuate it, but he lives *in* it, so that the soul also is *alive*. Grace in the soul is as much from Christ, as the light in a glass, held out in the sunbeams, is from the sun. But this represents the manner of the communication of grace to the soul but in part; because the glass remaining as it was, the *nature* of it not being at all changed, it is as much without any lightsomeness in its nature as ever. But the soul of a saint receives light from the sun of righteousness in such a manner, that its *nature* is changed, and it becomes properly a luminous thing. Not only does the sun shine in the saints, but they also become little suns, partaking of the nature of the fountain of their light. In this respect, the manner of their derivation of light, is like that of the lamps in the tabernacle, rather than that of a reflecting glass; which though they were lit up by fire from heaven, yet thereby became themselves burning, shining things. The saints do not only drink of the water of life, that flows from the original fountain; but this water becomes a fountain of water in them, springing up there, and flowing out of them, John iv. 14. and chap. vii. 38, 39. Grace is compared to a seed implanted, that not only is *in* the ground, but has *hold* of it; has *root* there, *grows* there, and is an abiding *principle* of life and nature there.

As it is with spiritual discoveries and affections given at first conversion, so it is in all subsequent illuminations and affections of that kind, they are all *transforming*. There is a like divine power and energy in them, as in the first discoveries: and they still reach the bottom of the heart, and affect and alter the very nature of the soul, in proportion to the degree in which they are given. And a transformation of nature is continued and carried on by them, to the end of life, until it is brought to perfection in glory. Hence the progress of the work of grace in the hearts of the saints, is represented in Scripture as a continued conversion and renovation of nature. So the apostle exhorts those that were at Rome, *beloved of God, called to be saints*—the subjects of God's redeeming *mercies*—to be *transformed by the renewing of their mind*, Rom. xii. 1, 2. "I beseech you therefore, by the mercies of God, that ye present your bodies a living sacrifice;—and be not conformed to this world: but be ye *transformed* by the renewing of your mind." (Compared with chap. i. 7.) So the apostle, writing to the *saints and faithful in Christ Jesus*, who were at Ephesus, (Eph. i. 1.)—who "were once dead in trespasses and sins, but now quickened, raised up, made to sit together in heavenly places in Christ, and created in Christ Jesus unto good works; who were once far off, but now made nigh by the blood of Christ: who were no more strangers and foreigners, but fellow-citizens with the saints, and of the household of God; who were built together for an habitation of God through the Spirit;"—tells them, "that he ceased not to pray for them, that God would give them the Spirit of wisdom and revelation, in the knowledge of Christ: the eyes of their understanding being enlightened, that they might know (or experience) what was the exceeding greatness of God's power towards them that believe, according to the working of his mighty power, which he wrought in Christ, when he raised him from the dead, and set him at his own right hand in the heavenly places," Eph. i, 16, to the end. In this the apostle has respect to the glorious power and work of God in converting and renewing the soul; as is most plain by the sequel. So the apostle exhorts the same persons "to put off the old man, which is corrupt according to the deceitful lusts: and be renewed in the spirit of their minds: and put on the new man, which after God is created in righteousness and true holiness," Eph. iv. 22, 23, 24.

There is a sort of high affections which leave persons without any appearance of an abiding effect. They go off suddenly; so that from the very height of their emotion, and seeming rapture, they pass at once to be quite dead, and void of all sense and activity. It surely is not wont to be thus with high gracious affections;* they leave a sweet savour and relish of divine things on the heart, and a stronger bent of the soul towards God and holiness. As Moses's face not only shone while he was in the mount, extraordinarily conversing with God, but it continued to shine *after* he came down from the mount. When men have been conversing with Christ in an extraordinary manner, a sensible effect of it *remains* upon them; there is something remarkable in their disposition and frame, of which if we take knowledge, and trace to its cause, we shall find it is because they have been with Jesus, Acts iv. 13.

SECT. VIII.

Truly gracious affections differ from those that are false and delusive, in that they naturally beget and promote such a spirit of love, meekness, quietness, forgiveness, and mercy, as appeared in Christ.

THE evidence of this in the Scripture is very abundant. If we judge of the nature of Christianity, and the proper spirit of the gospel, by the word of God, this spirit is what may, by way of eminency, be called *the christian spirit*; and may be looked upon as the true and distinguishing disposition of the hearts of Christians, as such. When some of the disciples of Christ said something, through inconsideration and infirmity, that was not agreeable to such a spirit, he told them that *they knew not what manner of spirit they were of*, Luke ix. 55. implying, that this spirit of which I am speaking, is the proper spirit of his religion and kingdom. All real disciples of Christ have this spirit in them; and not only so, but they *are of* this spirit; it is the spirit by which they are so possessed and governed, that it is their true and proper character. This is evident by what the wise man says, Prov. xvii. 27. (having respect plainly to such a spirit as this,) "A man of understanding is of an excellent spirit;" and by the particular description Christ gives of the qualities and temper of such as are truly blessed, that shall obtain mercy, and are God's children and heirs, Matt. v. "Blessed are the meek: for they shall inherit the earth. Blessed are the merciful: for they shall obtain mercy. Blessed are the peace-makers: for they shall be called the children of God." And that this spirit is the special character of the elect of God, is manifest by Col. iii. 12, 13. "Put on therefore as the elect of God, holy and beloved, bowels of mercies, kindness, humbleness of mind, meekness, long-suffering; forbearing one another, and forgiving one another." The apostle discoursing of that temper and disposition which he speaks

* "Do you think the Holy Ghost comes on a man, as on Balaam, by immediate acting, and then leaves him, and then he has nothing?—Shepard's *Parable*, Part I. p. 126.

of, as the most excellent and essential thing in Christianity—*that* without which none are true Christians, and the most glorious profession and gifts are nothing, calling this spirit by the name of *charity*—describes it thus; (1 Cor. xiii. 4, 5.) " Charity suffereth long, and is kind; charity envieth not; charity vaunteth not itself; is not puffed up; doth not behave itself unseemly; seeketh not her own; is not easily provoked; thinketh no evil." And the same apostle, (Gal. v.) designedly declaring the distinguishing marks and fruits of true christian grace, chiefly insists on the things that appertain to such a temper and spirit, (ver. 22, 23.) " The fruit of the Spirit is love, joy, peace, long-suffering, gentleness, goodness, faith, meekness, temperance." And so does the apostle James in describing true grace, or *that wisdom that is from above,* with that declared design, that others who are of a contrary spirit may not deceive themselves—and lie against the truth, in professing to be Christians, when they are not—James iii. 14—17. " If ye have bitter envying and strife in your hearts, glory not, and lie not against the truth. This wisdom descendeth not from above, but is earthly, sensual, devilish. For where envying and strife is, there is confusion, and every evil work. But the wisdom that is from above, is first pure, then peaceable, gentle, and easy to be entreated, full of mercy and good fruits."

Every thing that appertains to holiness of heart, does indeed belong to the nature of true Christianity, and the character of Christians; but a spirit of holiness, as appearing in some particular graces, may more especially be called the christian spirit or temper. Some amiable qualities and virtues more especially agree with the nature of the gospel constitution, and christian profession; because there is a special agreeableness in them with those divine *attributes* which God has more remarkably manifested and glorified in the work of redemption by Jesus Christ, the grand subject of the christian revelation. There is also a special agreeableness with those *virtues* which were so wonderfully exercised by Jesus Christ towards us in that affair, and the blessed example he hath therein set us. And they are peculiarly agreeable to the special drift and *design* of the work of redemption, the *benefits* we thereby receive, and the *relation* that it brings us into, to God and one another. And what are these virtues but such as humility, meekness, love, forgiveness, and mercy; which belong to the character of Christians, as such?

These things are spoken of as what are especially the character of Jesus Christ himself, the great head of the christian church. They are so spoken of in the prophecies of the Old Testament; as in that cited Matt. xxi. 5. " Tell ye the daughter of Sion, Behold, thy King cometh unto thee, meek, and sitting upon an ass, and a colt, the foal of an ass." So Christ himself speaks of them, Matt. xi. 29. " Learn of me, for I am meek and lowly in heart." The same appears by the name by which Christ is so often called in Scripture, viz. THE LAMB. And as these things are especially the character of Christ; so they are also especially the character of Christians. Christians are *Christ-like;* none deserve the name who are not so in their prevailing character. " The new man is renewed, after the image of him that created him," Col. iii. 10. All true Christians " behold as in a glass the glory of the Lord, and are changed into the same image, by his Spirit," 2 Cor. iii. 18. The elect are all " predestinated to be conformed to the image of the Son of God, that he might be the first-born among many brethren," Rom. viii. 29. " As we have borne the image of the first man, that is earthy, so we must also bear the image of the heavenly: for as is the earthy, such are they also that are earthy; and as is the heavenly, such are they also that are heavenly," 1 Cor. xv. 47—49. Christ is full of grace; and Christians all receive of his fulness, and grace for grace; *i. e.* there is grace in Christians *answering* to grace in Christ, such an answerableness as there is between the wax and the seal. There is character for character; such kind of graces, such a spirit and temper; the same things that belong to Christ's character belong to theirs. In that disposition wherein Christ's character in a special manner consists, does his image in a special manner consist. Christians who shine by reflecting the light of the Sun of righteousness, shine with the same sort of brightness, the same mild, sweet, and pleasant beams. These lamps of the spiritual temple, enkindled by fire from heaven, burn with the same sort of flame. The branch is of the same nature with the stock and root, has the same sap, and bears the same sort of fruit. The members have the same kind of life with the head. It would be strange if Christians should not be of the same temper and spirit with that of Christ; when they are *his flesh and his bone,* yea, are *one spirit,* 1 Cor. vi. 17. and so live, that it is *not they that live, but Christ that lives in them.* A christian spirit is Christ's *mark,* which he sets upon the souls of his people; his *seal* in their foreheads, bearing his image and superscription. Christians are the followers of Christ, as they are obedient to that call of Christ, Matt. xi. 28, 29. " Come to me, and learn of me, for I am meek and lowly of heart." They follow him as the Lamb; Rev. xiv. 4. " These are they which follow the Lamb whithersoever he goeth." True Christians are as it were clothed with the meek, quiet, and loving temper of Christ; for *as many as are in Christ, have put on Christ.* And in this respect *the church is clothed with the sun,* not only by being clothed with his imputed righteousness, but also by being adorned with his graces, Rom. xiii. 14. Christ the great Shepherd is himself a lamb, and believers are also lambs; all the flock are lambs; John xxi. 15. " Feed my lambs." Luke x. 3. " I send you forth as lambs in the midst of wolves." The redemption of the church by Christ from the power of the devil, was typified of old by David's delivering the *lamb* out of the mouth of the lion and the bear.

That such virtue is the very nature of the christian spirit, or the spirit that worketh in Christ and in his members, is evident by this, that *the dove* is the very symbol or emblem, chosen of God to represent it. Those things are the fittest emblems of other things, which best represent *that* which is most distinguishing in their nature. The Spirit that descended on Christ, when he was anointed of the Father, descended on him *like a dove.* The dove is a noted emblem of meekness, harmlessness, peace, and love. But the same Spirit that descended on the head of the church, descends to the members. " God hath sent forth the Spirit of his Son into their hearts," Gal. iv. 6. And " if any man have not the Spirit of Christ, he is none of his." Rom. viii. 9. There is but one Spirit to the whole mystical body, head and members, (1 Cor. vi. 17. Eph. iv. 4.) Christ breathes his own Spirit on his disciples, John xx. 22. As Christ was anointed with the Holy Ghost, descending on him like a dove, so Christians " have an anointing from the Holy One," 1 John ii. 20, 27. They are anointed with the same oil; it is the same " precious ointment on the head, that goes down to the skirts of the garments." And on both it is a spirit of peace and love: Ps. cxxxiii. 1, 2. " Behold, how good and pleasant it is, for brethren to dwell together in unity! It is like the precious ointment upon the head, that ran down upon the beard, even Aaron's beard, that went down to the skirts of his garments." The oil on Aaron's garments, had the same sweet and inimitable odour with that on his head; the smell of the same sweet spices. Christian affections, and a christian behaviour, are the flowing out of the savour of Christ's sweet ointments. Because the church has a dove-like temper and disposition, therefore it is said of her that she has doves' eyes, Cant. i. 15. " Behold thou art fair, my love; behold, thou art fair, thou hast doves' eyes." And chap. iv. 1. " Behold, thou art fair, my love, behold, thou art fair, thou hast doves' eyes within thy locks." The same is said of Christ, chap. vi. 12. " His eyes are as the eyes of doves." And the church is frequently compared to a dove, Cant. ii. 14. " O my dove, that art in the clefts of the rock."—Chap. v. 2. " Open to me, my love, my dove." And chap. vi. 9. " My dove, my undefiled is but one." Ps. lxviii. 13. " Ye shall be as the wings of a dove covered with silver, and her feathers with yellow gold." And lxxiv. 19. " O deliver not the soul of thy turtle-dove unto the multitude of the wicked." The dove that Noah sent out of the ark—that could find no rest for the sole of her foot until she returned—was a type of a true saint.

Meekness is so much the character of the saints, that *the meek* and *the godly* are used as synonymous terms in Scripture: so Ps. xxxvii. 10, 11. the wicked and the meek are set in opposition, as wicked and godly, "Yet a little while and the wicked shall not be: but the meek shall inherit the earth." So Ps. cxlvii. 6. "The Lord lifteth up the meek: he casteth the wicked down to the ground."

It is doubtless very much on this account, that Christ represents all his disciples, though the heirs of heaven, as *little children*: Matt. xix. 14. "Suffer little children to come unto me, and forbid them not; for of such is the kingdom of heaven." Matt. x. 42. "Whosoever shall give to drink unto one of those little ones a cup of cold water, in the name of a disciple, verily I say unto you, he shall in no wise lose his reward." Matt. xviiii. 6. "Whoso shall offend one of these little ones," &c. Ver. 10. "Take heed that ye despise not one of these little ones." Ver. 14. "It is not the will of your Father which is in heaven, that one of these little ones should perish." John xiii. 33. "Little children, yet a little while I am with you." Little children are innocent and harmless; they do not much mischief in the world; men need not be afraid of them; their anger does not last long, they do not lay up injuries in high resentment, entertaining deep and rooted malice. So Christians, in malice are children, 1 Cor. xiv. 20. Little children are not guileful and deceitful, but plain and simple; they are not versed in the arts of fiction and deceit; and are strangers to artful disguises. They are yielding and flexible, and not wilful and obstinate; do not trust to their own understanding, but rely on the instructions of parents, and others of superior understanding. Here is therefore a fit and lively emblem of the followers of the Lamb. Persons being thus like little children, is not only a thing highly commendable, what Christians aim at, and which some of extraordinary proficiency attain; but it is their *universal* character, and absolutely *necessary* in order to enter into the kingdom of heaven; Matt. xviii. 3. "Verily I say unto you, Except ye be converted, and become as little children, ye shall not enter into the kingdom of heaven." Mark x. 15. "Verily I say unto you, Whosoever shall not receive the kingdom of God as a little child, he shall not enter therein."

But here some may be ready to say, Is there no such thing as christian fortitude, and boldness for Christ, being good soldiers in the christian warfare, and coming out bold against the enemies of Christ and his people?

To which I answer, there doubtless is such a thing. The whole christian life is fitly compared to a warfare. The most eminent Christians are the best soldiers, endued with the greatest degrees of christian fortitude. And it is the duty of God's people to be stedfast, and vigorous in their opposition to the designs and ways of such as are endeavouring to overthrow the kingdom of Christ, and the interest of religion. But yet many persons seem to be quite mistaken concerning the nature of christian fortitude. It is an exceeding diverse thing from a brutal fierceness, or the boldness of beasts of prey. True christian fortitude consists in strength of mind, through grace, exerted in two things; in ruling and suppressing the *evil* passions and affections of the mind; and in stedfastly and freely exerting and following *good* affections and dispositions, without being hindered by sinful fear, or the opposition of enemies. But the *passions restrained*, and kept under in the exercise of this christian strength and fortitude, are those very passions that are vigorously and violently *exerted* in a false boldness for Christ. And those affections which are vigorously exerted in true fortitude, are those christian holy affections, that are directly contrary to the others. Though christian fortitude appears in withstanding and counteracting enemies without us; yet it much more appears in resisting and suppressing the enemies that are within us; because they are our worst and strongest enemies, and have greatest advantage against us. The strength of the good soldier of Jesus Christ appears in nothing more, than in stedfastly maintaining the holy, calm meekness, sweetness, and benevolence of his mind, amidst all the storms, injuries, strange behaviour, and surprising acts and events, of this evil and unreasonable world. The Scripture seems to intimate that true fortitude consists chiefly in this, Prov. xvi. 32. "He that is slow to anger, is better than the mighty; and he that ruleth his spirit, than he that taketh a city."

The surest way to make a right judgment of what is a holy fortitude in fighting with God's enemies, is to look to the Captain of all God's hosts, our great leader and example, and see wherein his fortitude and valour appeared, in his chief conflict. View him in the greatest battle that ever was or ever will be fought with these enemies, when he fought with them all alone, and of the people there was none with him. See *how* he exercised his fortitude in the highest degree, and got that glorious victory which will be celebrated in the praises and triumphs of all the hosts of heaven, through all eternity. Behold Jesus Christ in his last sufferings, when his enemies in earth and hell made their most violent attack upon him, compassing him round on every side, like roaring lions. Doubtless here we shall see the fortitude of a holy warrior and champion in the cause of God, in its highest perfection and greatest lustre, and an example fit for the soldiers to follow, that fight under this Captain. But how did he show his holy boldness and valour at that time? Not in the exercise of any fiery passions; not in fierce and violent speeches, vehemently declaiming against the intolerable wickedness of opposers, *giving them their own* in plain terms; but in not opening his mouth when afflicted and oppressed, in going as a lamb to the slaughter, and, as a sheep before his shearers is dumb, not opening his mouth; praying that the Father would forgive his cruel enemies, because they knew not what they did; nor shedding others' blood, but with all-conquering patience and love shedding his own. Indeed one of his disciples, who made a forward pretence to *boldness for Christ*, and confidently declared he would sooner die with Christ than deny him, began to lay about him with a sword: but Christ meekly rebukes him, and heals the wound he gives. And never was the patience, meekness, love, and forgiveness of Christ, in so glorious a manifestation, as at that time. Never did he appear so much a *Lamb*, and never did he show so much of the *dove-like* spirit, as at that time. If therefore we see any of the followers of Christ, in the midst of the most violent, unreasonable, and wicked opposition, maintaining the humility, quietness, and gentleness of a lamb, and the harmlessness, love, and sweetness of a dove, we may well judge that here is *a good soldier of Jesus Christ*.

When persons are fierce and violent, and exert their sharp and bitter passions, it shows *weakness*, instead of strength and fortitude. 1 Cor. iii. at the beginning, "And I, brethren, could not speak unto you as unto spiritual, but as unto carnal, even as unto babes in Christ.—For ye are yet carnal; for whereas there is among you envying, and strife, and divisions, are ye not carnal, and walk as men?"

There is a pretended boldness for Christ that arises from no better principle than pride. A man may be forward to expose himself to the dislike of the world, and even to provoke their displeasure, out of pride. For it is the nature of spiritual pride to cause men to seek distinction and singularity; and so oftentimes to set themselves at war with those whom they call carnal, that they may be more highly exalted among their party. True boldness for Christ is universal, and carries men above the displeasure of friends and foes; so that they will forsake all rather than Christ; and will rather offend all parties, and be thought meanly of by all, than offend Christ. And that duty which tries whether a man is willing to be despised by those of his own party, and thought the least worthy to be regarded by them, is a more proper trial of his boldness for Christ, than his being forward to expose himself to the reproach of opposers. The apostle declined to seek glory, not only of heathens and Jews, but of Christians; as he declares, 1 Thess. ii. 26.* He is bold for Christ, who has christian fortitude enough to confess his fault openly, when he has committed one that requires it, and as it were to come down upon his knees before opposers. Such things as these are much greater evidence of holy boldness, than resolutely and fiercely confronting opposers.

As some are much mistaken concerning the nature of

* Mr. Shepard, speaking of hypocrites affecting applause, says, "Hence men forsake their friends, and trample under foot the scorns of the world: they have credit elsewhere. To maintain their interest in the love of godly men, they will suffer much." *Parable of the Ten Virgins*, Part I. p. 180.

true *boldness* for Christ, so they are concerning christian *zeal*. It is indeed a flame, but a sweet one; or rather it is the heat and fervour of a sweet flame. For the flame of which it is the heat, is no other than that of divine love, or christian charity; which is the sweetest and most benevolent thing that can be, in the heart of man or angel. Zeal is the fervour of this flame, as it ardently and vigorously goes out towards the good that is its object; and so consequently in opposition to the evil that is contrary to, and impedes it. There is indeed opposition, vigorous opposition, that is an attendant of it; but it is against *things*, and not *persons*. Bitterness against the *persons* of men is no part of, but is contrary to it; insomuch that the warmer true zeal is, and the higher it is raised, so much the further are persons from such bitterness, and so much fuller of love both to the evil and to the good. It is no other, in its very nature and essence, than the fervour of christian love. And as to what opposition there is in it to *things*, it is *firstly* and chiefly against the *evil things* in the person *himself* who has this zeal; against the enemies of God and holiness in his own heart; (as these are most in his view, and what he has most to do with;) and but *secondarily* against the sins of others. And therefore there is nothing in a true christian zeal contrary to the spirit of meekness, gentleness, and love; the spirit of a little child, a lamb and dove, that has been spoken of; but is entirely agreeable to, and tends to promote it.

But I would say something particularly concerning this christian spirit as exercised in these three things, *forgiveness*, *love*, and *mercy*. The Scripture is very clear and express concerning the absolute *necessity* of each of these, as belonging to the temper and character of every Christian. A *forgiving* spirit is necessary, or a disposition to overlook and forgive injuries. Christ gives it to us both as a negative and positive evidence; and is express in teaching us, that if we are of such a spirit, it is a sign we are in a state of forgiveness and favour ourselves; and that if we are not of such a spirit, we are not forgiven of God; and seems to take special care that we should always bear it on our minds. Matt. vi. 12, 14, 15. "Forgive us our debts, as we forgive our debtors. For, if ye forgive men their trespasses, your heavenly Father will also forgive you. But if ye forgive not men their trespasses, neither will your Father forgive your trespasses." Christ expresses the same at another time, Mark xi. 25, 26. and again in Matt. xviii. 22, to the end, in the parable of the servant, who owed his lord ten thousand talents, and who would not forgive his fellow-servant a hundred pence; and therefore was delivered to the tormentors. In the application of the parable Christ says, ver. 35. "So likewise shall my heavenly Father do, if ye from your hearts forgive not every one his brother their trespasses."

And that all true saints are of a *loving*, benevolent, and beneficent temper, the Scripture is very plain and abundant. Without it, the apostle tells us, though we should speak with the tongues of men and angels, we are as a sounding brass, or a tinkling cymbal: and though we have the gift of prophecy, and understand all mysteries, and all knowledge; yet without this spirit we are nothing. There is no one virtue, or disposition of mind, so often and so expressly insisted on, as marks laid down in the New Testament, whereby to know true Christians. It is often given as a sign peculiarly distinguishing, by which all may know Christ's disciples, and by which they may know themselves; and is often laid down, both as a negative and positive evidence. Christ calls the law of love, by way of eminence, *his commandment*, John xiii. 34. "A new commandment I give unto you, that ye love one another; as I have loved you, that ye also love one another." And chap. xv. 12. "This is my commandment, that ye love one another, as I have loved you." And ver. 17. "These things I command you, that ye love one another." And says, chap. xiii. 35. "By this shall all men know that ye are my disciples, if ye have love one to another." And chap. xiv. 21. (still with a special reference to this which he calls *his* commandment,) "He that hath my commandments, and keepeth them, he it is that loveth me." The beloved disciple, who had so much of this sweet temper himself, abundantly insists on it, in his epistles. Not one of the apostles is so express in laying down signs of grace, for professors to try themselves by, as he; and in his signs, he insists scarcely on any thing but a spirit of christian love, and an agreeable practice: 1 John ii. 9, 10. "He that saith he is in the light, and hateth his brother, is in darkness even until now. He that loveth his brother abideth in the light, and there is none occasion of stumbling in him." Chap. iii. 14. "We know that we are passed from death unto life, because we love the brethren: he that loveth not his brother, abideth in death." Ver. 18, 19, "My little children, let us not love in word and in tongue, but in deed, and in truth. And hereby we know that we are of the truth, and shall assure our hearts before him." Ver. 23, 24. "This is his commandment, that we should love one another. And he that keepeth his commandments, dwelleth in him, and he in him: and hereby we know that he abideth in us, by the Spirit which he hath given us." Chap. iv. 7, 8. "Beloved, let us love one another: for love is of God: and every one that loveth is born of God, and knoweth God. He that loveth not, knoweth not God; for God is love." Ver. 12, 13. "No man hath seen God at any time. If we love one another, God dwelleth in us, and his love is perfected in us. Hereby know we that we dwell in him, because he hath given us of his Spirit." Ver. 16. "God is love; and he that dwelleth in love, dwelleth in God, and God in him." Ver. 20. "If a man say, I love God, and hateth his brother, he is a liar: for he that loveth not his brother whom he hath seen, how can he love God whom he hath not seen?"

And the Scripture is as plain as possible, that none are true saints, but those who are of a disposition to *pity* and *relieve* their fellow-creatures, who are poor, indigent, and afflicted: Psal. xxxvii. 21. "The righteous showeth mercy, and giveth." Ver. 26. "He is ever merciful, and lendeth." Psal. cxii. 5. "A good man showeth favour and lendeth." Ver. 9. "He hath dispersed abroad, and given to the poor." Prov. xiv. 31. "He that honoureth God, hath mercy on the poor." Prov. xxi. 26. "The righteous giveth, and spareth not." Jer. xxii. 16. "He judged the cause of the poor and needy, then it was well with him: was not this to know me? saith the Lord." Jam. i. 27. "Pure religion and undefiled before God and the Father, is this, To visit the fatherless and widows in their affliction," &c. Hos. vi. 6. "For I desired mercy and not sacrifice; and the knowledge of God, more than burnt-offerings." Matt. v. 7. "Blessed are the merciful: for they shall obtain mercy." 2 Cor. viii. 8. "I speak not by commandment, but by occasion of the forwardness of others, and to prove the sincerity of your love." Jam. ii. 13—16. "For he shall have judgment without mercy, that hath showed no mercy.—What doth it profit, my brethren, though a man say he hath faith, and have not works? can faith save him? If a brother or sister be naked, and destitute of daily food; and one of you say unto them, Depart in peace, be you warmed and filled: notwithstanding ye give them not those things which are needful to the body; what doth it profit?" 1 John iii. 17. "Whoso hath this world's good, and seeth his brother have need, and shutteth up his bowels of compassion from him, how dwelleth the love of God in him?" Christ in that description he gives us of the day of judgment, Matt. xxv. (which is the most particular in all the Bible,) represents, that judgment will be passed at that day, according as men have been of a merciful spirit and practice, or otherwise. Christ's design in giving such a description of the process of that day, is plainly to possess all his followers with the apprehension, that unless this was their spirit and practice, there was no hope of their being accepted and owned by him at that day. We find in Scripture, that a *righteous man* and a *merciful man* are synonymous expressions; Isa. lvii. 1. "The righteous perisheth, and no man layeth it to heart; and merciful men are taken away, none considering that the righteous is taken away from the evil to come."

Thus we see how full, clear, and abundant, the evidence from Scripture is, that those who are truly gracious, are under the government of that lamb-like, dove-like Spirit of Jesus Christ, and that this is essentially and eminently the nature of the saving grace of the gospel, and the proper spirit of true Christianity. We may therefore undoubtedly determine, that all truly christian affections are attended with such a spirit: and that this is the natural tendency of the fear and hope, the sorrow and the joy, the confidence and the zeal of true Christians.

None will understand me, that true Christians have no remains of a contrary spirit, and can never, in any instances, be guilty of a behaviour not agreeable to such a spirit. But this I affirm, and shall affirm until I deny the Bible to be any thing worth, that every thing in Christians that belongs to true Christianity, is of this tendency, and works this way; and that there is no true Christian upon earth, but is so under the prevailing power of such a spirit, that he is properly denominated from it, and it is truly and justly his character. Therefore, ministers and others have no warrant from Christ to encourage persons of a contrary character and behaviour, to think they are converted, because they tell a fair story of illuminations and discoveries. In so doing, they would set up their own wisdom against Christ's, and judge *against* that rule by which Christ has declared all men should know his disciples. Some persons place religion so much in certain transient illuminations and impressions, (especially if they are in such a particular method,) and so little in the spirit and temper, that they greatly deform religion, and form notions of Christianity quite different from what it is, as delineated in the Scriptures. The Scripture knows no true Christians, of a sordid, selfish, cross, and contentious spirit. Nothing can be a greater absurdity, than a morose, hard, close, high-spirited, spiteful, true Christian. We must learn the way of bringing men to rules; and not rules to men, and so strain the rules of God's word, in order to take in ourselves, and some of our neighbours, until we make them wholly of none effect

It is true, allowances must be made for men's natural temper; but we must not allow men, that once were wolves and serpents, to be now converted, without any remarkable change in the spirit of their mind. The change made by true conversion, is wont to be most remarkable, with respect to the past notorious wickedness of the person. Grace has as great a tendency to restrain and mortify such sins, as are contrary to the spirit that has been spoken of, as it has to mortify drunkenness or lasciviousness. Yea, the Scripture represents the change wrought by gospel-grace, as especially appearing in an alteration of the former sort; Isa. xi. 6—9. "The wolf shall dwell with the lamb, and the leopard shall lie down with the kid: and the calf, and the young lion, and the fatling together, and a little child shall lead them. And the cow and the bear shall feed, their young ones shall lie down together: and the lion shall eat straw like the ox. And the sucking child shall play on the hole of the asp, and the weaned child shall put his hand on the cockatrice' den. They shall not hurt nor destroy in all my holy mountain: for the earth shall be full of the knowledge of the Lord, as the waters cover the sea." And to the same purpose is Isa. lxv. 25. Accordingly we find, that in the primitive times of the christian church, converts were remarkably changed in this respect; Tit. iii. 3, &c. "For we ourselves also were sometimes foolish, disobedient, deceived, serving divers lusts and pleasures, living in malice and envy, hateful, and hating one another. But after that the kindness and love of God our Saviour toward man appeared,—he saved us by the washing of regeneration, and renewing of the Holy Ghost." And Col. iii. 7, 8. "In the which ye also walked some time, when ye lived in them. But now ye also put off all these; anger, wrath, malice, blasphemy, filthy communication out of your mouth."

SECT. IX.

Gracious affections soften the heart, and are attended with a christian tenderness of spirit.

FALSE affections, however persons may seem to be melted by them while they are new, have a tendency in the end to harden the heart. A disposition to some kind of passions may be established; such as imply self-seeking, self-exaltation, and opposition to others. But false affections, with the delusion that attends them, finally tend to stupify the mind, and shut it up against those affections wherein tenderness of heart consists. The effect of them at last is, that persons in the settled frame of their minds, become less affected with their present and past sins, and less conscientious with respect to future sins; less moved with the warnings and cautions of God's word, or chastisements in his providence; more careless of the frame of their hearts, and the manner and tendency of their behaviour; less quick-sighted to discern what is sinful, and less afraid of the appearance of evil, than they were while under legal awakenings and fears of hell. Now they have been the subjects of impressions and affections, have a high opinion of themselves, and look on their state to be safe, they can be much more easy than before, though living in the neglect of duties that are troublesome and inconvenient.—They are much more slow and partial in complying with difficult commands; and are not alarmed at the appearance of their own defects and transgressions. They are emboldened to favour themselves more, with respect to the labour and painful exactness in their walk, and more easily yield to temptations, and the solicitations of their lusts; and have far less care of their behaviour, when they come into the holy presence of God, in the time of public or private worship. Formerly it may be, under legal convictions, they took much pains in religion, and denied themselves in many things: but now, thinking themselves out of the danger of hell, they very much put off the burden of the cross, and save themselves the trouble of difficult duties, allowing themselves more of the enjoyment of their ease and lusts.

Such persons as these, instead of embracing Christ as their *Saviour from sin*, trust in him as the *saviour of their sins;* instead of flying to him as their refuge *from their spiritual enemies*, they make use of him as the defence *of their spiritual enemies*, *from God*, and to strengthen them against him. They make Christ the minister of sin, the great officer and vicegerent of the devil, to strengthen his interest, and make him above all things in the world strong against JEHOVAH; so that they may sin against him with good courage, and without any fear, being effectually secured from restraints by his most solemn warnings and most awful threatenings. They trust in Christ to preserve to them the quiet enjoyment of their sins, and to be their shield to defend them from God's displeasure; while they come close to him, even to his bosom, the place of his children, to fight against him, with their mortal weapons, hid under their skirts.* However, some of these, at the same time, make a great profession of love to God, and assurance of his favour, and great joy in tasting the sweetness of his love.

After this manner *they* trusted in Christ, of whom the apostle Jude speaks, who *crept in* among the saints *unknown;* but were really "ungodly men, turning the grace of God into lasciviousness," Jude 4. These are they

* "These are hypocrites that believe, but fail in regard of the use of the gospel, and of the Lord Jesus. And these we read of, Jude 3. *viz.* of some men *that did turn grace into wantonness.* For therein appears the exceeding evil of a man's heart, that not only the law, but also the glorious gospel of the Lord Jesus, works in him all manner of unrighteousness. And it is too common for men at the first work of conversion, Oh then to cry for grace and Christ, and afterwards grow licentious, live and lie in the breach of the law, and take their warrant for their course from the gospel."—Shepard's *Parable*, Part I. p. 126.

Again, p. 232. Mr. Shepard speaks of such hypocrites as those, "who, like strange eggs being put into the same nest, where honest men have lived, they have been hatched up; and when they are young, keep their nest, and live by crying and opening their mouths wide after the Lord, and the food of his word; but when their wings are grown, and they have got some affections, some knowledge, some hope of mercy, are hardened thereby to fly from God." And adds, "Can that man be good, whom God's grace makes worse?"

Again, Part II. p. 167. "When men fly to Christ in times of peace, that so they may preserve their sins with greater peace of conscience; so that sin makes them fly to Christ, as well as misery; not that they may destroy and abolish sin, but they may be preserved in their sins with peace; then men may be said to apprehend Christ only by a seeming faith.—Many an heart secretly saith this, If I can have my sin, and peace, and conscience quiet for the present, and God merciful to pardon it afterward; hence he doth rely (as he saith) only on the mercy of God in Christ: and now this hardens and blinds him, and makes his faith secure, and his faith is sermon proof, nothing stirs him—And were it not for their faith they should despair, but this keeps them up. And now they think if they have any trouble of mind, the devil troubles them; and so make Christ and faith protectors of sin, not purifiers from sin: which is most dreadful; turning grace to wantonness, as they did sacrifice. So these would sin under the shadow of Christ, because the shadow is good and sweet, Mic. iii. 11. They had subtle sly ends in good duties; for therein may lie a man's sin: yet they lean upon the Lord.—When money-changers came into the temple, *You have made it a den of thieves.* Thieves when hunted fly to their den or cave, and there they are secure against all searchers, and hue and cries: so here. But Christ whipped them out. So when men are pursued with cries and fears of conscience, away to Christ they go as to their den: not as saints, to pray and lament out the life of their sin there; but to preserve their sin. This is vile; will the Lord receive such?"

that trust in their being righteous; and because God has promised that the *righteous shall surely live*, or certainly be saved, are therefore emboldened to *commit iniquity*, whom God threatens in Ezek. xxxiii. 13. "When I shall say to the righteous, that he shall surely live: if he trust to his own righteousness, and commit iniquity; all his righteousness shall not be remembered, but for his iniquity that he hath committed, he shall die for it."

Gracious affections are of a quite contrary tendency; they turn a heart of stone more and more into a heart of flesh. Holy love and hope are principles vastly more efficacious upon the heart, to make it tender, and to fill it with a dread of sin, or whatever might displease and offend God; and to engage it to watchfulness, and care, and strictness, than a slavish fear of hell. Gracious affections, as was observed before, flow out of a contrite heart, or (as the word signifies) a bruised heart, bruised and broken with godly sorrow; which makes the heart tender, as bruised flesh is tender, and easily hurt. Godly sorrow has much greater influence to make the heart tender, than mere legal sorrow from selfish principles.

The tenderness of the heart of a true Christian, is elegantly signified by our Saviour, in his comparing such a one to a *little child*. The flesh of a little child is very tender: so is the heart of one that is new-born. This is also represented in what we are told of Naaman's cure of his leprosy, by his washing in Jordan, by the direction of the prophet; which was undoubtedly a type of the renewing of the soul, by washing in the laver of regeneration. We are told, 2 Kings v. 14. that "he went down, and dipped himself seven times in Jordan, according to the saying of the man of God; and his flesh came again like unto the flesh of a little child." Not only is the *flesh* of a little child tender, but his *mind* is tender. A little child has his heart easily moved, wrought upon, and bowed: so is a Christian in spiritual things. A little child is apt to be affected with sympathy, to weep with them that weep, and cannot well bear to see others in distress: so it is with a Christian; John xi. 35. Rom. xii. 15. 1 Cor. xii. 26. A little child is easily won by kindness: so is a Christian. A little child is easily affected with grief at temporal evils, his heart is melted, and he falls a-weeping; thus tender is the heart of a Christian, with regard to the evil of sin. A little child, is easily affrighted at the appearance of outward evils, or any thing that threatens its hurt: so is a Christian apt to be alarmed at the appearance of moral evil, and any thing that threatens the hurt of the soul. A little child when it meets enemies, or fierce beasts, is not apt to trust its own strength, but flies to its parents: for refuge so a saint is not self-confident in engaging spiritual enemies, but flies to Christ. A little child is apt to be suspicious of evil in places of danger, afraid in the dark, afraid when left solitary, or far from home: so is a saint apt to be sensible of his spiritual dangers, jealous of himself, full of fear when he cannot see his way plain before him, afraid to be left alone, and to be at a distance from God; Prov. xxviii. 14. "Happy is the man that feareth alway; but he that hardeneth his heart, shall fall into mischief." A little child is apt to be afraid of superiors, and to dread their anger, and tremble at their frowns and threatenings: so is a true saint with respect to God; Psal. cxix. 120. "My flesh trembleth for fear of thee, and I am afraid of thy judgments." Isa. lxvi. 2. "To this man will I look, even to him that is poor, and trembleth at my word. Ver. 5. Hear ye the word of the Lord, ye that tremble at his word." Ezra ix 4. "Then were assembled unto me every one that trembled at the words of the God of Israel." Chap. x. 3. "According to the counsel of my lord, and of those that tremble at the commandment of our God." A little child approaches superiors with awe: so do the saints approach God with holy awe and reverence; Job xiii. 11. "Shall not his excellency make you afraid? and his dread fall upon you? Holy fear is so much the nature of true godliness, that it is called in Scripture by no other name more frequently, than the *fear of God*.

Hence gracious affections do not tend to make men bold, forward, noisy, and boisterous; but rather to *speak trembling;* Hos. xiii. 1. "When Ephraim spake trembling, he exalted himself in Israel; but when he offended in Baal, he died." It tends to clothe them with a kind of holy fear in all their behaviour towards God and man; agreeable to Psal. ii. 11. 1 Pet. iii. 15. 2 Cor. vii. 15. Eph. vi. 5. 1 Pet. iii. 2. Rom. xi. 20.

But, is there no such thing as a holy boldness in prayer, and the duties of divine worship? There is doubtless such a thing; and it is chiefly to be found in eminent saints, persons of great degrees of faith and love. But this holy boldness is not in the least opposite to *reverence;* though it be to *disunion* and *servility*. It abolishes or lessens that disposition which arises from *moral distance* or *alienation;* and also *distance of relation*, as that of a slave: but not at all, that which becomes the *natural distance*, whereby we are infinitely inferior. No boldness in poor sinful worms of the dust, who have a right view of God and themselves, will prompt them to approach God with less fear and reverence, than spotless and glorious angels in heaven, who cover their faces before his throne, Isa. vi. 1, &c. Rebecca, (who in her marriage with Isaac, in almost all its circumstances, was manifestly a great type of the church, the spouse of Christ,) when she meets Isaac, alights from her camel, takes a vail, and covers herself; although she was brought to him as his bride, to be with him, in the nearest relation, and most intimate union.* Elijah, that great prophet, who had so much holy familiarity with God, at a time of special nearness to him, even when he conversed with him in the mount, wrapped his face in his mantle. Which was not because he was terrified with any servile fear, by the terrible *wind,* and *earthquake,* and *fire;* but after these were all over, and God spake to him as a friend, *in a still small voice;* 1 Kings xix. 12, 13. "And after the fire, a still small voice; and it was so, when Elijah heard it, he wrapped his face in his mantle." And Moses, with whom God spake face to face, as a man speaks with his friend, and who was distinguished above all the prophets, in the familiarity with God to which he was admitted—at a time when he was brought nearest of all, when God showed him his glory in that same mount, where he afterwards spake to Elijah—"made haste, and bowed his head towards the earth, and worshipped," Exod. xxxiv. 8. There is in some persons a most unsuitable and unsufferable boldness, in their addresses to the great Jehovah—an affectation of holy boldness, and ostentation of eminent nearness and familiarity—the very thoughts of which would make them shrink into nothing, with horror and confusion, if they saw the distance that is between God and them. They are like the Pharisee, that boldly drew near, in confidence of his own eminence in holiness. Whereas, if they saw their vileness, they would be more like the publican, that "stood afar off, and durst not so much as lift up his eyes to heaven: but smote upon his breast, saying, God be merciful to me a sinner." It becomes such sinful creatures as we, to approach a holy God (although with faith, and without terror, yet) with contrition, penitent shame, and confusion of face. It is foretold that this should be the disposition of the church, at the time of her highest privileges on earth, in her latter day of glory, when God should remarkably comfort her, by revealing to her his covenant-mercy; Ezek. xvi. 60, &c. "I will establish unto thee an everlasting covenant. Then thou shalt remember thy ways, and be ashamed. And I will establish my covenant with thee, and thou shalt know that I am the Lord: that thou mayest remember and be confounded, and never open thy mouth any more because of thy shame, when I am pacified toward thee for all that thou hast done, saith the Lord God." The woman we read of in the 7th chapter of Luke, who was an eminent saint and had much of that true love which casts out fear, (by Christ's own testimony, ver. 47.) approached Christ in an acceptable manner when she came with humble modesty, reverence, and shame. She stood at his feet, weeping *behind him*, as not being fit to appear before his face, and washed his feet with her tears.

One reason why gracious affections are attended with this tenderness of spirit, is, that true grace tends to pro-

* Dr. Ames, in his Cases of Conscience, Book III. chap. iv. speaks of a holy modesty in the worship of God, as one sign of true humility.

mote convictions of conscience. Persons are wont to have some convictions of conscience before they have any grace: and if afterwards they are truly converted, have true repentance, joy, and peace in believing; this has a tendency to put an end to *terrors*, but has no tendency to put an end to *convictions of sin*; it rather increases them. Grace does not stupify a man's conscience; but makes it more sensible, more easily and thoroughly to discern the sinfulness of that which is sinful, and to receive a greater conviction of the heinous and dreadful nature of sin. The conscience becomes susceptive of a quicker and deeper sense of sin, and the man is more convinced of his own sinfulness, and the wickedness of his heart; consequently grace has a tendency to make him more jealous of his heart. Grace tends to give the soul a further and *better conviction* of the *same* things concerning sin, that it was convinced of under a legal work of the Spirit; *viz.* its great contrariety to the will, and law, and honour of God, the greatness of God's hatred of it, and displeasure against it, and the dreadful punishment it exposes to and deserves. And not only so, but it convinces the soul of something further concerning sin, of which it saw nothing, while only under *legal convictions;* and that is, the infinitely hateful nature of sin, and its dreadfulness upon that account. And this makes the heart tender with respect to sin; like David's heart, that smote him when he had cut off Saul's skirt. The heart of a true penitent is like a burnt child that dreads the fire. Whereas, on the contrary, he that has had a counterfeit repentance, and false comforts and joys, is like iron that has been suddenly heated and quenched; it becomes much harder than before. A false conversion puts an end to convictions of conscience; and so, either takes away or much diminishes that conscientiousness which was manifested under a work of the law.

All gracious affections have a tendency to promote this christian tenderness of heart. Not only godly sorrow, but even a gracious joy does this. Psal. ii. 11. "Serve the Lord with fear, and rejoice with trembling." As also a gracious hope; Psal. xxxiii. 18. "Behold, the eye of the Lord is upon them that fear him; upon them that hope in his mercy." And Psal. cxlvii. 11. "The Lord taketh pleasure in them that fear him, in those that hope in his mercy." Yea, the most confident and assured hope, that is truly gracious, has this tendency. The higher a holy hope is raised, the more there is of this christian tenderness. The banishing of servile fear by a holy assurance, is attended with a proportionable increase of a reverential fear. The diminishing of the fear of God's displeasure in future punishment, is attended with a proportionable increase of fear of his displeasure *itself;* a diminished fear of hell, with an increase of the fear of sin. The vanishing of jealousies concerning the person's state, is attended with a proportionable increase of jealousy of his heart, in a distrust of its strength, wisdom, stability, faithfulness, &c. The less apt he is to be afraid of natural evil—having *his heart fixed, trusting in God*, and so, *not afraid of evil tidings*—the more apt is he to be alarmed with the appearance of moral evil, or the evil of sin. As he has more holy boldness, so he has less of self-confidence, or a forward assuming boldness, and more modesty. As he is more sure than others of deliverance from hell, so he has a greater sense of its desert. He is less apt than others to be shaken in faith; but more apt to be moved with solemn warnings, with God's frowns, and with the calamities of others. He has the firmest comfort, but the softest heart: richer than others, but poorest of all in spirit. He is the tallest and strongest saint, but the least and tenderest child among them.

SECT. X.

Another thing wherein those affections that are truly gracious and holy, differ from those that are false, is beautiful symmetry and proportion.

NOT that the symmetry of the virtues and gracious affections of the saints, in this life, is perfect: it oftentimes is in many things defective, through the imperfection of grace, want of proper instructions, errors in judgment, some particular unhappiness of natural temper, defects in education, and many other disadvantages that might be mentioned. But yet there is in no wise that monstrous disproportion in gracious affections, and the various parts of true religion in the saints, that is very commonly to be observed in the false religion and counterfeit graces of hypocrites.

In the truly holy affections of the saints is found that proportion, which is the natural consequence of the universality of their sanctification. They have the whole image of Christ upon them: they have *put off the old man*, and have *put on the new man* entire in all his parts and members. *It hath pleased the Father that in Christ all fulness should dwell:* there is in him every grace; *he is full of grace and truth:* and they that are Christ's *of his fulness receive, and grace for grace;* (John i. 14, 16.) There is every grace in them which is in Christ: *grace for grace;* that is, grace answerable to grace: there is no grace in Christ, but there is its image in believers to answer it. The image is a *true* image; and there is something of the same beautiful proportion in the image, which is in the original; there is feature for feature, and member for member. There is symmetry and beauty in God's workmanship. The natural body which God hath made, consists of many members; and all are in a beautiful proportion: so the new man consists of various graces and affections. The body of one that was born a perfect child, may fail of exact proportion through distemper, weakness, or injury of some of its members; yet the disproportion is in no measure like that of those who are born monsters.

It is with hypocrites, as it was with Ephraim of old, at a time when God greatly complains of their hypocrisy; Hos. vii. "Ephraim is a cake not turned," half roasted and half raw: there is commonly no manner of uniformity in their affections. There is in many of them a great partiality, with regard to the several kinds of religious affections; great affections in some things, and no proportion in others. A holy hope and holy fear go together in the saints, Psal. xxxiii. 18. and cxlvii. 11. But in some of these there is the most confident hope, while they are void of reverence, self-jealousy, and caution, and while they to a great degree cast off fear. In the saints, joy and holy fear go together, though the joy be never so great: as it was with the disciples, in that joyful morning of Christ's resurrection, Matt. xxviii. 8. "And they departed quickly from the sepulchre, with fear and *great* joy."* But many of these rejoice without trembling: their joy is truly opposite to godly fear.

But particularly, one great difference between saints and hypocrites is this, that the joy and comfort of the former is attended with godly sorrow and mourning for sin. They have not only sorrow to prepare them for their first comfort, but after they are comforted, and their joy is established. As it is foretold of the church of God, that they should mourn and loathe themselves for their sins, after they were returned from the captivity, and were settled in the land of Canaan, the land of rest, the land flowing with milk and honey, Ezek. xx. 42, 43. "And ye shall know that I am the Lord, when I shall bring you into the land of Israel, into the country for the which I lifted up mine hand to give it to your fathers. And there shall ye remember your ways, and all your doings, wherein ye have been defiled, and ye shall loathe yourselves in your own sight, for all your evils that ye have committed;" (also Ezek. xvi. 61—63.) A true saint is like a little child in this respect: he never had any godly sorrow before he was born again; but since, has it often in exercise. A little child, before it is born, and while it remains in darkness, never cries; but as soon as ever it sees the light, it begins to cry; and thenceforward is often crying. Although Christ hath borne our griefs, and carried our sorrows, so that we are freed from the *sorrow of punishment*, and may now sweetly feed upon the comforts Christ hath purchased for us; yet that hinders not but that our feeding on these comforts should be attended with the *sorrow of repentance*. Thus of old,

* "Renewed care and diligence follow the sealings of the Spirit. Now is the soul at the foot of Christ, as Mary was at the sepulchre, *with fear and great joy.* He that travels the road with a rich treasure about him, is afraid of a thief in every bush." Flavel's *Sacramental Meditations*, Med. 4.

the children of Israel were commanded evermore to feed upon the paschal lamb with bitter herbs.* True saints are spoken of in Scripture, not only as those that *have* mourned for sin, but as those that *do* mourn, whose manner it is still to mourn; Matt. v. 4. "Blessed are they that mourn: for they shall be comforted."

Not only is there often in hypocrites, an essential deficiency, as to the various kinds of religious affections; but also a strange partiality and disproportion, in the same affections, with regard to different objects.—Thus as to the affection of *love*, some make high pretences, and a great show of love to God and Christ, and it may be have been greatly affected with what they have heard or thought concerning them: but they have not a spirit of love and benevolence towards men, but are disposed to contention, envy, revenge, and evil-speaking; and will, it may be, suffer an old grudge to rest in their bosoms towards a neighbour for seven years together, if not twice seven years; living in real ill-will and bitterness of spirit towards him. And it may be in their dealings with their neighbours, they are not very strict and conscientious in observing the rule of *doing to others, as they would that they should do to them*: 1 John iv. 20. "If a man say, I love God, and hateth his brother, he is a liar: for he that loveth not his brother whom he hath seen, how can he love God whom he hath not seen?" On the other hand, there are others who appear as if they had a great deal of benevolence to men, who are very good-natured and generous in their way; but have no love to God.

And as to love to men, there are some who have flowing affections to some; but their love is far from being of so extensive and universal a nature, as a truly christian love is.—They are full of dear affections to some, and full of bitterness towards others. They are knit to their own party, those who approve, those who love, and admire them; but are fierce against those that oppose and dislike them. Matt. v. 45, 46. "Be like your Father which is in heaven; for he maketh his sun to rise on the evil and on the good. For if ye love them which love you, what reward have ye? do not even the publicans the same?" Some show a great affection to their neighbours, and pretend to be ravished with the company of the children of God *abroad*: but at the same time are uncomfortable and churlish towards their near relations *at home*, and are very negligent of relative duties. And as to the great love to sinners and opposers of religion, and the great concern for their souls, that some express, even to extreme agony—singling out a particular person from among a multitude for its object—while at the same time there is no general compassion to sinners in equally miserable circumstances, but what is in a monstrous disproportion; this seems not to be of the nature of a gracious affection. Not that I suppose it to be at all strange, that pity to the perishing souls of sinners should be to a degree of agony, if other things are answerable; or that a truly gracious compassion to souls should be exercised much more to some persons than others who are equally miserable, especially on some particular occasions. Many things may happen to fix the mind, and affect the heart, with respect to a particular person, at such a juncture; and without doubt some saints have been in great distress for the souls of particular persons, so as to be, as it were, in travail for them. But when persons appear, at particular times, in agonies for the soul of some single person, far beyond what has been usual in eminent saints, but appear to be far inferior to them in a spirit of meek and fervent love, charity, and compassion to mankind in general; I say, such agonies are greatly to be suspected, because the Spirit of God is wont to give graces and gracious affections in a beautiful symmetry and proportion.

And as there is a monstrous disproportion in the love of some, in its exercises towards *different* persons, so there is in their seeming exercises of love towards the *same* persons. Some men show a love to others as to their outward man, they are liberal of their worldly substance, and often give to the poor; but have no love to or concern for the *souls* of men. Others pretend a great love to men's souls, but are not compassionate and charitable towards their *bodies*. To make a great show of love, pity, and distress for souls, costs them nothing; but in order to show mercy to men's bodies, they must part with money. But a true christian love to our brethren, extends both to their souls and bodies; and herein is like the love and compassion of Jesus Christ. He showed mercy to men's souls, by laboriously preaching the gospel to them; and to their bodies, in going about doing good, healing all manner of sickness and diseases among the people. We have a remarkable instance of Christ's compassion at once both to men's souls and bodies, in Mark vi. 34, &c. "And Jesus, when he came out, saw much people, and was moved with compassion toward them, because they were as sheep not having a shepherd: and he began to teach them many things." Here was his compassion to their souls. And in the sequel, we have an account of his compassion to their bodies; he fed five thousand of them with five loaves and two fishes, because they had been a long while *having nothing to eat*. And if the compassion of professing Christians towards others does not work in the same ways, it is a sign that it is no true christian compassion.

And furthermore, it is a sign that affections are not of the right sort, if persons seem to be much affected with the bad qualities of their fellow-Christians, (as the coldness and lifeliness of other saints,) but are in no proportion affected with their own defects and corruptions. A true Christian may be affected with the coldness and unsavouriness of other saints, and may mourn much over it: but at the same time, he is not so apt to be affected with the badness of any body's heart, as his own; this is most in his view; this he is most quick-sighted to discern; to see its aggravations, and to condemn. A lesser degree of virtue will bring him to pity himself, and be concerned at his own calamities, than is needful rightly to be affected with those of others; and if men have not attained to the less, we may determine they never attained to the greater.

And here by the way, I would observe, that it may be laid down as a general rule, That if persons pretend to high attainments in religion, who have never yet arrived to the lesser, it is a sign of a vain pretence. If persons pretend, that they have got beyond mere *morality*, to live a *spiritual* and *divine* life; but really have not come to be so much as *moral* persons: or pretend to be greatly affected with the wickedness of their hearts, and are not affected with the palpable violations of God's commands in their practice, which is a lesser attainment, their pretences are vain. If they pretend to be brought to be even willing to be damned for the glory of God, but have no forwardness to suffer a little in their estates and names, and worldly convenience, for the sake of their duty: or finally pretend that they are not afraid to venture their souls upon Christ, and commit their all to God, trusting to his bare word, and the faithfulness of his promises, for

* "If repentance accompanies faith, it is no presumption to believe. Many know the sin, and hence believe in Christ, trust in Christ, and there is an end of their faith. But what confession and sorrow for sin? what more love to Christ follows this faith? Truly none. Nay, their faith is the cause why they have none. For they think, if I trust in Christ to forgive me, he will do it; and there is an end of the business. Verily this hedge faith, this bramble-faith, that catches hold on Christ, and pricks and scratches Christ, by more impenitency, more contempt of him, is mere presumption; which shall one day be burnt up and destroyed by the fire of God's jealousy. Fye upon that faith, that serves only to keep a man from being tormented before his time! Your sins would be your sorrows, but that your faith quiets you. But if faith be accompanied with repentance, mourning for sin, more esteem of God's grace in Christ; so that nothing breaks thy heart more than the thoughts of Christ's unchangeable love to one so vile, and this love makes thee love much, and love him the more; as thy sin increaseth, so thou desirest thy love's increase; and now the stream of thy thoughts run, how thou mayst live to him that died for thee: this was Mary's faith, who sat at Christ's feet weeping, washing them with her tears, and loving much, because much was forgiven."—Shepard's *Sound Believer*, p. 128, 129.

"You shall know godly sorrow (says Dr. Preston, in his discourse on Paul's conversion) by the continuance of it; it is constant: but worldly sorrow is but a passion of the mind; it changes, it lasts not. Though for the present it may be violent and strong, and work much outwardly; yet it comes but by fits, and continues not: like a land-flood, which violently, for the present, overflows the banks; but it will away again; it is not always thus. But godly sorrow is like a spring, that still keeps running both winter and summer, wet and dry, in heat and cold, early and late. So this godly sorrow is the same in a regenerate man still; take him when you will, he is still sorrowing for sin. This godly sorrow stands like the centre of the earth, which removes not, but still remains."

"I am persuaded, many a man's heart is kept from breaking and mourning, because of this. He saith (it may be) that he is a vile sinner; but I trust in Christ, &c. If they do go to Christ to destroy their sin, this makes them more secure in their sin. For (say they) I cannot help it, and Christ must do all. Whereas faith makes the soul mourn after the Lord the more." Shepard's *Parable of the Ten Virgins*, Part II. p. 168.

their eternal welfare; but at the same time, have not confidence enough in God, to dare to trust him with a little of their estates, bestowed to pious and charitable uses: I say, when it is thus with persons, their pretences are manifestly vain. He that is on a journey, and imagines he has got far beyond such a place in his road, and never yet came to it, must be mistaken. He has not yet arrived at the *top* of the hill, who never yet got half-way thither. But this by the way.

What has been observed of the affections of *love*, is applicable also to *other* religious affections. Those that are true, extend in some proportion to their due and proper objects: but the false, are commonly strangely disproportionate. So it is with religious *desires* and longings; these in the saints, are toward those things that are spiritual and excellent in general, and in some proportion to their excellency, importance, or necessity, or the near concern they have in them: but in false longings, it is often far otherwise. They will strangely run, with impatient vehemence, after something of less importance, when other things of greater importance are neglected. Thus for instance, some persons are attended with a vehement inclination, an unaccountably violent pressure, to declare to others what they experience, and to exhort them; when there is at the same time no inclination, in any proportionable measure, to other things, to which true Christianity has as great, yea, a greater tendency; as pouring out the soul before God in secret, earnest prayer and praise to him, more conformity to him, living more to his glory, &c. We read in Scripture of *groanings that cannot be uttered*, and *soul-breakings for the longing it hath;* and *longings, thirstings*, and *pantings*, much more frequently to these latter things, than the former.

And so as to *hatred* and *zeal;* when these are from right principles, they are against sin in general, in some proportion to the degree of sinfulness; Psal. cxix. 104. "I hate every false way." So ver. 128. But a false hatred and zeal against sin, is against some particular sin only. Thus some seem to be very zealous against profaneness, and pride in apparel, who themselves are notorious for covetousness, closeness, and it may be backbiting, envy towards superiors, turbulency of spirit towards rulers, and rooted ill-will to those who have injured them. False zeal is against the sins of others; while he that has true zeal, exercises it chiefly against his own sins; though he shows also a proper zeal against prevailing and dangerous iniquity in others. Some pretend to have a great abhorrence of their own inward corruption; and yet make light of sins in practice, and seem to commit them without much restraint or remorse; though these imply sin, both in heart and life.

As there is a much greater disproportion in the exercises of false affections, than of true, as to different objects; so there is also, as to different *times*. For although true Christians are not always alike—yea, there is very great difference, at different times, and the best have reason to be greatly ashamed of their unsteadiness—yet there is in no wise the instability and inconstancy of the false-hearted, in those who are true *virgins, that follow the Lamb whithersoever he goeth*. The righteous man is truly said to be one *whose heart is fixed, trusting in God*, (Psal. cxii. 7.) and whose *heart is established with grace;* (Heb. xiii. 9.) Job xvii. 9. "The righteous shall hold on his way, and he that hath clean hands shall wax stronger and stronger." It is spoken of as a note of the hypocrisy of the Jewish church, that they *were as a swift dromedary, traversing her ways*.

If therefore persons are religious only by fits and starts, if they now and then seem to be raised up to the clouds in their affections, and then suddenly fall down again, lose all, and become quite careless and carnal, and this is their manner of carrying on religion; if they appear greatly moved, and mightily engaged in religion, only in extraordinary seasons—as in the time of a remarkable out-pouring of the Spirit, or other uncommon dispensations of Providence, or upon the real or supposed receipt of some great mercy, &c.—but quickly return to such a frame, that their hearts are chiefly upon other things, and the prevailing stream of their affections is ordinarily towards the things of this world, they clearly evince their unsoundness. When they are like the children of Israel in the wilderness, who had their affections highly raised by what God had done for them at the Red sea, and sang his praises, and soon fell a lusting after the flesh-pots of Egypt; but then again when they came to mount Sinai, and saw the great manifestations God made of himself there, seemed to be greatly engaged again, and mightily forward to enter into covenant with God, saying, *All that the Lord hath spoken will we do, and be obedient*, but then quickly made them a golden calf; I say, when it is thus with persons, it is a sign of the unsoundness of affections.* They are like the waters in the time of a shower of rain, which, during the shower, and a little after, run like a brook, and flow abundantly; but are presently quite dry: and when another shower comes, then they will flow again. Whereas a true saint is like a stream from a living spring; which though it may be greatly increased by a shower of rain, and diminished in time of drought, yet constantly runs: (John iv. 14. "The water that I shall give him, shall be in him a well of water, springing up," &c.) or like a tree planted by such a stream, that has a constant supply at the root, and is always green, even in time of the greatest drought; Jer. xvii. 7, 8. "Blessed is the man that trusteth in the Lord, and whose hope the Lord is. For he shall be as a tree planted by the waters, and that spreadeth out her roots by the river, and shall not see when heat cometh, but her leaf shall be green, and shall not be careful in the year of drought, neither shall cease from yielding fruit." Many hypocrites are like comets, that appear for a while with a mighty blaze; but are very unsteady and irregular in their motion, (and are therefore called wandering stars, Jude 13.) their blaze soon disappears, and they appear but once in a great while. But true saints are like the fixed stars, which, though they rise and set, and are often clouded, yet are stedfast in their orb, and shine with a constant light. Hypocritical affections are like a violent motion; as that of the air moved with winds, (Jude 12.) But gracious affections are more a natural motion; like the stream of a river, which, though it has many turns, may meet with obstacles, and run more freely and swiftly in some places than others; yet in the general, with a steady and constant course, tends the same way, until it gets to the ocean.

And as there is a strange unevenness and disproportion in false affections, at different *times;* so there often is in different *places*. Some are greatly affected when in company; but have nothing that bears any manner of proportion to it in secret, in close meditation, prayer and conversing with God when alone, and separated from all the world.† A true Christian doubtless delights in

* Dr. Owen (on the Spirit, Book III. chap. ii. § 18.) speaking of a common work of the Spirit, says, "This work operates greatly on the affections: we have given instances, in fear, sorrow, joy, and delight, about spiritual things, that are stirred up and acted thereby: but yet it comes short in two things, of a thorough work upon the affections themselves. For, 1st, It doth not *fix* them. And, 2dly, It doth not *fill* them. 1. It is required that our affections be fixed on heavenly and spiritual things, and true grace will effect it; Col. iii. 1, 2. "If ye be risen with Christ, seek those things which are above, where Christ sitteth on the right hand of God. Set your affections on things above." The joys, the fears, the hopes, the sorrows, with reference to spiritual and eternal things, which the work before mentioned doth produce, are evanid, uncertain, unstable, not only as to the degrees, but as to the very being of them. Sometimes they are as a river ready to overflow its banks, men cannot but be pouring them out on all occasions; and sometimes as waters that fail, no drop comes from them. Sometimes they are hot, and sometimes cold; sometimes up, and sometimes down; sometimes all heaven, and sometimes all world; without equality, without stability. But true grace fixeth the affections on spiritual things. As to the degrees of their exercise, there may be and is in them a great variety, according as they may be excited, aided, assisted by grace and the means of it; or obstructed and impeded, by the interposition of temptations and diversions. But the constant bent and inclination of renewed affections, is unto spiritual things; as the Scripture every where testifieth, and as experience doth confirm."

"There is (says Dr. Preston) a certain love, by fits, which God accepts not; when men come and offer to God great promises, like the waves of the sea, as big as mountains: Oh, they think, they will do much for God! But their minds change; and they become as those high waves, which at last fall level with the other waters. If a man should proffer thee great kindnesses; and thou shouldst afterwards come to him to make use of him, and he should look strangely upon thee, as if he were never acquainted with thee; how wouldst thou esteem of such love? If we are now on, now off, in our love, God will not esteem of such love." *Discourse on the Divine Love of Christ*.

Mr. Flavel, speaking of these changeable professors, says, "These professors have more of the moon than of the sun; little light, less heat, and many changes. They deceive many, yea, they deceive themselves, but cannot deceive God. They want that ballast and establishment in themselves, that would have kept them tight and steady." *Touchstone of Sincerity*, chap. ii. § 2.

† "The Lord is neglected secretly, yet honoured openly; because there is no wind in their chambers to blow their sails; and therefore there they stand still. Hence many men keep their profession, when they lose their

religious fellowship and christian conversation, and finds much to affect his heart in it; but he also delights at times to retire from all mankind, to converse with God in solitude. And this also has its peculiar advantages for fixing his heart, and engaging his affections. True religion disposes persons to be much alone in solitary places, for holy meditation and prayer. So it wrought in Isaac, Gen. xxiv. 63. And which is much more, so it wrought in Jesus Christ. How often do we read of his retiring into mountains and solitary places, for holy converse with his Father! It is difficult to conceal great affections, but yet gracious affections are of a much more silent and secret nature, than those that are counterfeit. So it is with the gracious *sorrow* of the saints for their *own* sins.* Thus the future gracious mourning of true penitents, at the beginning of the latter-day glory, is represented as being so secret, as to be hidden from the companions of their bosom; Zech. xii. 12, 13, 14. "And the land shall mourn, every family apart; the family of the house of David apart, and their wives apart; the family of the house of Nathan apart, and their wives apart; the family of the house of Levi apart, and their wives apart; the family of Shimei apart, and their wives apart; all the families that remain, every family apart, and their wives apart." So it is with their sorrow for the sins of *others*. The saints' pains and travail for the souls of sinners is chiefly in secret places; Jer. xiii. 17. "If ye will not hear it, my soul shall weep in secret places for your pride, and mine eye shall weep sore, and run down with tears, because the Lord's flock is carried away captive." So it is with gracious *joys*: they are *hidden manna*, in this respect, as well as others, Rev. ii. 17. The psalmist seems to speak of his sweetest comforts, as those which he had in secret; Psal. lxiii. 5, 6. "My soul shall be satisfied, as with marrow and fatness; and my mouth shall praise thee with joyful lips: when I remember thee upon my bed, and meditate on thee in the night-watches." Christ calls forth his spouse away from the world into retired places, that he may give her his sweetest love; Cant. vii. 11, 12. "Come, my beloved, let us go forth into the field; let us lodge in the villages;—there will I give thee my loves." The most eminent divine favours which the saints obtained, that we read of in Scripture, were in their retirement. The principal manifestations that God made of himself, and his covenant-mercy to Abraham, were when he was alone, apart from his numerous family; as any one will judge that carefully reads his history. Isaac received that special gift of God, Rebekah, who was so great a comfort to him, and by whom he obtained the promised seed, walking alone, meditating in the field. Jacob was retired for secret prayer, when Christ came to him; and he wrestled with him, and obtained the blessing. God revealed himself to Moses in the bush, when he was in a solitary place in the desert, in mount Horeb, Exod. iii. And afterwards, when God showed him his glory, and he was admitted to the highest degree of communion with God that ever he enjoyed; he was alone, in the same mountain, and continued there forty days and forty nights, and then came down with his face shining. God came to those great prophets, Elijah and Elisha, and conversed freely with them, chiefly in their retirement. Elijah conversed alone with God at mount Sinai, as Moses did. And when Jesus Christ had his greatest prelibation of his future glory, when he was transfigured; it was not when he was with the multitude, or with the twelve disciples, but retired into a solitary place in a mountain, with only three select disciples, whom he charged that they should tell no man, until he was risen from the dead. When the angel Gabriel came to the blessed virgin, and when the Holy Ghost came upon her, and the power of the Highest overshadowed her, she seems to have been alone, in this matter hid from the world; her nearest and dearest earthly friend Joseph, who had betrothed her, knew nothing of the matter. And she that first partook of the joy of Christ's resurrection, was alone with Christ at the sepulchre, John xx. And when the beloved disciple was favoured with those wonderful visions of Christ, and his future dispensations towards the church and the world, he was alone in the isle of Patmos. Not but that we have also instances of great privileges that the saints have received when with others; there is much in christian conversation, and social and public worship, tending greatly to refresh and rejoice the hearts of the saints. But this is all that I aim at by what has been said, to show that it is the nature of true grace, however it loves christian society in its place, in a peculiar manner to delight in retirement, and secret converse with God. So that if persons appear greatly engaged in social religion, and but little in the religion of the closet, and are often highly affected when with others, and but little moved when they have none but God and Christ to converse with, it looks very darkly upon their religion.

SECT. XI.

Another great and very distinguishing difference is, that the higher gracious affections are raised, the more is a spiritual appetite and longing of soul after spiritual attainments increased: on the contrary, false affections rest satisfied in themselves.†

The more a true saint loves God with a gracious love, the more he desires to love him, and the more uneasy is he at his want of love to him: the more he hates sin, the more he desires to hate it, and laments that he has so much remaining love to it. The more he mourns for sin, the more he longs to mourn; the more his heart is broken, the more he desires it should be broken. The more he thirsts and longs after God and holiness, the more he longs to long, and breathe out his very soul in longings after God. The kindling and raising of gracious affections is like kindling a flame; the higher it is raised, the more ardent it is; and the more it burns, the more vehemently does it tend and seek to burn. So that the spiritual appetite after holiness, and an increase of holy affections, is much more lively and keen in those that are eminent in holiness, than others; and more when grace and holy affections are in their most lively exercise, than at other times. It is as much the nature of one that is spiritually new-born, to thirst after growth in holiness, as it is the nature of a new-born babe to thirst after the mother's breast; who has the sharpest appetite, when best in health; 1 Pet. ii. 2, 3. "As new-born babes, desire the sincere milk of the word, that ye may grow thereby: if so be that ye have tasted that the Lord is gracious." The most that the saints have in this world, is but a taste, a prelibation of that future glory which is their proper fulness; it is only an earnest of their future inheritance; (2 Cor. i. 22. and v. 5. and Eph. i. 14.) The most eminent saints in this state are but children, compared with their future, which is their proper, state of maturity and perfection; as the apostle observes, 1 Cor. xiii. 10, 11. The greatest eminence and perfection that the saints arrive at in this world, has no tendency to satiety, or to abate their desires after more; but, on the contrary, makes them more eager to

affection. They have by the one a name to live, (and that is enough,) though their hearts be dead. And hence so long as you love and commend them, so long they love you; but if not, they will forsake you. They were warm only by another's fire, and hence having no principle of life within, soon grow dead. This is the water that turns a Pharisee's mill." Shepard's *Parable*, Part I. p. 180.

"The hypocrite (says Mr. Flavel) is not for the closet, but the synagogue, Matt. vi. 5, 6. It is not his meat and drink to retire from the clamour of the world, to enjoy God in secret." *Touchstone of Sincerity*, chap. vii. § 2.

Dr. Ames, in his Cases of Conscience, Lib. III. chap. v. speaks of it as a thing by which sincerity may be known, "That persons be obedient in the absence, as well as in the presence, of lookers on; in secret, as well, yea more, than in public;" alleging Phil. ii. 12. and Matt. vi. 6.

* Mr. Flavel, in reckoning up those things, wherein the sorrow of saints is distinguished from the sorrow of hypocrites, about their sins, says, "Their troubles for sin are more private and silent troubles than others are; their sore runs in the night." *Touchstone of Sincerity*, chap. vi. § 5.

† "Truly there is no work of Christ that is right, (says Mr. Shepard,) but it carries the soul to long for more of it." *Par. Ten Virg.* Part I. p. 136.

And again, "There is in true grace an infinite circle: a man by thirsting receives, and receiving thirsts for more. But hence the Spirit is not poured out abundantly on churches; because men shut it out, by shutting in and contenting themselves with their common graces and gifts; Matt. vii. 29. Examine if it be not so." *Ibid.* p. 182.

And in p. 210. he says, "This I say, True grace, as it comforts, so it never fills, but puts an edge on the appetite; more of that grace, Lord! Thus Paul, Phil. iii. 13, 14. Thus David, *Out of my poverty I have given*, &c. 1 Chron. xxix. 3, 17, 18. It is a sure way never to be deceived in lighter strokes of the Spirit, to be thankful for any, but to be content with no measure of it. And this cuts the thread of difference, between a superficial lighter stroke of the Spirit, and that which is sound."

press forwards; as is evident by the apostle's words, Phil. iii. 13—15. "Forgetting those things which are behind, and reaching forth unto those things which are before, I press toward the mark. Let us therefore, as many as be *perfect*, be thus minded."

The reasons of it are, that the more persons have of holy affections, the more they have of that spiritual taste which I have spoken of elsewhere; whereby they perceive the excellency, and relish the divine sweetness, of holiness. And the more grace they have, while in this state of imperfection, the more they see their imperfection and emptiness, and distance from what ought to be; and so the more do they see their need of grace; as I showed at large before, when speaking of the nature of evangelical humiliation. And besides, grace, as long as it is imperfect, is of a growing nature, and in a growing state. And we see it to be so with all living things, that while they are in a state of imperfection, and in their growing state, their nature seeks after growth; and so much the more, as they are more healthy and prosperous. Therefore the cry of every true grace, is like that cry of true faith, Mark ix. 24. "Lord, I believe, help thou my unbelief." And the greater spiritual discoveries and affections the true Christian has, the more does he become an earnest supplicant for grace, and spiritual food, that he may grow; and the more earnestly does he pursue after it, in the use of proper means and endeavours; for true and gracious longings after holiness, are no idle ineffectual desires.

But here some may object, How is this consistent with what all allow, that spiritual enjoyments are of a soul-satisfying nature?

I answer, Its being so will appear to be not at all inconsistent with what has been said, if it be considered in what manner spiritual enjoyments are said to be of a soul-satisfying nature. Certainly they are not of a cloying nature, so that he who has any thing of them, though but in a very imperfect degree, desires no more. But spiritual enjoyments are of a soul-satisfying nature in the following respects. 1. They in their kind and nature, are fully adapted to the nature, capacity, and need of the soul of man. So that those who find them, desire *no other kind* of enjoyments; they sit down fully contented with that kind of happiness which they have, desiring no change, nor inclining to wander about any more, saying, *Who will show us any good?* the soul is never cloyed, never weary; but perpetually giving up itself, with all its powers, to this happiness. But not that those who have something of this happiness, desire no more of the same. 2. They are satisfying also in this respect, that they answer the expectation of the appetite. When the appetite is high to any thing, the expectation is consequently so. Appetite to a particular object, implies expectation in its nature. This expectation is not satisfied by worldly enjoyments; the man expected to have a great accession of happiness, but he is disappointed. But it is not so with spiritual enjoyments; they fully answer and satisfy the expectation. 3. The gratification and pleasure of spiritual enjoyments is permanent. It is not so with worldly enjoyments. They in a sense satisfy particular appetites; but the appetite in being satisfied, is glutted, and then the pleasure is over: and as soon as that is over, the general appetite of human nature after happiness returns; but is empty, and without any thing to satisfy it. So that the glutting of a particular appetite, does but take away from, and leave empty, the general thirst of nature. 4. Spiritual good is satisfying, as there is enough in it to satisfy the soul, as to the degree, if obstacles were but removed, and the enjoying faculty duly applied. There is room enough here for the soul to extend itself; here is an infinite ocean. If men be not satisfied here, as to degree of happiness, the cause is with themselves; it is because they do not open their mouths wide enough.

But these things do not argue that a soul has no appetite excited after more of the same, when it has tasted a little; or that the appetite will not increase, until it comes to fulness of enjoyment: as bodies attracted to the earth, tend to it more strongly, the nearer they come to the attracting body, and are not at rest out of the centre. Spiritual good is of a satisfying nature; and for that very reason, the soul that tastes, and knows its nature, will thirst after it, and a fulness of it, that it may be satisfied. And the more one experiences and knows this excellent, unparalleled, exquisite, and satisfying sweetness, the more earnestly will he hunger and thirst for more, until he comes to perfection. And therefore this is the nature of spiritual affections, that the greater they be, the greater the appetite and longing is, after grace and holiness.

But with those joys, and other religious affections, that are false and counterfeit, it is otherwise. If before there was a great desire, of some sort, after grace; as these affections rise, *that* desire ceases, or is abated. It may be before, while the man was under legal convictions, and much afraid of hell, he earnestly longed that he might obtain spiritual light in his understanding, faith in Christ, and love to God: but now, when these false affections deceive him, and make him confident that he is converted, and his state good, there are no more earnest longings after light and grace; for his end is answered; he is confident that his sins are forgiven him, and that he shall go to heaven; and so he is satisfied. And especially when false affections are raised very high, do they put an end to longings after grace and holiness. The man now is far from appearing to himself a poor empty creature; on the contrary, he is rich, and increased with goods, and hardly conceives of any thing more excellent, than what he has already attained.

Hence there is an end to many persons' earnestness in seeking, after they have once obtained that which they call their conversion; or at least, after they have had those high affections, that make them fully confident of it. Before, while they looked upon themselves as in a state of nature, they were engaged in seeking after God and Christ, and cried earnestly for grace, and strove in the use of means: but now they act as though they thought their work was done; they live upon their first work, or some high past experiences; and there is an end to their crying, and striving after God and grace.* Whereas the holy principles that actuate a true saint, have a far more powerful influence to stir him up to earnestness in seeking God

* "It is usual to see a false heart most diligent in seeking the Lord, when he has been worst, and most careless when it is best. Hence many at first conversion, sought the Lord earnestly: afterwards affections and endeavours die; that now they are good as the word can make them.—An hypocrite's last end is to satisfy himself: hence he has enough. A saint's is to satisfy Christ: hence he never has enough." Shepard's *Parable*, Part I. p. 157.

"Many a man, it may be, may say, I have nothing in myself, and all is in Christ; and comfort himself there; and so falls asleep. Hands off! and touch not this ark, lest the Lord slay thee: a Christ of clouts would serve your turn as well." *Ibid.* p. 71.

"An hypocrite's light goes out, and grows not. Hence many ancient standers take all their comfort from their first work, and droop when in old age." *Ibid.* p. 77.

And p. 93, 94. Mr. Shepard, mentioning the characters of those that have a dead hope, says, "They that content themselves with any measure of holiness and grace, they look not for Christ's coming and company. For saints that do look for him, though they have not that holiness and grace they would have, yet they rest not satisfied with any measure; 1 John iii. 3. "He that hath this hope, purifieth himself as he is pure."—That saints content not themselves with any dressings, until made glorious, and so fit for fellowship with that spouse.—When a man leaves not, until he gets such a measure of faith and grace, and now when he has got this, contents himself with this, as a good sign that he shall be saved, he looks not for Christ. Or when men are heavily laden with sin; then close with Christ; and then are comforted, sealed, and have joy that fills them; and now the work is done.—And when men shall not content themselves with any measure; but wish they had more, if grace would grow, while they tell clocks and sit idle; and so God must do all: but do not purge themselves, and make work of it."

Again, p. 109. "There is never a hypocrite living, but closeth with Christ for his own ends: for he cannot work beyond his principle. Now when men have served their own turns out of another man, away they go, and keep that which they have. An hypocrite closeth with Christ, as a man with a rich shop; he will not be at cost to buy all the shop, but so much as serves his turn. Commonly men in horror, seek so much of Christ as will ease them; and hence profess, and hence seek for so much of Christ as will credit them; and hence their desires after Christ are soon satisfied. *Appetitus finis est infinitus.*"

"Woe to thee that canst paint such a Christ in thy head, and receive such a Christ into thy heart, as must be a pander to your sloth. The Lord will revenge this wrong done to his glory, with greater sorrows than ever any felt: to make Christ not only meat and drink to feed, but clothes to cover your sloth—Why what can we do? what can we do?—Why as the first Adam conveys not only guilt, but power; so the second conveys both righteousness and strength." *Ibid.* p. 158.

"When the Lord hath given some light and affection, and some comfort and some reformation, now a man grows full here. Saints do for God; and carnal hearts do something too; but a little fills them, and quiets them, and so damns them. And hence men at the first work upon them, are very diligent in the use of means; but after that, they be brought to neglect prayer, sleep out sermons, and to be careless, sapless, lifeless." *Ibid.* p. 210.

"It is an argument of want of grace, when a man saith to himself, as the glutton said to his soul, "Take thy rest, for thou hast goods laid up for many years." So thou hast repentance and grace, and peace enough *for many years:* and hence the soul takes its rest, grows sluggish and negligent. Oh, if you die in this case, this night thy soul will be taken away to hell." *Ibid.* p. 227.

and holiness, than servile fear. Hence seeking God is spoken of as one of the distinguishing characters of the saints; and *those that seek God*, is one of the names by which the godly are called in Scripture: Ps. xxiv. 6. "This is the generation of them that seek him, that seek thy face, O Jacob." Ps. lxix. 6. "Let not those that seek thee, be confounded for my sake." Ver. 32. "The humble shall see this, and be glad; and your heart shall live that seek God." And lxx. 4. "Let all those that seek thee, rejoice, and be glad in thee: and let such as love thy salvation say continually, The Lord be magnified." And the Scriptures every where represent the seeking, striving, and labour of a Christian, as being chiefly *after* his conversion, and his conversion as being but the beginning of his work. And almost all that is said in the New Testament, of men's watching, giving earnest heed to themselves, running the race that is set before them, striving and agonizing, wrestling not with flesh and blood, but principalities and powers, fighting, putting on the whole armour of God, and standing, having done all to stand, pressing forward, reaching forth, continuing instant in prayer, crying to God day and night; I say, almost all that is said in the New Testament of these things, is spoken of and directed to the saints. Where these things are applied to sinners' seeking conversion once, they are spoken of the saints' prosecution of the great business of their high calling ten times. But many in these days have got into a strange anti-scriptural way, of having all their striving and wrestling over *before* they are converted; and so having an easy time of it afterwards, to sit down and enjoy their sloth and indolence; as those that now have a supply of their wants, and are become rich and full. But when the Lord *fills the hungry with good things, these rich* are like to be *sent away empty*, Luke i. 53.

But doubtless there are some hypocrites, that have only false affections, who will think they are able to stand this trial; and will readily say, that they desire not to rest satisfied with past attainments, but to be pressing forward; they desire more, they long after God and Christ, desire more holiness, and seek it. But the truth is, their desires are not properly the desires of appetite after holiness, for its own sake, or for its moral excellency and holy sweetness; but only for by-ends. They long after clearer discoveries, that they may be better satisfied about the state of their souls; or because in great discoveries self is gratified, in being made so much of by God, and so exalted above others; they long to *taste* the love of God, (as they call it,) rather than to have *more* love to God. Or, it may be, they have a kind of forced, fancied, or made longings; because they think they must long for more grace, otherwise it will be a dark sign upon them. But such things as these are far different from the natural, and as it were necessary, appetite and thirsting of the new man after God and holiness. There is an inward burning desire that a saint has after holiness, as natural to the new creature, as vital heat is to the body. There is a holy breathing and panting after the Spirit of God to increase holiness, as natural to a holy nature, as breathing is to a living body. And holiness or sanctification is more directly the object of it, than any manifestation of God's love and favour. This is the meat and drink that is the object of the spiritual appetite; John iv. 34. "My meat is to do the will of him that sent me, and to finish his work." Where we read in Scripture of the desires, longings, and thirstings of the saints, righteousness and God's laws are much more frequently mentioned, as the object of them, than any thing else. The saints *desire the sincere milk of the word*, not so much to testify God's love to them, as *that they may grow thereby* in holiness. I have shown before, that holiness is that good which is the immediate object of a spiritual taste. But undoubtedly the same sweetness that is the chief object of a spiritual taste, is also the chief object of a spiritual appetite. Grace is the godly man's treasure; Isa. xxxiii. 6. "The fear of the Lord is his treasure." Godliness is the gain of which he is covetous, 1 Tim. vi. 6. Hypocrites long for discoveries, more for the present comfort of the discovery, and the high manifestation of God's love in it, than for any sanctifying influence of it. But neither a longing after great discoveries, or after great tastes of the love of God, nor longing to be in heaven, nor longing to die, are in any measure so distinguishing marks of true saints, as longing after a more holy heart, and living a more holy life.

SECT. XII.

Gracious and holy affections have their exercise and fruit in christian practice.

I mean, they have that influence and power upon him who is the subject of them, that they cause that a practice, which is universally conformed to, and directed by christian rules, should be the practice and business of his life.

This implies three things; 1. That his behaviour or practice in the world, be universally conformed to and directed by christian rules. 2. That he makes a business of such a holy practice above all things; that it be a business which he is chiefly engaged in, and devoted to, and pursues with highest earnestness and diligence; so that he may be said to make this practice of religion eminently *his work and business*.—And, 3. That he persists in it to the end of life: so that it may be said, not only to be his business at certain seasons, the business of Sabbath-days, or certain extraordinary times, or the business of a month, or a year, or of seven years, or his business under certain circumstances; but the *business of his life*; it being that business which he perseveres in through all changes, and under all trials, as long as he lives. The necessity of each of these, in all true Christians, is most clearly and fully taught in the word of God.

1. It is necessary that men should be universally obedient:* 1 John iii. 3, &c. "Every man that hath this hope in him, purifieth himself, even as he is pure.—And ye know that

* "He that pretends to godliness, and turns aside to crooked ways, is an hypocrite: for those that are really godly, do live in a way of obedience; Psal. cxix. 1, 2, 3. "Blessed are the undefiled in the way, that walk in the law of the Lord.—They also do iniquity." Luke i. 6. "They were both righteous before God, walking in all the commandments of the Lord blameless." But such as live in ways of sin, are dissemblers: for all such will be rejected in the day of judgment; Matth. vii. 23. "Depart from me ye that work iniquity". The like we have Luke xiii. 27. If men live in a way of disobedience, they do not love God; for love will make men keep God's commandments; I John v. 3. "Herein is love, that we keep his commandments: and his commandments are not grievous." If men live in a way of disobedience, they have not a spirit of faith; for faith sanctifies men; Acts xxvi. 18. "Sanctified by faith that is in me." If men live in a way of disobedience, they are not Christ's sheep; for his sheep hear his voice; John x. 27. Men that live in a way of disobedience are not born of God; 1 John iii. 9. "He that is born of God, sinneth not." Men that live in a way of disobedience are the servants of sin; John viii. 34. "He that committeth sin, is the servant of sin."—A course of external sin is an evidence of hypocrisy; whether it be a sin of omission or commission.—If men live in the neglect of known duties, or in the practice of known evils, that will be their condemnation; let the sin be what it will; let it be profaneness, uncleanness, lying, or injustice.—If men allow themselves in malice, envy, wanton thoughts, profane thoughts, that will condemn them; though those corruptions do not break out in any scandalous way. These thoughts are an evidence of a rotten heart; Tit. iii. 3. "We ourselves were sometimes foolish, disobedient, deceived, serving divers lusts and pleasures, living in malice and envy, hateful, and hating one another." If a man allows himself, though he thinks he doth not, in malice and envy, he is an hypocrite: though his conscience disallows it, yet if his heart allows it, he is no saint.—Some make pretences to godliness, whereby they do not only deceive others, but (which is a great deal worse) deceive themselves also: but this will condemn them, that they live in a course of sin, and so must go with ungodly men; Ps. cxxv. 5. "As for such as turn aside unto their crooked ways, the Lord will lead them forth with the workers of iniquity." If there be a great change in a man's carriage, and he be reformed in several particulars, yet if there be one evil way, the man is an ungodly man; where there is piety there is universal obedience. A man may have great infirmities, yet be a godly man. So it was with Lot, David, and Peter: but if he lives in a way of sin, he does not render his godliness only suspicious, but it is full evidence against him. Men that are godly have respect to all God's commandments, Psal. cxix. 6. There be a great many commands, and if there be one of them that a man has not respect unto, he will be put to shame another day. If a man lives in one evil way, he is not subject to God's authority: but then he lives in rebellion; and that will take off all his pleas, and at once cut off all his pretences; and he will be condemned in the day of judgment.—One way of sin is exception enough against the man's salvation. Though the sin that he lives in be but small: such persons will not be guilty of perjury, stealing, drunkenness, fornication; they look upon them to be heinous things, and they are afraid of them; but they do not much matter it, if they oppress a little in a bargain, if they commend a thing too much when they are about to sell it, if they break a promise, if they spend the Sabbath unprofitably, if they neglect secret prayer, if they talk rudely and reproach others; they think these are but small things. if they can keep clear of great transgressions, they hope that God will not insist upon small things.—But indeed all the commands of God are established by divine authority: a small shot may kill a man, as well as a cannon bullet: a small leak may sink a ship. If a man lives in small sins, that shows he has no love to God, no sincere care to please and honour God. Little sins are of a damning nature, as well as great: if they do not deserve so much punishment as greater, yet they do deserve damnation. There is contempt of God in all sins; Matt. v. 19. "He that shall break one of the least of these commands, and shall teach men so, shall be called the least in the kingdom of God." Prov. xix. 16. "He that keepeth the commandment, keepeth his own soul; but he that despiseth his way, shall die." If a man says, this is a great command, and so lays weight on it and another is a little commandment, and so does not regard it, but will allow himself to break it, he is in a perishing condition."—Stoddard's *Way to Know Sincerity and Hypocrisy*.

he was manifested to take away our sins; and in him is no sin. Whosoever abideth in him, sinneth not: whosoever sinneth, hath not seen him, neither known him.—He that doth righteousness, is righteous, even as he is righteous: he that committeth sin, is of the devil. Chap. v. 18. We know that whosoever is born of God, sinneth not, but he that is begotten of God, keepeth himself, and that wicked one toucheth him not." John xv. 14. "Ye are my friends if ye do whatsoever I command you." James ii. 10. "Whosoever shall keep the whole law, and yet offend in one point, he is guilty of all." 1 Cor. vi. 9. "Know ye not that the unrighteous shall not inherit the kingdom of God? Be not deceived: neither fornicators, nor idolaters, &c. shall inherit the kingdom of God." Gal. v. 19, 20. "Now the works of the flesh are manifest, which are these, adultery, fornication, uncleanness, lasciviousness, idolatry, witchcraft, hatred, variance, emulations, wrath, strife, envyings, murders, drunkenness, revellings, and such like: of the which I tell you before, as I have also told you in time past, that they which do such things, shall not inherit the kingdom of God." Which is as much as to say, they that do any sort of wickedness. Job xxxi. 3—7. "Is not destruction to the wicked? and a strange punishment to the workers of iniquity? Doth not he see my ways, and count all my steps? Let me be weighed in an even balance, that God may know mine integrity. If my step hath turned out of the way, and mine heart walked after mine eyes, and if any blot hath cleaved to my hands," &c. Ezek. xxxiii. 15. "If he walk in the statutes of life, without committing iniquity, he shall surely live." If one member only be corrupt, and we do not cut it off, it will carry the whole body to hell, Matt. v. 29, 30. Saul was commanded to slay all God's enemies, the Amalekites; and he slew all but Agag, and the saving him alive proved his ruin. Caleb and Joshua entered into God's promised rest, because they *wholly* followed the Lord, (Numb. xiv. 24. and xxxii. 11, 12. Deut. i. 36. Josh. xiv. 6, 8, 9, 14.) Naaman's hypocrisy appeared in that—however he seemed to be greatly affected with gratitude to God for healing his leprosy, and engaged to serve him, yet—in one thing he desired to be excused. And Herod, though he feared John, observed him, heard him gladly, and did many things; yet was condemned, in that in one thing he would not hearken to him, even in parting with his beloved Herodias. So that it is necessary that men should part with their dearest iniquities, which are as their right hand and right eyes; sins that most easily beset them, and to which they are most exposed by their natural inclinations, evil customs, or particular circumstances, as well as others. As Joseph would not make known himself to his brethren who had sold him, until Benjamin the beloved child of the family was delivered up; no more will Christ reveal his love to us, until we part with our dearest lusts, and until we are brought to comply with the most difficult duties, and those to which we have the greatest aversion.

And it is of importance to observe, that in order to a man's being universally obedient, his obedience must not only consist in *negatives*, or in universally avoiding wicked practices; but he must also be universal in the *positives* of religion. Sins of omission are as much breaches of God's commands, as sins of commission. Christ, in Matt. xxv. represents those on the left hand, as being condemned and cursed to everlasting fire, for sins of omission, *I was an hungred, and ye gave me no meat, &c.* A man therefore cannot be said to be universally obedient, and of a christian conversation, only because he is no thief, oppressor, fraudulent person, drunkard, tavern-haunter, whore-master, rioter, night-walker, nor unclean, profane in his language, slanderer, liar, furious, malicious, nor reviler. He is falsely said to be of a conversation becoming the gospel, who goes thus far, and no farther; but, in order to this, it is necessary that he should also be of a serious, religious, devout, humble, meek, forgiving, peaceful, respectful, condescending, benevolent, merciful, charitable, and beneficent walk and conversation. Without such things as these, he does not obey the laws of Christ, laws that he and his apostles abundantly insist on, as of greatest importance and necessity.

2. In order to men's being true Christians, it is necessary that they prosecute the business of religion, and the service of God, with great earnestness and diligence, as the work to which they devote themselves, and make the main business of their lives. All Christ's *peculiar people*, not only do good works, but are *zealous of good works*, Tit. ii. 14. No man can do the service of two masters at once. They who are God's true servants, give up themselves to his service, and make it as it were their whole work, therein employing their whole hearts, and the chief of their strength; Phil. iii. 13. "This one thing I do." Christians in their effectual calling, are not called to idleness, but to labour in God's vineyard, and spend their day in doing a great and laborious service. All true Christians comply with this call, (as is implied in its being an effectual call,) and do the work of Christians; which is every where in the New Testament compared to those exercises, wherein men are wont to exert their strength with the greatest earnestness, as running, wrestling, fighting. All true Christians are good and faithful soldiers of Jesus Christ, and *fight the good fight of faith:* for none but those who do so, ever *lay hold on eternal life.* Those who *fight as those who beat the air,* never win the crown of victory. *They that run in a race, run all; but one wins the prize:* and they that are slack and negligent in their course, do not *so run, as that they may obtain.* The kingdom of heaven is not to be taken but by violence. Without earnestness there is no getting along in that narrow way that leads to life; and so no arriving at that state of glorious life and happiness to which it leads. Without earnest labour, there is no ascending the steep and high hill of Zion; and so no arriving at the heavenly city on the top of it. Without a constant laboriousness, there is no stemming the swift stream in which we swim, so as ever to come to that fountain of water of life, that is at the head of it. There is need that we should *watch and pray always,* in order to our *escaping those* dreadful *things* that are coming on the ungodly, and our *being counted worthy to stand before the Son of man.* There is need of our *putting on the whole armour of God, and doing all to stand,* in order to our avoiding a total overthrow, and being utterly destroyed by the *fiery darts of the devil.* There is need that we should *forget the things that are behind,* and *be reaching forth to the things that are before, and pressing towards the mark, for the prize of the high calling of God, in Christ Jesus our Lord,* in order to our obtaining that prize. Slothfulness in the service of God, in his professed servants, is as damning as open rebellion: for the *slothful servant* is a *wicked servant,* and shall be cast into outer darkness, among God's open enemies. Matt. xxv. 26, 30. They that are *slothful,* are not *followers of them, who through faith and patience inherit the promises;* Heb. vi. 11, 12. "And we desire that every one of you do show the same diligence, to the full assurance of hope unto the end: that ye be not slothful, but followers of them, who through faith and patience inherit the promises." And all they who follow *that cloud of witnesses* who are gone before to heaven, do *lay aside every weight, and the sin that easily besets them, and run with patience the race that is set before them,* Heb. xii. 1. That true faith by which persons rely on the righteousness of Christ and the work he hath done for them, and truly feed and live upon him, is evermore accompanied with a spirit of earnestness in the christian work and course. Which was typified of old, by the manner of the children of Israel's feeding on the paschal lamb; Exod. xii. 11. "And thus shall ye eat it, with your loins girded, your shoes on your feet, and your staff in your hand: and ye shall eat it in haste; it is the Lord's passover."

3. Every true Christian perseveres in this way of universal obedience, diligent and earnest service of God, through all the various kinds of trials that he meets with, to the end of life. That all true saints, all who obtain eternal life, do thus persevere in the practice of religion, and the service of God, is a doctrine so abundantly taught in the Scripture, that particularly to rehearse all the texts which imply it would be endless. I shall content myself with referring to some in the margin.*

* Deut. v. 29. Deut. xxxii. 18, 19, 20. 1 Chron. xxviii. 9. Psal. lxxviii. 7, 8, 10, 11, 35, 36, 37, 41, 42, 56, &c. Psal. cvi. 3, 12–15. Psal. cxxv. 4, 5. Prov. xxvi. 11. Isa. lxiv. 5. Jer. xvii. 13. Ezek. iii. 20. and xviii. 24. and xxxiii. 12, 13. Matt. x. 22. and xiii. 4–8. with verses 19–23. and xxv. 8.

But *that* in persevering obedience, which is chiefly insisted on in the Scripture, as a special note of the truth of grace, is the continuance of professors in the practice of their duty, and being stedfast in a holy walk, through the various *trials* that they meet with.

By *trials* here I mean, those things which a professor meets with in his course, that especially render his continuance in duty, and faithfulness to God, difficult to nature. These things are called in Scripture by the name of *trials*, or *temptations*, which are words of the same signification. These are of various kinds: there are many things that render continuance in the way of duty difficult, by their tendency to cherish and foment, or to stir up and provoke, lusts and corruptions. Many things make it hard to continue in the way of duty, by their being of an alluring nature, and having a tendency to entice persons to sin; or by their tendency to take off restraints, and embolden them in iniquity. Other things are trials of the soundness and stedfastness of professors, by their tendency to make their duty appear terrible to them, and so to drive them from it: such as the sufferings to which their duty will expose them; pain, ill-will, contempt, and reproach, or loss of outward possessions and comforts. If persons, after they have made a profession of religion, live any considerable time in this world, which is so full of changes, and so full of evil, it cannot be otherwise, than that they should meet with many trials of their sincerity and stedfastness. And besides, it is God's providential manner, to bring trials on his professing friends and servants designedly, that he may manifest them; and may exhibit sufficient matter of conviction of the state in which they are to their own consciences; and oftentimes, to the world. This appears by innumerable scriptures; some are referred to in the margin.*

True saints may be guilty of some kinds and degrees of backsliding, may be foiled by particular temptations, and fall into sin, yea, great sins: but they can never fall away so as to grow weary of religion and the service of God, and habitually to dislike and neglect it, either on its own account, or on account of the difficulties that attend it; as is evident by Gal. vi. 9. Rom. ii. 7. Heb. x. 36. Isa. xliii. 22. Mal. i. 13. They can never backslide so as to continue no longer in a *way* of universal obedience; or so, that it shall cease to be their *manner* to observe all the rules of Christianity, and do all duties required, even the most difficult, and in the most difficult circumstances.† This is abundantly manifest by the things observed already. Nor can they ever fall away, so as habitually to be more engaged in other things than in the business of religion: or so that it should become their way and manner to serve something else more than God; or so as statedly to cease to serve God, with such earnestness and diligence, as still to be habitually devoted and given up to the business of religion; unless those words of Christ can fall to the ground, *Ye cannot serve two masters;* and those of the apostle, *He that will be a friend of the world, is the enemy of God;* and unless a saint can change his God, and yet be a true saint. Nor can a true saint ever fall away so, that ordinarily there shall be no remarkable difference in his walk and behaviour since his conversion, from what was before. They who are truly converted are new men, new creatures; new, not only within, but without; they are sanctified throughout, in spirit, soul, and body; old things are passed away, all things are become new. They have new hearts, new eyes, new ears, new tongues, new hands, new feet; *i. e.* a new conversation and practice; they walk in newness of life, and continue to do so to the end of life. And they that fall away, show visibly that they never were risen with Christ.‡ And especially when men's opinion of their being converted, and so in a safe estate, is the very cause of their failure, it is a most evident sign of their hypocrisy.§ And this is the case, whether their falling away be into their former sins, or into some new kind of wickedness, having the corruption of nature only turned into a new channel, instead of its being mortified. As when persons that think themselves converted, though they do not return to former profaneness and lewdness; yet from the high opinion they have of their experiences, graces, and privileges, gradually settle more and more in a self-righteous and spiritually proud temper of mind, and in such a manner of behaviour and conversation, as naturally arises therefrom. When it is thus with men, however far they may seem to be from their former evil practices, this alone is enough to condemn them, and may render their last state far worse than the first. For this seems to be the very case of the Jews of that generation of whom Christ speaks, Matt. xii. 43—45. They had been awakened by John the Baptist's preaching, and brought to a reformation of their former licentious courses, whereby the unclean spirit was as it were turned out, and the house swept and garnished; yet being *empty* of God and of grace, full of themselves, and exalted in an exceeding high opinion of their own righteousness and eminent holiness, they became habituated to an answerably self-exalting behaviour. They changed the sins of publicans and harlots, for those of the Pharisees; and in the issue, had seven devils worse than the first.

Thus I have explained what exercise and fruit I mean, when I say, that gracious affections have their exercise and fruit in christian practice. The reason why gracious affections have such a tendency and effect, appears from many things that have already been observed in the preceding parts of this discourse.

The reason of it appears particularly from this, that *gracious affections arise from those operations and influences which are spiritual*, and that the inward principle from whence they flow, is something *divine*, a communication of God, a participation of the divine nature, Christ living in the heart, the Holy Spirit dwelling there, in union with the faculties of the soul, as an internal vital principle, exerting his own proper nature in the exercise of those faculties. This is sufficient to show us why true

and xxiv. 12, 13. Luke ix. 62. and xii. 35. &c. and xxii. 28. and xvii. 32. John viii. 30, 31. and xv. 6, 7, 8, 10, 16. Rom. ii. 7. and xi. 22. Col. i. 22, 23. Heb. iii. 6, 12, 14. and vi. 11, 12. and x. 35, &c. James i. 25. Rev. ii. 13, 26. and ii. 10. 1 Tim. ii. 15. 2 Tim. iv. 4—8.

* Gen. xxii. 1. Exod. xv. 25. and xvi. 4. Deut. viii. 2, 15, 16. and xiii. 3. Judg. ii. 22. and iii. 1, 4. Job xxiii. 10. Psal. lxvi. 10, 11. Ezek. iii. 20. Dan. xii. 10. Zech. xiii. 9. Matt. viii. 19, 20. and xviii. 21, 22. Luke i. 35. 1 Cor. xi. 19. 2 Cor. viii. 8. Jam. i. 12. 1 Pet. iv. 12. 1 John ii. 19. Heb. xi. 17. Rev. iii. 10.

† "One way of sin is exception enough against men's salvation, though their temptations be great. Some persons delight in iniquity; they take pleasure in rudeness, and intemperate practices: but there be others, that do not delight in sin; when they can handsomely avoid it, they do not choose it; except they be under some great necessity, they will not do it. They are afraid to sin; they think it is dangerous, and have some care to avoid it: but sometimes they force themselves to sin; they are reduced to difficulties, and cannot tell how well to avoid it; it is a dangerous thing not to do it. If Naaman do not bow himself in the house of Rimmon, the king will be in a rage with him, take away his office, it may be take away his life, and so he complies; 2 Kings v. 18.—So Jeroboam forced himself to set up the calves at Dan and Bethel: he thought that if the people went up to Jerusalem to worship, they would return to Rehoboam, and kill him; therefore he must think of some expedient to deliver himself in this strait; 1 Kings xii. 27, 28. He was driven by appearing necessity to take this wicked course.—So the stony-ground hearers were willing to retain the profession of the true religion; but the case was such, that they thought they could not well do it; Matt. xiii. 21. "When tribulation or persecution ariseth because of the word, by and by he is offended." So Achan and Gehazi had singular opportunities to get an estate; if they live twenty years they are not like to have such an advantage; and they force themselves to borrow a point, and break the law of God. They lay a necessity on estate, and liberty, and life, but not upon obedience. If a man be willing to serve God in ordinary cases, but excuse himself when there be great difficulties, he is not godly. It is a small matter to serve God when men have no temptation; but Lot was holy in Sodom, Noah was righteous in the old world. Temptations try men, but they do not force men to sin: and grace will establish the heart in a day of temptation.—They are blessed that do endure temptation, James i. 12. But they are cursed that fall away in a day of temptation." Stoddard's *Way to know Sincerity and Hypocrisy.*

‡ "Hence we learn what verdict to pass and give in concerning those men that decay and fall off from the Lord. They never had oil in the vessel; never had a dram of grace in their heart. Thus 1 John ii. 19. "If they had been of us, they would no doubt have continued with us." It seems they were such men, which were so eminent and excellent, as that there were no brands nor marks upon them, to give notice to the churches, that they were marked out for apostacy; but were only discovered to be unsound, by their apostacy; and this was argument good enough." Shepard's *Parable*, Part I. p. 226.

§ "When a man's rising is the cause of his fall, or seals a man up in his fall, or at least the cause through his corruption. Ex. Gr. Time was, a man lived a loose, careless, carnal life; by the ministry of some word, or reading of some book, or speaking with some friend, he comes to be convinced of his misery and woful condition, and sees no good nor grace in himself; he hath been even hitherto deceived: at last he comes to get some light, some taste, some sorrows, some heart to use the means, some comfort and mercy, and hope of life: and when it is thus with him, now he falls; he grows full and falls; and this rising is the cause of his fall; his light is darkness and death to him; and grows to a form of knowledge; his rising makes him fall to formality, and then to profaneness; and so his tasting satisfies him; his sorrows empty his heart of sorrows for sin; and his sorrows for his falls harden his heart in his falls; and all the means of recovering him harden him.—Look as it is in diseases; if the physic and meat turn to be poison, then there is no hope of recovery; a man is sick to death now. The saint's little measure makes him forget what is behind." Shepard's *Parable*, Part I. p. 226.

grace should have such activity, power, and efficacy. No wonder that what is divine, is powerful and effectual; for it has omnipotence on its side. If God dwells in the heart, and be vitally united to it, he will show that he is a God by the efficacy of his operation. Christ is not in the heart of a saint as in a sepulchre, as a dead saviour that does nothing; but as in his temple, one that is alive from the dead. For in the heart where Christ savingly is, there he lives, and exerts himself after the power of that endless life, that he received at his resurrection. Thus every saint who is the subject of the benefit of Christ's sufferings, is made to know and experience the power, of his resurrection. The Spirit of Christ, which is the immediate spring of grace in the heart, is all life, all power all act; 2 Cor. ii. 4.—"In demonstration of the Spirit, and of power." 1 Thess. i. 5. "Our gospel came not unto you in word only, but also in power, and in the Holy Ghost."—1 Cor. iv. 20. "The kingdom of God is not in word, but in power." Hence saving affections, though oftentimes they do not make so great a noise and show as others; yet have in them a secret solidity, life, and strength, whereby they take hold of and carry away the heart, leading it into a kind of captivity, 2 Cor. x. 5. gaining a full and stedfast determination of the will for God and holiness; Psal. cx. 3. "Thy people shall be willing in the day of thy power." And thus it is that holy affections have a governing power in the course of a man's life. A statue may look very much like a real man, and a beautiful man; yea it may have, in its appearance to the eye, the resemblance of a very lively, strong, and active man: but yet an inward principle of life and strength is wanting; and therefore it does nothing, it brings nothing to pass, there is no action or operation to answer the show. False discoveries and affections do not go deep enough, to reach and govern the spring of men's actions and practice. The seed in the stony ground had not deepness of earth; the root did not go deep enough to bring forth fruit. But gracious affections go to the very bottom of the heart, and take hold of the very inmost springs of life and activity. Herein chiefly appears the power of true godliness, viz. in its being effectual in practice. And the efficacy of godliness in this respect, is what the apostle respects, when he speaks of the power of godliness, 2 Tim. iii. 5. for he there is particularly declaring, how some professors of religion would notoriously fail in the practice of it, and then the 5th verse observes, that in being thus of an unholy practice, they deny the *power* of godliness, though they have the *form* of it. Indeed the power of godliness is exerted in the first place *within* the soul; in the sensible, lively exercise of gracious affections there. Yet the principal *evidence* of this power is in those exercises of holy affections that are practical; conquering the will, the lusts, and corruptions of men, and carrying them on in the way of holiness, through all temptation, difficulty, and opposition.

Again, the reason why gracious affections have their exercise and effect in christian practice, appears from this, that *the first objective ground of gracious affections, is the transcendently excellent and amiable nature of divine things, as they are in themselves, and not any conceived relation they bear to self, or self-interest.* This shows why holy affections will cause men to be holy in their practice universally. What makes men partial in religion is, that they seek themselves, and not God, in their religion, and close with religion, not for its own excellent nature, but only to serve a turn. He that closes with religion only to serve a turn, will close with no more of it than he imagines serves that turn: but he that closes with religion for its own excellent and lovely nature, closes with all that has that nature: he that embraces religion for its own sake, embraces the whole of religion. This also shows why gracious affections will cause men to practise religion perseveringly, and at all times. Religion may alter greatly in process of time, as to its consistence with men's private interest, in many respects; and therefore he that complies with it only from selfish views, is liable, in the changes of time, to forsake it: but the excellent nature of religion, as it is in itself, is invariable; it is always the same, at all times, and through all changes; it never alters in any respect.

The reason why gracious affections issue in holy practice, also further appears from the kind of excellency which is the foundation of all holy affections, *viz. their moral excellency, or the beauty of their holiness.* No wonder that a love to holiness, for holiness' sake, inclines persons to practise holiness, and to practise every thing that is holy. Seeing holiness is the main thing that excites, draws, and governs all gracious affections, no wonder that all such affections tend to holiness. That which men love, they desire to have, to be united to, and possessed of. That beauty which men delight in, they desire to be adorned with. Those acts which men delight in, they necessarily incline to do.

And what has been observed of *divine teaching and leading of the Spirit of God*, shows the reason of this tendency of gracious affections to an universally holy practice. For as has been observed, the Spirit of God in this his divine teaching and leading, gives the soul a natural relish of the sweetness of that which is holy, and of every thing that is holy, so far as it comes in view, and excites a disrelish and disgust of every thing that is unholy.

The same also appears from what has been observed of the nature of that *spiritual knowledge*, which is the foundation of all holy affection, as consisting in *a sense and view of that excellency in divine things, which is supreme and transcendent.* For hereby these things appear above all others, worthy to be chosen and adhered to. By the sight of the transcendent glory of Christ, true Christians see him worthy to be followed; and so are powerfully drawn after him; they see him worthy that they should forsake all for him. By the sight of that superlative amiableness, they are thoroughly disposed to be subject to him, and engaged to labour with earnestness and activity in his service, and made willing to go through all difficulties for his sake. And it is the discovery of this divine excellency of Christ, that makes them constant to him: for it makes so deep an impression upon their minds, that they cannot forget him; they will follow him whithersoever he goes, and it is in vain for any to endeavour to draw them away from him.

The reason of this practical tendency and issue of gracious affections, further appears, from what has been observed of such affections being *attended with a thorough conviction of the reality and certainty of divine things.* No wonder that they who were never thoroughly convinced that there is any reality in religion, will never be at the labour and trouble of such an earnest, universal, and persevering practice of religion, through all difficulties, self-denials and sufferings, in a dependence on that, of which they are not convinced. But on the other hand, they who are thoroughly convinced of the certain truth of those things, must needs be governed by them in their practice; for the things revealed in the word of God are so great, and so infinitely more important than all others, that it is inconsistent with human nature, that a man should fully believe their truth, and not be influenced by them above all things in his practice.

Again, the reason of this expression and effect of holy affections in the practice, appears from what has been observed of *a change of nature, accompanying such affections.* Without a change of nature, men's practice will not be thoroughly changed. Until the tree be made good, the fruit will not be good. Men do not gather grapes of thorns, nor figs of thistles. The swine may be washed, and appear clean for a little while, but yet, without a change of nature, he will still wallow in the mire. Nature is a more powerful principle of action, than any thing that opposes it: though it may be violently restrained for a while, it will finally overcome that which restrains it. It is like the stream of a river, it may be stopped a while with a dam, but if nothing be done to dry the fountain, it will not be stopped always; it will have a course, either in its old channel, or a new one. Nature is a thing more constant and permanent, than any of those things that are the foundation of carnal men's reformation and righteousness. When a natural man denies his lust, lives a strict, religious life, and seems humble, painful, and earnest in religion; it is not natural, it is all a force against nature; as when a stone is violently thrown upwards. But that force will be gradually spent; nature will remain in its full strength, and so prevails again, and the stone returns downwards. As long as corrupt nature is not mortified, but the principle left whole in a man, it is a vain thing to expect that it should not govern. But if the old nature be indeed mortified, and a new heavenly nature infused; then may it well be expected, that men will walk in newness of life, and continue to do so to the end of their days.

The reason of this practical exercise and effect of holy affections, may also be partly seen, from what has been said of that *spirit of humility, which attends them*. Humility is that wherein a spirit of obedience much consists. A proud spirit is rebellious, but an humble spirit is a submissive, obediential spirit. We see among men, that the servant who is of a haughty spirit, is not apt in every thing to be submissive and obedient to the will of his master; but it is otherwise with the servant who is of a lowly spirit.

That *lamb-like, dove-like spirit*, that has been spoken of, which accompanies all gracious affections, fulfils (as the apostle observes, Rom. xiii. 8, 9, 10. and Gal. v. 14.) all the duties of the second table of the law; wherein christian practice very much consists, and the external practice of Christianity.

And the reason why gracious affections are attended with strict, universal, and constant obedience, further appears, from what has been observed of that *tenderness of spirit*, which accompanies the affections of true saints, causing in them so quick and lively a sense of pain, through the presence of sin, and such a dread of the appearance of evil.

One great reason why the christian practice which flows from gracious affections, is universal, constant, and persevering, appears from what has been observed of those affections themselves from whence this practice flows, being universal and constant, in all kinds of holy exercises, and towards all objects, in all circumstances, and at all seasons, *in a beautiful symmetry and proportion*.

And much of the reason why holy affections are expressed and manifested in such an earnestness, activity, engagedness, and perseverance in holy practice, appears from what has been observed, of the spiritual appetite and longing after further attainments in religion, which evermore attends true affection, and does not decay, but increases as those affections increase. Thus we see how the tendency of holy affections to such a christian practice as has been explained, appears from each of those characteristics of holy affection, before spoken of.

And this point may be further illustrated and confirmed, if it be considered, that the Holy Scriptures abundantly place sincerity and soundness in religion, in making a full choice of God as our only Lord and portion, forsaking all for him, and in a full determination of the will for God and Christ, on counting the cost; in our hearts closing and complying with the religion of Jesus Christ, with all that belongs to it, embracing it with all its difficulties, as it were hating our dearest earthly enjoyments, and even our own lives, for Christ; giving up ourselves with all that we have, wholly, and for ever unto Christ, without keeping back any thing, or making any reserve. In one word, sincerity consists in the great duty of *self-denial* for Christ; or in denying, *i. e.* as it were disowning and renouncing, ourselves for him, making ourselves nothing that he may be all. See the texts to this purpose referred to in the margin.* Now surely having a heart to forsake all for Christ, tends to actually forsaking all for him, so far as there is occasion, and we have the trial. Having a heart to deny ourselves for Christ, tends to denying ourselves in deed, when Christ and self-interest stand in competition. A giving up of ourselves, with all that we have, in our hearts, without making any reserve there, tends to our behaving ourselves universally as his, as subject to his will, and devoted to his ends. Our hearts entirely closing with the religion of Jesus, with all that belongs to it, and as attended with all its difficulties, upon a deliberate counting of the cost, tends to an universal closing with the same in act and deed, and actually going through all the difficulties we meet with in the way of religion, and so holding out with patience and perseverance.

The tendency of grace in the heart to holy practice, is very direct, and the connexion most natural, close, and necessary. True grace is not an inactive thing; there is nothing in heaven or earth of a more active nature; for it is life itself, the most active kind, even spiritual and divine life. It is no barren thing; there is nothing in the universe that in its nature has a greater tendency to fruit. Godliness in the heart has as direct a relation to practice, as a fountain has to a stream, or as the luminous nature of the sun has to beams sent forth, or as life has to breathing, or the beating of the pulse, or any other vital act; or as a habit or principle of action has to action: for it is the very nature and notion of grace, that it is a principle of holy action or practice. Regeneration, which is that work of God in which grace is infused, has a direct relation to practice; for it is the very end of it, with a view to which the whole work is wrought. All is calculated and framed, in this mighty and manifold change wrought in the soul, so as directly to tend to this end; Eph. ii. 10. "For we are his workmanship, created in Christ Jesus unto good works." Yea it is the very end of the redemption of Christ; Tit. ii. 14. "Who gave himself for us, that he might redeem us from all iniquity, and purify unto himself a peculiar people, zealous of good works." 2 Cor. v. 15. "He died for all, that they which live, should not henceforth live unto themselves, but unto him who died for them, and rose again." Heb. ix. 14. "How much more shall the blood of Christ, who through the eternal Spirit, offered himself without spot to God, purge your conscience from dead works to serve the living God?" Col. i. 21, 22. "And you that were sometimes alienated, and enemies in your mind by wicked works, yet now hath he reconciled, in the body of his flesh through death, to present you holy and unblamable, and unreprovable in his sight." 1 Pet. i. 18. "For as much as ye know that ye were not redeemed with corruptible things, as silver and gold, from your vain conversation." Luke i. 74, 75. "That he would grant unto us, that we being delivered out of the hands of our enemies, might serve him without fear, in holiness and righteousness before him, all the days of our life." God often speaks of holy practice, as the end of that great typical redemption, the redemption from Egyptian bondage; as Exod. iv. 23. "Let my son go, that he may serve me." (So chap. iv. 23. and vii. 16. and viii. 1, 20. and ix. 1, 13. and x. 3.) And this is also declared to be the end of election; John xv. 16. "Ye have not chosen me, but I have chosen you, and ordained you, that you should go and bring forth fruit, and that your fruit should remain." Eph. i. 4. "According as he hath chosen us in him, before the foundation of the world, that we should be holy, and without blame before him in love." Chap. ii. 10. "Created unto good works, which God hath fore-ordained that we should walk in them." Holy practice is as much the end of all that God does about his saints, as fruit is the end of all the husbandman does about the growth of his field or vineyard: as the matter is often represented in Scripture; (Matt. iii. 10. chap. xiii. 8, 23—30, 38. chap. xxi. 19, 33, 34. Luke xiii. 6. John xv. 1, 2, 4, 5, 6, 8. 1 Cor. iii. 9. Heb. vi. 7, 8. Isa. v. 1—8. Cant. viii. 11, 12. Isa. xxvii. 2, 3.)† And therefore every thing in a true Christian is calculated to reach this end. This fruit of holy practice, is that to which every grace, every discovery, and every individual thing which belongs to christian experience, has a direct tendency.‡

* Matt. v. 29, 30. Chap. vi. 24. Chap. viii. 19—22. Chap. iv. 18–22. Chap. x. 37, 38, 39. Chap. xiii. 44, 45, 46. Chap. xvi. 24, 25, 26. Chap. xviii. 8, 9. Chap. xix. 21, 27, 28, 29. Luke v. 27, 28. Chap. x. 42. Chap. xii. 33, 34. Chap. xiv. 16—20, 25–33. Chap. xvi. 13. Acts iv. 34, 35. with Chap. v. 1—11. Rom. vi. 3–8. Gal. ii. 20. Chap. vi. 14. Philip. iii. 7—10. Jam. i. 8, 9, 10. Chap. iv. 4. 1 John ii. 15. Rev. xiv. 4. Gen. xii. 1—4. with Heb. xi. 8, 9, 10. Gen. xxii. 12. and Heb. xi. 17. Chap. xi. 24–27. Deut. xiii. 6. and Chap. xxxiii. 9. Ruth. i. 6—16. with Psal. xlv. 10, 11. and 2 Sam. xv. 19—22. Psal. lxxxiii. 25. Psal. xvi. 5, 6. Lam. iii. 24. Jer. x. 16.

† "To profess to know much is easy; but to bring your affections into subjection, to wrestle with lusts, to cross your wills and yourselves, upon every occasion, this is hard. The Lord looketh that in our lives we should be serviceable to him, and useful to men. That which is within, the Lord and our brethren are never the better for it: but the outward obedience, flowing thence, glorifieth God, and does good to men. The Lord will have this done. What else is the end of our planting and watering, but that the trees may be filled with sap? And what is the end of that sap, but that the trees may bring forth fruit? What careth the husbandman for leaves and barren trees?"—Dr. Preston *of the Church's Carriage*.

‡ "What is the end of every grace, but to mollify the heart, and make it pliable to some command or other? Look, how many commandments, so many graces there are in virtue and efficacy, although not so many several names are given them. The end of every such grace is to make us

The constant and indissoluble connexion there is between a christian principle and profession in the true saints, and the fruit of holy practice in their lives, was typified of old in the frame of the golden candlestick in the temple. It is beyond doubt that the golden candlestick, with its seven branches and seven lamps, was a type of the church of Christ. The Holy Ghost himself has been pleased to put that matter out of doubt, by representing his church by such a golden candlestick with seven lamps, in the fourth chapter of Zechariah, and representing the seven churches of Asia by seven golden candlesticks, in the first chapter of the Revelation. That golden candlestick in the temple was every where, throughout its whole frame, made with *knops and flowers*, Exod. xxv. 31, to the end, and chap. xxxvii. 17—24. The word translated *knop*, in the original signifies apple or pomegranate. There was a *knop and a flower, a knop and a flower;* wherever there was a flower, there was an apple or pomegranate with it; the flower and the fruit were constantly connected, without fail. The flower contained the principles of the fruit, and a beautiful promising appearance of it; and it never was a deceitful appearance; the principle or show of fruit, had evermore real fruit attending it, or succeeding it. So it is in the church of Christ: there is the gracious principle of fruit in the heart; and there is an amiable profession, signified by the open flowers of the candlestick; and there is answerable fruit, in holy practice, constantly attending this principle and profession. Every branch of the golden candlestick, thus composed of golden apples and flowers, was crowned with a burning, shining lamp on the top of it. For it is by this means that the saints shine as lights in the world, by making a fair and good profession of religion, and having their profession evermore joined with answerable fruit in practice: agreeable to that of our Saviour, Matt. v. 15, 16. "Neither do men light a candle, and put it under a bushel, but on a candlestick, and it giveth light unto all that are in the house. Let your light so shine before men, that they may *see your good works*, and glorify your Father which is in heaven." A fair and beautiful profession, and golden fruits accompanying one another, are the amiable ornaments of the true church of Christ. Therefore we find that apples and flowers were not only the ornaments of the candlestick in the temple, but of the temple itself, which is a type of the church; which the apostle tells us, *is the temple of the living God.* See 1 Kings vi. 18. "And the cedar of the house within was carved with knops, and open flowers." The ornaments and crown of the pillars, at the entrance of the temple, were of the same sort: they were lilies and pomegranates, or flowers and fruits, mixed together, 1 Kings vii. 18, 19. So it is with all those that are *as pillars in the temple of God, who shall go no more out*, or never be ejected as intruders; as it is with all true saints; Rev. iii. 12. "Him that overcometh, will I make a pillar in the temple of my God, and he shall go no more out."

Much the same thing seems to be signified by the ornaments on the skirt of the ephod, the garment of Aaron the high priest; which were golden bells and pomegranates. That these skirts of Aaron's garment represent the church, or the saints, (that are as it were the garment of Christ,) is manifest; for they are evidently so spoken of, Psal. cxxxiii. 1, 2. "Behold, how good and how pleasant it is, for brethren to dwell together in unity! It is like the precious ointment upon the head, that ran down upon the beard, even Aaron's beard, that went down to the skirts of his garments." That ephod of Aaron signified the same with the seamless coat of Christ our great High Priest. As Christ's coat had no seam, but was woven from the top throughout, so was the ephod, Exod. xxxix. 22. As God took care in his providence, that Christ's coat should not be rent; so God took special care that the ephod should not be rent; (Exod. xxviii. 32. and chap. xxxix. 23.) The golden bells on this ephod, by their precious matter and pleasant sound, well represent the good profession that the saints make; and the pomegranates, the fruit they bring forth. And as in the hem of the ephod, bells and pomegranates were constantly connected, as is once and again observed, there was "a golden bell and a pomegranate, a golden bell and a pomegranate," (Exod. xxviii. 34. and chap. xxxix. 26.) so it is in the true saints; their good profession and their good fruit, constantly accompany one another: the fruit they bring forth in life, evermore answers the pleasant sound of their profession.

Again, the very same thing is represented by Christ, in his description of his spouse, Cant. vii. 2. "Thy belly is like an heap of wheat, set about with lilies." Here again are beautiful flowers, and good fruit, accompanying one another. The lilies were fair and beautiful flowers, and the wheat was good fruit.

As this fruit of christian practice is evermore found in true saints, according as they have opportunity and trial, so it is found in them only; none but true Christians do live such an obedient life, so universally devoted to their duty, and given up to the business of a Christian, as has been explained. All unsanctified men are *workers of iniquity:* they are of their father the devil, and the lusts of their father they will do.—There is no hypocrite that will go through with the business of religion, will both begin and finish the tour. They will not endure the trials God is wont to bring on the professors of religion, but will turn aside to their crooked ways; they will not be thoroughly faithful to Christ in their practice, and follow him whithersoever he goes. Whatever lengths they may go in religion in some instances, though they may appear exceeding strict, and mightily engaged in the service of God for a season; yet they are servants to sin; the chains of their old task-masters are not broken. Their lusts yet have a reigning power in their hearts; and therefore to these masters they will bow down again.* Dan. xii. 10. "Many shall be purified, and made white, and tried: but the

obedient; as the end of temperance is chastity, to bow the heart to these commands, *Be ye sober, &c. not in chambering and wantonness, &c.* When the Lord commandeth us not to be angry with our brother, the end of meekness, and why the Lord infuseth it, is to keep us from unadvised rash anger. So faith, the end of it is to take Jesus Christ, to make us obedient to the command of the gospel, which commands us to believe in him. So as all graces do join together, but to frame and fashion the soul to obedience; then so much obedience as is in your lives, so much grace in your hearts, and no more. Therefore ask your hearts, how subject you are to the Lord in your lives? It was the counsel that Francis Spira gave to them about him, saith he, Learn all of me to take heed of severing faith and obedience: I taught justification by faith, but neglected obedience; and therefore is this befallen me. I have known some godly men, whose comfort on their death-beds hath been not from the inward acts of their minds, which apart considered, might be subject to misapprehensions, but from the course of obedience in their lives, issuing thence. Let Christians look to it, that in all their conversation, as they stand in every relation, as scholars, tradesmen, husbands, wives, look to this, that when they come to die, they have been subject in all things. This will yield comfort." Dr. Preston's *Church's Carriage.*

* "No unregenerate man, though he go never so far, let him do never so much, but he lives in some one sin or other, secret or open, little or great. Judas went far, but he was covetous: Herod went far, but he loved his Herodias. Every dog hath his kennel; every swine hath his swill; and every wicked man his lust." Shepard's *Sincere Convert*, 1st edition, p. 96.

"There is never an unsound heart in the world, but as they say of witches, they have some familiar that sucks them, so they have some lust that is beloved of them, some beloved there is they have given a promise to never to forsake." Shepard's *Parable*, Part. I. p. 15.

"No man that is married to the law, but his fig-leaves cover some nakedness. All his duties ever brood some lust. There is some one sin or other the man lives in; which either the Lord discovers, and he will not part with, as the young man; or else is so spiritual, he cannot see all his life-time. Read through the strictest of all, and see this, Matt. xxiii. *Painted sepulchres.* Paul that was blameless, yet (Eph. ii. 3. Tit. iii. 3.) *served divers lusts and pleasures.* And the reason is, the law is not the ministration of the Spirit, 2 Cor. iii. 8, 9. which breaks off from every sin. There is no law that can give life, Gal. iii. 21. and hence many men have strong resolutions, and break all again. Hence men sin and sorrow, and pray again, and then go with more ease in their sin. Examine thyself; is there any living lust with thy righteousness? It is sure, it is a righteousness thou art married to, and never wert yet matched to Christ." Shepard's *Parable*, Part I. p. 19, 20.

"No hypocrite, though he closeth with Christ, and for a time grow up in knowledge of and communion with Christ, but he hath at that time hidden lusts and thorns that overgrow his growings, and choke all at last, and in conclusion meditates a league between Christ and his lusts, and seeks to reconcile them together." Shepard's *Parable*, Part I. p. 109.

"—Their faith is in such a party, as never was yet thoroughly rent from sin. And here is the great wound of the most cunning hypocrites living. Let a man be cast down as low as hell with sorrow, and lie under chains, quaking in apprehension of terror to come; let a man then be raised up to heaven in joy, not able to live; let a man reform and shine like an earthly angel: yet if not rent from lust, that either you did never see it, or if so, you have not followed the Lord to remove it, but proud, dogged, worldly, sluggish still, false in your dealings, cunning in your tradings, devils in your families, images in your churches; you are objects of pity now, and shall be of terror at the great day. For where sin remains in power, it will bring faith, and Christ, and joy into bondage and service of itself." Shepard's *Parable*, Part I. p. 125.

"Methinks it is with the best hypocrites, as it is with divers old merchants: they prize and desire the gain of merchandise; but to be at the trouble to prepare the ship, to put themselves upon the hazard and dangers of the ship, to go and fetch the treasure that they prize, this they will never do. So many prize and desire earnestly the treasures of heaven; but to be at the trouble of a heaven-voyage to fetch this treasure, to pass through the valley of Baca, tears, temptations, the powers of darkness, the breaches, wicked will do wickedly: and none of the wicked shall understand." Isa. xxvi. 10. "Let favour be showed to the wicked, yet will he not learn righteousness: in the land of uprightness will he deal unjustly." Isa. xxxv. 8. "And an high-way shall be there, and a way, and it shall be called The way of holiness; the unclean shall not pass over it." Hos. xiv. 9. "The ways of the Lord are right, and the just shall walk in them: but the transgressors shall fall therein." Job xxvii. 8, 9, 10. "What is the hope of the hypocrite?—Will he delight himself in the Almighty? will he always call upon God?" An unsanctified man may hide his sin, and may in many things and for a season refrain from sin; but he will not be brought finally to renounce, and give it a bill of divorce: sin is too dear to him, for him to be willing for that; "Wickedness is sweet in his mouth: and therefore he hides it under his tongue; he spares it, and forsakes it not; but keeps it still within his mouth," Job xx. 12, 13. Herein chiefly consists the straitness of the gate, and the narrowness of the way that leads to life; on account of which, carnal men will not go in thereat, *viz.* that it is a way of utterly denying and finally renouncing all ungodliness, and so a way of *self-denial* or *self-renunciation.*

Many natural men, under the means used, and God's strivings with them, do by their sins as Pharaoh did by his pride and covetousness; these he gratified by their keeping the children of Israel in bondage, when God strove with him to let the people go. When God's hand pressed Pharaoh sore, and he was exercised with fears of God's future wrath, he entertained some thoughts of letting the people go, and promised he would do it: but from time to time he broke his promises, when he saw there was respite. When God filled Egypt with thunder and lightning, and the fire ran along the ground, then Pharaoh is brought to confess his sin with seeming humility, and to have a great resolution to let the people go, Exod. ix. 27, 28. "And Pharaoh sent, and called for Moses and Aaron, and said unto them, I have sinned this time: the Lord is righteous, and I and my people are wicked: entreat the Lord (for it is enough) that there be no more mighty thunderings and hail; and I will let you go, and ye shall stay no longer." So sinners are sometimes by thunders and lightnings, and great terrors of the law, brought to a seeming work of humiliation, and to an appearance of parting with their sins; but are no more thoroughly brought to a disposition to dismiss them, than Pharaoh was to let the people go. Pharaoh in the struggle between his conscience and his lusts, was for contriving that God might be served, and he to enjoy his lusts, that were gratified by the slavery of the people. Moses insisted that Israel's God should be served: Pharaoh was willing to consent to that; but would have it done without his parting with the people; "Go sacrifice to your God in the land," says he, Exod. viii. 25. So, many sinners are for contriving to serve God, and enjoy their lusts too. Moses objected against complying with Pharaoh's proposal, because serving God, and yet continuing in Egypt under their task-masters, did not agree together, and were inconsistent. After this Pharaoh consented to let the people go, provided they would not go *far* away: he was not willing to part with them finally, and therefore would have them within reach. So do many hypocrites with respect to their sins. Afterwards Pharaoh consented to let the *men* go, if they would leave the *women* and *children*, Exod. x. 8—10. And then after that, when God's hand was yet harder upon him, he consented that they should go, even *women* and *children*, as well as *men*, provided they would leave their *cattle* behind: but he was not willing to let them go, and all that they had, Exod. x. 24. So it oftentimes is with sinners; they are willing to part with some of their sins, but not all; they are brought to part with the more gross acts of sin, but not to part with their lusts, in lesser indulgencies of them. Whereas we must part with all our sins, little and great; and all that belongs to them, *men, women, children,* and *cattle:* they must all be let go, with *their young, and with their old, with their sons, and with their daughters, with their flocks, and with their herds, there must not be an hoof left behind:* as Moses told Pharaoh, with respect to the children of Israel. At last, when it came to extremity, Pharaoh consented to let the people all go, and all that they had; but he was not stedfastly of that mind; he soon repented, and pursued after them again. The reason was, that those lusts of pride and covetousness, which were gratified by Pharaoh's dominion over the people, and the gains of their service, were never really mortified in him, but only violently restrained. And thus, he being guilty of backsliding, after his seeming compliance with God's commands, was destroyed without remedy. Thus there may be a forcing parting with ways of disobedience to the commands of God, that may seem to be universal, as to what appears for a little season: but because it is a mere force, without the mortification of the inward principle of sin, they will not persevere in it; but will return as the dog to his vomit; and so bring on themselves dreadful and remediless destruction. There were many false disciples in Christ's time, that followed him for a while; but none of them followed him to the end; some on one occasion, and some on another, went back and walked no more with him.*

From what has been said, it is manifest, that christian practice, or a holy life, is *a great and distinguishing sign* of true and saving grace. But I may go further, and assert, that it is *the chief* of all the signs of grace, both as an evidence of the sincerity of professors UNTO OTHERS, and also to their OWN CONSCIENCES.

But then it is necessary that this be rightly taken, and that it be well understood and observed, in what sense and manner christian practice is the *greatest sign* of grace. Therefore, to set this matter in a clear light, I will endeavour particularly and distinctly to prove, that christian practice is the *principal sign* by which Christians are to judge, both of their own and others' sincerity of godliness; withal observing some things that are needful to be particularly noted, in order to a right understanding of this matter.

opposition, and contradictions of a sinful unbelieving heart, good and evil report, to pass from one depth and wave to another, this the best hypocrite fails in; and hence loses all at last. And this I conceive to be one of the great differences between the strong desires and esteems of hypocrites and saints.—Look, as it is with men that have two trades, or two shops; one is as much as ever they can follow or tend: they are forced at last to put off one, and they must neglect one; so here. That spirit of sloth and slumber, which the Lord ever leaves the best hypocrite to, so mightily oppresseth all their senses, that they cannot use effectually all means to accomplish their ends. And hence a man desires the end, but has it not; Prov. xiii. 4." Shepard's *Parable*, Part I. p. 150, 151.

"Read through all the Scripture; constantly, never any hypocrites but they had this brand, Matt. vii. 23. *You workers of iniquity.*" Shepard's *Parable*, Part I. p. 195.

"A carnal man may hit upon some good duty that God commands, and refrain from some sin that God forbids; but to go through, he cannot: to take up reproach and disgrace, to lose his credit, to forsake his friends, to lose honour, and riches, and pleasures; this he will not do, until he be humbled." Dr. Preston *on Paul's Conversion.*

"So it is with men, because they want humiliation. Therefore their *profession* and *they* do not continue, but part willingly one from another. They will do some things, but not all things: and they will forego some things, but not all things.—And therefore our Saviour saith, Luke xiv. "He that will not forsake all for my sake, is not worthy of me." He is not worth the saving, that prizes not me above all things whatsoever. And a man will not prize Christ, nor forsake all things for Christ, until he be humbled." *Ibid.*

* "The counterfeit and common grace of foolish virgins, after some time of glorious profession, will certainly go out and be quite spent. It consumes in the using, and shining, and burning.—Men that have been most forward, decay; their gifts decay, life decays.—It is so, after some time of profession: for at first, it rather grows than decays and withers: but afterward they have enough of it, it withers and dies.—The Spirit of God comes upon many hypocrites, in abundant and plentiful measure of awakening grace; it comes upon them, as it did upon Balaam, and as it is in overflowing waters, which spread far, and grow very deep, and fill many empty places.—Though it doth come upon them so, yet it doth never rest within, so as to dwell there, to take up an eternal mansion for himself.—Hence it doth decay by little and little; until at last it is quite gone. As ponds filled with rain-water, which comes upon them; not spring water, that riseth up within them: it drys up by little and little, until quite dry." Shepard's *Parable*, Part II. p. 58, 59.

"Some men may apprehend Christ, neither out of fear of misery nor only to preserve some sin; but God lets in light and heat of the blessed beams of the glorious gospel of the Son of God: and therefore there is mercy, rich, free, sweet, for damned, great, vile sinners: Good Lord, saith the soul, what a sweet ministry, word, God, and gospel is this! and there rests. This was the frame of the stony-ground; which heard the word, and received it with joy, and for a time believed. And this is the case of thousands, that are much affected with the promise and mercy of Christ, and hang upon free grace for a time: but as it is with sweet smells in a room, they continue not long; or as flowers, they grow old and withered, and then fall. In time of temptation, lust, and world, and sloth, is more sweet than Christ, and all his gospel is." Shepard's *Parable*, Part II. p. 168.

"Never any carnal heart, but some root of bitterness did grow up at last in this soil." Shepard's *Parable*, Part I. p. 195.

"We shall see in experience: take the best professors living; though they may come, as they and others judged, to the Lord, and follow the Lord; yet they will in time depart. The Spirit never was given effectually to draw them, nor yet to keep them." Shepard's *Parable*, Part I. p. 205.

SECT. XIII.

Christian practice or holy life, is a manifestation and sign of the sincerity of a professing Christian, to the eye of his neighbours and brethren.

AND that this is the *chief sign* of grace in this respect, is very evident from the word of God. Christ, who knew best how to give us rules to judge of others, has repeated, and inculcated the rule, that we should know them by their fruits; Matt. vii. 16. "Ye shall know them by their fruits." And then after arguing the point, and giving clear reasons, why men's fruits must be the chief evidence of what sort they are, in the following verses, he closes by repeating the assertion; ver. 20. "Wherefore by their fruits ye shall know them." Again, chap. xii. 33. "Either make the tree good, and his fruit good; or else make the tree corrupt, and his fruit corrupt."—As much as to say, it is a very absurd thing, for any to suppose that the tree is good, and yet the fruit bad; that the tree is of one sort, and the fruit of another; for the proper evidence of the nature of the tree is its fruit. Nothing else can be intended by that last clause in the verse, "For the tree is known by its fruit," than that the tree is chiefly known by its fruit, that this is the main and most proper diagnostic by which one tree is distinguished from another. So Luke vi. 44. "Every tree is known by his own fruit." Christ no where says, Ye shall know the tree by its leaves or flowers; or ye shall know men by their talk, by the good story they tell of their experiences, by the manner and air of their speaking, or emphasis and pathos of expression; or ye shall know them by their speaking feelingly, or by abundance of talk, or by many tears and affectionate expressions, or by the affections ye feel in your hearts towards them: but by *their fruits shall ye know them; the tree is known by its fruit; every tree is known by its own fruit.* And as this is the evidence that Christ has directed us mainly to look at it in others, in judging of them, so it is the evidence that Christ has mainly directed us to give to others, whereby they may judge of us; Matt. v. 16. "Let your light so shine before men, that others seeing your good works, may glorify your Father which is in heaven." Here Christ directs us to manifest our godliness to others. Godliness is as it were a light that shines in the soul: Christ directs that this light should not only shine within, but that it should *shine* out *before men*, that they may see it. But which way shall this be? It is by our good works. Christ doth not say, that others hearing your good words, your good story, or your pathetical expressions; but *that others seeing your good* WORKS, *may glorify your Father which is in heaven.* Doubtless when Christ gives us a rule how to make our light shine, that others may have evidence of it, his rule is the best. And the apostles mention a christian practice, as the principal ground of their esteem of persons as true Christians. As the apostle Paul, in the 6th chapter of Hebrews. There the apostle, in the beginning of the chapter, speaks of persons who have great common illuminations, who have *been enlightened, and have tasted of the heavenly gift, and were made partakers of the Holy Ghost, and have tasted the good word of God, and the powers of the world to come, who afterwards fall away*, and are like barren ground, *that is nigh unto cursing, whose end is to be burned:* and then he immediately adds in the 9th verse, (expressing his charity for the christian Hebrews, as having that saving grace, which is better than all these common illuminations,) "But, beloved, we are persuaded better things of you, and things that accompany salvation: though we thus speak." And then in the next verse, he tells them what was the reason he had such good thoughts of them: he does not say, that it was because they had given him a good account of a work of God upon their souls, and talked very experimentally; but it was their work, and labour of love; "for God is not unrighteous, to forget your work, and labour of love, which ye have showed towards his name, in that ye have ministered to the saints, and do minister." And the same apostle speaks of faithfully serving God in practice, as the proper proof to others of men's loving Christ above all, and preferring his honour to their private interest, Phil. ii. 21, 22. "For all seek their own, not the things which are Jesus Christ's: but ye know the proof of him, that as a son with the father, he hath served with me in the gospel." So the apostle John expresses the same, as the ground of his good opinion of Gaius, 3 John 3—6. "For I rejoiced greatly when the brethren came and testified of the truth that is in thee." But how did the brethren testify of the truth that was in Gaius? and how did the apostle judge of the truth that was in him? it was not because they testified that he had given them a good account of the steps of his experiences, and talked like one that felt what he said, and had the very language of a Christian: but they testified, "that he walked in the truth:" as it follows, "even as thou walkest in the truth. I have no greater joy than to hear that my children walk in the truth. Beloved, thou dost faithfully whatsoever thou dost to the brethren, and to strangers: which have borne witness of thy charity before the church." Thus the apostle explains what the brethren had borne witness of, when they *came and testified of his walking in the truth.* And the apostle seems in this same place, to give it as a rule to Gaius how he should judge of others. In verse 10. he mentions one Diotrephes, that did not conduct himself well, and led away others after him; and then in the 11th verse, he directs Gaius to beware of such, and not to follow them: and gives him a rule whereby he may know them, exactly agreeable to that rule Christ had given before, "by their fruits ye shall know them." says the apostle, "Beloved, follow not that which is evil, but that which is good. He that doth good, is of God: but he that doth evil, hath not seen God." And I would further observe, that the apostle James, expressly comparing that way of showing others our faith and Christianity by our practice or works, with other ways of showing our faith without works, or not by works, does plainly and abundantly prefer the former; Jam. ii. 18. "Yea, a man may say, Thou hast faith, and I have works: show me thy faith without thy works, and I will show thee my faith by my works." A manifestation of our faith *without works*, or in a way diverse from works, is a manifestation of it in *words*, whereby a man professes faith. As the apostle says, ver. 14. "What doth it profit, my brethren, though a man *say* he hath faith?"—Therefore here are two ways of manifesting to our neighbour what is in our hearts; one by what we *say*, and the other by what we *do*. But the apostle abundantly prefers the latter as the best evidence. Now certainly all accounts we give of ourselves in words, our saying that we have faith, and that we are converted; telling the manner how we came to have faith, the steps by which it was wrought, and the discoveries and experiences that accompanied it, are still but manifesting our faith by what we *say;* it is but showing our faith by our *words;* which the apostle speaks of as falling vastly short of manifesting of it by what we do, and showing our faith by our *works.*

And as the Scripture plainly teaches, that practice is the best evidence of the sincerity of professing Christians; so reason teaches the same thing. Reason shows, that men's deeds are better and more faithful interpreters of their minds, than their words. The common sense of all mankind, through all ages and nations, teaches them to judge of men's hearts chiefly by their practice, in other matters: as, whether a man be a loyal subject, a true lover, a dutiful child, or a faithful servant. If a man professes a great deal of love and friendship to another, reason teaches all men, that such a profession is not so great an evidence of his being a real and hearty friend, as his appearing a friend in deeds; being faithful and constant to his friend, in prosperity and adversity, ready to lay out himself, and deny himself, and suffer in his personal interest, to do him a kindness. A wise man will trust to such evidences of the sincerity of friendship, further than a thousand earnest professions and solemn declarations, and most affectionate expressions of friendship in words. And there is equal reason, why practice should also be looked upon as the best evidence of friendship towards Christ. Reason says the same that Christ said, in John xiv. 21. "He that hath my commandments, and keepeth them, he it is that loveth me." Thus if we see a man, who in the course of his life seems to follow and imitate Christ, and greatly to exert and deny himself for his honour, and to promote his kingdom and interest in the world; reason teaches, that this is an evidence of love to Christ, more to be depended on, than if a man only *says* he has love to him, and tells of his inward experiences, what strong love he felt, and how his heart was drawn out in love at such and such a time; when it may be there appears but little imitation of Christ in his behaviour. He seems backward to do any great matter for him, or to put himself out of his way for the promoting of his kingdom, but seems to be apt to excuse himself whenever he is called to deny himself for Christ. So if a man, in declaring his experiences, tells how he found his heart weaned from the world, and saw the vanity of it, so that all looked as nothing to him at such and such times, and professes that he gives up all to God, and calls heaven and earth to witness to it: but yet in his practice is violent in pursuing the world, what he gets he keeps close, is exceeding loth to part with much of it to charitable and pious uses, it comes from him almost like his heart's blood. But there is another professing Christian, that says not a great deal, yet in his behaviour appears ready at all times to forsake the world, whenever it stands in the way of his duty, and is free to part with it at any time, to promote religion and the good of his fellow-creatures. Reason teaches, that the latter gives far the most credible manifestation of a heart weaned from the world. And if a man appears to walk humbly before God and men, and to be of a conversation that savours of a broken heart, appearing patient and resigned to God under affliction, and meek in his behaviour amongst men; this is a better evidence of humiliation, than if a person only *tells* how great a sense he had of his own unworthiness—how he was brought to lie in the dust, quite emptied of himself, and to see himself all over filthy and abominable, &c. &c.—but yet acts as if he looked upon himself one of the first and best of saints, and by just right the head of all the Christians in the town. He is assuming, self-willed, and impatient of the least contradiction or opposition; we may be assured in such a case, that a man's practice comes from a lower place in his heart, than his profession. So (to mention no more instances) if a professor of Christianity manifest in his behaviour a tender spirit towards others in calamity, ready to bear their burdens with them, willing to spend his substance for them, and to suffer many inconveniences in his worldly interest to promote the good of others' souls and bodies; is not this a more credible manifestation of a spirit of love to men, than only a man's *telling* what love he felt to others at certain times—how he pitied their souls, how his soul was in travail for them, and how he felt a hearty love and pity to his enemies—when in his behaviour he seems to be of a very selfish spirit, close and niggardly, all for himself, and none for his neighbours, and perhaps envious and contentious? Persons in a pang of affection may think they have a willingness of heart for great things, to do much and to suffer much, and so may profess it very earnestly and confidently, when really their hearts are far from it. Thus many in their affectionate pangs have thought themselves willing to be damned eternally for the glory of God. Passing affections easily produce words; and words are cheap; and godliness is more easily feigned in words than in actions. Christian practice is a costly laborious thing. The self-denial that is required of Christians, the narrowness of the way that leads to life, does not consist in words, but in practice.. Hypocrites may much more easily be brought to *talk* like saints than to *act* like saints.

Thus it is plain, that christian practice is the best sign or manifestation of the true godliness of a professing Christian, to the eye of his *neighbours*. But then, the following things should be well observed, that this matter may be rightly understood:

First, It must be observed, that when the Scripture speaks of christian practice, as the best evidence to others of sincerity and truth of grace, *a profession of Christianity* is not excluded, but supposed. The rules mentioned, were rules given to the followers of Christ, to guide them in their thoughts of *professing Christians,* and those that offered themselves as some of their society, whereby they might judge of the truth of their *pretences*, and the sincerity of the *profession* they made; and not for the trial of heathens, or those who made no pretence to Christianity, and with whom Christians had nothing to do. This is as plain as possible in that great rule which Christ gives in the 7th of Matthew, "By their fruits ye shall know them." He there gives a rule how to judge of professed Christians, yea those who made a very high profession, "false prophets, who come in sheep's clothing," as ver. 15. So that passage of the apostle James, chap. ii. 18. "Show me thy faith without thy works, and I will show thee my faith by my works." It is evident, that both these sorts of persons, offering to give these diverse evidences of their faith, are *professors* of faith; this is implied in each offering to give evidences of the faith professed. And it is evident by the preceding verses, that the apostle is speaking of professors of faith in Jesus Christ. So it is very plain that the apostle John, in those passages observed in his third epistle, is speaking of *professing* Christians. Though in these rules, the christian *practice* of professors be spoken of as the greatest and most distinguishing sign of their sincerity, much more evidential than their profession itself; yet a profession of Christianity is plainly pre-supposed. It is not the main thing in the evidence, nor any thing distinguishing; yet it is a thing requisite and necessary in it. As having an animal body, is not any thing distinguishing of a man from other creatures, and is not the main thing in the evidence of human nature; yet it is a thing requisite and necessary in the evidence. So that if any man should say plainly that he was not a Christian, and did not believe that Jesus was the Son of God, or a person sent of God; these rules of Christ and his apostles do not at all oblige us to look upon him as a sincere Christian, let his visible practice and virtues be what they will. And not only do these rules take no place with respect to a man that explicitly denies Christianity, and is a professed deist, Jew, heathen, or open infidel; but also with respect to a man that only forbears to make a profession of Christianity: because these rules were given us only to judge of professing Christians; fruits must be joined with open flowers; bells and pomegranates go together.

But here will naturally arise this inquiry, viz. When a man may be said to profess Christianity? or, what profession may properly be called a profession of Christianity? I answer in two things:

1. In order to a man's being properly said to make a profession of *Christianity*, there must undoubtedly be a *profession* of all that is necessary to his being a Christian, or of so much as belongs to the *essence* of Christianity. Whatsoever is essential in Christianity itself, the profession of that is essential in the profession of Christianity. The profession must be of the thing professed. For a man to *profess* Christianity, is for him to declare that he *has* it. And therefore so much as belongs to the true denomination of a thing; so much is essential to a true declaration of *that* thing. If we *take* only a part of Christianity, and leave out a part which is essential to it, what we take is not Christianity; because something of the essence of it is wanting. So if we *profess* only a part, and leave out a part that is essential, that which we profess is not Christianity. Thus in order to a profession of Christianity, we must profess that we believe that Jesus is the Messiah; for this reason, because such a belief is essential to Christianity. And so we must profess, either expressly or implicitly, that Jesus satisfied for our sins, and other essential doctrines of the gospel, because a belief of these things also are essential to Christianity. But there are other things as essential to religion, as an orthodox belief; which it is therefore as necessary that we should profess, in order to our being truly said to profess Christianity. Thus it is essential to Christianity that we repent of our sins, that we be convinced of our own sinfulness, that we are sensible we have justly exposed ourselves to God's wrath; that our hearts renounce all sin, that we do with our whole hearts embrace Christ as our only Saviour, that we love him above all, are willing for his sake to forsake all, and that we give up ourselves to be entirely and for ever his, &c. Such things as these as much belong to the *essence* of christianity, as the belief of any of the doctrines of the gospel; and therefore the *profession* of them as much belongs to a christian profession. Not that in order to persons being professing Christians, it is necessary that there should be an explicit profession of every individual

thing that belongs to christian grace or virtue: but certainly, there must be a profession, either express or implicit, of what is of the essence of religion. And as to those things that Christians should *express* in their profession, we ought to be guided by the precepts of God's word, or by scripture-examples of public professions of religion, which God's people have made from time to time.

Thus they ought to profess their repentance of sin: as of old, when persons were initiated as professors, they came, confessing their sins, manifesting their humiliation for sin, Matt. iii. 6. And the baptism they were baptized with, was called *the baptism of repentance*, Mark i. 3. And John, when he had baptized them, exhorted them to "bring forth fruits meet for repentance," Matt. iii. 8. *i. e.* agreeable to that repentance which they had professed; encouraging them, that if they did so, they should escape the wrath to come, and be gathered as wheat into God's garner, Matt. iii. 7, 8—10, 12. So the apostle Peter says to the Jews, Acts ii. 38. "Repent, and be baptized:" which shows, that repentance is a qualification that must be *visible*, in order to baptism; and therefore ought to be publicly *professed*. So when the Jews that returned from captivity, entered publicly into covenant, it was with confession, or public profession of repentance of their sins, Neh. ix. 2. This profession of repentance should include or imply a profession of conviction, that God would be just in our damnation: (see Neh. ix. 33—35. and chap. x.) They should profess their faith in Jesus Christ, that they embrace Christ, rely upon him as their Saviour with their whole hearts, and joyfully entertain his gospel. Thus Philip, in order to his baptizing the eunuch, required him to profess, that he *believed with all his heart*. They who were received as visible Christians, at that great out-pouring of the Spirit, which began at the day of Pentecost, appeared *gladly to receive the gospel*: Acts ii. 41. "Then they that gladly received the word, were baptized: and the same day there were added unto them about three thousand souls." They should profess that they rely only on Christ's righteousness and strength, that they are devoted to him as their only Lord and Saviour, and that they rejoice in him as their only righteousness and portion. It is foretold, that all nations should be brought publicly to make this profession, Isa. xlv. 22, &c. "Look unto me, and be ye saved, all the ends of the earth: for I am God, and there is none else. I have sworn by myself, the word is gone out of my mouth in righteousness, and shall not return, that unto me every knee shall bow, every tongue shall swear. Surely, shall one say, In the Lord have I righteousness and strength: even unto him shall men come, and all that are incensed against him shall be ashamed. In the Lord shall all the seed of Israel be justified, and shall glory." They should profess to give up themselves entirely to Christ, and to God through him; as the children of Israel, when they publicly recognised their covenant with God; Deut. xxvi. 17. "Thou hast avouched the Lord this day to be thy God, and to walk in his ways, and to keep his statutes, and his commandments, and his judgments, and to hearken unto his voice." They ought to profess a willingness of heart to embrace religion with all its difficulties, and to walk in a way of obedience to God universally and perseveringly; (Exod. xix. 8. and xxiv. 3, 7. Deut. xxvi. 16—18. 2 Kings xxiii. 3. Neh. x. 28, 29. Ps. cxix. 57, 106.) They ought to profess, that all their hearts and souls are in these engagements to be the Lord's, and for ever to serve him; 2 Chron. xv. 12—14. God's people swearing *by* his name, or *to* his name, as it might be rendered, (by which seems to be signified their solemnly giving up themselves to him in covenant, and vowing to receive him as their God, and to be entirely his, to obey and serve him,) is spoken of as a duty to be performed by all God's visible Israel; (Deut. vi. 13. and x. 20. Ps. lxiii. 11. Isa. xix. 18. chap. xlv. 23, 24. compared with Rom. xiv. 11. and Phil. ii. 10, 11. Isa. xlviii. 1, 2. and lxv. 15, 16. Jer. iv. 2. and v. 7. and xii. 16. Hos. iv. 15. and x. 4.) Therefore, in order to persons being entitled to full esteem and charity, with their neighbours, as being sincere professors of Christianity; by those fore-mentioned rules of Christ and his apostles, there must be a visibly holy life, with a profession, either expressing, or plainly implying, such things as those which have been now mentioned. We are to *know them by their fruits:* that is, we are by their fruits to know whether they be what they profess to be; not that we are to know by their fruits, that they have something in them, to which they do not so much as pretend. Moreover,

2. That profession of these things, which is properly called a christian profession, and which must be joined with christian practice, in order to persons being entitled to the benefit of those rules, must be made (as to what appears) *understandingly:* that is, they must be persons that appear to have been so far instructed in the principles of religion, as to be in an ordinary capacity to *understand* the proper import of what is expressed in their profession. For sounds are no significations or declarations of any thing, any further than men understand the meaning of their own sounds.

But in order to persons making a proper profession of Christianity, such as the Scripture directs, and such as the followers of Christ should require, in order to the acceptance of professors, with full charity, as of their society; it is not necessary they should give an account of the *particular steps* and method, by which the Holy Spirit, sensibly to them, wrought those great essentials of Christianity in their hearts. There is no footstep in the Scripture of any such way of the apostles, or primitive ministers and Christians, requiring any such relation, in order to their receiving and treating others as their christian brethren; or of their first examining them concerning the particular method and order of their experiences. They required of them a profession of the things wrought; but no account of the *manner* of working was required of them. Nor is there the least shadow in the Scripture of any such custom in the church of God, from Adam to the death of the apostle John.

I am far from saying, that it is not requisite that persons should give any sort of account of their experiences to their brethren. For persons to profess those things wherein the essence of Christianity lies, is the same thing as to profess that they *experience* those things. Thus for persons solemnly to *profess*, that, in a sense and full conviction of their own utter sinfulness, misery, and impotence, and totally undone state as in themselves—their just desert of God's utter rejection and eternal wrath, without mercy, and the utter insufficiency of their own righteousness, or any thing in them, to satisfy divine justice, or recommend them to God's favour—they do only and entirely depend on the Lord Jesus Christ, and his satisfaction and righteousness; it is the same thing as to profess, that they *experience* those particulars. When any *profess*, that they do with all their hearts believe the truth of the gospel of Christ; and that, in a full conviction and sense of his sufficiency and perfect excellency as a Saviour, as exhibited in the gospel, they do with their whole souls cleave to him, and acquiesce in him, as the refuge and rest of their souls, and the fountain of their comfort; that they repent of their sins, and utterly renounce all sin, and give up themselves wholly to Christ, willingly subjecting themselves to him as their King; that they give him their hearts and their whole man; and are willing and resolved to have God for their whole and everlasting portion; what is it but saying, that they *experience* those things? Again, if any *profess*, in a dependence on God's promises of a future eternal enjoyment of him in heaven, to renounce all the enjoyments of this vain world, selling all for this great treasure and future inheritance, and to comply with every command of God, even the most difficult and self-denying, and devote their whole lives to God's service; what is it but a declaration of so much *experience?* Once more, when any profess, that, in the forgiveness of those who have injured them, and a general benevolence to mankind, their hearts are united to the people of Jesus Christ as their people, cleave to them and love them as their brethren, and worship and serve God, and follow Christ, in union and fellowship with them, being willing and resolved to perform all incumbent duties, as members of the same family of God and mystical body of Christ; I say, for persons solemnly to profess such things as these, as in the presence of God, is the same thing, as to profess that they are conscious to, or do *experience*, such things in their hearts.

Nor do I suppose, that persons giving an account of their experience of particular exercises of grace, with the times and circumstances, gives no advantage to others in forming a judgment of their state; or that persons may not fitly be inquired of concerning these, especially in cases of great importance, where all possible satisfaction is to be desired and sought after, as in the case of ordination or approbation of a minister. It may give advantage in forming a judgment, in several respects; and among others in this, that hereby we may be better satisfied, that the professor speaks honestly and understandingly, in what he professes; and that he does not make the profession in mere formality. In order to a profession of Christianity being accepted to any purpose, there ought to be good reason, from the circumstances of the profession, to think, that the professor does not make such a profession out of a mere customary compliance with a prescribed form, using words without any distinct meaning, or in a very lax and ambiguous manner, as confessions of faith are often subscribed; but that the professor understandingly and honestly signifies what he is conscious of in his own heart; otherwise his profession can be of no significance, and no more to be regarded than the sound of things without life. But indeed (whatever advantage an account of particular exercises may give in judging of this) it must be owned, that the professor having been previously thoroughly instructed by his teachers, and giving good proof of his sufficient knowledge, together with a practice agreeable to his profession, is the best evidence of this.

Nor do I suppose, but that, if a person—who is inquired of about particular passages, times, and circumstances of his christian experience—seems to be able to give a distinct account of the manner of his first conversion, in such a method as has been frequently observable in true conversion, so that things seem sensibly and distinctly to follow one another in the order of time, according to the order of nature: it is an illustrating circumstance which, among other things, adds lustre to the evidence he gives his brethren of the truth of his experiences.

But what I speak of as unscriptural, is insisting on a particular account of the *distinct method* and steps, wherein the Spirit of God did sensibly proceed, in first bringing the soul into a state of salvation, as a thing *requisite* in order to receiving a professor into full charity as a real Christian; so as, for the want of such relation to disregard other things, in the evidence which persons give to their neighbours of their Christianity, that are vastly more important and essential.

Secondly, That we may rightly understand how christian practice is the *greatest* evidence that *others* can have of the sincerity of a professing Christian, it is needful that what was said before, showing what christian practice is, should be borne in mind; and that it should be considered how far this may be visible to others. Merely that a professor of Christianity is, what is commonly called, an honest, moral man, (*i. e.* having no special transgression or iniquity that might bring a blot on his character,) is no great evidence of the sincerity of his profession. This is not *making his light shine before men*. This is not that *work and labour of love showed towards Christ's name*, which gave the apostle such persuasion of the sincerity of the professing Hebrews, (Heb. vi. 9, 10.) We may see nothing in a man, *but that he may be* a good man; there may appear nothing in his life and conversation inconsistent with his being godly, and yet neither any great positive evidence *that he is* so. But there may be great positive appearances of holiness in men's visible behaviour; their life devoted to the service of God. They may appear to follow the example of Jesus Christ, and come up in a great measure to those excellent rules in the 5th, 6th, and 7th chapters of Matthew, and 12th of Romans, and many other parts of the New Testament. There may be a great appearance of their being *universal* in their obedience to Christ's commands and the rules of the gospel; in the performance of the duties of the first table, manifesting the fear and love of God; and also universal in fulfilling rules of love to men, love to saints, and love to enemies; rules of meekness and forgiveness, rules of mercy and charity, and looking not only at our own things, but also at the things of others; rules of doing good to men's souls and bodies, to particular persons and to the public; rules of temperance and mortification, and of an humble conversation; rules of bridling the tongue, and improving it to glorify God and bless men, showing that in their tongues is the law of kindness. They may appear to walk as Christians, in all *places*, and at all *seasons;* in the house of God, and in their families, among their neighbours, on Sabbath-days, and every day, in business and in conversation, towards friends and enemies, towards superiors, inferiors, and equals. Persons in their visible walk may appear to be very earnestly engaged in the service of God and mankind, much to labour and lay out themselves in this work of a Christian, and to be very constant and stedfast in it, under all circumstances and temptations. There may be great manifestations of a spirit to deny themselves, and suffer for God and Christ, the interest of religion, and the benefit of their brethren. There may be great appearances in a man's walk, of a disposition to forsake any thing, rather than to forsake Christ, and to make every thing give place to his honour. There may be great manifestations in a man's behaviour of such religion as this being his element, and of his placing the delight and happiness of his life in it; and his conversation may be such, as to carry with him a sweet odour of christian graces and heavenly dispositions, wherever he goes. And when it is thus in the professors of Christianity, here is an evidence to others of their sincerity in their profession, to which all other manifestations are not worthy to be compared.

There is doubtless a great variety in the degrees of evidence that professors exhibit of their sincerity, in their life and practice; as there is a variety in the fairness and clearness of accounts persons give of the manner and method of their experiences: but undoubtedly such a manifestation as has been described, of a christian spirit in practice, is vastly beyond the fairest and brightest story of particular steps and passages of experience, that ever was told. And in general, a manifestation of the sincerity of a christian profession in practice, is far better than a relation of experiences.—But yet,

Thirdly, It must be noted, agreeable to what was formerly observed, that no external appearances whatsoever, that are visible to the world, are infallible evidences of grace. The manifestations that have been mentioned, are the best that mankind can have; and they are such as oblige Christians entirely to embrace professors as saints, to love and rejoice in them as the children of God; and they are sufficient to give as great satisfaction concerning them as ever is needful to guide them in their conduct, or for any purpose that needs to be answered in this world. But nothing that appears to them in their neighbour, can be sufficient to beget an *absolute certainty* concerning the state of his soul. They see not his heart, nor can they see all his external behaviour; for much of it is in *secret*, and hid from the eye of the world: and it is impossible certainly to determine, how far a man may go in many external appearances and imitations of grace, from other principles. Though undoubtedly, if others could see so much of what belongs to men's practice, as their own consciences may know of it, it might be an infallible evidence of their state, as will appear from what follows.

SECT. XIV.

Christian practice is a distinguishing and sure evidence of grace to persons' own consciences.

This is very plain in 1 John ii. 3. "Hereby we do know that we know him, if we keep his commandments." And the testimony of our consciences, with respect to our good deeds, is spoken of as that which may give us assurance of our own godliness; 1 John iii. 18, 19. "My little children, let us not love in word, neither in tongue, but in deed (in the original it is ΕΡΓΩ, *in work*) and in truth. And hereby we know that we are of the truth, and shall assure our hearts before him." And the apostle Paul, (Heb. vi.) speaks of *the work and labour of love* of the christian Hebrews, as that which both gave him a persuasion that they had something above the highest common illuminations, and also as that evidence which tended to give them the highest assurance of hope concerning themselves; ver. 9, &c. "But, beloved, we are persuaded better things of you, and things that accompany salvation, though we thus speak. For God is not unrighteous, to forget your work and labour of love, which ye have showed towards his name, in that ye have ministered to the saints, and do minister. And we desire that every one of you do show the same diligence, to the full assurance of hope unto the end." So the apostle directs the Galatians to examine their behaviour or practice, that they might have rejoicing in themselves, in their own happy state; Gal. vi. 4. "Let every man prove his own work, so shall he have rejoicing in himself, and not in another." And the psalmist says, Psal. cxix. 6. "Then shall I not be ashamed, when I have respect unto all thy commandments;" *i. e.* then shall I be bold, and assured, and stedfast in my hope. And in that of our Saviour, Matt. vii. 19, 20. "Every tree that bringeth not forth good fruit, is hewn down and cast into the fire. Wherefore by their fruits ye shall know them." Though Christ gives this, first, as a rule by which we should judge of others, yet in the words that next follow, he plainly shows, that he intends it also as a rule by which we should judge ourselves; "Not every one that saith unto me, Lord, Lord, shall enter into the kingdom of heaven: but he that *doth the will* of my Father which is in heaven. Many will say to me in that day, Lord, Lord, &c.——And then will I profess unto them, I never knew you: depart from me, *ye that work iniquity*. Therefore, whosoever heareth these sayings of mine, and *doth* them, I will liken him unto a wise man which built his house upon a rock.——And every one that heareth these sayings of mine, and *doth them not*, shall be likened unto a foolish man which built his house upon the sand." I shall have occasion to mention other texts that show the same thing, hereafter.

But for the greater clearness in this matter, I would, *first*, show how christian practice, doing good works, or keeping Christ's commandments, is to be taken, when the Scripture represents it as a sure sign to our *own* consciences, that we are real Christians. And, *secondly*, will prove, that this is the chief of all evidences that men can have of their own sincere godliness.

First, I would show how christian practice, or keeping Christ's commandments, is to be taken, when the Scripture represents it as a sure evidence to our own consciences, that we are sincere Christians.

And here I would observe, that we cannot reasonably suppose, when the Scripture in this case speaks of good works, good fruit, and keeping Christ's commandments, that it has respect merely to what is *external*, or the motion and action of the body, without including respect to any aim or intention of the agent, or any act of his understanding or will. For consider men's actions so, and they are no more good works or acts of obedience, than the regular motions of a clock; nor are they considered as any human actions at all. The actions of the body, taken thus, are neither acts of obedience, nor disobedience; any more than the motions of the body in a convulsion. But the obedience and fruit that is spoken of, is the obedience and fruit of the man; and therefore not only the acts of the body, but the obedience of the soul, consisting in the acts and practice of the soul. Not that I suppose, that when the Scripture speaks, in this case, of gracious works, fruit, and practice, that in these expressions is included all inward piety and holiness of heart, both principle and exercise, both spirit and practice: because then, in these things being given as signs of a gracious principle in the heart, the same thing would be given as a sign of itself, and there would be no distinction between root and fruit. But only the gracious exercise and holy act of the soul is meant, and given as the sign of the holy principle, and good estate. Neither is every kind of inward exercise of grace meant; but the practical exercise, that exercise of the soul, and exertion of inward holiness, which there is in an obediential act; or that exertion of the mind, and act of grace, which issues and terminates in what they call the imperate acts of the will; in which something is directed and commanded by the soul to be done, and brought to pass in practice.

Here, for a clearer understanding, I would observe, that there are two kinds of exercises of grace. 1. There are what some call *immanent* acts; that is, those exercises of grace that remain within the soul, that begin and are terminated there, without any immediate relation to any thing to be done outwardly, or to be brought to pass in practice. Such are the exercises of grace, which the saints often have in *contemplation;* when the exercise in the heart does not directly proceed *to*, or terminate *in*, any thing beyond the thoughts of the mind: however they may tend to practice (as all exercises of grace do) more remotely. 2. There are acts of grace, that are more strictly called *practical*, or effective exercises; because they immediately respect something to be *done*. They are the exertions of grace in the commanding acts of the will, directing the outward actions. As when a saint gives a cup of cold water to a disciple, in and from the exercise of the grace of charity; or voluntarily endures persecution, in the way of his duty, immediately from the exercise of a supreme love to Christ. Here is the exertion of grace producing its effect in outward actions. These exercises of grace are practical and productive of good works, not only because they are of a *productive nature*, (for so are all exercises of true grace,) but they are the *producing* acts. This is properly the exercise of grace in the act of the will; and this is properly the practice of the soul. And the soul is the immediate actor of no other practice but this: the motions of the body follow from the laws of union between the soul and body, which God, and not the soul, has fixed, and does maintain. The act of the soul, and the exercise of grace, exerted in the performance of a good work, is the good work itself, so far as the soul is concerned in it, or so far as it is the soul's good work. The determinations of the will, are indeed our very actions, so far as they are properly ours, as Dr. Doddridge observes.* In this practice of the soul, is included the aim and intention of the soul which is the agent. For not only should we not look on the motions of a statue, doing justice or distributing alms by clock-work, as any acts of obedience to Christ in that statue; but neither would any body call the voluntary actions of a man, externally and materially agreeable to a command of Christ, by the name of obedience to Christ, if he had never heard of Christ, or any of his commands, or had no thought of his commands in what he did.—If the acts of obedience and good fruits spoken of, be looked upon, not as mere motions of the body, but as acts of the soul; the whole exercise of the spirit of the mind, in the action, must be taken in, with the end acted for, and the respect the soul then has to God, &c. otherwise they are no acts of denial of ourselves, or obedience to God, or service done to him, but something else. Such effective exercises of grace as these, many of the martyrs have experienced in a high degree. And all true saints live a life of such acts of grace as these, as they all live a life of gracious works, of which these operative exertions of grace are the life and soul. And this is the obedience and fruit that God mainly looks at, as he looks at the soul, more than the body; as much as the soul, in the constitution of human nature, is the superior part. As God looks at the obedience and practice of the man, he looks at the practice of the soul; for the soul is the man in God's sight, "For the Lord seeth not as man seeth, for he looketh on the heart."

And thus it is, that obedience, good works, and good fruit, are to be taken, when given in Scripture as a sure evidence to our own consciences of a true principle of grace; even as including the obedience and practice of the soul, as preceding and governing the actions of the body. When practice is given in Scripture as the main evidence of our true Christianity to *others*, then is meant *that* in our practice which is visible to them, even our outward actions: but when practice is given as a sure evidence of our real Christianity to our own *consciences*, then is meant *that* in our practice which is visible to our own consciences; which is not only the motion of our

* Scripture-doctrine of Salvation, Sermon I. p. 11.

bodies, but the exertion and exercise of the soul, which directs and commands that motion; which is more directly and immediately under the view of our own consciences, than the act of the body. And that this is the intent of Scripture, not only does the nature and reason of the thing show, but it is plain by the Scripture itself. Thus it is evident that when Christ at the conclusion of his sermon on the mount, speaks of *doing* or practising those sayings of his, as the grand sign of professors being true disciples; *without* which he likens them to a man that built his house upon the sand; and *with* which, to a man that built his house upon a rock; he has respect, not only to the outward behaviour, but to the inward exercise of the mind in that behaviour. This is evident by observing what those preceding sayings of his are; "Blessed are the poor in spirit; blessed are they that mourn; blessed are the meek; blessed are they that do hunger and thirst after righteousness; blessed are the merciful; blessed are the pure in heart; whosoever is angry with his brother without a cause, &c.; whosoever looketh on a woman to lust after her, &c.; love your enemies; take no thought for your life," and others of the like nature, which imply inward exercises: and when Christ says, John xiv. 21. "He that hath my commandments, and keepeth them, he it is that loveth me;" he has evidently a special respect to that command several times repeated in the same discourse, (which he calls, by way of eminence, *his commandment,) that they should love one another, as he had loved them.* (See chap. xiii. 34, 35. and chap. xv. 10, 12, 13, 14.) But this command respects chiefly an exercise of the mind or heart, though exerted in practice. So when the apostle John says, 1 John ii. 3. "Hereby we do know that we know him, if we keep his commandments; he has plainly a principal respect to the same command, as appears by what follows, ver. 7—11. and 2d Epist. ver. 5, 6.: and when we are told in Scripture that men shall at the last day be judged *according to their works,* and *all shall receive according to the things done in the body;* it is not to be understood only of *outward* acts; for if so, why is God so often spoken of as searching the hearts and trying the reins, *that he may render to every one according to his works?* as Rev. ii. 23. "And all the churches shall know that I am he which searcheth the reins and hearts: and I will give unto every one according to his works." Jer. xvii. 10. "I the Lord search the heart, I try the reins, even to give every man according to his ways, and according to the fruit of his doings." But if by *his ways, and the fruit of his doings,* is meant only the actions of his body, what need of *searching the heart and reins,* in order to know them? Hezekiah in his sickness pleads his practice as an evidence of his title to God's favour, as including not only his outward actions, but what was in his heart, Isa. xxxviii. 3. "Remember now, O Lord, I beseech thee, how I have walked before thee in truth, and with a perfect heart."

Though in this great evidence of sincerity that the Scripture gives us, what is inward is of greatest importance; yet what is outward is included and intended, as connected with the practical exertion of grace in the will, directing and commanding the actions of the body. And hereby are effectually cut off all pretensions that any man can have to evidences of godliness, who externally lives wickedly; because the great evidence lies in that inward exercise and practice of the soul, which consists in the act of the will, commanding outward acts. But it is known, that these commanding acts of the will are not one way, and the actions of the bodily organs another: for the unalterable law of nature is, that they should be united, as long as soul and body are united, and the organs are not so destroyed as to be incapable of those motions that the soul commands. Thus it would be ridiculous for a man to plead, that the commanding act of his will was to go to the public worship, while his feet carry him to a tavern or brothel-house; or that the commanding act of his will was to give such a piece of money he had in his hand to a poor beggar, while his hand at the same instant kept it back, and held it fast.

Secondly, I proceed to show, that christian practice, taken in the sense explained, is *the chief* of all the evidences of a saving sincerity in religion, to the consciences of the professors of it; much to be preferred to the method of the first convictions, enlightenings, and comforts in conversion; or any immanent discoveries or exercises of grace whatsoever, that begin and end in contemplation.* The evidence of this appears by the following arguments.

Argument I. *Reason* plainly shows, that those things which put it to the proof, what men will actually cleave to in their *practice,* when left to follow their own choice and inclinations, are the proper trial what they do really prefer in their hearts. Sincerity in religion, as observed already, consists in setting God highest in the heart, in choosing him before other things, in having a heart to sell all for Christ, &c.—But a man's actions are the proper trial what a man's heart prefers. As for instance, when God and other things come to stand in competition, God is as it were set before a man on one hand, and his worldly interest or pleasure on the other; his behaviour in such case, in actually cleaving to the one and forsaking the other, is the proper trial which he prefers. Sincerity consists in forsaking all for Christ in heart; but to forsake all for Christ in heart, is the very same thing as to have a heart to forsake all for Christ. The proper trial whether a man has a heart to forsake all for Christ, is his being actually put to it, Christ and other things coming in competition, that he *must* practically cleave to one and forsake the other. To forsake all for Christ in heart, is the same thing as to have a heart to forsake all for Christ when *called* to it: but the highest proof to ourselves and others, that we have a heart to forsake all for Christ when called to it, is *actually doing* it when or so far as called to it. To follow Christ in heart, is to have a heart to follow him. To deny ourselves in heart for Christ, is the same thing as to have a *heart* to deny ourselves for him in *fact.* The main and most proper proof of a man having a *heart* to any thing, concerning which he is at liberty to follow his own inclinations, is his *doing* it. When a man is at liberty whether to speak or keep silence, the most proper evidence of his having a *heart* to speak, is his *speaking.* When a man is at liberty whether to walk or sit still, the proper proof of his having a heart to walk, is his walking. Godliness consists not in a heart to *intend* to do the will of God, but in a heart to do it. The children of Israel in the wilderness had the former, of whom we read, Deut. v. 27—29. "Go thou near, and hear all that the Lord our God shall say; and speak thou unto us all that the Lord our God shall speak unto thee, and we will hear it, and do it. And the Lord heard the voice of your words, when ye spake unto me; and the Lord said unto me, I have heard the voice of the words of this people, which they have spoken unto thee: they have well said all that they have spoken. O that there were such an *heart* in them, that they would fear me, and keep all my commandments always, that it might be well with them, and with their children for ever!" The people manifested that they had *a heart to* INTEND *to keep God's commandments,* and to be very forward in those intentions; but God manifests, that this was far from being the thing he desired, wherein true godliness consists, even *a heart actually to keep them.*

It is therefore exceedingly absurd, and even ridiculous,

* "Look upon John, Christ's beloved disciple and bosom companion; he had received the anointing to know him that is true, *and he knew that he knew him,* 1 John ii. 3. But how did he know that? He might be deceived; (as it is strange to see what a melancholy fancy will do, and the effects of it; as honest men are reputed to have weak brains, and never saw the depths of the secrets of God;) what is his *last* proof? *Because we keep his commandments.*" Shepard's *Parable,* Part I. p. 131.

"A man may know his present union to the Lord Jesus, by a work; 1 John ii. 4. *He that saith, I know him, and keeps not his commandments, is a liar.*—Yes, that is true negatively; but may a man, ought a man, to see or know his union positively by this? Ans. ver. 5. Many said they did know and love the Lord, but *he that keeps his words.*—O they are sweet! It is heaven to cleave to him in every command; it is death to depart from any command: *hereby know we that we are in him.* If it were possible to ask of angels, how they know they are not devils, they would answer, the Lord's will is ours." Shepard's *Parable,* Part I. p. 134.

"If the question be, Whom doth the Lord Jesus love? you need not go to heaven for it, the word is nigh thee, *Those that love Christ.* Who are those? *Those that keep his commandments.*" Shepard's *Parable,* Part I. p. 138.

"Will you have Christ to sit in heaven, and not look that he subdue your lusts by the work of his grace, and so sway your hearts? You despise his kingdom then. Do you seek for pardon in the blood of Christ, and never look for the virtue and end of that blood to wash you and make you without spot, &c.? You despise his priesthood and blood then. Do you look for Christ to do work for you, and you not do Christ's work, and bring forth fruit to him? You despise his honour then, John xv. 8. If I were to discover a hypocrite, or a false heart, this I would say, It is he that shall set up Christ, but loathe his work." Shepard's *Parable,* Part I. p. 140.

for any to pretend that they have a good heart, while they live a wicked life, or do not bring forth the fruit of universal holiness in their practice. For it is proved in fact, that such men do not love God above all. It is foolish to dispute against plain fact and experience. Men that live in ways of sin, and yet flatter themselves that they shall go to heaven, or expect to be received hereafter as holy persons, without a holy life and practice, act as though they expected to make a fool of their Judge. Which is implied in what the apostle says, Gal. vi. 7. "Be not deceived; God is not mocked: for whatsoever a man soweth, that shall he also reap." As much as to say, "Do not deceive yourselves with an expectation of reaping life everlasting hereafter, if you sow not to the Spirit here; it is in vain to think that God will be made a fool of by you, that he will be imposed upon with shadows instead of substance, and with vain pretences, instead of that good fruit which he expects; when the contrary to what you pretend appears plainly in your life, before his face." In this manner the word *mock* is sometimes used in Scripture. Thus Delilah says to Samson, *Behold, thou hast mocked me, and told me lies*, Judges xvi. 10, 13. *i. e.* "Thou hast baffled me, intending to make a fool of me, as if I might be easily turned off with any vain pretence, instead of the truth." So it is said that Lot, when he told his sons-in-law that God would destroy that place, *he seemed as one that mocked to his sons-in-law*, Gen. xix. 14. *i. e.* he seemed as one that would make a game of them, as though they were credulous fools. But the great Judge, whose eyes are as a flame of fire, will not be mocked or baffled with any pretences, without a holy life. If in his name men have prophesied and wrought miracles, and have had faith so that they could remove mountains, and cast out devils, and however high their religious affections have been, however great resemblances they have had of grace, and though their hiding-place has been so dark and deep, that no human skill nor search could find them out; yet if they are *workers* or *practisers of iniquity*, they cannot hide their hypocrisy from their Judge; Job xxxiv. 22. "There is no darkness, nor shadow of death, where the *workers of iniquity* may hide themselves." Would a wise prince suffer himself to be mocked by a subject, who should pretend that he was loyal, and should tell his prince that he had an entire affection for him, and that at such and such a time he had experience of it, and felt his affections strongly working towards him, and should come expecting to be accepted and rewarded by his prince, as one of his best friends on that account, though he lived in rebellion against him, following some pretender to his crown, and from time to time stirring up sedition against him? Or, would a master suffer himself to be shammed and gulled by a servant, that should pretend to great experiences of love and honour towards him in his heart, and a great sense of his worthiness and kindness, when at the same time he refused to obey and serve him?

Argument II. As *reason* shows, that those things which occur in the course of life, which put it to the proof whether men will prefer God to other things in *practice*, are the proper trial of the sincerity of their *hearts;* so the same are represented as the proper trial of the sincerity of professors, in the *Scripture.* There we find that such things are called by that very name, *trials* or *temptations*, both words of the same signification.——The things that put it to the proof, whether men will prefer God to other things in practice, are the difficulties of religion, or those things which occur that make the practice of duty difficult, and cross to other principles besides the love of God; because in them, God and other things are both set before men together, for their actual and practical choice; and it comes to this, that we cannot hold to both, but one or the other must be forsaken. And these things are all over the Scripture called by the name of *trials* or *proofs.** And they are called by this name, because hereby professors are tried and proved of what sort they be, whether they be really what they profess and appear to be; and because in them the reality of the supreme love of God is brought to the test of experiment and fact; they are the proper proofs, in which it is truly determined by experience, whether men have a thorough disposition of heart to cleave to God or no; Deut. viii. 2. "And thou shalt remember all the way which the Lord God led thee these forty years in the wilderness, to humble thee, and to prove thee, whether thou wouldst keep his commandments, or no." Judg. ii. 21, 22. "I also will not henceforth drive out any from before them, of the nations which Joshua left when he died: that through them I may prove Israel, whether they will keep the way of the Lord." So chap. iii. 1, 4. and Exod. xvi. 4. And the Scripture, when it calls these difficulties of religion by the name of temptations or trials, explains itself to mean thereby, the trial or experiment of their *faith*, James i. 2, 3. "My brethren, count it all joy when ye fall into divers temptations; knowing this, that the trying of your faith worketh patience." 1 Pet. i. 6, 7. "Now for a season—ye are in heaviness, through manifold temptations; that the trial of your faith being much more precious than of gold," &c. So the apostle Paul speaks of that expensive duty of parting with our substance to the poor, as the proof of the *sincerity* of the love of Christians, 2 Cor. viii. 8. And the difficulties of religion are often represented in Scripture as being the trial of professors, in the same manner that the furnace is the proper trial of gold and silver; Psal. lxvi. 10, 11. "Thou, O God, hast proved us: thou hast tried us, as silver is tried: thou broughtest us into the net, thou laidest affliction upon our loins." Zech. xii. 9. "And I will bring the third part of them through the fire; and I will refine them as silver is refined: and I will try them as gold is tried." That which has the colour and appearance of gold, is put into the furnace to try whether it be what it seems to be, real gold or no. So the difficulties of religion are called trials, because they try those that have the profession and appearance of saints, whether they are what they appear to be, real saints. If we put true gold into the furnace, we shall find its great value and preciousness; so the truth and inestimable value of the virtues of a true Christian appear, when under these trials; 1 Pet. i. 7. "That the trial of your faith being much more precious than of gold that perisheth, might be found unto praise, and honour, and glory." True and pure gold will come out of the furnace in full weight: so true saints when tried come forth as gold, Job xxiii. 10. Christ distinguishes true grace from counterfeit by this, that it is *gold tried in the fire*, Rev. iii. 17, 18. So that it is evident that these things are called *trials* in Scripture, principally as they try or prove the *sincerity* of professors. And from what has been now observed, it is evident that they are the most proper trial or proof of their sincerity; inasmuch as the very meaning of the word *trial*, as it is ordinarily used in Scripture, is the difficulty occurring in the way of a professor's duty, as an experiment of his sincerity. If *trial of sincerity* be the proper name of these difficulties of religion, then doubtless these difficulties of religion are *properly and eminently* the trial of sincerity; for they are doubtless eminently what they are called by the Holy Ghost: God gives things their name from that which is eminently their nature. And if it be so, that these things are the proper and eminent trial, proof, or experiment of the sincerity of professors; then certainly the result of the trial or experiment (that is, persons' behaviour or practice under such trials) is the proper and eminent evidence of their sincerity. For they are called trials or proofs only with regard to the result, and because the effect is eminently the *proof*, or *evidence.* And this is the most proper proof and evidence to the *conscience* of those that are the subjects of these trials. For when God is said by these things to *try men, and prove them, to see what is in their hearts, and whether they will keep his commandments or no:* we are not to understand, that it is for his *own* information, or that he may obtain evidence himself of their sincerity; (for he needs no trials for his information;) but chiefly for their conviction, and to exhibit evidence to their consciences.† Thus when God is said to prove Israel by the difficulties they met with in the wilderness, and by the

* 2 Cor. viii 2. Heb. xi. 36. 1 Pet. i. 7. Chap. iv. 12. Gen. xxii. 1. Deut. viii. 2, 16. Chap. xiii 3. Exod. xv. 35. Chap. xvi. 4. Judges ii. 22. Chap. iii. 1, 4. Psal. lxvi. 10, 11 Dan. xii. 10. Rev. iii. 10. Job xxiii. 10. Zech. xiii. 2. James i. 12. Rev. ii. 10. Luke viii. 13. Acts xx. 19. James i. 2, 3. 1 Pet. i. 5.

† "I am persuaded, as Calvin is, that all the several trials of men, are to show them to themselves, and to the world, that they be but counterfeits; and to make saints known to themselves the better.—Rom. v. 5. *Tribulation works trial, and that hope.* Prov. xvii. 3. If you will know whether it will hold weight, the trial will tell you.—Shepard's *Parable*, Part I. p. 191.

difficulties they met with from their enemies in Canaan, to know what was in their hearts, whether they would keep his commandments, or no; it must be understood, that it was to discover them to *themselves*, that they might know what was in their own hearts. So when God tempted or tried Abraham with that difficult command of offering up his son, it was not for his satisfaction, whether he feared God or no, but for Abraham's own greater satisfaction and comfort, and the more clear manifestation of the favour of God to him. When Abraham had proved faithful under this trial, God says to him, *Now I know that thou fearest God, seeing that thou hast not withheld thy son, thine only son from me.* Which plainly implies, that in this practical exercise of Abraham's grace under this trial, was a clearer evidence of the truth of his grace, than ever was before; and the greatest evidence to Abraham's conscience; because God himself gives it to Abraham as such, for his comfort and rejoicing; and speaks of it to him, as what might be the greatest evidence to his conscience of his being upright in the sight of his Judge. Which proves what I say, that *holy practice* under trials, is the *highest evidence* of the sincerity of professors to their *own consciences*. And we find that Christ frequently took the same method to convince the consciences of those that pretended friendship to him, and to show them what they were. This was the method he took with the rich young man, Matt. xix. 16, &c. He seemed to show a great respect to Christ; he came kneeling to him, and called him *good master*, and made a great profession of obedience to the commandments; but Christ tried him by bidding him *go and sell all that he had, and give to the poor, and come and take up his cross, and follow him;* telling him, *that then he should have treasure in heaven.* So he tried another, Matt. viii. 20. He made a great profession of respect to Christ: says he, *Lord, I will follow thee whithersoever thou goest.* Christ immediately puts his friendship to the proof, by telling him that *the foxes had holes, and the birds of the air had nests, but that the Son of man had not where to lay his head.* And thus Christ is wont still to try professed disciples in general, in the course of his providence. So the seed sown in every kind of ground, stony ground, thorny ground, and good ground, which in all appears alike, when it first springs up; yet is tried, and the difference is made to appear by the burning heat of the sun.

Seeing therefore that these are the things which God employs to try us, it is undoubtedly the surest way, in order to pass a right judgment, to try ourselves by the same things. These trials are not for *his* information, but for *ours;* therefore we ought to receive our information from thence. The surest way to know our gold, is to examine it in God's furnace, where he tries it for that very end, that *we may see* what it is. If we have a mind to know whether a building stands strong or no, we must look upon it when the wind blows. If we would know whether that which appears in the form of wheat, has the real substance of wheat, or be only chaff, we must observe it when it is winnowed. If we would know whether a staff be strong, or a rotten broken reed, we must observe it when it is leaned on, when weight is borne upon it. If we would weigh ourselves justly, it must be in God's appointed scales.* These trials in the course of our practice, are as it were the balances in which our hearts are weighed, or in which Christ and the world, or Christ and his competitors, as to the esteem and regard they have in our hearts, are weighed, or are put into opposites scales, by which there is opportunity to see which preponderates. When a man is brought to the dividing of paths, the one of which leads to Christ, and the other to the objects of his lusts, to see which way he will go; when set as it were between Christ and the world, Christ on the right hand, and the world on the left, so that if he goes to one he must leave the other: this is just the same thing as laying Christ and the world in two opposite scales; and his going to the one, and leaving the other, is just the same thing, as the sinking of one scale, and rising of the other. A man's practice, therefore, under the trials of God's providence, is as much the proper experiment and evidence of the superior inclination of his heart, as the motion of the balance, with different weights in opposite scales, is the proper experiment of the superior weight.

Argument III. Another argument, that holy practice, in the sense which has been explained, is the highest kind of evidence of the truth of grace to the consciences of Christians, is, that in *practice*, grace in scripture style is said to be *made perfect*, or to be *finished*. So the apostle James says, Jam. ii. 22. "Seest thou how faith wrought with his works, and by works was faith made perfect," or finished? So the love of God is said to be made perfect, or finished, in keeping his commandments; 1 John ii. 4, 5. "He that saith, I know him, and keepeth not his commandments, is a liar; and the truth is not in him: but whoso keepeth his word, in him verily is the love of God perfected." The commandment of Christ which the apostle has a special respect to, is that which respects deeds of love to our brethren; as appears by the following verses. Again, the love of God is said to be *perfected*, in the same sense, chap. iv. 12. "If we love one another, God dwelleth in us, and his love is perfected in us." Here doubtless the apostle has still respect to loving one another, in the same manner that he had explained in the preceding chapter, speaking of loving one another as a *sign* of the love of God, ver. 17, 18. "Whoso hath this world's good, and shutteth up his bowels, &c. how dwelleth the love of God in him? My little children, let us not love in word, neither in tongue, but in deed, (or in work,) and in truth." By thus *loving in work*, the apostle says *the love of God is* PERFECTED *in us*. Grace is said to be *perfected* or *finished* in holy practice, as therein it is brought to its proper effect, and to that exercise which is the *end* of the principle; the tendency and design of grace herein is reached, and its operation completed and crowned. The tree is not perfected in the seed being planted in the ground; in the first quickening of the seed, and in its putting forth root and sprout; nor is it perfected when it comes up out of the ground; in bringing forth leaves; nor yet in putting forth blossoms: but when it has brought forth good ripe *fruit*, then it is *perfected*, therein it reaches its *end*, the design is *finished:* all that belongs to the tree is *completed* and brought to its proper effect in the *fruit*. So is grace in its practical exercises. Grace is said to be made perfect or finished in its work or fruit, in the same manner as it is said of sin, Jam. i. 15. "When

* Dr. Sibbs, in his *Bruised Reed*, says, "When Christ's will cometh in competition with any worldly loss or gain, yet if then, in that particular case, the heart will stoop to Christ, it is a true sign. For the truest trial of the power of grace, is in such particular cases as touch us nearest; for there our corruption maketh the greatest head. When Christ came home to the young man in the gospel, he lost a disciple of him."

Mr. Flavel speaks of a holy practice under trials, as the greatest evidence of grace. "No man (says he) can say what he is, whether his grace be true or false, until they be *tried*, and examined by those things, which are to them as fire is to gold." *Touchstone of Sincerity*, chap. iv. sect. 1. Again, speaking of great difficulties and sufferings in the way of duty, wherein a person must actually part with what is dearest of a worldly nature, or with his duty; he says, "That such sufferings as these will discover the falseness and rottenness of men's hearts, cannot be doubted; if you consider, that this is the fire designed by God for this very use and purpose, to separate the gold from the dross. So you will find it, 1 Pet. iv. 12.—'Beloved, think it not strange concerning the fiery trial that is to try you,' *i. e.* The very design and aim of Providence in permitting and ordering them, is to try you. Upon this account you find the hour of persecution (in a suitable notion) called the hour of temptation or probation, Rev. iii. 10. For then, professors are sifted to the very bran, searched to the very bottom principles. This is 'the day that burns as an oven; all that do wickedly shall be as stubble,' Mal. iv. i. For in that day the predominant interest must appear and be discovered, it can be concealed no longer. 'No man can serve two masters,' saith Christ, Luke xvi. 13. A man may serve many masters, if they all command the same thing, or things subordinate to each other: but he cannot serve two masters, if their commands clash and interfere with each other; and such are the commands of Christ and the flesh in a suffering hour:—thus the two interests come in full opposition. And now have but patience and wait a little, and you will discern which is predominant. A dog follows two men, while they both walk one way, and you know not which of the two is his master: stay but a little, until their path parts, and then you shall quickly see who is his master: so it is in this case." *Ibid.* chap viii. § 3. And in another chapter he says, "Great numbers of persons are deceived and destroyed by trusting to seeming untried grace. This was the miserable condition of the Laodicean professors; they reckoned themselves rich, but were really poor: all is not gold that glisters: their gold (as they accounted it) was never tried in the fire. If a man's whole estate lay in some precious stone, suppose a rich diamond, how is he concerned to have it thoroughly tried, to see whether it will bear a smart stroke with the hammer, or fly like a Bristol diamond!" *Ibid.* chap. x. § 3. Again, in the same place, "The promises of salvation are made over to tried grace, and that only as will endure the trial."

"The Lord will try you. God hath his trying times; and they were never sent, but to discover who were dross, who were gold. And the main end of all God's trials, is to discover this truth that I now am pressing upon you. Some have a thorough work; and now the trial discovers the truth, as in Abraham, Heb. xi. 17. Some have a superficial work, and they fall in trial, as in Saul; and it doth discover it was but an overly work. For this is the question God makes, Is it thorough, or no? Ay, saith the carnal heart; Yes, saith a gracious heart. Hence it is strange to see what men will do when a *trial* comes." Shepard's *Parable*, Part I. p. 219.

"There is an hour of temptation which tries men, which will discover men indeed." Shepard's *Parable*, Part II. p. 60.

lust hath conceived, it bringeth forth sin; and sin when it is finished, bringeth forth death." Here are three steps; *first*, sin in its *principle* or habit, the being of lust in the heart; and *nextly*, here is its conceiving, consisting in the *immanent exercises* of it in the mind; and *lastly*, here is the fruit that was conceived actually brought forth, in the wicked work and *practice*. And this the apostle calls the *finishing* or *perfecting* of sin: for the word in the original is the same that is translated *perfected* in those forementioned places.

Now certainly, if grace be in this manner made perfect in its fruit, if these practical exercises of grace are those wherein grace is brought to its proper effect and end, and the exercises wherein whatsoever belongs to its design, tendency, and operation, is completed and crowned; then these exercises must be the highest evidences of grace, above all other exercises. Certainly the proper nature and tendency, of every principle, must appear best and most fully, in its most perfect exercises, or in those wherein its nature is most completely exerted, and its tendency most fully answered and crowned, in its proper effect and end. If we would see the proper nature of any thing whatsoever, and see it in its full distinction from other things, let us look upon it in the *finishing* of it. The apostle James says, *by works is faith made perfect*; and introduces this as an argument to prove that works are the chief evidence of faith, whereby the sincerity of the professors of faith is justified, Jam. ii. And the apostle John, after he had once and again told us, that love was made perfect in keeping Christ's commandments, observes, 1 John iv. 18. "That perfect love casteth out fear;" meaning (at least in part) love made perfect in this sense; agreeable to what he had said in the foregoing chapter, "That by love in deed, or work, we know that we are of the truth, and shall assure our hearts," ver. 18, 19.

Argument IV. Another thing which makes it evident, that holy *practice* is the principal evidence that we ought to use in judging both of our own and others' sincerity, is, that this evidence is *above all others* insisted on in Scripture. A common acquaintance with the Scripture, together with a little attention and observation, will be sufficient to show to any one, that this is ten times more insisted on as a note of true piety, throughout the Scripture, from the beginning of Genesis to the end of Revelations, than any thing else. And in the New Testament, where Christ and his apostles do expressly, and of declared purpose, lay down signs of true godliness, this is almost wholly insisted on. It may be observed, that Christ and his apostles do not only *often* say those things, in discoursing on the great doctrines of religion, which do show what the nature of true godliness must be, or from whence the nature and signs of it may be inferred by just consequence—and often occasionally mention many things which appertain to godliness—but they also often *of set purpose* give signs and marks for the trial of professors, putting them upon trying themselves by the signs they give, introducing what they say with such like expressions as these; "By this you shall know that you know God: By this are manifest the children of God, and the children of the devil: He that hath this, builds on a good foundation; he that hath it not, builds on the sand: Hereby we shall assure our hearts: He is the man that loveth Christ," &c. But I can find no place, where either Christ or his apostles in this manner give signs of godliness, (though the places are many) but where christian practice is almost the only thing insisted on. Indeed in many of these places, *love to the brethren* is spoken of as a sign of godliness: and (as I have observed before) there is no one virtuous affection or disposition so often expressly spoken of as a sign of true grace, as our having love one to another: but then the Scriptures explain themselves to intend chiefly this love as exercised and expressed in *practice*, or in deeds of love. So does the apostle John (who above all others insists on love to the brethren as a sign of godliness) most expressly explain himself, in that 1 John iii. 14, &c. "We know that we have passed from death unto life, because we love the brethren: he that loveth not his brother, abideth in death.—Whoso hath this world's good, and seeth his brother have need, and shutteth up his bowels of compassion from him, how dwelleth the love of God in him? My little children, let us love, not in word, neither in tongue, but in deed (*i. e.* in deeds of love) and in truth. And hereby we know that we are of the truth, and shall assure our hearts before him." So that when the Scripture so much insists on our loving one another, as a great sign of godliness, we are not thereby to understand the immanent workings of affection which men feel one to another, so much as the soul's practising all the duties of the second table of the law; all which the New Testament tells us again and again, a true love one to another comprehends; Rom. xiii. 8, and 10. Gal. v. 14. Matt. xxii. 39, 40. So that really, there is no place in the New Testament, where the declared design is to give signs of godliness, but that holy practice, or keeping Christ's commandments, is the mark insisted on. Which is an invincible argument, that it is the *chief* of all the evidences of godliness: unless we suppose, that Christ and his apostles did not know how to choose signs so well as we could have chosen for them. But if we make the word of Christ our rule, then undoubtedly those marks which Christ and his apostles chiefly lay down, that we might try ourselves by them, those same marks we ought especially to receive, and chiefly to use, in the trial of ourselves.* And surely those things which Christ and his apostles *chiefly* insisted on in the rules they gave, *ministers* ought chiefly to insist on in the rules they give. To insist *much* on those things on which the Scripture insists little, and to insist very *little* on those things on which the Scripture insists much, is a dangerous thing; because it is going out of God's way, and is to judge ourselves, and guide others, in an *unscriptural* manner. God knew which way of leading and guiding souls was safest and best for them; he insisted so much on some things, because he knew it to be needful that they should be insisted on; and let other things more alone, as a wise God, because he knew it was not best for us, so much to lay the weight of the trial there. As the Sabbath was made for man, so the Scriptures were made for man; and they are by infinite wisdom fitted for our use and benefit. We should therefore make them our guide in all things, in our thoughts of religion, and of ourselves. And for us to make that great which the Scripture makes little, and that little which the Scripture makes great, tends to give us a monstrous idea of religion; and (at least indirectly and gradually) to lead us wholly away from the right rule, and from a right opinion of ourselves, and to establish delusion and hypocrisy.

Argument V. Christian practice *is plainly spoken of* in the *word of God*, as the main evidence of the truth of grace, not only to others, but to men's own consciences. It is only *more* spoken of and insisted on than other signs, but in many places where it is spoken of, it is represented as the chief of all evidences. This is plain in the manner of expression from time to time. If God were now to speak from heaven to resolve our doubts concerning signs of godliness, and should give some particular sign, that by it all might know whether they were sincerely godly or not, with such emphatical expressions as these, The man who hath such a qualification or mark, *that is the man who is a true saint; that is the very man; by this you may know; this is the thing by which it is manifest who are saints and who are sinners; such men as these are saints indeed*: should not we look upon it as a thing beyond doubt, that this was given as a special, and eminently distinguishing, note of true godliness? But this is the very case with respect to the sign of grace I am speaking of; God has again and again uttered himself in his word in this very manner, concerning christian practice, as John xiv. "He that hath my commandments, and keepeth them, *he it is that loveth me.*" This Christ gives to the disciples, not so much to guide them in judging others, but to apply to themselves for their own comfort after his departure, as appears by every word of the context. And by the way I would observe, that not only the emphasis with which Christ utters himself is remarkable, but also his so much insisting on, and repeating the matter, as he does in the context; ver. 15. "If ye love me, keep my commandments." Ver. 23. "If a man love me, he will keep my words." And ver.

* "It is a sure rule, (says Dr. Preston,) that what the Scriptures bestow much words on, we should have much thought on; and what the Holy Ghost urgeth most, we should prize most."—*Church's Carriage.*

24. "He that loveth me not, keepeth not my sayings." And in the next chapter over and over; ver. 2. "Every branch in me that beareth not fruit, he taketh away; and every branch that beareth fruit, he purgeth it." Ver. 8. "Herein is my Father glorified, that ye bear much fruit, so shall ye be my disciples." Ver. 14. "Ye are my friends, if ye do whatsoever I command you." We have this mark laid down with the same emphasis again, John viii. 31. "If ye continue in my word, *then* are ye my disciples *indeed*." And again, 1 John ii. 3. "*Hereby* we do know that we know him, if we keep his commandments." And ver. 5. "Whoso keepeth his word, *in him verily* is the love of God perfected: *hereby* know we that we are in him." And chap. iii. 18, 19. "Let us love in deed, and in truth: *hereby* we know that we are of the truth." What is translated *hereby*, would have been a little more emphatical, if it had been rendered more literally from the original, BY THIS *we do know*.—And how evidently is holy practice spoken of as the grand note of distinction between the children of God and the children of the devil, in ver. 10. of the same chapter? "In this the children of God are manifest, and the children of the devil." Speaking of a holy and a wicked practice, as may be seen in all the context: as ver. 3. "Every man that hath this hope in him, purifieth himself, even as he is pure." Ver. 6—10. "Whosoever abideth in him, sinneth not: whosoever sinneth, hath not seen him, neither known him. Little children, let no man deceive you: he that doth righteousness, is righteous, even as he is righteous: he that committeth sin is of the devil.—Whosoever is born of God sinneth not.—Whosoever doth not righteousness, is not of God." So we have the like emphasis, 2 John 6. "*This is love*, that we walk after his commandments:" that is, (as we must understand it,) *This is the proper evidence of love.* So 1 John v. 3. "*This is the love of God*, that we keep his commandments." So the apostle James speaking of the proper evidences of true and pure religion, says, Jam. i. 27. "Pure religion and undefiled before God and the Father, *is this*, To visit the fatherless and widows in their affliction, and to keep himself unspotted from the world." We have the like emphatical expressions used about the same thing in the Old Testament: Job xxviii. 28. "And unto man he said, Behold, the fear of the Lord, that is wisdom, and to depart from evil is understanding." Jer. xxii. 15, 16. "Did not thy father eat and drink, and do judgment and justice?—He judged the cause of the poor and needy; was not this to know me? saith the Lord." Psal. xxxiv. 11, &c. "Come, ye children, unto me, and I will teach you the fear of the Lord.—Keep thy tongue from evil, and thy lips from speaking guile: depart from evil, and do good; seek peace and pursue it." Psal. xv. at the beginning, "Who shall abide in thy tabernacle? who shall dwell in thy holy hill? He that walketh uprightly," &c. Psal. xxiv. 3, 4. "Who shall ascend into the hill of the Lord? and who shall stand in his holy place? He that hath clean hands, and a pure heart," &c. Psal. cxix. 1. "Blessed are the undefiled in the way, who walk in the law of the Lord." Ver. 6. "Then shall I not be ashamed, when I have respect to all thy commandments." Prov. viii. 13. "The fear of the Lord is to hate evil."

The Scripture never uses such emphatical expressions concerning any other signs of hypocrisy, and unsoundness of heart, as concerning an *unholy practice*. So Gal. vi. 7. "Be not deceived; God is not mocked: for whatsoever a man soweth, that shall he also reap." 1 Cor. vi. 9, 10. "Be not deceived: neither fornicators, nor idolaters, &c. shall inherit the kingdom of God." Eph. v. 5, 6. "For this ye know, that no whoremonger, nor unclean person, &c. hath any inheritance in the kingdom of Christ, and of God. Let no man deceive you with vain words." 1 John iii. 7, 8. "Little children, let no man deceive you: he that doth righteousness, is righteous, even as he is righteous: he that committeth sin, is of the devil." Chap. ii. 4. "He that saith, I know him, and keepeth not his commandments, is a liar, and the truth is not in him." And chap. i. 6. "If we say that we have fellowship with him, and walk in darkness, we lie, and do not the truth." James i. 26. "If any man among you seem to be religious, and bridleth not his tongue, but deceiveth his own heart, this man's religion is vain." Chap. iii. 14, 15. "If ye have bitter envying and strife in your hearts, glory not, and lie not against the truth. This wisdom descendeth not from above, but is earthly, sensual, devilish." Psal. cxxv. 5. "As for such as turn aside unto their crooked ways, the Lord shall lead them forth with the workers of iniquity." Isa. xxxv. 8. "An high-way shall be there, and it shall be called the way of holiness: the unclean shall not pass over it." Rev. xxi. 27. "And there shall in no wise enter into it, whatsoever worketh abomination, or maketh a lie." And in many places, "Depart from me, I know you not, ye that work iniquity."

Argument VI. Another thing which makes it evident, that holy practice is the chief of all the signs of the sincerity of professors, not only to the world, but to their own consciences, is, that this is the grand evidence which will hereafter be made use of, before the judgment-seat of God; according to which his judgment will be regulated, and the state of every professor of religion unalterably determined. In the future judgment, there will be an open trial of professors; and evidences will be made use of in the judgment. For God's future judging of men, in order to their eternal retribution, will not be his trying and finding out, and passing a judgment upon, the state of men's hearts, in his *own* mind; but it will be a *declarative* judgment: and the end of it will be, not God's forming a judgment within himself, but the *manifestation* of his judgment, and the righteousness of it, to men's own consciences and to the world. And therefore the day of judgment is called *the day of the* revelation *of the righteous judgment of God*, Rom. ii. 5. And the end of God's future trial and judgment of men, as to the part that each one in particular is to have in the judgment, will be especially the clear manifestation of God's righteous judgment to his conscience.* And therefore though God needs no medium, whereby to make the truth evident to himself, yet evidences will be exhibited in his future judging of men. And doubtless the evidences used in their trial, will be such as are best fitted to serve the *ends* of the judgment; viz. the manifestation of the righteous judgment of God, not only to the world, but to men's own consciences. But the Scriptures abundantly teach us, that the grand evidences which the Judge will make use of in the trial, for these ends, according to which the judgment of every one shall be regulated, and the irreversible sentence passed, will be men's works, or *practice*, in this world: Rev. xx. 12. "And I saw the dead, small and great, stand before God: and the books were opened: and the dead were judged out of those things which were written in the books, according to their works." So ver. 13. "And the sea gave up the dead which were in it; and death and hell gave up the dead which were in them: and they were judged every man according to their works." 2 Cor. v. 10. "For we must all appear before the judgment-seat of Christ; that every one may receive the things done in his body, whether it be good or bad." So men's practice is the *only* evidence that Christ represents the future judgment as regulated by, in that most particular description of the day of judgment, which we have in the Holy Bible.† The Judge, then, will not examine men as to the method of their experiences, or set every man to tell his story of the *manner* of his conversion; but his *works* will be brought forth, as evidences of what he is, what he has done in darkness and in light; Eccl. xii. 14. "For God will bring every work into judgment, with every secret thing, whether it be good, or whether it be evil." In the *trial* of professors at the future judgment, God will call in the same evidences, to manifest them to themselves and to the world, which he makes use of to manifest them, in the temptations or trials of his providence here, *viz.* their *practice*, in cases wherein Christ and other things come into actual and immediate competition. God, then, for the manifestation of his righteous judgment, will weigh professors in a balance that is *visible;* the same that he weighs men in now; which has been already described.

Hence we may undoubtedly infer, that men's works

* As is manifest by Matt. xviii. 31. to the end. Chap. xx. 8—15. Chap. xxii. 11, 12, 13. Chap. xxv. 19—30. and ver. 35, to the end. Luke xix. 15—23.

† See Matt. xxv. at the latter end. See also Rom. ii. 6—13. Jer. xvii. 10. Job xxxiv. 11. Prov. xxiv. 12. Jer. xxxii. 19. Rev. xxii. 12. Matt. xvi. 27 Rev. ii. 23. Ezek. xxxiii. 20 1 Pet. i. 17.

(taken in the sense explained) are the highest evidences by which they ought to try themselves. Certainly that which our Supreme Judge will *chiefly* use, when we come to stand before him, we should chiefly adopt, in order to judge ourselves by.* If it had not been revealed in what manner and by what evidence the Judge would proceed with us hereafter, how natural would it be for one to say, "O that I knew what token God will chiefly look for, and insist upon, in the last and decisive judgment; and which he expects that all should be able to *produce*, who would then be accepted of him, and according to which sentence shall be passed; that I might know what evidence especially to seek after now, as I would be sure not to fail then." And seeing God has so plainly and abundantly revealed what this evidence is, surely, if we act wisely, we shall regard it as of the greatest importance.

Now from all that has been said, I think it abundantly manifest, that christian *practice* is the most proper evidence of the gracious sincerity of professors, to *themselves* and *others;* and the chief of all the marks of grace, the sign of signs, and evidence of evidences, that which seals and crowns all other signs.—I had rather have the testimony of my conscience, that I have such a saying of my Supreme Judge on my side, as that, John xiv. 21. "He that hath my commandments, and keepeth them, he it is that loveth me;" than the judgment and fullest approbation of all the wise, sound, and experienced divines, that have lived this thousand years, on the most exact and critical examination of my experiences, as to the *manner* of my conversion. Not that there are no *other* good evidences of a state of grace but this. There may be other exercises of grace, besides these efficient exercises, which the saints may have in contemplation, that may be very satisfying to them: but yet this is the *chief* and most proper evidence. There may be several good evidences that a tree is a fig-tree; but the *highest* and most proper evidence of it is, that it actually *bears* figs. It is possible, that a man may have a good assurance of a state of grace, at his first conversion, before he has had opportunity to gain assurance by this great evidence I am speaking of.—If a man hears that a great treasure is offered him, in a distant place, on condition that he will prize it so much, as to be willing to leave what he possesses at home, and go a journey for it, over the rocks and mountains that are in the way, to the place where it is; it is possible the man may be well assured, that he values the treasure to the degree spoken of, as soon as the offer is made him; he may feel a willingness to go for the treasure, beyond all doubt: but yet, this does not hinder but that his *actual going* for it, is the *highest* and most proper evidence of his being willing, not only to others, but to himself. But then as an evidence to himself, his outward actions, and the motions of his body in his journey, are not considered alone, exclusive of the action of his mind, and a consciousness within himself, of the thing that moves him, and the end he goes for; otherwise his bodily motion is no evidence to him, of his prizing the treasure. In such a manner is christian practice the most proper evidence of a saving value of *the pearl of great price, and treasure hid in the field.*

Christian practice is the *sign of signs,* in this sense, that it is the great evidence which confirms and crowns all other signs of godliness. There is no *one* grace of the Spirit of God, but that christian practice is the most proper evidence of the truth of it. As it is with the members of our bodies, and all our utensils, the proper proof of their soundness and goodness is in the *use* of them; so it is with our graces, (which are given to be used in practice, as much as our hands and feet, or the tools with which we work, the proper trial and proof of them is in their exercise in practice. Most of the things we use are serviceable to us, and so have their serviceableness proved, in some pressure, straining, agitation, or collision. So it is with a bow, a sword, an axe, a saw, a cord, a chain, a staff, a foot, a tooth, &c. And those which are so weak, as not to bear the strain or pressure we need, to which we put them, are good for nothing. So it is with all the virtues of the mind. The proper trial and proof of them, is in their being exercised under those temptations and trials that God brings us under, in the course of his providence, and in being put to such service as strains hard upon the principles of nature.

Practice is the proper proof of the true and saving *knowledge of God:* as appears by that of the apostle already mentioned, "Hereby we know that we know him, that we keep his commandments." It is in vain for us to "profess that we know God, *if* in works we deny him," Tit. i. 16. And if we "know God, but glorify him not as God;" our knowledge will only *condemn,* and not *save* us, Rom. i. 21. The great note of that knowledge which saves and makes happy, is, that it is *practical;* John xiii. 17. "If ye know these things, happy are ye if ye do them." Job xxviii. 28. "To depart from evil is understanding."

Holy practice is the proper evidence of *repentance.* When the Jews professed repentance, when they came confessing their sins to John, preaching the baptism of repentance for the remission of sins; he directed them to the right way of getting and exhibiting proper evidences of the truth of their repentance when he said to them, "Bring forth fruits meet for repentance," Matt. iii. 8. Which was agreeable to the practice of the apostle Paul; see Acts xxvi. 20. Pardon and mercy are constantly promised to him who has this evidence of true repentance, that he forsakes his sin; Prov. xxviii. 13. and Isa. lv. 7. and many other places.

Holy practice is the proper evidence of a *saving faith.* It is evident that the apostle James speaks of *works,* as what eminently justifies faith, or (which is the same thing) justifies the professors of faith, and vindicate and manifest the sincerity of their profession, not only to the world, but to their own consciences: as is evident by the instance he gives of Abraham, James ii. 21—24. And in ver. 20, and 26. he speaks of the practical and working nature of faith, as the very life and soul of it; in the same manner, that the active nature and substance, which is in the body of a man, is the life and soul of it. And if so, practice is the proper evidence of the life and soul of true faith, by which it is distinguished from a dead faith. For doubtless, practice is the most proper evidence of a practical nature, and operation the most proper evidence of an operative nature.

Practice is the best evidence of a saving *belief of the truth.* That is spoken of as the proper evidence of the *truth being in* a professing Christian, that *he walks in the truth,* 3 John 3. "I rejoiced greatly when the brethren came and testified of the truth that is in thee, even as thou walkest in the truth."

Practice is the most proper evidence of a true *coming to Christ,* and *accepting* of and *closing* with him. A true and saving coming to Christ, is (as Christ often teaches) a coming so as to forsake all for him. And, as observed before, to forsake all for Christ in heart, is the same thing as to have a heart actually to forsake all; but the proper evidence of having a heart actually to forsake all, is indeed actually to forsake all when called to it. If a prince make suit to a woman in a far country, that she would forsake her own people, and father's house, and come to him, in order to be his bride; the proper evidence of the compliance of her heart with the king's suit, is her actually forsaking her own people, and father's house, and coming to him. By this, her compliance with the king's suit is made perfect, in the same sense that the apostle James says, *by works is faith made perfect.*† Christ promises eternal life, on condition of our coming to him: but it is such a coming as he directed the young man to, who came to inquire, "what he shall do, that he might have eternal life:" Christ bid him "go and sell all that he had, and come to him, and follow him." If he had consented in his heart to the proposal, (and had therein come to Christ in his

* "That which God maketh a rule of his own judgment, as that by which he judgeth of every man, that is a sure rule for every man to judge himself by. That which we shall be judged by at the last day is a sure rule to apply to ourselves for the present. Now by our obedience and works he judgeth us. He will give to every man according to his works." Dr. Preston's *Church's Carriage.*

† "Our real taking of Christ, appears in our actions and works; Isa. i. 19. 'If ye consent and obey, ye shall eat the good things of the land.' That is, If ye will consent to take JEHOVAH for your Lord and King: *if ye give consent;* there is the first thing; but that is not enough; *but if ye also obey.* The consent that standeth in the inward act of the mind, the truth of it will be seen in your obedience, in the acts of your lives. *If ye consent and obey, ye shall eat the good things of the land;* that is, you shall take of all that he hath that is convenient for you: for then you are married to him in truth, and have an interest in all his goods." Dr. Preston's *Church's Carriage.*

heart,) the proper *evidence* of it would have been his *doing* of it: and therein his coming to Christ would have been *made perfect*. When Christ called Levi the publican, when sitting at the receipt of custom, and in the midst of his worldly gains; the closing of Levi's heart with this invitation of his Saviour to come to him, was manifested, and made perfect, by his actually rising up, leaving all, and following him, Luke v. 27, 28. Christ and other things are set before us together, for us practically to cleave to one, and forsake the other: in such a case, a practical cleaving to Christ, is a practical *acceptance* of Christ; as much as a beggar's reaching out his hand, and taking a gift offered, is his practical acceptance of the gift. Yea, that act of the soul which cleaves to Christ in practice, is itself the most perfect coming of the soul to Christ.

Practice is the most proper evidence of *trusting in Christ for salvation*. The proper signification of the word *trust*, according to the more ordinary use of it, both in common speech and in the Holy Scriptures, is the emboldening and encouragement of a person's mind, to run some venture in practice, or in something that he does, on the credit of another's sufficiency and faithfulness. And therefore the proper evidence of his trusting, is *the venture he runs in what he does*. He is not properly said to run any venture in a dependence on any thing, who *does* nothing on that dependence, or whose practice is no otherwise than if he had no dependence. For a man to run a venture in *dependence* on another, is for him to *do something* from that dependence, by which he seems to expose himself, and which he would not do were it not for that dependence. And therefore it is in complying with the difficulties and seeming dangers of christian practice, in a dependence on Christ's sufficiency and faithfulness to bestow eternal life, that persons are said to venture themselves upon Christ, and trust in him for happiness and life. They depend on such promises as that, Matt. x. 39. "He that loseth his life for my sake shall find it." And so they part with all, and venture their all, in a dependence on Christ's sufficiency and truth. And this is the scripture notion of *trusting* in Christ, in the exercise of a saving faith in him. Thus Abraham, the father of believers, trusted in Christ, and by faith forsook his own country, in a reliance on the covenant of grace which God established with him, Heb. xi. 8, 9. Thus also "Moses, by faith refused to be called the son of Pharaoh's daughter, choosing rather to suffer affliction with the people of God, than to enjoy the pleasures of sin for a season," Heb. xi. 23, &c. So *by faith* others exposed themselves to be *stoned*, and *sawn in sunder*, or *slain with the sword*; endured the *trial of cruel mockings and scourgings, bonds and imprisonments, and wandered about in sheep-skins and goat-skins, being destitute, afflicted, tormented*. And in this sense the apostle Paul trusted in Christ, and committed himself to him, venturing himself, and his whole interest, in a dependence on the ability and faithfulness of his Redeemer, under great persecutions, and in suffering the loss of all things; 2 Tim. i. 12. "For the which cause I also suffer these things: nevertheless I am not ashamed: for I know whom I have believed, and I am persuaded that he is able to keep that which I have committed unto him against that day."

If a man should have word brought him from the king of a distant land, that he intended to make him his heir, if upon receiving the tidings he immediately leaves his native land and friends, and all he has in the world, to go to that country, in a dependence on what he hears; then he may be said to venture himself and all he has in the world upon it. But if he only sits still, and hopes for the promised benefit, inwardly pleasing himself with the thoughts of it; he cannot properly be said to *venture* himself upon it; he runs no venture in the case; he does nothing, otherwise than he would do, if he had received no such tidings, by which he would be exposed to any suffering, in case all should fail. So he that on the credit of what he hears of a future world, and in dependence on the report of the gospel, concerning life and immortality, forsakes all, or does so at least so far as there is occasion, making every thing entirely give place to his eternal interest; he, and he only, may properly be said to venture himself on the report of the gospel. And this is the proper evidence of a true *trust* in Christ for salvation.

Practice is the proper evidence of a *gracious love*, both to God and men. The texts that plainly teach this, have been so often mentioned already, that it is needless to repeat them.

Practice is the proper evidence of *humility*. That expression and manifestation of humility of heart which God insists on, we should regard as the proper expression and manifestation of it: but this is *walking humbly:* Micah vi. 8. "He hath showed thee, O man, what is good, and what doth the Lord require of thee, but to do justly, to love mercy, and to walk humbly with thy God?"

This is also the proper evidence of the true *fear of God*. Prov. viii. 13. "The fear of the Lord is to hate evil." Psal. xxxiv. 11, &c. "Come, ye children, hearken unto me, and I will teach you the fear of the Lord.—Keep thy tongue from evil, and thy lips from speaking guile: depart from evil, and do good; seek peace and pursue it." Prov. iii. 7. "Fear the Lord, and depart from evil." Prov. xvi. 6. "By the fear of the Lord, men depart from evil." Job i. 8. "Hast thou considered my servant Job,—a perfect and an upright man, one that feareth God, and escheweth evil?" Chap. ii. 3. "Hast thou considered my servant Job,—a perfect and an upright man, one that feareth God, and escheweth evil? and still he holdeth fast his integrity, although thou movedst me against him." Psal. xxxvi. 1. "The transgression of the wicked saith within my heart, there is no fear of God before his eyes."

So practice, in rendering again according to benefits received, is the proper evidence of true *thankfulness*. Psal. cxvi. 12. "What shall I render to the Lord, for all his benefits towards me?" 2 Chron. xxxii. 25. "But Hezekiah rendered not again, according to the benefit done unto him." Paying our vows unto God, and ordering our conversation aright, seem to be spoken of, as the proper expression and evidence of true thankfulness in the 50th Psalm, ver. 14. "Offer unto God thanksgiving, and pay thy vows to the Most High." Ver. 23. "Whoso offereth praise, glorifieth me: and to him that ordereth his conversation aright, will I show the salvation of God."

The proper evidence of *gracious desires and longings*, and what distinguishes them from those that are false and vain, is, that they are not idle wishes, like Balaam's; but effectual in practice, stirring up persons earnestly and thoroughly to seek the things they look for. Psal. xxvii. 4. "One thing have I desired of the Lord, that will I seek after." Psal. lxiii. 1, 2. "O God, thou art my God, early will I seek thee: my soul thirsteth for thee, my flesh longeth for thee in a dry and thirsty land, where no water is, to see thy power and thy glory." Ver. 8. "My soul followeth hard after thee." Cant. i. 4. "Draw me, we will run after thee."

Practice is the proper evidence of a gracious hope. 1 John iii. 3. "Every man that hath this hope in him purifieth himself, even as he is pure." Patient continuance in well-doing, through the difficulties and trials of the christian course, is often mentioned as the proper expression and fruit of a christian hope; 1 Thess. i. 3. "Remembering without ceasing your work of faith, and labour of love, and patience of hope." 1 Pet. i. 13, 14. "Wherefore gird up the loins of your mind, be sober, and hope to the end, for the grace that is to be brought unto you, at the revelation of Jesus Christ; as obedient children," &c. Psal. cxix. 166. "Lord, I have hoped in thy salvation, and done thy commandments." Psal. lxxviii. 7. "That they might set their hope in God, and not forget the works of the Lord: but keep his commandments."

A cheerful practice of our duty, or doing the will of God, is the proper evidence of a truly *holy joy*. Isa. lxiv. 5. "Thou meetest him that rejoiceth, and worketh righteousness." Psal. cxix. 111, 112. "Thy testimonies have I taken for my heritage for ever; for they are the rejoicing of my heart. I have inclined mine heart to perform thy statutes alway, even unto the end." Ver. 14. "I have rejoiced in the way of thy testimonies, as much as in all riches." 1 Cor. xiii. 6. "Charity rejoiceth not in iniquity, but rejoiceth in the truth." 2 Cor. viii. 2. "The abundance of their joy, abounded unto the riches of their liberality."

Practice also is the proper evidence of Christian *for-*

titude. The trial of a good soldier is not in his chimney corner, but in the field of battle; 1 Cor. ix. 25 26. 2 Tim. ii. 3—5.

And as the fruit of holy practice is the chief evidence of the truth of grace; so the degree in which experiences have influence on a person's practice, is the surest evidence of the degree of that which is spiritual and divine in his experiences. Whatever pretences persons may make to great discoveries, great love and joys, they are no further to be regarded, than they have influence on their practice. Not but that allowances must be made for the natural temper. But that does not hinder, but that the degree of grace is justly measured, by the degree of the effect in practice. For the effect of grace is as great, and the alteration as remarkable, in a person of a very ill natural temper, as another. Although a person of such a temper, will not behave himself so well, with the same degree of grace, as another; the diversity from what was before conversion, may be as great: because a person of a good natural temper did not behave himself so ill, before conversion.

Thus I have endeavoured to represent the evidence there is, that christian practice is *the chief* of all the signs of saving grace. And before I conclude this discourse, I would say something briefly, in answer to two objections, that may possibly be made by some, against what has been said upon this head.

Object. 1. Some may be ready to say, this seems to be contrary to an opinion much received among good people; that professors should judge of their state chiefly by their inward experience, and that *spiritual experiences* are the main evidences of true grace.

I answer, It is doubtless a true opinion, and justly much received among good people, that professors should chiefly judge of their state by their *experience.* But it is a great mistake, that what has been said is at all *contrary* to that opinion. The chief sign of grace to the consciences of Christians being christian practice, in the sense explained, and according to what has been shown to be the true notion of christian practice, is not at all inconsistent with *christian experience* being the chief evidence of grace. Christian or holy practice is *spiritual* practice; and that is not the motion of a body, that knows not how, nor when, nor wherefore it moves: but spiritual practice in man, is the practice of a spirit and body jointly; or the practice of a spirit, animating, commanding, and actuating a body to which it is united, and over which it has power given it by the Creator. And therefore the main thing in this holy practice is the *holy acts* of the mind, directing and governing the motions of the body. And the motions of the body are to be looked upon as belonging to christian practice, only secondarily, and as they are dependent and consequent on the acts of the soul. The exercises of grace which Christians are conscious of, are what they *experience* within themselves; and herein therefore lies christian experience: and this christian experience consists as much in those operative exercises of grace in the will, immediately concerned in the management of the behaviour of the body, as in other exercises. These inward exercises are not the less a part of christian experience, because they have outward behaviour immediately connected with them. A strong act of love to God is not the less a part of spiritual experience, because it is the act that immediately produces and effects some self-denying and expensive outward action, which is much to the honour and glory of God.

To speak of christian experience and practice, as if they were two things, properly and entirely distinct, is to make a distinction without consideration or reason. Indeed all christian experience is not properly called practice; but all christian practice is properly experience. And the distinction that is made between them, is not only an unreasonable, but an unscriptural distinction. Holy practice is one kind or part of christian experience; and both reason and Scripture represent it as the chief, and most important, and most distinguishing part of it. So it is represented in Jer. xxii. 15, 16. "Did not thy father eat and drink, and do justice and judgment?—He judged the cause of the poor and needy:—was not this to know me? saith the Lord." Our inward acquaintance with God, surely belongs to the head of experimental religion; but this God represents as consisting chiefly in that experience which there is in holy practice. So the exercises of those graces of the love of God, and the fear of God, are a part of experimental religion; but these the Scripture represents as consisting chiefly in practice, in those fore-mentioned texts.—1 John v. 3. "This is the love of God, that we keep his commandments." 2 John 6. "This is love, that we walk after his commandment." Psal. xxxiv. 11, &c. "Come, ye children, and I will teach you the fear of the Lord:—Depart from evil, and do good." Such experiences as these Hezekiah took comfort in chiefly, on his sick-bed; when he said, "Remember, O Lord, I beseech thee, how I have walked before thee in truth, and with a perfect heart." And such experiences as these the psalmist chiefly insists upon, in the 119th Psalm, and elsewhere. Such experiences as these the apostle Paul mainly insists upon, as Rom. i. 9. "God is my witness, whom I serve with my spirit in the gospel of his Son." 2 Cor. i. 12. "For our rejoicing is this, the testimony of our conscience, that, by the grace of God, we have had our conversation in the world. Chap. iv. 13. We having the same spirit of faith, according as it is written, I have believed, and therefore have I spoken: we also believe, and therefore speak. Chap. v. 7. We walk by faith, not by sight. Ver. 14. The love of Christ constraineth us. Chap. vi. 4—7. In all things approving ourselves as the ministers of God, in much patience, in afflictions, in necessities, in distresses,—in labours, in watchings, in fastings. By pureness, by knowledge, by kindness, by the Holy Ghost, by love unfeigned,—by the power of God." Gal. ii. 20. "I am crucified with Christ: nevertheless I live: yet not I, but Christ liveth in me: and the life which I now live in the flesh, I live by the faith of the Son of God." Phil. iii. 7, 8. "But what things were gain to me, those I counted loss for Christ. Yea, doubtless, and I count all things but loss, for the excellency of the knowledge of Christ Jesus my Lord, and do count them but dung that I may win Christ." Col. i. 29. "Whereunto I also labour, striving according to his working, which worketh in me mightily." 1 Thess. ii. 2. "We were bold in our God, to speak unto you the gospel of God with much contention. Ver. 8—10. Being affectionately desirous of you, we were willing to have imparted unto you, not the gospel of God only, but also our own souls, because ye were dear unto us. For ye remember, brethren, our labour and travail, labouring night and day.—Ye are witnesses, and God also, how holily, and justly, and unblamably we behaved ourselves among you." And with such experiences as these this blessed apostle chiefly comforted himself, when he was going to martyrdom, 2 Tim. iv. 6, 7. "For I am now ready to be offered, and the time of my departure is at hand. I have fought a good fight, I have finished my course, I have kept the faith."

And not only does the most important and distinguishing part of christian experience, lie in spiritual practice; but such is the nature of that sort of exercises of grace, wherein spiritual practice consists, that nothing is so properly called by the name of *experimental religion.* For that experience, which exercises of grace prove effectual at the very point of trial—wherein God proves which we will actually cleave to, Christ or our lusts—is the proper *experiment* of the truth and power of our godliness; wherein its victorious power and efficacy in producing its proper effect, and reaching its end, is found *by experience.* This is properly christian experience, wherein the saints have opportunity to see, by actual *experience* and *trial,* whether they have a heart to do the will of God, and to forsake other things for Christ, or no. As that is called experimental philosophy, which brings opinions and notions to the test of fact; so is that properly called experimental religion, which brings religious affections and intentions to the like test.

There is a sort of external religious practice, without inward experience; which in the sight of God is esteemed good for nothing. And there is what is called experience, without practice, being neither accompanied nor followed with a christian behaviour; and this is worse than nothing. Many persons seem to have very wrong notions of christian experience, and spiritual discoveries. Whenever a person finds a heart to treat God as God, at the time he has the trial, and finds his disposition effectual in the experiment, that is the most proper and most distinguishing experience. And to have at such a time that sense of divine things, that apprehension of the truth, importance and excellency of the things of religion, which then sways and prevails, and governs his heart and hands; this is the most excellent spiritual light, and these are the most distinguishing discoveries. Religion consists much in holy affection; but those exercises of affection which are most distinguishing of true religion, are these practical exercises. Friendship between earthly friends consists much in affection; but yet those strong exercises of affection, that actually carry them through fire and water for each other, are the highest evidences of true friendship.

There is nothing in what has been said, contrary to what is asserted by some sound divines; when they say, that there are no sure evidences of grace, but the acts of grace. For that doth not hinder but that these operative productive acts, those exercises of grace, which are effectual in practice, may be the highest evidences. Nor does it hinder but that, when there are many of these acts and exercises, following one another in a course, under various trials of every kind, the evidence is still heightened; as one act confirms another. A man by once seeing his neighbour, may have good evidence of his presence; but by seeing him from day to day, and conversing with him in a course, in various circumstances, the evidence is established. The disciples, when they first saw Christ after his resurrection, had good evidence that he was alive: but by conversing with him for forty days, and his *showing himself to them alive, by many infallible proofs*, they had yet higher evidence.*

The *witness* or seal of the Spirit consists in the *effect* of the Spirit of God in the heart, in the implantation and *exercises* of grace there, and so consists in *experience*. And it is beyond doubt, that this seal of the Spirit is the highest kind of evidence of the saints' adoption, that ever they obtain. But in these exercises of grace in practice, God gives witness, and sets to his seal, in the most conspicuous, eminent, and evident manner. It has been abundantly found to be true in fact, by the experience of the christian church, that Christ commonly gives by his Spirit the greatest and most joyful evidences to his saints of their sonship, in those effectual *exercises* of grace under *trials*, of which we have spoken; as is manifest in the full assurance and unspeakable joys of many of the martyrs. Agreeable to 1 Pet. iv. 14. "If ye are reproached for the name of Christ, happy are ye; for the Spirit of glory and of God resteth upon you." And Rom. v. 2, 3. "We rejoice in hope of the glory of God, and glory in tribulations." And agreeable to what the apostle Paul often declares of what he experienced in his trials. When the apostle Peter, in my text, speaks of the *joy unspeakable, and full of glory*, which the Christians to whom he wrote experienced; he has respect to what they found under persecution, as appears by the context. Christ thus manifesting himself, as the friend and saviour of his saints cleaving to him under trials, seems to have been represented of old by his coming and manifesting himself to Shadrach, Meshach, and Abednego, in the furnace. And when the apostle speaks of the *witness* of the Spirit, in Rom. viii. 15—17. he has a more immediate respect to what the Christians experienced in their exercises of love to God, while suffering persecution; as is plain by the context. He is, in the foregoing verses, encouraging the christian Romans under their sufferings, that though their bodies be dead because of sin, yet they should be raised to life again. But it is more especially plain by the verse immediately following, ver. 18. "For I reckon, that the sufferings of this present time are not worthy to be compared with the glory that shall be revealed in us." So the apostle has evidently respect to their persecutions, in all that he says to the end of the chapter. So when the apostle speaks of the *earnest of the Spirit*, which God had given to him, 2 Cor. v. 5. the context shows plainly that he has respect to what was given him in his great trials and sufferings. And in that promise of "the white stone, and new name, to him that overcomes," Rev. ii. 17. it is evident Christ has a special respect to a benefit that Christians should obtain by *overcoming*, when tried, in that day of persecution. This appears by ver. 13. and many other passages in this epistle to the seven churches of Asia.

Object. 2. Some also may be ready to object against what has been said of christian practice being the chief evidence of the truth of grace, that this is a *legal* doctrine; and that this making practice a thing of such great importance in religion, magnifies *works*, and tends to lead men to make too much of their *own doings*, to the diminution of the glory of free grace, and does not seem well to consist with that great gospel-doctrine of *justification by faith alone*.

But this objection is altogether without reason. Which way is it inconsistent with the *freeness* of God's grace, that holy practice should be a *sign* of God's grace? It is our works being the *price* of God's favour, and not their being the *sign* of it, that is the thing which is inconsistent with the freeness of that favour. Surely the beggar's looking on the money he has in his hands, as a *sign* of the kindness of him who gave it to him, is in no respect inconsistent with the *freeness* of that kindness. It is his having money in his hand as the *price* of a benefit, that is the thing which is inconsistent with the free kindness of the giver. The notion of the *freeness* of the grace of God to sinners, as that is revealed and taught in the gospel, is not, that no holy and amiable qualifications or actions in us shall be a *fruit*, and so a *sign*, of that grace; but that it is not the *worthiness* or loveliness of any qualification or action of ours which recommends us to that grace. Free grace implies, that kindness is shown to the unworthy and unlovely; that there is great excellency in the benefit bestowed, and no excellency in the subject as the price of it; that goodness goes forth, and flows out, from the fulness of God's nature, the fulness of the fountain of good, without any amiableness in the object to draw it. And this is the notion of justification *without works*, (as this doctrine is taught in the Scripture,) that it is not the worthiness or loveliness of our works, or any thing in us, which is in any wise accepted with God, as a *balance* for the guilt of sin, or a recommendation of sinners to his acceptance as heirs of life. Thus we are justified only by the righteousness of *Christ*, and not by *our* righteousness. And when works are opposed to faith in this affair, and it is said that we are justified by faith and not by works; thereby is meant, that it is not the worthiness or amiableness of our works, or any thing in us, which recommends us to an interest in Christ and his benefits; but that we have this interest only by faith, or by our souls *receiving* Christ, or adhering to and closing with him. But that the worthiness or amiableness of nothing in us recommends and brings us to an interest in Christ, is no argument that nothing in us is a *sign* of an interest in Christ.

If the doctrines of free grace and justification by faith alone, be inconsistent with the importance of *holy practice* as a *sign* of grace; then they are equally inconsistent with the importance of *any thing* whatsoever in us as a sign of grace; and holiness, or any grace in us, or any *experiences*; for it is as contrary to the doctrines of free grace and justification by faith alone, that any of *these* should be the righteousness which we are justified by, as that *holy practice* should be so. It is with holy works, as it is with holy qualifications: it is inconsistent with the freeness of gospel-grace, that a title to salvation should be given to men for the loveliness of any of their holy qualifications, as much as that it should be given for the holiness of their works. It is inconsistent with the gospel-doctrine of free grace, that an interest in Christ and his benefits should be given for the loveliness of a man's *true holiness*; the amiableness of his renewed, sanctified, heavenly heart; his

* "The more these visible exercises of grace are renewed, the more certain you will be. The more frequently these actings are renewed, the more abiding and confirmed your assurance will be. A man that has been assured of such visible exercises of grace, may quickly after be in doubt, whether he was not mistaken. But when such actings are renewed again and again, he grows more settled and established about his good estate. If a man see a thing once, that makes him sure; but if afterwards he fear he was deceived, when he comes to see it again, he is more sure he was not mistaken. If a man read such passages in a book, he is sure it is so. Some months after, some may bear him down, that he was mistaken, so as to make him question it himself: but when he looks, and reads it again, he is abundantly confirmed. The more men's grace is multiplied, the more their peace is multiplied; 2 Pet i. 2. 'Grace and peace be multiplied unto you, through the knowledge of God and Jesus our Lord." Stoddard's *Way to know Sincerity and Hypocrisy.*

love to God, his experience of joy in the Holy Ghost, self-emptiness, a spirit to exalt Christ above all, and to give all glory to him, and a heart devoted unto him. I say, it is inconsistent with the gospel-doctrine of free grace, that a title to Christ's benefits should be given out of regard to the loveliness of *any* of these, or that any of these should be our *righteousness* in the affair of justification. And yet this does not hinder the importance of these things as *evidences* of an interest in Christ. Just so it is with respect to holy actions and works. To make light of works because we are not *justified* by them, is the same thing in effect as to make light of all religion, all grace and holiness, yea, true evangelical holiness, and all gracious experience: for *all* is included, when the Scripture says, we are not justified by *works*. By works in this case is meant all our own righteousness, religion, or holiness, and every thing that *is in us;* all the good we do, and are conscious of; all external acts, all internal exercises of grace, all experiences, and all those holy and heavenly things wherein the life, power, and very essence of religion consist; all those great things which Christ and his apostles mainly insisted on in their preaching, and endeavoured to promote, as of the greatest consequence in the hearts and lives of men, and all good dispositions, exercises, and qualifications of every kind whatsoever; and even *faith itself*, considered as a part of our holiness. For we are justified by none of these things: if we were, we should, in a scripture sense, be justified by *works*. And therefore if it be not legal, and contrary to the evangelical doctrine of justification without works, to insist on any of these, as of great importance in evidence of an interest in Christ; then no more is it thus, to insist on the importance of holy practice. It would be *legal* to suppose, that holy practice *justifies* by entitling us to Christ's benefits; but it is not legal to suppose, that holy practice justifies the sincerity of a believer, as the proper *evidence* of it. The apostle James did not think it legal to say, that *Abraham our father was justified by works*, in this sense. The Spirit that indited the Scripture, did not think the great importance and absolute necessity of holy practice, in this respect, to be inconsistent with the freeness of grace; for it commonly teaches them both together; as in Rev. xxi. 6, 7. God says, "I will give unto him that is athirst, of the fountain of the water of life freely;" and then adds in the very next words, "He that overcometh shall inherit all things;" as though behaving well in the christian race and warfare, were the condition of the promise. So in the next chapter, the 14th and 15th verses, Christ says, "Blessed are they that do his commandments, that they may have right to the tree of life, and enter in through the gates into the city:" and then declares, 15th ver. *how they that are of a wicked practice* shall be excluded. Yet in the two following verses, with very great solemnity, Christ invites all to come, and take of the water of life freely; "I am the root and the offspring of David, the bright and morning star.—And the Spirit and the bride say, Come. And let him that heareth, say, Come. And let him that is athirst, come: and whosoever will, let him come and take of the water of life freely." So chap. iii. 20, 21. "Behold, I stand at the door and knock: If any man hear my voice, and open the door, I will come in to him, and sup with him, and he with me." But then it is added in the next words, "To him that overcometh will I grant to sit with me in my throne." And in that great invitation, Matt. xi. "Come unto me, all ye that labour, and are heavy laden, and I will give you rest;" Christ adds in the next words, "Take my yoke upon you, and learn of me, for I am meek and lowly in heart: and ye shall find rest unto your souls: for my yoke is easy, and my burden is light:" as though taking the burden of Christ's service, and imitating his example, were necessary in order to the promised rest. So in that great invitation to sinners to accept of free grace; Isa. lv. "Ho, every one that thirsteth, come ye to the waters, and he that hath no money: come ye, buy and eat, yea, come, buy wine and milk without money, and without price:" even there, in the continuation of the same invitation, the sinner's forsaking his wicked practice is spoken of as necessary to the obtaining of mercy; ver. 7. "Let the wicked forsake his way, and the unrighteous man his thoughts: and let him return unto the Lord, and he will have mercy upon him, and to our God, for he will abundantly pardon." So the riches of divine grace in the justification of sinners, is set forth with the necessity of holy practice, Isa. i. 16, &c. "Wash ye, make you clean, put away the evil of your doings from before mine eyes, cease to do evil, learn to do well, seek judgment, relieve the oppressed, judge the fatherless, plead for the widow. Come now, let us reason together, saith the Lord: though your sins be as scarlet, they shall be as white as snow; though they be red like crimson, they shall be as wool." And in that most solemn invitation of wisdom, Prov. ix. after it is represented what great provision is made; and how all things were ready, the house built, the beasts killed, the wine mingled, the table furnished, and the messengers sent forth to invite the guests; then we have the free invitation, ver. 4—6. "Whoso is simple, let him turn in hither: as for him that wanteth understanding, (*i.e.* has no righteousness,) she saith to him, Come, eat of my bread, and drink of the wine which I have mingled." But then in the next breath it follows, "Forsake the foolish, and live; and go in the way of understanding:" as though forsaking sin, and going in the way of holiness, were necessary in order to life. So that the *freeness* of grace, and the *necessity* of holy practice, which are thus joined together in Scripture, are not inconsistent. Nor does it at all diminish the honour and importance of faith, that its exercises and effects in practice should be esteemed its chief signs; any more than it lessens the importance of life, that action and motion are esteemed its chief signs.

So that in what has been said of the importance of holy practice as the main sign of sincerity, there is nothing legal; nothing derogatory to the freedom and sovereignty of gospel-grace; nothing in the least clashing with the gospel-doctrine of justification by faith alone without the works of the law; nothing in the least tending to lessen the glory of the Mediator and our dependence on his righteousness; nothing infringing on the special prerogatives of faith in the affair of our salvation; nothing in any wise detracting from the glory of God and his mercy, exalting man, or diminishing his dependence and obligation. So that if any are against the importance of holy practice as explained, it must be only from a senseless aversion to the letters and sound of the word *works;* when there is no reason in the world to be given for it, but what may be given with equal force, why they should have an aversion to the words *holiness, godliness, grace, religion, experience,* and even *faith* itself: for to make a righteousness of any of these, is as legal, and as inconsistent with the way of the new covenant, as to make a righteousness of holy practice.*

It is greatly to the hurt of religion, for persons to insist little on those things which the Scripture insists most upon, as of most importance in the evidence of our interest in Christ, under a notion that to lay weight on these things is legal, and an old covenant-way. To neglect the exercises and effectual operations of grace in *practice,* and insist almost wholly on discoveries, and the method of the immanent exercises of conscience and grace in contemplation—depending on an ability to make nice distinctions in these matters, and a faculty of accurate discerning in them, from philosophy or experience—is highly injurious. It is in vain to seek for any better or any further signs, than those which the Scriptures have most expressly mentioned, and most frequently insisted on, as signs of godliness. They who pretend to a greater accuracy in giving signs—or, by their extraordinary experience, or insight into the nature of things, to give more distinguishing marks, which

* "You say you know Christ, and the love and good-will of Christ towards you, and that he is the propitiation for your sins. How do you know this? 'He that saith I know him, and keepeth not his commandments, is a liar,' 1 John ii. 4. True, might some reply, he that keeps not the commands of Christ, hath thereby a sure evidence that he knows him not, and that he is not united to him; but is this any evidence that we do know him, and that we are united to him, if we do keep his commandments? Yes, verily, saith the apostle, "Hereby we do know that we know him, if we keep his commandments." And again, ver. 5. "Hereby know we that we are in him." What can be more plain? What a vanity is it to say, that this is running upon a covenant of works?—O beloved, it is a sad thing to hear such questions and such cold answers also, that sanctification possibly may be an evidence. May be? Is it not certain? Assuredly, to deny it, is as bad as to affirm that God's own promises of favour are not sure evidences thereof, and consequently that they are lies and untruths.—Our Saviour, who was no legal preacher, pronounceth, and consequently evidenceth, blessedness, by eight or nine promises, expressly made to such persons, as had inherent graces, Matt. v. 3, 4, &c."—Shepard's *Sound Believer*, p. 221, 222, 223.

shall more thoroughly search out and detect the hypocrite—are but subtle to darken their own minds, and the minds of others; their refinings, and nice discerning, are in God's sight but refined foolishness, and sagacious delusion. Here are applicable those words of Agur, Prov. xxx. 5, 6. "Every word of God is pure; he is a shield to them that put their trust in him: add thou not unto his words, lest he reprove thee, and thou be found a liar." Our wisdom and discerning, with regard to the hearts of men, is not much to be trusted. We can see but a little way into the nature of the soul, and the depths of man's heart. The ways are many whereby persons' affections may be moved without any supernatural influence; the natural springs of the affections are various and secret. Many things have oftentimes a joint influence on the affections; the imagination, natural temper, education, the common influences of the Spirit of God; a surprising concourse of affecting circumstances, an extraordinary coincidence of things in the course of men's thoughts, together with the subtle management of invisible malicious spirits. No philosophy or experience will ever be sufficient to guide us safely through this labyrinth and maze, without our closely following the clue which God has given us in his word. God knows his own reasons, why he insists on some things, and plainly sets them forth as what we should try ourselves by, rather than others. It may be it is because he knows that these things are attended with less perplexity, and that we are less liable to be deceived by them than others. He best knows our nature, and the nature and manner of his own operations; and he best knows the way of our safety. He knows what allowances to make for different states of his church, different tempers of particular persons, and varieties in the manner of his own operations; how far nature may resemble grace, and how far nature may be mixed with grace; what affections may rise from imagination, and how far imagination may be mixed with spiritual illumination. And therefore it is our wisdom not to take his work out of his hands; but to follow him, and lay the stress of the judgment of ourselves there, where he has directed us. If we do otherwise, no wonder if we are bewildered, confounded, and fatally deluded. But if we had got into the way of looking chiefly at those things which Christ, his apostles, and prophets chiefly insisted on—while judging of ourselves and others, chiefly regarding *practical* exercises and effects of grace, not neglecting other things—it would have been of manifold happy consequence. This would above all things tend to the conviction of deluded hypocrites, and to prevent the delusion of those whose hearts were never brought to a thorough compliance with the strait and narrow way which leads to life. It would tend to deliver us from innumerable perplexities, arising from various inconsistent schemes about methods and steps of experience; it would greatly tend to prevent professors neglecting strictness of life, and tend to promote their engagedness and earnestness in their christian walk; and it would become fashionable for men to show their Christianity, more by an amiable distinguished behaviour, than by an abundant and excessive declaring of their experiences. We should then get into the way of appearing lively in religion, more by being lively in the *service* of God and our generation, than by the forwardness of our *tongues*, and making a business of proclaiming on the house-tops the holy and eminent acts and exercises of our own hearts. Then Christians who are intimate friends, would talk together of their experiences and comforts, in a manner better becoming christian humility and modesty, and more to each other's profit; their tongues not running before their hands and feet, after the prudent example of the blessed apostle, 2 Cor. xii. 6. Many occasions of spiritual pride would be cut off, and so a great door shut against the devil; and a great many of the main stumbling-blocks against experimental and powerful religion would be removed. Religion would be declared and manifested in such a way as—instead of hardening spectators, and exceedingly promoting infidelity and atheism—would above all things tend to convince men that there is a reality in religion, and greatly awaken them, and win them, by convincing their consciences of the importance and excellency of religion. Thus the light of professors would so shine before men, that others seeing their good works, would glorify their Father which is in heaven!

APPENDIX

TO THE TREATISE OF THE AFFECTIONS, IN TWO LETTERS.*

LETTER I.

TO MR. GILLESPIE, IN ANSWER TO OBJECTIONS.

Northampton, Sept. 4, 1747.

Rev. and Dear Sir,

I received your letter of Nov. 24, 1746, though very long after it was written. I thank you for it, and for your offering me a correspondence with you. Such an offer I shall gladly embrace, and esteem it a great privilege, more especially from the character I have received of you from Mr. Abercrombie, who I perceive was intimately acquainted with you.

As to the objections you make against some things contained in my late book *on Religious Affections*, I am sorry you did not read the book through, before you made them; if you had, perhaps the difficulties would not have appeared quite so great. As to what is contained in the 74th and 75th pages, I suppose there is not the least difference of opinion between you and me, unless it be concerning the signification and propriety of expressions. I am fully of your mind, and always was without the least doubt of it; "That every one, both saint and sinner, is indispensably bound, at all seasons, by the divine authority, to believe instantly on the Lord Jesus, and that the command of the Lord, 1 John iii. 23. that we should believe on the name of his Son Jesus Christ, as it is a prescription of the moral law, no less binds the sinner to immediate performance, than the commandment not to kill, to keep the Sabbath-day, or any other duty, as to the *present* performance of which, in way of duty, all agree the sinner is bound; and that men are bound to trust the divine faithfulness, be their case with respect to light and darkness, sight, &c. what it will; and that no situation they can be in, looses them from obligation to glorify the Lord at all seasons, and expecting the fulfilment of his words; and that the sinner that is without spiritual light or sight is bound to believe, and that it is a duty *at that very time* incumbent on him to believe." But I conceive that there is a great deal of difference between these two things, viz. its being a man's duty that is without spiritual light or sight to believe, and its being his duty to believe without spiritual light or sight, or to believe while he yet remains without spiritual light or sight. Just the same difference that is between these two things, viz. its being *his* duty that has no faith to believe, and its being his duty to believe without faith, or to believe without believing. I trust there is none will assert the latter, because of the contradiction that it implies. As it is not proper to say, it is a man's duty to believe without faith, because it implies a contra-

* These Letters were first printed in the "Quarterly Magazine," Edinb.

diction, so I think it equally improper to say it is a man's duty to believe without these things that are essentially implied in faith, because that also implies a contradiction. But a spiritual sight of Christ or knowledge of Christ is essentially implied in the very nature and notion of faith, and therefore it is absurd to talk of believing on Christ without spiritual light or sight. It is the duty of a man that is without these things that essentially belong to faith, to believe, and it is the duty of a man that is without these things that essentially belong to love, to love God; because it is an indispensable obligation that lies on all men at all times, and in all circumstances, to love God: but yet it is not a duty to love God without loving him, or continuing without those things that essentially belong to his love. It is the duty of those that have no sense of the loveliness of God, and have no esteem of him, to love him, and they be not in the least excused by the want of this sense and esteem, in not loving him one moment; but yet it would be properly nonsense to say it is their duty to love him without any sense of his loveliness or any esteem of him. It is indeed their duty this moment to come out of their disesteem and stupid wicked insensibility of his loveliness, and to love him. I made the distinction (I thought) very plainly, in the midst of those sentences you quote as exceptionable. I say expressly, p. 74. "It is truly the duty of those who are in darkness to come out of darkness into light and believe; but, that they should confidently believe and trust, while they yet remain without spiritual light or sight, is an anti-scriptural and absurd doctrine." The misunderstanding between us, dear Sir, I suppose to be in the different application of the particle *without*, in my use of it, and your understanding of it, or what we understand as spoken of and supposed in the expression, *without spiritual light or sight*. As I use it, I apply it to the act of believing, and I suppose it to be very absurd to talk of an act of faith *without* spiritual light and sight, wherein I suppose you will allow me to be in the right. As you understand it, it is applied to duty or obligation, and you suppose it to be not at all absurd to talk of an obligation to believe without spiritual light or sight, but that the obligation remains full where there is no spiritual light or sight, wherein I allow you are in the right. I think, Sir, if you read what I have said in my book on this head again, it will be exceeding apparent to you, that it is thus that I apply the preposition *without*, and not as you before understood it. I thought I had very plainly manifested that what I meant by *being in darkness* was a being in spiritual blindness, and so in a dead, stupid, carnal, and unchristian frame and way, and not what is commonly called a being without the light of God's countenance, under the hidings of his face. We have a great number of people in these parts that go on that supposition in their notions and practice, that there really is such a thing as such a manner of believing, such a kind of faith as this, *viz.* a confident believing and firm trusting in God in the dark, in the sense mentioned, that is to be sought after, and is the subject matter of divine prescription, and which many actually have; and indeed there are innumerable instances of such as are apparently in a most senseless, careless, negligent, apostate, and every way unchristian and wicked frame, that yet, encouraged by this principle, do retain an exceeding strong confidence of their good state, and count that herein they do their duty and give much glory to God, under the notion of trusting God in the dark, and hoping against hope, and not trusting on their own righteousness; and they suppose it would show a legal spirit to do otherwise. I thought it would be manifest to every reader that I was arguing against such a sort of people.

You say, "It merits consideration whether the believer should ever doubt of his state, on any account whatever, because doubting, as opposed to believing, is absolutely sinful." Here, Sir, you seem to suppose that a person's doubting of his own good estate, is the proper opposite of faith, and these and some other expressions in your letter seem to suppose that doubting of one's good estate and unbelief is the same thing, and so, that being confident of one's good estate and faith are the same thing. This I acknowledge I don't understand; I don't take faith, and a person's believing that they have faith, to be the same thing. Nor do I take unbelief, or being without faith, and doubting whether they have it, to be the same thing, but entirely different. I should have been glad either that you had taken a little more notice of what I say on this head, p. 76, 77. or that you had said something to convince me that I am wrong in this point. *The exercise of faith is doubtless the way to be delivered from darkness, deadness, backsliding*, &c. or rather is the deliverance; as forsaking sin is the way to deliverance from sin, and is the deliverance itself. The exercise of grace is doubtless the way to deliverance from a graceless frame, that consists in the want of the exercise of grace. But as to what you say, or seem to intimate, of a person's being confident of his own good estate, as being the way to be delivered from darkness, deadness, backsliding, and prevailing iniquity, I think, whoever supposes this to be God's method of delivering his saints, when sunk into an evil, careless, carnal, and unchristian frame, first to assure them of their good estate and his favour, while they yet remain in such a frame, and to make *that* the means of their deliverance, does surely mistake God's method of dealing with such persons. Among all the multitudes I have had opportunity to observe, I never knew one dealt with after this manner. I have known many brought back from great declension, that appeared to me to be true saints, but it was in a way very diverse from this. *In the first place*, conscience has been awakened, and they have been brought into great fear of the wrath of God, having his favour hid, and they have been the subjects of a kind of new work of humiliation, brought to a great sense of their deserving of God's wrath, even while they have yet feared it, before God has delivered them from the apprehension of it, and comforted them with a renewed sense of his favour.

As to what I say of the necessity of universal obedience, or of one way of known sin, (*i. e.* so as properly to be said to be the way and manner of the man,) being exception enough against a man's salvation; I should have known better what to have said further about it, if you had briefly shown how the scriptures that I mention, and the arguments I deduce from them, are insufficient for the proof of this point. I confess they appear to me to prove it as fully as any thing concerning the necessary qualifications of a true saint can be proved from Scripture.

You object against my saying, p. 276. "Nor can a true saint ever fall away, so that it shall come to this, that ordinarily there shall be no remarkable difference in his walk and behaviour since his conversion, from what was before." This, I think, implies no more than that his walk over the same ground, in like circumstances, and under like trials, will have a remarkable difference. As to the instance you mention of David and Solomon, I don't know that the Scripture gives us any where so much of a history of their walk and behaviour before their conversion, as to put us into any proper capacity of comparing their after walk with their former. These examples are uncertain. But I think those doctrines of the Scripture are not uncertain, which I mention in the place you cite, to confirm the point, which teach that converts are new men, new creatures, that they are renewed not only within but without, that old things are passed away, and all things become new, that they walk in newness of life, that the members of their bodies are new, that whereas they before were the servants of sin, and yielded their members servants of iniquity, now they yield them servants of righteousness unto holiness.

As to those doubts and cases of difficulty you mention, I should think it very needless for a divine of your character, to apply yourself to me for a solution of difficulties, for whom it would be more proper to learn of you. However, since you are pleased to insist on my giving my mind upon them, I would observe, as to the first case you mention, of a person incessantly harassed by Satan, &c. you don't say of what nature the temptations are that he is harassed with. But I think it impossible to give proper advice and direction without knowing this. Satan is to be resisted in a very different manner, in different kinds of onsets. When persons are harassed with those strange, horrid injections, that melancholic persons are often subject to, he is to be resisted in a very different manner, from what is proper in case of violent temptation to gratify some worldly lust. In the former case, I should by no means advise a person to resist the devil by entering the lists with him, and vehemently engaging their mind in an earnest dispute and violent struggle with the grand adversary, but rather by diverting the mind from his frightful suggestions, by going on stedfastly and diligently in the ordinary course of duty, without allowing themselves time and leisure to attend to the devil's sophistry, or viewing his frightful representations, committing themselves to God by prayer in this way, without anxiety about what had been suggested. That is the best way of resisting the devil, that crosses his design most; and he more effectually disappoints him in such cases, that treats him with neglect, than he that attends so much to him, as to engage in a direct conflict, and goes about to try his strength and skill with him, in a violent dispute or combat. The latter course rather gives him advantage, than any thing else. It is what he would; if he can get persons thus engaged in a violent struggle, he gains a great point. He knows that melancholic persons are not fit for it. By this he gains that point of diverting and taking off the person from the ordinary course of duty, which is one great thing he aims at; and by this, having gained the person's attention to what he says, he has opportunity to use all his craft and subtlety, and by this struggle he raises melancholic vapours to a greater degree, and further weakens the person's mind, and gets him faster and faster in his snares, deeper and deeper in the mire. He increases the person's anxiety of mind, which is the very thing by which mainly he fulfils all his purposes with such persons.

Concerning the other difficulty you mention relating to the verifying of Rom. viii. 20. "All things shall work together for good," &c. in a saint that falls under backsliding and spiritual decays, &c. it seems to be a matter of some difficulty to understand exactly how this is to be taken, and how far it may from hence be inferred, that the temptations the saints meet with from Satan, and an evil world, and their own declensions and sins, shall surely work for their good. However, since you desire my thoughts, I would express them, such as they are, as follows.

In order rightly to state this matter, there are two things may be laid down, as positions of certain and indubitable truth concerning this doctrine of the apostle.

First, The meaning cannot be that God's dispensations and disposals towards each saint are the best for him, most tending to his happiness, *of all that are possible*: or that all things that are ordered for him, or done by God with respect to him, are in all respects better for him than any thing else that God could have ordered or done, issuing in the highest good and happiness, that it is possible he should be brought to; for that would be as much as to say, that God will bestow on every one of his elect, as much happiness as he can (confer,) in the utmost exercise of his omnipotence, and this sets aside all these different degrees of grace and holiness here, and glory hereafter, which he bestows according to his sovereign pleasure.

All things may work together for good to the saints. All may be of benefit to them, and may have a concurring tendency to their happiness, and may all finally issue in it, and yet not tend to or issue in the highest degree of good and happiness possible. There is a certain measure of holiness and happiness, that each one of the elect is eternally appointed to, and all things that relate to him work together to bring to pass *this appointed measure of good*. The text and context speak of God's *eternal purpose* of good to the elect, predestinating them to a conformity to his Son in holiness and happiness; and the implicit reasoning of the apostle leads us to suppose that all things will purely concur to bring to effect God's eternal purpose. And therefore from his reasoning it may be inferred, that all things will tend to and work together to bring to pass, that degree of good that God has purposed to bestow upon them, and not any more. And indeed it would be in itself unreasonable to suppose any thing else but this; inasmuch as God is the supreme orderer of all things, doubtless all things shall be so ordered, that with one consent, they shall help to bring to pass his ends, aims, and purposes; but surely not to bring to pass what he does not aim at, and never intended. God in his government of the world is carrying on his own designs in every thing; but he is not carrying on that which is not his design, and therefore there is no need of supposing, that all the circumstances, means, and advantages of every saint, are the best in every respect that God could have ordered for him, or that there could have been no circumstances or means that he could have been the subject of, that would with God's usual blessing have issued in his greater good. Every saint is as it were a living stone, that in this present state of preparation, is fitting for the place appointed for him in the heavenly temple. And in this sense all things undoubtedly work together for good to every one that is called according to God's purpose. He is, all the while he lives in this world, by all the dispensations of Providence towards him, fitting for the particular mansion in glory, that is appointed and prepared for him, or hewing for his appointed place in the heavenly building.

Secondly, Another thing which is no less certain and demonstrable than the position that has been already laid down, and indeed follows from it, is this, When it is said, "all things work together for good," &c. hereby cannot be intended that all things, *both positive and negative, are best for them*, or that it is so universally, that not only every positive thing that the saints are the subjects of, or are concerned in, will work for their good, but also that when any thing is absent or withheld from them by God in his providence, that absence or withholding is also for their good in that sense, or to be better for them than the presence or bestowment would have been; for this would have the same absurd consequence that was mentioned before, viz. That God makes every saint as happy as possibly he can. And besides, if so, it would follow that God's withholding greater degrees of the sanctifying influences of his Spirit is for the saints' good, and that it is best for them to live and die so low in grace as they do, which would be as much as to say that it is for their good to have no more good, or that it is for their happiness to have no more happiness here and hereafter. If we take good notice of the apostle's discourse in Rom. viii. it will be apparent that his words imply no such thing. All God's creatures, and all that God does in disposing of them, is for the good of the saint. But it will not thence follow, that all God's forbearing to do is also for his good, or that it is best for him that God does no more for him.

Therefore, the following things I humbly conceive to be the truth, concerning the sins and temptations of the saints being for their good.

1. That all things whatsoever are for the good of the saints, things negative as well as positive, in this sense, that *God intends that some benefit to them shall arise from every thing*, so that something of the grace and love of God will hereafter be seen to have been exercised towards them in every thing. At the same time, the sovereignty of God will also be seen, with regard to the measure of the good or benefit aimed at, in that some other things, if God had seen cause to order them, would have produced a higher benefit. And with regard to negative disposals, consisting not in God's doing, but forbearing to do, not in giving, but withholding, some benefit in some respect or other, will ever accrue to the saints, even from these; though sometimes the benefit will not be equal to the benefit withheld, if it had been bestowed. As for instance, when a saint lives and dies comparatively low in grace. There is some good improvement shall be made, even of this, in the eternal state of the saint, whereby he shall receive a real benefit, though the benefit shall not be equal to the benefit of a higher degree of holiness, if God had bestowed it.

2. God carries on a design of love to his people, and to each individual saint, not only in all things that they are the subjects of while they live, but also in all his works and disposals, and in all his acts from eternity to eternity.

3. That the sin, in general, of the saints, is for their good, and for the best in this respect, viz. that it is a thing that, through the sovereign grace of God, and his infinite wisdom, will issue in a high advancement of their eternal happiness, that they have been sinful, fallen creatures, and not from the beginning perfectly innocent and holy, as the elect angels; and that they shall obtain some additional good on occasion of all the sin they have been the subjects of, or have committed, beyond what they would have had, if they never had been fallen creatures.

4. The sin of the saints in this sense cannot be for their good, that it should finally be best for them, that while they lived in this world, their restoration and recovery from the corruption they became subject to by the fall, was no greater, the mortification of sin, and spiritual vivification of their soul, carried on to no greater degree, that they remained so deficient, as to love to God, christian love to men, humility, heavenly-mindedness, and that they were so barren, and did so few good works, and consequently, that in general, they had so much sin, and of the exercises of it, and not more holiness, and of the exercises and fruits of that, for in proportion as one of these is more, the other will be less, as infallibly as darkness is more or less in proportion to the diminution or increase of light. It cannot finally be better for the saints, that in general, while they live, they had so much sin of heart and life, rather than more holiness of heart and life. Because the reward of all at last will be according to their works, and he that sowed sparingly shall reap sparingly, and he that sowed bountifully shall reap bountifully, and he that builds wood, hay, and stubble, shall finally suffer loss, and have a less reward, than if he had built gold, silver, and precious stones though he himself shall be saved. But notwithstanding this,

5. The sins and falls of the saints may be for their good, and for the better, in this respect, that the issue may be better than if the temptation had not happened, and so the occasion not given, either for the sin of yielding to the temptation, or the virtue of overcoming it: and yet not in the respect (with regard to their sins or falls in general) that it should be better for them in the issue, that they have yielded to the temptation offered, than if they had overcome. For the fewer victories they obtain over temptation, the fewer are their good works, and particularly of that kind of good works to which a distinguished reward is promised in Rev. ii. and iii. and in many other parts of Scripture. The word of God represents the work of a Christian in this world as a warfare, and it is evident in the Scripture that he who acquits himself as the best soldier shall win the greatest prize. Therefore, when the saints are brought into backslidings and decays, by being overcome by temptations, the issue of their backslidings may be some good to them. They may receive some benefit by occasion of it, beyond what they would have received if that temptation had never prevailed, and yet their backslidings in general may be a great loss to them in the following respect, *viz.* That they shall have much less reward, than if the temptations had been overcome, and they notwithstanding had persevered in spiritual vigour and diligence. But yet this don't hinder, but that,

6. It may be so ordered by a sovereign and all-wise God, that the saints' falls and backslidings, through their being overcome by temptations in some particular instances, may prove best for them, not only in that the issue may be greater good to them, than they would have received if the temptation had not happened, but even greater in that instance, than if the temptation had been overcome. It may be so ordered that their being overcome by that temptation, shall be the occasion of their having greater strength, and on the whole, obtaining more and greater victories, than if they had not fallen in that instance. But this is no where promised, nor can it be so, that, in the general, it should prove better for them that they were foiled so much, and overcome so little, in the course of their lives, and that finally their decay is so great, or their progress so small. From these things it appears,

7. That the saying of the apostle, *all things work together for good to them that love God,* though it be fulfilled in some respects to all saints, and at all times, and in all circumstances, yet it is fulfilled more especially and eminently to the saints *continuing in the exercise of love to God,* not falling from the exercises, or failing in the fruits, of divine love in times of trial. Then it is, that temptations, enemies, and suffering, will be best for them, working that which is most for their good every way, and they shall be more than conquerors over tribulation, distress, persecution, famine, nakedness, peril, and sword, Rom. viii. 35—37.

8. As God is carrying on a design of love to each individual saint, in all his works and disposals whatsoever, as was observed before, so the particular design of love to them that he is carrying on, is to fit them for, and bring them to, their appointed place in the heavenly temple, or to that individual, precise happiness and glory in heaven, that his eternal love designed for them, and no other (for God's design of love or of happiness to them, is only just what it is, and is not different from itself). And to fulfil this particular design of love, every thing that God does, or in any respect disposes, whether it be positive, privative, or negative, contributes, because doubtless every thing that God does, or in any respect offers, tends to fulfil his aims and designs. Therefore, undoubtedly,

9. All the while the saint lives in the world, he is fitting for his appointed mansion in glory, and hewing for his place in the heavenly building. And all his temptations, though they may occasion, for the present, great spiritual wounds, yet at last, they shall be an occasion of his being more fitted for his place in glory. And therefore we may determine, that however the true saint may die, in some respects, under decays, under the decay of comfort, and of the exercise of some religious affections, yet every saint dies at that time when his habitual fitness for his place in the heavenly temple is most complete, because otherwise, all things that happen to him while he lives, would not work together to fit him for that place.

10. God brings his saints at the end of their lives to this greatest fitness for their place in heaven, not by diminishing grace in their hearts, but by increasing it, and carrying on the work of grace in their souls. If it be not so, that cannot be true, that where God *has begun a good work he will perform it, or carry it on to the day of Christ,* for if they die with a less degree of grace than they had before, then it ceases to be carried on before the day of Christ comes. If grace is finally diminished, then Satan so far finally obtains the victory. He finally prevails to diminish the fire in the smoking flax, and then how is that promise verified, that God *will not quench the smoking flax, till he bring forth judgment unto victory?* So that it must needs be, that although saints may die under decay in some respects, yet they never die under a real habitual decay of the work of grace in general. If they fall, they shall rise again before they die, and rise higher than before, if not in joy, and some other affections, yet in greater degrees of spiritual knowledge, self-emptiness, trust in God, and solidity and ripeness of grace.

If these things that have been observed are true, then we may infer from them these corollaries.

1*st,* That notwithstanding the truth of that saying of the apostle, Rom. viii. 28. the saints have cause to lament their leanness and barrenness, and that they are guilty of so much sin, not only as it is to the dishonour of God, but also as that which is like to be to their own eternal loss and damage.

2*dly,* That nothing can be inferred from the forementioned promise tending to set aside, or make void, the influence of motives to earnest endeavours to avoid all sin, to increase in holiness, and abound in good works, from an aim at a high and eminent degree of glory and happiness in the future world.

3*dly,* That though it is to the eternal damage of the saints, ordinarily, when they yield to, and are overcome by temptations, yet Satan and other enemies of the saints by whom these temptations come, are always wholly disappointed in their temptation, and baffled in their design to hurt the saints, inasmuch as the temptation and the sin that comes by it, is for the saints' good, and they receive a greater benefit in the issue, than if the temptation had not been, and yet less than if the temptation had been overcome.

As to Mr. Boston's View of the Covenant of Grace, I have had some opportunity with it, and I confess I did not understand his scheme delivered in that book. I have read his Fourfold State of Man, and liked it exceeding well. I think he herein shows himself to be a truly great divine.

Hoping that you will accept my letter with candour, and remember me in your prayers, I subscribe myself

Your affectionate and obliged Brother
and Servant,
JONATHAN EDWARDS.

LETTER II.

TO MR. GILLESPIE, IN ANSWER TO OBJECTIONS.

Northampton, April 2, 1750.

Rev. and Dear Sir,

I RECEIVED your favour of September 19, 1748, the last summer, and would now heartily thank you for it. I suppose it might come in the same ship with letters I had from my other correspondents in Scotland, which I answered the last summer; but it did not come to hand till a long time after most of the others, and after I had finished and sent away my answers to them, and that opportunity for answering was past. I have had no leisure or opportunity to write any letters to Scotland from that time till now, by reason of my peculiar and very extraordinary circumstances, on account of the controversy that has arisen between me and my people, concerning the profession that ought to be made by persons that come to christian sacraments, which is likely speedily to issue in a separation between me and my congregation. This controversy, in the progress of it, has proved not only a controversy between me and my people, but between me and a great part of New England; there being many far and near that are warmly engaged in it. This affair has unavoidably engaged my mind, and filled up my time, and taken me off from other things. I need the prayers of my friends, that God would be with me, and direct and assist me in such a time of trial, and mercifully order the issue.

As to the epistolary controversy, dear Sir, between you and me, about FAITH and DOUBTING, I am sorry it should *seem* to be greater than it is, through misunderstanding of one another's meaning, and that the *real* difference between us is so great as it is, in some part of the controversy.

As to the dispute about believing without spiritual light or sight, I thought I expressed my meaning in my last letter very plainly, but I kept no copy, and it might perhaps be owing to my dulness that I thought so. However, I perceive I was not understood. I cannot find out by any thing you say to me on this head, that we really differ in sentiments, but only in words. I acknowledge with you that "all are bound to believe the divine testimony, and trust in Christ; and that want of spiritual light or sight does not loose from the obligation one is laid under by the divine command, to believe instantly on Christ, at all seasons, nor excuse him, in any degree, for not believing. Even when one wants the influence and grace of the Spirit, still he is bound to believe. Ability is not the rule of duty." I think the obligation to believe, lies on a person *who is remaining without spiritual light or sight*, or even in darkness. No darkness, no blindness, no carnality or stupidity, excuses him a moment from having as strong and lively faith and love as ever was exercised by the apostle Paul, or rather renders it not sinful in him that he is at that same moment without such a faith and love;—and yet I believe it is absurd, and of very hurtful consequence, to urge persons to believe in the dark, in the manner and in the sense in which many hundreds have done in *America*, who plainly intend, a believing strongly with such a sort of strong faith or great confidence as is consistent with continuing still, even in the time of these strong acts of faith, without spiritual light; carnal, stupid, careless, and senseless. Their doctrine evidently comes to this, both in sense and effect, that it is a mere duty strongly to believe with a lightless and sightless faith, or to have a confident, although a blind, dark, and stupid faith. And such a faith has indeed been promoted exceedingly by their doctrine, and has prevailed with its dreadful effects, answerable to the nature of the cause. We have had, and have to this day, multitudes of such strong believers, whose bold, proud, and stupid confidence, attended with a very wicked behaviour, has given the greatest wound to the cause of truth and vital religion that ever it suffered in America.

As to what follows in your letter, concerning a person's believing himself to be in a good state, and its being properly of the nature of faith: in this there seems to be some real difference between us. But, perhaps, there would be none, if distinctness were well observed in the use of words. If by a man's believing that he is in a good estate, be meant no more than his believing that he does believe in Christ, does love God, &c. I think there is nothing of the nature of faith in it; because knowing it, or believing it, depends on our own immediate sensation or consciousness, and not on divine testimony. True believers, in the hope they entertain of salvation, make use of the following syllogism, *whosoever believes shall be saved: I believe, therefore*, &c. Assenting to the major proposition is properly of the nature of faith, because the ground of my assent to that is divine testimony; but my assent to the minor proposition, I humbly conceive, is not of the nature of faith, because that is not grounded on divine testimony, but my own consciousness. The testimony that is the proper ground of faith is in the word of God, Rom. x. 17. "Faith cometh by hearing, and hearing by the word of God." There is such a testimony given us in the word of God, that "He that believeth shall be saved." But there is no such testimony in the word of God, as that such an individual person in such a town in *Scotland* or *New England*, believes. There is such a proposition in the Scripture, as that *Christ loves those that love him*, and therefore, this every one is bound to believe, and affirm: believing this on divine testimony is properly of the nature of faith, and for any one to doubt of it, is properly of the heinous sin of unbelief. But there is no such proposition in the Scripture, nor is it any part of the gospel of Christ, that such an individual person in Northampton loves Christ. If I know that I have complacence in Christ, I know it the same way that I know I have complacence in my wife and children, *viz.* by the testimony of my own heart or inward consciousness. Evangelical faith has the gospel of Christ for its foundation; but that I love Christ is a proposition not contained in the gospel of Christ.

And therefore, that we may not dispute in the dark, it is necessary, that we should explain what we mean by a person's believing he is in a good estate. If thereby we mean only believing the minor of the foregoing syllogism, or such like syllogisms, I believe or I love God, it is not in the nature of faith. But if by a man's believing himself to be in a good estate, be understood his believing not only the minor, but the consequence, *therefore I shall be saved*, or *therefore God will never leave me nor forsake me;* then a man's believing his good estate, partakes of the nature of faith; for these consequences depend on divine testimony in the word of God and the gospel of Jesus Christ. Yea, I would observe farther, that a man's judging of the faith or love he finds in himself, whether they are that sort of faith and love which he finds to be saving, may depend on his reliance on scripture rules and marks which are divine testimonies, which he may be tempted not to rely upon, from the consideration of his great unworthiness. But his judging that he has those individual inward acts of understanding, and exercises of heart, depends on inward sensations, and not on any testimony of the word of God. The knowing present acts depends on immediate consciousness, and the knowing past acts depends on memory. And therefore the fulness of my satisfaction, that I now have such an inward act or exercise of mind, depends on the strength of sensation; and my satisfaction, that I have had them heretofore, depends on the clearness of my memory, and not on the strength of my reliance on any divine testimony; and so my doubting whether I have, or have had, such individual inward acts, is not of the nature of unbelief, though it may arise from unbelief *indirectly;* because, if I had had more faith, the actings of it would have been more sensible, and the memory of them more clear, and so I should have been better satisfied that I had them.

God seems to have given Abraham's servant a revelation, that the damsel in whom he found such marks, *viz.* coming to draw water with a pitcher to that well, her readiness to give him and his camels drink, &c. should be Isaac's wife, and therefore his assenting to *this* was of the nature of faith, having divine testimony for its foundation. But his believing that Rebekah was the damsel that had these individual marks, his knowing that she came to draw water, and that she let down her pitcher, &c. was not of the nature of faith. His knowing *this* was not from divine testimony, but from the testimony of his own senses. (Vide Gen. xxiv.)

You speak of "a saint's doubting of his good estate as a part of unbelief, and the opposite of faith, considered in its full compass and latitude, as one branch of unbelief, one ingredient in unbelief; and of assurance of a man's good estate, as one thing that belongs to the exercise of faith." I do not know whether I take your meaning in these expressions. If you mean, that a person's believing himself to be in a good estate is one thing that appertains to the essence of saving faith, or that saving faith, in all that belongs to its essence, yea its perfection, cannot be without implying it, I must humbly ask leave to differ from you. That a believing that I am in a good estate, is no part or ingredient in the essence of saving faith, is evident by this, that the essence of saving faith must be complete in me, before it can be true that I am in a good estate. If I have not as yet acted faith, yea if there be any thing wanting in me to make up the essence of saving faith, then I am not as yet in a state of salvation, and therefore can have no ground to believe that I am so. Any thing that belongs to the essence of saving faith is prior, in the order of nature, to a man's being in a [believing] state of salvation, because it is saving faith that brings him into such a state. And therefore believing that he is in such a state cannot be one thing that is essential or necessary in order to his being in such a state; for that would imply a contradiction. It would be to suppose a man's believing that he is in a good estate to be prior, in the order of nature, to his being in a good estate. But a thing cannot be both prior and posterior, antecedent and consequent, with respect to the very same thing. The real truth of a proposition is in the order of nature first, before its being believed to be true. But till a man has already all that belongs to the essence of saving faith, that proposition, *that he is in a good* [believing] *estate*, is not as yet true. All the propositions contained in the gospel, all divine testimonies that we have in God's word, are true already, are already laid for a foundation for faith, and were laid long ago. But that proposition, *I am in a good estate*, not being one of them, is not true till I have first believed; and therefore this proposition cannot be believed to be true, till saving faith be first complete. Therefore the completeness of the act of saving faith will not make it take in a belief of this proposition, nor will the strength or perfection of the act cause it to imply this. If a man, in his first act of faith, has ever so great a conviction of God's sufficiency and faithfulness, and let his reliance on the divine testimony be ever so strong and perfect, all will have no tendency to make him believe this proposition, *I am in a good estate*, to be true, till it be true, which it is not till the first act of faith is complete, and has made it true. A belief of divine testimony in the first act of faith, may be to any assignable degree of strength and perfection, without believing that proposition, for there is no such divine testimony then extant, nor is there any such truth extant, but in consequence of the first act of faith. Therefore, (as I said) saving faith may be, with all that belongs to its essence, and that in the highest perfection, without implying a belief of my own good estate. I do not say it can be without having this immediate *effect*. But it is rather the *effect* of faith, than a *part*, *branch*, or *ingredient* of faith. And so I do not dispute whether a man's doubting of his good state may be a consequence of unbelief, (I doubt not but it is in those who are in a good state,) because, if men had the exercise of faith in such a degree as they ought to have, it could not but be very sensible and plain that they had it. But yet I think this doubting of a good state is entirely a different thing from the sin of unbelief itself, and has nothing of the nature of unbelief in it, *i. e.* if we take doubting one's good state in the sense in which I have before explained it, *viz.* for doubting whether I have such individual principles and acts in my soul. Take it in a complex sense, and it may have the sin of unbelief in it; *e. g.* If, although I doubt not that I have such and such qualifications, I yet doubt of those consequences, for which I have divine testimony or promise; as when a person doubts not that he loves Christ, yet doubts whether *he shall receive a crown of life*. The doubting of this consequence is properly the sin of unbelief.

You say, dear Sir, "The Holy Ghost requires us to believe the reality of his work in us in all its parts just as it is;" and, a little before, "The believer's doubting whether or not he has faith, is sinful; because it is belying the Holy Ghost, denying his work in him, so there is no sin to which that doubting can so properly be reduced as unbelief."

Here I would ask leave thus to express my thoughts in a diversity from yours. I think, if it be allowed to be sinful for a believer to doubt whether he has faith, that this doubting is not the sin of unbelief on any such account as you mention, *viz.* as belying or denying any testimony of the Holy Ghost. There is a difference between doubting of the being of some *work* of the Holy Ghost, and denying the *testimony* of the Holy Ghost, as there is a difference between doubting concerning some other works of God, and denying the testimony of God. It is the work of God to give a man great natural abilities; and if we suppose God *requires* such a man *to believe the reality of his work in all its parts just as it is*, and so that it is sinful for him at all to doubt of his natural abilities being just as good as they are, yet this is no belying any testimony of God, though it be doubting of a work of God, and so is diverse from the sin of unbelief. So, if we suppose a very eminent saint is to blame in doubting whether he has so much grace as he really has; he indeed *does not believe the reality of God's work in him, in all its parts, just as it is*, yet he is not therein guilty of the sin of unbelief, against any testimony of God, any more than the other.

I acknowledge, that for a true saint in a carnal and careless frame, to doubt of his good state, is sinful, *more indirectly*, as the cause of it is sinful, *viz.* the lowness and insensibility of the actings of grace in him, and the prevalence of carnality and stupidity. 'Tis sinful to be without assurance, or, (as we say,) *it is his own fault*, he sinfully deprives himself of it; or foregoes it, as a servant's being without his tools is his sin, when he has carelessly lost them, or as it is his sin to be without strength of body, or without the sight of his eyes, when he has deprived himself of these by intemperance. Not that weakness or blindness of body, in their own nature, are sin, for they are qualities of the body, and not of mind, the subject in which sin is inherent. It is indirectly the duty of a true saint *always* to rejoice in the light of God's countenance, because sin is the cause of his being without this joy at any time, and therefore it was *indirectly* David's sin that he was not rejoicing in the light of God's countenance, at the very time when he was committing the great iniquities of adultery and murder. But yet it is not directly a believer's duty to rejoice in the light of God's countenance, when God hides his face. But it rather then becomes him to be troubled and to mourn. So there are perhaps many other privileges of saints that are their duty indirectly, and the want of them is sinful, not simply, but complexly considered. Of this kind I take the want of assurance of my good estate to be.

I think no words of mine, either in my book or letter, implied that a person's deliverance from a bad frame does not begin with renewed acts of faith or trusting in God. If they did, they implied what I never intended. Doubtless if a saint comes out of an ill frame, wherein grace is asleep and inactive, it must be by renewed actings of grace. It is very plainly impossible, that grace should begin to cease to be inactive, in any other way, than by its beginning to be active. It must begin with the renewed actings of some grace or other, and I know nothing that I have said to the contrary, but that the grace that shall first begin sensibly to revive shall be faith, and that this shall lead the way to the renewed acting of all other graces, and to the farther acting of faith itself. But a person's coming out of a carnal, careless, dead frame, by, or in the reviving of grace in his soul, is quite another thing from a saint's having a strong exercise of faith, or strong hope, or strong exercise of any other grace, while yet remaining in a carnal, careless, dead frame; or, in other words, in a frame wherein grace is so far from being in strong exercise, that it is asleep, and in a great measure without exercise.

There is a *holy hope*, a truly *christian hope*, that the Scripture speaks of, that is reckoned among the graces of the Spirit: and I think I should never desire or seek any other hope; for I believe no other hope has any holy or good tendency. Therefore *this* hope, *this* grace of hope alone, can properly be called a duty. But it is just as absurd to talk of the exercise of this holy hope, the strong exercise of this grace of the Spirit, in a carnal, stupid, careless frame, such *a frame yet remaining*, as it would be to talk of the strong exercises of love to God, or heavenly-mindedness, or any other grace, remaining in such a frame. It is doubtless proper, earnestly to exhort those who are in such a frame to come out of it, in and by the strong exercises of all grace; but I should not think it proper to press a man earnestly to maintain strong hope, *notwithstanding* the prevailing and continuance of great carnality and stupidity (which is plainly the case of the people I opposed). For this is plainly to press people to an unholy hope, a strong hope that is no christian grace, but strong and wicked presumption; and the promoting of this has most evidently been the effect of such a method of dealing with souls in innumerable multitudes of awful instances.

You seem, Sir, to suppose, that God's manner of dealing with his saints, *while in a secure and careless frame*, is *first* to give assurance of their good state *while they remain in such a frame*, and to make use of that assurance as a mean to bring them out of such a frame. Here, again, I must beg leave to differ from you, and to think, that none of the instances or texts you adduce from Scripture, do at all prove the point. I think it is God's manner, first to awaken their consciences, and to bring them to reflect upon themselves, and to bring them to feel their own calamity which they have brought upon themselves by so departing from God, (by which an end is put to their carelessness and security,) and again earnestly and carefully to seek God's face before they find him, and before God restores the comfortable and joyful sense of his favour; and I think this is abundantly evident both by Scripture and experience. You much insist on *Jonah* as a clear instance of the thing you lay down. You observe that he says, chap. ii. "I said, I am cast of thy sight, yet will I look again towards thy holy temple." Ver. 5, 7. "When my soul fainted within me; I remembered the Lord, and my prayer came in unto thee, even into thine holy temple." You speak of these words as expressing an assurance of his good state and of God's favour; (I will not now dispute whether they do or not;) and you speak of this exercise of assurance, &c. as *his practice in an evil frame, and in a careless frame; for he slept securely in the sides of the ship*, manifesting *dismal security, awful carelessness in a carnal frame*. That Jonah was in a careless secure frame when he was asleep in the sides of the ship, I do not deny. But, dear Sir, does that prove that he remained still in a careless secure frame, when in his heart he said these things in the fish's belly, chap. ii. 4, 7.? does it prove that he remained careless after he was awakened, and saw the furious storm, and owned it was the fruit of God's anger towards him for his sins? and does it prove, that he still remained careless after the whale had swallowed him, when he seemed to himself to be *in the belly of hell?* when *the water compassed him about, even to the soul*, and, as he says, *all God's waters and billows passed over him, and he was ready to despair when he went down to the bottoms of the mountains*, was ready to think God had cast him out of his sight, and confined him in a prison, that he could never escape, *the earth with her bars was about him, for ever, and his soul fainted within him.* He was brought into *this* condition *after* his sleeping securely in the sides of the ship, *before* he said, "I will look again towards thine holy temple," &c. He was evidently first awakened out of carelessness and security, and brought into distress, before he was comforted.

The other place you also much insist on, concerning the people of Israel, is very much like this. Before God comforted them with the testimonies of his favour, after their backslidings, he first, by severe chastisements, together with the awakening influences of his Spirit, brought them out of their *carelessness* and carnal *security*. It appears by many scriptures, that this was God's way of dealing with that people. So Hos. chap. ii. God first "hedged up her ways with thorns, and made a wall that she could not find her paths. And took away her corn and wine, and wool and flax, destroyed her vines and fig-trees, and caused her mirth to cease;" and, by this means, brought her to herself, brought her out of her security, carelessness, and deep sleep, very much as the prodigal son was brought to himself. God "brought her first into the wilderness, before he spake comfortably to her, and opened to her a door of hope." By her distress first brought her to say, "I will go and return to my first husband;" and then, when God spake comfortably to her, she called him "*Ishi*, my husband;" and God did as it were renewedly betroth her unto him. That passage Hosea ii. is very parallel with Jer. iii. One place serves well to illustrate and explain the other, and that it was God's way of dealing with his people Israel, after their apostacy and carnal security, *first* to awaken them, and under a sense of their sin and misery to bring them solicitously to seek his face, before he gave them sensible evidence of his favour; and not to awaken out of security, by first making manifest his favour to them.*

And, besides, I would observe, that in Jer. iii. the prophecy is not concerning the recovery of backsliding saints or the mystical church, which, though she had corrupted herself, still continued to be God's wife: it is concerning apostate Israel, that had forsaken and renounced her husband, and gone after other lovers, and whom God had renounced, put away, and given her a bill of divorce, (ver. 8.) so that her recovery could not be by giving her assurance of her good estate as still remaining his wife, and that God was already married unto her, for that was not true, and is not consistent with the context. And whereas it is said, ver. 14. "Return, O backsliding children, saith the Lord; for I am married unto you, and I will take you one of a city," &c. *I am married*, in the Hebrew, is in the preterperfect tense; but you know, Sir, that in the language of prophecy, the preter tense is very commonly put for the future; and whereas it is said, ver. 19. "How shall I put thee among the children? And I said, Thou shalt call me, My father." I acknowledge this expression here, my Father, and that Rom. viii. 15. is the language of faith. It is so two ways: 1st, It is such language of the soul as is the immediate effect of a lively faith. I acknowledge, that the lively exercises of faith do naturally produce satisfaction of a good state *as their immediate effect*. 2nd, It is language which, in another sense, does properly and naturally express the very act of faith itself, yea, the first act of faith in a sinner, before which he never was in a good state. As thus, supposing a man in distress, pursued by his enemies that sought his life, should have the gates of several fortresses set open before him, and should be called to from each of them to fly thither for refuge; and viewing them all, and one appearing strong and safe, but the rest insufficient, he should accept the invitation to that one, and fly thither, with this language, "This is my fortress; this is my refuge. In vain is salvation looked for from the other. Behold I come to thee; this is my sure defence." Not that he means that he is already within the fortress, and so in a good estate. But this is my chosen fortress, in the strength of which I trust, and to which I betake myself for safety. So if a woman were at once to be solicited by many lovers, to give herself to them in a married state, and beholding the superior excellencies of one far above all the rest, should betake herself to him, with this language, "This is my husband, behold I come unto thee, thou art my spouse." Not that she means that she is already married to him, but that he is her chosen husband, &c. Thus God offers himself to sinners as their Saviour, God, and Father; and the language of the heart of him that accepts the offer by active faith, is, "Thou art my Saviour; in vain is salvation hoped for from others that offer themselves. Thou art my God and Father." Not that he is already his child, but he chooses him, and comes to him, that he may be one of

* This is evident by many scriptures; as, Lev. xxvi. 40—42. Deut. xxxii. 36—39. 1 Kings viii. 21, 22. chap. i. 4—8. Ezek. xx. 35, 36, 37. Hos. v. 15. with chap. vi. 1—3. chap. xiii. 9, 10, chap. xiv. throughout.

his children; as in Jer. iii. 19. Israel calls God his Father, as the way to be *put among the children*, and to be one of them, and not as being one already; and in ver. 21, 22, 23. she is not brought out of a careless and secure state by knowing that the Lord is her God, but she is first brought to consideration and sense of her sin and misery, weeping and supplications for mercy and conviction of the vanity of other saviours and refuges, not only before she has assurance of her good estate, but before she is brought to fly to God for refuge, that she may be in a good estate.

As to the instance of Job, I would only say this: I think while in his state of sore affliction, though he had some great exercises of infirmity and impatience under his extreme trials, yet he was very far from being in such a frame as I intended, when I spoke of a *secure, careless, carnal* frame, &c. I doubt not, nor did I ever question it, that the saints' hope and knowledge of their good state, is in many cases of excellent benefit, to help them against temptation and the exercises of corruption.

With regard to the case of extraordinary temptation, and buffeting of Satan, which you mention, I do not very well know what to say further. I have often found my own insufficiency as a counsellor in such like cases, wherein melancholy and bodily distemper have so great a hand, and give Satan so great advantage, as appears to me in the case you mention. If the Lord do not help, whence should we help? If some christian friends of such afflicted and (as it were) possessed persons, would, from time to time, pray and fast for them, it might be a proper exercise of christian charity, and the likeliest way I know for relief. I kept no copy of my former letter to you, and so do not remember fully what I have already said concerning this case. But this I have often found with such melancholy people, that the greatest difficulty does not lie in giving them good advice, but in persuading them to take it. One thing I think of great importance, which is, that such persons should go on in a steady course of performance of all duties, both of their general and particular calling, without suffering themselves to be diverted from it by any violence of Satan, or specious pretence of his whatsoever, properly ordering, proportioning, and timing all sorts of duties, duties to God, public, private, and secret, and duties to man, relative duties, of business and conversation, family duties, duties of friendship and good neighbourhood, duly proportioning labour and rest, intentness and relaxation, without suffering one duty to crowd out or intrench upon another. If such persons could be persuaded to this, I think, in this way, they would be best guarded against the devil, and he would soonest be discouraged, and a good state of body would be most likely to be gained, and persons would act most as if they trusted and rested in God, and would be most in the way of his help and blessing.

With regard to what you write concerning immediate revelations, I have thought of it, and I find I cannot say any thing to purpose, without drawing out this letter to a very extraordinary length, and I am already got to such length, that I had need to ask your excuse. I have written enough to tire your patience.

It has indeed been with great difficulty that I have found time to write much. If you knew my extraordinary circumstances, I doubt not, you would excuse my not writing any more. I acknowledge the subject you mention is very important. Probably if God spares my life, and gives me opportunity, I may write largely upon it. I know not how Providence will dispose of me, I am going to be cast on the wide world, with my large family of ten children.—I humbly request your prayers for me under my difficulties and trials.

As to the state of religion in this place and this land, it is at present very sorrowful and dark. But I must, for a more particular account of things, refer you to my letter to Mr. M'Lauren, of Glasgow, and Mr. Robe. So, asking a remembrance in your prayers, I must conclude, by subscribing myself, with much esteem and respect,

Your obliged Brother and Servant,

JONATHAN EDWARDS.

P. S. *July* 3, 1750. Having had no leisure to finish the preparation of my letters to Scotland before this time, by reason of the extraordinary troubles, hurries, and confusions of my unusual circumstances, I can now inform you, that the controversy between me and my people, that I mentioned in the beginning of my letter, has issued in a separation. An ecclesiastical council was called on the affair, who sat here the week before last, who, by a majority of one voice, determined an immediate separation to be necessary; and accordingly my pastoral relation to my people was dissolved on June 22. If I can procure the printed accounts from Boston of the proceedings of the council, I will give order to my friend there to enclose them with this letter, and direct them to you.—I desire your prayers, that I may take a suitable notice of the frowns of Heaven on me and this people, (between whom was once so great an union,) in bringing to pass such a separation between us; and that these troubles may be sanctified to me, that God would overrule this event for his own glory, (which doubtless many adversaries will rejoice and triumph in,) that God would open a door for my future usefulness, and provide for me and my numerous family, and take a fatherly care of us in our present unsettled, uncertain circumstances, being cast on the wide world.

J. E.

A

FAITHFUL NARRATIVE

OF THE

SURPRISING WORK OF GOD,

IN THE

CONVERSION OF MANY HUNDRED SOULS,

IN NORTHAMPTON,

AND THE

NEIGHBOURING TOWNS AND VILLAGES OF NEW HAMPSHIRE, IN NEW ENGLAND;

IN A

LETTER TO THE REV. DR. COLMAN, OF BOSTON.

PREFACE

BY THE FIRST EDITORS, DR. ISAAC WATTS, AND DR. JOHN GUYSE.

THE friendly correspondence which we maintain with our brethren of New England, gives us now and then the pleasure of hearing some remarkable instances of divine grace in the conversion of sinners, and some eminent examples of piety in that American part of the world. But never did we hear or read, since the first ages of Christianity, any event of this kind so surprising as the present Narrative hath set before us. The Rev. and worthy Dr. Colman, of Boston, had given us some short intimations of it in his letters; and upon our request of a more large and particular account, Mr. Edwards, the happy and successful minister of Northampton, which was one of the chief scenes of these wonders, drew up this history in an epistle to Dr. Colman.

There were some useful sermons of the venerable and aged Mr. Wm. Williams, published late in New England, which were preached in that part of the country during this season of the glorious work of God in the conversion of men; to which Dr. Colman subjoined a most judicious and accurate abridgment of this epistle: and a little after, by Mr. Edwards's request, he sent the original to our hands, to be communicated to the world under our care here in London.

We are abundantly satisfied of the truth of this narrative, not only from the pious character of the writer, but from the concurrent testimony of many other persons in New England; *for this thing was not done in a corner.* There is a spot of ground, as we are here informed, wherein there are twelve or fourteen towns and villages, chiefly situate in New Hampshire, near the banks of the river of Connecticut, within the compass of thirty miles, wherein it pleased God, two years ago, to display his free and sovereign mercy in the conversion of a great multitude of souls in a short space of time, turning them from a formal, cold, and careless profession of Christianity, to the lively exercise of every christian grace, and the powerful practice of our holy religion. The great God has seemed to act over again the miracle of Gideon's fleece, which was plentifully watered with the dew of heaven, while the rest of the earth round about it was dry, and had no such remarkable blessing.

There has been a great and just complaint for many years among the ministers and churches in Old England, and in New, (except about the time of the late earthquake there,) that the work of conversion goes on very slowly, that the Spirit of God in his saving influences is much withdrawn from the ministrations of his word, and there are few that receive the report of the gospel, with any eminent success upon their hearts. But as the gospel is the same divine instrument of grace still, as ever it was in the days of the apostles, so our ascended Saviour now and then takes a special occasion to manifest the divinity of this gospel by a plentiful effusion of his Spirit where it is preached: then sinners are turned into saints in numbers, and there is a new face of things spread over a town or a country. *The wilderness and the solitary places are glad, the desert rejoices and blossoms as the rose;* and surely concerning this instance we may add, that *they have seen the glory of the Lord* there, *and the excellency of our God;* they have *seen the out-goings of God our King in his sanctuary.*

Certainly it becomes us, who profess the religion of Christ, to take notice of such astonishing exercises of his power and mercy, and give him the glory which is due, when he begins to accomplish any of his promises concerning the latter days: and it gives us further encouragement to pray, and wait, and hope for the like display of his power in the midst of us. *The hand of God is not shortened that it cannot save,* but we have reason to fear that *our iniquities,* our coldness in religion, and the general carnality of our spirits, have raised a wall of separation between God and us: and we may add, the pride and perverse humour of infidelity, degeneracy, and apostacy from the christian faith, which have of late years broken out amongst us, seem to have provoked the Spirit of Christ to absent himself much from our nation. "Return, O Lord, and visit thy churches, and revive thine own work in the midst of us."

From such blessed instances of the success of the gospel, as appear in this narrative, we may learn much of the way of the Spirit of God in his dealing with the souls of men, in order to convince sinners, and restore them to his favour and his image by Jesus Christ, his Son. We acknowledge that some particular appearances in the work of conversion among men may be occasioned by the ministry which they sit under, whether it be of a more or less evangelical strain, whether it be more severe and affrighting, or more gentle and persuasive. But wheresoever God works with power for salvation upon the minds of men, there will be some discoveries of a sense of sin, of the danger of the wrath of God, and the all-sufficiency of his Son Jesus, to relieve us under all our spiritual wants and distresses, and a hearty consent of soul to receive him in the various offices of grace, wherein he is set forth in the Holy Scriptures. And if our readers had opportunity (as we have had) to peruse several of the sermons which were preached during this glorious season, we should find that it is the common plain protestant doctrine of the Reformation, without stretching towards the antinomians on the one side, or the Arminians on the other, that the Spirit of God has been pleased to honour with such illustrious success.

We are taught also by this happy event, how easy it will be for our blessed Lord to make a full accomplishment of all his predictions concerning his kingdom, and to spread his dominion from sea to sea, through all the nations of the earth. We see how easy it is for him with one turn of his hand, with one word of his mouth, to awaken whole countries of stupid and sleeping sinners, and kindle divine life in their souls. The heavenly influence shall run from door to door, filling the hearts and lips of every inhabitant with importunate inquiries, *What shall we do to be saved?* And *how shall we escape the wrath to come?* And the name of Christ the Saviour shall diffuse itself like a rich and vital perfume to multitudes that were ready to sink and perish under the painful sense of their own guilt and danger. Salvation shall spread through all the tribes and ranks of mankind, as the lightning from heaven in a few moments would communicate a living flame through ten thousand lamps and torches placed in a proper situation and neighbourhood. Thus *a nation shall be born in a day* when our Redeemer please, and his faithful and obedient subjects shall become as numerous as the spires of grass in a meadow newly mown, and refreshed with the showers of heaven. But the pleasure of this agreeable hint bears the mind away from our theme.

Let us return to the present narrative: It is worthy of our observation, that this great and surprising work does not seem to have taken its rise from any sudden and distressing calamity of public terror that might universally impress the minds of a people: here was no storm, no earthquake, no inundation of water, no desolation by fire, no pestilence or any other sweeping distemper, nor any cruel invasion by their Indian neighbours, that might force the inhabitants into a serious thoughtfulness, and a religious temper, by the fears of approaching death and judgment. Such scenes as these have sometimes been made happily effectual to awaken sinners in Zion, and the formal professor and the hypocrite have been terrified with the thoughts of divine wrath breaking in upon them, *Who shall dwell with everlasting burnings?* But in the present case the immediate hand of God in the work of his Spirit appears much more evident, because there is no such awful and threatening Providence attending it.

It is worthy also of our further notice, that when many profane sinners, and formal professors of religion, have been affrighted out of their present carelessness and stupidity by some astonishing terrors approaching them, those religious appearances have not been so durable, nor the real change of heart so thoroughly effected; many of this sort of sudden converts have dropped their religious concerns in a great measure when their fears of the threatening calamity were vanished. But it is a blessed confirmation of the truth of this present work of grace, that the persons who were divinely wrought upon in this season continue still to profess serious religion, and to practise it without returning to their former follies.

It may not be amiss in this place to take notice, that a very surprising and threatening Providence has this last year attended the people of Northampton, among whom this work of divine grace was so remarkable: which Providence at first might have been construed by the unthinking world to be a signal token of God's displeasure against that town, or a judgment from heaven upon the people; but soon afterwards, like Paul's shaking the viper off from his hand, it discovered the astonishing care and goodness of God expressed towards a place where such a multitude of young converts were assembled: nor can we give a better account of it than in the language of this very gentleman, the Rev. Mr. Edwards, minister of that town, who wrote the following Letter, which was published in New England.

Northampton, March 19, 1737.

"We in this town, were the last Lord's Day the spectators, and many of us the subjects, of one of the most amazing instances of divine preservation, that perhaps was ever known in the land. Our meeting-house is old and decayed, so that we have been for some time building a new one, which is yet unfinished. It has been observed of late, that the house we have hitherto met in, has gradually spread at bottom; the cells and walls giving way, especially in the foreside, by reason of the weight of timber at top, pressing on the braces that are inserted into the posts and beams of the house. It has done so more than ordinarily this spring; which seems to have been occasioned by the heaving of the ground through the extreme frosts of the winter past, and its now settling again on that side which is next the sun, by the spring thaws. By this means, the under-pinning has been considerably disordered; which people were not sensible of till the ends of the joists which bore up the front gallery, were drawn off from the girts on which they rested by the walls giving way. So that in the midst of the public exercise in the forenoon, soon after the beginning of sermon, the whole gallery—full of people, with all the seats and timber, suddenly and without any warning—sunk, and fell down with the most amazing noise upon the heads of those that sat under, to the astonishment of the congregation. The house was filled with dolorous shrieking and crying; and nothing else was expected than to find many people dead, and dashed to pieces.

"The gallery in falling seemed to break and sink first in the middle; so that those who were upon it were thrown together in heaps before the front door. But the whole was so sudden, that many of them who fell, knew nothing at the time what it was that had befallen them. Others in the congregation thought it had been an amazing clap of thunder. The falling gallery seemed to be broken all to pieces before it got down; so that some who fell with it, as well as those who were under, were buried in the ruins; and were found pressed under heavy loads of timber, and could do nothing to help themselves.

"But so mysteriously and wonderfully did it come to pass, that every life was preserved; and though many were greatly bruised, and their flesh torn, yet there is not, as I can understand, one bone broken or so much as put out of joint, among them all. Some who were thought to be almost dead at first, were greatly recovered; and but one young woman seems yet to remain in dangerous circumstances, by an inward hurt in her breast: but of late there appears more hope of her recovery.

"None can give account, or conceive, by what means people's lives and limbs should be thus preserved, when so great a multitude were thus imminently exposed. It looked as though it was impossible but that great numbers must instantly be crushed to death, or dashed in pieces. It seems unreasonable to ascribe it to any thing else but the care of Providence, in disposing the motions of every piece of timber, and the precise place of safety where every one should sit, and fall, when none were in any capacity to care for their own preservation. The preservation seems to be most wonderful, with respect to the women and children in the middle ally, under the gallery, where it came down first, and with greatest force, and where there was nothing to break the force of the falling weight.

"Such an event may be a sufficient argument of a divine Providence over the lives of men. We thought ourselves called to set apart a day to be spent in the solemn worship of God, to humble ourselves under such a rebuke of God upon us in time of public service in his house by so dangerous and surprising an accident; and to praise his name for so wonderful, and as it were miraculous, a preservation. The last Wednesday was kept by us to that end; and a mercy in which the hand of God is so remarkably evident, may be well worthy to affect the hearts of all who hear it."

Thus far the letter.

But it is time to conclude our Preface. If there should be any thing found in this narrative of the surprising conversion of such numbers of souls, where the sentiments or the style of the relater, or his inferences from matters of fact, do not appear so agreeable to every reader, we hope it will have no unhappy influence to discourage the belief of this glorious event. We must allow every writer his own way; and must allow him to choose what particular instances he would select from the numerous cases which came before him. And though he might have chosen others perhaps, of more significancy in the eye of the world, than the *woman* and the *child*, whose experiences he relates at large; yet it is evident he chose that of the woman, because she was dead, and she is thereby incapable of knowing any honours or reproaches on this account. And as for the child, those who were present, and saw and heard such a remarkable and lasting change, on one so very young, must necessarily receive a stronger impression from it, and a more agreeable surprise, than the mere narration of it can communicate to others at a distance. Children's language always loses its striking beauties at second-hand.

Upon the whole, whatever defects any reader may find or imagine in this narrative, we are well satisfied, that such an eminent work of God ought not to be concealed from the world: and as it was the reverend author's opinion, so we declare it to be ours also, that it is very likely that this account of such an extraordinary and illustrious appearance of divine grace in the conversion of sinners, may, by the blessing of God, have a happy effect upon the minds of men, towards the honour and enlargement of the kingdom of Christ, much more than any supposed imperfection in this representation of it can do injury.

May the worthy writer of this epistle, and all those his reverend brethren in the ministry, who have been honoured in this excellent and important service, go on to see their labours crowned with daily and persevering success! May the numerous subjects of this surprising work hold fast what they have received, and increase in every christian grace and blessing! May a plentiful effusion of the blessed Spirit, also, descend on the British isles, and all their American plantations, to renew the face of religion there! And we entreat our readers in both Englands, to join with us in our hearty addresses to the throne of grace, that this wonderful discovery of the hand of God in saving sinners, may encourage our faith and hope of the accomplishment of all his words of grace, which are written in the Old Testament and in the New, concerning the large extent of this salvation in the latter days of the world. *Come, Lord Jesus, come quickly*, and spread thy dominion through all the ends of the earth. *Amen.*

ISAAC WATTS.
JOHN GUYSE.

London,
Oct. 12, 1737.

A FAITHFUL NARRATIVE,

&c. &c.

REV. AND HONOURED SIR,

HAVING seen your *letter* to my honoured uncle Williams of Hatfield, of July 20, wherein you inform him of the *notice* that has been taken of the late *wonderful work of God*, in this and some other towns in this country, by the Rev. Dr. Watts, and Dr. Guyse, of London, and the congregation to which the last of these preached on a monthly day of solemn prayer; as also, of your desire to be more perfectly acquainted with it, by some of us on the spot: and having been since informed by my uncle Williams that you desire me to undertake it; I would now do it, in as *just and faithful a manner* as in me lies.

SECT. I.

A general introductory statement.

THE people of the country, in general, I suppose, are as sober, orderly, and good sort of people, as in any part of New England; and I believe they have been preserved the freest by far of any part of the country, from *error*, and variety of *sects* and opinions. Our being so far *within* the land, at a distance from sea-ports, and in a corner of the country, has doubtless been *one reason* why we have not been so much corrupted with *vice*, as most other parts. But without question, the *religion* and good order of the county, and purity in *doctrine*, has, under God, been very much owing to the great abilities, and eminent piety, of my venerable and honoured grandfather Stoddard. I suppose we have been the freest of any part of the land from unhappy *divisions* and *quarrels* in our ecclesiastical and religious affairs, till the late lamentable *Springfield contention*.*

Being much separated from other parts of the province, and having comparatively but little intercourse with them, we have always managed our ecclesiastical affairs within ourselves. It is the way in which the country, from its infancy, has gone on, by the practical agreement of all; and the way in which our peace and good order has hitherto been maintained.

The town of Northampton is of about 82 years standing, and has now about 200 families; which mostly dwell

* The *Springfield* Contention relates to the settlement of a minister there, which occasioned too warm debates between some, both pastors and people, that were for it, and others that were against it, on account of their different apprehensions about his principles, and about some steps that were taken to procure his ordination.

more *compactly* together than any town of such a size in these parts of the country. This probably has been an occasion, that both our *corruptions* and *reformations* have been, from time to time, the more *swiftly* propagated from one to another through the town. Take the town in general, and so far as I can judge, they are as *rational* and *intelligent* a people as most I have been acquainted with. Many of them have been *noted* for religion; and particularly remarkable for their distinct *knowledge* in things that relate to *heart* religion, and christian *experience*, and their great *regards* thereto.

I am the *third minister* who has been settled in the town. The Rev. Mr. Eleazer Mather, who was the *first*, was ordained in July, 1669. He was one whose heart was *much* in his work, and abundant in *labours* for the good of precious souls. He had the high esteem and great love of his people, and was blessed with no small *success*. The Rev. Mr. Stoddard who succeeded him, came first to the town the November after his death; but was not ordained till September 11, 1672, and died February 11, 1728-9. So that he continued in the work of the ministry here, from his first coming to town, near 60 years. And as he was eminent and *renowned* for his gifts and grace; so he was blessed, from the beginning, with *extraordinary success* in his ministry, in the conversion of many souls. He had *five harvests*, as he called them. The *first* was about 57 years ago; the *second* about 53; the *third* about 40; the *fourth* about 24; the *fifth* and last about 18 years ago. *Some* of these times were much more remarkable than others, and the ingathering of souls more plentiful. Those about 53, and 40, and 24 years ago, were much greater than either the *first* or the *last*: but in *each* of them, I have heard my grandfather say, the greater part of the *young* people in the town, seemed to be mainly concerned for their eternal salvation.

After the *last* of these, came a far more degenerate time, (at least among the young people,) I suppose, than ever before. Mr. Stoddard, indeed, had the comfort, before he died, of seeing a time where there were no small appearances of a divine work among some, and a considerable *ingathering* of souls, even after I was settled with him in the *ministry*, which was about *two* years before his death; and I have reason to *bless God* for the great advantage I had by it. In these *two* years there were nearly *twenty* that Mr. Stoddard hoped to be savingly converted; but there was nothing of any general awakening. The greater part seemed to be at that time very insensible of the things of religion, and engaged in other cares and pursuits. Just after my grandfather's death, it seemed to be a time of extraordinary dulness in religion. *Licentiousness* for some years greatly prevailed among the *youth* of the town; they were many of them very much addicted to *night-walking*, and frequenting the *tavern*, and *lewd* practices, wherein some, by their example, exceedingly corrupted others. It was their manner very frequently to get together, in conventions of both *sexes* for mirth and jollity, which they called *frolics*; and they would often spend the greater part of the *night* in them, without regard to any *order* in the families they belonged to: and indeed *family government* did too much fail in the town. It was become very customary with many of our young people to be *indecent* in their carriage at *meeting*, which doubtless would not have prevailed in such a degree, had it not been that my *grandfather*, through his *great age*, (though he retained his *powers* surprisingly to the *last*,) was not so able to *observe* them. There had also long prevailed in the town a spirit of contention between *two parties*, into which they had for many years been *divided*; by which they maintained a *jealousy* one of the other, and were prepared to *oppose* one another in all public affairs.

But in *two* or *three* years after Mr. Stoddard's death, there began to be a sensible amendment of these evils. The *young people* showed more of a disposition to hearken to counsel, and by degrees left off their *frolics*; they grew observably more *decent* in their attendance on the public worship, and there were more who manifested a *religious concern* than there used to be.

At the latter end of the year 1733, there appeared a very unusual flexibleness, and yielding to advice, in our young people. It had been too long their manner to make the *evening after the sabbath*,* and after our public *lecture*, to be especially the times of their *mirth*, and company-keeping. But a *sermon* was now preached on the sabbath before the *lecture*, to show the *evil tendency* of the practice, and to persuade them to reform it; and it was urged on *heads* of *families* that it should be a thing *agreed* upon among them, to govern their families, and keep their children at home, at these times. It was also more *privately* moved, that they should meet together the next day, in their several neighbourhoods, to know each other's minds; which was accordingly done, and the *motion* complied with throughout the town. But *parents* found little or no occasion for the exercise of government in the case. The *young people* declared themselves *convinced* by what they had heard from the *pulpit*, and were willing of themselves to comply with the counsel that had been given: and it was *immediately*, and, I suppose, almost *universally*, complied with; and there was a thorough *reformation* of these disorders thenceforward, which has continued ever since.

Presently after this, there began to appear a *remarkable religious concern* at a little village belonging to the congregation called Pascommuck, where a few families were settled, at about three miles distance from the main body of the town. At this place, a number of persons seemed to be savingly wrought upon. In the April following, *anno* 1734, there happened a very *sudden and awful death of a young man* in the bloom of his youth; who being violently seized with a *pleurisy*, and taken immediately very *delirious*, died in about *two days*; which (together with what was preached publicly on that occasion) *much affected* many young people. This was followed with another death of a young married woman, who had been considerably *exercised* in mind, about the salvation of her *soul*, before she was ill, and was in great *distress* in the beginning of her illness; but seemed to have *satisfying evidences* of God's saving *mercy* to her, before her death; so that she died very full of *comfort*, in a most earnest and moving manner *warning*, and counselling others. This seemed to *contribute* to render solemn the spirits of many young persons; and there began evidently to appear more of a *religious concern* on people's minds.

In the fall of the year I proposed it to the *young people*, that they should agree among themselves to spend the *evenings after lectures* in *social* religion, and to that end divide themselves into several companies to meet in various parts of the town; which was accordingly done, and those *meetings* have been since continued, and the *example* imitated by *elder* people. This was followed with the death of an *elderly* person, which was attended with many *unusual* circumstances, by which many were much moved and affected.

About this time began the great *noise*, in this part of the country, about *Arminianism*, which seemed to appear with a very *threatening* aspect upon the interest of religion here. The friends of vital piety trembled for fear of the issue; but it seemed, contrary to their fear, strongly to be *overruled* for the promoting of religion. Many who looked on themselves as in a *Christless* condition, seemed to be awakened by it, with fear that God was about to withdraw from the land, and that we should be given up to *heterodoxy* and corrupt principles; and that then their *opportunity* for obtaining salvation would be past. Many who were brought a little to *doubt* about the *truth* of the *doctrines* they had hitherto been taught, seemed to have a kind of trembling *fear* with their doubts, lest they should be led into *by-paths*, to their eternal undoing; and they seemed, with much concern and engagedness of mind, to inquire what was indeed the way in which they must come to be accepted with God. There were some things said *publicly* on that occasion, concerning *justification by faith alone*.

Although great *fault* was found with *meddling* with the *controversy* in the pulpit, by such a person, and at that time—and though it was ridiculed by many *elsewhere*—yet it proved a word spoken in season here; and was most

* It must be noted, that it has never been our manner, to observe the *evening* that *follows* the sabbath, but that which *precedes* it, as part of the holy time.

evidently attended with a very remarkable *blessing* of heaven to the souls of the people in this town. They received thence a general satisfaction, with respect to the main thing in question, which they had been in trembling doubts and concern about; and their minds were engaged the more earnestly to seek that they might come to be accepted of God, and saved in the way of the gospel, which had been made evident to them to be the true and only way. And *then* it was, in the latter part of *December, that the Spirit of God* began extraordinarily to set in, and *wonderfully* to work amongst us; and there were, very *suddenly*, one after another, five or six persons, who were to all appearance savingly converted, and some of them wrought upon in a very remarkable manner.

Particularly, I was surprised with the relation of a *young woman*, who had been one of the greatest company-keepers in the whole town. When she came to me, I had never heard that she was become in any wise serious, but by the conversation I then had with her, it appeared to me, that what she gave an account of, was a glorious work of God's infinite power and sovereign grace; and that God had given her a *new* heart, truly broken and sanctified. I could not then doubt of it, and have seen much in my acquaintance with her since to confirm it.

Though the work was *glorious*, yet I was filled with concern about the *effect* it might have upon others. I was ready to conclude, (though too rashly,) that some would be *hardened* by it, in carelessness and looseness of life; and would take occasion from it to open their mouths in *reproaches* of religion. But the *event* was the *reverse*, to a wonderful degree. God made it, I suppose, the *greatest occasion of awakening* to others, of any thing that ever came to pass in the town. I have had abundant opportunity to know the effect it had, by my private conversation with many. The news of it seemed to be almost like a *flash of lightning*, upon the hearts of young people, all over the town, and upon many others. Those persons amongst us, who used to be *farthest* from seriousness, and that I most feared would make an ill improvement of it, seemed greatly to be *awakened* with it. Many went to talk with her, concerning what she had met with; and what appeared in her seemed to be to the satisfaction of all that did so.

Presently upon this, a great and earnest concern about the great things of religion, and the eternal world, became *universal* in all parts of the town, and among persons of all degrees, and all ages. The noise amongst the *dry bones* waxed louder and louder; all other talk but about spiritual and eternal things, was soon thrown by; all the conversation, in all companies and upon all occasions, was upon these things only, unless so much as was necessary for people carrying on their ordinary secular business. Other discourse than of the things of religion, would scarcely be tolerated in any company. The minds of people were wonderfully taken off from the *world*, it was treated amongst us as a thing of very little consequence. They seemed to follow their worldly business, more as a part of their duty, than from any disposition they had to it; the *temptation* now seemed to lie on that hand, to *neglect* worldly affairs too much, and to spend too much time in the immediate exercise of religion. This was exceedingly misrepresented by reports that were spread in distant parts of the land, as though the people here had wholly thrown by all worldly business, and betook themselves entirely to reading and praying, and such like religious exercises.

But although people did not ordinarily neglect their worldly business; yet *religion* was with all sorts the great concern, and the *world* was a thing only by the bye. The only thing in their view was to get the kingdom of heaven, and every one appeared pressing into it. The engagedness of their hearts in this great concern could not *be hid*, it appeared in their very *countenances*. It then was a dreadful thing amongst us to lie out of Christ, in danger every day of dropping into hell; and what persons' minds were intent upon, was to *escape for their lives*, and to *fly from wrath to come.* All would eagerly lay hold of opportunities for their souls; and were wont very often to meet together in private houses, for religious purposes: and such meetings when appointed were greatly thronged.

There was scarcely a single person in the town, old or young, left unconcerned about the great things of the eternal world. Those who were wont to be the vainest and loosest, and those who had been most disposed to think and speak slightly of vital and experimental religion, were now generally subject to great awakenings. And the work of *conversion* was carried on in a most *astonishing* manner, and increased more and more; souls did as it were come by flocks to Jesus Christ. From day to day, for many months together, might be seen evident instances of sinners brought *out of darkness into marvellous light*, and delivered *out of an horrible pit, and from the miry clay, and set upon a rock*, with a *new song of praise to God in their mouths.*

This work of God, as it was carried on, and the number of true saints multiplied, soon made a glorious alteration in the town: so that in the spring and summer following, *anno* 1735, the town seemed to be full of the presence of God: it never was so full of *love*, nor of *joy*, and yet so full of distress, as it was then. There were remarkable tokens of God's presence in almost every house. It was a time of joy in *families* on account of salvation being brought unto them; *parents* rejoicing over their children as new born, and *husbands* over their wives, and *wives* over their husbands. *The goings of God* were then *seen in his sanctuary*, God's *day* was *a delight*, and his *tabernacles* were *amiable.* Our public assemblies were then beautiful: the congregation was *alive* in God's service, every one earnestly intent on the public worship, every *hearer* eager to drink in the words of the *minister* as they came from his mouth; the assembly in general were, from time to time, *in tears* while the word was preached; *some* weeping with sorrow and distress, *others* with joy and love, *others* with pity and concern for the souls of their neighbours.

Our public *praises* were then greatly enlivened; God was then served in our *psalmody*, in some measure, in the *beauty of holiness.* It has been observable, that there has been scarce *any part* of divine worship, wherein good men amongst us have had *grace so drawn forth*, and their hearts *so lifted up* in the ways of God, as *in singing* his praises. Our congregation excelled all that ever I knew in the *external* part of the duty before, the men generally carrying regularly, and well, *three parts of music*, and the *women* a part by themselves; but now they were evidently wont to sing with *unusual elevation* of heart and voice, which made the duty pleasant indeed.

In all *companies*, on *other* days, on whatever *occasions* persons met together, *Christ* was to be heard of, and seen in the midst of them. Our *young people*, when they met, were wont to spend the time in talking of the *excellency* and dying *love* of Jesus Christ, the glory of the way of *salvation*, the wonderful, free, and sovereign grace of God, his glorious work in the *conversion* of a soul, the *truth* and certainty of the great things of God's word, the sweetness of the views of his *perfections*, &c. And even at *weddings*, which formerly were mere occasions of mirth and jollity, there was now no discourse of any thing but religion, and no appearance of any but *spiritual mirth*. Those amongst us who had been *formerly converted*, were greatly enlivened, and renewed with fresh and extraordinary incomes of the Spirit of God; though some much more than others, *according to the measure of the gift of Christ.* Many who before had laboured under *difficulties* about their own state, had now their *doubts* removed by more satisfying experience, and more clear discoveries of God's love.

When this work first appeared, and was so extraordinarily carried on amongst *us* in the winter, *others* round about us seemed not to know what to make of it. Many scoffed at and ridiculed it; and some compared what we called conversion, to certain *distempers*. But it was very observable of many, who occasionally came amongst us from abroad with disregardful hearts, that what they saw here cured them of such a temper of mind. *Strangers* were generally surprised to find things so much *beyond* what they had heard, and were wont to tell others that the state of the town could not be conceived of by those who had not seen it. The notice that was taken of it by the people who came to town on occasion of the *court* that sat here in the beginning of March, was very observable. And those who came from the neighbourhood to our public *lectures*, were for the most part remarkably affected. Many who came to town, on one occasion or other, had their consciences smitten, and awakened; and went home with wounded hearts, and with those impressions that never wore off till they had hopefully a saving issue; and those who before had serious thoughts, had their awakenings and convictions greatly increased. There were many instances of persons who came from abroad on visits, or on business, who had not been long here before, to all appearance, they were savingly wrought upon; and partook of that shower of divine blessing which God rained down here, and went home rejoicing; till at length the *same work* began evidently to appear and prevail in several other towns in the *county*.

In the month of March, the people in *South-Hadley* begun to be seized with deep concern about the things of religion; which very soon became universal. The work of God has been very wonderful *there;* not much, if any thing, short of what it has been here, in proportion to the size of the place. About the same time, it began to break forth in the west part of *Suffield*, (where it also has been very great,) and it soon spread into all parts of the town. It next appeared at *Sunderland*, and soon overspread the town: and I believe was, for a season, not less remarkable than it was here. About the same time it began to appear in a part of *Deerfield*, called *Green River*, and afterwards filled the town, and there has been a *glorious* work there. It began also to be manifest, in the south part of *Hatfield*, in a place called the *Hill*, and the *whole town*, in the second week in April, seemed to be seized, as it were at once, with concern about the things of religion; and the work of God has been *great* there. There has been also a very general awakening at *West-Springfield*, and *Long Meadow;* and in *Enfield* there was for a time a pretty general concern amongst some who before had been very loose persons. About the same time that this appeared at *Enfield*, the Rev. Mr. Bull, of *Westfield*, informed me, that there had been a great alteration *there*, and that more had been done in *one week*, than in *seven years* before. Something of this work likewise appeared in the first precinct in *Springfield*, principally in the north and south extremes of the parish. And in *Hadley* old town, there gradually appeared so much of a work of God on souls, as at another time would have been thought worthy of much notice. For a *short* time there was also a very great and general concern, of the like nature, at *Northfield*. And wherever this concern appeared, it seemed not to be *in vain:* but in every place God brought saving blessings with him, and his *word* attended with his *Spirit* (as we have all reason to think) returned *not void*. It might well be said at that time, in all parts of the county, *who are these that fly as a cloud, and as doves to their windows?*

As what *other* towns heard of and found in this, was a great means of awakening *them;* so *our* hearing of such a swift and extraordinary propagation, and extent of this work, did doubtless for a time serve to uphold the work amongst us. The continual news kept alive the talk of religion, and did greatly quicken and rejoice the hearts of God's people, and much awakened those who looked on themselves as still *left behind*, and made them the more earnest that they also might *share* in the great blessings that others had obtained.

This remarkable *pouring out of the Spirit of God*, which thus extended from one end to the other of this county, was not confined to it, but many places in Connecticut have partaken in the same mercy. For instance, the first parish in Windsor, under the pastoral care of the Rev. Mr. Marsh, was thus blest about the same time as we in Northampton, while we had *no knowledge* of each other's circumstances. There has been a very great ingathering of souls to *Christ* in that place, and something considerable of the same work begun afterwards in East Windsor, my honoured father's parish, which has *in times past* been a place favoured with mercies of this nature, *above any* on this western side of New England, excepting Northampton; there having been *four* or *five* seasons of the *pouring out of the Spirit* to the *general* awakening of the people there, since my father's settlement amongst them.

There was also the *last* spring and summer a wonderful work of God carried on at *Coventry*, under the ministry of the Rev. Mr. Meacham. I had opportunity to converse with some Coventry people, who gave me a very remarkable account of the surprising *change* that appeared in the most rude and vicious persons there. The like was also very great at the same time in a part of Lebanon, called the *Crank*, where the Rev. Mr. Wheelock, a young gentleman, is lately settled: and there has been much of the same at Durham, under the ministry of the Rev. Mr. Chauncey; and to appearance no small ingathering of souls there. Likewise amongst many of the young people in the first precinct in *Stratford*, under the ministry of the Rev. Mr. Gould; where the work was much promoted by the remarkable conversion of a young woman who had been a great company-keeper, as it was here.

Something of this work appeared in several other *towns* in those parts, as I was informed when I was there, the last *fall*. And we have since been acquainted with something very remarkable of this nature at another parish in Stratford, called *Ripton*, under the pastoral care of the Rev. Mr. Mills. There was a considerable revival of religion last summer at *Newhaven* old town, as I was once and again informed by the Rev. Mr. Noyes, the minister there, and by others: and by a letter which I very lately received from Mr. Noyes, and also by information we have had other ways. This flourishing of religion still continues, and has lately much increased. Mr. Noyes writes, that *many this summer have been added to the church*, and particularly mentions several young persons that belong to the principal families of that town.

There has been a degree of the same work at a part of *Guildford;* and very considerable at *Mansfield*, under the ministry of the Rev. Mr. Eleazar Williams; and an unusual religious concern at *Tolland;* and something of it at *Hebron*, and *Bolton*. There was also no small effusion of the Spirit of God in the north parish in *Preston*, in the eastern part of Connecticut, of which I was informed, and saw something, when I was the last autumn at the house, and in the congregation of the Rev. Mr. Lord, the minister there; who, with the Rev. Mr. Owen, of Groton, came up hither in May, the last year, on purpose to see the work of God. Having heard various and contradictory accounts of it, they were careful when here to satisfy themselves; and to that end particularly conversed with many of our people; which they declared to be entirely to their satisfaction; and that the *one half had not been told them*, nor could be told them. Mr. Lord told me that, when he got home, he informed his congregation of what he had seen, and that they were greatly affected with it; and that it proved the beginning of the same work amongst them, which prevailed till there was a *general* awakening, and many instances of persons, who seemed to be remarkably converted. I also have lately heard that there has been something of the work at *Woodbury*.

But this shower of divine blessing has been yet more *extensive:* there was no small degree of it in some part of the *Jerseys;* as I was informed when I was at New York, (in a long journey I took at that time of the year for my health,) by some people of the Jerseys, whom I saw. Especially the Rev. William Tennent, a minister who seemed to have such things much at heart, told me of a very great awakening of many in a place called the *Mountains*, under the ministry of one Mr. Cross; and of a very considerable revival of religion in another place under the ministry of his brother the Rev. Gilbert Tennent; and also at another place, under the ministry of a very pious young gentleman, a Dutch minister, whose name as I remember was Freelinghousa.

This seems to have been a very *extraordinary* dispensation of providence; God has in many respects gone out of, and much beyond, his usual and *ordinary way*. The work in this town, and some others about us, has been extraordinary on account of the *universality* of it, affecting all sorts, sober and vicious, high and low, rich and poor, wise and unwise. It reached the most considerable families and persons, to all appearance, as much as others. In former stirrings of this nature, the bulk of the *young* people have been greatly affected; but *old men* and *little children* have been so now. Many of the *last* have, of their own accord, formed themselves into *religious societies*, in different parts of the town. A loose careless person could scarcely be found in the whole neighbourhood; and if there was *any one* that seemed to remain senseless or unconcerned, it would be spoken of as a *strange* thing.

This dispensation has also appeared very extraordinary in the *numbers* of those on whom we have reason to hope it has had a saving effect. We have about *six hundred and twenty communicants*, which include almost all our adult persons. The church was very *large* before; but persons never *thronged* into it, as they did in the late extraordinary time.—Our *sacraments* are eight weeks asunder, and I received into our communion about a *hundred* before one sacrament, *fourscore* of them at one time, whose appearance, when they presented themselves together to make an open explicit *profession* of Christianity, was very affecting to the congregation. I took in near *sixty* before the next sacrament day: and I had very sufficient evidence of the conversion of their souls, through divine grace, though it is not the custom here, as it is in many other churches in this country, to make a credible relation of their inward experiences the ground of admission to the Lord's supper.

I am far from pretending to be able to determine how many have lately been the subjects of such mercy; but if I may be allowed to declare any thing that appears to me probable in a thing of this nature, I hope that more than 300 souls were savingly brought home to Christ, in this town, in the space of half a year, and about the same number of males as females. By what I have heard Mr. Stoddard say, this was far from what has been usual in years past; for he observed that in his time, many more women were converted than men. Those of our young people who are on other accounts most considerable, are mostly, as I hope, truly pious, and leading persons in the ways of religion. Those who were formerly loose young persons, are generally, to all appearance, become true lovers of God and Christ, and spiritual in their dispositions. I hope that by far the greater part of persons in this town, above sixteen years of age, are such as have the saving knowledge of Jesus Christ. By what I have heard I suppose it is so in some other places; particularly at *Sunderland* and *South Hadley*.

This has also appeared to be a very extraordinary dispensation, in that the Spirit of God has so much extended not only his *awakening*, but *regenerating* influences, both to *elderly* persons, and also to those who are *very young*. It has been heretofore rarely heard of, that *any* were converted past middle age; but now we have the same ground to think, that *many such* have at this time been savingly changed, as that *others* have been so in more early years. I suppose there were upwards of *fifty* persons converted in this town above forty years of age; more than *twenty* of them above fifty; about *ten* of them above sixty; and *two* of them above seventy years of age.

It has heretofore been looked on as a strange thing, when any have seemed to be savingly wrought upon and remarkably changed in their *childhood*. But now, I suppose, near *thirty* were, to appearance, savingly wrought upon, between ten and fourteen years of age; *two* between nine and ten, and *one* of about four years of age; and because I suppose this last will be with most difficulty believed, I will hereafter give a particular account of it. The influences of God's Holy Spirit have also been very remarkable on children in some *other* places; particularly at *Sunderland, South Hadley*, and the west part of *Suffield*. There are several *families* in this town who are *all* hopefully pious. Yea, there are several numerous families, in which, I think, we have reason to hope that all the children are truly godly, and most of them lately become so. There are very few *houses* in the whole town, into which salvation has not lately come, in one or more instances. There are several *negroes*, who from what was seen in them then, and what is discernible in them since, appear to have been truly born again in the late remarkable season.

God has also seemed to have gone out of his usual way, in the *quickness* of his work, and the swift progress his Spirit has made in his operations on the hearts of many. It is wonderful that persons should be so *suddenly*, and yet so *greatly* changed. Many have been taken from a loose and careless way of living, and seized with strong convictions of their guilt and misery, and in a very little time old things have passed away, and all things have become new with them.

God's work has also appeared very extraordinary in the *degrees* of his influences; in the degrees both of *awakening* and conviction, and also of *saving light, love*, and *joy*, that many have experienced. It has also been very extraordinary in the *extent* of it, and its being so swiftly propagated from town to town. In former times of the pouring out of the Spirit of God on this town, though in some of them it was very remarkable, it reached no further then, the neighbouring towns all around continued unmoved.

This work seemed to be at its greatest height in this town, in the former part of the spring, in March and April. At that time, God's work in the conversion of souls was carried on amongst us in so wonderful a manner, that, so far as I can judge, it appears to have been at the rate, at least, of four persons in a day; or near thirty in a week, take one with another, for five or six weeks together. When God in so remarkable a manner took the work into his own hands, there was as much done in a *day or two* as at ordinary times, with all endeavours that men can use, and with such a blessing as we commonly have, is done in a *year*.

I am very sensible, how apt many would be, if they should see the account I have here given, presently to think with themselves that I am very fond of making a great many converts, and of magnifying the matter; and to think that, for want of judgment, I take every religious pang, and enthusiastic conceit, for saving conversion. I do not much wonder, if they should be apt to think so; and, for this reason, I have forborne to publish an account of this great work of God, though I have often been solicited. But having now a special call to give an account of it, upon mature consideration I thought it might not be beside my duty to declare this amazing work, as it appeared to me to be indeed divine, and to conceal no part of the glory of it; leaving it with God to take care of the credit of his own work, and running the venture of any censorious thoughts, which might be entertained of me to my disadvantage. That *distant* persons may be under as great advantage as may be to judge for themselves of this matter, I would be a little more large and particular.

SECT. II.

The manner of conversion various, yet bearing a great analogy.

I THEREFORE proceed to give an account of the *manner* of persons being wrought upon; and here there is a *vast variety*, perhaps as manifold as the subjects of the operation; but yet in many things there is a *great analogy* in all.—Persons are first awakened with a sense of their miserable condition by nature, the danger they are in of perishing eternally, and that it is of great importance to them that they speedily escape and get into a better state. Those who before were secure and senseless, are made sensible how much they were in the way to ruin, in their former courses. *Some* are more *suddenly* seized with convictions—it may be, by the news of others' conversion, or something they hear in public, or in private conference—their consciences are smitten, as if their hearts were pierced through with a dart. *Others* are awakened more *gradually*, they begin at first to be something more thoughtful and considerate, so as to come to a conclusion in their minds, that it is their best and wisest way to delay no longer, but to improve the present opportunity. They have accordingly set themselves seriously to meditate on those things that have the most awakening tendency, on purpose to obtain *convictions*; and so their awakenings have *increased*, till a sense of their misery, by God's Holy Spirit setting in therewith, has had fast hold of them. *Others* who before had been somewhat religious, and concerned for their salvation, have been awakened in a new manner; and made sensible that their slack and dull way of seeking, was never like to attain that purpose.

These awakenings when they have first seized on persons, have had two effects; *one* was, that they have brought them immediately to quit their sinful practices; and the looser sort have been brought to forsake and dread their former vices and extravagancies. When once the Spirit of God began to be so wonderfully poured out in a general way through the town, people had soon done with their old quarrels, backbitings, and intermeddling with other men's matters. The tavern was soon left empty, and persons kept very much at home; none went abroad unless on necessary business, or on some religious account, and every day seemed in many respects like a Sabbath-day. The *other* effect was, that it put them on earnest application to the means of salvation, reading, prayer, meditation, the ordinances of God's house, and private conference; their cry was, *What shall we do to be saved?* The place of resort was now altered, it was no longer the tavern, but the minister's house that was thronged far more than ever the tavern had been wont to be.

There is a very great *variety*, as to the *degree* of fear and trouble that persons are exercised with, before they attain any comfortable evidences of pardon and acceptance with God. Some are from the beginning carried on with abundantly more encouragement and hope than others. Some have had *ten* times less trouble of mind than others, in whom yet the issue seems to be the same. Some have had such a sense of the displeasure of God, and the great danger they were in of damnation, that they could not sleep at nights; and many have said that when they have laid down, the thoughts of sleeping in such a condition have been frightful to them; they have scarcely been free from terror while asleep, and they have awakened with fear, heaviness, and distress, still abiding on their spirits. It has been very common, that the deep and fixed concern on persons' minds, has had a painful influence on their bodies, and given disturbance to animal nature.

The awful apprehensions persons have had of their misery, have for the most part been *increasing*, the nearer they have approached to deliverance; though they often pass through many changes and alterations in the frame and circumstances of their minds. Sometimes they think themselves wholly senseless, and fear that the Spirit of God has left them, and that they are given up to judicial hardness; yet they appear very deeply exercised about that fear, and are in great earnest to obtain *convictions* again.

Together with those fears, and that exercise of mind which is rational, and which they have just ground for, they have often suffered many needless distresses of thought, in which *Satan* probably has a great hand, to entangle them, and block up their way. Sometimes the distemper of melancholy has been evidently mixed; of which, when it happens, the tempter seems to take great advantage, and puts an unhappy bar in the way of any good effect. One knows not how to deal with such persons; they turn every thing that is said to them the wrong way, and most to their own disadvantage. There is nothing that the devil seems to make so great a handle of, as a melancholy humour; unless it be the real corruption of the heart.

But it is very remarkable, that there has been far less of this mixture at this time of extraordinary blessing, than there was wont to be in persons under awakenings at other times; for it is evident that many who before had been exceedingly involved in such difficulties, seemed now strangely to be set at liberty. Some persons who had before, for a long time, been exceedingly entangled with peculiar temptations of one sort or other, unprofitable and hurtful distresses, were soon helped over former stumbling-blocks, that hindered their progress towards saving good; convictions have wrought more kindly, and they have been successfully carried on in the way to life. And thus *Satan* seemed to be restrained, till towards the latter end of this wonderful time, when God's Holy Spirit was about to withdraw.

Many times persons under great awakenings were concerned, because they thought they were *not* awakened, but miserable, hard-hearted, senseless, sottish creatures still, and sleeping upon the brink of hell. The sense of the *need* they have to be awakened, and of their comparative hardness, grows upon them with their awakenings; so that they seem to themselves to be very *senseless*, when indeed most *sensible*. There have been some instances of persons who have had as great a sense of their danger and misery, as their natures could well subsist under, so that a little more would probably have destroyed them; and yet they have expressed themselves much amazed at their own *insensibility* and sottishness, at such an extraordinary time.

Persons are sometimes brought to the borders of despair, and it looks as black as midnight to them a little before the day dawns in their souls. Some few instances there have been, of persons who have had such a sense of God's wrath for sin, that they have been overborne; and made to *cry out* under an astonishing sense of their guilt, wondering that God suffers such guilty wretches to live upon earth, and that he doth not immediately send them to hell. Sometimes their guilt doth so stare them in the face, that they are in exceeding terror for fear that God will instantly do it; but more commonly their distresses under legal awakenings have not been to such a degree. In some, these terrors do not seem to be so sharp, when near comfort, as before; their convictions have not seemed to work so much that way, but to be led further down into their own hearts, to a further sense of their own universal depravity and deadness in sin.

The corruption of the heart has discovered itself in various exercises, in the time of legal convictions; sometimes it appears in a great struggle, like something roused by an enemy, and Satan the old inhabitant seems to exert himself, like a serpent disturbed and enraged. Many in such circumstances, have felt a great spirit of envy towards the godly, especially towards those who are thought to have been lately converted, and most of all towards acquaintance and companions, *when they* are thought to be converted. Indeed, some have felt many heart-risings against God, and murmurings at his way of dealing with mankind, and his dealings with themselves in particular. It has been much insisted on, both in public and private, that persons should have the utmost dread of such envious thoughts; which if allowed tend exceedingly to quench the Spirit of God, if not to provoke him finally to forsake them. And when such a spirit has much prevailed, and persons have not so earnestly strove against it as they ought to have done, it has seemed to be exceedingly to the hinderance of the good of their souls. But in some other instances, where persons have been much terrified at the sight of such wickedness in their hearts, God has brought good to them out of evil; and made it a means of convincing them of their own desperate sinfulness, and bringing them off from all self-confidence.

The drift of the Spirit of God in his *legal* strivings with persons, have seemed most evidently to be, to bring to a conviction of their *absolute dependence* on his sovereign power and grace, and an universal necessity of a mediator. This has been effected by leading them more and more to a sense of their exceeding wickedness and guiltiness in his sight; their pollution, and the insufficiency of their own righteousness; that they can in no wise help themselves, and that God would be wholly just and righteous in rejecting them and all that they do, and in casting them off for ever. There is however, a vast variety, as to the *manner* and distinctness of such convictions.

As they are gradually more and more convinced of the corruption and wickedness of their hearts; they seem to themselves to grow worse and worse, harder and blinder, and more desperately wicked, instead of growing better. They are ready to be discouraged by it, and oftentimes never think themselves so *far off* from good, as when they are *nearest*. Under the sense which the Spirit of God gives them of their sinfulness, they often think that they differ from all others; their hearts are ready to sink with the thought, that they are the worst of all, and that none ever obtained mercy who were so wicked as they.

When awakenings *first begin*, their consciences are commonly most exercised about their *outward* vicious course, or other acts of sin; but *afterwards*, are much more burdened with a sense of heart-sins, the dreadful corruption of their nature, their enmity against God, the pride of their hearts, their unbelief, their rejection of Christ, the stubbornness and obstinacy of their wills; and the like. In many, God makes much use of their own experience, in the course of their awakenings and endeavours after saving good, to convince them of their own vile emptiness and universal depravity.

Very often under first awakenings, when they are brought to reflect on the sin of their past lives, and have something of a terrifying sense of God's anger, they set themselves to walk more strictly, and confess their sins, and perform many religious duties, with a secret hope of appeasing God's anger, and making up for the sins they have committed. And oftentimes, at first setting out, their affections are so moved, that they are full of tears, in their confessions and prayers; which they are ready to make very much of, as though they were some atonement, and had power to move correspondent affections in God too. Hence they are for a while big with expectation of what God will do for them; and conceive they grow better apace, and shall soon be thoroughly converted. But these affections are but short-lived; they quickly find that they fail, and then they think themselves to be grown worse again. They do not find such a prospect of being soon converted, as they thought: instead of being *nearer*, they seem to be *farther* off; their hearts they think are grown harder, and by this means their fears of perishing greatly increase. But though they are disappointed, they renew their attempts again and again; and still as their attempts are multiplied, so are their disappointments. All fails, they see no token of having inclined God's heart to them, they do not see that he hears their prayers at all, as they expected he would; and sometimes there have been great temptations arising hence to leave off seeking, and to yield up the case. But as they are still more terrified with fears of perishing, and their former hopes of prevailing on God to be merciful to them in a great measure fail; sometimes their religious affections have turned into heart-risings against God, because he will not pity them, and seems to have little regard to their distress, and piteous cries, and to all the pains they take. They think of the mercy God has shown to *others;* how soon and how easily others have obtained comfort, and those too who were worse than they, and have not laboured so much as they have done; and sometimes they have had even dreadful blasphemous thoughts, in these circumstances.

But when they reflect on these wicked workings of heart against God—if their convictions are continued, and the Spirit of God is not provoked utterly to forsake them—they have more distressing apprehensions of the anger of God towards *those* whose hearts work after such a sinful manner about *him ;* and it may be, have great fears that they have committed the *unpardonable* sin, or that God will surely never show mercy to them who are such vipers; and are often tempted to leave off in despair. But then perhaps by something they read or hear of the infinite mercy of God, and all-sufficiency of Christ for the chief of sinners, they have some encouragement and hope renewed; but think that as yet they are not fit to come to Christ; they are so wicked that Christ will never accept of them. And then it may be they set themselves upon a new course of fruitless endeavours, in their own strength, to make themselves better; and still meet with new disappointments. They are earnest to inquire, what they shall do? They do not know but there is something else to be done, in order to their obtaining converting grace, that they have never done yet. It may be they hope, that they are something better than they were; but then the pleasing dream all vanishes again. If they are told, that they trust too much to their own strength and righteousness, they cannot unlearn this practice all at once, and find not yet the appearance of any good, but all looks as dark as midnight to them. Thus they wander about from mountain to hill, seeking rest, and finding none. When they are beat out of *one* refuge, they fly to *another ;* till they are as it were debilitated, broken, and subdued with legal humblings; in which God gives them a conviction of their own utter helplessness and insufficiency, and discovers the true remedy in a clearer knowledge of Christ and his gospel.

When they begin to seek salvation, they are commonly profoundly ignorant of themselves; they are not sensible how blind they are, and how little they can do *towards* bringing themselves to see spiritual things aright, and *towards* putting forth gracious exercises in their own souls. They are not sensible how remote they are from love to God, and other holy dispositions, and how dead they are in sin. When they see unexpected pollution in their own hearts, they go about to wash away their own defilements, and make themselves clean; and they weary themselves in vain, till God shows them that it is in vain, and that their help is not where they have sought it.

But some persons continue wandering in such a kind of labyrinth, ten times as long as others, before their own experience will convince them of their insufficiency; and so it appears not to be their own experience only, but the convincing influence of God's Holy Spirit with their experience, that attains the effect. God has of late abundantly shown, that he does not need to wait to have men convinced by long and often repeated fruitless trials; for in multitudes of instances he has made a shorter work of it. He has so awakened and convinced persons' consciences, and made them so sensible of their exceeding great vileness, and given them such a sense of his wrath against sin, as has quickly overcome all their vain self-confidence, and borne them down into the dust before a holy and righteous God.

There have been some who have not had great terrors, but have had a very quick work. Some of those who have not had so deep a conviction of these things *before* their conversion, have much more of it *afterwards.* God has appeared far from limiting himself to *any certain method* in his proceedings with sinners under legal convictions. In *some* instances, it seems easy for our reasoning powers to discern the methods of divine wisdom, in his dealings with the soul under awakenings; in *others,* his footsteps cannot be traced, and his ways are past finding out. Some who are *less distinctly* wrought upon, in what is preparatory to grace, appear *no less eminent* in gracious experiences afterwards.

There is in nothing a greater difference, in different persons, than with respect to the *time* of their being under trouble; some but a few days, and others for months or years. There were many in this town, who had been, before this effusion of the Spirit upon us, for years, and some for many years, concerned about their salvation. Though probably they were not thoroughly awakened, yet they were concerned to such a degree as to be very uneasy, so as to live an uncomfortable disquieted life. They continued in a way of taking considerable pains about their salvation; but had never obtained any comfortable evidence of a good state. Several such persons, in this extraordinary time, have received light; but many of them were some of the *last.* They first saw multitudes of others rejoicing, with songs of deliverance in their mouths, who before had seemed wholly careless and at ease, and in pursuit of vanity; while they had been bowed down with solicitude about their souls. Yea, some had lived licentiously, and so continued till a little before they were converted; and yet soon grew up to a holy rejoicing in the infinite blessings God had bestowed upon *them.*

Whatever minister has a like occasion to deal with souls, in a flock under such circumstances, as this was in the last year, I cannot but think he will soon find himself under a necessity, greatly to insist upon it with them, that God is under no manner of *obligation* to show mercy to any natural man, whose heart is not turned to God: and that a man can challenge nothing either in *absolute justice,* or by *free promise,* from any thing he does before he has believed on *Jesus Christ,* or has true repentance begun in him. It appears to me, that if I had taught those who came to me under trouble, any other doctrine, I should have taken a most direct course utterly to undo them. I should have directly crossed what was plainly the drift of the Spirit of God in his influences upon them; for if they had believed what I said, it would either have promoted *self-flattery* and *carelessness,* and so put an end to their awakenings; or cherished and established their contention and strife with God, concerning his dealings with them and others, and blocked up their way to that *humiliation* before the Sovereign Disposer of life and death, whereby God is wont to prepare them for his consolations. And yet those who have been under awakenings have oftentimes plainly stood in need of being encouraged, by being told of the infinite and all-sufficient mercy of God in Christ;

and that it is God's manner to succeed diligence, and to bless his own means, that so *awakenings and encouragements, fear and hope*, may be duly mixed, and proportioned to preserve their minds in a just medium between the two extremes of *self-flattery* and *despondence*, both which tend to slackness and negligence, and in the end to security. I think I have found that no discourses have been more *remarkably blessed*, than those in which the doctrine of God's *absolute sovereignty*, with regard to the salvation of sinners, and his *just liberty*, with regard to answering the prayers, or succeeding the pains, of natural men, continuing such, have been insisted on. I never found so much immediate saving fruit, in any measure, of any discourses I have offered to my congregation, as some from these words, Rom. iii. 19. "That every mouth may be stopped;" endeavouring to show from thence, that it would be just with God for ever to reject and cast off mere natural men.

As to those in whom awakenings seem to have a saving issue, commonly the first thing that appears after their legal troubles, is a conviction of the *justice of God* in their *condemnation*, appearing in a sense of their own exceeding sinfulness, and the vileness of all their performances. In giving an account of this, they expressed themselves very variously; some, that they saw God was *sovereign*, and might receive others and reject them; some, that they were convinced, God might justly bestow *mercy* on every person in the town, in the world, and damn themselves to all eternity; some, that they see God may justly have no regard to all the pains they have taken, and all the prayers they have made; some, that if they should seek, and take the utmost pains all their lives, God might justly cast them into hell at last, because all their labours, prayers, and tears cannot make an atonement for the least sin, nor merit any blessing at the hands of God. Some have declared themselves to be in the hands of God, that he may dispose of them just as he pleases; some, that God may glorify himself in their damnation, and they wonder that God has suffered them to live so long, and has not cast them into hell long ago.

Some are brought to this conviction by a great sense of their sinfulness, in general, that they are such vile wicked creatures in heart and life: *others* have the sins of their lives in an extraordinary manner set before them, multitudes of them coming just then fresh to their memory, and being set before them with their aggravations. Some have their minds especially fixed on some particular wicked practice they have indulged. Some are especially convinced by a sight of the corruption and wickedness of their hearts. Some, from a view they have of the horridness of some particular exercises of corruption, which they have had in the time of their awakening, whereby the enmity of the heart against God has been manifested. Some are convinced especially by a sense of the sin of *unbelief*, the opposition of their hearts to the way of salvation by Christ, and their obstinacy in rejecting him and his grace.

There is a great deal of difference as to *distinctness* here; some, who have not so clear a sight of God's justice in their condemnation, yet mention things that plainly imply it. They find a disposition to acknowledge God to be just and righteous in his threatenings; and that they are undeserving: and many times, though they had not so particular a sight of it at the beginning, they have very clear discoveries of it soon afterwards, with great humblings in the dust before God.

Commonly persons' minds immediately before this discovery of God's justice are exceedingly restless, in a kind of struggle and tumult, and sometimes in mere anguish; but generally, as soon as they have this conviction, it immediately brings their minds to a calm, an unexpected quietness and composure; and most frequently, though not always, *then* the pressing weight upon their spirits is taken away, and a general hope arises, that some time or other God will be gracious, even before any distinct and particular discoveries of mercy. Often they then come to a conclusion within themselves, that they will lie at God's feet, and wait his time; and they rest in that, not being sensible that the Spirit of God has now brought them to a frame whereby they are prepared for mercy. For it is remarkable, that persons when they first have this sense of the justice of God, rarely, at the time, think any thing of its being that *humiliation* they have often heard insisted on, and that others experience.

In many persons, the first conviction of the justice of God in their condemnation, which they *take particular notice of*, and probably the first distinct conviction of it that they *have*, is of such a nature, as seems to be *above* any thing merely legal. Though it be after legal humblings, and much of a sense of their own helplessness, and of the insufficiency of their own duties; yet it does not appear to be forced by mere legal terrors and convictions; but rather from a high exercise of grace, in saving repentance, and evangelical humiliation. For there is in it a sort of complacency of soul, in the *attribute* of God's justice, as displayed in his threatenings of eternal damnation to sinners. Sometimes at the discovery of it, they can scarcely forbear crying out, IT IS JUST! IT IS JUST! Some express themselves, that they see the glory of God would *shine bright* in their own condemnation; and they are ready to think that if they are damned, they could take part with God against themselves, and would glorify his justice therein. And when it is thus, they commonly have some evident sense of free and all-sufficient grace, though they give no *distinct* account of it; but it is manifest, by that great degree of hope and encouragement they then conceive, though they were never so sensible of their own vileness and ill-deservings as they are at that time.

Some, when in such circumstances, have felt that sense of the *excellency* of God's justice, appearing in the vindictive exercises of it, against such sinfulness as theirs was; and have had such a *submission* of mind in their *idea* of this attribute, and of those exercises of it—together with an exceeding loathing of their own unworthiness, and a kind of indignation against themselves—that they have sometimes almost called it a *willingness to be damned*; though it must be owned they had not clear and distinct ideas of damnation, nor does any word in the Bible require such self-denial as this. But the truth is, as some have more clearly expressed it, that salvation has appeared *too good for them, that they were worthy of nothing but condemnation*, and they could *not tell how to think of salvation being bestowed upon them*, fearing it was *inconsistent with the glory of God's majesty, that they had so much contemned and affronted*.

That calm of spirit that some persons have found after their legal distresses, continues some time before any special and delightful manifestation is made to the soul of the grace of God as revealed in the gospel. But very often some comfortable and sweet view of a merciful God, of a sufficient Redeemer, or of some great and joyful things of the gospel, immediately follows, or in a very little time: and in some, the first sight of their just desert of hell, and God's sovereignty with respect to their salvation, and a discovery of all-sufficient grace, are so near, that they seem to go as it were together.

These gracious discoveries given, whence the first special comforts are derived, are in many respects very various. More frequently, Christ is distinctly made the object of the mind, in his all-sufficiency and willingness to save sinners; but some have their thoughts more especially fixed on God, in some of his sweet and glorious attributes manifested in the gospel, and shining forth in the face of Christ. Some view the all-sufficiency of the mercy and grace of God; some, chiefly the infinite power of God, and his ability to save them, and to do all things for them; and some look most at the truth and faithfulness of God. In *some*, the truth and certainty of the gospel in general is the first joyful discovery they have; in *others*, the certain truth of some particular promises; in some, the grace and sincerity of God in his invitations, very commonly in some particular invitation in the mind, and it now appears real to them that God does indeed invite them. Some are struck with the glory and wonderfulness of the dying love of Christ; and some with the sufficiency and preciousness of his blood, as offered to make an atonement for sin; and others with the value and glory of his obedience and righteousness. In some the excellency and loveliness of Christ, chiefly engages their thoughts; in some his divinity, that he is indeed *the Son of the living God*; and in others, the excellency of the way of salvation by Christ, and the suitableness of it to their necessities.

Some have an apprehension of these things so given, that it seems more natural to them to express it by *sight* or *discovery ; others* think what they experience better expressed by the *realizing conviction*, or a *lively* or *feeling sense of heart ;* meaning, as I suppose, no other difference but what is merely circumstantial or gradual.

There is, often, in the mind, some *particular* text of Scripture, holding forth some evangelical ground of consolation ; sometimes a *multitude* of texts, gracious invitations and promises flowing in one after another, filling the soul more and more with comfort and satisfaction. Comfort is first given to some, while *reading* some portion of Scripture ; but in some it is attended with *no particular scripture* at all, either in *reading* or *meditation.* In *some, many divine things* seem to be discovered to the soul as it were at once ; *others* have their minds especially fixing on some *one thing* at first, and afterwards a sense is given of *others ;* in *some* with a swifter, and *others* a slower, succession, and sometimes with interruptions of much darkness.

The way that grace seems sometimes first to appear, after legal humiliation, is in earnest longings of soul after God and Christ : to know God, to love him, to be humble before him, to have communion with Christ in his benefits ; which longings, as they express them, seem evidently to be of such a nature as can arise from nothing but a sense of the superlative excellency of divine things, with a spiritual taste and relish of them, and an esteem of them as their highest happiness and best portion. Such longings as I speak of, are commonly attended with firm resolutions to pursue this good for ever, together with a hoping, waiting disposition. When persons have begun in such frames, commonly other experiences and discoveries have soon followed, which have yet more clearly manifested a change of heart.

It must needs be confessed that Christ is not *always distinctly* and *explicitly* thought of in the first sensible act of grace, (though most commonly he is,) but sometimes he is the object of the mind only *implicitly.* Thus sometimes when persons have seemed evidently to be stripped of all their own righteousness, and to have stood self-condemned as guilty of death, they have been comforted with a joyful and satisfying view, that the mercy and grace of God is sufficient for them—that their sins, though never so great, shall be no hinderance to their being accepted ; that there is mercy enough in God for the whole world, and the like—when they give no account of any particular or distinct thought of Christ. But yet, when the account they give is duly weighed, and they are a little interrogated about it, it appears that the revelation of mercy in the gospel, is the ground of their encouragement and hope ; and that it is indeed the mercy of God *through Christ* that is discovered to them, and that it is depended on *in him,* and not in any wise moved by any thing *in them.*

Sometimes disconsolate souls have been revived, and brought to rest in God, by a sweet sense of his grace and faithfulness, in some special invitation or promise ; in which nevertheless there is no particular mention of Christ, nor is it accompanied with any distinct thought of him in their minds : but yet, it is not received as *out of Christ,* but as one of the invitations or promises made of God to poor sinners *through* his Son *Jesus.* And such persons afterwards have had clear and distinct discoveries of *Christ,* accompanied with lively and special actings of faith and love towards him.

Frequently, when persons have first had the gospel-ground of relief discovered to them, and have been entertaining their minds with the sweet prospect, they have thought nothing at that time of their being *converted.* To see, that there is an all-sufficiency in God, and such plentiful provision made in Christ, after they have been borne down, and sunk with a sense of their guilt and fears of wrath, exceedingly refreshes them. The view is joyful to them ; as it is in its own nature glorious, gives them quite new and delightful *ideas* of God and Christ, greatly encourages them to seek conversion. This begets in them a strong resolution to devote themselves and their whole lives to God and his Son, and patiently to wait till God shall see fit to make all effectual ; and very often entertain a strong persuasion, that he will in his own time do it for them.

There is wrought in them a holy repose of soul in God through Christ, with a secret disposition to fear and love him, and to hope for blessings from him in this way. Yet, they have no imagination that they are now *converted,* it does not so much as come into their minds : and very often the reason is, that they do not see that they *accept* of this sufficiency of salvation they behold in Christ, having entertained a wrong notion of *acceptance ;* not being sensible that the obedient and joyful entertainment which their hearts give to this discovery of grace, is a real acceptance of it. They know not that the sweet complacence they feel in the mercy and complete salvation of God, as it includes pardon and sanctification, and is held forth to them only through Christ, is a true *receiving* of this mercy, or a plain *evidence* of their receiving it. They expected I know not what kind of *act of soul,* and perhaps they had no distinct *idea* of it themselves.

And indeed it appears very plainly in some of them, that *before* their own conversion they had very *imperfect ideas* what conversion was. It is all new and strange, and what there was no clear conception of before. It is most evident, as they themselves acknowledge, that the expressions used to describe conversion, and the graces of God's Holy Spirit—such as *a spiritual sight of Christ, faith in Christ, poverty of spirit, trust in God,* &c.—did not convey those distinct *ideas* to their minds, which they were intended to signify. Perhaps to some of them it was but little more than the names of *colours* are to convey the ideas to one that is *blind* from his birth.

In this town there has always been a great deal of talk about conversion and spiritual experiences ; and therefore people in general had formed a notion in their own minds what these things were. But when they come to be the *subjects* of them, they find themselves much confounded in their notions, and overthrown in many of their former conceits. And it has been very observable, that persons of the greatest understanding, and who had studied most about things of this nature, have been more confounded than others. Some such persons declare, that all their former wisdom is brought to nought, and that they appear to have been mere babes, who knew nothing. It has appeared, that none have stood more in need of instruction, even of their fellow-Christians, concerning their own circumstances and difficulties, than they : and it seems to have been with delight, that they have seen themselves thus brought down, and become *nothing ;* that free grace and divine power may be *exalted* in them.

It was very wonderful to see how persons' *affections* were sometimes moved—when God did as it were suddenly open their eyes, and let into their minds a sense of the greatness of his grace, the fulness of *Christ,* and his readiness to save—after having been broken with apprehensions of divine wrath, and sunk into an abyss, under a sense of guilt which they were ready to think was beyond the mercy of God. Their joyful surprise has caused their hearts as it were to leap, so that they have been ready to break forth into laughter, tears often at the same time issuing like a flood, and intermingling a loud weeping. Sometimes they have not been able to forbear crying out with a loud voice, expressing their great admiration. In some, even the view of the glory of God's sovereignty, in the exercises of his grace, has surprised the soul with such sweetness, as to produce the same effects. I remember an instance of one, who, reading something concerning God's *sovereign* way of saving sinners, as being self-moved—having no regard to men's *own righteousness* as the motive of his grace, but as magnifying himself and abasing man, or to that purpose—felt such a sudden rapture of joy and delight in the consideration of it : and yet then he suspected himself to be in a Christless condition, and had been long in great distress for fear that God would not have mercy on him.

Many continue a long time in a course of gracious exercises and experiences, and do not think themselves to be converted, but conclude otherwise ; and none knows how long they would continue so, were they not helped by particular instructions. There are undoubted instances of some who have lived in this way for many years together; and these circumstances had various consequences, with various persons, and with the same persons, at various times. Some continue in great encouragement and hope, that they shall obtain mercy in a stedfast resolution to persevere in seeking it, and in an humble waiting in it before God. But very often, when the lively sense of the sufficiency of *Christ* and the riches of divine grace, begins to vanish, upon a withdrawment of divine influences, they return to greater distress than ever. For they have now a far greater sense of the misery of a natural condition than before, being in a new manner sensible of the reality of eternal things, the greatness of God, his excellency, and how dreadful it is to be separated from him, and to be subject to his wrath; so that they are sometimes swallowed up with darkness and amazement. Satan has a vast advantage in such cases to ply them with various temptations, which he is not wont to neglect: in such a case, persons very much need a guide to lead them to an understanding of what we are taught in the word of God concerning the nature of grace, and to help them to apply it to themselves.

I have been much blamed and censured by many, that I should make it my practice, when I have been satisfied concerning persons' good estate, to signify it to them. This has been greatly misrepresented abroad, as innumerable other things concerning us, to prejudice the country against the whole affair. But let it be noted, that what I have undertaken to judge of, has rather been *qualifications*, and declared experiences, than *persons*. Not but that I have thought it my duty, as a pastor, to assist and instruct persons in applying scripture-rules and characters to their *own* case; (in which, I think, many greatly need a guide;) and I have, where the case appeared plain, used freedom in signifying my hope of them to others. But I have been far from doing this concerning all that I have had some hopes of; and I believe have used much more caution than many have supposed. Yet I should account it a great calamity to be deprived of the comfort of rejoicing with those of my flock, who have been in great distress, whose circumstances I have been acquainted with, when there seems to be good evidence that those who were dead are alive, and that those who were lost are found. I am sensible the practice would have been safer in the hands of one of a riper judgment and greater experience: but yet, there seemed to be an absolute necessity of it on the forementioned accounts; and it has been found what God has most remarkably owned and blessed amongst us, both to the persons themselves, and to others.

Grace in many persons, through this ignorance of their state, and their looking on themselves still as the objects of God's displeasure, has been like the trees in winter, or like seed in the spring suppressed under a hard clod of earth. Many in such cases have laboured to their utmost to divert their minds from the pleasing and joyful views they have had, and to suppress those consolations and gracious affections that arose thereupon. And when it has once come into their minds to inquire, whether or no this was not true grace, they have been much afraid lest they should be deceived with common illuminations and flashes of affection, and *eternally* undone with a false hope. But when they have been better instructed, and so brought to allow of *hope*, this has awakened the gracious disposition of their hearts into life and vigour, as the warm beams of the sun in the spring have quickened the seeds and productions of the earth. Grace being now at liberty, and cherished with hope, has soon flowed out to their abundant satisfaction and increase.

There is no one thing that I know of which God has made such a means of promoting his work amongst us, as the news of others' conversion. This has been owned in awakening sinners, engaging them earnestly to seek the same blessing, and in quickening saints. Though I have thought that a minister declaring his judgment about particular persons' experiences, might from these things be justified; yet I often signify to my people, how unable man is to know another's heart, and how unsafe it is to depend merely on the judgment of others. I have abundantly insisted, that a manifestation of sincerity in *fruits brought forth*, is better than any manifestation they can make of it in *words* alone: and that without this, all pretences to spiritual experiences are vain. This all my congregation can witness. And the people in general have manifested an extraordinary dread of being deceived; being exceeding fearful lest they should build wrong. Some of them have been backward to receive hope, even to a great extreme, which has occasioned me to dwell longer on this part of the narrative.

Conversion is a great and glorious work of God's power, at once changing the heart, and infusing life into the dead soul; though the grace then implanted more gradually displays itself in some than in others. But as to fixing on the *precise time* when they put forth the very first act of grace, there is a great deal of difference in different persons; in some it seems to be very discernible when the very time was; but others are more at a loss. In *this respect*, there are very many who do not know, even when they have it, that *it is* the grace of conversion, and sometimes do not think it to be so till a long time after. Many, even when they come to entertain great hopes that they are converted, if they remember what they experienced in the first exercises of grace, they are at a loss whether it was any more than a common illumination; or whether some *other* more clear and remarkable experience which they had afterwards, was not the *first* of a saving nature. The manner of God's work on the soul, sometimes especially, is very *mysterious;* and it is with the kingdom of God as to its manifestation in the heart of a convert, as is said, Mark iv. 26, 27, 28. "So is the kingdom of God, as if a man should cast seed into the ground, and should sleep, and rise, night and day, and the seed should spring, and grow up, he knoweth not how; for the earth bringeth forth of herself, first the blade, then the ear, then the full corn in the ear."

In *some*, converting light is like a glorious brightness suddenly shining *upon* a person, and all *around* him: they are in a remarkable manner brought *out of darkness into marvellous light*. In many *others* it has been like the dawning of the day, when at first but a *little* light appears, and it may be is presently hid with a cloud; and then it appears again, and shines a little *brighter*, and gradually increases, with intervening darkness, till at length it breaks forth more clearly from behind the clouds. And many are, doubtless, ready to *date* their conversion wrong, throwing by those lesser degrees of light that appeared at *first* dawning, and calling some more remarkable experience they had *afterwards*, their conversion. This often, in a great measure, arises from a wrong understanding of what they have always been taught, that conversion is a *great* change, wherein *old things are done away, and all things become new*, or at least from a false inference from that doctrine.

Persons commonly at first conversion, and afterwards, have had many texts of Scripture brought to their minds, which are exceeding suitable to their circumstances, often come with great power, as the word of God or of *Christ* indeed; and many have a multitude of sweet invitations, promises, and doxologies flowing in one after another, bringing great light and comfort with them, filling the soul brimful, enlarging the heart, and opening the mouth in religion. And it seems to me necessary to suppose, that there is an immediate influence of the Spirit of God, oftentimes, in bringing texts of Scripture to the mind. Not that I suppose it is done in a way of immediate revelation, without any use of the memory; but yet there seems plainly to be an immediate and extraordinary influence, in leading their thoughts to such and such passages of Scripture, and exciting them *in the memory*. Indeed in some, God seems to bring texts of scripture to their minds no otherwise than by leading them into such frames and meditations, as *harmonize* with those scriptures; but in many persons there seems to be something more than this.

Those who, while under legal convictions, have had the greatest terrors, have not always obtained the greatest light and comfort; nor have they always light most suddenly communicated; but yet, I think, the *time* of conversion has generally been most sensible in such persons. Oftentimes, the first sensible change after the extremity of terrors, is a calmness, and then the light gradually comes in; *small glimpses* at first, after their midnight darkness, and *a word or two of comfort*, as it were softly spoken to them. They have a *little taste* of the sweetness of divine grace, and the love of a Saviour; when terror and distress of conscience begin to be turned into an humble, meek sense of their own unworthiness before God. There is felt, inwardly, sometimes a disposition to praise God; and after a little while the light comes in more clearly and powerfully. But yet, I think, more frequently, great terrors have been followed with more sudden and great light and comfort; when the sinner seems to be as it were subdued and brought to a calm, from a kind of tumult of mind, then God lets in an extraordinary sense of his great mercy through a Redeemer.

Converting influences very commonly bring an extraordinary conviction of the *reality* and certainty of the great things of religion; though in some this is much greater some time *after* conversion, than at first. They have that sight and taste of the divine excellency there is in the gospel, which is more effectual to convince them, than reading many volumes of arguments without it. It seems to me, that in many instances, when the glory of christian truths has been set before persons, and they have at the same time as it were seen, and tasted, and felt the divinity of them, they have been as far from doubting their truth, as they are from doubting whether there be a sun, when their eyes are open in the midst of a clear hemisphere, and the strong blaze of his light overcomes all objections. And yet, many of them, if we should ask them *why* they believed those things to be true, would not be able well to express or communicate a sufficient reason to satisfy the inquirer; and perhaps would make no other answer but that they *see them to be true*. But a person might soon be satisfied, by a particular conversation with them, that what they mean by such an answer is, that they have *intuitively* beheld, and *immediately felt*, most illustrious and powerful evidence of divinity in them.

Some are thus convinced of the truth of the *gospel* in general, and that the Scriptures are the word of God: others have their minds more especially fixed on some particular *great doctrine* of the gospel, some particular truths that they are *meditating* on, or *reading* of, in some portion of Scripture. Some have such convictions in a much more remarkable manner than others: and there are some who never had such a special sense of the certainty of divine things impressed upon them, with such inward evidence and strength, have yet very clear exercises of grace; *i. e.* of love to God, repentance, and holiness. And if they be more particularly examined, they appear plainly to have an inward firm persuasion of the reality of divine things, such as they did not use to have before their conversion. And those who have the most *clear* discoveries of divine truth, in the manner that has been mentioned, cannot have this *always* in view. When the sense and relish of the divine excellency of these things fades, on a withdrawment of the Spirit of God, they have not the medium of the conviction of their truth at command. In a dull frame, they cannot recall the *idea* and inward sense they had, perfectly to mind; things appear very dim to what they did before. And though there still remains an habitual strong persuasion; yet not so as to exclude temptations to unbelief, and all possibility of doubting. But then, at particular times, by God's help, the same sense of things revives again, like fire that lay hid in ashes. I suppose the *grounds* of such a conviction of the truth of divine things to be just and *rational;* but yet, in some, God makes use of their own reason much more sensibly than in others. Oftentimes persons have (so far as could be judged) received the first saving conviction from *reasoning* which they have heard *from the pulpit;* and often in the course of reasoning they are led into *in their own meditations*.

The arguments are the *same* that they have heard hundreds of times; but *the force of the arguments,* and *their conviction by them,* is altogether new; they come with a new and before unexperienced power. *Before,* they *heard it* was so, and they *allowed it* to be so; but now they *see it* to be so indeed. Things now look exceeding plain to them, and they wonder they did not see them before.

They are so greatly taken with their new discovery, and things appear so plain and so rational to them, that they are often at first ready to think they can convince others; and are apt to engage in talk with every one they meet with, *almost* to this end; and when they are disappointed, are ready to wonder that their reasonings seem to make no more impression.

Many fall under such a mistake as to be ready to doubt of their good estate, because there was so much use made of their *own reason* in the convictions they have received; they are afraid that they have no illumination above the natural force of their own faculties: and many make that an objection against the *spirituality* of their convictions, that it is so *easy* to see things as they now see them. They have often heard, that conversion is a work of mighty power, manifesting to the soul what neither man nor angel can give such a conviction of; but it seems to them that these things are so plain and easy, and rational, that any body can see them. If they are asked, why they never saw thus before; they say, it seems to them it was because they never *thought* of it. But very often these difficulties are soon removed by those of another nature; for when God withdraws, they find themselves as it were blind again, they for the present lose their realizing sense of those things that looked so plain to them, and, by all they can do, they cannot recover it, till God renews the influences of his Spirit.

Persons after their conversion often speak of religious things as seeming *new* to them; that preaching is a *new* thing; that it seems to them they never heard preaching before; that the Bible is a *new* book: they find there *new* chapters, *new* psalms, *new* histories, because they see them in a new light. Here was a remarkable instance of an aged woman, of above seventy years, who had spent most of her days under Mr. *Stoddard's* powerful ministry. Reading in the New Testament concerning *Christ's* sufferings for sinners, she seemed to be astonished at what she read, as what was *real* and very *wonderful*, but quite *new* to her. At first, before she had time to turn her thoughts, she wondered within herself, that she had never heard of it before; but then immediately recollected herself, and thought she had often *heard of it*, and *read* it, but never till now *saw it as real*. She then cast in her mind, how *wonderful* this was, that the Son of God should undergo such things for sinners, and how she had spent her time in ungratefully sinning against so good a God, and such a Saviour; though she was a person, apparently, of a very blameless and inoffensive life. And she was so overcome by those considerations, that her nature was ready to fail under them: those who were about her, and knew not what was the matter, were surprised, and thought she was a dying.

Many have spoken much of their hearts being drawn out in *love* to God and Christ; and of their minds being wrapt up in delightful contemplation of the glory and wonderful grace of God, the excellency and dying love of *Jesus Christ;* and of their souls going forth in longing desires *after God and Christ*. Several of our young children have expressed much of this; and have manifested a willingness to leave father and mother and all things in the world, to go and be with Christ. Some persons having had such longing desires after Christ, or which have risen to such degree, as to take away thei natural strength. Some have been so overcome with a sense of the dying love of Christ, to such poor, wretched, and unworthy creatures, as to weaken the body. Several persons have had so great a sense of the glory of God, and excellency of Christ, that nature and life seemed almost to *sink* under it; and in all probability, if God had showed them a little more of himself, it would have dissolved their frame. I have seen some, and conversed with them in such frames, who have certainly been perfectly sober, and very remote from any thing like *enthusiastic* wildness. And they have talked, when able to speak, of the glory of God's perfections, the wonderfulness of his grace in Christ, and their own unworthiness, in such a manner as cannot be perfectly expressed after them. Their sense of their exceeding littleness and vileness, and their disposition to abase themselves before God, has appeared to be great *in proportion* to their light and joy.

Such persons amongst us as have been thus distinguished with the most extraordinary discoveries, have commonly nowise appeared with the assuming, self-conceited, and self-sufficient airs of enthusiasts; but exceedingly the contrary. They are eminent for a spirit of meekness, modesty, self-diffidence, and a low opinion of themselves. No persons appear so sensible of their need of instruction, and so eager to receive it, as some of them; nor so ready to think *others better than themselves.* Those that have been considered as converted amongst us, have *generally* manifested a longing to *lie low,* and in the dust before God; withal complaining of their not being able to lie low enough.

They speak much of their sense of excellency in the way of salvation by free and sovereign grace, through the righteousness of Christ alone; and how it is with delight that they renounce their own righteousness, and rejoice in having no account made of it. Many have expressed themselves to this purpose, that it would lessen the satisfaction they hope for in heaven to have it by their *own righteousness,* or in any other way than as bestowed by *free grace,* and for *Christ's sake alone.* They speak much of the inexpressibleness of what they experience, how their *words* fail, so that they cannot declare it. And particularly they speak with exceeding admiration of the superlative excellency of that pleasure and delight which they sometimes enjoy; how a *little* of it is sufficient to pay them for *all* the pains and trouble they have gone through in seeking salvation; and how far it exceeds all earthly pleasures. Some express much of the sense which these spiritual views give them of the *vanity* of earthly enjoyments, how mean and worthless all these things appear to them.

Many, while their minds have been filled with *spiritual* delights, have as it were forgot their food; their bodily appetite has failed, while their minds have been entertained with *meat to eat that others knew not of.* The light and comfort which some of them enjoy, give a new relish to their *common blessings,* and cause all things about them to appear as it were beautiful, sweet, and pleasant. All things abroad, the sun, moon, and stars, the clouds and sky, the heavens and earth, appear as it were with a cast of *divine glory* and sweetness upon them. Though this joy include in it a delightful sense of the safety of their own state, yet frequently, in times of their highest spiritual entertainment, this seems not to be the chief object of their fixed thought and meditation. The supreme attention of their minds is to the glorious excellencies of God and Christ; and there is very often a ravishing sense of God's love accompanying a sense of his excellency. They rejoice in a sense of the faithfulness of God's promises, as they respect the future, eternal enjoyment of him.

The unparalleled joy that many of them speak of, is what they find when they are lowest in the dust, emptied most of themselves, and as it were annihilating themselves before God; when they are nothing, and God is all; seeing their own unworthiness, depending not at all on themselves, but alone on Christ, and ascribing all glory to God. Then their souls are most in the enjoyment of satisfying rest; excepting that, at such times, they apprehend themselves to be not sufficiently self-abased; for then above all times do they long to be lower. Some speak much of the exquisite sweetness, and rest of soul, that is to be found in the exercise of resignation to God, and humble submission to his will. Many express earnest longings of soul to praise God; but at the same time complain that they cannot praise him as they would, and they want to have others help them in praising him. They want to have *every one* praise God, and are ready to call upon *every thing* to praise him. They express a longing desire to live to God's glory, and to do something to his honour; but at the same time complain of their insufficiency and barrenness; that they are *poor and impotent creatures, can do nothing of themselves, and are utterly insufficient to glorify their Creator and Redeemer.*

While God was so remarkably present amongst us by his Spirit, there was no book so delightful as the Bible; especially the Book of Psalms, the Prophecy of Isaiah, and the New Testament. Some, by reason of their love to God's word, at times, have been wonderfully delighted and affected at the sight of a Bible; and *then,* also, there was *no time* so prized as the Lord's day, and *no place* in this world so desired as God's house. Our converts *then* remarkably appeared united in dear affection to one another, and many have expressed much of that spirit of love which they felt toward all mankind; and particularly to those who had been least friendly to them. Never, I believe, was so much done in confessing injuries, and making up differences, as the last year. Persons, after their own conversion, have commonly expressed an exceeding great desire for the conversion of others. Some have thought that they should be willing to *die* for the conversion of any soul, though of one of the meanest of their fellow-creatures, or of their worst enemies; and many have, indeed, been in great distress with desires and longings for it. This work of God had also a good effect to unite the people's affections much to their minister.

There are some persons whom I have been acquainted with, but more especially two, that belong to other towns, who have been swallowed up exceedingly with a sense of the awful greatness and *majesty* of God; and both of them told me to this purpose, that if at the time, they had entertained the least fear that they were not at peace with this so great a God, they should certainly have died.

It is worthy to be remarked, that some persons, by their conversion, seem to be greatly helped as to their *doctrinal* notions of religion. It was particularly remarkable in one, who, having been taken captive in his childhood, was trained up in Canada, in the popish religion. Some years since he returned to this his native place, and was in a measure brought off from popery; but seemed very awkward and dull in receiving any clear notion of the protestant scheme, till he was *converted;* and then he was remarkably altered in this respect.

There is a vast difference, as observed, in the *degree,* and also in the particular *manner,* of persons' experiences, both *at* and *after* conversion; *some* have grace working more sensibly in one way, *others* in another. *Some* speak more fully of a conviction of the *justice* of God in their condemnation; *others,* more of their consenting to the way of salvation by *Christ;* and some, more of the actings of love to God and *Christ.* Some more of acts of affiance, in a sweet and assured conviction of the truth and faithfulness of God in his promises; others, more of their choosing and resting in God, as their whole and everlasting portion; and of their ardent and longing desire after God, to have communion with him; and others, more of their abhorrence to themselves for their past sins, and earnest longings to live to God's glory for the time to come. But it seems evidently to be the *same work,* the *same habitual change* wrought in the heart; it all tends the same way, and to the *same end;* and it is plainly the *same spirit* that breathes and acts in *various* persons. There is an endless *variety* in the particular manner and circumstances in which persons are wrought on; and an opportunity of seeing so much will show, that God is further from confining himself to a particular method in his work on souls, than some imagine. I believe it has occasioned some good people amongst us, who were before too ready to make their own experience a rule to others, to be less censorious and more *extended in their charity;* and this is an excellent advantage indeed. The work of God has been *glorious* in its variety; it has the more displayed the manifold and unsearchable wisdom of God, and wrought more charity among his people.

There is a great difference among those who are converted, as to the degree of *hope and satisfaction* they have concerning their own *state.* Some have a high degree of satisfaction in this matter almost constantly; and yet it is rare that any enjoy so full an assurance of their interest in Christ, that self-examination should seem needless to them; unless it be at particular seasons, while in the actual enjoyment of some great discovery God gives of his glory and rich grace in Christ, to the drawing forth of extraordinary acts of grace. But the greater part, as they sometimes fall into dead frames of spirit, are frequently exercised with scruples and fears concerning their condition.

They generally have an awful apprehension of the dreadful nature of a false hope; and there has been observable in most a great caution, lest in giving an account of their experiences, they should say *too much,* and use too strong terms. Many, after they have related their experiences, have been greatly afflicted with fears, lest they have played the hypocrite, and used stronger terms than their case would fairly allow of; and yet could not find how they could correct themselves.

I think the main ground of the doubts and fears, that persons after their conversion have been exercised with, about their own state, has been, that they have found so much corruption remaining in their hearts. At first, their souls seem to be all alive, their hearts are fixed, and their affections flowing; they seem to live quite above the world, and meet with but little difficulty in religious exercises; and they are ready to think it will always be so. Though they are truly abased under a sense of their vileness, by reason of former acts of sin; yet they are not then sufficiently sensible, what corruption still remains in their hearts; and therefore, are *surprised* when they find that they begin to be in dull and dead frames, troubled with wandering thoughts at the time of public and private worship, and utterly unable to keep themselves from them. When they find themselves unaffected, while yet there is the greatest occasion to be affected; and when they feel worldly dispositions working in them—pride, envy, stirrings of revenge, or some ill spirit towards some person that has injured them, as well as other workings of indwelling sin—their hearts are almost sunk with the disappointment; and they are ready presently to think that they are mere hypocrites.

They are ready to argue, If God had, indeed, done such great things for them, as they hoped, such ingratitude would be inconsistent with it. They complain of the hardness and wickedness of their hearts; and say there is so much corruption, that it seems to them *impossible there should be any goodness there*. Many of them seem to be much more sensible how corrupt their hearts are, than before they were converted; and some have been too ready to be impressed with fear, that instead of becoming better, they are grown much worse, and make it an argument against the goodness of their state. But in truth, the case seems plainly to be, that now they feel the pain of their own wound; they have a watchful eye upon their hearts, that they did not use to have. They take more notice of what sin is there, which is now more burdensome to them; they strive more against it, and feel more of its strength.

They are somewhat surprised that they should in this respect find themselves so different from the *idea* they generally had entertained of godly persons. For, though grace be indeed of a far more excellent nature than they imagined; yet, those who are godly have much less of it, and much more remaining corruption, than they thought. They never realized it, that persons were wont to meet with such difficulties, after they were once converted. When they are thus exercised with doubts about their state, through the deadness of their frames; as long as these frames last, they are commonly unable to satisfy themselves of the *truth* of their grace, by all their self-examination. When they hear of the signs of grace laid down for them to try themselves by, they are often so clouded, that they do not know how to apply them. They hardly know whether they have such and such things or no, and whether they have experienced them or not. That which was the sweetest, best, and most distinguishing in their experiences, they cannot recover a sense of. But on a return of the influences of the Spirit of God, to revive the lively actings of grace, the light breaks through the cloud, and doubting and darkness soon vanish away.

Persons are often revived out of their dead and dark frames, by religious conversation: while they are talking of divine things, *or ever they are aware*, their souls are carried away into holy exercises with abundant pleasure. And oftentimes, while relating their past experiences to their christian brethren, they have a sense of them revived, and the same experiences in a degree again renewed. Sometimes, while persons are exercised in mind with several objections against the goodness of their state, they have scriptures one after another coming to their minds, to answer their scruples, and unravel their difficulties, exceedingly apposite and proper to their circumstances. By these means, their darkness is scattered; and often, before the bestowment of any new remarkable comforts, especially after long-continued deadness and ill frames, there are *renewed humblings*, in a great sense of their own exceeding vileness and unworthiness, as before their first comforts were bestowed.

Many in the country have entertained a mean thought of this great work, from what they have heard of *impressions* made on persons' *imaginations*. But there have been exceeding great misrepresentations, and innumerable false reports, concerning that matter. It is not, that I know of, the profession or opinion of *any one person in the town*, that any weight is to be laid on any thing seen with the bodily eyes. I know the *contrary* to be a received and established principle amongst us. I cannot say that there have been no instances of persons who have been ready to give too much heed to vain and useless *imaginations;* but they have been easily corrected, and I conclude it will not be wondered at, that a congregation should need a guide in such cases, to assist them in distinguishing *wheat* from *chaff*. But such impressions on the imaginations as have been more usual, seem to me to be plainly no other than what is to be expected in human nature in such circumstances, and what is the *natural result* of the strong exercise of the mind, and impressions on the heart.

I do not suppose, that they themselves imagined they saw any thing with their *bodily* eyes; but only have had within them *ideas* strongly impressed, and as it were lively pictures in their minds. For instance, some when in great terrors, through fear of hell, have had lively ideas of a dreadful furnace. Some, when their hearts have been strongly impressed, and their affections greatly moved with a sense of the beauty and excellency of *Christ*, have had their imaginations so wrought upon, that, together with a sense of his glorious spiritual perfections, there has arisen in the mind an *idea* of one of glorious majesty, and of a sweet and gracious aspect. Some, when they have been greatly affected with *Christ's* death, have at the same time a lively *idea of Christ* hanging upon the cross, and his blood running from his wounds. Surely such things will not be wondered at by them who have observed, how any strong affections about temporal matters will excite lively *ideas* and pictures of different things in the mind.

The vigorous exercises of the mind, doubtless, more strongly impress it with imaginary *ideas* in some than others, which probably may arise from the difference of constitution, and seems evidently in some, partly to arise from their peculiar circumstances. When persons have been exercised with extreme terrors, and there is a sudden change to light and joy, the imagination seems more susceptive of strong *ideas;* the inferior powers, and even the frame of the body, are much more affected, than when the same persons have as great spiritual light and joy afterwards; of which it might, perhaps, be easy to give a reason. The forementioned Reverend Messrs. *Lord* and *Owen*—who, I believe, are esteemed persons of learning and discretion where they are best known—declared, that they found these *impressions* on persons' *imaginations* quite different things from what fame had before represented to them, and that they were what none need to wonder at—or to that purpose.

There have indeed been some few instances of *impressions* on persons' *imaginations*, which have been somewhat mysterious to me, and I have been at a loss about them. For, though it has been exceeding evident to me, by many things that appeared both then and afterwards, that they indeed had a greater sense of the spiritual excellency of divine things accompanying them; yet I have not been able well to satisfy myself, whether their imaginary *ideas* have been more than could naturally arise from their spiritual sense of things. However, I have used the utmost caution in such cases; great care has been taken both in public and in private to teach persons the difference between what is *spiritual* and what is merely *imaginary*. I have often warned persons not to lay the stress of their hope on any *ideas* of any outward glory, or any external thing whatsoever, and have met with no opposition in such instructions. But it is not strange if some weaker persons, in giving an account of their experiences, have not so prudently distinguished between the *spiritual* and *imaginary* part; of which some who have not been well affected to religion might take advantage.

There has been much talk in many parts of the country, as though the people have symbolized with the *quakers*, and the *quakers themselves* have been moved with such reports; and some came here, once and again, hoping to find good waters to fish in; but without the least success, and have left off coming. There have also been reports spread about the country, as though the first occasion of so remarkable a concern was an apprehension that the world was near to an end; which was altogether a false report. Indeed, after this concern became so general and extraordinary, as related, the minds of some were filled with speculation, what so great a dispensation of Divine Providence might forebode; and some reports were heard from abroad, as though certain divines and others thought the conflagration was nigh; but such reports were never generally looked upon worthy of notice.

The work which has now been wrought on souls, is evidently the same that was wrought in my venerable predecessor's days; as I have had abundant opportunity to know, having been in the ministry here two years with him, and so conversed with a considerable number whom my grandfather thought to be savingly converted at that time; and having been particularly acquainted with the experiences of many who were converted under his ministry before. And I know no one of them, who in the least doubts of its being the same spirit and the same work. Persons have now no otherwise been subject to impressions on their imaginations than formerly: the work is of the same nature, and has not been attended with any extraordinary circumstances, excepting such as are analogous to the extraordinary degree of it before described. And God's people who were formerly converted, have now partaken of the same shower of divine blessing—in the *renewing, strengthening, edifying influences* of the Spirit of God—that others have in his *converting influences;* and the work here has also been plainly the same with that of other places which have been mentioned, as partaking of the same blessing. I have particularly conversed with persons, about their experiences, who belong to all parts of the country, and in various parts of *Connecticut*, where a religious concern has lately appeared; and have been informed of the experiences of many others by their own pastors.

It is easily perceived by the foregoing account, that it is very much the practice of the people here, to converse freely one with another about their spiritual experiences; which many have been disgusted at. But however our people *may have*, in some respects, gone to extremes in it, it is, doubtless, a practice that the circumstances of this town, and neighbouring towns, have naturally led them into. Whatsoever people have their minds engaged to such a degree in the same affair, that it is ever uppermost in their thoughts, they will naturally make it the subject of conversation when they get together, in which they will grow more and more free. Restraints will soon vanish; and they will not conceal from one another what they meet with. And it has been a practice which, in the general, has been attended with many good effects, and what God has greatly blessed amongst us: but it must be confessed, there may have been some ill consequences of it; which yet are rather to be laid to the *indiscreet management* of it than to the *practice itself;* and none can wonder, if among such a multitude some fail of exercising so much *prudence* in choosing the time, manner, and occasion of such discourse, as is desirable.

SECT. III.

This work further illustrated in particular instances.

BUT to give a clear *idea* of the nature and manner of the operation of God's Spirit, in this wonderful effusion of it, I would give an account of two *particular instances.* The first is an *adult person*, a young woman whose name was ABIGAIL HUTCHINSON. I fix upon her especially, because she is now dead, and so it may be more fit to speak freely of her than of living instances: though I am under far greater disadvantages, on other accounts, to give a full and clear narrative of her experiences, than I might of some others; nor can any account be given but what has been retained in the memories of her friends, of what they have heard her express in her lifetime.

She was of an intelligent family: there could be nothing in her education that tended to *enthusiasm*, but rather to the contrary extreme. It is in nowise the temper of the family to be ostentatious of experiences, and it was far from being her temper. She was before her conversion, to the observation of her neighbours, of a sober and inoffensive conversation; and was a still, quiet, reserved person. She had long been infirm of body, but her infirmity had never been observed at all to incline her to be notional or fanciful, or to occasion any thing of religious melancholy. She was under awakenings scarcely a week, before there seemed to be plain evidence of her being savingly converted.

She was first awakened in the winter season, on *Monday*, by something she heard her brother say of the necessity of being in good earnest in seeking regenerating grace, together with the news of the conversion of the young woman before mentioned, whose conversion so generally affected most of the young people here. This news wrought much upon her, and stirred up a spirit of envy in her towards this young woman, whom she thought very unworthy of being distinguished from others by such a mercy; but withal it engaged her in a firm resolution to do her utmost to obtain the same blessing. Considering with herself what course she should take, she thought, that she had not a sufficient knowledge of the principles of religion, to render her capable of conversion; whereupon she resolved thoroughly to search the Scriptures; and accordingly immediately began at the beginning of the Bible, intending to read it through. She continued thus till *Thursday:* and then there was a sudden alteration, by a great increase of her concern, in an extraordinary sense of her own sinfulness, particularly the sinfulness of her *nature*, and wickedness of her heart. This came upon her, as she expressed it, as a flash of lightning, and struck her into an exceeding terror. Upon which she left off reading the Bible, in course, as she had begun; and turned to the New Testament, to see if she could not find some relief there for her distressed soul.

Her *great terror*, she said, *was, that she had sinned against God:* her distress grew more and more for three days; until she saw *nothing but blackness of darkness before her, and* her *very flesh trembled for fear of God's wrath:* she *wondered and was astonished at herself, that she had been so concerned for her body, and had applied so often to physicians to heal that, and had neglected her soul.* Her sinfulness appeared with a very awful aspect to her, especially in three things; *viz.* her *original sin*, and her sin in *murmuring* at God's providence—in the weakness and afflictions she had been under—and in want of duty to *parents*, though others had looked upon her to excel in dutifulness. On *Saturday*, she was so earnestly engaged in reading the Bible and other books, that she continued in it, searching for something to relieve her, till her eyes were so dim, that she could not know the letters. While she was thus engaged in reading, prayer, and other religious exercises, she thought of those words of Christ, wherein he warns us not to be *as the heathen*, that *think they shall be heard for their much speaking;* which, she said, led her to see that she had trusted to her own prayers and religious performances, and now she was put to a *nonplus*, and knew not which way to turn herself, or where to seek relief.

While her mind was in this posture, her heart, she said, seemed to fly to the *minister* for refuge, hoping, that *he* could give her some relief. She came the same day to her brother, with the countenance of a person in distress, expostulating with him, why he had not told her more of her sinfulness, and earnestly inquiring of him what she should do. She seemed that day to feel in herself an enmity against the Bible, which greatly affrighted her. Her sense of her own exceeding sinfulness continued increasing from *Thursday* till *Monday* and she gave this account of it: That it had been her opinion, till now, she was not guilty of *Adam's* sin, nor any way concerned in it, because she was not *active* in it; but that now she saw she was guilty of that sin, and all over *defiled* by it; and the sin which she brought into the world with her, was alone sufficient to condemn her.

On the *Sabbath-day* she was so ill, that her friends thought it not best that she should go to public worship, of which she seemed very desirous: but when she went to bed on the *Sabbath* night, she took up a resolution, that she would the next morning go to the *minister*, hoping to find some relief there. As she awaked on *Monday* morning, a little before day, she wondered within herself at the easiness and calmness she felt in her mind, which was of that kind she never felt before. As she thought of this, such words as these were in her mind: *The words of the Lord are pure words, health to the soul, and marrow to the bones*: and then these words, *The blood of Christ cleanses from all sin;* which were accompanied with a lively sense of the excellency of *Christ*, and his sufficiency to satisfy for the sins of the whole world. She then thought of that expression, *It is a pleasant thing for the eyes to behold the sun;* which words then seemed to her to be very applicable to Jesus Christ. By these things her mind was led into such contemplations and views of Christ, as filled her exceeding full of joy. She told her brother, in the morning, that she had *seen (i. e.* in realizing views by faith) *Christ the last night*, and that she had *really thought that she had not knowledge enough to be converted;* but, says she, *God can make it quite easy!* On *Monday* she felt all day a constant sweetness in her soul. She had a repetition of the same discoveries of Christ three mornings together, and much in the same manner, at each time, waking a little before day; but brighter and brighter every day.

At the last time, on *Wednesday* morning, while in the enjoyment of a spiritual view of Christ's glory and fulness, her soul was filled with distress for Christless persons, to consider what a miserable condition they were in. She felt a strong inclination immediately to go forth to warn sinners; and proposed it the next day to her brother to assist her in going from house to house; but her brother restrained her, by telling her of the unsuitableness of such a method. She told one of her sisters that day, that she loved *all mankind, but especially the people of God.* Her sister asked her, Why she loved all mankind? She replied, *Because God had made them.* After this, there happened to come into the shop where she was at work, three persons who were thought to have been lately converted: her seeing of them, as they stepped in one after another, so affected her, and so drew forth her love to them, that it overcame her, and she almost fainted. When they began to talk of the things of religion, it was more than she could bear; they were obliged to cease on that account. It was a very frequent thing with her to be overcome with a flow of affection to them whom she thought godly, in conversation with them, and sometimes only at the sight of them.

She had many extraordinary discoveries of the glory of God and Christ; sometimes, in some particular attributes, and sometimes in many. She gave an account, that once, as those four words passed through her mind, WISDOM, JUSTICE, GOODNESS, *and* TRUTH, her soul was filled with a sense of the glory of each of these divine attributes, but especially the last. *Truth*, said she, *sunk the deepest!* And, therefore, as these words passed, this was repeated, TRUTH, TRUTH! Her mind was so swallowed up with a sense of the glory of God's *truth* and other perfections, that she said, *it seemed as though her life was going*, and that she *saw it was easy with God to take away her life by discoveries of himself.* Soon after this she went to a private religious meeting, and her mind was full of a sense and view of the glory of God all the time. When the exercise was ended, some asked her concerning what she had experienced; and she began to give an account, but as she was relating it, it revived such a sense of the same things, that her strength failed; and they were obliged to take her and lay her upon the bed. Afterwards she was greatly affected, and rejoiced with these words, *Worthy is the Lamb that was slain!*

She had several days together a sweet sense of the excellency and loveliness of *Christ* in his *meekness*, which disposed her continually to be repeating over these words, which were sweet to her, MEEK AND LOWLY IN HEART, MEEK AND LOWLY IN HEART. She once expressed herself to one of her sisters to this purpose, that she had continued *whole days and whole nights*, in a constant ravishing view of the *glory of God and Christ, having enjoyed as much as her life could bear.* Once, as her brother was speaking of the dying love of Christ, she told him, she had such a sense of it, that the mere mentioning of it was ready to overcome her.

Once, when she came to me, she said, that at such and such a time, she thought she saw as much of God, and had as much joy and pleasure, as was *possible in this life;* and that yet, afterwards, God discovered himself far more abundantly. She saw the same things as before, yet more clearly, and in a far more excellent and delightful manner; and was filled with a more exceeding sweetness. She likewise gave me such an account of the sense she once had, from day to day, of the glory of Christ, and of God, in his various attributes, that it seemed to me she dwelt for days together in a kind of *beatific vision* of God; and seemed to have, as I thought, as immediate an intercourse with him, as a child with a father. At the same time, she appeared most remote from any high thought of herself, and of her own sufficiency; but was like a *little child*, and expressed a great desire to be instructed, telling me that she longed very often to come to me for instruction, and wanted to live at my house, that I might tell her what was her duty.

She often expressed a sense of the glory of God appearing in the trees, the growth of the fields, and other works of God's hands. She told her sister who lived near the heart of the town, that she once thought it a pleasant thing to live in the middle of the town, *but now*, says she, *I think it much more pleasant to sit and see the wind blowing the trees, and to behold in the country what* GOD *has made.* She had sometimes the powerful breathings of the Spirit of God on her soul, while reading the Scripture; and would express her sense of the certain truth and divinity thereof. She sometimes would appear with a pleasant smile on her countenance; and once, when her sister took notice of it, and asked why she smiled, she replied, *I am brim-full of a sweet feeling within!* She often used to express how *good and sweet it* was *to lie low before God, and the lower* (says she) *the better!* and that it was *pleasant to think of lying in the dust, all the days of her life, mourning for sin.* She was wont to manifest a great sense of her own meanness and dependence. She often expressed an exceeding compassion, and pitiful love, which she found in her heart towards persons in a Christless condition. This was sometimes so strong, that, as she was passing by such in the streets, or those that she feared were such, she would be overcome by the sight of them. She once said, that she *longed to have the whole world saved*, she wanted, as it were, *to pull them all* to her; she could *not bear to have one lost.*

She had great longings to die, that she might be with Christ: which increased until she thought she did not know how to be patient to wait till God's time. But once, when she felt those longings, she thought with herself, *If I long to die, why do I go to physicians?* Whence she concluded that her longings for death were not well regulated. After this she often put it to herself, which she should choose, whether to live or to die, to be sick or to be well; and she found she could not tell, till at last she found herself disposed to say these words; *I am quite willing to live, and quite willing to die; quite willing to be sick, and quite willing to be well; and quite willing for any thing that God will bring upon me! And then*, said she, *I felt myself perfectly easy*, in a full submission to the will of God. She then lamented much, that she had been so eager in her longings for death, as it argued want of such a resignation to God as ought to be. She seemed henceforward to continue in this resigned frame till death.

After this, her illness increased upon her: and once after she had before spent the greater part of the night in extreme pain, she waked out of a little sleep with these words in her heart and mouth; *I am willing to suffer for Christ's sake, I am willing to spend and be spent for Christ's sake; I am willing to spend my life, even my very life, for*

Christ's sake! And though she had an extraordinary resignation, with respect to life or death, yet the thoughts of dying were exceeding sweet to her. At a time when her brother was reading in Job, concerning worms feeding on the dead body, she appeared with a pleasant smile; and being asked about it, she said, It was sweet to her to think of *her* being in such circumstances. At another time, when her brother mentioned the danger there seemed to be, that the illness she laboured under, might be an occasion of her death, it filled her with joy that almost overcame her. At another time, when she met a company following a corpse to the grave, she said, it was sweet to her to think, that they would in a little time follow her in like manner.

Her illness, in the latter part of it, was seated much in her throat; and an inward swelling filled up the pipe, so that she could swallow nothing but what was perfectly liquid, and but very little of that, with great and long strugglings. That which she took in fled out at her nostrils, till at last she could swallow nothing at all. She had a raging appetite for food; so that she told her sister, when talking with her about her circumstances, that the worst bit would be sweet to her; but yet, when she saw that she could not swallow it, she seemed to be as perfectly contented without it, as if she had no appetite. Others were greatly moved to see what she underwent, and were filled with admiration at her unexampled patience. At a time when she was striving in vain to get down a little of something liquid, and was very much spent with it; she looked up on her sister with a smile, saying, *O sister, this is for my good!* At another time, when her sister was speaking of what she underwent, she told her, that she *lived a heaven upon earth for all that.* She used sometimes to say to her sister, under her extreme sufferings, *It is good to be so!* Her sister once asked her, why she said so; *why*, says she, *because God would have it so: it is best that things should be as God would have them: it looks best to me.* After her confinement, as they were leading her from the bed to the door, she seemed overcome by the sight of things abroad, as showing forth the glory of the Being who had made them. As she lay on her death-bed, she would often say these words, *God is my friend!* And once looking upon her sister, with a smile, said, *O sister, How good it is! How sweet and comfortable it is to consider, and think of heavenly things!* and used this argument to persuade her sister to be much in such meditations.

She expressed, on her death-bed, an exceeding longing, *both for persons in a natural state, that they might be converted; and for the godly, that they might see and know more of God.* And when those who looked on themselves as in a Christless state came to see her, she would be greatly moved with compassionate affection. One in particular, who seemed to be in great distress about the state of her soul, and had come to see her from time to time, she desired her sister to persuade not to come any more, because the sight of her so wrought on her compassions, that it overcame her nature. The same week that she died, when she was in distressing circumstances as to her body, some of the neighbours who came to see her, asked if she was willing to die? She replied, that she was *quite willing either to live or die; she was willing to be in pain; she was willing to be so always as she was then, if that was the will of God.* She *willed what God willed.* They asked her whether she was willing to die that night? She answered, *Yes, if it be God's will.* And seemed to speak all with that perfect composure of spirit, and with such a cheerful and pleasant countenance, that it filled them with admiration.

She was very weak a considerable time before she died, having pined away with famine and thirst, so that her flesh seemed to be dried upon her bones; and therefore could say but little, and manifested her mind very much by signs. She said she had *matter enough to fill up all her time with talk, if she had but strength.* A few days before her death, some asked her, Whether she *held her integrity still?* Whether she was not *afraid of death?* she answered to this purpose, that she had not the least degree of fear of death. They asked her *why she would be so confident?* She answered, *If I should say otherwise, I should speak contrary to what I know. There is*, said she, *indeed, a dark entry, that looks something dark, but on the other side there appears such a bright shining light, that I cannot be afraid!* She said not long before she died, that she *used to be afraid how she should grapple with death; But*, says she, *God has showed me that he can make it easy in great pain.* Several days before she died, she could scarcely say any thing but just *Yes*, and *No*, to questions that were asked her; for she seemed to be dying for three days together. But seemed to continue in an admirably sweet composure of soul, without any interruption, to the last; and died as a person that went to sleep, without any struggling, about noon, on *Friday, June* 27, 1735.

She had long been infirm, and often had been exercised with great pain; but she died chiefly of famine. It was, doubtless, partly owing to her bodily weakness, that her nature was so often overcome, and ready to sink with gracious affection; but yet the truth was, that she had more grace, and greater discoveries of God and Christ, than the present frail state did well consist with. She wanted to be where strong grace might have more liberty, and be without the clog of a weak body; there she longed to be, and there she doubtless now is. She was looked upon amongst us, as a very eminent instance of christian experience; but this is but a very broken and imperfect account I have given of her: her eminency would much more appear, if her experiences were fully related, as she was wont to express, and manifest them, while living. I once read this account to some of her pious neighbours, who were acquainted with her, who said, to this purpose, that the *picture* fell much short of the *life*; and particularly that it much failed of duly representing her *humility*, and that admirable *lowliness of heart*, that at all times appeared in her. But there are, blessed be God! many living instances, of much the like nature, and in some things no less extraordinary.

But I now proceed to the *other instance*, that of the *little child* before mentioned. Her name is Phebe Bartlet,* daughter of William Bartlet. I shall give the account as I took it from the mouth of her parents, whose veracity none who know them doubt of.

She was born in *March*, 1731. About the latter end of *April*, or beginning of *May*, 1735, she was greatly affected by the talk of her brother, who had been hopefully converted a little before, at about eleven years of age, and then seriously talked to her about the great things of religion. Her parents did not know of it at that time, and were not wont, in the counsels they gave to their children, particularly to direct themselves to her, being so young, and, as they supposed, not capable of understanding. But after her brother had talked to her, they observed her very earnestly listen to the advice they gave to the other children; and she was observed very constantly to retire, several times in a day, as was concluded, for secret prayer. She grew more and more engaged in religion, and was more frequent in her closet; till at last she was wont to visit it five or six times a day: and was so engaged in it, that nothing would at any time divert her from her stated closet exercises. Her mother often observed and watched her, when such things occurred as she thought most likely to divert her, either by putting it out of her thoughts, or otherwise engaging her inclinations; but never could observe her to fail. She mentioned some very remarkable instances.

She once of her own accord spake of her unsuccessfulness, in that she could not find God, or to that purpose. But on *Thursday*, the last day of *July*, about the middle of the day, the child being in the closet, where it used to retire, its mother heard it speaking aloud; which was unusual, and never had been observed before. And her voice seemed to be as of one exceedingly importunate and engaged; but her mother could distinctly hear only these words, spoken in a childish manner, but with extraordinary earnestness, and out of distress of soul, PRAY, BLESSED LORD, *give me salvation!* I PRAY, BEG, *pardon all my sins!* When the child had done prayer, she came out of the closet, sat down by her mother, and cried out aloud.

* She was living in March, 1789, and maintained the character of a true convert.

Her mother very earnestly asked her several times, what the matter was, before she would make any answer; but she continued crying, and writhing her body to and fro, like one in anguish of spirit. Her mother then asked her, whether she was afraid that God would not give her salvation. She then answered, *Yes, I am afraid I shall go to hell!* Her mother then endeavoured to quiet her, and told her she *would not have her cry*, she *must be a good girl, and pray every day, and* she *hoped God would give her salvation.* But this did not quiet her at all; she continued thus earnestly crying, and taking on for some time, till at length she suddenly ceased crying, and began to smile, and presently said with a smiling countenance, *Mother, the kingdom of heaven is come to me!* Her mother was surprised at the sudden alteration, and at the speech; and knew not what to make of it; but at first said nothing to her. The child presently spake again, and said, *there is another come to me, and there is another, there is three;* and being asked what she meant, she answered, *one is, Thy will be done, and there is another, Enjoy him for ever;* by which it seems, that when the child said, *there is three come to me;* she meant three passages of her catechism that came to her mind.

After the child had said this, she retired again into her closet; and her mother went over to her brother's, who was next neighbour; and when she came back, the child, being come out of the closet, meets her mother with this cheerful speech; *I can find God now!* referring to what she had before complained of, that she could not find God. Then the child spoke again and said, *I love God!* her mother asked her, *how well* she loved God, whether she loved God *better than her father and mother*, she said, *Yes.* Then she asked her, whether she loved God *better than her little sister* Rachel. She answered, *Yes, better than any thing!* Then her elder sister, referring to her saying she could *find God now*, asked her, where she could *find God.* She answered, *In heaven. Why,* said she, *have you been in heaven? No,* said the child. By this it seems not to have been any imagination of any thing seen with bodily eyes, that she called God, when she said, I can find God now. Her mother asked her, whether she was *afraid of going to hell,* and if that had made her cry? She answered, *Yes, I was; but now I shan't.* Her mother asked her, whether she thought that God had given her salvation: she answered, *Yes.* Her mother asked her, *When?* She answered, *To-day.* She appeared all that afternoon exceeding cheerful and joyful. One of the neighbours asked her, how she felt herself? She answered, *I feel better than I did.* The neighbour asked her, what made her feel better. She answered, *God makes me.* That evening, as she lay a-bed, she called one of her little cousins to her, who was present in the room, as having something to say to him; and when he came, she told him, that *Heaven was better than earth.* The next day, her mother asked her *what God made her for?* She answered, *To serve him;* and added, *Every body should serve God, and get an interest in Christ.*

The same day the elder children, when they came home from school, seemed much affected with the extraordinary change that seemed to be made in *Phebe.* And her sister *Abigail* standing by, her mother took occasion to counsel her, now to improve her time, to prepare for another world. On which *Phebe* burst out in tears, and cried out, *Poor Nabby!* Her mother told her, she would not have her cry, she hoped that God would give *Nabby* salvation; but that did not quiet her, she continued earnestly crying for some time. When she had in a measure ceased, her sister *Eunice* being by her, she burst out again, and cried, *Poor Eunice!* and cried exceedingly; and when she had almost done, she went into another room, and there looked up on her sister *Naomi*: and burst out again, crying, *Poor Amy!* Her mother was greatly affected at such a behaviour in a child, and knew not what to say to her. One of the neighbours coming in a little after, asked her what she had cried for. She seemed at first backward to tell the reason: her mother told her she might tell that person, for he *had given her an apple*: upon which she said, she *cried because she was afraid they would go to hell.*

At night, a certain minister, who was occasionally in the own, was at the house, and talked with her of religious things. After he was gone, she sat leaning on the table, with tears running from her eyes; and being asked what made her cry, she said, It was *thinking about God.* The next day, being *Saturday*, she seemed great part of the day to be in a very affectionate frame, had four turns of crying and seemed to endeavour to curb herself, and hide her tears, and was very backward to talk of the occasion. On the *Sabbath-day* she was asked, whether she believed in God; she answered, *Yes.* And being told that Christ was the Son of God, she made ready answer, and said, *I know it.*

From this time there appeared a very remarkable abiding change in the child. She has been very strict upon the Sabbath; and seems to long for the Sabbath-day before it comes, and will often in the week time be inquiring how long it is to the Sabbath-day, and must have the days between particularly counted over, before she will be contented. She seems to love God's house, and is very eager to go thither. Her mother once asked her, why she had such a mind to go? whether it was not to see fine folks? She said, No, *it* was *to hear Mr. Edwards preach.* When she is in the place of worship, she is very far from spending her time there as children at her age usually do, but appears with an attention that is very extraordinary for such a child. She also appears very desirous at all opportunities to go to private religious meetings; and is very still and attentive at home, during prayer, and has appeared affected in time of family-prayer. She seems to delight much in hearing religious conversation. When I once was there with some strangers, and talked to her something of religion, she seemed more than ordinarily attentive; and when we were gone, she looked out very wistfully after us, and said, *I wish they would come again!* Her mother asked her, *why?* Says she, *I love to hear 'em talk.*

She seems to have very much of the fear of God before her eyes, and an extraordinary dread of sinning against him; of which her mother mentioned the following remarkable instance. Some time in *August*, the last year, she went with some bigger children, to get some plums in a neighbour's lot, knowing nothing of any harm in what she did; but when she brought some of the plums into the house, her mother mildly reproved her, and told her that she *must not get plums without leave, because it was sin*: God had *commanded her not to steal.* The child seemed greatly surprised, and burst out in tears, and cried out, *I wont have these plums!* and turning to her sister *Eunice*, very earnestly said to her, *Why did you ask me to go to that plum-tree? I should not have gone, if you had not asked me.* The other children did not seem to be much affected or concerned; but there was no pacifying *Phebe.* Her mother told her, she might go and ask leave, and then it would not be sin for her to eat them; and sent one of the children to that end; and, when she returned, her mother told her, that the owner had given leave, now she might eat them, and it would not be stealing. This stilled her a little while; but presently she broke out again into an exceeding fit of crying. Her mother asked her, *what made her cry again? Why she cried now, since* they had asked leave? *What* it was that troubled her now? And asked her several times very earnestly, before she made any answer; but at last said, *it was because,* BECAUSE IT WAS SIN. She continued a considerable time crying; and said she would not go again *if Eunice asked her an hundred times;* and she retained her aversion to that fruit for a considerable time, under the remembrance of her former sin.

She sometimes appears greatly affected, and delighted with texts of Scripture that come to her mind. Particularly about the beginning of *November*, that text came to her mind, Rev. iii. 20. "Behold, I stand at the door, and knock: If any man hear my voice, and open the door, I will come in, and sup with him, and he with me." She spoke of it to those of the family, with a great appearance of joy, a smiling countenance, and elevation of voice; and afterwards she went into another room, where her mother overheard her talking very earnestly to the children about it; and particularly heard her say to them, three or four times over, with an air of exceeding joy and admiration, *Why it is to* SUP WITH GOD. Some time about the middle of winter, very late in the night, when all were a-bed, her mother perceived that she was awake, and heard her, as though she was weeping. She called to her, and asked her what was the matter. She answered with a low voice, so that her mother could not hear what she said; but thinking that it might be occasioned by some spiritual affection, said no more to her: but perceived her to lie awake, and to continue in the same frame, for a considerable time. The next morning, she asked her, whether she did not cry the last night. The child answered, *Yes, I did cry a little, for I was thinking about God and Christ, and they loved me.* Her mother asked her, whether *to think of God and Christ loving her made her cry?* she answered, *Yes, it does sometimes.*

She has often manifested a great concern for the good of others' souls: and has been wont many times affectionately to counsel the other children. Once, about the latter end of *September*, the last year, when she and some others of the children were in a room by themselves, husking Indian corn, the child, after a while, came out and sat by the fire. Her mother took notice that she appeared with a more than ordinary serious and pensive countenance; but at last she broke silence, and said, I have been talking to *Nabby* and *Eunice.* Her mother asked her, what she had said to them. Why, said she, I *told them they must pray, and prepare to die;* that they had *but a little while to live in this world, and they must be always ready.* When *Nabby* came out, her mother asked her, whether she had said that to them. Yes, said she, *she said that, and a great deal more.* At other times, the child took opportunities to talk to the other children about the great concern of their souls, so as much to affect them. She was once exceeding importunate with her mother to go with her sister *Naomi* to pray: her mother endeavoured to put her off; but she pulled her by the sleeve, and seemed as if she would by no means be denied. At last her mother told her, that *Amy must go and pray by herself; but,* says the child, *she will not go;* and persisted earnestly to beg of her mother to go with her.

She has discovered an uncommon degree of a spirit of charity, particularly on the following occasion. A poor man that lives in the woods, had lately lost a cow that the family much depended on; and being at the house, he was relating his misfortune, and telling of the straits and difficulties they were reduced to by it. She took much notice of it, and it wrought exceedingly on her compassion. After she had attentively heard him awhile, she went away to her father, who was in the shop, and entreated him to give that man a cow: and told him, that *the poor man had no cow!* that *the hunters, or something else, had killed his cow!* and entreated him to give him one of theirs. Her father told her, that they could not spare one. Then she entreated him to let him and his family come and live at his house: and had much more talk of the same nature, whereby she manifested bowels of compassion to the poor.

She has manifested great love to her minister: particularly when I returned from my long journey for my health, the last *fall.* When she heard of it, she appeared very joyful at the news, and told the children of it, with an elevated voice, as the most joyful tidings; repeating it over and over, *Mr.* Edwards *is come home! Mr.* Edwards *is come home!* She still continues very constant in secret prayer, so far as can be observed, for she seems to have no desire that others should observe her when she retires, being a child of a reserved temper. Every night, before she goes to bed, she will say her catechism, and will by no means miss. She never forgot it but once, and then, after she was a-bed, thought of it, and cried out in tears, *I han't said my catechism!* and would not be quieted till her mother asked her the catechism as she lay in bed. She sometimes appears to be in doubt about the condition of her soul; and when asked, whether she thinks that she is prepared for death, speaks something doubtfully about it. At other times she seems to have no doubt, but when asked, replies, *Yes,* without hesitation.

In the former part of this great work of God amongst us, till it got to its height, we seemed to be wonderfully smiled upon and blessed in all respects. *Satan* seemed to be unusually restrained; persons who before had been involved in melancholy, seemed to be as it were waked up out of it; and those who had been entangled with extraordinary temptations, seemed wonderfully freed. And not only so, but it was the most remarkable time of health that ever I knew since I have been in the town. We ordinarily have several bills put up, every sabbath, for sick persons; but now we had not so much as one for many sabbaths together. But after this it seemed to be otherwise.

When this work of God appeared to be at its greatest height, a poor weak man who belongs to the town, being in great spiritual trouble, was hurried with violent temptations to cut his own throat, and made an attempt, but did not do it effectually. He, after this, continued a considerable time exceedingly overwhelmed with melancholy; but has now for a long time been very greatly delivered, by the light of God's countenance lifted up upon him, and has expressed a great sense of his sin in so far yielding to temptation; and there are in him all hopeful evidences of his having been made a subject of saving mercy.

In the latter part of May, it began to be very sensible that the Spirit of God was gradually withdrawing from us, and after this time *Satan* seemed to be more let loose, and raged in a dreadful manner. The first instance wherein it appeared, was a person putting an end to his own life by cutting his throat. He was a gentleman of more than common understanding, of strict morals, religious in his behaviour, and a useful and honourable person in the town; but was of a family that are exceedingly prone to the disease of melancholy, and his mother was killed with it. He had, from the beginning of this extraordinary time, been exceedingly concerned about the state of his soul, and there were some things in his experience that appeared very hopeful; but he durst entertain no hope concerning his own good estate. Towards the latter part of his time, he grew much discouraged, and melancholy grew again upon him, till he was wholly overpowered by it, and was in a great measure past a capacity of receiving advice, or being reasoned with to any purpose. The devil took the advantage, and drove him into despairing thoughts. He was kept awake at nights, meditating terror, so that he had scarce any sleep at all for a long time together; and it was observed at last, that he was scarcely well capable of managing his ordinary business, and was judged delirious by the coroner's inquest. The news of this extraordinarily affected the minds of people here, and struck them as it were with astonishment. After this, multitudes in this and other towns seemed to have it strongly suggested to them, and pressed upon them, to do as this person had done. And many who seemed to be under no melancholy, some pious persons who had no special darkness or doubts about the goodness of their state—nor were under any special trouble or concern of mind about any thing spiritual or temporal—had it urged upon them as if somebody had spoke to them, *Cut your own throat, now is a good opportunity.* Now! now! So that they were obliged to fight with all their might to resist it, and yet no reason suggested to them why they should do it.

About the same time, there were two remarkable instances of persons led away with strange enthusiastic delusions; one at *Suffield,* and another at *South Hadley.* That which has made the greatest noise in the country was the conduct of the man at *South Hadley;* whose delusion was, that he thought himself divinely instructed to direct a poor man in melancholy and despairing circumstances, to say certain words in prayer to God, as recorded in Psal. cxvi. 4. for his own relief. The man is esteemed a pious man; I have seen this error of his; had a particular acquaintance with him; and I believe none would question his piety who had such acquaintance. He gave me a particular account of the *manner* how he was deluded, which is too long to be here inserted; but, in short, he exceedingly rejoiced, and was elevated with the extraordinary work carried on in this part of the country; and was possessed with an opinion, that it was the beginning of the glorious times of the church spoken of in Scripture. He had read it as the opinion of some divines, that many in these times should be endued with extraordinary gifts of the Holy Ghost, and had embraced the notion, though he had at first no apprehensions that any besides ministers would have such gifts. But he since exceedingly laments the dishonour he has done to God, and the wound he has given religion in it, and has lain low before God and man for it.

After these things, the instances of conversion were rare here in comparison of what they had before been, though that remarkable instance before noticed of the little child, was after this. The Spirit of God not long after this time, appeared very sensibly withdrawing from all parts of the country, though we have heard of the work going on in some places of *Connecticut,* and that it continues to be carried on even to this day. But religion remained here, and I believe in some other places, the main subject of conversation for several months after. And there were some turns, wherein God's work seemed to revive, and we were ready to hope that all was going to be renewed again; yet, in the main, there was a gradual decline of that general, engaged, lively spirit in religion, which had been. Several things have happened since, which have diverted people's minds, and turned their conversation more to other affairs; particularly, his excellency the Governor's coming up, and the *committee of general court,* on the treaty with the *Indians.*—Afterwards, the *Springfield* controversy; and since that, our people in this town have been engaged in the building of a new meeting-house. Some other occurrences might be mentioned, that have seemed to have this effect. But as to those who have been thought converted at this time, they generally seem to have had an abiding change wrought on them. I have had particular acquaintance with many of them since; and they generally appear to be persons who have a new sense of things, new apprehensions and views of God, of the divine attributes of *Jesus Christ,* and the great things of the gospel. They have a new sense of their truth, and they affect them in a new manner; though it is very far from being always alike with them, neither can they revive a sense of things when they please. Their hearts are often touched, and sometimes filled, with new sweetnesses and delights; there seems to express an inward ardour and burning of heart, like to which they never experienced before; sometimes, perhaps, occasioned only by the mention of *Christ's* name, or some one of the divine perfections. There are new appetites, and a new kind of breathings and pantings of heart, *and groanings that cannot be uttered.* There is a new kind of inward labour and struggle of soul towards heaven and holiness.

Some who before were very rough in their temper and manners, seemed to be remarkably softened and sweetened. And some have had their souls exceedingly filled, and overwhelmed with light, love, and comfort, long since the work of God has ceased to be so remarkably carried on in a general way; and some have had much greater experiences of this nature than they had before. There is still a great deal of religious conversation continued in the town, amongst young and old; a religious disposition appears to be still maintained amongst our people, by their holding frequent private religious meetings; and all sorts are generally worshipping God at such meetings, on Sabbath-nights, and in the evening after our public lecture. Many children in the town still keep up such meetings among themselves. I know of no one young person in the town who has returned to former ways of *looseness* and *extravagance* in any respect; but we still remain a *reformed* people, and God has evidently made us a new people.

I cannot say that there has been *no instance* of any one person who has conducted himself unworthily; nor am I so vain as to imagine that we have not been mistaken in our good opinion concerning any; or that there are none who pass amongst us for sheep, that are indeed wolves in sheep's clothing; and who probably may, some time or other, discover themselves by their fruits. We are not so *pure,* but that we have great cause to be humbled and ashamed that we are so *impure;* nor so religious, but that those who watch for our halting, may see things in us, whence they may take occasion to reproach us and religion. But in the main, there has been a *great and marvellous work of conversion and sanctification* among the people here; and they have paid all due respect to those who have been blest of God to be the instruments of it. Both old and young have shown a forwardness to hearken not only to my counsels, but even to my reproofs, from the pulpit.

A great part of the country have not received the most favourable thoughts of this affair; and to this day many retain a jealousy concerning it, and prejudice against it. I have reason to think that the meanness and weakness of the instrument, that has been made use of in this town, has prejudiced many against it; nor does it appear to me strange that it should be so. But yet the circumstance of this great work of God, is analogous to other circumstances of it. God has so ordered the manner of the work in many respects, as very signally and remarkably to show it to be his own peculiar and immediate work; and to secure the glory of it wholly to his own almighty power, and sovereign grace. And whatever the circumstances and means have been, and though we are so unworthy, yet *so* hath it pleased God to work! And we are evidently a people blessed of the Lord! For here, *in this corner of the world,* God dwells, and manifests his glory.

Thus, Reverend Sir, I have given a *large* and *particular* account of this remarkable affair; and yet, considering how manifold God's works have been amongst us, it is but a very *brief* one. I should have sent it much sooner, had I not been greatly hindered by illness in my family, and also in my own person. It is probably much larger than you *expected,* and, it may be, than you *would have chosen.* I thought that the extraordinary nature of the thing, and the innumerable misrepresentations which have gone abroad of it, many of which, doubtless, have reached your ears, made it necessary that I should be particular. But I would leave it entirely with your wisdom to make what use of it you think best, to send a part of it to England, or all, or none, if you think it not worthy; or otherwise to dispose of it as you may think most for God's glory, and the interest of religion. If you are pleased to send any thing to the Rev. Dr. Guyse, I should be glad to have it signified to him, as my humble desire, that since he and the congregation to which he preached, have been pleased to take so much notice of us, as they have, that they would also think of us at the throne of grace, and seek there for us, that God would not forsake us, but enable us to bring forth fruit answerable to our profession, and our mercies; and that our "light may so shine before men, that others seeing our good works, may glorify our Father which is in heaven."

When I first heard of the notice the Rev. Dr. Watts and Dr. Guyse took of God's mercies to us, I took occasion to inform our congregation of it in a discourse from these words—*A city that is set upon a hill cannot be hid.* And having since seen a particular account of the notice which the Rev. Dr. Guyse and his congregation took of it, in a letter you wrote to my honoured uncle Williams, I read that part of your letter to the congregation, and laboured as much as in me lay to enforce their duty from it. The congregation were very sensibly moved and affected at both times.

I humbly request of you, Reverend Sir, your prayers for *this county,* in its present melancholy circumstances, into which it is brought by the Springfield quarrel; which, doubtless, above all things that have happened, has tended to put a stop to the glorious work here, and to prejudice this country against it, and hinder the propagation of it. I also ask your prayers for *this town,* and would particularly beg an interest in them for *him* who is,

Honoured Sir,

With humble respect,

Your obedient Son and Servant,

JONATHAN EDWARDS.

Northampton,
Nov. 6, 1736.

SOME THOUGHTS

CONCERNING

THE PRESENT REVIVAL OF RELIGION

IN NEW ENGLAND,

AND THE

WAY IN WHICH IT OUGHT TO BE ACKNOWLEDGED AND PROMOTED;

HUMBLY OFFERED TO THE PUBLIC,

IN A TREATISE ON THAT SUBJECT.

Isa. xl. 3.—Prepare ye the way of the Lord, make straight in the desert a high-way for our God.

THE PREFACE.

In the ensuing treatise, I condemn ministers assuming, or taking too much upon them, and appearing as though they supposed that they were the persons to whom it especially belonged to dictate, direct, and determine; but perhaps shall be thought to be very guilty of it myself. And some, when they read this treatise, may be ready to say, that while I condemn this in others, I have the monopoly of it.——I confess that I have taken a great deal of liberty freely to express my thoughts concerning almost every thing appertaining to the wonderful work of God that has of late been carried on in the land, and to declare what has appeared to me to be the mind of God concerning the duty and obligations of all sorts of persons, and even those that are my superiors and fathers, ministers of the gospel, and civil rulers. But yet I hope the liberty I have taken is not greater than can be justified. In a free nation, such liberty of the press is allowed, that every author takes leave, without offence, freely to speak his opinion concerning the management of public affairs, and the duty of the legislature, and those that are at the head of the administration, though vastly his superiors. As at this day, private subjects offer their sentiments to the public, from the press, concerning the management of the war with Spain; freely declaring what they think to be the duty of the parliament, and the principal ministers of state, &c. We in New England are now engaged in a more important war. And I am sure, if we consider the sad jangling and confusion that has attended it, we shall confess that it is highly requisite somebody should speak his mind, concerning the way in which it ought to be managed. Not only a few of the many particulars, which are the matter of strife, should be debated, on the one side and the other, in pamphlets (as has of late been done, with heat and fierceness enough)—which do not tend to bring the contention in general to an end, but rather to inflame it, and increase the uproar—but something should be published to bring the affair in general, and the many things that attend it, which are the subjects of debate, under a particular consideration. And certainly it is high time that this was done. If private persons may speak their minds without arrogance; much more may a minister of the kingdom of Christ speak freely about things of this nature, which do so nearly concern the interest of the kingdom of his Lord and Master, at so important a juncture. If some elder minister had undertaken this, I acknowledge it would have been more proper; but I have heard of no such thing like to be done. I hope therefore I shall be excused for undertaking such a work. I think that nothing I have said can justly be interpreted, as though I would impose my thoughts upon any, or did not suppose that others have equal right to think for themselves. We are not accountable one to another for our thoughts; but we must all give an account to Him who searches our hearts, and has doubtless his eye especially upon us at such an extraordinary season as this. If I have well confirmed my opinion concerning this work, and the way in which it should be acknowledged and promoted, with Scripture and reason, I hope those who read it will receive it as a manifestation of the mind and will of God. If others would hold forth further light to me in any of these particulars, I hope I should thankfully receive it. I think I have been made in some measure sensible, and much more of late than formerly, of my need of more wisdom than I have. I make it my rule to lay hold of light and embrace it, wherever I see it, though held forth by a child or an enemy. If I have assumed too much in the following discourse, and have spoken in a manner that savours of a spirit of pride, no wonder that others can better discern it than I myself. If it be so, I ask pardon, and beg the prayers of every christian reader, that I may have more light, humility, and zeal; and that I may be favoured with such measures of the divine Spirit, as a minister of the gospel stands in need of, at such an extraordinary season.

THOUGHTS ON THE REVIVAL, &c.

PART I.

SHOWING THAT THE EXTRAORDINARY WORK WHICH HAS OF LATE BEEN GOING ON IN THIS LAND, IS A GLORIOUS WORK OF GOD.

THE error of those who have had ill thoughts of the great religious operation on the minds of men, which has been carried on of late in *New England*, (so far as the ground of such an error has been in the understanding, and not in the disposition,) seems fundamentally to lie in three things: *First*, In judging of this work *a priori*. *Secondly*, In not taking the Holy Scriptures as a whole rule whereby to judge of such operations. *Thirdly*, In not justly separating and distinguishing the good from the bad.

SECT. I.

We should not judge of this work by the supposed causes, but by the effects.

THEY have greatly erred in the way in which they have gone about to try this work, whether it be a work of the Spirit of God or no, *viz.* in judging of it *a priori;* from the way that it *began*, the *instruments* that have been employed, the *means* that have been used, and the methods that have been taken and succeeded, in carrying it on. Whereas, if we duly consider the matter, it will evidently appear that such a work is not to be judged of *a priori*, but *a posteriori*. We are to observe the *effect* wrought; and if, upon examination of that, it be found to be agreeable to the word of God, we are bound to rest in it as God's work; and shall be like to be rebuked for our arrogance, if we refuse so to do till God shall explain to us how he has brought this effect to pass, or why he has made use of such and such means in doing it. These texts are enough to cause us, with trembling, to forbear such a way of proceeding in judging of a work of God's Spirit: Isa. xl. 13, 14. "Who hath directed the Spirit of the Lord, or being his counsellor hath taught him? With whom took he counsel, and who instructed him, and taught him in the path of judgment, and taught him knowledge, and showed to him the way of understanding?" John iii. 8. "The wind bloweth where it listeth, and thou hearest the sound thereof; but canst not tell whence it cometh, and whither it goeth." We hear the sound, we perceive the effect, and from thence we judge that the wind does indeed blow; without waiting, before we pass this judgment, first to be satisfied what should be the cause of the wind's blowing from such a part of the heavens, and how it should come to pass that it should blow in such a manner, at such a time. To judge *a priori*, is a wrong way of judging of any of the works of God. We are not to resolve that we will first be satisfied how God brought this or the other effect to pass, and why he hath made it thus, or why it has pleased him to take such a course, and to use such and such means, before we will acknowledge his work, and give him the glory of it. This is too much for the *clay* to take upon it with respect to the *potter*. "God gives not account of his matters: His judgments are a great deep: He hath his way in the sea, and his path in the great waters, and his footsteps are not known; and who shall teach God knowledge, or enjoin him his way, or say unto him, What dost thou? We know not what is the way of the Spirit, nor how the bones do grow in the womb of her that is with child; even so we know not the works of God who maketh all." No wonder therefore if those that go this forbidden way to work, in judging of the present wonderful operation, are perplexed and confounded. We ought to take heed that we do not expose ourselves to the calamity of those who pried into the ark of God, when God mercifully returned it to *Israel*, after it had departed from them.

Indeed God has not taken that course, nor made use of those means, to begin and carry on this great work, which men in their wisdom would have thought most advisable, if he had asked their counsel; but quite the contrary. But it appears to me that the great God has wrought like himself, in the manner of his carrying on this work; so as very much to show his own glory, exalt his own sovereignty, power, and all-sufficiency. He has poured contempt on all that human strength, wisdom, prudence, and sufficiency which men have been wont to trust, and to glory in; so as greatly to cross, rebuke, and chastise the pride and other corruptions of men; Isa. ii. 17. "And the loftiness of man shall be bowed down, and the haughtiness of men shall be made low, and the Lord alone shall be exalted in that day." God doth thus, in intermingling in his providence so many stumbling-blocks with this work: in suffering so much of human weakness and infirmity to appear; and in ordering so many things that are mysterious to men's wisdom: in pouring out his Spirit chiefly on the common people, and bestowing his greatest and highest favours upon them, admitting them nearer to himself than the great, the honourable, the rich, and the learned; agreeable to that prophecy, Zech. xii. 7. "The Lord also shall save the tents of Judah first, that the glory of the house of David, and the glory of the inhabitants of Jerusalem, do not magnify themselves against Judah." Those who dwelt in the tents of *Judah* were the common people, who dwelt in the country, and were of inferior rank. The inhabitants of *Jerusalem* were their citizens, their men of wealth and figure; and *Jerusalem* also was the chief place of the habitation or resort of their priests and Levites, and their officers and judges; there sat the great *Sanhedrim*. The house of *David* was the highest rank of all, the royal family, and the great men about the king.—It is evident by the context, that this prophecy has respect to something further than saving the people out of the *Babylonish* captivity.

God in this work has begun at the lower end, and he has made use of the weak and foolish things of the world to carry it on. Some of the ministers chiefly employed, have been mere babes in age and standing; and some of them not so high in reputation among their brethren as many others; and God has suffered their infirmities to appear in the sight of others, so as much to displease them; and at the same time it has pleased God greatly to succeed them, while he has not so succeeded others who are generally reputed vastly their superiors. Yea, there is reason to think that it has pleased God to make use of the infirmities of some, particularly their imprudent zeal, and censorious spirit, to chastise the deadness, negligence, earthly-mindedness, and vanity found among ministers in the late times of declension and deadness, wherein wise virgins and foolish, ministers and people, have sunk into a deep sleep. These things in ministers of the gospel, that go forth as the ambassadors of Christ, and have the care of immortal souls, are extremely abominable to God; vastly more hately in his sight than all the imprudence and intemperate heats, wildness and distraction (as some call it) of these zealous preachers. A supine carelessness, and a vain, carnal, worldly spirit in a minister of the gospel, is the worst madness and distraction in the sight of God. God may also make use at this day of the unchristian censoriousness of some preachers, the more to humble and purify some of his own children and true servants that have been wrongfully censured, to fit them for more eminent service and future honour.

SECT. II.

We should judge by the rule of Scripture

ANOTHER foundation-error of those who do not acknowledge the divinity of this work is, not taking the Holy Scriptures as *whole*, and in itself a sufficient rule to judge of such things by. They who have one certain consistent rule to judge by, are like to come to some clear determination; but they who have half a dozen different rules, instead of justly and clearly determining, do but perplex and darken themselves and others. They who would learn the true measure of any thing, and will have many different measures to try it by, have a task that they will not accomplish.—Those of whom I am speaking will indeed make some use of Scripture, so far as they think it serves their turn, but do not make use of it *alone* as a rule sufficient by itself, but make as much and a great deal more use of other things, diverse and wide from it, by which to judge of this work. For,

I. Some make *philosophy*, instead of the Holy Scriptures, their rule of judging of this work; particularly the philosophical notions they entertain of the nature of the soul, its faculties and affections. Some are ready to say, "There is but little sober solid religion in this work; it is little else but flash and noise. Religion now all runs out into transports and high flights of the passions and affections." In their philosophy, the affections of the soul are something diverse from the will, and not appertaining to the noblest part of the soul. They are ranked among the meanest principles that belong to men as partaking of animal nature, and what he has in common with the brute creation, rather than any thing whereby he is conformed to angels and pure spirits. And though they acknowledge that a good use may be made of the affections in religion, yet they suppose that the substantial part of religion does not consist in them, but that they are something adventitious and accidental in Christianity.

But these gentlemen, I cannot but think, labour under great mistakes, both in their philosophy and divinity. It is true, distinction must be made in the affections or passions. There is a great deal of difference in high and raised affections, which must be distinguished by the skill of the observer. Some are much more solid than others. There are many exercises of the affections that are very flashy, and little to be depended on; and oftentimes a great deal appertains to them, or rather is the effect of them, that has its seat in animal nature, and is very much owing to the constitution and frame of the body; and that which sometimes more especially obtains the name of passion, is nothing solid or substantial. But it is false philosophy to suppose this to be the case with all exercises of affection in the soul, or with all great and high affections; and false divinity to suppose that religious affections do not appertain to the substance and essence of Christianity. On the contrary, it seems to me that the very life and soul of all true religion consists in them.

I humbly conceive that the affections of the soul are not properly distinguished from the will, as though they were two faculties. All acts of the affections are in some sense acts of the will, and all the acts of the will are acts of the affections. All exercises of the will are, in some degree or other, exercises of the soul's appetition or aversion; or which is the same thing, of its love or hatred. The soul wills one thing rather than another, or chooses one thing rather than another, no otherwise than as it loves one thing more than another; but love and hatred are affections of the soul. Therefore all acts of the will are truly acts of the affections; though the exercises of the will do not obtain the name of passions, unless the will, either in its aversion or opposition, be exercised in a high degree, or in a vigorous and lively manner.—All will allow that true virtue or holiness has its seat chiefly in the heart, rather than in the head. It therefore follows, from what has been said already, that it consists chiefly in holy *affections*. The things of religion take place in men's hearts, no further than they are *affected* with them. The informing of the understanding is all vain, any farther than it *affects* the heart, or, which is the same thing, has influence on the *affections*.

Those gentlemen, who make light of these raised affections in religion, will doubtless allow that true religion and holiness, as it has its seat in the heart, is capable of very high degrees, and high exercises in the soul. For instance; they will probably allow, that the holiness of the heart or will is capable of being raised to a hundred times as great a degree of strength as it is in the most eminent saint on earth, or to be exerted in a hundred times so vigorous exercises of the heart; and yet be true religion or holiness still. Now therefore I would ask them, by what name they will call these high and vigorous exercises of the will or heart? Are they not high affections? What can they consist in, but in high acts of love; strong and vigorous exercises of benevolence and complacence; high, exalting, and admiring thoughts of God and his perfections; strong desires after God, &c.?—And now, what are we come to but high and raised affections? yea, those very affections that before they objected against, as worthy of little regard?

All will allow that there is nothing but solid religion in heaven; but there, holiness is raised to an exceeding great height, to strong, high, exalted exercises of heart. Now, what other strong and high exercises of the heart, or of holiness as it has its seat in their hearts, can we devise for them, but holy affections, high degrees of actings of love to God, rejoicing in God, admiration of God, &c.?—Therefore these things in the saints and angels in heaven are not to be despised and cashiered by the name of great heats and transports of the passions.—And it will doubtless be yet further allowed, that the more eminent the saints are on earth, the stronger their grace, and the higher its exercises are, the more they are like the saints in heaven, *i. e.* (by what has been just now observed,) the more they have of high or raised affections in religion.

Though there are false affections in religion, and in some respects raised high; yet undoubtedly there are also true, holy, and solid affections; and the higher these are raised, the better. And, when they are raised to an exceeding great height, they are not to be suspected merely because of their degree, but on the contrary to be esteemed. Charity, or divine love, is in Scripture represented as the sum of all the religion of the heart; but this is only a holy *affection*. And therefore, in proportion as this is firmly fixed in the soul, and raised to a great height, the more eminent a person is in holiness. Divine love or charity is represented as the sum of all the religion of heaven, and that wherein mainly the religion of the church in its more perfect state on earth shall consist, when knowledge, and tongues, and prophesyings shall cease; and therefore the higher this holy affection is raised in the church of God, or in a gracious soul, the more excellent and perfect is the state of the church, or a particular soul.

If we take the Scriptures for our rule, then the greater and higher our exercises of love to God, delight and complacency in him, desires and longings after him, delight in his children, love to mankind, brokenness of heart, abhorrence of sin, and self-abhorrence for it; the more we have of the peace of God which passeth all understanding, and joy in the Holy Ghost, unspeakable and full of glory: the higher our admiring thoughts of God, exulting and glorying in him; so much the higher is Christ's religion, or that virtue which he and his apostles taught, raised in the soul.

It is a stumbling to some, that religious affections should seem to be so powerful, or that they should be so violent, (as they express it,) in some persons. They are therefore ready to doubt whether it can be the Spirit of God; or, whether this vehemence be not rather a sign of the operation of an evil spirit. But why should such a doubt arise? What is represented in Scripture as more powerful in its effects than the Spirit of God? which is therefore called "the power of the Highest," Luke i. 35. and its saving effect in the soul is called "the power of godliness." So we read of the "demonstration of the Spirit and of power," 1 Cor. ii. 4. And it is said to operate in the minds of men with the "exceeding greatness of divine power," and "according to the working of God's mighty power," Eph. i. 19. So we read of "the effectual working of his power," Eph. iii. 7. "the power that worketh in Christians," v. 20. the *glorious power* of God in the operations of the Spirit, Col. i. 11. and *the work of faith*, wrought *with power*, 2 Thess. i. 11. In 2 Tim. i. 7. the Spirit of God is called "the Spirit of power, and of love, and of a sound mind."—So the Spirit is represented by a mighty wind, and by fire, things most powerful in their operation.

II. Many are guilty of not taking the Holy *Scriptures* as a *sufficient* and *whole* rule, whereby to judge of this work. They judge by those things which the Scripture does not give as any signs or marks whereby to judge one way or the other, *viz.* the effects that religious exercises and affections of mind have upon the body. Scripture-rules respect the state of the mind, moral conduct, and voluntary behaviour; and not the physical state of the body. The design of the Scripture is to teach us divinity, and not physic and anatomy. Ministers are made the watchmen of men's souls, and not their bodies; and therefore the great rule which God has committed into their hands, is to make them divines, and not physicians.—Christ knew what instructions and rules his church would stand in need of, better than we do; and, if he had seen it needful in order to the church's safety, he doubtless would have given to ministers rules for judging of bodily effects. He would have told them how the pulse should beat under such and such religious exercises of mind; when men should look pale, and when they should shed tears; when they should tremble, and whether or no they should ever be faint or cry out; or whether the body should ever be put into convulsions. He probably would have put some book into their hands, that should have tended to make them excellent anatomists and physicians. But he has not done it, because he did not see it to be needful.—He judged, that if ministers thoroughly did their duty as watchmen and overseers of the state and frame of men's souls, and of their voluntary conduct, according to the rules he had given, his church would be well provided for as to its safety in these matters. And therefore those ministers of Christ, and overseers of souls, who are full of concern about the involuntary motions of the fluids and solids of men's bodies, and who from thence are full of doubts and suspicions of the cause—when nothing appears but that the state and frame of their minds, and their voluntary behaviour, is good, and agreeable to God's word—go out of the place that Christ has set them in, and leave their proper business, as much as if they should undertake to tell who are under the influence of the Spirit by their looks, or their gait. I cannot see which way we are in danger, or how the devil is like to get any notable advantage against us, if we do but thoroughly do our duty with respect to those two things, *viz.* the state of persons' *minds*, and their moral *conduct;* seeing to it that they be maintained in an agreeableness to the rules that Christ has given us. If things are but kept right in these respects, our fears and suspicions arising from extraordinary bodily effects seem wholly groundless.

The most specious thing alleged against these extraordinary effects on the body, is, That the body is impaired, and that it is hard to think that God, in the merciful influences of his Spirit on men, would wound their bodies, and impair their health. But if it were in multiplied instances (which I do not suppose it is) that persons received a lasting wound to their health by extraordinary religious impressions made upon their minds, yet it is too much for us to determine that God shall never bring an outward calamity, in bestowing a vastly greater spiritual and eternal good. *Jacob* in doing his duty in wrestling with God for the blessing, and even at the same time that he received the blessing from God, suffered a great outward calamity from his hand. God gave him the blessing, but sent him away halting on his thigh, and he went lame all his life after. And yet this is not mentioned as if it were any diminution of the great mercy of God to him, when God blessed him, and he received his name *Israel*, because as a prince he had power with God, and had prevailed.

But, say some, The operations of the Spirit of God are of a benign nature; nothing is of a more kind influence on human nature than the merciful breathings of God's own Spirit. But it has been generally supposed and allowed in the church of God, till now, that there is such a thing as being sick of love to Christ, or having the bodily strength weakened by strong and vigorous exercises of love to him. And however kind to human nature the influences of the Spirit of God are, yet nobody doubts but that divine and eternal things, as they may be discovered, would overpower the nature of man in its present weak state; and that therefore the body, in its present weakness, is not fitted for the views, and pleasures, and employments of heaven. Were God to discover but a little of that which is seen by saints and angels in heaven, our frail natures would sink under it. Let us rationally consider what we profess to believe of the infinite greatness of divine wrath, divine glory, the divine infinite love and grace in Jesus Christ, and the infinite importance of eternal things; and then how reasonable it is to suppose, that if God a little withdraw the veil, to let light into the soul—and give a view of the great things of another world in their transcendent and infinite greatness—that human nature, which is as the grass, a shaking leaf, a weak withering flower, should totter under such a discovery! Such a bubble is too weak to bear a weight so vast. Alas! what is man that he should support himself under a view of the awful wrath or infinite glory and love of JEHOVAH! No wonder therefore that it is said, "No man can see me and live;" and, "Flesh and blood cannot inherit the kingdom of God." That external glory and majesty of Christ which Daniel saw, when "there remained no strength in him, and his comeliness was turned in him into corruption," Dan. x. 6—8. and which the apostle John saw, when he fell at his feet as dead; was but a shadow of that spiritual majesty of Christ which will be manifested in the souls of the saints in another world, and which is sometimes, in a degree, manifested to the soul in this world. And if beholding the image of this glory did so overpower human nature, is it unreasonable to suppose that a sight of the spiritual glory itself, should have as powerful an effect? The prophet Habakkuk, speaking of the awful manifestations God made of his majesty and wrath, at the Red sea, and in the wilderness, and at mount Sinai, where he gave the law; and of the merciful influence and strong impression God caused it to have upon him, to the end that he might be saved from that wrath, and rest in the day of trouble; says, Hab. iii. 16. "When I heard, my belly trembled, my lips quivered at the voice, rottenness entered into my bones, I trembled in myself, that I might rest in the day of trouble." This is an effect similar to what the discovery of the same majesty and wrath has had upon many in these days; and to the same purposes, *viz.* to give them rest in the day of trouble, and save them from that wrath. The psalmist also speaks of such an effect as I have often seen on persons under religious affections of late, Psal. cxix. 131.

God is pleased sometimes, in dealing forth spiritual blessings to his people, in some respects to exceed the capacity of the vessel in its present scantiness; so that he not only fills it, but makes their *cup to run over;* (Psal. xxiii. 5.) and pours out a blessing, sometimes, in such manner and measure that there is not room enough to receive it. (Mal. iii. 10.) He gives them riches more than they can carry away; as he did to Jehoshaphat and his people in a time of great favour, by the word of his prophet Jahaziel in answer to earnest prayer, when the people blessed the Lord in the valley of Berachah, 2 Chron. xx. 25, 26. It has been with the disciples of Christ, for a long season, a time of great emptiness on spiritual accounts. They have gone hungry, and having been toiling in vain, during a dark night with the church of God; as it was with the disciples of old, when they had toiled all night for something to eat, and caught nothing, Luke v. 5. and John xxi. 3. But now, the morning being come, Jesus appears to his disciples, and takes a compassionate notice of their wants, and says to them, *Children, have ye any meat?* and gives some of them such abundance of food, that they are not able to draw their net; yea, so that their net breaks, and their vessel is overloaded, and begins to sink; as it was with the disciples of old, Luke v. 6, 7. and John xxi. 6.

We cannot determine that God never shall give any person so much of a discovery of himself, not only as to weaken their bodies, but to take away their lives. It is supposed by very learned and judicious divines, that Moses's life was taken away after this manner; and this has also been supposed to be the case with some other saints. Yea, I do not see any solid sure grounds any have to determine, that God shall never make such strong impressions on the mind by his Spirit, that shall be an occasion of so impairing the frame of the body, that persons shall be deprived of the use of reason. As I said before, it is too much for us to determine, that God will not bring an outward calamity in bestowing spiritual and eternal blessings; so it is too much for us to determine how great an outward calamity he will bring. If God gives a great increase of discoveries of himself, and of love to him, the benefit is infinitely greater than the calamity, though the life should presently after be taken away; yea, though the soul should lie for years in a deep sleep, and then be taken to heaven: or, which is much the same thing, if it be deprived of the use of its faculties, and be as inactive and unserviceable, as if it lay in a deep sleep for some years, and then should pass into glory. We cannot determine how great a calamity distraction is, considered with all its consequences; and all that might have been consequent if the distraction had not happened; nor indeed whether, thus considered, it be any calamity at all, or whether it be not a mercy, by preventing some great sin, &c. It is a great fault in us to limit a sovereign all-wise God, whose judgments are a great deep, and his ways past finding out, where he has not limited himself, and in things concerning which he has not told us what his way shall be. It is remarkable, considering in what multitudes of instances, and to how great a degree, the frame of the body has been overpowered of late, that persons' lives have, notwithstanding, been preserved. The instances of those who have been deprived of reason, have been very few, and those, perhaps all of them, persons under the peculiar disadvantage of a weak, vaporous habit of body. A merciful and careful divine hand is very manifest in it, that the ship, though in so many instances it has begun to sink, yet has been upheld, and has not totally sunk. The instances of such as have been deprived of reason are so few, that certainly they are not enough to cause alarm, as though this work was like to be of baneful influence; unless we are disposed to gather up all that we can to darken it, and set it forth in frightful colours.

There is one particular kind of exercise by which many have been overpowered, that has been especially stumbling to some; and that is, their deep distress for the souls of others. I am sorry that any put us to the trouble of defending such a thing as this. It seems like mere trifling in so plain a case, to enter into a particular debate, in order to determine whether there be any thing in the greatness and importance of the case that will bear a proportion to the greatness of the concern manifested. Men may be allowed, from no higher a principle than common humanity, to be very deeply concerned, and greatly exercised in mind, at seeing others in great danger of, or being burnt up in a house on fire. And it will be allowed to be equally reasonable, if they saw them in danger of a calamity ten times greater, to be still much more concerned; and so much more still, if the calamity was still vastly greater. Why then should it be thought unreasonable, and looked on with a suspicious eye, as if it must come from some bad cause, when persons are extremely concerned at seeing others in a very great danger of suffering the fierceness and wrath of almighty God to all eternity? Besides, it will doubtless be allowed that those who have great degrees of the Spirit of God, which is a Spirit of love, may well be supposed to have vastly more love and compassion to their fellow-creatures, than those who are influenced only by common humanity. Why should it be thought strange that those who are full of the Spirit of Christ, should be proportionably, in their love to souls, like to Christ? He had so strong a love and concern for them, as to be willing to drink the dregs of the cup of God's fury; and, at the same time that he offered up his blood for souls, he offered up also, as their high priest, strong crying and tears, with an extreme agony, wherein the soul of Christ was as it were in travail for the souls of the elect; and therefore, in saving them, he is said to see of the *travail* of his soul. As such a spirit of love and concern for souls was the spirit of Christ, so it is that of the church. Therefore the church, in desiring and seeking that Christ might be brought forth in the souls of men, is represented, Rev. xii. as a "woman crying, travailing in birth, and pained to be delivered." The spirit of those who have been in distress for the souls of others, so far as I can discern, seems not to be different from that of the apostle, who travailed for souls, and was ready to *wish himself accursed from Christ*, for others; and that of the psalmist, Psal. cxix. 53. "Horror hath taken hold upon me, because of the wicked that forsake thy law." And ver. 136. "Rivers of waters run down mine eyes, because they keep not thy law." And that of the prophet *Jeremiah*, Jer. iv. 19. "My bowels! my bowels! I am pained at my very heart! my heart maketh a noise in me! I cannot hold my peace! because thou hast heard, O my soul, the sound of the trumpet, the alarm of war!" And so chap. ix. 1. and xiii. 17. xiv. 17. and Isa. xvii. 4. We read of *Mordecai*, when he saw his people in danger of being destroyed with a temporal destruction, Esth. iv. 1. that "he rent his clothes, and put on sackcloth with ashes, and went out in the midst of the city, and cried with a loud and bitter cry." And why then should persons be thought to be distracted, when they cannot forbear crying out, at the consideration of the misery of those who are going to eternal destruction.

III. Another thing that some make their rule to judge of this work by, instead of the Holy Scriptures, is *history*, or former observation. Herein they err two ways:

First, If there be any thing extraordinary in the circumstances of this work, which was not observed in former times, theirs is a rule to reject this work which God has not given them, and they limit God, where he has not limited himself. And this is especially unreasonable in this case: for whosoever has well weighed the wonderful and mysterious methods of divine wisdom in carrying on the work of the new creation—or in the progress of the work of redemption, from the first promise of the seed of the woman to this time—may easily observe that it has all along been God's manner to open new scenes, and to bring forth to view things new and wonderful—such as eye had not seen, nor ear heard, nor entered into the heart of man or angels—to the astonishment of heaven and earth, not only in the revelations he makes of his mind and will, but also in the works of his hands. As the old creation was carried on through six days, and appeared all complete, settled in a state of rest, on the seventh; so the new creation, which is immensely the greatest and most glorious work, is carried on in a gradual progress, from the fall of man, to the consummation of all things. And as in the progress of the old creation, there were still new things accomplished; new wonders every day in the sight of the angels, the spectators of that work—while those morning-stars sang together, new scenes were opened, till the whole was finished—so it is in the progress of the new creation. So that that promise, Isa. lxiv. 4. "For since the beginning of the world, men have not heard, nor perceived by the ear, neither hath the eye seen, O God, besides thee, what he hath prepared for him that waiteth for him." Though it had a glorious fulfilment in the days of Christ and his apostles, as the words are applied, 1 Cor. ii. 9. yet it always remains to be fulfilled, in things that are yet behind, till the new creation is finished, at Christ's delivering up the kingdom to the Father. And we live in those latter days, wherein we may be especially warranted to expect that things will be accomplished, concerning which it will be said, *Who hath heard such a thing? who hath seen such things?*

Besides, those things in this work, which have been chiefly complained of as new, are not so new as has been generally imagined. Though they have been much more frequent lately, in proportion to the uncommon degree, extent, and swiftness, and other extraordinary circumstances, of the work, yet they are not *new* in their kind; but are of the same nature as have been found, and well approved of, in the church of God before, from time to time.—We have a remarkable instance in Mr. *Bolton*, that noted minister of the church of *England*, who after being awakened by the preaching of the famous Mr. *Perkins*, minister of Christ in the university of *Cambridge*, was the subject of such terrors as threw him to the ground, and caused him to roar with anguish. The pangs of the new birth in him were such, that he lay pale and without sense, like one dead; as we have an account in the *Fulfilment of the Scripture*, the 5th edition, p. 103, 104. We have an account in the same page of another, whose comforts under the sun-shine of God's presence were so great, that he could not forbear crying out in a transport, and expressing in exclamations the great sense he had of forgiving mercy and his assurance of God's love. And we have a remarkable instance, in the life of Mr. *George Trosse*, written by himself, (who, of a notoriously vicious profligate liver, became an eminent saint and minister of the gospel,) of terrors occasioned by awakenings of conscience, so overpowering the body, as to deprive him, for some time, of the use of reason.

Yea, such extraordinary external effects of inward impressions have not been found merely in here and there a single person, but there have been times wherein many have been thus affected, in some particular parts of the church of God; and such effects have appeared in congregations, in many at once. So it was in the year 1625, in the west of *Scotland*, on a time of great outpouring of the Spirit of God. It was then a frequent thing for many to be so extraordinarily seized with terror in hearing the word, by the Spirit of God convincing them of sin, that they fell down, and were carried out of the church, and they afterwards proved most solid and lively Christians; as the author of the *Fulfilling of the Scripture* informs us, p. 185. The same author in the preceding page, informs of many in *France* that were so wonderfully affected with the preaching of the gospel, in the time of those famous divines *Farel* and *Viret*, that for a time they could not follow their secular business: and, p. 186. of many in *Ireland*, in a time of great outpouring of the Spirit there, in the year 1628, that were so filled with divine comforts, and a sense of God, that they made but little use of either meat, drink, or sleep; and professed that they did not feel the need thereof. The same author gives a similar account of Mrs. *Katharine Brettergh*, of *Lancashire*, in *England*, (p. 391, 392.) After great distress, which very much affected her body, God did so break in upon her mind with light and discoveries of himself, that she was forced to burst out, crying, "O the joys, the joys, the joys that I feel in my soul! O they be wonderful, they be wonderful! The place where I now am is sweet and pleasant! How comfortable is the sweetness I feel, that delights my soul! The taste is precious; do you not feel it? Oh so sweet as it is!" And at other times, "O my sweet Saviour, shall I be one with thee, as thou art one with the Father? And dost thou so love me that am but dust, to make me partaker of glory with Christ? O how wonderful is thy love! And O that my tongue and heart were able to sound forth thy praises as I ought!" At another time she burst forth thus; "Yea, Lord, I feel thy mercy, and I am assured of thy love! And so certain am I thereof, as thou art that God of truth; even so certainly do I know myself to be thine, O Lord my God; and this my soul knoweth right well!" Which last words she again doubled. To a grave minister, one Mr. *Harrison*, then with her, she said, "My soul hath been compassed with the terrors of death, the sorrows of hell were upon me, and a wilderness of woe was in me; but blessed, blessed, blessed be the Lord my God! he hath brought me to a place of rest, even to the sweet running waters of life. The way I now go in is a sweet and easy way, strewed with flowers; he hath brought me into a place more sweet than the garden of *Eden*, O the joy, the joy, the delights and joy that I feel! O how wonderful!"

Great outcries under awakenings were more frequently heard of in former times in the country than they have been of late, as some aged persons now living do testify: particularly I think fit here to insert a testimony of my honoured father, of what he remembers formerly to have heard.—"I well remember that one Mr. *Alexander Allen*, a *Scots* gentleman of good credit, that dwelt formerly in this town, showed me a letter that came from *Scotland*, that gave an account of a sermon preached in the city of *Edinburgh* (as I remember) in the time of the sitting of the general assembly of divines in that kingdom, that so affected the people, that there was a great and loud cry made throughout the assembly. I have also been credibly informed, and how often I cannot now say, that it was a common thing, when the famous Mr. *John Rogers* of *Dedham*, in *England*, was preaching, for some of his hearers to cry out; and, by what I have heard, I conclude that it was usual for many that heard that very awakening and rousing preacher of God's word, to make a great cry in the congregation.

(Signed) TIMOTHY EDWARDS."

Windsor, *May* 5, 1742.

Mr. *Flavel* gives a remarkable instance of a man whom he knew, that was wonderfully overcome with divine comforts; which it is supposed he knew, as the apostle *Paul* knew the man that was caught up to the third heaven. He relates, that "As the person was travelling alone, with his thoughts closely fixed on the great and astonishing things of another world, his thoughts began to swell higher and higher, like the water in *Ezekiel's* vision, till at last they became an overflowing flood. Such was the intenseness of his mind, such the ravishing tastes of heavenly joys, and such his full assurance of his interest therein, that he utterly lost all sight and sense of this world, and the concernments thereof; and for some hours knew not where he was, nor what he was about; but, having lost a great quantity of blood at the nose, he found himself so faint, that it brought him a little more to himself. And after he had washed himself at a spring, and drank of the water for his refreshment, he continued to the end of his journey, which was thirty miles; and all this while was scarce sensible: and says, he had several trances of considerable continuance. The same blessed frame was preserved all that night, and, in a lower degree, great part of the next day; the night passed without one wink of sleep; and yet he declares he never had a sweeter night's rest in all his life. Still, *adds the story*, the joy of the Lord overflowed him, and he seemed to be an inhabitant of another world. And he used for many years after to call that day one of the days of heaven; and professed that he understood more of the life of heaven by it, than by all the books he ever read, or discourses he ever entertained about it."

There have been instances before now, of persons crying out in transports of divine joy in *New England*. We have an instance in Capt. *Clap's* memoirs, (published by the Rev. Mr. *Prince*,) not of a silly woman or child, but a man of solid understanding, that, in a high transport of spiritual joy, was made to cry out aloud on his bed. His words, p. 9. are, "God's Holy Spirit did witness (I do believe) together with my spirit, that I was a child of God; and did fill my heart and soul with such full assurance that Christ was mine, that it did so transport me, as to make me cry out upon my bed, with a loud voice, *He is come, he is come!*"

There has, before now, been both crying out and falling, even in this town, under awakenings of conscience, and in the pangs of the new birth; and also in one of the neighbouring towns, more than seven years ago, a great number together cried out and fell down under conviction; and in most of whom there was an abiding good issue. And the Rev. Mr. *Williams* of *Deerfield* gave me an account of an aged man in that town, many years before that, who being awakened by his preaching, cried out aloud in the congregation. There have been many instances, before now, of persons in this town fainting with joyful discoveries made to their souls, and once several together. And there have been several instances here of persons waxing cold and benumbed, with their hands clinched, yea, and their bodies in convulsions, being overpowered with a strong sense of the astonishingly great and excellent things of God and the eternal world.

Secondly, Another way that some err in making history and former observation their rule instead of the Holy Scripture, is in comparing some external, accidental circumstances of this work, with what has appeared sometimes in enthusiasts. They find an agreement in some such things, and so they reject the whole work, or at least the substance of it, concluding it to be enthusiasm. Great use has been made to this purpose of many things that are found amongst the *quakers;* however totally and essentially different in its nature this work is, and the principles upon which it is built, from the whole religion of the *quakers.* To the same purpose, some external appearances that were found amongst the *French prophets,* and other enthusiasts in former times, have been of late trumped up with great assurance and triumph.

IV. I would propose it to be considered, whether or no some, instead of making the Scriptures their only rule to judge of this work, do not make their own *experience* the rule, and reject such and such things as are now professed and experienced, because they themselves never felt them. Are there not many, who, chiefly on this ground, have entertained and vented suspicions, if not peremptory condemnations, of those extreme terrors, and those great, sudden, and extraordinary discoveries of the glorious perfections of God, and of the beauty and love of Christ? Have they not condemned such vehement affections, such high transports of love and joy, such pity and distress for the souls of others, and exercises of mind that have such great effects, merely, or chiefly, because they knew nothing about them by experience? Persons are very ready to be suspicious of what they have not felt themselves. It is to be feared that many good men have been guilty of this error; which however does not make it the less unreasonable. And perhaps there are some who upon this ground do not only reject these extraordinary things, but all such conviction of sin, discoveries of the glory of God, excellency of Christ, and inward conviction of the truth of the gospel, by the immediate influence of the Spirit of God, now supposed to be necessary to salvation.—These persons who thus make their own experiences their rule of judgment, instead of bowing to the wisdom of God, and yielding to his word as an infallible rule, are guilty of casting a great reflection upon the understanding of the Most High.

SECT. III.

We should distinguish the good from the bad, and not judge of the whole by a part.

ANOTHER foundation-error of those who reject this work, is, their not duly distinguishing the good from the bad, and very unjustly judging of the whole by a part; and so rejecting the work in general, or in the main substance of it, for the sake of some accidental evil in it. They look for more in men because subject to the operations of a good spirit, than is justly to be expected from them for that reason, in this imperfect state, where so much blindness and corruption remains in the best. When any profess to have received light and comforts from heaven, and to have had sensible communion with God, many are ready to expect that now they appear like angels, and not still like poor, feeble, blind, and sinful worms of the dust. There being so much corruption left in the hearts of God's own children, and its prevailing as it sometimes does, is indeed a mysterious thing, and always was a stumbling-block to the world; but will not be so much wondered at by those who are well versed in, and duly mindful of, two things, *viz. First,* The word of God, which teaches the state of true Christians in this world; and, *Secondly,* Their own hearts, at least if they have any grace, and have experience of its conflicts with corruption. True saints are the most inexcusable, in making a great difficulty of much blindness and many sinful errors in those who profess godliness. If all our conduct, both open and secret, should be known, and our hearts laid open to the world; how should we be even ready to flee from the light of the sun, and hide ourselves from the view of mankind! And what great allowances would we need that others should make for us? Perhaps much greater than we are willing to make for others.

The great weakness of the greater part of mankind, in any affair that is new and uncommon, appears in not distinguishing, but either approving or condemning all in the lump. They who highly approve of the affair in general, cannot bear to have any thing at all found fault with; and, on the other hand, those who fasten their eyes upon some things in the affair that are amiss, and appear very disagreeable to them, at once reject the whole. Both which errors oftentimes arise from the want of persons having a due acquaintance with themselves. It is rash and unjust when we proceed thus in judging either of a particular person, or a people. Many, if they see any thing very ill in a particular person, a minister or private professor, will at once brand him as a hypocrite. And, if there be two or three of a people or society that behave themselves very irregularly, the whole must bear the blame of it. And if there be a few, though it may not be above one in a hundred, that professed, and had a show of being the happy partakers of what are called the saving benefits of this work, but afterwards give the world just grounds to suspect them, the whole work must be rejected on their account; and those in general, that make the like profession, must be condemned for their sakes.

So careful are some persons lest this work should be defended, that now they will hardly allow that the influences of the Spirit of God on the heart can so much as indirectly, and *accidentally,* be the occasion of the exercise of corruption, and the commission of sin. Thus far is true, that the influence of the Spirit of God in his *saving* operations will not be an occasion of increasing the corruption of the heart in general; but on the contrary of weakening it: but yet there is nothing unreasonable in supposing, that, at the same time that it weakens corruption in general, it may be an occasion of turning what is left into a new channel. There may be more of some kinds of the exercise of corruption than before; as that which tends to stop the course of a stream, if it do it not wholly, may give a new course to so much of the water as gets by the obstacle. The influences of the Spirit, for instance, may be an occasion of new ways of the exercise of *pride,* as has been acknowledged by orthodox divines in general. That spiritual discoveries and comforts may, through the corruption of the heart, be an occasion of the exercise of spiritual pride, was not used to be doubted, till now it is found to be needful to maintain the war against this work.

They who will hardly allow that a work of the Spirit of God can be a remote occasion of any sinful behaviour or unchristian conduct, I suppose will allow that the truly gracious influences of the Spirit of God, yea, and a high degree of love to God, is consistent with these two things, *viz.* a considerable degree of remaining corruption, and also many errors in judgment in matters of religion. And this is all that need to be allowed, in order to its being most demonstratively evident, that a high degree of love to God may *accidentally* move a person to that which is very contrary to the mind and will of God. For a high degree of love to God will strongly move a person to do that which he believes to be agreeable to God's will; and therefore, if he be mistaken, and be persuaded that that is agreeable to the will of God, which indeed is very contrary to it, then his love will accidentally, but strongly, incline him to that, which is indeed very contrary to the will of God.—They who are studied in logic have learned, that the *nature* of the cause is not to be judged of by the nature of the effect, nor the nature of the effect from the nature of the cause, when the cause is only *causa sine qua non,* or an occasional cause; yea, that, in such a case, oftentimes the nature of the effect is quite contrary to the nature of the cause.

True disciples of Christ may have a great deal of false zeal, such as the disciples had of old, when they would have fire called for from heaven to come down on the *Samaritans,* because they did not receive them. And even so eminently holy, and great, and divine a saint as *Moses*—who conversed with God as a man speaks with his friend, and concerning whom God gives his testimony, that he *was very meek, above any man upon the face of the earth*—

may be rash and sinful in his zeal, when his spirit is stirred by the hard-heartedness and opposition of others. He may speak very unadvisedly with his lips, and greatly offend God, and shut himself out from the possession of the good things that God is about to accomplish for his church on earth; as Moses was excluded Canaan, though he had brought the people out of Egypt, Psal. cvi. 32, 33. And men, even in those very things wherein they are influenced by a truly pious principle, may, through error and want of due consideration and caution, be very rash with their zeal. It was a truly good spirit which animated that excellent generation of Israel in Joshua's time; Josh. xxii. and yet they were rash and heady with their zeal, to gather all Israel together to go so furiously to war with their brethren of the two tribes and half, about their building the altar *Ed*, without first inquiring into the matter, or so much as sending a messenger to be informed. So the Christians of the circumcision, with warmth and contention condemned Peter for receiving Cornelius, Acts xi. This their heat and censure was unjust, and Peter was wronged in it; but there is every appearance in the story, that they acted from a real zeal and concern for the will and honour of God. So the primitive Christians, from their zeal for and against unclean meats, censured and condemned one another. This was a bad effect, and yet the apostle bears them witness, or at least expresses his charity towards them, that both sides acted from a good principle, and true respect to the Lord, Rom. xiv. 6. The zeal of the Corinthians with respect to the incestuous man, though the apostle highly commends it, yet he at the same time saw that they needed a caution, lest they should carry it too far, to an undue severity, so as to fail of christian meekness and forgiveness, 2 Cor. ii. 6—11. and chapter vii. 11, to the end.——Luther, that great reformer, had a great deal of bitterness with his zeal.

It surely cannot be wondered at by considerate persons, when multitudes all over the land have their affections greatly moved, that great numbers should run into many errors and mistakes with respect to their duty, and consequently, into many practices that are imprudent and irregular. I question whether there be a man in *New England*, of the strongest reason and greatest learning, but what would be put to it to keep master of himself, thoroughly to weigh his words, and to consider all the consequences of his behaviour, so as to conduct himself in all respects prudently, if he were so strongly impressed with a sense of divine and eternal things, and his affections so exceedingly moved, as has been frequent of late among the common people. How little do they consider human nature, who look upon it so insuperable a stumbling-block, when such multitudes of all kinds of capacities, natural tempers, educations, customs, and manners of life, are so greatly and variously affected, that imprudences and irregularities of conduct should abound; especially in a state of things so uncommon, and when the degree, extent, swiftness, and power of the operation is so very extraordinary, and so new, that there has not been time and experience enough to give birth to rules for people's conduct, and the writings of divines do not afford rules to direct us in such a state of things!

A great deal of noise and tumult, confusion and uproar, darkness mixed with light, and evil with good, is always to be expected in the beginning of something very glorious in the state of things in human society, or the church of God. After nature has long been shut up in a cold dead state, when the sun returns in the spring, there is, together with the increase of the light and heat of the sun, very tempestuous weather, before all is settled calm and serene, and all nature rejoices in its bloom and beauty. It is in the new creation as it was in the old; the Spirit of God first moved upon the face of the waters, which was an occasion of great uproar and tumult. Things were then gradually brought to a settled state, till at length all stood forth in that beautiful, peaceful order, when the heavens and the earth were finished, and God saw every thing that he had made, and behold it was very good. When God is about to bring to pass something great and glorious in the world, nature is in a ferment and struggle, and the world as it were in travail. When God was about to introduce the *Messiah* into the world, and a new, glorious dispensation, he *shook the heavens and the earth*, and he *shook all nations*. There is nothing that the church of God is in Scripture more frequently represented by than vegetables; as a tree, a vine, corn, &c. which gradually bring forth their fruit, and are first green before they are ripe. A great revival of religion is expressly compared to this gradual production of vegetables, Isa. lxi. 11. "As the earth bringeth forth her bud, and as the garden causeth the things that are sown in it to spring forth; so the Lord God will cause righteousness and praise to spring forth before all the nations." The church is in a special manner compared to a palm-tree, (Cant. vii. 7, 8. Exod. xv. 27. 1 Kings vi. 29. Psal. xcii. 12.) of which it is observed, That the fruit of it, though very sweet and good when ripe, has, while unripe, a mixture of poison.

The weakness of human nature has always appeared in times of great revival of religion, by a disposition to run to extremes, and get into confusion; and especially in these three things, enthusiasm, superstition, and intemperate zeal. So it appeared in the time of the reformation very remarkably, and even in the days of the apostles. Many were exceedingly disposed to lay weight on those things that were very chimerical, giving heed to fables, (1 Tim. i. 4. and iv. 7. 2 Tim. ii. 16. and ver. 23. and Tit. i. 14. and iii. 9.) Many, as ecclesiastical history informs us, fell off into the most wild enthusiasm, and extravagant notions of spirituality, and extraordinary illumination from heaven beyond others; and many were prone to superstition, will-worship, and a voluntary humility, giving heed to the commandments of men, being fond of an unprofitable bodily exercise, as appears by many passages in the apostles' writings. And what a proneness then appeared among professors to swerve from the path of duty, and the spirit of the gospel, in the exercises of a rash indiscreet zeal, censuring and condemning ministers and people; one saying, I am of *Paul;* another, I am of *Apollos;* another, I am of *Cephas.*—They judged one another for differences of opinion about smaller matters, unclean meats, holy days and holy places, and their different opinions and practices respecting civil intercourse and communication with their heathen neighbours. And how much did vain jangling, disputing, and confusion prevail, through undue heat of spirit, under the name of a religious zeal! (1 Tim. vi. 4, 5. 2 Tim ii. 16. and Tit. iii. 9.) and what a task had the apostles to keep them within bounds, and maintain good order in the churches! How often do they mention their irregularities! The prevailing of such like disorders seems to have been the special occasion of writing many of their epistles. The church in that great effusion of the Spirit, and under strong impressions, had the care of infallible guides, that watched over them day and night; but yet, so prone were they, through the weakness and corruption of human nature, to get out of the way, that irregularity and confusion arose in some churches, where there was an extraordinary outpouring of the Spirit, to a very great height, even in the apostles' lifetime, and under their eye. And though some of the apostles lived long to settle the state of things, yet, presently after their death the christian church ran into many superstitions and childish notions and practices, and in some respects into a great severity in their zeal. And let any wise person, that has not in the midst of the disputes of the present day got beyond the calmness of consideration, impartially consider, to what lengths we may reasonably suppose many of the primitive Christians, in their heat of zeal, and under their extraordinary impressions, would soon have gone, if they had not had inspired guides. Is it not probable, that the church of *Corinth* in particular, by an increase of their irregularities and contentions, would in a little time have been broken to pieces, and dissolved in a state of the utmost confusion? And yet this would have been no evidence that there had not been a most glorious and remarkable outpouring of the Spirit in that city. But as for us, we have no infallible apostle to guide and direct us, to rectify disorders, and reclaim us when we are wandering; but every one does what is right in his own eyes; and they that err in judgment, and are got into a wrong path, continue to wander, till experience of the mischievous issue convinces them of their error.

If we look over this affair, and seriously weigh it in its circumstances, it will appear a matter of no great difficulty to account for the errors that have been gone into, supposing the work in general to be from a very great outpouring of the Spirit of God. It may easily be accounted for, that many have run into just such errors as they have. It is known, that some who have been great instruments to promote this work were very young. They were newly awaked out of sleep, and brought out of that state of darkness, insensibility, and spiritual death, in which they had been ever since they were born. A new and wonderful scene opens to them; and they have in view the reality, the vastness, the infinite importance, and nearness of spiritual and eternal things; and at the same time are surprised to see the world asleep about them. They have not the advantage of age and experience, and have had but little opportunity to study divinity, or to converse with aged experienced Christians and divines. How natural is it then for such to fall into many errors with respect to the state of mankind, with which they are so surprised, and with respect to the means and methods of their relief? Is it any wonder that they have not at once learned how to make allowances, and that they do not at once find out that method of dealing with the world, which is adapted to the mysterious state and nature of mankind? Is it any wonder that they cannot at once foresee the consequences of things, what evils are to be guarded against, and what difficulties are like to arise?

We have been long in a strange stupor: The influences of the Spirit of God upon the heart have been but little felt, and the nature of them but little taught; so that they are in many respects new to great numbers of those who have lately fallen under them. And is it any wonder that they who never before had experience of the supernatural influence of the Divine Spirit upon their souls, and never were instructed in the nature of these influences, do not so well know how to distinguish one extraordinary new impression from another, and so (to themselves insensibly) run into enthusiasm, taking every strong impulse or impression to be divine? How natural is it to suppose, that among the multitudes of illiterate people who find themselves so wonderfully changed, and brought into such new circumstances, many should pass wrong and very strange judgments of both persons and things about them! Now they behold them in a new light, and in their surprise they go further from the judgment that they were wont to make of them than they ought, and, in their great change of sentiments, pass from one extreme to another. And why should it be thought strange, that those who scarce ever heard of any such thing as an outpouring of the Spirit of God before; or, if they did, had no notion of it; do not know how to behave themselves in such a new and strange state of things? And is it any wonder that they are ready to hearken to those who have instructed them, who have been the means of delivering them from such a state of death and misery as they were in before, or have a name for being the happy instruments of promoting the same work among others? Is it unaccountable that persons in these circumstances are ready to receive every thing they say, and to drink down error as well as truth from them? And why should there be all indignation, and no compassion, towards those who are thus misled?

These persons are extraordinarily affected with a new sense, and recent discovery, of the greatness and excellency of the Divine Being, the certainty and infinite importance of eternal things, the preciousness of souls, and the dreadful danger and madness of mankind, together with a great sense of God's distinguishing kindness and love to them. Is it any wonder that now they think they must exert themselves, and do something extraordinary for the honour of God and the good of souls? They know not how to sit still, and forbear speaking and acting with uncommon earnestness and vigour. And in these circumstances, if they be not persons of more than common steadiness and discretion, or have not some person of wisdom to direct them, it is a wonder if they do not proceed without due caution, and do things that are irregular, and that will, in the issue, do much more hurt than good.

Censuring others is the worst disease with which this affair has been attended. But this is indeed a time of great temptation to this sinful error. When there has been a long-continued deadness, and many are brought out of a state of nature in so extraordinary a manner, and filled with such uncommon degrees of light, it is natural for such to form their notions of a state of grace wholly from what they experience. Many of them know no other way; for they never have been taught much about a state of grace, the different degrees of grace, and the degrees of darkness and corruption with which grace is compatible, nor concerning the manner of the influences of the Spirit in converting a soul, and the variety of the manner of his operations. They therefore forming their idea of a state of grace only by their own experience, no wonder that it appears an insuperable difficulty to them to reconcile such a state, of which they have this idea, with what they observe in professors about them. It is indeed in itself a very great mystery, that grace should be compatible with so much and such kind of corruption as sometimes prevails in the truly godly; and no wonder that it especially appears so to uninstructed new converts, who have been converted in an extraordinary manner.

Though censoriousness is very sinful, and is most commonly found in hypocrites and persons of a pharisaical spirit, yet it is not so inconsistent with true godliness as some imagine. We have remarkable instances of it in those holy men of whom we have an account in the book of Job. Not only were Job's three friends, who seem to have been eminently holy men, guilty of it, in very unreasonably censuring the best man on earth—very positively determining that he was an unconverted man—but Job himself, who was not only a man of true piety, but excelled all men in piety, and particularly excelled in an humble, meek, and patient spirit, was guilty of bitterly censuring his three friends, as wicked, vile hypocrites, Job xvi. 9—11. "He teareth me in his wrath who hateth me, he gnasheth upon me with his teeth; mine enemy sharpeneth his eyes upon me: they have gaped upon me with their mouth.—God hath delivered me to the ungodly, and turned me over into the hands of the wicked." He is very positive that they are hypocrites, and shall be miserably destroyed as such, Job xvii. 2—4. "Are there not mockers with me? and doth not mine eye continue in their provocation? Lay down now, put me in surety with thee; who is he that will strike hands with me? For thou hast hid their heart from understanding, therefore shalt thou not exalt them." And again, ver. 8—10. "Upright men shall be astonished at this, and the innocent shall stir up himself against the hypocrite; the righteous also shall hold on his way, and he that hath clean hands shall be stronger and stronger. But as for you all, do you return and come now, for I cannot find one wise man (*i. e.* one good man) among you."

Thus, I think, the errors and irregularities that attend this work may be accounted for, from the consideration of the infirmity and common corruption of mankind, together with the circumstances of the work, though we should suppose it to be the work of God. And it would not be a just objection in any to say, if these powerful impressions and great affections are from the Spirit of God, why does not the same Spirit give strength of understanding and capacity in proportion, to those persons who are the subjects of them; so that strong affections may not, through their error, drive them to an irregular and sinful conduct? I do not know that God has any where obliged himself to do it. The end of the influences of God's Spirit is, to make men spiritually wise to salvation, which is the most excellent wisdom; and he has also appointed means for our gaining such degrees of other knowledge as we need, to conduct ourselves regularly, which means should be carefully used. But the end of the influence of the Spirit of God is not to increase men's natural capacities, nor has God obliged himself immediately to increase civil prudence in proportion to the degrees of spiritual light.

If we consider the errors that attend this work, not only as from man and his infirmity, but also as from God and by his permission and disposal, they are not strange, upon the supposition of its being, as to the substance of it, a work of God. If God intends this great revival of religion to be the dawning of a happy state of his church on earth, it may be an instance of the divine wisdom, in the beginning of it, to suffer so many irregularities and errors in conduct, to which he knew men in their present weak state were most exposed, under great religious affections, and when animated with great zeal. For it is very likely to be of excellent benefit to his church, in the continuance and progress of the work afterwards. Their experience, in the first setting out, of the mischievous consequences of these errors, and smarting for them in the beginning, may be a happy defence to them afterwards, for many generations, from these errors, which otherwise they might continually be exposed to. As when *David* and all *Israel* went about to bring back the ark into the midst of the land, after it had been long absent, first in the land of the *Philistines*, and then in *Kirjath-jearim*, in the utmost borders of the land; they at first sought not the Lord after the due order, and they smarted for their error: but this put them upon studying the law, and more thoroughly acquainting themselves with the mind and will of God, and seeking and serving him with greater circumspection. The consequence was glorious, viz. their seeking God in such a manner as was accepted of him. The ark of God ascended into the heights of *Zion*, with great and extraordinary rejoicings of the king and all the people, without any frown or rebuke from God intermixed; and God dwelt thenceforward in the midst of the people for those glorious purposes expressed in the 68th Psalm.

It is very analogous to the manner of God's dealing with his people, to permit a great deal of error, and suffer the infirmity of his people to appear, in the beginning of a glorious work of his grace, for their felicity, to teach them what they are, to humble them, and fit them for that glorious prosperity to which he is about to advance them, and the more to secure to himself the honour of such a glorious work. For, by man's exceeding weakness appearing in the beginning of it, it is evident that God does not lay the foundation of it in man's strength or wisdom.—And as we need not wonder at the errors that attend this work, if we look at the hand of men who are guilty of them, and the hand of God in permitting them: so neither shall we see cause to wonder if we consider them with regard to the hand that Satan has in them. For, as the work is much greater than any other that ever has been in *New England;* so, no wonder that the devil is more alarmed and enraged, that he exerts himself more vigorously against it, and more powerfully endeavours to tempt and mislead the subjects and promoters of it.

SECT. IV.

The nature of the work in general.

Whatever imprudences there have been, and whatever sinful irregularities; whatever vehemence of the passions, and heats of the imagination, transports, and ecstasies: whatever error in judgment, and indiscreet zeal; and whatever outcries, faintings, and agitations of body; yet, it is manifest and notorious, that there has been of late a very uncommon influence upon the minds of a very great part of the inhabitants of *New England*, attended with the best effects. There has been a great increase of seriousness, and sober consideration of eternal things; a disposition to hearken to what is said of such things, with attention and affection; a disposition to treat matters of religion with solemnity, and as of great importance; to make these things the subject of conversation; to hear the word of God preached, and to take all opportunities in order to it; to attend on the public worship of God, and all external duties of religion, in a more solemn and decent manner; so that there is a remarkable and general alteration in the face of *New England* in these respects. Multitudes in all parts of the land, of vain, thoughtless, regardless persons, are quite changed, and become serious and considerate. There is a vast increase of concern for the salvation of the precious soul, and of that inquiry, *What shall I do to be saved?* The hearts of multitudes had been greatly taken off from the things of the world, its profits, pleasures, and honours. Multitudes in all parts have had their consciences awakened, and have been made sensible of the pernicious nature and consequences of sin, and what a dreadful thing it is to be under guilt and the displeasure of God, and to live without peace and reconciliation with him. They have also been awakened to a sense of the shortness and uncertainty of life, and the reality of another world and future judgment, and of the necessity of an interest in Christ. They are more afraid of sin, more careful and inquisitive that they may know what is contrary to the mind and will of God, that they may avoid it, and what he requires of them, that they may do it, more careful to guard against temptations, more watchful over their own hearts, earnestly desirous of knowing and of being diligent in the use of the means that God has appointed in his word, in order to salvation. Many very stupid, senseless sinners, and persons of a vain mind, have been greatly awakened.

There is a strange alteration almost all over *New England* amongst young people: by a powerful invisible influence on their minds, they have been brought to forsake, in a general way, as it were at once, those things of which they were extremely fond, and in which they seemed to place the happiness of their lives, and which nothing before could induce them to forsake; as their frolicking, vain company-keeping, night-walking, their mirth and jollity, their impure language, and lewd songs. In vain did ministers preach against those things before, in vain were laws made to restrain them, and in vain was all the vigilance of magistrates and civil officers; but now they have almost every where dropt them as it were of themselves. And there is great alteration amongst old and young as to drinking, tavern-haunting, profane speaking, and extravagance in apparel. Many notoriously vicious persons have been reformed, and become externally quite new creatures. Some that are wealthy, and of a fashionable, gay education; some great beaus and fine ladies, that seemed to have their minds swallowed up with nothing but the vain shows and pleasures of the world, have been wonderfully altered, have relinquished these vanities, and are become serious, mortified, and humble in their conversation. It is astonishing to see the alteration there is in some towns, where before there was but little appearance of religion, or any thing but vice and vanity. And now they are transformed into another sort of people; their former vain, worldly, and vicious conversation and dispositions seem to be forsaken, and they are, as it were, gone over to a new world. Their thoughts, their talk, and their concern, affections, and inquiries are now about the favour of God, an interest in Christ, a renewed sanctified heart, and a spiritual blessedness, acceptance, and happiness in a future world.

Now, through the greatest part of *New England*, the holy Bible is in much greater esteem and use than before. The great things contained in it are much more regarded, as things of the greatest consequence, and are much more the subjects of meditation and conversation: and other books of piety that have long been of established reputation, as the most excellent, and most tending to promote true godliness, have been abundantly more in use. The Lord's day is more religiously and strictly observed. And much has been lately done at making up differences, confessing faults one to another, and making restitution: probably more within two years, than was done in thirty years before. It has been undoubtedly so in many places. And surprising has been the power of this spirit, in many instances, to destroy old grudges, to make up long-continued breaches, and to bring those who seemed to be in a confirmed irreconcilable alienation, to embrace each other in a sincere and entire amity. Great numbers under this influence have been brought to a deep sense of their own sinfulness and vileness; the sinfulness of their lives, the heinousness of their disregard of the authority of the great God, and of their living in contempt of a Saviour. They have lamented their former negligence of their souls, and their neglecting and losing precious time. The sins of their life have been extraordinarily set before them; and they have had a great sense of their hardness of heart, their enmity against that which is good, and proneness to all evil; and also of the worthlessness of their own religious performances, how unworthy of God's regard were their prayers, praises, and all that they did in religion. It has been a common thing, that persons have had such a sense of their own sinfulness, that they have thought themselves to be the worst of all, and that none ever was so vile as they. And many seem to have been greatly convinced that they were utterly unworthy of any mercy at the hands of God, however miserable they were, and though they stood in extreme necessity of mercy; and that they deserved nothing but eternal burnings. They have been sensible that God would be altogether just and righteous in inflicting endless damnation upon them, at the same time that they have had an exceedingly affecting sense of the dreadfulness of such endless torments, and apprehended themselves to be greatly in danger of it. And many have been deeply affected with a sense of their own ignorance and blindness, and exceeding helplessness, and so of their extreme need of the divine pity and help.

Multitudes in *New England* have lately been brought to a new and great conviction of the truth and certainty of the things of the gospel; to a firm persuasion that Christ Jesus is the Son of God, and the great and only Saviour of the world; and that the great doctrines of the gospel touching reconciliation by his blood, and acceptance in his righteousness, and eternal life and salvation through him, are matters of undoubted truth. They have had a most affecting sense of the excellency and sufficiency of this Saviour, and the glorious wisdom and grace of God shining in this way of salvation; and of the wonders of Christ's dying love, and the sincerity of Christ in the invitations of the gospel. They have experienced a consequent affiance and sweet rest of soul in Christ, as a glorious Saviour, a strong rock and high tower; accompanied with an admiring and exalted apprehension of the glory of the divine perfections, God's majesty, holiness, sovereign grace, &c.—with a sensible, strong, and sweet love to God, and delight in him, far surpassing all temporal delights, or earthly pleasures; and a rest of soul in him, as a portion and the fountain of all good. And this has been attended with an abhorrence of sin, and self-loathing for it, and earnest longings of soul after more holiness and conformity to God, with a sense of the great need of God's help in order to holiness of life; together they have had a most dear love to all that are supposed to be the children of God, and a love to mankind in general, and a most sensible and tender compassion for the souls of sinners, and earnest desires of the advancement of Christ's kingdom in the world. And these things have appeared with an abiding concern to live a holy life, and great complaints of remaining corruption, and a longing to be more free from the body of sin and death. And not only do these effects appear in new converts, but great numbers of those who were formerly esteemed the most sober and pious people, have, under the influence of this work, been greatly quickened, and their hearts renewed with greater degrees of light, renewed repentance and humiliation, and more lively exercises of faith, love, and joy in the Lord. Many have been remarkably engaged to watch, and strive, and fight against sin; to cast out every idol, sell all for Christ, give up themselves entirely to God, and make a sacrifice of every worldly and carnal thing to the welfare and prosperity of their souls. And there has of late appeared in some places an unusual disposition to bind themselves to it in a solemn covenant with God. And now, instead of meetings at taverns and drinking-houses, and of young people in frolics and vain company, the country is full of meetings of all sorts and ages of persons—young and old, men, women, and little children—to read and pray, and sing praises, and to converse of the things of God and another world. In very many places the main of the conversation in all companies turns on religion, and things of a spiritual nature. Instead of vain mirth among young people, there is now either mourning under a sense of the guilt of sin, or holy rejoicing in Christ Jesus: and, instead of their lewd songs, there are now to be heard from them songs of praise to God, and the Lamb that was slain to redeem them by his blood. And there has been this alteration abiding on multitudes all over the land, for a year and a half, without any appearance of a disposition to return to former vice and vanity.

And, under the influences of this work, there have been many of the remains of those wretched people and dregs of mankind, the poor *Indians*, that seemed to be next to a state of brutality, and with whom, till now, it seemed to be to little more purpose to use endeavours for their instruction and awakening, than with the beasts. Their minds have now been strangely opened to receive instruction, and been deeply affected with the concerns of their precious souls; they have reformed their lives, and forsaken their former stupid, barbarous, and brutish way of living; and particularly that sin to which they have been so exceedingly addicted, their drunkenness. Many of them to appearance brought truly and greatly to delight in the things of God, and to have their souls very much engaged and entertained with the great things of the gospel. And many of the poor *negroes* also have been in like manner wrought upon and changed. Very many little children have been remarkably enlightened, and their hearts wonderfully affected and enlarged, and their mouths opened, expressing themselves in a manner far beyond their years, and to the just astonishment of those who have heard them. Some of them for many months, have been greatly and delightfully affected with the glory of divine things, and the excellency and love of the Redeemer, with their hearts greatly filled with love to and joy in him; and they have continued to be serious and pious in their behaviour.

The divine power of this work has marvellously appeared in some instances I have been acquainted with; in supporting and fortifying the heart under great trials, such as the death of children, and extreme pain of body; and in wonderfully maintaining the serenity, calmness, and joy of the soul, in an immoveable rest in God, and sweet resignation to him. And some under the blessed influences of this work have, in a calm, bright, and joyful frame of mind, been carried through the valley of the shadow of death.

And now let us consider:——Is it not strange that in a christian country, and such a land of light as this is, there are many at a loss to conclude whose work this is, whether the work of God or the work of the devil? Is it not a shame to *New England* that such a work should be much doubted of here? Need we look over the histories of all past times, to see if there be not some circumstances and external appearances that attend this work, which have been formerly found amongst enthusiasts? Whether the *Montanists* had not great transports of joy, and whether the *French prophets* had not agitations of body? Blessed be God! he does not put us to the toil of such inquiries. We need not say, Who shall ascend into heaven, to bring us down something whereby to judge of this work? Nor does God send us beyond the seas, nor into past ages, to obtain a rule that shall determine and satisfy us: but we have a rule near at hand, a sacred book that God himself has put into our hands, with clear and infallible marks, sufficient to resolve us in things of this nature; which book I think we must reject, not only in some particular passages, but in the substance of it, if we reject such a work as has now been described, as not being the work of God. The whole tenor of the gospel proves it; all the notion of religion that the Scripture gives us confirms it.

I suppose there is scarcely a minister in this land, but from Sabbath to Sabbath is used to pray that God would pour out his Spirit, and work a reformation and revival of religion in the country, and turn us from our intemperance, profaneness, uncleanness, wordliness, and other sins; and we have kept from year to year, days of public fasting and prayer to God, to acknowledge our backslidings, and humble ourselves for our sins, and to seek of God forgiveness and reformation: and now when so great and extensive a reformation is so suddenly and wonderfully accomplished, in those very things that we have sought to God for, shall we not acknowledge it? or, do it with great coldness, caution, and reserve, and scarcely take any notice of it in our public prayers and praises, or mention it but slightly and cursorily, and in such a manner as carries an appearance as though we would contrive to say as little of it as ever we could, and were glad to pass from it? And that because the work is attended with a mixture of error, imprudences, darkness, and sin; because some persons are carried away with impressions, and are indiscreet, and too censorious with their zeal; and because there are high transports of religious affections; and some effects on their bodies of which we do not understand the reason.

SECT. V.

The nature of the work in a particular instance.

I HAVE been particularly acquainted with many persons who have been the subjects of the high and extraordinary transports of the present day. But in the highest transports I have been acquainted with, and where the affections of admiration, love, and joy, so far as another could judge, have been raised to the highest pitch, the following things have been united, *viz.* A very frequent dwelling for some considerable time together, in views of the glory of the divine perfections and Christ's excellencies; so that the soul has been as it were perfectly overwhelmed, and swallowed up with light and love, a sweet solace, and a rest and joy of soul altogether unspeakable. The person has more than once continued for five or six hours together, without interruption, in a clear and lively view or sense of the infinite beauty and amiableness of Christ's person, and the heavenly sweetness of his transcendent love. So that (to use the person's own expressions) the soul remained in a kind of heavenly elysium, and did as it were swim in the rays of Christ's love, like a little mote swimming in the beams of the sun that come in at a window. The heart was swallowed up in a kind of glow of Christ's love coming down as a constant stream of sweet light, at the same time the soul all flowing out in love to him; so that there seemed to be a constant flowing and reflowing from heart to heart. The soul dwelt on high, was lost in God, and seemed almost to leave the body. The mind dwelt in a pure delight that fed and satisfied it; enjoying pleasure without the least sting, or any interruption. And, (so far as the judgment and word of a person of discretion may be taken, speaking upon the most deliberate consideration,) what was enjoyed in a single minute of the whole space, which was many hours, was worth more than all the outward comfort and pleasure of the whole life put together; and this without being in any trance, or at all deprived of the exercise of the bodily senses. And this heavenly delight has been enjoyed for years together; though not frequently so long together to such a height. Extraordinary views of divine things, and the religious affections, were frequently attended with very great effects on the body. Nature often sunk under the weight of divine discoveries, and the strength of the body was taken away. The person was deprived of all ability to stand or speak. Sometimes the hands were clinched, and the flesh cold, but the senses remaining. Animal nature was often in a great emotion and agitation, and the soul so overcome with admiration, and a kind of omnipotent joy, as to cause the person, unavoidably, to leap with all the might, with joy and mighty exultation. The soul at the same time was so strongly drawn towards God and Christ in heaven, that it seemed to the person as though soul and body would, as it were of themselves, of necessity mount up, leave the earth, and ascend thither.

These effects on the body were not owing to the influence of example, but began about seven years ago, when there was no such enthusiastical season as many account this, but it was a very dead time through the land. They arose from no distemper catched from Mr. *Whitefield*, or Mr. *Tennant*, because they began before either of them came into the country.—Near three years ago, they greatly increased, upon an extraordinary self-dedication, renunciation of the world, and resignation of all to God; which were made in a great view of God's excellency, in high exercise of love to him, and rest and joy in him. Since that time they have been very frequent; and began in a yet higher degree, and greater frequency, about a year and a half ago, upon another new resignation of all to God, with a yet greater fervency and delight of soul; the body often fainting with the love of Christ.—These effects appeared in a higher degree still, the last winter, upon another resignation to and acceptance of God, as the only portion and happiness of the soul, wherein the whole world, with the dearest enjoyments in it, were renounced as dirt and dung. All that is pleasant and glorious, and all that is terrible in this world, seemed perfectly to vanish into nothing, and nothing to be left but God, in whom the soul was perfectly swallowed up, as in an infinite ocean of blessedness.—Since this time there have often been great agitations of body, and an unavoidable leaping for joy; and the soul as it were dwelling, almost without interruption, in a kind of paradise; and very often, in high transports, disposed to speak to others concerning the great and glorious things of God, and Christ, and the eternal world, in a most earnest manner, and with a loud voice, so that it is next to impossible to avoid it. These effects on the body did not arise from any bodily distemper or weakness, because the greatest of all have been in a good state of health.

This great rejoicing has been with trembling, *i. e.* attended with a deep and lively sense of the greatness and majesty of God, and the person's own exceeding littleness and vileness. Spiritual joys in this person never were attended with the least appearance of laughter, or lightness, either of countenance or manner of speaking; but with a peculiar abhorrence of such appearances in spiritual rejoicings. These high transports, when past, have had abiding effects in the increase of sweetness, rest, and humility which they have left upon the soul; and a new engagedness of heart to live to God's honour, and watch and fight against sin. And these things took place not in the giddy age of youth, nor in a new convert, or unexperienced Christian, but in one that was converted above twenty-seven years ago; and neither converted nor educated in that enthusiastic town of *Northampton*, (as some may be ready to call it,) but in a town and family which none, that I know of, suspected of enthusiasm. And these effects were found in a Christian that has been long, in an uncommon manner, growing in grace, and rising, by very sensible degrees, to higher love to God, weanedness from the world, mastery over sin and temptation, through great trials and conflicts, long-continued strugglings and fighting with sin, earnest and constant prayer and labour in religion, and engagedness of mind in the use of all means, attended with a great exactness of life.—Which growth has been attended, not only with a great increase of religious affections, but with a wonderful alteration of outward behaviour, in many things, visible to those who are most intimately acquainted, so as lately to have become as it were a new person; and particularly in living so much more above the world, and in a greater degree of stedfastness and strength in the way of duty and self-denial, maintaining the christian conflict against temptations, and conquering from time to time under great trials; persisting in an unmoved, untouched calm and rest, under the changes and accidents of time. The person had formerly, in lower degrees of grace, been subject to unsteadiness, and many ups and downs, in the frame of mind, being under great disadvantages, through a vaporous habit of body, and often subject to melancholy, and at times almost over-borne with it, it having been so even from early youth; but strength of grace and divine light has of a long time wholly conquered these disadvantages, and carried the mind, in a constant manner, quite above all such effects.—Since that resignation spoken of before, made near three years ago, every thing of that nature seems to be overcome and crushed by the power of faith and trust in God, and resignation to him; the person has remained in a constant uninterrupted rest, humble joy in God, and assurance of his favour, without one hour's melancholy or darkness, from that day to this; vapours have had great effects on the body, such as they used to have before, but the soul has been always out of their reach. And this stedfastness and constancy has remained through great outward changes and trials; such as times of the most extreme pain, and apparent hazard of immediate death.

These transporting views and rapturous affections are not attended with any enthusiastic disposition to follow impulses, or any supposed prophetical revelations; nor have they been observed to be attended with any appearance of spiritual pride, but very much of a contrary disposition, an increase of humility and meekness, and a disposition in honour to prefer others. And it is worthy to be remarked, that when these discoveries and holy affections were evidently at the greatest height—which began early in the morning of the holy Sabbath, and lasted for days together, melting all down in the deepest humility and poverty of spirit, reverence and resignation, and the sweetest meekness, and universal benevolence—these two things were felt in a remarkable manner, *viz. First,* a peculiar aversion to judging other professing Christians of good standing in the visible church, with respect to their conversion or degrees of grace; or at all intermeddling with that matter, so much as to determine against and condemn others in the thoughts of the heart. Such want of candour appeared hateful, as not agreeing with that lamb-like humility, meekness, gentleness, and charity, which the soul then, above other times, saw to be beautiful. The disposition then felt was, on the contrary, to prefer others to self, and to hope that they saw more of God and loved him better; though before, under smaller discoveries, and feebler exercises of divine affection, there had been a disposition to censure and condemn others. *Secondly*, another thing that was felt at that time, was a very great sense of the importance of moral social duties, and how great a part of religion lay in them. There was such a new sense and conviction of this, beyond what had been before, that it seemed to be as it were a clear discovery then made to the soul. But, in general, there has been a very great increase of a sense of these two things, as divine views and divine love have increased.

The things already mentioned have been attended also with the following things, *viz.* An extraordinary sense of the awful majesty, greatness, and holiness of God, so as sometimes to overwhelm soul and body; a sense of the piercing all-seeing eye of God, so as sometimes to take away the bodily strength; and an extraordinary view of the infinite terribleness of the wrath of God; together with a sense of the ineffable misery of sinners who are exposed to this wrath. Sometimes the exceeding pollution of the person's own heart, as a sink of all manner of abomination, and the dreadfulness of an eternal hell of God's wrath, opened to view both together. There was a clear view of a desert of that misery, and that by the pollution of the best duties; yea, only by the irreverence, and want of humility, that attended once speaking of the holy name of God, when done in the best manner that ever it was done. The strength of the body was very often taken away with a deep mourning for sin, as committed against so holy and good a God; sometimes with an affecting sense of actual sin, sometimes especially indwelling sin, and sometimes the consideration of the sin of the heart as appearing in a particular thing, as for instance, in that there was no greater forwardness and readiness to self-denial for God and Christ, who had so denied himself for us. Yea, sometimes the consideration of sin that was in only speaking one word concerning the infinitely great and holy God, has been so affecting as to overcome the strength of nature. There has been a very great sense of the certain truth of the great things revealed in the gospel; an overwhelming sense of the glory of the work of redemption, and the way of salvation by Jesus Christ; of the glorious harmony of the divine attributes appearing therein, as that wherein mercy and truth are met together, and righteousness and peace have kissed each other. A sight of the fulness and glorious sufficiency of Christ, has been so affecting as to overcome the body. A constant immovable trust in God through Christ, with a great sense of his strength and faithfulness, the sureness of his covenant and the immutability of his promises, made the everlasting mountains and perpetual hills to appear as mere shadows to these things.

Sometimes the sufficiency and faithfulness of God, as the covenant God of his people, appeared in these words, I AM THAT I AM, in so affecting a manner as to overcome the body. A sense of the glorious, unsearchable, unerring wisdom of God in his works, both of creation and providence, was such as to swallow up the soul, and overcome the strength of the body. There was a sweet rejoicing of soul at the thoughts of God being infinitely and unchangeably happy, and an exulting gladness of heart that God is self-sufficient, and infinitely above all dependence, and reigns over all, and does his will with absolute and uncontrollable power and sovereignty. A sense of the glory of the Holy Spirit, as the great Comforter, was such as to overwhelm both soul and body; only mentioning the word the COMFORTER, has immediately taken away all strength; that word, as the person expressed it, seemed great enough to fill heaven and earth. There was a most vehement and passionate desire of the honour and glory of God's name; a sensible, clear, and constant preference of it, not only to the person's own temporal interest, but to his spiritual comfort in this world. There was a willingness to suffer the hidings of God's face, and to live and die in darkness and horror, if God's honour should require it, and to have no other reward for it but that God's name should be glorified, although so much of the sweetness of the light of God's countenance had been experienced. A great lamenting of ingratitude and the defect of love to God, took away bodily strength; and there were very often vehement longings and faintings after more love to Christ, and greater conformity to him; especially longing after these two things, *viz.* to be more perfect in *humility* and *adoration*. The flesh and heart seem often to cry out for lying low before God, and adoring him with greater love and humility. The thoughts of the perfect humility with which the saints in heaven worship God, and fall down before his throne, have often overcome the body, and set it into a great agitation. The person felt a great delight in singing praises to God and Jesus Christ, and longing that this present life may be, as it were, one continued song of praise to God. There was a longing, as the person expressed it, to sit and sing this life away; and an overcoming pleasure in the thoughts of spending an eternity in that exercise. Together with living by faith to a great degree, there was a constant and extraordinary distrust of our own strength and wisdom; a great dependence on God for his help in order to the performance of any thing to God's acceptance, and being restrained from the most horrid sins.

A sense of the black ingratitude of true saints, as to coldness and deadness in religion, and their setting their hearts on the things of this world, has overcome the bodily frame. There was an experience of great longing that all the children of God might be lively in religion, fervent in their love, and active in the service of God; and, when there have been appearances of it in others, rejoicing so in beholding the pleasant sight, that the joy of soul has been too great for the body.—The person took pleasure in the thoughts of watching and striving against sin, fighting through the way to heaven, and filling up this life with hard labour, and bearing the cross for Christ, as an opportunity to give God honour; not desiring to rest from labours till arrived in heaven, but abhorring the thoughts of it, and seeming astonished that God's own children should be backward to strive and deny themselves for God. There were earnest longings that all God's people might be clothed with humility and meekness, like the Lamb of God, and feel nothing in their hearts but love and compassion to all mankind; and great grief when any thing to the contrary appeared in any of the children of God, as bitterness, fierceness of zeal, censoriousness, or reflecting uncharitably on others, or disputing with any appearance of heat of spirit: a deep concern for the good of others' souls; a melting compassion to those that looked on themselves as in a state of nature, and to saints under darkness, so as to cause the body to faint. There was found an universal benevolence to mankind, with a longing as it were to embrace the whole world in the arms of pity and love; and ideas of suffering from enemies the utmost conceivable rage and cruelty, with a disposition felt to fervent love and pity in such a case, so far as it could be realized in thought. Sometimes a disposition was felt to a life given up to mourning alone in a wilderness over a lost and miserable world; compassion towards them being often to that degree, that would allow of no support or rest, but in going to God, and pouring out the soul in prayer for them. Earnest desires were felt that the work of God, now in the land, may be carried on, and that with greater purity, and freedom from all bitter zeal, censoriousness, spiritual pride, hot disputes, &c. and a vehement and constant desire for the setting up of Christ's kingdom through the earth, as a kingdom of holiness, purity, love, peace, and happiness to mankind

The soul often entertained, with unspeakable delight, the thoughts of heaven, as a world of love; where love shall be the saints' eternal food, where they shall dwell in the light, and swim in an ocean of love, and where the very air and breath will be nothing but love; love to the people of God, or God's true saints, as having the image of Christ, and as those who will in a very little time shine in his perfect image. The strength was very often taken away with longings that others might love God more, and serve God better, and have more of his comfortable presence, than the person that was the subject of these longings; desiring to follow the whole world to heaven, or that every one should go before, and be higher in grace and happiness, not by this person's diminution, but by others' increase. This experience included a delight in conversing on religious subjects, and in seeing Christians together, talking of the most spiritual and heavenly things in religion, in a lively and feeling manner; and very frequently the person was overcome with the pleasure of such conversation. A great sense was often expressed, of the importance of the duty of charity to the poor, and how much the generality of Christians come short in the practice of it. There was also a great sense of the need ministers have of much of the Spirit of God, at this day especially; and there were most earnest longings and wrestlings with God for them, so as to take away the bodily strength. It also included the greatest, fullest, longest continued, and most constant assurance of the favour of God and of a title to future glory, that ever I saw any appearance of in any person, enjoying, especially of late, (to use the person's own expression,) *the riches of full assurance.* Formerly there was a longing to die with something of impatience; but lately, since that resignation forementioned, about three years ago, an uninterrupted entire resignation to God with respect to life or death, sickness or health, ease or pain, which has remained unchanged and unshaken, when actually under extreme and violent pains, and in times of threatenings of immediate death. But notwithstanding this patience and submission, the thoughts of death and the day of judgment are always exceeding sweet to the soul. This resignation is also attended with a constant resignation of the lives of dearest earthly friends, and sometimes when some of their lives have been imminently threatened; the person often expressing the sweetness of the liberty of having wholly left the world, and renounced all for God, and having nothing but God, in whom is an infinite fulness. These things have been attended with a constant sweet peace and calm, and serenity of soul, without any cloud to interrupt it; a continual rejoicing in all the works of God's hands, the works of nature, and God's daily works of providence, all appearing with a sweet smile upon them; a wonderful access to God by prayer, as it were seeing him, and immediately conversing with him, as much oftentimes (to use the person's own expressions) as if Christ were here on earth, sitting on a visible throne, to be approached to and conversed with.

There have been frequent, plain, sensible, and immediate answers of prayer, all tears wiped away, all former troubles and sorrows of life forgotten, and all sorrow and sighing fled away—excepting grief for past sins, and for remaining corruption, and that Christ is loved no more, and that God is no more honoured in the world; and a compassionate grief towards fellow-creatures—a daily sensible doing and suffering every thing for God, for a long time past, eating, working, sleeping, and bearing pain and trouble for God, and doing all as the service of love, with a continual uninterrupted cheerfulness, peace, and joy. Oh how good, said the person once, is it to work for God in the day-time, and at night to lie down under his smiles! High experiences and religious affections in this person have not been attended with any disposition at all to neglect the necessary business of a secular calling, to spend the time in reading and prayer, and other exercises of devotion; but worldly business has been attended with great alacrity, as part of the service of God: the person declaring that, it being done thus, it was found to be as good as prayer. These things have been accompanied with exceeding concern and zeal for moral duties, and that all professors may with them adorn the doctrine of God their Saviour; and an uncommon care to perform relative and social duties, and a noted eminence in them; a great inoffensiveness of life and conversation in the sight of others; a great meekness, gentleness, and benevolence of spirit and behaviour; and a great alteration in those things that formerly used to be the person's failings; seeming to be much overcome and swallowed up by the late great increase of grace, to the observation of those who are most conversant and most intimately acquainted.

In times of the brightest light and highest flights of love and joy, there was found no disposition to the opinion of being now perfectly free from sin, (according to the notion of the *Wesleys* and their followers, and some other high pretenders to spirituality in these days,) but exceedingly the contrary. At such times especially, it was seen how loathsome and polluted the soul is; soul and body, and every act and word, appearing like rottenness and corruption in that pure and holy light of God's glory. The person did not slight instruction or means of grace any more for having had great discoveries; on the contrary, never was more sensible of the need of instruction than now. And one thing more may be added, *viz.* That these things have been attended with a particular dislike of placing religion much in dress, and spending much zeal about those things that in themselves are matters of indifference, or an affecting to show humility and devotion by a mean habit, or a demure and melancholy countenance, or any thing singular and superstitious.

SECT. VI.

This work is very glorious.

Now if such things are enthusiasm, and the fruits of a distempered brain, let my brain be evermore possessed of that happy distemper! If this be distraction, I pray God that the world of mankind may be all seized with this benign, meek, beneficent, beatifical, glorious distraction! If agitations of body were found in the *French prophets*, and ten thousand prophets more, it is little to their purpose who bring it as an objection against such a work as this, unless their purpose be to disprove the whole of the christian religion. The great affections and high transports, that others have lately been under, are in general of the same kind with those in the instance that has been given, though not to so high a degree, and many of them not so pure and unmixed, and so well regulated. I have had opportunity to observe many instances here and elsewhere; and though there are some instances of great affections in which there has been a great mixture of nature with grace, and, in some, a sad degenerating of religious affections; yet there is that uniformity observable, which makes it easy to be seen, that in general it is the same spirit from whence the work in all parts of the land has originated. And what notions have they of religion, that reject what has been described, as not true religion! What shall we find to answer those expressions in Scripture, "The peace of God that passeth all understanding; rejoicing with joy unspeakable and full of glory, in believing in and loving an unseen Saviour;—All joy and peace in believing; God's shining into our hearts, to give the light of the knowledge of the glory of God, in the face of Jesus Christ; With open face, beholding as in a glass the glory of the Lord, and being changed into the same image, from glory to glory, even as by the Spirit of the Lord;—Having the love of God shed abroad in our hearts, by the Holy Ghost given to us;—Having the Spirit of God and of glory rest upon us;—A being called out of darkness into marvellous light; and having the day-star arise in our hearts:"—I say, if those things which have been mentioned, do not answer these expressions, what else can we find out that does answer them? Those that do not think such things as these to be the fruits of the true Spirit, would do well to consider what kind of spirit they are waiting and praying for, and what sort of fruits they expect he should produce when he comes. I suppose it will generally be allowed, that there is such a thing as a glorious outpouring of the Spirit of God to be expected, to introduce very joyful and glorious times upon religious accounts; times wherein holy love and joy will be raised to a great height in true Christians: but, if those things be rejected, what is left that we can find wherewith to patch up a notion, or form an idea, of the high, blessed, joyful religion of these times? What is there sweet, excellent, and joyful, of a religious nature, that is entirely of a different nature from these things?

Those who are waiting for the fruits, in order to determine whether this be the work of God or no, would do well to consider, what they are waiting for: whether it be not to have this wonderful religious influence subside, and then to see how they will behave themselves? That is, to have grace subside, and the actings of it in a great measure to cease, and to have persons grow cold and dead; and then to see whether, after that, they will behave themselves with that exactness and brightness of conversation, that is to be expected of lively Christians, or those that are in the vigorous exercises of grace. There are many that will not be satisfied with any exactness or laboriousness in religion now, while persons have their minds much moved, and their affections are high; for they lay it to their flash of affection, and heat of zeal, as they call it; they are waiting to see whether they will carry themselves as well when these affections are over; that is, they are waiting to have persons sicken and lose their strength, that they may see whether they will then behave themselves like healthy strong men. I would desire that they would also consider, whether they be not waiting for more than is reasonably to be expected, supposing this to be really a great work of God, and much more than has been found in former great outpourings of the Spirit of God, that have been universally acknowledged in the christian church? Do not they expect fewer instances of apostacy and evidences of hypocrisy in professors, than were after that great outpouring of the Spirit in the apostles' days, or that which was in the time of the reformation? And do not they stand prepared to make a mighty argument of it against this work, if there should be *half* so many? And, they would do well to consider how *long* they will wait to see the good fruit of this work, before they will determine in favour of it. Is not their waiting unlimited? The visible fruit that is to be expected of a pouring out of the Spirit of God on a country, is a visible reformation in that country. What reformation has lately been brought to pass in *New England*, by this work, has been before observed. And has it not continued long enough already, to give reasonable satisfaction? If God cannot work on the hearts of a people after such a manner, as reasonably to expect it should be acknowledged in a year and a half, or two years' time; yet surely it is unreasonable that our expectations and demands should be unlimited, and our waiting without any bounds.

As there is the clearest evidence, from what has been observed, that this is the work of God; so it is evident that it is a very great and wonderful and exceeding glorious work.—This is certain, that it is a great and wonderful event, a strange revolution, an unexpected, surprising overturning of things, suddenly brought to pass; such as never has been seen in *New England*, and scarce ever has been heard of in any land. Who that saw the state of things in *New England* a few years ago, would have thought that in so short a time there would be such a change? This is undoubtedly either a very great work of God, or a great work of the devil, as to the main substance of it. For though, undoubtedly, God and the devil may work together at the same time, and in the same land; and Satan will do his utmost endeavour to intrude, and, by intermingling his work, to darken and hinder God's work; yet God and the devil do not work together in producing the same event, and in effecting the same change in the hearts and lives of men. But it is apparent that as to some things wherein the main substance of this work consists, there is a likeness and agreement every where: now this is either a wonderful work of God, or a mighty work of the devil: and so is either a most happy event, greatly to be admired and rejoiced in, or a most awful calamity. Therefore, if what has been said before be sufficient to determine it to be, as to the main, the work of God, then it must be acknowledged to be a very wonderful and glorious work of God.

Such a work is, in its nature and kind, the most glorious of any work of God whatsoever, and is always so spoken of in Scripture. It is the work of redemption (the great end of all the other works of God, and of which the work of creation was but a shadow) in the event, success, and end of it: it is the work of new creation, which is infinitely more glorious than the old. I am bold to say, that the work of God in the conversion of one soul, considered together with the source, foundation, and purchase of it, and also the benefit, end, and eternal issue of it, is a more glorious work of God than the creation of the whole material universe. It is the most glorious of God's works, as it above all others manifests the glory of God; it is spoken of in Scripture, as that which shows *the exceeding greatness of God's power*, and *the glory and riches of divine grace*, and wherein Christ has the most glorious triumph over his enemies, and wherein God is mightily exalted. And it is a work above all others glorious, as it concerns the happiness of mankind; more happiness, and a greater benefit to man, is the fruit of each single drop of such a shower, than all the temporal good of the most happy revolution, or all that a people could gain by the conquest of the world.

This work is very glorious both in its *nature*, and in its *degree* and *circumstances*. It will appear very glorious, if we consider the unworthiness of the people who are the subjects of it; what obligations God has laid us under by the special privileges we have enjoyed for our souls' good, and the great things God did for us at our first settlement in the land; how he has followed us with his goodness to this day, and how we have abused his goodness; how long we have been revolting more and more, (as all confess,) and how very corrupt we were become at last; in how great a degree we had forsaken the fountain of living waters; how obstinate we have been under all manner of means that God has used to reclaim us; how often we have mocked God with hypocritical pretences of humiliation, as in our annual days of public fasting, and other things, while, instead of reforming, we only grew worse and worse; and how dead a time it was every where before this work began. If we consider these things, we shall be most stupidly ungrateful, if we do not acknowledge God's visiting us as he has done, as an instance of the glorious triumph of free and sovereign grace.

The work is very glorious, if we consider the *extent* of it; being in this respect vastly beyond any that ever was known in *New England*. There has formerly sometimes been a remarkable awakening and success of the means of grace, in some particular congregations; and this used to be much noticed, and acknowledged to be glorious, though the towns and congregations round about continued dead: but now God has brought to pass a new thing, he has wrought a great work, which has extended from one end of the land to the other, besides what has been wrought in other *British* colonies in *America*.

The work is very glorious in the great *numbers* that have, to appearance, been turned from sin to God, and so, delivered from a wretched captivity to sin and Satan, saved from everlasting burnings, and made heirs of eternal glory. How high an honour and great a reward of their labours, have some eminent persons of note in the church of God signified that they should esteem it, if they should be made the instruments of the conversion and eternal salvation of but *one* soul! And no greater event than that, is thought worthy of great notice in heaven among the hosts of glorious angels, who rejoice and sing on such an occasion. Now, when there are many thousands of souls thus converted and saved, shall it be esteemed worth but little notice, and be mentioned with coldness and indifference here on earth, by those among whom such a work is wrought

The work has been very glorious and wonderful in many *circumstances* and events of it, wherein God has in an uncommon manner made his hand visible and his power conspicuous; as in the extraordinary degrees of awakening, and the suddenness of conversions in innumerable instances. How common a thing has it been for a great part of a congregation to be at once moved by a mighty invisible power! and for six, eight, or ten souls to be converted to God (to all appearance) in an exercise, in whom the visible change still continues! How great an alteration has been made in some towns, yea, some populous towns, the change still abiding! And how many very vicious persons have been wrought upon, so as to become visibly new creatures! God has also made his hand very visible, and his work glorious, in the multitudes of little children that have been wrought upon. I suppose there have been some hundreds of instances of this nature of late, any one of which formerly would have been looked upon so remarkable, as to be worthy to be recorded, and published through the land. The work is very glorious in its influences and effects on many who have been very ignorant and barbarous, as I before observed of the *Indians and negroes.*

The work is also exceeding glorious in the high attainments of Christians, in the extraordinary degrees of light, love, and spiritual joy, that God has bestowed upon great multitudes. In this respect also, the land in all parts has abounded with such instances, any one of which, if they had happened formerly, would have been thought worthy to be noticed by God's people throughout the *British* dominions. The *New Jerusalem* in this respect has begun to come down from heaven, and perhaps never were more of the prelibations of heaven's glory given upon earth.

There being a great many errors and sinful irregularities mixed with this work of God, arising from our weakness, darkness, and corruption, does not hinder this work of God's power and grace from being very glorious. Our follies and sins in some respects manifest the glory of it. The glory of divine power and grace is set off with the greater lustre, by what appears at the same time of the weakness of the earthen vessel. It is God's pleasure to manifest the weakness and unworthiness of the subject, at the same time that he displays the excellency of his power and the riches of his grace. And I doubt not but some of these things which make some of us here on earth to be out of humour, and to look on this work with a sour displeased countenance, heighten the songs of the angels, when they praise God and the Lamb for what they see of the glory of God's all-sufficiency, and the efficacy of Christ's redemption. And how unreasonable is it that we should be backward to acknowledge the glory of what God has done, because the devil, and we in hearkening to him, have done a great deal of mischief!

PART II.

SHOWING THE OBLIGATIONS THAT ALL ARE UNDER TO ACKNOWLEDGE, REJOICE IN, AND PROMOTE THIS WORK; AND THE GREAT DANGER OF THE CONTRARY.

SECT. I.

The danger of lying still, and keeping long silence, respecting any remarkable work of God.

THERE are many things in the word of God, showing that when God remarkably appears in any great work for his church, and against his enemies, it is a most dangerous thing, and highly provoking to God, to be slow and backward to acknowledge and honour God in the work. Christ's people are in Scripture represented as his army; he is the Lord of hosts, the Captain of the host of the Lord, as he called himself when he appeared to *Joshua*, with a sword drawn in his hand, Joshua v. 13—15. the Captain of his people's salvation: and therefore it may well be highly resented, if they do not resort to him when he orders his banner to be displayed; or if they refuse to follow him when he blows the trumpet, and gloriously appears going forth against his enemies. God expects that every living soul should have his attention roused on such an occasion, and should most cheerfully yield to the call, and heedfully and diligently obey it. Isa. xviii. 3. "All ye inhabitants of the world, and dwellers on the earth, see ye when he lifteth up an ensign on the mountains; and when he bloweth the trumpet, hear ye." Especially should all *Israel* be gathered after their Captain, as we read they were after *Ehud*, when he blew the trumpet in mount *Ephraim,* when he had slain *Eglon* king of *Moab*, Judges iii. 27, 28. How severe is the martial law in such a case, when any of the army refuses to obey the sound of the trumpet, and follow his general to the battle! God at such a time appears in peculiar manifestations of his glory; and therefore, not to be affected and animated, and to lie still, and refuse to follow God, will be resented as a high contempt of him. Suppose a subject should stand by, and be a spectator of the solemnity of his prince's coronation, and should appear silent and sullen, when all the multitude were testifying their loyalty and joy with loud acclamations; how greatly would he expose himself to be treated as a rebel, and quickly to perish by the authority of the prince that he refuses to honour!

At a time when God manifests himself in such a great work for his church, there is no such thing as being neuters; there is a necessity of being either for or against the king that then gloriously appears. When a king is crowned, and there are public manifestations of joy on that occasion, there is no such thing as standing by as an indifferent spectator; all must appear as loyal subjects, and express their joy on that occasion, or be accounted enemies. So when God, in any great dispensation of his providence, remarkably sets his King on his holy hill of Zion, Christ in an extraordinary manner comes down from heaven to the earth, and appears in his visible church in a great work of salvation for his people. When Christ came down from heaven in his incarnation, and appeared on earth in his human presence, there was no such thing as being neuters, neither on his side nor against him. Those who sat still and said nothing, and did not declare for him, and come and join with him, after he, by his word and works, had given sufficient evidence who he was, were justly looked upon as his enemies. Matt. xii. 30. "He that is not with me is against me; and he that gathereth not with me, scattereth abroad." So it is when Christ comes to carry on the work of redemption in the application of it, as well as in its revelation and purchase. If a king should come into one of his provinces, which had been oppressed by its foes, where some of his subjects had fallen off to the enemy, and joined with them against their lawful sovereign and his loyal subjects; I say, if the royal sovereign himself should come into the province, and should ride forth there against his enemies, and should call upon all who were on his side to come and gather themselves to him; there would be no such thing, in such a case, as standing neuter. They who lay still and staid at a distance would undoubtedly be looked upon and treated as rebels. So in the day of battle, when two armies join, there is no such thing for any present as being of neither party, all must be on one side or the other; and they who are not found with the conqueror in such a case, must expect to have his weapons turned against them, and to fall with the rest of his enemies.

When God manifests himself with such glorious power in a work of this nature, he appears especially determined to put honour upon his Son, and to fulfil his oath that he has sworn to him, that he would make every knee to bow, and every tongue to confess to him. God hath had it much on his heart, from all eternity, to glorify his dear and only-begotten Son; and there are some special seasons that he appoints to that end, wherein he comes forth with omnipotent power to fulfil his promise and oath to him. Now these are times of remarkable pouring out of his Spirit, to advance his kingdom; such is a day of his power, wherein his people shall be made willing, and he shall rule in the midst of his enemies; these especially are the times wherein God declares his firm decree, that his Son shall reign on his holy hill of *Zion*. And therefore those who at such a time do not kiss the Son, as he then manifests himself, and appears in the glory of his majesty and grace, expose themselves to *perish from the way*, and to be *dashed in pieces with a rod of iron.*

As such is a time wherein God eminently *sets his King on his holy hill of Zion,* so it is a time wherein he remarkably fulfils that in Isa. xxviii. 16. "Therefore thus saith the Lord God, Behold, I lay in Zion for a foundation, a stone, a tried stone, a precious corner-stone, a sure foundation." Which the two apostles *Peter* and *Paul* (1 Pet. ii. 6—8. and Rom. ix. 33.) join with that prophecy, Isa. viii. 14, 15. "And he shall be for a sanctuary; but for a stone of stumbling, and for a rock of offence to both the houses of Israel, for a gin and for a snare to the inhabitants of Jerusalem. And many among them shall stumble and fall, and be broken, and be snared, and be taken." As signifying that both are fulfilled together. Yea, both are joined together by the prophet *Isaiah* himself; as you may see in the context of that forementioned place, Isa. xxviii. 16. In ver. 13. preceding, it is said, "But the word of the Lord was unto them, precept upon precept, precept upon precept, line upon line, line upon line, here a little and there a little; that they might go, and fall backward, and be broken, and snared, and taken." And accordingly, when Christ is in a peculiar and eminent manner manifested and magnified, by a glorious work of God in his church, as a foundation and a sanctuary for some, he is remarkably a stone of stumbling and a rock of offence, a gin and a snare, to others. They who continue long to stumble and to be offended and insnared in their minds, at such a great and glorious work of Christ, in God's account, stumble at Christ, and are offended in him; for the work is that by which he makes Christ manifest, and shows his glory, and by which he makes *the stone that the builders refused, to become the head of the corner.* This shows how dangerous it is to continue always stumbling at such a work, for ever doubting of it, and forbearing fully to acknowledge it, and give God the glory of it. Such persons are in danger to *go, and fall backward, and be broken, and snared, and taken*, and to have Christ *a stone of stumbling* to them, that shall be an occasion of their ruin; while he is to others *a sanctuary*, and a *sure foundation.*

The prophet *Isaiah* (Isa. xxix. 14.) speaks of God's proceeding to do a marvellous work and a wonder, which should stumble and confound the wisdom of the wise and prudent; which the apostle in Acts xiii. 41. applies to the glorious work of salvation wrought in those days by the redemption of Christ, and that glorious outpouring of the Spirit to apply it which followed. The prophet in the context of that place in Isa. xxix. speaking of the same thing, and of the prophets and rulers and seers, those wise and prudent whose eyes God had closed, says to them, ver. 9. "Stay yourselves and wonder." In the original it is, "Be ye slow and wonder." I leave it to others to consider whether it be not natural to interpret it thus, "Wonder at this *marvellous work;* let it be a strange thing, a great mystery that you know not what to make of, and that you are very slow and backward to acknowledge, long delaying to come to a determination concerning it." And what persons are in danger, and are thus slow to acknowledge God in such a work, we learn from the apostle in that forementioned place, Acts xiii. 41. "Behold, ye despisers, and wonder and perish; for I work a work in your days, a work which you shall in nowise believe, though a man declare it unto you."

The church of Christ is called upon greatly to rejoice, when at any time Christ remarkably appears, coming to his church, to carry on the work of salvation, to enlarge his own kingdom, and to deliver poor souls out of the pit wherein there is no water. Zech. ix. 9, 10, 11. "Rejoice greatly, O daughter of Zion; shout, O daughter of Jerusalem; behold, thy King cometh unto thee; he is just, and having salvation:—His dominion shall be from sea to sea.—As for thee also, by the blood of thy covenant, I have sent forth thy prisoners out of the pit wherein is no water." Christ was pleased to give a notable typical or symbolical representation of such a great event as is spoken of in that prophecy, in his solemn entry into the literal Jerusalem, which was a type of the church or daughter of Zion; probably intending it as a figure and prelude of that great actual fulfilment of this prophecy, that was to be after his ascension, by the pouring out of the Spirit in the days of the apostles, and that more full accomplishment that should be in the latter ages of the christian church. We have an account, that when Christ made this his solemn entry into Jerusalem, and the whole multitude of the disciples were rejoicing and praising God, with loud voices, for all the mighty works that they had seen, the Pharisees from among the multitude said to Christ, *Master, rebuke thy disciples;* but we are told, Luke xix. 39, 40. Christ "answered and said unto them, I tell you, that if these should hold their peace, the stones would immediately cry out." Signifying, that if Christ's professing disciples should be unaffected on such an occasion, and should not appear openly to acknowledge and rejoice in the glory of God therein appearing, it would manifest such fearful hardness of heart that the very stones would condemn them. Should not this make those consider, who have held their peace so long since Christ has come to our Zion having salvation, and so wonderfully manifested his glory in this mighty work of his Spirit, and so many of his disciples have been *rejoicing and praising God with loud voices?*

It must be acknowledged, that so great and wonderful a work of God's Spirit, is a work wherein God's hand is remarkably *lifted up*, and wherein he displays his *majesty*, and shows great *favour* and mercy to sinners, in the glorious opportunity he gives them, and by which he makes our land to become much more a *land of uprightness.* Therefore that place, Isa. xxvi. 10, 11. shows the great danger of not seeing God's hand, and acknowledging his glory and majesty, in such a work; "Let favour be showed to the wicked, yet will he not learn righteousness: In the land of uprightness he will deal unjustly, and will not behold the majesty of the Lord. Lord, when thy hand is lifted up, they will not see; but they shall see, and be ashamed for their envy at the people; yea, the fire of thine enemies shall devour them."

SECT. II.

The latter-day glory, is probably to begin in America.

It is not unlikely that this work of God's Spirit, so extraordinary and wonderful, is the dawning, or, at least, a prelude of that glorious work of God, so often foretold in Scripture, which, in the progress and issue of it, shall renew the world of mankind. If we consider how long since the things foretold as what should precede this great event, have been accomplished; and how long this event has been expected by the church of God, and thought to be nigh by the most eminent men of God in the church; and withal consider what the state of things now is, and has for a considerable time been, in the church of God, and the world of mankind; we cannot reasonably think otherwise, than that the beginning of this great work of God must be near. And there are many things that make it probable that this work will begin in *America.*—It is signified that it shall begin in some very remote part of the world, with which other parts have no communication but by navigation, in Isa. lx. 9. "Surely the isles shall wait for me, and the ships of *Tarshish* first, to bring my sons from far." It is exceeding manifest that this chapter is a prophecy of the prosperity of the church, in its most glorious state on earth, in the latter days; and I cannot think that any thing else can be here intended but *America* by the isles that are far off, from whence the first-born sons of that glorious day shall be brought. Indeed, by *the isles*, in prophecies of gospel-times, is very often meant *Europe.* It is so in prophecies of that great spreading of the gospel that should be soon after Christ's time, because it was far separated from that part of the world where the church of God had till then been, by the sea. But *this* prophecy cannot have respect to the conversion of *Europe*, in the time of that great work of God, in the primitive ages of the christian church; for it was not fulfilled then. The isles and ships of *Tarshish*, thus understood, did not wait for God first; that glorious work did not begin in *Europe*, but in *Jerusalem*, and had for a considerable time been very wonderfully carried on in *Asia*, before it reached *Europe.* And as it is not *that* work of God which is chiefly intended in this chapter, but some more glorious work that should be in the latter ages of the christian church; therefore, some other part of the world is here intended by the isles, that should be, as *Europe* then was, far separated from that part of the world where the church had before been, and with which it can have no communication but by the ships of *Tarshish*. And what is chiefly intended is not the *British* isles, nor any isles near the other continent; for they are spoken of as at a great distance from that part of the world where the church had till then been. This prophecy therefore seems plainly to point out *America*, as the first-fruits of that glorious day.

God has made as it were two worlds here below, two great habitable continents, far separated one from the other: The latter is as it were now but newly created; it has been, till of late, wholly the possession of *Satan*, the church of God having never been in it, as it has been in the other continent, from the beginning of the world. This new world is probably now discovered, that the new and most glorious state of God's church on earth might commence there; that God might in it begin a new world in a spiritual respect, when he creates the *new heavens* and *new earth*.

God has already put that honour upon the other continent, that Christ was born there literally, and there made the *purchase of redemption*. So, as Providence observes a kind of equal distribution of things, it is not unlikely that the great spiritual birth of Christ, and the most glorious *application of redemption*, is to begin in this. The elder sister brought forth *Judah*, of whom Christ came, and so she was the mother of Christ; but the younger sister, after long barrenness, brought forth *Joseph* and *Benjamin*, the beloved children. *Joseph* who had the most glorious apparel, the coat of many colours; who was separated from his brethren, and was exalted to great glory out of a dark dungeon—who fed and saved the world when ready to perish with famine, and was as a fruitful bough by a well, whose branches ran over the wall, and was blessed with all manner of blessings and precious things of heaven and earth, through the good-will of him that dwelt in the bush—was, as by the horns of an unicorn, to push the people together, to the ends of the earth, *i. e.* conquer the world. See Gen. xlix. 22, &c. and Deut. xxxiii. 13, &c. And *Benjamin*, whose mess was five times so great as that of any of his brethren, and to whom Joseph, that type of Christ, gave wealth and raiment far beyond all the rest, Gen. xlv. 22.

The other continent hath slain Christ, and has from age to age shed the blood of the saints and martyrs of Jesus, and has often been as it were deluged with the church's blood. God has therefore probably reserved the honour of building the glorious temple to the daughter that has not shed so much blood, when those times of the peace, prosperity, and glory of the church, typified by the reign of Solomon, shall commence.

The *Gentiles* first received the true religion from the *Jews*: God's church of ancient times had been among them, and Christ was of them. But, that there may be a kind of equality in the dispositions of providence, God has so ordered it, that when the *Jews* come to be admitted to the benefits of the evangelical dispensation, and to receive their highest privileges of all, they should receive the gospel from the *Gentiles*. Though Christ was of them, yet they have been guilty of crucifying him; it is therefore the will of God, that the Jews should not have the honour of communicating the blessings of the kingdom of God in its most glorious state to the *Gentiles;* but on the contrary, they shall receive the gospel in the beginning of that glorious day from the *Gentiles*. In some analogy to this, I apprehend, God's dealings will be with the two continents. *America* has received the true religion of the old continent; the church of ancient times has been there, and Christ is from thence. But that there may be an equality, and inasmuch as that continent has crucified Christ, they shall not have the honour of communicating religion in its most glorious state to us, but we to them.

The old continent has been the source and original of mankind, in several respects. The first parents of mankind dwelt there; and there dwelt *Noah* and his sons; there the second *Adam* was born, and crucified and raised again: and 'tis probable that, in some measure to balance these things, the most glorious renovation of the world shall originate from the new continent, and the church of God in that respect be from hence. And so it is probable that will come to pass in spirituals, which has taken place in temporals, with respect to *America;* that whereas, till of late, the world was supplied with its silver, and gold, and earthly treasures from the old continent, now it is supplied chiefly from the new; so the course of things in spiritual respects will be in like manner turned.—And it is worthy to be noted, that *America* was discovered about the time of the reformation, or but little before: which reformation was the first thing that God did towards the glorious renovation of the world, after it had sunk into the depths of darkness and ruin, under the great antichristian apostacy. So that, as soon as this new world stands forth in view, God presently goes about doing some great thing in order to make way for the introduction of the church's latter-day glory—which is to have its first seat in, and is to take its rise from, that new world.

It is agreeable to God's manner, when he accomplishes any glorious work in the world, in order to introduce a new and more excellent state of his church, to begin where no foundation had been already laid, that the power of God might be the more conspicuous; that the work might appear to be entirely God's, and be more manifestly a creation out of nothing; agreeable to Hos. i. 10. "And it shall come to pass, that in the place where it was said unto them, Ye are not my people, there it shall be said unto them, Ye are the sons of the living God." When God is about to turn the earth into a paradise, he does not begin his work where there is some good growth already, but in the wilderness, where nothing grows, and nothing is to be seen but dry sand and barren rocks; that the light may shine out of darkness, the world be replenished from emptiness, and the earth watered by springs from a droughty desert; agreeable to many prophecies of Scripture, as Isa. xxxii. 15. "Until the Spirit be poured from on high, and the wilderness become a fruitful field." And chap. xli. 18, 19. "I will open rivers in high places, and fountains in the midst of the valleys: I will make the wilderness a pool of water, and the dry land springs of water. I will plant in the wilderness the cedar, the shittah-tree, and the myrtle, and oil-tree: I will set in the desert the fir-tree, and the pine, and the box-tree together." And chap. xliii. 20. "I will give waters in the wilderness, and rivers in the desert, to give drink to my people, my chosen." And many other parallel scriptures might be mentioned. Now as, when God is about to do some great work for his church, his manner is to begin at the lower end; so, when he is about to renew the whole habitable earth, it is probable that he will begin in this utmost, meanest, youngest, and weakest part of it, where the church of God has been planted last of all; and so the first shall be last, and the last first; and that will be fulfilled in an eminent manner in Isa. xxiv. 19. "From the uttermost part of the earth have we heard songs, even glory to the righteous."

There are several things that seem to me to argue, that the Sun of righteousness, the Sun of the new heavens and new earth, when he rises—and *comes forth as the bridegroom* of his church, *rejoicing as a strong man to run his race, having his going forth from the end of heaven, and his circuit to the end of it, that nothing may be hid from the light and heat of it*,*—shall rise in the west, contrary to the course of things in the old heavens and earth. The movements of Providence shall in that day be so wonderfully altered in many respects, that God will as it were change the course of nature, in answer to the prayers of his church; as he caused the sun to go from the west to the east, when he promised to do such great things for his church; a deliverance out of the hand of the king of *Assyria*, is often used by the prophet *Isaiah*, as a type of the glorious deliverance of the church from her enemies in the

* It is evident that the Holy Spirit, in those expressions in Psal. xix. 4, 6. has respect to something else besides the natural sun, and that a regard is had to the Sun of righteousness, who by his light converts the soul, makes wise the simple, enlightens the eyes, and rejoices the heart; and by his preached gospel enlightens and warms the world of mankind; by the psalmist's own application in ver. 7. and the apostle's application of ver. 4. in Rom. x. 18.

latter days. The resurrection as it were of *Hezekiah*, the king and captain of the church, (as he is called, 2 Kings xx. 5.) is given as an earnest of the church's resurrection and salvation, Isa. xxxviii. 6. and is a type of the resurrection of Christ. At the same time there is a resurrection of the sun, or coming back and rising again from the west, whither it had gone down; which is also a type of the Sun of righteousness. The sun was brought back ten degrees; which probably brought it to the meridian. The Sun of righteousness has long been going down from east to west; and probably when the time comes of the church's deliverance from her enemies, so often typified by the *Assyrians*, the light will rise in the west, till it shines through the world like the sun in its meridian brightness.

The same seems also to be represented by the course of the waters of the sanctuary, Ezek. xlvii. which was from west to east; which waters undoubtedly represented the Holy Spirit, in the progress of his saving influences, in the latter ages of the world: for it is manifest, that the whole of those last chapters of *Ezekiel* treat concerning the glorious state of the church at that time. And if we may suppose that this glorious work of God shall begin in any part of *America*, I think, if we consider the circumstances of the settlement of *New England*, it must needs appear the most likely, of all *American* colonies, to be the place whence this work shall principally take its rise. And, if these things be so, it gives us more abundant reason to hope that what is now seen in *America*, and especially in *New England*, may prove the dawn of that glorious day: and the very uncommon and wonderful circumstances and events of this work, seem to me strongly to argue that God intends it as the beginning or forerunner of something vastly great.

SECT. III.

The danger of not acknowledging and encouraging, and especially of deriding, this work.

I HAVE thus long insisted on this point, because, if these things are so, it greatly manifests how much it behoves us to encourage and promote this work, and how dangerous it will be to forbear so doing. It is very dangerous for God's professing people to lie still, and not to come to the help of the Lord, whenever he remarkably pours out his Spirit, to carry on the work of redemption in the application of it; but above all, when he comes forth, to introduce that happy day of God's power and salvation, so often spoken of. That is especially the appointed season of the application of redemption. The appointed time of Christ's reign. The reign of Satan as god of this world lasts till then; but afterwards will be the proper time of actual redemption, or new creation, as is evident by Isa. lxv. 17, 18, &c. and lxvi. 12. and Rev. xxi. 1. All the outpourings of the Spirit of God before this, are as it were by way of anticipation. There was indeed a glorious season of the application of redemption in the first ages of the christian church, which began at *Jerusalem*, on the day of *Pentecost;* but that was not the proper time of ingathering. It was only as it were the feast of first-fruits; the ingathering is at the end of the year, or in the last ages of the christian church, as is represented, Rev. xiv. 14—16. and will probably as much exceed what was in the first ages of the christian church, though that filled the *Roman* empire, as that exceeded all that had been before, under the Old Testament, confined only to the land of *Judea*.

The great danger of not appearing openly to acknowledge, rejoice in, and promote that great work of God, in bringing in that glorious harvest, is represented in Zech. xiv. 16, 17, 18, 19. "And it shall come to pass, that every one that is left, of all the nations which came against Jerusalem, shall even go up from year to year to worship the King, the Lord of hosts, and to keep the feast of tabernacles. And it shall be, that whoso will not come up of all the families of the earth unto Jerusalem, to worship the King, the Lord of hosts, even upon them shall be no rain. And if the family of *Egypt* go not up, and come not, that have no rain; there shall be the plague wherewith the Lord will smite the heathen that come not up to keep the feast of tabernacles. This shall be the punishment of *Egypt*, and the punishment of all nations that come not up to keep the feast of tabernacles." It is evident by all the context, that the glorious day of the church of God in the latter ages of the world, is the time spoken of. The *feast of tabernacles* here seems to signify that glorious spiritual feast which God shall then make for his church, the same that is spoken of, Isa. xxv. 6. and the great spiritual rejoicings of God's people at that time. There were three great feasts in *Israel* at which all the males were appointed to go up to *Jerusalem;* the feast of the *passover;* and the feast of the *first-fruits*, or the feast of *Pentecost;* and the feast of *ingathering*, at the end of the year, or the feast of *tabernacles*. In the first of these, *viz. the feast of the passover*, was represented the *purchase* of redemption by Jesus Christ; for the paschal lamb was slain at the time of that feast. The other two that followed it were to represent the two great seasons of the *application* of the purchased redemption. In the former of them, *viz. the feast of the first-fruits*, which was called the feast of *Pentecost*, was represented that time of the outpouring of the Spirit in the first ages of the christian church, for the bringing in the *first-fruits* of Christ's redemption, which began at *Jerusalem* on the day of *Pentecost*. The other, which was the feast of *ingathering*, at the end of the year--which the children of *Israel* were appointed to keep on occasion of their gathering in their corn and their wine, and all the fruit of their land, and was called the *feast of tabernacles*—represented the other more joyful and glorious season of the application of Christ's redemption, which is to be in the latter days. Then will be the great day of ingathering of the elect, the proper and appointed time of gathering in God's fruits, when the angel of the covenant shall thrust in his sickle, and gather the harvest of the earth; and the clusters of the vine of the earth shall also be gathered. This was upon many accounts the greatest feast of the three. There were much greater tokens of rejoicings in this feast than any other. The people then dwelt in booths of green boughs, and were commanded to take boughs of goodly trees, branches of palm-trees, and the boughs of thick trees, and willows of the brook, and to rejoice before the Lord their God. This represents the flourishing, beautiful, pleasant state of the church, rejoicing in God's grace and love, and triumphing over all her enemies. The tabernacle of God was first set up among the children of *Israel*, at the time of the *feast of tabernacles;* but, in that glorious time of the christian church, God will above all other times set up his tabernacle amongst men, Rev. xxi. 3. "And I heard a great voice out of heaven, saying, The tabernacle of God is with men, and he will dwell with them, and they shall be his people, and God himself shall be with them, and be their God."

The world is supposed to have been created about the time of year wherein the *feast of tabernacles* was appointed; so, in that glorious time God will create a new heaven and a new earth. The temple of *Solomon* was dedicated at the time of the *feast of tabernacles*, when God descended in a pillar of cloud, and dwelt in the temple; so, at this happy time, the temple of God shall be gloriously built up in the world, and God shall in a wonderful manner come down from heaven to dwell with his church. Christ is supposed to have been born at the feast of tabernacles; so, at the commencement of that glorious day, Christ shall be born; then, above all other times, shall "the woman clothed with the sun, with the moon under her feet, that is in travail, and pained to be delivered, bring forth her son, to rule all nations," Rev. xii. The *feast of tabernacles* was the last feast that *Israel* had in the whole year, before the face of the earth was destroyed by the winter; presently after the rejoicings of that feast were past, a tempestuous season began, Acts xxvii. 9. "Sailing was now dangerous, because the feast was now already past." So this great feast of the christian church will be the last feast she shall have on earth; soon after it is past, this lower world will be destroyed. At the *feast of tabernacles*, *Israel* left their houses to dwell in booths or green tents; which signifies the great weanedness of God's people from the world, as pilgrims and strangers on the earth, and their great joy therein. *Israel* were prepared for the *feast of tabernacles* by the *feast of trumpets*, and the day of atonement, both in the same month; so, way shall be made for the joy of the church of God, in its glorious state on earth, by the extraordinary preaching of the gospel, deep repentance and humiliation for past sins, and for the great and long-continued deadness and carnality of the visible church. Christ, at the great *feast of tabernacles*, stood in *Jerusalem*, and "cried, saying, If any man thirst, let him come unto me and drink: he that believeth on me, as the scripture hath said, out of his belly shall flow rivers of living waters:" signifying the extraordinary freedom and riches of divine grace towards sinners at that day, and the extraordinary measures of the Holy Spirit that shall be then given; agreeable to Rev. xxi. 6. and xxii. 17.

It is threatened (Zech. xiv.) that those who at that time shall not come to keep this feast, *i. e.* that shall not acknowledge God's glorious works, praise his name, and rejoice with his people—but who should stand at a distance, as unbelieving and disaffected—*upon them shall be no rain;* they shall have no share in the shower of divine blessing that shall then descend on the earth, the spiritual rain spoken of, Isa. xliv. 3. but God would give them over to hardness of heart and blindness of mind. The curse is denounced against such, in a manner still more awful, ver. 12. "And this shall be the plague wherewith the Lord shall smite all the people that have fought against *Jerusalem:* their flesh shall consume away while they stand upon their feet, and their eyes shall consume away in their holes, and their tongue shall consume away in their mouth." Here also, in all probability, is intended a spiritual judgment, or a plague and curse from God upon the soul, rather than upon the body; that such persons, who at that time shall oppose God's people in his work, shall in an extraordinary manner be given over to a state of spiritual death and ruin, that they shall remarkably appear dead while alive, and shall be as walking rotten corpses while they go about amongst men. The great danger of not joining with God's people at that glorious day is also represented, Isa. lx. 12. "For the nation and kingdom that will not serve thee shall perish; yea, those nations shall be utterly wasted."

Most of the great temporal deliverances wrought for *Israel* of old, were typical of the great spiritual works of God for the salvation of souls, and the deliverance and prosperity of his church, in gospel days; and especially they represented that greatest of all deliverances of God's church in the latter days; which is above all others the proper season of actual redemption of men's souls. But it may be observed, that if any appeared to oppose God's work in those great temporal deliverances; or if there were any of his professing people, who on such occasions lay still, stood at a distance, or did not arise and acknowledge God in his work, and appear to promote it; it was what in a remarkable manner incensed God's anger, and brought his curse upon such persons.—When God wrought that great work of bringing the children of *Israel* out of *Egypt*, (which was a type of God's delivering his church out of the spiritual *Egypt* at the time of the fall of *Antichrist*, as is evident by Rev. xi. 8. and xv. 3.) how highly did he resent it, when the *Amalekites* appeared as opposers in that affair! and how dreadfully did he curse them for it! Exod. xvii. 14, 15, 16. "And the Lord said unto *Moses*, Write this for a memorial in a book, and rehearse it in the ears of *Joshua;* for I will utterly put out the remembrance of *Amalek* from under heaven. And *Moses* built an altar, and called the name of it *Jehovah-nissi*. For he said, Because the Lord will have war with *Amalek* from generation to generation." And accordingly we find that God remembered it a long time after, 1 Sam. xv. 3. And how highly did God resent it in the *Moabites* and *Ammonites*, that they did not lend a helping hand, and encourage and promote the affair! Deut. xxiii. 3, 4. "An Ammonite or Moabite shall not enter into the congregation of the Lord; even to their tenth generation, shall they not enter into the congregation of the Lord for ever: because they met you not with bread and with water in the way, when ye came forth out of Egypt." And how were the children of *Reuben*, and the children of *Gad*, and the half-tribe of *Manasseh* threatened, if they did not go and help their brethren in their wars against the *Canaanites!* Num. xxxii. 20—23. "And Moses said unto them, if ye will do this thing, if ye will go armed before the Lord to war, and will go all of you armed over Jordan before the Lord, until he hath driven out his enemies from before him, and the land be subdued before the Lord; then afterward ye shall return, and be guiltless before the Lord, and before Israel; and this land shall be your possession before the Lord. But if ye will not do so, behold, ye have sinned against the Lord; and be sure your sin will find you out."

That was a glorious work which God wrought for *Israel*, when he delivered them from the *Canaanites*, by the hand of *Deborah* and *Barak*. Almost every thing about it showed a remarkable hand of God. It was a prophetess, one immediately inspired by God, that called the people to the battle, and conducted them in the whole affair. The people seem to have been miraculously animated and encouraged in the matter, when they willingly offered themselves, and gathered together to the battle; they jeoparded their lives in the high places of the field, without being pressed or hired, when one would have thought they should have but little courage for such an undertaking. For what could a number of poor, weak, defenceless slaves do, without *a shield or spear to be seen among forty thousand of them*, to go against a great prince, with his mighty host, and nine hundred chariots of iron? And the success wonderfully showed the hand of God; which makes *Deborah* exultingly to say, Judg. v. 31. "O my soul, thou hast trodden down strength!" Christ with his heavenly host was engaged in that battle; and therefore it is said, ver. 20. "They fought from heaven, the stars in their courses fought against Sisera." The work of God therefore, in this victory and deliverance which Christ and his host wrought for *Israel*, was a type of what he will accomplish for his church in that great last conflict of the church with her open enemies, that shall introduce the church's latter-day glory; as appears by Rev. xvi. 16. (speaking of that great battle,) "And he gathered them together into a place, called in the *Hebrew* tongue, *Armageddon*," *i. e.* the mountain of *Megiddo;* alluding, as is supposed by expositors, to the place where the battle was fought with the host of *Sisera*, Judg. v. 19. "The kings came and fought, the kings of *Canaan*, in *Taanach*, by the waters of *Megiddo*." Which can signify nothing else than that this battle, which Christ and his church shall have with their enemies, is the antitype of the battle that was fought there. But what a dreadful curse from Christ did some of God's professing people *Israel* bring upon themselves, by lying still at that time, and not putting to a helping hand! Judg. v. 23. "Curse ye *Meroz*, said the angel of the Lord, curse ye bitterly the inhabitants thereof: because they came not to the help of the Lord, to the help of the Lord against the mighty." The angel of the Lord was the captain of the host; he that had led *Israel*, and fought for them in that battle, who is very often called *the angel of the Lord*, in Scripture; the same that appeared to *Joshua* with a sword drawn in his hand, and told him that he was *come as the captain of the host of the Lord:* and the same glorious captain who is represented as leading forth his hosts to that battle, of which this was the type, Rev. xix. 11, &c. It seems the inhabitants of *Meroz* were unbelieving concerning this great work; they would not hearken to *Deborah's* pretences, nor did it enter into them that such a poor defenceless company should ever prevail against those that were so mighty. They did not acknowledge the hand of God, and therefore stood at a distance, and did nothing to promote the work; but what a bitter curse from God did they bring upon themselves by it!—It is very probable that one great reason why the inhabitants of *Meroz* were so unbelieving concerning this work, was, that they argued *a priori;* they did not like the beginning of it, it being a woman that first led the way, and had the chief conduct in the affair; nor could they believe that such despicable instruments, as a company of unarmed slaves, were ever like to effect so great a thing; and pride and unbelief wrought together, in not being willing to follow *Deborah* to the battle.

It was another glorious work of God that he wrought for *Israel*, in the victory that was obtained by *Gideon* over the *Midianites* and *Amalekites*, and the children of the east, when they came up against *Israel* like grasshoppers, a multitude that could not be numbered. This also was a remarkable type of the victory of Christ and his church over his enemies, by the pouring out of the Spirit with the preached gospel; as is evident by the manner in which *Gideon* was immediately directed of God, which was not by human sword or bow, but by blowing of trumpets, and by lights in earthen vessels. We read that, on this occasion, *Gideon* called the people together to help in this great affair; and that accordingly great numbers resorted to him, and came to the help of the Lord, Judg. vii. 23, 24. But the inhabitants of *Succoth* and *Penuel* were unbelieving, and would not acknowledge the hand of God in that work, though it was so great and wonderful, nor would they join to promote it. *Gideon* desired their help, when he was pursuing after *Zeba* and *Zalmunna;* but they despised his pretences, and his confidence of the Lord being on his side, to deliver those two great princes into the hands of such a despicable company as he and his three hundred men, and would not own the work of God, nor afford *Gideon* any assistance. God proceeded in this work in a way that was exceeding cross to their pride. And they also refused to own the work, because they argued *a priori;* they could not believe that God would do such great things by such a despicable instrument, one of such a poor, mean family in *Manasseh,* and he the least in his father's house; and the company that was with him appeared very wretched, being but three hundred men, and they weak and faint. But we see how they suffered for their folly, in not acknowledging and appearing to promote this work of God: *Gideon,* when he returned from the victory, *took them, and taught them with the briers and thorns of the wilderness, and beat down the tower of* Penuel, (he brought down their pride and their false confidence,) *and slew the men of the city,* Judg. viii. This in all probability *Gideon* did, as moved and directed by the angel of the Lord, that is Christ, who first called him, and sent him forth in this battle, and instructed and directed him in the whole affair.

The return of the ark of God to dwell in *Zion,* in the midst of the land of *Israel,* after it had been long absent—first in the land of the *Philistines,* and then in *Kirjath-jearim,* in the utmost borders of the land—strikingly represented the return of God to a professing people, in the spiritual tokens of his presence, after long absence from them. The ark ascending up into a mountain, typified Christ's ascension into heaven. It is evident by the psalms that were penned on that occasion, especially the 68th *Psalm,* that the exceeding rejoicings of *Israel* on that occasion represented the joy of the church of Christ on his returning to it, after it has been in a low and dark state, to revive his work, bringing his people *back,* as it were, *from* Bashan, *and from the depth of the sea;* scattering their spiritual enemies, and causing that *though they had lien among the pots, yet they should be as the wings of a dove, covered with silver, and her feathers with yellow gold;* and giving the blessed tokens of his presence in his house, that his people may *see the goings of God their King in the sanctuary.* The gifts of which *David,* with such royal bounty, distributed amongst the people on that occasion, (2 Sam. vi. 18, 19. and 1 Chron. xvi. 2, 3.) represent spiritual blessings that Christ liberally sends down on his church, by the outpourings of the Spirit. See Ps. lxviii. 1, 3, 13, 18—24. And we have an account how that all the people, from *Shihor* of *Egypt,* even unto the entering in of *Hemath,* gathered together, and appeared to join and assist in that great affair; and that all Israel "brought up the ark of the covenant of the Lord, with shouting, and with sound of the cornet, and with trumpets, and with cymbals, making a noise with psalteries and harps," 1 Chron. xiii. 2, 5. and xv. 28. And not only the men, but the women of *Israel,* the daughters of *Zion* appeared, as publicly joining in the praises and rejoicings on that occasion, 2 Sam. vi. 19. But we read of one of *David's* wives, even *Michal, Saul's* daughter, whose heart was not engaged in the affair, and did not appear with others to rejoice and praise God on this occasion, but kept away, and stood at a distance, as disaffected, and disliking the management. She despised and ridiculed the transports and extraordinary manifestations of joy; and the curse that she brought upon herself by it was that of being barren to the day of her death. Let this be a warning to us: let us take heed, in this day of the bringing up of the ark of God, that, while we are in visibility and profession the spouse of the spiritual *David,* we do not show ourselves to be indeed the children of falsehearted and rebellious *Saul,* by our standing aloof, and our not joining in the joy and praises of the day, disliking and despising the joys and affections of God's people because they are so high in degree, and so bring the curse of perpetual barrenness upon our souls.

Let us take heed that we be not like the son of the bond-woman, born after the flesh, that persecuted him that was born after the Spirit, and mocked at the feasting and rejoicings that were made for *Isaac* when he was weaned; let we should be cast out of the family of *Abraham,* as he was, Gen. xxi. 8, 9. That affair contained spiritual mysteries, and was typical of things that come to pass in these days of the gospel; as is evident by the apostle's testimony, Gal. iv. 22, &c. And particularly it seems to have been typical of two things;

First, The weaning of the church from its milk of carnal ordinances, ceremonies, shadows, and beggarly elements upon the coming of Christ, and pouring out of the Spirit in the days of the apostles. The church of Christ, in the times of the Old Testament, was in its minority, even as a babe; and the apostle tells us that babes must be fed with milk, and not with strong meat: but when God weaned his church from these carnal ordinances, on the ceasing of the legal dispensation, a glorious gospel-feast was provided for souls, and God fed his people with spiritual dainties, filled them with the Spirit, and gave them joy in the Holy Ghost. *Ishmael* in mocking at the time of *Isaac's* feast, by the apostle's testimony, represented the carnal *Jews,* the children of the literal *Jerusalem,* who, when they beheld the rejoicings of Christians in their spiritual and evangelical privileges, were filled with envy, deriding, contradicting, and blaspheming, (Acts ii. 13. and chap. xiii. 45. and xviii. 6.) and therefore were cast out of the family of *Abraham,* and out of the land of *Canaan,* to wander through the earth.

Secondly, This weaning of *Isaac* seems also to represent the conversion of sinners, which is several times represented in Scripture by the weaning of a child; as in Ps. cxxxi. and Isa. xxviii. 9. because in conversion the soul is weaned from the enjoyments of the world, which are as it were the breast of our mother earth; and is also weaned from the covenant of our first parents, which we as naturally hang upon, as a child on its mother's breast. And the great feast that *Abraham* made on that occasion represents the spiritual feast, the heavenly privileges, and holy joys and comforts, which God gives to souls at their conversion. Now is a time when God in a remarkable manner is bestowing the blessings of such a feast: let every one take heed that he do not now show himself to be the son of the bond-woman, and born after the flesh, by standing and deriding, with mocking *Ishmael;* lest they be cast out as he was, and it be said concerning them, "These sons of the bond-woman shall not be heirs with the sons of the free-woman." Do not let us stumble at these things, because they are so great and extraordinary; for *if* we "have run with the footmen, and they have wearied us, how shall we contend with horses?" There is doubtless a time coming when God will accomplish things vastly greater and more extraordinary than these.

And that we may be warned not to continue doubting and unbelieving concerning this work, because of the extraordinary degree of it, and the suddenness and swiftness of the accomplishment of the great things that pertain to it; let us consider the example of the unbelieving lord in *Samaria,* who could not believe so extraordinary a work of God to be accomplished so suddenly as was declared to him. The prophet *Elisha* foretold that the great famine in *Samaria* should very suddenly, even in one day, be turned into an extraordinary plenty; but the work was too great and too sudden for him to believe; says he, "If the Lord should make windows in heaven, might this thing be?" And the curse that he brought upon himself by it was, that he saw it with his eyes, and did not eat thereof, but miserably perished, and was trodden down as the mire of the streets, when others were feasting and rejoicing, 2 Kings vii.

When God redeemed his people from their *Babylonish* captivity, and they rebuilt *Jerusalem*, it was, as is universally owned, a remarkable type of the spiritual redemption of God's church; and particularly of the great deliverance of the christian church from spiritual *Babylon*, and their rebuilding the spiritual *Jerusalem*, in the latter days; and therefore they are often spoken of as one by the prophets. And this probably was the main reason that it was so ordered in Providence, and particularly noted in Scripture, that the children of *Israel*, on that occasion, kept the greatest *feast of tabernacles* that ever had been kept in *Israel* since the days of *Joshua*, when the people were first settled in *Canaan*. (Neh. viii. 16, 17.) For at that time happened that restoration of *Israel*, which had the greatest resemblance of that great restoration of the church of God, of which the *feast of tabernacles* was the type, of any that had been since *Joshua* first brought the people out of the wilderness, and settled them in the good land. But we read of some that opposed the *Jews* in that affair, weakened their hands, ridiculed God's people, the instruments employed in that work, despised their hopes, and made as though their confidence was little more than a shadow, and would utterly fail them: "What do these feeble Jews? (say they,) will they fortify themselves? will they sacrifice? will they make an end in a day? will they revive the stones out of the heaps of the rubbish which are burnt? Even that which they build, if a fox go up, he shall even break down their stone wall." Let not us be in any measure like them, lest it be said to us, as *Nehemiah* said to them, Neh. ii. 20. "We his servants will arise and build; but you have no portion, nor right, nor memorial in *Jerusalem*." And lest we bring *Nehemiah's* imprecations upon us, chap. iv. 5. "Cover not their iniquity, and let not their sin be blotted out from before thee; for they have provoked thee to anger before the builders."

As persons will greatly expose themselves to the curse of God, by opposing, or standing at a distance, and keeping silence at such a time as this; so for persons to arise, and readily to acknowledge God, and honour him in such a work, and cheerfully and vigorously to exert themselves to promote it, will be to put themselves much in the way of the divine blessing. What a mark of honour does God put upon those in *Israel*, that willingly offered themselves, and came to the help of the Lord against the mighty, when the angel of the Lord led forth his armies, and they fought from heaven against *Sisera!* Judg. v. 2, 9, 14—18. And what a great blessing is pronounced on *Jael*, the wife of *Heber* the *Kenite*, for her appearing on the Lord's side, and for what she did to promote that work! "Blessed above women shall *Jael* the wife of *Heber* the *Kenite* be, blessed shall she be above women in the tent." And what a blessing is pronounced on those which shall have any hand in the destruction of *Babylon*, which was the head city of the kingdom of *Satan*, and of the enemies of the church of God! Psal. cxxxvii. 9. "Happy shall he be that taketh and dasheth thy little ones against the stones." What a particular and honourable notice is taken, in the records of God's work, of those that arose and appeared as *David's* helpers, to introduce him into the kingdom of *Israel!* 1 Chron. xii. The host of those who thus came to the help of the Lord, in that glorious revolution in *Israel*, by which the kingdom of that great type of the *Messiah* was set up in *Israel*, is compared to the host of God, (ver. 22.) "At that time, day by day, there came to *David* to help him, until it was a great host, like the host of God." And doubtless it was intended to be a type of the host that shall appear with the spiritual *David*, as his helpers, when he shall come to set up his kingdom in the world; the same host that we read of, Rev. xiv. 14. The Spirit of God then pronounced a special blessing on *David's* helpers, as co-workers with God, ver. 18. "Then the Spirit came upon *Amasai*, who was chief of the captains, and he said, Thine are we, *David*, and on thy side, thou son of *Jesse*: Peace, peace be unto thee, and peace be to thine helpers; for thy God helpeth thee." So we may conclude, that God will much more give his blessing to such as come to the help of the Lord, when he sets his own dear Son as King on his holy hill of *Zion*. They shall be received by Christ, and he will put peculiar honour upon them, as *David* did on those his helpers; as we have an account in the following words, ver. 18. "Then *David* received them, and made them captains of the band." It is particularly noted of those that came to *David* to *Hebron*, ready armed to the war, to turn the kingdom of *Saul* to him, according to the word of the Lord, that "they were men that had understanding of the times, to know what *Israel* ought to do," ver. 23, and 32. Wherein they differed from the *Pharisees* and other *Jews*, who did not come to the help of the Lord, at the time that the great Son of *David* appeared to set up his kingdom in the world. These Christ condemns, because they had not "understanding of those times," Luke xii. 56. "Ye hypocrites, ye can discern the face of the sky, and of the earth; but how is it that ye do not discern these times;" so it will always be, when Christ remarkably appears on earth, on a design of setting up his kingdom here; many will not understand the times, nor what *Israel* ought to do, and so will not come to turn about the kingdom to *David*.

The favourable notice that God will take of such as appear to promote the work of God, at such a time as this, may also be argued from such a very particular notice being taken in the sacred records, of those that helped in rebuilding the wall of *Jerusalem*, upon the return from the *Babylonish* captivity, Nehem. chap. iii.

SECT. IV.

The obligations of rulers, ministers, and all sorts to promote this work.

At such a time as this, when God is setting his King on his holy hill of *Zion*, or establishing his dominion, or showing forth his regal glory from thence, he expects that his visible people, without exception, should openly appear to acknowledge him in such a work, and bow before him, and join with him. But especially does he expect this of civil *rulers*: God's eye is especially upon them, to see how they behave themselves on such occasions. When a new king comes to the throne, if he comes from abroad, and enters into his kingdom, and makes his solemn entry into the royal city, it is expected that all sorts should acknowledge him; but above all others is it expected that the great men, and public officers of the nation, should then make their appearance, and attend on their sovereign, with suitable congratulations, and manifestations of respect and loyalty. If such as these stand at a distance at such a time, it will be much more noticed; and will awaken the prince's jealousy and displeasure much more, than such a behaviour in the common people. And thus it is, when that eternal Son of God, and heir of the world—by whom kings reign, and princes decree justice, and whom his Father has appointed to be King of kings—comes as it were from far, and in the spiritual tokens of his presence enters into the royal city *Zion*. God has his eye at such a time, especially, upon those princes, nobles, and judges of the earth, spoken of, Prov. viii. 16. to see how they behave themselves, whether they bow to him, who is made the head of all principality and power. This is evident by Psal. ii. 6, 7, 10—12. "Yet have I set my King upon my holy hill of *Zion*. I will declare the decree: the Lord hath said unto me, Thou art my Son, this day have I begotten thee.—Be wise now therefore, O ye kings: be instructed, ye judges of the earth. Serve the Lord with fear, and rejoice with trembling. Kiss the Son, lest he be angry and ye perish from the way, when his wrath is kindled but a little." There seems to be in the words an allusion to a new king coming to the throne, and making his solemn entry into the royal city, when it is expected that all, especially men in public office and authority, should manifest their loyalty, by some open and visible tokens of respect, *by the way*, as he passes along; and those that refuse or neglect it, are in danger of being immediately struck down, and perishing *from the way*, by which the king goes in solemn procession.

The day wherein God, in an eminent manner, sends forth the rod of Christ's strength out of *Zion*, that he may rule in the midst of his enemies, the day of his power wherein his people shall be made willing, is also eminently a day of his wrath, especially to such rulers as oppose him, or will not bow to him. It will prove a day wherein he "shall strike through kings, and fill the places with the dead bodies, and wound the heads over many countries," Psal. cx. And thus it is, that when the Son of God "girds his sword upon his thigh, with his glory and his majesty, and in his majesty rides prosperously, because of truth, meekness, and righteousness, his right hand teaches him terrible things." They were the princes of *Succoth* especially who suffered punishment, when the inhabitants of that city refused to come to the help of the Lord. When *Gideon* was pursuing after *Zebah* and *Zalmunna*, we read that *Gideon* took the *elders* of the city, and thorns of the wilderness, and briers, and with them he taught the men of *Succoth*. It is especially noticed, that the rulers and chief men of *Israel*, were called upon to assist in the affair of bringing up the ark of God; they were chiefly consulted, and were principal in the management of the affair, 1 Chron. xiii. 1. "And *David* consulted with the captains of thousands and hundreds, and with every leader." And chap. xv. 25. "So *David* and the elders of *Israel*, and the captains over thousands, went to bring up the ark of the covenant of the Lord, out of the house of *Obed-Edom*, with joy." So 2 Sam. vi. 1. And so it was when the ark was brought into the temple, (1 Kings viii. 1, 3. and 2 Chron. v. 2, 4.)

And as rulers, by neglecting their duty at such a time, will especially expose themselves to God's great displeasure; so by fully acknowledging God in such a work, and by cheerfully and vigorously exerting themselves to promote it, they will especially be in the way of receiving peculiar honours and rewards at God's hands. It is noted of the princes of *Israel*, that *they* especially appeared to honour God with their princely offering, on occasion of setting up the tabernacle of God in the congregation of *Israel*. I have observed already that this was done at the time of the *feast of tabernacles*, and was a type of the tabernacle of God being with men, and his dwelling with men in the latter days. And with what abundant particularity is it noted of each prince, how much he offered to God on that occasion, for their everlasting honour, in the 7th chapter of *Numbers!* And so, with how much favour and honour does the Spirit of God take notice of those princes in *Israel*, who came to the help of the Lord, in the war against *Sisera!* Judg. v. 9. "My heart is towards the governors of *Israel*, that offered themselves willingly among the people." And, (ver. 14.) "Out of *Machir* came down governors." (ver. 15.) "And the princes of *Issachar* were with *Deborah*." And in the account we have of rebuilding the wall of *Jerusalem*, Neh. iii. it is particularly noted what a hand one and another of the rulers had in this affair; such a part of the wall was repaired by the ruler of the half-part of *Jerusalem*, and such a part by the ruler of the other half-part of *Jerusalem*, and such a part by the ruler of part of *Beth-haccerem*, and such a part by the ruler of part of *Mizpah*, and such a part by the ruler of the half-part of *Bethzur;* and such a part by the ruler of *Mizpah*, ver. 9—19. And there it is particularly noted of the rulers of one of the cities, that they put not their necks to the work of the Lord, though the common people did; and they are stigmatized for it in the sacred records, to their everlasting reproach, (v. 5.) "And next unto them the *Tekoites* repaired; but their nobles put not their necks to the work of the Lord." So the Spirit of God, with special honour, takes notice of princes and rulers of several tribes, who assisted in bringing up the ark, Psal. lxviii. 27.

And I humbly desire it may be considered, whether we have not reason to fear, that God is provoked with this land, because no more notice has been taken of the late glorious work by the civil authority; that no more has been done by them as a public acknowledgment of God in this work, and no more improvement of their authority to promote it. This might have been done, either by appointing a day of public thanksgiving to God for so unspeakable a mercy, or a day of fasting and prayer, to humble ourselves before God for our past deadness and unprofitableness under the means of grace, and to seek the continuance and increase of the tokens of his presence. Can it be pleasing to God, that the civil authority have not so much as entered upon any public consultation, what should be done to advance the present revival of religion, and great reformation that is begun in the land? Is there not danger that such a behaviour, at such a time, will be interpreted by God, as a denial of Christ? If but a new governor comes into a province, how much is there done, especially by those who are in authority, to put honour upon him! They arise, appear publicly, and go forth to meet, to address, and congratulate him, and with great expense to attend and aid him! If the authority of the province, on such an occasion, should all sit still, and say and do nothing, and take no notice of the arrival of their new governor, would there not be danger of its being interpreted by him, and his prince that sent him, as a denial of his authority, or a refusing to receive and honour him as their governor? And shall the head of the angels, and Lord of the universe, come down from heaven, in so wonderful a manner, into a land; and shall all stand at a distance, and be silent and inactive on such an occasion? I would humbly recommend it to our rulers to consider whether God does not now say to them, "Be wise now, ye rulers; be instructed, ye judges of *New England:* kiss the Son, lest he be angry, and ye perish from the way."

It is prophesied, Zech. xii. 8. that, in the glorious day of the christian church, the house of *David*, or the rulers in God's "Israel, shall be as God, as the angel of the Lord, before his people." But how can such rulers expect to have any share in this glorious promise, who do not so much as openly acknowledge God in the work of that Spirit, by whom the glory of that day is to be accomplished? The days are coming, when the saints shall reign on earth, and all dominion and authority shall be given into their hands: but, if our rulers would partake of this honour, they ought, at such a day as this, to bring their glory and honour into the spiritual *Jerusalem*, agreeable to Rev. xxi. 24.

But, above all others, is God's eye upon the *ministers* of the gospel, as expecting of them, that they should arise, acknowledge, and honour him in such a work as this, and do their utmost to encourage and promote it. For this is the very business to which they are called and devoted; it is the office to which they are appointed, as co-workers with Christ. They are his ambassadors and instruments, to awaken and convert sinners, and establish, build up, and comfort saints; it is the business they have been solemnly charged with, before God, angels, and men, and to which they have given up themselves by the most sacred vows. These especially are the officers of Christ's kingdom, who, above all other men upon earth, represent his person; into whose hands Christ has committed the sacred oracles, holy ordinances, and all his appointed means of grace, to be administered by them. They are the stewards of his household, into whose hands he has committed its provision; the immortal souls of men are committed to them, as a flock of sheep are committed to the care of a shepherd, or as a master commits a treasure to the care of a servant, of which he must give an account. It is expected of them, above all others, that they should have understanding of the times, and know what *Israel* ought to do; for it is their business to acquaint themselves with things pertaining to the kingdom of God, and to teach and enlighten others in the same. We who are employed in the sacred work of the gospel ministry, are the watchmen over the city, to whom God has committed the keys of the gates of *Zion;* and if, when the rightful King of *Zion* comes to deliver his people from the enemy that oppresses them, we refuse to open the gates to him, how greatly shall we expose ourselves to his wrath! We are appointed to be the captains of the host in this war; and if a general will highly resent it in a private soldier, if he refuses to follow him when his banner is displayed, and his trumpet blown; how much more will he resent it in the officers of his army! The work of the gospel-ministry, consisting in the administration of God's word and ordinances, is the principal means that God has appointed for carrying on his work on the souls of men; and it is his revealed will, that whenever that glorious revival of religion, and reformation of the world, so often spoken of in his word, is accomplished, it should be principally by the labours of his ministers. Therefore, how heinous will it be in the sight of God, if, when a work of that nature is begun, we appear unbelieving, slow, backward, and disaffected! There was no sort of persons among the *Jews* treated with such manifestations of God's great displeasure, and severe indignation, for not acknowledging Christ, and the work of his Spirit, in the days of Christ and his apostles, as the ministers of religion. See how Christ deals with them for it, Matt. xxiii. With what gentleness did Christ treat publicans and harlots, in comparison of them!

When the tabernacle was erected in the camp of *Israel*, and God came down from heaven to dwell in it, the priests were above all others concerned, and busily employed in the solemn transactions of that occasion, Lev. viii. and ix. And so it was at the time of the dedication of the temple by *Solomon*, (1 Kings viii. and 2 Chron. v. vi. and vii.) which was at the time of the feast of tabernacles, the same as when the tabernacle was erected in the wilderness. And the *Levites* were primarily and most immediately concerned in bringing up the ark into mount *Zion;* the business properly belonged to them, and the ark was carried upon their shoulders, 1 Chron. xv. 2. "Then *David* said, None ought to carry the ark of God but the *Levites;* for them hath the Lord chosen to carry the ark of God, and to minister unto him for ever." And (ver. 11, 12.) "And *David* called for *Zadock* and *Abiathar* the priests, and for the *Levites*, for *Uriel*, *Asaiah*, and *Joel*, *Shemaiah*, and *Eliel*, and *Amminadab*, and said unto them, Ye are the chief of the fathers of the *Levites;* sanctify yourselves, both ye and your brethren, that you may bring up the ark of the Lord God of *Israel*, unto the place that I have prepared for it." So we have an account that the priests led the way in rebuilding the wall of *Jerusalem*, after the *Babylonish* captivity, Neh. iii.

Though ministers preach never so good doctrine, and be never so painful and laborious in their work, yet if they show to their people that they are not well-affected to this work, but are doubtful and suspicious of it, they will be very likely to do their people a great deal more hurt than good. For the very fame of such a great and extraordinary work of God, if their people were suffered to believe it to be his work, and the example of other towns, together with what preaching they might hear occasionally, would be likely to have a much greater influence upon the minds of their people to awaken and animate them in religion, than all other labours with them. Besides, their ministers' opinion will not only beget in them a suspicion of the work they hear of abroad, whereby the mighty hand of God that appears in it loses its influence upon their minds; but it will also tend to create a suspicion of every thing of the like nature, that shall appear among themselves, as being something of the same distemper that is become so epidemical in the land. And what is this, in effect, but to create a suspicion of all vital religion, and to put the people upon talking against and discouraging it, wherever it appears, and knocking it on the head as fast as it rises. We, who are ministers, by looking on this work from year to year with a displeased countenance, shall effectually keep the sheep from their pasture, instead of doing the part of shepherds by feeding them; and our people had a great deal better be without any settled minister at all, at such a day as this.

We who are in this sacred office had need to take heed what we do, and how we behave ourselves at this time: a less thing in a *minister* will hinder the work of God, than in *others*. If we are very silent, or say but little about the work, in our public prayers and preaching, or seem carefully to avoid speaking of it in our conversation, it will be interpreted by our people, that we, who are their guides, to whom they are to have their eye for spiritual instruction, are suspicious of it; and this will tend to raise the same suspicions in them; and so the forementioned consequences will follow. And if we really hinder and stand in the way of the work of God, whose business above all others it is to promote it, how can we expect to partake of the glorious benefits of it? And, by keeping others from the benefit, we shall keep them out of heaven; therefore those awful words of Christ to the *Jewish* teachers, should be considered by us, Matt. xxiii. 13. "Woe unto you, for you shut up the kingdom of heaven;——for ye neither go in yourselves, neither suffer ye them that are entering, to go in." If we keep the sheep from their pasture, how shall we answer it to the great Shepherd, who has bought the flock with his precious blood, and has committed the care of them to us? I would humbly desire of every minister that has thus long remained disaffected to this work, and has had contemptible thoughts of it, to consider whether he has not hitherto been like *Michal*, without any child, or at least in a great measure barren and unsuccessful in his work: I pray God it may not be a perpetual barrenness, as hers was.

The times of Christ's remarkably appearing in behalf of his church, to revive religion, and advance his kingdom in the world, are often spoken of in the prophecies of Scripture, as times wherein he will remarkably execute judgments on such ministers or shepherds as do not feed the flock, but hinder their being fed, and so will deliver his flock from them, (Jer. xxiii. throughout, and Ezek. xxxiv. throughout, and Zech. x. 3. and Isa. lvi. 7, 8, 9, &c.) I observed before, that Christ's solemn, magnificent entry into *Jerusalem*, seems to be designed as a representation of his glorious coming into his church, the spiritual *Jerusalem;* and therefore it is worthy to be noted, to our present purpose, that Christ at that time cast out all them who sold and bought in the temple, and overthrew the tables of the money-changers, and the seats of them that sold doves; signifying that, when he should come to set up his kingdom on earth, he would cast out those out of his house, who, instead of being faithful ministers, officiated there only for worldly gain. Not that I determine, that all ministers who are suspicious of this work, do so; but I mention these things to show why it is to be expected, that a time of a glorious outpouring of the Spirit of God to revive religion, will be a time of remarkable judgments on those ministers who do not serve the end of their ministry.

The example of the unbelieving lord in *Samaria* should especially be for the warning of ministers and rulers. At the time when God turned an extreme famine into great plenty, by a wonderful work of his, the king appointed this lord to have the charge of the gate of the city; where he saw the common people, in multitudes, entering with great joy and gladness, loaden with provision, to feed and feast their almost famished bodies; but he himself, though he saw it with his eyes, never had one taste of it, but, being weak with famine, sunk down in the crowd, and was trodden to death, as a punishment of God for his not giving credit to that great and wonderful work of God, when sufficiently manifested to him to require his belief.—Ministers are those whom the King of the church has appointed to have the charge of the gate at which his people enter into the kingdom of heaven, there to be entertained and satisfied with an eternal feast, *i. e.* ministers have the charge of the house of God, which is the gate of heaven.

They should especially take heed of a spirit of envy towards other ministers, whom God is pleased to use for carrying on this work more than they; and that they do not from such a spirit, reproach some preachers who have the true spirit, as though they were influenced by a false spirit—or were bereft of reason, were mad, and proud, false pretenders, and deserved to be put in prison or the stocks, as disturbers of the peace—lest they expose themselves to the curse of *Shemaiah* the *Nehelamite*, who envied the prophet *Jeremiah*, and in this manner reviled him, in his letter to *Zephaniah* the priest, Jer. xxix. 26, 27. "The Lord hath made thee priest in the stead of *Jehoiada* the priest, that ye should be officers in the house of the Lord, for every man that is mad, and maketh himself a prophet, that thou shouldest put him in prison, and in the stocks. Now therefore, why hast thou not reproved *Jeremiah* of *Anathoth*, which maketh himself a prophet to you?" His curse is denounced in the 32d ver. "Therefore thus saith the Lord, Behold, I will punish *Shemaiah* the *Nehemalite*, and his seed: he shall not have a man to dwell among his people, neither shall he behold the good that I will do for my people, saith the Lord, because he hath taught rebellion against the Lord." All superiors or elders should take heed, that at this day they be not like the elder brother, who could not bear that the prodigal should be sumptuously entertained, and would not join in the joy of the feast. He was like *Michal*, *Saul's* daughter, offended at the music and dancing that he heard; the transports of joy displeased him; it seemed to him to be an unseemly and unseasonable noise; and therefore stood at a distance, sullen, and much offended, and full of invectives against the young prodigal.

It is our wisest and best way, fully, and without reluctance, to bow to the great God in this work, and to be entirely resigned to him, with respect to the manner in which he carries it on, and the instruments he is pleased to use. Let us not show ourselves out of humour, and sullenly refuse to acknowledge the work in its full glory, because we have not had so great a hand in promoting it, or have not shared so largely in its blessings, as some others. Let us not refuse to give all that honour which belongs to others as instruments, because they are young, or are upon other accounts much inferior to ourselves and others; and may appear to us very unworthy that God should put so much honour upon them. When God comes to accomplish any great work for his church, and for the advancement of the kingdom of his Son, he always fulfils that scripture, Isa. ii. 17. "And the loftiness of man shall be bowed down, and the haughtiness of man shall be made low, and the Lord alone shall be exalted in that day." If God has a design of carrying on this work, every one, whether he be great or small, must either bow to it, or be broken before it. It may be expected that God's hand will be upon every thing that is high, and stiff, and strong in opposition; as in Isa. ii. 12—15. "For the day of the Lord of hosts shall be upon every one that is proud and lofty, and upon every one that is lifted up, and he shall be brought low; and upon all the cedars of *Lebanon*, that are high and lifted up, and upon all the oaks of *Bashan*, and upon all the high mountains, and upon all the hills that are lifted up, and upon every high tower, and upon every fenced wall."

Not only magistrates and ministers, but *every living soul*, is now obliged to arise and acknowledge God in this work, and put to his hand to promote it, as they would not expose themselves to God's curse. All sorts of persons throughout the whole congregation of *Israel*, great and small, rich and poor, men and women, helped to build the tabernacle in the wilderness; some in one way, others in another; each one according to his capacity: every one whose heart stirred him up, and every one whom his spirit made willing; all sorts contributed and all sorts were employed in that affair, in labours of their hands, both men and women. Some brought gold and silver, others blue, purple, and scarlet, and fine linen; others offered an offering of brass; others, with whom was found shittim-wood, brought it an offering to the Lord: the rulers brought onyx-stones, and spice, and oil; and some brought goats' hair, some rams' skins, and others badgers' skins. (See Exod. xxxv. 20, &c.) And we are told, ver. 29. "The children of *Israel* brought a willing offering unto the Lord, every man and woman, whose heart made them willing." And thus it ought to be in this day of building the tabernacle of God; with such a willing and cheerful heart ought every man, woman, and child, to do something to promote this work: those who have not onyx-stones, or are not able to bring gold or silver, yet may bring goats' hair.

As all sorts of persons were employed in building the tabernacle in the wilderness, so the whole congregation of *Israel* were called together to set up the tabernacle in *Shiloh*, after they came into *Canaan*, Josh. xviii. 1. and the whole congregation of *Israel* were gathered together, to bring up the ark of God from *Kirjath-jearim*. Again, they were all assembled to bring it up out of the house of *Obed-Edom* into *mount Zion;* so again, all *Israel* met together to assist in the great affair of the dedication of the temple, and bring the ark into it. So we have an account, how that all sorts assisted in the rebuilding the wall of *Jerusalem*, not only the proper inhabitants of *Jerusalem*, but those that dwelt in other parts of the land; not only the priests and rulers, but the *Nethinims* and merchants, husbandmen and mechanics, and even women, Neh. iii. 5, 12, 26, 31, 32. And we have an account of one and another, that he repaired over against his house, ver. 10, 23, 28. and one that repaired over against his chamber, ver. 30. So now, at this time of the rebuilding the wall of *Jerusalem*, every one ought to promote the work of God within his own sphere, and by doing what belongs to him, in the place in which God has set him. Men in a private capacity may repair over against their houses; and even those that have not the government of families, and have but a part of a house belonging to them, should repair each one over against his chamber. Every one should be engaged to do the utmost that lies in his power, labouring with watchfulness, care, and diligence, with united hearts, and united strength, and the greatest readiness to assist one another in this work; as God's people rebuilt the wall of *Jerusalem*, who were so diligent in the work, that they wrought from break of day till the stars appeared, and did not so much as put off their clothes in the night. They wrought with great care and watchfulness; with one hand they laboured in the work, and with the other they held a weapon, besides the guard they set to defend them. They were so well united in it, that they appointed one to stand ready with a trumpet in his hand, that, if any were assaulted in one part, those in the other parts, at the sound of the trumpet, might resort to them, and help them. Neh. iv.

Great care should be taken that the *press* should be improved to no purpose contrary to the interest of this work. We read, that when God fought against *Sisera*, for the deliverance of his oppressed church, *they that handle the pen of the writer* came to the help of the Lord in that affair, Judges v. 14. Whatever sort of men in *Israel* were intended, yet, as the words were indicted by a spirit that had a perfect view of all events to the end of the world, and had a special eye in this song, to that great event of the deliverance of God's church in the latter days, of which this deliverance of *Israel* was a type, it is not unlikely that they have respect to *authors*, who should fight against the kingdom of *Satan* with their pens. Those therefore that publish pamphlets to the disadvantage of this work, and tend either directly or indirectly to bring it under suspicion, and to discourage or hinder it, would do well thoroughly to consider whether this be not indeed the work of God; and whether, if it be, it is not likely that God will go forth as fire, to consume all that stand in his way; and whether there be not danger that the fire kindled in them will scorch the authors.

When a people oppose Christ in the work of his Holy Spirit, it is because it touches them in something that is dear to their carnal minds, and because they see the tendency of it is to cross their pride, and deprive them of the objects of their lusts. We should take heed that at this day we be not like the *Gadarenes*, who—when Christ came into their country in the exercise of his glorious power and grace, triumphing over a legion of devils, and delivering a miserable creature that had long been their captive—were all alarmed, because they lost their swine by it; and a whole multitude of the country came, and besought him to depart out of their coasts. They loved their filthy swine better than Jesus Christ; and had rather have a legion of devils in their country with their herd of swine, than Jesus Christ without them.

This work may be opposed in other ways, besides by directly speaking against the whole of it. Persons may say that they believe there is a good work carried on in the country; and may sometimes bless God, in their public prayers, in general terms, for any awakenings or revivals of religion there have lately been in any part of the land; and may pray that God would carry on his own work, and pour out his Spirit more and more; and yet, as I apprehend, be in the sight of God great opposers of his work. Some will express themselves after this manner, who are so far from acknowledging and rejoicing in the infinite mercy and glorious grace of God in causing so happy a change, that they look on the religious state of the country, take it on the whole, much more sorrowful than it was ten years ago; and whose conversation, to those who are well acquainted with them, evidently shows, that they are more out of humour with the state of things, and enjoy themselves less, than they did before ever this work began. If it be manifestly thus with us, and our talk and behaviour with respect to this work be such as has though but an indirect tendency to beget ill thoughts and suspicions in others concerning it, we are opposers of the work of God.

Instead of coming to the help of the Lord, we shall actually fight against him, if we are abundant in insisting on and setting forth the blemishes of the work; so as to manifest that we rather choose and are more forward to take notice of what is amiss, than what is good and glorious in the work. Not but that the errors committed ought to be observed and lamented, and a proper testimony borne against them, and the most probable means should be used to have them amended; but insisting much upon them, as though it were a pleasing theme, or speaking of them with more appearance of heat of spirit, or with ridicule, or an air of contempt, than grief for them, has no tendency to correct the errors; but has a tendency to darken the glory of God's power and grace appearing in the substance of the work, and to beget jealousies and ill thoughts in the minds of others concerning the whole of it. Whatever errors many zealous persons have ran into, yet if the work, in the substance of it, be the work of God, then it is a joyful day indeed; it is so in heaven, and ought to be so among God's people on earth, especially in that part of the earth where this glorious work is carried on. It is a day of great rejoicing with Christ himself, the good Shepherd, when he finds his sheep that was lost, lays it on his shoulders rejoicing, and calls together his friends and neighbours, saying, *Rejoice with me.* If we therefore are Christ's friends, now it should be a day of great rejoicing with us. If we viewed things in a just light, so great an event as the conversion of such a multitude of sinners, would draw and engage our attention much more than all the imprudences and irregularities that have been; our hearts would be swallowed up with the glory of this event, and we should have no great disposition to attend to any thing else. The imprudences and errors of poor feeble worms do not prevent great rejoicing, in the presence of the angels of God, over so many poor sinners that have repented; and it will be an argument of something very ill in us, if they prevent our rejoicing.

Who loves, in a day of great joy and gladness, to be much insisting on those things that are uncomfortable? Would it not be very improper, on a king's coronation-day, to be much in taking notice of the blemishes of the royal family? Or would it be agreeable to the bridegroom, on the day of his espousals, the day of the gladness of his heart, to be much insisting on the blemishes of his bride? We have an account, how at the time of that joyful dispensation of Providence, the restoration of the church of *Israel* after the *Babylonish* captivity, and at the time of the feast of tabernacles, many wept at the faults which were found amongst the people, but were reproved for taking so much notice of the blemishes of that affair, as to overlook the cause of rejoicing. Neh. viii. 9—12. "And *Nehemiah* which is the *Tirshatha*, and *Ezra* the priest the scribe, and the *Levites* that taught the people, said unto all the people, This day is holy unto the Lord your God, mourn not nor weep: for all the people wept, when they heard the words of the law. Then he said unto them, Go your way, eat the fat, and drink the sweet, and send portions unto them for whom nothing is prepared; for this day is holy unto the Lord; neither be you sorry, for the joy of the Lord is your strength. So the *Levites* stilled all the people, saying, Hold your peace, for the day is holy, neither be you grieved. And all the people went their way to eat, and to drink, and to send portions, and to make great mirth, because they had understood the words that were declared unto them."

God doubtless now expects, that all sorts of persons in *New England*, rulers, ministers, and people, high and low, rich and poor, old and young, should take great notice of his hand in this mighty work of his grace, and should appear to acknowledge his glory in it, and greatly to rejoice in it, every one doing his utmost, in the place where God has set them in, to promote it. And God, according to his wonderful patience, seems to be still waiting to give us opportunity thus to acknowledge and honour him. But, if we finally refuse, there is not the least reason to expect any other than that his awful curse will pursue us, and that the pourings out of his wrath will be proportionable to the despised outpourings of his Spirit and grace.

PART III.

SHOWING, IN MANY INSTANCES, WHEREIN THE SUBJECTS, OR ZEALOUS PROMOTERS, OF THIS WORK, HAVE BEEN INJURIOUSLY BLAMED.

This work, which has lately been carried on in the land, is the work of God, and not the work of man. Its beginning has not been of man's power or device, and its being carried on depends not on our strength or wisdom; but yet God expects of all, that they should use their utmost endeavours to promote it, and that the hearts of all should be greatly engaged in this affair. We should improve our utmost strength in it. however vain human strength is without the power of God; and so he no less requires that we should improve our utmost care, wisdom, and prudence, though human wisdom, of itself, be as vain as human strength. Though God is wont to carry on such a work, in such a manner as many ways to show the weakness and vanity of means and human endeavours in themselves; yet, at the same time, he carries it on in such a manner as to encourage diligence and vigilance in the use of proper means and endeavours, and to punish the neglect of them. Therefore, in our endeavours to promote this great work, we ought to use the utmost caution, vigilance, and skill, in the measures we take in order to it. A great affair should be managed with great prudence. This is the most important affair that ever *New England* was called to be concerned in. When a people are engaged in war with a powerful and crafty nation, it concerns them to manage an affair of such consequence with the utmost discretion. Of what vast importance then must it be, that we should be vigilant and prudent in the management of this great war with so great a host of subtle and cruel enemies. We must either conquer or be conquered; and the consequence of the victory, on one side, will be our eternal destruction in both soul and body in hell, and on the other side, our obtaining the kingdom of heaven, and reigning in it in eternal glory! We had need always to stand on our watch, and to be well versed in the art of war, and not be ignorant of the devices of our enemies, and to take heed lest by any means we be beguiled through their subtlety.

Though the devil be strong, yet, in such a war as this, he depends more on his craft than his strength. The course he has chiefly taken, from time to time, to clog, hinder, and overthrow revivals of religion in the church of God, has been by his subtle, deceitful management, to beguile and mislead those that have been engaged therein; and in such a course God has been pleased, in his holy and sovereign providence, to suffer him to succeed, oftentimes, in a great measure, to overthrow that which in its beginning appeared most hopeful and glorious. The work now begun, as I have shown, is eminently glorious, and, if it should go on and prevail, it would make *New England* a kind of heaven upon earth. Is it not therefore a thousand pities that it should be overthrown, through wrong and improper management, which we are led into by our subtle adversary, in our endeavours to promote it?—My present design is to take notice of some things at which offence has been taken beyond just bounds.

I. One thing that has been complained of is, ministers addressing themselves rather to the *affections* of their hearers than to their understandings, and striving to raise their passions to the utmost height, rather by a very affectionate manner of speaking, and a great appearance of earnestness in voice and gesture, than by clear reasoning, and informing their judgment: by which means it is objected that the affections are moved, without a proportionable enlightening of the understanding.

To which I would say, I am far from thinking that it is not very profitable for ministers, in their preaching, to endeavour clearly and distinctly to explain the doctrines of religion, and unravel the difficulties that attend them, and to confirm them with strength of reason and argumentation, and also to observe some easy and clear method in their discourses, for the help of the understanding and memory; and it is very probable that these things have been of late too much neglected by many ministers. Yet I believe that the objection made, of affections raised without enlightening the understanding, is in a great measure built on a mistake, and confused notions that some have about the nature and cause of the affections, and the manner in which they depend on the understanding. All affections are raised either by light *in the understanding*, or by some error and delusion *in the understanding*: for all affections do certainly arise from some apprehension in the understanding; and that apprehension must either be agreeable to truth, or else be some mistake or delusion; if it be an apprehension or notion that is agreeable to truth, then it is *light in the understanding*. Therefore the thing to be inquired into is, whether the apprehensions or notions of divine and eternal things, that are raised in people's minds by these affectionate preachers, whence their affections are excited, be apprehensions agreeable to truth, or whether they are mistakes. If the former, then the affections are raised the way they should be, *viz.* by informing the mind, or conveying light to the understanding. They go away with a wrong notion, who think that those preachers cannot affect their hearers by enlightening their understandings, except by such a distinct and learned handling of the doctrinal points of religion, as depends on human discipline, or the strength of natural reason, and tends to enlarge their hearers' learning, and speculative knowledge in divinity. The manner of preaching without this, may be such as shall tend very much to set divine and eternal things in a right view, and to give the hearers such ideas and apprehensions of them as are agreeable to truth, and such impressions on their hearts as are answerable to the real nature of things. And beside the words that are spoken, the manner of speaking has a great tendency to this. I think an exceeding affectionate way of preaching about the great things of religion, has in itself no tendency to beget false apprehensions of them; but on the contrary, a much greater tendency to beget true apprehensions of them, than a moderate, dull, indifferent way of speaking of them. An appearance of affection and earnestness in the manner of delivery, though very great indeed, if it be agreeable to the nature of the subject—and be not beyond a proportion to its importance, and worthiness of affection, and if there be no appearance of its being feigned or forced—has so much the greater tendency to beget true ideas or apprehensions in the minds of the hearers concerning the subject spoken of, and so to enlighten the understanding: and that for this reason, That such a way or manner of speaking of these things does, in fact, more truly represent them, than a more cold and indifferent way of speaking of them. If the subject be in its own nature worthy of very great affection, then speaking of it with very great affection is most agreeable to the nature of that subject, or is the truest representation of it, and therefore has most of a tendency to beget true ideas of it in the minds of those to whom the representation is made. And I do not think ministers are to be blamed for raising the affections of their hearers too high, if that which they are affected with be only that which is worthy of affection, and their affections are not raised beyond a proportion to their importance, or worthiness of affection. I should think myself in the way of my duty, to raise the affections of my hearers as high as possibly I can, provided that they are affected with nothing but truth, and with affections that are not disagreeable to the nature of the subject. I know it has long been fashionable to despise a very earnest and pathetical way of preaching; and they only have been valued as preachers, who have shown the greatest extent of learning, strength of reason, and correctness of method and language. But I humbly conceive it has been for want of understanding or duly considering human nature, that such preaching has been thought to have the greatest tendency to answer the ends of preaching; and the experience of the present and past ages abundantly confirms the same. Though, as I said before, clearness of distinction and illustration, and strength of reason, and a good method, in the doctrinal handling of the truths of religion, is many ways needful and profitable, and not to be neglected; yet an increase in speculative knowledge in divinity is not what is so much needed by our people as something else. Men may abound in this sort of light, and have no heat. How much has there been of this sort of knowledge, in the christian world, in this age! Was there ever an age, wherein strength and penetration of reason, extent of learning, exactness of distinction, correctness of style, and clearness of expression, did so abound? And yet, was there ever an age, wherein there has been so little sense of the evil of sin, so little love to God, heavenly-mindedness, and holiness of life, among the professors of the true religion? Our people do not so much need to have their heads stored, as to have their hearts touched; and they stand in the greatest need of that sort of preaching, which has the greatest tendency to do this.

Those texts, Isa. lviii. 1. "Cry aloud, spare not, lift up thy voice like a trumpet, and show my people their transgression, and the house of Jacob their sins." And, Ezek. vi. 11. "Thus saith the Lord God, Smite with thine hand, and stamp with thy foot, and say, Alas, for all the evil abominations of the house of Israel!" I say, these texts (however the use that some have made of them has been laughed at) will fully justify a great degree of *pathos*, and manifestation of zeal and fervency in preaching the word of God. They may indeed be abused, so as to countenance that which would be odd and unnatural amongst us, not making due allowance for difference of manners and customs in different ages and nations; but, let us interpret them how we will, they at least imply, that a most affectionate and earnest manner of delivery, in many cases, becomes a preacher of God's word.

Preaching of the word of God is commonly spoken of in Scripture, in such expressions as seem to import a loud and earnest speaking; as in Isa. xl. 2. "Speak ye comfortably to Jerusalem, and cry unto her, that her iniquity is pardoned." And ver. 3. "The voice of him that crieth in the wilderness, Prepare ye the way of the Lord,"—ver. 6. "The voice said, Cry. And he said, What shall I cry? All flesh is grass, and all the goodliness thereof as the flower of the field." Jer. ii. 2. "Go and cry in the ears of Jerusalem, saying, Thus saith the Lord," &c. Jonah i. 2. "Arise, go to Nineveh, that great city, and cry against it." Isa. lxi. 1, 2. "The Spirit of the Lord God is upon me, because the Lord hath anointed me to preach good tidings to the meek—to proclaim liberty to the captives, and the opening of the prison to them that are bound: to proclaim the acceptable year of the Lord, and the day of vengeance of our God." Isa. lxii. 11. "Behold, the Lord hath proclaimed unto the end of the world, Say ye to the daughter of Zion, Behold, thy salvation cometh," &c. Rom. x. 18. "Their sound went into all the earth, and their words to the end of the world." Jer. xi. 6. "Proclaim all these words in the cities of Judah, and in the streets of Jerusalem, saying, Hear ye the words of this covenant, and do them." So, chap. xix. 2. and vii. 2. Prov. viii. 1. "Doth not wisdom cry, and understanding put forth her voice?" ver. 3, 4. "She crieth at the gates, at the entry of the city, at the coming in at the doors. Unto you, O men, I call, and my voice is to the sons of men." And chap. i. 20. "Wisdom crieth without, she uttereth her voice in the streets." Chap. ix. 3. "She hath sent forth her maidens, she crieth upon the high places of the city." John vii. 37. "In the last day, that great day of the feast, Jesus stood and cried, saying, If any man thirst, let him come unto me and drink."

It seems to be foretold, that the gospel should be especially preached in a loud and earnest manner, at the introduction of the prosperous state of religion in the latter days. Isa. xl. 9. "O Zion, that bringest good tidings, get thee up into the high mountain! O Jerusalem, that bringest good tidings, lift up thy voice with strength! Lift it up, and be not afraid! Say unto the cities of Judah, Behold your God!" Isa. lii. 7, 8. "How beautiful upon the mountains are the feet of him that bringeth good tidings!—Thy watchmen shall lift up the voice." Isa. xxvii. 13. "And it shall come to pass in that day, that the great trumpet shall be blown, and they shall come which were ready to perish."—And this will be one way by which the church of God will cry at that time like a travailing woman, when Christ mystical is going to be brought forth; as Rev. xii. at the beginning. It will be by ministers, as her mouth, that Christ will then cry like a travailing woman, as in Isa. xlii. 14. "I have long time holden my peace, I have been still and refrained myself: now will I cry like a travailing woman." Christ cries by his ministers, and the church cries by her officers. And it is worthy to be noted, that the word commonly used in the New Testament which we translate *preach*, properly signifies to *proclaim aloud like a crier*.

II. Another thing that some ministers have been greatly blamed for, and I think unjustly, is speaking *terror* to them who are already under great terrors, instead of comforting them. Indeed, if ministers in such a case go about to terrify persons with that which is not true, or to affright them by representing their case worse than it is, or in any respect otherwise than it is, they are to be condemned; but if they terrify them only by still holding forth more light to them, and giving them to understand more of the truth of their case, they are altogether to be justified. When consciences are greatly awakened by the Spirit of God, it is but light imparted, enabling men to see their case, in some measure, as it is; and, if more light be let in, it will terrify them still more. But ministers are not therefore to be blamed, that they endeavour to hold forth more light to the conscience, and do not rather alleviate the pain they are under, by intercepting and obstructing the light that shines already. To say any thing to those who have never believed in the Lord Jesus Christ, to represent their case any otherwise than exceeding terrible, is not to preach the word of God to them; for the word of God reveals nothing but truth; but this is to delude them. Why should we be afraid to let persons who are in an infinitely miserable condition, know the truth, or bring them into the light, for fear it should terrify them? It is light that must convert them, if ever they are converted. The more we bring sinners into the light, while they are miserable, and the light is terrible to them, the more likely it is that afterward the light will be joyful to them. The ease, peace, and comfort, which natural men enjoy, have their foundation in darkness and blindness; therefore as that darkness vanishes, and light comes in, their peace vanishes, and they are terrified. But that is no good argument why we should endeavour to hold their darkness, that we may uphold their comfort. The truth is, that as long as men reject Christ, and do not savingly believe in him, however they may be awakened, and however strict, and conscientious, and laborious they may be in religion, they have the wrath of God abiding on them, they are his enemies, and the children of the devil; (as the Scripture calls all who are not savingly converted, Matt. xiii. 38. 1 John iii. 10.) and it is uncertain whether they shall ever obtain mercy. God is under no obligation to show them mercy, nor will he, if they fast and pray and cry never so much: and they are then especially provoking God, under those terrors, that they stand it out against Christ, and will not accept of an offered Saviour, though they see so much need of him. And seeing this is the truth, they should be told so, that they may be sensible what their case indeed is.

To blame a minister for thus declaring the truth to those who are under awakenings, and not immediately administering comfort to them, is like blaming a surgeon, because when he has begun to thrust in his lance, whereby he has already put his patient to great pain, and he shrinks and cries out with anguish, he is so cruel that he will not stay his hand, but goes on to thrust it in further, till he comes to the core of the wound. Such a compassionate physician, who as soon as his patient began to flinch, should withdraw his hand, and go about immediately to apply a plaister, to skin over the wound, and leave the core untouched, would heal the hurt slightly, crying, *Peace, peace, when there is no peace.*

Indeed something besides terror is to be preached to them whose consciences are awakened. They are to be told that there is a Saviour provided, who is excellent and glorious; who has shed his precious blood for sinners, and is every way sufficient to save them; who stands ready to receive them, if they will heartily embrace him; for this is also the truth, as well as that they now are in an infinitely dreadful condition. This is the word of God. Sinners, at the same time that they are told how miserable their case is, should be earnestly invited to come and accept of a Saviour, and yield their hearts unto him, with all the winning, encouraging arguments, that the gospel affords. But this is to induce them to escape from the misery of their condition, not to make them think their present condition to be less miserable than it is, or to abate their uneasiness and distress, while they are in it. That would be the way to quiet them, and fasten them there, and not to excite them to flee from it. Comfort in one sense, is to be held forth to sinners under awakenings of conscience, *i. e.* comfort is to be offered to them in Christ, on their fleeing *from their present miserable state* to him. But comfort is not to be administered to them, *in their present state*, or while out of Christ. No comfort is to be administered to them, from any thing in *them*, any of their qualifications, prayers, or other performances, past, present, or future; but ministers should, in such cases, strive to their utmost to take all such comforts from them, though it greatly increases their terror. A person who sees himself ready to sink into hell, is prone to strive, some way or other, to lay God under some obligation to him; but he is to be beat off from every thing of that nature, though it greatly increases his terror, to see himself wholly destitute of any refuge, or any thing of his own to lay hold of; as a man that sees himself in danger of drowning, is in terror, and endeavours to catch hold on every twig within his reach, and he that pulls away those twigs from him increases his terror; yet if they are insufficient to save him, and by being in his way prevents his looking to that which will save him, to pull away them is necessary to save his life.

If sinners are in distress from any error they embrace, or mistake they are under, that is to be removed. For instance, if they are in terror, from an apprehension that they have committed the unpardonable sin, or that those things have happened to them which are certain signs of reprobation, or any other delusion, such terrors have no tendency to do them any good; for these terrors are from temptation, and not from conviction. But that terror which arises from conviction, or a sight of truth, is to be increased; for those who are most awakened, have great remaining stupidity. It is from remaining blindness and darkness that they see no more, and that remaining blindness is a disease which we should endeavour to remove. I am not afraid to tell sinners who are most sensible of their misery, that their case is indeed as miserable as they think it to be, and a thousand times more so; for this is the truth. Some may be ready to say, that though it be the truth, yet the truth is not to be spoken at all times, and seems not to be seasonable then. But it seems to me, such truth is never more seasonable than at such a time, when Christ is beginning to open the eyes of conscience. Ministers ought to act as co-workers with him; to take that opportunity, and to the utmost to improve that advantage, and strike while the iron is hot. When the light has begun to shine, then they should remove all obstacles, and use all proper means, that it may come in more fully. And experience abundantly shows, that to take this course is not of a hurtful tendency, but very much the contrary. I have seen, in very many instances, the happy effects of it, and oftentimes a very speedy happy issue; and never knew any ill consequence, in case of real conviction, and when distress has been only from thence.

I know of but one case, wherein the truth ought to be withheld from sinners in distress of conscience, and that is the case of melancholy: and it is not to be withheld from them, as if the truth tends to do them hurt; but because, if we speak the truth to them, sometimes they will be deceived, and led into error by it, through that strange disposition there is in them to take things wrong. So that, though what is spoken is truth, yet as it is heard, received, and applied by them, it is falsehood; as it will be, unless the truth be spoken with abundance of caution and prudence, and consideration of their disposition and circumstances. But the most awful truths of God's word ought not to be withheld from public congregations, because it may happen that some such melancholic persons may be in it: any more than the Bible is to be withheld from the christian world, because it is manifest that there are a great many melancholic persons in christendom that exceedingly abuse the awful things contained in the Scripture, to their own wounding. Nor do I think that to be of weight, which is made use of by some, as a great and dreadful objection against the terrifying preaching that has of late been in *New England*, *viz.* That there have been some instances of melancholic persons who have so abused it, that the issue has been the murder of themselves. The objection from hence is no stronger against awakening preaching, than it is against the Bible itself. There are hundreds, and probably thousands, of instances, of persons who have murdered themselves under religious melancholy. These murders probably never would have been, if the world had remained in a state of heathenish darkness. The Bible has not only been the occasion of these sad effects, but of thousands, and I suppose millions, of other cruel murders committed in the persecutions that have been raised, which never would have been if it had not been for the Bible. Many whole countries have been as it were deluged with innocent blood, which would not have been if the gospel never had been preached in the world. It is not a good objection against any kind of preaching, that some men abuse it greatly to their hurt. It has been acknowledged by all divines, as a thing common in all ages, and all christian countries, that a very great part of those who sit under the gospel abuse it. It proves an occasion of their far more aggravated damnation, and so of eternally murdering their souls; which is an effect infinitely more terrible than the murder of their bodies. It is as unjust to lay the blame of these self-murders to those ministers who have declared the awful truths of God's word in the most lively and affecting manner, as it would be to lay the blame of hardening men's hearts, and blinding their eyes, and their more dreadful eternal damnation, to the prophet *Isaiah* or Jesus Christ, because this was the consequence of their preaching with respect to many of their hearers; Isa. vi. 10. John ix. 39. Matt. xiii. 14. Though a few have abused the awakening preaching to their own temporal death; yet it may be to one such instance, there have been hundreds, yea thousands, who have been saved, by this means, from eternal death.

What has more especially given offence to many, and raised a loud cry against some preachers, as though their conduct were intolerable, is their frighting poor innocent children with talk of hell-fire, and eternal damnation. But if those who complain so loudly of this, really believe what is the general profession of the country, *viz.* That all are by nature the children of wrath, and heirs of hell—and that every one that has not been born again, whether he be young or old, is exposed every moment to eternal destruction—then such a complaint and cry as this bewrays a great deal of weakness and inconsideration. Innocent as children seem to us, yet, if they are out of Christ, they are not so in the sight of God; but are in a most miserable condition, as well as grown persons: and they are naturally very senseless and stupid, being *born as the wild ass's colt*, and need much to awaken them. Why should we conceal the truth from them? Will those children who have been dealt tenderly with in this respect, and lived and died insensible of their misery till they come to feel it in hell, ever thank parents and others for their tenderness, in not letting them know their danger? If parents' love towards their children were not blind, it would affect them much more to see their children every day exposed to eternal burnings, and yet senseless, than to see them suffer the distress of that awakening which is necessary in order to their escape, and that tends to their being eternally happy as the children of God. A child that has a dangerous wound may need the painful lance, as well as grown persons; and that would be a foolish pity, in such a case, that should hold back the lance, and throw away the life——I have seen the happy effects of dealing plainly and thoroughly with children in the concerns of their souls, without sparing them at all, in many instances; and never knew any ill consequence of it, in any one instance.

III. Another thing, against which a great deal has been said, is having so frequent *religious meetings*, and spending so much time in religion. Indeed, there are none of the externals of religion but what are capable of excess; and I believe it is true, that there has not been a due proportion observed of late. We have placed religion too much in the external duties of the first table; we have abounded in religious meetings, in praying, reading, hearing, singing, and religious conference; and there has not been a proportionable increase of zeal for deeds of charity, and other duties of the second table; though it must be acknowledged that they are also much increased. But yet it appears to me, that this objection has been in the general groundless. Though worldly business must be done, and persons ought not to neglect that of their particular callings; yet it is to the honour of God, that a people should be so much in outward acts of religion, as to carry in it a visible, public appearance of a great engagedness of mind, especially at such an extraordinary time. When God appears unusually present with a people in wonderful works of power and mercy, they should spend more time than usual in religious exercises, to put honour upon that God who is then extraordinarily present, and to seek his face. Thus it was with the christian church in *Jerusalem*, on occasion of that extraordinary pouring out of the Spirit, soon after Christ's ascension, Acts ii. 46. "And they continued daily with one accord in the temple, and breaking bread from house to house;" and at *Ephesus*, where the Christians attended public religious exercises, every day, for two years together, Acts xix. 8, 9, 10. "And he went into the synagogue, and spake boldly for the space of three months, disputing and persuading the things concerning the kingdom of God. But when divers were hardened, and believed not, but spake evil of that way before the multitude, he departed from them, and separated the disciples, disputing daily in the school of one *Tyrannus*. And this continued by the space of two years; so that all they that dwelt in *Asia*, heard the word of the Lord, both *Jews* and *Greeks*." And as to the grand objection of, *six days shalt thou labour;* all that can be understood by it, and all that the very objectors themselves understand by it, is, that we *may* follow our secular labours in those six days that are not the Sabbath, and *ought* to be diligent in them: not but that sometimes we may turn from them, even within those six days, to keep a day of fasting or thanksgiving, or to attend a lecture; and that more frequently or rarely, as God's providence and the state of things shall call us, according to the best of our discretion.

Though secular business, as I said before, ought not to be neglected; yet I cannot see how it can be maintained, that religion ought not to be attended, lest it should injure our temporal affairs, on any other principle than that of infidelity.—None object against injuring one temporal affair for the sake of another of much greater importance: And therefore, if eternal things are as real as temporal things, and are indeed of infinitely greater importance; then why may we not voluntarily suffer, in some measure, in our temporal concerns, while we are seeking eternal riches, and immortal glory? It is looked upon as no way improper for a whole nation to spend a considerable time, and much of their outward substance, on some extraordinary temporal occasion, for the sake only of the ceremonies of a public rejoicing; and it would be thought dishonourable to be very exact about what we spend, or careful lest we injure our estates, on such an occasion. And why should we be exact only with Almighty God, so that it should be a crime to be otherwise than scrupulously careful lest we injure ourselves in our temporal interest, to put honour upon him, and seek our own eternal happiness? We should take heed that none of us be in any wise like *Judas*, who greatly complained of needless expense, and waste of outward substance, to put honour upon Christ, when *Mary* broke her box, and poured the precious ointment on his head. He *had indignation* within himself on that account, and cries out, "Why was this waste of ointment made? For it might have been sold for more than three hundred pence, and have been given to the poor," Mark xiv. 3, &c. and John xii. 4, &c.

Besides, if the matter be justly examined, I believe it will be found, that the country has lost no time from their temporal affairs by the late revival of religion, but have rather gained; and that more time has been saved from frolicking and tavern-haunting, idleness and unprofitable visits, vain talk, fruitless pastimes, and needless diversions, than has lately been spent in extraordinary religion; and probably five times as much has been saved in various ways, as has been spent by religious meetings. The great complaint made against so much time being spent in religion, cannot be in general from a real concern that God may be honoured, and his will done, and the best good of men promoted; as is very manifest from this, that now there is a much more earnest and zealous outcry made in the country against this extraordinary religion, than was before against so much time spent in tavern-haunting, vain company-keeping, night-walking, and other things, which wasted both our time and substance and injured our moral virtue.

The frequent preaching that has lately obtained, has in a particular manner been objected against as unprofitable and prejudicial. It is objected, that, when sermons are heard so very often, one sermon tends to thrust out another; so that persons lose the benefit of all. They say, two or three sermons in a week is as much as they can remember and digest.—Such objections against frequent preaching, if they be not from an enmity against religion, are for want of duly considering the way that sermons usually profit an auditory. The main benefit obtained by preaching is by impression made upon the mind at the time, and not by an effect that arises afterwards by a remembrance of what was delivered. And though an after-remembrance of what was heard in a sermon is oftentimes very profitable; yet, for the most part, that remembrance is from an impression the words made on the heart at the time; and the memory profits, as it renews and increases that impression. A frequent inculcating the more important things of religion in preaching, has no tendency to rase out such impressions, but to increase them, and fix them deeper and deeper in the mind, as is found by experience. It never used to be objected against, that persons upon the Sabbath, after they have heard two sermons on that day, should go home, and spend the remaining part of the Sabbath in reading the Scriptures, and printed sermons; which, in proportion as it has a tendency to affect the mind at all, tends as much to drive out what they have heard, as if they heard another sermon preached. It seems to have been the practice of the apostles to preach every day, in places where they went; yea, though sometimes they continued long in one place, Acts ii. 42, 46. and xix. 8, 9, 10. They did not avoid preaching one day, for fear they should thrust out of the minds of their hearers what they had delivered the day before; nor did Christians avoid going every day to hear, for fear of any such bad effect; Acts ii. 42, 46.

There are some things in Scripture that seem to signify that there should be preaching in an extraordinary frequency, at the time when God should introduce the flourishing state of religion in the latter days; as Isa. lxii. 1, 2. "For Zion's sake will I not hold my peace, and for Jerusalem's sake I will not rest, until the righteousness thereof go forth as brightness, and the salvation thereof as a lamp that burneth. And the Gentiles shall see thy righteousness, and all kings thy glory." And ver. 5, 6. "For as a young man marrieth a virgin, so shall thy sons marry thee: And as a bridegroom rejoiceth over the bride, so shall thy God rejoice over thee. I have set watchmen upon thy walls, O Jerusalem, which shall never hold their peace day nor night." The destruction of the city of *Jericho* is evidently, in all its circumstances, intended by God as a great type of the overthrow of Satan's kingdom. The priests blowing with trumpets, represents ministers preaching the gospel. The people compassed the city seven days, the priests blowing the trumpets. But, when the day was come that the walls of the city were to fall, the priests were more frequent and abundant in blowing their trumpets; there was as much done in one day then, as had been done in seven days before; they compassed the city seven times that day, blowing their trumpets, till at length it came to one long and perpetual blast, and then the walls of the city fell down flat. The extraordinary preaching that shall be at the beginning of that glorious jubilee of the church, is represented by the extraordinary sounding of trumpets, throughout the land of *Canaan*, at the beginning of the year of jubilee. And the reading of the law before all *Israel*, in the year of release, at the feast of tabernacles; and the crowing of the cock at break of day, which brought Peter to repentance; seem to me to be intended to signify the awakening of God's church out of their lethargy, wherein they had denied their Lord, by the extraordinary preaching of the gospel that shall be at the dawning of the day of the church's light and glory. And there seems at this day to be an uncommon hand of Divine Providence, in animating, enabling, and upholding some ministers in such abundant labours.

IV. Another thing, wherein I think some ministers have been injured, is in being very much blamed for making so much of outcries, faintings, and other bodily effects; speaking of them as tokens of the presence of God, and arguments of the success of preaching; seeming to strive to their utmost to bring a congregation to that pass, and seeming to rejoice in it, yea, even blessing God for it when they see these effects.

Concerning this I would observe, in the *first* place, That there are many things, with respect to cryings out, falling down, &c. charged on ministers, that they are not guilty of. Some would have it, that they speak of these things as certain evidences of a work of the Spirit of God on the hearts of their hearers, or that they esteem these bodily effects themselves to be the work of God, as though the Spirit of God took hold of and agitated the bodies of men; and some are charged with making these things essential, and supposing that persons cannot be converted without them; whereas I never yet could see the person that held either of these things.

But for speaking of such effects as probable tokens of God's presence, and arguments of the success of preaching, it seems to me they are not to be blamed; because I think they are so indeed. And therefore when I see them excited by preaching the important truths of God's word, urged and enforced by proper arguments and motives, or as consequent on other means that are good, I do not scruple to speak of them, and to rejoice in them, and bless God for them as such; and for this reason, *viz.* That from time to time, upon proper inquiry and examination, and observation of the consequences and fruits, I have found that these are all evidences of the persons in whom these effects appear, being under the influences of God's Spirit, in such cases. Crying out, in such a manner, and with such circumstances, as I have seen them from time to time, is as much an evidence to me, of the general cause it proceeds from, as language. I have learned the meaning of it the same way that persons learn the meaning of language, *viz.* by use and experience. I confess that when I see a great crying out in a congregation, in the manner that I have seen it, when those things are held forth to them which are worthy of their being greatly affected by them, I rejoice in it, much more than merely in an appearance of solemn attention, and a show of affection by weeping; and that because when there have been those outcries, I have found from time to time a much greater and more excellent effect. To rejoice that the work of God is carried on calmly, without much ado, is in effect to rejoice that it is carried on with less power, or that there is not so much of the influence of God's Spirit.—For though the degree of the influence of the Spirit of God on *particular persons*, is by no means to be judged of by the degree of external appearances, because of the different constitutions, tempers, and circumstances of men; yet, if there be a very powerful influence of the Spirit of God on a mixed multitude, it will cause some way or other a great visible commotion.

And as to ministers aiming at such effects, and striving by all means to bring a congregation to that pass, that there should be such an uproar among them; I suppose none aim at it any otherwise, than as they strive to raise the affections of their hearers to such a height as very often appears in these effects. And if those affections are commonly good, and it be found by experience that such a degree of them commonly has a good effect, I think they are to be justified in so doing.

V. Again, some ministers have been blamed for keeping persons together, that have been under great affections, which have appeared in such extraordinary outward manifestations.—Many think this promotes confusion; that persons in such circumstances do but discompose each others' minds, and disturb the minds of others; and that therefore it is best they should be dispersed; and that when any in a congregation are strongly seized, that they cannot forbear outward manifestations of it, they should be removed, that others' minds may not be diverted.

I cannot but think that those who thus object go upon quite wrong notions of things. For though persons ought to take heed that they do not make an ado without necessity; for this will be the way in time to have such appearances lose all their effect; yet the unavoidable manifestations of strong religious affections tend to a happy influence on the minds of bystanders, and are found by experience to have an excellent and durable effect. And so to contrive and order things, that others may have opportunity and advantage to observe them, has been found to be blessed, as a great means to promote the work of God; and to prevent their being in the way of observation, is to prevent the effect of that which God makes use of as a principal means of carrying on his work at such an extraordinary time, *viz.* example; which is often spoken of in Scripture, as one of the chief means by which God would carry on his work in the prosperity of religion in the latter days.—I have mentioned some texts already to this purpose, in what I published before, of *the marks of a work of the true Spirit;* but would here mention some others. In Zech. ix. 15, 16. those that in the latter days should be filled in an extraordinary manner with the Holy Spirit, so as to appear in outward manifestations, and making a noise, are spoken of as those that God, in these uncommon circumstances, will set up to the view of others, as a prize or ensign, by their example and the excellency of their attainments, to animate and draw others, as men gather about an ensign, and run for a prize, a crown and precious jewels, set up in their view. The words are; "And they shall drink and make a noise as through wine, and they shall be filled like bowls, and as the corners of the altar. And the Lord their God shall save them in that day as the flock of his people; for they shall be as the stones of a crown, lifted up as an ensign upon his land." (I shall have occasion to say something more of this scripture afterwards.) Those that make the objection I am upon, instead of suffering this ensign to be in public view, are for having it removed, and hid in some corner. To the like purpose is that, Isa. lxii. 3. "Thou shalt be a crown of glory in the hand of the Lord, and a royal diadem in the hand of thy God." Here it is observable, that it is not said, thou shalt be a crown *upon the head*, but *in the hand*, of the Lord; *i. e.* held forth, in thy beauty and thy excellency, as a prize, to be bestowed upon others that shall behold thee, and be animated by the brightness and lustre which God shall endow thee with. The great influence of the example of God's people, in their bright and excellent attainments, to propagate religion in those days, is further signified in Isa. lx. 3. "And the Gentiles shall come to thy light, and Kings to the brightness of thy rising." With ver. 22. "A little one shall become a thousand, and a small one a strong nation." And Zech. x. 8, 9. "And they shall increase, as they have increased: and I will sow them among the people." And Hos. ii. 23. "And I will sow her unto me in the earth." So Jer. xxxi. 27.

VI. Another thing that gives great disgust to many, is the disposition that persons show, under great affections, to speak so much; and, with such earnestness and vehemence, to be setting forth the greatness, and wonderfulness, and importance of divine and eternal things; and to be so passionately warning, inviting, and entreating others.

Concerning which I would say, that I am far from thinking that such a disposition should be wholly without any limits or regulation (as I shall more particularly show afterwards); and I believe some have erred, in setting no bounds, and indulging and encouraging this disposition without any kind of restraint or direction. But yet it seems to me, that such a disposition in general is what both reason and Scripture will justify. Those who are offended at such things, as though they were unreasonable, are not just. Upon examination it will probably be found, that they have one rule of reasoning about temporal things, and another about spiritual things. They do not at all wonder, if a person on some very great and affecting occasion, an occasion of extraordinary danger or great joy, that eminently and immediately concerns him and others—is disposed to speak much, and with great earnestness, especially to those with whom he is united in the bonds of dear affection, and great concern for their good. And therefore, if they were just, why would not they allow it in spiritual things? and much *more* in them, agreeably to the vastly greater importance and more affecting nature of spiritual things, and the concern which true religion causes in men's minds for the good of others, and the disposition it gives and excites to speak God's praises, to show forth his infinite glory, and talk of all his glorious perfections and works?

That a very great and proper sense of the importance of religion, and the danger sinners are in, should sometimes cause an almost insuperable disposition to speak and warn others, is agreeable to Jer. vi. 10, 11. "To whom shall I speak and give warning, that they may hear? Behold, their ear is uncircumcised, and they cannot hearken: Behold, the word of the Lord is unto them a reproach; they have no delight in it. Therefore I am full of the fury of the Lord; I am weary with holding in: I will pour it out upon the children abroad, and upon the assembly of the young men together; for even the husband with the wife shall be taken, the aged, with him that is full of days." And that true Christians, when they come to be as it were waked out of sleep, and to be filled with a sweet and joyful sense of the excellent things of religion, by the preaching of the gospel, or by other means of grace, should be disposed to be much in speaking of divine things, though before they were dumb, is agreeable to what Christ says to his church, Cant. vii. 9. "And the roof of thy mouth is like the best wine, for my beloved, that goeth down sweetly, causing the lips of those that are asleep to speak." The roof of the church's mouth is the officers in the church, that preach the gospel; their word is to Christ's beloved like the best wine, that goes down sweetly; extraordinarily refreshing and enlivening the saints, causing them to speak, though before they were mute and asleep. It is said by some, that the subjects of this work, when they get together, talking loud and earnestly in their pretended great joys, several in a room talking at the same time, make a noise just like a company of drunken persons. On which I would observe, that it is foretold that God's people should do so, in that forementioned place, Zech. ix. 15—17. of which I shall now take more particular notice. The words are as follows; "The Lord of hosts shall defend them, and they shall devour and subdue with sling stones, and they shall drink and make a noise as through wine, and they shall be filled like bowls, and as the corners of the altar. And the Lord their God shall save them in that day as the flock of his people; for they shall be as the stones of a crown, lifted up as an ensign upon his land. For how great is his goodness, and how great is his beauty! Corn shall make the young men cheerful, and new wine the maids." The words are very remarkable: Here it is foretold, that at the time when Christ shall set up an universal kingdom upon earth (ver. 20.) the children of Zion shall drink, till they are filled like the vessels of the sanctuary. And, if we would know with what they shall be thus filled, the prophecy does in effect explain itself; they shall be filled as the vessels of the sanctuary that contained the drink-offering, which was wine. And yet the words imply, that it shall not literally be wine that they shall drink and be filled with, because it is said, They shall drink, and make a noise, *as through wine*, as if they had drank wine; which implies that they had not literally done it. And therefore we must understand the words, that they shall drink into that, and be filled with that, which the wine of the drink-offering typically represented, which is the Holy Spirit, as well as the blood of Christ, that new wine that is drank in our heavenly Father's kingdom. They shall be filled with the Spirit, which the Apostle sets in opposition to a being drunk with wine, Eph. v. 18. "This is the new wine spoken of, ver. 17. It is the same with that *best wine*, spoken of in *Canticles*, "that goes down sweetly, causing the lips of those that are asleep to speak." It is here foretold, that the children of Zion, in the latter days, should be filled with that which should make them cheerful, and cause them to make a noise as through wine, and by which these joyful happy persons shall be as the stones of a crown lifted up as an ensign upon God's land, being made joyful in the extraordinary manifestations of the beauty and love of Christ; as it follows, "How great is his goodness! and how great is his beauty!" And it is further remarkable that, as is here foretold, it should be thus especially amongst young people; "Corn shall make the young men cheerful, and new wine the maids." It would be ridiculous to understand this of literal bread and wine. Without doubt, the same spiritual blessings are signified by bread and wine here, which were represented by *Melchizedek's* bread and wine, and are signified by the bread and wine in the Lord's supper. One of the marginal readings is, "shall make the young men to speak;" which is agreeable to that in Canticles, of the "best wines causing the lips of those that are asleep to speak."

We ought not to be, in any measure, like the unbelieving *Jews* in Christ's time, who were disgusted both with crying out with distress, and with joy. When the poor blind man cried out before all the multitude, "Jesus, thou Son of David, have mercy on me!" and continued instantly thus doing, the multitude rebuked him, and charged him that he should hold his tongue, Mark x. 46—48. and Luke xviii. 38, 39. They looked upon it to be a very indecent noise that he made; a thing very ill becoming him, to cause his voice to be heard so much, and so loud, among the multitude. And when Christ made his solemn and triumphant entry into *Jerusalem*, (which, I have before observed, was a type of the glory and triumph of the latter days,) the whole multitude of the disciples, especially young people, began to rejoice and praise God with a loud voice, for all the mighty works that they had seen, saying, "Blessed be the King that cometh in the name of the Lord! peace in heaven, and glory in the highest!" The *Pharisees* said to Christ, "Master, rebuke thy disciples." They did not understand such great transports of joy; it seemed to them a very unsuitable and indecent noise and clamour that they made, a confused uproar, many crying out together, as though they were out of their wits; they wondered that Christ would tolerate it. But what says Christ? "I tell you, that if these should hold their peace, the stones would immediately cry out." The words seem to intimate, that there was cause enough to constrain those whose hearts were not harder than the very stones, to cry out, and make a noise; which is something like that other expression, of "causing the lips of those that are asleep to speak."

When many, under great religious affections, are earnestly speaking together of divine wonders, in various parts of a company, to those who are next them; some attending to one, and others to another; there is something very beautiful in it, provided they do not speak so as to drown each others' voices, that none can hear what any say. There is a greater and more affecting appearance of a joint engagedness of heart, in the love and praises of God; and I had rather see it, than to see one speaking alone, and all attending to what he says; it has more of the appearance of conversation. When a multitude meets on any occasion of temporal rejoicing, freely and cheerfully to converse together, they are not wont to observe the ceremony of but one speaking at a time, while all the rest in a formal manner set themselves to attend to what he says. That would spoil all conversation, and turn it into the formality of set speeches. It is better for lay persons, speaking one to another of the things of God, when they meet together, to speak after the manner of christian conversation, than to observe the formality of but one speaking at a time, the whole multitude silently and solemnly attending to what he says; which would carry in it too much of the air of the authority and solemnity of preaching. The apostle says, 1 Cor. xiv. 29, 30, 31. "Let the prophets speak, two or three, and let the others judge: If any thing be revealed to another that sitteth by, let the first hold his peace: For ye may all prophesy, one by one, that all may learn, and all may be comforted;" but this does not reach the present case, because what the apostle is speaking of is the solemnity of their religious exercises in public worship, and persons speaking in the church by immediate inspiration, and in the use of the gift of prophecy, or some gift of inspiration, in the exercises of which they acted as extraordinary ministers of Christ.

VII. Another thing that some have found fault with, is abounding so much in singing in religious meetings. Objecting against such a thing as this, seems to arise from a suspicion already established of this work. They doubt of the pretended extraordinary love and joys that attend this work, and so find fault with the manifestations of them. If they thought persons were truly the subjects of an extraordinary degree of divine love, and heavenly rejoicing in God, I suppose they would not wonder at their having a disposition to be much in praise. They object not against the saints and angels in heaven singing praises and *hallelujahs* to God, without ceasing day or night; and therefore doubtless will allow that the more the saints on earth are like them in their dispositions, the more they will be disposed to do like them. They will readily own that the generality of Christians have great reason to be ashamed that they have so little thankfulness, and are no more in praising God, whom they have such infinite cause to praise. And why therefore should Christians be found fault with, for showing a disposition to be much in praising God, and manifesting a delight in that heavenly exercise? To complain of this, is to be too much like the *Pharisees*, who were disgusted when the multitude of the disciples began to rejoice, and with loud voices to praise God, and cry, *Hosanna*, when Christ was entering into *Jerusalem*.

There are many things in Scripture, that seem to intimate that praising God, both in speeches and songs, will be what the church of God will very much abound in, in the approaching glorious day. So on the seventh day of compassing the walls of *Jericho*, when the priests blew with the trumpets in an extraordinary manner, the people shouted with a great shout, and the wall of the city fell down flat. So the ark was brought back from its banishment, with extraordinary shouting and singing of the whole congregation of *Israel*. And the places in the prophecies of Scripture, signifying that the church of God, in the glorious *Jubilee* that is foretold, shall greatly abound in singing and shouting forth the praises of God, are too many to be mentioned. And there will be cause enough for it: I believe it will be a time wherein both heaven and earth will be much more full of joy and praise than ever they were before.

But what is more especially found fault with, in the singing that is now practised, is making use of hymns of human composure. I am far from thinking that the book of Psalms should be thrown by in our public worship, but that it should always be used in the christian church to the end of the world: but I know of no obligation we are under to *confine* ourselves to it. I can find no command or rule of God's word, that does any more confine us to the words of the Scripture in our singing, than it does in our praying; we speak to God in both. And I can see no reason why we should limit ourselves to such particular forms of words, that we find in the Bible, in speaking to him by way of praise, in metre, and with music, than when we speak to him in prose, by way of prayer and supplication. And it is really *needful* that we should have some other songs besides the Psalms of *David*. It is unreasonable to suppose that the christian church should for ever, and even in times of her greatest light, in her praises of God and the Lamb, be confined only to the words of the Old Testament, wherein all the greatest and most glorious things of the gospel, that are infinitely the greatest subjects of her praise, are spoken of under a veil, and not so much as the name of our glorious Redeemer ever mentioned, but in some dark figure, or as hid under the name of some type. And as to our making use of the words of others, and not those that are conceived by ourselves, it is no more than we do in all our public prayers; the whole worshipping assembly, excepting one only, makes use of the words that are conceived by him who speaks for the rest.

VIII. Another thing that many have disliked, is the religious meetings of children to read and pray together, and perform religious exercises by themselves. What is objected is children's want of that knowledge and discretion which is requisite in order to a decent and profitable management of religious exercises. But it appears to me the objection is not sufficient. Children, as they have the nature of men, are inclined to society; and those of them who are capable of society one with another, are capable of the influence of the Spirit of God in its active fruits. And if they are inclined by a religious disposition, which they have from the Spirit of God, in order to improve their society one with another, in a religious manner, and to religious purposes, who should forbid them? If they have not discretion to observe method in their religious performances, or to speak sense in all that they say in prayer, they may notwithstanding have a good meaning, and God understands them, and it does not spoil or interrupt their devotion one with another. We who are adults have defects in our prayers, that are a thousand times worse in the sight of God, and are a greater confusion, and more absurd nonsense in his eyes, than their childish indiscretions. There is not so much difference before God, between children and grown persons, as we are ready to imagine; we are all poor, ignorant, foolish babes, in his sight. Our adult age does bring us so much nearer to God as we are apt to think. God in this work has shown a remarkable regard to little children; never was there such a glorious work amongst persons in their childhood, as has been of late, in *New England*. He has been pleased in a wonderful manner to perfect praise out of the mouths of babes and sucklings; and many of them have more of that knowledge and wisdom that pleases him, and renders their religious worship acceptable, than many of the great and learned men of the world: it is they, in the sight of God, who are the ignorant and foolish children; these are grown men, and an hundred years old, in comparison with them. It is to be hoped that the days are coming, prophesied of, Isa. lxv. 20. when "the child shall die an hundred years old."

I have seen many happy effects of children's religious meetings; and God has seemed often remarkably to own them in their meetings, and really descended from heaven to be amongst them: I have known several probable instances of children's being converted at such meetings. I should therefore think, that if children appear to be really moved to it by a religious disposition, and not merely from a childish affectation of imitating grown persons, they ought by no means to be discouraged or discountenanced. But yet it is fit that care should be taken of them by their parents and pastors, to instruct and direct them, and to correct imprudent conduct and irregularities if they are perceived, or any thing by which the devil may pervert and destroy the design of their meetings.—All should take heed that they do not find fault with and despise the religion of children, from an evil principle, lest they should be like the chief priests and scribes, who were sore displeased at the religious worship and praises of little children, and the honour they gave Christ in the temple. We have an account of it, and of what Christ said upon it, in Matt. xxi. 15, 16. "And when the chief priests and scribes saw the wonderful things that he did, and the children crying in the temple, and saying, Hosanna to the Son of *David*, they were sore displeased, and said unto him, Hearest thou what those say? And *Jesus* saith unto them, Yea, have ye never read, Out of the mouths of babes and sucklings thou hast perfected praise?"

PART IV.

SHOWING WHAT THINGS ARE TO BE CORRECTED OR AVOIDED, IN PROMOTING THIS WORK, OR IN OUR BEHAVIOUR UNDER IT.

HAVING thus observed, in some instances, wherein the conduct of those that have appeared to be the subjects of this work, or have been zealous to promote it, has been objected against or complained of without or beyond just cause; I proceed now to show what things ought to be corrected or avoided.

Many, who are zealous for this glorious work of God, are heartily sick of the great noise there is in the country about *imprudences* and *disorders*; they have heard it so often from the mouths of opposers, that they are prejudiced against the sound. And they look upon it, that what is called being *prudent* and *regular*, so much insisted on, is no other than being asleep, or cold and dead, in religion; and that the great imprudence, so much blamed, is only being alive and engaged in the things of God. They are therefore rather confirmed in any practice, than brought off from it, by the clamour they hear against it, as imprudent and irregular. And, to tell the truth, the cry of irregularity and imprudence has been much more in the mouths of those who have been enemies to the main of the work than others; for they have watched for the halting of the zealous, and eagerly catched at any thing that has been wrong, and have greatly insisted on it, made the most of it, and magnified it; especially have they watched for errors in zealous preachers, who are much in reproving and condemning the wickedness of the times. They would therefore do well to consider that scripture, Isa. xxix. 20, 21. "The scorner is consumed, and all that watch for iniquity are cut off, that make a man an offender for a word, and lay a snare for him that reproveth in the gate, and turn aside the just for a thing of nought." They have not only too much insisted on the magnified real errors, but have very injuriously charged them as guilty in things wherein they have been innocent, and have done their duty. This has so prejudiced the minds of some, that they have been ready to think that all that which has been said about errors and imprudences was injurious and from an ill spirit. It has confirmed them, that there is no such thing as any prevailing imprudences; and it has made them less cautious and supicious of themselves, lest they should err.—Herein the devil has had an advantage put into his hands, and has taken it; and, doubtless, has been too subtle for some of the true friends of religion. That would be strange indeed, if in so great a commotion and revolution, and such a new state of things, wherein so many have been engaged, none have been guilty of any imprudence. It would be such a revival of religion as never was, if among so many men, not guided by infallible inspiration, there had not been many notable errors in judgment and conduct; our young preachers, and young converts, must in general vastly exceed *Luther*, the head of the reformation, who was guilty of a great many excesses in that great affair in which God made him the chief instrument.

If we look back into the history of the church of God in past ages, we may observe that it has been a common device of the devil, to overset a revival of religion; when he finds he can keep men quiet and secure no longer, then he drives them to excesses and extravagances. He holds them back as long as he can; but when he can do it no longer, then he will push them on, and, if possible, run them upon their heads. And it has been by this means chiefly that he has been successful, in several instances, to overthrow most hopeful and promising beginnings. Yea, the principal means by which the devil was successful, by degrees, to overset the grand religious revival of the world, in the primitive ages of Christianity, and in a manner to overthrow the christian church through the earth, and to make way for the great Antichristian apostacy, that masterpiece of all the devil's works, was to improve the indiscreet zeal of Christians, to drive them into those three extremes of *enthusiasm, superstition*, and *severity towards opposers;* which should be enough for an everlasting warning to the christian church.

Though the devil will do his diligence to stir up the open enemies of religion, yet he knows what is for his interest so well, that, in a time of revival of religion, his main strength shall be tried with the friends of it; and he will chiefly exert himself in his attempts to mislead them. One truly zealous person, in the time of such an event, that seems to have a great hand in the affair, and draws the eyes of many upon him, may do more (through Satan's being too subtle for him) to hinder the work, than a hundred great, and strong, and open opposers. In the time of the great *work* of Christ, his hands, with which he *works*, are often wounded in the house of his friends, and his work hindered chiefly by them: so that if any one inquires, as in Zech. xiii. 6. "What are those wounds in thine hands?" he may answer, "Those with which I was wounded in the house of my friends."

The errors of the friends of the work of God, and especially of the great promoters of it, give vast advantage to the enemies of such a work. Indeed there are many things which are no errors, but are only duties faithfully and thoroughly done, that wound the minds of such persons more than real errors: but yet one real error gives opposers as much advantage, and hinders and clogs the work as much, as ten that are only supposed ones. Real errors do not fret and gall the enemies of religion so much as those things that are strictly right; but they encourage them more, they give them liberty, and open a gap for them; so that some who before kept their enmity burning in their own breasts, and durst not show themselves, will on such an occasion take courage, and give themselves vent, and their rage will be like that of an enemy let loose. Those who lay still before, having nothing to say but what they would be ashamed of, (agreeable to Tit. ii. 8.) when they have such a weapon put into their hands, will fight with all violence. And indeed the enemies of religion would not know what to do for weapons to fight with, were it not for the errors of its friends; and so must soon fall before them. Besides, in real errors, things that are truly disagreeable to the rule of God's word, we cannot expect the divine protection, and that God will appear on our side, as if our errors were only supposed ones.

Since therefore the errors of the friends and promoters of such a glorious work of God are of such dreadful consequence; and seeing the devil, being sensible of this, is so assiduous, watchful, and subtle in his attempts with them, and has thereby been so successful to overthrow religion heretofore; certainly such persons ought to be exceeding circumspect and vigilant, diffident and jealous of themselves, and humbly dependent on the guidance of the good Shepherd. 1 Pet. iv. 7. "Be sober, and watch unto prayer." And chap. v. 8. "Be sober, be vigilant; because your adversary the devil, as a roaring lion, walketh about." For persons to go on resolutely, in a kind of heat and vehemence, despising admonition and correction, being confident that they must be in the right because they are full of the Spirit, is directly contrary to the import of these words, be *sober*, be *vigilant*.

It is a mistake I have observed in some, by which they have been greatly exposed to their wounding, that they think they are in no danger of going astray, or being misled by the devil, because they are near to God; and so have no jealous eye upon themselves, and neglect vigilance and circumspection, as needless in their case. They say, they do not think that God will leave them to dishonour him, and wound religion as long as they keep near to him. And I believe so too, as long as they keep near to God, so as to maintain an universal and diligent watch, and care to do their duty, avoid sin and snares with diffidence in themselves, and humble dependence and prayerfulness. But not merely because they are receiving blessed communications from God, in refreshing views of him; if at the same time they let down their watch, and are not jealous over their own hearts, by reason of its remaining blindness and corruption, and a subtle adversary.—It is a grand error for persons to think they are out of danger from the devil, and a corrupt, deceitful heart, even in their highest flights, and most raised frames of spiritual joy. For persons, in such a confidence, to cease to be jealous of themselves, and to neglect watchfulness and care, is a presumption by which I have known many wofully insnared. However highly we may be favoured with divine discoveries and comforts, yet, as long as we are in the world, we are in the enemies' country; and therefore that direction of Christ to his disciples is never out of date in this world, Luke xxi. 36. "Watch and pray always, that you may be accounted worthy to escape all these things, and to stand before the Son of man." It was not out of date with the disciples to whom it was given, after they came to be full of the Holy Ghost, and *out of their bellies flowed rivers of living water*, by that great effusion upon them that began on the day of *Pentecost*. And though God stands ready to protect his people, especially those that are near to him; yet he expects of all great care and labour, and that we should put on the whole armour of God, that we may stand in the evil day. To whatever spiritual privileges we are raised, we have no warrant to expect protection in any other way; for God has appointed this whole life, to be all as a race or a battle; the state of rest, wherein we shall be so out of danger as to have no need of watching and fighting, is reserved for another world. I have known it in abundance of instances, that the devil has come in very remarkably, even in the midst of the most excellent frames. It may seem a great mystery that it should be so; but it is no greater mystery, than that Christ should be taken captive by the devil, and carried into the wilderness, immediately after the heavens had been opened to him, and the Holy Ghost descended like a dove upon him, and when he heard that comfortable, joyful voice from the Father, saying, "This is my beloved Son, in whom I am well pleased." In like manner Christ in the heart of a Christian, is oftentimes as it were taken, and carried captive into a wilderness, presently after heaven has been as it were opened to the soul, and the Holy Ghost has descended upon it like a dove, and when God has been sweetly owning the believer, and testifying his favour to him as his beloved child.

It is therefore a great error and sin in some persons, at this day, that they are fixed in some things which others account errors, and will not hearken to admonition and counsel, but are confident that they are in the right, because God is much with them. There were some such in the apostles' days. The apostle *Paul*, writing to the *Corinthians*, was sensible that some of them would not be easily convinced that they had been in any error, because they looked upon themselves as spiritual, or full of the Spirit of God, 1 Cor. xiv. 37, 38. "If any man think himself to be a prophet, or *spiritual*, let him acknowledge that the things that I write unto you are the commandment of the Lord; but if any man be ignorant, let him be ignorant."

And although those who are spiritual amongst us have no infallible apostle to admonish them, yet let me entreat them, by the love of Christ, calmly and impartially to weigh what may be said to them by one who is their hearty and fervent friend, (though an inferior worm,) in giving his humble opinion concerning the errors that have been committed, by the zealous friends or promoters of this great work of God. In speaking of past errors, and those we are in danger of, I would, in the

First place, take notice of the *causes* whence the errors that attend a great revival of religion usually arise; and, as I go along, take notice of some particular errors that arise from each of those causes.

Secondly, Observe some errors that have been owing to the influence of several of those causes conjunctly.

The errors that attend a great revival of religion usually arise from these three things; 1. Undiscerned spiritual pride; 2. Wrong principles; and 3. Ignorance of Satan's advantages and devices.

SECT. I.

One cause of errors attending a great revival of religion, is undiscerned spiritual pride.

THE first and the worst cause of errors, that prevail in such a state of things, is *spiritual pride*. This is the main door by which the devil comes into the hearts of those who are zealous for the advancement of religion. It is the chief inlet of smoke from the bottomless pit, to darken the mind and mislead the judgment. This is the main handle by which the devil has hold of religious persons, and the chief source of all the mischief that he introduces, to clog and hinder a work of God.—This cause of error is the main spring, or at least the main support, of all the rest. Till this disease is cured, medicines are in vain applied to heal other diseases. It is by this that the mind defends itself in other errors, and guards itself against light, by which it might be corrected and reclaimed. The spiritually proud man is full of light already, he does not need instruction, and is ready to despise the offer of it. But, if this disease be healed, other things are easily rectified. The humble person is like a little child, he easily receives instruction; he is jealous over himself, sensible how liable he is to go astray, and therefore, if it be suggested to him that he does so, he is ready most narrowly and impartially to inquire. Nothing sets a person so much out of the devil's reach as humility, and so prepares the mind for true divine light without darkness, and so clears the eye to look on things as they truly are; Ps. xxv. 9. "The meek will he guide in judgment. And the meek will he teach his way." Therefore we should fight, neither with small nor with great, but with the king of *Israel*. Our first care should be to rectify the heart, and pull the beam out of our eye, and then we shall see clearly.

I know that a great many things at this day are very injuriously laid to the pride of those that are zealous in the cause of God. When any person appears, in any respect, remarkably distinguished in religion from others; if he professes those spiritual comforts and joys that are greater than ordinary, or appears distinguishingly zealous in religion; if he exerts himself more than others in the cause of religion, or seems to be distinguished with success; ten to one but it will immediately awaken the jealousy of those about him. They will suspect (whether they have cause or no) that he is very proud of his goodness, and affects to have it thought that nobody is so good as he; and all his talk is heard, and all his behaviour beheld, with this prejudice. Those who are themselves cold and dead, and especially such as never had any experience of the power of godliness on their own hearts, are ready to entertain such thoughts of the best Christians; which arises from a secret enmity against vital and fervent piety. But zealous Christians should take heed lest this prove a snare to them, and the devil take advantage from it, to blind their eyes from beholding what there is indeed of this nature in their hearts, and make them think, because they are charged with pride wrongfully and from an ill spirit, in many things, that therefore it is so in every thing. Alas, how much pride have the best of us in our hearts! It is the worst part of the body of sin and death; the first sin that ever entered into the universe, and the last that is rooted out: it is God's most stubborn enemy!

The corruption of nature may all be resolved into two things, *pride* and *worldly-mindedness*, the *devil* and the *beast*, or *self* and the *world*. These are the two pillars of *Dagon's* temple, on which the whole house leans. But the former of these is every way the worst part of the corruption of nature; it is the first-born son of the devil, and his image in the heart of man chiefly consists in it. It is the last thing in a sinner that is overborne by conviction, in order to conversion; and here is the saint's hardest conflict; the last thing over which he obtains a good degree of conquest, that which most directly militates against God, and is most contrary to the Spirit of the Lamb of God. It is most like the devil its father, in a serpentine deceitfulness and secrecy; it lies deepest, is most active, and is most ready secretly to mix itself with every thing.

And, of all kinds of pride, spiritual pride is upon many accounts the most hateful, it is most like the devil; most like the sin he committed in a heaven of light and glory, where he was exalted high in divine knowledge, honour, beauty, and happiness. Pride is much more difficult to be discerned than any other corruption, because its nature very much consists in a person's having too high a thought of himself. No wonder that he who has too high a thought of himself, does not know it; for he necessarily thinks that the opinion he has of himself has just grounds, and therefore is not too high; if he thought such an opinion of himself was without just grounds, he would therein cease to have it. Those that are spiritually proud, have a high conceit of these two things, *viz.* their *light*, and their *humility*; both which are a strong prejudice against a discovery of their pride. Being proud of their *light*, that makes them not jealous of themselves; he who thinks a clear light shines around him, is not suspicious of an enemy lurking near him unseen; and then, being proud of their *humility*, that makes them least of all jealous of themselves in that particular, *viz.* as being under the prevalence of pride. There are many sins of the heart that are very secret in their nature, and difficultly discerned. The psalmist says, Psal. xix. 12. "Who can understand his errors,? cleanse thou me from secret faults." But spiritual pride is the most secret of all sins. The heart is deceitful and unsearchable in nothing so much as in this matter; and there is no sin in the world, that men are so confident in. The very nature of it is to work self-confidence, and drive away jealousy of any evil of that kind. There is no sin so much like the devil as this for secrecy and subtlety, and appearing in a great many shapes undiscerned and unsuspected. It appears as an angel of light; takes occasion to arise from every thing; it perverts and abuses every thing, and even the exercises of real grace, and real humility, as an occasion to exert itself: it is a sin that has, as it were, many lives; if you kill it, it will live still; if you mortify and suppress it in one shape, it rises in another; if you think it is all gone, yet it is there still. There are a great many kinds of it, that lie in different forms and shapes, one under another, and encompass the heart like the coats of an onion; if you pull off one, there is another underneath. We had need therefore to have the greatest watch imaginable over our hearts with respect to this matter, and to cry most earnestly to the great searcher of hearts for his help. He that trusts his own heart is a fool.

God's own people should be the more jealous of themselves with respect to this particular at this day, because the temptations that many have to this sin are exceeding great. The great and distinguishing privileges to which God admits many of his saints, and the high honours he puts on some ministers, are great trials of persons in this respect. It is true, that great degrees of the spiritual presence of God tends greatly to mortify pride and corruption; but yet, though in the experience of such favours there be much to restrain pride one way, there is much to tempt and provoke it another; and we shall be in great danger thereby, without great watchfulness and prayerfulness. The angels that fell, while in heaven had great honours and high privileges, in beholding the face of God, and viewing his infinite glory, to cause in them exercises of humility, and to keep them from pride; yet, through want of watchfulness in them, their great honour and heavenly privilege proved to be to them an undoing temptation to pride, though they had no principle of pride in their hearts to expose them. Let no saint therefore, however eminent, and however near to God, think himself out of danger. He that thinks himself most out of danger, is indeed most in danger. The apostle *Paul*, who doubtless was as eminent a saint as any now, was not out of danger, even just after he was admitted to see God in the third heavens, 2 Cor. xii. and yet doubtless, what he saw in heaven of the ineffable glory of the Divine Being, had a direct tendency to make him appear exceeding little and vile in his own eyes.

Spiritual pride in its own nature is so secret, that it is not so well discerned by immediate intuition on the thing itself, as by the effects and fruits of it; some of which I would mention, together with the contrary fruits of pure christian humility. Spiritual pride disposes to speak of other persons' sins, their enmity against God and his people, the miserable delusion of hypocrites, and their enmity against vital piety, and the deadness of some saints, with bitterness, or with laughter and levity, and an air of contempt; whereas pure christian humility rather disposes, either to be silent about them, or to speak of them with grief and pity. Spiritual pride is very apt to suspect others; whereas an humble saint is most jealous of himself, he is so suspicious of nothing in the world as he is of his own heart. The spiritually proud person is apt to find fault with other saints, that they are low in grace; and to be much in observing how cold and dead they are; and being quick to discern and take notice of their deficiencies. But the eminently humble Christian has so much to do at home, and sees so much evil in his own heart, and is so concerned about it, that he is not apt to be very busy with other hearts; he complains most of himself, and complains of his own coldness and lowness in grace. He is apt to esteem others better than himself, and is ready to hope that there is nobody but what has more love and thankfulness to God than he, and cannot bear to think that others should bring forth no more fruit to God's honour than he. Some who have spiritual pride mixed with high discoveries and great transports of joy, disposing them in an earnest manner to talk to others, are apt, in such frames, to be calling upon other Christians about them, and sharply reproving them for their being so cold and lifeless. There are others, who in their raptures are overwhelmed with a sense of their own vileness; and, when they have extraordinary discoveries of God's glory, are all taken up about their own sinfulness; and though they also are disposed to speak much and very earnestly, yet it is very much in blaming themselves, and exhorting fellow-Christians, but in a charitable and humble manner. Pure christian humility disposes a person to take notice of every thing that is good in others, and to make the best of it, and to diminish their failings; but to gave his eye chiefly on those things that are bad in himself, and to take much notice of every thing that aggravates them.

In a contrariety to this, it has been the manner in some places, or at least the manner of some persons, to speak of almost every thing that they see amiss in others, in the most harsh, severe, and terrible language. It is frequent with them to say of others' opinions, or conduct, or advice —or of their coldness, their silence, their caution, their moderation, their prudence, &c.—that they are from the devil, or from hell; that such a thing is devilish, or hellish, or cursed, and that such persons are serving the devil, or the devil is in them, that they are soul-murderers, and the like; so that the words *devil* and *hell* are almost continually in their mouths. And such kind of language they will commonly use, not only towards wicked men, but towards them whom they themselves allow to be the true children of God, and also towards ministers of the gospel and others who are very much their superiors. And they look upon it as a virtue and high attainment thus to behave themselves. *Oh*, say they, *we must be plain-hearted and bold for Christ, we must declare war against sin wherever we see it, we must not mince the matter in the cause of God and when speaking for Christ*. And to make any distinction in persons, or to speak the more tenderly, because that which is amiss is seen in a superior, they look upon as very mean for a follower of Christ when speaking in the cause of his Master. What a strange device of the devil is here, to overthrow all christian meekness and gentleness, and even all show and appearance of it, and to defile the mouths of the children of God, and to introduce the language of common sailors among the followers of Christ, under a cloak of high sanctity and zeal, and boldness for Christ! And it is a remarkable instance of the weakness of the human mind, and how much too cunning the devil is for us!

The grand defence of this way of talking is, That they say no more than what is true; they only speak the truth without mincing the matter; and that true Christians who have a great sight of the evil of sin, and acquaintance with their own hearts, know it to be true, and therefore will not be offended to hear such harsh expressions concerning them and their sins. It is only (say they) hypocrites, or cold and dead Christians, that are provoked and feel their enmity rise on such an occasion. But it is a grand mistake to think that we may commonly use all such language as represents the worst of each other, according to strict truth. It is really true, that every kind of sin, and every degree of it, is devilish and from hell, and is cursed, hellish, and condemned or damned. And if persons had a full sight of their hearts, they would think no terms too bad for them; they would look like beasts, like serpents, and like devils to themselves; they would be at a loss for language to express what they see in themselves. The worst terms they could think of would seem as it were faint to represent what they see in themselves. But shall a child therefore, from time to time, use such language concerning an excellent and eminently holy father or mother, as, That the devil is in them; that they have such and such devilish, cursed dispositions; that they commit every day hundreds of hellish, damned acts; and that they are cursed dogs, hell-hounds, and devils? And shall the meanest of the people be justified, in commonly using such language concerning the most excellent magistrates, or the most eminent ministers? I hope nobody has gone to this height. But the same pretences of boldness, plain-heartedness, and declared war against sin, will as well justify these things as the others. If we proceed in such a manner, on such principles as these, what a face will be introduced upon the church of Christ, the little beloved flock of that gentle Shepherd the Lamb of God! What a sound shall we bring into the house of God, into the family of his dear little children! How far off shall we soon banish that lovely appearance of humility, sweetness, gentleness, mutual honour, benevolence, complacence, and an esteem of others above themselves, which ought to clothe the children of God all over! Not but that Christians should watch over one another, and in any wise reprove one another, and do it plainly and faithfully; but it does not thence follow that dear brethren in the family of God, in rebuking one another, should use worse language than *Michael* the archangel durst use when rebuking the devil himself.

Christians who are but fellow-worms, ought at least to treat one another with as much humility and gentleness as Christ, who is infinitely above them, treats them. But how did Christ treat his disciples when they were so cold towards him, and so regardless of him, at the time when his soul was exceeding sorrowful even unto death—and he in a dismal agony was crying and sweating blood for them—and they would not watch with him and allow him the comfort of their company one hour in his great distress, though he once and again desired it of them? One would think that then was a proper time, if ever, to have reproved them for a devilish, hellish, cursed, and damned slothfulness and deadness. But after what manner does Christ reprove them? Behold his astonishing gentleness! Says he, *What, could ye not watch with me one hour? The spirit indeed is willing, but the flesh is weak.* And how did he treat *Peter* when he was ashamed of his Master, while he was made a mocking stock and a spitting stock for him? Why, he looked upon him with a look of love, and melted his heart. And though we read that Christ once *turned, and said unto Peter*, on a certain occasion, *Get thee behind me, Satan;* and this may seem like an instance of harshness and severity in reproving *Peter;* yet I humbly conceive that this is by many taken wrong, and that this is indeed no instance of Christ's severity in his treatment of *Peter*, but on the contrary, of his wonderful gentleness and grace, distinguishing between *Peter* and the devil in him, not laying the blame of what *Peter* had then said, or imputing it to him, but to the devil that influenced him. Christ saw the devil then present, secretly influencing *Peter* to do the part of a tempter to his Master; and therefore Christ turned him about to *Peter*, in whom the devil then was, and spake to the devil, and rebuked him. Thus the grace of Christ does not behold iniquity in his people, imputes not what is amiss in them to them, but to sin that dwells in them, and to *Satan* that influences them.

Spiritual pride often disposes persons to singularity in external appearance, to affect a singular way of speaking, to use a different sort of dialect from others, or to be singular in voice, countenance, or behaviour. But he that is an eminently humble Christian, though he will be firm to his duty, however singular—going in the way that leads to heaven alone, though all the world forsake him—yet he delights not in singularity for singularity's sake. He does not affect to set up himself to be viewed and observed as one distinguished, as desiring to be accounted better than others—despising their company, or conformity to them—

but on the contrary is disposed to become all things to all men, to yield to others, and conform to them and please them, in every thing but sin. Spiritual pride commonly occasions a certain stiffness and inflexibility in persons, in their own judgment and their own ways; whereas the eminently humble person, though he be inflexible in his duty, and in those things wherein God's honour is concerned; and with regard to temptation to those things he apprehends to be sinful, though in never so small a degree, he is not at all of a yielding spirit, but is like a brazen wall; yet in other things he is of a pliable disposition, not disposed to set up his own opinion, or his own will; he is ready to pay deference to others' opinions, loves to comply with their inclinations, and has a heart that is tender and flexible, like a little child. Spiritual pride disposes persons to affect separation, to stand at a distance from others, as being better than they; and loves the show and appearance of the distinction. But, on the contrary, the eminently humble Christian is ready to look upon himself as not worthy that others should be united to him —to think himself more brutish than any man, and worthy to be cast out of human society—and especially unworthy of the society of God's children.—And though he will not be a companion with one that is visibly Christ's enemy—but delights most in the company of lively Christians, choosing such for his companions, and will be most intimate with them, not delighting to spend much time in the company of those who seem to relish no conversation but about worldly things—yet he does not love the appearance of an open separation from visible Christians, as being a kind of distinct company from them who are one visible company with him by Christ's appointment; and will as much as possible shun all appearances of a superiority, or distinguishing himself as better than others. His universal benevolence delights in the appearance of union with his fellow-creatures, and will maintain it as much as he possibly can without giving open countenance to iniquity, or wounding his own soul. And herein he follows the example of his meek and lowly Redeemer, who did not keep up such a separation and distance as the *Pharisees*, but freely ate with publicans and sinners, that he might win them.

The eminently humble Christian is as it were clothed with lowliness, mildness, meekness, gentleness of spirit and behaviour, and with a soft, sweet, condescending, winning air and deportment; these things are just like garments to him, he is clothed all over with them. 1 Pet. v. 5. "And be clothed with humility." Col. iii. 12. "Put on therefore, as the elect of God, holy and beloved, bowels of mercies, kindness, humbleness of mind, meekness, long-suffering." Pure christian humility has no such thing as roughness, or contempt, or fierceness, or bitterness in its nature; it makes a person like a little child, harmless and innocent, that none need to be afraid of; or like a lamb, destitute of all bitterness, wrath, anger, and clamour; agreeable to Eph. iv. 31. With such a spirit as this ought especially zealous ministers of the gospel to be clothed, and those that God is pleased to employ as instruments in his hands of promoting his work. They ought indeed to be thorough in preaching the word of God, without mincing the matter at all; in handling the sword of the Spirit, as the ministers of the Lord of hosts, they ought not to be mild and gentle; they are not to be gentle and moderate in searching and awakening the conscience, but should be sons of thunder. The word of God, which is in itself sharper than any two-edged sword, ought not to be sheathed by its ministers, but so used that its sharp edges may have their full effect, even to the dividing asunder soul and spirit, joints and marrow. Yet they should do it without judging particular persons, leaving it to conscience and the Spirit of God to make the particular application. But all their conversation should savour of nothing but lowliness and good-will, love and pity to all mankind; so that such a spirit should be like a sweet odour diffused around them wherever they go. They should be like lions to guilty consciences, but like lambs to men's persons. This would have no tendency to prevent the awakening of men's consciences, but on the contrary would have a very great tendency to awaken them. It would make way for the sharp sword to enter; it would remove the obstacles, and make a naked breast for the arrow.—Yea, the amiable Christ-like conversation of such ministers in itself, would terrify the consciences of men, as well as their terrible preaching; both would co-operate to subdue the hard, and bring down the proud heart. If there had been constantly and universally observable such a behaviour as this in itinerant preachers, it would have terrified the consciences of sinners ten times as much as all the invectives and the censorious talk there has been concerning particular persons, for their opposition, hypocrisy, delusion, pharisaism, &c. These things in general have rather stupified sinners' consciences; they take them up, and make use of them as a shield, wherewith to defend themselves from the sharp arrows of the word that are shot by these preachers. The enemies of the present work have been glad of these things with all their hearts. —Many of the most bitter of them are probably such as in the beginning of this work had their consciences something galled and terrified with it; but these errors of awakening preachers are the things they chiefly make use of as plaisters to heal the sore that was made in their consciences.

Spiritual pride takes great notice of opposition and injuries that are received, and is apt to be often speaking of them, and to be much in taking notice of their aggravations, either with an air of bitterness or contempt. Whereas pure and unmixed christian humility, disposes a person rather to be like his blessed Lord, when reviled, dumb, not opening his mouth, but committing himself in silence to him that judgeth righteously. The eminently humble Christian, the more clamorous and furious the world is against him, the more silent and still will he be; unless it be in his closet, and there he will not be still.—Our blessed Lord Jesus seems never to have been so silent as when the world compassed him round, reproaching, buffeting, and spitting on him, with loud and virulent outcries, and horrid cruelties. There has been a great deal too much talk of late, among many of the true and zealous friends of religion, about opposition and persecution. It becomes the followers of the Lamb of God, when the world is in an uproar about them, and full of clamour against them, not to raise another noise to answer it, but to be still and quiet. It is not beautiful, at such time, to have pulpits and conversation ring with the sound of *persecution, persecution*, or with abundant talk about *Pharisees*, carnal persecutors, and the seed of the serpent.—Meekness and quietness among God's people, when opposed and reviled, would be the surest way to have God remarkably to appear for their defence. It is particularly observed of *Moses*, on occasion of *Aaron* and *Miriam* envying him, and rising up in opposition against him, that he "was very meek, above all men upon the face of the earth," Num. xii. 3. Doubtless because he remarkably showed his meekness on that occasion, being wholly silent under the abuse. And how remarkable is the account that follows of God's being as it were suddenly roused to appear for his vindication! What high honour did he put upon *Moses!* and how severe were his rebukes of his opposers! The story is very remarkable, and worthy every one's observation. Nothing is so effectual to bring God down from heaven in the defence of his people, as their patience and meekness under sufferings. When Christ "girds his sword upon his thigh, with his glory and majesty, and in his majesty rides prosperously, his right hand teaching him terrible things, it is because of truth, and MEEKNESS, and righteousness," Psal. xlv. 3, 4. "God will cause judgment to be heard from heaven; the earth shall fear and be still, and God will arise to judgment, to save all the *meek* of the earth," Psal. lxxvi. 8, 9. "He will lift up the *meek*, and cast the wicked down to the ground," Psal. cxlvii. 6. "He will reprove with equity for the *meek of the earth*, and will smite the earth with the rod of his mouth, and with the breath of his lips will he slay the wicked," Isa. xi. 4. The great commendation that Christ gives the church of *Philadelphia* is, "Thou hast kept the word of my patience," Rev. iii. 10. And we may see what reward he promises her, in the preceding verse, "Behold, I will make them of the synagogue of Satan, which say they are Jews and are not, but do lie; behold, I will make them to come and worship at thy feet, and to know that I have loved thee." And thus it is that we might expect to have Christ appear for us, if under all the reproaches we are loaded with, we behaved ourselves with a lamb-like meekness and gentleness. But if our spirits are raised, and we are vehement and noisy with our complaints under colour of christian zeal, this will be to take upon us our own defence, and God will leave it with us, to vindicate our cause as well as we can; yea, if we go on in a way of bitterness, and high censuring, it will be the way to have him rebuke us, and put us to shame before our enemies.

Here some may be ready to say, "It is not in our own cause that we are thus vehement, but it is in the cause of God, and the apostle directed the primitive Christians to *contend earnestly for the faith once delivered to the saints.*" But how was it that the primitive Christians contended earnestly for the faith? They defended the truth with arguments and a holy conversation, but yet gave their reasons with meekness and fear. They contended earnestly for the faith, by fighting violently against their own unbelief, and the corruptions of their hearts: yea, they resisted unto blood striving against sin; but the blood that was shed in this earnest strife, was their own blood, and not the blood of their enemies. It was *in the cause of God* that *Peter* was so fierce, and drew his sword, and began to smite with it; but Christ bids him put up his sword again, telling him that they that take the sword shall perish by the sword; and, while *Peter* wounds, Christ heals. They contend the most violently, and are the greatest conquerors in a time of persecution, who bear it with the greatest meekness and patience. Great humility improves even the reflections and reproaches of enemies, to put upon serious self-examination, whether or no there be not some just cause; whether they have not in some respect given occasion to the enemy to speak reproachfully. Whereas spiritual pride improves such reflections to make them the more bold and confident, and to go the greater lengths in that for which they are found fault with. I desire it may be considered, whether there has been nothing amiss of late among the true friends of vital piety in this respect; and whether the words of *David*, when reviled by *Michal*, have not been misinterpreted and misapplied to justify them in it, when he said, "I will be yet more vile, and will be base in mine own sight." The import of his words is, that he would humble himself yet more before God, being sensible that he was far from being sufficiently abased; and he signifies this to *Michal*, that he longed to be yet lower, and had designed already to abase himself more in his behaviour.—Not that he would go the greater length, to show his regardlessness of her revilings; that would be to exalt himself, and not to abase himself as more vile in his own sight.

Another effect of spiritual pride is a certain unsuitable and self-confident boldness before God and men. Thus some, in their great rejoicings before God, have not paid a sufficient regard to that rule in Psal. ii. 11. They have not rejoiced with a reverential trembling, in a proper sense of the awful majesty of God, and the awful distance between him and them. And there has also been an improper boldness before men, that has been encouraged and defended, by a misapplication of that scripture, Prov. xxix. 25. "The fear of man bringeth a snare." As though it became all persons, high and low, men, women, and children, in all religious conversation, wholly to divest themselves of all manner of shamefacedness, modesty, or reverence towards man; which is a great error, and quite contrary to Scripture. There is a fear of reverence that is due to some men, Rom. xiii. 7. "Fear to whom fear, honour to whom honour." And there is a fear of modesty and shamefacedness in inferiors towards superiors, which is amiable, and required by christian rules, 1 Pet. iii. 2. "While they behold your chaste conversation coupled with fear;" and 1 Tim. ii. 9. "In like manner also, that women adorn themselves in modest apparel, with shamefacedness and sobriety." The apostle means that this virtue shall have place, not only in civil communication, but also in spiritual communication, and in our religious concerns and behaviour, as is evident by what follows, ver. 11, 12. "Let the women learn in silence, with all subjection. But I suffer not a woman to teach, nor to usurp authority over the man, but to be in silence." Not that I would hence infer that women's mouths should be shut up from christian conversation; but all that I mean from it at this time is, that modesty, or shamefacedness, and reverence towards men, ought to have some place, even in our religious communication one with another. The same is also evident by 1 Pet. iii. 15. "Be ready always to give an answer to every man that asketh you a reason of the hope that is in you, with meekness and fear." It is well if that very fear and shamefacedness, which the apostle recommends, have not sometimes been condemned, under the name of a *cursed fear of man.*

It is beautiful for persons, when they are at prayer as the mouth of others, to make God only their fear and their dread, and to be wholly forgetful of men present, who, let them be great or small, are nothing in the presence of the great God. And it is beautiful for a minister, when he speaks in the name of the Lord of hosts, to be bold, and to put off all fear of men. And it is beautiful in private Christians, though they are women and even children, to be bold in professing the faith of Christ, in the practice of all religion, and in owning God's hand in the work of his power and grace, without any fear of men; though they should be reproached as fools and madmen, frowned upon by great men, and cast off by parents and all the world. But for private Christians, women and others, to instruct, rebuke, and exhort, with a like sort of boldness as becomes a minister when preaching, is not beautiful. Some have been bold in things that have really been errors; and have gloried in their boldness in practising them, though odd and irregular. And those who have gone the greatest lengths in these things, have been by some most highly esteemed, as appearing bold for the Lord Jesus Christ, and fully on his side; while others who have professed to be godly, and who have condemned such things, have been spoken of as enemies of the cross of Christ, or at least very cold and dead; and thus many, that of themselves were not inclined to such practices, have by this means been driven on, being ashamed to be behind, and accounted poor soldiers for Christ.

Another effect of spiritual pride is to make the subject of it *assuming*. It oftentimes makes it natural to persons so to act and speak, as though in a special manner it belonged to them to be taken notice of and much regarded. It is very natural to a person that is much under the influence of spiritual pride, to take all the respect that is paid him. If others show a disposition to submit to him, and yield him the deference of a preceptor, he is open to it, and freely admits it; yea, it is natural for him to expect such treatment, and to take much notice if he fails of it, and to have an ill opinion of others that do not pay him that which he looks upon as his prerogative.—He is apt to think that it belongs to him to speak, and to clothe himself with a judicial and dogmatical air in conversation, and to take it upon him, as what belongs to him, to give forth his sentence, and to determine and decide. Whereas pure christian humility *vaunteth not itself, doth not behave itself unseemly*, and is apt to *prefer others in honour*. One under the influence of spiritual pride is more apt to instruct others, than to inquire for himself, and naturally puts on the airs of a master. Whereas one that is full of pure humility, naturally has on the air of a disciple; his voice is, "What shall I do? What shall I do that I may live more to God's honour? What shall I do with this wicked heart?" He is ready to receive instruction from any body, agreeable to Jam. i. 19. "Wherefore, my beloved brethren, let every man be swift to hear, slow to speak." The eminently humble Christian thinks he wants help from every body, whereas he that is spiritually proud thinks that every body wants his help. Christian humility, under a sense of others' misery, entreats and beseeches; but spiritual pride affects to command and warn with authority. There ought to be the utmost watchfulness against all such appearances of spiritual pride, in all that profess to have been the subjects of this work, and especially in the promoters of it, but above all in itinerant preachers. The most eminent gifts, and highest tokens of God's favour and blessing, will not excuse them.—Alas! what is man at his best estate! What is the most highly-favoured Christian, or the most eminent and successful minister, that he should now think he is sufficient for something, and somebody to be regarded; and that he should go forth, and act among his fellow-creatures as if he were wise, and strong, and good!

Ministers who have been the principal instruments of carrying on this glorious revival of religion, and whom God has made use of to bring up his people as it were out of *Egypt*, should take heed, that they do not provoke God, as *Moses* did, by assuming too much to themselves, and by their intemperate zeal to shut them out from seeing the good things that God is going to do for his church in this world. The fruits of *Moses's* unbelief, which provoked God to shut him out of *Canaan*, and not to suffer him to partake of those great things God was about to do for *Israel*, were chiefly these two things:—*First*, His mingling bitterness with his zeal. He had a great zeal for God, and he could not bear to see the intolerable stiff-neckedness of the people, that they did not acknowledge the work of God, and were not convinced by all his wonders that they had seen. But human passion was mingled with his zeal, Psal. cvi. 32, 33. "They angered him also at the waters of strife; so that it went ill with *Moses* for their sakes: because they provoked his spirit, so that he spake unadvisedly with his lips." *Hear now, ye rebels*, says he, with bitterness of language.—*Secondly*, He behaved himself, and spake, with an assuming air. He assumed too much to himself; *Hear now, ye rebels, must we fetch water out of this rock?* Spiritual pride wrought in *Moses* at that time. His temptations to it were very great; for he had had great discoveries of God, and had been privileged with intimate and sweet communion with him, and God had made him the instrument of great good to his church. But though he was so humble a person. and, by God's own testimony, meek above all men upon the face of the whole earth, yet his temptations were too strong for him. Which surely should make our young ministers, that have of late been highly favoured, and have had great success, exceeding careful, and distrustful of themselves. Alas! how far are we from having the strength of holy, meek, aged *Moses!* The temptation at this day is exceeding great to both those errors that *Moses* was guilty of. There is great temptation to bitterness and corrupt passion with zeal; for there is so much unreasonable opposition made against this glorious work of God, and so much stiff-neckedness manifested in multitudes of this generation, notwithstanding all the great and wonderful works in which God has passed before them, that it greatly tends to provoke the spirits of such as have the interest of this work at heart, so as to move them to speak unadvisedly with their lips. And there is also great temptation to an assuming behaviour in some persons. When a minister is greatly succeeded from time to time, and so draws the eyes of the multitude upon him, when he sees himself followed, resorted to as an oracle—and people ready to adore him, and as it were to offer sacrifice to him, as it was with *Paul* and *Barnabas* at *Lystra*—it is almost impossible for a man to avoid taking upon him the airs of a master, or some extraordinary person; a man had need to have a great stock of humility, and much divine assistance, to resist the temptation. But the greater our dangers are, the more ought to be our watchfulness, prayerfulness, and diffidence, lest we bring ourselves into mischief. Fishermen who have been very successful, having caught a great many fish, had need to be careful that they do not at length begin to burn incense to their net. And we should take warning by *Gideon*, who after God had highly favoured and exalted him, and made him the instrument of working a wonderful deliverance for his people, at length made a god of the spoils of his enemies, which became a snare to him and to his house, so as to prove the ruin of his family.

All young ministers, in this day of bringing up the ark of God, should take warning by the example of a young *Levite* in *Israel*, *Uzza* the son of *Abinadab*. He seemed to have a real concern for the ark of God, and to be zealous and engaged in his mind on that joyful occasion of bringing it up. God made him an instrument to bring the ark out of its long-continued obscurity in *Kirjath-jearim*, and he was succeeded to bring it a considerable way towards mount *Zion;* but for his want of humility, reverence, and circumspection, and assuming or taking too much upon him, God broke forth upon him, and smote him for his error, so that he never lived to see and partake of the great joy of his church on occasion of the carrying up the ark into mount *Zion*, and the great blessings of heaven upon *Israel* consequent upon it. Ministers employed to carry on this work, have been chiefly of the younger sort, who have doubtless (as *Uzza* had) a real concern for the ark; and it is evident that they are much animated and engaged in their minds (as he was) in this joyful day of bringing up the ark.—They are afraid what will become of the ark under the conduct of its ministers: they see it shakes, and they are afraid these blundering oxen will throw it. Some of them, it is to be feared, have been over-officious on this occasion, have assumed too much to themselves, and have been bold to put forth their hand to take hold of the ark, as though they were the only fit and worthy persons to defend it. If young ministers had great humility, without a corrupt mixture, it would dispose them especially to treat aged ministers with respect and reverence, as their fathers, notwithstanding that a sovereign God may have given themselves greater assistance and success, 1 Pet. v. 5. "Likewise, ye younger, submit yourselves unto the elder; yea, all of you be subject one to another; and be clothed with humility; for God resisteth the proud, and giveth grace to the humble." Lev. xix. 32. "Thou shalt rise up before the hoary head, and honour the face of the old man, and fear thy God; I am the Lord."

As spiritual pride disposes persons to assume much to themselves, so it also disposes them to treat others with neglect. On the contrary, pure christian humility disposes persons to honour all men, agreeable to that rule, 1 Pet. ii. 17. There has been in some, who I believe are true friends of religion, too great appearance of this fruit of spiritual pride, in their treatment of those whom they looked upon to be carnal men; and particularly in refusing to enter into any discourse or reasoning with them. Indeed to spend a great deal of time in jangling and warm debates about religion, is not the way to propagate, but to hinder it; and some are so dreadfully set against this work, that it is a dismal task to dispute with them; all that one can say is utterly in vain. I have found it so by experience. To enter into disputes about religion, at some times, is quite unseasonable; particularly in meetings for religious conference, or exercises of worship. But yet we ought to be very careful that we do not refuse to discourse with men, with any appearance of a supercilious neglect, as though we counted them not worthy to be regarded; on the contrary, we should condescend to carnal men, as Christ has condescended to us, to bear with our unteachableness and stupidity.—He still follows us with instructions, line upon line, and precept upon precept, saying, *Come, let us reason together:* setting light before us, and using all manner of arguments with us, and waiting upon such dull scholars, as it were hoping that we should receive light. We should be ready with meekness and calmness, without hot disputing, to give our reasons, why we think this work is the work of God, to carnal men when they ask us, and not turn them by as not worthy to be talked with; as the apostle directed the primitive Christians to be ready to give a reason of the christian faith, and hope to the enemies of Christianity, 1 Pet. iii. 15. "Be ready always to give an answer to every man that asketh you a reason of the hope that is in you, with meekness and fear." And we ought not to condemn all reasoning about things of religion under the name of carnal reason. For my part, I desire no better than that those who oppose this work should fairly submit to have the cause betwixt us tried by strict reasoning.

One qualification that the Scripture speaks of once and again, as requisite in a minister, is, that he should be (διδακτικος) *apt to teach*, 1 Tim. iii. 2. And the apostle seems to explain what he means by it, in 2 Tim. ii. 24, 25. or at least there expresses one thing that he intends by it, *viz.* That a minister should be ready, meekly to condescend to and instruct opposers; "And the servant of the Lord must not strive, but be gentle unto all men, apt to teach, patient, in meekness instructing those that oppose themselves, if God peradventure will give them repentance, to the acknowledging of the truth."

SECT. II.

Another cause of errors in conduct attending a religious revival, is the adoption of wrong principles.

One erroneous principle, than which scarce any has proved more mischievous to the present glorious work of God, is a notion that it is God's manner in these days, to guide his saints, at least some that are more eminent, by inspiration, or immediate revelation. They suppose he makes known to them what shall come to pass hereafter, or what it is his will that they should do, by impressions made upon their minds, either with or without texts of Scripture; whereby something is made known to them, that is not taught in the Scripture. By such a notion the devil has a great door opened for him; and if once this opinion should come to be fully yielded to, and established in the church of God, Satan would have opportunity thereby to set up himself as the guide and oracle of God's people, and to have *his* word regarded as their infallible rule, and so to lead them where he would, and to introduce what he pleased, and soon to bring the Bible into neglect and contempt.——Late experience, in some instances, has shown that the tendency of this notion is to cause persons to esteem the Bible as in a great measure useless.

This error will defend and support errors. As long as a person has a notion that he is guided by immediate direction from heaven, it makes him incorrigible and impregnable in all his misconduct. For what signifies it, for poor blind worms of the dust, to go to argue with a man, and endeavour to convince him and correct him, that is guided by the immediate counsels and commands of the great JEHOVAH? This great work of God has been exceedingly hindered by this error; and, till we have quite taken this handle out of the devil's hands, the work of God will never go on without great clogs and hinderances.—Satan will always have a vast advantage in his hands against it, and as he has improved it hitherto, so he will do still. And it is evident, that the devil knows the vast advantage he has by it, that makes him exceeding loth to let go his hold.

It is strange what a disposition there is in many well-disposed and religious persons to fall in with and hold fast this notion. It is enough to astonish one, that such multiplied, plain instances of the failing of such supposed revelations in the event, do not open every one's eyes. I have seen so many instances of the failing of such impressions, that would almost furnish a history. I have been acquainted with them when made under all kinds of circumstances, and have seen them fail in the event, when made with such circumstances as have been fairest and brightest, and most promising. They have been made upon the minds of apparently eminent saints, and with an excellent heavenly frame of spirit yet continued, and made with texts of Scripture that seemed exceeding apposite, yea, many texts following one another, extraordinarily and wonderfully brought to the mind, and the impressions repeated over and over; and yet all has most manifestly come to nothing, to the full conviction of the persons themselves. God has in so many instances of late, in his providence, covered such things with darkness, that one would think it should be enough quite to blank the expectations of those who have been ready to think highly of such things. It seems to be a testimony of God, that he has no design of reviving revelations in his church, and a rebuke from him to the groundless expectations of it.

It seems to me that Zech. xiii. 5. is a prophecy concerning ministers of the gospel in the latter and glorious day of the christian church (which is evidently spoken of in this and the foregoing chapters). The words, I apprehend, are to be interpreted in a spiritual sense. *I am an husbandman:* The work of ministers is very often, in the New Testament, compared to the business of the husbandmen, that take care of God's husbandry, to whom he lets out his vineyard, and sends them forth to labour in his field, where one plants and another waters, one sows and another reaps; so ministers are called labourers in God's harvest. And as it is added, *Men taught me to keep cattle from my youth;* so the work of a minister is very often in Scripture represented by the business of a shepherd or pastor. And whereas it is said, *I am no prophet; but man taught me from my youth:* it is as much as to say, I do not pretend to have received my skill, whereby I am fitted for the business of a pastor or shepherd in the church of God, by immediate inspiration, but by education, by being trained up to the business by human learning, and instructions received from my youth or childhood, by ordinary means.

And why cannot we be contented with the divine oracles, that holy, pure word of God, which we have in such abundance and clearness, now since the canon of Scripture is completed? Why should we desire to have any thing added to them by impulses from above? Why should we not rest in that standing rule that God has given to his church, which, the apostle teaches us, is surer than a voice from heaven? And why should we desire to make the Scripture speak more to us than it does? Or why should any desire a higher kind of intercourse with heaven, than by having the Holy Spirit given in his sanctifying influences, infusing and exciting grace and holiness, love and joy, which is the highest kind of intercourse that the saints and angels in heaven have with God, and the chief excellency of the glorified man Christ Jesus?

Some that follow impulses and impressions indulge a notion, that they do no other than follow the guidance of God's word, because the impression is made with a text of Scripture that comes to their mind. But they take that text as it is impressed on their minds, and improve it as a new revelation to all intents and purposes; while the text, as it is in the Bible, implies no such thing, and they themselves do not suppose that any such revelation was contained in it before. Suppose, for instance, that text should come into a person's mind with strong impression, Acts ix. 6. "Arise, and go into the city; and it shall be told thee what thou must do;" and he should interpret it as an immediate signification of the will of God, that he should now forthwith go to such a neighbouring town, and there he should meet with a further discovery of his duty. If such things as these are revealed by the impression of these words, it is to all intents a new revelation, not the less because certain words of Scripture are made use of in the case. Here are propositions or truths entirely new, that those words do not contain. These propositions, That it is God's mind and will that such a person by name should arise at such a time, and go to such a place, and that there he should meet with discoveries, are entirely new propositions, wholly different from those contained in that text of Scripture. They are no more implied in the words themselves, without a new revelation, than it is implied that he should arise and go to any other place, or that any other person should arise and go to that place. The propositions, supposed to be now revealed, are as really different from those contained in that scripture, as they are from the propositions contained in that text, Gen. v. 6. "And Seth lived an hundred and five years, and begat Enos." This is quite a different thing from the Spirit's enlightening the mind to understand the words of God, and know what is contained and revealed in them, and what consequences may justly be drawn from them, and to see how they are applicable to our case and circumstances; which is done without any new revelation, only by enabling the mind to understand and apply a revelation already made.

Those texts of Scripture, that speak of the children of God as *led by the Spirit*, have been by some brought to defend such impulses; particularly Rom. viii. 14. "For as many as are led by the Spirit of God, they are the sons of God:" And Gal. v. 18. "But if ye are led by the Spirit, ye are not under the law." But these texts themselves confute them that bring them; for it is evident that the leading of the Spirit which the apostle speaks of is peculiar to the children of God, and that natural men cannot have; for he speaks of it as a sure evidence of their being the sons of God, and not under the law. But a leading or directing of a person by immediately revealing to him where he should go, or what shall hereafter come to pass, or what shall be the future consequence of his doing thus or thus, if there be any such thing in these days, is not of the nature of the gracious leading of the Spirit of

God, peculiar to God's children. It is no more than a common gift; there is nothing in it but what natural men are capable of, and many of them have had in the days of inspiration. A man may have ten thousand such revelations and directions from the Spirit of God, and yet not have a jot of grace in his heart. It is no more than the gift of prophecy, which immediately reveals what will be, or should be hereafter; but this is only a common gift, as the apostle expressly shows, 1 Cor. xiii. 2, 8. If a person has any thing revealed to him from God, or is directed to any thing by a voice from heaven, or a whisper, or words immediately suggested to his mind, there is nothing of the nature of grace merely in this: it is of the nature of a common influence of the Spirit, and is but dross in comparison of the excellency of that gracious leading of the Spirit that the saints have. Such a way of being directed where one shall go, and what he shall do, is no more than what *Balaam* had from God, who from time to time revealed to him what he should do; so that he was in this sense led by the Spirit for a considerable time. There is *a more excellent way* in which the Spirit leads *the sons of God*, that natural men cannot have; and that is, by inclining them to do the will of God, and go in the shining path of truth and christian holiness, from a holy, heavenly disposition, which the Spirit of God gives them, and which inclines and leads them to those things that are excellent and agreeable to God's mind, whereby they "are transformed by the renewing of their minds, and prove what is that good, and acceptable, and perfect will of God," Rom. xii. 2. And so the Spirit of God does in a gracious manner teach the saints their duty; and he teaches them in a higher manner than ever *Balaam*, or *Saul*, or *Judas*, were taught. The Spirit of God enlightens them with respect to their duty, by making their eye single and pure, whereby the whole body is full of light. The sanctifying influence of the Spirit of God rectifies the taste of the soul, whereby it savours those things that are of God, and naturally relishes and delights in those things that are holy and agreeable to God's mind; and, like one of a distinguishing taste, it chooses those things that are good and wholesome, and rejects those that are evil. The sanctified ear tries words, and the sanctified heart tries actions, as the mouth tastes meat. And thus the Spirit of God leads and guides the meek in his way, agreeable to his promises; he enables them to understand the commands and counsels of his word, and rightly to apply them. Christ blames the *Pharisees* that they had not this holy distinguishing taste, to discern and distinguish what was right and wrong, Luke xii. 57. "Yea, and why even of your own selves judge ye not what is right?"

The leading of the Spirit which God gives his children, and which is peculiar to them, is that teaching them his statutes, and causing them to understand the way of his precepts, which the psalmist so very often prays for, especially in the 119th Psalm: and not in giving them *new statutes* and *new precepts*. He graciously gives them eyes to see, and ears to hear, and hearts to understand; he causes them to understand the fear of the Lord, and so "brings the blind by a way they knew not, and leads them in paths that they had not known, and makes darkness light before them, and crooked things straight." So the assistance of the Spirit in praying and preaching seems by some to have been greatly misunderstood, and they have sought after a miraculous assistance of inspiration, by the immediate suggesting of words to them, by such gifts and influences of the Spirit, in praying and teaching, as the apostle speaks of, 1 Cor. xiv. 14, 26. (which many natural men had in those days,) instead of a gracious holy assistance of the Spirit of God, which is the far *more excellent way;* (as 1 Cor. xii. 31. and xiii. 1.) the gracious and most excellent assistance of the Spirit of God in praying and preaching, is not by immediately suggesting words to the apprehension, which may be with a cold, dead heart; but by warming the heart, and filling it with a great sense of things to be spoken, and with holy affections, that these may suggest words. Thus indeed the Spirit of God may be said, indirectly and mediately, to suggest words to us, to indite our petitions for us, and to teach the preacher what to say; he fills the heart, and that fills the mouth. We know that when men are greatly affected in any matter, and their hearts are very full, it fills them with matter for speech, and makes them eloquent upon that subject; and much more have spiritual affections this tendency, for many reasons that might be given. When a person is in a holy and lively frame in secret prayer, or in christian conversation, it will wonderfully supply him with matter, and with expressions, as every true Christian knows; and it has the like tendency to enable a person in public prayer and preaching. And, if he has these holy influences of the Spirit on his heart in a high degree, nothing in the world will have so great a tendency to make both the matter and manner of his public performances excellent and profitable. But, since there is no immediate suggesting of words from the Spirit of God to be expected or desired, they who neglect and despise study and premeditation, in order to a preparation for the pulpit, in such an expectation, are guilty of presumption: though doubtless it may be lawful for some persons, in some cases, (and they may be called to it,) to preach with very little study; and the Spirit of God, by the heavenly frame of heart that he gives them, may enable them to do it to excellent purpose. Besides this most excellent way of the Spirit of God assisting ministers in public performances, which (considered as the preacher's privilege) far excels inspiration, there is a common assistance which natural men may have in these days, and which the godly may have intermingled with a gracious assistance, which is also very different from inspiration, and that is, his assisting natural principles; as the natural apprehension, reason, memory, conscience, and natural affection.

But, to return to the head of impressions and immediate revelations; many lay themselves open to a delusion by expecting direction from heaven in this way, and waiting for it. In such a case it is easy for persons to imagine that they have it. They are perhaps at a loss concerning something, undetermined what they shall do, or what course they shall take in some affair; and they pray to God to direct them, and make known to them his mind and will: and then, instead of expecting to be directed, by being assisted in considering the rules of God's word, his providence, and their circumstances, to look on things in a true light, and justly to weigh them, they are waiting for some secret immediate influence, unaccountably swaying their minds, and turning their thoughts or inclinations that way in which God would have them to go. Hereby they are exposed to two things; *first*, they lay themselves open to the devil, and give him a fair opportunity to lead them where he pleases; for they stand ready to follow the first extraordinary impulse that they shall have, groundlessly concluding it is from God. And, *secondly*, they are greatly exposed to be deceived by their own imaginations: for such an expectation awakens and quickens the imagination; and that oftentimes is called an uncommon impression, that is no such thing; and they ascribe that to the agency of some invisible being, which is owing only to themselves.

Again, another way that many have been deceived, is by drawing false conclusions from true premises. Many true and eminent saints have been led into mistakes and snares, by arguing that they have prayed in faith. They have indeed been greatly assisted in prayer for such a particular mercy, and have had the true spirit of prayer in exercise in their asking it of God: but they have concluded more from these premises than is a just consequence from them. That they have thus prayed is a sure sign that their prayer is accepted and heard, and that God will give a gracious answer according to his own wisdom, and that the particular thing asked shall be given, or that which is equivalent; this is a just consequence from it.—But it is not inferred by any new revelation now made, but by the promises made to the prayer of faith in the Holy Scriptures. But that God will answer them in that individual thing they ask, if it be not a thing promised in God's word, or they do not certainly know that it is what will be most for the good of God's church, and the advancement of Christ's kingdom and glory, nor whether it will be best for them, is more than can be justly concluded from it. If God remarkably meets with one of his children while he is praying for a particular mercy of great importance, for himself or some other person, or any society of men, and does by the influences of his Spirit greatly humble him, and empty him of himself in his prayer, and manifests himself remarkably in his excellency, sovereignty, and all-sufficient power and grace in Jesus Christ—and in a remarkable manner enables the person to come to him for that mercy, poor in spirit, and with humble resignation to God, and with a great degree of faith in the divine sufficiency, and the sufficiency of Christ's mediation—that person has indeed a great deal the more reason to hope that God will grant that mercy, than otherwise he would have. The greater probability is justly inferred, agreeable to the promises of the Holy Scripture, in that such prayer is accepted and heard; and it is much more probable that a prayer that is heard will be returned with a particular mercy that is asked, than one that is not so. And there is no reason at all to doubt, but that God sometimes especially enables to the exercises of faith, when the minds of his saints are engaged in thoughts of, and prayer for, some particular blessing they greatly desire; *i. e.* God is pleased especially to give them a believing frame, a sense of his fulness, and a spirit of humble dependence on him, at such times. When they are thinking of and praying for such mercy, he gives them a particular sense of his ability, and of the sufficiency of his power to overcome obstacles, and the sufficiency of his mercy and of the blood of Christ for the removal of the guilt that is in the way of the bestowment of such a mercy, in particular. When this is the case, it makes the probability still much greater, that God intends to bestow the particular mercy sought, in his own time, and his own way. But here is nothing of the nature of a revelation in the case, but only a drawing rational conclusions from the particular manner and circumstances of the ordinary gracious influences of God's Spirit. And as God is pleased sometimes to give his saints particular exercises of faith in his sufficiency, with regard to particular mercies; so he is sometimes pleased to make use of his word in order to it, and helps the actings of faith with respect to such a mercy. The strengthening of their faith in God's sufficiency, in this case, is therefore a just improvement of such scriptures; it is no more than what those scriptures, as they stand in the Bible, hold forth. But to take them as new whispers or revelations from heaven, is not making a just improvement of them. If persons have thus a spirit of prayer remarkably given them, concerning particular mercy, from time to time, so as evidently to be assisted to act faith in God, in that particular, in a very distinguishing manner; the argument in some cases may be very strong, that God does design to grant that mercy, not from any revelation now made of it, but from such a kind and manner of the ordinary influence of his Spirit with respect to that thing.

But here a great deal of caution and circumspection must be used in drawing inferences of this nature. There are many ways by which persons may be misled and deluded. The ground on which some expect that they shall receive the thing they have asked for, is rather a strong imagination, than any true humble faith in the divine sufficiency. They have a strong persuasion that the thing asked shall be granted, (which they can give no reason for,) without any remarkable discovery of that glory and fulness of God and Christ, that is the ground of faith. And sometimes the confidence that their prayers shall be answered, is only a self-righteous confidence, and no true faith. They have a high conceit of themselves as eminent saints, and special favourites of God, and have also a high conceit of the prayers they have made, because they were much enlarged and affected in them; and hence they are positive in it, that the thing will come to pass. And sometimes, when once they have conceived such a notion, they grow stronger and stronger in it; and this they think is from an immediate divine hand upon their minds to strengthen their confidence; whereas it is only by their dwelling in their minds on their own excellency, and high experiences, and great assistances, whereby they look brighter and brighter in their own eyes. Hence it is found by observation and experience, that nothing in the world exposes so much to enthusiasm as spiritual pride and self-righteousness.

In order to drawing a just inference from the supposed assistance we have had in prayer for a particular mercy, and judging of the probability of the bestowment of that individual mercy, many things must be considered. We must consider the importance of the mercy sought, and the principle whence we so earnestly desire it; how far it is good, and agreeable to the mind and will of God; the degree of love to God that we exercised in our prayer; the degree of discovery that is made of the divine sufficiency, and the degree in which our assistance is manifestly distinguishing with respect to that mercy.—And there is nothing of greater importance in the argument than the degree of humility, poverty of spirit, self-emptiness, and resignation to the holy will of God, exercised in seeking that mercy. Praying for a particular mercy with much of these things, I have often seen blessed with a remarkable bestowment of the particular thing asked for. From what has been said, we may see which way God may, only by the ordinary gracious influences of his Spirit, sometimes give his saints special reason to hope for the bestowment of a particular mercy they prayed for, and which we may suppose he oftentimes gives eminent saints, who have great degrees of humility, and much communion with God. And here, I humbly conceive, some eminent servants of Jesus Christ that we read of in ecclesiastical story, have been led into a mistake; and, through want of distinguishing such things as these from immediate revelations, have thought that God has favoured them, in some instances, with the same kind of divine influences that the apostles and prophets had of old.

Another erroneous principle that some have embraced, and which has been a source of many errors in their conduct, is, That persons ought always to do whatsoever the Spirit of God (though but indirectly) inclines them to. Indeed the Spirit of God is in itself infinitely perfect, and all his immediate actings, simply considered, are perfect, and there can be nothing wrong in them; and therefore all that the Spirit of God inclines us to directly and immediately, without the intervention of any other cause that shall pervert and misimprove what is from him, ought to be done. But there may be many things, disposition to do which may indirectly be from the Spirit of God, that we ought not to do. The disposition in general may be good, and from the Spirit of God; but the particular determination of that disposition, as to particular actions, objects, and circumstances, may be from the intervention or interposition of some infirmity, blindness, inadvertence, deceit, or corruption of ours. So that although the disposition in general ought to be allowed and promoted, and all those actings of it that are simply from God's Spirit, yet the particular ill direction or determination of that disposition, which is from some other cause, ought not to be followed.

As for instance, the Spirit of God may cause a person to have a dear love to another, and so a great desire of and delight in his comfort, ease, and pleasure. This disposition in general is good, and ought to be followed; but yet through the intervention of indiscretion, or some other bad cause, it may be ill directed, and have a bad determination, as to particular acts; and the person indirectly, through that real love he has to his neighbour, may kill him with kindness; he may do that out of sincere goodwill to him, which may tend to ruin him.—A good disposition may, through some inadvertence or delusion, strongly incline a person to that which, if he saw all things as they are, would be most contrary to that disposition. The true loyalty of a general, and his zeal for the honour of his prince, may exceedingly animate him in war; but this good disposition, through indiscretion and mistake, may push him forward to those things that give the enemy great advantage, and may expose him and his army to ruin, and may tend to the ruin of his master's interest.

The apostle does evidently suppose that the Spirit of God, in his extraordinary, immediate, and miraculous influences on men's minds, may in some respect excite inclinations, which, if gratified, would tend to confusion, and therefore must sometimes be restrained, and in their exercise must be under the government of discretion, 1 Cor. xiv. 31—33. " For ye may all prophesy one by one, that all may learn, and all may be comforted. And the spirits of the prophets are subject to the prophets. For God is not the author of confusion, but of peace, as in all the churches of the saints." Here by *the spirits of the prophets*, according to the known phraseology of the apostle, is meant the Spirit of God acting in the prophets, according to those special gifts with which each one was endued: and here it is plainly implied that the Spirit of God, thus operating in them, may be an occasion of their having sometimes an inclination to do that, in the exercise of those gifts, which it was not proper, decent, or profitable that they should; and that therefore the inclination, though indirectly from the Spirit of God, should be restrained; and that it ought to be subject to the discretion of the prophets, as to the particular time and circumstances of its exercise.

I make no doubt but that it is possible for a minister to have by the Spirit of God such a sense of the importance of eternal things, and of the misery of mankind—so many of whom are exposed to eternal destruction—together with such a love to souls, that he might find in himself a disposition to spend all his time, day and night, in warning, exhorting, and calling upon men; and so that he must be obliged as it were to do violence to himself ever to refrain, so as to give himself any opportunity to eat, drink, or sleep. And so I believe there may be a disposition, in like manner, indirectly excited in lay-persons, through the intervention of their infirmity, to do what only belongs to ministers; yea, to do those things that would not become either ministers or people. Through the influence of the Spirit of God, together with want of discretion, and some remaining corruption, women and children might feel themselves inclined to break forth aloud to great congregations, warning and exhorting the whole multitude; and to scream in the streets, or to leave their families, and go from house to house, earnestly exhorting others; but yet it would by no means follow that it was their duty to do these things, or that they would not have a tendency to do ten times as much hurt as good.

Another wrong principle, from whence have arisen errors in conduct, is, that whatsoever is found to be of present and immediate benefit, may and ought to be practised, without looking forward to future consequences. Some persons seem to think that it sufficiently justifies any thing they say or do, that it is found to be for present edification; it assists and promotes their present affection, and therefore they think they should not concern themselves about future consequences, but leave them with God. Indeed in things that are in themselves our duty, being required by moral rules, or absolute positive commands of God, they must be done, and future consequences must be left with God; our discretion takes no place here: but in other things we are to be governed by discretion, and must not only look at the present good, but our view must be extensive, and we must look at the consequences of things. It is the duty of ministers especially to exercise this discretion. In things wherein they are not determined by an absolute rule, and not enjoined them by a wisdom superior to their own, Christ has left them to their own discretion, with that general rule, that they should exercise the utmost wisdom they can obtain, in pursuing that which, upon the best view of the consequences of things, will tend most to the advancement of his kingdom. This is implied in those words of Christ to his disciples, when he sent them forth to preach the gospel, Matt. x. 16. "Be ye wise as serpents."

The Scripture always represents the work of a gospel-minister by those employments that especially require a wise foresight of, and provision for, future events and consequences. So it is compared with the business of a steward, which in an eminent manner requires forecast; as, for instance, a wise laying in of provision for the supply of the needs of a family, according to its future necessities. So it is compared to the husbandman, that almost wholly consists in things done with a view to the future fruits and consequences of his labour. The husbandman's discretion and forecast is eloquently set forth in Isa. xxviii. 24, 25, 26. "Doth the plowman plow all day to sow? doth he open and break the clods of his ground? When he hath made plain the face thereof, doth he not cast abroad the fitches, and scatter the cummin, and cast in the principal wheat, and the appointed barley, and the rye in their place? For his God doth instruct him to discretion, and doth teach him." So the work of the ministry is compared to that of a wise builder or architect, who has a comprehensive view; and for whom it is necessary, that, when he begins a building, he should have at once a view of the whole frame, and all the future parts of the structure, even to the pinnacle, that all may be fitly framed together. So also it is compared to the business of a trader or merchant, who is to gain by trading; a business that exceedingly requires forecast, and without which it is never like to be followed with success for any long time. So it is represented by the business of a fisherman, which depends on peculiar skill; and to that of a soldier, which perhaps, above any other secular business, requires great foresight, and a wise provision for future events and consequences.

And particularly, ministers ought not to be careless how much they discompose the minds of natural men, or how great an uproar they raise in the carnal world, and so lay blocks in the way of the propagation of religion. This certainly is not to follow the example of the zealous apostle *Paul*, who though he would not depart from his duty to please carnal men, yet, wherein he might with a good conscience, exceedingly laid out himself to please them. He avoided raising in the multitude prejudices, oppositions, and tumults against the gospel; and looked upon it as of great consequence. 1 Cor. x. 32, 33. "Give none offence, neither to the Jews, nor to the Gentiles, nor to the church of God: even as I please all men in all things, not seeking mine own profit, but the profit of many, that they may be saved." Yea, he declares that he laid himself out so much for this, that he made himself a kind of a servant to all sorts of men, conforming to their customs and various humours in every thing wherein he might, even in the things that were very burdensome to him, that he might not fright men away from Christianity, and cause them to stand as it were braced and armed against it, but on the contrary, if possible, might with condescension and friendship win and draw them to it; 1 Cor. ix. 19—23. And agreeable hereto are the directions he gives to others, both ministers and people: So he directs the christian *Romans, not to please themselves, but every one please his neighbour, for his good, to edification,* Rom. xv. 1, 2, and to *follow after the things that make for peace,* chap. xiv. 19. And he expresses it in terms exceeding strong, Rom. xii. 18. "If it be possible, as much as lieth in you, live peaceably with all men." And he directs ministers to endeavour, if possible, to gain opposers by a meek, condescending treatment, avoiding all appearance of strife or fierceness, 2 Tim. ii. 24—26. To the like purpose, the same apostle directs Christians to *walk in wisdom towards them that are without,* Eph. iv. 5. and to avoid giving offence to others, if we can, "that our good may not be evil spoken of," Rom. xiv 16. So that it is evident, the most zealous and most successful propagator of vital religion that ever was, looked upon it to be of great consequence to endeavour, as much as possible, by all the methods of lawful meekness and gentleness, to avoid raising the prejudice and opposition of the world against religion.—When we have done our utmost, there will be opposition enough to vital religion, against which the carnal mind of man has such an enmity. We should not therefore needlessly increase and raise that enmity. The apostle, though he took so much pains to please men, had persecution almost every where raised against him. A fisherman is careful not needlessly to ruffle and disturb the water, lest he should drive the fish away from his net; but he will rather endeavour if possible to draw them into it. Such a fisherman was the apostle, 2 Cor. xii. 15, 16. "And I will very gladly spend and be spent for you; though the more abundantly I love you, the less I be loved. But be it so, I did not burden you, nevertheless, being crafty, I caught you with guile."

The necessity of suffering persecution, in order to being a true Christian, has undoubtedly by some been carried to an extreme, and the doctrine has been abused. It has been looked upon as necessary to uphold a man's credit amongst others as a Christian, that he should be persecuted. I have heard it made an objection against the sincerity of particular persons, that they were no more hated and reproached. And the manner of glorying in persecution, or the cross of Christ, has in some been very wrong, bearing too much the appearance of lifting up themselves in it, that they were very much hated and reviled, more than most, as an evidence of their excelling others, in being good soldiers of Jesus Christ. Such an improvement of the doctrine of the enmity between the seed of the woman and the seed of the serpent, and of the necessity of persecution, becoming credible and customary, has a direct tendency to cause those that would be accounted true Christians, to behave themselves so towards those that are not well-affected to religion, as to provoke their hatred, or at least to be but little careful to avoid it, and not very studiously and earnestly to strive (after the apostle's example and precepts) to please them to their edification, and by meekness and gentleness to win them, and by all possible means to live peaceably with them.

I believe that saying of our Saviour, "I came not to send peace on earth, but division," has been abused; as though when we see great strife arise about religion, violent heats of spirit against the truly pious, and a loud clamour and uproar against the work of God, it was to be rejoiced in, because it is that which Christ came to send. It has almost been laid down as a maxim by some, That the more division and strife, the better sign; which naturally leads persons to seek and provoke it, or leads them to such a manner of behaviour, such a roughness and sharpness, or such an affected neglect, as has a natural tendency to raise prejudice and opposition; instead of striving as the apostle did to his utmost, by all meekness, gentleness, and benevolence of behaviour, to prevent or assuage it.—Christ came to send a sword on earth, and to cause division, no otherwise than he came to send damnation; for Christ, that is set for the glorious restoration of some, is set for the fall of others, and to be a stone of stumbling and rock of offence to them, and an occasion of their vastly more aggravated and terrible ruin. And this is always the consequence of a great revival of vital religion; it is the means of the salvation of some, and the more aggravated damnation of others. But certainly this is no just argument that men's exposedness to damnation is not to be lamented, or that we should not exert ourselves to our utmost, in all the methods that we can devise, that others might be saved, and to avoid all such behaviour towards them as tends to lead them down to hell.

I know there is naturally a great enmity in the heart of man against vital religion; and I believe there would have been a great deal of opposition against this glorious work of God in *New England*, if the subjects and promoters of it had behaved themselves never so agreeably to Christian rules; and I believe if this work goes on and spreads much in the world, so as to begin to shake kingdoms and nations, it will dreadfully stir up the rage of earth and hell, and will put the world into the greatest uproar that ever it was in since it stood. I believe Satan's dying struggles will be the most violent; but yet a great deal might be done to restrain this opposition, by a good conformity to that of the apostle, Jam. iii. 13. "Who is a wise man, and endued with knowledge? let him show out of a good conversation his works with meekness of wisdom." And I also believe that if the rules of christian charity, meekness, gentleness, and prudence had been duly observed by the generality of the zealous promoters of this work, it would have made three times the progress that it has; *i. e.* if it had pleased God in such a case to give a blessing to means in proportion as he has done.

Under this head of carelessness about future consequences, it may be proper to say something of introducing things new and strange, and that have a tendency by their novelty to shock and surprise people. Nothing can be more evident from the New Testament, than that such things ought to be done with great caution and moderation, to avoid the offence that may be thereby given, and the prejudices that might be raised, to clog and hinder the progress of religion. Yea, it ought to be thus in things that are in themselves good and excellent, and of great weight, provided they are not things of absolute duty, which though they may appear to be innovations, yet cannot be neglected without immorality or disobedience to the commands of God. What great caution and moderation did the apostles use in introducing things that were new, and abolishing things that were old, in their day! How gradually were the ceremonial performances of the law of *Moses* removed and abolished among the christian *Jews!* and how long did even the apostle *Paul* himself conform to those ceremonies which he calls weak and beggarly elements! yea, even to the rite of circumcision, (Acts xvi. 3.) that he might not prejudice the *Jews* against Christianity! So it seems to have been very gradually that the *Jewish* sabbath was abolished, and the christian sabbath introduced, for the same reason. And the apostles avoided teaching Christians in those earlier days, at least for a great while, some high and excellent divine truths, because they could not bear them yet, 1 Cor. iii. 1, 2. Heb. v. 11, to the end. Thus strictly did the apostles observe the rule that their blessed Master gave them, of not putting new wine into old bottles, lest they should burst the bottles, and lose the wine. And how did Christ himself, while on earth, forbear so plainly to teach his disciples the great doctrines of Christianity, concerning his satsifaction, and the nature and manner of a sinner's justification and reconciliation with God, and the particular benefits of his death, resurrection, and ascension! because, in that infant state of the disciples, their minds were not prepared for such instructions; and therefore the more clear and full revelation of these things was reserved for the time when their minds should be further enlightened and strengthened by the outpouring of the Spirit after his ascension; John xvi. 12, 13. "I have yet many things to say unto you, but ye cannot bear them now. Howbeit, when he the Spirit of truth is come, he will guide you into all truth." And Mark iv. 33. "And with many such parables spake he the word unto them, as they were able to bear it."—These things might be enough to convince any one, that does not think himself wiser than Christ and his apostles, that great prudence and caution should be used in introducing things into the church of God, that are very uncommon, though in themselves excellent, lest by our rashness and imprudent haste we hinder religion much more than we help it.

Persons influenced by indiscreet zeal are always in too much haste; they are impatient of delays, and therefore are for jumping to the uppermost step first, before they have taken the preceding steps; whereby they expose themselves to fall and break their bones. They are delighted to see the building rise, and all their endeavour and strength is employed in advancing its height, without taking care proportionably of the bottom; whereby the whole is in danger of coming to the ground. Or they are for putting on the cupola and pinnacle before the lower parts of the building are done; which tends at once to put a stop to the building, and hinder its ever being a complete structure. Many that are thus imprudent and hasty with their zeal, have a real eager appetite for that which is good; but like children, are impatient to wait for the fruit, and therefore snatch it before it is ripe. Oftentimes in their haste they overshoot their mark, and frustrate their own end; they put that which they would obtain further out of reach than it was before, and establish and confirm that which they would remove. Things must have time to ripen. The prudent husbandman waits till the harvest is ripe, before he reaps. We are now just beginning to recover out of a dreadful disease; but to feed a man recovering from a fever with strong meat at once, is the ready way to kill him. The reformation from popery was much hindered by this hasty zeal. Many were for immediately rectifying all disorders by force, which was condemned by *Luther*, and was a great trouble to him. See *Sleiden's* Hist. of the Reformation, p. 52, &c. and book v. throughout. It is a vain prejudice that some have lately imbibed against such rules of prudence and moderation; but they will be forced to come to them at last; they will find themselves unable to maintain their cause without them; and, if they will not hearken before, experience will convince them at last, when it will be too late for them to rectify their mistake.

Another error, arising from an erroneous principle, is a wrong notion that they have an attestation of Divine Providence to persons, or things. We go too far, when we look upon the success that God gives to some persons, in making them the instruments of doing much good, as a testimony of God's approbation of those persons and all the courses they take. It has been a main argument to defend the conduct of some ministers, who have been blamed as imprudent and irregular, that God has blessed them, and given them great success; and that however men charge them as guilty of wrong things, yet that God is with them, and then who can be against them? And probably some of those ministers themselves, by this very means, have had their ears stopt against all that has been said to convince them of their misconduct. But there are innumerable ways by which persons may be misled, in forming a judgment of the mind and will of God, from the events of providence. If a person's success be a reward of something in him that God approves, yet it is no argument that he approves of every thing in him. Who can tell how far the divine grace may go in greatly rewarding some small good in a person, a good meaning, something good in his disposition; while he at the same time, in sovereign mercy, hides his eyes from a great deal that is bad, which it is his pleasure to forgive, and not to mark against the person, though in itself it be very ill? God has not told us after what manner he will proceed in this matter, and we go upon most uncertain grounds when we undertake to determine. It is an exceeding difficult thing to know how far love or hatred are exercised towards persons or actions by all that is before us. God was pleased in his sovereignty to give such success to *Jacob* in that which, from beginning to end, was a deceitful, lying contrivance and proceeding of his. In that way he obtained a blessing that was worth infinitely more than the fatness of the earth and the dew of heaven, given to *Esau* in his blessing; yea, worth more than all that the world can afford. God was for a while with *Judas*, so that by God's power accompanying him, he wrought miracles and cast out devils; but this could not justly be interpreted as God's approbation of his person, or the thievery in which he lived at the same time.

The dispensations and events of providence, with their reasons, are too little understood by us, to be as our rule, instead of God's word; *God has his way in the sea, and his path in the mighty waters, and his footsteps are not known, and he gives us no account of any of his matters.* And therefore we cannot safely take the events of his providence as a revelation of his mind concerning a person's conduct and behaviour; we have no warrant so to do. God has never appointed those things to be our rule. We have but one rule to go by, and that is his holy word; and when we join any thing else with it, as having the force of a rule, we are guilty of that which is strictly forbidden, Deut. iv. 2. Prov. xxx. 6. and Rev. xxii. 18. They who make what they imagine is pointed forth to them in providence, the rule of behaviour, do err, as well as those that follow impulses and impressions. We should put nothing in the room of the word of God. It is to be feared that some have been greatly confirmed and imboldened, by the great success that God has given them, in some things that have really been contrary to the rules of God's holy word. If so, they have been guilty of presumption, and abusing God's kindness to them, and the great honour he has put upon them. They have seen that God was with them, and made them victorious in their preaching; and this, it is to be feared, has been abused by some to a degree of self-confidence. This has much taken off all jealousy of themselves; they have been bold therefore to go great lengths, in a presumption that God was with them, and would defend them, and finally baffle all that found fault with them.

Indeed there is a voice of God in his providence, that may be interpreted and well understood by the rule of his word; and providence may, to our dark minds and weak faith, confirm the word of God, as it fulfils it. But to *improve* divine providence thus, is quite a different thing from making a *rule* of providence. Good use may be made of the events of providence, of our own observation and experience, and human histories, and the opinion of eminent men; but finally all must be brought to *one rule, viz.* the word of God, and that must be regarded as our *only rule.*

Nor do I think that they go upon sure ground, who conclude they have not been in an error in their conduct, because at the time of their doing a thing for which they have been blamed and reproached by others, they were favoured with special comforts of God's Spirit. God's bestowing special mercies on a person, is no sign that he approves of every thing he sees in him at that time. *David* had the presence of God while he lived in polygamy; and *Solomon* had some very high favours, and peculiar smiles of Heaven, and particularly at the dedication of the temple, while he greatly multiplied wives to himself, and horses, and silver, and gold; all contrary to the most express command of God to the king, in the law of *Moses*, Deut. xvii. 16, 17. We cannot tell how far God may hide his eyes from beholding iniquity in *Jacob*, and seeing perverseness in *Israel*. We cannot tell what are the reasons of God's actions any further than he interprets for himself. God sometimes gave some of the primitive Christians the extraordinary influence of his Spirit when they were out of the way of their duty, and even while they were abusing it; as is plainly implied, 1 Cor. xiv. 31, 33.—Suppose a person has done a thing for which he is reproached, and that reproach be an occasion of his feeling sweet exercises of grace in his soul, I do not think that a certain evidence that God approves of the thing he is blamed for: for undoubtedly a mistake may be the occasion of stirring up the exercise of grace. If a person, through mistake, thinks he has received some particular great mercy, that mistake may be the occasion of stirring up the sweet exercises of love, and true thankfulness to God. Suppose one that is full of love to God should hear what he deems credible tidings, concerning a remarkable deliverance of a child or a dear friend, or of some glorious thing done for the city of God, no wonder if, on such an occasion, the sweet actings of love to God, and delight in God, should be excited, though indeed afterwards it should prove a false report that he had heard. So, if one that loves God is much maligned and reproached for doing what he thinks God required and approves, no wonder that it is sweet to such an one to think that God is his friend, though men are his enemies; no wonder at all, that this is an occasion of his betaking himself to God as his sure friend, and find sweet complacence in him; though he be indeed in a mistake concerning that which he thought was agreeable to God's will. As I have before shown that the exercise of a truly good affection may be the occasion of error, and may indirectly incline a person to do that which is wrong; so, on the other hand, error, or a doing that which is wrong, may be an occasion of the exercise of a truly good affection. The reason of it is this, that however all exercises of grace be from the Spirit of God, yet he dwells and acts in the hearts of the saints, in some measure, after the manner of a vital, natural principle, a principle of new nature in them; whose exercises are excited by means, in some measure, as other natural principles are. Though grace is not in the saints as a *mere natural principle*, but as a sovereign agent, and so its exercises are not *tied to means*, by an immutable law of nature, as in mere natural principles; yet God has so constituted, that grace should dwell so in the hearts of the saints, that its exercises should have some degree of connexion with means, after the manner of a principle of nature.

Another erroneous principle that has been an occasion of some mischief and confusion, is, That external order in matters of religion, and use of the means of grace, is but little to be regarded. It has been spoken lightly of, under the names of ceremonies and dead forms, &c. and is probably the more despised by some, because their opposers insist so much upon it, and because they are so continually hearing from them the cry of *disorder and confusion.*——It is objected against the importance of external order, that God does not look at the outward form, he looks at the heart. But that is a weak argument against its importance, that true godliness does not consist in it; for it may be equally made use of against all the outward means of grace whatsoever. True godliness does not consist in ink and paper, but yet that would be a foolish objection against the importance of ink and paper in religion, when without it we could not have the word of God. If any external means at all are needful, any outward actions of a public nature, or wherein God's people are jointly concerned in public society, without doubt external order is needful. The management of an external affair that is public, or wherein a multitude is concerned, without order, is in every thing found impossible.—Without order there can be no general direction of a multitude to any particular designed end, their purposes will cross and hinder one another. A multitude cannot act in union one with another without order; confusion separates and divides them, so that there can be no concert or agreement. If a multitude would help one another in any affair, they must unite themselves one to another in a regular subordination of members, in some measure as it is in the natural body; by this means they will be in some capacity to act with united strength. And thus Christ has appointed that it should be in the visible church, as 1 Cor. xii. 14, &c. and Rom. xii. 4—8. Zeal without order will do but little, or at least it will be effectual but a little while. Let a company, however zealous against the enemy, go forth to war without any order, every one rushing forward as his zeal shall drive him, all in confusion; if they gain something at first onset, by surprising the enemy, yet how soon do they come to nothing, and fall an easy helpless prey to their adversaries! Order is one of the most necessary of all external means of the spiritual good of God's church; and therefore it is requisite even in heaven itself, where there is the least need of any external means of grace. Order is maintained amongst the glorious angels there. And the necessity of it for carrying on any design, wherein a multitude are concerned, is so great that even the devils in hell are driven to something of it, that they may carry on the designs of their kingdom. And it is very observable, that those irrational creatures for whom it is needful that they should act in union, and join as a multitude together to carry on any work for their preservation—by a wonderful instinct that God has put into them—observe and maintain a most regular and exact order among themselves; such as bees and some others. And order in the visible church is not only necessary for carrying on the designs of Christ's glory and the church's prosperity, but it is absolutely necessary to its defence; without it, it is like a city without walls, and can be in no capacity to defend itself from any kind of mischief. And so, however it be an external thing, yet is not to be despised on that account; for though it be not the food of souls, yet it is in some respect their defence. The people of *Holland* would be very foolish to despise the dikes that keep out the sea from overwhelming them, under the names of dead stones and vile earth, because the matter of which they are built is not good to eat. It seems to be partly on this foundation that some have seemed to act on that principle, That the power of judging and openly censuring others should not be reserved in the hands of particular persons, or consistories appointed thereto, but ought to be left at large, for any body that pleases to take it upon them, or that think themselves fit for it. But more of this afterwards.

On this foundation also, an orderly attending on the stated worship of God in families, has been made too light of; and it has been in some places too much a common and customary thing to be absent from family-worship, and to be abroad late in the night at religious meetings, or to attend religious conversation. Not but that this may be done on certain extraordinary occasions; I have seen the case to be such in many instances, that I have thought did afford sufficient warrant for persons to be absent from family-prayer, and to be from home till very late in the night. But we should take heed that it do not become a custom or common practice; if so, we shall soon find the consequences to be very ill. It seems to be on the same foundation—the supposed unprofitableness of external order—that it has been thought by some, there is no need of religious services and performances being limited to any certain office in the church; (of which more afterwards; and also, that those officers themselves, particularly that of the gospel-ministry, need not be limited, as it used to be, to persons of a liberal education; but some of late have been for having others, whom they have supposed to be persons of eminent experience, publicly licensed to preach, yea and ordained to the work of the ministry; and some ministers have seemed to favour such a thing. But how little do they seem to look forward, and consider the unavoidable consequences of opening such a door! If once it should become a custom, or a thing generally approved and allowed of, to admit uneducated persons to the work of the ministry, because of their remarkable experiences, and good understanding, how many lay-persons would soon appear as candidates for the work of the ministry; I doubt not but that I have been acquainted with scores that would have desired it. And how shall we know where to stop? If one is admitted because his experiences are remarkable, another will think his experiences also remarkable; and we perhaps shall not be able to deny but that they are nearly as great. If one is admitted because, besides experiences, he has good natural abilities, another by himself, and many of his neighbours, may be thought equal to him. It will be found of absolute necessity that there should be some certain, visible limits fixed, to avoid bringing odium upon ourselves, and breeding uneasiness and strife amongst others; and I know of none better, and indeed no other that can well be fixed, than what the prophet *Zechariah* fixes, *viz.* That those only should be appointed to be pastors or shepherds in God's church, that "have been taught to keep cattle from their youth," or that have had an education for that purpose. Those ministers who would break over these limits, and make a practice of it, would break down that fence which they themselves, after they have been wearied with the ill consequences, would be glad to have somebody else build up for them. Not but that there may probably be some persons in the land, who have had no education at college, that are in themselves better qualified for the work of the ministry, than some others who have taken their degrees, and are now ordained. But yet I believe the breaking over those bounds which have hitherto been set, in ordaining such persons, would in its consequences be a greater calamity than the missing such persons in the work of the ministry. Opening a door for the admission of unlearned men to the work of the ministry, though they should be persons of extraordinary experience, would on some accounts be especially prejudicial at such a day as this; because such persons, for want of extensive knowledge, are oftentimes forward to lead others into those things which a people are in danger of at such a time, above all others; *viz.* impulses, vain imaginations, superstition, indiscreet zeal, and such like extremes.

Another erroneous principle that some have been, at least, in danger of, is, that ministers, because they speak as Christ's ambassadors, may assume the same style, and speak as with the same authority, that the prophets of old did, yea that Jesus Christ himself did in the 23d of Matthew, "Ye serpents, ye generation of vipers," &c.; and that not only when they are speaking to the people, but also to their brethren in the ministry. The principle is absurd, because it makes no difference in the degrees and orders of messengers, though God has made a very great difference; for though they all come in some respect in the name of God, and with something of his authority, yet certainly there is a vast difference in the *degree* of authority with which God has invested them. Jesus Christ was sent into the world as God's messenger, and so was one of his apostles; and so also is an ordinary pastor of a church: but yet it does not follow, that because Jesus Christ and an ordinary minister are both messengers of God, that therefore an ordinary minister, in his office, is vested with an equal degree of authority that Christ was in his. As there is a great difference in their authority, and as Christ came as God's messenger in a vastly higher manner, so another style became him, more authoritative than is proper for us worms of the dust, though we also are messengers of inferior degree. It would be strange if God, when he has made so great a difference in the degree in which he has invested different messengers with his authority, should make no difference as to the outward appearance and show of authority. Though God has put great honour upon ministers, and they may speak as his ambassadors, yet he never intended that they should have the same outward appearance of authority and majesty, either in their behaviour or speech, as his Son shall have, when he comes to judgment at the last day; though both come in the name of the Lord. Alas! can it enter into the hearts of worms of the dust, that it is fit and suitable it should be so?

SECT. III.

A third cause of errors in conduct, is, being ignorant or unobservant of some things, by which the devil has special advantage.

AND here I would particularly notice some things with respect to the *inward experiences* of Christians themselves. And something with regard to the *external effects* of experiences.

I. *Inward experiences.* There are *three* things I would notice with regard to the *experiences* of Christians, by which the devil has many advantages against us.

1. The first thing is the *mixture* there oftentimes is in the experiences of true Christians; whereby when they have truly gracious experiences, and divine and spiritual discoveries and exercises, they have something else mixed with them, besides what is spiritual. There is a mixture of that which is natural, and that which is corrupt, with that which is divine. The great imperfection of grace, the feebleness and infancy of the new nature, and the great remains of corruption, together with our circumstances in this world, where we are encompassed with what tends to pollute us, expose to this. And indeed it is not to be supposed that Christians ever have any experiences in this world that are wholly pure, entirely spiritual, without any mixture of what is natural and carnal. The beam of light, as it comes from the fountain of light upon our hearts, is pure; but, as it is reflected thence, it is mixt. The seed as sent from heaven, and planted in the heart, is pure; but, as it springs up out of the heart, is impure: yea, there is commonly a much greater mixture than persons for the most part seem to imagine. I have often thought that the experiences of true Christians are very frequently as it is with some sorts of fruits, which are enveloped in several coverings of thick shells or pods, that are thrown away by him that gathers the fruit, and but a very small part of the whole bulk is the pure kernel that is good to eat.

The things, of all which there is frequently some mixture with gracious experiences, yea with very great and high experiences, are these three; *human or natural affection and passions; impressions on the imagination;* and a degree of *self-righteousness* or *spiritual pride.* There is very often with that which is spiritual a great mixture of that affection or passion which arises from natural principles; so that nature has a very great hand in those vehement motions and flights of the *passions* that appear. Hence the same degrees of divine communications from heaven shall have vastly different effects, in what outwardly appears, in persons of different natural tempers. The great mixture of that which is natural with that which is spiritual, is very manifest in the peculiar effects that divine influences have in some certain families, or persons of such a blood, in distinguishing the operations of the passions and affections, and the manner of their outward expressions. I know some remarkable instances of this. The same is also evident by the different effects of divine communications on the same person at different times, and in different circumstances. The novelty of things, or the sudden transition from an opposite extreme, and many other things that might be mentioned, greatly contribute to the raising of the passions. And sometimes there is not only a mixture of that which is common and natural with gracious experience, but even that which is animal, what is in a great measure from the body, and is properly the result of the animal frame. In what true Christians feel of affections towards God, all is not always purely holy and divine; every thing that is felt in the affections does not arise from spiritual principles, but common and natural principles have a very great hand; an improper self-love may have a great share in the effect: God is not loved for his own sake, or for the excellency and beauty of his own perfections, as he ought to be; nor have these things in any wise that proportion in the effect that they ought to have. So, in the love true Christians have one to another, very often there is a great mixture of what arises from common and natural principles, with grace. Self-love has a great hand; the children of God are not loved purely for Christ's sake, but there may be a great mixture of that natural love which many sects of heretics have boasted of, who have been greatly united one to another, because they were of their company, on their side, against the rest of the world; yea, there may be a mixture of natural love to the opposite sex, with christian and divine love. So there may be a great mixture in that sorrow for sin which the godly have, and also in their joys; natural principles may greatly contribute to what is felt, a great many ways, as might easily be shown. There is nothing that belongs to christian experience more liable to a corrupt mixture than zeal. Though it be an excellent virtue, a heavenly flame, when it is pure; yet as it is exercised in those who are so little sanctified, and so little humbled, as we are in the present state, it is very apt to be mixed with human passion, yea with corrupt, hateful affections, pride and uncharitable bitterness, and other things that are not from heaven, but from hell.

Another thing often mixed with what is spiritual in the experiences of Christians, is an impression on the *imagination;* whereby godly persons, together with a spiritual understanding of divine things, and conviction of their reality and certainty, and a deep sense of their excellency or great importance upon their hearts, have strongly impressed on their minds external ideas or images of things. A degree of imagination in such a case, is unavoidable, and necessarily arises from human nature, as constituted in the present state; and often is of great benefit; but, when it is in too great a degree, it becomes an impure mixture that is prejudicial. This mixture very often arises from the constitution of the body. It commonly greatly contributes to the other kind of mixture mentioned before, *viz.* of natural affections and passions; it helps to raise them to a great height.

Another thing that is often mixed with the experiences of true Christians, which is the worst mixture of all, is a degree of self-righteousness or spiritual pride. This is often mixed with the joys of Christians. Their joy is not purely the joy of faith, or a rejoicing in Christ Jesus, but is partly a rejoicing in themselves. There is oftentimes in their elevations a looking upon themselves, and a viewing their own high attainments; they rejoice partly because they are taken with their own experiences and great discoveries, which makes them in their own apprehensions so to excel; and this heightens all their passions, and especially those effects that are more external. There is a much greater mixture of these things in the experiences of some Christians than others; in some the mixture is so great, as very much to obscure and hide the beauty of grace in them, like a thick smoke that hinders all the shining of the fire.

These things we ought to be well aware of, that we may not take all for gold that glisters, and that we may know what to countenance and encourage, and what to discourage; otherwise Satan will have a vast advantage against us, for he works in the corrupt mixture. Sometimes, for want of persons distinguishing the ore from the pure metal, those experiences are most admired by the persons themselves and by others, that are not the most excellent. The great external effects, and vehemence of the passions, and violent agitations of the animal spirits, is sometimes much owing to the corrupt mixture, (as is very apparent in some instances,) though it be not always so. I have observed a great difference among those of high affections, who seem disposed to be earnestly talking to those about them. Some insist much more, in their talk, on what they behold in God and Christ, the glory of the divine perfections, Christ's beauty and excellency, and wonderful condescension and grace, and their own unworthiness, and the great and infinite obligations that they themselves and others are under to love and serve God; others insist almost wholly on their own high privileges, their assurance of God's love and favour, and the weakness and wickedness of opposers, and how much they are above their reach. The latter may have much of the presence of God, but their experiences do not appear to be so solid and unmixed as the former. And there is a great deal of difference in persons' earnestness in their talk and behaviour. In some it seems to come from the fulness of their hearts, and from the great sense they have of truth. They have a deep sense of the certainty and infinite greatness, excellency, and importance of divine and eternal things, attended with all appearances of great humility

In others their earnestness seems to arise from a great mixture of human passion, and an undue and intemperate agitation of the spirits, which appears by their earnestness and vehemence not being proportioned to the nature of the subject they insist on, but they are violent in every thing they say, as much when they are talking of things of smaller importance, as when speaking of things of greater weight. I have seen it thus in an instance or two, in which this vehemence at length issued in distraction. And there have been some few instances of a more extraordinary nature still, even of persons finding themselves disposed earnestly to talk and cry out, from an unaccountable kind of bodily pressure, without any extraordinary view of any thing in their minds, or sense of any thing upon their hearts; wherein probably there was the immediate hand of the devil.

2. Another thing, by which the devil has great advantage, is the unheeded *defects* there sometimes are in the experiences of true Christians, connected with those high affections wherein there is much that is truly good. I do not mean that defect or imperfection of degree which is in every holy disposition and exercise in this life, in the best of the saints; but I aim at experiences being especially defective in some particular thing that ought to be in them; which, though it be not an essential defect, or such as is in the experiences of hypocrites, which renders them utterly vain, monstrous, and altogether abominable to God, is such as maims and deforms the experience. The essence of truly christian experiences is not wanting, but that is wanting which is very needful in order to the proper beauty of the image of Christ in such a person's experiences. Things are very much out of a due proportion; there is indeed much of some things, but at the same time there is so little of some other things that should bear a proportion, that the defect very much deforms the Christian, and is truly odious in the sight of God. What I observed before was something *too much*, something mixed, not belonging to the Christian as such; what I speak of now is something *not enough*, something wanting that does belong to the Christian as such. The one deforms the Christian as a monstrous excrescence; by the other the new creature is maimed, some member in a great measure is wanting, or so small and withering as to be very much out of due proportion. This is another spiritual calamity that the saints are liable to through the great imperfection of grace in this life. Thus the chicken in the egg, in the beginning of its formation, has indeed the rudiments or lineaments of all the parts; yet some few parts only are plainly seen, when others are hid, so that without a microscope it appears very monstrous. When this deficiency and disproportion is great, as sometimes it is in real saints, it is not only a great deformity in itself, but has many ill consequences; it gives the devil great advantage, leaves a door open for corruption, exposes to very deformed and unlovely actions, and issues oftentimes in the great wounding of the soul.

For the better understanding of this matter, we may observe, that God, in the revelation that he has made of himself to the world by Jesus Christ, has taken care to give a proportionable manifestation of two kinds of excellencies or perfections of his nature, *viz.* those that especially tend to possess us with awe and reverence, and to search and humble us; and those that tend to win, to draw, and encourage us. By *the one*, he appears as an infinitely great, pure, holy, and heart-searching judge; by *the other*, as a gentle and gracious father and a loving friend. By the one, he is a pure, searching, and burning flame; by the other, a sweet, refreshing light. These two kinds of attributes are as it were admirably tempered together in the revelation of the gospel. There is a proportionable manifestation of justice and mercy, holiness and grace, majesty and gentleness, authority and condescension. God hath thus ordered that his diverse excellencies, as he reveals himself in the face of Jesus Christ, should have a proportionable manifestation, herein providing for our necessities. He knew it to be of great consequence that our apprehensions of these diverse perfections of his nature should be duly proportioned one to another. A defect on the one hand, *viz.* having a discovery of his love and grace, without a proportionable discovery of his awful majesty, his holy and searching purity, would tend to spiritual pride, carnal confidence, and presumption; and a defect on the other hand, *viz.* having a discovery of his holy majesty, without a proportionable discovery of his grace, tends to unbelief, a sinful fearfulness and spirit of bondage. And therefore herein chiefly consists that deficiency of experiences that I am now speaking of. The revelation God has made of himself in his word, and the provision made for our spiritual welfare in the gospel, are perfect; but the actual light and communications we have, are many ways exceeding imperfect and maimed. And experience plainly shows, that Christians may have high manifestations in some respects, and yet their circumstances may be unhappy in this regard, that their discoveries are no more general. There is a great difference among Christians in this respect: some have much more general discoveries than others, who are upon many accounts the most amiable Christians. Christians may have experiences that are very high, and yet there may be very much of this deficiency and disproportion. Their high experiences are truly from the Spirit of God, but sin comes in by the defect, (as indeed all sin is originally from a defective, privative cause,) and in such a case high discoveries, at the same time that they are enjoyed, may be and sometimes are the occasion, or *causa sine qua non*, of sin. Sin may come in at the back door, the gap that is left open; as spiritual pride often does. And many times the Spirit of God is quenched by this means, and God punishes the pride and presumption that rises, by bringing such darkness, and suffering such awful consequences and horrid temptations, as are enough to make one's hair stand on end to hear them.—Christians therefore should diligently observe their own hearts as to this matter, and should pray to God that he would give them experiences in which one thing may bear a proportion to another, that God may be honoured and their souls edified thereby; and ministers should have an eye to this, in their private dealings with the souls of their people.

It is chiefly from such a defect of experiences that some things have arisen which have been pretty common among true Christians of late, though supposed by many to have risen from a good cause; as particularly, talking of divine and heavenly things, and expressing divine joys, with laughter or light behaviour. I believe in many instances such things have arisen from a good cause, as their *causa sine qua non*. High discoveries and gracious joyful affections have been the *occasion* of them; but the proper *cause* has been sin, even that odious defect in their experience, whereby there has been wanting a sense of the awful and holy majesty of God as present with them, and their nothingness and vileness before him, proportionable to the sense they have had of God's grace and the love of Christ. And the same is true in many cases of unsuitable boldness; a disposition to speak with authority, intemperate zeal, and many other things that sometimes appear under great religious affections. And sometimes the vehemence of the motion of the animal spirits, under great affections, is owing in considerable measure to experiences being thus partial. I have known it in several instances, that persons have been greatly affected with the dying love of Christ, and the consideration of the happiness of the enjoyment of him in heaven, and other things of that nature, and their animal spirits at the same time have been in great emotion; but in the midst of it they have had such a deep sense of the awful, holy majesty of God, as at once composed them, and quieted animal nature, without diminishing their comfort, but only has made it of a better and more solid nature. When they have had a sense both of the majesty and grace of God, one thing has as it were balanced another, and caused a more happy sedateness and composure of body and mind.

From these things we may learn how to judge of experiences, and to estimate their goodness. Those are not always the best which are attended with the most violent affections, and most vehement motions of the animal spirits, or have the greatest effects on the body. Nor are they always the best, that most dispose persons to abound in talk to others, and to speak in the most vehement manner, though these things often arise from the greatness of spiritual experiences. But those are the most excellent experiences that are qualified as follows: 1. That have the *least mixture*, or are the most purely spiritual. 2. That are the *least deficient* and partial, in which the diverse things that appertain to christian experience are proportionable one to another. And, 3. That are raised to the *highest degree*. It is no matter how high they are raised if they are qualified as before mentioned, the higher the better. Experiences, thus qualified, will be attended with the most amiable behaviour, will bring forth the most solid and sweet fruits, will be the most durable, and will have the greatest effect on the abiding temper of the soul.

If God is pleased to carry on this work, and it should prove to be the dawning of a general revival of the christian church, it may be expected that the time will come before long, when the experiences of Christians shall be much more generally thus qualified. We must expect green fruits before we have ripe ones. It is probable that hereafter the discoveries which the saints shall have of divine things, will be in a much higher degree than yet have been; but yet shall be so ordered of an infinitely wise and all-sufficient God, that they shall not have so great an effect, in proportion, on the body, and will be less oppressive to nature. The outward manifestations will rather be like those that were in *Stephen*, when he was full of the Holy Ghost, when "all that sat in the council, looking stedfastly on him, saw his face as it had been the face of an angel." Their inward fulness of the Spirit of God, in his divine, amiable, and sweet influences, shall as it were shine forth in a heavenly aspect, and the manner of speech and behaviour.—But,

3. There is another thing concerning the experiences of Christians, of which it is of yet greater importance that we should be aware, than of the preceding, and that is the *degenerating of experiences*. What I mean is something diverse from the mere decay of experiences, or their gradually vanishing, by persons losing their sense of things; *viz.* experiences growing by degrees worse and worse in their kind, more and more partial and deficient; in which things are more out of due proportion, and also have more and more of a corrupt mixture; the spiritual part decreases, and the other useless and hurtful parts greatly increase. This I have seen in very many instances; and great are the mischiefs that have risen through want of being more aware of it.

There is commonly, as I observed before, in high experiences, besides that which is spiritual, a mixture of three things, *viz.* natural or common affections, workings of the imagination, and a degree of self-righteousness or spiritual pride. Now it often comes to pass, that through persons not distinguishing the wheat from the chaff, and for want of watchfulness and humble jealousy of themselves—and by laying great weight on the natural and imaginary part, yielding to it, and indulging it, whereby that part grows and increases, and the spiritual part decreases—the devil sets in, and works in the corrupt part, and cherishes it to his utmost. At length the experiences of some persons, who began well, come to little else but violent motions of carnal affections, with great heats of the imagination, a great degree of enthusiasm and swelling of spiritual pride: very much like some fruits which bud, blossom, and kernel well, but afterwards are blasted with an excess of moisture; so that though the bulk is monstrously great, yet there is little else in it but what is useless and unwholesome. It appears to me very probable, that many of the heresies that have arisen, and sects that have appeared in the christian world, in one age and another, with wild enthusiastic notions and practices, began at first by this means, that it was such a degenerating of experiences which first gave rise to them, or at least led the way to them.—Nothing in the world so much exposes to this, as an unheeded spiritual pride and self-confidence, and persons being conceited of their own stock, without an humble, daily, and continual dependence on God. And this very thing seems to be typified of old, by the corrupting of the *manna*. Some of the children of *Israel*, because they had gathered a store of *manna*, trusted in it; there being, as they apprehended, sufficient in the store they had gathered and laid up, without humbly looking to heaven, and stooping to the earth, for daily supplies; and the consequence was, that their *manna* bred worms and stank, Exod. xvi. 20. Pride above all things promotes this degeneracy of experiences, because it grieves and quenches the Spirit of the Lamb of God; and so it kills the spiritual part, cherishes the natural part, inflames the carnal affections, and heats the imagination.—The unhappy subject of such a degeneracy, for the most part, is not sensible of his own calamity; but because he finds himself still violently moved, has greater heats of zeal, and more vehement motions of his animal spirits, thinks himself fuller of the Spirit of God than ever. But indeed it is with him, as the apostle says of the *Galatians*, Gal. iii. 3. "Having begun in the Spirit, they are made perfect by the flesh."

By the mixture there is of *common* affection with love to God, the love of true Christians is liable to degenerate, and to be more and more built on a supposition of being his high and peculiar favourites, and less and less on an apprehension of the excellency of God's nature as he is in himself. So the joy of Christians, by reason of the mixture there is with spiritual joy, is liable to degenerate, and to become little else but joy in self, joy in a person's own supposed eminency, and distinction from others in the favour of God. So zeal, that at first might be in great part spiritual, yet, in a long continuance of opposition and controversy, may degenerate more and more into human and proud passion, and may come to bitterness, and even a degree of hatred. And so love to the brethren may by degrees come to little else but fondness, and zeal for a party; yea, through a mixture of a natural love to the opposite sex, may degenerate more and more, till it issues in that which is criminal and gross. And I leave it with those who are better acquainted with ecclesiastical history, to inquire whether such a degeneracy of affections as this, might not be the first thing that led the way, and gave occasion to the rise, of the abominable notions of some sects that have arisen, concerning the community of women. However that is, yet certainly the mutual embraces and kisses of persons of different sexes, under the notion of christian love and holy kisses, are utterly to be disallowed and abominated, as having the most direct tendency quickly to turn Christian love into unclean and brutish lust, which will not be the better, but ten times the worse, for being christened by the name of *christian love*. I should also think it advisable, that meetings of young people, of both sexes, in the evening, by themselves, without a minister, or any elder people amongst them, for religious exercises, should be avoided. For though for the present, while their minds are greatly solemn with lively impressions, and a deep sense of divine things, there may appear no ill consequence; yet we must look to the further end of things, and guard against future dangers, and advantages that Satan might gain against us. As a lively, solemn sense of divine things on the minds of young persons may gradually decay, so there will be danger that an ill improvement of these meetings may gradually prevail; if not in any unsuitable behaviour while together in the meeting, yet, when they break up to go home, they may naturally consort together in couples, for other than religious purposes; and it may at last so terminate, that young persons may go to such meetings, chiefly for the sake of such an opportunity for company-keeping.

The *defect* there sometimes is in the experiences of Christians exposes them to degenerate, as well as the mixture that they have. Deficient maimed experiences do sometimes become more and more so. The mind being wholly intent upon those things that are in view, and those that are most wanting being neglected, there is less and less of them, and so the gap for corruption to come in grows wider and wider. And commonly both these causes operate together.—We had need to be *jealous over ourselves with a godly jealousy*, as the apostle was over the christian *Corinthians*, *lest by any means, as the serpent beguiled Eve through his subtilty, so our minds should be corrupted from the simplicity that is in Christ.* God indeed will never suffer his true saints totally and finally to fall away, but yet may punish their pride and self-confidence, by suffering them to be long led into a dreadful wilderness, by the subtle serpent, to the great wounding of their own souls and the interest of religion.

Before I dismiss this head of the degenerating of experiences, I would mention one thing more that tends to it; and that is, persons aiming in their experience to go beyond the rule of God's word, *i. e.* aiming at that *which is indeed*, in some respect, beyond the rule. Thus some persons have endeavoured utterly to root out and abolish all natural affection, or any special affection or respect to their near relations, under a notion that no other love ought to be allowed but spiritual love, and that all other love is to be abolished as carnal, and that it becomes Christians to love none upon the account of any thing else but the image of God; and that therefore love should go out to one and another only in that proportion in which the image of God is seen in them. They might as well argue that a man ought utterly to disallow of, and endeavour to abolish, all love or appetite to his daily food, under a notion that it is a carnal appetite, and that no other appetite should be tolerated but spiritual appetites. Why should the saints strive after that, as a high attainment in holiness, which the apostle in Rom. i. 31. mentions as one instance wherein the heathen had got to the most horrid pass in wickedness, *viz. being without natural affection?* Some have doubted whether they might pray for the conversion and salvation of the souls of their children, any more than for the souls of others; because the salvation of the souls of others would be as much to God's glory, as the salvation of their children; and they have supposed that to pray most for their own, would show a selfish disposition. So they have been afraid to tolerate a compassionate grief and concern for their nearest friends, for fear it would be an argument of want of resignation to God.—It is true, there is great danger of persons setting their hearts too much upon their earthly friends; our love to earthly friends ought to be under the government of the love of God, and should be attended with a spirit of submission and resignation to his will, and every thing should be subordinated to his glory. But that is no argument that these affections should be entirely abolished. The Creator of the world has put them in us, for the good of mankind, and because he saw they would be needful for them, as they must be united in society in the present state, and are of great use when kept in their proper place; and to endeavour totally to root them out, would be to reproach and oppose the wisdom of the Creator. Nor is the being of these natural inclinations, if well regulated, inconsistent with any part of our duty to God, or any argument of a sinful selfishness, any more than our natural abhorrence of pain, and the natural inclination to ease that was in the man Christ Jesus himself.

It is the duty of parents to be more concerned and to pray more for the salvation of their children, than for the children of their neighbours; as it is the duty of a minister to be more concerned for the salvation of the souls of his flock, and to pray more for them, than those of other congregations, because they are committed to his care. So our near friends are more committed to our care than others, and our near neighbours, than those that live at a great distance; and the people of our land and nation are more, in some sense, committed to our care than the people of *China*, and we ought to pray more for them, and to be more concerned that the kingdom of Christ should flourish among them, than in another country, where it would be as much, and no more, for the glory of God. Compassion ought to be especially exercised towards friends, Job vi. 14. Christ did not frown upon a special affection and compassion for near friends; but rather countenanced and encouraged it, from time to time, in those who, in the exercise of such an affection and compassion, applied to him for relief for their friends; as in the instances of the woman of *Canaan, Jairus, Mary* and *Martha*, the centurion, the widow of *Nain*, and many others. The apostle *Paul*, though as much resigned and devoted to God, and under the power of his love, perhaps, as any mere man that ever lived, had a peculiar concern for his countrymen the *Jews*, the rather on that account, that they were his *brethren and kinsmen according to the flesh*. He had a very high degree of compassionate grief for them, insomuch that he tells us he had great heaviness and continual sorrow of heart for them, and could wish himself accursed from Christ for them.—Many things are proper for the saints in heaven, which are not suitable to our state in this world: and for Christians, in these and other instances, to affect to go beyond the present state of mankind, and what God has appointed as fit for it, is an instance of that which the wise man calls *being righteous overmuch*, and has a tendency to open a door for Satan, and to cause religious affections to degenerate into something very unbecoming Christians.—Thus I have, as I proposed, taken notice of some things with regard to the inward experiences of Christians, by which *Satan* has an advantage. I now proceed,

II. To take notice of something with regard to the *external effects* of experiences, which also gives *Satan* an advantage. What I refer to, is the secret and unaccountable influence that custom has upon persons, with respect to the external effects and manifestations of the inward affections of the mind. By custom I mean, both a person's being accustomed to a thing in himself, in his own common, allowed, and indulged practice; and also the countenance and approbation of others amongst whom he dwells, by their general voice and practice. It is well known, and appears sufficiently by what I have said already in this treatise and elsewhere, that I am far from ascribing all the late uncommon effects and outward manifestations of inward experiences to custom and fashion, as some do; I know it to be otherwise, if it be possible for me to know any thing of this nature by the most critical observation, under all manner of opportunities of observing. But yet this also is exceeding evident by experience, that custom has a strange influence in these things. I know it by the different manners and degrees of external effects and manifestations of great affections and high discoveries, in different towns, according to what persons are gradually led into, and to which they are insensibly habituated, by example and custom; and also in the same place, at different times, according to their conduct. If some person conducts them, that much countenances and encourages such kind of outward manifestations of great affections, they naturally and insensibly prevail, and grow by degrees unavoidable; but, when afterwards they come under another kind of conduct, the manner of external appearances will strangely alter. And yet it seems to be without any proper design or contrivance of those in whom there is this alteration; it is not properly affected by them, but the influence of example and custom is secret and insensible to the persons themselves. These things have a vast influence in the manner of persons manifesting their joys, whether with smiles and an air of lightness, or whether with more solemnity and reverence; and so they have a great influence as to the dispositions persons have under high affections to abound in talk; and also as to the manner of their speaking, the loudness and vehemence of their speech. It would, however, be exceeding unjust, and against all the evidence of fact and experience, and the reason of things, to ascribe to custom all dispositions to be much in speaking to others, and to speak in a very earnest manner. It is manifest that example and custom has some way or other, a secret and unsearchable influence on those actions that are involuntary, in different places, and in the same places at different times.

It would be very unreasonable, and prejudicial to the interest of religion, to frown upon all these extraordinary external effects and manifestations of great religious affections.—A measure of them is natural, necessary, and beautiful, and the effect in no wise disproportioned to the spiritual cause, and is of great benefit to promote religion. Yet I think they greatly err who suppose that these things should be wholly unlimited, and that all should be encouraged in going to the utmost length that they feel themselves inclined to. There ought to be a general restraint upon these things, and there should be a prudent care taken of persons in such extraordinary circumstances. They should be moderately advised at proper seasons, not to make more ado than there is need of, but rather to hold a restraint upon their inclinations; otherwise extraordinary outward effects will grow upon them, they will be more and more natural and unavoidable, and the extraordinary outward show will increase, without any increase of the internal cause. Persons will find themselves under a kind of necessity of making a great ado, with less and less affection of soul, till at length almost any slight emotion will set them going; and they will be more and more violent and boisterous, and will grow louder and louder, till their actions and behaviour become indeed very absurd. These things experience proves. Thus I have taken notice of the more general causes whence the errors that have attended this great revival of religion have risen, and under each head have observed some particular errors that have flowed from these fountains.

SECT. IV.

Some particular errors that have risen from several of the preceding causes—Censuring others.

In some cases perhaps they have been chiefly owing to one, and in others to another, and in others to the influence of several, or all conjunctly. And here the first thing I would take notice of is, censuring professing Christians of good standing in the visible church, as unconverted. I need not repeat what I have elsewhere said to show this to be against the plain, frequent, and strict prohibitions of the word of God. It is the worst disease that has attended this work, most contrary to the spirit and rules of Christianity, and of the worst consequences.—There is a most unhappy tincture that the minds of many, both ministers and people, have received that way. The manner of many has been, when they first enter into conversation with any person that seems to make any pretences to religion, to fix a judgment of him, from his manner of talking of religious things, whether he be converted, or experimentally acquainted with vital piety, or not; and then to treat him accordingly, and freely to express their thoughts of him to others, especially those of whom they have a good opinion, as true Christians, and accepted as brethren and companions in Christ. Or if they do not declare their minds expressly, yet by their manner of speaking of them, at least to their friends, they will show plainly what their thoughts are. So, when they have heard any minister pray or preach, their first work has been to observe him on a design of discerning him, whether he be a converted man or no; whether he prays like one that feels the saving power of God's Spirit in his heart, and whether he preaches like one that knows what he says. It has been so much the way in some places, that many new converts do not know but it is their duty to do so, they know no other way. And when once persons yield to such a notion, and give in to such a humour, they will quickly grow very discerning in their own apprehension, and think they can easily tell a hypocrite. And when once they have passed their censure, every thing seems to confirm it; they see more and more in the person they have censured, that seems to them to show plainly that he is an unconverted man. And then, if the person censured be a minister, every thing in his public performances seems dead and sapless, and to do them no good at all, but on the contrary to be of a deadening influence, and poisonous to the soul; yea, it seems worse and worse to them, his preaching grows more and more intolerable. Which is owing to a secret, strong prejudice, that steals in more and more upon the mind, as experience plainly and certainly shows. When the Spirit of God was wonderfully poured out in this place more than seven years ago, and near thirty souls in a week, take one with another, for five or six weeks together, were to appearance brought home to Christ, and all the town seemed to be alive and full of God, there was no such notion or humour prevailing here. When ministers preached here, as very many did at that time, young and old, our people did not go about to discern whether they were men of experience or not; they did not know that they must. Mr. Stoddard never brought them up in that way; it did not seem natural to them to go about any thing of that nature, nor did any such thing enter into their hearts; but, when any minister preached, the business of every one was to listen and attend to what he said, and apply it to his own heart, and make the utmost improvement of it. And it is remarkable, that never did there appear such a disposition in the people to relish, approve of, and admire ministers' preaching as at that time. Such expressions as these were frequent in the mouths of one and another, on occasion of the preaching of strangers here, *viz. That they rejoiced there were so many such eminent ministers in the country; and they wondered they never heard the fame of them before. They were thankful that other towns had so good means;* and the like. And scarcely ever did any minister preach here, but his preaching did some remarkable service; as I had good opportunity to know, because at that time I had particular acquaintance with most of the persons in the town, in their soul-concerns. That it has been so much otherwise of late in many places in the land is another instance of the secret and powerful influence of custom and example.

There has been an unhappy disposition in some ministers toward their brethren in the ministry in this respect, which has encouraged and greatly promoted such a spirit among some of their people. A wrong improvement has been made of Christ's scourging the buyers and sellers out of the temple. It has been expected by some, that Christ was now about thus to purge his house of unconverted ministers; and this has made it more natural to them to think that they should do Christ service, and act as co-workers with him, to put to their hand, and endeavour by all means to cashier those ministers that they thought to be unconverted. Indeed it appears to me probable that the time is coming when awful judgments will be executed on unfaithful ministers, and that no sort of men in the world will be so much exposed to divine judgments. But then we should leave that work to Christ, who is the searcher of hearts, and to whom vengeance belongs; and not, without warrant, take the scourge out of his hand into our own. There has been too much of a disposition in some, as it were, to give ministers over as reprobates, being looked upon as wolves in sheeps' clothing; which has tended to promote and encourage a spirit of bitterness towards them, and to make it natural to treat them too much as if they knew God hated them. If God's children knew that others were reprobates, it would not be required of them to love them; we may hate those that we know God hates; as it is lawful to hate the devil, and as the saints at the day of judgment will hate the wicked.* Some have been too apt to look for fire from heaven upon particular ministers; and this has naturally excited that disposition to call for it, which Christ rebuked in his disciples at *Samaria*. For my part, though I believe no sort of men on earth are so exposed to spiritual judgments as wicked ministers, yet I feel no disposition to treat any minister as if I supposed that he was finally rejected of God; for I cannot but hope that there is coming a day of such great grace, a time so appointed for magnifying the riches and sovereignty of divine mercy, beyond what ever was, that a great number of unconverted ministers will obtain mercy. There were no sort of persons in Christ's time that were so guilty, and so hardened, and towards whom Christ manifested such great indignation, as the priests and scribes; and there were no such persecutors of Christ and his disciples as they. And yet in that great outpouring of the Spirit that began on the day of *Pentecost*, though it began with the common people, yet in the progress of the work, after awhile, "a great company of priests in *Jerusalem* were obedient to the faith," Acts vi. 7. And *Saul*, one of the most violent of all the persecuting *Pharisees*, became afterwards the greatest promoter of the work of God that ever was. I hope we shall yet see in many instances a fulfilment of that in Isa. xxix. 24. "They also that erred in spirit shall come to understanding, and they that murmured shall learn doctrine."

Nothing has been gained by this practice. The end that some have aimed at in it has not been obtained, nor is ever like to be. Possibly some have openly censured ministers, and encouraged their people's uneasiness under them, in hopes that the uneasiness would be so general, and so

* In these expressions our excellent author is not sufficiently guarded.—Our *knowing* or *not knowing* persons to be reprobates, in any sense of that term, is no sufficient *standard* of obligation to hate or to love them, in the way of benevolence. The obligation to love or to hate is founded on the *nature* of the *object*, as good or bad. But here we are liable to err, for want of discriminating between a *person* and his *criminal qualities*. Now every criminal object should be regarded by us a *being* possessed of physical powers; but this existence and these powers, being the product of divine bounty, deserve our benevolent approbation, not our hatred. On the other hand, every criminal object, or agent, is chargeable with criminal *designs* and hateful *qualities* exclusively his own; and these alone deserve our hatred. In no other sense but this latter can it be truly said that God hates the workers of iniquity, wicked men, or even the devil. But if so, in no other sense or degree ought we to hate them. Had our author been scientifically acquainted with that principle which accounts for the true origin of moral evil, he would have seen the impropriety of his statement.—W.

great, that unconverted ministers in general would be cast off, and then things would go on happily. But there is no likelihood of it. The devil indeed has obtained his end; this practice has bred a great deal of unhappiness among ministers and people, has spoiled Christians' enjoyment of Sabbaths, and made them their most uneasy, uncomfortable, and unprofitable days, and has stirred up great contention, and set all in a flame. In one place and another, where there was a glorious work of God's Spirit begun, it has in a great measure knocked all on the head, and their ministers hold their places. Some have aimed at a better end in censuring ministers; they have supposed it to be a likely means to awaken them. Whereas indeed no one thing has had so great a tendency to prevent the awakening of disaffected ministers in general; and no one thing has actually had such influence to lock up the minds of ministers against any good effect of this great work of God in the land. I have known instances of some who seemed to be much moved by the first appearance of this work, but since have seemed to be greatly deadened by what has appeared of this nature. And, if there be one or two instances of ministers who have been awakened by it, there are ten to one on whom it has had a contrary influence. The worst enemies of this work have been inwardly caused by this practice; they have made a shield of it to defend their consciences, and have been glad that it has been carried to so great a length; at the same time that they have looked upon it, and improved it, as a door opened for them to be more bold in opposing the work in general.

There is no such dreadful danger of natural men being undone by our forbearing thus to censure them, and carrying it towards them as visible Christians. It will be no bloody hell-peopling charity, as some seem to suppose, when we only allow them to be worthy of a public charity, on their profession and good external behaviour; any more than *Judas* was in danger of being deceived, by Christ's treating him a long time as a disciple, and sending him forth as an apostle. Christ did not then take it upon him to act as the judge and searcher of hearts, but only as the head of the visible church. Indeed such a charity as this may be abused by some, as every thing is, and will be, that is in its own nature proper, and of never so good tendency. I say nothing against dealing thoroughly with conscience, by the most convincing and searching dispensation of the word of God. I do not desire *that* sword should be sheathed, or gently handled by ministers; but let it be used as a two-edged sword, to pierce, even to the dividing asunder soul and spirit, joints and marrow; let conscience be dealt with, without any compliments; let ministers handle it in flaming fire, without having any more mercy on it, than the furnace has on those metals that are tried in it. But we should let men's persons alone: let the word of God judge them, but let us not take it upon us till we have a warrant for it.

Some have been ready to censure ministers because they seem, in comparison of some other ministers, to be very cold and lifeless in their ministerial performances. But then it should be considered, that, for ought we know, God may hereafter raise up ministers of so much more excellent and heavenly qualifications, and so much more spiritual and divine in their performances, that there may appear as great a difference between them, and those who now seem the most lively, as there is now between them, and others that are called dead and sapless. And those that are now called lively ministers may appear to their hearers, when they compare them with others who shall excel them, as wretchedly mean, and their performances poor, dead, dry things; and many may be ready to be prejudiced against them, as accounting them good for nothing, and, it may be, calling them soul-murderers. What a poor figure may we suppose the most lively of us, and those that are most admired by the people, make in the eyes of one of the saints of heaven, any otherwise than as their deadness, deformity, and rottenness is hid by the veil of Christ's righteousness!

Another thing that has been supposed to be sufficient warrant for openly censuring ministers as unconverted, is their opposing this work of God that has lately been carried on in the land. And there can be no doubt with me but that opposition against this work may be such, as to render either ministers or people truly scandalous, and expose them to public ecclesiastical censure; and that ministers hereby may utterly defeat the design of their ministry, (as I observed before,) and so give their people just cause of uneasiness. I should not think that any person had power to oblige me constantly to attend the ministry of one who did from time to time plainly pray and preach against this work, or speak reproachfully of it frequently in his public performances, after all christian methods had been used for a remedy, and to no purpose.—But to determine how far opposing this work is consistent with a state of grace, is, as experience shows, a very difficult thing: who can tell how far, and for how long time, some persons of good experience in their own souls may proceed, through prejudices they have received from the errors that have been mixed with this work, or through some peculiar disadvantages they are under to behold things in a right view, by reason of the persons they converse with, or their own cold and dead frames? I have seen what abundantly convinces me, that the business is too high for me; I am glad that God has not committed such a difficult affair to me; I can joyfully leave it wholly in his hands, who is infinitely fit for it, without meddling at all with it myself. We may represent it as exceeding dangerous to oppose this work, for this we have good warrant in the word of God; but I know of no necessity we are under to determine whether it be possible for those that are guilty of it to be in a state of grace or no.

God seems so strictly to have forbidden our judging our brethren in the visible church, not only because he knew that we were infinitely too weak, fallible, and blind, to be well capacitated for it, but also because he knew that it was not a work suited to our proud hearts; that it would be setting us vastly too high, and making us too much of lords over our fellow-creatures. Judging our brethren, and passing a condemnatory sentence upon them, seems to carry in it an act of *authority*, especially to sentence them with respect to that state of their hearts, on which depends their liableness to eternal damnation. This is evident by such interrogations as the following, to hear which from God's mouth, is enough to make us shrink into nothing with shame and confusion, under a sense of our own blindness and worthlessness, Rom. xiv. 4. "Who art thou that judgest another man's servant? to his own master he standeth or falleth." And James iv. 12. "There is one lawgiver that is able to save and to destroy; who art thou that judgest another?" Our wise and merciful Shepherd has graciously taken care not to lay in our way such a temptation to pride; he has cut up all such poison out of our pasture; and therefore we should not desire to have it restored. Blessed be his name, that he has not laid such a temptation in the way of my pride! I know that, in order to be fit for this business, I must not only be vastly more knowing, but more humble than I am.—Though I believe some of God's own children have of late been very guilty in this matter, yet, by what is said of it in the Scripture, it appears to me very likely, that God will awfully rebuke that practice. May it in sovereign and infinite mercy be prevented, by the deep and open humiliation of those that have openly practised it!

As this practice ought to be avoided, so should all such open, visible marks of distinction and separation that imply it, (as particularly, distinguishing such as we have judged to be in a converted state with the compellations of *brother* or *sister*,) any further than there is a visible ecclesiastical distinction. In those places where it is the manner to receive such, and such only, to the communion of the visible church, as recommend themselves by giving a satisfying account of their inward experiences, there Christians may openly distinguish such persons, in their speech and ordinary behaviour, with a visible separation, without being inconsistent with themselves. I do not now pretend to meddle with that controversy, whether such an account of experience be requisite to church-fellowship. But certainly, to admit persons to communion with us as brethren in the visible church, and then visibly to reject them, and to make an open distinction between them and others, by different names or appellations, is to be inconsistent with ourselves. It is to make a visible church within a visible church, and visibly to divide between sheep and goats, setting one on the right hand, and the other on the left.—This bitter root of censoriousness must be totally rooted out, as we would prepare the way of the Lord. It has nourished and upheld many other things contrary to the humility, meekness, and love of the gospel. The minds of many have received an unhappy turn, with their religion: there is a certain point or sharpness, a disposition to a kind of warmth, that does not savour of that meek, lamb-like, sweet disposition that becomes Christians. Many have now been so long habituated to it, that they do not know how to get out of it; but we must get out of it; the point and sharpness must be blunted, and we must learn another way of manifesting our zeal for God.

Some have a way of reflecting on others, and censuring them in open prayer; which, though it has a fair show of love, is indeed the boldest way of reproaching others imaginable; because there is implied in it an appeal to the most high God, concerning the truth of their censures and reflections.—And some have a way of joining a sort of imprecations with their petitions for others, though but conditional ones, that appear to me wholly needless and improper. They pray that others may either be converted or removed. I never heard nor read of any such thing practised in the church of God till now, unless it be with respect to some of the most visibly and notoriously abandoned enemies of the church of God. This is a sort of cursing men in our prayers, adding a curse with our blessing; whereas the rule is, *Bless, and curse not*. To pray that God would kill another, is to curse him as *Elisha* cursed the children who came out of *Bethel*. And the case must be very great and extraordinary indeed to warrant it, unless we were prophets, and did not speak our own words, but words indited by the immediate inspiration of the Spirit of God. It is pleaded, that if God has no design of converting others, it is best for them and others, that they should be immediately taken away and sent to hell before they have contracted more guilt. To which I would say, that so it was best for those children who met *Elisha*, seeing God had no design of converting them, to die immediately, as they did; but yet *Elisha's* imprecating that sudden death upon them, was cursing them; and therefore would not have been lawful for one who did not speak in the name of the Lord as a prophet.—And then, if we give way to such things as these, where shall we stop? A child that suspects he has an unconverted father and mother, may pray openly that his father and mother may either be converted, or taken away and sent to hell now quickly, before their guilt is greater. For unconverted parents are as likely to poison the souls of their family in their manner of training them up, as unconverted ministers are to poison their people. And so it might come to be a common thing all over the country, for children to pray after this manner concerning their parents, brethren and sisters concerning one another, husbands concerning their wives, and wives concerning their husbands; and so for persons to pray concerning all their unconverted friends and neighbours. And not only so, but we may also pray concerning all those saints who are not lively Christians, that they may either be enlivened or taken away; if that be true which is often said by some at this day, that these cold dead saints do more hurt than natural men, and lead more souls to hell, and that it would be well for mankind if they were all dead.

How needless are such petitions or imprecations as these! What benefit is there of them? Is it not sufficient for us to pray that God would provide for his church and the good of souls, take care of his own flock, and give it needful means and advantages for its spiritual prosperity? Does God need to be directed by us in what way he shall do it? What need we ask of God to do it by killing such and such persons, if he do not convert them? unless we delight in the thoughts of God's answering us in such terrible ways, and with such awful manifestations of his wrath to our fellow-creatures.—And why do not ministers direct sinners to pray for themselves, that God would either convert them or kill them, and send them to hell now, before their guilt is greater? In this way we should lead persons in the next place to self-murder: for many probably would soon begin to think, that what they may pray for, they may seek by the use of means.

Some, with whom I have discoursed about this way of praying, have said, That the Spirit of God, as it were, forces out such words from their mouths, when otherwise they should not dare to utter them. But such kind of impulse does not look like the influence of the Spirit of God. The Spirit of God indeed sometimes strongly inclines men to utter words; not by putting expressions into the mouth, and urging to utter them, but by filling the heart with a sense of divine things, and holy affections, whence the mouth speaks. That other way of being urged to use certain expressions, by an unaccountable force, is very probably from the influence of the devil.

SECT. V.

Of errors connected with lay-exhorting.

ANOTHER thing, in the management of which there has been much error and misconduct, is lay-exhorting; about which there has been abundance of disputing, jangling, and contention. In the midst of these disputes, I suppose that all are agreed as to these two things, *viz.* 1. That all exhorting one another by lay-men is not unlawful or improper; but, on the contrary, that such exhorting is a christian duty. And, 2. I suppose also, all will allow that there is some kind or way of exhorting and teaching which belongs only to *the office of teachers*. All will allow that God has appointed such an office as that of *teachers* in the christian church, and therefore doubtless will allow that something or other is proper and peculiar to that office, or some business of *teaching* that does not belong as much to others as to them. If there be any way of teaching that is peculiar to that office, then for others to take that upon them, is to invade the office of a minister; which doubtless is very sinful, and is often so represented in Scripture. But the great difficulty is to settle the bounds, and to tell exactly how far lay-men may go, and when they exceed their limits; which is a matter of so much difficulty, that I do not wonder if many in their zeal have transgressed. The two ways of teaching and exhorting, the one of which ought ordinarily to be left to ministers, and the other of which may and ought to be practised by the people, may be expressed by those two names of *preaching*, and *exhorting* in way of *christian conversation*. But then a great deal of difficulty and controversy arises to determine what is *preaching*, and what is *christian conversation*. However, I will humbly offer my thoughts concerning this subject of lay-exhorting, as follows.

I. The common people, in exhorting one another, ought not to clothe themselves with the like authority with that which is proper for ministers. There is a certain authority that ministers have and should exercise in teaching, as well as in governing the flock. Teaching is spoken of in Scripture as an act of authority, 1 Tim. ii. 12. In order to a man's preaching, special authority must be committed to him, Rom. x. 15. "How shall they preach, except they be sent?" Ministers in this work of teaching and exhorting are clothed with authority, as Christ's messengers, Mal. ii. 7. as representing him, and so speaking in his name, and in his stead, 2 Cor. v. 18—20. And it seems to be the most honourable thing that belongs to the office of a minister of the gospel, that to him is committed the word of reconciliation, and that he has power to preach the gospel, as Christ's messenger, and speaking in his name. The apostle seems to speak of it as such, 1 Cor. i. 16, 17. Ministers therefore, in the exercise of this power, may clothe themselves with authority in speaking, or may teach others in an authoritative manner, Tit. ii. 15. "These things speak and exhort, and rebuke with all authority: Let no man despise thee." But the common people, in exhorting one another, ought not thus to exhort in an authoritative manner. There is a great deal of difference between teaching as a *father* amongst a company of children, and counselling in a *brotherly* way, as the children may kindly counsel and admonish one another. Those that are mere brethren ought not to assume authority in exhorting, though one may be better, and have more experience, than another. Lay-men ought not to exhort as though they were the ambassadors or messengers of Christ, as ministers do; nor should they exhort, warn, and charge *in his name*, according to the ordinary import of such an expression, when applied to teaching.—Indeed in one sense, a Christian ought to do every thing he does in religion in the name of Christ, *i. e.* he ought to act in a dependence on him as his head and mediator, and do all for his glory. But the expression, as it is usually understood, when applied to teaching or exhorting, is speaking in Christ's stead, and as having a message from him.

Persons may clothe themselves with authority in speaking, either by the authoritative words they make use of, or in the manner and authoritative air of their speaking. Though some may think that this latter is a matter of indifference, or at least of small importance, yet there is indeed a great deal in it; a person may go much out of his place, and be guilty of a great degree of assuming, in the manner of his speaking those words, which, as they might be spoken, might be proper for him.—The same words, spoken in a different manner, may express what is very diverse. Doubtless there may be as much hurt in the manner of a person's speaking, as there may in his looks; but the wise man tells us, that "an high look is an abomination to the Lord," Prov. xxi. 4. Again, a man may clothe himself with authority, in the circumstances under which he speaks; as for instance, if he sets himself up as a *public teacher*. Here I would have it observed, that I do not suppose that a person is guilty of this, merely because he speaks in the hearing of many. Persons may speak only in a way of conversation, and yet speak in the hearing of a great number, as they often do in their common conversation about temporal things, at feasts and entertainments, where women as well as others converse freely together, in the hearing it may be of a great number, and yet without offence. And if their conversation on such occasions should turn on spiritual things, and they should speak as freely and openly, I do not see why it would not be as harmless. Nor do I think, that besides a great number being present, persons speaking with a very earnest and loud voice, is for them to set up themselves as public teachers, if they do it from no contrivance or premeditated design, or as purposely directing themselves to a congregation or multitude. But persons speaking in conversation, or when all freely converse one with another—directing themselves to none but those that are near them, and fall in their way—in that earnest and pathetic manner, to which the subject naturally leads, and as it were constrains them: I say, that for persons to do thus, though many happen to hear them, does not appear to me to be setting themselves up as public teachers. Yea, suppose all this happens to be in a meeting-house; I do not think that this much alters the case, provided the solemnity of public service and divine ordinances be over; and provided also that they speak in no authoritative way, but in an humble manner, becoming their degree and station, though they speak very earnestly and pathetically.—Indeed modesty might in ordinary cases restrain some persons (as women and those that are young) from so much as speaking when a great number are present, at least, when some of those present are much their superiors, unless they are spoken to. And yet, the case may be so extraordinary as fully to warrant it. If something very extraordinary happens to persons, or if they are in extraordinary circumstances; as if a person be struck with lightning in the midst of a great company, or if he lies a-dying, it appears to none any violation of modesty for him to speak freely before those that are much his superiors. I have seen some women and children in such circumstances, on religious accounts, that it has appeared to me no more a transgressing the laws of humility and modesty for them to speak freely, let who will be present, than if they were in danger of dying.

But then may a man be said to set up himself as a public teacher, when in a set speech, of design, he directs himself to a multitude, as looking that they should compose themselves to attend to what he has to say. And much more when this is a contrived and premeditated thing, without any thing like a constraint by an extraordinary sense or affection; and more still, when meetings are appointed on purpose to hear lay-persons exhort, and they take it as their business to be speakers, while they expect that others should come, and compose themselves, and attend as hearers. When private Christians take it upon them in private meetings to act as the masters or presidents of the assembly, and accordingly from time to time to teach and exhort the rest, this has the appearance of authoritative teaching.

When private Christians, who are no more than mere brethren, exhort and admonish one another, it ought to be in an humble manner, rather by way of entreaty, than with authority; and the more, according as the station of persons is lower. Thus it becomes women, and those that are young, ordinarily to be at a greater distance from any appearance of authority in speaking than others. Thus much at least is evident by 1 Tim. ii. 9, 11, 12. That lay-persons ought not to exhort one another as clothed with authority, is a general rule; but it cannot justly be supposed to extend to heads of families in their own families. Every christian family is a little church, and the heads of it are its authoritative teachers and governors. Nor can it extend to schoolmasters among their scholars; and some other cases might perhaps be mentioned, that ordinary discretion will distinguish, where a man's circumstances do properly clothe him with authority, and render it fit and suitable for him to counsel and admonish others in an authoritative manner.

II. No man but a minister duly appointed to that sacred calling, ought to follow teaching and exhorting *as a calling*, or so as to neglect that which is his *proper calling*. Having the office of a teacher in the church of God implies two things: 1. A being invested with the *authority* of a teacher; and 2. A being called to the *business* of a teacher, to make it the business of his life. Therefore that man who is not a minister, taking either of these upon him, invades the office of a minister. Concerning assuming the authority of a minister I have spoken already. But if a lay-man do not assume authority in his teaching, yet if he forsakes his proper calling, or doth so at least in a great measure, and spends his time in going about from house to house to counsel and exhort, he goes beyond his line, and violates christian rules. Those that have the office of teachers or exhorters, have it for their calling, and should make it their business, as a business proper to their office; and none should make it their business but such, Rom. xii. 3—8. "For I say, through the grace given unto me, to every man that is among you, not to think of himself more highly than he ought to think; but to think soberly, according as God hath dealt to every man the proportion of faith. For as we have many members in one body, and all members have not the same office; so we being many, are one body in Christ.—He that teacheth let him wait on teaching, or he that exhorteth, on exhortation." 1 Cor. xii. 29. "Are all apostles? are all prophets? are all teachers?" 1 Cor. vii. 20. "Let every man abide in the same calling wherein he was called." 1 Thess. iv. 11. "And that ye study to be quiet, and to do your own business, and to work with your own hands, as we commanded you."

It will be a very dangerous thing for lay-men, in either of these respects, to invade the office of a minister. If this be common among us, we shall be in danger of having a stop put to the work of God, of the ark turning aside from us, before it comes to mount *Zion*, and of God making a breach upon us; as of old there was an unhappy stop put to the joy of the congregation of *Israel*, in bringing up the ark of God, because others carried it besides the *Levites*. And therefore *David*, when the error was found out, says, 1 Chron. xv. 2. "None ought to carry the ark of God, but the *Levites* only; for them hath the Lord chosen to carry the ark of God, and to minister unto him for ever." And because one presumed to touch the ark who was not of the sons of *Aaron*, therefore the Lord made a breach upon them, and covered their day of rejoicing with a cloud in his anger.—Before I dismiss this head of lay-exhorting, I would take notice of three things relating to it, upon which there ought to be a restraint.

1. Speaking in the time of the solemn worship of God; as public prayer, singing, or preaching, or administration of the sacrament of the holy supper, or any duty of social worship. This should not be allowed. I know it will

be said, that in some cases, when persons are exceedingly affected, they cannot help it; and I believe so too; but then I also believe, and know by experience, that there are several things which contribute to that inability, besides merely and absolutely the sense of divine things upon their hearts. Custom and example, or the thing being allowed, have such an influence, that they actually help to make it impossible for persons under strong affections to avoid speaking. If it was disallowed, and persons at the time that they were thus disposed to break out, had this apprehension, that it would be very unbecoming for them so to do, it would contribute to their ability to avoid it. Their inability arises from their strong and vehement disposition: and, so far as that disposition is from a good principle, it would be weakened by this thought, *viz.* "What I am going to do, will be for the dishonour of Christ and religion." And so the inward vehemence, that pushed them forward to speak, would fall, and they would be enabled to avoid it. This experience confirms.

2. There ought to be a moderate restraint on the loudness of persons' talking under high affections; for, if there be not, it will grow natural and unavoidable for persons to be louder and louder, without any increase of their inward sense; till it becomes natural to them, at last, to scream and halloo to almost every one they see in the streets, when they are much affected. But this is certainly very improper, and what has no tendency to promote religion. The man Christ Jesus, when he was upon earth, had doubtless as great a sense of the infinite greatness and importance of eternal things, and the worth of souls, as any have now; but there is not the least appearance in his history, of his taking any such course, or manner of exhorting others.

3. There should also be some restraint on the abundance of talk, under strong affections; for, if persons give themselves an unbounded liberty to talk just so much as they feel an inclination to, they will increase and abound more and more in talk, beyond the proportion of their sense or affection; till at length it will become ineffectual on those that hear them, and, by the commonness of their abundant talk, they will defeat their own end.

SECT. VI.

Of errors connected with singing praises to God.

ONE thing more of which I would take notice, before I conclude this part, is the mismanagement of singing praises to God. I believe it to have been one fruit of the extraordinary degrees of the sweet and joyful influence of the Spirit of God, that there has appeared such a disposition to abound in this divine exercise; not only in appointed solemn meetings, but when Christians occasionally meet together at each other's houses. But the mismanagement I have respect to is a way of performing it, without almost any appearance of that reverence and solemnity with which all visible, open acts of divine worship ought to be attended. It may be two or three are in a room singing hymns of praise to God, others talking at the same time, others about their work, with little more appearance of regard to what is doing, than if only singing a common song for their amusement and diversion. There is danger, if such things are continued, that a mere nothing be made of this duty, to the great violation of the third commandment. Let Christians abound as much as they will in this holy, heavenly exercise, in God's house and in their own houses; but, let it be performed as a holy act, wherein they have immediately and visibly to do with God. When any social open act of devotion or solemn worship of God is performed, God should be reverenced as present. As we would not have the ark of God depart from us, nor provoke God to make a breach upon us, we should take heed that we handle the ark with reverence.

With respect to companies singing in the streets, going to or coming from the place of public worship, I would humbly offer my thoughts in the following particulars:

1. The rule of Christ, concerning *putting new wine into old bottles,* does undoubtedly take place in things of this nature, supposing the thing in itself is good, but not essential, and not particularly enjoined or forbidden. For things so very new and uncommon, and of so open and public a nature, to be suddenly introduced and set up and practised in many parts of the country, without the matter being so much as first proposed to any public consideration, or giving any opportunity for the people of God to weigh the matter, or to consider any reasons that might be offered to support it, is putting new wine into old bottles with a witness; as if it were with no other design than to burst them directly. Nothing else can be expected to be the consequence of this than uproar and confusion, great offence, and unhappy mischievous disputes, even among the children of God themselves. Not that what is good in itself, and is new, ought to be forborne, till there is nobody that will like it; but it ought to be forborne till the visible church of God is so prepared for it, at least, that there is a probability it will not do more hurt than good, or hinder the work of God more than promote it; as is more evident from Christ's rule, and the apostles' practice. If it be brought in when the country is so unprepared, that the shock and surprise, the contention and prejudice against religion it is like to occasion, will do more to hinder religion, than the practice is like to promote it, then the fruit is picked before it is ripe. And, indeed, such a hasty endeavour to introduce an innovation, supposing it to be good in itself, is the likeliest way to retard the effectual introduction of it; it will hinder its being extensively introduced, much more than it will promote it, and so will defeat its own end. But,

2. As to the thing itself, if a considerable part of a congregation have occasion to go in company together to a place of public worship, and they should join together in singing praises to God, as they go, I confess, that after long consideration—and endeavouring to view the thing every way with the utmost diligence and impartiality I am capable of—I cannot find any valid objection against it. As to the common objection from Matt. vi. 5. "And when thou prayest, thou shalt not be as the hypocrites are; for they love to pray standing in the synagogues, and in the corners of the streets, that they may be seen of men;" it is strong against a single person singing in the streets, or in the meeting-house by himself, as offering to God personal worship. But as it is brought against a considerable company, their thus publicly worshipping God, appears to me to have no weight at all; it is of no more force against a company's thus praising God in the streets, than against their praising him in the synagogues, or meeting-houses; for the streets and the synagogues are both put together in these words of our Saviour, as parallel in the case. It is evident that Christ speaks of personal, and not public worship. If to sing in the streets be ostentatious, then it must be because it is a public place, and it cannot be done there without being very open; but it is no more public than the synagogue or meeting-house is when full of people. Some worship is in its nature private, as that which is proper to particular persons, or families, or private societies, and has respect to their particular concerns: but that which I now speak of, is performed under no other notion than a part of God's public worship, without any relation to any private, separate society, and in which every visible Christian has equal liberty to join, if it be convenient for him, and he has a disposition, as in the worship that is performed in the meeting-house. When persons are going to the house of public worship, to serve God there with the assembly of his people, they are upon no other design than that of putting public honour upon God; that is the business they go from home upon; and, even in their walking the streets on this errand, they appear in a public act of respect to God; and therefore, if they go in company with public praise, it is not being public when they ought to be private. It is one part of the beauty of public worship, that it be *very public;* the more public it is, the more open honour it puts upon God: and especially is it beautiful in *public praise;* for the very notion of publicly praising God, is to declare abroad his glory, to publish his praise, to make it known, and proclaim it aloud, as is evident by innumerable expressions of Scripture. It is fit that God's honour should not be con-

cealed, but made known in the great congregation, and proclaimed before the sun, and upon the house-tops, before kings and all nations, and that his praises should be heard to the utmost ends of the earth.

I suppose none will condemn singing God's praises, merely because it is performed in the open air; and, if it may be performed by a company in the open air, doubtless they may do it moving, as well as standing still. So the children of *Israel* praised God, when they went to mount *Zion* with the ark of God; and the multitude praised Christ, when they entered with him into *Jerusalem*, a little before his passion. The children of *Israel* were wont, from year to year, to go up to *Jerusalem* in companies, from all parts of the land, three times in the year, when they often used to manifest the engagedness of their minds by travelling all night, and manifested their joy and gladness by singing praises with great decency and beauty, as they went towards God's holy mountain; as is evident by Isa. xxx. 29. " Ye shall have a song as in the night, when a holy solemnity is kept, and gladness of heart, as when one goeth with a pipe to come into the mountain of the Lord, to the mighty One of Israel." And Ps. xlii. 4. " When I remember these things, I pour out my soul in me; for I had gone with the multitude, I went with them to the house of God; with the voice of joy and praise, with a multitude that kept holy-day." Ps. c. 4. " Enter into his gates with thanksgiving, and into his courts with praise." When God's people are going to his house, the occasion is so joyful to a Christian in a lively frame, that the duty of singing praises seems to be peculiarly beautiful on such an occasion. So that if the state of the country were ripe for it, and there should be frequent occasions for a considerable part of a congregation to go together to the places of public worship, and there was in other respects a proportionable appearance of fervency of devotion, it appears to me that it would be ravishingly beautiful, if such things were practised all over the land, and would have a great tendency to enliven, animate, and rejoice the souls of God's saints, and greatly to propagate vital religion. I believe the time is coming when the world will be full of such things.

3. It seems to me to be requisite that there should be the consent of the governing part of the worshipping societies, to which persons have joined themselves, and of which they own themselves a part, in order to the introducing of things in public worship, so new and uncommon, and not essential, nor particularly commanded, into the places where those worshipping societies belong. The peace and union of such societies seems to require it. They have voluntarily united themselves to these worshipping societies, to the end that they might be one in the affairs of God's public worship, and have obliged themselves in covenant to act as brethren, mutual assistants, and members of one body in those affairs. All are hereby naturally and necessarily led to be concerned with one another, in matters of religion and God's worship; and this is a part of the public worship, that must be performed from time to time in the view of the whole, being performed at a time when they are meeting together for mutual assistance in worship, and therefore that which all must unavoidably be in some measure concerned in, at least so as to show their approbation and consent, or open dislike and separation from them in it. Hence charity, and a regard to the union and peace of such societies, seems to require a consent of the governing part, in order to the introducing any thing of this nature. Certainly if we are of the spirit of the apostle *Paul*, and have his discretion, we shall not set up any such practice without it. He, for the sake of peace, conformed in things wherein he was not particularly forbidden, to the *Jews* when among them; and so, when among those that were without the law, he conformed to them wherein he might.——To be sure, those go much beyond proper limits, who, coming from abroad, do immediately of their own heads, in a strange place, set up such a new and uncommon practice among a people.

In introducing any thing of this nature among a people, their minister especially ought to be consulted, and his voice taken, as long as he is owned for their minister. Ministers are pastors of worshipping societies, and their heads and guides in the affairs of public worship. They are called in Scripture, " those that rule over them;" and their people are commanded " to obey them, because they watch for their souls, as those that must give account." If it belongs to these shepherds and rulers to direct and guide the flock in any thing at all, it belongs to them so to do in the circumstantials of their public worship.—Thus I have taken particular notice of many of those things that have appeared to me to be amiss in the management of our religious concerns relating to the present revival of religion, and have taken liberty freely to express my thoughts upon them. Upon the whole it appears manifest to me, that things have as yet never been set a-going in their right channel; if they had, and means had been blessed in proportion as they have been now, this work would have so prevailed, as before this time to have carried all before it, and have triumphed over *New England* as its conquest.

The devil, in driving things to these extremes, besides the present hinderance of the work of God, has, I believe, had in view a twofold mischief, in the issue of things; one, with respect to those that are cold in religion, to carry things to such an extreme in order that people in general, having their eyes opened by the great excess, might be tempted entirely to reject the whole work, as being all nothing but delusion and distraction. And another, with respect to those of God's children who have been very warm and zealous out of the way, to sink them down in unbelief and darkness. The time is coming, I doubt not, when the greater part of them will be convinced of their errors; and then probably the devil will take advantage to lead them into a dreadful wilderness, to puzzle and confound them about their own experiences, and the experiences of others; and to make them to doubt of many things that they ought not, and even to tempt them with atheistical thoughts. I believe, if all true Christians over the land should now at once have their eyes opened fully to see all their errors, it would seem for the present to damp religion. The dark thoughts that it would at first occasion, and the inward doubts, difficulties, and conflicts that would rise in their souls, would deaden their lively affections and joys, and would cause an appearance of a present decay of religion. But yet it would do God's saints great good in their latter end; it would fit them for more spiritual and excellent experiences, more humble and heavenly love, and unmixed joys, and would greatly tend to a more powerful, extensive, and durable prevalence of vital piety. I do not know but we shall be in danger, after our eyes are fully opened to see our errors, to go to contrary extremes. The devil has driven the *pendulum* far beyond its proper point of rest; and when he has carried it to the utmost length that he can, and it begins by its own weight to swing back, he probably will set in, and drive it with the utmost fury the other way; and so give us no rest; and if possible prevent our settling in a proper medium. What a poor, blind, weak, and miserable creature is man, at his best estate! We are like poor helpless sheep; the devil is too subtle for us. What is our strength! What is our wisdom! How ready are we to go astray! How easily are we drawn aside into innumerable snares, while in the mean time we are bold and confident, and doubt not but we are right and safe! We are foolish sheep in the midst of subtle serpents and cruel wolves, and do not know it. Oh how unfit are we to be left to ourselves! And how much do we stand in need of the wisdom, the power, the condescension, patience, forgiveness, and gentleness of our good Shepherd!

PART V.

SHOWING POSITIVELY, WHAT OUGHT TO BE DONE TO PROMOTE THIS WORK.

IN considering means and methods for promoting this glorious work of God, I have already observed, in some instances, wherein there has been needless objecting and complaining; and have also taken notice of many things amiss, that ought to be amended. I now proceed to show positively, what ought to be done, or what courses (according to my humble opinion) ought to be taken to promote this work. The obligations that all are under, with one consent, to do their utmost, and the great danger of neglecting it, were observed before.—I hope that some, upon reading what was said under that head, will be ready to say, What shall we do? To such readers I would now offer my thoughts, in answer to such an inquiry.

SECT. I.

We should endeavour to remove stumbling-blocks.

THAT which I think we ought to set ourselves about, in the first place, is to remove stumbling-blocks. When God is revealed as about to come gloriously to set up his kingdom in the world, this is proclaimed, " Prepare ye the way of the Lord, make straight in the desert a high-way for our God," Isa. xl. 3. And again, Isa. lvii. 14. " Cast ye up, cast ye up; prepare the way; take up the stumbling-block out of the way of my people." And, chap. lxii. 10. " Go through, go through the gates; prepare you the way of the people; cast up, cast up the highway; gather out the stones."

And, in order to this, there must be a great deal done at confessing of faults, on both sides. For undoubtedly many and great are the faults that have been committed, in the jangling and confusions, and mixtures of light and darkness, that have been of late. There is hardly any duty more contrary to our corrupt dispositions, and mortifying to the pride of man; but it must be done. Repentance of faults is, in a peculiar manner, a proper duty, when the kingdom of heaven is at hand, or when we especially expect or desire that it should come; as appears by *John* the *Baptist's* preaching. And if God does now loudly call upon us to repent, then he also calls upon us to make proper manifestations of our repentance. I am persuaded that those who have openly opposed this work, or have from time to time spoken lightly of it, cannot be excused in the sight of God, without openly confessing their fault therein; especially ministers. If they have any way, either directly or indirectly, opposed the work, or have so behaved, in their public performances or private conversation, as to prejudice the minds of their people against the work; if hereafter they shall be convinced of the goodness and divinity of what they have opposed, they ought by no means to palliate the matter, or excuse themselves, and pretend that they always thought so, and that it was only such and such imprudences that they objected against. But they ought openly to declare their conviction, and condemn themselves for what they have done; for it is Christ that they have spoken against, in speaking lightly of and prejudicing others against this work; yea, it is the Holy Ghost. And though they have done it ignorantly and in unbelief, yet, when they find out who it is that they have opposed, undoubtedly God will hold them bound publicly to confess it.

And on the other side, if those who have been zealous to promote the work have in any of the fore-mentioned instances openly gone much out of the way, and done that which is contrary to christian rules, whereby they have openly injured others, or greatly violated good order, and so done that which has wounded religion, they must publicly confess it, and humble themselves; as they would gather out the stones, and prepare the way of God's people. They who have laid great stumbling-blocks in others' way, by their *open transgression*, are bound to remove them by their *open repentance*.

Some probably will be ready to object against this, that the opposers will take advantage by this to behave themselves insolently, and to insult both them and religion. And indeed, to the shame of some, they have taken advantage by such things; as of the good spirit that Mr. *Whitfield* showed in his retractations, and some others. But if there are some imbittered enemies of religion, that stand ready to improve every thing to its disadvantage, yet that ought not to hinder doing an enjoined christian duty; though it be in the manifestation of humility and repentance, after a fault openly committed. To stand it out, in a visible impenitence of a real fault, to avoid such an inconvenience, is to do evil in order to prevent evil. Besides, the danger of evil consequence is much greater on the other side: to commit sin, and then stand in it, is what will give the enemy the greatest advantage. For Christians to act like Christians, in openly humbling themselves when they have openly offended, in the end brings the greatest honour to Christ and religion; and in this way are persons most likely to have God appear for them.

Again, at such a day as this, God especially calls his people to the exercise of extraordinary meekness and mutual forbearance. Christ appears as it were coming in his kingdom, which calls for great moderation in our behaviour towards all men; Phil. iv. 5. " Let your moderation be known unto all men: The Lord is at hand." The awe of the Divine Majesty, that appears present or approaching, should dispose us to it, and deter us from the contrary. For us to be judging one another, and behaving with fierceness and bitterness one towards another, when he who is the searcher of all hearts, to whom we must all give an account, appears so remarkably present, is exceeding unsuitable. Our business at such a time should be at home, searching and condemning ourselves, and taking heed to our own behaviour. If there be glorious prosperity to the church of God approaching, those that are the most meek will have the largest share in it. For, when Christ " rides forth in his glory and his majesty," it is " because of truth, meekness, and righteousness," Psal. xlv. 3, 4. and, when God remarkably " arises to execute judgment," it is " to save all the meek of the earth," Psal. lxxvi. 9. and it is " the meek" that " shall increase their joy in the Lord," Isa. xxix. 19. And, when the time comes that God will give this lower world into the hands of his saints, it is " the meek that shall inherit the earth." Psal. xxxvii. 11. and Matt. v. 9. " But with the froward, God will show himself unsavoury."

Those therefore that have been zealous for this work, and have greatly erred and been injurious with their zeal, ought not to be treated with bitterness. There is abundant reason to think, that most of them are the dear children of God, for whom Christ died; and therefore that they will see their error. As to those things, wherein we see them to be in an error, we have reason to say of them as the apostle, Phil. iii. 15. " If any are otherwise minded, God shall reveal this unto them." Their errors should not be made use of to excite indignation towards them, but should influence all who hope we are the children of God, to humble ourselves, and become more entirely dependent on the Lord Jesus Christ, when we see those who are God's own people so ready to go astray. And those ministers who have been judged, and injuriously dealt with, will do the part of Christ's disciples, not to judge and revile again, but to receive such injuries with meekness and forbearance, and making a good improvement of them, more strictly examining their hearts and ways, and committing themselves to God. This will be the way to have

God vindicate them in his providence, if they belong to him. We have not yet seen the end of things; nor do we know who will be most vindicated, and honoured of God, in the issue. Eccl. vii. 8. "Better is the end of a thing, than the beginning thereof; and the patient in spirit is better than the proud in spirit."—Contrary to this mutual meekness, is each party's stigmatizing one another with odious names, as is done in many parts of *New England;* which tends greatly to widen and perpetuate the breach. Such distinguishing names of reproach do as it were divide us into two armies, separated, and drawn up in battle-array; which greatly hinders the work of God.

And as such an extraordinary time as this does especially require of us the exercise of great forbearance *one towards another;* so there is peculiarly requisite in God's people the exercise of great patience, in waiting *on God,* under any special difficulties and disadvantages they may be under as to the means of grace. The beginning of a revival of religion will naturally and necessarily be attended with a great many difficulties of this nature; many parts of the reviving church will, for a while, be under great disadvantages, by reason of what remains of the old disease, of a general corruption of the visible church. We cannot expect that, after a long time of degeneracy and depravity in the state of things in the church, all should come to rights at once; it must be a work of time. And for God's people to be over-hasty and violent, in such a case, being resolved to have every thing rectified at once, or else forcibly to deliver themselves by breaches and separations, is the way to hinder things coming to rights as they otherwise would. It is the way to keep them back, and to break all in pieces. Indeed the difficulty may be so intolerable as to allow of no delay, and God's people cannot continue in the state wherein they were, without violations of God's absolute commands: but otherwise, though the difficulty may be very great, another course should be taken. God's people should have recourse directly to the throne of grace, to represent their difficulties before the great Shepherd of the sheep, who has the care of all the affairs of his church; and, when they have done, they should wait patiently upon him. If they do so, they may expect that in his time he will appear for their deliverance: but if, instead of that, they are impatient, and take the work into their own hands, they will betray their want of faith, will dishonour God, and have reason to fear that he will leave them to manage their affairs for themselves as well as they can. If they had waited on Christ patiently, continuing still instant in prayer, they might have had him appearing for them, much more effectually to deliver them. *He that believeth shall not make haste.* And it is for those that are found patiently waiting on the Lord, under difficulties, that he will especially appear, when he comes to do great things for his church; as is evident by Isa. xxx. 18. chap. xl. at the latter end, and xlix. 23. and Psal. xxxvii. 9. and many other places.

I have somewhere, not long since, met with an exposition of those words of the spouse, several times repeated in the book of *Canticles, I charge you, O daughters of* Jerusalem, *that ye stir not up, nor awake my love, till he please.* It was the only satisfying exposition that ever I met with, and was to this purpose, *viz.* That when the church of God is under great difficulties, and in distress, and Christ does not appear for her help, but seems to neglect her, as though he were asleep, God's people, or the daughters of *Jerusalem,* in such a case, should not show a hasty spirit, and, not having patience to wait for Christ to awake for their help till his time comes, take indirect courses for their own deliverance, and use violent means for their escape, before Christ appears to open the door for them; and so, as it were, *stir up, and awake Christ,* before his time. When the church is in distress, and God seems not to appear for her in his providence, he is very often represented in Scripture as being asleep; as Christ was asleep in the ship, when the disciples were tossed by the storm, and the ship covered with waves. And God's appearing for his people's help, is represented as his awaking out of sleep, Psal. vii. 6. xxxv. 23. xliv. 23. lix. 4. lxxiii. 20. Christ has an appointed time for his thus awaking out of sleep; and his people ought to wait upon him, and not, in an impatient fit, stir him up before his time. It is worthy to be observed, how strict this charge is given to the daughters of *Jerusalem;* it is repeated three times over in the book of Canticles, chap. ii. 7.—iii. 5.—viii. 4. In the 2d chapter and six first verses, are represented the support Christ gives his church, while she is in a suffering state, *as the lily among thorns.* In the 7th verse is represented her patience in waiting for Christ, to appear for her deliverance, when she charges the daughters of *Jerusalem* not to stir up, nor awake her love till he please, *by the roes, and the hinds of the field;* which are creatures of a gentle, harmless nature. They are not beasts of prey, do not devour one another, do not fight with their enemies, but flee from them; and are of a pleasant loving nature, Prov. v. 19. In the next verse, we see the church's success, in this way of waiting under sufferings, with meekness and patience; Christ soon awakes, speedily appears, and swiftly comes; "The voice of my beloved! Behold, he cometh, leaping upon the mountains, skipping upon the hills!"

SECT. II.

What must be done more directly to advance this work.

What has been mentioned hitherto, has relation to the behaviour we are obliged to, as we would prevent the hinderances of the work; but, besides these, there are things that must be *done,* more directly to advance it. And here it concerns every one, in the first place, to look into his own heart, and see to it that he be a partaker of the benefits of the work himself, and that it be promoted in his own soul. Now is a most glorious opportunity for the good of souls. It is manifestly with respect to a time of great revival of religion in the world, that we have that gracious, earnest, and moving invitation proclaimed in the 55th of Isa. "Ho, every one that thirsteth," &c. as is evident by the foregoing chapter, and what follows in the close of this. In the 6th verse, it is said, "Seek ye the Lord while he may be found, call upon him while he is near." And it is with special reference to such a time, that Christ proclaims as he does, Rev. xxi. 6. "I will give unto him that is athirst, of the fountain of the water of life freely." And chap. xxii. 17. "And the Spirit and the bride say, Come; and let him that heareth say, Come; and let him that is athirst come: and whosoever will, let him take the water of life freely." And it seems to be with reference to such a time, which is typified by the *feast of tabernacles,* that Jesus, at that feast, stood and cried, as we have an account, John vii. 37, 38. "In the last day, that great day of the feast, Jesus stood and cried, saying, If any man thirst, let him come unto me and drink. He that believeth on me, out of his belly shall flow rivers of living water." And it is with special reference to God's freeness and readiness to bestow grace at such a time, that it is said in Isa. lx. 11. of the spiritual *Jerusalem,* "Thy gates shall be open continually, they shall not be shut day nor night."

And though I judge not those who have opposed this work, and would not have others judge them, yet, if any such shall happen to read this treatise, I would take the liberty to entreat them to leave off troubling themselves so much about others, and to look into their own souls, and see to it that they are the subjects of a true, saving work of the Spirit of God.—If they have reason to think they never have been, or if it be but a very doubtful hope that they have, then how can they have any heart to be fiercely engaged about the mistakes and the supposed false hopes of others? And I would now beseech those who have hitherto been somewhat inclining to *Arminian* principles, seriously to weigh the matter with respect to this work, and consider, whether, if the Scriptures are the word of God, the work that has been described in the first part of this treatise must not be, as to the substance of it, the work of God, and the flourishing of that religion which is taught by Christ and his apostles. Can any good medium be found, where a man can rest with any stability, between owning this work, and being a deist? If indeed this be the work of God, does it not entirely overthrow their scheme of religion; and does it not infinitely concern them, as they would be partakers of eternal salvation, to relinquish their scheme? Now is a good time for *Arminians* to change their principles. I would now, as one of the friends of this work, humbly invite them to come and join with us, and be on our side; and, if I had the authority of *Moses*, I would say to them as he did to *Hobab*, Num. x. 29. "We are journeying unto the place, of which the Lord said, I will give it you; come thou with us, and we will do thee good: for the Lord hath spoken good concerning Israel."

As the benefit and advantage of the good improvement of such a season is very great, so the danger of neglecting and misimproving it is proportionably great. It is abundantly evident by the Scripture, that as a time of great outpouring of the Spirit is a time of great favour to those who are partakers of the blessing, so it is always a time of remarkable vengeance to others. So in Isa. lxi. 2. what is called, *the acceptable year of the Lord*, is also called, *the day of vengeance of our God*. So it was amongst the *Jews*, in the apostles' days. The apostle in 2 Cor. vi. 2. says of that time, that it was *the accepted time, and day of salvation;* and Christ says of the same time, Luke xxi. 22. "These are the days of vengeance." While the blessings of the kingdom of heaven were given to some, there was an *axe laid at the root of the trees, that those that did not bear fruit, might be hewn down, and cast into the fire,* Matt. iii. 9—11. Then was glorified both the goodness and severity of God, in a remarkable manner, Rom. xi. 22. The harvest and the vintage go together: at the same time that the earth is reaped, and God's elect are gathered into his garner, "the angel that has power over fire, thrusts in his sickle, and gathers the cluster of the vine of the earth, and casts it into the great wine-press of the wrath of God," Rev. xiv. So it is foretold, in reference to the beginning of the glorious times of the christian church, that as "the hand of the Lord is known towards his servants, so shall his indignation be towards his enemies," Isa. lxvi. 14. So when that glorious morning shall appear, wherein "the Sun of righteousness shall arise to the elect with healing in his wings, the day shall burn as an oven to the wicked," Mal. iv. 1—3. There is no time like it for the increase of guilt, and treasuring up wrath, and desperate hardening of the heart, if men stand it out; which is the most awful judgment, and fruit of divine wrath, that can be inflicted on any mortal. So that a time of great grace, and the fruits of divine mercy, is evermore also a time of divine vengeance, on those that neglect and misimprove such a season.

The state of the present revival of religion has an awful aspect upon those that are advanced in years. The work has been chiefly amongst the young; and comparatively but few others have been made partakers of it. And indeed it has commonly been so, when God has begun any great work for the revival of his church; he has taken the young people, and has cast off the old and stiff-necked generation. There was a remarkable outpouring of the Spirit of God on the children of *Israel* in the wilderness, but chiefly on the younger generation, *their little ones, that they said should be a prey*, the generation that entered into *Canaan* with *Joshua*. That generation seems to have been the most excellent that ever was in the church of *Israel*. There is no generation, of which there is so much good, and so little evil, spoken in Scripture, as might be shown. In that generation, such as were under twenty years when they went out of *Egypt*, was that *kindness of youth*, and *love of espousals*, spoken of, Jer. ii. 2, 3. But the old generation were passed by; they remained obstinate and stiff-necked, were always murmuring, and would not be convinced by all God's wondrous works that they beheld. God by his awful judgments executed in the wilderness, and the affliction which the people suffered there, convinced and humbled the younger generation, and fitted them for great mercy; as is evident by Deut. ii. 16. but he destroyed the old generation; "he swore in his wrath that they should not enter into his rest, and their carcasses fell in the wilderness." When it was a time of great mercy, and of God's Spirit on their children, it was remarkably a day of vengeance unto them; as appears by the 90th Psalm. Let the old generation in this land take warning from hence, and take heed that they do not refuse to be convinced by all God's wonders that he works before their eyes, and that they do not continue for ever objecting, murmuring, and cavilling against the work of God, lest, while he is bringing their children into a land flowing with milk and honey, he should swear in his wrath concerning them, that their carcasses shall fall in the wilderness.

So when God had a design of great mercy to the *Jews*, in bringing them out of the *Babylonish* captivity, and returning them to their own land, there was a blessed outpouring of the Spirit upon them in *Babylon*, to bring them to deep conviction and repentance, and to cry earnestly to God for mercy; which is often spoken of by the prophets. But it was not upon the *old* generation, that were carried captive. The captivity continued just long enough for that perverse generation to waste away and die in their captivity, at least those of them that were adult persons when carried captive. The heads of families were exceeding obstinate, and would not hearken to the earnest repeated warnings of the prophet *Jeremiah;* but he had greater success among the young people; as appears by Jer. vi. 10, 11. "To whom shall I speak and give warning, that they may hear? Behold, their ear is uncircumcised, and they cannot hearken: behold, the word of the Lord is unto them a reproach; they have no delight in it. Therefore I am full of the fury of the Lord; I am weary with holding in: I will pour it out upon the children abroad, and upon the assembly of the young men together: for even the husband with the wife (*i. e.* the heads of families, and parents of these children) shall be taken, the aged, with him that is full of days." Blessed be God! there are some of the elder people that have been made partakers of this work. And those that are most awakened by these warnings of God's word, and the awful frowns of his providence, will be most likely to be made partakers hereafter. It infinitely concerns them to take heed to themselves, that they may be partakers of it; for how dreadful will it be to go to hell, after having spent so many years in doing nothing but treasuring up wrath!

But above all others does it concern us who are ministers, to see to it that we have experience of the saving operations of the same Spirit that is now poured out on the land. How sorrowful and melancholy is the case, when it is otherwise! For one to stand at the head of a congregation of God's people, as representing Christ and speaking in his stead; and to act the part of a shepherd and guide to a people in such a state of things, when many are under great awakenings, many are converted, and many of God's saints are filled with divine light, love, and joy: to undertake to instruct and lead them all under these various circumstances; to be put to it continually to play the hypocrite, and force the airs of a saint in preaching; and from time to time in private conversation, and particular dealing with souls, to undertake to judge of their circumstances: to try to talk with persons of experience, as if he knew how to converse with them, and had experience as well as they; to make others believe that he rejoices when others are converted; and to force a pleased and joyful countenance and manner of speech, when there is nothing in the heart: what sorrowful work is here! Oh how miserable must such a person feel! What a wretched bondage and slavery is this! What pains, and how much art, must such a minister use to conceal himself! And how weak are his hands! What infinite provocation of the most high God, and displeasure of his Lord and Master, he incurs, by continuing a secret enemy to him in his heart, in such circumstances! I think there is a great deal of reason from the Scripture to conclude, that no sort of men in the world will be so low in hell as ungodly ministers. Every thing spoken of in Scripture, as that which aggravates guilt, and heightens divine wrath, meets in them. And what great disadvantages are unconverted ministers under, to oppose any irregularities, imprudences, or intemperate zeal, which they may see in those who are the children of God, when they are conscious to themselves that they have no zeal at all! If enthusiasm and wildness comes in like a flood, what poor, weak instruments are such ministers to withstand it! With what courage can they open their mouths, when they look inward, and consider how it is with them!

We who are ministers, not only have need of some true experience of the saving influence of the Spirit of God upon our heart, but we need a double portion at such a time as this. We need to be as full of light as a glass that is held out in the sun; and, with respect to love and zeal, we need to be like the angels, who are a flame of fire. The state of the times extremely requires a fulness of the divine spirit in ministers, and we ought to give ourselves no rest till we have obtained it. And, in order to this, I should think ministers, above all persons, ought to be much in prayer and fasting, both in secret and one with another. It seems to me, that it would become the circumstances of the present day, if ministers in a neighbourhood would often meet together, and spend days in fasting and fervent prayer among themselves, earnestly seeking extraordinary supplies of divine grace from heaven. And how desirable that, on their occasional visits one to another, instead of spending away their time in sitting and smoking, in diverting, or worldly, unprofitable conversation—telling news, and making their remarks on this and the other trifling subject—they would spend their time in praying together, singing praises, and religious conference. How much do many of the common people shame many of us who are in the work of the ministry, in these respects! Surely we do not behave ourselves so much like christian ministers, and the disciples and ambassadors of Christ, as we ought to do. And, while we condemn zealous persons for censuring ministers at this day, it ought not to be without deep reflections upon, and great condemnation of, ourselves; for indeed we do very much to provoke censoriousness, and lay a great temptation before others to the sin of judging. And if we can prove that those who are guilty of it transgress the scripture-rule, our indignation should be chiefly against ourselves.

Ministers, at this day in a special manner, should act as fellow-helpers in their great work. It should be seen that they are animated and engaged, that they exert themselves with one heart and soul, and with united strength, to promote the present glorious revival of religion; and to that end should often meet together, and act in concert. And if it were a common thing in the country, for ministers to join in public exercises, and second one another in their preaching, I believe it would be of great service. I mean that ministers having consulted one another as to their subjects before they go to the house of God, should there (two or three of them) in short discourses earnestly enforce each other's warnings and counsels. Such appearance of united zeal in ministers would have a great tendency to awaken attention, and to impress and animate the hearers; as has been found by experience in some parts of the country.—Ministers should carefully avoid weakening one another's hands: and therefore every thing should be avoided, by which their interest with their people might be diminished, or their union with them broken. Therefore, if ministers have not forfeited their acceptance in that character in the visible church, by their doctrine or behaviour, their brethren in the ministry ought studiously to endeavour to heighten the esteem and affection of their people towards them, that they may have no temptation to repent their admitting other ministers to preach in their pulpits.

Two things exceeding needful in ministers, as they would do any great matters to advance the kingdom of Christ, are *zeal* and *resolution*. Their influence and power, to bring to pass great effects, is greater than can well be imagined. A man of but an ordinary capacity will do more with them, than one of ten times the parts and learning without them; more may be done with them in a few days, or at least weeks, than can be done without them in many years. Those who are possessed of these qualities commonly carry the day, in almost all affairs. Most of the great things that have been done in the world, the great revolutions that have been accomplished in the kingdoms and empires of the earth, have been chiefly owing to them. The very appearance of a thoroughly engaged spirit, together with a fearless courage and unyielding resolution, in any person that has undertaken the managing of any affair amongst mankind, goes a great way towards accomplishing the effect aimed at. It is evident that the appearance of these in *Alexander* did three times as much towards conquering the world, as all the blows that he struck. And how much were the great things that *Oliver Cromwell* did owing to these! And the great things that Mr. *Whitfield* has done, every where, as he has run through the *British* dominions, (so far as they are owing to means,) are very much owing to the appearance of these things which he is eminently possessed of. When the people see these in a person, to a great degree, it awes them, and has a commanding influence upon their minds. It seems to them that they must yield; they naturally fall before them, without standing to contest or dispute the matter; they are conquered as it were by surprise. But while we are cold and heartless, and only go on in a dull manner, in an old formal round, we shall never do any great matters. Our attempts, with the appearance of such coldness and irresolution, will not so much as make persons think of yielding. They will hardly be sufficient to put it into their minds; and if it be put into their minds, the appearance of such indifference and cowardice does as it were call for and provoke opposition.—Our misery is want of zeal and courage; for not only through want of them does all fail that we seem to attempt, but it prevents our *attempting* any thing very remarkable for the kingdom of Christ. Hence oftentimes, when any thing very considerable is proposed to be done for the advancement of religion or the public good, many difficulties are in the way, and a great many objections are started, and it may be it is put off from one to another; but nobody does any thing. And after this manner good designs or proposals have often failed, and have sunk as soon as proposed. Whereas, if we had but Mr. *Whitfield's* zeal and courage, what could not we do, with such a blessing as we might expect!

Zeal and courage will do much in persons of but an ordinary capacity; but especially would they do great things, if joined with great abilities. If some great men who have appeared in our nation, had been as eminent in divinity as they were in philosophy, and had engaged in the christian cause with as much zeal and fervour as some others have done, and with a proportional blessing of heaven, they would have conquered all *Christendom*, and turned the world upside down. We have many ministers in the land that do not want abilities, they are persons of bright parts and learning; they should consider how much is expected and will be required of them by their Lord and Master, how much they might do for Christ, and what great honour and glorious a reward they might receive, if they had in their hearts a heavenly warmth, and divine heat proportionable to their light.

With respect to candidates for the ministry, I will not undertake particularly to determine what kind of examination or trial they should pass under, in order to their admission to that sacred work. But I think this is evident from the Scripture, that another sort of trial with regard to their virtue and piety is requisite, than is required in order to persons being admitted into the visible church. The apostle directs, *that hands be laid suddenly on no man;* but that they should *first be tried*, before they are admitted to the work of the ministry; but it is evident that persons were suddenly admitted by baptism into the visible church, on profession of their faith in Christ, without such caution or strictness in their probation. And it seems to me, those would act very unadvisedly, that should enter on that great and sacred work, before they had comfortable satisfaction concerning themselves, that they have had a saving work of God on their souls.

And though it may be thought that I go out of my proper sphere, to intermeddle in the affairs of the colleges; yet I will take the liberty of an *Englishman* that speaks his mind freely concerning public affairs, and the liberty of a minister of Christ, (who doubtless may speak his mind as freely about things that concern the kingdom of his Lord and Master,) to give my opinion, in some things, with respect to those societies; the original and main design of which is to train up persons, and fit them for the work of the ministry. And I would say in general, that it appears to me care should be taken, some way or other, that those societies should be so regulated, that they should, in fact, be nurseries of piety. Otherwise they are fundamentally ruined and undone as to their main design and most essential end. They ought to be so constituted, that vice and idleness should have no living there. They are intolerable in societies, whose main design is, to train up youth in christian knowledge and eminent piety, to fit them to be pastors of the flock of the blessed Jesus. I have heretofore had some acquaintance with the affairs of a college, and experience of what belonged to its tuition and government; and I cannot but think that it is practicable enough, so to constitute such societies, that there should be no residing there, without being virtuous, serious, and diligent. It seems to me a reproach to the land, that ever it should be so with our colleges, that, instead of being places of the greatest advantages for true piety, one cannot send a child thither without great danger of his being infected as to his morals. It is perfectly intolerable; and any thing should be done, rather than it should be so. If we pretend to have any colleges at all, under any notion of training up youth for the ministry, there should be some way found out, that should certainly prevent its being thus. To have societies for bringing persons up to be ambassadors of Jesus Christ, and to lead souls to heaven, and to have them places of so much infection, is the greatest nonsense and absurdity imaginable.

And as thorough and effectual care should be taken that vice and idleness be not tolerated in these societies, so certainly their design requires that extraordinary means should be used in them for training up the students in vital religion, and experimental and practical godliness; so that they should be holy societies, the very place should be as it were sacred. They should be, in the midst of the land, fountains of piety and holiness. There is a great deal of pains taken to teach the scholars human learning; there ought to be as much and more care thoroughly to educate them in religion, and lead them to true and eminent holiness. If the main design of these nurseries is to bring up persons to teach Christ, then it is of the greatest importance that there should be care and pains taken to bring those who are there educated to the knowledge of Christ. It has been common in our public prayers, to call these societies, *the schools of the prophets;* and, if they are schools to train up young men to be *prophets*, certainly there ought to be extraordinary care taken to train them up to be *Christians*.—And I cannot see why it is not on all accounts fit and convenient for the governors and instructors of the colleges particularly, singly, and frequently, to converse with the students about the state of their souls; as is the practice of the Rev. Dr. *Doddridge*, one of the most noted of the present dissenting ministers in *England*, who keeps an academy at *Northampton*, as he himself informs the Rev. Mr. *Wadsworth* of *Hartford* in *Connecticut*, in a letter dated at *Northampton, March* 6th, 1741. The original of which letter I have seen, and have by me an extract of it, sent me by Mr. *Wadsworth;* which is as follows:

"Through the divine goodness, I have every year the pleasure to see some plants taken out of my nursery, and set in neighbouring congregations; where they generally settle with an unanimous consent, and that to a very remarkable degree, in some very large and once divided congregations. A circumstance in which I own and adore the hand of a wise and gracious God; and cannot but look upon it as a token for good. I have at present a greater proportion of pious and ingenious youth under my care, than I ever before had: so that I hope the church may reasonably expect some considerable relief from hence, if God spare their lives a few years, and continue to them those gracious assistances which he has hitherto mercifully imparted.—I will not, *Sir*, trouble you at present with a large account of my method of academical education: only would observe, that I think it of vast importance to instruct them carefully in the Scriptures; and not only endeavour to establish them in the great truths of Christianity, but to labour to promote their practical influence on their hearts. For which purpose, I frequently converse with each of them alone, and conclude the conversation with prayer. This does indeed take up a great deal of time; but I bless God, it is amply repaired in the pleasure I have in seeing my labour is not in vain in the Lord."

There are some who are not ministers, nor are concerned immediately in those things that appertain to their office, or in the education of persons for it, who are under great advantages to promote such a glorious work as this. Some laymen, though it be not their business publicly to exhort and teach, are in some respects under greater advantage to encourage and forward this work than ministers; as particularly great men, or those who are high in honour and influence. How much might such do to encourage religion, and open the way for it to have free course, and bear down opposition, if they were but inclined! There is commonly a certain unhappy shyness in great men with respect to religion, as though they were ashamed of it, or at least ashamed to do much at it; whereby they dishonour and doubtless greatly provoke the King of kings, and very much wound religion among the common people. They are careful of their honour, and seem to be afraid of appearing openly forward and zealous in religion, as though it were what would debase their character, and expose them to contempt.—But, in this day of bringing up the ark, they ought to be like *David*, that great king of *Israel*, who *made himself vile* before the ark; and as he was the highest in honour and dignity among God's people, so he thought it became him to appear foremost in the zeal and activity manifested on that occasion; thereby animating and encouraging the whole congregation to praise the Lord, and rejoice before him with all their might. And though it diminished him in the eyes of scoffing *Michal*, yet it did not at all abate the honour and esteem of the congregation of *Israel*, but advanced it; as appears by 2 Sam. vi. 22.

Rich men have a talent in their hands, in the disposal and improvement of which they might very much promote such a work as this, if they were so disposed. They are far beyond others in advantages to do good, and lay up for themselves treasures in heaven. What a thousand pities it is that, for want of a heart, they commonly have no share at all there, but heaven is peopled mostly with the poor of this world! One would think that our rich men who call themselves Christians, might devise some notable things to do with their money, to advance the kingdom of their professed Redeemer, and the prosperity of the souls of men, at this time of such extraordinary advantage for it. It seems to me, that in this age most of us have but very narrow penurious notions of Christianity, as it respects our use and disposal of our temporal goods. The primitive Christians had not such notions; they were trained up by the apostles in another way.—God has greatly distinguished some of the inhabitants of *New England* from others, in the abundance he has given them of the good things of this life. If they could now be persuaded to lay out some considerable part of that which God has given them for his honour, and lay it up in heaven, instead of spending it for their own honour, or laying it up for their posterity, they would not repent of it afterwards. How liberally did the heads of the tribes contribute to their wealth at the setting up the tabernacle, though it was in a barren wilderness! These are the days of erecting the tabernacle of God amongst us. We have a particular account how the goldsmiths and the merchants helped to rebuild the wall of *Jerusalem*, Neh. iii. 32. The days are coming, and I believe not very far off, when the sons of "Zion shall come from far, bringing their silver and their gold with them, unto the name of the Lord their God, and to the holy One of *Israel;*" when the merchants of the earth shall trade for Christ, more than for themselves, and "their merchandise and hire shall be holiness to the Lord, and shall not be treasured or laid up for posterity, but shall be for them that dwell before the Lord, to eat sufficiently, and for durable clothing;" when "the ships of *Tarshish* shall bring *the wealth of the distant parts of the earth* to the place of God's sanctuary, and to make the place of his feet glorious; and the abundance of the sea shall be converted to the use of God's church, and she shall suck the milk of the Gentiles, and suck the breasts of kings." The days are coming, when the great and the rich men of the word "shall bring their honour and glory into the church," and shall, as it were, strip themselves in order to spread their garments under Christ's feet, as he enters triumphantly into *Jerusalem;* and when those that will not do so shall have no glory, and their silver and gold shall be cankered, and their garments moth-eaten. For the saints shall then inherit the earth, and they shall reign on it; and those that honour God he will honour, and those that despise him shall be lightly esteemed.—If some of our rich men would give one quarter of their estates to promote this work, they would act a little as if they were designed for the kingdom of heaven, and as rich men will act by and by who shall be partakers of the spiritual wealth and glories of that kingdom.

Great things might be done for the advancement of the kingdom of Christ at this day by those who have ability, by establishing *funds* for the support and propagation of religion; by supporting some who are eminently qualified with gifts and grace in *preaching the gospel* in certain parts of the country, which are more destitute of the means of grace; by searching out children of promising abilities, and their hearts full of love to Christ, but of poor families, (as doubtless there are such now in the land,) and *bringing them up for the ministry;* and by *distributing books,* that are remarkably fitted to promote vital religion, and have a great tendency to advance this work.—Or if they would only bear the trouble and expense of sending such books into various parts of the land to be *sold,* it might be an occasion that ten times so many of those books should be bought, as otherwise would be—by establishing and supporting *schools* in poor towns and villages; which might be done on such a foundation, as not only to bring up children in common learning, but also might very much tend to their conviction and conversion, and being trained up in vital piety. Doubtless something might be done this way in old towns and more populous places, that might have a great tendency to the flourishing of religion in the rising generation.

SECT. III.

Of some particulars that concern all in general.

And here, the first thing I shall mention is *fasting and prayer.* It seems to me, that the circumstances of the present work loudly call upon God's people to abound in this; whether they consider their own *experience,* or the riches of God's *grace.* God has lately given them an experience of the worth of his presence, and of the blessed fruits of the effusions of his Spirit, to excite them to pray for the continuance, increase, and greater extent of such blessings; and they have great encouragement to pray for the out-pouring of his Spirit, and the carrying on of this work, by the great manifestations he has lately made of the freeness and riches of his grace. There is much in what we have seen of the glorious works of God's power and grace, to put us in mind of the yet greater things of this nature that he has spoken of in his word, and to excite our longings, and our hopes of their approach. Beside, we should consider the great opposition that *Satan* makes against this work, the many difficulties with which it is clogged, and the distressing circumstances that some parts of God's church in this land are under at this day, on one account and another.

So is God's will, through his wonderful grace, that the prayers of his saints should be one great and principal means of carrying on the designs of Christ's kingdom in the world. When God has something very great to accomplish for his church, it is his will that there should precede it the extraordinary prayers of his people; as is manifest by Ezek. xxxvi. 37. "I will yet, for this, be inquired of by the house of *Israel,* to do it for them:" (see the context.) And it is revealed that, when God is about to accomplish great things for his church, he will begin by remarkably pouring out the spirit of grace and supplication, Zech. xii. 10. If we are not to expect that the devil should go out of a particular person, under a bodily possession, without extraordinary prayer, *or prayer and fasting;* how much less should we expect to have him cast out the land, and the world, without it!

I am sensible that somewhat considerable has been done in duties of this nature in some places, but I do not think so much as God in the present dispensations of his providence calls for. I should think the people of God in this land, at such a time as this is, would be in the way of their duty while doing three times as much at fasting and prayer as they do; not only, nor principally, for the pouring out of the Spirit on those places to which they belong; but that God would appear for his church, and, in mercy to miserable men, carry on his work in the land, and in the world, and fulfil the things he has spoken of in his word, that his church has been so long wishing, and hoping, and waiting for. "They that make mention of the Lord," at this day, ought not to "keep silence," and should "give God no rest, till he establish, and till he make *Jerusalem* a praise in the earth;" agreeable to Isa. lxii. 6, 7. Before the first great out-pouring of the Spirit of God on the christian church, which began at *Jerusalem,* the disciples gave themselves to incessant prayer, Acts i. 13, 14. There is a time spoken of, wherein God will remarkably and wonderfully appear for the deliverance of his church from all her enemies, and when he will *avenge his own elect:* and Christ reveals that this will be in answer to their incessant prayers, or "crying day and night," Luke xviii. 7. In *Israel,* the *day of atonement,* which was their great day of fasting and prayer, preceded and made way for the glorious and joyful *feast of tabernacles.* When Christ is mystically born into the world, to rule over all nations, it is represented in the 12th chap. of Rev. as being in consequence of the church's "crying, and travailing in birth, and being pained to be delivered." One thing here intended doubtless is, her crying and agonizing in prayer.

God seems at this very time to be waiting for this from us. When he is about to bestow some great blessing on his church, it is often his manner, in the first place, so to order things in his providence, as to show his church their great need of it, and to bring them into distress for want of it, and so put them upon crying earnestly to him for it. Let us consider God's present dispensations towards his church in this land: a glorious work of his grace has been begun and carried on; and he has of late suffered innumerable difficulties to arise, that in a great measure clog and hinder it, and bring many of God's dear children into great distress. And yet he does not wholly forsake the work of his hand; there are remarkable tokens of his presence still to be seen, here and there; as though he was not forward to forsake us, and (if I may so say) as though he had a mind to carry on his work, but only was waiting for something that he expected in us, as requisite in order to it. And we have a great deal of reason to think, that one thing at least is, that we should further acknowledge the greatness and necessity of such a mercy, and our dependence on God for it, in earnest and importunate prayers to him. And by the many errors that have been run into, by the wounds we have thereby given ourselves and the cause that we would promote, and the mischief and confusion we have thereby made, God has hitherto been remarkably showing us our great and universal dependence on him, and exceeding need of his help and grace; which should engage our cries to him for it.

There is no way that Christians in a private capacity can do so much to promote the work of God, and advance the kingdom of Christ, as by prayer. By this even women, children, and servants may have a public influence. Let persons in other respects be never so weak, and never so mean, and under never so poor advantages to do much for Christ and the souls of men; yet, if they have much of the spirit of grace and supplication, in this way they may have power with him who is infinite in power, and has the government of the whole world. A poor man in his cottage may have a blessed influence all over the world. God is, if I may so say, at the command of the prayer of faith; and in this respect is, as it were, under the power of his people; *as princes, they have power with God, and prevail.* Though they may be private persons, their prayers are put up in the name of a Mediator who is a public person, being the Head of the whole church, and the Lord of the universe. If they have a great sense of the importance of eternal things, and a concern for the precious souls of men, they need not regret it that they are not preachers; they may go in their earnestness and agonies of soul, and pour out their souls before one who is able to do all things. Before him they may speak as freely as ministers; they have a great High Priest, through whom they may come boldly at all times, and may vent themselves before a prayer-hearing Father without restraint.

If the people of God at this day, instead of spending time in fruitless disputing, in talking about opposers, judging them, and animadverting upon the unreasonableness of their talk and behaviour, and its inconsistence with true experience, would be more silent in this way, and open their mouths much more before God, and spend more time in fasting and prayer, they would be more in the way of a blessing. And if some Christians who have been complaining of their ministers, and struggling in vain to deliver themselves from the difficulties complained of under their ministry, had said and acted less before men, and had applied themselves with all their might to cry to God for their ministers, had as it were risen and stormed heaven with their humble, fervent, and incessant prayers for them, they would have been much more in the way of success.

God in his providence appearing in the present state of things, does especially call on his people in *New England* to be very much in praying to him for the pouring out of the Spirit upon *ministers* in the land. For though it is not for us to determine concerning particular ministers, how much they have of the Spirit of God; yet in the general it is apparent, that there is at this day need of very great degrees of the presence of God with the ministry in *New England*, much greater degrees of it than have hitherto been granted; they need it for themselves, and the church of God stands in extreme need of it.

On days of fasting and prayer, wherein the whole congregation is concerned, if the day, besides what is spent in our families, was not wholly spent in the meeting-house, but part of it in particular praying companies or societies, it would have a tendency to animate and engage devotion, more than if the whole day were spent in public, where the people are no way active themselves in the worship, any otherwise than as they join with the minister. The inhabitants of many of our towns are now divided into particular praying societies; most of the people, young and old, have voluntarily associated themselves in distinct companies, for mutual assistance in social worship, in private houses. What I intend therefore is, that days of prayer should be spent partly in these distinct praying companies. Such a method as *this*, has been several times proved, *viz*. In the forenoon, after the duties of the family and closet, as early as might be, all the people of the congregation have gathered in their particular religious societies; companies of men by themselves, and companies of women by themselves; young men by themselves, and young women by themselves; and companies of children in all parts of the town by themselves, as many as were capable of social religious exercises; the boys by themselves, and the girls by themselves: and about the middle of the day, at an appointed hour, all have met together in the house of God, to offer up public prayers, and to hear a sermon suitable to the occasion; and then, they have retired from the house of God again into their private societies, and spent the remaining part of the day in praying together there, excepting so much as was requisite for the duties of the family and closet in their own houses.—And it has been found to be of great benefit, to assist and engage the minds of the people in the duties of the day.

I have often thought it would be very desirable, and very likely to be followed with a great blessing, if there could be some contrivance for an agreement of all God's people in *America*, who are well-affected to this work, to deep a day of fasting and prayer; wherein we should all unite on the same day, in humbling ourselves before God for our past long-continued lukewarmness and unprofitableness; not omitting humiliation for the errors that so many of God's people—though zealously affected towards this work—through their infirmity and remaining blindness and corruption have run into: and together with thanksgivings to God for so glorious and wonderful a display of his power and grace in the late out-pourings of his Spirit, to address the Father of mercies, with prayers and supplications, and earnest cries, that he would guide and direct his own people, and that he would continue and still carry on this work, and more abundantly and extensively pour out his Spirit, and particularly upon ministers; and that he would bow the heavens and come down, and erect his glorious kingdom through the earth.—Some perhaps may think that its being all on the same day, is a circumstance of no great consequence; but I cannot be of that mind. Such a circumstance makes the union and agreement of God's people in his worship the more visible, and puts the greater honour upon God, and would have a great tendency to assist and enliven the devotions of Christians. It seems to me, it would mightily encourage and animate God's saints in humbly and earnestly seeking to God for such blessings which concern them all; and that it would be much for the rejoicing of all, to think, that at the same time such multitudes of God's dear children, far and near, were sending up their cries to the same common Father, for the same mercies. Christ speaks of agreement in asking, as what contributes to the prevalence of the prayers of his people, Matt. xviii. 19. "Again I say unto you, that if any two of you shall agree on earth, as touching any thing that they shall ask, it shall be done for them of my Father which is in heaven." If the agreement, or united purpose and appointment, of but two of God's children, would contribute much to the prevalence of their prayers; how much more the agreement of so many thousands! Christ delights greatly in the union of his people, as appears by his prayer in the 17th of John; and especially is the appearance of their union in worship lovely and attractive unto him.

I doubt not but such a thing as I have now mentioned is practicable without a great deal of trouble. Some considerable number of ministers might meet together, and draw up the proposal, wherein a certain day should be fixed at a sufficient distance, endeavouring therein to avoid any other public day that might interfere with the design in any of the provinces, and the business of the day should be particularly mentioned. These proposals should be published, and sent abroad into all parts, with a desire, that as many ministers as are disposed to fall in with them, would propose the matter to their congregations, and, having taken their consent, would subscribe their names, together with the places of which they are ministers, and send back the proposals thus subscribed to the printer. The hands of many ministers might be to one paper. The printer having received the papers, thus subscribed, from all the provinces, might print the proposals again, with all the names; thus they might be sent abroad again with the names, that God's people might know who are united with them in the affair. One of the ministers of *Boston* might be desired to have the oversight of printing and dispersing the proposals. In such a way, perhaps, might be fulfilled, in some measure, such a general mourning and supplication of God's people as is spoken of, Zech. xii. at the latter end, with which the church's glorious day is to be introduced.—And such a day might be something like the *day of atonement* in *Israel*, before the joyful *feast of tabernacles*.

One thing more I would mention concerning fasting and prayer, wherein I think there has been a neglect in ministers; and that is, That although they recommend and much insist on the duty of secret prayer, in their preaching, so little is said about secret fasting. It is a duty recommended by our Saviour to his followers, just in like manner as secret prayer is; as may be seen by comparing Matt. vi. 5, 6, with ver. 16—18. Though I do not suppose that secret fasting is to be practised in a stated manner, and steady course, like secret prayer; yet it seems to me a duty that all professing Christians should practise, and frequently practise. There are many occasions, of both a spiritual and temporal nature, that properly require it; and there are many particular mercies we desire for ourselves or friends, that it would be proper in this manner to seek of God.

Another thing I would also mention, wherein it appears to me that there has been an omission, with respect to the external worship of God. There has been of late a great increase of preaching the word, of social prayer, and of singing praises. These external duties of religion are attended much more frequently than they used to be; yet I cannot understand that there is any increase of the administration of the Lord's supper, or that God's people do any more frequently commemorate the dying love of their Redeemer, in this sacred memorial of it, than they used to do. I do not see why an increase of love to Christ should not dispose Christians as much to increase in this as in those other duties; or why it is not as proper that Christ's disciples should abound in this duty, in this joyful season, which is spiritually supper-time, a feast-day with God's saints, wherein Christ is so abundantly manifesting his dying love to souls, and is dealing forth so liberally of the precious fruits of his death. It seems plain by the Scripture, that the primitive Christians were wont to celebrate this memorial of the sufferings of their dear Redeemer every Lord's day; and so I believe it will be again in the church of Christ, in days that are approaching. And whether we attend this holy and sweet ordinance so often now, or no; yet I cannot but think it would become us, at such a time as this, to attend it much oftener than is commonly done in the land.

But another thing I would mention, which it is of much greater importance that we should attend to, and that is the duty incumbent upon God's people at this day, to take heed, that while they abound in external duties of devotion, such as praying, hearing, singing, and attending religious meetings, there be a proportionable care to abound in moral duties, such as acts of righteousness, truth, meekness, forgiveness, and love towards our neighbour; which are of much greater importance in the sight of God than all the externals of his worship. Our Saviour was particularly careful that men should be well aware of this, Matt. ix. 13. "But go ye and learn what that meaneth, I will have mercy, and not sacrifice." And chap. xii. 7. "But if ye had known what this meaneth, I will have mercy and not sacrifice, ye would not have condemned the guiltless."

The internal acts and principles of the worship of God, or the worship of the heart, in love and fear, trust in God, and resignation to him, &c. are the most essential and important of all duties of religion whatsoever; for therein consists the essence of all religion. But of this inward religion there are two sorts of external manifestations or expressions. To one sort belong outward acts of worship, such as meeting in religious assemblies, attending sacraments and other outward institutions, honouring God with gestures, such as bowing, or kneeling before him, or with words, in speaking honourably of him in prayer, praise, or religious conference. To the other sort belong expressions of our love to God, by obeying his moral commands, self-denial, righteousness, meekness, and christian love, in our behaviour among men. The latter are of vastly the greatest importance in the christian life; God makes little account of the former, in comparison of them; they are abundantly more insisted on, by the prophets of the Old Testament, and Christ and his apostles in the New. When these two kinds of duties are spoken of together, the latter are evermore greatly preferred; as in Isa. i. 12—18. and Amos v. 21, &c. and Mic. vi. 7, 8. and Isa. lviii. 5, 6, 7. and Zech. vii. ten first verses, and Jer. ii. seven first verses, and Matt. xv. 3, &c. Often, when the times were very corrupt in Israel, the people abounded in the former kind of duties, but were at such times always notoriously deficient in the latter; as the prophets complain, Isa. lviii. four first verses, Jer. vi. 13, compared with ver. 20. hypocrites and self-righteous persons do much more commonly abound in the former kind of duties than the latter; as Christ remarks of the *Pharisees,* Matt. xxiii. 14, 25—34. When the Scripture directs us to *show our faith by our works,* it is principally the latter sort are intended; as appears by Jam. ii. from ver. 8, to the end, and 1 John 2d chap. ver. 3, 7—11. And we are to be judged, at the last day, especially by these latter sort of works; as is evident by the account we have of the day of judgment, in the 25th of Matt. External acts of worship, in words and gestures, and outward forms, are of little use, but as signs of something else, or as they are a profession of inward worship. They are not so properly showing our religion by our deeds; for they are only showing our religion by words, or an outward profession. But he that shows religion in the other sort of duties, shows it in something more than a profession of words, he shows it in deeds. And though deeds may be hypocritical, as well as words; yet in themselves they are of greater importance, for they are much more profitable to ourselves and our neighbour. We cannot express our love to God by doing any thing that is profitable to him; God would therefore have us do it in those things that are profitable to our neighbours, whom he has constituted his receivers. Our goodness extends not to God, but to our fellow-Christians. The latter sort of duties put greater honour upon God, because there is greater self-denial in them. The external acts of worship, consisting in bodily gestures, words, and sounds, are the cheapest part of religion, and least contrary to our lusts. The difficulty of thorough, external religion, does not lie in them. Let wicked men enjoy their covetousness, their pride, their malice, envy, and revenge, their sensuality and voluptuousness, in their behaviour amongst men, and they will be willing to compound the matter with God, and submit to what forms of worship you please, and as many as you please. This was manifest in the *Jews* in the days of the prophets, the *Pharisees* in Christ's time, and the *Papists* and *Mahometans* at this day.

At a time when there is an apparent approach of any glorious revival of God's church, he especially calls his professing people to the practice of moral duties, Isa. lvi. 1. "Thus saith the Lord, Keep ye judgment, and do justice; for my salvation is near to come, and my righteousness to be revealed." So when *John* preached that "the kingdom of heaven was at hand," and cried to the people, "Prepare ye the way of the Lord, make his paths straight," Luke iii. 4. the people asked him, "What they should do?" He answers, "He that hath two coats, let him impart to him that hath none; and he that hath meat, let him do likewise." The publicans said, "What shall we do?" He answers, "Exact no more than that which is appointed you." And the soldiers asked him, "What shall we do?" He replies, "Do violence to no man, neither accuse any falsely; and be content with your wages," ver. 10—14.

God's people at such time as this, ought especially to abound in deeds of charity, or alms-giving. We generally, in these days, seem to fall far below the true spirit and practice of Christianity with regard to this duty, and seem to have but little notion of it, so far as I can understand the New Testament.—At a time when God is so liberal of spiritual things, we ought not to be strait-handed towards him, and sparing of our temporal things. So far as I can judge by the Scripture, there is no external duty whatsoever, by which persons will be so much in the way, not only of receiving temporal benefits, but also spiritual blessings, the influences of God's Holy Spirit in the heart, in divine discoveries and spiritual consolations. I think it would be unreasonable to understand those promises, made to this duty, in the 58th chap. of Isaiah, in a sense exclusive of spiritual discoveries and comforts; Isa. lviii. 7, &c.—"Is it not to deal thy bread to the hungry, and that thou bring the poor that are cast out, to thy house? when thou seest the naked, that thou cover him, and that thou hide not thyself from thine own flesh? Then shall thy light break forth as the morning, and thy health shall spring forth speedily; and thy righteousness shall go before thee; the glory of the Lord shall be thy rere-ward. Then shalt thou call, and the Lord shall answer; thou shalt cry, and he shall say, Here I am: if thou take away from the midst of thee the yoke, the putting forth of the finger, and speaking vanity: and if thou draw out thy soul to the hungry, and satisfy the afflicted soul; then shall thy light rise in obscurity, and thy darkness be as the noon-day. And the Lord shall guide thee continually, and satisfy thy soul in drought, and make fat thy bones: and thou shalt be like a watered garden, and like a spring of water, whose waters fail not." So that giving to the poor is the way to receive spiritual blessings, is manifest by Psal. cxii. 4, &c. "Unto the upright there ariseth light in the darkness: he is gracious, and full of compassion, and righteous. A good man showeth favour, and lendeth; he will guide his affairs with discretion. Surely he shall not be moved for ever; the righteous shall be in everlasting remembrance. He shall not be afraid of evil tidings: his heart is fixed, trusting in the Lord. His heart is established, he shall not be afraid, until he see his desire upon his enemies. He hath dispersed, he hath given to the poor; his horn shall be exalted with honour." That this is one likely means to obtain assurance, is evident by 1 John iii. 18, 19. "My little children, let us not love in word, neither in tongue, but in deed, and in truth. And hereby we know that we are of the truth, and shall assure our hearts before him."

We have a remarkable instance in *Abraham*, of God rewarding deeds of charity with sweet discoveries of himself. He had been remarkably charitable to his brother *Lot*, and the people redeemed out of captivity with him, by exposing his life to rescue them. He had re-taken not only the persons, but all the spoil that had been taken by *Chedorlaomer* and the confederate kings. The king of *Sodom* offered him, that, if he would give him the persons, he might take the goods to himself; but *Abraham* refused to take any thing, even so much as a thread or shoe-latchet, but returned all.—He might have greatly enriched himself if he had taken the spoil to himself, for it was the spoil of five wealthy kings and their kingdoms, yet he did not covet it. The king and people of *Sodom* were now become objects of charity, having been stript of all by their enemies; therefore *Abraham* generously bestowed all upon them, as we have an account in Gen. xiv. and four last verses. He was soon rewarded for it, by a blessed discovery that God made of himself to him; as in the next words: "After these things the word of the Lord came unto *Abraham* in a vision, saying, Fear not, *Abraham*: I am thy shield, and thy exceeding great reward." "I am thy shield to defend thee in battle, as I have now done: and though thou hast charitably refused to take any reward for exposing thy life to rescue this people, yet fear not, thou shalt not be a loser, thou shalt have a reward; I am thy exceeding great reward."

When Christ was upon earth, he was poor, and an object of charity; and, during the time of his public ministry he was supported by the charity of some of his followers, and particularly certain women, of whom we read Luke viii. 2, 3. And these women were rewarded, by being peculiarly favoured with gracious manifestations which Christ made of himself to them. He discovered himself first to them after his resurrection, before the twelve disciples: they first saw a vision of glorious angels, who spake comfortably to them; and then Christ himself appeared to them, and spake peace to them, saying, "All hail, be not afraid; and they were admitted to come and hold him by the feet, and worship him," Matt. xxviii. And though we cannot be charitable in *this way* to Christ, who in his exalted state is infinitely above the need of our charity; yet we may be charitable to him even now, as well as they then. For though Christ is not here, yet he has left others in his room, to be his receivers; and they are the poor. Christ is yet poor in his members; and he that gives to them, lends to the Lord: and Christ tells us, that he shall look on what is done to them, as done to him.

Rebekah, in her marriage with *Isaac*, was undoubtedly a remarkable type of the church, in her espousals to the Lord Jesus. She obtained her husband in doing deeds of charity; agreeable to the prayer of *Abraham's* servant, who desired that this might be the thing to distinguish the virgin who was to be *Isaac's* wife. So *Cornelius* was brought to the knowledge of Christ in this way. "He was a devout man, and one that feared God, with all his house; which gave much alms to the people, and prayed to God alway. And an angel appeared to him, and said to him, Thy prayers and thine alms are come up for a memorial before God; and now send men to *Joppa*, and call for one *Simon*, whose surname is *Peter*," &c. Acts x. at the beginning. And we have an account of the following parts of the chapter, how God, by *Peter's* preaching, revealed Christ to *Cornelius* and his family, and of the Holy Ghost descending upon them, and filling their hearts with joy and their mouths with praises.

Some may possibly object, That for persons to do deeds of charity, in hope of obtaining spiritual blessings and comforts in this way, would seem to show a self-righteous spirit, as though they would offer something to God to purchase these favours. But, if this be a good objection, it may be made against every duty whatsoever. All external duties of the first table will be excluded by it, as well as those of the second. First-table duties have as direct a tendency to raise self-righteous persons' expectations of receiving something from God, on account of them, as second-table duties; and on some accounts more, for those duties are more immediately offered *to God*, and therefore persons are more ready to expect something *from God* for them. But no duty is to be neglected, for fear of making a righteousness of it. And I have always observed, that those professors who are most partial in their duty—exact and abundant in external duties of the first table, and slack as to those of the second—are the most self-righteous.

If God's people in this land were once brought to abound in such deeds of love, as much as in praying, hearing, singing, and religious meetings and conference, it would be a most blessed omen. Nothing would have a greater tendency to bring the God of love down from heaven to earth; so amiable would be the sight in the eyes of our loving and exalted Redeemer, that it would soon as it were fetch him down from his throne in heaven, to set up his tabernacle with men on the earth, and dwell with them. I do not remember ever to have read of any remarkable outpouring of the Spirit, that continued any long time, but what was attended with an abounding in this duty. We know it was so with that great effusion of the Spirit which began at *Jerusalem* in the apostles' days. And so it was in the late remarkable revival of religion in *Saxony*, which began by the labours of the famous professor *Franck*, and has now been carried on for above thirty years, and has spread its happy influences into many parts of the world; it was begun, and has been carried on, by a wonderful practice in this duty. And the remarkable blessing that God has given Mr. *Whitfield*, and the great success with which he has crowned him, may well be thought to be very much owing to his laying out himself so abundantly in charitable designs. And it is foretold, that God's people shall abound in this duty at the time of the great outpouring of the Spirit that shall be in the latter days, Isa. xxxii. 5, 8. "The vile person shall no more be called liberal, nor the churl said to be bountiful—But the liberal deviseth liberal things, and by liberal things shall he stand."

To promote a reformation, with respect to all sorts of duties among a professing people, one proper means, and that which is recommended by frequent scripture examples, is their solemn, public renewing of their covenant with God.—And doubtless it would greatly tend to promote this work in the land, if the congregations of God's people could generally be brought to this. Suppose a draught of a covenant be made by their ministers, wherein there should be an express mention of those particular duties that the people of the respective congregations have been observed to be most prone to neglect, those particular sins into which they have heretofore especially fallen, or of which it may be apprehended they are especially in danger, whereby they may prevent or resist the motions of God's Spirit. Suppose the matter be fully proposed and explained to the people, and, after sufficient opportunity for consideration, they be led, all that are capable of understanding, particularly to subscribe the covenant. Suppose also all appear together on a day of prayer and fasting, publicly to own it before God in his house, as their vow to the Lord; hereby congregations of Christians would do what would be beautiful in itself, what would put honour upon God, and be very profitable to themselves. Such a thing was attended with a very wonderful blessing in *Scotland*, and followed with a great increase of the blessed tokens of the presence of God, and remarkable outpourings of his Spirit; as the author of the *Fulfilling of the Scripture* informs, p. 186. 5th edition.—A people must be taken when they are in a good mood, when considerable religious impressions prevail among them; otherwise innumerable will be their objections and cavils against it.

One thing more I would mention, which, if God should still carry on this work, would tend much to promote it; and that is, That a history should be published once a month, or once a fortnight, of its progress, by one of the ministers of *Boston*, who are near the press, and are most conveniently situated to receive accounts from all parts. It has been found by experience, that the tidings of remarkable effects of the power and grace of God in any place, tend greatly to awaken and engage the minds of persons in other places. It is a great pity, therefore, but that some means should be used for the most speedy, most extensive, and certain information of such things; that the country be not left to the slow, partial, and doubtful information, and false representations, of common report.

Thus I have (I hope, by the help of God) finished what I proposed. I have taken the more pains in it, because it appears to me that now God is giving us the most happy season to attempt an universal reformation that ever was given in *New England.* And it is a thousand pities, that we should fail of that which would be so glorious, for want of being sensible of our opportunity, of being aware of those things that tend to hinder it, of taking improper courses to obtain it, or of not being sensible in what way God expects we should seek it. If it should please God to bless any means for convincing the country of his hand in this work, for bringing them fully and freely to acknowledge his glorious power and grace in it; and for bringing them to engage with one heart and soul, and by due methods, to endeavour to promote it, it would be a dispensation of Divine Providence that would have a most glorious aspect, happily signifying the approach of great and glorious things to the church of God, and justly causing us to hope that Christ would speedily come to set up his kingdom of light, holiness, peace, and joy on earth, as is foretold in his word. *Amen;* even so come, Lord Jesus!

AN HUMBLE INQUIRY

INTO THE

RULES OF THE WORD OF GOD,

CONCERNING

THE QUALIFICATIONS

REQUISITE

TO A COMPLETE STANDING AND FULL COMMUNION

IN THE VISIBLE

CHRISTIAN CHURCH.

Behold now I have opened my mouth :—My words shall be of the uprightness of my heart.——Job xxxiii. 2, 3.

Confitebatur [*Lutherus*] dolorem suum, quod ab ipsis reflorescentis Evangelii Primordiis, quosvis absque Discrimine ad Cœnam Dominicam admisisset, quodque Disciplinam, Fratrum Disciplinæ similem, apud suos non constituisset.—Quia objiciebatur, Fratres non habere Ecclesiam apertam;—Responsum fuit, Sancta dare non Sanctis prohibuisse Christum :—Errorem [in *Papatu*] corrigi non posse *aliter quam ut certa Probatione, nec illa subitanea, Cordium Arcana revelentur*, Novitiique diu et caute tum informentur, tum explorentur.—*Ratio Discipl. Fratr.* Bohem.

THE AUTHOR'S PREFACE.

My appearing in this public manner on that side of the question, which is defended in the following sheets, will probably be surprising to many; as it is well known, that Mr Stoddard, so great and eminent a divine, and my venerable predecessor in the pastoral office over the church in Northampton, as well as my own grandfather, publicly and strenuously appeared in opposition to the doctrine here maintained.

However, I hope it will be not taken amiss that I think as I do, merely because I herein differ from him, though so much my superior, and one whose name and memory I am under distinguishing obligations, on every account, to treat with great respect and honour. Especially may I justly expect, that it will not be charged on me as a crime, that I do not think in every thing just as he did, since none more than he himself asserted this scriptural and protestant maxim, that we ought to *call no man on earth master*, or make the authority of the greatest and holiest of mere men the ground of our belief of any doctrine in religion. Certainly we are not obliged to think any man infallible, who himself utterly disclaims infallibility. Very justly Mr. Stoddard observes in his *Appeal to the Learned*, p. 97. "All protestants agree, that there is no infallibility at Rome; and I know nobody else pretends to any, since the apostles' days." And he insists, in his *preface* to his *sermon* on the same subject, That it argues no want of a due respect in us to our *forefathers*, for us to *examine* their opinions. Some of his words in that *preface* contain a good apology for me, and are worthy to be repeated on this occasion. They are as follows:

"It may possibly be a *fault* (says Mr. Stoddard) to depart from the ways of our *fathers*: but it may also be a *virtue*, and an eminent act of obedience, to depart from them in *some* things. Men are wont to make a great *noise*, that we are bringing in innovations, and depart from the *old way*: but it is beyond me, to find out wherein the *iniquity* does lie. We may see cause to *alter some practices of our fathers*, without despising *them*, without priding ourselves in our wisdom, without apostacy, without abusing the advantages God has given us, without a spirit of compliance with corrupt men, without inclination to superstition, without making disturbance in the church of God: and there is no reason, that it should be turned as a *reproach* upon us. Surely it is *commendable* for us to *examine* the practices of our fathers; we have no sufficient reason to take practices upon *trust* from them. Let them have as high a character as belongs to them; yet we may not look upon their principles as *oracles*. Nathan himself missed it in his conjecture about *building the house of God*. He that believes principles because *they* affirm them, makes *idols* of them. And it would be no *humility*, but *baseness* of spirit, for us to judge ourselves *incapable* to examine the principles that have been handed down to us. If we be by any means *fit to open the mysteries of the gospel*, we are capable to judge of *these* matters: and it would *ill* become us, so to indulge ourselves in *ease*, as to *neglect* the examination of received principles. If the practices of our fathers in any particulars were *mistaken*, it is *fit* they should be *rejected*; if they be not, they will bear examination. If we be forbidden to examine their practice, that will cut off all hopes of *reformation*."

Thus, in these very reasonable and apposite sayings, Mr. Stoddard, *though dead, yet speaketh*: and here (to apply them to my own case) he tells *me*, that I am not at all blamable, for not *taking his principles on trust*; that notwithstanding *the high character* justly *belonging to him,* I ought not to *look on his principles as oracles,* as though he could *not miss it,* as well as Nathan himself *in his conjecture about building the house of God;* nay, surely, that I am even *to be commended, for examining his practice,* and judging for myself; that *it would ill become me* to do otherwise; that this *would be no manifestation of humility,* but rather show a *baseness of spirit;* that if I *be not capable to judge for myself in these matters, I am by no means fit to open the mysteries of the gospel;* that if I *should believe his principles, because he advanced them, I should be guilty of making him an idol.*—Also he tells his and my flock, with all others, that it *ill becomes them, so to indulge their ease, as to neglect examining received principles and practices;* and that it is *fit, mistakes in any particulars be rejected:* that if in some things I differ in my judgment from him, it would be very unreasonable, on this account, to *make a great noise, as though I were bringing in innovations, and departing from the old way;* that I *may see cause to alter some practices of my grandfather and predecessor, without despising* him, *without priding myself in my wisdom, without apostacy, without despising the advantages God has given me, without inclination to superstition, and without making disturbance in the church of God;* in short, that *it is beyond him to find out wherein the iniquity of my so doing lies;* and that *there is no reason why it should be turned as a reproach upon me.* Thus, I think, he sufficiently vindicates my conduct in the present case, and warns all with whom I am concerned, not to be at all displeased with me, or to find the least fault with me, merely because I examine for myself, have a judgment of my own, and am for practising in some particulars different from him, how positive soever he was that his judgment and practice were right. It is reasonably hoped and expected, that they who have a great regard to his judgment, will impartially regard his judgment, and hearken to his admonition in these things.

I can seriously declare, that an affectation of making a show as if I were something wiser than that excellent person, is exceeding distant from me, and very far from having the least influence in my appearing to oppose, in this way of the press, an opinion which he so earnestly maintained and promoted. Sure I am, I have not affected to vary from his judgment, nor in the least been governed by a spirit of contradiction, neither indulged a cavilling humour, in remarking on any of his arguments or expressions.—I have formerly been of *his opinion,* which I imbibed from his books, even from my childhood, and have in my proceedings conformed to *his practice;* though never without some difficulties in my view, which I could not solve. Yet, however, a distrust of my own understanding, and deference to the authority of so venerable a man, the seeming strength of some of his arguments, together with the success he had in his ministry, and his great reputation and influence, prevailed for a long time to bear down my scruples.—But the difficulties and uneasiness on my mind increasing, as I became more studied in divinity, and as I improved in experience; this brought me to closer diligence and care to *search the Scriptures,* and more impartially to examine and weigh the arguments of my *grandfather,* and such other authors as I could get on his side of the question. By which means, after long searching, pondering, viewing, and reviewing, I gained satisfaction, became fully settled in the opinion I now maintain, as in the discourse here offered to public view; and dared to proceed no further in a practice and administration inconsistent therewith: which brought me into peculiar circumstances, laying me under an inevitable necessity publicly to declare and maintain the opinion I was thus established in; as also to do it from the press, and to do it at this time without delay.

It is far from a pleasing circumstance of this publication, that it is against what my honoured *grandfather* strenuously maintained, both from the pulpit and press. I can truly say, on account of this and some other considerations, it is what I engage in with the greatest reluctance that ever I undertook any public service in my life. But the state of things with me is so ordered, by the sovereign disposal of the great Governor of the world, that my doing this appeared to me very necessary and altogether unavoidable. I am conscious, not only is the interest of religion concerned in this affair, but my own reputation, future usefulness, and my very subsistence, all seem to depend on my freely opening and defending myself, as to my principles, and agreeable conduct in my pastoral charge; and on my doing it from the press: in which way alone am I able to state and justify my opinion, to any purpose, before the country, (which is full of noise, misrepresentations, and many censures concerning this affair,) or even before my own people, as all would be fully sensible, if they knew the exact state of the case.—I have been brought to this necessity in divine providence, by such a situation of affairs and coincidence of circumstances and events, as I choose at present to be silent about; and which it is not needful, nor perhaps expedient, for me to publish to the world.

One thing among others that caused me to go about this business with so much backwardness, was the fear of a bad improvement some ill-minded people might be ready, at this day, to make of the doctrine here defended; particularly that wild enthusiastical sort of people, who have of late gone into unjustifiable *separations,* even renouncing the ministers and churches of the land in general, under pretence of setting up a pure church. It is well known, that I have heretofore publicly remonstrated, both from the pulpit and press, against very many of the notions and practices of this kind of people: and shall be very sorry if what I now offer to the public, should be any occasion of their encouraging or strengthening themselves in those notions and practices. To prevent which, I would now take occasion to declare, I am still of the same mind concerning them that I have formerly manifested. I have the same opinion concerning the religion and inward experiences chiefly in vogue among them, as I had when I wrote my *Treatise on Religious Affections,* and when I wrote my *Observations and Reflections on Mr. Brainerd's Life.* I have no better opinion of their notion of a *pure church* by means of a *spirit of discerning,* their *censorious outcries* against the standing ministers and churches in general, their *lay ordinations,* their *lay preachings,* and *public exhortings,* and administering *sacraments;* their assuming, self-confident, contentious, uncharitable, *separating spirit;* their going about the country, as *sent by the Lord,* to make proselytes; with their many other extravagant and wicked ways. My holding the doctrine that is defended in this discourse, is no argument of any change of my opinion concerning them; for when I wrote those two books before mentioned, I was of the same mind concerning the qualifications of communicants at the Lord's table that I am of now.

However, it is not unlikely, that some will still exclaim against my principles, as being of the same pernicious tendency with those of the *Separatists.* To such I can only by a solemn protestation aver the sincerity of my aims, and the great care I have exercised to avoid whatsoever is erroneous, or might be in any respect mischievous. But as to my success in these my upright aims and endeavours, I must leave it to every reader to judge for himself, after he has carefully perused and impartially considered the following discourse: which, considering the nature and importance of the subject, I hope all serious readers will accompany with their earnest prayers to the *Father of lights,* for his gracious direction and influence. And, *to Him be glory in the churches by Christ Jesus.*

J. E.

A PREFACE

BY HIS AMERICAN FRIENDS.

THOUGH the doctrine here maintained by our dear and reverend brother, was brought over hither by the pious and judicious fathers of this country from the Puritans in England, and held by them and their successors in our churches above threescore years without dissension; yet some good and learned men have since gone into another way of thinking in this matter. And as the WORD OF GOD is our only rule of judging, and this only can bind the conscience in religion, it must needs concern every man to search the Scriptures, that he may come to as satisfying a knowledge as may be, whether he has a right to the Lord's supper, and whether it be his immediate duty to partake of it, or admit of others. And for all that we had hitherto read on this subject, it seemed to us, there wanted further searchings and discoveries.

And though we have not all had opportunity to read the composure following; yet we apprehend the reverend Author singularly qualified to manage this important argument, from his great acquaintance with the Scriptures, and diligent application to the study of them, with a special aim to find the mind of CHRIST and settle his judgment in this particular; both to get more light himself, and communicate the same to others. And we have this peculiar motive to excite attention to what he writes, that he is so far from arguing from the prejudice or influence of education, that being brought up in the contrary way of thinking, and more inclined thereto from a special veneration of his reverend grandfather; yet on carefully searching the sacred volumes, he was obliged to yield to those convictions they produced in him, and change his judgment.

The following Treatise contains the substance of those convictions, or the particular reasons of this alteration. And if those who are now in his former way of thinking, would with due seriousness, humility, calmness, diligence, and impartiality, search the Scriptures, and consider his arguments derived from them, looking up to GOD through CHRIST, and subjecting their minds entirely to him, they may either see and yield to the same convictions, and find cause to change their judgments also, or will at least continue their fraternal affection to the worthy Author, and others in the same sentiments with him.

We heartily pray that the reverend Author and his flock may for a long time be happy together; that their cordial love and tenderness to each other may continue and operate in mutual and all lawful condescensions and forbearances under different sentiments in these particulars; that every one may be open to light, and guard against all prejudice, precipitance, and passion; that they may be very watchful against the devices of Satan to disunite or disaffect them; that they may study the things that make for peace and edification.—And the GOD of light, love, and peace, will continue with them.

THOMAS PRINCE.
JOHN WEBB.
THOMAS FOXCROFT.
M. BYLES.

Boston,
August 11, 1746.

ADVERTISEMENT TO THE EDINBURGH EDITION.

A NARRATIVE of the transactions to which the following Treatise refers, may be read in the account of the Author's Life, which was printed originally at Boston, New England, in 1765, and lately reprinted at Glasgow. The works of the Author are now very well known in this country. The world, it is apprehended, owe no small obligation to Dr. John Erskine, one of the ministers of this city, who first introduced them to their acquaintance.

There are very few persons attentive to the subjects on which President Edwards has written who will not acknowledge, that he has cast much light upon them. And nothing will prevent Christians from considering the present Treatise as one of the most able and interesting parts of his works, but prejudice and indifference about the subject of it. His own opinion of it may be seen in his Preface. It will there appear, if persons should even be inattentive to its internal evidence, that it called forth the complete extent of his abilities, and was the fruit of dependence on the Father of lights for instruction and preservation from error.

The whole of his works are now reprinted in Britain, excepting only his Defence of this Treatise, against the Objections of Mr. Solomon Williams. If the present performance, which is exceedingly scarce, meets with encouragement, the publisher intends to print it also.

Edinburgh, May 15, 1790.

AN

HUMBLE INQUIRY, &c.

PART I.

THE QUESTION STATED AND EXPLAINED.

THE main question I would consider, and for the negative of which I would offer some arguments in the following discourse, is this; *Whether, according to the rules of* CHRIST, *any ought to be admitted to the communion and privileges of members of the visible church of* CHRIST *in complete standing, but such as are in profession, and in the eye of the church's christian judgment, godly or gracious persons?*

When I speak of members of the visible church of Christ, *in complete standing,* I would be understood of those who are received as the proper immediate subjects of all the external privileges Christ has appointed for the ordinary members of his church. I say *ordinary members,* in distinction from any peculiar privileges and honours of church-officers and rulers. All allow, there are some that are in some respect in the church of God, who are not members in complete standing, in the sense that has been explained. All that acknowledge infant baptism, allow infants, who are the proper subjects of baptism, and are baptized, to be in some sort members of the christian church; yet none suppose them to be members in such standing as to be the proper immediate subjects of all ecclesiastical ordinances and privileges: but that some further qualifications are requisite in order to this, to be obtained, either in a course of nature, or by education, or by divine grace. And some who are baptized in infancy, even after they come to be adult, may yet remain for a season short of such a standing as has been spoken of; being destitute of sufficient knowledge, and perhaps some other qualifications, through the neglect of parents, or their own negligence, or otherwise; or because they carelessly neglected to qualify themselves for ecclesiastical privileges by making a public profession of the christian faith, or owning the christian covenant, or forbear to offer themselves as candidates for these privileges; and yet not be cast out of the church, or cease to be in any respect its members: this, I suppose, will also be generally allowed.

One thing mainly intended in the foregoing question is, whether any adult persons but such as are in the profession and appearance endowed with the christian grace or piety, ought to be admitted to *the christian sacraments.* Particularly, whether they ought to be admitted to the *Lord's supper;* and, if they are such as were not baptized in infancy, ought to be admitted to *baptism.* Adult persons having those qualifications that oblige others to receive them as the proper immediate subjects of the christian sacraments, is a main thing intended in the question, by being such as *ought to be admitted to the communion and privileges of members of the visible church, in complete standing.* There are many adult persons that by the allowance of all are in some respects within the church of God, who are not members in good standing, in this respect. There are many, for instance, that have not at present the qualifications proper to recommend them to the *Lord's supper:* there are many scandalous persons, who are under suspension. The late venerable *Mr. Stoddard,* and many other great divines, suppose, that even excommunicated persons are still members of the church of God; and some suppose, the worshippers of Baal in Israel, even those who were bred up such from their infancy, remained still members of the church of God. And very many protestant divines suppose, that the members of the church of Rome, though they are brought up and live continually in gross idolatry, and innumerable errors and superstitions that tend utterly to make void the gospel of Christ, still are in the visible church of Christ: yet, I suppose, no orthodox divines would hold these to be properly and regularly qualified for the Lord's supper. It was therefore requisite, in the question before us, that a distinction should be made between the members of the visible church *in general,* and members *in complete standing.*

It was also requisite, that such a distinction should be made in the question, to avoid lengthening out this discourse exceedingly, with needless questions and debates concerning the state of baptized infants; that is *needless* as to my present purpose. Though I have no doubts about the doctrine of infant baptism; yet God's manner of dealing with such infants as are regularly dedicated to him in baptism, is a matter liable to great disputes and many controversies, and would require a large dissertation by itself to clear it up; which, as it would extend this discourse beyond all bounds, so it appears not necessary in order to a clear determination of the present question. The revelation of God's word is much plainer and more express concerning adult persons, that act for themselves in religious matters, than concerning infants. The Scriptures were written for the sake of adult persons, or those that are capable of knowing what is written. It is to such the apostle speaks in the Epistles, and to such only does God speak throughout his word; and the Scriptures especially speak for the sake of these, and about those *to whom* they speak. And therefore if the word of God affords us light enough concerning those spoken of in the question, as I have stated it, clearly to determine the matter with respect to them, we need not wait till we see all doubts and controversies about baptized infants cleared and settled, before we pass a judgment with respect to the point in hand. The denominations, characters, and descriptions, which we find given in the Scripture to visible Christians, and to the visible church, are principally with an eye to the church of Christ in its adult state and proper standing. If any one was about to describe that kind of birds called doves, it would be most proper to describe grown doves, and not young ones in the egg or nest, without wings or feathers. So if any one should describe a palm-tree or olive-tree by their visible form and appearance, it would be presumed that they described those of these kinds of trees in their natural and proper state; and not as just peeping from the ground, or as thunder-struck or blown down. And therefore I would here give notice, once for all, that when in the ensuing discourse I use such like phrases as *visible saints, members of the visible church,* &c. I, for the most part, mean persons that are *adult* and in *good standing.*

The question is not, whether Christ has made converting grace or piety *itself* the condition or rule of his people's admitting any to the privileges of members in full communion with them. There is no one qualification of the *mind* whatsoever, that Christ has properly made the term of this; not so much as a common belief that *Jesus* is the *Messiah,* or a belief of the being of a God. It is the credible *profession* and *visibility* of these things, that is the church's rule in this case. Christian *piety* or godliness may be a qualification requisite to communion in the christian sacraments, just in the same manner as a *belief* that Jesus is the Messiah, and the Scriptures the word of God, are requisite qualifications; and in the same manner as some kind of *repentance* is a qualification in one that has been suspended for being grossly scandalous, in order to his coming again to the Lord's supper; and yet godliness *itself* not be properly the rule of the church's proceeding, in like manner as such a belief and repentance, as I have mentioned, are not their rule. It is a *visibility* to the eye of a christian judgment, that is the rule of the church's proceeding in each of these cases.—There are two *distinctions* must be here observed. As,

1. We must distinguish between such qualifications as are requisite to give a person a right to ecclesiastical privileges in *foro ecclesiæ*, or a right to be admitted by the *church* to those privileges; and those qualifications that are a proper and good foundation for a man's *own* conduct in coming and offering himself as a candidate for immediate admission to these privileges. There is a difference between these. Thus, for instance, a *profession* of the belief of a future state and of revealed religion, and some other things that are internal and out of sight, and a visibility of these things to the eye of a christian judgment, is all relating to these things, that is requisite to give a man a right in *foro ecclesiæ*, or before the church; but it is the real existence of these things, that is what lays a proper and *good* foundation for his making this profession, and so demanding these privileges. None will suppose, that he has good and proper ground for such a conduct, who does not believe another world, nor believe the Bible to be the word of God. And then,

2. We must distinguish between that which *nextly* brings an obligation on a man's conscience to seek admission to a christian ordinance, and that which is a good foundation for the dictate of an enlightened well-informed conscience, and so is properly a *solid* foundation of a right in him to act thus. Certainly this distinction does really take place among mankind in innumerable cases. The dictates of men's consciences are what bring them under a most *immediate* obligation to act; but it is that which is a good foundation for such a dictate of an *enlightened* conscience, that alone is a *solid* foundation of a right in him so to act. Believing the doctrine of the Trinity *with all the heart*, in some sense, (let us suppose a moral sense,) is one thing requisite in order to a person's having a solid foundation of a right in him to go and demand baptism in the name of the Trinity; but his *best judgment* or dictate of his conscience, concerning his believing this doctrine with this sincerity, or with all his heart, may be sufficient to bring an obligation on his conscience. Again, when a delinquent has been convicted of scandal, it is repentance in some respect sincere, (some a moral sincerity,) that is a proper foundation of a right in him to offer himself for forgiveness and restoration; but it is the dictate of his conscience or his *best judgment* concerning his sincerity, that is the thing which immediately obliges him to offer himself. It is repentance *itself*, that is the proper qualification fundamental of his right, and without which he cannot have a proper right; for though he may be deceived, and think he has real repentance when he has not, yet he has not properly a right to be deceived; and perhaps deceit in such cases is always owing to something blamable, or the influence of some corrupt principle: but yet his best judgment brings him under obligation. In the same manner, and no otherwise, I suppose that christian *grace itself* is a qualification requisite in order to a proper solid ground of a right in a person to come to the christian sacraments. But of this I may say something more when I come to answer objections.

When I speak, in the question, of being godly or gracious in the eye of a christian judgment, by *christian judgment* I intend something further than a kind of mere *negative* charity, implying that we forbear to censure and condemn a man, because we do not know but that he may be godly, and therefore forbear to proceed on the foot of such a censure or judgment in our treatment of him: as we would kindly entertain a stranger, not knowing but in so doing we entertain an angel or precious saint of God. But I mean *a positive judgment*, founded on some positive appearance, or visibly, some outward manifestations that ordinarily render the thing probable. There is a difference between suspending our judgment, or forbearing to condemn, or having some hope that *possibly* the thing may be so, and so hoping the best; and a positive judgment in favour of a person. For having some hope, only implies that a man is not in utter despair of a thing, though his prevailing opinion may be otherwise, or he may suspend his opinion. Though we cannot know a man believes that *Jesus* is the *Messiah*, yet we expect some positive manifestation or visibility of it, to be a ground of our charitable judgment: so I suppose the case is here.

When I speak of christian *judgment*, I mean a judgment wherein men do properly exercise reason, and have their reason under the due influence of love and other christian principles; which do not blind reason, but regulate its exercises; being not contrary to reason, though they be very contrary to censoriousness, or unreasonable niceness and rigidness.

I say *in the eye of the* Church's *christian judgment*, because it is properly a visibility to the eye of the public charity, and not of a private judgment, that gives a person a right to be received as a visible saint by the public. If any are known to be persons of an honest character, and appear to be of good understanding in the doctrines of Christianity, and particularly those doctrines that teach the grand condition of salvation, and the nature of true saving religion, and publicly and seriously profess the great and main things wherein the essence of true religion or godliness consists, and their conversation is agreeable; this justly recommends them to the good opinion of the public, whatever suspicions and fears any particular person, either the minister, or some other, may entertain, from what he in particular has observed, perhaps from the manner of his expressing himself in giving an account of his experiences, or an obscurity in the order and method of his experiences, &c. The minister in receiving him to the communion of the church, is to act as a public officer, and in behalf of the public society, and not merely for himself, and therefore is to be governed, in acting, by a proper visibility of godliness in the eye of the public.

It is not my design, in holding the negative of the foregoing question, to affirm, that all who are regularly admitted as members of the visible church in complete standing, ought to be believed to be godly or gracious persons, when taken *collectively*, or considered in the gross, by the judgment of any person or society. This may not be, and yet each person taken singly may visibly be a gracious person to the eye of the judgment of Christians in general. These two are not the same thing, but vastly diverse; and the latter may be, and yet not the former. If we should know so much of a thousand persons one after another, and from what we observed in them should have a prevailing opinion concerning each one of them, singly taken, that they were indeed pious, and think the judgment we passed, when we consider each judgment apart, to be right; it will not follow, when we consider the whole company collectively, that we shall have so high an opinion of our own judgment, as to think it probable, there was not one erroneous judgment in the whole thousand. We all have innumerable judgments about one thing or other, concerning religious, moral, secular, and philosophical affairs, concerning past, present, and future matters, reports, facts, persons, things, &c. And concerning all the many thousand dictates of judgment that we have, we think them every one right, taken singly; for if there was any one that we thought wrong, it would not be our judgment; and yet there is no man, unless he is stupidly foolish, who when he considers all in the gross, will say he thinks that his every opinion he is of, concerning all persons and things whatsoever, important and trifling, is right, without the least error. But the more clearly to illustrate this matter, as it relates to visibility, or probable appearances of holiness in professors: supposing it had been found by experience concerning precious stones, that such and such external marks were *probable* signs of a diamond; and supposing, by putting together a great number of experiments, the probability is *as ten to one*, that, take one time with another, *one in ten* of the stones which have these marks (and no visible signs to the contrary) proves to be not a true diamond. Then it will follow, that when I find a particular stone with these marks, and nothing to the contrary, there is a probability of *ten to one*, concerning that stone, that it is a diamond; and so concerning each stone that I find with these marks: but if we take *ten* of these together, it is as probable as not, that some *one* of the ten is spurious; because, if it were not as likely as not, that *one to ten* is false, or if taking *one ten* with another, there were not *one in ten* that was false, then the probability of those, that have these marks, being true diamonds, would be more than *ten to one*, contrary to the supposition; because that is what we mean by a probability of *ten to one*, that they are not false, *viz.* that take one *ten* with another there will be *one* false stone among them, and no more. Hence if we take a *hundred* such stones together, the probability will be just *ten to one*, that there is *one* false among them; and as likely as not that there are *ten* false ones in the whole hundred. And the probability of the individuals must be much greater than *ten* to one, even a probability of more than a *hundred* to one, in order to its making it probable that every one is true. It is an easy mathematical demonstration. Hence the negative of the foregoing question by no means implies a pretence of any scheme, that shall be effectual to keep all hypocrites out of the church, and for the establishing in that sense *a pure church*.

When it is said, those who are admitted, &c. ought to be by profession *godly* or *gracious* persons; it is not meant, they should merely *profess* or *say* that they are converted or are gracious persons, that they *know* so, or *think* so; but that they profess the great things wherein christian piety consists, *viz.* a supreme respect to God, faith in Christ, &c. Indeed it is necessary, as men would keep a good conscience, that they should think that these things are in them, which they profess to be in them; otherwise they are guilty of the horrid wickedness of wilfully making a lying profession. Hence it is supposed to be necessary, in order to men's regularly and with a good conscience coming into communion with the church of Christ in the christian sacraments, that they themselves should suppose the essential things, belonging to christian piety, to be in them.

It does not belong to the present question, to consider and determine what the nature of christian piety is, or wherein it consists: this question may be properly determined, and the determination demonstrated, without entering into any controversies about the nature of conversion, &c. Nor does an asserting the negative of the question determine any thing how particular the profession of godliness ought to be, but only that the more essential things, which belong to it, ought to be professed. Nor is it determined, but that the public professions made on occasion of persons' admission to the Lord's supper, in some of our churches, who yet go upon that principle, that persons need not esteem themselves truly gracious in order to a coming conscientiously and properly to the Lord's supper; I say, it is not determined but that some of these professions are sufficient, if those that made them were taught to use the words, and others to understand them, in no other than their proper meaning, and principle and custom had not established a meaning very diverse from it, or perhaps an use of the words without any distinct and clear determinate meaning.

PART II.

REASONS FOR THE NEGATIVE OF THE FOREGOING QUESTION.

HAVING thus explained what I mean, when I say, *That none ought to be admitted to the communion and privileges of members of the visible church of Christ in complete standing, but such as are in profession, and in the eye of the church's christian judgment, godly or gracious persons*: I now proceed to observe some things which may tend to evince the truth of this position.

SECT. I.

None ought to be admitted as members of the visible church of Christ but visible and professing saints.

I BEGIN with observing, I think it is both evident by the word of God, and also granted on all hands, that none ought to be admitted as members of the visible church of Christ but *visible* and *professing saints*, or visible and professing Christians.—We find the word *saint*, when applied to men, used two ways in the New Testament. The word in some places is so used as to mean those that are *real* saints, who are converted, and are truly gracious persons; as 1 Cor. vi. 2. "Do ye not know that the saints shall judge the world?" Eph. i. 18. "The riches of the glory of his inheritance in the saints." Chap. iii. 17, 18. "That Christ may dwell in your hearts by faith, that ye being rooted and grounded in love, may be able to comprehend with all saints, what is the breadth," &c. 2 Thess. i. 10. "When he shall come to be glorified in his saints, and admired in all them that believe." So Rev. v. 8. chap. viii. 4. and xi. 18. and xiii. 10. and xiv. 12. and xix. 8. In other places the word is used so as to have respect not only to real saints, but to such as were saints in *visibility*, *appearance*, and *profession*; and so were outwardly, as to what concerns their acceptance among men and their outward treatment and privileges, of the company of saints. So the word is used in very many places, which it is needless to mention, as every one acknowledges it.

In like manner we find the word *Christian* used two ways: the word is used to express the same thing as "a righteous man that shall be saved," 1 Pet. iv. 16—18. Elsewhere it is so used as to take in all that were Christians by profession and outward appearance; Acts xi. 26. So there is a twofold use of the word *disciples* in the New Testament. There were disciples in name, profession, and appearance; and there were those whom Christ calls *disciples indeed*, John viii. 30, 31.—The word is ἀληθῶς, *truly*. The expression plainly supposes this distinction of true or real disciples, and those who were the same in pretence and appearance. See also Luke xiv. 25—27. and John xv. 8. The same distinction is signified, in the New Testament, by those that *live*, being alive from the dead, and risen with Christ, (2 Cor. iv. 11. Rom. vi. 11. and elsewhere,) and those who *have a name to live*, having only a pretence and appearance of life. And the distinction of the visible church of Christ into these two, is plainly signified of the growth of the good ground, and that in the stony and thorny ground, which had the same appearance and show with the other, till it came to wither away; and also by the two sorts of virgins, Matt. xxv. who both had a show, profession, and visibility of the same thing. By these things, and many others which might be observed, it appears, that the distinction of *real* and *visible* or professing saints is scriptural, and that the visible church was made up of these two, and that none are according to Scripture admitted into the visible church of Christ, but those who are visible and professing saints or Christians. And it is the more needless to insist longer upon it, because it is not a thing in controversy; so far as my small reading will inform me, it is owned by all protestants. To be sure, the most eminent divine in New England who has appeared to maintain the Lord's supper to be properly a converting ordinance, was very full in it. In his *Appeal to the Learned*, in the title-page, and through the Treatise, he supposes that all who come to the Lord's supper, must be *visible saints*, and sometimes speaks of them as *professing saints*, page 85, 86: and supposes that it is requisite in order to their being admitted to the communion of the Lord's table, that they make a personal public profession of their faith and repentance to the just satisfaction of the church, page 93, 94. In these things the whole of the position that I would prove is in effect granted. If it be allowed (as it is allowed on all sides) that none ought to be admitted to the communion of the christian visible church, but visible and professing saints or Christians, if these words are used in any propriety of speech, or in any agreement with scripture representations, the whole of that which I have laid down is either implied or will certainly follow.

As *real* saints are the same with real converts, or really gracious persons, so *visible* saints are the same with visible converts, or those that are visibly converted and gracious persons. *Visibility* is the same with *manifestation* or *appearance* to our view and apprehension. And therefore to be visibly a gracious person, is the same thing as to be a truly gracious person to our view, apprehension, or esteem. The distinction of *real* and *visible* does not only take place with regard to saintship or holiness, but with regard to innumerable other things. There is visible and real truth, visible and real honesty, visible and real money, visible and real gold, visible and real diamonds, &c. &c. *Visible* and *real* are words that stand related one to another, as the words *real* and *seeming*, or *true* and *apparent*. Some seem to speak of *visibility* with regard to saintship or holiness, as though it had no reference to the *reality*, or as though it were a distinct reality by itself; as though by visible saints were not meant those who to appearance are real saints or disciples indeed, but properly a distinct sort of saints, which is an absurdity. There is a distinction between real money and visible money, because all that is esteemed money and passes for money is not real money, but some is false and counterfeit. By visible money, is not meant that which is taken and passes for a different sort from true money, but that which is esteemed and taken as real money, or which has that appearance that recommends it to men's judgment and acceptance as true money; though men may be deceived, and some of it may finally prove not to be so.

There are not properly two sorts of saints spoken of in Scripture. Though the word *saints* may be said indeed to be used two ways in Scripture, or used so as to reach two sorts of persons; yet the word has not properly two significations in the New Testament, any more than the word *gold* has two significations among us: the word gold among us is so used as to extend to several sorts of substances; it is true, it extends to true gold, and also to that which only appears to be gold, and is reputed such, and by that appearance or visibility some things that are not *real* obtain the *name* of gold; but this is not properly through a diversity in the signification of the word, but by a diversity of the application of it, through the imperfection of our discerning. It does not follow that there are properly two sorts of saints, because some who are not *real* saints, do by the show and appearance they make obtain the *name* of saints, and are reputed such, and whom by the rules of Scripture (which are accommodated to our imperfect state) we are directed to receive and treat as saints; any more than it follows that there are two sorts of honest men, because some who are not truly honest men, yet being so seemingly or visibly, do obtain the name of honest men, and ought to be treated by us as such. So there are not properly two distinct churches of Christ, one the real, and another the visible; though they that are visibly or seemingly of the one only church of Christ, are many more than they who are really of his church; and so the visible or seeming church is of larger extent than the real.

Visibility is a relative thing, and has relation to an eye that views or beholds. Visibility is the same as appearance or exhibition to the eye; and to be a visible saint is the same as to appear to be a real saint in the eye that beholds; not the eye of God, but the eye of man. Real saints or converts are those that are so in the eye of God; visible saints or converts are those who are so in the eye of man; not his bodily eye, for thus no man is a saint any more in the eye of a man than he is in the eye of a beast; but the eye of his mind, which is his judgment or esteem. There is no more visibility of holiness in the brightest professor to the eye of our bodies, without the exercise of the reason and judgment of our minds, than may be in a machine. But nothing short of an apparent probability, or a probable exhibition, can amount to a visibility to the eye of man's reason or judgment. The eye which God has given to *man* is the eye of reason: and the eye of a *Christian* is reason sanctified, regulated, and enlightened, by a principle of christian love. But it implies a contradiction to say, that that is visible to the eye of reason, which does not appear probable to reason. And if there be a man that is in this sense a visible saint, he is in the eye of a rational judgment a real saint. To say a man is visibly a saint, but not visibly a real saint, but only visibly a visible saint, is a very absurd way of speaking; it is as much as to say, he is to appearance an appearing saint; which is in effect to say nothing, and to use words without signification. The thing which must be visible and probable, in order to *visible saintship*, must be saintship *itself*, or real grace and true holiness; not visibility of saintship, not unregenerate morality, not mere moral sincerity. To pretend, or in any respect to exhibit, moral sincerity, makes nothing visible beyond what is pretended to or exhibited. For a man to have that visibly, which if he had it really, and have nothing more, would not make him a real saint, is not to be visibly a saint.

Mr. Stoddard, in his *Appeal to the Learned*, seems to express the very same notion of visibility, and that visibility of saintship which is requisite to persons coming to the Lord's supper, that I have here expressed. In page 10, he makes a distinction between being *visibly* circumcised in heart, and being *really* so; evidently meaning by the latter, saving *conversion;* and he allows the former, *viz.* a visibility of *heart-circumcision*, to be necessary to a coming to the Lord's supper. So that according to him, it is not a visibility of *moral sincerity* only, but a visibility of *circumcision of heart*, or saving conversion, that is a necessary requisite to a person's coming to the Lord's table. And in what manner this must be *visible*, he signifies elsewhere, when he allows, that it must be so *to a judgment of charity; a judgment of rational charity*. This he expressly allows over and over; as in page 2, 3, 28, 33, 73, and 95: and *having reason to look upon them as such*, page 28. And towards the close of his book, he declares himself stedfastly of the mind, that it is requisite those be not admitted to the Lord's supper, who do not *make a personal and public profession of their* faith *and* repentance, *to the just satisfaction of the church*, page 93, 94. But how he reconciled these passages with the rest of his Treatise, I would modestly say, I must confess myself at a loss. And particularly, I cannot see how they consist with what this venerable and ever-honoured author says, page 16, in these words; "Indeed by the rule that God has given for admissions, if it be carefully attended, *more* unconverted persons will be admitted than converted." I would humbly inquire, how those visible qualifications can be the ground of a *rational judgment*, that a person is *circumcised in heart*, which nevertheless, at the same time, we are sensible are so far from being any probable signs of it, that they are *more* frequently without it than with it. The appearance of that thing surely cannot imply an appearing probability of another thing, which at the same time we are sensible is most frequently, and so most probably, without that other thing.

Indeed I can easily see, how that may seem visible, and appear probable, to God's people, by reason of the imperfect and dark state they are in, and so may oblige their charity, which yet is not real, and which would not appear at all probable to *angels*, who stand in a clearer light. And the different degrees of light, in which God's church stands, in different *ages*, may make a difference in this respect. The church under the New Testament being favoured by God with a vastly greater light in divine things, than the church under the Old Testament, that might make some difference, as to the kind of profession of religion that is requisite, under these different dispensations, in order to a visibility of holiness; also a proper visibility may fail in the greater number in some extraordinary case, and in exempt circumstances. But how those signs can be a ground of a *rational judgment* that a thing is, which, at that very time, and under that degree of light we then have, we are sensible do *oftener* fail than not, and this ordinarily, I own myself much at a loss. Surely nothing but *appearing reason* is the ground of a *rational judgment*. And indeed it is impossible in the nature of things, to form a *judgment*, which at that very time we think to be not only without, but against, *probability*.

If it be said, that although persons do not profess that wherein *sanctifying grace* consists, yet seeing they profess to believe the *doctrines* of the *gospel*, which God is wont to make use of in order to sanctification, and are called the *doctrine which is according to godliness;* and since we see nothing in their *lives* to make us determine, that they have not had a proper effect on their *hearts*, we are obliged in charity to hope, that they are *real saints*, or *gracious* persons, and to treat them accordingly, and so to receive them into the christian church, and to its special ordinances.

I answer, this objection does in effect suppose and grant the very thing mainly in dispute. For it supposes, that a *gracious character* is the thing that ought to be aimed at in admitting persons into the communion of the church; and so that it is needful to have this charity for persons, or such a favourable notion of them, in order to our receiving them as properly qualified members of the society, and properly qualified subjects of the special privileges to which they are admitted. Whereas, the doctrine taught is, that sanctifying grace is not a necessary qualification, and that there is no need that the person himself, or any other, should imagine he is a person so qualified. The assigned reason is, because it is no qualification requisite in itself; the ordinance of the Lord's supper is as proper for them that are not qualified as for those that are; it being according to the design of the institution a *converting* ordinance, and so an ordinance as much intended for the good of the *unconverted*, as of the *converted;* even as it is with the preaching of the gospel. Now if the case be so, why is there any talk about a *charitable hoping* they are converted, and so admitting them? What need of any charitable hope of such a qualification, in order to admitting them to an ordinance that is as proper for those who are without this qualification, as for those that have it? We need not have any charitable hope of any such qualification in order to admit a person to hear the word preached. What need have we to aim at any thing beyond the proper qualifications? And what need of any charitable opinion or hope of any thing further? Some sort of belief, that *Jesus* is the *Messiah*, is a qualification properly requisite to a coming to the Lord's supper; and therefore it is necessary that we should have a charitable *hope*, that those have such a belief whom we admit; though it be not necessary that we should *know* it, it being what none can know of another. But as to grace or christian piety, it clearly follows, on the principles which I oppose, that no kind of visibility or appearance, whether direct or indirect, whether to a greater or less degree, no charity or hope of it, have any thing at all to do in the affair of admission to the Lord's supper; for, according to them, it is properly a *converting* ordinance. What has any visibility or hope of a person being already in health to do, in admitting him into an hospital for the use of those means that are appointed for the healing of the sick, and bringing them to health? And therefore it is needless here to dispute about the nature of visibility; and all arguing concerning a profession of christian doctrines, and an orderly life being a sufficient ground of public charity, and an obligation on the church to treat them as saints, are wholly impertinent and nothing to the purpose. For on the principles which I oppose, there is no need of any ground for *treating them as saints*, in order to admitting them to the Lord's supper, the very design of which is *to make them saints*, any more than there is need of some ground of treating a sick man as being a man in health, in order to admitting him into an hospital. Persons, by the doctrine that I oppose, are not taught to offer themselves as candidates for church communion under any such notion, or with any such pretence, as their being gracious persons; and therefore surely when those that teach them, receive them to the ordinance, they do not receive them under any such notion, nor has any appearance, hope, or thought of it, any thing to do in the case.

The apostle speaks of the members of the christian church, as those that made a *profession of godliness*. 2 Cor. ix. 13. "They glorified God for your *professed* subjection to the gospel of Christ." 1 Tim. ii. 9, 10. "In like manner also that women adorn themselves in modest apparel—not with costly array; but which becometh women *professing* godliness, with good works." The apostle is speaking of the women that were members of that great church of Ephesus, which Timothy for the present had the care of; and he speaks of them as supposing that they all *professed godliness*. By the allowance of all, *profession* is one thing belonging to the visibility of Christianity or holiness, in the members of the visible church. Visible holiness is an appearance or exhibition of holiness, by those things which are external, and so fall under our notice and observation, and these are two, *viz. profession*, and outward *behaviour* agreeable to that profession. That profession which belongs to visible saintship, must be a profession of *godliness*, or real saintship; for a profession makes nothing visible beyond what is professed. What is it to be a saint by profession, but to be by profession a true saint? For to be by profession a false saint, is to be by profession no saint; and only to profess that, which if never so true, is nothing peculiar to a saint, is not to be a professing saint.

In order to a man's being properly a *professing Christian*, he must profess the *religion of Jesus Christ:* and he surely does not profess the religion that was taught by Jesus Christ, if he leaves out of his profession the most essential things that belong to that religion. That which is most essential in that religion itself, the profession of that is essential in a profession of that religion; for (as I have observed elsewhere) that which is most essential in a thing, in order to its being truly denominated that thing, the same is essentially necessary to be expressed or signified in any exhibition or declaration of that thing, in order to its being truly denominated a declaration or exhibition of that thing. If we take a more inconsiderable part of Christ's religion, and leave out the main and most essential, surely what we have cannot be properly called the religion of Jesus Christ: so if we profess only a less important part, and are silent about the most important and essential part, it cannot be properly said that we profess the religion of Jesus Christ. And therefore we cannot in any propriety be said to profess Christ's religion, unless we profess those things wherein consist piety of heart, which is vastly the most important and essential part of that religion, and is in effect all; being that without which all the rest that belongs to it, is nothing, and wholly in vain. But they who are admitted to the Lord's supper, proceeding on the principles of those who hold it to be a *converting* ordinance, do in no respect profess christian piety, neither in whole nor in part, neither explicitly nor implicitly, directly nor indirectly; and therefore are not professing Christians, or saints by profession. I mean, though they may be godly persons, yet as they come to the ordinance without *professing godliness*, they cannot properly be called *professing saints*.

Here it may be said, that although no *explicit* and *formal* profession of those things which belong to true piety, be required of them; yet there are many things they do, that are a *virtual* and *implicit* profession of these things: such as their owning the christian covenant, their owning God the Father, Son, and Holy Ghost to be their God; and by their visibly joining in the public prayers and singing God's praises, there is a show and implicit profession of supreme respect to God and love to him; by joining in the public confessions, they make a show of repentance; by keeping Sabbaths and hearing the word, they make a show of a spirit of obedience; by offering to come to sacraments, they make a show of love to Christ and a dependence on his sacrifice.

To this I answer; It is a great mistake, if any one imagines, that all these external performances are of the nature of a *profession*, of any thing that belongs to *saving grace*, as they are commonly used and understood. None of them are so, according to the doctrines that are taught and embraced, and the customs that are established, in such churches as proceed on the footing of the principles forementioned. For what is *professing*, but exhibiting, uttering, or declaring, either by intelligible words, or by other established signs that are equivalent? But in such churches, neither their publicly saying, that they *avouch*

God the Father, Son, and Holy Ghost, to be their God, and that they *give themselves up to him,* and *promise to obey all his commands,* nor their coming to the Lord's supper, or to any other ordinances, are taken for expressions or signs, of any thing belonging to the essence of christian piety. But on the contrary, the public doctrine, principle, and custom in such churches, establishes a *diverse* use of these words and signs. People are taught, that they may use them all, and not so much as make any pretence to the least degree of *sanctifying grace;* and this is the established custom. So they are used, and so they are understood. And therefore whatever some of these words and signs may *in themselves* most properly and naturally import, they entirely cease to be significations of any such thing among people accustomed to understand and use them otherwise; and so cease to be of the nature of a profession of christian piety. There can be no such thing among such a people, as either an explicit or implicit *profession of godliness,* by any thing which (by their established doctrine and custom) an *unregenerate* man may and ought to say and perform, knowing himself to be so. For let the words and actions otherwise signify what they will, yet people have in effect agreed among themselves, that persons who use them need not intend them so, and that others need not understand them so. And hence they cease to be of the nature of any pretension to grace. And surely it is an absurdity to say, that men openly and solemnly profess grace, and yet do not so much as pretend to it. If a certain people should agree, and it should be an established principle among them, that men might and ought to use such and such words to their neighbours, which according to their proper signification were a profession of entire love and devoted friendship towards the man they speak to, and yet not think that he has any love in his heart to him, yea, and know at the same time that he had a reigning enmity against him; and it was known that this was the established principle of the people; would not these words, whatever their proper signification was, entirely cease to be any profession or testimony of friendship to his neighbour? To be sure, there could be no visibility of it to the eye of reason.

Thus it is evident, that those who are admitted into the church on the principles that I oppose, are not *professing saints,* nor *visible saints;* because that thing which alone is truly saintship, is not what they profess, or pretend, or have any visibility of, to the eye of a christian judgment. Or if they in fact be visible and professing saints, yet they are not admitted *as such;* no profession of true saintship, nor any manner of visibility of it, has any thing to do in the affair.

There is one way to evade these things, which has been taken by some. They plead, Although it be true, that the Scripture represents the members of the visible church of Christ as professors of *godliness;* and they are abundantly called by the name of *saints* in Scripture, undoubtedly because they *were saints by profession, and in visibility, and the acceptance of others,* yet this is not with any reference to *saving* holiness, but to quite another sort of *saintship, viz. moral sincerity;* and that this is the real saintship, discipleship, and godliness, which is professed, and visible in them, and with regard to which, as having an appearance of it to the eye of reason, they have the name of *saints, disciples,* &c. in Scripture.—It must be noted, that in this objection the visibility is supposed to be of *real* saintship, discipleship, and godliness, but only another sort of *real godliness,* than that which belongs to those who shall finally be owned by Christ as his people, at the day of judgment.

To which I answer, This is a mere *evasion;* the only one, that ever I saw or heard of; and I think the only one possible. For it is certain, they are not professors of sanctifying grace, or true saintship: the principle proceeded on being, that they need make no pretence to that; nor has any visibility of saving holiness any thing to do in the affair. If then they have any holiness at all, it must be of another sort. And if this evasion fails, all fails, and the whole matter in debate must be given up. Therefore I desire that this matter may be impartially considered and examined to the very bottom; and that it may be thoroughly inquired, whether this distinction of these two sorts of *real Christianity, godliness,* and *holiness,* is a distinction of which Christ in his word is the author; or whether it be a human invention of something which the New Testament knows nothing of, devised to serve and maintain an hypothesis.—And here I desire that the following things may be observed:

1. According to this hypothesis, the words *saints, disciples,* and *Christians,* are used *four* ways in the New Testament, as applied to four sorts of persons. (1.) To those that in *truth* and *reality* are the *heirs of eternal life,* and that shall judge the world, or have indeed that saintship which is saving. (2.) To those who *profess* this, and pretend to and make a fair show of a supreme regard to Christ, and to renounce the world for his sake, but have not real ground for these pretences and appearances. (3.) To those who, although they have not saving grace, yet have that other sort of *real godliness,* or *saintship, viz. moral sincerity* in religion; and so are properly a sort of *real saints, true Christians, sincerely godly persons,* and *disciples indeed,* though they have no saving grace. And, (4.) To those who make a *profession* and have a *visibility* of this *latter* sort of sincere Christianity, and are nominally such kind of saints, but are not so indeed.—So that here are two sorts of *real* Christians, and two sorts of *visible* Christians; two sorts of *invisible* and real churches of Christ, and two sorts of *visible* churches. Now will any one that is well acquainted with the New Testament say, there is in that the least appearance or shadow of such a four-fold use of the words, *saints, disciples,* &c.? It is manifest by what was observed before, that these words are there used but *two* ways; and that those of mankind to whom these names are applied, are there distinguished into but *two* sorts, *viz.* Those who have *really* a saving interest in Christ, spiritual conformity and union to him, and those who have a *name* for it, as having a profession and appearance of it. And this is further evident by various representations, which we there find of the visible church; as in the company of *virgins* that went forth to meet the bridegroom, we find a distinction of them into but *two* sorts, *viz.* The wise that had both *lamps* and *oil;* and those who had *lamps* indeed like the wise virgins, (therein having an external show of the same thing,) but really had no *oil;* signifying that they had the same profession and outward show of religion, and entertained the same hopes with the wise virgins. So when the visible church is represented by the husbandman's floor, we find a distinction but of two sorts, *viz.* the *wheat* and the *chaff.* And, when the church is compared to the husbandman's field, we find a distinction but of two sorts, the *wheat* and the *tares,* which (naturalists observe) appear exactly like the wheat, till it comes to bring forth its fruit; representing, that those who are only visible Christians, have an appearance of the nature of *wheat,* which shall be gathered into Christ's barn, that is, of the *nature* of saving grace.

2. It is evident, that those who had the name of *disciples* in the times of the New Testament, bore that name with reference to a visibility of the *same relation* to Christ, which they had who should be *finally owned as his.* This is manifest, John viii. 30, 31. "As he spake these words, many believed on him. Then said Jesus to those Jews which believed on him, If ye continue in my word, then are ye my *disciples indeed.*" (Compare Luke xiv. 25, 26, 27. and John xv. 8.) The phrase, *disciples indeed,* is relative; and has reference to a *visibility, pretence,* or *name,* only, to which it is set in opposition; which makes it evident, that those who then bore the name of *disciples,* had a visibility and pretence of *discipleship indeed.* For true discipleship is not properly set in opposition to any thing else but a pretence to the *same thing,* that is not true. The phrase, *gold indeed,* is in opposition to something that has the appearance of that *same metal,* and not to an appearance of *brass.* If there were another sort of real discipleship in those days, besides saving discipleship, persons might be Christ's *disciples indeed,* or *truly,* (as the word in the original is,) without *continuing in his word,* and without selling all that they had, and without hating father and mother and their own lives, for his sake. By this it appears, that those who bore the name of disciples in those times were distinguished into but two sorts, *disciples in name* or visibility, and *disciples indeed;* and that the visi-

bility and profession of the former was of the discipleship of the latter.

3. The same thing is evident by 1 John ii. 19. "They went out from us, because they were not of us: If they had been of us, they would no doubt have continued with us."—The words naturally suggest and imply, that those professing Christians, who at last proved *false*, did, before they *went out*, seem to belong to the society of the *true* saints, or those endued with persevering grace and holiness. They seemed to be of their number, and so were accepted in the judgment of charity.

4. The name that visible Christians had in the days of the New Testament, was of *saving Christianity*, and not of *moral sincerity;* for they had *a name to live*, though many of them were *dead*, Rev. iii. 1. Now it is very plain what that is in religion which is called by the name of *life*, all over the New Testament, *viz.* saving grace; and I do not know that any thing else, of a religious nature, is ever so called.

5. The visibility of saintship in the apostles' days, was not of *moral sincerity*, but *gracious* sincerity, or saving saintship. For they are spoken of as being visibly of the number of those saints who shall judge the world, and judge angels. 1 Cor. vi. 1, 2, 3. "Dare any of you, having a matter against another, go to law before the unjust, and not before the *saints?* Do ye not know, that the *saints shall judge the world?* And if the world shall be judged BY YOU, are ye unworthy to judge the smallest matters? Know ye not that WE *shall judge angels?*" These things manifestly imply, that if the christian Corinthians were what they supposed they were, what they professed to be, and what they were accepted to be, they were some of those saints who at the day of judgment should judge angels and men.

6. That the visibility was not only of moral sincerity but saving grace, is manifest, because the apostle speaks of visible christians as visible "members of Christ's body, of his flesh, and of his bones, *and* one spirit with him, *and* temples of the Holy Ghost," Eph. v. 30. and 1 Cor. vi. 16, 19. And the apostle Peter speaks of visible Christians as those who were visibly such *righteous* persons as should be *saved;* and that are distinguished from the *ungodly*, and *them that obey not the gospel, who shall perish.* 1 Pet. iv. 16, 17, 18. "Yet if any man suffer as a Christian, let him not be ashamed, but let him glorify God on this behalf. For the time is come that judgment must begin at the house of God; "and if it first begin at US," (*us* Christians, comprehending himself, and those to whom he wrote, and all of that sort,) "what shall the end of them be that obey not the gospel of God? And if the *righteous* scarcely be *saved*, where shall the *ungodly* and *sinners* appear?"

7. That the visibility was not merely of moral sincerity, but of that sort of saintship which the saints in *heaven* have, is manifest by this, that they are often spoken of as visibly *belonging* to *heaven*, and as of the *society* of the saints in heaven. So the apostle in his Epistle to the Ephesians speaks of them as visibly of the same *household* or *family of God*, a part of which is in *heaven*. Chap. ii. 19. "Now therefore ye are no more strangers and foreigners, but fellow-citizens with the saints, and of the *household* of God." Together with the next chapter, verse 15. "Of whom the whole family in heaven and earth is named." Where the context and continuation of discourse demonstrates, that he is still speaking of the same *family* or *household* he had spoken of in the latter part of the preceding chapter. So all visible Christians are spoken of as visibly the children of the church which is in *heaven*. Gal. iv. 26. "Jerusalem which is above, is free, which is the mother of us all." The same apostle speaks of visible Christians as being visibly come to the *heavenly city*, and having joined the glorious *company of angels* there, and as visibly belonging to the "general assembly and church of the first-born, that are written in heaven, and to the spirits of just men made perfect," Heb. xii. 22, 23. And elsewhere they are spoken of as being visibly of the number of those who have their "names written in the book of life," Rev. iii. 5. and xxii. 19. They who truly have their names written in the book of life, are God's true saints, that have saving grace: as is evident by Rev. xiii. 8. "And all that dwell on the earth, shall worship him, whose names are not *written in the book of life* of the Lamb slain from the foundation of the world." And chap. xx. 12. "And another book was opened, which was the book of life." Ver. 15. "And whosoever was not found written in the book of life, was cast into the lake of fire." We are told in the conclusion of this chapter, how they were disposed of whose names were not written in the book of life; and then the prophet proceeds, in the next chapter, to tell us, how they were disposed whose names were found there written, *viz.* that they were admitted into the New Jerusalem. Verse 27. "And there shall in no wise enter into it any thing that defileth, neither whatsoever worketh abomination, or maketh a lie; but they which are written in the Lamb's book of life." And yet in the next chapter it is implied, that some who were not truly gracious persons, and some that should finally perish, were visibly of the number of those that had both a *part* in the New Jerusalem, and also their *names* written in the *book of life.* Verse 19. "And if any man shall take away from the words of the book of this prophecy, God shall take away his part out of the *book of life,* and out of *the holy city.*"

8. That *baptism,* by which the primitive converts were admitted into the church, was used as an exhibition and token of their being visibly "regenerated, dead to sin, alive to God, having the old man crucified, being delivered from the reigning power of sin, being made free from sin, and become the servants of righteousness, those servants of God that have their fruit unto that holiness whose end is everlasting life;" as is evident by Rom. vi. throughout. In the former part of the chapter, he speaks of the Christian Romans, as "dead to sin, *being* buried with Christ in baptism, having their old man crucified with Christ," &c. He does not mean only, that their baptism laid them under special *obligations* to these things, and was a mark and token of their engagement to be thus *hereafter;* but was designed as a mark, token, and exhibition, of their being *visibly* thus *already.* As is most manifest by the apostle's prosecution of his argument in the following part of the chapter. Verse 14. "For sin shall not have dominion over you, for ye are not under the law, but under grace." Verse 17, 18. "God be thanked, ye were the servants of sin, but ye have obeyed from the heart that form of doctrine which was delivered you. Being then made free from sin, ye became the servants of righteousness." Verse 22. "But now being made free from sin, and become servants to God, ye have your fruit unto holiness, and the end everlasting life."

9. It is evident, that it is not only a visibility of moral sincerity in religion, which is the scripture qualification of admission into the christian church, but a visibility of regeneration and renovation of heart, because it was *foretold* that God's people and the ministers of his house in the days of the Messiah, should not admit into the christian church any that were not visibly *circumcised in heart.* Ezek. xliv. 6—9. "And thou shalt say to the rebellious, even to the house of Israel, Thus saith the Lord God, O ye house of Israel, let it suffice you of all your abominations, in that ye have brought into my sanctuary strangers *uncircumcised in heart,* and uncircumcised in flesh, to be in my sanctuary to pollute it, *even my house,* when ye offer my bread, the fat, and the blood; and they have broken my covenant, because of all your abominations: and ye have not kept the charge of mine holy things, but ye have set keepers of my charge in my sanctuary for yourselves. Thus saith the Lord, No stranger *uncircumcised in heart, nor uncircumcised in flesh,* shall enter into my sanctuary, of any stranger that is among the children of Israel."

The venerable author of the *Appeal to the Learned,* says, page 10. "That this scripture has no particular reference to the Lord's supper." I answer, though I do not suppose it has merely a reference to that ordinance, yet I think it manifest, that it has a reference to admitting persons into the *christian church,* and to *external church privileges.* It might be easy to prove, that these nine last chapters of Ezekiel must be a vision and prophecy of the state of things in the church of God in the Messiah's days; but I suppose it will not be denied, it being a thing wherein divines are so generally agreed. And I suppose, none will dispute but that by the *house of God and his sanctuary,* which it is here foretold the *uncircumcised in heart* should not be admitted into in the days of the gospel, is meant the same *house, sanctuary*, or *temple* of God, that the prophet had just before been speaking of, in the foregoing part of the same chapter, and been describing throughout the four preceding chapters. But we all know, that the New Testament *house of God* is his *church*. Heb. iii. 3. "For this man was counted worthy of more glory than Moses, inasmuch as he who builded the *house*, hath more honour than the *house*." Verse 6. "But Christ as a Son over his own *house*, whose *house* are we," &c. 2 Tim. ii. 20. "In a great *house* there are not only vessels of gold and silver, but also of wood and of earth," &c. 1 Tim. iii. 15. "That thou mayest know how thou oughtest to behave thyself in the *house of God*, which is the *church* of the living God." Eph. ii. 20, 21. "And are built upon the foundation of the prophets and apostles, Jesus Christ himself being the chief corner-stone; in whom all the building fitly framed together, groweth into an holy temple in the Lord." 1 Cor. iii. 9. "Ye are God's building." Verse 16. "Know ye not, that ye are the temple of God?" 1 Pet. ii. 5. "Ye also as lively stones are built up a spiritual *house*." Chap. iv. 17. "For the time is come, that judgment must begin at the *house* of God: and if it begin at us, what shall the end be?" &c. Heb. x. 21. "And having an high priest over the *house* of God." Ezekiel's temple is doubtless the same which it is foretold the Messiah should build. Zech. vi. 12, 13. "The man whose name is the Branch—he shall build the *temple* of the Lord, even he shall build the *temple* of the Lord." And what the temple that Christ builds is, the apostle tells us, Heb. iii. 3, 6. The temple that Ezekiel in his vision was bid to observe the measures of, as *measured with a reed*, (Ezek. xl. 3, 4.) we have reason to think, was the same the apostle John in his vision was bid to *measure with a reed*, Rev. xi. 1. And when it is here foretold, that the *uncircumcised in heart* should not enter into the Christian *sanctuary* or church, nor have communion in the offerings of *God's bread, of the fat and blood*, that were made there, I think so much is at least implied, that they should not have communion in those ordinances of the christian sanctuary, in which that *body* and *blood of Christ* were symbolically represented, which used of old to be symbolically represented by the fat and the blood. For the admission into the christian church here spoken of, is an admission into the *visible*, and not the *mystical*, church; for such an admission is spoken of as is made by the officers of the church. And I suppose it will not be doubted, but that by *circumcision of heart* is meant the spiritual renewing of the heart; not any common virtues, which do not in the least change the nature, and mortify the corruption of the heart; as is held by all orthodox divines, and as Mr. Stoddard in particular abundantly insisted. However, if any body disputes it, I desire that the Scripture may be allowed to speak for itself; for it very often speaks of *circumcision of heart*, and this every where, both in the Old Testament and New, manifestly signifies that great change of heart that was typified by the ceremony of *circumcision of the flesh*. The same which afterwards was signified by *baptism*, viz. *regeneration*, or else the progress of that work in sanctification; as we read of the *washing of regeneration*, &c. The apostle tells us what was signified both by circumcision and baptism, Col. ii. 11, 12. "In whom also ye are *circumcised* with the *circumcision* made without hands, in putting off the sins of the flesh by the *circumcision* of Christ, buried with him in *baptism*; wherein also you are risen with him, through the faith of the operation of God." Where I would observe by the way, he speaks of all the members of the church of Colosse as visibly *circumcised with this circumcision*; agreeable to Ezekiel's prophecy, that the members of the christian church shall visibly have this *circumcision*. The apostle speaks, in like manner, of the members of the church of Philippi as spiritually *circumcised*, (*i. e.* in profession and visibility,) and tells wherein this circumcision appeared. Philip. iii. 3. "For we are *the circumcision*, which worship God in the spirit, and rejoice in Christ Jesus, and have no confidence in the flesh." And in Rom. ii. 28, 29. the apostle speaks of this christian and Jewish circumcision together, calling the former the *circumcision of the heart*. "But he is not a Jew which is one outwardly, neither is that circumcision which is outward in the FLESH; but he is a Jew, which is one inwardly, and *circumcision* is that of THE HEART, in the spirit, not in the letter; whose praise is not of men, but of God." And whereas in this prophecy of Ezekiel it is foretold, that none should enter into the christian sanctuary or church, but such as are *circumcised in heart and circumcised in flesh;* thereby I suppose is intended, that none should be admitted but such as were visibly *regenerated*, as well as *baptized* with outward baptism.

By what has been observed, I think it abundantly evident, that the *saintship, godliness, and holiness*, of which, according to Scripture, professing Christians and visible saints do make a profession and have a visibility, is not any religion and virtue that is the result of common grace, or moral sincerity, (as it is called,) but saving grace.—Yet there are many other clear evidences of the same thing, which may in some measure appear in all the following part of this discourse.

SECT. II.

All who are capable of it are bound to make an explicit open profession of the true religion.

I COME to another reason, why I answer the question at first proposed, in the negative, viz. That it is a duty which in an ordinary state of things is required of all that are capable of it, *to make an explicit open profession of the true religion, by owning God's covenant;* or, in other words, *professedly and verbally to unite themselves to God in his covenant, by their own public act.*

Here I would *(first)* prove this point; and then *(secondly)* draw the consequence, and show how this demonstrates the thing in debate.

First, I shall endeavour to establish this point, *viz.* That it is the duty of God's people thus publicly to own the *covenant;* and that it was not only a duty in Israel of old, but is so in the christian church, and to the end of the world; and that it is a duty required of *adult* persons before they come to sacraments. And this being a point of great consequence in this controversy, but a matter seldom handled, (though it seems to be generally taken for granted,) I shall be the more particular in the consideration of it.

This not only seems to be in itself most consonant to reason, and is a duty generally allowed in New England, but is evidently a great institution of the word of God, appointed as a very important part of that public religion by which God's people should give honour to his name. This institution we have in Deut. vi. 13. "Thou shalt fear the Lord thy God, and serve him, and shalt swear by his name." It is repeated, chap. x. 20. "Thou shalt fear the Lord thy God, him shalt thou serve, and to him shalt thou cleave, and swear by his name." In both places it might have been rendered; *thou shalt swear in his name*, or *into his name*. In the original, *bishmo*, with the prefix *beth*, which signifies *in* or *into*, as well as *by*. And whereas, in the latter place, in our translation, it is said, *to him shalt thou cleave and swear by his name.* The words are thus in the Hebrew, *ubho thidhbák ubhishmo tisshàbhéang*. The literal translation of which is, *into him shalt thou cleave*, [*or unite*,] *and into his name shalt thou swear*. There is the same prefix, *beth*, before *him*, when it is said, *Thou shalt cleave to him*, as before *his name*, when it is said, *Thou shalt swear by his name*. *Swearing into God's name*, is a very emphatical and significant way of expressing a person's taking on himself, by his own solemn profession, the name of God, as one of his people; or by swearing to or covenanting with God, uniting himself by his own act to the people *that is called by his name*. The figure of speech is something like that by which Christians in the New Testament are said to be baptized εις το ονομα, INTO THE NAME *of the Father, the Son, and the Holy Ghost*. So Christians are said to *be baptized into Christ*, Gal. iii. 17. This swearing by the name, or into the name, of the Lord, is so often, and in such a manner, spoken of by the prophets as a great duty of God's solemn public worship, as much as praying or sacrificing, that it would be unreasonable to understand it only, or chiefly, of occasionally taking an oath before a court of judicature, which, it may be, one tenth part of the people never had occasion to do once in their lives. If we well consider the matter, we shall see abundant reason to be satisfied, that the thing intended in this institution was publicly covenanting with God. Covenanting in Scripture is very often called by the name of *swearing*, and a *covenant* is called *an oath*.* And particularly *God's covenant* is called *his oath*, Deut. xxxix. 12. " That thou shouldst enter into *covenant* with the Lord thy God, and into his *oath*." Ver. 14. " Neither with you only do I *make* this *covenant* and this *oath*." 1 Chron. xvi. 15, 16. " Be ye mindful always of his *covenant*:—Even of the *covenant* which he made with Abraham, and his *oath* unto Isaac." 2 Chron. xv. 12." And they entered into *covenant* to seek the Lord God of their fathers." Ver. 14, 15. " And they *sware* unto the Lord with a loud voice: and all Judah rejoiced at the *oath*." Swearing *to the Lord*, or swearing *in* or *into the* name of the Lord, are equipollent expressions in the Bible. The prefixes *beth* and *lamed* are evidently used indifferently in this case to signify the same thing, Zeph. i. 5. " That swear by the Lord, and that swear by Malcham." The word translated *to the Lord*, is *Laihovah*, with the prefix *lamed;* but *to Malcham*, is *Bemalcham* with the prefix *beth*, *into Malcham*. In 1 Kings xviii. 32. it is said, " Elijah built an altar in the name of the Lord;" *beshem*. Here the prefix *beth* is manifestly of the same force with *lamed*, in 1 Kings viii. 44. " The house I have built *for thy name* or *to thy name;" leshem*.

God's people in swearing to his name, or into his name, according to the institution, solemnly professed two things, *viz.* their *faith* and *obedience*. The former part of this profession of religion was called, *Saying, the Lord liveth*. Jer. v. 2. " And though they say, the Lord liveth, yet surely they swear falsely." Verse 7. " They have sworn by them that are no gods:" that is, they had openly professed idol-worship. Chap. iv. 2. " Thou shalt swear, the Lord liveth, in truth, in judgment, and in righteousness; and the nations shall bless themselves in him, and in him shall they glory." (Compare this with Isaiah xlv. 23, 24, 25.) Jer. xliv. 26. " Behold I have sworn by my great name, saith the Lord, that my name shall no more be named in the mouth of any man of Judah in all the land of Egypt, *saying, the Lord liveth:" i. e.* They shall never any more make any profession of the true God, and of the true religion, but shall be wholly given up to heathenism. See also Jer. xii. 16. and xvi. 14, 15. and xxiii. 7, 8. Hos. iv. 15. Amos viii. 14. and ver. 5.

These words, CHAI JEHOVAH, Jehovah liveth, summarily comprehend a profession of faith in that all-sufficiency and immutability of God, which is implied in the name JEHOVAH, and which attributes are very often signified in Scripture by God's being the LIVING GOD, as is very manifest from Josh. iii. 10. 1 Sam. xvii. 26, 36. 2 Kings xix. 4, 16. Dan. vi. 26. Psalm xviii. 46. and innumerable other places.

The other thing professed in swearing into the Lord was obedience, called, *Walking in the name of the Lord*. Micah iv. 5. " All people will walk every one in the name of his god, and we will walk in the name of the Lord our God for ever and ever." Still with the prefix *beth*, *beshem*, as they were said to swear *beshem*, in the name, or into, the name of the Lord.

This institution, in Deuteronomy, of swearing into the name of the Lord, or visibly and explicitly uniting themselves to him in covenant, was not prescribed as an extraordinary duty, to be performed on a return from a general apostacy, and some other extraordinary occasions: but is evidently mentioned in the institution, as a part of the public worship of God to be performed by all God's people, properly belonging to the visible worshippers of Jehovah; and so it is very often mentioned by the prophets, as I observed before, and could largely demonstrate, if there was occasion for it, and would not too much lengthen out this discourse.

And this was not only an institution belonging to Israel under the Old Testament, but also to Gentile converts, and Christians under the New Testament. Thus God declares concerning the Gentile nations, Jer. xii. 16. " If they will diligently learn the ways of my people, to SWEAR BY MY NAME, THE LORD LIVETH, as they taught my people to swear by Baal: then shall they be built in the midst of my people," *i. e.* They shall be added to my church; or as the apostle Paul expresses it, Eph. ii. 19—22. " They shall be no more strangers and foreigners, but fellow-citizens with the saints, and of the household of God, and be built upon the foundation of Christ; in whom all the BUILDING fitly framed together, &c.—In whom they also shall be BUILDED for an habitation of God through the Spirit." So it is foretold, that the way of public covenanting should be the way of the Gentiles joining themselves to the church in the days of the gospel, Isa. xliv. 3—5. " I will pour water upon him that is thirsty, and floods upon the dry ground; I will pour my Spirit upon thy seed, and my blessing upon thine offspring, and they shall spring up as among the grass, as willows by the water-courses; one shall say, I am the Lord's, and another shall call himself by the name of Jacob, and another shall subscribe with his hand unto the Lord,"—as subscribing an instrument whereby they bound themselves to the Lord. This was subscribing and covenanting themselves into the name of Israel, and *swearing into the name of the Lord*, in the language of those forementioned texts in Deuteronomy. So taking hold of God's covenant, is foretold as the way in which the sons of the stranger in the days of the gospel should be joined to God's church, and brought into God's sanctuary, and to have communion in its worship and ordinances, in Isa. lvi. 3, 6, 7. So in Isa. xix. 18. the future conversion of the Gentiles in the days of the gospel, and their being brought to profess the true religion, is expressed by saying, that they should SWEAR TO THE LORD OF HOSTS. " In that day shall five cities in the land of Egypt speak the language of Canaan, and swear to the Lord of hosts." So in Jer. xxiii. 5—8. it seems to be plainly foretold, that after Christ is come, and has wrought out his great redemption, the same way of publicly professing faith in the all-sufficient and immutable God, by swearing, The Lord liveth, should be continued, which was instituted of old; but only with this difference, that whereas formerly they covenanted with God as their Redeemer out of Egypt, now they shall as it were forget that work, and have a special respect to a much greater redemption. " Behold, the days come, saith the Lord, that I will raise unto David a righteous Branch.—Therefore they shall no more say, The Lord liveth, which brought up the children of Israel out of the land of Egypt; but, The Lord liveth, which brought up, and which led the seed of the house of Israel out of the north country," &c.

Another remarkable place wherein it is plainly foretold, that the like method of professing religion should be continued in the days of the gospel, is Isaiah xlv. 22—25. " Look unto me, and be ye saved, all ye ends of the earth; for I am God, and there is none else: I have sworn by myself, the word is gone out of my mouth in righteousness, and shall not return, that unto me every knee shall bow, EVERY TONGUE SHALL SWEAR: surely shall one say, In the Lord have I righteousness and strength: even to him shall men come:—in the Lord shall all the seed of Israel be justified, and shall glory." This prophecy will have its last fulfilment at the day of judgment; but it is plain, that the thing most directly intended is the conversion of the Gentile world to the christian religion. What is here called *swearing*, the apostle, in citing this place, once and again calls *confessing;* Rom. xiv. 11.—" Every tongue shall confess to God." Philip. ii. 10.—" That every tongue should confess that Jesus Christ is Lord." Which is the word commonly used in the New Testament, to signify making a public profession of religion. So Rom. x. 9, 10. " If thou shalt confess with thy mouth the Lord Jesus, and shalt believe in thine heart, that God hath raised him from the dead, thou shalt be saved: for with the heart man believeth unto righteousness, and with the mouth confession is made unto salvation." Where a public *profession of religion* with the mouth is evidently spoken of as a great duty of all Christ's people, as well as *believing in him;* and ordinarily requi-

* As Gen. xxi 23, to the end. xxvi. 28, to the end. xxxi. 44, 53. Josh. ii. 12, &c. 1 Sam. xx. 16, 17, 42. 2 Kings xi. 4. Eccl. viii. 2. Ezek. xvi. 59. xvii. 16. and many other places.

site to salvation; not that it is necessary in the same manner that faith is, but in like manner as baptism is. Faith and verbal profession are jointly spoken of here as necessary to salvation, in the same manner as faith and baptism are, in Mark xvi. 16. "He that *believeth* and is *baptized*, shall be saved." And I know no good reason why we should not look on moral profession and covenanting with Christ, in those who are capable of it, as much of a stated duty in the christian church, and an institution universally pertaining to the followers of Christ, as baptism.

And if explicit, open covenanting with God be a great duty required of all, as has been represented, then it ought to be expected of persons before they are admitted to the privileges of the adult in the church of Christ. Surely it is proper, if this explicit covenanting takes place at all, that it should take place before persons come to those ordinances wherein they, by their own act, publicly confirm and seal this covenant. This public transaction of covenanting, which God has appointed, ought to have existence, before we publicly confirm and seal this transaction. It was that by which the Israelites of old were introduced into the communion of God's nominal or visible church and holy city: as appears by Isaiah xlviii. 1, 2. "Hear ye this, O house of Jacob, which ARE CALLED BY THE NAME OF ISRAEL, and are come forth out of the waters of Judah, WHICH SWEAR BY THE NAME OF THE LORD, and make mention of the God of Israel, but not in truth nor in righteousness: FOR THEY CALL THEMSELVES OF THE HOLY CITY," &c. When, and after what manner particularly, the Israelites ordinarily performed this explicit covenanting, I do not know that we can be certain. But, as it was first done on occasion of God's first promulgating his law or covenant at mount Sinai—on a repetition or renewed promulgation of it on the plains of Moab—on the public reading of the law in Josiah's time (2 Kings xxiii. 3.)—on after the return from the captivity—and on the public reading of it at the feast of tabernacles (Neh. viii. ix. and x.) so it appears to me most likely, that it was done every seventh year, when the law or covenant of God was, by divine appointment, read in the audience of all the people at the feast of tabernacles; at least by all who then heard the law read the first time, and who never had publicly owned the covenant of God before. There are good evidences that they never had communion in those ordinances which God had appointed as seals of his covenant, wherein they themselves were to be active, such as their sacrifices, &c. till they had done it. It is plainly implied in Psal. l. that it was the manner in Israel vocally to own *God's covenant*, or to *take it into their mouths*, before they sealed that covenant in their sacrifices. See ver. 16. taken with the preceding part of the psalm, from ver. 5. And that they did it before they partook of the passover, (which indeed was one of their sacrifices,) or entered into the sanctuary for communion in the temple-worship, is confirmed by the words of Hezekiah, when he proclaimed a passover, 2 Chron. xxx. 8. "Now be ye not stiff-necked, as your fathers were; but yield yourselves unto the Lord, (in the Hebrew, Give the hand to the Lord,) and enter into his sanctuary, which he hath sanctified for ever, and serve the Lord your God." *To give the hand*, seems to be a Hebrew phrase for entering into covenant, or obliging themselves by covenant, Ezra x. 19. "And they gave their hands that they would put away their wives." And, as has been already observed, it was foretold that Christians should in this way be admitted to communion in the privileges of the church of Christ.—Having thus established the *premises* of the argument, I now come to the *consequence*.

SECT. III.

That none ought to be admitted to the privileges of adult persons in the church of Christ, but such as make a profession of real piety.

THE covenant to be owned or professed, is *God's covenant*, which he has revealed as the method of our spiritual union with him, and our acceptance as the objects of his eternal favour; which is no other than the *covenant of grace;* at least it is so, without dispute, in these days of the gospel. To own this covenant, is to profess the consent of our *hearts* to it; and that is the sum and substance of true piety. It is not only professing the assent of our understandings that we understand there is such a covenant, or that we understand we are obliged to comply with it; but it is to profess the consent of our *wills*, it is to manifest *that we do comply with it*. There is mutual profession in this affair, a profession on Christ's part, and a profession on our part; as it is in *marriage*. And it is the same sort of profession that is made on both sides, in this respect, that each professes a consent of *heart*. Christ in his word declares an entire consent of heart as to what he offers; and the visible Christian, in the answer that he makes to it in his christian profession, declares a consent and compliance of heart to his proposal. Owning the covenant is professing to make the transaction of that covenant our own. The transaction of that covenant is that of espousals to Christ; on our part, it is giving our souls to Christ as his spouse. There is no one thing that the covenant of grace is so often compared to in Scripture, as the marriage-covenant; and the visible transaction, or mutual profession, there is between Christ and the visible church, is abundantly compared to the mutual profession there is in marriage. In marriage the bride professes to yield to the bridegroom's suit, and to take him for her husband, renouncing all others, and to give up herself to him to be entirely and for ever possessed by him as his wife. But he that professes this towards Christ, professes saving faith. They that openly covenanted with God according to the tenor of the institution, Deut. x. 20. visibly united themselves to God in the union of that covenant. They professed on their parts the union of the covenant of God, which was the covenant of grace. It is said in the institution, "Thou shalt cleave to the Lord, and swear by his name;" or as the words more literally are, "Thou shalt unite unto the Lord, and swear into his name." So in Isaiah lvi. it is called a "joining themselves to the Lord." But the union, cleaving, or joining of that covenant, is saving faith, the grand condition or the covenant of Christ, by which we are in Christ. This is what [on our part] brings us *into the Lord*. For a person explicitly or professedly to enter into the union or relation of the covenant of grace with Christ, is the same as professedly to do that which on our part is the uniting act, and that is the act of faith. To profess the covenant of grace, is to profess it, not as a spectator, but as one immediately concerned in the affair, as a party in the covenant professed; and this is to profess *that* in the covenant which belongs to us *as a party*, or to profess *our part* in the covenant; and that is the soul's believing acceptance of the Saviour. Christ's part is salvation, our part is a saving faith in him; not a feigned, but unfeigned faith; not a common, but special and saving faith; no other faith is the condition of the covenant of grace.

I know the distinction made by some, between the *internal* and *external covenant;* but, I hope, the divines that make this distinction, would not be understood, that there are really and properly *two* covenants of grace; but only that those who profess the one only covenant of grace, are of two sorts. There are those who comply with it *internally* and really, and others who do so only *externally*, that is, in profession and visibility. But he that externally and visibly complies with the covenant of grace, appears and professes to do so really.—There is also this distinction concerning the covenant of grace; it is exhibited two ways, the one *externally*, by the preaching of the word, the other *internally* and spiritually, by enlightening the mind rightly to understand the word. But it is with the *covenant*, as it is with the call of the gospel: he that really complies with the *external* call, has the *internal* call; so he that truly complies with the *external* proposal of God's covenant, as visible Christians profess to do, does indeed perform the inward condition of it. But the New Testament affords no more foundation for supposing two real and properly distinct covenants of grace, than it does to suppose two sorts of real Christians.

When those persons who were baptized in infancy properly own their baptismal covenant, the meaning is, that they now, being capable to act for themselves, do professedly and explicitly make their parents' act, in giving them up to God, their own, by expressly giving themselves up to God. But this no person can do, without either being deceived, or dissembling and professing what he himself supposes to be a falsehood, unless he supposes that in his heart he consents to be God's. A child of christian parents never does that for himself which his parents did for him in infancy, till he gives himself wholly to God. But surely he does not do it, who not only keeps back a part, but the chief part, his heart and soul. He that keeps back his heart, does in effect keep back all; and therefore, if he be sensible of it, is guilty of solemn wilful mockery, if at the same time he solemnly and publicly professes that he gives himself up to God. If there are any words used by such, which in their proper signification imply that they give themselves up to God; and if these words, as they intend them to be understood, and as they are understood by those that hear them, according to their established use and custom among that people, do not imply, that they do it really, but do truly reserve or keep back the chief part; it ceases to be a profession of giving themselves up to God, and so ceases to be a professed covenanting with God. The thing which they profess belongs to no existing covenant of God; for God has revealed no such covenant, in which our transacting of it is a giving up ourselves to him with reserve, or holding back our souls, our chief part, and in effect our all. And therefore, although such public and solemn professing may be a very unwarrantable and great abuse of words, and taking God's name in vain, it is no professed covenanting with God.

One thing, as observed, that belonged to Israel's *swearing into the name of the Lord*, was *saying, The Lord liveth;* whereby they professed their faith in God's all-sufficiency, immutability, and faithfulness. But if they really had such a faith, it was a saving grace. To them who indeed trust in the all-sufficiency of God, he will surely be an all-sufficient portion; and them who trust in God's immutability and faithfulness, he surely will never leave nor forsake. There were two ways of swearing *Jehovah liveth*, that we read of in Scripture; one we read of, Jer. ii. 2. "Thou shalt swear, The Lord liveth, in truth, in judgment, and in righteousness:" and the other way is *swearing falsely*, which we read of in the next chapter, verse 2, 3. "And though they say, The Lord liveth, yet surely they swear falsely." And certainly none ought to do this. It follows, "O Lord, are not thine eyes upon the truth?" *i. e.* God desires sincerity of heart in those that profess religion. Here a gracious sincerity is opposed to a false profession; for when it is said, "O Lord, are not thine eyes upon the truth?" the expression is parallel with Ps. li. 6. "Behold thou desirest truth in the inward parts." 1 Sam. xvi. 7. "Man looketh on the outward appearance, but the Lord looketh on the heart." Ps. xi. 7. "His countenance doth behold the upright." But these texts speak of a gracious sincerity. Those spoken of, Jer. iv. 2. that "sware, The Lord liveth, in truth, in judgment, and righteousness," were gracious persons, who had a thorough conversion to God, as appears by the preceding verse, "If thou wilt return, O Israel, saith the Lord, return unto me;" *i. e.* Do not do as Judah was charged with doing in the foregoing chapter, verse 10. "Judah hath not turned unto me with her whole heart, but feignedly." Do not do thus, "but if thou wilt return, return unto me." And then it is added in the second verse, "And thou shalt swear, The Lord liveth, in truth," &c.; that is, then your profession of religion will be worth regarding, you will be indeed what you pretend to be, you will be Israelites indeed, in whose profession is no guile. They who said, "The Lord liveth, in truth, in judgment, and in righteousness;" said, The Lord liveth, as David did, Ps. xviii. 46. "The Lord liveth, and blessed be my Rock." And as the apostle says he did, 1 Tim. iv. 10. "We trust in the living God, who is the Saviour of all men, especially of those that believe." And as he would have Timothy exhort rich men to do, chap. vi. 17. "That they trust not in uncertain riches, but in the living God." When the apostle speaks of a profession of our faith in Christ, as one duty which all Christians ought to perform as they seek salvation, it is the profession of a *saving faith*. His words plainly imply it: "If thou shalt confess with thy mouth the Lord Jesus, and shalt believe in thine heart that God hath raised him from the dead, thou shalt be saved." The faith which was to be *professed with the mouth*, was the same which the apostle speaks of *as in the heart*, but that is saving faith. The latter is yet plainer in the following words; "for with the heart man believeth unto righteousness, and with the mouth confession is made unto salvation." Believing unto righteousness, is saving faith; but it is evidently the same faith which is spoken of, as *professed with the mouth*, in the next words in the same sentence. And that the Gentiles, in professing the christian religion, or swearing to Christ, should profess saving faith, is implied, Isa. xlv. 23, 24.—"Every tongue shall swear; surely shall one say, In the Lord have I righteousness and strength;" *i. e.* should profess entirely to depend on Christ's righteousness and strength.

For persons merely to promise, that they will believe in Christ, or that they will hereafter comply with the conditions and duties of the covenant of grace, is not to own that covenant. Such persons do not profess now to enter into the covenant of grace with Christ, or into the relation of that covenant to Christ. All they do at present, is to say, they will do it hereafter; they profess, that they will hereafter obey that command of God, to *believe on the name of his Son Jesus Christ*. But what is such a profession good for, and what credit is to be given to such promises of *future obedience;* when at the same time they pretend no other at present, than to live and continue in rebellion against those great commands which give no allowance or licence for delay? They who do thus, instead of properly owning the covenant, do rather for the present visibly reject it. It is not unusual, in some churches, where the doctrine I oppose has been established, for persons at the same time that they come into the church, and pretend to own the covenant, freely to declare to their neighbours, they have no imagination that they have any true faith in Christ, or love to him. Such persons, instead of being professedly united to Christ, in the union of the covenant of grace, are rather visibly destitute of the love of Christ; and so, instead of being qualified for admission to the Lord's supper, are rather exposed to that denunciation of the apostle, 1 Cor. xvi. 22. "If any man love not the Lord Jesus Christ, let him be Anathema Maran-atha."

That outward covenanting, which is agreeable to scripture-institution, is not only a promising what is future, (though that is not excluded,) but a professing what is *present*, as it is in the marriage-covenant. For a woman to promise, that she will hereafter renounce all other men for the sake of him who makes suit to her, and will in some future time accept of him for her husband, is not for her now to enter into the marriage-covenant with him. She that does this with a man, professes now to accept of him, renouncing all others; though promises of hereafter behaving towards him as a wife, are also included in the transaction. It seems the primitive converts to Christianity, in the profession they made of religion, in order to their admission into the christian church, and in their visibly entering into covenant, in order to the initiating seal of the covenant in baptism, did not *explicitly* make any promises of any thing future. They only professed the present sentiments and habit of their minds, they professed that they *believed in Christ*, and so were admitted into the church by baptism; and yet undoubtedly they were, according to forementioned prophecies, admitted in the way of public covenanting. As the covenant-people of God, they owned the covenant, before the seal of the covenant was applied. Their professing faith in Christ was visibly owning the covenant of grace, because faith in Christ was the grand condition of that covenant. Indeed, if the faith which they professed in order to baptism, was only an historical or doctrinal faith, (as some suppose,) or any common faith, it would not have been any visible entering into the covenant of grace; for a common faith is not the condition of that covenant; nor would there properly have been any covenanting in the case. If we suppose, the faith they professed was the grace by which the soul is united to Christ, their profession was a covenanting in this respect also, that it implied an engagement of future obedience; for true faith in Christ includes in its nature an acceptance of him as our Lord and King, and devoting ourselves to his service. But a profession of historical faith implies no profession of accepting Christ as our King, nor engagement to submit to him as such.

When the Israelites publicly covenanted with God, according to the institution in Deuteronomy, they did not only promise something future, but professed something present; they *avouched Jehovah to be their God*, and also promised to keep his commands. Thus it was in that solemn covenant-transaction between God and the people on the plains of Moab; which is summarily described, Deut. xxvi. 17, 18. "Thou hast avouched the Lord this day to be thy God, and to walk in his ways, and to keep his statutes, and his commandments, and his judgments, and to hearken unto his voice; and the Lord hath avouched thee this day to be his peculiar people, as he hath promised thee, and that thou shouldst keep all his commandments." The people in avouching God for their God, professed a compliance with the terms of the covenant of grace; as summarily expressed in those words, "I will be thy God, and thou shalt be my people." They that avouch the Lord to be their God, profess to accept of Jehovah as their God; and that is to accept him as the object of their supreme respect and trust. For that which we choose as the object of our highest regard, that, and that only, do we take *as our God*. None therefore that value and love the world more than Jehovah, can, without lying, or being deceived, avouch Jehovah to be their God. And none that do not trust in Christ, but trust more in their own strength or righteousness, can avouch Christ to be their Saviour. To avouch God to be our God, is to profess that he is our God *by our own act; i. e.* That we choose him to be our chief good and last end, the supreme object of our esteem and regard, to whom we devote ourselves. And if we are sensible that we do not do this *sincerely*, we cannot profess that we actually do it; for he that does not do it sincerely, does not do it at all. There is no room for the distinction of a moral sincerity and gracious sincerity in this case. A supreme respect of heart to God, or a supreme love to him, which is real, is but of one sort. Whoever does with any reality at all make God the object of the supreme regard of his heart, is certainly a gracious person. And whoever does not make God the supreme object of his respect with a gracious sincerity, certainly does not do it with any sincerity. I fear, while leading people in many of our congregations, who have no thought of their having the least spark of true love to God in their hearts, to say, publicly and solemnly, that *they avouch God the Father, Son, and Holy Ghost, to be their God*, and that *they give themselves up to him*, we have led them to say they know not what. To be sure, they are very obscure expressions, if they mean any thing that a carnal man does, under the reigning power of sin and enmity against God.

Here possibly it may be objected, that it is unreasonable to suppose any such thing should be intended, in the profession of the congregation in the wilderness, as a gracious respect to God, that which is the condition of God's covenant, when we have reason to think that so few of them were truly gracious. But I suppose, upon mature consideration, this will not appear at all unreasonable. It is no more unreasonable to suppose this people to make a profession of that respect to God, which they had not in their hearts now, than at other times when we are informed they did so, as in Ezek. xxxiii. 31. "They come unto thee as the people cometh, and they sit before thee as my people:" [*i. e.* as though they were my saints, as they profess to be:] "For with their mouth they show much love, but their heart goeth after their covetousness." So in the apostle's time, people professed that to be in their hearts towards God, which was not there. The apostle is speaking of them, when he says, Tit. i. 16. "They profess that they know God, but in works they deny him." This was common among that people; God declares them to be an *hypocritical nation*, Isaiah x. 6. And it is certain, this was the case with them in the wilderness; they there professed that respect to God which they had not; as is evident by Psal. lxxviii. 36, 37. "They did flatter him with their mouth, and they lied unto him with their tongues; for their heart was not right with him, neither were they stedfast in his covenant." In owning the covenant with God, they professed *their heart was right with him*, because it is mentioned as an evidence of their having *lied* or dealt falsely in their profession, that *their heart was not right with him*, and so proved not stedfast in God's covenant, which they had owned. If their *heart* had been *right with God*, they would have been truly pious persons; which is a demonstration, that what they professed was true piety. It also appears that if they had had such a heart in them, as they pretended to have, they would have been truly pious persons, Deut. v. where we have a rehearsal of their covenanting at mount Sinai: Concerning this it is said, verse 28, 29. "And the Lord heard the voice of your words, when ye spake unto me; and the Lord said unto me, They have well said all that they have spoken. O that there were such an heart in them, that they would fear me, and keep all my commandments always, that it might be well with them and with their children for ever." The people were mistaken about their disposition and preparation of heart to go through the business of God's service, as the man in the parable, who undertook to build a tower without counting the cost. Nor need it seem at all incredible, that the generation who covenanted at mount Sinai, should, the greater part of them, be deceived, and think their *hearts* thoroughly disposed to give up themselves for ever to God, if we consider how much they had strongly to move their *affections*. They saw the wonders wrought in Egypt and at the Red sea, where they were led through on dry ground, and the Egyptians miraculously destroyed; whereby their affections were greatly raised, and they *sang God's praises*. And particularly they now saw at mount Sinai, the astonishing manifestations of God's majesty. Probably the greater part of the sinners among them were deceived with false affections; and if there were others less affected and not deceived, it is not incredible that they, in those circumstances, should wilfully dissemble in their profession, and so in a more gross sense *flatter God with their lips, and lie to him with their tongues*. And these things are more credible concerning a generation peculiarly left to hardness and blindness of mind in divine matters, and peculiarly noted in the book of Psalms for hypocrisy. And the generation of their children, who owned the covenant on the plains of Moab, had much to move their affections; they saw the awful judgments of God on their fathers. God had brought them through the wilderness, and subdued Sihon king of the Amorites and Og the king of Bashan before them.—They had heard Moses's affecting rehearsal of the whole series of God's wonderful dealings with them, together with his most pathetic exhortations. But it was also a time of great revival of religion and powerful influence of the Spirit of God, and that generation was probably the most excellent that ever was in Israel. There is more good and less hurt spoken of them, than of any other generation that we have any account of in Scripture.* A very great part of them swore in truth, in judgment, and in righteousness. And no wonder that others at such a time fell in, either *deceiving*, or *being deceived*, with common affections; as is usual in times of great works of God for his church, and of the flourishing of religion. In succeeding generations, as the people grew more corrupt, I suppose, their covenanting or swearing into the name of the Lord degenerated into a matter of mere form and ceremony; even as subscribing religious articles seems to have done with the church of England; and as, it is to be feared, owning the covenant, as it is called, has too much done in New England; it being visibly a prevailing custom for persons to neglect this, till they come to be married, and then to do it for their credit's sake, and that their children may be baptized. And I suppose, there was commonly a great laxness in Israel among the priests who had the conduct of this affair. There were many things in the nature of that comparatively carnal dispensation, which negatively gave occasion for such things: that is, whereby it had by no means so great a tendency to prevent such irregularities, as the more excellent dispensation introduced by Christ and his

* See Num. xiv. 31. Deut. i. 39. and viii. 15, 16. Josh. xxii. 2. and ver. 11, to the end, and xxiii. 8. Deut. iv. 4. Josh. xxiv. 31. Judg. ii. 17, 22. Psal lxviii. 14. Jer. ii. 2, 3, 21. and xxxi. 2, 3. Hos. ix. 10.

apostles. And though these things were testified against by the prophets, before the Babylonish captivity; yet God, who is only wise, did designedly in a great measure wink at these and many other great irregularities in the church, till *the time of reformation* should come, which the Messiah was to have the honour of introducing. But of these things I may perhaps have occasion to say something more, when I come to answer the objection concerning the passover.

Now to return to the argument from the nature of covenanting with God, or owning God's covenant. As to the promises, which are herein either explicitly or implicitly made; these imply a profession of true piety. For, in the covenant of grace universal obedience is engaged, obedience to all the commands of God; and the performance of inward spiritual duties is as much engaged, as external duties; and in some respects much more. Therefore he that visibly makes the covenant of grace his own, promises to perform those internal duties, and to perform all duties with a gracious sincerity. We have no warrant, in our profession of God's covenant, to *divide* the duties of it, to take some, and leave out others: especially to leave out those great commands, *of believing with the heart*, of *loving the Lord our God with all our heart and with all our soul, and our neighbour as ourselves.* He that leaves out these, in effect leaves out all; for these are the sum of our whole duty, and of all God's commands. If we leave these out of our profession, surely it is not the covenant of grace which we profess. The Israelites, when they covenanted with God at mount Sinai, and said, when God had declared to them the ten commandments, "All that the Lord hath spoken will we do, and be obedient;" promised, that as they *professed to know God*, they would *in works* not *deny*, but own and honour him, and would conform to those *two great commandments*, which are the sum of all the ten, and concerning which God said, "These words which I command thee this day, shall be in thine heart," Deut. vi. 6.—And when they covenanted on the plains of Moab, they promised to keep and do God's commands, "with all their heart, and with all their soul," as is very evident by Deut. xxvi. 16, 17. So it was also when the people owned their covenant in Asa's time, 2 Chron. xv. 12. "They entered into a covenant to seek the Lord God of their fathers, with all their heart, and with all their soul." We have also another remarkable instance, 2 Kings xxiii. 3. and 2 Chron. xxxiv. 31.

Now he who is wholly under the power of a *carnal mind*, which is *not subject to the law of God, nor indeed can be*, cannot promise these things without either great deceit, or the most manifest and palpable absurdity. Promising supposes the person to be conscious to himself, or persuaded of himself, that he has *such a heart in him;* for his lips pretend to declare his heart. The nature of a promise implies intention or design. And proper real intention implies will, disposition, and compliance of heart. But no natural man is properly willing to do these duties, nor does his heart comply with them: and to make natural men believe otherwise, tends greatly to their hurt. A natural man may be willing, from self-love, and from sinister views, to use means and take pains that he may obtain a willingness or disposition to these duties: but that is a very different thing from actually being willing, or truly having a disposition to them. So he may promise, that he will, from some considerations or other, take great pains to obtain such a heart; but this is not the promise of the covenant of grace. Men may make many religious promises to God some way relating to the covenant of grace, which yet are not themselves the promises of that covenant; nor is there any thing of the nature of covenanting in the case, because although they should actually fulfil their promises, God is not obliged by promise to them. If a natural man promises to do all that it is possible for a natural man to do in religion, and fulfils his promises, God is not obliged, by any covenant that he has entered into with man, to perform any thing at all for him, respecting his saving benefits. And therefore he that promises these things only, enters into no covenant with God; because the very notion of entering into covenant with any being, is entering into a mutual agreement, doing or engaging that which, if done, the other party becomes engaged on his part. The New Testament informs us but of one covenant God enters into with mankind through Christ, and that is the covenant of grace; in which God obliges himself to nothing in us that is exclusive of *unfeigned faith*, and the spiritual duties that attend it. Therefore if a natural man makes never so many vows, that he will perform all external duties, and will pray for help to do spiritual duties, and for an ability and will to comply with the covenant of grace, from such principles as he has, he does not *lay hold of God's covenant*, nor properly enter into any covenant with God. For we have no opportunity to covenant with God in any other way, than that which he has revealed; he becomes a covenant-party in no other covenant. It is true, every natural man that lives under the gospel, is obliged to comply with the terms of the covenant of grace; and if he promises to do it, his promise may increase his obligation, though he *flattered God with his mouth, and lied to him with his tongue*, as the children of Israel did in promising. But it will not thence follow, that they ought knowingly to make a lying promise, or that ministers and churches should countenance them in so doing.

Indeed there is no natural man but what deceives himself, if he thinks he is truly willing to perform external obedience to God, universally and perseveringly through the various trials of life. And therefore in promising it, he is either very deceitful, or is like the foolish deceived man that undertook to *build* when he had not wherewith to *finish*. And if it be known by the church, before whom he promises to *build* and *finish*, that at the same time he does not pretend to have a *heart* to finish, his promise is worthy of no credit or regard from them, and can make nothing *visible* to them but his presumption.

A great confirmation of what has been said under this head of covenanting, is Psal. l. 16. "But unto the wicked God saith, What hast thou to do, to declare my statutes, or that thou shouldest take my covenant in thy mouth?" This term, the wicked, in the more general use of it in Scripture, is applied in that extent as to include all ungodly or graceless persons, all that are under the reigning power of sin, and are the objects of God's anger, or exposed to his eternal vengeance; as might easily be made to appear by a particular enumeration of texts all over the Bible. All such are in Scripture called, *workers of iniquity, the children of the wicked one*, Matt. xiii. 38. All such are said to be *of the devil*, 1 John iii. 8. And to be *the children of the devil*, verse 10. *The righteous* and *the wicked* are, in a multitude of places in Scripture, evidently opposed one to the other, and distinguished as *saints* and *sinners, holy* and *unholy*, those that *fear God* and those that *fear him not*, those that *love him* and those that *hate him.* All mankind are in Scripture divided by these distinctions, and the Bible knows of no *neuters* or third sort.

Indeed those who are really wicked, may be visibly righteous, righteous in profession and outward appearance. But a sort of men who have no saving grace, and yet are not really wicked, the Scripture is entirely ignorant of. It is reasonable to suppose, that by *wicked men*, in this psalm, is meant all that *hate instruction*, and *reject God's word*, (Psal. l. 17.) and not merely such as are guilty of particular crimes mentioned, verse 17—20. stealing, adultery, fraud, and backbiting. Though only some particular ways of wickedness are mentioned, yet we are not to understand that all others are excluded; yea the words, in the conclusion of the paragraph, are expressly applied to all that forget God in such a manner as to expose themselves to be torn in pieces by God's wrath in hell, verse 22. "Now consider this, ye that forget God, lest I tear you in pieces, and there be none to deliver." We can no more justly argue, that because some gross sins are here specified, that no sinners are meant but such as live in those or other gross sins, than we can argue from Rev. xxii. 14, 15. that none shall be shut out of heaven but those who have lived in the gross sins there mentioned; "Blessed are they that do his commandments, that they may have right to the tree of life, and may enter in through the gates into the city: for without are dogs, and sorcerers, and murderers, and idolaters, and whosoever loveth and maketh a lie." Nothing is more common in Scripture, than—in the descriptions it gives both of the godly and ungodly, together with their general character—to insert some particular excellent practices of the one to which grace tends, and some certain gross sins of the other for which there is a foundation in the reigning corruption of their hearts. So, *lying* is mentioned as part of the character of all natural men, Psal. lviii. 3, 4. (there called *wicked men*, as in Psal. l.) "The wicked are estranged from the womb; they go astray as soon as they be born, speaking lies: their poison is like the poison of a serpent," &c. So it is said of the wicked, Psal. x. 2, 3, 4, 7. "His mouth is full of cursing and bitterness." This the apostle, Rom. iii. cites as a description of all natural men. So it is said of the *wicked*, Psal. cxl. 3. "They have sharpened their tongues as a serpent; adders' poison is under their lips;" which the same apostle, in the same place, also cites as what is said of all natural men. The very same gross sins which are here mentioned in the fiftieth psalm, are from time to time inserted in Solomon's descriptions of the *wicked man*, as opposed to the *righteous*, in the book of Proverbs. Particularly, the sins mentioned in the 19th verse of that psalm, "Thou givest thy mouth to evil, and thy tongue frameth deceit;" are thus mentioned, as belonging to the character of the *wicked man*, Prov. xii. 5, 6. "The thoughts of the *righteous* are right; but the counsels of the *wicked* are deceit. The words of the *wicked* are to lie in wait for blood; but the mouth of the *upright* shall deliver them." Nevertheless it is plain, that the wise man in this book, in his distinction of the *righteous* and the *wicked*, means the same as *godly* and *ungodly*. Only reading the two foregoing chapters will be enough to satisfy any of this. Observe chap. x. 3, 7, 16, 20, 21, 24, 28—32. and xi. 3, 5, 9, 11, 18—23, 30, 31. besides innumerable other like texts all over the book. In chap. i. 16. it is said of sinners, "Their feet run to evil, and make haste to shed blood." This the apostle, in Rom. iii. 15. cites as belonging to the description of all natural men. So in the description of the wicked, Prov. iv. 14—19. it is said that "they sleep not unless they have done mischief; that they drink the wine of violence," &c. and yet by the wicked there is meant the same with the graceless man; as appears by the *antithesis* there made between him and the just, or righteous, "whose path is as the shining light, that shineth more and more to the perfect day."

As a further evidence that by the wicked in Psal. l. 16. is meant the same as the ungodly or graceless, it is to be observed, here is a pretty manifest *antithesis*, or opposition between the wicked, and the saints, that shall be gathered to Christ at the day of judgment, ver. 5. There God speaking of his coming to judgment, says, "Gather my SAINTS together, those that have made a COVENANT with me by sacrifice:" and then, after showing the insufficiency of the sacrifices of beasts, implying that it is a greater sacrifice by which these saints make a COVENANT with him, it is added, "But to the wicked" [that are not in the number of my saints] "God doth say, What hast thou to do, to take my COVENANT into thy mouth?" Approving of the *covenanting* of the former, but disapproving the *covenanting* of the latter. As to the gathering of God's saints, there mentioned, if we consider the foregoing and the following verses, it is evidently the same with the gathering of his elect, when Christ comes in the clouds of heaven, Matt. xxiv. 30, 31. and with the gathering of the righteous, as his wheat into his barn, at the day of judgment, Matt. xiii. And therefore there is as much reason to suppose, that by the wicked, which are opposed to them, is meant all graceless persons, as there is to understand the *doers of iniquity*, Matt. xiii. as opposed to the righteous, which shall then "shine forth as the sun in the kingdom of their Father," ver. 43.—And there is one thing more which still further confirms me in my construction of Psal. l. 16. which is, That the plain reason here given against wicked men taking God's covenant into their mouths, holds good with respect to all graceless men, *viz.* Because they do not comply with, but reject, the very covenant, which they with their mouths profess to own and consent to. Ver. 17. "Seeing thou hatest instruction, and castest my words behind thee;" as much as to say, "Thou rejectest and hast a reigning enmity against my statutes, with which thou declarest and professest a compliance." And this is the spirit and practice of all who live in the sin of unbelief and rejection of Christ; they live in a way that is altogether inconsistent with the covenant of grace; for against the sum and substance of the condition and engagement of that covenant every natural man is under the reigning power of enmity, and lives in contradiction to it. Therefore, I think, it follows, that they who know it is thus with them, have *nothing to do to take God's covenant into their mouths.*

SECT. IV.

The nature of things seems to afford no good reason why the people of Christ should not openly profess a proper respect to him in their hearts, as well as a true notion of him in their heads, or a right opinion of him in their judgments, and this is confirmed by scripture testimony.

I CAN conceive of nothing reasonably to be supposed as the design or end of a public profession of religion, that does not as much require a profession of honour, esteem, and friendship of heart towards Christ, as an orthodox opinion about him; or why the former should not be as much expected and required in order to be admitted into the company of his friends and followers, as the latter. It cannot be because the former in itself is not as important as the latter; seeing the very essence of religion itself consists in the former, and without it the latter is wholly vain, and makes us never the better; neither happier in ourselves, nor more acceptable to God.—One end of a public profession of religion is giving public honour to God. But surely the profession of inward esteem and a supreme respect of heart towards God more directly tends to it, than the declaring of right speculative notions of him. We look upon it that our friends do the more especially and directly put honour upon us, when upon proper occasions they stand ready not only to own the truth of such and such facts concerning us, but also to testify their high esteem and cordial and entire regard to us. When persons only manifest their doctrinal knowledge of religion, and express the assent of their judgments, but at the same time make no pretence but that they are wholly destitute of all true love to God, and are under the dominion of enmity against him, their profession is, in some respects, very greatly to God's dishonour: for they leave reason for the public greatly to suspect that they *hold the truth in unrighteousness*, and that they are some of those who have both seen and hated Christ and his Father, John xv. 24. Who of all persons have the greatest sin, and are most to God's dishonour.

I am at a loss, how that *visibility of saintship*, which the honoured author of *The Appeal to the Learned*, supposes to be all that is required in order to admission to the Lord's supper, can be much to God's honour, *viz.* Such a visibility as leaves reason to believe, that the greater part of those who have it, are enemies to God in their hearts, and inwardly the servants of sin. Such a visibility of religion as this, seems rather to increase a visibility of wickedness in the world, and so of God's dishonour, than any thing else; *i. e.* it makes more wickedness visible to the eye of a human judgment, and gives men reason to think, there is more wickedness in the world than otherwise would be visible to them. Because we have reason to think, that those who live in a rejection of Christ, under the light of the gospel, and the knowledge and common belief of its doctrine, have vastly greater sin and guilt than other men. And that venerable divine himself did abundantly teach this.

Christ came into the world to engage in a war with God's enemies, *sin* and *Satan;* and a great war there is maintained between them; and the contest is, who shall have the possession of OUR HEARTS. Now it is reasonable, under these circumstances, that we should declare on whose side we are, whether on Christ's side, or on the side of his enemies. If we would be admitted among Christ's friends and followers, it is reasonable, that we should profess we are *on the Lord's side*, and that we yield OUR HEARTS to him, and not to his rivals. And this seems plainly to be the design and nature of a public profession of Christ. If *this* profession is not made, no profession is made that is worth regarding, in such a case as this, and to any such purpose as being admitted among his visible friends. There is no being on Christ's side, in this case, but with an *undivided heart* preferring him to all his rivals, and renouncing them all for his sake. The case admits of no neutrality, or lukewarmness, or a middle sort of persons with a moral sincerity, or such a common faith as is consistent with loving sin and the world better than Christ. *He that is not with me* (says Christ) *is against me.* And therefore none profess to be on Christ's side, but they who profess to renounce his rivals. For those who would be called Christians, to profess no higher regard to Christ than what will admit of a superior regard to the world, is more absurd than if a woman pretending to marry a man, and take him for her husband, should profess to take him in some sort, but yet not pretend to take him in such a manner as is inconsistent with her allowing other men a fuller possession of her, and greater intimacy with her, than she allows him. The nature of the case, as it stands between us and Jesus Christ, is such, that an open solemn profession of being entirely for him, and giving him the possession of our hearts, renouncing all competitors, is more requisite in this, than a like profession in any other case. The profession of an intermediate sort of state of our mind, is very disagreeable to the nature of Christ's work and kingdom in the world, and all that belongs to the designs and ends of his administrations; and for ministers and churches openly to establish such a profession of Christ as part of his public service, which does not imply more than lukewarmness, is, I fear, to make a mere sham of a solemn public profession of Christianity, and seems to be wholly without warrant from the word of God, and greatly to his dishonour.

It cannot be justly pretended, as a reason why the *opinion concerning doctrines* should be professed, and not *friendship* or *respect of heart*, that the former is more *easily discerned* and known by us than the latter. For though it be true, that men may be at a loss concerning the latter, yet it is as true they may be so concerning the former too. They may be at a loss in many cases concerning the fulness of the determination of their own inclination and choice; and so they may concerning the fulness of the determination of their judgment. I know of nothing in human nature that hinders the acts of men's wills being properly subject to their own consciousness, any more than the acts of their judgment; nor of any reason to suppose that men may not discern their own *consent*, as well as their *assent*. The Scripture plainly supposes gracious dispositions and acts to be things properly under the eye of conscience. 2 Cor. xiii. 5. "Know ye not your ownselves?" John xxi. 15. "Simon, son of Jonas, lovest thou me?" and many other places. Nor is the nature of godliness less made known, that the true doctrines of religion. Piety of heart, in the more essential things belonging to it, is as clearly revealed, as the doctrines concerning the nature of God, the person of the Messiah, and the method of his redemption.

We find in Scripture, that all those of God's professing people or visible saints who are not *truly pious*, are represented as *counterfeits*, as having *guile*, *disguise*, and a *false appearance*, as making *false pretences*, and as being *deceitful* and *hypocrites.*—Thus Christ says of Nathanael, John i. 47. "Behold an Israelite indeed, in whom is no guile;" that is, a truly gracious person; implying, that those of God's professing people, who are not gracious, are *guileful*, and deceitful in their profession. So sinners in Zion, or in God's visible church, are called *hypocrites.* Isa. xxxiii. 14. "The sinners in Zion are afraid, fearfulness hath surprised the *hypocrites.*" Isa. xi. 17. "Every one is an *hypocrite* and an evil-doer." So they are called *lying children*, Isa. xxx. 9. and chap. lix. 13. and are represented as *lying*, in pretending to be of *the temple* or church of God. Jer. vii. 2, 4. "Hear the word of the Lord, all ye of Judah, that enter in at these gates to worship the Lord.—Trust ye not in lying words, saying, The temple of the Lord, the temple of the Lord, the temple of the Lord are these." These are spoken of as falsely calling themselves of the *holy city*, Isa. xlviii. 1, 2. They are called *silver-dross*, and *reprobate* or *refuse silver*, (Ezek. xxii. 18. Jer. vi. 30.) which glisters and shows like true silver, but has not its inward worth. So they are compared to *adulterated wine*, Isa. i. 22. and to *trees* full of *leaves*, bidding fair for fruitfulness, Matt. xxi. 19. *Clouds* that look as if they were full of rain, yet bring nothing but *wind*, Jude 12. *Wells without water*, that do but cheat the thirsty traveller, 2 Pet. ii. 13. A deceitful bow, that appears good, but fails the archer, Psal. lxxviii. 57. Hos. vii. 16.—Mr. Stoddard, in his *Appeal to the Learned*, from time to time, supposes all *visible saints*, who are not truly pious, to be *hypocrites*, as in page 15, 17, 18.

Now what ground or reason can there be thus to represent those to be *visible saints*, or members of God's visible church, who are not *truly pious*, if the profession of such does not imply any pretence to *true piety*; and when they never made a pretence to any thing more than *common grace*, or *moral sincerity*, which many of them *truly have*, and therefore are not at all *hypocritical* or deceitful in their pretences, and are as much *without guile*, in what they make a profession of, as Nathanael was? The psalmist speaking of sincere piety, calls it *truth in the inward parts.* Psal. li. 6. "Behold, thou desirest truth in the inward parts." It is called *truth* with reference to some *declaration* or *profession* made by God's visible people; but on the hypothesis which I oppose, *common grace* is as properly *truth in the inward parts*, in this respect, as saving grace. God says concerning Israel, Deut. xxxii. 5. "Their spot is not the spot of his children." God here speaks of himself, as it were, disappointed; the words having reference to some *profession* they had made. For why should the remark be made, after this manner, that *spots* appeared upon them, and showed marks that they were not his *children*, if they never *pretended* to be his children, and never were accepted under any such notion to any of the privileges of his people?

God is pleased to represent himself in his word as if he *trusted* the profession of his visible people, and as *disappointed* when they did not approve themselves as his faithful, stedfast, and thorough friends. Isa. lxiii. 8, 9, 10. "For he said, Surely they are my people, children that will not lie. So he was their Saviour: in all their affliction he was afflicted. But they rebelled and vexed his Holy Spirit: therefore he was turned to be their enemy." The same is represented in many other places. I suppose that God speaks after this manner, because, in his present external dealings with his visible people, he does not act in the capacity of the Searcher of hearts, but accommodates himself to their nature, and the present state and circumstances of his church, and speaks to them and treats them after the manner of men, and deals with them in their own way.* But supposing the case to be even thus, there would be no ground for such representations, if there were no profession of true godliness. When God is represented as trusting that men will be his faithful friends, we must understand that he trusts to their pretences. But how improperly would the matter be so represented, if there were no pretences to trust to, no pretences of any real thorough friendship! However there may be a profession of some common affection that is morally sincere, yet there is no pretence of loving him more than, yea not so much as, his enemies.—What reason to trust that they will be faithful to God as their master, when the religion they profess amounts to no more than serving two masters? What reason to trust that they will be stable in their ways, when they do not pretend to be of a single heart, and all know that the double-minded persons used to be unstable in all their ways? Those who only profess *moral sincerity* or common grace, do not pretend to love God above the world. And such grace is what God and man know is liable to *pass away as the early dew, and the morning cloud.*—If what men profess amounts to nothing beyond *lukewarmness*, it is not to be expected, that they will be *faithful to the death.* If men do not pretend to have any oil in their vessels, what cause can there be to trust that their lamps will not *go out?* If they do not pretend to have any *root* in them, what cause is there for any disappointment when they wither away.

* This distinction is too vague. A more satisfactory reason is, that the very nature of *moral government* requires this mode of treatment. See "An Essay on Equity and Sovereignty," throughout.—W.

When God, in the forementioned place, Isa. lxiii. represents himself as trusting Israel's profession, and saying, "Surely they are my people, children that will not lie;" it cannot be understood, as if he trusted that they were *his people* in that sense, in which the ten tribes were called God's people after they had given up themselves to idolatry for two or three hundred years together without once repenting. But, *surely they are my sincere saints and children*, as they profess to be, Israelites indeed, without guile; they would not do so evil a thing as to make a *lying profession*. This seems to be the plain import of the words. It therefore shows that the profession they made was of real vital godliness.

The eight first verses of the fifty-sixth chapter of Isaiah, I think, afford good evidence, that such qualifications are requisite in order to the privileges of a visible church state, as I have insisted on.—In the four preceding chapters we have a prophecy of gospel-times, the blessed state of things which the Messiah should introduce. The prophecy of the same times is continued in the former part of this chapter. Here we have a prophecy of the abolishing of the *ceremonial law*, which was a *wall of separation*, that kept two sorts of persons, (*viz.* eunuchs and Gentiles,) out from the ordinances of the church or congregation of the Lord, (for the words *congregation* and *church* are the same,) the place of whose meeting was *in God's house within God's walls*, ver. 5. and *on God's holy mountain*, ver. 7. That in the ceremonial law which especially kept out the Gentiles, was the law of circumcision; and the law that the eunuch shall not enter into the congregation or church of the Lord, we have in Deut. xxiii. 1. Now here it is foretold, that in the days when "God's salvation shall be come, and his righteousness revealed," by the coming of the Messiah, this wall of separation should be broken down, this ceremonial law removed out of the way; (but still taking care to note, that the law of the Sabbath shall be continued, as not being one of those ceremonial observances which shall be abolished;) and then it is declared, what is the great qualification which should be looked at in those blessed days, when these external ceremonial qualifications of circumcision and soundness of body should no more be insisted on, *viz.* piety of heart and practice, "joining themselves to the Lord, loving the name of the Lord, to be his servants, choosing the things that please him," &c. Ver. 3, &c. "Neither let the son of the stranger that hath joined himself to the Lord, speak, saying, The Lord hath utterly separated me from his people; neither let the eunuch say, Behold, I am a dry tree; for thus saith the Lord unto the eunuchs that keep my Sabbaths, and choose the things that please me, and take hold of my covenant, even unto them will I give in my house, and within my walls, a place, and a name better than of sons and of daughters; I will give unto them an everlasting name, that shall not be cut off. Also the sons of the stranger that join themselves to the Lord, to serve him, and to love the name of the Lord, to be his servants, every one that keepeth the Sabbath from polluting it, and taketh hold of my covenant: even them will I bring to my holy mountain, and make them joyful in my house of prayer; their burnt-offerings and their sacrifices shall be accepted upon mine altar: for mine house shall be called an house of prayer for all people. The Lord God which gathered the outcasts of Israel, saith, Yet will I gather others to him besides those that are gathered unto him."

SECT. V.

The representations which Christ makes of his visible church, from time to time, in his discourses and parables, make the thing manifest which I have laid down.

THIS is required by the representation which Christ makes in the latter end of Matthew vii. of the final issue of things with respect to the different sorts of members of his visible church. Those that only say, *Lord, Lord*, and those who *do the will of his Father which is in heaven; those who build their house upon a rock*, and *those who build upon the sand*. They are all (of both kinds) evidently such as have pretended to a high honour and regard to Christ, have claimed an interest in him, and accordingly hoped to be finally acknowledged and received as his. Those visible Christians who are not true Christians cry, *Lord, Lord;* that is, are forward to profess respect and claim relation to him; and will be greatly disappointed hereafter in not being owned by him. They shall then come and cry, *Lord, Lord*. This compellation, *Lord*, is commonly given to Jesus Christ in the New Testament, as signifying the special relation which Christ stood in to his disciples, rather than his universal dominion. They shall then come and earnestly claim relation, as it is represented of Israel of old, in the day of their distress, and God's awful judgments upon them, Hos. viii. 2. "Israel shall cry unto me, My God, we know thee." To *know* does not here intend speculative knowledge, but knowing as one *knows his own*, with a peculiar respect and interest. These false disciples shall not only claim an interest in Christ, but shall plead and bring arguments to confirm their claim; "Lord, Lord, have we not prophesied in thy name, and in thy name have cast out devils, and in thy name have done many wonderful works?" It is evidently the language of those that are dreadfully disappointed. "Then (says Christ) I will profess unto them, I never knew you; depart from me, ye that work iniquity:" *q. d.* "Though they profess a relation to me, I will profess none to them; though they plead that they know me, and have an interest in me, I will declare to them that I never owned them as any of mine; and will bid them depart from me as those that I will never own, nor have any thing to do with in such a relation as they claim." Thus all the hopes they had lived in, of being hereafter received and owned by Christ as in the number of his friends and favourites, are dashed in pieces.—This is further illustrated by what follows, in the comparison of the wise man who built his house on a rock; representing those professed disciples who build their hope of an interest in him on a sure foundation, whose house shall stand in the trying day: and the foolish man who built his house on the sand; representing those professed disciples or hearers of his word, who build their opinion and hope of an interest in him on a false foundation, whose house in the great time of trial shall have a dreadful fall, their vain hope shall issue in dismal disappointment and confusion.

On the whole, it is manifest that all visible Christians or saints, all Christ's professing disciples or hearers that profess him to be their Lord, according to the scripture notion of professing Christ, are such as profess a "saving interest in him and relation to him, and live in the hope of being hereafter owned as those that are so interested and related."—By *those that hear Christ's sayings*, in this place, are not meant merely auditors of the word preached; for there are many such who make no pretence to an interest in Christ, and have no such hope or opinion built on any foundation at all; but those who profess to hearken, believe, and yield submission to the word of Christ. This is confirmed by the manner in which the matter is expressed in Luke vi. "Whosoever cometh to me, and heareth my sayings, and doth them, I will show you to whom he is like:" *i. e.* Whosoever visibly comes to me, and is one of my professed disciples, &c.

This matter is confirmed by that parallel representation that Christ gives us in Luke xiii. 25—29. of his final disposal of the two different sorts of persons that are in the kingdom or church of God; *viz.* those who shall be allowed in his church or kingdom when it comes to its state of glory, and those who though they have visibly been in it, shall be thrust out of it. It is represented of the latter, that they shall then come and claim relation and interest, and cry, "Lord, Lord, open to us;" and "Christ shall answer, and say, I know you not whence you are." As much as to say, "Why do you claim relation and acquaintance with me? You are strangers to me, I do not own you." "Then (it is said) they shall begin to say, We have eaten and drank in thy presence, and thou hast taught in our streets." As much as to say, "This is a strange thing, that thou dost not own us! We are exceedingly surprised, that thou shouldst account us as strangers that have no part in thee, when we have eaten and drank in thy presence," &c. And when he shall finally insist upon it, that he does not own them, and will have nothing to do with them as his, "then there shall be weeping and gnashing of teeth;" then they shall be filled with dismal disappointment, confusion, and despair, when they shall see Abraham, Isaac, and Jacob, and all the prophets, in the kingdom of God, with whom they expected to dwell for ever there, and they themselves thrust out. By this it is evident, that those visible members of the kingdom of God, that hereafter shall be cast out of it, are such as look upon themselves now interested in Christ and the eternal blessings of his kingdom, and make that profession.

The same is manifest by the parable of the ten virgins, Matt. xxv. In the first verse it is said, "The kingdom of heaven (*i. e.* the church of Christ) is likened unto ten virgins." The two sorts of virgins evidently represent the two sorts of members of the visible church of Christ; the wise, those who are true Christians; and the foolish, those who are apparent but not true Christians. The foolish virgins were to all appearance the children of the bride-chamber; such as had accepted of the invitation to the wedding, which represents the invitations of the gospel, wherein the bridegroom and bride say, *Come.* They herein had testified the same respect to the bridegroom and bride that the wise had. The parable naturally leads us to suppose, that they were to appearance every way of the same society with the wise, pretended to be the same sort of persons, in like manner interested in the bridegroom, and that they were received by the wise under such a notion. They made a profession of the very same kind of honour and regard to the bridegroom, in going forth to meet him with their lamps, as his friends to show him respect, and had the same hopes of enjoying the privileges and entertainments of the wedding: there was a difference with respect to oil in their vessels, but there was no difference with respect to their lamps. One thing intended by their lamps, as I suppose is agreed by all, is their profession. This is the same in both; and in both it is a profession of grace, as a lamp (from its known end and use) is a manifestation or show of oil. Another thing signified by the blaze of their lamps seems to be the light of hope. Their lamps signify in general the appearance of grace or godliness, including both the appearance of it to the view or judgment of others, and also to their own view, and the judgment they entertain of themselves. Their lamps shone, not only in the eyes of others, but also in their own eyes. This is confirmed because on hearing the midnight cry, they find their *lamps are gone out;* which seems most naturally to represent, that however hypocrites may maintain their hopes while they live, and while their judge is at a distance, yet when they come to be alarmed by the sound of the last trumpet, their hopes will immediately expire and vanish away, and very often fail them in the sensible approaches of death. *Where is the hope of the hypocrite, when God takes away his soul?* But till the midnight cry the foolish virgins seem to entertain the same hopes with the wise. When they first went forth with the wise virgins, their lamps shone in their own eyes, and in the eyes of others, in like manner with the lamps of the wise virgins.—So that by this parable it also appears, that all visible members of the christian church, or kingdom of heaven, are those that profess to be gracious persons, as looking on themselves, and at least pretending, to be such.

And that true piety is what persons ought to look at in themselves as the qualification that is proper in coming into the visible church of Christ, and taking the privileges of its members, I think, is evident also from the parable of the *marriage,* which the king made for his son, Matt. xxii. particularly the 11th and 12th verses, "And when the king came in to see the guests, he saw there a man which had not on a wedding-garment: and he saith unto him, Friend, how camest thou in hither, not having on a wedding-garment? and he was speechless."—Mr. Stoddard says, (*Appeal,* page 4, 5.) "Here is a representation of the day of judgment; and such persons as come for salvation without a *wedding-garment* shall be rejected in that day. So that here being nothing said about the *Lord's supper,* all arguing from this scripture falls to the ground." Upon which I take leave to observe, that the king's coming in to see the guests, means Christ's visiting his professing church at the day of judgment, I make no doubt; but, that the guests coming into the king's house means persons coming for salvation at the day of judgment, I am not convinced. If it may properly be represented, that any reprobates will come for salvation at the day of judgment, they will not do so *before* the king appears; but Christ will appear *first,* and *then* they will come and cry to him for salvation.—Whereas, in this parable, the guests are represented as gathered together in the king's house before the king appears, and the king as coming in and finding them there; where they had entered while the day of grace lasted, while the door was kept open, and invitations given forth; and not like those who come for salvation at the day of judgment, Luke xiii. 25. who come "after the door is shut, and stand without knocking at the door." I think it is apparent beyond all contradiction, that by the guests coming into the king's house at the invitation of the servants, is intended Jews and Gentiles coming into the *christian church,* at the preaching of Christ's apostles and others, making profession of godliness, and expecting to partake of the eternal marriage supper. I showed before, that what is called the house of God in the New Testament, is his church. In this parable, the king first sends forth his servants to *call them that were bidden,* and they would not come; and they having repeatedly rejected the invitation, and evil-entreated the servants, the king sent forth his armies and burnt up their city; representing the Jews being first invited, and rejecting the invitations of the gospel, and persecuting Christ's ministers, and so provoking God to give up Jerusalem and the nation to destruction. Then the king sends forth his servants into the *highways,* to call in all sorts; upon which many flocked into the king's house; hereby most plainly representing the preaching the gospel to the Gentiles, and their flocking into the *christian church.* This gathering of the Gentiles into the king's house, is BEFORE the day of judgment, and the man without the wedding-garment among them. It fitly represents the resorting that should be to the christian church, during the day of grace, through all ages; but by no means signifies men's coming for salvation *after* the day of grace is at an end, at Christ's appearing in the clouds of heaven. Let this parable be compared with that parallel place, Luke xiv. 16—24. The company gathered to the marriage in this parable, plainly represents the same thing with the company of virgins gathered to the marriage in the other parable, Matt. xxv. *viz.* the company of visible saints, or the company belonging to the visible kingdom of heaven; and therefore both parables are introduced alike with these words, "The kingdom of heaven is like unto," &c. As to the man's being cast out of the king's house when the *king comes in to see his guests,* it is agreeable to other representations made of false Christians being thrust out of God's kingdom at the day of judgment; the "servant's not abiding in the house for ever, though the son abideth ever;" God's "taking away their part out of the holy city, and blotting their names out of the book of life," &c.

Mr. Stoddard says, "This person that had not a *wedding-garment,* was a *reprobate;* but every one that partakes of the Lord's supper without grace is not a reprobate." I answer, all that will be found in the king's house without grace *when the king comes in to see the guests,* are doubtless reprobates.

If it be questioned, whether by the *wedding-garment* be meant true piety, or whether hereby is not intended *moral sincerity,* let the Scripture interpret itself; which elsewhere tells us plainly what the wedding-garment is at the marriage of the Son of God: Rev. xix. 7, 8. "The marriage of the Lamb is come, and his wife hath made herself ready. And to her was granted that she should be arrayed in fine linen, clean and white; for the fine linen is the righteousness of saints." None, I suppose, will say, this righteousness that is so pure, is the common grace of lukewarm professors, and those that go about to serve God and mammon. The same wedding-garment we have an account of in Psal. xlv. 13, 14. "The king's daughter is all glorious within, her clothing is of wrought gold: she shall be brought unto the king in raiment of needle-work." But we need go no where else but to the parable itself; that alone determines the matter. The wedding-garment spoken of as that without which professors will be excluded from among God's people at the day of judgment, is not *moral sincerity*, or common grace, but special saving grace. If common grace were the wedding-garment intended, not only would the king cast out those whom he found *without* a wedding-garment, but also many *with* a wedding-garment: for all such as shall be found then with no better garment than *moral sincerity*, will be bound hand and foot, and cast into outer darkness; such a wedding-garment as this will not save them. So that true piety, unfeigned faith, or the righteousness of Christ which is upon every one that believeth, is doubtless the wedding-garment intended. But if a person has good and proper ground to proceed on in *coming into the king's house*, that knows he is *without* this wedding-garment, why should the king upbraid him, saying, "How camest thou in hither, not having a wedding-garment?" And why should he be speechless, when asked such a question? Would he not have had a good answer to make? *viz.* "Thou thyself hast given me leave to come in hither, *without a wedding-garment*." Or this, "Thy own word is my warrant; which invited such as had only common grace, or *moral sincerity*, to come in."

SECT. VI.

What took place, in fact, in the manner and circumstances of the admission of members into the primitive christian church, and the profession they made in order to their admission, as recorded in the Acts of the Apostles, will further confirm the point.

We have an account, concerning these, of their being first awakened by the preaching of the apostles and other ministers, and earnestly inquiring *what they should do to be saved*, and of their being directed to *repent and believe on the Lord Jesus*, as the way to have their sins blotted out, and to be saved; and then, upon their *professing* that they did believe, of their being baptized and admitted into the christian church. Now can any reasonably imagine, that these primitive converts, when they made that profession in order to their admission, had any such *distinction* in view as that which some now make, of *two sorts* of real Christianity, two sorts of sincere faith and repentance, one with *a moral* and another with a *gracious* sincerity? Or that the apostles, who disciplined them and baptized them, had instructed them in any such distinction? The history informs us of their teaching them but *one* faith and repentance; *Believing in Christ that they might be saved*, and *repentance for the remission of sins*; and it would be unreasonable to suppose, that a thought of any lower or other kind entered into the heads of these converts, when immediately upon their receiving such instructions they professed *faith* and *repentance*; or that those who admitted them understood them as meaning any other but what they professed.

Let us particularly consider what we are informed concerning those multitudes, whose admission we have an account of in Acts ii. We are told concerning the three thousand first converts, that they were greatly awakened by the preaching of the apostles, *pricked in their hearts*, made sensible of their guilt and misery; "and said to Peter, and the rest of the apostles, Men and brethren, what shall we do?" *i. e.* What shall we do to be *saved*, and that our *sins may be remitted?* Upon which they directed them what they should do, *viz.* "Repent, and be baptized, in the name of the Lord Jesus, for the remission of sins." They are here directed into the way of salvation, *viz.* faith and repentance, with a proper profession of these.—*Then*, we are told, that *they which gladly received the word were baptized;* that is, They which appeared gladly to receive the word, or manifested and professed a cordial and cheerful compliance with the calls of the word, with the directions which the apostles had given them. The manifestation was doubtless by some profession, and the profession was of *that repentance for the remission of sins*, and *that faith in Christ*, which the apostles had directed them to, in answer to their inquiry, *what they should do to be saved?* I can see no ground to suppose they thought of any lower or other kind. And it is evident by what follows, that these converts now looked upon it that they had complied with these directions, and so were at peace with God. Their business now is to rejoice and praise God from day to day; "They continued stedfastly in the apostles' doctrine and fellowship—continuing daily with one accord in the temple, and breaking bread from house to house, they did eat their meat with gladness and singleness of heart, praising God." The account of them now is not as of persons under awakenings, weary and heavy-laden sinners, under an awful sense of guilt and wrath, *pricked in their hearts*, as before; but of persons whose sorrow was turned into joy, looking on themselves as now in a good estate. And in the last verse it is said, "The Lord added to the church daily such as should be saved;" in the original it is τους σωζομενυς, *the saved;* οι σωζομενοι was a common appellation given to all visible Christians, or to all members of the visible christian church. It is as much as to say, *the converted*, or *the regenerate.* Being converted is in Scripture called being saved, because it is so in effect; they were "passed from death to life," John v. 24. Tit. i. 4. "According to his mercy he SAVED us, by the washing of REGENERATION, and renewing of the Holy Ghost." 2 Tim. i. 9. "Who hath SAVED us, and called us with an holy calling." Not that all who were added to the visible church were indeed regenerated, but they were so in profession and repute, and therefore were so in name. 1 Cor. i. 18. "The preaching of the cross is to them that perish, foolishness; but unto us [*i. e.* us Christians] which are SAVED [τοις σωζομενοις] it is the power of God." So those that from time to time were added to the primitive church, were all called οι σωζομενοι, *the saved.* Before, while under awakenings, they used to inquire of their teachers, what they should do to be saved; and the directions that used to be given them, were to *repent* and *believe in Christ;* and before they were admitted into the church, they professed that they did so; and thenceforward, having visibly complied with the terms proposed, they were called THE SAVED; it being supposed, that they now had obtained what they inquired after when they asked what they should do to be saved. Accordingly we find that Christ's ministers treated them no more as miserable perishing sinners, but as true converts; not setting before them their sin and misery to awaken them, and to convince them of the necessity of a Saviour, exhorting them to fly from the wrath to come, and seek conversion to God; but exhorting them to *hold fast the profession of their faith*, to *continue in the grace of God*, and persevere in holiness; endeavouring by all means to confirm and strengthen them in grace. Thus when a great number believed and turned to the Lord at Antioch, Barnabas was sent to them; "who, when he came, and had seen the grace of God, was glad, and exhorted them all, that with purpose of heart they should cleave to the Lord." Acts xi. 23. See also Acts xiii. 43. and xiv. 22. and xv. 32, 41. and xx. 32. And when the apostles heard of the conversion of the Gentiles to the christian faith, visible by their profession when they joined themselves to the christian church, they supposed and believed that God had given them saving repentance, and a heart-purifying faith. Acts xi. 18. "When they heard these things, they held their peace, and glorified God, saying, Then hath God also granted unto the Gentiles REPENTANCE unto LIFE." Chap. xv. 9. "And put no difference between us and them, purifying their hearts by FAITH."

If any should here object, that when such multitudes were converted from Judaism and heathenism, and received into the christian church in so short a season, it was impossible there should be *time* for each one to say so much in his public profession, as to be any credible exhibition of true godliness to the church: I answer, This objection will soon vanish, if we particularly consider how the case was with those primitive converts, and how they were dealt with by their teachers. It was apparently the manner of the first preachers of the gospel, when their hearers were awakened and brought in good earnest to inquire what they should do to be saved, then particularly to instruct them in the way of salvation, and explain to them what qualifications must be in them, or what they must do in order to their being saved, agreeable to Christ's direc tion, Mark xvi. 15, 16. This we find was the method they took with the *three thousand*, in the second chapter of Acts, ver. 37--40. And it seems, they were particular and full in it: they said much more to them than the words recorded. It is said, ver. 40. "With many other words did Peter testify and exhort." And this we find to be the course Paul and Silas took with the jailor, chap. xvi. Who also gave more large and full instructions than are rehearsed in the history. And when they had thus instructed them, they doubtless saw to it, either by themselves or some others who assisted them, that their instructions were *understood* by them, before they proceeded to baptize them. For I suppose, none with whom I have to do in this controversy, will maintain, from the apostles' example, that we ought not to insist on a good degree of doctrinal knowledge in the way and terms of salvation, as requisite to the admission of members into the church. And after they were satisfied that they well understood these things, it took up no great time to make a profession of them, or to declare that they did, or found in themselves, those things they had been told of as necessary to their salvation. After they had been well informed what saving faith and repentance were, it took up no more time to profess *that* faith and repentance, than any other.—In this case not only the converts' words, but the words of the preacher, which they consented to, and in effect made their own, are to be taken into their profession. For persons that are known to be of an honest character, and manifestly qualified with good doctrinal knowledge of the nature of true godliness, in the more essential things which belong to it, solemnly to profess they have or do those things, is to make as credible a profession of godliness as I insist upon. And we may also well suppose, that more words were uttered by the professors, and with other circumstances to render them credible, than are recorded in that very brief history, which we have of the primitive church in the Acts of the Apostles; and also we may yet suppose one thing further, *viz.* that in that extraordinary state of things so particular a profession was not requisite in order to the church's satisfaction, either of doctrines *assented* to, or of the *consent* and disposition of the heart, as may be expedient in a more ordinary state of things; for various reasons that might be given, would it not too much lengthen out this discourse.

One thing which makes it very evident, that the inspired ministers of the primitive christian church looked upon *saving faith* as the proper matter of the profession requisite in order to admission into the church, is the story of Philip and the eunuch, in Acts viii. For when the eunuch desires to be baptized, Philip makes answer, ver. 37. "If thou believest with all thine heart, thou mayst." Which words certainly imply, that *believing with all his heart* was requisite in order to his coming to this ordinance properly and in a due manner. I cannot conceive what should move Philip to utter these words, or what he should aim at in them, if at the same time he supposed, that the eunuch had no need to look at any such qualification in himself, or at all to inquire whether he had such a faith, in order to determine whether he might present himself as the subject of *baptism*.

It is said by some, that Philip intended nothing more by *believing with all his heart*, than that he believed that doctrine, that *Jesus Christ was the Son of God*, with a *moral sincerity* of persuasion. But here again I desire, that the Scripture may be allowed to be its own interpreter. The Scripture very much abounds with such phrases as this, *with all the heart*, or *with the whole heart*, in speaking of religious matters. And the manifest intent of them is to signify a gracious simplicity and godly sincerity. Thus, 1 Sam. xii. 20. "Turn not aside from following the Lord, but serve the Lord with all your heart." So ver. 24. "Only fear the Lord, and serve him in truth, with all your heart." 1 Kings viii. 23. "Who keepest covenant and mercy with thy servants, that walk before thee with all their heart." Chap. xiv. 8. "My servant David, who kept my commandments, and who followed me with all his heart." 2 Kings x. 31. "But Jehu took no heed to walk in the law of the Lord God of Israel with all his heart." 2 Chron. xxii. 9. "Jehoshaphat sought the Lord with all his heart." Chap. xxxi. 20, 21. "Hezekiah wrought that which was good and right and truth before the Lord his God; and in every work that he began in the service of the house of God, and in the law, and in the commandments, to seek his God, he did it with all his heart." Ps. ix. 1. "I will praise thee, O Lord, with my whole heart." Ps. lxxxvi. 12. "I will praise thee, O Lord my God, with all my heart, and will glorify thy name." Ps. cxi. 1. "I will praise thee, O Lord, with my whole heart, in the assembly of the upright." And cxix. 2. "Blessed are they that keep his testimonies, and that seek him with the whole heart." Ver. 10. "With my whole heart have I sought thee." Ver. 34. "Give me understanding, and I shall keep thy law, yea, I shall observe it with my whole heart." Ver. 69. "The proud have forged a lie against me, but I will keep thy precepts with my whole heart." Jer. xxiv. 7. "And I will give them an heart to know me—for they shall return unto me with their whole heart." Joel ii. 12, 13. "Turn ye even unto me with all your heart—and rend your heart, and not your garments." And we have the like phrases in innumerable other places. And I suppose that not so much as one place can be produced, wherein there is the least evidence or appearance of their being used to signify any thing but a *gracious sincerity*. And indeed it must be a very improper use of language, to speak of those as performing acts of religion *with all their hearts*, whose heart the Scriptures abundantly represent as under the reigning power of sin and unbelief—and as those that do not give God their hearts, but give them to other things—as those who go about to *serve two masters*, and who *draw near to God with their lips*, but have at the same time their hearts *far from him*, running more after other things; and who have not a single eye, nor single heart. The word *believe*, in the New Testament, answers to the word *trust* in the Old; and therefore the phrase used by Philip, of *believing with all the heart*, is parallel to that in Prov. iii. "Trust in the Lord with all thine heart." And believing with the heart is a phrase used in the New Testament, to signify saving faith.—Rom. x. 9, 10. "If thou shalt believe in thine heart, that God hath raised him from the dead, thou shalt be saved; for with the heart man believeth unto righteousness." The same is signified by obeying the form of doctrine from the heart, Rom. vi. 17, 18. "But God be thanked, that ye were the servants of sin, but ye have obeyed from the heart that form of doctrine which was delivered you; being then made free from sin, ye became the servants of righteousness." Here it is manifest, that saving faith is intended by obeying the form of doctrine from the heart. And the same is signified as if it had been said, "ye have believed with the heart" the form of doctrine. But Philip uses a yet stronger expression, he does not only say, if thou believest with the heart, or from the heart, but with ALL thine heart. Besides, for any to suppose, that those same persons which the Scriptures represent in some places as under the power of an evil heart of unbelief—as double-minded with regard to their faith, (James i. 6, 7, 8.) who, though they *believe for a while*, have their hearts like a *rock*, in which faith has *no root*, (Luke viii.)—and yet that this same sort of persons are in other scriptures spoken of *as believing with all their heart;* I say, for any to suppose this, would be to make the voice of God's word not very harmonious and consonant to itself.—And one thing more I would observe on this head, there is good reason to suppose, that Philip, while he sat in the chariot with the eunuch, and (as we are told) *preached unto him Jesus*, had showed to him the way of salvation—had opened to him the way of getting an interest in Christ, or obtaining salvation by him, *viz. believing in him*, agreeable to Christ's own direction, Mark xvi. 15, 16. and agreeable to what we find to be the manner of the first preachers of the gospel. And therefore, when after this discourse he puts it to the eunuch, whether he *believed with all his heart;* it is natural to suppose, that he meant whether he found his *heart* acquiescing in the gospel-way of salvation, or whether he sincerely exercised that *belief in Christ* which he had been inculcating; and it would be natural for the eunuch so to understand him.

Here if it be objected, that the eunuch's answer and the profession he hereupon made, (wherein he speaks nothing of his *heart*, but barely says,) *I believe that Jesus Christ is the Son of God*, shows that he understood no more by the inquiry, than whether he gave his *assent* to that *doctrine*: to this I answer; we must take this confession of the eunuch together with Philip's words, to which they were a reply, and expound the one by the other. Nor is there any reason but to understand it in the same sense in which we find the words of the like confession elsewhere in the New Testament, and as the words of such a confession were wont to be used in those days; as particularly the words of Peter's confession, Matt. xvi. 16. "And Simon Peter answered and said, Thou art Christ, the Son of the living God." Which was a profession of saving faith, as appears by what Christ says upon it. And we read, 1 Cor. xii. 3. "No man can say, that Jesus is the Lord, but by the Holy Ghost." Not but that a man might make a profession in these words without the Holy Ghost, but he could not do it heartily, or WITH ALL HIS HEART. So 1 John iv. 15. "Whosoever shall confess that Jesus is the Son of God, God dwelleth in him, and he in God." *i. e.* Whoever makes this christian confession (this profession which all Christians were wont to make) cordially, or *with his whole heart*, God dwells in him, &c. But it was *thus* that the eunuch was put upon making this confession.

SECT. VII.

The epistles of the apostles to the churches, prove what has been asserted.

It is apparent by the epistles of the apostles to the primitive *christian churches*, their *manner of addressing and treating* them throughout all those epistles, and what they say *to* them and *of* them, that all those churches were *constituted* of members *so qualified* as has been represented, having such a *visibility* of *godliness* as has been insisted on. Those who were reputed to be *real saints*, were taken into the church under a *notion* of their being truly pious persons, made that *profession*, and had this *hope* of themselves; and that *natural* and *graceless* men were not admitted designedly, but *unawares*, and beside the aim of the primitive churches and ministers; and that such as remained in good standing, and free from an offensive behaviour, continued to have the reputation and esteem of real saints, with the apostles, and one with another.

There were numbers indeed in these churches, who after their admission fell into an offensive behaviour; of some of whom the apostles in their epistles speak doubtfully; others that had behaved themselves very scandalously, they speak of in language that seems to suppose them to be wicked men.—The apostle Paul, in his epistles to the Corinthians, oftentimes speaks of some among them that had embraced heretical opinions, and had behaved themselves in a very disorderly and schismatical manner, whom he represents as exposed to censure, and to whom he threatens excommunication. On occasion of so many offences of this kind appearing among them that for a while had been thought well of, he puts them all upon *examining* themselves, whether they were indeed *in the faith*, and whether *Christ* was truly *in them*, as they and others had supposed, 2 Cor. xiii.—And the same apostle speaks of great numbers among the Galatians, who had made a high profession, and were such as he had thought well of when they were first admitted into the church, but since had given him cause to *doubt* of their state, by giving heed to seducers, that denied the great gospel-doctrine of *justification by faith alone*: yet notwithstanding, the apostle speaks of them in such language as shows surprise and disappointment, and implies that he had looked upon them as true Christians, and hoped that his labours among them had had a saving effect upon them. Gal. i. 6. "I marvel that ye are so soon removed from him that called you into the grace of Christ, unto another gospel." Chap. iv. 11. "I am afraid of you, lest I have bestowed upon you labour in vain." And ver. 20. "I desire to be present with you now, and change my voice; for I stand in doubt of you." As much as to say, "I have heretofore addressed you with the voice of love and charity, as supposing you the dear children of God; but now I begin to think of speaking to you in other language." In the same chapter, to show them what little reason he had to expect that they would come to this, he puts them in mind of the *great profession* they had made, and the extraordinary appearances there had formerly been in them of fervent piety.—Ver. 15. "Where is the blessedness you spake of? For I bear you record, that if it had been possible, you would have plucked out your own eyes, and have given them unto me." The apostle James, in his epistle, speaks of scandalous persons among the *twelve tribes that were scattered abroad*; some that were men of *unbridled tongues*; some that seem to have been a kind of antinomians in their principles, and of a very bitter and violent spirit, that reproached, condemned, and *cursed* their brethren, and raised *wars* and *fightings* among professing Christians, and were also very unclean in their practice, *adulterers* and *adulteresses*, chap. iv. 4. And in the fifth chapter of his epistle, he seems to speak to the unbelieving Jews, who persecuted the Christians, ver. 6.—And the apostles also often speak of some who had once been admitted into the church, *crept in unawares*, but who apostatized from Christianity, and finally proved notoriously wicked men.——But otherwise, and as to such members of the visible church as continued in the same good standing and visibility of Christianity, wherein they were admitted, it is evident by the epistles of the apostles, they were all in the eye of a christian judgment *truly pious* or *gracious* persons. And here I desire the following things may be particularly observed.

The apostles continually, in their epistles, speak to them and of them, as supposing and judging them to be gracious persons. Thus the apostle Paul, in his epistle to the Romans, chap. i. 7. speaks of the members of that church as *beloved of God*. In chap. vi. 17, 18, &c. he "thanks God, that they had obeyed from the heart that form of doctrine which had been delivered them,—were made free from sin, and become the servants of righteousness," &c. The apostle in giving thanks to God for this, must not only have a kind of *negative charity* for them, as not knowing but that they were gracious persons, and so *charitably hoping* (as we say) that it was so; but he seems to have formed a *positive judgment* that they were such. His thanksgiving must at least be founded on rational probability; since it would be but a mocking of God, to give him *thanks* for bestowing a mercy which at the same time he did not see reason positively to believe was bestowed. In chap. vii. 4—6. the apostle speaks of them as those that once *were in the flesh*, and *were under the law*, but now *delivered from the law, and dead to it*. In chap. viii. 15, and following verses, he tells them, *they had received the Spirit of adoption*, and speaks of them as *having the witness of the Spirit that they were the children of God, heirs of God, and joint heirs with Christ*. And the whole of his discourse, to the end of the chapter, implies, that he esteemed them truly gracious persons. In chap. ix. 23, 24. he speaks of the christian Romans, together with all other Christians, both Jews and Gentiles, as *vessels of mercy*. In chap. xiv. 6, 7, 8. speaking of the difference that then was among professing Christians, in point of regard to the ceremonial institutions of the law, he speaks of both parties as acting from a gracious principle, and as those that lived to the Lord, and should die unto the Lord; "He that regardeth the day, regardeth it unto the Lord, &c. For none of us liveth to himself, and no man [*i. e. none of us*] dieth to himself. For whether we live, we live unto the Lord, or whether we die, we die unto the Lord: whether we live therefore or die, we are the Lord's." In chap. xv. 14. he says, "I myself also am persuaded of you, my brethren, that ye are full of goodness." His being thus persuaded implies a positive judgment of charity.

And the same apostle in his first epistle to the Corinthians, directs it "to the church at Corinth, that are sanctified in Christ Jesus, called to be saints, with all that in every place call on the name of the Lord Jesus;" *i. e.* to all visible Christians through the world, or all the members of Christ's visible church every where. And continuing his speech, chap. i. 8. he speaks of them as those "that God would confirm to the end, that they may be blameless in the day of our Lord Jesus Christ:" plainly speaking of them all as persons, in christian esteem, savingly converted. In the next verse, he speaks of the *faithfulness of God* as engaged thus to preserve them to salvation, *having called them to the fellowship of his Son.* And in the 30th verse, he speaks of them as having a saving interest in Christ; "Of him are ye in Christ Jesus; who of God is made unto us wisdom, righteousness, sanctification, and redemption." In chap. iii. 21—23. he says to the members of the church of Corinth, "All things are yours, whether Paul, or Apollos, or Cephas, or the world, or life, or death, or things present, or things to come; all are yours, and ye are Christ's." In chap. iv. 15. he tells them, *he had begotten them through the gospel.* In chap. vi. 1—3. he speaks of them as "those who shall judge the world, and shall judge angels." And in verse 11. he says to them, "Ye are washed, ye are sanctified, ye are justified, in the name of the Lord Jesus, and by the Spirit of God." And in chap. xv. 49, to the end, he speaks of them as having an interest, with him and other Christians, in the happiness and glory of the *resurrection of the just.* And in his second epistle, chap. i. 7. he says to them, "Our hope of you is stedfast; knowing that as you are partakers of the sufferings, so shall ye be also of the consolation." This stedfast hope implies a positive judgment. We must here understand the apostle to speak of such members of the church of Corinth, as had not visibly backslidden. Again, in the 14th and 15th verses, he speaks of a *confidence* which he had, that they *should be his rejoicing in the day of the Lord Jesus.* In all reason we must conclude, there was a visibility of grace, carrying with it an apparent probability in the eyes of the apostle, which was the ground of this his *confidence.* Such an apparent probability, and his confidence as built upon it, are both expressed in chap. iii. 3, 4. "Ye are manifestly declared to be the epistle of Christ, ministered by us; written not with ink, but with the Spirit of the living God; not in tables of stone, but in the fleshy tables of the heart; and such trust have we through Christ to God-ward." And in ver. 18. the apostle speaks of them, with himself and other Christians, as *all with open face beholding, as in a glass, the glory of the Lord,* and *being changed into the same image, from glory to glory.*

And in the epistle to the churches of Galatia. chap. iv. 26. the apostle speaks of visible Christians, as visibly belonging to heaven, the Jerusalem *which is above.* And, ver. 28, 29. represents them to be the *children of the promise, as Isaac was;* and *born after the Spirit.* In the 6th verse of the same chapter, he says to the christian Galatians, "Because ye are sons, God hath sent forth the Spirit of his Son into your hearts, crying, Abba, Father." And chap. vi. 1. he speaks of those of them that had not fallen into scandal, as *spiritual persons.*

In his epistle to that great church at Ephesus, he *blesses God* on behalf of its members, as being, together with himself and all *the faithful in Christ Jesus,* "Chosen in him before the foundation of the world, to be holy and without blame before him in love, being predestinated to the adoption of children by Jesus Christ to himself, according to the good pleasure of his will, to the praise of the glory of his grace, wherein God had made them accepted in the beloved: in whom they had redemption through his blood, the forgiveness of sins." In chap. i. 13, 14. he thus writes to them, "In whom ye also trusted —In whom after ye believed, ye were sealed with that Holy Spirit of promise, which is the earnest of our inheritance, until the redemption of the purchased possession." And in chap. ii. at the beginning; "You hath he quickened, who were dead in trespasses and sins." With much more, showing that they were, in a charitable esteem, regenerated persons, and heirs of salvation.

So in the epistle to the church at Philippi, the apostle tells them, that he "thanks God upon every remembrance of them, for their fellowship in the gospel; being confident of this very thing, that he which had begun a good work in them, would perform it until the day of Christ: even *(says he)* as it is meet for me to think this of you all." If it was meet for him to think this of them, and to be confident of it, he had at least some appearing rational probability to found his judgment and confidence upon; for surely it is not *meet* for reasonable creatures to think at random, and be confident without reason. In ver. 25, 26. he speaks of his "confidence that he should come to them for their furtherance and joy of faith, that their rejoicing might be more abundant in Christ Jesus." Which words certainly suppose that they were persons who had already received Christ, and comfort in him; had already obtained faith and joy in Christ, and only needed to have it increased.

In the epistle to the members of the church at Colosse, the apostle saluting them in the beginning of the epistle, "gives thanks for their faith in Christ Jesus, and love to all saints, and the hope laid up for them in heaven;" and speaks of "the gospel bringing forth fruit in them, since the day they knew the grace of God in truth;" *i. e.* since the day of their saving conversion. In chap. i. 8. he speaks of "their love in the Spirit;" and ver. 12—14. as "made meet to be partakers of the inheritance of the saints in light; *as* being delivered from the power of darkness, and translated into the kingdom of God's dear Son; *as* having redemption through Christ's blood, and the forgiveness of sins." In chap. iii. at the beginning, he speaks of them as "risen with Christ; *as* being dead; [*i. e. to the law, to sin, and the world;*] *as having* their life hid with Christ in God;" and being such as, "when Christ their life should appear, should appear with him in glory." In ver. 7. he speaks of them as "having once walked and lived in lusts, but as having now put off the old man with his deeds, and put on the new man, which is renewed in knowledge, after the image of him that created him."

In the first epistle to the members of the church at Thessalonica, in words annexed to his salutation, chap. i. he declares what kind of visibility there was of their *election of God,* in the appearance there had been of true and saving conversion, and their consequent holy life, ver. 3—7. And in the beginning of the second epistle, he speaks of their *faith and love greatly increasing;* and in ver. 7. expresses his *confidence* of meeting them in eternal *rest,* when *the Lord Jesus Christ should be revealed from heaven with his mighty angels.* And in chap. ii. 13. he *gives thanks to God, that from the beginning he had chosen them to salvation.*

In the epistle to the christian Hebrews, though the apostle speaks of some that once belonged to their churches, but had apostatized and proved themselves hypocrites; yet concerning the rest that remained in good standing, he says, chap. vi. 9. "I am persuaded better things of you, and things that accompany salvation." Where we may again note, his being thus *persuaded* evidently implies a positive judgment. And in chap. xii. 22, &c. he speaks of them as visibly belonging to the glorious society of *heaven.* And in chap. xiii. 5, 6. he speaks of them as those who may *boldly say, The Lord is my helper.*

The apostle James, writing to the Christians of *the twelve tribes which were scattered abroad,* speaks of them as regenerated persons, meaning, as I observed before, those which were in good standing. Chap. i. 18. "Of his own will begat he us by the word of truth, that we should be a kind of first-fruits of his creatures." The apostle Peter writing to the Jewish Christians, scattered throughout Pontus, Galatia, Cappadocia, Asia, and Bithynia, (large countries, and therefore they must in the whole be supposed to be a great multitude of people,) to all these, gives the title of *elect,* according to the foreknowledge of God the Father, through sanctification of the Spirit unto obedience, and sprinkling of the blood of Jesus Christ. And in the verses next following, speaks of them as regenerated, "or begotten again to a lively hope, to an inheritance incorruptible," &c. And as "kept by the power of God through faith unto salvation." And says to them in ver. 8, 9. "Whom *(namely, Christ)* having not seen, ye love; in whom though now ye see him not, yet believing, ye rejoice with joy unspeakable and full of glory; receiving the end of your faith, even the salvation of your souls." And in ver. 18, to the end, the apostle speaks of them as "redeemed from their vain conversation, by the precious blood of Christ.—And as having purified their souls in obeying the truth through the Spirit.—Being born again of incorruptible seed," &c. And in the former part of chap. ii. he speaks of them as "living stones, coming to Christ, and on him built up a spiritual house, an holy priesthood, to offer up spiritual sacrifices, acceptable to God through Jesus Christ.—*And as* those that believe, to whom

Christ is precious.——*As* a chosen generation, a royal priesthood, a holy nation, a peculiar people, called out of darkness into marvellous light." The church at Babylon, occasionally mentioned in chap. v. 13. is said to be *elected together with them.* And in his second epistle (which appears by chap. iii. 1. to be written to the same persons) the inscription is, *To them which have obtained like precious faith with us, i. e.* with the apostles and servants of Christ. And in the third chapter, he tells them, both his epistles were designed to *stir up their* PURE *minds.*

In the first epistle of John, written (for ought appears) to professing Christians in general, chap. ii. 12, &c. the apostle tells them, " He writes to them because their sins were forgiven, because they had known him that was from the beginning.—Because they had overcome the wicked one," &c. In ver. 20, 21. he tells them, they have an unction from the Holy One, and know all things; and that he did not write to them because they had not known the truth, but because they had known it, &c. And in ver. 27. he says, " The anointing which ye have received of him, abideth in you, and ye need not that any man should teach you; but as the same anointing teacheth you of all things, and is true, and is no lie; and even as it hath taught you, ye shall abide in him." And in the beginning of chap. iii. he addresses them as those " who were the sons of God, who when he should appear should be like him, because they should see him as he is." In chap. iv. 4. he says, " Ye are of God, little children, and have overcome," &c.

The apostle Jude, in his general epistle, speaks much of apostates and their wickedness; but to other professing Christians, that had not fallen away, he says, ver. 20, 21. " But ye, beloved, building up yourselves on your most holy faith, praying in the Holy Ghost, keep yourselves in the love of God, looking for the mercy of our Lord Jesus Christ unto eternal life:" plainly supposing, that they had professed faith with love to God our Saviour, and were by the apostle considered as his friends and lovers. ——Many other passages to the like purpose might be observed in the epistles, but these may suffice.

Now how unaccountable would these things be, if the members of the primitive christian churches were not admitted into them under any such notion as their being really godly persons and heirs of eternal life, nor with any respect to such a character appearing on them; and that they themselves joined to these churches without any such pretence, as having no such opinion of themselves!

But it is particularly evident that they had such an opinion of themselves, as well as the apostles of them, by many things the apostles say in their epistles. Thus, in Rom. viii. 15, 16. the apostle speaks of them as " having received the Spirit of adoption, the Spirit of God bearing witness with their spirits, that they were the children of God."—And chap. v. 2. of " their rejoicing in hope of the glory of God."—In 1 Cor. i. 7. he speaks of them as " waiting for the coming of the Lord Jesus." In chap. xv. 17. the apostle says to the members of the church at Corinth, " If Christ be not raised, your faith is vain, ye are yet in your sins:" plainly supposing, that they hoped their sins were forgiven.—In Philip. i. 25, 26. the apostle speaks of his coming to Philippi, to " increase their joy of faith, and that their rejoicing in Christ might be more abundant:" implying, (as was observed before,) that they had received comfort already, in some degree, as supposing themselves to have a saving interest in Christ.—In 1 Thess. i. 10. he speaks of the members of the church at Thessalonica as " waiting for Christ from heaven, *as one* who had delivered them from the wrath to come."—In Heb. vi. 9, 10. he speaks of the christian Hebrews as having that " hope which was an anchor of their souls."—The apostle Peter, 1 Epist. i. 3—9. speaks of the visible Christians he wrote to, as being " begotten to a lively hope, of an inheritance incorruptible, &c.—Wherein they greatly rejoiced," &c.— And even the members of the church of Laodicea, the very worst of all the seven churches of Asia, yet looked upon themselves as truly gracious persons, and made that profession; they " said *they* were rich, and increased in goods, and knew not that they were wretched and miserable," &c. Rev. iii. 17.

It is also evident, that the members of these primitive churches had this judgment one of another, and of the members of the visible church of Christ in general. In 1 Thess. iv. 13, &c. the apostle exhorts the christian Thessalonians, in mourning for their deceased friends who were visible Christians, *not to sorrow* as the hopeless heathen were wont to do for their departed friends; upon this consideration, that they had reason to expect to meet them again in *glorious* circumstances at the day of judgment, never to part more. The ground of *comfort* concerning their dead friends, is evidently something *more* than such a *hope* as we ought to have of all that profess christian *doctrines*, and are not *scandalous* in life, whom we must forbear to censure, because we do not know but they are true saints.—The members of the church of Sardis, next to Laodicea, the worst of the seven churches of Asia, yet *had a name that they lived;* though Christ, who speaks to these seven churches from heaven, in the character of the Searcher of hearts, (see Rev. ii. 23.) explicitly tells them, that *they were dead;* perhaps all in a dead frame, and the most in a dead state.

These things evidently show, how all the christian churches through the world were *constituted* in those days; and what sort of *holiness* or *saintship* it was, that all visible Christians in good standing had a *visibility* and *profession* of, in that apostolic age; and also what sort of visibility of this they had, *viz.* not only that which gave them right to a kind of *negative charity*, or freedom from censure, but that which might justly induce a *positive* judgment in their favour. The churches to whom these epistles were written, were all the principal churches in the world; some of them very large, as the churches at Corinth and Ephesus. Some of the epistles were directed to all the churches through large countries where the gospel had great success, as the epistle to the Galatians. The epistle to the Hebrews was written to all the Jewish Christians in the land of Canaan, in distinction from the Jews that lived in other countries, who were called Hellenists or Grecians, because they generally spake the Greek tongue. The epistles of Peter were written to all the christian Jews through many countries, Pontus, Galatia, Cappadocia, Asia, and Bithynia; containing great numbers of Jews, beyond any other Gentile countries. The epistle of James was directed to all christian Jews, scattered abroad through the whole world. The epistles of John and Jude, for ought appears in those epistles, were directed to all visible Christians through the whole world. And the apostle Paul directs the first epistle to the Corinthians, not only to the members of that church, but to all professing Christians on the face of the earth: 1 Cor. i. 2. and chap. xiv. 33. calling them *all churches of the saints.* And by what Christ says to the churches of Sardis and Laodicea in the Apocalypse, of whom more evil is said than of any christian churches spoken of in the New Testament, it appears that even the members of those churches looked on themselves as in a state of salvation, and had such a name with others.

Here possibly some may object, and say, It will not follow from the apostles speaking to and of the members of the primitive church after the manner which has been observed, as though they supposed them to be *gracious* persons, that therefore a *profession* and *appearance* of this was looked upon in those days as a requisite *qualification* for admission into the visible church; because another reason may be given for it, *viz.* Such was the *extraordinary* state of things at that day, that the *greater part* of those converted from heathenism and Judaism to Christianity, were *hopefully gracious persons*, by reason of its being a day of such large communications of divine grace, and such great and unavoidable sufferings of professors, &c.—And the apostles knowing those facts, might properly speak to and of the churches, as if they were societies of truly gracious persons, because there was just ground on such accounts, to *think* the greater part of them to be so; although no profession or visibility of this was requisite in their members by the *constitution* of those churches, and the door of admission was as open for *others* as for such.

But this cannot be a satisfactory nor a true account of the matter, if we consider the following things.

(1.) The apostles in the very *superscription* or direction of their letters to these churches, and in their *salutation* at the beginning of their epistles, speak of them as gracious persons. For instance, the apostle Peter, in the direction of his first letter to all professing Jewish Christians through many countries, says thus, "To the strangers scattered through Pontus, &c. elect, according to the foreknowledge of God the Father, through sanctification of the Spirit unto obedience, and sprinkling of the blood of Jesus Christ." And in his directing his second epistle to the same persons, he says, "Simon Peter, a servant and an apostle of Jesus Christ, to them that have obtained like precious faith with us," &c. And the apostle Paul directs his epistle to the Romans thus, "To them that be at Rome, beloved of God." So he directs his first epistle to the Corinthians thus, "Unto the church of God which is at Corinth, to them that are sanctified in Christ Jesus." In what sense he means *sanctified*, his following words show, ver. 4—9. The same was before observed of words *annexed* to the apostle's salutations, in the beginning of several of the epistles. This shows, that the apostles extend this *character* as far as they do the *epistles* themselves. Which surely would be very improper, and not agreeable to truth, if the apostles at the same time knew very well that such a character did not belong to members of churches, as such, and that they were not received into those churches with any regard to such a character, or upon the account of any right they had to be esteemed such persons. In the superscription of letters to societies of men, we are wont to give them that *title* or *denomination* which properly belongs to them as members of such a body. Thus, if one should write to the Royal Society in London, or the Royal Academy of Sciences at Paris, it would be proper and natural to give them the title of Learned; for whether every one of the members truly deserve the epithet, or not, yet the title is agreeable to their *profession*, and what is known to be aimed at, and is professedly insisted on, in the admission of members. But if one should write to the House of Commons, or to the East-India Company, and in his superscription give them the title of Learned, this would be very improper, and ill-judged; because that character does not belong to their profession as members of that body, and *learning* is not a qualification insisted on in their admission of members. Nor would it excuse the impropriety, though the writer might, from his special acquaintance, know it to be fact, that the greater part of them were men of learning. To inscribe a letter to them, would be something strange; but more strange, if it should appear, by various instances, to be a custom so to direct letters to such societies; as it seems to be the manner of the apostles, in their epistles to christian churches, to address them under titles which imply a profession and visibility of *true holiness*.

(2.) The apostle John, in his general epistle, very plainly manifests, that all to whom he wrote were *supposed* to have true grace, inasmuch as he declares this to be the qualification he respects in writing to them; and lets them know, he writes to them for that reason, because they are supposed to be persons of the character of such as *have known God, overcome the wicked one*, and *have had their sins forgiven them*. 1 John ii. 12—14, 21.

(3.) The apostles, when speaking of visible Christians, as a *society*, and what belongs to such a kind of society, speak of it as visibly (*i. e.* in profession and reputation) a *society* of gracious persons. So the apostle Peter speaks of them as a spiritual house, an holy and royal priesthood, an holy nation, a peculiar people, a chosen or elect generation, called out of darkness into marvellous light, 1 Pet. ii.—The apostle Paul also speaks of them as the family of God, Eph. ii. 19. And in the next chapter he explains himself to mean that family a part of which is *in heaven*; *i. e.* they were by profession a part of that divine family.

(4.) The apostle Paul speaks often and expressly of the members of the churches to whom he wrote, as all of them in esteem and visibility truly gracious persons. Philip. i. 6. "Being confident of this very thing, that he which has begun a good work in you will perform it until the day of the Lord Jesus Christ: even as it is meet for me to think this of YOU ALL" (that is, all singly taken, not collectively, according to the distinction before observed). So Gal. iv. 26. "Jerusalem which is above, which is the mother of us ALL." Rom. vi. "As many of us as have been baptized into Christ, have been baptized into his death." Here he speaks of all that have been baptized; and in the continuation of the discourse, explaining what is here said, he speaks of their "being dead to sin, no longer under the law, but under grace; having obeyed the form of doctrine from the heart, being made free from sin, and become the servants of righteousness," &c. Rom. xiv. 7, 8. "None of us liveth to himself, and no man dieth to himself;" (taken together with the context;) 2 Cor. iii. 18. "We ALL with open face beholding as in a glass," &c.; and Gal. iii. 26. "Ye are ALL the children of God by faith."

(5.) It is evident, that even in those churches where the greater part of the members were not true saints, as in those degenerate churches of Sardis and Laodicea, which we may suppose were become very lax in their admissions and discipline; yet they looked upon themselves as truly gracious persons, and had with others the reputation of such.

(6.) If we should suppose, that, by reason of the extraordinary state of things in that day, the apostles had reason to think the greater part of the members of churches to be true Christians, yet unless profession and appearance of true Christianity was their proper qualification and the ground of their admission—and unless it was supposed that all of them esteemed themselves true Christians—it is altogether unaccountable that the apostles in their epistles to them never make any express particular distinction between those different sorts of members. If the churches were made up of persons who looked on themselves in so different a state—some the children of God, and others the children of the devil, some the high favourites of heaven and heirs of eternal glory, others the children of wrath, being under condemnation to eternal death, and every moment in danger of dropping into hell—why do the apostles make no *distinction* in their manner of addressing them, and in the counsels, reproofs, and warnings they gave them? Why do they never direct their speech to the *unconverted* members of churches, in particular, in a manner tending to awaken them, and make them sensible of the miserable condition they were in, and press them to seek the converting grace of God? It is to be considered, that the apostle Paul was very particularly acquainted with the circumstances of most of those churches to whom he wrote; for he had been among them, was their spiritual father, had been the instrument of gathering and founding those churches, and they had received all their instructions and directions relating to Christianity and their soul-concerns from him; nor can it be questioned but that many of them had opened the case of their souls to him. And if he was sensible, that there was a number among them who made no pretensions to a regenerate state, and that none had reason to judge them to be in such a state, he knew that the sin of such—who lived in the rejection of a Saviour, even in the very house of God, in the midst of gospel-light, and in violation of the most sacred vows—was peculiarly aggravated, and their guilt and state peculiarly dreadful. Why should he therefore never particularly and distinctly point his addresses to such, applying himself to them in much compassion to their souls, and putting them in mind of their awful circumstances? But instead of this, we observe him continually lumping all together, and indifferently addressing the whole body, as if they were all in happy circumstances, expressing his charity for them all, and congratulating them all in their glorious and eternal privilege. Instead of speaking to them in such a manner as should have a tendency to alarm them with a sense of danger, we see him, on the contrary, calling on all without distinction to rejoice. Philip. iii. 1. "Finally, my brethren, rejoice in the Lord." So, 2 Cor. xiii. 11. "Finally, brethren, be of good comfort." Philip. iv. 4. "Rejoice in the Lord alway, and again I say, Rejoice." The matter is insisted upon, as though rejoicing were a duty especially proper for them, and what they had the highest reason for. The apostle not only did not preach terror to those to whom he wrote, but is careful to guard them against fears of God's wrath. In 1 Thess. v. at the beginning, the apostle observes, how that Christ will come on ungodly men "as a thief in the night; and when they shall say, Peace and safety, then sudden destruction shall come upon them, as travail on a woman with child, and they shall not escape:" then immediately he uses caution, that the members of the church at Thessalonica should not take this to themselves, and be terrified, as though they were in danger; and says, in the next words, "But ye, brethren, are not in darkness, that that day should overtake you as a thief; ye are all the children of light, and the children of the day." Ver. 9—11. "For God hath not appointed us to wrath, but to obtain salvation by our Lord Jesus Christ; who died for us, that whether we wake or sleep, we should live together with him. Wherefore comfort yourselves together, and edify one another; even as also ye do." And ver. 16. "Rejoice evermore." How diverse is this way of treating churches, from the method in which faithful ministers are wont to deal with their congregations, wherein are many that make no pretence to true piety, and from the way in which Mr. Stoddard was wont to deal with his congregation. And how would he have undoubtedly judged such a way of treating them the most direct course in the world eternally to undo them! And shall we determine that the apostle Paul was one of those prophets, who *daubed with untempered mortar, and sewed pillows under all arm-holes, and healed the hurt* of immortal souls *slightly, crying, Peace, peace, when there was no peace.*—These things make it most evident, that the primitive churches were not constituted as those modern churches, where persons knowing and owning themselves *unregenerate,* are admitted, on principle.

If it be here objected, that the apostle sometimes exhorts those to whom he writes, to *put off the old man,* and *put on the new man,* and to *be renewed in the spirit of their minds,* &c. as exhorting them to seek conversion: I answer, that the meaning is manifestly this, That they should mortify the *remains* of corruption, or the old man, and turn more and more from sin to God. Thus he exhorts the Ephesians to be *renewed,* &c. Eph. iv. 22, 23. whom yet he had before in the same epistle abundantly represented as savingly renewed already; as has been before observed. And the like might be shown of other instances.

(7.) It is clear, not only that the greater part of the members of the primitive churches were to appearance true Christians; but that they were taken in *under that notion,* and because there appeared in them grounds of such an *estimation* of them. When any happened to be admitted that were otherwise, it was *beside their aim;* inasmuch as when others were admitted, they are represented as *brought* or *crept in unawares.* Thus the matter is represented by the apostles. Jude, ver. 4. "There are certain men crept in unawares—ungodly men, turning the grace of God into lasciviousness." Gal. ii. 4. "False brethren, unawares brought in." If it be said, these here spoken of were openly scandalous persons and heretics: I answer, they were not openly scandalous when they were brought in; nor is there any reason to think they were heretics when admitted, though afterwards they turned apostates. Mr. Stoddard says, It does not follow that *all* hypocrites crept in unawares because some did. (*Appeal,* p. 17.) To which I would humbly say, It must be certainly true with respect to all hypocrites who were admitted, either that the church which admitted them was *aware* they were such, or else was not. If there were some of whom the church was *aware* that they were hypocrites, at the time when they were taken in, then the church, in admitting them, did not follow the *rule* that Mr. Stoddard often declares himself to suppose ought to be followed in admitting members, *viz.* to admit none but what *in a judgment of rational charity are true Christians.* (*Appeal,* p. 2, 3, 10, 28, 33, 67, 73, 93, 94.) But that not only heretics and designing dissemblers *crept in unawares,* but that all *false brethren,* all church-members not truly gracious, did so, appears by such being represented as *bastards* in a family, who are false children and false heirs, brought into it *unawares,* and imposed upon the disposers of those privileges *by stealth.*—Heb. xii. 8. "If ye are without chastisement, whereof all are partakers, then are ye *bastards,* and not sons."

Thus it is abundantly manifest, from the apostolical writings, how the visible church of Christ, through the whole world, was at first constituted, under the direction of the apostles themselves, who regulated it according to the infallible guidance of the Spirit of their great Lord and Master.—And doubtless, as the christian church was constituted *then,* so it ought to be constituted *now.* What better rule have we for our ecclesiastical regulations in other respects, than what was done in the *primitive* churches, under the *apostles'* own direction; as particularly the standing officers of the church, presbyters and deacons, the method of introducing ministers in their ordination, &c.? In this matter that I have insisted on, I think the Scripture is abundantly more full, than in those other things.

SECT. VIII.

The Scripture represents the visible church of Christ, as a society having its several members united by the bond of christian brotherly love.

BESIDES that general benevolence or charity which the saints have to mankind, and which they exercise towards both the evil and the good in common, there is a *peculiar* and very *distinguishing* kind of affection, that every true Christian *experiences* towards those whom he looks upon as truly *gracious* persons. The soul, at least at times, is very sensibly and sweetly knit to such persons, and there is an ineffable *oneness of heart* with them; whereby, to use the scripture phrase, (Acts iv. 32.) "They are of one heart and one soul:" which holy affection is exercised towards others on account of the spiritual image of God in them, their supposed relation to God as his children, and to Christ as his members, and to them as their spiritual brethren in Christ. This sacred affection is a very good and distinguishing note of true grace, much spoken of as such in Scripture, under the name of φιλαδελφια, *the love of the brethren,* or *brotherly love;* and is called by Christ, "the receiving a righteous man in the name of a righteous man; and receiving one of Christ's little ones in the name of a disciple, or because he belongs to Christ;" (Matt. x. 41, 42. Mark ix. 41.) and a "loving one another as Christ has loved them;" (John xiii. 34. and xv. 13—15.) having a peculiar image of that *oneness* which is between Christ himself and his saints. Compare John xvii. 20, to the end.

This *love* the apostles are often directing Christians to exercise towards fellow-members of the visible church; as in Rom. xii. 10. "Be ye kindly affectioned one to another with *brotherly* love." The words are much more emphatical in the original, and represent in a more lively manner, that peculiar *endearment* there is between *gracious* persons, or those that look on one another as such; τη φιλαδελφια εις αλληλυς φιλοσοργοι. The expressions properly signify, *cleaving one to another with brotherly, natural, strong endearment.* With the like emphasis and energy does the apostle Peter express himself, 1 Epist. i. 22. "Seeing ye have purified your souls in obeying the truth through the Spirit, unto unfeigned love of the brethren, (εις φιλαδελφιαν ανυποκριτον,) see that ye love one another with a pure heart fervently." Again, chap. iii. 8. "Finally, be ye all of one mind, having compassion one of another, love as brethren, be pitiful, be courteous." The words in the Greek are much more significant, elegant, and forcible; παντες ομοφρονες, συμπαθεις, φιλαδελφοι, ευσπλαγχνοι, φιλοφρονες. The same peculiar endearment the apostle has doubtless respect to in chap. iv. "Above all things have fervent charity among yourselves." And from time to time, he considers it as a note of their piety. Col. i. 4. "We heard of your faith in Christ Jesus, and of the love which ye have to all saints." 1 Thess. iv. 9. "As touching *brotherly love,* ye need not that I write unto you; for ye yourselves are taught of God to love one another." So Philem. 5. "Hearing of thy love and faith, which thou hast towards the Lord Jesus Christ, and towards all saints." And this is what he exhorts to, Heb. xiii. 1. "Let *brotherly love* continue." 1 Thess. v. 26. "Greet all the brethren with an holy kiss." Compare 1 Cor. xvi. 20. 2 Cor. xiii. 12. and 1 Pet. v. 14.

This φιλαδελφια, or *love to the brethren,* is that virtue which the apostle John so much insists on in his first epistle, as one of the most distinguishing *characteristics* of true grace, and a peculiar evidence that *God dwelleth in us,* and *we in God.* By which must needs be understood a love to saints *as* saints, or on account of the spiritual image of God supposed to be in them, and their spiritual relation to God; according as it has always been understood by orthodox divines. No reasonable doubt can be made, but that the apostle John, in this epistle, has respect to the same sort of *love*, which Christ prescribed to his disciples, in that which he called by way of eminency HIS COMMANDMENT, and HIS NEW COMMANDMENT, which he gave as a great *mark* of their being truly his *disciples*, as this same apostle gives an account in his gospel; and to which he plainly refers, when speaking of *the love of the brethren* in his epistle, chap. ii. 7, 8. and iii. 23. But that *love*, which Christ speaks of in his *new commandment*, is spoken of as between those that *Christ loves*, or is supposed *to love;* and which has *his love* to them for its ground and pattern. And if this φιλαδελφια, this *love of the brethren*, so much spoken of by Christ, and by the apostles Paul and John, be not that *peculiar* affection which gracious persons or true saints have one to another, which is so great a part, and so remarkable an exercise, of true grace, *where* is it spoken of at all in the New Testament?

We see how often the apostles exhort visible Christians to exercise this affection to all other members of the visible church of Christ, and how often they speak of the members of the visible church as actually thus *united*, in places already mentioned. In 2 Cor. ix. 14. the apostle speaks of the members of *other* churches *loving* the members of the church of Corinth, with this peculiar endearment and oneness of heart, for *the grace of God* in them; "And by their prayer for you, which long after you, for the exceeding grace of God in you." The word translated *long after*, is επιποθουντων; which properly signifies to love with an *exceeding* and *dear* love. And this is represented as the *bond* that unites all the members of the visible church; Acts iv. 32. "And the multitude of them that believed were of one heart and one soul." This is the same thing which elsewhere is called being of *one mind:* 1 Pet. iii. 8. "Finally, be ye all of one mind." And being of *the same mind;* 1 Cor. i. 10. "That ye be perfectly joined together in the same mind." And Philip. iv. 2. "I beseech Euodias, and beseech Syntyche, that they be *of the same mind* in the Lord." And being *like-minded*, (the word is the same in the Greek,) Rom. xv. 5, 6. "Now the God of patience and consolation grant you to be *like-minded* one towards another; that ye may with *one mind*, and one mouth, glorify God, even the Father of our Lord Jesus Christ." There is reason to think, that it is this *oneness of mind*, or being *of one heart and soul*, is meant by that *charity* which the apostle calls the *bond of perfectness*, Col. iii. 14. and represents as the bond of union between all the *members* of the *body*, in Eph. iv. 15, 16. "But speaking the truth in *love*, may grow up into him in all things, which is the head, even Christ; from whom the whole body *fitly joined together, and compacted* by that which every joint supplieth, according to the effectual working in the measure of every part, maketh increase of the body, unto the edifying itself in *love*."

Herein seems much to consist the nature of *scandal* in the members of a church, *viz.* such an offence as is a wound and interruption to this kind of *affection*, being a stumbling-block to a christian judgment, in regard of its esteem of the offender as a *real Christian*, and what much lessens the visibility of his christian character. And therefore when scandal is removed by visible *repentance*, the church is directed to *confirm their love* to the offender, 2 Cor. ii. 8.

Now this intimate affection towards others as *brethren in Christ* and *fellow-members* of him, must have some apprehension of the understanding, some judgment of the mind, for its foundation. To say, that we must thus *love* others as visible members of Christ, if any thing *else* be meant, than that we must love them *because* they are visibly, or *as* they appear to our judgment, real members of Christ, is in effect to say, that we must thus love them without any foundation at all. In order to a real and fervent affection to another, on account of some amiableness of qualification or relation, the mind must first judge there is that amiableness in the object. The affections of the mind are not so at command that we can make them strongly to go forth to an object *as* having such loveliness, when at the same time we do not positively *judge* any such thing concerning them, but only *hope* it may be so, because we see no sufficient reason to determine the contrary. There must be a *positive* dictate of the understanding, and some degree of satisfaction of the judgment, to be a ground of that *oneness of heart and soul*, which is agreeable to scripture representations of φιλαδελφια, or *brotherly love*. And a supposition only of that *moral sincerity and virtue*, or *common grace*, which some insist upon, though it may be a sufficient ground of this intimate affection to them as *brethren* in the family of a heavenly Father,—this fervent love to them *in the bowels of Jesus Christ*. For *gospel-sinners* and domestic *enemies* in the house of God, Christians know, are of all others the most hateful enemies to Christ.

It well agrees with the wisdom of Christ, with that peculiar favour he has manifested to his saints, and with his dealings towards them in many other respects, to suppose, he has made provision in his institutions, that they might have the comfort of uniting with such as their hearts are united with, in some special religious exercises and duties of worship, and visible intercourse with their Redeemer; that they should join with those concerning whom they can have some satisfaction of mind, that they are cordially united with them in adoring and expressing their *love* to their common Lord and Saviour, that they may *with one mind, with one heart, and one soul*, as well as *with one mouth, glorify him;* as in the forementioned Rom. xv. 5, 6. compared with Acts iv. 32. This seems to be what this heavenly affection naturally inclines to. And how eminently fit and proper for this purpose is the sacrament of the *Lord's supper*, the christian church's great feast of *love;* wherein Christ's people sit together as *brethren* in the family of God, at their Father's table, to feast on the love of their Redeemer, commemorating his sufferings for them, and his dying love to them, and sealing their love to him and one another!—It is hardly credible, that Christ has so ordered things as that there are no instituted social acts of worship, wherein *his saints* are to manifest their respect to him, but such as wherein they ordinarily are obliged *(if the rule for admissions be carefully attended)* to join with a society of fellow-worshippers, concerning whom they have no reason to think but that the *greater part* of them are *unconverted*, (and are more provoking enemies to that Lord they love and adore, than most of the very heathen,) which Mr. Stoddard supposes to be the case with the members of the visible church. *Appeal*, p. 16.

SECT. IX.

It is necessary, that those who partake of the Lord's supper, should judge themselves truly and cordially to accept of CHRIST, *as their only Saviour and chief good; for of this the actions which communicants perform at the Lord's table, are a solemn profession.*

THERE is in the Lord's supper a mutual solemn *profession* of the two parties transacting the covenant of grace, and visibly united in that covenant; the Lord Christ by his minister, on the one hand, and the communicants (who are professing believers) on the other. The administrator of the ordinance acts in the quality of Christ's minister, acts in his name, as representing him; and stands in the place where Christ himself stood at the first administration of this sacrament, and in the original institution of the ordinance. Christ, by the speeches and actions of the minister, makes a solemn profession of his part in the covenant of grace: he exhibits the sacrifice of his body broken and his blood shed; and in the minister's offering the sacramental bread and wine to the communicants, Christ presents himself to the believing communicants, as their propitiation and bread of life; and by these outward signs confirms and seals his sincere engagements to be their Saviour and food, and to impart to them all the benefits of his propitiation and salvation. And they, in receiving what is offered, and eating and drinking the symbols of Christ's body and blood, also profess their part in the covenant of grace: they profess to embrace the promises and lay hold of the hope set before them, to receive the atonement, to receive Christ as their spiritual food, and to feed upon him in their hearts by faith. Indeed what is professed on both sides is the *heart:* for Christ, in offering himself, professes the willingness of *his heart* to be theirs who truly receive him; and the communicants, on their part, profess the willingness of *their hearts* to receive him, which they declare by significant actions. They profess to take Christ as their spiritual food, and bread of life. To accept of Christ as our *bread of life*, is to accept of him *as our Saviour and portion;* as food is both the means of preserving life, and is also the refreshment and comfort of life. The signification of the word *manna*, that great type of this bread of life, is a *portion.* That which God offers to us as our food, he offers as our portion; and that which we accept as our food, we accept as our portion. Thus the Lord's supper is plainly a *mutual* renovation, confirmation, and seal of the covenant of grace: both the covenanting parties *profess* their consent to their respective parts in the covenant, and each affixes his *seal* to his profession. And there is in this ordinance the very same thing acted over in profession and sensible signs, which is spiritually transacted between Christ and his spouse in the covenant that unites them. Here we have from time to time the glorious *bridegroom* exhibiting himself with his great love that is stronger than death, appearing clothed in robes of grace, and engaging himself, with all his glory and love, and its infinite benefits, to be theirs, who receive him: and here we have his *spouse* accepting this bridegroom, choosing him for her friend, her only Saviour and portion, and relying on him for all his benefits. And thus the covenant-transaction of this spiritual marriage is confirmed and sealed, from time to time. The *actions* of the communicants at the Lord's table have as expressive and significant a language, as the most solemn words. When a person in this ordinance *takes* and *eats* and *drinks* those things which represent Christ, the plain meaning and implicit profession of these his actions, is this, "I take this crucified Jesus as my Saviour, my sweetest food, my chief portion, and the life of my soul, consenting to acquiesce in him as such, and to hunger and thirst after him only, renouncing all other saviours, and all other portions, for his sake." The actions, *thus interpreted*, are a proper renovation and ratification of the covenant of grace; and no otherwise. And those that take and eat and drink the sacramental elements at the Lord's table with any *other* meaning, I fear, *know not what they do.*

The *actions* at the Lord's supper thus implying, in their nature and signification, a renewing and confirming of the covenant, there is a declarative explicit covenanting supposed to *precede* it; which is the *profession* of religion, before spoken of, that qualifies a person for admission to the Lord's supper. And doubtless there is, or ought to be, as much explicitly professed in *words*, as is implicitly professed in these *actions;* for by these significant actions, the communicant sets his seal but to his *profession.* The established signs in the Lord's supper are fully equivalent to words; they are a renewing and reiterating the same thing which was done *before;* only with this difference, that now it is done by *speaking signs*, whereas before it was by *speaking sounds.* Our taking the bread and wine is as much a *professing* to accept of Christ, at least, as a woman's taking a *ring* of the bridegroom in her marriage is a profession and seal of her taking him for her husband. The sacramental elements in the Lord's supper represent Christ as a party in covenant, as truly as a *proxy* represents a prince to a foreign lady in her marriage; and our taking those elements is as truly a professing to accept of Christ, as in the other case the lady's taking the proxy is her professing to accept the prince as her husband. Or the matter may more fitly be represented by this similitude: it is as if a prince should send an ambassador to a woman in a foreign land, proposing marriage, and by his ambassador should send her his *picture*, and should desire her to manifest her acceptance of his suit, not only by professing her acceptance in words to his ambassador, but in token of her sincerity openly to take or accept that picture, and to seal her profession, by thus representing the matter over again by a symbolical action.

To suppose persons ought thus solemnly to *profess* that which at the same time they do not at all imagine they experience in themselves, and do not really pretend to, is a very great absurdity. For a man sacramentally to make *such a profession of religion*, proceeding avowedly on the foot of *such doctrine*, is to profess that which he *does not* profess; his *actions* being no established *signs* of the *thing* supposed to be professed, nor carrying in them the least pretension to it. And therefore doing thus can be no man's duty; unless it be men's duty to make a solemn profession of that which in truth they make *no* profession of. The Lord's supper is most evidently a *professing* ordinance; and the communicants' *profession* must be such as is adjusted to the nature and design of the ordinance; which nothing short of *faith in the blood of Christ* will answer, even *faith unfeigned*, which *worketh by love.* A profession therefore exclusive of this, is essentially defective, and quite unsuitable to the character of a *communicant.*

When the apostle says, 1 Cor. xi. 28. "Let a man examine himself, and so let him eat;" it seems most reasonable to understand it of *trying himself* with regard to the *truth* of his *Christianity*, or the reality of his grace; the same as 2 Cor. xiii. 5. where the same word is used in the original. The Greek word (δοκιμαζετω) will not allow of what some have supposed to be the apostle's meaning, *viz.* that a man should consider and inquire into his *circumstances*, and the necessities of his case, that he may know what are the wants for the supply of which he should go to the Lord's table. The word properly signifies *proving* or *trying* a thing with respect to its *quality* and *goodness*, or in order to determine whether it be *true* and *of the right sort.* And so the word is always used in the New Testament; unless that sometimes it is used metonymically, and in such places is variously translated, either *discerning*, or *allowing*, *approving*, *liking*, *&c.* these being the effects of *trial.* Nor is the word used more frequently in the New Testament for any sort of trial whatever, than for the trial of professors with regard to their *grace* or *piety.* The word (as Dr. Ames in his Catecheseos Sciagraphia, and Mr. Willard in his Body of Divinity, observe) is borrowed from goldsmiths, properly signifying the *trial* they make of their silver and gold, whether it be *genuine* or *counterfeit:* and with a manifest allusion to this original application of the word, is often used in the New Testament for *trying* the piety of professors. It is used with this view in all the following texts: 1 Pet. i. 7. "That the *trial* of your faith, being much more precious than of gold that perisheth, though it be *tried* by fire, might be found unto praise," &c. 1 Cor. iii. 13. "The fire shall *try* every man's work of what sort it is." James i. 3. "The *trying* of your faith worketh patience." 1 Thess. ii. 4. "God who *trieth* our hearts." The same word is used in 2 Cor. viii. 8. "To *prove* the sincerity of your love." So, Gal. vi. 3, 4. "If any man thinketh himself to be something, when he is nothing, he deceiveth himself: but let every man *prove* his own work." In all these places there is the same word in the Greek with that in the text now under consideration.

When the apostle directs professing Christians to *try themselves*, using this word indefinitely, as properly signifying the examining or proving of a thing whether it be *genuine* or *counterfeit*, the most natural construction of his advice is, that they should *try themselves* with respect to their spiritual state and religious profession, whether they are *disciples indeed*, real and genuine Christians, or whether they are not false and hypocritical professors. As if a man should bring a piece of metal that had the colour of gold, with the impress of the king's coin, to a goldsmith, and desire him to *try* that money, without adding any words to limit his meaning, would not the goldsmith naturally understand, that he was to try whether it was true gold or true money?

But here it is said by some, that the *context* of the passage under debate (1 Cor. xi. 28.) plainly *limits* the meaning of the word in that place; the apostle there speaking of those things that had appeared among the communicants at Corinth, which were of a *scandalous* nature, so doubtless unfitting them for the Lord's supper; and therefore when the apostle directs them to *examine* or prove themselves, it is but just, to suppose his meaning to be, that they should try whether they be not disqualified by *scandal.*—To this I answer, though the apostle putting the Corinthians upon trying themselves, was on *occasion* of mentioning some scandalous practices found among them, yet this is by no means any argument of its being only his meaning, that they should *try themselves* whether they were *scandalous* persons; and not, that they should try whether they were *genuine Christians.* The very nature of *scandal* (as was observed before) is, that which tends to obscure the visibility of the piety of professors, and wound others' charity towards them, by bringing the reality of their grace into doubt; and therefore what could be more natural, than for the apostle, when mentioning such scandals among the Corinthians, to put them upon trying the state of their souls, and proving their sincerity? This is certainly the case in this apostle's directing the same persons to *prove themselves,* 2 Cor. xiii. 5. using the same word there which he uses here, and giving his direction on the like occasion. For in the second epistle (as well as in the first) his putting them on *examining* and *proving themselves,* was on occasion of his mentioning some *scandals* found among them; as is plain from the foregoing context. And yet there it is expressly said, that the thing concerning which he directs them to *prove* themselves, is, whether they be *in the faith,* and whether *Christ is in them.* Nor is there any thing more in the preceding context of one place, than in that of the other, obliging or leading us to understand the apostle to intend only a trying whether they were *scandalous,* and not whether they were sincere Christians.

And as to the words following in the next verse; "For he that eateth and drinketh unworthily, eateth and drinketh judgment to himself, not discerning the Lord's body:"—these words by no means make it evident, (as some hold,) that what the apostle would have them examine themselves about, is, whether they have *doctrinal knowledge,* sufficient to understand, that the bread and wine in the sacrament signify the body and blood of Christ: but on the contrary, to interpret the apostle in this sense only, is unreasonable, upon several accounts. (1.) None can so much as attempt such an *examination,* without *first knowing,* that the Lord's body and blood *is signified* by these elements. For merely a man putting this question to himself, *Do I understand that this bread and this wine signify the body and blood of Christ?* supposes him already to know it from a previous information; and therefore to exhort persons to such an examination, would be absurd. And then, (2.) It is incredible, that there should be any such *gross ignorance* in a number of the communicants in the Corinthian church, if we consider what the Scripture informs us concerning that church. St. Paul was an able and thorough instructor and spiritual father, who founded that church, brought them out of their heathenish darkness, and initiated them in the christian religion. He had instructed them in the nature and ends of gospel-ordinances, and continued at Corinth, constantly labouring in the word and doctrine for a long while, no less than a *year and six months;* and, we may well suppose, administered the Lord's supper among them every Lord's day; for the apostle speaks of it as the manner of that church to communicate at the Lord's table with such frequency, 1 Cor. xvi. 2. And the Corinthian church, when the apostle wrote this epistle, was noted for excelling in *doctrinal knowledge;* as is evident by chap i. 5—7. and several other passages in the epistle. Besides, the communicants were expressly told at every communion, every week, when the bread and wine were delivered to them in the administration, that the bread signified the body, and that the wine signified the blood, of Christ. And, (3.) The apostle by his argument in chap. x. 16. supposes the Corinthians doctrinally acquainted with this subject already. It therefore appears to me much more reasonable, to apprehend the case to be thus: the offensive behaviour of the communicants at Corinth gave the apostle reason to suspect, that some of them came to the Lord's table without a proper impression and true sense of the great and glorious things there signified; having no habitual hunger or relish for the spiritual food there represented, no inward vital and experimental taste of that *flesh of the Son of man,* which is *meat indeed.* The word translated *discerning,* signifies to *discriminate* or *distinguish.* The *taste* is the proper sense whereby to discern or distinguish food, Job xxxiv. 3. And it is by a spiritual *sense* or *taste* we discern or distinguish spiritual food. Heb. v. 14.—"Those who by reason of use, have their senses exercised to discern both good and evil:" προς διακρισιν, &c. a word of the same root with that rendered *discerning,* in 1 Cor. xi. 29. He that has no habitual relish of that spiritual food, which is represented and offered at the Lord's table; he that has no spiritual taste, wherewith to perceive any thing more at the Lord's supper, than in common food; or that has no higher view, than with a little seeming devotion to eat bread, in the way of an ordinance, but without regarding in his heart the spiritual meaning and end of it, and without being at all suitably affected by the dying love of Christ therein commemorated; such a one may most truly and properly be said *not to discern the Lord's body.*—When therefore the apostle exhorts to *self-examination* as a preparative for the sacramental supper, he may well be understood to put professors upon inquiring whether they have such a principle of *faith,* by means whereof they are habitually in a capacity and disposition of mind to *discern the Lord's body,* practically and spiritually, (as well as speculatively and notionally,) in their communicating at the Lord's table: which is what none can do who have a faith short of that which is justifying and saving. It is only a living faith that capacitates men to *discern the Lord's body* in the sacrament with that spiritual sensation or spiritual gust, which is suitable to the nature and design of the ordinance, and which the apostle seems principally to intend.

PART III.

OBJECTIONS ANSWERED.

OBJECT. I.

THE Scripture calls the members of the visible church by the name of *disciples, scholars,* or *learners:* and that suggests to us this notion of the visible church, that it is the *school* of Christ, into which persons are admitted in order to their *learning of Christ,* and coming to spiritual attainments, in the use of the means of teaching, discipline, and training up, established in the school. Now if this be a right notion of the visible church, then reason shows that no other qualifications are necessary in order to being members of this *school,* than such a *faith* and *disposition of mind* as are requisite to persons' putting themselves under Christ as their *Master* and *Teacher,* and subjecting themselves to the *orders* of the school. But a *common faith* and *moral sincerity* are sufficient for this.—Therefore the Scripture leads us to suppose the visible church to be *properly constituted* of those who have these qualifications, though they have not *saving faith* and *true piety.*

ANSWER 1. I own, the Scripture calls the members of the visible church by the name of *disciples;* but deny, that it *therefore* follows that the church of which they are members, is duly and properly constituted of those who have not true piety. Because, if this consequence was good, then it would equally follow, that not only the *visible,* but also the *invisible* or *mystical,* church is properly constituted of those who have not unfeigned faith and true piety. For the members of the mystical church, *as such,* and to denote the special character of such, are called *disciples;* Luke xiv. 26, 27, 33. and John viii. 31. and xiii. 35. and xv. 8. This shows, that in the argument I am answering, there is no connexion between the premises and the conclusion. For the force of the objection consists in this, that the members of the visible church are called *disciples* in Scripture: this is the sum total of the premises: and if there be any connexion between the premises and the conclusion, it must lie in the truth of this proposition; *The church whose members are called by the name of* disciples, *as signifying their state and quality as members of that society, that church is properly and fitly constituted, not only of persons truly pious, but of others that have merely a common faith and virtue.* But this proposition, we have seen, is not true; and so there is no connexion between the former and latter part of it, which are the same with the premises and conclusion of this argument.

2. Though I do not deny, that the visible church of Christ may fitly be represented as a school of Christ, where persons are trained up in the use of means, in order to *some* spiritual attainments: yet it will not hence necessarily follow, that this is in order to *all* good attainments; for it will not follow but that certain good attainments may be *pre-requisite,* in order to a *place* in the school. The church of Christ is a school appointed for the training up Christ's *little children,* to greater degrees of knowledge, higher privileges, and greater serviceableness in this world, and more meetness for the possession of their eternal inheritance. But there is no necessity of supposing, that it is in order to fit them to become Christ's children, or to be introduced into his family; any more than there is a necessity of supposing, because a prince puts his children under tutors, that therefore it must be in order to their being of the royal family. If it be necessary, that there should be a church of Christ appointed as a school of instruction and discipline, to bring persons to *all* good attainments whatsoever, then it will follow, that there must be a visible church constituted of *scandalous* and *profane* persons and *heretics,* and all in common that assume the christian name, that so means may be used with them in order to bring them to *moral sincerity,* and an acknowledgment of the christian faith.

3. I grant, that no other qualifications are necessary in order to being members of that school of Christ which is his visible church, than such as are requisite in order to *their subjecting themselves to Christ as their Master and Teacher,* and *subjecting themselves to the laws and orders of his school:* nevertheless I deny, that a *common faith* and *moral sincerity* are sufficient for this; because none do truly subject themselves to Christ *as their Master,* but such as having their *hearts purified by faith,* are delivered from the reigning power of *sin:* for we cannot subject ourselves to obey *two* contrary *masters* at the same time. None submit to Christ as *their Teacher,* but those who truly receive him as their Prophet, to teach them by his word and Spirit; giving up themselves to his teachings, *sitting* with *Mary* at *Jesus' feet to hear his word;* and hearkening more to his dictates, than those of their blind and deceitful lusts, and relying on his wisdom more than their own. The Scripture knows nothing of an ecclesiastical school constituted of *enemies of the cross of Christ,* and appointed to bring such to be reconciled to him and submit to him as their Master. Neither have they who are not truly pious persons, any true disposition of heart to submit to the *laws* and *orders* of Christ's school, the rules which his word prescribes to all his scholars; such as, *to love their Master* supremely; *to love one another as brethren;* and *to love their book, i. e.* their Bible, more than vain trifles and amusements, yea, above gold and silver; *to be faithful to the interest of the Master and of the school;* to *depend on his teachings;* to *cry to him for knowledge; above all their gettings, to get understanding,* &c.

4. Whatever ways of constituting the church may to us seem fit, proper, and reasonable, the *question* is, not what constitution of Christ's church seems convenient to *human* wisdom, but what constitution is actually established by *Christ's* infinite wisdom. Doubtless, if men should set their wits to work, and proceed according to what seems good in their sight, they would greatly alter Christ's constitution of his church, to make it more convenient and beautiful, and would adorn it with a vast variety of ingenious inventions; as the church of Rome has done. The question is, whether this *school* of Christ which they talk of, made up very much of those who pretend to no experiences or attainments but what consist with their being *enemies* of Christ in their hearts, and who in reality love the vilest lust better than him, be that church of Christ which in the New Testament is denominated *his city, his temple, his family, his body,* &c. by which names the visible church of Christ is there frequently called.

I acknowledge, that *means* of Christ's appointment, are to be used with those who are Christ's, and do not profess themselves any other, to change their *hearts,* and bring them to be Christ's *friends* and *disciples.* Such means are to be used with all sorts of persons, with Jews, Mahometans, heathens, with nominal Christians that are heretical or vicious, the profane, the intemperate, the unclean, and all other enemies of Christ; and these means to be used constantly, and laboriously. Scandalous persons need to go to *school,* to learn to be Christians, as much as other men. And there are many persons that are not *morally sincere,* who from selfish and sinister views consent ordinarily to go to church, and so be in the way of means. And none ought to forbid them thus going to Christ's *school,* that they may be taught by him, in the ministry of the gospel. But yet it will not follow, that such a *school* is the *church* of *Christ.* Human laws can put persons, even those who are very vicious, into the *school* of Christ, in that sense; they can oblige them constantly to be present at public teaching, and attend on the means of grace appointed by Christ, and dispensed in his name: but human laws cannot join men to the *church* of Christ, and make them members of his body.

OBJECT. II.

Visible saintship in the scripture sense cannot be the same with that which has been supposed and insisted on, because Israel of old were called *God's people,* when it is certain the greater part of them were far from having any *such* visible holiness as this. Thus the *ten tribes* were called God's people, Hos. iv. 6. after they had revolted from the true worship of God, and had obstinately continued in their idolatrous worship at Bethel and Dan for about two hundred and fifty years, and were at that time, a little before their captivity especially, in the height of their wickedness. So the Jews are called *God's people,* in Ezek. xxxvi. 20. and other places, at the time of their captivity in Babylon, a time when most of them were abandoned to all kinds of the most horrid and open impieties, as the prophets frequently represent. Now it is certain, that the people at that time were not called *God's people* because of any visibility of true piety to the eye of reason or of a rational charity, because most of them were grossly wicked, and declared their sin as Sodom. And in the same manner wherein the Jews of old were *God's people,* are the members of the visible christian Gentile church *God's people;* for they are spoken of as *graffed into the same olive-tree,* from whence the former were *broken off by unbelief.*

Answ. 1. The argument proves too much, and therefore nothing at all. Those whom I oppose in this controversy, will in effect as much oppose themselves in it, as me. The objection, if it has any force, equally militates against their and my notion of visible saintship. For those Jews, which it is alleged were called God's people, and yet were so notoriously, openly, and obstinately wicked, had neither any visibility of true piety, nor yet of that *moral sincerity* in the profession and duties of the true religion, which the opponents themselves suppose to be requisite in order to a proper visible holiness, and a due admission to the privileges and ordinances of the church of God. None will pretend, that these obstinate idolaters and impious wretches had those qualifications which are now requisite in order to an admission to the *christian* sacraments. And therefore to what purpose can they bring this objection? which, if it proves any thing, overthrows my scheme and their own both together, and both in an equally effectual manner. And not only so, but will thoroughly destroy the schemes of all *protestants* through the world, concerning the qualifications of the subjects of christian ordinances. And therefore the support of what I have laid down against those whom I oppose in this controversy, requires no further answer to this objection. Nevertheless, for greater satisfaction, I would here observe further:

2. That such appellations as God's *people*, God's *Israel*, and some other like phrases, are used and applied in Scripture with considerable *diversity* of intention. Thus, we have a plain distinction between the *house of Israel* and the *house of Israel*, in Ezek. xx. 38—40. By the house of *Israel* in the 39th verse is meant literally the nation or family of *Israel;* but by the house of *Israel* in the 40th verse seems to be intended the *spiritual house*, the body of God's visible saints, that should attend the ordinances of his public worship in gospel-times. So likewise there is a distinction made between the *house of Israel*, and *God's disciples* who should profess and visibly adhere *to his law and testimony*, in Isa. viii. 14—17. And though the whole nation of the Jews are often called *God's people* in those degenerate times wherein the prophets were sent to reprove them, yet at the same time they are charged as *falsely calling themselves of the holy city*, Isa. xlviii. 2. And God often tells them, they are rather to be reckoned among aliens, and as children of the Ethiopians, or posterity of the ancient Canaanites, on account of their grossly wicked and scandalous behaviour. See Amos ix. 7, &c. Ezek. xvi. 2, 3, &c. ver. 45, &c. Isa. i. 10.

It is evident that God sometimes, according to the methods of his marvellous mercy and long-suffering towards mankind, has a merciful respect to a degenerate church, become exceeding corrupt, and constituted of members who have not those qualifications which ought to be insisted on. God continues still to have respect to them so far as not utterly to forsake them, or wholly to deny his confirmation of and blessing on their administrations. And not being utterly renounced of God, their administrations are to be looked upon as in some respect valid, and the society as in some sort a people or church of God. This was the case with the church of Rome, at least till the Reformation and council of Trent; for till then we must own their baptisms and ordinations to be valid.—The church that the pope sits in, is called, *The temple of God*, 2 Thess. ii. 4.

And with regard to the people of Israel, it is very manifest, that something diverse is oftentimes intended by that nation being *God's people*, from their being visible saints, visibly holy, or having those qualifications which are requisite in order to a due admission to the ecclesiastical privileges of such. That *nation*, that *family of Israel according to the flesh*, and *with regard to that external and carnal qualification*, were in some sense adopted by God to be his *peculiar people*, and his *covenant people*. This is not only evident by what has been already observed, but also indisputably manifest from Rom. ix. 3, 4, 5. "I have great heaviness and continual sorrow of heart; for I could wish that myself were accursed from Christ for my brethren, my kinsmen, ACCORDING TO THE FLESH, who are Israelites, to whom pertaineth the ADOPTION, and the glory, and the COVENANTS, and the giving of the law, and the service of God, and the PROMISES; whose are the fathers; and of whom, as concerning the flesh, Christ came." It is to be noted, that the privileges here mentioned are spoken of as belonging to the Jews, not now as visible saints, not as professors of the true religion, not as members of the visible church of Christ; but only as people of *such a nation*, such a blood, such an external and carnal relation to the patriarchs their ancestors, *Israelites* ACCORDING TO THE FLESH. For the apostle is speaking here of the *unbelieving Jews*, professed unbelievers, that were out of the christian church, and open visible enemies to it, and such as had no right to the external privileges of Christ's people. So, in Rom. xi. 28, 29. this apostle speaks of the same *unbelieving Jews*, as in some respect an *elect people*, and interested in the *calling*, *promises*, and *covenants* God formerly gave to their forefathers, and as still *beloved* for their sakes. "As concerning the gospel, they are enemies for your sake; but as touching the election, they are beloved for the fathers' sakes: for the gifts and calling of God are without repentance." These things are not privileges belonging to the Jews now as a people of the right religion, or in the true church of visible worshippers of God; but as a people of such a pedigree or blood; and that even after the ceasing of the Mosaic administration. But there were privileges more especially belonging to them under the Old Testament: they were a *family* that God had chosen in distinction from all others, to show special favour to above all other *nations*. It was manifestly agreeable to God's design to constitute things so under the Old Testament, that the means of grace and spiritual privileges and blessings should be—though not wholly, yet in a great measure—confined to a *particular family*, much more than those privileges and blessings are confined to any posterity or blood now under the gospel. God purposely by these favours distinguished *that nation* not only from those who were not professed worshippers of the true God, but also in a great measure *from other nations*, by a constituted wall of separation. This was not merely a wall between professors and non-professors, but between NATION and NATIONS. God, if he pleases, may by his sovereignty annex his blessing, and in some measure fix it, for his own reasons, to a particular blood, as well as to a particular place or spot of ground, to a certain building, to a particular heap of stones, or altar of brass, to particular garments, and other external things. And it is evident, that he actually did affix his blessing to that particular external family of Jacob, very much as he did to the city Jerusalem, where he chose to place his name, and to mount Zion *where he commanded the blessing*. God did not so affix his blessing to Jerusalem or mount Zion, as to limit himself, either by confining the blessing wholly to that place, never to bestow it elsewhere; nor by obliging himself always to bestow it on those that sought him there; nor yet obliging himself never to withdraw his blessing from thence, by forsaking his dwelling-place there, and leaving it to be a common or profane place. But he was pleased to make it the seat of his blessing in a peculiar manner, in great distinction from other places. In like manner did he fix his blessing to the progeny of Jacob. It was a family which he delighted in, and which he blessed in a peculiar manner, and to which in a great measure he confined the blessing; but not so as to limit himself, or so as to oblige himself to bestow it on all of that blood, or not to bestow it on others that were not of that blood. He affixed his blessing both to the place and nation, by sovereign election, Psal. cxxxii. 13—15. He annexed and fixed his blessing to both by covenant.

To that nation he fixed his blessing by his covenant with the patriarchs. Indeed the main thing, the substance and marrow of that covenant which God made with Abraham and the other patriarchs, was the *covenant of grace*, which is continued in these days of the gospel, and extends to all his spiritual seed, of the Gentiles as well as Jews: but yet that covenant with the patriarchs contained other things that were appendages to that everlasting covenant of grace; promises of lesser matters, subservient to the grand promise of the future seed, and typical of things appertaining to him. Such were those that annexed the blessing to the land of Canaan, and the progeny of Isaac and Jacob. Just so it was also as to the covenant God made with David. 2 Sam. vii. and Psal. cxxxii. If we consider that covenant with regard to its marrow and soul, it was the covenant of grace: but there were other subservient promises which were typical of its benefits; such were promises of blessings to the nation of Israel, of continuing the temporal crown to David's posterity, and of fixing the blessing to Jerusalem or mount Zion, as the place which he chose to set his name there. And in this sense it was that the *very family* of Jacob were *God's people by covenant*, and his *chosen people;* even when they were no visible saints, when they lived in idolatry, and made no profession of the true religion.

On the whole, it is evident that the *very nation* of Israel, not as visible saints, but *as the progeny of Jacob according to the flesh*, were in some respect a *chosen people*, a *people of God*, a *covenant people*, an *holy nation;* even as Jerusalem was a *chosen city*, the *city of God*, a *holy city*, and a city that God had engaged *by covenant* to dwell in.

Thus a sovereign and all-wise God was pleased to ordain

things with respect to *the nation* of Israel. Perhaps we may not be able to give all the reasons of such a constitution; but some of them seem to be pretty manifest; as,

1. The great and main end of separating one particular nation from all others, as God did *the nation* of Israel, was to prepare the way for the coming of the *Messiah*. God's covenant with Abraham and the other patriarchs implied that the Messiah should be *of their blood*, or their seed *according to the flesh*. And therefore it was requisite that *their progeny according to the flesh* should be fenced in by a wall of separation, and made *God's people*. If the Messiah had been born of some of the *professors of Abraham's religion*, but of some other nation, that religion being propagated from nation to nation, as it is now under the gospel, it would not have answered the covenant with Abraham, for the Messiah to have been born of Abraham's seed only in this sense. The *Messiah* being by covenant so related to Jacob's *progeny according to the flesh*, God was pleased, agreeable to the nature of such a covenant, to show great respect to that people on account of that external relation. Therefore the apostle mentions it as one great privilege, that of them *according to the flesh* Christ came, Rom. ix. 5. As the introducing of the *Messiah* and his salvation and kingdom was the special design of all God's dealings and peculiar dispensations towards that people, the natural result of this was, that great account should be made of their being *of that nation*, in God's covenant dealings with them.

2. That nation was a *typical nation*. There was then literally a *land*, which was a type of heaven, the true dwelling-place of God; and an *external city*, which was a type of the spiritual city of God; *an external temple of God*, which was a type of his spiritual temple. So there was an *external people and family of God*, by carnal generation, which was a type of his spiritual progeny. And the covenant by which they were made a people of God, was a type of the covenant of grace; and so is sometimes represented as a marriage-covenant. God, agreeably to the nature of that dispensation, showed a great regard to external and carnal things in those days, as types of spiritual things. What a great regard God did show then to external qualifications for privileges and services, appears in this, that there is ten times so much said in the books of Moses about such qualifications in the institutions of the passover and tabernacle services, as about any moral qualifications whatsoever. And so much were such typical qualifications insisted on, that even by the law of Moses, the congregation of the Lord, or church of visible worshippers of God, and the number of public professors of the true religion who were visible saints, were not the same. Some were of the latter, that were not of the former; as the eunuchs, who were excluded the congregation, though never so externally religious, yea truly pious; and so also bastards, &c.

3. It was the sovereign pleasure of God to choose the posterity of *Jacob according to the flesh*, to reserve them for special favours to the end of time. And therefore they are still kept a distinct nation, being still reserved for distinguishing mercy in the latter day, when they shall be restored to the church of God. God is pleased in this way to testify his regard to their holy ancestors, and his regard to their external relation to Christ. Therefore the apostle still speaks of them as an *elect nation*, and *beloved for the fathers' sakes*, even after they were broken off from the good olive by unbelief. God's covenant with Abraham is in some sense in force with respect to that people, and reaches them even to this day; and yet surely they are not God's covenant people, in the sense that visible Christians are. See Lev. xxvi. 42.

If it be said, It was often foretold by the prophets, that in gospel-days other *nations* should be the people of God, as well as the *nation* of the Jews: and when Christ sent forth his apostles, he bid them go and *disciple all nations*.

I answer; By a common figure of speech the prevailing part of a nation are called *the nation*, and what is done to them is said to be done to the nation, and what is done *by* them is said to be done *by* that nation. And it is to be hoped, that the time is coming when the prevailing part of many nations, yea of every nation under heaven, will be regularly brought into the visible church of Christ. If by *nations* in these prophecies we understand any other than the prevailing part, and it be insisted on that we must understand it of all the people belonging to those nations; there never yet has been any nation in this sense regularly brought into the visible church of Christ, even according to the scheme of those whom I oppose. For there never yet has been a whole nation outwardly moral. And besides, what Mr. Blake says in his *Treatise of the Covenant*, page 238. may be applied here, and serve as an answer to this objection: "The prophecies of the Old Testament (says he) of the glory of the New-Testament times, are in Old-Testament phrases, by way of allusion to the worship of those times, set forth to us." In Rev. xxi. 24. *nations* are spoken of, as having an interest in the *New Jerusalem*, which yet is represented as perfectly pure, without the least degree of pollution and defilement, ver. 27. And as for the command to the apostles, to *disciple all nations*, it was a direction to them as to what they should attempt, not a prediction of what they should bring to pass in their day. For they never brought one-half of any one nation into the visible christian church, nor any at all in one-half of the nations in the world, it is very probable.

If it should be further objected, that it is an evidence that Gentile Christians are visible saints, according to the New-Testament notion of visible saintship, in the very same manner as the whole Jewish nation were till they were broken off by their obstinate rejection of the Messiah; that the Gentile Christians are represented as being *grafted into the same olive*, from whence the Jews were *broken off by unbelief*, Rom. xi. 17, &c.

I would inquire, What any one can intend by this objection? Whether it be this, *viz.* That we ought to insist on no higher or better qualifications, in admitting persons as members of the christian church, and to all its privileges, than the whole Jewish nation in Christ's time possessed, till they had obstinately persisted in their rejection of him? If this is *not* intended, the objection is nothing to the purpose: or, if this *be* intended, neither then is it to the purpose of those with whom I have especially to do in this controversy, who hold *orthodoxy*, *knowledge* of the fundamental doctrines of religion, *moral sincerity*, and a *good conversation*, to be qualifications, which ought to be insisted on, in order to a visible church-state. For a very great part of those Jews were destitute of these qualifications; many of them were Sadducees, who denied a future state; others of them Herodians, who were occasional conformists with the Romans in their idolatries; the prevailing sect among them were Pharisees, who openly professed the false doctrine of justification by the works of the law and external privileges, that *leaven of the Pharisees*, which Christ warns his disciples to beware of. Many of them were scandalously *ignorant*, for their teachers had taken away the key of knowledge. Multitudes were grossly *vicious*, for it was a generation in which all manner of sin and wickedness prevailed.

I think that text in Rom. xi. can be understood no otherwise, in any consistence with plain fact, than that the Gentile Christians succeeded the Jews, who had been, either in themselves or ancestors, the children of Abraham, with respect to a visible interest in the covenant of grace, until they were broken off from the church, and ceased to be visible saints by their open and obstinate unbelief. Indeed their ancestors had all been thus broken off from the church of visible saints; for every branch or family of the stock of Jacob had been in the church of visible saints, and each branch withered and failed through unbelief. This was the highest and most important sense, in which any of the Jews were externally the children of Abraham, and implied the greatest privileges. But there was another sense, in which the whole nation, including even those of them who were no visible saints, were his children, which (as has been shown) implied great privileges, wherein christian Gentiles do not succeed them, though they have additional ecclesiastical privileges, vastly beyond the Jews.

Whether I have succeeded, in rightly explaining these matters, or no, yet my failing in it is of no great importance with regard to the strength of the objection, that occasioned my attempting it; which was, that scandalously *wicked* men among the Jews are called *God's people*, &c. The objection, as I observed, is as much against the scheme of those whom I oppose, as against my scheme; and therefore it as much concerns *them*, to find out some explanation of the matter, that shall show something else is intended by it, than their having the qualifications of visible saints, as it does me; and a failing in such an attempt as much affects and hurts their cause, as it does mine.

OBJECT. III.

Those in Israel, who made no profession of piety of heart, did according to divine institution partake of the *passover;* a Jewish *sacrament*, representing the same things, and a seal of the very same covenant of grace, with the *Lord's supper;* and particularly, it would be unreasonable to suppose, that all made a profession of godliness whom God commanded to keep that first *passover* in Egypt, which the whole congregation were required to keep, and there is no shadow of any such thing as all first making a solemn public profession of those things wherein true piety consists: and so the people in general partook of the *passover*, from generation to generation; but it would be improbable to suppose, that they all professed a supreme regard to God in their hearts.

ANSW. 1. The affair of the Israelites' participation of the *passover*, and particularly that first *passover* in Egypt, is attended with altogether as much difficulty in regard to the qualifications which the *objectors* themselves suppose requisite in communicants at the Lord's table, as with regard to those which I insist upon; and if there be any argument in the case, it is fully as strong an argument against *their* scheme, as mine.

One thing they insist upon as a requisite qualification for the Lord's supper, is a public profession of religion as to the essential *doctrines* of it. But there is no more public profession of this kind, preceding that passover in Egypt, than of a profession of godliness. Here, not to insist on the great doctrines of the *fall of man*, of our *undone state by nature*, of the *Trinity*, of our *dependence on the free grace of God for justification*, &c. let us take only those two doctrines of a *future state of rewards and punishments*, and the doctrine of *the Messiah to come*, that Messiah who was represented in the *passover*. Is there any more appearance, in sacred story, of the people making a public profession in Egypt of these doctrines, before they partook of the passover, than of their making profession of the love of God? And is there any more probability of the former, than of the latter? *Another* thing which they on the other side suppose necessary to a due attendance on the Lord's supper, is, that when any have openly been guilty of gross sins, they should before they come to this sacrament, openly *confess* and *humble* themselves for their faults. Now it is evident by many scriptures, that a great part of the children of Israel in Egypt had been guilty of joining with the Egyptians in worshipping their false gods, and had lived in *idolatry*. But the history in Exodus gives us no account of any public solemn confession of, or humiliation, for this great sin, before they came to the passover. Mr. Stoddard observes, (*Appeal*, p. 58, 59.) that there was in the church of Israel a way appointed by God for the removal of scandals; men being required in that case to offer up their *sacrifices*, attended with *confession* and visible signs of *repentance*. But where do we read of the people offering up sacrifices in Egypt, attended with confession, for removing the scandal of that most heinous sin of *idolatry* they had lived in? Or is there any more probability of their publicly professing their repentance and humiliation for their sin, before their celebrating the passover, than of their publicly professing to love God above all? *Another* thing which they suppose to be requisite in order to admission to the Lord's table, and about which they would have a particular care to be taken, is, that every person admitted give evidence of a competent *knowledge* in the doctrines of religion, and none be allowed to partake who are grossly ignorant. Now there is no more appearance of this with regard to the congregation in Egypt, than of a *profession of godliness;* and it is as difficult to suppose it. There is abundant reason to suppose, that vast numbers in that nation, consisting of more than a million of adult persons, had been brought up in a great degree of ignorance, amidst their slavery in Egypt, where the people seem to have almost forgotten the true God and the true religion. And though pains had been taken by Moses, now for a short season, to instruct the people better; yet it must be considered, it is a very great work, to take a whole nation under such degrees of ignorance and prejudice, and bring every one of them to a competent degree of knowledge in religion; and a greater work still for Moses both thus to instruct them, and also by examination or otherwise, to come to a just satisfaction, that all had indeed attained to such knowledge.

Mr. Stoddard insists, that if grace be requisite in the Lord's supper, it would have been as much so in the *passover*, inasmuch as the chief thing which the *passover* (as well as the Lord's supper) represents, is Christ's sufferings. But if, on this account, the same qualifications are requisite in both ordinances, then it would be as requisite that the partakers should have knowledge to *discern the Lord's body*, (in Mr. Stoddard's sense of 1 Cor. xi. 29.) in the *passover*, as in the Lord's supper. But this certainly is as difficult to suppose, as that they professed godliness. For how does it appear, that the people in general who partook of the *passover*—knew that it signified the death of the *Messiah*, and the way in which he should make atonement for sin by his blood? Does it look very likely that they should know this, when Christ's own disciples had not knowledge thus to *discern the Lord's body* in the *passover*, of which they partook from year to year with their Master? Can it be supposed, they actually knew Christ's death and the design of it to be thereby signified, when they did not so much as realize the fact itself, that Christ was to die, at least not till the year before the last passover? Besides, how unreasonable would it be, to suppose, that the Jews understood what was signified, pertaining to Christ and salvation by him, in all those many kinds of sacrifices, which they attended and partook of, and all the vast variety of ceremonies belonging to them; all which sacrifices were sacramental representations of Christ's death, as well as the sacrifice of the passover! The apostle tells us, that all these things had *a shadow of good things to come*, the things concerning *Christ;* and yet there are many of them, which the church of Christ to this day does not understand; though we are under a thousand times greater advantage to understand them, than they were. For we have the *New Testament*, wherein God uses *great plainness of speech*, to guide us, and live in days wherein the *vail* which Moses put over his face is taken away in Christ, and the vail of the temple rent, and have the substance and antitype plainly exhibited, and so have opportunity to compare these with those shadows.

If it be objected, as a difficulty that lies against our supposing a profession of godliness requisite to a participation of the *passover*, that they who were *uncircumcised* were expressly forbidden to partake, and if conversion was as important and a more important qualification than circumcision, why were not the *unregenerate* as expressly forbidden? I answer; Why were not *scandalous* sinners as expressly forbidden? And why was not *moral sincerity* as expressly required as circumcision?

If it be objected, that they were *all* expressly and strictly required to keep the passover; but if grace was requisite, and God knew that many of the partakers would have no grace, why would he give such universal orders?

I answer; When God gave those commands, he knew that the commands, in all their strictness, would reach many persons who in the time of the *passover* would be without so much as *moral sincerity* in religion. Every man in the nation, from the first institution till the death of Christ, were all (excepting such as were ceremonially unclean, or on a journey) strictly required to keep the feast of *passover;* and yet God knew that multitudes would be without the qualification of *moral seriousness* in religion. It would be very unreasonable to suppose, that every single person in the nation was morally serious, even in the very best time, or that ever there was such a happy day with any nation under heaven, wherein all were morally sincere in religion. How much then was it otherwise many times with that nation, which was so prone to corruption, and so often generally involved in gross wickedness! But the strict command of God to keep the *passover* reached the morally *insincere*, as well as others; they are no where excepted, any more than the *unconverted*. And as to any general commands of God's word, these no more required men to turn from a state of moral insincerity before they came to the *passover*, than they required them to turn from a graceless state.

But further, I reply, that God required them all to keep the *passover*, no more strictly than he required them all to *love* the Lord their God with their whole heart. And if God might strictly command this, he might also strictly command them to keep that ordinance wherein they were especially to profess it, and seal their profession of it. That *evil generation* were not expressly forbidden to keep the *passover* in succeeding years, for the whole *forty years* during which they went on provoking God, very often by gross sin and open rebellion; but still the express and strict commands for the whole congregation to keep the *passover* reached them, nor were they released from their obligation.

If it be said, that we must suppose multitudes in Israel attended the *passover*, from age to age, without such a *visibility* of *piety* as I have insisted on; and yet we do not find their attending this ordinance charged on them as a *sin*, in Scripture: I answer; We must also suppose that multitudes in Israel, from age to age, attended the passover, who lived in *moral insincerity*, yea and *scandalous wickedness*. For the people in general very often notoriously corrupted themselves, and declined to ways of open and great transgression; and yet there is reason to think, that in these times of corruption, for the most part, they held *circumcision* and the *passover;* and we do not find their attending on these ordinances under such circumstances, any more expressly charged on them as a sin, than their coming without piety of heart. The *ten tribes* continued constantly in *idolatry* for about 250 years, and there is a ground to suppose, that in the mean time they ordinarily kept up circumcision and the passover. For though they worshipped God by images, yet they maintained most of the ceremonial observances of the law of Moses, called *the manner of the God of the land*, which their priests taught the Samaritans who were settled in their stead, 2 Kings xvii. 26, 27. Nevertheless we do not find Elijah, Elisha, or other prophets, reproving them for attending these ordinances without the required moral qualifications. Indeed there are some things in the writings of the prophets, which may be interpreted as a reproof of this; but no more as a reproof of this, than of attending God's ordinances without a gracious sincerity and true piety of heart and life.

How many seasons were there, wherein the people in general fell into and lived in *idolatry*, that scandal of scandals, in the times of the judges, and of the kings both in Judah and Israel! But still amidst all this wickedness, they continued to attend the sacrament of *circumcision*. We have every whit as much evidence of it, as that they attended the *passover* without a profession of godliness. We have no account of their ever leaving it off at such seasons, nor any hint of its being renewed (as a thing which had ceased) when they came to reform. Though we have so full an account of the particulars of Josiah's reformation, after the long and scandalous reign of Manasseh, there is no hint of any reviving of *circumcision*, or returning to it after a cessation. And where have we an account of the people being once reproved for attending this holy sacrament while thus involved in *scandalous* sin, in all the Old Testament? And where is this once charged on them as a sin, any more than in the case of unconverted persons attending the sacrament of the *passover?* *

ANSW. 2. Whatever was the case with respect to the qualifications for the sacraments of the Old-Testament dispensation, I humbly conceive it is nothing to the purpose in the present argument, nor needful to determine us with respect to the qualifications for the sacraments of the *christian* dispensation, which is a matter of such plain fact in the New Testament. Far am I from thinking the Old Testament to be like an old almanack out of use; nay, I think it is evident from the New Testament, that some things which had their first institution under the Old Testament, are continued under the New; for instance, the acceptance of the infant-seed of believers as children of the covenant with their parents; and probably some things belonging to the order and discipline of christian churches, had their first beginning in the Jewish synagogue. But yet all allow that the Old-Testament *dispensation* is out of date, with its ordinances; and I think, in a matter pertaining to the constitution and order of the *New-Testament church*—a matter of fact, wherein the *New Testament* itself is express, full, and abundant—to have recourse to the Mosaic dispensation for rules or precedents to determine our judgment, is quite needless, and out of reason. There is perhaps no part of divinity attended with so much intricacy, and wherein orthodox divines do so much differ, as the stating of the precise agreement and difference between the two dispensations of Moses and of Christ.† And probably the reason why God has left it so intricate, is, because our understanding the ancient dispensation, and God's design in it, is not of so great importance, nor does it so nearly concern us. Since God uses great plainness of speech in the New Testament, which is as it were the charter and municipal law of the christian church, what need we run back to the ceremonial and typical institutions of an antiquated dispensation, wherein God's declared design was, to deliver divine things in comparative obscurity, hid under a veil, and involved in clouds?

We have no more occasion for going to search among the types, dark revelations, and carnal ordinances of the Old Testament, to find out whether this matter of fact concerning the constitution and order of the New-Testament church be true, than we have occasion for going there to find out whether any other matter of fact, of which we have an account in the New Testament, be true; as particularly, whether there were such officers in the primitive church as *bishops* and *deacons*, whether *miraculous* gifts of the Spirit were common in the apostles' days, whether the believing Gentiles were received into the primitive christian church, and the like.

ANSW. 3. I think, nothing can be alleged from the Holy Scripture, sufficient to prove a *profession of godliness* to be not a qualification requisite in order to a due and regular participation of the *passover*.

Although none of the requisite moral qualifications for this Jewish sacrament, are near so clearly made known in the Old Testament, as the qualifications for the *christian* sacraments are in the New; and although a supposed visibility of either moral sincerity or sanctifying grace, is involved in some obscurity and difficulty; yet I would humbly offer what appears to me to be the truth concerning that matter, in the things that follow.

(1.) Although the people in Egypt before the *first passover*, probably made no *explicit* public profession at all, either of their *humiliation for their former idolatry* or of *present devotedness of heart to God;* it being before any particular institution of an express public profession, either of godliness, or repentance in case of scandal: yet I think, there was some sort of *public manifestation*, or *implicit profession* of both.—Probably in Egypt they implicitly professed the same things, which they afterwards professed more expressly and solemnly in the *wilderness*. The Israelites in Egypt had very much to affect their hearts, before the last plague, in the great things that God had done for them; especially in some of the latter plagues, wherein they were so remarkably distinguished from the Egyptians. They seem now to be brought to a tender frame, and a disposition to show much respect to God; (see Exod. xii. 27.) and were probably now very forward to profess themselves devoted to him, and true penitents.

(2.) After the institution of an *explicit public profession* of devotedness to God, or (which is the same thing) of true piety of heart, this was wont to be required in order to a partaking of the *passover* and other sacrifices and sa-

* Let the reader here take notice of what is observed in the conclusion of my answer to the objection from the instance of Judas.

† On this "precise agreement and difference," Dr. Owen has written with admirable clearness in his Exposition to the Epistle to the Hebrews and the prefixed exercitation.—W.

craments that adult persons were admitted to. Accordingly all the adult persons that were circumcised at Gilgal, had made this profession a little before on the plains of Moab. Not that all of them were truly gracious; but seeing they all had a profession and visibility, Christ in his dealings with his church as to external things, acted not as the Searcher of hearts, but as the Head of the visible church, accommodating himself to the present state of mankind; and therefore he represents himself in Scripture as *trusting* his people's profession; as I formerly observed.

(3.) In *degenerate* times in Israel, both priests and people were very *lax* with respect to covenanting with God, and professing devotedness to him; and these professions were used, as public professions commonly are still in corrupt times, merely as matters of *form* and *ceremony*, at least by great multitudes.

(4.) Such was the nature of the Levitical dispensation, that it had in no measure so great a tendency to preclude and prevent *hypocritical professions*, as the *New-Testament dispensation;* particularly, on account of the vastly greater *darkness* of it. For the covenant of grace was not then so fully revealed, and consequently the nature of the conditions of that covenant was not then so well known. There was then a far more obscure revelation of those great duties of repentance towards God and faith in the Mediator, and of those things wherein true holiness consists, and wherein it is distinguished from other things. Persons then had not equal advantage to know their own hearts, while viewing themselves in this comparatively dim light of Moses's law, as now they have in the clear sun-shine of the gospel. In that state of the minority of the church, the nature of true piety, as consisting in the *Spirit of adoption*, or ingenuous filial love to God, and as distinguished from a *spirit of bondage*, servile fear, and self-love, was not so clearly made known. The Israelites were therefore the more ready to mistake for true piety, that moral seriousness and those warm affections and resolutions that resulted from that *spirit of bondage*, which showed itself in Israel remarkably at mount Sinai; and to which through all the Old-Testament times, they were especially incident.

(5.) God was pleased in a great measure *to suffer* (though he did not properly *allow*) a *laxness* among the people, with regard to the visibility of holiness, and the moral qualifications requisite to an attendance on their sacraments. This he also did in many other cases of great irregularity, under that dark, imperfect, and comparatively carnal dispensation; such as polygamy, putting away their wives at pleasure, the revenging of blood, killing the man-slayer, &c. And he *winked at* their worshipping in high places in Solomon's time, (1 Kings iii. 4, 5.) the neglect of keeping the feast of tabernacles according to the law, from Joshua's time till after the captivity, (Neh. viii. 17.) and the neglect of the synagogue-worship, or the public service of God in particular congregations, till after the captivity,* though the light of nature, together with the general rules of the law of Moses, did sufficiently teach and require it.

(6.) It seems to be foretold in the prophecies of the Old Testament, that there would be a great *alteration* in this respect, in the days of the gospel; that under the new dispensation there should be far *greater purity* in the church. Thus, in the forementioned place in Ezekiel it is foretold, that "those who are [*visibly*] uncircumcised in heart, should NO MORE enter into God's sanctuary." Again, Ezek. xx. 37, 38. "And I will cause you to pass under the rod, and will bring you into the bond of the covenant; and I will purge out from among you the rebels, and them that transgress against me." It seems to be a prophecy of the greater purity of those who are visibly *in covenant with God*. Isa. iv. 3. "And it shall come to pass that he that is left in Zion, and he that remaineth in Jerusalem, shall be called holy, even every one that is written among the living [*i. e. has a name to live*, or is enrolled among the saints] in Jerusalem." Isa. lii. 1. "Put on thy beautiful garments, O Jerusalem, the holy city; from henceforth there shall NO MORE come to thee the uncircumcised and the unclean." Zech. xiv. 21. "And in that day, there shall be NO MORE the Canaanite in the house of the Lord."

(7.) This is just such an alteration as might reasonably be expected from what we are taught of the whole *nature* of the *two dispensations*. As the one had *carnal ordinances*, (so they are called Heb. ix. 10.) the other a *spiritual* service; (John iv. 24.) the one an *earthly* Canaan, the other a *heavenly;* the one an *external* Jerusalem, the other a *spiritual;* the one an *earthly* high priest, the other a *heavenly;* the one a *worldly* sanctuary, the other a *spiritual;* the one a *bodily* and *temporal* redemption, (which is all that they generally discerned or understood in the *passover,)* the other a *spiritual* and *eternal*. And agreeably to these things, it was so ordered in providence, that Israel, the congregation that should enter this *worldly* sanctuary, and attend these *carnal* ordinances, should be much more a *worldly, carnal* congregation, than the New-Testament congregation. One reason of such a difference seems to be this, *viz.* That the *Messiah* might have the honour of introducing a state of greater purity and spiritual glory. Hence God is said to find *fault* with that ancient dispensation of the covenant, Heb. viii. 7, 8. And the time of introducing the new dispensation is called the time of *reformation*, Heb. ix. 10. And one thing, wherein the amendment of what God found fault with in the former dispensation should consist, the apostle intimates, is the greater *purity* and *spirituality* of the church, Heb. viii. 7, 8, 11.

OBJECT. IV.

It is not reasonable to suppose, that the multitudes which John the Baptist baptized, made a *profession* of saving grace, or had any such *visibility* of true piety, as has been insisted on.

ANSW. Those whom John baptized, *came to him confessing their sins*, making a profession of some kind of *repentance;* and it is not reasonable to suppose, the repentance they professed was specifically or in kind *diverse* from that which he had instructed them in, and called them to, which is called *repentance for the remission of sins;* and that is saving repentance. John's baptism is called *the baptism of repentance for the remission of sins:* I know not how such a phrase can be reasonably understood any otherwise, than so as to imply, that his *baptism* was some exhibition of that *repentance*, and a seal of the profession of it. Baptism is a seal of some sort of religious profession, in adult persons: but the very name of John's baptism shows, that it was a seal of a profession of *repentance for the remission of sins*. It is said, Luke iii. 3. "John PREACHED the baptism of repentance for the remission of sins." What can be understood by this, but *his preaching* that men should now speedily *turn to God*, by true *repentance* and *faith* in the promised Saviour, and *come and confess their sins*, and openly declare this repentance towards God, and faith in the Lamb of God, and that they should confirm and seal this their profession by *baptism*, as well as therein receive the seal of God's willingness to *remit the sins* of such as had this faith and repentance. Accordingly, we are told, the *people came and were baptized of him, confessing their sins*, manifesting and professing that sort of *repentance* and *faith* which he *preached*. They had no notion of any *other sort* of repentance put into their heads, that they could suppose John *called* them to profess in *baptism*, but this accompanied with *faith* in the Lamb whom he called them to behold; for he *preached* no other to them. The people that John baptized, professed both *repentance for the remission of sins*, and also *faith in the Messiah;* as is evident by Acts xix. 4, 5. "John verily baptized with the baptism of repentance, saying unto the people, that they should believe on him that should come after him;" *i. e.* on *Christ Jesus*. "When they heard this [John's preaching] they were baptized in the name of the Lord *Jesus*."

If it be objected here, that we are told, Matt. iii. 5, 6. "There went out to him Jerusalem, and all Judea, and

* *Prid. Connect.* Part I. p. 354—536. and 555, 556. 9th Edit. The word translated *synagogues*, Psal. lxxiv. 8. signifies *assemblies;* and is supposed by the generality of learned men to relate to another sort of assemblies.

all the region round about Jordan, and were baptized of him in Jordan, confessing their sins;" and that it is not to be imagined, *all* these made any credible profession of saving repentance and faith: I answer; No more is to be understood by these expressions, according to the phraseology of the Scripture, than that there was a very great resort of people from these places to John. Nor is any more to be understood by the like term of universality in John iii. 26. "They came to John, and said unto him, Rabbi, he that was with thee beyond Jordan, to whom thou barest witness, behold, the same baptizeth, and ALL MEN come to him;" that is, there was a great resort to him from all quarters. It is in nowise unreasonable to suppose, there was indeed a very great number of people that came to John from the places mentioned, who being exceedingly moved by his preaching, in that time of extraordinary outpouring of the Spirit, made profession of the faith and repentance which John preached. Doubtless there were many more professors than real converts: but still in the great resort to John, there were many of the latter character; as we may infer from the prophecy: as appears by Luke, i. 16, 17. "And many of the children of Israel shall he turn to the Lord their God. And he shall go before him in the spirit and power of Elias, to turn the hearts of the fathers to the children, and of the disobedient to the wisdom of the just, to make ready a people prepared for the Lord." And from that account of fact in Mark xi. 12. "From the days of John the Baptist until now, the kingdom of heaven suffereth violence, and the violent take it by force." And in Luke xvi. 16. "The law and the prophets were until John: since that time the kingdom of God is preached, and *every man* presseth into it." Here the expression is no less universal, than that which is objected in Matt. iii. 5, 6. As to those wicked Pharisees, that so much opposed Christ, some of them I suppose had been baptized by John, and then had a great show of repentance and faith; but they afterwards apostatized, and were much worse than ever before: therefore Christ speaks of them as being like a *house* from *which the unclean spirit* is visibly turned out for *a while*, and is *left empty, swept, and garnished*, but afterward is *repossessed*, and has many devils instead of one, Luke xi. 24, &c. Yet as to the greater part of these Pharisees, they were not baptized by John; as appears by Luke vii. 29, 30.

If it be further objected, that John in baptizing such multitudes could not have *time* to be sufficiently informed of those he baptized, whether their profession of godliness was *credible*, or no: I answer; That we are not particularly informed of the circumstances of his teaching, and of the assistance he was favoured with, and the means he had of information, concerning those whom he baptized: but we may be sure of one thing, *viz.* He had as much opportunity to inquire into the credibility of their profession, as he had to inquire into their *doctrinal* knowledge and *moral* character; which my opponents suppose to be necessary, as well as I: and this is enough to silence the present objection.

OBJECT. V.

Christ says, Matt. xx. 16. and again, chap. xxii. 14. that *many are called, but few are chosen.* By which it is evident, that there are *many* who belong to the *visible church*, and yet but *few* real and true *saints;* and that it is ordinarily thus, even under the *New Testament*, and in days of gospel-light: and therefore that *visibility* of *saintship*, whereby persons are visible saints in a scripture sense, cannot imply an apparent probability of their being *real* saints, or truly gracious persons.

Answ. In these texts, by those that are *called*, are not meant those who are *visible saints*, and have the requisite qualifications for christian sacraments; but all such as have the *external call* of the word of God, and have its offers and invitations made to them. And it is undoubtedly true, and has been matter of fact, for the most part, that of those *called* in this sense, *many* have been but *only* called, and never truly obedient to the call, *few* have been true saints. So it was in the Jewish nation, to which the parable in the twentieth of Matthew has a special respect; in general they had the *external call* of God's word, and attended many religious duties, in hopes of God's favour and reward, which is called *labouring in God's vineyard;* and yet but *few* of them eventually obtained salvation; nay, great multitudes of those who were *called* in this sense, were *scandalous* persons, and gross hypocrites. The Pharisees and Sadducees were *called*, and they *laboured in the vineyard*, in the sense of the parable; for which they expected great rewards, above the Gentile converts or proselytes; wherefore their *eye was evil* towards them, and they could not bear that they should be made *equal* to them. But still these Pharisees and Sadducees had not generally the intellectual and moral qualifications, that my opponents suppose requisite for *christian* sacraments; being generally scandalous persons, denying some fundamental principles of religion, and explaining away some of its most important precepts. Thus, *many* in christendom are called, by the outward call of God's word, and yet *few* of them are in a state of salvation: but not all who sit under the sound of the gospel, and hear its invitations, are fit to come to *sacraments.*

That by those who are *called*, in this saying of our Saviour, is meant those that have the *gospel-offer*, and not those who belong to the society of *visible saints*, is evident beyond all dispute, in Matt. xxii. 14. By the *many that are called*, are plainly intended the many that are *invited to the wedding*. In the foregoing parable, we have an account of those who from time to time were *bidden*, or CALLED, (for the word is the same in the original,) ver. 3. "And sent forth his servants to CALL them that were CALLED, [καλεσαι τȣς κεκλημενȣς,] and they would not come." This has respect to the Jews, who refused not only savingly to come to Christ, but refused so much as to come into the visible church of Christ. Ver. 4. "Again he sent forth other servants, saying, Tell them which are bidden, [or CALLED,] Behold I have prepared my dinner," &c. Ver. 8. "They which were bidden [or CALLED] were not worthy," Ver. 9. "Go ye therefore into the high-ways, and as many as ye shall find, bid [or CALL, καλεσατε] to the marriage," or nuptial banquet; representing the preaching of the gospel to the Gentiles; who upon it came into the *king's house*, *i. e.* the visible church, and among them *one that had not a wedding-garment, who was bound hand and foot, and cast out when the king came:* and then, at the conclusion, Christ adds this remark, ver. 14. "For many are CALLED *or* bidden [κλητοι,] but few are chosen;" which must have reference, not only to the *man* last mentioned, who came into the wedding-house, the christian visible church, *without a wedding-garment*, but to those also mentioned before, who were *called*, but would not so much as *come into the king's house*, or join to the visible christian church. To suppose this saying to have reference only to that *one man* who came without *a wedding-garment*, (representing one that comes into the visible church, but is not a true saint,) would be to make the introduction of this aphorism, and its connexion with what went before, very strange and unintelligible, thus, "*Multitudes* came into the king's house, who were *called*, and the house was full of guests; but among them was found *one* man who was not *chosen; for many are* called, *but few are* chosen."

OBJECT. VI.

When the servants of the householder, in the parable of the wheat and tares (Matt. xiii.) unexpectedly found *tares* among the wheat, they said to their master, "Wilt thou that we go and gather them up? But he said, Nay, lest while ye gather up the tares, ye root up also the wheat with them; let both grow together until the harvest." Which shows the mind of Christ, that we ought not to make a *distinction* between true saints and others in this world, or aim at admitting true saints *only* into the visible church, but ought to let *both* be *together* in the church till the day of *judgment.*

Answ. 1. These things have no reference to *introduction* into the field, or *admission* into the visible church, as though no care nor measures should be taken to prevent *tares* being *sown;* or as though the servants who had the charge of the field, would have done well to have taken *tares*, appearing to be such, and *planted* them in the field amongst the wheat: no, instead of this, the parable plainly implies the contrary. But the words cited have wholly respect to a CASTING OUT and purging the field, *after* the tares had been introduced *unawares*, and *contrary to design*, through men's infirmity and Satan's procurement. Concerning purging the *tares* out of the field, or casting men out of the church, there is no difference between me and those whom I oppose in the present controversy: and therefore it is impossible there should be any objection from that which Christ says here concerning this matter against *me*, but what is as much of an objection against *them;* for we both hold the same thing. It is agreed on all hands, that adult persons, actually admitted to communion in the visible church, however they may behave themselves so as to bring their spiritual state into suspicion, yet ought not to be *cast out*, unless they are obstinate in *heresy* or *scandal;* lest, while we go about to root out the *tares*, we should root out the *wheat* also. And it is also agreed on all hands, that when those represented under the name of *tares* bring forth such evil fruit, such scandalous and obstinate wickedness, as is plainly and visibly inconsistent with the being of true grace, they ought to be *cast out*. And therefore it is impossible that this objection should be any thing to the purpose.

Answ. 2. I think this parable, instead of being a just objection *against* the doctrine I maintain, is on the contrary a clear evidence *for* it.

For (1.) the parable shows plainly, that if any are introduced into the field of the householder, or church of Christ, who prove to be not *wheat*, (*i. e.* not true saints,) they are brought in *unawares*, or contrary to design. If *tares* are as properly to be *sown* in the field, as is the *wheat*, which must be the case if the Lord's supper be a *converting* ordinance; then surely no care ought to be taken to introduce *wheat* only, and no respect ought to be had more to the qualities of *wheat* in sowing the field, than the qualities of *tares;* nor is there any more impropriety in the *tares* having a place there, than the *wheat*. But this surely is altogether inconsistent with the scope of the parable.

(2.) This parable plainly shows, that those who are in the visible church, have at first a *visibility*, or appearance to human sight of *true grace*, or of the nature of true saints. For it is observed, *tares* have this property, that when they first appear, and till the products of the field arrive to some maturity, they have such a resemblance of *wheat*, that it is next to impossible to *distinguish* them.

OBJECT. VII.

Christ himself administered the Lord's supper to Judas, whom he knew at the same time to be *graceless;* which is a full evidence, that grace is not *in itself* a requisite qualification in order to coming to the Lord's supper; and if it be not requisite in itself, a *profession* of it cannot be requisite.

Answ. 1. It is to me apparent, that Judas was not present at the administration of the Lord's supper. It is true, he was present at the passover, and *dipped with Christ in the* paschal *dish*. The three former evangelists do differ in the order of the account they give of this *dipping in the dish*.—Luke gives an account of it *after* his account of the Lord's supper, Luke xxii. 21. But Matthew and Mark both give an account of it *before*. (Matt. xxvi. 23. Mark xiv. 20.) And the like might be shown in other instances of these three evangelists differing one from another in the *order* of their narratives; one places those things in his history after others, which another places first. These sacred historians do not undertake to declare precisely the *date* of every incident, but regard more the truth of facts, than the order of time. However, in the present case, the nature of the thing speaks for itself, and shows, that *Judas's dipping with Christ in the dish*, or *his hand being with Christ on the table*, or *receiving a sop dipped in the dish*, must be in that order wherein Matthew and Mark place it in their history, *viz.* at the *passover*, antecedent to the Lord's supper. For there is no such thing in the Lord's supper as *dipping of sops*, and *dipping together in the dish;* but there was in the passover, where all had their hands together in the dish, and dipt their sops in the bitter sauce. None of these three evangelists give us any account of the time when Judas went out: but John—who is vastly more particular as to what passed that night, and is every where more exact as to the order of time than the other evangelists—is very precise as to the time, *viz.* that *Jesus when he gave him the sop*, at the same time sent him away, bidding him *do quickly what he intended to do;* and accordingly *when he had received the sop, he went immediately out*, John xiii. 27—30. Now this sop being at the *passover*, it is evident he was not present at the *Lord's supper* which followed. Many of the best expositors are of this opinion, such as Van Mastricht, Dr. Doddridge, and others.

Answ. 2. If Judas was there, I deny the consequence. As I have observed once and again concerning the Lord's dealings with his people under the Old Testament, so under the New the same observation takes place. Christ did not come to *judge the secrets of men*, nor did ordinarily act in his external dealings with his disciples, and in the administration of ordinances, as the *Searcher of hearts;* but rather as the Head of the visible church, proceeding according to what was exhibited in profession and visibility; herein setting an example to his ministers, who should stand in his place when he was gone, and act in his name in the administration of ordinances. Judas had made the same profession of regard to his Master, and of forsaking all for him, as the other disciples: and therefore Christ did not openly renounce him till he himself had destroyed his profession and visibility of saintship, by public scandalous apostacy. Supposing then the presence of Judas at the Lord's supper, this affords no consequence in favour of what I oppose.

Answ. 3. If they with whom I have to do in this controversy, are not contented with the answers already given, and think there is a remaining difficulty in this matter lying against *my scheme*, I will venture to tell them, that this difficulty lies full as hard against *their own scheme;* and if there be any strength at all in the argument, it is to all intents of the same strength against the need of those *qualifications* which they themselves suppose to be necessary in order to an approach to the Lord's table. For although they do not think renewing saving grace necessary, yet they suppose *moral seriousness* or (as they variously speak) *moral sincerity* in religion to be necessary. They suppose it to be requisite, that persons should have some kind of serious principle and view in coming to the Lord's table; some intention of subjecting themselves to Christ, and of seeking and serving him, in general; and in particular some religious end in coming to the sacramental supper, some religious respect to Christ in it. But now did not Christ at that time perfectly know, that Judas had none of these things? He knew he had nothing of *sincerity* in the christian religion, or of regard to *Christ* in that ordinance, of any sort whatsoever; he knew, that *Satan* had *entered into him* and filled his heart, and that he was then cherishing in himself a malignant spirit against his Master, excited by the reproof Christ had lately given him, (compare John xii. 8. with Matt. xxvi. 8—16. and Mark xiv. 4—11.) and that he had already formed a traitorous, murderous design against him, and was now in the prosecution of that bloody design, having actually just before been to the chief priests, and agreed with them to *betray* him for thirty pieces of silver. (See Matt. xxvi. 14, 15, 16. Mark xiv. 10, 11. Luke xxii. 3—6. and John xiii. 2.) Christ knew these things, and knew that Judas was utterly unqualified for the *holy* sacrament of the Lord's supper; though it had not yet been made known to the church, or the disciples.—Therefore it concerns those on the contrary part in this controversy, to find out some solution of this difficulty, as much as it does me; and they will find they have as much need to take refuge in the solution already given, in one or other of the two preceding answers to this objection.

By the way I would observe, that Christ's not excluding Judas from the passover, under these circumstances, *knowing* him to be thus *unqualified*, without so much as *moral sincerity*, &c. is another thing that effectually enervates all the strength of the objection against me, from the *passover*. For Judas did not only in common with others fall under God's strict command, in the law of Moses, to keep this feast, without any exception of his case there to be found; but *Christ* himself, with his own hand, gave him the *sop*, a part of the paschal feast; even although at the same instant he had in view the man's secret wickedness and hypocrisy, the traitorous design which was then in his heart, and the horrid conspiracy with the chief priests, which he had already entered into, and was now prosecuting. This was then in Christ's mind, and he intimated it to him, at the same moment when he gave him the sop, saying, "What thou doest, do quickly." This demonstrates, that the objection from the *passover* is no stronger argument against my scheme, than the scheme of those whom I oppose; because it is no stronger against the necessity of *sanctifying grace*, the qualification for christian sacraments, which I insist upon, than it is against the necessity of *moral seriousness* or *sincerity*, the qualification which they insist upon.

OBJECT. VIII.

If *sanctifying grace* be a requisite qualification in order to due access to christian sacraments, God would have given some *certain rule*, whereby those who are to admit them, might know whether they have such grace, or not.

ANSW. This objection was obviated in my stating the question. However, I will say something further to it in this place; and would observe, that if there be any strength in this objection, it lies in the truth of this proposition, *viz. That whatever qualifications are requisite in order to persons' due access to christian sacraments, God has given some* certain rule, *whereby those who admit them, may know whether they have those qualifications, or not.* If this proposition is not true, then there is no force at all in the argument. But I dare say, there is not a divine, nor Christian of common sense, on the face of the earth, that will assert and stand to it, that this proposition is true. For none will deny, that some sort of belief of the being of a God, some sort of belief that the Scriptures are the word of God, that there is a future state of rewards and punishments, and that Jesus is the Messiah, are qualifications requisite in order to a due access to christian sacraments; and yet God has given those who are to admit persons no *certain rule*, whereby they may know whether they *believe* any one of these things. Neither has he given his ministers or churches any *certain rule*, whereby they may know whether any person that offers himself for admission to the sacrament, has any degree of *moral sincerity, moral seriousness* of spirit, or any inward moral qualification whatsoever. These things have all their existence in the soul, which is out of our neighbour's view. Not therefore a *certainty*, but a *profession* and *visibility*, of these things, must be the rule of the church's proceeding; and it is as good and as reasonable a rule of judgment concerning *saving grace*, as it is concerning any other internal invisible qualifications, which cannot be certainly known by any but the subject himself.

OBJECT. IX.

If *sanctifying grace* be requisite to a due approach to the Lord's table, then no man may come but he that *knows* he has such grace. A man must not only *think* he has a right to the Lord's supper, in order to his lawful partaking of it; but he must *know* he has a right. If nothing but *sanctification* gives him a *real right* to the Lord's supper, then nothing short of the *knowledge* of sanctification gives him a *known right* to it: only an *opinion* and *probable hopes* of a right will not warrant his coming.

ANSW. 1. I desire those who insist on this as an invincible argument, to consider calmly whether they themselves ever *did*, or ever *will*, stand to it. For here these two things are to be observed:

(1.) If no man may warrantably come to the Lord's supper, but such as *know* they have a *right*, then no *unconverted* persons may come unless they not only *think*, but *know*, it is the *mind of God*, that unconverted persons should come, and *know* that he does not require *grace* in order to their coming. For unless they know that men may come *without grace*, they cannot *know* that they themselves have a *right* to come, *being without grace*. And will any one assert and stand to it, that of necessity all adult persons, of every age, rank, and condition of life, must be so versed in this controversy, as to have a certainty in this matter, in order to their coming to the Lord's supper? It would be most absurd for any to assert it to be a point of easy proof, the evidence of which is so clear and obvious to every one of every capacity, as to supersede all occasion for their being studied in divinity, in order to a certainty of its truth, that persons may come to the sacred table of the Lord, notwithstanding they *know* themselves to be *unconverted!* Especially considering, that the contrary to this opinion has been in general the judgment of protestant divines and churches, from the Reformation to this day; and that the most of the greatest divines that have ever appeared in the world, who have spent their lives in the diligent prayerful study of divinity, have been fixed in the reverse of that opinion. This is sufficient at least to show, that this opinion is not so plain as not to be a disputable point; and that the evidence of it is not so obvious to persons of the lowest capacity and little inquiry, as that all may come to a certainty in the matter, without difficulty and without study. I would humbly ask here, What has been the case in fact in *our* churches, who have practised for so many years on this principle? Can it be pretended, or was it ever supposed, that the communicants in general, even persons of mean intellects and low education, not excepting the very boys and girls of sixteen years old, that have been taken into the church, had so studied divinity, as not only to *think*, but *know*, that our pious forefathers, and almost all the protestant and christian divines in the world, have been in an *error* in this matter? And have people ever been taught the *necessity* of this previous knowledge? Has it ever been insisted upon, that before persons come to the Lord's supper, they must look so far into the case of a *right* to the Lord's supper, as to come not only to a full settled opinion, but even *certainty*, in this point? And has any one minister or church in their admissions ever proceeded on the supposition, that all whom they took into communion were so versed in this controversy, as this comes to? Has it ever been the manner to examine them as to their thorough acquaintance with this particular controversy? Has it been the manner to put by those who had only an opinion and not a certainty; even as the *priests* who could not find their *register*, were put by, till the matter could be determined by Urim and Thummim? And I dare appeal to every minister, and every member of a church that has been concerned in admitting communicants, whether they ever imagined, or it ever entered into their thought, concerning each one to whose admission they have consented, that they had looked so much into this matter, as not only to have settled their *opinion*, but to be arrived to a proper *certainty?*

(2.) I desire it may be remembered, that the venerable author of the *Appeal to the Learned*, did in his ministry ever teach such doctrine from whence it will unavoidably follow, that no one *unconverted* man in the world can *know* he has a warrant to come to the Lord's supper. For if any unconverted man has a warrant to worship his Maker in this way, it must be because God has given him such warrant by the revelation of his mind in the Holy Scriptures. And therefore if any unconverted man not only *thinks, but knows*, he has a warrant from God, he must of consequence, not only *think*, but *know*, that the Scriptures are the word of God. But I believe all that survive of the stated hearers of that eminent divine, and all who were acquainted with him, well remember it to be a doctrine which he often taught and much insisted on, that no natural man *knows* the Scripture to be the word of God; that although such may *think* so, yet they do not *know* it; and that at best they have but a *doubtful opinion*: and he often would express himself thus; *No natural man is thoroughly convinced, that the Scriptures are the word of God; if they were convinced, they would be gained.* Now if so, it is impossible any natural man in the world should ever *know*, it is his right, in his present condition, to come to the Lord's supper. True, he may *think* it is his right, he may have that *opinion*: but he cannot *know* it; and so must not come, according to this argument. For it is only the *word of God* in the Holy Scriptures, that gives a man a *right* to worship the Supreme Being in this sacramental manner, and to come to him in this way, or any other, as one in covenant with him. The Lord's supper being no branch of natural worship, reason without institution is no ground of duty or right in this affair. And hence it is plainly impossible for those that do not so much as *know* the Scriptures are the word of God, to *know* they have any good ground of duty or right in this matter. Therefore, supposing unconverted men have a real right, yet since they have no *known* right, they have no warrant (according to the argument before us) to take and use their right; and what good then can their right do them? Or how can they excuse themselves from presumption, in claiming a *right*, which they do not *know* belongs to them?—It is said, a *probable hope* that persons are regenerate, will not warrant them to come; if they come, they take a liberty to do that which they do not *know* God gives them leave to do, which is horrible presumption in them. But if this be good arguing, I may as well say, a *probable opinion* that unregenerate men may communicate, will not warrant such to do it. They must have *certain knowledge* of this; else their *right* being uncertain, they run a dreadful venture in coming.

ANSW. 2. Men are liable to doubt concerning their *moral sincerity*, as well as saving grace. Suppose an unconverted man, sensible of his being under the reigning power of sin, was about to appear solemnly to *own the covenant*, (as it is commonly called,) and to profess to give up himself to the service of God in an universal and persevering obedience; and suppose at the same time he knew, that if he sealed this profession at the Lord's supper, without *moral sincerity*, (supposing him to understand the meaning of that phrase,) he should *eat and drink judgment* to himself; and if accordingly, his conscience being awakened, he was *afraid of God's judgment;* in this case, I believe, the man would be every whit as liable to doubts about his *moral sincerity*, as godly men are about their gracious sincerity. And if it be not matter of fact, that natural men are so often exercised and troubled with doubts about their *moral sincerity*, as godly men are about their regeneration, I suppose it to be owing only to this cause, *viz.* that godly men being of more tender consciences than those under the dominion of sin, are more afraid of God's judgments, and more ready to tremble at his word. The divines on the other side of the question, suppose it to be requisite, that communicants should believe the fundamental doctrines of religion *with all their heart*, (in the sense of Acts viii. 37.) the doctrine of *Three Persons and one God*, in particular. But I think there can be no reasonable doubt, that natural men—who have so weak and poor a kind of faith in these mysteries—if they were indeed as much afraid of the terrible consequences of their being deceived in being not *morally sincere* in their profession of the truth, as truly gracious men are wont to be of delusion concerning their experience of a work of grace—or whether they are evangelically sincere in choosing God for their portion—the former would be as frequently exercised with doubts in the one case, as the latter in the other. And I very much question, whether any divine on the other side of the controversy would think it necessary, that natural men in professing those things should mean that they *know* they are *morally sincere*, or intend any more than that they trust they have that sincerity, so far as they know their own hearts. If a man should come to them, proposing to join with the church, and tell them, though indeed he was something afraid whether he believed the doctrine of the Trinity *with all his heart*, (meaning in a moral sense,) yet that he had often *examined* himself as to that matter with the utmost impartiality and strictness he was capable of, and on the whole he found reasons of probable hope, and his preponderating thought of himself was, that he was *sincere* in it; would they think such an one ought to be rejected, or would they advise him not to come to the sacrament, because he did not certainly *know* he had this sincerity, but only *thought* he had it?

ANSW. 3. If we suppose sanctifying grace requisite in order to be properly qualified, according to God's word, for an attendance on the Lord's supper; yet it will not follow, that a man must *know* he has this qualification, in order to his being capable of *conscientiously* attending it. If he *judges* that he has it, according to the best light he can obtain, on the most careful examination, with the improvement of such helps as he can get, the advice of his pastor, &c. he may be bound in *conscience* to attend. And the reason is this; Christians partaking of the Lord's supper is not a matter of mere *claim*, or *right* and *privilege*, but a matter of *duty* and *obligation;* being an affair wherein God has a *claim* and *demand on us*. And as we ought to be careful, on the one hand, that we proceed on good grounds in taking to ourselves a privilege, lest we take what we have no good claim to; so we should be equally careful, on the other hand, to proceed on good grounds in what we withhold from another, lest we do not withhold that from him which is his due, and which he justly challenges from us. Therefore in a case of this complex nature, where a thing is both a matter of *right* or *privilege* to us, and also a matter of *obligation* to another, or a *right* of his from us, the danger of proceeding *without* right and truth is equal both ways; and consequently, if we cannot be absolutely sure either way, here the best judgment we can form, after all proper endeavours to know the truth, must govern and determine us; otherwise we shall designedly do that whereby, according to our own judgment, we run the greatest risk; which is certainly contrary to reason. If the question were only what a man has a *right to*, he might forbear till he were sure: but the question is, not only whether *he* has right to attend the supper, but whether *God* also has not a right to his attendance there? Supposing it were merely a privilege which I am allowed but not commanded, in a certain *specified case*, then, supposing I am uncertain *whether that be the case with me or no*, it will be safest to abstain. But supposing I am not only forbidden to take it, unless that be the case with me, but positively commanded and required to take it, if that be the case in fact, then it is equally dangerous to *neglect* on uncertainties, as to *take* on uncertainties. In such a critical situation, a man must act according to the best of his judgment on his case; otherwise he wilfully runs into that which he thinks the greatest danger of the two.

Thus it is in innumerable cases in human life. I shall give one plain instance: A man ought not to take upon him the work of the *ministry*, unless *called* to it in the providence of God; for a man has no right to *take this honour to himself, unless called of God.* Now let us suppose a young man, of a liberal education, and well accomplished, to be at a loss whether it is the will of God that he should follow the work of the ministry; and he examines himself, and examines his circumstances, with great seriousness and solemn prayer, and well considers and weighs the appearances in divine providence: and yet when he has done all, he is not come to a proper certainty, that God calls him to this work; but however, it looks so to him, according to the best light he can obtain, and the most careful judgment he can form: now such an one appears *obliged in conscience* to give himself to this work. He must by no means neglect it under a notion that he must not *take this honour to himself*, till he *knows* he has a *right* to it; because, though it be indeed a *privilege*, yet it is not a matter of *mere* privilege, but a matter of duty too; and if he neglects it *under these circumstances*, he neglects what, according to his own best judgment, he *thinks* God requires of him, and calls him to; which is to sin against his *conscience*.

As to the case of the *priests*, that could not find their

register, (Ezra ii.) alleged in *the Appeal to the Learned*, p. 64. it appears to me of no force in this argument; for if those *priests* had never so great *assurance* in themselves of their pedigree being good, or of their being descended from *priests*, and should have *professed* such assurance, yet it would not have availed. Nor did they abstain from the *priesthood*, because they wanted satisfaction themselves, but they were subject to the judgment of the *Sanhedrim*. God had never made any profession of the parties themselves, but the visibility of the thing, and evidence of the fact to their own eyes, as the rule to judge of the qualification; this matter of *pedigree* being an external object, ordinarily within the view of man; and not any qualification of heart. But this is not the case with regard to requisite qualifications for the *Lord's supper*. These being many of them internal invisible things, seated in the mind and heart, such as the *belief* of a Supreme Being, &c. God has made a credible *profession* of these things the rule to direct in admission of persons to the ordinance. In making this profession they are determined and governed by their own judgment of themselves, and not by any thing within the view of the church.

OBJECT. X.

The natural consequence of the doctrine which has been maintained, is the bringing multitudes of persons of a *tender conscience* and true piety into great *perplexities*; who being at a loss about the state of their souls, must needs be as much in suspense about their duty: and it is not reasonable to suppose, that God would order things so in the revelations of his will, as to *bring his own people into such perplexities*.

ANSW. 1. It is for *want* of the like tenderness of conscience which the godly have, that the other doctrine which insists on *moral sincerity*, does not naturally bring those who are received to communion on those principles, into the same *perplexities*, through their doubting of their *moral sincerity*, of their believing mysteries *with all their heart*, &c. as has been already observed. And being *free* from perplexity, only through *stupidity* and hardness of heart, is *worse* than being in the greatest perplexity through tenderness of conscience.

ANSW. 2. Suppposing the doctrine which I have maintained, be indeed the doctrine of *God's word*, yet it will not follow, that the *perplexities* true saints are in through doubting of their state, are effects owing to the *revelations of God's word*. Perplexity and distress of mind, not only on occasion of the Lord's supper, but innumerable other occasions, is the natural and unavoidable consequence of true Christians *doubting of their state*. But shall we therefore say, that all these perplexities are owing to the *word of God?* No, it is not owing to God, nor to any of his revelations, that true saints ever doubt of their state; his revelations are plain and clear, and his rules sufficient for men to determine their own condition by. But, for the most part, it is owing to their own *sloth*, and giving way to their *sinful* dispositions. Must God's institutions and revelations be answerable for all the perplexities men bring on themselves, through their own negligence and unwatchfulness? It is wisely ordered that the saints should escape perplexity in no other way than that of great strictness, diligence, and maintaining the lively, laborious, and self-denying exercises of religion.

It might as well be said, it is unreasonable to suppose that God should order things so as to bring his own people into such perplexities, as doubting saints are wont to be exercised with, in the sensible approaches of *death*; when their doubts tend to vastly greater *perplexity*, than in their approaches to the Lord's table. If Christians would more thoroughly *exercise themselves unto godliness*, labouring always to *keep a conscience void of offence both towards God and towards man*, it would be the way to have the comfort and taste the sweetness of religion. If they would *so run, not as uncertainly; so fight, not as they that beat the air;* it would be the way for them to escape perplexity, both in ordinances and providences, and to rejoice and enjoy God in both.—Not but that doubting of their state sometimes arises from other causes, besides want of watchfulness; it may arise from melancholy, and some other peculiar disadvantages. But however, it is not owing to God's revelations nor institutions; which, whatsoever we may suppose them to be, will not prevent the perplexities of *such* persons.

ANSW. 3. It appears to me reasonable to suppose, that the doctrine I maintain, if *universally* embraced by God's people—however it might be an accidental occasion of *perplexity* in many instances, through their own infirmity and sin—would, on the whole, be a happy occasion of much more *comfort* to the saints than trouble, as it would have a tendency, on every return of the Lord's supper, to put them on the strictest examination and trial of the state of their souls, agreeable to that rule of the apostle, 1 Cor. xi. 28. The *neglect* of which great duty of frequent and thorough *self-examination*, seems to be one main cause of the darkness and perplexity of the saints, and the reason why they have so little comfort in ordinances, and so little comfort in general.—Mr. Stoddard often taught his people, that *assurance* is *attainable*, and that those who are true saints might know it, if they would; *i. e.* if they would use proper means and endeavours in order to it.—And if so, then certainly it is not just, to charge those perplexities on *God's institutions*, which arise through *men's negligence;* nor would it be just on the supposition of God's institutions being such as I suppose them to be.

OBJECT. XI.

You may as well say, that unsanctified persons may not attend *any* duty of divine worship whatsoever, as that they may not attend the Lord's supper; for all duties of worship are *holy* and *require holiness*, in order to an acceptable performance of them, as well as that.

ANSW. If this argument has any foundation at all, it has its foundation in the supposed truth of the following *propositions, viz. Whosoever is qualified for admission to one duty of divine worship, is qualified for admission to all;* and *he that is unqualified for one, and may be forbidden one, is unqualified for all, and ought to be allowed to attend none.* But certainly these propositions are not true. There are many *qualified* for some duties of worship, and may be *allowed* to attend them, who yet are *not* qualified for some others, nor by any means to be admitted to them. As every body grants, the unbaptized, the excommunicated, heretics, scandalous livers, &c. may be admitted to hear the *word* preached; nevertheless they are not to be allowed to come to the Lord's supper. Even excommunicated persons remain still under the law of the Sabbath, and are not to be forbidden to observe the Lord's day. Ignorant persons, such as have not knowledge sufficient for an approach to the Lord's table, yet are not excused from the duty of prayer: they may pray to God to instruct them, and assist them in obtaining knowledge. They who have been educated in Arianism and Socinianism, and are not yet brought off from these fundamental errors, and so are by no means to be admitted to the Lord's supper, yet may pray to God to assist them in their studies, and guide them into the truth, and for all other mercies which they need. Socrates, that great Gentile philosopher, who worshipped the true God, as he was led by the light of nature, might pray to God, and he attended his duty when he did so; although he knew not the revelation which God had made of himself in his word. That great philosopher, Seneca, who was contemporary with the apostle Paul, held one Supreme Being, and had in many respects right notions of the divine perfections and providence, though he did not embrace the gospel, which at that day was preached in the world: yet might pray to that Supreme Being whom he acknowledged. And if his brother Gallio at Corinth, when Paul preached there, had prayed to this Supreme Being to guide him into the truth, that he might know whether the doctrine Paul preached was true, he therein would have acted very becoming a reasonable creature, and any one would have acted unreasonably in forbidding him;

but yet surely neither of these men was qualified for the christian sacrament. So that it is apparent there is and ought to be a *distinction* made between duties of worship, with respect to qualifications for them; and that which is a sufficient qualification for admission to one duty, is not so for all. And therefore the position is not true, which is the foundation whereon the whole weight of this argument rests. To say, that although it be true there ought to be a distinction made, in admission to duties of worship, with regard to some qualifications, yet sanctifying grace is not one of those qualifications that make the difference; would be but giving up the argument, and a perfect begging the question.

It is said, there can be *no reason* assigned, why unsanctified persons may attend *other* duties of worship, and not the *Lord's supper*. But I humbly conceive this must be an inadvertence. For there is a reason very obvious from that necessary and very notable *distinction* among duties of worship, which follows:

1. There are *some duties* of worship, that imply a *profession of God's covenant;* whose very nature and design is an exhibition of those vital active principles and inward exercises, wherein consists the *condition of the covenant of grace,* or that union of soul to God, which is the union between Christ and his spouse, entered into by an inward hearty consenting to that covenant. Such are the christian *sacraments,* whose very design is to make and confirm a *profession* of compliance with that covenant, and whose very nature is to exhibit or express the uniting acts of the soul: those sacramental duties therefore cannot be attended by any whose hearts do not really consent to that covenant, and whose souls do not truly close with Christ, without either their being self-deceived, or else wilfully making a false profession, and lying in a very aggravated manner.

2. There are *other duties,* which are *not* in their own nature an exhibition of a *covenant-union* with God, or of any compliance with the condition of the *covenant of grace;* but are the expression of *general virtues,* or virtues in their largest extent, including both special and common. Thus *prayer,* or asking mercy of God, is in its own nature *no* profession of a compliance with the *covenant* of grace. It is an expression of some belief of the being of a God, some sense of our wants, and of a need of God's help, some sense of our dependence, &c. but not merely such a sense of these things as is spiritual and saving. Indeed there are some prayers proper to be made by *saints,* and many things proper to be expressed by them in prayer, which imply the profession of a spiritual union of heart to God through Christ; but such as no heathen, no heretic, nor natural man whatever, can or ought to make. Prayer in general, and asking mercy and help from God, is no more a profession of consent to the *covenant* of grace, than reading the Scriptures, or meditation, or performing any duty of morality and natural religion. A Mahometan may as well ask mercy, as hear instruction: and any natural man may as well express his desires to God, as hear when God declares his will to him. It is true, when an unconverted man prays, the *manner* of his doing it is sinful: but when a natural man, knowing himself to be so, comes to the Lord's supper, the very *matter* of what he does, in respect of the profession he there makes, and his pretension to lay hold of God's covenant, is a *lie,* and a lie told in the most solemn manner.

In a word, the venerable Mr. Stoddard himself, in his *Doctrine of Instituted Churches,* has taught us to distinguish between *instituted* and *natural* acts of religion: the *word* and prayer he places under the head of moral duty, and considers as *common* to all; but the *sacraments,* according to what he says there, being *instituted,* are of *special* administration, and must be *limited* agreeable to the institution.

OBJECT. XII.

The Lord's supper has a proper *tendency* to promote men's *conversion,* being an affecting representation of the greatest and most important things of God's word: it has a proper *tendency* to awaken and humble sinners; here being a discovery of the terrible anger of God for sin, by the infliction of the curse upon Christ, when sin was imputed to him; and the representation here made of the dying love of Christ has a *tendency* to draw the hearts of sinners from sin to God, &c.

Answ. Unless it be an evident truth, that *what the Lord's supper may have tendency to promote, the same it was appointed to promote,* nothing follows from this argument. If the argument affords any consequence, the consequence is built on the *tendency* of the Lord's supper. And if the consequence be good and strong on this foundation, as drawn from such premises, then wherever the *premises hold,* the *consequence* holds; otherwise it must appear, that the *premises* and *consequence* are not connected. And now let us see how it is in *fact.* Do not *scandalous* persons need to have these very effects wrought in their hearts which have been mentioned? Yes, surely; they need them in a special manner: they need to be awakened; they need to have an affecting discovery of that terrible wrath of God against sin, which was manifested in a peculiar manner by the terrible effects of God's wrath in the sufferings of his own incarnate Son. Gross sinners need this in some respect more than others. They need to have their hearts broken by an affecting view of the great and important things of God's word. They need especially to fly to Christ for refuge, and therefore need to have their hearts drawn. And seeing the *Lord's supper* has so great a *tendency* to promote these things, if the consequence from the *tendency* of the Lord's supper, as inferring the end of its *appointment,* be good, then it must be a consequence also well inferred, that the Lord's supper was appointed for the reclaiming and bringing to repentance *scandalous* persons.

To turn this off, by saying, *Scandalous persons are expressly forbid,* is but giving up the argument, and begging the question. It is giving up the argument; since it allows the *consequence* not to be good. For it allows, that notwithstanding the proper *tendency* of the Lord's supper to promote a design, yet it may be the Lord's supper was not appointed with a view to promote that end.—And it is a begging the question; since it supposes, that *unconverted men are not evidently forbidden,* as well as scandalous persons; which is the thing in controversy. If they be *evidently* forbid, that is as much to reasonable creatures (who need nothing but good evidence) as if they were *expressly* forbidden.—To say here, that the *Lord's supper is a converting ordinance only to orderly members,* and that *there is another ordinance appointed for bringing scandalous persons to repentance,* this is no solution of the difficulty; but is only another instance of yielding up the argument, and begging the question. For it plainly concedes, that the *tendency* of an ordinance does not prove it *appointed* to all the ends, which it seems to have a tendency to promote; and also supposes, that there is not any *other* ordinance, appointed for converting sinners that are moral and orderly in their lives, *exclusive of this,* which is the thing in question.

It is at best but very precarious arguing from the seeming *tendency* of things, to the *divine appointment,* or God's will and disposition with respect to the *use* of those things. Would it not have had a great *tendency* to convince the scribes and Pharisees, and to promote their conversion, if they had been admitted into the mount when Christ was *transfigured?* But yet it was not the will of Christ, that they should be admitted there, or any other but Peter, James, and John. Would it not have had a very great *tendency* to convince and bring to repentance the unbelieving Jews, if they had been allowed to see and converse freely with Christ after his *resurrection,* and see him *ascend* into heaven? But yet it was the will of God, that none but *disciples* should be admitted to these privileges. Might it not have had a good *tendency,* if *all* that were sincere followers of Christ, women as well as men, had been allowed to be *present* at the institution of the *Lord's supper?* But yet it is commonly thought, none were admitted beside the *apostles.*

Indeed the ever honoured author of the *Appeal to the Learned* has supplied me with the true and proper answer to this objection, in the following words, p. 27, 28. " The efficacy of the Lord's supper does depend upon the blessing of God. *Whatever* TENDENCY *ordinances have in their* OWN NATURE *to be serviceable* to men, yet they will not prevail any further than God doth bless them. "The weapons of our warfare are mighty through God," 2 Cor. x. 4. It is God that teaches men to profit, and makes them profitable and serviceable to men's souls. There is reason to hope for a divine blessing on the *Lord's supper*, when it is administered to those that it *ought* to be administered to; God's *blessing* is to be expected in God's *way*. If men act according to their own humours and fancies, and do not keep in the way of *obedience*, it is presumption to expect God's blessing, Matt. xv. 9. "In vain do they worship me, teaching for doctrines the commandments of men." But when *they* are admitted to the Lord's supper that *God would have to be* admitted, there is ground to hope that he will make it profitable."

OBJECT. XIII.

All that are members of the *visible church* and in the *external covenant*, and neither ignorant nor scandalous, are commanded to perform all *external covenant duties;* and particularly they are commanded to attend the *Lord's supper*, in those words of Christ, *This do in remembrance of me.*

ANSW. This argument is of no force, without first taking for granted the very thing in question. For this is plainly supposed in it, that however these commands are given to such as are in the *external covenant*, yet they are given *indefinitely*, but with exceptions and reserves, and do not immediately reach *all* such; they do not reach those who are *unqualified*, though they be in the *external covenant*. Now the question is, *Who* are these that are *unqualified?* The objection supposes, that only *ignorant* and *scandalous* persons are so. But *why* are they only supposed unqualified; and not *unconverted* persons too? *Because* it is taken for granted, that these are *not* unqualified. And thus the grand point in question is supposed, instead of being proved. Why are these limitations only singled out, *neither ignorant nor scandalous;* and not others as well? The answer must be, because these are *all* the limitations which the Scripture makes: but this now is the very thing in question. Whereas, the business of an argument is to *prove*, and not to suppose, or to take for granted, the very thing which is to be proved.

If it be here said, It is with good reason that those who are *ignorant* or *scandalous* alone are supposed to be excepted in God's command, and obligations of the *covenant;* for the covenant spoken of in the objection, is the *external covenant*, and this requires only *external duties;* which alone are what lie within the reach of man's *natural power*, and so in the reach of his *legal power:* God does not command or require what men have no natural power to perform, and which cannot be performed before something else, some antecedent duty, is performed, which antecedent duty is not in their natural power.

I reply, Still things are but *supposed*, which should be proved, and which want confirmation.

(1.) It is *supposed*, that those who have *externally* (*i. e.* by oral profession and promise) entered into God's covenant, are thereby obliged to no more than the external duties of that covenant: which is not proved, and I humbly conceive, is certainly not the true state of the case. They who have *externally* entered into God's covenant, are by external profession and engagements entered into that one only *covenant of grace*, which the Scripture informs us of; and therefore are obliged to fulfil the duties of *that* covenant, which are chiefly *internal*. The children of Israel, when they *externally* entered into covenant with God at mount Sinai, promised to perform all the duties of the covenant, to obey all the *ten commandments* spoken by God in their hearing, and written in tables of stone, which were therefore called *The Tables of the Covenant;* the sum of which ten commands was, *to love the Lord their God with all their heart, and with all their soul, and to love their neighbour as themselves;* which principally at least are *internal* duties. In particular, they promised *not to covet;* which is an *internal* duty.—They promised to *have no other god before the Lord;* which implied, that they would in their hearts regard no other being or object whatever above God, or in equality with him, but would give him their supreme respect.

(2.) It is *supposed*, that God does not *require impossibilities* of men, in this sense, that he does not require those things of them which are out of their *natural* power, and particularly that he does not require them to be *converted*. But this is not proved; nor can I reconcile it with the tenor of the scripture revelation. And the chief advocates for the doctrine I oppose, have themselves abundantly asserted the contrary. The venerable author fore-mentioned, as every body knows, that knew him, always taught, that God justly requires men to be *converted*, to repent of their sins, and turn to the Lord, to close with Christ, and savingly to believe in him; and that in refusing to accept of Christ and turn to God, they disobeyed the divine *commands*, and were guilty of the most heinous sin; and that their moral *inability* was no excuse.

(3.) It is *supposed*, that God does not command men to do those things which are not to be done till *something else* is done, that is not within the reach of men's *natural ability*. This also is not proved; nor do I see how it can be true, even according to the principles of those who insist on this objection. The fore-mentioned memorable divine ever taught, that God commandeth natural men without delay to *believe* in Christ: and yet he always held, that it was impossible for them to believe till they had by a *preceding* act submitted to the *sovereignty* of God; and yet he held, that men never could do this of *themselves*, till humbled and bowed by powerful convictions of God's Spirit. Again, he taught, that God commandeth natural men to *love* him with all their heart: and yet he held, that this could not be till men had first *believed* in Christ; the exercise of love being a fruit of faith; and believing in Christ, he supposed not to be within the reach of man's *natural* ability. Further, he held, that God requireth of all men holy, spiritual, and acceptable *obedience;* and yet that such obedience is not within the reach of their *natural ability;* and not only so, but that there must first be *love* to God, before there could be new obedience, and that this love to God is not within the reach of men's *natural ability*. Yet, before this love there must be *faith*, which faith is not within the reach of man's *natural power;* and still, before faith there must be the *knowledge* of God, which knowledge is not in *natural* men's reach: and, once more, even before the knowledge of God there must be a thorough *humiliation*, which humiliation men could not work in themselves by any natural power of their own. Now, must it needs be thought, notwithstanding all these *unreasonable* things, that God should *command* those whom he has nourished and brought up, to honour him by giving an open testimony of *love* to him; only because wicked men cannot *testify* love till they *have* love, and love is not in their *natural power?* And is it any good *excuse* in the sight of God, for one who is under the highest obligations to him, and yet refuses him suitable honour by openly *testifying* his love of him, to plead that he has no love to testify; but on the contrary, has an infinitely unreasonable hatred? God may most reasonably require a proper testimony and profession of love to him; and yet it may also be reasonable to suppose, at the same time, he forbids men to lie; or to declare that they have love, when they have none: because, though it be supposed, that God requires men to testify love to him, yet he requires them to do it in a right way, and in the true order, *viz.* first *loving* him, and then *testifying* their love.

(4.) I do not see how it can be true, that a natural man has not a *legal* power to be converted, accept of Christ, love God, &c. By a *legal power* to do a thing, is plainly meant such power as brings a person properly within the reach of a *legal obligation*, or the obligation of a law or command to do that thing. But he that has such natural faculties, as render him a proper subject of moral government, may properly be *commanded*, and put under the obligation of a *law* to do things so reasonable; notwithstanding any native aversion and moral inability in him to do his duty, arising from the power of sin. This also, I must observe, was a known doctrine of Mr. Stoddard's, and what he ever taught.

OBJECT. XIV.

Either *unsanctified* persons may lawfully come to the Lord's supper, or it is unlawful for them to *carry themselves as saints;* but it is not unlawful for them to carry themselves as saints.

Answ. It is the duty of unconverted men both to *become* saints, and to behave as saints. The scripture rule is, *Make the tree good, that the fruit may be good.* Mr. Stoddard himself never supposed, that the fruit of *saints* was to be expected from men, or could possibly be brought forth by them in truth, till they *were* saints.

And I see not how it is true, that unconverted men ought, in *every* respect, to do those *external* things, which it is the duty of a godly man to do. It is the duty of a godly man, conscious of his having given his heart unto the Lord, to profess his love to God and his esteem of him above all, his unfeigned faith in Christ, &c. and in his closet-devotions to thank God for these graces as the fruit of the Spirit in him. But it is not the duty of another that really has no faith, nor love to God, to do thus. Neither any more is it a natural man's duty to profess these things in the *Lord's supper.*—Mr. Stoddard taught it to be the duty of converts, on many occasions, to profess their faith and love and other graces *before men*, by relating their *experiences* in conversation: but it would be great wickedness, for such as know themselves to be not *saints*, thus to do; because they would speak falsely, and utter lies in so doing. Now, for the like reason, it would be very sinful, for men to profess and seal their *consent* to the covenant of grace in the *Lord's supper,* when they know at the same time that they do *not* consent to it, nor have their *hearts* at all in the affair.

OBJECT. XV.

This scheme will *keep out* of the church some *true saints;* for there are some such who determine against themselves, and their prevailing judgment is, that they are *not* saints: and we had better let in several hypocrites, than exclude one true child of God.

Answ. I think, it is much better to insist on some *visibility* to reason, of *true saintship*, in admitting members, even although this, through men's infirmity and darkness, and Satan's temptations, be an occasion of some true saints abstaining; than by express liberty given, to open the door to as many as please, of those who have *no visibility* of real saintship, and make no profession of it, nor pretension to it; and that because this method tends to the ruin and great reproach of the christian church, and also to the ruin of the persons admitted.

1. It tends to the *reproach* and *ruin* of the christian *church.* For *by the rule which God hath given for admissions, if it be carefully attended,* (it is said,) MORE *unconverted than converted persons, will be admitted.* It is then *confessedly* the way to have the greater part of the members of the christian church *ungodly* men; yea, so much greater, that the godly shall be but *few* in comparison of the ungodly; agreeable to their interpretation of that saying of Christ, *many are called, but few are chosen.* Now, if this be an exact state of the case, it will demonstrably follow, on scripture principles, that opening the door so wide has a direct tendency to bring into christian churches such as are without even *moral sincerity*, and do not make religion at all their business, neglecting and casting off secret prayer and other duties, and living a life of carnality and vanity, so far as they can, consistently with avoiding *church-censures;* which possibly may be sometimes to a great degree. Ungodly men may be morally sober, serious, and conscientious, and may have what is called *moral sincerity*, for a while; and even may have these things in a considerable measure, when they first come into the church: but if their hearts are not changed, there is no probability at all of these things continuing long. The Scripture has told us, that this *their goodness* is apt to vanish *like the morning cloud and early dew.* How can it be expected but that their religion should in a little time *wither away*, when it has *no root?* How can it be expected, that the *lamp* should burn long, without *oil in the vessel* to feed it? If *lust* be unmortified, and left in reigning power in the heart, it will sooner or later prevail; and at length sweep away *common grace* and *moral sincerity*, however excited and maintained for a while by conviction and temporary affections. It will happen to them according to the *true proverb, The dog is returned to his vomit; and the swine that was washed, to his wallowing in the mire.* It is said of the hypocrite, *Will he delight himself in the Almighty? Will he always call upon God?*—And thus our churches will be likely to be such congregations as the psalmist said he *hated*, and *would not sit with.* Psal. xxvi. 4, 5. "I have not sat with vain persons, nor will I go in with dissemblers; I have hated the congregation of evil-doers, nor will I sit with the wicked."—This will be the way to have the Lord's table ordinarily furnished with such guests as allow themselves to live in known sin, meeting together only to crucify Christ afresh, instead of commemorating his crucifixion with the repentance, faith, gratitude, and love of friends. And this is the way to have the governing part of the church such as are not even conscientious men, and are careless about the honour and interest of religion. And the direct tendency of that is, in process of time, to introduce a prevailing negligence in discipline, and carelessness in seeking ministers of a pious and worthy character. And the next step will be, the church being filled with persons openly vicious in manners, or else scandalously erroneous in opinions. It is well if this be not already the case in fact with some churches that have long professed and practised on the principles I oppose. And if these principles should be professed and proceeded on by christian churches every where, the natural tendency of it would be, to have the greater part of what is called the church of Christ, through the world, made up of vicious and erroneous persons. And how greatly would this be to the reproach of the christian church, and of the holy name and religion of Jesus Christ in the sight of all nations!*

And now is it not better, to have a few real living Christians kept back through darkness and scruples, than to open a door for letting in such universal ruin as this? To illustrate it by a familiar comparison; Is it not better, when England is at war with France, to keep out of the British realm a few loyal Englishmen, than to give leave for as many treacherous Frenchmen to come in as please?

2. This way tends to the eternal ruin of the *parties admitted;* for it lets in such, yea, it persuades such to come in, as *know themselves to be impenitent and unbelieving*, in a dreadful manner to *take God's name in vain; in vain to worship him,* and abuse sacred things, by performing those external acts and rites in the name of God, which are instituted for declarative signs and professions of repentance toward God, faith in Christ, and love to him, at the same time that *they know* themselves destitute of those things which they profess to have. And is it not better, that some *true saints*, through their own weakness and misunderstanding, should be kept away from the Lord's table, which will not keep such out of heaven, than voluntarily to bring in multitudes of *false professors* to partake unworthily, and in effect to seal their own condemnation.

OBJECT. XVI.

You *cannot keep out hypocrites,* when all is said and done; but *as many* graceless persons will be likely to get

* And this by the way answers another *objection*, which some have made, *viz.* That the way I plead for, tends to keep the church of Christ *small*, and hinder the growth of it. Whereas, I think, the contrary tends to keep it small, as it is the wickedness of its members, that above all things in the world prejudices mankind against it; and is the chief stumbling-block, that hinders the propagation of Christianity, and so the growth of the christian church. But holiness would cause the light of the church to shine so as to induce others to resort to it.

into the church in the way of a *profession of godliness*, as if nothing were insisted on, but a freedom from public *scandal*.

ANSW. It may possibly be so in some places through the misconduct of ministers and people, by remissness in their inquiries, carelessness as to the proper matter of a profession, or setting up some mistaken rules of judgment; neglecting those things which the Scripture insists upon as the most essential articles in the character of a *real saint;* and substituting others in the room of them; such as impressions on the imagination, instead of renewing influences on the heart; pangs of affection, instead of the habitual temper of the mind; a certain method and order of impressions and suggestions, instead of the nature of things experienced, &c. But to say, that in churches where the nature, the notes, and evidences of *true Christianity*, as described in the Scriptures, are well understood, taught, and observed, *there* as many *hypocrites* are likely to get in; or to suppose, that *there* as many persons of an honest character, who are well instructed in these rules, and well conducted by them—and judging of themselves by these rules, do think themselves true saints, and accordingly make profession of godliness, and are admitted as saints in a judgment of rational charity—are likely to be carnal, unconverted men, as of those who make no such pretence and have no such hope, nor exhibit any such evidences to the eye of a judicious charity, is not so much an objection against the doctrine I am defending, as a reflection upon the Scripture itself, with regard to the rules it gives, either for persons to judge of their own state, or for others to form a charitable judgment, as if they were of little or no service. We are in miserable circumstances indeed, if the rules of God's holy word in things of such infinite importance, are so ambiguous and uncertain, like the heathen oracles. And it would be very strange, if in these days of the gospel, when God's mind is revealed with such great plainness of speech, and the canon of Scripture is completed, it should ordinarily be the case in fact, that those who, having a right doctrinal understanding of the Scripture, and judging themselves by its rules, do probably conclude or seriously hope of themselves, that they are real saints, are *as many* of them in a state of sin and condemnation, as others who have no such rational hope concerning their good estate, nor pretend to any special experiences in religion.

OBJECT. XVII.

If a *profession of godliness* be a thing required in order to admission into the church, there being some *true saints* who *doubt* of their state, and from a *tender conscience* will not dare to make such a profession; and there being *others*, that have no grace, nor much tenderness of conscience, but great *presumption* and *forwardness*, who will boldly make the highest profession of religion, and so will get admittance: it will hence come to pass, that the very thing, which will in effect procure for the *latter* an admission, rather than the former, will be their *presumption* and *wickedness*.

ANSW. 1. It is no sufficient objection against the *wholesomeness* of a rule established for regulating the *civil* state of mankind, that in *some* instances men's *wickedness* may take *advantage* by that *rule*, so that even their *wickedness* shall be the very thing, which, by an abuse of that rule, procures them temporal *honours* and *privileges*. For such is the present state of man in this evil world, that good rules, in many instances, are liable to be thus abused and perverted. As for instance, there are many human laws, accounted wholesome and necessary, by which an accused or suspected person's own solemn profession of *innocency*, upon *oath*, shall be the condition of acquittance and impunity; and the want of such a protestation or profession shall expose him to the punishment. And yet, by an abuse of these rules, in some instances, nothing but the horrid sin of *perjury*, or that most presumptuous wickedness of false swearing, shall be the very thing that acquits a man: while another of a more tender conscience, who *fears an oath*, must suffer the penalty of the law.

2. Those rules, by all wise lawgivers, are accounted wholesome, which prove of *general* good tendency, notwithstanding any bad consequences arising in some particular instances. And as to the ecclesiastical rule now in question, of admission to sacraments on a *profession of godliness*, when attended with requisite circumstances; although in particular instances it may be an occasion of some *tender-hearted* Christians *abstaining*, and some *presumptuous* sinners being *admitted*, yet that does not hinder but that a proper *visibility* of holiness to the eye of reason, or a *probability* of it in a judgment of rational christian charity, may this way be maintained, as the proper qualification of candidates for admission. Nor does it hinder but that it may be reasonable and wholesome for mankind, in their outward conduct, to regulate themselves by such probability; and that this should be a reasonable and good rule for the church to regulate themselves by in their admissions; notwithstanding it may happen in particular instances, that things are *really* diverse from, yea the very reverse of, what they are *visibly*. Such a *profession* as has been insisted on, when attended with *requisite circumstances*, carries in it a rational credibility in the judgment of christian charity: for it ought to be attended with an honest and sober character, and with evidences of good doctrinal knowledge, and with all proper, careful, and diligent instructions of a prudent pastor. And though the pastor is not to act as a *searcher of the heart*, or a *lord of conscience* in this affair, yet that hinders not but that he may and ought to inquire particularly into the experiences of the souls committed to his care and charge, that he may be under the best advantages to instruct and advise them, to apply the teachings and rules of God's word unto them, for their self-examination, to be *helpers of their joy*, and promoters of their salvation. However, finally, not any pretended extraordinary skill of *his* in discerning the heart, but the person's *own* serious profession concerning what he finds in his own soul, after he has been well instructed, must regulate the public conduct with respect to him, where there is no other external visible thing to contradict and overrule it. And a serious profession of godliness, under these circumstances, carries in it a visibility to the eye of the church's rational and christian judgment.

3. If it be still insisted on, that a *rule* of admission into the church cannot be *good*, if liable to such *abuse* as that forementioned, I must observe, This will overthrow the rules that the *objectors* themselves go by in their admissions. For they insist upon it, that a man must not only have knowledge and be free of scandal, but must appear *orthodox* and profess the common faith. Now *presumptuous lying*, for the sake of the honour of being in the church, having children baptized, and voting in ecclesiastical affairs, may possibly be the very thing that brings some men into the church by this rule; while greater *tenderness of conscience* may be the very thing that keeps others out. For instance, a man who secretly in his mind gives no credit to the commonly received doctrine of the *Trinity*, yet may, by pretending an assent to it, and in hypocrisy making a public profession of it, get into the church; when at the same time another that equally disbelieves it, but has a more tender conscience than to allow himself in solemnly telling a lie, may by that very means be kept off from the communion.

OBJECT. XVIII.

It seems hardly reasonable to suppose, that the only wise God has made men's *opinion of themselves*, and a *profession* of it, the term of their admission to church-privileges; when we know, that very often the *worst* men have the *highest* opinion of themselves.

ANSW. 1. It must be granted me, that in fact this is the case, if any proper *profession* at all is expected and required, whether it be of *sanctifying grace*, or of *moral sincerity*, or any thing else that is *good:* and to be sure, nothing is *required* to be professed, or is *worthy* to be professed, any further than it is *good*.

ANSW. 2. If *some* things, by the confession of all, must be *professed*, *because* they are *good*, and of great importance; then certainly it must be very unreasonable, to say, that those things wherein true *holiness* consists are *not* to be professed, or that a profession of them should *not* be required, because they are *good*, even in the highest degree, and infinitely the most important and most necessary things of any in the world. And it is unreasonable to say, that it is the less to be expected we should profess sincere friendship to Christ, *because* friendship to Christ is the most *excellent* qualification of any whatsoever, and the contrary the most odious. How absurd is it to say this, merely under a notion that for a man to *profess* what is so good and so reasonable, is to profess a *high opinion of himself!*

ANSW. 3. Though some of the *worst* men are apt to entertain the *highest opinion of themselves*, yet their self-conceit is no *rule* to the church; but the apparent *credibility* of men's *profession* is to be the ground of ecclesiastical proceedings.

OBJECT. XIX.

IF it be necessary that *adult* persons should make a profession of godliness, in order to their own admission to *baptism*, then undoubtedly it is necessary in order to their *children* being baptized on their account. For parents cannot convey to their children a right to this sacrament by virtue of any qualifications *lower* than those requisite in order to their own right: children being admitted to baptism only as being, as it were, parts and members of their parents. And besides, the act of parents in offering up their *children* in a sacrament, which is a seal of the *covenant of grace*, is in them a solemn attending that sacrament *as* persons *interested* in the covenant, and a public manifestation of their approving and consenting to it, as truly as if they then offered up *themselves* to God in that ordinance. Indeed it implies a renewed offering up themselves with their children, and devoting both jointly to God in covenant; *themselves*, with their children, as *parts of themselves*. But now what fearful work will such doctrine make amongst us! We shall have multitudes *unbaptized*, who will be without the external badge of Christianity, and so in that respect will be like heathens. And this is the way to have the land full of persons who are destitute of that which is spoken of in Scripture as ordinarily requisite to men's *salvation;* and it will bring a *reproach* on vast multitudes, with the families they belong to. And not only so, but it will tend to make them profane and heathenish; for by thus treating our children, as though "they had no part in the Lord, *we shall* cause them to cease from fearing the Lord;" Josh. xxii. 24, 25.

ANSW. 1. As to children being *destitute* of that which is spoken of in Scripture as one thing ordinarily *requisite to salvation ;* I would observe, that *baptism* can do their souls no good any otherwise than through God's *blessing* attending it: but we have no reason to expect his blessing with baptism, if administered to those that it does *not* belong to by *his institution.*

ANSW. 2. As to the *reproach*, which will be brought on parents and children, by children going without baptism, through the parents neglecting a profession of godliness, and so visibly remaining among the unconverted; if any insist on this objection, I think it will savour of much *unreasonableness* and even *stupidity*.

It will savour of an *unreasonable* spirit. Is it not enough, if God freely offers men to own their children and to give them the honour of baptism, in case the parents will turn from sin and relinquish their enmity against him, heartily give up themselves and their children to him, and take upon them the profession of godliness?—If men are truly *excusable*, in not turning to God through Christ, in not believing with the heart, and in not confessing with the mouth, why do not we openly plead that they are so? And why do we not teach sinners, that they are *not to blame* for continuing among the enemies of Christ, and neglecting and despising his great salvation? If they are not at all excusable in this, and it be wholly owing to their own indulged lusts, that they refuse sincerely to give up themselves and their children to God, then how unreasonable is it for them to complain that their children are denied the honour of having God's mark set upon them as some of his? If parents are angry at this, such a temper shows them to be very insensible of their own vile treatment of the blessed God. Suppose a prince send to a traitor in prison, and upon opening the prison doors make him the offer, that if he would come forth and submit himself to him, he should not only be pardoned himself, but both he and his children should have such and such badges of honour conferred upon them; and yet the rebel's enmity and stoutness of spirit against his prince is such, that he cannot find in his heart to comply with the gracious offer, will he have any cause to be angry, that his children have not those badges of honour given them? Besides, it is very much owing to *parents*, that there are so many *young* people who can make no profession of godliness. They have themselves therefore to blame, if proceeding on the principles which have been maintained, there is like to rise a generation of unbaptized persons. If ancestors had thoroughly done their duty to their posterity in instructing, praying for, and governing their children, and setting them good examples, there is reason to think, the case would have been far otherwise.

Insisting on this objection would savour of much *stupidity*. For the objection seems to suppose the country to be full of those that are *unconverted*, and so exposed every moment to eternal damnation; yet it seems we do not hear such great and general complaints and lamentable outcries concerning this. Now why is it looked upon so dreadful, to have great numbers going without the *name* and honourable *badge* of Christianity, when at the same time it is no more resented and laid to heart, that such multitudes go without the *thing*, which is infinitely more dreadful? Why are we so silent about this? What is the *name* good for, without the *thing?* Can parents bear to have their children go about the world in the most odious and dangerous state of soul, in reality the children of the devil, and condemned to eternal burnings; when at the same time they cannot bear to have them disgraced by going without the honour of being *baptized?* A high honour and privilege this is; yet how can parents be contented with the *sign*, exclusive of the *thing* signified? Why should they covet the external honour for their children, while they are so careless about the spiritual blessing? Does not this argue a senselessness of their own misery, as well as of their children's, in being in a *Christless* state? If a man and his child were both together bitten by a viper, dreadfully swollen, and like to die, would it not argue *stupidity* in the parent, to be anxiously concerned only about his child's having on a dirty garment in such circumstances, and angry at others for not putting some outward ornament upon it? But the difference in this present case is infinitely greater, and more important. Let parents pity their poor children because they are without baptism; and pity themselves who are in danger of everlasting misery, while they have no interest in the covenant of grace, and so have no right to covenant favours and honours, for themselves nor children. No religious honours, to be obtained in any other way than by real religion, are much worth contending for. And in truth, it is no honour at all to a man, to have merely the outward *badges* of a Christian, without *being* a Christian indeed; any more than it would be an honour to a man that has no learning, but is a mere dunce, to have a degree at college; or than it is for a man who has no valour, but is a grand coward, to have an honourable commission in an army; which only serves, by lifting him up, to expose him to deeper reproach, and sets him forth as the more notable object of contempt.

ANSW. 3. Concerning the *tendency* of this way of confining baptism to professors of godliness and their children, to promote *irreligion* and *profaneness;* I would observe, *first*, That *Christ* is best able to *judge* of the tendency of his own *institutions*. *Secondly*, I am bold to say, that supposing this principle and practice to have such a tendency, is a great *mistake*, contrary to Scripture and plain reason and experience. Indeed such a tendency it would have, to shut men out from *having any part in the Lord,* (in the sense of the two tribes and half, Josh. xxii. 25.) or to fence them out by such a partition-wall as formerly was between Jews and Gentiles; and so to shut them out as to tell them, if they were never so much disposed to serve God, he was not ready to accept them; according to the notion the Jews seem to have had of the uncircumcised Gentiles.—But to forbear giving men honours to which they have no title, and not to compliment them with the name and badge of God's people and children, while they pretend to nothing but what is consistent with their being his enemies, this has no such tendency. But the contrary has very much this tendency. For is it not found by constant experience through all ages, that blind, corrupt mankind, in matters of religion, are strongly disposed to rest in a *name* instead of the *thing;* in the shadow, instead of the substance; and to make themselves easy with the former, in the neglect of the latter? This over-valuing of common grace, and *moral sincerity,* as it is called; this building so much upon them, making them the conditions of enjoying the seals of God's covenant, and the appointed privileges, and honourable and sacred badges, of God's children; this, I cannot but think, naturally tends to sooth and flatter the pride of vain man, while it tends to aggrandize those things in men's eyes, which they of themselves are strongly disposed to magnify and trust in, without such encouragements to prompt them to it, yea, against all discouragements and dissuasives that can possibly be used with them.

This way of proceeding greatly tends to establish the negligence of *parents,* and to confirm the stupidity and security of wicked *children.*—If *baptism* were *denied* to all children, whose parents did not *profess godliness,* and in a judgment of rational charity appear *real saints,* it would tend to excite pious heads of families to more thorough care and pains in the religious education of their children, and to more fervent prayer for them, that they might be converted in *youth,* before they enter into a married state; and so if they have children, the entail of the covenant be secured.—And it would tend to awaken *young* people themselves, as yet unconverted, especially when about to settle in the world. Their having no right to christian privileges for their children, in case they should become parents, would tend to lead them at such a time seriously to reflect on their own awful state; which, if they do not get out of it, must lay a foundation for so much calamity and reproach to their families. And if after their becoming *parents,* they still remain unconverted, the melancholy thought of their children going without so much as the external mark of Christians, would have a continual tendency to affect them with their own sin and folly in neglecting to turn to God, by which they bring such visible calamity and disgrace on themselves and families. They would have this additional motive continually to stir them up to seek grace for themselves and their children. Whereas, the contrary practice has a natural tendency to quiet the minds of persons, both in their own and their children's unregeneracy. Yea, may it not be suspected, that the way of baptizing the children of such as never make any proper profession of godliness, is an expedient originally invented for that very end, to give ease to ancestors with respect to their posterity, in times of general declension and degeneracy?

This way of proceeding greatly tends to establish the stupidity and irreligion of *children,* as well as the negligence of parents. It is certain, that unconverted parents do never truly give up their children to God; since they do not truly give up themselves to him. And if neither of the parents appear truly pious, in the judgment of rational charity, there is not in this case any ground to expect that the children will be *brought up in the nurture and admonition of the Lord,* or that they will have any thing worthy the name of a christian education, how solemnly soever the parents may promise it. The faithfulness of Abraham was such as might be trusted in this matter. See Gen. xviii. 19. But men that are not so much as visibly godly, upon what grounds are they to be trusted? How can it be reasonably expected, that they should faithfully bring up their children for GOD, who were never sincerely willing that their children or themselves should be his? And it will be but presumption, to expect that those children who are never given up to God, nor brought up for him, should prove religious, and be God's children. There is no manner of reason to expect any other than that such children ordinarily will grow up in irreligion, whether they are baptized or not. And for persons to go about with the name and visible seal of God, and the sacred badge of Christianity upon them, having had their bodies, by a holy ordinance, consecrated to God as his temples, yet living in irreligion and ways of wickedness; this serves to tend exceedingly to harden them, and establish in them an habitual contempt of sacred things. Such persons, above all men, are like to be the most hardened and abandoned, and reclaimed with most difficulty: as it was with the wicked Jews, who were much more confirmed in their wickedness, than those heathen cities of Tyre and Sidon. To give that which is holy to those who are profane, or whom we have no reason, from the circumstances of parentage and education, to expect will be otherwise, is not the way to make them better, but worse. It is the way to have them habitually *trample* holy things *under their feet,* and increase in contempt of them, yea, even to *turn again and rend us,* and be more mischievous and hurtful enemies of that which is good, than otherwise they would be.

OBJECT. XX.

Some *ministers* have been greatly *blessed* in the other way of proceeding, and some men have been *converted at the Lord's supper.*

ANSW. Though we are to eye the providence of God, and not disregard his *works,* yet to interpret them to a sense, or to apply them to an use, inconsistent with the scope of the *word* of God, is a misconstruction and misapplication of them. God has not given us his *providence,* but his *word,* to be our governing *rule.* God is sovereign in his dispensations of providence; he bestowed the blessing on Jacob, even when he had a lie in his mouth. He was pleased to meet with Solomon, and make known himself to him, and bless him in an extraordinary manner, while he was worshipping in a *high place.* He met with Saul, when in a course of violent opposition to him, and out of the way of his duty in the highest degree, going to Damascus to persecute Christ; and even then bestowed the greatest blessing upon him, that perhaps ever was bestowed on a mere man. The conduct of Divine Providence, with its reasons, is too little understood by us, to be improved as our rule. "God has his way in the sea, his path in the mighty waters, and his footsteps are not known: and he gives none account of any of his matters." But God has given us his *word,* to this very end, that it might be our *rule;* and therefore has so ordered it that it may be understood by us. And strictly speaking, this is our *only* rule. If we join any thing else to it, as making it our *rule,* we do that which we have no warrant for, yea, that which God himself has forbidden. See Deut. iv. 2. Prov. xxx. 6. And with regard to God's blessing and succeeding ministers, have not some had remarkable experience of it in the way which I plead for, as well as some who have been for the way I oppose? However, we cannot conclude, that God sees nothing at all *amiss* in ministers, because he *blesses* them. In general, he may see those things in them which are very right and excellent; these he approves and regards, while he overlooks and pardons their mistakes in opinion or practice, and, notwithstanding these, is pleased to crown their labours with his blessing.

As to the two last arguments in the *Appeal to the Learned,* concerning the subjects of the christian sacraments, their being members of the *visible church,* and not the *invisible;* the force of those arguments depends entirely on the resolution of this question, Who are *visible saints?* or what adult persons are regularly admitted to the privileges of members of the *visible church?* Which question has already been largely considered; and, I think, it has been demonstrated that they are those who exhibit a credible profession and visibility of *gospel holiness* or vital piety, and not merely of *moral sincerity.* So that there is no need of further debating the point in this place.

I might here mention many things not yet noticed, which some object as *inconveniences* attending the scheme I have maintained. If men should set up their own wit and wisdom in opposition to God's revealed will, there is no end of objections of this kind, which might be raised against any of God's institutions. Some have found great fault even with the *creation* of the world, as being very inconveniently done, and have imagined that they could tell how it might be mended in a great many respects. But however God's altar may appear homely to us, yet if we lift up our hand to mend it, we shall pollute it. Laws and institutions are given for the *general good*, and not to avoid every particular inconvenience. And however it may so happen, that sometimes inconveniences (real or imaginary) may attend the scheme I have maintained; yet, I think, they are in no measure equal to the manifest conveniences and happy tendencies of it, or to the palpable inconveniences and pernicious consequences of the other.—I have already mentioned some things of this aspect, and would here briefly observe some others.

Thus, the way of making such a difference between outward duties of *morality* and *worship*, and those great inward duties of our *love of God* and *acceptance of Christ*, that the former must be *visible*, but that there need be *no exhibition* nor *pretence* of the latter, in order to persons being admitted into the visible family of God; and that under a notion of the latter being *impossibilities*, but the other being *within men's power;* this, I think, has a direct tendency to confirm in men an *insensibility* of the heinousness of unbelief and enmity against God our Saviour, which are the source and sum of all wickedness. It tends to prevent their coming under an humbling *conviction* of the greatness and utter inexcusableness of these sins, which men must be brought to if ever they obtain salvation. Indeed it is a way that not only has this tendency, but has actually and apparently this effect, and that to a great degree.

The effect of this method of proceeding in the churches in New England, which have fallen into it, is actually this.—There are some that are received into these churches under the notion of their being in the judgment of rational charity *visible saints* or *professing saints,* who yet at the same time are actually open *professors* of heinous *wickedness;* I mean, the wickedness of living in known impenitence and unbelief, the wickedness of living in enmity against God, and in the rejection of Christ under the gospel. Or, which is the same thing, they are such as freely and frequently acknowledge, that they do not profess to be as yet *born again*, but look on themselves as really *unconverted*, as having never unfeignedly accepted of Christ; and they do either explicitly or implicitly number themselves among those that *love not the Lord Jesus Christ;* of whom the apostle says, let such be *Anathema Maran-atha!* And accordingly it is known, all over the town where they live, that they make no pretensions to any *sanctifying grace* already obtained; nor of consequence are they commonly looked upon as any other than *unconverted* persons. Now, can this be judged the comely *order* of the gospel? or shall God be supposed the *author* of such *confusion?*

In this way of church-proceeding, God's own children and the true disciples of Christ are obliged to receive those as their *brethren*, admit them to the *communion of saints*, and embrace them in the highest acts of christian society, even in their great *feast of love*, where they feed together on the body and blood of Christ, whom yet they have no reason to look upon otherwise than as *enemies of the cross of Christ*, and haters of their heavenly Father and dear Redeemer. For they make no pretension to any thing at all inconsistent with those characters; yea, in many places, as I said before, freely professing this to be actually the case with them.

Christ often forbids the members of his church to *judge one another*. But in this way of ecclesiastical proceeding, it is done continually, and looked upon as no hurt; a great part of those admitted into the church are by others of the same communion judged *unconverted*, *graceless* persons; and it is impossible to avoid it, while we stretch not beyond the bounds of a *rational* charity.

This method of proceeding must inevitably have one of these two consequences: either there must be *no public notice* at all given of it, when so signal a work of grace is wrought, as a sinner being brought to repent and turn to God, and hopefully become the subject of saving conversion; or else this notice must be given in the way of *conversation*, by the *persons themselves*, frequently, freely, and in all companies, declaring their own experiences. But surely, either of these consequences must be very unhappy.—The former is so, *viz.* forbidding and preventing any *public* notice being given on earth of the *repentance of a sinner*, an event so much to the honour of God, and so much taken notice of in *heaven*, causing *joy in the presence of the angels of God*, and tending so much to the advancement of religion in the world. For it is found by experience, that scarce any one thing has so great an influence to awaken sinners, and engage them to seek salvation, and to quicken and animate saints, as the tidings of a sinner's repentance, or hopeful conversion. God evidently makes use of it as an eminent means of advancing religion in a time of remarkable revival. And to take a course effectually to prevent its being notified on earth, appears to me a counteracting of God, in that which he ever makes use of as a chief means of the propagation of true piety, and which we have reason to think he will make use of as one principal means of the conversion of the world in the glorious latter day.—But now as to the *other* way—the way of giving notice to the public of this event, by particular persons *themselves* publishing their own experiences, from time to time and from place to place, on all occasions and before all companies—I must confess, it is a practice that appears to me attended with many inconveniences, yea, big with mischiefs. The abundant trial of this method lately made, and the large experience we have had of the evil consequences of it, is enough to put all sober and judicious people for ever out of conceit with it. I shall not pretend to enumerate all the mischiefs attending it, which would be very tedious; but shall now only mention two things. One is, the bad effect it has upon the persons themselves that practise it, in the great tendency it has to spiritual *pride;* insensibly begetting and establishing an evil habit of mind in that respect, by the frequent return of the temptation, and this many times when they are not guarded against it, and have no time, by consideration and prayer, to fortify their minds. And then it has a very bad effect on the minds of *others* that hear their communication, and so on the state of religion in general, in this way. It being thus the custom for persons of all sorts, young and old, wise and unwise, superiors and inferiors, freely to tell their own experiences before all companies, it is commonly done very *injudiciously*, often very rashly and foolishly, out of season, and in circumstances tending to defeat any good end. Even sincere Christians too frequently in their conversation insist mainly on those things that are no part of their *true spiritual experience;* such as impressions on their imagination, suggestions of facts by passages of Scripture, &c.; in which case *children* and weak persons that hear, are apt to form their notions of religion and true piety by such experimental communications, and much more than they do by the most solid and judicious instructions they hear from the pulpit. This is found to be one of the devices whereby Satan has an inexpressible advantage to ruin the souls of men, and utterly to confound the interest of religion.—This matter of making a public profession of godliness or piety of heart, is certainly a very important affair, and ought to be under some *public regulation*, and under the direction of *skilful guides*, and not left to the management of every man, woman, and child, according to their humour or fancy. And when it is done, it should be done with great seriousness, preparation, and prayer, as a solemn act of public respect and honour to God, in his house and in the presence of his people. Not that I condemn, but greatly approve of, persons speaking sometimes of their religious experiences in private conversation, to proper persons and on proper occasions, with modesty and discretion, when the glory of God and the benefits or just satisfaction of others require it of them.

In a word, the practice of promiscuous admission—or that way of taking all into the *church* indifferently, *as visi-*

ble saints, who are not either ignorant or scandalous—and at the same time that custom taking place of persons publishing their own *conversion* in common *conversation;* where these two things meet together, they unavoidably make *two* distinct kinds of *visible churches,* or different bodies of professing saints, one within another, openly distinguished one from another, as it were by a visible dividing line. One company consisting of those who are *visibly gracious* Christians, and open *professors of godliness;* another consisting of those who are *visibly moral* livers, and only profess common virtues, without pretending to any special and spiritual experiences in their hearts, and who therefore are not reputed to be converts. I may appeal to those acquainted with the state of the churches, whether this be not actually the case in some, where this method of proceeding has been long established. But I leave the judicious reader to make his own remarks on this case, and to determine, whether there be a just foundation in Scripture or reason for any such state of things; which to me, I confess, carries the face of glaring absurdity.

And now I commit this whole discourse (under God's blessing) to the reader's candid reflection and impartial judgment. I am sensible, it will be very difficult for many to be truly impartial in this affair; their prejudices being very great against the doctrine which I have maintained. And, I believe, I myself am the person, who, above all other upon the face of the earth, have had most in my circumstances to prejudice me against this doctrine, and to make me unwilling to receive conviction of its truth. However, the clear evidence of God's mind in his word, as things appear to me, has constrained me to think and act as I have now done. I dare not go contrary to such texts as these, Lev. x. 10. Jer. xv. 19. Ezek. xxii. 26. and xliv. 6—8. And having been fully persuaded in my own mind, as to what is the scripture rule in this matter, after a most careful, painful, and long search, I am willing, in the faithful prosecution of what appears to me of such importance and so plainly the mind and will of God, to resign to his providence, and leave the event in his hand.

It may not be improper to add here, as I have often had suggested to me the probability of my being *answered* from the press: If any one shall see cause to undertake this, I have these reasonable requests to make to him, *viz.* That he would avoid the ungenerous and unmanly artifices used by too many polemic writers, while they *turn aside to vain jangling,* in *carping* at incidental passages, and displaying their wit upon some minute particulars, or less material things, in the author they oppose, with much *exclamation,* if possible to excite the ignorant and unwary reader's disrelish of the author, and to make him appear contemptible, and so to get the victory that way; perhaps dwelling upon, and glorying in, some pretended *inconsistencies* in some parts of the discourse, without ever entering thoroughly into the *merits of the cause,* or closely encountering any of the main arguments. If any one opposes me from the press, I desire he would attend to the true state of the question, and endeavour fairly to take off the force of each argument, by answering the same directly, and distinctly, with calm and close reasoning; avoiding (as much as may be) both dogmatical assertion and passionate reflection. Sure I am, I shall not envy him the applause of a victory over me, however signal and complete, if only gained by superior light and convincing evidence.—I would also request him to set his *name* to his performance, that I may in that respect stand on even ground with him before the world, in a debate wherein the public is to judge between us. This will be the more reasonable, in case he should mingle any thing of accusation with his arguing. It was *the manner* even of the heathen Romans, and reputed by them but just and equal, *to have accusers face to face.*

May the GOD of all grace and peace unite us more in judgment, affection, and practice, that with *one heart,* and *one mouth,* we may glorify his name through *Jesus Christ.* AMEN.

APPENDIX.

Being a LETTER *to the* AUTHOR, *in answer to his request of information concerning the opinion of Protestant Divines and Churches in general, of the Presbyterians in Scotland and Dissenters in England in particular, respecting* FIVE QUESTIONS *that relate to this controversy.*

REV. AND DEAR SIR,

IF you look into Mr. Baxter's controversial writings against Mr. Blake, you will meet with such accounts of principles and facts, as I think may reasonably give an inquirer much satisfaction as to the common judgment of protestant churches and divines in the points you mention. I particularly refer you to his FIVE DISPUTATIONS *of Right to Sacraments, and the true Nature of Visible Christianity;* where all or the most of your *queries* are considered and answered, with a multitude of *testimonies* produced in favour of sentiments contrary to those of your excellent predecessor, the late *Mr. Stoddard.* I have not said this from any disposition to excuse myself from the labour of making some further inquiry, if it be thought needful. And as it may show my willingness to gratify your desire, I will now say something on your *questions* distinctly, but with as much brevity as I can.

QUEST. I. *What is the general opinion respecting that* SELF-EXAMINATION *required in* 1 Cor. xi. 28. *Whether communicants are not here directed to examine themselves concerning the* truth of grace, *or their real godliness?*

ANSW. This construction of the text, as far as I have had opportunity to inquire, appears to me very generally received; if I may judge by what many celebrated *expositors* have said on the place, and by what many famous divines have written in treatises of *preparation* for the Lord's supper, besides what is contained in public *confessions, catechisms, directories,* &c. I think Dr. Reynolds, in his *Meditations on the Lord's Supper,* has summarily expressed the common judgment of Calvinists in these strong lines of his: "The *sacrament* is but a *seal* of the *covenant;* and the covenant essentially includes *conditions;* and the condition on our part is *faith.* No faith, no *covenant;* no covenant, no *seal;* no seal, no *sacrament.*—The *matter* then of this *trial* (says he) must be that *vital qualification,* which predisposeth a man for receiving of these holy mysteries; and that is *faith.*"

However, I may venture to be confident, that Mr. Stoddard's gloss on the text, who tells us in his controverted *sermon,* "The meaning is, that a man must *come solemnly* to that ordinance, *examining what* NEED *he has of it,*" is quite foreign from the current sense of Calvinist writers. And, though he makes a different comment in his *Appeal to the Learned,* saying, "The *examination* called for is, whether they *understood the nature* of the ordinance, that so they may *solemnly consider what they have to do* when they wait upon God in it," neither can I find any appearance of a general consent of the learned and orthodox to this *new gloss,* at least as exhibiting the full meaning of the text. I might easily confront it with numerous authorities: but the *Palatine Catechism,* and that of the *Westminster Assembly,* with the common explanations and catechizings upon them, may be appealed to as *instar omnium.* And I shall only add here, if it be allowed a just expectation that the *candidate* for the communion *examine himself* about the *same* things at least as the *pastor,* to whom he applies for admission, ought to make the subject of his examination, then it was worth while to hear the opinion of those unnamed *ministers in New England,* (among whom the late Dr. Colman, I have reason to think, was the principal,) that answered Dr. Mather's *Order of the Gospel,* (anno 1700,) who, in the *Postscript* to their *Review,* thus express themselves: "*We highly approve*—that the proponant of the Lord's table be *examined* of his baptismal vow; *his sense* of spiritual wants, sinfulness, and wretchedness; *his hope, faith, experiences,* resolutions through the grace of God." This, I think, is something beyond Mr. Stoddard.

Quest. II. *Whether it be the general opinion of those aforesaid, that some who* know *themselves to be* unregenerate, *and under the reigning power of sin,* ought *notwithstanding, in such a state, to come to the Lord's table?*

Answ. I am aware, Sir, though you have seen fit to take no notice of it to me, that Mr. Stoddard (in his *Doctrine of Instituted Churches*) is peremptory in the *affirmative;* but I have met with no author among Calvinists, at home or abroad, consenting with him, unless it be Mr. Blake, and some that were for a promiscuous admission, with little or no limitation. If divines in general, of the Calvinistic character, were for such a latitude as Mr. Stoddard's, what can we suppose to be the reason, that in treating on the *Lord's supper*, they so constantly consider it as one of the *rights of the church, belonging to the truly faithful alone, exclusively of all others?* Why do we hear them declaring, *It is certain that the right of external fellowship resides in the faithful only: and as to the rest, they are in that communion only by accident, and it is also only by accident that they are suffered there; but being what they are, they have not any part in the rights of that society properly belonging to them?* If they thought the sacrament instituted for *conversion*, why do we never find them recommending it as a *converting* ordinance, and urging persons to come to it with that view, who *know* themselves to be in an *unconverted state?* If they thought that any such have a *right before God*, and may come to it *with a good conscience*, why do we find them so solemnly *warning* all that are truly *convinced* of their remaining yet in a *natural* state, to *refrain* coming to the Lord's table in their unbelief and impenitence; as if they judged it a *sinful* and *dangerous* thing for them to come under such circumstances? I know Mr. Stoddard, in his *Appeal*, disputes the *fact*. But it has occurred to me in abundance of instances, while reviewing my authors on this occasion.

Among the foreign protestants in Germany, France, &c. I shall name but two out of many instances before me. The *Heidelberg* or *Palatine Catechism*, which had the solemn approbation of the synod of Dort, and was especially praised by the divines of Great Britain; which has been in a manner universally received and taught, formerly in Scotland, and still all over Holland, and by reason of its excellency has been translated into no less than *thirteen* several languages; this is most express in claiming the *Lord's supper* for a special privilege of such as have *true faith* and *repentance;* and forbidding it to *hypocrites*, as well as scandalous persons, declaring that none such ought to come. See the *eighty-first* and other questions and answers, with Ursin's Latin *Explications*, and De Witte's English *Catechizings* thereon. Here, Sir, indeed you have the judgment of a multitude in one. Another celebrated book is Claude's *Historical Defence of the Reformation;* in which I meet with repeated declarations of the same sentiments, perfectly on the *negative* side of the question in hand, but, I think, too many and too long to be here transcribed.—The language of some of them I have just now had occasion to make use of.

As for the church of Scotland, I find they have adopted the Westminster Confession, Catechisms, and Directory, which debar all *ignorant* and *ungodly* persons from the Lord's table, and require every one to *examine* himself, not only as to his knowledge, but also his *faith, repentance, love, new obedience*, &c.—In their *books of discipline*, I observe sundry passages that appropriate the sacrament to the *truly penitent and faithful*, as the only proper subjects. Their *national covenant*, renewed from time to time, has this clause; to the which [true reformed kirk] we join ourselves willingly, in doctrine, faith, religion, discipline, and use of the holy sacraments, *as lively members* of the same *in Christ* our Head, &c. And among the *divines* of Scotland, I find many in their sermons, sacramental speeches, and other discourses, declaring themselves strongly on the *negative* part in the question before us, advising to strictness in admission to the Lord's supper, renouncing the opinion of its being a *converting ordinance*, inviting only the sincere friends of Christ to it, and frequently *warning* professors conscious of reigning sin and hypocrisy to forbear approaching the Lord's table. I might bring much to this purpose from Mr. Andrew Gray's book of sermons, published anno 1716; and his sermons printed anno 1746; with a preface by Mr. Willison.—So from Mr. Ebenezer Erskine's synodical sermon, anno 1732.—And from Mr. Ralph Erskine's sermon on Isa. xlii. 6. and his discourse on fencing the tables, annexed to his sermon on John xvi. 15.—So from Mr. Willison's synodical sermon, anno 1733; where he sets down a variety of searching questions (no less than twenty-seven) which he advises to be put to proponants, and their answers to be waited for, before they are admitted.—The anonymous author of *a Defence of National Churches against the Independents*, (who is reputed to be Mr. Willison,) asserts it as a presbyterian principle, that none have *right before God* to the complete communion of the church, but such as have *grace;* and that none are to be admitted but those who are *saints*, at least in profession; such as profess to accept of the offers of Christ's grace, &c. and confess themselves to be *sincere*. Mr. Aytone, in his *Review* against Mr. Glas, owns that the Lord's supper is not a formal mean of *conversion*, but of further growth and nourishment to those *already* converted. In the same strain is Mr. Nasmith's *Treatise of the Entail of the Covenant.*—And Mr. Warden's *Essay on Baptism.* In a word, I find Mr. Currie (in his synodical sermon, anno 1732) testifying of the ministers in Scotland, that they are *tender* (*i. e.* circumspect and cautious) *in admitting people to the holy table of the Lord;* knowing the *design* of the ordinance is *not conversion*, but *confirmation;* and he observes, that all who approve themselves to God here, will a thousand times rather choose to have, was it but *one table* or *half* a table of honest communicants, *true believers* and *real saints*, than have a *hundred* tables, by admitting any that are *unworthy*, (or *Christless* souls, as he anon characterizes them,) of whom there are not moral evidences of their *fitness* for this holy ordinance. And for the commendable practice of the church of Scotland, in being *pointed* and *particular* in *debarring* the unworthy from this ordinance, (says he,) God forbid ever it turn into desuetude. I think I may here not unfitly subjoin those remarkable passages in Mr. Anderson's excellent *Defence of the Presbyterians*, against Mr. Rhind; where he informs us, *they look upon this holy ordinance as the common privilege of the faithful;* and therefore they usually fence the Lord's table, in the words of Scripture, 1 Cor. vi. 9. or some such-like. To exclude the *impenitent* from the *privilege* of gospel-mysteries; to debar those from the *Lord's table*, whom the Lord has, by the express sentence of his word, debarred out of the *kingdom of heaven*, is what every one, who is not quite lost in impiety, must own to be not only *lawful*, but a *duty*. Upon which I beg leave to observe, according to this principle I do not see but that a man who with apparent signs of credibility *confesses* himself habitually impenitent, ought to be debarred from the Lord's table: and surely, by parity of reason, he that *knows* himself to be unregenerate, ought to *refrain* coming, since there can be no true repentance without regeneration. I think we have no just grounds to suppose Mr. Stoddard's principle in this matter has hitherto any general prevalence in the church of Scotland.

And now to pass over to England, neither do I find reason to think the *dissenters* there in general are for Mr. Stoddard's latitude. The *Assembly of Divines* pronounce all the *ungodly*, as well as ignorant, *unworthy* of the Lord's table; direct to *preparation* for it, by examining ourselves of our *being in Christ*, &c. And though they declare this sacrament appointed for the relief even of the *weak* and *doubting* Christian, who *unfeignedly* desires to be *found in Christ;* and having directed *such* a one to bewail his unbelief and labour to have his doubts resolved, they assert that *so doing* he may and ought to come to the Lord's supper, to be *further strengthened:* yet I do not find any appearance of a hint, as if others who *know* themselves to be in a natural state, or are conscious of their being certainly graceless, may and ought to come to this ordinance, that they may be *converted*. Nay, they expressly declare of ALL *ungodly* persons, that while they remain such, they *cannot* without great sin against Christ partake of those holy mysteries.—As to particular divines, I find multitudes of them among the dissenters, in later as well as former times, expressing the same sentiments: distinguishing between natural and instituted duties, between initial and confirming means, between special ordinances and common: and declaring the Lord's supper a *disciple-privilege*, peculiar to such as have *disciple-properties*, and admonishing as well the *close hypocrite*, as the more gross, of the *sin and danger* of coming to it in his unregenerate state, impenitent and unbelieving. Thus Mr. Bolton, in his discourse on *the Wedding Supper and the Wedding Garment*, warns the *graceless* not to come to the Lord's supper; affirming, that an *unsanctified presence* will be found as bad as a *profane absence*.—Mr. Baxter, in his *Five Disputations*, has much that runs in the same strain; so in his *Reformed Liturgy*, and in his *Christian Concord*, where we have his brethren joining their testimony with his. Likewise Mr. Charnock, in his discourse of *the Subjects of the Lord's Supper*—Mr. Palmer, in his *Scripture-Rail to the Lord's Table*—Mr. Saunders, in his *Anti-Diatribe*—Mr. Langley, in his *Suspension Reviewed*—Mr. Doolittle, Mr. Henry, Dr. Earle, and others, in their books on the *Lord's Supper*—Mr. Shower, in his *Sacramental Discourses*—Mr. Flavel, in his sermon on *Gospel-Unity*, and other pieces—Mr. Philip Henry, and Mr. Trosse, in the accounts of their *Lives*—Dr. Calamy, in his discourse on *Vows*, and his *Defence of Nonconformity*—Mr. Simon Browne, in the Continuation of *Henry's Exposition*, on 1 Cor. xi. 28—Dr. Harris, in his discourse on *Self-Dedication*—Dr. Jennings, in his sermons to *Young People*.—I could, from all these authors, cite passages much to the purpose: but it would be too tedious. Yet I will give you a few hints from some others.—Dr. Williams, in his *Gospel-Truth Stated*, says, Though a man had it revealed to him that he is one of the *elect*, yet so long as he remains *unregenerate*, he has no right to partake of the Lord's supper.—Dr. Guyse, in his late sermon at Mr. Gibbons's ordination, observes, that men being *church-members* supposes them *already* to have a *good work begun* in them, and to be partakers of christian *love*, even such as proceeds from *faith*, in a prevailing degree; and persons (says he) that have nothing of this, *ought not* to be church-members.—Mr. Hall, in his *Exhortation* on the same occasion, remarks, that the seals of the covenant are to be used as *discriminating* signs of the real separation of true believers from the world; and urges to have the fence kept up, which Christ has set about his church, that it may appear to be a body wholly *distinct* from the world: God's house being erected for the entertainment, not of *hypocrites* and dead sinners, but of the living in Jerusalem.—But says Dr. Watts, in his *Humble Attempt*, it is true, this cannot be practised universally and perfectly here on earth, so as to prevent some *secret* sinners making their way into our separate congregations, and joining with us in the most solemn ordinances; yet he declares such *not really worthy* of any room or place in the house of God.—And in his *Holiness of Times, Places, and People*, the Doctor observes, The *visible* christian church is founded on a *supposition*, that the members of it are, or should appear to be, members of the *invisible*: and *none* (says he) are to be admitted into the *visible* church, or esteemed complete members of it, but those who make such a declaration and profession of their faith in Christ and their avowed subjection to him, as may be supposed in a judgment of charity to manifest them to be real believers, true subjects of his spiritual kingdom, and members of the *invisible* church.—I find Dr. Doddridge in the same sentiments, by what he says in his *Family Expositor*. Thus, on the case of Ananias and Sapphira, he has this note, The *church* is never *happier*, than when the *sons of falsehood* are *deterred* from intruding into it: if its *members* are *less numerous*, it is a sufficient balance, that it is *more pure*. And on Simon's case, he pronounces it to be *in vain* for men to *profess* themselves *Christians*, in vain to submit to *baptism*, &c. if their *heart* be not *right with God*. And *such persons* being admitted to *distinguishing* ordinances, he calls an evil, in the present state of things unavoidable; wishing for the *happy medium*, between *prostituting divine ordinances* by a foolish credulity, and *defrauding the children of the household of their bread*, by a rigorous severity and mistaken caution. He every where represents the Lord's supper as the sacrament of *nutrition*, a reviving and nourishing ordinance; but never that I can find, as a *regenerating* or *converting* one. Upon the case of Judas, the Doctor observes, that if he had truly stated the order of the story, then Judas certainly *went out* before the *Eucharist* was instituted: and indeed one cannot reasonably suppose, Christ would have commanded him to *drink of this cup* as the *blood shed for* him *for the remission of sins*, when he had just before been declaring in effect, that *his* sins should *never* be forgiven.—By which observation, I think, Dr. Doddridge has quite demolished one of the most plausible pleas in favour of the secret and conscious hypocrite's claim to the Lord's supper.

In fine, even those who appear advocates for a latitude in admissions to the communion, I observe, generally in the course of the argument offer such *distinctions*, or make such *concessions*, as seem by fair consequence a giving up of the point, at least as stated in the present question. For they usually distinguish between a right *in foro Dei* and *in foro ecclesiæ*; accordingly treat these as two different questions, *Who ought to come?* and, *Who ought to be admitted?* considering the latter as an *ecclesiastical* case, and here they assert a *latitude*; but the former, as a case of *conscience*, of private reference only, and here they grant a *limitation*. How large soever their principles, while taking the case in its *ecclesiastical* view, yet I have met with very few divines, that taking it as a *private case of conscience*, have gone Mr. Stoddard's length, in asserting, that *some unsanctified men have right before God to the Lord's supper*, and *may come with a good conscience*, yea, *ought to come*, notwithstanding they *know* themselves at the same time to be in a *natural* condition. This he declares in his *Doctrine of Instituted Churches*, and confirms in his *Sermon and Appeal*. But then he has made some *concessions*, which seem to be subversive of his opinion. For he expressly allows, that the *sacrament* by institution supposes communicants to be *visible saints;* and this title of *visible saints* he assigns to "such as have a visible union to Christ, such as are in the judgment of rational charity believers, such as carry themselves so that there is reason to look upon them to be saints." Now, taking the case as a *private case of conscience*, (in which light only Mr. Stoddard professes to have designed to consider it in his sermon, and not at all as an *ecclesiastical* case,) I think, this *visibility of saintship* immediately respects the *proponant* for the Lord's table, and must be referred to his own *private judgment* of himself. But then, how can there be a *visibility of saintship* in the eye of the man's own conscience, when at the same time he *knows* himself to be in a *natural* condition? Or how can a man come to the Lord's table with a good *conscience*, as having *right before God*, while he cannot form so much as a judgment of *rational charity* for himself; seeing he carries so, in the view of his own *conscience*, that he has no *reason* to look on himself to be a *saint*, nay, even *knows* he is still in a natural state, and therefore in the eye of his own impartial judgment is not such a one as the *sacrament* by institution *supposes* the communicant to be? Moreover, Mr. Stoddard, in describing visible saints, inserts into their character *a serious profession of the true religion*, which he sometimes calls *a profession of faith and repentance, morally sincere*: and in his *Doctrine of Instituted Churches*, (p. 19.) he lays down a remarkable *position*, in these words, SUCH A PROFESSION AS BEING SINCERE MAKES A MAN A REAL SAINT, BEING MORALLY SINCERE MAKES A MAN A VISIBLE SAINT. Now according to this, it seems to me, the *profession* itself, whether evangelically or morally sincere, is always of a *uniform tenor;* having one and the same thing for the *matter* of it; and not respecting, in the different cases, a religion *specifically* different, or a faith and repentance of a higher and a lower *kind*. But then it is quite beyond me to comprehend, how a man who *knows* himself to be in a *natural* condition, can be so much as *morally* sincere in his *profession*, while it is in its matter and tenor *such a profession as being* (evangelically) *sincere makes a man a real saint*. For if he *knows* himself to be in a *natural* condition, he then as certainly *knows* he hath not (in the principle or exercise) that *faith and repentance*, which is the just matter of *such a profession:* and how therefore can he be reasonably supposed, with any degree of *moral sincerity*, to make *such a profession*, when for the matter of it, it is the very *same* profession he would make, if he *knew* himself to be a *real saint?* Can a person in any sound gospel sense profess himself a *saint* or *believing penitent*, and herein *speak the truth* with a common *moral honesty*, while yet he *knows* himself to be destitute of all such *characters* in the sight of God and conscience, being still in a *natural* condition, and under the dominion of *unbelief* and *impenitence*? For my own part, I must confess this a difficulty in Mr. Stoddard's scheme, that I am not capable of solving. His favourite hypothesis, I think, must fall, if his *position* stands, and his *concessions* be abode by; which serve clearly to determine the present *question* in the *negative*, agreeable to the general sense of protestant churches and divines.

Quest. III. *Whether it be not the general opinion, that persons admitted to the Lord's table ought to* PROFESS saving faith and repentance; *meaning that faith and repentance, which are the terms of the* covenant of grace?

Answ. I believe, after what has been already offered, we need be at no loss to know the mind of the generality respecting the subject of this inquiry. Were there occasion for it, I could easily produce a *cloud of witnesses*, to evidence that the general opinion is on the *affirmative* side, in this question. Repeated searches have been made by diligent and impartial inquirers, who though of varying judgment and practice in church-discipline, yet agree in their reports: and from them I will give you the following attestations.

Mr. Lob (in his *True Dissenter*) tells us, It is the judgment of all the *Nonconformists*, that nothing less than the *profession* of *saving faith*, credibly significant of the thing professed, gives right to church-communion. And this he declares to be the rule of *all protestants* in general. He brings even Mr. Humphrey (though opposite in judgment) for his voucher: who acknowledges, that the *visible church* is defined by a *profession* of true, regenerate faith, and of no less than that, according to the most *general* opinion of *protestant divines*. He speaks of it as the *common opinion*, that a profession of no less than true grace or justifying faith is the *rule of admission* to the church-sacraments. And though Mr. Humphrey went off from the received opinion, yet could he not come into Mr. Blake's notions in this matter, who also had gone off from it, nor hope for their vindication: hence he makes that challenge, *What man is there, that dares revive Mr. Blake's cause, and defend it against Mr. Baxter's* RIGHT *to sacraments?*

Mr. Baxter in this his book very copiously argues a *profession* of *saving faith*, as the rule of admission to the sacraments, and much insists on its being so by the unanimous consent of judicious divines. He tells us, Mr. Gataker in his books has largely proved this by a multitude of quotations from protestant writers. And he adds his own testimony, repeatedly saying, It is indeed their *most common* doctrine—It is the *common protestant* doctrine. And again, Certain I am, this is the *common* doctrine of reformed divines. He subjoins, I must profess, that I do not know of *any one protestant* divine, reputed orthodox, of the contrary judgment, before Dr. Ward and Mr. Blake, though some papists and Arminians I knew of that mind. And again, (beside Sir Henry Vane,) he says, *All* that I know of, since Dr. Ward, is Mr. Blake, Mr. Humphrey, and one John Timson; and John Timson, Mr. Humphrey, and Mr. Blake. He alleges Mr. Vines, as thus witnessing in the case on his side. To this purpose *all our learned divines* have given their suffrage: I need not authors or churches. It is so plain a case, that I wonder those [of the contrary opinion] have not taken notice of it, *there is an army to a man against them*.

Mr. Langley, in his *Suspension Reviewed*, observes, The *concurrent judgment* of divines, English and foreign, episcopal and presbyterian, that a man of vast and digested reading, the learned Mr. Baxter, hath demonstrated at large in SIXTY *testimonies*; sundry of which have *many* in them, being the judgment of many *churches* and many *learned* men therein; and more might easily be brought. In short, he calls it the *old protestant* doctrine asserted against the *papists*; and wonders at the confidence of the men, who tell us, against our own eyes, that it is a *novelism*.

To these attestations I subjoin that of our Mr. Mitchel, (in his Introduction before the *Defence of the Synod*, 1662,) who while asserting a different latitude of the two sacraments, yet pleads for strictness in admissions to the Lord's table; and testifies, It is most evident, that *godly reforming divines* have in their doctrine *unanimously* taught, and in their practice (many of them) endeavoured, a *strict selection* of those who should be admitted to the *Lord's supper*. I think it may be not improperly observed here, that in a manuscript, drawn up by this eminent person for his own satisfaction, and inserted in the account of his life, he has left his solemn testimony against a lax *mode* of *profession*, (exclusive of all examinations and confessions, of a practical and experimental nature,) as having been found by plentiful experience a *nurse* of *formality* and *irreligion*. At the same time declaring his judgment, with a particular eye to the churches of *New England*, that the *power of godliness* will be *lost*, if only *doctrinal* knowledge and *outward* behaviour come to be accounted sufficient for a title to all church-privileges; and the use of *practical confessions* and *examinations* of men's *spiritual* estate be laid aside. For (says he) that which people see to be publicly required and held in reputation, *that* will they look after, and usually *no more*. In another place he observes, this will not only lose the power of godliness, but in a little time bring in *profaneness* and *ruin the churches*, these two ways. (1.) *Election of ministers* will soon be carried by a formal looser sort. (2.) The exercise of *discipline* will by this means be impossible.—And discipline failing, profaneness riseth like a flood. Agreeably he says elsewhere; Certain it is, that we stand for the *purity* of the churches, when we stand for *such qualifications* as we do, in those whom we would admit to *full communion*; and do withstand those notions and reasonings that would infer a *laxness* therein, which hath apparent *peril* in it. In sum, (says he,) we make account that we shall be near about the *middle-way* of church reformation, if we keep *baptism* within the compass of the *non-excommunicable*, and the *Lord's supper* within the compass of those that have (unto charity) somewhat of the *power* of godliness, or grace in *exercise*. For Mr. Mitchel, as he thought *faith in the special and lively* EXERCISE *thereof* necessary to a safe and comfortable participation of the *Lord's supper*, so he judged an *appearance* of this unto rational charity, judging by *positive sensible* signs and evidences, justly required in order to admission into *full communion*. Whereas, he thought *baptism* annexed to *initial* faith, or faith in the *being* of it; the charitable judgment whereof (says he) runs upon a great *latitude;* and he conceived the same *strictness*, as to outward signs, not necessary unto a charitable probable judgment, or hope of the *being* of faith, which entitles to baptism, as of that *growth* and *special exercise* of faith, which is requisite to the Lord's supper. These are the main *distinctions*, on which he grounded his opinion of a *different* latitude of the two sacraments. For I must observe, as strenuously as he pleads for a various extent, as to the subjects of them, he never supposes any adult regularly admittable to either sacrament, but such as in ecclesiastical reputation sustain the character of *believers;* such as in the account of a rational charity (judging by probable signs) have the being of *regeneration*; or as he variously expresses it, have *true faith*, in the judgment of charity; and do in *some measure* perform the duties of faith and obedience, as to *church-visibility* and *charitable hope;* and therefore are such as the church ought to receive and hold as *heirs of the grace of life*, according to the rules of christian charity. Though it seems Mr. Shepard before him speaks of his *church charity* and *experimental charity;* so Mr. Mitchel had his *positive* charity and his *negative*, and conducted his judgment and administrations accordingly, in admitting persons to the one sacrament or the other. I should not have been so prolix and particular here, but that I thought it might serve to prepare the way for a more easy, short, and intelligible answer to your remaining queries.

Quest. IV. *Whether it be the general opinion of protestant churches and divines, in the case of* adult *persons, that the terms of admission to* both *sacraments are the* same?

Answ. I presume, Sir, the question does not respect a sameness in the *degree* of qualifications, experiences, and evidences; but only a sameness in *kind*, or for the substance and general nature of things. I suppose, you had no view here to any such critical *distinction* as that before mentioned, between an *initial* faith and a *grown* faith; or between the simple *being* of faith, which entitleth to baptism, and the *special exercise* of faith, which fits for the Lord's supper; nor aim at a nice adjustment of the several *characters of visibility*, or *motives of credibility*, in the one case and the other, but only intend in general to inquire, whether persons admittable to one or other sacrament, ought to profess *true justifying faith*, and not be admitted on the profession of any faith of a kind *inferior* and *specifically* different. Now, taking this to be the scope of your question, I have good reason to apprehend, that the *generality* of protestant churches and divines, of the Calvinistic persuasion especially, have declared themselves for the *affirmative*.

I think all that hold the *visible* christian church ought to consist of such as make a *visible and credible profession of faith and holiness*, and *appear to rational charity real members of the church invisible*, (which is the common language of protestants,) are to be understood as in principle exploding the conceit of a conscious unbeliever's right before God to special church-ordinances, and as denying the apparent unbeliever's right before the church to admission, whether to one sacrament or the other. I observe, *Eadem est ratio utriusque sacramenti*, is a maxim (in its general notion) espoused by the several contending parties in this controversy about a right to sacraments.

That a credible profession of saving faith and repentance is necessary to *baptism*, in the case of the adult, I can show, by the authority of Claude's approved *Defence of the Reformation*, to be the general opinion of French protestants; and by the Palatine Catechism, by the Leyden Professors' *Synopsis*, &c. to be the prevailing judgment of the reformed in Germany, Holland, and foreign parts.

And for the *Dissenters in England*, that they are in general of the same judgment, I might prove from the *Assembly of Divines*' Confession, Catechisms, and Directory; and from the Heads of Agreement assented to by the *United Ministers*, formerly distinguished by the names of *Presbyterian* and *Congregational*; as also by a large induction of particular instances among divines of every denomination, would it not carry me to too great a length. I find Mr. Lob (in his *True Dissenter*) assuring us in general, "It is held by the dissenters, that nothing less than the *profession of a saving faith* gives a right to *baptism*." Nor do I see, by their writings of a later date and most in vogue, any just grounds to suppose a general change of sentiments among them. I will mention two or three moderns of distinguished name. Dr. Harris (in his *Self-Dedication*) tells us, The nature of the Lord's supper plainly supposes *faith*; and that none but *real* Christians have right in the sight of God; though a credible *profession* entitles to it in the sight of the church, who cannot know the heart. And he declares it the *same faith*, which qualifies the adult, both for *baptism* and for the *Lord's supper*; there being the same common nature to both sacraments, and the latter only a *recognising* the former. The late Dr. Watts (in his *Holiness of Times, Places, and People*) says, The christian church receives none but upon profession of *true* faith in Christ, and *sincere* repentance; none but those who profess to be members of the *invisible* church, and in a judgment of charity are to be so esteemed. Our *entrance* into it is appointed to be by a visible *profession* of our being *born of God*, of real faith in Christ, of true repentance, and inward holiness. In fine, to name no more, Dr. Doddridge (in his *Family Expositor*, on Acts viii. 37.) supposes a credible *profession* of their *faith in Christ* required of the adult in apostolic times, in order to their being admitted to *baptism*; even such (says he) as implied their cordially subjecting their souls to the gospel, and their being come to a point, so as to give up themselves to Christ *with all their heart*.

And for the church of Scotland, Mr. Anderson, who well understood their principles and practice, assures us, (in his *Defence* of them,) that *presbyterians* will not baptize without a previous profession or sponsion. To the adult (says he) it is not only necessary (as it is also in infants) that they be *internally sanctified*, but also that they make an *outward profession*, of which baptism is the badge and token. To justify this, he observes concerning the *catechumens* in primitive times, that during all that state they were probationers, not only as to their knowledge, but piety; and were obliged, before they could be admitted to *baptism*, to give moral evidences of the *grace of God in their hearts*. And he advances it as a *presbyterian* principle, that *faith* and *repentance* are *prerequired* to baptism, in adult persons at least. By this he points out the true *matter* of baptismal profession: and then in opposition to such as pretend baptism to be a *converting* ordinance, he observes, If they can have *faith* and *repentance* without the *Spirit* and spiritual *regeneration*, which they say is not obtained but *in* and *by baptism*, I do not see why they may not go to *heaven* without the Spirit and spiritual regeneration: for I am sure, *repentance* toward God and *faith* toward our Lord Jesus Christ, is the sum of the gospel.—Mr. Warden, another of their noted writers, (in his *Essay on Baptism*,) says in the name of *presbyterians*, We think that baptism *supposeth* men *Christians*; else they have *no right* to baptism, the seal of Christianity; all seals, in their nature, supposing the *thing* that is sealed. He that is of adult age, is to *profess* his *faith* in Christ, and his *compliance* with the whole device of salvation, *before* he can have the seal of the covenant administered to him. The author of the *Defence of National Churches*, (thought to be Mr. Willison,) says, I know nothing more requisite to admission to the Lord's supper, *in foro ecclesiastico*, than unto baptism in an adult person; they being both seals of the same covenant. And he thinks the objects of church-fellowship are "all who profess to accept the offers of Christ's grace, with subjection to his ordinances, and a suitable walk, and who confess themselves sincere."

I have reserved Mr. Baxter for my last witness, because his attestation is comprehensive and of a general aspect. In his *Disputations of Right to Sacraments*, and other writings, he repeatedly declares, "It hath been the constant principle and practice of the *universal* church of Christ, to require a *profession* of saving *faith* and *repentance*, as necessary before they would *baptize*; and not to baptize any upon the profession of any *lower* kind of faith. He must shut his eyes against the fullest evidence of history and church-practice, who will deny this. I desire those otherwise-minded to help me to an instance of any *one* approved baptism, since Christ's time or his apostles, upon the account of a *faith* that was *short* of *justifying*, and not upon the profession of a justifying faith. Hitherto this is not done by them, but the contrary is fully done by others, and yet they confidently except against my opinion as a *novelty*. Mr. Gataker's books have multitudes of sentences recited out of our *protestant* divines, that affirm this which they call *new*. It is indeed the common *protestant* doctrine, that the sacraments do *presuppose* remission of sins, and our faith; that they are instituted to signify these *as in being*; and do solemnize and publicly own and confirm the mutual covenant *already* entered in heart. The Jesuits themselves do witness this to be the ordinary *protestant* doctrine.—It seems not necessary to mention the judgment of our reformed divines, as expressed in any of their particular sayings, when their public confessions and practices are so satisfactory herein." Mr. Baxter, however, recites a multitude of their testimonies; producing the judgment of Luther, Calvin, Beza, Pet. Martyr, Piscator, Melancthon, Altingius, Junius, Polanus, Zanchius, Ursinus, Paræus, Bucanus, Musculus, Professores Leyd. et Salm. Wollebius, Vossius, Wendeline, Keckerman, Bullinger, Alsted, Deodate, Dr. Ames, Dr. Moulin; The Catechism of the Church of England, and English Divines; Bp. Usher, Dr. Willet, Dr. Fulk, Dr. Prideaux, Dr. Whitaker, Mr. Yates, Perkins, Cartwright, &c.; The Scottish Church in their Heads of Church-policy, and Divines of Scotland; Mr. Gillespie, Mr. Rutherford, and Mr. Wood; The Westminister Assembly of Divines, their Confession, Catechisms, and Directory; The Annot. of some of those Divines, &c. And for the *reformed* churches in general (Mr. Baxter observes) it is past all question, by their constant *practice*, that they require the profession of a *saving* christian faith, and take not up with any *lower*. And respecting the then practice in England, he says, This is manifest by our daily administration of baptism. I never heard (says he) any man baptize an infant but upon the parent's, or susceptor's, or offerer's *profession* of a *justifying faith*.

This leads to your last inquiry.

QUEST. V. *Whether it be the general opinion, that the* same qualifications *are required in a* parent *bringing his child to baptism, as in an* adult *person for his own admission to this ordinance?*

ANSW. Here, Sir, I suppose you intend only the same qualifications in *kind;* or a profession and visibility, in some degree, of the *same sort* of faith and repentance; meaning that which is truly evangelical and saving. And understanding you in this sense, I am persuaded, by all I can observe, that the generality of protestants are in the *affirmative;* not assenting to a specific and essential difference, whatever circumstantial and gradual disparity they may allow, between the two cases you mention.

Mr. Baxter, speaking of the judgment and practice of the christian *fathers*, tells us, that faith (justifying faith, and not another kind of faith) was supposed to be in the parent, for himself and his seed: because the condition or qualification of the infant is but this, that he be the *seed* of a *believer*. And he thinks the generality of the *reformed* are in these sentiments. He declares his own judgment in full concurrence herewith, and backs the same with a variety of arguments, in his *Five Disputations*, and other writings. He observes, it seems strange to him that any should imagine, a *lower* belief in the parent will help his *child* to a title to baptism, than that which is necessary to *his own*, if he were unbaptized; because mutual consent is necessary to mutual covenant, and the covenant *must* be mutual. No man hath right to God's part, that refuseth his own: they that have no right to remission of sins, have no right given them by God to baptism. If God be not at all actually obliged in covenant to any *ungodly* man, then he is not obliged to give him baptism: but God is not obliged so to him. *Most of our divines* make the contrary doctrine Pelagianism, that God should be obliged to man in a state of nature in such a covenant. If the parent's title be questionable, (says he,) the infant's is so too; because the ground is the same: and it is from the parent that the child must derive it; nor can any man give that which he hath not. We ought not (says he) to baptize those persons, or their children, as theirs, who are visible members of the kingdom of the devil, or that do not so much as profess their forsaking the devil's kingdom: but such are all that profess not a saving faith. If such are not visibly *in* the kingdom of the devil, at least they are not visibly *out* of it. All that are duly baptized, are baptized *into* Christ: therefore they are supposed to possess that *faith* by which men are united or ingrafted into Christ: but that is only justifying faith. Tell me (says he) where any man was ever said in Scripture to be united to Christ, without saving faith, or profession of it. In a word, Mr. Baxter takes occasion to declare himself in this manner: If Mr. Blake exacts not a profession of *saving* faith and repentance, I say he makes *foul work* in the church. And when such *foul work* shall be voluntarily *maintained*, and the word of God abused for the *defilement* of the church and ordinances of God, it is a greater scandal to the *weak*, and to the *schismatics*, and a greater reproach to the church, and a sadder case to considerate men, than the too common pollutions of others, which are merely through *negligence*, but not justified and defended.

We are told by other impartial inquirers, that *all the reformed* do in their directories and practices require *professions*, as well as promises, of *parents* bringing their children to baptism; even professions of present faith and repentance, as well as promises of future obedience; and these not merely of the moral, but the evangelical kind. The judgment of the church of Scotland may be known by their adopting the Confession, Catechisms, and Directory of the *Assembly of Divines;* who, when they require a *parental profession*, (as in their *Catechisms*, &c.) intend it not of any *lower* kind, than a true gospel faith and obedience. The mind of the *dissenters* may be very much judged of by the *reformed liturgy*, presented in their name upon King Charles's restoration; where parents' *credible profession* of their faith, repentance, and obedience, is required in order to the baptism of their children. I might bring further evidence from the writings of particular divines among them, ancient and modern; but I must for brevity omit this. Only I will give you a specimen in two or three hints. Mr. Charnock, that great divine, observes, "Baptism *supposes* faith in the adult, and the profession of faith in the parent for his child." The late eminent Dr. Watts, in his *Holiness of Times, Places, and People*, thus declares himself, with respect to the *infants of true believers:* "In my opinion, so far as they are any way members of the *visible* christian church, it is upon *supposition* of their being (with their *parents*) members of the *invisible* church of God."

On the whole, as to our fathers here in New England, it is true, they asserted a *baptism-right* in parents for themselves and children, whom yet they excluded from full communion; the ground of which difference was hinted before: and they denied a *parity of reason* between the *two cases* now in view, on some accounts. Their chief ground was, that *adult baptism* requires a measure of visible *moral fitness* or inherent holiness in the recipient; whereas, *infant baptism* requires nothing visible in its subject, but a *relative fitness* or federal holiness, the *formalis ratio* of infant membership, accruing from God's charter of grace to his church, taking in the infant seed with the believing parent. Baptism they supposed to run parallel with regular membership; and the child of such a parent entitled to this covenant-seal in its own right, on the foot of a distinct personal membership, derivative in point of *being*, but independent for its *duration*, and for the *privileges* annexed to it by divine institution. However, they certainly owned *parental profession*, as belonging to the due order and just manner of administration, both *meet* and *needful*. Accordingly they provided, that *parents* claiming covenant-privileges for their children, should own their covenant-state, have a measure of covenant-qualifications, and do covenant-duties, in some degree, to the satisfaction of a rational charity. And it ought to be remembered, they have left it as their solemn judgment, that even taking *baptism-right* for a right of *fitness in foro ecclesiastico*, still the parents whose children they claimed *baptism* for, were such as must be allowed to have a title to it for *themselves*, in case they had remained unbaptized: looking upon them, although not duly fitted for the sacrament of communion and confirmation, yet sufficiently so for the sacrament of union and initiation; professors in their infancy *parentally*, and now *personally*, in an initial way; appearing Abraham's children, in some measure of *truth*, to a judicious charity; justly therefore baptizable, in their persons and offspring, by all the rules of the gospel. I am not here to argue upon the justness of this scheme of thought on the case; but only to represent the fact in a genuine light.

I have no room, Sir, for any further remarks. But must conclude, with christian salutes, and the tender of every brotherly office, from

Your very affectionate Friend
and humble Servant,
THOMAS FOXCROFT.

Boston,
June 26, 1749.

MISREPRESENTATIONS CORRECTED,

AND

TRUTH VINDICATED,

IN

A REPLY

TO THE

REV. MR. SOLOMON WILLIAMS'S BOOK,

ENTITLED,

THE TRUE STATE OF THE QUESTION CONCERNING THE QUALIFICATIONS NECESSARY TO LAWFUL COMMUNION IN THE CHRISTIAN SACRAMENTS.

Prov. xii. 17. He that speaketh truth, showeth forth righteousness.
Chap. xxii. 20, 21. Have I not written to thee excellent things in counsels and knowledge; that I might make thee know the certainty of the words of truth, that thou mightest answer the words of truth to them that send unto thee?

THE PREFACE.

SINCE I have been so repeatedly charged by Mr. *Williams* with indecent and injurious treatment of Mr. *Stoddard*, (whom doubtless I ought to treat with much respect,) I may expect, from what appears of Mr. *Williams's* disposition this way, to be charged with ill treatment of *him* too. I desire therefore that it may be justly considered by the reader, what is, and what is not, injurious or unhandsome treatment of an author in a controversy. And here I would crave leave to say, that I humbly conceive, a distinction ought to be made between opposing and exposing a *cause*, or the *arguments* used to defend it, and reproaching *persons*. He is a weak writer indeed, who undertakes to confute an opinion, but dares not expose the nakedness and absurdity of it, nor the weakness or inconsistence of the methods taken and arguments used by any to maintain it, for fear he should be guilty of speaking evil of these things, and be charged with reproaching them. If an antagonist is angry at this, he thereby gives his readers too much occasion of suspicion towards himself, as chargeable with weakness, or bitterness.

I therefore now give notice, that I have taken full liberty in this respect; only endeavouring to avoid pointed and exaggerating expressions. If to set forth what I suppose to be the true absurdity of Mr. *Williams's* scheme, or any part of it, that it may be viewed justly in all its nakedness; withal observing the *weakness* of the defence he has made, not fearing to show *wherein* it is weak, and how the badness of his *cause* obliges him to be *inconsistent* with himself, inconsistent with his own professed principles in religion, and with things conceded and asserted by him in the book especially under consideration; and declaring particularly wherein I think his arguments fail, whether it be in *begging the question*, or being impertinent and *beside* the question, or arguing in effect against himself; also observing wherein Mr. W. has made *misrepresentations* of words or things; I say, if to do these things be reproaching *him*, and injurious treatment of him, then I have injured him.—But I think I should be foolish, if I were afraid to do *that* (and to do it as thoroughly as I can) *which must be the design* of my writing, if I write at all in opposition to his tenets, and to the defence he makes of them.

Indeed if I misrepresent what he says, in order to make it appear in the worst colours; altering his words to another sense, to make them appear more ridiculous; or adding other words, that carry the sense beyond the proper import of his words, to heighten the supposed absurdity, and give me greater advantage to exclaim; if I set myself to aggravate matters, and strain them beyond bounds, making mighty things of mere trifles: or if I use exclamations and invectives, instead of arguments; then Mr. W. might have just cause to complain, and the reader would have just reason for disgust. But whether I have done so, or not, must be judged by the reader; of whom I desire nothing more than the most impartial and exact consideration of the merits of the cause, and examination of the force and weight of every argument. I desire, that no bitter reproachful invectives, no vehement exclamations, no supercilious assuming words and phrases, may be taken for reasoning, on either side. If the reader thinks he finds any such in what I have written, I am willing he should set them aside as nothing worth; carefully distinguishing between them, and the strength of the argument. I desire not, that the cause should be judged of by the skill which either Mr. *W.* or *I* do manifest, in flinging one at another.

If in places where the argument pinches most, and there is the greatest appearance of strong reason, in Mr. W's. book, I do, (as some other disputants,) instead of entering thoroughly into the matter, begin to flounce and fling, and divert the reader's attention to the argument, by the noise of big words, or magisterial and disdainful expressions; let the reader take it (as justly he may) for a shrewd sign of a consciousness of the weakness of my cause in that particular, or at least of a distrust of my own ability to defend myself well in the reader's apprehension, and to come off with a good grace any other way.

In this case, I shall not think it any injustice done me by the reader, though he suspects that I feel myself pressed, and begin to be in trouble, for fear I should not seem to come off like a champion, if I should trust to mere reasoning. I can uprightly say, I never have endeavoured by such means to evade a proper consideration of any part of Mr. W.'s reasoning; nor have designedly contrived, in this or any other method, to free myself from the trouble of a just answer to any thing material in his book; and I have been especially careful to speak most particularly to the main parts of his scheme, and such of his reasonings as I could suppose those of his readers who are on his side, would be most likely to have their chief dependence on, and to think most difficult to be answered.

With regard to my *method* in this reply, I judged it most convenient to reduce my remarks on Mr. W.'s principles, and the parts of his scheme, and kinds of arguing, which repeatedly appear in various parts of his book, to their *proper heads.* I thought this tended to give the reader a clearer and more comprehensive view of the whole controversy, and the nature of the arguments; and that it also would make my work the shorter. For otherwise, I must have had the same things, or things of the same nature, to have observed often, as I found them repeated in different parts of this book, and the same remarks to make over and over again.—And that the reader may not be without any advantages which he might have had in the other method, of keeping, in my reply, to the order in which things lie in the book answered, following my author from one page and paragraph to another, I have therefore subjoined a table, by which the reader may readily turn to what is said on each particular, that is wont to be brought into this debate, on one side or the other.*

With regard to my *citations* from Mr. W.'s book, I have never designedly altered his words: and where I have for brevity's sake referred to any sentiment of his, without citing the words at large, I have used care not to change or heighten the sense, or in any respect to vary from the just import of what he delivers. And that the reader may himself more easily and readily judge of the fairness of my citations and references, I have mentioned the *page*, and the *part* of the page, where the thing referred to is to be found: supposing each page to be divided into five equal parts, I have noted the several parts of the page by the letters *a. b. c. d. e.* So that when I have referred to the *top* of the page, or the first fifth part of it, I have mentioned the number of the page, and added the letter *a.* to the number: and if the *middle*, or third fifth part, then I have added the letter *c.*—and so of the rest, as the reader will see. I have ever done thus, unless the thing referred to is to be found through the whole or great part of the page. I have also done the same very often, where I have occasion to cite other authors. Only when I have *before* quoted the same thing, I am not always so exact and particular in noting the place again, in my *second* quotation or reference.

MISREPRESENTATIONS CORRECTED,

AND

TRUTH VINDICATED.

PART I.

THE GENERAL MISREPRESENTATIONS MR. WILLIAMS MAKES CONCERNING THE BOOK HE WRITES AGAINST.

SECT. I.

Concerning the design of my writing and publishing my book, and the question debated in it.

MR. WILLIAMS asserts it to be my professed and declared *design*, in writing the book which he has undertaken to answer, to oppose Mr. Stoddard. He has taken a great liberty in this matter. He charges me with a declared design of writing in opposition to Mr. Stoddard, no less than nine or ten times in his book. And he does not content himself merely with saying, there are passages in my Preface, or elsewhere, whence this may be *inferred;* but he says expressly, that I profess to be disputing against Mr. Stoddard's doctrine, (p. 14. *d.*) That I tell my readers, I am disputing against Mr. Stoddard's question, (p. 37. *d.*) That I tell them so in my Preface, (p. 107. *d.*) That I often declare that I am opposing Mr. Stoddard's opinion, (p. 132. *d.*) And on this foundation he charges me with blotting a great deal of paper, disserving the cause of truth by changing the question, and putting it in such terms as Mr. S. expressly disclaims, and then confuting it as Mr. S——d's principle; unfair treatment of Mr. S. (p. 2. *d. e.*)—surprisingly going off from Mr. S——d's argument to cast an odium upon it, treating Mr. S. and his doctrine in such a manner as to reproach him and his principles, tending to render them odious to the unthinking multitude, and telling a manifest untruth, (p. 14. *d.* and 15. *c. d.*) Whereas, I never once signified it to be the thing I aimed at, to oppose Mr. Stoddard, or appear as *his* antagonist. But the very reverse was true; and meddling with him, or what he had said, I studied to avoid, as much as the circumstances of the debate with my people would allow, who had been taught by him, and who so greatly and continually alleged against me the things which he had said. Nor is there any appearance in those passages Mr. W. cites from my preface, that this was the thing I aimed at. Nay, one of those passages which he produces to prove it, shows the contrary: as it shows, that what I wrote being not consistent with, but opposite to, what Mr. S. had maintained, was an unsought for and unpleasing circumstance of that publication. My words are, "It is far from a pleasing circumstance of this publication, that it is against what my honoured grandfather strenuously maintained, both from the pulpit and the press." Certainly my *regretting* and *excusing* such an unavoidable circumstance was a thing exceeding diverse from

* This is now incorporated with the General Index.

giving notice to the world, that the thing I aimed at was to set myself up as Mr. Stoddard's antagonist, and to write an answer to, and confute, what he had written. It will, at first sight, be manifest to every impartial reader, that the design of my *Preface* was not to state the subject and intention of the book. This is done professedly, and very particularly afterwards, in the first part of the essay itself. And if I might have common justice, surely I might be allowed to tell my own opinion, and declare my own design, without being so confidently and frequently charged with *misrepresenting* my own thoughts and intentions.

The very *nature of the case* is such as must lead every impartial person to a conviction, that the design of my writing must be to defend myself, in that controversy which I had with my people at *Northampton;* as it is notorious and publicly known, that *that controversy* was the occasion of my writing; and that therefore my business must be to defend that opinion or position of *mine* which I had declared to them, which had been the occasion of the controversy, and so the grand subject of debate between us; whether this were exactly agreeable to any words that might be found in Mr. Stoddard's writings on the subject, or not. Now this opinion or position was the same with that which I expressed in the first part of my book. In such terms I expressed myself to the committee of the church, when I first made that declaration of my opinion, which was the beginning of the controversy, and when writing in defence of my opinion was first proposed. And this was the point continually talked of in all conversation at *Northampton,* for more than two years, even till Mr. W.'s book came out. The controversy was, *Whether there was any need of making a credible profession of godliness, in order to persons being admitted to full communion; whether they must profess having faith, or whether a profession of common faith were not sufficient; whether persons must be esteemed truly godly, and must be taken in under that notion, or whether if they appeared morally sincere, that were not sufficient?* And when my book came abroad, there was no objection made, that I had not truly expressed the subject of debate in stating the question: but the subject of debate afterwards, in parish meetings, church-meetings, and in all conversation, was the question laid down in my book. No suggestion existed among them, that the profession persons made in Mr. Stoddard's way, was taken as a profession of *real* godliness, or gospel-holiness; or that they were taken in *under a notion of their being truly pious persons,* as Mr. W. would have it. There was no suggestion, that the dispute was only about the *degree of evidence;* but what was the thing to be made *evident;* whether *real godliness,* or *moral sincerity?* It was constantly insisted on, with the greatest vehemence, that it was not saving religion, which needed to be *professed,* or *pretended to;* but another thing, religion of a lower kind. The public *acts* of the church and parish, from time to time, show, that the point in controversy was, *Whether the professors of godliness, only, ought to be admitted?* Public votes of which I made a record, were several times passed to know the church's mind concerning the admission of *those who are able and willing to make a profession of godliness;* using these terms. And once it was passed, That *such should not be admitted in the way of publicly making such a profession.* And at another time the vote passed, *That the admission of such persons in such a way* (described in the same words) *should not be referred to the judgment of certain neighbouring ministers.* At another time, it was insisted on by the parish, in a parish-meeting, That I should put a vote in the church, in these words, *Whether there be not a dispute between* Mr. Edwards *pastor of the church, and the church, respecting the question he hath argued in his book last published.* And accordingly the vote was put and affirmed, in a church-meeting, in the same terms. And this was the question I insisted on in my public lectures at *Northampton,* appointed for giving the reasons of my opinion. My doctrine was in these words, *It is the mind and will of God, that none should be admitted to full communion in the church of Christ, but such as in profession, and in the eye of a reasonable judgment, are truly saints, or godly persons.* The town was full of objections against those sermons; but none, as ever I heard, objected, that my doctrine was *beside the controversy.*—And this was all along the point of difference between me and the neighbouring *ministers.* This was the grand subject of debate with them, at a meeting of ministers, appointed on purpose for conference on the subject. It was wholly concerning the matter of profession, or the *thing* to be exhibited and made evident or visible; and not about the *manner* of professing, and the *degree* of evidence. And this was the doctrine directly opposed by Mr. A—y, one of the neighbouring ministers, whom my people had got as their champion to defend their cause in the pulpit at *Northampton.* Thus one of the corollaries he drew from his doctrine (as it was taken from his mouth in writing) was, That "a man may be a visible saint, and yet there be no sufficient grounds for our charity, that he is regenerate." Quite contrary to what Mr. W. maintains. Another of his corollaries was in these words, "A minister or church may judge a man a saint, and upon good grounds, and not have grounds to judge him regenerate." He proposed this inquiry, "Do not such as join themselves to the church, covenant not only to be visible saints, but saints in heart?" The answer was in the *negative;* quite contrary to Mr. W. Another was, "*Does not a visible saint imply a visibility of grace, or an appearance of it?*" The answer was, "Not always."—Quite contrary to Mr. W. Another was, "Is it not hypocrisy in any man, to make a profession of religion, and join himself to the church, and not have grace?" The answer was in the *negative;* also quite contrary to Mr. W.—But these sermons of Mr. A—y were highly approved by the generality of the people of *Northampton,* as agreeable to their minds.

And the controversy, as I have stated it in my book, was that in which the church and I appeared before the *council,* who determined our separation, when we each of us declared our sentiments before them. The point of difference was entirely the *matter* of profession, and the *thing* to be made *visible:* not the *degree* of evidence or *visibility.* No hint was given as though we both agreed, that true piety or gospel-holiness was the thing to be made visible, and that such only should be received as are truly godly persons in the eye of the church's judgment, (as Mr. W. holds,) and that we only differed about the proper grounds of such a judgment.

And therefore it is apparent, this controversy and its consequences, were the ground of my separation from my people; and not any thing like the controversy which Mr. W. professes to manage in his answer. This controversy, when it came out in Mr. W—'s book, was new in *Northampton,* and entirely alien from all the dispute which had filled that part of the country, and a great part of *New England,* with noise and uproar, for about two years and a half. The thing which Mr. W. over and over allows to be true, was the very same, both in effect and in terms, which the people had been most vehemently fighting against, from week to week, and from month to month, during all this time. And therefore the design of my writing led and obliged me to maintain that position or doctrine of mine, which was the occasion of this debate.

And be it so, that I did suppose this position was contrary to Mr. Stoddard's opinion, and was opposed by him,* and therefore thought fit in my *Preface* to excuse myself to the world for differing from him; did this oblige me, in all that I wrote for maintaining my position, to keep myself strictly to the words which he had expressed *his question* in, and to regulate and limit myself in every argument I used, and objection I answered, by the terms which he made use of in proposing his opinion and arguments? And if I have not done it, do I therefore deserve to be charged before the world with *changing the question,* with *unfair treatment of Mr. Stoddard,* with *surprisingly going off from his argument,* with *disserving the cause of truth,* &c.

It would have been no great condescension in Mr. W. if he had allowed that *I* knew what the question was, which was disputed between me and my people, as well

* Whether I was mistaken in this, will appear in the sequel.

as *he*, in a distant part of the country. Yea, if he had acknowledged, that I was as likely as he, to understand Mr. Stoddard's real sentiments and practice; since I was in the ministry two years with him, as co-pastor of the same church, and was united with him in ecclesiastical administrations, in admitting members, and in examining them as to their qualifications. I have stood for more than twenty-three years in a pastoral relation to his church, most intimately acquainted with the nature of its constitution, its sentiments and method of administration, and all its religious concerns. I have myself been immediately concerned in the admission of more than three quarters of its present members, and have had the greatest occasion to look into their way of admission, and have been acquainted with every living member that Mr. S. had admitted before my coming; and have been particularly informed, by many of them, of the manner of Mr. S——d's conduct in admitting them, their own apprehensions concerning the terms of their admission, and the profession they made in order to it; and also the sentiments of the whole of that large town, who were born and brought up under his ministry, concerning his constant doctrine and practice, relating to the admission of members, from their infancy.—Whereas, Mr. W. from his youth had lived in another part of the country, at seventy miles distance.

SECT. II.

Mr. Williams's misrepresentations of the principles and tenets, delivered in the book which he undertakes to answer.

MR. W. very greatly misrepresents my opinion, and the principles I maintain in my book, in many respects.

I. He says, (p. 5. *d.*) "The whole argument, and indeed the whole controversy, turns upon this single point, *viz.* What is that *evidence*, which by divine appointment the church is to have, of the *saintship* of those who are admitted to the outward privileges of the covenant of grace? Mr. *Edwards* seems to suppose, this must be the *highest* evidence a man can give of sincerity; and I apprehend it to be the *lowest* evidence the nature of the thing will admit."—But this is very strange, since I had particularly declared in my *stating of the question*, (p. 5.) that the evidence I insisted on, was *some outward manifestation, that ordinarily rendered the thing probable.* Which shows, that all I insisted on, was only, that the evidence should amount to *probability*. And if the nature of the case will admit of some *lower* kind of evidence than this, or if there be any such thing as a sort of evidence that does not so much as amount to *probability*, then it is possible that I may have some controversy with him and others about the degree of evidence. Otherwise it is hard to conceive, how he should contrive to make out a controversy with me.

But that the reader may better judge, whether Mr. W. truly represents me as supposing that the evidence which should be insisted on, is *the highest evidence a man can give of sincerity*, I would here insert an extract of a *Letter* which I wrote to the Rev. Mr. *Peter Clark* of *Salem-Village*, a twelvemonth before Mr. W—'s book was published. The original is doubtless in Mr. *Clark's* hands. In that letter, I declare my sentiments in the following words:

"It does not belong to the controversy between me and my people, how particular or large the profession should be that is required. I should not choose to be confined to exact limits as to that matter. But rather than contend, I should content myself with a few words, briefly expressing the cardinal virtues, or acts implied in a hearty compliance with the covenant of grace; the profession being made (as should appear by inquiry into the person's doctrinal knowledge) understandingly; if there were an external conversation agreeable thereto. Yea, I should think that such a person, solemnly making such a profession, had a right to be received as the object of a public charity, however he himself might scruple his own conversion, on account of his not remembering the time, not knowing the method, of his conversion, or finding so much remaining sin, &c. And (if his own scruples did not hinder*) I should think a minister or church had no right to debar such a professor, though he should say, he did not think himself converted. For I call that a profession of godliness, which is a profession of the great things wherein godliness consists, and not a profession of his own opinion of his good estate."—*Northampton, May* 7, 1750.

In like manner, I explained my opinion, very particularly and expressly, before the *council* that determined my separation from my people, and before the church, in a very public manner in the meeting-house, many people being present, near a year before Mr. W—'s book was published. And to make it the more sure, that what I maintained might be well observed, I afterwards sent in the foregoing extract of my letter to Mr. *Clark of Salem-Village*, into the council. And, as I was informed, it was particularly taken notice of in the council, and handed round among them, to be read by them.

The same *council*, having heard that I had made certain draughts of the *covenant*, or forms of a public *profession* of religion, which I stood ready to accept of from the candidates for communion, they, for their further information, sent for them. Accordingly I sent them four distinct draughts or forms, which I had drawn up about a twelvemonth before, (near two years before the publishing of Mr. W—'s book,) as what I stood ready to accept of (any one of them) rather than contend and break with my people.—The two shortest of those forms were as follows.

One of them was;

"I hope, I do truly find a heart to give up myself wholly to God, according to the tenor of that covenant of grace which was sealed in my baptism, and to walk in a way of that obedience to all the commandments of God, which the covenant of grace requires, as long as I live."

The other,

"I hope, I truly find in my heart a willingness to comply with all the commandments of God, which require me to give up myself wholly to him, and to serve him with my body and my spirit; and do accordingly now promise to walk in a way of obedience to all the commandments of God, as long as I live."

Now the reader is left to judge, whether I insist, as Mr. W. represents, that persons must not be admitted without the *highest* evidence a man *can* give of sincerity.

II. Mr. W. is abundant in suggesting and insinuating to his readers, that the opinion laid down in my book is, That persons ought not to be admitted to a communion without an absolute and peremptory determination in those who admit them, that they are truly godly; because I suppose it to be necessary, that there should be a *positive* judgment in their favour.

Here I desire the reader to observe, that the word *positive* is used in two senses. (1.) Sometimes it is put in opposition to *doubtful* or *uncertain*: and then it signifies the same as *certain, peremptory*, or *assured.* But, (2.) The word *positive* is very often used in a very different sense; not in opposition to *doubtful*, but in opposition to *negative*: and so understood, it signifies very much the same as *real* or *actual.* Thus, we often speak of a *negative good*, and a *positive good.* A *negative good* is a mere negation or absence of *evil;* but a *positive good* is something more,—some *real, actual good*, instead of evil. So there is a *negative charity*, and a *positive charity.* A *negative* charity is a mere absence of an ill judgment of a man, or forbearing to condemn him. Such a charity a man may have towards any stranger he transiently sees in the street, that he never saw or heard any thing of before. A *positive charity* is something further than merely not condemning, or not judging ill, it implies a *good thought* of a man. The reader will easily see that the word *positive*, taken in this sense, is an ex-

* I added this, because I supposed that such persons as judge themselves unconverted, if of my principles respecting qualifications for communion, would scruple coming, and could not come with a good conscience: but if they were of Mr. S—d's principles, *viz.* That unconverted men might lawfully come, neither a man's being of that opinion, nor his judging himself unconverted, would hinder my receiving him who exhibited proper evidence to the church of his being a convert

ceeding different thing from *certain* or *peremptory*. A man may have something more than a mere *negative* charity towards another, or a mere forbearing to condemn him, he may actually entertain some *good thought* of him, and yet there may be no proper *peremptoriness*, no pretence of any *certainty* in the case.

Now it is in this sense I use the phrase *positive judgment, viz.* In opposition to a mere *negative charity;* as I very plainly express the matter, and particularly and fully explain myself in *stating the question*. In my *Inquiry* (p. 5.) I have the following words: "By *christian judgment*, I intend something further than a kind of mere *negative* charity, implying that we forbear to censure and condemn a man, because we do not know but that he may be godly, and therefore forbear to proceed on the foot of such a censure or judgment in our treatment of him; as we would kindly entertain a stranger, not knowing but, in so doing, we entertain an angel, or precious saint of God: but I mean a *positive judgment*, founded on some *positive* appearance or visibility, some outward manifestation that ordinarily renders the thing probable. There is a difference between suspending our judgment, or forbearing to condemn, or having some hope that possibly the thing may be so, and so hoping the best, and a *positive* judgment in favour of a person. For having some hope, only implies, that a man is not in utter despair of a thing; though his prevailing opinion may be otherwise, or he may suspend his opinion."

Here, I think, my meaning is very plainly and carefully explained. However, inasmuch as the word *positive* is sometimes used for *peremptory or certain*, Mr. W. catches at the term, and lays fast hold of the advantage he thinks this gives him, and is abundant, all over his book, in representing as though I insisted on a *positive judgment* in this sense. So he applies the word, referring to my use of it, from time to time. Thus, (p. 69. *b.*) "If there be any thing in this argument, I think it must be what I have observed, *viz.* That a Christian must make a *positive judgment* and determination, that another man is a saint, and this judgment must have for its ground something which he supposes is, at least ordinarily, a *certain* evidence of his saintship, and by which gracious sincerity is *certainly* distinguished from every thing else." And, (p. 141. *a.*) "The notion of men's being able and fit to determine *positively* the condition of other men, or the *certainty* of their gracious state, has a direct tendency to deceive the souls of men." And thus Mr. W. makes mention of a *positive judgment* above forty times in his book, with reference to my use of it, and to my declared opinion of its necessity; and every where plainly uses the phrase in *that* sense, for *absolute* and *peremptory*, in opposition to *doubtfulness;* continually insinuating, that this is what I professedly insist on. Whereas every *act* of the judgment whatsoever, is a *positive* judgment in the sense in which I have fully declared I use it, *viz.* in opposition to *negative;* which is no act, but a mere withholding of the act of the judgment, or forbearing any actual judgment.* Mr. W. himself does abundantly suppose, that there must be a *positive* judgment in *this* sense. He grants the very thing, though he rejects the term. For he holds, there must be such a visibility as makes persons to appear to be real saints. (p. 5. *b.*)—He allows, that the moral image of God or Christ must appear, or be supposed to be in them, as the ground and reason of our charity; and that there must be some apprehension, some judgment of mind, of the saintship of persons, for its foundation. (p. 68. *c. d. e.* and 69. *a.* 71. *d.*)—That they must have such a character appearing in them. (p. 55. *e.*)—That there must be a judgment founded on moral evidence of gospel-holiness. (p. 139. *d.*)

III. Mr. W. to make my scheme appear the more ridiculous, more than once represents it as my opinion, that in order to persons being admitted into the church, there must be a judgment of their being regenerate, founded on such a degree of evidence, as that it shall not be liable to be mistaken more than *once in ten times*. Thus, (p. 63. *c.*) "Mr. *Edwards* himself supposes, in his own scheme, when he has made a positive judgment that every one singly whom he admits into the church is regenerate; yet when taken collectively, it is probable *one in ten* will be an hypocrite." (So, p. 71. *b.*) "If any thing be intended to the purpose for which this argument is brought, I conceive, it must mean, that there must be such a *positive judgment* of the real holiness of persons, as is not mistaken more than once in ten times."—Now, I desire the reader to observe what is the whole ground, on which he makes such a representation. In explaining my opinion, in the beginning of my *Inquiry*, (p. 6.) I desired it might be observed, that I did not suppose we ought to expect any such degree of *certainty* of the godliness of those who are admitted into the church, as that when the whole number admitted are taken collectively, or considered in the gross, we should have any reason to suppose every one to be truly godly; though we might have charity for each one that was admitted, taken *singly*, and by himself. And to show, that such a thing was possible, I endeavoured to illustrate it by a comparison, or supposed case of *probability of ten to one*, in the example of certain stones, with such probable marks of a *diamond*, as by experience had been found not to fail more than *once in ten times*. In which case, if a particular stone were found with those marks, there would be a probability of *ten to one*, with respect to that stone, singly taken, that it was genuine: but if ten such were taken together, there would not be the same probability that every one of them was so; but in this case, it is as likely as not, that some one in the ten is spurious. Now it is so apparent, that this particular degree of probability of *ten to one* is mentioned only as a *supposed case*, for illustration, and because, in a particular example, some number or other must be mentioned, that it would have been an affront to the sense of my readers to have added any caution, that he should not understand me otherwise. However, Mr. W. has laid hold of this, as a good handle by which he might exhibit my scheme to the world in a ridiculous light; as though I had declared it my real opinion, that there must be the probability of just *ten to one*, of true godliness, in order to persons' admission into the church. He might with as much appearance of sense and justice, have asserted concerning all the supposed cases in books of arithmetic, that the authors intend these cases should be understood as real *facts*, and that they have written their books, with all the sums and numbers in them, as books of *history;* and if any cases mentioned there only as examples of the several rules, are unlikely to be true accounts of fact, therefore have charged the authors with writing a *false* and *absurd* history.

IV. Another thing, yet further from what is honourable in Mr. W. is this; That, whereas I said as above, that there ought to be a prevailing opinion concerning those that are admitted, *taken singly, or by themselves*, that they are truly godly or gracious, though when we look on the whole number in the gross, we are far from determining that every one is a true saint, and that not one of the judgments we have passed, has been mistaken; Mr. W. because I used the phrase *singly taken*, has laid hold on the expression, and from thence has taken occasion to insinuate to his readers, as if my scheme were so very extravagant, that according to this, when a great multitude are admitted, their admitters must be confident of EVERY ONE's being *regenerated*. Hence he observes, (p. 98. *c.*) "There is no appearance, that *John* made a positive judgment that *every one* of these people were regenerated." Plainly using the

* Mr. *John Glas*, in his *Observes upon the original Constitution of the Christian Church*, (p. 55, 56.) says as follows, "You seem to have a great prejudice at what you call *positive evidences*, and judging upon them in the admission of church-members. And I am at some loss to understand what you mean by them, though I have heard the expression frequently, among people of your opinion, used to express some very ill thing. If you mean by *positive evidences*, infallible evidences of a thing that none but God infallibly knows, and can assure a man's own conscience of, with respect to a man himself: I think it would be a very great evil for a man to require such evidence to found his judgment of charity, concerning another man's faith and holiness, or concerning his being an object of *brotherly love*. And I think, he is bound by the law of Christ to form his judgment in this matter upon less evidence. But if you mean *positive evidence* in opposition to *negative*, which is no evidence, I must own, I know not how to form a judgment of charity without some *positive* evidence. And is not a *credible profession* something *positive?*—Is not a credible profession of the faith, love, and hope that is in Christ, or of Christianity, a *positive evidence* of a man's being an object of *brotherly love*, which evidence ought to be the ground of my *judgment of charity* concerning him, that he is a Christian, a believer in Christ, a brother for whom Christ died? If it be otherwise, and if there be no evidence upon which I can charitably judge, that a man is a brother for whom Christ died, then tell me, how I can evidence my love to Jesus Christ, in the labour of love towards my brother, whom I have seen; and my love to God, in my love to them that are begotten of him."

expression as a very strong one; leading the reader to suppose, that I insist the evidence shall be so clear, that when such a vast multitude as *John* baptized are viewed, the admitter should be peremptory in it, that his judgment has not failed so much as in a *single* instance; the very *reverse* of what I had expressed. In like manner, Mr. W. treats the matter from time to time. As in p. 55. *a.* "The thing to be proved from hence is, that the apostles and primitive Christians, not only thought that these persons were Christians, by reason of their external calling, and professed compliance with the call; but had formed a positive judgment concerning EVERY ONE OF THEM SINGLY, that they were real saints." Here the expression is plainly used as a very strong one; as implying much more than esteeming so great a multitude, when taken in the gross, to be generally true saints, and with a manifest design to carry the same idea in the mind of the reader as was before mentioned. See another like instance, p. 62. *c.*

V. However, my opinion is not represented bad enough yet; but to make it appear still worse, Mr. W. is bold to strain his representation of it to that height, as to suggest that what I insist on, is a *certainty* of others' regeneration; though this be so diverse from what I had largely explained in stating the question, and plainly expressed in other parts of my book,* and also inconsistent with his own representations in other places. For if what I insist on be a probability that *may fail once in ten times*, as he says it is, p. 63. *a.* then it is not a *certainty* that I insist on; as he suggests, p. 141. *a.*—Speaking of the evil consequences of my opinion, he says, "The notion of men's being able and fit to determine positively the condition of other men, or the certainty of their gracious estate, has a direct tendency to deceive the souls of men." So again in p. 69. And he suggests, that I require more than *moral evidence*, in p. 6. *c.* and p. 139. *d.*

VI. Mr. W. represents me as insisting on some way of judging the state of such as are admitted to communion, *by their inward and spiritual experiences*, diverse from judging *by their profession and behaviour*. So, p. 7. *b.* "If *their outward profession and behaviour* be the ground of this judgment, then it is not *the inward experience of the heart*." P. 55. *b.* "Which judgment must be founded on something beyond and beside their external calling, and *visible profession* to comply with it, and to be separated for God: and therefore this judgment must be founded, either upon revelation, or a personal acquaintance with *their experiences*," &c. In like manner he is abundant, from one end of his book to the other, in representing as though I insisted on judging men *by their inward and spiritual experiences*, in some peculiar manner. Which is something surprising, since there is not so much as a word said about *relating, or giving an account of, experiences*, or what is commonly so called, as a term of communion. Mr. W. (p. 6. *a.*) pretends to quote two passages of mine, as an evidence, that this is what I insist on. One is from the 5th page of my book. It is true, I there say thus, "It is a visibility to the eye of the public charity, and not a private judgment, that gives a person a right to be received as a visible saint by the public." And I there say, "A public and serious profession of the great and main things wherein the essence of true religion or godliness consists, together with an honest character, an agreeable conversation, and good understanding of the doctrines of Christianity, and particularly those doctrines that teach the grand condition of salvation, and the nature of true saving religion; this justly recommends persons to the good opinion of the public; whatever suspicions and fears any particular person, either the minister, or some other, may entertain, from what he in particular has observed; perhaps the manner of his expressing himself *in giving an account of his experiences*, or an obscurity in the order and method of his *experiences*," &c.—But the words do not imply, it may be demanded of the candidate, that he should give an account of his experiences to the minister, or any body else, as the term of his admission into the church: nor had I respect to any such thing. But I knew it was the manner in many places for those who hoped they were godly persons, to converse with their neighbours, and especially with their minister, about their experiences; whether it was required of them in order to their coming into the church, or no; and particularly, I was sensible, that this was the manner at *Northampton*, for whose sake especially I wrote; and I supposed it the way of many ministers, and people, to judge of others' state, openly and publicly, by the order and method of their experiences, or the manner of their relating them. But this I condemn in the very passage that Mr. W. quotes; and very much condemn in other writings of mine which have been published; and have ever loudly condemned, and borne my testimony against.

There is one passage more, which Mr. W. adds to the preceding, and fathers on me, to prove that I require *an account of experiences* in order to admission; pretending to rehearse my words, with marks of quotation, saying as follows, (p. 6. *a.*) and as he further explains himself elsewhere; "The proper visibility which the public is to have of a man's being a saint, must be on some account of his experience of those doctrines which teach the nature of true saving religion."—I have made long and diligent search for such a passage in my writings, but cannot find it. Mr. W. says, *I thus explain myself elsewhere;* but I wish he had mentioned in what place.

If there be such a sentence in some of my writings, (as I suppose there is not,) it will serve little to Mr. W—'s purpose. If we take the word *experience* according to the common acceptation of it in the English language, *viz.* a person's perceiving or knowing any thing by trial or experiment, or by immediate sensation or consciousness within himself: in this sense, I own, it may from what I say in my book be inferred, that a man's profession of his experience should be required as a term of communion. And so it may be as justly and as plainly inferred, that Mr. W. himself insists on a profession of experience as a term of communion; experience of a deep conviction of a man's undone state without Christ; experience of a persuasion of his judgment and conscience, that there is no other way of salvation; experience of unfeigned desires to be brought to the terms of the covenant. For such things as these, he says, must be professed. So, p. 75. *d. e.* and in innumerable other places. There is no such thing possible as a man's professing any thing within himself or belonging to his own mind, either good or bad, either common or saving, unless it be something that he *finds*, or (which is the same thing) *experiences*, within himself.

I know the word *experience* is used by many in a sort of peculiar sense, for the particular order and method of what passes within the mind and heart in conversion. And in this sense, Mr. W. knows, I disclaim the notion of making *experiences* a term of communion. I say, he knows it, because (in p. 6. *a.*) he quotes and rehearses the very words wherein I do expressly disclaim it. And I am very large and particular in testifying against it in my book on *Religious Affections*: (a book I have good reason to think Mr. W. has seen and read, having been thus informed by a man of his own principles, that had it from his mouth.) There, in p. 300. *e.* and 301. *a.* I say as follows: "In order to persons making a proper profession of Christianity, such as the Scripture directs to, and such as the followers of Christ should require in order to the acceptance of the professors with full charity, as of their society, it is not necessary they should give an account of the particular *steps* and *method*, by which the Holy Spirit, sensibly to them, wrought, and brought about those great essential things of Christianity in their hearts. There is no footstep in the Scripture of any such way of the apostles, or primitive ministers and Christians, requiring any such relation in order to their receiving and treating others as their christian brethren, to all intents and purposes; or of their first examining them concerning the particular method and order of their *experiences*.—They required of them a profession of the things wrought; but no account of the manner of working was required of them. Nor is there the least shadow in the Scripture of any such custom in the

* In stating the question, p. 5. *b.* I explained the requisite visibility, to be *some outward manifestation, that ordinarily renders the thing probable.* To the like purpose, is what I say in p. 10. *e.* and p. 11. *a. b. e.* and p. 12. *a. b. c.* And in p. 106. *e.* I say expressly, "Not a *certainty*, but a profession and visibility of these things, must be the rule of the church's proceeding.

church of God, from *Adam* to the death of the apostle *John*." To the same purpose again I express myself in p. 302. *d*. And in the *Preface* to the book that Mr. W. writes against, I make particular mention of this book *on Religious Affections*, wherein these things are said; and there declare expressly, that when I wrote that book, I was of the same mind concerning the qualifications of communicants that I am of now.—But,

VII. To make my scheme still more obnoxious and odious, Mr. W. once and again insinuates, that I insist on an account of such inward FEELINGS, as are by men supposed to be the certain discriminating marks of grace, (so p. 7. *b*. and 141. *e*.) though I never once used the phrase any where in my book.—I said not a word about *inward feelings*, from one end of it to the other. Nor is any *inward feeling* at all more implied in my scheme, than in his. But however Mr. W. knew that these phrases, *experiences*, and *inward feelings*, were become odious of late to a great part of the country; and especially the latter of them, since *Mr. Whitfield* used it so much. And he well knew, that to tack these phrases to my scheme, and to suggest to his readers that these were the things I professed to insist on, would tend to render me and my scheme contemptible. If he says, Though I use not that phrase, yet the things I insist on, are such as are *inwardly felt*; such as saving repentance, faith, &c. I answer, these things are no more *inward feelings*, than the things he himself insists on; such as a *deep conviction* of a man's undone state, *unfeigned fervent desires* after Christ, a *fixed resolution* for Christ, *engagedness* for heaven, &c.

VIII. Mr. W. abundantly, in almost all parts of his book, represents my principles to be such as suppose *men* to be the SEARCHERS *of others' hearts*. For which I have given no other ground, than only supposing that some such qualifications are necessary in order to communion, which have their seat *in the heart*, and so not to be intuitively seen by others; and that such qualifications must, by profession and practice, be made so visible or credible to others, that others may rationally judge they are there. And Mr. W. supposes the same thing as much as I. In p. 111. *c*. he expressly speaks of the qualifications necessary to communion, as being *in the heart*, and not possible to be known any other way than by their being *seen* there; and also often allows, that these qualifications must be exhibited, and made *visible*, by a credible profession, and answerable practice. Yea, he goes further, he even supposes that those who admit them to sacraments, ought to be *satisfied* by their profession, that they *really have these qualifications*. Thus he says, p. 54. *c*. "The baptizer *ought to be satisfied* by a person's profession, that he *really believes the gospel*, and that Jesus Christ is the Son of God, the Saviour."

IX. Mr. W. is not contented with all these representations of my scheme, but will have it appear more absurd and monstrous still; and therefore represents me as maintaining that it is not the *visible profession of experiences*, that I suppose the ground of the church's judgment; but these *experiences and inward feelings themselves*, by having *the heart turned inside out*, and viewing them immediately *in the heart itself*, and *judging upon the next and immediate actings of the heart*.—Here, I only desire the reader to read down Mr. W.'s 7th page, and make his own reflections.

X. Whereas, in p. 16. of my book, I observed it to be the opinion of some, that "Although the members of the visible church are saints in profession and visibility, and in the acceptance of others, yet this is not with reference to saving holiness, but quite another sort of saintship, *viz. moral sincerity*; and that this is the *real saintship, discipleship*, and *godliness*, that is professed and visible in them," &c. Mr. W. (p. 4, 5.) says, He does not remember that he ever heard of this, or that anybody thought of it, before he saw it in my book; and represents it as *a poor man of straw*, of my own framing; and he insists upon it, that *it is allowed on all hands*, that the visibility must be *with reference to saving holiness*.

I will not say, that Mr. W. knew it to be a false representation which he here makes; but this I will say, that he ought to have been better informed, before he had thus publicly ridiculed this as a fiction of *mine*; especially considering the opportunities and advantages he has had to know otherwise: this being the notion that had been (as was before observed) so loudly and publicly insisted on, for more than two years, by the people of *Northampton*, and by the neighbouring ministers, and those of them that were Mr. W.'s near relatives; as he has abundant opportunities to be fully informed, having withal had great inducements to inquire. Besides, that this has been the universal opinion of all that part of the country (who thought themselves Mr. Stoddard's followers) for more than twenty years, is a fact as notorious, as that the people there generally believe Mr. Stoddard's doctrine of the necessity of a work of conversion in order to get to heaven.—And this is the opinion professedly maintained in a pamphlet published in *Boston*, (anno 1741,) entitled, *A Right to the Lord's Supper considered*: a piece which has long been well known among Mr. W.'s nearest relatives, and in good repute with them; as I have had occasion to observe. This pamphlet insists expressly and abundantly, that *moral sincerity* is the REAL *discipleship and holiness*, with respect to which visible Christians are called *disciples* and *saints* in Scripture. Particularly see pages 9, 10, 13, and 14. And which is more strange yet, Mr. Blake, the great author Mr. W. makes so much use of, and in a book which I know he has long been the possessor of, speaks much of a profession of religion that has respect only to a dogmatical, historical faith, a common faith, a faith true indeed (as he says) in its kind, but short of that which is justifying and saving, and a profession which goes no further, as that which entitles to sealing ordinances. See Blake on the Covenant, p. 241, 244, 245. The same author again and again distinguishes between *justifying faith* and *faith of profession*; as in p. 284, 285, 286. And which is more than all this, Mr. W. (as will appear in the sequel) abundantly contends for the same thing himself, though against himself, and although he charges me (p. 35. *d*.) with a great misrepresentation, in supposing that according to the scheme of my opposers, the profession required in those that are admitted, does not imply a pretence to any thing more than moral sincerity and common grace.

PART II.

AN EXAMINATION OF MR. WILLIAMS'S SCHEME, IN THE VARIOUS PARTS OF IT.

SECT. I.

Mr. W—'s Concessions.

MR. W. allows, that, in order to a man's coming to sacraments, he ought solemnly to profess and declare, that he is really and heartily convinced of the divine truth of the gospel, (p. 30. *e*. p. 36. *a*. p. 32. *c*. p. 84. *a*.) That he does sincerely, and with all his heart, believe the gospel,* (p. 49. *e*.) And that they which admit him, ought to be satisfied he really believes the gospel, that Jesus is the Son of God, the Saviour. (p. 54. *c*.) That he should pro-

* When I first proposed to a certain candidate for communion at *Northampton*, the publicly making this profession, *viz. That he believed the truth of the gospel with all his heart*, many of the people cried out, that I insisted on what no saint on earth could profess, and that this amounted to a profession of absolute perfection. Hence many reports spread about the country, that I insisted on perfection as a term of communion.

fess and declare he believes in Christ, and that the gospel is indeed the revelation of God. (p. 5. *c.*) He allows, that none ought to be admitted, but such as openly profess and declare a hearty consent to the covenant of grace, and compliance with the call of the gospel, and submission to the proposals of it, and satisfaction with that device for our salvation that is revealed in the gospel, and with the offer which God makes of himself to be our God in Christ Jesus,* and that they fall in with the terms of salvation proposed in the gospel, and renounce all other ways. (p. 5. *c.* p. 8. *a.* p. 9. *b. c.* p. 11. *a.* p. 18. *e.* p. 55. *a.* p. 32. *c.*) He plainly supposes it not to be lawful for them that are lukewarm in religion, or those that serve two masters, to come to sacraments. (p. 32. *b.* p. 35. *d. e.* p. 36. *c.*) He supposes, that there must be a real determination of a man's judgment and affection for the word of God. (p. 55. *c.*) That there ought to be a profession of subjection to Christ with all the heart, (p. 10. *d.*) and of a devotedness to the service of God. (p. 49. *d.*) And a professed giving up themselves to Christ, to be taught, ruled, and led by him in the gospel-way to salvation; (p. 31. *e.* and 32. *a.*) And that communicants ought to declare, that they do, with all their hearts, cast themselves upon the mercy of God, to help them to keep covenant; (p. 125. *b.*) That they ought to profess a proper respect to Christ in their hearts, as well as a true notion of him in their heads; (p. 31. *d.*) That they must make a profession that imparts a pretence of real friendship to Christ, and love to God above the world. (p. 36. *c.*) That none ought to be admitted but visible saints, and that this visibility must be such as to a judgment of rational charity makes them appear as real saints, wise virgins, and endowed with gospel holiness: (p. 5. *a. b.* p. 41. *e.* p. 42. *b.* p. 139. *a. d.* p. 14. *a.*) That there should be a charitable presumption, that the Spirit of God has taken hold of them, and turned their hearts to God. (p. 52. *c.*) That they should be such persons as are in the eye of a christian judgment truly gracious persons, supposed and believed in charity to be those to whom God has given saving repentance, and a heart-purifying faith; (p. 65. *e.* and p. 47. *b. c.*) Such as have the moral image of Christ appearing in them, or supposed to be in them, and are to be loved on that account. (p. 68. *c.*) He allows, that there ought to be some apprehension, some judgment of the mind, that they are Christians and saints, and have the moral image of God in them.† (p. 68. *c. d. e.* p. 69. *a.* and 71. *d.*) He allows, that they must be taken into the church under a notion of their being godly, and with respect to such a character appearing on them: and very often insists, that they themselves must make such a pretence. (p. 55. *c. d. e.* ‡ p. 132. *a. c. d. e.* p. 136. *d.* p. 143. *c.*) So he allows, that they must not only be endowed with christian piety in appearance; but that they must be so in profession. (p. 3. *a.* p. 41. *e.* p. 44. *d.*) That they make a show of being wise virgins by the nature and purport of their profession. (p. 42. *b.*) And he insists with great strenuousness, over and over, upon its being their scheme, that they ought to make a profession of real saintship. (p. 132. *a. c. d.*) Yea, he holds, that there must be not only some visibility and profession of real piety, but moral evidence of it. (p. 139. *d.*) He often uses notes of distinction, distinguishing between *moral sincerity* and *real piety;* and insists much upon it as belonging to their scheme, that there must be a visibility of the latter, as thus distinguished from the former. So, he rejects with great contempt any suggestion of its being the scheme of my opposers, that *moral sincerity* is that saintship, which is to be professed and made visible; and in distinction from this, he asserts, that it is *real holiness.* (p. 4. *d. e.* and p. 5. *a. b.*) And again (p. 35. *c.*) he uses a note of distinction, and insists that the opposers of my opinion hold, that communicants must make a profession of something MORE than common grace and moral sincerity. And again (p. 139. *a. d.*) he uses notes of discrimination, and says, that they must exhibit a credible profession of gospel-holiness, and NOT MERELY of moral sincerity; and says, it is NOT the visibility of moral sincerity, BUT the moral evidence of gospel-sincerity, which God's word makes the rule of judging.—And as he holds, that communicants must profess gospel-holiness, so he seems to suppose that these professors must judge this of themselves; several things he says, seem plainly to imply it. This appears evidently implied in that interrogation put by Mr. W. (p. 35. *e.*) "Mr. S. rightly supposes all visible saints who are not truly pious, to be hypocrites; and the Scripture supposes and calls them so too: but will it therefore follow, that all hypocrites know they are so?" And he in effect asserts, that men should look at such a qualification, as sanctifying grace, in themselves, and inquire whether they have it, or no, in order to determine whether they should present themselves to gospel-ordinances: for he greatly finds fault with me for suggesting, as if those of a different opinion from me supposed, that persons have no manner of need to look at any such qualification in themselves, or at all inquire, whether they have it, in order to present themselves to sacraments. He refers to that passage in my book, (p. 55. *d.*) "I cannot conceive what should move *Philip* to utter those words, or what he should aim at in them, if he at the same time supposed that the eunuch had no manner of need to look at any such qualification in himself, or at all to inquire whether he had such a faith, or no, in order to determine whether he might present himself as the subject of baptism." It is plain, the qualification I have respect to, is *grace,* or *saving faith.* And so Mr. W. himself understands me; as appears by his reflections, (p. 49. *c. d. e.*) where, after quoting this passage, he consigns me over to another judgment, for suggesting that my opposers hold what I had there expressed, and for "representing the matter, as if they looked on it as no matter whether a person coming to gospel ordinances had any GRACE or no, and that he had no manner of need to inquire any thing about his sincerity."§

SECT. II.

Some plain consequences of the foregoing concessions.

IF it be as Mr. W. says, that the church ought to admit none to their holy communion, in special ordinances, but visible saints, and that this visibility must be such as to a

* Mr. W. cites Mr. *Guthrie* (pref. p. 4. *c. e.*) as on *his* side, when he speaks of such a profession, as that which is to be made.

† By this it appears, when Mr. W. speaks of the church's *rational judgment that persons have real holiness,* and the like, he does not mean merely treating them as such, in public administrations, and external conduct: for here he speaks not of the external conduct, but of *the apprehension of the understanding, and judgment of the mind;* and this as the foundation of the affection of the heart.

‡ Mr. W—'s words (p. 55. *d. e.*) are pretty remarkable: "The reader (says he) will judge, whether the manner of Mr. Edwards's treating the question, and representing the opinion of Mr. Stoddard and others, in the words I have quoted above, be not *unaccountable;* though this is neither the first nor the last time of his treating the matter in such a manner: as if Mr. Stoddard and his adherents supposed persons were to be admitted without any notion of their being godly, or any respect to such a character appearing on them, and that they themselves are without such a pretence."—Whereas, Mr. Stoddard expressly maintains, that men may be *duly qualified,* and *fit matter* for church-membership, without saving grace. (*Appeal,* p. 15, 16.) And that they *may* and *ought to come, though they know themselves to be in a natural condition.* (*Doct. of Instituted Churches,* p. 21. See also his *Sermon* on the subject, p. 13.) And according to Mr. Stoddard, communicants are not so much as *supposed* godly persons. This (*Appeal,* p. 43.) he says expressly, that *by the institution communicants at the Lord's supper are not supposed to be real saints.* And also asserts (*Appeal,* p. 76.) that we are not obliged to *believe* visible saints to be real saints. And it seems by what he says in his *Appeal,* (p. 17.) the church may admit persons to communion, when at the same time *they are aware that they are hypocrites.* For there, in answer to Dr. *Mather,* who had cited certain texts to prove, that when hypocrites do come into the church, they come in *unawares;* he says, *but neither of the places he cites proves that* all *hypocrites come in unawares.* And in the next page he says, *The discovery of men's hypocrisy is not the reason of their being cast out.* Still evidently on the same foundation, that some known hypocrites are *fit* to be admitted; for he says, (p. 15. *d.*) *Such as being admitted may not be cast out, are fit to be admitted.* And these things are agreeable to what I know Mr. *Stoddard's* church and congregation have universally supposed to be his constant doctrine and practice among them. Thus it was, without one dissenting voice among them, during the twenty-four years that I lived with them. And now the reader is desired to judge, as Mr. W. would have him, whether my representing it to be the opinion of Mr. S. and his adherents, that persons might *be admitted into the church without any notion of their being godly, or any respect to such a character appearing on them,* be unaccountable.—By these things it is evident, Mr. S——d's scheme was far from being what Mr. W. represents it to be, and pretends to maintain as his. And if the question he had to controvert with me, were Mr. S——d's question, as he asserts; yet he greatly mistakes *the true state of the question,* though that be given as the title of his book.

§ Now let all that have been acquainted with the controversy between me and my people at *Northampton,* consider these things, which Mr. W. earnestly insists do belong to *his* scheme: and judge whether they be agreeable to the scheme which my opposers *there* have so vehemently and long contended for; yea, whether they are not very opposite to it; or whether in these things Mr. W. has not entirely yielded up, yea, vehemently asserted, the chief things concerning which they contested with me; and so, whether he has at all helped *their* cause by writing his book, or rather, on the contrary, has fought against them.

judgment of rational charity, makes them appear as real saints, and those that are admitted must be such as profess real saintship, gospel-holiness, in distinction from moral sincerity; then the whole of my *first* argument, from the nature of a *visibility* and *profession* of Christianity, is allowed by him, in both *premises* and *consequences*. And indeed Mr. W. does not only do thus consequentially, but he is express in it. In (p. 4. *c.*) taking notice of this argument, he says, "The sense and force of it wholly lies in this compass; a *visible saint* is one that to the view, appearance, and judgment of the church, is a *real saint;* and since none but *visible saints* are to be admitted by the church, therefore none are to be admitted but such as *appear* to the view and judgment of the church to be *real saints*." But these things, which Mr. W. himself allows as the sum of the argument, both premises and consequence, are expressly allowed by him in what there follows.

2. If there must be a visibility and profession of *real piety*, in distinction from *moral sincerity*, so that it can be truly said, as Mr. W. says with discretive terms, and notes of discrimination, that NOT MERELY the one must be professed, BUT the other; and that MORE than moral sincerity must be professed, &c.—Then it follows (or rather it is the same thing) that men must profess religion with some *discrimination*, or marks of difference in their words, distinguishing what is professed from moral sincerity; contrary to what Mr. W. strenuously and frequently asserts, (p. 6. *c. d.* and p. 9. *c.* and many other places.) For if the profession is made in words that signify no *difference*, then nothing *different* is signified or professed by those words; and so nothing MORE; contrary to what Mr. W. also asserts

3. If it be as Mr. W. says, that the Scripture has determined none ought to be admitted, but such as make an open profession and declaration of a hearty consent to the terms of the covenant of grace, such as covenant with God with their whole hearts, and profess gospel-holiness: then the whole of my *second* argument, concerning *explicit covenanting with God*, is expressly allowed, in both *premises* and *consequence;* though Mr. W. seems at the same time, with much labour and earnestness, to militate against it. For the *premises* are, that *all ought openly and explicitly to own God's covenant, or consent to the terms of it*. This is the same thing that he asserts, as above. And the *consequence*, or thing which I inferred from it, was, that all that are admitted ought to make a profession of real godliness: and this also he expressly and often allows.

4. Since it is supposed, that in order to admission, men ought to profess real friendship to Christ, and love to him above the world, and to profess a proper respect to Christ in their hearts, as well as true notion of him in their heads; and that they ought to profess gospel-holiness, and not merely moral sincerity: therefore the whole of what belongs to my *third* argument, is allowed, both *premises* and *consequence*. The *premises* were, that *the nature of things affords as much reason for professing a proper respect to Christ in the heart, as a true notion of him in the head*. This he allows. What I endeavoured to *infer* from hence, was, that *therefore men ought to profess true piety, and not only moral sincerity:* and this is also allowed by him.

5. It appears, that the whole of my *fourth* argument, both *premises* and *consequence*, is allowed. The *premises* were, that *the Scripture reckons all visible saints who are not truly pious, to be hypocrites*. This Mr. W. expressly allows, (p. 25. *e.*) The *consequence* I inferred, was, that visible saints are such as make a profession of true godliness, and not only moral sincerity. This also is very fully allowed by him, (p. 139. *a.*)

6. Since it is supposed, that when Christ's rules are attended, they that come to sacraments, *do not know themselves to be hypocrites*, but most *look at such a qualification in themselves*, as grace, and make such a *pretence*, and *profess gospel holiness:* therefore all is in effect allowed, that I endeavoured from the latter part of the 7th chapter of *Matthew*, which was to show, that professing Christians in general, all those that said, *Lord, Lord*, both those that built on the *sand*, and those that built on a *rock*, were such as imagined themselves to have a saving interest in Christ, and *pretended* to be his real disciples, and made such a *profession*. The same was what I endeavoured to show from the parable of the *ten virgins*. And therefore all that I argued from thence is in like manner allowed.

7. Hence, in vain is all the opposition Mr. W. makes to what I allege from the *Acts of the Apostles*, from the story of the *eunuch* and other parts of that book, concerning the manner and circumstances of the admission of members into the primitive christian church, and the profession they made; seeing he grants the main point I endeavoured to prove by it, *viz.* That they *did make*, and all adult persons that are admitted into the church *must make*, a profession *of something* MORE *than moral sincerity*, even *gospel-holiness*.

8. Hence, in vain is all he says in opposition to my *eighth* argument, taken from the manner of the apostles' treating and addressing the primitive churches in their *epistles;* since he does either expressly or virtually grant each of those three things, which he himself reckons up as the sum of what I intend under that argument, *viz.* (1.) That the apostles speak to the churches, and of them, as supposing and judging them to be gracious persons. (2.) That the members of these churches had such an opinion of themselves. (3.) That they had this judgment one of another. Mr. W. allows all these. He abundantly allows and asserts, that the members of churches are such as are supposed, and rationally judged, to be gracious persons, by those that admit them; that they are taken in under that notion, and from respect to such a character appearing on them; and that they are rationally judged to be so by their fellow-Christians; and that they must look at such a character in themselves, and must make such a pretence.

9. Since Mr. W. abundantly allows, that visible Christians must be believed in charity to be truly pious; and that they are such as have the moral image of Christ appearing in them, and supposed to be in them, and that they are to be loved on that account: therefore very impertinent and inconsistent is the opposition he makes to my *ninth* argument, from the nature of that *brotherly love* required towards all visible Christians; which was to show, that visible Christians by the rule of Christ were to be apprehended to be true Christians.

10. In like manner, vain and to no purpose is the opposition he makes to my *tenth* argument, from the nature of *sacramental actions*, supposed in their intent and signification to be a solemn profession of those things wherein real piety consists, *viz.* a cordial acceptance of Christ and his benefits; from thence arguing, that a profession of these things is necessary, and so inferring, that those who perform these actions, should suppose themselves truly to accept of Christ: since both these things are in effect granted, that communicants must judge that they have sanctifying grace, and also that they must profess gospel-holiness, a compliance with the call of the gospel, and falling in with the terms of salvation proposed, &c.

11. In vain also is the opposition he makes to my *eleventh* argument, from 1 Cor. xi. 28. "Let a man examine himself; and so let him eat."—Inferring from thence, that a man ought to inquire concerning such a qualification in himself, as grace, in order to know whether he may come to the sacrament of the Lord's supper. Since Mr. W. himself plainly supposes this very thing. That men ought to look at such a qualification in themselves, as grace, and to inquire whether they have it, in order to determine whether they may present themselves to christian sacraments.

12. If it be true, according to Mr. W.'s representation of his own scheme, That persons may not be admitted to sacraments, but under a notion of their being truly godly, and with respect to such a character appearing on them; and that persons themselves had need to look at such a qualification in themselves, and inquire whether they have it, in order to determine whether they may come to sacraments; it must be because if they find they have it *not*, they *may not* come, or (which is the same thing) *it is not lawful* for them to come. For it would be ridiculous to say that others must look at such a qualification in them, and must not admit them but from respect to such a cha-

racter on them; and that they themselves also must look at such a qualification in themselves, and inquire whether they have it in order to determine whether they MAY come; when yet they *may* come whether they have it or no, and have as much of a lawful right without it as with it. So that Mr. W. has in effect determined against himself the grand point, which he himself insists on, as the point in dispute, according to *the true state of the question*. And therefore,

13. It follows from the foregoing concessions, that Mr. W. is inconsistent with himself in all his arguings that men may come to sacraments without such a qualification or character as that of true piety. Because God has given no certain rule by which sacraments may be restrained to such;* or because that otherwise none might come but those that know they have such a character;† or because the contrary doctrine tends to bring saints into great perplexities in their attendance on sacraments;‡ or from the lawfulness of unregenerate men's attending other duties.§ If there be any force in this arguing from other duties to an attendance on sacraments, then the argument will infer, that men must not be admitted to other duties, but under the notion of their being truly godly, and from respect to such a character appearing on them, &c.—as Mr. W. insists with regard to christian sacraments. And so if these things which Mr. W. concedes and asserts, are true, in vain is all arguing from the like tendency in sacraments to convert men, as in other duties;‖ and in vain is it to argue the lawfulness of men's coming without this character, from their obligation to perform external covenant-duties,¶ and to carry themselves like saints;** and in vain is all arguing from the pretended bad consequences of the contrary doctrine.††

14. The opposition Mr. W. makes to my argument from Isaiah lvi. especially those words, ver. 6, 7. "The sons of the stranger that join themselves to the Lord, to love the Lord, and be his servants—will I bring into my holy mountain"—to prove that none have a right in the sight of God to the privileges of the christian church, but those that love God, and are truly pious; I say, the opposition Mr. W. makes to this argument is frivolous, since he in effect grants the same thing, (as above,) yea, expressly allows, that they must make pretences of being God's real friends, and loving God more than the world, p. 36. *c.*

15. If it be true, as Mr. W. allows and abundantly asserts, that in order to persons being admitted to holy communion in special ordinances, the Scripture has determined, that there must be an open profession and declaration of a person's believing, or of a personal believing, *in Christ*, (which is the same thing,) and of a hearty consent to the terms of the covenant of grace,‡‡ and that therein must be a profession of gospel-holiness: then nothing to the contrary avails that great argument of his, taken from the state of baptized infants, that they are already in the church, and in covenant, and are members in complete standing, &c. and that therefore no owning the covenant or professing godliness can be demanded of them:§§ and in vain is all that he has said to prove this in his discourse on the *wheat* and *tares*.‖‖

16. To what purpose is it, to object from the parable now mentioned, that the church ought not to make a distinction between *wheat* and *tares*, in their admission of members, by pretending to discern the difference? When it is so apparent, that there is no pretence to any proper discerning in the case, nor any other distinction pleaded, than what is made by a judgment of charity. According to Mr. W—'s own scheme, churches are obliged to make a distinction, in the rational judgment they pass, and to admit none, but what they judge to be true saints; so that those who are *wheat*, in the eye of their judgment, only are to be admitted, and such as are *tares*, in the eye of their judgment, are to be excluded.

17. What is said by Mr. W. of the visible church being the *school of Christ*, and men being admitted into it as disciples or scholars, some of them in order to attain grace, (p. 81, and 83.) is nothing to the purpose, if it be as Mr. W. allows and asserts, that in order to be admitted into this *school*, they must be supposed, in a reasonable judgment, to have this attainment already, and make a pretence to it, and a solemn profession of it, and must give moral evidence that they have it, and must be admitted into the school under no other notion than that of their being already possessed of it.

18. If it be as Mr. W. expressly says, That persons are not visible saints without a credible profession, visibility, and moral evidence, not only of moral sincerity, but true holiness, (p. 139.) then all is wholly insignificant and vain, that is said to prove, that the children of *Israel* were visible saints without any evidence of such holiness, by reason of the idolatry and gross and open wickedness of vast multitudes of them, who are yet called God's people. And so likewise, all that is said to prove, that the members of the primitive christian church had no other visibility of saintship than they, because they are grafted into the same olive; and also all that Mr. W. has said to prove, that many of the members of the primitive churches were as grossly wicked as they.

19. Since according to Mr. W. the terms of admission to the Jewish ordinances, were the same as to christian ordinances, the like profession and the same visibility of saintship required, and no other; as he strenuously asserts, (p. 57. *e.* p. 61. *e.* and p. 65. *c.*) it will therefore follow from his foregoing concessions and assertions, that none were, by God's appointment, to come to the passover, and to have their children circumcised, but such as openly professed and declared that they were convinced of the truth of God's word, and believed it with all their hearts; and professed a hearty consent to the terms of the covenant of grace: such as covenanted with God with their whole hearts, and gave up all their hearts and lives to Christ; such as subjected themselves to Christ with their whole hearts, and gave up themselves to him, to be ruled, taught, and led by him; such as with all their hearts cast themselves on the mercy of God to enable them to keep covenant; such as professed to love God above the world, and professed more than common faith and moral sincerity, even true holiness, real piety; and who gave moral evidence, that they had such a qualification; and were received to the passover, &c. under that notion, and with respect to such a character appearing in them, and apprehended to be in them. And if these things are so, what is become of the argument from the passover and circumcision, against the necessity of the qualifications I have insisted on?

20. To what purpose does Mr. W. insist, (p. 98. *a.*) That we read not a word in Scripture about John the Baptist's making any inquiry, whether the people he baptized made a credible profession of true piety? when he himself insists, that in order to admission to christian sacraments, men must make a credible profession of true piety. And why does he urge, (p. 96. *e.* and p. 97.) That the profession the people made which John baptized did not imply that they had saving repentance, but only an engagement to repent, hereafter? when he himself holds, that in order to admission to sacraments, men must profess something more than common grace, and not only promise it hereafter.

21. It makes nothing to any point in controversy between Mr. W. and me, whether Judas partook of the Lord's supper or no, since according to the fore-mentioned principles, as well as mine, he could not be admitted there under any other notion than that of being truly pious, and from respect to such a character appearing on him, and a credible profession of gospel-holiness; and since he might not lawfully come without some qualifications he had not, *viz.* such a friendship for Christ, as is above lukewarmness, and above serving two masters, Christ and Mammon, and a giving up all his heart and life to Christ, and a real determination of his judgment and affections for Christ's word, &c.

22. If it be true, as Mr. W. allows, that ministers and churches ought not to admit adult persons to sacraments, without a pious character appearing on them, and their professing and exhibiting moral evidence of gospel-holiness, then no good argument can be brought against such a way of admission, from the success of ministers in another way, or in any way whatsoever.

* See Mr. W.'s book, p. 106, &c. † Ibid. p. 108, &c. ‡ P. 120, &c. § P. 123, &c. ‖ P. 126, &c. ¶ P. 128, &c. ** P. 131. †† P. 131, &c. ‡‡ See how Mr. W. expresses himself, p. 5. *b. c.* §§ See especially, p. 3. ‖‖ P. 99, 100.

Besides these plain and obvious consequences of Mr. W.'s concessions, some other consequences will hereafter be observed under particular heads.

Thus Mr. W. has in effect given up every point belonging to the whole controversy, every thing material insisted on through that whole book which he undertakes to answer. He has established every part of my scheme, and every particular argument I have used to confirm it; and answered, or overthrown every argument which he brings, or pretends to support, against it. And I should have no further occasion to say any thing in reply to him, if he had not really, through great part of his performance, argued for other things, opposite to those that have been rehearsed, which he so strenuously insists belong to his scheme. That arguing may seem to support another scheme, though nothing akin to his, any otherwise than as it is indeed a mixture of many schemes, one clashing with and destroying another; as will appear in the ensuing part of this reply.

SECT. III.

The inconsistence of the fore-mentioned concessions with the lawfulness of unsanctified persons coming to the Lord's supper, and their right to sacraments in the sight of God.

MR. W. in the book under consideration, which he entitles the true state of the question, insists upon it that the question to be debated is the question Mr. Stoddard debated in his dispute with Dr. Mather; in whose scheme Mr. W. declares himself to be. Mr. S. in his dispute with Dr. Mather asserted, that it was lawful for some unsanctified men to come to the Lord's supper, and that they had a right so to do in the sight of God. And he declares that this was the point in dispute between him and Dr. Mather; as in *Appeal*, p. 20. "That which I am to show is, that some unsanctified men have a right before God to the Lord's supper." So Mr. Blake (who is so great an author with Mr. W.) says in his treatise *on the covenant*, p. 244. "That faith which is the condition of the promise, is not the condition *in foro Dei* [before God] of a title to the seal." And there (in the next p.) he insists, that it is a common faith, that is believed by men not justified, which gives this title. Agreeable to these things Mr. W. says, (p. 132. *d.*) Some men have a lawful right to the sacrament without sanctification. Which is the same thing as to say, They have a right in the sight of God. For if they have no right in the sight of God to come to the Lord's supper, then it is not lawful in the sight of God that they should come.

Here I would lay down this as a maxim;

There is some inward religion and virtue or other, some sincerity of heart, either moral or saving, that is necessary to a right to sacraments in the sight of God, and in order to a lawful coming to them. No man, I trust, will say, that a man has a right in God's sight, who has no sort of seriousness of mind; and that merely outward sounds and motions give him this right in God's sight, without regard to any property or quality of mind, and though this outward show is joined with the most horrid and resolved secret irreligion and wickedness. Mr. W. in particular utterly disclaims such doctrine as this, and always maintains that in order to men's lawful coming, they must be *morally sincere;* as in his Preface, and also in p. 25. *d. e.* p. 27. *c.* p. 30. *d.* p. 35. *e.* p. 111.—In p. 115. he supposes, that if a man makes a doubt of his moral sincerity, no divine will advise him to come till he knows.

Having observed this, I now desire it may be considered, whether it be reasonable to suppose, as Mr. W. does, that God would give men that are without grace, a lawful right to sacraments, so that this qualification itself should be nothing necessary to a proper and rightful claim to these ordinances; and yet that he would wholly forbid them to come, and others to admit them, without their making some pretence to it, and exhibiting moral evidence that they have it: that moral sincerity is the qualification which by God's own appointment invests persons with a lawful right to sacraments, and that by his institution nothing more is requisite to a lawful right; and yet that he has commanded them not to come, nor others to allow them to come, without making a profession of something *more* than moral sincerity, as Mr. W. says. Mr. W. supposes that God requires us, before we admit persons, to seek credible evidence of true piety, and to see to it that we have reasonable ground to believe they have it; otherwise, not to allow them to come; and yet that God does not look on such a qualification requisite in itself, when all is done, and that he has given them as true and lawful a right to come without it, as with it. If God insists upon it, as Mr. W. supposes, that members should be admitted under no other notion than of their being truly godly, and from respect to such a character appearing on them, is it not plain, that God looks on such a character in itself requisite, in order to a person's being a rightful subject of such a privilege? If the want of this qualification do not in the least hinder a person's lawful right to a thing, on what account can the want of an appearance of it and pretence to it, warrant and oblige others to hinder his taking possession of that thing?

That we should be obliged to require a credible pretence and evidence of the being of a thing, in order to a certain purpose, the being of which is not requisite to that purpose; or that some evidence of a thing should be necessary, and yet withal no necessity there should be any foundation of such evidence, in the being of the thing to be made evident; that it should be necessary for us to seek evidence that something is true, and yet there be no need in order to the intended purpose, that there be any such truth to be made evident;—if these things are the dictates of common sense, I am willing all that are possessed of any degree of common sense should be judges.

If God has plainly revealed, that gospel-holiness is not necessary in itself in order to men's lawful right to sacraments, as Mr. W. greatly insists, then his churches need not *believe it to be necessary;* yea, it is their duty *to believe that it is* not *necessary*, as it is their duty to believe what God says to be true. But yet Mr. W. holds, that God forbids his churches to admit any to sacraments, unless they first have some rational evidence obliging them *to believe that they have gospel-holiness.* Now how palpable is the inconsistence, that we must be obliged to believe men have a qualification in order to our suffering them to come, which yet at the same time we need not believe to be necessary for them to have in order to their coming, but which God requires us to believe to be unnecessary! Or in other words, that God has made it necessary for us to believe or suppose men are truly pious, in order to our lawfully allowing them to take the sacraments, and yet at the same time requires us to believe no such thing as their being pious is necessary in order to their lawfully taking the sacraments!

Mr. Stoddard (whose principles Mr. W. in Preface, p. 3. *a.* declares himself to be fully established in) not only says, that some unsanctified men have a right before God to the Lord's supper, but strongly asserts, over and over, that they are FIT to be admitted to the Lord's supper, that they are DULY QUALIFIED, FIT MATTER for church-membership. —(*Appeal*, p. 15, 16.) And Mr. W. argues that such qualifications as some unsanctified men have, are SUFFICIENT to bring them into the church. Now if it be so, what business have we to demand evidence or pretence of any thing further? What case in the world can be mentioned parallel to it, in any nation or age? Are there any such kind of laws or regulations to be found in any nation, city, or family; in any society, civil, military or academic, stated or occasional, that the society should be required to insist on some credible pretence and evidence of a certain qualification, in order to persons being admitted to the privileges of the society; prohibiting their being admitted *under any other notion* than as persons possessed of that qualification, or *without a respect in their admission to such a character appearing on them:* and yet at the same time, by the laws of that very society, that qualification is not necessary; but persons are declared, without any such qualification, to have a LAWFUL RIGHT, to be FIT MATTER, to be DULY QUALIFIED, and to have SUFFICIENT qualifications to be admitted to these privileges, without that qualification?

If some men have a right in the sight of God to sacraments without true piety, and are *fit* and *duly qualified* without it, in his sight and by his institution, and yet the church must not admit them unless they are truly pious in their sight; then the eye of man must require higher terms, than the infinitely holy eye of God himself; they must look for something that the eye of God looks not for, and which he judges them duly qualified without.

Mr. W. when speaking of the evidence, on which he supposes the church ought to judge persons to be real saints, from time to time adds, that on such evidence "The church is obliged, in their external carriage, *to treat them as saints*, and admit them to the external privileges of the church."—So, p. 9. *d.* p. 12. *a.* &c. p. 13. *a. b.* and p. 14. *c.* and in other places. But what does he mean by treating them *as saints*, in admitting them to the external privileges of the church? If *sinners* have as much of a lawful right to these privileges, as *saints*, then why is giving them these privileges, a treating them *as saints*, any more than as *sinners?* If it belongs to an ignorant child, to be admitted into school, as much as one that is learned, then how is it treating him as one that is learned, to admit him? Mr. W. (p. 11. *d. e.*) giving a reason why he that professes conviction of the truth of the gospel, &c. ought to be admitted to sacraments, says, "Though this conviction may be only by moral evidence and common illumination, yet—the church knows not but it is done on a divine and gracious discovery." But how can this be a reason? What if the church *did know* that it was not on a gracious discovery, if the man has a right in the sight of God without, and God has made it his duty to come to sacraments without it? Surely the church have no right to forbid him to do that which God has given him a right to do, and made it his duty to do; as Mr. S. says, (*Doct. of Inst. Churches*, p. 20. *b.*) The church may not hinder any man from doing his duty.

Therefore if this be Mr. S——d's question, Whether some unsanctified men may lawfully come to the Lord's supper, and if this be the grand point in dispute, the thing which Mr. W. undertakes to maintain, as he often declares, then it is most plainly evident, that in conceding and asserting those things forementioned, he does in effect abundantly give up that which he himself insists on as the grand point in controversy; and so makes void and vain all his own labour, and for himself effectually confutes all that he has written.

SECT. IV.

Concerning Mr. W.'s notion of a public profession of godliness in terms of an indeterminate and double signification.

ACCORDING to Mr. W. the profession of godliness must be in words not of a determinate meaning, or without any discrimination in the meaning of the words, obliging us to understand them of saving religion. (p. 6. *c. d.*) They must make an open declaration of their sincere consent to the terms of the covenant, without any discrimination, by which it can be determined, that the consent signified by the words is a gracious consent. (p. 9. *c.*) And without any marks of difference, or any distinction in the words, whereby we can be enabled to judge when they mean a saving faith, and when a different one. (p. 10. *c. e.* p. 50. *e.* and p. 53. *c.*) That nothing should be expressed in the words of the profession, but what some unsanctified men may say, and speak true. (p. 47. *e.*) He supposes, that the primitive Christians in the profession they made of faith, did not speak only in that sense, *viz.* so as to signify justifying faith; and that the persons admitted did not understand that their profession was understood by those that admitted them, only in that sense. (p. 58. *c.*)

Agreeable to this notion of making a profession in words of indiscriminate meaning, and professing godliness without godliness, and yet speaking true, Mr. W. (in p. 44. *d. e.*) allows, that men must be by profession godly persons, in order to come to the sacrament; and yet in the next sentence he denies, that christian grace itself is requisite in the person who is to come to the sacrament, or that the dictate of his conscience that he has it, is the thing that gives him a right to offer himself. And agreeable to this last clause, Mr. Stoddard (of whose opinion Mr. W. professes himself fully to be) expressly maintains, that a man may and ought to come to the Lord's supper, though he knows himself to be in a natural condition. (*Doct. of Inst. Churches*, p. 21. See also his sermon on this controversy, p. 13.) So that putting these things together, it must be agreeable to Mr. W.'s scheme, that a man has a right to make a profession of godliness, without having godliness, and without any dictate of his conscience that he has the thing he professes, yea, though he knows he has not! And all this is made out by the doctrine of professing godliness in words that are ambiguous, and of two meanings.

This notion of a solemn profession of godliness, in words of a double meaning, *without any marks of difference in their signification*, is the great peculiarity of Mr. W.'s scheme; and in all his controversy with me, this appears to be the main hinge, the crisis of the whole affair. Therefore I would particularly consider it. And for the greater distinctness and clearness, I will lay down certain *positions*, as of most evident truth; observing some of their no less plain and evident consequences.

I. Words declare or profess nothing any otherwise than by their signification: for to declare or profess something by words, is to signify something by words. And therefore, if nothing is signified by words of a pretended profession, nothing is really professed; and if something be professed, no more is professed than the words of the profession signify or import.

II. If a man declare or profess any particular thing by words which have no distinguishing signification, or without any signs or discriminating marks by which men may be enabled to distinguish what he means, his words are vain to the pretended purpose, and wholly fail of answering the end of words, which is to convey the thing meant to others' understanding, or to give notice to others of the thing supposed or understood.*

Therefore to use words thus in common conversation, is to act in a vain trifling manner, more like children than men: but to use words thus in the sacred services of God's house, and solemn duties of his worship, is something much worse than children's play. But thus Mr. W. expressly declares, words are to be used in a public profession of religion. (p. 10. *c.*) "And these words are so used in such cases, without any marks of difference, whereby we are enabled to judge when they mean a saving faith, and when a different one."

III. A profession made in words that are either equivocal, or general, equally signifying several distinct things, without any marks of difference or distinction, by which we are enabled to judge what is meant, is not a profession or signification of *any one* of those several things; nor can they afford any rational ground of understanding or apprehending any *particular thing*. Thus for instance, if a man using an equivocal term, should say, that such an evening a king was in that room, without any marks of difference or discrimination whatsoever, by which others could discern whether, by a *king*, he meant the ruler of a kingdom, or a king used in a game of chess; the words thus used would be no declaration, that the head of a kingdom was there at such a time; nor would they give any notice of any such thing to those to whom he spoke, or give them any rational ground to understand or judge any such thing.

Or if a man should use a *general* term, comprehending various particular sorts, without at all distinguishing or pointing forth any one particular sort, he thereby professes no one particular sort. Thus if a man professes that he has metal in his pocket, not saying what sort of metal, whether gold, silver, brass, iron, lead, or tin; his words are no profession that he has gold.

So if a man professes sincerity or religion, designedly

* The Apostle *Paul* says, 1 Cor. xiv. 7. "Even things without life, giving sound, whether pipe or harp, except they give a distinction in the sounds, how shall it be known what is piped or harped?" ——Mr. *Locke* says, *Hum. Und.* Vol. 2. Edit. 7. p. 103. "He that uses words of any language without distinct ideas in his mind, to which he applies them, does so far as he uses them in discourse, only make a noise without any sense or signification."

using terms of double signification, or (which comes to the same thing) of general signification, equally signifying two entirely distinct things, either *moral sincerity*, or *real piety*, his words are no profession of real piety; he makes no credible profession, and indeed no profession at all of *gospel holiness*.

IV. If a man who knows himself to be destitute of any certain qualification, yet makes a profession or pretence in words of double meaning, equally signifying that qualification, and something else very different, with a design to recommend himself to others' judgment and apprehension, as possessed of that qualification, he is guilty of deceitful equivocation, *viz.* using words of double meaning, or capable of double application, with a design to induce others to judge something to be true, which is not true. But he that would recommend himself by such terms to others' opinion or judgment, as being what he at the same time knows he is not, endeavours to induce them to believe what he knows is not true, which is to deceive them.*

But if the scheme which Mr. W. undertakes to defend were true, it would follow that such a kind of equivocation as this, (be it far from us to suppose it,) is what the infinitely wise and holy God has instituted to be publicly used in the solemn services of his house, as the very condition of persons' admission to the external privileges of his people! For Mr. W. abundantly asserts, that persons must be *esteemed* in the *judgment* and *apprehension* of others to have true piety; and that one thing that must *be done in order to it*, one thing pertaining to the moral evidence that *recommends* them to this judgment, is the profession they make of religion, (p. 5. p. 139. p. 47. *b, c.* p. 132. p. 44. *d.*) In p. 42. speaking of the profession of visible Christians, he has these words, "And it is from the nature and purport of this profession, we say, the church is to judge the members to be wise virgins, or what they make a show of." And Mr. W. insists upon it, that according to Christ's institution, this must be in words equally signifying true godliness, and something else, without any discrimination or marks of difference.—This is the scheme! And certainly such a doctrine of deceitful equivocation in the public exercises of religion, is more agreeable to the principles and practices of a religion I am loth to name, than the true religion of Jesus Christ.

Mr. W. says, (p. 35. *d.*) "I am at a loss to conceive how it will help the cause of truth to represent those who are of Mr. S—'s opinion, as teaching men that they may enter into covenant with God with known and allowed guile." Supposing I had made such a representation, I can tell him how it would have helped the cause of truth, (as it would be speaking nothing but the truth,) if he be one of *Mr. Stoddard's* opinion, (as he says he is,) and represents his own opinion truly.

But let the unreasonableness of this notion of professing gospel-holiness in words of two meanings, without any discrimination or mark of difference, be a little further considered. Since it is allowed, that *gospel-holiness* is the thing which is to be exhibited in the profession, and there are words which signify this by a determinate meaning, why must they needs be avoided, and words of doubtful and double signification only be made use of?† Since the design of the profession is to exhibit to others' understanding that very thing; if the proper and distinguishing names of that must nevertheless be avoided in the profession, and for this very reason, that they point forth to others' understanding that very thing by a determinate meaning; then we are brought to this gross absurdity, *viz.* That the end of a profession is to exhibit to others' understanding and reasonable judgment a *particular qualification;* but at the same time such words only must be used as do not distinctly point forth to others' understanding and judgment that *particular qualification.* The church are to seek and demand a profession, that shall *determine their rational judgment;* but yet are designedly to avoid such a profession as shall *determine their understandings.*—Be it far from us to attribute to the allwise God any such an absurd and inconsistent constitution.

Mr. W. says, *charity obliges the church to understand the words of the professors in the most favourable sense.* But charity does not oblige us to understand their words in any other sense than that in which they professedly use them. But in churches which professedly act on Mr. W.'s scheme, (if any such there be,) the professors who are admitted, professedly use ambiguous words, or words equally signifying two entirely distinct things, without discrimination or marks of difference; and therefore charity obliges us to understand their words no otherwise, than as signifying that they have one or other of those two things; and not that they have one in particular: for their words do not signify this, in the sense they professedly use them. If a man that is indebted to me, professes that he has either gold or brass, which he promises to pay me; or if he uses an equivocal or general term, that equally, and without marks of difference, signifies either one or the other; charity may oblige me to believe what he says, which is, that he has either gold or brass: but no charity obliges me to believe that he has gold, which he does not say.

Mr. W. in his description of such a profession as Christ has instituted, in order to admission to sacraments, often mentions two things, *viz.* A profession of something *present*, a present believing in Christ, and cordial consent to the terms of the covenant of grace, &c. And a promise of something *future*. And with regard to the latter, he is very full in it, that what is promised for time to come is saving faith, repentance, and obedience.‡ Now what reason can be given why we should use words of double meaning in the former part of the profession more than in the latter? Seeing Mr. W. allows that we must *profess* gospel-holiness as well as *promise* it, and seeing we may and must make use of words of indiscriminate and double meaning in professing present gospel-holiness, why should not we do so too in promising what is future; and so equivocate in our solemn vows and oaths as the papists do? If Mr. W. says it is very hard for men to discern the discrimination between moral sincerity and gospel-holiness; I answer, there is as much need to discern the difference in order understandingly to promise gospel-holiness with discrimination, as to profess it with discrimination.

Mr. W. says, (p. 8. *b. c.*) "It is a received rule among mankind, in all public judgments, to interpret words in the most extensive and favourable sense that the nature of the words or expressions will bear." I know not what he means: but if he means, (as he must, if he means any thing to the purpose,) that it is a received rule amongst mankind, to trust, or accept, or at all regard any professions or declarations that men make, with professed design, in words of double and indiscriminate meaning, without any marks of difference by which their meaning can be known, for that very end that they may be used with a safe conscience, though they have no dictates of their own consciences, that they have what others are to believe they have; I say, if this be a received rule among mankind, it is a rule that mankind has lately received from Mr. W. Heretofore mankind, societies or particular persons, would have been counted very foolish for regarding such professions. Is this the way in earthly kingdoms, in professions of allegiance to temporal princes, in order to their admission to the privileges of good subjects? Do they choose equivocal terms to put into their oaths of allegiance, to that end that men may use them and speak true, though they are secret enemies?—There are two competitors for the kingdom of this world, *Christ* and *Satan;* the design of a public profession of religion is, to declare on which side men are. And is it agreeable to the custom of mankind in such cases, to make laws that no other than ambiguous words shall be used, or to accept of such in declarations of this kind? There are two competitors for the kingdom of *Great Britain*, King George, and the *Pretender:* is it the constitution of King George and the *British* parliament, that men should take oaths of allegiance, contrived in words of indeterminate signification, to the end that men who are in their hearts enemies to King George, and friends to the Pretender, may use

* "To advance a dubious proposition, knowing it will be understood in a sense different from what you give it in your mind, is an *equivocation*, in breach of good faith and sincerity." *Chambers's* Dictionary, under the word *Equivocation.*

† Mr. W. (p. 6. *d. e.*) speaks of a profession in terms of indiscriminate signification, when not contradicted in life, as *The sole, entire evidence, which the church, as a church, is to have, by divine appointment, in order to that public judgment it is to make of the saintship of men.*

‡ Pref. (p. 3. *d. e.* and 5. *d.* p. 24. *b.* 25. *b.* 22. *d.* 27. *a.* 58. *d.* 69. *d.*

them and speak true? And certainly mankind, those of them that have common sense, never in any affairs of life look on such professions as worth a rush. Would Mr. W. himself, if tried, in any affair wherein his temporal interest is concerned, trust such professions as these? If any man with whom he has dealings, should profess to him that he had pawned for him, in a certain place, a *hundred pounds*, evidently, yea professedly, using the expression as an ambiguous one, so that there is no understanding by it, what is pawned there, whether a *hundred pound* in money, or a hundred weight of stones: if he should inquire of the man what he meant, and he should reply, You have no business to *search my heart*, or to *turn my heart inside out;* you are obliged in charity to understand my words *in the most favourable sense;* would Mr. W. in this case stick to his own *received rule?* would he regard such a profession, or run the venture of one *sixpence* upon it? Would he not rather look on such a man as affronting him, and treating him as though he would make a fool of him? And would not he know, that every body else would think him a fool, if he should suffer himself to be gulled by such professions, in things which concern his own private interest? And yet it seems, this is the way in which he thinks he ought to conduct himself as a minister of Christ, and one intrusted by him in affairs wherein his honour and the interests of his kingdom are concerned.

And now I desire it may be judged by such as are possessed of human understanding, and are not disabled by prejudice from exercising it, whether this notion of Mr. W.'s, of making a solemn profession of gospel-holiness in words of indiscriminate meaning, be not too absurd to be received by the reason God has given mankind.—This peculiar notion of his is apparently the life and soul of his scheme; the main pillar of his temple, on which the whole weight of the building rests; which if it be broken, the whole falls to the ground, and buries the builder, or at least his work, in its ruins. For if this notion of his be disproved, then inasmuch as it is agreed, that true godliness must be professed, it will follow, that it must be professed in words properly signifying the thing by a determinate meaning, which therefore no ungodly men can use, and speak true; and that therefore men must have true godliness in order to a right in the sight of God to make such profession, and to receive the privileges depending thereon: which implies and infers all those principles of mine which Mr. W. opposes in his book, and confutes all that he says in opposition to them.

SECT. V.

Showing that Mr. Williams, in supposing that unsanctified men may profess such things, as he allows must be professed, and yet speak true, is inconsistent with Mr. Stoddard, and with himself.

MR. W. denies, that in order to men being admitted to sacraments, they need make any peculiar profession, distinguished from what an unregenerate man may make, (p. 44. *c*. p. 50. *e*. 6. *c*. *d*. *e*. 9. *c*. 10. *c*. *e*. 45. *e*. 46. *a*. and 53. *e*.) or that they need to profess any thing but what an unregenerate man may say, and speak true. (p. 47. *c*.) And that they need make no profession but what is compatible with an unregenerate state. (p. 8. *d*. *e*.) And yet the reader has seen what things he says all must profess in order to come to sacraments. One thing he says they must profess, is a real conviction of the heart, of the divine truth of God's word; that they do sincerely and with all their hearts believe the gospel. And these things, he says, are agreeable to the opinion of Mr. Stoddard, and the doctrine he taught. (p. 32. *b*. *c*. and p. 36. *a*.) Let us compare these things with the doctrine Mr. S. taught. Mr. S. taught, that natural men do not believe the gospel, (*Benef. of the Gosp*. p. 89. *b*.) that they do not properly believe the word of God. (*Guide to Christ*, p. 26. *d*.) That they do not believe the testimony of God, do not lay weight on the word of God; that they do not believe the report of the gospel. (*Safety of Ap*. Edit. 2. p. 229. *c*. *e*.) that they do not receive God's testimony, nor lay weight on it. (*Ibid*. p. 99.) That there is no man, how great soever his profession, how large soever his knowledge, that continues in a natural condition, who thoroughly believes that truth; *i. e.* that men may be saved by Christ's righteousness. (*Ibid*. p. 4. *d*. and p. 5. *d*. *e*.) That common illumination does not convince men of the truth of the gospel. (*Benef. of the Gosp*. p. 148, 149.) How then could it be the doctrine Mr. S. taught, that natural men may really and with all their hearts believe and be convinced of the truth of the gospel?

And Mr. W. himself, in his sermons on *Christ a King and Witness*, (p. 114, 115.) says, "man since the fall is naturally ignorant of divine truth, and an enemy to it, and full of prejudices against the truth:" and further, (*ibid*. p. 114.) "The renewing of the Holy Ghost makes an universal change of the heart and life.——He knows the doctrine contained in the Bible in a new manner.—Before, he had a view of the truth as a *doubtful uncertain thing;* he received it as a thing which was probably true;—and perhaps for the most part it appeared something likely to answer the end proposed.—But now the gospel appears to him *divinely true* and *real*," &c. But how do these things consist with men being, before conversion, sincerely and with all their hearts convinced of the divine truth of the gospel? Can that be, and yet men *view it as a doubtful uncertain thing*, as not yet appearing to them *divinely true and real?*

Again, Mr. W. supposes, that some unsanctified men may speak true, and profess a hearty consent to the terms of the covenant of grace, a compliance with the call of the gospel, submission to the proposals of it, satisfaction with that device for our salvation that is revealed in the gospel, and with the offer which God makes of himself to be our God in Christ Jesus, a fervent desire of Christ and the benefits of the covenant of grace, and an earnest purpose and resolution to seek salvation on the terms of it, (p. 11. *c*.) and a falling in with the terms of salvation proposed in the gospel, with a renouncing of all other ways, (which he speaks of as agreeable to Mr. Stoddard's opinion, p. 32. *b*. *c*.) Quite contrary to the current doctrine of Calvinistic divines; contrary to the opinion of Mr. Guthrie, whom he cites as a witness in his favour, (pref. p. 4.) who insists on satisfaction with that device for our salvation which is revealed in the gospel, and with the offer which God makes of himself to be our God in Christ, as the peculiar nature of saving faith. And contrary to the principles of Mr. Perkins (another author he quotes as his voucher) delivered in these very words, which Mr. W. cites in the present point, (p. 11.) "That a desire of the favour and mercy of God in Christ, and the means to attain that favour, is a special grace of God, and hath the promise of blessedness:—That wicked men cannot sincerely desire these means of eternal life, *faith, repentance*, mortification, reconciliation," &c. And it is exceedingly contrary to the constant doctrine of Mr. Stoddard, (though he says it was his opinion,) who ever insisted, that all unconverted sinners under the gospel are so far from heartily consenting to the covenant of grace—and complying with the call of the gospel, and falling in with the terms of salvation proposed in it, renouncing all other ways, as Mr. W. supposes—that they are wilful rejecters of Christ, despisers of the gospel, and obstinate refusers of offered mercy. So he says, "The man that has but common grace—sets himself against the way of salvation which God prescribes." (*Nat. of Sav. Conv.*) "In awakened sinners, it is not merely from weakness, but from pride and sturdiness of spirit, that they do not come to Christ." (*Safety of Ap*. p. 229. *c*. *d*.) And in other places he says, that it is *from the hardness and stubbornness of natural men's hearts*, that they do not comply with the gospel; That *there is a mighty opposition in their hearts to believe in Christ*, because it is *cross to their haughty spirits;* That they are *enemies to this way of salvation;* That they *are dreadfully averse to come to Christ*. (See Book *of three Sermons*, p. 84. *Guide to Christ*, p. 55. *c*. *Safety of Ap*. p. 106. and 194. *e*.)

And this scheme of our author is in a glaring manner contrary to the doctrine of Mr. Williams himself, in his sermon on Isa. xlv. 11. (p. 25, 26, 27.) Speaking to those *whose natures remain unrenewed and unsanctified* (see his words p. 25. *d.*) he says, p. 27. *b. c.* "You are opposing all the means of your own deliverance and salvation. The offers of grace, the allurements and invitations of the great Saviour of the world, have all been ineffectual to persuade you to accept of deliverance from a slavery you are willingly held in. Nay, you strive against the liberty of the sons of God, and labour to find out all manner of difficulties and hinderances in the way of it. If you pray for it, you do not desire it should yet come, but would stay a while longer." And are these the persons who can truly profess, that they comply with the call of the gospel, and submit to the proposals of it, and are satisfied with the device for our salvation, and with the offers of the gospel, and consent to the terms of the covenant of grace *with all their hearts*, renouncing all other ways? It is not much more easy to make these things consist with what he says in his answer to Mr. Croswell, (p. 26. *b. c.*) He there says, "There is not a son nor daughter of Adam excluded from salvation, who will accept Christ upon God's offer, and take him in his person and offices, and whole work of redemption, to be their Saviour, and they find themselves willing to accept of Christ as so offered to them, and PLEASED WITH THAT DEVICE for their salvation, and heartily choosing him to be to them, and in them, wisdom, righteousness, sanctification, and redemption." (See also to the same purpose, *Ibid.* p. 32. *e.* and p. 33. *a. b.* and p. 94. *c.*)

Mr. W. though he holds, that it is lawful for some unsanctified men to come to sacraments, yet supposes it not to be lawful for those that are *lukewarm* in religion to come. (p. 35. *d. e.*) So that according to his scheme some unsanctified professors are above *lukewarmness*: that is to say, their hearts within them are truly hot or fervent with christian zeal, and they such as Christ will never spue out of his mouth; in a great inconsistence with the Scripture. He suggests, that it is an injury done to the cause of truth, in me, to represent Mr. Stoddard as being of another opinion. (p. 35. *c. d. e.*) But let us see whether such a representation be an injury to truth or no. Mr. S. taught, that natural men have *no sincerity in them.* (*Guide to Christ*, p. 60, 61.) That their hearts are dead as a stone, that there is no disposition or inclination to any thing that is good, but a total emptiness of all goodness. (*Ibid.* p. 63. *b.*) That some of them have considerable shows of goodness, there is an appearance of good desires, &c. but there is nothing of goodness in all this; that all they do is in hypocrisy. (*Benef. of the Gos.* p. 73. *d. c.*) That they are acted by a lust of self-love in all their religion; —If they are swept and garnished, they are empty: there may be some similitude of faith and love, but no reality, not a spark of goodness in their hearts; though corruption may be restrained, yet it reigns. He speaks abundantly to the same purpose in his sermon, entitled, *Natural men are under the government of self-love.*

And Mr. W. himself, in his sermon on Psal. xci. 1. describing carnal men, by which he means the same with unconverted men, (as is evident through the book, particularly p. 36. *c.*) says, p. 27, 28. that to such "Religion looks like a dull unpleasant kind of exercises, and so different from the sensual joys and pleasures which they choose, that they *hate* to set about it, as long as they dare let it alone; and would do as *little* as ever they can at it: —That when they durst not let it alone any longer, they set about it, but would fain despatch it as *soon* and as *easily* as they can; because it seems to them a *miserable uncomfortable* sort of life. Ask your own conscience, (says he,) see if this be not the *truth* of the case."—Now let the reader judge, whether this be a description of persons whom it would be injurious to represent as having nothing above *lukewarmness*.

Another thing, which Mr. W. supposes must be professed in order to come to sacraments, and therefore according to him is what an unsanctified man can profess, and speak *true*, is, "That they *with all their hearts cast themselves upon the mercy of God*, to help them to keep covenant." (p. 31. *e.* and p. 32. *a.*) And yet elsewhere he mentions a depending on Christ for things of this nature, as a discriminating mark of a true Christian. (Ser. on *Christ a King and Witness*, p. 19. *c.*) Under a use of examination, he there says, "Do you depend on Christ to protect you from all your spiritual enemies, to restore you to holiness, to subdue all your heart to the will of God, to make you partakers of his image and moral perfections, and in that way to preserve and lead you to your true perfection and eternal happiness."

Mr. W. supposes (p. 36. *a. b. c.*) that the profession men must make in order to come to sacraments, implies real friendship to God, loving God more than his enemies, loving him above the world; and therefore according to Mr. W. unsanctified men may make this profession also, and speak true: contrary to the whole current of Scripture, which represents unsanctified men as *the enemies of God, those that have not the love of God in them*, under the power of a *carnal mind*, &c.—And contrary to the unanimous voice of all sound divines, yea, of the whole christian world. Mr. W. in the forementioned place blames me, that I had intimated (as he supposes) that the profession which Mr. Stoddard taught to be necessary, did not imply real friendship, and loving God above his enemies, and above the world. Let us then compare this with Mr. S—d's doctrine, as extant in his writings. He speaks of it as a property of saving grace, wherein it specifically differs from common grace, that a true love to God prizes God above all the world. (*Nat. of Sav. Conv.* p. 7. *b. c.*) That every natural man prefers vain and base things before God. (*Ibid.* p. 96. *b.*) That they are all enemies to God, and the very being of God. (*Ibid.* p. 5. *c. d.* and p. 97.) That their hearts are full of enmity to God. (*Ibid.* p. 55. *e.*) That they have an aversion to those gracious actions of loving God, and trusting in Christ, and are under the dominion of a contrary inclination. (*Ibid.* p. 67.) That those of them whose consciences are enlightened, and are reforming their lives, have no love; and that it is a burden to them that they suspect there is such a God, that they wish there was not such an one. And that they are haters of God, and are so addicted to their own interest, that they have a bitter spirit towards God, have an ill affection to him, and are adversaries to his felicity. (*Ibid.* p. 97. *Three Serm.* p. 38, 39.) That they are governed by a spirit of self-love, and are wholly destitute of love to God; that some of them confess that they have but little love to God; but indeed they have not one spark of love to God in their hearts. (*Three Serm.* p. 48.) That they set their interest at the right hand of God's glory,—as if God's honour were not to be regarded, compared with their interest, &c. &c. (*Ibid.* p. 63, 64.)

So Mr. W. himself (*Christ a King and Witness*, p. 145. *e.*) plainly supposes, that before conversion men love the world more than God. For, speaking of the nature of the change wrought in conversion, he says, things are quite turned about, God and Christ are got into the place the world had before. Again (*Ibid.* p. 18. *b.*) he says, "You must know that there is no man who is not either a true subject to Christ, or his enemy. That man who does not submit to Christ as his King and Lord, by bearing true faith and allegiance to him, is the enemy of Christ and his kingdom. Such are all they who will not depend on him, believe in him, give up themselves and all to him." And again, (p. 106. *e.* 107. *a.*) "Man since the fall has a natural unlikeness to God, and hates the holiness and purity of the divine nature." And in his sermon on Isa. xlv. 11. he says to his hearers, If your nature remain unrenewed and unsanctified,—you are the enemies of God and Christ by wicked works, and an impure heart.—But yet now it seems, some of these may profess real friendship to Christ, and loving him above the world, and speak true.

And these things are no less inconsistent with what Mr. W. says in the very book under consideration. He here says, (p. 36.) "Why should any divine now tell us, that these same professions do not imply that there are any pretences of any real friendship, that they import no pretence of loving God more, yea, not so much, as his enemies, no pretence to love God above the world?" When he himself is the divine that tells us so, or plainly supposes so in this very book of his. For, in p. 8, 9. having mentioned the profession communicants may be required to make, he then says, that such a profession contains all that is essential to true religion in it; and if this is the fruit of the love of God, it is true godliness: plainly supposing, that persons may have these things without the love of God; as the reader will see more evidently if he views the place. So that the profession must imply real friendship, and love to God, even above the world; and yet must contain only such things as may be with or without the love of God indiscriminately.

Mr. W. allows, that in order to come to sacraments men ought to profess a subjection to Christ with all their hearts, (p. 10. *d.*) and to be devoted to the service of God, (p. 49. *d.*) and to give up themselves to Christ, to be taught, ruled, and led by him in a gospel-way to salvation, (p. 31. *e.* and p. 32. *a.*) And though he and Mr. Stoddard taught, that it is lawful for some unsanctified men to come to sacraments, yet Mr. W. supposes it to be unlawful for any to come to sacraments *serving two masters;* and says Mr. S. taught that they ought to covenant with God with their whole hearts, and give up all their hearts and lives to Christ. We are therefore to understand Mr. W. that some unsanctified men can profess all these things, and speak true. Strange doctrine for a christian divine! Let us see whether Mr. S. taught such doctrine. He taught that faith in Christ is the first act of obedience that any sinner does perform; that it is by faith that a man first gives himself to be God's servant. (*Safety of App.* p. 228. *e.* p. 229. *a.*) That all those who are not converted, are under the dominion of sin, enemies to God. (*Ibid.* p. 5. *c. d.*) That there is no obedience to God in what they do, who have only common grace; that they do not attend the will of God. (*Ibid.* p. 7. *d.*) That all ungodly men are servants of Satan, and live in a way of rebellion against God. (*Ibid.* p. 94. *b.*) That they are enemies to the authority of God; to the wisdom, power, and justice of God, yea to the very being of God; they have a preparedness of heart to all wickedness that is committed in the world, if God did not restrain them; that if they were in the circumstances that the fallen angels are in they would be as the very devils. (*Ibid.* p. 95.) That their hearts are like the hearts of devils, as full of sin as a toad is full of poison, having no inclination to any thing that is good. (*Guide to Christ*, p. 68. see also *Benef. of the Gos.* p. 130. *a. b.*) That they utterly neglect the end they were made for, and make it their business to serve themselves; they care not whether God's glory sinks or swims. (*Three Sermons*, p. 62.) That they hate God, because God crosses them in his laws. (*Ibid.* p. 38. *c.*) These are the men, which Mr. W. supposes must, and may (some of them) truly profess a subjection to Christ with all their hearts, and to be devoted to Christ; and the men that Mr. S. taught, might covenant with God with their whole hearts, and give up all their hearts and lives to Christ. Mr. Stoddard taught, that men that have but common grace, go quite in another path than that which God directs to—That they set themselves against the way of salvation God prescribes. (*Safety*, p. 10.) That man in his natural state is an enemy to the way of salvation; that he is an enemy to the law of God, and the gospel of Jesus Christ. (*Ibid.* p. 106. *b. c.*) But yet these, if we believe Mr. W. may *truly* profess a subjection to Christ with all their hearts, and give up themselves to him, to be taught, ruled, and led by him in a gospel-way of salvation. Yet if we believe him, we must have the trouble of disbelieving him again; for in these things he is as inconsistent with himself, as he is with Mr. S. For in his sermon on Isa. xlv. 11. (p. 26, 27.) he says to those whose natures are *unrenewed and unsanctified,* " If you are without Christ, you are in a state of slavery to sin, led about of divers lusts, and under the reigning power and dominion of your corruptions, which debase your souls, and bring them down from the dignity of their nature, to the vilest, most shameful, and accursed bondage. And by means of sin, ye are in bondage to the devil, the most hateful and accursed enemy of God and your own souls;* —and are opposing all the means of your own deliverance. The offers of grace, the calls and invitations of the gospel, have all been ineffectual to persuade you to accept of deliverance from a slavery you are willingly held in. Nay, you strive against the liberty of the sons of God." And yet some of these are (if we believe what Mr. W. now says) subject to Christ with all their hearts, give up all their hearts and lives to Christ, and give up themselves to be taught, ruled, and led by him in a gospel-way to salvation.—Mr. W. in his sermons on *Christ a King and Witness*, (p. 81.) under a use of examination, giving marks of trial, says, " Have you unreservedly given up your souls and bodies to him? [*viz.* Christ.] You must be all Christ's, and have NO OTHER MASTER. You must be given to him without reserve, both in body and spirit, which are his." But now it seems, these are no discriminating evidences of true piety: he says, (*Ibid.* p. 118.) " A man naturally hates God should reign." And (p. 119. *c.*) speaking of the natural man, he says, " He hates to be controlled, and in all things subjected to God;—he really owns no God but himself." But if so, then certainly he is not subject to God with all his heart.

Our author in the book more especially attended to, says, (p. 31. *d. e.*) He knows of nobody who has any controversy with me in what he calls my loose way of arguing, in my saying, " The nature of things seems to afford no good reason why the people of Christ should not openly profess a proper respect to him in their hearts, as well as a true notion of him in their heads." And then, in that and the following page, proceeds to show what respect Mr. S. and those that think with him, suppose men must profess in order to come to the Lord's supper; and (in p. 33. *a.*) speaks of such a profession as is equally honourable to Christ with a profession of saving grace. And, as according to Mr. W. no profession discriminating what is professed from common grace, can be required, so common grace must be supposed to be a *proper respect to Christ in the heart*. Now let us see what Mr. S. says. " There is (says he) an opposition between saving and common grace;—they have a contrariety one to another, and are at war one with the other, and would destroy one the other.—Common graces are LUSTS, and do oppose saving grace." (*Nat. of Sav. Conv.* p. 9. *d. e.*) " Men that are in a natural condition, such of them as are addicted to morality and religion, are serving their LUSTS therein. The most orderly natural men do live an *ungodly* life;—yea, their *very religion is iniquity*." (*Ibid.* p. 96, 97.)—" Their best works are not only sinful, but *properly sins;* they are acted by a SPIRIT OF LUST in all that they do." (*Saf. of App.* p. 168. *d.*)—" Moral virtues do not render men acceptable to God; for though they look like virtues, yet they are LUSTS." (*Ibid.* p. 81.)—Now the question plainly is, Whether *lust* can be *a proper respect to Christ in the heart?* And, Whether a *profession* which implies *no more* in it, be equally honourable to Christ, as a credible profession of a *gracious* respect to him?

SECT. VI.

Concerning visibility without apparent probability.

MR. STODDARD (*Appeal*, p. 16.) says thus: " Such persons as the *apostles* did admit into gospel churches, are *fit* to be admitted into them; but they admitted *many* that had not a thorough work of regeneration. Indeed by the *rule* that God has given for admissions, if carefully attended, *more* unconverted persons will be admitted, than converted."

This passage I took notice of in my book, where I say, " I would humbly inquire, How those visible qualifications can be the ground of a rational judgment, that a person is circumcised in heart, which nevertheless at the same time, we are sensible, are so far from being probable signs of it, that they are more frequently without it than with it," &c. This seems to be a terrible thing in Mr. W.'s way, which he strikes at from time to time; and is an impediment he boggles at exceedingly. One while he pretends, he can give a sufficient answer. (p. 7, 8.) At another time he pretends, that I remove the difficulty myself. (p. 12.) Then again, in the same page, he pretends to solve the difficulty; and then in the next page pretends, that if the case be as I say, *That we cannot form a rational judgment that a thing is, which, at the same time, and under that degree of light we then stand in, it more probably is a mistaken one than not,* yet it can argue nothing to the case;

* And yet now it seems, some such do serve but one master, and give up themselves to Christ to be led by him.

seeing the judgment we do form, is directed by a rule which is appointed for us. But still as if not satisfied with these answers and remarks, he seems afterwards to suggest, that Mr. S. did not express this as *his own* sentiment, but as Mr. Cotton's, as a gentleman of the same principles with Mr. Mather, using it as *argumentum ad hominem*. See p. 33.

In p. 34. *a.* he expressly says, " Mr. S. does not say, That when the rule which God has given for admissions is carefully attended, it leaves reason to believe, that the greater part of those who are admitted, are *enemies to God*," &c.—True, he does not say this in terms; but he says, " more *unconverted* persons will be admitted, than converted :"—which is equivalent. And (p. 133. *a.*) Mr. W. presumes confidently to affirm, that Mr. S. says this [the thing forementioned] not with peculiar relation to his own scheme, but only as an application of a saying of Mr. Cotton's, who was of a different opinion, and said upon a different scheme; to show, that upon their own principles, the matter will not be mended. But this is contrary to the most plain fact. For Mr. S. having said, *The apostles admitted many* unconverted, he immediately adds the passage in dispute, *indeed by the rule*, &c. plainly expressing his own sentiment; though he *backs* it with a saying of Mr. Cotton's. So, Mr. Cotton's words come in as a confirmation of Mr. S—d's; and not Mr. S—d's as an *application* of Mr. Cotton's. However, Mr. W. delivers the same sentiment *as his own*, once and again, in his book: he delivers it as his own sentiment, (p. 34.) that probably many more hypocrites, than real saints, do make such a profession, as that which must be accepted. He delivers it as his own sentiment, (p. 61. *e.*) That the apostles judged it likely, that of the Christians taken into the church under their direction, as many were hypocrites in proportion to their number, as to those that were taken into the *Jewish* church. And as to the latter, he delivers it as his sentiment, (p. 24. *a.*) that the body of the people were not regenerate. So that, according to his own sentiments, when the apostolical rule of taking in is observed, the body of those who are admitted will be hypocrites.

Now therefore, I desire that this matter may be examined to the very bottom.—And here let it be considered, whether the truth of the following things be not incontestable.

1. If *indeed by the rule God has given for admissions, when it is carefully attended, more unconverted persons will be admitted, than converted;* then it will follow, That just such a visibility or visible appearance of saintship as the *rule requires*, is more frequently *without* real saintship, than *with* it.

2. If Mr. S. and Mr. W. had just reason from the Holy Scripture, and Divine Providence, to *think thus*, and to publish such a sentiment, and the christian church has good reason to believe them; then God has given the christian church in its present state (dark and imperfect as it is) good reason to *think so* too.

3. If Christ by the rule he has given for admissions, requires his churches to receive such a visibility or appearance, which he has given the same churches at the same time reason to judge to be an appearance that *for the most part* is without godliness, or more frequently connected with ungodliness; then he requires them to receive such an appearance, as he at the same time has given them reason to think does not imply a *probability* of godliness, but is attended rather with a probability of ungodliness. For that is the notion of probability; *an appearance, which so far as we have means to judge, is for the most part connected with the thing.** Therefore the sign or appearance, let it be what it will, implies a *probability* of that which we have reason to think it is *for the most part* connected or attended with. Where there is only probability without certainty, there is a *peradventure* in the case on both sides; or in vulgar language, the supposition on both sides stands a chance to be true. But that side which most commonly proves true in such a case, stands the best chance; and therefore properly on that side lies the *probability*.

4. That cannot be a *credible* visibility or appearance, which is not a *probable* appearance. To say, a thing is *credible* and not *probable*, is a contradiction. And it is impossible rationally to judge a thing true, and at the same time rationally to judge a thing most probably not true. Therefore it is absurd (not to say worse) to talk of any *divine institution*, leading us thus to judge. It would be to suppose, that God by his institution has made that judgment rational, which he at the same time makes improbable, and therefore irrational.

This notion of admitting members into the church of Christ without and against *probability* of true piety, is not only very inconsistent with itself, but very inconsistent with what the common light of mankind teaches in their dealings one with another. Common sense teaches all mankind, in admission of members into societies, at least societies formed for very great and important purposes, to admit none but those concerning whom there is an *apparent probability*, that they are the hearty friends of the society, and of the main designs and interests of it; and especially not to admit such concerning whom there is a greater probability of their being habitual fixed enemies. But thus it is, according to Mr. S.'s and Mr. W.'s doctrine, as well as the doctrine of the Scripture, with all *unsanctified* men, in regard to the church of Christ. They are enemies to the head of the society, enemies to his honour and authority, and the work of salvation in the way of the gospel; the upholding and promoting of which is the main design of the society. The church is represented in Scripture as the *household of God*, in a peculiar manner intrusted with the care of his name and honour in the world, the interests of his kingdom, the care of his jewels, and most precious things. And would not common sense teach an earthly prince not to admit into his *household*, such as he had no reason to look upon so much as probable friends and loyal subjects in their hearts; but rather friends and slaves in their hearts to his enemies and competitors for his crown and dignity? The visible church of Christ is often represented as his *city* and his *army*. Now would not common sense teach the inhabitants of a besieged city to open the gates to none, but those concerning whom there is at least an *apparent probability* of their not being enemies? And would any imagine, that in a militant state of things it is a likely way to promote the interest of the war, to fill up the army with such as are more likely to be on the enemies' side in their hearts, than on the side of their lawful and rightful prince, and his faithful soldiers and subjects.

SECT. VII.

Concerning the Lord's supper being a converting ordinance.

THOUGH Mr. W. holds, that none are to be admitted to the Lord's supper, but such as make a credible profession of *real godliness*, and are to be admitted under that *notion*, and with *respect* to such a character appearing on them; yet he holds at the same time, that the Lord's supper is a *converting ordinance*, an ordinance designed for the bringing of some men that have no such a character, to be of such a character, (p. 14. *c. d.* p. 15. p. 35. *a. b.* p. 83. *b.* p. 100. *e.* 101. *a.* 126, 127.) It is evident, that the meaning of those divines who speak of the Lord's supper as a converting ordinance, is not merely that God in his sovereign providence will use it as an *occasion* of the conversion of some; but that it is a converting *means by his institution given to men*, appointing them to use it for this purpose. Thus Mr. Stoddard expressly declares, That the Lord's supper is INSTITUTED to be a means of regeneration, (*Doct. of Inst. Churches*, p. 22. *a.*) INSTITUTED for the conversion of sinners, as well as the confirmation of saints; (*Appeal*, p. 70. *c.* p. 71. *a.*) that the direct end of it is conversion, when the subject that it is administered unto

* Mr. Locke thus defines *probability*. (*Hum. Und.* 7th Edit. 8vo. Vol. II. p. 273.) " Probability is nothing but the appearance of such an agreement or disagreement, by the intervention of proofs, whose connexion is not constant and immutable, or at least is not perceived to be so; but is, or appears FOR THE MOST PART to be so; and is enough to induce the mind to judge the proposition to be true, or false, rather than the contrary. And Mr. W. himself (p. 139.) says, " It is *moral evidence* of gospel sincerity, which God's word makes the church's *rule*," &c. Now does such an appearance, as we have reason at the same time to think is *more frequently* without gospel-holiness than with it, amount to moral evidence of gospel-sincerity?

stands in need of conversion. (*Ibid.* p. 73, 74.) And thus Mr. W. after Mr. S. speaks of the Lord's supper *as by Christ's* APPOINTMENT *a proper means of conversion* of some that are unconverted; (p. 100. *e.* 101. *a.*) so he speaks of it as *instituted* for the conversion of sinners. (p. 126, and 127.)

Now if so, what need of men being, to rational charity, converted already, in order to their coming to the Lord's supper? Is it reasonable to suppose God would *institute* this ordinance *directly for that end,* that sinners might be *converted* by it; and then charge his ministers and churches not to admit any that they had not reasonable ground to think were converted already?—Mr. W. (in p. 83. *b.*) supposes two ends of Christ's appointing the communion of the christian church; that such as have grace already should be under proper advantages to gain more, and that those who have none, should be under proper advantages to attain grace. But this ill consists with other parts of his scheme.—If a king should erect an *hospital* for the help of the poor, and therein has two ends; *one,* the nourishing of such as are in health, and the *other,* the healing of the sick; and furnishes the hospital accordingly, with proper food for the healthy, and proper remedies for the sick: but at the same time charges the officers, to whom he commits the care of the hospital, by no means to admit any, unless it be under a notion of their being in health, and from respect to such a qualification in them, and unless they have reasonable ground and moral evidence to induce them to believe that they are well: and if this pretence should be made to justify such a conduct, that the hospital was indeed designed for the healing of the *sick,* yet it was designed to confer this benefit only on such diseased people as were *hypocrites,* and made a profession and pretence of being in health; will any man presume to say, that such a conduct is agreeable to the dictates of the understanding of rational beings? And to suppose, that such should be the conduct of the infinitely wise God, is as unscriptural, as it is unreasonable. We often read in God's word, of men's being convinced of their wickedness, and confessing their sins, as a way to be healed and cleansed from sin: but where do we read of men's pretending to more goodness than they have, and making a hypocritical profession and show of goodness, in order to their becoming good men?* Where have we a divine institution, that any who are *wolves* should put on *sheep's clothing,* and so come to his people, that they may believe them to be *sheep,* and under this notion receive them into the flock, to the end that they may truly become *of his sheep?*

But to examine this matter, of the Lord's supper being a converting ordinance to ungodly men professing godliness, a little more exactly. If Christ has appointed the Lord's supper to be a converting ordinance to some such as these, then he has appointed it either only for such of them as are mistaken, and think themselves godly when they are not; or he has appointed it not only for such, but also for such as are *sensible they are ungodly.*

If it be appointed as a converting ordinance only for such as are mistaken, and think themselves converted; then here is an institution of Christ, which never can, in any one instance, be made use of to the end for which he has appointed men to use it. It cannot be used for this end by *those who admit* members, and administer the ordinance: for they, as Mr. W. says, must admit none but such as they are bound by the rule of Christ to look upon as godly men already, and to administer the sacrament to them under that notion, and with respect to such a character. Neither can it be used to such a purpose by any of the *communicants:* for by the supposition, they must be all such as think they are converted already, and also come *under that notion.* So that by this scheme of things, here is an institution appointed to be upheld and used in the church, which the institution itself makes void and impossible. For, as was observed before, the notion of a converting ordinance has not reference to any secret decree of God, how *he* in his sovereign pleasure *will sometimes use it;* but to his *institution given to men,* appointing the end for which *they should use it.* Therefore, on the present supposition, the institution appoints the Lord's supper to be used in some cases for the conversion of sinners, but at the same time forbids its being either given or received under any other notion than that of the communicant's being converted already: which is in effect to forbid its being either given or received for the conversion of the communicant, in any one instance. So that the institution effectually destroys and disannuls itself.—But God forbid, that we should ascribe any such inconsistent institutions to the Divine Head of the church!

Or if the other part of the disjunction be taken, and it be said, the Lord's supper is appointed for the conversion of some *that are sensible they are ungodly* or *unconverted,* the consequence is no less absurd, on Mr. W.'s principles. For then the scheme is this. The institution requires some men to make a pretence of *real piety,* and to make a public solemn profession of *gospel-holiness,* which at the same time they are *sensible* they have not; and this, to the end that others may look upon them to be *real saints,* and receive them to the Lord's supper *under that notion:* not putting on a disguise, and making a show of what they have not, through mistake, but doing it consciously and wilfully, to the honour and glory of God: and all this strictly required of them, as the *instituted means* of their becoming real saints, and the children of God!

Mr. W. says, (p. 14. *d.*) "Since it is *God's will,* that his church should admit all such visible saints, [*viz.* such as he had been speaking of,] it follows, that the Lord's supper is a *converting* ordinance to such of them as are *unconverted.*" But Mr. W. is mistaken as to his consequence. The Lord's supper is not instituted to be a converting ordinance to *all* unconverted men, whom it is *God's will* the church should admit. For it may be the church's duty, and so God's will, to admit those that live *secretly* in the grossest wickedness, as adultery, uncleanness, deism, &c. Such men as these may make a fair profession, and the church may be ignorant of their secret wickedness, and therefore may have no warrant to reject them: but yet it will not follow, that God by his institution has given *such* a lawful right to the Lord's supper, having appointed it to be a *converting* ordinance to them.

SECT. VIII.

The notion of moral sincerity's being the qualification, which gives a lawful right to christian sacraments, examined.

THOUGH our author disdains the imputation of any such notion, as that of men's being called visible and professed saints from respect to a visibility and profession of *moral sincerity:* yet it is manifest, that in his scheme (whether consistently or no, others must judge) *moral sincerity* is the qualification which entitles, and gives a lawful right, to sacraments. For he holds, that it is lawful for unsanctified men, who have this qualification, to come to sacraments; and that it is not lawful for them to come without it. Therefore I desire this notion may be thoroughly examined.

And for the greater clearness, let it be observed what *sincerity* in general is. Now *sincerity,* in the general notion of it, is *an honest conformity of some profession or outward show of some inward property or act of mind, to the truth and reality of it.* If there be a show or pretence of what *is not,* and has *no real existence,* then the pretence is altogether vain; it is only a pretence, and nothing else: and therefore is a pretence or show without any *sincerity,* of any kind, either moral or gracious.

I now proceed to offer the following arguments against

* Mr. Williams (p. 42.) owns that persons must make a profession wherein they make a show of being wise virgins, in order to come into the visible church. And (p. 35. *e.*) he owns, that all visible saints who are not truly pious, are hypocrites. Again, it may be observed, he abundantly insists, that men who have no more than common grace and moral sincerity, may lawfully come to sacraments; and yet by what he says, (p. 35. *e.*) they must profess more. So that men who have no more must profess more; and this, it seems, according to divine institution!—Again he says, (p. 35. *a. b. c.*) That one end God designed by appointing men to be brought into the church, is, that through divine grace they might effectually be brought to Christ, *to give him the whole possession of their hearts;* and yet in the very next paragraph (p. 35. *e.* and 36. *a.*) he speaks of it as unlawful for men to come to sacraments till they *give up all their hearts to Christ.*

the notion of *moral sincerity* being the qualification, which gives a lawful right to sacraments.

I. There is no such thing as moral sincerity, in the *covenant of grace*, distinct from gracious sincerity. If any sincerity at all be requisite in order to a title to the seals of the covenant of grace, doubtless it is the sincerity which belongs to that covenant. But there is only one sort of sincerity which belongs to that covenant; and that is a gracious sincerity. There is but one sort of faith belonging to that covenant; and that is saving faith in Jesus Christ, called in Scripture *unfeigned faith*. As for the faith of devils, it is not the faith of the covenant of grace.

Here the distinction of an *internal and external* covenant, will not help at all; as long as the covenant, of which the sacraments are seals, is a *covenant of salvation*, or a covenant proposing terms of eternal salvation. The sacraments are seals of such a covenant. They are seals of the *New Testament in Christ's blood*, (Matt. xxvi. 28. Luke xxii. 28.) *a Testament which has better promises than the Old*, (Heb. viii. 6.) and which the apostle tells us, *makes us heirs of the eternal inheritance*. (Heb. ix. 15.)—Mr. W. himself speaks of the covenant sealed in baptism, as *the covenant proposing terms of salvation*. (p. 23. *b*. c.) So he speaks of the covenant entered into by a visible people, as the covenant *in which God offers everlasting happiness*. (p. 24, 25.) But there is no other religion, no other sincerity, belonging to this covenant *of salvation*, but that which *accompanies salvation*, or is *saving religion and sincerity*. As it is written, (Psal. li. 6.) "Behold, thou desirest truth in the inward parts."

There is what may be called a *moral sincerity*, in distinction from saving, in many moral things; as in loving our friends and neighbours, in loving our country, in choosing the *protestant* religion before the *popish*, in a conscientious care to do many duties, in being willing to take a great deal of pains in religion, in being sorry for the commission of such and such acts of wickedness, &c. But there are some duties, which, unless they are done with a *gracious sincerity*, they cannot be done at all. As Mr. Stoddard observes, (*Safety of Ap.* p. 216.) "There are some duties which cannot be done but from a *gracious respect to God*." Thus, there is but one sort of sincerity in loving God as God, and setting our hearts on him as our highest happiness, loving him above the world, and loving holiness above all the objects of our lusts. He that does not these things with a gracious sincerity, never really doth them at all. He that truly does them, is certainly a godly man; as we are abundantly assured by the word of God. So, there is but one sort of *sincere and cordial consent to the covenant of grace*, but one sort of *giving all our hearts to Jesus Christ;* which things Mr. W. allows to be necessary, to come to sacraments. That to which a man's heart is full of reigning enmity, he cannot with any reality at all cordially consent to and comply with: but the hearts of *unsanctified* men are full of reigning enmity to the covenant of grace, according to the doctrine of Scripture, and according to the doctrine of Mr. S. and Mr. W. too, as we have seen before.

However, if there were any such thing, as being heartily willing to accept of Christ, and a giving all our hearts to Christ, without a saving sincerity, this would not be a complying with the terms of a covenant of salvation. For it is self-evident, that only something which is *saving*, is a compliance with the terms of *salvation*. Now Mr. W. himself often allows (as has been observed) that persons must comply with the terms of the covenant of grace, in order to come to sacraments.—Yet because he also in effect denies it, I shall say something further in confirmation of it.

1. The sacraments are covenant privileges. Mr. W. himself calls them so. (p. 5. *a*. *b*.) Covenant privileges are covenant benefits, or benefits to which persons have a right by the covenant. But persons can have no right to any of the benefits of a covenant, without compliance with its terms. For that is the very notion of the terms of a covenant, *viz*. Terms of an interest in the benefits of that covenant. It is so in all covenants whatsoever; if a man refuses to comply with its conditions, he can claim nothing by that covenant.

2. If we consider the sacraments as seals of the covenant, the same thing is evident, *viz*. That a man can have no right to them without a compliance with the terms. The sacraments are not only seals of the offer *on God's part*, or ordinances God has appointed as confirmations of the truth of his covenant, as Mr. W. seems to insist. (p. 74, 75.) For considered merely as seals and confirmations of the truth of the gospel, they are (as miracles and other evidences of the christian religion) seals equally given to *Christians, Jews, Deists*, moral and vicious, and the whole world that knows of them. Whereas, it is manifest, in the nature of the thing, sacraments are seals of the covenant *to be applied to the communicant*, and of which he is the immediate subject, in a peculiar manner, *as a party in covenant*. Otherwise, what need would there be of his being one of God's *covenant people*, in any sense whatsoever?

But now it is not reasonable to suppose, that the seal of the covenant belongs to any man, *as a party in the covenant*, who will not accept of and comply with the covenant. He that rejects the covenant, and will not comply with it, has no interest in it. And he that has no interest in the covenant, has no right to the seals; for the covenant and seals go together. It is so in all covenants among mankind; after a man has come into a bargain proposed and offered by another, yielding to the terms of it, he has a right to have the bargain *sealed*, and confirmed to him, as a *party in the covenant;* but not before.

And if what the communicant does be a seal *on his part* also, as the nature of the thing demonstrates, seeing he is active in the matter, and as Mr. W. seems willing to allow, (p. 75.) it will follow, with equal evidence, that a man cannot lawfully partake, unless he yields to and complies with the covenant. To what purpose is a man's sealing an instrument or contract, but to confirm it *as his own act and deed*, and to declare his compliance with his part of the contract. As when a servant seals his indenture, it is a testimony and ratification of his compliance as to the proposed contract with his master. And if a covenant of friendship be proposed between two parties, and they both put their seal to it, hereby they both testify and declare their mutual friendship.

It has been already observed, that *unsanctified* men, while such, cannot with any sincerity at all testify a *present* cordial compliance with the covenant of grace: and as they cannot do this, so neither can they with any sincerity promise a *future* compliance with that covenant. Mr. W. often allows, that in order to christian communion men must *promise* a compliance with the covenant, in its spiritual and saving duties; that they will believe and repent in the sense of the covenant, willingly accept of Christ and his salvation, love him and live to him, and will do it immediately, henceforward, from this moment. (p. 25. *c*. *e*. p. 26. *a*. p. 28. *a*. *c*. and p. 76. *a*. *b*.) But how absurd is this! when at the same instant, while they are making and uttering these promises, they are entirely *averse* to any such thing; being then enemies to Christ, willingly rejecting him, opposing his salvation, striving against it, labouring to find out all manner of difficulties and hinderances in the way of it, not desiring it should come yet, &c. which our author, in a place forecited, says is the case with all unsanctified men.

And when unsanctified men promise, that they will spend the rest of their lives in universal *obedience* to Christ, there is no sincerity in such promises; because there is not *such a heart* in them. There is no man but a true disciple of Christ, that is willing thoroughly to *deny himself* for him, and *follow him* in a way of obedience to all his commands, unto the end, through all difficulties which Christ has given his followers reason to expect, or commanded them to prepare for; as is evident by Christ's frequent declarations. (Luke xiv. 25—33. Matt. x. 37, 38, 39. chap. xiii. 44, 45, 46. and many parallel places.) If an unsanctified man thinks he is willing, he does not know his own heart. If he professes to be willing, he does not know what he says. The difficulty and cost of it is not in his view: and therefore he has no proper willingness to comply with the cost and difficulty. That which he is willing for, with a moral sincerity, is something else, which is a great deal easier, and less cross to flesh and blood. Suppose a king should propose to a subject his building him such a tower, promising him a certain reward. If the subject should undertake it, *not counting the cost*, thinking with himself that the king meant another sort of tower, much cheaper; and should be willing only to build that cheap one, which he imagined in his own mind; when he would by no means have consented to build so costly a tower as the king proposed, if he had understood him right: such a man could not be said properly to be willing to comply with his prince's proposal, with any sincerity at all. For what he consents to with a moral sincerity, is *not the thing* which the king proposed.

The promises of unsanctified men are like the promises of the man we read of, (Luke ix. 57, 58.) who said, "Lord, I will follow thee whithersoever thou goest." To whom Christ replied, "The foxes have holes, and the birds of the air have nests, but the Son of man hath not where to lay his head." When he made his promise, he probably quite mistook the thing, and did not imagine, that to follow Christ wherever he went, would be to follow him in such poverty and hardship. I suppose, the rich *young man* we read of (Mark x. 17, &c.) might have what is called *moral sincerity*. But he had no sincerity in the *covenant of grace*. When he came to Christ to know *what he should do to have eternal life*, it is probable he ignorantly thought himself willing to yield himself to Christ's direction. Yet when it came to a trial, and Christ told him he must *go and sell all that he had and give to the poor*, it proved that he had no sincerity of willingness at all for any such thing.—So that it is evident, however unsanctified men may be morally sincere in some things, yet they have no sincerity of any sort in *that covenant*, of which the sacraments are seals; and that moral sincerity, distinct from gracious, in *this covenant*, is a mere imagination, there being indeed no such thing.

II. Another argument against this notion of moral sincerity, giving a right to church communion, is this: a quality that is *transient* and *vanishing*, can be no qualification of fitness for a *standing* privilege. Unsanctified men may be very serious, greatly affected, and much engaged in religion; but the Scripture compares their religion to a *lamp* not supplied with oil, which will go out, and to a *plant* that has *no root* nor *deepness of earth*, which will soon wither; and compares such unsanctified men to the *dog* that will *return to his vomit*, and to the *sow* which, though washed ever so clean, yet her nature not being changed, will *return to her wallowing in the mire*.

Mr. W. allows, that persons in order to come to sacraments, must have deep convictions, an earnest concern to obtain salvation, &c. Now every one who is in any degree acquainted with religious matters, knows that such convictions are not wont to last a great while, if they have no saving issue. Mr. S. in his sermon on the danger of speedy degeneracy, (p. 11.) says, "Unconverted men *will grow weary* of religious duties." And our author himself, (p. 78. c.) speaking of those professors in the primitive churches that fell away to heresy and other wickedness, takes notice that the apostle *observes*, IT WILL BE SO, *that they which are approved, might be made manifest*: and says Mr. W. upon it, evil and unsanctified men, by such sins, will discover their hypocrisy.

Now seeing this is the case with moral sincerity and common religion, how can it be a qualification for a standing privilege? Nothing can be a fitness for a *durable privilege*, but a *durable qualification*. For no qualification has any fitness or adaptedness for more than it extends to; as a short scabbard cannot be fit for a long sword. If a man going a journey in the night, needs a lamp to light him in his way, who will pretend that a flaming wick without oil, which will last but a few rods, is fit for his purpose? Or if a man were building a house for himself and family, should he put into the frame pieces of timber known to be of such a nature as that they would probably be rotten in a few months; or should he take blocks of ice, instead of hewn stone, because during a present cold season they seemed to be hard and firm; and withal should for a covering put only leaves that will soon fade away, instead of tiles or shingles, that are solid and lasting; would not every spectator ridicule his folly?

If it should be said, that unsanctified men, when they *lose* their moral sincerity, may be *cast out* again: this is far from helping the case, or showing that such men were ever *fit* to be admitted. To say, a piece of timber, though not of a durable nature, is *fit* to be put into the frame of a building, because when it begins to rot, it may be pulled out again, is so far from proving that it was ever fit to be put in, that the speedy necessity of pulling it out rather proves the contrary. If we had the power of constituting a human body, or it were left to us to add members to our own bodies, as there might be occasion; we should not think such a member was *fit* to be added to the frame, that had already radically seated in it a cancer or gangrene, by which it could last but a little while itself, and would endanger the other members; though it were true, that when the disease should prevail, there were surgeons which might be procured to cut that member off.

But to consider a little further this point of *moral sincerity* qualifying persons for the privileges of the church. I would lay down this proposition as a thing of clear evidence: *those persons have no fitness in themselves to* come *to the privileges of the church, who, if they were known, would not be fit to be* admitted *by others*. For to say, they are *fit* to be members, and yet *not* fit to be allowed to be members, is apparently absurd. But they who have no better fitness than moral sincerity, if that were *known*, would not be fit to be admitted by others; as is allowed by Mr. W. For he holds, that in order to be fit to be admitted by others, they must credibly appear to them to have something *more* than moral sincerity, even gospel-holiness. And it is evident in itself, as well as allowed by Mr. W. that if such were *known*, they would not be *fit* to be admitted, *only* on their moral sincerity, and the profession and promises they make from such a principle; and that for this reason, because such a principle alone *would not be fit to be trusted*. God himself has taught his church, that the religion of unsanctified men is not fit to be trusted; as a lamp without *oil*, and a plant without *root*, are things not to be trusted.—God has directly taught his church to expect, that such religion will fail; and that such men, having no higher principle, will return to their wickedness. Job xxvii. 8, 9, 10. "The hypocrite—will he delight himself in the Almighty? will he always call upon God?"—Dan. xii. 10. "The wicked will do wickedly." And therefore God does not require his church to accept their profession and promises. If he has taught us not to credit their profession and promises, then certainly he has taught us not to accept them.

III. Another argument against this supposed rule of allowing and requiring unsanctified men with moral sincerity, to come to sacraments, is this. *That rule*, which if fully attended, would naturally bring it to pass, that the *greater part* of communicants would be *unfit*, even according to that very rule, cannot be a *divine* rule. But this supposed rule of *moral sincerity* is such a rule. For if this rule be universally attended, then all unsanctified men, who have present convictions of conscience sufficient to make them *morally sincere*, must come into the communion of the church. But this conviction and common religion, if it do not issue in conversion, (as has been observed,) commonly vanishes away in a short time. And yet still these persons, if not convicted of open scandal, are left in the communion of the church, and remain there, *without even moral sincerity*.—Experience gives us abundant reason to think, that of those who some time or other have considerable convictions of conscience, so as to make them for the present to be what is called *morally sincere*, but few are savingly converted.* And if all these must be admitted, (as they must, if this rule be fully attended,) then their convictions going away, and their sincerity vanishing with it, it will hereby be brought about, that the Lord's table is chiefly surrounded with the *worst* sort of morally insincere persons, *viz.* stupid backsliders, that are in themselves far *worse* than they were before, according to the scripture account, Matt. xii. 45. and 2 Pet. ii. 20. —And this as the natural consequence of the forementioned rule, appointing *moral sincerity* to be the qualification for communion. Thus this supposed rule supplants its own design.

* How small a proportion are there of the vast multitudes, that in the time of the late religious commotion through the land had their consciences awakened who give hopeful abiding evidences of a saving conversion to God!

IV. Another argument, that moral sincerity is not the qualification to which God has annexed a lawful right to sacraments, is, that this qualification is *not at all inconsistent* with a man's living at the same time in the most *heinous wickedness*, in a superlative degree contrary to the christian religion.

It was before observed to be a thing evident in itself, and allowed by Mr. W. that there are some *sins*, which, while wilfully continued and lived in, though secretly, do wholly *disqualify* persons for christian sacraments, and make it *unlawful* for men to partake of them. Now if it be thus with some sins, doubtless it is because of the *heinousness* of those sins, the high degree of wickedness which is in them. And hence it will follow, that those sins which are in themselves most heinous, and most contrary to the christian religion, do especially disqualify persons for christian sacraments, when wilfully lived in.

Let it therefore now be considered, whether it will not follow from these premises, that for men to live in enmity against God and Christ, and in wilful unbelief and rejection of Christ, (as the Scriptures teach, and as Mr. S. and Mr. W. too assert, is the case with all unsanctified men under the gospel,) wholly *disqualifies* them for christian sacraments. For it is very manifest, by Scripture and reason, that to live in these things, is to live in some of the *most heinous* kinds of wickedness; as is allowed by *Calvinistic* divines in general, and by Mr. S. in particular, who says, (*Safety of Ap.* p. 224. *d.*) "You *cannot anger God more by any thing*, than by continuing in the neglect of Christ. This is the *great controversy* God has with sinners; not that they have been guilty of these and those particular transgressions, but that they abide in the rejection of the gospel." Again, he says, (*ibid.* p. 249. *e.*) "*The great sin*, that God is angry with you for, is your *unbelief*. Despising the gospel is *the great provoking sin.*"

A man's continuing in hatred of his *brother*, especially a fellow-communicant, is generally allowed to disqualify for communion. The apostle compares it to *leaven* in the passover, 1 Cor. v. 6, 7, 8. But now certainly it is as bad, and as contrary to the nature and design of christian sacraments, for a man to live in hatred of Christ, and to remain a *hateful and accursed enemy* (if I may use Mr. W.'s own language) to the glorious Redeemer and Head of the christian church.

None will deny, that *lying* and *perjury* are very gross and heinous sins, and (if known) very scandalous: and therefore it follows from what was observed before, that such sins, if lived in, though secretly, do disqualify persons for christian sacraments in God's sight. But by our author's own account, all unsanctified men that partake of the Lord's supper, live in *lying* and *perjury*, and go on to renew these crimes continually; since while they continue ungodly men, they live in a constant violation of their promise and oath. For Mr. W. often lays it down, that all who enter into covenant with God, promise spiritual duties, such as repentance, faith, love, &c. And that they promise to perform these *henceforward*, even from the *present moment*, unto the *end of life*; (see p. 25. *c. e.* 26. *a.* 28. *a. c.* 76. *a. b.*) and that they not only promise, but *swear* to do this. (p. 18. *d.* 100. *c.* 101. *a.* 129. *a.* 130. *c.* 140. *b.*) But for a man to violate the promises he makes in covenanting with God, Mr. W. once and again speaks of it as *lying*. (p. 24. *d. e.* p. 130. *c.*) And if so, doubtless their breaking the oath they swear to God is *perjury*.—Now lying to *men* is bad; but lying to God is worse. (Acts v. 4.) And without doubt, perjury towards God is the *worst* sort of perjury. But if unsanctified men, when they entered into covenant with God, promised and swore, that they would *immediately* and *thenceforward* accept of Christ as their Saviour, and love him, and live to him; then while they continue in a wilful rejection of him (which according to Mr. W. all unregenerate men do) they live continually in the violation of their promise and oath.*

I would observe one thing further under this head, *viz.* That ungodly men which live under the gospel, notwithstanding any moral sincerity they may have, are worse, and more provoking enemies to God, than the very heathen, who never sinned against gospel-light and mercy. This is very manifest by the Scriptures, particularly Matt. x. 13, 14. Amos iii. 2. Rom. ii. 9. 2 Pet. ii. 21. Rev. iii. 15, 16.

I had suggested, concerning Mr. Stoddard's doctrine of admitting more unconverted than converted by attending Christ's rule, that this supposes it to be the case of the members of the visible church, that the greater part of them are more provoking enemies to God than most of the heathen. Mr. W. represents himself as greatly alarmed at this: he calls it an extraordinary passage, and puts five questions about it to my serious consideration. (p. 72, 73.) The first and chief question is this; "Did Mr. S. ever say in the *Appeal*, or any where else, of most of our fellow-worshippers at the sacrament, that we have no reason to think concerning them, but that they are more provoking enemies to the Lord, whom Christians love and adore, than most of the very *heathen?*" His three next questions are to represent the heinousness of such supposed ill treatment of Mr. S.—And I think will be sufficiently answered, by what I shall offer in reply to the first.

I will tell him what Mr. S. said. Speaking to such as do not come to Christ, living under the gospel, he said, (*Safety of Ap.* p. 234, 235.) "You may not think to escape as the *heathen* do: your load will be heavier, and your fire will be hotter, and your judgment sorer, than the judgment of other men. God will proportion every man's misery to his iniquity. And as you have enjoyed greater light and love, so you must expect more amazing and exquisite wrath, than other men. Conscience has more to accuse you of and condemn you for; and so has God: and you will sink down deeper into hell than other men. You are treasuring up a greater measure of wrath, than others, against the day of wrath. You will wish you had lived in the *darkest* corners of the earth among *Scythians and barbarians.*"—

And Mr. W. must allow me to remind him of what another divine has said, and that is himself. In his sermon on Isa. xlv. 11. (p. 25, 26.) he says, "It is to be feared, there are great numbers here present, that are in an *unconverted, unrenewed, unpardoned state;* strangers from God, and enemies to him. Yet you now look with great pity and compassion on that poor *captive*, for whom we have now been offering up our earnest prayers,† who has been so long in a pitiable and sorrowful condition, and who is now in the thickness of *popish* darkness and superstition.—If you are out of Christ, and destitute of true faith in him, if your natures remain *unrenewed and unsanctified*, what is your state better than hers, which looks so sorrowful and distressing? Rather, is it not *worse?* When you consider, that in the fulness of the means of grace which you have enjoyed all your days, you are as

* Here I would observe, that not only in the general do unsanctified men, notwithstanding their moral sincerity, thus live in the most heinous wickedness; but particularly, according to Mr. W.'s own doctrine, their very attendance on the outward ordinances and duties of worship, is the vilest, most flagrant, and abominable impiety. In his sermons on *Christ a King and Witness*. (p. 77, 78.) he says, "If a man could perform all the outward acts of worship and obedience, which the Bible requires, from the beginning to the end of it, and not do them from *faith in Christ, and love to God*, and not express by them the thoughts, desires, and actings of his soul; they would be so far from being that obedience which Christ requires, that they would be a *mocking of God*, and *hateful to him*. These outward acts ought to be no other, and in religion are designed to stand for nothing else, but to be representations of a man's soul, and the acts of that. And when they are not so, they are in their own nature a lie, and false pretence of something within, which is not there: Therefore the Lord abhors them, and reckons these false pretences the vilest wickedness.———Now when a man performs all outward obedience and worship, but it does not come from his *heart*, he practically denies the omniscience of Christ, while he puts before him a show and pretence of something for the reality; and so he belies his own profession. And all this, be it more or less, whatever it pretends to be of religion, instead of being that which Christ requires, is entirely different from it, yea, infinitely contrary to it. And those same actions, which when they are the language of the *heart*, and flow from it, are pleasing and acceptable to God and Jesus Christ, are true obedience to him; when they do not, are reckoned the most flagrant and abominable impiety, and threatened with the severest damnation of hell."—Now, who can believe, that God has, by his own holy institution, made that sort of sincerity, which is nothing better than what is consistent with such a lying, vile, abominable, flagrantly wicked pretence and show of religion as this, the very thing that gives a right, even in his sight, to christian sacraments.

I might here also observe, that if moral sincerity or common grace gives a right to sacraments in the sight of God, then that which (according to Mr. S—d's doctrine before observed) is a SPIRIT of LUST, that which is contrary to, and at war with, and would destroy saving grace, is the thing which gives a right in the sight of God to christian sacraments.

† Mrs. Eunice Williams, brought up in Canada, among the Caghnawaga Indians, sister to the then pastor of the church in Mansfield, where this sermon was preached, upon a day of prayer kept on her account; she being then in that place on a visit.

far from any saving knowledge of Jesus Christ, as those who have lived in the dregs and abyss of *popish* ignorance, and know not what to believe, but what the church, that is, *antichrist*, tells them. If you die thus, your misery will be *aggravated inconceivably* beyond theirs: which Christ has plainly enough shown us, when he upbraided the cities wherein most of his mighty works were done, and tells them how much in the comparison they fall below Tyre and Sidon," (heathen cities, notorious for luxury, debauchery, and the grossest idolatry,) "and Sodom; for whom it should be *more tolerable* than for them."

The same author says also, even in the book under consideration, (p. 86.) "That the unbelief and impieties of *visible saints*, is what they will be punished for *above all men in the world*."

And now, I think it may be proper for Mr. W. himself to answer his 5th question, which he puts to my serious consideration, *viz.* "What honour is it to our Lord Jesus Christ, to treat visible saints in such a manner, when at the same time it is his revealed will they should be outwardly treated as visible saints?"

SECT. IX.

A view of what Mr. W. says concerning the public covenanting of professors.

I. MR. W. often speaks with contempt, of my supposing it to be a duty required of such as come to sacraments, that they should *explicitly own the covenant*, and disputes largely against it. (p. 15, 16, 17, 18, 19, 20, 21, 22. and many other places.) He says concerning me, (p. 22. *a. b.*) "It is very unhappy, that this good gentleman should use the Scripture in such a manner, to prove a divine institution which never had an existence; and after all that is said, is but a mere imagination and chimera; it being evident, there never was any such divine institution for the church under the Old Testament, binding particular persons *publicly and explicitly to own the covenant*, in order to their enjoying the outward ordinances of it." However, it falls out something happily for me, that I am not quite alone in the chimera, but have Mr. W. himself to join me in it; who abundantly asserts the same thing, (p. 5. *c.* p. 8. *a.* p. 9. *b. c.* and many other places,) who uses the Scripture in the same manner, and supposes the same divine institution; and who, (in p. 5. *b. c.* of the treatise in hand,) having stated the following inquiry, "What is that evidence, which by DIVINE APPOINTMENT the church is to have, of the saintship of those who are admitted to the outward privileges of the covenant of grace?" makes this answer to it: "The SCRIPTURE has determined the matter thus, that the open profession and declaration of a PERSON's believing in Christ,—and a hearty consent to the terms of the covenant of grace, and engagement on his part to fulfil it," &c. "is the sole and entire ground of that public judgment, which the church is to make of the real saintship of professors." It is manifest, he cannot intend merely that they should be the *posterity* of such as thus owned the covenant, or *declared their consent to it*, and so are looked upon as those that owned the covenant in their ancestors, at the beginning of the covenant line; (though sometimes he seems to suppose, this is all that is necessary, as I shall take particular notice by and by;) for here he expressly speaks of a *personal* owning the covenant, or the *open profession and declaration of a* PERSON's consent to the covenant. And thus he often speaks of the same matter, in like manner, as a *personal* thing, or what is done by the person judged of, and received. (See p. 10. *c. d.* 31. *e.* 32. *e.* 33. *a.* 34. *b. c.* 73. *b.* 84. *a.* 139. *a.*) And in the second page of his *preface*, he declares himself fully established in Mr. S——d's doctrine concerning this affair of qualifications for the Lord's supper; who expressly declare it to be *his* judgment, that "It is requisite, that persons be not admitted unto communion in the Lord's supper, without making a PERSONAL and public profession of their faith and repentance." (*Appeal*, p. 93, 94.)

And as Mr. W. holds, that there must be a *public personal owning of the covenant*; so he also maintains, that this profession must be *explicit*, or *express*. He says, (p. 20. *d. e.*) "Since we have no direction in the Bible, at what time nor in what manner any *personal explicit* covenanting should be performed,—it appears plain to a demonstration, that the people knew nothing of any such institution; as I suppose, the christian church never did, till Mr. Edwards discovered it." But if I was the first discoverer, he should have owned, that since I have discovered it, he himself, and all my opposers, have seen cause to follow me, and receive my discovery. For so the case seems to be, if he gives us a true account (in p. 132. *b.*) where he rejects, with indignation, the imputation of any other opinion. "How often (says he) has Mr. Edwards said, none but visible saints are to be admitted? Do not ALL Mr. Edwards's OPPOSERS say, that NO MAN is to be admitted, who does not profess his hearty belief of the gospel, and the earnest and sincere purpose of his heart, so far as he knows it, to obey all God's commands, and keep his COVENANT? NONE, who do not make as full and EXPRESS a profession as the *Israelites* did, or was ever required by Christ or his apostles, in any instances that can be produced in the Bible, of bodies of men or particular persons admitted into visible covenant with God?"—He had before spoken of the WORDS which the Israelites used in their entering into covenant with God. (p. 5. *d.*) Which must refer to their entering into covenant in the *wilderness;* for we have no account of any *words* at all used by that nation, *at their entering into covenant*, if not there. And this he sometimes speaks of as the covenant they made, when God *took them into covenant*. (p. 8. *d.* 36. *d. e.* 37. *a. b.*) And (p. 20.) he allows *that to be an instance of explicit covenanting*: but ridicules *my* pretending to show, *that explicit covenanting was a divine institution for all;* when, he says, we have an account of but four instances of any *explicit* covenanting with God by the Jews, and those on most extraordinary occasions, and by *the body of the people*. But what matter is it, whether there were four, or but two, or only that one instance in the wilderness? when he himself with such earnestness declares, that all my opposers hold, *every man* must make as full and express a profession of the covenant as ever the *Israelites* did, or was ever required, in any instance that can be produced in the Bible, whether of *bodies of men* or *particular persons*' admission, &c. If this be so, and what he said before be also true, then all *Israel*, even every individual person among them, that ever was admitted to the privileges of the church, throughout all their generations, by his own confession and assertion, did personally make as *explicit* a profession of the covenant, as the body of the people did in that instance in the *wilderness*. And not only so, but the same must every individual person do, that ever comes to sacraments, through all ages, to the end of the world.—Thus Mr. W. fights hard to beat down himself. But I will not say in his own language, that in so doing *he fights hard to beat down a poor man of straw*.

If any should say, that Mr. W. when speaking of an *express profession*, does not mean a *profession in words, but only in actions;* such as an outward attendance on ordinances and duties of worship: I answer, if such actions are a profession, yet certainly they are not an *express profession;* they are no more than an *implicit profession*. And besides, it is very plain, the profession he speaks of is a *profession in words*. Thus (p. 36. *b.*) when describing the profession which ought to be made, he says, "It is in as strong WORDS, as were used by any whom the apostles admitted." And elsewhere (as was before noted) he often insists, that a profession should be made in WORDS without any discrimination as to their meaning. Which shows, it is a profession in *words*, that he designs. And although (p. 104. *e.*) he speaks of a performance of the outward duties of morality and worship, as the only way that God ever appointed of making real saintship visible: yet this is only another instance of his great *inconsistence* with himself; as appears by what has already been observed, and appears further by this, that when he speaks of a profession of consent to the terms of the covenant, &c. he often speaks of it as a profession which ought to be made in order to admission to these ordinances. (p. 5. *b. c.* 10. *a* 35. *e.* 36. *a. b. c.* 132. *b.* and other places.) If so, then how can the *attendance* itself, on these ordinances of worship, be all the profession which is to be made? Must men *first come to ordinances, in order to admission to ordinances?* And moreover, Mr. W. himself distinguishes between *engaging and swearing to keep covenant* in the public profession, and attending on the ordinances and duties of worship, which he speaks of as belonging to the *fulfilment of the engagement and oath.* (p. 130.) And *lastly* I would observe, though it could be consistently made out (which it never can) that Mr. W. does not mean a professing in *words,* it would be nothing to the purpose. If it be in words, or in other signs which are equivalent to words, and which are a *full and express profession,* (as Mr. W. says,) it is exactly the same thing as to my purpose, and the consequence of the argument, which was, that real godliness must be professed. And indeed this very thing which I endeavoured to prove by all that I said on this head, is expressly again and again allowed by Mr. W. Yet he makes a great ado, as if there was a vast difference between him and me in this affair of public covenanting with God; and as though my notions of it were very singular, absurd, and mischievous.

II. Mr. W. says a great deal in opposition to me, to show that *swearing by God's name, swearing to the Lord,* and the like, do not mean *covenanting with God:* but yet (in p. 18.) in the midst of his earnest dispute against it, he owns it.—I mentioned several prophecies, referring to the *Gentile* converts in the days of the gospel, which foretell that they should *swear by God's name, swear to the Lord of hosts, &c.* as a prediction of the Gentiles *publicly covenanting with God;* using that as one thing which confirmed, that this was commonly the meaning of such phrases in the Old Testament. But Mr. W. despises my interpretation of these prophecies, and my argument from them. Nevertheless, in his reply, he owns the very thing: he in effect owns, that entering into covenant, and owning the covenant, is what is meant by these prophecies; mentioning this, plainly with approbation, as the universal sense of protestant commentators. His words are, (p. 18. *d. e.*) "As to all these prophecies, which Mr. Edwards has quoted, referring to the Gentiles, and their *swearing by the name of the Lord,* the sense of protestant commentators upon them, I think, universally is, that when the Gentiles in God's appointed time should be brought into covenant with God, it should be as the Jews were, by being persuaded to consent to the terms of the covenant of grace, and engaging themselves to God, to be faithful to him, and keep covenant with him. He who heartily consents to the terms of the *covenant of grace,* gives up himself to the Lord, *gives the hand to the Lord,* engages to own and serve him; which is the thing signified in all those metaphorical phrases, which describe or point out this event, in the Old-Testament language."

III. Mr. W. in these last-cited words, explains the phrase of *giving the hand to the Lord,* as signifying engaging themselves to God in covenant, and consenting to the terms of the covenant, and yet in the next page but two, he contemns and utterly disallows my interpreting the same phrase in the same manner. Mr. W. says, (p. 21. *c.*) "As to the words of *Hezekiah,* when he called the *Israelites* to the passover, bidding them *yield or give the hand to the Lord; and in Ezra, they gave the hand to put away their wives;* which he thinks to be a *Hebrew* phrase for entering into covenant; it carries its own confutation with it."

IV. Mr. W. often speaks of the professions made by the ancient Israelites and Jewish Christians, when they entered into covenant, and were admitted into the church. Whereas, according to the doctrine of the same author, in the same book, we have no account of any profession made by either, on any such occasion. For he insists, that the children of such as are in covenant, are born in covenant; and are not admitted into covenant, any otherwise than as they were seminally in their ancestors; and that the profession of their ancestors, at the head of the covenant line, is that *individual profession, which brings them into covenant.* His words are, (p. 135. *e.* 136. *a. b. c.*) "It is one and the same individual profession and engagement, which brings them and their children into covenant. And if there is one instance in the Bible, where God ever took any man into covenant, and not his children at the same time, I should be glad to see it. It is by virtue of their being in covenant, that they have a right to the seals. And if *these* children are not cast out of covenant by God, *their* children have as good a right to the seals as they had. It is God's will, that his mark and seal should be set upon them, AND THEIR CHILDREN, AND THEIR CHILDREN FOR EVER, till God casts them out of covenant. It is certain, they have an interest in the covenant, and they have a right to the privileges of the covenant so long as they remain in covenant; and that is, till God cuts them off, and casts them out."

And accordingly he supposes, that *John the Baptist* never inquired into the doctrinal knowledge of those he baptized, because they *were already in covenant with God,* and members of his visible church, and not yet turned out: and he suggests, that *John* knew many of them not to be of a good moral character. (p. 98.) So he largely insists, that the *three thousand Jews* and proselytes that the apostles baptized, (Acts ii.) were not taken into covenant, but only *continued in covenant.* (p. 46, 47.) So he supposes the *eunuch,* before *Philip* baptized him, was a member of the church, and in covenant with God. (p. 50.) Though he inconsistently mentions those same persons in the 2d of Acts, and the *eunuch,* as *admitted into the church* by the apostles, and primitive ministers. (p. 9. *e.* p. 10. *a.* p. 59. *a.*) And so (p. 8. *d.* p. 26. *a.*) he mentions God's *taking all Israel* into covenant: he mentions the *profession* which the *Israelites* made, (p. 25. *e.*) and (p. 5. *d.*) he speaks of the *words which the* Israelites *used, in their entering into covenant with God.* And (p. 36. *d. e.* p. 37. *a. b.*) he speaks of their profession in *Moses's* time, *which God trusted so far as to admit them into covenant.* Whereas indeed, according to Mr. W. they *were not taken in,* nor did they *enter into covenant,* neither in the plains of *Moab,* nor at mount *Sinai.* He says expressly, that they were *in* covenant before that time, when in *Egypt,* being taken in their ancestors, *Abraham, Isaac, and Jacob.* (p. 91. *b.*) But then we read of *no words* that these patriarchs *used at their entering into covenant.*—And it will undoubtedly follow, on Mr. W.'s principles, that we must go further back still for *Israel's* being taken into covenant; we must go up even to *Adam* himself, the first father of mankind, who was visibly in covenant, and so his posterity, in the line of *Noah's* ancestors, without the line being broken by a visible *cutting off,* and *casting out* by God, as we have all reason to suppose. And after the flood, we have reason to think, God had a covenant race continued in *Shem's* posterity, especially in the line of *Abraham's* ancestors. And though *Terah, Abraham's* father, was tainted with the then prevailing idolatry; yet there is no appearance of the line being then *cut off,* in the way Mr. W. speaks of, by God's visibly *casting him out.* On the contrary, God took a special fatherly care of him and his children, in bringing them from *Ur* of the *Chaldees,* the land of graven images, to *Haran.* (Gen. xi. 31.) And God is called the God of the father of *Abraham* and *Nahor,* that is, the God of *Terah.* (Gen. xxxi. 53.) And if it be said, that in *Abraham* began a new dispensation of the covenant; so that *Abraham* might properly on that account be said to be *taken into covenant,* as though his ancestors had not been in covenant: I answer, The alteration of the dispensation was in no measure so great as that after Christ's resurrection and ascension; and yet Mr. W. will not allow, that the Jewish converts, received (Acts ii.) on this new dispensation, were any more than *continued in covenant,* and in the church. So that, according to Mr. W.'s scheme, it must be Adam's profession of religion, that was *the individual profession* which made all his posterity, in the line of the church, even to the apostles' days, *visible saints,* or (as he himself explains visible saintship) such as we have rational ground to think are real saints, possessed of *gospel-holiness;* and on that account have a right to sacraments. For so he says it is with the children of them that are in covenant, and their children, and their children *for ever,* till cut off and cast out by God.

So that now we have the scheme in a true view of it.—The *Pharisees and Sadducees that John baptized,* whom Mr. W. supposes *John* knew to be not of a good moral character, and whose doctrinal knowledge he did not inquire into before he baptized them; because they had before been admitted in their ancestors; even *these were visible saints*, and such as John had rational ground to think had sufficient doctrinal knowledge and were orthodox and *real saints*, having moral evidence that they had *gospel-holiness*, because Adam their original ancestor made a profession of religion, in words of double meaning, without any marks of distinction or discrimination, by which any might know their meaning.

And if we should go back no further than Abraham, it would not much mend the matter; supposing the case had been so, that we had the words of both Abraham's and Adam's profession written down in our Bibles: whereas, we have neither; no, nor have we the words of the profession of any one person, either in the Old Testament or New, at their being *taken into* the church, if the things which Mr. W. says are true; though he speaks so often of professions, and words of professions, and declarations, made on such occasions, as if we had an express account of them in Scripture.

V. As our author abundantly maintains, that unsanctified men in covenanting with God, may and do promise the exercise of saving faith, repentance, love, &c.; so he holds, that they promise to begin the exercise of these graces *immediately, from this moment*, and to live in them *from henceforth*. (p. 25. *c. e.* and 26. *a.* and 28. *a. c.* 76. *a. b.*)

Now I desire this matter may be looked into, and thoroughly examined.—Not only the Holy Scriptures, and agreeable to them, Mr. Stoddard, and sound divines in general, teach us, but Mr. W. himself maintains, that men who are unsanctified do *for the present refuse* and *oppose* these things. In a forecited place of his sermon on Isaiah xlv. 11. our author says, that unregenerate and unsanctified men oppose all means for bringing them to these things, are willingly without them, and labour to find out all manner of difficulties and hinderances in the way of them; and if they pray for them, do not desire they should come yet, but would stay a while longer. Now, how is this consistent with such persons promising, with any *sincerity* at all, that they will comply with and perform these things *immediately, from henceforth*, without staying *one moment* longer? If God calls a man *this moment* to yield his whole heart to him in faith, love, and new obedience; and if he in answer to the call solemnly promises and swears* to God, that he will immediately comply with the call, without the least delay, and does it with any sincerity, how does he now willingly refuse, oppose, and struggle against it, as choosing to *stay a while longer?*

Besides, such promises and oaths of unregenerate men must not only be contrary to sincerity, but very *presumptuous*, upon these two accounts. (1.) Because herein they take an oath to the Most High, which, it is ten thousand to one, they will break as soon as the words are out of their mouths, by continuing still unconverted; yea, an oath which they are breaking even while they are uttering it. And what folly and wickedness is it for men to take such oaths! and how contrary to the counsel given by the wise man, in Eccl. v. 2—6.! And to what purpose should ungodly men be encouraged to utter such promises and oaths before the church, for the church's acceptance; which are so far from being worthy to be credited, or a fulfilment of them to be expected, that it is many thousands, and perhaps millions, of times more likely to be otherwise? That is, it is so much more likely they will not be converted the very next *moment*.—(2.) When an unconverted man makes such a promise, he promises what he has not to give, or that for which he has no sufficiency. There is indeed a sufficiency in God to enable him; but he has no claim to it. For God's helping a man savingly to believe in Christ is a *saving blessing*: and Mr. W. himself owns, that a man cannot by promise claim any saving blessings, till he has fulfilled the conditions of the covenant of grace. (p. 22. *e.* and 28. *e.*) So that in vain it is said by Mr. W. (p. 27. *e.*) "I pray that it may be thoroughly considered what is propounded in the covenant of grace, and on what *stock* a man is to finish." Meaning (as appears by the sequel) the *stock* of God's sufficiency. To what purpose is this said? when the covenant of grace promises or makes over no such *stock* to him who has no interest in the promises of it, as having not yet complied with the condition of its promises. Nor does an unconverted man promise any thing in an humble dependence on that *stock;* no such men do *lay hold on God's strength*, or trust in God's sufficiency. For this is a discriminating mark of a true saint; as our author himself observes, in that forecited passage in his Sermons *on Christ a King and Witness*, p. 19. *c.*

I would here take notice of it as remarkable, that though Mr. W. had owned that a natural man can claim no saving blessings by God's *promise*, yet to help out his scheme of a natural man engaging and promising, even with an oath, the exercises of saving grace, he (in p. 27, 28. especially p. 28. *e.*) speaking of the *great encouragement* on which unsanctified men can promise these things, supposes God has given *such encouragement* to them who promise and engage themselves to God, with that degree of earnestness and sincerity which he often speaks of as requisite to communion, that we have reason to determine that God never will fail of bestowing on them saving grace; so that they shall fulfil their promises. I say, he supposes that we have reason to determine this, because he himself determines it. His words are these:—"Though there be no promise of saving good, exclusive of faith, yet there being a command and encouragement, there are suitable springs of his endeavour and hope, in his engaging himself to God, and casting himself upon his mercy with all the earnestness and sincerity he can. *God* NEVER *will be worse than his encouragement*, nor do less than he has encouraged; and he has said, *To him that hath shall be given.*" Now if this be so, and if this will make it out, that an unconverted man who is *morally sincere* may reasonably, on this *encouragement*, promise immediately to believe and repent, though this be not in his own power; then it will follow, that whenever an unconverted man covenants, with such moral sincerity as gives a lawful right to sacraments, *God* NEVER *will fail* of giving him converting grace *that moment*, to enable him *from thenceforward* to believe and repent, as he promises. And if this be so, and none may lawfully covenant with God *without* moral sincerity, (as Mr. W. also says,) then it will follow, that *never* any one person comes, nor can come, lawfully to the Lord's supper, in an unconverted state; because when they enter into covenant lawfully, (supposing them not converted before,) God always converts them in the moment of their covenanting, *before* they come to the Lord's table.—And if so, what is become of all this grand dispute about the lawfulness of persons coming to the Lord's table, who have not converting grace?

VI. Mr. W. greatly misrepresents me from time to time, as though I had asserted, that *it is impossible for an unsanctified man to enter into covenant with God;* and that those who were sanctified among the *Israelites*, did not enter into covenant with God; that the pretended covenanting of such is *not covenanting, but only lying, wilful lying;* and that no natural man can own the covenant, *but that he certainly lies, knows he lies*, and *designedly lies, in all these things, when he says them.* (p. 26. *d.* 22. *d.* 24. *d.* 31. *a. b. c.* 21. *c.*) Whereas, I never said nor supposed any such thing. I never doubted but that multitudes of unsanctified persons, and in all ages of the christian church, and in this age, and here in *New England*, have entered visibly, and in profession, into the covenant of grace, and have owned that covenant, and promised a compliance with all the duties of it, without known or wilful lying; for this reason, because they were deceived, and did not know their own hearts: and that they (however deceived) were under the obligations of the covenant, and bound by their engagements and promises. And that in *that* sense, they were God's covenant people, that by their own binding act they were engaged to God in covenant; though such an act, performed without habitual holiness, be an unlawful one. If a thing be externally devoted to God, by doing what ought not to have been done, the thing devoted may, by that act, be the Lord's: as it was with the censers of *Korah* and his company. (Num. xvi. 37, 38.)

* It must be observed, that Mr. W. often speaks of the promise which an unregenerate man makes in covenanting with God, as his oath. P. 18. *d.* p. 100. p. 101. *a.* p. 129. *a.* p. 130. *c.* p. 143. *b.*

What I asserted, was, that none could profess a compliance with the covenant of grace, and avouch Jehovah to be their God, and Christ to be their Saviour, *i. e.* that they are so by their own act and choice, and yet love the world more than Jehovah without lying, or being deceived.* And that he who is wholly under the power of a carnal mind, which is not subject to the law of God, nor indeed can be, cannot promise to love God with all his heart and with all his soul, without either great deceit, or the most manifest and palpable absurdity. Inasmuch as promising supposes the person to be conscious to himself, or persuaded of himself, that he has such a heart in him; because his lips pretend to declare his heart, and the nature of a promise implies real intention, will, and compliance of heart.† And what can be more evident than these propositions? Surely they that reject the covenant of grace *in their hearts* (as Mr. W. owns all unsanctified men do) cannot own it *with their lips*, without either *deceiving* or *being deceived*. Words cannot be a true signification of more than is in the mind. *Inward covenanting*, as Mr. S. taught, is by an act of saving faith. (*Safety of Ap.* p. 85. *e.* 86. *a.*) And *outward covenanting* is an expression of *inward covenanting;* therefore, if it be not attended with *inward covenanting*, it is a false expression. And Mr. W. in effect owns the same thing; for he says, (p. 21. *b.*) "That there is no doubt they who are wilful obstinate sinners, deal *deceitfully* and *falsely* when they pretend to covenant with God." But so do all unregenerate sinners under the gospel, according to Mr. Stoddard and his own doctrine. And thus the very point, about which he contests so earnestly and so long, and with so many great words, is, in the midst of it all, given up fully, by his own concession.

VII. Mr. W. is greatly displeased with my saying (as above) that none who are under the power of a carnal mind can visibly own the covenant, *without lying* or *being deceived*, &c. And he finds great fault with my gloss on Psal. lxxviii. 36, 37. "They did flatter him with their mouth, and lied to him with their tongue:" which I interpret, as though they lied in pretending that respect to God, which indeed they had not. (p. 35. *a.* of my *Inquiry.*) But he insists, that what is meant is only *their lying in breaking their promise.* (p. 24. *e.*) And he insists upon it, (as has been observed already,) that natural men may covenant with God and *speak true.* But it seems he has wonderfully changed his mind of late; for a little while ago he declared elsewhere *for* the very same things which he here inveighs *against*, and spoke of natural men's profession and pretence of respect to God, as being actually a lie in its own nature; and not only becoming so by their breaking covenant afterwards. Particularly, it is remarkable, he has thus interpreted this very text now in dispute. In his sermons on *Christ a King and Witness*, speaking of the outward acts of *worship* done by those that do not love God nor believe in Christ, he expressly says, (p. 77.) 'They are in their *own nature* a lie; a false pretence of something *within*, that is not there.—See (says Mr. W.) this interpretation of it, in Psal. lxxviii. 34—37. "They did flatter him with their mouths; they lied to him with their tongues,"' &c.—(*Ibid.* p. 74. *b. e.*) "Christ's visible church are such as visibly and outwardly profess to be his subjects, and act outwardly as if they believed on him. But these outward acts in themselves are not that religion and obedience, which Christ requires; nay, of themselves, they have no religion in them; and Christ has nothing to do with them, *but as* they are the fruits and expressions of the heart, as they are the language and index of the mind and conscience, and outward declarations of the inward frame, tempers and acting, of the soul. If they are *not so*, they are so far from having any religion in them, that they are *hateful* to him, being only the visible resemblance, the pretence and *feigning*, of religion; *i. e.* they are *mockery, hypocrisy*, FALSEHOOD, AND LIES; and belong not to the kingdom of Christ, but of the *devil.*"—Let the reader now compare this with my gloss on the text.

Thus I have considered the various parts and principles of Mr. W.'s scheme, which are the foundations on which he builds all his superstructure, and the ground on which he proceeds in all his reasonings, through his book; and many particulars in his answers and arguments have been already considered.—Mr. W. says thus, (p. 135. *a.*) "I own, that at present I have no more expectation to see the scheme which Mr. Edwards aims to establish, defended upon *Calvinistic* principles, than the doctrine of *transubstantiation.*" On which I shall only say, it might perhaps be thought very impertinent in me, to tell my readers what I do or what I do not expect, concerning *his* scheme. Every reader, that has reason enough of his own not to take the big words and confident speeches of others for demonstration, is now left to judge for himself, whose scheme is most akin to the doctrine of *transubstantiation*, for inconsistence and self-contradiction. Nevertheless, I will proceed to consider our author's reasonings a little more particularly, in the ensuing part.

PART III.

CONTAINING SOME REMARKS ON MR. WILLIAMS'S EXCEPTIONABLE WAY OF REASONING, IN SUPPORT OF HIS OWN SCHEME, AND IN OPPOSITION TO THE CONTRARY PRINCIPLES.

SECT. I.

General observations upon his way of arguing, and answering arguments; with some instances of the first method excepted against.

Mr. W. endeavours to support his own opinion, and to confute the book he pretends to answer, by the following methods.

1. By frequently *misrepresenting what I say*, and then disputing or exclaiming against what he wrongfully charges as *mine.*

2. By misrepresenting what *others* say in their writings, whose opinions he pretends to *espouse.*

3. By *seeming to oppose* and *confute* arguments, and yet only saying things which have no *reference* at all to them, but relate entirely to *other* matters, that are altogether *foreign* to the argument in hand.

4. By advancing *new* and *extraordinary notions;* which are both manifestly contrary to *truth*, and also contrary to the *common apprehensions* of the christian church in all ages.

5. By making use of peremptory and confident *assertions*, instead of arguments.

6. By using great *exclamation*, in the room of arguing; as though he would amuse and alarm his readers, and excite terror in them, instead of rational conviction.

7. By wholly *overlooking* arguments, *and not answering at all;* pretending, that there is no argument, nothing to answer; when the case is manifestly far otherwise.

8. By frequently turning off an argument with this reflection, that it is *begging the question;* when there is not the least show or pretext for it.

9. By very frequently *begging the question* himself, or doing that which is *equivalent.*

10. By often alleging and insisting on things in which he is *inconsistent* with himself.

* See my Inquiry, p. 33, 34.

† Ibid. p. 37, 38.

As to the *first* of these methods used by Mr. W. *i. e.* his *misrepresenting what I say,* and then disputing or exclaiming against what he injuriously charges as mine, many instances have been already observed: I now would take notice of some other instances.

In p. 15. *c.* He charges me with "affirming vehemently, in a number of repetitions, that the doctrine taught is, that no manner of pretence to any visible holiness is made or designed to be made." These he cites as my words, marking them with notes of quotation. Whereas I never said or thought any such thing, but the contrary. I knew, that those whose doctrine I opposed, declared that *visible holiness* was necessary: and take particular notice of it, (p. 8.) where I say, "It is granted on all hands, that none ought to be admitted, as members of the visible church of Christ, but visible saints:" and argue on this supposition for fifteen pages together, in that same part of my book where Mr. W. charges me with asserting the contrary. What I say is, that people are taught, that *they come into the church without any pretence to sanctifying grace,* (p. 15. *d.*) I do not say, without a pretence to *visible holiness.* Thus Mr. W. alters my words, to make them speak something not only diverse but contrary to what I do say, and say very often; and so takes occasion, or rather *makes* an occasion, to charge me before the world, with telling a *manifest untruth.* (p. 15. *d.*)

Again, Mr. W. in answering my argument concerning *brotherly love,* (p. 70. *e.* 71. *a.*) represents me as arguing, "That in the exercise of christian love described in the gospel, there is such an union of hearts, as there cannot be of a saint to an unsanctified man." Which is a thing I never said, and is quite contrary to the sentiments which I have abundantly declared. I indeed speak of that *brotherly love,* as what cannot be of a saint to one that is not *apprehended* and *judged* to be sanctified. But that notion of a peculiar love, which cannot be to an unsanctified man—or without the reality of holiness in the person beloved—is what I ever abhorred, and have borne a most loud and open and large testimony against, again and again, from the press,* and did so in the preface to that very book which Mr. W. writes against.

In p. 74. *a. b.* Mr. W. represents me as supposing, that in the sacrament of the Lord's supper, both the covenanting parties, *viz.* Christ and the communicant, seal to the truth of the communicant's faith; or that both seal to this as true, that the communicant does receive Christ. Whereas, by me, no such thing was ever thought; nor is any thing said that has such an aspect. What I say, is very plain and express, (p. 75.) "That Christ by his minister professes his part of the covenant, presents himself, and professes the willingness of his heart to be theirs who receive him. That on the other hand, the communicant in receiving the offered symbols, professes his part in the covenant, and the willingness of his heart to receive Christ who is offered." How different is this from both parties sealing to the truth of the communicant's faith!

In p. 76, 77, and 80. he greatly misrepresents my argument from 1 Cor. xi. 28. "Let a man examine himself," &c. as though I supposed, the Greek word translated *examine,* must necessarily imply an examination to approbation; that it signifies to approve; and that a man's examination must mean his approving himself to himself to be sanctified. This representation he makes over and over, and builds his answer to the argument upon it; and in opposition to this, he says, (p. 77. *c.*) "Wherever the word means to examine to approbation, it is not used in its natural sense, but metonymically." Whereas, there is not the least foundation for such a representation: no such thing is said or suggested by me, as if I supposed that the meaning of the word is to *approve,* or to *examine to approbation.* What I say is, that it properly signifies *proving or trying a thing, whether it be true and of the right sort.* (p. 77. *d.*) And, in the same place, I expressly speak of the word (in the manner Mr. W. does) as not used in its natural sense, but metonymically, when it is used to signify *approve.* So that Mr. W.'s representation is not only diverse from, but contrary to, what I say. Indeed I suppose (as well I may) that when the apostle directs persons to try themselves with respect to their qualifications for the Lord's supper, he would not have them come, if upon trial they find themselves not qualified. But it would be ridiculous to say, that I therefore suppose the meaning of the word, *try* or *examine,* is to *approve,* when it is evident that the *trying* is only in order to knowing whether a thing is to be *approved,* or *disapproved.*

In p. 98. *b.* on the argument from *John's* baptism, Mr. W. alters my words, bringing them the better to comport with the odious representation he had made of my opinion, *viz.* that I required giving an account of *experiences,* as a term of communion; he puts in words as mine which are not mine, and distinguishes them with marks of quotation; charging me with representing it as "probable that *John* had as much time to inquire into their experiences as into their doctrinal knowledge."—Whereas, my words are these, (p. 101. *a.*) *He had as much opportunity to inquire into the credibility of their profession, as he had to inquire into their doctrinal knowledge and moral character.*

In p. 118. *d.* (and to the like purpose, p. 134. *c.*) our author represents me, and others of my principles, as holding, That the gospel does peremptorily sentence men to damnation for eating and drinking without sanctifying grace. But surely Mr. W. would have done well to have referred to the place in my Inquiry, where any thing is said that has such an appearance. For, I find nothing that I have said in that book, or any other writing of mine, about the gospel peremptorily sentencing such men to damnation, or signifying how far I thought they were exposed to damnation, or expressing my sentiments more or less about the matter.

In p. 130. *e.* and 131. *a.* Mr. W. says, "When one sees with what epithets of honour Mr. Edwards in some parts of his book has complimented Mr. Stoddard, it must look like a strange medley to tack to them;—That he was a weak beggar of his question; a supposer of what was to be proved; taking for granted the point in controversy; inconsistent with himself; ridiculously contradicting his own arguments." These expressions, which Mr. W. speaks of as tacked to those honourable epithets, he represents as expressions which I had used concerning Mr. Stoddard. And his readers that have not consulted my book, will doubtless take it so from his manner of representation. Whereas, the truth is, no one of these expressions is used concerning Mr. S. any where in my book; nor is there one disrespectful word spoken of him there. All the ground Mr. W. had to make such a representation, was, that in answering *arguments* against my opinion I endeavoured to show them to be *weak,* (though I do not find that I used that epithet,) and certainly for one to pretend to answer arguments, and yet allow them to be strong, would be to show *himself* to be very weak. In answering some of these arguments, and endeavouring to show wherein the inconclusiveness of them lay, I have sometimes taken notice that the defect lay in what is called *begging the question,* or supposing the thing to be proved. And if I had said so concerning Mr. S——d's arguments, speaking of them *as his,* I do not know why it should be represented as any *personal* reflection, or unhandsome dishonourable treatment of *him.* Every inconclusive argument is weak; and the business of a disputant is to show wherein the weakness lies: but to speak of *arguments* as weak, is not to call *men* weak.——All the ground Mr. W. has to speak of me as saying, that Mr. S. *ridiculously contradicted his own arguments,* is, that (in p. 11.) citing some passages out of Mr. S——d's *Appeal,* I use these words; "But how he reconciled these passages with the rest of his treatise, I would modestly say, I must confess myself at a loss." And particularly I observed, that I could not see how they consist with what he says, p. 16. and so proceed to mention one thing which appears to me not well to consist with them. But certainly this is not indecently to reflect on Mr. S. any more than Mr. W. indecently reflects on the *first reformers,* in his answer to Mr. *Croswell,* (p. 74, 75.) where speaking of their doctrine of a particular persuasion as of the essence of saving faith, he says, They are found inconsistent with themselves, and their doctrine lighter than vanity. And

* *Marks of a Work of the True Spirit,* p. 101, 102, 103, 104. *Thoughts on the Revival of Religion,* from p. 292 to 303. *Nature of Religious Affections,* p. 85 – 87. Preface to *Inquiry into Qualifications for Communion,* p. 5.

again, (p. 82.) If ever, (says Mr. W.) any men were confuted from their own concessions, these divines are. And more to the like purpose.—Which gives me a fair occasion to express the like *wonder* at him, as he does at me, (p. 131. *a.*) but I forbear *personal* reflections.

Mr. W. (in the same p. *d.*) has these words; "And to say, that all unsanctified men do profess and seal their consent to the covenant of grace in the Lord's supper, when they *know* at the same time they do not consent to it, nor have their heart at all in the affair,—is something *worse* than begging the question,"—that is, as I suppose, (the same that he charged me with before,) *telling a manifest untruth*. By which he plainly suggests, that I have said thus. Whereas, I no where say, nor in any respect signify that I suppose, all unsanctified communicants do KNOW that they do not consent to the covenant of grace. I never made any doubt, but that multitudes of unsanctified communicants are deceived, and think they do consent to it.

In p. 132. *d.* he says of me, "The author endeavours to show, that the admitting unsanctified persons tends to the ruin and reproach of the christian church; and to the ruin of the persons admitted." But how widely different is this from what I express in the place he refers to! (*Inq.* p. 121. *c.*) That which I say there, is, that "by express liberty given, to open the door to as many as please, of those who have *no visibility* of real saintship, and make no profession of it, nor pretension to it, is a method which tends to the ruin and great reproach of the christian church, and also to the ruin of the persons admitted." I freely grant, and show abundantly in my book, it is never to be expected, that all unsanctified men can be kept out, by the most exact attendance on the rules of Christ, by those that admit members.

In p. 136. *d.* Mr. W. wholly without grounds speaks of me as representing, that "unconverted men make pretension to nothing but what God's enemies have, remaining in open and avowed rebellion against him." Whereas, I suppose that some natural men do profess, and profess truly, *many things*, which those have not, who are *open* and *avowed* enemies of God. They may truly profess that sort of moral sincerity, in many things belonging to morality and religion, which avowed enemies have not: nor is there any sentence or word in my book, which implies or intimates the contrary.

In p. 141. *c. d.* Mr. W. evidently insinuates, that I am one of those who "If men live never so strictly conformable to the laws of the gospel, and never so diligently seek their own salvation, to outward appearance, yet do not stick to speak of them, and act openly towards them, as persons giving no more public evidence, that they are not the enemies of God and haters of Jesus Christ, than the very worst of the heathen." But surely every one that has read my book, every one that knows my constant conduct, and manner of preaching, as well as writing, and how much I have written, said, and done, against judging and censuring persons of an externally moral and religious behaviour, must know how injurious this representation of me is.

SECT. II.

Instances of the second thing mentioned as exceptionable in Mr. W.'s method of managing this controversy; viz. His misrepresenting what is said in the writings of others, that he supposes favour his opinion.

PERHAPS instances enough of this have already been taken notice of; yet I would now mention some others.

In what he says in reply to my answer to the eighth *objection*, he says, (p. 108.) "Mr. Stoddard does not say, If sanctifying grace be necessary to a person's lawful partaking of the Lord's supper, then God would have given some certain rule, whereby those WHO ARE TO ADMIT THEM, may know whether they have such grace or not." Mr. W. there intimates (as the reader may see) as if Mr. S. spake so, that it is to be understood *disjunctively*, meaning, he would *either* have given some certain rule to the church who admit them, *or* else to the persons themselves: so that by one means or other, the *Lord's supper might be restrained to converted men.* And he exclaims against me for representing as though Mr. Stoddard's argument were concerning a *certain rule, whereby those who are to admit them, may know whether they have grace,* (see the foregoing page,) and speaks of it as nothing akin to Mr. S.'s argument. Now let the reader take notice of Mr. S.'s words, and see whether his argument be not something *akin* to this. He says expressly, (*Appeal*, p. 75.) "God does not bind his CHURCH to impossibilities. If he had made such an ordinance, he would give gifts to his CHURCH, to distinguish sincere men from hypocrites, whereby the ordinance might have been attended.—The *minor* is also evident: he has given no such rule to his CHURCH, whereby it may be restrained to converted men. This appears, because by the rule that they are to go by, they are allowed TO GIVE the Lord's supper to many unconverted men. For all visible signs are common to men converted, and unconverted." So that Mr. S. in fact does say, If sanctifying grace be necessary to a person's lawful partaking of the Lord's supper, then God would have given some certain rule, whereby the church [those who are to admit them] may know, whether they have grace, or not. Though Mr. W. denies it, and says, this is nothing akin to Mr. S.'s argument; contrary to the plainest fact.

In p. 99. Mr. W. replying to my answer to the sixth objection, misrepresents Mr. *Hudson*, in the following passage. "This, (*i. e.* baptism,) says Mr. *Hudson*, makes them members of the body of Christ. And as for a particular explicit covenant, besides the general imposed on churches, I find no mention of it, no example, nor warrant for it, in all the Scripture."—Here Mr. W. is still manifestly endeavouring to discredit my doctrine of *an explicit owning the covenant of grace;* and he so manages and alters Mr. *Hudson's* words, as naturally leads the reader to suppose, that Mr. *Hudson* speaks against this: whereas, he says not a word about it. What Mr. H. speaks of, is not an explicit owning the covenant of grace, or baptismal covenant; but a *particular church-covenant*, by which a particular society bind themselves explicitly, one to another, jointly to carry on the public worship. Mr. *Hudson's* words are, (p. 19.) "I dare not make a *particular explicit holy covenant to be the* FORM *of a* PARTICULAR *church, as this description seemeth to do;* because I find no mention of any such covenant, besides the general imposed on churches, nor example, nor warrant for it, in all the Scripture." And then afterwards Mr. *Hudson* says, "but it is the general covenant sealed by *baptism*, and not this, that makes them members of the body of Christ."—Mr. W. by citing distant passages in Mr. *Hudson*, and joining them, in his own way, by particles and conjunctions, which Mr. *Hudson* does not use, and leaving out these words—*To be the form of a particular church, as this description seemeth to do,*—quite blinds the mind of his reader, as to Mr. *Hudson's* true sense, which is nothing to Mr. W.'s purpose.—Mr. *Hudson* says not a word here against, or about an *express or explicit covenanting*, or owning the covenant in my sense: but in other places, in the same book, he speaks of it, and for it, as necessary for *all Christians.* Thus, (p. 69. *b. c.*) "There is one individual EXPRESS, eternal covenant; not only on God's part,—but also it is one external, visible covenant, on men's part; which *all Christians*, as Christians, *enter into*, by their PROFESSED acceptance, and EXPRESS restipulation, and promised subjection and obedience; though not altogether in one place, or at one time." He speaks again to the same purpose, p. 100.

SECT. III.

Instances of the third thing observed in Mr. W.'s manner of arguing, viz. His pretending to oppose and answer arguments, by saying things which have no reference to them, but relate to other matters, perfectly foreign to the subject of the argument.

SUCH is his answer (p. 37, &c.) to my argument from Isa. lvi. Particularly from those words, 6. 7. "Also the sons of the stranger, that join themselves to the Lord, to serve him, to love the name of the Lord, to be his servants,—even them will I bring to my holy mountain, and make them joyful in my house of prayer," &c. For I say nothing under that argument, (as Mr. W. in his answer presumes,) which supposes any *antithesis* or opposition here between the state of the Gentiles and eunuchs *under the Old Testament, and under the gospel, as to terms of acceptance with God:* nor any opposition, as to a greater necessity of sanctifying grace, to the lawful partaking of ordinances, under the gospel, than under the law; as Mr. W. also supposes in his arguings on this head. But the *opposition* I speak of, as plainly pointed forth in the chapter, is this: That whereas under the law, *not only* piety of heart and practice were required, but something *else*, even soundness of body and circumcision, it is foretold, that under the gospel, piety of heart and practice *only* should be required; that although they were eunuchs or uncircumcised, yet if it appeared that they *loved the name of the Lord*, &c. they should be admitted.

So when I argued, that Christ, in the latter part of the 7th chap. of Matt. representing the final issue of things, with regard to the visible church in general, speaks of all as those who had looked on themselves to be interested in him as their Lord and Saviour, and had an opinion of their good estate; though the hope of some was built on the *sand*, and others on a *rock*:—Mr. W. in his reply, (p. 40, 41.) entirely overlooks the argument, and talks about other things. He says, Christ does not find fault with those that cried, Lord, Lord, for entering into covenant, but for not keeping covenant. (p. 41. *b.*) Here he runs back to another thing, relating to another argument, to which this has no reference, which he dwells wholly upon; and says nothing to the argument I use in that place.

So in his reply to what I say on the parable of the *wheat and tares*, (p. 98, &c.) he has entirely overlooked the argument. He says, to vindicate the objection, (p. 99.) "Which we think shows us the mind and will of Christ in this matter is, that his servants shall proceed only on certain established rules of his visible kingdom, and not upon any private rules of judging about them."—Whereas, I never said, or supposed, that Christ's servants must not *proceed on certain established rules of his visible kingdom*, or that they ought to go upon *any private rules of judging;* but particularly and largely expressed my mind to the contrary, in explaining the question; (*Inq.* p. 5.) "That it is properly a visibility to the eye of the *public* charity, and not of a *private* judgment, that gives a right to be received as visible saints by the public." And repeat the same thing again, p. 125. *c. d.*

And as to what Mr. W. says in this place about *infants* being *born in the church*, it entirely diverts the reader to another point (which I shall hereafter particularly consider) wholly distinct from the subject of the argument; which is about rules of *admission into the church*, whenever they are admitted. If persons are born in the church in complete standing, as Mr. W. supposes, then they are not *admitted* at all, but in their *ancestors*. But, however, the question returns, whether ancestors that are *unsanctified*, can have a lawful right to come into the church? Mr. W. holds they may. The subject of the argument is about *bringing in* tares into the field, *whenever they are brought in*, whether sooner or later; and whether *tares* have a lawful right, by warrant from Christ, to be in the *field;* supposing this to intend the church of Christ. The argument I produced to the contrary was, that the tares were introduced contrary to the owner's design, through men's infirmity and Satan's procurement. Which argument, being entirely overlooked by my opponent, I desire it may be now particularly considered.

When the *devil* brought in the *tares*, it is manifest, he brought in something that did not belong there; and therein counteracted the owner of the field, and did it under that very notion of crossing his design. *An enemy* (says the parable) *hath done this.* But how does this consist with the tares having a lawful right, by the owner's warrant and appointment, to have a standing in his field? If Christ by his institution has, in mercy to unsanctified men, given them a lawful right to come into the church, that it may be a means of their conversion; then it is a work of his kindness, as the compassionate Redeemer of souls, to bring them in; and not the doing of the great *enemy* and destroyer of souls. If the great Physician of souls has built his church, as an infirmary, in compassion to those that are sick, for this end, that they may be brought in and healed there; shall it be said with surprise, when such are found there, *How came those sick people* HERE? And shall the compassionate Physician, who built the hospital, make answer, *An enemy hath done this?*

Besides, if Christ has appointed that unsanctified men should come into the church, in order to their conversion, it would be an instance of the faithfulness of his servants to bring in such. But the bringing in tares into the field, is not represented as owing to the faithfulness and watchfulness of the servants; but on the contrary, is ascribed to their sleepiness and remissness. They were brought in while they slept, who ought to have done the part of watchmen, in keeping them out, and preventing the designs of the subtle enemy that brought them in.—Perhaps some would be ready to make the reflection that those churches whose practice is agreeable to the loose principles Mr. W. espouses, do that at noon-day, in the presence of God, angels, and men, which the devil did in the dead of the night, *while men slept!*

Again, Mr. W. in his reply to my argument from that *christian brotherly love*, which is required towards all members of the visible church, goes entirely off from the argument, to things quite alien from it. His first answer (p. 69. *c.*) is, that *the exercise of this christian love is not the term of communion or admission into the visible church:* which is perfectly foreign to the business. For the argument respects *the object* of this love, *viz.* visible saints, *that are to be thus beloved;* and not at all the qualifications of the *inherent subject* of it, or the *person that exercises this love.* If they that are admitted, are to be loved *as true saints*, or *for the image of Christ appearing in them, or supposed to be in them*, (as Mr. W. allows (p. 68. *c.*) then it will follow, that none are to be admitted, but such as can reasonably be the objects of christian love, or be loved *as true saints*, and as those who *have the image of Christ appearing in them.* Whether the exercise of this love be the term of communion, or not; yet if we are commanded to exercise this love to all that are admitted to communion, then it will certainly follow, that some reasonable ground for being thus beloved, must be a term of communion in such as are admitted. To suppose it appointed, that we should love all that are admitted as true saints, and yet that it is not appointed that such as are admitted should exhibit any reasonable grounds for such a love, is certainly to suppose very inconsistent appointments.*

Mr. W.'s second answer (p. 70. *b.*) is no less impertinent; *viz. That men's right to communion in gospel-ordinances does not depend upon the corruptions of other men*, in their forbearing to love them. As if my argument were, that unless men are *actually loved*, as true saints, they have no right to communion! Whereas, the argument was very diverse, *viz.* That unless men have *a right to be so loved*, they have no right to communion. If men have an appearance, to reason, of being true saints, they may have a right to be loved as true saints, and to be admitted as such; however corrupt and void of love other men are: but without such an appearance to reason, it is no corruption, not to love them as true saints; unless it be corrupt, not to act without reason.†—As to Mr. W.'s third answer,

* "The apostles looked on all those, whom they gathered into churches or christian congregations to eat the Lord's supper, as having the truth dwelling in them: and so they behoved, every one of them, to look upon one another: seeing they could not love one another as brethren in the truth, without acknowledging that truth as dwelling in them. And so we see the apostles, in their writings to the churches, supposing all their members objects of this brotherly love.—Christ's visible church then is the congregation of those whom the apostle could call the saints and faithful in Christ Jesus."—*Glass's Notes on Scripture Texts*, Numb. 5. p. 32.

† A good argument might also be drawn from the corruption of unsanctified men; for that they are all so under the power of corruption, that they are not able to love saints, or any one else, with truly christian love. Agreeable to what Mr. Stoddard says in his three sermons, (p. 40.) "Men are obliged to love their neighbours as themselves. But no natural men do in any measure live up to that rule; but men are great enemies one to another, hateful and hating one another. They do but little good one to another: they do a great deal of hurt one to another." Now is it reasonable to suppose, that such men have the proper qualifications, by divine institution, for a lawful right to be members of the visible family of God?

and the misrepresentation it is built upon, it has already been taken notice of.

In Mr. W.'s reply to my answer to the first objection, (p. 81, &c.) he wholly leaves the argument, and writes in support and defence of other matters, quite different from those which I mentioned, or had any concern with. The objection which I mentioned, and which had been much insisted on by some against my opinion, was, That church-members are called disciples, or scholars; a name, that gives us a notion of the visible church as a school; and leads us to suppose, that all who profess that sort of faith and sincerity, which implies a disposition to seek christian learning and spiritual attainments, are qualified for admission. But Mr. W. says nothing at all in support of this objection. In answer to it, I endeavoured to show, that the name disciples given to church-members, does not argue that unsanctified persons are fit to be members. He says nothing to show that it does. He says, if it will not follow from Christ's visible church being represented as Christ's school, that it is in order to *all* good attainments; *yet it is in order to all that they have not yet attained.* Which is nothing to the purpose, but foreign to the thing in debate, *viz. Whether sanctifying grace is one of those things which are not yet attained by those that are lawfully in the church.* He there says nothing to prove that it is; and especially to prove it from the meaning of the word, disciples; which was the argument in hand. He insists, that men may be sufficiently subject to Christ as their master and teacher, in order to be in his school or church, without grace: but then the thing to be proved, was, that church-members being called disciples makes this evident, in order to support the argument or objection I was upon: which argument is entirely neglected throughout all his discourse under this head.

So in his reply to my answer to the eleventh objection, (p. 123, &c.) he wholly neglects the argument, and labours to support a different one. I endeavoured, without concerning myself about the words of any argument in Mr. Stoddard's *Appeal*, to answer an argument abundantly used at Northampton against my doctrine, of unsanctified men not having a right to come to the Lord's supper; which was this, "You may as well say, that unsanctified men may not attend any other duty of worship:" and particularly, "You may as well forbid them to pray."—As for Mr. S.'s objection, in these words, "If unsanctified men may attend all other ordinances or duties of worship, then they may lawfully attend the Lord's supper;" it was an argument I was not obliged to attend to in the words in which he delivered it, because it was not an argument brought against *my* scheme of things, but one very diverse: since it is not my opinion, that unsanctified men may attend *all other ordinances, or duties of worship, besides the Lord's supper;* for I do not suppose, such may offer themselves to *baptism;* which Mr. S. takes for granted, in his argument. And therefore what Mr. W. says in support of it, is quite beside the business. As to the argument I was concerned with, taken especially from the lawfulness of unsanctified men *praying*, to prove, that therefore it must be lawful for them to come to the Lord's supper, certainly if there be any consequence in it, the consequence depends on the truth of this supposition, *that the same thing which makes it lawful for a man to* pray, *also makes it lawful for him to come to the Lord's supper.* And seeing this position is proved to be not true, the argument falls to the ground. And Mr. W.'s nice observations and distinctions, of a *non obstante*, and a *simply and per se*, are nothing to the purpose.

This good reason (with several others) may be given, why the same that makes it lawful for a man to pray and hear the word, will not make it lawful for him to partake of sacraments, *viz.* that the sacraments are not only duties, but *covenant privileges*, and are never lawfully given or received but under that notion. Whereas, it is not so with prayer and hearing the word: and therefore they who have no interest in the *covenant of grace*, and are in no respect God's *covenant people*, may lawfully hear the word and pray. But it is agreed on all hands, that they who are not in some respect God's *covenant people*, may not come to sacraments: and the reason is this, because sacraments are *covenant privileges*. And this same reason will prove, that none but true believers, or those that have saving faith, the only condition of the *covenant of grace*, have a right to sacraments. For, as was observed before, the condition of any covenant is the condition of all the benefits or privileges of that covenant. (See Part II. sect. 8.

SECT. IV.

The fourth thing observed in Mr. W.'s method of managing the controversy, particularly considered, viz. His advancing new and extraordinary notions, not only manifestly contrary to truth, but also to the common and received principles of the christian church.

THUS it is with regard to many things which have already been taken notice of. As, that men may be ungodly, and yet truly profess to love God more than the world; that men may be professors of religion and have no true grace, and yet not be lukewarm, but serve God as their only master; that such may profess to be subject to Christ with all their hearts, and to give up all their hearts and lives to Christ, and speak true, &c. &c.

I shall now take notice of another remarkable instance, *viz.* That Mr. W. in his reply to my argument from the epithets and characters given by the apostles to the members of visible christian churches, in their epistles, represents, (p. 56. *d.*) That there "is no *difference in all the epithets and characters, which I had heaped up from the New Testament*," from those that are given in the Old Testament, to the whole body of the Jewish church; which he elsewhere abundantly suppose to be the whole body of the Jewish nation; yea, even in their *worst* times, till the nation was rejected and cast off by God from being any longer his people; as I shall have occasion particularly to observe afterwards.

That it may be the more easily judged, how manifestly this is contrary to truth, I shall here repeat some of those *epithets* and *characters* I before mentioned, to which Mr. W. has reference. This is very manifest concerning most of them; but that I may not be tedious, I will now rehearse but a few instances: *viz.* Being "made free from sin, and becoming the servants of righteousness:" Having "the spirit of adoption:" Being "the children of God, heirs of God, joint-heirs with Christ:" Being "vessels of mercy, prepared unto glory:" Being such "as do not live to themselves, nor die to themselves; but live to the Lord, and die unto the Lord;" and who "living and dying are the Lord's:" Being those that have "all things for theirs, whether Paul, or Apollos, or Cephas, or the world, or life, or death, or things present, or things to come; because they are Christ's:" Being "begotten through the gospel:" Being such as "shall judge the world:" Being "washed, sanctified, justified in the name of the Lord Jesus, and by the Spirit of our God:" Being "manifestly declared to be the epistle of Christ, written not with ink, but by the Spirit of the living God; not in tables of stone, but in fleshly tables of the heart:" Being such as "behold as in a glass the glory of the Lord, and are changed into the same image, from glory to glory:" Being "chosen in Christ before the foundation of the world, that they should be holy and without blame before him in love; and predestinated unto the adoption of children:" Being "sealed by that holy spirit of promise:" Being "quickened, though once dead in trespasses and sins:" Being "made meet to be partakers of the inheritance of the saints in light:" Being "dead, and having their life hid with Christ in God;" and being those who, "when Christ who is our life shall appear, shall also appear with him in glory; having put off the old man with his deeds, and having put on the new man, which is renewed in knowledge, after the image of him that created him:" Being "begotten again to a living hope—to an inheritance incorruptible, and undefiled, and that fadeth not away, reserved in heaven for them; who are kept by the power of God through faith unto salvation; who love Christ, though they have not seen him; in whom, though now they see him not, yet believing, they rejoice with joy unspeakable and full of glory; having purified their souls in obeying the truth through the Spirit; knowing him that is from the beginning; having their sins forgiven; having overcome the wicked one; having an unction from the Holy One, by which they know all things; who are now the sons of God; and who, when Christ shall appear, shall be like him, because they shall see him as he is."

Now let the christian reader judge, with what face of reason our author could represent as though there were nothing in all these epithets and characters, more than used of old to be given to the whole nation of the *Jews*, and that even in times of their greatest corruption and apostacy, till the nation was rejected of God! One would think, there is no need of arguing the matter with any that have read the Bible.

This representation of Mr. W.'s is not only very contrary to truth, but also to the common sentiments of the *christian church*. Though I pretend not to be a person of great reading, yet I have read enough to warrant this assertion. I never yet (as I remember) met with any author that went the same length in this matter with Mr. W. but Mr. Taylor, of *Norwich*, in *England*, the author who lately has been so famous for his corrupt doctrine. In his piece which he calls *A Key to the Apostolic Writings*, where he delivers his scheme of religion, (which seems scarcely so agreeable to the christian scheme, as the doctrine of many of the wiser *heathen*,) he delivers the same opinion, and insists largely upon it; it being a main thing to establish his whole scheme. And it evidently appears, in the manner of his delivering it, that he is sensible it is exceeding far from what has hitherto been the commonly received sentiment in the christian world. He supposes that as all those epithets and characters belong to the whole nation of the *Jews*, even in their most corrupt times, so they belong to all *christendom*, even the most vicious parts of it; that the most vicious men, who are baptized, and profess to believe Jesus to be the *Messiah*, are "chosen before the foundation of the world, predestinated according to the foreknowledge of God, regenerated, justified, sanctified, children of God, heirs of God, joint-heirs with Christ, the spouse of Christ, the temple of God, made to sit together in heavenly places in Christ, being the family of heaven," &c. &c. And certainly he may with as good reason, and with the same reason, suppose this of all *christendom*, even the most vicious parts of it, as of the whole nation of the *Jews*, however corrupt, till there was a national rejection of them.

Indeed, it is manifest there is no other way of evading the force of the argument from the epistles, but by falling into Taylor's scheme. If his scheme of religion be not true, then it is plain as any fact in the New Testament, that all the christian churches, through the whole earth, in the apostles' days, were constituted in the manner that I insist on. The Scripture says ten times as much to demonstrate this matter, as it does about the manner of discipline, officers and government of the church, or about the several parts of the public worship, or the sanctification of the christian sabbath.

SECT. V.

Instances of the fifth and sixth particulars, in Mr. W.'s method of disputing, viz. his using confident and peremptory assertions, and great exclamations, instead of arguments.

WE have an instance of the *former*, in his reply to my answer to the 14th objection, *viz.* That *it is not unlawful for unsanctified men to carry themselves like saints.* I objected against this, if thereby be meant, that they may lawfully carry themselves externally like saints in all respects, remaining ungodly; and mentioned some things which belonged to the external duty of godly men, which no ungodly man, remaining such, may do To which Mr. W. makes no reply; but to prove the point says, "Mr. St—d knew, and all divines know, That the external carriage of some unsanctified men *is* to the outward appearance, and the public judgment of the church, the same with the carriage of the saints; and they know they are *bound* to such a behaviour." And this peremptory confident assertion is all the argument he brings to prove the thing asserted.

Again, I observe, that sometimes Mr. W. uses *great exclamation*, as though he intended to alarm, and excite terror in his readers, and raise their indignation; though they are perhaps never likely to know *for what*. We have two very remarkable instances of this, (p. 136 and 137.) where he says, "I shall further take notice of two *extraordinary* and *surprising* passages, if I understand them. And I have with great diligence tried to find out the meaning of them. One is p. 129. between the 17th and 23d lines; if it be rightly printed."—He does not quote my words: this mighty exclamation would have become too flat, and appeared ridiculous, if he had.—The passage referred to is in these words—"Indeed such a tendency (*i. e.* a tendency to irreligion and profaneness) it would have, to shut men out from having any part in the Lord, in the sense of the two tribes and half, Josh. xxii. 25. or to fence them out by such a partition-wall, as formerly was between Jews and Gentiles; and so to shut them out as to tell them, if they were never so much disposed to serve God, he was not ready to accept them: according to the notion the Jews seem to have had of the uncircumcised Gentiles." That is, plainly to shut them out so as to tell them, that let them have hearts never so well and piously disposed to love and serve God, their love and service could not be accepted.—This doubtless would have a tendency to discourage religion in men. And how the owning of it, is an owning my scheme to have such a tendency, I do not know. Mr. W. might as well have picked out any other sentence through all the 136 pages of the book, and called it an *extraordinary passage*, and stood astonished over it, and told how he was ready to doubt whether it was *rightly printed*, and what *great diligence* he had used *to find out the meaning of it!*

The other extraordinary passage he stands thunderstruck with, is in these words; "May it not be suspected, that this way of baptizing the children of such as never make any proper profession of godliness, is an expedient originally invented for that very end, to give ease to ancestors with respect to their posterity, in times of great declension and degeneracy?"—Mr. W. knows, that through the whole of my book I suppose, this practice of baptizing the children of such as are here spoken of, is *wrong;* and so does *he* too; for he abundantly allows, that persons in order to be admitted to the privileges of visible saints, must make a profession of real piety, or gospel-holiness. And if it be wrong, as we are both agreed, then surely it is nothing akin to blasphemy, to suspect that it arose from some bad cause.

SECT. VI.

Instances of the seventh particular observed in Mr. W.'s way of disputing, viz. His wholly overlooking arguments, pretending there is no argument, nothing to answer; when the case is far otherwise.

THUS in his reply to my tenth argument, which was this, "It is necessary, that those who partake of the Lord's supper, should judge themselves truly and cordially to accept of Christ as their Saviour, and chief good; for this is what the actions, which communicants perform at the Lord's table, are a solemn profession of." I largely endeavoured (in p. 75, 76, and 77.) to prove this, from the nature of those significant actions, of receiving the symbols of Christ's body and blood when offered, representing their accepting the thing signified, as their spiritual food, &c. To all which Mr. W. says, (p. 74. *a.*) "I do not find that Mr. Edwards has said any thing to prove the proposition, which is the whole argument offered here in proof of the point proposed to be proved, but only gives his opinion, or paraphrase, of the purport and nature of the sacramental actions."—Since Mr. W. esteems it no argument, I desire it may be considered impartially whether there be any argument in it or no.

These sacramental actions all allow to be *significant* actions: they are a signification and profession of something: they are not actions without a meaning. And all allow, that these external actions signify something *inward* and *spiritual*. And if they signify any thing spiritual, they doubtless signify those spiritual things which they *represent*. But what *inward* thing does the outward taking or accepting the body and blood of Christ represent, but the *inward* accepting Christ's body and blood, or an accepting him in the heart? And what *spiritual* thing is the outward feeding on Christ in this ordinance a sign of, but a *spiritual* feeding on Christ, or the soul's feeding on him? Now there is no other way of the soul's feeding on him, but by that *faith*, by which Christ becomes our spiritual food, and the refreshment and vital nourishment of our souls. The *outward eating and drinking* in this ordinance is a sign of *spiritual eating and drinking*, as much as the *outward bread* in this ordinance is a sign of *spiritual bread;* or as much as the *outward drink* is a sign of *spiritual drink*. And doubtless those actions, if they are a profession of any thing at all, are a profession of the things they signify.* To say, that these significant actions are appointed to be a *profession* of something, but not to be a profession of the *things* they are appointed to *signify*, is as unreasonable as to say, that certain sounds or words are appointed to be a profession of something, but not to be a profession of the things signified by those words.

Again, Mr. W. in his reply to my answer to the *second objection*, with like contempt passes over the main argument which I offered, to prove that the nation of *Israel* were called *God's people*, and *covenant people*, in another sense besides a being visible saints. My argument (in p. 85, 86.) was this: That it is manifest, something diverse from being visible saints, is often intended by that nation being called *God's people*, and that the family of *Israel according to the flesh*—not with regard to any moral and religious qualifications—were in some sense adopted by God, to be his peculiar and covenant people; from Rom. ix. 3, 4, 5.—"I could wish myself accursed from Christ for my brethren according to the flesh; who are *Israelites;* to whom pertaineth the adoption, and the glory, and the COVENANTS, and the giving of the law, and the service of God, and the promises; whose are the fathers," &c. I observed, that these privileges are spoken of as belonging to the *Jews*, not now as visible saints, not as professors of the true religion, not as members of the visible church of Christ, (which they did not belong to,) but only as a people of such a nation, such a blood, such an external carnal relation to the patriarchs, their ancestors; *Israelites according to the flesh:* inasmuch as the apostle is speaking here of the *unbelieving Jews*, professed unbelievers, that were out of the christian church, and open visible enemies to it; and such as had no right at all to the external privileges of Christ's people.—I observed further, that in like manner this apostle in Rom. xi. 28, 29. speaks of the same *unbelieving Jews*, that were enemies to the gospel, as in some respect an elect people, and interested in the calling, promises, and covenants, God formerly gave their forefathers, and are still beloved for their sakes. "As concerning the gospel, they are enemies for your sakes; but as touching the election, they are beloved for the fathers' sakes. For the gifts and calling of God are without repentance."

All that Mr. W. says, which has any reference to these things, is, "That he had read my explication of the name of *the people of God*, as given to the people of *Israel*, &c. But that he confesses, it is perfectly unintelligible to him." The impartial reader is left to judge, whether the matter did not require some other answer.

SECT. VII.

What is, and what is not, begging the question; and how Mr. W. charges me, from time to time, with begging the question, without cause.

AMONG the particulars of Mr. W.'s method of disputing, I observed, that *he often causelessly charges me with begging the question, while he frequently begs the question himself, or does that which is equivalent.*

But that it may be determined with justice and clearness, who does, and who does not, beg the question, I desire it may be particularly considered, what that is which is called *begging the question* in a dispute.—This is more especially needful for the sake of illiterate readers. And here,

1. Let it be observed, that merely to suppose something in a dispute, without bringing any argument to prove it, is not begging the question: for this is done necessarily, in every dispute, and even in the best and clearest demonstrations. One point is proved by another, till at length the matter is reduced to a point that is supposed to need no proof; either because it is self-evident, or is a thing wherein both parties are agreed, or so clear that it is supposed it will not be denied.

2. Nor is begging the question the same thing as offering a weak argument, to prove the point in question. It is not all weak arguing, but one *particular way* of weak arguing, that is called *begging the question*.

3. Nor is it the same thing as *missing the true question*, and bringing an argument that is impertinent, or *beside the question*.

But the thing which is called *begging the question*, is the making use of the very point in debate, or the thing to be proved, as an argument to prove itself. Thus, if I were endeavouring to prove that none but godly persons might come to sacraments, and should take this for an argument to prove it, that none might come but such as have saving faith, taking this for granted; I should then beg the question: for this is the very point in question, whether a man must have saving faith or no? It is called begging the question, because it is a depending as it were on the courtesy of the other side, to grant me the point in question, without offering any argument as the price of it.

And whether the point I thus take for granted, be the main point in question, in the general dispute, or some subordinate point, something under consideration, under a particular argument; yet if I take this particular point for granted, and then make use of it to prove itself, it is begging the question.

Thus if I were endeavouring, under this general controversy between Mr. W. and me, to prove that particular point, that we ought to love all the members of the church as true saints; and should bring this as a proof of the point, that we ought to love all the members of the church as true Christians, taking this for granted; this is only the same thing, under another term, as the thing to be proved; and therefore is no argument at all, but only begging the question.

Or if the point I thus take for granted, and make use of as an argument, be neither the general point in controversy, nor yet the thing nextly to be proved under a particular argument; yet if it be some known controverted point between the parties, it is begging the question, or equivalent to it: for it is begging a thing known to be in question in the dispute, and using it as if it were a thing allowed.

I would now consider the instances, wherein Mr. W. asserts or suggests that I have begged the question.

In p. 30. *d. e.* and 31. *a. b.* he represents the force of my reasoning as built on a supposition, that there is no unsanctified man, but what knows he has no desire of salvation by Christ, no design to fulfil the covenant of grace, but designs to live in stealing, lying, adultery,—or some other known sin: and then says, "Is it not manifest, that such sort of reasoning is a mere quibbling with words, and begging the question?" And so insinuates, that I have thus begged the question. Whereas, I nowhere say or suppose this which he speaks of, nor any thing like it. But on the contrary, often say, what supposes an unsanctified man may think he is truly godly,

* Mr. Stoddard owns, that the sacramental actions, both in baptism and the Lord's supper, signify saving faith in Christ. *Safety of App.* p. 120. "By baptism is signified our fellowship with Christ in his sufferings. That is signified hereby, that we have an interest in the virtue of his sufferings, that his sufferings are made over unto us, and that we do participate in the good and benefit of them.——It was John the Baptist's manner, before he baptized persons, to teach them that they must believe on Christ. And the apostles and apostolical men would not baptize any adult persons but such as professed to believe on Christ.—He that believeth and is baptized, shall be saved. Baptism is mentioned as the evidence of faith."—So concerning the Lord's supper, *ibid.* p. 122. *e.* 123. *a.* "In this ordinance we are invited to put our trust in the death of Christ. Take, eat; this is my body: and drink ye all of it. When the body feeds on the sacramental bread and wine, the soul is to do that which answers unto it; The soul is to feed on Christ crucified; which is nothing else but the acting faith on him."

and that he has truly upright and gracious designs and desires.—Nor does any argument of mine depend on any such supposition. Nay, under the argument he speaks of, I expressly suppose the contrary, *viz.* That unsanctified men who visibly enter into covenant, may be deceived.

In p. 38. *a.* Mr. W. makes a certain representation of my arguing from Isaiah lvi. and then says upon it, "It is no arguing, but only begging the question." But as has been already shown, that which he represents as my argument from that scripture, has no relation to my argument.

In p. 59. in opposition to my arguing from the Epistles, that the apostles treated those members of churches which they wrote to, as those who had been received on a positive judgment, *i. e.* (as I explain myself,) a proper and affirmative opinion, that they were real saints; Mr. W. argues, that the apostles could make no such judgment of them, without either personal converse, or revelation; unless it be supposed to be founded on a presumption, that ministers who baptized them, would not have done it, unless they had themselves made such a positive judgment concerning their state: and then adds these words, This may do for this scheme, but only it is a begging the question. Whereas, it is a point that never has been in question in this controversy, as ever I knew, whether *some ministers or churches* might reasonably and affirmatively suppose, the members of *other churches* they are united with, were admitted on evidence of proper qualifications, (whatever they be, whether common or saving,) trusting to the faithfulness of other ministers and churches. Besides, this can be no point in question between me and Mr. W. unless it be a point in question between him and himself. For he holds, as well as I, that persons ought not to be received as visible Christians, without moral evidence (which is something positive, and not a mere negation of evidence of the contrary) of *gospel-holiness*.

In p. 82. of my book I suppose, that none at all do truly subject themselves to Christ as their master, but those who graciously subject themselves to him, and are delivered from the reigning power of sin. Mr. W. suggests, (p. 83. *d.*) that herein I beg the question. For which there is no pretext, not only as this is no known point in controversy between the parties in this debate; but also as it is a point I do not take for granted, but offer this argument to prove it, that they who have no grace, *are under the reigning power of sin*, and no man can truly subject himself to two such contrary masters, at the same time, as Christ and sin. I think this argument sufficient to obtain the point, without begging it. And besides, this doctrine, that they who have no grace do not truly subject themselves to Christ, was no point in question between me and Mr. W. But a point wherein we were fully agreed, and wherein he had before expressed himself as fully, and more fully, than I. In his sermons on *Christ a King and Witness*, (p. 18. *b.*) he speaks of all such as do not depend on Christ, believe in him, and give up themselves and all to him, as not true subjects to Christ; but enemies to him, and his kingdom. We have expressions to the same purpose again, in p. 74. and 91. and in p. 94. *d. e.* of the same book, he says, "It is utterly inconsistent with the nature of the obedience of the gospel, that it should be a *forced subjection.*—No man is a *subject* of Christ, who does not make the laws and will of Christ his choice, and desire to be governed by him, and to live in subjection to the will of Christ, as *good* and *fit*, and *best* to be the rule of his living, and *way to his happiness.* A forced obedience to Christ is *no obedience. It is in terms a contradiction.* Christ draws men with the cords of love, and the bands of a man. Our Lord has himself expressly determined this point." There are other passages in the same book to the same purpose. So that I had no need to beg this point of Mr. W. since he had given it largely, and that in full measure, and over and over again, without begging.

In p. 120. *b.* he observes, "That to say, such a profession of internal invisible things is the rule to direct the church in admission,—is to hide the parallel, and beg the question. For the question here is about the persons' right to come, and not about the church's admitting them." Here Mr. W. would make us believe, that he does not know what begging the question is: for it is evident, his meaning is, that my saying so is *beside the question.* But to say something beside the question, is a different thing from begging the question, as has been observed. My saying, that *a profession of invisible things* is the church's rule in admission, is not begging the question: because it is not, nor ever was, any thing in question. For Mr. S. and Mr. W. himself are full in it, that a profession of *invisible things*, such as a believing that Christ is the Son of God, &c. is the church's rule. Yea, Mr. W. is express in it, that a credible profession and visibility of *gospel-holiness* is the church's rule, p. 139. Nor is my saying as above, *beside the question then in hand*, relating to the church of Israel admitting to the priesthood, those that could not find their register. For that wholly relates to the rule of admission to the priesthood, and not to the priests' *assurance of their own right.* For, as I observed, if the priests had been never so fully assured of their pedigree, yet if they could not demonstrate it to others, by a public register, it would not have availed for their admission.

Again, in p. 124. *e.* Mr. W. charges me with begging the question, in supposing that sacraments are duties of worship whose very nature and design is an exhibition of those vital and active principles and inward exercises, wherein consists the condition of the covenant of grace. He charges the same thing as a begging the question, p. 131. *d.*—But this is no begging the question, for two reasons; (1.) Because I had before proved this point, by proofs which Mr. W. has not seen cause to attempt to answer, as has been just now observed, in the last section. (2.) This, when I wrote, was no point in question, wherein Mr. W. and I differed; but wherein we were agreed, and in which he had declared himself as fully as I, in his sermons on *Christ a King and Witness*; p. 76. *c.* "When we attend sacraments (says he) we are therein visibly to profess our receiving Christ, and the graces of his Spirit, and the benefits of his redemption, on his own terms and offer, and giving up the all of our souls to him, on his call, covenant, and engagement." And in the next preceding page but one, in a place forecited, he speaks of these acts "as mockery, hypocrisy, falsehood, and lies, if they are not the expressions of faith and hope, and spiritual acts of obedience." So that I had no manner of need to come to Mr. W. as a beggar for these things, which he had so plentifully given me, and all the world that would accept them, years before.

SECT. VIII.

Showing how Mr. W. often begs the question himself.

THE question is certainly begged in that argument which Mr. W. espouses and defends, *viz.* That the Lord's supper has a proper tendency to promote men's conversion. In the prosecution of the argument Mr. W. implicitly yields, that it is not the apparent natural tendency alone, that is of any force to prove the point; but the apparent tendency under this circumstance, *that there is no express prohibition.* And thus it is allowed, that in the case of express prohibition with respect to the scandalous and morally insincere, no seeming tendency in the nature of the thing proves the ordinance to be intended for the conviction and conversion of such. So that it is a thing supposed in this argument, that all morally insincere persons are expressly forbidden, but unsanctified persons not so. Now when it is supposed, that morally insincere persons are expressly forbidden, the thing meant cannot be, that they are forbidden in those very words; for no such prohibition is to be found: nor are men that live in sodomy, bestiality, and witchcraft, any where expressly forbidden in this sense. But the thing intended must be, that they are very evidently forbidden, by plain implication, or consequence. But then the whole weight of the argument lies in this *supposition*, that unsanctified persons are not also plainly and evidently forbidden; which is the very point in question. And therefore to make this the ground of an argument to prove this point, is a manifest *begging the question.* And what Mr. W. says to the contrary, (p. 127. *a.*) that Mr. Stoddard had proved this point before, avails nothing: for let it be never so much proved before, yet, after all, to take this very point and make use of it *as a further argument* to prove itself, is certainly *begging the question*. The notion of bringing a new argument is bringing additional proof: but to take a certain point, supposed to be already proved, to prove itself with over again, certainly does not add any thing to the evidence.

Mr. W. says, my supposing *unconverted* persons, as such, to be as evidently forbidden, as *scandalous* persons, is as much begging the question. I answer, So it would be, if I made that point an argument to prove itself with, after Mr. W.'s manner. But this is far from being the case in fact.

And the question is again most certainly begged, in that other thing said to support this argument, *viz.* That though the Lord's supper may seem to have a tendency to convert scandalous sinners, yet there is another ordinance appointed for that. Here the meaning must be, that there is another ordinance *exclusive* of the Lord's supper; otherwise it is nothing to the purpose. For they do not deny but that there are other ordinances for the conversion of sinners, who are morally sincere, as well as of those who are scandalous. But the question is, Whether other ordinances are appointed for their conversion *exclusive* of the Lord's supper; or, whether the Lord's supper be one ordinance appointed for their conversion? This is the grand point *in question*. And to take this point as the foundation of an argument, to prove this same point, is plainly begging the question. And it is also giving up the argument from the tendency, and resting the whole argument on another thing.

Mr. W. again plainly begs the question in his reply, (p. 127. *c. d.*) That God's prohibition is an argument, that God saw there was no such tendency for their conversion. His so saying supposes again, that there is no evident prohibition of unsanctified persons. In which he again flies to the very point in question, and rests the weight of his reasoning upon it.

Just in the same manner Mr. W. begs the question in espousing and making use of that argument, That all in external covenant, and neither ignorant nor scandalous, are commanded to perform all external covenant duties. Here it is supposed, that scandalous persons, (which, according to Mr. W.'s scheme, must include all that have not moral sincerity,) though in the external covenant, are expressly, that is, *evidently, excepted and forbidden*: and that unsanctified men are not also *evidently forbidden*; which is the point in question. For if unsanctified men, though in external covenant, are as evidently forbidden and excepted, as scandalous men that are in external covenant, then the argument touches not one any more than the other. So that the argument is entirely a castle in the air, resting on nothing but itself. The grand thing to be proved, first taken for granted, and then made an argument to prove itself!

In explaining the nature of *begging the question*, I observed, that it is *begging the question*, or equivalent to it, whether the point that is taken for granted, and made an argument of, be the main point in controversy, or some particular known disputed point between the controverting parties: I will now illustrate this by an example. It is a known disputed point in this controversy, whether in the parable concerning the *man without the wedding garment*, the king condemned the man for coming into the church without *grace*. Now supposing that I, because I look on the matter as very clear, should, besides using it as one distinct argument, also make it the basis of other arguments; and should use it in opposition to the strongest arguments of my opposers, as if it were sufficient to stop their mouths, without offering any proper solution of those arguments: as, in case I were pressed with the argument from the passover, if I should fly to *the man without the wedding garment*; and should say, It is certain, this argument from the passover can be of no force against the express word of God in the 22nd of Matt. For there *it is plain as any fact that ever the sun shone upon*, that the king condemns the man for coming into the church *without a wedding garment*; and it is plain as the sun at noonday, that the wedding garment is *grace*.—And if when the argument from *Judas's* partaking of the Lord's supper is alleged, I should again fly to *the man without a wedding garment*, and say, whatever reasons Christ might have for admitting *Judas*, yet it is plainly revealed, in Matt. xxii. 12. that God does not approve of men coming into the church without a *wedding garment*. This would be a *beggarly* impertinent way of disputing, thus to answer one argument by throwing another in the way, which is contested, and the validity of which is denied. It is fair, that I should have liberty to use the argument concerning *the wedding garment*, in its place, and make the most of it: but to use it as the support of other arguments, is to produce no additional proof. And thus, from time to time, to produce the disputed hypothesis of one argument, for answer to the arguments of my antagonist, instead of solving those arguments, is flying and hiding from arguments, instead of answering them: instead of defending the fortress which is attacked, it is dodging and flying from one refuge to another.

Mr. W. acts this part from time to time, in the use he makes of his great argument from the *Old-Testament* church and its ordinances. Thus (in p. 8.) he takes this method to answer my argument from the nature of visibility and profession, insisting that the *Israelites* avouching and covenanting was a thing compatible with *ungodliness;* which he knows is a disputed point in this controversy, and what I deny.—Again, he makes use of the same thing, in answer to my argument from the nature of covenanting with God. (p. 23, 24.) And again he brings it in, (p. 25. *e.* 26. *a.*) answering what I say, by confidently asserting that concerning the church of *Israel*, which he knows is disputed, and I deny; *viz.* That the covenanting of *Israel* did not imply a profession that they did already believe and repent: as in these words, "This was never intended nor understood, in the profession which the *Israelites* made; but that they *would* immediately and from thenceforth comply with the terms of the covenant; and by the help of God, offered in it, *would* fulfil it. *I am sure*, this was what they professed; and *I am sure*, God declared he took them into covenant with him." And the same thing is brought in again to answer the same argument. (p. 31. *c.*)—The same thing is thrown in, once and again, as an answer to what I say of the unreasonableness of accepting such professions as leave room to judge the greater part of the professors to be enemies of God. (p. 34. *b. c.*) The same thing is cast in as a sufficient block in the way of my arguing from the unreasonableness of accepting such professions, as amount to nothing more than *lukewarmness*. (p. 36. *d. e.*) The same is brought in, and greatly insisted on, to stop my mouth, in arguing from the Epistles. (p. 56, 57.) The same is brought in again, to enervate my argument concerning *brotherly love*. (p. 69. *d.*) And this is made use of as the support of other arguments; as that from the name *disciples*, and about the church being the *school of Christ;* and to confute what I say, in answer to that argument. (p. 84. *a.*) The same is brought in as a support of the eleventh objection, and a confutation of my answer to that. (p. 125. *c. d. e.*) And again, in reply to what I say in answer to the nineteenth objection. (p. 137. *b. c.*)

Another thing, near akin to *begging the question*, is resting the weight of arguments on things asserted without proof; which, though they do not properly make a part of the controversy, yet are things not allowed by those on the other side.—Thus does Mr. W. in his arguing from the success of the Lord's supper in the *conversion* of sinners. (p. 137, 138.) Supposing, not only that the Lord's supper has been the *occasion* of the conversion of many, but that their communicating was the *means* of it. This he offers nothing to prove, and it is not allowed by those on the other side.* And it is what would be very hard to prove: if many were converted *at* the Lord's table, (which yet is not evident,) it would not prove, that their *partaking* was

* Thus that very eminent divine, and successful minister of Christ, the late Dr. Doddridge, in his *Sermons on Regeneration*, speaking of the means of regeneration (p. 251. *e.* 252. *a.*) says, "I do not mention the administration of sacraments, upon this occasion; because, though they have so noble and effectual a tendency to improve men's minds in piety, and to promote christian edification; yet I do not remember to have heard of any instance, in which they have been the means of men's conversion; which is the less to be wondered at, as they are appointed for a very different end."

the means of their conversion; it might be only what they saw and heard there, which others may see and hear, that do not partake.

SECT. IX.

Mr. W.'s inconsistence with himself, in what he says in answer to my third and fourth arguments, and in his reply to my arguments from the Acts, and the Epistles.

THE *last* thing observed in Mr. W.'s way of disputing, is his alleging and insisting on things wherein he is inconsistent with himself. His inconsistencies are of many sorts. Sometimes he alleges those things that are inconsistent with the doctrine of those whose principles he pretends to maintain.—He abundantly urges those things against my scheme, which are in like manner against his own. He often argues against those things which he allows, and strenuously insists on. He denies what he affirms, and affirms what he utterly denies; laying down and urging those things which are contrary to what he says in other books; and sometimes contrary to what he says in the same book. Yielding up the thing wherein the argument lies, yet strenuously maintaining the argument.—Allowing both premises and consequence, yet finding fault, and opposing. Sometimes he urges things which are contrary to what he says under *different* arguments; and sometimes contrary to what he says under the *same* argument. Sometimes he contradicts himself in the plain sense and meaning of what he says; at other times even in plain terms. Sometimes in effect contradicting himself in the same breath, and in the same sentence.

These various kinds of inconsistence have many of them been already observed. And will further appear by a particular consideration of what he says on several heads, in what remains.

In my third argument, I insisted, that it could not be much to God's honour, for men to profess the assent of their judgment to the true religion, without pretending to any real friendship or love to God in their hearts. Mr. W. in opposition, (p. 34. *d. e.*) speaks of it as an honour to God, that secret hypocrites openly declare their conviction of the truth of God's word, &c. as *in the multitude of subjects is the king's honour.* And yet he himself represents the matter quite otherwise in his sermons on *Christ a King and Witness;* there (p. 87. *a.*) he has these words, "to promote the kingdom of Christ, is not to do that which may prevail with men to make pretences that they are Christians, or that they own Jesus Christ as their Saviour, and to call him Lord, Lord, when really he is not so."

In answer to my fourth argument (p. 35. *d.*) Mr. W. says, I make great misrepresentation of the matter, in insinuating that according to Mr. S—d's scheme, (of which scheme he declares himself to be,) they who are admitted make a pretence of NO MORE than moral sincerity, and common grace. And yet he insists, that when *Philip* required a profession of the *eunuch's* faith his question designed NO MORE than an assent of the understanding, (p. 51. *a. b.*) which he there distinguishes from saving faith: and says, that it is morally certain that his inquiry amounted to NO MORE. And yet in his discourse on the same head (p. 49. *c.*) he inveighs against me for supposing it a consequence of the opinion of my opposers, that the *eunuch*, in order to come to sacraments, had no need to look at any such qualification in himself as saving faith.——Certainly the *eunuch* in making answer to *Philip's* inquiry, had no need to look at *any more* than *Philip* inquired after. In p. 50. *a.* he says, "It does not seem at all probable, that *Philip* INQUIRED ANY THING about the regeneration or sanctification of the *eunuch.*" And yet in the next preceding sentence, he refers me over to another judgment, for representing as though my opposers supposed, that it was no matter whether a person coming to gospel-ordinances had any grace or not, and had no manner of need to inquire any thing about his sincerity.

And though he highly blames me for insinuating, as above, that my opposers require a pretence of NO MORE than common grace and moral sincerity; yet in opposition to my insisting on a profession of saving faith, speaking of the profession which the *apostles* required, he says, (p. 58. *c.*) "It is certain, that a profession in these words, which was wont to be required, do sometimes import NO MORE than a conviction of the understanding on moral evidence." So he says concerning those whose admission into the christian church we have an account of in Acts ii. (p. 45. *e.*) "There is not one word said about ANY OTHER FAITH, but believing that *Jesus* was the *Messiah.*" And if so, then certainly NO MORE was professed.

In p. 35. *e.* he allows, that all visible saints who are not truly pious, are *hypocrites;* and yet maintains, that the profession they make is no more than what they may make and speak HONESTLY and TRULY. (p. 105. *d.* and 47. *c.*) How then are they all hypocrites, if they are *honestly and truly* what they profess to be?

In supporting the argument from *John's* baptism, he insists, that the profession the people made, did *not* imply, that they *had savingly repented:* and that *John* openly supposed, that their profession did *not* imply it, in what he said to them. (p. 97. *a. b. c.*)—And (p. 98. *a. b.*) he says, "We read not a word of *John's* inquiring whether these people made a credible profession of true piety." And he there manifestly suggests, that *John* knew they were not pious, as *he knew they were a generation of vipers.* Yet how often elsewhere does Mr. W. insist, that men in order to come to sacraments *must* make a credible profession of true piety and gospel-holiness, and that they must in a judgment of charity be supposed to have real godliness?

In answer to my argument from the instance of the converts in Acts ii. Mr. W. speaking of their convictions, and being *pricked in their hearts,* (p. 45. *c. d. e.*) says, "They *were convinced that Jesus was the true Messiah* and Saviour, whom God had promised to *Israel,*—whereupon convinced of their sin, they cry out, *What shall we do?* To which the apostles reply, *Repent and be baptized,—in the name of the Lord Jesus Christ for the remission of sins.*—There is not one word said about any other faith, but *believing that Jesus was the Messiah.*"—And in the two next pages Mr. W. insists, that their *gladly receiving the word* can by no necessity from the text imply more, than that they now *believed that Jesus was the Messiah,* and that it was matter of joy to them that the *Messiah* was come.—So that we have this *inconsistent* account of the matter from Mr. W. that these people are first *convinced that Jesus is the Messiah,* and this is cause of *distress* to them: and they ask, *what they shall do?* Hereupon the apostles direct them *to believe that Jesus is the Messiah;* which they believed *already,* before they asked the question: but however, when they heard this, *they believed that Jesus was the Messiah.* They now found it out, as a *new* thing they did not know of before, and are *glad* at the joyful discovery; though just before they believed the same thing, and the discovery filled them with distress.

In p. 47. *b.* whereas it is said concerning these new converts,—"That such were added to the church, as were *the saved,*"—Mr. W. says, the like appellation is given to the whole church of Israel. And in this and the foregoing page, he insists, that these converts were before *in* the church of *Israel,* and were not now *admitted,* but only *continued* as some of God's people. But if these things were so, they were *the saved* before their conversion to Christianity, as much as after; and others that were in the *Jewish* church, that were not yet converted to Christianity, were as much *the saved* as they. And then why is their being *saved* spoken of as what was now brought to pass, and as a thing that distinguished the believing *Jews* from others?

In the same page, *c.* Mr. W. says, "we do not dispute but that the apostles *supposed* and *believed* in charity, so far as they had any thing to do to suppose or believe any thing about it, that God had given these persons saving repentance, and a heart-purifying faith." And yet in p. 61. he speaks of the apostles as supposing the contrary of many of those that had been admitted into the primitive church; in that they speak of them, as such *temples* of God as might be *destroyed:* "which (says Mr. W.) cannot be true of sanctified persons, unless they can fall from grace."

In his answer to the argument from *Philip* and the *eunuch* he supposes, that *believing with all the heart* is only such a belief of the doctrine of Christianity as *unsanctified* men may have. And yet in that forementioned place, (*Christ a King and Witness*, p. 144.) he says, a man before he is renewed by the Holy Ghost, has a view of the truth as a doubtful uncertain thing. And in the book now especially attended to, he in effect owns the thing, which he earnestly disputes against in reply to this argument. He greatly insists, that the phrase, *with all the heart*, does not signify gracious sincerity; and yet he owns it does. (p. 51. *e.* and 52. *a. b.*) He owns, that according to the usual way of speaking *among mankind*, both in our days, and also in the times when the Scriptures were written, "GOD *requires* men to give him their hearts, intending by it such a sincerity as God will own and accept; which be sure (says he) is nothing less than a *gracious sincerity;* which never can be, unless the whole soul and all its faculties be engaged for God." Then afterwards adds, "But how will this any ways prove, that *when men* use the same expressions, it must necessarily be understood in the same sense?" And yet in the same breath, he had observed that GOD in thus using the phrase, uses it according to the usual manner of speaking AMONG MANKIND. He gives this reason, why the phrase need not be understood in the same sense when used *by men*, that men are not searchers of hearts. But the argument is about the phrase as Philip put it to the eunuch's own conscience, which was or ought to be a searcher of his heart.

And by the way I must observe, that Mr. W. would have done well, if he was able, to have reconciled these repugnant things, taken notice of in my book; "That with the heart man believeth to righteousness," and that if men believe with the heart that God raised Christ from the dead, they shall be saved; agreeable to Rom. x. 9, 10. And yet that men may believe this with their heart, yea, and with all their heart, and still not believe to righteousness, nor ever be saved. So likewise that "whoever shall confess that Jesus is the Son of God, God dwelleth in him, and he in God;" as in 1 John iv. 15. And that "whosoever believeth that Jesus is the Christ, is born of God," 1 John v. 1. And yet, that a man *may believe* this very thing "with all his heart, and confess it with his mouth;" and this in the language of the same apostles and primitive ministers; and still not *be born of God*, nor have a spark of grace in him.

It may also be worthy to be considered, whether it be reasonable to suppose, that the faith which a man must profess, in order to being in the visible kingdom of *Christ*, and not in the visible kingdom of the *devil*, must not be some other sort of faith than that which the *devil* has: that seeing the very design of a public profession of religion is to declare on which side we are, whether on Christ's, or on the devil's, no other faith is required to be professed, than such as Satan himself has, and such as is not at all inconsistent with being a willing, cursed servant and slave of the devil, and enemy to Christ; as Mr. W. says all unsanctified men are.

Mr. W. in his reply to my argument from the *epistles*, (p. 55.) speaks of it as an *unaccountable* thing, that I should represent as if according to the principles of my opposites, the primitive Christians were not admitted under any such notion of their being REALLY godly persons, or with any respect to such a character:* and yet in his discourse on the same head, he abundantly insists, that it was not REAL holiness, but only FEDERAL holiness, which was the qualification to which the apostles had respect in admitting them; expressly, from time to time, distinguishing *federal* holiness from *real*. In p. 56. *e.* and 57. *a.* "It makes it evident (says he) that this manner of treating churches and bodies of men, and such expressions used to them and of them, are to be understood in NO OTHER SENSE, than to signify FEDERAL holiness."—So in p. 60 he affirms the same thing, once and again, distinguishing *federal holiness from real.* He says, they formed no positive judgment of their REAL piety.—And knew nothing at all about them, but only that they were FEDERALLY holy. And again, "They did not make a positive judgment, that these persons were REALLY godly; and the high characters they gave them, and the hopes they expressed concerning them, could be understood in *no other sense* than as holding forth a FEDERAL holiness."—So that by this, they expressed no HOPES concerning any thing more than their *federal holiness*, as distinguished from *real.* And he argues earnestly, through the two next pages, that they could not be looked upon, many of them, as having *real holiness.* How does this consist with their being treated as visible saints; under the notion of their having real holiness, and from respect to such a character appearing on them? or with none being visible saints, but such as have a credible visibility of *gospel-holiness?*

So in p. 63. *b.* he speaks of the gross scandals of many of those to whom the apostles wrote, as an absolute proof, that they considered them only as *federally holy;* which he in the same place distinguishes from *real holiness.* Then how were they treated (as he insists) as those that had the character of REAL PIETY appearing on them, and as making a credible profession of gospel-holiness, and real Christianity? Which, he abundantly allows, all must make in order to being visible saints. See also p. 64. *e.*

In p. 58. Mr. W. insists, that it does not appear, that those who were admitted into the primitive church, made a declaration that they had saving faith, but ONLY that they engaged to that faith.—But how does this consist with what he abundantly says elsewhere, that they must *pretend* to real piety, make a profession of gospel-holiness, exhibit moral evidence, that they have such holiness, &c.? These things are something else besides *engaging to* saving faith and gospel-holiness *for the future.*

* So in p. 132. c. he exclaims against me thus; "After all this, to repeat it again and again, that these persons have no visibility to reason of REAL saintship, &c. I think, gives better ground to retort Mr. Edwards's words."

SECT. X.

The unreasonableness and inconsistence of Mr. W.'s answer to my argument from the man without a wedding garment, and concerning brotherly love, and from 1 Cor. xi. 28. *and of what he says in support of the* 15th *objection.*

MR. W. in answering my argument from Matt. xxii. 11. allows that the *king's house*, into which the guest came, is the visible church. (p. 43. *c.* and 44. *d.*) So that the man's *coming in hither*, is his coming into the visible church. Nor does he at all dispute but that by *the wedding garment* is meant saving grace; (for truly the thing is too evident to be disputed;) and yet he says, (p. 43. *b. c.*) "We read nothing of Christ condemning the man for coming into the church without saving grace." So that Mr. W.'s answer amounts plainly to this; the king, when he comes to judgment, will say, I do not at all condemn thee for coming in hither without a wedding garment; but friend, how camest thou in hither without a wedding garment? And no wonder; the case is too plain to allow of any other than such a lamentable refuge as this is.—If the *wedding garment* be saving grace, which is not denied; and if coming into the *king's house* be coming into the visible church, as Mr. W. owns; then if the king condemns the man for coming into the house without a *wedding garment*, he condemns him for coming into the visible church without saving grace.

It is plain, the thing the man is blamed for, is something else than simply *a being without grace*, or without a *wedding garment.* The king's words have respect to this as it stands in *connexion with coming into the king's house.* If Christ has commanded men who are *not converted*, to come into the church, *that they may be converted*, he will never say to them, upon their obeying this command, *Friend, how camest thou in hither before thou wast converted?* Which would be another thing than blaming him simply for not being converted. If a man, at his own cost, sets up a school, in order to teach ignorant children to read; and accordingly ignorant children should go thither in order to learn to read, would he come into the school, and say in anger to an ignorant child that he found there, *How camest thou in hither, before thou hadst learnt to read?* Did the apostle Paul ever rebuke the heathen, who came to hear him preach the gospel, saying, *How came you hither to hear me preach, not having grace?* This would have been unreasonable, because preaching is an ordinance appointed to that end, that men might obtain grace. And so, in Mr. W.'s scheme, is the *Lord's supper*.—Can we suppose, that Christ will say to men in indignation, at the day of judgment, *How came you to presume to use the means I appointed for your conversion, before you were converted!*

It is true, the servants were to invite all, *both bad and good*, to come to the feast, and to *compel them to come in:* but this does not prove, that bad men, *remaining in their badness*, have a lawful right to come. The servants were to invite the vicious, as well as the moral; they were to invite the heathen, who were especially meant by them that were *in the highways and hedges:* yet it will not follow, that the heathen, while *remaining heathen*, have a lawful right to come to christian sacraments. But heathen men must turn from their heathenism, and come: so likewise wicked men must turn from their wickedness, and come.

I endeavoured to prove, that *that brotherly love*, which is required towards the members of the *christian church* in general, is such a love as is required to those *only* whom we have reason to look upon as *true saints*. Mr. W. disputes, through two pages, (p. 66, 67.) against the force of my reasoning to prove this point; and yet when he has done, he allows the point. He allows it (p. 68. *d, e.*) as an undisputed thing, that it is the image of God and Christ appearing or supposed to be in others, that is the ground and reason of this love. And so again (p. 71. *d. e.*) he grants, that there must be some apprehension, and judgment of the mind, of the saintship of persons, in order to this brotherly love. Indeed he pretends to differ from me in this, that he denies the need of any *positive judgment:* but doubtless the judgment or apprehension of the mind must be as positive as the *love* founded on that apprehension and judgment of the mind.

In p. 78, 79. he seems to insist, that what the apostle calls *unworthy communicating*, is eating in a greedy, disorderly, and irreverent manner: as though men might communicate without grace, and yet not communicate *unworthily*, in the apostle's sense. But if so, the apostle differed much in his sense of things from Mr. W.—The latter says, in his sermon on *Christ a King and Witness*, (p. 77, 78.) "These outward acts of worship, when not performed from faith in Christ, and love to God, are *mocking* God—in their own nature a *lie*—the *vilest wickedness;*—instead of being that religion, which Christ requires, it is *infinitely contrary* to it—the most *flagrant and abominable impiety, and threatened with the severest damnation.*" Is not this a communicating *unworthily* enough of all reason?

In p. 132, 133. Mr. W. strenuously opposes me in my supposition, that the way of freely allowing all that have only *moral sincerity* to come into the church, tends to the *reproach and ruin* of the church. On the contrary, he seems to suppose it tends to the establishing and building up of the church. But I desire that what Mr. Stoddard says, in his sermon on *the danger of speedy degeneracy*, may be considered under this head. He there largely insists, that the prevailing of unconverted men and unholy professors among a people, is the principal thing that brings them into danger of *speedy degeneracy* and corruption. He says, that where this is the case, there will be many bad examples, that will corrupt others; and that unconverted men will indulge their children in evil, will be negligent in their education; and that by this means their children will be very corrupt and ungoverned;* that by this means the godly themselves that are among them, will be tainted, as sweet liquor put into a corrupt vessel will be tainted; that thus a people will grow blind, will not much regard the warnings of the word, or the judgments of God; and that they will grow weary of religious duties after awhile; and that many of their leading men will be carnal; and that this will expose a people to have carnal ministers and other leading men in the town and church.

And I desire also, that here may be considered what Mr. W. himself says, in that passage forecited, (p. 86, 87.) of his sermons on *Christ a King and Witness;* where, in explaining what it is to promote the kingdom of Christ, he says negatively, "That it is not to do that which may prevail on men to make *pretences*, that they are Christians, and that they own Jesus Christ as their Saviour, and to *call him Lord, Lord*, when *really* he is not so." Which he supposes is the case with all unsanctified professors; for in the same book, he abundantly declares, that they who make such pretences, and have not true faith and love, make *false* and *lying* pretences; as has been several times observed.

SECT. XI.

The impertinence of arguments, that are in like manner against the schemes of both the controverting parties: And this exemplified in what Mr. W. says concerning the notion of Israel being the people of God, and his manner of arguing concerning the members of the primitive christian church.

Inasmuch as in each of the remaining instances of Mr. W.'s arguing, that I shall take notice of, he insists upon and urges arguments which are in like manner against his *own* scheme, as against mine, I desire, that such a way of arguing may be a little particularly considered.

And here I would lay down this as a maxim of undoubted verity; *That an argument, brought to support one scheme against another, can avail nothing to the purpose it is brought for, if it is at the same time against the scheme it would* support, *in like manner as against that which it would* destroy.

It is an old and approved maxim, *That argument which proves too much, proves nothing, i. e.* If it proves too much for him that brings it—proves against himself in like manner as against his opponent—then it is nothing to help his cause.—The reason of it is plain: the business of a dispute is to make one cause good against another, to make one scale heavier than the other. But when a man uses an argument which takes *alike* out of *both* scales, this does not at all serve to make *his* side preponderate, but leaves the balance just as it was.

Arguments brought by any man in a dispute, if they be not altogether impertinent, are against the *difference* between him and his opponent, or against his opponent's *differing from him:* for wherein there is *no difference*, there is no *dispute*.—But that can be no argument against his opponent *differing* from him, which is only an argument against what is *common to both*, and taken from some difficulty that *both* sides equally share in. If I charge supposed absurdities or difficulties against him that *differs* from me, as an argument to show the unreasonableness of his *differing;* and yet the difficulty is not owing to his *differing* from me, inasmuch as the same would lie against him, if he *agreed* with me, my conduct herein is both very impertinent and injurious.

If one in a dispute insists on an argument, that lies equally against his own scheme as the other, and yet will stand to it that his argument is *good*, he in effect stands to that his own scheme is *not good;* he supplants himself, and gives up his own cause, in opposing his adversary; in holding fast *his argument*, he holds fast what is *his own overthrow;* and in insisting that his argument is *solid* and *strong*, he in effect insists that his own scheme is *weak* and *vain*. If my antagonist will insist upon it, that his argument is good, that he brings *against me*, which is in like manner *against himself;* then I may take the same argument, in my turn, and use it against him, and he can have nothing to answer; but has stopped his own mouth, having owned the argument to be conclusive.—Now such sort of arguments as these Mr. W. abundantly uses.

For instance, the argument taken from the whole nation of *Israel* being called *God's people*, and every thing that Mr. W. alleges, pertaining to this matter, is in like manner

* If we have reason to expect it will be thus with ungodly parents, with respect to their children, then certainly such cannot reasonably expect ministers and churches should admit their children to baptism, in a dependence that they do give them up to God, and will bring them up in the nurture and admonition of the Lord, if they make no profession that implies more than moral sincerity; and none but what wicked men may as well make as the godly, and speak true.

against *his own* scheme as against mine: and that, let the question be what it will; whether it be about the qualifications which make it lawful for the church to *admit*, or about the lawfulness of persons *coming* to sacraments; whether it be about the *profession they should make before men*, or the *internal qualification they must have in the sight of God*. And what Mr. W. says to the contrary, does not at all deliver the argument from this embarrassment and absurdity. After all he has said, the argument, if any thing related to the controversy, is plainly this, That because the whole nation of Israel were God's *visible people*, (which is the same as visible saints,) therefore the scripture notion of *visible saintship* is of larger extent than mine; and the Scripture supposes those to be visible saints, which my scheme does not suppose to be so.

But if this be Mr. W.'s argument, then let us see whether it agrees any better with *his own* scheme. Mr. Blake (Mr. W.'s great author) in his book *on the Covenant*, (p. 190. *b.*) insists, that Israel at the very WORST is owned as God's covenant people, and were called God's people; and (p. 149. *e.*) that all the congregation of Israel, and every one of them, are called holy, and God's own people, even Korah and his company.—And (p. 253. *e.* 254. *a.*) he urges, that every one who is descended from Jacob, even the WORST of Israel, in their *lowest* state and condition, were God's people in covenant, called by the name of God's people. And Mr. W. herein follows Mr. Blake, and urges the same thing; that this nation was God's covenant people, and were called God's people, at the time that they were carried captive into *Babylon*, (p. 24. *d.*) when they were undoubtedly *at their worst*, more corrupt than at any other time we read of in the Old Testament; being represented by the prophets, as overrun with abominable idolatries, and other kinds of the most gross, heaven-daring impieties, most obstinate, abandoned, pertinacious, and irreclaimable in their rebellion against God, and against his word by his prophets. But yet these, it is urged, are called the *people of God;* not agreeable to my notion of visible saintship, but agreeable to Mr. W.'s. What his notion of *visible saints* is, he tells us in p. 139. He there says expressly, that he "does not suppose persons to be visible saints, unless they exhibit a credible profession and visibility of *gospel-holiness*." Now do those things said about those vile wretches in Israel, agree with this? Did they exhibit moral evidence of *gospel-holiness?* —But if we bring the matter lower still, and say, the true notion of visible saintship is a credible appearance and moral evidence of *moral sincerity;* does this flagrant, open, abandoned, obstinate impiety consist with moral evidence of such sincerity as that? It is as apparent therefore, in Mr. W.'s scheme as mine, that when these are called *God's people*, it is in some other sense than that wherein the members of the christian church are called *visible saints*. And indeed the body of the nation of Israel, in those corrupt times, were so far from being God's church of visibly pious persons, visibly endowed with *gospel-holiness*, that *that* people, as to the body of them, were visibly and openly declared by God, to be a *whore* and a *witch*, and her children *bastards*, or *children of adultery*. Isa. lvii. 3. "Draw near hither, ye sons of the sorceress, the seed of the adulterer and the whore." We have the like in other places. And so the body of the same people in Christ's time—which Mr. W. supposes even then to be branches of the *true olive*, in the same manner as the members of the christian church were in the apostles' times—are visibly declared not to be God's children, or children of the true church, but bastards, or an adulterous brood. Matt. xii. 39. "An evil and adulterous generation seeketh after a sign." Ver. 45. "Even so shall it be with this wicked generation." And certainly the people were then, visibly and in the eyes of men, such as Christ had visibly and openly, and in the sight of men, declared them to be.

If the question be not concerning the *visibility* which makes it *lawful for others to admit persons*, but concerning the *qualifications which render it lawful for them to come*, still the objection is no more against *my* scheme than against Mr. W.'s. He (in p. 84—86.) says, that such openly scandalous persons *ought not to be admitted into the church;* insinuating, that these scandalous people among the *Jews* were *otherwise* when they were *admitted at first:* but that being taken in, and not cast out again, *it was lawful for them to be there*, and they had a lawful right to the privileges of the church. But this supposition, that all who are lawfully *admitted* by others, may lawfully *come* into the church, and lawfully *continue* to partake of its privileges *till cast out*, is utterly inconsistent with Mr. W.'s own scheme. For according to his scheme, it is not lawful for men that are not *morally sincere*, to partake of the privileges of the church; but yet such may in some cases be lawfully admitted by others; for he maintains, that in admitting them, they are not to act as *searchers of hearts*, even with regard to their moral sincerity; and so argues, (p. 106.) that Christ might give *Judas* the sacrament, when not morally sincere. If Christ as head of the visible church might admit *Judas* to his table, when he knew he was not morally sincere, and when it was not lawful for *Judas* himself to come; then it is lawful for men to admit some, for whom it is not lawful to be there; contrary to Mr. W.'s assertion in p. 86. *b.*

It is true, that persons may become grossly scandalous, after having been regularly admitted on Mr. W.'s principles, on a profession in words of indiscriminate signification. And so they may after being regularly admitted, according to my principles, on a credible profession of gospel-holiness in words of a determinate meaning: and therefore the gross wickedness of such apostates as we read of in Scripture, is no more an objection against my principles, than his.

Just in the same manner is Mr. W.'s arguing (p. 59—63.) concerning the members of churches mentioned in the *epistles*, equally against his own scheme and mine. He largely insists on it, that the apostle speaks of many of them as grossly scandalous, notoriously wicked persons, idolaters, heretics, fornicators, adulterers, adulteresses, &c. &c. In his arguing from these things, he is inconsistent with his own principles, two ways. (1.) Such a character is as plainly inconsistent with the character he insists on as necessary to render it lawful for persons themselves to come to sacraments, as mine. And, (2.) It is utterly inconsistent with what he often declares to be his notion of *visible saintship*, necessary to a being admitted by others; so no more an argument against my opinion of *visible saintship*, than his own.

SECT. XII.

The great argument from the Jewish sacraments, of the Passover, and Circumcision, considered.

As has been observed concerning the argument from the *Jewish* nation, so the argument from the *Jewish* ordinances, if it be against my scheme, is as plainly, in every respect, against Mr. W.'s.—This grand argument, as plainly expressed, or implied, in Mr. Stoddard's words (which Mr. W. insists I should attend to,) is this:

God did expressly command all the nation of *Israel* to be *circumcised;* and he also expressly commanded the whole nation to come to the *passover;* excepting such as were ceremoniously unclean, or on a journey. Therefore it was lawful for unsanctified men to come. (See Mr. S.'s *sermon* on the controv. p. 8. and *Appeal*, p. 51.) The want of sanctification never was alleged by any man as a reason for forbearing the passover. (*Appeal*, p. 51.) Unsanctified persons attending this ordinance is never charged on them as a sin in Scripture. (*Ibid.*) Jesus Christ himself partook of the passover with *Judas;* which proves it to be lawful for unsanctified men to come to the passover. But such as might lawfully come to the *passover*, may lawfully come to the *Lord's supper*.

Now let us consider what are the qualifications, which are necessary, according to Mr. W.'s scheme, to a lawful coming to christian sacraments; and then see whether this objection, in every part of it, and every thing that belongs to it, be not as plainly and directly against *his own* scheme, as mine.

According to Mr. W. it is not lawful for a man to come unless he is *morally sincere*. (*Pref.* p. 2 and 3. p. 21. *b.* 25. *d.* *e.* 30. *d.* 35. *e.* 36. *a.* 111. *b.* *c.* 115. *b.*) And, according as he has explained that moral sincerity, which is necessary in order to come to sacraments, it implies "a real conviction of the judgment and conscience of the truth of the great things of religion, a deep conviction of a man's undone state without Christ, and an earnest concern to obtain salvation by him,—a fervent desire of Christ and the benefits of the covenant of grace, with an earnest purpose and resolution to seek salvation on the terms of it;—a man's being willing to do the utmost that he can, by the utmost improvement of his natural and moral power, in the most earnest and diligent use of the ordinances of salvation;—being resolved for Christ, coming to a point, being engaged for heaven;—having a settled determination of the judgment and affections for God;—giving up all his heart and life to Christ," &c. &c.* Such moral sincerity as this is necessary, according to Mr. W. to be found in professing Christians, in order to their lawful coming to christian sacraments. And he says, they are received into the church, on like terms, by entering into covenant in like manner, as the Jews; and that their holiness, both real and federal, is the same with theirs. (p. 56, 57. p. 61. *e.* p. 65. *c.*) So that according to this scheme, none but those that had such qualifications as these, such a sincerity and engagedness in religion as this, might lawfully come to the *passover*.—But now, do the things alleged agree any better with this scheme, than with mine? If the case be so, to what purpose is it alleged, that God, in Numb. ix. expressly commanded all of that perverse, rebellious, and obstinate generation in the wilderness, and the whole nation of *Israel* in all generations, to keep the *passover*, excepting such as were ceremonially unclean or on a journey, without the exception of any other? Was every one else of such a character as is above described? Was every one under deep convictions, and persons of such earnest engagedness in religion, of such settled strong resolution to give up their utmost strength and all their heart and life to God, &c.? Mr. W. suggests, that those who had not moral sincerity are expressly excepted from the command. (p. 93. *d.*) But I wish he had mentioned the place of Scripture. He cites Mr. Stoddard, who says, God appointed sacrifice to be offered for scandal, with confession. But where did God appoint *sacrifice*, for the *want* of such *sincerity*, for the *want* of such deep conviction, earnest desire, and fixed resolution, as Mr. W. speaks of? And where are such as are without these things, *expressly excepted* from the command to keep the *passover?* Besides, there were many scandalous sins, for which *no sacrifice* was appointed: as *David's* murder and adultery, and the sin of idolatry—which the nation in general often fell into—and many other gross sins. Nor was there any precept for *deferring* the keeping of the *passover*, in case of scandalous wickedness, or moral uncleanness, till there should be opportunity for cleansing by *sacrifice*, &c. as was in the case of ceremonial uncleanness.

Mr. S. says, The want of sanctification was never alleged by any man as a reason for forbearing the passover. Where do we read in any part of the Bible, that the *want* of such deep conviction, &c. as Mr. W. speaks of, or indeed any scandalous moral uncleanness, was ever alleged by any man, as a reason for forbearing to eat the *passover?* —Mr. S. urges, that unsanctified persons attending the *passover* was never charged on them as a *sin*. And where do we read of persons coming without such *moral sincerity* being any more charged on them as a *sin*, than the other? We have reason to think, it was a common thing for parents that had no such *moral sincerity*, yea, that were grossly and openly wicked, to have their children *circumcised;* for the body of the people were often so: but where is this charged as a *sin?* Mr. S. says, (*Serm.* p. 7.) *Ishmael* was circumcised, but yet a carnal person. And there is as much reason to say, he was *not* of the character Mr. W. insists on, under deep convictions, having earnest desires of grace, a full and fixed determination, with all his heart, to the utmost of his power, to give his whole life to God, &c.—Mr. S. says, (*Serm.* p. 8.) Hezekiah sent to invite the people of Ephraim and Manasseh, and other tribes, to celebrate the passover, though they had lived in idolatry for some ages. But if so, this was as much of an evidence, that they were not of such a character as Mr. W. insists on, as that they were without sanctifying grace.—Mr. W. says, (p. 91. *c.*) The Israelites had carefully attended the seal of circumcision, from the time of its institution, till the departure out of Egypt. But surely most of them at the same time were without Mr. W.'s moral sincerity; for it is abundantly manifest, that the body of the people fell away to idolatry in *Egypt*. (See Levit. xvii. 7. Josh. xxiv. 14. Ezek. xx. 8. and xxiii. 3, 8, 27.) And there is not the least appearance of any more *exception*, either in the precepts or history of the Old Testament, of the case of *moral insincerity*, in such as attended these ordinances, than of ungodliness, or an unsanctified state.

Mr. S. urges, that *Jesus Christ himself partook of the passover with* Judas; and thence he would argue, that it was lawful for an *unregenerate* person to partake of the *Lord's supper*. But there can be no argument, in any sort, drawn from this, to prove that it is lawful for men to partake of the Lord's supper without *sanctifying grace*, any more than that it is lawful for them to partake without *moral sincerity*: for it is every whit as evident, that Judas was at that time without moral sincerity, as that he was unregenerate. We have no greater evidence, in all the scripture history, of the moral insincerity of any one man, than of Judas, at the time when he partook of the *passover* with Christ; he having just then bargained with the high priest to *betray* him, and being then in prosecution of the horrid design of the murder of the Son of God.

If any thing contrary to my principles could be argued from all Israel being required, throughout their generations, to come to the *passover and circumcision*, it would be this; that all persons, of all sorts, throughout all *christendom*, might lawfully come to *baptism* and the *Lord's Supper;* godly and ungodly, the knowing and the ignorant, the moral and the vicious, orthodox and heretical, protestants and papists alike. But this does not agree with Mr. W.'s principles, any better than with mine.

SECT. XIII.

Concerning Judas's partaking of the Lord's supper.

I THINK, we have a remarkable instance of tergiversation, in what Mr. W. says in support of the argument from Judas's partaking of the Lord's supper. By those on his side of the question, it is insisted upon, as a clear evidence of its being lawful for unsanctified men to come to the Lord's table, that Christ gave the Lord's supper to Judas, when he knew he was unsanctified. In answer to which I showed, that this is just as much against their own principles, as mine; because Christ knew as perfectly that he was not *morally sincere*, as that he was not *graciously sincere;* and they themselves hold, that it is not lawful for such as are not morally sincere, to partake. Mr. W. ridicules this, as very impertinent and strange; because Christ did not know this as head of the visible church, but only as omniscient God and searcher of hearts. And what does this argue? Only, that although Judas was really not fit to come, yet, inasmuch as Christ, acting as king of the visible church, did not know it, *he might admit him:* but not, that it was lawful for Judas himself to come, who knew his own heart in this matter, and knew his own perfidiousness and treachery; Mr. W. denies, that it is lawful for such to come, as have no moral sincerity. So that here the question is changed; from, *who may lawfully come, to who may lawfully be admitted?* Mr. W. abundantly insists, that the question is not, *who shall be admitted? but, who may lawfully come?* Not, whether it be lawful to admit those who have not a visibility of saintship, or do not appear to be true saints? but whether those who are not true saints, may lawfully partake? And this he insists upon in his discourse on this very argument, (p. 104, *c. d.*) And to prove this latter point, *viz.* That *those who are not real saints, may lawfully come*, the instance of Judas's coming to the Lord's supper is produced as an undeniable evidence. But when it is answered, that the argument does not prove this, any more than that the morally insincere may lawfully come; because Judas was

* P. 10. *d.* 11 *c. d.* 30. *e.* 31. *a. e.* 35. *e.* 36. *a.* 53 *b* 83. *d.* 125. *b.* and many other places.

morally insincere: then Mr. W. (p. 106.) to shelter himself, evidently changes the question, at once, to that which he had so much exclaimed against as *not the question.* Now, to serve his turn, the question is not, whether Judas might *lawfully come?* but, whether Christ might *lawfully admit him,* acting on a public visibility? And he makes an occasion to cry out against me, as talking *strangely,* and soon forgetting that I had said, Christ in this matter did not act as searcher of hearts. Whereas, let the question be what it will, the argument from Judas's partaking, (should the fact be supposed,) if it proves any thing relating to the matter, is perfectly, and in every respect, against the one, just as it is against the other. If the question be about *profession and visibility* to others, and who others may *lawfully admit,* then Judas's being admitted, (if he was admitted,) no more proves, that men may be admitted without a visibility and profession of godliness, than without a visibility of moral sincerity. For it no more appears, that he was without a profession and visibility of the former, than of the latter. But if the question is not about *visibility to others,* or who others *may admit,* but who may *lawfully come,* then Judas's coming no more proves, that a man may come without grace, than without moral necessity; because he was in like manner without both: and Christ knew as perfectly, that he was without the one, as the other; and was not ignorant of the one case, as king of the visible church, any more than of the other. So that there is no way to support this argument, but to hide the question, by shifting and changing it; to have one question in the premises, and to slip in another into the conclusion. Which is according to the course Mr. W. takes. In the premises, (p. 104, 105.) he expressly mentions Mr. S——d's question, as now in view: and agreeably must here have this for his question, *whether it was lawful for a man so qualified to come to the Lord's supper?* Who, according to Mr. W.'s own doctrine, (p. 111.) ought to act as a discerner of his own heart. But in his conclusion, (p. 106.) he has this for his question, *whether Christ might lawfully admit a man so qualified,* therein not acting as the searcher of hearts?——What shuffling is this!

SECT. XIV.

Concerning that great argument, which Mr. W. urges in various parts of his book, of those being born in the church, who are children of parents that are in covenant.

It is hard to understand distinctly what Mr. W. would be at, concerning this matter, or what his argument is. He often speaks of parents that are in covenant, as born in covenant, and so born in the church. For to be in covenant, is the same with him as to be members of the visible church. (See p. 98. *c.* 88. *d.* 89. *b.* 59. *e.* 60. *a.* 136. *b.*) And he speaks of them as admitted into the church in their ancestors, and by the profession of their ancestors. (p. 135. *e.* 136. *a.*) Yea, for ought I can see, he holds that they were born members in COMPLETE STANDING in the visible church. (p. 3.)

And yet he abundantly speaks of their being ADMITTED into the church, and MADE members, after they are born, *viz.* by their baptism. And his words (unless we will suppose him to speak nonsense) are such as will not allow us to understand him, merely, that baptism is a sign and public acknowledgment of their having been admitted in their ancestors, in preceding generations. For he speaks of baptism as the ONLY rite (or way) of admission into the visible church, applying it to the baptism of children; and as that which MAKES them members of the body of Christ. (p. 99. *c. d.*) And he grants, that it was ordained for the ADMISSION of the party baptized into the visible church. (p. 99. *e.* p. 100. *a.*) That baptism is an admission; and that they were thus before admitted, (p. 100. *c.*) still speaking of the baptism of infants, and of admission of members into churches.—But surely these things do not harmonize with the doctrine of their first receiving being in the church—as a branch receives being in the tree, and grows in it and from it—or their being *born in the covenant, born in the house of God.* And yet these repugnant things are uttered as it were in the same breath by Mr. W. (p. 99.) And he joins them together in the same line, (p. 46. *e.*) in these words,—"Baptism instituted by him, as a rite of ADMISSION into his church, and being CONTINUED in covenant with God."—Certainly, being then admitted into the church, and being continued in covenant (or in the church) into which they were admitted before, are not the same thing, nor consistent one with another. If infants are born members in complete standing, as it seems Mr. W. holds, then their baptism does nothing towards making them members; nor is there any need of it to make the matter more complete.

Again, (p. 3. *b.* where he also speaks of infants as members having a complete standing in the church,) he maintains, that nothing else is requisite in order to *communion and privileges of members in complete standing,* but only that they should be *capable* hereof, and *should desire* the same, and should not be *under censure, or scandalously ignorant or immoral.* (See also p. 100. *c. d.* to the same purpose.) Mr. W says this in opposition to my insisting on something further, *viz.* making a profession of godliness. And yet he himself insists on something *further,* as much as I; which has been observed before. For he abundantly insists on a *personal, explicit profession and open declaration* of believing that the gospel is indeed the revelation of God, and of a hearty consent to the terms of the covenant of grace, &c. And speaks of the whole controversy as turning upon that single point, of the degree of evidence to be given, and the kind of profession to be made, whether in words of indiscriminate meaning? (See p. 5. *b. c.* p. 6. *c. d.*) And consequently not, whether they must make any profession at all, having been completely admitted before, in the profession of their ancestors?

Therefore, if the infants of visible believers are born in the church, and are already members in complete standing, and do not drop out of the church, and fall from a complete standing, when they grow up; and therefore if they are not ignorant nor immoral, and desire full communion, *nothing else* can be required of them: and it will hence follow, contrary to my principles, that they cannot be required to make a profession in words of discriminate meaning: but then, it also equally follows, contrary to his principles, that neither can they be required to make a profession in words of indiscriminate meaning. If nothing else besides those forementioned things is necessary, then no profession is necessary, in any words at all, neither of determinate nor indeterminate signification. So that Mr. W. in supposing some personal profession to be necessary, gives up and destroys this grand argument.

But if he did not give it up by this means, it would not be tenable on other principles belonging to his scheme; such as its being necessary in order to a being admitted to sacraments, that persons should have a visibility that recommends them to the reasonable judgment and apprehension of the minds of others, as true Christians, really pious persons, and that there should be such a profession as exhibits moral evidence of this. For who will say, that the individual profession of an ancestor, a thousand or fifteen hundred years ago, is a credible exhibition and moral evidence of the real piety of his present posterity, without any personal explicit profession of any thing about religion, in any one of the succeeding generations. And if Mr. W. had not said, there must be a credible exhibition of *gospel-holiness,* but only some common faith or virtue; yet no such thing is made visible to a rational judgment and apprehension of mind, by this means. How, for instance, does it make *orthodoxy* visible? What reasonable ground is there in it, at such a day as this in England, to believe concerning any man, that he believes the doctrine of the Trinity, and all other fundamental doctrines, with full conviction, and with all his heart, because he descended from an ancestor that made a good profession, when the ancient Britons or Saxons were converted from heathenism, and because withal he is free from open scandalous immorality, and appears willing to attend duties of public worship? If an attendance on these public duties was in its own nature a profession of orthodoxy, or even piety; yet the reason of mankind teaches them the need of joining *words and actions* together in public manifestations of the mind, in cases of importance: speech being the great and peculiar talent, which God has given to mankind, as the special means and instrument of the manifestation of their minds one to another. Thus, treaties among men are not concluded and finished, only with actions, without words. Feasting together was used of old, as a testimony of peace and covenant friendship; as between Isaac and Abimelech, Laban and Jacob, but not without a verbal profession. Giving the hand, delivering the ring, &c. are to express a marriage agreement and union; but still a profession in words is annexed. So we allow it to be needful, after persons have fallen into scandal, that in manifesting repentance there should be a verbal profession, besides attending duties of worship. Earthly princes will not trust a profession of allegiance in actions only, such as bowing, kneeling, keeping the king's birth-day, &c. but they require also a profession in words, and an oath of allegiance is demanded. Yea, it is thought to be reasonably demanded, in order to men's coming to the actual possession and enjoyment of those privileges *they are born heirs to*. Thus the eldest sons of noblemen in Great Britain, are born heirs to the honours and estate of their fathers; yet this no way hinders but they may be obliged, when they come to ripeness of age, in order to being invested in the actual possession, to take the oath of allegiance: though in order to their lawfully doing it, it may be necessary they should believe in their hearts, that King George is the lawful prince, and that they should not be enemies to him, and friends to the Pretender.

But moreover, if this objection of Mr. W. about infants being born in the church be well considered, it will appear to be all *beside the question*, and so nothing to the purpose. It is not to the purpose of either of the *questions*, Mr. W.'s or mine. The *question as I have stated it*, is concerning them that may be *admitted members in complete standing;* not about them that have a *complete standing in the church already*, and so are no candidates for *admission;* which, he says, is the case of these infants. And *the question as he often states it* is concerning them that may *lawfully come*. And this objection, from infants being *born in the church*, as it must be understood from Mr. W. does not touch this *question*. For when Mr. W. objects, *that some persons are born in the church, and therefore may lawfully come to sacraments*, he cannot be understood to mean, *that their being born in the church alone is sufficient;* but that, *besides* this, persons must have some virtue or religion, of one sort or other, in order to their *lawful coming*. For he is full in it, that it is not lawful for men to come without moral virtue and sincerity. Therefore the *question* comes to this in the result: seeing persons, besides their being born in covenant, must have some sort of virtue and religion, in order to a lawful coming to the Lord's supper, *what sort of virtue and religion that is*, whether *common or saving?* Now this *question* is not touched by the present objection. Merely persons being *born in covenant*, is no more evidence of their having moral sincerity, than saving grace. Yea, there is more reason to suppose the latter, than the former without it, in the infant children of believing parents. For the Scripture gives us ground to think, that some infants have the habit of saving grace, and that they have a new nature given them. But no reason at all to think, that ever God works any mere moral change in them, or infuses any habits of moral virtue without saving grace.—And we know, they cannot come by moral habits in infancy, any other way than by immediate infusion. They cannot obtain them by human instruction, nor contract them by use and custom. And especially there is no reason to think, that the children of such as are visible saints, according to Mr. W's scheme, have any goodness infused into them by God, of any kind. For in his scheme, all that are morally sincere may lawfully receive the privileges of visible saints; but we have no scripture grounds to suppose, that God will bless the children of such parents as have nothing more than moral sincerity, with either common or saving grace. There are no promises of the covenant of grace made to such parents, either concerning themselves, or their children. The covenant of grace is a conditional covenant; as both sides in this controversy suppose. And therefore, by the supposition, men have no title to the promises without the condition. And as saving faith is the condition, the promises are all made to *that*, both those which respect persons themselves, and those that respect their seed. As it is with many covenants or bargains among men; by these, men are often entitled to possessions for themselves and their heirs: yet they are entitled to no benefits of the bargain, neither for themselves, nor their children, but by complying with the terms of the bargain. So with respect to the covenant of grace, the apostle says, (Acts ii. 39.) "The promise is to you and to your children." So the apostle says to the *jailor*, (Acts xvi. 31.) "Believe on the Lord Jesus Christ, and thou shalt be saved, and thy house." And we find many promises, all over the Bible, made to the righteous, that God will bless their seed for their sakes. Thus, Psal. cxii. 2. "The generation of the upright shall be blessed." Psal. lxix. 35, 36. "For God will save Zion;—The seed also of his servants shall inherit it; and they that love his name shall dwell therein." (See also Prov. xiv. 26. Psal. cii. 28. Psal. ciii. 17, 18. Exod. xx. 5, 6. Deut. vii. 9.) Supposing these to be what are called indefinite promises; yet do they extend to any but the *seed of the righteous?* Where are any such promises made to the children of unsanctified men, the enemies of God, and slaves of the devil, (as Mr. W. owns all unsanctified men are,) whatever moral sincerity and common religion they may have?

The baptism of infants is the seal of these promises made to the seed of the righteous: and on these principles, some rational account may be given of infant baptism; but there is no account can be given of it on Mr. W.'s scheme, no warrant can be found for it in Scripture; for they are *promises*, that are the warrant for *privileges:* but there are no promises of God's word to the seed of morally sincere men, and only half Christians. Thus this argument of Mr. W.'s, let us take it which way we will, has nothing but what is as much, yea, much more, against his scheme, than against mine.

However, if this were not the case, but all the show or pretence of strength there is in the argument, lay directly and only against *me*, yet the strength of it, if tried, will avail to prove nothing at all. The pretended argument, so far as I can find it out, is this; *The children of visible saints are born in covenant; and being already in covenant, they must have a right to the privileges of the covenant, without any more ado: such therefore have a right to come to the Lord's supper, whether they are truly godly or not.*

But the show of argument there is here, depends on the ambiguity of the phrase, *being in covenant;* which signifies two distinct things: either, (1.) *Being under the obligation and bond of the covenant;* or, (2.) *Being conformed to the covenant, and complying with the terms of it.* Being the subject of the obligations and engagements of the covenant, is a thing quite distinct from being conformed to these obligations, and so being the subject of the conditions of the covenant.

Now it is not being in covenant in the former, but the latter sense, that gives a right to the privileges of the covenant. The reason is plain, because compliance and conformity to the terms of a covenant, is the thing which gives right to all the benefits; and not merely being under ties to that compliance and conformity. Privileges are not annexed merely to obligations, but to compliance with obligations.

Many that do not so much as visibly comply with the conditions of the covenant, are some of God's covenant people in *that* sense, that they are under the bonds and engagements of the covenant; so were Korah and his company; so were many gross idolaters in *Israel*, that lived openly in that sin; and so may heretics, deists, and atheists be God's covenant people. They may still be held under the bonds of their covenant engagements to God; for their great wickedness and apostacy does not free them from the obligation of the solemn promises and engagements they formerly entered into. But yet being in covenant merely in this sense, gives them no right to any privileges of the covenant. In order to that, they must be in covenant in another sense; they must cordially consent to the covenant; which indeed Mr. W. himself owns, when he acknowledges, that in order to come to sacraments, men must profess a cordial consent to, and compliance with the conditions of the covenant of grace.* And if Mr. W. inquires, Why those children that were born in the covenant, are not *cast out*, when in adult age they make no such profession; certainly, it as much concerns *him* to answer, as me; for it is as much his doctrine, as mine, that they must profess such consent.——But I am willing to answer nevertheless.—They are not cast out, because it is a matter held in suspense, whether they do cordially consent to the covenant, or not; or whether their making no such profession do not arise from some other cause. And none are to be excommunicated, without some positive evidence against them. And therefore they are left in the state they were in, in infancy, not admitted actually to partake of the Lord's supper (which actual participation is a new positive privilege) for want of a profession, or some evidence, beyond what is merely negative, to make it visible that they do consent to the covenant. For it is reasonable to expect some appearance more than what is negative, of a proper qualification, in order to being admitted to a privilege beyond what they may have hitherto actually received. A negative charity may be sufficient for a negative privilege, such as freedom from censure and punishment; but something more than a negative charity, is needful to actual admission to a new positive privilege.

SECT. XV.

A particular examination of Mr. W.'s defence of the ninth objection, or that boasted argument, that if it be not lawful for unconverted men to come to the Lord's supper, then none may come but they that know themselves to be converted.

THIS argument has been greatly gloried in, as altogether invincible. Mr. W. seems to have been alarmed, and his spirits raised to no small degree of warmth, at the pretence of an answer to it: and he uses many big words and strong expressions in his reply; such as, It is absolutely certain—It is beyond my power to comprehend, and I believe beyond the power of any man to tell me—this I assert and stand to—as plain as the sun—a contradiction of the Bible, of the light of nature, and of the common sense of mankind, &c. &c. But let us get away from the noise of a torrent, and bring this matter to the test of calm reasoning, and examine it to the very bottom.

Here let it be considered, wherein precisely the argument consists.——If it has any strength in it, it consists in this proposition, *viz.* That it is not lawful for men to come to sacraments, without a known right. This is a proposition Mr. S. himself reduces the argument to, in his *Appeal*, p. 62, 63. And it is very evident, that the whole strength of the argument rests on the supposed truth of this proposition.

And here let it be noted, what sort of *knowledge* of a right Mr. S. and Mr. W. mean in this argument. It is *knowledge* as distinguished from such an *opinion*, or *hope*, as is *founded on probability*. Thus Mr. S. expressly insists, that a man must not only THINK he has a right, but he must KNOW it —(*Appeal*, p. 62.) And again, (p. 63.) Probable hopes will not warrant him to come.

Mr. W. uses many peremptory strong expressions (p. 109.) to set forth the certainty of that which never was denied; *viz.* That a man cannot know he has a right, unless he knows he has the qualification which gives him a right. But this is not the thing in question: The point is, *Whether a man may not have a lawful right, or may not lawfully come, and yet not know his right, with such a knowledge and evidence as is beyond probability?* This is the thing asserted, and herein lies the argument. And the negative of this cannot be maintained, in order to maintain Mr. W.'s scheme, without the grossest absurdity; it being a position, which, according to Scripture, reason, Mr. S.'s doctrine, and Mr. W.'s own, effectually destroys his scheme.

To this purpose, I observed, If this proposition be true, that no man may come, save he who not only thinks but *knows* he has a right, then it will follow, that no unconverted person may come, unless he *knows* that doctrine to be true, *That unconverted men may have a right.* Because an unconverted man cannot know, that he himself has a right, unless he knows that doctrine which Mr. S. maintained, to be true, *viz.* That men may have a right, though they are unconverted. And consequently no one unconverted man may lawfully come to the Lord's supper, unless he is so knowing in this point of controversy, as not only to think, and have probable evidence, that this opinion is right, but *knows* it to be so.—Mr. W. endeavours to help the matter by a distinction, of different kinds of knowledge: and by the help of this distinction would make it out, that common people in general, and even boys and girls of sixteen years old, may with ease know, that his doctrine about unsanctified men's lawful coming to the Lord's supper, is true. And we must understand him (as he is defending Mr. S.'s argument) that they may know it with that evidence which is distinguished from probability; and this according to Mr. W. himself, is *certainty;* which he speaks of as above *a thousand probabilities.* (See p. 118. *c.*) But how miserable is this; to pretend, that his doctrine about qualifications for sacraments, is so far from a disputable point, that it is of such plain and obvious evidence to common people, and even children, that without being studied in divinity, they may not only *think* it to be *exceeding probable*, but *know* it to be *true!* When it is an undeniable fact, that multitudes of the greatest ability and piety, that have spent their lives in the study of the Holy Scriptures, have never so much as *thought* so.

Again, I observed, that according to Mr. S.'s doctrine, *not one* unconverted man in the world can *know*, that he has *warrant* to come to the Lord's supper; because, if he has any warrant, God has given him warrant in the *Scriptures*: and therefore if any unconverted man, not only *thinks*, but *knows*, that he has warrant from God, he must of consequence not only *think*, but *know*, the Scriptures to be the word of GOD. Whereas it was the constant doctrine of Mr. S. that no unconverted man *knows* the Scriptures to be the word of God.†—But Mr. W. would make it out, that Mr. S. did hold, unconverted men might *know* the Scriptures to be the word of God; but only not know it with *a gracious knowledge, such as effectually bowed* men's *hearts, and influenced them to a gracious obedience.* (p. 113. *b.*) But let us see whether it was so, or not. Mr. S. in his *Nature of Saving Conversion* (p. 73.) says, "The carnal man is *ignorant* of the divine authority of the word of God;—His wound is, that he *does not know certainly* the divine authority of these institutions; he *does not know* but they are the inventions of men." Again (*ibid.* p. 74.) he says, "The carnal man is *uncertain* of those things that are the foundation of his reasonings. He thinks there is *a great probability* of the truth of these things; but he has *no assurance.* His principles are grounded on an *uncertain* proposition." And he observes, (p. 20.) "Men when converted, do not look on it as probable, that the word is his word, as they did before; but they have assurance of the truth of it."—So elsewhere, (*Guide to Christ*, p. 26.) "They that have not grace, *do not properly believe* the word of GOD."—And in another book, (*Safety of Ap.* p. 6.) "The gospel always works effectually where it is believed and received as the truth of GOD."—In another book, (*Benef. of the Gos.* p. 149.) "Common illumination does not convince men of the truth of the gospel."—In his discourse on the *Virtue of Christ's Blood*, (p. 27.) speaking of such as have no interest in the blood of Christ, he says, "They are strangers to the divine authority of the word of GOD." Again, (*ibid.* p. 16.) "Before [*i. e.* before saving faith] they were at a loss whether the word was the word of GOD."—To the like

* If it be said here, Those who have been born of baptized ancestors, though they do not comply with the terms of the covenant, are in covenant, in this sense, that they have a right to the promises of the covenant conditionally, in case they will hereafter comply: I answer, So are all mankind in covenant, God may be said to have bound himself to them all conditionally; and many have these promises declared to them, that still remain Jews, Mahometans, or heathens.

† I did not say, that it was also a doctrine according to Scripture; for there was no occasion for this, among those with whom I had chiefly to do in this controversy; with whom I knew it was a point as much settled and uncontroverted, as any doctrine of Mr. S. whatever. And I knew it to be the current doctrine of orthodox divines; who ever allow this doctrine to be implied in such texts as those, John xvii. 7. 1 John iv. 15, 16. Chap. v. 1, 10. and many others.

purpose are many other passages in his writings. (See *Nat. of Sav. Conv.* p. 72. *Safety of Ap.* p. 6, 7, 99, 107, 186, 187, 229.—*Benef. of the Gosp.* p. 89.)

So that here, if it be true, that some unconverted men have a divine warrant to come to the Lord's supper; and if the thing which is the foundation of this argument, be also true, *viz.* That in order to men's warrantably coming to the Lord's supper, they must not only *think* but *know* they have a right; then it must be true likewise, that they not only *think* but *know*, that the Scripture, wherein this warrant is supposed to be delivered, is the word of God. And then we have the following propositions to make hang together: that unconverted men are ignorant of the Scripture's being the word of God, are uncertain of it, have no assurance of it, are not convinced of it, do not properly believe it, are at a loss whether it be the word of God, or not; and yet they not only think, but know, that the Scriptures are the word of God, and that the gospel, which is the charter of all christian privileges, is divine; they have a knowledge of it, which is above all probable hope or thought, and attended with evidence above a thousand probabilities.

And now let it be considered, whether this agrees better with Mr. W.'s own doctrine, concerning men's knowing the truth and divine authority of the gospel, in what has been before cited from his sermons on *Christ a King and Witness.* Where he expressly says, that man, since the fall, is ignorant of the divine truth, and full of prejudices against it; has a view of the truth contained in the Bible, as a doubtful uncertain thing; receives it as what is probably true; sees it as a probable scheme, and something likely to answer the end proposed: but that after conversion it appears divinely true and real. (See p. 114, 115, and 144.) Then unconverted men only looked on the truth of the word of God, as probable, something likely, yet as a doubtful uncertain thing; but now they not only think but know it to be true.

No distinction, about the different kinds of knowledge, or the various ways of knowing, will ever help these absurdities, or reconcile such inconsistencies. If there be any such sort of *knowing*, as is contra-distinguished to probable *thinking*, and to such opinion as is built on *a thousand probabilities*, which yet is inconsistent with being ignorant, not believing, being uncertain, nor assured, nor convinced, only looking on a thing probable, looking on it doubtful and uncertain, it must certainly be a new and very strange sort of knowledge.

But this argument, that is so clear and invincible, must have such supports as these, or must quite sink to the earth. It is indeed a remarkable kind of argument. It is not only as much against the scheme it is brought to support, as against that which it would confute; but abundantly more so. For if it were the case in truth, that none might come to the Lord's supper, but they that *know* they have a right, yet it would be no direct and proper proof, that *unconverted* men might come. It would indeed prove, that many *godly* men might *not* come; which, it is true, would bring some difficulty on the scheme *opposed;* yet would be no proof against it. But it is direct and perfect demonstration against the scheme it would *support:* it demonstrates according to the Scripture, and according to the doctrine of those that urge the argument, that not one unconverted man in the world may lawfully come to the Lord's supper; as no one of them certainly *knows* the gospel to be divine, and so no one *knows* the charter to be authentic, in which alone the right of any to christian privileges is conveyed; hence no one unsanctified man is *sure* of his right; and therefore (as they draw the consequence) no one unsanctified man may come to the Lord's supper. And so it follows, that the more strongly Mr. W. stands to this argument, the more peremptory and confident his expressions are concerning it, the more violently and effectually does he supplant himself.

And this position, *that a man must not take any privilege, till he not only thinks, but knows, he has a right,* is not only unreasonable, as used by Mr. W. against me, when indeed it is ten times as much against himself; but it is unreasonable in itself, as it is an argument, which if allowed and pursued, will prove, that a man may do nothing at all, never move hand or foot, for his own advantage, unless he first, not only *thinks*, but *knows*, it is his duty. Mr. W. himself owns (p. 116.) that all the *duties*, which God requires of us in his instituted worship, are *privileges*, as well as the Lord's supper: and so is every other duty, which we are to do for our own benefit. But all human actions are, upon the whole, either *good* or *evil:* every thing that we do as rational creatures, is either a duty, or a sin; and the neglect of every thing that is our duty is forbidden. So that we must never so much as take a step, or move a finger, upon only a probable judgment and hope; but must first *know* it to be our duty, before we do it: nay, we must neither move, nor voluntarily forbear to move, without a *certainty* of our duty in the case, one way or other!

As to its being *alike difficult* for men to know or be assured of their moral sincerity, as of their real sanctification, I shall speak to that under the next head; whereby it will appear again, another way, that this argument is vastly more against Mr. W.'s scheme than mine.

SECT. XVI.

A consideration of Mr. W.'s defence on the 10th objection, against the doctrine of the unlawfulness of unsanctified men coming to the Lord's supper, that it tends to the great perplexity and torment of many godly men in their attendance on this ordinance.

My *first* reply to this objection was, that it is for want of like tenderness of conscience, that the other doctrine which insists on *moral sincerity*, does not naturally bring such as are received on those principles, into as great *perplexities.*—Mr. W. in his animadversions upon it says, "This is an assertion which I take to be contrary to common sense, and the experience of mankind: and the allowing of it to be true, must overthrow the law of nature, and cast infinite reproach upon the author of it."

These are strong expressions; but let us bring the matter to the test of reason.—The necessary qualification, on Mr. W.'s principles, is moral sincerity, and a *certain degree* of moral sincerity. For there is scarcely any man, that lives under the light of the gospel, and is not an atheist, or deist, but what has *some degree* of moral sincerity, in some things pertaining to Christianity and his duty; some degree of common faith, some degree of conviction of the need of Christ, some desire of him, and moral willingness though from selfish considerations, to be good; and some purpose to endeavour a conformity to the covenant of grace, and to seek salvation on the terms of it. But how shall a man know what is a *sufficient degree* of these things? Mr. W. has determined the matter thus; that his belief of the doctrine of the gospel, and moral willingness, to be conformed to the covenant of grace, must be *with his* WHOLE *heart*, (p. 49. *e.* p. 5. *c.* 36. *a.*) And that his conviction of his undone state without Christ must be *deep;* and his desire of Christ and his benefits *fervent*, and his purpose *earnest*, (p. 75. *c.* p. 11. *c.*) so as to induce him to enter into covenant with ALL the earnestness he can, and engage him to use endeavours with ALL the strength and power that he has. (p. 83. *e.* p. 32. *d.* p. 36. *a.*)

Now how exceeding *difficult* must it be for unsanctified men to determine, with any assurance, whether they have moral sincerity to *such a degree!*—How difficult for them to know, whether their convictions are thus *deep!* Every one that is used to deal with souls under conviction, knows, that when they are indeed under deep convictions, they are especially apt to complain of the *hardness* of their hearts, and to think their convictions are *not* deep.—How difficult to determine, with any assurance, whether their assent rises so high, that they can truly be said to *believe with all their hearts!* Whether their moral willingness to be conformed to the covenant of grace, be *with their whole heart!* And whether they are really engaged *with all the solicitude they can*, and are willing to do *all that they can!* These things, I am pretty sure, are of vastly more difficult determination, than whether a man has any true holiness, or not. For in the former case, the determination is concerning the degree of things, that are capable of an infinite variety of degrees; some of which are nearer to, and others are further from, the lowest *sufficient* degree: and consequently some of the degrees that are not sufficient, may yet be very near; which renders the matter of very difficult determination; unspeakably more so, that when what is to be distinguished, is the *nature* of things, which *in all degrees* is widely diverse, and even contrary to that which it is to be distinguished from: as is the case between saving and common grace; which Mr. W. himself acknowledges.* It is more easy to distinguish *light* from darkness, than to determine the precise *degree* of light; and so it is more easy to determine, whether a man be alive or dead, than whether there be exactly such a certain *degree* of vigour and liveliness.

This *moral sincerity*, which Mr. W. insists on, is a most indeterminate uncertain thing; a phrase without any certain precise meaning; and must for ever remain so. It being not determined, *how much* men must be morally sincere; *how much* they must believe with a moral sincerity; whether the deeply awakened and convinced sinner must believe, that God is absolutely sovereign *with respect to his salvation*, and that Christ is perfectly sufficient to *save him in particular;* and to what *degree* of moral assent and consent, he must believe and embrace these things, and comply with the terms of the covenant of grace; whether he must be willing to obey all God's commands, the most difficult, as well as the most easy, and this in all circumstances, even the most difficult that can arise in providence; or whether only in some circumstances; and what, and how many. The Scripture gives us many infallible rules, by which to distinguish between saving grace, and common. But I know of no rules given in the Bible, by which men may certainly determine this *precise degree* of moral sincerity. So that if *grace* is not the thing which gives a right to sacraments in the sight of God, we have no certain rule in the Bible, commensurate to the understanding of mankind, by which to determine when we have a right, and when not.—Now let the impartial reader judge, which scheme lays the greatest foundation for *perplexity* to communicants of tender consciences, concerning their qualifications for the Lord's supper; and whether this argument drawn from such a supposed *tendency* to such perplexity (if there be any force in it) is not vastly more against Mr. W.'s scheme, than mine.

And here by the way, let it be noted, that by these things it is again demonstrated, that the *ninth objection*, the great argument considered in the preceding section, concerning the necessity of a *known right*, in order to a lawful partaking, is exceedingly more against Mr. W.'s principles, than mine; inasmuch as, on his principles, it is so much more difficult for men to know, whether they have a right, or have the prescribed qualification, or not.

I answered this argument in the second place, by alleging, that this doctrine of the necessity of saving grace in order to a right to the Lord's supper, is not properly the cause of the perplexities of doubting saints, in their attendance on this ordinance; though it may be the occasion: but that their own *negligence* and *sin* is the true cause; and that this doctrine is no more the cause of these perplexities, than the doctrine of the necessity of saving grace in order to salvation, is the cause of the perplexity of doubting saints when they come to *die*. Upon which Mr. W. says, There is no shadow of resemblance of these cases, because death is no ordinance, &c. But if death is no ordinance, yet it is the required duty of the saints to yield themselves to the Lord, and resign to the will of God, in their death. And in this respect, the cases are exactly parallel, that perplexities are just so much the consequence of the respective doctrines, in one case, as in the other; that is, the perplexities of a doubting saint on a *death-bed*, the difficulty and trouble he meets with in resigning himself to the will of God in dying, is just in the same manner the consequence of the doctrine of the necessity of saving grace in order to eternal salvation, as the perplexities of a doubting saint at the Lord's table are the consequence of the doctrine of the necessity of saving grace in order to a right to the Lord's supper. And this is sufficient for my purpose.

Mr. W. himself says, in his answer to Mr. Croswell, (p. 122. c.) " Although there are comparatively few that obtain assurance; yet it is through their own sloth and negligence that they do not. We fully agree with Mr. Perkins, that a man in this life may ordinarily be infallibly certain of his salvation. So Mr. Stoddard (in his sermon on *one good sign*—) says, " There is no necessity, that the people of God should lie under darkness and temptation; they may obtain assurance."—Now, if this be the case, then certainly there is no justice in laying the temptation and uneasiness, which is the effect of sloth and negligence, to the doctrine I maintain, in those that embrace it. It is a wise dispensation of God, that he has so ordered things, that comfort in ordinances, and in all duties, and under all providences, should be to be obtained in a way of diligence; and that slothfulness should be the way to perplexity and uneasiness, and should be a way hedged up with thorns, agreeable to Prov. xv. 19.—That it is so ordered, is for the good of the saints, as it tends to turn them out of this thorny path, into the way of diligence. And so this doctrine, as it has this tendency, has a tendency in the end to that solid peace and comfort, which is the happy fruit of their holy diligence. And that, and not the saints' perplexity, is properly the effect of this doctrine.

SECT. XVII.

Containing some further observations on what is said by Mr. W. in support of the 13th objection, concerning God's commanding all the members of the visible church, that are not ignorant nor scandalous, to attend all external covenant duties.

It has been already demonstrated (sect. 8th of this third part) that in this argument the question is begged, notwithstanding what Mr. W. has said to the contrary, which sufficiently overthrows the whole argument. Nevertheless, that I may pass by nothing, which those who are on Mr. W.'s side may be likely to think material, I will here make some further observations on this objection, as represented and supported by Mr. W.

The chief thing, that has the plausible appearance of argument in what Mr. S. and Mr. W. say on this head, is this; " That for God to require all who are in covenant to come to the Lord's supper, and yet to forbid them to come unconverted, is to suppose, that he both commands them and forbids them at the same time." And this is thought to be the more manifest, inasmuch as *conversion is not in men's power*. Though it is not denied, but that God justly requires men to be converted, or to be truly holy. (See p. 129, 130.)

To this I would say,

(1.) If when they speak of commanding and forbidding at the same time, they mean God's commanding and forbidding the same thing at the same time, no such consequence follows from my principles. For that thing, and that only, which I suppose God requires of any, is to come to the Lord's supper with a sanctified heart; and that this God requires at *all times*, and never forbids at *any time;* and that to come without this qualification, is what he *always* forbids, and requires at *no time*. So that *what* he requires, at the same time he forbids something, is not the *same thing* that he forbids; but a very different and contrary one. And it is no absurdity, to suppose, that God requires one thing, and forbids a contrary thing at the same time.

To illustrate this by an example: It was the duty of the *Jews* at *Jerusalem*, openly to *confess* Christ, to own him as the *Messiah*, at that hour when he was led away to be crucified, and openly to testify their adoring respect to him on that extraordinary occasion. But yet they did not believe him to be the *Messiah*, and could not believe it, (many of them at least,) since they looked on his present abject circumstances as a demonstration, that he was not the *Messiah*. It was beyond their power, at least at once, in that instant, to give their assent, with all their hearts, to such a supposition. Nor was it in their power, to exercise

* See his serm. on *Christ a King and Witness*, (p. 84. e.) where he says, " notwithstanding the visible likeness of nominal and real Christians, there is a wide difference, as there is between the subjects of Christ and the slaves of the devil."

an adoring respect to him: for, besides their strong prejudices, most of them were judicially hardened, and given up to a spirit of unbelief and obstinate rejection of him; as appears by that account, (John xii. 39, 40.) "Therefore they could not believe, because that *Esaias* said again, He hath blinded their eyes, and hardened their heart, that they should not see with their eyes," &c. (See also Luke xix. 41, 42. and Matt. xiii. 14, 15.) And yet it would have been unlawful for them to have made a lying profession; to profess, that they believed him to be the *Messiah*, and that they received and loved him as such, when at the same time they hated him, and did not believe he was the *Messiah*.—But here is no requiring and forbidding the same thing at the same time: for the only thing required of them was, to have faith and love, and to testify it; which was not at all forbidden.

(2.) None of the difficulties, which Mr. S. or Mr. W. object—either God's supposed requiring impossibilities, or his requiring and forbidding at the same time—do follow, any more on *my* principles, than on Mr. W.'s. Mr. W. maintains, that God calls men *this moment* to enter into covenant with him, and commands them to do it. (p. 28. *c.*) One thing implied in this, according to his own frequent explanation of visibly entering into covenant, is professing a belief of the fundamental doctrines of Christianity. Now therefore, we will suppose a man to be a candidate for baptism, who has been brought up in *Arianism;* and is strongly persuaded, that the doctrine of the Trinity is not true: yet he is this moment required to profess that doctrine; but has no ability in a moment to believe the doctrine, because he does not at present see the evidence of it. For as Mr. W. himself says, (Sermon on *Christ a King and Witness*, p. 91. *d. e.* and 92. *a.*) "The understanding cannot be brought to yield its assent to any truth, which it does not see the truth or apprehend the evidence of.——If you would hire him with cart-loads or ship-loads of gold and silver; if you should imprison him, whip him, burn him; you cannot make him believe a thing to be true, which he apprehends to be incredible, or which he sees no sufficient reason to believe." Now therefore what shall the man do, on Mr. W.'s principles? He is commanded to profess the doctrine of the Trinity, which must be professed in order to be lawfully baptized in the name of the Trinity; and on Mr. W.'s principles, he is commanded to do it *this moment.* Yet also on his principles, if the man professes it, and is not morally sincere, or knows he does not believe it, he is guilty of *horrible falsehood and prevarication;* which God doubtless forbids. Therefore here is certainly as much of an appearance of commanding and forbidding the same thing at the same time, as in the other case.

Every husbandman in *Israel*, that lived even in Christ's time, was required to offer a basket of the first-fruits; and was commanded when he offered it, solemnly to make that profession, concerning the principal facts relating to the redemption out of *Egypt*,—which is prescribed in Deut. xxvi. 5—10. "A *Syrian* ready to perish was my father," &c. Now supposing there had been an *Israelite*, who did not believe the truth of all these facts, which came to pass so many ages before, (as there are now many in *christendom*, who do not believe the facts concerning *Jesus Christ*,) and continued in his unbelief, till the very moment of his offering: God peremptorily requires him to make this profession; yet none will say, that he may lawfully profess these things, at the same time when he does not believe them to be true. However, here is no commanding and forbidding the same thing at the same time: because, though God required the *Jews* to make this profession, yet the thing required was *to believe it* and *profess it.* Though some might not believe it, nor be able for the present to believe it; yet this inability arose from depravity and wickedness of heart, which did not at all excuse their unbelief, for *one moment.** Mr. W. himself owns, (p. 129. *b. c.*) that God may require those things which are out of men's natural power.

Now this may be laid down as a truth, of easy and plain evidence; if God may require what wicked men, while such, are unable to perform, then he may also require those things which are connected with it, and dependent on it, and which, if the other be done, they would be able to do, and might do, and without which they may not do it. So, if God may require an unsanctified man to love him, then he may require him to testify and profess his love, as I suppose Christians do in the act of partaking of the Lord's supper; and yet it may not be lawful for him to testify and profess love, when he has it not.†

* This instance may show us, that God's requiring all *Israel* to enter into covenant with God, and seal their covenant in the passover, will not prove, that it was lawful for any to avouch the Lord to be their God, and promise and swear they would perform universal and persevering obedience, when at the same moment they had no love to God, and even then, while speaking the words, continued in an habitual wilful disobedience to God's commands, and were willing slaves to the devil. Nor will it follow, from these commands given to the *Israelites*, concerning their covenanting with God, and sealing their covenant, that God ever did, since the foundation of the world, appoint or command any other covenanting with him, than as giving up themselves wholly and without reserve, both soul and body, both heart and life; or that ever he appointed or commanded any covenanting, wherein men give a part, and keep back a part, give him the outside, and keep back the noblest and best part, the heart, will, and affections, for sin and Satan; or that there is any such covenant of God in being; or that such covenanting has not always been as much without foundation in any institution of God, as any of the spurious sacraments of the church of *Rome;* or that it has not always been strictly forbidden of God; or that it is not absolutely and in itself sinful and unlawful, as truly as the act of Ananias and Sapphira.

† Much of the controversy discussed in this book (and the preceding one) which was agitated with great warmth in the American churches, and which is not unfrequently started among congregational churches in Great Britain, seems to originate in the want of clearly stating the *scriptural design* of entering into full communion. If this be not previously settled, there is but little hope of a satisfactory adjustment. Without entering here into the *minutiæ* of proofs, the following particulars are submitted to the reader's consideration, as probably calculated to aid his inquiries.

1. The *chief* end of every human society, as well as of every intelligent being, ought to be this, *viz.* To glorify God, or to represent him as *glorious* in all his perfections and ways. No human society, of whatever kind, is exempt from this obligation. For a society is only an aggregate of individuals; and as every individual is obliged to do this in all his actions, he is therefore thus obliged in his *social* capacity. This obligation arises from the respective *natures* of God and the creature, and it is clearly enjoined in the Holy Scripture. "Whatsoever ye do, do all to the glory of God"—But,

2. The distinguishing *subordinate end* or special design of any society, must designate its *peculiar nature*, whereby it is best adapted to promote that end. Though every society is bound to seek the one chief end, yet every social union is not adapted to answer all social ends. Societies of a religious, moral, charitable, scientific, or political design, must have members of a corresponding character, otherwise the proposed end cannot be answered. The qualifications of the members must have an *aptitude* to promote the design.

3. The distinguishing design of a society denominated a *church*, evidently, is *to promote religion.* Numbers are united by divine appointment, to *maintain* religion—to exhibit before the world real Christianity—to *encourage* those who seek the right way—to edify one another—and the like. Such particulars we gather from the sacred Scriptures. "Striving together for the faith of the gospel."—"That ye may be blameless and harmless, the sons of God (resembling him) without rebuke (or, cause of rebuke) in the minds of a crooked and perverse nation, among whom ye shine as lights in the world, holding forth the word of life."—A church of Christ is appointed to shine in a dark world, to be blameless and harmless among the crooked and perverse, to imitate God, as far as practicable, while among the children of the wicked one, to give no offence to those who are without or those who are within the church, to hold forth, and hold fast, the word of life, by doctrine, by discipline, and by practice. "Him that is weak in the faith receive you, but not to doubtful disputations." Provided a person be desirous of christian fellowship, and is possessed of so much knowledge, so much experienced efficacy of truth, and so much good conduct, as is calculated to answer, in a prevailing degree, the design of a church being at all formed, let him not be rejected. "Wherefore comfort yourselves together, and edify one another, even as also ye do?" This is done by mutual instructions, exhortations, prayers, and praises; by watchful discipline, and the exercise of religious gifts; by friendly offices, and acts of christian kindness.

4. The preceding particulars are produced only as *instances;* but in order accurately to ascertain the special end of christian fellowship, in full communion, *all* the passages contained in the New Testament relating to the subject ought to be included. For until the revealed special design for which a church of Christ is instituted be ascertained, it is obviously not possible to ascertain the precise nature of the society, and consequently the qualifications of its members. However,

5. We will suppose that, by an appeal to all the passages of the New Testament, the precise *design* is known; from whence the *nature* of a church is deduced: the question returns,—Is there any *general rule* that may form an invariable standard by which all qualifications of candidates may be measured? There undoubtedly is, for this plain reason, because a church is a society instituted for *specific ends*, revealed in the New Testament. Now as these ends are matter of divine *record*, and not of human opinion, the *standard* is *invariable.*

6. We will further suppose, that the *general rule*, by which to measure qualifications for full communion, is *The scriptural design for which a gospel church in full communion is divinely instituted.* No party, however they may differ about other things, can object to this rule, with any colour of reason. To deny its claim, they must either subvert the evident principles of all voluntary societies, or else hold, that a christian church is not instituted in the New Testament for any specific end. But this no reasonable person, much less a serious Christian, will maintain. Hence,

7. Those candidates for full communion, and only those, who are conformed *to this rule*, are fully qualified. But here it is of essential importance to observe, that though a *rule* is, and from its very nature must be, fixed and invariable, the qualifications of individuals are variable things, admitting of more or less conformity to it. The conjectures of men, however ingenious and plausible, cannot be admitted as a *rule*, because they are *variable;* but the rule must be deduced from the *design* itself of instituting a church, which is evidently a matter of pure divine pleasure, and which could not be known without a revelation from God. A *rule*, then, must be sought from the sacred oracles by an induction of particulars relating to the point in question, and from their harmonious agreement: and it is the business of every christian church, minister and member, to search the Scriptures in order to ascertain it. To contend about *qualifications*,

AN APPENDIX.

Being a Letter to the people of the first church and congregation in Northampton.

DEAR BRETHREN,

THOUGH I am not now your pastor, yet having so long stood in that relation to you, I look on myself obliged, notwithstanding all that has of late passed between us, still to maintain a special concern for your spiritual welfare. And as your present circumstances appear to me very evidently attended with some peculiar dangers, threatening the great wounding of the interest of vital religion among you; which probably most of you are not well aware of; I look on myself called to point forth your danger to you, and give you warning. What I now especially have respect to, is the danger I apprehend you are in, from the contents of that book of Mr. W. of *Lebanon*, to which the foregoing performance is a reply; which I perceive has been written and published very much by your procurement and at your expense; and so (it may naturally be supposed and expected) is dispersed in your families, and will be valued and much used by you as a book of great importance. What I regard, is not so much the danger you are in of being established by that book in your former principles, concerning the admission of members; (though I think these principles are indeed very opposite to the interest of true piety in churches;) but what I now mean is the danger there is, that while you are making much of that book as a means to maintain Mr. Stoddard's doctrine concerning the terms of communion, you, and especially your children, will by the contents of it be led quite off from *other* religious principles and doctrines, which Mr. S. brought you up in, and always esteemed as of vastly greater importance, than his particular tenet about the Lord's supper; and be naturally led into notions and principles, which *he* ever esteemed as of fatal tendency to the souls of men.

By the way, I would have it observed, that when I take notice of these things in his book, my aim is not to beget in you an ill opinion of Mr. W. as though he were as corrupt in his settled persuasion, as one would be ready to think, if he were to judge only by things delivered in *some parts* of this book; and especially if it should be supposed, that he embraced all the *consequences* of what he here maintains. Men often do not see or allow the plain consequences of their own doctrines. And therefore, though I charge very pernicious consequences on some *things* he says, yet I do not charge *him* with embracing these consequences: nor will I undertake to explain how it could come to pass, that he should maintain things now in *this* book, in opposition to me, which are so contrary to the good and sound doctrines he has formerly delivered in *other* books. Let that be as it will, and however orthodox the principles may be, which he more ordi-

before this is agreed upon, is to contend about the dimensions of different things, before a standard is fixed upon which to measure them. But the constituent parts of the qualifications in candidates cannot be found in Scripture; they must, most evidently, be sought in the *characters* of the individuals, which are indefinitely variable. To suppose that the character, or the *actual attainment*, of each candidate is revealed in Scripture, is too absurd to be maintained by any rational mind. Therefore,

8. What remains for a church to do in judging of qualifications, is to *compare* the *proficiency* of the candidate, with the scriptural *rule*. The former, admitting of indefinite degrees of approximation to the standard, must be learnt from the person himself, from his conduct, and from the testimony of others. His profession, his declared experience of divine truth, his deportment in society, in short, his general character, is to be viewed, in comparison with the evident design of God in forming a church.

9. Should it be objected, that different persons, or churches, might fix on a different standard, by *adding* more texts of Scripture out of which a various general result would arise; it is answered, that therefore this is the point to be first settled. When any disagree about the rule, they cannot of course agree about the qualifications. There are many texts, however, such as those above produced, concerning which there can be no disagreement. The rule therefore should be admitted, *as far as it goes*. A measure of a foot long may, as far as it goes, be a standard of straightness and of measure, as well as a yard or a fathom. Or, to change the comparison, a small measure of capacity may be equally accurate, to a certain degree, as a larger measure. Let the church of small attainments act charitably, and wait for brighter evidence. If any lack wisdom, let them ask of God, who giveth liberally. "Let us therefore, as many as be perfect, be thus minded; and if in any thing ye be otherwise minded, God shall reveal even this unto you. Nevertheless, *whereto we have already attained*, let us walk by the same rule, let us mind the same thing."

10. The scriptural rule is not only invariable, but also perfect in its kind, as dictated by infinite wisdom for the noblest ends. But no human character, in the present state, is perfect, so as to comport universally with the standard. Therefore no candidate for communion is perfectly qualified; that is, his qualifications are only comparative. One may be qualified in a greater, and another in a smaller degree. One is qualified to fill his place eminently, another moderately well. One may be strong, and another weak in the faith. Yet he who is weak in the faith may be comparatively qualified. Therefore,

11. Since qualifications are so various, and admit of indefinite approximations to the perfect standard, or deviations from it, we are bound to accede to another conclusion, *viz.* That whatever kind or degree of qualification appears to *befriend*, rather than to oppose, to *honour*, rather than to discredit, the scriptural design of full communion, ought to be admitted by the church. When a candidate for communion is proposed to a church, its immediate business is to consult the scriptural design of communion; and then to consider how far the qualifications of the candidate appear to befriend and to honour it.

12. From the premises it follows, that to reason from qualifications for communion in the Jewish church, to those for full communion in a gospel church, must needs be uncertain and inconclusive; except it could be first proved, that the revealed design of each was the same. But it requires no great labour to show by an induction of particulars, that the design was very different; and consequently, that what would be a suitable qualification for the one, would not be so for the other.

13. We may further infer, that when a church requires a probable evidence of grace as the measuring rule of admission, and directs nearly all its attention to ascertain this point, its proceedings are irregular, unscriptural, and therefore unwarrantable. The rule of judging, as before shown, must be found in the Scripture, and not in the candidate.

14. We may further infer from the preceding observations, that a *probable evidence of grace* in a candidate, is not the *precise ground* of the qualification, however *desirable* that evidence may be. Yet, because ordinarily, and most probably, the absence of saving grace implies the absence of the precise ground of answerableness to the scriptural design of full communion, such probable evidence is of great importance. However nice this distinction may appear to some, the want of attending to it seems to have constituted the chief difference between our author and his antagonists. And, in fair investigation, another question, different from what was agitated, ought to have been first settled, *viz.* Whether *any person*, who is not visibly the subject of saving grace, can "befriend, rather than oppose, can *honour*, rather than discredit, the scriptural design of full communion?" Fairly to answer this question in the negative, it is not enough to prove, that such a person cannot *fully answer* the scriptural design. But it ought to be proved, that no person destitute of such probable evidence of saving grace, in any circumstances whatever, can be found, who might befriend and honour the scriptural design of communion, rather than the contrary. This is the real hinge of the controversy.

15. It is an unscriptural notion, too much taken upon trust, that the immediate business of a church, is to form an opinion respecting the spiritual state of a person before God; as, whether he is the subject of saving grace—whether he has a principle of sincerity—whether his motives are spiritually pure, &c. Whereas, a church ought not to act the part of a jury on the candidate's real state towards *God*, but on his state towards the *church*. They are to determine, whether he is or is not *eligible* to answer the scriptural ends of such a society, and indeed of that particular church. For, as the circumstances of divers churches may be very different, there may be cases, where the same person may be eligible to one church, and not to another. In one church he may *promote* its welfare, in another *hinder* it. This may greatly depend on his peculiar tenets, and the zeal with which he may be disposed to maintain them. In one society he may be a source of disquiet and confusion, but in another the reverse.

16 Hence it is evident, that a visibility of saving grace, though it claims the christian love and respect of the church, does not in all cases constitute eligible qualifications. For, whatever has an evident tendency to produce disputes, animosities, and divisions in a church, ought to be kept out of it. But the admission of a person who appeared zealous for sentiments and customs opposite to those held by the church, would have this apparent tendency, notwithstanding his possessing a visibility of grace, on other accounts. Therefore, though a visibility of grace, in some cases, may be sufficiently plain, yet an apparent failure in other respects may be sufficient to show that a person is not qualified for full communion. In short, if the church have good reason to think, that his admission would do more harm than good, he should be deemed *unqualified* for membership in that society, though he may be entitled to a charitable opinion, or even christian love, on other accounts: and, on the contrary, if the church have good reason to think, that his admission would do more good than harm, he should be deemed *qualified* for membership—even though he may be less entitled to a charitable opinion of his state towards God, than the other.

COROLLARIES.

1. Any candidate who appears, in the charitable judgment of a christian church, likely to give a favourable representation of Christianity to the church and the world—to encourage the desirous, by his knowledge and tempers—and to give and receive christian edification in that communion—is, in the scripture sense, *qualified* for full communion.

2. Personal religion, in the sight of God, is to be deemed necessary only *for the sake* of enabling the candidate to answer such ends,—as far as *membership* is concerned; but, as final salvation is concerned, personal religion is indispensably necessary, this connexion being clearly revealed, as well as founded in the nature of things.

3. A christian minister may consistently exercise holy jealousy over some church-members, and warn them of the danger of hypocrisy, without threatening them with exclusion from their membership; because only their *overt-acts* (including sentiments, tempers, and conduct,) are the object of discipline, as they were of admission.

4. Some persons, though in a safe state towards God, may not answer the forementioned ends of membership, better than others who are not in such a state.

5. A person may be qualified for the society of heaven, while not qualified for full communion in a christian church; because the natures of the two societies are different, and consequently the scriptural ends of their admission into each. For infants, and idiots, &c. may be qualified by grace for the society of heaven; but are totally unqualified for full communion in the church on earth.

6 Were christian churches to act always on these principles, much bitter strife and useless discussions would be avoided, in the admission and exclusion of members. For, in neither the one nor the other, would the church pronounce on the state of the persons towards God; for when any were *admitted*, no handle would be afforded to the presumption, that membership below is a qualification for heaven—and when any were excluded, no occasion would be given to the excommunicated person, or to the world, to pass the censure of uncharitableness on the church; for every voluntary society has a right to judge, according to its own appropriate rules, who is, and who is not, qualified to promote its welfare.—W.

narily maintains; yet the *ill and unsound* things he delivers here, may do nevertheless hurt to you and your children, who may read this book without having in view the more wholesome doctrines of his other writings.

For instance, you have ever been taught, that *unconverted men do not really believe the gospel, are never truly convinced of its truth*; and that it is of great importance that sinners should be sensible of the unbelief and atheism of their hearts. But contrary to this, Mr. W.'s book abundantly teaches you and your children this notion, *That unsanctified men may really be convinced of the divine truth of the gospel, and believe it with all their hearts.*

You have been ever taught, that Christless sinners, especially when under some more slight awakenings, are very ready to flatter themselves that they are willing to accept of Christ as their Saviour; but that they must be brought off from their vain imagination, and be brought to see that the fault is in their own wills, and that their not being interested in Christ is owing to their obstinacy and perverseness, and wilful wicked refusal of God's terms; on which account they are wholy inexcusable, and may justly be cast off by God. But contrary to these things, this book of Mr. W. abundantly teaches you, that men in an unconverted state, may indeed cordially consent to the terms of the covenant of grace, may comply with the call of the gospel, may submit to its proposals, may have satisfaction in the offer God makes of himself as our God in Christ, may fall in with the terms of salvation propounded in the gospel, and renounce all other ways, and may sincerely and earnestly desire salvation in this way: and that some unconverted men are not wilful obstinate sinners. (p. 21. *b.*) Which doctrines, if embraced and retained by your children as true, will tend for ever to hinder that conviction of the opposition and obstinacy of the heart, which Mr. S. ever taught you to be of such importance in order to the soul's humiliation, and thorough conviction of the justice of God in its damnation.

You have ever been taught, that the hearts of natural men are wholly corrupt, entirely destitute of any thing spiritually good, not having the least spark of love to God, and as much without all things of this nature, as a dead corpse is without life: nevertheless, that it is hard for sinners to be convinced of this; that they are exceeding prone to imagine, there is some goodness in them, some respect to God in what they do; yet that they must be brought off from such a vain conceit of themselves, and come to see themselves utterly depraved and quite dead in sin.—But now this book of Mr. W. leads you to quite other notions; it leads you to suppose, that some natural men are above lukewarmness in religion, that they may truly profess to be the real friends of Christ, and to love God, more than his enemies, and above the world.

It was a doctrine greatly inculcated on you by Mr. S. as supposing it of great importance for all to be convinced of it, that natural men *are not subject to the law of God, nor indeed can be*; that they never do truly serve God, but are wholly under the dominion of sin and Satan.—But if sinners believe Mr. W.'s book, they will not be convinced of these things; nay, they will believe quite contrary things, *viz.* That sinners, while in a state of nature, may have a cordial subjection to Jesus Christ, and may be subject to him with all their hearts, and may be so devoted to the service of Christ as to be above those that serve two masters, may give up themselves to be taught, ruled, and led by him in a gospel-way of salvation, and may give up all their hearts and lives to him.—And is it likely, while sinners believe these doctrines of Mr. W. that they will ever be brought to a thorough humiliation, in a conviction of their being wholly under the power of enmity against God, which Mr. S. taught you to be of such great importance?

You know it was always a doctrine greatly insisted on by Mr. S. as a thing of the utmost consequence, that sinners who are seeking converting grace, should be thoroughly sensible of God's being under no manner of obligation, from any desires, labours, or endeavours of theirs, to bestow his grace upon them; either in justice, or truth, or any other way; but that when they have done all, God is perfectly at liberty, whether to show them mercy, or not; that they are wholly in the hands of God's sovereignty. (See *Guide to Christ*, p. 75. *c. d.* and *Benef. of the Gosp.* p. 64. and p. 75, 76.)—Whereas, if a sinner seeking salvation believes Mr. W.'s book, it will naturally lead him to think quite otherwise. He (in p. 28.) speaking of such sincerity and earnestness of endeavours as may be in natural men, to qualify them to come to the sacrament, and of the great encouragement God has given, that he will bestow his saving grace on such as use such endeavours, adds these words, (near the bottom of the page,) "God never will be worse than his encouragement, nor do less than he has encouraged; and he has said, *to him that hath shall be given.*" Naturally leading the awakened sinner, who is supposed to have moral sincerity enough to come to the sacrament, to suppose, that God is not wholly at liberty; but that he has given so much encouragement, that it may be depended upon he will give his grace; and that it would not be reasonable or becoming of God to do otherwise; because if God should do so, he would *be worse than his encouragement*, and would not fulfil that word of his, *to him who hath shall be given.* And how will this tend effectually to prevent the sinner looking on God as absolutely at liberty, and prevent his resigning himself wholly into the hands of God, and to his sovereign pleasure!

It is a doctrine which has ever been taught you, and used for the warning, awakening, and humbling of gospel sinners, that they have greater guilt, and are exposed to a more terrible punishment, than the *heathen.*—But this is spoken of by Mr. W. as an unsufferable treatment of *visible saints;* naturally tending to alleviate and smooth the matter in the consciences of those that are not scandalous persons, though they live in unbelief and the rejection of Christ under gospel light and mercy.

If you will believe what Mr. W. says, (p. 56.) those blessed *epithets* and *characters* in the epistles of the apostles, which you always, from the first foundation of the town, have been taught to be peculiar and glorious expressions and descriptions of the blessed qualifications and state of true saints, and heirs of eternal happiness; such as "being elected, chosen before the foundation of the world, predestinated to the adoption of children through Jesus Christ; quickened, and made alive to God, *though once dead in trespasses and sins;* washed, sanctified, justified;—made to sit together in heavenly places in Christ; begotten again, to an inheritance incorruptible, undefiled;"—with innumerable others the like:—I say if you believe Mr. W. you have been quite mistaken all your days, and misled by all your ministers; these things are no more than were said of the whole nation of the *Jews*, even in their worst times! Which is (as I have observed) exactly agreeable to the strange opinion of Mr. Taylor, of *Norwich, in England*, that author who has so corrupted multitudes in *New England*. Thus you are at once deprived of all the chief texts in the Bible, that hitherto have been made use of among you, as teaching the discriminating qualifications and privileges of the truly pious, and the nature and benefits of a real conversion; too much paving the way for the rest of *Taylor's* scheme of religion, which utterly explodes the doctrines you have been formerly taught concerning eternal election, conversion, justification; and so, of a natural state of death in sin; and the whole doctrine of original sin, and of the mighty change made in the soul by the redemption of Christ applied to it.

And this, taken with those other things which I have observed, in conjunction with some other things which have lately appeared in *Northampton*, tend to lead the young people among you apace into a liking to the new, fashionable, lax schemes of divinity, which have so greatly prevailed in *New England* of late; as wide as the East is from the West, from those great principles of religion, which have always been taught, and have been embraced, and esteemed most precious, and have justly been accounted very much your glory by others.

If this book of Mr. W. with all these things, is made much of by you, and recommended to your children, as of great importance to defend the principles of the town, how far has your zeal for that one tenet, respecting natural men's right to the Lord's supper, transported you, and made you forget your value and concern for the most precious and important doctrines of Jesus Christ, taught you by Mr. Stoddard, which do most nearly concern the very vitals of religion!

I beseech you, brethren, seasonably to consider how dark the cloud is that hangs over you, and how melancholy the prospect (especially with regard to the rising generation) in many respects. I have long been intimately acquainted with your religious circumstances, your notions and principles, your advantages and dangers; having had perhaps greater opportunity for it than any other person on earth.—Before I left you, it was very evident, that *Arminianism*, and other loose notions in religion, and Mr. Taylor's in particular, began to get some footing among you; and there were some things special in your circumstances, that threatened a great prevailing of such like notions: which if they should by degrees generally prevail, will doubtless by degrees put an end to what used to be called saving religion.

Therefore let me entreat you to take the friendly warning I now give you, and stand on your guard against the encroaching evil. If you are not inclined to hearken to me, from any remaining affection to one whose voice and counsels you once heard with joy, and yielded to with great alacrity; yet let me desire you not to refuse, as you would act the part of friends to yourselves and your dear children.

I am,

Dear Brethren,

He who was once (as I hope through grace)

Your faithful pastor,

And devoted servant for Jesus' sake,

J. E.

A HISTORY

OF THE

WORK OF REDEMPTION,

CONTAINING

THE OUTLINES OF A BODY OF DIVINITY,

INCLUDING

A VIEW OF CHURCH HISTORY,

IN A METHOD ENTIRELY NEW.

PREFACE.

It has long been desired by the friends of Mr. Edwards, that a number of his manuscripts should be published; but the disadvantage under which all posthumous publications must necessarily appear, and the difficulty of getting any considerable work printed in this infant country hitherto, have proved sufficient obstacles to the execution of such a proposal. The first of these obstacles made me doubt, for a considerable time after these manuscripts came into my hands, whether I could, consistently with that regard which I owe to the honour of so worthy a parent, suffer any of them to appear in the world. However, being diffident of my own sentiments, and doubtful whether I were not over-jealous in this matter, I determined to submit to the opinion of gentlemen, who are friends both to the character of Mr. Edwards and to the cause of truth. The consequence was, that they gave their advice for publishing them.

The other obstacle was removed by a gentleman in the church of Scotland, who was formerly a correspondent of Mr. Edwards. He engaged a bookseller to undertake the work, and also signified his desire that these following discourses in particular might be made public.

Mr. Edwards had planned a body of divinity, in a new method, and in the form of a history; in which he was first to show how the most remarkable events, in all ages from the fall to the present times, recorded in sacred and profane history, were adapted to promote the work of redemption; and then to trace, by the light of scripture prophecy, how the same work should be yet further carried on even to the end of the world. His heart was so much set on executing this plan, that he was considerably averse to accept the presidentship of Prince-town college, lest the duties of that office should put it out of his power.

The outlines of that work are now offered to the public, as contained in a series of sermons, preached at Northampton in 1739,* without any view to publication. On that account, the reader cannot reasonably expect all that from them, which he might justly have expected, had they been written with such a view, and prepared by the author's own hand for the press.

As to elegance of composition, which is now esteemed so essential to all publications, it is well known, that the author did not make that his chief study. However, his other writings, though destitute of the ornaments of fine language, have it seems that solid merit, which has procured both to themselves and to him a considerable reputation in the world, and with many, a high esteem. It is hoped that the reader will find in these discourses many traces of plain good sense, sound reasoning, and thorough knowledge of the sacred oracles, and real unfeigned piety: and that, as the plan is new, and many of the sentiments uncommon, they may afford entertainment and improvement to the ingenious, the inquisitive, and the pious reader; may confirm their faith in God's government of the world, in our holy christian religion in general, and in many of its peculiar doctrines; may assist in studying with greater pleasure and advantage the historical and prophetical books of Scripture; and may excite to a conversation becoming the gospel.

That this volume may produce these happy effects in all who shall peruse it, is the hearty desire and prayer of

The reader's most humble servant,

JONATHAN EDWARDS.

Newhaven, Feb. 25, 1773.

ADVERTISEMENT.

They who have a relish for the study of the Scriptures, and have access to peruse the following sheets, will, I am persuaded, deem themselves indebted to the Rev. Mr. Edwards of Newhaven, for consenting to publish them. Though the acute philosopher and deep divine appears in them, yet they are in the general better calculated for the instruction and improvement of ordinary Christians, than those of President Edwards's writings, where the abstruse nature of the subject, or the subtle objections of opposers of the truth, led him to more abstract and metaphysical reasonings. The manuscript being intrusted to my care, I have not presumed to make any change in the sentiments or composition. I have, however, taken the liberty to reduce it from the form of sermons, which it originally bore, to that of a continued treatise; and I have so altered and diversified the marks of the several divisions and subdivisions, that each class of heads might be easily distinguished.

JOHN ERSKINE.

Edinburgh, April 29, 1774.

* This is necessary to be remembered by the reader, in order to understand some chronological observations in the following work.

A HISTORY

OF THE

WORK OF REDEMPTION.

GENERAL INTRODUCTION.

ISAIAH li. 8.

For the moth shall eat them up like a garment, and the worm shall eat them like wool: but my righteousness shall be for ever, and my salvation from generation to generation.

THE design of this chapter is to comfort the church under her sufferings, and the persecutions of her enemies; and the argument of consolation insisted on, is the constancy and perpetuity of God's mercy and faithfulness towards her, which shall be manifest in continuing to work salvation for her, protecting her against all assaults of her enemies, and carrying her safely through all the changes of the world, and finally, crowning her with victory and deliverance.

In the text, this happiness of the church of God is set forth by comparing it with the contrary fate of her enemies that oppress her. And therein we may observe,

I. How short-lived the power and prosperity of the church's enemies is: "The moth shall eat them up like a garment, and the worm shall eat them like wool;" *i. e.* however great their prosperity is, and however great their present glory, they shall by degrees consume and vanish away by a secret curse of God, till they come to nothing; and all their power and glory, and so their persecutions, eternally cease, and they be finally and irrecoverably ruined: as the finest and most glorious apparel will in time wear away, and be consumed by moths and rottenness. We learn who those are that shall thus consume away, by the foregoing verse, *viz.* those that are the enemies of God's people: "Hearken unto me, ye that know righteousness, the people in whose heart is my law, fear ye not the reproach of men, neither be ye afraid of their revilings.

II. The contrary happy lot and portion of God's church; expressed in these words, "My righteousness shall be for ever, and my salvation from generation to generation." Who shall have the benefit of this, we also learn by the preceding verse, *viz.* They *that know righteousness*, and *the people in whose heart is God's law;* or, in one word, the church of God. And concerning their happiness, we may observe, wherein it consists; in its continuance.

1. Wherein it CONSISTS, *viz.* In God's righteousness and salvation towards them. By God's righteousness here, is meant his faithfulness in fulfilling his covenant promises to his church, or his faithfulness towards his church and people, in bestowing the benefits of the covenant of grace upon them. Though these benefits are bestowed of free and sovereign grace, as being altogether undeserved; yet as God has been pleased, by the promises of the covenant of grace, to bind himself to bestow them, they are bestowed in the exercise of God's righteousness or justice. And therefore the apostle says, Heb. vi. 10. "God is not unrighteous, to forget your work and labour of love." And 1 John i. 9. "If we confess our sins, he is faithful and just to forgive us our sins, and to cleanse us from all unrighteousness." So the word *righteousness* is very often used in Scripture for God's covenant faithfulness; as in Nehem. ix. 8. "Thou hast performed thy words, for thou art righteous." So we are often to understand righteousness and covenant mercy for the same thing; as Psal. xxiv. 5. "He shall receive the blessing from the Lord, and righteousness from the God of his salvation." Psal. xxxvi. 10. "Continue thy loving-kindness to them that know thee, and thy righteousness to the upright in heart." And Psal. li. 14. "Deliver me from blood-guiltiness, O God, thou God of my salvation; and my tongue shall sing aloud of thy righteousness." Dan. ix. 16. "O Lord, according to thy righteousness, I beseech thee, let thine anger and thy fury be turned away."—And so in innumerable other places.

The other word here used is *salvation.* Of these two, God's righteousness and his salvation, the one is the cause, of which the other is the effect. God's righteousness, or covenant mercy, is the root, of which his salvation is the fruit. Both of them relate to the covenant of grace. The one is God's covenant mercy and faithfulness, the other intends that work of God by which this covenant mercy is accomplished in the fruits of it. For salvation is the sum of all those works of God by which the benefits that are by the covenant of grace are procured and bestowed.

2. We may observe its *continuance*, signified here by two expressions; *for ever*, and *from generation to generation.* The latter seems to be explanatory of the former. The phrase *for ever*, is variously used in Scripture. Sometimes thereby is meant *as long as a man lives.* It is said, that the servant who had his ear bored through with an awl to the door of his master should be his *for ever.* Sometimes thereby is meant during the *continuance of the Jewish state.* Of many of the ceremonial and Levitical laws it is said, that they should be statutes *for ever.* Sometimes it means *as long as the world shall stand*, or to the end of the generations of men. Thus, Eccles. i. 4. "One generation passeth away, and another cometh; but the earth abideth for ever." Sometimes thereby is meant *to all eternity.* So it is said, "God is blessed for ever," Rom. i. 25. And so it is said, John vi. 51. "If any man eat of this bread, he shall live *for ever.*"—And which of these senses is here to be understood, the next words determine, *viz. to the end of the world*, or to the end of the generations of men. It is said in the next words, "and my salvation *from generation to generation.*" Indeed the *fruits* of God's salvation shall remain after the end of the world, as appears by the 6th verse: "Lift up your eyes to the heavens, and look upon the earth beneath: for the heavens shall vanish away like smoke, and the earth shall wax old like a garment, and they that dwell therein shall die in like manner, but my salvation shall be for ever, and my righteousness shall not be abolished." But the work of salvation itself toward the church shall continue to be wrought till then: till the end of the world God will go on to accomplish deliverance and salvation for the church, from all her enemies; for that is what the prophet is here speaking of. *Till the end of the world;* till her enemies cease to be, as to any power to molest the church. And this expression *from generation to generation*, may deter-

mine us as to the time which God continues to carry on the work of salvation for his church, both with respect to the beginning and end. It is from generation to generation, *i. e.* throughout all generations; beginning with the generations of men on the earth, and not ending till these generations end.—And therefore we deduce from these words this

DOCTRINE.

The work of redemption is a work that God carries on from the fall of man to the end of the world.

The generations of mankind on the earth which began after the fall, by ordinary generation, are partakers of the corruption of nature that followed from it; and these generations, by which the human race is propagated, shall continue to the end of the world. These two are the limits of the generations of men on the earth; the fall of man, and the end of the world, or the day of judgment. The same are the limits of the work of redemption, as to those progressive works of God, by which that redemption is brought about and accomplished, though not as to the *fruits* of it; for they shall be to eternity.

The work of redemption and the work of salvation are the same thing. What is sometimes in Scripture called God's *saving* his people, is in other places called his *redeeming* them. So Christ is called both the *Saviour* and the *Redeemer* of his people.

Before entering on the proposed History of the Work of Redemption, I would explain the *terms* made use of in the doctrine;—and show what those *things* are that are designed to be accomplished by this great work of God.

First. I would show in what sense the terms of the doctrine are used;—particularly the word *redemption;*—and, how this is a work of God, carried on from the fall of man to the end of the world.

I. The use of the word *redemption.*—And here it may be observed, that the work of redemption is sometimes understood in a more *limited* sense, for the *purchase* of salvation; for the word strictly signifies, a purchase of deliverance. If we take the word in this *restrained* sense, the work of redemption was not so long in doing; but was begun and finished with Christ's humiliation. It was begun with Christ's incarnation, carried on through his life, and finished with the time of his remaining under the power of death, which ended in his resurrection. And so we say, that on the day of his resurrection Christ finished the work of redemption, *i. e.* then the purchase was finished, and the work itself, and all that appertained to it, was *virtually* done and finished, but not *actually.*

But sometimes the work of redemption is taken more *largely*, as including all that God accomplishes tending to this end; not only the purchase itself, but also all God's works that were properly preparatory to the purchase, and accomplishing the success of it. So that the whole dispensation, as it includes the preparation and purchase, the application and success of Christ's redemption, is here called the work of *redemption.* All that Christ does in this great affair as Mediator, in any of his offices, either of prophet, priest, or king; either when he was in this world, in his human nature, or before, or since. And it includes not only what Christ the Mediator has done, but also what the Father, or the Holy Ghost, have done, as united or confederated in this design of redeeming sinful men; or, in one word, all that is wrought in execution of the external covenant of redemption. This is what I call the work of redemption in the *doctrine;* for it is all but one work, one design. The various dispensations or works that belong to it, are but the several parts of one scheme. It is but one design that is formed, to which all the offices of Christ directly tend, and in which all the persons of the Trinity conspire. All the various dispensations that belong to it are united; and the several wheels are one machine, to answer one end, and produce one effect.

II. When I say, this work is *carried on* from the fall of man to the end of the world; in order to the full understanding of my meaning in it, I would desire two or three things to be observed.

1. That it is not meant, that nothing was done in order to it *before* the fall of man. Some things were done before the world was created, yea from eternity. The persons of the Trinity were, as it were, confederated in a design, and a covenant of redemption. In this covenant the Father had appointed the Son, and the Son had undertaken the work; and all things to be accomplished in the work were stipulated and agreed. There were things done at the *creation* of the world, in order to that work; for the world itself seems to have been created in order to it. The work of creation was in order to God's works of providence. So that if it be inquired, which are greatest, the works of creation or those of providence? I answer, the works of providence; because those of providence are the *end* of his works of creation; as the building of a house, or the forming of a machine, is for its *use.* But God's main work of providence is this of redemption, as will more fully appear hereafter.

The creation of heaven was in order to the work of redemption; as a habitation for the redeemed; Matt. xxv. 34. "Then shall the King say unto them on his right, Come, ye blessed of my Father, inherit the kingdom prepared for you from the foundation of the world." Even the *angels* were created to be employed in this work. And therefore the apostle calls them, "ministering spirits, sent forth to minister for them who shall be heirs of salvation," Heb. i. 14. As to this *lower world*, it was doubtless created to be a stage upon which this great and wonderful work of redemption should be transacted: and therefore, as might be shown, in many respects this lower world is wisely fitted, in its formation, for such a state of man as he is in since the fall, under a possibility of redemption. So that when it is said, that the work of redemption is carried on from the fall of man to the end of the world, it is not meant, that all that ever was done in order to redemption has been done since the fall. Nor,

2. Is it meant that there will be no remaining fruits of this work *after* the end of the world. That glory and blessedness that will be the sum of all the fruits, will remain to all the saints for ever. The work of redemption is not a work always doing and never accomplished. The *fruits* of it are eternal, but the *work* has an issue. In the issue the end will be obtained; which end will last for ever. As those things which were in order to this work—God's electing love, and the covenant of redemption—never had a beginning; so the fruits of this work never will have an end. And therefore,

3. When it is said in the doctrine, that this is a work that God is *carrying on* from the fall of man to the end of the world, what I mean is, that those things which belong to this work itself, and are parts of the scheme, are all this while accomplishing. There were some things done preparatory to its beginning, and the fruits of it will remain after it is finished. But the work itself was begun immediately upon the fall, and will continue to the end of the world. The various dispensations of God during this space, belong to the same work, and to the same design, and have all one issue; and therefore are all to be reckoned but as several successive motions of one machine, to bring about in the conclusion one great event.

And here also we must distinguish between the parts of *redemption* itself, and the parts of the *work* by which that redemption is wrought out. There is a difference between the parts of the *benefits*, and the parts of the *work* of God by which those benefits were procured and bestowed. For example, the redemption of Israel out of Egypt, considered as the benefit which they enjoyed, consisted of two parts, *viz.* their deliverance from their former Egyptian bondage and misery, and their being brought into a more happy state, as the servants of God, and heirs of Canaan. But there are many more things which are *parts* of that work. To this belongs his calling of Moses, his sending him to Pharaoh, and all the signs and wonders he wrought in Egypt, and his bringing such terrible judgments on the Egyptians, and many other things.

Such is this work by which God effects redemption, and it is carried on from the fall of man to the end of the world, in two respects.

1. With respect to the *effect* wrought on the souls of the redeemed; which is common to all ages. This effect is the application of redemption with respect to the souls of

particular persons, in converting, justifying, sanctifying, and glorifying them. By these things they are actually redeemed, and receive the benefit of the work in its effects. And in this sense the work of redemption is carried on in all ages, from the fall of man to the end of the world. The work of God in converting souls, opening blind eyes, unstopping deaf ears, raising dead souls to life, and rescuing the miserable captives out of the hands of Satan, was begun soon after the fall of man, has been carried on in the world ever since to this day, and will be to the end of the world. God has always had such a church in the world. Though oftentimes it has been reduced to a very narrow compass, and to low circumstances; yet it has never wholly failed.

And as God carries on the work of converting the souls of fallen men through all ages, so he goes on to justify them, to blot out all their sins, and to accept them as righteous in his sight, through the righteousness of Christ. He goes on to adopt and receive them from being the children of Satan, to be his own children; to carry on the work of his grace which he has begun in them, to comfort them with the consolations of his Spirit, and to bestow upon them, when their bodies die, that eternal glory which is the fruit of Christ's purchase. What is said, Rom. viii. 30. "Whom he did predestinate, them he also called; and whom he called, them he also justified; and whom he justified, them he also glorified:" is applicable to all ages, from the fall to the end of the world.

And the way of effecting this, is carried on by repeating continually the same work over again, though in different persons, from age to age. But,

2. The work of redemption with respect to the grand design in general, as it respects the universal subject and end, is carried on—not merely by repeating or renewing the same effect in the different subjects of it, but—by many successive works and dispensations of God, all tending to one great effect, united as the several parts of a scheme, and all together making up one great work. Like a temple that is building; first, the workmen are sent forth, then the materials are gathered, the ground is fitted, and the foundation laid; then the superstructure is erected, one part after another, till at length the top-stone is laid, and all is finished. Now the work of redemption in this large sense, may be compared to such a building. God began it immediately after the fall, and will proceed to the end of the world. Then shall the top-stone be brought forth, and all will appear complete and glorious.

This work is carried on in the *former* respect, as being an effect common to all ages; and in the *latter* respect—the grand design in general—not only by that which is common to all ages, but by successive works wrought in different ages. All are parts of one great scheme, whereby one work is brought about by various steps, one step in one age, and another in another. It is this last that I shall chiefly insist upon, though not excluding the former; for one necessarily supposes the other.

Having thus explained what I mean by the *terms* of the doctrine; I now proceed,

SECONDLY, to show what is the *design* of this great work, or what *things* are designed to be accomplished by it. In order to see how any design is carried on, we must first know what it is. To know for instance, how a workman proceeds, and to understand the various steps he takes in order to accomplish a piece of work, we need to be informed what he *intends* to accomplish; otherwise we may stand by, seeing him do one thing after another, and be quite puzzled, because we see nothing of his scheme. Suppose an architect, with a great number of hands, were building some great palace; and one that was a stranger to such things should stand by, and see some men digging in the earth, others bringing timber, others hewing stones, and the like, he might see that there was a great deal done; but if he knew not the *design*, it would all appear to him confusion. And therefore, that the great works and dispensations of God which belong to this great affair of redemption may not appear like confusion to you, I would set before you briefly the *main things* designed to be accomplished.

I. It is to put all God's enemies under his feet, and that his goodness may finally appear triumphant over all evil. Soon after the world was created, evil entered into the world in the fall of the angels and man. Presently after God had made rational creatures, there were enemies who rose up against him from among them; and in the fall of man evil entered into this lower world; where also God's enemies rose up against him. Satan endeavoured to frustrate his design in the creation of this lower world, to destroy his workmanship, to wrest the government of it out of his hands, to usurp the throne, and set up himself as the God of this world, instead of him who made it. To these ends he introduced sin into the world; and having made man God's enemy, he introduced guilt, and death, and the most dreadful misery.

Now one great design of God, in the affair of redemption, was to subdue those enemies: 1 Cor. xv. 25. "He must reign till he hath put all enemies under his feet." Things were originally so planned, that he might disappoint, confound, and triumph over Satan; and that he might be bruised under Christ's feet, Gen. iii. 15. The promise was given, that the seed of the woman should bruise the serpent's head. It was a part of God's original design in this work, to destroy the works of the devil, and confound him in all his purposes: 1 John iii. 8. "For this purpose was the Son of God manifested, that he might destroy the works of the devil." It was a part of his design, to triumph over sin, and over the corruptions of men, and to root them out of the hearts of his people, by conforming them to himself. He designed also, that his grace should triumph over man's guilt, and sin's infinite demerit. Again, it was a part of his design, to triumph over death; and however this is the last enemy that shall be destroyed, yet that shall finally be vanquished and destroyed. Thus God appears glorious above all evil, and triumphant over all his enemies by the work of redemption.

II. God's design was perfectly to restore all the ruins of the fall, so far as concerns the elect part of the world, by his Son; and therefore we read of the *restitution of all things*, Acts iii. 21. "Whom the heaven must receive, until the times of the restitution of all things; and of the times of refreshing from the presence of the Lord Jesus." Acts iii. 19. "Repent ye therefore and be converted, that your sins may be blotted out, when the times of refreshing shall come from the presence of the Lord."

Man's *soul* was ruined by the fall; the image of God was defaced; man's nature was corrupted, and he became dead in sin. The design of God was, to restore the soul of man to life and the divine image in conversion, to carry on the change in sanctification, and to perfect it in glory. Man's body was ruined; by the fall it became subject to death. The design of God was, to restore it from this ruin, and not only to deliver it from death in the resurrection, but to deliver it from mortality itself, in making it like unto Christ's glorious body. The *world* was ruined, as to man, as effectually as if it had been reduced to *chaos* again; all heaven and earth were overthrown. But the design of God was, to restore all, and as it were to create a new heaven and a new earth: Isa. lxv. 17. "Behold, I create new heavens, and a new earth; and the former shall not be remembered, nor come into mind." 2 Pet. iii. 13. "Nevertheless we, according to his promise, look for new heavens, and a new earth, wherein dwelleth righteousness."

The work by which this was to be done, was begun immediately after the fall, and so is carried on till all is finished, when the whole world, heaven and earth, shall be restored. There shall be, as it were, new heavens, and a new earth, in a spiritual sense, at the end of the world. Thus it is represented, Rev. xxi. 1. "And I saw a new heaven, and a new earth; for the first heaven and the first earth were passed away."

III. Another great design of God in the work of redemption, was to gather together in one all things in Christ, in heaven and in earth, *i. e.* all elect creatures; to bring all elect creatures, in heaven and in earth, to an union one to another in one body, under one head, and to unite all together in one body to God the Father. This was begun soon after the fall, and is carried on through all ages, and shall be finished at the end of the world.

IV. God designed by this work to perfect and complete the *glory* of all the elect by Christ—glory, "such as eye hath not seen, nor ear heard, nor has ever entered into the heart of man." He intended to bring them to perfect excellency and beauty in his holy image, which is the proper beauty of spiritual beings; and to advance them to a glorious degree of honour, and raise them to an ineffable height of pleasure and joy. Thus he designed to glorify the whole church of elect men in soul and body, and with them to bring the glory of the elect angels to its highest elevation under one head.

V. In all this God designed to accomplish the glory of the blessed Trinity in an eminent degree. God had a design of glorifying himself from eternity; yea, to glorify each person in the Godhead. The *end* must be considered as first in order of nature, and then the means; and therefore we must conceive, that God having professed this end, had then as it were the means to choose; and the principal mean that he adopted was this great work of redemption. It was his design in this work to glorify his only-begotten Son, Jesus Christ; and by the Son to glorify the Father: John xiii. 31, 32. "Now is the Son of man glorified, and God is glorified in him. If God be glorified in him, God also shall glorify him in himself, and shall straightway glorify him." It was his design that the Son should thus be glorified, and should glorify the Father by what should be accomplished by the Spirit to the glory of the Spirit, that the whole Trinity, conjunctly, and each person singly, might be exceedingly glorified. The work that was the appointed means of this, was begun immediately after the fall, and is carried on till, and finished at, the end of the world, when all this intended glory shall be fully accomplished in all things

HAVING thus explained the *terms* in the doctrine, and shown what *things* are to be accomplished by this great work of God, I proceed now to the proposed history; that is, to show how what was designed by the work of redemption has been accomplished, in the *various steps* of this work, from the fall of man to the end of the world.

In order to this, I would divide this whole space of time into three periods:——the

1st, reaching from the fall of man to the incarnation of Christ;—the

2d, from Christ's incarnation till his resurrection; or the whole time of Christ's humiliation;—the

3d, from thence to the end of the world.

Some may be ready to think this a very unequal division; and so indeed it is in some respects, because the second period, although so much shorter than either of the other—being but between thirty and forty years, whereas both the other contain thousands—in this affair is more than both the others.—I would therefore proceed to show distinctly how the work of redemption is carried on through each of these periods in their order, under three propositions.

I. That from the fall of man to the incarnation of Christ, God was doing those things which were preparatory to his coming, as forerunners and earnests of it.

II. That the time from Christ's incarnation to his resurrection, was spent in procuring and purchasing redemption.

III. That the space of time from the resurrection of Christ to the end of the world, is all taken up in bringing about or accomplishing the great effect or success of that purpose.

In a particular consideration of these three propositions, the great truth taught in the doctrine may perhaps appear in a clear light.

PERIOD I.

FROM THE FALL TO THE INCARNATION.

THE great works of God in the world during this whole space of time, were all preparatory. There were many great changes and revolutions in the world, and they were all only the turning of the wheels of providence to make way for the coming of Christ, and what he was to do in the world. Hither tended especially all God's great works towards his church. The church was under various dispensations of providence, and in very various circumstances, before Christ came; but all these dispensations were to prepare the way for his coming. God wrought salvation for the souls of men through all that space of time, though the number was very small to what it was afterwards; and all this was by way of anticipation. All the souls that were saved before Christ came, were only the earnests of the future harvest.

God wrought many deliverances for his church and people before Christ came; but these were only so many images and forerunners of the great salvation. The church during that space of time enjoyed the light of divine revelation. They had in a degree the light of the gospel. But all these revelations were only so many earnests of the great light that he should bring who came to be the light of the world. That whole space of time was the time of night, wherein the church of God was not indeed wholly without light; but it was like the light of the moon and stars; a dim light in comparison of the light of the sun, and mixed with a great deal of darkness. It had no glory by reason of the glory that excelleth, 2 Cor. iii. 10. The church had indeed the light of the sun, but it was only as reflected from the moon and stars. The church all that while was a minor. Gal. iv. 1—3. "Now I say, that the heir as long as he is a child, differeth nothing from a servant, though he be lord of all; but is under tutors and governors, until the time appointed of the Father. Even so we, when we were children, were in bondage under the elements of the world."

But here, for the greater clearness and distinctness, I shall subdivide this period into parts:

1st, From the fall to the flood.
2d, From thence to the calling of Abraham.
3d, From thence to Moses.
4th, From thence to David.
5th, From David to the captivity in Babylon.
6th, From thence to the incarnation of Christ.

PART I.

FROM THE FALL TO THE FLOOD.

THOUGH this period was the most distant from Christ's incarnation; yet then was this glorious building begun.

I. As soon as man fell, Christ entered on his mediatorial work. Then it was that he began to execute the work and office of a mediator. He had undertaken it before the world was made. He stood engaged with the Father to appear as man's mediator, and to take on that office when there should be occasion, from all eternity. But now the time was come. Christ the eternal Son of God clothed himself with the mediatorial character, and therein presented himself before the Father. He immediately stepped in between a holy, infinite, offended Majesty, and offending mankind. He was accepted in his interposition; and so wrath was prevented from going forth in the full execution of that amazing curse that man had brought on himself.

It is manifest that Christ began to exercise the office of *mediator* between God and man as soon as ever man fell, because mercy began to be exercised towards man immediately. There was mercy in the forbearance of God, that he did not destroy him, as he did the angels when they fell. But there is no mercy exercised toward fallen man but through a mediator. If God had not in mercy restrained Satan, he would immediately have seized on his prey. Christ began to do the part of an *intercessor* for man as soon as he fell; for there is no mercy exercised towards man but what is obtained through Christ's intercession. From that day Christ took on him the care of the church, in the exercise of all his offices. He undertook to *teach* mankind in the exercise of his *prophetical* office; to *intercede* for fallen man in his *priestly* office; and to *govern* the church and the world as a king. He from that time took upon him the care of defending his elect church from all their enemies. When Satan, the grand enemy, had conquered and overthrown man, the business of resisting and conquering him was committed to Christ. He thenceforward undertook to manage that subtle powerful adversary. He was then appointed the Captain of the Lord's hosts, the Captain of their salvation. Henceforward this lower world, with all its concerns, devolved upon the Son of God: for when man had sinned, God the Father would have no more to do *immediately* with this world of mankind, that had apostatized from and rebelled against him. He would henceforward act only through a mediator, either in teaching men, or in governing, or bestowing any benefits on them.

And therefore, when we read in sacred history what God did, from time to time, towards his church and people, and how he revealed himself to them, we are to understand it especially of the second person of the Trinity. When we read of God appearing after the fall, in some visible form or outward symbol of his presence, we are ordinarily, if not universally, to understand it of the second person of the Trinity. John i. 18. "No man hath seen God at any time; the only begotten Son, which is in the bosom of the Father, he hath declared him." He is therefore called "the image of the invisible God," Col. i. 15. intimating, that though God the Father be invisible, yet Christ is his image or representation, by which he is seen.

Yea, not only this lower world devolved on Christ, that he might have the care and government of it, and order it agreeably to his design of redemption, but also in some respect the whole universe. The *angels* from that time are subject to him in his mediatorial office, as is manifest by the scripture history, wherein we have accounts of their acting as ministering spirits in the affairs of the church.

And therefore we may suppose, that immediately on the fall of Adam, it was made known in heaven among the angels, that God had a design of redemption with respect to fallen man; that Christ had now taken upon him the office and work of a mediator between God and man; and that they were to be subservient to him in this office. And as Christ, in this office, has been solemnly installed the King of heaven, and is thenceforward, as God-man, the Light, the Sun of heaven, (agreeable to Rev. xxi. 23.) so this revelation made in heaven among the angels, was as it were the first dawning of this light there. When Christ ascended into heaven after his passion, and was solemnly enthroned, then this Sun rose in heaven, even the Lamb that is the light of the New Jerusalem.

II. Presently upon this the gospel was first revealed on earth, in these words, Gen. iii. 15. "And I will put enmity between thee and the woman, and between thy seed and her seed: it shall bruise thy head, and thou shalt bruise his heel." We must suppose, that God's intention of redeeming fallen man was first signified in heaven, before it was signified on earth, because the business of the angels as ministering spirits of the Mediator required it; for as soon as ever Christ had taken on him the work of a mediator, it was requisite that the angels should be ready immediately to be subservient to him in that office: so that the light first dawned in heaven; but very soon after the same was signified on earth. In those words of God there was an intimation of another surety to be appointed for man, after the first surety had failed. This was the first revelation of the covenant of grace; the first dawning of the light of the gospel on earth.

This lower world before the fall enjoyed noon-day light; the light of the knowledge of God, the light of his glory, and the light of his favour. But when man fell, all this light was at once extinguished, and the world reduced back again to total darkness; a worse darkness than that which was in the beginning of the world, (Gen. i. 2.) *Darkness was upon the face of the deep*, a darkness a thousand times more remediless than that. Neither men nor angels could find out any way whereby this darkness might be scattered. It appeared in its blackness when *Adam* and his wife saw that they were naked, and sewed fig-leaves; when they heard the voice of the Lord God, walking in the garden, and hid themselves among the trees. When God first called them to an account, and said to *Adam*, "What is this that thou hast done? Hast thou eaten of the tree, whereof I commanded thee, that thou shouldst not eat?" Then we may suppose that their hearts were filled with shame and terror. But these words of God, (Gen. iii. 15.) were the first dawning of gospel light, after this dismal darkness. Before this there was not one glimpse of light, any beam of comfort, or the least hope. It was an obscure yet comprehensive revelation of the gospel; not indeed made to *Adam* or *Eve* directly, but contained in what God said to the serpent.

Here was a certain intimation of a merciful design by "the seed of the woman," which was like the first glimmerings of the light in the east when the day first dawns. This intimation of mercy was given, even before sentence was pronounced on either *Adam* or *Eve*, from tenderness to them, lest they should be overborne with a sentence of condemnation, without having any thing held forth whence they could gather any hope.

One of those great things that were intended to be done by the work of redemption, is more plainly intimated, *viz.* God subduing his enemies under the feet of his Son. God's design of this was now first declared. Satan probably had triumphed greatly in the fall of man, as though he had defeated the designs of God in his creation. But in these words God gives him a plain intimation, that he should not finally triumph, but that a complete victory and triumph should be obtained over him by the seed of the woman.

This revelation of the gospel was the first thing that Christ did in his prophetical office. From the fall of man to the incarnation of Christ, God was doing those things that were preparatory to Christ's coming to effect redemption, and were forerunners and earnests of it. And one of those things was to foretell and promise it, as he did from age to age, till Christ came. This was the first promise given, the first prediction that ever was made of it.

III. Soon after this, the custom of sacrificing was appointed, to be a standing type of the sacrifice of Christ, till he should come, and offer up himself a sacrifice to God. Sacrificing was not a custom first established by the Levitical law, for it had been a part of God's instituted worship from the beginning. We read of the patriarchs, Abraham, Isaac, and Jacob, offering sacrifice, and before them Noah, and Abel. And this was by divine appointment; for it was part of God's worship in his church, which was offered up in faith, and which he accepted. This proves that it was by his institution; for sacrificing is no part of natural worship. The light of nature doth not teach men to offer up beasts in sacrifice to God; and seeing it was not enjoined by the law of nature, to be acceptable to God, it must be by some positive command or institution; for God has declared his abhorrence of such worship as is taught by the precept of men without his institution. (Isa. xxix. 13.) And such worship as hath not a warrant from divine institution, cannot be offered up in faith, because faith has no foundation where there is no divine appointment. Men have no warrant to hope for God's acceptance, in that which is not of his appointment, and in that to which he hath not promised his acceptance: and therefore it follows, that the custom of offering sacrifices to God was instituted soon after the fall; for the Scripture teaches us, that Abel offered "the firstlings of his flock, and of the fat thereof," Gen. iv. 4. and that he was accepted of God in this offering, Heb. xi. 4. And there is nothing in the story intimating that the institution was first given when Abel offered up that sacrifice to God; but rather that Abel only complied with a custom already established.

It is very probable that sacrifice was instituted immediately after God had revealed the covenant of grace, (Gen. iii. 15.) as the foundation on which the custom of sacrificing was built. That promise was the first stone laid towards this glorious building, the work of redemption; and the next stone, the institution of sacrifices, to be a type of the *great sacrifice*.

The next thing that we have an account of, after God had pronounced sentence on the serpent, on the woman, and on the man, was, that God made them coats of skins, and clothed them; which, by the generality of divines, are thought to be the skins of beasts slain in sacrifice. For we have no account of any thing else that should be the occasion of man's slaying beasts, except to offer them in sacrifice, till after the flood. Men were not wont to eat the flesh of beasts as their common food till after the flood. The first food of man before the fall, was the fruit of the trees of paradise; and after the fall, his food was the produce of the field: Gen. iii. 18. "And thou shalt eat the herb of the field." The first grant that he had to eat flesh, as his common food, was after the flood: Gen. ix. 3. "Every moving thing that liveth shall be meat for you; even as the green herb have I given you all things." So that it is likely that these skins with which Adam and Eve were clothed, were the skins of their sacrifices. God's clothing them with these was a lively figure of their being clothed with the righteousness of Christ. It was God that gave them this clothing; for it is said, *God made them coats of skins, and clothed them.* The righteousness with which we are clothed, is of God. It is he only clothes the naked soul.

Our first parents, who were naked, were clothed at the expense of life. Beasts were slain, in order to afford them clothing. So doth Christ, to afford clothing to our naked souls. The tabernacle in the wilderness, which signified the church, was covered with rams' skins died red, as though they were dipped in blood, to signify that Christ's righteousness was wrought out through the pains of death, under which he shed his precious blood.

We observed before, that the light that the church enjoyed from the fall of man, till Christ came, was like the light which we enjoy in the night; not the light of the sun directly, but as reflected from the moon and other luminaries; which light prefigured Christ, the Sun of righteousness that was afterwards to arise. This light they had chiefly two ways; one was by predictions of Christ to come; the other was by types and shadows, whereby his coming and redemption were prefigured. The first thing that was done to prepare the way for Christ in the former of these ways, was in that promise noticed in the foregoing particular; and the first thing of the latter kind, was that institution of sacrifices that we are now upon. As that promise in Gen. iii. 15. was the first dawn of gospel-light after the fall in *prophecy;* so the institution of *sacrifices* was the first hint of it in types. The former was done in pursuance of Christ's prophetical office; in the latter, Christ exhibited himself in his priestly office.

The institution of sacrifices was a great thing done towards preparing the way for Christ's coming, and working out redemption. For the sacrifices of the Old Testament were the main of all the Old-Testament types of Christ and his redemption; and it tended to establish in the minds of God's visible church the necessity of a a propitiatory sacrifice, in order to the Deity's being satisfied for sin; and so prepared the way for the reception of the glorious gospel, that reveals the great sacrifice in the visible church, and not only so, but through the world of mankind. For from this institution of sacrifices all nations derived the custom of sacrificing to the gods, to atone for their sins. No nation, however barbarous, was found without it. This is a great evidence of the truth of the christian religion; for no nation except the Jews, could tell how they came by this custom, or to what purpose it was to offer sacrifices to their deities. The light of nature did not teach them any such thing. That did not teach them that the gods were hungry, and fed upon the flesh which they burnt in sacrifice; and yet they all had this custom; of which no other account can be given, but that they derived it from Noah, who had it from his ancestors, on whom God had enjoined it as a type of the great sacrifice of Christ. However, by this means all nations of the world had their minds possessed with this notion, that an atonement or sacrifice for sin was necessary; and a way was made for their more readily receiving the great doctrine of the gospel, the atonement and sacrifice of Christ.

IV. God soon after the fall began actually to *save* the souls of men through Christ's redemption. In this, Christ, who had lately taken upon him the work of mediator between God and man, did first begin that work, wherein he appeared in the exercise of his *kingly* office, as in the sacrifices he was represented in his *priestly* office, and in the first prediction of redemption by Christ he had appeared in the exercise of his *prophetical* office. In that prediction the light of Christ's redemption first began to dawn in the prophecies of it; in the institution of sacrifices it first began to dawn in the *types of it;* in this, *viz.* his beginning actually to save men, it first began to dawn in the *fruit* of it.

It is probable, therefore, that Adam and Eve were the first fruits of Christ's redemption; it is probable by God's manner of treating them, by his comforting them as he did, after their awakenings and terror. They were awakened, and ashamed with a sense of their guilt, after their eyes were opened, and they saw that they were naked, and sewed fig-leaves to cover their nakedness; as the sinner, under the first awakenings, is wont to endeavour to hide the nakedness of his soul, by a fancied righteousness of his own. Then they were further terrified and awakened, by hearing the voice of God as he was coming to condemn them. Their coverings of fig-leaves do not answer the purpose; but notwithstanding these, they ran to hide themselves among the trees of the garden, because they were naked, not daring to trust to their fig-leaves to hide their nakedness from God. Then they were further awakened by God's calling of them to a strict account. But while their terrors were raised to such a height, and they stood, as we may suppose, trembling and astonished before their Judge, without any expedient whence they could gather any hope, then God took care to hold forth some encouragement, to keep them from the dreadful effects of despair under their awakenings, by giving a hint of a design of mercy by a Saviour, even before he pronounced sentence against them. And when after this he proceeded to pronounce sentence, whereby we may suppose their terrors were further raised, God soon after took care to encourage them, and to let them see, that he had not wholly cast them off, by taking a fatherly care of them in their fallen, naked, and miserable state, by making them coats of skins and clothing them. Which also manifested an acceptance of those sacrifices that they offered to God; which were types of what God had promised, when he said, *The seed of the woman shall bruise the serpent's head.* This promise, there is reason to think, they believed and embraced. Eve seems plainly to express her hope in and dependence on that promise, in what she says at the birth of Cain, Gen. iv. 1. "I have gotten a man from the Lord;" *i. e* as God has promised, that my seed should bruise the serpent's head; so now has God given me this pledge and token of it, and I have a seed born. She plainly owns, that this child was from God, and hoped that her promised seed was to be of this, her eldest son; though she was mistaken, as *Abraham* was with respect to *Ishmael*, as *Isaac* was with respect to *Esau*, and as *Samuel* was with respect to the first-born of *Jesse*. And especially does what she said at the birth of Seth, express her hope and dependence on the promise of God; (ver. 25.) "For God hath appointed me another seed, instead of Abel, whom Cain slew."

Thus it is exceeding probable, if not evident, that as Christ took on him the work of mediator as soon as man fell; so that he now immediately began his work of redemption in its *effect*, and that he immediately encountered his great enemy the devil, whom he had undertaken to conquer, and rescued those two first captives out of his hands; therein baffling him, soon after his triumph over them, whereby he had made them his captives. And though he seemed sure of them and all their posterity, Christ the Redeemer soon showed him, that he was mistaken. He let him see it, in delivering those first captives, and so soon gave him an instance of the fulfilment of that threatening, "The seed of the woman shall bruise the serpent's head;" and in this instance a presage of his subduing all his enemies under his feet.

After this we have another instance of redemption in one of their children, righteous Abel, as the Scripture calls him; whose soul perhaps was the first that went to heaven through Christ's redemption. In him we have at least the first recorded instance of the death of a redeemed person. If he was the first, then as the redemption of Christ began to dawn before in the souls of men in their conversion and justification, in him it first began to dawn in glorification; and in him the angels began first to do the part of ministering spirits to Christ, in going forth to conduct to glory the souls of the redeemed. And in him the elect angels in heaven had the first opportunity to see so wonderful a thing as the soul of one of the fallen race of mankind, that had been sunk by the fall into such an abyss of sin and misery, brought to heaven, and in the enjoyment of heavenly glory, which was a much greater thing than if they had seen him returned to the earthly paradise. Thus they saw the glorious effect of Christ's redemption, in the great honour and happiness that was procured for sinful, miserable creatures.

V. The next remarkable thing that God did in further carrying on this great redemption, was the first uncommon pouring out of the Spirit, through Christ, in the days of *Enos.* We read, Gen. iv. 26. "Then began men to call upon the name of the Lord." The meaning of those words has been considerably controverted among divines. We cannot suppose the meaning is, that then first men performed the duty of prayer. Prayer is a duty of natural religion, and a duty to which a spirit of piety does most naturally lead men. Prayer is the very breath of a spirit of piety; we cannot suppose therefore, that holy men before, for above two hundred years, had lived without prayer. Therefore some divines think, that the meaning is, that then men first began to perform public worship, or to call upon the name of the Lord in public assemblies. However, thus much must necessarily be understood by it, *viz.* that there was something *new* in the visible church of God with respect to calling upon the name of the Lord; that there was a great *addition* to the performance of this duty; and that in some respect or other it was carried far beyond what it ever had been before, which must be the consequence of a remarkable pouring out of the Spirit of God.

If it was now first that men were stirred up to meet in assemblies to assist one another in seeking God, so as they never had done before; it argues something extraordinary as the cause, and could be from nothing but the uncommon influences of God's Spirit. We see by experience, that a remarkable pouring out of God's Spirit is always attended with such an effect, *viz.* a great increase of the performance of the duty of prayer. When the Spirit of God begins a work on men's hearts, it immediately sets them to calling on the name of the Lord. As it was with Paul after the Spirit of God had arrested him; *Behold, he prayeth!* so it has been in all remarkable effusions of the Spirit of God recorded in Scripture; and so it is foretold it will be in the latter days. It is foretold, that the Holy Spirit will be poured out as a spirit of grace and supplication, Zech. xii. 10. See also Zeph. iii. 9. "For then will I turn to the people a pure language, that they may all call upon the name of the Lord, to serve him with one consent."

And when it is said, "Then began men to call upon the name of the Lord," no more can be intended by it, than that this was the *first remarkable* season of this nature that ever was. It was the beginning, or the first, of such a work of God. In this manner such an expression is commonly used in Scripture: so, 1 Sam. xiv. 35. "And Saul built an altar unto the Lord; the same was the first altar that he built unto the Lord." In the Hebrew it is, as you may see in the margin, *that altar he began to build unto the Lord.* Heb. ii. 3. "How shall we escape if we neglect so great salvation, which first began to be spoken by the Lord?"

It may here be observed, that from the fall of man, to our day, the work of redemption in its effect has mainly been carried on by remarkable communications of the Spirit of God. Though there be a more constant influence of God's Spirit always in some degree attending his ordinances; yet the way in which the greatest things have been done towards carrying on this work, always have been by remarkable effusions, at special seasons of mercy, as may fully appear hereafter in our further prosecution of our subject. And this in the days of *Enos,* was the first remarkable pouring out of the Spirit of God that ever was. There had been a saving work of God on the hearts of some before; but now God was pleased to bring in a harvest of souls to Christ; so that in this we see that great building, of which God laid the foundation immediately after the fall of man, carried on further, and built higher, than ever it had been before.

VI. The next thing I shall notice, is the eminently holy life of *Enoch,* who, we have reason to think, was a saint of greater eminency than any that had been before him; so that in this respect the work of redemption was carried on to a still greater height. With respect to its effect in the visible church in *general,* we observed above how it was carried higher in the days of *Enos* than ever it had been before. Probably Enoch was one of the saints of that harvest; for he lived all the days that he did live on earth, in the days of *Enos.* And with respect to the *degree* to which this work was carried in the soul of a *particular person,* it was raised to a greater height in Enoch than ever before. His soul, built on Christ, was built up in holiness to a greater height than any preceding instance. He was a wonderful instance of Christ's redemption, and of the efficacy of his grace.

VII. In *Enoch's* time, God more expressly revealed the coming of Christ than he had before done. Jude, ver. 14, 15. "And Enoch also, the seventh from Adam, prophesied of these, saying, Behold, the Lord cometh with ten thousand of his saints, to execute judgment upon all, and to convince all that are ungodly among them, of their ungodly deeds which they have ungodly committed, and of all their hard speeches which ungodly sinners have spoken against him." Here Enoch prophesies of the coming of Christ. It does not seem to be confined to any *particular* coming of Christ; but it has respect in general to Christ's coming in his kingdom, and is fulfilled in a degree in both his first and second coming; and indeed in *every* remarkable manifestation Christ has made of himself in the world, for the saving of his people, and the destroying of his enemies. It is very parallel in this respect with many other prophecies of the Old Testament; and, in particular, with that great prophecy of Christ's coming in his kingdom, whence the Jews principally took their notion of the kingdom of heaven, Daniel vii. 10. "A fiery stream issued, and came forth from before him: thousand thousands ministered unto him, and ten thousand times ten thousand stood before him: the judgment was set, and the books were opened." And ver. 13, 14. "I saw in the night visions, and behold, one like the Son of man, came with the clouds of heaven, and came to the Ancient of days, and they brought him near before him. And there was given him dominion, and glory, and a kingdom, that all people, nations, and languages, should serve him: his dominion is an everlasting dominion, which shall not pass away, and his kingdom that which shall not be destroyed." And though it is not unlikely that *Enoch* might have a more immediate respect in this prophecy to the approaching destruction of the old world by the flood, which was a remarkable resemblance of Christ's destruction of all his enemies at his second coming, yet it doubtless looked beyond the type to the antitype.

And as this prophecy of Christ's coming is more express than any preceding it; so it is an instance of the increase of that gospel-light which began to dawn presently after the fall of man; and of that building which is the subject of our present discourse, being yet further carried on, and built up higher than it had been before.

And here, by the way, I would observe, that the increase of gospel-light, and the progress of the work of redemption, as it respects the church in general, from its erection to the end of the world, is very similar to the progress of the same work and the same light, in a particular soul, from the time of its conversion, till it is perfected and crowned in glory. Sometimes the light shines brighter, and at other times more obscurely; sometimes grace prevails, at other times it seems to languish for a great while together; now corruption prevails, and then grace revives again. But in general grace is growing: from its first infusion, till it is perfected in glory, the kingdom of Christ is building up in the soul. So it is with respect to the great affair in general, as it relates to the universal subject of it, and as it is carried on from its first beginning, till it is perfected at the end of the world.

VIII. The next remarkable thing towards carrying on this work, was the translation of Enoch into heaven. (Gen. v. 24.) "And Enoch walked with God, and he was not; for God took him." Moses, in giving an account of the genealogy of those that were of the line of *Noah*, does not say concerning *Enoch*, he lived so long and he died, as he does of the rest; but, *he was not, for God took him*; *i. e.* he translated him; in body and soul carried him to heaven without dying, as it is explained in Heb. xi. 5. "By faith Enoch was translated that he should not see death." By this wonderful work of God, the work of redemption was carried to a greater height, in several respects, than it had been before.

When showing what God aimed at in the work of redemption, or what were the main things he intended to bring to pass; among other things I mentioned the perfect restoration of the ruins of the fall, with respect to the elect, both in soul and body. Now this translation of *Enoch* was the first instance of restoration with respect to the *body*. There had been many instances of restoring the *soul* of man by Christ's redemption, but none of redeeming and actually saving the body, till now. All the *bodies* of the elect are to be saved as well as their *souls*. At the end of the world, all their bodies shall actually be redeemed; those that then shall have been dead, by a resurrection; and others, that then shall be living, by causing them to undergo a glorious change. There was a number of the bodies of saints raised and glorified, at the resurrection of Christ; and before that there was an instance of a body glorified in Elijah. But the first instance of all was this of Enoch.

By this, the work of redemption was carried on still further; as, this wonderful work of God afforded a great increase of gospel-light to the church, hereby it had a clearer manifestation of a future state, and of the glorious reward of the saints in heaven. We are told, 2 Tim. i. 10. "That life and immortality are brought to light by the gospel." What was said in the Old Testament of a future state, is very obscure, in comparison with the more full, plain, and abundant revelation given of it in the New. But yet even in those early days, the church of God, in this instance, was favoured with an instance of it set before their eyes, in that one of their brethren was actually taken up to heaven without dying; which we have all reason to think the church of God knew then, as they afterwards knew Elijah's translation. And as this was a clearer manifestation of a future state than the church had enjoyed before, so it was a pledge or earnest of that future glorification of all the saints which God intended through the redemption of Jesus Christ.

IX. The next thing that I shall observe, was the upholding of the church of God in that family from which Christ was to proceed during that great and general defection which preceded the flood. The church of God, in all probability, was small, in comparison with the rest of the world, from the time that mankind began to multiply; or from the time, (Gen iv. 16.) "When Cain went out from the presence of the Lord, and dwelt in the land of Nod;" which being interpreted, is the land of *banishment*. The church seems to have been kept up chiefly in the posterity of *Seth*: for this was the seed that God appointed instead of *Abel* whom *Cain* slew. But we cannot reasonably suppose that *Seth's* posterity were one fiftieth part of the world: "For Adam was one hundred and thirty years old when Seth was born." But *Cain*, who seems to have been the leader of those that were not of the church, was *Adam's* eldest child, and probably was born soon after the fall, which doubtless was soon after *Adam's* creation; so that there was time for *Cain* to have many sons before *Seth* was born; besides many other children, that probably Adam and Eve had before this time, agreeably to God's blessing, "Be fruitful, and multiply, and replenish the earth;" and many of these children might have children. The history of *Cain* before *Seth* was born, seems to imply, that there were great numbers of men on the earth: Gen. iv. 14, 15. "Behold, thou hast driven me out this day from the face of the earth: and from thy face shall I be hid, and I shall be a fugitive and a vagabond in the earth; and it shall come to pass, that every one that findeth me shall slay me. And the Lord said unto him, Therefore whosoever slayeth Cain, vengeance shall be taken on him seven-fold. And the Lord set a mark upon Cain, lest any finding him should kill him." And all who existed when *Seth* was born, must be supposed to stand in equal capacity of multiplying their posterity with him; and therefore, *Seth's* posterity were but a small part of the inhabitants of the world.

But after the days of *Enos* and *Enoch*, (for *Enoch* was translated before *Enos* died,) the church of God greatly diminished, in proportion as multitudes of the line of *Seth*, born in the church of God, fell away, and joined with the wicked world, principally by means of intermarriages with them: as Gen. vi. 1, 2, 4. "And it came to pass, when men began to multiply on the face of the earth, and daughters were born unto them, that the sons of God saw the daughters of men, that they were fair; and they took them wives of all which they chose.—There were giants in the earth in those days; and also after that, when the sons of God came in unto the daughters of men, and they bare children to them, the same became mighty men, which were of old men of renown." By the *sons of God* here, are doubtless meant the children of the church. It is a denomination often given them in Scripture. They intermarried with the wicked world, and so had their hearts led away from God: and there was a great and continual defection from the church. The church, that used to be a restraint on the wicked world, diminished exceedingly, and so wickedness went on without restraint. Satan, that old serpent the devil, that tempted our first parents, and set up himself as the God of this world, raged exceedingly; and every imagination of the thoughts of man's heart was only evil continually, and the earth was filled with violence. It seemed to be deluged with wickedness then, as it was with water afterwards; and mankind in general were swallowed up in it. And now Satan made a most violent and potent attempt to devour the church of God; and had almost done it. But yet God restored it in the midst of all this flood of wickedness and violence. He kept it up in that line of which Christ was to proceed. He would not suffer it to be destroyed, for a blessing was in it. There was a particular family, a root whence the branch of righteousness was afterwards to shoot forth. And therefore, however the branches were lopped off, and the tree seemed to be destroyed; yet God, in the midst of all, kept alive this root, by his wonderful redeeming power and grace, so that the gates of hell could not prevail against it.

Thus I have shown how God carried on the great affair of redemption; how the building went on during this first period, from the fall of man, till God brought the flood on the earth. And I would observe, that though the Mosaic history during that space be very short, yet it is exceedingly comprehensive and instructive. And it may also be profitable for us here to observe, the efficacy of that purchase of redemption which had such great effects so many ages before Christ actually appeared.

PART II.

FROM THE FLOOD TO THE CALLING OF ABRAHAM.

I PROCEED now to show how the same work was carried on *from the beginning of the flood till the calling of Abraham*. For though that mighty, universal deluge overthrew the world: yet it did not overthrow this building of God, the work of redemption. This went on; and instead of being overthrown, continued to be built up, in order to a further preparation for the great Saviour's coming into the world, for the redemption for his people.

I. The flood itself was a work of God that belonged to this great affair, and tended to promote it. All the mighty works of God from the fall of man to the end of the world, are reducible to this work; and if seen in a right view, will appear as parts of it; and so many steps for carrying it on; and doubtless so great a work, so remarkable and universal a catastrophe, as the deluge was, cannot be excepted. Thereby God removed out of the way the enemies and obstacles that were ready to overthrow it.

Satan seems to have been in a dreadful rage just before the flood, and his rage then doubtless was, as it always has been, chiefly against the church of God to overthrow it; and he had filled the earth with violence and rage against it. He had drawn over almost all the world to be on his side, and they listed under his banner against Christ and his church. We read, that *the earth was filled with violence;* and doubtless that violence was chiefly against the church, in fulfilment of what was foretold, *I will put enmity between thy seed and her seed.* Their enmity and violence was so great, and the enemies of the church so numerous, the whole world being against it, that it was come to the last extremity. Noah's reproofs, and his preaching of righteousness, were utterly disregarded. God's Spirit had striven with them a hundred and twenty years, but all in vain; and the church was reduced to so narrow limits, as to be confined to one family. There was no prospect of any thing else but of their totally swallowing up the church, and that in a very little time; and so wholly destroying that small root that had the blessing in it, whence the Redeemer was to proceed.

And therefore, God's destroying those enemies of the church by the flood belongs to this affair of redemption; for it was one thing that was done in fulfilment of the covenant of grace, as it was revealed to *Adam:* "I will put enmity between thee and the woman, and between thy seed and her seed; it shall bruise thy head." This was only a destruction of the seed of the serpent in the midst of their most violent rage against the seed of the woman, when in the utmost peril by them.

We read in Scripture of scarce any destruction of nations but that one main reason given for it is, their enmity and injuries against God's church; and doubtless this was one main reason of the destruction of all nations by the flood. The giants that were in those days, in all likelihood, got themselves renown by their great exploits against heaven, and against Christ and his church, the remaining sons of God that had not corrupted themselves.

We read, that just before the world shall be destroyed by fire, "the nations that are in the four quarters of the earth, shall gather together against the church as the sand of the sea, and shall go up on the breadth of the earth, and compass the camp of the saints about, and the beloved city; and then fire shall come down from God out of heaven, and devour them," Rev. xx. 8, 9. And it seems there was that which was very parallel to it, just before the world was destroyed by water. And therefore their destruction was a work of God that did as much belong to the work of redemption, as the destruction of the *Egyptians* belonged to the redemption of the children of Israel out of Egypt, or as the destruction of Sennacherib's mighty army, that had compassed about Jerusalem to destroy it, belonged to God's redemption of that city from them.

By means of this flood, all the enemies of God's church, against whom that little handful had no strength, were swept off at once. God took their part, appeared for them against their enemies, and drowned those of whom they had been afraid, in the flood of water, as he drowned the enemies of Israel that pursued them in the Red sea.

Indeed God could have taken other methods to deliver his church: he could have converted all the world instead of drowning it; and so he could have taken another method than drowning the *Egyptians* in the Red sea. But that is no argument, that the method he did take, was not a method to show his redeeming mercy to them.

By the deluge the enemies of God's people were dispossessed of the earth, and the whole earth was given to Noah and his family to possess it in quiet; as God made room for the *Israelites* in *Canaan*, by casting out their enemies from before them. And God thus taking the possession of the enemies of the church, and giving it all to his church, was agreeable to that promise of the covenant of grace: Ps. xxxvii. 9—11. "For evil-doers shall be cut off: but those that wait upon the Lord, they shall inherit the earth. For yet a little while and the wicked shall not be: yea, thou shalt diligently consider his place, and it shall not be. But the meek shall inherit the earth, and shall delight themselves in the abundance of peace."

II. Another thing belonging to the same work, was God's wonderfully preserving that family of which the Redeemer was to proceed, when all the rest of the world was drowned. God's drowning the world, and saving *Noah* and his family, were both reducible to this great work. The saving of *Noah* and his family belonged to it two ways, *viz.* as from that family the Redeemer was to proceed, and it was the mystical body of Christ that was there saved. The manner of saving those persons, when all the world besides was so overthrown, was very wonderful. It was a wonderful type of the redemption of Christ, of that redemption that is sealed by the baptism of water, and is so spoken of in the New Testament, as 1 Pet. iii. 20, 21. "Which sometimes were disobedient, when once the long-suffering of God waited in the days of Noah, while the ark was a preparing, wherein few, that is, eight souls, were saved by water. The like figure whereunto, even baptism, doth also now save us, (not the putting away of the filth of the flesh, but the answer of a good conscience towards God,) by the resurrection of Jesus Christ." That water which washed away the filth of the world, that cleared the world of wicked men, was a type of the blood of Christ, that takes away the sin of the world. That water which delivered Noah and his sons from their enemies, is a type of the blood that delivers God's church from their sins, their worst enemies. That water which was so plentiful and abundant, that it filled the world, and reached above the tops of the highest mountains, was a type of that blood, which is sufficient for the whole world; sufficient to bury the highest mountains of sin. The ark, that was the refuge and hiding-place of the church in this time of storm and flood, was a type of Christ, the true hiding-place of the church from the storms and floods of God's wrath.

III. The next thing I would observe is, the *new grant* of the earth God made to Noah and his family immediately after the flood, as founded on the covenant of grace. The sacrifice of Christ was represented by Noah's building an altar to the Lord, and offering a sacrifice of every clean beast, and every clean fowl. And we have an account of God accepting this sacrifice: and thereupon he blessed Noah, and established his covenant with him, and with his seed, promising to destroy the earth in like manner no more; signifying that it is by the sacrifice of Christ, God's favour is obtained, and his people are in safety from destroying judgments, and obtain the blessing of the Lord. And God now, on occasion of this sacrifice that Noah offered, gives him and his posterity a new grant of the earth; a new power of dominion over the creatures, as founded on that sacrifice, and so founded on the covenant of grace. And so it is to be looked upon as a different grant from that which was made to Adam, Gen. i. 28. "And God blessed them, and God said unto them, Be fruitful, and multiply, and replenish the earth, and subdue it; and have dominion over the fish of the sea, and over the fowl of the air, and over every living thing that moveth upon the earth." That grant was not founded on the covenant of *grace;* for it was given to Adam while he was under the covenant of *works,* and therefore was antiquated when that covenant ceased. Hence it came to pass, that the earth was taken away from mankind by the flood: for the first grant was forfeited; and God had never made another after that, till after the flood. If the first covenant had not been broken, God never would have drowned the world, and so have taken it away from mankind; for then the first grant made to mankind would have stood good. But that being broken, God after a while destroyed the earth, when the wickedness of man was great.

But after the flood, on Noah's offering a sacrifice that represented the sacrifice of Christ, God in smelling a sweet savour, or accepting the sacrifice—as it was a representation of the true sacrifice of Christ, which is a sweet savour indeed to God—gives Noah a new grant of the earth, founded on that covenant of grace which is by the sacrifice of Christ, with a promise annexed, that now the earth should no more be destroyed, till the consummation of all things; (Gen. viii. 20—22. and chap. ix. 1—3, 7.) The reason why such a promise, that God would no more destroy the earth, was added to this grant made to Noah, and not to that made to Adam, was because this was founded on the covenant of grace, of which Christ was the surety, and therefore could not be broken. And therefore it comes to pass now, that though the wickedness of man has dreadfully raged, and the earth has been filled with violence and wickedness, one age after another, and much more dreadful and aggravated wickedness, being against so much greater light and mercy; especially in these days of the gospel: yet God's patience holds out; God does not destroy the earth: his mercy and forbearance abides according to his promise; and his grant established with Noah and his sons abides firm and good, being founded on the covenant of grace.

IV. On this God renews with Noah and his sons the covenant of grace, Gen. ix. 9, 10. "And I, behold, I establish my covenant with you, and with your seed after you, and with every living creature that is with you," &c.; which was the covenant of grace; of which even the brute creation have this benefit, that it shall never be destroyed again until the consummation of all things. By this expression in Scripture, *my covenant*, is commonly to be understood the covenant of grace. The manner of expression, *I will establish my covenant with you, and with your seed after you*, shows plainly, that it was a covenant already in being, and that Noah would understand by that denomination the covenant of grace.

V. God's disappointing the design of building the city and tower of Babel belongs to the great work of redemption. For that was undertaken in opposition of this great building of God of which we are speaking. Men's going about to build such a city and tower was an effect of the corruption into which mankind were now fallen. This city and tower was set up in opposition to the city of God, as the god to whom they built it, was their pride. Being sunk into a disposition to forsake the true God, the first idol they set up in his room, was their own fame. And as this city and tower had their foundation laid in the pride and vanity of men, and the haughtiness of their minds, so it was built on a foundation exceedingly contrary to the nature of the kingdom of Christ, and his redeemed city, which has its foundation laid in humility.

Therefore God saw that it tended to frustrate the design of that great building which was founded in Christ's humiliation: and therefore the thing displeased the Lord, and he baffled and confounded the design. God will frustrate and confound all other designs, that are set up in opposition to the great work of redemption.

Isaiah, (chap. ii.) representing God setting up the kingdom of Christ in the world, foretells how, in order to it, he will bring down the haughtiness of men, and how the day of the Lord shall be on *every high tower*, and upon *every fenced wall*, &c. Christ's kingdom is established, by bringing down every high thing to make way for it, 2 Cor. x. 4, 5. "For the weapons of our warfare are mighty through God, to the pulling down of strong holds, casting down imaginations, and every high thing that exalteth itself against the knowledge of God." What is done in a particular soul, to make way for the setting up of Christ's kingdom, is to destroy Babel in that soul.

They intended to have built Babel up to heaven. However, that building of which we speak shall reach to heaven indeed, the highest heavens, at the end of the world, when it shall be finished: and therefore God would not suffer the building of his enemies, in opposition to it, to prosper. If they had prospered in building that city and tower, it might have kept the world of wicked men, the enemies of the church, together, as that was their design. They might have remained united in one vast, powerful city; and so have been too powerful for the city of God.

This Babel is the same with the city of Babylon; for Babylon in the original is Babel. But Babylon is always spoken of in Scripture as chiefly opposite to the city of God, as a powerful and terrible enemy, notwithstanding this great check put to the building of it in the beginning. But it probably would have been vastly more powerful, and able to vex if not to destroy the church of God, if it had not been thus checked.

Thus it was in kindness to his church, and in prosecution of the great design of redemption, that God put a stop to the building of the city and tower of Babel.

VI. The dispersing of the nations, and dividing the earth among its inhabitants, immediately after God had caused the building of Babel to cease. This was done so as most to suit the great design of redemption. And particularly, God therein had an eye to the future propagation of the gospel among the nations. They were so placed, their habitation so limited, round about the land of Canaan, as most suited that design. Deut. xxxii. 8. "When the Most High divided to the nations their inheritance, when he separated the sons of Adam, he set the bounds of the people according to the number of the children of Israel." Acts xvii. 26, 27. "And hath made of one blood all nations of men, for to dwell on all the face of the earth, and hath determined the times before appointed, and the bounds of their habitation; that they should seek the Lord, if haply they might feel after him, and find him." The land of Canaan was the most conveniently situated of any place in the world, for the purpose of spreading revealed light among the nations in general. The Roman empire, the chief part of the civilized world, in the apostolic age, was in the countries round about Jerusalem. The devil seeing the advantage of this situation of the nations for promoting the great work of redemption, and the disadvantage of it with respect to the interests of his kingdom, afterward led away many nations into the remotest parts of the world, to get them out of the way of the gospel. Thus he led some into America; and others into northern cold regions, that are almost inaccessible.

VII. Another thing I would mention in this period, was God's preserving the true religion in that line from which Christ was to proceed, when the world in general apostatized to idolatry, and the church was in imminent danger of being swallowed in the general corruption. Although God had lately wrought so wonderfully for the deliverance of his church, and had shown so great mercy towards it, as for its sake even to destroy all the rest of the world; and although he had lately renewed and established his covenant of grace with Noah and his sons; yet so prone is the corrupt heart of man to depart from God, and to sink into the depths of wickedness, darkness, and delusion, that the world soon after the flood fell into gross idolatry; so that before Abraham the distemper was become almost universal. The earth was become very corrupt at the time of the building of Babel; even God's people themselves, that line of which Christ was to come. Josh. xxiv. 2. "Your fathers dwelt on the other side of the flood in old time, even Terah the father of Abraham, and the father of Nahor; and THEY SERVED OTHER GODS." The other side of the flood means beyond the river Euphrates, where the ancestors of Abraham lived.

We are not to understand, that they were *wholly* drawn off to idolatry, to forsake the true God. For God is said to be the God of Nahor: Gen. xxxi. 53. "The God of Abraham, and the God of Nahor, the God of their father, judge betwixt us." But they partook in some measure of the general and almost universal corruption of the times; as Solomon was in a measure infected with idolatrous corruption; and as the children of Israel in Egypt are said to serve other gods, though there was the true church of God among them; and as there were images kept for a considerable time in the family of Jacob, the corruption being brought from Padan-Aram, whence he fetched his wives.

This was the second time that the church was almost brought to nothing by the corruption and general defection of the world from true religion. But still the true religion was kept up in the family from which Christ was to proceed. Which is another instance of God's remarkably preserving his church in a time of a general deluge of wickedness; and wherein, although the god of this world raged, and had almost swallowed up God's church, yet he did not suffer the gates of hell to prevail against it.

PART III.

FROM THE CALLING OF ABRAHAM TO MOSES.

I PROCEED now to show how the work of redemption was carried on from *the calling of Abraham to Moses.* And,

I. It pleased God now to separate that person of whom Christ was to come, from the rest of the world, that his church might be upheld in his family and posterity till that time. He called Abraham out of his own country, and from his kindred, to go into a distant country, that God should show him; and brought him first out of Ur of the Chaldees to Charran, and then to the land of Canaan.

It was before observed, that the idolatrous corruption of the world was now become general; mankind were almost wholly overrun with idolatry. God therefore saw it necessary, in order to uphold true religion in the world, that there should be a family separated from all others. It proved to be high time to take this course, lest the church of Christ should wholly be carried away with the apostacy. For Abraham's own country and kindred had most of them fallen off; and without some extraordinary interposition of Providence, in all likelihood, in a generation or two more, the true religion in this line would have been extinct. And therefore God called Abraham, the person in whose family he intended to uphold the true religion, out of his own country, and from his kindred, to a far distant country, that his posterity might there remain a people separate from all the rest of the world; that so the true religion might be upheld there, while all mankind besides were swallowed up in heathenism.

The land of the Chaldees, whence Abraham was called, was the country about Babel. Babel, or Babylon, was the chief city of Chaldea. Learned men suppose by what they gather from the most ancient accounts of things, that it was in this land idolatry first began; that Babel and Chaldea were the original and chief seats of the worship of idols, whence it spread into other nations. And therefore the land of the Chaldeans, the country of Babylon, is in Scripture called *the land of graven images;* Jer. l. 35, 38. "A sword is upon the Chaldeans, saith the Lord, and upon the inhabitants of Babylon, and upon her princes, and upon her wise men.—A drought is upon her waters, and they shall be dried up; for it is the land of graven images, and they are mad upon their idols." God calls Abraham out of this idolatrous country, to a great distance from it. And when he came there, he gave him no inheritance in it, no not so much as to set his foot on; but he remained a stranger and a sojourner, that he and his family might be kept separate from all the world.

This was a new thing: God had never taken such a method before. His church had not in this manner been separated from the rest of the world till now; but were wont to dwell with them, without any bar or fence to keep them separate; the mischievous consequence of which had been found once and again. Before the flood, the effect of God's people living intermingled with the wicked world, without any remarkable wall of separation, was, that the sons of the church joined in marriage with others, and thereby almost all soon became infected, and the church was almost brought to nothing. The method that God then took to fence the church was, to drown the wicked world, and save the church in the ark. Before Abraham was called, the world was become corrupt again. But now God took another method; he did not destroy the wicked world, and save Abraham, and his wife, and Lot, but calls these persons to go and live separate from the rest of the world.

This was a new and great thing, that God did toward the work of redemption. It was about the middle of the space of time between the fall of man and the coming of Christ; about two thousand years before the great Redeemer was to appear. But by this calling of Abraham, the ancestor of Christ, a foundation was laid for upholding the church in the world, till Christ should come. For the world having become idolatrous, there was a necessity in order to this, that the seed of the woman should be thus separated from it.

And then it was needful that there should be a particular nation separated from the rest of the world, to receive the types and prophecies that were to be given of Christ, to prepare the way for his coming; that to them might be committed the oracles of God; that by them the history of God's great works of creation and providence might be preserved; that Christ might be born of this nation; and that from hence the light of the gospel might shine forth to the rest of the world. These ends could not well be obtained, if God's people, through all these two thousand years, had lived intermixed with the heathen world. So that the calling of Abraham may be looked upon as a kind of new foundation laid for the visible church of God, in a more distinct and regular state. Abraham, being the person in whom this foundation is laid, is represented in Scripture as though he were the father of all the church, the father of all them that believe; a root whence the visible church rose as a tree, distinct from all other plants. Of this tree Christ was the branch of righteousness; and from it, after Christ came, the natural branches were broken off, and the Gentiles were grafted in. So that Abraham still remains the father, the root of the church. It is the same tree which, from that small beginning in Abraham's time, has in these days of the gospel spread its branches over a great part of the earth, and will fill the whole in due time, and at the end of the world shall be transplanted from an earthly soil into the paradise of God.

II. There accompanied this a more particular and full revelation and confirmation of the covenant of grace than ever before. There had been before this two particular and solemn editions or confirmations of this covenant; one, to our first parents, soon after the fall; the other, to Noah and his family, soon after the flood. And now there is a third, at and after the calling of Abraham. It is now revealed to Abraham, not only that Christ should come; but that he should be his seed; and promised, that all the families of the earth should be blessed in him. And God repeated the promises of this to Abraham. The first promise was when he first called him, Gen. xii. 2. "And I will make of thee a great nation, and I will bless thee, and make thy name great; and thou shalt be a blessing." The same promise was renewed after he came into the land of Canaan, (chap. xiii. 14, &c.) Again after Abraham had returned from the slaughter of the kings, (chap. xv. 5, 6.) And a fourth time, after his offering up Isaac, (chap. xxii. 16—18.)

In this renewal of the covenant of grace with Abraham, several particulars concerning it were revealed more fully than before; not only that Christ was to be of Abraham's seed, but also, the calling of the Gentiles, that all nations should be brought into the church, all the families of the earth made blessed. And then the great condition of the covenant of grace, which is faith, was now more fully made known. Gen. xv. 5, 6. "And he said unto him, So shall thy seed be. And Abraham believed God, and it was counted unto him for righteousness." Which is much noticed in the New Testament, as that for which Abraham was called the father of believers.

And as there was now a further revelation of the covenant of grace, so there was a further confirmation of it by seals and pledges; particularly, circumcision, which was a seal of the covenant of grace, as appears by the first institution of it, Gen. xvii. It there appears to be a seal of that covenant by which God promised to make Abraham a father of many nations, (ver. 5, 9, 10.) And we are expressly taught, that it was *a seal of righteousness of faith,* Rom. iv. 11. Speaking of Abraham, the apostle says, *he received the sign of circumcision, a seal of the righteousness of faith.*

Abraham's family and posterity must be kept separate from the rest of the world, till Christ should come; and this sacrament was the principal wall of separation. Besides, God gave Abraham a remarkable pledge of the fulfilment of the promise he had made him, in his victory over Chedorlaomer and the kings that were with him. Chedorlaomer seems to have been a great emperor, who reigned over a great part of the world at that day; and though he had his seat at Elam, which was not much, if any thing, short of a thousand miles distant from the land of Canaan, yet he extended his empire so as to reign over many parts of the land of Canaan, as appears by chap. xiv. 4—7. It is supposed by learned men, that he was a king of the Assyrian empire at that day, which had been before begun by Nimrod at Babel. And as it was the honour of kings in those days to build cities for the seat of their empire, (Gen. x. 10—12.) so it is conjectured, that he had gone forth and built him a city in Elam, and made that his seat; and that those other kings who came with him, were his deputies in the several cities and countries where they reigned. But yet as mighty an empire as he had, and as great an army as he came with, Abraham, only with his trained servants, that were born in his house, conquered and subdued this mighty emperor, the kings that came with him, and all their army. This he received of God as a pledge of what he had promised, *viz.* the victory that Christ his seed should obtain over the nations of the earth, whereby he should possess the gates of his enemies. It is plainly spoken of as such in the 41st of Isaiah. In that chapter is foretold the future glorious victory the church shall obtain over the nations of the world, (ver. 1, 10, 15.) This victory of Abraham over such a great emperor and his mighty forces, is spoken of as a pledge and earnest of victory to the church, (ver. 2, 3.) "Who raised up the righteous man from the east, called him to his foot, gave the nations before him, and made him rule over kings? He gave them as the dust to his sword, and as driven stubble to his bow. He pursued them, and passed safely; even by the way that he had not gone with his feet."

Another remarkable confirmation Abraham received of the covenant of grace, was when he returned from the slaughter of the kings; when Melchisedec the king of Salem, the priest of the most high God, that great type of Christ, met him, and blessed him, and brought forth bread and wine. The bread and wine signified the same blessings of the covenant of grace, that the bread and wine does in the sacrament of the Lord's supper. As Abraham had a seal of the covenant in circumcision that was equivalent to baptism, so now he had a seal of it equivalent to the Lord's supper. And Melchisedec's coming to meet him with such a seal of the covenant of grace, on the occasion of this victory, evinces, that it was a pledge of God's fulfilment of the same covenant. (Gen xiv. 19, 20.)

Another confirmation of the covenant of grace, was the vision he had, in the deep sleep that fell upon him, of the smoking furnace, and burning lamp, that passed between the parts of the sacrifice, (Gen. xv.) The sacrifice signified that of Christ. The smoking furnace that passed through the midst of that sacrifice first, signified the sufferings of Christ. But the burning lamp that followed, which shone with a clear bright light, signifies the glory that followed Christ's sufferings, and was procured by them.

Another remarkable pledge that God gave Abraham of the fulfilment of the covenant of grace, was his giving of that child of whom Christ was to come, in his old age, (Heb. xi. 11, 12. and Rom. iv. 18, &c.) and his delivering Isaac, after he was laid upon the wood of the sacrifice to be slain. This was a confirmation of Abraham's faith in the promise that God had made of Christ, that he should be of Isaac's posterity; and was a representation of the resurrection of Christ. (Heb. xi. 17—19.) And because this was given as a confirmation of the covenant of grace, therefore God renewed that covenant with Abraham on this occasion, (Gen. xxiv. 15, &c.)

Thus you see how much more fully the covenant of grace was revealed and confirmed in Abraham's time than ever it had been before; by means of which Abraham seems to have had a clear view of Christ the great Redeemer, and the future things that were to be accomplished by him. And therefore Christ informs us, that "Abraham rejoiced to see his day, and he saw it, and was glad," John viii. 56. So great an advance did it please God now to make in this building, which he had been carrying on from the beginning of the world.

III. The next thing is God's preserving the patriarchs for so long a time in the midst of the wicked inhabitants of Canaan, and from all other enemies. The patriarchs, Abraham, Isaac, and Jacob, were those of whom Christ was to proceed; and they were now separated from the world, that in them his church might be upheld. Therefore, in preserving them, the great design of redemption was carried on. He preserved them, and kept the inhabitants of the land where they sojourned from destroying them; which was a remarkable dispensation of providence. For the inhabitants of the land were at that day very wicked, though they grew more wicked afterwards. This appears by Gen. xv. 16. "In the fourth generation they shall come hither again; for the iniquity of the Canaanites is not yet full:" as much as to say, though it be very great, yet it is not yet full. And their great wickedness also appears by Abraham and Isaac's aversion to their children marrying any of the daughters of the land. Abraham, when he was old, could not be content till he had made his servant swear that he would not take a wife for his son of the daughters of the land. And Isaac and Rebecca were content to send away Jacob to so great a distance as Padan-Aram, to take him a wife thence. And when Esau married some of the daughters of the land, we are told, that they were *a grief of mind to Isaac and Rebecca.*

Another argument of their great wickedness, was the instances we have in Sodom and Gomorrah, Admah and Zeboim, which were some of the cities of Canaan, though they were probably most notoriously wicked; and likely to have the most bitter enmity against these holy men; agreeable to what was declared at first, "I will put enmity between thee and the woman, and between thy seed and her seed." Their holy lives were a continual condemnation of their wickedness. Besides, it could not be otherwise, but that they must be much in reproving their wickedness, as we find Lot was in Sodom; who, we are told, vexed his righteous soul with their unlawful deeds, and was to them a preacher of righteousness.

And they were the more exposed to them, being strangers and sojourners in the land, and having as yet no inheritance there. Men are more apt to find fault with strangers, and to be irritated by any thing in them that offends, as they were with Lot in Sodom. He very gently reproved their wickedness; and they say upon it, "This fellow came in to sojourn, and he will needs be a ruler and a judge;" and threatened what they would do to him.

But God wonderfully preserved Abraham and Lot, Isaac and Jacob, and their families, amongst them, though they were few in number, and they might quickly have destroyed them; which is taken notice of as a wonderful instance of God's preserving mercy towards his church, Psal. cv. 12, &c. "When they were but a few men in number; yea, very few, and strangers in it. When they went from one nation to another, from one kingdom to another people. He suffered no man to do them wrong; yea, he reproved kings for their sakes, saying, Touch not mine anointed, and do my prophets no harm."

This preservation was, in some instances especially, very remarkable; when the people of the land were greatly irritated and provoked; as they were by Simeon and Levi's treatment of the Shechemites, in Gen. xxxiv. 30, &c. God then strangely preserved Jacob and his family, restraining the provoked people by an unusual terror on their minds, Gen. xxxv. 5. "And the terror of God was upon the cities that were round about them, and they did not pursue after the sons of Jacob."

And God preserved them, not only from the Canaanites, but from all others that intended mischief to them. He preserved Jacob and his company, when pursued by Laban, full of rage, and a disposition to overtake him as an enemy. God met him, rebuked him, and said to him, "Take heed that thou speak not to Jacob either good or bad." How wonderfully did he also preserve him from Esau his brother, when he came forth with an army, with a full design to cut him off! How did God, in answer to his prayer, when Jacob wrestled with Christ at Penuel, wonderfully turn Esau's heart, and make him, instead of meeting him as an enemy with slaughter and destruction, to meet him as a friend and brother, doing him no harm!

And thus was this handful, this little root that had the blessing of the Redeemer in it, preserved in the midst of enemies and dangers; which was not unlike to preserving the ark in the midst of the tempestuous deluge.

IV. The next thing I would mention is, the awful destruction of Sodom and Gomorrah, and the neighbouring cities. This tended to promote the great work designed two ways: First, as it tended powerfully to restrain the inhabitants of the land from injuring those holy strangers that God had brought to sojourn amongst them. Lot was one of those strangers; he came into the land with Abraham; and Sodom was destroyed for their abusive disregard of Lot, the preacher of righteousness. And their destruction came upon their committing a most injurious and abominable insult on Lot, and the strangers that were come into his house, even those angels, whom they probably took to be some of Lot's former acquaintance come to visit him. They in a most outrageous manner beset Lot's house, intending a monstrous abuse and act of violence on those strangers, and threatening to serve Lot worse than them.

But in the midst of this God smote them with blindness; and the next morning the city and the country about it was overthrown in a most terrible storm of fire and brimstone; which dreadful destruction, as it was in the sight of the rest of the inhabitants of the land, and therefore greatly tended to restrain them from hurting those holy strangers any more; it doubtless struck a dread and terror on their minds, and made them afraid to hurt them, and probably was one principal means to restrain them, and preserve the patriarchs. And when that reason is given, why the inhabitants of the land did not pursue after Jacob, when they were so provoked by the destruction of the Shechemites, *viz. that the terror of the Lord was upon them;* it is very probable, that this was the terror which was set home upon them. They remembered the amazing destruction of Sodom, and the cities of the plain, that came upon them for their abusive treatment of Lot, and so durst not hurt Jacob and his family, though they were so much provoked to it.

Another way that this awful destruction tended to promote this great affair of redemption, was, that hereby God remarkably exhibited the terrors of his law, to make men sensible of their need of redeeming mercy. The work of redemption never was carried on without this. The law, from the beginning, is made use of as a schoolmaster to bring men to Christ.

But under the Old Testament there was much more need of some extraordinary, visible, and sensible manifestation of God's wrath against sin, than in the days of the gospel; since a future state, and the eternal misery of hell, is more clearly revealed, and since the awful justice of God against the sins of men has been so wonderfully displayed in the sufferings of Christ. And therefore the revelation that God gave of himself in those days, used to be accompanied with much more terror than it is in these days of the gospel. So when God appeared at mount Sinai to give the law, it was with thunders and lightnings, and a thick cloud, and the voice of the trumpet exceeding loud. Some external, awful manifestations of God's wrath against sin were on some accounts especially necessary before the giving of the law: and therefore, before the flood, the terrors of the law handed down by tradition from Adam served for that purpose. Adam lived nine hundred and thirty years himself, to proclaim God's awful threatenings denounced in the covenant made with him, and how dreadful the consequences of the fall were; and others, that conversed with Adam, lived till the flood. And the destruction of the world by the flood served to exhibit the terrors of the law, and manifested the wrath of God against sin; in order to make men sensible of the absolute necessity of redeeming mercy. And some that saw the flood were alive in Abraham's time.

But this was now in a great measure forgotten; therefore God was pleased again, in a most amazing manner, to show his wrath against sin, in the destruction of these cities; which was the liveliest image of hell of any thing that ever had been; and therefore the apostle Jude says, "They suffer the vengeance of eternal fire," Jude 7. God rained storms of fire and brimstone upon them; probably by thick flashes of lightning. The streams of brimstone burnt up all these cities; so that they perished in the flames of divine wrath. By this might be seen the dreadful wrath of God against the ungodliness and unrighteousness of men; which tended to show the necessity of redemption, and so to promote that great work.

V. God again renewed and confirmed the covenant of grace to Isaac and Jacob. To Isaac in these words; Gen. xxvi. 3, 4. "And I will perform the oath which I sware unto Abraham thy father; and I will make thy seed to multiply as the stars of heaven, and will give unto thy seed all these countries; and in thy seed shall all the nations of the earth be blessed." And afterwards to Jacob; first, in Isaac blessing him and his seed, wherein he acted and spoke by extraordinary divine direction, Gen. xxvii. 29. "Let people serve thee, and nations bow down to thee; be lord over thy brethren, and let thy mother's sons bow down to thee: Cursed be every one that curseth thee, and blessed be he that blesseth thee." And therefore Esau, not included in this blessing, missed of being blessed as an heir of the benefits of the covenant of grace.

This covenant was again renewed and confirmed to Jacob at Bethel, in his vision of the ladder that reached to heaven; which was a symbol of the way of salvation by Christ. The stone that Jacob rested on was a type of Christ, the stone of Israel, which the spiritual Israel rests upon; as is evident, because it was anointed, and made use of as an altar. But we know that Christ is the anointed of God, and is the only true altar. While Jacob was resting on this stone, and saw this ladder, God appears to him as his covenant God, and renews the covenant of grace with him; as in Gen. xxviii. 14. "And thy seed shall be as the dust of the earth; and thou shalt spread abroad to the west, and to the east, and to the north, and to the south; and in thee and in thy seed shall all the families of the earth be blessed."

Jacob had another remarkable confirmation of this covenant at Penuel, where he wrestled with God, and prevailed; where Christ appeared to him in the form of that nature which he was afterwards to receive in a personal union with his divine nature.—And God renewed his covenant with him again, after he left Padan-Aram, and was come up to Bethel, and where he had the vision of the ladder; as you may see in Gen. xxxv. 10, &c.

Thus the covenant of grace was now renewed much oftener than it had been before. The light of the gospel now began to shine much brighter, as the time of Christ's appearing drew nearer.

VI. The next thing I would observe, is God's remarkably preserving the family of which Christ was to proceed from perishing by famine, by the instrumentality of Joseph. When there was a seven-years famine approaching, God was pleased, by a wonderful providence, to send Joseph into Egypt, there to provide for Jacob and his family, and to keep the holy seed alive, which otherwise would have perished. Joseph was sent into Egypt for that end, as he observes, Gen. l. 20. "But as for you, ye thought evil against me; but God meant it unto good, to save much people alive." How often had this holy root, that had in it the future branch of righteousness, the glorious Redeemer, been in danger of being destroyed! But God wonderfully preserved it.

This salvation of the house of Israel, by the hand of Joseph, was upon some accounts very much a resemblance of the salvation of Christ. The children of Israel were saved by Joseph their kinsman and brother, from perishing by famine; as he that saves the souls of the spiritual Israel from spiritual famine is their near kinsman, and one that is not ashamed to call them brethren. Joseph was a brother they had hated, sold, and as it were killed; for they had designed to kill him. So Christ is one that we naturally hate, and by our wicked lives, have sold for the vain things of the world, and by our sins have slain. Joseph was first in a state of humiliation; he was a servant, as Christ appeared in the form of a servant; and then was cast into a dungeon, as Christ descended into the grave. When he rose out of the dungeon, he was in a state of great exaltation, at the king's right hand as his deputy, to reign over all his kingdom, to provide food, to preserve life; and being in this state of exaltation, he dispenses food to his brethren, and so gives them life. So Christ was exalted at God's right hand to be a Prince and Saviour to his brethren, received gifts for men, even for the rebellious, them that had hated and sold him.

VII. After this there was a prophecy of Christ, on some accounts more particular than any before, in Jacob's blessing his son Judah. This was more particular as it showed of whose posterity he was to be. When God called Abraham, it was revealed that he was to be of Abraham's posterity. Before, we have no account of any revelation concerning Christ's pedigree confined to narrower limits than the posterity of Noah: after this it was confined to still narrower limits; for though Abraham had many sons, yet it was revealed, that Christ was to be of Isaac's posterity. And then it was limited still more; for when Isaac had two sons, it was revealed that Christ was to be of Israel's posterity. And now, though Israel had twelve sons, yet it is revealed that Christ should be of Judah's posterity. Christ is the lion of the tribe of Judah. Respect is chiefly had to his great acts, when it is said here, Gen. xlix. 8. "Judah, thou art he whom thy brethren shall praise; thy hand shall be in the neck of thine enemies; thy father's children shall bow down before thee. Judah is a lion's whelp; from the prey, my son, thou art gone up: he stooped down, he couched as a lion, and as an old lion; who shall rouse him up?" And then this prediction is more particular concerning the time of Christ's coming, as in ver. 10. "The sceptre shall not depart from Judah, nor a lawgiver from between his feet, until Shiloh come; and unto him shall the gathering of the people be." The prophecy here, of the calling of the Gentiles consequent on Christ's coming, seems to be more plain than any had been before, in the expression, "to him shall the gathering of the people be." Thus you see how that gospel-light which dawned immediately after the fall of man, gradually increases.

VIII. The work of redemption was carried on in this period, in God's wonderfully preserving the children of Israel in Egypt, when the power of Egypt was engaged utterly to destroy them. They seemed to be wholly in the hands of the Egyptians; they were their servants, and were subject to the power of Pharaoh: and Pharaoh set himself to weaken them with hard bondage. And when he saw that did not do, he set himself to extirpate their race, by commanding that every male child should be drowned. But after all that Pharaoh could do, God wonderfully preserved them; and not only so, but increased them exceedingly; so that, instead of being extirpated, they greatly multiplied.

IX. Here is to be observed, not only the preservation of the nation, but God's wonderfully preserving and upholding his invisible church in that nation, when in danger of being overwhelmed in the idolatry of Egypt. The children of Israel being long among the Egyptians, and servants under them, and so not having advantages to keep God's ordinances among themselves, and maintain any public worship or instruction, whereby the true religion might be upheld, and there being now no written word, they by degrees, in a great measure, lost the true religion, and borrowed the idolatry of Egypt; and the greater part of the people fell away to the worship of their gods. This we learn by Ezek. xx. 6, 7, 8. and by chap. xxiii. 8.

This now was the third time that God's church was almost swallowed up and carried away with the wickedness of the world; once before the flood; the other time, before the calling of Abraham; and now, the third time, in Egypt. But yet God did not suffer his church to be quite overwhelmed: he still saved it, like the ark in the flood, and as he saved Moses in the midst of the waters, in an ark of bulrushes, where he was in the utmost danger of being swallowed up. The true religion was still kept up with some; and God had still a people among them, even in this miserable, corrupt, and dark time. The parents of Moses were true servants of God, as we may learn by Heb. xi. 23. "By faith Moses, when he was born, was hid three months of his parents, because they saw that he was a proper child; and they were not afraid of the king's commandment."

I have now shown how the work of redemption was carried on from the calling of Abraham to Moses; in which we have seen many great things done towards this work, and a great advancement of this building, beyond what had preceded.

PART IV.

FROM MOSES TO DAVID.

I PROCEED to the time which reaches from Moses to David.

I. The first thing that offers itself is the redemption of the church of God out of Egypt; the most remarkable of all in the Old Testament, the greatest pledge and forerunner of the future redemption by Christ, and much more insisted on in Scripture than any other of those redemptions. And indeed it was the greatest type of Christ's redemption of any providential event whatsoever. This was by Jesus Christ, for it was wrought by him who appeared to Moses in the bush; the person that sent Moses to redeem that people. But that was Christ, as is evident, because he is called *the angel of the Lord*, Exod. iii. 2, 3. The bush represented the human nature of Christ, who is called the *branch*. This bush grew on mount Sinai or Horeb, a word that signifies a dry place, as the human nature of Christ was a root out of a dry ground. The bush burning with fire, represented the sufferings of Christ, in the fire of God's wrath. It burned, and was not consumed; so Christ, though he suffered extremely, yet perished not; but overcame at last, and rose from his sufferings. Because this great mystery of the incarnation and sufferings of Christ was here represented, therefore Moses says, *I will turn aside, and behold this great sight*. A great sight he might well call it, when there was represented, *God manifest in the flesh*, suffering a dreadful death, and rising from the dead.

This was the glorious Redeemer who redeemed the church out of Egypt, from under the hand of Pharaoh; as Christ, by his death and sufferings, redeemed his people from Satan, the spiritual Pharaoh. He redeemed them from hard service and cruel drudgery; so Christ redeems his people from the cruel slavery of sin and Satan. He redeemed them, as it is said, *from the iron furnace;* so Christ redeems his church from a furnace of fire and everlasting burnings.—He redeemed them with a strong hand and outstretched arm, and great and terrible judgments on their enemies; so Christ with mighty power triumphs over *principalities and powers*, and executes terrible judgments on his church's enemies, bruising the serpent's head. He saved them, when others were destroyed, by the sprinkling of the blood of the paschal lamb; so God's church is saved from death by the sprinkling of the blood of Christ, when the rest of the world is destroyed. God brought forth the people sorely against the will of the Egyptians, when they could not bear to let them go; so Christ rescues his people out of the hands of the devil, sorely against his will, when his proud heart cannot bear to be overcome.

In that redemption, Christ did not only redeem the people from the Egyptians, but he redeemed them from the devils, the gods of Egypt; for before, they had been in a state of servitude to the gods of Egypt, as well as to the men. And Christ, the seed of the woman, did now, in a very remarkable manner, fulfil the curse on the serpent, in bruising his head: Exod. xii. 12. "For I will pass through the land of Egypt this night, and will smite all the first-born in the land of Egypt, both man and beast, and against all the gods of Egypt will I execute judgment." Hell was as much, nay more engaged in that affair, than Egypt was. The pride and cruelty of Satan, that old serpent, was more concerned in it than Pharaoh's. He did his utmost against the people, and to his utmost opposed their redemption. But it is said, that when God redeemed his people out of Egypt, he "broke the heads of the dragons in the waters, and broke the head of leviathan in pieces, and gave him to be meat for the people inhabiting the wilderness," Ps. lxxiv. 12—14. God forced their enemies to let them go, that they might serve him; as Zacharias observes with respect to the church under the gospel, Luke i. 74, 75.

The people of Israel went out with a high hand, and Christ went before them in a pillar of cloud and fire. There was a glorious triumph over earth and hell in that deliverance. When Pharaoh and his hosts, and Satan by them, pursued the people, Christ overthrew them in the Red sea; the Lord triumphed gloriously; the horse and his rider he cast into the sea, and there they slept their sleep, and never followed the children of Israel any more. The Red sea represented Christ's blood, because the apostle compares the children of Israel's passage through the Red sea to baptism, 1 Cor. x. 1, 2.—But we all know that the water of baptism represents Christ's blood.

Thus Christ, the angel of God's presence, in his love and his pity, redeemed his people, and carried them in the days of old as on eagles' wings, so that none of their proud and spiteful enemies, neither Egyptians nor devils, could touch them.

This was quite a new thing that God did towards this great work of redemption. God never had done any thing like it before; Deut. iv. 32, 34. This was a great advancement of the work, that had been begun and carried on from the fall of man; a great step taken in Divine Providence towards a preparation for Christ's coming into the world, and working out his great and eternal redemption: for this was the people of whom Christ was to come. And now we may see how that plant flourished which God had planted in Abraham. Though the family of which Christ was to come, had been in a degree separated from the rest of the world before, in the calling of Abraham; yet that separation appeared not to be sufficient. For though by that separation, they were kept, as strangers and sojourners, from being united with other people in the same political societies; yet they remained mixed among them, by which means they had been in danger of wholly losing the true religion, and of being overrun with the idolatry of their neighbours. God now, therefore, by this redemption, separated them as a nation from all others, to subsist by themselves in their own political and ecclesiastical state, without having any concern with the heathen nations, that the church of Christ might be upheld, and might keep the oracles of God; that in them might be kept up those types and prophecies of Christ, and those histories and other divine previous instructions, which were necessary to prepare the way for Christ's coming.

II. As this people were separated to be God's peculiar people, so all other people upon the face of the whole earth were wholly rejected and given over to heathenism. This was one thing that God ordered in his providence to prepare the way for Christ's coming, and the great salvation he was to accomplish; for it was only to prepare the way for the more glorious and signal victory and triumph of Christ's power and grace over the wicked and miserable world, and that Christ's salvation of mankind might become the more sensible. This is the account the Scripture itself gives us of the matter, Rom. xi. 30, 32. The apostle, speaking to the Gentiles that had formerly been heathens, says, "As ye in times past have not believed God, yet have now obtained mercy through their unbelief; even so have these also now not believed, that through your mercy they also may obtain mercy. For God hath concluded them all in unbelief, that he might have mercy upon all:" *i. e.* It was the will of God, that the whole world, Jews and Gentiles, should be concluded in visible and professed unbelief, that so God's mercy and Christ's salvation towards them all might be visible. For the apostle is not speaking only of that unbelief that is natural to all God's professing people as well as others, but that which appears, and is visible; such as the Jews fell into, when they openly rejected Christ, and ceased to be a professing people. The apostle observes, how that first the Gentiles, even the Gentile nations, were included in a professed unbelief and open opposition to the true religion, before Christ came, to prepare the way for the calling of the Gentiles, which was soon after Christ came, in order that God's mercy might be the more visible to them; and that the Jews were rejected, and apostatized from the visible church, to prepare the way for the calling of the Jews, which shall be in the latter days. So that it may be seen concerning all nations, Jews and Gentiles, that are redeemed by Christ, from being visibly aliens from the commonwealth of Israel, without hope, and without God in the world.

We cannot certainly determine precisely at what time

the apostacy of the Gentile nations from the true God, or their being concluded in visible unbelief, became universal. Their falling away was a gradual thing, as we observed before. It was general in Abraham's time, but not universal: for then we find Melchizedec, one of the kings of Canaan, was priest of the most high God. And after this the true religion was kept up for a while among some of the rest of Abraham's posterity, besides the family of Jacob; and also in some of the posterity of Nahor, as we have instances in Job, and his three friends, and Elihu. The land of Uz, where Job lived, was possessed by the posterity of Uz, or Huz, the son of Nahor, Abraham's brother, of whom we read, Gen. xxii. 21. Bildad the Shuhite was of the offspring of Shuah, Abraham's son by Keturah, Gen. xxv. 1, 2. and Elihu the Buzite, was of Buz the son of Nahor, the brother of Abraham. So the true religion lasted among some other people, besides the Israelites, a while after Abraham. But it did not last long: and it is probable that their total rejection, and giving up to idolatry, was about the time when God separated the children of Israel from Egypt to serve him. For they are often put in mind on that occasion, that God had now separated them to be his peculiar people; or to be distinguished from all other people upon earth, to be his people alone; to be his portion, when others were rejected. This seems to imply, that God now chose them in such a manner, as was accompanied with a visible rejection of all other nations in the world; that God visibly came, and took up his residence with them, forsaking all other nations. As the first calling of the Gentiles, after Christ came, was accompanied with a rejection of the Jews; so the first calling of the Jews to be God's people, when they left Egypt, was accompanied with a rejection of the Gentiles.

Thus all the nations in the world, except the Israelites, and those who embodied themselves with them, were given up to idolatry; and so continued till Christ came, which was about fifteen hundred years. They were concluded so long a time in unbelief, that there might be a thorough proof of the necessity of a Saviour; that it might appear by so long a trial, past all contradiction, that mankind were utterly insufficient to deliver themselves from that gross darkness and misery, and subjection to the devil; that all the wisdom of the heathen philosophers could not deliver them from their darkness, for the greater glory to Jesus Christ, who, when he came, enlightened and delivered them by his glorious gospel. Herein the wonderful wisdom of God appeared, in thus preparing the way for Christ's redemption. This the Scripture teaches us, 1 Cor. i. 21. "For after that, in the wisdom of God, the world by wisdom knew not God, it pleased God by the foolishness of preaching to save them that believe."

III. The next thing done towards the work of redemption, is God's giving the moral law in so awful a manner at mount Sinai. This was another new step taken in this great affair. Deut. iv. 33. "Did ever people hear the voice of God speaking out of the midst of the fire, as thou hast heard, and live?" And it was a great thing, whether we consider it as a new exhibition of the covenant of works, or given as a rule of life.

The covenant of works was here exhibited as a schoolmaster to lead to Christ, not only for the use of that nation, under the Old Testament, but for the use of God's church throughout all ages of the world. It is an instrument that the great Redeemer makes use of to convince men of their sin, misery, and helpless state, and of God's awful and tremendous majesty and justice as a lawgiver, in order to make men sensible of the necessity of Christ as a Saviour. This work of redemption, in its saving effect on men's souls, in all its progress, is not carried on without the use of this law delivered at Sinai.

It was given in an awful manner, with a terrible voice, exceedingly loud and awful, so that all the people in the camp trembled; and even Moses himself, though so intimate a friend of God, said, "I exceedingly fear and quake." The voice was accompanied with thunders and lightnings, the mountain burning with fire to the midst of heaven, and the earth itself shaking and trembling. This was done in order to make all sensible how great that authority, power, and justice were, that stood engaged to exact the fulfilment of this law, and to see it fully executed. Here might be understood, how strictly God would require the fulfilment; and how terrible his wrath would be against every transgressor. Men, being sensible of these things, might thoroughly prove their own hearts, and know how impossible it is for them to obtain salvation by the works of the law, and be assured of their absolute need of a mediator.

If we regard the law given at mount Sinai—not as a covenant of works, but—as a rule of life, it is employed by the Redeemer, from that time to the end of the world, as a directory to his people, to show them the way in which they must walk, as they would go to heaven: for a way of sincere and universal obedience to this law is the narrow way that leads to life.

IV. The next thing observable in this period, was God's giving the *typical* law, those precepts that did not properly belong to the *moral* law. Not only those laws which are commonly called *ceremonial*, which prescribe the ceremonies and circumstances of the Jewish worship, and their ecclesiastical state; but also those that were political, for regulating the Jewish commonwealth, commonly called *judicial* laws, were many of them typical. The giving this typical law was another great thing that God did in this period, tending to build up the glorious structure of redemption. There had been many typical events of providence before, that represented Christ and his redemption, and some typical ordinances, as particularly those two of sacrifices and circumcision: but now, instead of representing the great Redeemer in a few institutions, God enacts a law full of typical representations of good things to come. By these, that nation were directed every year, month, and day, in their religious actions, and in their conduct, in all that appertained to their ecclesiastical and civil state, to something of Christ; one observance exhibiting one doctrine, or one benefit; another, another; so that the whole nation by this law was, as it were, constituted in a typical state. Thus the gospel was abundantly held forth to that nation; so that there is scarce any doctrine of it, but is particularly taught and exhibited by some observance of this law; though it was in shadows, and under a vail, as Moses put a vail on his face when it shone.—To this typical law belong all the precepts which relate to building the tabernacle, set up in the wilderness, and all its form, circumstances, and utensils.

V. About this time was given to the church the first written word of God. This was another great thing done towards the affair of redemption, a new and glorious advancement of the building; which God has given for the regulation of faith, worship, and practice to the end of the world. This rule grew, and was added to from that time, for many ages, till it was finished, and the canon of Scripture completed by the apostle John. It is not very material, whether the first written word was the ten commandments, written on the tables of stone with the finger of God, or the book of Job; and whether the book of Job was written by Moses, as some suppose, or by Elihu, as others. If it was written by Elihu, it must have been before this period; but yet could not be far from it, as appears by considering whose posterity the persons spoken of in it were, together with Job's great age, before it was written.

The written word of God is the main instrument employed by Christ, in order to carry on his work of redemption in all ages. There was a necessity now of the word of God being committed to writing, for a steady rule to God's church. Before this, the church had the word by tradition, either by immediate tradition from eminent men inspired, that were living, or else by tradition from former generations, which might be had with tolerable certainty in ages preceding this, by reason of men's long lives. Noah might converse with Adam, and receive traditions from him; and Noah lived till about Abraham's time: and the sons of Jacob lived a considerable time to deliver the revelations made to Abraham, Isaac, and Jacob, to their posterity in Egypt. But the distance from the beginning of things was become now so great, and the lives of men become so short—being brought down to the present standard about the time of Moses—and God having now separated a nation to be a peculiar people, to be the keepers of the oracles of God; God saw it to be a convenient time now to commit his word to writing, to remain henceforward for a steady rule throughout all ages. And therefore, besides the book of Job, Christ wrote the ten commandments on tables of stone, with his own finger. After this, the whole law, as containing the substance of the five books of Moses, was by God's special command committed to writing, which was called " the book of the law," and was laid up in the tabernacle, to be kept there for the use of the church, Deut. xxxi. 24—26.

VI. God was pleased now wonderfully to represent the progress of his redeemed church through the world to their eternal inheritance, by the journey of the children of Israel through the wilderness, from Egypt to Canaan. Here all the various steps of the redemption of the church by Christ were represented, from the beginning to its consummation in glory. The state they are redeemed from is represented by Egypt, and their bondage there, which they left. The purchase of their redemption was represented by the sacrifice of the paschal lamb, which was offered up that night in which God slew all the first-born of Egypt. The beginning of the application of the redemption of Christ's church in their conversion, was represented by Israel's going out of Egypt, and passing through the Red sea in so extraordinary and miraculous a manner. The travel of the church through this evil world, and the various changes through which the church passes, was represented by the journey of the Israelites through the wilderness. The manner of their being conducted by Christ, was represented by the Israelites being led by the pillar of cloud by day, and the pillar of fire by night. The manner of the church's being supported in their progress, supplied with spiritual food, and daily communications from God, was represented by his supplying the children of Israel with *manna* from heaven, and water out of the rock. The dangers that the saints must meet with in their course through the world, were represented by the fiery flying serpents in the wilderness. The conflicts the church has with her enemies, were represented by their battle with the Amalekites and others. And innumerable other particulars might be mentioned, which were lively images of what the church and saints meet with in all ages of the world. That these things were typical, is manifest from 1 Cor. x. 11. " Now all these things happened unto them for ensamples, and they were written for our admonition, upon whom the ends of the world are come." Here the apostle is speaking of those very things which we have now mentioned, and he says expressly, that they happened unto them for *types;* so it is in the original.

VII. Another thing here must not be omitted, which was a great and remarkable dispensation of Providence, respecting the whole world of mankind, in this period; *viz.* the shortening of man's life. It was now brought down from being between nine hundred and a thousand years, to about seventy or eighty. The life of man began to be shortened immediately after the flood. It was brought down the first generation to six hundred years, and the next to between four and five hundred years. So the life of man gradually grew shorter and shorter, till about the time of the great mortality which was in the congregation of Israel, after they had murmured at the report of the spies, and their carcasses fell in the wilderness, whereby all the men of war died. Then the life of man was reduced to its present standard, as Moses observes in that psalm which he wrote on occasion of that mortality: Psal. xc. 10. " The days of our years are threescore years and ten; and if by reason of strength they be fourscore years, yet is their strength labour and sorrow; for it is soon cut off, and we fly away."

Man's life being cut so very short, tended to prepare the way for poor, short-lived men, the more joyfully to entertain the glad tidings of everlasting life, *brought to light by the gospel;* and more readily to embrace a Saviour, that purchases and offers such a blessing. If men's lives were still commonly about nine hundred years, how much less would be the inducement to regard the proffers of a future life; how much greater the temptation to rest in the things of this world, and to neglect any other life but this! This probably contributed greatly to the wickedness of the antediluvians. But now how much greater motives have men to seek redemption, and a better life than this, by the great Redeemer, since the life of man is not one twelfth part of what it used to be, and men now universally die at the age when formerly they used to be but setting out in the world.

VIII. The same work was carried on in preserving that people, of whom Christ was to come, from totally perishing in the wilderness, by a constant miracle of forty years' continuance. I observed before how God preserved those of whom the Redeemer was to proceed in a very wonderful manner; as Noah and his family from the flood; Abraham, Isaac, and Jacob, with their families, from the wicked inhabitants of Canaan; and Jacob and his family from perishing by the famine, by Joseph in Egypt. But this preservation of Israel in the wilderness, was on some accounts more remarkable than any of them; for it was by a continual miracle of so long duration. There was, as may be fairly computed, at first two millions of souls in that congregation. But if miraculous support had been withheld, they must all have perished, in less than a month's time, so that there would not have been one of them left. But yet this vast multitude subsisted for forty years together, in a dry barren wilderness, without sowing, reaping, or tillage. Their bread was daily rained down to them out of heaven, and they were furnished with water out of a rock; and the same clothes with which they came out of Egypt, lasted all that time. Never was any instance like this, of a nation being so upheld for so long a time together. Thus God upheld his church by a continual miracle, and kept alive that people in whom was the blessing, the great Redeemer of the world.

IX. God was pleased, during this time, to give a further revelation of Christ the Redeemer in the predictions of him. Three prophecies deserve particular notice. The first is that of Balaam, Numb. xxiv. 17—19. "I shall see him, but not now; I shall behold him, but not nigh: there shall come a Star out of Jacob, and a Sceptre shall rise out of Israel, and shall smite the corners of Moab, and destroy all the children of Sheth. And Edom shall be a possession, Seir also shall be a possession for his enemies, and Israel shall do valiantly. Out of Jacob shall come he that shall have dominion, and shall destroy him that remaineth of the city." This is a plainer prophecy of Christ, especially with regard to his kingly office, than any former one. But we have another, that God gave by Moses, plainer still, especially with regard to his prophetical office, in Deut. xviii. 18, &c. "I will raise up a prophet from among their brethren, like unto thee, and will put my words in his mouth, and he shall speak unto them all that I command him," &c. This is a plainer prophecy of Christ than any before. All the preceding prophecies were in figurative, mystical language. The first prophecy was so, That the seed of the woman should bruise the serpent's head. The promises made to Abraham, Isaac, and Jacob, That *in their seed all the families of the earth should be blessed,* were also mystical; and not so particular, because the expression, *thy seed,* is general, and not plainly limited to any particular person. The prophecy of Jacob in blessing Judah, Gen. xlix. 8. is in mystical language; and so is that of Balaam, which speaks of Christ under the figurative expression of a *star.* But this is a plain prophecy, without being veiled at all in any mystical language.

There are several things contained in this prophecy of Christ. Here is his mediatorial office in general, ver. 16. Here it is revealed how he should be a person to stand between them and God, a being of such awful majesty, holiness, and justice, that they could not have come to him, and have intercourse with him immediately, without a mediator to stand between them; because, if they came to such a sin-revenging God immediately, they should die; God would prove a consuming fire to them. And here is a particular revelation of Christ with respect to his prophetical office: "I will raise them up a prophet from among their brethren, like unto thee," &c. And further, it is revealed what kind of a prophet he should be; a prophet like unto Moses, who was the head and leader of all the people, and who, under God, had been their redeemer, to bring them out of the house of bondage. He was their shepherd, by whom God led them through the Red sea and the wilderness, was an intercessor for them with God, and was both a prophet and a king in the congregation; for Moses had the power of a king among them. It is said of him, Deut. xxxiii. 5. that *he was king in Jeshurun,* was the prophet by whom God built up his church, and delivered his instructions of worship. Thus Christ was to be a prophet like unto Moses; so that this is both the plainest and fullest prophecy of Christ that ever had been from the beginning of the world to this time.

The next prophecy respects the calling of the Gentiles, which should be after Christ's coming, Deut. xxxii. 21. Here is a very plain prophecy of the rejection of the Jews and calling the Gentiles. As they moved *God* to jealousy, by that which was not God, by casting him off, and taking others, that were no gods, in his room; so God declares that he will move *them* to jealousy in like manner, by casting them off, and taking others, who had not been his people, in their room. The apostle Paul takes notice of this prophecy, as foretelling the calling of the Gentiles, in Rom. x. 19, 20. "But I say, Did not Israel know? First, Moses saith, I will provoke you to jealousy by them that are no people, and by a foolish nation I will anger you. But Esaias is very bold, and saith, I was found of them that sought me not; I was made manifest to them that asked not after me."

Thus you see how the light of the gospel, which first began to dawn and glimmer immediately after the fall, gradually increases the nearer we come to Christ's time.

X. Another thing by which God carried on this work in this time, was a remarkable pouring out of his Spirit on the young generation in the wilderness. The generation that was grown up when they came out of Egypt, from twenty years old and upward, was a very froward and perverse generation. They were tainted with the idolatry and wickedness of Egypt, and were not weaned from it. Ezek. xx. 6—8. Hence they made the golden calf in imitation of the idolatry of Egypt, that was wont to worship a bull or an ox; and therefore cattle are called *the abomination of the Egyptians, i. e.* their idol. With this generation God was exceeding angry, and swore in his wrath, that they should not enter into his rest. But the younger generation, who were under twenty years old when they came out of Egypt, were not so, Numb. xiv. 31. "But your little ones, whom ye said should be a prey, them will I bring in; and they shall know the land that ye have despised." This was the generation with whom the covenant was renewed, as we have an account in Deuteronomy, and that entered into the land of Canaan. This generation God was pleased to make a people to his praise, and they were eminent for piety; as appears by many things said about them; particularly, Jer. ii. 2, 3. "I remember thee, the kindness of thy youth, the love of thine espousals, when thou wentest after me in the wilderness, in a land that was not sown. Israel was holiness to the Lord, and the first-fruits of his increase." Here the generation that went after God in the wilderness, is spoken of with very high commendations, as eminent for holiness. Their love to God is distinguished like the love of a bride at her espousals, when they followed him through that dreadful wilderness, after they went back from Kadesh-Barnea, Deut. viii. 15. "Who led thee through the great and terrible wilderness, wherein were fiery serpents, and scorpions, and drought, where there was no water." Though this generation had a much greater trial, than the generation of their fathers had before they came to Kadesh-Barnea, yet they never murmured against God, as their fathers had done: but their trials had a contrary effect upon them, to awaken, convince, and humble them, and fit them for great mercy. They were awakened by those awful judgments of God inflicted on their fathers, whereby their carcasses fell in the wilderness. God poured out his Spirit with those awakening providences, and their own travel in the wilderness, and the word preached to them by Moses; whereby they were humbled, and at length multitudes of them were savingly converted; as Deut. viii. 2, 3. "And thou shalt remember the way which the Lord thy God led thee these forty years in the wilderness, to humble thee, and to prove thee, to know what was in thine heart, whether thou wouldst keep his commandments, or no. And he humbled thee," &c. And ver. 15. "Who led thee through that great and terrible wilderness,—that he might humble thee, and that he might prove thee, to do thee good at thy latter end." And therefore it is said, Hos. xiii. 5. "I did know thee in the wilderness, in the land of great drought." God allured them, and brought them into that wilderness, and spake comfortably to them, as it was foretold that he would do afterwards, Hos. ii. 14.

Those terrible judgments that were executed in the congregation after their turning back from Kadesh-Barnea, in the matter of Korah, and the matter of Peor, were chiefly on the *old* generation, whom God consumed in the wilderness. Those rebellions were chiefly among the elders of the congregation, who were given up to their hearts' lust; and they walked in their own counsels, and God was grieved with their manners forty years in the wilderness.

That this younger congregation were eminent for piety, appears by all their history. The former generation were wicked, and were followed with curses; but this was holy, and wonderful blessings followed them. God did great things for them; he fought for them, and gave them the possession of Canaan. And it is God's manner, when he hath very great mercies to bestow on a visible people, first, to fit them for such mercies, and then to confer them. So it was here: they believed in God, and by faith overcame Sihon and Og, and the giants of Canaan; and are commended for cleaving to the Lord: Josh. xxiii. 8. Joshua says unto them, "Cleave unto the Lord, as ye have done unto this day." But when Joshua and all that generation were dead, there arose another that knew not the Lord. This pious generation showed a laudable and fervent zeal for God on several occasions; as on occasion of Achan's sin; but especially when they suspected the two tribes and a half had set up an altar in opposition to the altar of burnt-offering. There never was any generation of Israel of which so much good and so little evil is mentioned. It is further observable, that in the time of this generation was the second general circumcision, whereby the reproach of Israel was fully rolled away, and they became pure; and when afterwards they were polluted by Achan, they purged themselves again.

The men of the former generation being dead, and God having sanctified this to himself, he solemnly renewed his covenant with them, as we have a particular account in the 29th chapter of Deuteronomy. We find that such solemn renovations of the covenant commonly accompanied any remarkable pouring out of the Spirit, causing a general reformation: so we find it was in Hezekiah's and Josiah's times. It is questionable whether there ever was a time of so great a flourishing of religion in the Israelitish church, as in that generation; and as, in the christian church, religion was in its most flourishing circumstances in the day of its espousals, in the apostles' days, so it seems to have been with the Jewish church in the days of its first establishment in the times of Moses and Joshua.

Thus God, at this time, gloriously advanced the work of redemption, both by his word and Spirit. Hereby the work of redemption was promoted, not only as it was in itself a glorious instance of redemption in its application, but as this was what God used for the orderly establishment of the Israelitish church, when it was first settled in the regular observance of God's ordinances in Canaan: even as the pouring out of the Spirit, in the beginning of the christian church, was a great means for establishing the christian church in all succeeding ages.

XI. The next thing I would observe, was God's bringing the people of Israel by Joshua, and settling them in that land where Christ was to be born, and which was the great type of the heavenly Canaan, which Christ has purchased. Joshua was of Joseph's posterity, and was an eminent type of Christ, and is therefore called the shepherd, the stone of Israel. Gen. xlix. 24. Being such a type, he bore the name of Christ. *Joshua* and *Jesus* are the same name, the one Hebrew, the other Greek: and therefore, in the New Testament, originally written in Greek, Joshua is called Jesus, Acts vii. 45. "Which also our fathers brought in with Jesus," *i. e.* Joshua; Heb. iv. 8. "If Jesus had given them rest, he would not have spoken of another day;" *i. e.* if Joshua had given them rest.

God wonderfully gave his people possession of this land, conquering its former inhabitants, and the mighty giants, as Christ conquered the devil. He first conquered the great kings on the eastern side of Jordan, Sihon king of the Amorites, and Og king of Bashan; and then divided the river Jordan, as before he had done the Red sea; causing the walls of Jericho to fall down at the sound of the trumpets of the priests. That sound typified the sound of the gospel by the preaching of gospel ministers, the walls of the accursed city Jericho, signifying the walls of Satan's kingdom. After this he wonderfully destroyed the mighty host of the Amorites under the five kings, causing the sun and moon to stand still, to help the people against their enemies, at the prayer of the typical Jesus; plainly intimating, that God would make the whole course of nature to be subservient to the affair of redemption; and that every thing should give place to the welfare of God's redeemed people.

Thus did Christ show his great love to his elect, that he would make the course of nature to give place to their happiness and prosperity; and showed that the sun and moon, and all things visible and invisible, were theirs by his purchase. At the same time, Christ fought as the captain of their host, and cast down great hailstones upon their enemies, by which more were slain than by the sword of Israel. And after this Christ gave the people a mighty victory over a yet greater army in the northern part of the land, gathered together at the waters of Merom, as the sand of the sea-shore, Josh. xi. 4.

Thus God gave the people whence Christ was to proceed, the land where he was to be born; where he was to live, preach, and work miracles; to die, and rise again; and whence he was to ascend into heaven, as the land which was a great type of heaven.

XII. Another thing that God did towards carrying on this affair, was his actually setting up his stated worship among the people, as it had been before instituted in the wilderness. This worship was appointed at mount Sinai; it was to make way for the coming of Christ; and the innumerable ceremonial observances of it were typical of him and his redemption. But there were many parts of their instituted worship that could not be observed in the wilderness, by reason of their unsettled state there. And there were many precepts that respected the land of Canaan, and their places of habitation there; which therefore could not be put in practice, till they came into that land. But now, when this was brought to pass, God set up his tabernacle in the midst of his people, as he had before promised them, Lev. xxvi. 11. "I will set my tabernacle amongst you." The tabernacle was set up at Shiloh, Josh. xviii. 1. and the priests and the Levites had their offices appointed them, and the cities of refuge, and now the people were in a condition to observe their feasts of the first-fruits, and their feasts of ingathering, and to bring all their tithes and appointed offerings to the Lord; and most parts of God's worship were set up, though there were some things that were not observed till afterwards.

XIII. The next thing was God's wonderfully preserving that people, from this time forward, when all the males went up, three times in the year, to the place where God's ark was. The people of Israel were generally surrounded with enemies, who sought all opportunities to destroy them, and dispossess them of their land. Till David's time, there were great numbers in the land of the remains of the Canaanites, and the other former inhabitants of the land, who were bitter enemies to the people of Israel: and these had, three times in the year, a fair opportunity of overrunning their country, and getting possession of their cities, when only the women, and those who were not able to go up, were left behind. And yet they were remarkably preserved throughout all generations at such seasons, agreeably to the promise, Exod. xxxiv. 24. "Neither shall any man desire thy land, when thou shalt go up to appear before the Lord thy God thrice in the year." So wonderfully did God order affairs, and influence the hearts of their enemies. They were full of enmity against Israel, desired to dispossess them of their land, and often had so fair an opportunity, that the whole country was left naked and empty of all that could resist them. It would have been only for them to go and take possession;

and yet we never read, in all their history, of any of their enemies taking these opportunities against them; which could be no less than a continual miracle, which God, for the preservation of his church, kept up for so many generations. It was surely a wonderful dispensation of Divine Providence to maintain and promote God's great design of redemption.

XIV. God's preserving his church and the true religion from being wholly extinct in the frequent apostacies of the Israelites in the time of the judges. How prone was that people to forsake the true God, who had done such wonderful things for them, and to fall into idolatry! and how did the land, from time to time, seem to be almost overrun with it! But yet God never suffered his true worship to be totally rooted out: his tabernacle stood, the ark was preserved, the book of the law was kept from being destroyed, God's priesthood was upheld, and he still had a church among the people. Time after time, when religion seemed to be almost gone, then God granted a revival, and sent some angel, or raised up some eminent person, to be an instrument of their reformation.

XV. God's preserving that nation from being destroyed, although they were so often subdued and brought under the dominion of their enemies. It was a wonder, not only that the true religion was not wholly rooted out, and so the church destroyed that way; but also that the very nation in which that church was, was not utterly destroyed; they were so often brought under the power of their enemies. One while they were subdued by Chushan-rishathaim king of Mesopotamia, another while they were brought under the Moabites; now they *were sold into the hand* of Jabin king of Canaan; then they were under the dominion of the Midianites; now they were sorely distressed by the children of Ammon; and then by the Philistines. But yet God, in all these dangers, preserved them, and kept them from being wholly overthrown. From time to time, when it was come to extremity, and God saw that they were upon the very brink of ruin, then he raised up a deliverer, agreeable to Deut. xxxii. 36. " For the Lord shall judge his people, and repent himself for his servants; when he seeth their power is gone, and there is none shut up or left."—Those remarkable dispensations of Providence are very elegantly set forth by the psalmist, Psal. cvi. 34, &c.—These deliverers were all types of Christ, the great redeemer and deliverer of his church; and some of them very remarkably so; as, Barak, Jephthah, Gideon, and Samson, in very many particulars; and above all in the acts of Samson, as might be shown, were it not that this would take up too much time.

XVI. It is observable, that when Christ appeared to manage the affairs of his church in this period, he often appeared in the form of that nature which he took upon him in his incarnation. So he seems to have appeared repeatedly to Moses, and particularly at that time when God spake to him face to face, as a man speaketh to his friend, and he beheld the similitude of the Lord, (Numb. xii. 8.) after he had besought him to show him his glory; which was the most remarkable vision that ever he had of Christ. There was a twofold discovery that Moses had of Christ: one was spiritual, made to his mind, by the word that was proclaimed, " The Lord, the Lord God, merciful and gracious, long-suffering, and abundant in goodness and truth, keeping mercy for thousands, forgiving iniquity and transgression and sin, and that will by no means clear the guilty; visiting the iniquity of the fathers upon the children, and upon the children's children, unto the third and to the fourth generation," Exod. xxxiv. 6, &c. Another was external; which was that which Moses saw, when Christ passed by, and put him in a cleft of the rock. What he saw was doubtless a glorious human form, in which Christ appeared to him, and in all likelihood the form of his glorified human nature, in which he should afterwards appear. He saw not his face; for it is not to be supposed that any man could subsist under a sight of the glory of Christ's human nature as it now appears.

So it was a human form in which Christ appeared to the seventy elders, of which we have an account, Exod. xxiv. 9, 11. " Then went up Moses and Aaron, Nadab and Abihu, and seventy of the elders of Israel. And they saw the God of Israel: and there was under his feet, as it were a paved work of sapphire-stone, and as it were the body of heaven in his clearness. And upon the nobles of the children of Israel he laid not his hand: also they saw God, and did eat and drink." So Christ appeared afterwards to Joshua in the form of the human nature, Josh. v. 13, 14. " And it came to pass when Joshua was by Jericho, he lift up his eyes, and looked, and behold, there stood a man over against him, with his sword drawn in his hand: and Joshua went unto him, and said unto him, Art thou for us, or for our adversaries? And he said, Nay, but as captain of the host of the Lord am I now come." And so he appeared to Gideon, Judg. vi. 11, &c. and so also to Manoah, Judg. xiii. 17—21. Here Christ appeared to Manoah in a representation both of his incarnation and death; of his incarnation, in that he appeared in a human form; and of his death and sufferings, represented by the sacrifice of a kid, and by his ascending up in the flame of the sacrifice; intimating, that it was he that was the great sacrifice, that must be offered up to God for a sweet savour, in the fire of his wrath, as that kid was burned and ascended up in the flame. *Thus Christ appeared, time after time, in the form of that nature he was afterwards to assume; because he now appeared on the same design and to carry on the same work.*

XVII. Another thing I would mention, done in this period towards the work of redemption, is the beginning of a succession of prophets, and erecting a school of the prophets, in Samuel's time. There was something of this spirit of prophecy in Israel after Moses, before Samuel. Joshua and many of the judges had a degree of it. Deborah was a prophetess; and some of the high-priests were inspired with this spirit; particularly Eli. That space of time was not wholly without instances of those that were set apart of God especially to this office, and so were called prophets. Such an one we read of Judg. vi. 8. " The Lord sent a prophet unto the children of Israel, which said unto them," &c. Such an one he seems to have been of whom we read, 1 Sam. ii. 27. " And there came a man of God to Eli," &c.

But there was no such *order* of men upheld in Israel, for any constancy, before Samuel; the want of it is taken notice of in 1 Sam. iii. 1. " And the word of the Lord was precious in those days; there was no open vision." But in Samuel there was begun a *succession* of prophets, maintained continually from that time, at least with very little interruption, till the spirit of prophecy ceased, about Malachi's time: and therefore Samuel is spoken of in the New Testament as the beginning of this succession of prophets, Acts iii. 24. " And all the prophets from Samuel, and those that follow after, as many as have spoken, have foretold of these days." After Samuel was Nathan, and Gad, Iddo, and Heman, Asaph, and others. And afterwards, in the latter end of Solomon's reign, we read of Ahijah; and in Jeroboam and Rehoboam's time we read of prophets; and so continually one prophet succeeded another till the captivity. In the writings of those prophets who are inserted in the canon of Scripture, we read of prophets as being a constant order of men upheld in the land. And even during the captivity there were prophets still, as Ezekiel and Daniel; and after the captivity, as Zechariah, Haggai, and Malachi.

And because God intended a constant succession of prophets from Samuel's time, therefore in his time was begun a school of the prophets; that is, a school of young men, trained up under some great prophet, who was their master and teacher in the study of divine things, and the practice of holiness, to fit them for this office as God should call them to it. Those young men were called *the sons of the prophets;* and oftentimes they are termed *prophets.* These at first were under the tuition of Samuel. Thus we read of Samuel's being appointed over them, 1 Sam. xix. 20. " And when they saw the company of the prophets prophesying, and Samuel standing as appointed over them." The company of prophets of whom we read 1 Sam. x. 5. were the same. Afterwards we read of their being under Elijah. Elisha was one of these sons; but he desired to have a double portion of his spirit, as his successor, as the eldest son was wont to have a double portion of the estate of his father; and therefore the sons of the prophets, when they perceived that the spirit of Elijah rested on Elisha, submitted themselves to him, and owned him for their master, as they had done Elijah before him, 2 Kings ii. 15. "And when the sons of the prophets which were to view at Jericho, saw him, they said, The spirit of Elijah doth rest on Elisha. And they bowed themselves to the ground before him." Elisha being their master, or teacher, he had the care of them; as you may see, 2 Kings iv. 38. "And Elisha came unto Gilgal, and there was a dearth in the land, and the sons of the prophets were sitting before him: and he said unto his servant, Set on the great pot, and seethe pottage for the sons of the prophets." In Elijah's and Elisha's time, there were several places where there resided companies of these sons of the prophets; as at Bethel, at Jericho, and at Gilgal, unless that at Gilgal and Jericho were the same: and possibly that which is called *the college*, where the prophetess Huldah resided, was another at Jerusalem; see 2 Kings xxii. 14. It is there said of Huldah the prophetess, that *she dwelt in Jerusalem, in the college*. They had houses built, where they used to dwell together; and therefore those at Jericho being multiplied, and finding their house too little for them, desired leave of their master and teacher Elisha, that they might go and hew timber to build a bigger; as you may see, 2 Kings vi. 1, 2. At some times there were numbers of these sons of the prophets in Israel; for when Jezebel cut off the prophets of the Lord, it is said, that Obadiah took a hundred of them, and hid them by fifty in a cave, 1 Kings xviii. 4.

These schools of the prophets being set up by Samuel, and afterwards kept up by such as Elijah and Elisha, must be of divine appointment; and accordingly we find, that those sons of the prophets were often favoured with a degree of inspiration, while they continued under tuition; and God commonly when he called any prophet to the constant exercise of the prophetical office, and to some extraordinary service, took them out of these schools; though not universally. Hence the prophet Amos, speaking of his being called to the prophetical office, says, that he had not been educated in the schools of the prophets, and was not one of the sons of the prophets, Amos vii. 14, 15. But Amos taking notice of it as remarkable, that he should be so called, shows that it was God's ordinary manner to take his prophets out of these schools; for therein he did but bless his own institution.

Now this remarkable dispensation of Providence—God beginning a constant succession of prophets in Samuel's time, which was to last for many ages; and to that end establishing a school of the prophets under Samuel, thenceforward to be continued in Israel—was a step that God took in the great affair of redemption. For the main business of this succession of prophets was, to foreshow Christ, and the glorious redemption he was to accomplish, and so to prepare the way for his coming; as appears by that forementioned place, Acts iii. 24. and Acts x. 43. "To him give all the prophets witness;" and Acts iii. 18. "But those things which God before had showed by the mouth of all his prophets, that Christ should suffer, he hath so fulfilled."

The Old-Testament church was not wholly without light, but had not the light of the sun directly, only as reflected. Now these prophets were the luminaries that reflected the light of the sun; and accordingly they spoke abundantly of Jesus Christ, as appears by what we have of their prophecies in writing. And they made it very much their business, when they studied in their schools or colleges, and elsewhere, to search out the work of redemption; agreeable to what the apostle Peter says of them, 1 Pet. i. 10, 11. "Of which salvation the prophets have inquired, and searched diligently, who prophesied of the grace that should come unto you; searching what, or what manner of time the Spirit of Christ that was in them did signify, when it testified beforehand the sufferings of Christ, and the glory that should follow." We are told, that the church of the Redeemer is built on the foundation of the prophets and apostles, the Redeemer himself being the chief corner-stone, Eph. ii. 20.

This was the first thing of the nature that ever was done in the world; and it was a great thing that God did towards further advancing this great building of redemption. There had been before occasional prophecies of Christ, as was shown; but now the time drawing nearer when the Redeemer should come, it pleased God to appoint a certain order of men, in constant succession, whose main business it should be, to point out Christ and his redemption, and as his forerunners to prepare the way for his coming; and God established schools, wherein multitudes were instructed and trained up to that end, Rev. xix. 10. "I am thy fellow-servant, and of thy brethren that have the testimony of Jesus; for the testimony of Jesus is the spirit of prophecy."

PART V.

FROM DAVID TO THE BABYLONISH CAPTIVITY.

I COME now to the *fifth period* of the times of the Old Testament, beginning with *David*, and extending to the *Babylonish captivity;* and would now proceed to show how the work of redemption was therein carried on.—And here,

I. The first thing to be noticed, is God's anointing that person who was to be the ancestor of Christ, to be king over his people. The dispensations of Providence through the last period, respect the *people* whence Christ was to proceed; but now the Scripture leads us to consider God's providence towards that particular *person* whence Christ was to descend, *viz.* David. It pleased God at this time remarkably to select out this person, from all the thousands of Israel, and to put a most honourable mark of distinction upon him, by anointing him to be king over his people. It was only God that could find him out. His father's house is spoken of as being little in Israel, and he was the youngest of all the sons of his father, and was least expected by Samuel to be the man whom God had chosen. God had before, in the former ages of the world, remarkably distinguished the persons from whom Christ was to come; as Seth, and Noah, and Abraham, and Isaac, and Jacob. But the last that we have any account of God's marking out in any notable manner, the very person of whom Christ was to come, was in Jacob's blessing his son Judah; unless we reckon Nahshon's advancement in the wilderness to be the head of the tribe of Judah. But this distinction of the person of whom Christ was to come, in David, was very honourable; for it was God's anointing him to be king over his people. And there was something further denoted by David's anointing, than was in the anointing of Saul. God anointed Saul to be king *personally;* but God intended something further by sending Samuel to anoint David, *viz.* to establish the crown of Israel in him and his *family*, as long as Israel continued to be a kingdom; and not only so, but what was infinitely more still, establishing the crown of his universal church, his spiritual Israel, in his seed, to the end of the world, and through eternity.

This was a great dispensation of God, and a great step taken towards a further advancing of the work of redemption, according as the time drew near wherein Christ was to come. David, as he was the ancestor of Christ, so he was the greatest personal type of Christ of all under the Old Testament. The types of Christ were of three sorts; instituted, providential, and personal. The ordinance of *sacrificing* was the greatest of the *instituted* types; the redemption out of *Egypt* was the greatest of the *providential;* and David the greatest of the *personal* ones. Hence Christ is often called David in the prophecies of Scripture; as Ezek. xxxiv. 23, 24. "And I will set up one shepherd over them, and he shall feed them, even my servant David; —My servant David a prince among them;" and so in many other places. He is very often spoken of as the seed and the son of David.

David being the ancestor and great type of Christ, his being solemnly anointed by God to be king over his people, that the kingdom of his church might be continued in his family for ever, may in some respects be looked on as an anointing of Christ himself. Christ was as it were anointed in him; and therefore Christ's anointing and David's anointing are spoken of under one scripture, Psal. lxxxix.

20. " I have found David my servant; with my holy oil have I anointed him." And David's throne and Christ's are spoken of as one: Luke i. 32. " And the Lord shall give him the throne of his father David." Acts ii. 30. " David—knowing that God had sworn with an oath to him, that of the fruit of his loins, according to the flesh, he would raise up Christ to sit on his throne."

Thus God beginning the kingdom of his church in the house of David, was, as it were, a new establishing of the kingdom of Christ; the beginning of it in a state of such visibility as it thenceforward continued in. It was planting the root, whence that branch of righteousness was afterwards to spring up, the everlasting king of his church; and therefore this everlasting king is called *the branch from the stem of Jesse.* Isa. xi. 1. " And there shall come forth a rod out of the stem of Jesse, and a branch shall grow out of his roots." Jer. xxiii. 5. " Behold, the days come, saith the Lord, that I will raise up unto David a righteous branch, and a king shall reign and prosper." So chap. xxxiii. 15. " In those days, and at that time, I will cause the branch of righteousness to grow up unto David, and he shall execute judgment and righteousness in the land." So Christ, in the New Testament, is called the root and offspring of David, Rev. xxii. 16.

It is observable, that God anointed David after Saul to reign in his room. He took away the crown from him and his family, who was higher in stature than any of his people, and was in their eyes fittest to bear rule; to give it to David, who was low of stature, and in comparison of despicable appearance. So God was pleased to show how Christ, who appeared despicable, without form or comeliness, and was despised and rejected of men, should take the kingdom from the great ones of the earth. And also it is observable, that David was the youngest of Jesse's sons, as Jacob the younger brother supplanted Esau, and got the birthright and blessing from him; and as Pharez, brother of Christ's ancestor, supplanted Zarah in the birth; and as Isaac, another of the ancestors of Christ, cast out his elder brother Ishmael: thus was that frequent saying of Christ fulfilled, " The last shall be first, and the first last."

II. The next thing I would observe, is God's preserving David's life, by a series of wonderful providences, till Saul's death. I before took notice of the wonderful preservation of other particular persons who were the ancestors of Christ; as Noah, Abraham, Isaac, Jacob; and have observed how, in their preservation, the work of redemption itself may be looked upon as preserved from being defeated, and the whole church, which is redeemed through him, from being overthrown. But the preservation of David was no less remarkable than that of any others already noticed. How often was there but a step between him and death. The first instance of it we have in his encountering a lion and a bear, when they had caught a lamb out of his flock, which, without miraculous assistance, could at once have rent this young stripling in pieces, as easily as they could the lamb that he delivered from them. So the root and offspring of David was preserved from the roaring lion that goes about seeking whom he may devour, and conquered him, and rescued the souls of men, that were as lambs in the mouth of this lion. Another remarkable instance was, in preserving him from that mighty giant Goliath, who was strong enough to have torn him to pieces, and given his flesh to the beasts of the field, and to the fowls of the air, as he threatened. But God preserved him, and gave him the victory over Goliath, so that he cut off his head with his own sword, and thus was made the deliverer of Israel. So Christ slew the spiritual Goliath with his own weapon, the cross, and delivered his represented people. And how remarkably did God preserve David from being slain by Saul, when he first sought his life! He gave him his daughter to be a snare to him, that the hand of the Philistines might be upon him, requiring of him a hundred foreskins of the Philistines, that so his life might be exposed to them. The same divine care was evident in preserving him afterwards, when Saul spake to Jonathan, and to all his servants, to kill David; and in inclining Jonathan, instead of his killing him, as his father commanded, to love him as his own soul, and to be a great instrument of his preservation, even so as to expose his own life to preserve David; though one would have thought that none would have been more willing to have David killed than Jonathan, seeing that he was competitor with him for the crown. Again, Saul threw a javelin at him, to smite him even to the wall; and sent messengers to his house, to watch, and to kill him, when Michal, Saul's daughter, let him down through a window. He afterwards sent messengers, once and again, to Naioth in Ramah, to take him, and they were remarkably prevented by miraculous impressions of the Spirit of God; and afterwards, when Saul, being resolute in the affair, went himself, he also was among the prophets. How wonderfully was David's life preserved at Gath among the Philistines, when he went to Achish the king of Gath, and was there in the hands of the Philistines, who, one would have thought, would have despatched him at once, he having so much provoked them by his exploits against them. He was again wonderfully preserved at Keilah, when he had entered into a fenced town, where Saul thought he was sure of him. And how wonderfully was he preserved from Saul, when he pursued and hunted him in the mountains! How remarkably did God deliver him in the wilderness of Maon, when Saul and his army were compassing David about! How was he delivered in the cave of Engedi, when, instead of Saul's killing David, God delivered Saul into his hands in the cave! David cut off his skirt, and might as easily have cut off his head. He was delivered in like manner in the wilderness of Ziph; and afterwards preserved in the land of the Philistines, though David had fought against the Philistines, and conquered them at Keilah, since he was last among them. This, one would think, would have been sufficient warning to them not to trust him, or let him escape a second time, if ever they had him in their hands again; but yet now, when they had a second opportunity, God wonderfully turned their hearts to befriend and protect, instead of destroying him.

Thus was the precious seed that virtually contained the Redeemer, and all the blessings of his redemption, wonderfully preserved, when hell and earth were conspired to destroy it. How often does David himself take notice of this, with praise and admiration, in the book of Psalms!

III. About this time, the written word of God, or the canon of Scripture, was augmented by Samuel. I have before observed, that the canon of Scripture was begun and the first written rule of faith and manners was given to the church, about the time of Moses. Joshua probably enlarged it, and wrote the last chapter of Deuteronomy, and most of the book of Joshua. Others think that Joshua, Judges, Ruth, and part of the first book of Samuel, were written by Samuel. However that was, of this we have good evidence, that Samuel made an addition to the canon of Scripture; for Samuel is manifestly mentioned in the New Testament, as one of the prophets whose writings we have in Scripture, Acts iii. 24. " Yea and all the prophets from Samuel, and those that follow after, as many as have spoken, have likewise foretold of these days." By that expression, " as many as have spoken," is meant, as many as have spoken by writing.

And the way that Samuel spoke of these times of Christ and the gospel, was by giving the history of those things that typified, and pointed to them, particularly what he wrote concerning David. The Spirit of God moved him to commit those things to writing, chiefly because they pointed to Christ, and the times of the gospel; and, as was said before, this was the main business of all that succession of prophets that began in Samuel. That Samuel added to the canon of the Scriptures seems further to appear from 1 Chron. xxix. 29. " Now the acts of David the king, first and last, behold they are written in the book of Samuel the seer."

Whether the book of Joshua was written by Samuel or not, yet it is the general opinion of divines, that the books of Judges and Ruth, and part of the first book of Samuel, were penned by him. The book of Ruth was penned for this reason, that though it seemed to treat of private affairs, yet the persons chiefly spoken of were of the family whence David and Christ proceeded, and so pointed to what the apostle Peter observed of Samuel and the other prophets, in the third chapter of Acts. These additions to the canon of the Scripture, the great and main instrument of the application of redemption, are to be considered as a further continuation of that work, and an addition made to that great building.

IV. Another thing God did towards this work, at that time, was his inspiring David to show forth Christ and his redemption, in divine songs, which should be for the use of the church, in public worship, throughout all ages. David was himself endued with the spirit of prophecy. He is called *a prophet,* Acts ii. 29, 30. "Let me freely speak to you of the patriarch David, that he is both dead and buried, and his sepulchre is with us unto this day; therefore being a prophet, and knowing that God had sworn with an oath," &c. So that herein he was a type of Christ, that he was both a *prophet* and a *king.*

The oil that was used in anointing David was a type of the Spirit of God; and the type and the antetype were given both together; as we are told, 1 Sam. xvi. 13. "Then Samuel took the horn of oil, and anointed him in the midst of his brethren; and the Spirit of the Lord came upon David from that day forward:" and it is probable, that it now came upon him in its prophetical influences. One way that this Spirit influenced him was by inspiring him to show forth Christ, and the glorious things of his redemption, in divine songs, sweetly expressing the breathings of a pious soul, full of admiration of the glorious things of the Redeemer, inflamed with divine love and elevated praise; and therefore he is called the sweet psalmist of Israel, 2 Sam. xxiii. 1. The main subjects of these songs were the glorious things of the gospel; as is evident by the interpretation that is often put upon them, and the use that is made of them in the New Testament: for there is no one book of the Old Testament that is so often quoted in the New, as the book of Psalms. Joyfully did this holy man sing of those great things of Christ's redemption, that had been the hope and expectation of God's church and people from the beginning; and joyfully did others follow him in it, as Asaph, Heman, Ethan, and others; for the book of Psalms was not all penned by David, though the greater part of it was. Hereby the canon of the Scripture was further enlarged by an excellent portion of divine writ.

This was a great advancement that God made in this building; and the light of the gospel, which had been gradually growing, was exceedingly increased by it: for whereas before there was but here and there a prophecy given of Christ in a great many ages, here Christ is spoken of by his ancestor David abundantly, in multitudes of songs, speaking of his incarnation, life, death, resurrection, ascension into heaven, his satisfaction, intercession; his prophetical, kingly, and priestly office; his glorious benefits in this life and that which is to come; his union with the church, and the blessedness of the church in him; the calling of the Gentiles, the future glory of the church near the end of the world, and Christ's coming to the final judgment. All these things, and many more, concerning Christ and his redemption, are abundantly spoken of in the book of Psalms.

This was also a glorious advancement of the affair of redemption, as God hereby gave his church a book of divine songs for their use in that part of their public worship, *viz.* singing his praises, throughout all ages to the end of the world. It is manifest the book of Psalms was given of God for this end. It was used in the church of Israel by God's appointment: this is manifest by the title of many of the Psalms, in which they are inscribed to the chief musician, *i. e.* to the man that was appointed to be the leader of divine songs in the temple, in the public worship of Israel. So David is called *the sweet psalmist of Israel,* because he penned psalms for the use of the church of Israel; and accordingly we have an account that they were actually made use of in the church of Israel for that end, even ages after David was dead; as 2 Chron. xxix. 30. "Moreover, Hezekiah the king, and the princes, commanded the Levites to sing praises unto the Lord, with the words of David, and of Asaph the seer." And we find that the same are appointed in the New Testament to be made use of in the christian church, in their worship: Eph. v. 19. "Speaking to yourselves in psalms, hymns, and spiritual songs." Col. iii. 16. "Admonishing one another in psalms, hymns, and spiritual songs." So they have been, and will, to the end of the world, be made use of in the church to celebrate the praises of God. The people of God were wont sometimes to worship God by singing songs to his praise before; as they did at the Red sea; and they had Moses's prophetical song, in the 32d chapter of Deuteronomy, committed to them for that end; and Deborah, Barak, and Hannah sung praises to God: but now first did God commit to his church a book of divine songs for their constant use.

V. The next thing I would notice, is God's actually exalting David to the throne of Israel, notwithstanding all the opposition made to it. God was determined to do it, and he made every thing give place that stood in its way. He removed Saul and his sons out of the way; and first set David over the tribe of Judah; then, having removed Ishbosheth, set him over all Israel. Thus did God fulfil his word to David. He took him from the sheep-cote, and made him king over his people Israel, Psal. lxxviii. 70, 71. And now the throne of Israel was established in that family in which it was to continue for ever.

VI. Now first it was that God proceeded to choose a particular city out of all the tribes of Israel to place his name. There is several times mention made in the law of Moses, of the children of Israel bringing their oblations to the place which God should choose; as Deut. xii. 5—7. and other places; but God had never proceeded to do it till now. The tabernacle and ark were never fixed, but sometimes in one place, and sometimes in another; but now God proceeded to choose Jerusalem. The city of Jerusalem was never thoroughly conquered, or taken out of the hands of the Jebusites, till David's time. It is said in Joshua xv. 63. "As for the Jebusites, the inhabitants of Jerusalem, the children of Judah could not drive them out: but the Jebusites dwell with the children of Judah at Jerusalem unto this day." But now David wholly subdued it, as we have an account in 2 Sam. v. And now God proceeded to choose that city *to place his name there,* as appears by David's bringing up the ark thither soon after; and therefore this is mentioned afterwards as the first time God proceeded to choose a city to that end. 2 Chron. vi. 5, 6. and chap. xii. 13. Afterwards God proceeded to show David the very place where he would have his temple built, *viz.* in the threshing-floor of Araunah the Jebusite.

This city of Jerusalem is therefore called the *holy city;* and it was the greatest type of the church of Christ in all the Old Testament. It was redeemed by David, the captain of the hosts of Israel, out of the hands of the Jebusites, to be God's city, the holy place of his rest for ever, where he would dwell. So Christ, the Captain of his people's salvation, redeems his church out of the hands of devils, to be his holy and beloved city. And therefore how often does the Scripture, when speaking of Christ's redemption of his church, call it by the names of Zion and Jerusalem! This was the city that God had appointed to be the place of the first gathering and erecting of the christian church after Christ's resurrection, of that remarkable effusion of the Spirit of God on the apostles and primitive Christians, and the place whence the gospel was to sound forth into all the world; the place of the first christian church, that was to be, as it were, the mother of all other churches through the world; agreeable to that prophecy, Isa. ii. 3, 4. "Out of Zion shall go forth the law, and the word of the Lord from Jerusalem: and he shall judge among the nations, and shall rebuke many people," &c. Thus God chose mount Zion whence the gospel was to be sounded forth, as the law had been from mount Sinai.

VII. The next thing to be observed here, is God's solemnly renewing the covenant of grace with David, and promising that the Messiah should be of his seed. We have an account of it in the 7th chapter of the second book of Samuel. It was done on occasion of the thoughts David entertained of building God a house. On this occasion God sends Nathan the prophet to him, with the glorious promises of the covenant of grace. It is especially contained in these words, (ver. 16.) "And thy house and thy kingdom shall be established for ever before thee; thy throne shall be established for ever." Which promise has respect to Christ, the seed of David, and is fulfilled in him only: for the kingdom of David has long since ceased, any otherwise than as it is upheld in Christ.

That this covenant, now established with David by Nathan the prophet, was the covenant of grace, is evident by the plain testimony of Scripture, Isa. lv. 1—3. There we have Christ inviting sinners to come to the waters, &c. And in the 3d verse, he says, " Incline your ear, and come unto me; hear and your souls shall live; and I will make with you an everlasting covenant, even the sure mercies of David." Here Christ offers to poor sinners, if they will come to him, to give them an interest in the same everlasting covenant that he had made with David, conveying to them the same sure mercies. But what is that covenant, in which sinners obtain an interest when they come to Christ, but the covenant of grace?

This was the fifth solemn establishment of the covenant of grace with the church after the fall. The covenant of grace was revealed and established all along. But there had been particular seasons, wherein God had in a very solemn manner renewed this covenant with his church, giving forth a new edition and establishment of it, revealing it in a new manner. The first was with Adam; the second with Noah; the third with the patriarchs, Abraham, Isaac, and Jacob; the fourth was in the wilderness by Moses; and now the fifth is made to David.

This establishment of the covenant of grace, David always esteemed the greatest smile of God upon him, the greatest honour put upon him; he prized it, and rejoiced in it above all the other blessings of his reign. You may see how joyfully and thankfully he received it, when Nathan came to him with the glorious message, 2 Sam. vii. 18, &c. And so David, in his last words, declares this to be all his salvation, and all his desire; 2 Sam. xxiii. 5. " He hath made with me an everlasting covenant, ordered in all things and sure: for this is all my salvation, and all my desire."

VIII. It was by David that God first gave his people Israel the possession of the whole promised land. I have before shown, how God giving possession of the promised land belonged to the covenant of grace. This was done in a great measure by Joshua, but not fully. Joshua did not wholly subdue that part of the promised land that was strictly called the land of Canaan, and that was divided by lot to the several tribes; but there were great numbers of the old inhabitants left unsubdued, as we read in the books of Joshua and Judges; and there were many left to prove Israel, and to be as thorns in their sides. There were the Jebusites in Jerusalem, and many of the Canaanites, and the whole nation of the Philistines, who all dwelt in that part of the land that was divided by lot, and chiefly in that which belonged to the tribes of Judah and Ephraim.

And thus these remains of the old inhabitants of Canaan continued unsubdued till David's time; but he wholly subdued them all. Which is agreeable to what St. Stephen observes, Acts vii. 45. " Which also our fathers brought in with Jesus (*i. e.* Joshua) into the possession of the Gentiles, whom God drove out before the face of our fathers, unto the days of David." They were till the days of David in driving them out, before they had wholly subdued them. But David entirely brought them under. He subdued the Jebusite, the whole nation of the Philistines, and all the rest of the remains of the seven nations of Canaan; 1 Chron. xviii. 1. " Now after this it came to pass, that David smote the Philistines, and subdued them, and took Gath and her towns out of the hands of the Philistines."

After this, all the remains of the former inhabitants of Canaan were made bond-servants to the Israelites. The posterity of the Gibeonites became servants before, hewers of wood, and drawers of water, for the house of God. But Solomon, David's son and successor, put all the other remains of the seven nations of Canaan to bond-service; at least made them pay a tribute of bond-service, 1 Kings ix. 20—22. And hence we read of the children of Solomon's servants, after the return from the Babylonish captivity, Ezra ii. 55. and Neh. xi. 3. They were the children or posterity of the seven nations of Canaan, that Solomon had subjected to bond-service.

Thus David subdued the whole land of Canaan, strictly so called. But then that was not one half, nor quarter, of the land God had promised to their fathers. The land often promised to their fathers, included all the countries from the river of Egypt to the river Euphrates. These were the bounds of the land promised to Abraham, Gen. xv. 19. " In that same day the Lord made a covenant with Abram, saying, Unto thy seed have I given this land, from the river of Egypt, unto the great river, the river Euphrates." So again God promised at mount Sinai, Exod. xxiii. 31. " And I will set thy bounds from the Red sea even unto the sea of the Philistines, and from the desert unto the river: for I will deliver the inhabitants of the land into your hand; and thou shalt drive them out before thee." So again, Deut. xi. 24. " Every place whereon the soles of your feet shall tread, shall be yours: from the wilderness, and Lebanon, from the river, the river Euphrates, even unto the uttermost sea, shall your coast be." Again, the same promise is made to Joshua: Josh. i. 3, 4. " Every place that the sole of your feet shall tread upon, have I given unto you, as I said unto Moses; from the wilderness and this Lebanon, even unto the great river, the river Euphrates, all the land of the Hittites, and unto the great sea, towards the going down of the sun, shall be your coast." But the land of which Joshua gave the people possession, was but a little part of this land. And the people never had possession of it, till now when God gave it them by David.

This large country did not only include that Canaan which was divided by lot to those who came in with Joshua, but the land of the Moabites and Ammonites, the land of the Amalekites, and the rest of the Edomites, and the country of Zobah. All these nations were subdued and brought under the children of Israel by David. And he put garrisons in the several countries, and they became David's servants, as we have a particular account in the 8th chapter of 2d Samuel: and David extended their border to the river Euphrates, as was promised; see the 3d verse: " And David smote also Hadadezer the son of Rehob, king of Zobah, as he went to recover his border at the river Euphrates." And accordingly we read, that Solomon his son reigned over all the region on this side the river, 1 Kings iv. 24. " For he had dominion over all the region on this side the river, from Tiphsah even unto Azzah, over all the kings on this side the river." This Artaxerxes king of Persia takes notice of long after: Ezra iv. 20. "There have been mighty kings also over Jerusalem, which have ruled over all countries beyond the river; and toll, tribute, and custom was paid unto them."

So that Joshua, that eminent type of Christ, did but begin the work of giving Israel the possession of the promised land; but left it to be finished by that much greater type and ancestor of Christ, even David, who subdued far more of that land than ever Joshua had done. And in this extent of his and Solomon's dominion was some resemblance of the great extent of Christ's kingdom; which is set forth by this very thing, Psal. lxxii. 8. " He shall have dominion also from sea to sea, and from the river unto the ends of the earth." See also 1 Kings viii. 56.

IX. God by David perfected the Jewish worship, and added to it several new institutions. The law was given by Moses, but yet all the institutions of the Jewish worship were not given by Moses; some were added by divine direction. So this greatest of all personal types of Christ did not only perfect Joshua's work, in giving Israel the possession of the promised land, but he also finished Moses's work, in perfecting the instituted worship of Israel. Thus there must be a number of typical prophets, priests, and princes, to complete one figure or shadow of Christ the antetype, he being the substance of all the types and shadows. Of so much more glory was Christ accounted worthy, than Moses, Joshua, David, and Solomon, and all the great prophets, priests, and princes, judges, and saviours of the Old Testament put together.

The ordinances of David are mentioned as of parallel validity with those of Moses, 2 Chron. xxiii. 18. " Also Jehoiada appointed the offices of the house of the Lord by the hand of the priests the Levites, whom David had distributed in the house of the Lord, to offer the burnt-offerings of the Lord, as it is written in the law of Moses, with rejoicing and with singing, as it was ordained by David." The worship of Israel was perfected by David, by the addition he made to the ceremonial law, (1 Chron. xxiii. &c.) consisting in the several orders and courses into which the Levites were divided, and the work and business to which he appointed them, different from what Moses had appointed them to; and also in the divisions of the priests, the sons of Aaron, into four and twenty courses, assigning to every course their business in the house of the Lord, and their particular stated times of attendance there. He also appointed some of the Levites to a new office, that of singers, particularly ordering and regulating them in that office, (1 Chron. xxv.) Others of the Levites he appointed by law to the several services of porters, treasurers, officers, and judges: and these ordinances of David were kept up thenceforth in the church of Israel, as long as the Jewish church lasted. Thus we find the several orders of priests, and the Levites, the porters, and singers, after the captivity. And we find the courses of the priests appointed by David still continuing in the New Testament; Zacharias the father of John the Baptist was a priest of the course of Abia; which is the same with the course of Abijah appointed by David, 1 Chron. xxiv. 10.

Thus David as well as Moses was made like to Christ the Son of David, in this respect, that by him God gave, in a manner, a new ecclesiastical establishment, and new institutions of worship. David did not only add to the institutions of Moses, but by those additions he abolished some of the old institutions that had been in force till that time; particularly those laws which appointed the business of the Levites, which we have in the 3d and 4th chapters of Numbers, which very much consisted in their charge of the several parts and utensils of the tabernacle. But those laws were now abolished; and they were no more to carry those things, as they had been used to do. But David appointed them to other work instead of it; 1 Chron. xxiii. 26. "And also unto the Levites, they shall no more carry the tabernacle, nor any vessels of it for the service thereof:" a sure evidence that the ceremonial law given by Moses is not perpetual, as the Jews suppose; but might be wholly abolished by Christ: for if David, a type of the Messiah, might abolish the law of Moses in part, much more might the Messiah himself abolish the whole.

David, by God's appointment, abolished all use of the tabernacle built by Moses, and of which he had the pattern from God: for God now revealed it to David to be his will, that a temple should be built instead of the tabernacle. This was a great presage of what Christ, the Son of David, would do when he should come, *viz.* abolish the whole Jewish ecclesiastical constitution, which was but as a movable tabernacle, to set up the spiritual gospel-temple, which was to be far more glorious, of greater extent, and was to last for ever. David had the pattern of all things pertaining to the temple showed him, even in like manner as Moses had the pattern of the tabernacle: and Solomon built the temple according to that pattern which he had from his father David, which *he* received from God. 1 Chron. xxviii. 11, 12. "Then David gave to Solomon his son the pattern of the porch, and of the houses thereof, and of the treasuries thereof, and of the upper chambers thereof, and of the inner parlours thereof, and of the place of the mercy-seat, and the pattern of all that he had by the Spirit, of the courts of the house of the Lord, and of all the chambers round about, of the treasuries of the house of God, and of the treasuries of the dedicated things." And, ver. 19. "All this, said David, the Lord made me understand in writing by his hand upon me, even all the works of this pattern."

X. The canon of Scripture seems at or after the close of David's reign to be added to by the prophets Nathan and Gad. It appears probable by the Scriptures, that they carried on the history of the two books of Samuel from the place where Samuel left it, and finished them. These seem to be called *the book of Samuel the seer, and Nathan the prophet, and Gad the seer*, 1 Chron. xxix. 29 "Now the acts of David the king, first and last, behold, they are written in the book of Samuel the seer, and in the book of Nathan the prophet, and in the book of Gad the seer."

XI. The next thing I would notice, is God's wonderfully continuing the kingdom of his visible people in the line of Christ's legal ancestors, as long as they remained an independent kingdom. Thus it was without any interruption worth notice. Indeed the kingdom of all the tribes of Israel was not kept in that line; but the dominion of that part in which the true worship of God was upheld, who were God's visible people, was always kept in the family of David, as long as there was any such thing as an independent king of Israel; according to his promise to David; and not only in the *family* of David, but always in that *part* of David's posterity whence Christ was legally descended. So that Christ's legal ancestor was always on the throne, excepting Jehoahaz, who reigned three months, and Zedekiah; as you may see in Matthew's genealogy of Christ.

Christ was *legally* descended from the kings of Judah, though not *naturally*. He was both legally and naturally descended from David. He was naturally descended from Nathan the son of David; for Mary his mother was one of the posterity of David by Nathan, as you may see in Luke's genealogy: but Joseph, the reputed and legal father of Christ, was naturally descended of Solomon and his successors, as we have an account in Matthew's genealogy. Jesus Christ, though he was not the natural son of Joseph, yet by the law and constitution of the Jews, was Joseph's heir; because he was the lawful son of Joseph's lawful life, conceived while she was his legally espoused wife. The Holy Ghost raised up seed to him. A person, by the law of Moses, might be the legal son and heir of another, whose natural son he was not; as sometimes a man raised up seed to his brother: a brother, in some cases, was to build up a brother's house; so the Holy Ghost built up Joseph's house. Joseph being in the direct line of the kings of Judah, of the house of David, he was in this respect the legal heir of the crown of David; and Christ being legally his first-born son, he was his heir; and so Christ, by the law, was the proper heir of the crown of David, and is therefore said to sit upon the throne of his father David.

The crown of God's people was wonderfully kept in the line of Christ's legal ancestors. When David was old, and not able any longer to manage the affairs of the kingdom, Adonijah, one of his sons, set up to be king, and seemed to have obtained his purpose. All things for a while seemed fair on his side, and he thought himself strong. But Adonijah was not the ancestor of Joseph, the legal father of Christ; and therefore how wonderfully did Providence work here! what a strange and sudden revolution! All Adonijah's kingdom and glory vanished away as soon as it was begun; and Solomon, the legal ancestor of Christ, was established in the throne.

And after Solomon's death, when Jeroboam had conspired against the family, and Rehoboam carried himself in such a manner that it was a wonder *all Israel* was not provoked to forsake him, (as ten tribes actually did,) and set up Jeroboam in opposition to him; and though he was a wicked man, and deserved to have been rejected altogether from being king; yet he being the legal ancestor of Christ, God kept the kingdom of the two tribes, in which the true religion was upheld, in his possession. And though his son Abijam was another wicked prince; yet God still continued the crown in the family, and gave it to Abijam's son, Asa. And afterwards, though many of the kings of Judah were very wicked men, and horribly provoked God, as particularly Jehoram, Ahaziah, Ahaz, Manasseh, and Amon; yet God did not take away the crown from their family, but gave it to their sons, because they were the ancestors of Christ. God's remembering his covenant established with David, is given as the reason why God did thus, notwithstanding their wicked lives; 1 Kings xv. 4. speaking of Abijam's wickedness, it is said, "Nevertheless, for David's sake did the Lord his God give him a lamp in Jerusalem, to set up his son after him, and to establish Jerusalem:" so, 2 Chron. xxi. 7. speaking of Jehoram's great wickedness, it is said, "Howbeit the Lord would not destroy the house of David, because of the covenant he had made with David, and as he promised to give a light unto him, and to his sons for ever."

The crown of the ten tribes was changed from one family to another continually. First, Jeroboam took it; but the crown descended only to his son Nadab. Then Baasha, who was of another family, took it; and it remained in his posterity but one generation after his death. And then Zimri, who was his servant, and not of his posterity, took it; from whom Omri, who was of another family, took it. The crown continued in his family for three successions: and then Jehu, who was of another family, took it. The crown continued in his family for three or four successions; and then Shallum, that was of another family, took it. The crown did not descend at all to his posterity; but Menahem, who was of another family, took it; and it remained in his family but one generation after him. Then Pekah, who was of another family, took it: and after him Hoshea, that was still of another family, took it. So great a difference was there between the crown of Israel and the crown of Judah; the one was continued evermore in the same family, and with very little interruption, in one right line; the other was continually tossed about from one family to another, as if it were the sport of fortune. The reason was not, because the kings of Judah, at least many of them, were better than the kings of Israel; but the one had the blessing in them; they were the ancestors of Christ, whose right it was to sit on the throne of Israel. But with the kings of Israel it was not so; and therefore Divine Providence exercised a continual care, through all the changes that happened through so many generations, and such a long space of time, to keep the crown of Judah in one direct line, in fulfilment of the everlasting covenant he had made with David, the mercies of which covenant were sure mercies; but in the other case there was no such covenant, and so no such interposing care of Providence.

And here it must not be omitted, that there was once a very strong conspiracy of the kings of Syria and Israel, in the time of that wicked king of Judah, Ahaz, to dispossess him and his family of the throne of Judah, and to set one of another family, even the son of Tabeal, on it; as Isa. vii. 6. "Let us go up against Judah, and vex it, and let us make a breach therein for us, and set a king in the midst of it, even the son of Tabeal." And they seemed very likely to accomplish their purpose. There seemed to be so great a likelihood of it, that the hearts of the people sunk within them; they gave up the cause. It is said, "The heart of Ahaz and his people was moved as the trees of the wood are moved with the wind." And on this occasion God sent the prophet Isaiah to encourage the people, and tell them that it should not come to pass. And because it looked so much like a lost cause to Ahaz and the people, therefore God directs the prophet to give them this sign of it, *viz.* that Christ should be born of the *legal seed of Ahaz*, as Isa. vii. 14. "Therefore the Lord himself shall give you a sign: behold, a virgin shall conceive, and bear a son, and shall call his name Immanuel." This was a good sign, and a great confirmation of the truth of what God promised by Isaiah, *viz.* that the kings of Syria and Israel should never accomplish their purpose of dispossessing the family of Ahaz of the crown of Judah, and setting up the son of Tabeal; for Christ the Immanuel was to be of them.

XII. The building of the temple was a great type of three things, *viz.* of Christ, especially his human nature; of the church; and of heaven. The tabernacle seemed rather to represent the church in its movable, changeable state, in this world. But that beautiful, glorious, costly structure, the temple, that succeeded the tabernacle, seems especially to represent the church in its glorified state in heaven. This temple was built according to the direction and the pattern shown by the Holy Ghost to David, in the place where was the threshing-floor of Ornan the Jebusite, in mount Moriah, 2 Chron. iii. 1.; the same mountain (and probably in the very same place) where Abraham offered up his son Isaac; for that is said to be in the land of Moriah, Gen. xxii. 2. and was called *the mountain of the Lord*, as this of the temple was, Gen. xxii. 14. "And Abraham called the name of that place Jehovah-jireh; as it is said to this day, In the mount of the Lord it shall be seen."

This was the house where Christ dwelt, till he came to dwell in human nature. That his body was the antetype of this temple, appears from what he says, "Destroy this temple, and in three days I will raise it up," speaking of the temple of his body, John ii. 19, 20. This continued to be the house of God, the place of worship for his church, till Christ came; the place that God chose, where all their sacrifices were offered up, till the great sacrifice came. Into this temple the Lord came, even the messenger of the covenant. Here he often delivered his heavenly doctrine, and wrought miracles; here his church was gathered by the pouring out of the Spirit, after his ascension. Luke xxiv. 53. "And they were continually in the temple, praising and blessing God." And (Acts ii. 46.) respecting the multitudes that were converted by that great effusion of the Spirit on the day of Pentecost, it is said, "And they continued daily with one accord in the temple." And the sacred historian (Acts v. 42.) speaking of the apostles, says, "And daily in the temple, and in every house, they ceased not to teach and preach Jesus Christ." And thence the sound of the gospel went forth, and the church was spread into all the world.

XIII. It is here worthy to be observed, that in Solomon's reign, after the temple was finished, the Jewish church was risen to its highest external glory. The Jewish church, as to its ordinances and constitution, is compared to the moon, Rev. xii. 1. "And there appeared a great wonder in heaven, a woman clothed with the sun, and the moon under her feet, and upon her head a crown of twelve stars." This church was like the moon in many other respects, but especially that it waxed and waned like the moon. From its first formation, which was in the covenant made with Abraham, when this moon began to appear, it had been gradually increasing in its glory. This time, wherein the temple was finished and dedicated, was about the middle between the calling of Abraham and the coming of Christ, and now it was full moon. After this the glory of the Jewish church gradually decreased, till Christ came; as I shall have occasion to show more particularly.

Now the church of Israel was in its highest external glory. Now Israel was multiplied exceedingly, so that they seemed to have become like the sand on the sea-shore, 1 Kings iv. 20. Now the kingdom of Israel was firmly established in the right family, the family of which Christ was to come. Now God had chosen the city where he would place his name; and had fully given his people the possession of the promised land.—They now possessed the dominion of it all, in quietness and peace, even from the river of Egypt, to the great river Euphrates; all those nations which had formerly been their enemies, quietly submitted to them; none pretended to rebel against them. Now the Jewish worship in all its ordinances was fully settled: instead of a movable tabernacle, they had a glorious temple; the most magnificent, beautiful, and costly structure, that ever had been, or has been since. Now the people enjoyed peace and plenty, and sat every man under his vine and fig-tree, eating and drinking and making merry, 1 Kings iv. 20. They were in the highest pitch of earthly prosperity, silver being as plenty as stones, and the land full of gold and precious stones, and other precious foreign commodities, which were brought by Solomon's ships from Ophir and other parts of the world. Now they had a king reigning over them who was the wisest of men, and probably the greatest earthly prince that ever was: their fame went abroad into all the earth, so that they came from the utmost parts of the earth to see their glory and their happiness.

Thus God was pleased, in one of Messiah's ancestors, remarkably to shadow forth the kingdom of Christ and himself reigning in his glory. David, a man of war, a man who had shed much blood, and whose life was full of troubles and conflicts, was a more suitable representation of Christ in his state of humiliation, wherein he was conflicting with his enemies. But Solomon, a man of peace, was a representation more especially of Christ exalted, triumphing and reigning in his kingdom of peace. And the happy glorious state of the Jewish church at that time, remarkably represented two things:—1. A glorious state of the church on earth, in the latter ages of the world; those days of peace, when nation shall not lift sword against nation, nor learn war any more. 2. The future glorified state of the church in heaven. The earthly Canaan never was so lively a type of the heavenly Canaan as it was then, when the happy people of Israel indeed enjoyed it as a land flowing with milk and honey.

XIV. After this the glory of the Jewish church gradually declined more and more till Christ came; yet the work of redemption went on. Whatever failed or declined, God still carried on this work from age to age; this building was advancing higher and higher. It went on, even during the decline of the Jewish church, towards a further preparation of things for the coming of Christ, as well as during its increase; for so wonderfully were things ordered by the infinitely wise Governor of the world, that whatever happened was ordered for good to this general design, and made a means of promoting it. When the Jews flourished, and were in prosperity, he made *that* to contribute to the promoting of this design; and when they were in adversity, God made this also contribute to the same. While the Jewish church was in its increasing state, the work of redemption was carried on by their increase; and when they came to their declining state, from Solomon's time till Christ, God carried on the work of redemption by *that*. The very decline itself, was one thing that God employed as a further preparation for Christ's coming.

As the moon, from the time of its full, is approaching nearer and nearer to her conjunction with the sun; so her light is still more and more decreasing, till at length, when the conjunction comes, it is wholly swallowed up in the light of the sun. So it was with the Jewish church from the time of its highest glory in Solomon's time. In the latter end of Solomon's reign, the state of things began to darken, by his corrupting himself with idolatry, which much obscured the glory of this mighty and wise prince; and troubles also began to arise in his kingdom. After his death the kingdom was divided, and ten tribes revolted, and withdrew their subjection from the house of David, apostatizing also from the true worship of God in the temple at Jerusalem, and setting up the golden calves of Bethel and Dan. And presently after this the number of the ten tribes was greatly diminished in the battle of Jeroboam with Abijah, wherein there fell down slain of Israel five hundred thousand chosen men; which loss the kingdom of Israel probably never in any measure recovered.

The ten tribes finally apostatized from the true God under Jeroboam. The kingdom of Judah was greatly corrupted, and from that time forward more generally in a corrupt state than otherwise. In Ahab's time the kingdom of Israel did not only worship the calves of Bethel and Dan, but the worship of Baal was introduced. Before, they pretended to worship the true God by these images, the calves of Jeroboam; but now Ahab introduced gross idolatry, and the direct worship of false gods in the room of the true God; and soon after, the worship of Baal was introduced into the kingdom of Judah, *viz.* in Jehoram's reign, by his marrying Athaliah, the daughter of Ahab. After this God began to cut Israel short, by finally destroying and sending into captivity that part which was beyond Jordan, 2 Kings x. 32, &c. Then Tiglath-Pileser subdued and enslaved all the northern parts, 2 Kings xv. 29.; and at last all the ten tribes were subdued by Salmaneser, and they were finally carried away captive out of their own land. After this also the kingdom of Judah was carried captive into Babylon, and a great part of the nation never returned. Those who returned were but a small number, compared with what had been carried captive; and for the most part after this they were dependent on the power of other states. They were subject one while to the kings of Persia, then to the monarchy of the Grecians, and then to the Romans. And before Christ's time, the Jewish church was become exceeding corrupt, overrun with superstition and self-righteousness. And how small a flock was the church of Christ in the days of his incarnation!

God, by this gradual decline of the Jewish state and church from Solomon's time, prepared the way for the coming of Christ several ways.

1. The decline of the glory of this legal dispensation, made way for the introduction of the more glorious dispensation of the gospel. The evangelical dispensation was so much more glorious, that the legal dispensation had no glory in comparison with it. The ancient dispensation, even as it was in Solomon's time, was but an inferior glory, compared with the spiritual glory of the dispensation introduced by Christ. The church, under the Old Testament, was a child under tutors and governors, and God dealt with it accordingly. Those pompous externals are called by the apostle, *weak and beggarly elements*. It was fit that those things should be diminished as Christ approached; as John the Baptist, the forerunner of Christ, speaking of Christ, says, "He must increase, but I must decrease," John iii. 30. It is fit that the twinkling stars should gradually withdraw their glory, when the sun is approaching towards his rising point. The glory of the Jewish dispensation must be gradually diminished, to prepare the way for the more joyful reception of the spiritual glory of the gospel. If the Jewish church, when Christ came, had been in the same external glory that it was in, in the reign of Solomon, men would have their eyes so dazzled with it, that they would not have been likely, joyfully to exchange such great external grandeur, for only the spiritual glory of the despised Jesus. Again,

2. This gradual decline of the glory in the Jewish state, tended to make the glory of God's power, in the great effects of Christ's redemption, the more conspicuous. God's people being so diminished and weakened by one step after another, till Christ came, was very much like the diminishing of Gideon's army. God told Gideon, that the people with him were *too many* for the conquest of the Midianites, lest Israel should vaunt itself, saying, "My own hand hath saved me." And therefore all that were fearful were commanded to return; and there returned twenty and two thousand, and there remained ten thousand. But still they were too many; and then, by trying the people at the water, they were reduced to three hundred men. So the people in Solomon's time were too many, and mighty, and glorious for Christ; therefore he diminished them; first, by sending off the ten tribes; then he diminished them by the captivity into Babylon; and then they were further diminished by their great and general corruption when Christ came; so that Christ found very few godly persons among them. With a small handful of disciples, Christ conquered the world. Thus high things were brought down, that Christ might be exalted.

3. This prepared the way for Christ's coming, as it made the salvation of those Jews who were saved by Christ to be more sensible and visible. Though the greater part of the Jewish nation was rejected, and the Gentiles called in their room; yet a great many thousands of the Jews were saved by Christ after his resurrection, Acts xxi. 20. They being taken from so low a state under temporal calamity in their bondage to the Romans, and from a state of so great superstition and wickedness, it made their redemption the more sensibly and visibly glorious.

XV. I would here take notice of the additions which were made to the canon of Scripture in or soon after the reign of Solomon. There were considerable additions made by Solomon himself, who wrote the books of Proverbs and Ecclesiastes, probably near the close of his reign. His Song of Songs, as it is called, is wholly on the subject we are upon, *viz.* Christ and his redemption, representing the high and glorious relation, union, and love, that is between Christ and his redeemed church. And the sacred history seems, in Solomon's reign, and some of the next succeeding, to have been enlarged by the prophets Nathan and Ahijah, Shemaiah and Iddo. It is probable that part of the history which we have in the first of Kings, was written by them. (See 2 Chron. ix. 29. xii. 15. xiii. 22.)

XVI. God wonderfully upheld his church and the true religion through this period. It was very wonderful, considering the many and great apostacies of that people to idolatry. When the ten tribes had generally and finally forsaken the true worship, God kept up the true religion in the kingdom of Judah; and when *they* corrupted themselves, as they very often did exceedingly, and idolatry was ready totally to swallow up all, yet God kept the lamp alive. When things seemed to be come to an extremity, and religion at its last gasp, he was often pleased to grant blessed revivals by remarkable outpourings of his Spirit, particularly in Hezekiah's and Josiah's time.

XVII. God remarkably kept the book of the law from being lost in times of general and long-continued neglect of it. The most remarkable instance of this kind was its preservation in the time of the great apostacy, during the greatest part of the long reign of Manasseh, which lasted fifty-five years, and the reign of Amon his son. This while the law was so much neglected, and such a careless and profane management of the affairs of the temple prevailed, that the book which used to be laid up by the side of the ark in the Holy of Holies, was lost for a long time; and nobody knew where it was. But yet God preserved it from being finally lost. In Josiah's time, when they came to repair the temple, it was found buried in rubbish. It had been lost so long that Josiah himself seems to have been much a stranger to it. (See 2 Kings xxii. 8, &c.)

XVIII. God remarkably preserved the tribe of which Christ was to proceed, from being ruined through the many and great dangers of this period. The visible church of Christ from Solomon's reign was mainly in the tribe of Judah. The tribe of Benjamin, which was annexed to them, was but a very small tribe, and that of Judah exceeding large; and as Judah took Benjamin under his protection when he went into Egypt to bring corn, so the tribe of Benjamin seemed to be under the covert of Judah ever after. And though, on occasion of Jeroboam's setting up the calves at Bethel and Dan, the Levites resorted to Judah out of all the tribes of Israel, (2 Chron. xi. 13.) yet they were also small, and not reckoned among the tribes. Many of the ten tribes, it is true, on that occasion, for the sake of worshipping God in the temple, left their inheritances in their several tribes, and settled in Judah, and so were incorporated with them, as we have account in the chapter just quoted, (ver. 16.) yet the tribe of Judah was so much the prevailing part, that they were called by one name, *Judah*. Therefore God said to Solomon, 1 Kings xi. 13. "I will not rend away all the kingdom: but will give one tribe to thy son, for David my servant's sake, and for Jerusalem's sake, which I have chosen." So when the ten tribes were carried captive, it is said, there was none left but the tribe of Judah: 2 Kings xvii. 18. "Therefore the Lord was very wroth with Israel, and removed them out of his sight: there was none left but the tribe of Judah only." Whence they were all called *Jews*, a word derived from *Judah*.

This was the tribe of which Christ was to come; and in this chiefly did God's visible church consist, from Solomon's time. This people, over whom the kings who were legal ancestors of Christ, and of the house of David, reigned, was wonderfully preserved from destruction during this period, when they often seemed to be upon the brink of ruin, and just ready to be swallowed up. So it was in Rehoboam's time, when Shishak king of Egypt came against Judah with a vast force. Of this we read in the beginning of the 12th chapter of 2 Chronicles. So it was again in Abijah's time, when Jeroboam set the battle in array against him with eight hundred thousand chosen men; a mighty army! 2 Chron. xiii. 3. Then God wrought deliverance to Judah, out of regard to the covenant of grace established with David, as is evident by ver. 4 and 5. and the victory they obtained was because the Lord was on their side, as you may see, ver. 12. So it was again in Asa's time, when Zerah the Ethiopian came against him with a larger army of a thousand thousand and three hundred chariots, 2 Chron. xiv. 9. On this occasion Asa cried to the Lord, and trusted in him, being sensible that it was nothing with him to help those that had no power: (ver. 11.) "And Asa cried unto the Lord his God, and said, Lord, it is nothing with thee to help, whether with many, or with those that have no power." And accordingly God gave them a glorious victory over this mighty host.

So again it was in Jehoshaphat's time, when the children of Moab, and the children of Ammon, and the inhabitants of mount Seir, combined together against Judah with a mighty army, a force vastly superior to any that Jehoshaphat could raise; and Jehoshaphat and his people were greatly afraid: yet they set themselves to seek God on this occasion, and trusted in him; and God told them by one of his prophets, that they need not fear them, nor should they have any occasion to fight in this battle, they should only *stand still and see the salvation of the Lord*. And according to his direction, they only stood still, and sang praises to God; and God made their enemies do the work themselves, by killing one another; and the children of Judah had nothing to do, but to gather the spoil, which was more than they could carry away. (2 Chron. xx.)

So it was again in Ahaz's time, when Rezin the king of Syria, and Pekah the son of Remaliah, the king of Israel, conspired against Judah, and seemed to be sure of their purpose; of which we have spoken already. So it was again in Hezekiah's time, when Sennacherib, that great king of Assyria, and head of the greatest monarchy then in the world, came up against all the fenced cities of Judah, after he had conquered most of the neighbouring countries. He sent Rabshakeh, the captain of his host, against Jerusalem, who in a very proud and scornful manner insulted Hezekiah and his people, as being sure of victory; and the people were trembling for fear, like lambs before a lion. Then God sent Isaiah the prophet to comfort them, and assure them that their enemies should not prevail; as a token of which he gave them this sign, *viz.* that the earth, for two years successively, should bring forth food of itself, from the roots of the old stalks, without their ploughing or sowing; and then the third year they should sow and reap, and plant vineyards, and eat the fruit of them, and live on the fruits of their labour, as they were wont to do before. (See 2 Kings xix. 29.) This is mentioned as a type of what is promised in ver. 30, 31. "And the remnant that is escaped of the house of Judah, shall yet again take root downward, and bear fruit upward. For out of Jerusalem shall go forth a remnant, and they that escape, out of mount Zion: the zeal of the Lord of hosts shall do this." The corn springing again after it had been cut off with the sickle, and bringing forth another crop from the roots, represents the church reviving again, and flourishing, like a plant after it had seemingly been cut down past recovery. When the enemies of the church have done their utmost, and seem to have gained their point; when they have overthrown the church, so that its being is scarcely visible, but is like a living root hid under ground; there is in it a secret life that will cause it to flourish again, and to take root downward, and bear fruit upward. This was now fulfilled. The king of Assyria had already carried captive the ten tribes; and Sennacherib had also taken all the fenced cities of Judah, and ranged the country round about, and Jerusalem only remained: and Rabshakeh had in his own imagination already swallowed that up, as he had also in the fearful apprehensions of the Jews themselves. But God wrought a wonderful deliverance; he sent an angel, that in one night smote a hundred fourscore and five thousand in the enemy's camp.

XIX. In the reign of Uzziah, and the following reigns, God was pleased to raise up a set of eminent prophets, who should commit their prophecies to writing, and leave them for the use of his church in all ages. We before observed, how that God began a constant succession of prophets in Israel in Samuel's time, and many of these prophets wrote by divine inspiration, and so added to the canon of Scripture. But none of them are supposed to have written *books of prophecies* till now. Several of them wrote *histories* of the wonderful dispensations of God towards his church. This we have observed already of Samuel, who is supposed to have written Judges and Ruth, and part of the first of Samuel, if not the book of Joshua. And Nathan and Gad seem to have written the rest of the two books of Samuel: and Nathan, with Ahijah and Iddo, wrote the history of Solomon, which is probably that which we have in the first book of Kings. The history of Israel seems to have been further carried on by Iddo and Shemaiah: 2 Chron. xii. 15. "Now the acts of Rehoboam, first and last, are they not written in the book of Shemaiah the prophet, and Iddo the seer, concerning genealogies?" And after that the history seems to have been further carried on by the prophet Jehu, the son of Hanani: 2 Chron. xx. 34. "Now the rest of the acts of Jehoshaphat, first and last, behold they are written in the book of Jehu son of Hanani, who is mentioned in the book of the kings of Israel." 1 Kings xvi. 1, 7. And then it was further continued by the prophet Isaiah: 2 Chron. xxvi. 22. "Now the rest of the acts of Uzziah, first and last, did Isaiah the prophet the son of Amos write." He probably did it as well in the second book of Kings, as in the book of his prophecy. And the history was carried on and finished by other prophets after him.

Thus the prophets, even from Samuel's time, had been adding to the canon of Scripture by their historical writings. But now, in the days of Uzziah, did God first raise up a set of great prophets, not only to write histories, but to write books of their prophecies. The first of these is thought to be Hosea the son of Beeri, and therefore his prophecy, or the word of the Lord by him, is called *the beginning of the word of the Lord;* Hos. i. 2. "The beginning of the word of the Lord by Hosea;" that is, the beginning, or the first part, of the written word of that kind, *viz.* that which is written in books of prophecy. He prophesied in the days of Uzziah, Jotham, Ahaz, and Hezekiah, kings of Judah, and in the days of Jeroboam, the son of Joash, king of Israel. There were many other witnesses for God raised up about the same time to commit their prophecies to writing, Isaiah, Amos, Jonah, Micah, Nahum, and probably some others: and so from that time forward God seemed to continue a succession of *writing* prophets.

This was a great dispensation of Providence, and a great advance made in the affair of redemption, which will appear, if we consider, that the main business of the prophets was to point out Christ and his redemption. They were all forerunners of the great prophet. The main end why the spirit of prophecy was given them was, that they might give testimony to Jesus Christ, the great Redeemer, who was to come. Therefore, the testimony of Jesus, and the spirit of prophecy, are spoken of as the same thing; Rev. xix. 10. "And I fell at his feet to worship him: and he said unto me, See thou do it not: I am thy fellow-servant, and of thy brethren that have the testimony of Jesus: worship God: for the testimony of Jesus is the spirit of prophecy." And therefore we find, that the great and main thing that the most of the prophets in their written prophecies insist upon, is Christ and his redemption, and the glorious times of the gospel. And though many other things were spoken of in their prophecies, yet they seem to be only as introductory to their prophecy of these great things. Whatever they predict, here their prophecies commonly terminate.

These prophets, inspired by the Spirit of Christ, wrote chiefly to prepare the way for his coming, and to exhibit the glory that should follow. And in what an exalted strain do they all speak of those things! Many other things they speak of in men's usual language. But when they enter upon this subject, what a joyful heavenly sublimity is there in their language! Some of them are very particular and full in their predictions of these things, and above all the prophet Isaiah, who is therefore deservedly called the *evangelical prophet*. He seems to teach the glorious doctrines of the gospel almost as plainly as the apostles did. The apostle Paul therefore takes notice, that the prophet Esaias is very *bold*, Rom. x. 20. *i. e.* according to the meaning of the word in the New Testament, is very *plain*, he speaks out very plainly and fully; so being *very bold* is used 2 Cor. iii. 12. we use *great boldness of speech*, or *boldness*, as in the margin.

How plainly and fully does the prophet Isaiah describe the manner and circumstances, the nature and end, of the sufferings and sacrifice of Christ, in the 53d chapter of his prophecy! There is scarce a chapter in the New Testament itself which is more full upon it. And how much, and in what a glorious strain, does the same prophet speak, from time to time, of the glorious benefits of Christ, the unspeakable blessings which shall redound to his church through his redemption! Jesus Christ, of whom this prophet spoke so much, once appeared to him in the form of the human nature, the nature he should afterwards take upon him. We have an account of it in the 6th chapter of his prophecy at the beginning: "I saw also the Lord sitting on a throne, high and lifted up, and his train filled the temple," &c. This was Christ, as we are expressly told in the New Testament. (See John xii. 39—41.)

And if we consider the abundant prophecies of this and the other prophets, what a great increase is there of gospel light! How plentiful are the revelations and prophecies of Christ, compared with what they were in the first period of the Old Testament, from Adam to Noah; or to what they were in the second, from Noah to Abraham; or to what they were before Moses, or in the time of Moses, Joshua, and the Judges! This dispensation was also a glorious advance of the work of redemption by the great additions that were made to the canon of scripture. Great part of the Old Testament was written now from the days of Uzziah to the captivity into Babylon. And how excellent are those portions of it! What a precious treasure have those prophets committed to the church of God, tending greatly to confirm the gospel of Christ! and which has been of great comfort and benefit to God's church in all ages since, and doubtless will be to the end of the world.

PART VI.

FROM THE BABYLONISH CAPTIVITY TO THE COMING OF CHRIST.

I COME now to the *last subordinate period* of the Old Testament, *viz.* that which begins with *the Babylonish captivity*, and extends to *the coming of Christ*, being near six hundred years; and shall endeavour to show how the work of redemption was carried on through this period.—But before I enter upon particulars, I would observe three things wherein this period is distinguished from the preceding ones.

1. Though we have no account of a great part of this period in the scripture history, yet the events of it are more the subject of scripture prophecy, than any of the preceding periods. There are two ways wherein the Scriptures give account of the events by which the work of redemption is carried on; one is by *history*, and another is by *prophecy;* and in one or the other of these ways we have in the Scriptures an account how the work of redemption is carried on from the beginning to the end. Although the Scriptures do not contain a proper *history* of the whole, yet the whole chain of great events, by which this affair hath been carried on from the commencement to the finishing of it, is found either in history or *prophecy*. And it is to be observed, that where the Scripture is wanting in one of these ways, it is made up in the other. Where scripture history fails, there prophecy takes place; so that the account is still carried on, and the chain is not broken, till we come to the very last link of it in the consummation of all things.

And accordingly it is observable of this space of time, that though it is so much less the subject of scripture history, than most of the preceding periods, (there being above four hundred years of which the Scriptures give us no history,) yet its events are more the subject of prophecy, than those of all the preceding periods put together. Most of those remarkable prophecies of the book of Daniel, and most of those in Isaiah, Jeremiah, and Ezekiel, against Babylon, Tyrus, Egypt, and many other nations, were fulfilled in this period.

Hence the reason why the Scriptures give us no history of so great a part of this time, is not because the events were not so important, or less worthy of notice, than those of the foregoing periods; for they were great and remarkable. But there are several reasons which may be given for it. One is, that it was the will of God that the spirit of prophecy should cease in this period, (for reasons that may be given hereafter,) so that there were no prophets to write the history of these times; and therefore God designing this, took care that the great events of this period should not be without mention in his word. It is observable, that the *writing* prophets in Israel, were raised up at the latter end of the foregoing period, and at the beginning of this; for the time was now approaching, when, the spirit of prophecy having ceased, there was to be no inspired history, and therefore no other scripture account but what was given in prophecy.

Another reason may be, for the suspension of inspired history, that God in his providence took care, that there should be authentic and full accounts of the events of this period preserved in *profane* history. It is very worthy of notice, that with respect to the events of the five preceding subordinate periods, of which the Scriptures give the history, profane history gives us no account, or at least of but very few of them. There are many fabulous and uncertain accounts of things that happened before; but the commencement of *authentic* profane history is judged to be but about a hundred years before Nebuchadnezzar's time. The learned Greeks and Romans used to call the ages before that *the fabulous age;* but the times after that they called *the historical age.* And from about that time to the coming of Christ, we have undoubted accounts in profane history of the principal events; accounts that wonderfully agree with the many prophecies that relate to those times.

Thus the great God, who disposes all things, took care to give an *historical* account of things from the beginning of the world, through all those former ages concerning which profane history is silent; and ceased not till he came to those ages in which profane history related things with some certainty. And concerning those times he gives us abundant account in *prophecy*, that by comparing profane history with those prophecies, we might see the agreement.

2. This last period of the Old Testament seems to have been remarkably distinguished from all others by great revolutions among the nations of the earth, to make way for the kingdom of Christ. The time now drawing nigh wherein Christ, the great King and Saviour of the world, was to come, great and mighty were the changes that were brought to pass in order to it. The way had been preparing for the coming of Christ from the fall of man, through all the foregoing periods; but now, the time drawing nigh, things began to ripen apace for his coming; and therefore Divine Providence now wrought wonderfully. The greatest revolutions that any history has recorded, since the flood, fell out in this period. Almost all the nations far and near, within the knowledge of the Jews, were overturned again and again. All lands were in their turn subdued, captivated, and as it were emptied, and turned upside down, and that most of them repeatedly, in this period; agreeable to that prophecy, Isa. xxiv. 1. "Behold, the Lord maketh the earth empty; he maketh it waste, and turneth it upside down, and scattereth abroad the inhabitants thereof."

This began with God's visible church, in their captivity by the king of Babylon. And then the cup from them went round to all other nations, agreeable to what God revealed to the prophet Jeremiah, xxv. 15—27. Here special respect seems to be had to the great revolutions in the times of the Babylonish empire. But after that there were three general overturnings before Christ came, in the succession of the three great monarchies of the world, after the Babylonish empire. The king of Babylon is represented in Scripture as overturning the world: but after that, the Babylonish empire was overthrown by Cyrus, who founded the Persian empire in the room of it; which was of much greater extent than the Babylonish empire in its greatest glory. Thus the world was overturned the second time. And then, the Persian empire was overthrown by Alexander, and the Grecian set up, which was still of much greater extent than the Persian. And thus there was a general overturning of the world a third time. After that, the Grecian empire was overthrown by the Romans, and the Roman empire was established; which vastly exceeded all the foregoing empires in power and extent of dominion. And so the world was overturned the fourth time.

These several monarchies, and the great revolutions of the world under them, are abundantly spoken of in the prophecies of Daniel. They are represented in Nebuchadnezzar's image of gold, silver, brass, and iron, and Daniel's interpretation of it, (Dan. ii.) in the vision of the four beasts, and the angel's interpretation of it, (Dan. vii.) And the succession of the Persian and Grecian monarchies is more particularly represented in the 8th chapter, in Daniel's vision of the ram and the he-goat, and again in the 11th chapter.

Beside these four general overturnings, the world was kept in a constant tumult between whiles; and indeed in a continual convulsion through this whole period. Before, the face of the earth was comparatively in quietness; though there were many great wars among the nations, yet we read of no such mighty and universal convulsions and overturnings as there were in this period. The nations of the world, most of them, had long remained on their lees, without being emptied from vessel to vessel, as is said of Moab, Jer. xlviii. 11. Now these great overturnings were because the time of the great Messiah drew nigh. That they were to prepare the way for Christ's coming, is evident by Scripture, particularly by Ezek. xxi. 27. "I will overturn, overturn, overturn it, and it shall be no more, until he come whose right it is, and I will give it him." The prophet, by repeating the word *overturn* three times, has respect to three overturnings, as in the Revelation, viii. 13. The repetition of the word *woe* three times, signifies three distinct woes; as appears by what follows, ix. 12. "One woe is past;" and xi. 14. "The second woe is past, and behold the third woe cometh quickly."

It must be noted, that the prophet Ezekiel prophesied in the time of the Babylonish captivity; and therefore there were three great and general overturnings to come after this prophecy, before Christ came; the first by the Persians, the second by the Grecians, the third by the Romans; and then Christ, whose right it was to take the diadem, and reign, should come. Here these great overturnings are evidently spoken of as preparatory to the coming and kingdom of Christ. But to understand the words aright, we must note the particular expression, "I will overturn, overturn, overturn *it*," *i. e.* the diadem and crown of Israel, or the supreme temporal dominion over God's visible people. This God said should be no more, *i. e.* the crown should be taken off, and the diadem removed, as it is said in the foregoing verse. The supreme power over Israel should be no more in the royal line of David, to which it properly belonged, but should be removed away, and given to others, and overturned from one to another: first the supreme power over Israel should be in the hands of the Persians; then it should be overturned, and be in the hands of the Grecians; and then it should be overturned again, and come into the hands of the Romans, and be no more in the line of David, till that very person should come, who was the Son of David, whose proper right it was, and then God would give it to him.

That those great shakings and revolutions of the nations of the world, were all to prepare the way for Christ's coming, and setting up his kingdom in the world, is further manifest by Haggai ii. 6, 7. "For thus saith the Lord of hosts, Yet once, it is a little while, and I will shake the heavens, and the earth, and the sea, and the dry land: and I will shake all nations, and the desire of all nations shall come, and I will fill this house with glory, saith the Lord of hosts." And again, ver. 21—23. It is evident by this, that these great revolutions and shakings of the nations, whereby the thrones of kingdoms and their armies were overthrown, and every one came down by the sword of his brother, were to prepare the way for the coming of him who is the desire of all nations.

The great changes and troubles that have sometimes been in the visible church of Christ, (Rev. xii. 2.) are compared to the church's being in travail to bring forth Christ: so these great troubles and mighty revolutions, were, as it were, the world's being in travail to bring forth the Son of God. The apostle, in the 8th of Romans, represents the whole creation as groaning and travailing in pain together until now, to bring forth the liberty and manifestation of the children of God.—So the world as it were travailed in pain, and was in continual convulsions, for several hundred years together, to bring forth the first-born child, and the only-begotten Son of God. And those mighty revolutions were as so many pangs and throes in order to it. The world being so long a time kept in a state of war and bloodshed, prepared the way for the coming of the Prince of peace, as it showed the great need the world stood in of such a prince, to deliver the world from its miseries.

It pleased God to order it in his providence, that earthly power and dominion should be raised to its greatest height, and appear in its utmost glory, in those four great monarchies that succeeded one another, and that every one should be greater and more glorious than the preceding, before he set up the kingdom of his Son. By this it appeared how much more glorious his spiritual kingdom was than the most glorious temporal kingdom. The strength and glory of Satan's kingdom in these four mighty monarchies, appeared in its greatest height: for, being the monarchies of the heathen world, the strength of them was the strength of Satan's kingdom. God suffered Satan's kingdom to rise to so great a height of power and magnificence before his Son came to overthrow it, in order to prepare the way for the more glorious triumph of his Son. Goliath must have on all his splendid armour when the stripling David comes against him with a sling and a stone, for the greater glory of David's victory. God suffered one of those great monarchies to subdue another, and erect itself on the other's ruins, appearing still in greater strength, and the last to be strongest and mightiest of all; that so Christ, in overthrowing that, might as it were overthrow them all at once. The stone cut out of the mountain without hands, is represented as destroying the whole image, the gold, the silver, the brass, the iron, and the clay; so that all became as the chaff of the summer threshing-floor.

These mighty empires were suffered thus to overthrow the world, and destroy one another. And though their power was so great, yet they could not uphold themselves, but fell one after another, and came to nothing; even the last of them, which was the strongest, and had swallowed up the earth. It pleased God thus to show in them the instability and vanity of all earthly power and greatness; which served as a foil to set forth the glory of the kingdom of his Son, which never shall be destroyed, Dan. ii. 44. "In the days of these kings shall the God of heaven set up a kingdom, which shall never be destroyed; and the kingdom shall not be left to other people, but it shall break in pieces and consume all these kingdoms, and it shall stand for ever." So greatly does this kingdom differ from all those kingdoms: they vanish away, and are left to other people; but this shall not be so left, but shall stand for ever. God suffered the devil to do his utmost, and to establish his interest, by setting up the greatest, strongest, and most glorious kingdoms in the world, before the despised Jesus overthrew him and his empire. Christ came into the world to bring down the high things of Satan's kingdom, that the hand of the Lord might be on every one that is proud and lofty, and every high tower, and every lofty mountain; as the prophet Isaiah says, chap. ii. 12, &c. And therefore these things were suffered to rise very high, that Christ might appear so much the more glorious in being above them. Thus wonderfully did the great and wise Governor of the world prepare the way for the erecting of the glorious kingdom of his beloved Son Jesus.

3. Another thing for which this last space of time before Christ was particularly remarkable, was the wonderful preservation of the church through all those overturnings. The preservation of the church was on some accounts more remarkable through this period, than through any of the foregoing. It was very wonderful that the church, which now was so weak, and in so low a state, and mostly subject to the dominion of heathen monarchies, should be preserved for five or six hundred years together, while the world was so often overturned, and the earth was rent in pieces, and made so often empty and waste, and the inhabitants of it came down so often every one by the sword of his brother. I say, it was wonderful that the church in its weak and low state, being but a little handful of men, should be preserved in all these great convulsions; especially considering that the land of Judea, the chief place of the church's residence, lay in the midst of the contending parties, was very much the seat of war amongst them, and was often overrun and subdued. It was sometimes in the hands of one people, and sometimes another, and very much the object of the envy and hatred of all heathen nations. It was often almost ruined by them, often great multitudes of its inhabitants being slain, and the land in a great measure depopulated; and those who had them in their power, often intended the utter destruction of the whole nation. Yet they were upheld; they were preserved in their captivity in Babylon, in all the dangers they passed through under the kings of Persia, in the much greater dangers under the empire of the Greeks, and afterwards when the world was trodden down by the Romans.

Their preservation through this period was also peculiarly remarkable, in that we never read of the church suffering persecution in any former period in any measure to such a degree as they did in this, under Antiochus Epiphanes, of which more afterwards. This wonderful preservation of the church through all these overturnings of the world, gives light and confirmation to what we read in the beginning of the 46th psalm: "God is our refuge and strength, a very present help in trouble.—Therefore will not we fear, though the earth be removed, and though the mountains be carried into the midst of the sea; though the waters thereof roar, and be troubled; though the mountains shake with the swelling thereof." Thus I have taken notice of some *general* things wherein this last period of the Old-Testament times was distinguished. I come now to consider how the work of redemption was carried on in *particulars*.

I. The first thing that here offers, is the captivity of the Jews into Babylon. This was a great dispensation of Providence, and such as never was before. The children of Israel in the time of the judges, had often been brought under their enemies; and many particular persons were carried captive at other times. But never had there been any such thing as destroying the whole land, the sanctuary, and the city of Jerusalem, and all the cities and villages of the land, and carrying the whole body of the people out of their own land into a country many hundred miles distant, and leaving the land of Canaan empty of God's visible people. The ark had once forsaken the tabernacle of Shiloh, and was carried captive into the land of the Philistines: but never had there been any such thing as burning the sanctuary, utterly destroying the ark, carrying away all the sacred vessels and utensils, breaking up all their stated worship in the land, and the land lying waste and empty for so many years together. How lively are those things set forth in the Lamentations of Jeremiah! The work of redemption was promoted by this remarkable dispensation in these following ways.

1. It finally cured that nation of their idolatry. The prophet Isaiah, speaking of the setting up of the kingdom of Christ, chap. ii. 18. speaks of the abolishing of idolatry as one thing that should be done to this end: "and the idols he shall utterly abolish." When the time was drawing near, that God would abolish heathen idolatry, through the greater part of the known world, as he did by the preaching of the gospel, it pleased him first to abolish heathenism among his own people; which he did by their captivity into Babylon. This was a presage of that abolition of idols, which God was about to bring to pass by Christ through so great a part of the heathen world.

This nation, that was addicted to idolatry for so many ages, notwithstanding all reproofs, warnings, corrections, and all the judgments God inflicted on them for it; were now finally cured. So that however some might fall into this sin afterwards, as they did about the time of Antiochus's persecution, yet the nation, as a nation, never showed any propensity to this sin any more. This was a remarkable and wonderful change in that people, and what directly promoted the work of redemption, as it was a great advancement of the interest of religion.

2. One thing that prepared the way for Christ's coming, and for setting up the glorious dispensation of the gospel, was the taking away many of those things wherein consisted the glory of the Jewish dispensation. In order to introduce the glorious dispensation of the gospel, the external glory of the Jewish church must be diminished. This the Babylonish captivity did many ways.

First, it removed the temporal dominion of the house of David, *i. e.* the supreme and independent government of themselves. It took away the crown and diadem from the nation. The time now approaching when Christ, the great and everlasting King of his church, was to reign, it was time for the typical kings to withdraw. As God said by Ezekiel, chap. xxi. 26. "He removed the crown and diadem, that it might be no more, till he should come whose right it was." The Jews henceforward were always dependent on the governing power of other nations, until Christ came, for near six hundred years; except about ninety years, during which space they maintained a sort of independence by continual wars under the dominion of the Maccabees and their posterity.

Again, by the captivity, the glory and magnificence of the temple were taken away, and the temple that was built afterwards was nothing in comparison with it. Thus it was meet, that when the time drew nigh that the glorious antetype of the temple should appear, that the typical temple should have its glory withdrawn.

Moreover, they lost by the captivity the two tables of the testimony delivered to Moses, on which God with his own finger wrote the ten commandments on mount Sinai. These seem to have been preserved in the ark till the captivity.—These were in the ark when Solomon placed the ark in the temple, 1 Kings viii. 9. "There was nothing in the ark, save the two tables of stone, which Moses put there at Horeb." We have no reason to suppose any other, but that they remained there as long as that temple stood. But the Jews speak of these as finally lost at that time; though the same commandments were preserved in the book of the law. These tables also were withdrawn on the approach of their antetype.

Another thing that was lost was the Urim and Thummim. This is evident by Ezra ii. 63. "And the Tirshatha said unto them, that they should not eat of the most holy things, till there should stand up a priest with Urim and Thummim." We have no account that this was ever restored; though the ancient writings of the Jews say the contrary. What this Urim and Thummim was, I shall not now inquire; but only observe, that it was something by which the high priest inquired of God, and received immediate answers from him, or by which God gave forth immediate oracles on particular occasions. This was now withdrawn, the time approaching when Christ, the antetype of the Urim and Thummim, the great word and oracle of God, was to come.

Another thing that the ancient Jews say was wanting in the second temple, was the Shechinah, or cloud of glory over the mercy-seat. This was promised to be in the tabernacle: Lev. xvi. 2. "For I will appear in the cloud upon the mercy-seat." And we read elsewhere of the cloud of glory descending into the tabernacle, Exod. xl. 35. and so we do likewise with respect to Solomon's temple. But we have no account that this cloud of glory was in the second temple. And the ancient accounts of the Jews say, that there was no such thing in the second temple. This was needless in the second temple, considering that God had promised that he would fill this temple with glory another way, *viz.* by Christ's coming into it; which was afterwards fulfilled. See Haggai ii. 7. "I will shake all nations, and the desire of all nations shall come, and I will fill this house with glory, saith the Lord of hosts."

When Moses built the tabernacle and altar in the wilderness, and the first sacrifices were offered on it, fire came down from heaven, and consumed the burnt-offering, as in Lev. ix. 24. also when Solomon built the temple, and offered the first sacrifices, 2 Chron. vii. 1. And this fire was never to go out, but to be kept alive with the greatest care, as God commanded, Lev. vi. 13. "The fire shall ever be burning upon the altar; it shall never go out." And there is no reason to suppose the fire kindled in Solomon's time ever went out till the temple was destroyed by the Babylonians. But then it was extinguished, and never was restored. We have no account of its being given on building the second temple, as we have at the building of the tabernacle and first temple. But the Jews, after their return, were forced to make use of their common fire instead of it, according to the ancient tradition of the Jews. Thus the lights of the Old Testament go out on the approach of the glorious Sun of righteousness.

3. The captivity into Babylon occasioned the dispersion of the Jews through the greater part of the known world, before the coming of Christ. For the whole nation being carried away far out of their own land, and continuing in a state of captivity for so long a time, they got possessions, built houses, and settled themselves in the land of their captivity, agreeable to the direction that Jeremiah gave them, (Jer. xxix.) And therefore, when Cyrus gave them liberty to return to the land where they had formerly dwelt, many of them never returned; they were not willing to leave their settlements and possessions there, to go into a desolate country, many hundred miles distant, which none but the old men among them had ever seen; and therefore they were but a small number that returned, as we see in the books of Ezra and Nehemiah. Great numbers tarried behind, though they still retained the same religion with those that returned, so far as it could be practised in a foreign land. Those messengers that we read of in the 7th chapter of Zechariah, that came to inquire of the priests and prophets in Jerusalem, Sherezer and Regem-melech, are supposed to be messengers sent from the Jews that remained still in Babylon.

Those Jews who remained in that country were soon, by the great changes that happened in the world, dispersed thence into all the adjacent countries. Hence we find, that in Esther's time, which was after the return from the captivity, the Jews were dispersed throughout all parts of the vast Persian empire, which extended from India to Ethiopia; Esth. iii. 8. "And Haman said unto king Ahasuerus, There is a certain people scattered abroad, and dispersed among the people in all the provinces of thy kingdom," &c. And so they continued dispersed till Christ came, and till the apostles went forth to preach the gospel. But yet these dispersed Jews retained their religion. Their captivity, as before observed, thoroughly cured them of their idolatry; and it was their manner, as many of them as could, to go up to Jerusalem at their great feasts. Hence we read in the 2nd chapter of Acts, that at the great feast of Pentecost, there were Jews abiding at Jerusalem out of every nation under heaven. These had come up from all countries where they were dispersed, to worship at that feast. And hence we find, in their history, that wherever the apostles went preaching through the world, they found Jews. They came to one city, and to another city, and went into the synagogue of the Jews.

Antiochus the Great, about two hundred years before Christ, on a certain occasion, transplanted two thousand families of Jews from the country about Babylon into Asia the Less; and so they and their posterity, many of them, settled in Pontus, Galatia, Phrygia, Pamphylia, and in Ephesus; and from thence settled in Athens, and Corinth, and Rome. Whence came the synagogues in those places in which the apostle Paul preached.—Now, this dispersion of the Jews through the world before Christ came, did many ways prepare the way for his coming, and setting up his kingdom in the world.

This was a means of raising a general expectation of the Messiah through the world, about the time that he actually came. For the Jews, wherever they were dispersed, carried the Holy Scriptures with them, and so the prophecies of the Messiah; and being conversant with the nations among whom they lived, they, by that means, became acquainted with these prophecies, and with the expectations of the Jews concerning their glorious Messiah. Hence, the birth of such a glorious person in Judea, about that time, began to be the general expectation of all nations, as appears by the writings of learned heathens, which are still extant; particularly the famous poet Virgil, who lived in Italy a little before Christ, has a poem about the expectation of a great prince that was to be born, and the happy times of righteousness and peace he was to introduce; some of it very much in the language of the prophet Isaiah.

Another way by which this dispersed state of the Jews prepared the way for Christ was, that it showed the necessity of abolishing the Jewish dispensation, and introducing a new dispensation of the covenant of grace. It showed the necessity of abolishing the ceremonial law, and the old Jewish worship: for, by this means, the observance of that ceremonial law became impracticable even by the Jews themselves. The ceremonial law was adapted to the state of a people dwelling together in the same land, where was the city which God had chosen; where was the temple, the only place where they might offer sacrifices; and where alone it was lawful for their priests and Levites to officiate, where they were to bring their first-fruits, where were their cities of refuge, and the like. But by this dispersion, many of the Jews lived more than a thousand miles distant, when Christ came; which made the observance of their laws of sacrifices, and the like, impracticable. And though their forefathers might be to blame in not going up to the land of Judea when they were permitted by Cyrus, yet the case was now, as to many of them at least, become impracticable; which showed the necessity of introducing a new dispensation, that should be fitted, not only to one particular land, but to the general circumstances and use of all nations of the world.

Again, this universal dispersion of the Jews contributed to make the facts concerning Jesus Christ publicly known through the world. For, as observed before, the Jews who lived in other countries, used frequently to go up to Jerusalem at their three great feasts, from year to year; by which means, they could not but become acquainted with the wonderful things that Christ did in that land. We find that the great miracle of raising Lazarus excited the curiosity of those foreign Jews who came up at the feast of the passover to see Jesus; John xii. 19—21. These Greeks were foreign Jews and proselytes, as is evident by their coming to worship at the feast of the passover. The Jews who lived abroad among the Greeks, and spoke their language, were called *Greeks, Hellenists*, and *Grecians*, Acts vi. 1. These were not Gentile Christians; for this occurred before the calling of the Gentiles.

By the same means the Jews who went up from other countries became acquainted with Christ's crucifixion. Thus the disciples going to Emmaus say to Christ, whom they did not know, Luke xxiv. 18. "Art thou only a stranger in Jerusalem, and hast not known the things which have come to pass there in these days;" plainly intimating, that the things concerning Jesus were so publicly known to all men, that it was wonderful to find any man unacquainted with them. And so afterwards they became acquainted with the news of his resurrection; and when they returned into their own countries, they carried the news with them, and made these *facts* public through the world, as before they had made the *prophecies* of them.

After this, those foreign Jews who came to Jerusalem, took great notice of the pouring out of the Spirit at Pentecost, and the wonderful effects of it; and many of them were converted by it. There were Parthians, Medes, Elamites, and the dwellers in Mesopotamia, and in Egypt, and the parts of Libya about Cyrene, and the strangers of Rome, Jews and proselytes, Cretes and Arabians. And so they not only carried back the news of these facts, but Christianity itself, into their own countries with them; which contributed much to the spreading of it through the world.

Again, the dispersion of the Jews opened a door for the introduction of the apostles in all places where they came to preach the gospel. For almost in all places where they came to preach the gospel, they found synagogues of the Jews, where the Holy Scriptures were wont to be read, and the true God worshipped; which was a great advantage to the apostles in spreading the gospel through the world. For their way was, into whatever city they came, first to go into the synagogue of the Jews, (they being of the same nation,) and there to preach the gospel unto them. And hereby their new doctrine was taken notice of by their Gentile neighbours, whose curiosity excited them to hear what they had to say; which became a fair occasion to the apostles to preach the gospel to them. This is the account we have in the Acts of the Apostles. And these Gentiles had been before, many of them, prepared in some measure, by the knowledge they had of the Jewish religion, of their worship of one God, their prophecies, and expectation of a Messiah. This knowledge they derived from the Jews, who had long been their neighbours; which opened the door for the gospel to have access to them. And the work of the apostles with them was doubtless much easier, than if they never had heard any thing before of such a person as the apostles preached, or any thing about the worship of one only true God. So many ways did the Babylonish captivity greatly prepare the way for Christ's coming.

II. The next particular that I would notice is, the addition made to the canon of Scripture in the time of the captivity, in those two remarkable portions of Scripture, the prophecies of Ezekiel and Daniel. Christ appeared to each of these prophets in the form of that nature which he was afterwards to take upon him. The prophet Ezekiel gives an account of his thus appearing to him repeatedly, as Ezek. i. 26. "And above the firmament that was over their heads, was the likeness of a throne, as the appearance of a sapphire-stone, and upon the likeness of the throne was the likeness as the appearance of a man above upon it;" and so chap. viii. 1, 2. So Christ appeared to the prophet Daniel: Dan. viii. 15, 16. "There stood before me as the appearance of a man. And I heard a man's voice between the banks of Ulai, which called, and said, Gabriel, make this man to understand the vision." There are several things which make it evident, that this was Christ; but I cannot now stand to mention particulars. Christ appeared again as a man to this prophet, Dan. x. 5, 6. "Then I lift up mine eyes and looked, and behold, a certain man clothed in linen, whose loins were girded with fine gold of Uphaz: his body also was like the beryl, and his face as the appearance of lightning, and his eyes as lamps of fire, and his arms and his feet like in colour to polished brass, and the voice of his words like the voice of a multitude." Comparing this vision with that of the apostle John in the 1st chapter of Revelation, makes it manifest that this person was Christ. And the prophet Daniel, in the historical part of his book, gives an account of a very remarkable appearance of Christ in Nebuchadnezzar's furnace, with Shadrach, Meshach, and Abednego. Dan. iii. 25. "Lo, I see four MEN loose,—and the form of the fourth is like the Son of God."

Christ not only appeared here in the form of the human nature, but he appeared in a furnace, saving those persons who believed on him from that furnace; by which is represented to us, how Christ, by coming himself into the furnace of God's wrath, saves those that believe in him from that furnace, so that it has no power on them; and the wrath of God never reaches or touches them, so much as to singe the hair of their head.

These two prophets, in many respects, were more particular concerning the coming of Christ, and his glorious gospel-kingdom, than any of the prophets had been before. They mention those three great overturnings of the world that should be before he came. Ezekiel is particular in several places concerning the coming of Christ. The prophet Daniel is more particular in foretelling the time of Christ's coming than ever any prophet had been before, (chap. ix.) He foretold, that it should be seventy weeks, *i. e.* seventy weeks of years, or seventy times seven years, which is four hundred and ninety years, from the decree to rebuild and restore the state of the Jews, till the Messiah should be crucified. This must be reckoned from the commission given to Ezra by Artaxerxes, whereby the very particular time of Christ's crucifixion was pointed out, which never had been before. (Ezra vii.)

The prophet Ezekiel is very particular in the mystical description of the gospel-church, in his vision of the temple and city, towards the latter part of his prophecy. The prophet Daniel points out the order of particular events that should come to pass relating to the christian church after Christ was come, as the rise of Antichrist, the continuance of his reign, his fall, and the glory that should follow.—Thus does the gospel-light still increase, the nearer we come to the time of Christ's birth.

III. The next particular I would mention is, the destruction of Babylon, and the overthrow of the Chaldean empire by Cyrus. The destruction of Babylon took place on that night in which Belshazzar the king, and the city in general, were drowned in a drunken festival, which they kept in honour of their gods, when Daniel was called to read the hand-writing on the wall, Dan. v. 30. and it was brought about in such a manner, as wonderfully to show the hand of God, and remarkably to fulfil his word by his prophets, which I cannot now stand particularly to relate. Now that great city, which had long been an enemy to the city of God, was destroyed, after it had stood ever since the first building of Babel, which was about seventeen hundred years. If the check which was put to the building of this city at its beginning, whereby they were prevented from carrying it to that extent and magnificence they intended, promoted the work of redemption, much more did this destruction of it.

This was a remarkable instance of God's vengeance on the enemies of his redeemed church; for God brought destruction on Babylon for the injuries they did to God's children, as is often set forth in the prophets. It also promoted the work of redemption, as thereby God's people who were held captive by them, were set at liberty to return to their own land in order to rebuild Jerusalem; and therefore Cyrus is called God's shepherd, Isa. xliv. and xlv. 1. And these are over and above those ways wherein the setting up and overthrowing the four monarchies of the world did promote the work of redemption.

IV. What next followed was the return of the Jews to their own land, and the rebuilding of Jerusalem and the temple. Cyrus, as soon as he had destroyed the Babylonish, and erected the Persian empire on its ruins, made a decree in favour of the Jews, that they might return to their own land, and rebuild their city and temple. This return of the Jews out of the Babylonish captivity is, next to the redemption out of Egypt, the most remarkable of all the Old-Testament redemptions, and most insisted on in Scripture, as a type of the great redemption of Jesus Christ. It was under the hand of one of the legal ancestors of Christ, *viz.* Zerubbabel, the son of Shealtiel, whose Babylonish name was Sheshbazzar. He was the governor of the Jews, and their leader in their first return out of captivity; and, together with Joshua the son of Josedek the high priest, had the chief hand in rebuilding the temple. This redemption was brought about by the hand of Zerubbabel and Joshua the priest, as the redemption out of Egypt was brought about by the hand of Moses and Aaron.

The return out of the captivity was a remarkable dispensation of Providence. It was remarkable, that the heart of a heathen prince, Cyrus, should be so inclined to favour such a design. He not only gave the people liberty to return, and rebuild the city and temple, but gave charge that they should be helped with silver and gold, with goods, and beasts, as we read in Ezra i. 4. And afterwards God wonderfully inclined the heart of Darius to further the building of the house of God with his own tribute-money, and gave command to their bitter enemies, the Samaritans, who had been striving to hinder them, to help them without fail, by furnishing them with all that they needed in order to it, and to supply them day by day. He made a decree, that whosoever failed of it, timber should be pulled down out of his house, and he hanged thereon, and his house made a dunghill, (Ezra vi.) After this, God inclined the heart of Artaxerxes, another king of Persia, to promote the work of preserving the state of the Jews, by his ample commission to Ezra, (Ezra vii.) He helped them abundantly with silver and gold out of his own bounty, and offered more, as should be needful, out of the king's treasure-house, commanding his treasurers beyond the river Euphrates to give more, as should be needed, unto a hundred talents of silver, a hundred measures of wheat, a hundred baths of wine, a hundred baths of oil, and salt, without prescribing how much. He gave leave to establish magistrates in the land; freeing the priests of toll, tribute, custom, and other things, which render this decree by Artaxerxes the most full and ample in the Jews' favour of any that had been given for the restoring of Jerusalem; and therefore, in Daniel's prophecy, this is called *the decree* for restoring and building Jerusalem; and hence the seventy weeks are dated.

After this, another favourable commission was granted by the king of Persia to Nehemiah, (chap. ii.)—It was remarkable, that the hearts of heathen princes should be so inclined. It was the effect of *his* power, who hath the hearts of kings in his hands, and turneth them whithersoever he will; and it was a remarkable instance of his favour to his people.

Another remarkable circumstance of this restitution of the state of the Jews to their own land was, that it was accomplished against so much opposition of their bitter indefatigable enemies, the Samaritans, who, for a long time together, with all the malice and craft they could exercise, opposed the Jews in this affair, and sought their destruction. One while they were opposed by Bishlam, Mithridath, Tabeel, Rehum, and Shimshai, as in Ezra iv. and then by Tatnai, Shetharboznai, and their companions, as in chap. v. and afterwards by Sanballat and Tobiah, as we read in the book of Nehemiah.

We have showed before, how the settlement of the people in this land in Joshua's time promoted the work of redemption. On the same accounts does their restitution belong to the same work. The re-settlement of the Jews in the land of Canaan belongs to this work, as it was a necessary means of preserving the Jewish church and dispensation in being, till Christ should come. If it had not been for this restoration of the Jewish church, temple, and worship, the people had remained without any temple, or land of their own, that should be as it were their head-quarters, a place of worship, habitation, and resort. The whole constitution, which God had done so much to establish, would have been in danger of utterly failing, long before the six hundred years had expired, which was from about the time of the captivity till Christ. And so all that preparation which God had been making for the coming of Christ, from the time of Abraham, would have been in vain. Now that very temple was built that God would fill with glory by Christ's coming into it, as the prophets Haggai and Zechariah told the Jews in order to encourage them in building it.

V. The next particular I would observe, is the addition made to the canon of the Scriptures soon after the captivity by the prophets Haggai and Zechariah, who were prophets sent to encourage the people in their work of rebuilding the city and temple; and the main argument they use to that end, is the approach of the coming of Christ. Haggai foretold that Christ should be of Zerubbabel's legal posterity. This seems to be the last and most particular revelation of the descent of Christ, till the angel Gabriel was sent to reveal it to his mother Mary.

VI. The next thing I would take notice of, was the pouring out of the Spirit of God that accompanied the ministry of Ezra the priest after the captivity. That there was such an effusion of the Spirit of God, that accompanied Ezra's ministry, is manifest by many things in the books of Ezra and Nehemiah. Presently after Ezra came up from Babylon, with the ample commission which Artaxerxes gave him, whence Daniel's seventy weeks began, he set himself to reform the vices and corruptions he found among the Jews; and his great success in it we have an account of in the 10th chapter of Ezra. So that there appeared a very general and great mourning of the congregation of Israel for their sins, which was accompanied with a solemn covenant that the people entered into with God; and this was followed with a great and general reformation, as we have there an account. And the people about the same time, with great zeal, earnestness, and reverence, gathered themselves together to hear the word of God read by Ezra; and gave diligent attention, while Ezra and the other priests preached to them, by reading and expounding the law, and were greatly affected in the hearing of it. They wept when they heard the words of the law, and set themselves to observe it, and kept the feast of tabernacles, as the Scripture observes, after such a manner as it had not been kept since the days of Joshua the son of Nun, (Neh. viii.) After this, having separated themselves from all strangers, they solemnly observed a fast, by hearing the word, confessing their sins, and renewing their covenant with God. And they manifested their sincerity in that transaction, by actually reforming many abuses in religion and morals; as we learn from the 9th and following chapters of Nehemiah.

It is observable, that it has been God's manner, on every remarkable new establishment of the state of his visible church, to afford a remarkable outpouring of his Spirit. So it was on the first establishment of the church of the

Jews at their coming into Canaan under Joshua; so it was now in this second settlement of the church in the time of Ezra; and so it was on the first establishment of the christian church after Christ's resurrection; God wisely and graciously laying the foundation of those establishments in a work of the Holy Spirit, for the lasting benefit of his church, thenceforward continued in those establishments. And this pouring out of the Spirit, was a final cure of the nation of that particular sin which just before they especially run into, *viz.* intermarrying with the Gentiles: for however inclined to it they were before, they ever after showed an aversion to it.

VII. Ezra added to the canon of the Scriptures. He wrote the book of Ezra; and he is supposed to have written the two books of Chronicles, at least of compiling them, if he was not the author of the materials, or all the parts, of these writings. That these books were written, or compiled and completed, after the captivity, the things contained in the books themselves make manifest; for the genealogies contained therein, are brought down below the captivity; as 1 Chron. iii. 17, &c. We have there an account of the posterity of Jehoiachin for several successive generations. And there is mention in these books of this captivity into Babylon, as of a thing past, and of things that were done on the return of the Jews after the captivity, (1 Chron. ix.) The chapter is mostly filled up with an account of things that came to pass *after* the captivity into Babylon, as you may see by comparing it with what is said in the books of Ezra and Nehemiah. And that Ezra was the person who compiled these books, is probable by this, because they conclude with words that we know are the words of Ezra's history. The two last verses are Ezra's words in the history he gives in the two first verses of the book of Ezra.

VIII. Ezra is supposed to have collected all the books of which the Holy Scriptures did then consist, and disposed them in their proper order. Ezra is often spoken of as a noted and eminent scribe of the law of God, and the canon of Scripture in his time was manifestly under his special care. The Jews, from the first accounts we have from them, have always held, that the canon of Scripture, so much of it as was then extant, was collected, and orderly disposed and settled, by Ezra; and that from him they have delivered it down in the order in which he disposed it, till Christ's time; when the christian church received it from them, and have delivered it down to our times. The truth of this is allowed as undoubted by divines in general.

IX. The work of redemption was carried on and promoted in this period, by greatly multiplying the copies of the law, and appointing the constant public reading of them in all the cities of Israel in their synagogues. It is evident, that before the captivity, there were but few copies of the law. The original was laid up beside the ark; and the kings were required to write out a copy of it for their use, and the law was required to be read to the whole congregation of Israel once every seventh year. And we have no account of any other stated public reading of the law before the captivity but this. And it is manifest by several things that might be mentioned, that copies of the law were exceeding rare before the captivity. But after this, the constant reading of the law was set up in every synagogue throughout the land. First, they began with reading the law, and then they proceeded to establish the constant reading of the other books of the Old Testament. And lessons were read out of the Old Testament, as made up of both the law and the other parts of the Scripture then extant, in all the synagogues, which were set up in every city, and wherever the Jews in any considerable number dwelt. Thus we find it was in the time of Christ and the apostles. Acts xv. 21. "Moses of old time hath in every city them that preach him, being read in the synagogues every sabbath-day." This custom is universally supposed, both by Jews and Christians, to be begun by Ezra. There were doubtless public assemblies before the captivity. They used to assemble at the temple at their great feasts, and were directed, when they were at a loss about any thing in the law, to go to the priest for instruction; and they used also to resort to the prophets' houses: and we read of synagogues in the land before, Psal. lxxiv. 8. But it is not supposed that they had copies of the law for constant public reading and expounding through the land before. This was one great means of their being preserved from idolatry.

X. The next thing I would mention, is God's remarkably preserving the church and nation of the Jews, when they were in imminent danger of being universally destroyed by Haman, as in the book of Esther. This series of providence was very wonderful in preventing this destruction. Esther was doubtless born for this end, to be the instrument of this remarkable preservation.

XI. After this the canon of Scripture was further enlarged in the books of Nehemiah and Esther; the one by Nehemiah himself. Whether the other was written by Nehemiah, or Mordecai, or Malachi, is not of importance for us to know, so long as it is one of those books that were always admitted and received as a part of their canon by the Jews, and was among those books which the Jews called their Scriptures in Christ's time, and as such was approved by him. For Christ often in his speeches to the Jews, manifestly approves and confirms those books, which amongst them went by the name of the *Scriptures*, as might easily be shown.

XII. After this the canon of the Old Testament was completed and sealed by Malachi. The manner of his concluding his prophecy seems to imply, that they were to expect no more prophecies, and no more written revelations from God, till Christ should come. For in the last chapter he prophesies of Christ's coming; ver. 2, 3. "But unto you that fear my name, shall the Sun of righteousness arise with healing in his wings; and ye shall go forth and grow up as calves of the stall. And ye shall tread down the wicked; for they shall be as ashes under the soles of your feet, in the day that I shall do this, saith the Lord of hosts." Then we read in ver. 4. "Remember ye the law of Moses my servant, which I commanded unto him in Horeb for all Israel, with the statutes and judgments," *i. e.* Remember and improve what ye have; keep close to your written rule, as expecting no more additions to it, till the night of the Old Testament is over, and the Sun of righteousness shall at length arise.

XIII. Soon after this, the spirit of prophecy ceased among that people till the time of the New Testament. Thus the Old-Testament light, the stars of the long night, began apace to hide their heads, the time of the Sun of righteousness now drawing nigh. We before observed, how the kings of the house of David ceased before the true king and head of the church came; and how the cloud of glory withdrew, before Christ, the brightness of the Father's glory, appeared. And now the spirit of prophecy ceased. The time of the great prophet of God was now so nigh, it was time for their typical prophets to be silent.

We have now gone through the time of which we have any historical account in the writings of the Old Testament; and the last thing mentioned, by which the work of redemption was promoted, was the ceasing of the spirit of prophecy.—I now proceed to show how the work of redemption was carried on through the remaining times before Christ. In this we have not that thread of scripture history to guide us that we have had hitherto; but have these three things, *viz.* the prophecies of the Old Testament, human histories, and some occasional evidence of things which happened in those times, in the New Testament. Therefore,

XIV. The next particular that I shall mention under this period, is the destruction of the Persian empire, and setting up of the Grecian empire by Alexander. This came to pass about sixty or seventy years after the times wherein the prophet Malachi is supposed to have prophesied, and about three hundred and thirty years before Christ. This was the third revolution that came to pass in this period, and was greater and more remarkable than either of the foregoing. It was very remarkable on account of the suddenness of that conquest which Alexander made, and the greatness of the empire he set up, which much exceeded in extent all the foregoing.

This event is much spoken of in the prophecies of Daniel. This empire is represented by the third kingdom of brass in Daniel's interpretation of Nebuchadnezzar's dream,

Dan. ii. And in Daniel's vision of the four beasts, it is represented by the third beast that was like a leopard, that had on his back four wings of a fowl, to represent the swiftness of its conquest, chap. vii. and is more particularly represented by the he-goat in the 8th chapter, that came from the west on the face of the whole earth, and touched not the ground, to represent how swiftly Alexander overran the world. The angel himself expressly interprets this he-goat to signify the king of Grecia, ver. 21. "The rough goat is the king of Grecia; and the great horn that is between his eyes is the first king," *i. e.* Alexander himself.

After Alexander had conquered the world, he soon died; and his dominion did not descend to his posterity, but four of his principal captains divided his empire between them. Now that being broken, and four stood up for it, four kingdoms stand up out of the nation, but not in his power; as in the 11th chapter of Daniel. The angel after foretelling the Persian empire, proceeds to foretell Alexander, ver. 3. "And a mighty king shall stand up, that shall rule with great dominion, and do according to his will." Then he foretells, in the 4th verse, the dividing of his kingdom between his four captains: "And when he shall stand up, his kingdom shall be broken, and shall be divided toward the four winds of heaven; and not to his posterity, nor according to his dominion which he ruled: for his kingdom shall be plucked up, even for others besides those." Of these four captains, one had Egypt and the neighbouring countries on the *south* of Judea; and another had Syria and the neighbouring countries *north* of Judea; and these two are called *the kings of the north and of the south.* (Dan. xi.)

Now, this setting up of the Grecian empire did greatly prepare the way for Christ's coming, and for the erection of his kingdom. Besides the ways common to others in this period, there is one peculiar to this revolution, which remarkably promoted the work of redemption; and that was, that it made the Greek language common in the world. To have one common language understood and used through the greater part of the world, must greatly prepare the way for the setting up of Christ's kingdom. This gave advantage for spreading the gospel through all nations, with vastly greater ease, than if every nation had a distinct language, and did not understand each other. For though some of the first preachers of the gospel had the gift of tongues, so that they could preach in any language; yet all had not this particular gift; and they who had could not exercise it when they would, but only at special seasons, when the Spirit of God was pleased to inspire them in this way. And the churches in different and distant parts of the world, as at Jerusalem, Antioch, Galatia, Corinth, &c. could not have had that communication of which we have an account in the book of Acts, without a common language.—After the Grecian empire was set up, many in all these countries well understood the Greek language; which wonderfully opened the door for mutual communication between those churches which were so far separated one from another.

Again, making the Greek language common through so great a part of the world, did wonderfully make way for the kingdom of Christ, because it was the language in which the New Testament was to be originally written. The apostles propagated the gospel through many scores of nations; and if those nations could not have understood the Bible any otherwise than as it was translated into so many languages, it would have rendered the spreading of the gospel vastly more difficult. But by the Greek being made common to all, they all understood the New Testament of Jesus Christ in the language in which the apostles and evangelists originally wrote it. As soon as ever it was written by its original penmen, it immediately lay open to the world in a language that was commonly understood.

XV. The next thing I notice is the translating of the Old Testament into the Greek language, which was commonly understood by the Gentiles. This is commonly called the Septuagint, or the translation of the Seventy; and is supposed to have been made about fifty or sixty years after Alexander's conquests. This is the first translation that ever was made of the Scriptures that we have any credible account of. The canon of the Old Testament had been completed by the prophet Malachi but about a hundred and twenty years before in its original. Hitherto the Scriptures had remained locked up among the Jews in the Hebrew tongue, which was understood by no other nation; but now it was translated into a language that was commonly understood by the nations of the world.

This translation of the Old Testament is still extant, and is of great use. The Jews have many fables about the occasion and manner of this translation; but the truth of the case is supposed to be this, that multitudes of the Jews living in other parts of the world besides Judea, and being born and bred among the Greeks, the Greek became their common language. These not understanding the original Hebrew, they procured the Scriptures to be translated for their use into the Greek language: and so henceforward the Jews, in all countries, except Judea, were wont in their synagogues to make use of this translation instead of the Hebrew.

This translation of the Scriptures into a language so commonly understood through the world, greatly prepared the way for setting up Christ's kingdom in the world. For the apostles commissioned to preach through the world, made great use of the scriptures of the Old Testament, and especially of the prophecies concerning Christ that were contained in them. By means of this translation, and by the Jews being scattered every where, they had the Scriptures at hand in a language understood by the Gentiles. Hence they principally made use of this translation in their preaching and writings wherever they went. In all the numerous quotations out of the Old Testament in their writings, they are made almost every where in the very words of the Septuagint. The sense is the same as in the original Hebrew; though the words are different. But yet this makes it evident, that the apostles in their preaching and writings, commonly made use of this translation. And this translation was principally used in christian churches through most nations of the world, for several hundred years after Christ.

XVI. The next thing is the wonderful preservation of the church when it was eminently threatened and persecuted under the Grecian empire. The first time they were threatened was by Alexander himself. When besieging the city of Tyre, he sent to the Jews for assistance and supplies for his army. Out of a conscientious regard to their oath to the king of Persia, they refused; but he being a man of a very furious spirit, agreeable to the scripture representation of the rough he-goat, marched against them, with a design to cut them off. When he met the priests going out to him in their priestly garments, God wonderfully turned his heart to spare them, and favour them, as he did the heart of Esau when he met Jacob.

After this, one of the kings of Egypt, a successor of one of Alexander's four captains, entertained a design of destroying the nation of the Jews;* but was remarkably and wonderfully prevented by a stronger interposition of Heaven for their preservation.

But the most wonderful preservation of them all in this period was under the cruel persecution of Antiochus Epiphanes, king of Syria, and successor of another of Alex-

* On the death of Alexander the Great, Ptolemy Lagus assumed the regal title in Egypt. He was succeeded by Ptolemy Philadelphus, Evergetes, and Philopater. This last, no doubt, is the person to whom our author here alludes. He was a cruel tyrant, revengeful and debauched. Having been at Jerusalem, during his expedition to Syria, and having been denied an entrance into the temple, he was greatly enraged against the whole body of the Jews. There were great numbers of them at Alexandria; these he degraded into slaves. The only condition by which a mark of disgrace with hot iron, and consequent slavery, could be avoided, was to offer sacrifice to his gods. Out of many thousands, only three hundred yielded by base compliance. These being excommunicated by their brethren, roused Philopater into greater fury He meditated nothing less than the utter ruin of the whole nation, beginning with those of Alexandria. He ordered them to be brought into the Hippodrome, an immense place without the city where the people usually assembled to see public races and diversions, and gave a peremptory injunction that five hundred elephants should be let loose upon them in that place. The first appointed day, the king, who was to have been present, overslept himself after a nocturnal debauch. The second passed by a similar disappointment. On the third day the king came to the Hippodrome, and the elephants were let loose upon the defenceless Jews.—But, by a wonderful providence, these animals turned upon the spectators and soldiers, and great numbers were killed by them. This, attended with some other circumstances of affright, induced the tyrant to desist from his cruel purpose.—W.

ander's four captains. The Jews were at that time subject to the power of Antiochus; and he being enraged against them, long strove to his utmost utterly to destroy them, and root them out; at least all of them that would not forsake their religion, and worship his idols. He did indeed in a great measure waste the country, and depopulate the city of Jerusalem; and profaned the temple, by setting up his idols in some parts of it; and persecuted the people with insatiable cruelty; so that we have no account of any persecution like this before. Many of the particular circumstances of this persecution would be very affecting were there time to insist on them. This cruel persecution began about a hundred and seventy years before Christ. It is spoken of in the prophecy of Daniel, Dan. viii. 9, 25. xi. 31—38. and in the New Testament, Heb. xi. 36—38.

Antiochus intended not only to extirpate the Jewish religion, but, as far as in him lay, the very nation; and particularly laboured to the utmost to destroy all copies of the law. And considering how weak they were, in comparison with a king of such vast dominion, the providence of God appears very wonderful in defeating his design. Many times the Jews seemed to be on the very brink of ruin, just ready to be wholly swallowed up; and their enemies often thought themselves sure of obtaining their purpose. They once came against the people with a mighty army, with a design of killing all, except the women and children, and of selling these for slaves; and so confident were they of obtaining their purpose, and others of purchasing, that above a thousand merchants came with the army, with money in their hands, to buy the slaves that should be sold. But God wonderfully stirred up and assisted one Judas, and others his successors, called the Maccabees, who, with a small handful in comparison vanquished their enemies time after time, and delivered their nation. This also was foretold by Daniel, xi. 32. Speaking of Antiochus's persecution, he says, "And such as do wickedly against the covenant, shall be corrupt by flatteries: but the people that do know their God, shall be strong and do exploits."

God afterwards brought this Antiochus to a fearful, miserable end, by a loathsome disease, under dreadful torments of body and horrors of mind; which was foretold, (Dan. xi. 45.) in these words, "Yet he shall come to his end, and none shall help him." After his death, there were attempts still to destroy the church; but God baffled them all.

XVII. The next thing is the destruction of the Grecian, and setting up of the Roman, empire. This was the fourth revolution in this period. And though it was brought to pass more gradually than the setting up of the Grecian empire, yet it far exceeded that, and was much the greatest and largest temporal monarchy that ever was in the world; so that the Roman empire was commonly called *all the world;* as in Luke ii. 1. "And there went out a decree from Cæsar Augustus, that all the world should be taxed:" *i. e.* all the Roman empire.

This empire is spoken of as much the strongest and greatest of any of the four: Dan. ii. 40. "And the fourth kingdom shall be strong as iron: forasmuch as iron breaketh in pieces, and subdueth all things: and as iron that breaketh all these, shall it break in pieces, and bruise." Dan. vii. 7, 19, 23. The time when the Romans first conquered and subdued the land of Judea, was between sixty and seventy years before Christ. Soon after this, the Roman empire was established in its greatest extent; and the world continued subject to it henceforward till Christ came, and many hundred years after.

The nations being thus united under one monarchy when Christ came, and when the apostles went forth to preach the gospel, greatly prepared the way for the spreading of the gospel, and the setting up of Christ's kingdom in the world.—For the world being thus subject to one government, it opened a general communication, and so opportunity was given for the more swift propagation of the gospel. Thus we find it in the British dominions, the communication is quick from one part to another. There are innumerable difficulties in travelling through different nations, that are under different independent governments, which there are not in travelling through different parts of the same realm, or different dominions of the same prince. So the world being under one government, that of the Romans, facilitated the apostles' travelling.

XVIII. About the same time learning and philosophy were risen to their greatest height in the heathen world.—Almost all the famous philosophers among the heathen, were after the captivity into Babylon. Almost all the wise men of Greece and Rome flourished in this time. What these philosophers in general chiefly professed as their business, was to inquire, wherein man's chief happiness lay, and how to obtain it. They seemed earnestly to busy themselves in this inquiry, and wrote multitudes of books about it, many of which are still extant; but they were exceedingly divided, there having been reckoned several hundreds of different opinions which they had concerning it. Thus they wearied themselves in vain, wandering in the dark, not having the glorious gospel to guide them. God was pleased to suffer men to do the utmost that they could with human wisdom, and to try the utmost extent of their own understandings in order to find out the way to happiness, before the true light came to enlighten the world. God suffered these great philosophers to try what they could do for six hundred years together; and then it proved by the events of so long a time, that all they could do was in vain; the world not becoming wiser, better, or happier under their instructions, but growing more and more foolish, wicked, and miserable. He suffered this, that it might be seen how far reason and philosophy could go in their highest ascent, that the necessity of a divine teacher might more convincingly appear. God was pleased to make foolish the wisdom of this world—to show men the folly of their best wisdom—by the doctrines of his glorious gospel, which were above the reach of all their philosophy. See 1 Cor. i. 19—21.

After God had showed the vanity of human learning, when set up in the room of the gospel, God was pleased to make it subservient to the purposes of Christ's kingdom, as a handmaid to divine revelation. Thereby the vanity of human wisdom was shown, and the necessity of the gospel appeared; and hereby a handmaid was prepared to the gospel. An instance of this we have in the apostle Paul, who was famed for his much learning, (Acts xxvi. 24.) being skilled in the learning not only of the Jews, but also of the philosophers. This he improved to subserve the gospel; as he did in disputing with the philosophers at Athens, Acts xvii. 22, &c. By his learning he knew how to accommodate himself in his discourses to learned men, having read their writings; and he cites their own poets. Dionysius, a philosopher, was converted by him, and was made a great instrument of promoting the gospel. And there were many others in that and the following ages, who were eminently useful by their human learning in promoting the interests of Christ's kingdom.

XIX. Just before Christ was born, the Roman empire was raised to its greatest height, and also settled in peace. About four and twenty years before Christ, Augustus Cæsar, the first Roman emperor, began to rule as emperor of the world. Till then the Roman empire had of a long time been a commonwealth under the government of the senate: but then it became an absolute monarchy. This personage, as he was the first, so he was the greatest of all the Roman emperors: he reigned in the greatest glory. Thus the power of the heathen world, which was Satan's visible kingdom, was raised to its greatest height, after it had been strengthening itself more and more from the days of Solomon, which was about a *thousand years.* Now the heathen world was in its greatest glory for strength, wealth, and learning.

God did two things to prepare the way for Christ's coming, wherein he took a contrary method from that which human wisdom would have taken. He brought his own visible people very low, and made them weak; but the heathen, his enemies, he exalted to the greatest height, for the more glorious triumph of the cross of Christ. With a small number in their greatest weakness, he conquered his enemies in their greatest glory. Thus Christ triumphed over principalities and powers in his cross.

Augustus Cæsar had been for many years establishing his empire, and subduing his enemies, till the very year that Christ was born: when, all his enemies being subdued, his dominion over the world seemed to be gloriously settled. All was established in peace; in token whereof the Romans shut the temple of Janus, which was an established symbol among them of there being universal peace throughout the empire. And this universal peace, which was begun that very year in which Christ was born, lasted twelve years, even till the year that Christ disputed with the doctors in the temple.

Thus the world, after it had been, as it were, in a continual convulsion for so many hundred years together—like the four winds striving together on the tumultuous raging ocean, whence arose those four great monarchies—was now established in the greatest height of the fourth and last monarchy, and settled in quietness. Now all things are ready for the birth of Christ. This remarkable universal peace, after so many ages of tumult and war, was a fit prelude for ushering the glorious Prince of peace into the world.

Thus I have gone through the first grand period of the whole space between the fall of man and the end of the world, *viz.* from the fall to the time of the incarnation of Christ; and have shown the truth of the first proposition, *viz.* That *from the fall of man to the incarnation of Christ*, God was doing those things which were preparatory to Christ's coming, and were forerunners of it.

PART VII.

IMPROVEMENT OF THE FIRST PERIOD.

BEFORE I proceed to the next period, I would make some few remarks, by way of improvement upon what has been said under this.

I. From what has been said, we may strongly argue, that Jesus of Nazareth is indeed the Son of God, and the Saviour of the world; and so that the christian religion is the true religion, seeing that Christ is the very person so evidently pointed at, in all the great dispensations of Divine Providence from the very fall of man, and was so undoubtedly in so many instances foretold from age to age, and shadowed forth in a vast variety of types and figures. If we seriously consider the course of things from the beginning, and observe the motions of all the great wheels of providence, we shall discern that they all tend hither. They are all as so many lines, whose course, if it be observed and accurately followed, will be found to centre here. It is so very plain in many things, that it would argue stupidity to deny it. This person, sent from God, came into the world with his commission and authority, to do his work, and to declare his mind. The Governor of the world, in all his great works towards Jews and Gentiles, down to the time of Christ's birth, has declared it. It is a plain and evident truth, that he who was born at Bethlehem, who dwelt at Nazareth and Capernaum, and who was crucified without the gates of Jerusalem, must be the great Messiah. Blessed are all they that believe in and confess him, and miserable are all that deny him. This shows the unreasonableness of the deists, who deny revealed religion, and of the Jews, who deny that this Jesus is the Messiah foretold and promised to their fathers.

Here should any object, That it may be, some cunning men contrived this history, and these prophecies, on purpose to prove that he is the Messiah. To such it may be replied, How could such a thing be contrived by cunning men to point to Jesus Christ, long before he ever was born? How could they know that any such person would be born? And how could their subtlety help them to foresee and point at an event that was to come to pass many ages afterwards? For no fact can be more evident, than that the Jews had those writings long before Christ was born: as they have them still in great veneration, in all their dispersions through the world. They would never have received such a contrivance from Christians, to prove Jesus to be the Messiah, whom they always denied; and much less would they have been made to believe that they always had those books in their hands, if they had been an imposition.

II. What has been said, affords a strong argument for the divine authority of the books of the Old Testament, from that admirable harmony there is in them, whereby they all point to the same thing. For we may see by what has been said, how all the parts of the Old Testament, though written by so many different penmen, and in ages so distant, harmonize one with another. All agree in one, and centre in the same event; which it was impossible for any one of them to know, but by divine revelation.

Now, if the Old Testament was not inspired by God, what account can be given of such an agreement? for if these books were written without any divine direction, then none of these penmen knew that there would come such a person as Jesus Christ into the world; his coming was only a mere figment of their own brain: and if so, how happened it, that this figment of theirs came to pass? How came a vain imagination of theirs, which they foretold without any manner of ground for their prediction, to be exactly fulfilled? and especially how did they come all to agree in it, all pointing exactly to the same thing, though many of them lived so many hundred years distant one from another?—This admirable consent and agreement in a future event, is therefore a clear and certain evidence of the divine authority of those writings.

III. Hence we may learn how weak and ignorant the objection is, against the Old Testament being the word of God, because it consists so much of warlike histories and civil transactions. Here, say some, we have histories of their kings and rulers, their wars with neighbouring nations, and the changes that happened in their state and government: but other nations used to keep histories of their public affairs, as well as they; why then should we think that these histories which the Jews kept are the word of God, more than those of other people? What has been said, shows the folly and vanity of such an objection. For hereby it appears, that the case of these histories is very different from that of all others. This history alone gives us an account of the first original of all things; and this alone deduces things down to us in a wonderful series from that original, giving an idea of the grand scheme of Divine Providence, as tending to its great end. And, together with the doctrines and prophecies contained in it, the same book gives a view of the whole series of the great events of Divine Providence, from the origin to the consummation of all things; exhibiting an excellent and glorious account of the wise and holy designs of the supreme Governor in all.—No common history has had such penmen. This history was all written by men who came with evident signs and testimonies of their being prophets of the most high God, immediately inspired.—And though *histories*, yet containing those great events of providence by which it appears how God has been carrying on the glorious work of redemption from age to age, they are no less full of divine instruction, and those things that show forth Christ, and his glorious gospel, than the other parts of the Holy Scriptures.

To object against a book's being divine, merely because it is historical, is a poor fancy; as if that could not be the word of God which gives an account of what is past; or as though it were not reasonable to suppose, that God, in a revelation he should give mankind, would give us any relation of the dispensations of his own providence. If so, it must be because his works are not worthy to be related: or because the scheme of his government, and the series of his dispensations towards his church, and the world he has made, is not worthy that any record should be kept of it.

The objection, That it is a common thing for nations and kingdoms to write histories and keep records of their wars, and the revolutions that come to pass in their territories, is so far from being a weighty objection against the historical part of Scripture, as though it were not the word of God, that it is a strong argument in favour of it. For if the light of nature teaches all civilized nations to keep records of the events of *their* government and the series of their administrations, and to publish histories for the information of others, how much more may we expect that God would give the world a record of the dispensations of *his* government, which doubtless is infinitely more worthy of a history for our information? If wise kings have taken care that there should be good histories written of the nations over which they have reigned, shall we think it incredible, that Jesus Christ should take care that his church, which is his nation, his peculiar people, should have in their hands a certain infallible history of their nation, and of his government of them?

If it had not been for the history of the Old Testament, how woefully should we have been left in the dark about many things which the church of God needs to know! How ignorant should we have been of God's dealings towards mankind, and towards his church, from the beginning! We should have been wholly in the dark about the creation of the world, the fall of man, the first rise and continued progress of the dispensations of grace towards fallen mankind. We should have known nothing how God at first set up a church in the world, and how it was preserved; after what manner he governed it from the beginning; how the light of the gospel first began to dawn in the world; how it increased, and how things were preparing for the coming of Christ.

If we are Christians, we belong to that building of God that has been the subject of our discourse: but if it had not been for the history of the Old Testament, we should never have known what was the first occasion of God's going about this building, how the foundation of it was laid, and how it has gone on from the beginning. The times of the history of the Old Testament are mostly such as no other history includes; and therefore, if God had not taken care to give and preserve an account of these things for us, we should have been wholly without them.

Those that object against the authority of the Old-Testament history, may as well object against Moses's account of the creation; for, in the former, we have a history of a work no less important, *viz.* the work of redemption. Yea, this is a far greater and more glorious work. If it be inquired which of the two works, that of creation, or that of providence, is greatest? it must be answered, the work of providence; but the work of redemption is the greatest of the works of providence.—And let those who make this objection consider what part of the Old-Testament history can be spared, without making a great breach in that thread or series of events by which this glorious work has been carried on.——This leads me to observe,

IV. That, from what has been said, we may see much of the wisdom of God in the composition of the Scriptures of the Old Testament, *i. e.* in the parts of which it consists. Let us briefly take a view of the several parts of it, and of the need there was of them.

It was necessary, for instance, that we should have some account of the creation of the world, of our first parents, and their primitive state; of the fall, of the old world, and its degeneracy; of the universal deluge, and the origin of nations after this destruction of mankind.

It seems necessary, moreover, that there should be some account of the succession of the church of God from the beginning. God suffered all the world to degenerate, and took one nation only to be his people, to preserve the true worship and religion till the Saviour of the world should come. In them the world was gradually prepared for that great light, and those wonderful things of which he was to be the author. Thus they were a typical nation, that in them God might shadow forth and teach, as under a vail, all the future glories of the gospel. It was therefore necessary that we should have some account of this; how it was first effected by the call of Abraham, and by their being bond-slaves in Egypt, and how they were brought to Canaan. It was necessary that we should have some account of the revelation which God made of himself to that people, in giving their law, in the appointment of their typical worship, wherein the gospel is vailed, and of the formation of their civil and ecclesiastical state.

It seems exceeding necessary that we should have some account of their being actually brought to Canaan, the country promised them and where they always dwelt; that we should have a history of the successions of the church of Israel, and of those providences towards them, which were most considerable and fullest of gospel mystery; that we should have some account of the promised external glory of that nation under David and Solomon, and a very particular account of David, whose history is so full of the gospel, and in whom began the race of their kings; and that we should have some account of the building of the temple, which was also full of gospel-mystery.

And it is a matter of great consequence, that we should have some account of Israel's dividing from Judah, and of the ten tribes' captivity and utter rejection, and therefore a brief history of them till that time; that we should have an account of the succession of the kings of Judah, and of the church, till their captivity into Babylon; of their return from captivity, and resettlement in their own land, with the origin of the last state of the church before Christ came.

A little consideration will convince any one, that all these things were necessary, and that none of them could be spared; and in the general, that it was necessary we should have a history of God's church till such times as are within the reach of human histories. It was of vast importance that we should have an inspired history of those times of the Jewish church, wherein there was kept up a more extraordinary intercourse between God and them, while he used to dwell among them as it were visibly, revealing himself by the Shechinah, by Urim and Thummim, and by prophecy, and so more immediately to order their affairs. And it was necessary that we should have some account of the great dispensations of God in prophecy, after the finishing of inspired history; for which it was needful that there should be a number of prophets raised who should foretell the coming of the Son of God, and the nature and glory of his kingdom, as so many harbingers to make way for him, and that their prophecies should remain in the church.

It was also a matter of great consequence that the church should have a book of divine songs given by inspiration from God, wherein there should be a lively representation of the true spirit of devotion, of faith, hope, and divine love, of joy, resignation, humility, obedience, repentance, &c. as in the Psalms; also that we should have from God such books of moral instructions as we have in Proverbs and Ecclesiastes, relating to the affairs and state of mankind, and the concerns of human life, containing rules of true wisdom and prudence for our conduct in all circumstances; and that we should have particularly a song representing the great love between Christ and his spouse the church, adapted to the disposition and holy affections of a true christian soul towards Christ, and representing his grace and marvellous love to, and delight in, his people, as in Solomon's Song. It is important that we should have a book to teach us how to conduct ourselves under affliction, seeing the church of God here is in a militant state, and God's people through much tribulation enter into the kingdom of heaven. The church is for a long time under trouble, meets with fiery trials, and extreme sufferings, before her time of peace and rest in the latter ages of the world. Therefore God has given us a book most proper in these circumstances, the book of Job; and though written on occasion of the afflictions of a particular saint, it was probably at first given to the church in Egypt under her afflictions there; and is made use of by the apostle to comfort Christians under persecutions, James v. 11. "Ye have heard of the patience of Job, and have seen the end of the Lord; that the Lord is very pitiful, and of tender mercy." God was also pleased, in this book of Job, to give some view of the ancient divinity before the giving of the law.

Thus, from this brief review, I think it appears, that every part of the scriptures of the Old Testament is very useful and necessary, and no part of it can be spared without loss to the church. And therefore the wisdom of God is conspicuous in ordering, that the scriptures of the Old Testament should consist of those very books of which they do consist.

Before I dismiss this particular, I would add, that it is very observable, that the history of the Old Testament is large and particular where the great affair of redemption required it; even where there was most done towards this work, most to typify Christ, and to prepare the way for him. Thus it is very particular in the history of Abraham and the other patriarchs; but very short in the account we have of the time which the children of Israel spent in Egypt. It is large in the account of the redemption out of Egypt, and the first settling of the affairs of the Jewish church and nation in the time of Moses and Joshua; but much shorter in the times of the judges. So again, it is large and particular in the times of David and Solomon, and then very short in the history of the ensuing reigns. Thus the accounts are large and short, just as there is more or less of the affair of redemption to be seen in them.

V. From what has been said, we may see, that Christ and his redemption are the great subject of the whole Bible. Concerning the New Testament, the matter is plain; and by what has been said, it appears to be so also with respect to the Old Testament. Christ and his redemption is the great subject of the prophecies of the Old Testament, as has been shown. It has also been shown, that he is the great subject of the songs of the Old Testament; and the moral rules and precepts are all given in subordination to him. Christ and his redemption are also the great subject of the history of the Old Testament from the beginning all along; and even the history of the creation is brought in as an introduction to the history of redemption that immediately follows it. The whole book, both Old Testament and New, is filled up with the gospel; only with this difference, that the Old Testament contains the gospel under a vail, but the New contains it unvailed, so that we may see the glory of the Lord with open face.

VI. By what has been said, we may see the usefulness and excellency of the Old Testament. Some are ready to look on the Old Testament as being out of date, and as if we in these days of the gospel have but little to do with it. But this is a very great mistake, arising from want of observing the nature and design of the Old Testament, which, if it were observed, would appear full of the gospel of Christ, and would in an excellent manner illustrate and confirm the glorious doctrines and promises of the New Testament. Those parts of the Old Testament which are commonly looked upon as containing the least divine instruction, are mines and treasures of gospel-knowledge; and the reason why they are thought to contain so little is, because persons do but superficially read them. The treasures which are hid underneath are not observed. They only look on the top of the ground, and suddenly pass a judgment that there is nothing there. But they never dig into the mine: if they did, they would find it richly stored with what is more valuable than silver and gold, and would be abundantly requited for their pains.

What has been said, may show us what a precious treasure God has committed into our hands, in that he has given us the Bible. How little do most persons consider what a privilege they enjoy, in the possession of that holy book, the Bible, which they have in their hands, and may converse with as they please. What an excellent book is this, and how far exceeding all human writings! It reveals God to us, and gives us a view of the grand design and glorious scheme of providence from the beginning of the world, either in history or prophecy. It reveals the great Redeemer, his glorious redemption, and the various steps by which God accomplishes it from the first foundation to the top-stone! Shall we prize a history which gives us a clear account of some great earthly prince, or mighty warrior, as of an Alexander, a Cæsar, or a Marlborough? and shall we not prize the history that God gives us of the glorious kingdom of his Son Jesus Christ, the Prince and Saviour, and of the great transactions of that King of kings, and Lord of armies, the Lord mighty in battle; and what he has wrought for the redemption of his chosen people?

VII. What has been said, may make us sensible how much most persons are to blame for their inattentive, unobservant way of reading the Scriptures. How much profitable matter do the Scriptures contain, if it were but observed! The Bible is the most comprehensive book in the world. But what will all this signify to us, if we read it without observing what is the drift of the Holy Ghost in it? The psalmist, (Psal. cxix. 18.) begs of God, "That he would enlighten his eyes that he might behold wondrous things out of his law." The Scriptures are full of wondrous things. Those histories which are too commonly read as if they were only private concerns of particular persons, such as of Abraham, Isaac, Jacob, and Joseph; of Ruth, Joshua, the Judges, David and the Israelitish princes, are accounts of vastly greater things, things of greater importance and more extensive concernment, than they who read them are commonly aware of.

The histories of Scripture are but too commonly read, as if they were written only to entertain men's fancies, when the infinitely great things contained in them are passed over without notice. Whatever treasures the Scriptures contain, we shall be never the better for them if we do not observe them. He that has a Bible, and does not observe what it contains, is like a man who has a box full of silver and gold, and does not know it, nor observe that it is any thing more than a vessel filled with common stones. He will be never the better for his treasure; and so might as well be without it. He who has plenty of the choicest food stored up in his house, and does not know it, will never taste what he has, and will be as likely to starve as if his house were empty.

VIII. What has been said, may show us how great a person Jesus Christ is, and how great his errand into the world, seeing there was so much done to prepare the way for his coming. God had been preparing the way for him through all ages of the world from the very beginning. If we had notice of a certain stranger being about to come into a country, and should observe that a great preparation was made for him, great things were done, many alterations made in the state of the whole country, many hands employed, persons of great note engaged in making the preparation; and all the affairs and concerns of the country ordered so as to be subservient to the design of entertaining that person, it would be natural for us to think, surely this is some extraordinary person, and it is some very great business that he is coming upon. How great a person then must he be, for whose coming the great God of heaven and earth, and Governor of all things, spent four thousand years in preparing the way! Soon after the world was created, and from age to age, he has been doing great things, bringing mighty events to pass, accomplishing wonders without number, often overturning the world in order to it. He has been causing every thing in the state of mankind, and all revolutions and changes in the habitable world, from generation to generation, to be subservient to this great design.—Surely this must be some great and extraordinary person, and a great work indeed it must needs be, about which he is coming.

We read, (Matt. xxi. 8—10.) when Christ was coming into Jerusalem, and multitudes ran before him, having cut down branches of palm-trees, and strewed them in the way; and others spread their garments in the way, crying, "Hosanna to the Son of David," that the whole city was moved, saying, Who is this? They wondered who that extraordinary person should be, that there should be such preparation made on occasion of his coming into the city. But if we consider, what great things were done in all ages to prepare the way for Christ's coming, and how the world was often overturned to make way for it, much more may we cry out, Who is this? What great person is this? and say, (as in Psal. xxiv. 8, 10.) "Who is this King of glory," that God should show such respect, and put such vast honour upon him? Surely this person is honourable in God's eyes, and greatly beloved of him; and surely it is a grand errand upon which he is sent.

PERIOD II.

FROM CHRIST'S INCARNATION TO HIS RESURRECTION.

HAVING shown how the work of redemption was carried on through the first period, from the fall of man to the incarnation of Christ, I come now to the second period, *viz.* the time of Christ's humiliation, or the space from his incarnation to his resurrection. And this is the most remarkable article of time that ever was or ever will be. Though it was but between thirty and forty years, yet more was done in it than had been done from the beginning of the world to that time. We have observed, that all which had been done from the fall to the incarnation of Christ, was only preparatory for what was now done. And it may also be observed, that all which was done before the beginning of time, in the eternal counsels between the persons of the blessed Trinity, chiefly respected this period. We therefore now proceed to consider the *second proposition, viz.*

That during the time of Christ's humiliation, from his incarnation to his resurrection, the purchase of redemption was made.

Though many things had been done in the affair of redemption, though millions of sacrifices had been offered; yet nothing was done to *purchase* redemption before Christ's incarnation. No part of the purchase was made, no part of the price was offered till now. But as soon as Christ was incarnate, the purchase began.—And the whole time of Christ's humiliation, till the morning that he rose from the dead, was taken up in this purchase. Then the purchase was entirely and completely finished. As nothing was done before Christ's incarnation, so nothing was done after his resurrection, to purchase redemption for men. Nor will there ever be any thing more done to all eternity. That very moment when the human nature of Christ ceased to remain under the power of death, the utmost farthing was paid of the price of salvation for every one of the elect.

But for the more orderly and regular consideration of the great things done by our Redeemer to purchase redemption for us, I would speak of his becoming incarnate to capacitate himself for this purchase;—and of the purchase itself.

PART I.

OF CHRIST'S INCARNATION.

CHRIST became incarnate, or, which is the same thing, became man, to put himself in a capacity for working out our redemption. For though Christ, as God, was infinitely sufficient for the work, yet to his being in an immediate capacity for it, it was needful that he should not only be God, but man. If Christ had remained only in the divine nature, he would not have been in a capacity to have purchased our salvation; not from any imperfection of the divine nature, but by reason of its absolute and infinite perfection: for Christ, merely as God, was not capable either of that obedience or suffering that was needful. The divine nature is not capable of *suffering;* for it is infinitely above all suffering. Neither is it capable of *obedience* to that law which was given to man. It is as impossible that one who is only God, should obey the law that was given to man, as it is that he should suffer man's punishment.

And it was necessary not only that Christ should take upon him a *created* nature, but that he should take upon him *our* nature. It would not have sufficed for Christ to have become an *angel*, and to have obeyed and suffered in the angelic nature. But it was necessary that he should become a *man*, upon three accounts.

1. *It was needful in order to answer the law, that the very nature to which the law was given, should obey it.* Man's law could not be answered, but by being obeyed by man. God insisted upon it, that the law which he had given to man shall be honoured, and fulfilled by the nature of man, otherwise the law could not be answered for men. The words, "Thou shalt not eat thereof," &c. were spoken to the race of mankind, to the human nature; and therefore the human nature must fulfil them.

2. *It was needful to answer the law that the nature that sinned should die.* These words, "Thou shalt surely die," respect the human nature. The same nature to which the command was given, was that to which the threatening was directed.

3. *God saw meet, that the same world which was the stage of man's fall and ruin, should also be the stage of his redemption.* We read often of his coming into the world to save sinners, and of God's sending him into the world for this purpose.—It was needful that he should come into this sinful, miserable, undone world, in order to restore and save it. For man's recovery, it was needful that he should come down to man, to man's proper habitation, and that he should tabernacle with us: John i. 14. "The Word was made flesh, and dwelt among us."

Concerning the incarnation of Christ, I would observe these following things.

I. The incarnation itself; in which especially two things are to be considered, *viz.*

1. His conception; which was in the womb of one of the race of mankind, whereby he became truly the Son of man, as he was often called. He was one of the posterity of Adam, a child of Abraham, and a son of David, according to God's promise. But his conception was—not in the way of ordinary generation, but—by the power of the Holy Ghost. Christ was formed in the womb of the Virgin, of the substance of her body, by the power of the Spirit of God. So that he was the immediate son of the woman, but not the immediate son of any male whatsoever; and so was the seed of the woman, and the son of a virgin, one that had never known man.

2. His birth.—Though the conception of Christ was supernatural, yet after he was conceived, his human nature was gradually perfected in the womb of the virgin, in a way of natural progress; and so his birth was in the way of nature. But his conception being supernatural, by the power of the Holy Ghost, he was both conceived and born without sin.

II. The second thing I would observe concerning the incarnation of Christ, is the fulness of the time in which it was accomplished. It was after things had been preparing for it from the very first fall of mankind, and when all things were ready. It came to pass at a time, which in infinite wisdom was the most fit and proper: Gal. iv. 4. "But when the fulness of time was come, God sent forth his Son, made of a woman, made under the law."

It was now the most proper time on every account. Any time before the flood would not have been so fit a time. For then the mischief and ruin that the fall brought on mankind, was not so fully seen. The curse did not so fully come on the earth before the flood, as it did afterwards: for though the ground was cursed in a great measure before, yet it pleased God that the curse should once, before the restoration by Christ, be executed in an universal destruction, even of the very form of the earth, that the dire effects of the fall might be seen before the recovery. Though mankind were mortal before the flood, yet their lives were almost a thousand years in length, a kind of immortality in comparison with what the life of man is now. It pleased God, that the curse, *Dust thou art, and unto dust thou shalt return,* should have its full accomplishment, and be executed in its greatest degree on mankind, before the Redeemer came to purchase a never-ending life.

It would not have been so fit a time for Christ to come, before Moses; for till then mankind were not so universally apostatized from the true God; they were not fallen universally into heathenish darkness; and so the need of Christ, the light of the world, was not so evident. The woful consequence of the fall with respect to man's mortality, was not so fully manifest till then; for man's life was not so shortened as to be reduced to the present standard, till about Moses's time.

It was most fit that the time of the Messiah's coming should not be till all nations, but the children of Israel, had lain long in heathenish darkness; that the remedilessness of their disease might by long experience be seen, and so the absolute necessity of the heavenly Physician.

Another reason why Christ did not come soon after the flood probably was, that the earth might be full of people, that he might have the more extensive kingdom, that the effects of his light, power, and grace, might be glorified, and that his victory over Satan might be attended with the more glory in the multitude of his conquests. It was also needful that the coming of Christ should be many ages after Moses, that the church might be prepared by the Messiah's being long prefigured, foretold, and expected. It was not proper that Christ should come before the Babylonish captivity, because Satan's kingdom was not then come to its height. The heathen world before that consisted of lesser kingdoms. But God saw meet that the Messiah should come in the time of one of the four great monarchies. Nor was it proper that he should come in the time of the Babylonish, the Persian, or the Grecian monarchy. It was the will of God that his Son should make his appearance in the world in the time of the Roman, the greatest and strongest monarchy, which was Satan's visible kingdom in the world; that, by overcoming this, he might visibly overcome Satan's kingdom in its greatest strength and glory, and so obtain the more complete triumph over Satan himself.

It was not proper that Christ should come before the Babylonish captivity. For, before that, we have not histories of the state of the heathen world, to give us an idea of the need of a Saviour. Besides, learning did not much flourish, and so there had not been opportunity to show the insufficiency of human learning and wisdom to reform and save mankind. Again, the Jews were not dispersed over the world, as they were afterwards; and so things were not prepared in this respect for the coming of Christ. The necessity of abolishing the Jewish dispensation was not then so apparent as it was afterwards, by reason of the dispersion of the Jews; neither was the way prepared for the propagation of the gospel, as it was afterwards, by the same dispersion. Many other things might be mentioned, by which it would appear, that no other season before that very time in which Christ came, would have been proper for his appearing.

III. The next thing that I would observe concerning the incarnation of Christ, is the greatness of this event. Christ's incarnation was a greater and more wonderful thing than ever had yet come to pass. The creation of the world was a very great thing, but not so great as the incarnation of Christ. It was a great thing for God to make the creature, but not so great as for the Creator himself to become a creature. We have spoken of many great things that were accomplished between the fall of man and the incarnation of Christ: but God becoming man was greater than all. Then the greatest person was born that ever was or ever will be.

IV. Next observe, concerning the incarnation of Christ, the remarkable circumstances of it. He was born of a poor virgin; a pious holy person, but poor, as appeared by her offering at her purification: Luke ii. 24. "And to offer a sacrifice according to that which is said in the law of the Lord, A pair of turtle-doves, or two young pigeons." Which refers to Lev. v. 7. "And if she be not able to bring a lamb, then she shall bring two turtle-doves or two young pigeons." And this poor virgin was espoused to a husband who was but a poor man. Though they were both of the royal family of David, which was the most honourable, and Joseph was the rightful heir to the crown; yet the family was reduced to a very low state; which is represented by the tabernacle of David being fallen, Amos ix. 11. "In that day will I raise up the tabernacle of David that is fallen, and close up the breaches thereof, and I will raise up his ruins, and I will build it as in the days of old."

He was born in the town of Bethlehem, as was foretold: (Mic. v. 2.) and there was a very remarkable providence of God to bring about the fulfilment of this prophecy, the taxing of all the world by Augustus Cæsar, (Luke ii.) He was born in a very low condition, even in a stable, and laid in a manger.

V. Observe the concomitants of this great event.—And,

1. The return of the *Spirit;* which indeed began a little before, but yet was given on occasion of his birth. I have before observed how the spirit of prophecy ceased, not long after Malachi. From about the same time visions and immediate revelations ceased also. But on this occasion, they were granted anew, and the Spirit in these operations returns again. The first revealed instance of its restoration is the vision of Zacharias, the father of John the Baptist, (Luke i.) The next is the vision which the Virgin Mary had, (*ibid.*) The third is the vision which Joseph had, (Matt. i.) In the next place, the Spirit was given to Elisabeth, (Luke i. 41.) Next, it was given to Mary, as appears by her song, (Luke i. 46, &c.) Then to Zacharias again, (*ibid.* ver. 64.) Then it was sent to the shepherds, (Luke ii. 9.) Then it was given to Simeon, (Luke ii. 25.) Then to Anna, (ver. 36.) Then to the wise men in the east. Then to Joseph again, directing him to flee into Egypt; and after that directing his return.

2. The next concomitant of Christ's incarnation is, the great notice that was taken of it in heaven, and on earth. How it was noticed by the glorious inhabitants of the heavenly world, appears by their joyful songs on this occasion, heard by the shepherds in the night. This was the greatest event of Providence that ever the angels had beheld. We read of their singing praises when they saw the formation of this lower world: Job xxxviii. 7. "When the morning-stars sang together, and all the sons of God shouted for joy." And so they do, on this much greater occasion, the birth of the Son of God, who is the Creator of the world.

The glorious angels had all along expected this event. They had taken great notice of the prophecies and promises of these things: for we are told, that they desire to look into the affairs of redemption, 1 Pet. i. 12. They had been the ministers of Christ in this affair of redemption, in all the several steps of it from the very fall of man; as in God's dealings with Abraham, with Jacob, and with the Israelites. And doubtless they had long joyfully expected the coming of Christ; but now they see it accomplished, and therefore greatly rejoice, and sing praises on this occasion.

Notice was taken of it by Elisabeth and the Virgin Mary before the birth of Christ; not to say by John the Baptist before he was born, when he leaped in his mother's womb as it were for joy, at the voice of the salutation of Mary. Elisabeth and Mary most joyfully praise God together, with Christ and his forerunner in their wombs, and the Holy Spirit in their souls. And afterwards what joyful notice is taken of this event by the shepherds, and by those holy persons, Zacharias, and Simeon, and Anna! How do they praise God on the occasion! Thus the inhabitants of heaven, and the church on earth, unite in their joy and praise on this occasion.

Great part of the universe takes joyful notice of the incarnation of Christ. Heaven takes notice of it, and the inhabitants sing for joy. This lower world of mankind, both Jews and Gentiles, take notice of it. It pleased God to put honour on his Son, by wonderfully stirring up some of the wisest of the Gentiles to come a long journey to see and worship him at his birth. They were led by a miraculous star, signifying the birth of that glorious person who is the bright and morning-star, going before, and leading them to the very place where the young child was. Some think they were instructed by the prophecy of Balaam, who dwelt in the eastern parts, and who foretold Christ's coming as a star that should rise out of Jacob. Or they might be instructed by that general expectation there was of the Messiah's coming about that time, from the prophecies the Jews had of him in their dispersions in all parts of the world.

3. The next concomitant of the birth of Christ was his circumcision. But this may more properly be spoken of under another head, and so I will not insist upon it now.

4. The next concomitant was his first coming into the second temple, when an infant, on occasion of the purification of the blessed Virgin. We read, Hagg. ii. 7. "The desire of all nations shall come, and I will fill this house, (or temple) with glory." And in Mal. iii. 1. "The Lord, whom ye seek, shall suddenly come to his temple, even the messenger of the covenant." And now was the first instance of the fulfilment of these prophecies.

5. The last concomitant I shall mention is the sceptre's departing from Judah, in the death of Herod the Great. The sceptre had never totally departed from Judah till now. Judah's sceptre was greatly diminished in the revolt of the ten tribes in Jeroboam's time; and the sceptre departed from Israel or Ephraim at the time of the captivity of the ten tribes by Shalmaneser. But it remained in the tribe of Judah, under the kings of the house of David. And when the tribes of Judah and Benjamin were carried captive by Nebuchadnezzar, the sceptre of Judah ceased for a little while, till the return from the captivity under Cyrus: and then, though they were not an independent government, as they had been before, but owed fealty to the kings of Persia; yet their governor was of themselves, who had the power of life and death, and they were governed by their own laws; and so Judah had a lawgiver from between his feet during the Persian and Grecian monarchies. Towards the latter part of the Grecian monarchy, the people were governed by kings of their own, of the race of the Maccabees, for near a hundred years; and after that they were subdued by the Romans. But yet the Romans suffered them to be governed by their own laws, and to have a king of their own, Herod the Great, who reigned about forty years, and governed with proper kingly authority, only paying homage to the Romans. But presently after Christ was born he died, as we have an account, Matt. ii. 19. and Archelaus succeeded him; but was soon put down by the Roman emperor; and then the sceptre departed from Judah. There were no more temporal kings of Judah after that, neither had that people their governors from the midst of themselves, but were ruled by a Roman governor sent among them; and they ceased to have the power of life and death among themselves. Hence the Jews say to Pilate, "It is not lawful for us to put any man to death," John xviii. 31. Thus the sceptre departed from Judah when Shiloh came.

PART II.

THE PURCHASE OF REDEMPTION.

Having thus considered Christ's coming into the world, and his taking on him our nature, to put himself in a capacity for the purchase of redemption, I come now to show what is intended by the *purchase* of redemption—to make some general *observations* concerning those things by which this purchase was made—and then to consider those things more particularly which Christ did and suffered, by which that purchase was made.

SECT. I.

The purchase itself, what?

By Christ purchasing redemption, two things are intended, his *satisfaction*, and his *merit*. All is done by the price that Christ lays down, which does two things: it pays our debt, and so it *satisfies*; it procures our title to happiness, and so it *merits*. The *satisfaction* of Christ is to free us from *misery*, and the *merit* of Christ is to purchase *happiness* for us.

The word *purchase*, in this connexion, is taken either more strictly or more largely. It is oftentimes used more strictly, to signify only the merit of Christ; and sometimes more largely, to signify both his satisfaction and merit. Indeed most of the words used in this affair have various significations. Thus sometimes divines use *merit* for the whole price that Christ offered, both satisfactory, and positively meritorious. And so the word *satisfaction* is sometimes used, not only for his propitiation, but also for his meritorious obedience. For in some sense, not only suffering the penalty, but positively obeying, is needful to satisfy the law. The reason of this various use of these terms seems to be, that satisfaction and merit do not differ so much really as relatively. They both consist in paying a valuable price, a price of infinite value: but only that price, as it respects a debt to be paid, is called *satisfaction;* and as it respects a positive good to be obtained, is called *merit*. The difference between paying a debt and making a positive purchase is more relative than essential. He who lays down a price to pay a debt, does in some sense make a purchase: he purchases liberty from the obligation. And he who lays down a price to purchase a good, does as it were make satisfaction: he satisfies the conditional demands of him to whom he pays it. This may suffice concerning what is meant by the purchase of Christ.

SECT. II.

Some general observations concerning those things by which this purchase was made.

1. And here observe, That whatever in Christ had the nature of *satisfaction*, was by virtue of the *suffering* or humiliation that was in it; but whatever had the nature of *merit*, was by virtue of the *obedience* or righteousness there was in it. The satisfaction of Christ consists in his answering the demands of the law on man, which were *consequent* on the breach of the law. These were answered by *suffering* the penalty of the law. The merit of Christ consists in what he did to answer the demands, which were *prior* to man's breach of the law, or to fulfil what the law demanded before man sinned, which was *obedience*.

The satisfaction or propitiation of Christ consists either in his *suffering* evil, or his being subject to *abasement*. Christ did not only make satisfaction by proper suffering, but by whatever had the nature of humiliation and abasement of circumstances. Thus he made satisfaction by continuing under the power of death, while he lay buried in the grave; though neither his body nor soul properly endured any suffering after he was dead. Whatever Christ was subject to that was the judicial fruit of sin, had the nature of satisfaction for sin. But not only proper suffering, but all abasement and depression of the state and circumstances of mankind below its primitive honour and dignity, such as his body remaining under death, his body and soul remaining separate, &c. are the judicial fruits of sin. And all that Christ did in his state of humiliation, that had the nature of obedience, moral virtue or goodness, had the nature of merit, in it, and was part of the price with which he purchased happiness for the elect.

2. Both Christ's satisfaction for sin, and also his meriting happiness by his righteousness, were carried on through the *whole time* of his humiliation. Christ's satisfaction for sin was not by his last sufferings only, though it was principally by them; but all his sufferings, and all his humiliation, from the first moment of his incarnation to his resurrection, were propitiatory or satisfactory. Christ's satisfaction was chiefly by his death, because his sufferings and humiliation in that was greatest. But all his other sufferings, and all his other humiliation, all along had the nature of satisfaction; the mean circumstances in which he was born; his being born of a poor virgin, in a stable, and laid in a manger; his taking the human nature upon him in its low state, and under those infirmities brought upon it by the fall; his being born in the form of sinful flesh, &c. And so all his sufferings in his infancy and

childhood, and all that labour, contempt, reproach, temptation, and difficulty of any kind which he suffered through the whole course of his life, was of a propitiatory and satisfactory nature.—And so his purchase of happiness by his righteousness was also carried on through the whole time of his humiliation till his resurrection: not only in that obedience he performed through the course of his life, but also in the obedience he performed in laying down his life.

3. It was by the *same things* that Christ hath satisfied God's justice, and also purchased eternal happiness. He did not make satisfaction by some things, and then work out righteousness by other different things; but in the *same acts* by which he wrought out righteousness, he also made satisfaction, but only taken in a different relation. One and the same act of Christ, considered with respect to the obedience there was in it, was part of his righteousness, and purchased heaven: but considered with respect to the self-denial, and difficulty, and humiliation, with which he performed it, had the nature of satisfaction for sin, and procured our pardon. Thus his going about doing good, preaching the gospel, and teaching his disciples, was a part of his righteousness, and the purchase of heaven, as it was done in obedience to the Father; and the same was a part of his satisfaction, as he did it with great labour, trouble, and weariness, and under great temptations exposing himself hereby to reproach and contempt. So his laying down his life had the nature of satisfaction to God's offended justice, considered as his bearing punishment in our stead: but considered as an act of obedience to God, who had given him this command, that he should lay down his life for sinners, it was a part of his righteousness and purchase, and as much the principal part of his righteousness as it was the principal part of his satisfaction. And to instance in his circumcision, what he suffered in it, had the nature of satisfaction: the blood that was shed therein was propitiatory blood; but as it was a conformity to the law of Moses, it was part of his meritorious righteousness. Though it was not properly the act of human nature, he being an infant; yet the human nature being the subject of it, and being the act of his *person*, it was accepted as an act of his obedience, as our mediator.—And even his being born in such a low condition, has the nature of satisfaction by reason of the humiliation that was in it; and of righteousness, as it was the act of his *person* in obedience to the Father, what the will of the human nature did acquiesce in, though there was no act of the will of the human nature prior to it.—These things may suffice to have been observed in general, concerning the purchase Christ made of redemption.

SECT. III.

Those things in particular by which the purchase was made.—Christ's obedience and righteousness.

I NOW proceed to consider the things that passed during the time of Christ's humiliation, and first, with respect to his *obedience and righteousness*. And this is subject to a threefold distribution. I shall therefore consider his obedience, with respect to the *laws* which he obeyed—the *different stages of his life* in which he performed it—and the *virtues he exercised* in his obedience.

I. The first distribution of the acts of Christ's righteousness is with respect to *the laws which he obeyed*. But here it must be observed in general, that all the precepts which Christ obeyed may be reduced to one law, and that is what the apostle calls *the law of works*, Rom. iii. 27. Every command that Christ obeyed may be reduced to that great and everlasting law of God that is contained in the covenant of works, that eternal rule of right which God had established between himself and mankind. Christ came into the world to fulfil and answer the covenant of works; that is, the covenant that is to stand for ever as a rule of judgment. The covenant that we had broken, was the covenant that must be fulfilled.

This law of works indeed includes all the laws of God that ever have been given to mankind; for it is a general rule of the law of works, and indeed of the law of nature, That God is to be obeyed, and that he must be submitted to in whatever positive precept he is pleased to give. It is a rule of the law of works, That men should obey their *earthly* parents: and it is certainly as much a rule of the same law, That we should obey our *heavenly* Father: and so the law of works requires obedience to all the positive commands of God. It required Adam's obedience to that positive command, Not to eat of the forbidden fruit; and it required obedience of the Jews to all the positive commands of their institution. When God commanded Jonah to arise and go to Nineveh, the law of works required him to obey: and so it required Christ's obedience to all the positive commands which God gave him.

But, more particularly, *the commands of God which Christ obeyed*, were of three kinds; they were such as he was subject to either merely *as man*, or *as he was a Jew*, or purely *as Mediator*.

1. He obeyed those commands which he was subject to merely as *man*. These were the commands of the moral law, which was the same with that which was given at mount Sinai, written in two tables of stone, which are obligatory on mankind of all ages and all nations of the world.

2. He obeyed all those laws he was subject to as he was *a Jew*. Thus he was subject to the ceremonial law, and was conformed to it. He was conformed to it in his being circumcised the eighth day; and he strictly obeyed it in going up to Jerusalem to the temple three times a year; at least after he was come to the age of twelve years, which seems to have been the age when the males began to go up to the temple. And so Christ constantly attended the service of the temple, and of the synagogues.

To this head of his obedience may be reduced his submission to John's baptism. For it was a special command to the Jews, to go forth to John the Baptist, and be baptized of him; and therefore Christ, being a Jew, was subject to this command: and therefore, when he came to be baptized of John, and John objected, that he had more need to come to him to be baptized of him, he gives this reason for it, That it was needful that he should do it, *that he might fulfil all righteousness*. (See Matt. iii. 13—15.)

3. Christ was subject to *the mediatorial law;* or that which related purely to his mediatorial office. Such were the commands which the Father gave him to teach such doctrines, to preach the gospel, to work such miracles, to call such disciples, to appoint such ordinances, and finally to lay down his life: for he did all these things in obedience to the commands he had received of the Father, as he often tells us, (John x. 18. xiv. 31.) These commands he was not subject to merely as man; for they did not belong to other men: nor yet was he subject to them as a Jew; for they were no part of the Mosaic law: but they were commands he had received of the Father, that purely respected his mediatorial office.

Christ's righteousness, by which he merited heaven for himself, and all who believe in him, consists principally in his obedience to this mediatorial law: for in fulfilling this law consisted his chief work and business in the world. The history of the evangelists is chiefly taken up in giving an account of his obedience to this law. This part of his obedience was attended with the greatest difficulty; and therefore his obedience in it was most meritorious. What Christ had to do in the world by virtue of his being Mediator, was infinitely more difficult than what he had to do merely as a man, or as a Jew. To his obedience to this mediatorial law belongs his going through his last sufferings, beginning with his agony in the garden, and ending with his resurrection.

As the obedience of the first Adam, wherein his righteousness would have consisted, if he had stood, would have mainly consisted in his obedience to that special law to which he was subject as moral head and surety of mankind, even the command of abstaining from the tree of knowledge of good and evil; so the obedience of the second Adam, wherein his righteousness consists, lies mainly in his obedience to that special law to which he was subject as mediator and surety for man.

Before I proceed to the next distribution of Christ's righteousness, I would observe three things concerning his obedience to these laws.

1. He performed that obedience to them which was in every respect *perfect*. It was perfect with respect to the *work* commanded; and the *principle* from which he obeyed. It was perfect with respect to the *ends* he acted for; he never had any by-ends, but aimed perfectly at such as the law of God required. It was perfect with respect to the *manner* of performance: every circumstance of each act was perfectly conformed to the command. It was perfect with respect to the *degree* of the performance: he acted wholly up to the rule.—It was perfect with respect to the *constancy* of obedience, without any interruption; and with respect to *perseverance*. He held out in perfect obedience to the very end, in all the changes he passed through, and all the trials that were before him.

The meritoriousness of Christ's obedience, depends on the perfection of it. If it had failed in any instance, it could not have been meritorious: for imperfect obedience is not accepted as any obedience at all in the sight of the law of works, to which Christ was subject. That is not accepted as obedience to a law that does not fully answer it.

2. Christ's obedience was performed through the greatest trials and temptations that ever any obedience was. His obedience was attended with the greatest difficulties, and most extreme abasement; which was another thing that rendered it more meritorious and thankworthy. To obey another when his commands are easy, is not so worthy, as it is to obey when it cannot be done without great difficulty.

3. He performed this obedience with infinite *respect* to God, and the honour of his law. The obedience he performed was with infinitely greater love to God, and regard to his authority, than that of angels. The angels perform their obedience with a sinless perfection of love; but Christ performed his with infinite love. Though the human nature of Christ was not capable of love absolutely infinite, yet Christ's obedience in that nature, is the obedience of his person, as God-man; and therefore there was infinite love manifest in that obedience. And this, together with the infinite dignity of the person who obeyed, rendered his obedience infinitely meritorious.

II. The second distribution of the acts of Christ's obedience, is with respect to *the different parts of his life*, wherein they were performed. And in this respect they may be divided into those which were performed in private life, and those which were performed in his public ministry.

1st, Those acts he performed during his *private life*.—He was perfectly obedient in his childhood. He infinitely differed from other children, who, as soon as they begin to act, begin to sin and rebel. He was subject to his earthly parents, though he was Lord of all, Luke ii. 51. and was found about his Father's business even when a child, Luke ii. 42.—He then began to fulfil the mediatorial law, which the Father had given him. He continued his private life for about thirty years, dwelling at Nazareth in the house of his reputed father Joseph, where he served God in a private capacity, and in following a mechanical trade, the business of a carpenter.

2dly, Those acts which he performed during his *public ministry*, which began when he was about thirty years of age, and continued for the three last years and a half of his life.—Most of the evangelic history is taken up in giving an account of what passed during that time. Indeed all the history of Matthew, except the two first chapters; the whole of Mark; all the gospel of John; and all of Luke, except the two first chapters; excepting also what we find in the evangelists concerning the ministry of John the Baptist. Christ's first appearing in his public ministry, is what is often called his *coming* in Scripture. Thus John speaks of Christ's coming as future, though he had been born long before.

Concerning the public ministry of Christ, I would observe the following things.

1. The *forerunner* of Christ's coming in his public ministry was John the Baptist. He came preaching repentance for the remission of sins, to make way for Christ's coming, agreeable to the prophecies of him, Isa. xl. 3—5. and Matt. iv. 5, 6. It is supposed that John the Baptist began his ministry about three years and a half before Christ; so that John's ministry and Christ's put together, made seven years, which was the last of Daniel's weeks; and this time is intended in Dan. ix. 27. "He will confirm the covenant with many for one week." Christ came in the midst of this week of years, as Daniel foretold, "And in the midst of the week he shall cause the sacrifice and the oblation to cease."

John the Baptist's ministry consisted principally in preaching the law, to awaken and convince men of sin, to prepare them for the coming of Christ, and to comfort them, as the law is to prepare the heart for the entertainment of the gospel. A very remarkable outpouring of the Spirit of God attended John's ministry; and the effect of it was, that Jerusalem, and all Judea, and all the region round about Jordan, were awakened and convinced. They went out to him, and submitted to his baptism, confessing their sins. John was the greatest of all the prophets who came before Christ, Matt. xi. 11. "Among those that are born of women, there hath not risen a greater than John the Baptist;" *i. e.* he had the most honourable office. He was as the morning-star, which is the harbinger of the approaching day, and forerunner of the rising sun. The other prophets were stars that gave light in the night; but those stars went out on the approach of the gospel-day. Now the coming of Christ being very nigh, the morning-star comes before him, the brightest of all the stars, as John the Baptist was, in the sense mentioned, the greatest of all the prophets. And when Christ came in his public ministry, the light of that morning-star decreased too; as we see, when the sun rises, it diminishes the light of the morning-star. So John the Baptist says of himself, John iii. 30. "He must increase, but I must decrease." And soon after Christ began his public ministry, John the Baptist was put to death; as the morning-star is visible a little while after the sun is risen, yet soon goes out.

2. Christ's entrance on his public ministry was by *baptism*, followed with the *temptation* in the wilderness. His baptism was as it were his solemn inauguration, by which he entered on his ministry; and was attended with his being anointed with the Holy Ghost, in a solemn and visible manner, the Holy Ghost descending upon him symbolically, in a visible shape like a dove, attended with a voice from heaven, saying, "This is my beloved Son, in whom I am well pleased," Matt. iii. 16, 17. After this he was led by the devil into the wilderness. Satan made a violent attack upon him at his first entrance on his work; and now he had a remarkable trial of his obedience; but he got the victory. He who had such success with the first Adam, had none with the second.

3. I would take notice of the *work* in which Christ was employed during his ministry. And here are *three* things chiefly to be noticed, *viz.* his preaching, his working of miracles, and his calling and appointing disciples and ministers of his kingdom.

(1.) His *preaching* the gospel. Great part of the work of his public ministry consisted in this; and much of that obedience by which he purchased salvation for us, was in his speaking those things which the Father commanded him. He more clearly and abundantly revealed the mind and will of God, than ever it had been revealed before. He came from the bosom of the Father, perfectly knew his mind, and was in the best capacity to reveal it. As the sun, as soon as it is risen, begins to shine; so Christ, as soon as he came into his public ministry, began to enlighten the world with his doctrine. As the law was given at mount Sinai, so Christ delivered his evangelical doctrine, (full of blessings, and not curses,) to a multitude on a mountain, Matt. v.—vii.

When he preached, he did not teach as the scribes, but as one having authority; so that his hearers were astonished at his doctrine. He did not reveal the mind and will of God in the style of the prophets, as, "Thus saith the Lord;" but in such a style as this, "I say unto you," "Verily, verily, I say unto you." He delivered his doctrines, not only as the doctrines of God the Father, but as his own doctrines. He gave forth commands, not (as the prophets were wont to do) as God's commands, but as his own. He spake in such a style as this, "This is my commandment," John xv. 12. "Ye are my friends, if ye do whatsoever I command you," *ibid.* 14.

(2.) Another thing that Christ was employed in during

the course of his ministry, was *working miracles.* Concerning which we may observe,—Their *multitude.* Besides particular instances, we often have an account of multitudes coming at once with diseases, and his healing them. They were *works of mercy.* In them was displayed not only his infinite power and greatness, but his infinite mercy and goodness. He went about doing good, healing the sick, restoring sight to the blind, hearing to the deaf, and the proper use of their limbs to the lame and halt; feeding the hungry, cleansing the leprous, and raising the dead.

They were almost all of them *such as had been spoken of as the peculiar works of God,* in the Old Testament. So with respect to stilling the sea, Psal. cvii. 29. "He maketh the storm a calm, so that the waves thereof are still;" walking on the sea in a storm, Job ix. 8. "Which alone—treadeth upon the waves of the sea;" and casting out devils, Psal. lxxiv. 14. "Thou breakest the heads of leviathan in pieces." So as to feeding a multitude in a wilderness: Deut. viii. 16. "Who fed thee in the wilderness with manna;" telling man's thoughts, Amos iv. 13. "Lo, he that declareth unto man what is his thought—the Lord, the God of hosts is his name;" and raising the dead, Psal. lxviii. 20. "Unto God the Lord belong the issues from death." So as to opening the eyes of the blind, Psal. cxlvi. 8. "The Lord openeth the eyes of the blind;" healing the sick, Psal. ciii. 3. "Who healeth all thy diseases;" and lifting up those who are bowed together, Psal. cxlvi. 8. "The Lord raiseth them that are bowed down."

They were in general such works as were *images of the great work which he came to work on man's heart;* representing that inward, spiritual cleansing, healing, renovation, and resurrection, of which all his redeemed are the subjects.—*He wrought them by his own power, and not as the other prophets did.* They were wont to work all their miracles in the name of the Lord; but Christ wrought in his own name. Moses was forbidden to enter into Canaan, because he seemed by his speech to assume to himself the honour of working only one miracle. Nor did Christ work miracles as the *apostles* did; but by his own authority and will: Thus, saith he, "I will, be thou clean," Matt. viii. 3. And in the same strain he put the question, "Believe ye that I am able to do this?" Matt. ix. 28.

(3) Another thing that Christ did in the course of his ministry, was to *call his disciples.* He called many disciples, whom he employed as ministers. He sent seventy at one time in this work: but there were twelve that he set apart as apostles, who were the grand ministers of his kingdom, and as it were the twelve foundations of his church. (See Rev. xxi. 14.) These were the main instruments of setting up his kingdom in the world, and therefore shall sit on twelve thrones, judging the twelve tribes of Israel.

4. I would observe how he *finished* his ministry. And this was, in giving his dying *counsels* to his disciples, and all that should be his disciples, which we have recorded particularly in the 14th, 15th, and 16th chapters of John's gospel.—In instituting a solemn *memorial* of his death, the sacrament of the Lord's supper, wherein we have a representation of his body broken, and of his blood shed.—In *offering* up himself a *sacrifice* to God in his last sufferings. This act he did as God's minister, as God's anointed priest; and it was the greatest act of his public ministry, the greatest act of his obedience, by which he purchased heaven for believers. The priests of old used to do many other things as God's ministers; but the highest execution of their office was their actually offering sacrifice on the altar. So the greatest thing that Christ did in the execution of his priestly office, and the greatest thing that he ever did, and the greatest thing that ever was done, was the offering up himself a sacrifice to God. Herein he was the antetype of all that had been done by all the priests, in all their sacrifices and offerings, from the beginning of the world.

III. The third distribution of the acts by which Christ purchased redemption, regards *the virtues that he exercised and manifested* in them. Christ in doing his work for our redemption, exercised every possible virtue and grace. Indeed there are some particular virtues that sinful man may have, which were not in Christ; not from any defect of virtue, but because his virtue was perfect, and without defect. Such is the virtue of repentance, brokenness of heart for sin, mortification, and denying of lust. Christ had no sin of his own to repent of, nor any lust to deny. But all virtues which do not presuppose sin, were in him in a higher degree than in any mere creature. Every virtue in him was perfect. Virtue itself was greater in him than in any other; and it was under greater advantages to shine in him than in any other. Strict virtue shines most when most tried: but never any virtue had such trials as Christ's had.

The virtue that Christ exercised in his work may be divided into three sorts, *viz.* the virtues which more immediately respect *God,* those which immediately respected *himself,* and those which immediately respect *men.*

1. Those *virtues which more immediately respect God.* There appeared in him a holy *fear* and *reverence* towards God the Father. Christ had a greater trial of his virtue in this respect than any other had, from the honourableness of his person. This was the temptation of the angels that fell to cast off their worship of God and reverence of his majesty, that they were beings of such exalted dignity themselves. But Christ was infinitely more worthy and honourable than they; for he was the eternal Son of God, and his person was equal to the person of the Father: and yet, as he had taken on him the office of mediator, and the nature of man, he was full of reverence towards God. He manifested a wonderful *love* toward God. The angels give great testimonies of their love towards God, in their constancy and agility in doing his will; and many saints have given great testimonies of their love, who, from love to God, endured great labours and sufferings: but none ever such testimonies of love to God as Christ has given. He manifested the most wonderful *submission* to the will of God. Never was any one's submission so tried as his was. And he manifested the most wonderful spirit of *obedience* that ever was manifested.

2. In this work he most wonderfully manifested those *virtues which more immediately respected himself;* as humility, patience, and contempt of the world. Christ, though he was the most excellent and honourable, yet was the most *humble;* yea, he was the most humble of all creatures. No angel or man ever equalled him in humility, though he was the highest in dignity and honourableness. Christ would have been under the greatest temptations to pride, if it had been possible for any thing to be a temptation to him. The temptation of the angels that fell was the dignity of their nature, and the honourableness of their circumstances; but Christ was infinitely more honourable than they. The human nature of Christ was so honoured as to be in the same person with the eternal Son of God, who was equal with God; and yet that human nature was not at all lifted up with pride. Nor was the man Christ Jesus at all lifted up with pride with all those wonderful works which he wrought, of healing the sick, curing the blind, lame, and maimed, and raising the dead. And though he knew that God had appointed him to be the king over heaven and earth, angels and men, as he says, Matt. xi. 27. "All things are delivered unto me of my Father;" though he knew he was such an infinitely honourable person, and thought it not robbery to be equal with God; and though he knew he was the heir of the Father's kingdom: yet such was his humility, that he did not disdain to be abased and depressed down into lower and viler circumstances and sufferings than ever any other elect creature was; so that he became least of all, and lowest of all. The proper trial and evidence of humility, is stooping or complying with those acts or circumstances, when called to it, which are very low, and contain great abasement. But none ever stooped so low as Christ, if we consider either the infinite height that he stooped from, or the great depth to which he stooped. Such was his humility, that though he knew his infinite worthiness of honour, and of being honoured ten thousand times as much as the highest prince on earth, or angel in heaven; yet he did not think it too much when called to it, to be bound as a malefactor, to become the laughing-stock of the vilest of men, to be crowned with thorns, to have a mock robe put upon him, and to be crucified like a slave and male-

factor, as one of the meanest and worst of vagabonds and miscreants, and an accursed enemy of God and men, who was not fit to live. And this was not for himself, but for some of the meanest and vilest of creatures, even some of those accursed wretches that crucified him. Was not this a wonderful manifestation of humility, when he cheerfully and most freely submitted to this abasement?—And how did his *patience* shine forth under all the terrible sufferings which he endured; when he was dumb, and opened not his mouth, but went as a lamb to the slaughter!—And what *contempt* of the glory of this world was there, when he rather chose this meanness, and suffering, than to be invested with the external glories of an earthly prince, as the multitude often solicited him!

3. Christ, in a wonderful manner, exercised those *virtues which more immediately respect other men.* And these may be summed up under two heads, *viz.* meekness, and love.

Christ's *meekness* was his humble calmness of spirit under the provocations that he met with. The greatness of provocation lies in two things, *viz.* in the degree of opposition by which the provocation is given; and, secondly, in the degree of the unreasonableness of that opposition, or in its being very causeless, and without reason, and the great degree of obligation to the contrary. Now, if we consider both these things, no man ever met with such provocations as Christ did, when he was upon earth. How much he was hated, what abuses he suffered from the vilest of men; how great his sufferings, and how spiteful and contemptuous they were in offering him those abuses! How causeless and unreasonable were these abuses, how undeserving he was of them, yea how much deserving of the contrary, *viz.* of love, and honour, and good treatment at their hands! If we consider these things, no man ever met with a thousandth part of the provocation that Christ met with from men: and yet how meek was he under all! how composed and quiet his spirit! how far from being in a ruffle and tumult! When he was reviled, he reviled not again; and as a sheep before her shearers is dumb, so he opened not his mouth. No appearance was there of a revengeful spirit: on the contrary, what a spirit of forgiveness did he exhibit! so that he fervently and effectually prayed for their forgiveness, when they were in the highest act of provocation that ever they perpetrated, *viz.* nailing him to the cross: Luke xxiii. 34. "Father, forgive them; for they know not what they do."

And never did there appear such an instance of *love* to men. Christ's love to men, especially in going through his last sufferings, and offering up his life and soul under those sufferings, which was his greatest act of love, was far beyond all parallel. There have been very remarkable manifestations of love in some of the saints, as in the apostle Paul, the apostle John, and others; but the love to men that Christ showed when on earth, as much exceeded the love of all other men, as the ocean exceeds a small stream.

And it is to be observed, that all the virtues which appeared in Christ shone brightest in the close of his life, under the trials he met with then. Eminent virtue always shows brightest in the fire. Pure gold shows its purity chiefly in the furnace. It was chiefly under those trials which Christ underwent in the close of his life, that his love to God, his honour of God's majesty, his regard to the honour of his law, his spirit of obedience, his humility, contempt of the world, his patience, meekness, and spirit of forgiveness towards men, appeared. Indeed every thing that Christ did to work out redemption for us appears mainly in the close of his life. Here mainly is his satisfaction for sin, and here chiefly is his merit of eternal life for sinners, and here chiefly appears the brightness of his example, which he hath set us for imitation.—Thus we have taken a brief view of the things whereby the purchase of redemption was made with respect to his *righteousness* that appeared in them.

SECT. IV.

Christ's sufferings and humiliation.

Among those things in particular by which the purchase was made. we must reckon the sufferings and humiliation to which Christ was subject, whence arose the satisfaction he made for sin.

I. He was subject to uncommon humiliation and suffering in his *infancy.* His mother not only suffered in bearing him, but when her travail came upon her, it is said, "there was no room in the inn," Luke ii. 7. She was forced to betake herself to a stable; where Christ was born. And we may conclude, that his mother's circumstances in other respects were proportionably strait and difficult, and that she was destitute of the conveniences necessary for so young an infant which others were wont to have. Besides, he was persecuted in his infancy. They began to seek his life as soon as he was born. Herod, the chief man of the land, was so engaged to kill him, that, in order to it, he killed all the children in Bethlehem, and in all the coasts thereof, from two years old and under. And Christ suffered banishment in his infancy, was driven out of his native country into Egypt, and without doubt suffered much by being carried so long a journey, when he was so young, into a strange country.

II. Christ was subject to great humiliation in his *private* life at Nazareth. He there led a servile, obscure life, in a mean, laborious occupation; for he is called not only the *carpenter's son,* but the *carpenter:* Mark vi. 3. "Is not this the carpenter, the brother of James and Joses, and Juda, and Simon?" By hard labour he earned his bread before he ate it, and so suffered that curse which God pronounced on Adam, Gen. iii. 13. "In the sweat of thy face shalt thou eat bread." Let us consider how great a degree of humiliation the glorious Son of God, the Creator of heaven and earth, was subject to in this, that for about thirty years he should live a private obscure life among labouring men, and all this while be overlooked, not taken notice of in the world, more than other common labourers. Christ's humiliation in some respects was greater in private life than in the time of his public ministry. There were many manifestations of his glory in the word he preached, and the miracles he wrought: but the first thirty years of his life he spent among ordinary men, as it were in silence. There was not any thing to make him to be taken notice of more than any ordinary mechanic, only the spotless purity and eminent holiness of his life; and that was in a great measure hid in obscurity; so that he was little taken notice of till after his baptism.

III. Christ was the subject of great humiliation and suffering during his *public* life, from his baptism till the night wherein he was betrayed.

1. He suffered great *poverty,* so that he had not *where to lay his head,* (Matt. viii. 20. compared with John xviii. 1, 2. and Luke xxi. 27. and chap. xxii. 30.) So that what was spoken of Christ in Cant. v. 2. "My head is filled with dew, and my locks with the drops of the night," was literally fulfilled. And through his poverty he doubtless was often tried with hunger, thirst, and cold. Matt. iv. 2. xxi. 18. His mother and natural relations were poor, not able to help him; and he was maintained by the charity of some of his disciples while he lived. So we read in Luke viii. at the beginning, of certain women that followed him, and ministered unto him of their substance. He was so poor, that he was not able to pay the demanded tribute, without a miracle. See Matt. xvii. 27. And when he ate his last passover, it was not at his own charge, but that of another, as appears by Luke xxii. 7, &c. And from his poverty he had no grave of his own to be buried in. It was the manner of the Jews, unless they were poor, to prepare themselves a sepulchre while they lived. But Christ had no land of his own, though he was possessor of heaven and earth; and therefore was buried by Joseph of Arimathea's charity, and in his tomb, which he had prepared for himself.

2. He suffered great hatred and *reproach.* He was despised and rejected of men; one of little account, slighted for his low parentage, and his mean city Nazareth. He was reproached as a glutton and drunkard, a friend of publicans and sinners; was called a deceiver of the people; sometimes was called a madman, and a Samaritan, and one possessed with a devil. (John vii. 20. viii. 48. and x. 20.) He was called a blasphemer, and was accounted by many a wizard, or one that wrought miracles by the black art, and by communication with Beelzebub.

They excommunicated him, and agreed to excommunicate any man that should own him. (John ix. 22.) They wished him dead, and were continually seeking to murder him; sometimes by force, and sometimes by craft. They often took up stones to stone him, and once led him to the brow of a hill, intending to throw him down the precipice, to dash him in pieces against the rocks.

He was thus hated and reproached by his own visible people: John i. 11. "He came to his own, and his own received him not." And he was principally despised and hated by those who were in chief repute, and were their greatest men. Indeed the hatred was general. Into whatever part of the land he went, he met with hatred and contempt; in Capernaum, and Jericho; in Jerusalem, which was the holy city, even when he went to the temple to worship; also in Nazareth, his own city, among his own relations, and his old neighbours.

3. He suffered the buffetings of Satan in an uncommon manner. One time in particular, he had a long conflict with the devil, when he was in the wilderness forty days, with wild beasts and devils; and was so exposed to the devil's power, that he was carried about by him from place to place, while he was otherwise in a very suffering state.—So much for the humiliation and suffering of Christ's public life, from his baptism to the night wherein he was betrayed.

IV. I come now to his last humiliation and sufferings, from the evening of the night wherein he was betrayed to his resurrection. And here was his greatest humiliation and suffering, by which principally he made satisfaction to the justice of God for the sins of men. First, his life was sold by one of his own disciples for thirty pieces of silver; which was the price of the life of a servant, Exod. xxi. 32. Then he was in dreadful agony in the garden. There came such a dismal gloom upon his soul, that he began to be sorrowful and very heavy, and said, that his "soul was exceeding sorrowful, even unto death, and was sore amazed." So violent was the agony of his soul, as to force the blood through the pores of his skin; so that while his soul was overwhelmed with amazing sorrow, his body was clotted with blood. The disciples, who used to be as his friends and family, at this time above all appeared cold towards, and unconcerned for him, at the same time that his Father's face was hid from him. Judas, to whom Christ had been so very merciful, and who was treated as one of his family or familiar friends, comes and betrays him in the most deceitful, treacherous manner. The officers and soldiers apprehend and bind him; his disciples forsake him, and flee; his own best friends do not stand by him to comfort him in this time of his distress. He is led away as a malefactor to appear before the priests and scribes, his venomous, mortal enemies, that they might sit as his judges. Now they had got him into their hands, they sat up all night, to have the pleasure of insulting him. But because they aimed at nothing short of his life, they set themselves to find some colour to put him to death, and seek for witnesses against him. When none appeared, they set some to bear false witness; and when their witness did not agree together, they examined him, in hope to catch something out of his own mouth. They hoped he would say, that he was the Son of God, and then they thought they should have enough. But because they see they are not like to obtain this, they adjure him, in the name of God, to say whether he was or not: and when he confessed that he was, then it was a time of rejoicing with them, which they show, by spitting in his face, blindfolding him, and striking him in the face with the palms of their hands, and then bidding him prophesy who it was that struck him; thus ridiculing him for pretending to be a prophet. And the very servants have a hand in the sport: Mark xiv. 65. "And the servants did strike him with the palms of their hands."

During the sufferings of the night, Peter, one of the chief of his own disciples, instead of standing by to comfort, appears ashamed to own him, and denies and renounces him with oaths and curses. And after the chief priests and elders had finished the night in so shamefully abusing him, in the morning, (the morning of the most wonderful day that ever was,) they led him away to Pilate, to be condemned to death by him, because they had not the power of life and death in their own hands. He is brought before Pilate's judgment-seat, and there the priests and elders accuse him as a traitor. And when Pilate, upon examining into the matter, declared he found no fault in him, the Jews were but the more fierce and violent to have him condemned. Upon which Pilate, after clearing him, very unjustly brings him upon a second trial; and then not finding any thing against him, acquits him again. Pilate treats him as a poor worthless fellow; but is ashamed on so little pretence to condemn him as a traitor.

And then he was sent to Herod to be tried by him, and was brought before his judgment-seat; his enemies followed, and virulently accused him before Herod. Herod does not condemn him as a traitor, or one that would set up for a king, but looks upon him as Pilate did, as a poor worthless creature, not worthy to be noticed, and makes a mere laugh of the Jews accusing him as dangerous to Cæsar, as one setting up to be a king against him; and therefore, in derision, dresses him up in a mock robe, makes sport of him, and sends him back through the streets of Jerusalem to Pilate with the mock robe on.

Then the Jews prefer Barabbas before him, and are instant and violent with loud vociferations to Pilate, to crucify him. So Pilate, after he had cleared him twice, and Herod once, very unrighteously brings him on trial the third time, to try if he could not find something sufficient to crucify him. Christ was stripped and scourged: thus he gave his back to the smiters. After that, though Pilate still declared that he found no fault in him; yet so unjust was he, that for fear of the Jews he delivered Christ to be crucified. But before they execute the sentence, his spiteful and cruel enemies take the pleasure of mocking him again; they get round him, and make a set business of it. They stripped him, put on him a scarlet robe, a reed in his hand, and a crown of thorns on his head. Both Jews and Roman soldiers were united in the transaction; they bow the knee before him, and in derision cry, "Hail, king of the Jews." They spit upon him also, take the reed out of his hand, and smite him on the head. After this they led him away to crucify him, made him carry his own cross, till he sunk under it, his strength being spent; and then they laid it on one Simon a Cyrenian.

At length, being come to mount Calvary, they execute the sentence which Pilate had so unrighteously pronounced. They nail him to his cross by his hands and feet, then raise it erect, and fix one end in the ground, he being still suspended on it by the nails which pierced his hands and feet. Now Christ's sufferings are come to the extremity: now the cup, which he so earnestly prayed might pass from him, is come; he must, he does drink it. In those days crucifixion was the most tormenting kind of death by which any were wont to be executed. There was no death wherein the person experienced so much of mere torment: and hence the Roman word, which signifies *torment*, is taken from this kind of death.——Besides what our Lord endured in this excruciating corporeal death, he endured vastly more in his soul. Now was that travail of his soul, of which we read in the prophet; now it pleased God to bruise him, and to put him to grief; now he poured out his soul unto death, as in Isa. liii. And if the mere forethought of this cup made him sweat blood, how much more dreadful and excruciating must the drinking of it have been! Many martyrs have endured much in their bodies, while their souls have been joyful, and have sung for joy, whereby they have been supported under the sufferings of their outward man, and have triumphed over them. But this was not the case with Christ; he had no such support; but his sufferings were chiefly those of the mind, though the other were extremely great. In his crucifixion Christ did not sweat blood, as he had done before; not because his agony was now not so great, but his blood had vent another way. But though he did not sweat blood, yet such was the sufferings of his soul, that probably it rent his vitals; when his side was pierced, there came forth blood and water. And so here was a kind of literal fulfilment of that in Psal. xxii. 14. "I am poured out like water;—my heart is like wax, it is melted in the midst of my bowels."

Now under all these sufferings the Jews still mock him; and wagging their heads say, "Thou that destroyest the temple, and buildest it in three days, save thyself: if thou be the Son of God, come down from the cross." And even the chief priests, scribes, and elders, joined in the cry, saying, "He saved others, himself he cannot save." And probably the devil at the same time tormented him to the utmost of his power; and hence it is said, Luke xxii. 53. "This is your hour, and the power of darkness."

Under these sufferings, Christ, having cried out once and again with a loud voice, at last said, IT IS FINISHED, (John xix. 30.) "and bowed the head, and gave up the ghost." And thus was finished the greatest and most wonderful thing that ever was done. Now the angels beheld the most wonderful sight that ever they saw. Now was accomplished the main thing that had been pointed at by the various institutions of the ceremonial law, by all the typical dispensations, and by all the sacrifices from the beginning of the world.

Christ being thus brought under the power of death, continued under it till the morning of next day but one. Then was finished that great work, the purchase of our redemption, for which such great preparation had been made from the beginning of the world. Then was finished all that was required in order to satisfy the threatenings of the law, and all that was necessary in order to satisfy divine justice; then the utmost that vindictive justice demanded, even the whole debt, was paid. Then was finished the whole of the purchase of eternal life. And now there is no need of any thing more to be done towards a purchase of salvation for sinners; nor has ever any thing been done since, nor will any thing more be done for ever and ever.

PART III.

IMPROVEMENT OF THE SECOND PERIOD.

IN surveying the history of redemption, we have now shown how this work was carried on through the two former of the three main periods into which this whole space of time was divided, *viz.* from the fall to the incarnation of Christ, and from thence to the end of the time of Christ's humiliation. In the first of these periods, we have particularly explained how God prepared the way for Christ's appearing and purchasing redemption; and in the second period, how that purchase was made and finished. I would now make some *improvement* of what has been said on both these subjects considered conjunctly.

SECT. I.

An use of reproof.

I BEGIN with an use of reproof; a reproof of unbelief, of self-righteousness, and of a careless neglect of the salvation of Christ.

1. How greatly do these things reprove those who do not believe in, but reject, the Lord Jesus Christ! *i. e.* all those who do not heartily receive him. Persons may receive him in profession outwardly, and may wish that they had some of those benefits that Christ has purchased, and yet their hearts not receive him. They may be hearty in nothing that they do towards Christ; they may have no high esteem of, nor any sincere respect to, Christ; they may never have opened the door of their heart to him, but have kept him shut out all their days, ever since the salvation has been offered to them. Though their hearts have been opened to others, their door flung wide open to them, with free admittance at all times; though they have been embraced, and the thrones of their hearts have been allowed them; yet Christ has always been shut out, and they have been deaf to all his calls. They never could find an inclination of heart to receive him, nor would they ever trust in him.

Let me now call upon such to consider, how great is their sin, in thus rejecting Jesus Christ. You slight the glorious person, for whose coming God made such great preparation in such a series of wonderful providences from the beginning of the world, and whom, after all things were made ready, God sent into the world, bringing to pass a thing before unknown, *viz.* the union of the divine nature with the human in one person. You have been guilty of slighting that great Saviour, who, after such preparation, actually accomplished the purchase of redemption; and who, after he had spent three or four and thirty years in poverty, labour, and contempt, in purchasing redemption, at last finished the purchase by closing his life under such extreme sufferings as you have heard; and so by his death, and continuing for a time under the power of death, completed the whole. This is the person you reject and despise. You make light of all the glory of his person, and of all the glorious love of God the Father, in sending him into the world, and all his wonderful love appearing in the whole of this affair. That precious stone which God hath laid in Zion for a foundation in such a manner, and by such wonderful works as you have heard, is a stone set at nought by you.

Sinners sometimes are ready to wonder why unbelief should be looked upon as a great sin; but if you consider what you have heard, how can you wonder? If this Saviour is so great, and this work so great, and such great things have been done in order to it; truly there is no cause of wonder that the rejection of this Saviour is so provoking to God. It brings greater guilt than the sins of the worst of heathens, who never heard of those things, nor have had this Saviour offered to them.

II. What has been said, affords matter of reproof to those who, instead of believing in Christ, trust in themselves for salvation. Is it not a common thing with men to take it upon themselves to do that great work which Christ came into the world to do? to trust in their prayers, their good conversations, the pains they take in religion, the reformation of their lives, and their self-denial, in order to recommend them to God, to make some atonement for their past sins? Let such consider three things:

1. How *great* a thing that is which you take upon you. It is to do the work of the great Saviour of the world.—Though you are poor, worthless, vile, and polluted, yet you arrogantly take upon you that very work for which the only-begotten Son of God became man; and in order to which God employed four thousand years in all the great dispensations of his providence, aiming chiefly to make way for Christ's coming to do this work. This is the work that you foolishly think yourself sufficient for; as though your prayers, and other performances, were excellent enough for this purpose. Consider how vain is the thought which you entertain of yourself. How must such arrogance appear in the sight of Christ, whom it cost so much. It was not to be obtained even by him, so great and glorious a person, at a cheaper rate than his going through a sea of blood, and passing through the midst of the furnace of God's wrath. And how vain must your arrogance appear in the sight of God, when he sees you imagining yourself sufficient, and your worthless, polluted performance excellent enough, for the accomplishing of that work of his own Son, to prepare the way for which he was employed in ordering all the great affairs of the world for so many ages!

2. If there be ground for you to trust, as you do, in your own righteousness, then all that Christ did to purchase salvation, and all that God did from the fall of man to prepare the way for it, is *in vain.* Your self-righteousness charges God with the greatest folly, as though he has done all things in vain, to bring about an accomplishment of what you alone, with your poor polluted prayers, and the little pains you take in religion, are sufficient to accomplish for yourself. For if you can appease God's anger, and commend yourself to him by these means, then you have no need of Christ; Gal. ii. 21. "If righteousness come by the law, then Christ is dead in vain."

If you can do this by your prayers and good works, Christ might have spared his pains; he might have spared his blood; he might have kept within the bosom of his Father, without coming down into this evil world to be despised, reproached, and persecuted to death. God needed not to have busied himself, as he did for four thousand years, causing so many changes in the state of the world all that while, in order to bring about that which you can accomplish in a few days, only with the trouble of a few religious performances. Consider, what greater folly could you have devised to charge upon God than this, that all those things were done so needlessly; when, instead of all this, he might only have called you forth, and committed the business to you, which you think you can do so easily. Alas! how blind are natural men! and especially how vain are the thoughts which they have of themselves! How ignorant of their own littleness and pollution! What great things do they assume to themselves!

3. You that trust to your own righteousness, arrogate to yourselves the honour of the *greatest* thing that ever God himself did. You seem not only sufficient to perform *divine* works, but such is your pride and vanity, that you are not content without taking upon you to do the very *greatest* work that ever God himself wrought. You see by what has been said, how God has subordinated all his other works to this of redemption. God's works of providence are greater than those of creation; and all his works of providence, from the beginning of the generations of men, were in order to make way for the purchasing of redemption. To take on yourself to work out redemption, is a greater thing than if you had taken it upon you to create a world. What a figure you would make, if you should seriously go about to create a world: or decking yourself with majesty, should pretend to speak the word of power, and call an universe out of nothing, intending to go on in order, and say, "Let there be light; Let there be a firmament," &c. But then consider, that in attempting to work out redemption for yourself, you attempt a *greater* thing than this, and are *serious* in it, and will not be dissuaded from it. You strive in it, are full of the thought that you are sufficient for it, and big with hopes of accomplishing it.

You take upon you to do the very greatest and *most difficult* part of this work, *viz.* to purchase redemption. Christ can accomplish other parts of this work without cost; but this part cost him his life, as well as innumerable pains and labours. Yet this is that part which self-righteous persons go about to accomplish for themselves. If all the angels in heaven had been sufficient for this work, would God have set himself to effect such things as he did in order to it? and would he ever have sent his own Son, the Creator of the angels, into the world, to have done and suffered such things?

What self-righteous persons take to themselves, is the same work that Christ was engaged in when he was in his agony and bloody sweat, and when he died on the cross, which was the greatest thing that ever the eyes of angels beheld. Great as it is, they imagine they can do the same that Christ accomplished by it. Their self-righteousness does in effect charge Christ's offering up himself in these sufferings, as the greatest instance of folly that ever men or angels saw, instead of being the most glorious display of the divine wisdom and grace. Yea, self-righteousness makes all that Christ did through the whole course of his life, all that he said and suffered, and his incarnation itself, and not only so, but all that God had been doing in the great dispensations of his providence from the beginning of the world to that time, as nothing but a scene of the most wild, extreme, and transcendent folly.

Is it any wonder, then, that a self-righteous spirit is so represented in Scripture, and spoken of, as that which is most fatal to the souls of men? And is it any wonder, that Christ is represented in Scripture as being so provoked with the Pharisees and others, who trusted in themselves that they were righteous, and were proud of their goodness, and thought that their own performances were a valuable price of God's favour and love?

Let persons hence be warned against a self-righteous spirit. You that are seeking salvation, and taking pains in religion, take heed to yourselves that you do not trust in what you do. Harbour no such thoughts, that God now, seeing how much you are reformed, how you are sometimes affected, will be pacified towards you, and will not be so angry for your former sins; that you shall gain on him by such things, and draw his heart to show you mercy. If you entertain the thought, that God is *obliged* to do it, and does not act justly if he refuse to regard your prayers and pains; if you quarrel with God, and complain of him for not doing it, this shows what your opinion is of your own righteousness, *viz.* that it is a valuable price of salvation, and ought to be accepted of God as such. Such complaining of God, and quarrelling with him, for not taking more notice of your righteousness, plainly shows that you are guilty of arrogance, thinking yourself sufficient to offer the price of your own salvation.

III. What has been said on this subject, affords matter of reproof to those who carelessly *neglect* the salvation of Christ. These live a senseless kind of life, neglect the business of religion and their own souls, not taking any course to get an interest in Christ, or what he has done and suffered, or any part in that glorious salvation he has purchased. They have their minds taken up about the gains of the world, or the vanities and pleasures of youth, and make light of what they hear of Christ's salvation, to that degree, that they do not at present so much as seek after it. Let me here apply myself to you in some expostulatory interrogations.

1. Shall so many prophets, and kings, and righteous men, have their minds so much taken up with the prospect, that the purchase of salvation was to be wrought out in ages long after their death; and will you neglect it when actually accomplished? You have heard what great account the church in all ages made of the future redemption of Christ; how joyfully they expected it, how they spoke of it, how they studied and searched into these things, how they sung joyful songs, and had their hearts greatly engaged about it, though they did not expect that it would be accomplished till many ages after their death, 1 Pet. i. 10—12. How much did Isaiah and Daniel, and other prophets, speak concerning this redemption! And how much were their hearts engaged, and their attention and study fixed upon it! How was David's mind taken up in this subject! He declared that it was all his salvation, and all his desire; 2 Sam. xxiii. 5. How did he employ his voice and harp in celebrating it, and the glorious display of divine grace therein exhibited! and all this although they beheld it not as yet accomplished, but saw that it was to be brought to pass so long a time after their day.——And before this, how did Abraham and the other patriarchs rejoice in the prospect of Christ's day, and the redemption which he was to purchase! And even the saints before the flood were affected and elated in the expectation of this glorious event, though it was then so long future, and it was so very faintly and obscurely revealed to them.

Now these things are declared to you as actually fulfilled. The church now has seen accomplished all those great things which they so joyfully prophesied of; and you are abundantly shown how those things were accomplished: Matt. xiii. 17. "Verily I say unto you, that many prophets and righteous men have desired to see those things which ye see, and have not seen; and to hear those things which ye hear, and have not heard them." And yet, when these things are thus abundantly set before you as already accomplished, how light do you make of them! How unconcerned are you about them, following other things, and not so much as feeling any interest in them! Indeed your sin is extremely aggravated in the sight of God. God has put you under great advantages for your eternal salvation, far greater than those saints of old enjoyed. He has put you under a more glorious dispensation; has given you a more clear revelation of Christ and his salvation; and yet you neglect all these advantages, and go on in a careless course of life, as though nothing had been done, no such proposals and offers had been made you.

2. Have the angels been so engaged about this salvation which is by Christ ever since the fall of man, though they are not immediately concerned in it, and will you who need it, and have it offered to you, be so careless about it? You have heard how the angels at first were subjected to Christ as mediator, and how they have all along been ministering spirits to him in this affair. In all the great dispensations which you have heard of from the beginning of the world, they have been active and as a flame of fire

in this affair, being most diligently employed as ministering spirits to minister to Christ in this great affair of man's redemption. And when Christ came, how engaged were their minds! They came to Zacharias, to inform him of the coming of Christ's forerunner.—They came to the Virgin Mary, to inform her of the approaching birth of Christ. They came to Joseph, to warn him of the danger which threatened the new-born Saviour, and to point out to him the means of safety. And how were their minds engaged at the time of the birth of Christ! The whole multitude of the heavenly hosts sang praises upon the occasion, saying, "Glory to God in the highest, on earth peace, good will towards men." And afterwards, from time to time, they ministered to Christ when on earth; at the time of his temptation, of his agony in the garden, at his resurrection, and at his ascension. All these things show, that they were greatly engaged in this affair; and the Scripture informs us, that they pry into these things: 1 Pet. i. 12. "Which things the angels desire to look into." And how are they represented in the Revelation as being employed in heaven in singing praises to him that sitteth on the throne, and to the Lamb! Now, shall these take so much notice of this redemption, and of the purchaser, who need it not for themselves, and have no immediate concern or interest in it, or offer of it; and will you, to whom it is offered, and who are in such extreme necessity of it, neglect and take no notice of it?

3. Did Christ labour so hard, and suffer so much to procure this salvation, and is it not worth the while for you to be at some labour in seeking it? Did our salvation lie with such weight on the mind of Christ, as to induce him to become man, to suffer even death itself, in order to procure it? And is it not worth the while for you, who need this salvation, and must perish eternally without it, to take earnest pains to obtain an interest in it after it is procured, and all things are ready?

4. Shall the great God be so concerned about this salvation, as often to overturn the world to make way for it; and when all is done, is it not worth your seeking after? What great, what wonderful things has he done; removing and setting up kings, raising up a great number of prophets, separating a distinct people from the rest of the world, overturning nations and kingdoms, and often the state of the world; and so has continued bringing about one change and revolution after another for forty centuries in succession, to make way for the procuring of this salvation! And when at the close of these ages, the great Saviour comes, passing through a long series of reproach and suffering, and then suffering all the waves and billows of God's wrath for men's sins, insomuch that they overwhelmed his soul; after all these things done to procure salvation for sinners, is it not worthy of your being so much concerned about it, but that it should be thrown by, and made nothing of, in comparison of worldly gain, gay clothing, or youthful diversions, and other such trifling things?

O! that you who live negligent of this salvation, would consider what you do! What you have heard from this subject, may show you what reason there is in that exclamation of the apostle, Heb. ii. 3. "How shall we escape if we neglect so great salvation?" And in Acts xiii. 41. "Behold, ye despisers, and wonder, and perish; for I work a work in your days, a work which you shall in no wise believe, though a man declare it unto you." God looks on you as great enemies of the cross of Christ, as adversaries and despisers of all the glory of this great work. And if God has made such account of the glory of salvation as to destroy many nations, in order to prepare the way for the glory of his Son in this affair; how little account will he make of the lives and souls of ten thousand such opposers and despisers as you, who continue impenitent, when your welfare stands in the way of that glory! Why surely you shall be dashed to pieces as a potter's vessel, and trodden down as the mire of the streets. God may, through wonderful patience, bear with hardened careless sinners for a while; but he will not long bear with such despisers of his dear Son, and his great salvation, the glory of which he has had so much at heart, before he will utterly consume without remedy or mercy.

SECT. II.

An use of encouragement.

I WILL conclude with a second use, of encouragement to burdened souls to put their trust in Christ for salvation. To all such as are not careless and negligent, but make seeking an interest in Christ their main business, being sensible in some measure of their necessity, and afraid of the wrath to come; to such, what has been said on this subject holds forth great matter of encouragement, to venture their souls on the Lord Jesus Christ. And as motives proper to excite you so to do, let me lead you to consider two things in particular.

1. The *completeness* of the purchase which has been made. You have heard, that this work of purchasing salvation was wholly finished during the time of Christ's humiliation. When Christ rose from the dead, and was exalted from that abasement to which he submitted for our salvation, the purchase of eternal life was completely made, so that there was no need of any thing more to be done in order to it. But now the servants were sent forth with a message, Matt. xxii. 4. "Behold, I have prepared my dinner: my oxen and my fatlings are killed, and all things are ready: come unto the marriage." Therefore, are your sins many and great? Here is enough done by Christ to procure their pardon. There is no need of any righteousness of yours to obtain your pardon and justification: no, you may come freely, without money and without price. Since therefore there is such a free and gracious invitation given you, come, come naked as you are; come as a poor condemned criminal; come and cast yourself down at Christ's feet, as one justly condemned, and utterly helpless. Here is a complete salvation wrought out by Christ, and through him offered to you. Come, therefore, accept of it, and be saved.

2. For Christ to reject one that thus comes to him, would be to frustrate all those great things which God brought to pass from the fall of man to the incarnation of Christ. It would also frustrate all that Christ did and suffered while on earth; yea, it would frustrate the incarnation itself. All the great things done were for that end, that those might be saved who should come to Christ. Therefore you may be sure Christ will not be backward in saving those who come to him, and trust in him; for he has no desire to frustrate himself in his own work. Neither will God the Father refuse you; for he has no desire to frustrate himself in all that he did for so many hundreds and thousands of years, to prepare the way for the salvation of sinners by Christ. Come, therefore, hearken to the sweet and earnest calls of Christ to your soul. Do as he invites and as he commands you, Matt. xi. 28—30. "Come unto me, all ye that labour, and are heavy laden, and I will give you rest. Take my yoke upon you, and learn of me; and ye shall find rest unto your souls. For my yoke is easy, and my burden is light."

PERIOD III.

FROM CHRIST'S RESURRECTION TO THE END OF THE WORLD.

IN discoursing on this subject, we have already shown how the work of redemption was carried on through the *two first* of the THREE PERIODS into which we divided the whole space of time from the fall to the end of the world. We are now come to the *third* and last period, beginning with Christ's resurrection; and would show, that the space of time from the end of Christ's humiliation to the end of the world is all taken up in bringing about the great effect or success of Christ's purchase.

SECT. I.

Scriptural representations of this period.

NOT but that there were great effects and glorious success of Christ's purchase of redemption before, even from the beginning of the generations of men. But all that success which was before, was only preparatory, by way of anticipation, as some few fruits are gathered before the harvest. There was no more success before Christ came, than God saw needful to prepare the way for his coming. The proper time of the success or effect of Christ's redemption is after the purchase has been made, as the proper time for the world to enjoy the light of the sun is the day-time, after the sun is risen, though we may have some small matter of it reflected from the moon and planets before. And even the success of Christ's redemption while he himself was on earth, was very small in comparison of what it was after.

But, Christ having finished that greatest and most difficult of all works, now is come the time for obtaining the end, the glorious effect of it. Having gone through the whole course of his sufferings and humiliation, Christ is never to suffer any more. But now is the time for him to obtain the joy that was set before him. Having made his soul an offering for sin, now is the time for him to see his seed, to have a portion with the great, and to divide the spoil with the strong.

One design of Christ in what he did in his humiliation, was to lay a foundation for the overthrow of Satan's kingdom; and now is come the time to effect it, as Christ, a little before his crucifixion, said, John xii. 31. "Now is the judgment of this world; now shall the prince of this world be cast out." Another design was, to gather together in one all things in Christ. Now is come the time for this also: John xii. 32. "And I, if I be lifted up, will draw all men unto me;" which is agreeable to Jacob's prophecy of Christ, that "when Shiloh should come, to him should the gathering of the people be," Gen. xlix. 10. Another design is the salvation of the elect. Now when his sufferings are finished, and his humiliation perfected, the time is come for that also: Heb. v. 8, 9. "Though he was a Son, yet learned obedience by the things which he suffered: and being made perfect, he became the author of eternal salvation unto all them that obey him." Another design was, to accomplish by these things great glory to the persons of the Trinity. John xvii. 1. "Father, the hour is come; glorify thy Son, that thy Son also may glorify thee." Another design was the glory of the saints. John xvii. 11. "As thou hast given him power over all flesh, that he should give eternal life to as many as thou hast given him." And all the dispensations of God's providence henceforward, even to the final consummation of all things, are to give Christ his reward, and fulfil his end in what he did and suffered upon earth, and to fulfil the joy that was set before him.

Before I enter on the consideration of any particular things accomplished in this period, I would briefly observe how the times of this period are represented in Scripture.

I. The times of this period, for the most part, are in the Old Testament called *the latter days*. We often, in the prophets of the Old Testament, read of things that should come to pass *in the latter days*, and sometimes *in the last days*, evidently referring to gospel times. They are called *the latter days*, and *the last days;* because this is the last period of the series of God's providences on earth, the last period of the great work of redemption; which is as it were the sum of God's works of providence; the last dispensation of the covenant of grace on earth.

II. The whole time of this period is sometimes in Scripture called *the end of the world*, 1 Cor. x. 11. "Now all these things happened unto them for ensamples; and they are written for our admonition, upon whom the ends of the world are come." And the apostle, Heb. ix. 26. in this expression of *the end of the world*, means the whole of the gospel-day, from the birth of Christ to the day of judgment: "But now once in the end of the world, hath he appeared, to put away sin by the sacrifice of himself." This space of time may well be called *the end of the world;* for this whole time is taken up in bringing things to their great end and issue. Before, things were in a kind of preparatory state; but now they are in a finishing state. An end is now brought to the former carnal state of things, which by degrees vanishes, and a spiritual state begins to be established more and more. Particularly, an end is brought to the former state of the *church*, which may be called its worldly state, in which it was subject to carnal ordinances, and the rudiments of the world. Then an end is brought to the Jewish *commonwealth*, in the destruction of their city and country. After that, an end is brought to the old *heathen empire* in Constantine's time. The next step is the finishing of *Satan's visible kingdom* in the world, upon the fall of Antichrist, and the calling of the Jews. And last will come the destruction of the outward frame of the world itself, at the conclusion of the day of judgment. Heaven and earth began to *shake*, in order to a dissolution, according to the prophecy of Haggai, before Christ came, that so only those things which cannot be shaken may remain, *i. e.* that those things which are to come to an end may terminate, and that only those things may remain which are to remain eternally.

In the first place, the carnal ordinances of the *Jewish worship* came to an end, in order to make way for the establishment of that spiritual worship, which is to endure to all eternity: John iv. 21. "Jesus saith unto the woman, Believe me, the hour cometh, when ye shall neither in this mountain, nor yet at Jerusalem, worship the Father." Ver. 23. "But the hour cometh, and now is, when the true worshippers shall worship the Father in spirit and in truth: for the Father seeketh such to worship him." This is one instance of the temporary world coming to an end, and the eternal world beginning. And then, the outward *temple* and the *city* Jerusalem came to an end, to give place to the setting up of the spiritual temple and city, which are to last for ever. Another instance of removing those things which are ready to vanish away, that those things which cannot be shaken may remain, is the bringing to an end the old heathen empire, to make way for the empire of Christ, which shall last to all eternity. After that, upon the fall of Antichrist, an end is put to Satan's visible kingdom on earth, to establish Christ's kingdom, which is an eternal kingdom; as the prophet Daniel says, chap. vii. 27. "And the kingdom and dominion, and the greatness of the kingdom under the whole heaven, shall be given to the people of the saints of the Most High, whose kingdom is an everlasting kingdom, and all dominions shall serve and obey him;" which is another instance of the ending of the temporary world, and the beginning of the eternal one. And then, lastly, the very frame of this corruptible world shall come to an end, to make way for the church to dwell in another dwelling-place, which shall last to eternity.

Because the world is thus coming to an end by various steps and degrees, the apostle perhaps uses this expression, that (not the *end* but) the *ends* of the world are come on us; as though the world has several endings one after another.—The gospel-dispensation is a finishing state: it is all spent in finishing things off which before had been preparing, or abolishing things which before had stood. It is all spent as it were in summing things up, and bringing them to their issues, and their proper fulfilment. Now all the old types are fulfilled, and the predictions of all the prophets from the beginning of the world shall be accomplished in this period.

III. That state of things which is attained in the events of this period is called *a new heaven and a new earth:* Isa. lxv. 17, 18. "For behold, I create new heavens, and a new earth: and the former shall not be remembered, nor come into mind. But be you glad and rejoice for ever in that which I create: for behold, I create Jerusalem a rejoicing, and her people a joy." And chap. lxvi. 22. "For as the new heavens and the new earth which I make, shall remain before me; so shall your seed and your name remain." See also chap. li. 16. As the former state of things, or the old world, by one step after another, is through this period coming to an end; so the new state of things, or the new world, which is a spiritual world, is beginning and setting up. In consequence of each of these finishings of the old state of things, there is the beginning of a new and eternal state. So that which accompanied the destruction of the literal Jerusalem, was an establishing of the spiritual. So with respect to the destruction of the old heathen empire, and all the other endings of the old state of things; till at length the very outward frame of the world itself shall come to an end; and the church shall dwell in heaven, which will be a new habitation. Then shall the utmost be accomplished that is meant by the new heavens and the new earth. (See Rev. xxi. 1.)

The end of God's creating the world, was to prepare a kingdom for his Son, (for he is appointed heir of the world,) which should remain to all eternity. So far as the *kingdom of Christ is set up* in the world, *so far* is the world brought to its end, and the eternal state of things set up—*so far* are all the great changes and revolutions of the world brought to their everlasting issue, and all things come to their ultimate period—*so far* are the waters of the long channel of divine providence, which has so many branches, and so many windings, emptied into their proper ocean, which they have been seeking from the beginning of their course, and so are come to their rest. So far as Christ's kingdom is established in the world, *so far* are things wound up and settled in their everlasting state, and a period put to the course of things in this changeable world; *so far* are the first heavens and the first earth come to an end, and the new heavens and the new earth, the everlasting heavens and earth, established in their room.—This leads me to observe,

IV. That the state of things which is attained by the events of this period, is what is so often called *the kingdom of heaven*, or *the kingdom of God*. We very often read in the New Testament of the kingdom of heaven. John the Baptist preached, that the kingdom of heaven was at hand; and so did Christ and his disciples after him; referring to something that the Jews in those days expected, and called by that name. They seem to have taken their expectation and the name chiefly from that prophecy of Daniel in Nebuchadnezzar's dream, Dan. ii. 44. "And in the days of these kings shall the God of heaven set up a kingdom;" together with chap. vii. 13, 14.

Now this *kingdom of heaven* is that evangelical state of things in the church, and in the world, wherein consists the success of Christ's redemption in this period. There had been often great kingdoms set up before; as the Babylonish, the Persian, the Grecian, and the Roman monarchies. But Christ came to set up the last, which is not an earthly kingdom, but a heavenly, John xviii. 36. "My kingdom is not of this world." This is the kingdom of which Christ speaks, Luke xxii. 29. "My Father hath appointed to me a kingdom." This kingdom began soon after Christ's resurrection, and is accomplished in *various steps* from that time to the end of the world. Sometimes by *the kingdom of heaven*, is meant not only that *spiritual* state of the church which began soon after Christ's resurrection; but also that *more perfect* state which shall obtain after the downfall of Antichrist; and sometimes that *glorious* and blessed state to which the church shall be received at the day of judgment. So 1 Cor. xv. 50. "This I say, that flesh and blood cannot inherit the kingdom of God."—Under this head I would observe several things particularly, for the clearer understanding of what the Scripture says concerning this period.

1. The setting up of the kingdom of Christ is chiefly accomplished by four successive great events, each of which is in Scripture called *Christ's coming in his kingdom*. The *first* is Christ's appearing in those wonderful dispensations of providence in the apostles' days, in setting up his kingdom, and destroying its enemies, which ended in the destruction of Jerusalem. This is called Christ's coming in his kingdom, Matt. xvi. 28. "Verily I say unto you, there be some standing here, which shall not taste of death till they see the Son of man coming in his kingdom." (And Matt. xxiv.) The *second* is that which was accomplished in Constantine's time, in the destruction of the heathen Roman empire. This is represented as Christ's coming, and is compared to his coming to judgment, (Rev. vi. at the latter end.) The *third* is that which is to be accomplished at the destruction of Antichrist. This also is represented as Christ's coming in his kingdom in the 7th chapter of Daniel, and in other places. The *fourth* and last is his coming to the last judgment, which is the event principally signified in Scripture by *Christ's coming in his kingdom*.

2. Each of the three former of these is a lively image, or type, of the fourth and last, *viz*. Christ's coming to the final judgment, as the principal dispensations of providence before were types of his first coming.——As Christ's last coming to judgment is accompanied with the resurrection of the dead, so is each of the three foregoing with a spiritual resurrection. That coming of Christ which ended in the destruction of Jerusalem, was preceded by a glorious *spiritual* resurrection of souls in the calling of the Gentiles through the preaching of the gospel. Christ's coming in Constantine's time, was accompanied with a glorious *spiritual* resurrection of the greater part of the known world, in a restoration of it to a visible church state, from a state of heathenism. Christ's coming at the destruction of Antichrist, will be attended with a *spiritual* resurrection of the church after it had been long as it were dead, in the times of Antichrist. This is called the *first resurrection* in the 20th chapter of Revelation.

Again, as Christ in the last judgment will gloriously manifest himself coming in the glory of his Father, so in each of the three foregoing events Christ gloriously manifested himself in sending judgments upon his enemies, and in showing favour to his church. As the last coming of Christ will be attended with a literal gathering together of the elect from the four winds of heaven, so were each of the preceding attended with a spiritual gathering in of the elect. As this gathering together of the elect will be effected by God's angels with a great sound of a trumpet; (Matt. xxiv. 31.) so were each of the preceding spiritual ingatherings effected by the trumpet of the gospel, sounded by the ministers of Christ. As there shall precede the last appearance of Christ, a time of great degeneracy and wickedness, so this has been, or will be, the case with each of the other appearances. Before each of them is a time of great opposition to the church: before the first, by the Jews; before the second, in Constantine's time, by the heathen; before the third, by Antichrist; and before the last, by Gog and Magog, as described in the Revelation.

By each of these comings of Christ, God works a glorious *deliverance* for his church. The *first*, which ended in the destruction of Jerusalem, was attended with bringing the church into the glorious state of the gospel. The *second*, which was in Constantine's time, was accompanied with an advancement of the church into a state of liberty from persecution, the countenance of civil authority, and her triumph over heathen persecutors. The *third*, which shall be at the downfall of Antichrist, will be accompanied with an advancement of the church into that state of the glorious prevalence of truth, liberty, peace, and joy, which we so often read of in the prophetical parts of Scripture. The *last* will be attended with the advancement of the church to consummate glory in heaven.

Each of these comings of Christ is accompanied with a terrible *destruction* of the wicked, and the enemies of the church: the *first*, with the destruction of the persecuting Jews, which was amazingly terrible; the *second*, with dreadful judgments on the heathen persecutors of the church; the *third*, with the awful destruction of Antichrist, the most cruel and bitter enemy that ever the church had; the *fourth*, with divine wrath and vengeance on all the ungodly.—Further, there is in *each* of these comings of Christ an ending of the old, and a beginning of new, heavens and a new earth; or an end of a temporal state of things, and a beginning of an eternal state.

3. I would observe, that each of those four great dispensations which are represented as Christ's coming in his kingdom, are but so many steps and degrees of the accomplishment of one event. They are not the setting up of so many distinct kingdoms of Christ; but only several degrees of the accomplishment of that one event prophesied of, Dan. vii. 13, 14. "And I saw in the night-visions, and

behold, one like the Son of man came with the clouds of heaven, and came to the Ancient of days, and they brought him near before him. And there was given him dominion, and glory, and a kingdom, that all people, nations, and languages, should serve him: his dominion is an everlasting dominion, and his kingdom that which shall not be destroyed." This is what the Jews expected, and called "the coming of the kingdom of heaven;" and what John the Baptist and Christ had respect to, when they said, "The kingdom of heaven is at hand." This great event is accomplished by several steps.

4. When Christ came with the preaching of the apostles, to set up his kingdom in the world, which dispensation ended with the destruction of Jerusalem, then it was accomplished in a *glorious* degree; when the heathen empire was destroyed in Constantine's time, it was fulfilled in a *further* degree; when Antichrist shall be destroyed, it will be accomplished in a *yet higher* degree; but when the end of the world is come, then will it be accomplished in its *most perfect* degree of all. And because these four great events are but images one of another, and the three former but types of the last, and since they are all only several steps of the accomplishment of the same thing; hence we find them all from time to time prophesied of under one, as in the prophecies of Daniel, and in the 24th chapter of Matthew, where some things seem more applicable to one of them, and others to another.

Thus it appears, that as there are several steps of the accomplishment of the kingdom of Christ, so in each one of them the event is accomplished in a further degree than in the foregoing. That in the time of Constantine was a greater and further accomplishment of the kingdom of Christ, than that which ended in the destruction of Jerusalem; that which shall be at the fall of Antichrist, will be a further accomplishment of the same thing, than that which took place in the time of Constantine; and so on with regard to each: so that the kingdom of Christ is gradually prevailing and growing by these several great steps of its fulfilment, from the time of Christ's resurrection, to the end of the world.

5. The great providences of God between these four events, are to make way for the kingdom and glory of Christ in the great event following. Those dispensations of providence towards the church and the world, before the destruction of the heathen empire in the time of Constantine, seem all to have been to make way for the glory of Christ, and the happiness of the church in that event. And so the great providences after that, till the destruction of Antichrist, and the beginning of the glorious times of the church which follow, seem all calculated to prepare the way for the greater glory of Christ and his church in that event; and the following ones to the end of the world, seem to be for the greater manifestation of Christ's glory at the consummation of all things.—Thus I thought it needful to observe those things in general concerning this last period, before I take notice of *particular* providences by which the work of redemption is carried on through this period, in their order.

Before I proceed, I will briefly answer an INQUIRY, *viz.* Why the setting up of Christ's kingdom after his humiliation, should be so gradual, since God could easily have finished it at once?—Though it would be presumption in us to pretend to declare all the ends of God in this, yet doubtless much of his wisdom may be seen in it; and particularly in these two things.

1. In this way the glory of God's wisdom is more visible to the observation of creatures. If it had been done at once, or in a very short time, there would not have been such opportunities for creatures to perceive and observe the particular steps of divine wisdom, as when the work is gradually accomplished, and one effect of his wisdom is held forth to observation after another. It is wisely determined of God, to accomplish his great design by a wonderful and long series of events, that the glory of his wisdom may be displayed, in the whole series of events, that the glory of his perfection may be seen, in particular successive manifestations. If all that glory which appears in these events had been manifested at once, it would have been too much for us; it would have overpowered our sight and capacities.

2. Satan is more gloriously triumphed over.—God could easily, by an act of almighty power, at once have crushed Satan. But by giving him time to use his utmost subtlety to hinder the success of what Christ had done and suffered, he is not defeated merely by surprise, but has large opportunity to ply his utmost power and subtlety again and again, to strengthen his own interest all that he can by the work of many ages. Thus God destroys and confounds him, and sets up Christ's kingdom time after time, in spite of all his subtle machinations and great works, and by every step advances it still higher and higher, till at length it is fully set up, and Satan perfectly and eternally vanquished.—I now proceed to take notice of the particular events, whereby, from the end of Christ's humiliation to the end of the world, the success of Christ's purchase has been or shall be accomplished.

SECT. II.

How Christ was capacitated for effecting his purpose.

As the incarnation of Christ was necessary in order to his being in a near capacity for the *purchase* of redemption; so his resurrection and ascension were requisite in order to the *success* of his purchase.

I. His *resurrection.* It was necessary in order to Christ's obtaining the end and effect of his purchase of redemption, that he should rise from the dead. For God the Father had committed the whole affair of redemption to his Son, that he should not only purchase it as priest, but actually bring it about as king; and that he should do this as God-man. God the Father would have nothing to do with fallen man in a way of mercy but by a mediator. But in order that Christ might accomplish the success of his own purchase as God-man, it was necessary that he should rise from the dead. Therefore Christ, after he had finished this purchase by death, rises from the dead, to fulfil the end of his purchase. This matter God the Father had committed unto him, that he might, as Lord of all, manage all to his own purposes: Rom. xiv. 9. "For to this end Christ both died, and rose, and revived, that he might be Lord both of the dead and of the living."

Indeed Christ's resurrection (and so his ascension) was part of the success of what Christ did and suffered in his humiliation. For though Christ did not properly purchase *redemption* for himself, yet he purchased *eternal life* and glory for himself, as a reward of what he did and suffered: Phil. ii. 8, 9. "He humbled himself, and became obedient unto death, even the death of the cross. Wherefore God also hath highly exalted him." And it may be looked upon as part of the success of Christ's purchase, since he did not rise as a *private* person, but as the *head* of the elect church; so that they did, as it were, all rise with him. Christ was justified in his resurrection, *i. e.* God acquitted and discharged him hereby, as having done and suffered enough for the sins of all the elect: Rom. iv. 25. "Who was delivered for our offences, and raised again for our justification." And God put him in possession of eternal life, as the head of the church, as a sure earnest that they should follow. For when Christ rose from the dead, that was the beginning of eternal life in him. His life before his death was a mortal life, a temporal life; but after his resurrection it was an eternal life: Rom. vi. 9. "Knowing that Christ being raised from the dead, dieth no more; death hath no more dominion over him." Rev. i. 18. "I am he that liveth, and was dead; and behold, I am alive for evermore, Amen."——But he was put in possession of this eternal life, as the head of the body; so that the whole church, as it were, rises in him. And now he who lately suffered so much, is to suffer no more for ever, but has entered into eternal glory.

This resurrection of Christ is the most *joyful* event that ever came to pass; because hereby Christ rested from the great and difficult work of purchasing redemption, and received God's testimony, that it was finished. The death of Christ was the greatest and most wonderful event that ever came to pass; but that has a great deal in it that is sorrowful. But by the resurrection of Christ, that sorrow is turned into joy. The Head of the church, in that great event, enters on the possession of eternal life; and the whole church is, as it were, *begotten again to a lively hope*, 1 Pet. i. 3. Weeping had continued for a night, but now joy cometh in the morning. This is the day of his reigning, as the head of the church, and all the church reigns with him. This day was worthy to be commemorated with the greatest joy. Ps. cxviii. 24. "This is the day which the Lord hath made, we will rejoice and be glad in it." And therefore this, above all other days, is appointed to the end of the world, to be weekly sanctified, as a day of holy rest and joy, that the church therein may rest and rejoice with her Head. And as the 3d chapter of Genesis is the most sorrowful chapter in the Bible; so those chapters in the evangelist, that give an account of the resurrection of Christ, may be looked upon as the most joyful. These give an account of the finishing of the purchase of redemption, and the beginning of the glory of the Head of the church, as the greatest seal and earnest of the eternal glory of all the members.

It is further to be observed, that the day of the gospel most properly begins with the resurrection of Christ. Till Christ rose from the dead, the Old-Testament dispensation remained: but now it ceases, all being fulfilled that was shadowed forth in the typical ordinances of that dispensation. Here most properly is the end of the Old-Testament night; and Christ rising from the grave with joy and glory, was like the sun rising after a long night of darkness, appearing in joyful light to enlighten the world. Now that joyful dispensation begins, that glorious dispensation, of which the prophets testified so much. Now the gospel-sun is risen in his glory, *and with healing in his wings*, that those who fear God's name, may *go forth, and grow up as calves of the stall*.

II. Christ's *ascension* into heaven. In this I would include his sitting at the right hand of God. For Christ's ascension was nothing else, but ascending to God's right hand in glory. A deliverer of a people as their king, in order that he may be under the best capacity for it, is first installed in his throne. We are told, that Christ was exalted for this end, that he might accomplish the success of his redemption: Acts v. 31. "Him hath God exalted with his right hand, for to give repentance unto Israel, and the remission of sins."

Christ's ascension into heaven was, as it were, his solemn coronation, when the Father set him upon the throne, and invested him with the glory of that kingdom which he had purchased for himself, that he might thereby obtain the success of his redemption in conquering all his enemies: Ps. cx. 1. "Sit thou at my right hand, until I make thine enemies thy footstool." Christ entered into heaven, in order to obtain the success of his purchase, as the high priest of old, after he had offered sacrifice, entered into the holy of holies with the blood of the sacrifice, in order to obtain the success of the sacrifice which he had offered. See Heb. ix. 12. He entered into heaven, there to make intercession for his people, to plead the sacrifice which he had made in order to the success of it, Heb. vii. 25.—And as he ascended into heaven, God the Father did in a visible manner set him on the throne as king of the universe. He then put the angels all under him, and subjected to him heaven and earth, that he might govern them for the good of the people for whom he died, Eph. i. 20—22.—And as Christ rose from the dead, so he ascended into heaven, as the head of the body, and forerunner of all the church; and they, as it were, ascend with him: so that we are both raised up together, and made to sit together in heavenly places in Christ, Eph. ii. 6.

The day of Christ's ascension was doubtless a joyful, glorious day in heaven. And as heaven received Christ, God-man, as its king, so doubtless it received a great accession of glory and happiness. So that the times in both parts of the church, that part which is in heaven, and that which is on earth, are become more glorious since Christ's humiliation than before.—So much for those things whereby Christ was put into the best capacity for obtaining the success of redemption.

SECT. III.

Established means of success.

Consider those dispensations of Providence, by which the *means of this success* were established after Christ's resurrection.

I. The abolishing the *Jewish dispensation*. This indeed was gradually done, but it began from the time of Christ's resurrection, in which the abolition of it is founded. For the *Jewish* dispensation was not fitted for the practice of the world in general, or for a church of God dwelling in all parts of the world: nor would it have been practicable by them. It would have been impossible for men living in all parts of the world to go to Jerusalem three times a year, as was prescribed in that constitution. When therefore God had a design of enlarging his church, as he did after Christ's resurrection, it was necessary that this dispensation should be abolished. If it had been continued, it would have been a great block and hinderance to the enlargement of the church. Besides, their ceremonial law, by reason of its burdensomeness, and great peculiarity of some of its rites, was a wall of partition between the Jews and Gentiles, and would have kept the Gentiles from complying with the true religion. This wall therefore was broken down to make way for the more extensive success of the gospel; as Eph. ii. 14, 15.

II. The next thing in order of time seems to be the appointment of the *christian sabbath*. For though this was gradually established in the christian church, yet those things by which the revelation of God's mind and will was made, began on the day of Christ's resurrection, by his appearing then to his disciples, John xx. 19. And afterwards, his appearing was from time to time on that day rather than any other, John xx. 26. This appointment was confirmed by his sending down the Holy Spirit so remarkably on that day, Acts ii. 1. and afterwards by directing, that the public worship of Christians should be on that day, which may be concluded from Acts xx. 7. 1 Cor. xvi. 1, 2. and Rev. i. 10. And so the day of the week on which Christ rose from the dead, that joyful day, is appointed to be the day of the church's holy rejoicing to the end of the world, and the day of their stated public worship. And this is a very great and principal means of the success which the gospel has had in the world.

III. The next thing was Christ's appointment of the *gospel-ministry*, by commissioning and sending forth his apostles to teach and baptize all nations. Of these things we have an account in Matt. xxviii. 19, 20. "Go ye, therefore, and teach all nations, baptizing them in the name of the Father, and of the Son, and of the Holy Ghost; teaching them to observe all things whatsoever I have commanded you; and lo, I am with you alway, even unto the end of the world."——There were three things done by this one commission of Christ to his apostles, *viz.*

1. The appointment of the *office* of the gospel-ministry.—For this commission which Christ gives to his apostles, in the most essential parts of it, belongs to all ministers; and the apostles, by virtue of it, were ministers or elders of the church.

2. Something peculiar in this commission, *viz.* to go forth *from one nation to another*, preaching the gospel in all the world. The apostles had something above what belonged to their ordinary character as ministers; they had an extraordinary power of teaching and ruling, which extended to all the churches; and not only all the churches which then were, but all that should be to the end of the world by their ministry. And so the apostles were, in subordination to Christ, made foundations of the christian church. See Eph. ii. 20. and Rev. xxi. 14.

3. Here is an appointment of Christian *baptism*. This ordinance indeed had a beginning before; John the Baptist and Christ baptized. But now especially by this institution is it established as an ordinance to be upheld in the christian church to the end of the world.——The ordinance of the Lord's supper had been established before, just before Christ's crucifixion.

IV. The next thing to be observed, is the enduing the apostles, and others, with extraordinary and *miraculous gifts* of the Holy Ghost; such as the gift of tongues, the gift of healing, of prophecy, &c. The Spirit of God was poured out in great abundance in this respect; so that not only ministers, but a very great part of the Christians through the world were endued with them, both old and young; not only officers, and more honourable persons, but the meaner sort of people, servants, and handmaids, agreeable to Joel's prophecy, Joel ii. 28, 29. of which prophecy the apostle Peter takes notice, that it is accomplished in this dispensation, Acts ii. 11.

How wonderful a dispensation was this! Under the Old Testament but few had such honours put upon them by God. Moses indeed wished that all the Lord's people were prophets, Numb. xi. 29. whereas Joshua thought it much that Eldad and Medad prophesied. But now we find the wish of Moses fulfilled. And this continued in a very considerable degree to the end of the apostolic age, or the first hundred years after the birth of Christ, which is therefore called *the age of miracles*.

This was a great means of the success of the gospel, and of establishing the christian church, not only in that age, but in all ages to the end of the world. For Christianity being established through so great a part of the known world by miracles, it was after that more easily continued by tradition; and by means of these extraordinary gifts of the Holy Ghost, the apostles and others were enabled to write the New Testament, to be an infallible and perpetual rule of faith and manners to the church. And these miracles recorded in those writings are a standing proof of the truth of Christianity to all ages.

V. The next thing is the revealing of those glorious doctrines fully and plainly, which had under the Old Testament been obscurely revealed. The doctrine of Christ's satisfaction and righteousness, his ascension and glory, and the way of salvation, were under the Old Testament in a great measure hid under the vail of types and shadows, and more obscure revelations, as Moses put a vail on his face to hide the shining of it; but now the vail of the temple is rent from the top to the bottom. Christ, the antetype of Moses, shines; his face is without a vail; 2 Cor. iii. 12, 13, and 18. Now these glorious mysteries, which were in a great measure kept secret from the foundation of the world, are clearly revealed. Eph. iii. 3—5. Rom. xvi. 25. "According to the revelation of the mystery which was kept secret since the world began, but now is made manifest;" and, Col. i. 26. "Even the mystery which hath been hid from ages and generations, but now is made manifest to his saints."

Thus the Sun of righteousness, after it is risen, begins to shine forth clearly, and not by a dim reflection as before.—Christ, before his death, revealed many things more clearly than ever they had been in the Old Testament: but the great mysteries of Christ's redemption, reconciliation by his death, and justification by his righteousness, were not so plainly revealed before Christ's resurrection. Christ gave this reason for it, that he would not put new wine into old bottles; and it was gradually done even after his resurrection. In all likelihood, Christ much more clearly instructed them personally after his resurrection, and before his ascension; as we read that he continued with them forty days, speaking of the things pertaining to the kingdom, Acts i. 3. and that "he opened their understandings, that they might understand the scriptures," Luke xxiv. 45. But the clear revelation of these things was principally after the pouring out of the Spirit on the day of Pentecost, agreeable to Christ's promise, John xvi. 12, 13. "I have yet many things to say unto you, but ye cannot bear them now. Howbeit, when the Spirit of truth is come, he shall guide you into all truth." This clear revelation of the mysteries of the gospel, as they are delivered, we have chiefly through the hands of the apostle Paul, by whose writings a child may come to know more of the doctrines of the gospel, in many respects, than the greatest prophets knew under the darkness of the Old Testament.

Thus we see how the light of the gospel, which began to dawn immediately after the fall, and gradually increased through all the ages of the Old Testament, is now come to the light of perfect day, as the brightness of the sun shining forth in his unvailed glory.

VI. The next thing that I would observe, is the appointment of the office of deacons in the christian church, which we have an account of in the 6th chapter of the Acts, to take care for the outward supply of the members of Christ's church, and the exercise of that great christian virtue charity.

VII. The calling, qualifying, and sending the apostle Paul. This was begun in his conversion as he was going to Damascus, and was one of the greatest means of the success of Christ's redemption that followed: for this success was more by the labours, preaching, and writings of this apostle, than all the other apostles put together. For, as he says, 1 Cor. xv. 10. he *laboured more abundantly than they all*. As he was the apostle of the Gentiles, so it was mainly by his ministry that the Gentiles were called and the gospel spread through the world. Our nation, and the other nations of Europe, have the gospel among them chiefly through his means; and he was more employed by the Holy Ghost in revealing the glorious doctrines of the gospel by his writings, for the use of the church in all ages, than all the other apostles taken together.

VIII. The next thing I would observe, is the institution of ecclesiastical councils, for deciding controversies, and ordering the affairs of the church of Christ, of which we have an account in the 15th chapter of Acts.

IX. The last thing I shall mention under this head, is the committing the New Testament to writing. This was all written after the resurrection of Christ by the apostles themselves, except the gospels of Mark and Luke, and the book of the Acts. He that wrote the gospel of Mark, is supposed to be the son of Mary, in whose house they were praying for Peter, when he, brought out of prison by the angel, came and knocked at the door; of which we read, Acts xii. 12. "And when he had considered the thing, he came to the house of Mary the mother of John, whose surname was Mark, where many were gathered together, praying." He was the companion of the apostles Barnabas and Paul: Acts xv. 37. "And Barnabas determined to take with them John, whose surname was Mark."—He was Barnabas's sister's son, and seems some time to have been a companion of the apostle Paul: Col. iv. 10. "Aristarchus, my fellow-prisoner, saluteth you, and Marcus, sister's son to Barnabas; touching whom ye received commandment: if he come unto you, receive him." The apostles seem to have made great account of him, as appears by those places, and also by Acts xii. 25. "And Barnabas and Saul returned from Jerusalem, and took with them John, whose surname was Mark;" and Acts xiii. 5. "And when they were at Salamis, they preached the word of God in the synagogues of the Jews; and they had also John to their minister;" and 2 Tim. iv. 11. "Only Luke is with me: take Mark and bring him with thee; for he is profitable to me for the ministry."

He who wrote the gospel of Luke and the book of Acts, was a great companion of the apostle Paul. Beside the last-mentioned place, he speaks of himself as accompanying Paul in his travels, and therefore speaks in the first person plural; We went to such a place; We set sail, &c. He was greatly beloved by the apostle Paul: he is that beloved physician spoken of, Col. iv. 14. The apostle ranks Mark and Luke among his fellow-labourers, Philemon 24. "Marcus, Aristarchus, Demas, Lucas, my fellow-labourers."

The books of the New Testament are either historical, doctrinal, or prophetical. The *historical* books are the writings of the four evangelists, giving us the history of Christ, his purchase of redemption, his resurrection and ascension; and the Acts of the Apostles, giving an account of the great things by which the christian church was first established and propagated. The *doctrinal* books are the epistles; most of which we have from the great apostle Paul. And we have one *prophetical* book, which takes place after the end of the history of the whole Bible, and gives an account of the great events which were to come to pass, by which the work of redemption was to be carried on to the end of the world.

All these books are supposed to have been written before the destruction of Jerusalem, excepting those which were written by the apostle John, who lived the longest of all the apostles, and who wrote after the destruction of Jerusalem, as is supposed. To this beloved disciple it was that Christ revealed those wonderful things which were to come to pass in his church to the end of time; and he was the person who put the finishing hand to the canon of Scripture, and sealed the whole of it. So that now the canon of Scripture, that great and standing written rule, which was begun about Moses's time, is completed and settled, and a curse denounced against him that adds any thing to it, or diminishes any thing from it. And so all the stated means of grace were finished in the apostolical age, or before the death of the apostle John, and are to remain unaltered to the day of judgment. Thus far we have considered those things by which the means of grace were given and established in the christian church.

SECT. IV.

How the success was carried on.

From Christ's resurrection till the fall of Antichrist, is the appointed day of Zion's troubles. During this space of time, some part or other of the church is under persecution; and great part of the time, the whole church, or at least the generality of God's people, have been persecuted. For the first three hundred years after Christ, the church was for the most part in a state of great affliction, the object of reproach and persecution; first by the Jews, and then by the heathen.—After this, from the beginning of Constantine's time, the church had rest and prosperity for a little while; which is represented in Rev. vii. at the beginning, by the angel's holding the four winds for a little while. But presently after, the church again suffered persecution from the Arians. After that, Antichrist rose, the church was driven away into the wilderness, was kept down in obscurity, contempt, and suffering, for a long time before the Reformation by Luther and others. And since the Reformation, the church's persecutions have been beyond all that ever were before. And though some parts of God's church sometimes have had rest, yet to this day, for the most part, the true church is very much kept under by its enemies, and some parts of it under grievous persecution. And so we may expect it will continue till the fall of Antichrist. Then will come the appointed day of the church's prosperity on earth, the set time in which God will favour Zion, the time when the saints shall not be kept under by wicked men, but wherein they shall reign, as it is said, Rev. v. 10. "And the kingdom shall be given to the people of the saints of the Most High," Dan. vii. 27.

The suffering state of the church is in Scripture represented as a state of the church's travail, (John xvi. 20, 21. and Rev. xii. 1, 2.) striving to bring forth that glory and prosperity which shall be after the fall of Antichrist, and then shall she bring forth her child. This is a long time of the church's trouble and affliction, though it be but for a little season, in comparison of the eternal prosperity of the church. Hence under the long continuance of this affliction, she cries out, (Rev. vi. 10.) "How long, O Lord, holy and true, dost thou not judge and avenge our blood on them that dwell on the earth?" And we are told, that "white robes were given unto every one of them; and it was said unto them, that they should rest yet for a little season, until their fellow-servants also, and their brethren that should be killed as they were, should be fulfilled." So, Dan. xii. 6. "How long shall it be to the end of these wonders."

It is to be observed, that during the time of these sufferings of the church, the main instrument of their sufferings has been the Roman government. Rome therefore in the New Testament is called *Babylon;* because, as of old the troubles of the city of Jerusalem were mainly from that adverse city Babylon, so the troubles of the christian church, the spiritual Jerusalem, during the long time of its tribulation, are mainly from Rome. Before the time of Constantine, the troubles of the christian church were from heathen Rome: since that time, its troubles have been mainly from antichristian Rome. And as of old, the captivity of the Jews ceased on the destruction of Babylon, so the time of the trouble of the christian church will cease with the destruction of the church of Rome, that spiritual Babylon.

PART I.

THE SUCCESS OF REDEMPTION FROM THE RESURRECTION OF CHRIST TO THE DESTRUCTION OF JERUSALEM.

I would now show, how the success of Christ's purchase of redemption was carried on from Christ's resurrection to the destruction of Jerusalem. In speaking of this I would, 1. take notice of the success itself; and, 2. the opposition made against it by its enemies; and, 3. the terrible judgments of God on those enemies.

I. I would observe the *success itself.* Soon after Christ had entered into the holy of holies with his own blood, there began a glorious success of what he had done and suffered.—Having undermined the foundation of Satan's kingdom, it began to fall apace. Swiftly did it hasten to ruin, which might well be compared to Satan's falling like lightning from heaven. Satan before had exalted his throne very high in this world, even to the very stars of heaven, reigning with great glory in his heathen Roman empire; but never before had he such a downfall as he had soon after Christ's ascension. He had, we may suppose, been very lately triumphing in a supposed victory, having brought about the death of Christ, which he doubtless gloried in as the greatest feat that ever he did; and probably imagined he had totally defeated God's design by him. But he was quickly made sensible, that he had only been ruining his own kingdom, when he saw it tumbling so fast so soon after, as a consequence of the death of Christ. For Christ, having ascended, and received the Holy Spirit, poured it forth abundantly for the conversion of thousands and millions of souls.

Never had Christ's kingdom been so set up in the world. There probably were more souls converted in the age of the apostles, than had been before from the beginning of the world till that time. Thus God so soon begins gloriously to accomplish his promise to his Son, wherein he had promised, That he should see his seed, and that the pleasure of the Lord should prosper in his hand, if he would make his soul an offering for sin. And,

1. Here is to be observed the success which the gospel had among the *Jews;* for God first began with them. He being about to reject the main body of that people, first calls in his elect from among them. It was so in former great and dreadful judgments of God on that nation; the bulk of them were destroyed, and only a remnant saved, or reformed. The bulk of the ten tribes was rejected, when they left the true worship of God under Jeroboam, and afterwards more fully in Ahab's time; but yet there was a remnant of them reserved. Many left their possessions in these tribes, and settled in the tribes of Judah and Benjamin. And afterwards there were seven thousand in Ahab's time, who had not bowed the knee to Baal. From the captivity into Babylon, only a remnant of them ever returned to their own land. So now the greater part of the people were rejected entirely, but some few were saved. And therefore the Holy Ghost compares this reservation of a number that were converted by the preaching of the apostles, to those former remnants: Rom. ix. 27. "Esaias also crieth concerning Israel, Though the number of the children of Israel be as the sand of the sea, a remnant shall be saved."—See Isa. x. 22.

The glorious success of the gospel among the Jews after Christ's ascension, began by the pouring out of the Spirit upon the day of Pentecost. (Acts ii.) So wonderful was this effusion, and so remarkable and swift the effect of it, that we read of three thousand who were converted to the christian faith in one day, Acts ii. 41. and probably the greater part of these were savingly converted. And after this, we read of God's adding to the church daily such as should be saved, (ver. 47.) Soon after, we read, that the number of them were about five thousand. Thus were not only a multitude converted, but the church was then eminent in piety, as appears by Acts ii. 46, 47. iv. 32.

Thus the christian church was first formed from the nation of Israel; and therefore, when the Gentiles were called, they were *added* to the christian church of Israel, as the proselytes of old were to the Mosaic church of Israel. They were only *grafted* on the stock of Abraham, and were not a distinct tree; for they were all still the seed of Abraham and Israel; as Ruth the Moabitess, and Uriah the Hittite, and other proselytes of old, were the same people, and ranked as the seed of Israel.

The christian church began at Jerusalem, and from thence was propagated to all nations: so that this church of Jerusalem was the mother of all other churches in the world; agreeable to the prophecy, Isa. ii. 3, 4. "Out of Zion shall go forth the law, and the word of the Lord from Jerusalem: and he shall judge among the nations, and rebuke many people." So that the whole church of God is still his spiritual Jerusalem.

After this, we read of many thousands of Jews in Jerusalem that believed, Acts xxi. 20. And we read of multitudes of Jews who were converted in other cities of Judea, and in other parts of the world. For it was the manner of the apostles to go first into the synagogues of the Jews, and preach the gospel to them, and many in one place and another believed; as in Damascus, Antioch, and many other places.

In this pouring out of the Spirit, at the Pentecost, began that first great dispensation which is called *Christ's coming in his kingdom.* Christ's coming thus in a spiritual manner for the glorious erection of his kingdom in the world, is represented as his coming down from heaven, whither he had ascended, John xiv. 18. "I will not leave you comfortless; I will come unto you." And ver. 28. "Ye have heard how I said unto you, I go away, and come again unto you." And thus the apostles began to see the kingdom of heaven come with power, as he promised them, Mark ix. 1.

2. After the success of the gospel had been so gloriously begun among the Jews, the Spirit of God was next wonderfully poured out on the *Samaritans;* who were the posterity of those whom the king of Assyria removed from different parts of his dominions, and settled in the land which had been inhabited by the ten tribes, whom he carried captive. These had received the five books of Moses, and practised most of the Mosaic rites, and so were a sort of *mongrel Jews.* We do not find them reckoned as Gentiles in the New Testament: for the calling of the Gentiles is spoken of as a new thing after this, beginning with the conversion of Cornelius. But yet it was an instance of making those a people who were no people: for they had corrupted the religion of Moses, and did not go up to Jerusalem to worship. They had another temple of their own in mount Gerizim; which is the mountain of which the woman of Samaria speaks, when she says, *Our fathers worshipped in this mountain.* Christ there does not approve of their separation from the Jews; but says, that they worshipped they knew not what, and that salvation is of the Jews. But now salvation is brought from the Jews to them by the preaching of Philip, (excepting that before Christ had some success among them,) with whose preaching there was a glorious pouring out of the Spirit of God in the city of Samaria; where we are told, that "the people believed Philip preaching the things concerning the kingdom of Christ, and were baptized, both men and women; and that there was great joy in that city," Acts viii. 8—12.

Thus Christ had a glorious harvest in Samaria; according to what he said to his disciples at Jacob's well, three or four years before, on occasion of the people of Samaria appearing at a distance in the fields coming to the place where he was. John iv. 35, 36. The disposition which the people of Samaria showed towards Christ and his gospel, showed that they were ripe for the harvest; and now the harvest is come by Philip's preaching. There used to be a most bitter enmity between the Jews and Samaritans; but now, by their conversion, the christian Jews and Samaritans are all happily united: for in Christ Jesus is neither Jew nor Samaritan, but Christ is all in all. This was a glorious instance of the wolf dwelling with the lamb, and the leopard lying down with the kid.

3. The next thing to be observed is the calling the Gentiles. This was a great and glorious dispensation, much spoken of in the Old Testament, and by the apostles, as a most glorious event. This was begun in the conversion of Cornelius and his family, greatly to the admiration of Peter, who was used as the instrument of it, and of those who were with him, Acts x. and xi. The next instance was the conversion of great numbers of Gentiles in Cyprus, Cyrene, and Antioch, by the disciples who were scattered abroad by the persecution which arose about Stephen, Acts xi. 19—21. And presently upon this the disciples began to be called Christians first at Antioch, (ver. 26.)

After this vast multitudes of Gentiles were converted in different parts of the world, chiefly by the ministry of the apostle Paul. Multitudes flocked into the church of Christ in a great number of cities where the apostle came. So the number of Gentile members of the christian church soon far exceeded that of its Jewish members; yea, in less than ten years' time after Paul was sent forth from Antioch to preach to the Gentiles, it was said of him and his companions, that they had turned the world upside down: Acts xvii. 6. "These that have turned the world upside down are come hither also." But the most remarkable instance, seems to be that in *Ephesus,* which was a very great city, Acts xix. There was also a very extraordinary ingathering of souls at *Corinth,* one of the greatest cities in all Greece. And after this many were converted in *Rome,* the chief city of all the world; and the gospel was propagated into all parts of the Roman empire. Thus the gospel-sun which had lately risen on the Jews, now rose upon, and began to enlighten, the heathen world, after they had continued in gross heathenish darkness for so many ages.

This was a great and new thing, such as never had been before. All nations but the Jews, and a few who had occasionally joined them, had been rejected from about the time of Moses. The Gentile world had been covered with the thick darkness of idolatry; but now at the joyful sound of the gospel, they began in all parts to forsake their idols, and to cast them to the moles and to the bats. They now learned to worship the true God, and to trust in his Son Jesus Christ. God owned them for his people; and those who had so long been afar off, were made nigh by the blood of Christ. Men, from being heathenish and brutish, became the children of God; were called out of Satan's kingdom of darkness, and brought into God's marvellous light. In almost all countries throughout the known world there were christian assemblies, and joyful praises were sung to the true God, and Jesus Christ the glorious Redeemer. Now that great building which God began soon after the fall of man, rises gloriously in a new manner; now Daniel's prophecies concerning the last kingdom, which should succeed the four heathenish monarchies, begins to be fulfilled; now the stone cut out of the mountain without hands, began to smite the image on its feet, and to break it in pieces, and to make great advances towards filling the earth; and now God gathers together his elect from the four winds of heaven, by the preaching of the apostles and other ministers, (the angels of the christian church sent forth with the great sound of the gospel-trumpet,) before the destruction of Jerusalem, agreeable to what Christ foretold, Matt. xxiv. 31.

II. I would proceed now, in the second place, to take notice of the *opposition* which was made to this success of Christ's purchase by the enemies of it.——Satan, who lately was so ready to triumph and exult, as though he had gained the victory in putting Christ to death, now finding himself fallen into the pit which he had digged, and finding his kingdom falling so fast, and seeing Christ's kingdom make such amazing progress, was filled with the greatest confusion and astonishment: and hell seemed to be effectually alarmed to make the most violent opposition against it. And, first, the devil stirred up the Jews, who had before crucified Christ, to persecute the church: for it is observable, that the persecution which the church suffered during this period, was mostly from the Jews. Thus we read in the Acts, when the Holy Ghost was poured out at Pentecost, how the Jews mocked, and said, *These men are full of new wine;* and how the scribes and Pharisees, and the captain of the temple, were alarmed, and bestirred themselves to oppose and persecute the apostles. They first apprehended and threatened them, and afterwards imprisoned and beat them; and breathing out threatenings and slaughter against the disciples of the Lord, they stoned Stephen in a tumultuous rage; and were not content to persecute those that they could find in Judea, but sent abroad to Damascus and other places, to persecute all that they could find every where. Herod, who was chief among them, stretched forth his hands to vex the church, and killed James with the sword, and proceeded to take Peter also, and cast him into prison.

So in other countries we find, that almost wherever the apostles came, the Jews opposed the gospel in a most malignant manner, contradicting and blaspheming. How many things did the blessed apostle Paul suffer at their hands! How violent and blood-thirsty did they show themselves towards him, when he came to bring alms to his nation! In this persecution and cruelty was fulfilled that saying of Christ, Matt. xxiii. 34. "Behold, I send you prophets, and wise men, and scribes; and some of them ye shall kill and crucify, and some of them shall ye scourge in your synagogues, and persecute them from city to city."

III. I proceed to take notice of the *judgments* which were executed on those enemies of Christ, the persecuting Jews.

1. The bulk of the people were given up to judicial blindness of mind and hardness of heart. Christ denounced such a woe upon them in the days of his flesh; Matt. xiii. 14, 15.——This curse was also denounced on them by the apostle Paul, Acts xxviii. 25, 26, 27. and under this curse, this judicial blindness and hardness, they remain to this very day, having been subject to it for about seventeen hundred years, being the most awful instance of such a judgment, and monument of God's terrible vengeance, of any people. That they should continue from generation to generation so obstinately to reject Christ, so that it is a very rare thing that any one of them is converted to the christian faith—though their own Scriptures of the Old Testament, which they acknowledge, are so full of plain testimonies against them—is a remarkable evidence of their being dreadfully left of God.

2. They were rejected from being any longer God's visible people. They were broken off from the stock of Abraham, and since that have no more been reputed his seed, than the Ishmaelites or Edomites, who are as much his natural seed as they. The greater part of the two tribes were now cast off, as the ten tribes had been before, and another people were taken in their room, agreeable to the predictions of their own prophets; Deut. xxxii. 21. "They have moved me to jealousy with that which is not God; they have provoked me to anger with their vanities; and I will move them to jealousy with those which are not a people, I will provoke them to anger with a foolish nation;" and Isaiah lxv. 1. "I am sought of them that asked not for me; I am found of them that sought me not."——They were visibly rejected by God's directing his apostles to turn away from them, and let them alone; Acts xiii. 46, 47. "Then Paul and Barnabas waxed bold, and said, It was necessary that the word of God should first have been spoken to you: but seeing ye put it from you, and judge yourselves unworthy of everlasting life, lo, we turn to the Gentiles: for so hath the Lord commanded us." And so Acts xviii. 6. and xxviii. 28.

Thus far we have had the scripture history to guide us: henceforward we shall have the guidance only of scripture prophecy, and human histories.

3. The third and last judgment of God on those enemies of the success of the gospel which I shall mention, is the terrible destruction of their city and country by the Romans.—They had great warnings and many means used with them before this destruction. First, John the Baptist warned them, and told them, that the axe was laid at the root of the tree; and that every tree which should not bring forth good fruit, should be hewn down, and cast into the fire. Then Christ warned them very particularly, and told them of their approaching destruction, at the thoughts of which he wept over them. And then the apostles after Christ's ascension abundantly warned them. But they proved obstinate, and went on in their opposition to Christ and his church, and in their bitter persecuting practices. Their so malignantly persecuting the apostle Paul, of which we have an account towards the end of the Acts of the Apostles, is supposed to have been not more than seven or eight years before their destruction.

After this, God was pleased to give them one more very remarkable warning by the apostle Paul, in his epistle to the Hebrews, written, it is supposed, about four years before their destruction; wherein the plainest and clearest arguments are set before them from their own law, and from their prophets, for whom they professed such a regard, to prove that Christ Jesus must be the Son of God, that all their law typified him, and that the Jewish dispensation must needs have ceased. For though the epistle was more immediately directed to the christian Hebrews, yet the matter of the epistle plainly shows that the apostle intended it for the use and conviction of the unbelieving Jews. And in this epistle he mentions particularly the approaching destruction, chap. x. 25. "So much the more, as ye see the day approaching;" and in ver. 27. he speaks of the approaching judgment and *fiery indignation which should devour the adversaries.*

But the generality of them, refusing to receive conviction, God soon destroyed with such terrible circumstances, as the destruction of no country or city since the foundation of the world can parallel; agreeable to what Christ foretold, Matt. xxiv. 21. "For then shall be tribulation, such as was not from the beginning of the world to this time, no, nor ever shall be." The first destruction of Jerusalem by the Babylonians was very terrible, as it is in a most affecting manner described by the prophet Jeremiah, in his Lamentations; but that was nothing to the dreadful misery and wrath which they suffered in this destruction. God, as Christ foretold, brought on them all the righteous blood that had been shed from the foundation of the world. Thus the enemies of Christ are made his footstool after his ascension, agreeable to God's promise in Psalm cx. and he rules them with a rod of iron. The briars and thorns set themselves against him in battle: but he went through them; he burned them together.

This destruction of Jerusalem was in all respects agreeable to what Christ had foretold of it, Matt. xxiv. as appears by the account which Josephus gives of it, who was then present, who had a share in the calamity, and who wrote the history of their destruction. Many circumstances resembled the destruction of the wicked at the day of judgment; by his account, it was accompanied with many fearful sights in the heavens, and with a separation of the righteous from the wicked. Their city and temple were burnt, and razed to the ground; and the ground on which the city stood was ploughed, so that one stone was not left upon another, Matt. xxiv. 2.

The people had ceased for the most part to be an independent government after the Babylonish captivity; but the sceptre entirely departed from Judah on the death of Archelaus, when Judea was made a Roman province. After this, they were cast off from being the people of God; but now their very city and land are utterly destroyed, and they carried away from it; and so have continued in their dispersions through the world for now above sixteen hundred years.

Thus there was a final end put to the Old-Testament world: all was finished with a kind of day of judgment, in which the people of God were saved, and his enemies terribly destroyed.—Thus does he who was so lately mocked, despised, and spit upon by these Jews, and whose followers they so malignantly persecuted, appear gloriously exalted over his enemies.

PART II.

THE SUCCESS OF REDEMPTION FROM THE DESTRUCTION OF JERUSALEM, TO THE TIME OF CONSTANTINE.

Jerusalem was destroyed about the year of our Lord sixty-eight, and so before that generation passed away which was contemporary with Christ. The destruction of the heathen empire under Constantine, was about two hundred and sixty years after this. In showing how the success of the gospel was carried on through this time, I would, 1. Take notice of the opposition made against it by the Roman empire. 2. How the work of the gospel went on notwithstanding all that opposition. 3. The peculiar circumstances of tribulation and distress that the church was in just before their deliverance by Constantine; and 4. The great revolution in Constantine's time.

I. I would briefly show what *opposition* was made against the gospel, and the kingdom of Christ, by the Roman empire. This opposition was mainly after the destruction of Jerusalem, though it began before; but that which was before the destruction of Jerusalem, was mainly by the Jews. When Jerusalem was destroyed, the Jews were much incapacitated for troubling the church; therefore the devil turns his hand elsewhere, and uses other instruments. The opposition which was made in the Roman empire against the kingdom of Christ was chiefly of two kinds.

1. They employed all their learning, philosophy, and wit, in opposing it. Christ came into the world in an age wherein learning and philosophy were at their height in the Roman empire. The gospel, which held forth a crucified Saviour, was not at all agreeable to the notions of the philosophers.—The christian scheme of trusting in such a crucified Redeemer, appeared foolish and ridiculous to them. Greece was a country the most famous for learning of any in the Roman empire; but the apostle observes, that the doctrine of Christ crucified appeared foolishness to the Greeks, 1 Cor. i. 23. and therefore the wise men and philosophers opposed the gospel with all the wit they had. We have a specimen of their manner of opposing, in their treatment of the apostle Paul at Athens, which was, and had been for many ages, the chief seat of philosophers in all the whole world. We read in Acts xvii. 18. that the philosophers of the Epicureans and Stoics encountered him, saying, "What will this babbler say? He seemeth to be a setter forth of strange gods." Thus they were wont to deride and ridicule Christianity; and, after the destruction of Jerusalem, several philosophers published books against it. The chief of these were Celsus and Porphyry, who wrote with a great deal of virulence and contempt, much after the manner of the deists of the present age. As great enemies and despisers as they were of the Christian religion, they never denied the facts recorded of Christ and his apostles in the New Testament, particularly the miracles which they wrought, but allowed them. They lived too near the times of these miracles to deny them; for they were so publicly done, and so lately, that neither Jews nor heathens in those days appeared to deny them; but they ascribed them to the power of magic.

2. The authority of the Roman empire employed all their strength, time after time, to persecute, and if possible to root out, Christianity. This they did in ten general successive persecutions. We have heretofore observed that Christ came into the world when the strength of heathen dominion and authority was the greatest under the Roman monarchy. All the strength of this monarchy was employed for a long time to oppose and persecute the christian church, and if possible to destroy it, in ten successive attempts, which are called *the ten heathen persecutions.*

The *first* of these, which was the persecution under Nero, was a little before the destruction of Jerusalem, in which the apostle Peter was crucified, and the apostle Paul beheaded, soon after he wrote his second epistle to Timothy. When he wrote that epistle, he was a prisoner at Rome under Nero, and says, chap. iv. 6, 7. "I am now ready to be offered, and the time of my departure is at hand. I have fought a good fight, I have finished my course, I have kept the faith." There were many thousands of other Christians slain in that persecution.—The other nine persecutions were all after the destruction of Jerusalem. Some of these were very terrible indeed, and far exceeded the first persecution under Nero. One emperor after another set himself with the utmost rage to root out the christian church from the earth, that there should not be so much as the name of Christian left in the world. Thousands, yea millions, were put to cruel deaths in them; for they spared neither sex nor age.

In the *second* general persecution, (under Domitian,) that which was next after the destruction of Jerusalem, the apostle John was banished to the isle of Patmos, where he had those visions which he has recorded in the Revelation. Under that persecution it was reckoned, that about forty thousand suffered martyrdom; which yet was nothing to what were put to death under some succeeding persecutions. Ten thousand suffered that one kind of cruel death, crucifixion, in the *third* persecution under the emperor Adrian. Under the *fourth* persecution, which began about the year of Christ one hundred and sixty-two, many suffered martyrdom in England, the land of our forefathers, where Christianity had been planted, it is supposed, in the days of the apostles. And in the *later* persecutions, the Roman emperors being vexed at the frustration of their predecessors, who were not able to extirpate Christianity, or hinder its progress, were enraged to be the more violent in their attempts.

Thus a great part of the first three hundred years after Christ was spent in violent and cruel persecutions of the church by the Roman powers. Satan was very unwilling to quit his hold of so great and distinguished a part of the world, as the countries contained in the Roman empire, of which he had had the quiet possession for so many ages: and therefore, when he saw it going so fast out of his hands, he bestirred himself to his utmost. All hell was raised to oppose it with its utmost power.

Satan thus exerting himself by the power of the heathen Roman empire, is called *the great red dragon*, having seven heads and ten horns, fighting against the woman clothed with the sun. (Rev. xii.) And this terrible conflict between the church of Christ, and the powers of the heathen empire before Constantine, is represented (verse 7) by the war between Michael and his angels, and the dragon and his angels: "And there was war in heaven; Michael and his angels fought, and the dragon fought and his angels."

II. I would take notice what success the gospel had in the world before the time of Constantine, notwithstanding all this opposition.—Though the learning and power of the Roman empire were so great, and both were employed to the utmost against Christianity; yet all was in vain. They could neither root it out, nor stop its progress. In spite of all, the kingdom of Christ wonderfully prevailed, and Satan's heathen kingdom mouldered and consumed away before it, agreeable to the text, "The moth shall eat them up like a garment, and the worm shall eat them like wool." And it was very observable that, for the most part, the more they persecuted the church, the more it increased; insomuch that it became a common saying, The blood of the martyrs is the seed of the church.—Herein the church of Christ proved to be like a palm-tree; of which it is remarked, that the greater weight is hung to its branches, the more it grows and flourishes. On this account probably the church is compared to a palm-tree, Cant. vii. 7. "This thy stature is like to a palm-tree." Justin Martyr, an eminent father in the christian church, says, that in his days there was no part of mankind, whether Greeks or barbarians, or by what name soever they were called, even the most rude and unpolished nations, where prayers and thanksgivings were not made to the great Creator of the world, through the name of the crucified Jesus. Tertullian, another eminent father in the christian church, who lived in the beginning of the following age, testifies, that in his days the christian religion had extended itself to the utmost bounds of the then known world, in which he reckons Britain; and thence demonstrates, that the kingdom of Christ was then more extensive than any of the four great monarchies. He moreover says, that though the Christians were strangers of no long standing, yet they had filled all places of the Roman dominions, their cities, islands, castles, corporations, councils, armies, tribes, the palace, senate, and courts of judicature; only they had left to the heathen their temples. He adds, that if they should all agree to retire out of the Roman empire, the world would be amazed at the solitude and desolation that would ensue upon it, there would be so few left; and that the Christians were enough to be able easily to defend themselves, if they were disposed to rise up in arms against the heathen magistrates.—And Pliny, a heathen who lived in those days, says, that multitudes, of each sex, of every age and quality, were become Christians. This superstition, says he, having infected and overrun not the city only, but towns and countries, the temples and sacrifices are generally desolate and forsaken.

And it was remarked by both heathen and christian writers in those days, that the famous heathen oracles in their temples—where princes and others for many past ages had been wont to inquire and receive answers with an audible voice from their gods, which were indeed answers from the devil—were now struck dumb, and gave no more answers: and particularly the oracle at Delphos, the most famous in the whole world, which both Greeks and Romans used to consult, began to cease to give any answers, even from the birth of Christ. The false deity who was worshipped, and who used to give answers from his oracle in that temple, being once inquired of, why he did not now give answers as he was wont to do? made this reply, (as several heathen historians who lived about those times relate,) There is a Hebrew boy, who is king of the gods, who has commanded me to leave this house, and begone to hell, and therefore you are to expect no more answers. And many heathen writers who lived about that time, speak much of the oracles being silenced, at which they wondered, not knowing what the cause should be. Plutarch wrote a particular treatise about it, which is still extant. And Porphyry, who opposed the christian religion, has these words, "It is no wonder if the city for these many years has been overrun with sickness; Esculapius, and the rest of the gods, having withdrawn their converse with men: for since Jesus began to be worshipped, no man has received any public help or benefit by the gods." Thus did the kingdom of Christ prevail against the kingdom of Satan.

III. I now proceed to take notice of the peculiar circumstances of tribulation and distress just before Constantine the Great came to the throne. This distress they suffered under the *tenth* heathen persecution, which, as it was the last, so it was by far the heaviest and most severe. The church before this, after the ceasing of the *ninth* persecution, had enjoyed a time of quietness for about forty years together; but abusing their liberty, they began to grow cold and lifeless in religion, and contentions prevailed among them; by which they offended God to suffer this dreadful trial to come upon them. And Satan having lost ground so much, notwithstanding all his attempts, now seemed to bestir himself with more than ordinary rage. Those who were then in authority set themselves with the utmost violence to root out Christianity, by burning all Bibles, and destroying all Christians; and therefore they did not stand to try or convict them in a formal process, but fell upon them wherever they could. Sometimes they set fire to houses where multitudes were assembled, burning them altogether; at other times they slaughtered such multitudes that their persecutors were quite spent with the labour of killing and tormenting them; and in some populous places, so many were slain together, that the blood ran like torrents. It is related, that seventeen thousand martyrs were slain in one month's time; and that during the continuance of this persecution, in the province of Egypt alone, no less than one hundred and forty-four thousand Christians died by the violence of their persecutors, besides seven hundred thousand that died through the fatigues of banishment, or the public works to which they were condemned.

This persecution lasted for ten years together, and as it exceeded all the foregoing persecutions, in the number of martyrs, so it exceeded them in the variety and multitude of inventions of torture and cruelty. Some authors who lived at that time, say, they were innumerable, and exceed all account and expression. This persecution in particular was very severe in England; and is that which was foretold in Rev. vi. 9, 10. "And when he had opened the fifth seal, I saw under the altar the souls of them that were slain for the word of God, and for the testimony which they held. And they cried with a loud voice, saying, How long, O Lord, holy and true, dost thou not judge and avenge our blood on them that dwell on the earth?" And at the end of the ten years, during which this persecution continued, the heathen persecutors thought they had finished their work, and boasted that they had utterly destroyed the name and superstition of the Christians, and had restored and propagated the worship of the gods.

Thus it was the darkest time with the christian church, just before the break of day. They were brought to the greatest extremity before God appeared for their glorious deliverance, as the bondage of the Israelites in Egypt was the most severe and cruel just before their deliverance by the hand of Moses. Their enemies thought they had swallowed them up, and sealed their destruction, as Pharaoh and his host thought when they had hemmed in the children of Israel at the Red sea.

IV. I come now, in the fourth place, to the great revolution by Constantine, which was in many respects like Christ's appearing in the clouds of heaven to save his people, and judge the world. The people of Rome being weary of the government of those tyrants to whom they had lately been subject, sent to Constantine, who was then in the city of York in England, to come and take the throne. He was encouraged, it is said, by a vision of a pillar of light in the heavens, in the form of a cross, in the sight of his whole army, with this inscription, Εν τουτω νικα, *In this overcome;* and the night following, by Christ's appearing to him in a dream with the same cross in his hand, who directed him to make a cross like that to be his royal standard, that his army might fight under that banner, and assured him that he should overcome. Accordingly he overcame his enemies, took possession of the imperial throne, embraced the christian religion, and was the first christian emperor that ever reigned. He came to the throne about three hundred and twenty years after Christ. There are several things which I would take notice of which attended, or immediately followed, Constantine's coming to the throne.

1. The christian church was thereby wholly delivered from persecution. Now the day of her deliverance came after such a dark night of affliction: weeping had continued for a night, but now deliverance and joy came in the morning. Now God appeared to judge his people, and repented himself for his servants, when he saw their power was gone, and that there was none shut up or left. Christians had no persecutions now to fear. Their persecutors now were all put down, and their rulers were some of them Christians like themselves.

2. God now appeared to execute terrible judgments on their enemies. Remarkable are the accounts which history gives of the fearful ends to which the heathen emperors, princes, generals, captains, and other great men were brought, who had exerted themselves in persecuting the Christians; dying miserably, one after another, under exquisite torments of body, and horrors of conscience, with a most visible hand of God upon them. So that what now came to pass might very fitly be compared to their hiding themselves in the dens and rocks of the mountains.

3. Heathenism now was in a great measure abolished throughout the Roman empire. Images were now destroyed, and heathen temples pulled down. Images of gold and silver were melted down, and coined into money. Some of the chief of their idols, which were curiously wrought, were brought to Constantinople, and there drawn with ropes up and down the streets for the people to behold and laugh at. The heathen priests were dispersed and banished.

4. The christian church was brought into a state of great peace and prosperity. Now all heathen magistrates were put down, and only Christians were advanced to places of authority all over the empire. They had now christian presidents, christian governors, christian judges and officers, instead of their old heathenish ones. Constantine set himself to put honour upon christian bishops or ministers, and to build and adorn churches; and now large and beautiful christian churches were erected in all parts of the world, instead of the old heathen temples.

This revolution was the greatest change in the face of things that ever came to pass in the world since the flood. —Satan, the prince of darkness, that king and god of the heathen world, was cast out. The roaring lion was conquered by the Lamb of God, in the strongest dominion that he ever had. This was a remarkable accomplishment of Jer. x. 11. "The gods that have not made the heavens and the earth, even they shall perish from the earth, and from under these heavens."—The chief part of the world was now brought utterly to cast off their gods and their old religion, to which they had been accustomed much longer than any of their histories give an account of. They had been accustomed to worship the gods so long, that they knew not any beginning of it. It was formerly spoken of as a thing unknown for a nation to change their gods, Jer. ii. 10, 11. but now the greater part of the nations of the known world were brought to cast off all their former gods. That multitude of gods which they worshipped, were all forsaken. Thousands of them were cast away for the worship of the true God, and Christ the only Saviour: and there was a most remarkable fulfilment of Isa. ii. 17, 18. "And the loftiness of man shall be bowed down, and the haughtiness of men shall be made low: and the Lord alone shall be exalted in that day. And the idols he shall utterly abolish." And since that, those gods which were once so famous in the world, as Jupiter, and Saturn, and Minerva, and Juno, &c. are only heard of as things of old. They have had no temples, no altars, no worshippers, for many hundred years.

Now is come the end of the old heathen world in its principal part, the Roman empire. And this great revolution, with that terrible destruction of the great men who had been persecutors, is compared, (Rev. vi.) to the end of the world, and Christ coming to judgment; and is most immediately signified under the sixth seal, which followed upon the souls under the altar crying, How long, O Lord, holy and true, dost thou not avenge our blood on them that dwell on the earth? This vision of the sixth seal, by the general consent of expositors, has respect to this downfall of the heathen Roman empire; though it has a more remote respect to the day of judgment of which this was a type. The day of judgment cannot be what is immediately intended; because we have an account of many events which were to come to pass after those of the sixth seal.

What came to pass now is also represented by the devil's being cast out of heaven to the earth. In his great strength and glory, over that mighty Roman empire, he had exalted his throne up to heaven. But now he fell like lightning from heaven, and his kingdom was confined to the meaner and more barbarous nations, or to the lower parts of the world. This is the event foretold, Rev. xii. 9, &c. "And the great dragon was cast out, that old serpent, called the devil and Satan, which deceiveth the whole world: he was cast out into the earth, and his angels were cast out with him," &c. Satan had formerly tempted Christ, and promised to give him the glory of the kingdoms of the world; but now he is obliged to give it to him even against his will. This was a glorious fulfilment of that promise which God made to his Son, Isa. liii. 12. "Therefore will I divide him a portion with the great, and he shall divide the spoil with the strong; because he hath poured out his soul unto death: and he was numbered with the transgressors, and he bare the sin of many, and made intercession for the transgressors." This was a great fulfilment of prophecies concerning the glorious time of the gospel, and particularly those of Daniel. Now it pleased the Lord God of heaven to set up a kingdom on the ruins of Satan's kingdom; and such honour does the Father put upon Christ for the disgrace he suffered when on earth.

From what has been said of the success of the gospel from Christ's ascension to the time of Constantine, we may deduce a strong argument for the truth of the christian religion, and that the gospel of Jesus Christ is really from God. Particularly,

1. We may gather from what has been said, that it is the gospel, and that only, which has actually been the means of bringing the world to the knowledge of the true God. That those are no gods whom the heathen worshipped, and that there is but one only God, is what, now since the gospel has so taught us, we can see to be truth by our own reason. It is plainly agreeable to the light of nature; and it can be easily shown by reason to be demonstrably true. The very deists themselves acknowledge, that it can be demonstrated, that there is one God, and but one, who has made and governs the world. But now it is evident that it is the gospel, and that only, which has actually been the means of bringing men to the knowledge of this truth. It was not the instructions of philosophers; they tried in vain: *The world by wisdom knew not God.* Till the gospel and the Holy Scriptures came abroad, all the world lay in ignorance of the true God, and in the greatest darkness with respect to religion, embracing the absurdest opinions and practices, which all civilized nations now acknowledge to be childish fooleries. The light of nature, their own reason, and all the wisdom of learned men, signified nothing till the Scriptures came. But when these came abroad, they were successful to bring the world to an acknowledgment of the one only true God, and to worship and serve him.

And hence it is, that all that part of the world which now acknowledges one only true God—Christians, Jews, Mahometans, and even deists—originally came to own him. It is owing to this that they are not in general at this day left in heathenish darkness. They have it all, either immediately from the Scriptures, or by tradition from their fathers, who had it first from the Scriptures. And doubtless those who now despise the Scriptures, and boast of the strength of their own reason, as being sufficient to lead into the knowledge of the one true God, if the gospel had never come abroad in the world to enlighten their forefathers, would have been as sottish and brutish idolaters as the world in general was before the gospel came abroad. The Mahometans, who own but one true God, at first borrowed the notion from the Scriptures: for the first Mahometans had been educated in the christian religion, and apostatized from it. And this is evident, that the Scriptures were designed of God to be the proper means to bring the world to the knowledge of himself, rather than human reason, or any thing else. For it is unreasonable to suppose, that the gospel, and that only which God never designed as the proper mean for obtaining this effect, should actually obtain it; and that after human reason, which he designed as the proper mean, had been tried for a great many ages without any effect. If the Scriptures be not the word of God, then they are nothing but darkness and delusion, yea, the greatest delusion that ever was. Now, is it reasonable to suppose, that God in his providence would make use of falsehood and delusion, to bring the world to the knowledge of himself, and that no part of it should be brought to the knowledge of him any other way?

2. The gospel prevailing as it did against such powerful opposition, plainly shows the hand of God. The Roman government, that so violently set itself to hinder the success of the gospel, and to subdue the church of Christ, was the most powerful that ever was in the world; and not only so, but they seemed to have the church in their hands. The Christians who were under their command, never took up arms to defend themselves; they armed themselves with nothing but patience, and such like spiritual weapons: and yet this mighty power could not conquer, but, on the contrary, Christianity conquered them. The Roman empire had subdued many mighty and potent kingdoms; they subdued the Grecian monarchy, though it made the utmost resistance: and yet they could not conquer the church which was in their hands; but, on the contrary, were subdued and finally triumphed over by the church.

3. No other sufficient cause can possibly be assigned for this propagation of the gospel, but only God's own power.—There was certainly some reason. Here was a great and wonderful effect; and this effect was not without some cause.—Now, what other cause can be devised but only the divine power? It was not the outward strength of the instruments which were employed in it. At first, the gospel was preached only by a few fishermen, who were without power and worldly interest to support them. It was not their craft and policy that produced this wonderful effect; for they were poor illiterate men. It was not the agreeableness of the story they had to tell to the notions and principles of mankind. This was no pleasant fable: a crucified God and Saviour was to the Jews a stumbling-block, and to the Greeks foolishness. It was not the agreeableness of their doctrines to the dispositions of men: for nothing is more contrary to the corruptions of men than the pure doctrines of the gospel. This effect therefore can have proceeded from no other cause than the power and agency of God: and if the

power of God was thus exercised to cause the gospel to prevail, then the gospel is his word; for surely God does not use his almighty power to promote a mere imposture and delusion.

4. This success is agreeable to what Christ and his apostles foretold.——Matt. xvi. 18. "Upon this rock will I build my church: and the gates of hell shall not prevail against it." John xii. 24. "Verily, verily, I say unto you, Except a corn of wheat fall into the ground, and die, it abideth alone: but if it die, it bringeth forth much fruit." And ver. 31, 32. "Now is the judgment of this world: now shall the prince of this world be cast out. And I, if I be lifted up from the earth, will draw all men unto me." John xvi. 8. "When he (the Comforter) is come, he will reprove the world of sin, of righteousness, and of judgment,—because the prince of this world is judged."

So the apostle Paul, in 1 Cor. chap. i. 21—28. declares, how that after the world by wisdom knew not God, it pleased God, by the foolishness of preaching, to save them that believe; and that God chose the foolish things of the world to confound the wise; and weak things of the world, to confound the things which are mighty; and base things of the world, and things which are despised, yea and things which are not, to bring to nought things that are.——If any man foretells a thing, very likely in itself to come to pass, from causes which can be foreseen, it is no great argument of a revelation from God: but when a thing is foretold which is very unlikely ever to come to pass, is entirely contrary to the common course of things, and yet it does come to pass just agreeable to the prediction, this is a strong argument that the prediction was from God. Thus the consideration of the *manner* of the propagation and success of the gospel during the time which has been spoken of, affords great evidence that the Scriptures are the word of God.

PART III.

THE SUCCESS OF REDEMPTION FROM THE TIME OF CONSTANTINE TO THE RISE OF ANTICHRIST.

I am now to show how the success of Christ's redemption is carried on from the overthrow of the heathen Roman empire in the time of Constantine the Great, till the rise of Antichrist. And in order to a more clear view of the great works of God in accomplishing the success of Christ's redemption, and our seeing the glory of them, it will be necessary, as in the foregoing periods, to consider not only the success itself, but the opposition made to it.

I. The *opposition*. Satan, the great red dragon, after so sore a conflict with Michael and his angels for the greater part of three hundred years, was at last entirely routed and vanquished; so that he was cast down, as it were, from heaven to the earth. Yet he does not give over his opposition to the woman, the church of Christ, concerning which all this conflict had been; but is still in a rage, renews his attempts, and has recourse to new devices against the church. The serpent, after he is cast out of heaven to the earth, casts out of his mouth water as a flood, to cause the woman to be carried away of the flood. The opposition that he made to the church of Christ before the rise of Antichrist, was principally of two sorts. It was either by corrupting the church of Christ with heresies, or by new endeavours to restore paganism.

1. After the destruction of the heathen Roman empire, Satan infested the church with *heresies*. Though there had been so glorious a work of God in delivering the church from her heathen persecutors, and overthrowing the heathen empire; yet the days of the church's travail not being ended, and the set time of her prosperity not being yet come, (as being what was to succeed the fall of Antichrist,) therefore the peace and prosperity which the church enjoyed in Constantine's time, was but very short. It was a respite, which gave the church a time of peace and silence, as it were, *for half an hour*, wherein the four angels held the four winds from blowing till the servants of God should be sealed in their foreheads. But the church soon began to be greatly infested with heresies; the two principal, and those which did most infest the church, were the Arian and Pelagian.

The *Arians* began soon after Constantine came to the throne. They denied the doctrine of the Trinity, the divinity of Christ and the Holy Ghost, and maintained, that they were but mere creatures. This heresy increased more and more in the church, and prevailed like a flood which threatened to overthrow all, and entirely to carry away the church, insomuch that before the close of the fourth century, the greater part of the christian church were become Arians. Some emperors, the successors of Constantine, were Arians; so that being the prevailing party, and having the civil authority on their side, they raised a great persecution against the true church of Christ; so that this heresy might well be compared to a flood out of the mouth of the serpent, which threatened to overthrow all, and quite carry away the woman.

The *Pelagian* heresy arose in the beginning of the next century. It began by one Pelagius, who was born in Britain: his British name was Morgan. He denied original sin and the influence of the Spirit of God in conversion, and held the power of free will, and many other things of like tendency; and this heresy did for a while greatly infest the church. Pelagius's principal antagonist, who wrote in defence of the orthodox faith, was St. Augustin.

2. The other kind of opposition which Satan made against the church, was in his endeavours to restore *paganism*. His first attempt was by Julian the apostate. Julian was nephew to Constantine the Great. When Constantine died, he left his empire to three sons; and after their death, Julian the apostate reigned in their stead. He had been a professed Christian; but he fell from Christianity, and turned pagan; and therefore is called *the apostate*. When he came to the throne, he used his utmost endeavours to overthrow the christian church, and set up paganism again in the empire. He put down the christian magistrates, and set up heathens in their room. He rebuilt the heathen temples, set up the heathen worship, and became a most notorious persecutor of the Christians. He used to call Christ, by way of reproach, *the Galilean*. He was killed with a lance in his wars with the Persians. When he saw that he was mortally wounded, he took a handful of his blood, and threw it up towards heaven, crying out, "Thou hast overcome, O Galilean." He is commonly thought by divines to have committed the unpardonable sin.

Another way that Satan attempted to restore paganism in the Roman empire, was by *the invasions and conquest of heathen nations*. For in this space of time, the Goths and Vandals, and other barbarous nations from the north, invaded the empire, and obtained great conquests. They even overran the empire, and in the fifth century took the city of Rome, and finally conquered and took possession of the western half of the empire, and divided it amongst them. It was divided into ten kingdoms, with which began the ten horns of the beast; for we are told, that the ten horns are ten kings, who should rise in the latter part of the Roman empire: these are also represented by the ten toes of Nebuchadnezzar's image. The invasion and conquests of these heathen nations are supposed to be foretold in the 8th chapter of Revelation, in what came to pass under the sounding of the four first trumpets. Now by their means heathenism was again for a while restored after it had been rooted out.—So much for the opposition of Satan against the success of the gospel during this space before the rise of Antichrist. I proceed,

II. To show what *success* there was of the gospel in this space, notwithstanding this opposition.

1. I would observe, that the opposition of Satan in those things was baffled. Though the dragon cast out of his mouth such a flood after the woman to carry her away, yet he could not obtain his design; but the earth helped the woman, and opened her mouth, and swallowed up the flood which the dragon cast out of his mouth. These heresies, which for a while so much prevailed, after a while dwindled away, and orthodoxy was again restored.

2. The gospel, during this space of time, was further

propagated amongst many barbarous nations in the confines of the Roman empire. In the time of Constantine there was a considerable propagation of the gospel in the East Indies, chiefly by the ministry of one Frumentius. Great numbers of the Iberians were converted to Christianity by a christian woman of eminent piety, whom they had taken captive. And some account is given of several other barbarous nations who were not within the Roman empire, that great numbers of them were brought to receive the gospel by the teaching and example of captives whom they had taken in war. About the year of Christ three hundred and seventy-two, the gospel was propagated among the barbarous inhabitants of Arabia; and among some of the northern nations; particularly, a prince of the Goths about this time became Christian, and a great number of his people with him. Towards the latter end of this century, the gospel was also further propagated among the Persians; and also the Scythians, a barbarous people, whom the apostle mentions, Col. iii. 11. "Barbarian, Scythian, bond nor free."

And after this, about the year four hundred and thirty, there was a remarkable conversion of *the Burgundians* to the christian faith. Now the gospel began to be propagated in Ireland; and the Irish, who till now had been heathen, began to receive the christian faith. About the same time it was further propagated among some barbarous people in Scotland, and in some other places. In the next century, *Zathus*, a heathen king, who ruled over the *Colchians*, was brought to renounce his heathenism, and to embrace the christian religion. Several other barbarous nations are recorded to have renounced heathenism and embraced Christianity about this time, that I cannot stand to mention.—Thus I have briefly considered the principal events of Providence which concern the success of the gospel of Christ from Constantine to the rise of Antichrist.

PART IV.

THE SUCCESS OF REDEMPTION FROM THE RISE OF ANTICHRIST TO THE REFORMATION.

I COME now to the darkest and most dismal day that ever the christian church saw, and probably the darkest that ever it will see; from the rise of Antichrist till the Reformation by Luther and others. The true church in this space was for many hundred years in a state of great obscurity; like the woman in the wilderness, she was almost hid from sight and observation. In speaking of the events of this space of time, I would, 1. Take notice of the great machinations and works of Satan against the kingdom of Christ; 2. How the church of Christ was upheld during this time.

I. I would take notice of the great machinations and works of Satan against the kingdom of Christ during this time. Satan had done great things against the christian church before, but had been baffled once and again. Michael and his angels had obtained a glorious victory How terrible was his opposition during the continuance of the heathen empire; and how glorious was Christ's victory and triumph over him in the time of Constantine! It pleased God now to prepare the way for a yet more glorious victory over him; he is suffered to renew his strength, and to do the utmost that his power and subtlety can effect. He has a long time to lay his schemes, to establish his interest, and make his matters strong. God suffers him to carry his designs a great length indeed, almost to the swallowing up of his church; and to exercise a high, proud, and almost uncontrolled dominion in the world, a long time before Christ finally conquers, and utterly ruins his visible kingdom. This he will do in the time of the destruction of Antichrist: thus gloriously triumphing over Satan, after he has done to the utmost of his power and subtlety; after he has lifted himself highest of all, and dealt most proudly.

The two great works of the devil, in this space of time, against the kingdom of Christ, are his creating his Antichristian and Mahometan kingdoms; which both together comprehend the ancient Roman empire; the kingdom of Antichrist the Western, and the Mahometan kingdom the Eastern, empire. As the Scriptures in the book of Revelation represent it, it is in the destruction of these that the glorious victory of Christ, at the introduction of the glorious times of the church, will mainly consist. And here let us briefly observe how Satan erects and maintains these two great kingdoms of his in opposition to the kingdom of Christ.

1. With respect to the kingdom of *Antichrist.* This seems to be the masterpiece of all the contrivances of the devil against the kingdom of Christ, and is evidently so spoken of in Scripture. Antichrist is *that* man of sin, (2 Thess. ii. 3.) emphatically, as though he were so eminently. He is called *Antichrist,* which signifies the opponent or adversary of Christ, not because he is the *only* opponent of Christ; for the apostle John observes, that in his days there were *many* Antichrists. But yet this is called *the Antichrist,* as though there were none but he, because he was so eminently, and above all others. So this contrivance of the devil, is called *the mystery of iniquity,* 2 Thess. ii. 7. We find no enemy of Christ one half so much spoken of in the prophecies of Revelation as this; and the destruction of no enemy is spoken of as so glorious, and so happy for the church.

This is a contrivance to turn the ministry of the christian church into a ministry of the devil, and the angels of the churches into fallen angels. In the tyranny, superstition, idolatry, and persecution, which he sets up, he contrives to make an image of ancient paganism, and more than to restore what was lost by the overthrow of paganism in the time of Constantine. By these means, the head of the beast, which was wounded unto death in Constantine, has his deadly wound healed in Antichrist, Rev. xiii. 3. And the dragon, that formerly reigned in the heathen Roman empire, being cast out thence, after the beast with seven heads and ten horns rises up out of the sea, gives him his power, and seat, and great authority; and all the world wonders after the beast.

I am far from pretending to determine the time when the reign of Antichrist began, which is a point that has been so much controverted among divines and expositors. It is certain that the twelve hundred and sixty days, or years, which are so often in Scripture mentioned as the time of the continuance of Antichrist's reign, did not commence before the year of Christ four hundred and seventy-nine; because if they did, they would have ended, and Antichrist would have fallen before now. The rise of Antichrist was gradual. The christian church corrupted itself in many things presently after Constantine's time; growing more and more superstitious in its worship, and by degrees bringing in many ceremonies into the worship of God, till at length they brought in the worship of saints, and set up images in their churches. The clergy in general, and especially the bishop of Rome, assumed more and more authority to himself. In the primitive times, he was only a minister of a congregation; then a standing moderator of a presbytery; then a diocesan bishop; then a metropolitan, which is equivalent to an archbishop; then a patriarch. Afterwards he claimed the power of universal bishop over the whole christian church; wherein he was opposed for a while, but afterwards was confirmed in it by the civil power of the emperor in the year six hundred and six. After that he claimed the power of a temporal prince, and so was wont to carry two swords, to signify that both the temporal and spiritual sword was his. He claimed more and more authority, till at length, as Christ's vicegerent on earth, he claimed the very same power that Christ would have done, if he was present on earth reigning on his throne; or the same power that belongs to God, and was used to be called *God on earth;* to be submitted to by all the princes of christendom. He claimed power to crown princes, and to degrade them at his pleasure; and this power was owned: yea, kings and emperors used to kiss his feet. The emperors received their crowns at his hands; and princes were wont to dread the displeasure of the pope, as they would dread a thunderbolt from heaven. If the pope was pleased to excommunicate a prince, all his subjects were at once freed from their allegiance to him; and obliged not to own him any more, on pain of excommunication; and not only so, but any man might kill him wherever he found him. Further, the pope was believed to have power to damn men at pleasure; for whoever died under his excommunication, was looked upon as certainly damned. Several emperors were actually deposed, and ejected, and died miserably by his means; and if the people of any state or kingdom did not please him, he had power to lay that state or kingdom under an interdict, which was a sentence pronounced by the pope against that state or kingdom, whereby all sacred administrations among them could have no validity. There could be no valid baptisms, or sacraments, or prayers, or preaching, or pardons, till that interdict was taken off; so that that people remained, in their apprehension, in a miserable, damnable state, and therefore dreaded it as they would a storm of fire and brimstone from heaven. And in order to execute his wrath on a prince or people with whom he was displeased, other princes must also be put to a great deal of trouble and expense.

And as the pope and his clergy robbed the people of their ecclesiastical and civil liberties and privileges, so they also robbed them of their estates, drained all christendom of their money. They engrossed most of their riches into their own coffers, by vast revenues, besides pay for pardons and indulgences, baptisms and extreme unctions, deliverance out of purgatory, and a hundred other things.—See how well this agrees with the prophecies, 2 Thess. ii. 3, 4. Dan. vii. 20, 21. Rev. xiii. 6, 7. and chap. xvii. 3, 4.

During this time also superstition and ignorance more and more prevailed. The Holy Scriptures by degrees were taken out of the hands of the laity, the better to promote the unscriptural and wicked designs of the pope and the clergy; and instead of promoting knowledge among the people, they industriously promoted ignorance. It was a received maxim among them, That ignorance is the mother of devotion: and so great was the darkness of those times, that learning was almost extinct in the world. The very priests themselves, most of them, were barbarously ignorant as to any commendable learning, or any other knowledge, than their hellish craft in oppressing and tyrannizing over the souls of the people.—The superstition and wickedness of the church of Rome, kept growing worse and worse till the very time of the Reformation, and the whole christian world were led away into this great defection, excepting the remains of the christian church in the Eastern empire that had not been utterly overthrown by the Turks. The Greek church, and some others, were also sunk into great darkness and gross superstition, excepting also those few that were the people of God, who are represented by the woman in the wilderness, and God's two witnesses, of which more hereafter.—This is one of those two great kingdoms which the devil in this period erected in opposition to the kingdom of Christ, and was the greatest and chief.

2. The Mahometan kingdom is another of mighty power and vast extent, set up by Satan against the kingdom of Christ. He set this up in the Eastern empire, as he did that of Antichrist in the Western.

Mahomet was born in the year of Christ five hundred and seventy, in Arabia. When he was about forty years of age, he began to boast that he was the great prophet of God; and proceeded to teach his new-invented religion, of which he was to be worshipped as the head next under God. He published his Alcoran, which he pretended he received from the angel Gabriel; and being a subtle crafty man, possessed of considerable wealth, and living among a people who were very ignorant, and greatly divided in their opinions on religious matters, he by subtlety and fair promises of a sensual paradise, gained a number to be his followers. He set up for their prince, and propagated his religion by the sword, and made it meritorious of paradise to fight for him. By such means his party grew, and went on fighting till they conquered and brought over the neighbouring countries; and so his party gradually increased till they overran a great part of the world. First, the Saracens were some of his followers, who were a people of Arabia, where Mahomet lived, and who about the year seven hundred, dreadfully wasted the Roman empire.—They overran a great many countries belonging to the empire, and continued their conquests for a long time. These are supposed to be meant by the locusts mentioned in the 9th chapter of Revelation.

And then the Turks, who were originally different from the Saracens, became followers of Mahomet, and conquered all the Eastern empire. They began their empire about the year of Christ twelve hundred and ninety-six; began to invade Europe in the year thirteen hundred; took Constantinople, and so became masters of all the Eastern empire, in the year fourteen hundred and fifty-three. And thus all the cities and countries where stood those famous churches of which we read in the New Testament, as Jerusalem, Antioch, Ephesus, Corinth, &c. now became subject to the Turks. These are supposed to be prophesied of by the horsemen in the 9th chapter of Revelation, beginning with the 15th verse. And the remains of the Christians in those parts of the world, who are mostly of the Greek church, are in miserable slavery under these Turks; are treated with a great deal of barbarity and cruelty, and are become mostly very ignorant and superstitious.

Thus I have shown what great works of Satan were wrought during this space of time in opposition to the kingdom of Christ.

II. I come now to show how the church of Christ was upheld through this dark time.

1. It is to be observed, that towards the former part of this space of time, some of the nations of christendom held out a long time before they complied with the corruptions and usurpations of the church of Rome. Though all the world wondered after the beast, yet all nations did not fall in at once. Many of the principal corruptions of the church of Rome were brought in with a great deal of struggle and opposition; and particularly, when the pope gave out, that he was universal bishop, many churches greatly opposed him in it; and it was a long time before they would yield to his exorbitant claims. And so, when the worship of images was first brought into the churches, there were many who greatly opposed it, and long held out against it. And so with respect to other corruptions of the church of Rome. Those who dwelt nearer to the city of Rome complied sooner; but some that were more remote, were a long time before they could be induced to put their necks under the yoke: and particularly a great part of the churches in England, Scotland, and France, retained the ancient purity of doctrine and worship much longer than many others who were nearer the chief seat of Antichrist.

2. In every age of this dark time, there appeared particular persons in all parts of christendom, who bore a testimony against the corruptions and tyranny of the church of Rome.—There is no one age of Antichrist, even in the darkest times, but ecclesiastical historians mention many by name who manifested an abhorrence of the pope, and his idolatrous worship, and pleaded for the ancient purity of doctrine and worship. God was pleased to maintain an uninterrupted succession of many witnesses through the whole time, in Germany, France, Britain, and other countries; private persons and ministers, some magistrates and persons of great distinction.—And there were numbers in every age who were persecuted and put to death for this testimony.

3. Besides these particular persons dispersed, there was a certain people called the *Waldenses*, who lived separate from all the rest of the world, and constantly bore a testimony against the church of Rome through all this dark time. The place where they dwelt was the Vaudois, or the five valleys of Piedmont, a very mountainous country, between Italy and France; it was compassed about with those exceeding high mountains, *the Alps*, which were almost impassable, and therefore the valleys were almost inaccessible. There this people lived for many ages, in a state of a separation from all the world, having very little to do with any other people. And there they served God in the ancient purity of his worship, and never submitted to the church of Rome. This probably was the place especially meant in the 12th chapter of Revelation, 6th verse, as prepared of God for the woman, that they should feed her there during the reign of Antichrist.

Some of the popish writers themselves own, that this people never submitted to the church of Rome. One of the popish writers, speaking of the Waldenses, says, The heresy of the Waldenses is the oldest heresy in the world. It is supposed that they first betook themselves to this place among the mountains, to hide themselves from the severity of the heathen persecutions which existed before Constantine the Great. And thus the woman fled into the wilderness from the face of the serpent, Rev. xii. 6, 14. "And to the woman were given two wings of a great eagle, that she might fly into the wilderness, into her place: where she is nourished for a time, and times, and half a time, from the face of the serpent." The people being settled there, their posterity continued from age to age: and being, as it were, by natural walls, as well as by God's grace, separated from the rest of the world, they never partook of the overflowing corruption.

These especially were those virgins who were not defiled, when other churches prostituted themselves; but they kept themselves pure for Christ alone. They followed the Lamb, their spiritual husband, whithersoever he went: they followed him into this hideous wilderness, Rev. xiv. 4, 5.——Their doctrine and worship appear to be the same with the protestant doctrine and worship; and by the confession of popish writers, they were a people remarkable for the strictness of their lives, for charity and other christian virtues. They lived in external poverty in this hideous country; but they chose this rather than comply with the great corruptions of the rest of the world.

Living in so secret a place, it was a long time before they were noticed. But at last, falling under observation, the Romanists went out in mighty armies against them, fell upon them with insatiable cruelty, barbarously massacring and putting to death men, women, and children, with all imaginable tortures. Their enemies continued persecuting them with but little intermission for several hundred years; by which means many were driven out of the valleys of Piedmont. These fled into all parts of Europe, carrying with them their doctrine, to which many were brought over. Their persecutors could not by all their cruelties extirpate the church of God; so fulfilling his word, "that the gates of hell should not prevail against it."

4. Towards the latter part of this dark time, several noted divines openly appeared to defend the truth, and bear testimony against the corruptions of the church of Rome.—The first and principal of these was a certain English divine, *John Wickliff*, who appeared about one hundred and forty years before the Reformation; he strenuously opposed the popish religion, taught the same doctrine that the Reformers afterwards did, and had many followers in England. He was hotly persecuted in his lifetime, yet died in peace; but after he was buried, his bones were dug up by his persecutors, and burnt. His followers remained in considerable numbers in England till the Reformation; they were cruelly persecuted, and multitudes were put to death for their religion.

Wickliff had many disciples, not only in England, but in other parts of Europe, whither his books were carried; and particularly in Bohemia, among whom were two eminent divines, *John Huss*, and *Jerom*, a divine of Prague, the chief city of Bohemia. These strenuously opposed the church of Rome, and had many who adhered to them. They were both burnt by the papists for their doctrine; and their followers in Bohemia were cruelly persecuted, but never extirpated till the Reformation.

PART V.

THE SUCCESS OF REDEMPTION FROM THE REFORMATION TO THE PRESENT TIME.

THUS having gone through the dark time of the church, I come now to consider that part which begins with the Reformation, and reaches to the present time. And here I would, 1. Speak of the Reformation itself; 2. The opposition which the devil has made to the Reformed church; 3. What success there has lately been of the gospel in one place and another; 4. What the state of things is now in the world with regard to the church of Christ, and the success of his purchase.

I. The first thing to be taken notice of is the *Reformation itself.* This was begun in Germany, about the year fifteen hundred and fifteen, by the preaching of Martin Luther, who being stirred in his spirit to see the horrid practices of the popish clergy—and having set himself diligently to inquire after truth by the study of the Holy Scriptures, and the writings of the ancient fathers of the church—very openly and boldly decried the corruptions and usurpations of the Romish church in his preaching and writings. He had soon a great number who fell in with him; among whom was the Elector of Saxony, the sovereign prince of the country to which he belonged. This greatly alarmed the church of Rome; it rallied all its force to oppose him and his doctrine, and fierce wars and persecutions were raised against it. But yet it went on by the labours of Luther and Melancthon in Germany, Zuinglius in Switzerland, and other eminent divines, who were contemporary with Luther; particularly Calvin, who appeared after the beginning of the Reformation, but was one of the most eminent reformers.

Many of the princes of Germany soon fell in with the Reformed religion, and many other states and kingdoms in Europe, as England, Scotland, Sweden, Denmark, Norway, great part of France, Poland, Lithuania, Switzerland, and the Low Countries. So that it is thought, that heretofore about half christendom were of the protestant religion; though since, the papists have gained ground: so that the protestants now have not so great a proportion.

Thus God began gloriously to revive his church again, and advance the kingdom of his Son; after such a dismal night of darkness from the rise of Antichrist to that time. There had been many endeavours used by the witnesses for the truth for a reformation before. But now, when God's appointed time was come, his work went on with a swift and wonderful progress; and Antichrist, who had been rising higher and higher from his beginning till that time, was swiftly and suddenly brought down; he fell half-way towards utter ruin, and never has been able to rise again to his former height. A certain late expositor, (Mr. Lowman,) who explains the five first vials in the 16th chapter of Revelation with greater probability perhaps than any who went before him, explains the fifth vial, which was poured out on the seat of the beast, of what came to pass in the Reformation; having explained the four preceding vials of certain great judgments which God brought on the popish dominions before the Reformation. It is said, Rev. xvi. 10. that "the fifth angel poured out his vial on the seat of the beast;" in the original, it is *the throne of the beast;* "and his kingdom was full of darkness, and they gnawed their tongues for pain, and blasphemed the God of heaven because of their pains and their sores, and repented not of their deeds." He poured out his vial upon the throne of the beast, *i. e.* on the authority and dominion of the pope: so the word *throne* is often used in Scripture; so 1 Kings i. 37. "As the Lord hath been with my lord the king, even so be he with Solomon, and make his throne greater than the throne of my lord King David;" *i. e.* make his dominion and authority greater, and his kingdom more glorious.

But now, in the Reformation, the vials of God's wrath were poured out on the throne of the beast, till it was terribly shaken and diminished. The pope's authority and dominion was so greatly diminished, both as to extent and degree, that he lost about half his dominions; besides that authority, even in popish dominions, which he had before He is not regarded, and his power is dreaded in no measure as it was wont to be. The powers of Europe have learned not to put their necks under the pope's feet. He is as a lion that has lost his teeth, in comparison of what he was once. And when the pope and his clergy, enraged to see their authority so diminished at the Reformation, laid their heads together, and joined their forces to destroy the Reformation; their policy, which was wont to serve them so well, failed. They found their kingdom full of darkness, so that they could do nothing, any more than the Egyptians, who rose not from their seats for three days. The Reformed church was defended as Lot and the angels were in Sodom, by smiting the Sodomites with darkness or blindness, so that they could not find the door. God then fulfilled that in Job v. 11, &c. "To set up on high those that be low; that those which mourn may be exalted to safety. He disappointeth the devices of the crafty, so that their hands cannot perform their enterprise. He taketh the wise in their own craftiness; and the counsel of the froward is carried headlong. They meet with darkness in the day-time, and grope in the noon-day as in the night. But he saveth the poor from the sword, from their mouth, and from the hand of the mighty."—Those proud enemies of God's people being so disappointed, and finding themselves so unable to uphold their own dominion and authority, were made as it were to gnaw their tongues for pain, or to bite them for mere rage.

II. I proceed to show what *opposition* has been made by Satan and his adherents, to this success of Christ's purchase by the Reformation; observing as we go along, how far they have been baffled, and how far they have been successful.

The opposition which Satan has made against the Reformed religion has been principally of the following kinds, *viz.* that which was made, 1. by a general council of the church of Rome; 2. by secret plots and devices; 3. by open wars and invasions; 4. by cruel oppression and persecution; and, 5. by bringing in corrupt opinions.

1. The first opposition that I shall notice is that which was made by the clergy of the church of Rome in a *general council.* This was the famous council of Trent, which the pope called a little while after the Reformation. In that council, there met together six cardinals, thirty-two archbishops, two hundred and twenty-eight bishops, besides innumerable others of the Romish clergy. This council, in all their sittings, including the times of intermission, was held for twenty-five years together. Their main business all this while was to concert measures for establishing the church of Rome against the reformers, and for destroying the Reformation. But it proved that they were not able to perform their enterprise. The Reformed church, notwithstanding their great council, remained, and still remains. So that the council of the froward is carried headlong; their kingdom is full of darkness, and they weary themselves to find the door.

Thus the church of Rome, instead of repenting of their deeds, when such clear light was held forth to them by Luther and other servants of God, persisted, by general agreement in council, in their vile corruptions and wickedness, and obstinate opposition to the kingdom of Christ. The doctrines and practices of the church of Rome, which were chiefly condemned by the Reformed, were confirmed by the decrees of their council; and the corruptions, in many respects, were carried higher than ever before. They uttered blasphemous reproaches and curses against the Reformed religion, and all the Reformed church was excommunicated and anathematized by them. According to the prophecy, *they blasphemed God.* Thus God hardened their hearts, [*i. e.* left them to do so,] intending to destroy them.

2. The papists have often endeavoured to overthrow the Reformation by *secret plots* and conspiracies. There were many plots against the life of Luther. The papists were contriving to despatch him out of their way; and he, being a very bold man, often very much exposed himself in the cause of Christ: but yet they were wonderfully prevented from hurting him, and he at last died in his bed in peace. There have been innumerable schemes secretly laid for the overthrow of the protestant religion; one of the most considerable, and which seemed to be the most likely to have taken effect, was that in the time of King James II. of England. There was at that time a strong conspiracy between the king of England and Lewis XIV. of France, who were both papists, to extirpate the Northern heresy, as they called the protestant religion, not only out of England, but out of all Europe; and they had laid their schemes so, that they seemed to be almost sure of their purpose. They looked upon it, that if the Reformed religion were suppressed in the British realms, and in the Netherlands, which were the strongest part, and chief defence of the protestant interest, they should have easy work with the rest. And just as their matters seemed to be come to a head, and their enterprise ripe for execution, God in his providence, suddenly dashed all their schemes in pieces by the Revolution, at the coming in of King William and Queen Mary; by which all their designs were at an end. Now the protestant interest was more strongly established, by the crown of England being transferred to the protestant house of Hanover, and a papist being, by the constitution of the nation, for ever rendered incapable of wearing the crown of England. Thus they groped in darkness at noon-day as in the night, and their hands could not perform their enterprise, and their kingdom was full of darkness, and they gnawed their tongues for pain.

After this, there was a deep design laid to bring the same thing to pass in the latter end of Queen Anne's reign, by the bringing in of the popish Pretender; which was no less suddenly and totally baffled by Divine Providence; as all the plots against the Reformation by bringing in the Pretender have been.

3. The Reformation has often been opposed by *open wars* and invasions. The emperor of Germany declared war with the duke of Saxony, and the principal men who favoured and received Luther's doctrine. But they could not obtain their end; they could not suppress the Reformation. For the same end, some time after, the king of Spain maintained a long war with Holland and the Low Countries. But those cruel wars issued greatly to the disadvantage of the Romish church, as they occasioned the setting up of one of the most powerful protestant states in Europe. The design of the Spanish invasion of England in Queen Elizabeth's time, was to suppress and root out the Reformed religion; and therefore they brought in their fleet all manner of instruments of cruelty wherewith to torture the protestants who would not renounce the protestant religion. But their design was totally baffled, and their mighty fleet in a great measure ruined.

4. Satan has opposed the Reformation with *cruel persecutions.* The persecutions with which the protestants have been harassed by the church of Rome, have in many respects been far beyond any of the heathen persecutions. So that Antichrist has proved the greatest and most cruel enemy to the church of Christ that ever was in the world, in this, as well as in all other respects; agreeable to the description given of the church of Rome, Rev. xvii. 6. "And I saw the woman drunken with the blood of the saints, and with the blood of the martyrs of Jesus." And, chap. xviii. 24. "And in her was found the blood of prophets, and of saints, and of all them that were slain upon the earth."

The heathen persecutions had been very dreadful: but now persecution by the church of Rome was improved, and studied, and cultivated, as an art or science. Such ways of afflicting and tormenting were found out, as are beyond the invention of ordinary men, or men unstudied in those things: and beyond the invention of all former ages. And that persecution might be managed the more effectually, there were certain societies of men established in various parts of the popish dominions, whose business it should be to study, and improve, and practise persecution in its highest perfection, *viz. the courts of inquisition.* The particular histories of the Romish persecution, and their courts of inquisition, will give that idea which a few words cannot express.

When the Reformation began, the beast with seven heads and ten horns began to rage in a dreadful manner. The church of Rome renewed its persecution of the poor Waldenses, and great multitudes of them were cruelly tortured and put to death. Soon after the Reformation, there were terrible persecutions in various parts of Germany; and especially in Bohemia, which lasted for thirty years together; in which so much blood was shed for the sake of religion, that a certain writer compares it to the plenty of waters of the great rivers of Germany. The countries of Poland, Lithuania, and Hungary, were in like manner deluged with protestant blood.

By means of these and other cruel persecutions, the protestant religion was in a great measure suppressed in

Bohemia, the Palatinate, and Hungary, which before were protestant countries. Thus was fulfilled what was foretold of the little horn, Dan. vii. 20, 21. "—and of the ten horns that were in his head, and of the other which came up, and before whom three fell, even of that horn that had eyes, and a mouth that spake very great things, whose look was more stout than his fellows. I beheld, and the same horn made war with the saints, and prevailed against them." And what was foretold of the beast having seven heads and ten horns, Rev. xiii. 7. "And it was given unto him to make war with the saints, and to overcome them; and power was given him over all kindreds, and tongues, and nations."

Holland and the other Low Countries were for many years a scene of nothing but the most affecting and amazing cruelties, being deluged with the blood of protestants, under the merciless hands of the Spaniards, to whom they were then in subjection. But in this persecution, the devil in a great measure failed of his purpose; as it issued in a great part of the Netherlands casting off the Spanish yoke, and setting up a wealthy and powerful protestant state, to the great defence of the protestant cause ever since.

France is also another country, which since the Reformation, in some respects, perhaps more than any other, has been a scene of dreadful cruelties suffered by the protestants. After many cruelties had been exercised towards the protestants in that kingdom, there was begun a persecution of them in the year fifteen hundred and seventy-one, in the reign of Charles IX. king of France. It began with a cruel massacre, wherein seventy thousand protestants were slain in a few days, as the king boasted: and in all this persecution, he slew, as is supposed, three hundred thousand martyrs. And it is reckoned, that about this time, within thirty years, there were martyred in this kingdom, for the protestant religion, thirty-nine princes, one hundred and forty-eight counts, two hundred and thirty-four barons, one hundred and forty-seven thousand five hundred and eighteen gentlemen, and seven hundred and sixty thousand common people.

But all these persecutions were, for exquisite cruelty, far exceeded by those which followed in the reign of Lewis XIV. which indeed are supposed to exceed all others; and being long continued, by reason of the long reign of that king, they almost wholly extirpated the protestant religion out of that kingdom, where had flourished a multitude of famous protestant churches all over the kingdom. Thus it was given to the beast to make war with the saints, and to overcome them.

There was also a terrible persecution in England in Queen Mary's time, wherein great numbers in all parts of the kingdom were burnt alive. And after this, though the protestant religion has been for the most part established by law in England, yet there have been very severe persecutions by the high-churchmen, who symbolize in many things with the papists. Such was that which occasioned our forefathers to flee from their native country, and to come and settle in this land, which was then a hideous howling wilderness. And these persecutions were continued with little intermission till King William came to the throne.

Scotland has also been the scene, for many years together, of cruelties and blood by the hands of high-churchmen, such as came very little short of the popish persecution in Queen Mary's days, and in many things much exceeded it, which continued till they were delivered by King William.

Ireland also has been as it were overwhelmed with protestant blood. In the days of King Charles I. of England, above two hundred thousand protestants were cruelly murdered in that kingdom in a few days; the papists, by a secret agreement, rising at an appointed time, intending to kill every protestant in the kingdom at once.

Besides these, there have been very cruel persecutions in Italy, and Spain, and other places, which I shall not stand to relate.—Thus did the devil, and his great minister Antichrist, rage with such violence and cruelty against the church of Christ! and thus did the whore of Babylon make herself drunk with the blood of the saints and martyrs of Jesus! By these persecutions the protestant church has been much diminished. Yet have they not been able to prevail; but still the protestant church is upheld, and Christ fulfils his promise, that "the gates of hell shall not prevail against it."

5. The last kind of opposition that Satan has made to the Reformation is by *corrupt opinions*. The first opposition of this kind was by the sect of the *Anabaptists*, which began about four or five years after the Reformation itself. This sect, as it first appeared in Germany, were vastly more extravagant than the present Anabaptists are in England. They held a great many exceeding corrupt opinions. One tenet of theirs was, that there ought to be no civil authority, and that it was lawful to rebel against it. And on this principle, they refused to submit to magistrates, or any human laws; and gathered together in vast armies, to defend themselves against their civil rulers, and put all Germany into an uproar, and so kept it for some time.

The next opposition of this kind to the Reformation was that which was made by *enthusiasts*. Those are called enthusiasts who falsely pretend to be inspired by the Holy Ghost as the prophets were. These began in Germany about ten years after Luther began the Reformation; and there arose various sects of them who were exceeding wild and extravagant. The followers of these are the Quakers in England, and other parts of the British dominions.

The next to these were the *Socinians*, who had their beginning chiefly in Poland, by the teaching of *Lælius Socinus*, and *Faustus Socinus*. They held, that Christ was a mere man, and denied Christ's satisfaction and most of the fundamental doctrines of the christian religion. Their heresy has since been greatly propagated among protestants in Poland, Germany, Holland, England, and other places.

After these arose the *Arminians*. They take their name from a Dutchman, whose name was *Jacobus Van Harmin*, which, turned into Latin, is called *Jacobus Arminius*; and from his name the whole sect are called *Arminians*. This Jacobus Arminius was first a minister at Amsterdam, and then a professor of divinity in the university of Leyden. He had many followers in Holland. There was upon this a synod of all the reformed churches called together, who met at Dort in Holland. The synod of Dort condemned them; but yet they spread and prevailed. They began to prevail in England in the reign of Charles I. especially in the church of England. The church of England divines before that were almost universally Calvinists: but since that, Arminianism has gradually more and more prevailed, till they are become almost universally Arminians. And not only so, but Arminianism has greatly prevailed among the dissenters, and has spread greatly in New England, as well as Old.

Since this, *Arianism* has been revived. Arianism, a little after Constantine's time, almost swallowed up the christian world, like a flood out of the mouth of the serpent which threatened to swallow up the woman. And of late years, this heresy has been revived in England, and greatly prevails there, both in the church of England, and among dissenters. These hold, that Christ is but a mere creature, though they grant that he is the greatest of all creatures.

Another thing which has of late exceedingly prevailed among protestants, and especially in England, is deism. The deists wholly cast off the christian religion, and are professed infidels. Indeed they own the being of God; but deny any revealed religion, or any word of God at all; and say, that God has given mankind no other light to walk by but their own reason. With these opinions our nation, which is the principal nation of the Reformation, is very much overrun, and they prevail more and more. Thus much concerning the opposition that Satan has made against the Reformation.

III. I proceed now to show what *success* the gospel has had in these later times of the Reformed church. This success may be reduced to three heads: 1. Reformation in doctrine and worship in countries called Christian; 2. Propagation of the gospel among the heathen; 3. Revival of religion in the power and practice of it.

1. As to the first, *viz*. reformation in *doctrine*, the most considerable success of late has been in the empire of

Muscovy, which is a country of vast extent. The people of this country, so many of them as call themselves Christians, professed to be of the Greek church; but were barbarously ignorant, and very superstitious, till of late years. Their late emperor, Peter the Great, set himself to reform his dominions, took great pains to bring them out of their darkness, and to have them instructed in religion. To that end, he set up schools of learning, ordered the Bible to be printed in the language of the country, made a law that every family should keep the Holy Scriptures in their houses, that every person should be able to read the same, and that no person should be allowed to marry till they were able to read the Scriptures. He also reformed the churches of his country of many of their superstitions, whereby the religion professed and practised in Muscovy is much nearer to that of the protestants than formerly it used to be. This emperor gave great encouragement to the exercise of the protestant religion in his dominions. And since that, Muscovy is become a land of light, in comparison of what it was fifty years past.

2. As to the second kind of success which the gospel has lately had, *viz.* its *propagation* among the heathen, I would take notice of three things.

(1.) The propagation of the gospel among the heathen here in *America*. This American continent, which is a very great part of the world, and, together with its neighbouring seas adjoining, takes up one side of the globe, was wholly unknown to all christian nations till these latter times. It was not known that there was any such part of the world, though it was very full of people: and therefore the devil had this part of the world as it were secure to himself, out of the reach of the light of the gospel, and so out of the way of molestation in his dominion over them. Here the many nations of Indians worshipped him as God from age to age, while the gospel was confined to the opposite side of the globe. It is probably supposed, from some remaining accounts, that the occasion of first peopling America was this; that the devil, being alarmed and surprised by the wonderful success of the gospel the first three hundred years after Christ, and by the downfall of the heathen empire in the time of Constantine—and seeing the gospel spread so fast, and fearing that his heathenish kingdom would be wholly overthrown through the world—led away a people from the other continent into America, that they might be quite out of the reach of the gospel, that here he might quietly possess them, and reign over them as their god.—Many writers intimate, that some of the Indian nations, when the Europeans first came into America, had a tradition among them, that their god first led them into this continent, and went before them in an ark.

However, it is certain that the devil did here quietly enjoy his dominion over the poor Indians for many ages. But in later times God has sent the gospel into these parts, and now the christian church is set up here in New England, and in other parts of America, where before had been nothing but the grossest heathenish darkness. Great part of America is now full of Bibles, and full of at least the *form* of the worship of the true God and Jesus Christ, where the name of Christ before had not been heard of for many ages, if at all. And though there has been but a small propagation of the gospel among the heathen here, in comparison of what were to be wished for; yet there has been something worthy of notice.—There was something remarkable in New England, both at first and of late, and in other parts of America among many Indians, of an inclination to be instructed in the christian religion.

However small the propagation of the gospel among the heathen here in America has been hitherto; yet I think we may well look upon the discovery of so great a part of the world, and bringing the gospel into it, as one thing by which Divine Providence is preparing the way for the future glorious times of the church; when Satan's kingdom shall be overthrown, throughout the whole habitable globe, on every side, and on all its continents. When those times come, then doubtless the gospel shall have glorious success, and all the inhabitants of this new-discovered world shall become subjects of the kingdom of Christ, as well as all the other ends of the earth. In all probability, Providence has so ordered it, that the mariner's compass (which is an invention of later times, whereby men are enabled to sail over the widest ocean, when before they durst not venture far from land) should prove a preparation for what God intends to bring to pass in the glorious times of the church, *viz.* the sending forth the gospel wherever any of the children of men dwell, how far soever off, and however separated by wide oceans from those parts of the world which are already christianized.

(2.) There has of late years been a very considerable propagation of the gospel among the heathen in the dominions of *Muscovy*. I have already observed the reformation which has lately been among those who are called *Christians* there: but I now speak of the heathen. Great part of the vast dominions of the emperor of Muscovy are gross heathens. The greater part of Great Tartary, a heathen country, has in later times been brought under the Muscovite government; and there have been of late great numbers who have renounced their heathenism, and have embraced the christian religion.

(3.) There has been lately a very considerable propagation of the christian religion among the heathen in the *East Indies*; particularly, many in *Malabar* have been brought over to the christian protestant religion, chiefly by the labours of certain missionaries sent thither to instruct them by the king of Denmark, who have brought over many heathens to the christian faith, and have set up schools among them, and a printing-press to print Bibles and other books for their instruction, in their own language, with great success.

3. The last kind of success which I shall notice, is the *revivals* of the power and practice of religion. And here I shall take notice of but two instances.

(1.) There has been not long since a remarkable revival of the power and practice of religion in *Germany*, through the endeavours of an eminent divine there, *August Herman Frank*, professor of divinity at Halle in Saxony. Being a person of eminent charity, the great work that God wrought by him, began with his setting on foot a charitable design. It began only with his placing an alms-box at his study-door, into which some poor mites were thrown, whereby books were bought for the instruction of the poor. And God was pleased so wonderfully to smile on his design, and so to pour out a spirit of charity on that occasion, that he was enabled in a little time to erect public schools for the instruction of poor children, and an orphan-house for their supply and instruction.—At last, near five hundred children were maintained and instructed in learning and piety by the charity of others; and the number continued to increase more and more for many years. This was accompanied with a wonderful reformation and revival of religion, and a spirit of piety, in the city and university of Halle; and thus it continued. Which also had great influence in many other places in Germany. Their example seemed remarkably to stir up multitudes to their imitation.

(2.) Another thing, which it would be ungrateful in us not to notice, is that remarkable pouring out of the Spirit of God which has been of late in this part of *New England*, of which we, in this town, have had such a share. But it is needless for me particularly to describe it, seeing *you* have so lately been eye-witnesses of it, and I hope multitudes are sensible of the benefit. Thus I have mentioned the more remarkable instances of the success which the gospel has lately had in the world.

IV. I proceed now to the last thing proposed to be considered, relating to the success of Christ's redemption during this space, *viz.* what is the *present state* of things now in the world, with regard to the church of Christ, and the success of his purchase. And this I would do, by showing how things are now compared with the first times of the Reformation.—And, 1. I would show wherein the state of things is altered for the worse; and, 2. How it is altered for the better.

1. I would show wherein the state of things is altered from what it was in the beginning of the Reformation, for the *worse;* and it is so especially in these three respects.

(1.) The reformed church is much *diminished*. The Reformation, in former times, was supposed to take place through one half of christendom, excepting the Greek church; or that there were as many protestants as papists. But now it is not so; the protestant church is much diminished. Heretofore there have been multitudes of protestants in *France;* many famous protestant churches were planted all over that country, who used to meet together in synods, and maintain a very regular discipline. The protestant church of France was a great part of the glory of the Reformation. But now it is far otherwise: this church is all broken and scattered, and there are now but very few protestant assemblies in all that kingdom. The protestant interest is also greatly diminished in *Germany.* There were formerly several sovereign protestant princes, whose successors are now papists; as, particularly the Elector Palatine, and the Elector of Saxony. The kingdom of *Bohemia* was formerly a protestant kingdom, but is now in the hands of the papists. *Hungary* was formerly a protestant country; but the protestants there have been greatly reduced, and in a great measure subdued, by persecutions. And the protestant interest has no way of late remarkably gained ground of the church of Rome.

(2.) Another thing wherein the state of things is altered for the worse compared with the former times of the Reformation, is the prevailing of *licentiousness* in principles and opinions.—There is not now that spirit of orthodoxy which then prevailed: there is very little appearance of zeal for the mysterious and spiritual doctrines of Christianity; and they never were so held in contempt, as they are in the present age; and especially in England, the principal kingdom of the Reformation. In this kingdom, those principles on which the power of godliness depends, are in a great measure exploded, and Arianism, Socinianism, Arminianism, and Deism, prevail, and carry almost all before them. History gives no account of any age wherein there was so great an infidel apostacy of those who had been brought up under the light of the gospel; never was there such a disavowal of all revealed religion; never any age wherein there was so much scoffing at and ridiculing the gospel of Christ by those who have been brought up under the gospel-light.

(3.) Another thing wherein things are altered for the worse, is, that there is much less of the prevalency of the power of *godliness,* than there was at the beginning of the Reformation. A glorious out-pouring of the Spirit of God accompanied the first Reformation, not only to convert multitudes in so short a time from popery to the true religion, but to turn many to God and true godliness. But now there is an exceeding great decay of vital piety; yea, it seems to be despised, called *enthusiasm,* and *fanaticism.* Those who are truly religious, are commonly looked upon to be beside their right mind; and vice and profaneness dreadfully prevail, like a flood which threatens to bear down all before it.—But I proceed now to show,

2. In what respects things are altered for the *better* from what they were in the first Reformation.

(1.) The power and influence of the *pope* is much diminished. Although, since the former times of the Reformation, he has gained ground in extent of dominion; yet he has lost in degree of influence. The vial which in the beginning of the Reformation was poured out on the throne of the beast, to the great diminishing of his power and authority in the world, has continued running ever since. The pope, soon after the Reformation, became less regarded by the princes of Europe than he had been before; and so he has been since less and less. Many of the popish princes themselves seem now to regard him very little more than they think will serve their own designs; of which there have been several remarkable proofs and instances of late.

(2.) There is far less *persecution* now than there was in the first times of the Reformation. Some parts of the protestant church are at this day under persecution, and so probably will be till the day of the church's suffering and travail is at an end, which will not be till the fall of Antichrist. But it is now in no measure as it was heretofore. There does not seem to be the same *spirit* of persecution prevailing; it is become more out of fashion even among the popish princes. The wickedness of the enemies of Christ, and the opposition against his cause, seem to run in another channel. The humour now is to despise and *laugh* at all religion; and there seems to be a spirit of indifferency about it. However, so far the state of things is better than it has been, that there is so much less of persecution.

3. There is a great increase of *learning.* In the dark times of popery, before the Reformation, learning was so far decayed, that the world seemed to be overrun with barbarous ignorance. Their very priests were many of them grossly ignorant. Learning began to revive with the Reformation, owing very much to the art of printing which was invented a little before this period. Since then, learning has increased more and more, and at this day is undoubtedly raised to a vastly greater height than ever it was before: and though no good use is made of it by the greater part of learned men, yet the increase of learning in itself is a thing to be rejoiced in, because it is a good, and, if duly applied, an excellent handmaid to divinity. It is a talent which, if God gives men a heart, affords them great advantage to do great things for the advancement of the kingdom of Christ, and the good of the souls of men. That learning and knowledge should greatly increase before the glorious times, seems to be foretold, Dan. xii. 4. "But thou, O Daniel, shut up the words, and seal the book, even to the time of the end: many shall run to and fro, and knowledge shall be increased." And however little now learning is applied to the advancement of religion; yet we may hope that the days are approaching wherein God will make great use of it for the advancement of the kingdom of Christ.

God in his providence now seems to be acting over again the same part which he did a little before Christ came. When Christ came into the world, learning greatly prevailed; and yet wickedness never prevailed more than then. God was pleased to suffer human learning to come to such a height before he sent forth the gospel into the world, that the world might see the insufficiency of all their own wisdom for the obtaining the knowledge of God, without the gospel of Christ, and the teaching of his Spirit. When, in the wisdom of God, the world by wisdom knew not God, it pleased God, by the foolishness of preaching, to save them that believe. And when the gospel came to prevail first without the help of man's wisdom, then God was pleased to make use of learning as a handmaid. So now, learning is at a great height in the world, far beyond what it was in the age when Christ appeared; and now the world, by their learning and wisdom, do not know God; and they seem to wander in darkness, are miserably deluded, stumble and fall in matters of religion, as in midnight darkness. Trusting to their learning, they grope in the day-time as in the night. Learned men are exceedingly divided in their opinions concerning the matters of religion, running into all manner of corrupt opinions, pernicious and foolish errors. They scorn to submit their reason to divine revelation, to believe any thing that is above their comprehension; and so being wise in their own eyes, they become fools, and even vain in their imaginations; they turn the truth of God into a lie, and their foolish hearts are darkened. See Rom. i. 21, &c.

But yet, when God has sufficiently shown men the insufficiency of human wisdom and learning for the purposes of religion, and when the appointed time comes for that glorious outpouring of the Spirit of God, when he will himself by his own immediate influence enlighten men's minds; then may we hope that God will make use of the great increase of learning as a handmaid of religion, as a means of the glorious advancement of the kingdom of his Son. Then shall human learning be subservient to the understanding of the Scriptures, and to a clear explanation and a glorious defence of the doctrines of Christianity. And there is no doubt, that God in his providence has of late given the world the art of printing, and such a great increase of learning, to prepare for what he designs to accomplish for his church in the approaching days of its prosperity. And thus the wealth of the wicked is laid up for the just, Prov. xiii. 22.

PART VI.

IMPROVEMENT OF PAST EVENTS.

HAVING now shown how the work of redemption has been carried on from the fall of man to the present time, before I proceed any further, I would make some APPLICATION.

I. From what has been said, we may see great evidence of the truth of the christian religion, and that *the Scriptures are the word of God.* There are three arguments of this, which may be drawn from what has been said.

1. It may be argued from that violent and inveterate *opposition* there has always appeared of the wickedness of the world against this religion. The religion that the church of God has professed from the first, has always been the same. Though the dispensations have been altered, yet the religion which the church has professed has always, as to its essentials, been the same. The church of God, from the beginning, has been one society. The christian church is manifestly the same society continued, that was before Christ came; grafted on the same root, built on the same foundation. The revelation on which both have depended, is essentially the same: for as the christian church is built on the Holy Scriptures, so was the Jewish church. Though now the Scriptures are enlarged by the addition of the New Testament, still it is essentially the same revelation with that which was given in the Old Testament, only the subjects of divine revelation are now more clearly revealed in the New Testament than they were in the Old. The sum of both the Old Testament and New, is Christ and his redemption. The ground-work of the religion of the church of God, both before and since Christ has appeared, is the same great scheme of redemption by the Son of God. The church that was before the Israelitish church, was still the same society, and it was essentially the same religion that was professed and practised in it. Thus it was from Noah to Abraham, and thus it was before the flood; for *this* also was built on the foundation of those revelations of Christ which were given to Adam, and Enoch. So that the church of God has always been built on those divine revelations, and were always essentially the same, and they are summarily comprehended in the Holy Scriptures. Ever since Moses's time the church has been built on the Scriptures themselves.

So that the opposition which has been made to the church of God in all ages, has always been against the same religion, and the same revelation. Now therefore the violent and perpetual opposition that has ever been made by the corruption and wickedness of mankind against this church, is a strong argument of the truth of this religion, and this revelation, upon which this church has always been built. Contraries are well argued one from another. We may well and safely argue, that a thing is good, according to the degree of opposition in which it stands to evil, or the degree in which evil opposes it, and is an enemy to it. Now it is evident by the things which you have heard concerning the church of Christ, and that holy religion of Jesus Christ which it has professed, that the wickedness of the world has had a perpetual hatred to it, and has made most violent opposition against it.

That the church of God has always met with great opposition in the world, none can deny. This is plain by profane history as far as that reaches; and before that, divine history gives us the same account. The church of God, its religion and worship, began to be opposed in the time of Cain and Abel; and was so when the earth was filled with violence in Noah's time. After this, how was the church opposed in Egypt! and how was Israel always hated by the nations round about, agreeable to Jer. xii. 9. "Mine heritage is unto me as a speckled bird, the birds round about are against her." And after the Babylonish captivity, how was this church persecuted by Antiochus Epiphanes and others! How was Christ persecuted when he was on earth! and how were the apostles and other Christians persecuted by the Jews, before the destruction of Jerusalem by the Romans! How violent were that people against the church! and how dreadful was the opposition of the heathen world against the Christian church after this before Constantine! How great was their spite against the true religion! And since that, how yet more violent, and spiteful, and cruel, has been the opposition of Antichrist against the church!

There is no other such instance of opposition. History gives no account of any other body of men that have been so hated, and so maliciously and insatiably pursued and persecuted, nor any thing like it. No other religion ever was so maligned age after age. The nations of other professions have enjoyed their religions in peace and quietness, however they have differed from their neighbours. One nation has worshipped one sort of gods, and others another, without molesting or disturbing one another about it. All the spite and opposition has been against this religion, which the church of Christ has professed. All other religions have seemed to show an implacable enmity to this; and men have seemed to have, from one age to another, such a spite against it, that they have seemed as though they could never satisfy their cruelty. They put their inventions upon the rack to find out torments that should be cruel enough; and yet, after all, never seemed to be satisfied. Their thirst has never been satisfied with blood.

So that it is out of doubt, that this religion, and these Scriptures, have always been malignantly opposed in the world. The only question that remains is, What it is that has made this opposition? whether or not it has been good or bad? whether it be the wickedness and corruption of the world, or not, that has done this? But of this there can be no greater doubt than that of the other, if we consider how causeless this cruelty has always been, who the opposers have been, and the manner in which they have opposed. The opposition has chiefly been from heathenism and popery; which are the fruits of the blindness, corruption, and wickedness of men, as the very deists themselves confess. The light of nature shows, that the religion of *heathens*, consisting in the worship of idols, and sacrificing their children to them, and in obscene and abominable rites and ceremonies, is wickedness. And the superstitions, idolatries, and usurpations of the church of *Rome*, are no less contrary to the light of nature. By this appears, that this opposition which has been made against the church of God, has been made by wicked men. And with regard to the opposition of the *Jews* in Christ's and the apostles' time, it was in a most corrupt time of that nation, when the people were generally become exceeding wicked, as some of the Jewish writers themselves, Josephus and others, who lived about that time, expressly declare. And that it has been mere wickedness that has made this opposition, is manifest from the *manner* of opposition; the extreme violence, injustice, and cruelty, with which the church of God has been treated. It seems to show the hand of malignant infernal spirits.

Now what reason can be assigned, why the corruption and wickedness of the world should so implacably set itself against this religion of Jesus Christ, and against the Scriptures, but only that they are contrary to wickedness, and consequently are good and holy? Why should the enemies of Christ, for so many thousand years together, manifest such a mortal hatred of this religion, but only that it is the cause of God? If the Scriptures be not the word of God, and the religion of the church of Christ be not the true religion, then it must follow, that it is a most wicked religion; nothing but a pack of lies and abominable delusions, invented by the enemies of God. And if so, it is not likely that the enemies of God, and the wickedness of the world, would have maintained such a perpetual and implacable enmity against it.

2. It is a great argument that the christian church and its religion is from God, that it has been *upheld* hitherto through all opposition and dangers. That the church of God and the true religion, which has been so continually and violently opposed, with so many endeavours to overthrow it—and which has so often been brought to the brink of ruin, through the greatest part of six thousand years—has yet been upheld, most remarkably shows the hand of God in favour of the church. If duly considered, it will

appear one of the greatest wonders and miracles that ever came to pass. There is nothing like it upon the face of the earth. There is no other society of men that has stood as the church has. As to the old world before the flood, that was overthrown by a deluge of waters; but yet the church of God was preserved. Satan's visible kingdom on earth was then once entirely overthrown; but the visible kingdom of Christ never has been overthrown. All those ancient human kingdoms and monarchies of which we read, are long since come to an end; the Moabites, the Ammonites, the Edomites, &c. The great empire of proud Babylon was overthrown by the Persians; then the Persian empire was overthrown by the Greeks; after this the Grecian empire was overthrown by the Romans; and, finally, the Roman empire fell a sacrifice to various barbarous nations. Here is a remarkable fulfilment of the text, "The moth has eaten them up like a garment, and the worm has eaten them like wool; but God's church remains."

Never were there so many and so potent endeavours to destroy any thing else, as there has been to destroy the church. Other kingdoms and societies of men, which have appeared to be ten times as strong as the church, have been destroyed with a hundredth part of the opposition which the church of God has met with: which shows, that it is God who has been its protector. For it is most plain, that it has not upheld itself by its own strength. For the most part, it has been a very weak society. The children of Israel were but a handful of people, in comparison of the many who often sought their overthrow. So in Christ's time, and in the beginning of the christian church, they were but a remnant: whereas the whole multitude of the Jewish nation were against them. And so in the beginning of the Gentile church, they were but a small number in comparison with the heathen, who sought their overthrow. In the dark times of Antichrist, before the Reformation, they were but a handful; and yet their enemies could not overthrow them. And commonly, the enemies of the church have not only had the greatest number on their side, but they have had the strength in other respects. They have commonly had all the civil authority on their side. So in Egypt, the civil authority was for the Egyptians, and the church were only their slaves, and in their hands; and yet they could not overthrow them. And so it was in the time of Antiochus Epiphanes, and Julian the apostate, the authority was all on the side of the persecutors, and the church was under their dominion; yet all their cruelty could not extirpate it. And for a great many ages, the civil authority was all on the side of Antichrist, and the church seemed to be in their hands.

And not only has the strength of its enemies been greater than that of the church, but ordinarily the church has not used what strength they have had in their own defence, but have committed themselves wholly to God. In the time of the Jewish persecutions before the destruction of Jerusalem by the Romans, and of the heathen persecutions before Constantine, the Christians did not pretend to make any forcible resistance to their heathen persecutors. So it has been for the most part under the popish persecutions; and yet they have never been able to overthrow the church of God; but it stands to this very day.

And this is still the more exceeding wonderful, if we consider how often the church has been brought to the brink of ruin, and the case seemed to be desperate. In the time of the old world, when wickedness so prevailed as that but one family was left, yet God wonderfully appeared, and overthrew the wicked world with a flood, and preserved his church. At the Red sea, when Pharaoh and his host thought they were quite sure of their prey, God appeared, destroyed them, and delivered his church. Under the tenth and last heathen persecution, their persecutors boasted that now they had done the business for the Christians, and overthrown the christian church; yet in the midst of their triumph, the christian church rises out of the dust and prevails, and the heathen empire totally falls before it. So when the christian church seemed ready to be swallowed up by the Arian heresy, when Antichrist rose and prevailed, and all the world wondered after the beast; when the church for many hundred years was reduced to a small number, and the power of the world was engaged to destroy those little remnants; yet they could never fully accomplish their design, and at last God wonderfully revived his church by the Reformation, made it to stand as it were on its feet in the sight of its enemies, and raised it out of their reach. And when the popish powers plotted the overthrow of the Reformed church, and seemed just about to bring their matters to a conclusion, then God wonderfully appeared for the deliverance of his church, as at the Revolution by King William. Presently after the darkest times, God has made his church most gloriously to flourish.

If such a preservation of the church of God, from the beginning of the world hitherto, attended with such circumstances, is not sufficient to show a divine hand in favour of it, what can be devised that would be sufficient? But if this be from the divine hand, then God owns the church, and owns that revelation and those Scriptures on which she is built; and so it will follow, that their religion is the true religion, or God's religion, and that the Scriptures, which they make their rule, are his word.

3. We may draw this further argument for the divine authority of the Scriptures from what has been said, *viz.* that God has *fulfilled* those things which are foretold in the Scriptures.—I have already observed in general, as I went along, how the prophecies of Scripture were fulfilled: I shall now single out but *two instances* of the fulfilment of scripture prophecy.

(1.) One is in *preserving* his church from being ruined. I have just now shown what an evidence this is of the divine authority of the Scriptures in itself considered; I now speak of it as a fulfilment of scripture prophecy. This is abundantly foretold and promised in the Scriptures; particularly in the text. There it is foretold, that other things shall fail, other kingdoms and monarchies, which set themselves in opposition, should come to nothing: "The moth should eat them up like a garment, and the worm should eat them like wool." It is here foretold, that God's covenant mercy to his church should continue for ever; and so it hath hitherto proved, though the church has passed through so many dangers. The same is promised, Isa. liv. 17. "No weapon that is formed against thee, shall prosper; and every tongue that shall rise against thee in judgment, thou shalt condemn." And again, Isa. xlix. 14—16. "But Zion said, The Lord hath forsaken me, and my Lord hath forgotten me. Can a woman forget her sucking child, that she should not have compassion on the son of her womb? yea, they may forget, yet will I not forget thee. Behold, I have graven thee upon the palms of my hands, thy walls are continually before me." The same is promised in Isa. lix. 21. xliii. 1, 2. and Zech. xii. 2, 3. So Christ promised the same, when he says, "On this rock will I build my church, and the gates of hell shall not prevail against it." Now if this be not from God, and the Scriptures be not the word of God, and the church of Christ built on the foundation of this word be not of God, how could the persons who foretold this, know it? for if the church were not of God, it was a very unlikely thing ever to come to pass. For they foretold great opposition and dangers, that other kingdoms should come to nought, and that the church should often be almost swallowed up; and yet that the church should remain. Now how could they foresee so unlikely a thing but by divine inspiration?

(2.) The other remarkable instance is, the *fulfilment* of scripture prophecy, concerning *Antichrist*. The way that this Antichrist should arise, is foretold, *viz.* by the falling away of the christian church into a corrupt state: 2 Thess. ii. 3. "For that day shall not come, except there come a falling away first, and that man of sin be revealed, the son of perdition."—And it is prophesied, that this man of sin should set himself up in the temple or visible church of God, pretending to be vested with divine power, as head of the church, (ver. 4.) And all this is exactly come to pass in the church of Rome. Again, it is intimated, that the rise of Antichrist should be *gradual*, (ver. 7.) "For the mystery of iniquity doth already work: only he who now letteth, will let, until he be taken out of the way." This also came to pass.—Again, it is prophesied of this mighty enemy of the christian church, that he should be a great prince or monarch of the Roman empire: so he is represented in Daniel as a horn of the fourth beast, or fourth monarchy, as the angel himself explains it, (Daniel vii.) This also came to pass.——Yea it is prophesied, that the seat of this pretended vicar of God, and head of the church, should be the city of Rome itself. It is said expressly, that the spiritual whore, or false church, should have her seat on seven mountains or hills; Rev. xvii. 9. "The seven heads are seven mountains, on which the woman sitteth:" and (ver. 18.) "The woman which thou sawest, is that great city, which reigneth over the kings of the earth;" which it is certain was at that time the city of Rome. This prophecy also has come to pass.

Further, it was prophesied, that this Antichrist should reign over peoples, and multitudes, and nations, and tongues, Rev. xvii. 15. and that all the world should wonder after the beast, Rev. xiii. 3. This also was verified in the church of Rome. It was foretold that this Antichrist should be remarkable for the sin of pride, pretending to great things, and assuming very much to himself: (2 Thess. ii. 4.) "That he should exalt himself above all that is called God, or that is worshipped." So Rev. xiii. 5. "And there was given unto him a mouth speaking great things, and blasphemies." Dan. vii. 8, 20. the *little horn* is said to have *a mouth speaking very great things*, and his look to be *more stout than his fellows*. This also was verified in the pope, and the church of Rome.——It was also prophesied, that Antichrist should be an exceeding cruel persecutor, Dan. vii. 21. The same horn "made war with the saints, and prevailed against them:" Rev. xiii. 7. "And it was given unto him to make war with the saints, and to overcome them." Rev. xvii. 6. "And I saw the woman drunken with the blood of the saints, and with the blood of the martyrs of Jesus." This also came to pass in the church of Rome.—It was foretold, that Antichrist should excel in craft and policy: Dan. vii. 8. "In this horn were eyes like the eyes of a man." And ver. 20. "Even of that horn that had eyes." This also marks the church of Rome.——It was foretold, that the kings of christendom should be subject to antichrist: Rev. xvii. 12, 13. "And the ten horns which thou sawest, are ten kings, which have received no kingdom as yet; but received power as kings one hour with the beast. These have one mind, and shall give their power and strength unto the beast." This also came to pass with respect to the Romish church.——It was foretold, that he should perform pretended miracles and lying wonders: 2 Thess. ii. 9. "Whose coming is after the working of Satan, with all power, and signs, and lying wonders." Rev. xiii. 13, 14. "And he doth great wonders, so that he maketh fire come down from heaven on the earth, in the sight of men, and deceiveth them that dwell on the earth, by the means of those miracles which he had power to do in the sight of the beast." This also designates the church of Rome. Fire coming down from heaven, seems to have reference to their excommunications, which were dreaded like fire from heaven.——It was foretold that he should forbid to marry, and to abstain from meats: 1 Tim. iv. 3. "Forbidding to marry, and commanding to abstain from meats, which God hath created to be received with thanksgiving." This also is exactly fulfilled in the church of Rome.——It was foretold that he should be very rich, and arrive at a great degree of earthly splendour and glory: Rev. xvii. 4. "And the woman was arrayed in purple, and scarlet colour, and decked with gold and precious stones, and pearls, having a golden cup in her hand." And so chap. xviii. 7, 12, 13, 16. What can more expressly describe the church of Rome?——It was foretold, that he should forbid any to buy or sell, but those that had his mark: Rev. xiii. 17. "And that no man might buy or sell, save he that had the mark, or the name of the beast, or the number of his name." This also is fulfilled in the church of Rome.——It was foretold that he should sell the souls of men, Rev. xviii. 13. where, in enumerating the articles of his merchandise, *the souls of men* are specifically mentioned as one. Is not this also exactly fulfilled in the same church?——It was foretold, that Antichrist would not suffer the bodies of God's people to be buried: Rev. xi. 8, 9. "And their dead bodies shall lie in the street of the great city,—and they—shall not suffer their dead bodies to be put in graves." How literally has this come to pass with respect to the church of Rome!——I might mention many other things which were foretold of Antichrist, and show that they were fulfilled most exactly in the pope and the church of Rome. How strong an argument is this, that the Scriptures are the word of God!

II. From what has been said, we may learn what the spirit of true Christians is, *viz. a spirit of suffering*. Seeing God has so ordered it in his providence, that his church should for so long a time be in a suffering state, yea, often in a state of extreme suffering, we may conclude, that the spirit of the true church is a suffering spirit, otherwise God never would have ordered for it so much suffering; for doubtless God accommodates the state and circumstances of the church to the spirit that he has given her. No wonder therefore that Christ so much inculcated upon his disciples, that *they must deny themselves, and take up their cross, if they would follow him*.

And what spirit has the church shown and exercised under her sufferings? She has actually, under those terrible persecutions through which she has passed, rather chosen to undergo those dreadful torments, and to sell all for the pearl of great price, to suffer all that her bitterest enemies could inflict, than to renounce Christ and his religion. History affords a great number of remarkable instances, sets in view a great cloud of witnesses. This abundantly confirms the necessity of possessing a spirit to sell all for Christ, to renounce our own ease, our own worldly profit, our honour, and our all, for *him*, and for the gospel.

Let us inquire whether we are of such a spirit. How does it prove upon trial? Does it prove in fact that we are willing to deny ourselves, and renounce our own worldly interest, and to pass through the trials to which we are called in providence? Alas, how small are our trials, compared with those of many of our fellow-Christians in former ages! And I would on this occasion apply that in Jer. xii. 5. "If thou hast run with the footmen, and they have wearied thee, then how canst thou contend with horses?" If you have not been able to endure the light trials to which you have been called, how would you be able to endure the far greater trials to which the church has been called in former ages? Every true Chrisuan has *the spirit of a martyr*, and would suffer as a martyr, if he were called to it in providence.

III. Hence we learn what great *reason* we have assuredly to expect the fulfilment of what yet *remains* to be fulfilled of things foretold in Scripture. The Scriptures foretell many great things yet to be fulfilled before the end of the world; but what great difficulties seem to be in the way! We seem at present to be very far from such a state as is foretold in the Scriptures; but yet we have abundant reason to expect, that these things, however seemingly difficult, will be accomplished in their season. We see the faithfulness of God to his promises hitherto; how true he has been to his church, and how he has remembered his mercy from generation to generation. We may say concerning what God has done hitherto for his church, as Joshua said to the children of Israel, Josh. xxiii. 14. "That not one thing hath failed of all that the Lord our God hath spoken concerning his church;" but all things are hitherto come to pass agreeable to the divine prediction. This should strengthen our faith in those promises, and encourage us, and stir us up to earnest prayer to God for the accomplishment of the great and glorious things which yet remain to be fulfilled.

PART VII.

THE SUCCESS OF REDEMPTION FROM THE PRESENT TIME TO THE FALL OF ANTICHRIST.

I COME now to show how the success of Christ's redemption will be carried on from the present time, till Antichrist is fallen, and Satan's visible kingdom on earth is destroyed.—With respect to this space of time, we have nothing to guide us but the prophecies of Scripture.

Through most of the time from the fall of man to the destruction of Jerusalem by the Romans, we had scripture history to guide us; and from thence to the present time we had prophecy, together with the accomplishment of it in providence, as related in human histories. But henceforward we have *prophecy alone* to guide us. And here I would pass by those things that are only conjectured, or that are surmised by some from those prophecies which are doubtful in their interpretation, and shall insist only on those things which are more evident.

We know not what particular events are to come to pass before that glorious work of God's Spirit begins, by which Satan's kingdom is to be overthrown. By the consent of most divines, there are but few things, if any at all, foretold to be accomplished before the *beginning* of that glorious work of God. But some think that the slaying of the witnesses, (Rev. xi. 7, 8.) is not yet accomplished; and there is a difference of opinion with respect to the pouring out of the seven vials, (Rev. xvi.) how many are *already*, or how many *remain* to be poured out. A late expositor, indeed, whom I have before mentioned, seems to make it evident, that all are already poured out but two, *viz.* the *sixth* on the river Euphrates, and the *seventh* into the air. I will not now stand to inquire, what is intended by the pouring out of the sixth vial on the river Euphrates, that the way of the kings of the east may be prepared; but would only say, that it seems to be something *immediately preparatory* to the destruction of spiritual Babylon, as the drying up of the river Euphrates, which ran through the midst of old Babylon, was what prepared the way of the kings of the Medes and Persians, (the kings of the east,) to come in under the walls, and destroy that city.

But whatever this be, it does not appear that it is any thing which shall be accomplished before that work of God's Spirit is *begun*, by which, as it goes on, Satan's visible kingdom on earth shall be utterly overthrown. And therefore I would proceed directly to consider what the Scripture reveals concerning the work of God itself, by which he will bring about this great event, as being the next thing to be accomplished that we are certain of from the prophecies of Scripture.

I. I would observe some things *in general* concerning it.

1. We have all reason to conclude from the Scriptures, that just before this work of God begins, it will be a *very dark time* with respect to the interests of religion in the world. It has been so before preceding glorious revivals of religion: when Christ came, it was an exceeding degenerate time among the Jews; and so it was a very dark time before the Reformation. And not only so, but it seems to be foretold in Scripture, that it shall be a time of but little religion, when Christ shall come to set up his kingdom in the world. Thus when Christ spake of his coming, to encourage his elect, who cry to him day and night, in Luke xviii. 8. he adds, "Nevertheless, when the Son of man cometh, shall he find faith on the earth?" Which seems to denote a great prevalency of infidelity just before Christ's coming to avenge his suffering church.—Though Christ's coming at the last judgment is not here to be excluded, yet there seems to be a special respect to his coming to deliver his church from their long-continued suffering, persecuted state, which is accomplished only at his coming at the destruction of Antichrist. Then will be accomplished the following passages, Rev. vi. 10. "How long, O Lord, holy and true, dost thou not judge and avenge our blood on them that dwell on the earth?" and Rev. xviii. 20. "Rejoice over her, thou heaven, and ye holy apostles, and prophets, for God hath avenged you on her."

It is *now* a very dark time with respect to the interests of religion, wherein there is but a little faith, and a great prevailing of infidelity on the earth. There is now a remarkable fulfilment of that in 2 Pet. iii. 3. "Knowing this, that there shall come in the last days scoffers, walking after their own lusts." And so Jude 17, 18. "But, beloved, remember ye the words which were spoken before of the apostles of our Lord Jesus Christ; how that they told you there should be mockers in the last time, who should walk after their own ungodly lusts." Whether the times shall be any darker still, or how much darker, before the beginning of this glorious work of God, we cannot tell.

2. There is no reason from the word of God to think any other, than that this great work of God will be wrought, though very swiftly, yet *gradually*. As the children of Israel were *gradually* brought out of the Babylonish captivity, first one company, and then another, and *gradually* rebuilt their city and temple; and as the heathen Roman empire was destroyed by a *gradual*, though a very swift, prevalency of the gospel; so, though there are many things which seem to hold forth that the work of God would be exceeding swift,—and many great and wonderful events should very suddenly be brought to pass, and some great parts of Satan's visible kingdom should have a very sudden fall,—yet all will not be accomplished at once, as by some great miracle, like the resurrection of the dead. But this work will be accomplished by *means*, by the preaching of the gospel, and the use of the ordinary means of grace, and so shall be *gradually* brought to pass. Some shall be converted, and be the means of others' conversion. God's Spirit shall be poured out first to raise up instruments, and then those instruments shall be used with success. And doubtless one nation shall be enlightened and converted, and one false religion and false way of worship exploded, after another. By the representation in Dan. ii. 3, 4. the stone cut out of the mountain without hands *gradually* grows. So Christ teaches us, that the kingdom of heaven is like a grain of mustard seed, Matt. xiii. 31, 32. and like leaven hid in three measures of meal, ver. 33. The same representation we have in Mark iv. 26, 27, 28. and in the vision of the waters of the sanctuary, Ezek. xlvii.—The Scriptures hold forth, that there should be several successive great and glorious events by which this glorious work should be accomplished. The angel speaking to the prophet Daniel of those glorious times, mentions two glorious periods, at the end of which glorious things shall be accomplished: Dan. xii. 11. "And from the time that the daily sacrifice shall be taken away, and the abomination that maketh desolate set up, there shall be a thousand two hundred and ninety days." But then he adds in the next verse, "Blessed is he that waiteth, and cometh to the thousand three hundred and five and thirty days;" intimating, that something very glorious should be accomplished at the end of the former period, but something much more glorious at the end of the latter.

II. I now proceed to show *how* this glorious work shall be accomplished.

1. The Spirit of God shall be gloriously poured out for the wonderful *revival and propagation* of religion. This great work shall be accomplished, not by the authority of princes, nor by the wisdom of learned men, but by God's Holy Spirit: Zech. iv. 6, 7. "Not by might, nor by power, but by my Spirit, saith the Lord of hosts. Who art thou, O great mountain? before Zerubbabel thou shalt become a plain, and he shall bring forth the head-stone thereof with shoutings, crying, Grace, grace unto it." So the prophet Ezekiel, speaking of this great work of God, says, chap. xxxix. 29. "Neither will I hide my face any more from them; for I have poured out my Spirit on the house of Israel, saith the Lord God." We know not where this pouring out of the Spirit shall begin, or whether in many places at once; or whether, what hath already taken place, be not some forerunner and beginning of it.

This pouring out of the Spirit of God, when it is begun, shall soon bring great multitudes to forsake that vice and wickedness which now so generally prevails; and shall cause that vital religion, which is now so despised and laughed at in the world, to revive. The work of conversion shall break forth, and go on in such a manner as never has been hitherto; agreeable to Isa. xliv. 3, 4, 5.——God, by pouring out his Holy Spirit, will furnish men to be glorious instruments of carrying on this work; will fill them with knowledge and wisdom, and fervent zeal for the promoting the kingdom of Christ, and the salvation of souls, and propagating the gospel in the world. The gospel shall begin to be preached with abundantly greater clearness and power than had heretofore been. This great work of God shall be brought to pass by the preaching of the gospel, as is represented in Rev. xiv. 6, 7, 8. that before

Babylon falls, the gospel shall be powerfully preached and propagated in the world.

This was typified of old by the sounding of the silver trumpets in Israel in the beginning of their jubilee: Lev. xxv. 9. "Then shalt thou cause the trumpet of the jubilee to sound on the tenth day of the seventh month; on the day of atonement shall ye make the trumpet sound throughout all your land. The glorious times which are approaching, are the church's jubilee, which shall be introduced by the sounding of the silver trumpet of the gospel, as is foretold in Isa. xxvii. 13. "And it shall come to pass in that day, that the great trumpet shall be blown, and they shall come which were ready to perish in the land of Assyria, and the outcasts of the land of Egypt, and shall worship the Lord in the holy mount at Jerusalem." And there shall be a glorious pouring out of the Spirit with this clear and powerful preaching of the gospel, to make it successful for reviving those holy doctrines of religion which are now chiefly ridiculed in the world, and turning many from heresy, from popery, and from other false religions; and also for turning many from their vice and profaneness, and for bringing vast multitudes savingly home to Christ.

The work of conversion shall go on in a wonderful manner, and spread more and more. Many shall flow together to the goodness of the Lord, one multitude after another continually, as in Isa. lx. 4, 5. "Lift up thine eyes round about, and see; all they gather themselves together, they come to thee; thy sons shall come from far, and thy daughters shall be nursed at thy side. Then thou shalt see and flow together." And so ver. 8. "Who are these that fly as a cloud, and as the doves to their windows?" And as the gospel shall be preached to every tongue, and kindred, and nation, and people, before the fall of Antichrist; so we may suppose, that it will be gloriously successful to bring in multitudes from every nation: and shall spread more and more with wonderful swiftness. (See Isa. lxvi. 7—9.)

2. This pouring out of the Spirit of God will not affect the overthrow of Satan's visible kingdom, till there has first been a violent and *mighty opposition* made. In this the Scripture is plain, that when Christ is thus gloriously coming forth, when the destruction of Antichrist is ready at hand, and Satan's kingdom begins to totter, the powers of the kingdom of darkness will rise up, and mightily exert themselves. Thus after the pouring out of the sixth vial, which was to dry up the river Euphrates, to prepare the way for the destruction of spiritual Babylon, (Rev. xvi.) the powers of hell will be mightily alarmed, and will stir up themselves to oppose the kingdom of Christ, before the seventh vial shall be poured out, which shall give them a final and complete overthrow. The beloved disciple informs us (ver. 13, 14.) that "three unclean spirits like frogs shall go forth unto the kings of the earth, to gather them together to the battle of the great day of God Almighty." This seems to be the last and greatest effort of Satan to save his kingdom from being overthrown; though perhaps he may make as great towards the end of the world to regain it.

When the Spirit begins to be so gloriously poured forth, when the devil sees such multitudes flocking to Christ in one nation and another, when the foundations and pillars of his kingdom are ready to come to swift and sudden destruction, all hell will be greatly alarmed. Satan has ever had a dread of having his kingdom overthrown, and has been doing great works to prevent it, especially since the day of Constantine the Great. To this end he set up those mighty kingdoms of Antichrist and Mahomet, and brought in all the heresies, superstitions, and corrupt opinions in the world. But when he sees all begin to fail, it will rouse him exceedingly. If Satan of old dreaded being cast out of the Roman empire, how much more does he dread being cast out of the whole world!

It seems, in this last great opposition, all the forces of Antichrist, and Mahometanism, and heathenism, will be united; all the forces of Satan's visible kingdom through the whole world of mankind. And therefore it is said, that "spirits of devils shall go forth unto the kings of the earth, and of the whole world, to gather them together to the battle of the great day of God Almighty." And these spirits are said to come out of the mouth of the *dragon*, and out of the mouth of the *beast*, and out of the mouth of the *false prophet*; *i. e.* there shall be the spirit of popery, the spirit of Mahometanism, and the spirit of heathenism all united. By the beast is meant Antichrist; by the dragon, in this book, is commonly meant the devil, as he reigns over his heathen kingdom: by the false prophet, is sometimes meant the pope and his clergy; but here an eye seems to be had to Mahomet, whom his followers call the great prophet of God. This will be as it were the dying struggles of the old serpent; a battle wherein he will fight as one that is almost desperate.

We know not particularly in what manner this opposition shall be made. It is represented as a battle; it is called *the battle of the great day of God Almighty*. There will be some way or other a mighty struggle between Satan's kingdom and the church, and probably in all ways of opposition that can be; and doubtless great opposition by external force. The princes of the world who are on the devil's side shall join hand in hand; for it is said, "The kings of the earth are gathered together to battle," Rev. xix. 19. And probably there will be great opposition by subtle disputers and carnal reasoning, persecution, virulent reproaches, craft, and subtlety. The devil now doubtless will ply his skill, as well as strength, to the utmost; and those who belong to his kingdom, will every where be stirred up, and engaged to make an united violent opposition against this holy religion, which they see prevailing so mightily in the world.——But,

3. Christ and his church shall in this battle obtain a complete and *entire victory* over their enemies. They shall be totally routed and overthrown in this their last effort. When the powers of hell and earth are thus gathered together against Christ, and his armies shall come forth against them by his word and Spirit, in how august and glorious a manner is this advance of Christ with his church described, Rev. xix. 11, &c. And to represent how great the victory they should obtain, and how mighty the overthrow of their enemies, it is said, (ver. 17, 18.) that "all the fowls of heaven are called together, to eat the great supper given them, of the flesh of kings, and captains, and mighty men," &c. and then, in the following verses, we have a distinct account of the victory and overthrow.

In this victory, the seventh vial shall be poured out. It is said, Rev. xvi. 16. of the great army that should be gathered together against Christ: "And he gathered them together into a place called in the Hebrew tongue, *Armageddon*;" then it is said, "And the seventh angel poured out his vial into the air; and there came a great voice out of the temple of heaven, from the throne, saying, It is done." Now the business is done for Satan and his adherents. When this victory is obtained, all is in effect done. Satan's last and greatest opposition is conquered; all his measures are defeated; the pillars of his kingdom broken asunder, and will fall of course. The devil is utterly baffled and confounded, and knows not what else to do. He now sees his antichristian, Mahometan, and heathenish kingdoms through the world, all tumbling down. He and his most powerful instruments are taken captive. Now that is in effect done, for which the church of God had been so long waiting and hoping, and so earnestly crying to God, saying, "How long, O Lord, holy and true?"

The angel who set his right foot on the sea, and his left foot on the earth, lift up his hand to heaven, and swore by *him that liveth for ever and ever*, &c. that when the seventh angel should come to sound, the time should be no longer.—And now the time is come; now the seventh trumpet sounds, and the seventh vial is poured out, both together; intimating, that now all is finished as to the overthrow of Satan's visible kingdom on earth. This victory shall be by far the greatest that ever was obtained over Satan and his adherents. By this blow, with which the stone cut out of the mountain without hands shall strike the image of gold, and silver, and brass, and iron, and clay, it shall all be broken to pieces. This will be a finishing blow to the image, so that it shall become as the chaff of the summer threshing-floor.

In this victory will be a most glorious display of divine power. Christ shall therein appear in the character of

King of kings, and Lord of lords, as in Rev. xix. 16. Now Christ shall dash his enemies, even the strongest and proudest of them, in pieces; as a potter's vessel shall they be broken to shivers.—Then shall strength be shown out of weakness, and Christ shall cause his church to thresh the mountains, as in Isa. xli. 15.—"Behold, I will make thee a new sharp threshing-instrument having teeth: thou shalt thresh the mountains, and beat them small, and shalt make the hills as chaff." And then shall be fulfilled Isa. xlii. 13—15.

III. Consequent on this victory, Satan's visible kingdom on earth shall be *destroyed*. When Satan is conquered in this last battle, the church of Christ will have easy work of it; as when Joshua and the children of Israel had obtained that great victory over the five kings of the Amorites. When God sent great hail-stones on their enemies, they had easy work of subduing the cities and country to which they belonged. So it was also after the other great battle that Joshua had with a great multitude at the waters of Merom. After this glorious victory of Christ and his church over their enemies, the chief powers of Satan's kingdom, they shall destroy that kingdom in all those cities and countries to which they belonged. After this the word of God shall have a speedy and swift progress through the earth; as it is said, that on the pouring out of the seventh vial, "the cities of the nations fell, and every island fled away, and the mountains were not found," Rev. xvi. 19, 20.—When once the stone cut out of the mountain without hands had broken the image in pieces, it was easy to abolish all the remains of it. The very wind will carry it away as the chaff of the summer threshing-floor. Because Satan's visible kingdom on earth shall now be destroyed, therefore it is said, that the seventh vial by which this shall be done, shall be poured out into the air; which is represented in Scripture as the special seat of his kingdom; for he is called "the prince of the power of the air," Eph. ii. 2. Now is come the time for punishing leviathan, that piercing serpent, of which we read in Isa. xxvii. 1. "In that day the Lord with his sore and great and strong sword, shall punish leviathan the piercing serpent, even leviathan, that crooked serpent, and he shall slay the dragon that is in the sea."

Concerning this overthrow of Satan's visible kingdom on earth, I would show wherein it will chiefly consist, with its extent and universality.

1. I would show wherein this overthrow of Satan's kingdom will chiefly consist. I shall mention the particular things in which it will consist, without pretending to determine in what order they shall come to pass, or which shall be accomplished first, or whether they shall be accomplished together.

(1.) *Heresies, infidelity*, and *superstition*, among those who have been brought up under the light of the gospel, will then be abolished; and particularly deism, which is now so bold and *confident in infidelity*, shall be driven away, and vanish to nothing. All shall agree in the same great and important doctrines of the gospel; Zech. xiv. 9. "And the Lord shall be king over all the earth: in that day shall there be one Lord, and his name one." Then shall be abolished all superstitious modes of worship, and all shall cordially agree in worshipping God in his own way: Jer. xxxii. 39. "And I will give them one heart, and one way, that they may fear me for ever, for the good of them, and of their children after them."

(2.) The kingdom of *Antichrist* shall be utterly overthrown. His dominion has been much brought down already by the vial poured out on his throne in the Reformation; but then it shall be utterly destroyed. Then shall be proclaimed, "Babylon is fallen, is fallen." When the seventh angel sounds, "the time, times, and half a time, shall be out; and the time shall be no longer." Then shall be accomplished concerning Antichrist the things which are written (Rev. xviii.) of the spiritual Babylon, the idolatrous Roman government, that has for so many ages been the great enemy of the christian church, first under heathenism, then under popery.—That proud city which lifted herself up to heaven, in her pride and haughtiness; that cruel, bloody city, shall come down to the ground. Then shall that be fulfilled, Isa. xxvi. 5. "For he bringeth down them that dwell on high, the lofty city he layeth it low, he layeth it low, even to the ground, he bringeth it even to the dust." She shall be thrown down with violence, like a great millstone cast into the sea, and shall be found no more at all, and shall become a habitation of devils, and the hold of every foul spirit, and a cage of every unclean and hateful bird. Now shall she be stripped of all her glory, and riches, and ornaments, and shall be cast out as an abominable branch, and shall be trodden down as the mire of the streets. All her policy and craft, in which she so abounded, shall not save her. All the strength and wisdom of this great whore shall fail her, and there shall be none to help her. The kings of the earth, who before gave their power and strength to the beast, shall now hate the whore, and shall make her desolate and naked, and shall eat her flesh, and burn her with fire, Rev. xvii. 16.

(3.) Satan's *Mahometan* kingdom shall be utterly overthrown. The locusts and horsemen in the 9th of Revelation, have their appointed and limited time set them there, and the false prophet shall be taken and destroyed. And then—though Mahometanism has been so vastly propagated in the world, and is upheld by such a great empire—this smoke, which has ascended out of the bottomless pit, shall be utterly scattered before the light of that glorious day, and the Mahometan empire shall fall at the sound of the great trumpet which shall then be blown.

(4.) *Jewish infidelity* shall then be overthrown. However obstinate they have been now for above seventeen hundred years in their rejection of Christ, and however rare have been the instances of individual conversions, ever since the destruction of Jerusalem—but they have, against the plain teachings of their own prophets, continued to approve of the cruelty of their forefathers in crucifying Christ—yet, when this day comes, the thick vail that blinds their eyes shall be removed, 2 Cor. iii. 16. and divine grace shall melt and renew their hard hearts, "and they shall look on him whom they have pierced, and they shall mourn for him as one mourneth for his only son, and shall be in bitterness as one that is in bitterness for his first-born," Zech. xii. 10, &c. And then shall the house of Israel be saved: the Jews in all their dispersions shall cast away their old infidelity, and shall have their hearts wonderfully changed, and abhor themselves for their past unbelief and obstinacy. They shall flow together to the blessed Jesus, penitently, humbly, and joyfully owning him as their glorious King and only Saviour, and shall with all their hearts, as with one heart and voice, declare his praises unto other nations.

Nothing is more certainly foretold than this national conversion of the Jews, in Rom. xi. There are also many passages of the Old Testament which cannot be interpreted in any other sense, which I cannot now stand to mention. Besides the prophecies of the calling of the Jews, we have a remarkable providential seal of the fulfilment of this great event, by a kind of continual miracle, *viz.* their being preserved a distinct nation in such a dispersed condition for above sixteen hundred years. The world affords nothing else like it. There is undoubtedly a remarkable hand of providence in it. When they shall be called, that ancient people, who alone were God's people for so long a time, shall be his people again, never to be rejected more. They shall then be gathered into one fold together with the Gentiles; and so also shall the remains of the ten tribes, wherever they be, and though they have been rejected much longer than the Jews, be brought in with their brethren. The prophecies of Hosea especially seem to hold this forth, that in the future glorious times of the church, both Judah and Ephraim, or Judah and the ten tribes, shall be brought in together, and shall be united as one people, as they formerly were under David and Solomon; (Hos. i. 11, &c.)—Though we do not know the time in which this conversion of Israel will come to pass; yet thus much we may determine by Scripture, that it will be before the glory of the Gentile part of the church shall be fully accomplished; because it is said, that their coming in shall be life from the dead to the Gentiles, (Rom. xi. 12, 15.)

(5.) Then shall also Satan's *heathenish* kingdom be overthrown. Gross heathenism now possesses a great part of the earth, and there are supposed to be more heathens now in the world, than of all other professions taken together. But then the heathen nations shall be enlightened with the glorious gospel. There will be a wonderful spirit of pity towards them, and zeal for their instruction and conversion put into multitudes, and many shall go forth and carry the gospel unto them. Then shall the joyful sound be heard among them, and the Sun of righteousness shall arise with his glorious light shining on those vast regions of the earth that have been covered with heathenish darkness for many thousand years. Many of them doubtless ever since the times of Moses and Abraham, have lain thus in a miserable condition, under the cruel tyranny of the devil, who has all this while blinded and befooled them, domineered over them, and made a prey of them. Now the glad tidings of the gospel shall sound there, and they shall be brought out of darkness into marvellous light.

It is promised, that heathenism shall thus be destroyed in many places. God has said, That the gods that have not made these heavens and this earth, shall perish from the earth, and from under these heavens, Jer. x. 11. and that he will utterly abolish idols, Isa. ii. 18.——Then shall the many nations of Africa, who now seem to be in a state but little above the beasts, and in many respects much below them, be visited with glorious light, and delivered from all their darkness, and shall become a civil, christian, understanding, and holy people.—Then shall the vast continent of America, which now in great part is covered with barbarous ignorance and cruelty, be every where covered with glorious gospel-light and christian love; and instead of worshipping the devil as now they do, they shall serve God, and praises shall be sung every where to the Lord Jesus Christ, the blessed Saviour of the world. So we may expect it will be in that great and populous part of the world, the East Indies, which are now mostly inhabited by the worshippers of the devil. Then the kingdom of Christ will be established in those continents which have been more lately discovered towards the north and south poles, where men differ very little from the wild beasts, except in impiety. The same will be the case with respect to those countries which have never yet been discovered. Thus will be gloriously fulfilled Isa. xxxv. 1. "The wilderness and the solitary place shall be glad for them: and the desert shall rejoice, and blossom as the rose." (See also ver. 6, 7.)

2. Having thus shown wherein this overthrow of Satan's kingdom will consist, I come now to observe its *universal extent*. The visible kingdom of Satan shall be overthrown, and the kingdom of Christ set up on the ruins of it, every where throughout the whole habitable globe. Now shall the promise made to Abraham be fulfilled, That in him and in his seed *all the families of the earth shall be blessed;* and Christ now shall become *the desire of all nations*, agreeable to Haggai ii. 7.—Now the kingdom of Christ shall in the most strict and literal sense be extended to all nations, and the whole earth. There are many passages of Scripture that can be understood in no other sense. What can be more universal than Isa. xi. 9. "For the earth shall be full of the knowledge of the Lord, as the waters cover the sea." As much as to say, As there is no part of the channel or cavity of the sea, but what is covered with water; so there shall be no part of the world of mankind but what shall be covered with the knowledge of God. So it is foretold in Isa. xlv. 22. that *all the ends of the earth* shall look to Christ, and be saved. And to show that the words are to be understood in the most universal sense, it is said in the next verse, "I have sworn by myself, the word is gone out of my mouth in righteousness, and shall not return, that unto me every knee shall bow, every tongue shall swear."—So the most universal expression is used, Dan. vii. 27. "And the kingdom and dominion, and the greatness of the kingdom under the whole heaven, shall be given to the people of the saints of the most high God."

When the devil was cast out of the Roman empire, because that was the highest and principal part of the world, and the other nations that were left were low and mean in comparison, it was represented as Satan's being cast out of heaven to the earth, Rev. xii. 9.; but it is represented that he shall be cast out of the earth too, and shut up in hell, Rev. xx. 1, 2, 3.—This is the greatest revolution by far that ever came to pass: therefore it is said in Rev. xvi. 17, 18. that on the pouring out of the seventh vial, "there was a great earthquake, such as was not since men were upon earth, so mighty an earthquake and so great." And this is the third great dispensation of Providence which is in Scripture compared to Christ's coming to judgment, Rev. xvi. 15. There, after the sixth vial, and after the devil's armies were gathered together to their great battle, and just before Christ's glorious victory over them, it is said, "Behold I come quickly; blessed is he that watcheth, and keepeth his garments." So it is called *Christ's coming*, 2 Thess. ii. 8. Speaking of Antichrist it is said, "And then shall that Wicked be revealed, whom the Lord shall consume with the spirit of his mouth, and shall destroy with the brightness of his coming." See also Dan. vii. 13, 14. where Christ's coming to set up his kingdom on earth, and to destroy Antichrist, is called *coming with clouds of heaven*. And this is more like Christ's last coming to judgment, than any of the preceding dispensations which are so called. The dispensation is so much greater and more universal, and so more like the day of judgment, which respects the whole world. The great spiritual resurrection of the church of God accompanying it, resembles the general resurrection at the end of the world more than any other. (See Rev. xx. 4.)

Terrible judgments and fearful destruction shall now be executed on God's enemies. There will doubtless at the introducing of this dispensation be a visible and awful hand of God against blasphemers, deists, obstinate heretics, and other enemies of Christ, terribly destroying them, with remarkable tokens of wrath and vengeance. More especially will this dispensation be attended with terrible judgments on Antichrist; the cruel persecutors who belong to the church of Rome, shall in a most awful manner be destroyed; which is compared to a casting of Antichrist into the burning flame, Dan. vii. 11. and to casting him alive into the lake that burns with fire and brimstone, Rev. xix. 20.

Then shall this cruel persecuting church suffer those judgments from God, which shall be far more dreadful than her persecutions of the saints, agreeable to Rev. xviii. 6, 7.——The judgments which God shall execute on the enemies of the church, are so great, that they are compared to God's sending great hail-stones from heaven upon them, every one of the weight of a talent, as it is said on the pouring out of the seventh vial, Rev. xvi. 21. "And there fell upon men a great hail out of heaven, every stone about the weight of a talent: and men blasphemed God, because of the plague of the hail; for the plague thereof was exceeding great." And now shall be that treading of the wine-press spoken of, Rev. xiv. 19, 20.

This shall put an end to the church's suffering state, and shall be attended with their glorious and joyful praises. The church's afflicted state has been continued, excepting some short intermissions, from the resurrection of Christ to this time; but now shall a final end be put to her suffering state. Indeed after this, near the end of the world, the church shall be greatly threatened; but it is said, it shall be but for *a little season*, Rev. xx. 3. for as the times of the church's rest have been but short, before the long day of her afflictions are at an end; so whatever affliction she may suffer after this, will be very short. In every other respect, the day of the church's afflictions and persecution shall now come to a final end. The Scriptures, in many places, speak of this time as the end of the suffering state of the church. So Isa. li. 22. "Behold, I have taken out of thine hand the cup of trembling, even the dregs of the cup of my fury, thou shalt no more drink it again." Then shall be proclaimed to the church, Isa. xl. 1, 2. "Comfort ye, comfort ye my people, saith your God. Speak ye comfortably to Jerusalem, and cry unto her, that her warfare is accomplished, that her iniquity is pardoned: for she hath received of the Lord's hand double for all her sins." Also Isa. liv. 8, 9. and lx. 20. belong to this time. "The Lord shall be thine everlasting light, and the days of thy mourning shall be ended." And so Zeph. iii. 15. "The Lord hath taken away thy judgments, he hath cast out thine enemy: the King of

Israel, even the Lord, is in the midst of thee: thou shalt not see evil any more."

The time before this, had been the church's sowing-time, wherein she sowed in tears and in blood; but now is her harvest, wherein she will come again rejoicing, bringing her sheaves with her. Now the time of travail of the woman clothed with the sun is at an end; now she hath brought forth her son: for this glorious setting up of the kingdom of Christ through the world, is what the church had been in travail for, with such terrible pangs, for so many ages: Isa. xxvi. 17.—"Like as a woman with child that draweth near the time of her delivery, is in pain, and crieth out in her pangs; so have we been in thy sight, O Lord." (See Isa. lx. 20. and lxi. 10, 11.) And now the church shall forget her sorrow, since a man-child is born into the world: now succeed her joyful praise and triumph. Her praises shall then go up to God from all parts of the earth; (as Isa. xlii. 10—12.) and praise shall not only fill the earth, but also heaven. The church on earth, and the church in heaven, shall both gloriously rejoice and praise God, as with one heart, on that occasion. Without doubt it will be a time of very distinguished joy and praise among the holy prophets and apostles, and the other saints in heaven: Rev. xviii. 20. "Rejoice over her, thou heaven, and ye holy apostles and prophets, for God hath avenged you on her." See how universal these praises will be in Isa. xliv. 23. "Sing, O ye heavens, for the Lord hath done it: shout, ye lower parts of the earth: break forth into singing, ye mountains, O forest, and every tree therein: for the Lord hath redeemed Jacob, and glorified himself in Israel." See what joyful praises are sung to God on this occasion by the universal church in heaven and earth, in the beginning of the 19th chapter of Revelation.

This dispensation is above all preceding ones like Christ's coming to judgment, in that it so puts an end to the former state of the world, and introduces the everlasting kingdom of Christ. Now Satan's visible kingdom shall be overthrown, after it had stood ever since the building of Babel; the old heavens and the old earth shall in a greater measure pass away, and the new heavens and new earth be set up in a far more glorious manner, than ever before.—Thus I have shown how the success of Christ's purchase has been carried on through the times of the afflicted state of the christian church, from Christ's resurrection till Antichrist is fallen, and Satan's visible kingdom on earth is overthrown.

PART VIII.

THE SUCCESS OF REDEMPTION THROUGH THAT SPACE WHEREIN THE CHRISTIAN CHURCH SHALL, FOR THE MOST PART, BE IN A STATE OF PEACE AND PROSPERITY.

In order to describe this part, I would speak, *first*, of the prosperous state of the church through the greatest part of this period; and, *secondly*, of the great apostacy there shall be towards the close of it.

I. I would speak of the *prosperous state* of he church through the greater part of this period. And in the general, I would observe two things,

1. That this is most properly the time of the kingdom of *heaven upon earth*. Though the kingdom of heaven was in a degree set up soon after Christ's resurrection, and in a further degree in the time of Constantine; and though the christian church in all ages of it is called *the kingdom of heaven;* yet this is the principal time of the kingdom of heaven upon earth, the time principally intended by the prophecies of Daniel whence the Jews took the name of *the kingdom of heaven.*

2. Now is the principal fulfilment of all the prophecies of the Old Testament which speak of the glorious times of the gospel in the latter days. Though there has been a glorious fulfilment of those prophecies already, in the times of the apostles, and of Constantine; yet the expressions are too high to suit any other time entirely, but that which is to succeed the fall of Antichrist. This is most properly the glorious day of the gospel. Other times are only forerunners and preparatory to this: those were the seed-time, but this is the harvest. But more particularly,

(1.) It will be a time of great light and *knowledge.* The present, are days of darkness, in comparison of those days.—The light of that glorious time shall be so great, that it is represented as though there should then be no night, but only day; no evening nor darkness. So Zech. xiv. 6, 7. "And it shall come to pass in that day, that the light shall not be clear, nor dark. But it shall be one day, which shall be known to the Lord, not day, nor night; but it shall come to pass, that at evening-time it shall be light."—It is further represented, as though God would then give such light to his church, that it should so much exceed the glory of the light of the sun and moon, that they should be ashamed: Isa. xxiv. 23. "Then the moon shall be confounded, and the sun ashamed, when the Lord of hosts shall reign in mount Zion, and in Jerusalem, and before his ancients gloriously."

There is a kind of vail now cast over the greater part of the world, which keeps them in darkness; but then this vail shall be destroyed: Isa. xxv. 7. "And he will destroy in this mountain the face of the covering cast over all people, and the vail that is spread over all nations." Then all countries and nations, even those which are now most ignorant, shall be full of light and knowledge. Great knowledge shall prevail every where. It may be hoped, that then many of the Negroes and Indians will be divines, and that excellent books will be published in Africa, in Ethiopia, in Tartary, and other now the most barbarous countries; and not only learned men, but others of more ordinary education, shall then be very knowing in religion: Isa. xxxii. 3, 4. "The eyes of them that see, shall not be dim; and the ears of them that hear, shall hearken. The heart also of the rash shall understand knowledge." Knowledge then shall be very universal among all sorts of persons; Jer. xxxi. 34. "And they shall teach no more every man his neighbour, and every man his brother, saying, Know the Lord: for they shall all know me, from the least of them unto the greatest of them."

There shall then be a wonderful unravelling of the difficulties in the doctrines of religion, and clearing up of seeming inconsistencies: "So crooked things shall be made straight, and rough places shall be made plain, and darkness shall become light before God's people." Difficulties in Scripture shall then be cleared up, and wonderful things shall be discovered in the word of God, which were never discovered before. The great discovery of those things in religion which had been before kept hid, seems to be compared to removing the vail, and discovering the ark of the testimony to the people, which before used to be kept in the secret part of the temple, and was never seen by them. Thus at the sounding of the seventh angel, when it is proclaimed, "that the kingdoms of this world are become the kingdoms of our Lord and of his Christ," it is added, that "the temple of God was opened in heaven, and there was seen in his temple the ark of his testament." So great shall be the increase of knowledge in this time, that heaven shall be as it were opened to the church of God on earth.

(2.) It shall be a time of great *holiness.* Now vital religion shall every where prevail and reign. Religion shall not be an empty profession, as it now mostly is, but holiness of heart and life shall abundantly prevail. Those times shall be an exception from what Christ says of the ordinary state of the church, *viz.* that there shall be *but few saved;* for now holiness shall become general: Isa. lx. 21. "Thy people also shall be all righteous." Not that there will be none remaining in a Christless condition; but that visible wickedness shall be suppressed every where, and true holiness shall become general, though not universal. It shall be a wonderful time, not only for the multitude of godly men, but for eminency of grace: Isa. lxv. 20. "There shall be no more thence an infant of days, nor an old man that hath not filled his days: for the child shall die an hundred years old, but the sinner being an hundred years old, shall be accursed." Zech. xii. 8. "He that is feeble among them at that day shall be as David; and the house of David shall be as God, as the angel of the Lord before them." And holiness shall then be as it were inscribed on every thing, on all men's common business and employments, and the common utensils of life: all shall be dedicated to God, and applied to holy purposes: every thing shall then be done to the glory of God: Isa. xxiii. 18. "And her merchandise and her hire shall be holiness to the Lord." (And so Zech. xiv. 20, 21.)—And as God's people then shall be eminent in holiness of heart, so they shall be also in holiness of life and practice.

(3.) It shall be a time wherein *religion* shall in every respect be *uppermost* in the world. It shall be had in great esteem and honour. The saints have hitherto for the most part been kept under, and wicked men have governed. But now they will be uppermost. The kingdom shall be given into the hands of the saints of the "most high God," Dan. vii. 27. And "they shall reign on earth," Rev. v. 10. They shall live and "reign with Christ a thousand years," Rev. xx. 4. In that day, such persons as are eminent for true piety and religion, shall be chiefly promoted to places of trust and authority. Vital religion shall then take possession of kings' palaces and thrones; and those who are in highest advancement shall be holy men: Isa. xlix. 23. "And kings shall be thy nursing-fathers, and their queens thy nursing-mothers." Kings shall employ all their power, and glory, and riches, for the advancement of the honour and glory of Christ, and the good of his church: Isa. lx. 16. "Thou shalt also suck the milk of the Gentiles, and shalt suck the breasts of kings." And the great men of the world, and the rich merchants, and others who have great wealth and influence, shall devote all to Christ and his church: Psal. xlv. 12. "The daughter of Tyre shall be there with a gift, even the rich among the people shall entreat thy favour."

(4.) Those will be times of *great peace and love.* There shall then be universal peace and a good understanding among the nations of the world, instead of confusion, wars, and bloodshed. Isa. ii. 4. "And he shall judge among the nations, and shall rebuke many people: and they shall beat their swords into plough-shares, and their spears into pruning-hooks: nation shall not lift up sword against nation, neither shall they learn war any more." It is represented as if all instruments of war should be destroyed, having become useless: Psal. xlvi. 9. "He maketh wars to cease unto the end of the earth: he breaketh the bow, and cutteth the spear in sunder, he burneth the chariot in the fire." (See also Zech. ix. 10.) Then shall all nations dwell quietly and safely, without fear of any enemy. Isa. xxxii. 18. "And my people shall dwell in a peaceable habitation, and in sure dwellings, and in quiet resting-places." (Also Zech. viii. 10, 11.)

Then shall malice, and envy, and wrath, and revenge, be suppressed every where; and peace and love shall prevail between one man and another; which is most elegantly set forth in Isa. xi. 6—10. Then shall there be peace and love between rulers and ruled. Rulers shall love their people, and with all their might seek their best good; and the people shall love their rulers, shall joyfully submit to them, and give them that honour which is their due. So shall there be happy love between ministers and their people: Mal. iv. 6. "And he shall turn the heart of the fathers to the children, and the heart of the children to their fathers." Then shall flourish in an eminent manner those christian virtues of meekness, forgiveness, long-suffering, gentleness, goodness, and brotherly-kindness, those excellent fruits of the Spirit. Men, in their temper and disposition, shall then be like the Lamb of God, the lovely Jesus. The body shall be conformed to the head.

Then shall all the world be united in one amiable society. All nations, in all parts of the world, on every side of the globe, shall then be knit together in sweet harmony. All parts of God's church shall assist and promote the spiritual good of one another. A communication shall then be upheld between all parts of the world to that end; and the art of navigation, which is now applied so much to favour men's covetousness and pride, and is used so much by wicked debauched men, shall then be consecrated to God, and applied to holy uses. (See Isa. lx. 5—9.) And then men will be abundant in expressing their love one to another, not only in words, but in deeds of charity, Isa. xxxii. 5. "The vile person shall be no more called liberal, nor the churl said to be bountiful;" but (ver. 8.) "the liberal deviseth liberal things, and by liberal things shall he stand."

(5.) It will be a time of *excellent order* in the church of Christ. The true government and discipline of the church will then be settled and put into practice. All the world shall then be as one church, one orderly, regular, beautiful society. And as the body shall be one, so the members shall be in beautiful proportion to each other. Then shall that be verified in Psal. cxxii. 3. "Jerusalem is builded as a city that is compact together."

(6.) The church of God shall then be *beautiful and glorious* on these accounts; yea, it will appear in the perfection of beauty: Isa. lx. 1. "Arise, shine, for thy light is come, and the glory of the Lord is risen upon thee." Isa. lxi. 10. "He hath covered me with the robe of righteousness, as a bridegroom decketh himself with ornaments, and as a bride adorneth herself with her jewels." On these accounts, the church will then be the greatest image of heaven itself.

(7.) That will be a time of the greatest *temporal prosperity.* Such a spiritual state as we have just described, has a natural tendency to health and long life; and that this will actually be the case, is evident by Zech. viii. 4. "Thus saith the Lord of hosts, There shall yet old men and old women dwell in the streets of Jerusalem, and every man with his staff in his hand for very age." It has also a natural tendency to procure ease, quietness, pleasantness, and cheerfulness of mind, also wealth, and a great increase of children; as is intimated in Zech. viii. 5. "And the streets of the city shall be full of boys and girls playing in the streets thereof."——But further, the temporal prosperity of the people of God will also be promoted by a remarkable blessing from heaven: Isa. lxv. 21. "They shall build houses, and inhabit them; and they shall plant vineyards, and eat the fruit of them." And in Mic. iv. 4. "But they shall sit every man under his vine, and under his fig-tree, and none shall make them afraid." Zech. vii. 12. "For the seed shall be prosperous, the vine shall give her fruit, and the ground shall give her increase, and the heavens shall give their dew, and I will cause the remnant of this people to possess all these things." (See also Jer. xxxi. 12, 13. and Amos ix. 13.) Yea then they shall receive all manner of tokens of God's presence, acceptance, and favour: Jer. xxxiii. 9. "And it shall be to me a name of joy, a praise and an honour before all the nations of the earth, which shall hear all the good that I do unto them: and they shall fear and tremble for all the goodness and for all the prosperity that I procure unto it." Even the days of Solomon were but an image of those days, as to the temporal prosperity which shall be obtained in them.

(8.) It will also be a time of great rejoicing: Isa. xxxv. 10. "And the ransomed of the Lord shall return and come to Zion with songs, and everlasting joy upon their heads: they shall obtain joy and gladness, and sorrow and sighing shall flee away." Chap. lv. 12. "For ye shall go out with joy, and be led forth with peace: the mountains and the hills shall break forth before you." Chap. lxvi. 11. "That ye may suck, and be satisfied with the breasts of her consolations: that ye may milk out, and be delighted with the abundance of her glory." Chap. xii. 3. "With joy shall ye draw water out of the wells of salvation." That will be the church's glorious wedding-day with Christ upon earth: Rev. xix. 7. "Let us be glad and rejoice, and give honour to him; for the marriage of the Lamb is come, and his wife hath made herself ready." Ver. 9. "Blessed are they which are called to the marriage-supper of the Lamb."

The Scriptures every where represent this prosperity to be of long continuance. The former intervals of rest and prosperity, as we before observed, are represented to be but short; but the representations of this state are quite different: Rev. xx. 4. "And I saw the souls of them that were beheaded for the witness of Jesus,—and they lived and reigned with Christ *a thousand years.*" Isa. lx. 15. "Whereas thou hast been forsaken and hated, so that no man went through thee, I will make thee an eternal excellency, a joy of *many generations.*"—This may suffice as to the prosperous state of the church through the greater part of the period from the destruction of Satan's visible kingdom in the world to Christ's appearing in the clouds of heaven to judgment.

II. I now come to speak of the *great apostacy* there should be towards the close of this period, and how the church should, for a short time, be threatened by her enemies. And this I shall do under three particulars.

1. A little before the end of the world, a *great part of the world* shall fall away from Christ and his church. It is said, Rev. xx. 3. that Satan should be cast into the bottomless pit, and shut up, and have a seal set upon him, that he should deceive the nations no more *till the thousand years should be fulfilled;* and that afterward he must be loosed out of his prison for a little season. Accordingly we are told, (ver. 7, 8.) that when the thousand years are expired, Satan shall be loosed out of his prison, and go forth to deceive the nations, which are in the four quarters of the earth, Gog and Magog. This intimates, that the apostacy would be very general. The nations of the four quarters of the earth shall be deceived; and the number of those who shall now turn enemies to Christ shall be vastly great, as the army of Gog and Magog is represented in Ezek. It is said, (Rev. xx. 8.) that the number of them is as the sand of the sea, and that they went up on the breadth of the earth, as if they were an army large enough to reach from one side of the earth to the other.

Thus after a happy and glorious season, such a long day of light and holiness, of love and peace, and joy, it shall again be a dark time. Satan shall begin to set up his dominion again in the world; and this world shall again become a scene of darkness and wickedness. The bottomless pit shall be opened, and devils shall come up again out of it, and a dreadful smoke shall ascend to darken the world. And the church of Christ, instead of extending to the utmost bounds of the world, as it did before, shall be reduced to narrow limits. The world of mankind being continued so long in a state of great prosperity shall now begin to abuse their prosperity, to serve their lust and corruption. This we learn from Luke xvii. 26, &c.

2. Those apostates shall make *great opposition* to the church of God. The church shall be threatened with a sudden and entire overthrow by them. It is said, Satan shall gather them together to battle, as the sand on the seashore; and they went up on the breadth of the earth, and compassed the camp of the saints about, and the beloved city. So that this beloved city shall seem just ready to be swallowed up by them: for her enemies shall not only threaten her, but shall actually have gathered together against her; and not only so, but shall have besieged her, shall have compassed her about on every side.—However, there is nothing in the prophecy which seems to hold forth, that the church had actually fallen into their hands, as it had fallen into the hands of Antichrist, to whom it was given to make war with the saints, and to overcome them. God will never suffer this to take place after the fall of Antichrist; for then the day of her mourning shall be ended, alarmingly threatened with utter and sudden destruction.

3. Now the state of things will seem most remarkably to call for Christ's immediate appearance to *judgment.* For then the world shall be filled with the most aggravated wickedness. For much the greater part of the world shall have become visibly wicked and open enemies to Christ, and their wickedness shall be dreadfully aggravated by their apostacy. Before the fall of Antichrist, most of the world was full of visibly wicked men. But the greater part of these are poor heathens, who never enjoyed the light of the gospel; and others are those that have been bred up in the Mahometan or popish darkness. But these have apostatized from the christian church, the visible kingdom of Christ, in which they enjoyed the great light and privileges of glorious times, which shall be incomparably greater than the light and privileges which the church of God enjoys now. This apostacy will be most like the apostacy of the devils of any that ever had before been: for the devils apostatized, and turned enemies to Christ, though they enjoyed the light of heaven; and these will apostatize, and turn enemies to him, though they have enjoyed the light and privileges of the glorious times of the church. That such should turn open and avowed enemies to Christ, and should seek the ruin of his church, will cry aloud for such immediate vengeance as was executed on the devils when they fell.

The wickedness of the world will remarkably call for Christ's immediate appearing in flaming fire to take vengeance on them, because of the way in which they shall manifest their wickedness. This will be by scoffing and blaspheming Christ and his holy religion; and particularly, they will scoff at the notion of Christ's coming to judgment, of which the church shall be in expectation. For now doubtless will be the greatest fulfilment of 2 Pet. iii. 3, 4. "Knowing this first, that there shall come in the last days scoffers, walking after their own lusts, and saying, Where is the promise of his coming? For since the fathers fell asleep, all things continue as they were from the beginning of the creation." They shall be in no expectation of the coming of Christ to judgment, and shall laugh at the notion. They shall trample all such things under foot, and shall give up themselves to their lusts, or to eat and drink, and wallow in sensual delights, as though they were to be here for ever. They shall despise the warnings the church shall give them of the coming of Christ to judgment, as the people of the old world despised what Noah told them of the approaching flood, and as the people of Sodom did when Lot said to them, *The Lord will destroy this city.* Their wickedness on this account will cry aloud to heaven for Christ's appearing in flaming fire to take vengeance of his enemies; and because they shall exercise their wickedness in a wicked design and violent attempt against the holy city of God, wherein, for so long a time, so much of the religion of Christ had been seen.

And the great number of the wicked is another thing which shall especially call for Christ's coming: for the world then will doubtless be exceeding full of people, having continued so long in so great a state of prosperity, without such terrible desolating extremities, as wars, pestilences, and the like, to diminish them. And the major part of this world, which shall be so populous, will be wicked contemptuous apostates from God. Undoubtedly the world then will be by far fuller of wickedness than ever it was before, from its foundation. And if the wickedness of the old world, when men began to multiply on the earth, called for the destruction of the world by a deluge of *water,* this wickedness will as much call for its destruction by a deluge of *fire.*

Again, the circumstances of the church at that day will also eminently call for the immediate appearing of Christ, as they will be compassed about by their blasphemous murderous enemies, just ready to be swallowed up by them. And it will be a most distressing time with the church, excepting the comfort they will have in the hope of deliverance from God: for all other help will seem to fail. The case will be come to the last extremity, and there will be an immediate need that Christ should come to their deliverance. And though the church shall be so eminently threatened, yet so will Providence order it, that it shall be preserved till Christ shall appear in his immediate presence, coming in the glory of his Father with all his holy angels. And then will come the time when all the elect shall be gathered in. That work of conversion which has been carried on from the beginning of the church after the fall through all those ages, shall be carried on no more. There never shall another soul be converted. Every one of those many millions, whose names were written in the book of life before the foundation of the world, shall be brought in; not one soul shall be lost. And the mystical body of Christ, which has been growing since it first began in the days of Adam, will be complete as to the number of parts, having every one of its members. In this respect, the work of redemption will now be finished. And now the end for which the means of grace have been instituted shall be obtained.—All that effect which was intended, shall now be accomplished.

PART IX.

THE GENERAL JUDGMENT.

Thus I have shown how the success of Christ's redemption has been accomplished during the continuance of the christian church under the means of grace. We have seen what great revolutions there have been, and are to be, during this space of time; how the great wheels of Providence have gone round for the accomplishment of that kind of success of Christ's purchase, which consists in the bestowment of grace on the elect. In the prosecution of the subject, we are come to the time when all the wheels have gone round; the course of things in this state of it is finished, and all things are ripe for Christ's coming to judgment.

The success of Christ's purchase is of two kinds, consisting either in grace or glory. The success consisting in the former of these, is to be seen in those works of God which are wrought during those ages that the church is continued under the means of grace; and the success, consisting in the latter, will chiefly be accomplished at the day of judgment.—Having already shown how the *former* kind of success has been accomplished, I come now to the *latter, viz.* that kind of success which is accomplished in the bestowment of *glory* on the church at the day of judgment.——And here I would mention two or three things in *general*, concerning this kind of success of Christ's purchase.

1. How *great* the success of Christ's purchase is, appears chiefly in this very thing. The success of Christ's purchase summarily consists in the *salvation* of the elect. But this bestowment of *glory* is eminently called *their salvation*: Heb. ix. 28. " To them that look for him, shall he appear the second time, without sin unto salvation."—So it is called *redemption*, being eminently that wherein the redemption of the church consists. So in Eph. iv. 30. " Sealed unto the day of redemption ;" and Luke xxi. 28. and Eph. i. 14. " Redemption of the purchased possession."

2. All that precedes this, while the church is under the means of grace, is only to make way for the success which is to be accomplished in the bestowment of glory. The *means* of grace, and God's *grace* itself, is bestowed on the elect to make them meet for glory.

3. All those glorious things which were brought to pass for the church while under the means of grace, are but images and shadows of this. So were those glorious things which were accomplished for the church in the days of Constantine the Great; and so is all that glory which is to succeed the fall of Antichrist. However great, it is all but a shadow of what will be bestowed at the day of judgment. But I hasten more particularly to show how this kind of success will be accomplished.

I. Christ will appear in the glory of his Father, with all his holy angels, coming in the clouds of heaven. When the world is thus revelling in their wickedness, and compassing the holy city, just ready to destroy it, then shall the glorious Redeemer make his appearance. He through whom this redemption has all along been carried on, shall appear in the sight of the world; the light of his glory shall break forth; the whole world shall immediately have notice of it, and they shall lift up their eyes and behold this wonderful sight. *Every eye shall see him*, (Rev. i. 7.) Christ shall appear coming in his human nature, in that same body (now glorified) which was brought forth in a stable, and laid in a manger, which afterwards was so cruelly used, and nailed to the cross.

Men shall now lift up their eyes, and see him coming in such majesty and glory as now is to us utterly inconceivable. The glory of the sun in a clear firmament, will be but darkness in comparison of it; and all the glorious angels and archangels shall attend him; thousand thousands ministering to him, and ten thousand times ten thousand round about him.—How different a person will he then appear from what he did at his first coming, when he was as a root out of a dry ground, a poor, despised, afflicted man! How different now is his appearance, in the midst of those glorious angels, principalities, and powers, in heavenly places, attending him as his ordinary servants, from what it was when in the midst of a ring of soldiers, with his mock robe and his crown of thorns, buffeted and spit upon, or hanging on the cross between two thieves, with a multitude of his enemies triumphing over him!

This will be a most unexpected sight to the wicked world: it will come as a cry at midnight: they shall be taken in the midst of their wickedness, and it will give them a dreadful alarm. It will at once break up their revels, their eating, and drinking, and carousing. It will put a quick end to the design of the great army that will then be compassing the camp of the saints: it will make them let drop their weapons out of their hands. The world, which will then be very full of people, most of whom will be wicked men, will then be filled with dolorous shrieking and crying; for all the kindreds of the earth shall wail because of him, (Rev. i. 7.) And where shall they hide themselves? How will the sight of that awful majesty terrify them when taken in the midst of their wickedness! Then they shall see who he is, what kind of a person he is, whom they have mocked and scoffed at, and whose church they have been endeavouring to overthrow. This sight will change their voice. The voice of their laughter and singing, while they are marrying and giving in marriage, and the voice of their scoffing, shall be changed into hideous, hellish yelling. Their countenances shall be changed from a show of carnal mirth, haughty pride, and contempt of God's people; they shall put on ghastly terror and amazement; and trembling and chattering of teeth shall seize upon them.

But with respect to the saints, it shall be a joyful and most glorious sight to them: for this sight will at once deliver them from all fear of their enemies, who were before compassing them about, just ready to swallow them up. Deliverance shall come in their extremity: the glorious Captain of their salvation shall appear for them, at a time when no other help appeared. Then shall they lift up their heads, and their redemption shall be drawing nigh, (Luke xxi. 28.) Christ will appear with infinite majesty, yet at the same time they shall see infinite love in his countenance. And thus to see their Redeemer coming in the clouds of heaven, will fill their hearts full of gladness. Their countenances also shall be changed, not as the countenances of the wicked, but from being sorrowful, to be exceedingly joyful and triumphant. And now the work of redemption will be finished in another sense, *viz.* that the whole church shall be completely and eternally freed from all persecution and molestation from wicked men and devils.

II. The last trumpet shall sound, and the dead shall be raised, and the living changed. God sent forth his angels with a great sound of a trumpet, to gather together his elect from the four corners of the earth in a mystical sense, before the destruction of Jerusalem; *i. e.* he sent forth the apostles, and others, to preach the gospel all over the world. And so in a mystical sense the great trumpet was blown at the beginning of the glorious times of the church. But now the great trumpet is blown in a more literal sense, with a mighty sound which shakes the earth. There will be a great signal given by a mighty sound made, which is called *the voice of the archangel*, as being the angel of greatest strength, 1 Thess. iv. 16. " For the Lord himself shall descend from heaven with a shout, with the voice of the archangel, and with the trump of God." On the sound of the great trumpet, the dead shall be raised every where. Now the number of the dead is very great. How many has death cut down since the world has stood. But then the number will be much greater, the world shall have stood longer, and through most of the remaining time it will doubtless be much fuller of inhabitants than ever it has been. All these shall now rise from the dead. The graves shall be opened in all parts of the world, and the sea shall give up the innumerable dead that are in it, (Rev. xx. 13.)

And now all the inhabitants that ever shall have been upon the face of the earth, shall all appear upon earth at once. Among these will be Adam and Eve, the first parents of mankind, Abel, and Seth, and Methuselah, and all the saints who were their contemporaries; Noah and Abraham, Isaac and Jacob, the prophets of Israel and holy confessors. Among them will appear all the holy apostles of Jesus Christ, and all the saints of their times; all the holy martyrs who fell under furious persecutions. There will be found all who belonged to the church in its wilderness-state, during the dark times of Antichrist, and all who have suffered under his persecuting cruelty, with all the saints of past and the present time, and that shall be to the end of the world.—Now also all the enemies of the church in all the ages shall appear again; all the wicked heathens, and Jews, and Mahometans, and papists. Sinners of all sorts; demure hypocrites, profane sensualists, heretics, deists, and all cruel persecutors, and all who shall have died in sin, shall come together.

And at the same time that the dead are raised, the living shall be changed. The bodies of the wicked who shall then be living, shall be so changed as to fit them for eternal torment; and the bodies of all the living saints shall be changed to be like unto Christ's glorious body, 1 Cor. xv. 51, 52, 53.——The bodies of the saints shall be so changed as to render them for ever incapable of pain, or affliction, or uneasiness; and all that dulness and heaviness, and all that deformity, which their bodies had before, shall be put off; and they shall put on strength and beauty, activity, and incorruptible unfading glory. And in such glory shall the bodies of all the risen saints appear.

And now the work of redemption shall be finished in another respect, *viz.* that all the elect shall now be actually redeemed both in soul and body. Before this, the work of redemption, as to its actual success, was but incomplete; for only the *souls* of the redeemed were actually saved and glorified, excepting in some few instances: but now all the *bodies* of the saints shall be saved and glorified together; all the elect shall be glorified in the whole man, the soul and body in union.

III. Now shall the saints be caught up in the clouds to meet the Lord in the air, and all wicked men and devils shall be arraigned before the judgment-seat. When the dead saints are raised, then the whole church, consisting of all the elect through all ages, will stand together on the earth, at least all excepting those few whose bodies were glorified before; and then they shall all mount up as with wings to meet Christ. It seems that Christ, when he comes to judgment, will not come quite to the ground, but his throne will be fixed in the airy region, whence he may be seen by all that vast multitude that shall be gathered before him. The saints therefore shall ascend up to their Saviour. Thus the apostle tells us, that when the dead in Christ are raised, and the living changed, then those who are alive and remain, shall be caught up together with them, to meet the Lord in the air, and so shall we be ever with the Lord, 1 Thess. iv. 16, 17. What a wonderful sight will that be, when all the many millions of saints are thus mounting up.

Then shall the work of redemption be finished in another respect: then shall the whole church be perfectly and for ever delivered from this present evil world; shall take their everlasting leave of this earth, where they have been strangers, and which has been for the most part a scene of trouble and sorrow: where the devil has reigned as god, and has greatly molested them, and which has been such a scene of wickedness and abomination, where Christ their Lord has been cruelly used; and where they have been so hated, reproached, and persecuted. They shall leave it, and shall never set foot on it again. And there shall be an everlasting separation made between them and wicked men. Before, they were mixed together, and it was impossible in many instances to determine their characters; but now all shall become visible; both saints and sinners shall appear in their true characters and forms.—Then shall all the church be seen ascending to the right hand of Christ. What a mighty cloud of them will there be!

And then also the work of redemption will be finished in another respect, *viz.* that then the church shall all be gathered together. They all belonged to one society before, but yet were greatly separated with respect to the place of their habitation. Some were in heaven, and some on earth; and those who were on earth were separated, many of them by wide oceans, and vast continents. But now they shall all be gathered together, never to be separated any more. And not only shall all the members of the church now be gathered together, but all shall be gathered unto their Head, into his immediate glorious presence, never to be separated from him any more.

At the same time, all wicked men and devils shall be brought before the judgment-seat of Christ. These shall be gathered to the left hand of Christ, and, as it seems, will still remain upon the earth, and shall not be caught up into the air, as the saints shall be. The devil, that old serpent, shall now be dragged up out of hell. He, that first procured the fall and misery of mankind, and has so set himself against their redemption—and has all along shown himself such an inveterate enemy to the Redeemer—shall never more have any thing to do with the church of God, nor be suffered in the least to afflict or molest any member of it for ever. Instead of that, now he must be judged, and receive the due reward of his deeds. Now is come the time which he has always dreaded; the time wherein he must be judged, and receive his full punishment. He who by his temptation maliciously procured Christ's crucifixion, and triumphed as though he had obtained the victory, even *he* shall see the consequences of that death which he procured. Now he must stand before that same Jesus, to be judged, condemned, and eternally destroyed by him. If Satan, the prince of hell, trembles at the thought of it thousands of years beforehand, how much more will he tremble, proud and stubborn as he is, when he comes to stand at Christ's bar!

Then shall he also stand at the bar of the saints, whom he has so hated, afflicted, and molested: for the saints shall judge him with Christ: 1 Cor. vi. 3. "Know ye not that we shall judge angels?" Now shall he be as it were subdued under the church's feet, agreeable to Rom. xvi. 20.—Satan, when he first tempted our first parents to sin, deceitfully and lyingly told them, that they should be as gods: but little did he think that they should indeed be so far *as gods,* as to be assessors with God to judge him. Much less did he think, that one of that *nature* which he then tempted, one of the posterity of those very *persons* whom he tempted, should actually be united to God; that as God he should judge the world, and that he himself must stand trembling and astonished before his judgment-seat. But thus all the devils in hell, who have so opposed Christ and his kingdom, shall now at last stand in utmost amazement and horror before Christ and his church, who shall appear to condemn them.

Now also shall all Christ's other enemies be brought to appear before him. Now shall proud scribes and Pharisees, who had such a malignant hatred of Christ while in his state of humiliation, and who persecuted him to death, be made to come. Now those before whose judgment-seat Christ once stood, as a malefactor at their bar—and those who mocked him, buffeted him, and spit in his face—shall see Christ in his awful glory, as forewarned, Matt. xxvi. 64, 65. Then *Christ* was before *their* judgment-seat; but now it is *their* turn to stand before *his* judgment-seat with inconceivable horror and amazement, with ghastly countenances, quaking limbs, chattering teeth, and knees smiting one against another.

Now also all the cruel enemies and persecutors of the church that have been in all ages, shall come in sight together. Pharaoh and the Egyptians, Antiochus Epiphanes, the malignant scribes and Pharisees, the persecuting heathen emperors, Julian the apostate, the cruel persecuting popes and papists, Gog and Magog, shall all appear at once before the judgment-seat of Christ. They and the saints who have in every age been persecuted by them, shall come in sight, and must now confront one another before the great Judge. And now shall the saints on their glorious thrones be made the judges of those unjust kings and rulers who before judged and condemned them, and put them to cruel death. Now shall those persecutors behold the glory to which they are arrived, whom they before so cruelly despised, and so cruelly treated. Thus wonderfully will the face of things be altered; now will all things be coming to rights.

IV. The righteousness of the church shall be manifested, and all the wickedness of their enemies shall be brought to light. Those saints who had been the objects of hatred, reproach, and contempt in the world; reviled and condemned by their persecutors without a cause, shall now be fully vindicated. They shall now appear clothed with the glorious robe of Christ's righteousness. It shall be most manifest before the world, that Christ's righteousness is theirs, and they shall gloriously shine forth in it. Then shall their inherent holiness be made manifest, and all their good works be brought to light. The good things which they did in secret shall now be manifested openly. Those holy ones of God, who had been treated as the filth and offscouring of the earth, as if not fit to live, as worse than beasts or devils, shall now appear to have been the excellent of the earth. Now God will bring forth their righteousness as the light, and their judgment as the noon-day. And now it shall appear who *indeed* were those wicked persons that were not fit to live; when all the wickedness of the enemies of Christ and his church, their pride, their malice, their cruelty, their hatred of true religion, shall be set forth in all its horrid acts, in its proper colours.

And now the righteous may be heard before this great Judge, who could not be heard before those unjust judges. Now they shall declare their cause, and rise up in judgment against their persecutors, and shall declare how they had been treated by them. And now all the wickedness of the wicked shall be brought to light; even all their *secret* wickedness, and their very hearts shall be opened to view, and as it were turned inside out, before the bright light of that great day. Things which have been spoken in the ear, in the closet, and done in the dark, shall be manifested in the light, and proclaimed before angels and men.

V. The sentence shall be pronounced on the righteous and the wicked. Christ, the glorious Judge, shall pass that blessed sentence on the church at his right hand, " Come, ye blessed of my Father, inherit the kingdom prepared for you from the foundation of the world." This sentence shall be pronounced with infinite love, and the voice will cause every heart to flow with joy. Thus Christ shall pronounce a sentence of justification on millions, who before had a sentence of condemnation passed upon them by their persecuting rulers. He will thus put honour upon those who have been before despised: he will own them for his, and will put a crown of glory upon their heads before the world; and then shall they shine forth as the sun with Jesus Christ in glory and joy, in the sight of all their enemies.

And then shall the sentence of condemnation be passed on the wicked, " Depart, ye cursed, into everlasting fire, prepared for the devil and his angels." Thus shall the church's enemies be condemned; in which sentence of condemnation, the holy martyrs, who have suffered from them, shall concur. When the words of this sentence are pronounced, they will strike every heart of those at the left hand with inconceivable horror and amazement. Every syllable of it will be more terrible than a stream of lightning through their hearts. What horrible shrieking, quaking, gnashing of teeth, distortions of countenance, hideous looks, hideous actions, and hideous voices, will be seen through all that vast throng!

VI. Upon this, Christ and all his saints, and all the holy angels ministering to them, shall leave this lower world, and ascend towards the highest heavens. Christ shall ascend in as great glory as he descended, and in some respects greater: for now he shall ascend with his elect church with him, glorified in body and soul. Christ's first ascension to heaven soon after his own resurrection was very glorious. But this his second ascension, with his mystical body, his whole church, shall be far more glorious. The redeemed church shall all ascend with him in a most joyful and triumphant manner: and all their enemies and persecutors, who shall be left behind to be consumed, shall see the sight, and hear their songs.—And thus Christ's church shall for ever leave this accursed world, to go into the highest heavens, the paradise of God, the kingdom prepared for them from the foundation of the world.

VII. When they are gone, this world shall be set on fire, and be turned into a great furnace, wherein all the enemies of Christ and his church shall be tormented for ever and ever. This is manifest by 2 Pet. iii. 7. " But the heavens and the earth which are now, by the same word are kept in store, reserved unto fire against the day of judgment, and perdition of ungodly men." When Christ and his church are ascended to a distance from this world—that miserable company of the wicked being left behind, to have their sentence executed upon them here—then, this whole lower world shall be set on fire, either from heaven, or by fire breaking out of the bowels of the earth, or both, as it was with the water in the time of the deluge. However, this lower world shall be set all on fire.—How will it strike the wicked with horror, when the fire begins to lay hold upon them, and they find no way to escape from it! What shrieking and crying will there be among those many millions, when they begin to enter into this great furnace, when the whole world shall be a furnace of the fiercest and most raging heat! insomuch that the apostle Peter says, (2 Pet. iii. 10, 12.) that " the heavens shall pass away with a great noise, and the elements shall melt with fervent heat, the earth also, and the works that are therein, shall be burnt up; and the heavens being on fire shall be dissolved, and the elements shall melt with fervent heat." And so fierce shall be its heat, that it shall burn the earth into its very centre; which seems to be what is meant, Deut. xxxii. 22. " For a fire is kindled in my anger, and shall burn unto the lowest hell, and shall consume the earth with her increase, and set on fire the foundations of the mountains."

And here shall all the persecutors of the church of God burn in everlasting fire, who had before burnt the saints at the stake; and shall suffer torments far beyond all that their utmost wit and malice could inflict on the saints. And here the bodies of all the wicked shall burn, and be tormented to all eternity, and never be consumed; and the wrath of God shall be poured out on their souls. Though the souls of the wicked in hell do now suffer dreadful punishment, yet their punishment will be so increased at the day of judgment, that what they suffered before, is, in comparison of it, as an imprisonment to the execution which follows it. And now the devil, that old serpent, shall receive his full punishment; now that for fear of which he before trembled, shall fully come upon him. This world, which formerly used to be the place of his kingdom, where he set up himself as God, shall now be the place of his complete punishment, of full and everlasting torment.—And in this, one design of the work of redemption, *viz.* putting Christ's enemies under his feet, shall be perfectly accomplished. His enemies shall now be made his footstool, in the fullest degree. Now shall be the most perfect fulfilment of Gen. iii. 15. " It shall bruise thy head."

VIII. At the same time, all the church shall enter with Christ, their glorious Lord, into the highest heavens, and there shall enter on the state of their highest and eternal blessedness and glory. While the lower world, which they have left under their feet, is seized with the fire of God's vengeance, and flames are kindling upon it, and the wicked are entering into everlasting fire, the whole church shall enter, with their glorious Head, and all the holy angels attending, in a joyful manner, into the eternal paradise of God, the palace of the great Jehovah, their heavenly Father. The gates shall open wide for them to enter, and there Christ will bring them into his chambers in the highest sense. Here Christ will bring them, and present them in glory to his Father, saying, " Here am I, and the children which thou hast given me;" as much as to say, Here am I, with every one of those whom thou gavest me from eternity to take the care of, that they might be redeemed and glorified, and to redeem whom I have done and suffered so much, and to make way for whose redemption I have for so many ages been accomplishing such great changes. Here they are now perfectly redeemed in body and soul; I have delivered them from all the ill fruits of the fall, and freed them from all their enemies; I have brought them all together into one glorious society, and united them all in myself; I have openly justified them before all angels and men, and here I have brought them all away from that accursed world where they have suffered so much, and have brought them before thy throne: I have done all that for them which thou hast appointed me: I have perfectly cleansed them in my blood, and here they are in perfect holiness, shining with thy perfect image.

And then the Father will accept of them, own them all for his children, and welcome them to the eternal and perfect inheritance and glory of his house, and will on this occasion give more glorious manifestations of his love than ever before, and will admit them to a more full and perfect enjoyment of himself.

Now shall be the marriage of the Lamb in the most perfect sense. The commencement of the glorious times of the church on earth, after the fall of Antichrist, is represented as the marriage of the Lamb; but after this we read of another marriage of the Lamb, at the close of the day of judgment.—After the beloved disciple had given an account of the day of judgment, (Rev. xx. xxi.) he gives an account, that he saw the holy city, the new Jerusalem, prepared as a bride adorned for her husband. Christ shall bring his church into his Father's house in heaven, as his bride, without spot or wrinkle, or any such thing.

The bridegroom and the bride shall then enter into heaven, both having on their wedding-robes, attended with all the glorious angels. And there they enter on the feast and joys of their marriage before the Father; they shall then begin an everlasting wedding-day. This shall be the day of the gladness of Christ's heart, wherein he will greatly rejoice, and all the saints shall rejoice with him. Christ shall rejoice over his bride, and the bride shall rejoice in her husband, in the state of her consummate and everlasting blessedness, of which we have a particular description in the 21st and 22d chapters of Revelation.

And now the whole work of redemption is finished. Now the top-stone of the building is laid. In the progress of our discourse, we have followed the church of God in all her great changes, all her tossings to and fro, all her storms and tempests through the many ages of the world. We have seen her enter the harbour, and landed in the highest heavens, in complete and eternal glory. We have gone through the several ages of time, as the providence and word of God have led us. We have seen all the church's enemies fixed in endless misery, and have seen the church presented in her perfect redemption before her Father in heaven, there to enjoy this most unspeakable and inconceivable glory and blessedness; and there we leave her to enjoy this glory throughout the never-ending ages of eternity.

Now all Christ's enemies will be perfectly put under his feet, and he shall have his most perfect triumph over sin and Satan, and all his instruments, and death, and hell. Now shall all the promises made to Christ by God the Father before the foundation of the world, the promises of the covenant of redemption, be fully accomplished. Christ shall now perfectly have obtained the joy set before him, for which he undertook those great sufferings in his state of humiliation. Now shall all the hopes and expectations of the saints be fulfilled. The state of the church before, was progressive and preparatory: but now she is arrived to her most perfect state of glory. All the glory of the church on earth, is but a faint shadow of this her consummate glory in heaven.

Now Christ the great Redeemer shall be most perfectly glorified, God the Father shall be glorified in him, and the Holy Ghost shall be most fully glorified in the perfection of his work on the hearts of all the church.—And now shall that new heaven and new earth, or the renewed state of things, be completely finished, after the material frame of the old heavens and old earth is destroyed: Rev. xxi. 1. " And I saw a new heaven, and a new earth: for the first heaven and the first earth were passed away."—And now will the great Redeemer have perfected every thing that appertains to the work of redemption, which he began so soon after the fall of man. And who can conceive of the triumph of those praises which shall be sung in heaven on this great occasion, so much greater than that on the fall of Antichrist. The beloved disciple John (Rev. xix.) seems to want expressions to describe those praises, and says, " It was as the voice of many waters, and as the voice of mighty thunderings, saying, Alleluia: for the Lord God omnipotent reigneth." But much more inexpressible will those praises be, which will be sung in heaven after the final consummation of all things. How shall the praises of that vast and glorious multitude be as mighty thunderings indeed!

How are all the former things passed away, and what a glorious state are things fixed in to remain to all eternity!—And as Christ, when he first entered upon the work of redemption, had the kingdom committed to him of the Father, and as he took on himself the administration of the affairs of the universe, to manage all so as to subserve the purposes of this affair; so now, the work being finished, he will deliver up the kingdom to God even the Father, 1 Cor. xv. 24. " Then cometh the end, when he shall have delivered up the kingdom to God, even the Father; when he shall have put down all rule, and all authority and power." Not that Christ shall cease to reign after this; for it is said, Luke i. 33. " He shall reign over the house of Jacob for ever, and of his kingdom there shall be no end;" and Dan. vii. 14. " His dominion is an everlasting dominion, which shall not pass away, and his kingdom that which shall not be destroyed." But the meaning is, that Christ shall deliver up that kingdom or dominion which he has over the world, as the Father's delegate or vicegerent, which the Father committed to him, to be managed in subserviency to this great design of redemption. The end of this commission, or delegation, which he had from the Father, seems to be to subserve this particular design of redemption; and therefore, when that design is fully accomplished, the commission will cease, and Christ will deliver it up to the Father, from whom he received it.

PART X.

IMPROVEMENT OF THE WHOLE.

I PROCEED now to enter upon some improvement of the whole that has been said from this doctrine.

I. Hence we may learn how great a work is this of redemption. We have now had it, though in a very imperfect manner, set forth, in its whole progress, from its first beginning after the fall, to its consummation. We have seen how God has carried on this building, by a long succession of wonderful works, advancing it higher and higher from one age to another, till the top-stone is laid. And now let us consider how great a work this is. Do men, when they behold some great edifices, admire their magnificence; how well may we admire the greatness of this building of God, which he builds up age after age! There are three things exhibited to us in what has been said, which especially show the *greatness* of the work of redemption.

1. The greatness of those *particular events*, and dispensations of Providence, by which it is accomplished. How great are those things which God has done, which are but so many parts of this great work! What great things were done in the world to *prepare the way* for Christ's coming to purchase, and what great things were done in the actual purchase of redemption! What a wonderful thing was accomplished to put Christ in an immediate capacity for this purchase, *viz.* his *incarnation*, that God should become man! And what great things were done in that purchase, that a person, who is the eternal Jehovah, should live upon earth for four or five and thirty years together, in a mean, despised condition, that he should spend his life in such labours and sufferings, and that at last he should die upon the cross! And what great things have been done to accomplish the *success* of Christ's redemption! what great things to put him into a capacity to accomplish this success! For this purpose he rose from the dead, and ascended into heaven, and all things were made subject to him. How many miracles have been wrought, what mighty revolutions have been brought to pass in the world already, and how much greater shall be brought to pass, in order to it!

2. The *number* of those great events by which God carries on this work, shows the greatness of the work. Those mighty revolutions are so many as to fill up many ages. The particular wonderful events by which the work of creation was carried on filled up six days; but the great dispensations by which the work of redemption is

carried on, are so many, that they fill up six or seven thousand years at least, as we have reason to conclude from the word of God.——There were great things wrought in this affair before the flood, and in the flood the world was once destroyed by water, and God's church was so wonderfully preserved from it in order to carry on this work. And after the flood, what great things did God work relating to the resettling of the world, to the building of Babel, the dispersing of the nations, the shortening of the days of man's life, the calling of Abraham, the destruction of Sodom and Gomorrah, and that long series of wonderful providences relating to Abraham, Isaac, Jacob, and Joseph; and those wonders in Egypt, and at the Red sea, in the wilderness, and in Canaan in Joshua's time, and by a long succession of wonderful providences from age to age towards the nation of the Jews.

What great things were wrought by God, in so often overturning the world before Christ came, to make way for his coming! What great things were done also in Christ's time, and after that, in overturning Satan's kingdom in the heathen empire, and in so preserving his church in the dark times of popery, and in bringing about the Reformation!—How many great and wonderful things will be effected in accomplishing the glorious times of the church, and at Christ's last coming on the day of judgment, in the destruction of the world, and in carrying the whole church into heaven!

3. The *glorious issue* of this whole affair, in the perfect and eternal destruction of the wicked, and in the consummate glory of the righteous. And now let us once more take a view of this building, now all is finished and the top-stone laid. It appeared in a glorious height in the apostle's time, and much more glorious in the time of Constantine, and will appear much more glorious still after the fall of Antichrist; but at the consummation of all things, it appears in an immensely more glorious height than ever before. Now it appears in its greatest magnificence, as a complete lofty structure, whose top reaches to the heaven of heavens; a building worthy of the great God, the King of kings.

And from what has been said, one may argue, that the work of redemption is the greatest of all God's works of which we have any notice, and it is the end of all his other works.—It appears plainly from what has been said, that this is the principal of all God's works of providence, and that all are subordinate to the great affair of redemption. We see that all the revolutions in the world are to subserve this grand design. This shows how much greater the work of redemption is, than the work of creation: because it is the end of it; as the use of a house is the end of the building it. But the work of redemption, is the sum of all God's works of providence; all are subordinate to it: so the work of the new creation is more excellent than the old. So it ever is, that when one thing is removed by God to make way for another, the new one excels the old. Thus the temple excelled the tabernacle; the new covenant the old; the new dispensation of the gospel the dispensation of Moses; the throne of David the throne of Saul; the priesthood of Christ the priesthood of Aaron; the new Jerusalem the old; and so the new creation far excels the old.

God has used the creation for no other purpose, but to subserve the designs of this affair. To answer this end, he hath created and disposed of mankind, to this the angels, to this the earth, to this the highest heavens. God created the world to provide a spouse and a kingdom for his Son: and the setting up of the kingdom of Christ, and the spiritual marriage of the spouse to him, is what the whole creation labours and travails in pain to bring to pass. This work of redemption is so much the greatest of all the works of God, that all other works are to be looked upon either as parts of it, or appendages to it, or are some way reducible to it; and so all the decrees of God some way or other belong to that eternal covenant of redemption which was between the Father and the Son before the foundation of the world. Every decree of God is some way or other reducible to that covenant. And seeing this work of redemption is so great, we need not wonder that the angels desire to look into it. And we need not wonder that so much is made of it in Scripture, that it is so much insisted on in the histories, and prophecies, and songs of the Bible; for the work of redemption is the great subject of the whole, its doctrines, its promises, its types, its songs, its histories, and its prophecies.

II. Hence we may learn how God is the Alpha and Omega, the beginning and ending of all things. Such are the characters and titles we find often ascribed to him in Scripture. Isa. xli. 4. "Who hath wrought and done it, calling the generations from the beginning? I the Lord, the first, and with the last, I am he." And particularly does the Scripture ascribe such titles to God, where it speaks of providence, as it relates to, and is summed up in, the great work of redemption; (as Isa. xliv. 6, 7. and xlviii. 9—12.) Therefore, when Christ reveals the future great events of providence relating to his church and people, to his disciple John, he often reveals himself under this character. Rev. i. 8. "I am Alpha and Omega, the beginning and the ending, saith the Lord, which is, and which was, and which is to come, the Almighty." So again, ver. 10, 11. "I heard behind me a great voice as of a trumpet, saying, I am Alpha and Omega, the first and the last." Alpha and Omega being the names of the first and the last letters of the Greek alphabet, it signifies the same as his being the first and the last, and the beginning and the ending: as Rev. xxi. 6. "And he said unto me, It is done. I am Alpha and Omega, the beginning and the end." And so chapter xxii. 12, 13. "And behold, I come quickly; and my reward is with me, to give every man according as his work shall be. I am Alpha and Omega, the beginning and the end, the first and the last."

We have seen on what design God began the course of his providence in the beginning of the generations of men; and how he has all along carried things on agreeably to the same design without ever failing; and how at last the conclusion and final issue of things are to God; and therefore may well now cry out with the apostle, Rom. xi. 33. "O the depth of the riches both of the wisdom and knowledge of God! how unsearchable are his judgments, and his ways past finding out!" and ver. 36. "For of him, and through him, and to him, are all things: to whom be glory for ever. Amen."

We have seen how other things came to an end one after another; how states, and kingdoms, and empires, fell, and came to nothing, even the greatest and strongest of them; we have seen how the world has been often overturned, and will be more remarkably yet; we have seen how it was first destroyed by water, and how at last it shall be utterly destroyed by fire: but yet God remains the same through all ages. He was before the beginning of this course of things, and he will be after the end of them; (Psal. cii. 25, 26.) Thus God is he *who is*, and *who was*, and *who is to come*.

We have seen, in a variety of instances, how all other gods perish. Those in the nations about Canaan, and throughout the Roman empire, are all destroyed, and their worship long since overthrown. We have heard how Antichrist, who has called himself a god on earth; how Mahomet, who claims religious honours; how all the gods of the heathen through the world, will come to an end; and how Satan, the great dragon, that old serpent, who has set up himself as god of this world, will be cast into the lake of fire, there to suffer his complete punishment: but Jehovah remains, his kingdom is an everlasting kingdom, and of his dominion there is no end. We have seen what mighty changes there have been in the world; but God is unchangeable, *the same yesterday, to-day, and for ever*.

We began at the head of the stream of divine providence, and have traced it through its various windings, till we are come to the end where it issues. As it began in God, so it ends in him. God is the infinite ocean into which it empties itself.—Providence is like a mighty wheel, whose circumference is so high that it is dreadful, with the glory of the God of Israel above upon it; as it is represented in Ezekiel's vision. We have seen the revolution of this wheel, and how as it was from God, its return has been to God again. All the events of divine providence are like the links of a chain; the first link is from God, and the last is to him.

III. We may see by what has been said, how Christ has in all things the pre-eminence. For he is the great

Redeemer; and therefore the work of redemption being the sum of God's works of providence, shows the glory of our Lord Jesus Christ, as being above all, and through all, and in all. That God intended the world for his Son's use in the affair of redemption is one reason why he created the world by him, Eph. iii. 9—12. What has been said, shows how all the *purposes* of God are purposed in Christ; and how he is before all, and above all. All things consist in him, are governed by him, and are for him, Colos. i. 15—18. God makes him his first-born, higher than the kings of the earth, and sets his throne above their thrones. God has always upheld his kingdom, when others have come to an end; that appears at last above all, however greatly opposed for so many ages. All other kingdoms fall, but his kingdom is the last, and never gives place to any other.

We see, that whatever changes there are, and however highly Christ's enemies exalt themselves, yet he reigns in uncontrolled power and immense glory: in the end, his people are all perfectly saved and made happy, and all his enemies become his footstool.—And thus God gives the world to his Son for his inheritance.

IV. The consideration of what has been said, may greatly serve to show us the consistency, order, and beauty, of God's works of providence. If we behold events in any other view, all will look like confusion, like the tossing of waves; things will look as though one confused revolution came to pass after another, merely by blind chance, without any regular or certain end. But if we consider the events of providence in the light in which they have been set before us, and in which the Scriptures set them before us, they appear an orderly series of events, all wisely directed in excellent harmony and consistence, tending all to one end. The wheels of providence are not turned round by blind chance, but are full of eyes round about, (as Ezekiel represents them,) and are guided by the Spirit of God: where the Spirit goes, they go. All God's works of providence, through all ages, meet at last, as so many lines meeting in one centre.

God's work of providence, like that of creation, is but one. The events of providence are not so many distinct, independent works; but rather so many different parts of one work, one regular scheme. They are all united, just as the several parts of one building: there are many stones, many pieces of timber, but all are so joined, and fitly formed together, that they make but one building; they have all but one foundation, and are united at last in one top-stone.

God's providence may not unfitly be compared to a large and long river, having innumerable branches, beginning in different regions, and at a great distance one from another, and all conspiring to one common issue. After their very diverse and apparent contrary courses, they all collect together, the nearer they come to their common end, and at length discharge themselves at one mouth into the same ocean. The different streams of this river are apt to appear like mere confusion to us, because of our limited sight, whereby we cannot see the whole at once. A man who sees but one or two streams at a time, cannot tell what their course tends to. Their course seems very crooked, and different streams seem to run for a while different and contrary ways: and if we view things at a distance, there seem to be innumerable obstacles and impediments in the way, as rocks and mountains, and the like; to hinder their ever uniting, and coming to the ocean; but yet if we trace them, they all unite at last, all come to the same issue, disgorging themselves in one into the same great ocean. Not one of all the streams fail.

V. From the whole that has been said, we may strongly argue, that the Scriptures are the word of God, because they alone inform us what God aims at, in his works. God doubtless is pursuing some design, and carrying on some scheme, in the various changes and revolutions which from age to age came to pass in the world. It is most reasonable to suppose, that there is some certain great design to which Providence subordinates all great successive changes in affairs. It is reasonable to suppose, that all revolutions, from the beginning of the world to the end of it, are but the various parts of the same scheme, all conspiring to bring to pass that great event which the great Creator and Governor of the world has ultimately in view; and that the scheme will not be finished, nor the design fully accomplished, and the great and ultimate event fully brought to pass, till the end of the world, and the last revolution is brought about.

Now there is nothing else that informs us what this scheme and design of God in his works is, but the Holy Scriptures.—Nothing else pretends to set in view the whole series of God's works of providence from beginning to end, and to inform us how all things were from God at first, for what end they are, how they were ordered from the beginning, how they will proceed to the end of the world, what they will come to at last, and how then all things shall be to God. Nothing else but the Scriptures has any pretence for showing any manner of regular scheme or drift in those revolutions which God orders from age to age. Nothing else pretends to show what God would effect by the things which he has done, is doing, and will do; what he seeks and intends by them. Nothing else pretends to show, with any distinctness or certainty, how the world began, or to tell us the true original of things. Nothing but the Scriptures set forth how God governed the world from the beginning of the generations of men upon the earth, in an orderly history; and nothing else sets before us how he will govern it to the end, by an orderly prophecy of future events; agreeable to the challenge which God makes to the gods, and prophets, and teachers of the heathen, in Isa. xli. 22, 23, "Let them bring them forth, and show us what shall happen: let them show the former things what they be, that we may consider them, and know the latter end of them; or declare us things for to come. Show the things that are to come hereafter, that we may know that ye are gods."

Reason shows, that it is fit and requisite, that the intelligent and rational beings of the world should know something of God's scheme and design in his works: for they doubtless are principally concerned. God's great design in his works, is doubtless concerning his reasonable creatures, rather than brute beasts and lifeless things. The revolutions by which God's great design is brought to pass, are doubtless chiefly among them, and concern their state, and not the state of things without life or reason. And therefore surely it is requisite, that they should know something of it; especially since reason teaches, that God has given his rational creatures a capacity of seeing him in his works; for this end, that they may see God's glory in them, and give him that glory. But how can they see God's glory in his works, if they do not know what his design in them is, and what he aims at by what he is doing in the world?

Further, it is fit that mankind should be somewhat informed of God's design in the government of the world, because they are made capable of actively falling in with that design, of promoting it, and acting herein as his friends and subjects. It is therefore reasonable to suppose, that God has given mankind some revelation to inform them of this: but there is nothing else that does it but the Bible. In the Bible this is done. Here we may learn the first original of things, and have an orderly account of the scheme of God's works from the beginning, through those ages that are beyond the reach of all other histories. Here we are told what God aims at in the whole, what is the great end, how he has contrived the grand design, and the great things he would accomplish.—Here we have a most rational excellent account of this matter, worthy of God, and exceedingly showing forth the glory of his perfections, his majesty, his wisdom, his glorious holiness, grace, and love; and his exaltation above all, as the first and the last.

Here we are shown the various parts of the work of providence, and how all are connected together in a regular, beautiful, and glorious frame. In the Bible, we have an account of the whole scheme of providence, from the beginning of the world to the end of it, either in history or prophecy, and are told what will become of things at last; how they will issue in the subduing of God's enemies, and in the salvation and glory of his church, and setting up of the everlasting kingdom of his Son.

How rational, worthy, and excellent a revelation is this! and how excellent a book is the Bible, which contains so much beyond all other books in the world! and what characters are here of its being indeed a divine book! a book that the great Jehovah has given to mankind for their instruction, without which we should be left in miserable darkness and confusion.

VI. From what has been said, we may see the glorious *majesty* and *power* of God in this affair of redemption. His glorious power appears in upholding his church for so long a time, and carrying on this work; upholding it oftentimes when it was but as a little spark, or as smoking flax, in which the fire was almost extinct, and the powers of earth and hell combined to destroy it. Yet God has never suffered them to quench it, and finally will bring forth judgment unto victory. God glorifies his strength in his church's weakness; in causing his people, who are like a number of little infants, finally to triumph over all earth and hell; so that they shall tread on the lion and adder; the young lion and dragon shall they trample under foot. The glorious power of God appears in conquering his many and mighty enemies by that person who was once an infant in a manger, and appeared as a poor, weak, despised man. He conquers them, and triumphs over them in their own weapon, the cross.

The glorious majesty of God appears in conquering all those mighty enemies of the church one age after another; in conquering Satan, that proud and strong spirit, and all his hellish host; in bringing him down under foot, long after he had vaunted himself as god of this world, and when he did his utmost to support himself in his kingdom. Christ, our Michael, has overcome him, the devil was cast out, and there was found no more place for him in heaven; but he was cast out into the earth, and his angels were cast out with him.—He is conquered in that kingdom wherein his pride, and subtlety, and cruelty, above all appears, *viz.* the kingdom of Antichrist. And the glorious power of God appears in thus conquering the devil, and bringing him under foot, after long time given him to strengthen himself to his utmost. He was once overthrown in his heathen Roman empire, after he had been making himself strong in those parts of the world, ever since the building of Babel. It appears also in overthrowing his kingdom more fatally and universally all over the world, after he had another opportunity to strengthen himself to his utmost for many ages, by setting up those two great kingdoms of Antichrist and Mahomet, and to establish his interest in the heathen world. We have seen how these kingdoms of God's enemies look strong, as though it was impossible to overthrow them; yet, when God appears, they seem to melt away, as the fat of lambs before the fire, and are driven away as the chaff before the whirlwind.

Those mighty kingdoms of Antichrist and Mahomet, which have made such a figure for so many ages, and have trampled the world under foot, when God comes to appear, will vanish away like a shadow, and will disappear of themselves, as the darkness in a room does, when the light is brought in. What are God's enemies in his hands? How is their greatest strength weakness when he rises up! and how weak will they all appear together at the day of judgment! Thus we may apply those words in the song of Moses, Exod. xv. 6. "Thy right hand, O Lord, is become glorious in power: thy right hand, O Lord, hath dashed in pieces the enemy." And how great doth the majesty of God appear in overturning the world from time to time, to accomplish his designs, and at last in causing the earth and heavens to flee away, for the advancement of the glory of his kingdom!

VII. From what has been said, we may see the glorious *wisdom* of God. It shows the wisdom of God in creating the world, in that he has created it for such an excellent use, to accomplish in it so glorious a work. And it shows the wisdom of Divine Providence, that he brings such great good out of such great evil, in making the fall and ruin of mankind, which in itself is so sorrowful and deplorable, an occasion of accomplishing such a glorious work as redemption, and of erecting such a glorious building, whose top should reach unto heaven, and of bringing his elect to a state of such unspeakable happiness. And how glorious doth the wisdom of God appear in that long course and series of great changes in the world, in bringing such order out of confusion, in so frustrating the most subtle machinations, and in causing the greatest works of Satan, those in which he has most glorified himself, to be wholly turned into occasions of so much the more glorious triumph of his Son Jesus Christ! And how wonderful is the wisdom of God, in bringing all such manifold and various changes and overturnings in the world to such a glorious period at last, and in so directing all the wheels of Providence by his skilful hand, that every one of them conspires, as the manifold wheels of a most curious machine, at last to strike out such an excellent issue, such a manifestation of the divine glory, such happiness to his people, and such a glorious and everlasting kingdom to his Son!

VIII. From what has been said, we may see the stability of God's *mercy* and *faithfulness* to his people; how he never forsakes his inheritance, and remembers his covenant to them through all generations. Now we may see what reason there was for the words of the text, "The moth shall eat them up like a garment, and the worm shall eat them like wool; but my righteousness shall endure for ever and ever, and my salvation from generation to generation." And now we may see abundant reason for that name of God which he reveals to Moses, Exod. iii. 14. "And God said unto Moses, *I am that I am:*" *i. e.* I am the same that I was when I entered into covenant with Abraham, Isaac, and Jacob, and ever shall be the same: I shall keep covenant for ever: I am self-sufficient, all sufficient, and immutable.

And now we may see the truth of Psalm xxxvi. 5, 6. "Thy mercy, O Lord, is in the heavens; and thy faithfulness reacheth unto the clouds. Thy righteousness is like the great mountains; thy judgments are a great deep." And if we consider what has been said, we need not wonder that the psalmist, in the 136th Psalm, so often repeats this, "For his mercy endureth for ever;" as if he were in an ecstasy at the consideration of the perpetuity of God's mercy to his church, delighted to think of it, and knew not how but continually to express it. Let us with like pleasure and joy celebrate the everlasting duration of God's mercy and faithfulness to his church and people, and let us be comforted by it under all the dark circumstances of the church of God, and all the uproar and confusions that are in the world, and all the threatenings of the church's enemies. And let us take encouragement earnestly to pray for those glorious things which God has promised to accomplish for his church.

IX. Hence we may learn how *happy* a society the church of Christ is. For all this great work is for them. Christ undertook it for their sakes, and for their sakes he carries it on; it is because he has loved them with an everlasting love. For their sakes he overturns states and kingdoms. For their sakes he shakes heaven and earth. He gives men for them, and people for their life. Since they have been precious in God's sight, they have been honourable; and therefore he first gives the blood of his own Son, and then gives the blood of all their enemies, many thousands and millions, all nations that stand in their way, as a sacrifice to their good.

For their sakes he made the world, and for their sakes he will destroy it; for their sakes he built heaven, and for their sakes he makes his angels ministering spirits. Therefore the apostle says, 1 Cor. iii. 21, &c. "All things are yours: whether Paul, or Apollos, or Cephas, or the world, or life, or death, or things present, or things to come; all are yours." How blessed is this people who are redeemed from among men, and are the first-fruits unto God, and to the Lamb; who have God in all ages for their protection and help! Deut. xxxiii. 29. "Happy art thou, O Israel: who is like unto thee, O people saved by the Lord, the shield of thy help, and who is the sword of thy excellency! and thine enemies shall be found liars unto thee, and thou shalt tread upon their high places."

Let who will prevail now, let the enemies of the church exalt themselves as much as they will, these are the people that shall finally prevail. The last kingdom shall finally be theirs; the kingdom shall finally be given into their hands, and shall not be left to other people. We have seen to what a blessed issue things shall finally be brought, and what glory they shall arrive at, and remain in possession of, for ever and ever; after all the kingdoms of the world are come to an end, and the earth is removed, and mountains are carried into the depth of the sea, or where the sea was, and this lower earth shall all be dissolved. O happy people, and blessed society! Well may they spend an eternity in praises and hallelujahs to him who hath loved them, and will love them to eternity.

X. And, lastly, hence all wicked men, all that are in a Christless condition, may see their exceeding *misery*. You that are such, whoever you are, shall have no part or lot in this matter. You are never the better for any of these things: yea, your guilt is but so much the greater, and the misery you are exposed to so much the more dreadful. You are some of those against whom God, in the progress of the work, exercises so much manifest wrath; some of those enemies who are liable to be made Christ's footstool, to be ruled with a rod of iron, and to be dashed in pieces. You are some of the seed of the serpent, to bruise the head of which is one great design of all this work. Whatever glorious things God accomplishes for his church, they will not be glorious to you. The most glorious times of the church are always the most dismal to the wicked and impenitent. (Isa. lxvi. 14.)—— And so we find, wherever glorious things are foretold concerning the church, there terrible things are foretold concerning the wicked, its enemies. So it ever has been in remarkable deliverances wrought for the church, there has been also a remarkable execution of wrath on its enemies. When God delivered the children of Israel out of Egypt; at the same time he remarkably poured out his wrath on Pharaoh and the Egyptians. When he brought them into Canaan by Joshua, and gave them that good land, he remarkably executed wrath upon the Canaanites. When they were delivered out of their Babylonish captivity, signal vengeance was inflicted on the Babylonians. When the Gentiles were called, and the elect of God were saved by the preaching of the apostles, Jerusalem and the persecuting Jews were destroyed in a most awful manner. I might observe the same concerning the glory accomplished to the church in the days of Constantine, at the overthrow of Satan's visible kingdom in the downfall of Antichrist, and at the day of judgment. In all these instances, and especially in the last, there have been, or will be, exhibited most awful tokens of the divine wrath against the wicked.

God will indeed make use of you in this affair; but it will be for the glory of his justice, and not of his mercy. The enemies of God are reserved for the triumph of Christ's glorious power in overcoming and punishing them. You are some of those who shall be consumed with this accursed world after the day of judgment, when Christ and his church shall triumphantly and gloriously ascend to heaven.—Therefore let all who are in a Christless condition seriously consider these things, and not be like the foolish people of the old world, who would not take warning, when Noah told them, that the Lord was about to bring a flood of waters upon the earth; or like the people of Sodom, who would not regard, when Lot told them, that God would destroy that city, and would not flee from the wrath to come, and so were consumed in that terrible destruction.

And now I would say, to conclude my whole discourse on this subject, "These sayings are faithful and true, and blessed is he that keepeth these sayings. Behold Christ cometh quickly, and his reward is with him, to render to every man according as his work shall be. And he that is unjust, shall be unjust still; and he that is filthy, shall be filthy still; and he that is holy, shall be holy still. Blessed are they that do his commandments, that they may have right to the tree of life, and may enter in through the gates into the city: for without are dogs, and sorcerers, and whoremongers, and murderers, and idolaters, and whosoever loveth and maketh a lie. He that testifieth these things, saith, Surely I come quickly.—Amen; even so come, Lord Jesus."

FIVE DISCOURSES

ON

IMPORTANT SUBJECTS,

NEARLY CONCERNING THE GREAT AFFAIR

OF THE

SOUL'S ETERNAL SALVATION,

VIZ.

I. JUSTIFICATION BY FAITH ALONE.
II. PRESSING INTO THE KINGDOM OF GOD.
III. RUTH'S RESOLUTION.
IV. THE JUSTICE OF GOD IN THE DAMNATION OF SINNERS.
V. THE EXCELLENCY OF JESUS CHRIST

DELIVERED AT NORTHAMPTON,

CHIEFLY AT THE TIME OF THE LATE WONDERFUL POURING OUT OF THE SPIRIT OF GOD THERE.

Deut. iv. 9.—Take heed to thyself, and keep thy soul diligently, lest thou forget the things which thine eyes have seen, and lest they depart from thy heart all the days of thy life.

PREFACE.

THE following discourses were all, excepting the last, delivered in the time of the late wonderful work of God's power and grace in this place, and are now published * on the earnest desire of those to whom they were preached. These particular discourses are fixed upon, and designed for the press, rather than others that were delivered in that remarkable season, by *their* election. What has determined them in their choice, is the experience they hope they have had of special benefit to their souls from *these discourses*. Their desire to have them in their hands from the press has been long manifested, and often expressed to me; their earnestness in it is evident from this, that though it be a year of the greatest public charge to them that ever has been, by reason of the expense of building a new meeting-house, yet they chose rather to be at this additional expense now, though it be very considerable, than to have it delayed another year. I am fully sensible that their value for these discourses has arisen more from the frame in which they heard them, and the good which, through the sovereign blessing of God, they have received, than any real worth in them. And whatever the discourses are in themselves, yet those who heard them are not to be blamed or wondered at, if that is dear to them, which they hope God has made a means of saving and everlasting benefit. They have much insisted on this argument with me, to induce me to comply with their desire, *viz.* that they hoped the reading of these discourses would have a tendency in some measure to renew the same effect in them that was wrought in the hearing, and revive the memory of that great work of God, which this town has so much cause ever to remember; which argument has been of principal weight with me, to incline me to think it to be my duty to comply with their desire; though I cannot say there are no other considerations concurring to induce me to it.

With respect to the discourse on *justification*, besides the desire of my people to make it public, I have been advised to it by certain reverend gentlemen, my fathers, that happened to be the hearers of it (or, at least, part of it) when preached, whose opinion and advice, in such an affair, I thought should be of as great weight with me as of most that I was acquainted with.

The beginning of the late work of God in this place was so circumstanced, that I could not but look upon it as a remarkable testimony of God's approbation of the doctrine of *justification by faith alone*, here asserted and vindicated. —By the noise that had a little before been raised in this county concerning that doctrine, people here seemed to have their minds put into an unusual ruffle; some were brought to doubt of that way of acceptance with God, which from their infancy they had been taught to be the only way; and many were engaged more thoroughly to look into the grounds of those doctrines in which they had been educated.—The following discourse of justification, that was preached (though not so fully as it is here printed) at two public lectures, seemed to be remarkably blessed, not only to establish the judgments of many in this truth, but to engage their hearts in a more earnest pursuit of justification, in that way that had been explained and defended; and *at that time*, while I was greatly reproached for defending this doctrine in the pulpit, and just upon my suffering a very open abuse for it, God's work wonderfully brake forth amongst us, and souls began to flock to Christ, as the Saviour in whose righteousness alone they hoped to be justified. So that this was the doctrine on which this work in its beginning was founded, as it evidently was in the whole progress of it.

* *Viz.* at Boston, 1738.

A great objection that is made against the old protestant doctrine of *justification by faith alone*, and the scheme of those divines that have chiefly defended it, by those that value themselves upon the new fashioned divinity, is, that the scheme is too much incumbered with speculative niceties, and subtle distinctions, that, they say, serve only to involve the subject in endless controversy and dispute; whereas, their scheme, they suppose, is a plain, easy, and natural account of things. But their prejudice against distinctions in divinity, I humbly conceive, is carried to a great extreme. So great, so general, and loud a cry has been raised by modern philosophers and divines against the subtle distinctions of the schoolmen, for their learned impertinence, that many are ready to start at any thing that looks like nice distinction, and to condemn it for nonsense without examination. Upon the same account, we might expect to have St. Paul's epistles, that are full of very nice distinctions, called nonsense and unintelligible jargon, had not they the good luck to be universally received by all Christians as part of the Holy Scriptures.

Our discovering the absurdity of the impertinent and abstruse distinctions of the school divines, may justly give us a distaste of *such distinctions* as have a show of learning in obscure words, but convey no light to the mind; but I can see no reason why we should also discard those that are clear and rational, and can be made out to have their foundation in truth, although they may be such as require some diligence and attention of mind clearly to apprehend them. So much of the Scripture scheme of justification as is absolutely necessary to salvation, may be very plain, and level with the understandings of the weakest Christians; but it does not therefore follow, that the Scripture teaches us no more about it that would be exceeding profitable for us to know, and by gaining the knowledge of which, we may obtain a more full and clear understanding of this doctrine, and be better able to solve doubts that may arise concerning it, and to defend it from the sophistry and cavils of subtle opposers.

It is so in most of the great doctrines of Christianity, that are looked upon as first principles of the christian faith, that though they contain something that is easy, yet they also contain great mysteries; and there is room for progress in the knowledge of them, and doubtless will be to the end of the world. But it is unreasonable, to expect that this progress should be made in the knowledge of things that are high and mysterious, without accurate distinction and close application of thought: and it is also unreasonable, to think that this doctrine, of the justification of a sinner by a mediator, should be without mysteries. We all own it to be a matter of pure revelation, above the light of natural reason, and that it is what the infinite wisdom of God revealed in the gospel mainly appears in, that he hath found out such a way of reconciliation of which neither men nor angels could have thought. And after all, shall we expect that this way, when found out and declared, shall contain nothing but what is obvious to the most cursory and superficial view, and may be fully and clearly comprehended without some diligence, accuracy, and careful distinction?

If the distinctions I have made use of in handling this subject are found to be inconsistent, trivial, and unscriptural niceties, tending only to cloud the subject, I ought to be willing that they should be rejected; but if on due examination they are found both scriptural and rational, I humbly conceive that it will be unjust to condemn them, merely because they are distinctions, under a notion that niceness in divinity never helps it, but always perplexes and darkens it. It is to God's own revelation that I make my appeal, by which alone we can know in what way he will be pleased again to receive into favour those who have offended him and incurred his displeasure. If there be any part of the scheme here laid down, or any distinction here used, not warranted by Scripture, let it be rejected; and if any opposite scheme can be found that is more easy and plain, having fewer and more rational distinctions, and not demonstrably inconsistent with itself, and with the word of God, let it be received. Let the Arminian scheme of justification by our own virtue be as *plain* and natural as it will, if at the same time it is *plainly* contrary to the certain and demonstrable doctrine of the gospel, as contained in the Scriptures, we are bound to reject it, unless we reject the Scriptures themselves as perplexed and absurd, and make ourselves wiser than God, and pretend to know his mind better than himself.

This discourse on justification is printed much larger than it was preached; but the practical discourses that follow have but little added to them, and now appear in that very plain and unpolished dress in which they were first prepared and delivered; which was mostly at a time when the circumstances of the auditory they were preached to, were enough to make a minister neglect, forget, and despise such ornaments as politeness and modishness of style and method, when coming as a messenger from God to souls deeply impressed with a sense of their danger of God's everlasting wrath, to treat with them about their eternal salvation.——However unable I am to preach or write politely, if I would, yet I have this to comfort me under such a defect, that God has showed us he does not need such talents in men to carry on his own work, and that he has been pleased to smile upon and bless a very plain unfashionable way of preaching. And have we not reason to think, that it ever has been, and ever will be, God's manner, to bless the foolishness of preaching to save them that believe, let the elegance of language and excellency of style be carried to never so great a height, by the learning and wit of the present and future ages?

What is published at the end, concerning the excellency of Christ, is added on my own motion; thinking that a discourse on such an evangelical subject would properly follow others that were chiefly awakening, and that something of the excellency of the Saviour was proper to succeed those things that were to show the necessity of *salvation*. I pitched upon that particular discourse, partly because I had been earnestly importuned for a copy of it for the press, by some in another town in whose hearing it was occasionally preached.

I request every reader's candid acceptance and due improvement of what is here offered; and especially would earnestly beseech the people of my own charge, not to fail of improving these discourses to those purposes that they have mentioned to me as the ends for which they desired to have them published, that I may have no cause to repent of my labour in transcribing, nor they of their cost in printing them. Happy would it be for us, and an unspeakable mercy of heaven, if God should bless what is here printed, so to revive the memory of the past great work of God amongst us, and the lively impressions and sense of divine things that persons then had on their minds, and to cause us to lament our declensions, so that the same work might renewedly break forth and go on amongst us! Surely we have seen much to excite our longings after such a mercy, and to encourage us to cry to God for it!

DISCOURSE I.

JUSTIFICATION BY FAITH ALONE.

ROM. iv. 5.

But to him that worketh not, but believeth on him that justifieth the ungodly, his faith is counted for righteousness.

THE following things may be noted in this verse:

1. That justification respects a man as ungodly. This is evident by these words,——*that justifieth the ungodly;* which cannot imply less, than that God, in the act of justification, has no regard to any thing in the person justified, as godliness, or any goodness in him; but that immediately before this act, God beholds him only as an ungodly creature; so that godliness in the person to be justified is not so antecedent to his justification as to be the ground of it. When it is said that God justifies the ungodly, it is absurd to suppose that our godliness, taken as some goodness in us, is the ground of our justification; as, when it is said that Christ gave sight to the blind, to suppose that sight was prior to, and the ground of, that act of mercy in Christ; or as, if it should be said that such an one by his bounty has made a poor man rich, to suppose that it was the wealth of this poor man that was the ground of this bounty towards him, and was the price by which it was procured.

2. It appears, that *by him that worketh not*, in this verse, is not meant one who merely does not conform to the ceremonial law; because *he that worketh not* and *the ungodly*, are evidently synonymous expressions, or what signify the same, as appears by the manner of their connexion; if not, to what purpose is the latter expression, *the ungodly*, brought in? The context gives no other occasion for it, but to show, that by the grace of the gospel, God in justification has no regard to any godliness of ours. The foregoing verse is, " Now to him that worketh, is the reward not reckoned of grace, but of debt." In *that* verse, it is evident, gospel grace consists in the reward being given *without works;* and in *this* verse, which immediately follows it, and in sense is connected with it, gospel-grace consists in a man's being justified as *ungodly*. By which it is most plain, that by *him that worketh not*, and him that is *ungodly*, are meant the same thing; and that therefore not only works of the ceremonial law are excluded in this business of justification, but works of morality and godliness.

3. It is evident in the words, that by the faith here spoken of, by which we are justified, is not meant the same thing as a course of obedience or righteousness, since the expression by which this faith is here denoted, is *believing on him that justifies the ungodly*.——They that oppose the Solifidians, as they call them, greatly insist on it, that we should take the words of Scripture concerning this doctrine in their most natural and obvious meaning; and how do they cry out, of our clouding this doctrine with obscure metaphors, and unintelligible figures of speech? But is this to interpret Scripture according to its most obvious meaning, when the Scripture speaks of our *believing on him that justifies the ungodly*, or the *breakers of his law*, to say, that the meaning of it is performing a course of obedience to his law, and avoiding the breaches of it? Believing on God as a *justifier*, certainly is a different thing from submitting to God as a *lawgiver;* especially believing on him as a justifier of *the ungodly*, or *rebels against the lawgiver*.

4. It is evident that the subject of justification is looked upon as destitute of any righteousness in himself, by that expression, *it is counted or imputed to him for righteousness*.—The phrase, as the apostle uses it here and in the context, manifestly imports, that God of his sovereign grace is pleased, in his dealings with the sinner, so to regard one that has no righteousness, that the consequence shall be the same as if he had. This however may be from the respect it bears to some thing that is indeed righteous. It is plain that this is the force of the expression in the preceding verses. In the last verse but one, it is manifest, the apostle lays the stress of his argument for the free grace of God—from that text of the Old Testament about Abraham—on the word *counted* or *imputed;* and this is the thing that he supposed God to show his grace in, *viz.* in this *counting* something for righteousness, in his consequential dealings with Abraham, that was no righteousness in itself. And in the next verse which immediately precedes the text, " Now to him that worketh, is the reward not reckoned of grace, but of debt," the word there translated *reckoned*, is the same that in the other verses is rendered *imputed*, and *counted:* and it is as much as if the apostle had said, "As to *him that works*, there is no need of any gracious *reckoning* or *counting* it for righteousness, and causing the reward to follow as if it were a righteousness; for if he has works, he has that which is a righteousness in itself, to which the reward properly belongs." This is further evident by the words that follow, verse 6. " Even as David also described the blessedness of the man unto whom God imputeth righteousness without works." What can here be meant by imputing righteousness without works, but imputing righteousness to him that has none of his own? verse 7, 8. " Saying, Blessed are they whose iniquities are forgiven, and whose sins are covered: blessed is the man to whom the Lord will not impute sin." How are these words of David to the apostle's purpose? or how do they prove any such thing, as that righteousness is imputed without works, unless it be because the word *imputed* is used, and the subject of the imputation is mentioned as a sinner, and consequently destitute of a moral righteousness? For David says no such thing, as that he is forgiven without the works of the ceremonial law; there is no hint of the ceremonial law, or reference to it, in the words.—I will therefore venture to infer this *doctrine* from the words, for the subject of my present discourse, *viz.*

That we are justified only by faith in Christ, and not by any manner of virtue or goodness of our own.

Such an assertion as this, I am sensible, many would be ready to call absurd, as betraying a great deal of ignorance, and containing much inconsistence; but I desire every one's patience till I have done.

In handling this doctrine, I would,

I. Explain the *meaning* of it, and show how I would be understood by such an assertion.

II. Proceed to the consideration of the evidence of the *truth* of it.

III. Show how evangelical obedience is concerned in this affair.

IV. Answer objections.

V. Consider the importance of the doctrine.

I. I would explain the meaning of the doctrine, or show in what sense I assert it, and would endeavour to evince the truth of it: which may be done in answer to these two inquiries, *viz.* 1. What is meant by being justified? 2. What is meant when it is said, that this is, " by faith alone, without any manner of virtue or goodness of our own?"

First, I would show what justification is, or what I suppose is meant in Scripture by being justified.

A person is said to be *justified*, when he is approved of God as free from the guilt of sin and its deserved punishment, and as having that righteousness belonging to him that entitles to the reward of life. That we should take the word in such a sense, and understand it as the judge's accepting a person as having both a negative and positive righteousness belonging to him, and looking on him therefore as not only free from any obligation to punishment, but also as just and righteous, and so entitled to a positive reward, is not only most agreeable to the etymology and natural import of the word, which signifies to pass one for righteous in judgment, but also manifestly agreeable to the force of the word as used in Scripture.

Some suppose that nothing more is intended in Scripture by justification, than barely the remission of sins. If so, it is very strange, if we consider the nature of the case; for it is most evident, and none will deny, that it is with respect to the rule or law of God we are under, that we are said in Scripture to be either justified or condemned. Now what is it to justify a person as the subject of a law or rule, but to judge him as standing right with respect to that rule? To justify a person in a particular case, is to approve of him as standing right, as subject to the law in that case; and to justify in general is to pass him in judgment, as standing right in a state correspondent to the law or rule in general: but certainly, in order to a person's being looked on as standing right with respect to the rule in general, or in a state corresponding with the law of God, more is needful than not having the guilt of sin; for whatever that law is, whether a new or an old one, doubtless something positive is needed in order to its being answered. We are no more justified by the voice of the law, or of him that judges according to it, by a mere pardon of sin, than Adam, our first surety, was justified by the law, at the first point of his existence, before he had fulfilled the obedience of the law, or had so much as any trial whether he would fulfil it or no. If Adam had finished his course of perfect obedience, he would have been justified: and certainly his justification would have implied something more than what is merely negative; he would have been approved of, as having fulfilled the righteousness of the law, and accordingly would have been adjudged to the reward of it. So Christ, our second surety, (in whose justification all whose surety he is, are virtually justified,) was not justified till he had done the work the Father had appointed him, and kept the Father's commandments through all trials; and then in his resurrection he was justified. When he had been put to death in the flesh, but quickened by the spirit, 1 Pet. iii. 18. then he that was manifest in the flesh was justified in the spirit, 1 Tim. iii. 16.; but God, when he justified him in raising him from the dead, did not only release him from his humiliation for sin, and acquit him from any further suffering or abasement for it, but admitted him to that eternal and immortal life, and to the beginning of that exaltation that was the reward of what he had done. And indeed the justification of a believer is no other than his being admitted to communion in the justification of this head and surety of all believers; for as Christ suffered the punishment of sin, not as a private person, but as our surety; so when after this suffering he was raised from the dead, he was therein justified, not as a private person, but as the surety and representative of all that should believe in him. So that he was raised again not only for his own, but also for our justification, according to the apostle, Rom. iv. 25. "Who was delivered for our offences, and raised again for our justification." And therefore it is that the apostle says, as he does in Rom. viii. 34. "Who is he that condemneth? It is Christ that died, yea rather, that is risen again."

But that a believer's justification implies not only remission of sins, or acquittance from the wrath due to it, but also an admittance to a title to that glory which is the reward of righteousness, is more directly taught in the Scripture, particularly in Rom. v. 1, 2. where the apostle mentions both these as joint benefits implied in justification: "Therefore being justified by faith, we have peace with God through our Lord Jesus Christ, by whom also we have access into this grace wherein we stand, and rejoice in hope of the glory of God." So remission of sin, and inheritance among them that are sanctified, are mentioned together as what are jointly obtained by faith in Christ, Acts xxvi. 18. "That they may receive forgiveness of sins, and inheritance among them that are sanctified, through faith that is in me." Both these are without doubt implied in that passing from death to life, which Christ speaks of as the fruit of faith, and which he opposes to condemnation, John v. 24. "Verily I say unto you, he that heareth my word, and believeth on him that sent me, hath everlasting life, and shall not come into condemnation; but is passed from death unto life." I proceed now,

Secondly, To show what is meant when it is said, that this justification is by faith only, and not by any virtue or goodness of our own.

This inquiry may be subdivided into two, *viz.*

1. How it is by *faith*. 2. How it is by faith *alone*, without any manner of goodness of ours.

1. How justification is by *faith*.—Here the great difficulty has been about the import and force of the particle *by*, or what is that influence that faith has in the affair of justification that is expressed in Scripture by being justified by faith.

Here, if I may humbly express what seems evident to me, though faith be indeed the condition of justification so as nothing else is, yet this matter is not clearly and sufficiently explained by saying that faith is the condition of justification; and that because the word seems ambiguous, both in common use, and also as used in divinity. In one sense, Christ alone performs the condition of our justification and salvation; in another sense, faith is the condition of justification; in another sense, other qualifications and acts are conditions of salvation and justification too. There seems to be a great deal of ambiguity in such expressions as are commonly used, (which yet we are forced to use,) such as condition of salvation, what is required in order to salvation or justification, the terms of the covenant, and the like; and I believe they are understood in very different senses by different persons. And besides, as the word condition is very often understood in the common use of language, faith is not the only thing in us that is the condition of justification; for by the word condition, as it is very often (and perhaps most commonly) used, we mean any thing that may have the place of a condition in a conditional proposition, and as such is truly connected with the consequent, especially if the proposition holds both in the affirmative and negative, as the condition is either affirmed or denied. If it be that with which, or which being supposed, a thing shall be, and without which, or it being denied, a thing shall not be, we in such a case call it a condition of that thing. But in this sense faith is not the only condition of salvation or justification; for there are many things that accompany and flow from faith, with which justification shall be, and without which it will not be, and therefore are found to be put in Scripture in conditional propositions with justification and salvation, in multitudes of places; such are love to God, and love to our brethren, forgiving men their trespasses, and many other good qualifications and acts. And there are many other things besides faith, which are directly proposed to us, to be pursued or performed by us, in order to eternal life, which if they are done, or obtained, we shall have eternal life, and if not done, or not obtained, we shall surely perish. And if faith was the only condition of justification in this sense, I do not apprehend that to say faith was the condition of justification, would express the sense of that phrase of Scripture, of being justified by faith. There is a difference between being justified by a thing, and that thing universally, necessarily, and inseparably attending justification; for so do a great many things that we are not said to be justified by. It is not the inseparable connexion with justification that the Holy Ghost would signify (or that is naturally signified) by such a phrase, but some particular influence that faith has in the affair, or some certain dependence that effect has on its influence.

Some, aware of this, have supposed, that the influence or dependence might well be expressed by faith's being the *instrument* of our justification; which has been misunderstood, and injuriously represented, and ridiculed by those that have denied the doctrine of justification by faith alone, as though they had supposed faith was used as an instrument in the hand of God, whereby he performed and brought to pass that act of his, *viz.* approving and justifying the believer. Whereas it was not intended that faith was the instrument wherewith God justifies, but the instrument wherewith we receive justification; not the instrument wherewith the justifier acts in justifying, but wherewith the receiver of justification acts in accepting justification. But yet, it must be owned, this is an obscure way of speaking, and there must certainly be some impropriety in calling it an instrument wherewith we receive or accept justification; for the very persons who thus explain the matter, speak of faith as being the reception or acceptance itself; and if so, how can it be the instrument of reception or acceptance? Certainly there is a difference between the act and the instrument. Besides, by their own descriptions of faith, Christ, the mediator by whom, and his righteousness by which, we are justified, is more directly the object of this acceptance and justification, which is the benefit arising therefrom more indirectly; and therefore, if faith be an instrument, it is more properly the instrument by which we receive Christ, than the instrument by which we receive justification.

But I humbly conceive we have been ready to look too far to find out what that influence of faith in our justification is, or what is that dependence of this effect on faith, signified by the expression of being justified by faith, overlooking that which is most obviously pointed forth in the expression, *viz.* that (there being a mediator that has purchased justification) faith in this mediator is that which renders it a meet and suitable thing, in the sight of God, that the believer, rather than others, should have this purchased benefit assigned to him.—There is this benefit purchased, which God sees it to be a more meet and suitable thing that it should be assigned to some rather than others, because he sees them differently qualified: that qualification wherein the meetness to this benefit, as the case stands, consists, is that in us by which we are justified. If Christ had not come into the world and died, &c. to purchase justification, no qualification whatever in us could render it a meet or fit thing that we should be justified. But the case being as it now stands, *viz.* that Christ has actually purchased justification by his own blood for infinitely unworthy creatures, there may be certain qualifications found in some persons, which, either from the relation it bears to the mediator and his merits, or on some other account, is the thing that in the sight of God renders it a meet and condecent thing, that they should have an interest in this purchased benefit, and of which if any are destitute, it renders it an unfit and unsuitable thing that they should have it. The wisdom of God in his constitutions doubtless appears much in the fitness and beauty of them, so that those things are established to be done that are fit to be done, and that those things are connected in his constitution that are agreeable one to another. So God justifies a believer according to his revealed constitution, without doubt, because he sees something in this qualification that, as the case stands, renders it a fit thing that such should be justified; whether it be because faith is the instrument, or as it were the hand, by which he that has purchased justification is apprehended and accepted, or because it is the acceptance itself, or whatever else. To be justified, is to be approved of God as a proper subject of pardon, with a right to eternal life; and therefore, when it is said that we are justified by faith, what else can be understood by it, than that faith is that by which we are rendered approvable, fitly so, and indeed, as the case stands, proper subjects of this benefit?

This is something different from faith being the *condition* of justification, though inseparably connected with justification. So are many other things besides faith; and yet nothing in us but faith renders it meet that we should have justification assigned to us; as I shall presently show in answer to the next inquiry, *viz.*

2. How this is said to be by faith *alone*, without any manner of virtue or goodness of our own. This may seem to some to be attended with two difficulties, *viz.* how this can be said to be by faith alone, without any virtue or goodness of ours, when faith itself is a virtue, and one part of our goodness, and is not only some manner of goodness of ours, but is a very excellent qualification, and one chief part of the inherent holiness of a Christian? And if it be a part of our inherent goodness or excellency (whether it be this part or any other) that renders it a condecent or congruous thing that we should have this benefit of Christ assigned to us, what is this less than what they mean who talk of a merit of congruity? And moreover, if this part of our christian holiness qualifies us, in the sight of God, for this benefit of Christ, and renders it a fit or meet thing, in his sight, that we should have it, why should not other parts of holiness, and conformity to God, which are also very excellent, and have as much of the image of Christ in them, and are no less lovely in God's eyes, qualify us as much, and have as much influence to render us meet, in God's sight, for such a benefit as this? Therefore I answer,

When it is said, that we are not justified by any righteousness or goodness of our *own*, what is meant is, that it is not out of respect to the excellency or goodness of any qualifications or acts in us whatsoever, that God judges it meet that this benefit of Christ should be ours; and it is not, in any wise, on account of any excellency or value that there is in faith, that it appears in the sight of God a meet thing, that he who believes should have this benefit of Christ assigned to him, but purely from the relation faith has to the person in whom this benefit is to be had, or as it unites to that mediator, in and by whom we are justified. Here, for the greater clearness, I would particularly explain myself under several propositions.

(1.) It is certain that there is some union or relation that the people of Christ stand in to him, that is expressed in Scripture, from time to time, by being *in Christ*, and is represented frequently by those metaphors of being members of Christ, or being united to him as members to the head, and branches to the stock,* and is compared to a marriage union between husband and wife. I do not now pretend to determine of what sort this union is; nor is it necessary to my present purpose to enter into any manner of disputes about it. If any are disgusted at the word *union*, as obscure and unintelligible, the word *relation* equally serves my purpose. I do not now desire to determine any more about it, than all, of all sorts, will readily allow, *viz.* that there is a peculiar *relation* between true Christians and Christ, which there is not between him and others; and which is signified by those metaphorical expressions in Scripture, of being in Christ, being members of Christ, &c.†

* "Our Saviour compares his mystical body, that is his church, to a vine, which his Father, whom he compares to a husbandman, hath planted; *I am the true vine, and my Father is the husbandman.* To represent to us the union that is betwixt Christ and all true Christians, and the influence of grace and spiritual life, which all that are united to him do derive and receive from him, he sets it forth to us by the resemblance of a vine and branches. As there is a natural vital union between the vine and the branches, so there is a spiritual union between Christ and true Christians; and this union is the cause of our fruitfulness in the works of obedience and a good life. There are some indeed that seem to be grafted into Christ by an outward profession of Christianity, who yet derive no influence from him, so as to bring forth fruit, because they are not vitally united to him"—*Dr. Tillotson in his 3rd vol. of Serm.* p. 307.

By this it appears that the vital union between Christ and true Christians, which is much more of a mystery than the relative union, and necessarily implies it, was not thought an unreasonable doctrine by one of the greatest divines on the other side of the question in hand.

† The word "*union*," in this connexion, is both more intelligible and more appropriate, than the word *relation*; since in this connexion the latter is the consequence of the former. As the doctrine of a *vital union* to Christ is fundamentally important in Christianity, and inseparable from the doctrine of justification; and as our author passes it over with so much brevity, a few observations upon it in this place may appear the more needful.

1. The Scriptures are not only full of the *fact*, but they abound with *illustrations* of it. The first part of John xv. is full and explicit to this purpose.

2. What the Scriptures assert, and illustrate, is abundantly corroborated by the *reasonableness* of the thing. To suppose the reality of *vital religion* without a corresponding *vital union*, is to suppose an important effect without an adequate cause, as shall be further shown.

3. The question then is, What is the *immediate* cause of this vital union? Now as the union subsisting is between the Spirit of *Christ*, and *man*, the immediate *cause* must be in the *one* or the *other* of these, or in *both* at the same instant, or in *neither*. If the immediate cause be in MAN, he makes his approach to Christ either as a *carnal* or a *spiritual* man, for there is no conceivable medium. But the idea of a *carnal* man uniting himself to Christ in order to form a vital union, is both unscriptural and unreasonable. It is *unscriptural*; for the scripture asserts that "The carnal mind is enmity

(2.) This *relation* or *union* to Christ, whereby Christians are said to be in Christ, (whatever it be,) is the ground of their right to his benefits. This needs no proof; the reason of the thing, at first blush, demonstrates it. It is exceeding evident also by Scripture, 1 John v. 12. "He that hath the Son, hath life; and he that hath not the Son, hath not life." 1 Cor. i. 30. "Of him are ye in Christ Jesus, who of God is made unto us—righteousness." First we must be *in him*, and then he will be made righteousness or justification to us. Eph. i. 6. "Who hath made us accepted in the beloved." Our being *in him* is the ground of our being accepted. So it is in those unions to which the Holy Ghost has thought fit to compare this. The *union* of the members of the body with the head, is the ground of their partaking of the life of the head; it is the *union* of the branches to the stock, which is the ground of their partaking of the sap and life of the stock; it is the *relation* of the wife to the husband, that is the ground of her joint interest in his estate; they are looked upon, in several respects, as one in law. So there is a legal union between Christ and true Christians; so that (as all except Socinians allow) one, in some respects, is accepted for the other by the Supreme Judge.

(3.) And thus it is that faith is the qualification in any person that renders it meet in the sight of God that he should be looked upon as having Christ's satisfaction and righteousness belonging to him, *viz.* because it is that in him which, *on his part*, makes up this union between him and Christ. By what has been just now observed, it is a person's being, according to scripture phrase, *in Christ*, that is the ground of having his satisfaction and merits belong to him, and a right to the benefits procured thereby. The reason of it is plain; it is easy to see how our having Christ's merits and benefits belonging to us, follows from our having (if I may so speak) *Christ himself* belonging to us, or our being united to him. And if so, it must also be easy to see how, or in what manner, that in a person, which *on his part* makes up the *union* between his soul and Christ, should be the thing on the account of which God looks on it as meet that he should have Christ's merits belonging to him. It is a very different thing for God to assign to a particular person a right to Christ's merits and benefits from regard to a qualification in him in this respect, from his doing it for him out of respect to the *value* or loveliness of that qualification, or as a reward of its excellency.

As there is nobody but what will allow that there is a peculiar *relation* between Christ and his true disciples, by which they are in some sense in Scripture said to be *one;* so I suppose there is nobody but what will allow, that there may be something that the true Christian does *on his part*, whereby he is *active* in coming into this relation or union; some *uniting* act, or that which is done towards this union or relation (or whatever any please to call it) *on the Christian's part*. Now faith I suppose to be this act.

I do not now pretend to define justifying faith, or to determine precisely how much is contained in it, but only to determine thus much concerning it, *viz.* That it is that by which the soul, which before was separate and alienated from Christ, unites itself to him, or ceases to be any longer in that state of alienation, and comes into that forementioned union or relation to him; or, to use the scripture phrase, it is that by which the soul comes to Christ,

against God;" how then can it be the cause of a vital union? "Of *him* are ye in Christ Jesus;"—"and you hath he quickened, who were dead in trespasses and sins;"—it is not therefore the carnal man that unites himself to Christ, or quickens himself in order to effect it. It is also *unreasonable;* for it supposes a glorious effect without an *adequate* cause. The effect is *spiritual*, while the cause is *carnal*, which are not only different but even directly *opposite*. What ideas can be more contradictory, or sentiment more unreasonable?

4. The supposition of *two simultaneous causes*, the one being the Spirit of Christ, and the other the carnal man, involves the same inconsistency. For how can the mere circumstance of *time*, irrespective of *causal* influence, make any difference? If the carnal mind be adequate to unite itself to Christ at *one time*, why not at *another* time as well, except some *causal* influence makes the difference? For surely no one can suppose that some individual moment of time, as distinguished from others preceding, constitutes the *cause* of difference.

5. To suppose a *spiritual* man, whether by the exercise of his faith or by any other mental act, in the *cause* of a vital union, is no less inconsistent than the former suppositions. For how came he to be a *spiritual* man without a spiritual causal influence? But if such influence be admitted as a predisposing cause of his vital acts, it is incumbent on the objector to show that such causal influence *may* take place *without* vital union. This, I am persuaded, no one can do. It is contrary to all analogy, and to every sound principle of true philosophy. It is contrary to Christian experience and revealed statements. What effect in *physical* nature can be produced, which does not imply a causal *union?* Does not the divine energy pervade all second causes in the way of *union* with them, in order to the production of their effects? and what *miraculous* effects have ever been produced without a present *uniting* cause? For instance, when Lazarus came forth from death to life, was there not an *uniting* causal influence to produce the change? and if we appeal to an experienced intelligent Christian, will he not own, will he not maintain, according to his views of revealed truth, that the powerful, the quickening, and uniting presence, the vital and transforming energy of the Spirit of God or of Christ in him, was the cause of his own vitality? Nay, would he not be shocked to hear any one maintain the contrary?

6. Perhaps it may be thought, that—though in the great laboratory of physical nature, in the bowels of the earth and in the surrounding atmosphere, a *causal union* be necessary to produce *chemical* effects; and that though in all works of mechanism a *causal union* is requisite to the existence of *mechanical* effects; and that, moreover, though the sun by his light and heat produces an effect upon objects by a *causal union* with them; yet, what shall we say of one body affecting a change of situation in another, at an immense distance? Does not the sun powerfully attract all the planets that surround him, however distant? and how can this be by *causal union?* This objection admits of two answers.

7. *First*, it has never been *proved*, that there is *no causal union* between these bodies adequate to the effect; while on the contrary several philosophers have at least attempted to show its existence. The solar system, for ought we know, may be perfectly mechanical, though we should never be able to perceive the intermediate parts.

8. *Secondly*, as the universe in general depends on the *causal presence* of the first cause, so must every part of it; Scripture and reason assure us that IN GOD we *live*, and *move*, and have our *being*. Therefore, whether there be any *intermediate* cause of gravitation or not, between the effect and the first cause, a *causal union* is still necessary to the effect. What difference there is, lies *against* the objector. For if there be no *intermediate* cause of gravitation, the presence, the energy, the *causal union* of the first cause is proportionally the *more immediate*.

9. Having shown that neither the carnal man nor the spiritual man is the immediate cause of the union subsisting between Christ and the Christian, it remains to be ascertained, what else is the cause? If it be not man it must be the DIVINE SPIRIT, either as the Spirit of the *Father* or of *Christ*. In one view this difference is not very material, but in another it is of considerable importance. Allow it to be from the Holy Spirit, in either sense, it secures the great point of salvation by *grace*, in opposition to our own *merit*. But, as it respects the nature of Christ's mediation, and particularly his federal headship and suretiship, it is of moment to ascertain, whether he or the Father, economically, be the *immediate cause* of the vital union.

10. The Scripture fully declares that the influence of the Spirit on the minds of men is from *Christ*. The Lord from heaven is a *quickening Spirit*—he *quickeneth* whom he will—he *sends* the Holy Ghost—he *gives* repentance, or the spirit of repentance—in him was life, (without whom nothing was created,) and this life is the true light of men—he *shines* into the heart—his *grace* and *strength* constitute our sufficiency—&c. These and other passages innumerable show, that quickening influence proceeds from his fulness of life and grace.

11. That other passages ascribe spiritual effects to the Holy Spirit, or the Spirit of God, is of no force, except with such as deny the divine nature of Christ, who are confuted on other grounds. But supposing his divine nature in union with humanity, the Spirit of God is the Spirit of Christ, and *vice versa*. And in the divine economy of grace, Christ is the head or source of influence to the church. It is he who gives gifts to the rebellious, who endows with the spirit of life, and who bestows the living water to which divine influence is compared.

12. And how beautifully consistent must this appear when we consider, that as a covenant head he is the *surety* of his chosen people! The office of a surety engages to perform what is requisite in behalf of a person or persons as required by another. Thus Jesus not only brought in an everlasting righteousness in behalf of his people as their federal perfection, in lieu of those who could never attain to it by any obedience of their own; but it also belonged to his office to secure for them a voluntary, penitential, believing obedience to the equitable requisitions of the divine Governor. This can be effected only by divine influence, and that influence must needs proceed from him as the immediate cause; otherwise we make the creditor and surety to be the very same. God, as governor, *demands obedience* from all the subjects of his government; and Christ, as the surety of those who were given him, *enables* them to comply with those demands, that is, to *submit*, to repent, to believe with the heart, to love God, and to walk with him.

13. From the premises it follows plainly, that the *immediate cause* of vital union is the SPIRIT OF CHRIST, which he bestows in the exercise of his office as the federal head of influence, and in virtue of his suretiship for his church and people. He as the true vine communicates life to the branches, and as the head of his church brings dead souls to be his living members. Faith is a *fruit* of the Spirit, and not the *cause* of a spiritual existence. Yet,

14. We maintain that *faith* forms a *consequent* union. Man being a subject of moral government, and therefore a free agent, at liberty to choose his end and means of happiness for which he is accountable; and God in infinite mercy proposing Jesus as the way, the truth, and the life; the all-sufficient and only Saviour of sinners—in whom we are required to believe and to trust with confidence, and whom we are encouraged to receive into our hearts, that he may dwell there by faith—the regenerate soul, by *believing*, *unites* itself to this object.

15. The former union is the immediate effect of *sovereign favour;* the latter union is the immediate effect of *exercised* grace; in the performance of an incumbent *duty*, or the discharge of moral *obligation*. Now since men are exhorted, warned, directed, reasoned, and expostulated with, on the ground of what they *ought* to do or abstain from doing, the Scripture abounds with such addresses. But lest any false inferences should be drawn, derogatory from the honours of sovereign grace, we are assured that every good and perfect gift cometh from the Father of lights. When we have done all we are unprofitable servants. Work out your own salvation, says Paul, with fear and trembling; for it is God who worketh in you both to will and to do of his own good pleasure. No one can come unto me except the Father who hath sent me draw him, that is, without divine influence; and whosoever cometh unto me, I will in no wise cast out. Ye have not chosen me, but I have chosen you. Ye are saved by grace, through faith, and that not of yourselves, it is the gift of God. Among many other parts of Scripture where *grace* and *obligation* are strikingly intermixed, and illustrative of the preceding remarks, the reader is particularly referred to the *sixth* and *fifteenth* chapters of St. John's Gospel.

16. *Coroll.* The old mode, adopted by many orthodox divines, of distinguishing the *vital union* between Christ and his people, first, on *his part*, and secondly, on *their part*, is founded on Scripture and the reason of the thing; and the former is the *cause* of the latter. And therefore, as the cause must ever *precede* the effect, the *first* union not only *may* be prior to the *second*, as in the *case* of happy infants, but also *must* be so in the case of adults.—W

and *receives* him: and this is evident by the Scriptures using these very expressions to signify faith. John vi. 35—39. "He that *cometh* to me, shall never hunger; and he that *believeth* on me, shall never thirst. But I said unto you, that ye also have seen me and believe not. All that the Father giveth me, shall *come to* me; and him that *cometh to* me, I will in no wise cast out. For I came down from heaven, not to do mine own will, but the will of him that sent me." Ver. 40. "And this is the will of him that sent me, that every one which seeth the Son, and *believeth* on him, may have everlasting life; and I will raise him up at the last day." Chap. v. 38—40.——"Whom he hath sent, him ye *believe* not. Search the Scriptures, for—they are they which testify of me. And ye will not *come unto me*, that ye might have life." Ver. 43, 44. "I am come in my Father's name, and ye *receive* me not: if another shall come in his own name, him ye will *receive*. How can ye *believe*, which receive honour one of another—?" Chap. i. 12. "But as many as *received* him, to them gave he power to become the sons of God, even to them that *believe* on his name." If it be said that these are obscure figures of speech, which, however they might be well understood of old among those who commonly used such metaphors, are with difficulty understood now. I allow, that the expressions of *receiving* Christ and *coming* to Christ, are metaphorical expressions; and if I should allow them to be obscure metaphors, yet thus much at least is certainly plain in them, *viz.* that faith is that by which those who before were separated, and at a distance from Christ, (that is to say, were not so related and united to him as his people are,) cease to be any longer at such a distance, and come into that relation and nearness; unless they are so unintelligible, that nothing at all can be understood by them.

God does not give those that believe an union with or an interest in the Saviour as a *reward* for faith, but only because faith is the soul's *active* uniting with Christ, or is itself the very act of unition, *on their part*. God sees it fit, that in order to an union being established between two intelligent active beings or persons, so as that they should be looked upon as one, there should be the mutual act of both, that each should receive other, as actively joining themselves one to another. God, in requiring this in order to an union with Christ as one of his people, treats men as reasonable creatures, capable of act and choice; and hence sees it fit that they only who are one with Christ by their own act, should be looked upon as one *in law*. What is *real* in the union between Christ and his people, is the foundation of what is *legal*; that is, it is something really in them, and between them, uniting them, that is the ground of the suitableness of their being accounted as one by the Judge. And if there be any *act* or qualification in believers of that uniting nature, that it is meet on that account the Judge should look upon them and accept them as one, no wonder that upon the account of the same act or qualification, he should accept the satisfaction and merits of the one for the other, as if these were their own satisfaction and merits. This necessarily follows, or rather is implied.

And thus it is that faith justifies, or gives an interest in Christ's satisfaction and merits, and a right to the benefits procured thereby, *viz.* as it thus makes Christ and the believer *one* in the acceptance of the Supreme Judge. It is by faith that we have a title to eternal life, because it is by faith that we have the Son of God, by whom life is. The apostle John in these words, 1 John v. 12. "He that hath the Son, hath life," seems evidently to have respect to those words of Christ of which he gives an account in his gospel, chap. iii. 36. "He that believeth on the Son, hath everlasting life; and he that believeth not the Son, shall not see life." And where the Scripture speaks of faith as the soul's receiving or coming to Christ, it also speaks of this receiving, coming to, or joining with, Christ, as the ground of an interest in his benefits. To as many as received him, "to them gave he power" to become the sons of God. Ye will not come unto me "that ye might have life." And there is a wide difference between its being suitable that Christ's satisfaction and merits should be theirs who believe, because an interest in that satisfaction and merit is a fit *reward* of faith—or a suitable testimony of God's respect to the amiableness and excellency of that grace—and its being suitable that Christ's satisfaction and merits should be theirs, because Christ and they are so united, that in the eyes of the Judge they may be looked upon and taken as one.

Although, on account of faith in the believer, it is in the sight of God fit and congruous, both that he who believes should be looked upon as in Christ, and also as having an interest in his merits, in the way that has been now explained; yet it appears that this is very wide from a *merit of congruity*, or indeed any *moral* congruity at all to either.* There is a twofold fitness to a state; I know

* The term here used, "*moral* congruity," is not happily chosen. Indeed our author, in the next sentence, professes himself to be *at a loss* what terms to use which may clearly convey the necessary distinction. By "*moral*" congruity or fitness he seems to mean *personal perfection*, or a perfection of state personally considered, without relation to a surety, or the righteousness which God has provided. But this is an acceptation of the term "moral" so unusual as to throw great perplexity into the argument. Beside, when *contrasted* with *believing*, it leaves the reader to suppose that *to believe* is not a *moral act*. But the supposition that "believing with the heart unto righteousness" is not a *moral* act, as contradistinguished from a *natural* one, leads to an endless confusion of ideas. Surely, to *believe* God's testimony concerning his Son and his righteousness is, if any thing be, a *moral* act of obedience to divine authority. How then can it be called a *natural* fitness only, as contrasted with what is *moral?* Nor is the distinction at all necessary in order to avoid the apprehended consequence of assigning to faith any *merit* of congruity. A few observations on this intricate subject may probably assist the reader in seeking scriptural and consistent notions.

1. Justification implies a *charge*, a *plea*, and a virtual declaration of *approval*.

2. The *charge* against Adam and all his posterity is twofold, including a breach of *covenant*, or a failure in federal *perfection;* and also *disobedience* in transgressing a divine *rule*. These considerations are perfectly distinct in their nature. A rule may be momentarily transgressed for a long series of years, as it was by Adam, and constantly is by his rebellious descendants, but a federal failure was, from the nature of perfect righteousness, the *very first act* of delinquency.

3. No *plea* can be valid against a *federal* delinquency, as was the case in Adam, but a participation of a *federal perfection*. Nothing less can answer the charge, and nothing more is requisite. This averts condemnation, and entitles to a virtual *approval* in reference to *that part* of the charge.

4. No *plea* can be valid against *disobedience* to divine authority, or the *rule* of moral government, but a *personal*, voluntary, actual compliance with that authoritative rule of government; which we find by divine revelation to be, in reference to fallen man, *submission* to the righteousness of God; or, as differently expressed, *believing* on the Son of God, *receiving* him as the Lord *our righteousness*, &c.

5. No man has possessed a *federal perfection*, except by *imputation*, beside the first Adam while he obeyed without failure, and the second Adam when he completed his work of humiliation. For no eminence of grace in a mere descendant of Adam could possibly attain to federal perfection, from the very nature of such perfection. Nor indeed can the perfect obedience of glorified saints rise higher than a conformity to the divine law as a *rule;* their federal perfection is still derived from their *union* to Christ, and a consequent *imputation*, which implies a virtual *approval*. Hence,

6. The *federal perfection* of Messiah is the proper and *sole ground* of an actual interest in reconciliation and justification. In other words, the righteousness of Christ, his perfect obedience unto death as our substitute, is that *alone* on account of which we can stand before God with acceptance, in reference to the charge of a federal failure in Adam.

7. An *actual interest* in this federal perfection is obtained only by a *vital* or an *effectual union* to the Lord our righteousness. This is plain from Scripture, and is perfectly rational. It is compared to the union of a vine and its branches, the head and members of the human body, &c. That a participation of nature between Christ and us, or an effectual *union*, is requisite for a ground of imputation is evident, not only from scriptural comparisons, and the rational consistence of such an idea, but also from the fact of the Saviour's *incarnation*. Without *this union* to us, our sin could not have been *imputed* to him; and without a vital union, his righteousness could not be imputed to us. This is fairly and fully implied in many parts of Scripture, as might be shown if necessary.—From whence it is plain, that *union* is the indispensable ground of *imputation*.

8. Whoever is the subject of a *vital union* to Christ, is in a *justified* state, as partaker of a *federal perfection*, prior to the performance of any moral duty whatever. But in order to explain and prove this it is requisite to attend to the following particulars.

9. Union to Christ is of *two kinds*, on *his* part by his SPIRIT; and on *our* part by FAITH, as explained in a preceding note. In the former, we are *passive;* and in the latter, we are *active*. In the one, *he acts* as a sovereign dispenser of benefits; in the other *we act* as accountable creatures.

10. By the order both of nature and of time, the *union* begins with *him* who is a quickening Spirit; and that of faith is consequent upon the other, and is the proper *effect* of it.

11. By *his* uniting act, which may be termed effectual calling, the enmity of sin is destroyed in the soul, and the Spirit of Christ is imparted, which as occasion offers, will manifest itself as the Spirit of faith, of love, &c. Hence,

12. To the soul *thus* in Christ, whether infant or adult, there is no condemnation arising from federal delinquency; for this charge is answered by the *union* on his part; and righteousness is imputed.

13. From the premises it follows, that the generally received theological maxim is perfectly just and plain, *viz.* that justification and regeneration are *simultaneous.*—*Union* is the immediate cause of both; and because the one is a *relative* and the other a *vital* effect, there is no interference as to the order of time. Thus an union of a tree and a branch by ingrafture, is attended with two *simultaneous* effects, the one *relative* and the other *vital;* it is *related* to the tree as a branch, and at the same time partakes of the vital sap. The union, however, must precede both, as to nature and time.

14. But where two effects are *both real*, as distinguished from *relative*, the one *must* precede the other, both as to nature and time. Thus union precedes vitality, and this of necessity must precede vital acts; and *regeneration*, as the act of the Spirit of Christ, must necessarily precede *believing*, which is one mode by which a vital principle *operates*. For to suppose

not how to give them distinguishing names, otherwise than by calling the one a *moral*, and the other a *natural*, fitness. A person has a moral fitness for a state, when his moral excellency commends him to it, or when his being put into such a good state is but a suitable testimony of regard to the moral excellency, or value, or amiableness of any of his qualifications or acts. A person has a natural fitness for a state, when it appears meet and condecent that he should be in such a state or circumstances, only from the natural concord or agreeableness there is between such qualifications and such circumstances; not because the qualifications are lovely or unlovely, but only because the qualifications and the circumstances are like one another, or do in their nature suit and agree or unite one to another. And it is on this latter account only that God looks on it fit by a natural fitness, that he whose heart sincerely unites itself to Christ as his Saviour, should be looked upon as united to that Saviour, and so having an interest in him; and not from any moral fitness there is between the excellency of such a qualification as faith, and such a glorious blessedness as the having an interest in Christ. God's bestowing Christ and his benefits on a soul in consequence of faith, out of regard only to the natural concord there is between such a qualification of a soul, and such an union with Christ, and interest in him, makes the case very widely different from what it would be, if he bestowed this from regard to any moral suitableness. For, in the former case, it is only from God's love of order that he bestows these things on the account of faith: in the latter, God doth it out of love to the grace of faith itself. God will neither look on Christ's merits as ours, nor adjudge his benefits to us, till we be in Christ: nor will he look upon us as being in him, without an active unition of our hearts and souls to him; because he is a wise being, and delights in order, and not in confusion, and that things should be together or asunder according to their nature; and his making such a constitution is a testimony of his love of order.* Whereas if it were out of regard to any moral fitness or suitableness between faith and such blessedness, it would be a testimony of his love to the act or qualification itself. The one supposes this divine constitution to be a manifestation of God's regard to the beauty of the act of faith: the other only supposes it to be a manifestation of his regard to the beauty of that order that there is in uniting those things that have a natural agreement, and congruity, and unition of the one with the other. Indeed a moral suitableness or fitness to a state includes a natural: for, if there be a moral suitableness that a person should be in such a state, there is also a natural suitableness; but such a natural suitableness as I have described, by no means necessarily includes a moral.

This is plainly what our divines intend when they say, that faith does not justify as a *work*, or a righteousness, *viz.* that it does not justify as a part of our moral goodness or excellency, or that it does not justify as man was to have been justified by the covenant of works, which was, to have a title to eternal life given him of God, in testimony of his pleasedness with his works, or his regard to the inherent excellency and beauty of his obedience. And this is certainly what the apostle Paul means, when he so much insists upon it, that we are not justified by works, *viz.* that we are not justified by them as good works, or by any goodness, value, or excellency of our works. For the proof of this I shall at present mention but one thing, and

that the operation produces, or is prior to the principle, either in nature or in time, is a direct contradiction.

15. If the preceding steps of these remarks be thoroughly weighed, it will be found, that justification, according to Scripture, and just reasoning upon it, has for its *foundation* the federal perfection of Messiah, and takes place as the immediate *result* of union to him.

16. But since this union is *twofold*, the one as the *effect* of the other, that is, union by *faith* is the effect of union by the *Spirit* of Christ, and these, *cause and effect*, cannot possibly be sumultaneous, there must necessarily be a *twofold justification* as the result of the corresponding unions. Though in that union which is first in the order of nature and of time, the person, whether infant or adult, is *passive;* the result however is the imputation of righteousness, which is Messiah's federal perfection, and which entitles to life eternal. And by that union which is the effect of the other, and consequently posterior to it in the order both of nature and of time, (and of which infants *cannot* be partakers,) that is, by the union effected by believing, the *result* is the *imputation* of the *same righteousness* in circumstances totally different.

17. These two different circumstances, clearly perceived, will develope the seeming difficulty. In the first, the person, whether infant or adult, is the *passive possessor* of decreed benefits, union, righteousness, and life; in the second circumstance, the adult person, as a free and accountable agent, is required to *determine for himself* on what to found his plea of acceptance with God. If he found his plea on his own *obedience* past or intended, whether moral, ceremonial, or both; he shows at once both *ignorance* and *rebellion. Ignorance*, that he supposes it even possible for him, by his own obedience, to attain to that federal perfection which is justly required by the righteous Governor; and also in that he does not perceive the love and wisdom, the superabounding grace and wonderful mercy, of God as a sovereign Benefactor in providing the needful remedy. *Rebellion*, in that he rejects the counsel of God, and resists, by obstinate unbelief, the divine *authority* requiring submission to this righteousness as the way to favour and life. Hence,

18. As all reasonings, expostulations, threats, promises and encouragements; all testimonies, declarations, appeals, inducements, and sanctions, are addressed to men as *moral agents*, with whom, in the business of accountability, it rests, what mode they will adopt for obtaining acceptance with God—whether by *doing* the work themselves, or by *believing* his testimony and receiving his gift—it fully accounts for *justification by faith* being the great point argued in the apostolic writings.

19. And it further appears, that justification by *faith alone* should be strenuously urged by all gospel ministers, while they have to do continually with persons whose inquiry is, "What shall we *do* to be saved?" To such as thus *inquire* after the way of salvation, who *seek* acceptance with God, who are about to *choose* for themselves "the way they will take," what answer can be given, in effect, but what is contained in the apostle's words? "To him that *worketh not*, but *believeth* on him that justifieth the ungodly, his faith is counted for righteousness." The above statement not only *agrees* with these words, but also, as I humbly conceive, *explains* their import; and the embarrassment respecting the office and influence of faith in justification is removed, without expunging faith, or the act of believing, from the class of moral duties.

20. It may be objected, If there be any justification *before* believing, then an *unbeliever* may be justified; whereas the Scripture saith, "He that believeth not is condemned already." This objection arises from a mistaken notion of the true meaning of such passages of Scripture. Condemnation, in the real import of Scripture, is levelled against the *rejecters* of Christ, or of the divine testimony, and these *only*, considered as free agents in seeking acceptance with God and final happiness. These, *not believing* in Christ, while prevailingly devoted to Moses or Mahomet, moral obedience or ceremonies, or indeed any other object whatever, *reject* in fact the testimony of God and his righteousness, and expose themselves to a *double* condemnation. They are condemned as being *destitute* of a perfect righteousness, and also for their actual *disobedience* to the divine authority. The sentence of the *law* is against them, both as a covenant and as a rule; and the *gospel* which they reject will be a witness to prove the wickedness of their heart. But this can never take place in one who is vitally united to Christ. All allow that *infants not believing* are not to be ranked with *unbelievers*. To them no testimony is proposed, and therefore no testimony is *rejected* by them. Nor does any *adult* united to Christ *reject* the divine testimony, even *before* he believes. Let but the *object* of faith be presented to him, and his vital union *secures* the *exercise* of the living principle towards the proposed object in proportion as the terms are understood. A testimony not *presented*, or one presented in an *unknown tongue*, cannot be believed, notwithstanding the principle of faith. The existence of a principle does not necessarily imply its exercise, whether it be sense, reason, or faith. Men are not necessarily conversant with the objects of sense, *because* they possess the senses requisite for these purposes; nor are they always *exercising* the powers of the mind, however essential these powers are to human nature. In like manner, *not exercising* faith is a very different thing from not possessing the *principle.* A vital union and the *spirit* of faith are inseparably and *essentially* connected; but a vital union and believing are connected *secundum quid*, in *certain circumstances.* Without the circumstances of adult age, or a capacity of understanding, *believing* is impracticable. But how absurd would it be to say, that a sinner *cannot* be justified *because* he has not arrived at a certain advanced portion of *understanding*, or has not learned some *language;* as if a title to heaven depended on age, or knowing a language! And equally absurd is it to suppose that Christ *cannot* effect a vital union *because* the sinner's voluntary consent to it is wanting; as if God's high sovereignty were bound by the human will! That God *requires* the sinner's consent, as a matter of *obligation*, is a solemn fact; but God has not laid *himself* under any obligation that he will never unite a soul to Christ for justification of life but by the sinner's previous consent. He has declared, however, that the *continued unbeliever*, who is properly a wilful *rejecter* of Christ and his righteousness, shall be *condemned* Hence it is evident, that to make believing *essential* to a vital union, on the part of Christ; and to make the *exercise* of faith on a divine testimony *essential* to its existence, are erroneous conclusions, derogatory to gospel grace, and founded on wrong notions of moral government.

20. To make this, if possible, still more plain, the gospel finds men, as apostatized with Adam, in a state of *condemnation;* infants and adults alike are under the condemnatory sentence which is the result of a breach of covenant. This evil can be removed, and a restoration to favour be effected, only by an act of *sovereign grace*, whereby Christ becomes *vitally united* to the soul. Without this vital union there is, there can be, no faith. This being the case, a vital union is formed *before* faith can have any ground of existence; and consequently a justification which is a *necessary result* of this union takes place. For to him who is thus in Christ Jesus there is *no condemnation;* but he is passed from death unto life, as an object of *mere grace and mercy.* In *this* respect, an adult and an infant are perfectly on a par, while justified and regenerated for the kingdom of God. But God, in the character of a *moral governor*, has a further claim on every free agent; he exhibits to the view, and solicits, yea demands, a *voluntary compliance* with the plan of mercy through the blessed Redeemer, who was delivered for our offences, and was raised again for our justification. The regenerate person that is capable of acting for himself, as the subject of commands and invitations, complies; he becomes an *active recipient* of the appointed righteousness, which he now *pleads* in opposition to all charges presented against him. By *faith*, or believing God's testimony, he makes his appeal, and by faith alone he is *justified.* An investigation of the *rationale* of christian doctrines is not necessary for *popular* use, but may be peculiarly useful as a *guard* against inconsistencies, and a means of strengthening our attachment to those doctrines.—W.

* This order, however, is a *law* to us, and compliance with it necessarily imports *moral* obedience; though the *object* received is the obedience of another. No one has room to expect success in his endeavours, but by complying with the divine requisition; and that requisition is, that we *submit* to the perfection of Messiah. And an act of submission to the righteousness of faith may well be an act of moral excellence, though that excellence has nothing *meritorious* on account of which a perfect righteousness should be imputed. A thing may have moral *goodness* without moral *perfection.* But in order to deny to faith the latter, it is not necessary to deprive it of the former. If we consistently maintain, that the moral excellence of faith constitutes *no part* of our justifying righteousness, it is all that the argument requires, in order to establish the conclusion intended.—W

that is, the apostle from time to time speaking of our not being justified by works, as the thing that excludes all boasting, Eph. ii. 9. Rom. iii. 27. and chap. iv. 2. Now which way do works give occasion for boasting, but as good? What do men use to boast of, but of something they suppose good or excellent? And on what account do they boast of any thing, but for the supposed excellency that is in it?

From these things we may learn in what manner faith is the only condition of justification and salvation. For though it be not the only condition, so as alone truly to have the place of a condition in an hypothetical proposition, in which justification and salvation are the consequent, yet it is the condition of justification in a manner peculiar to it, and so that nothing else has a parallel influence with it; because faith includes the whole act of unition to Christ as a Saviour. The entire active uniting of the soul, or the whole of what is called coming to Christ, and receiving of him, is called faith in Scripture; and however other things may be no less excellent than faith, yet it is not the nature of any other graces or virtues directly to close with Christ as a mediator, any further than they enter into the constitution of justifying faith, and do belong to its nature.

Thus I have explained my meaning, in asserting it as a doctrine of the gospel, that we are justified by *faith only*, without any manner of goodness of our own.

I now proceed,

II. To the proof of it; which I shall endeavour to produce in the following arguments.

First, Such is our case, and the state of things, that neither faith, nor any other qualifications, or act or course of acts, does or can render it suitable that a person should have an interest in the Saviour, and so a title to his benefits, on account of any excellency therein, or any other way, than as something in him may unite him to the Saviour. It is not suitable that God should give fallen man an interest in Christ and his merits, as a testimony of his respect to any thing whatsoever as a loveliness in him; and that because it is not meet, till a sinner is actually justified, that any thing in him should be accepted of God, as any excellency or amiableness of his person; or that God, by any act, should in any manner or degree testify any pleasedness with him, or favour towards him, on the account of any thing inherent in him: and that for two reasons:

1. The nature of things will not admit of it. And this appears from the infinite guilt that the sinner till justified is under; which arises from the infinite evil or heinousness of sin. But because this is what some deny, I would therefore first establish that point, and show that sin is a thing that is indeed properly of infinite heinousness; and then show the consequence, that it cannot be suitable, till the sinner is actually justified, that God should by any act testify pleasedness with or acceptance of any excellency or amiableness of his person.

That the evil and demerit of sin is infinitely great, is most demonstrably evident, because what the evil or iniquity of sin consists in, is the violating of an obligation, or doing what we should not do; and therefore by how much the greater the obligation is that is violated, by so much the greater is the iniquity of the violation. But certainly our obligation to love or honour any being is great in proportion to the greatness or excellency of that being, or his worthiness to be loved and honoured. We are under greater obligations to love a more lovely being than a less lovely; and if a being be infinitely excellent and lovely, our obligations to love him are therein infinitely great. The matter is so plain, it seems needless to say much about it.

Some have argued exceeding strangely against the infinite evil of sin, from its being committed against an infinite object, that then it may as well be argued, that there is also an infinite value or worthiness in holiness and love to God, because that also has an infinite object; whereas the argument, from parity of reason, will carry it in the reverse. The sin of the creature against God is ill deserving in proportion to the distance there is between God and the creature; the greatness of the object, and the meanness of the subject, aggravates it. But it is the reverse with regard to the worthiness of the respect of the creature to God; it is worthless (and not worthy) in proportion to the meanness of the subject. So much the greater the distance between God and the creature, so much the less is the creature's respect worthy of God's notice or regard. The unworthiness of sin or opposition to God rises and is great in proportion to the dignity of the object and inferiority of the subject; but on the contrary, the value of respect rises in proportion to the value of the subject; and that for this plain reason, *viz.* that the evil of disrespect is in proportion to the obligation that lies upon the subject to the object; which obligation is most evidently increased by the excellency and superiority of the object. But on the contrary, the worthiness of respect to a being is in proportion to the obligation that lies on him who is the object, (or rather the reason he has,) to regard the subject, which certainly is in proportion to the subject's value or excellency. Sin or disrespect is evil or heinous in proportion to the degree of what it denies in the object, and as it were takes from it, *viz.* its excellency and worthiness of respect; on the contrary, respect is valuable in proportion to the value of what is given to the object in that respect, which undoubtedly (other things being equal) is great in proportion to the subject's value, or worthiness of regard; because the subject in giving his respect, can give no more than himself: so far as he gives his respect, he gives himself to the object; and therefore his gift is of greater or lesser value in proportion to the value of himself.

Hence, (by the way,) the love, honour, and obedience of Christ towards God, has infinite value, from the excellency and dignity of the person in whom these qualifications were inherent; and the reason why we needed a person of infinite dignity to obey for us, was because of our infinite comparative meanness, who had disobeyed, whereby our disobedience was infinitely aggravated. We needed one, the worthiness of whose obedience might be answerable to the unworthiness of our disobedience; and therefore needed one who was as great and worthy as we were unworthy.

Another objection (that perhaps may be thought hardly worth mentioning) is, that to suppose sin to be infinitely heinous, is to make all sins equally heinous; for how can any sin be more than infinitely heinous? But all that can be argued hence is, that no sin can be greater with respect to that aggravation, the worthiness of the object against whom it is committed. One sin cannot be more aggravated than another in *that* respect, because the aggravation of every sin is infinite; but that does not hinder, that some sins may be more heinous than others in *other* respects: as if we should suppose a cylinder infinitely long, it cannot be greater in that respect, *viz.* with respect to the length of it; but yet it may be doubled and trebled, and made a thousand-fold more, by the increase of other dimensions. Of sins that are all infinitely heinous, some may be more heinous than others; as well as of divers punishments that are all infinitely dreadful calamities, or all of them infinitely exceeding all finite calamities, so that there is no finite calamity, however great, but what is infinitely less dreadful, or more eligible, than any of them, yet some of them may be a thousand times more dreadful than others. A punishment may be infinitely dreadful by reason of the infinite duration of it; and therefore cannot be greater with respect to *that* aggravation of it, *viz.* its length of continuance, but yet may be vastly more terrible on other accounts.

Having thus, as I imagine, made it clear, that all sin is infinitely heinous, and consequently that the sinner, before he is justified, is under infinite guilt in God's sight; it now remains that I show the consequence, or how it follows from hence, that it is not suitable that God should give the sinner an interest in Christ's merits, and so a title to his benefits, from regard to any qualification, or act, or course of acts in him, on the account of any excellency or goodness whatsoever therein, but only as uniting to Christ; or (which fully implies it) that it is not suitable that God, by any act, should, in any manner or degree, testify any acceptance of, or pleasedness with, any thing, as any virtue, or excellency, or any part of loveliness, or valuableness in his person, until he is actually already interested in Christ's merits. From the premises it follows, that before the sinner is already interested in

Christ, and justified, it is impossible God should have any acceptance of or pleasedness with the person of the sinner, as in any degree lovely in his sight, or indeed less the object of his displeasure and wrath. For, by the supposition, the sinner still remains infinitely guilty in the sight of God; for guilt is not removed but by pardon: but to suppose the sinner already pardoned, is to suppose him already justified; which is contrary to the supposition. But if the sinner still remains infinitely guilty in God's sight, that is the same thing as still to be beheld of God as infinitely the object of his displeasure and wrath, or infinitely hateful in his eyes; and if so, where is any room for any thing in him, to be accepted as some valuableness or acceptableness of him in God's sight, or for any act of favour of any kind towards him, or any gift whatsoever to him, in testimony of God's respect to and acceptance of something of him lovely and pleasing? If we should suppose that a sinner could have faith, or some other grace in his heart, and yet remain separate from Christ; and that he is not looked upon as being in Christ, or having any relation to him, it would not be meet that such true grace should be accepted of God as any loveliness of his person in the sight of God. If it should be accepted as the loveliness of the person, that would be to accept the person as in some degree lovely to God; but this cannot be consistent with his still remaining under infinite guilt, or infinite unworthiness in God's sight, which that goodness has no worthiness to balance. While God beholds the man as separate from Christ, he must behold him as he is in himself; and so his goodness cannot be beheld by God, but as taken with his guilt and hatefulness, and as put in the scales with it; and so his goodness is nothing; because there is a finite on the balance against an infinite whose proportion to it is nothing. In such a case, if the man be looked on as he is in himself, the excess of the weight in one scale above another, must be looked upon as the quality of the man. These contraries being beheld together, one takes from another, as one number is substracted from another; and the man must be looked upon in God's sight according to the remainder. For here, by the supposition, all acts of grace or favour, in not imputing the guilt as it is, are excluded, because that supposes a degree of pardon, and that supposes justification, which is contrary to what is supposed, *viz.* that the sinner is not already justified; and therefore things must be taken strictly as they are; and so the man is still infinitely unworthy and hateful in God's sight, as he was before, without diminution, because his goodness bears no proportion to his unworthiness, and therefore when taken together is nothing.

Hence may be more clearly seen the force of that expression in the text, of believing on him that *justifieth the ungodly*; for though there is indeed something in man that is really and spiritually good, prior to justification, yet there is nothing that is accepted as any godliness or excellency of the person, till after justification. Goodness or loveliness of the person in the acceptance of God, in any degree, is not to be considered as prior but posterior in the order and method of God's proceeding in this affair. Though a respect to the natural suitableness between such a qualification, and such a state, does go before justification, yet the acceptance even of faith as any goodness or loveliness of the believer, follows justification. The goodness is on the forementioned account justly looked upon as nothing, until the man is justified: and therefore the man is respected in justification, as in himself altogether hateful.—Thus the nature of things will not admit of a man having an interest given him in the merits or benefits of a Saviour, on the account of any thing as a righteousness, or a virtue, or excellency in him.

2. A divine constitution antecedent to that which establishes justification by a Saviour, (and indeed to any need of a Saviour,) stands in the way of it, *viz.* that original constitution or law which man was put under; by which constitution or law the sinner is condemned, because he is a violator of that law; and stands condemned, till he has actually an interest in the Saviour, through whom he is set at liberty from that condemnation. But to suppose that God gives a man an interest in Christ in *reward* for his righteousness or virtue, is inconsistent with his still remaining under condemnation till he has an interest in Christ; because he supposes, that the sinner's virtue is accepted, and he accepted for it, before he has an interest in Christ; inasmuch as an interest in Christ is given as a reward of his virtue. But the virtue must first be accepted, before it is rewarded, and the man must first be accepted for his virtue, before he is rewarded for it with so great and glorious a reward; for the very notion of a reward, is some good bestowed in testimony of respect to and acceptance of virtue in the person rewarded. It does not consist with the honour of the majesty of the King of heaven and earth, to accept of any thing from a condemned malefactor, condemned by the justice of his own holy law, till that condemnation be removed. And then, such acceptance is inconsistent with, and contradictory to, such remaining condemnation; for the law condemns him that violates it, to be totally rejected and cast off by God. But how can a man continue under this condemnation, *i. e.* continue utterly rejected and cast off by God, and yet his righteousness or virtue be accepted, and he himself accepted on the account of it, so as to have so glorious a reward as an interest in Christ bestowed as a testimony of that acceptance?

I know that the answer will be, that we now are not subject to that constitution which mankind were at first put under; but that God, in mercy to mankind, has abolished that rigorous constitution, and put us under a new law, and introduced a more mild constitution; and that the constitution or law itself not remaining, there is no need of supposing that the condemnation of it remains, to stand in the way of the acceptance of our virtue. And indeed there is no other way of avoiding this difficulty. The condemnation of the law must stand in force against a man, till he is actually interested in the Saviour who has satisfied and answered the law, so as effectually to prevent any acceptance of his virtue, either before, or even in order to, such an interest, unless the law or constitution itself be abolished. But the scheme of those modern divines by whom this is maintained, seems to contain a great deal of absurdity and self-contradiction: they hold, that the old law given to Adam, which requires perfect obedience, is entirely repealed, and that instead of it we are put under a new law, which requires no more than imperfect sincere obedience, in compliance with our poor, infirm, impotent circumstances since the fall, whereby we are unable to perform that perfect obedience that was required by the first law; for they strenuously maintain, that it would be unjust in God to require any thing of us that is beyond our present power and ability to perform; and yet they hold, that Christ died to satisfy for the imperfections of our obedience, that so our imperfect obedience might be accepted instead of perfect. Now, how can these things hang together? I would ask, What law these imperfections of our obedience are a breach of? If they are a breach of no law, then they are not sins; and if they be not sins, what need of Christ's dying to satisfy for them? but if they are sins, and so the breach of some law, what law is it? They cannot be a breach of their new law, for that requires no other than imperfect obedience, or obedience with imperfections; and they cannot be a breach of the old law, for that they say is entirely abolished, and we never were under it; and we cannot break a law that we never were under. They say it would not be just in God to exact of us perfect obedience, because it would not be just in God to require more of us than we can perform in our present state, and to punish us for failing of it; and therefore, by their own scheme, the imperfections of our obedience do not deserve to be punished. What need therefore of Christ's dying to satisfy for them? What need of Christ's suffering to satisfy for that which is no fault, and in its own nature deserves no suffering? What need of Christ's dying to purchase that our imperfect obedience should be accepted, when according to their scheme it would be unjust in itself that any other obedience than imperfect should be required? What need of Christ's dying to make way for God's accepting such an obedience, as it would in itself be unjust in him not to accept? Is there any need of Christ's dying to persuade God not to do unjustly? If it be said, that Christ died to satisfy that law for us, that so we might not be under that law, but might be delivered from it, that so there might be room for us to be under a more mild law; still I would inquire, What need of Christ's dying that we might not be under a law that (according to their scheme) it would in itself be unjust that we should be under, because in our present state we are not able to keep it? What need of Christ's dying that we might not be under a law that it would be unjust that we should be under, whether Christ died or no?

Thus far I have argued principally from reason, and the nature of things:—I proceed now to the

Second argument, which is, That this is a doctrine which the Holy Scriptures, the revelation that God has given us of his mind and will—by which alone we can never come to know how those who have offended God can come to be accepted of him, and justified in his sight—is exceeding full. The apostle Paul is abundant in teaching, that "we are justified by faith alone, without the works of the law!" There is no one doctrine that he insists so much upon, and that he handles with so much distinctness, explaining, giving reasons, and answering objections.

Here it is not denied by any, that the apostle does assert, that we are justified by faith, without the works of the law, because the words are express; but only it is said, that we take his words wrong, and understand that by them that never entered into his heart, in that when he excludes the works of the law, we understand him of the whole law of God, or the rule which he has given to mankind to walk by; whereas all that he intends is the ceremonial law.

Some that oppose this doctrine indeed say, that the apostle sometimes means that it is by faith, *i. e.* a hearty embracing the gospel in its first act only, or without any preceding holy life, that persons are admitted into a justified state; but, say they, it is by a persevering obedience that they are continued in a justified state, and it is by this that they are finally justified. But this is the same thing as to say, that a man on his first embracing the gospel is conditionally justified and pardoned. To pardon sin, is to free the sinner from the punishment of it, or from that eternal misery that is due to it; and therefore if a person is pardoned, or freed from this misery, on his first embracing the gospel, and yet not finally freed, but his actual freedom still depends on some condition yet to be performed, it is inconceivable how he can be pardoned otherwise than conditionally; that is, he is not properly actually pardoned, and freed from punishment, but only he has God's promise that he shall be pardoned on future conditions. God promises him, that now, if he perseveres in obedience, he shall be finally pardoned, or actually freed from hell; which is to make just nothing at all of the apostle's great doctrine of justification by faith alone. Such a conditional pardon is no pardon or justification at all, any more than all mankind have, whether they embrace the gospel or no; for they all have a promise of final justification on conditions of future sincere obedience, as much as he that embraces the gospel. But not to dispute about this, we will suppose that there may be something or other at the sinner's first embracing the gospel, that may properly be called justification or pardon, and yet that final justification, or real freedom from the punishment of sin, is still suspended on conditions hitherto unfulfilled; yet they who hold that sinners are thus justified on embracing the gospel, suppose that they are justified by this, no otherwise than as it is a leading act of obedience, or at least as virtue and moral goodness in them, and therefore would be excluded by the apostle as much as any other virtue or obedience, if it be allowed that he means the moral law, when he excludes works of the law. And therefore, if that point be yielded, that the apostle means the moral, and not only the ceremonial, law, their whole scheme falls to the ground.

And because the issue of the whole argument from those texts in St. Paul's epistles depends on the determination of this point, I would be particular in the discussion of it.

Some of our opponents in this doctrine of justification, when they deny, that by the law the apostle means the moral law, or the whole rule of life which God has given to mankind, seem to choose to express themselves thus, that the apostle only intends the Mosaic dispensation. But this comes to just the same thing as if they said, that the apostle only means to exclude the works of the ceremonial law; for when they say, that it is intended only that we are not justified by the works of the Mosaic dispensation, if they mean any thing by it, it must be, that we are not justified by attending and observing what is Mosaic in that dispensation, or by what was peculiar to it, and wherein it differed from the christian dispensation; which is the same as that which is ceremonial and positive, and not moral, in that administration. So that this is what I have to disprove, *viz.* that the apostle, when he speaks of works of the law in this affair, means only works of the ceremonial law, or those observances that were peculiar to the Mosaic administration.

And here it must be noted, that nobody controverts it with them, whether the works of the ceremonial law be not included, or whether the apostle does not particularly argue against justification by circumcision, and other ceremonial observances; but all in question is, whether, when he denies justification by works of the law, he is to be understood only of the ceremonial law, or whether the moral law be not also implied and intended; and therefore those arguments which are brought to prove that the apostle meant the ceremonial law, are nothing to the purpose, unless they prove that the apostle meant those *only*.

What is much insisted on is, that it was the judaizing Christians being so fond of circumcision, and other ceremonies of the law, and depending so much on them, which was the very occasion of the apostle's writing as he does against justification by the works of the law. But supposing it were so, that their trusting in works of the ceremonial law were the sole *occasion* of the apostle's writing, (which yet there is no reason to allow, as may appear afterwards,) if their trusting in a particular work, as a work of righteousness, was all that gave occasion to the apostle to write, how does it follow, that therefore the apostle did not upon that occasion write against trusting in *all works* of righteousness whatsoever? Where is the absurdity of supposing that the apostle might take occasion, from his observing some to trust in a certain work as a work of righteousness, to write to them against persons trusting in any works of righteousness at all, and that it was a very proper occasion too? Yea, it would have been unavoidable for the apostle to have argued against trusting in a particular work, in the quality of a work of righteousness, which quality was general, but he must therein argue against trusting in works of righteousness in general. Supposing it had been some other particular sort of works that was the occasion of the apostle's writing, as for instance, works of charity, and the apostle should hence take occasion to write to them not to trust in their works, could the apostle by that be understood of no other works besides works of charity? Would it have been absurd to understand him as writing against trusting in any work at all, because it was their trusting to a particular work that gave occasion to his writing?

Another thing alleged, as an evidence that the apostle means the ceremonial law—when he says, we cannot be justified by the works of the law—is, that he uses this argument to prove it, *viz.* that the law he speaks of was given so long after the covenant with Abraham, in Gal. iii. 17. "And this I say, that the covenant that was confirmed before of God in Christ, the law which was four hundred and thirty years after, cannot disannul." But, say they, it was only the Mosaic administration, and not the covenant of works, that was given so long after. But the apostle's argument seems manifestly to be mistaken by them. The apostle does not speak of a law that began to exist four hundred and thirty years after; if he did, there would be some force in their objection; but he has respect to a certain solemn transaction, well known among the Jews by the phrase "the giving of the law," which was at mount Sinai, (Exod. xix. xx.) consisting especially in God's giving the ten commandments (which is the moral law) with a terrible voice, which law he afterwards gave in tables of stone. This transaction the Jews in the apostle's time misinterpreted; they looked upon it as God's establishing that law as a rule of justification. Against this conceit of theirs the apostle brings this invincible argument, *viz.* that God would never go about to disannul his covenant with Abraham, which was plainly a covenant of grace, by a transaction with his posterity, that was so long after it, and was plainly built upon it. He would not overthrow a covenant of grace that he had long before established with Abraham, for him and his seed, (which is often mentioned as the ground of God's making them his people,) by now establishing a covenant of works with them at mount Sinai, as the Jews and judaizing Christians supposed.

But that the apostle does not mean only works of the ceremonial law, when he excludes works of the law in justification, but also of the moral law, and all works of obedience, virtue, and righteousness whatsoever, may appear by the following things.

1. The apostle does not only say, that we are not justified by the works of the law, but that we are not justified by *works*, using a general term; as in our text, "to him that worketh not, but believeth on him that justifieth," &c.; and in the 6th verse, "God imputeth righteousness without works;" and chap. xi. 6. "And if by grace, then is it no more of works, otherwise grace is no more grace: but if it be of works, then it is no more grace; otherwise work is no more work." So, Eph. ii. 8, 9. "For by grace are ye saved, through faith,——not of works;" by which, there is no reason in the world to understand the apostle of any other than works in general, as correlates of a reward, or good works, or works of virtue and righteousness. When the apostle says, we are justified or saved not by works, without any such term annexed, as the law, or any other addition, to limit the expression, what warrant have any to confine it to works of a particular law or institution, excluding others? Are not observances of other divine laws works, as well as of that? It seems to be allowed by the divines in the Arminian scheme, in their interpretation of several of those texts where the apostle only mentions works, without any addition, that he means our own good works in general; but then, they say, he only means to exclude any proper merit in those works. But to say the apostle means one thing when he says, we are not justified by works, and another when he says, we are not justified by the works of the law, when we find the expressions mixed and used in the same discourse, and when the apostle is evidently upon the same argument, is very unreasonable; it is to dodge, and fly from Scripture, rather than open and yield ourselves to its teachings.

2. In the third chapter of Romans, our having been guilty of breaches of the moral law, is an argument that the apostle uses, why we cannot be justified by the works of the law. Beginning with the 9th verse, he proves out of the Old Testament, that all are under sin: "There is none righteous, no not one: their throat is as an open sepulchre; with their tongues they have used deceit: their mouth is full of cursing and bitterness; and their feet swift to shed blood." And so he goes on, mentioning only those things that are breaches of the moral law; and then when he has done, his conclusion is, in the 19th and 20th verses, "Now we know that whatsoever things the law saith, it saith to them that are under the law, that every mouth may be stopped, and all the world may become guilty before God. Therefore, by the deeds of the law, shall no flesh be justified in his sight." This is most evidently his argument, because all had sinned, (as it was said in the 9th verse,) and been guilty of those breaches of the moral law that he had mentioned, (and it is repeated over again, verse 23.) "For all have sinned, and come short of the glory of God;" therefore none at all can be justified by the deeds of the law. Now if the apostle meant only, that we are not justified by the deeds of the ceremonial law, what kind of arguing would that be, "Their mouth is full of cursing and bitterness, their feet are swift to shed blood?" therefore they cannot be justified by the deeds of the Mosaic administration. They are guilty of the breaches of the moral law; and therefore they cannot be justified by the deeds of the ceremonial law! Doubtless, the apostle's argument is, that the very same law they have broken, can never justify them as observers of it, because every law necessarily condemns its violators. And therefore our breaches of the moral law argue no more, than that we cannot be justified by that law we have broken.

And it may be noted, that the apostle's argument here is the same that I have already used, *viz.* that as we are in ourselves, and out of Christ, we are under the condemnation of that original law or constitution that God established with mankind; and therefore it is no way fit that any thing we do, any virtue or obedience of ours, should be accepted, or we accepted on the account of it.

3. The apostle, in all the preceding part of this epistle, wherever he has the phrase, *the law*, evidently intends the moral law principally. As in the 12th verse of the foregoing chapter: "For as many as have sinned without law, shall also perish without law." It is evidently the written moral law the apostle means, by the next verse but one: "For when the Gentiles, which have not the law, do by nature the things contained in the law;" that is, the moral law that the Gentiles have by nature. And so the next verse, "Which show the work of the law written in their hearts." It is the moral law, and not the ceremonial, that is written in the hearts of those who are destitute of divine revelation. And so in the 18th verse, "Thou approvest the things that are more excellent, being instructed out of the law." It is the moral law that shows us the nature of things, and teaches us what is excellent; 20th verse, "Thou hast a form of knowledge and truth in the law." It is the moral law, as is evident by what follows, verse 22, 23. "Thou that sayest a man should not commit adultery, dost thou commit adultery? Thou that abhorrest idols, dost thou commit sacrilege? Thou that makest thy boast of the law, through breaking the law, dishonourest thou God?" Adultery, idolatry, and sacrilege, surely are the breaking of the moral, and not the ceremonial law. So in the 27th verse, "And shall not uncircumcision which is by nature, if it fulfil the law, judge thee, who by the letter and circumcision dost transgress the law?" *i. e.* the Gentiles, that you despise because uncircumcised, if they live moral and holy lives, in obedience to the moral law, shall condemn you though circumcised. And so there is not one place in all the preceding part of the epistle, where the apostle speaks of the law, but that he most apparently intends principally the moral law; and yet when the apostle, in continuance of the same discourse, comes to tell us, that we cannot be justified by the works of the law, then they will needs have it, that he means only the ceremonial law. Yea, though all this discourse about the moral law, showing how the Jews as well as Gentiles have violated it, is evidently preparatory and introductory to that doctrine, chap. iii. 20. "That no flesh," that is, none of mankind, neither Jews nor Gentiles, "can be justified by the works of the law."

4. It is evident that when the apostle says, we cannot be justified by the works of the law, he means the moral as well as ceremonial law, by his giving this reason for it, that "by the law is the knowledge of sin," as Rom. iii. 20. "By the deeds of the law shall no flesh be justified in his sight; for by the law is the knowledge of sin." Now that law by which we come to the knowledge of sin, is the moral law chiefly and primarily. If this argument of the apostle be good, "that we cannot be justified by the deeds of the law, because it is by the law that we come to the knowledge of sin;" then it proves that we cannot be justified by the deeds of the moral law, nor by the precepts of Christianity; for by them is the knowledge of sin. If the reason be good, then where the reason holds, the truth holds. It is a miserable shift, and a violent force put upon the words, to say that the meaning is, that by the law of circumcision is the knowledge of sin, because circumcision signifying the taking away of sin, puts men in mind of sin. The plain meaning of the apostle is, that as the law most strictly forbids sin, it tends to convince us of sin, and bring our own consciences to condemn us, instead of justifying of us; that the use of it is to declare to us our own guilt and unworthiness, which is the reverse of justifying and approving of us as virtuous or worthy. This is the apostle's meaning, if we will allow him to be his own expositor; for he himself, in this very epistle, explains to us how it is that by the law we have the knowledge of sin, and that it is by the law's forbidding sin, chap. vii. 7. "I had not known sin, but by the law; for I had not known lust, except the law had said, Thou shalt not covet." There the apostle determines two things; first, That the way in which "by the law is the knowledge of sin," is by the law's forbidding sin: and secondly, which is more directly still to the pur-

pose, he determines that it is the moral law by which we come to the knowledge of sin; "for," says he, "I had not known lust, except the law had said, Thou shalt not covet." Now it is the moral, and not the ceremonial law, that says, "Thou shalt not covet." Therefore, when the apostle argues, that by the deeds of the law no flesh living shall be justified, because by the law is the knowledge of sin, his argument proves, (unless he was mistaken as to the force of his argument,) that we cannot be justified by the deeds of the moral law.

5. It is evident that the apostle does not mean only the ceremonial law, because he gives this reason why we have righteousness, and a title to the privilege of God's children, not by the law, but by faith, "that the law worketh wrath." Rom. iv. 13—16. "For the promise that he should be the heir of the world, was not to Abraham, or to his seed through the law, but through righteousness of faith. For if they which are of the law be heirs, faith is made void, and the promise made of none effect. Because the law worketh wrath: for where no law is, there is no transgression. Therefore it is of faith, that it might be by grace." Now the way in which the law works wrath, by the apostle's own account, in the reason he himself annexes, is by forbidding sin, and aggravating the guilt of the transgression; "for," says he, "where no law is, there is no transgression:" And so, chap. vii. 13. "That sin by the commandment might become exceeding sinful." If, therefore, this reason of the apostle be good, it is much stronger against justification by the moral law than the ceremonial law; for it is by transgressions of the moral law chiefly that there comes wrath: for they are most strictly forbidden, and most terribly threatened.

6. It is evident that when the apostle says, we are not justified by the works of the law, that he excludes all our own virtue, goodness, or excellency, by that reason he gives for it, *viz.* "That boasting might be excluded." Rom. iii. 26, 27, 28. "To declare, I say, at this time his righteousness: that he might be just, and the justifier of him which believeth in Jesus. Where is boasting then? It is excluded. By what law? of works? Nay; but by the law of faith. Therefore we conclude, that a man is justified by faith without the deeds of the law." Eph. ii. 8, 9. "For by grace are ye saved, through faith; and that not of yourselves; it is the gift of God: not of works, lest any man should boast." Now what are men wont to boast of, but what they esteem their own goodness or excellency? If we are not justified by works of the ceremonial law, yet how does that exclude boasting, as long as we are justified by our own excellency, or virtue and goodness of our own, or works of righteousness which we have done?

But it is said, that boasting is excluded, as circumcision was excluded, which was what the Jews especially used to glory in, and value themselves upon, above other nations.

To this I answer, that the Jews were not only used to boast of circumcision, but were notorious for boasting of their moral righteousness. The Jews of those days were generally admirers and followers of the Pharisees, who were full of their boasts of their moral righteousness; as we may see by the example of the Pharisee mentioned in the 18th of Luke, which Christ mentions as describing the general temper of that sect: "Lord," says he, "I thank thee, that I am not as other men, an extortioner, nor unjust, nor an adulterer." The works that he boasts of were chiefly moral works: he depended on the works of the law for justification; and therefore Christ tells us, that the publican, that renounced all his own righteousness, "went down to his house justified rather than he." And elsewhere, we read of the Pharisees praying in the corners of the streets, and sounding a trumpet before them when they did alms. But those works which they so vainly boasted of were *moral* works. And not only so, but what the apostle in this very epistle condemns the Jews for, is their boasting of the moral law. Chap. ii. 22, 23. "Thou that sayest a man should not commit adultery, dost thou commit adultery? Thou that abhorrest idols, dost thou commit sacrilege? Thou that makest thy boast of the law, through breaking the law, dishonourest thou God?" The law here mentioned that they made their boast of, was that of which adultery, idolatry, and sacrilege, were the breaches, which is the moral law. So that this is the boasting which the apostle condemns them for; and therefore, if they were justified by the works of this law, then how comes he to say that their boasting is excluded? And besides, when they boasted of the rites of the ceremonial law, it was under a notion of its being a part of their own goodness or excellency, or what made them holier and more lovely in the sight of God than other people; and if they were not justified by this part of their own supposed goodness or holiness, yet if they were by another, how did that exclude boasting? How was their boasting excluded, unless all goodness or excellency of their own was excluded?

7. The reason given by the apostle why we can be justified only by faith, and not by the works of the law, in the 3d chapter of Gal. *viz.* "That they that are under the law, are under the curse," makes it evident that he does not mean only the ceremonial law. In that chapter the apostle had particularly insisted upon it, that Abraham was justified by faith, and that it is by faith only, and not by the works of the law, that we can be justified, and become the children of Abraham, and be made partakers of the blessing of Abraham: and he gives this reason for it in the 10th verse: "For as many as are of the works of the law, are under the curse; for it is written, Cursed is every one that continueth not in all things which are written in the book of the law to do them." It is manifest that these words, cited from Deuteronomy, are spoken not only with regard to the ceremonial law, but the whole law of God to mankind, and chiefly the moral law; and that all mankind are therefore as they are in themselves under that curse, not only while the ceremonial law lasted, but now since that has ceased. And therefore all who are justified, are redeemed from that curse, by Christ's bearing it for them; as in verse 13. "Christ hath redeemed us from the curse of the law, being made a curse for us: for it is written, Cursed is every one that hangeth on a tree." Now therefore, either its being said, that he is cursed who continueth not in all things which are written in the book of the law to do them, is a good reason why we cannot be justified by the works of that law of which it is so said; or it is not: if it be, then it is a good reason why we cannot be justified by the works of the moral law, and of the whole rule which God has given to mankind to walk by; for the words are spoken of the moral as well as the ceremonial law, and reach every command or precept which God has given to mankind; and chiefly the moral precepts, which are most strictly enjoined, and the violations of which in both the New Testament and the Old, and in the books of Moses themselves, are threatened with the most dreadful curse.

8. The apostle in like manner argues against our being justified by our own righteousness, as he does against being justified by the works of the law; and evidently uses the expressions, of our *own righteousness*, and *works of the law*, promiscuously, and as signifying the same thing. It is particularly evident by Rom. x. 3. "For they being ignorant of God's righteousness, and going about to establish their own righteousness, have not submitted themselves unto the righteousness of God." Here it is plain that the same thing is asserted as in the two last verses but one of the foregoing chapter. "But Israel, which followed after the law of righteousness, hath not attained to the law of righteousness. Wherefore? because they sought it, not by faith, but as it were by the works of the law." And it is very unreasonable, upon several accounts, to suppose that the apostle, by their own righteousness, intends only their ceremonial righteousness. For when the apostle warns us against trusting in our own righteousness for justification, doubtless it is fair to interpret the expression in an agreement with other scriptures, where we are warned, not to think that it is for the sake of our own righteousness that we obtain God's favour and blessing: as particularly in Deut. ix. 4—6. "Speak not thou in thine heart, after that the Lord thy God hath cast them out from before thee, saying, For my righteousness the Lord hath brought me in to possess this land: but for the wickedness of these nations the Lord doth drive them out from before thee. Not for thy righteousness, or for the uprightness of thine heart, dost thou go to possess their land: but for the wickedness of these nations, the Lord thy God doth drive

them out from before thee, and that he may perform the word which he sware unto thy fathers, Abraham, Isaac, and Jacob. Understand therefore, that the Lord thy God giveth thee not this good land to possess it, for thy righteousness; for thou art a stiff-necked people." None will pretend that here the expression *thy righteousness,* signifies only a ceremonial righteousness, but all virtue or goodness of their own; yea, and the inward goodness of the heart, as well as the outward goodness of life; which appears by the beginning of the 5th verse, "Not for thy righteousness, or for the uprightness of thy heart;" and also by the antithesis in the 6th verse, "Not for thy righteousness, for thou art a stiff-necked people." Their stiff-neckedness was their moral wickedness, obstinacy, and perverseness of heart. By righteousness, therefore, on the contrary, is meant their moral virtue, and rectitude of heart and life. This is what I would argue from hence, that the expression of *our own righteousness,* when used in Scripture with relation to the favour of God—and when we are warned against looking upon it as that by which that favour, or the fruits of it, are obtained—does not signify only a ceremonial righteousness, but all manner of goodness of our own.

The Jews also, in the New Testament, are condemned for trusting in their own righteousness in this sense; Luke xviii. 9, &c. "And he spake this parable unto certain that trusted in themselves that they were righteous." This intends chiefly a moral righteousness; as appears by the parable itself, in which we have an account of the prayer of the Pharisee, wherein the things that he mentions as what he trusts in, are chiefly moral qualifications and performances, *viz.* That he was not an extortioner, unjust, nor an adulterer, &c.

But we need not go to the writings of other penmen of the Scripture. If we will allow the apostle Paul to be his own interpreter, he—when he speaks of our own righteousness as that by which we are not justified or saved—does not mean only a ceremonial righteousness, nor does he only intend a way of religion and serving God, of our own choosing, without divine warrant or prescription; but by our own righteousness he means the same as a righteousness of our own doing, whether it be a service or righteousness of God's prescribing, or our own unwarranted performing. Let it be an obedience to the ceremonial law, or a gospel obedience, or what it will, if it be a righteousness of our own doing, it is excluded by the apostle in this affair, as is evident by Titus iii. 5. "Not by works of righteousness which we have done."—But I would more particularly insist on this text; and therefore this may be the

9th argument, That the apostle, when he denies justification by works, works of the law, and our own righteousness, does not mean works of the ceremonial law only. Tit. iii. 3—7. "For we ourselves also were sometimes foolish, disobedient, deceived, serving divers lusts and pleasures, living in malice and envy, hateful, and hating one another. But after that the kindness and love of God our Saviour toward man appeared, not by works of righteousness which we have done, but according to his mercy he saved us, by the washing of regeneration, and renewing of the Holy Ghost; which he shed on us abundantly, through Jesus Christ our Saviour: that being justified by his grace we should be made heirs according to the hope of eternal life." Works of righteousness that we have done are here excluded, as what we are neither saved nor justified by. The apostle expressly says, we are not saved by them; and it is evident that when he says this, he has respect to the affair of justification. And that he means, we are not *saved* by them in not being *justified* by them, as by the next verse but one, which is part of the same sentence, "That being justified by his grace, we should be made heirs according to the hope of eternal life."

It is several ways manifest, that the apostle in this text, by "works of righteousness which we have done," does not mean only works of the ceremonial law. It appears by the 3d verse, "For we ourselves also were sometimes foolish, disobedient, deceived, serving divers lusts and pleasures, living in malice and envy, hateful, and hating one another." These are breaches of the moral law, that the apostle observes they lived in before they were justified: and it is most plain that it is this which gives occasion to the apostle to observe, as he does in the 5th verse, that it was not by works of righteousness which they had done, that they were saved or justified.

But we need not go to the context, it is most apparent from the words themselves, that the apostle does not mean only works of the ceremonial law. If he had only said, it is not by our own works of righteousness; what could we understand by works of righteousness, but only righteous works, or, which is the same thing, good works? And to say, that it is by our own righteous works that we are justified, though not by one particular kind of righteous works, would certainly be a contradiction to such an assertion. But, the words are rendered yet more strong, plain, and determined in their sense, by those additional words, *which we have done;* which shows that the apostle intends to exclude all our own righteous or virtuous works universally. If it should be asserted concerning any commodity, treasure, or precious jewel, that it could not be procured by money, and not only so, but, to make the assertion the more strong, it should be asserted with additional words, that it could not be procured by money that men possess; how unreasonable would it be, after all, to say, that all that was meant was, that it could not be procured with brass money.

And what renders the interpreting of this text, as intending works of the ceremonial law, yet more unreasonable, is, that these works were indeed no works of righteousness at all, but were only falsely supposed to be so by the Jews. And this our opponents in this doctrine also suppose is the very reason why we are not justified by them, because they are not works of righteousness, or because (the ceremonial law being now abrogated) there is no obedience in them. But how absurd is it to say, that the apostle, when he says we are not justified by works of righteousness that we have done, meant only works of the ceremonial law, and that for that very reason, because they are not works of righteousness? To illustrate this by the forementioned comparison: If it should be asserted, that such a thing could not be procured by money that men possess, how ridiculous would it be to say, that the meaning only was, that it could not be procured by counterfeit money, and that for that reason, because it was not money. What scripture will stand before men, if they will take liberty to manage scripture thus? Or what one text is there in the Bible that may not at this rate be explained all away, and perverted to any sense men please?

But further, if we should allow that the apostle intends only to oppose justification by works of the ceremonial law in this text, yet it is evident by the expression he uses, that he means to oppose it under that notion, or in that quality, of their being works of righteousness of our own doing. But if the apostle argues against our being justified by works of the ceremonial law, under the notion of their being of that nature and kind, *viz.* works of our own doing; then it will follow, that the apostle's argument is strong against, not only those, but all of that nature and kind, even all that are of our own doing.

If there were no other text in the Bible about justification but this, this would clearly and invincibly prove, that we are not justified by any of our own goodness, virtue, or righteousness, or for the excellency or righteousness of any thing that we have done in religion; because it is here so fully and strongly asserted; but this text abundantly confirms other texts of the apostle, where he denies justification by works of the law. No doubt can be rationally made, but that the apostle, when he shows, that God does not save us by "works of righteousness that we have done," verse 5. and that so we are "justified by grace," verse 7. herein opposing salvation by works, and salvation by grace—means the *same* works as he does in other places, where he in like manner opposes works and grace: as in Rom. xi. 6. "And if by grace, then it is no more of works: otherwise grace is no more grace. But if it be of works, then is it no more grace: otherwise work is no more work." And the same works as in Rom. iv. 4. "Now to him that worketh, is the reward not reckoned of grace, but of debt." And the same works that are spoken of in the context of the 24th verse of the foregoing chapter, which the apostle there calls "works of the law, being justified freely by his grace." And of the 4th chapter, 16th verse, "Therefore it is of faith, that it might be by grace." Where in the context the righteousness of faith is opposed to the righteousness of the law: for here God's saving us according to his mercy, and justifying us by grace, is opposed to saving us by works of righteousness that we have done; in the same manner as in those places, justifying us by his grace, is opposed to justifying us by works of the law.

10. The apostle could not mean only works of the ceremonial law, when he says, we are not justified by the works of the law, because it is asserted of the saints under the Old Testament as well as New. If men are justified by their sincere obedience, it will then follow that formerly, before the ceremonial law was abrogated, men were justified by the works of the ceremonial law, as well as the moral. For if we are justified by our sincere obedience, then it alters not the case, whether the commands be moral or positive, provided they be God's commands, and our obedience be obedience to God. And so the case must be just the same under the Old Testament, with the works of the moral law and ceremonial, according to the measure of the virtue of obedience there was in either. It is true, their obedience to the ceremonial law would have nothing to do in the affair of justification, unless it was sincere; and so neither would the works of the moral law. If obedience was the thing, then obedience to the ceremonial law, while that stood in force, and obedience to the moral law, had just the same sort of concern, according to the proportion of obedience that consists in each; as now under the New Testament, if obedience is what we are justified by, that obedience must doubtless comprehend obedience to all God's commands now in force, to the positive precepts of attendance on baptism and the Lord's supper, as well as moral precepts. If obedience be the thing, it is not because it is obedience to such a kind of commands, but because it is *obedience*. So that by this supposition, the saints under the Old Testament were justified, at least in part, by their obedience to the ceremonial law.

But it is evident that the saints under the Old Testament were not justified, in any measure, by the works of the ceremonial law. This may be proved, proceeding on the foot of our adversaries' own interpretation of the apostle's phrase, "the works of the law," and supposing them to mean by it only the works of the ceremonial law. To instance in David, it is evident that he was not justified in any wise by the works of the ceremonial law, by Rom. iv. 6—8. "Even as David also describeth the blessedness of the man unto whom God imputeth righteousness without works, saying, Blessed are they whose iniquities are forgiven, and whose sins are covered. Blessed is the man to whom the Lord will not impute sin." It is plain that the apostle is here speaking of justification, from the preceding verse, and all the context; and the thing spoken of, *viz.* forgiving iniquities and covering sins, is what our adversaries themselves suppose to be justification, and even the whole of justification. This David, speaking of himself, says (by the apostle's interpretation) that he had *without* works. For it is manifest that David, in the words here cited, from the beginning of the 32d Psalm, has a special respect to himself: he speaks of his own sins being forgiven and not imputed to him; as appears by the words that immediately follow. "When I kept silence, my bones waxed old; through my roaring all the day long. For day and night thy hand was heavy upon me: my moisture is turned into the drought of summer. I acknowledged my sin unto thee, and mine iniquity have I not hid; I said, I will confess my transgressions unto the Lord; and thou forgavest the iniquity of my sin." Let us therefore understand the apostle which way we will respecting works, when he says, "David describes the blessedness of the man to whom the Lord imputes righteousness without works," whether of all manner of works, or only works of the ceremonial law, yet it is evident at least, that David was not justified by works of the ceremonial law. Therefore here is the argument: if our own obedience be that by which men are justified, then under the Old Testament, men were justified partly by obedience to the ceremonial law (as has been proved); but the saints under the Old Testament were not justified partly by the works of the ceremonial law; therefore men's own obedience is not that by which they are justified.

11. Another argument that the apostle, when he speaks of the two opposite ways of justification, one by the works of the law, and the other by faith, does not mean only the works of the ceremonial law, may be taken from Rom. x. 5, 6. "For Moses describeth the righteousness which is of the law, that the man which doth those things, shall live by them. But the righteousness which is of faith, speaketh on this wise," &c.—Here two things are evident.

First, That the apostle here speaks of the same two opposite ways of justification, one by the righteousness which is of the law, the other by faith, that he had treated of in the former part of the epistle; and therefore it must be the same law that is here spoken of. The same law is here meant as in the last verses of the foregoing chapter, where he says, the Jews had "not attained to the law of righteousness. Wherefore? Because they sought it, not by faith, but as it were by the works of the law;" as is plain, because the apostle is still speaking of the same thing; the words are a continuation of the same discourse, as may be seen at first glance, by any one that looks on the context.

Secondly, It is manifest that Moses, when he describes the righteousness which is of the law, or the way of justification by the law, in the words here cited, "He that doth those things, shall live in them," does not speak only, nor chiefly, of the works of the ceremonial law; for none will pretend that God ever made such a covenant with man, that he who kept the ceremonial law should live in it, or that there ever was a time, that it was chiefly by the works of the ceremonial law that men lived and were justified. Yea, it is manifest by the forementioned instance of David, mentioned in the 4th of Romans, that there never was a time wherein men were justified in any measure by the works of the ceremonial law, as has been just now shown. Moses therefore, in those words which, the apostle says, are a description of the righteousness which is of the law, cannot mean only the ceremonial law. And therefore it follows, that when the apostle speaks of justification by the works of the law, as opposite to justification by faith, he does not mean only the ceremonial law, but also the works of the moral law, which are the things spoken of by Moses, when he says, "He that doth those things, shall live in them." And these are the things which the apostle in this very place is arguing that we cannot be justified by; as is evident by the last verses of the preceding chapter; "But Israel, which followed after the law of righteousness, hath not attained to the law of righteousness. Wherefore? Because they sought it, not by faith, but as it were by the works of the law," &c. And in the 3d verse of this chapter, "For they being ignorant of God's righteousness, and going about to establish their own righteousness, have not submitted themselves unto the righteousness of God."

And further, how can the apostle's description that he here gives from Moses, of this exploded way of justification by the works of the law, consist with the Arminian scheme, of a way of justification by the virtue of a sincere obedience, that still remains as the true and only way of justification under the gospel? It is most apparent that it is the design of the apostle to give a description of both the legal rejected and the evangelical valid ways of justification, in that wherein they are distinguished the one from the other. But how is it, that "he who doth those things, shall live in them," *that* wherein the way of justification by the works of the law is distinguished from that in which Christians under the gospel are justified, according to their scheme; for still, according to them, it may be said, in the same manner, of the precepts of the gospel, he that doth these things, shall live in them. The difference lies only in the things to be done, but not at all in that the doing of them is not the condition of living in them, just in the one case, as in the other. The words, "He that doth them, shall live in them," will serve just as well for a description of the latter as the former. By the apostle's saying, the righteousness of the law is described thus, he that doth these things, shall live in them; but the righteousness of faith saith thus, plainly intimates that the righteousness of faith saith otherwise, and in an opposite manner. Besides, if these words cited from Moses are actually said by him of the moral law as well as ceremonial, as it is most evident they are, it renders it still more absurd to suppose them mentioned by the apostle, as the very note of distinction between justification by a ceremonial obedience, and a moral sincere obedience, as the Arminians must suppose.

Thus I have spoken to a second argument, to prove that we are not justified by any manner of virtue or goodness of our own, *viz.* that to suppose otherwise, is contrary to the doctrine directly urged, and abundantly insisted on, by the apostle Paul in his epistles.

I now proceed to a

Third argument, *viz.* That to suppose that we are justified by our own sincere obedience, or any of our own virtue or goodness, derogates from gospel grace.

That scheme of justification that manifestly takes from or diminishes the grace of God, is undoubtedly to be rejected; for it is the declared design of God in the gospel to exalt the freedom and riches of his grace, in that method of justification of sinners, and way of admitting them to his favour, and the blessed fruits of it, which it declares. The Scripture teaches, that the way of justification appointed in the gospel-covenant, is appointed for that end, that free grace might be expressed, and glorified; Rom. iv. 16. "Therefore it is of faith, that it might be by grace." The exercising and magnifying of free grace in the gospel-contrivance for the justification and salvation of sinners, is evidently the chief design of it. And this freedom and riches of grace in the gospel is every where spoken of in Scripture as the chief glory of it. Therefore that doctrine which derogates from the free grace of God in justifying sinners, as it is most opposite to God's design, so it must be exceedingly offensive to him.

Those who maintain, that we are justified by our own sincere obedience, pretend that their scheme does not diminish the grace of the gospel; for they say, that the grace of God is wonderfully manifested in appointing such a way and method of salvation by sincere obedience, in assisting us to perform such an obedience, and in accepting our imperfect obedience, instead of perfect.

Let us therefore examine that matter, whether their scheme, of a man's being justified by his own virtue and sincere obedience, does derogate from the grace of God or no; or whether free grace is not more exalted in supposing, as we do, that we are justified without any manner of goodness of our own. In order to this, I will lay down this self-evident

Proposition, that whatsoever that be by which the abundant benevolence of the giver is expressed, and gratitude in the receiver is obliged, that magnifies free grace. This I suppose none will ever controvert or dispute.—And it is not much less evident, that it doth both show a more abundant benevolence in the giver when he shows kindness without goodness or excellency in the object, to move him to it; and that it enhances the obligation to gratitude in the receiver.

1. It shows a more abundant goodness in the giver, when he shows kindness without any excellency in our persons or actions that should move the giver to love and beneficence. For it certainly shows the more abundant and overflowing goodness, or disposition to communicate good, by how much the less loveliness or excellency there is to entice beneficence. The less there is in the receiver to draw good-will and kindness, it argues the more of the principle of good-will and kindness in the giver. One that has but little of a principle of love and benevolence, may be drawn to do good, and to show kindness, when there is a great deal to draw him, or when there is much excellency and loveliness in the object to move good-will; when he whose goodness and benevolence is more abundant, will show kindness where there is less to draw it forth; for he does not so much need to have it drawn from without, he has enough of the principle within to move him of itself. Where there is most of the principle, there it is most sufficient for itself, and stands in least need of something without to excite it. For certainly a more abundant goodness more easily flows forth with less to impel or draw it, than where there is less; or, which is the same thing, the more any one is disposed of himself, the less he needs from without himself, to put him upon it, or stir him up to it. And therefore his kindness and goodness appears the more exceeding great, when it is bestowed without any excellency or loveliness at all in the receiver, or when the receiver is respected in the gift, as wholly without excellency. And much more still when the benevolence of the giver not only finds nothing in the receiver to draw it, but a great deal of hatefulness to repel it. The abundance of goodness is then manifested, not only in flowing forth without any thing extrinsic to put it forward, but in overcoming great repulsion in the object. And then does kindness and love appear most triumphant, and wonderfully great, when the receiver is not only wholly without all excellency or beauty to attract it, but altogether, yea infinitely, vile and hateful.

2. It is apparent also that it enhances the obligation to gratitude in the receiver. This is agreeable to the common sense of mankind, that the less worthy or excellent the object of benevolence, or the receiver of kindness, is, the more he is obliged, and the greater gratitude is due. He therefore is most of all obliged, that receives kindness without any goodness or excellency in himself, but with a total and universal hatefulness. And as it is agreeable to the common sense of mankind, so it is agreeable to the word of God. How often does God in the Scripture insist on this argument with men, to move them to love him, and to acknowledge his kindness! How much does he insist on this as an obligation to gratitude, that they are so sinful, and undeserving, and ill deserving!

Therefore it certainly follows, that the doctrine which teaches, that God, when he justifies a man, and shows him such great kindness as to give him a right to eternal life, does not do it for any obedience, or any manner of goodness, of his; but that justification respects a man as ungodly, and wholly without any manner of virtue, beauty, or excellency. I say, this doctrine does certainly more exalt the free grace of God in justification, and man's obligation to gratitude for such a favour, than the contrary doctrine, *viz.* That God, in showing this kindness to man, respects him as sincerely obedient and virtuous, and as having something in him that is truly excellent and lovely, and acceptable in his sight, and that this goodness or excellency of man is the very fundamental condition of the bestowment of that kindness on him, or of distinguishing him from others by that benefit. But I hasten to a

Fourth argument for the truth of the doctrine, That to suppose a man is justified by his own virtue or obedience, derogates from the honour of the Mediator, and ascribes that to man's virtue which belongs only to the righteousness of Christ: it puts man in Christ's stead, and makes him his own saviour, in a respect in which Christ only is his Saviour. And so it is a doctrine contrary to the nature and design of the gospel, which is to abase man, and to ascribe all the glory of our salvation to Christ the Redeemer. It is inconsistent with the doctrine of the imputation of Christ's righteousness, which is a gospel-doctrine.

Here I would *explain* what we mean by the *imputation* of Christ's righteousness. *Prove* the thing intended by it to be true. *Show* that this doctrine is utterly inconsistent with the doctrine of our being justified by our own virtue or sincere obedience.

First, I would explain what we mean by the imputation of Christ's righteousness. Sometimes the expression is taken by our divines in a larger sense, for the imputation of all that Christ did and suffered for our redemption, whereby we are free from guilt, and stand righteous in the sight of God; and so implies the imputation both of Christ's satisfaction and obedience. But here I intend it in a stricter sense, for the imputation of that righteousness or moral goodness that consists in the obedience of Christ. And by that righteousness being *imputed* to us, is meant no other than this, that the righteousness of Christ is accepted for us, and admitted instead of that perfect inherent righteousness which ought to be in ourselves. Christ's perfect obedience shall be reckoned to our account, so that we shall have the benefit of it, as though we had performed it ourselves. And so we suppose that a title to eternal life is given us as the reward of this righteousness. The Scripture uses the word *impute* in this sense, *viz.* for reckoning any thing belonging to any person, to another person's account: as Philemon 18. "If he hath wronged thee, or oweth thee ought, put that on mine account." In the original it is τουτο ἐμοὶ ελλογα: *impute that to me.* It is a word of the same root with that which is translated *impute*, Rom. iv. 6. "To whom God imputeth righteousness without works." And it is the very same word that is used, Rom. v. 13. that is translated *impute*, "sin is not imputed when there is no law."

The opposers of this doctrine suppose that there is an absurdity in supposing that God imputes Christ's obedience to us, it is to suppose that God is mistaken, and thinks that we performed that obedience which Christ performed. But why cannot that righteousness be reckoned to our account, and be accepted for us, without any such absurdity? Why is there any more absurdity in it, than in a merchant's transferring debt or credit from one man's account to another, when one man pays a price for another, so that it shall be accepted as if that other had paid it? Why is there any more absurdity in supposing that Christ's obedience is imputed to us, than that his satisfaction is imputed? If Christ has suffered the penalty of the law in our stead, then it will follow, that his suffering that penalty is imputed to us, that is accepted for us, and in our stead, and is reckoned to our account, as though we had suffered it. But why may not his obeying the law of God be as rationally reckoned to our account, as his suffering the penalty of the law? Why may not a price to bring into debt, be as rationally transferred from one person's account to another, as a price to pay a debt? Having thus explained what we mean by the imputation of Christ's righteousness, I proceed,

Secondly, To prove that the righteousness of Christ is thus imputed.

1. There is the very same need of Christ's obeying the law in our stead, in order to the reward, as of his suffering the penalty of the law in our stead, in order to our escaping the penalty; and the same reason why one should be accepted on our account, as the other. There is the same need of one as the other, that the law of God might be answered: one was as requisite to answer the law as the other. It is certain, that was the reason why there was need that Christ should suffer the penalty for us, even that the law might be answered; for this the Scripture plainly teaches. This is given as the reason why Christ was made a curse for us, that the law threatened a curse to us, Gal. iii. 10, 13. But the same law that fixes the curse of God as the consequence of not continuing in all things written in the law to do them, verse 10. has as much fixed doing those things as an antecedent of living in them, (as verse 12.) There is as much connexion established in one case as in the other. There is therefore exactly the same need, from the law, of perfect obedience being fulfilled in order to our obtaining the reward, as there is of death being suffered in order to our escaping the punishment; or the same necessity by the law, of perfect obedience preceding life, as there is of disobedience being succeeded by death. The law is, without doubt, as much of an established rule in one case as in the other.

Christ by suffering the penalty, and so making atonement for us, only removes the guilt of our sins, and so sets us in the same state that Adam was in the first moment of his creation: and it is no more fit that we should obtain eternal life only on that account, than that Adam should have the reward of eternal life, or of a confirmed and unalterable state of happiness, the first moments of his existence, without any obedience at all. Adam was not to have the reward merely on account of his being innocent; if so, he would have had it fixed upon him at once, as soon as ever he was created; for he was as innocent then as he could be. But he was to have the reward on account of his activeness in obedience; not on account merely of his not having done ill, but on account of his doing well.

So on the same account we have not eternal life merely as void of guilt, which we have by the atonement of Christ; but on the account of Christ's activeness in obedience, and doing well. Christ is our second federal head, and is called the second Adam, 1 Cor. xv. 22. because he acted that part for us which the first Adam should have done. When he had undertaken to stand in our stead, he was looked upon and treated as though he were guilty with our guilt; and by his bearing the penalty, he did as it were free himself from this guilt. But by this the second Adam did only bring himself into the state in which the first Adam was on the first moment of his existence, *viz.* a state of mere freedom from guilt; and hereby indeed was free from any obligation to suffer punishment: but this being supposed, there was need of something further, even a positive obedience, in order to his obtaining, as our second Adam, the reward of eternal life.

God saw meet to place man first in a state of trial, and not to give him a title to eternal life as soon as he had made him; because it was his will that he should first give honour to his authority, by fully submitting to it, in will and act, and perfectly obeying his law. God insisted upon it, that his holy majesty and law should have their due acknowledgment and honour from man, such as became the relation he stood in to that Being who created him, before he would bestow the reward of confirmed and everlasting happiness upon him; and therefore God gave him a law that he might have opportunity, by giving due honour to his authority in obeying it, to obtain this happiness. It therefore became Christ—seeing that, in assuming man to himself, he sought a title to this eternal happiness for him after he had broken the law—that he himself should become subject to God's authority, and be in the form of a servant, that he might do that honour to God's authority for him, by his obedience, which God at first required of man as the condition of his having a title to that reward. Christ came into the world to render the honour of God's authority and law consistent with the salvation and eternal life of sinners; he came to save them, and yet withal to assert and vindicate the honour of the lawgiver, and his holy law. Now, if the sinner, after his sin was satisfied for, had eternal life bestowed upon him without active righteousness, the honour of his law would not be sufficiently vindicated. Supposing this were possible, that the sinner himself could, by suffering, pay the debt, and afterwards be in the same state that he was in before his probation, that is to say, negatively righteous, or merely without guilt; if he now at last should have eternal life bestowed upon him, without performing that condition of obedience; then God would recede from his law, and would give the promised reward, and his law never have respect and honour shown to it, in that way of being obeyed. But now Christ, by subjecting himself to the law, and obeying it, has done great honour to the law, and to the authority of God who gave it. That so glorious a person should become subject to the law, and fulfil it, has done much more to honour it, than if mere man had obeyed it. It was a thing infinitely honourable to God, that a person of infinite dignity was not ashamed to call him his God, and to adore and obey him as such. This was more to God's honour than if any mere creature, of any possible degree of excellence and dignity, had so done.

It is absolutely necessary, that in order to a sinner's being justified, the righteousness of some other should be reckoned to his account; for it is declared, that the person justified is looked upon as (in himself) ungodly; but God neither will nor can justify a person without a righteousness; for justification is manifestly a *forensic* term, as the word is used in Scripture, and a judicial thing, or the act of a judge. So that if a person should be justified without a righteousness, the judgment would not be according to truth. The sentence of justification would be a false sentence, unless there be a righteousness performed that is by the judge properly looked upon as his. To say, that God does not justify the sinner without sincere, though an imperfect, obedience, does not help the case; for an imperfect righteousness before a judge is no righteousness. To accept of something that falls short of the rule, instead of something else that answers the rule, is no judicial act, or act of a judge, but a pure act of sovereignty. An imperfect righteousness is no righteousness before a judge; for "righteousness (as one observes) is a relative thing, and has always relation to a law. The formal nature of righteousness, properly understood, lies in a conformity of actions to that which is the rule and measure of them." Therefore that only is righteousness in the sight of a judge that answers the law.* The law is the judge's rule: if he pardons and hides what really is, and so does not pass sentence according to what things are in themselves, he either does not act the part of a judge, or else judges falsely. The very notion of judging is to determine what is, and what is not, in any one's case. The judge's work is twofold; it is to determine first what is fact, and then whether what is in fact be according to rule, or according to the law. If a judge has no rule or law established beforehand, by which he should proceed in judging, he has no foundation to go upon in judging, he has no opportunity to be a judge; nor is it possible that he should do the part of a judge. To judge without a law or rule by which to judge, is impossible; for the very notion of judging, is to determine whether the object of judgment be according to rule; and therefore God has declared, that when he acts as a judge, he will not justify the wicked, and cannot clear the guilty; and, by parity of reason, cannot justify without righteousness.

And the scheme of the old law's being abrogated, and a new law introduced, will not help at all in this difficulty; for an imperfect righteousness cannot answer the law of God we are under, whether that be an old or a new one; for every law requires perfect obedience to itself. Every rule whatsoever requires perfect conformity to itself; it is a contradiction to suppose otherwise. For to say, that there is a law that does not require perfect obedience to itself, is to say that there is a law that does not require all that it requires. That law that now forbids sin, is certainly the law that we are now under, (let that be an old or a new one,) or else it is not sin. That which is not forbidden, and is the breach of no law, is no sin. But if we are now forbidden to commit sin, then it is by a law that we are now under; for surely we are neither under the forbiddings nor commanding of a law that we are not under. Therefore, if all sin is now forbidden, then we are now under a law that requires perfect obedience; and therefore nothing can be accepted as a righteousness in the sight of our Judge, but perfect righteousness. So that our Judge cannot justify us, unless he sees a perfect righteousness, some way belonging to us, either performed by ourselves, or by another, and justly and duly reckoned to our account.

God doth, in the sentence of justification, pronounce a man perfectly righteous, or else he would need a further justification after he is justified. His sins being removed by Christ's atonement, is not sufficient for his justification; for justifying a man, as has been already shown, is not merely pronouncing him innocent, or without guilt, but standing right with regard to the rule that he is under, and righteous unto life: but this, according to the established rule of nature, reason, and divine appointment, is a positive, perfect righteousness.

As there is the same need that Christ's obedience should be reckoned to our account, as that his atonement should; so there is the same reason why it should. As if Adam had persevered, and finished his course of obedience, we should have received the benefit of his obedience, as much as now we have the mischief of his disobedience; so in like manner, there is reason that we should receive the benefit of the second Adam's obedience, as of his atonement of our disobedience. Believers are represented in Scripture as being so in Christ, as that they are legally one, or accepted as one, by the Supreme Judge: Christ has assumed our nature, and has so assumed all in that nature that belongs to him, into such an union with himself, that he is become their head, and has taken them to be his members. And therefore, what Christ has done in our nature, whereby he did honour to the law and authority of God by his acts, as well as the reparation to the honour of the law by his sufferings, is reckoned to the believer's account; so as that the believer should be made happy, because it was so well and worthily done by his Head, as well as freed from being miserable, because he has suffered for our ill and unworthy doing.

When Christ had once undertaken with God to stand for us, and put himself under our law, by that law he was obliged to suffer, and by the same law he was obliged to obey: by the same law, after he had taken man's guilt upon him, he himself, being our surety, could not be acquitted till he had suffered, nor rewarded till he had obeyed: but he was not acquitted as a private person, but as our head, and believers are acquitted in his acquittance; nor was he accepted to a reward for his obedience, as a private person, but as our head, and we are accepted to a reward in his acceptance. The Scripture teaches us, that when Christ was raised from the dead, he was justified; which justification, as I have already shown, implies both his acquittance from our guilt, and his acceptance to the exaltation and glory that was the reward of his obedience: but believers, as soon as they believe, are admitted to partake with Christ in this his justification: hence we are told, that he was "raised again for our justification," Rom. iv. 25. which is true, not only of that part of his justification that consists in his acquittance, but also his acceptance to his reward. The Scripture teaches us, that he is exalted, and gone to heaven to take possession of glory in our name, as our forerunner, Heb. vi. 20. We are, as it were, both raised up together with Christ, and also made to sit together with Christ in heavenly places, and in him, Eph. ii. 6.

If it be objected here, that there is this reason, why what Christ suffered should be accepted on our account, rather than the obedience he performed, that he was obliged to obedience for himself, but was not obliged to suffer but only on our account; to this I answer, That Christ was not obliged, on his own account, to undertake to obey. Christ, in his original circumstances, was in no subjection to the Father, being altogether equal with him: he was under no obligation to put himself in man's stead, and under man's law; or to put himself into any state of subjection to God whatsoever. There was a transaction between the Father and the Son, that was antecedent to Christ's becoming man, and being made under the law, wherein he undertook to put himself under the law, and both to obey and to suffer; in which transaction these things were already virtually done in the sight of God; as is evident by this, that God acted on the ground of that transaction, justifying and saving sinners, as if the things undertaken had been actually performed long before they were performed indeed. And therefore, without doubt, in order to estimate the value and validity of what Christ did and suffered, we must look back to that transaction, wherein these things were first undertaken, and virtually done in the sight of God, and see what capacity and circumstances Christ acted in them, and we shall find that

* That perfect obedience, is what is called righteousness in the New Testament, and that this righteousness, or perfect obedience, is by God's fixed unalterable rule the condition of justification, is, from the plain evidence of truth, confessed by a certain great man, whom nobody will think to be blinded by prejudice in favour of the doctrine we are maintaining, and one who did not receive this doctrine. M. Locke, in his *Reasonableness of Christianity, as delivered in the Scriptures*, vol. 2. of his works, p. 474. writes thus: "To one that thus unbiassed reads the Scripture, what *Adam* fell from, is visible, was the state of perfect obedience, which is called *justice* in the New Testament, though the word, which in the original signifies justice, be translated *righteousness.*" Ibid. p. 476. 477. "For righteousness, or an exact obedience to the law, seems by the Scripture to have a claim of right to eternal life; Rom. iv. 4. *To him that worketh, i. e.* does the works of the law, *is the reward not reckoned of grace but of debt.*—On the other side, it seems the unalterable purpose of divine justice, that no unrighteous person, no one that is guilty of any breach of the law, should be in paradise; but that the wages of sin should be to every man, as it was to Adam, an exclusion of him out of that happy state of immortality, and bring death upon him. And this is so conformable to the eternal and established law of right and wrong, that it is spoke of too as it could not be otherwise.--Here then we have the standing and fixed measures of life and death; immortality and bliss belong to the righteous. Those who have lived in an exact conformity to the law of God are out of the reach of death; but an exclusion from paradise and loss of immortality, is the portion of sinners, of all those who have any way broke that law, and failed of a complete obedience to it, by the guilt of any one transgression. And thus mankind, by the law, are put upon the issues of life or death, as they are righteous or unrighteous, just or unjust, *i. e.* exact performers or transgressors of the law." Again, in p. 477. "The was of works then in short is, that law which requires perfect obedience, without any remission or abatement; so that by that law a man cannot be just or justified, without an exact performance of every tittle. Such a perfect obedience in the New Testament, is termed δικαιοσυνη, which we translate *righteousness.*" In which last passage it is also to be noted, that Mr. Locke, by the law of works, does not understand the ceremonial law, but the covenant of works; as he more fully expresses himself in the next paragraph but one. "Where this law of works was to be found, the New Testament tells us, *viz.* in the law delivered by Moses: John i. 17. *The law was given by Moses, but grace and truth came by Jesus Christ.* Chap. vii. 19. *Did not Moses give you the law*, says our Saviour, *and yet none of you keep the law?* And this is the law which he speaks of—verse 28. *This do, and thou shalt live.* This is that which St Paul so often styles *the law*, without any other distinction: Rom. ii. 13. *Not the hearers of the law are just before God, but the doers of the law are justified.* It is needless to quote any more places, his epistles are all full of it, especially this to the Romans."

Christ was under no manner of obligation, either to obey the law, or to suffer its penalty. After this he was equally under obligation to both; for henceforward he stood as our surety or representative: and therefore this consequent obligation may be as much of an objection against the validity of his suffering the penalty, as against his obedience. But if we look to that original transaction between the Father and the Son, wherein both these were undertaken and accepted as virtually done in the sight of the Father, we shall find Christ acting with regard to both, as one perfectly in his own right, and under no manner of previous obligation to hinder the validity of either.

2. To suppose that all Christ does is only to make atonement for us by suffering, is to make him our Saviour but in part. It is to rob him of half his glory as a Saviour. For if so, all that he does is to deliver us from hell; he does not purchase heaven for us. The adverse scheme supposes that he purchases heaven for us, in that he satisfies for the imperfections of our obedience, and so purchases that our sincere imperfect obedience might be accepted as the condition of eternal life; and so purchases an opportunity for us to obtain heaven by our own obedience. But to purchase heaven for us only in this sense, is to purchase it in no sense at all; for all of it comes to no more than a satisfaction for our sins, or removing the penalty by suffering in our stead. For all the purchasing they speak of, that our imperfect obedience should be accepted, is only his satisfying for the sinful imperfection of our obedience; or (which is the same thing) making atonement for the sin that our obedience is attended with. But that is not purchasing heaven, merely to set us at liberty again, that we may go and get heaven by what we do ourselves: all that Christ does is only to pay a debt for us; there is no positive purchase of any good. We are taught in Scripture that heaven is purchased for us; it is called the *purchased possession*, Eph. i. 14. The gospel proposes the eternal inheritance, not to be acquired, as the first covenant did, but as already acquired and purchased. But he that pays a man's debt for him, and so delivers him from slavery, cannot be said to purchase an estate for him, merely because he sets him at liberty, so that henceforward he has an opportunity to get an estate by his own hand-labour. So that according to this scheme, the saints in heaven have no reason to thank Christ for purchasing heaven for them, or redeeming them to God, and making them kings and priests, as we have an account that they do, in Rev. v. 9.

3. Justification by the righteousness and obedience of Christ, is a doctrine that the Scripture teaches in very full terms; Rom. v. 18, 19. "By the righteousness of one, the free gift came upon all men unto justification of life. For as by one man's disobedience many were made sinners; so, by the obedience of one, shall many be made righteous." Here in one verse we are told, that we have justification by Christ's righteousness; and, that there might be no room to understand the righteousness spoken of, merely of Christ's atonement by his suffering the penalty, in the next verse it is put in other terms, and asserted, that it is by Christ's obedience we are made righteous. It is scarcely possible any thing should be more full and determined: the terms, taken singly, are such as fix their own meaning, and taken together, they fix the meaning of each other. The words show that we are justified by that righteousness of Christ which consists in his obedience, and that we are made righteous or justified by that obedience of his, that is, his righteousness, or moral goodness before God.

Here possibly it may be objected, that this text means only, that we are justified by Christ's passive obedience.

To this I answer, whether we call it active or passive, it alters not the case as to the present argument, as long as it is evident by the words, that it is not merely under the notion of an atonement for disobedience, or a satisfaction for unrighteousness, but under the notion of a positive obedience, and a righteousness, or moral goodness, that it justifies us, or makes us righteous; because both the words *righteousness* and *obedience* are used, and used too as the opposites to sin and disobedience, and an offence. "Therefore as by the offence of one, judgment came upon all men to condemnation; even so, by the righteousness of one, the free gift came upon all men to justification of life. For as by one man's disobedience many were made sinners; so, by the obedience of one, shall many be made righteous." Now, what can be meant by righteousness, when spoken of as the opposite to sin, or moral evil, but moral goodness? What is the righteousness that is the opposite of an offence, but the behaviour that is well pleasing? and what can be meant by obedience, when spoken of as the opposite of disobedience, or going contrary to a command, but a positive obeying and an actual complying with the command? So that there is no room for any invented distinction of active and passive, to hurt the argument from this scripture; for it is evident by it, as any thing can be, that believers are justified by the righteousness and obedience of Christ, under the notion of his moral goodness;—his positive obeying, and actual complying with the commands of God, and that behaviour which, because of its conformity to his commands, was well-pleasing in his sight. This is all that ever any need to desire to have granted in this dispute.

By this it appears, that if Christ's dying be here included in the words *righteousness* and *obedience*, it is not merely as a propitiation, or bearing a penalty of a broken law in our stead, but as his voluntary submitting and yielding himself to those sufferings, was an act of obedience to the Father's commands, and so was a part of his positive righteousness, or moral goodness.

Indeed all obedience considered under the notion of righteousness, is something active, something done in voluntary compliance with a command; whether it may be done without suffering, or whether it be hard and difficult; yet as it is obedience, righteousness, or moral goodness, it must be considered as something voluntary and active. If any one is commanded to go through difficulties and sufferings, and he, in compliance with this command, voluntarily does it, he properly obeys in so doing; and as he voluntarily does it in compliance with a command, his obedience is as active as any whatsoever. It is the same sort of obedience, a thing of the very same nature, as when a man, in compliance with a command, does a piece of hard service, or goes through hard labour; and there is no room to distinguish between such obedience of it, as if it were a thing of quite a different nature, by such opposite terms as active and passive: all the distinction that can be pretended, is that which is between obeying an easy command and a difficult one. But is there from hence any foundation to make two species of obedience, one active and the other passive? There is no appearance of any such distinction ever entering into the hearts of any of the penmen of Scripture.

It is true, that of late, when a man refuses to obey the precept of a human law, but patiently yields himself up to suffer the penalty of the law, it is called *passive* obedience: but this I suppose is only a modern use of the word *obedience;* surely it is a sense of the word that the Scripture is a perfect stranger to. It is improperly called obedience, unless there be such a precept in the law, that he shall yield himself patiently to suffer, to which his so doing shall be an active voluntary conformity. There may in some sense be said to be a conformity of the law in a person's suffering the penalty of the law; but no other conformity to the law is properly called obedience to it, but an active voluntary conformity to the precepts of it. The word *obey* is often found in Scripture with respect to the law of God to man, but never in any other sense.

It is true that Christ's *willingly* undergoing those sufferings which he endured, is a great part of that obedience or righteousness by which we are justified. The sufferings of Christ are respected in Scripture under a twofold consideration, either merely as his being substituted for us, or put into our stead, in suffering the penalty of the law; and so his sufferings are considered as a satisfaction and propitiation for sin; or as he, in obedience to a law or command of the Father, voluntarily submitted himself to those sufferings, and actively yielded himself up to bear them; and so they are considered as his righteousness, and a part of his active obedience. Christ underwent death in obedience to the command of the Father, Psalm xl. 6, 7, 8. "Sacrifice and offering thou didst not desire, mine ears hast thou opened: burnt-offering and sin-offering hast thou not required. Then said I, Lo, I come: in the volume of the book it is written of me: I delight to do thy will, O my God; yea, thy "law is within my heart." John x. 17, 18. "I lay down my life, that I might take it again. No man taketh it from me, but I lay it down of myself: I have power to lay it down, and I have power to take it again. This commandment have I received of my Father." John xviii. 11. "The cup which my Father hath given me, shall I not drink it?" And this is part, and indeed the principal part, of that active obedience by which we are justified.

It can be no just objection against this, that the command of the Father to Christ that he should lay down his life, was no part of the law that we had broken; and therefore, that his obeying this command could be no part of that obedience that he performed for us, because we needed that he should obey no other law for us, but only that which we had broken or failed of obeying. For although it must be the same legislative authority, whose honour is repaired by Christ's obedience, that we have injured by our disobedience; yet there is no need that the law which Christ obeys should be precisely the same that Adam was to have obeyed, in that sense, that there should be no positive precepts wanting, nor any added. There was wanting the precept about the forbidden fruit, and there was added the ceremonial law. The thing required was perfect obedience. It is no matter whether the positive precepts were the same, if they were equivalent. The positive precepts that Christ was to obey, were much more than equivalent to what was wanting, because infinitely more difficult, particularly the command that he had received to lay down his life, which was his principal act of obedience, and which, above all other, is concerned in our justification. As that act of disobedience by which we fell, was disobedience to a positive precept that Christ never was under, *viz.* that of abstaining from the tree of knowledge of good and evil; so that act of obedience by which principally we are redeemed, is obedience to a positive precept that Adam never was under, *viz.* the precept of laying down his life. It was suitable that it should be a positive precept, that should try both Adam's and Christ's obedience. Such precepts are the greatest and most proper trial of obedience; because in them, the mere authority and will of the legislator is the sole ground of the obligation, (and nothing in the nature of the things themselves,) and therefore they are the greatest trial of any person's respect to that authority and will.

The law that Christ was subject to, and obeyed, was in some sense the same that was given to Adam. There are innumerable particular duties required by the law only conditionally; and in such circumstances, are comprehended in some great and general rule of that law. Thus, for instance, there are innumerable acts of respect and obedience to men, which are required by the law of nature, (which was a law given to Adam,) which yet are not required absolutely, but upon many pre-requisite conditions; as, that there be men standing in such relations to us, and that they give forth such commands, and the like. So many acts of respect and obedience to God are included, in like manner, in the moral law conditionally, or such and such things being supposed; as Abraham's going about to sacrifice his son, the Jews' circumcising their children when eight days old, and Adam's not eating the forbidden fruit; they are virtually comprehended in that great general rule of the moral law, that we should obey God, and be subject to him in whatsoever he pleases to command us. Certainly the moral law does as much require us to obey God's positive commands, as it requires us to obey the positive commands of our parents. And thus all that Adam, and all that Christ was commanded, even his observing the rites and ceremonies of the Jewish worship, and his laying down his life, was virtually included in this same great law.*

It is no objection against the last-mentioned thing, even Christ's laying down his life, it being included in the moral law given to Adam, because that law itself allowed of no occasion for any such thing; for the moral law virtually includes all right acts, on all possible occasions, even occasions that the law itself allows not: thus we are obliged by the moral law to mortify our lusts, and repent of our sins, though that law allows of no lust to mortify, or sin to repent of.

There is indeed but one great law of God, and that is the same law that says, "if thou sinnest, thou shalt die;" and "cursed is every one that continues not in all things contained in this law to do them." All duties of positive institution are virtually comprehended in this law: and therefore, if the Jews broke the ceremonial law, it exposed them to the penalty of the law, or covenant of works, which threatened, "thou shalt surely die." The law is the eternal and unalterable rule of righteousness between God and man, and therefore is the rule of judgment, by which all that a man does shall be either justified or condemned; and no sin exposes to damnation, but by the law. So now he that refuses to obey the precepts that require an attendance on the sacraments of the New Testament, is exposed to damnation, by virtue of the law or covenant of works. It may moreover be argued, that all sins whatsoever are breaches of the law or covenant of works, because all sins, even breaches of the positive precepts, as well as others, have atonement by the death of Christ: but what Christ died for, was to satisfy the law, or to bear the curse of the law; as appears by Gal. iii. 10—13. and Rom. vii. 3, 4.

So that Christ's laying down his life might be part of that obedience by which we are justified, though it was a positive precept not given to Adam. It was doubtless Christ's main act of obedience, because it was obedience to a command that was attended with immensely the greatest difficulty, and so to a command that was the greatest trial of his obedience. His respect shown to God in it, and his honour to God's authority, was proportionably great. It is spoken of in Scripture as Christ's principal act of obedience. Philip. ii. 7, 8. "But made himself of no reputation, and took upon him the form of a servant, and was made in the likeness of men: and being found in fashion as a man, he humbled himself, and became obedient unto death, even the death of the cross." Heb. v. 8. "Though he were a son, yet learned he obedience by the things that he suffered." It was mainly by this act of obedience that Christ purchased so glorious a reward for himself; Philip. ii. 8, 9. "He became obedient unto death, even the death of the cross. Wherefore God also hath highly exalted him, and given him a name which is above every name." And it therefore follows from what has been already said, that it is mainly by this act of obedience that believers in Christ also have the reward of glory, or come to partake with Christ in his glory. We are as much saved by the death of Christ, as his yielding himself to die was an act of obedience, as we are, as it was a propitiation for our sins: for as it was not the only act of obedience that merited, he having performed meritorious acts of obedience through the whole course of his life; so neither was it the only suffering that was propitiatory; all his sufferings through the whole course of his life being propitiatory, as well as every act of obedience meritorious. Indeed this was his principal suffering; and it was as much his principal act of obedience.

Hence we may see how that the death of Christ did not only make atonement, but also merited eternal life; and hence we may see how by the blood of Christ we are not only redeemed from sin, but redeemed unto God; and therefore the Scripture seems every where to attribute the whole of salvation to the blood of Christ. This precious blood is as much the main price by which heaven is purchased, as it is the main price by which we are redeemed from hell. The positive righteousness of Christ, or that price by which he merited, was of equal value with that

* Thus Mr. Locke in his ***Reasonableness of Christianity, as delivered in the Scriptures***, vol. 2d of his Works, p. 478. "Nay, ***whatever God requires any where to be done***, without making any allowance for faith, that is a part of the law of works. So that forbidding Adam to eat of the tree of knowledge, was part of the law of works. Only we must take notice here, that some of God's positive commands being for peculiar ends, and suited to particular circumstances of times, places, and persons, have a limited and only temporary obligation, by virtue of God's positive injunction: such was that part of Moses's law which concerned the outward worship or political constitution of the Jews, and is called the ceremonial and judaical law." Again, p. 479. "Thus then, as to the law in short, the civil and ritual part of the law delivered by Moses obliges not Christians, though to the Jews it were a part of the law of works; it being a part of the law of nature, that men ought to obey every positive law of God, whenever he shall please to make any such addition to the law of his nature."

by which he satisfied; for indeed it was the same price. He spilled his blood to satisfy, and by reason of the infinite dignity of his person, his sufferings were looked upon as of infinite value, and equivalent to the eternal sufferings of a finite creature. And he spilled his blood out of respect to the honour of God's majesty, and in submission to his authority, who had commanded him so to do: and his obedience therein was of infinite value; both because of the dignity of the person that performed it, and because he put himself to infinite expense to perform it, whereby the infinite degree of his regard to God's authority appeared.

One would wonder what Arminians mean by Christ's merits. They talk of Christ's merits as much as any body, and yet deny the imputation of Christ's positive righteousness. What should there be that any one should merit or deserve any thing by, besides righteousness or goodness? If any thing that Christ did or suffered, merited or deserved any thing, it was by virtue of the goodness, or righteousness, or holiness of it. If Christ's sufferings and death merited heaven, it must be because there was an excellent righteousness and transcendent moral goodness in that act of laying down his life. And if by that excellent righteousness he merited heaven for us; then surely that righteousness is reckoned to our account, that we have the benefit of it, or, which is the same thing, it is imputed to us.

Thus, I hope, I have made it evident, that the righteousness of Christ is indeed imputed to us. I proceed now to the

Third and last thing under this argument, That this doctrine, of the imputation of Christ's righteousness, is utterly inconsistent with the doctrine of our being justified by our own virtue or sincere obedience. If acceptance to God's favour, and a title to life, be given to believers as the reward of Christ's obedience, then it is not given as the reward of our own obedience. In what respect soever Christ is our Saviour, that doubtless excludes our being our own saviours in that same respect. If we can be our own saviours in the same respect that Christ is, it will thence follow, that the salvation of Christ is needless in that respect; according to the apostle's reasoning, Gal. v. 4. "Christ is rendered of no effect unto you, whosoever of you are justified by the law." Doubtless, it is Christ's prerogative to be our Saviour in that sense wherein he is our Saviour. And therefore, if it be by his obedience that we are justified, then it is not by our own obedience.

Here perhaps it may be said, that a title to salvation is not directly given as the reward of our obedience; for that is not by any thing of ours, but only by Christ's satisfaction and righteousness; but yet an interest in that satisfaction and righteousness is given as a reward of our obedience.

But this does not at all help the case; for this is to ascribe as much to our obedience as if we ascribed salvation to it directly, without the intervention of Christ's righteousness. For it would be as great a thing for God to give us Christ, and his satisfaction and righteousness, in reward for our obedience, as to give us heaven immediately; it would be as great a reward, and as great a testimony of respect to our obedience. And if God gives as great a thing as salvation for our obedience, why could he not as well give salvation itself directly? and then there would have been no need of Christ's righteousness. And indeed if God gives us Christ, or an interest in him, properly in reward of our obedience, he does really give us salvation in reward for our obedience: for the former implies the latter; yea, it implies it, as the greater implies the less. So that indeed it exalts our virtue and obedience more, to suppose that God gives us Christ in reward of that virtue and obedience, than if he should give salvation without Christ.

The thing that the Scripture guards and militates against, is our imagining that it is our own goodness, virtue, or excellency, that instates us in God's acceptance and favour. But to suppose that God gives us an interest in Christ in reward for our virtue, is as great an argument that it instates us in God's favour, as if he bestowed a title to eternal life as its direct reward. If God gives us an interest in Christ as a reward of our obedience, it will then follow, that we are instated in God's acceptance and favour by our own obedience, antecedent to our having an interest in Christ. For a rewarding any one's excellency, evermore supposes favour and acceptance on the account of that excellency: it is the very notion of a reward, that it is a good thing, bestowed in testimony of respect and favour for the virtue or excellency rewarded. So that it is not by virtue of our interest in Christ and his merits, that we first come into favour with God, according to this scheme; for we are in God's favour before we have any interest in those merits; in that we have an interest in those merits given as a fruit of God's favour for our own virtue. If our interest in Christ be the fruit of God's favour, then it cannot be the ground of it. If God did not accept us, and had no favour for us for our own excellency, he never would bestow so great a reward upon us, as a right in Christ's satisfaction and righteousness. So that such a scheme destroys itself; for it supposes that Christ's satisfaction and righteousness are necessary for us to recommend us to the favour of God; and yet supposes that we have God's favour and acceptance before we have Christ's satisfaction and righteousness, and have these given as a fruit of God's favour.

Indeed, neither salvation itself, nor Christ the Saviour, are given as a reward of any thing in man: they are not given as a reward of faith, nor any thing else of ours: we are not united to Christ as a reward of our faith, but have union with him by faith, only as faith is the very act of uniting or closing *on our part*. As when a man offers himself to a woman in marriage, he does not give himself to her as a *reward* of her receiving him in marriage. Her receiving him is not considered as a worthy deed in her for which he rewards her by giving himself to her; but it is by her receiving him that the union is made, by which she hath him for her husband. It is *on her part* the unition itself. By these things it appears how contrary to the gospel of Christ their scheme is, who say that faith justifies as a principle of obedience, or as a leading act of obedience; or (as others) the sum and comprehension of all evangelical obedience. For by this, the obedience or virtue that is in faith gives it its justifying influence; and that is the same thing as to say, that we are justified by our own obedience, virtue, or goodness.

Having thus considered the evidence of the truth of the doctrine, I proceed now to the

III. Thing proposed, *viz.* "To show in what sense the acts of a christian life, or of evangelical obedience, may be looked upon to be concerned in this affair."

From what has been said already, it is manifest that they cannot have any concern in this affair as good works, or by virtue of any moral goodness in them; not as works of the law, or as that moral excellency, or any part of it, which is the fulfilment of that great, universal, and everlasting law or covenant of works which the great lawgiver has establish d, as the highest and unalterable rule of judgment, which Christ alone answers, or does any thing towards it.

It having been shown out of the Scripture, that it is only by faith, or the soul's receiving and uniting to the Saviour who has wrought our righteousness, that we are justified; it therefore remains, that the acts of a christian life cannot be concerned in this affair any otherwise than as they imply, and are the expressions of, faith, and may be looked upon as so many acts of reception of Christ the Saviour. But the determining what concerns acts of christian obedience can have in justification in this respect, will depend on the resolving of another point, *viz.* Whether any other act of faith besides the first act, has any concern in our justification, or how far perseverance in faith, or the continued and renewed acts of faith, have influence in this affair. And it seems manifest that justification is by the first act of faith, in some respects, in a peculiar manner, because a sinner is actually and finally justified as soon as he has performed one act of faith; and faith in its first act does, virtually at least, depend on God for perseverance, and entitles to this among other benefits. But yet the perseverance of faith is not excluded in this affair; it is not only certainly connected with justification, but it is not to be excluded from that on which the justification of a sinner has a dependence, or that by which he is justified.

I have shown that the way in which justification has a

dependence on faith, is, that it is the qualification on which the congruity of an interest in the righteousness of Christ depends, or wherein such a fitness consists. But the consideration of the perseverance of faith cannot be excluded out of this congruity or fitness, for it is congruous that he that believes in Christ should have an interest in Christ's righteousness, and so in the eternal benefits purchased by it, because faith is that by which the soul hath union or oneness with Christ; and there is a natural congruity in it, that they who are one with Christ should have a joint interest with him in his eternal benefits; but yet this congruity depends on its being an abiding union. As it is needful that the branch should abide in the vine, in order to its receiving the lasting benefits of the root; so it is necessary that the soul should abide in Christ, in order to its receiving those lasting benefits of God's final acceptance and favour. John xv. 6, 7. "If a man abide not in me, he is cast forth as a branch. If ye abide in me, and my words abide in you, ye shall ask what ye will, and it shall be done unto you." Ver. 9, 10. "Continue ye in my love. If ye keep (or abide in) my commandments, ye shall abide in my love: even as I have kept my Father's commandments, and abide in his love." There is the same reason why it is necessary that the union with Christ should remain, as why it should be begun; why it should continue to be, as why it should once be. If it should be begun without remaining, the beginning would be in vain. In order to the soul's being now in a justified state, and now free from condemnation, it is necessary that it should now be in Christ, and not merely that it should once have been in him. Rom. viii. 1. "There is no condemnation to them which are in Christ Jesus." The soul is saved in Christ, as being now in him, when the salvation is bestowed, and not merely as remembering that it once was in him. Philip. iii. 9. "That I may be found in him, not having mine own righteousness, which is of the law, but that which is through the faith of Christ, the righteousness which is of God by faith." 1 John ii. 28. "And now, little children, abide in him; that when he shall appear, we may have confidence, and not be ashamed before him at his coming." In order to persons being blessed after death, it is necessary not only that they should once be in him, but that they should die in him. Rev. xiv. 13. "Blessed are the dead that die in the Lord."—And there is the same reason why faith, the uniting qualification, should remain, in order to the union's remaining; as why it should once be, in order to the union's once being.

So that although the sinner is actually and finally justified on the first acts of faith, yet the perseverance of faith, even then, comes into consideration, as one thing on which the fitness of acceptance to life depends. God, in the act of justification, which is passed on a sinner's first believing, has respect to perseverance, as being virtually contained in that first act of faith; and it is looked upon, and taken by him that justifies, as being as it were a property in that faith. God has respect to the believer's continuance in faith, and he is justified by that, as though it already were, because by divine establishment it shall follow; and it being by divine constitution connected with that first faith, as much as if it were a property in it, it is then considered as such, and so justification is not suspended; but were it not for this, it would be needful that it should be suspended, till the sinner had actually persevered in faith.

And that it is so, that God in the act of final justification which he passes at the sinner's conversion, has respect to perseverance in faith, and future acts of faith, as being virtually implied in the first act, is further manifest by this, *viz.* That in a sinner's justification, at his conversion there is virtually contained a forgiveness as to eternal and deserved punishment, not only of all past sins, but also of all future infirmities and acts of sin that they shall be guilty of; because that first justification is decisive and final. And yet pardon, in the order of nature, properly follows the crime, and also follows those acts of repentance and faith that respect the crime pardoned, as is manifest both from reason and Scripture. David, in the beginning of Psalm xxxii. speaks of the forgiveness of sins which were doubtless committed long after he was first godly, as being consequent on those sins, and on his repentance and faith with respect to them; and yet this forgiveness is spoken of by the apostle in the 4th of Romans, as an instance of justification by faith. Probably the sin David there speaks of is the same that he committed in the matter of Uriah, and so the pardon the same with that release from death, or eternal punishment, which the prophet Nathan speaks of, 2 Sam. xii. 13. "The Lord also hath put away thy sin; thou shalt not die." Not only does the manifestation of this pardon follow the sin in the order of time, but the pardon itself, in the order of nature, follows David's repentance and faith with respect to this sin; for it is spoken of in the 32d Psalm, as depending on it.

But inasmuch as a sinner, in his first justification, is for ever justified and freed from all obligation to eternal punishment; it hence of necessity follows, that future faith and repentance are beheld, in that justification, as virtually contained in that first faith and repentance; because repentance of those future sins, and faith in a Redeemer, with respect to them, or, at least, the continuance of that habit and principle in the heart that has such an actual repentance and faith in its nature and tendency, is now made sure by God's promise.—If remission of sins, committed after conversion, in the order of nature, follows that faith and repentance that is after them, then it follows that future sins are respected in the first justification, no otherwise than as future faith and repentance are respected in it. And future repentance and faith are looked upon by him that justifies, as virtually implied in the first repentance and faith, in the same manner as justification from future sins is virtually implied in the first justification; which is the thing that was to be proved.

And besides, if no other act of faith could be concerned in justification but the first act, it will then follow, that Christians ought never to seek justification by any other act of faith. For if justification is not to be obtained by after acts of faith, then surely it is not a duty to seek it by such acts: and so it can never be a duty for persons after they are once converted, by faith to seek to God, or believingly to look to him, for the remission of sin, or deliverance from the guilt of it, because deliverance from the guilt of sin is part of what belongs to justification. And if it be not proper for converts by faith to look to God through Christ for it, then it will follow, that it is not proper for them to pray for it; for christian prayer to God for a blessing, is but an expression of faith in God for that blessing; prayer is only the voice of faith. But if these things are so, it will follow that the petition in the Lord's prayer, *forgive us our debts*, is not proper to be put up by disciples of Christ, or to be used in christian assemblies; and that Christ improperly directed his disciples to use that petition, when they were all of them, except Judas, converted before. The debt that Christ directs his disciples to pray for the forgiveness of, can mean nothing else but the punishment that sin deserves, or the debt that we owe to divine justice, the ten thousand talents we owe our Lord. To pray that God would forgive our debts, is undoubtedly the same thing as to pray that God would release us from obligation to due punishment; but releasing from obligation to the punishment due to sin, and forgiving the debt that we owe to divine justice, is what appertains to justification.

And then to suppose that no after acts of faith are concerned in the business of justification, and so that it is not proper for any ever to seek justification by such acts, would be for ever to cut off those Christians that are doubtful concerning their first act of faith, from the joy and peace of believing. As the business of a justifying faith is to obtain pardon and peace with God, by looking to God, and trusting in him for these blessings; so the joy and peace of that faith is in the apprehension of pardon and peace obtained by such a trust. This a Christian that is doubtful of his first act of faith cannot have from that act, because, by the supposition, he is doubtful whether it be an act of faith, and so whether he did obtain pardon and peace by that act. The proper remedy, in such a case, is now by faith to look to God in Christ for these blessings: but he is cut off from this remedy, because he is uncertain whether he has warrant so to do; for he does not know but that he has believed already; and if so, then he has no warrant to look to God by faith for these blessings now, because, by the supposition, no new act of faith is a proper means of obtaining these blessings. And so he can never properly obtain the joy of faith; for there are acts of true faith that are very weak, and the first act may be so as well as others: it may be like the first motion of the infant in the womb; it may be so weak an act, that the Christian, by examining it, may never be able to determine whether it was a true act of faith or no; and it is evident from fact, and abundant experience, that many Christians are for ever at a loss to determine which was their first act of faith. And those saints who have had a good degree of satisfaction concerning their faith, may be subject to great declensions and falls, in which case they are liable to great fears of eternal punishment; and the proper way of deliverance, is to forsake their sin by repentance, and by faith now to come to Christ for deliverance from the deserved eternal punishment; but this it would not be, if deliverance from that punishment was not this way to be obtained.

But what is a still more plain and direct evidence of what I am now arguing for, is, that the act of faith which Abraham exercised in the great promise of the covenant of grace that God made to him, of which it is expressly said, Gal. iii. 6. "It was accounted to him for righteousness"—the grand instance and proof that the apostle so much insists upon throughout the 4th chapter of Romans, and 3d chapter of Galatians, to confirm his doctrine of justification by faith alone—was not Abraham's first act of faith, but was exerted long after he had by faith forsaken his own country, Heb. xi. 8. and had been treated as an eminent friend of God.

Moreover, the apostle Paul, in the 3d chapter of Philip. tells us how earnestly he sought justification by faith, or to win Christ and obtain that righteousness which was by the faith of him, in what he did after his conversion. Verse 8, 9. "For whom I have suffered the loss of all things, and do count them but dung that I may win Christ, and be found in him, not having mine own righteousness which is of the law, but that which is through the faith of Christ, the righteousness which is of God by faith." And in the two next verses he expresses the same thing in other words, and tells us how he went through sufferings, and became conformable to Christ's death, that he might be a partaker with Christ in the benefit of his resurrection; which the same apostle elsewhere teaches us, is especially justification. Christ's resurrection was his justification; in this, he that was put to death in the flesh, was justified by the Spirit; and he that was delivered for our offences, rose again for our justification. And the apostle tells us in the verses that follow in that 3d chapter of Philippians, that he thus sought to attain the righteousness which is through the faith of Christ, and so to partake of the benefit of his resurrection, still as though he had not already attained, but that he continued to follow after it.

On the whole, it appears, that the perseverance of faith is necessary, even to the congruity of justification; and that not the less, because a sinner is justified, and perseverance promised, on the first act of faith, but God, in that justification, has respect, not only to the past act of faith, but to his own promise of future acts, and to the fitness of a qualification beheld as yet only in his own promise. And that perseverance in faith is thus necessary to salvation, not merely as a *sine qua non*, or as an universal concomitant of it, but by reason of such an influence and dependence, seems manifest by many scriptures: I would mention two or three; Heb. iii. 6. "Whose house are we, if we hold fast the confidence, and the rejoicing of the hope firm unto the end." Verse 14. "For we are made partakers of Christ, if we hold the beginning of our confidence stedfast unto the end." Chap. vi. 12. "Be ye followers of them, who through faith and patience inherit the promises." Rom. xi. 20. "Well, because of unbelief they were broken off; but thou standest by faith. Be not high minded, but fear."

And, as the congruity to a final justification depends on perseverance in faith, as well as the first act, so oftentimes the manifestation of justification in the conscience, arises a great deal more from after acts, than the first act. And all the difference whereby the first act of faith has a concern in this affair that is peculiar, seems to be, as it were, only an accidental difference, arising from the circumstance of time, or its being first in order of time; and not from any peculiar respect that God has to it, or any influence it has of a peculiar nature, in the affair of our salvation.

And thus it is that a truly christian walk, and the acts of an evangelical, child-like, believing obedience, are concerned in the affair of our justification, and seem to be sometimes so spoken of in Scripture, *viz.* as an expression of a persevering faith in the Son of God, the only Saviour. Faith unites to Christ, and so gives a congruity to justification, not merely as remaining a dormant principle in the heart, but as being and appearing in its active expressions. The obedience of a Christian, so far as it is truly evangelical, and performed with the Spirit of the Son sent forth into the heart, has all relation to Christ, the Mediator, and is but an expression of the soul's believing unition to Christ. All evangelical works are works of that faith that worketh by love; and every such act of obedience, wherein it is inward, and the act of the soul, is only a new effective act of reception of Christ, and adherence to the glorious Saviour. Hence that of the apostle, Gal. ii. 20. "I live; yet not I, but Christ liveth in me; and the life that I now live in the flesh, is by the faith of the Son of God." And hence we are directed, in whatever we do, whether in word or deed, to do all in the name of the Lord Jesus Christ, Col. iii. 17.

And that God in justification has respect, not only to the first act of faith, but also to future persevering acts, as expressed in life, seems manifest by Rom. i. 17. "For therein is the righteousness of God revealed from faith to faith: as it is written, The just shall live by faith." And Heb. x. 38, 39. "Now the just shall live by faith; but if any man draw back, my soul shall have no pleasure in him. But we are not of them who draw back unto perdition; but of them that believe, to the saving of the soul."

So that as was before said of faith, so may it be said of a child-like believing obedience, it has no concern in justification by any virtue or excellency in it; but only as there is a reception of Christ in it. And this is no more contrary to the apostle's frequent assertion of our being justified without the works of the law, than to say that we are justified by faith; for faith is as much a work, or act of christian obedience, as the expressions of faith, in spiritual life and walk. And therefore, as we say that faith does not justify as a work, so we say of all these effective expressions of faith.

This is the reverse of the scheme of our modern divines, who hold, that faith justifies only as an act or expression of obedience; whereas, in truth, obedience has no concern in justification, any otherwise than as an expression of faith.

I now proceed to the

IV. Thing proposed, *viz.* To answer objections.

Object. 1. We frequently find promises of eternal life and salvation, and sometimes of justification itself, made to our own virtue and obedience. Eternal life is promised to obedience, in Rom. ii. 7. "To them, who by patient continuance in well doing, seek for glory, honour, and immortality; eternal life:" and the like in innumerable other places. And justification itself is promised to that virtue of a forgiving spirit or temper in us, Matt. vi. 14. "For, if ye forgive men their trespasses, your heavenly Father will also forgive you: but if ye forgive not men their trespasses, neither will your Father forgive your trespasses." All allow that justification in great part consists in the forgiveness of sins.

To this I answer,

1. These things being promised to our virtue and obedience, argues no more, than that there is a connexion between them and evangelical obedience; which, I have already observed, is not the thing in dispute. All that can be proved by obedience and salvation being connected in the promise, is, that obedience and salvation are connected in fact; which nobody denies; and whether it be owned or denied, is, as has been shown, nothing to the purpose. There is no need that an admission to a title to salvation, should be given on the account of our obedience, in order to the promises being true. If we find such a promise, that he that obeys shall be saved, or he that is holy shall be justified; all that is needful, in order to such promises being true, is, that it be really so, that he that obeys shall be saved, and that holiness and justification shall indeed go together. That proposition may be a truth, that he that obeys shall be saved; because obedience and salvation are

connected together in fact; and yet an acceptance to a title to salvation not be granted upon the account of any of our own virtue or obedience. What is a promise, but only a declaration of future truth, for the comfort and encouragement of the person to whom it is declared? Promises are conditional propositions; and, as has been already observed, it is not the thing in dispute, whether other things besides faith may not have the place of the condition in such propositions wherein pardon and salvation are the consequent.

2. Promises may rationally be made to signs and evidences of faith, and yet the thing promised not be upon the account of the sign, but the thing signified. Thus, for instance, human government may rationally make promises of such and such privileges to those that can show such evidences of their being free of such a city, or members of such a corporation, or descended of such a family; when it is not at all for the sake of that which is the evidence or sign, in itself considered, that they are admitted to such a privilege, but only and purely for the sake of that which it is an evidence of. And though God does not stand in need of signs to know whether we have true faith or not, yet our own consciences do; so that it is much for our comfort that promises are made to signs of faith. Finding in ourselves a forgiving temper and disposition, may be a most proper and natural evidence to our consciences, that our hearts have, in a sense of our own utter unworthiness, truly closed and fallen in with the way of free and infinitely gracious forgiveness of our sins by Jesus Christ; whence we may be enabled, with the greater comfort, to apply to ourselves the promises of forgiveness by Christ.

3. It has been just now shown, how that acts of evangelical obedience are indeed concerned in our justification itself, and are not excluded from that condition that justification depends upon, without the least prejudice to that doctrine of justification by faith, without any goodness of our own, that has been maintained; and therefore it can be no objection against this doctrine, that we have sometimes in Scripture promises of pardon and acceptance made to such acts of obedience.

4. Promises of particular benefits implied in justification and salvation, may especially be fitly made to such expressions and evidences of faith as they have a peculiar natural likeness and suitableness to. As forgiveness is promised to a forgiving spirit in us; obtaining mercy is fitly promised to mercifulness in us, and the like: and that upon several accounts, they are the most natural evidences of our heart's closing with those benefits by faith; for they do especially show the sweet accord and consent that there is between the heart and these benefits; and by reason of the natural likeness that there is between the virtue and the benefit, the one has the greater tendency to bring the other to mind; the practice of the virtue tends the more to renew the sense, and refresh the hope, of the blessing promised; and also to convince the conscience of the justice of being denied the benefit, if the duty be neglected. Besides the sense and manifestation of divine forgiveness in our own consciences—yea, and many exercises of God's forgiving mercy, (as it respects God's fatherly displeasure,) granted after justification, through the course of a Christian's life—may be given as the proper rewards of a forgiving spirit, and yet this not be at all to the prejudice of the doctrine we have maintained; as will more fully appear, when we come to answer another objection hereafter to be mentioned.

Object. 2. Our own obedience, and inherent holiness, is necessary to prepare men for heaven; and therefore is doubtless what recommends persons to God's acceptance, as the heirs of heaven.

To this I answer,

1. Our own obedience being necessary in order to a preparation for an actual bestowment of glory, is no argument that it is the thing upon the account of which we are accepted to a right to it. God may, and does do many things to prepare the saints for glory, after he has accepted them as the heirs of glory. A parent may do much to prepare a child for an inheritance in its education, after the child is an heir; yea, there are many things necessary to fit a child for the actual possession of the inheritance, yet not necessary in order to its having a right to the inheritance.

2. If every thing that is necessary to prepare men for glory must be the proper condition of justification, then perfect holiness is the condition of justification. Men must be made perfectly holy, before they are admitted to the enjoyment of the blessedness of heaven; for there must in no wise enter in there any spiritual defilement. And therefore, when a saint dies, he leaves all his sin and corruption when he leaves the body.

Object. 3. Our obedience is not only indissolubly connected with salvation, and preparatory to it, but the Scripture expressly speaks of bestowing eternal blessings as rewards for the good deeds of the saints. Matt. x. 42. "Whosoever shall give to drink unto one of these little ones a cup of cold water only, in the name of a disciple, he shall in no wise lose his reward." 1 Cor. iii. 8. "Every man shall receive his own reward, according to his own labour." And in many other places. This seems to militate against the doctrine that has been maintained, two ways: (1.) The bestowing a reward, carries in it a respect to a moral fitness in the thing rewarded to the reward; the very notion of a reward being a benefit bestowed in testimony of acceptance of, and respect to, the goodness or amiableness of some qualification or work in the person rewarded. Besides, the Scripture seems to explain itself in this matter, in Rev. iii. 4. "Thou hast a few names, even in Sardis, which have not defiled their garments; and they shall walk with me in white; for they are worthy." This is here given as the reason why they should have such a reward, "because they were worthy;" which, though we suppose it to imply no proper merit, yet it at least implies a moral fitness, or that the excellency of their virtue in God's sight recommends them to such a reward; which seems directly repugnant to what has been supposed, *viz.* that we are accepted, and approved of God, as the heirs of salvation, not out of regard to the excellency of our own virtue or goodness, or any moral fitness therein to such a reward, but only on account of the dignity and moral fitness of Christ's righteousness. (2.) Our being eternally rewarded for our own holiness and good works, necessarily supposes that our future happiness will be greater or smaller, in some proportion as our own holiness and obedience is more or less; and that there are different degrees of glory, according to different degrees of virtue and good works, is a doctrine very expressly and frequently taught us in Scripture. But this seems quite inconsistent with the saints all having their future blessedness as a reward of Christ's righteousness: for if Christ's righteousness be imputed to all, and this be what entitles each one to glory, then it is the same righteousness that entitles one to glory which entitles another. But if all have glory as the reward of the same righteousness, why have not all the same glory? Does not the same righteousness merit as much glory when imputed to one as when imputed to another?

In answer to the *first* part of this objection, I would observe, that it does not argue that we are justified by our good deeds, that we shall have eternal blessings in reward for them; for it is in consequence of our justification, that our good deeds become rewardable with spiritual and eternal rewards. The acceptableness, and so the rewardableness, of our virtue, is not antecedent to justification, but follows it, and is built entirely upon it; which is the reverse of what those in the adverse scheme of justification suppose, *viz.* that justification is built on the acceptableness and rewardableness of our virtue. They suppose that a saving interest in Christ is given as a reward of our virtue, or, (which is the same thing,) as a testimony of God's acceptance of our excellency in our virtue. But the contrary is true; that God's respect to our virtue as our amiableness in his sight, and his acceptance of it as rewardable, is entirely built on our interest in Christ already established. So that the relation to Christ, whereby believers in scripture language are said to be in Christ, is the very foundation of our virtues and good deeds being accepted of God, and so of their being rewarded; for a reward is a testimony of acceptance. For we, and all that we do, are accepted only in the beloved, Eph. i. 6. Our sacrifices are acceptable, only through our interest in him, and through his worthiness and preciousness being, as it were, made ours. 1 Pet. ii. 4, 5. "To whom coming, as unto a living stone, disallowed indeed of men, but chosen of God, and precious. Ye also as lively stones, are built up a spiritual house, an holy priesthood to offer up spiritual sacrifices, acceptable to God by Jesus Christ." Here being actually built on this stone, precious to God, is mentioned as all the ground of the acceptableness of our good works to God, and their becoming also precious in his eyes. So, Heb. xiii. 21. "Make you perfect in every good work to do his will, working in you that which is well pleasing in his sight, through Jesus Christ." And hence we are directed, whatever we offer to God, to offer it in Christ's name, as expecting to have it accepted no other way, than from the value that God has to that name. Col. iii. 17. "And whatsoever ye do in word or deed, do all in the name of the Lord Jesus, giving thanks to God and the Father by him." To act in Christ's name, is to act under him as our head, and as having him to stand for us, and represent us to God-ward.

The reason of this may be seen from what has been already said, to show it is not meet that any thing in us should be accepted of God as any excellency of our persons, until we are actually in Christ, and justified through him. The loveliness of the virtue of fallen creatures is nothing in the sight of God, till he beholds them in Christ, and clothed with his righteousness. 1. Because till then we stand condemned before God, by his own holy law, to his utter rejection and abhorrence. And, 2. Because we are infinitely guilty before him; and the loveliness of our virtue bears no proportion to our guilt, and must therefore pass for nothing before a strict judge. And, 3. Because our good deeds and virtuous acts themselves are in a sense corrupt; and the hatefulness of the corruption of them, if we are beheld as we are in ourselves, or separate from Christ, infinitely outweighs the loveliness of the good that is in them. So that if no other sin was considered but only that which attends the act of virtue itself, the loveliness vanishes into nothing in comparison of it; and therefore the virtue must pass for nothing, out of Christ. Not only are our best duties defiled, in being attended with the exercises of sin and corruption which precede, follow, and are intermingled with them; but even the holy acts themselves, and the gracious exercises of the godly, are defective. Though the act most simply considered is good, yet take the acts in their measure and dimensions, and the manner in which they are exerted, and they are sinfully defective; there is that defect in them that may well be called the corruption of them. That defect is properly sin, an expression of a vile sinfulness of heart, and what tends to provoke the just anger of God: not because the exercise of love and other grace is not equal to God's loveliness; for it is impossible the love of creatures (men or angels) should be so; but because the act is so very disproportionate to the occasion given for love or other grace, considering God's loveliness, the manifestation that is made of it, the exercises of kindness, the capacity of human nature, and our advantages (and the like) together.—A negative expression of corruption may be as truly sin, and as just cause of provocation, as a positive. Thus if a worthy and excellent person should, from mere generosity and goodness, exceedingly lay out himself, and with great expense and suffering save another's life, or redeem him from some extreme calamity; and if that other person should never thank him for it, or express the least gratitude any way; this would be a negative expression of his ingratitude and baseness; but is equivalent to an act of ingratitude, or positive exercise of a base unworthy spirit; and is truly an expression of it, and brings as much blame as if he by some positive act had much injured another person. And so it would be (only in a lesser degree) if the gratitude was but very small, bearing no proportion to the benefit and obligation: as if, for so great and extraordinary a kindness, he should express no more gratitude than would have been becoming towards a person who had only given him a cup of water when thirsty, or shown him the way in a journey when at a loss, or had done him some such small kindness. If he should come to his benefactor to express his gratitude, and should do after this manner, he might truly be said to act unworthily and odiously; he would show a most ungrateful spirit. His doing after such a manner might justly be abhorred by all; and yet the gratitude, that little there is of it, most simply considered, and so far as it goes, is good. And so it is with respect to our exercise of love, and gratitude, and other graces, towards God; they are defectively corrupt and sinful, and, take them as they are, in their manner and measure, might justly be odious and provoking to God, and would necessarily be so, were we beheld out of Christ. For in that this defect is sin, it is infinitely hateful; and so the hatefulness of the very act infinitely outweighs the loveliness of it; because all sin has infinite hatefulness and heinousness; but our holiness has but little value and loveliness, as has been elsewhere demonstrated.

Hence, though it be true that the saints are rewarded for their good works, yet it is for Christ's sake only, and not for the excellency of their works in themselves considered, or beheld separately from Christ; for so they have no excellency in God's sight, or acceptableness to him, as has now been shown. It is acknowledged that God, in rewarding the holiness and good works of believers, does in some respect give them happiness as a testimony of his respect to the loveliness of their holiness and good works in his sight; for that is the very notion of a reward. But it is in a very different sense from what would have been if man had not fallen; which would have been to bestow eternal life on man, as a testimony of God's respect to the loveliness of what man did, considered as in itself, and as in man separately by himself, and not beheld as a member of Christ. In which sense also, the scheme of justification we are opposing necessarily supposes the excellency of our virtue to be respected and rewarded; for it supposes a saving interest in Christ itself to be given as a reward of it.

Two things come to pass, relating to the saints' reward for their inherent righteousness, by virtue of their relation to Christ. 1. The guilt of their persons is all done away, and the pollution and hatefulness that attends and is in their good works, is hid. 2. Their relation to Christ adds a positive value and dignity to their good works in God's sight. That little holiness, and those faint and feeble acts of love, and other grace, receive an exceeding value in the sight of God, by virtue of God's beholding them as in Christ, and as it were members of one so infinitely worthy in his eyes; and that because God looks upon the persons as of greater dignity on this account. Isa. xliii. 4. "Since thou wast precious in my sight, thou hast been honourable." God, for Christ's sake, and because they are members of his own righteous and dear Son, sets an exceeding value upon their persons; and hence it follows, that he also sets a great value upon their good acts and offerings. The same love and obedience in a person of greater dignity and value in God's sight, is more valuable in his eyes than in one of less dignity. Love is valuable in proportion to the dignity of the person whose love it is; because, so far as any one gives his love to another, he gives himself, in that he gives his heart. But this is a more excellent offering, in proportion as the person whose self is offered is more worthy. Believers are become immensely more honourable in God's esteem by virtue of their relation to Christ, than man would have been considered as by himself, though he had been free from sin; as a mean person becomes more honourable when married to a king. Hence God will probably reward the little weak love, and poor and exceeding imperfect obedience of believers in Christ, with more glorious reward than he would have done Adam's perfect obedience. According to the tenor of the first covenant, the person was to be accepted and rewarded, only for the work's sake; but by the covenant of grace, the work is accepted and rewarded, only for the person's sake; the person being beheld antecedently as a member of Christ, and clothed with his righteousness. So that though the saints' inherent holiness is rewarded, yet this very reward is indeed not the less founded on the worthiness and righteousness of Christ. None of the value that their works have in his sight, nor any of the acceptance they have with him, is out of Christ, and out of his righteousness; but his worthiness as mediator is the prime and only foundation on which all is built, and the universal source whence all arises. God indeed doth great things out of regard to the saints' loveliness, but it is only as a secondary and derivative loveliness. When I speak of a derivative loveliness, I do not mean only, that the qualifications themselves accepted as lovely, are derived from Christ, from his power and purchase; but that the acceptance of them as a loveliness, and all the value that is set upon them, and all their connexion with the reward, is founded in, and derived from, Christ's righteousness and worthiness.

If we suppose that not only higher degrees of glory in heaven, but heaven itself, is in some respect given in reward for the holiness and good works of the saints, in this secondary and derivative sense, it will not prejudice the doctrine we have maintained. It is no way impossible that God may bestow heaven's glory wholly out of respect to Christ's righteousness, and yet in reward for man's inherent holiness, in different respects, and different ways. It may be only Christ's righteousness that God has respect to, for its own sake, the independent acceptableness and dignity of it being sufficient of itself to recommend all that believe in Christ to a title to this glory; and so it may be only by this that persons enter into a title to heaven, or have their prime right to it: and yet God may also have respect to the saints' own holiness, for Christ's sake, and as deriving a value from Christ's merit, which he may testify in bestowing heaven upon them. The saints being beheld as members of Christ, their obedience is looked upon by God as something of Christ's, it being the obedience of the members of Christ; as the sufferings of the members of Christ are looked upon, in some respect, as the sufferings of Christ. Hence the apostle, speaking of his sufferings, says, Col. i. 24. "Who now rejoice in my sufferings for you, and fill up that which is behind of the afflictions of Christ in my flesh." To the same purpose is Matt. xxv. 35, &c. I was an hungred, naked, sick, and in prison, &c. And so that in Rev. xi. 8. "And their dead bodies shall lie in the street of the great city, which spiritually is called Sodom and Egypt, where also our Lord was crucified."

By the merit and righteousness of Christ, such favour of God towards the believer may be obtained, as that God may hereby be already, as it were, disposed to make them perfectly and eternally happy. But yet this does not hinder, but that God in his wisdom may choose to bestow this perfect and eternal happiness in this way, *viz.* in some respect as a reward of their holiness and obedience. It is not impossible but that the blessedness may be bestowed as a reward for that which is done after that an interest is already obtained in that favour, which (to speak of God after the manner of men) disposes God to bestow the blessedness. Our heavenly Father may already have that favour for a child, whereby he may be thoroughly ready to give the child an inheritance, because he is his child; which he is by the purchase of Christ's righteousness: and yet that the Father may choose to bestow the inheritance on the child in a way of reward for his dutifulness, and behaving in a manner becoming a child. And so great a reward may not be judged more than a meet reward for his dutifulness; but that so great a reward is judged meet, does not arise from the excellency of the obedience absolutely considered, but from his standing in so near and honourable a relation to God, as that of a child, which is obtained only by the righteousness of Christ. And thus the reward, and the greatness of it, arises properly from the righteousness of Christ; though it be indeed in some sort the reward of their obedience. As a father might justly esteem the inheritance no more than a meet reward for the obedience of his child, and yet esteem it more than a meet reward for the obedience of a servant. The favour whence a believer's heavenly Father bestows the eternal inheritance, and his title as an heir, is founded in that relation he stands in to him as a child, purchased by Christ's righteousness; though he in wisdom chooses to bestow it in such a way, and therein to testify his acceptance of the amiableness of his obedience in Christ.

Believers having a title to heaven by faith antecedent to their obedience, or its being absolutely promised to them before, does not hinder but that the actual bestowment of heaven may also be a testimony of God's regard to their obedience, though performed afterwards. Thus it was with Abraham, the father and pattern of all believers: God bestowed upon him that blessing of multiplying his seed as the stars of heaven, and causing that in his seed all the families of the earth should be blessed, in reward for his obedience in offering up his son Isaac, Gen. xxii. 16, 17, 18. "And said, By myself have I sworn, saith the Lord, for because thou hast done this thing, and hast not withheld thy son, thine only son; that in blessing I will bless thee, and in multiplying I will multiply thy seed as the stars of heaven, and as the sand which is upon the sea shore; and thy seed shall possess the gate of his enemies; and in thy seed shall all the nations of the earth be blessed; because thou hast obeyed my voice." And yet the very same blessings had been from time to time promised to Abraham, in the most positive terms, and the promise, with great solemnity, confirmed and sealed to him; as chap. xii. 2, 3. chap. xiii. 16. chap. xv. 1, 4—7, &c. chap. xvii. throughout; chap. xviii. 10, 18.

From what has been said we may easily solve the difficulty arising from that text in Rev. iii. 4. "They shall walk with me in white, for they are worthy;" which is parallel with that text in Luke xx. 35. "But they which shall be accounted worthy to obtain that world, and the resurrection from the dead." I allow (as in the objection) that this worthiness does doubtless denote a moral fitness to the reward, or that God looks on these glorious benefits as a meet testimony of his regard to the value which their persons and performances have in his sight.

1. God looks on these glorious benefits as a meet testimony of his regard to the value which their persons have in his sight. But he sets this value upon their persons purely for Christ's sake. They are such jewels, and have such preciousness in his eyes, only because they are beheld in Christ, and by reason of the worthiness of the head they are the members of, and the stock they are grafted into. And the value that God sets upon them on this account is so great, that God thinks meet, from regard to it, to admit them to such exceeding glory. The saints, on account of their relation to Christ, are such precious jewels in God's sight, that they are thought worthy of a place in his own crown. Mal. iii. 17. Zech. ix. 16. So far as the saints are said to be valuable in God's sight, on whatever account, so far may they properly be said to be worthy, or meet for that honour which is answerable to the value or price which God sets upon them. A child or wife of a prince is worthy to be treated with great honour; and therefore if a mean person should be adopted to be a child of a prince, or should be espoused to a prince, it would be proper to say, that she was worthy of such and such honour and respect, and there would be no force upon the words in saying, that she ought to have such respect paid her, for she is worthy, though it be only on account of her relation to the prince that she is so.

2. From the value God sets upon their persons, for the sake of Christ's worthiness, he also sets a high value on their virtue and performances. Their meek and quiet spirit is of great price in his sight. Their fruits are pleasant fruits, their offerings are an odour of sweet smell to him; and that because of the value he sets on their persons, as has been already observed and explained. This preciousness or high valuableness of believers is a moral fitness to a reward; and yet this valuableness is all in the righteousness of Christ, that is the foundation of it. The thing respected is not excellency in them separately by themselves, or in their virtue by itself, but the value in God's account arises from other considerations; which is the natural import of Luke xx. 35. "They which shall be accounted worthy to obtain that world," &c. and Luke xxi. 36. "That ye may be accounted worthy to escape all these things that shall come to pass, and to stand before the Son of man." 2 Thess. i. 5. "That ye may be counted worthy of the kingdom of God, for which ye also suffer."

There is a vast difference between this scheme, and what is supposed in the scheme of those that oppose the doctrine of justification by faith alone. This lays the foundation of first acceptance with God, and all actual salvation consequent upon it, wholly in Christ and his righteousness. On the contrary, in their scheme, a regard to man's own excellency or virtue is supposed to be first, and to have the place of the first foundation in actual salvation, though not in that ineffectual redemption, which they suppose common to all. They lay the foundation of all discriminating salvation in man's own virtue and moral excellency. This is the very bottom stone in this affair; for they suppose that it is from regard to our virtue, that even a special interest in Christ itself is given. The foundation being thus contrary, the whole scheme becomes exceeding diverse and contrary; the one is an evangelical scheme, the other a legal one; the one is utterly inconsistent with our being justified by Christ's righteousness, the other not at all.

From what has been said, we may understand, not only how the forgiveness of sin granted in justification is indissolubly connected with a forgiving spirit in us, but how there may be many exercises of forgiving mercy granted in reward for our forgiving those who trespass against us. For none will deny but that there are many acts of divine forgiveness towards the saints, that do not presuppose an unjustified state immediately preceding that forgiveness. None will deny, that saints who never fell from a justified state, yet commit many sins which God forgives afterwards, by laying aside his fatherly displeasure. This forgiveness may be in reward for our forgiveness, without any prejudice to the doctrine that has been maintained, as well as other mercies and blessings consequent on justification.

With respect to the *second* part of the objection, that relates to the different degrees of glory, and the seeming inconsistence there is in it, that the degrees of glory in different saints should be greater or lesser according to their inherent holiness and good works, and yet, that every one's glory should be purchased with the price of the very same imputed righteousness,—I answer, That Christ, by his righteousness, purchased for every one complete and perfect happiness, according to his capacity. But this does not hinder but that the saints, being of various capacities, may have various degrees of happiness, and yet all their happiness be the fruit of Christ's purchase. Indeed it cannot be properly said, that Christ purchased any particular degree of happiness, so that the value of Christ's righteousness in the sight of God, is sufficient to raise a believer so high in happiness, and no higher, and so that if the believer were made happier, it would exceed the value of Christ's righteousness; but in general, Christ purchased eternal life, or perfect happiness for all, according to their several capacities. The saints are as so many vessels of different sizes, cast into a sea of happiness, where every vessel is full; this Christ purchased for all. But after all, it is left to God's sovereign pleasure to determine the largeness of the vessel; Christ's righteousness meddles not with this matter. Eph. iv. 4, 5, 6, 7. "There is one body, and one Spirit, even as ye are called in one hope of your calling; one Lord, one faith, one baptism," &c.—"But unto every one of us is given grace according to the measure of the gift of Christ." God may dispense in this matter according to what rule he pleases, not the less for what Christ has done: he may dispense either without condition, or upon what condition he pleases to fix. It is evident that Christ's righteousness meddles not with this matter; for what Christ did was to fulfil the covenant of works; but the covenant of works did not meddle at all with this. If Adam had persevered in perfect obedience, he and his posterity would have had perfect and full happiness; every one's happiness would have so answered his capacity, that he would have been completely blessed; but God would have been at liberty to have made some of one capacity, and others of another, as he pleased.—The angels have obtained eternal life, or a state of confirmed glory, by a covenant of works, whose condition was perfect obedience; but yet some are higher in glory than others, according to the several capacities that God, according to his sovereign pleasure, hath given them. So that it being still left with God, notwithstanding the perfect obedience of the second Adam, to fix the degree of each one's capacity by what rule he pleases, he hath been pleased to fix the degree of capacity, and so of glory, by the proportion of the saints' grace and fruitfulness here. He gives higher degrees of glory, in reward for higher degrees of holiness and good works, because it pleases him; and yet all the happiness of each saint is indeed the fruit of the purchase of Christ's obedience. If it had been but one man that Christ had obeyed and died for, and it had pleased God to make him of a very large capacity, Christ's perfect obedience would have purchased that his capacity should be filled, and then all his happiness might properly be said to be the fruit of Christ's perfect obedience; though, if he had been of a less capacity, he would not have had so much happiness by the same obedience; and yet would have had as much as Christ merited for him. Christ's righteousness meddles not with the degree of happiness, any otherwise than as he merits that it should be full and perfect, according to the capacity: and so it may be said to be concerned in the degree of happiness, as perfect is a degree with respect to imperfect; but it meddles not with degrees of perfect happiness.

This matter may be yet better understood, if we consider that Christ and the whole church of saints are, as it were, one body, of which he is the Head, and they members, of different place and capacity: now the whole body, head, and members, have communion in Christ's righteousness; they are all partakers of the benefit of it; Christ himself the Head is rewarded for it, and every member is partaker of the benefit and reward. But it does by no means follow, that every part should equally partake of the benefit, but every part in proportion to its place and capacity; the Head partakes of far more than other parts, and the more noble members partake of more than the inferior. As it is in a natural body that enjoys perfect health, the head, and the heart, and lungs, have a greater share of this health, they have it more seated in them, than the hands and feet, because they are parts of greater capacity; though the hands and feet are as much in perfect health as those nobler parts of the body. So it is in the mystical body of Christ, all the members are partakers of the benefit of the Head; but it is according to the different capacity and place they have in the body; and God determines that place and capacity as he pleases; he makes whom he pleases the foot, and whom he pleases the hand, and whom he pleases the lungs, &c. 1 Cor. xii. 18. "God hath set the members every one of them in the body, as it hath pleased him." God efficaciously determines the place and capacity of every member, by the different degrees of grace and assistance in the improvement of it in this world. Those that he intends for the highest place in the body, he gives them most of his Spirit, the greatest share of the divine nature, the Spirit and nature of Christ Jesus the Head, and that assistance whereby they perform the most excellent works, and do most abound in them.

Object. 4. It may be objected against what has been supposed, (*viz.* That rewards are given to our good works, only in consequence of an interest in Christ, or in testimony of God's respect to the excellency or value of them in his sight, as built on an interest in Christ's righteousness already obtained,) That the Scripture speaks of an interest in Christ itself, as being given out of respect to our moral fitness. Matt. x. 37, 38, 39. "He that loveth father or mother more than me, is not worthy of me: he that loveth son or daughter more than me, is not worthy of me: he that taketh not up his cross, and followeth after me, is not worthy of me: he that findeth his life, shall lose it," &c. Worthiness here at least signifies a moral fitness, or an excellency that recommends. And this place seems to intimate as though it were from respect to a moral fitness that men are admitted even to an union with Christ, and interest in him; and therefore this worthiness cannot be consequent on being in Christ, and by the imputation of his worthiness, or from any value that is in us, or in our actions in God's sight, as beheld in Christ.

To this I *answer*, That though persons when they are *accepted*, are not accepted as *worthy*, yet when they are *rejected*, they are rejected as *unworthy*. He that does not love Christ above other things, but treats him with such indignity, as to set him below earthly things, shall be treated as unworthy of Christ; his unworthiness of Christ, especially in that particular, shall be marked against him, and imputed to him. And though he be a professing Christian, and live in the enjoyment of the gospel, and has been visibly ingrafted into Christ, and admitted as one of his disciples, as Judas was; yet he shall be thrust out in wrath, as a punishment of his vile treatment of Christ. The forementioned words do not imply, that if a man does love Christ above father and mother, &c. that he would be *worthy*; the most they imply is, that such a visible Christian shall be treated and thrust out as unworthy. He that believes is not received for the worthiness or moral fitness of faith; but yet the visible Christian is cast out by God, for the unworthiness and moral unfitness of unbelief. A being accepted as one of Christ's, is not the reward of believing; but being thrust out from being one of Christ's disciples, after a visible admission as such, is properly a punishment of unbelief. John iii. 18, 19. "He that believeth on him, is not condemned; but he that believeth not, is condemned already, because he hath not believed in the name of the only begotten Son of God. And this is the condemnation, that light is come into the world, and men loved darkness rather than light, because their deeds were evil." Salvation is promised to faith as a free gift, but damnation is threatened to unbelief as a debt, or punishment due to unbelief. They who believed while in the wilderness, did not enter into Canaan, because of the worthiness of their faith; but God sware in his wrath, that they that believed not should not enter in, because of the unworthiness of their unbelief. Admitting a soul to an union with Christ is an act of free and sovereign grace; but excluding at death, and at the day of judgment, those professors of Christianity who have had the offers of a Saviour, and enjoyed great privileges as God's people, is a judicial proceeding, and a just punishment of their unworthy treatment of Christ. The design of this saying of Christ is to make them sensible of the unworthiness of their treatment of Christ, who professed him to be their Lord and Saviour, and set him below father and mother, &c. and not to show the worthiness of loving him above father and mother. If a beggar should be offered any great and precious gift, but as soon as offered, should trample it under his feet, it might be taken from him, as unworthy to have it. Or if a malefactor should have his pardon offered him, that he might be freed from execution, and should only scoff at it, his pardon might be refused him, as unworthy of it; though if he had received it, he would not have had it for his worthiness, or as being recommended to it by his virtue; for his being a malefactor supposes him unworthy, and its being offered him to have it only on accepting, supposes that the king looks for no worthiness, nothing in him for which he should bestow pardon as a reward. This may teach us how to understand Acts xiii. 46. "It was necessary that the word of God should first have been spoken unto you; but seeing ye put it from you, and judge yourselves unworthy of everlasting life, lo, we turn to the Gentiles."

Object. 5. It is objected against the doctrine of justification by faith alone, That repentance is evidently spoken of in Scripture as that which is in a special manner the condition of remission of sins; but remission of sins is by all allowed to be that wherein justification does (at least) in great part consist.

But it must certainly arise from a misunderstanding of what the Scripture says about repentance, to suppose that faith and repentance are two distinct things, that in like manner are the conditions of justification. For it is most plain from the Scripture, that the condition of justification, or that in us by which we are justified, is but one, and that is faith. Faith and repentance are not two distinct conditions of justification, nor are they two distinct things that together make one condition of justification; but faith comprehends the whole of that by which we are justified, or by which we come to have an interest in Christ, and there is nothing else has a parallel concern with it in the affair of our salvation. And this the divines on the other side themselves are sensible of, and therefore they suppose that the faith the apostle Paul speaks of, which he says we are justified by alone, comprehends in it repentance.

And therefore, in answer to the objection, I would say, That when repentance is spoken of in Scripture as the condition of pardon, thereby is not intended any particular grace, or act, properly distinct from faith, that has a parallel influence with it in the affair of our pardon or justification; but by repentance is intended nothing distinct from active conversion, (or conversion actively considered,) as it respects the term from which. Active conversion is a motion or exercise of the mind that respects two terms, *viz.* sin and God; and by repentance is meant this conversion, or active change of the mind, so far as it is conversant about the term from which, or about sin. This is what the word *repentance* properly signifies; which, in the original of the New Testament, is μετανοια, and signifies *a change of the mind,* or, which is the same thing, the turning or the conversion of the mind. Repentance is this turning, as it respects what is turned from. Acts xxvi. 20. "Whereupon, O king Agrippa, I showed unto them of Damascus, and at Jerusalem, and throughout all the coasts of Judea, and then to the Gentiles, that they should repent, and turn to God." Both these are the same turning, but only with respect to opposite terms: in the former, is expressed the exercise of mind about sin in this turning; in the other, the exercise of mind towards God.

If we look over the scriptures that speak of evangelical repentance, we shall presently see that repentance is to be understood in this sense; as Matt. ix. 13. "I am not come to call the righteous, but sinners to repentance." Luke xiii. 3. "Except ye repent, ye shall all likewise perish." And chap. xv. 7, 10. "There is joy in heaven over one sinner that repenteth," *i. e.* over one sinner that is converted. Acts xi. 18. "Then hath God also to the Gentiles granted repentance unto life." This is said by the Christians of the circumcision at Jerusalem, upon Peter's giving an account of the conversion of Cornelius and his family, and their embracing the gospel, though Peter had said nothing expressly about their sorrow for sin. And again, Acts xvii. 30. "But now commandeth all men every where to repent." And Luke xvi. 30. "Nay, father Abraham, but if one went to them from the dead, they would repent." 2 Pet. iii. 9. "The Lord is not slack concerning his promise, as some men count slackness, but is long-suffering to us-ward, not willing that any should perish, but that all should come to repentance." It is plain that in these and other places, by repentance is meant conversion.

Now it is true, that conversion is the condition of pardon and justification: but if it be so, how absurd is it to say, that conversion is one condition of justification, and faith another, as though they were two distributively distinct and parallel conditions! Conversion is the condition of justification, because it is that great change by which we are brought from sin to Christ, and by which we become believers in him: agreeable to Matt. xxi. 32. "And ye, when ye had seen it, repented not afterward, that ye might believe him." When we are directed to repent, that our sins may be blotted out, it is as much as to say, Let your minds and hearts be changed, that your sins may be blotted out. But if it be said, Let your hearts be changed, that you may be justified; and believe, that you may be justified; does it therefore follow, that the heart being changed is one condition of justification, and believing another? But our minds must be changed, that we may believe, and so may be justified.

And besides, evangelical repentance, being active conversion, is not to be treated of as a particular grace, properly and entirely distinct from faith, as by some it seems to have been. What is conversion, but the sinful, alienated soul's closing with Christ, or the sinner's being brought to believe in Christ? That exercise of soul in conversion that respects sin, cannot be excluded out of the nature of faith in Christ: there is something in faith, or closing with Christ, that respects sin, and that is evangelical repentance. That repentance which in Scripture is called, repentance for the remission of sins, is that very principle or operation of the mind itself that is called faith, so far as it is conversant about sin. Justifying faith in a Mediator is conversant about two things: it is conversant about sin or evil to be rejected and to be delivered from, and about positive good to be accepted and obtained by the Mediator; as conversant about the former of these, it is evangelical repentance, or repentance for remission of sins. Surely they must be very ignorant, or at least very inconsiderate, of the whole tenor of the gospel, who think that the repentance by which remission of sins is obtained, can be completed, as to all that is essential to it, without any respect to Christ, or application of the mind to the Mediator, who alone has made atonement for sin. Surely so great a part of salvation as remission of sins, is not to be obtained without looking or coming to the great and only

Saviour. It is true, repentance, in its more general abstracted nature, is only a sorrow for sin, and forsaking of it, which is a duty of natural religion; but evangelical repentance, or repentance for remission of sins, hath more than this essential to it; a dependence of soul on the Mediator for deliverance from sin, is of the essence of it.

That justifying repentance has the nature of faith, seems evident by Acts xix. 4. "Then said Paul, John verily baptized with the baptism of repentance, saying unto the people, that they should believe on him which should come after him, that is, on Christ Jesus." The latter words, "saying unto the people, that they should believe on him," &c. are evidently exegetical of the former, and explain how he preached repentance for the remission of sins. When it is said, that he preached repentance for the remission of sin, saying, that they should believe on Christ, it cannot be supposed but that his saying, that they should believe on Christ, was intended as directing them what to do that they might obtain the remission of sins. So, 2 Tim. ii. 25. "In meekness instructing those that oppose themselves; if God peradventure will give them repentance to the acknowledging of the truth." That acknowledging of the truth which there is in believing, is here spoken of as what is retained in repentance. And on the other hand, that faith includes repentance in its nature, is evident by the apostle's speaking of sin as destroyed in faith, Gal. ii. 18.—In the preceding verses the apostle mentions an objection against the doctrine of justification by faith alone, *viz.* that it tends to encourage men in sin, and so to make Christ the minister of sin. This objection he rejects and refutes with this, "If I build again the things that I destroyed, I make myself a transgressor." If sin be destroyed by faith, it must be by repentance of sin included in it; for we know that it is our repentance of sin, or the μετανοια, or turning of the mind from sin, that is our destroying our sin.

That in justifying faith which directly respects sin, or the evil to be delivered from by the Mediator, is as follows: a sense of our own sinfulness, and the hatefulness of it, and a hearty acknowledgment of its desert of the threatened punishment, looking to the free mercy of God in a Redeemer, for deliverance from it and its punishment.

Concerning this, here described, three things may be noted: 1. That it is the very same with that evangelical repentance to which remission of sins is promised in Scripture. 2. That it is of the essence of justifying faith, and is the same with that faith, so far as it is conversant about evil to be delivered from by the Mediator. 3. That this is indeed the proper and peculiar condition of remission of sins.

1. All of it is essential to evangelical repentance, and is indeed the very thing meant by that repentance, to which remission of sins is promised in the gospel. As to the former part of the description, *viz.* a sense of our own sinfulness, and the hatefulness of it, and a hearty acknowledgment of its desert of wrath, none will deny it to be included in repentance: but this does not comprehend the whole essence of evangelical repentance; but what follows does also properly and essentially belong to its nature, looking to the free mercy of God in a Redeemer, for deliverance from it, and the punishment of it. That repentance to which remission is promised, not only always has this with it, but it is contained in it, as what is of the proper nature and essence of it: and respect is ever had to this in the nature of repentance, whenever remission is promised to it; and it is especially from respect to this in the nature of repentance, that it has that promise made to it. If this latter part be missing, it fails of the nature of that evangelical repentance to which remission of sins is promised. If repentance remains in sorrow for sin, and does not reach to a looking to the free mercy of God in Christ for pardon, it is not that which is the condition of pardon, neither shall pardon be obtained by it. Evangelical repentance is an humiliation for sin before God; but the sinner never comes and humbles himself before God in any other repentance, but that which includes hoping in his mercy for remission: if sorrow be not accompanied with that, there will be no coming to God in it, but a flying further from him. There is some worship of God in justifying repentance; but that is not in any other repentance which has not a sense of and faith in the divine mercy to forgive sin; Psalm cxxx. 4. "There is forgiveness with thee, that thou mayest be feared." The promise of mercy to a true penitent, in Prov. xxviii. 13. is expressed in these terms, "Whoso confesseth and forsaketh his sins, shall have mercy." But there is faith in God's mercy in that confessing. The psalmist, (Psalm xxxii.) speaking of the blessedness of the man whose transgression is forgiven—and whose sin is covered, to whom the Lord imputes not sin—says, that while he kept silence his bones waxed old: but he acknowledged his sin unto God, his iniquity he did not hide; he said, he would confess his transgression to the Lord, and then God forgave the iniquity of his sin. The manner of expression plainly holds forth, that *then* he began to encourage himself in the mercy of God, but his bones waxed old while he kept silence; and therefore the apostle Paul, in the 4th of Romans, brings this instance, to confirm the doctrine of justification by faith alone, that he had been insisting on. When sin is aright confessed to God, there is always faith in that act. That confessing of sin which is joined with despair, as in Judas, is not the confession to which the promise is made. In Acts ii. 38. the direction given to those who were pricked in their heart with a sense of the guilt of sin, was to repent, and be baptized in the name of Jesus Christ for the remission of their sins. Being baptized in the name of Christ for the remission of sins, implied faith in Christ for the remission of sins. Repentance for the remission of sins was typified of old by the priest's confessing the sins of the people over the scape-goat, laying his hands on him, Lev. xvi. 21. denoting it is that repentance and confession of sin only that obtains remission, which is made over Christ the great sacrifice, and with dependence on him. Many other things might be produced from the Scripture, that in like manner confirm this point; but these may be sufficient.

2. All the forementioned description is of the essence of justifying faith, and not different from it, so far as it is conversant about sin, or the evil to be delivered from by the Mediator. For it is doubtless of the essence of justifying faith, to embrace Christ as a Saviour from sin and its punishment; and all that is contained in that act is contained in the nature of faith itself. But in the act of embracing Christ as a Saviour from our sin and its punishment, is implied a sense of our sinfulness, and a hatred of our sins, or a rejecting them with abhorrence, and a sense of our desert of punishment. Embracing Christ as a Saviour from sin, implies the contrary act, *viz.* rejecting sin. If we fly to the light to be delivered from darkness, the same act is contrary to darkness, *viz.* a rejecting of it. In proportion to the earnestness with which we embrace Christ as a Saviour from sin, in the same proportion is the abhorrence with which we reject sin, in the same act. Yea, suppose there be in the nature of faith, as conversant about sin, no more than the hearty embracing of Christ as a Saviour from the punishment of sin, this act will imply in it the whole of the above-mentioned description. It implies a sense of our own sinfulness. Certainly in the hearty embracing of a Saviour from the punishment of our sinfulness, there is the exercise of a sense that we are sinful. We cannot heartily embrace Christ as a Saviour from the punishment of that which we are not sensible we are guilty of. There is also in the same act, a sense of our desert of the threatened punishment. We cannot heartily embrace Christ as a Saviour from that which we are not sensible that we have deserved. For if we are not sensible that we have deserved the punishment, we shall not be sensible that we have any need of a Saviour from it, or, at least, shall not be convinced but that God who offers the Saviour, unjustly makes him needful; and we cannot heartily embrace such an offer. And further, there is implied in a hearty embracing Christ as a Saviour from punishment, not only a conviction of conscience, that we have deserved the punishment, such as the devils and damned have; but there is a hearty acknowledgment of it, with the submission of the soul, so as, with the accord of the heart, to own that God might be just in the punishment. If the heart rises against the act or judgment of God, in holding us obliged to the punishment, when he offers us his Son as a Saviour from the punishment, we cannot with the consent of the heart receive him in that

character: but if persons thus submit to the righteousness of so dreadful a punishment of sin, this carries in it a hatred of sin.

That such a sense of our sinfulness, and utter unworthiness, and desert of punishment, belongs to the nature of saving faith, is what the Scripture from time to time holds forth; as particularly in Matt. xv. 26—28. " But he answered and said, It is not meet to take the children's bread, and to cast it to dogs. And she said, Truth, Lord: yet the dogs eat of the crumbs which fall from their master's table. Then Jesus answered, and said unto her, O woman, great is thy faith."—And Luke vii. 6—9. " The centurion sent friends to him, saying unto him, Lord, trouble not thyself, for I am not worthy that thou shouldst enter under my roof. Wherefore neither thought I myself worthy to come unto thee; but say in a word, and my servant shall be healed: for I also am a man set under authority," &c.—" When Jesus heard these things, he marvelled at him, and turned him about, and said unto the people that followed him, I say unto you, I have not found so great faith, no, not in Israel." And also ver. 37, 38. " And behold, a woman in the city, which was a sinner, when she knew that Jesus sat at meat in the Pharisee's house, brought an alabaster-box of ointment, and stood at his feet behind him weeping, and began to wash his feet with tears, and did wipe them with the hairs of her head, and kissed his feet, and anointed them with the ointment." Together with ver. 50. " He said unto the woman, Thy faith hath saved thee; go in peace."

These things do not necessarily suppose that repentance and faith are words of just the same signification; for it is only so much in justifying faith as respects the evil to be delivered from by the Saviour, that is called repentance. Besides, both repentance and faith, take them only in their general nature, are entirely distinct; repentance is a sorrow for sin, and forsaking of it; and faith is a trusting in God's sufficiency and truth. But faith and repentance, as *evangelical* duties, or justifying faith, and repentance for remission of sins, contain more in them, and imply a respect to a mediator, and involve each other's nature;* though they still bear the name of faith and repentance, from those general moral virtues—that repentance, which is a duty of natural religion, and that faith, which was a duty required under the first covenant—that are contained in this evangelical act; which severally appear, when this act is considered with respect to its different terms and objects.

It may be objected here, that the Scripture sometimes mentions faith and repentance together, as if they were entirely distinct things; as in Mark i. 15. " Repent ye, and believe the gospel." But there is no need of understanding these as two distinct conditions of salvation, but the words are exegetical one of another. It is to teach us after what manner we must repent, *viz.* as believing the gospel, and after what manner we must believe the gospel, *viz.* as repenting. These words no more prove faith and repentance to be entirely distinct, than those fore-mentioned, Matt. xxi. 32. " And ye, when ye had seen it, repented not afterwards, that ye might believe him." Or those, 2 Tim. ii. 25. " If peradventure God will give them repentance to the acknowledging of the truth." The apostle, in Acts xix. 4. seems to have reference to these words of John the Baptist, " John baptized with the baptism of repentance, saying unto the people, that they should believe," &c. where the latter words, as we have already observed, are to explain how he preached repentance.

Another Scripture where faith and repentance are mentioned together, is Acts xx. 21. " Testifying both to the Jews, and also to the Greeks, repentance towards God, and faith towards the Lord Jesus Christ." It may be objected, that in this place, faith and repentance are not only spoken of as distinct things, but having distinct objects.

To this I answer, That faith and repentance, in their general nature, are distinct things: and repentance for the remission of sins, or that in justifying faith that respects the evil to be delivered from, so far as it regards that term, which is what especially denominates it repentance, has respect to God as the object, because he is the Being offended by sin, and to be reconciled, but that in this justifying act, whence it is denominated faith, does more especially respect Christ. But let us interpret it how we will, the objection of faith being here so distinguished from repentance, is as much of an objection against the scheme of those that oppose justification by faith alone, as against this scheme; for they hold that the justifying faith the apostle Paul speaks of, includes repentance, as has been already observed.

3. This repentance that has been described, is indeed the special condition of remission of sins. This seems very evident by the Scripture, as particularly, Mark i. 4. " John did baptize in the wilderness, and preach the baptism of repentance, for the remission of sins." So, Luke iii. 3. " And he came into all the country about Jordan, preaching the baptism of repentance, for the remission of sins." Luke xxiv. 47. " And that repentance and remission of sins should be preached in his name among all nations." Acts v. 31. " Him hath God exalted with his right hand to be a Prince and a Saviour, for to give repentance unto Israel, and forgiveness of sins." Chap. ii. 38. Repent, and be baptized every one of you in the name of Jesus Christ, for the remission of sins." And, chap. iii. 19. " Repent ye therefore, and be converted, that your sins may be blotted out." The like is evident by Lev. xxvi. 40—42. Job xxxiii. 27, 28. Psal. xxxii. 5. Prov. xxviii. 13. Jer. iii. 13. And 1 John i. 9. and other places.

And the reason may be plain from what has been said. We need not wonder that what in faith especially respects sin, should be especially the condition of remission of sins; or that this motion or exercise of the soul, as it rejects and flies from evil, and embraces Christ as a Saviour from it, should especially be the condition of being free from that evil; in like manner, as the same principle or motion, as it seeks good, and cleaves to Christ as the procurer of that good, should be the condition of obtaining that good. Faith with respect to good is accepting, and with respect to evil it is rejecting. Yea this rejecting evil is itself an act of acceptance; it is accepting freedom or separation from that evil; and this freedom or separation is the benefit bestowed in remission. No wonder that what in faith immediately respects this benefit, and is our acceptance of it, should be the special condition of our having it. It is so with respect to all the benefits that Christ has purchased. Trusting in God through Christ for such a particular benefit that we need, is the special condition of obtaining that benefit. When we need protection from enemies, the exercise of faith with respect to such a benefit, or trusting in Christ for protection from enemies, is especially the way to obtain that particular benefit, rather than trusting in Christ for something else; and so of any other benefit that might be mentioned. So prayer (which is the expression of faith) for a particular mercy needed, is especially the way to obtain that mercy.†—So that no argument can be drawn from hence against the doctrine of justification by faith alone. And there is that in the nature of repentance, which peculiarly tends to establish the contrary of justification by works: for nothing so much renounces our own worthiness and excellency, as repentance; the very nature of it is to acknowledge our own utter sinfulness and unworthiness, and to renounce our own goodness, and all confidence in self; and so to trust in the propitiation of the Mediator, and ascribe all the glory of forgiveness to him.

Object. 6. The last objection I shall mention, is that paragraph in the 3d chapter of James, where persons are said expressly to be justified by works: Ver. 21. " Was not Abraham our father justified by works?" Ver. 24. " Ye see then how that by works a man is justified, and not by faith only." Ver. 25. " Was not Rahab the harlot justified by works?"

In answer to this objection, I would,

1. Take notice of the great unfairness of the divines that

* Agreeable to this is what Mr. Locke says in his second *Vindication of the Reasonableness of Christianity*, &c. vol. ii. of his works, p. 630, 631. " The believing him therefore to be the Messiah is very often, with great reason, put both for faith and repentance too, which are sometimes set down singly, where one is put for both, as implying the other."

† If repentance justifies, or be that by which we obtain pardon of sin any other way than this, it must be either as a virtue or righteousness, or something amiable in us; or else it must be, that our sorrow and condemning what is past, is accepted as some atonement for it; both which are equally contrary to the gospel-doctrine of justification by Christ.

oppose us, in the improvement they make of this passage against us. All will allow, that in that proposition of St. James, "By works a man is justified, and not by faith only," one of the terms, either the word *faith*, or else the word *justify*, is not to be understood precisely in the same sense as the same terms when used by St. Paul; because they suppose, as well as we, that it was not the intent of the apostle James to contradict St. Paul in that doctrine of justification by faith alone, in which he had instructed the churches. But if we understand both the terms, as used by each apostle, in precisely the same sense, then what one asserts is a precise, direct, and full contradiction of the other, the one affirming and the other denying the very same thing. So that all the controversy from this text comes to this, *viz.* which of these two terms shall be understood in a diversity from St. Paul. They say that it is the word *faith;* for they suppose, that when the apostle Paul uses the word, and makes faith that by which alone we are justified, that then by it is understood a compliance with and practice of Christianity in general; so as to include all saving christian virtue and obedience. But as the apostle James uses the word faith in this place, they suppose thereby is to be understood only an assent of the understanding to the truth of gospel doctrines, as distinguished from good works, and that may exist separate from them, and from all saving grace. We, on the other hand, suppose that the word *justify* is to be understood in a different sense from the apostle Paul. So that they are forced to go as far in their scheme, in altering the sense of terms from Paul's use of them, as we. But yet at the same time that they freely vary the sense of the former of them, *viz.* faith, yet when we understand the latter, *viz.* justify, in a different sense from St. Paul, they exclaim against us. What necessity of framing this distinction, but only to serve an opinion? At this rate a man may maintain any thing, though never so contrary to Scripture, and elude the clearest text in the Bible! though they do not show us why we have not as good warrant to understand the word *justify* in a diversity from St. Paul, as they the word *faith.* If the sense of one of the words must be varied on either scheme, to make the apostle James's doctrine consistent with the apostle Paul's; and if varying the sense of one term or the other be all that stands in the way of their agreeing with either scheme; and if varying the sense of the latter be in itself as fair as of the former, then the text lies as fair for one scheme as the other, and can no more fairly be an objection against our scheme than theirs. And if so, what becomes of all this great objection from this passage in James?

2. If there be no more difficulty in varying the sense of one of these terms than another, from any thing in the text itself, so as to make the words suit with either scheme, then certainly that is to be chosen that is most agreeable to the current of Scripture, and other places where the same matter is more particularly and fully treated of; and therefore that we should understand the word *justify* in this passage of James, in a sense in some respects diverse from that in which St. Paul uses it. For by what has been already said, it may appear, that there is no one doctrine in the whole Bible more fully asserted, explained, and urged, than the doctrine of justification by faith alone, without any of our own righteousness.

3. There is a very fair interpretation of this passage of St. James, no way inconsistent with this doctrine of justification, which I have shown that other scriptures abundantly teach, which the words themselves will as well allow of, as that which the objectors put upon them, and much better agrees with the context; and that is, that works are here spoken of as justifying as evidences. A man may be said to be justified by that which clears him, or vindicates him, or makes the goodness of his cause manifest. When a person has a cause tried in a civil court, and is justified or cleared, he may be said in different senses to be justified or cleared, by the goodness of his cause, and by the goodness of the evidences of it. He may be said to be cleared by what evidences his cause to be good; but not in the same sense as he is by that which makes his cause to be good. That which renders his cause good, is the proper ground of his justification; it is by that that he is himself a proper subject of it; but evidences justify, only as they manifest that his cause is good in fact, whether they are of such a nature as to have any influence to render it so or no. It is by works that our cause appears to be good; but by faith our cause not only appears to be good, but becomes good; because thereby we are united to Christ. That the word *justify* should be sometimes understood to signify the former of these, as well as the latter, is agreeable to the use of the word in common speech; as we say such an one stood up to justify another, *i. e.* he endeavoured to show or manifest his cause to be good.—And it is certain that the word is sometimes used in this sense in Scripture, when speaking of our being justified before God; as where it is said, we shall be justified by our words, Matt. xii. 37. "For by thy words thou shalt be justified, and by thy words thou shalt be condemned." It cannot be meant that men are accepted before God on the account of their words; for God has told us nothing more plainly, than that it is the heart that he looks at; and that when he acts as judge towards men, in order to justifying or condemning, he tries the heart, Jer. xi. 20. "But, O Lord of hosts, that judgest righteously, that triest the reins and the heart, let me see thy vengeance on them; for unto thee have I revealed my cause." Psalm vii. 8, 9. "The Lord shall judge the people: judge me, O Lord, according to my righteousness, and according to mine integrity that is in me. O let the wickedness of the wicked come to an end; but establish the just; for the righteous God trieth the hearts and reins." Ver. 11. "God judgeth the righteous." And many other places to the like purpose. And therefore men can be justified by their words, no otherwise than as evidences or manifestations of what is in the heart. And it is thus that Christ speaks of the words in this very place, as is evident by the context, ver. 34, 35. "Out of the abundance of the heart the mouth speaketh. A good man out of the good treasure of the heart," &c. The words, or sounds themselves, are neither parts of godliness nor evidences of godliness, but as signs of what is inward.

God himself, when he acts towards men as judge, in order to a declarative judgment, makes use of evidences, and so judges men by their works. And therefore, at the day of judgment, God will judge men according to their works: for though God will stand in no need of evidence to inform him what is right, yet it is to be considered, that he will then sit in judgment, not as earthly judges do, to find out what is right in a cause, but to declare and manifest what is right: and therefore that day is called by the apostle, "the day of the revelation of the righteous judgment of God," Rom. ii. 5.

To be justified, is to be approved of and accepted: but a man may be said to be approved and accepted in two respects; the one is to be approved really, and the other to be approved and accepted declaratively. Justification is twofold; it is either the acceptance and approbation of the judge itself, or the manifestation of that approbation, by a sentence or judgment declared by the judge, either to our own consciences, or to the world. If justification be understood in the former sense, for the approbation itself, that is only that by which we become fit to be approved: but if it be understood in the latter sense, for the manifestation of this approbation, it is by whatever is a proper evidence of that fitness. In the former, only faith is concerned; because it is by that only in us that we become fit to be accepted and approved: in the latter, whatever is an evidence of our fitness, is alike concerned. And therefore, take justification in this sense, and then faith, and all other graces and good works, have a common and equal concern in it: for any other grace, or holy act, is equally an evidence of a qualification for acceptance or approbation, as faith.

To justify has always, in common speech, signified indifferently, either simply approbation, or testifying that approbation; sometimes one, and sometimes the other; because they are both the same, only as one is outwardly what the other is inwardly. So we, and it may be all nations, are wont to give the same name to two things, when one is only declarative of the other. Thus sometimes judging, intends only judging in our thoughts; at other times, testifying and declaring judgment. So such words as justify, condemn, accept, reject, prize, slight, approve, renounce, are sometimes put for mental acts, at other times, for an outward treatment. So in the sense in which the apostle James seems to use the word *justify* for *manifestative justification*, a man is justified not only by *faith*, but also by *works;* as a tree is manifested to be good, not only by immediately examining the tree, but also by the fruit,* Prov. xx. 11. "Even a child is known by his doing, whether his work be pure, and whether it be right."

The drift of the apostle does not require that he should be understood in any other sense; for all that he aims at, as appears by a view of the context, is to prove that good works are necessary. The error of those that he opposed was this, That good works were not necessary to salvation; that if they did but believe that there was but one God, and that Christ was the Son of God, and the like, and were baptized, they were safe, let them live how they would; which doctrine greatly tended to licentiousness. The evincing the contrary of this is evidently the apostle's scope.

And that we should understand the apostle, of works justifying as an *evidence*, and in a declarative judgment, is what a due consideration of the context will naturally lead us to.—For it is plain, that the apostle is here insisting on works, in the quality of a necessary manifestation and evidence of faith, or as what the truth of faith is made to appear by: as ver. 18. "Show me thy faith without thy works, and I will show thee my faith by my works." And when he says, ver. 26. "As the body without the spirit is dead, so faith without works is dead also." It is much more rational and natural to understand him as speaking of works, as the proper signs and evidences of the reality, life, and goodness of faith. Not that the very works or actions done are properly the life of faith, as the spirit in the body; but it is the active, working nature of faith, of which the actions or works done are the signs, that is itself the life and spirit of faith. The sign of a thing is often in scripture language said to be that thing; as it is in that comparison by which the apostle illustrates it. Not the actions themselves of a body, are properly the life or spirit of the body; but the active nature, of which those actions or motions are the signs, is the life of the body. That which makes men pronounce any thing to be alive, is, that they observe it has an active operative nature; which they observe no otherwise than by the actions or motions which are the signs of it. It is plainly the apostle's aim to prove, that if faith hath not works, it is a sign that it is not a good sort of faith; which would not have been to his purpose, if it was his design to show that it is not by faith alone, though of a right sort, that we have acceptance with God, but that we are accepted on the account of obedience as well as faith. It is evident, by the apostle's reasoning, that the necessity of works, is not from their having a parallel concern in our salvation with faith; but he speaks of works only as related to faith, and expressive of it; which, after all, leaves faith the alone fundamental condition, without any thing else having a parallel concern with it in this affair; and other things conditions, only as several expressions and evidences of it.

That the apostle speaks of works justifying only as a sign, or evidence, and in God's declarative judgment, is further confirmed by verse 21. "Was not Abraham our father justified by works, when he had offered up Isaac his son upon the altar?" Here the apostle seems plainly to refer to that declarative judgment of God concerning Abraham's sincerity, manifested to him, for the peace and assurance of his own conscience, after his offering up Isaac his son on the altar, Gen. xxii. 12. "Now I know that thou fearest God, seeing thou hast not withheld thy son, thine only son, from me." But here it is plain, and expressed in the very words of justification or approbation, that this work of Abraham offering up his son on the altar, justified him as an *evidence*. When the apostle James says, we are justified by works, he may and ought to be understood in a sense agreeable to the instance he brings for the proof of it: but justification in that instance appears by the words of justification themselves, to be by

* This distinction is just and scriptural as far as it goes, but it does not reach the bottom of the difficulty, since *believing* in order to justification is itself a part of *obedience*, and is expressly called "the obedience of faith." Hence justification by faith, in comparison of what precedes it, is only *manifestative*. The *tree* must be good, that is, the *person* must be vitally united to Christ, as the adequate cause of believing, otherwise he would be still carnal. The faith of a man spiritually dead or carnal, must needs be a *dead faith;* but to suppose that *such* faith unites to Christ, has neither Scripture nor any plausible reason to support it.

To him that is *in Christ Jesus* by a vital union, there is no condemnation; and as there is no medium between condemnation and justification, he who is *in Christ* is justified, or "accepted in the beloved" Saviour. That union which Christ effects by his quickening Spirit, makes the *tree good*, and believing with the heart, in order to receive the promised righteousness, is the *fruit* of a good tree. Therefore the justification which is received as the *consequence* of believing is only *manifestative* of *union;* even as justification by works, as asserted by St. James, is *manifestative* of a living *faith*. As without *works* there is no sufficient evidence of union to Christ on *our part*, so without *faith* in Christ as our complete righteousness, there is no sufficient evidence of union with him on *his part*.

The true Christian's works, are "works of faith and labours of love," performed in obedience to God's authority, directed to his glory, and inspired by gratitude for the blessings of his grace, and this is the *first* of all such works, called "the work of God," even to *believe* on Jesus Christ in whom alone is righteousness and life. By believing we receive the divine testimony respecting a *gratuitous* righteousness, and renounce all hope of obtaining justification by any other way.

The justifying *righteousness* is only *one*, but the appointed ways of becoming *interested* in it are divers. One way is by the will of *God* our Saviour, the other by the will of *man* the accountable agent, each in its own order. The will of God gives the *fundamental* interest, and the will of man the *consequent* and manifestative interest. In the first way, we are interested in Christ's righteousness by *one act continued*, commencing with, and permanent as, the primary vital union; in the other way, it is by *repeated acts*, commencing with the first act of faith in Christ, and repeated with every succeeding reception of him.

Among persons who have made any, even the smallest, progress in christian knowledge, there can be no dispute respecting the *fundamental cause* of justification. All such acknowledge, that the righteousness, or *federal perfection* of Jesus Christ, is that for the sake of which any of the fallen race of Adam can be justified. The difference of sentiment arises from the *appointed method* of obtaining an interest in this meritorious cause. For want of consideration, we too hastily infer, that if the Scripture states *one* appointed method, that it must be an *exclusive* appointment.—Hence one pleads from Scripture, and especially St. James's epistle, that this appointed method is by *works*, that is, evangelical obedience, of which faith is a leading part. Another pleads from Scripture, that it is by *faith*, not as an act of moral obedience, but as a suitable bond of union, to the exclusion of all works. And a third, from the same Scripture, pleads, that we are justified by an eternal immanent act of God, and that faith only brings us to *enjoy* a privilege which belongs to the elect from eternity.

Now each of these schemes overlooks the important truth, that the immediate ground of justification is the *vital union* between Christ and the soul. Justification from eternity *precedes* vital union; justification by works *denies* the fact of a vital union being an adequate ground of a justifying sentence; and justification by faith alone, or believing in Christ, to the exclusion of a *prior* vital union on the part of the Spirit, *confounds* the work of man and the work of God. This last being the most difficult part of the subject, I beg leave to make a few observations upon it.

1. The *claims* of God, in reference to justification, are *twofold*. In the first instance, he claims from man a *federal perfection;* and in the second instance, he claims *compliance* with his method of bestowing an interest in it. The former claim may be answered by the *surety*, and in fact is answered by *his act* of a vital union on his part. For by this he gives an *interest* in himself to the soul he savingly adopts. Thus there is no condemnation to you that are *in Christ Jesus*. But the latter claim can be answered only by the *believer* himself, when he actually receives Christ as his righteousness, and so answers the divine requisition. Thus, he that *believeth* in Christ is justified from all things. In the first instance, *Christ* pleads his own righteousness in behalf of the adopted sinner; in the last instance, the *believer* pleads the *same* righteousness in his own behalf.

2. The *obligations* of man, in reference to justification, are also of two kinds. In the first place, he stands obliged to be conformed to the law as a *covenant*, which demands a sinless perfection; and, in the second place, he is obliged to conform to the law as a *rule*. Now whatever God enjoins as a duty, is a part of this rule; whether it be to hate sin, to love God, to believe in Christ, or to observe whatever Christ hath commanded. Our obligation to be conformed to the law as a covenant, is discharged by *Christ only* as our surety; and our ability to discharge our obligation of being conformed to the law as a rule is from him. We are obliged to believe on him as our justifying righteousness, under pain of God's displeasure, but man will ever continue in unbelief until Christ slays his enmity, and enables him to believe. But to slay a sinner's enmity, to change his nature, or to give him ability to believe, is the effect of a vital union; for as there is no such ability without gracious influence, so there is no gracious influence without union to the source of spiritual life. When thus enabled, man exercises repentance towards God, and faith in our Lord Jesus Christ. Receiving him by *faith* alone, as our righteousness and life, the law is obeyed as the voice of God, requiring the *obedience* of faith.

3. The method of *mercy*, in reference to justification, includes the substitution of the Saviour, and our acceptance in him, without *any works* of righteousness on our part. In this respect, not by works of righteousness which we have done, whether faith, repentance, or any kind of obedience, but according to his mercy he saveth us—provides a Saviour and gives us a saving interest in him. Grace *provides*, and grace *applies* the remedy. Mercy imputes to Jesus our sins, and imputes to us his righteousness. He who knew no sin was by sovereign mercy made a sin-offering for us, that we might be made the righteousness of God in him. Mercy laid the foundation, and placed us on it, that we might become living stones on him; and in consequence find him to be precious.

4. The rule of *moral government*, in reference to justification, is, that we believe on the Lord Jesus Christ as the end of the law for righteousness. For this end is the gospel proclaimed to all nations, even for "the obedience of faith." This is the language of divine government, "He that believeth shall be saved; but he that believeth not shall be condemned." The unbeliever is condemned already, because he rejects the counsel of God, and neglects so great salvation. Mercy hath *provided* an adequate and all-sufficient remedy, and government requires our closing with it as the only ground of hope left us. An endeavour to set up our own obedience instead of the righteousness of Christ, is rebellion against the authority of God, and undervaluing his wisdom and grace. None deserve condemnation more than those who reject the only remedy. And even they who believe have no ground of boasting. For we are saved by grace, and justified by faith, and that is not of ourselves, but is the gift of God.—The influence of works in justification our author has well explained.—W

works as an evidence. And where this instance of Abraham's obedience is elsewhere mentioned in the New Testament, it is mentioned as a fruit and evidence of his faith. Heb. xi. 17. "By faith Abraham, when he was tried, offered up Isaac; and he that had received the promises, offered up his only-begotten son."

And in the other instance which the apostle mentions, ver. 25. "Likewise also was not Rahab the harlot justified by works, when she had received the messengers, and had sent them out another way?" The apostle refers to a declarative judgment, in that particular testimony which was given of God's approbation of her as a believer, in directing Joshua to save her when the rest of Jericho was destroyed, Josh. vi. 25. "And Joshua saved Rahab the harlot alive, and her father's household, and all that she had; and she dwelleth in Israel even unto this day: because she hid the messengers which Joshua sent to spy out Jericho." This was accepted as an evidence and expression of her faith. Heb. xi. 31. "By faith the harlot Rahab perished not with them that believed not, when she had received the spies with peace." The apostle in saying, "Was not Rahab the harlot justified by works?" by the manner of his speaking has reference to something in her history; but we have no account in her history of any other justification of her but this.

4. If, notwithstanding, any choose to take justification in St. James's precisely as we do in Paul's epistles, for God's acceptance or approbation itself, and not any expression of that approbation; what has been already said concerning the manner in which acts of evangelical obedience are concerned in the affair of our justification, affords a very easy, clear, and full answer. For if we take works as acts or expressions of faith, they are not excluded; so a man is not justified by faith only, but also by works; *i. e.* he is not justified only by faith as a principle in the heart, or in its first and more immanent acts, but also by the effective acts of it in life, which are the expressions of the life of faith, as the operations and actions of the body are of the life of that; agreeable to verse 26.

What has been said in answer to these objections, may also, I hope, abundantly serve for an answer to another objection, often made against this doctrine, *viz.* that it encourages licentiousness in life. For, from what has been said, we may see that the Scripture doctrine of justification by faith alone, without any manner of goodness or excellency of ours, does in no wise diminish either the necessity or benefit of a sincere evangelical universal *obedience.* Man's salvation is not only indissolubly connected with obedience, and damnation with the want of it, in those who have opportunity for it, but depends upon it in many respects. It is the way to salvation, and the necessary preparation for it; eternal blessings are bestowed in reward for it, and our justification in our own consciences and at the day of judgment, depends on it, as the proper evidence of our acceptable state; and that even in accepting of us as entitled to life in our justification, God has respect to this, as that on which the fitness of such an act of justification depends: so that our *salvation* does as truly depend upon it, as if we were justified for the moral excellency of it. And besides all this, the degree of our happiness to all eternity is suspended on, and determined by, the degree of this. So that this gospel-scheme of justification is as far from encouraging licentiousness, and contains as much to encourage and excite to strict and universal obedience, and the utmost possible eminency of holiness, as any scheme that can be devised, and indeed unspeakably more.

I come now to the

V. And last thing proposed, which is, to consider the "importance of this doctrine."

I know there are many who make as though this controversy was of no great importance; that it is chiefly a matter of nice speculation, depending on certain subtle distinctions, which many that make use of them do not understand themselves; and that the difference is not of such consequence as to be worth being zealous about; and that more hurt is done by raising disputes about it than good.

Indeed I am far from thinking that it is of absolute necessity persons should understand, and be agreed upon, all the distinctions needful particularly to explain and defend this doctrine against all cavils and objections. Yet all Christians should strive after an increase of knowledge; and none should content themselves without some clear and distinct understanding in this point. But we should believe in the general, according to the clear and abundant revelations of God's word, that it is none of our own excellency, virtue, or righteousness, that is the *ground* of our being received from a state of condemnation into a state of acceptance in God's sight, but only Jesus Christ, and his righteousness and worthiness, received by faith. This I think to be of great importance, at least in application to ourselves; and that for the following reasons.

1. The Scripture treats of this doctrine, as a doctrine of very great importance. That there is a certain doctrine of justification by faith, in opposition to justification by the works of the law, which the apostle Paul insists upon as of the greatest importance, none will deny; because there is nothing in the Bible more apparent. The apostle, under the infallible conduct of the Spirit of God, thought it worth his most strenuous and zealous disputing about and defending. He speaks of the contrary doctrine as fatal and ruinous to the souls of men, in the latter end of the 9th chapter of Romans, and beginning of the 10th. He speaks of it as subversive of the gospel of Christ, and calls it another gospel, and says concerning it, if any one, "though an angel from heaven, preach it, let him be accursed;" Gal. i. 6—9 compared with the following part of the epistle. Certainly we must allow the apostles to be good judges of the importance and tendency of doctrines; at least the Holy Ghost in them. And doubtless we are safe, and in no danger of harshness and censoriousness, if we only follow him, and keep close to his express teachings, in what we believe and say of the hurtful and pernicious tendency of any error. Why are we to blame, for saying what the Bible has taught us to say, or for believing what the Holy Ghost has taught us to that end that we might believe it?

2. The adverse scheme lays another foundation of man's salvation than God hath laid. I do not now speak of that ineffectual redemption that they suppose to be universal, and what all mankind are equally the subjects of; but, I say, it lays entirely another foundation of man's actual, discriminating salvation, or that salvation wherein true Christians differ from wicked men. We suppose the foundation of this to be Christ's worthiness and righteousness: on the contrary, that scheme supposes it to be men's own virtue; even so, that this is the ground of a saving interest in Christ itself. It takes away Christ out of the place of the bottom stone, and puts in men's own virtue in the room of him: so that Christ himself in the affair of distinguishing actual salvation, is laid upon this foundation. And the foundation being so different, I leave it to every one to judge whether the difference between the two schemes consists only in punctilios of small consequence. The foundation being contrary, makes the whole scheme exceeding diverse and opposite; the one is a gospel scheme, the other a legal one.

3. It is in this doctrine that the most essential difference lies between the covenant of grace and the first covenant. The adverse scheme of justification supposes that we are justified by our *works*, in the very same sense wherein man was to have been justified by his works under the first covenant. By that covenant our first parents were not to have had eternal life given them for any proper merit in their obedience; because their perfect obedience was a debt that they owed God. Nor was it to be bestowed for any proportion between the dignity of their obedience, and the value of the reward; but only it was to be bestowed from a regard to a moral fitness in the virtue of their obedience, to the reward of God's favour; and a title to eternal life was to be given them, as a testimony of God's pleasedness with their works, or his regard to the inherent beauty of their virtue. And so it is the very same way that those in the adverse scheme suppose that we are received into God's special favour now, and to those saving benefits that are the testimonies of it. I am sensible the divines of that side entirely disclaim the popish doctrine of *merit;* and are free to speak of our utter unworthiness, and the great imperfection of all our services. But after all, it is our *virtue,* im-

perfect as it is, that recommends men to God, by which good men come to have a saving interest in Christ, and God's favour, rather than others; and these things are bestowed in testimony of God's respect to their goodness. So that whether they will allow the term *merit* or no, yet they hold, that we are accepted by our own merit, in the same sense, though not in the same degree, as under the first covenant.

But the great and most distinguishing difference between that covenant and the covenant of grace is, that by the covenant of grace we are not thus justified by our own works, but only by faith in Jesus Christ. It is on this account chiefly that the new covenant deserves the name of a covenant of grace, as is evident by Rom. iv. 16. "Therefore it is of faith, that it might be by grace." And chap. iii. 20, 24. "Therefore by the deeds of the law there shall no flesh be justified in his sight;"——"Being justified freely by his grace, through the redemption that is in Jesus Christ." And chap. xi. 6. "And if by grace, then it is no more of works; otherwise grace is no more grace: but if it be of works, then it is no more grace; otherwise work is no more work." Gal. v. 4. "Whosoever of you are justified by the law, ye are fallen from grace." And therefore the apostle, in the same epistle to the Galatians, speaking of the doctrine of justification by works as another gospel, adds, "which is not another," chap. i. verse 6, 7. It is no gospel at all; it is law. It is no covenant of grace, but of works; not an evangelical, but a legal doctrine. Certainly that doctrine wherein consists the greatest and most essential difference between the covenant of grace and the first covenant, must be a doctrine of great importance. That doctrine of the gospel by which above all others it is worthy of the name of gospel, is doubtless a very important doctrine of the gospel.

4. This is the main thing for which fallen men stood in need of divine revelation, to teach us how we who have sinned may come to be again accepted of God; or, which is the same thing, how the sinner may be justified. Something beyond the light of nature is necessary to salvation chiefly on this account. Mere natural reason afforded no means by which we could come to the knowledge of this, it depending on the sovereign pleasure of the Being that we had offended by sin. This seems to be the great drift of that revelation which God has given, and of all those mysteries it reveals, all those great doctrines that are peculiarly doctrines of revelation, and above the light of nature. It seems to have been very much on this account, that it was requisite the doctrine of the Trinity itself should be revealed to us; that by a discovery of the concern of the several divine persons in the great affair of our salvation, we might the better understand and see how all our dependence in this affair is on God, and our sufficiency all in him, and not in ourselves; that he is all in all in this business, agreeable to 1 Cor. i. 29—31. "That no flesh should glory in his presence. But of him are ye in Christ Jesus, who of God is made unto us wisdom, and righteousness, and sanctification, and redemption: that, according as it is written, He that glorieth, let him glory in the Lord." What is the gospel, but only the glad tidings of a new way of acceptance with God unto life, a way wherein sinners may come to be free from the guilt of sin, and obtain a title to eternal life? And if, when this way is revealed, it is rejected, and another of man's devising be put in the room of it, without doubt, it must be an error of great importance, and the apostle might well say it was another gospel.

5. The contrary scheme of justification derogates much from the honour of God and the Mediator. I have already shown how it diminishes the glory of the Mediator, in ascribing that to man's virtue and goodness, which belongs alone to his worthiness and righteousness. By the apostle's sense of the matter it renders Christ needless. Gal. v. 4. "Christ is become of no effect to you, whosoever of you are justified by the law." If that scheme of justification be followed in its consequences, it utterly overthrows the glory of all the great things that have been contrived, and done, and suffered in the work of redemption. Gal. ii. 21. "If righteousness come by the law, Christ is dead in vain." It has also been already shown how it diminishes the glory of divine grace, (which is the attribute God hath especially set himself to glorify in the work of redemption,) and so that it greatly diminishes the obligation to gratitude in the sinner that is saved. Yea, in the sense of the apostle, it makes void the distinguishing grace of the gospel. Gal. v. 4. "Whosoever of you are justified by the law, are fallen from grace." It diminishes the glory of the grace of God and the Redeemer, and proportionably magnifies man. It makes the goodness and excellency of fallen man to be something, which I have shown are nothing. I have also already shown, that it is contrary to the truth of God in the threatening of his holy law, to justify the sinner for his virtue. And whether it were contrary to God's truth or no, it is a scheme of things very unworthy of God. It supposes that God, when about to lift up a poor forlorn malefactor condemned to eternal misery for sinning against his Majesty, and to make him unspeakably and eternally happy by bestowing his Son and himself upon him, as it were, sets all this to sale, for the price of his virtue and excellency. I know that those whom we oppose acknowledge, that the price is very disproportionate to the benefit bestowed; and say, that God's grace is wonderfully manifested in accepting so little virtue, and bestowing so glorious a reward for such imperfect righteousness. But seeing we are such infinitely sinful and abominable creatures in God's sight, and by our infinite guilt have brought ourselves into such wretched and deplorable circumstances—and all our righteousnesses are nothing, and ten thousand times worse than nothing, if God looks upon them as they are in themselves—is it not immensely more worthy of the infinite majesty and glory of God, to deliver and make happy such wretched vagabonds and captives, without any money or price of theirs, or any manner of expectation of excellency or virtue in them, in any wise to recommend them? Will it not betray a foolish exalting opinion of ourselves, and a mean one of God, to have thought of offering any thing of ours, to recommend us to the favour of being brought from wallowing, like filthy swine, in the mire of our sins, and from the enmity and misery of devils in the lowest hell, to the state of God's dear children in the everlasting arms of his love in heavenly glory; or to imagine that it is the constitution of God, that we should bring our filthy rags, and offer them to him as the *price* of this?

6. The opposite scheme does most directly tend to lead men to trust in their own righteousness for justification, which is a thing fatal to the soul. This is what men are of themselves exceeding prone to do, (and that though they are never so much taught the contrary,) through the partial and high thoughts they have of themselves, and their exceeding dulness of apprehending any such mystery as our being accepted for the righteousness of another. But this scheme directly teaches men to trust in their own righteousness for justification; in that it teaches them that this is indeed what they must be justified by, being the way of justification which God himself has appointed. So that if a man had naturally no disposition to trust in his own righteousness, yet if he embraced this scheme, and acted consistently, it would lead him to it. But that trusting in our own righteousness, is a thing fatal to the soul, is what the Scripture plainly teaches us. It tells us, that it will cause that Christ shall profit us nothing, and be of no effect to us, Gal. v. 2—4. For though the apostle speaks there particularly of circumcision, yet it is not merely being circumcised, but trusting in circumcision as a righteousness, that the apostle has respect to. He could not mean, that merely being circumcised would render Christ of no profit or effect to a person; for we read that he himself, for certain reasons, took Timothy and circumcised him, Acts xvi. 3. And the same is evident by the context, and by the rest of the epistle. And the apostle speaks of trusting in their own righteousness as fatal to the Jews, Rom. ix. 31, 32. "But Israel, which followed after the law of righteousness, hath not attained to the law of righteousness. Wherefore? Because they sought it not by faith, but as it were by the works of the law; for they stumbled at that stumbling-stone." Together with chap. x. verse 3. "For they being ignorant of God's righteousness, and going about to establish their own righteousness, have not submitted themselves unto the righteousness of God." And this is spoken of as fatal to the Pharisees, in the parable of the Pharisee and the publican, which Christ

spake to them in order to reprove them for trusting in themselves that they were righteous. The design of the parable is to show them, that the very publicans shall be justified, rather than they; as appears by the reflection Christ makes upon it, Luke xviii. 14. "I tell you, this man went down to his house justified rather than the other;" that is, this and not the other. The fatal tendency of it might also be proved from its inconsistence with the nature of justifying faith, and with the nature of that humiliation that the Scripture often speaks of as absolutely necessary to salvation; but these scriptures are so express, that it is needless to bring any further arguments.

How far a wonderful and mysterious agency of God's Spirit may so influence some men's hearts, that their practice in this regard may be contrary to their own principles, so that they shall not trust in their own righteousness, though they profess that men are justified by their own righteousness—or how far they may believe the doctrine of justification by men's own righteousness in general, and yet not believe it in a particular application of it to themselves—or how far that error which they may have been led into by education, or cunning sophistry of others, may yet be indeed contrary to the prevailing disposition of their hearts, and contrary to their practice—or how far some may seem to maintain a doctrine contrary to this gospel-doctrine of justification, that really do not, but only express themselves differently from others; or seem to oppose it through their misunderstanding of our expressions, or we of theirs, when indeed our real sentiments are the same in the main—or may seem to differ more than they do, by using terms that are without a precisely fixed and determinate meaning—or to be wide in their sentiments from this doctrine, for want of a distinct understanding of it; whose hearts, at the same time, entirely agree with it, and if once it was clearly explained to their understandings, would immediately close with it, and embrace it:—how far these things may be, I will not determine; but am fully persuaded that great allowances are to be made on these and such like accounts, in innumerable instances; though it is manifest, from what has been said, that the teaching and propagating contrary doctrines and schemes, is of a pernicious and fatal tendency.

DISCOURSE II.

PRESSING INTO THE KINGDOM OF GOD.

LUKE xvi. 16.

The law and the prophets were until John: since that time the kingdom of God is preached, and every man presseth into it.

IN these words two things may be observed: *First*, Wherein the work and office of John the Baptist consisted, *viz.* in preaching the kingdom of God, to prepare the way for its introduction to succeed the law and the prophets. By the law and the prophets, in the text, seems to be intended the ancient dispensation under the Old Testament, which was received from Moses and the prophets. These are said to be *until John;* not that the revelations given by them are out of use since that time, but that the state of the church, founded and regulated under God by them, the dispensation of which they were the ministers, and wherein the church depended mainly on light received from them, fully continued till John. He first began to introduce the New-Testament dispensation, or gospel-state of the church; which, with its glorious, spiritual, and eternal privileges and blessings, is often called the kingdom of heaven, or kingdom of God. John the Baptist preached, that the kingdom of God was at hand. "Repent," says he, "for the kingdom of heaven is at hand:"—"Since that time," says Christ, "the kingdom of God is preached." John the Baptist first began to preach it; and then, after him, Christ and his disciples preached the same. Thus Christ preached, Matt. iv. 17. "From that time Jesus began to preach, and to say, Repent, for the kingdom of heaven is at hand." So the disciples were directed to preach, Matt. x. 7. "And, as ye go, preach, saying, The kingdom of heaven is at hand." It was not John the Baptist, but Christ, that fully brought in, and actually established, this kingdom of God; but he, as Christ's forerunner to prepare his way before him, did the first thing that was done towards introducing it. The old dispensation was abolished, and the new brought in by degrees; as the night gradually ceases, and gives place to the increasing day which succeeds in its room. First the day-star arises; next follows the light of the sun itself, but dimly reflected, in the dawning of the day; but this light increases, and shines more and more, and the stars that served for light during the foregoing night, gradually go out, and their light ceases, as being now needless, till at length the sun rises, and enlightens the world by his own direct light, which increases as he ascends higher above the horizon, till the day-star itself gradually disappears; agreeable to what John says of himself, John iii. 30. "He must increase, but I must decrease." John was the forerunner of Christ, and harbinger of the gospel-day; much as the morning-star is the forerunner of the sun. He had the most honourable office of any of the prophets; the other prophets foretold Christ to come, he revealed him as already come, and had the honour to be that servant who should come immediately before him, and actually introduce him, and even to be the instrument concerned in his solemn inauguration, as he was in baptizing him. He was the greatest of the prophets that came before Christ, as the morning-star is the brightest of all the stars, Matt. xi. 11. He came to prepare men's hearts to receive that kingdom of God which Christ was about more fully to reveal and erect. Luke i. 17. "To make ready a people prepared for the Lord."

Secondly, We may observe wherein his success appeared, *viz.* in that since he began his ministry, every man pressed into that kingdom of God which he preached. The greatness of his success appeared in two things:

1. In the generalness of it, with regard to the subject, or the persons in whom the success appeared; *every man.* Here is a term of universality; but it is not to be taken as universal with regard to individuals, but kinds; as such universal terms are often used in Scripture. When John preached, there was an extraordinary pouring out of the Spirit of God that attended his preaching. An uncommon awakening, and concern for salvation, appeared on the minds of all sorts of persons; and even in the most unlikely persons, and those from whom such a thing might least be expected; as the Pharisees, who were exceeding proud, and self-sufficient, and conceited of their own wisdom and righteousness, and looked on themselves fit to be teachers of others, and used to scorn to be taught; and the Sadducees, who were a kind of infidels, that denied any resurrection, angel, or spirit, or any future state. So that John himself seems to be surprised to see them come to him, under such concern for their salvation; as in Matt. iii. 7. "But when he saw many of the Pharisees and Sadducees come to his baptism, he said unto them, O generation of vipers, who hath warned you to flee from the wrath to come?" And besides these, the publicans, who were some of the most infamous sort of men, came to him, inquiring what they should do to be saved. And the soldiers, who were doubtless a very profane, loose, and profligate sort of persons, made the same inquiry, Luke iii. 12, and 14. "Then came also publicans to be baptized, and said

unto him, Master, what shall we do? And the soldiers likewise demanded of him, saying, And what shall we do?"

2. His success appeared in the manner in which his hearers sought the kingdom of God; they pressed into it. It is elsewhere set forth by their being violent for the kingdom of heaven, and taking it by force. Matt. xi. 12. "From the days of John the Baptist until now, the kingdom of heaven suffers violence, and the violent take it by force."

The DOCTRINE that I observe from the words is this.—"It concerns every one that would obtain the kingdom of God, to be pressing into it."—In discoursing on this subject, I would,

First, Show *what* is that way of seeking salvation that seems to be pointed forth in the expression of *pressing into the kingdom of God.*

Secondly, Give the reasons *why* it concerns every one that would obtain the kingdom of God, to seek it in this way.—And then make application.

I. I would show what manner of seeking salvation seems to be denoted by "pressing into the kingdom of God."

1. This expression denotes *strength of desire.* Men in general who live under the light of the gospel, and are not atheists, desire the kingdom of God; that is, they desire to go to heaven rather than to hell. Most of them indeed are not much concerned about it; but on the contrary, live a secure and careless life. And some who are many degrees above these, being under some degrees of the awakenings of God's Spirit, yet are not pressing into the kingdom of God. But they that may be said to be truly so, have strong desires to get out of a natural condition, and to get an interest in Christ. They have such a conviction of the misery of their present state, and of the extreme necessity of obtaining a better, that their minds are as it were possessed with and wrapped up in concern about it. To obtain salvation is desired by them above all things in the world. This concern is so great that it very much shuts out other concerns. They used before to have the stream of their desires after other things, or, it may be, had their concern divided between this and them; but when they come to answer the expression in the text, of *pressing into the kingdom of God*, this concern prevails above all others; it lays other things low, and does in a manner engross the care of the mind. This seeking eternal life should not only be one concern that our souls are taken up about with other things; but salvation should be sought as the one thing needful, Luke x. 42. And as the one thing that is desired, Psalm xxvii. 4.

2. Pressing into the kingdom of heaven denotes earnestness and *firmness of resolution.* There should be strength of resolution, accompanying strength of desire, as it was in the psalmist, in the place just now referred to; "one thing have I desired, and that will I seek after." In order to a thorough engagedness of the mind in this affair, both these must meet together. Besides desires after salvation, there should be an earnest resolution in persons to pursue this good as much as lies in their power; to do all that in the use of their utmost strength they are able to do, in an attendance on every duty, and resisting and militating against all manner of sin, and to continue in such a pursuit.

There are two things needful in a person, in order to these strong resolutions; there must be a sense of the great importance and necessity of the mercy sought, and there must also be a sense of opportunity to obtain it, or the encouragement there is to seek it. The strength of resolution depends on the sense which God gives to the heart of these things. Persons without such a sense, may seem to themselves to take up resolutions; they may, as it were, force a promise to themselves, and say within themselves, "I will seek as long as I live, I will not give up till I obtain," when they do but deceive themselves. Their hearts are not in it; neither do they indeed take up any such resolution as they seem to themselves to do. It is the resolution of the mouth more than of the heart; their hearts are not strongly bent to fulfil what their mouth says. The firmness of resolution lies in the fulness of the disposition of the heart to do what is resolved to be done. Those who are pressing into the kingdom of God, have a disposition of heart to do every thing that is required, and that lies in their power to do, and to continue in it. They have not only earnestness, but steadiness of resolution: they do not seek with a wavering unsteady heart, by turns or fits, being off and on; but it is the constant bent of the soul, if possible, to obtain the kingdom of God.

3. By pressing into the kingdom of God is signified *greatness of endeavour.* It is expressed in Eccles. ix. 10. by doing what our hand finds to do *with our might.* And this is the natural and necessary consequence of the two forementioned things. Where there is strength of desire, and firmness of resolution, there will be answerable endeavours. Persons thus engaged in their hearts will "strive to enter in at the strait gate," and will be violent for heaven; their practice will be agreeable to the counsel of the wise man, in Prov. ii. at the beginning, "My son, if thou wilt receive my words, and hide my commandments with thee; so that thou incline thine ear unto wisdom, and apply thine heart to understanding; yea, if thou criest after knowledge, and liftest up thy voice for understanding; if thou seekest her as silver, and searchest for her as for hid treasures; then shalt thou understand the fear of the Lord, and find the knowledge of God." Here the earnestness of desire and strength of resolution is signified by inclining the ear to wisdom, and applying the heart to understanding; and the greatness of endeavour is denoted by crying after knowledge, and lifting up the voice for understanding; seeking her as silver, and searching for her as for hid treasures: such desires and resolutions, and such endeavours, go together.

4. Pressing into the kingdom of God denotes an engagedness and earnestness, that is *directly about that business* of getting into the kingdom of God. Persons may be in very great exercise and distress of mind, and that about the condition of their souls; their thoughts and cares may be greatly engaged and taken up about things of a spiritual nature, and yet not be pressing into the kingdom of God, nor towards it. The exercise of their minds is not directly about the work of *seeking* salvation, in a diligent attendance on the means that God hath appointed in order to it, but something else that is beside their business; it may be about God's decrees and secret purposes, prying into them, searching for signs whereby they may determine, or at least conjecture, what they are before God makes them known by their accomplishment. They distress their minds with fears that they be not elected, or that they have committed the unpardonable sin, or that their day is past, and that God has given them up to judicial and final hardness, and never intends to show them mercy; and therefore, that it is in vain for them to seek salvation. Or they entangle themselves about the doctrine of original sin, and other mysterious doctrines of religion that are above their comprehension. Many persons that seem to be in great distress about a future eternal state, get much into a way of perplexing themselves with such things as these. When it is so, let them be never so much concerned and engaged in their minds, they cannot be said to be pressing towards the kingdom of God; because their exercise is not in their *work*, but rather that which tends to *hinder* them in their work. If they are violent, they are only working violently to *entangle* themselves, and lay blocks in their own way; their pressure is not forwards. Instead of getting along, they do but lose their time, and worse than merely lose it; instead of fighting with the giants that stand in the way to keep them out of Canaan, they spend away their time and strength in conflicting with shadows that appear by the way-side.

Hence we are not to judge of the hopefulness of the way that persons are in, or of the probability of their success in seeking salvation, only by the greatness of the concern and distress that they are in; for many persons have needless distresses that they had much better be without. It is thus very often with persons overrun with the distemper of melancholy; whence the adversary of souls is wont to take great advantage. But then are persons in the most likely way to obtain the kingdom of heaven, when the intent of their minds, and the engagedness of their spirits, is about their *proper work* and business, and all the bent of their souls is to attend on God's means, and to do what he commands and directs them to. The apostle tells us, 1 Cor. ix. 26. "that he did not fight as those that beat the air." Our time is short enough; we had not need to spend it in that which is nothing to the purpose. There are real difficulties and enemies enough for persons to encounter, to employ all their strength; they had not need to waste it in fighting with phantoms.

5. By pressing into the kingdom of God is denoted a *breaking through opposition and difficulties.* There is in the expression a plain intimation of difficulty. If there were no opposition, but the way was all clear and open, there would be no need of pressing to get along. They therefore that are pressing into the kingdom of God, go on with such engagedness, that they break through the difficulties that are in their way. They are so set for salvation, that those things by which others are discouraged, and stopped, and turned back, do not stop them, but they press through them. Persons ought to be so resolved for heaven, that if by any means they *can* obtain, they *will* obtain. Whether those means be difficult or easy, cross or agreeable, if they are requisite means of salvation, they should be complied with. When any thing is presented to be done, the question should not be, Is it easy or hard? is it agreeable to my carnal inclinations or interest, or against them? But is it a required means of my obtaining an interest in Jesus Christ, and eternal salvation? Thus the apostle, Philip. iii. 11. "If by any means I might attain unto the resurrection of the dead." He tells us there in the context what difficulties he broke through, that he suffered the loss of all things, and was willingly made conformable even to Christ's death, though that was attended with such extreme torment and ignominy.

He that is pressing into the kingdom of God, commonly finds many things in the way that are against the grain; but he is not stopped by the cross that lies before him, but takes it up, and carries it. Suppose there be something incumbent on him to do, that is cross to his natural temper, and irksome to him on that account; suppose something that he cannot do without suffering in his estate, or that he apprehends will look odd and strange in the eyes of others, and expose him to ridicule and reproach, or any thing that will offend a neighbour, and get his ill-will, or something that will be very cross to his own carnal appetite—he will *press through such difficulties.* Every thing that is found to be a weight that hinders him in running this race he casts from him, though it be a weight of gold or pearls; yea, if it be a right hand or foot that offends him, he will cut them off, and will not stick at plucking out a right eye with his own hands. These things are insuperable difficulties to those who are not thoroughly engaged in seeking their salvation; they are stumbling-blocks that they never get over. But it is not so with him that presses into the kingdom of God. Those things (before he was thoroughly roused from his security) about which he was wont to have long parleyings and disputings with his own conscience—employing carnal reason to invent arguments and pleas of excuse—he now sticks at no longer; he has done with this endless disputing and reasoning, and presses violently through all difficulties. Let what will be in the way, heaven is what he must and will obtain, not if he can without difficulty, but if it be possible. He meets with temptation: the devil is often whispering in his ear, setting allurements before him, magnifying the difficulties of the work he is engaged in, telling him that they are insuperable, and that he can never conquer them, and trying all ways in the world to discourage him; but still he presses forward. God has given and maintains such an earnest spirit for heaven, that the devil cannot stop him in his course; he is not at leisure to lend an ear to what he has to say.—I come now,

II. To show *why* the kingdom of heaven should be sought in this manner.—It should be thus sought,

1. On account of the *extreme necessity* we are in of getting into the kingdom of heaven. We are in a perishing necessity of it; without it we are utterly and eternally lost. Out of the kingdom of God is no safety; there is no other hiding-place; this is the only city of refuge, in which we can be secure from the avenger that pursues all the ungodly. The vengeance of God will pursue, overtake, and eternally destroy, them that are not in this kingdom. All that are without this enclosure will be swallowed up in an overflowing fiery deluge of wrath. They may stand at the door and knock, and cry, Lord, Lord, open to us, in vain; they will be thrust back; and God will have no mercy on them; they shall be eternally left of him. His fearful vengeance will seize them; the devils will lay hold of them; and all evil will come upon them; and there will be none to pity or help; their case will be utterly desperate, and infinitely doleful. It will be a gone case with them; all offers of mercy and expressions of divine goodness will be finally withdrawn, and all hope will be lost. God will have no kind of regard to their well-being; will take no care of them to save them from any enemy, or any evil; but himself will be their dreadful enemy, and will execute wrath with fury, and will take vengeance in an inexpressibly dreadful manner. Such as shall be in this case will be lost and undone indeed! They will be sunk down into perdition, infinitely below all that we can think. For who knows the power of God's anger? And who knows the misery of that poor worm, on whom that anger is executed without mercy?

2. On account of the shortness and *uncertainty of the opportunity* for getting into this kingdom. When a few days are past, all our opportunity for it will be gone. Our day is limited. God has set our bounds, and we know not where. While persons are out of this kingdom, they are in danger every hour of being overtaken with wrath. We know not how soon we shall get past that line, beyond which there is no work, device, knowledge, nor wisdom; and therefore we should do what we have to do with our might, Eccles. ix. 10.

3. On account of the *difficulty* of getting into the kingdom of God. There are innumerable difficulties in the way; such as few conquer: most of them that try have not resolution, courage, earnestness, and constancy enough; but they fail, give up, and perish. The difficulties are too many and too great for them that do not violently press forward. They never get along, but stick by the way; are turned aside, or turned back, and ruined. Matt. vii. 14. "Strait is the gate, and narrow is the way, which leadeth unto life, and few there be that find it." Luke xiii. 24. "Strive to enter in at the strait gate; for many, I say unto you, will seek to enter in, and shall not be able."

4. The *possibility* of obtaining. Though it be attended with so much difficulty, yet it is not a thing impossible. Acts viii. 22. "If perhaps the thought of thine heart may be forgiven thee." 2 Tim. ii. 25. "If peradventure God will give them repentance to the acknowledging of the truth." However sinful a person is, and whatever his circumstances are, there is, notwithstanding, a possibility of his salvation. He himself is capable of it, and God is able to accomplish it, and has mercy sufficient for it; and there is sufficient provision made through Christ, that God may do it consistent with the honour of his majesty, justice, and truth. So that there is no want either of sufficiency in God, or capacity in the sinner, in order to this. The greatest and vilest, most blind, dead, hard-hearted sinner living, is a subject capable of saving light and grace. Seeing therefore there is such necessity of obtaining the kingdom of God, and so short a time, and such difficulty, and yet such a possibility, it may well induce us to press into it. Jonah iii. 8, 9.

5. It is meet that the kingdom of heaven should be thus sought, because of the *great excellency* of it. We are willing to seek earthly things, of trifling value, with great diligence, and through much difficulty; it therefore certainly becomes us to seek that with great earnestness which is of infinitely greater worth and excellence. And how well may God expect and require it of us, that we should seek it in such a manner, in order to our obtaining it!

6. Such a manner of seeking is *needful to prepare* persons for the kingdom of God. Such earnestness and thoroughness of endeavours, is the ordinary means that God makes use of to bring persons to an acquaintance with themselves, to a sight of their own hearts, to a sense of their own helplessness, and to a despair in their own strength and righteousness. And such engagedness and constancy in seeking the kingdom of heaven, prepare the soul to receive it the more joyfully and thankfully, and the more highly to prize and value it when obtained. So that it is

in mercy to us, as well as for the glory of his own name, that God has appointed such earnest seeking, to be the way in which he will bestow the kingdom of heaven.

APPLICATION.

The use I would make of this doctrine, is of *exhortation* to all Christless persons to press into the kingdom of God. Some of you are inquiring what you shall do? You seem to desire to know what is the way wherein salvation is to be sought, and how you may be likely to obtain it. You have now heard the way that the holy word of God directs to. Some are seeking, but it cannot be said of them that they are *pressing* into the kingdom of heaven. There are many that in time past have sought salvation, but not in this manner, and so they never obtained, but are now gone to hell. Some of them sought it year after year, but failed of it, and perished at last. They were overtaken with divine wrath, and are now suffering the fearful misery of damnation, and have no rest day nor night, having no more opportunity to seek, but must suffer and be miserable throughout the never-ending ages of eternity. Be exhorted, therefore, not to seek salvation as they did, but let the kingdom of heaven suffer violence from you.

Here I would first answer an *objection* or two, and then proceed to give some *directions* how to press into the kingdom of God.

Object. 1. Some may be ready to say, We cannot do this of ourselves; that strength of desire, and firmness of resolution, that have been spoken of, are out of our reach. If I endeavour to resolve and to seek with engagedness of spirit, I find I fail; my thoughts are presently off from the business, and I feel myself dull, and my engagedness relaxed, in spite of all I can do.

Ans. 1. Though earnestness of mind be not immediately in your power, yet the consideration of what has been now said of the *need* of it, may be a means of stirring you up to it. It is true, persons never will be thoroughly engaged in this business, unless it be by God's influence; but God influences persons by means. Persons are not stirred up to a thorough earnestness without some considerations that move them to it. And if persons can but be made sensible of the necessity of salvation, and also duly consider the exceeding difficulty of it, and the greatness of the opposition, and how short and uncertain the time is, but yet are sensible that they have an opportunity, and that there is a possibility of their obtaining, they will need no more in order to their being thoroughly engaged and resolved in this matter. If we see persons slack and unresolved, and unsteady, it is because they do not enough consider these things.

2. Though strong desires and resolutions of mind be not in your power, yet painfulness of endeavours is in your power. It is in your power to take pains in the use of means, yea very great pains. You can be very painful and diligent in watching your own heart, and striving against sin. Though there is all manner of corruption in the heart continually ready to work, yet you can very laboriously watch and strive against these corruptions; and it is in your power, with great diligence to attend the matter of your duty towards God and towards your neighbour. It is in your power to attend all ordinances, and all public and private duties of religion, and to do it with your might. It would be a contradiction to suppose that a man cannot do these things with all the might he has, though he cannot do them with more might than he has. The dulness and deadness of the heart, and slothfulness of disposition, do not hinder men being able to take pains, though it hinders their being willing. That is one thing wherein your laboriousness may appear, even striving against your own dulness. That men have a dead and sluggish heart, does not argue that they be not able to take pains; it is so far from that, that it gives occasion for pains. It is one of the difficulties in the way of duty, that persons have to strive with, and that gives occasion for struggling and labour. If there were no difficulties attended seeking salvation, there would be no occasion for striving; a man would have nothing to strive about. There is indeed a great deal of difficulty attending all duties required of those that would obtain heaven. It is an exceeding difficult thing for them to keep their thoughts; it is a difficult thing seriously, or to any good purpose, to consider matters of the greatest importance; it is a difficult thing to hear, or read, or pray attentively. But it does not argue that a man cannot strive in these things because they are difficult; nay, he could not strive therein if there were not difficulty in them. For what is there excepting difficulties that any can have to strive or struggle with in any affair or business? Earnestness of mind, and diligence of endeavour, tend to promote each other. He that has a heart earnestly engaged, will take pains; and he that is diligent and painful in all duty, probably will not be so long before he finds the sensibleness of his heart and earnestness of his spirit greatly increased.

Object. 2. Some may object, that if they are earnest, and take a great deal of pains, they shall be in danger of trusting to what they do; they are afraid of doing their duty for fear of making a righteousness of it.

Ans. There is ordinarily no kind of seekers that trust so much to what they do, as slack and dull seekers. Though all seeking salvation, that have never been the subjects of a thorough humiliation, do trust in their own righteousness; yet some do it much more fully than others. Some though they *trust* in their own righteousness, yet are not *quiet* in it. And those who are most disturbed in their self-confidence, (and therefore in the likeliest way to be wholly brought off from it,) are not such as go on in a remiss way of seeking, but such as are most earnest and thoroughly engaged; partly because in such a way conscience is kept more sensible. A more awakened conscience will not rest so quietly in moral and religious duties, as one that is less awakened. A dull seeker's conscience will be in a great measure satisfied and quieted with his own works and performances; but one that is thoroughly awakened cannot be stilled or pacified with such things as these. In this way persons gain much more knowledge of themselves, and acquaintance with their own hearts, than in a negligent, slight way of seeking; for they have a great deal more experience of themselves. It is experience of ourselves, and finding what we are, that God commonly makes use of as the means of bringing us off from all dependence on ourselves. But men never get acquaintance with themselves so fast, as in the most earnest way of seeking. They that are in this way have more to engage them to think of their sins, and strictly to observe themselves, and have much more to do with their own hearts, than others. Such a one has much more experience of his own weakness, than another that does not put forth and try his strength; and will therefore sooner see himself dead in sin. Such a one, though he hath a disposition continually to be flying to his own righteousness, yet finds rest in nothing; he wanders about from one thing to another, seeking something to ease his disquieted conscience; he is driven from one refuge to another, goes from mountain to hill, seeking rest and finding none; and therefore will the sooner prove that there is no rest to be found, nor trust to be put, in any creature whatsoever.

It is therefore quite a wrong notion that some entertain, that the more they do, the more they shall depend on it. Whereas the reverse is true; the more they do, or the more thorough they are in seeking, the less will they be likely to rest in their doings, and the sooner will they see the vanity of all that they do. So that persons will exceedingly miss it, if ever they neglect to do any duty either to God or man, whether it be any duty of religion, justice, or charity, under a notion of its exposing them to trust in their own righteousness. It is very true, that it is a common thing for persons, when they earnestly seek salvation, to trust in the pains that they take: but yet commonly those that go on in a more slight way, trust a great deal more securely to their dull services, than he that is pressing into the kingdom of God does to his earnestness. Men's slackness in religion, and their trust in their own righteousness, strengthen and establish one another. Their trust in what they have done, and what they now do, settles them in a slothful rest and ease, and hinders their being sensible of their need of rousing up themselves and pressing forward. And on the other hand, their negligence tends so to benumb them, and keep them in such ignorance of themselves, that the most miserable refuges are stupidly rested in as sufficient. Therefore we see, that when persons have been going on for a long time in such a way, and God afterwards comes more thoroughly to awaken them, and to stir them up to be in good earnest, he shakes all their old foundations, and rouses them out of their old resting-places; so that they cannot quiet themselves with those things that formerly kept them secure.

I would now proceed to give some *directions* how you should press into the kingdom of God.

1. Be directed to sacrifice *every thing* to your soul's eternal interest. Let seeking this be so much your bent, and what you are so resolved in, that you will make every thing give place to it. Let nothing stand before your resolution of seeking the kingdom of God. Whatever it be that you used to look upon as a convenience, or comfort, or ease, or thing desirable on any account, if it stands in the way of this great concern, let it be dismissed without hesitation; and if it be of that nature that it is likely always to be a hinderance, then wholly have done with it, and never entertain any expectation from it more. If in time past you have, for the sake of worldly gain, involved yourself in more care and business than you find to be consistent with your being so thorough in the business of religion as you ought to be, then get into some other way, though you suffer in your worldly interest by it. Or if you have heretofore been conversant with company that you have reason to think have been and will be a snare to you, and a hinderance to this great design in any wise, break off from their society, however it may expose you to reproach from your old companions, or let what will be the effect of it. Whatever it be that stands in the way of your most advantageously seeking salvation—whether it be some dear sinful pleasure, or strong carnal appetite, or credit and honour, or the good-will of some persons whose friendship you desire, and whose esteem and liking you have highly valued—and though there be danger, if you do as you ought, that you shall be looked upon by them as odd and ridiculous, and become contemptible in their eyes—or if it be your ease and indolence, and aversion to continual labour; or your outward convenience in any respect, whereby you might avoid difficulties of one kind or other—*let all go;* offer up all such things together, as it were, in one sacrifice, to the interest of your soul. Let nothing stand in competition with this, but make every thing to fall before it. If the flesh must be crossed, then cross it, spare it not, crucify it, and do not be afraid of being too cruel to it. Gal. v. 24. "They that are Christ's, have crucified the flesh, with the affections and lusts." Have no dependence on any worldly enjoyment whatsoever. Let salvation be the one thing with you. This is what is certainly required of you: and this is what many stick at; this giving up other things for salvation, is a stumbling-block that few get over. While others pressed into the kingdom of God at the preaching of John the Baptist, Herod was pretty much stirred up by his preaching. It is said, he heard him, and observed him, and did many things; but when he came to tell him that he must part with his beloved Herodias, here he stuck; this he never would yield to, Mark vii. 18—20. The rich young man was considerably concerned for salvation; and accordingly was a very strict liver in many things: but when Christ came to direct him to go and sell all that he had, and give to the poor, and come and follow him, he could not find in his heart to comply with it, but went away sorrowful. He had great possessions, and set his heart much on his estate, and could not bear to part with it. It may be, if Christ had directed him only to give away a considerable part of his estate, he would have done it; yea, perhaps, if he had bid him part with half of it, he would have complied with it: but when he directed him to throw up all, he could not grapple with such a proposal. Herein the straitness of the gate very much consists; and it is on this account that so many seek to enter in, and are not able. There are many that have a great mind to salvation, and spend great part of their time in wishing that they had it, but they will not comply with the necessary means.

2. Be directed to *forget the things that are behind;* that is, not to keep thinking and making much of what you have done, but let your mind be wholly intent on what you have to do. In some sense you ought to look back; you should look back on your sins. Jer. ii. 23. "See thy way in the valley, know what thou hast done." You should look back on the wretchedness of your religious performances, and consider how you have fallen short in them; how exceedingly polluted all your duties have been, and how justly God might reject and loathe them, and you for them. But you ought not to spend your time in looking back, as many persons do, thinking how much they have done for their salvation; what great pains they have taken, how that they have done what they can, and do not see how they can do more; how long a time they have been seeking, and how much more they have done than others, and even than such and such who have obtained mercy. They think with themselves how hardly God deals with them, that he does not extend mercy to them, but turns a deaf ear to their cries; and hence discourage themselves, and complain of God. Do not thus spend your time in looking on what is past, but look forward, and consider what is before you; consider what it is that you can do, and what it is necessary that you should do, and what God calls you still to do, in order to your own salvation. The apostle, in the 3d chapter to the Philippians, tells us what things he did while a Jew, how much he had to boast of, if any could boast; but he tells us, that he forgot those things, and all others that were behind, and reached forth towards the things that were before, pressing forwards towards the mark for the prize of the high calling of God in Christ Jesus.

3. Labour to get your *heart thoroughly disposed* to go on and hold out to the end. Many that seem to be earnest have not a heart thus disposed. It is a common thing for persons to appear greatly affected for a little while; but all is soon past away, and there is no more to be seen of it. Labour therefore to obtain a thorough willingness and preparation of spirit, to continue seeking, in the use of your utmost endeavours, without limitation; and do not think your whole life too long. And in order to this, be advised to two things.

(1.) Remember that if ever God bestows mercy upon you, he will use his sovereign pleasure about the *time when.* He will bestow it on some in a little time, and on others not till they have sought it long. If other persons are soon enlightened and comforted, while you remain long in darkness, there is no other way but for you to wait. God will act arbitrarily in this matter, and you cannot help it. You must even be content to wait, in a way of laborious and earnest striving, till his time comes. If you refuse, you will but undo yourself; and when you shall hereafter find yourself undone, and see that your case is past remedy, how will you condemn yourself for foregoing a great probability of salvation, only because you had not patience to hold out, and was not willing to be at the trouble of a persevering labour! And what will it avail before God or your own conscience to say, that you could not bear to be obliged to seek salvation so long, when God bestowed it on others that sought it but for a very short time? Though God may have bestowed the testimonies of his favour on others in a few days or hours after they have begun earnestly to seek it, how does that alter the case as to you, if there proves to be a necessity of your laboriously seeking many years before you obtain them? Is salvation less worth taking a great deal of pains for, because, through the sovereign pleasure of God, others have obtained it with comparatively little pains? If there are two persons, the one of which has obtained converting grace with comparative ease, and another that has obtained it after continuing for many years in the greatest and most earnest labours after it, how little difference does it make at last, when once salvation is obtained! Put all the *labour* and pains, the long-continued difficulties and strugglings, of the one in the scale against salvation, and how little does it substract; and put the ease with which the other has obtained in the scale with salvation, and how little does it add! What is either added or substracted is lighter than vanity, and a thing worthy of no consideration, when compared with that infinite benefit that is obtained. Indeed if you were ten thousand years, and all that time should strive and press forward with as great earnestness as ever a person did for one day, all this would bear no proportion to the importance of the benefit; and it will doubtless appear little to you, when once you come to be in actual possession of eternal glory, and to see what that eternal misery is which you have escaped. You must not think much of your pains, and of the length of time; you must press towards the kingdom of God, and do your utmost, and hold out to the end, and learn to make no account of it when you have done. You must undertake the business of seeking salvation upon these terms, and with no other expectations than this, that if ever God bestows mercy it will be in his own time; and not only so, but also that when you have done all, God will not hold himself obliged to show you mercy at last.

(2.) Endeavour now thoroughly to weigh in your mind the difficulty, and to *count the cost* of perseverance in seeking salvation. You that are now setting out in this business, (as there are many here who have very lately set about it;—Praised be the name of God that he has stirred you up to it!) be exhorted to attend this direction. Do not undertake in this affair with any other thought but of giving yourself wholly to it for the remaining part of your life, and going through many and great difficulties in it. Take heed that you do not engage secretly upon this condition, that you shall obtain in a little time, promising yourself that it shall be within this present season of the pouring out of God's Spirit, or with any other limitation of time whatsoever. Many, when they begin, (seeming to set out very earnestly,) do not expect that they shall need to seek very long, and so do not prepare themselves for it. And therefore, when they come to find it otherwise, and meet with unexpected difficulty, they are found unguarded, and easily overthrown. But let me advise you all who are now seeking salvation, not to entertain any self-flattering thoughts; but weigh the utmost difficulties of perseverance, and be provided for them, having your mind fixed in it to go through them, let them be what they will. Consider now beforehand, how tedious it would be, with utmost earnestness and labour, to strive after salvation for many years, in the mean time receiving no joyful or comfortable evidence of your having obtained. Consider what a great temptation to discouragement there probably would be in it; how apt you would be to yield the case; how ready to think that it is in vain for you to seek any longer, and that God never intends to show you mercy, in that he has not yet done it; how apt you would be to think with yourself, "What an uncomfortable life do I live! how much more unpleasantly do I spend my time than others that do not perplex their minds about the things of another world, but are at ease, and take the comfort of their worldly enjoyments!" Consider what a temptation there would probably be in it, if you saw others brought in that began to seek the kingdom of heaven long after you, rejoicing in a hope and sense of God's favour, after but little pains and a short time of awakening; while you, from day to day, and from year to year, seemed to labour in vain. Prepare for such temptations now. Lay in beforehand for such trials and difficulties, that you may not think any strange thing has happened when they come.

I hope that those who have given attention to what has been said, have by this time conceived, in some measure, what is signified by the expression in the text, and after what manner they ought to press into the kingdom of God. Here is this to induce you to a compliance with what you have been directed to; if you sit still, you die; if you go backward, behold you shall surely die; if you go forward, you may live. And though God has not bound himself to any thing that a person does while destitute of faith, and out of Christ, yet there is great probability, that in a way of hearkening to this counsel you will live; and that by pressing onward, and persevering, you will at last, as it were by violence, take the kingdom of heaven. Those of you who have not only heard the directions given, but shall through God's merciful assistance, practise according to them, are those that probably will overcome. These we may well hope at last to see standing with the Lamb on mount Sion, clothed in white robes, with palms in their hands; when all your labour and toil will be abundantly compensated, and you will not repent that you have taken so much pains, and denied yourself so much, and waited so long. This self-denial, this waiting, will then look little, and vanish into nothing in your eyes, being all swallowed up in the first minute's enjoyment of that glory that you will then possess, and will uninterruptedly possess and enjoy to all eternity.

4th direction. Improve the present season of the pouring out of the Spirit of God on this town. Prudence in any affair whatsoever consists very much in minding and improving our opportunities. If you would have spiritual prosperity, you must exercise prudence in the concerns of your souls, as well as in outward concerns when you seek outward prosperity. The prudent husbandman will observe his opportunities; he will improve seed-time and harvest; he will make his advantage of the showers and shines of heaven. The prudent merchant will discern his opportunities; he will not be idle on a market-day; he is careful not to let slip his seasons for enriching himself: So will those who prudently seek the fruits of righteousness, and the merchandise of wisdom, improve their opportunities for their eternal wealth and happiness.

God is pleased at this time, in a very remarkable manner, to pour out his Spirit amongst us; (glory be to his name!) You that have a mind to obtain converting grace, and to go to heaven when you die, now is your season! Now, if you have any sort of prudence for your own salvation, and have not a mind to go to hell, improve this season! Now is the accepted time! Now is the day of salvation! You that in time past have been called upon, and have turned a deaf ear to God's voice, and long stood out and resisted his commands and counsels, hear God's voice to-day, while it is called to-day! Do not harden your hearts at such a day as this! Now you have a special and remarkable price put into your hands to get wisdom, if you have but a heart to improve it.

God hath his certain days or appointed seasons of exercising both mercy and judgment. There are some remarkable times of wrath, laid out by God for his awful visitation, and the executions of his anger; which times are called days of vengeance, Prov. vi. 34. Wherein God will visit for sin, Exod. xxxii. 34. And so, on the contrary, God has laid out in his sovereign counsels seasons of remarkable mercy, wherein he will manifest himself in the exercises of his grace and loving-kindness, more than at other times. Such times in Scripture are called by way of eminency, accepted times, and days of salvation, and also days of God's visitation; because they are days wherein God will visit in a way of mercy; as Luke xix. 44. "And shall lay thee even with the ground, and thy children within thee; and they shall not leave in thee one stone upon another; because thou knewest not the time of thy visitation." It is such a time now in this town; it is with us a day of God's gracious visitation. It is indeed a day of grace with us as long as we live in this world, in the enjoyment of the means of grace; but such a time as this is especially, and in a distinguishing manner, a day of grace. There is a door of mercy always standing open for sinners; but at such a day as this, God opens an extraordinary door.

We are directed to seek the Lord while he may be found, and to call upon him while he is near, Isa. lv. 6. If you that are hitherto Christless, be not strangely besotted and infatuated, you will by all means improve such an opportunity as this to get heaven, when heaven is brought so near, when the fountain is opened in the midst of us in so extraordinary a manner. Now is the time to obtain a supply of the necessities of your poor perishing souls! This is the day for sinners that have a mind to be converted before they die, when God is dealing forth so liberally and bountifully amongst us; when conversion and salvation work is going on amongst us from sabbath to sabbath, and many are pressing into the kingdom of God! Now do not stay behind, but press in amongst the rest! Others have been stirred up to be in good earnest, and have taken heaven by violence; be entreated to follow their example, if you would have a part of the inheritance with them, and would not be left at the great day, when they are taken!

How should it move you to consider that you have this opportunity now in your hands! You are in the actual possession of it! If it were past, it would not be in your power to recover it, or in the power of any creature to bring it back for you; but it is not past; it is now, at this day. Now is the accepted time, even while it is called to-day! Will you sit still at such a time? Will you sleep in such a harvest? Will you deal with a slack hand, and stay behind out of mere sloth, or love to some lust, or lothness to grapple with some small difficulty, or to put yourself a little out of your way, when so many are flowing to the goodness of the Lord? You are behind still; and so you will be in danger of being left behind, when the whole number is completed that are to enter in, if you do not earnestly bestir yourself! To be left behind at the close of such a season as this, will be awful—next to being left behind on that day when God's saints shall mount up as with wings to meet the Lord in the air—and will be what will appear very threatening of it.

God is now calling you in an extraordinary manner: and it is agreeable to the will and word of Christ, that I should now, in his name, call you, as one set over you, and sent to you to that end; so it is his will that you should hearken to what I say, as his voice. I therefore beseech you in Christ's stead now to press into the kingdom of God! Whoever you are, whether young or old, small or great; if you are a great sinner, if you have been a backslider, if you have quenched the Spirit, be who you will, do not stand making objections, but arise, apply yourself to your work! Do what you have to do with your might. Christ is calling you before, and holding forth his grace, and everlasting benefits, and wrath is pursuing you behind; wherefore fly for your life, and look not behind you!

But here I would particularly direct myself to several sorts of persons.

I. To those sinners who are in a measure awakened, and are concerned for their salvation. You have reason to be glad that you have such an opportunity, and to prize it above gold. To induce you to prize and improve it, consider several things.

1. God has doubtless a design now to deal forth saving blessings to a number. God has done it to some already, and it is not probable that he has yet finished his work amongst us: we may well hope still to see others brought out of darkness into marvellous light. And therefore,

2. God comes this day, and knocks at many persons' doors, and at your door among the rest. God seems to be come in a very unusual manner amongst us, upon a gracious and merciful design; a design of saving a number of poor miserable souls out of a lost and perishing condition, and of bringing them into a happy state and eternal glory! This is offered to you, not only as it has always been in the word and ordinances, but by the particular influences of the Spirit of Christ awakening you! This special offer is made to many amongst us; and you are not passed over. Christ has not forgot you; but has come to your door; and there as it were stands waiting for you to open to him. If you have wisdom and discretion to discern your own advantage, you will know that now is your opportunity.

3. How much more easily converting grace is obtained at such a time, than at other times! The work is equally easy with God at all times; but there is far less difficulty in the way as to *men* at such a time, than at other times. It is, as I said before, a day of God's gracious visitation; a day that he has as it were set apart for the more liberally and bountifully dispensing of his grace; a day wherein God's hand is opened wide. Experience shows it. God seems to be more ready to help, to give proper convictions, to help against temptations, and let in divine light. He seems to carry on his work with a more glorious discovery of his power, and Satan is more chained up than at other times. Those difficulties and temptations that persons before stuck at, from year to year, they are soon helped over. The work of God is carried on with greater speed and swiftness, and there are often instances of sudden conversion at such a time. So it was in the apostles' days, when there was a time of the most extraordinary pouring out of the Spirit that ever was. How quick and sudden were conversions in those days! Such instances as that of the jailer abounded then, in fulfilment of that prophecy, Isa. lxvi. 7, 8. "Before she travailed, she brought forth: before her pain came, she was delivered of a man-child. Who hath heard such a thing? Who hath seen such things? For as soon as Zion travailed, she brought forth her children." So it is in some degree, whenever there is an extraordinary pouring out of the Spirit of God; more or less so, in proportion to the greatness of that effusion. There is seldom such quick work made of it at other times. Persons are not so soon delivered from their various temptations and entanglements; but are much longer wandering in a wilderness, and groping in darkness. And yet,

4. There are probably some here present that are now concerned about their salvation, that never will obtain. It is not to be supposed that all that are now moved and awakened, will ever be savingly converted. Doubtless there are many now seeking that will not be able to enter. When has it been so in times past, when there has been times of great outpourings of God's Spirit, but that many who for a while have inquired with others, what they should do to be saved, have failed, and afterwards grown hard and secure? All of you that are now awakened, have a mind to obtain salvation, and probably hope to get a title to heaven, in the time of this present moving of God's Spirit: but yet, (though it be awful to be spoken, and awful to be thought,) we have no reason to think any other, than that some of you will burn in hell to all eternity. You all are afraid of hell, and seem at present disposed to take pains to be delivered from it; and yet it would be unreasonable to think any other, than that some of you will have your portion in the lake that burns with fire and brimstone. Though there are so many that seem to obtain so easily, having been but a little while under convictions, yet, for all that, some never will obtain. Some will soon lose the sense of things they now have; though their awakenings seem to be very considerable for the present, they will not hold; they have not hearts disposed to hold on through very many difficulties. Some that have set out for heaven, and hope as much as others to obtain, are indeed but slighty and slack, even now, in the midst of such a time as this. And others, who for the present seem to be more in earnest, will probably, before long, decline and fail, and gradually return to be as they were before. The convictions of some seem to be great, while that which is the occasion of their convictions is new; which, when that begins to grow old, will gradually decay and wear off. Thus, it may be, the occasion of your awakening has been the hearing of the conversion of some person, or seeing so extraordinary a dispensation of Providence as this in which God now appears amongst us; but by and by the newness and freshness of these things will be gone, and so will not affect your mind as now they do; and it may be your convictions will go away with it.

Though this be a time wherein God doth more liberally bestow his grace, and so a time of greater advantage for obtaining it; yet there seems to be, upon some accounts, greater danger of backsliding, than when persons are awakened at other times. For commonly such extraordinary times do not last long; and then when they cease, there are multitudes that lose their convictions as it were together.

We speak of it as a happy thing, that God is pleased to cause such a time amongst us, and so it is indeed: but there are some to whom it will be no benefit; it will be an occasion of their greater misery; they will wish they had never seen this time; it will be more tolerable for those that never saw it, or any thing like it, in the day of judgment, than for them. It is an awful consideration, that there are probably those here, whom the great Judge will hereafter call to a strict account about this very thing, why they no better improved this opportunity, when he set open the fountain of his grace, and so loudly called upon them, and came and strove with them in particular, by the awakening influences of his Spirit; and they will have no good account to give to the Judge, but their mouths will be stopped, and they will stand speechless before him.

You had need therefore to be earnest, and very resolved in this affair, that you may not be one of those who shall thus fail, that you may so fight, as not uncertainly, and so run, as that you may win the prize.

5. Consider in what sad circumstances times of extraordinary effusion of God's Spirit commonly leave persons, when they leave them unconverted. They *find* them in a doleful, because in a natural, condition; but commonly *leave* them in a much more doleful condition. They are left dreadfully hardened, and with a great increase of guilt, and their souls under a more strong dominion and possession of Satan. And frequently seasons of extraordinary advantage for salvation, when they pass over persons, and they do not improve them, nor receive any good in them, seal their damnation. As such seasons leave them, God for ever leaves them, and gives them up to judicial hardness. Luke xix. 41, 42. "And when he was come near, he beheld the city, and wept over it, saying, If thou hadst known, even thou, the things which belong unto thy peace! but now they are hid from thine eyes."

6. Consider, that it is very uncertain whether you will ever see such another time as this. If there should be such another time, it is very uncertain whether you will live to see it. Many that are now concerned for their salvation amongst us, will probably be in their graves, and it may be in hell, before that time; and if you should miss this opportunity, it may be so with you. And what good will that do you, to have the Spirit of God poured out upon earth, in the place where you once lived, while you are tormented in hell? What will it avail you, that others are crying, What shall I do to be saved? while you are shut up for ever in the bottomless pit, and are wailing and gnashing your teeth in everlasting burnings?

Wherefore improve this opportunity, while God is pouring out his Spirit, and you are on earth, and while you dwell in that place where the Spirit of God is thus poured out, and you yourself have the awakening influences of it, that you may never wail and gnash your teeth in hell, but may sing in heaven for ever, with others that are redeemed from amongst men, and redeemed amongst us.

7. If you should see another such time, it will be under far greater disadvantages than now. You will probably then be much older, and will have more hardened your heart; and so will be under less probability of receiving good. Some persons are so hardened in sin, and so left of God, that they can live through such a time as this, and not be much awakened or affected by it; they can stand their ground, and be but little moved. And so it may be with you, by another such time, if there should be another amongst us, and you should live to see it. The case in all probability will be greatly altered with you by that time. If you should continue Christless and graceless till then, you will be much further from the kingdom of God, and much deeper involved in snares and misery; and the devil will probably have a vastly greater advantage against you, to tempt and confound you.

8. We do not know but that God is now gathering in his elect, before some great and sore judgment. It has been God's manner before he casts off a visible people, or brings some great and destroying judgments upon them, first to gather in his elect, that they may be secure. So it was before the casting off the Jews from being God's people. There was first a very remarkable pouring out of the Spirit, and gathering in of the elect, by the preaching of the apostles and evangelists, as we read in the beginning of the Acts: but after this harvest and its gleanings were over, the rest were blinded, and hardened; the gospel had little success amongst them, and the nation was given up, and cast off from being God's people, and their city and land was destroyed by the Romans in a terrible manner; and they have been cast off by God now for a great many ages, and still remain a hardened and rejected people. So we read in the beginning of the 7th chapter of the Revelations, that God, when about to bring destroying judgments on the earth, first sealed his servants in the forehead. He set his seal upon the hearts of the elect, gave them the saving influences and indwelling of his Spirit, by which they were sealed to the day of redemption. Rev. vii. 1—3. "And after these things, I saw four angels standing on the four corners of the earth, holding the four winds of the earth, that the wind should not blow on the earth, nor on the sea, nor on any tree. And I saw another angel ascending from the east, having the seal of the living God: and he cried with a loud voice to the four angels, to whom it was given to hurt the earth and the sea, saying, Hurt not the earth, neither the sea, nor the trees, till we have sealed the servants of our God in their foreheads."

And this may be the case now, that God is about, in a great measure, to forsake this land, and give up this people, and to bring most awful and overwhelming judgments upon it, and that he is now gathering in his elect, to secure them from the calamity. The state of the nation, and of this land, never looked so threatening of such a thing as at this day. The present aspect of things exceedingly threatens vital religion, and even those truths that are especially the foundation of it, out of this land. If it should be so, how awful will the case be with those that shall be left, and not brought in, while God continues the influences of his Spirit, to gather in those that are to be redeemed from amongst us!

9. If you neglect the present opportunity, and be finally unbelieving, those that are converted in this time of the pouring out of God's Spirit will rise up in judgment against you. Your neighbours, your relations, acquaintance, or companions that are converted, will that day appear against you. They will not only be taken while you are left, mounting up with joy to meet the Lord in the air—at his right hand with glorious saints and angels, while you are at the left with devils—but how they will rise up in judgment *against* you. However friendly you have been together, and have taken pleasure in one another's company, and have often familiarly conversed together, they will then surely appear against you. They will rise up as witnesses, and will declare what a precious opportunity you had, and did not improve; how you continued unbelieving, and rejected the offers of a Saviour, when those offers were made in so extraordinary a manner, and when so many others were prevailed upon to accept of Christ; how you was negligent and slack, and did not know the things that belonged to your peace, in that your day. And not only so, but they shall be your judges, as assessors with the great Judge; and as such will appear against you; they will be with the Judge in passing sentence upon you. 1 Cor. vi. 2. "Know ye not that the saints shall judge the world?" Christ will admit them to the honour of judging the world with him: "They shall sit with him in his throne," Rev. iii. 21. They shall sit with Christ in his throne of government, and they shall sit with him in his throne of judgment, and shall be judges with him when you are judged, and as such shall condemn you.

10. And *lastly*, You do not know that you shall live through the present time of the pouring out of God's Spirit. You may be taken away in the midst of it, or you may be taken away in the beginning of it; as God in his providence is putting you in mind, by the late instance of death in a young person in the town.* God has of late been very awful in his dealings with us, in the repeated deaths of young persons amongst us. This should stir every one up to be in the more haste to press into the kingdom of God, that so you may be safe whenever death comes. This is a blessed season and opportunity; but you do not know how little of it you may have. You may have much less of it than others; may by death be suddenly snatched away from all advantages that are here enjoyed for the good of souls. Therefore make haste, and escape for thy life. One moment's delay is dangerous; for wrath is pursuing, and divine vengeance hanging over every uncovered person.

Let these considerations move every one to be improving this opportunity, that while others receive saving good, and are made heirs of eternal glory, you may not be left behind, in the same miserable doleful circumstances in which you came into the world, a poor captive to sin and Satan, a lost sheep, a perishing, undone creature, sinking down into everlasting perdition; that you may not be one of them spoken of, Jer. xvii. 6. "That shall be like the heath in the desert, and shall not see when good comes." If you do not improve this opportunity, remember I have told you, you will hereafter lament it; and if you do not

* Joseph Clark's wife, a young woman lately married, that died suddenly the week before this was delivered.

lament it in this world, then I will leave it with you to remember it throughout a miserable eternity.

II. I would address myself to such as yet remain unawakened. It is an awful thing that there should be any one person remaining secure amongst us at such a time as this; but yet it is to be feared that there are some of this sort. I would here a little expostulate with such persons.

1. When do you expect that it will be more likely that you should be awakened and wrought upon than now? You are in a Christless condition; and yet without doubt intend to go to heaven; and therefore intend to be converted some time before you die; but this is not to be expected till you are first awakened, and deeply concerned about the welfare of your soul, and brought earnestly to seek God's converting grace. And when do you intend that this shall be? How do you lay things out in your own mind, or what projection have you about this matter? Is it ever so likely that a person will be awakened, as at such a time as this? How do we see many, who before were secure, now roused out of their sleep, and crying, What shall I do to be saved? But you are yet secure! Do you flatter yourself that it will be more likely you should be awakened when it is a dull and dead time? Do you lay matters out thus in your own mind, that though you are senseless when others are generally awakened, that yet you shall be awakened when others are generally senseless? Or do you hope to see another such time of the pouring out of God's Spirit hereafter? And do you think it will be more likely that you should be wrought upon then, than now? And why do you think so? Is it because then you shall be so much older than you are now, and so that your heart will be grown softer and more tender with age? or because you will then have stood out so much longer against the calls of the gospel, and all means of grace? Do you think it more likely that God will give you the needed influences of his Spirit then, than now, because then you will have provoked him so much more, and your sin and guilt will be so much greater? And do you think it will be any benefit to you, to stand it out through the present season of grace, as proof against the extraordinary means of awakening there are? Do you think that this will be a good preparation for a saving work of the Spirit hereafter?

2. What means do you expect to be awakened by? As to the awakening awful things of the word of God, you have had those set before you times without number, in the most moving manner that the dispensers of the word have been capable of. As to particular solemn warnings, directed to those that are in your circumstances, you have had them frequently, and have them now from time to time. Do you expect to be awakened by awful providences? Those also you have lately had, of the most awakening nature, one after another. Do you expect to be moved by the deaths of others? We have lately had repeated instances of these. There have been deaths of old and young: the year has been remarkable for the deaths of young persons in the bloom of life; and some of them very sudden deaths. Will the conversion of others move you? There is indeed scarce any thing that is found to have so great a tendency to stir persons up as this: and this you have been tried with of late in frequent instances; but are hitherto proof against it. Will a general pouring out of the Spirit, and seeing a concern about salvation amongst all sorts of people, do it? This means you now have, but without effect. Yea, you have all these things together; you have the solemn warnings of God's word, and awful instances of death, and the conversion of others, and see a general concern about salvation: but all together do not move you to any great concern about your own precious, immortal, and miserable soul. Therefore consider by what means it is that you expect ever to be awakened.

You have heard that it is probable some who are now awakened, will never obtain salvation; how dark then does it look upon you that remain stupidly unawakened! Those who are not moved at such a time as this, come to adult age, have reason to fear whether they are not given up to judicial hardness. I do not say they have reason to *conclude* it, but they have reason to fear it. How dark doth it look upon you, that God comes and knocks at so many persons' doors, and misses yours! that God is giving the strivings of his Spirit so generally amongst us, while you are left senseless!

3. Do you expect to obtain salvation without ever seeking it? If you are sensible that there is a necessity of your seeking in order to obtaining, and ever intend to seek, one would think you could not avoid it at such a time as this. Inquire therefore, whether you intend to go to heaven, living all your days a secure, negligent, careless life.——Or,

4. Do you think you can bear the damnation of hell? Do you imagine that you can tolerably endure the devouring fire, and everlasting burnings? Do you hope that you shall be able to grapple with the vengeance of God Almighty, when he girds himself with strength, and clothes himself with wrath? Do you think to strengthen yourself against God, and to be able to make your part good with him? 1 Cor. x. 22. "Do we provoke the Lord to jealousy? are we stronger than he?" Do you flatter yourself that you shall find out ways for your ease and support, and to make it out tolerably well, to bear up your spirit in those everlasting burnings that are prepared for the devil and his angels? Ezek. xxii. 14. "Can thine heart endure, or can thine hands be strong, in the days that I shall deal with thee?"—It is a difficult thing to conceive what such Christless persons think, that are unconcerned at such a time.

III. I would direct myself to them who are grown considerably into years, and are yet in a natural condition. I would now take occasion earnestly to exhort you to improve this extraordinary opportunity, and press into the kingdom of God. You have lost many advantages that once you had, and now have not the same advantages that others have. The case is very different with you from what it is with many of your neighbours. You, above all, had need to improve such an opportunity. Now is the time for you to bestir yourself, and take the kingdom of heaven!—Consider,

1. Now there seems to be a door opened for old sinners. Now God is dealing forth freely to all sorts: his hand is opened wide, and he does not pass by old ones so much as he used to do. You are not under such advantages as others who are younger; but yet, so wonderfully has God ordered it, that now you are not destitute of great advantage. Though old in sin, God has put a new and extraordinary advantage into your hands. O! improve this price you have to get wisdom! You that have been long seeking to enter in at the strait gate and yet remain without, now take your opportunity and press in! You that have been long in the wilderness, fighting with various temptations, labouring under discouragements, ready to give up the case, and have been often tempted to despair, now, behold the door that God opens for you! Do not give way to discouragements now; this is not a time for it. Do not spend time in thinking, that you have done what you can already, and that you are not elected, and in giving way to other perplexing, weakening, disheartening temptations. Do not waste away this precious opportunity in such a manner. You have no time to spare for such things as these; God calls you now to something else. Improve this time in seeking and striving for salvation, and not in that which tends to hinder it.—It is no time now for you to stand talking with the devil; but hearken to God, and apply yourself to that which he does now so loudly call you to.

Some of you have often lamented the loss of past opportunities, particularly, the loss of the time of youth, and have been wishing that you had so good an opportunity again; and have been ready to say, "O! if I was young again, how would I improve such an advantage!" That opportunity which you have had in time past is irrecoverable; you can never have it again: but God can give you other advantages of another sort, that are very great, and he is so doing at this day. He is now putting a new opportunity into your hands; though not of the same kind with that which you once had, and have lost, yet in some respects as great of another kind. If you lament your folly in neglecting and losing past opportunities, then do not be guilty of the folly of neglecting the opportunity which God now gives you. This opportunity you could not have purchased, if you would have given all that you had in the world for it. But God is putting it into your hands himself, of his own free and sovereign mercy, without your purchasing it. Therefore when you have it, do not neglect it.

2. It is a great deal more likely with respect to such persons than others, that this is their last time. There will be a last time of special offer of salvation to impenitent sinners.—"God's Spirit shall not always strive with man," Gen. vi. 3. God sometimes continues long knocking at the doors of wicked men's hearts; but there are the *last* knocks, and the *last* calls that ever they shall have. And sometimes God's last calls are the loudest; and then if sinners do not hearken, he finally leaves them. How long has God been knocking at many of your doors that are old in sin! It is a great deal more likely that these are his last knocks. You have resisted God's Spirit in times past, and have hardened your heart once and again; but God will not be thus dealt with always. There is danger, that if now, after so long a time, you will not hearken, he will utterly desert you, and leave you to walk in your own counsels.

It seems by God's providence, as though God had yet an elect number amongst old sinners in this place, that perhaps he is now about to bring in. It looks as though there were some that long lived under Mr. Stoddard's ministry, that God has not utterly cast off, though they stood it out under such great means as they then enjoyed. It is to be hoped that God will now bring in a remnant from among them. But it is the more likely that God is now about finishing with them, one way or other, for their having been so long the subjects of such extraordinary means. You have seen former times of the pouring out of God's Spirit upon the town, when others were taken and you left, others were called out of darkness into marvellous light, and were brought into a glorious and happy state, and you saw not good when good came. How dark will your circumstances appear, if you shall also stand it out through this opportunity, and still be left behind! Take heed that you be not of those spoken of, Heb. vi. 7, 8. that are like the "earth that has rain coming oft upon it, and only bears briers and thorns." As we see there are some pieces of ground, the more showers of rain fall upon them, the more fruitful seasons there are, the more do the briers, and other useless and hurtful plants, that are rooted in them, grow and flourish. Of such ground the apostle says, "It is rejected, and is nigh unto cursing, whose end is to be burned." The way that the husbandman takes with such ground, is, to set fire to it, to burn up the growth of it.—If you miss this opportunity, there is danger that you will be utterly rejected, and that your end will be to be burned. And if this is to be, it is to be feared, that you are not far from, but nigh unto, cursing.

Those of you that are already grown old in sin, and are now under awakenings, when you feel your convictions begin to go off, if ever that should be, then remember what you have now been told; it may well then strike you to the heart!

IV. I would direct the advice to those that are young, and now under their first special convictions. I would earnestly urge such to improve this opportunity, and press into the kingdom of God.—Consider two things,

1. You have all manner of advantages now centering upon you. It is a time of great advantage for all; but your advantages are above others. There is no other sort of persons that have now so great and happy an opportunity as you have.—You have the great advantage that is common to all who live in this place, *viz.* That now it is a time of the extraordinary pouring out of the Spirit of God. And have you not that great advantage, the awakening influences of the Spirit of God on you in particular? and besides, you have this peculiar advantage, that you are now in your youth. And added to this, you have another unspeakable advantage, that you now are under your first convictions. Happy is he that never has hardened his heart, and blocked up his own way to heaven by backsliding, and has now the awakening influences of God's Spirit, if God does but enable him thoroughly to improve them! Such above all in the world bid fair for the kingdom of God. God is wont on such, above any kind of persons, as it were easily and readily to bestow the saving grace and comforts of his Spirit. Instances of speedy and sudden conversion are most commonly found among such. Happy are they that have the Spirit of God with them, and never have quenched it, if they did but know the price they have in their hands!

If you have a sense of your necessity of salvation, and the great worth and value of it, you will be willing to take the surest way to it, or that which has the greatest probability of success; and that certainly is, thoroughly to improve your first convictions. If you do so, it is not likely that you will fail; there is the greatest probability that you will succeed.—What is it not worth, to have such an advantage in one's hands for obtaining eternal life? The present season of the pouring out of God's Spirit, is the first that many of you who are now under awakenings have ever seen, since you came to years of understanding. On which account, it is the greatest opportunity that ever you have had, and probably by far the greatest that ever you will have. There are many here present who wish they had such an opportunity, but they never can obtain it; they cannot buy it for money; but you have it in your possession, and can improve it if you will. But yet,

2. There is on some accounts greater danger that such as are in your circumstances will fail of thoroughly improving their convictions, with respect to stedfastness and perseverance, than others. Those that are young are more unstable than elder persons. They who never had convictions before, have less experience of the difficulty of the work they have engaged in; they are more ready to think that they shall obtain salvation easily, and are more easily discouraged by disappointments; and young persons have less reason and consideration to fortify them against temptations to backsliding. You should therefore labour now the more to guard against such temptations. By all means make but one work of seeking salvation! Make thorough work of it the first time! There are vast disadvantages that they bring themselves under, who have several turns of seeking with great intermissions. By such a course, persons exceedingly wound their own souls, and entangle themselves in many snares. Who are those that commonly meet with so many difficulties, and are so long labouring in darkness and perplexity, but those who have had several turns at seeking salvation; who have one while had convictions, and then have quenched them, and then have set about the work again, and have backslidden again, and have gone on after that manner? The children of Israel would not have been forty years in the wilderness, if they had held their courage, and had gone on as they set out; but they were of an unstable mind, and were for going back again into Egypt.—Otherwise, if they had gone right forward without discouragement, as God would have led them, they would have soon entered and taken possession of Canaan. They had got to the very borders of it when they turned back, but were thirty-eight years after that, before they got through the wilderness. Therefore, as you regard the interest of your soul, do not run yourself into a like difficulty, by unsteadiness, intermission, and backsliding; but press right forward, from henceforth, and make but one work of seeking, converting, and pardoning grace, however great, and difficult, and long a work that may be.

DISCOURSE III.

RUTH'S RESOLUTION.

Ruth i. 16.

And Ruth said, Entreat me not to leave thee, or to return from following after thee: for whither thou goest, I will go; and where thou lodgest, I will lodge: thy people shall be my people, and thy God my God.

The historical things in this book of Ruth, seem to be inserted in the canon of the Scripture, especially on two accounts:

First, Because Christ was of Ruth's posterity. The Holy Ghost thought fit to take particular notice of that marriage of Boaz with Ruth, whence sprang the Saviour of the world. We may often observe it, that the Holy Spirit who indited the Scriptures, often takes notice of little things, or minute occurrences, that do but remotely relate to Jesus Christ.

Secondly, Because this history seems to be typical of the calling of the Gentile church, and indeed of the conversion of every believer. Ruth was not originally of Israel, but was a Moabitess, an alien from the commonwealth of Israel: but she forsook her own people, and the idols of the Gentiles, to worship the God of Israel, and to join herself to that people. Herein she seems to be a type of the Gentile church, and also of every sincere convert. Ruth was the remote mother of Christ; he came of her posterity: so the church is Christ's mother, as she is represented, Rev. xii. at the beginning. And so also is every true Christian his mother. Matt. xii. 50. "Whosoever shall do the will of my Father which is in heaven, the same is my brother, and sister, and mother." Christ is what the soul is in travail with, at the new birth. Ruth forsook all her natural relations, and her own country, the land of her nativity, and all her former possessions there, for the sake of the God of Israel; as every true Christian forsakes all for Christ. Psalm xlv. 10. "Hearken, O daughter, and consider, and incline thine ear; forget also thine own people, and thy father's house."

Naomi was now returning out of the land of Moab, into the land of Israel, with her two daughters-in-law, Orpah and Ruth; who will represent to us two sorts of professors of religion: Orpah, those who indeed make a fair profession, and seem to set out well, but continue only for a while, and then turn back; Ruth, those who are sound and sincere, and therefore are stedfast and persevering in their way. Naomi, in the preceding verses, represents to her daughters the difficulties of their leaving their own country to go with her. And in this verse may be observed,

1. The remarkable conduct and behaviour of Ruth on this occasion; with what inflexible resolution she cleaves to Naomi, and follows her. When Naomi first arose to return from the country of Moab into the land of Israel, Orpah and Ruth both set out with her; and Naomi exhorts them both to return. And both wept, and seemed as if they could not bear the thoughts of leaving her, and appeared as if they were resolved to go with her. Verse 10. "And they said unto her, Surely we will return with thee unto thy people." Then Naomi says to them again, "Turn again, my daughters, go your way," &c. And then they were greatly affected again, and Orpah returned and went back. Now Ruth's stedfastness in her purpose had a greater trial, but yet is not overcome: "She clave unto her," verse 14. Then Naomi speaks to her again, verse 15. "Behold, thy sister-in-law is gone back unto her people, and unto her gods; return thou after thy sister-in-law." And then she shows her immovable resolution in the text and following verse.

2. I would particularly observe that wherein the virtuousness of this her resolution consists, *viz.* that it was for the sake of the God of Israel, and that she might be one of his people, that she was thus resolved to cleave to Naomi: "Thy people shall be my people, and thy God my God." It was for God's sake that she did thus; and therefore her so doing is afterwards spoken of as a virtuous behaviour in her, chap. ii. 11, 12. "And Boaz answered and said unto her, It hath fully been showed me, all that thou hast done unto thy mother-in-law since the death of thine husband; and how thou hast left thy father, and thy mother, and the land of thy nativity, and art come unto a people which thou knewest not heretofore. The Lord recompense thy work, and a full reward be given thee of the Lord God of Israel, under whose wings thou art come to trust." She left her father and mother, and the land of her nativity, to come and trust under the shadow of God's wings; and she had indeed a full reward given her, as Boaz wished; for besides immediate spiritual blessings to her own soul, and eternal rewards in another world, she was rewarded with plentiful and prosperous outward circumstances in the family of Boaz. And God raised up David and Solomon of her seed, and established the crown of Israel (the people that she chose before her own people) in her posterity; and, which is much more, of her seed he raised up Jesus Christ, in whom all the families of the earth are blessed.

From the words thus opened, I observe this for the subject of my present discourse:—"When those that we have formerly been conversant with, are turning to God, and joining themselves to his people, it ought to be our firm resolution, that we will not leave them; but that their people shall be our people, and their God our God."

It sometimes happens, that of those who have been conversant one with another—who have dwelt together as neighbours, and have been often together as companions, or united in their relation, and have been together in darkness, bondage, and misery, in the service of Satan—some are enlightened, and have their minds changed, are made to see the great evil of sin, and have their hearts turned to God. They are influenced by the Holy Spirit of God, to leave their company that are on Satan's side, and to join themselves with that blessed company that are with Jesus Christ. They are made willing to forsake the tents of wickedness, to dwell in the land of uprightness with the people of God.

And sometimes this proves a final parting or separation between them and those with whom they have been formerly conversant. Though it may be no parting in outward respects, they may still dwell, and converse one with another; yet in other respects, it sets them at a great distance. One is a child of God, and the other his enemy; one is in a miserable, and the other in a happy, condition; one is a citizen of the heavenly Zion, the other is under condemnation to hell. They are no longer together in those respects wherein they used to be together. They used to be of one mind to serve sin, and do Satan's work; now they are of contrary minds. They used to be together in worldliness and sinful vanity; now they are of exceeding different dispositions. They are separated as they are in different kingdoms; the one remains in the kingdom of darkness, the other is translated into the kingdom of God's dear Son. And sometimes they are finally separated in these respects: while one dwells in the land of Israel, and in the house of God; the other, like Orpah, lives and dies in the land of Moab.

Now it is lamentable, it is awful being parted so. It is doleful, when of those who have formerly been together in sin, some turn to God, and join themselves with his people, that it should prove a *parting* between them and their former companions and acquaintance. It should be our firm and inflexible resolution in such a case, that it shall be no parting, but that we will follow them, that their people shall be our people, and their God our God; and that for the following reasons:

I. Because their *God* is a glorious God. There is none like him, who is infinite in glory and excellency. He is the most high God, glorious in holiness, fearful in praises, doing wonders. His name is excellent in all the earth, and his glory is above the heavens. Among the gods there is none like unto him; there is none in heaven to be compared to him, nor are there any among the sons of the mighty that can be likened unto him. Their God is the fountain of all good, and an inexhaustible fountain; he is an all-sufficient God, able to protect and defend them, and do all things for them. He is the King of glory, the Lord strong and mighty, the Lord mighty in battle: a strong rock, and a high tower. There is none like the God of Jeshurun, who rideth on the heaven in their help, and in his excellency on the sky: the eternal God is their refuge, and underneath are everlasting arms. He is a God who hath all things in his hands, and does whatsoever he pleases: he killeth and maketh alive; he bringeth down to the grave and bringeth up; he maketh poor and maketh rich: the pillars of the earth are the Lord's. Their God is an infinitely holy God; there is none holy as the Lord. And he is infinitely good and merciful. Many that others worship and serve as gods, are cruel beings, spirits that seek the ruin of souls; but this is a God that delighteth in mercy; his grace is infinite, and endures for ever. He is love itself, an infinite fountain and ocean of it.

Such a God is their God! Such is the excellency of Jacob! Such is the God of them who have forsaken their sins and are converted! They have made a wise choice who have chosen this for their God. They have made a happy exchange indeed, that have exchanged sin, and the world, for such a God!

They have an excellent and glorious Saviour, who is the only-begotten Son of God; the brightness of his Father's glory; one in whom God from eternity had infinite delight; a Saviour of infinite love; one that has shed his own blood, and made his soul an offering for their sins, and one that is able to save them to the uttermost.

II. Their *people* are an excellent and happy people. God has renewed them, and stamped his own image upon them, and made them partakers of his holiness. They are more excellent than their neighbours, Prov. xii. 26. Yea, they are the excellent of the earth, Psalm xvi. 3. They are lovely in the sight of the angels; and they have their souls adorned with those graces that in the sight of God himself are of great price.

The people of God are the most excellent and happy society in the world. That God whom they have chosen for their God, is their Father; he has pardoned all their sins, and they are at peace with him; and he has admitted them to all the privileges of his children. As they have devoted themselves to God, so he has given himself to them. He is become their salvation, and their portion: his power and mercy, and all his attributes, are theirs. They are in a safe state, free from all possibility of perishing: Satan has no power to destroy them. God carries them on eagle's wings, far above Satan's reach, and above the reach of all the enemies of their souls. God is with them in this world; they have his gracious presence. God is for them; who then can be against them? As the mountains are round about Jerusalem, so Jehovah is round about them. God is their shield, and their exceeding great reward; and their fellowship is with the Father, and with his Son Jesus Christ: and they have the divine promise and oath, that in the world to come they shall dwell for ever in the glorious presence of God.

It may well be sufficient to induce us to resolve to cleave to those that forsake their sins and idols to join themselves with this people, that God is with them, Zech. viii. 23. "Thus saith the Lord of hosts, in those days it shall come to pass, that ten men shall take hold out of all languages of the nations, even shall take hold of the skirt of him that is a Jew, saying, We will go with you; for we have heard that God is with you." So should persons, as it were, take hold of the skirt of their neighbours and companions that have turned to God, and resolve that they will go with them, because God is with them.

III. *Happiness* is no where else to be had, but in their God, and with their people. There are that are called gods many, and lords many. Some make gods of their pleasures; some choose Mammon for their god; some make gods of their own supposed excellences, or the outward advantages they have above their neighbours: some choose one thing for their god, and others another. But men can be happy in no other but the God of Israel: he is the only fountain of happiness. Other gods cannot help in calamity; nor can any of them afford what the poor empty soul stands in need of. Let men adore those other gods never so much, and call upon them never so earnestly, and serve them never so diligently, they will nevertheless remain poor, wretched, unsatisfied, undone creatures. All other people are miserable, but that people whose God is the Lord.—The world is divided into two societies: *the people of God*, the little flock of Jesus Christ, that company that we read of, Rev. xiv. 4. "These are they which were not defiled with women; for they are virgins: these are they which follow the Lamb whithersoever he goeth: these were redeemed from among men, being the first-fruits unto God, and to the Lamb:" and, *those that belong to the kingdom of darkness*, that are without Christ, being aliens from the commonwealth of Israel, strangers from the covenant of promise, having no hope, and without God in the world. All that are of this latter company are wretched and undone; they are the enemies of God, and under his wrath and condemnation. They are the devil's slaves, that serve him blindfold, and are befooled and ensnared by him, and hurried along in the broad way to eternal perdition.

IV. When those that we have formerly been conversant with are turning to God and to his people, their *example* ought to influence us. Their example should be looked upon as the call of God to us, to do as they have done. God, when he changes the heart of one, calls upon another; especially does he loudly call on those that have been their friends and acquaintance. We have been influenced by their examples in evil; and shall we cease to follow them, when they make the wisest choice that ever they made, and do the best thing that ever they did? If we have been companions with them in worldliness, in vanity, in unprofitable and sinful conversation, it will be a hard case, if there must be a parting now, because we are not willing to be companions with them in holiness and true happiness. Men are greatly influenced by seeing one another's prosperity in other things. If those whom they have been much conversant with, grow rich, and obtain any great earthly advantages, it awakens their ambition, and eager desire after the like prosperity: how much more should they be influenced, and stirred up to follow them, and be like them, when they obtain that spiritual and eternal happiness, that is of infinitely more worth, than all the prosperity and glory of this world!

V. Our *resolutions* to cleave to and follow those that are turning to God, and joining themselves to his people, ought to be *fixed* and strong, because of the great difficulty of it. If we will cleave to them, and have their God for our God, and their people for our people, we must mortify and deny all our lusts, and cross every evil appetite and inclination, and for ever part with all sin. But our lusts are many and violent. Sin is naturally exceeding dear to us; to part with it is compared to plucking out our right eyes. Men may refrain from wonted ways of sin for a little while, and may deny their lusts in a partial degree, with less difficulty; but it is heart-rending work, finally to part with all sin, and to give our dearest lusts a bill of divorce, utterly to send them away. But this we must do, if we would follow those that are truly turning to God: yea, we must not only forsake sin, but must, in a sense, forsake all the world, Luke xiv. 33. "Whosoever he be of you that forsaketh not all that he hath, he cannot be my disciple." That is, he must forsake all in his heart, and must come to a thorough disposition and readiness actually to quit all for God, and the glorious spiritual privileges of his people, whenever the case may require it; and that without any prospect of any thing of the like nature, or any worldly thing whatsoever, to make amends for it; and all to go into a strange country, a land that has hitherto been unseen; like Abraham, who being called of God, "went out of his own country, and from his kindred, and from his father's house, for a land that God should show him, not knowing whither he went."

Thus, it was a hard thing for Ruth to forsake her native country, her father and mother, her kindred and acquaintance, and all the pleasant things she had in the land of Moab, to dwell in the land of Israel, where she never had been. Naomi told her of the difficulties once and again. They were too hard for her sister Orpah; the consideration of them turned her back after she was set out. Her resolution was not firm enough to overcome them. But so firmly resolved was Ruth, that she brake through all; she was stedfast in it, that, let the difficulty be what it would, she would not leave her mother-in-law. So persons had need to be very firm in their resolution to conquer the difficulties that are in the way of cleaving to them who are indeed turning from sin to God.

Our cleaving to them, and having their God for our God, and their people for our people, depends on our resolution and choice; and that in two respects.

1. The firmness of resolution in using means in order to it, is the way to have means effectual. There are means appointed in order to our becoming some of the true Israel, and having their God for our God; and the thorough use of these means is the way to have success; but not a slack or slighty use of them. And that we may be thorough, there is need of strength of resolution, a firm and inflexible disposition and bent of mind to be universal in the use of means, and to do what we do with our might, and to persevere in it. Matt. xi. 12. "The kingdom of heaven suffereth violence, and the violent take it by force."

2. A choosing of their God, and their people, with a full determination, and with the whole soul, is the condition of an union with them. God gives every man his choice in this matter: as Orpah and Ruth had their choice, whether they would go with Naomi into the land of Israel, or stay in the land of Moab. A natural man may choose deliverance from hell; but no man doth ever heartily choose God and Christ, and the spiritual benefits that Christ has purchased, and the happiness of God's people, till he is converted. On the contrary, he is averse to them; he has no relish of them; and is wholly ignorant of their inestimable worth and value.

Many carnal men seem to choose these things, but do it not really; as Orpah seemed at first to choose to forsake Moab to go into the land of Israel: but when Naomi came to set before her the difficulty of it, she went back; and thereby showed that she was not fully determined in her choice, and that her whole soul was not in it as Ruth's was.

APPLICATION.

The use that I shall make of what has been said, is to move sinners to this resolution, with respect to those amongst us that have lately turned to God, and joined themselves to the flock of Christ. Through the abundant mercy and grace of God to us in this place, it may be said of many of you that are in a Christless condition, that you have lately been left by those that were formerly with you in such a state. Some of those with whom you have formerly been conversant, have lately forsaken a life of sin and the service of Satan, and have turned to God, and fled to Christ, and joined themselves to that blessed company that are with him. They formerly were with you in sin and in misery; but now they are with you no more in that state or manner of life. They are changed, and have fled from the wrath to come; they have chosen a life of holiness here, and the enjoyment of God hereafter. They were formerly your associates in bondage, and were with you in Satan's business; but now you have their company no longer in these things. Many of you have seen those you live with, under the same roof, turning from being any longer with you in sin, to be with the people of Jesus Christ. Some of you that are husbands, have had your wives; and some of you that are wives, have had your husbands; some of you that are children, have had your parents; and parents have had your children; many of you have had your brothers and sisters; and many your near neighbours, and acquaintance, and special friends; many of you that are young have had your companions: I say, many of you have had those that you have been thus concerned with, leaving you, forsaking that doleful life and wretched state in which you still continue. God, of his good pleasure and wonderful grace, hath lately caused in this place multitudes to forsake their old abodes in the land of Moab, and under the gods of Moab, and go into the land of Israel, to put their trust under the wings of the Lord God of Israel. Though you and they have been nearly related, and have dwelt together, or have been often together and intimately acquainted, they have been taken, and you hitherto left! O let it not be the foundation of a final parting! But earnestly follow them; be firm in your resolution in this matter. Do not as Orpah did, who, though at first she made as though she would follow Naomi, yet when she had the difficulty set before her, went back: but say as Ruth, "I will not leave thee; but where thou goest, I will go: thy people shall be my people, and thy God my God." Say as she said, and do as she did. Consider the excellency of their God, and their Saviour, and the happiness of their people, the blessed state that they are in, and the doleful state you are in.

You are *old* sinners, who have lived long in the service of Satan, have lately seen some that have travelled with you in the paths of sin these many years, turning to God. They with you enjoyed great means and advantages, had calls and warnings with you, and with you passed through remarkable times of the pouring out of God's Spirit in this place, and hardened their hearts and stood it out with you, and with you have grown old in sin; yet you have seen some of them turning to God, *i. e.* you have seen those evidences of it in them, whence you may rationally judge that it is so. O! let it not be a final parting! You have been thus long together in sin, and under condemnation; let it be your firm resolution, that, if possible, you will be with them still, now they are in a holy and happy state, and that you will follow them into the holy and pleasant land.—You that tell of your having been seeking salvation for many years, (though, without doubt, in a poor dull way, in comparison of what you ought to have done,) have seen some old sinners and old seekers, as you are, obtaining mercy. God has lately roused them from their dulness, and caused them to alter their hand, and put them on more thorough endeavours; and they have now, after so long a time, heard God's voice, and have fled for refuge to the rock of ages. Let this awaken earnestness and resolution in you. Resolve that you will not leave them.

You who are in your *youth*, how many have you seen of your age and standing, that have of late hopefully chosen God for their God, and Christ for their Saviour! You have followed them in sin, and have perhaps followed them into vain company; and will you not now follow them to Christ?—And you who are *children*, know that there have lately been some of your sort who have repented of their sins, loved the Lord Jesus Christ, and trusted in him, and are become God's children, as we have reason to hope: let it stir you up to resolve to your utmost to seek and cry to God, that you may have the like change made in your hearts, that their people may be your people, and their God your God.

You who are great sinners, who have made yourselves distinguishingly guilty by the wicked practices you have lived in, know that there are some of your sort who have lately (as we have reason to hope) had their hearts broken for sin, and have forsaken it, and trusted in the blood of Christ for the pardon of it. They have chosen a holy life, and have betaken themselves to the ways of wisdom: let it excite and encourage you resolutely to cleave to them, and earnestly to follow them.

Let the following things be considered:

1. That your soul is as precious as theirs. It is immortal as theirs is; and stands in as much need of happiness, and can as ill bear eternal misery. You was born in the same miserable condition that they were, having the same wrath of God abiding on you. You must stand before the same Judge; who will be as strict in judgment with you as with them; and your own righteousness will stand you in no more stead before him than theirs; and therefore you stand in as absolute necessity of a Saviour as they. Carnal confidences can no more answer your end than theirs; nor

can this world or its enjoyments serve to make you happy without God and Christ, more than them. When the bridegroom comes, the foolish virgins stand in as much need of oil as the wise, Matt. xxv. at the beginning.

2. Unless you follow them in their turning to God, their conversion will be a foundation of an eternal separation between you and them. You will be in different interests, and in exceeding different states, as long as you live; they the children of God, and you the children of Satan; and you will be parted in another world; when you come to die, there will be a vast separation made between you. Luke xvi. 26. "And besides all this, between us and you there is a great gulf fixed: so that they which would pass from hence to you, cannot; neither can they pass to us, that would come from thence." And you will be parted at the day of judgment. You will be parted at Christ's first appearance in the clouds of heaven. While they are caught up in the clouds to meet the Lord in the air, to be ever with the Lord, you will remain below, confined to this cursed ground, that is kept in store, reserved unto fire, against the day of judgment, and perdition of ungodly men. You will appear separated from them, while you stand before the great judgment-seat, they being at the right hand, while you are set at the left. Matt. xxv. 32, 33. "And before him shall be gathered all nations; and he shall separate them one from another, as a shepherd divideth his sheep from the goats; and he shall set the sheep on his right hand, but the goats on the left." And you shall then appear in exceeding different circumstances: while you stand with devils, in the image and deformity of devils, and in ineffable horror and amazement, they shall appear in glory, sitting on thrones, as assessors with Christ, and as such passing judgment upon you, 1 Cor. vi. 2. And what shame and confusion will then cover you, when so many of your contemporaries, your equals, your neighbours, relations, and companions, shall be honoured, and openly acknowledged, and confessed by the glorious Judge of the universe, and Redeemer of saints, and shall be seen by you sitting with him in such glory. You shall appear to have neglected your salvation, and not to have improved your opportunities, and rejected the Lord Jesus Christ, the same person that will then appear as your great Judge, and you shall be the subjects of wrath, and, as it were, trodden down in eternal contempt and disgrace. Dan. xii. 2. "Some shall rise to everlasting life, and some to shame and everlasting contempt." And what a wide separation will the sentence then passed and executed make between you and them! When you shall be sent away out of the presence of the Judge with indignation and abhorrence, as cursed and loathsome creatures they shall be sweetly accosted and invited into his glory as his dear friends, and the blessed of his Father! When *you*, with all that vast throng of wicked and accursed men and devils, shall descend with loud lamentings, and horrid shrieks, into that dreadful gulf of fire and brimstone, and shall be swallowed up in that great and everlasting furnace; *they* shall joyfully, and with sweet songs of glory and praise, ascend with Christ, and all that beauteous and blessed company of saints and angels, into eternal felicity, in the glorious presence of God, and the sweet embraces of his love. You and they shall spend eternity in such a separation, and immensely different circumstances! You have been intimately acquainted and nearly related, closely united and mutually conversant in this world; and you have taken delight in each other's company! And shall it be—after you have been together a great while, each of you in undoing yourselves, enhancing your guilt, and heaping up wrath—that their so wisely changing their minds and their course, and choosing such happiness for themselves, should now at length be the beginning of such an exceeding and everlasting separation between you and them? How awful will it be to be parted so!

3. Consider the great encouragement that God gives you, earnestly to strive for the same blessing that others have obtained. There is great encouragement in the word of God to sinners to seek salvation, in the revelation we have of the abundant provision made for the salvation even of the chief of sinners, and in the appointment of so many means to be used with and by sinners, in order to their salvation; and by the blessing which God in his word connects with the means of his appointment. There is hence great encouragement for all, at all times, that will be thorough in using of these means. But now God gives extraordinary encouragement in his providence, by pouring out his Spirit so remarkably amongst us, and bringing savingly home to himself all sorts, young and old, rich and poor, wise and unwise, sober and vicious, old self-righteous seekers, and profligate livers: no sort are exempt. There is at this day amongst us the loudest call, and the greatest encouragement, and the widest door opened to sinners, to escape out of a state of sin and condemnation, that perhaps God ever granted in New England. Who is there that has an immortal soul, so sottish as not to improve such an opportunity, and that will not bestir himself with all his might? How unreasonable is negligence, and how exceeding unreasonable is discouragement, at such a day as this! Will you be so stupid as to neglect your soul now? Will any mortal amongst us be so unreasonable as to lag behind, or look back in discouragement, when God opens such a door? Let every person be thoroughly awake! Let every one encourage himself now to press forward, and fly for his life!

4. Consider how earnestly desirous they that have obtained are that you should follow them, and that their people should be your people, and their God your God. They desire that you should partake of that great good which God has given them, and that unspeakable and eternal blessedness which he has promised them. They wish and long it. If you do not go with them, and are not still of their company, it will not be for want of their willingness, but your own. That of Moses to Hobab is the language of every true saint of your acquaintance to you. Numb. x. 29. "We are journeying unto the place of which the Lord said, I will give it you: come thou with us, and we will do thee good; for the Lord hath spoken good concerning Israel." As Moses, when on his journey through the wilderness, following the pillar of cloud and fire, invited Hobab—with whom he had been acquainted in the land of Midian, where Moses had formerly dwelt with him—to go with him and his people to Canaan, to partake with them in the good that God had promised them; so do those of your friends and acquaintance invite you, out of a land of darkness and wickedness, where they have formerly been with you, to go with them to the heavenly Canaan. The company of saints, the true church of Christ, invite you. The lovely bride calls you to the marriage supper. She hath authority to invite guests to her own wedding; and you ought to look on her invitation and desire, as the call of Christ the bridegroom; for it is the voice of his Spirit in her, Rev. xxii. 17. "The Spirit and the bride say, Come." Where seems to be a reference to what has been said, chap. xix. 7—9. "The marriage of the Lamb is come, and his wife hath made herself ready. And to her was granted, that she should be arrayed in fine linen, clean and white; for the fine linen is the righteousness of saints. And he saith unto me, Write, blessed are they which are called to the marriage-supper of the Lamb." It is with respect to this her marriage-supper that she, from the motion of the Spirit of the Lamb in her, says, Come. So that you are invited on all hands; all conspire to call you. God the Father invites you: this is the King who has made a marriage for his Son; and he sends forth his servants, the ministers of the gospel, to invite the guests. And the Son himself invites you: it is he that speaks, Rev. xvii. 17. "And let him that heareth say, Come; and let him that is athirst, come; and whosoever will, let him come." He tells us who he is in the foregoing verse, "I Jesus, the root and offspring of David, the bright and morning star." And God's ministers invite you, and all the church invites you; and there will be joy in the presence of the angels of God that hour that you accept the invitation.

5. Consider what a doleful company will be left after this extraordinary time of mercy is over. We have reason to think that there will be a number left. We read that when Ezekiel's healing waters increased so abundantly, and the healing effect of them was so very general; yet there were certain places, where the waters came, that never were healed. Ezek. xlvii. 9—11. "And it shall come to

pass, that every thing that liveth, which moveth, whithersoever the rivers shall come, shall live. And there shall be a very great multitude of fish, because these waters shall come thither: for they shall be healed, and every thing shall live whither the river cometh. And it shall come to pass, that the fishers shall stand upon it, from En-gedi even unto En-eglaim; they shall be a place to spread forth nets: there fish shall be according to their kinds, as the fish of the great sea, exceeding many. But the miry places thereof, and the marishes thereof, shall not be healed, they shall be given to salt." And even in the apostles' times, when there was such wonderful success of the gospel wherever they came, there were some that did not believe. Acts xiii. 48. " And when the Gentiles heard this, they were glad, and glorified the word of the Lord: and as many as were ordained to eternal life, believed." And chap. xxviii. 24. " And some believed, and some believed not." So we have no reason to expect but there will be some left amongst us. It is to be hoped it will be but a small company: but what a doleful company will it be! How darkly and awfully will it look upon them! If you shall be of that company, how well may your friends and relations lament over you, and bemoan your dark and dangerous circumstances! If you would not be one of them, make haste, delay not, and look not behind you. Shall all sorts obtain, shall every one press into the kingdom of God, while you stay loitering behind in a doleful undone condition? Shall every one take heaven, while you remain with no other portion but this world? Now take up that resolution, that if it be possible you will cleave to them that have fled for refuge to lay hold of the hope set before them. Count the cost of a thorough, violent, and perpetual pursuit of salvation, and forsake all, as Ruth forsook her own country, and all her pleasant enjoyments in it. Do not do as Orpah did; who set out, and then was discouraged, and went back: but hold out with Ruth through all discouragement and opposition. When you consider others that have chosen the better part, let that resolution be ever firm with you: " Where thou goest, I will go; where thou lodgest, I will lodge: thy people shall be my people, and thy God my God."

DISCOURSE IV.

THE JUSTICE OF GOD IN THE DAMNATION OF SINNERS.

Rom. iii. 19.

—That every mouth may be stopped.—

The main subject of the doctrinal part of this epistle, is the free grace of God in the salvation of men by Jesus Christ; especially as it appears in the doctrine of justification by faith alone. And the more clearly to evince this doctrine, and show the reason of it, the apostle, in the first place, establishes that point, that no flesh living can be justified by the deeds of the law. And to prove it, he is very large and particular in showing, that all mankind, not only the Gentiles, but Jews, are under sin, and so under the condemnation of the law; which is what he insists upon from the beginning of the epistle to this place. He first begins with the Gentiles; and in the first chapter shows that they are under sin, by setting forth the exceeding corruptions and horrid wickedness that overspread the Gentile world: and then through the second chapter, and the former part of this third chapter, to the text and following verse, he shows the same of the Jews, that they also are in the same circumstances with the Gentiles in this regard. They had a high thought of themselves, because they were God's covenant people, and circumcised, and the children of Abraham. They despised the Gentiles as polluted, condemned, and accursed; but looked on themselves, on account of their external privileges, and ceremonial and moral righteousness, as a pure and holy people, and the children of God; as the apostle observes in the second chapter. It was therefore strange doctrine to them, that they also were unclean and guilty in God's sight, and under the condemnation and curse of the law. The apostle therefore, on account of their strong prejudices against such doctrine, the more particularly insists upon it, and shows that they are no better than the Gentiles; as in the 9th verse of this chapter, " What then? are we better than they? No, in no wise; for we have before proved both Jews and Gentiles, that they are all under sin." And, to convince them of it, he produces certain passages out of their own law, or the Old Testament, (to whose authority they pretended a great regard,) from the 9th verse to our text. And it may be observed, that the apostle, *first*, cites certain passages to prove that all mankind are *corrupt*, (ver. 10—12.) " As it is written, There is none righteous, no not one: There is none that understandeth, there is none that seeketh after God: They are all gone out of the way, they are together become unprofitable, there is none that doeth good, no not one." *Secondly*, The passages he cites next, are to prove, that not only are all corrupt, but each one *wholly* corrupt, as it were all over unclean, from the crown of the head to the soles of his feet; and therefore several particular parts of the body are mentioned, the throat, the tongue, the lips, the mouth, the feet, (ver. 13—15.) " Their throat is an open sepulchre; with their tongues they have used deceit; the poison of asps is under their lips; whose mouth is full of cursing and bitterness: their feet are swift to shed blood." And, *Thirdly*, He quotes other passages to show, that each one is not only all over corrupt, but corrupt to a desperate degree, (ver. 16—18.) by affirming the most pernicious tendency of their wickedness; " Destruction and misery are in their ways." And then by denying all goodness or godliness in them; " And the way of peace have they not known: There is no fear of God before their eyes." And then, lest the Jews should think these passages of their law do not concern them, and that only the Gentiles are intended in them, the apostle shows in the text, not only that they are not exempt, but that they especially must be understood: " Now we know that whatsoever things the law saith, it saith to them who are under the law." By those that are *under* the law are meant the Jews; and the Gentiles by those that are *without* law; as appears by the 12th verse of the preceding chapter. There is special reason to understand the law, as speaking to and of them, to whom it was immediately given. And therefore the Jews would be unreasonable in exempting themselves. And if we examine the places of the Old Testament whence these passages are taken, we shall see plainly that special respect is had to the wickedness of the people of that nation, in every one of them. So that the law shuts all up in universal and desperate wickedness, *that every mouth may be stopped;* the mouths of the Jews, as well as of the Gentiles, notwithstanding all those privileges by which they were distinguished from the Gentiles.

The things that the law says, are sufficient to stop the mouths of all mankind, in two respects.

1. To stop them from boasting of their righteousness, as the Jews were wont to do; as the apostle observes in the 23d verse of the preceding chapter.—That the apostle has respect to stopping their mouths in this respect, appears by the 27th verse of the context, " Where is boasting then? It is excluded." The law stops our mouths from making any plea for life, or the favour of God, or any positive good, from our own righteousness.

2. To stop them from making any excuse for ourselves, or objection against the execution of the sentence of the law, or the infliction of the punishment that it threatens. That this is intended, appears by the words immediately following, "That all the world may become guilty before God." That is, that they may appear to be guilty, and stand convicted before God, and justly liable to the condemnation of his law, as guilty of death, according to the Jewish way of speaking.

And thus the apostle proves, that no flesh can be justified in God's sight by the deeds of the law; as he draws the conclusion in the following verse; and so prepares the way for establishing the great doctrine of justification by faith alone, which he proceeds to do in the following part of the chapter, and of the epistle.

DOCTRINE.

"It is just with God eternally to cast off and destroy sinners."—For this is the punishment which the law condemns to.—The truth of this doctrine may appear by the joint consideration of two things, *viz.* Man's *sinfulness*, and God's *sovereignty*.

I. It appears from the consideration of man's sinfulness. And that whether we consider the infinitely evil nature of all sin, or how much sin men are guilty of.

1. If we consider the infinite evil and heinousness of sin in general, it is not unjust in God to inflict what punishment is deserved; because the very notion of deserving any punishment is, that it may be justly inflicted. A deserved punishment and a just punishment are the same thing. To say that one *deserves* such a punishment, and yet to say that he does not *justly* deserve it, is a contradiction; and if he justly deserves it, then it may be justly *inflicted.*

Every crime or fault deserves a greater or less punishment, in proportion as the crime itself is greater or less. If any fault deserves punishment, then so much the greater the fault, so much the greater is the punishment deserved. The faulty nature of any thing is the formal ground and reason of its desert of punishment; and therefore the more any thing hath of this nature, the more punishment it deserves. And therefore the terribleness of the degree of punishment, let it be never so terrible, is no argument against the justice of it, if the proportion does but hold between the heinousness of the crime and the dreadfulness of the punishment; so that if there be any such thing as a fault infinitely heinous, it will follow that it is just to inflict a punishment for it that is infinitely dreadful.

A crime is more or less heinous, according as we are under greater or less *obligations* to the contrary. This is self-evident; because it is herein that the criminalness or faultiness of any thing consists, that it is contrary to what we are obliged or bound to, or what *ought* to be in us. So the faultiness of one being hating another, is in proportion to his obligation to love him. The crime of one being despising and casting contempt on another, is proportionably more or less heinous, as he was under greater or less obligations to honour him. The fault of disobeying another, is greater or less, as any one is under greater or less obligations to obey him. And therefore if there be any being that we are under infinite obligations to love, and honour, and obey, the contrary towards him must be infinitely faulty.

Our obligation to love, honour, and obey any being, is in proportion to his loveliness, honourableness, and authority; for that is the very meaning of the words. When we say any one is very lovely, it is the same as to say, that he is one very much to be loved. Or if we say such a one is more honourable than another, the meaning of the words is, that he is one that we are more obliged to honour. If we say any one has great authority over us, it is the same as to say, that he has great right to our subjection and obedience.

But God is a being *infinitely* lovely, because he hath infinite excellency and beauty. To have infinite excellency and beauty, is the same thing as to have infinite loveliness. He is a being of infinite greatness, majesty, and glory; and therefore he is infinitely honourable. He is infinitely exalted above the greatest potentates of the earth, and highest angels in heaven; and therefore he is infinitely more honourable than they. His authority over us is infinite; and the ground of his right to our obedience is infinitely strong; for he is infinitely worthy to be obeyed himself, and we have an absolute, universal, and infinite dependence upon him.

So that sin against God, being a violation of infinite obligations, must be a crime infinitely heinous, and so deserving infinite punishment.—Nothing is more agreeable to the common sense of mankind, than that sins committed against any one, must be proportionably heinous to the dignity of the being offended and abused; as it is also agreeable to the word of God, 1 Sam. ii. 25. "If one man sin against another, the Judge shall judge him;" (*i. e.* shall judge him, and inflict a finite punishment, such as finite judges can inflict;) "but if a man sin against the Lord, who shall entreat for him?" This was the aggravation of sin that made Joseph afraid of it, Gen. xxxix. 9. "How shall I commit this great wickedness, and sin against God?" This was the aggravation of David's sin, in comparison of which he esteemed all others as nothing, because they were infinitely exceeded by it. Psalm li. 4. "Against thee, thee only have I sinned."—The *eternity* of the punishment of ungodly men renders it infinite: and it renders it no more than infinite; and therefore renders no more than proportionable to the heinousness of what they are guilty of.

If there be *any* evil or faultiness in sin against God, there is certainly *infinite* evil: for if it be any fault at all, it has an infinite aggravation, *viz.* that it is against an infinite object. If it be ever so small upon other accounts, yet if it be any thing, it has one infinite dimension; and so is an infinite evil. Which may be illustrated by this: if we suppose a thing to have infinite length, but no breadth and thickness, (a mere mathematical line,) it is nothing: but if it have *any* breadth and thickness, though never so small, and infinite length, the quantity of it is infinite; it exceeds the quantity of any thing, however broad, thick, and long, wherein these dimensions are all finite.

So that the objections made against the *infinite* punishment of sin, from the necessity, or rather previous certainty, of the futurition of sin, arising from the unavoidable original corruption of nature, if they argue any thing, argue against *any* faultiness at all: for if this necessity or certainty leaves *any* evil at all in sin, that fault must be *infinite* by reason of the infinite object.

But every such objector as would argue from hence, that there is no fault at all in sin, confutes himself, and shows his own insincerity in his objection. For at the same time that he objects, that men's acts are necessary, and that this kind of necessity is inconsistent with faultiness in the act, his own practice shows that he does not believe what he objects to be true: otherwise why does he at all *blame* men? Or why are such persons at all displeased with men, for abusive, injurious, and ungrateful acts towards them? Whatever they pretend, by this they show that indeed they do believe that there is no necessity in men's acts that is inconsistent with blame. And if their objection be this, that this previous certainty is by God's own ordering, and that where God orders an antecedent certainty of acts, he transfers all the fault from the actor on himself; their practice shows, that at the same time they do not believe this, but fully believe the contrary: for when they are abused by men, they are displeased with *men*, and not with *God* only.

The light of nature teaches all mankind, that when an injury is *voluntary*, it is faulty, without any consideration of what there might be previously to determine the futurition of that evil act of the will. And it really teaches this as much to those that object and cavil most as to others; as their universal practice shows. By which it appears, that such objections are insincere and perverse. Men will mention others' corrupt nature when they are injured, as a thing that aggravates their crime, and that wherein their faultiness partly consists. How common is it for persons, when they look on themselves greatly injured by another, to inveigh against him, and aggravate his baseness, by saying, "He is a man of a most perverse spirit: he is naturally of a selfish, niggardly, or proud and haughty temper: he is one of a base and vile disposition." And yet men's natural and corrupt dispositions are mentioned as an excuse for them, with respect to their sins against God, as if they rendered them blameless.

2. That it is just with God eternally to cast off wicked men, may more abundantly appear, if we consider how much sin they are guilty of. From what has been already said, it appears, that if men were guilty of sin but in one particular, that is sufficient ground of their eternal rejection and condemnation. If they are *sinners*, that is enough. Merely this, might be sufficient to keep them from ever lifting up their heads, and cause them to smite on their breasts, with the publican that cried, "God be merciful to me a sinner." But sinful men are full of sin; principles and acts of sin: their guilt is like great mountains, heaped one upon another, till the pile is grown up to heaven. They are totally corrupt, in every part, in all their faculties; in all the principles of their nature, their understandings, and wills; and in all their dispositions and affections. Their heads, their hearts, are totally depraved; all the members of their bodies are only instruments of sin; and all their senses, seeing, hearing, tasting, &c. are only inlets and outlets of sin, channels of corruption. There is nothing but sin, no good at all. Rom. vii. 18. "In me, that is, in my flesh, dwells no good thing." There is all manner of wickedness. There are the seeds of the greatest and blackest crimes. There are principles of all sorts of wickedness against men; and there is all wickedness against God. There is pride; there is enmity; there is contempt; there is quarrelling; there is atheism; there is blasphemy. There are these things in exceeding strength; the heart is under the power of them, is sold under sin, and is a perfect slave to it. There is hard-heartedness, hardness greater than that of a rock, or an adamant-stone. There is obstinacy and perverseness, incorrigibleness and inflexibleness in sin, that will not be overcome by threatenings or promises, by awakenings or encouragements, by judgments or mercies, neither by that which is terrifying nor that which is winning. The very blood of God our Saviour will not win the heart of a wicked man.

And there are actual wickednesses without number or measure. There are breaches of every command, in thought, word, and deed: a life full of sin; days and nights filled up with sin; mercies abused and frowns despised; mercy and justice, and all the divine perfections, trampled on; and the honour of each person in the Trinity trod in the dirt. Now if one sinful word or thought has so much evil in it, as to deserve eternal destruction, how do they deserve to be eternally cast off and destroyed, that are guilty of so much sin!

II. If with man's sinfulness, we consider God's *sovereignty*, it may serve further to clear God's justice in the eternal rejection and condemnation of sinners, from men's cavils and objections. I shall not now pretend to determine precisely, what things are, and what things are not, proper acts and exercises of God's holy sovereignty; but only, that God's sovereignty extends to the following things.

1. That such is God's sovereign power and right, that he is originally under no *obligation* to keep men from sinning; but may in his providence permit and *leave* them to sin. He was not obliged to keep either angels or men from falling. It is *unreasonable* to suppose, that God should be obliged, if he makes a reasonable creature capable of knowing his will, and receiving a law from him, and being subject to his moral government, at the same time to make it *impossible* for him to sin, or break his law. For if God be obliged to this, it destroys all use of any commands, laws, promises, or threatenings, and the very notion of any moral government of God over those reasonable creatures. For to what purpose would it be, for God to give such and such laws, and declare his holy will to a creature, and annex promises and threatenings to move him to his duty, and make him careful to perform it, if the creature at the same time has this to think of, that God is *obliged* to make it *impossible* for him to break his laws? How can God's threatenings move to care or watchfulness, when, at the same time, God is obliged to render it impossible that he should be exposed to the threatenings? Or, to what purpose is it for God to give a law at all? For according to this supposition, it is God, and not the creature, that is under law. It is the lawgiver's care, and not the subject's, to see that his law is obeyed; and this care is what the lawgiver is absolutely obliged to! If God be *obliged* never to *permit* a creature to fall, there is an end of all divine laws, or government, or authority of God over the creature; there can be no manner of use of these things.

God *may permit* sin, though the being of sin will *certainly* ensue on that permission: and so, by permission, he may dispose and order the event. If there were any such thing as chance, or mere contingence, and the very notion of it did not carry a gross absurdity, (as might easily be shown that it does,) it would have been very unfit that God should have left it to mere chance, whether man should fall or no. For chance, if there should be any such thing, is undesigning and blind. And certainly it is more fit that an event of so great importance, and which is attended with such an infinite train of great consequences, should be disposed and ordered by infinite *wisdom*, than that it should be left to blind *chance*.

If it be said, that God need not have interposed to render it impossible for man to sin, and yet not leave it to mere contingence or blind chance neither; but might have left it with man's *free will*, to determine whether to sin or no: I answer, if God did leave it to man's free will, without any *sort of disposal, or ordering* [or rather, *adequate cause*] in the case, whence it should be previously *certain* how that free will should determine, then still that first determination of the will must be merely contingent or by chance. It could not have any antecedent act of the will to determine it; for I speak now of the very first act or motion of the will, respecting the affair that may be looked upon as the prime ground and highest source of the event. To suppose this to be determined by a foregoing act is a contradiction. God's disposing this determination of the will by his *permission*, does not at all infringe the liberty of the creature. It is in no respect any more inconsistent with liberty, than mere chance or contingence. For if the determination of the will be from blind, undesigning chance, it is no more from the agent himself, or from the will itself, than if we suppose, in the case, a wise, divine disposal by permission.

2. It was fit that it should be at the ordering of the divine wisdom and good pleasure, whether every particular man should stand for himself, or whether the first father of mankind should be appointed as the moral and federal head and representative of the rest. If God has not liberty in this matter to determine either of these two as he pleases, it must be because determining that the first father of men should represent the rest, and not that every one should stand for himself, is *injurious* to mankind. For if it be not injurious, how is it unjust? But it is not injurious to mankind; for there is nothing in the nature of the case itself, that makes it better that each man should stand for himself, than that all should be represented by their common father; as the least reflection or consideration will convince any one. And if there be nothing in the nature of the thing that makes the former better for mankind than the latter, then it will follow, that they are not hurt in God's choosing and appointing the latter, rather than the former; or, which is the same thing, that it is not injurious to mankind.

3. When men are fallen, and become sinful, God by his sovereignty has a right to determine about their redemption as he pleases. He has a right to determine whether he will redeem any or not. He might, if he had pleased, have left all to perish, or might have redeemed all. Or, he may redeem some, and leave others; and if he doth so, he may take whom he pleases, and leave whom he pleases. To suppose that all have forfeited his favour, and deserved to perish, and to suppose that he may not leave any one individual of them to perish, implies a contradiction; because it supposes that such a one has a claim to God's favour, and is not justly liable to perish; which is contrary to the supposition.

It is meet that God should order all these things according to his own pleasure. By reason of his greatness and glory, by which he is infinitely above all, he is worthy to be sovereign, and that his pleasure should in all things take place. He is worthy that he should make himself his end, and that he should make nothing but his own wisdom his rule in pursuing that end, without asking leave or counsel of any, and without giving account of any of his matters. It is fit that he who is absolutely perfect, and infinitely wise, and the Fountain of all wisdom, should determine every thing [that he effects] by his own will, even things of the greatest importance. It is meet that he should be thus sovereign, because he is the first being, the eternal being, whence all other beings are. He is the Creator of all things; and all are absolutely and universally dependent on him; and therefore it is meet that he should act as the sovereign possessor of heaven and earth.

APPLICATION.

In the improvement of this doctrine, I would chiefly direct myself to sinners who are afraid of damnation, in a use of conviction. This may be matter of conviction to you, that it would be just and righteous with God eternally to reject and destroy you. This is what you are in danger of. You who are a Christless sinner, are a poor condemned creature: God's wrath still abides upon you; and the sentence of condemnation lies upon you. You are in God's hands, and it is uncertain what he will do with you. You are afraid what will become of you. You are afraid that it will be your portion to suffer eternal burnings; and your fears are not without grounds; you have reason to tremble every moment. But be you never so much afraid of it, let eternal damnation be never so dreadful, yet it is just. God may nevertheless do it, and be righteous, and holy, and glorious. Though eternal damnation be what you cannot bear, and how much soever your heart shrinks at the thoughts of it, yet God's justice may be glorious in it. The dreadfulness of the thing on your part, and the greatness of your dread of it, do not render it the less righteous on God's part. If you think otherwise, it is a sign that you do not see yourself, that you are not sensible what sin is, nor how much of it you have been guilty of. Therefore for your conviction, be directed,

First, To look over your past life: inquire at the mouth of conscience, and hear what that has to testify concerning it. Consider what you are, what light you have had, and what means you have lived under: and yet how you have behaved yourself! What have those many days and nights you have lived been filled up with? How have those years that have rolled over your heads, one after another, been spent? What has the sun shone upon you for, from day to day, while you have improved his light to serve Satan by it? What has God kept your breath in your nostrils for, and given you meat and drink, that you have spent your life and strength, supported by them, in opposing God, and rebellion against him?

How *many sorts* of wickedness have you not been guilty of! How manifold have been the abominations of your life! What profaneness and contempt of God has been exercised by you! How little regard have you had to the Scriptures, to the word preached, to sabbaths, and sacraments! How profanely have you talked, many of you, about those things that are holy! After what manner have many of you kept God's holy day, not regarding the holiness of the time, nor caring what you thought of in it! Yea, you have not only spent the time in worldly, vain, and unprofitable thoughts, but immoral thoughts; pleasing yourself with the reflection on past acts of wickedness, and in contriving new acts. Have not you spent much holy time in gratifying your lusts in your imaginations; yea, not only holy time, but the very time of God's public worship, when you have appeared in God's more immediate presence? How have you not only not attended to the worship, but have in the mean time been feasting your lusts, and wallowing yourself in abominable uncleanness! How many sabbaths have you spent, one after another, in a most wretched manner! Some of you not only in worldly and wicked thoughts, but also a very wicked outward behaviour! When you on sabbath-days have got along with your wicked companions, how has holy time been treated among you! What kind of conversation has there been! Yea, how have some of you, by a very indecent carriage, openly dishonoured and cast contempt on the sacred services of God's house, and holy day! And what you have done some of you alone, what wicked practices there have been in secret, even in holy time, God and your own consciences know.

And how have you behaved yourself in the time of family prayer! And what a trade have many of you made of absenting yourselves from the worship of the families you belong to, for the sake of vain company! And how have you continued in the neglect of secret prayer! therein wilfully living in a known sin, going abreast against as plain a command as any in the Bible! Have you not been one that has cast off fear, and restrained prayer before God?

What wicked carriage have some of you been guilty of towards your parents! How far have you been from paying that honour to them which God has required! Have you not even harboured ill-will and malice towards them? and when they have displeased you, have wished evil to them? yea, and shown your vile spirit in your behaviour? and it is well if you have not mocked them behind their backs; and, like the accursed Ham and Canaan, as it were, derided your parents' nakedness instead of covering it, and hiding your eyes from it. Have not some of you often disobeyed your parents, yea, and refused to be subject to them? Is it not a wonder of mercy and forbearance, that the proverb has not before now been accomplished on you, Prov. xxx. 17. "The eye that mocketh at his father, and refuseth to obey his mother, the ravens of the valley shall pick it out, and the young eagles shall eat it?"

What revenge and malice have you been guilty of towards your neighbours! How have you indulged this spirit of the devil, hating others, and wishing evil to them, rejoicing when evil befell them, and grieving at others' prosperity, and lived in such a way for a long time! Have not some of you allowed a passionate furious spirit, and behaved yourselves in your anger more like wild beasts than like Christians?

What covetousness has been in many of you! Such has been your inordinate love of the world, and care about the things of it, that it has taken up your heart; you have allowed no room for God and religion; you have minded the world more than your eternal salvation. For the vanities of the world you have neglected reading, praying, and meditation; for the things of the world you have broken the sabbath; for the world you have spent a great deal of your time in quarrelling. For the world you have envied and hated your neighbour; for the world you have cast God, and Christ, and heaven, behind your back; for the world you have sold your own soul. You have as it were drowned your soul in worldly cares and desires; you have been a mere earth-worm, that is never in its element but when grovelling and buried in the earth.

How much of a spirit of *pride* has appeared in you, which is in a peculiar manner the spirit and condemnation of the devil! How have some of you vaunted yourselves in your apparel! others in their riches! others in their knowledge and abilities! How has it galled you to see others above you! How much has it gone against the grain for you to give others their due honour! And how have you shown your pride by setting up your wills in opposing others, and stirring up and promoting division, and a party spirit in public affairs.

How *sensual* have you been! Are there not some here that have debased themselves below the dignity of human nature, by wallowing in sensual filthiness, as swine in the mire, or as filthy vermin feeding with delight on rotten carrion? What intemperance have some of you been guilty of! How much of your precious time have you spent away at the tavern, and in drinking companies, when you ought to have been at home seeking God and your salvation in your families and closets!

And what abominable *lasciviousness* have some of you been guilty of! How have you indulged yourself from day to day, and from night to night, in all manner of unclean imaginations! Has not your soul been filled with them, till it has become a hold of foul spirits, and a cage of every unclean and hateful bird? What foul-mouthed persons have some of you been, often in lewd and lascivious talk and unclean songs, wherein were things not fit to be spoken! And such company, where such conversation has been carried on, has been your delight. And with what unclean acts and practices have you defiled yourself! God and your own consciences know what abominable lasciviousness you have practised in things not fit to be named, when you have been alone; when you ought to have been reading, or meditating, or on your knees before God in secret prayer. And how have you corrupted others, as well as polluted yourselves! What vile uncleanness have you practised in company! What abominations have you been guilty of in the dark! Such as the apostle doubtless had respect to in Eph. v. 12. "For it is a shame even to speak of those things that are done of them in secret." Some of you have corrupted others, and done what in you lay to undo their souls, (if you have not actually done it,) and by your vile practices and example have made room for Satan, invited his presence, and established his interest, in the town where you have lived.

What *lying* have some of you been guilty of, especially in your childhood! And have not your heart and lips often disagreed since you came to riper years? What fraud, and deceit, and unfaithfulness, have many of you practised in your own dealings with your neighbours, of which your own heart is conscious, if you have not been noted by others.

And how have some of you behaved yourselves in your *family* relations! How have you neglected your children's souls! And not only so, but have corrupted their minds by your bad examples; and instead of training them up in the nurture and admonition of the Lord, have rather brought them up in the devil's service!

How have some of you attended that sacred ordinance of the Lord's supper without any manner of serious preparation, and in a careless slighty frame of spirits, and chiefly to comply with custom! Have you not ventured to put the sacred symbols of the body and blood of Christ into your mouth, while at the same time you lived in ways of known sins, and intended no other than still to go on in the same wicked practices? And, it may be, have sat at the Lord's table with rancour in your heart against some of your brethren that you have sat therewith. You have come even to that holy feast of love among God's children, with the leaven of malice and envy in your heart; and so have eat and drank judgment to yourself.

What stupidity and sottishness has attended your course of wickedness; which has appeared in your obstinacy under awakening dispensations of God's word and providence. And how have some of you backslidden after you have set out in religion, and quenched God's Spirit after he had been striving with you! And what unsteadiness, and slothfulness, and long misimprovement of God's strivings with you, have you been chargeable with!

Now, can you think when you have thus behaved yourself, that God is *obliged* to show you mercy? Are you not after all this ashamed to talk of its being hard with God to cast you off? Does it become one who has lived such a life to open his mouth to excuse himself, to object against God's justice in his condemnation, or to complain of it as hard in God not to give him converting and pardoning grace, and make him his child, and bestow on him eternal life? or to talk of his duties and great pains in religion, as if such performances were worthy to be accepted, and to draw God's heart to such a creature? If this has been your manner, does it not show how little you have considered yourself, and how little a sense you have had of your own sinfulness?

Secondly, Be directed to consider, if God should eternally reject and destroy you, what an agreeableness and exact mutual answerableness there would be between God so dealing with you, and your spirit and behaviour. There would not only be an equality, but a similitude. God declares, that his dealings with men shall be suitable to their disposition and practice. Psalm xviii. 25, 26. "With the merciful man, thou wilt show thyself merciful; with an upright man, thou wilt show thyself upright: with the pure, thou wilt show thyself pure; and with the froward, thou wilt show thyself froward." How much soever you dread damnation, and are affrighted and concerned at the thoughts of it; yet if God should indeed eternally damn you, you would be met with but in your own way; you would be dealt with exactly according to your own dealing. Surely it is but fair that you should be made to buy in the same measure in which you sell.

Here I would particularly show,—1. That if God should eternally destroy you, it would be agreeable to your treatment of *God*. 2. That it would be agreeable to your treatment of *Jesus Christ*. 3. That it would be agreeable to your behaviour towards your *neighbours*. 4. That it would be according to your own foolish behaviour towards *yourself*.

I. If God should for ever cast you off, it would be exactly agreeable to your treatment of *him*. That you may be sensible of this, consider,

1. You never have exercised the least degree of love to God; and therefore it would be agreeable to your treatment of him if he should never express any love to you. When God converts and saves a sinner, it is a wonderful and unspeakable manifestation of divine love. When a poor lost soul is brought home to Christ, and has all his sins forgiven him, and is made a child of God, it will take up a whole eternity to express and declare the greatness of that love. And why should God be *obliged* to express such wonderful love to you, who never exercised the least degree of love to him in all your life? You never have loved God, who is infinitely glorious and lovely; and why then is God under *obligation* to love you, who are all over deformed and loathsome as a filthy worm, or rather a hateful viper? You have no benevolence in your heart towards God; you never rejoiced in God's happiness; if he had been miserable, and that had been possible, you would have liked it as well as if he were happy; you would not have cared how miserable he was, nor mourned for it, any more than you now do for the devil's being miserable. And why then should God be looked upon as obliged to take so much care for your happiness, as to do such great things for it, as he doth for those that are saved? Or why should God be called hard, in case he should not be careful to save you from misery? You care not what becomes of God's glory; you are not distressed how much soever his honour seems to suffer in the world: and why should God care any more for your welfare? Has it not been so, that if you could but promote your private interest, and gratify your own lusts, you cared not how much the glory of God suffered? And why may not God advance his own glory in the ruin of your welfare, not caring how much your interest suffers by it? You never so much as stirred one step, sincerely making the glory of God your end, or acting from real respect to him; and why then is it hard if God do not do such great things for you, as the changing of your nature, raising you from spiritual death to life, conquering the powers of darkness for you, translating you out of the kingdom of darkness into the kingdom of his dear Son, delivering you from eternal misery, and bestowing upon you eternal glory? You were not willing to deny yourself for God; you never cared to put yourself out of your way for Christ; whenever any thing cross or difficult came in your way, that the glory of God was concerned in, it has been your manner to shun it, and excuse yourself from it. You did not care to hurt yourself for Christ, whom you did not see worthy of it; and why then must it be looked upon as a hard and cruel thing, if Christ has not been pleased to spill his blood and be tormented to death for such a sinner.

2. You have slighted God; and why then may not God justly slight you? When sinners are sensible in some measure of their misery, they are ready to think it hard that God will take no more notice of them; that he will see them in such a lamentable distressed condition, beholding their burdens and tears, and seem to slight it, and manifest no pity to them. Their souls they think are precious: it would be a dreadful thing if they should perish, and burn in hell for ever. They do not see through it, that God should make so light of their salvation. But then, ought they not to consider, that as their souls are precious, so is God's honour precious? The honour of the infinite God, the great King of heaven and earth, is a thing of as great importance, (and surely may justly be so esteemed by God,) as the happiness of you, a poor little worm. But yet you have slighted that honour of God, and valued it

no more than the dirt under your feet. You have been told that such and such things were contrary to the will of a holy God, and against his honour; but you cared not for that. God called upon you, and exhorted you to be more tender of his honour; but you went on without regarding him. Thus have you slighted God! And yet, is it hard that God should slight you? Are you more honourable than God, that he must be obliged to make much of you, how light soever you make of him and his glory?

And you have not only slighted God in time past, but you slight him still. You indeed now make a pretence and show of honouring him in your prayers, and attendance on other external duties, and by sober countenance, and seeming devoutness in your words and behaviour; but it is all mere dissembling. That downcast look and seeming reverence, is not from any honour you have to God in your heart, though you would have God take it so. You who have not believed in Christ, have not the least jot of honour to God; that show of it is merely forced, and what you are driven to by fear, like those mentioned in Psalm lxvi. 3. "Through the greatness of thy power shall thine enemies submit themselves to thee." In the original it is, "shall lie unto thee;" that is, yield feigned submission, and dissemble respect and honour to thee. There is a rod held over you that makes you seem to pay such respect to God. This religion and devotion, even the very appearance of it, would soon be gone, and all vanish away, if that were removed. Sometimes it may be you weep in your prayers, and in your hearing sermons, and hope God will take notice of it, and take it for some honour; but he sees it to be all hypocrisy. You weep for yourself; you are afraid of hell; and do you think that that is worthy of God to take much notice of you, because you can cry when you are in danger of being damned; when at the same time you indeed care nothing for God's honour.

Seeing you thus disregard so great a God, is it a heinous thing for God to slight you, a little, wretched, despicable creature; a worm, a mere nothing, and less than nothing; a vile insect, that has risen up in contempt against the Majesty of heaven and earth?

3. Why should God be looked upon as obliged to bestow salvation upon you, when you have been so ungrateful for the mercies he has bestowed upon you already? God has tried you with a great deal of kindness, and he never has sincerely been thanked by you for any of it. God has watched over you, and preserved you, and provided for you, and followed you with mercy all your days; and yet you have continued sinning against him. He has given you food and raiment, but you have improved both in the service of sin. He has preserved you while you slept; but when you arose, it was to return to the old trade of sinning. God, notwithstanding this ingratitude, has still continued his mercy; but his kindness has never won your heart, or brought you to a more grateful behaviour towards him. It may be you have received many remarkable mercies, recoveries from sickness, or preservations of your life when exposed by accidents, when if you had died, you would have gone directly to hell; but you never had any true thankfulness for any of these mercies. God has kept you out of hell, and continued your day of grace, and the offers of salvation, so long a time; while you did not regard your own salvation so much as in secret to ask God for it. And now God has greatly added to his mercy to you, by giving you the strivings of his Spirit, whereby a most precious opportunity for your salvation is in your hands. But what thanks has God received for it? What kind of returns have you made for all this kindness? As God has multiplied mercies, so have you multiplied provocations.

And yet now are you ready to quarrel for mercy, and to find fault with God, not only that he does not bestow more mercy, but to contend with him, because he does not bestow infinite mercy upon you, heaven with all it contains, and even himself, for your eternal portion. What ideas have you of yourself, that you think God is *obliged* to do so much for you, though you treat him ever so ungratefully for his kindness wherewith you have been followed all the days of your life.

4. You have voluntarily chosen to be with Satan in his enmity and opposition to God; how justly therefore might you be with him in his punishment! You did not choose to be on God's side, but rather chose to side with the devil, and have obstinately continued in it, against God's often repeated calls and counsels. You have chosen rather to hearken to Satan than to God, and would be with him in his work. You have given yourself up to him, to be subject to his power and government, in opposition to God; how justly therefore may God also give you up to him, and leave you in his power, to accomplish your ruin! Seeing you have yielded yourself to his will, to do as he would have you, surely God may leave you in his hands to execute his will upon you. If men will be with God's enemy, and on his side, why is God obliged to redeem them out of his hands, when they have done his work? Doubtless you would be glad to serve the devil, and be God's enemy while you live, and then to have God your friend, and deliver you from the devil, when you come to die. But will God be unjust if he deals otherwise by you? No, surely! It will be altogether and perfectly just, that you should have your portion with him with whom you have chosen to work; and that you should be in his possession to whose dominion you have yielded yourself; and if you cry to God for deliverance, he may most justly give you that answer, Judges x. 14. "Go to the gods which you have chosen."

5. Consider how often you have refused to hear God's calls to you, and how just it would therefore be, if he should refuse to hear you when you call upon him. You are ready, it may be, to complain that you have often prayed, and earnestly begged of God to show you mercy, and yet have no answer of prayer: One says, I have been constant in prayer for so many years, and God has not heard me. Another says, I have done what I can; I have prayed as earnestly as I am able; I do not see how I can do more; and it will seem hard if after all I am denied. But do you consider how often God has called, and you have denied him? God has called earnestly and for a long time; he has called and called again in his word, and in his providence, and you have refused. You was not uneasy for fear you should not show regard enough to his calls. You let him call as loud and as long as he would; for your part, you had no leisure to attend to what he said; you had other business to mind; you had these and those lusts to gratify and please, and worldly concerns to attend; you could not afford to stand considering of what God had to say to you. When the ministers of Christ have stood and pleaded with you, in his name, sabbath after sabbath, and have even spent their strength in it, how little was you moved! It did not alter you, but you went on still as you used to do; when you went away, you returned again to your sins, to your lasciviousness, to your vain mirth, to your covetousness, to your intemperance, and that has been the language of your heart and practice, Exod. v. 2. "Who is the Lord, that I should obey his voice?" Was it no crime for you to refuse to hear when God called? And yet is it now very hard that God does not hear your earnest calls, and that though your calling on God be not from any respect to him, but merely from self-love? The devil would beg as earnestly as you, if he had any hope to get salvation by it, and a thousand times as earnestly, and yet be as much of a devil as he is now. Are your calls more worthy to be heard than God's? Or is God more obliged to regard what you say to him, than you to regard his commands, counsels, and invitations to you? What can be more justice than this, Prov. i. 24, &c. "Because I have called, and ye refused, I have stretched out my hand, and no man regarded; but ye have set at nought all my counsel, and would none of my reproof: I will also laugh at your calamity, I will mock when your fear cometh; when your fear cometh as desolation, and your destruction cometh as a whirlwind; when distress and anguish cometh upon you. Then shall they call upon me, but I will not answer; they shall seek me early, but they shall not find me."

6. Have you not taken encouragement to sin against God, on that very presumption, that God would show you mercy when you sought it? And may not God justly refuse you that mercy that you have so presumed upon?

You have flattered yourself, that though you did so, yet God would show you mercy when you cried earnestly to him for it: how righteous therefore would it be in God, to disappoint such a wicked presumption! It was upon that very hope that you dared to affront the Majesty of heaven so dreadfully as you have done; and can you now be so sottish as to think that God is obliged not to frustrate that hope?

When a sinner takes encouragement to neglect secret prayer which God has commanded, to gratify his lusts, to live a carnal vain life, to thwart God, to run upon him, and contemn him to his face, thinking with himself, "If I do so, God would not damn me; he is a merciful God, and therefore when I seek his mercy he will bestow it upon me;" must God be accounted hard because he will not do according to such a sinner's presumption?

Cannot he be excused from showing such a sinner mercy when he is pleased to seek it, without incurring the charge of being unjust; if this be the case, God has no liberty to vindicate his own honour and majesty; but must lay himself open to all manner of affronts, and yield himself up to the abuses of vile men, though they disobey, despise, and dishonour him, as much as they will; and when they have done, his mercy and pardoning grace must not be in his own power and at his own disposal, but he must be obliged to dispense it at their call. He must take these bold and vile contemners of his Majesty, when it suits them to ask it, and must forgive all their sins, and not only so, but must adopt them into his family, and make them his children, and bestow eternal glory upon them. What mean, low, and strange thoughts have such men of God, who think thus of him! Consider, that you have injured God the more, and have been the worse enemy to him, for his being a merciful God. So have you treated that attribute of God's mercy! How just is it therefore that you never should have any benefit of that attribute!

There is something peculiarly heinous in sinning against the mercy of God more than other attributes. There is such base and horrid ingratitude, in being the worse to God because he is a being of infinite goodness and grace, that it above all things renders wickedness vile and detestable. This ought to win us, and engage us to serve God better; but instead of that, to sin against him the more, has something inexpressibly bad in it, and does in a peculiar manner enhance guilt, and incense wrath; as seems to be intimated, Rom. ii. 4, 5. "Or despisest thou the riches of his goodness, and forbearance, and long-suffering; not knowing that the goodness of God leadeth thee to repentance? But after thy hardness and impenitent heart, treasurest up unto thyself wrath against the day of wrath, and revelation of the righteous judgment of God."

The greater the mercy of God is, the more should you be engaged to love him, and live to his glory. But it has been contrariwise with you; the consideration of the mercies of God being so exceeding great, is the thing wherewith you have encouraged yourself in sin. You have heard that the mercy of God was without bounds, that it was sufficient to pardon the greatest sinner, and you have upon that very account ventured to be a very great sinner. Though it was very offensive to God, though you heard that God infinitely hated sin, and that such practices as you went on in were exceeding contrary to his nature, will, and glory, yet that did not make you uneasy; you heard that he was a very merciful God, and had grace enough to pardon you, and so cared not how offensive your sins were to him. How long have some of you gone on in sin, and what great sins have some of you been guilty of, on that presumption! Your own conscience can give testimony to it, that this has made you refuse God's calls, and has made you regardless of his repeated commands. Now, how righteous would it be if God should swear in his wrath, that you should never be the better for his being infinitely merciful!

Your ingratitude has been the greater, that you have not only abused the attribute of God's mercy, taking encouragement from it to continue in sin, but you have also presumed that God would exercise infinite mercy to you in particular; which consideration should have especially endeared God to you. You have taken encouragement to sin the more, from that consideration, that Christ came into the world and died to save sinners; such thanks has Christ had from you, for enduring such a tormenting death for his enemies! Now, how justly might God refuse that you should ever be the better for his Son's laying down his life! It was because of these things that you put off seeking salvation. You would take the pleasures of sin still longer, hardening yourself because mercy was infinite, and it would not be too late, if you sought it afterwards; now, how justly may God disappoint you in this, and so order it that it shall be too late.

7. How have some of you risen up against God, and in the frame of your minds opposed him in his sovereign dispensations! And how justly upon that account might God oppose you, and set himself against you! You never yet would submit to God; never willingly comply, that God should have dominion over the world, and that he should govern it for his own glory, according to his own wisdom. You, a poor worm, a potsherd, a broken piece of an earthen vessel, have dared to find fault and quarrel with God. Isaiah xlv. 9. "Woe to him that strives with his Maker. Let the potsherd strive with the potsherds of the earth: shall the clay say to him that fashioned it, What makest thou?" But yet you have ventured to do it. Rom. ix. 20. "Who art thou, O man, that repliest against God?" But yet you have thought you was big enough; you have taken upon you to call God to an account, why he does thus and thus; you have said to Jehovah, What dost thou?

If you have been restrained by fear from openly venting your opposition and enmity of heart against God's government, yet it has been in you; you have not been quiet in the frame of your mind; you have had the heart of a viper within, and have been ready to spit your venom at God. It is well if sometimes you have not actually done it, by tolerating blasphemous thoughts and malignant risings of heart against him; yea, and the frame of your heart in some measure appeared in impatient and fretful behaviour.—Now, seeing you have thus opposed God, how just is it that God should oppose you! Or is it because you are so much better, and so much greater than God, that it is a crime for him to make that opposition against you which you make against him? Do you think that the liberty of making opposition is your exclusive prerogative, so that you may be an enemy to God, but God must by no means be an enemy to you, but must be looked upon under obligation nevertheless to help you, and save you by his blood, and bestow his best blessings upon you?

Consider how in the frame of your mind you have thwarted God in those very exercises of mercy towards others that you are seeking for yourself. God exercising his infinite grace towards your neighbours, has put you into an ill frame, and it may be, set you in a tumult of mind. How justly therefore may God refuse ever to exercise that mercy towards you! Have you not thus opposed God showing mercy to others, even at the very time when you pretended to be earnest with God for pity and help for yourself? yea, and while you was endeavouring to get something wherewith to recommend yourself to God? And will you look to God still with a challenge of mercy, and contend with him for it notwithstanding? Can you who have such a heart, and have thus behaved yourself, come to God for any other than mere *sovereign mercy?*

II. If you should for ever be cast off by God, it would be agreeable to your treatment of *Jesus Christ*. It would have been just with God if he had cast you off for ever, without ever making you the offer of a Saviour. But God hath not done that; he has provided a Saviour for sinners, and offered him to you, even his own Son Jesus Christ, who is the only Saviour of men. All that are not forever cast off are saved by him. God offers men salvation through him, and has promised us, that if we come to him, we shall not be cast off. But if you have treated, and still treat, this Saviour after such a manner, that if you should be eternally cast off by God, it would be most agreeable to your behaviour towards him; which appears by this, *viz.* "That you reject Christ, and will not have him for your Saviour."

If God offers you a Saviour from deserved punishment, and you will not receive him, then surely it is just that you should go without a Saviour. Or is God obliged. because you do not like *this* Saviour, to provide you another? He has given an infinitely honourable and glorious person, even his only-begotten Son, to be a sacrifice for sin, and so provided salvation; and this Saviour is offered to you: now if you refuse to accept him, is God therefore unjust if he does not save you? Is he obliged to save you in a way of *your* own choosing, because you do not like the way of *his* choosing? Or will you charge Christ with injustice because he does not become your Saviour, when at the same time you will not have him when he offers himself to you, and beseeches you to accept of him as your Saviour?

I am sensible that by this time many persons are ready to object against this. If all should speak what they now think, we should hear a murmuring all over the meeting-house, and one and another would say, "I cannot see how this can be, that I am not willing that Christ should be my Saviour, when I would give all the world that he was my Saviour: how is it possible that I should not be willing to have Christ for my Saviour, when this is what I am seeking after, and praying for, and striving for, as for my life?"

Here therefore I would endeavour to convince you, that you are under a gross mistake in this matter. And, 1*st*, I would endeavour to show the grounds of your mistake. And, 2*dly*, To demonstrate to you, that you have rejected, and do wilfully reject, Jesus Christ.

1*st*, That you may see the weak grounds of your mistake, consider,

1. There is a great deal of difference between a willingness not to be damned, and a being willing to receive Christ for your Saviour. You have the former; there is no doubt of that: nobody supposes that you *love misery* so as to choose an eternity of it; and so doubtless you are willing to be saved from eternal misery. But that is a very different thing from being willing to come to Christ: persons very commonly mistake the one for the other, but they are quite two things. You may love the deliverance, but hate the deliverer. You tell of a willingness; but consider what is the object of that willingness. It does not respect Christ; the way of salvation by him is not at all the object of it; but it is wholly terminated on your escape from misery. The inclination of your will goes no further than self, it never reaches Christ. You are willing not to be miserable; that is, you love yourself, and there your will and choice terminate. And it is but a vain pretence and delusion to say or think, that you are willing to accept of Christ.

2. There is certainly a great deal of difference between a forced compliance and a free willingness. Force and freedom cannot consist together. Now that willingness, whereby you think you are willing to have Christ for a Saviour, is merely a forced thing. Your heart does not go out after Christ of itself, but you are forced and driven to seek an interest in him. Christ has no share at all in your heart; there is no manner of closing of the heart with him. This forced compliance is not what Christ seeks of you; he seeks a free and willing acceptance, Psalm cx. 3. "Thy people shall be willing in the day of thy power." He seeks not that you should receive him *against* your will, but *with* a free will. He seeks entertainment in your heart and choice.——And if you refuse thus to receive Christ, how just is it that Christ should refuse to receive you! How reasonable are Christ's terms, who offers to save all those that willingly, or with a good will, accept of him for their Saviour! Who can rationally expect that Christ should force himself upon any man to be his Saviour? Or what can be looked for more reasonable, than that all who would be saved by Christ, should heartily and freely entertain him? And surely it would be very dishonourable for Christ to offer himself upon lower terms. —But I would now proceed,

2*dly*, To show that you are not willing to have Christ for a Saviour. To convince you of it, consider,

1. How it is possible that you should be willing to accept of Christ as a Saviour from the desert of a punishment that you are not sensible you have deserved. If you are truly willing to accept of Christ as a Saviour, it must be as a sacrifice to make atonement for your guilt. Christ came into the world on this errand, to offer himself as an atonement, to answer for our desert of punishment. But how can you be willing to have Christ for a Saviour from a desert of hell, if you be not sensible that you have a desert of hell? If you have not really deserved everlasting burnings in hell, then the very offer of an atonement for such a desert is an imposition upon you. If you have no such guilt upon you, then the very offer of a satisfaction for that guilt is an injury, because it implies in it a charge of guilt that you are free from. Now therefore it is impossible that a man who is not convinced of his guilt can be willing to accept of such an offer; because he cannot be willing to accept the charge which the offer implies. A man who is not convinced that he has deserved so dreadful a punishment, cannot willingly submit to be charged with it. If he thinks he is willing, it is but a mere forced, feigned business; because in his heart he looks upon himself greatly injured; and therefore he cannot freely accept of Christ, under that notion of a Saviour from the desert of such a punishment; for such an acceptance is an implicit owning that he does deserve such a punishment.

I do not say, but that men may be willing to be saved from an undeserved punishment; they may rather not suffer it than suffer it. But a man cannot be willing to accept one at God's hands, under the notion of a Saviour from a punishment deserved from him which he thinks he has not deserved; it is impossible that any one should freely allow a Saviour under that notion. Such an one cannot like the way of salvation by Christ; for if he thinks he has not deserved hell, then he will think that freedom from hell is a debt; and therefore cannot willingly and heartily receive it as a free gift.—If a king should condemn a man to some tormenting death, which the condemned person thought himself not deserving of, but looked upon the sentence as unjust and cruel, and the king, when the time of execution drew nigh, should offer him his pardon, under the notion of a very great act of grace and clemency, the condemned person never could willingly and heartily allow it under that notion, because he judged himself unjustly condemned.

Now by this it is evident that you are not willing to accept of Christ as your Saviour; because you never yet had such a sense of your own sinfulness, and such a conviction of your great guilt in God's sight, as to be indeed convinced that you lay justly condemned to the punishment of hell. You never was convinced that you had forfeited all favour, and was in God's hands, and at his sovereign and arbitrary disposal, to be either destroyed or saved, just as he pleased. You never yet was convinced of the sovereignty of God. Hence are there so many objections arising against the justice of your punishment from original sin, and from God's decrees, from mercy shown to others, and the like.

2. That you are not sincerely willing to accept of Christ as your Saviour, appears by this, That you never have been convinced that he is sufficient for the work of your salvation. You never had a sight or sense of any such excellency or worthiness in Christ, as should give such great value to his blood and his mediation with God, as that it was sufficient to be accepted for such exceeding guilty creatures, who have so provoked God, and exposed themselves to such amazing wrath. Saying it is so, and allowing it to be as others say, is a very different thing from being really convinced of it, and a being made sensible of it in your own heart. The sufficiency of Christ depends upon, or rather consists in, his excellency. It is because he is so excellent a person that his blood is of sufficient value to atone for sin, and it is hence that his obedience is so worthy in God's sight; it is also hence that his intercession is so prevalent; and therefore those that never had any spiritual sight or sense of Christ's excellency, cannot be sensible of his sufficiency.

And that sinners are not convinced that Christ is sufficient for the work he has undertaken, appears most manifestly when they are under great convictions of their sin, and danger of God's wrath. Though it may be before they thought they could allow Christ to be sufficient, (for it is easy to allow any one to be sufficient for our defence at a time when we see no danger,) yet when they come to be sensible of their guilt and God's wrath, what discouraging thoughts do they entertain! How are they ready to draw towards despair, as if there were no hope or help for such wicked creatures as they! The reason is, They have no apprehension or sense of any other way that God's majesty can be vindicated, but only in their misery. To tell them of the blood of Christ signifies nothing, it does not relieve their sinking, despairing hearts. This makes it most evident that they are not convinced that Christ is sufficient to be their Mediator.—And as long as they are unconvinced of this, it is impossible they should be willing to accept of him as their Mediator and Saviour. A man in distressing fear will not willingly betake himself to a fort that he judges not sufficient to defend him from the enemy. A man will not willingly venture out into the ocean in a ship that he suspects is leaky, and will sink before he gets through his voyage.

3. It is evident that you are not willing to have Christ for your Saviour, because you have so mean an opinion of him, that you durst not trust his faithfulness. One that undertakes to be the Saviour of souls had need be faithful; for if he fails in such a trust, how great is the loss! But you are not convinced of Christ's faithfulness; as is evident, because at such times as when you are in a considerable measure sensible of your guilt and God's anger, you cannot be convinced that Christ is willing to accept of you, or that he stands ready to receive you, if you should come to him, though Christ so much invites you to come to him, and has so fully declared that he will not reject you, if you do come; as particularly, John vi. 37. "Him that cometh to me, I will in no wise cast out." Now, there is no man can be heartily willing to trust his eternal welfare in the hands of an unfaithful person, or one whose faithfulness he suspects.

4. You are not willing to be saved in that way by Christ, as is evident, because you are not willing that your own goodness should be set at nought. In the way of salvation by Christ men's own goodness is wholly set at nought; there is no account at all made of it. Now you cannot be willing to be saved in a way wherein your own goodness is set at nought, as is evident, since you make much of it yourself. You make much of your prayers and pains in religion, and are often thinking of them; how considerable do they appear to you, when you look back upon them! And some of you are thinking how much more you have done than others, and expecting some respect or regard that God should manifest to what you do. Now, if you make so much of what you do yourself, it is impossible that you should be freely willing that God should make nothing of it. As we may see in other things; if a man is proud of a great estate, or if he values himself much upon his honourable office, or his great abilities, it is impossible that he should like it, and heartily approve of it, that others should make light of these things and despise them.

Seeing therefore it is so evident, that you refuse to accept of Christ as your Saviour, why is Christ to be blamed that he does not save you? Christ has offered himself to you to be your Saviour in time past, and he continues offering himself still, and you continue to reject him, and yet complain that he does not save you.—So strangely unreasonable, and inconsistent with themselves, are gospel sinners!

But I expect there are many of you that still object. Such an objection as this, is probably now in the hearts of many here present.

Object. If I am not willing to have Christ for my Saviour, I cannot make myself willing.—But I would give an answer to this objection by laying down two things, that must be acknowledged to be exceeding evident.

1. It is no excuse, that you cannot receive Christ of yourself, unless you *would* if you could. This is so evident of itself, that it scarce needs any proof. Certainly if persons would not if they could, it is just the same thing as to the blame that lies upon them, whether they can or cannot. If you were willing, and then found that you could not, your being unable would alter the case, and might be some excuse; because then the defect would not be in your will, but only in your ability. But as long as you *will* not, it is no matter, whether you have ability or no ability.

If you are not willing to accept of Christ, it follows that you have no sincere willingness to be willing; because the will always necessarily approves of and rests in its own acts. To suppose the contrary would be to suppose a contradiction; it would be to suppose that a man's will is contrary to itself, or that he wills contrary to what he himself wills. As you are not willing to come to Christ, and cannot make yourself willing, so you have no sincere desire to be willing; and therefore may most justly perish without a Saviour. There is no excuse at all for you; for say what you will about your inability, the seat of your blame lies in your perverse *will*, that is an *enemy* to the Saviour. It is in vain for you to tell of your want of power, as long as your will is found defective. If a man should hate you, and smite you in the face, but should tell you at the same time, that he hated you so much, that he could not help choosing and willing so to do, would you take it the more patiently for that? Would not your indignation be rather stirred up the more?

2. If you would be willing if you could, that is no excuse, unless your willingness to be willing be *sincere*. That which is hypocritical, and does not come from the heart, but is merely forced, ought wholly to be set aside, as worthy of no consideration; because common sense teaches, that what is not hearty, but hypocritical, is indeed nothing, being only a show of what is not; but that which is good for nothing, ought to go for nothing. But if you set aside all that is not free, and call nothing a willingness, but a free hearty willingness, then see how the case stands, and whether or no you have not lost all your excuse for standing out against the calls of the gospel. You say you would make yourself willing to accept if you *could*; but it is not from any good principle that you are willing for that. It is not from any free inclination, or true respect to Christ, or any love to your duty, or any spirit of obedience. It is not from the influence of any real respect, or tendency in your heart, towards any thing good, or from any other principle than such as is in the hearts of devils, and would make them have the same sort of willingness in the same circumstances. It is therefore evident, that there can be no goodness in that *would* be willing to come to Christ: and that which has no goodness, cannot be an excuse for any badness. If there be no good in it, then it signifies nothing, and weighs nothing, when put into the scales to counterbalance that which is bad.

Sinners therefore spend their time in foolish arguing and objecting, making much of that which is good for nothing, making those excuses that are not worth offering. It is in vain to keep making objections. You stand justly condemned. The blame lies at your door: Thrust it off from you as often as you will, it will return upon you. Sew fig-leaves as long as you will, your nakedness will appear. You continue wilfully and wickedly rejecting Jesus Christ, and will not have him for your Saviour, and therefore it is sottish madness in you to charge Christ with injustice that he does not save you.

Here is the sin of unbelief! Thus the guilt of that great sin lies upon you! If you never had thus treated a Saviour, you might most justly have been damned to all eternity: it would but be exactly agreeable to your treatment of God. But besides this, when God, notwithstanding, has offered you his own dear Son, to save you from this endless misery you had deserved, and not only so, but to make you happy eternally in the enjoyment of himself, you have refused him, and would not have him for your Saviour, and still refuse to comply with the offers of the gospel; what can render any person more inexcusable? If you should now perish for ever, what can you have to say?

Hereby the justice of God in your destruction appears in two respects:

1. It is more abundantly manifest that it is *just* that you should be destroyed. Justice never appears so conspicuous as it does after refused and abused mercy. Justice in damnation appears abundantly the more clear and bright, after a wilful rejection of offered salvation. What can an offended prince do more than freely offer pardon to a condemned malefactor? And if he refuses to accept of it, will any one say that his execution is unjust?

2. God's justice will appear in your *greater* destruction.

Besides the guilt that you would have had if a Saviour never had been offered. You bring that great additional guilt upon you, of most ungratefully refusing offered deliverance. What more base and vile treatment of God can there be, than for you, when justly condemned to eternal misery, and ready to be executed, and God graciously sends his own Son, who comes and knocks at your door with a pardon in his hand, and not only a pardon, but a deed of eternal glory; I say, what can be worse, than for you, out of dislike and enmity against God and his Son, to refuse to accept those benefits at his hands? How justly may the anger of God be greatly incensed and increased by it! when a sinner thus ungratefully rejects mercy, his last error is worse than the first; this is more heinous than all his former rebellion, and may justly bring down more fearful wrath upon him.

The heinousness of this sin of rejecting a Saviour especially appears in two things:

1. The greatness of the benefits offered: which appears in the greatness of the deliverance, which is from inexpressible degrees of corruption and wickedness of heart and life, the least degree of which is infinitely evil; and from misery that is everlasting; and in the greatness and glory of the inheritance purchased and offered. Heb: ii. 3. "How shall we escape if we neglect so great salvation."

2. The wonderfulness of the way in which these benefits are procured and offered. That God should lay help on his own Son, when our case was so deplorable that help could be had in no mere creature; and that he should undertake for us, and should come into the world, and take upon him our nature, and should not only appear in a low state of life, but should die such a death, and endure such torments and contempt for sinners while enemies, how wonderful is it! And what tongue or pen can set forth the greatness of the ingratitude, baseness, and perverseness there is in it, when a perishing sinner that is in the most extreme necessity of salvation, rejects it, after it is procured in such a way as this! That so glorious a person should be thus treated, and that when he comes on so gracious an errand! That he should stand so long offering himself and calling and inviting, as he has done to many of you, and all to no purpose, but all the while be set at nought! Surely you might justly be cast into hell without one more offer of a Saviour! yea, and thrust down into the lowest hell! Herein you have exceeded the very devils; for they never rejected the offers of such glorious mercy; no, nor of any mercy at all. This will be the distinguishing condemnation of gospel-sinners, John iii. 18. "He that believeth not, is condemned already, because he hath not believed in the name of the only-begotten Son of God."—That outward smoothness of your carriage towards Christ, that appearance of respect to him in your looks, your speeches, and gestures, do not argue but that you set him at nought in your heart.. There may be much of these outward shows of respect, and yet you be like Judas, that betrayed the Son of man with a kiss; and like those mockers that bowed the knee before him, and at the same time spit in his face.

III. If God should for ever cast you off and destroy you, it would be agreeable to your treatment of *others*.—It would be no other than what would be exactly answerable to your behaviour towards your fellow-creatures, that have the same human nature, and are naturally in the same circumstances with you, and that you ought to love as yourself. And that appears especially in two things.

1. You have many of you been opposite in your spirit to the salvation of others. There are several ways that natural men manifest a spirit of opposition against the salvation of souls. It sometimes appears by a fear that their companions, acquaintance, and equals, will obtain mercy, and so become unspeakably happier than they. It is sometimes manifested by an uneasiness at the news of what others have hopefully obtained. It appears when persons envy others for it, and dislike them the more, and disrelish their talk, and avoid their company, and cannot bear to hear their religious discourse, and especially to receive warnings and counsels from them. And it oftentimes appears by their backwardness to entertain charitable thoughts of them, and by their being brought with difficulty to believe that they have obtained mercy, and a forwardness to listen to any thing that seems to contradict it. The devil hated to own Job's sincerity, Job i. 7, &c. and chap. ii. verses 3, 4, 5. There appears very often much of this spirit of the devil in natural men. Sometimes they are ready to make a ridicule of others' pretended godliness: they speak of the ground of others' hopes, as the enemies of the Jews did of the wall that they built. Neh. iv. 3. "Now Tobiah the Ammonite was by him, and he said, That which they build, if a fox go up, he shall even break down their stone-wall." There are many that join with Sanballat and Tobiah, and are of the same spirit with them. There always was, and always will be, an enmity betwixt the seed of the serpent and the seed of the woman. It appeared in Cain, who hated his brother, because he was more acceptable to God than himself; and it appears still in these times, and in this place. There are many that are like the elder brother, who could not bear that the prodigal when he returned should be received with such joy and good entertainment, and was put into a fret by it, both against his brother that had returned, and his father that made him so welcome. Luke xv.

Thus have many of you been opposite to the salvation of others, who stand in as great necessity of it as you. You have been against their being delivered from everlasting misery, who can bear it no better than you; not because their salvation would do you any hurt, or their damnation help you, any otherwise than as it would gratify that vile spirit that is so much like the spirit of the devil, who, because he is miserable himself, is unwilling that others should be happy. How just therefore is it that God should be opposite to your salvation! If you have so little love or mercy in you as to begrudge your neighbour's salvation, whom you have no cause to hate, but the law of God and nature requires you to love, why is God bound to exercise such infinite love and mercy to you, as to save you at the price of his own blood? you, whom he is no way bound to love, but who have deserved his hatred a thousand and a thousand times? You are not willing that others should be converted, who have behaved themselves injuriously towards you; and yet, will you count it hard if God does not bestow converting grace upon you that have deserved ten thousand times as ill of God, as ever any of your neighbours have of you? You are opposite to God's showing mercy to those that you think have been vicious persons, and are very unworthy of such mercy. Is others' unworthiness a just reason why God should not bestow mercy on them? and yet will God be heard, if, notwithstanding all your unworthiness, and the abominableness of your spirit and practice in his sight, he does not show you mercy? You would have God bestow liberally on you, and upbraid not; but yet when he shows mercy to others, you are ready to upbraid as soon as you hear of it: you immediately are thinking with yourself how ill they have behaved themselves; and it may be your mouths on this occasion are open, enumerating and aggravating the sins they have been guilty of. You would have God bury all your faults, and wholly blot out all your transgressions; but yet if he bestows mercy on others, it may be you will take that occasion to rake up all their old faults that you can think of. You do not much reflect on and condemn yourself for your baseness and unjust spirit towards others, in your opposition to their salvation; you do not quarrel with yourself, and condemn yourself for this; but yet you in your heart will quarrel with God, and fret at his dispensations, because you think he seems opposite to showing mercy to you. One would think that the consideration of these things should for ever *stop your mouth*.

2. Consider how you have promoted others' damnation. Many of you, by the bad examples you have set, by corrupting the minds of others, by your sinful conversation, by leading them into or strengthening them in sin, and by the mischief you have done in human society other ways that might be mentioned, have been guilty of those things that have tended to others' damnation. You have heretofore appeared on the side of sin and Satan, and have strengthened their interest, and have been many ways accessary to others' sins, have hardened their hearts, and thereby have done what has tended to the ruin of their souls.—Without doubt there are those here present who

have been in a great measure the means of others' damnation. One man may really be a means of others' damnation as well as salvation. Christ charges the scribes and Pharisees with this, Matt. xxiii. 13. "Ye shut up the kingdom of heaven against men; for ye neither go in yourselves, neither suffer ye them that are entering, to go in." We have no reason to think that this congregation has none in it who are cursed from day to day by poor souls that are roaring out in hell, whose damnation they have been the means of, or have greatly contributed to.—There are many who contribute to their own children's damnation, by neglecting their education, by setting them bad examples, and bringing them up in sinful ways. They take some care of their bodies, but take little care of their poor souls; they provide for them bread to eat, but deny them the bread of life, that their famishing souls stand in need of. And are there no such parents here who have thus treated their children? If their children be not gone to hell, no thanks to them; it is not because they have not done what has tended to their destruction. Seeing therefore you have had no more regard to others' salvation, and have promoted their damnation, how justly might God leave you to perish yourself!

IV. If God should eternally cast you off, it would but be agreeable to your own behaviour towards *yourself;* and that in two respects:

1. In being so *careless* of your own salvation. You have refused to take care for your salvation, as God has counselled and commanded you from time to time; and why may not God neglect it, now you seek it of him? Is God obliged to be more careful of your happiness, than you are either of your own happiness or his glory? Is God bound to take that care for you, out of love to you, that you will not take for yourself, either from love to yourself, or regard to his authority? How long, and how greatly, have you neglected the welfare of your precious soul, refusing to take pains and deny yourself, or put yourself a little out of your way for your salvation, while God has been calling upon you! Neither your duty to God, nor love to your own soul, were enough to induce you to do little things for your own eternal welfare; and yet do you now expect that God should do great things, putting forth almighty power, and exercising infinite mercy for it? You was urged to take care for your salvation, and not to put it off. You was told *that* was the best time before you grew older, and that it might be, if you would put it off, God would not hear you afterwards; but yet you would not hearken; you would run the venture of it. Now how justly might God order it so, that it should be too late, leaving you to seek in vain! You was told, that you would repent of it if you delayed; but you would not hear: how justly therefore may God give you cause to repent of it, by refusing to show you mercy now! If God sees you going on in ways contrary to his commands and his glory, and requires you to forsake them, and tells you that they tend to the destruction of your own soul, and therefore counsels you to avoid them, and you refuse; how just would it be if God should be provoked by it, henceforward to be as careless of the good of your soul as you are yourself!

2. You have not only neglected your salvation, but you have wilfully taken direct courses to *undo* yourself. You have gone on in those ways and practices which have directly tended to your damnation, and have been perverse and obstinate in it. You cannot plead ignorance; you had all the light set before you that you could desire. God told you that you was undoing yourself; but yet you would do it. He told you that the path you was going in led to destruction, and counselled you to avoid it; but you would not hearken. How justly therefore may God leave you to be undone! You have obstinately persisted to travel in the way that leads to hell for a long time, contrary to God's continual counsels and commands, till it may be at length you are got almost to your journey's end, and are come near to hell's gate, and so begin to be sensible of your danger and misery; and now account it unjust and hard if God will not deliver you! You have destroyed yourself, and destroyed yourself wilfully, contrary to God's repeated counsels, yea, and destroyed yourself in fighting against God. Now therefore, why do you blame any but *yourself* if you are destroyed? If you will undo yourself in opposing God, and while God opposes you by his calls and counsels, and, it may be too, by the convictions of his Spirit, what can you object against it, if God now leaves you to be undone? You would have your own way, and did not like that God should oppose you in it, and your way was to ruin your own soul; how just therefore is it, if, now at length, God ceases to oppose you, and falls in with you, and lets your soul be ruined; and as you would destroy yourself, so should put to his hand to destroy you too! The ways you went on in had a natural tendency to your misery: if you would drink poison in opposition to God, and in contempt of him and his advice, who can you blame but yourself if you are poisoned, and so perish? If you would run into the fire against all restraints both of God's mercy and authority, you must even blame yourself if you are burnt.

Thus I have proposed some things to your consideration, which, if you are not exceeding blind, senseless, and perverse, will *stop your mouth,* and convince you that you stand justly condemned before God; and that he would in no wise deal hardly with you, but altogether *justly,* in denying you any mercy, and in refusing to hear your prayers, though you pray never so earnestly, and never so often, and continue in it never so long. God may utterly disregard your tears and moans, your heavy heart, your earnest desires, and great endeavours; and he may cast you into eternal destruction, without any regard to your welfare, denying you converting grace, and giving you over to Satan, and at last cast you into the lake that burns with fire and brimstone, to be there to eternity, having no rest day or night, for ever glorifying his justice upon you in the presence of the holy angels, and in the presence of the Lamb.

Object. But here many may still object, (for I am sensible it is a hard thing to *stop* sinners' mouths,) "God shows mercy to others that have done these things as well as I, yea, that have done a great deal worse than I."

Ans. 1. That does not prove that God is any way *bound* to show mercy to you, or them either. If God bestows it on others, he does not so because he is bound to bestow it: he might if he had pleased, with glorious justice, have denied it them. If God bestows it on some, that does not prove that he is *bound* to bestow it on *any;* and if he is bound to bestow it on none, then he is not bound to bestow it on you. God is in debt to none; and if he gives to some that he is not in debt to, because it is his pleasure, that does not bring him into debt to others. It alters not the case as to you, whether others have it, or have it not: you do not deserve damnation the less, than if mercy never had been bestowed on any at all. Matt. xx. 15. "Is thine eye evil, because mine is good?"

2. If this objection be good, then the exercise of God's mercy is not in his *own right,* and his grace is not his own to give. That which God may not dispose of as he pleases, is not his own; for that which is one's own, is at his own disposal: but if it be not God's own, then he is not capable of making a gift or present of it to any one; it is impossible to give what is a *debt.*—What is it that you would make of God? Must the great God be tied up, that he must not use his own pleasure in bestowing his own gifts, but if he bestows them on one, must be looked upon obliged to bestow them on another? Is not God worthy to have the same right, with respect to the gifts of his grace, that a man has to his money or goods? Is it because God is not so great, and should be more in subjection than man, that this cannot be allowed him? If any of you see cause to show kindness to a neighbour, do all the rest of your neighbours come to you, and tell you, that you owe them so much as you have given to such a man? But this is the way that you deal with God, as though God were not worthy to have as absolute a property in his goods, as you have in yours.

At this rate God cannot make a present of any thing; he has nothing of his own to bestow: if he has a mind to show peculiar favour to some, or to lay some particular persons under peculiar obligations to him, he cannot do it; because he has no special gift at his own disposal. If this be the case, why do you pray to God to bestow saving grace upon you? If God does not do fairly to deny it you, because he bestows it on others, then it is not worth your while to pray for it, but you may go and tell him that he has bestowed it on others as bad or worse than you, and so *demand* it of him as a debt. And at this rate persons never need to *thank* God for salvation, when it is bestowed; for what occasion is there to thank God for that which was not at his own disposal, and that he could not fairly have denied? The thing at bottom is, that men have low thoughts of God, and high thoughts of themselves; and therefore it is that they look upon God as having so little right, and they so much. Matt. xx. 15. "Is it not lawful for me to do what I will with mine own?"

3. God may justly show greater respect to others than to you, for you have shown greater respect to others than to God. You have rather chosen to offend God than men. God only shows a greater respect to others, who are by nature your equals, than to you; but you have shown a greater respect to those that are infinitely inferior to God than to him. You have shown a greater regard to *wicked* men than to God; you have honoured them more, loved them better, and adhered to them rather than to him. Yea, you have honoured the devil, in many respects, more than God: you have chosen his will and his interest, rather than God's will and his glory: you have chosen a little worldly pelf, rather than God: you have set more by a vile lust than by him: you have chosen these things, and rejected God. You have set your heart on these things, and cast God behind your back: and where is the injustice if God is pleased to show greater respect to others than to you, or if he chooses others and rejects you? You have shown great respect to vile and worthless things, and no respect to God's glory; and why may not God set his love on others, and have no respect to your happiness? You have shown great respect to others, and not to God, whom you are laid under infinite obligations to respect above all; and why may not God show respect to others, and not to you, who never have laid him under the least obligation?

And will you not be ashamed, notwithstanding all these things, still to open your mouth, to object and cavil about the *decrees* of God, and other things that you cannot fully understand. Let the decrees of God be what they will, that alters not the case as to your *liberty*, any more than if God had only foreknown. And why is God to blame for decreeing things? Especially since he decrees nothing but *good*. How unbecoming an infinitely wise Being would it have been to have made a world, and let things run at random, without disposing events, or fore-ordering how they should come to pass? And what is that to you, how God has fore-ordered things, as long as your constant experience teaches you, that it does not hinder your doing what you choose to do. This you know, and your daily practice and behaviour amongst men declares that you are fully sensible of it, with respect to yourself and others. Still to object, because there are some things in God's dispensations above your understanding, is exceedingly unreasonable. Your own conscience charges you with great guilt, and with those things that have been mentioned, let the secret things of God be what they will. Your conscience charges you with those vile dispositions, and that base behaviour towards God, that you would at any time most highly resent in your neighbour towards you, and that not a whit the less for any concern those secret counsels and mysterious dispensations of God may have in the matter. It is in vain for you to exalt yourself against an infinitely great, and holy, and just God. If you continue in it, it will be to your eternal shame and confusion, when hereafter you shall see at whose door all the blame of your misery lies.

I will finish what I have to say to natural men in the application of this doctrine, with a *caution* not to improve the doctrine to *discouragement*. For though it would be *righteous* in God for ever to cast you off, and destroy you, yet it would also be just in God to save you, in and through Christ, who has made complete satisfaction for all sin. Rom. iii. 25, 26. "Whom God hath set forth to be a propitiation, through faith in his blood, to declare his righteousness for the remission of sins that are past, through the forbearance of God; to declare, I say, at this time his righteousness, that he might be just, and the justifier of him which believeth in Jesus." Yea, God may, through this Mediator, not only justly, but honourably, show you mercy. The blood of Christ is so precious, that it is fully sufficient to pay the debt you have contracted, and perfectly to vindicate the Divine Majesty from all the dishonour cast upon it, by those many great sins of yours that have been mentioned. It was as great, and indeed a much greater thing, for Christ to die, than it would have been for you and all mankind to have burnt in hell to all eternity. Of such dignity and excellency is Christ in the eyes of God, that, seeing he has suffered so much for poor sinners, God is willing to be at peace with them, however vile and unworthy they have been, and on how many accounts soever the punishment would be *just*. So that you need not be at all discouraged from seeking mercy, for there is enough in Christ.

Indeed it would not become the glory of God's majesty to show mercy to you, so sinful and vile a creature, for any thing that you have done; for such worthless and despicable things as your prayers, and other religious performances. It would be very dishonourable and unworthy of God so to do, and it is in vain to expect it. He will show mercy only on Christ's account, and that, according to his sovereign pleasure, on whom he pleases, when he pleases, and in what manner he pleases. You cannot bring him under *obligation* by your works; do what you will, he will not look on himself obliged. But if it be his pleasure, he can honourably show mercy through Christ to any sinner of you all, not one in this congregation excepted.—Therefore here is encouragement for you still to seek and wait, notwithstanding all your wickedness; agreeable to Samuel's speech to the children of Israel, when they were terrified with the thunder and rain that God sent, and when guilt stared them in the face, 1 Sam. xii. 20. "Fear not; ye have done all this wickedness; yet turn not aside from following the Lord, but serve the Lord with all your heart."

I would conclude this discourse by putting the godly in mind of the freeness and wonderfulness of the grace of God towards them. For such were the same of you.—The case was just so with you as you have heard; you had such a wicked heart, you lived such a wicked life, and it would have been most just with God for ever to have cast you off: but he has had mercy upon you; he hath made his glorious grace appear in your everlasting salvation. You had no love to God; but yet he has exercised unspeakable love to you. You have contemned God, and set light by him; but so great a value has God's grace set on you and your happiness, that you have been redeemed at the price of the blood of his own Son. You chose to be with Satan in his service; but yet God hath made you a joint heir with Christ of his glory. You was ungrateful for past mercies; yet God not only continued those mercies, but bestowed unspeakably greater mercies upon you. You refused to hear when God called; yet God heard you when you called. You abused the infiniteness of God's mercy to encourage yourself in sin against him; yet God has manifested the infiniteness of that mercy, in the exercises of it towards you. You have rejected Christ, and set him at nought; and yet he is become your Saviour. You have neglected your own salvation; but God has not neglected it. You have destroyed yourself; but yet in God has been your help. God has magnified his free grace towards you, and not to others; because he has chosen you, and it hath pleased him to set his love upon you.

O! what cause is here for praise! What obligations you are under to bless the Lord who hath dealt bountifully with you, and magnify his holy name! What cause for you to praise God in humility, to walk humbly before him. Ezek. xvi. 63. "That thou mayest remember and be confounded, and never open thy mouth any more, because of thy shame, when I am pacified toward thee for all that thou hast done, saith the Lord God!" You shall never open your mouth in boasting, or self-justification; but lie the lower before God for his mercy to you. You have reason, the more abundantly, to open your mouth in God's praises, that they may be continually in your mouth, both here and to all eternity, for his rich, unspeakable, and sovereign mercy to you, whereby he, and he alone, hath made you to differ from others.

DISCOURSE V.

THE EXCELLENCY OF CHRIST.

REV. v. 5, 6.

And one of the elders saith unto me, Weep not: behold, the Lion of the tribe of Juda, the Root of David, hath prevailed to open the book, and to loose the seven seals thereof. And I beheld, and, lo, in the midst of the throne, and of the four beasts, and in the midst of the elders, stood a Lamb as it had been slain——.

THE visions and revelations the apostle John had of the future events of God's providence, are here introduced with a vision of the book of God's decrees, by which those events were fore-ordained. This is represented (ver. 1.) as a book in the right hand of him who sat on the throne, "written within and on the back side, and sealed with seven seals." Books, in the form in which they were wont of old to be made, were broad leaves of parchment or paper, or something of that nature, joined together at one edge, and so rolled up together, and then sealed, or some way fastened together, to prevent their unfolding and opening. Hence we read of the roll of a book, Jer. xxxvi. 2. It seems to have been such a book that John had a vision of here; and therefore it is said to be "written within and on the back side," *i. e.* on the inside pages, and also on one of the outside pages, *viz.* that which was rolled in, in rolling the book up together. And it is said to be "sealed with seven seals," to signify that what was written in it was perfectly hidden and secret; or that God's decrees of future events are sealed, and shut up from all possibility of being discovered by creatures, till God is pleased to make them known. We find that seven is often used in Scripture as the number of perfection, to signify the superlative or most perfect degree of any thing; which probably arose from this, that on the seventh day God beheld the works of creation finished, and rested and rejoiced in them, as being complete and perfect.

When John saw this book, he tells us, he "saw a strong angel proclaiming with a loud voice, Who is worthy to open the book, and to loose the seals thereof? And no man in heaven, nor in earth, neither under the earth, was able to open the book, neither to look thereon." And that he wept much, because "no man was found worthy to open and read the book, neither to look thereon." And then tells us how his tears were dried up, *viz.* that "one of the elders said unto him, Weep not; Behold the Lion of the tribe of Judah hath prevailed," &c. as in the text. Though no man nor angel, nor any mere creature, was found either able to loose the seals, or worthy to be admitted to the privilege of reading the book; yet this was declared, for the comfort of this beloved disciple, that Christ was found both able and worthy. And we have an account in the succeeding chapters how he actually did it, opening the seals in order, first one, and then another, revealing what God had decreed should come to pass hereafter. And we have an account in this chapter, of his coming and taking the book out of the right hand of him that sat on the throne, and of the joyful praises that were sung to him in heaven and earth on that occasion.

Many things might be observed in the words of the text; but it is to my present purpose only to take notice of the two distinct appellations here given to Christ.

1. He is called a *Lion*. *Behold, the Lion of the tribe of Judah.* He seems to be called the Lion of the tribe of Judah, in allusion to what Jacob said in his blessing of the tribes on his death-bed; who, when he came to bless Judah, compares him to a lion, Gen. xlix. 9. "Judah is a lion's whelp; from the prey, my son, thou art gone up: he stooped down, he couched as a lion, and as an old lion; who shall rouse him up?" And also to the standard of the camp of Judah in the wilderness, on which was displayed a lion, according to the ancient tradition of the Jews. It is much on account of the valiant acts of David that the tribe of Judah, of which David was, is in Jacob's prophetical blessing compared to a lion; but more especially with an eye to Jesus Christ, who also was of that tribe, and was descended of David, and is in our text called "the Root of David;" and therefore Christ is here called "the Lion of the tribe of Judah."

2. He is called a *Lamb*. John was told of a Lion that had prevailed to open the book, and probably expected to see a lion in his vision; but while he is expecting, behold a Lamb appears to open the book, an exceeding diverse kind of creature from a lion. A lion is a devourer, one that is wont to make terrible slaughter of others; and no creature more easily falls a prey to him than a lamb. And Christ is here represented not only as a Lamb, a creature very liable to be slain, but a "Lamb as it had been slain," that is, with the marks of its deadly wounds appearing on it.

That which I would observe from the words, for the subject of my present discourse, is this, *viz.*——

"There is an admirable conjunction of diverse excellencies in Jesus Christ."

The lion and the lamb, though very diverse kinds of creatures, yet have each their peculiar excellencies. The lion excels in strength, and in the majesty of his appearance and voice: the lamb excels in meekness and patience, besides the excellent nature of the creature as good for food, and yielding that which is fit for our clothing, and being suitable to be offered in sacrifice to God. But we see that Christ is in the text compared to both; because the diverse excellencies of both wonderfully meet in him,—In handling this subject I would,

First, Show wherein there is an admirable conjunction of diverse excellencies in Christ.

Secondly, How this admirable conjunction of excellencies appear in Christ's acts.

And then make application.

First, I would show wherein there is an admirable conjunction of diverse excellencies in Jesus Christ. Which appears in three things:

I. There is a conjunction of such excellencies in Christ, as, in our manner of conceiving, are very diverse one from another.

II. There is in him a conjunction of such really diverse excellencies, as otherwise would have seemed to us utterly incompatible in the same subject.

III. Such diverse excellencies are exercised in him towards men that otherwise would have seemed impossible to be exercised towards the same object.

I. There is a conjunction of such excellencies in Christ, as, in our manner of conceiving, are very diverse one from another. Such are the various divine perfections and excellencies that Christ is possessed of. Christ is a divine person; and therefore has all the attributes of God. The difference between these is chiefly relative, and in our manner of conceiving them. And those which, in this sense, are most diverse, meet in the person of Christ. I shall mention two instances.

1. There do meet in Jesus Christ infinite highness and infinite condescension. Christ, as he is God, is infinitely great and high above all. He is higher than the kings of the earth; for he is King of kings, and Lord of lords. He is higher than the heavens, and higher than the highest angels of heaven. So great is he, that all men, all kings and princes, are as worms of the dust before him; all nations are as the drop of the bucket, and the light dust of the balance; yea, and angels themselves are as nothing

before him. He is so high, that he is infinitely above any need of us; above our reach, that we cannot be profitable to him; and above our conceptions, that we cannot comprehend him. Prov. xxx. 4. "What is his name, and what is his Son's name, if thou canst tell?" Our understandings, if we stretch them never so far, cannot reach up to his divine glory. Job xi. 8. "It is high as heaven, what canst thou do?" Christ is the Creator and great Possessor of heaven and earth. He is sovereign Lord of all. He rules over the whole universe, and doth whatsoever pleaseth him. His knowledge is without bound. His wisdom is perfect, and what none can circumvent. His power is infinite, and none can resist him. His riches are immense and inexhaustible. His majesty is infinitely awful.

And yet he is one of infinite condescension. None are so low or inferior, but Christ's condescension is sufficient to take a gracious notice of them. He condescends not only to the angels, humbling himself to behold the things that are done in heaven, but he also condescends to such poor creatures as men; and that not only so as to take notice of princes and great men, but of those that are of meanest rank and degree, "the poor of the world," James ii. 5. Such as are commonly despised by their fellow-creatures, Christ does not despise. 1 Cor. i. 28. "Base things of the world, and things that are despised, hath God chosen." Christ condescends to take notice of beggars, Luke xvi. 22. and people of the most despised nations. In Christ Jesus is neither "Barbarian, Scythian, bond nor free," Col. iii. 11. He that is thus high, condescends to take a gracious notice of little children, Matt. xix. 14. "Suffer little children to come unto me." Yea, which is more, his condescension is sufficient to take a gracious notice of the most unworthy, sinful creatures, those that have no good deservings, and those that have infinite ill-deservings.

Yea, so great is his condescension, that it is not only sufficient to take some gracious notice of such as these, but sufficient for every thing that is an act of condescension. His condescension is great enough to become their friend; to become their companion, to unite their souls to him in spiritual marriage. It is enough to take their nature upon him, to become one of them, that he may be one with them. Yea, it is great enough to abase himself yet lower for them, even to expose himself to shame and spitting; yea, to yield up himself to an ignominious death for them. And what act of condescension can be conceived of greater? Yet such an act as this, has his condescension yielded to, for those that are so low and mean, despicable and unworthy!

Such a conjunction of infinite highness and low condescension, in the same person, is admirable. We see, by manifold instances, what a tendency a high station has in men, to make them to be of a quite contrary disposition. If one worm be a little exalted above another, by having more dust, or a bigger dunghill, how much does he make of himself! What a distance does he keep from those that are below him! And a little condescension is what he expects should be made much of, and greatly acknowledged. Christ condescends to wash our feet; but how would great men, (or rather the bigger worms,) account themselves debased by acts of far less condescension!

2. There meet in Jesus Christ, infinite *justice* and infinite *grace*. As Christ is a divine person, he is infinitely holy and just; hating sin, and disposed to execute condign punishment for sin. He is the Judge of the world, and the infinitely just Judge of it, and will not at all acquit the wicked, or by any means clear the guilty.

And yet he is infinitely gracious and merciful. Though his justice be so strict with respect to all sin, and every breach of the law, yet he has grace sufficient for every sinner, and even the chief of sinners. And it is not only sufficient for the most unworthy to show them mercy, and bestow some good upon them, but to bestow the greatest good; yea, it is sufficient to bestow all good upon them, and to do all things for them. There is no benefit or blessing that they can receive, so great but the grace of Christ is sufficient to bestow it on the greatest sinner that ever lived. And not only so, but so great is his grace, that nothing is too much as the means of this good. It is sufficient not only to do great things, but also to suffer in order to it; and not only to suffer, but to suffer most extremely even unto death, the most terrible of natural evils; and not only death, but the most ignominious and tormenting, and every way the most terrible that men could inflict; yea, and greater sufferings than men could inflict, who could only torment the body. He had sufferings in his soul, that were the more immediate fruits of the wrath of God against the sins of those he undertakes for.

II. There do meet in the person of Christ such really diverse excellencies, which otherwise would have been thought utterly incompatible in the same subject; such as are conjoined in no other person whatever, either divine, human, or angelical; and such as neither men nor angels would ever have imagined could have met together in the same person, had it not been seen in the person of Christ. I would give some instances.

1. In the person of Christ do meet together infinite *glory* and lowest *humility*. Infinite glory, and the virtue of humility, meet in no other person but Christ. They meet in no created person; for no created person has infinite glory; and they meet in no other divine person but Christ. For though the divine nature be infinitely abhorrent to pride, yet humility is not properly predicable of God the Father, and the Holy Ghost, that exists only in the divine nature; because it is proper excellency only of a created nature; for it consists radically in a sense of a comparative lowness and littleness before God, or the great distance between God and the subject of this virtue; but it would be a contradiction to suppose any such thing in God.

But in Jesus Christ, who is both God and man, those two diverse excellencies are sweetly united. He is a person infinitely exalted in glory and dignity. Phil. ii. 6. "Being in the form of God, he thought it not robbery to be equal with God." There is equal honour due to him with the Father. John v. 23.—"That all men should honour the Son, even as they honour the Father." God himself says to him, "Thy throne, O God, is for ever and ever," Heb. i. 8. And there is the same supreme respect and divine worship paid to him by the angels of heaven, as to God the Father, (ver. 6.) "Let all the angels of God worship him."

But however he is thus above all, yet he is lowest of all in humility. There never was so great an instance of this virtue among either men or angels, as Jesus. None ever was so sensible of the distance between God and him, or had a heart so lowly before God, as the man Christ Jesus. Matt. xi. 29. What a wonderful spirit of humility appeared in him, when he was here upon earth, in all his behaviour! In his contentment in his mean outward condition, contentedly living in the family of Joseph the carpenter, and Mary his mother, for thirty years together, and afterwards choosing outward meanness, poverty, and contempt, rather than earthly greatness; in his washing his disciples' feet, and in all his speeches and deportment towards them; in his cheerfully sustaining the form of a servant through his whole life, and submitting to such immense humiliation at death!

2. In the person of Christ do meet together infinite *majesty* and transcendent *meekness*. These again are two qualifications that meet together in no other person but Christ. Meekness, properly so called, is a virtue proper only to the creature: we scarcely ever find meekness mentioned as a divine attribute in Scripture; at least not in the New Testament; for thereby seems to be signified, a calmness and quietness of spirit, arising from humility in mutable beings that are naturally liable to be put into a ruffle by the assaults of a tempestuous and injurious world. But Christ being both God and man, hath both infinite majesty and superlative meekness.

Christ was a person of infinite majesty. It is he that is spoken of, Psalm xlv. 3. "Gird thy sword upon thy thigh, O most mighty, with thy glory and thy majesty." It is he that is mighty, that rideth on the heavens, and his excellency on the sky. It is he that is terrible out of his holy places; who is mightier than the noise of many waters, yea, than the mighty waves of the sea: before whom a fire goeth, and burneth up his enemies round about; at whose presence the earth quakes, and the hills melt; who sitteth on the circle of the earth, and all the inhabitants thereof are as grasshoppers; who rebukes the sea, and maketh it dry, and drieth up the rivers; whose eyes are as a flame of fire; from whose presence, and from the glory of whose power, the wicked shall be punished with everlasting destruction; who is the blessed and only Potentate, the King of kings, and Lord of lords, who hath heaven for his throne, and the earth for his footstool, and is the high and lofty One who inhabits eternity, whose kingdom is an everlasting kingdom, and of whose dominion there is no end.

And yet he was the most marvellous instance of meekness, and humble quietness of spirit, that ever was; agreeable to the *prophecies* of him, Matt. xxi. 4, 5. "All this was done, that it might be fulfilled which was spoken by the prophet, saying, Tell ye the daughter of Sion, Behold, thy King cometh unto thee, meek, and sitting upon an ass, and a colt the foal of an ass." And, agreeable to what Christ declares of himself, Matt. xi. 29. "I am meek and lowly in heart." And agreeable to what was manifest in his behaviour: for there never was such an instance seen on earth, of a meek behaviour, under injuries and reproaches, and towards enemies; who, when he was reviled, reviled not again. He had a wonderful spirit of forgiveness, was ready to forgive his worst enemies, and prayed for them with fervent and effectual prayers. With what meekness did he appear in the ring of soldiers that were contemning and mocking him; he was silent, and opened not his mouth, but went as a lamb to the slaughter. Thus is Christ a Lion in majesty, and a Lamb in meekness.

3. There meet in the person of Christ the deepest *reverence* towards God and *equality* with God. Christ, when on earth, appeared full of holy reverence towards the Father. He paid the most reverential worship to him, praying to him with postures of reverence. Thus we read of his "kneeling down and praying," Luke xxii. 41. This became Christ, as one who had taken on him the human nature; but at the same time he existed in the divine nature; whereby his person was in all respects equal to the person of the Father. God the Father hath no attribute or perfection that the Son hath not, in equal degree, and equal glory. These things meet in no other person but Jesus Christ.

4. There are conjoined in the person of Christ infinite *worthiness* of good, and the greatest *patience* under sufferings of evil. He was perfectly innocent, and deserved no suffering. He deserved nothing from God by any guilt of his own; and he deserved no ill from men. Yea, he was not only harmless and undeserving of suffering, but he was infinitely worthy; worthy of the infinite love of the Father, worthy of infinite and eternal happiness, and infinitely worthy of all possible esteem, love, and service from all men. And yet he was perfectly patient under the greatest sufferings that ever were endured in this world. Heb. xii. 2. "He endured the cross, despising the shame." He suffered not from his Father for his faults, but ours; and he suffered from men not for his faults, but for those things on account of which he was infinitely worthy of their love and honour; which made his patience the more wonderful and the more glorious. 1 Pet. ii. 20, &c. "For what glory is it, if when ye be buffeted for your faults, ye shall take it patiently, but if when ye do well, and suffer for it, ye take it patiently; this is acceptable with God. For even hereunto were ye called; because Christ also suffered for us, leaving us an example, that we should follow his steps: who did no sin, neither was guile found in his mouth: who when he was reviled, reviled not again; when he suffered, he threatened not; but committed himself to him that judgeth righteously: who his own self bare our sins in his own body on the tree, that we being dead to sin, should live unto righteousness: by whose stripes ye were healed." There is no such conjunction of innocence, worthiness, and patience under sufferings, as in the person of Christ.

5. In the person of Christ are conjoined an exceeding spirit of *obedience*, with supreme *dominion* over heaven and earth. Christ is the Lord of all things in two respects: he is so, as God-man and Mediator; and thus his dominion is appointed, and given him of the Father. Having it by delegation from God, he is as it were the Father's vicegerent. But he is Lord of all things in another respect, *viz.* as he is (by his original nature) God; and so he is by natural right the Lord of all, and supreme over all as much as the Father. Thus, he has dominion over the world, not by delegation, but in his own right. He is not an under God, as the Arians suppose, but, to all intents and purposes, supreme God.

And yet in the same person is found the greatest spirit of obedience to the commands and laws of God that ever was in the universe; which was manifest in his obedience here in this world. John xiv. 31. "As the Father gave me commandment, even so I do." John xv. 10. "[illegible]en as I have kept my Father's commandments, and abide in his love." The greatness of his obedience appears in its perfection, and in his obeying commands of such exceeding difficulty. Never any one received commands from God of such difficulty, and that were so great a trial of obedience, as Jesus Christ. One of God's commands to him was, that he should yield himself to those dreadful sufferings that he underwent. See John x. 18. "No man taketh it from me, but I lay it down of myself."—"This commandment received I of my Father." And Christ was thoroughly obedient to this command of God. Heb. v. 8. "Though he were a Son, yet he learned obedience by the things that he suffered." Philip. ii. 8. "He humbled himself, and became obedient unto death, even the death of the cross." Never was there such an instance of obedience in man or angel as this, though he was at the same time supreme Lord of both angels and men.

6. In the person of Christ are conjoined absolute *sovereignty* and perfect *resignation*. This is another unparalleled conjunction. Christ, as he is God, is the absolute sovereign of the world; the sovereign disposer of all events. The decrees of God are all his sovereign decrees; and the work of creation, and all God's works of providence, are his sovereign works. It is he that worketh all things according to the counsel of his own will. Col. i. 16, 17. "By him, and through him, and to him, are all things." John v. 17. "The Father worketh hitherto, and I work." Matt. viii. 3. "I will, be thou clean."

But yet Christ was the most wonderful instance of resignation that ever appeared in the world. He was absolutely and perfectly resigned when he had a near and immediate prospect of his terrible sufferings, and the dreadful cup that he was to drink. The idea and expectation of this made his soul exceeding sorrowful, even unto death, and put him into such an agony, that his sweat was as it were great drops or clots of blood, falling down to the ground. But in such circumstances he was wholly resigned to the will of God. Matt. xxvi. 39. "O my Father, if it be possible, let this cup pass from me: nevertheless, not as I will, but as thou wilt." Verse 42. "O my Father, if this cup may not pass from me, except I drink it, thy will be done."

7. In Christ do meet together *self-sufficiency*, and an entire *trust* and reliance on God; which is another conjunction peculiar to the person of Christ. As he is a divine person, he is self-sufficient, standing in need of nothing. All creatures are dependent on him, but he is dependent on none, but is absolutely independent. His proceeding from the Father, in his eternal generation or filiation, argues no proper dependence on the *will* of the Father; for that proceeding was natural and *necessary*, and not arbitrary. But yet Christ entirely trusted in God: his enemies say that of him, "He trusted in God that he would deliver him," Matt. xxvii. 43. And the apostle testifies, 1 Pet. ii. 23. "That he committed himself to God."

III. Such diverse excellencies are expressed in him towards men, that otherwise would have seemed impossible to be exercised towards the same object; as particularly these three, justice, mercy, and truth. The same that are mentioned Psalm lxxxv. 10. "Mercy and truth are met together, righteousness and peace have kissed each other." The strict justice of God, and even his revenging justice, and that against the sins of men, never was so gloriously manifested as in Christ. He manifested an infinite regard to the attribute of God's justice, in that, when he had a mind to save sinners, he was willing to undergo such extreme sufferings, rather than that their salvation should be to the injury of the honour of that attribute. And as he is the Judge of the world, he doth himself exercise strict justice; he will not clear the guilty, nor at all acquit the wicked in judgment. Yet how wonderfully is infinite mercy towards sinners displayed in him! And what glorious and ineffable grace and love have been and are exercised by him, towards sinful men! Though he be the just Judge of a sinful world, yet he is also the Saviour of the world. Though he be a consuming fire to sin, yet he is the light and life of sinners. Rom. iii. 25, 26. "Whom God hath set forth to be a propitiation, through faith in his blood, to declare his righteousness for the remission of sins that are past, through the forbearance of God; to declare, I say, at this time his righteousness, that he might be just, and the justifier of him which believeth in Jesus."

So the immutable truth of God, in the threatenings of his law against the sins of men, was never so manifested as it is in Jesus Christ; for there never was any other so great a trial of the unalterableness of the truth of God in those threatenings, as when sin came to be imputed to his own Son. And then in Christ has been seen already an actual complete accomplishment of those threatenings, which never has been nor will be seen in any other instance; because the eternity that will be taken up in fulfilling those threatenings on others, never will be finished. Christ manifested an infinite regard to this truth of God in his sufferings. And, in his judging the world, he makes the covenant of works, that contains those dreadful threatenings, his rule of judgment. He will see to it, that it is not infringed in the least jot or tittle: he will do nothing contrary to the threatenings of the law, and their complete fulfilment. And yet in him we have many great and precious promises, promises of perfect deliverance from the penalty of the law. And this is the promise that he hath promised us, even eternal life. And in him are all the promises of God, yea, and Amen.

Having thus shown wherein there is an admirable conjunction of excellencies in Jesus Christ, I now proceed,

Secondly, To show how this admirable conjunction of excellencies appears in Christ's *acts*.

1. It appears in what Christ did in taking on him our nature. In this act, his infinite condescension wonderfully appeared, that he who was God should become man; that the word should be made flesh, and should take on him a nature infinitely below his original nature! And it appears yet more remarkably in the low circumstances of his incarnation: he was conceived in the womb of a poor young woman, whose poverty appeared in this, when she came to offer sacrifices of her purification, she brought what was allowed of in the law only in case of poverty; as Luke ii. 24. "According to what is said in the law of the Lord, a pair of turtle-doves, or two young pigeons." This was allowed only in case the person was so poor that she was not able to offer a lamb. Lev. xii. 8.

And though his infinite condescension thus appeared in the manner of his incarnation, yet his divine dignity also appeared in it; for though he was conceived in the womb of a poor virgin, yet he was conceived there by the power of the Holy Ghost. And his divine dignity also appeared in the holiness of his conception and birth. Though he was conceived in the womb of one of the corrupt race of mankind, yet he was conceived and born without sin; as the angel said to the blessed Virgin, Luke i. 35. "The Holy Ghost shall come upon thee, and the power of the Highest shall overshadow thee; therefore also that holy thing which shall be born of thee, shall be called the Son of God."

His infinite condescension marvellously appeared in the manner of his birth. He was brought forth in a stable, because there was no room for them in the inn. The inn was taken up by others, that were looked upon as persons of greater account. The blessed Virgin, being poor and despised, was turned or shut out. Though she was in such necessitous circumstances, yet those that counted themselves her betters would not give place to her; and therefore, in the time of her travail, she was forced to betake herself to a stable; and when the child was born, it was wrapped in swaddling-clothes, and laid in a manger. There Christ lay a little infant; and there he eminently appeared as a lamb. But yet this feeble infant, born thus in a stable, and laid in a manger, was born to conquer and triumph over Satan, that roaring lion. He came to subdue the mighty powers of darkness, and make a show of them openly; and so to restore peace on earth, and to manifest God's good-will towards men, and to bring glory to God in the highest; according as the end of his birth was declared by the joyful songs of the glorious hosts of angels appearing to the shepherds at the same time that the infant lay in the manger; whereby his divine dignity was manifested.

II. This admirable conjunction of excellencies appears in the acts and various passages of Christ's life. Though Christ dwelt in mean outward circumstances, whereby his condescension and humility especially appeared, and his majesty was veiled; yet his divine dignity and glory did in many of his acts shine through the veil, and it illustriously appeared, that he was not only the Son of man, but the great God.

Thus, in the circumstances of his infancy, his outward meanness appeared; yet there was something then to show forth his divine dignity, in the wise men's being stirred up to come from the east to give honour to him, their being led by a miraculous star, and coming and falling down and worshipping him, and presenting him with gold, frankincense, and myrrh. His humility and meekness wonderfully appeared in his subjection to his mother and reputed father when he was a child. Herein he appeared as a lamb. But his divine glory broke forth and shone when, at twelve years old, he disputed with doctors in the temple. In that he appeared, in some measure, as *the Lion of the tribe of Judah*.

And so, after he entered on his public ministry, his marvellous humility and meekness was manifested in his choosing to appear in such mean outward circumstances; and in being contented in them, when he was so poor that he had not where to lay his head, and depended on the charity of some of his followers for his subsistence; as appears by Luke viii. at the beginning. How meek, condescending, and familiar his treatment of his disciples; his discourses with them, treating them as a father his children; yea, as friends and companions. How patient, bearing such affliction and reproach, and so many injuries from the scribes and Pharisees, and others. In these things he appeared *as a Lamb*. And yet he at the same time did in many ways show forth his divine majesty and glory, particularly in the miracles he wrought, which were evidently divine works, and manifested omnipotent power, and so declared him to be *the Lion of the tribe of Judah*. His wonderful and miraculous works plainly showed him to be the God of nature; in that it appeared by them that he had all nature in his hands, and could lay an arrest upon it, and stop and change its course as he pleased. In healing the sick, and opening the eyes of the blind, and unstopping the ears of the deaf, and healing the lame; he showed that he was the God that framed the eye, and created the ear, and was the author of the frame of man's body. By the dead's rising at his command, it appeared that he was the author and fountain of life, and that "God the Lord, to whom belong the issues from death." By his walking on the sea in a storm, when the waves were raised, he showed himself to be that God spoken of in Job ix. 8. "That treadeth on the waves of the sea." By his stilling the storm, and calming the rage of the sea, by his powerful command, saying, "Peace, be still," he showed that he has the command of the universe, and that he is that God who brings things to pass by the word of his power, who speaks and it is done, who commands and it stands fast; Psalm lxv. 7. "Who stilleth the noise of the seas, the noise of their waves." And Psalm cvii. 29. "That maketh the storm a calm, so that the waves thereof are still." And Psalm lxxxix. 8, 9. "O Lord God of hosts, who is a strong Lord like unto thee, or to thy faithfulness round about thee? Thou rulest the raging of the sea: when the waves thereof arise, thou stillest them." Christ, by casting out devils, remarkably appeared as *the Lion of the tribe of Judah*, and showed that he was stronger than the roaring lion, that seeks whom he may devour. He commanded them to come out, and they were forced to obey. They were terribly afraid of him; they fall down before him, and beseech him not to torment them. He forces a whole legion of them to forsake their hold, by his powerful word; and they could not so much as enter into the swine without his leave. He showed the glory of his omniscience, by telling the thoughts of men; as we have often an account. Herein he appeared to be that God spoken of, Amos iv. 13. "That declareth unto man what is his thought." Thus, in the midst of his meanness and humiliation, his divine glory appeared in his miracles, John ii. 11. "This beginning of miracles did Jesus in Cana of Galilee, and manifested forth his glory."

And though Christ ordinarily appeared without outward glory, and in great obscurity, yet at a certain time he threw off the veil, and appeared in his divine majesty, so far as it could be outwardly manifested to men in this frail state, when he was transfigured in the mount. The apostle Peter, 2 Pet. i. 16, 17. was an "eye-witness of his majesty, when he received from God the Father honour and glory, when there came such a voice to him from the excellent glory, This is my beloved Son, in whom I am well pleased; which voice that came from heaven they heard, when they were with him in the holy mount."

And at the same time that Christ was wont to appear in such meekness, condescension, and humility, in his familiar discourses with his disciples, appearing therein as the Lamb of God; he was also wont to appear as *The Lion of the tribe of Judah*, with divine authority and majesty, in his so sharply rebuking the scribes and Pharisees, and other hypocrites.

III. This admirable conjunction of excellencies remarkably appears in his offering up himself a sacrifice for sinners in his last sufferings. As this was the greatest thing in all the works of redemption, the greatest act of Christ in that work; so in this act especially does there appear that admirable conjunction of excellencies that has been spoken of. Christ never so much appeared as a lamb, as when he was slain: "He came like a lamb to the slaughter," Isaiah liii. 7. Then he was offered up to God as a lamb without blemish, and without spot: then especially did he appear to be the anti-type of the lamb of the passover: 1 Cor. v. 7. "Christ our Passover sacrificed for us." And yet in that act he did in an especial manner appear as "*the Lion of the tribe of Judah*;" yea, in this above all other acts, in many respects, as may appear in the following things.

1. Then was Christ in the greatest degree of his humiliation, and yet by that, above all other things, his divine glory appears. Christ's humiliation was great, in being born in such a low condition, of a poor virgin, and in a stable. His humiliation was great, in being subject to Joseph the carpenter, and Mary his mother, and afterwards living in poverty, so as not to have where to lay his head; and in suffering such manifold and bitter reproaches as he suffered, while he went about preaching and working miracles. But his humiliation was never so great as it was in his last sufferings, beginning with his agony in the garden, till he expired on the cross. Never was he subject to such ignominy as then; never did he suffer so much pain in his body, or so much sorrow in his soul; never was he in so great an exercise of his condescension, humility, meekness, and patience, as he was in these last sufferings; never was his divine glory and majesty covered with so thick and dark a veil; never did he so empty himself and make himself of no reputation, as at this time. And yet, never was his divine glory so manifested, by any act of his, as in yielding himself up to these sufferings. When the fruit of it came to appear, and the mystery and ends of it to be unfolded in its issue, then did the glory of it appear; then did it appear as the most glorious act of Christ that ever he exercised towards the creature. This act of his is celebrated by the angels and hosts of heaven with peculiar praises, as that which is above all others glorious, as you may see in the context, (ver. 9, &c.) "And they sung a new song, saying, Thou art worthy to take the book, and to open the seals thereof: for thou wast slain, and hast redeemed us to God by thy blood, out of every kindred, and tongue, and people, and nation; and hast made us unto our God kings and priests: and we shall reign on the earth. And I beheld, and I heard the voice of many angels round about the throne, and the beasts, and the elders: and the number of them was ten thousand times ten thousand, and thousands of thousands; saying with a loud voice, Worthy is the Lamb that was slain, to receive power, and riches, and wisdom, and strength, and honour, and glory, and blessing."

2. He never in any act gave so great a manifestation of love to God, and yet never so manifested his love to those that were enemies to God, as in that act. Christ never did any thing whereby his love to the Father was so eminently manifested, as in his laying down his life, under such inexpressible sufferings, in obedience to his command, and for the vindication of the honour of his authority and majesty; nor did ever any mere creature give such a testimony of love to God as that was. And yet this was the greatest expression of his love to sinful men who were enemies to God; Rom. v. 10. "When we were enemies, we were reconciled to God, by the death of his Son." The greatness of Christ's love to such, appears in nothing so much as in its being dying love. That blood of Christ which fell in great drops to the ground, in his agony, was shed from love to God's enemies, and his own. That shame and spitting, that torment of body, and that exceeding sorrow, even unto death, which he endured in his soul, was what he underwent from love to rebels against God, to save them from hell, and to purchase for them eternal glory. Never did Christ so eminently show his regard to God's honour, as in offering up himself a victim to justice. And yet in this above all, he manifested his love to them who dishonoured God, so as to bring such guilt on themselves, that nothing less than his blood could atone for it.

3. Christ never so eminently appeared *for* divine justice, and yet never suffered so much *from* divine justice, as when he offered up himself a sacrifice for our sins. In Christ's great sufferings, did his infinite regard to the honour of God's justice distinguishingly appear; for it was from regard to *that* that he thus humbled himself. And yet in these sufferings, Christ was the mark of the vindictive expressions of that very justice of God. Revenging justice then spent all its force upon him, on account of our guilt; which made him sweat blood, and cry out upon the cross, and probably rent his vitals—broke his heart, the fountain of blood, or some other blood vessels—and by the violent fermentation turned his blood to water. For the blood and water that issued out of his side, when pierced by the spear, seems to have been extravasated blood; and so there might be a kind of literal fulfilment of Psalm xxii. 14. "I am poured out like water, and all my bones are out of joint: my heart is like wax, it is melted in the midst of my bowels." And this was the way and means by which Christ stood up for the honour of God's justice, *viz.* by thus suffering its terrible executions. For when he had undertaken for sinners, and had substituted himself in their room, divine justice could have its due honour no other way than by his suffering its revenges.—In this the diverse excellencies that met in the person of Christ appeared, *viz.* his infinite regard to God's justice, and such love to those that have exposed themselves to it, as induced him thus to yield himself a sacrifice to it.

4. Christ's holiness never so illustriously shone forth as it did in his last sufferings; and yet he never was to such a degree treated as guilty. Christ's holiness never had such a trial as it had then; and therefore never had so great a manifestation. When it was tried in this furnace, it came forth as gold, or as silver purified seven times. His holiness then above all appeared in his stedfast pursuit of the honour of God, and in his obedience to him. For his yielding himself unto death was transcendently the greatest act of obedience that ever was paid to God by any one since the foundation of the world.

And yet then Christ was in the greatest degree treated as a wicked person would have been. He was apprehended and bound as a malefactor. His accusers represented him as a most wicked wretch. In his sufferings before his crucifixion, he was treated as if he had been the worst and vilest of mankind; and then, he was put to a kind of death, that none but the worst sort of malefactors were wont to suffer, those that were most abject in their persons, and guilty of the blackest crimes. And he suffered as though guilty from God himself, by reason of our guilt imputed to him; for he who knew no sin, was made sin for us; he was made subject to wrath, as if he had been sinful himself. He was made a curse for us.

Christ never so greatly manifested his hatred of sin, as against God, as in his dying to take away the dishonour that sin had done to God; and yet never was he to such a degree subject to the terrible effects of God's hatred of sin, and wrath against it, as he was then. In this appears those diverse excellencies meeting in Christ, *viz.* love to God, and grace to sinners.

5. He never was so dealt with, as unworthy, as in his last sufferings; and yet it is chiefly on account of them that he is accounted worthy. He was therein dealt with as if he had not been worthy to live: they cry out, "Away with him! away with him! Crucify him." John xix. 15. And they prefer Barabbas before him. And he suffered from the Father, as one whose demerits were infinite, by reason of our demerits that were laid upon him. And yet it was especially by that act of his subjecting himself to those sufferings, that he merited, and on the account of which chiefly he was accounted worthy of the glory of his exaltation. Philip. ii. 8, 9. "He humbled himself, and became obedient unto death; wherefore God hath highly exalted him." And we see that it is on this account chiefly, that he is extolled as worthy by saints and angels in the context; "Worthy," say they, "is the Lamb that was slain." This shows an admirable conjunction in him of infinite dignity, and infinite condescension and love to the infinitely unworthy.

6. Christ in his last sufferings suffered most extremely from those towards whom he was then manifesting his greatest act of love. He never suffered so much from his Father, (though not from any hatred to him, but from hatred to our sins,) for he then *forsook* him, or took away the comforts of his presence; and then "it pleased the Lord to bruise him, and put him to grief," as Isaiah liii. 10. And yet never gave so great a manifestation of love to God as then, as has been already observed. So Christ never suffered so much from the hands of men as he did then; and yet never was in so high an exercise of love to men. He never was so ill treated by his disciples; who were so unconcerned about his sufferings, that they would not watch with him one hour, in his agony; and when he was apprehended, all forsook him and fled, except Peter, who denied him with oaths and curses. And yet then he was suffering, shedding his blood, and pouring out his soul unto death for them. Yea, he probably was then shedding his blood for some of them that shed his blood; for whom he prayed while they were crucifying him; and who were probably afterwards brought home to Christ by Peter's preaching. (Compare Luke xxiii. 34. Acts ii. 23, 36, 37, 41. and chap. iii. 17. and chap. iv. 4.) This shows an admirable meeting of justice and grace in the redemption of Christ.

7. It was in Christ's last sufferings, above all, that he was delivered up to the power of his enemies; and yet by these, above all, he obtained victory over his enemies. Christ never was so in his enemies' hands, as in the time of his last sufferings. They sought his life before; but from time to time they were restrained, and Christ escaped out of their hands; and this reason is given for it, that *his time was not yet come.* But now they were suffered to work their will upon him; he was in a great degree delivered up to the malice and cruelty of both wicked men and devils. And therefore when Christ's enemies came to apprehend him, he says to them, Luke xxii. 53. "When I was daily with you in the temple, ye stretched forth no hand against me: but this is your hour, and the power of darkness."

And yet it was principally by means of those sufferings that he conquered and overthrew his enemies. Christ never so effectually bruised Satan's head, as when Satan bruised his heel. The weapon with which Christ warred against the devil, and obtained a most complete victory and glorious triumph over him, was the cross, the instrument and weapon with which he thought he had overthrown Christ, and brought on him shameful destruction. Col. ii. 14, 15. "Blotting out the handwriting of ordinances,—nailing it to his cross: and having spoiled principalities and powers, he made a show of them openly, triumphing over them in it." In his last sufferings, Christ sapped the very foundations of Satan's kingdom; he conquered his enemies in their own territories, and beat them with their own weapons; as David cut off Goliah's head with his own sword. The devil had, as it were, swallowed up Christ, as the whale did Jonah; but it was deadly poison to him; he gave him a mortal wound in his own bowels. He was soon sick of his morsel, and was forced to do by him as the whale did by Jonah. To this day he is heart-sick of what he then swallowed as his prey. In those sufferings of Christ was laid the foundation of all that glorious victory he has already obtained over Satan, in the overthrow of his heathenish kingdom in the Roman empire, and all the success the gospel has had since; and also of all his future and still more glorious victory that is to be obtained in the earth. Thus Samson's riddle is most eminently fulfilled, Judges xiv. 14. "Out of the eater came forth meat, and out of the strong came forth sweetness." And thus the true Samson does more towards the destruction of his enemies at his death than in his life; in yielding up himself to death, he pulls down the temple of Dagon, and destroys many thousands of his enemies, even while they are making themselves sport in his sufferings; and so he whose type was the ark, pulls down Dagon, and breaks off his head and hands in his own temple, even while he is brought in there as Dagon's captive.

Thus Christ appeared at the same time, and in the same act, as both a lion and a lamb. He appeared as a lamb in the hands of his cruel enemies; as a lamb in the paws, and between the devouring jaws, of a roaring lion; yea, he was a lamb actually slain by this lion: and yet at the same time, as *the Lion of the tribe of Judah*, he conquers and triumphs over Satan, destroying his own devourer; as Samson did the lion that roared upon him, when he rent him as he would a kid. And in nothing has Christ appeared so much as a lion, in glorious strength destroying his enemies, as when he was brought as a lamb to the slaughter. In his greatest weakness he was most strong; and when he suffered most from his enemies, he brought the greatest confusion on his enemies.—Thus this admirable conjunction of diverse excellencies was manifest in Christ, in his offering up himself to God in his last sufferings.

IV. It is still manifest in his acts, in his present state of exaltation in heaven. Indeed, in his exalted state, he most eminently appears in manifestation of those excellencies, on the account of which he is compared to a lion; but still he appears as a lamb; Rev. xiv. 1. "And I looked, and lo, a Lion stood on mount Sion;" as in his state of humiliation he chiefly appeared as a lamb, and yet did not appear without manifestation of his divine majesty and power, as *the Lion of the tribe of Judah.* Though Christ be now at the right-hand of God, exalted as King of heaven, and Lord of the universe; yet as he still is in the human nature, he still excels in humility. Though the man Christ Jesus be the highest of all creatures in heaven, yet he as much excels them all in humility as he doth in glory and dignity; for none sees so much of the distance between God and him as he does. And though he now appears in such glorious majesty and dominion in heaven, yet he appears as a lamb in his condescending, mild, and sweet treatment of his saints there; for he is a Lamb still, even amidst the throne of his exaltation; and he that is the Shepherd of the whole flock is himself a Lamb, and goes before them in heaven as such. Rev. vii. 17. "For the Lamb, which is in the midst of the throne, shall feed them, and shall lead them unto living fountains of waters, and God shall wipe away all tears from their eyes." Though in heaven every knee bows to him, and though the angels fall down before him adoring him, yet he treats his saints with infinite condescension, mildness, and endearment. And in his acts towards the saints on earth, he still appears as a lamb, manifesting exceeding love and tenderness in his intercession for them, as one that has had experience of affliction and temptation. He has not forgot what these things are; nor has he forgot how to pity those that are subject to them. And he still manifests his lamb-like excellencies, in his dealings with his saints on earth, in admirable forbearance, love, gentleness, and compassion. Behold him instructing, supplying, supporting, and comforting them; often coming to them, and manifesting himself to them by his Spirit, that he may sup with them, and they with him. Behold him admitting them to sweet communion, enabling them with boldness and confidence to come to him, and solacing their hearts. And in heaven Christ still appears, as it were with the marks of his wounds upon him; and so appears as a Lamb as it had been slain; as he was represented in vision to St. John, in the text, when he appeared to open the book sealed with seven seals, which is part of the glory of his exaltation.

5. And *lastly*, this admirable conjunction of excellencies will be manifest in Christ's acts at the last judgment. He then, above all other times, will appear as *the Lion of the tribe of Judah* in infinite greatness and majesty, when he shall come in the glory of his Father, with all the holy angels, and the earth shall tremble before him, and the hills shall melt. This is he (Rev. xx. 11.) "that shall sit on a great white throne, before whose face the earth and heaven shall flee away." He will then appear in the most dreadful and amazing manner to the wicked. The devils tremble at the thought of that appearance; and when it shall be, the kings, and the great men, and the rich men, and the chief captains, and the mighty men, and every bond-man, and every free-man, shall hide themselves in the dens, and in the rocks of the mountains, and shall cry to the mountains and rocks to fall on them, to hide them from the face and wrath of the Lamb. And none can declare or conceive of the amazing manifestations of wrath in which he will then appear towards these; or the trembling and astonishment, the shrieking and gnashing of teeth, with which they shall stand before his judgment-seat, and receive the terrible sentence of his wrath.

And yet he will at the same time appear as a Lamb to his saints; he will receive them as friends and brethren, treating them with infinite mildness and love. There shall be nothing in him terrible to them; but towards them he will clothe himself wholly with sweetness and endearment. The church shall be then admitted to him as his bride; that shall be her wedding-day. The saints shall all be sweetly invited to come with him to inherit the kingdom, and reign in it with him to all eternity.

APPLICATION.

I. From this doctrine we may learn one reason why Christ is called by such a variety of names, and held forth under such a variety of representations, in Scripture. It is the better to signify and exhibit to us that variety of excellencies that meet together and are conjoined in him. Many appellations are mentioned together in one verse, Isaiah ix. 6. "For unto us a Child is born, unto us a Son is given, and the government shall be upon his shoulder: and his name shall be called Wonderful, Counsellor, the mighty God, the everlasting Father, the Prince of Peace." It shows a wonderful conjunction of excellencies, that the same person should be a Son, born and given, and yet be the everlasting Father, without beginning or end; that he should be a Child, and yet be he whose name is Counsellor, and the mighty God; and well may his name, in whom such things are conjoined, be called Wonderful.

By reason of the same wonderful conjunction, Christ is represented by a great variety of sensible things, that are on some account excellent. Thus in some places he is called a Sun, as Mal. iv. 2. in others a Star, Numb. xxiv. 17. And he is especially represented by the Morning-star, as being that which excels all other stars in brightness, and is the forerunner of the day, Rev. xxii. 16. And, as in our text, he is compared to a lion in one verse, and a lamb in the next, so sometimes he is compared to a roe or a young hart, another creature most diverse from a lion. So in some places he is called a rock, in others he is compared to a pearl. In some places he is called a man of war, and the Captain of our Salvation, in other places he is represented as a bridegroom. In the second chapter of Canticles, the 1st verse, he is compared to a rose and lily, that are sweet and beautiful flowers; in the next verse but one, he is compared to a tree bearing sweet fruit. In Isaiah liii. 2. he is called a Root out of a dry ground; but elsewhere, instead of that, he is called the Tree of Life, that grows (not in a dry or barren ground, but) "in the midst of the paradise of God," Rev. ii. 7.

II. Let the consideration of this wonderful meeting of diverse excellencies in Christ induce you to accept of him, and close with him as your Saviour. As all manner of excellencies meet in him, so there are concurring in him all manner of arguments and motives, to move you to choose him for your Saviour, and every thing that tends to encourage poor sinners to come and put their trust in him: his fulness and all-sufficiency as a Saviour gloriously appear in that variety of excellencies that has been spoken of.

Fallen man is in a state of exceeding great misery, and is helpless in it; he is a poor weak creature, like an infant cast out in its blood in the day that it is born. But Christ is *the Lion of the tribe of Judah;* he is strong, though we are weak; he hath prevailed to do that for us which no creature else could do. Fallen man is a mean despicable creature, a contemptible worm; but Christ, who has undertaken for us, is infinitely honourable and worthy. Fallen man is polluted, but Christ is infinitely holy; fallen man is hateful, but Christ is infinitely lovely; fallen man is the object of God's indignation, but Christ is infinitely dear to him. We have dreadfully provoked God, but Christ has performed that righteousness which is infinitely precious in God's eyes.

And here is not only infinite strength and infinite worthiness, but infinite condescension, and love and mercy, as great as power and dignity. If you are a poor, distressed sinner, whose heart is ready to sink for fear that God never will have mercy on you, you need not be afraid to go to Christ, for fear that he is either unable or unwilling to help you. Here is a strong foundation, and an inexhaustible treasure, to answer the necessities of your poor soul; and here is infinite grace and gentleness to invite and imbolden a poor, unworthy, fearful soul to come to it. If Christ accepts of you, you need not fear but that you will be safe; for he is a strong Lion for your defence. And if you come, you need not fear but that you shall be accepted; for he is like a Lamb to all that come to him, and receives them with infinite grace and tenderness. It is true he has awful majesty; he is the great God, and infinitely high above you; but there is this to encourage and imbolden the poor sinner, that Christ is man as well as God; he is a creature, as well as the Creator; and he is the most humble and lowly in heart of any creature in heaven or earth. This may well make the poor unworthy creature bold in coming to him. You need not hesitate one moment; but may run to him, and cast yourself upon him. You will certainly be graciously and meekly received by him. Though he is a lion, he will only be a lion to your enemies; but he will be a lamb to you. It could not have been conceived, had it not been so in the person of Christ, that there could have been so much in any Saviour, that is inviting and tending to encourage sinners to trust in him. Whatever your circumstances are, you need not be afraid to come to such a Saviour as this. Be you never so wicked a creature, here is worthiness enough; be you never so poor, and mean, and ignorant a creature, there is no danger of being despised; for though he be so much greater than you, he is also immensely more humble than you. Any one of you that is a father or mother, will not despise one of your own children that comes to you in distress: much less danger is there of Christ despising you, if you in your heart come to him. Here let me a little expostulate with the poor, burdened, distressed soul.

1. What are you afraid of, that you dare not venture your soul upon Christ? Are you afraid that he cannot save you; that he is not strong enough to conquer the enemies of your soul? But how can you desire one stronger than the "mighty God?" as Christ is called, Isa. ix. 6. Is there need of greater than infinite strength? Are you afraid that he will not be willing to stoop so low as to take any gracious notice of you? But then, look on him, as he stood in the ring of soldiers, exposing his blessed face to be buffeted and spit upon by them! Behold him bound with his back uncovered to those that smote him! And behold him hanging on the cross! Do you think that he that had condescension enough to stoop to these things, and that for his crucifiers, will be unwilling to accept of you if you come

to him? Or, are you afraid that if he does accept of you, that God the Father will not accept of him for you? But consider, will God reject his own Son, in whom his infinite delight is, and has been, from all eternity, and who is so united to him, that if he should reject him he would reject himself?

2. What is there that you can desire should be in a Saviour, that is not in Christ? Or, wherein should you desire a Saviour should be otherwise than Christ is? What excellency is there wanting? What is there that is great or good; what is there that is venerable or winning; what is there that is adorable or endearing; or, what can you think of that would be encouraging, which is not to be found in the person of Christ? Would you have your Saviour to be great and honourable, because you are not willing to be beholden to a mean person? And, is not Christ a person honourable enough to be worthy that you should be dependent on him; is he not a person high enough to be appointed to so honourable a work as your salvation? Would you not only have a Saviour of high degree, but would you have him, notwithstanding his exaltation and dignity, to be made also of low degree, that he might have experience of afflictions and trials, that he might learn by the things that he has suffered, to pity them that suffer and are tempted? And has not Christ been made low enough for you? and has he not suffered enough? Would you not only have him possess experience of the afflictions you now suffer, but also of that amazing wrath that you fear hereafter, that he may know how to pity those that are in danger, and afraid of it? This Christ has had experience of, which experience gave him a greater sense of it, a thousand times, than you have, or any man living has. Would you have your Saviour to be one who is near to God, that so his mediation might be prevalent with him? And can you desire him to be nearer to God than Christ is, who is his only-begotten Son, of the same essence with the Father? And would you not only have him near to God, but also near to you, that you may have free access to him? And would you have him nearer to you than to be in the same nature, united to you by a spiritual union, so close as to be fitly represented by the union of the wife to the husband, of the branch to the vine, of the member to the head; yea, so as to be one spirit? For so he will be united to you, if you accept of him. Would you have a Saviour that has given some great and extraordinary testimony of mercy and love to sinners, by something that he has done, as well as by what he says? And can you think or conceive of greater things than Christ has done? Was it not a great thing for him, who was God, to take upon him human nature; to be not only God, but man thenceforward to all eternity? But would you look upon suffering for sinners to be a yet greater testimony of love to sinners, than merely doing, though it be ever so extraordinary a thing that he has done? And would you desire that a Saviour should suffer more than Christ has suffered for sinners? What is there wanting, or what would you add if you could, to make him more fit to be your Saviour? But further, to induce you to accept of Christ as your Saviour, consider two things particularly.

(1.) How much Christ appears as the Lamb of God in his invitations to you to come to him and trust in him. With what sweet grace and kindness does he, from time to time, call and invite you; as Prov. viii. 4. "Unto you, O men, I call, and my voice is to the sons of men." And Isaiah lv. 1, 2, 3. "Ho, every one that thirsteth, come ye to the waters, and he that hath no money; come ye, buy and eat; yea, come, buy wine and milk without money, and without price." How gracious is he here in inviting every one that thirsts, and in so repeating his invitation over and over, "Come ye to the waters; come, buy and eat; yea, come!" Mark the excellency of that entertainment which he invites you to accept of, "Come, buy wine and milk!" your poverty, having nothing to pay for it, shall be no objection,—"Come, he that hath no money, come without money, and without price!" What gracious arguments and expostulations he uses with you! "Wherefore do ye spend money for that which is not bread? and your labour for that which satisfieth not? Hearken diligently unto me, and eat ye that which is good, and let your soul delight itself in fatness." As much as to say, It is altogether needless for you to continue labouring and toiling for that which can never serve your turn, seeking rest in the world, and in your own righteousness:—I have made abundant provision for you, of that which is really good, and will fully satisfy your desires, and answer your end, and stand ready to accept of you: you need not be afraid; if you will come to me, I will engage to see all your wants supplied, and you made a happy creature. As he promises in the third verse, "Incline your ear, and come unto me: Hear, and your soul shall live, and I will make an everlasting covenant with you, even the sure mercies of David." And so, Prov. ix. at the beginning. How gracious and sweet is the invitation there! "Whoso is simple, let him turn in hither;" let you be never so poor, ignorant, and blind a creature, you shall be welcome. And in the following words, Christ sets forth the provision that he has made for you, "Come, eat of my bread, and drink of the wine which I have mingled." You are in a poor famishing state, and have nothing wherewith to feed your perishing soul; you have been seeking something, but yet remain destitute. Hearken, how Christ calls you to eat of his bread, and to drink of the wine that he hath mingled! And how much like a lamb does Christ appear in Matt. xi. 28—30. "Come unto me, all ye that labour and are heavy laden, and I will give you rest. Take my yoke upon you, and learn of me, for I am meek and lowly in heart; and ye shall find rest to your souls. For my yoke is easy, and my burden is light." O thou poor distressed soul! whoever thou art, consider that Christ mentions thy very case, when he calls to them who labour and are heavy laden! How he repeatedly promises you rest if you come to him! In the 28th verse he says, "I will give you rest." And in the 29th verse, "Ye shall find rest to your souls." This is what you want. This is the thing you have been so long in vain seeking after. O how sweet would rest be to you, if you could but obtain it! Come to Christ, and you shall obtain it. And hear how Christ, to encourage you, represents himself as a lamb! He tells you, that he is meek and lowly in heart; and are you afraid to come to such a one? And again, Rev. iii. 20. "Behold, I stand at the door and knock: if any man hear my voice, and open the door, I will come in to him, and I will sup with him, and he with me." Christ condescends not only to call you to him, but he comes to you; he comes to your door, and there knocks. He might send an officer and seize you as a rebel and vile malefactor; but instead of that, he comes and knocks at your door, and seeks that you would receive him into your house, as your Friend and Saviour. And he not only knocks at your door, but he stands there waiting, while you are backward and unwilling. And not only so, but he makes promises what he will do for you, if you will admit him, what privileges he will admit you to; he will sup with you, and you with him." And again, Rev. xxii. 16, 17. "I am the root and the offspring of David, and the bright and morning star. And the Spirit and the bride say, Come. And let him that heareth, say, come. And let him that is athirst come. And whosoever will, let him take of the water of life freely." How does Christ here graciously set before you his own winning attractive excellency! And how does he condescend to declare to you not only his own invitation, but the invitation of the Spirit and the bride, if by any means he might encourage you to come! And how does he invite every one that will, that they may "take of the water of life freely," that they may take it as a free gift, however precious it be, and though it be the water of life!

(2.) If you do come to Christ, he will appear as a Lion, in his glorious power and dominion, to defend you. All those excellencies of his, in which he appears as a lion, shall be yours, and shall be employed for you in your defence, for your safety, and to promote your glory; he will be as a lion to fight against your enemies. He that touches you, or offends you, will provoke his wrath, as he that stirs up a lion. Unless your enemies can conquer this Lion, they shall not be able to destroy or hurt you; unless they are stronger than he, they shall not be able to hinder your happiness. Isa. xxxi. 4. "For thus hath the Lord spoken unto me, Like as the lion and the young lion roaring on his prey, when a multitude of shepherds is called forth against him, he will not be afraid of their voice, nor abase himself for the noise of them; so shall the Lord of hosts come down to fight for mount Zion, and for the hill thereof."

III. Let what has been said be improved to induce you to love the Lord Jesus Christ, and choose him for your friend and portion. As there is such an admirable meeting of diverse excellencies in Christ, so there is every thing in him to render him worthy of your love and choice, and to win and engage it. Whatsoever there is or can be desirable in a friend, is in Christ, and that to the highest degree that can be desired.

Would you choose for a friend a person of great dignity? It is a thing taking with men to have those for their friends who are much above them; because they look upon themselves honoured by the friendship of such. Thus, how taking would it be with an inferior maid to be the object of the dear love of some great and excellent prince. But Christ is infinitely above you, and above all the princes of the earth; for he is the King of kings. So honourable a person as this offers himself to you, in the nearest and dearest friendship.

And would you choose to have a friend not only great but good? In Christ infinite greatness and infinite goodness meet together, and receive lustre and glory one from another. His greatness is rendered lovely by his goodness. The greater any one is without goodness, so much the greater evil; but when infinite goodness is joined with greatness, it renders it a glorious and adorable greatness. So, on the other hand, his infinite goodness receives lustre from his greatness. He that is of great understanding and ability, and is withal of a good and excellent disposition, is deservedly more esteemed than a lower and lesser being, with the same kind inclination and good will. Indeed goodness is excellent in whatever subject it be found; it is beauty and excellency itself, and renders all excellent that are possessed of it; and yet most excellent when joined with greatness. The very same excellent qualities of gold render the body in which they are inherent more precious, and of greater value, when joined with greater than when with lesser dimensions. And how glorious is the sight, to see him who is the great Creator and supreme Lord of heaven and earth, full of condescension, tender pity and mercy, towards the mean and unworthy! His almighty power, and infinite majesty and self-sufficiency, render his exceeding love and grace the more surprising. And how do his condescension and compassion endear his majesty, power, and dominion, and render those attributes pleasant, that would otherwise be only terrible! Would you not desire that your friend, though great and honourable, should be of such condescension and grace, and so to have the way opened to free access to him, that his exaltation above you might not hinder your free enjoyment of his friendship?—And would you choose not only that the infinite greatness and majesty of your friend should be, as it were, mollified and sweetened with condescension and grace; but would you also desire to have your friend brought nearer to you? Would you choose a friend far above you, and yet as it were upon a level with you too? Though it be taking with men to have a near and dear friend of superior dignity, yet there is also an inclination in them to have their friend a sharer with them in circumstances. Thus is Christ. Though he be the great God, yet he has, as it were, brought himself down to be upon a level with you, so as to become man as you are, that he might not only be your Lord, but your brother, and that he might be the more fit to be a companion for such a worm of the dust. This is one end of Christ's taking upon him man's nature, that his people might be under advantages for a more familiar converse with him, than the infinite distance of the divine nature would allow of. And upon this account the church longed for Christ's incarnation, Cant. viii. 1. "O that thou wert my brother, that sucked the breasts of my mother! when I should find thee without, I would kiss thee, yea, I should not be despised." One design of God in the gospel, is to bring us to make God the object of our undivided respect, that he may engross our regard every way, that whatever natural inclination there is in our souls, he may be the centre of it; that God may be all in all. But there is an inclination in the creature, not only to the adoration of a Lord and Sovereign, but to complacence in some one as a friend, to love and delight in some one that may be conversed with as a companion. And virtue and holiness do not destroy or weaken this inclination of our nature. But so hath God contrived in the affair of our redemption, that a divine person may be the object even of this inclination of our nature. And in order hereto, such an one is come down to us, and has taken our nature, and is become one of us, and calls himself our friend, brother, and companion. Psal. cxxii. 8. "For my brethren and companions' sake, will I now say, Peace be within thee."

But is it not enough in order to invite and encourage you to free access to a friend so great and high, that he is one of infinite condescending grace, and also has taken your own nature, and is become man? But would you, further to imbolden and win you, have him a man of wonderful meekness and humility? Why, such an one is Christ! He is not only become man for you, but far the meekest and most humble of all men, the greatest instance of these sweet virtues that ever was, or will be. And besides these, he has all other human excellencies in the highest perfection. These, indeed, are no proper addition to his divine excellencies. Christ has no more excellency in his person, since his incarnation, than he had before; for divine excellency is infinite, and cannot be added to. Yet his human excellencies are additional *manifestations* of his glory and excellency to us, and are additional recommendations of him to our esteem and love, who are of finite comprehension. Though his human excellencies are but communications and reflections of his divine; and though this light, as reflected, falls infinitely short of the divine fountain of light in its immediate glory; yet the reflection shines not without its proper advantages, as presented to our view and affection. The glory of Christ in the qualifications of his human nature, appears to us in excellencies that are of our own kind, and are exercised in our own way and manner; and so, in some respects, are peculiarly fitted to invite our acquaintance and draw our affection. The glory of Christ as it appears in his divinity, though far brighter, more dazzles our eyes, and exceeds the strength of our sight or our comprehension; but, as it shines in the human excellencies of Christ, it is brought more to a level with our conceptions, and suitableness to our nature and manner, yet retaining a semblance of the same divine beauty, and a savour of the same divine sweetness. But as both divine and human excellencies meet together in Christ, they set off and recommend each other to us. It tends to endear the divine majesty and holiness of Christ to us, that these are attributes of one in our nature, one of us, who is become our brother, and is the meekest and humblest of men. It encourages us to look upon these divine perfections, however high and great; since we have some near concern in, and liberty freely to enjoy them. And on the other hand, how much more glorious and surprising do the meekness, the humility, obedience, resignation, and other human excellencies of Christ appear, when we consider that they are in so great a person, as the eternal Son of God, the Lord of heaven and earth!

By your choosing Christ for your friend and portion, you will obtain these two infinite benefits.

1. Christ will give himself to you, with all those various excellencies that meet in him, to your full and everlasting enjoyment. He will ever after treat you as his dear friend; and you shall ere long be where he is, and shall behold his glory, and dwell with him, in most free and intimate communion and enjoyment.

When the saints get to heaven, they shall not merely see Christ, and have to do with him as subjects and servants with a glorious and gracious Lord and Sovereign, but Christ will entertain them as friends and brethren. This we may learn from the manner of Christ's conversing with his disciples here on earth: though he was their sovereign Lord, and did not refuse, but required, their supreme respect and adoration, yet he did not treat them as earthly sovereigns are wont to do their subjects. He did not keep them at an awful distance; but all along conversed with them with the most friendly familiarity, as a father amongst a company of children, yea, as with brethren. So he did with the twelve, and so he did with

Mary, Martha, and Lazarus. He told his disciples, that he did not call them servants, but friends; and we read of one of them that leaned on his bosom: and doubtless he will not treat his disciples with less freedom and endearment in heaven. He will not keep them at a greater distance for his being in a state of exaltation; but he will rather take them into a state of exaltation with him. This will be the improvement Christ will make of his own glory, to make his beloved friends partakers with him, to glorify them in his glory, as he says to his Father, John xvii. 22, 23. "And the glory which thou hast given me, have I given them, that they may be one, even as we are one; I in them," &c. We are to consider, that though Christ is greatly exalted, yet he is exalted, not as a private person for himself only, but as his people's head; he is exalted in their name, and upon their account, as the first fruits, and as representing the whole harvest. He is not exalted that he may be at a greater distance from them, but that they may be exalted with him. The exaltation and honour of the head is not to make a greater distance between the head and the members; but the members have the same relation and union with the head they had before, and are honoured with the head; and instead of the distance being greater, the union shall be nearer and more perfect. When believers get to heaven, Christ will conform them to himself; as he is set down in his Father's throne, so they shall sit down with him on his throne, and shall in their measure be made like him.

When Christ was going to heaven, he comforted his disciples with the thought, that after a while, he would come again and take them to himself, that they might be with him. And we are not to suppose that when the disciples got to heaven, they found him keeping a greater distance than he used to do. No, doubtless, he embraced them as friends, and welcomed them to his and their Father's house, and to his and their glory. They who had been his friends in this world, who had been together with him here, and had together partaken of sorrows and troubles, are now welcomed by him to rest, and to partake of glory with him. He took them and led them into his chambers, and showed them all his glory; as he prayed, John xvii. 24. "Father, I will that they also whom thou hast given me, be with me, that they may behold the glory which thou hast given me." And he led them to his living fountains of waters, and made them partake of his delights; as he prays, John xvii. 13. "That my joy may be fulfilled in themselves;" and set them down with him at his table in his kingdom, and made them partake with him of his dainties, according to his promise, Luke xxii. 30. and led them into his banqueting house, and made them to drink new wine with him in the kingdom of his heavenly Father, as he foretold them when he instituted the Lord's supper, Matt. xxvi. 29.

Yea, the saints' conversation with Christ in heaven shall not only be as intimate, and their access to him as free, as of the disciples on earth, but in many respects much more so; for in heaven, that vital union shall be perfect, which is exceeding imperfect here. While the saints are in this world, there are great remains of sin and darkness, to separate or disunite them from Christ, which shall then all be removed. This is not a time for that full acquaintance, and those glorious manifestations of love, which Christ designs for his people hereafter; which seems to be signified by his speech to Mary Magdalene, when ready to embrace him, when she met him after his resurrection; John xx. 17. "Jesus saith unto her, Touch me not; for I am not yet ascended to my Father."

When the saints shall see Christ's glory and exaltation in heaven, it will indeed possess their hearts with the greater admiration and adoring respect, but will not awe them into any separation, but will serve only to heighten their surprise and joy, when they find Christ condescending to admit them to such intimate access, and so freely and fully communicating himself to them. So that if we choose Christ for our friend and portion, we shall hereafter be so received to him, that there shall be nothing to hinder the fullest enjoyment of him, to the satisfying the utmost cravings of our souls. We may take our full swing at gratifying our spiritual appetite after these holy pleasures. Christ will then say, as in Cant. v. 1. "Eat, O friends, drink, yea, drink abundantly, O beloved." And this shall be our entertainment to all eternity! There shall never be any end of this happiness, or any thing to interrupt our enjoyment of it, or in the least to molest us in it!

2. By your being united to Christ, you will have a more glorious union with and enjoyment of God the Father, than otherwise could be. For hereby the saints' relation to God becomes much nearer; they are the children of God in a higher manner than otherwise could be. For, being members of God's own Son, they are in a sort partakers of his relation to the Father: they are not only sons of God by regeneration, but by a kind of communion in the sonship of the eternal Son. This seems to be intended, Gal. iv. 4, 5, 6. "God sent forth his Son, made of a woman, made under the law, to redeem them that are under the law, that we might receive the adoption of sons. And because ye are sons, God hath sent forth the Spirit of his Son into your hearts, crying, Abba, Father." The church is the daughter of God, not only as he hath begotten her by his word and Spirit, but as she is the spouse of his eternal Son.

So we being members of the Son, are partakers in our measure of the Father's love to the Son, and complacence in him. John xvii. 23. "I in them, and thou in me,—Thou hast loved them as thou hast loved me." And ver. 26. "That the love wherewith thou hast loved me may be in them." And chap. xvi. 27. "The Father himself loveth you, because ye have loved me, and have believed that I came out from God." So we shall, according to our capacities, be partakers of the Son's enjoyment of God, and have his joy fulfilled in ourselves, John xvii. 13. And by this means we shall come to an immensely higher, more intimate and full enjoyment of God, than otherwise could have been. For there is doubtless an infinite intimacy between the Father and the Son; which is expressed by his being in the bosom of the Father. And saints being in him, shall, in their measure and manner, partake with him in it, and of the blessedness of it.

And thus is the affair of our redemption ordered, that thereby we are brought to an immensely more exalted kind of union with God, and enjoyment of him, both the Father and the Son, than otherwise could have been. For Christ being united to the human nature, we have advantage for a more free and full enjoyment of him, than we could have had if he had remained only in the divine nature. So again, we being united to a divine person, as his members, can have a more intimate union and intercourse with God the Father, who is only in the divine nature, than otherwise could be. Christ, who is a divine person, by taking on him our nature, descends from the infinite distance and height above us, and is brought nigh to us; whereby we have advantage for the full enjoyment of him. And, on the other hand, we, by being in Christ a divine person, do as it were ascend up to God, through the infinite distance, and have hereby advantage for the full enjoyment of him also.

This was the design of Christ, that he, and his Father, and his people, might all be united in one. John xvii. 21—23. "That they all may be one, as thou, Father, art in me, and I in thee; that they also may be one in us; that the world may believe that thou hast sent me. And the glory which thou hast given me, I have given them, that they may be one, even as we are one; I in them and thou in me, that they may be made perfect in one." Christ has brought it to pass, that those whom the Father has given him should be brought into the household of God; that he and his Father, and his people, should be as one society, one family; that the church should be as it were admitted into the society of the blessed Trinity.

THEOLOGICAL QUESTIONS.

1. How does it appear that something has existed from eternity?

2. How does it appear that this earth and the visible system are not from eternity?

3. How does it appear that the existence of man is derived and dependent?

4. How do you prove the natural perfections of God, *viz.* his intelligence, infinite power, foreknowledge, and immutability?

5. How do you prove his moral perfections, that he is a friend of virtue, or absolutely holy, true, just, and good?

6. How do you prove that the Scriptures are a revelation from God? And what are the evidences, internal and external?

7. How do you prove the divine mission of Christ?

8. How do you prove the divinity of Christ?

9. How do you prove the personality and divinity of the Holy Ghost?

10. How do you prove that the persons in the Trinity are one God?

11. Whence arose the Manichean notion of two Gods, and how is it confuted?

12. Whence arose the polytheism of the pagans, and how confuted?

13. Whence was it that the knowledge of the one true God, in which Noah was instructed, was not preserved among his posterity in all ages?

14. Why are not mankind in all ages (their internal faculties and external advantages being sufficient) united in right sentiments of the one true God?

15. Were the moral character of God and the moral law understood and loved, would there be any objections against revealed religion?

16. What is the true idea of God's decrees?

17. How do you prove absolute and particular election?

18. Did God decree the existence of sin?

19. Why did God decree sin?

20. In what sense did he introduce sin into the universe?

21. How do you reconcile this with the holiness and goodness of God?

22. What is necessary to constitute a moral agent?

23. Are men moral and free agents?

24. What is the difference between natural and moral power and inability?

25. How is absolute moral necessity, or inability, consistent with the free agency of men?

26. How is the doctrine of universal, absolute decrees, consistent with the free agency of men?

27. How do you prove an universal and special providence?

28. What is the covenant of redemption?

29. If man was created in original righteousness, how is that consistent with moral agency? It being said that a necessary holiness is no holiness.

30. What was the constitution under which Adam in innocency was placed?

31. Was Adam under the same necessity of falling that we are of sinning?

32. Are all intelligencies bound to love God supremely, sinners and devils?

33. Is the law holy, just, and good, and how is it proved?

34. Are they, who are under its curse, bound to delight in it?

35. How great is the demerit of sin?

36. Are the torments of hell eternal?

37. How do you reconcile them with the justice and infinite goodness of God?

38. How do you reconcile them with those texts which say Christ died for all men, that God will not that any should perish?

39. How does it appear that human nature is originally depraved?

40. Whence comes that depravity?

41. How is it proved to be total?

42. What is the covenant of grace?

43. Are the law and gospel inconsistent with each other?

44. Why was an atonement, and one so precious as the blood of Christ, necessary?

45. In what manner did Christ atone for sin?

46. To whom doth it belong to provide an atonement, God, or the sinner?

47. Did Christ redeem all men alike, elect and non-elect?

48. Can the offer of the gospel be made in sincerity to the non-elect?

49. How is redemption applied?

50. What is the office of the Holy Ghost in the work of redemption?

51. What is regeneration?

52. Whence arises the necessity of it?

53. What is true love to God?

54. What is true benevolence to men?

55. What is true repentance, and how distinguished from legal?

56. What is true faith?

57. What is pardon and justification? What is their foundation, and what is the influence of faith therein?

58. How are full satisfaction and free pardon consistent?

59. Is the sinner forgiven before he repents?

60. Is sanctifying grace needful at all to any man, unless with respect to that which is his duty, and in neglect of which he would be without excuse?

61. What is the sum of man's duty, and what the effect produced by the sanctifying influence of the Holy Spirit.

62. Can that holy volition in us, which is the effect of divine power, be wholly our act, or our duty?

63. How is it proved that unbelief is sin, and that all errors in moral matters are of a criminal nature?

64. Will the wicked heathens, Jews, infidels, and errorists of every kind, be without excuse at the day of judgment?

65. What is the essence of true virtue, or holiness?
66. Is there no virtue in the exercise of natural conscience, the moral sense, natural compassion, and generosity?
67. Is not self-love the root of all virtue?
68. Do not the unregenerate desire to be regenerated, and can they not properly pray for regenerating grace?
69. Do they not desire the heavenly happiness?
70. What is the utmost the unregenerate do in the use of the means of grace?
71. Is any duty done by them therein?
72. Do they grow better in the use of means?
73. To what are they to be exhorted?
74. What is the real advantage of the assiduous use of means to the unregenerate?
75. How do you prove that the institution of the Sabbath is of perpetual obligation?
76. How is it that the Sabbath is changed from the seventh to the first day of the week?
77. How do you prove that public worship is to be celebrated on the Sabbath?
78. What is the foundation of the duty of prayer, since God is omniscient and immutable?
79. How do you prove that family prayer is a duty?
80. To whom are the promises of the gospel made, to the regenerate, or unregenerate?
81. Are no encouragements given to the unregenerate?
82. How do you prove the saints' perseverance?
83. What is the nature of a christian church?
84. Who are fit for communion therein?
85. What is the nature and import of baptism?
86. How do you prove infant baptism?
87. What is the nature of the Lord's supper?
88. What are the rules and end of church discipline?
89. What is the character of a good minister of Christ?
90. In what does the happiness of heaven consist?

END OF THE FIRST VOLUME.